The NIV

Interlinear Hebrew-English Old Testament

The NIV

Interlinear Hebrew-English Old Testament

Volume 1 / Genesis - Deuteronomy

Edited by
John R. Kohlenberger III

THE NIV INTERLINEAR HEBREW-ENGLISH OLD TESTAMENT, VOL. 1

Grand Rapids, Michigan

Second printing 1980

Library of Congress Cataloging in Publication Data

Bible. O.T. Hebrew. 1979.
The NIV interlinear Hebrew-English Old Testament.

Bibliography: p.
1. Bible. O.T.—Interlinear translations. English. I. Kohlenberger, John R. II. Bible. O.T. English. New international. 1979. III. Title.
BS715 1979 221.4'4 79-23008
ISBN 0-310-38880-5 (v. 1)

Printed in the United States of America

CONTENTS

ACKNOWLEDGMENTS

Although the author's name alone appears on the cover, a long list of people made it possible for this volume to come together. I would like to single out just a few of the many who directly and indirectly saw me this far into the project.

First, I must mention John Van Diest of the Christian Supply Centers and Kin Millen of Zondervan, who first put me in touch with the publisher. And I must thank my editors, Bob DeVries and Paul Hillman, for the incredible faith and patient cooperation they have shown.

Next, as far as production goes, I must thank my parents, John and Doris, who arranged the difficult interlinear typesetting, and John Hemmingsen for the tedious and exacting work of setting the Hebrew and proofreading the translation.

I also extend my gratitude to the people who put me together—the faculties of Multnomah School of the Bible and Western Conservative Baptist Seminary. But I must single out from Western Drs. Ronald B. Allen and Ralph Alexander, who taught me to read Hebrew and to love the Old Testament (but who must not be criticized for my shortcomings), and from Multnomah Professor E. W. Goodrick, who has been my mentor and special friend throughout my entire Christian education and without whose encouragement I would not have taken this direction in biblical studies.

Above all, I must thank my wife, not only for her encouragement and her patience but also for her example of devotion to a lengthy project: our first child, Sarah Natanya, who was born in the midst of the preparation of this volume. It is to my wife, Carolyn, that I dedicate this book.

HOW TO USE THIS VOLUME

This preintroductory section is designed to acquaint English Bible students and beginning language students with the value and use of this (or any other) interlinear work by describing what it is, what it can do, and what it cannot do. The introduction that follows presents in more detail a technical discussion of the Hebrew text and the translation techniques underlying the interlinear version and is directed to those already familiar with the basics of textual criticism and Hebrew grammar.

What It Is

As the title implies, an interlinear Hebrew-English Old Testament is a book that interlines Hebrew with English; that is, it provides a line of English translation for each line of Hebrew. Furthermore, it matches these lines word-for-word so that each Hebrew word has a representative word or phrase translating it into English.

This interlinear is difficult to read as a line because Hebrew reads right to left whereas English reads left to right. In the past, interlinears have written their English lines right to left, thus making the reader work backwards whenever he read. In this interlinear each multiple-word phrase that translates a single Hebrew word is written normally in English—left to right—so that when the interlinear is used to read Hebrew a word at a time, its English rendering reads as English should. For example, in Genesis 12:2, the Hebrew word וַאֲבָרֶכְךָ in traditional interlinears would be rendered "you bless will I and," but in this volume it is "and-I-will-bless-you."

An interlinear *should* be read a word at a time, not as a version. No language can be translated into another language word by word and make sense. Anyone who has studied a foreign language knows that. Thus, for an interlinear to accurately represent the Hebrew (or Greek, for the New Testament), it must not represent itself as a version by itself. In most other Old or New Testament interlinears, words are numbered so they may be read in proper English order, and many words are supplied in brackets or italics because they are needed in English but do not come directly from the original language. This interlinear was *not* constructed in that way so that the reader can see a literal rendering for each Hebrew word. Also, by comparing the sum total of these English words and phrases with the version in the margin, he can see the sort of give and take that must go on in order to express in proper English idiom the thoughts generated by these words.

This brings us closer to defining what an interlinear is. It is a sourcebook both for word studies and for the study of Hebrew. It is a source for word studies because the reader can work from the New International Version, which parallels the interlinear text, and thus discover the Hebrew word that underlies the key words of the text. It is a source for the study of Hebrew because it provides an English translation for every Hebrew word; so the student of Hebrew can read large portions of the text without constant reference to dictionaries or grammar books. These processes will be explained further in the next section.

What It Can Do

Because it is based on the NIV, and the whole NIV is contained on the same page as the interlinear text, one can read from the major words of the English text into the interlinear text and find the Hebrew word that will begin a word study. Needless to say, if you do not know at least the Hebrew alphabet, this book will be of little value to you. Thus, I have included a chart of the alphabet and vowels with pronunciation as a bare-bones minimum of knowledge necessary to work with this text. It would be of great value, however, if you were to dabble in a beginning Hebrew grammar or, better yet, to learn the essentials of Hebrew sounds and grammar from E. W. Goodrick's *Do It Yourself Hebrew and Greek* (Portland: Multnomah, 1976; Grand Rapids: Zondervan, 1979). Goodrick's book has a companion cassette that pronounces all Hebrew sounds and slowly reads through the first two chapters of Genesis to apply the basic sounds to the actual words of the text.

Suppose you are reading "The Song of Moses" in Exodus 15 and you see the footnote in verse 4 that says the Hebrew meaning of the name *Red Sea* is really the "Sea of Reeds." As you look over to the interlinear text, you do not even find the word *red*. The last word in verse 4 is "Reed," its corresponding Hebrew word being סוּף. If this is not enough proof for you, you will want to take the next step of going to the Hebrew dictionaries (or lexicons) and the *Englishman's Hebrew and Chaldee Concordance of the Old Testament* (Grand Rapids: Zondervan, 1970).

Before you can use these tools, you will have to know the root form of the word. Hebrew (and Greek) words change their forms in many ways, depending on how they are used in a sentence, but the dictionaries list only the most basic form of each word. The book that will give you this form is called the *Analytical Hebrew and Chaldee Lexicon,* 2nd ed. (Grand Rapids: Zondervan, 1970). We find the form סוּף on page 574 and notice that it is indeed already in its basic form, for there is a definition after it (note that this is the word in the second column, a noun, and not the one in brackets in the first, which is a verb). The definitions given include "sea-weed," "sedge," "reed," "rush," and "bulrush," besides the proper name "Red Sea." If you go further and look in a larger lexicon like that of Brown, Driver, and Briggs (and you should!), you will discover that the word never refers to the color red at all, but only to water plants and the "arms" of the Red Sea—the gulfs of Suez and Akaba. BDB explains that the term *Red Sea* comes from the Greek translation of the Old Testament, for the Greeks called these bodies of water by their color, not by their vegetation.

If you do not want to accept someone else's opinion or interpretation, you can look for yourself at every verse in which the word occurs by finding סוּף in the *Englishman's Concordance.* Every occurrence of this word is listed on page 872. After looking them all up you will see that whenever the word is not used of the Red Sea, it refers to reeds or water plants in general. (This does not mean you cannot refer to this body of water as the Red Sea; it simply means that you now know the basis for the footnote in the NIV and can explain to someone else what the Hebrew word means.) Goodrick's book, mentioned earlier, will not only teach you how to sound out Hebrew words, it will also teach you how to do this kind of word study in both Hebrew and Greek.

Because it is a grammatically literal translation, this interlinear helps the student of Hebrew learn the language by allowing him to read the Hebrew text without constant reference to lexicons and grammars. When he is unable to identify the form or determine the meaning of a word, he merely has to glance at the English translation to see if it is a noun or a verb, a participle or an imperative, singular or plural, or whatever, and he will also see its definition. By comparing the interlinear rendering with the NIV, he will also see how the form functions, for the form in which Hebrew casts a word or phrase must often be changed in order to make good sense in English.

For example, the first word in Exodus 20:8, זָכוֹר, being an infinitive, is translated in the interlinear as "to-remember." But in the NIV it is rendered as an imperative, "Remember." The student would then understand (or discover in a grammar) that this infinitive is an The"imperitival infinitive," an emphatic way of expressing a command. The difference in form between the literal translation and that of the NIV does not mean that the NIV is neither literal nor accurate, but that a change in grammatical form was necessary in order to express the same idea in each language.

What It Cannot Do

This brings us to the third section: what an interlinear cannot do. First, it cannot be used by itself to "correct" or criticize a *real* translation. By "real translation" I mean one that was made for English-speaking people to read in normal English idiom, such as the NIV. As we saw in the preceding example, the form of grammar and even the number and order of words used in an expression may have to change from one language to the next. Because the interlinear supplies only a word-for-word grammatically literal equivalence, it cannot be used as a normal English translation. It is a sort of half-way point between the Hebrew original and its idiomatic English rendering. So, the English Bible student cannot use the interlinear *grammatically* as he can *lexically* (that is, as a source for word studies).

Second, in respect to word studies, the interlinear translation cannot fully and exactly express the Hebrew in every instance. It can give a definition for a word in its context but cannot provide a commentary on all of the subtle nuances and meanings of that word. For this, one must consult the lexicons and concordances. With the help of a concordance one can examine any word in every location in which it appears in Scripture, and with the lexicon he can obtain categorized definitions and even commentary on key passages. We have already seen this process in regard to the Red Sea.

Third, the interlinear cannot be an independent source of exegesis or interpretation. For example, בְּרֵאשִׁית, the first word in Genesis 1:1, is translated "in-beginning" (because there is no definite article present in the Hebrew), but this does not mean it should be interpreted as speaking of *a* beginning; i.e., one among many. An article is required in English, whether "a" or "the," even though the Hebrew has none, and the NIV has interpreted this verse to refer to *the* beginning (as have most other English versions). That decision cannot be challenged and refuted solely on the rendering of the Hebrew word in the interlinear.

In summary, the English Bible student can use this volume to locate and begin to study words in lexicons, concordances, and linguistically based commentaries and even glean a little information about Hebrew grammar by observing the style of translation. The student of Hebrew can use it more fully, as a companion to translation that provides both form and function and as a pedagogue to lead him to a better reading knowledge of Hebrew—even to the point where he outgrows the book altogether.

The introduction that follows explains more fully to the student of Hebrew how to use the interlinear as a help in understanding grammar. It does so by pointing out the techniques of translation that express the forms of the words. A careful reading of the introduction will give the student a better understanding of the book and a fuller, more satisfying use of it. At the end of the introduction is a list of books basic to the study of Hebrew and of the biblical languages in general.

The Hebrew Alphabet and Vowel System

The following table lists the alphabet in order, giving both pronunciation value (as used in modern Hebrew) and transliteration value (that is, the way the letter is represented in reference books in English characters).

Form	Final Form	Translit-eration	Name	Pronounced as in:
א		ʾ	ʾAleph	(silent)
בּ (ב)		b (bh or ḇ)	Beth	*b*all (*v*ery)
גּ (ג)		g (gh or g̱)	Gimel	*g*one (same)*
דּ (ד)		d (dh or ḏ)	Daleth	*d*og (same)*
ה		h	He	*h*at
ו		w or v	Vav	*v*ery
ז		z	Zayin	*z*eal
ח		ḥ or ch	Heth	Ba*ch* (the composer)
ט		ṭ	Teth	*t*en
י		y	Yod	*y*et
כּ (כ)	ך	k (kh or ḵ)	Kaph	*k*ing (like ח)
ל		l	Lamed	*l*ong
מ	ם	m	Mem	*m*en
נ	ן	n	Nun	*n*ew
ס		s	Samech	*s*ign
ע		ʿ	ʿAyin	(silent)
פּ (פ)	ף	p (ph or p̱)	Pe	*p*ea (*ph*one)
צ	ץ	s or ts	Tsadhe	hi*ts*
ק		q	Qoph	uni*q*ue
ר		r	Resh	*r*un
שׂ		ś	Sin	*s*o
שׁ		š or sh	Shin	*sh*ip
תּ (ת)		t (th or ṯ)	Tav	*t*oe (same)*

*Modern Hebrew does not distinguish the variant forms of the consonant in pronunciation.

The following charts gives the pronunciation value as used in modern Hebrew:

Hebrew Long Vowel	Name	Translit-eration	Sounds Like
ָ	qamets	ā	father
ֵ	tsere	ē	they
ִי	hireq yod	î	machine
וֹ, ֹ	holem	ô, ō	roll
וּ	shureq	û	tune

Hebrew Short Vowel	Name	Translit-eration	Sounds Like
ַ	pathah	a	father
ֶ	seghol	e	met
ִ	hireq	i	pin
ָ	qamets hatuph	o	roll
ֻ	qibbuts	u	tune

The following "half-vowels" require only a fraction of the effort put into pronouncing the regular vowels, much as the "e" in "the" in the phrase "the bee."

Hebrew	Name	Translit-eration	Pronunciation Value
ְ	sheva	^{e}	half an "eh" sound, or silent
ֲ	hateph pathah	^{a}	half an "ah" sound
ֱ	hateph seghol	^{e}	half an "eh" sound
ֳ	hateph qamets	^{o}	half an "oh" sound

The following examples are not necessarily Hebrew words. They are combinations of letters that make a sound similar to English words you know, thus you can associate these known sounds with letters in combination and learn to read words.

סָא	saw	נוֹת	note	כּוּל	cool	הֶנְפֶּק	henpeck
מַא	ma	טוֹי	toy	שׁוּת	shoot	לֶפְּרֶשִׁי	leprosy
פַּה	pa	שִׁיץ	sheets	טוּם	tomb	מֶלְתֶּד	melted
רַה	rah	פִּיק	peak	בֶּטִי	Betty	הַרְוִי	Harvey
שָׂע	saw	לִיק	leak	מַרוֹ	morrow	בָּלוּן	balloon
בַּט	bought	אֶב	ebb	לֱפֶּל	lapel	טַלֶרֵעת	tolerate
גָּט	got	בֶּד	bed	גֹּפֶר	gopher	כֻּקוּא	cuckoo
דַת	dot	הֶן	hen	סֻפֶּר	super	דִּילִיץ	deletes
כֹּת	coat	יֶס	yes	שֱלֻן	saloon	תֶּלֶפֹן	telephone
וֹת	vote	זֶן	zen	מֹרַן	moron	שָׁלוֹם	shalom

INTRODUCTION

The NIV Interlinear Hebrew-English Old Testament (NIVIHEOT) combines the best available Hebrew text and English version, bridged with a grammatically literal, word-for-word translation, to meet the needs of English Bible students as well as those of the beginning and intermediate students of Hebrew. As the interlinear translation is based on the vocabulary of the New International Version (NIV), the English Bible student may use the NIVIHEOT to identify the Hebrew word or phrase underlying any portion of his English text, thereby providing himself with the material for word studies or interaction with linguistically based commentaries. For the formal student of Hebrew, whether he is beginning or reviving his studies, the NIVIHEOT provides a word-for-word translation, which is of great help in learning Hebrew by permitting one to read large portions of the text without constant reference to lexicons and grammars. In addition, this translation is grammatically literal—a feature not found in any previous interlinear translation—which aids in the identification of nominal and verbal inflection, the first step of exegesis. The following discussion details these and other features characteristic of the Hebrew, English, and interlinear texts.

THE HEBREW TEXT

In contrast to the New Testament, where the best approximation of the original text is produced through the careful collation and evaluation of the thousands of available Greek manuscripts, the Old Testament is predominantly represented by one type of text (commonly known as the Masoretic Text [MT]), which has very few significant variations. As a result, all printed texts of the Hebrew Old Testament are virtually identical. Even in the critical editions of this century, deviations from the basic MT are not incorporated into the text but appear in footnotes. However, the existence of readings differing from the MT—as found in such early recensions and versions as the Samaritan Pentateuch, the Targums, the Septuagint and other Greek translations, the Syriac Peshitta, and the Latin Vulgate—as well as the existence of some untranslatable readings in the MT, prompt even conservative scholars to carefully suggest some changes in the Hebrew text.

In the desire to represent the basic MT, as well as to provide material for limited textual criticism, the NIVIHEOT uses as its Hebrew text the recently completed *Biblia Hebraica Stuttgartensia* (BHS), which reproduces the Leningrad Codex B19a (L), considered the oldest dated MS of the complete Hebrew Bible. Deviations from the text of B19a (L) in the NIVIHEOT are very few and conservative (in contrast to the textual footnotes of BHS, which are not reproduced), and these changes are based only on the translations and footnotes of the NIV, not on my independent judgment, as the following points indicate:

1) When the NIV adds to the MT, the suggested emendation and translation are entered into the text in brackets [ ] and are discussed in a footnote (e.g., Gen. 4:8).

2) When the NIV presents an alternative reading in the text based on versions, the conjectured Hebrew reading is printed in a footnote (e.g., Gen. 47:21).

3) When the NIV suggests an alternative spelling of a proper name or place-name based on the versions, whether reproduced in the text or suggested in the footnotes, the conjectured Hebrew reading is *not* supplied (e.g., Gen. 10:4). Readers wishing to see the suggested alternate spelling may consult the critical edition of BHS.

4) When the NIV suggests alternate readings from the versions in the footnotes, but not in the text, the conjectured Hebrew reading is *not* supplied (e.g., Gen. 1:26). Again, consult BHS.

5) There are many readings in B19a (L) that do not exactly agree with the majority of the Masoretic tradition. Most of these differences are idiosyncrasies of vowel pointing and the use of the *dagesh*. In the desire to represent the majority tradition, all such divergences in spelling noted in BHS are corrected in footnotes (e.g., Gen. 2:18).

The ancient textual variants noted within the MT, which occurred when the reading in the text (*Kethib*, "that which is written") was corrected for the proper pronunciation or spelling by a reading in the margin (*Qere*, "read!"), are indicated by the small circle (°) over the *Kethib* form. The *Qere* form is given in a footnote with its verse number preceded by the small circle. When there are more than one type of footnote on a page, the *Kethib-Qere* is always at the bottom of the page (e.g., Num. 12:3). The exception to this occurs when the *Qere* form is a different word or word division than the *Kethib*. In this case, a translation is supplied beneath the footnote (e.g., Gen. 30:11).

Four forms in the Hebrew Bible are always pronounced differently from the way they are pointed, yet are not noted as *Kethib-Qere*. Of these so-called *Qere perpetua*, three occur in this volume. (The fourth, יְרוּשָׁלַםִ, "Jerusalem," does not occur until the book of Joshua.)

1) יהוה, *Yahweh*, the proper name of God, is either pointed with the vowels of אֲדֹנָי, "Lord," (יְהֹוָה) or אֱלֹהִים, "God," (יֱהֹוִה) and is to be pronounced as the word whose vowels it borrows. This deliberate mispointing was an effort by the scribes to keep the name of God from being taken in vain (Exod. 20:7; Lev. 24:11) by making it unpronounceable. This device was misinterpreted in 1520 by one Galatinus who mixed the vowels of אֲדֹנָי with the consonants of יהוה, thus producing the hybrid form *Jehovah*, which has remained with us to this day.

2) הִוא occurs throughout the Pentateuch in place of הִיא, the normal spelling of the third person, feminine, singular pronoun ("she"). There is no clear explanation for this.

3) יִשָּׂשכָר, "Issachar," is consistently spelled in this unpronounceable form, the background of which is a mystery.

Although the *Kethib-Qere* and the *Qere perpetua* are included in the NIVIHEOT as normal features of the MT, textual notes are included only because of alternate readings in the NIV. Textual criticism, Greek or Hebrew, is the domain of the scholar and should not be dabbled in by beginning, intermediate, or even advanced students. For further discussion, the reader is referred to the excellent introduction to Old Testament textual criticism by Bruce Waltke, which appears in volume 1 of *The Expositor's Bible Commentary* (Grand Rapids: Zondervan, 1979). His article and extensive bibliography provides the interested student with a massive amount of material on this highly technical subject.

The English Text

The NIVIHEOT reproduces in the margin the text of the NIV, complete with its special indentations, section headings, and footnotes. The reason for the choice of the NIV is twofold. First, the desire to make this work a lasting standard necessitated the choice of the Hebrew and English texts most likely to remain standards. Second, the character of both the translation and the format of the NIV makes it a superior marginal text. Because it is fluid and idiomatic, yet accurate and dignified, the NIV provides a superb model of expressing in good colloquial English the thought forms generated by a literal translation of the Hebrew. Further, the structure of the text, often as significant as the grammar, is displayed by the special indentations and paragraphing that make more apparent the literary forms of poetry, letters, lists, and so forth, reminding the student that the text is woven into a unified and flowing whole and is not simply a collection of words.

The introduction prepared by the Committee on Bible Translation follows this introduction and explains more fully the presuppositions, goals, and methods underlying the translation and publication of the NIV.

The Interlinear Text

As previously mentioned, the interlinear text is based on the vocabulary of the NIV and is grammatically literal. In this regard, the NIVIHEOT presents a unique concept in interlinear translation. The interlinear translator is usually quite independent, choosing not only the vocabulary of his version but also the verbal and nominal forms into which they are cast. The result is a translation that is literal in the sense that it gives an English equivalent for every word of the original (if indeed *literal* means "word-for-word") but not literal in grammatical form (if literal also means matching each inflection of the original with a consistent approximation of that inflection in English). Thus, all interlinear translations contain English singulars translating plurals and vice versa, verbs translating nouns, finite verbs translating infinitives and participles, and so forth, so that the text will make better sense to the normal English reader. Even when this idiomatic translation is corrected by the grammatically literal rendering supplied in brackets, the impression remains that the interlinear rendering is the most accurate rendering possible, whereas in reality it is just another version, not necessarily more accurate or less accurate than any other English version.

In fact, an interlinear translation cannot be more accurate than a good idiomatic translation, for, as any linguist will testify, no two languages have identical word meanings or identical grammatical structures. Thus, accuracy in translation depends on "dynamic equivalence": the reproduction of the *meanings* and *impacts* generated by the words and grammar of the original language in the words and grammar of the receptor language best suited to recreate these meanings and impacts. Although in some cases a word-for-word translation produces the best dynamic equivalence, more often this effect must be generated through idiomatic rendering.

This does not preclude the role of the interlinear translation, for the meaning of the original language must first be discovered through the careful study of words and grammar before this meaning may be recast into the words and grammar of the receptor language. With this in mind, the NIVIHEOT attempts to supply this grammatically and lexically literal link between the words of the Hebrew text and the skillfully cast idioms of the NIV. The following discussion presents the format and features of the interlinear translation.

Word Choice and Word Order

Word Choice. Words have little meaning outside of the contexts in which they are used. Thus, the translator must see the whole context of a word before he can accurately render it with one of its many potential definitions. The NIV is the product of many brilliant scholars working many hours to establish the best contextual lexical choices; so it would be presumptuous to alter their word choices simply for the sake of novelty or to provide new synonyms. The vocabulary of the interlinear text, then, is taken from the NIV in most cases. Exceptions occur when (1) the limits of space in the interlinear text require a shorter word or phrase (e.g., "unleavened bread" instead of "bread made without yeast"), (2) Hebrew words are combined to produce a single English reading (e.g., "sons of Israel" instead of "Israelites"), and (3) the English renders the Hebrew with an idiom that cannot be matched word-for-word (e.g., "he lifted his eyes" instead of "he looked up"). This wording does not imply that it is the only viable option for any context; the thorough student will want to consult the standard lexicons of biblical Hebrew for more detailed discussion of words, idioms, and difficult readings. Although the words are taken from the NIV, the grammatical form of these words is determined strictly by the Hebrew form, as detailed below.

Word Order. The word order presents great difficulty because Hebrew reads right-to-left while English reads left-to-right. This problem is further complicated by the need to render most Hebrew words with more than one English word. Thus, all previous interlinears have forced the English reader not only to read the word-for-word translation backwards but also to read the phrases used to translate individual Hebrew words backwards. Whereas the first situation is unavoidable in an interlinear, the second is unnecessary. Why should the reader be made to read the translation of the word וְשָׁמַעְתָּ as "hear shall you and," when the phrase could be put in normal order "and you shall hear"? The NIVIHEOT chooses the latter format, believing that most readers will be reading the Hebrew one word at a time and would therefore prefer to read its translation in proper English word order.

A further difficulty found in most interlinears—especially the few that have appeared for portions of the Old Testament—is determining where the translation for one word ends and the translation for the next begins. To eliminate this confusion, the NIVIHEOT connects all the English words used to translate any one Hebrew word with hyphens. The example above appears as "and-you-shall-hear."

With these two features in the format, giving the translation of each Hebrew word in proper English word order and connecting multiple words with hyphens, the NIVIHEOT should prove to be the easiest to read of all existing interlinear translations of the Old Testament.

Translation techniques

Although this introduction is not intended as a primer for Hebrew grammar, the attempt to maintain grammatical literalness demands that the elements of Hebrew grammar be discussed in relation to the way they affect the translation. Underlying the following description is the presupposition that no English words will be supplied that are not direct translations of a Hebrew word and its inflected form. The NIV text given in the margin will provide the reader with English words necessary to construct a good translation; e.g., the indefinite article (a, an), which does not occur in Hebrew but is required in English. In this way the student can see where literal translation necessarily involves a degree of interpretation rather than being strictly a word-for-word equivalence. Also, no punctuation is provided in the interlinear text except to indicate interrogative pronouns and particles and the imperative form of verbs.

1. The Nominal System

Nouns in General. Hebrew nouns are rendered as English nouns unless the Hebrew nouns are also used as adjectives. In the latter case they are rendered as adjectives. Only proper names (e.g., Jacob), place-names (e.g., Canaan), and titles of God (e.g., Holy One) are capitalized.

Number. Hebrew singulars are rendered as singulars, even when the noun is a collective (e.g., Gen. 6:1, הָאָדָם, "the man" rather than "the men"). Hebrew duals are usually rendered simply as plurals, unless the dual demands the use of the number two (e.g., Exod. 25:10, אַמָּתַיִם, "two cubits"). Hebrew plurals are translated as plurals. If the plural is a fixed form denoting a singular object, it may be rendered as a singular (e.g., Gen. 1:1, אֱלֹהִים, "God").

Gender. Although English still preserves some gender distinctions in certain nouns—e.g., the female counterparts of the male actor, waiter, and god are the actress, waitress, and goddess—gender is not a universal feature of the language. Thus, gender will be seen consistently only in the pronouns and the verbal system, discussed below.

Case. Although case endings existed in Hebrew older than that of the MT, no case endings have survived in our existing manuscripts. Since case is therefore determined by context rather than by inflection, no special translation device is used to distinguish nominative, genitive, or accusative, even if the context demands an English preposition (e.g., Gen. 2:7, עָפָר, "dust" rather than "from the dust"). The NIV text will be of great value in providing the prepositions needed for good English translation when no preposition exists in the Hebrew context.

Absolute and construct structure. Possession and other genitive functions are expressed by the construct structure. The word in construct in Hebrew is indicated in the translation by the use of the word *of* as a suffix (e.g., Gen. 12:15, בֵּית פַּרְעֹה, "house-of Pharaoh"). When the inflection of a word does not change to indicate it is in construct, the Masoretic accentuation becomes the guide. But as it is not always an absolute determinant, many "judgment calls" in relation to this grammatical structure had to be made and criticisms and corrections are welcomed. (See *Article* below.)

Adjectives. Adjectives are rendered in the same way as nouns in regard to number and gender. Plurality is indicated by the addition of the word *ones* (e.g., Gen. 1:16, הַמְּאֹרֹת הַגְּדֹלִים, "the-lights the-great-ones").

Article. The Hebrew article is always translated by the English definite article (see example of Gen. 1:16 above). It is translated everywhere it appears, even when not needed in English (e.g., Gen. 22:9, הָאֱלֹהִים, "the-God"). It is never supplied in translation where it does not occur in Hebrew. As words in construct do not take the article, even when they are considered definite by being in construct to a proper name or a noun with the article, the English article is not supplied in translation (e.g., Gen. 1:2, וְרוּחַ אֱלֹהִים, "and-Spirit-of God" not "and-the-Spirit-of").

Numerals. Numerals are simply translated as numbers, whether ordinal or cardinal, without indication of gender.

Pronouns. Pronouns are consistently rendered according to person, number, and gender. As there is no neuter gender in Hebrew as there is in English, inanimate objects are referred to as "he" or "she," but not as "it." Although this will sound foreign to English ears, (e.g., Gen.

1:12), this gender distinction will often aid in the identification of a subject with its verb or a noun with its modifier, as they will share the same gender. In the translation pronominal suffixes are likewise suffixed to the word they modify (e.g., Gen. 6:18, בְּרִיתִי, "covenant-of-me"). Because no special pronouns are used in Hebrew to refer to God and because such reference is often a matter of interpretation, no pronouns are capitalized.

As English does not distinguish between second person masculine and feminine, singular and plural (using "you" for all four forms), or between third person plural, masculine and feminine (referring to both as "they"), the interlinear makes no differentation either. To introduce another typeface or to resort to archaic English (e.g., ye and thee) would draw undue attention to this matter and possibly confuse those unfamiliar with Hebrew. But for those who have not memorized these pronouns and wish to see the difference, the following chart shows all the possible spellings of these pronouns, both independent and suffixed:

	Independent	Suffixed
Second masc. sing.	אָֽתָּה, אַתָּה	ךָ', כָה'
Second fem. sing.	אָֽתְּ, אַתְּ	ךְ'
Second masc. plur.	אַתֶּם	כֶם'
Second fem. plur.	אַתֵּן, אַתֶּן, אַתֵּֽנָה	כֶן'
Third masc. plur.	הֵמָּה, הֵם	מוֹ', ם', הֶם'
Third fem. plur.	הֵנָּה, הֵן	נָה', ן', הֵן', הֶן'

Demonstratives. Demonstratives are translated consistently as to number, but gender is not indicated.

Interrogatives. As interrogatives introduce a question, they are always followed by a question mark, whether they are independent words (e.g., Gen. 4:9, אֵי, "where?") or the prefix הֲ (e.g., Gen. 4:7, הֲלוֹא, "not?").

Relatives. The Hebrew relatives אֲשֶׁר and (rarely) זוּ are translated by the English relative pronouns *that, which,* and *who.* If אֲשֶׁר expresses the idea of place, it is rendered "where."

2. The Verbal System

Stem or theme. The eight (or nine, counting Qal passive) Hebrew stems or themes have not been distinguished in translation. Their influence on verbs is seen, however, in the way in which the words are rendered (e.g., Lev. 11:36, יִטְמָא, "he-is-unclean" [Qal]; 11:43a, תִּטַּמְּאוּ, "you-make-yourselves-unclean" [Hithpa'el]; and 43b, וְנִטְמֵתֶם, "or-you-be-made-unclean" [Niphal]). Since this is not adequate material for parsing, the student who has not memorized the basic vowel patterns of the verbal system should consult the *Analytical Hebrew and Chaldee Lexicon*, 2nd. ed. (Grand Rapids: Zondervan, 1970) when in doubt about the inflection of a verb—or about any other part of speech for that matter.

Person, number, and gender. The person, number, and gender of all finite verbs are indicated by the use of pronouns as subjects, even when the subject is expressed by means of a noun or independent pronoun (e.g., Gen. 1:1, בָּרָא אֱלֹהִים, "he-created God"). The possibility of confusing the expressed subject with the object of the verb is usually eliminated by pronouns or the definite direct object indicator (see אֵת below). If these prove inadequate, consult the NIV translation.

Again, there is the problem of distinguishing second person, masculine and feminine, singular and plural, as well as third person plural, masculine and feminine (see *Pronouns* above). Consultation of the *Analytical Lexicon* or the following chart, which lists all the perfect and imperfect preformative and afformative indicators used consistently in all themes to distinguish person, number, and gender, should answer most questions.

	PERFECT		IMPERFECT	
	Singular	Plural	Singular	Plural
3rd masc.	(none)	''וּ	יִ''	יִ''וּ
3rd fem.	''ָה	''וּ	תִּ''	תִּ''נָה
2nd masc.	''תָּ	''תֶּם	תִּ''	תִּ''וּ
2nd fem.	''תְּ	''תֶּן	תִּ''ִי	תִּ''נָה
1st com.	''תִּי	''נוּ	אֶ''	נִ''

Tense, or aspect, and mood. Because the two major tenses, or aspects—perfect and imperfect—overlap so greatly in both time orientation and function, they are not distinguished in translation. The chart above or the *Analytical Lexicon* should prove sufficient for this distinction. The tense and the function expressed in the NIV have been used to translate this element of verbal inflection. However, in the interlinear text, simple past and simple present forms have consistently been used in place of perfective or continual forms in order to save space and to eliminate the confusion of a finite verb with a participle or infinitive (e.g., Gen. 2:21, וַיִּישַׁן, "and-he-slept" rather than "and-while-he-was-sleeping").

Jussive and cohortative forms are often indistinguishable from the imperfect; therefore the NIV serves as the guide in rendering these forms by their English counterparts (e.g., Gen. 33:15, אֶמְצָא־חֵן, "let-me-find favor").

Imperative forms are indicated by an exclamation mark (e.g., Gen. 12:1, לֶךְ, "go!") but are not distinguished as to number or gender. As the imperative uses the same afformatives as the imperfect, the chart above or the *Analytical Lexicon* will serve to make the necessary distinctions.

There is a further difficulty with stative verbs—verbs expressing a state of being rather than an activity—when they are inflected as Qal perfect, third person, masculine gender, singular number. In this form they are spelled exactly the same as their cognate adjectives and nouns. In choosing between these two possibilities, Lisowsky's *Konkordanz zum Hebraischen Alten Testamentum* (Stuttgart: Württembergische Bibelanstalt, 1958) has generally been followed (e.g., Lev. 5:2, טָמֵא, "unclean"; 11:25, וְטָמֵא, "and-he-will-be-unclean").

Infinitives. The infinitives, absolute and construct, are always prefixed with *to* in translation but are not distinguished (e.g., Gen. 2:17, מוֹת, "to-die"; cf. Gen. 25:32, לָמוּת, "to-die"). The preposition לְ, often prefixed to the infinitive construct, does not receive an additional *to* in translation, as seen in the previous example.

Participles. Participles are translated by English participles ending in *-ing* (e.g., Gen. 1:2, מְרַחֶפֶת, "hovering"). In the case of most passive participles and of words that do not have a participial form in English, the word *being* is used as a helper (e.g., Exod. 39:9, כָּפוּל, "being-doubled"). Gender is not indicated, but plurals are rendered with the addition of the word *ones* (e.g., Exod. 25:20, סֹכְכִים, "ones-over-shadowing").

There are two difficulties in regard to participles. First, many participial forms in Hebrew have become fixed as substantives (e.g., Gen. 14:18, כֹּהֵן, "priest") and are therefore rendered as nouns, though they could have been rendered as participles. Unfortunately, the lexicons are not in total agreement as to when a participle ceases to be a verbal noun and becomes a noun proper; therefore, in such instances I have often used my own judgment, well aware that my decisions will not be universally accepted. Second, not all English words ending in *-ing* are participles (e.g., Gen. 1:1, בְּרֵאשִׁית, "in-beginning"). When in doubt in either situation, consult the *Analytical Lexicon.*

3. Particles

Prepositions. Prepositions, prefixed or independent, are always translated, whether or not they are necessary in English (e.g., Gen. 27:27, וַיִּשַּׁק־לוֹ, "and-he-kissed on-him"). The exception to this, the ל prefixed to the infinitive construct, has been mentioned above. Some prepositions are fixed forms compounded from several Hebrew words but rendered with one term (e.g., Lev. 1:3, לִפְנֵי, "before"). The *Analytical Lexicon* will sort out the components, if needed.

Adverbs. Adverbs of manner or place are simply rendered with the words chosen by the NIV translators.

Negatives. Negatives are always rendered with "no" or "not." The substantive אַיִן is often rendered as a quasi-verb (e.g., Gen. 37:29, אֵין, "he-was-not").

Conjunctions. Conjunctions are usually rendered as in the NIV. The conjunction אִם is rendered as a negative when it appears in an abbreviated oath formula (e.g., Gen. 14:23, וְאִם־אֶקַּח, "and-not I-will-accept"), the full oath being something like, "May God punish me *if* I accept anything from you." As in the case of prepositions, although more rarely, some compounded conjunctions must be translated as a unit (e.g., Gen. 18:5, כִּי־עַל־כֵּן, "because").

Other particles and parts of speech. The following parts of speech are listed in alphabetical order and their specialized translations discussed.

אֵת, the definite direct object indicator, is never translated. When standing independently, it is rendered with three asterisks (***, e.g., Gen. 1:1). When prefixed or suffixed, only those components to which it is affixed are translated (e.g., Gen. 1:1, וְאֵת, "and"; Gen. 2:3, אֹתוֹ, "him").

ה ָ, the directive suffix, is translated as a preposition (e.g., Gen. 12:10, מִצְרַיְמָה, "to-Egypt").

הֵן, הִנֵּה, the interjection, is translated "see!" (e.g., Gen. 24:13).

יֵשׁ, the particle of existence (counter to אַיִן), is usually translated as a quasi-verb (e.g., Gen. 44:20, "he-is").

נָא is used to intensify, or make more politely formal, the cohortative, the jussive, the imperative, and some particles. It is always translated "now!" because the distinction between intensity and politeness is not always easy to determine.

4. Final Note

יהוה, the personal name of God, is always translated "Yahweh," against the practice of the NIV in rendering it as "LORD." On the one hand, this prevents confusion of this name with the title אֲדֹנָי ("my-

Lord"), for the idea of lordship is not an integral element of the name. On the other hand, perhaps the use of Yahweh in this work will encourage the reader to use the personal name of God in prayer and praise, as is intended by the most common imperative in the Scriptures, הַלְלוּ־יָהּ (e.g., Ps. 104:35, "praise Yahweh!"). For an excellent study of the significance and meaning of the name *Yahweh,* please consult "What Is in a Name?" by Ronald B. Allen in *God: What Is He Like?* (Wheaton: Tyndale House, 1977).

Bibliography

General

Nida, Eugene. *God's Word in Man's Language.* 1952. Reprint. Pasadena: Wm. Carey Library, 1973.

This book illustrates the necessity of dynamic equivalence in translation through the experience and difficulties encountered by missionary Bible translators.

Beekman, John, and Callow, John. *Translating the Word of God.* Grand Rapids: Zondervan, 1974.

This is a more technical discussion of the same materials treated by Nida, intended for a more scholarly reader.

Goodrick, E. W., *Do-it-Yourself Hebrew and Greek.* Portland: Multnomah, 1976; Grand Rapids: Zondervan, 1979.

This book introduces the student to the study of both biblical languages by providing information and exercises in the use of lexicons, grammars, interlinears, and other resources of linguistic study.

Grammars

LaSor, William Sanford. *Handbook of Biblical Hebrew.* Grand Rapids: Eerdmans, 1979.

This is the most recent and most demanding of all beginning Hebrew grammars. However, it is probably the finest and most thorough such grammar in print and will take the student far beyond the level of the other grammars and is even keyed to the best advanced grammar, that of Gesenius, Kautzsch, and Cowley (see below), for further study.

Mansoor, Menahem. *Biblical Hebrew: Step by Step.* Grand Rapids: Baker, 1978.

This grammar is superb for self-study of Hebrew and is used as the textbook for four hours of college credit in a correspondence course from the University of Wisconsin (Madison).

Williams, Ronald J. *Hebrew Syntax: An Outline.* 2nd ed. Toronto: University of Toronto Press, 1976.

This linguistically up-to-date grammar is valuable on the intermediate and advanced levels for dealing with the potential interpretations of word inflection and syntax.

Gesenius, Wilhelm; Kautzsch, E.; and Cowley, A. E. *Gesenius' Hebrew Grammar.* 2nd English ed. London: Oxford University Press, 1910.

This encyclopedic work is the finest advanced grammar in English and, despite its age, is still the final word in matters of inflection, syntax, and interpretation.

Lexicons

Brown, Francis; Driver, S. R.; and Briggs, Charles A. *A Hebrew and English Lexicon of the Old Testament.* Corrected edition. London: Oxford University Press, 1968.

This lexicon, though dated and difficult to use, is the finest lexicon for the classification of its definitions and the thoroughness of its biblical references.

Koehler, Ludwig; and Baumgartner, Walter. *Lexicon in Veteris Testamenti Libros.* Leiden: E. J. Brill, 1953, with *Supplementum,* 1958.

This two-volume work, available also from William B. Eerdmans Publishing Co, is the most up-to-date of Hebrew lexicons in English, though its definitions are translated from the German original and are awkward at times. William Holladay has produced an abridged reworking of this set under the title *A Concise Hebrew and Aramaic Lexicon of the Old Testament* (Grand Rapids: Eerdmans, 1971)—an edition which may prove more useful for beginning students. For those who read German, a third edition is in process and exists in two fascicles (1967 [א–טבח] and 1974 [טבח–נבט]) available from Brill.

Botterweck, G. Johannes, and Ringgren, Helmer. *Theological Dictionary of the Old Testament.* Grand Rapids: Eerdmans, 1974—.

This set, projected for ten volumes of which three are in print in English, combines lexicography with a full examination of the cognate languages to give lengthy expositions on significant words in the Old Testament. Although liberal in theological orientation, it is a rich source of data for the student of any theological persuasion.

NIV PREFACE

The New International Version is a completely new translation of the Holy Bible made by over a hundred scholars working directly from the best available Hebrew, Aramaic and Greek texts. It had its beginning in 1965 when, after several years of exploratory study by committees from the Christian Reformed Church and the National Association of Evangelicals, a group of scholars met at Palos Heights, Illinois, and concurred in the need for a new translation of the Bible in contemporary English. This group, though not made up of official church representatives, was transdenominational. Its conclusion was endorsed by a large number of leaders from many denominations who met in Chicago in 1966.

Responsibility for the new version was delegated by the Palos Heights group to a self-governing body of fifteen, the Committee on Bible Translation, composed for the most part of biblical scholars from colleges, universities and seminaries. In 1967 the New York Bible Society (now the New York International Bible Society) generously undertook the financial sponsorship of the project—a sponsorship that made it possible to enlist the help of many distinguished scholars. The fact that participants from the United States, Great Britain, Canada, Australia and New Zealand worked together gave the project its international scope. That they were from many denominations—including Anglican, Assemblies of God, Baptist, Brethren, Christian Reformed, Church of Christ, Evangelical Free, Lutheran, Mennonite, Methodist, Nazarene, Presbyterian, Wesleyan and other churches—helped to safeguard the translation from sectarian bias.

How it was made helps to give the New International Version its distinctiveness. The translation of each book was assigned to a team of scholars. Next, one of the Intermediate Editorial Committees revised the initial translation, with constant reference to the Hebrew, Aramaic or Greek. Their work then went to one of the General Editorial Committees, which checked it in detail and made another thorough revision. This revision in turn was carefully reviewed by the Committee on Bible Translation, which made further changes and then released the final version for publication. In this way the entire Bible underwent three revisions, during each of which the translation was examined for its faithfulness to the original languages and for its English style.

All this involved many thousands of hours of research and discussion regarding the meaning of the texts and the precise way of putting them into English. It may well be that no other translation has been made by a more thorough process of review and revision from committee to committee than this one.

From the beginning of the project, the Committee on Bible Translation held to certain goals for the New International Version: that it would be an accurate translation and one that would have clarity and literary quality and so prove suitable for public and private reading, teaching, preaching, memorizing and liturgical use. The Committee also sought to preserve some measure of continuity with the long tradition of translating the Scriptures into English.

In working toward these goals, the translators were united in their commitment to the authority and infallibility of the Bible as God's Word in written form. They believe that it contains the divine answer to the deepest needs of humanity, that it sheds unique light on our path in a dark world, and that it sets forth the way to our eternal well-being.

The first concern of the translators has been the accuracy of the translation and its fidelity to the thought of the biblical writers. They have weighed the significance of the lexical and grammatical details of the Hebrew, Aramaic and Greek texts. At the same time, they have striven for more than a word-for-word translation. Because thought patterns and syntax differ from language to language, faithful communication of the meaning of the writers of the Bible demands frequent modifications in sentence structure and constant regard for the contextual meanings of words.

A sensitive feeling for style does not always accompany scholarship. Accordingly the Committee on Bible Translation submitted the developing version to a number of stylistic consultants. Two of them read every book of both Old and New Testaments twice—once before and once after the last major revision—and made invaluable suggestions. Samples of the translation were tested for clarity and ease of reading by various kinds of people—young and old, highly educated and less well educated, ministers and laymen.

Concern for clear and natural English—that the New International Version should be idiomatic but not idiosyncratic, contemporary but not dated—motivated the translators and consultants. At the same time, they tried to reflect the differing styles of the biblical writers. In view of the international use of English, the translators sought to avoid obvious Americanisms on the one hand and obvious Anglicisms on the other. A British edition reflects the comparatively few differences of significant idiom and of spelling.

As for the traditional pronouns "thou," "thee" and "thine" in reference to the Deity, the translators judged that to use these archaisms (along with the old verb forms such as "doest," "wouldest" and "hadst") would violate accuracy in translation. Neither Hebrew, Aramaic nor Greek uses special pronouns for the persons of the Godhead. A present-day translation is not enhanced by forms that in the time of the King James Version were used in everyday speech, whether referring to God or man.

For the Old Testament the standard Hebrew text, the Masoretic Text as published in the latest editions of *Biblia Hebraica,* was used throughout. The Dead Sea Scrolls contain material bearing on an earlier stage of the Hebrew text. They were consulted, as were the Samaritan Pentateuch and the ancient scribal traditions relating to textual changes. Sometimes a variant Hebrew reading in the margin of the Masoretic Text was followed instead of the text itself. Such instances, being variants within the Masoretic tradition, are not specified by footnotes. In rare cases, words in the consonantal text were divided differently from the way they appear in the Masoretic Text. Footnotes indicate this. The translators also consulted the more important early versions—the Septuagint; Symmachus and Theodotion; the Vulgate; the Syriac Peshitta; the Targums; and for the Psalms the *Juxta Hebraica* of Jerome. Readings from these versions were occasionally followed where the Masoretic Text seemed doubtful and where accepted principles of textual criticism showed that one or more of these textual witnesses appeared to provide the correct reading. Such instances are footnoted. Sometimes vowel letters and vowel signs did not, in the judgment of the translators, represent the correct vowels for the original consonantal text. Accordingly some words were read with a different set of vowels. These instances are usually not indicated by footnotes.

The Greek text used in translating the New Testament was an eclectic one. No other piece of ancient literature has such an abundance of manuscript witnesses as does the New Testament. Where existing manuscripts differ, the translators made their choice of readings according to accepted principles of New Testament textual criticism. Footnotes call attention to places where there was uncertainty about what the original text was. The best current printed texts of the Greek New Testament were used.

There is a sense in which the work of translation is never wholly finished. This applies to all great literature and uniquely so to the Bible. In 1973 the New Testament in the New International Version was published. Since then, suggestions for corrections and revisions have been received from various sources. The Committee on Bible Translation carefully considered the suggestions and adopted a number of them. These are incorporated in the first printing of the entire Bible.

As in other ancient documents, the precise meaning of the biblical texts is sometimes uncertain. This is more often the case with the Hebrew and Aramaic texts than with the Greek text. Although archaeological and linguistic discoveries in this century aid in understanding difficult passages, some uncertainties remain. The more significant of these have been called to the reader's attention in the footnotes.

In regard to the divine name *YHWH,* commonly referred to as the *Tetragrammaton,* the translators adopted the device used in most English versions of rendering that name as "LORD" in capital letters to distinguish it from *Adonai,* another Hebrew word rendered "Lord," for which small letters are used. Wherever the two names stand together in the Old Testament as a compound name of God, they are rendered "Sovereign LORD."

Because for most readers today the phrase "the LORD of hosts" and "God of hosts" have little meaning, this version renders them "the LORD Almighty" and "God Almighty." These renderings convey the sense of the Hebrew, namely, "he who is sovereign over all the 'hosts' (powers) in heaven and on earth, especially over the 'hosts' (armies) of Israel." For readers unacquainted with Hebrew this does not make clear the distinction between *Sabaoth* ("hosts" or "Almighty"), and *Shaddai* (which can also be translated "Almighty"), but the latter occurs infrequently and is always footnoted. When *Adonai* and *YHWH Sabaoth* occur together, they are rendered "the Lord, the LORD Almighty."

As for other proper nouns, the familiar spellings of the King James Version are generally retained. Names traditionally spelled with "ch," except where it is final, are usually spelled in this translation with "k" or "c," since the biblical languages do not have the sound that "ch" frequently indicates in English—for example, in *chant.* For well-known names such as Zechariah, however, the traditional spelling has been retained. Variation in the spelling of names in the original languages has usually not been indicated. Where a person or place has two or more different names in the Hebrew, Aramaic or Greek texts, the more familiar one has generally been used, with footnotes where needed.

To achieve clarity the translators sometimes supplied words not in the original texts but required by the context. If there was uncertainty about such material, it is enclosed in brackets. Also for the sake of clarity or style, nouns, including some proper nouns, are sometimes substituted for pronouns, and vice versa. And though the Hebrew writers often shifted back and forth between first, second and third personal pronouns without change of antecedent, this translation often makes them uniform, in accordance with English style and without the use of footnotes.

Poetical passages are printed as poetry, that is, with indentation of lines and with separate stanzas. These are generally designed to reflect the structure of Hebrew poetry. This poetry is normally characterized by parallelism in balanced lines. Most of the poetry in the Bible is in the Old Testament, and scholars differ regarding the scansion of Hebrew lines. The translators determined the stanza divisions for the most part by analysis of the subject matter. The stanzas therefore serve as poetic paragraphs.

As an aid to the reader, italicized sectional headings are inserted in most of the books. They are not to be regarded as part of the NIV text, are not for oral reading, and are not intended to dictate the interpretation of the sections they head.

The footnotes in this version are of several kinds, most of which need no explanation. Those giving alternative translations begin with "Or" and generally introduce the alternative with the last word preceding it in the text, except when it is a single-word alternative; in poetry quoted in a footnote a slant mark indicates a line division. Footnotes introduced by "Or" do not have uniform significance. In some cases two possible translations were considered to have about equal validity. In other cases, though the translators were convinced that the translation in the text was correct, they judged that another interpretation was possible and of sufficient importance to be represented in a footnote.

In the New Testament, footnotes that refer to uncertainty regarding the original texts are introduced by "Some manuscripts" or similar expressions. In the Old Testament, evidence for the reading chosen is given first and evidence for the alternative is added after a semicolon (for example: Septuagint; Hebrew *father*). In such notes the term "Hebrew" refers to the Masoretic Text.

It should be noted that minerals, flora and fauna, architectural details, articles of clothing and jewelry, musical instruments and other articles cannot always be identified with precision. Also measures of capacity in the biblical period are particularly uncertain (see the table of weights and measures following the text).

Like all translations of the Bible, made as they are by imperfect man, this one undoubtedly falls short of its goals. Yet we are grateful to God for the extent to which he has enabled us to realize these goals and for the strength he has given us and our colleagues to complete our task. We offer this version of the Bible to him in whose name and for whose glory it has been made. We pray that it will lead many into a better understanding of the Holy Scriptures and a fuller knowledge of Jesus Christ the incarnate Word, of whom the Scriptures so faithfully testify.

The Committee on Bible Translation

The NIV

Interlinear Hebrew-English Old Testament

בְּרֵאשִׁית בָּרָא אֱלֹהִים אֵת הַשָּׁמַיִם וְאֵת הָאָרֶץ׃
the-earth and the-heavens *** God he-created in-beginning (1:1)

וְהָאָרֶץ הָיְתָה תֹהוּ וָבֹהוּ וְחֹשֶׁךְ עַל־ פְּנֵי
surface-of over and-darkness and-empty formless she-was now-the-earth (2)

תְהוֹם וְרוּחַ אֱלֹהִים מְרַחֶפֶת עַל־ פְּנֵי הַמָּיִם׃ וַיֹּאמֶר
and-he-said (3) the-waters surface-of over hovering God and-spirit-of deep

אֱלֹהִים יְהִי אוֹר וַיְהִי־ אוֹר׃ וַיַּרְא אֱלֹהִים אֶת־ הָאוֹר כִּי־
that the-light *** God and-he-saw (4) light and-he-was light let-him-be God

טוֹב וַיַּבְדֵּל אֱלֹהִים בֵּין הָאוֹר וּבֵין הַחֹשֶׁךְ׃
the-darkness and-between the-light between God and-he-separated good

וַיִּקְרָא אֱלֹהִים ׀ לָאוֹר יוֹם וְלַחֹשֶׁךְ קָרָא לָיְלָה
night he-called and-to-the-darkness day to-the-light God and-he-called (5)

וַיְהִי־ עֶרֶב וַיְהִי־ בֹקֶר יוֹם אֶחָד׃ וַיֹּאמֶר אֱלֹהִים
God and-he-said (6) first day morning and-he-was evening and-he-was

יְהִי רָקִיעַ בְּתוֹךְ הַמָּיִם וִיהִי מַבְדִּיל בֵּין
between separating and-let-him-be the-waters between expanse let-him-be

מַיִם לָמָיִם׃ וַיַּעַשׂ אֱלֹהִים אֶת־ הָרָקִיעַ וַיַּבְדֵּל
and-he-separated the-expanse *** God so-he-made (7) from-the-waters waters

בֵּין הַמַּיִם אֲשֶׁר מִתַּחַת לָרָקִיעַ וּבֵין הַמַּיִם
the-waters and-between to-the-expanse from-under which the-waters between

אֲשֶׁר מֵעַל לָרָקִיעַ וַיְהִי־ כֵן׃ וַיִּקְרָא אֱלֹהִים
God and-he-called (8) so and-he-was to-the-expanse from-above which

לָרָקִיעַ שָׁמָיִם וַיְהִי־ עֶרֶב וַיְהִי־ בֹקֶר יוֹם שֵׁנִי׃
second day morning and-he-was evening and-he-was sky to-the-expanse

וַיֹּאמֶר אֱלֹהִים יִקָּווּ הַמַּיִם מִתַּחַת הַשָּׁמַיִם אֶל־
to the-sky from-under the-waters let-them-be-gathered God and-he-said (9)

מָקוֹם אֶחָד וְתֵרָאֶה הַיַּבָּשָׁה וַיְהִי־ כֵן׃ וַיִּקְרָא
and he-called (10) so and-he-was the-dry-ground and-let-her-appear one place

אֱלֹהִים ׀ לַיַּבָּשָׁה אֶרֶץ וּלְמִקְוֵה הַמַּיִם קָרָא יַמִּים
seas he-called the-waters and-to-gathering-of land to-the-dry-ground God

וַיַּרְא אֱלֹהִים כִּי־ טוֹב׃ וַיֹּאמֶר אֱלֹהִים תַּדְשֵׁא הָאָרֶץ
the-earth let-her-produce God then-he-said (11) good that God and-he-saw

דֶּשֶׁא עֵשֶׂב מַזְרִיעַ זֶרַע עֵץ פְּרִי עֹשֶׂה פְּרִי לְמִינוֹ
to-kind-of-him fruit bearing fruit tree seed seed-bearing plant vegetation

אֲשֶׁר זַרְעוֹ־ בוֹ עַל־ הָאָרֶץ וַיְהִי־ כֵן׃ וַתּוֹצֵא
and-she-produced (12) so and-he-was the-land on in-him seed-of-him which

הָאָרֶץ דֶּשֶׁא עֵשֶׂב מַזְרִיעַ זֶרַע לְמִינֵהוּ וְעֵץ
and-tree to-kind-of-him seed seed-bearing plant vegetation the-land

The Beginning

1 In the beginning God
created the heavens and
the earth. [2]Now the earth
was[a] formless and empty,
darkness was over the surface of the deep, and the
Spirit of God was hovering
over the waters.
[3]And God said, "Let there be
light," and there was light.
[4]God saw that the light was
good, and he separated the
light from the darkness.
[5]God called the light "day"
and the darkness he called
"night." And there was
evening, and there was
morning—the first day.
[6]And God said, "Let there be
an expanse between the
waters to separate water
from water." [7]So God
made the expanse and sep-
arated the water under the
expanse from the water
above it. And it was so.
[8]God called the expanse
"sky." And there was eve-
ning, and there was morn-
ing—the second day.
[9]And God said, "Let the water
under the sky be gathered
to one place, and let dry
ground appear." And it
was so. [10]God called the dry
ground "land," and the
gathered waters he called
"seas." And God saw that
it was good.
[11]Then God said, "Let the
land produce vegetation:
seed-bearing plants and
trees on the land that bear
fruit with seed in it, according to their various
kinds." And it was so.
[12]The land produced vegetation: plants bearing seed
according to their kinds
and trees bearing fruit

[a]2 Or possibly *became*

עֹשֶׂה פְּרִי אֲשֶׁר זַרְעוֹ־ בוֹ לְמִינֵהוּ וַיַּרְא אֱלֹהִים
God and-he-saw to-kind-of-him in-him seed-of-him which fruit bearing

כִּי־ טוֹב׃ וַיְהִי־ עֶרֶב וַיְהִי־ בֹקֶר יוֹם שְׁלִישִׁי׃
third day morning and-he-was evening and-he-was (13) good that

וַיֹּאמֶר אֱלֹהִים יְהִי מְאֹרֹת בִּרְקִיעַ הַשָּׁמַיִם לְהַבְדִּיל
to-separate the-sky in-expanse-of lights let-him-be God and-he-said (14)

בֵּין הַיּוֹם וּבֵין הַלָּיְלָה וְהָיוּ לְאֹתֹת וּלְמוֹעֲדִים
and-for-seasons as-signs and-let-them-be the-night and-between the-day between

וּלְיָמִים וְשָׁנִים׃ וְהָיוּ לִמְאוֹרֹת בִּרְקִיעַ הַשָּׁמַיִם
the-sky in-expanse-of for-lights and-let-them-be (15) and-years and-for-days

לְהָאִיר עַל־ הָאָרֶץ וַיְהִי־ כֵן׃ וַיַּעַשׂ אֱלֹהִים אֶת־ שְׁנֵי
two-of *** God and-he-made (16) so and-he-was the-earth on to-give-light

הַמְּאֹרֹת הַגְּדֹלִים אֶת־ הַמָּאוֹר הַגָּדֹל לְמֶמְשֶׁלֶת הַיּוֹם
the-day for-governing-of the-great the-light *** the-great-ones the-lights

וְאֶת־ הַמָּאוֹר הַקָּטֹן לְמֶמְשֶׁלֶת הַלַּיְלָה וְאֵת הַכּוֹכָבִים׃
the-stars also the-night for-governing-of the-less the-light and

וַיִּתֵּן אֹתָם אֱלֹהִים בִּרְקִיעַ הַשָּׁמָיִם לְהָאִיר עַל־ הָאָרֶץ׃
the-earth on to-give-light the-sky in-expanse-of God them and-he-set (17)

וְלִמְשֹׁל בַּיּוֹם וּבַלַּיְלָה וּֽלֲהַבְדִּיל בֵּין
between and-to-separate and-over-the-night over-the-day and-to-govern (18)

הָאוֹר וּבֵין הַחֹשֶׁךְ וַיַּרְא אֱלֹהִים כִּי־ טוֹב׃ וַיְהִי־
and-he-was (19) good that God and-he-saw the-darkness and-between the-light

עֶרֶב וַיְהִי־ בֹקֶר יוֹם רְבִיעִי׃ וַיֹּאמֶר אֱלֹהִים יִשְׁרְצוּ
let-them-teem God and-he-said (20) fourth day morning and-he-was evening

הַמַּיִם שֶׁרֶץ נֶפֶשׁ חַיָּה וְעוֹף יְעוֹפֵף עַל־ הָאָרֶץ
the-earth above let-him-fly and-bird living breath-of creature the-waters

עַל־ פְּנֵי רְקִיעַ הַשָּׁמָיִם׃ וַיִּבְרָא אֱלֹהִים אֶת־ הַתַּנִּינִם
the-sea-creatures *** God so-he-created (21) the-sky expanse-of face-of across

הַגְּדֹלִים וְאֵת כָּל־ נֶפֶשׁ הַחַיָּה ׀ הָרֹמֶשֶׂת אֲשֶׁר שָׁרְצוּ
they-teem which the-moving the-living breath-of every-of and the-great-ones

הַמַּיִם לְמִינֵהֶם וְאֵת כָּל־ עוֹף כָּנָף לְמִינֵהוּ
to-kind-of-him wing bird-of every-of and to-kind-of-them the-waters

וַיַּרְא אֱלֹהִים כִּי־ טוֹב׃ וַיְבָרֶךְ אֹתָם אֱלֹהִים לֵאמֹר פְּרוּ
be-fruitful! to-say God them and-he-blessed (22) good that God and-he-saw

וּרְבוּ וּמִלְאוּ אֶת־ הַמַּיִם בַּיַּמִּים וְהָעוֹף יִרֶב
let-him-increase and-the-bird in-the-seas the-waters *** and-fill! and-increase!

בָּאָרֶץ׃ וַיְהִי־ עֶרֶב וַיְהִי־ בֹקֶר יוֹם חֲמִישִׁי׃ וַיֹּאמֶר
and-he-said (24) fifth day morning and-he-was evening and-he-was (23) on-the-earth

with seed in it according
to their kinds. And God
saw that it was good.
13And there was evening,
and there was morning–
the third day.
14And God said, "Let there be
lights in the expanse of the
sky to separate the day
from the night, and let
them serve as signs to
mark seasons and days
and years, 15and let them
be lights in the expanse of
the sky to give light on the
earth." And it was so.
16God made two great
lights–the greater light to
govern the day and the
lesser light to govern the
night. He also made the
stars. 17God set them in the
expanse of the sky to give
light on the earth, 18to govern the day and the night,
and to separate light from
darkness. And God saw
that it was good. 19And
there was evening, and
there was morning–the
fourth day.
20And God said, "Let the water
teem with living creatures,
and let birds fly above the
earth across the expanse of
the sky." 21So God created
the great creatures of the
sea and every living and
moving thing with which
the water teems, according
to their kinds, and every
winged bird according to
its kind. And God saw that
it was good. 22God blessed
them and said, "Be fruitful
and increase in number
and fill the water in the
seas, and let the birds increase on the earth." 23And
there was evening, and
there was morning–the
fifth day.

אֱלֹהִים תּוֹצֵא הָאָרֶץ נֶפֶשׁ חַיָּה לְמִינָהּ בְּהֵמָה
livestock to-kind-of-her living creature-of the-land let-her-produce God

וָרֶמֶשׂ וְחַיְתוֹ־ אֶרֶץ לְמִינָהּ וַיְהִי־ כֵן: (25) וַיַּעַשׂ
and-he-made (25) so and-he-was to-kind-of-her earth and-animal-of and-crawler

אֱלֹהִים אֶת־ חַיַּת הָאָרֶץ לְמִינָהּ וְאֶת־ הַבְּהֵמָה לְמִינָהּ
to-kind-of-her the-livestock and to-kind-of-her the-earth animal-of *** God

וְאֵת כָּל־ רֶמֶשׂ הָאֲדָמָה לְמִינֵהוּ וַיַּרְא אֱלֹהִים כִּי־טוֹב:
good that God and-he-saw to-kind-of-him the-ground crawler-of every-of and

(26) וַיֹּאמֶר אֱלֹהִים נַעֲשֶׂה אָדָם בְּצַלְמֵנוּ כִּדְמוּתֵנוּ
in-likeness-of-us in-image-of-us man let-us-make God then-he-said (26)

וְיִרְדּוּ בִדְגַת הַיָּם וּבְעוֹף הַשָּׁמַיִם
the-air and-over-bird-of the-sea over-fish-of and-let-them-rule

וּבַבְּהֵמָה וּבְכָל־ הָאָרֶץ וּבְכָל־ הָרֶמֶשׂ
the-crawler and-over-every-of the-earth and-over-all-of and-over-the-livestock

הָרֹמֵשׂ עַל־ הָאָרֶץ: (27) וַיִּבְרָא אֱלֹהִים ׀ אֶת־ הָאָדָם
the-man *** God so-he-created (27) the-ground along the-one-crawling

בְּצַלְמוֹ בְּצֶלֶם אֱלֹהִים בָּרָא אֹתוֹ זָכָר וּנְקֵבָה בָּרָא
he-created and-female male him he-created God in-image-of in-image-of-him

אֹתָם: (28) וַיְבָרֶךְ אֹתָם אֱלֹהִים וַיֹּאמֶר לָהֶם אֱלֹהִים פְּרוּ
be-fruitful! God to-them and-he-said God them and-he-blessed (28) them

וּרְבוּ וּמִלְאוּ אֶת־ הָאָרֶץ וְכִבְשֻׁהָ וּרְדוּ בִּדְגַת
over-fish-of and-rule! and-subdue-her! the-earth *** and-fill! and-increase!

הַיָּם וּבְעוֹף הַשָּׁמַיִם וּבְכָל־ חַיָּה הָרֹמֶשֶׂת עַל־
on the-one-crawling living and-over-every-of the-air and-over-bird-of the-sea

הָאָרֶץ: (29) וַיֹּאמֶר אֱלֹהִים הִנֵּה נָתַתִּי לָכֶם אֶת־ כָּל־ עֵשֶׂב ׀ זֹרֵעַ
seed-bearing plant every-of *** to-you I-give see! God then-he-said (29) the-ground

זֹרֵעַ זֶרַע אֲשֶׁר עַל־ פְּנֵי כָל־ הָאָרֶץ וְאֶת־ כָּל־ הָעֵץ אֲשֶׁר־ בּוֹ
in-it which the-tree every-of and the-earth whole-of face-of on which seed

פְרִי־ עֵץ זֹרֵעַ זָרַע לָכֶם יִהְיֶה לְאָכְלָה: (30) וּלְכָל־
and-to-every-of (30) for-food he-will-be for-you seed seeding tree fruit-of

חַיַּת הָאָרֶץ וּלְכָל־ עוֹף הַשָּׁמַיִם וּלְכֹל ׀ רוֹמֵשׂ
crawling-one and-to-every-of the-air bird-of and-to-every-of the-earth beast-of

עַל־ הָאָרֶץ אֲשֶׁר־ בּוֹ נֶפֶשׁ חַיָּה אֶת־ כָּל־ יֶרֶק עֵשֶׂב לְאָכְלָה
for-food plant green every-of *** life breath-of in-him which the-ground on

וַיְהִי־ כֵן: (31) וַיַּרְא אֱלֹהִים אֶת־כָּל־אֲשֶׁר עָשָׂה וְהִנֵּה־ טוֹב מְאֹד
very good and-see! he-made that all-of *** God and-he-saw (31) so and-he-was

וַיְהִי־ עֶרֶב וַיְהִי־ בֹקֶר יוֹם הַשִּׁשִּׁי: (2:1) וַיְכֻלּוּ
thus-they-were-done (2:1) the-sixth day-of morning and-he-was evening and-he-was

24And God said, "Let the land
produce living creatures
according to their kinds:
livestock, creatures that
move along the ground,
and wild animals, each according to its kind." And it
was so. 25God made the
wild animals according to
their kinds, the livestock
according to their kinds,
and all the creatures that
move along the ground ac-
cording to their kinds.
And God saw that it was
good.

26Then God said, "Let us
make man in our image, in
our likeness, and let them
rule over the fish of the sea
and the birds of the air,
over the livestock, over all
the earth,[b] and over all the
creatures that move along
the ground."

27So God created man in his
own image,
in the image of God he
created him;
male and female he
created them.

28God blessed them and
said to them, "Be fruitful
and increase in number;
fill the earth and subdue it.
Rule over the fish of the
sea and the birds of the air
and over every living creature that moves on the
ground."

29Then God said, "I give
you every seed-bearing
plant on the face of the
whole earth and every tree
that has fruit with seed in
it. They will be yours for
food. 30And to all the beasts
of the earth and all the
birds of the air and all the
creatures that move on the
ground—everything that
has the breath of life in
it—I give every green plant
for food." And it was so.

31God saw all that he had
made, and it was very
good. And there was eve-
ning, and there was morn-
ing—the sixth day.

[b]26 Hebrew; Syriac *all the wild animals*

הַשָּׁמַיִם וְהָאָרֶץ וְכָל־ צְבָאָם׃ וַיְכַל אֱלֹהִים
God and-he-finished (2) array-of-them and-all-of and-the-earth the-heavens

בַּיּוֹם הַשְּׁבִיעִי מְלַאכְתּוֹ אֲשֶׁר עָשָׂה וַיִּשְׁבֹּת בַּיּוֹם
on-the-day and-he-rested he-did which work-of-him the-seventh by-the-day

הַשְּׁבִיעִי מִכָּל־ מְלַאכְתּוֹ אֲשֶׁר עָשָׂה׃ וַיְבָרֶךְ אֱלֹהִים אֶת־
*** God and-he-blessed (3) he-did which work-of-him from-all-of the-seventh

יוֹם הַשְּׁבִיעִי וַיְקַדֵּשׁ אֹתוֹ כִּי בוֹ שָׁבַת מִכָּל־
from-all-of he-rested on-him because him and-he-made-holy the-seventh day-of

מְלַאכְתּוֹ אֲשֶׁר־ בָּרָא אֱלֹהִים לַעֲשׂוֹת׃ אֵלֶּה תוֹלְדוֹת הַשָּׁמַיִם
the-heavens generations-of these (4) to-do God he-created that work-of-him

וְהָאָרֶץ בְּהִבָּרְאָם בְּיוֹם עֲשׂוֹת יְהוָה אֱלֹהִים אֶרֶץ וְשָׁמָיִם׃
and-heavens earth God Yahweh to-make in-day when-to-be-created-them and-the-earth

וְכֹל ׀ שִׂיחַ הַשָּׂדֶה טֶרֶם יִהְיֶה בָאָרֶץ וְכָל־
and-any-of on-the-earth he-appeared not-yet the-field shrub-of and-any-of (5)

עֵשֶׂב הַשָּׂדֶה טֶרֶם יִצְמָח כִּי לֹא הִמְטִיר יְהוָה אֱלֹהִים עַל־
on God Yahweh he-sent-rain not for he-sprung-up not-yet the-field plant-of

הָאָרֶץ וְאָדָם אַיִן לַעֲבֹד אֶת־ הָאֲדָמָה׃ וְאֵד יַעֲלֶה
he-came-up but-stream (6) the-ground *** to-work was-not and-man the-earth

מִן־ הָאָרֶץ וְהִשְׁקָה אֶת־ כָּל־ פְּנֵי־ הָאֲדָמָה׃
the-ground surface-of whole-of *** and-he-watered the-earth from

וַיִּיצֶר יְהוָה אֱלֹהִים אֶת־ הָאָדָם עָפָר מִן־ הָאֲדָמָה וַיִּפַּח
and-he-breathed the-ground from dust the-man *** God Yahweh and-he-formed (7)

בְּאַפָּיו נִשְׁמַת חַיִּים וַיְהִי הָאָדָם לְנֶפֶשׁ חַיָּה׃
living into-being the-man and-he-became life breath-of into-nostrils-of-him

וַיִּטַּע יְהוָה אֱלֹהִים גַּן־ בְּעֵדֶן מִקֶּדֶם וַיָּשֶׂם שָׁם אֶת־
*** there and-he-put in-east in-Eden garden God Yahweh now-he-planted (8)

הָאָדָם אֲשֶׁר יָצָר׃ וַיַּצְמַח יְהוָה אֱלֹהִים מִן־ הָאֲדָמָה
the-ground from God Yahweh and-he-made-grow (9) he-formed whom the-man

כָּל־ עֵץ נֶחְמָד לְמַרְאֶה וְטוֹב לְמַאֲכָל וְעֵץ הַחַיִּים
the-life and-tree-of for-food and-good to-sight being-pleasant tree every-of

בְּתוֹךְ הַגָּן וְעֵץ הַדַּעַת טוֹב וָרָע׃ וְנָהָר
and-river (10) and-evil good the-knowledge and-tree-of the-garden in-middle-of

יֹצֵא מֵעֵדֶן לְהַשְׁקוֹת אֶת־ הַגָּן וּמִשָּׁם יִפָּרֵד
he-divided and-from-there the-garden *** to-water from-Eden flowing

וְהָיָה לְאַרְבָּעָה רָאשִׁים׃ שֵׁם הָאֶחָד פִּישׁוֹן הוּא הַסֹּבֵב
the-one-winding he Pishon the-first name-of (11) headstreams to-four and-he-became

אֵת כָּל־ אֶרֶץ הַחֲוִילָה אֲשֶׁר־ שָׁם הַזָּהָב׃ וּזֲהַב הָאָרֶץ
the-land and-gold-of (12) the-gold there where the-Havilah land-of all-of ***

2 Thus the heavens and
the earth were completed
in all their vast array.

2By the seventh day God had
finished the work he had
been doing; so on the seventh day he rested from all
his work. 3And God
blessed the seventh day
and made it holy, because
on it he rested[c] from all the
work of creating that he
had done.

Adam and Eve

4This is the account of the
heavens and the earth when
they were created.

When the LORD God made
the earth and the heavens, 5no
shrub of the field had yet appeared on the earth[d] and no
plant of the field had yet
sprung up; the LORD God had
not sent rain on the earth[d] and
there was no man to work the
ground, 6but streams[e] came up
from the earth and watered
the whole surface of the
ground. 7And the LORD God
formed man[f] from the dust of
the ground and breathed into
his nostrils the breath of life,
and man became a living being.

8Now the LORD God had
planted a garden in the east, in
Eden; and there he put the
man he had formed. 9And the
LORD God made all kinds of
trees grow out of the ground—
trees that were pleasing to the
eye and good for food. In the
middle of the garden were the
tree of life and the tree of the
knowledge of good and evil.

10A river watering the garden flowed from Eden, and
from there it divided; it had
four headstreams. 11The name
of the first is the Pishon; it
winds through the entire land
of Havilah, where there is
gold. 12(The gold of that land is

[c]3 Or *ceased* [d]5 Or *land*; also in verse 6
[e]6 Or *mist*
[f]7 The Hebrew for *man (adam)* sounds like and may be related to the Hebrew for *ground (adamah)*; it is also the name *Adam* (see Gen. 2:20).

הַהִוא טוֹב שָׁם הַבְּדֹלַח וְאֶבֶן הַשֹּׁהַם׃ וְשֵׁם־הַנָּהָר
the-river and-name-of (13) the-onyx and-stone-of the-resin there good the-that

הַשֵּׁנִי גִּיחוֹן הוּא הַסּוֹבֵב אֵת כָּל־אֶרֶץ כּוּשׁ׃ וְשֵׁם
and-name-of (14) Cush land-of all-of *** the-one-winding he Gihon the-second

הַנָּהָר הַשְּׁלִישִׁי חִדֶּקֶל הוּא הַהֹלֵךְ קִדְמַת אַשּׁוּר וְהַנָּהָר
and-the-river Asshur east-of the-one-running he Tigris the-third the-river

הָרְבִיעִי הוּא פְרָת׃ וַיִּקַּח יְהוָה אֱלֹהִים אֶת־הָאָדָם וַיַּנִּחֵהוּ
and-he-put-him the-man *** God Yahweh and-he-took (15) Euphrates he the-fourth

בְגַן־עֵדֶן לְעָבְדָהּ וּלְשָׁמְרָהּ׃ וַיְצַו יְהוָה
Yahweh and-he-commanded (16) and-to-care-for-her to-work-her Eden in-garden-of

אֱלֹהִים עַל־הָאָדָם לֵאמֹר מִכֹּל עֵץ־הַגָּן אָכֹל תֹּאכֵל׃
you-may-eat to-eat the-garden tree-of from-any-of to-say the-man to God

וּמֵעֵץ הַדַּעַת טוֹב וָרָע לֹא תֹאכַל מִמֶּנּוּ כִּי
for from-him you-must-eat not and-evil good the-knowledge but-from-tree-of (17)

בְּיוֹם אֲכָלְךָ מִמֶּנּוּ מוֹת תָּמוּת׃ וַיֹּאמֶר יְהוָה אֱלֹהִים
God Yahweh and-he-said (18) you-will-die to-die from-him to-eat-you in-day-of

לֹא־טוֹב הֱיוֹת הָאָדָם לְבַדּוֹ אֶעֱשֶׂהּ־* לּוֹ עֵזֶר כְּנֶגְדּוֹ׃
to-suit-him helper for-him I-will-make alone the-man to-be good not

וַיִּצֶר יְהוָה אֱלֹהִים מִן־הָאֲדָמָה כָּל־חַיַּת הַשָּׂדֶה
the-field beast-of every-of the-ground from God Yahweh now-he-formed (19)

וְאֵת כָּל־עוֹף הַשָּׁמַיִם וַיָּבֵא אֶל־הָאָדָם לִרְאוֹת מַה־
what to-see the-man to and-he-brought the-air bird-of every-of and

יִּקְרָא־לוֹ וְכֹל אֲשֶׁר יִקְרָא־לוֹ הָאָדָם נֶפֶשׁ חַיָּה
living creature the-man to-him he-named which and-all to-him he-would-name

הוּא שְׁמוֹ׃ וַיִּקְרָא הָאָדָם שֵׁמוֹת לְכָל־הַבְּהֵמָה
the-livestock to-all-of names the-man so-he-named (20) name-of-him that

וּלְעוֹף הַשָּׁמַיִם וּלְכֹל חַיַּת הַשָּׂדֶה וּלְאָדָם לֹא־
not but-for-Adam the-field beast-of and-to-every-of the-air and-to-bird-of

מָצָא עֵזֶר כְּנֶגְדּוֹ׃ וַיַּפֵּל יְהוָה אֱלֹהִים ׀ תַּרְדֵּמָה עַל־
upon deep-sleep God Yahweh so-he-made-fall (21) to-suit-him helper he-found

הָאָדָם וַיִּישָׁן וַיִּקַּח אַחַת מִצַּלְעֹתָיו וַיִּסְגֹּר בָּשָׂר
flesh and-he-closed from-ribs-of-him one-of and-he-took and-he-slept the-man

תַּחְתֶּנָּה׃ וַיִּבֶן יְהוָה אֱלֹהִים ׀ אֶת־הַצֵּלָע אֲשֶׁר־לָקַח מִן־
from he-took which the-rib *** God Yahweh then-he-made (22) place-of-her

הָאָדָם לְאִשָּׁה וַיְבִאֶהָ אֶל־הָאָדָם׃ וַיֹּאמֶר הָאָדָם
the-man and-he-said (23) the-man to and-he-brought-her into-woman the-man

זֹאת הַפַּעַם עֶצֶם מֵעֲצָמַי וּבָשָׂר מִבְּשָׂרִי לְזֹאת
to-this from-flesh-of-me and-flesh from-bones-of-me bone the-now this

good; aromatic resin[g] and
onyx are also there.) 13The
name of the second river is the
Gihon; it winds through the
entire land of Cush.[h] 14The
name of the third river is the
Tigris; it runs along the east
side of Asshur. And the fourth
river is the Euphrates.
15The LORD God took the
man and put him in the Garden of Eden to work it and
take care of it. 16And the LORD
God commanded the man,
"You are free to eat from any
tree in the garden; 17but you
must not eat from the tree of
the knowledge of good and
evil, for when you eat of it you
will surely die."
18The LORD God said, "It is
not good for the man to be
alone. I will make a helper
suitable for him."
19Now the LORD God had
formed out of the ground all
the beasts of the field and all
the birds of the air. He
brought them to the man to
see what he would name
them; and whatever the man
called each living creature,
that was its name. 20So the
man gave names to all the
livestock, the birds of the air
and all the beasts of the field.
But for Adam[i] no suitable
helper was found. 21So the
LORD God caused the man to
fall into a deep sleep; and
while he was sleeping, he took
one of the man's ribs[j] and
closed up the place with flesh.
22Then the LORD God made a
woman from the rib[k] he had
taken out of the man, and he
brought her to the man.
23The man said,

"This is now bone of my
bones
and flesh of my flesh;

g12 Or *good; pearls*
h13 Possibly southeast Mesopotamia
i20 Or *man*
j21 Or *took part of the man's side*
k22 Or *part*

*18 Most mss have no *mappiq* in the *he* (הָ).

יִקָּרֵא אִשָּׁה כִּי מֵאִישׁ לֻקֳחָה־ זֹּאת׃ עַל־ כֵּן
this for (24) this she-was-taken from-man for woman he-shall-be-called

יַעֲזָב־ אִישׁ אֶת־ אָבִיו וְאֶת־ אִמּוֹ וְדָבַק
and-he-will-unite mother-of-him and father-of-him *** man he-will-leave

בְּאִשְׁתּוֹ וְהָיוּ לְבָשָׂר אֶחָד׃ וַיִּהְיוּ שְׁנֵיהֶם
both-of-them and-they-were (25) one as-flesh and-they-will-be to-wife-of-him

עֲרוּמִּים הָאָדָם וְאִשְׁתּוֹ וְלֹא יִתְבֹּשָׁשׁוּ׃ וְהַנָּחָשׁ
now-the-serpent (3:1) they-felt-shame and-not and-wife-of-him the-man naked-ones

הָיָה עָרוּם מִכֹּל חַיַּת הַשָּׂדֶה אֲשֶׁר עָשָׂה יְהוָה אֱלֹהִים
God Yahweh he-made which the-field animal-of more-than-all-of crafty he-was

וַיֹּאמֶר אֶל־ הָאִשָּׁה אַף כִּי־ אָמַר אֱלֹהִים לֹא תֹאכְלוּ מִכֹּל
from-any-of you-must-eat not God he-said really indeed the-woman to and-he-said

עֵץ הַגָּן׃ וַתֹּאמֶר הָאִשָּׁה אֶל־ הַנָּחָשׁ מִפְּרִי
from-fruit-of the-serpent to the-woman and-she-said (2) the-garden tree-of

עֵץ־ הַגָּן נֹאכֵל׃ וּמִפְּרִי הָעֵץ אֲשֶׁר בְּתוֹךְ־
in-middle-of that the-tree but-from-fruit-of (3) we-may-eat the-garden tree-of

הַגָּן אָמַר אֱלֹהִים לֹא תֹאכְלוּ מִמֶּנּוּ וְלֹא תִגְּעוּ
you-must-touch and-not from-him you-must-eat not God he-said the-garden

בּוֹ פֶּן־ תְּמֻתוּן׃ וַיֹּאמֶר הַנָּחָשׁ אֶל־ הָאִשָּׁה לֹא־ מוֹת
to-die not the-woman to the-serpent and-he-said (4) you-will-die or on-him

תְּמֻתוּן׃ כִּי יֹדֵעַ אֱלֹהִים כִּי בְּיוֹם אֲכָלְכֶם מִמֶּנּוּ
from-him to-eat-you in-day that God knowing for (5) you-will-die

וְנִפְקְחוּ עֵינֵיכֶם וִהְיִיתֶם כֵּאלֹהִים יֹדְעֵי טוֹב
good knowing-of like-God and-you-will-be eyes-of-you and-they-will-be-opened

וָרָע׃ וַתֵּרֶא הָאִשָּׁה כִּי טוֹב הָעֵץ לְמַאֲכָל וְכִי
and-that for-food the-tree good that the-woman and-she-saw (6) and-evil

תַאֲוָה־ הוּא לָעֵינַיִם וְנֶחְמָד הָעֵץ לְהַשְׂכִּיל וַתִּקַּח
and-she-took to-gain-wisdom the-tree and-being-desirable to-the-eyes he pleasant

מִפִּרְיוֹ וַתֹּאכַל וַתִּתֵּן גַּם־ לְאִישָׁהּ עִמָּהּ
with-her to-husband-of-her also and-she-gave and-she-ate from-fruit-of-him

וַיֹּאכַל׃ וַתִּפָּקַחְנָה עֵינֵי שְׁנֵיהֶם וַיֵּדְעוּ כִּי
that and-they-realized both-of-them eyes-of and-they-were-opened (7) and-he-ate

עֵירֻמִּם הֵם וַיִּתְפְּרוּ עֲלֵה תְאֵנָה וַיַּעֲשׂוּ לָהֶם
for-themselves and-they-made fig leaf-of and-they-sewed they naked-ones

חֲגֹרֹת׃ וַיִּשְׁמְעוּ אֶת־ קוֹל יְהוָה אֱלֹהִים מִתְהַלֵּךְ בַּגָּן
in-the-garden walking God Yahweh sound-of *** then-they-heard (8) coverings

לְרוּחַ הַיּוֹם וַיִּתְחַבֵּא הָאָדָם וְאִשְׁתּוֹ מִפְּנֵי יְהוָה אֱלֹהִים
God Yahweh from-face-of and-wife-of-him the-man and-he-hid the-day in-cool-of

she shall be called
'woman,[l]'
for she was taken out of
man."

[24]For this reason a man will
leave his father and mother
and be united to his wife, and
they will become one flesh.
[25]The man and his wife were
both naked, and they felt no
shame.

The Fall of Man

3 Now the serpent was
more crafty than any of
the wild animals the LORD God
had made. He said to the
woman, "Did God really say,
'You must not eat from any
tree in the garden'?"
[2]The woman said to the serpent, "We may eat fruit from
the trees in the garden, [3]but
God did say, 'You must not eat
fruit from the tree that is in the
middle of the garden, and you
must not touch it, or you will
die.' "
[4]"You will not surely die,"
the serpent said to the woman.
[5]"For God knows that when
you eat of it your eyes will be
opened, and you will be like
God, knowing good and evil."
[6]When the woman saw that
the fruit of the tree was good
for food and pleasing to the
eye, and also desirable for
gaining wisdom, she took
some and ate it. She also gave
some to her husband, who
was with her, and he ate it.
[7]Then the eyes of both of them
were opened, and they realized they were naked; so they
sewed fig leaves together and
made coverings for them-
selves.
[8]Then the man and his wife
heard the sound of the LORD
God as he was walking in the
garden in the cool of the day,
and they hid from the LORD

[l]23 The Hebrew for *woman* sounds like the Hebrew for *man*.

בְּתוֹךְ עֵץ הַגָּן׃ (9) וַיִּקְרָא יְהוָה אֱלֹהִים אֶל־הָאָדָם וַיֹּאמֶר
and-he-said the-man to God Yahweh but-he-called (9) the-garden tree-of among

לוֹ אַיֶּכָּה׃ (10) וַיֹּאמֶר אֶת־קֹלְךָ שָׁמַעְתִּי בַּגָּן
in-the-garden I-heard sound-of-you *** and-he-answered (10) where-you? to-him

וָאִירָא כִּי־עֵירֹם אָנֹכִי וָאֵחָבֵא׃ (11) וַיֹּאמֶר מִי הִגִּיד לְךָ
to-you he-told who? and-he-said (11) so-I-hid I naked because and-I-was-afraid

כִּי עֵירֹם אָתָּה הֲמִן־הָעֵץ אֲשֶׁר צִוִּיתִיךָ לְבִלְתִּי אֲכָל־מִמֶּנּוּ
from-him to-eat not I-commanded-you that the-tree from? you naked that

אָכָלְתָּ׃ (12) וַיֹּאמֶר הָאָדָם הָאִשָּׁה אֲשֶׁר נָתַתָּה עִמָּדִי הִוא נָתְנָה־
she-gave she with-me you-put whom the-woman the-man and-he-said (12) you-ate

לִּי מִן־הָעֵץ וָאֹכֵל׃ (13) וַיֹּאמֶר יְהוָה אֱלֹהִים לָאִשָּׁה מַה־
what? to-the-woman God Yahweh and-he-said (13) and-I-ate the-tree from to-me

זֹּאת עָשִׂית וַתֹּאמֶר הָאִשָּׁה הַנָּחָשׁ הִשִּׁיאַנִי וָאֹכֵל׃
and-I-ate he-deceived-me the-serpent the-woman and-she-said you-did this

(14) וַיֹּאמֶר יְהוָה אֱלֹהִים ׀ אֶל־הַנָּחָשׁ כִּי עָשִׂיתָ זֹּאת אָרוּר
being-cursed this you-did because the-serpent to God Yahweh and-he-said (14)

אַתָּה מִכָּל־הַבְּהֵמָה וּמִכֹּל חַיַּת הַשָּׂדֶה עַל־גְּחֹנְךָ
belly-of-you on the-field animal-of and-above-all the-livestock above-all-of you

תֵלֵךְ וְעָפָר תֹּאכַל כָּל־יְמֵי חַיֶּיךָ׃ (15) וְאֵיבָה ׀
and-enmity (15) life-of-you days-of all-of you-will-eat and-dust you-will-crawl

אָשִׁית בֵּינְךָ וּבֵין הָאִשָּׁה וּבֵין זַרְעֲךָ
offspring-of-you and-between the-woman and-between between-you I-will-put

וּבֵין זַרְעָהּ הוּא יְשׁוּפְךָ רֹאשׁ וְאַתָּה תְּשׁוּפֶנּוּ
you-will-strike-him and-you head he-will-crush-you he offspring-of-her and-between

עָקֵב׃ (16) אֶל־הָאִשָּׁה אָמַר הַרְבָּה אַרְבֶּה עִצְּבוֹנֵךְ
pain-of-you I-will-increase to-increase he-said the-woman to (16) heel

וְהֵרֹנֵךְ בְּעֶצֶב תֵּלְדִי בָנִים וְאֶל־אִישֵׁךְ
husband-of-you and-to children you-will-bear in-pain and-childbearing-of-you

תְּשׁוּקָתֵךְ וְהוּא יִמְשָׁל־בָּךְ׃ (17) וּלְאָדָם אָמַר כִּי
because he-said and-to-Adam (17) over-you he-will-rule and-he desire-of-you

שָׁמַעְתָּ לְקוֹל אִשְׁתֶּךָ וַתֹּאכַל מִן־הָעֵץ אֲשֶׁר
which the-tree from and-you-ate wife-of-you to-voice-of you-listened

צִוִּיתִיךָ לֵאמֹר לֹא תֹאכַל מִמֶּנּוּ אֲרוּרָה הָאֲדָמָה
the-ground being-cursed from-him you-must-eat not to-say I-commanded-you

בַּעֲבוּרֶךָ בְּעִצָּבוֹן תֹּאכֲלֶנָּה כֹּל יְמֵי חַיֶּיךָ׃
life-of-you days-of all-of you-will-eat-her by-painful-toil because-of-you

(18) וְקוֹץ וְדַרְדַּר תַּצְמִיחַ לָךְ וְאָכַלְתָּ אֶת־עֵשֶׂב
plant-of *** and-you-will-eat for-you she-will-produce and-thistle and-thorn (18)

God among the trees of the
garden. 9 But the LORD God
called to the man, "Where are
you?"
10 He answered, "I heard you
in the garden, and I was afraid
because I was naked; so I hid."
11 And he said, "Who told
you that you were naked?
Have you eaten from the tree
that I commanded you not to
eat from?"
12 The man said, "The
woman you put here with
me—she gave me some fruit
from the tree, and I ate it."
13 Then the LORD God said to
the woman, "What is this you
have done?"

The woman said, "The ser-
pent deceived me, and I ate."
14 So the LORD God said to the
serpent, "Because you have
done this,

"Cursed are you above all
the livestock
and all the wild animals!
You will crawl on your
belly
and you will eat dust
all the days of your life.
15 And I will put enmity
between you and the
woman,
and between your
offspring[m] and hers;
he will crush[n] your head,
and you will strike his
heel."

16 To the woman he said,

"I will greatly increase
your pains in
childbearing;
with pain you will give
birth to children.
Your desire will be for your
husband,
and he will rule over
you."

17 To Adam he said, "Because
you listened to your wife and
ate from the tree about which
I commanded you, 'You must
not eat of it,'

"Cursed is the ground
because of you;
through painful toil you
will eat of it
all the days of your life.
18 It will produce thorns and
thistles for you,
and you will eat the
plants of the field.

[m] 15 Or *seed* [n] 15 Or *strike*

הַשָּׂדֶה׃ בְּזֵעַת אַפֶּיךָ תֹּאכַל לֶחֶם עַד שׁוּבְךָ
to-return-you until food you-will-eat brow-of-you by-sweat-of (19) the-field

אֶל־הָאֲדָמָה כִּי מִמֶּנָּה לֻקָּחְתָּ כִּי־עָפָר אַתָּה וְאֶל־עָפָר
dust and-to you dust for you-were-taken from-her since the-ground to

תָּשׁוּב׃ וַיִּקְרָא הָאָדָם שֵׁם אִשְׁתּוֹ חַוָּה כִּי הִוא
she because Eve wife-of-him name-of the-man and-he-named (20) you-will-return

הָיְתָה אֵם כָּל־חָי׃ וַיַּעַשׂ יְהוָה אֱלֹהִים לְאָדָם
for-Adam God Yahweh and-he-made (21) living all-of mother-of she-would-be

וּלְאִשְׁתּוֹ כָּתְנוֹת עוֹר וַיַּלְבִּשֵׁם׃ וַיֹּאמֶר׀
and-he-said (22) and-he-clothed-them skin garments-of and-for-wife-of-him

יְהוָה אֱלֹהִים הֵן הָאָדָם הָיָה כְּאַחַד מִמֶּנּוּ לָדַעַת טוֹב וָרָע
and-evil good to-know from-us like-one-of he-became the-man see! God Yahweh

וְעַתָּה׀ פֶּן־יִשְׁלַח יָדוֹ וְלָקַח גַּם מֵעֵץ הַחַיִּים
the-life from-tree-of also and-he-take hand-of-him he-reach-out lest and-now

וְאָכַל וָחַי לְעֹלָם׃ וַיְשַׁלְּחֵהוּ יְהוָה אֱלֹהִים מִגַּן־
from-garden-of God Yahweh so-he-sent-him (23) for-ever and-he-live and-he-eat

עֵדֶן לַעֲבֹד אֶת־הָאֲדָמָה אֲשֶׁר לֻקַּח מִשָּׁם׃ וַיְגָרֶשׁ
and-he-drove-out (24) from-there he-was-taken which the-ground *** to-work Eden

אֶת־הָאָדָם וַיַּשְׁכֵּן מִקֶּדֶם לְגַן־עֵדֶן אֶת־הַכְּרֻבִים וְאֵת
and the-cherubim *** Eden to-garden-of on-east and-he-placed the-man ***

לַהַט הַחֶרֶב הַמִּתְהַפֶּכֶת לִשְׁמֹר אֶת־דֶּרֶךְ עֵץ הַחַיִּים׃
the-life tree-of way-of *** to-guard the-one-flashing-around the-sword flame-of

וְהָאָדָם יָדַע אֶת־חַוָּה אִשְׁתּוֹ וַתַּהַר וַתֵּלֶד
and-she-bore and-she-conceived wife-of-him Eve *** he-knew and-the-man (4:1)

אֶת־קַיִן וַתֹּאמֶר קָנִיתִי אִישׁ אֶת־יְהוָה׃ וַתֹּסֶף
and-she-continued (2) Yahweh with man I-brought-forth and-she-said Cain ***

לָלֶדֶת אֶת־אָחִיו אֶת־הָבֶל וַיְהִי־הֶבֶל רֹעֵה צֹאן וְקַיִן
and-Cain flock keeping-of Abel now-he-was Abel *** brother-of-him *** to-bear

הָיָה עֹבֵד אֲדָמָה׃ וַיְהִי מִקֵּץ יָמִים וַיָּבֵא קַיִן
Cain and-he-brought days in-course-of and-he-was (3) soil working-of he-was

מִפְּרִי הָאֲדָמָה מִנְחָה לַיהוָה׃ וְהֶבֶל הֵבִיא גַם־הוּא
he also he-brought but-Abel (4) to-Yahweh offering the-soil from-fruit-of

מִבְּכֹרוֹת צֹאנוֹ וּמֵחֶלְבֵהֶן וַיִּשַׁע יְהוָה
Yahweh and-he-had-favor and-from-fat-of-them flock-of-him from-firstborn-of

אֶל־הֶבֶל וְאֶל־מִנְחָתוֹ׃ וְאֶל־קַיִן וְאֶל־מִנְחָתוֹ לֹא
not offering-of-him and-on Cain but-on (5) offering-of-him and-on Abel on

שָׁעָה וַיִּחַר לְקַיִן מְאֹד וַיִּפְּלוּ פָּנָיו׃
faces-of-him and-they-were-downcast very to-Cain so-he-was-angry he-had-favor

19By the sweat of your brow
you will eat your food
until you return to the
ground,
since from it you were
taken;
for dust you are
and to dust you will
return."

20Adam[o] named his wife
Eve,[p] because she would
become the mother of all the
living.
21The LORD God made gar-
ments of skin for Adam and
his wife and clothed them.
22And the LORD God said, "The
man has now become like one
of us, knowing good and evil.
He must not be allowed to
reach out his hand and take
also from the tree of life and
eat, and live forever." 23So the
LORD God banished him from
the Garden of Eden to work
the ground from which he had
been taken. 24After he drove
the man out, he placed on the
east side[q] of the Garden of
Eden cherubim and a flaming
sword flashing back and forth
to guard the way to the tree of
life.

Cain and Abel

4 Adam[o] lay with his wife
Eve, and she conceived
and gave birth to Cain.[r] She
said, "With the help of the
LORD I have brought forth[s] a
man." 2Later she gave birth to
his brother Abel.
Now Abel kept flocks, and
Cain worked the soil. 3In the
course of time Cain brought
some of the fruits of the soil as
an offering to the LORD. 4But
Abel brought fat portions from
some of the firstborn of his
flock. The LORD looked with
favor on Abel and his offering,
5but on Cain and his offering
he did not look with favor. So
Cain was very angry, and his
face was downcast.

[o]20,1 Or *The man* [p]20 *Eve* means *living.*
[q]24 Or *placed in front*
[r]1 *Cain* sounds like the Hebrew for *brought forth* or *acquired.*
[s]1 Or *have acquired*

וַיֹּאמֶר יְהוָה אֶל־קָיִן לָמָּה חָרָה לָךְ וְלָמָּה
and-why? to-you is-he-angry why? Cain to Yahweh then-he-said (6)

נָפְלוּ פָנֶיךָ׃ הֲלוֹא אִם־תֵּיטִיב שְׂאֵת
to-be-accepted you-do-right if not? (7) faces-of-you are-they-downcast

וְאִם לֹא תֵיטִיב לַפֶּתַח חַטָּאת רֹבֵץ וְאֵלֶיךָ תְּשׁוּקָתוֹ
desire-of-him and-for-you crouching sin at-the-door you-do-right not but-if

וְאַתָּה תִּמְשָׁל־בּוֹ׃ וַיֹּאמֶר קַיִן אֶל־הֶבֶל אָחִיו
brother-of-him Abel to Cain now-he-said (8) over-him you-must-master but-you

[נֵלְכָה הַשָּׂדֶה]* וַיְהִי בִּהְיוֹתָם בַּשָּׂדֶה
in-the-field while-to-be-them and-he-was *[the-field let-us-go]

וַיָּקָם קַיִן אֶל־הֶבֶל אָחִיו וַיַּהַרְגֵהוּ׃ וַיֹּאמֶר
and-he-said (9) and-he-killed-him brother-of-him Abel at Cain and-he-attacked

יְהוָה אֶל־קַיִן אֵי הֶבֶל אָחִיךָ וַיֹּאמֶר לֹא יָדַעְתִּי
I-know not and-he-replied brother-of-you Abel where? Cain to Yahweh

הֲשֹׁמֵר אָחִי אָנֹכִי׃ וַיֹּאמֶר מֶה עָשִׂיתָ קוֹל
voice-of you-did what? and-he-said (10) I brother-of-me keeping-of?

דְּמֵי אָחִיךָ צֹעֲקִים אֵלַי מִן־הָאֲדָמָה׃ וְעַתָּה
and-now (11) the-ground from to-me ones-crying brother-of-you bloods-of

אָרוּר אָתָּה מִן־הָאֲדָמָה אֲשֶׁר פָּצְתָה אֶת־פִּיהָ לָקַחַת
to-receive mouth-of-her *** she-opened which the-ground from you being-cursed

אֶת־דְּמֵי אָחִיךָ מִיָּדֶךָ׃ כִּי תַעֲבֹד אֶת־הָאֲדָמָה
the-ground *** you-work when (12) from-hand-of-you brother-of-you bloods-of ***

לֹא־תֹסֵף תֵּת־כֹּחָהּ לָךְ נָע וָנָד
and-wandering being-restless to-you crop-of-her to-yield she-will-continue not

תִּהְיֶה בָאָרֶץ׃ וַיֹּאמֶר קַיִן אֶל־יְהוָה גָּדוֹל עֲוֹנִי
punishment-of-me more Yahweh to Cain and-he-said (13) on-the-earth you-will-be

מִנְּשֹׂא׃ הֵן גֵּרַשְׁתָּ אֹתִי הַיּוֹם מֵעַל פְּנֵי הָאֲדָמָה
the-land face-of from-on today me you-drive see! (14) than-to-bear

וּמִפָּנֶיךָ אֶסָּתֵר וְהָיִיתִי נָע
being-restless and-I-will-be I will be hidden and-from-presence-of-you

וָנָד בָּאָרֶץ וְהָיָה כָל־מֹצְאִי יַהַרְגֵנִי׃
he-will-kill-me one-finding-me every-of and-he-will-be on-the-earth and-wandering

וַיֹּאמֶר לוֹ יְהוָה לָכֵן כָּל־הֹרֵג קַיִן שִׁבְעָתַיִם
seven-times Cain killing every-of not-so Yahweh to-him but-he-said (15)

יֻקָּם וַיָּשֶׂם יְהוָה לְקַיִן אוֹת לְבִלְתִּי הַכּוֹת־אֹתוֹ
him to-kill not mark on-Cain Yahweh then-he-put he-will-suffer-vengeance

כָּל־מֹצְאוֹ׃ וַיֵּצֵא קַיִן מִלִּפְנֵי יְהוָה
Yahweh from-presence-of Cain so-he-went-out (16) finding-him every-of

6Then the LORD said to Cain,
"Why are you angry? Why is
your face downcast? 7If you do
what is right, will you not be
accepted? But if you do not do
what is right, sin is crouching
at your door; it desires to have
you, but you must master it."
8Now Cain said to his brother Abel, "Let's go out to the
field."[t] And while they were
in the field, Cain attacked his
brother Abel and killed him.
9Then the LORD said to Cain,
"Where is your brother Abel?"
"I don't know," he replied.
"Am I my brother's keeper?"
10The LORD said, "What have
you done? Listen! Your brother's blood cries out to me from
the ground. 11Now you are under a curse and driven from
the ground, which opened its
mouth to receive your brother's blood from your hand.
12When you work the ground,
it will no longer yield its crops
for you. You will be a restless
wanderer on the earth."
13Cain said to the LORD, "My
punishment is more than I
can bear. 14Today you are driving me from the land, and I
will be hidden from your presence; I will be a restless wanderer on the earth, and whoever finds me will kill me."
15But the LORD said to him,
"Not so"[u]; if anyone kills Cain,
he will suffer vengeance seven
times over." Then the LORD
put a mark on Cain so that no
one who found him would kill
him. 16So Cain went out from
the LORD's presence and lived

[t]8 Samaritan Pentateuch, Septuagint, Vulgate and Syriac; Masoretic Text does not have *"Let's go out to the field."*
[u]15 Septuagint, Vulgate and Syriac; Hebrew *Very well*

***8 This Hebrew reading and translation is conjectured on the basis of the early versions listed above in note *t*.**

וַיֵּשֶׁב בְּאֶרֶץ־ נוֹד קִדְמַת־ עֵדֶן׃ וַיֵּדַע קַיִן אֶת־ אִשְׁתּוֹ
wife-of-him *** Cain and-he-knew (17) Eden east-of Nod in-land-of and-he-lived

וַתַּהַר וַתֵּלֶד אֶת־ חֲנוֹךְ וַיְהִי בֹּנֶה עִיר
city building and-he-was Enoch *** and-she-bore and-she-became-pregnant

וַיִּקְרָא שֵׁם הָעִיר כְּשֵׁם בְּנוֹ חֲנוֹךְ׃ וַיִּוָּלֵד
and-he-was-born (18) Enoch son-of-him after-name-of the-city name-of and-he-called

לַחֲנוֹךְ אֶת־עִירָד וְעִירָד יָלַד אֶת־ מְחוּיָאֵל וּמְחִיָּיאֵל יָלַד
he-fathered and-Mehujael Mehujael *** he-fathered and-Irad Irad *** to-Enoch

אֶת־ מְתוּשָׁאֵל וּמְתוּשָׁאֵל יָלַד אֶת־ לָמֶךְ׃ וַיִּקַּח־
and-he-married (19) Lamech *** he-fathered and-Methushael Methushael ***

לוֹ לֶמֶךְ שְׁתֵּי נָשִׁים שֵׁם הָאַחַת עָדָה וְשֵׁם הַשֵּׁנִית
the-second and-name-of Adah the-one name-of women two-of Lamech for-him

צִלָּה׃ וַתֵּלֶד עָדָה אֶת־ יָבָל הוּא הָיָה אֲבִי יֹשֵׁב אֹהֶל
tent living-of father-of he-was he Jabal *** Adah and-she-bore (20) Zillah

וּמִקְנֶה׃ וְשֵׁם אָחִיו יוּבָל הוּא הָיָה אֲבִי
father-of he-was he Jubal brother-of-him and-name-of (21) and-livestock-raiser

כָּל־ תֹּפֵשׂ כִּנּוֹר וְעוּגָב׃ וְצִלָּה גַם־הִוא יָלְדָה אֶת־תּוּבַל
Tubal *** she-bore she also and-Zillah (22) and-flute harp playing-of every-of

קַיִן לֹטֵשׁ כָּל־ חֹרֵשׁ נְחֹשֶׁת וּבַרְזֶל וַאֲחוֹת תּוּבַל־ קַיִן
Cain Tubal and-sister-of and-iron bronze tooling-of every-of forging Cain

נַעֲמָה׃ וַיֹּאמֶר לֶמֶךְ לְנָשָׁיו עָדָה וְצִלָּה שְׁמַעַן קוֹלִי
voice-of-me listen! and-Zillah Adah to-wives-of-him Lamech and-he-said (23) Naamah

נְשֵׁי לֶמֶךְ הַאְזֵנָּה אִמְרָתִי כִּי אִישׁ הָרַגְתִּי לְפִצְעִי וְיֶלֶד
and-youth for-wound-of-me I-killed man for word-of-me hear! Lamech wives-of

לְחַבֻּרָתִי׃ כִּי שִׁבְעָתַיִם יֻקַּם־ קָיִן וְלֶמֶךְ שִׁבְעִים
seventy then-Lamech Cain he-is-avenged seven-times if (24) for-injury-of-me

וְשִׁבְעָה׃ וַיֵּדַע אָדָם עוֹד אֶת־ אִשְׁתּוֹ וַתֵּלֶד בֵּן
son and-she-bore wife-of-him *** again Adam and-he-knew (25) and-seven

וַתִּקְרָא אֶת־ שְׁמוֹ שֵׁת כִּי שָׁת־ לִי אֱלֹהִים זֶרַע אַחֵר
another child God to-me he-granted for Seth name-of-him *** and-she-called

תַּחַת הֶבֶל כִּי הֲרָגוֹ קָיִן׃ וּלְשֵׁת גַּם־הוּא יֻלַּד־
he-was-born he also and-to-Seth (26) Cain he-killed-him since Abel in-place-of

בֵּן וַיִּקְרָא אֶת־ שְׁמוֹ אֱנוֹשׁ אָז הוּחַל לִקְרֹא בְּשֵׁם
on-name-of to-call he-began then Enosh name-of-him *** and-he-called son

יְהוָה׃ זֶה סֵפֶר תּוֹלְדֹת אָדָם בְּיוֹם בְּרֹא אֱלֹהִים אָדָם בִּדְמוּת
in-likeness-of man God to-create in-day Adam lines-of account-of this (5:1) Yahweh

אֱלֹהִים עָשָׂה אֹתוֹ׃ זָכָר וּנְקֵבָה בְּרָאָם וַיְבָרֶךְ אֹתָם
them and-he-blessed he-created-them and-female male (2) him he-made God

in the land of Nod,[v] east of
Eden.
17Cain lay with his wife, and
she became pregnant and
gave birth to Enoch. Cain was
then building a city, and he
named it after his son Enoch.
18To Enoch was born Irad, and
Irad was the father of Mehujael, and Mehujael was the father of Methushael, and Methushael was the father of Lamech.
19Lamech married two
women, one named Adah and
the other Zillah. 20Adah gave
birth to Jabal; he was the father of those who live in tents
and raise livestock. 21His
brother's name was Jubal; he
was the father of all who play
the harp and flute. 22Zillah also
had a son, Tubal-Cain, who
forged all kinds of tools out of[w]
bronze and iron. Tubal-Cain's
sister was Naamah.
23Lamech said to his wives,

"Adah and Zillah, listen to
me;
wives of Lamech, hear
my words.
I have killed[x] a man for
wounding me,
a young man for injuring
me.
24If Cain is avenged seven
times,
then Lamech
seventy-seven times."

25Adam lay with his wife
again, and she gave birth to a
son and named him Seth,[y]
saying, "God has granted me
another child in place of Abel,
since Cain killed him." 26Seth
also had a son, and he named
him Enosh.
At that time men began to
call on[z] the name of the LORD.

From Adam to Noah

5 This is the written account
of Adam's line.

When God created man, he
made him in the likeness of
God. 2He created them male
and female; at the time they
were created, he blessed them

[v]16 Nod means *wandering* (see verses 12 and 14).
[w]22 Or *who instructed all who work in*
[x]23 Or *I will kill*
[y]25 Seth probably means *granted.*
[z]26 Or *to proclaim*

וַיִּקְרָא אֶת־ שְׁמָם אָדָם בְּיוֹם הִבָּרְאָם׃
to-be-created-them in-day man name-of-them *** and-he-called

וַיְחִי אָדָם שְׁלֹשִׁים וּמְאַת שָׁנָה וַיּוֹלֶד
and-he-fathered year and-hundred-of thirty Adam and-he-lived (3)

בִּדְמוּתוֹ כְּצַלְמוֹ וַיִּקְרָא אֶת־ שְׁמוֹ שֵׁת׃
Seth name-of-him *** and-he-called in-image-of-him in-likeness-of-him

וַיִּהְיוּ יְמֵי־ אָדָם אַחֲרֵי הוֹלִידוֹ אֶת־ שֵׁת שְׁמֹנֶה מֵאֹת
hundreds eight Seth *** to-father-him after Adam days-of and-they-were (4)

שָׁנָה וַיּוֹלֶד בָּנִים וּבָנוֹת׃ וַיִּהְיוּ כָּל־ יְמֵי
days-of all-of and-they-were (5) and-daughters sons and-he-fathered year

אָדָם אֲשֶׁר־ חַי תְּשַׁע מֵאוֹת שָׁנָה וּשְׁלֹשִׁים שָׁנָה וַיָּמֹת׃
then-he-died year and-thirty year hundreds nine life which Adam

וַיְחִי־ שֵׁת חָמֵשׁ שָׁנִים וּמְאַת שָׁנָה וַיּוֹלֶד אֶת־
*** and-he-fathered year and-hundred years five Seth and-he-lived (6)

אֱנוֹשׁ׃ וַיְחִי־ שֵׁת אַחֲרֵי הוֹלִידוֹ אֶת־ אֱנוֹשׁ שֶׁבַע שָׁנִים
years seven Enosh *** to-father-him after Seth and-he-lived (7) Enosh

וּשְׁמֹנֶה מֵאוֹת שָׁנָה וַיּוֹלֶד בָּנִים וּבָנוֹת׃
and-daughters sons and-he-fathered year hundreds and-eight

וַיִּהְיוּ כָּל־ יְמֵי־ שֵׁת שְׁתֵּים עֶשְׂרֵה שָׁנָה וּתְשַׁע מֵאוֹת שָׁנָה
year hundreds and-nine year ten two Seth days-of all-of and-they-were (8)

וַיָּמֹת׃ וַיְחִי אֱנוֹשׁ תִּשְׁעִים שָׁנָה וַיּוֹלֶד אֶת־ קֵינָן׃
Kenan *** and-he-fathered year ninety Enosh and-he-lived (9) then-he-died

וַיְחִי אֱנוֹשׁ אַחֲרֵי הוֹלִידוֹ אֶת־ קֵינָן חֲמֵשׁ עֶשְׂרֵה שָׁנָה
year ten five Kenan *** to-father-him after Enosh and-he-lived (10)

וּשְׁמֹנֶה מֵאוֹת שָׁנָה וַיּוֹלֶד בָּנִים וּבָנוֹת׃
and-daughters sons and-he-fathered year hundreds and-eight

וַיִּהְיוּ כָּל־ יְמֵי אֱנוֹשׁ חָמֵשׁ שָׁנִים וּתְשַׁע מֵאוֹת שָׁנָה
year hundreds and-nine years five Enosh days-of all-of and-they-were (11)

וַיָּמֹת׃ וַיְחִי קֵינָן שִׁבְעִים שָׁנָה וַיּוֹלֶד אֶת־
*** and-he-fathered year seventy Kenan and-he-lived (12) then-he-died

מַהֲלַלְאֵל׃ וַיְחִי קֵינָן אַחֲרֵי הוֹלִידוֹ אֶת־מַהֲלַלְאֵל אַרְבָּעִים
forty Mahalalel *** to-father-him after Kenan and-he-lived (13) Mahalalel

שָׁנָה וּשְׁמֹנֶה מֵאוֹת שָׁנָה וַיּוֹלֶד בָּנִים וּבָנוֹת׃
and-daughters sons and-he-fathered year hundreds and-eight year

וַיִּהְיוּ כָּל־ יְמֵי קֵינָן עֶשֶׂר שָׁנִים וּתְשַׁע מֵאוֹת שָׁנָה
year hundreds and-nine years ten Kenan days-of all-of and-they-were (14)

וַיָּמֹת׃ וַיְחִי מַהֲלַלְאֵל חָמֵשׁ שָׁנִים וְשִׁשִּׁים שָׁנָה
year and-sixty years five Mahalalel and-he-lived (15) then-he-died

and called them "man.[a]"
[3]When Adam had lived 130
years, he had a son in his own
likeness, in his own image;
and he named him Seth. [4]Af-
ter Seth was born, Adam lived
800 years and had other sons
and daughters. [5]Altogether,
Adam lived 930 years, and
then he died.
[6]When Seth had lived 105
years, he became the father[b] of
Enosh. [7]And after he became
the father of Enosh, Seth lived
807 years and had other sons
and daughters. [8]Altogether,
Seth lived 912 years, and then
he died.
[9]When Enosh had lived 90
years, he became the father of
Kenan. [10]And after he became
the father of Kenan, Enosh
lived 815 years and had other
sons and daughters. [11]Alto-
gether, Enosh lived 905 years,
and then he died.
[12]When Kenan had lived 70
years, he became the father of
Mahalalel. [13]And after he
became the father of Mahalalel, Kenan lived 840 years and
had other sons and daughters.
[14]Altogether, Kenan lived 910
years, and then he died.
[15]When Mahalalel had lived

[a]2 Hebrew *adam*
[b]6 *Father* may mean *ancestor*; also in verses 7-26.

וַיּוֹלֶד אֶת־ יָרֶד׃ וַיְחִי מַהֲלַלְאֵל אַחֲרֵי הוֹלִידוֹ
to-father-him after Mahalalel and-he-lived (16) Jared *** and-he-fathered

אֶת־ יֶרֶד שְׁלֹשִׁים שָׁנָה וּשְׁמֹנֶה מֵאוֹת שָׁנָה וַיּוֹלֶד בָּנִים
sons and-he-fathered year hundreds and-eight year thirty Jared ***

וּבָנוֹת׃ וַיִּהְיוּ כָּל־ יְמֵי מַהֲלַלְאֵל חָמֵשׁ וְתִשְׁעִים
and-ninety five Mahalalel days-of all-of and-they-were (17) and-daughters

שָׁנָה וּשְׁמֹנֶה מֵאוֹת שָׁנָה וַיָּמֹת׃ וַיְחִי־ יֶרֶד שְׁתַּיִם
two Jared and-he-lived (18) and-he-died year hundreds and-eight year

וְשִׁשִּׁים שָׁנָה וּמְאַת שָׁנָה וַיּוֹלֶד אֶת־ חֲנוֹךְ׃ וַיְחִי־
and-he-lived (19) Enoch *** and-he-fathered year and-hundred-of year and-sixty

יֶרֶד אַחֲרֵי הוֹלִידוֹ אֶת־ חֲנוֹךְ שְׁמֹנֶה מֵאוֹת שָׁנָה וַיּוֹלֶד בָּנִים
sons and-he-fathered year hundreds eight Enoch *** to-father-him after Jared

וּבָנוֹת׃ וַיִּהְיוּ כָּל־ יְמֵי־ יֶרֶד שְׁתַּיִם וְשִׁשִּׁים שָׁנָה
year and-sixty two Jared days-of all-of and-they-were (20) and-daughters

וּתְשַׁע מֵאוֹת שָׁנָה וַיָּמֹת׃ וַיְחִי חֲנוֹךְ חָמֵשׁ וְשִׁשִּׁים
and-sixty five Enoch and-he-lived (21) then-he-died year hundreds and-nine

שָׁנָה וַיּוֹלֶד אֶת־ מְתוּשָׁלַח׃ וַיִּתְהַלֵּךְ חֲנוֹךְ אֶת־הָאֱלֹהִים אַחֲרֵי
after the-God with Enoch and-he-walked (22) Methuselah *** and-he-fathered year

הוֹלִידוֹ אֶת־ מְתוּשֶׁלַח שְׁלֹשׁ מֵאוֹת שָׁנָה וַיּוֹלֶד בָּנִים
sons and-he-fathered year hundreds three Methuselah *** to-father-him

וּבָנוֹת׃ וַיְהִי כָּל־ יְמֵי חֲנוֹךְ חָמֵשׁ וְשִׁשִּׁים שָׁנָה
year and-sixty five Enoch days-of all-of and-he-was (23) and-daughters

וּשְׁלֹשׁ מֵאוֹת שָׁנָה׃ וַיִּתְהַלֵּךְ חֲנוֹךְ אֶת־הָאֱלֹהִים וְאֵינֶנּוּ
then-he-was-not the-God with Enoch and-he-walked (24) year hundreds and-three

כִּי־ לָקַח אֹתוֹ אֱלֹהִים׃ וַיְחִי מְתוּשֶׁלַח שֶׁבַע וּשְׁמֹנִים שָׁנָה
year and-eighty seven Methuselah and-he-lived (25) God him he-took because

וּמְאַת שָׁנָה וַיּוֹלֶד אֶת־ לָמֶךְ׃ וַיְחִי מְתוּשֶׁלַח
Methuselah and-he-lived (26) Lamech *** and-he-fathered year and-hundred-of

אַחֲרֵי הוֹלִידוֹ אֶת־ לֶמֶךְ שְׁתַּיִם וּשְׁמוֹנִים שָׁנָה וּשְׁבַע מֵאוֹת שָׁנָה
year hundreds and-seven year and-eighty two Lamech *** to-father-him after

וַיּוֹלֶד בָּנִים וּבָנוֹת׃ וַיִּהְיוּ כָּל־ יְמֵי
days-of all-of and-they-were (27) and-daughters sons and-he-fathered

מְתוּשֶׁלַח תֵּשַׁע וְשִׁשִּׁים שָׁנָה וּתְשַׁע מֵאוֹת שָׁנָה וַיָּמֹת׃
then-he-died year hundreds and-nine year and-sixty nine Methuselah

וַיְחִי־ לֶמֶךְ שְׁתַּיִם וּשְׁמֹנִים שָׁנָה וּמְאַת שָׁנָה וַיּוֹלֶד
and-he-fathered year and-hundred-of year and-eighty two Lamech and-he-lived (28)

בֵּן׃ וַיִּקְרָא אֶת־ שְׁמוֹ נֹחַ לֵאמֹר זֶה יְנַחֲמֵנוּ
he-will-comfort-us this to-say Noah name-of-him *** and-he-called (29) son

65 years, he became the father
of Jared. [16]And after he became
the father of Jared, Mahalalel
lived 830 years and had other
sons and daughters. [17]Alto-
gether, Mahalalel lived 895
years, and then he died.
[18]When Jared had lived 162
years, he became the father of
Enoch. [19]And after he became
the father of Enoch, Jared
lived 800 years and had other
sons and daughters. [20]Alto-
gether, Jared lived 962 years,
and then he died.
[21]When Enoch had lived 65
years, he became the father of
Methuselah. [22]And after he
became the father of Me-
thuselah, Enoch walked with
God 300 years and had other
sons and daughters. [23]Alto-
gether, Enoch lived 365 years.
[24]Enoch walked with God;
then he was no more, because
God took him away.
[25]When Methuselah had
lived 187 years, he became the
father of Lamech. [26]And after
he became the father of Lamech, Methuselah lived 782
years and had other sons and
daughters. [27]Altogether, Methuselah lived 969 years, and
then he died.
[28]When Lamech had lived
182 years, he had a son. [29]He
named him Noah[c] and said,

[c]29 *Noah* sounds like the Hebrew for *comfort*.

מִמַּעֲשֵׂנוּ וּמֵעִצְּבוֹן יָדֵינוּ מִן־הָאֲדָמָה אֲשֶׁר אֵרְרָהּ
he-cursed-her which the-ground from hands-of-us and-in-toil-of in-labors-of-us

יְהוָה׃ וַיְחִי־לֶמֶךְ אַחֲרֵי הוֹלִידוֹ אֶת־נֹחַ חָמֵשׁ וְתִשְׁעִים
and-ninety five Noah *** to-father-him after Lamech and-he-lived (30) Yahweh

שָׁנָה וַחֲמֵשׁ מֵאֹת שָׁנָה וַיּוֹלֶד בָּנִים וּבָנוֹת׃ וַיְהִי
and-he-was (31) and-daughters sons and-he-fathered year hundreds and-five year

כָּל־יְמֵי־לֶמֶךְ שֶׁבַע וְשִׁבְעִים שָׁנָה וּשְׁבַע מֵאוֹת שָׁנָה
year hundreds and-seven year and-seventy seven Lamech days-of all-of

וַיָּמֹת׃ וַיְהִי־נֹחַ בֶּן־חֲמֵשׁ מֵאוֹת שָׁנָה וַיּוֹלֶד
and-he-fathered year hundreds five son-of Noah and-he-was (32) then-he-died

נֹחַ אֶת־שֵׁם אֶת־חָם וְאֶת־יָפֶת׃ וַיְהִי כִּי־הֵחֵל הָאָדָם
the-man he-began when and-he-was (6:1) Japheth and Ham *** Shem *** Noah

לָרֹב עַל־פְּנֵי הָאֲדָמָה וּבָנוֹת יֻלְּדוּ לָהֶם׃
to-them they-were-born and-daughters the-earth face-of on to-increase

וַיִּרְאוּ בְנֵי־הָאֱלֹהִים אֶת־בְּנוֹת הָאָדָם כִּי טֹבֹת
beautiful-ones that the-man daughters-of *** the-God sons-of and-they-saw (2)

הֵנָּה וַיִּקְחוּ לָהֶם נָשִׁים מִכֹּל אֲשֶׁר בָּחָרוּ׃ וַיֹּאמֶר
then-he-said (3) they-chose whom from-any wives for-them and-they-took they

יְהוָה לֹא־יָדוֹן רוּחִי בָאָדָם לְעֹלָם בְּשַׁגַּם הוּא
he for-indeed for-ever with-the-man spirit-of-me he-will-contend not Yahweh

בָשָׂר וְהָיוּ יָמָיו מֵאָה וְעֶשְׂרִים שָׁנָה׃ הַנְּפִלִים
the-Nephilim (4) year and-twenty hundred days-of-him and-they-will-be mortal

הָיוּ בָאָרֶץ בַּיָּמִים הָהֵם וְגַם אַחֲרֵי־כֵן אֲשֶׁר
when then after and-also the-those in-the-days on-the-earth they-were

יָבֹאוּ בְּנֵי הָאֱלֹהִים אֶל־בְּנוֹת הָאָדָם וְיָלְדוּ לָהֶם הֵמָּה
they to-them and-they-bore the-man daughters-of to the-God sons-of they-went

הַגִּבֹּרִים אֲשֶׁר מֵעוֹלָם אַנְשֵׁי הַשֵּׁם׃ וַיַּרְא יְהוָה כִּי רַבָּה
great how Yahweh and-he-saw (5) the-name men-of of-old which the-heroes

רָעַת הָאָדָם בָּאָרֶץ וְכָל־יֵצֶר מַחְשְׁבֹת
thoughts-of inclination-of and-every-of on-the-earth the-man wickedness-of

לִבּוֹ רַק רַע כָּל־הַיּוֹם׃ וַיִּנָּחֶם יְהוָה כִּי־
that Yahweh and-he-was-grieved (6) the-day all-of evil only heart-of-him

עָשָׂה אֶת־הָאָדָם בָּאָרֶץ וַיִּתְעַצֵּב אֶל־לִבּוֹ׃ וַיֹּאמֶר
so-he-said (7) heart-of-him to and-he-hurt on-the-earth the-man *** he-made

יְהוָה אֶמְחֶה אֶת־הָאָדָם אֲשֶׁר־בָּרָאתִי מֵעַל פְּנֵי הָאֲדָמָה
the-earth face-of from-on I-created whom the-man *** I-will-wipe-away Yahweh

מֵאָדָם עַד־בְּהֵמָה עַד־רֶמֶשׂ וְעַד־עוֹף הַשָּׁמַיִם כִּי נִחַמְתִּי כִּי
that I-am-grieved for the-air bird-of and-to crawler to animal to from-man

"He will comfort us in the labor and painful toil of our
hands caused by the ground
the LORD has cursed." 30After
Noah was born, Lamech lived
595 years and had other sons
and daughters. 31Altogether,
Lamech lived 777 years, and
then he died.
32After Noah was 500 years
old, he became the father of
Shem, Ham and Japheth.

The Flood

6 When men began to in-
crease in number on the
earth and daughters were
born to them, 2the sons of God
saw that the daughters of men
were beautiful, and they married any of them they chose.
3Then the LORD said, "My
Spirit will not contend with[d]
man forever, for he is mortal;
his days will be a hundred and
twenty years."
4The Nephilim were on the
earth in those days—and also
afterward—when the sons of
God went to the daughters of
men and had children by
them. They were the heroes of
old, men of renown.
5The LORD saw how great
man's wickedness on the
earth had become, and that
every inclination of the
thoughts of his heart was only
evil all the time. 6The LORD
was grieved that he had made
man on the earth, and his
heart was filled with pain. 7So
the LORD said, "I will wipe
mankind, whom I have
created, from the face of the
earth—men and animals, and
creatures that move along the
ground, and birds of the air—
for I am grieved that I have

[d]3 Or *My spirit will not remain in*

עֲשִׂיתִם׃ וְנֹחַ מָצָא חֵן בְּעֵינֵי יְהוָה׃ אֵלֶּה תּוֹלְדֹת

lines-of these (9) Yahweh in-eyes-of favor he-found but-Noah (8) I-made-them

נֹחַ נֹחַ אִישׁ צַדִּיק תָּמִים הָיָה בְּדֹרֹתָיו אֶת־הָאֱלֹהִים

the-God with in-contemporaries-of-him he-was blameless righteous man Noah Noah

הִתְהַלֶּךְ־ נֹחַ׃ וַיּוֹלֶד נֹחַ שְׁלֹשָׁה בָנִים אֶת־ שֵׁם אֶת־חָם וְאֶת־

and Ham *** Shem *** sons three Noah and-he-fathered (10) Noah he-walked

יָפֶת׃ וַתִּשָּׁחֵת הָאָרֶץ לִפְנֵי הָאֱלֹהִים וַתִּמָּלֵא

and-she-was-full the-God in-face-of the-earth now-she-was-corrupt (11) Japheth

הָאָרֶץ חָמָס׃ וַיַּרְא אֱלֹהִים אֶת־ הָאָרֶץ וְהִנֵּה נִשְׁחָתָה

she-was-corrupt and-see! the-earth *** God and-he-saw (12) violence the-earth

כִּי־ הִשְׁחִית כָּל־ בָּשָׂר אֶת־ דַּרְכּוֹ עַל־ הָאָרֶץ׃ וַיֹּאמֶר

so-he-said (13) the-earth on way-of-him *** person every-of he-corrupted for

אֱלֹהִים לְנֹחַ קֵץ כָּל־ בָּשָׂר בָּא לְפָנַי כִּי־ מָלְאָה

she-is-filled for before-me coming person every-of end-of to-Noah God

הָאָרֶץ חָמָס מִפְּנֵיהֶם וְהִנְנִי מַשְׁחִיתָם אֶת־ הָאָרֶץ׃

the-earth with destroying-them so-now-I from-face-of-them violence the-earth

עֲשֵׂה לְךָ תֵּבַת עֲצֵי־ גֹפֶר קִנִּים תַּעֲשֶׂה אֶת־הַתֵּבָה

the-ark *** you-make rooms cypress woods-of ark-of for-you make! (14)

וְכָפַרְתָּ אֹתָהּ מִבַּיִת וּמִחוּץ בַּכֹּפֶר׃ וְזֶה אֲשֶׁר תַּעֲשֶׂה

you-build how and-this (15) with-the-pitch and-outside on-inside her and-you-coat

אֹתָהּ שְׁלֹשׁ מֵאוֹת אַמָּה אֹרֶךְ הַתֵּבָה חֲמִשִּׁים אַמָּה רָחְבָּהּ

width-of-her cubit fifty the-ark length-of cubit hundreds three-of her

וּשְׁלֹשִׁים אַמָּה קוֹמָתָהּ׃ צֹהַר ׀ תַּעֲשֶׂה לַתֵּבָה וְאֶל־ אַמָּה

cubit and-to for-the-ark you-make roof (16) height-of-her cubit and-thirty

תְּכַלֶּנָּה* מִלְמַעְלָה וּפֶתַח הַתֵּבָה בְּצִדָּהּ תָּשִׂים

you-put in-side-of-her the-ark and-door-of from-above you-finish-her

תַּחְתִּיִּם שְׁנִיִּם וּשְׁלִשִׁים תַּעֲשֶׂהָ׃ וַאֲנִי הִנְנִי מֵבִיא

bringing now-I and-I (17) you-make and-third-ones second-ones lower-ones

אֶת־ הַמַּבּוּל מַיִם עַל־ הָאָרֶץ לְשַׁחֵת כָּל־ בָּשָׂר אֲשֶׁר־

that creature every-of to-destroy the-earth on waters the-flood-of ***

בּוֹ רוּחַ חַיִּים מִתַּחַת הַשָּׁמָיִם כֹּל אֲשֶׁר־ בָּאָרֶץ

on-the-earth that everything the-heavens from-under life breath-of in-him

יִגְוָע׃ וַהֲקִמֹתִי אֶת־ בְּרִיתִי אִתָּךְ

with-you covenant-of-me *** but-I-will-establish (18) he-will-perish

וּבָאתָ אֶל־הַתֵּבָה אַתָּה וּבָנֶיךָ וְאִשְׁתְּךָ וּנְשֵׁי־

and-wives-of and-wife-of-you and-sons-of-you you the-ark to and-you-will-enter

בָנֶיךָ אִתָּךְ׃ וּמִכָּל־ הָחַי מִכָּל־ בָּשָׂר

creature from-every-of the-living and-from-all-of (19) with-you sons-of-you

made them." [8]But Noah found favor in the eyes of the LORD.

[9]This is the account of Noah.

Noah was a righteous man, blameless among the people of his time, and he walked with God. [10]Noah had three sons: Shem, Ham and Japheth.

[11]Now the earth was corrupt in God's sight and was full of violence. [12]God saw how corrupt the earth had become, for all the people on earth had corrupted their ways. [13]So God said to Noah, "I am going to put an end to all people, for the earth is filled with violence because of them. I am surely going to destroy both them and the earth. [14]So make yourself an ark of cypress[e] wood; make rooms in it and coat it with pitch inside and out. [15]This is how you are to build it: The ark is to be 450 feet long, 75 feet wide and 45 feet high.[f] [16]Make a roof for it and finish[g] the ark to within 18 inches[h] of the top. Put a door in the side of the ark and make lower, middle and upper decks. [17]I am going to bring floodwaters on the earth to destroy all life under the heavens, every creature that has the breath of life in it. Everything on earth will perish. [18]But I will establish my covenant with you, and you will enter the ark—you and your sons and your wife and your sons' wives with you. [19]You

[e]*14* The meaning of the Hebrew for this word is uncertain.
[f]*15* Hebrew *300 cubits long, 50 cubits wide and 30 cubits high* (about 140 meters long, 23 meters wide and 13.5 meters high)
[g]*16* Or *Make an opening for light by finishing*
[h]*16* Hebrew *a cubit* (about 0.5 meter)

**16* Most mss have *dagesh* in the *lamed* (לּ־).

שְׁנַיִם מִכֹּל תָּבִיא אֶל־הַתֵּבָה לְהַחֲיֹת אִתָּךְ זָכָר וּנְקֵבָה
and-female male with-you to-keep-alive the-ark to you-shall-bring from-all two

יִהְיוּ׃ מֵהָעוֹף לְמִינֵהוּ וּמִן־הַבְּהֵמָה לְמִינָהּ
to kind-of-her the-animal and-from to-kind-of-him from-the-bird (20) they-shall-be

מִכֹּל רֶמֶשׂ הָאֲדָמָה לְמִינֵהוּ שְׁנַיִם מִכֹּל יָבֹאוּ
they-will-come from-all two to-kind-of-him the-ground crawler-of from-every-of

אֵלֶיךָ לְהַחֲיוֹת׃ וְאַתָּה קַח־לְךָ מִכָּל־מַאֲכָל אֲשֶׁר
that food from-every-of for-you take! and-you (21) to-keep-alive to-you

יֵאָכֵל וְאָסַפְתָּ אֵלֶיךָ וְהָיָה לְךָ וְלָהֶם לְאָכְלָה׃
as-food and-for-them for-you and-he-is for-you and-you-store he-is-eaten

וַיַּעַשׂ נֹחַ כְּכֹל אֲשֶׁר צִוָּה אֹתוֹ אֱלֹהִים כֵּן עָשָׂה׃
he-did so God him he-commanded that as-all Noah so-he-did (22)

וַיֹּאמֶר יְהוָה לְנֹחַ בֹּא־אַתָּה וְכָל־בֵּיתְךָ אֶל־הַתֵּבָה
the-ark into family-of-you and-whole-of you go! to-Noah Yahweh then-he-said (7:1)

כִּי־אֹתְךָ רָאִיתִי צַדִּיק לְפָנַי בַּדּוֹר הַזֶּה׃ מִכֹּל ׀
from-every-of (2) the-this in-the-generation before-me righteous I-found you for

הַבְּהֵמָה הַטְּהוֹרָה תִּקַּח־לְךָ שִׁבְעָה שִׁבְעָה אִישׁ וְאִשְׁתּוֹ
and-mate-of-him male seven seven with-you you-take the-clean the-animal

וּמִן־הַבְּהֵמָה אֲשֶׁר לֹא טְהֹרָה הִוא שְׁנַיִם אִישׁ וְאִשְׁתּוֹ׃ גַּם
also (3) and-mate-of-him male two she clean not that the-animal and-from

מֵעוֹף הַשָּׁמַיִם שִׁבְעָה שִׁבְעָה זָכָר וּנְקֵבָה לְחַיּוֹת זֶרַע עַל־
on kind to-keep-alive and-female male seven seven the-air from-bird-of

פְּנֵי כָל־הָאָרֶץ׃ כִּי לְיָמִים עוֹד שִׁבְעָה אָנֹכִי מַמְטִיר עַל־
on sending-rain I seven from-now to-days for (4) the-earth all-of face-of

הָאָרֶץ אַרְבָּעִים יוֹם וְאַרְבָּעִים לָיְלָה וּמָחִיתִי אֶת־כָּל־
every-of *** and-I-will-wipe-away night and-forty day forty the-earth

הַיְקוּם אֲשֶׁר עָשִׂיתִי מֵעַל פְּנֵי הָאֲדָמָה׃ וַיַּעַשׂ נֹחַ כְּכֹל
as-all Noah and-he-did (5) the-earth face-of from-on I-made that creature

אֲשֶׁר־צִוָּהוּ יְהוָה׃ וְנֹחַ בֶּן־שֵׁשׁ מֵאוֹת שָׁנָה
year hundreds six son-of and-Noah (6) Yahweh he-commanded-him that

וְהַמַּבּוּל הָיָה מַיִם עַל־הָאָרֶץ׃ וַיָּבֹא נֹחַ
Noah and-he-entered (7) the-earth on waters he-was and-the-flood

וּבָנָיו וְאִשְׁתּוֹ וּנְשֵׁי־בָנָיו אִתּוֹ אֶל־
into with-him sons-of-him and-wives-of and-wife-of-him and-sons-of-him

הַתֵּבָה מִפְּנֵי מֵי הַמַּבּוּל׃ מִן־הַבְּהֵמָה הַטְּהוֹרָה
the-clean the-animal from (8) the-flood waters-of from-face-of the-ark

וּמִן־הַבְּהֵמָה אֲשֶׁר אֵינֶנָּה טְהֹרָה וּמִן־הָעוֹף וְכֹל אֲשֶׁר־
that and-all the-bird and-from clean she-is-not that the-animal and-from

are to bring into the ark two of
all living creatures, male and
female, to keep them alive
with you. [20]Two of every kind
of bird, of every kind of animal and of every kind of creature that moves along the
ground will come to you to be
kept alive. [21]You are to take
every kind of food that is to be
eaten and store it away as food
for you and for them."
[22]Noah did everything just
as God commanded him.

7 The LORD then said to
Noah, "Go into the ark,
you and your whole family,
because I have found you
righteous in this generation.
[2]Take with you seven[i] of every
kind of clean animal, a male
and its mate, and two of every
kind of unclean animal, a
male and its mate, [3]and also
seven of every kind of bird,
male and female, to keep their
various kinds alive throughout the earth. [4]Seven days
from now I will send rain on
the earth for forty days and
forty nights, and I will wipe
from the face of the earth
every living creature I have
made."
[5]And Noah did all that the
LORD commanded him.
[6]Noah was six hundred
years old when the floodwaters came on the earth. [7]And
Noah and his sons and his
wife and his sons' wives entered the ark to escape the waters of the flood. [8]Pairs of clean
and unclean animals, of birds
and of all creatures that move

[i]2 Or *seven pairs;* also in verse 3

רֹמֵשׂ עַל־ הָאֲדָמָה׃ שְׁנַיִם שְׁנַיִם בָּאוּ אֶל־ נֹחַ אֶל־ הַתֵּבָה זָכָר
male the-ark to Noah to they-came pair pair (9) the-ground on moving

וּנְקֵבָה כַּאֲשֶׁר צִוָּה אֱלֹהִים אֶת־ נֹחַ׃ וַיְהִי לְשִׁבְעַת
after-seven-of and-he-was (10) Noah *** God he-commanded just-as and-female

הַיָּמִים וּמֵי הַמַּבּוּל הָיוּ עַל־ הָאָרֶץ׃ בִּשְׁנַת
in-year-of (11) the-earth on they-came the-flood and-waters-of the-days

שֵׁשׁ־ מֵאוֹת שָׁנָה לְחַיֵּי־ נֹחַ בַּחֹדֶשׁ הַשֵּׁנִי בְּשִׁבְעָה־עָשָׂר יוֹם
day ten on-seven the-second in-the-month Noah to-life-of year hundreds six

לַחֹדֶשׁ בַּיּוֹם הַזֶּה נִבְקְעוּ כָּל־ מַעְיְנֹת תְּהוֹם רַבָּה
great deep springs-of all-of they-burst the-that on-the-day to-the-month

וַאֲרֻבֹּת הַשָּׁמַיִם נִפְתָּחוּ׃ וַיְהִי הַגֶּשֶׁם עַל־
on the-rain and-he-fell (12) they-were-opened the-heavens and-floodgates-of

הָאָרֶץ אַרְבָּעִים יוֹם וְאַרְבָּעִים לָיְלָה׃ בְּעֶצֶם הַיּוֹם הַזֶּה
the-that the-day on-very-of (13) night and-forty day forty the-earth

בָּא נֹחַ וְשֵׁם־ וְחָם וָיֶפֶת בְּנֵי־ נֹחַ וְאֵשֶׁת נֹחַ
Noah and-wife-of Noah sons-of and-Japheth and-Ham and-Shem Noah he-entered

וּשְׁלֹשֶׁת נְשֵׁי־ בָנָיו אִתָּם אֶל־ הַתֵּבָה׃ הֵמָּה
they (14) the-ark into with-them sons-of-him wives-of and-three-of

וְכָל־ הַחַיָּה לְמִינָהּ וְכָל־ הַבְּהֵמָה
the-livestock and-every-of to-kind-of-her the-animal and-every-of

לְמִינָהּ וְכָל־ הָרֶמֶשׂ הָרֹמֵשׂ עַל־ הָאָרֶץ
the-ground on the-one-crawling the-crawler and-every-of to-kind-of-her

לְמִינֵהוּ וְכָל־ הָעוֹף לְמִינֵהוּ כֹּל צִפּוֹר כָּל־ כָּנָף׃
wing every-of bird every-of to-kind-of-him the-bird and-every-of to-kind-of-him

וַיָּבֹאוּ אֶל־ נֹחַ אֶל־ הַתֵּבָה שְׁנַיִם שְׁנַיִם מִכָּל־ הַבָּשָׂר
the-creature from-every-of pair pair the-ark into Noah to and-they-came (15)

אֲשֶׁר־ בּוֹ רוּחַ חַיִּים׃ וְהַבָּאִים זָכָר וּנְקֵבָה
and-female male and-the-ones-going-in (16) life breath-of in-him that

מִכָּל־ בָּשָׂר בָּאוּ כַּאֲשֶׁר צִוָּה אֹתוֹ אֱלֹהִים וַיִּסְגֹּר
then-he-shut-in God him he-commanded just-as they-came creature from-every-of

יְהוָה בַּעֲדוֹ׃ וַיְהִי הַמַּבּוּל אַרְבָּעִים יוֹם עַל־ הָאָרֶץ
the-earth on day forty the-flood and-he-came (17) after-him Yahweh

וַיִּרְבּוּ הַמַּיִם וַיִּשְׂאוּ אֶת־ הַתֵּבָה וַתָּרָם
and-she-rose the-ark *** and-they-lifted the-waters and-they-increased

מֵעַל הָאָרֶץ׃ וַיִּגְבְּרוּ הַמַּיִם וַיִּרְבּוּ מְאֹד
greatly and-they-increased the-waters and-they-rose (18) the-earth from-on

עַל־ הָאָרֶץ וַתֵּלֶךְ הַתֵּבָה עַל־ פְּנֵי הַמָּיִם׃
the-waters surface-of on the-ark and-she-floated the-earth on

along the ground, 9male and
female, came to Noah and entered the ark, as God had commanded Noah. 10And after the
seven days the floodwaters came on the earth.

11In the six hundredth year of Noah's life, on the seventeenth day of the second month—on that day all the springs of the great deep burst forth, and the floodgates of the heavens were opened. 12And
rain fell on the earth forty days and forty nights.

13On that very day Noah and his sons, Shem, Ham and Japheth, together with his wife and the wives of his three sons, entered the ark. 14They
had with them every wild animal according to its kind, all livestock according to their kinds, every creature that moves along the ground according to its kind and every bird according to its kind, everything with wings. 15Pairs
of all creatures that have the breath of life in them came to Noah and entered the ark.
16The animals going in were male and female of every living thing, as God had commanded Noah. Then the LORD shut him in.

17For forty days the flood kept coming on the earth, and as the waters increased they lifted the ark high above the earth. 18The waters rose and
increased greatly on the earth, and the ark floated on the surface of the water. 19They rose

וְהַמַּיִם גָּבְרוּ מְאֹד מְאֹד עַל־הָאָרֶץ וַיְכֻסּוּ
and-they-were-covered the-earth on greatly greatly they-rose and-the-waters (19)

כָּל־הֶהָרִים הַגְּבֹהִים אֲשֶׁר־תַּחַת כָּל־הַשָּׁמָיִם׃
the-heavens entire-of under that the-high-ones the-mountains all-of

חֲמֵשׁ עֶשְׂרֵה אַמָּה מִלְמַעְלָה גָּבְרוּ הַמָּיִם וַיְכֻסּוּ
and-they-were-covered the-waters they-rose from-above cubit ten five (20)

הֶהָרִים׃ וַיִּגְוַע כָּל־בָּשָׂר ׀ הָרֹמֵשׂ עַל־
on the-one-crawling creature every-of and-he-perished (21) the-mountains

הָאָרֶץ בָּעוֹף וּבַבְּהֵמָה וּבַחַיָּה
and-with-the-animal and-with-the-livestock with-the-bird the-earth

וּבְכָל־הַשֶּׁרֶץ הַשֹּׁרֵץ עַל־הָאָרֶץ וְכֹל
and-every-of the-earth on the-one-swarming the-swarmer and-with-every-of

הָאָדָם׃ כֹּל אֲשֶׁר נִשְׁמַת־רוּחַ חַיִּים בְּאַפָּיו
in-nostrils-of-him life spirit-of breath-of that everything (22) the-mankind

מִכֹּל אֲשֶׁר בֶּחָרָבָה מֵתוּ׃ וַיִּמַח אֶת־כָּל־
every-of *** and-he-was-wiped-out (23) they-died on-the-dry-land that from-everything

הַיְקוּם ׀ אֲשֶׁר ׀ עַל־פְּנֵי הָאֲדָמָה מֵאָדָם עַד־בְּהֵמָה עַד־רֶמֶשׂ וְעַד־
and-to crawler to animal to from-man the-earth face-of on that the-living

עוֹף הַשָּׁמַיִם וַיִּמָּחוּ מִן־הָאָרֶץ וַיִּשָּׁאֶר* אַךְ־
only and-he-was-left the-earth from and-they-were-wiped-out the-air bird-of

נֹחַ וַאֲשֶׁר אִתּוֹ בַּתֵּבָה׃ וַיִּגְבְּרוּ הַמַּיִם עַל־
over the-waters and-they-flooded (24) in-the-ark with-him and-whom Noah

הָאָרֶץ חֲמִשִּׁים וּמְאַת יוֹם׃ וַיִּזְכֹּר אֱלֹהִים אֶת־נֹחַ וְאֵת
and Noah *** God but-he-remembered (8:1) day and-hundred-of fifty the-earth

כָּל־הַחַיָּה וְאֶת־כָּל־הַבְּהֵמָה אֲשֶׁר אִתּוֹ בַּתֵּבָה
on-the-ark with-him that the-livestock every-of and the-animal every-of

וַיַּעֲבֵר אֱלֹהִים רוּחַ עַל־הָאָרֶץ וַיָּשֹׁכּוּ הַמָּיִם׃
the-waters and-they-receded the-earth over wind God and-he-sent

וַיִּסָּכְרוּ מַעְיְנֹת תְּהוֹם וַאֲרֻבֹּת הַשָּׁמָיִם
the-heavens and-floodgates-of deep springs-of and-they-were-closed (2)

וַיִּכָּלֵא הַגֶּשֶׁם מִן־הַשָּׁמָיִם׃ וַיָּשֻׁבוּ הַמַּיִם
the-waters and-they-receded (3) the-sky from the-rain and-he-stopped

מֵעַל הָאָרֶץ הָלוֹךְ וָשׁוֹב וַיַּחְסְרוּ הַמַּיִם
the-waters and-they-went-down and-to-recede to-continue the-earth from-on

מִקְצֵה חֲמִשִּׁים וּמְאַת יוֹם׃ וַתָּנַח הַתֵּבָה בַּחֹדֶשׁ
on-the-month the-ark and-she-rested (4) day and-hundred-of fifty at-end-of

הַשְּׁבִיעִי בְּשִׁבְעָה־עָשָׂר יוֹם לַחֹדֶשׁ עַל הָרֵי אֲרָרָט׃
Ararat mountains-of on to-the-month day ten in-seven the-seventh

greatly on the earth, and all
the high mountains under the
entire heavens were covered.
20The waters rose and covered
the mountains to a depth of
more than twenty feet.[j, k]
21Every living thing that
moved on the earth perished—
birds, livestock, wild animals,
all the creatures that swarm
over the earth, and all mankind. 22Everything on dry land
that had the breath of life in its
nostrils died. 23Every living
thing on the face of the earth
was wiped out; men and animals and the creatures that
move along the ground and
the birds of the air were wiped
from the earth. Only Noah
was left, and those with him
in the ark.

24The waters flooded the
earth for a hundred and fifty
days.

8 But God remembered
Noah and all the wild animals and the livestock that
were with him in the ark, and
he sent a wind over the earth
and the waters receded. 2Now
the springs of the deep and the
floodgates of the heavens had
been closed, and the rain had
stopped falling from the sky.
3The water receded steadily
from the earth. At the end of
the hundred and fifty days the
water had gone down, 4and on
the seventeenth day of the
seventh month the ark came
to rest on the mountains of

j20 Hebrew *fifteen cubits* (about 6.9 meters)
k20 Or *rose more than twenty feet, and the mountains were covered*

*23 Most mss have *dagesh* in the *yod* (יּ).

וְהַמַּיִם הָיוּ הָלוֹךְ וְחָסוֹר עַד הַחֹדֶשׁ
the-month until and-to-recede to-continue they-were and-the-waters (5)

הָעֲשִׂירִי בָּעֲשִׂירִי בְּאֶחָד לַחֹדֶשׁ נִרְאוּ רָאשֵׁי
tops-of they-became-visible to-the-month on-first on-the-tenth the-tenth

הֶהָרִים׃ וַיְהִי מִקֵּץ אַרְבָּעִים יוֹם וַיִּפְתַּח נֹחַ אֶת־
*** Noah and-he-opened day forty at-end-of and-he-was (6) the-mountains

חַלּוֹן הַתֵּבָה אֲשֶׁר עָשָׂה׃ וַיְשַׁלַּח אֶת־ הָעֹרֵב וַיֵּצֵא
and-he-went the-raven *** then-he-sent (7) he-made that the-ark window-of

יָצוֹא וָשׁוֹב עַד־ יְבֹשֶׁת הַמַּיִם מֵעַל הָאָרֶץ׃
the-earth from-on the-waters to-dry until and-to-return to-go-out

וַיְשַׁלַּח אֶת־ הַיּוֹנָה מֵאִתּוֹ לִרְאוֹת הֲקַלּוּ הַמַּיִם
the-waters they-receded? to-see from-with-him the-dove *** then-he-sent (8)

מֵעַל פְּנֵי הָאֲדָמָה׃ וְלֹא־ מָצְאָה הַיּוֹנָה מָנוֹחַ
place the-dove she-found but-not (9) the-ground surface-of from-on

לְכַף־ רַגְלָהּ וַתָּשָׁב אֵלָיו אֶל־ הַתֵּבָה כִּי־ מַיִם עַל־
over waters for the-ark to to-him so-she-returned foot-of-her for-sole-of

פְּנֵי כָל־ הָאָרֶץ וַיִּשְׁלַח יָדוֹ וַיִּקָּחֶהָ
and-he-took-her hand-of-him and-he-reached the-earth all-of surface-of

וַיָּבֵא אֹתָהּ אֵלָיו אֶל־ הַתֵּבָה׃ וַיָּחֶל עוֹד שִׁבְעַת
seven-of yet and-he-waited (10) the-ark to to-him her and-he-brought

יָמִים אֲחֵרִים וַיֹּסֶף שַׁלַּח אֶת־ הַיּוֹנָה מִן־ הַתֵּבָה׃
the-ark from the-dove *** to-send and-he-repeated more-ones days

וַתָּבֹא אֵלָיו הַיּוֹנָה לְעֵת עֶרֶב וְהִנֵּה עֲלֵה־
leaf-of and-see! evening in-time-of the-dove to-him when-she-returned (11)

זַיִת טָרָף בְּפִיהָ וַיֵּדַע נֹחַ כִּי־ קַלּוּ
they-receded that Noah then-he-knew in-beak-of-her freshly-plucked olive

הַמַּיִם מֵעַל הָאָרֶץ׃ וַיִּיָּחֶל עוֹד שִׁבְעַת יָמִים אֲחֵרִים
more-ones days seven-of yet and-he-waited (12) the-earth from-on the-waters

וַיְשַׁלַּח אֶת־ הַיּוֹנָה וְלֹא־ יָסְפָה שׁוּב־ אֵלָיו עוֹד׃
again to-him to-return she-repeated and-not the-dove *** and-he-sent

וַיְהִי בְּאַחַת וְשֵׁשׁ־ מֵאוֹת שָׁנָה בָּרִאשׁוֹן בְּאֶחָד
on-first on-the-first year hundreds and-six on-first and-he-was (13)

לַחֹדֶשׁ חָרְבוּ הַמַּיִם מֵעַל הָאָרֶץ וַיָּסַר נֹחַ
Noah and-he-removed the-earth from-on the-waters they-dried-up to-the-month

אֶת־ מִכְסֵה הַתֵּבָה וַיַּרְא וְהִנֵּה חָרְבוּ פְּנֵי
surfaces-of they-were-dry and-see! and-he-looked the-ark covering-of ***

הָאֲדָמָה׃ וּבַחֹדֶשׁ הַשֵּׁנִי בְּשִׁבְעָה וְעֶשְׂרִים יוֹם
day and-twenty on-seven the-second and-by-the-month (14) the-ground

Ararat. 5The waters continued
to recede until the tenth
month, and on the first day of
the tenth month the tops of
the mountains became visible.
6After forty days Noah
opened the window he had
made in the ark 7and sent out
a raven, and it kept flying back
and forth until the water had
dried up from the earth. 8Then
he sent out a dove to see if the
water had receded from the
surface of the ground. 9But the
dove could find no place to set
its feet because there was
water over all the surface of
the earth; so it returned to
Noah in the ark. He reached
out his hand and took the
dove and brought it back to
himself in the ark. 10He waited
seven more days and again
sent out the dove from the ark.
11When the dove returned to
him in the evening, there in
its beak was a freshly plucked
olive leaf! Then Noah knew
that the water had receded
from the earth. 12He waited
seven more days and sent the
dove out again, but this time it
did not return to him.
13By the first day of the first
month of Noah's six hundred
and first year, the water had
dried up from the earth. Noah
then removed the covering
from the ark and saw that the
surface of the ground was dry.
14By the twenty-seventh day
of the second month the earth

לַחֹדֶשׁ יָבְשָׁה הָאָרֶץ׃ וַיְדַבֵּר אֱלֹהִים אֶל־ נֹחַ לֵאמֹר׃
to-say Noah to God then-he-said (15) the-earth she-was-dry to-the-month

צֵא מִן־ הַתֵּבָה אַתָּה וְאִשְׁתְּךָ וּבָנֶיךָ וּנְשֵׁי־
and-wives-of and-sons-of-you and-wife-of-you you the-ark from come-out! (16)

בָנֶיךָ אִתָּךְ׃ כָּל־ הַחַיָּה אֲשֶׁר־ אִתְּךָ מִכָּל־
from-every-of with-you that the-living every-of (17) with-you sons-of-you

בָּשָׂר בָּעוֹף וּבַבְּהֵמָה וּבְכָל־ הָרֶמֶשׂ
the-crawler and-with-every-of and-with-the-animal with-the-bird creature

הָרֹמֵשׂ עַל־ הָאָרֶץ הוֹצֵא° אִתָּךְ וְשָׁרְצוּ
so-they-can-multiply with-you bring-out! the-ground on the-one-crawling

בָאָרֶץ וּפָרוּ וְרָבוּ עַל־ הָאָרֶץ׃
the-earth upon and-they-increase and-they-be-fruitful on-the-earth

וַיֵּצֵא־ נֹחַ וּבָנָיו וְאִשְׁתּוֹ וּנְשֵׁי־ בָנָיו
sons-of-him and-wives-of and-wife-of-him and-sons-of-him Noah so-he-came-out (18)

אִתּוֹ׃ כָּל־ הַחַיָּה כָּל־ הָרֶמֶשׂ וְכָל־ הָעוֹף
the-bird and-every-of the-crawler every-of the-animal every-of (19) with-him

כֹּל רוֹמֵשׂ עַל־ הָאָרֶץ לְמִשְׁפְּחֹתֵיהֶם יָצְאוּ מִן־ הַתֵּבָה׃
the-ark from they-came by-kinds-of-them the-earth on moving every-of

וַיִּבֶן נֹחַ מִזְבֵּחַ לַיהוָה וַיִּקַּח מִכֹּל ׀ הַבְּהֵמָה
the-animal from-every-of and-he-took to-Yahweh altar Noah then-he-built (20)

הַטְּהוֹרָה וּמִכֹּל הָעוֹף הַטָּהֹר וַיַּעַל
and-he-sacrificed the-clean the-bird and-from-every-of the-clean

עֹלֹת בַּמִּזְבֵּחַ׃ וַיָּרַח יְהוָה אֶת־ רֵיחַ הַנִּיחֹחַ
the-pleasant aroma-of *** Yahweh and-he-smelled (21) on-the-altar burnt-offerings

וַיֹּאמֶר יְהוָה אֶל־ לִבּוֹ לֹא־ אֹסִף לְקַלֵּל עוֹד אֶת־
*** again to-curse I-will-repeat not heart-of-him in Yahweh and-he-said

הָאֲדָמָה בַּעֲבוּר הָאָדָם כִּי יֵצֶר לֵב הָאָדָם רַע
evil the-man heart-of inclination-of though the-man because-of the-ground

מִנְּעֻרָיו וְלֹא־ אֹסִף עוֹד לְהַכּוֹת אֶת־ כָּל־
every-of *** to-destroy again I-will-repeat and-not from-childhood-of-him

חַי כַּאֲשֶׁר עָשִׂיתִי׃ עֹד כָּל־ יְמֵי הָאָרֶץ זֶרַע וְקָצִיר
and-harvest seedtime the-earth days-of all-of while (22) I-did just-as living

וְקֹר וָחֹם וְקַיִץ וָחֹרֶף וְיוֹם וָלַיְלָה לֹא יִשְׁבֹּתוּ׃
they-will-cease never and-night and-day and-winter and-summer and-heat and-cold

וַיְבָרֶךְ אֱלֹהִים אֶת־ נֹחַ וְאֶת־ בָּנָיו וַיֹּאמֶר לָהֶם
to-them and-he-said sons-of-him and Noah *** God then-he-blessed (9:1)

פְּרוּ וּרְבוּ וּמִלְאוּ אֶת־ הָאָרֶץ׃ וּמוֹרַאֲכֶם
and-fear-of-you (2) the-earth *** and-fill! and-increase! be-fruitful!

°17 ק היצא

was completely dry.
[15]Then God said to Noah,
[16]"Come out of the ark, you
and your wife and your sons
and their wives. [17]Bring out
every kind of living creature
that is with you—the birds,
the animals, and all the creatures that move along the
ground—so they can multiply
on the earth and be fruitful
and increase in number upon
it."
[18]So Noah came out, to-
gether with his sons and his
wife and his sons' wives. [19]All
the animals and all the creatures that move along the
ground and all the birds—
everything that moves on the
earth—came out of the ark,
one kind after another.
[20]Then Noah built an altar to
the LORD and, taking some of
all the clean animals and clean
birds, he sacrificed burnt
offerings on it. [21]The LORD
smelled the pleasing aroma
and said in his heart: "Never
again will I curse the ground
because of man, even though[l]
every inclination of his heart
is evil from childhood. And
never again will I destroy all
living creatures, as I have
done.

[22]"As long as the earth
endures,
seedtime and harvest,
cold and heat,
summer and winter,
day and night
will never cease."

God's Covenant With Noah

9 Then God blessed Noah
and his sons, saying to
them, "Be fruitful and increase in number and fill the
earth. [2]The fear and dread of

[l]21 Or *man, for*

וְחִתְּכֶם יִהְיֶה עַל כָּל־ חַיַּת הָאָרֶץ וְעַל כָּל־
every-of and-upon the-earth beast-of every-of upon he-will-be and-dread-of-you

עוֹף הַשָּׁמָיִם בְּכֹל אֲשֶׁר תִּרְמֹשׂ הָאֲדָמָה וּבְכָל־ דְּגֵי
fishes-of and-on-all-of the-ground she-moves that on-every the-air bird-of

הַיָּם בְּיֶדְכֶם נִתָּנוּ׃ כָּל־ רֶמֶשׂ אֲשֶׁר הוּא־ חַי
lives he that crawler every-of (3) they-are-given into-hand-of-you the-sea

לָכֶם יִהְיֶה לְאָכְלָה כְּיֶרֶק עֵשֶׂב נָתַתִּי לָכֶם אֶת־ כֹּל׃
everything *** to-you I-gave plant as-green for-food he-will-be to-you

אַךְ־ בָּשָׂר בְּנַפְשׁוֹ דָמוֹ לֹא תֹאכֵלוּ׃ וְאַךְ
and-surely (5) you-must-eat not blood-of-him with-life-of-him meat but (4)

אֶת־ דִּמְכֶם לְנַפְשֹׁתֵיכֶם אֶדְרֹשׁ מִיַּד כָּל־ חַיָּה
animal every-of from-hand-of I-will-demand for-lives-of-you blood-of-you ***

אֶדְרְשֶׁנּוּ וּמִיַּד הָאָדָם מִיַּד אִישׁ אָחִיו
fellow-of-him man from-hand-of the-man and-from-hand-of I-will-demand-him

אֶדְרֹשׁ אֶת־ נֶפֶשׁ הָאָדָם׃ שֹׁפֵךְ דַּם הָאָדָם בָּאָדָם
by-the-man the-man blood-of one-shedding (6) the-man life-of *** I-will-demand

דָּמוֹ יִשָּׁפֵךְ כִּי בְּצֶלֶם אֱלֹהִים עָשָׂה אֶת־ הָאָדָם׃
the-man *** he-made God in-image-of for he-shall-be-shed blood-of-him

וְאַתֶּם פְּרוּ וּרְבוּ שִׁרְצוּ בָאָרֶץ וּרְבוּ־
and-increase! on-the-earth multiply! and-increase! be-fruitful! and-you (7)

בָהּ׃ וַיֹּאמֶר אֱלֹהִים אֶל־ נֹחַ וְאֶל־ בָּנָיו אִתּוֹ לֵאמֹר׃
to-say with-him sons-of-him and-to Noah to God then-he-said (8) on-her

וַאֲנִי הִנְנִי מֵקִים אֶת־ בְּרִיתִי אִתְּכֶם וְאֶת־
and-with with-you covenant-of-me *** establishing see!-I now-I (9)

זַרְעֲכֶם אַחֲרֵיכֶם׃ וְאֵת כָּל־ נֶפֶשׁ הַחַיָּה אֲשֶׁר
that the-creature living-of every-of and-with (10) after-you descendants-of-you

אִתְּכֶם בָּעוֹף בַּבְּהֵמָה וּבְכָל־ חַיַּת
animal-of and-with-every-of with-the-livestock with-the-bird with-you

הָאָרֶץ אִתְּכֶם מִכֹּל יֹצְאֵי הַתֵּבָה לְכֹל
with-every-of the-ark ones-coming-out-of with-all-of with-you the-earth

חַיַּת הָאָרֶץ׃ וַהֲקִמֹתִי אֶת־ בְּרִיתִי אִתְּכֶם
with-you covenant-of-me *** and-I-establish (11) the-earth creature-of

וְלֹא־ יִכָּרֵת כָּל־ בָּשָׂר עוֹד מִמֵּי הַמַּבּוּל וְלֹא־
and-not the-flood by-waters-of ever life all-of he-will-be-cut-off and-not

יִהְיֶה עוֹד מַבּוּל לְשַׁחֵת הָאָרֶץ׃ וַיֹּאמֶר אֱלֹהִים זֹאת אוֹת־
sign-of this God and-he-said (12) the-earth to-destroy flood ever he-will-be

הַבְּרִית אֲשֶׁר־אֲנִי נֹתֵן בֵּינִי וּבֵינֵיכֶם וּבֵין כָּל־
every-of and-between and-between-you between-me making I that the-covenant

you will fall upon all the beasts of the earth and all the birds of the air, upon every creature that moves along the ground, and upon all the fish of the sea; they are given into your
hands. [3]Everything that lives and moves will be food for you. Just as I gave you the green plants, I now give you everything.
[4]"But you must not eat meat that has its lifeblood still in it.
[5]And for your lifeblood I will surely demand an accounting. I will demand an accounting from every animal. And from each man, too, I will demand an accounting for the life of his fellow man.

[6]"Whoever sheds the blood
of man,
by man shall his blood
be shed;
for in the image of God
has God made man.

[7]As for you, be fruitful and increase in number; multiply on the earth and increase upon it."
[8]Then God said to Noah and to his sons with him: [9]"I now
establish my covenant with you and with your descendants after you [10]and with every
living creature that was with you—the birds, the livestock and all the wild animals, all those that came out of the ark with you—every living creature on earth. [11]I establish my
covenant with you: Never again will all life be cut off by the waters of a flood; never again will there be a flood to destroy the earth."
[12]And God said, "This is the sign of the covenant I am making between me and you

נֶפֶשׁ חַיָּה אֲשֶׁר אִתְּכֶם לְדֹרֹת עוֹלָם׃ אֶת־ קַשְׁתִּי
rainbow-of-me *** (13) to-come for-generations with-you that creature living

נָתַתִּי בֶּעָנָן וְהָיְתָה לְאוֹת בְּרִית בֵּינִי וּבֵין
and-between between-me covenant for-sign-of and-she-will-be in-the-cloud I-set

הָאָרֶץ׃ וְהָיָה בְּעַנְנִי עָנָן עַל־ הָאָרֶץ
the-earth over cloud when-to-bring-me and-he-will-be (14) the-earth

וְנִרְאֲתָה הַקֶּשֶׁת בֶּעָנָן׃ וְזָכַרְתִּי אֶת־
*** and-I-will-remember (15) in-the-cloud the-rainbow and-she-appears

בְּרִיתִי אֲשֶׁר בֵּינִי וּבֵינֵיכֶם וּבֵין כָּל־ נֶפֶשׁ
living every-of and-between and-between-you between-me that covenant-of-me

חַיָּה בְּכָל־ בָּשָׂר וְלֹא־ יִהְיֶה עוֹד הַמַּיִם לְמַבּוּל
for-flood the-waters again he-will-become and-not kind with-every-of creature

לְשַׁחֵת כָּל־ בָּשָׂר׃ וְהָיְתָה הַקֶּשֶׁת בֶּעָנָן וּרְאִיתִיהָ
and-I-see-her in-the-cloud the-rainbow when-she-is (16) life all-of to-destroy

לִזְכֹּר בְּרִית עוֹלָם בֵּין אֱלֹהִים וּבֵין כָּל־ נֶפֶשׁ
living every-of and-between God between everlasting covenant to-remember

חַיָּה בְּכָל־ בָּשָׂר אֲשֶׁר עַל־ הָאָרֶץ׃ וַיֹּאמֶר אֱלֹהִים אֶל־ נֹחַ
Noah to God so-he-said (17) the-earth on that kind with-every-of creature

זֹאת אוֹת־ הַבְּרִית אֲשֶׁר הֲקִמֹתִי בֵּינִי וּבֵין כָּל־
all-of and-between between-me I-established that the-covenant sign-of this

בָּשָׂר אֲשֶׁר עַל־הָאָרֶץ׃ וַיִּהְיוּ בְנֵי־ נֹחַ הַיֹּצְאִים מִן־
from the-ones-coming Noah sons-of and-they-were (18) the-earth on that life

הַתֵּבָה שֵׁם וְחָם וָיָפֶת וְחָם הוּא אֲבִי כְנָעַן׃ שְׁלֹשָׁה
three (19) Canaan father-of he and-Ham and-Japheth and-Ham Shem the-ark

אֵלֶּה בְּנֵי־ נֹחַ וּמֵאֵלֶּה נָפְצָה כָל־ הָאָרֶץ׃
the-earth all-of she-was-populated and-from-these Noah sons-of these

וַיָּחֶל נֹחַ אִישׁ הָאֲדָמָה וַיִּטַּע כָּרֶם׃
vineyard and-he-planted the-soil man-of Noah and-he-proceeded (20)

וַיֵּשְׁתְּ מִן־ הַיַּיִן וַיִּשְׁכָּר וַיִּתְגַּל בְּתוֹךְ
inside and-he-lay-uncovered and-he-became-drunk the-wine from when-he-drank (21)

אָהֳלֹה׃ וַיַּרְא חָם אֲבִי כְנַעַן אֵת עֶרְוַת אָבִיו
father-of-him nakedness-of *** Canaan father-of Ham and-he-saw (22) tent-of-him

וַיַּגֵּד לִשְׁנֵי־ אֶחָיו בַּחוּץ׃ וַיִּקַּח שֵׁם
Shem but-he-took (23) on-the-outside brothers-of-him to-two-of and-he-told

וָיֶפֶת אֶת־ הַשִּׂמְלָה וַיָּשִׂימוּ עַל־ שְׁכֶם שְׁנֵיהֶם
two-of-them shoulder-of across and-they-laid the-garment *** and-Japheth

וַיֵּלְכוּ אֲחֹרַנִּית וַיְכַסּוּ אֵת עֶרְוַת אֲבִיהֶם
father-of-them nakedness-of *** and-they-covered backward and-they-walked

and every living creature with
you, a covenant for all generations to come: 13I have set my
rainbow in the clouds, and it
will be the sign of the covenant between me and the
earth. 14Whenever I bring
clouds over the earth and the
rainbow appears in the
clouds, 15I will remember my
covenant between me and you
and all living creatures of
every kind. Never again will
the waters become a flood to
destroy all life. 16Whenever the
rainbow appears in the
clouds, I will see it and
remember the everlasting covenant between God and all living creatures of every kind on
the earth."
17So God said to Noah, "This
is the sign of the covenant I
have established between me
and all life on the earth."

The Sons of Noah

18The sons of Noah who
came out of the ark were
Shem, Ham and Japheth.
(Ham was the father of Canaan.) 19These were the three
sons of Noah, and from them
came the people who were
scattered over the earth.
20Noah, a man of the soil,
proceeded[m] to plant a vineyard. 21When he drank some
of its wine, he became drunk
and lay uncovered inside his
tent. 22Ham, the father of Canaan, saw his father's nakedness and told his two brothers
outside. 23But Shem and
Japheth took a garment and
laid it across their shoulders;
then they walked in backward
and covered their father's

m20 Or *soil, was the first*

°21 ק אהלו

וּפְנֵיהֶם אֲחֹרַנִּית וְעֶרְוַת אֲבִיהֶם לֹא רָאוּ׃
they-saw not father-of-them and-nakedness-of backward and-faces-of-them

(24) וַיִּיקֶץ נֹחַ מִיֵּינוֹ וַיֵּדַע אֵת אֲשֶׁר־עָשָׂה־
he-did what *** and-he-found-out from-wine-of-him Noah when-he-awoke (24)

לוֹ בְּנוֹ הַקָּטָן׃ (25) וַיֹּאמֶר אָרוּר כְּנָעַן עֶבֶד
slave-of Canaan being-cursed and-he-said (25) the-young son-of-him to-him

עֲבָדִים יִהְיֶה לְאֶחָיו׃ (26) וַיֹּאמֶר בָּרוּךְ יְהוָה
Yahweh being-blessed also-he-said (26) to-brothers-of-him he-will-be slaves

אֱלֹהֵי שֵׁם וִיהִי כְנַעַן עֶבֶד לָמוֹ׃ (27) יַפְתְּ אֱלֹהִים
God may-he-enlarge (27) to-him slave Canaan and-may-he-be Shem God-of

לְיֶפֶת וְיִשְׁכֹּן בְּאָהֳלֵי־שֵׁם וִיהִי כְנַעַן עֶבֶד
slave Canaan and-may-he-be Shem in-tents-of and-may-he-live to-Japheth

לָמוֹ׃ (28) וַיְחִי־נֹחַ אַחַר הַמַּבּוּל שְׁלֹשׁ מֵאוֹת שָׁנָה וַחֲמִשִּׁים
and-fifty year hundreds three the-flood after Noah and-he-lived (28) to-him

שָׁנָה׃ (29) וַיְהִי כָּל־יְמֵי־נֹחַ תְּשַׁע מֵאוֹת שָׁנָה וַחֲמִשִּׁים
and-fifty year hundreds nine Noah days-of all-of and-they-were (29) year

שָׁנָה וַיָּמֹת׃ (10:1) וְאֵלֶּה תּוֹלְדֹת בְּנֵי־נֹחַ שֵׁם חָם וָיָפֶת
and-Japheth Ham Shem Noah sons-of lines-of and-these (10:1) then-he-died year

וַיִּוָּלְדוּ לָהֶם בָּנִים אַחַר הַמַּבּוּל׃ (2) בְּנֵי יֶפֶת גֹּמֶר
Gomer Japheth sons-of (2) the-flood after sons to-them and-they-were-born

וּמָגוֹג וּמָדַי וְיָוָן וְתֻבָל וּמֶשֶׁךְ וְתִירָס׃ (3) וּבְנֵי
and-sons-of (3) and-Tiras and-Meshech and-Tubal and-Javan and-Madai and-Magog

גֹּמֶר אַשְׁכְּנַז וְרִיפַת וְתֹגַרְמָה׃ (4) וּבְנֵי יָוָן אֱלִישָׁה
Elishah Javan and-sons-of (4) and-Togarmah and-Riphath Ashkenaz Gomer

וְתַרְשִׁישׁ כִּתִּים וְדֹדָנִים׃ (5) מֵאֵלֶּה נִפְרְדוּ אִיֵּי
maritime-ones-of they-spread from-these (5) and-Dodanim Kittim and-Tarshish

הַגּוֹיִם בְּאַרְצֹתָם אִישׁ לִלְשֹׁנוֹ לְמִשְׁפְּחֹתָם
by-clans-of-them with-language-of-him each into-territories-of-them the-peoples

בְּגוֹיֵהֶם׃ (6) וּבְנֵי חָם כּוּשׁ וּמִצְרַיִם וּפוּט וּכְנָעַן׃
and-Canaan and-Put and-Mizraim Cush Ham and-sons-of (6) within-nations-of-them

(7) וּבְנֵי כוּשׁ סְבָא וַחֲוִילָה וְסַבְתָּה וְרַעְמָה וְסַבְתְּכָא
and-Sabtecah and-Raamah and-Sabtah and-Havilah Seba Cush and-sons-of (7)

וּבְנֵי רַעְמָה שְׁבָא וּדְדָן׃ (8) וְכוּשׁ יָלַד אֶת־נִמְרֹד הוּא
he Nimrod *** he-fathered and-Cush (8) and-Dedan Sheba Raamah and-sons-of

הֵחֵל לִהְיוֹת גִּבֹּר בָּאָרֶץ׃ (9) הוּא־הָיָה גִבֹּר־צַיִד לִפְנֵי
before hunter mighty he-was he (9) on-the-earth mighty to-be he-was-first

יְהוָה עַל־כֵּן יֵאָמַר כְּנִמְרֹד גִּבּוֹר צַיִד לִפְנֵי יְהוָה׃
Yahweh before hunter mighty like-Nimrod he-is-said this for Yahweh

nakedness. Their faces were
turned the other way so that
they would not see their father's nakedness.
24When Noah awoke from
his wine and found out what
his youngest son had done to
him, 25he said,

"Cursed be Canaan!
The lowest of slaves
will he be to his
brothers."

26He also said,

"Blessed be the LORD, the
God of Shem!
May Canaan be the slave
of Shem.[n]
27May God extend the
territory of Japheth[o];
may Japheth live in the
tents of Shem,
and may Canaan be his[p]
slave."

28After the flood Noah lived
350 years. 29Altogether, Noah
lived 950 years, and then he
died.

The Table of Nations

10 This is the account of
Shem, Ham and
Japheth, Noah's sons, who
themselves had sons after the
flood.

The Japhethites

2The sons[q] of Japheth:
Gomer, Magog, Madai,
Javan, Tubal, Meshech
and Tiras.
3The sons of Gomer:
Ashkenaz, Riphath and
Togarmah.
4The sons of Javan:
Elishah, Tarshish, the
Kittim and the Roda-
nim.[r] 5(From these the
maritime peoples spread
out into their territories
by their clans within
their nations, each with
its own language.)

The Hamites

6The sons of Ham:
Cush, Mizraim,[s] Put and
Canaan.
7The sons of Cush:
Seba, Havilah, Sabtah,
Raamah and Sabtecah.
The sons of Raamah:
Sheba and Dedan.

8Cush was the father[t] of
Nimrod, who grew to be a
mighty warrior on the earth.
9He was a mighty hunter before the LORD; that is why it is
said, "Like Nimrod, a mighty

[n]26 Or *be his slave*
[o]27 *Japheth* sounds like the Hebrew for *extend.* [p]27 Or *their*
[q]2 *Sons* may mean *descendants* or *successors* or *nations*; also in verses 3, 4, 6, 7, 20-23, 29 and 31.
[r]4 Some manuscripts of the Masoretic Text and Samaritan Pentateuch (see also Septuagint and 1 Chron. 1:7); most manuscripts of the Masoretic Text *Dodanim*
[s]6 That is, Egypt; also in verse 13
[t]8 *Father* may mean *ancestor* or *predecessor* or *founder*; also in verses 13, 15, 24 and 26.

וַתְּהִי רֵאשִׁית מַמְלַכְתּוֹ בָּבֶל וְאֶרֶךְ וְאַכַּד
and-Akkad and-Erech Babylon kingdom-of-him first-of and-she-was (10)

וְכַלְנֵה בְּאֶרֶץ שִׁנְעָר׃ מִן־הָאָרֶץ הַהִוא יָצָא אַשּׁוּר
Assyria he-went-to the-that the-land from (11) Shinar in-land-of and-Calneh

וַיִּבֶן אֶת־נִינְוֵה וְאֶת־רְחֹבֹת עִיר וְאֶת־כָּלַח׃ וְאֶת־רֶסֶן בֵּין
between Resen and (12) Calah and Ir Rehoboth and Ninevah *** and-he-built

נִינְוֵה וּבֵין כָּלַח הִוא הָעִיר הַגְּדֹלָה׃ וּמִצְרַיִם יָלַד
he-fathered and-Mizraim (13) the-great the-city that Calah and-between Nineveh

אֶת־לוּדִים וְאֶת־עֲנָמִים וְאֶת־לְהָבִים וְאֶת־נַפְתֻּחִים׃ וְאֶת־פַּתְרֻסִים
Pathrusites and (14) Naphtuhites and Lehabites and Anamites and Ludites ***

וְאֶת־כַּסְלֻחִים אֲשֶׁר יָצְאוּ מִשָּׁם פְּלִשְׁתִּים וְאֶת־כַּפְתֹּרִים׃
Caphtorites and Philistines from-there they-came whom Casluhites and

וּכְנַעַן יָלַד אֶת־צִידֹן בְּכֹרוֹ וְאֶת־חֵת׃ וְאֶת־
and (16) Hittite and firstborn-of-him Sidon *** he-fathered and-Canaan (15)

הַיְבוּסִי וְאֶת־הָאֱמֹרִי וְאֵת הַגִּרְגָּשִׁי׃ וְאֶת־הַחִוִּי וְאֶת־
and the-Hivite and (17) the-Girgashite and the-Amorite and the-Jebusite

הַעַרְקִי וְאֶת־הַסִּינִי׃ וְאֶת־הָאַרְוָדִי וְאֶת־הַצְּמָרִי וְאֶת־
and the-Zemarite and the-Arvadite and (18) the-Sinite and the-Arkite

הַחֲמָתִי וְאַחַר נָפֹצוּ מִשְׁפְּחוֹת הַכְּנַעֲנִי׃ וַיְהִי
and-he-was (19) the-Canaanite clans-of they-scattered and-later the-Hamathite

גְּבוּל הַכְּנַעֲנִי מִצִּידֹן בֹּאֲכָה גְרָרָה עַד־עַזָּה בֹּאֲכָה
to-go-you Gaza as-far-as to-Gerar to-go-you from-Sidon the-Canaanite border-of

סְדֹמָה וַעֲמֹרָה וְאַדְמָה וּצְבֹיִם עַד־לָשַׁע׃ אֵלֶּה
these (20) Lasha as-far-as and-Zeboiim and-Admah and-Gomorrah to-Sodom

בְנֵי־חָם לְמִשְׁפְּחֹתָם לִלְשֹׁנֹתָם בְּאַרְצֹתָם
in-territories-of-them by-languages-of-them by-clans-of-them Ham sons-of

בְּגוֹיֵהֶם׃ וּלְשֵׁם יֻלַּד גַּם־הוּא אֲבִי כָּל־בְּנֵי־
sons-of all-of father-of he also he-was-born and-to-Shem (21) in-nations-of-them

עֵבֶר אֲחִי יֶפֶת הַגָּדוֹל׃ בְּנֵי שֵׁם עֵילָם וְאַשּׁוּר
and-Asshur Elam Shem sons-of (22) the-older Japheth brother-of Eber

וְאַרְפַּכְשַׁד וְלוּד וַאֲרָם׃ וּבְנֵי אֲרָם עוּץ וְחוּל וְגֶתֶר
and-Gether and-Hul Uz Aram and-sons-of (23) and-Aram and-Lud and-Arphaxad

וָמַשׁ׃ וְאַרְפַּכְשַׁד יָלַד אֶת־שָׁלַח וְשֶׁלַח יָלַד אֶת־
*** he-fathered and-Shelah Shelah *** he-fathered and-Arphaxad (24) and-Mash

עֵבֶר׃ וּלְעֵבֶר יֻלַּד שְׁנֵי בָנִים שֵׁם הָאֶחָד פֶּלֶג כִּי
because Peleg the-one name-of sons two-of he-was-born and-to-Eber (25) Eber

בְיָמָיו נִפְלְגָה הָאָרֶץ וְשֵׁם אָחִיו יָקְטָן׃
Joktan brother-of-him and-name-of the-earth she-was-divided in-days-of-him

hunter before the LORD." [10]The first centers of his kingdom were Babylon, Erech, Akkad and Calneh, in[u] Shinar.[v] [11]From that land he went to Assyria, where he built Nineveh, Rehoboth Ir,[w] Calah [12]and Resen, which is between Nineveh and Calah; that is the great city.

[13]Mizraim was the father of
the Ludites, Anamites, Lehabites, Naphtuhites,
[14]Pathrusites, Casluhites (from whom the Philistines came) and Caphtorites.

[15]Canaan was the father of
Sidon his firstborn,[x] and of the Hittites, [16]Jebusites, Amorites, Girgashites, [17]Hivites, Arkites, Sinites, [18]Arvadites, Zemarites and Hamathites.

Later the Canaanite clans scattered [19]and the borders of Canaan reached from Sidon toward Gerar as far as Gaza, and then toward Sodom, Gomorrah, Admah and Zeboiim, as far as Lasha.

[20]These are the descendants of Ham by their clans and languages, in their territories and nations.

The Semites

[21]Sons were also born to Shem, whose older brother was[y] Japheth; Shem was the ancestor of all the sons of Eber.

[22]The sons of Shem:
Elam, Asshur, Arphaxad, Lud and Aram.
[23]The sons of Aram:
Uz, Hul, Gether and Meshech.[z]
[24]Arphaxad was the father of[a] Shelah,
and Shelah the father of Eber.
[25]Two sons were born to Eber:
One was named Peleg,[b] because in his time the earth was divided; his brother was named Joktan.

[u]10 Or *Erech and Akkad—all of them in*
[v]10 That is, Babylonia
[w]11 Or *Nineveh with its city squares*
[x]15 Or *of the Sidonians, the foremost*
[y]21 Or *Shem, the older brother of*
[z]23 Septuagint (see also 1 Chron. 1:17); Hebrew *Mash*
[a]24 Hebrew; Septuagint *father of Cainan, and Cainan was the father of*
[b]25 *Peleg* means *division.*

וְיָקְטָן יָלַד אֶת־אַלְמוֹדָד וְאֶת־שָׁלֶף וְאֶת־חֲצַרְמָוֶת וְאֶת־
and Hazarmaveth and Sheleph and Almodad *** he-fathered and-Joktan (26)

יָרַח׃ וְאֶת־הֲדוֹרָם וְאֶת־אוּזָל וְאֶת־דִּקְלָה׃ וְאֶת־עוֹבָל וְאֶת־אֲבִימָאֵל וְאֶת־
and Abimael and Obal and (28) Diklah and Uzal and Hadoram and (27) Jerah

שְׁבָא׃ וְאֶת־אוֹפִר וְאֶת־חֲוִילָה וְאֶת־יוֹבָב כָּל־אֵלֶּה בְּנֵי יָקְטָן׃
Joktan sons-of these all-of Jobab and Havilah and Ophir and (29) Sheba

וַיְהִי מוֹשָׁבָם מִמֵּשָׁא בֹּאֲכָה סְפָרָה הַר
hill-country-of to-Sephar to-go-you from-Mesha region-of-them and-he-was (30)

הַקֶּדֶם׃ אֵלֶּה בְנֵי־שֵׁם לְמִשְׁפְּחֹתָם לִלְשֹׁנֹתָם
by-languages-of-them by-clans-of-them Shem sons-of these (31) the-east

בְּאַרְצֹתָם לְגוֹיֵהֶם׃ אֵלֶּה מִשְׁפְּחֹת בְּנֵי־נֹחַ
Noah sons-of clans-of these (32) by-nations-of-them in-territories-of-them

לְתוֹלְדֹתָם בְּגוֹיֵהֶם וּמֵאֵלֶּה נִפְרְדוּ הַגּוֹיִם
the-nations they-spread-out and-from-these in-nations-of-them by-lines-of-them

בָּאָרֶץ אַחַר הַמַּבּוּל׃ וַיְהִי כָל־הָאָרֶץ שָׂפָה אֶחָת
one language the-earth all-of now-he-had (11:1) the-flood after on-the-earth

וּדְבָרִים אֲחָדִים׃ וַיְהִי בְּנָסְעָם מִקֶּדֶם וַיִּמְצְאוּ
and-they-found to-east as-to-move-them and-he-was (2) common-ones and-words

בִקְעָה בְּאֶרֶץ שִׁנְעָר וַיֵּשְׁבוּ שָׁם׃ וַיֹּאמְרוּ אִישׁ אֶל־
to each and-they-said (3) there and-they-settled Shinar in-land-of plain

רֵעֵהוּ הָבָה נִלְבְּנָה לְבֵנִים וְנִשְׂרְפָה לִשְׂרֵפָה וַתְּהִי
and-she-was with-fire and-let-us-bake bricks let-us-make come! fellow-of-him

לָהֶם הַלְּבֵנָה לְאָבֶן וְהַחֵמָר הָיָה לָהֶם לַחֹמֶר׃
instead-of-mortar to-them he-was and-the-tar instead-of-stone the-brick to-them

וַיֹּאמְרוּ הָבָה ׀ נִבְנֶה־לָּנוּ עִיר וּמִגְדָּל וְרֹאשׁוֹ
and-top-of-him and-tower city for-us let-us-build come! then-they-said (4)

בַשָּׁמַיִם וְנַעֲשֶׂה־לָּנוּ שֵׁם פֶּן־נָפוּץ עַל־פְּנֵי
face-of over we-be-scattered lest name for-us so-let-us-make in-the-heavens

כָל־הָאָרֶץ׃ וַיֵּרֶד יְהוָה לִרְאֹת אֶת־הָעִיר וְאֶת־
and the-city *** to-see Yahweh but-he-came-down (5) the-earth whole-of

הַמִּגְדָּל אֲשֶׁר בָּנוּ בְּנֵי הָאָדָם׃ וַיֹּאמֶר יְהוָה הֵן עַם
people see! Yahweh and-he-said (6) the-man sons-of they-built that the-tower

אֶחָד וְשָׂפָה אַחַת לְכֻלָּם וְזֶה הַחִלָּם לַעֲשׂוֹת וְעַתָּה
then-now to-do to-begin-them and-this to-all-of-them same and-language one

לֹא־יִבָּצֵר מֵהֶם כֹּל אֲשֶׁר יָזְמוּ לַעֲשׂוֹת׃ הָבָה
come! (7) to-do they-plan that all for-them he-is-impossible nothing

נֵרְדָה וְנָבְלָה שָׁם שְׂפָתָם אֲשֶׁר לֹא
not so language-of-them there and-let-us-confuse let-us-go-down

26Joktan was the father of
Almodad, Sheleph,
Hazarmaveth, Jerah,
27Hadoram, Uzal, Diklah,
28Obal, Abimael, Sheba,
29Ophir, Havilah and
Jobab. All these were
sons of Joktan.

30The region where they lived
stretched from Mesha toward
Sephar, in the eastern hill
country.

31These are the sons of Shem
by their clans and languages,
in their territories and nations.

32These are the clans of
Noah's sons, according to
their lines of descent, within
their nations. From these the
nations spread out over the
earth after the flood.

The Tower of Babel

11 Now the whole world
had one language and
a common speech. 2As men
moved eastward,[c] they found
a plain in Shinar[d] and settled
there.

3They said to each other,
"Come, let's make bricks and
bake them thoroughly." They
used brick instead of stone,
and tar instead of mortar.
4Then they said, "Come, let us
build ourselves a city, with a
tower that reaches to the heavens, so that we may make a
name for ourselves and not be
scattered over the face of the
whole earth."

5But the LORD came down to
see the city and the tower that
the men were building. 6The
LORD said, "If as one people
speaking the same language
they have begun to do this,
then nothing they plan to do
will be impossible for them.
7Come, let us go down and
confuse their language so they

[c]2 Or *from the east;* or *in the east*
[d]2 That is, Babylonia

יִשְׁמְעוּ אִישׁ שְׂפַת רֵעֵהוּ׃ וַיָּפֶץ יְהוָה
Yahweh so-he-scattered (8) fellow-of-him language-of one they-will-understand

אֹתָם מִשָּׁם עַל־ פְּנֵי כָל־ הָאָרֶץ וַיַּחְדְּלוּ לִבְנֹת
to-build and-they-stopped the-earth all-of face-of over from-there them

הָעִיר׃ עַל־ כֵּן קָרָא שְׁמָהּ בָּבֶל כִּי־ שָׁם בָּלַל
he-confused there because Babel name-of-her he-calls this for (9) the-city

יְהוָה שְׂפַת כָּל־ הָאָרֶץ וּמִשָּׁם הֱפִיצָם יְהוָה
Yahweh he-scattered-them and-from-there the-earth whole-of language-of Yahweh

עַל־ פְּנֵי כָּל־ הָאָרֶץ׃ אֵלֶּה תּוֹלְדֹת שֵׁם שֵׁם בֶּן־
son-of Shem Shem lines-of these (10) the-earth whole-of face-of over

מְאַת שָׁנָה וַיּוֹלֶד אֶת־אַרְפַּכְשָׁד שְׁנָתַיִם אַחַר הַמַּבּוּל׃ וַיְחִי־
and-he-lived (11) the-flood after two Arphaxad *** and-he-fathered year hundred-of

שֵׁם אַחֲרֵי הוֹלִידוֹ אֶת־אַרְפַּכְשָׁד חֲמֵשׁ מֵאוֹת שָׁנָה וַיּוֹלֶד
and-he-fathered year hundreds five Arphaxad *** to-father-him after Shem

בָּנִים וּבָנוֹת׃ וְאַרְפַּכְשַׁד חַי חָמֵשׁ וּשְׁלֹשִׁים שָׁנָה וַיּוֹלֶד
and-he-fathered year and-thirty five life and-Arphaxad (12) and-daughters sons

אֶת־ שָׁלַח׃ וַיְחִי אַרְפַּכְשַׁד אַחֲרֵי הוֹלִידוֹ אֶת־ שֶׁלַח שָׁלֹשׁ
three Shelah *** to-father-him after Arphaxad and-he-lived (13) Shelah ***

שָׁנִים וְאַרְבַּע מֵאוֹת שָׁנָה וַיּוֹלֶד בָּנִים וּבָנוֹת׃ וְשֶׁלַח
and-Shelah (14) and-daughters sons and-he-fathered year hundreds and-four years

חַי שְׁלֹשִׁים שָׁנָה וַיּוֹלֶד אֶת־ עֵבֶר׃ וַיְחִי־ שֶׁלַח אַחֲרֵי
after Shelah and-he-lived (15) Eber *** and-he-fathered year thirty life

הוֹלִידוֹ אֶת־ עֵבֶר שָׁלֹשׁ שָׁנִים וְאַרְבַּע מֵאוֹת שָׁנָה וַיּוֹלֶד
and-he-fathered year hundreds and-four years three Eber *** to-father-him

בָּנִים וּבָנוֹת׃ וַיְחִי־ עֵבֶר אַרְבַּע וּשְׁלֹשִׁים שָׁנָה וַיּוֹלֶד
and-he-fathered year and-thirty four Eber and-he-lived (16) and-daughters sons

אֶת־ פָּלֶג׃ וַיְחִי־ עֵבֶר אַחֲרֵי הוֹלִידוֹ אֶת־ פֶּלֶג שְׁלֹשִׁים שָׁנָה
year thirty Peleg *** to-father-him after Eber and-he-lived (17) Peleg ***

וְאַרְבַּע מֵאוֹת שָׁנָה וַיּוֹלֶד בָּנִים וּבָנוֹת׃ וַיְחִי־
and-he-lived (18) and-daughters sons and-he-fathered year hundreds and-four

פֶלֶג שְׁלֹשִׁים שָׁנָה וַיּוֹלֶד אֶת־ רְעוּ׃ וַיְחִי־ פֶלֶג אַחֲרֵי
after Peleg and-he-lived (19) Reu *** and-he-fathered year thirty Peleg

הוֹלִידוֹ אֶת־ רְעוּ תֵּשַׁע שָׁנִים וּמָאתַיִם שָׁנָה וַיּוֹלֶד בָּנִים
sons and-he-fathered year and-two-hundred years nine Reu *** to-father-him

וּבָנוֹת׃ וַיְחִי רְעוּ שְׁתַּיִם וּשְׁלֹשִׁים שָׁנָה וַיּוֹלֶד אֶת־
*** and-he-fathered year and-thirty two Reu and-he-lived (20) and-daughters

שְׂרוּג׃ וַיְחִי רְעוּ אַחֲרֵי הוֹלִידוֹ אֶת־ שְׂרוּג שֶׁבַע שָׁנִים
years seven Serug *** to-father-him after Reu and-he-lived (21) Serug

will not understand each other."

[8]So the LORD scattered them from there over all the earth, and they stopped building the city. [9]That is why it was called Babel[e]—because there the LORD confused the language of the whole world. From there the LORD scattered them over the face of the whole earth.

From Shem to Abram

[10]This is the account of Shem.

Two years after the flood, when Shem was 100 years old, he became the father[f] of Arphaxad. [11]And after he became the father of Arphaxad, Shem lived 500 years and had other sons and daughters.

[12]When Arphaxad had lived 35 years, he became the father of Shelah. [13]And after he became the father of Shelah, Arphaxad lived 403 years and had other sons and daughters.[g]

[14]When Shelah had lived 30 years, he became the father of Eber. [15]And after he became the father of Eber, Shelah lived 403 years and had other sons and daughters.

[16]When Eber had lived 34 years, he became the father of Peleg. [17]And after he became the father of Peleg, Eber lived 430 years and had other sons and daughters.

[18]When Peleg had lived 30 years, he became the father of Reu. [19]And after he became the father of Reu, Peleg lived 209 years and had other sons and daughters.

[20]When Reu had lived 32 years, he became the father of Serug. [21]And after he became the father of Serug, Reu lived

[e]9 That is, Babylon; *Babel* sounds like the Hebrew for *confused*.

[f]10 *Father* may mean *ancestor*; also in verses 11-25.

[g]12,13 Hebrew; Septuagint (see also Gen. 10:24 and Luke 3:35, 36) *35 years, he became the father of Cainan. [13]And after he became the father of Cainan, Arphaxad lived 430 years and had other sons and daughters. When Cainan had lived 130 years, he became the father of Shelah. And after he became the father of Shelah, Cainan lived 330 years and had other sons and daughters*

וּמָאתַיִם שָׁנָה וַיּוֹלֶד בָּנִים וּבָנוֹת׃ וַיְחִי
and-he-lived (22) and-daughters sons and-he-fathered year and-two-hundred

שְׂרוּג שְׁלֹשִׁים שָׁנָה וַיּוֹלֶד אֶת־ נָחוֹר׃ וַיְחִי שְׂרוּג אַחֲרֵי
after Serug and-he-lived (23) Nahor *** and-he-fathered year thirty Serug

הוֹלִידוֹ אֶת־ נָחוֹר מָאתַיִם שָׁנָה וַיּוֹלֶד בָּנִים וּבָנוֹת׃
and-daughters sons and-he-fathered year two-hundred Nahor *** to-father-him

וַיְחִי נָחוֹר תֵּשַׁע וְעֶשְׂרִים שָׁנָה וַיּוֹלֶד אֶת־ תָּרַח׃
Terah *** and-he-fathered year and-twenty nine Nahor and-he-lived (24)

וַיְחִי נָחוֹר אַחֲרֵי הוֹלִידוֹ אֶת־ תֶּרַח תְּשַׁע־עֶשְׂרֵה שָׁנָה
year ten nine Terah *** to-father-him after Nahor and-he-lived (25)

וּמְאַת שָׁנָה וַיּוֹלֶד בָּנִים וּבָנוֹת׃ וַיְחִי־
and-he-lived (26) and-daughters sons and-he-fathered year and-hundred-of

תֶרַח שִׁבְעִים שָׁנָה וַיּוֹלֶד אֶת־ אַבְרָם אֶת־ נָחוֹר וְאֶת־ הָרָן׃
Haran and Nahor *** Abram *** and-he-fathered year seventy Terah

וְאֵלֶּה תּוֹלְדֹת תֶּרַח תֶּרַח הוֹלִיד אֶת־אַבְרָם אֶת־ נָחוֹר וְאֶת־
and Nahor *** Abram *** he-fathered Terah Terah lines-of and-these (27)

הָרָן וְהָרָן הוֹלִיד אֶת־לוֹט׃ וַיָּמָת הָרָן עַל־ פְּנֵי תֶּרַח
Terah life-of in Haran and-he-died (28) Lot *** he-fathered and-Haran Haran

אָבִיו בְּאֶרֶץ מוֹלַדְתּוֹ בְּאוּר כַּשְׂדִּים׃ וַיִּקַּח
and-he-took (29) Chaldeans in-Ur-of birth-of-him in-land-of father-of-him

אַבְרָם וְנָחוֹר לָהֶם נָשִׁים שֵׁם אֵשֶׁת־ אַבְרָם שָׂרָי וְשֵׁם אֵשֶׁת־
wife-of and-name-of Sarai Abram wife-of name-of wives to-them and-Nahor Abram

נָחוֹר מִלְכָּה בַּת־ הָרָן אֲבִי־ מִלְכָּה וַאֲבִי יִסְכָּה׃
Iscah and-father-of Milcah father-of Haran daughter-of Milcah Nahor

וַתְּהִי שָׂרַי עֲקָרָה אֵין לָהּ וָלָד׃ וַיִּקַּח תֶּרַח אֶת־
*** Terah and-he-took (31) child to-her not barren Sarai now-she-was (30)

אַבְרָם בְּנוֹ וְאֶת־לוֹט בֶּן־ הָרָן בֶּן־ בְּנוֹ וְאֵת שָׂרַי
Sarai and son-of-him son-of Haran son-of Lot and son-of-him Abram

כַּלָּתוֹ אֵשֶׁת אַבְרָם בְּנוֹ וַיֵּצְאוּ אִתָּם
together and-they-set-out son-of-him Abram wife-of daughters-in-law-of-him

מֵאוּר כַּשְׂדִּים לָלֶכֶת אַרְצָה כְּנַעַן וַיָּבֹאוּ עַד־ חָרָן
Haran to but-they-came Canaan to-land to-go Chaldeans from-Ur-of

וַיֵּשְׁבוּ שָׁם׃ וַיִּהְיוּ יְמֵי־ תֶרַח חָמֵשׁ שָׁנִים
years five Terah days-of and-they-were (32) there and-they-settled

וּמָאתַיִם שָׁנָה וַיָּמָת תֶּרַח בְּחָרָן׃ וַיֹּאמֶר יְהוָה
Yahweh and-he-said (12:1) in-Haran Terah and-he-died year and-two-hundred

אֶל־ אַבְרָם לֶךְ־ לְךָ מֵאַרְצְךָ וּמִמּוֹלַדְתְּךָ
and-from-people-of-you from-country-of-you for-you leave! Abram to

207 years and had other sons and daughters.
[22]When Serug had lived 30 years, he became the father of
Nahor. [23]And after he became the father of Nahor, Serug lived 200 years and had other sons and daughters.
[24]When Nahor had lived 29 years, he became the father of
Terah. [25]And after he became the father of Terah, Nahor lived 119 years and had other sons and daughters.
[26]After Terah had lived 70 years, he became the father of Abram, Nahor and Haran.

[27]This is the account of Terah.

Terah became the father of Abram, Nahor and Haran. And Haran became the father
of Lot. [28]While his father Terah was still alive, Haran died in Ur of the Chaldeans, in the
land of his birth. [29]Abram and Nahor both married. The name of Abram's wife was Sarai, and the name of Nahor's wife was Milcah; she was the daughter of Haran, the father of both Milcah and
Iscah. [30]Now Sarai was barren; she had no children.
[31]Terah took his son Abram, his grandson Lot son of Haran, and his daughter-in-law Sarai, the wife of his son Abram, and together they set out from Ur of the Chaldeans to go to Canaan. But when they came to Haran, they settled there.
[32]Terah lived 205 years, and he died in Haran.

The Call of Abram

12 The LORD had said to Abram, "Leave your country, your people and your

וּמִבֵּית אָבִיךָ אֶל־הָאָרֶץ אֲשֶׁר אַרְאֶךָּ׃
I-will-show-you that the-land to father-of-you and-from-house-of

וְאֶעֶשְׂךָ לְגוֹי גָּדוֹל וַאֲבָרֶכְךָ וַאֲגַדְּלָה
and-I-will-make-great and-I-will-bless-you great into-nation and-I-will-make-you (2)

שְׁמֶךָ וֶהְיֵה בְּרָכָה׃ וַאֲבָרְכָה מְבָרְכֶיךָ
ones-blessing-you and-I-will-bless (3) blessing and-be! name-of-you

וּמְקַלֶּלְךָ אָאֹר וְנִבְרְכוּ בְךָ כֹּל
all-of through-you and-they-will-be-blessed I-will-curse and-one-cursing-you

מִשְׁפְּחֹת הָאֲדָמָה׃ וַיֵּלֶךְ אַבְרָם כַּאֲשֶׁר דִּבֶּר אֵלָיו יְהוָה
Yahweh to-him he-told just-as Abram so-he-left (4) the-earth peoples-of

וַיֵּלֶךְ אִתּוֹ לוֹט וְאַבְרָם בֶּן־חָמֵשׁ שָׁנִים וְשִׁבְעִים שָׁנָה
year and-seventy years five son-of and-Abram Lot with-him and-he-went

בְּצֵאתוֹ מֵחָרָן׃ וַיִּקַּח אַבְרָם אֶת־שָׂרַי אִשְׁתּוֹ וְאֶת־לוֹט
Lot and wife-of-him Sarai *** Abram and-he-took (5) from-Haran when-to-go-him

בֶּן־אָחִיו וְאֶת־כָּל־רְכוּשָׁם אֲשֶׁר רָכָשׁוּ
they-accumulated that possessions-of-them all-of and brother-of-him son-of

וְאֶת־הַנֶּפֶשׁ אֲשֶׁר־עָשׂוּ בְחָרָן וַיֵּצְאוּ לָלֶכֶת אַרְצָה
to-land to-go and-they-set-out in-Haran they-acquired that the-people and

כְּנַעַן וַיָּבֹאוּ אַרְצָה כְּנָעַן׃ וַיַּעֲבֹר אַבְרָם בָּאָרֶץ
in-the-land Abram and-he-traveled (6) Canaan in-land and-they-arrived Canaan

עַד מְקוֹם שְׁכֶם עַד אֵלוֹן מוֹרֶה וְהַכְּנַעֲנִי אָז בָּאָרֶץ׃
in-the-land then and-the-Canaanite Moreh tree-of to Shechem site-of as-far-as

וַיֵּרָא יְהוָה אֶל־אַבְרָם וַיֹּאמֶר לְזַרְעֲךָ אֶתֵּן
I-will-give to-offspring-of-you and-he-said Abram to Yahweh but-he-appeared (7)

אֶת־הָאָרֶץ הַזֹּאת וַיִּבֶן שָׁם מִזְבֵּחַ לַיהוָה הַנִּרְאֶה
the-one-appearing to-Yahweh altar there so-he-built the-this the-land ***

אֵלָיו׃ וַיַּעְתֵּק מִשָּׁם הָהָרָה מִקֶּדֶם לְבֵית־אֵל
El to-Beth on-east to-the-hill from-there and-he-went-on (8) to-him

וַיֵּט אָהֳלֹה בֵּית־אֵל מִיָּם וְהָעַי מִקֶּדֶם וַיִּבֶן־
and-he-built on-east and the-Ai on-west El Beth tent-of-him and-he-pitched

שָׁם מִזְבֵּחַ לַיהוָה וַיִּקְרָא בְּשֵׁם יְהוָה׃ וַיִּסַּע
then-he-set-out (9) Yahweh on-name-of and-he-called to-Yahweh altar there

אַבְרָם הָלוֹךְ וְנָסוֹעַ הַנֶּגְבָּה׃ וַיְהִי רָעָב בָּאָרֶץ
in-the-land famine and-he-was (10) to-the-Negev and-to-continue to-go Abram

וַיֵּרֶד אַבְרָם מִצְרַיְמָה לָגוּר שָׁם כִּי־כָבֵד הָרָעָב
the-famine he-was-severe because there to-live to-Egypt Abram and-he-went-down

בָּאָרֶץ׃ וַיְהִי כַּאֲשֶׁר הִקְרִיב לָבוֹא מִצְרָיְמָה
into-Egypt to-enter he-was-about just-as and-he-was (11) in-the-land

father's household and go to the land I will show you.

[2]"I will make you into a great nation
and I will bless you;
I will make your name great,
and you will be a blessing.
[3]I will bless those who bless you,
and whoever curses you I will curse;
and all peoples on earth will be blessed through you."

[4]So Abram left, as the LORD had told him; and Lot went with him. Abram was seventy-five years old when he set out from Haran. [5]He took his wife Sarai, his nephew Lot, all the possessions they had accumulated and the people they had acquired in Haran, and they set out for the land of Canaan, and they arrived there.

[6]Abram traveled through the land as far as the site of the great tree of Moreh at Shechem. The Canaanites were then in the land, [7]but the LORD appeared to Abram and said, "To your offspring[h] I will give this land." So he built an altar there to the LORD, who had appeared to him.

[8]From there he went on toward the hills east of Bethel and pitched his tent, with Bethel on the west and Ai on the east. There he built an altar to the LORD and called on the name of the LORD. [9]Then Abram set out and continued toward the Negev.

Abram in Egypt

[10]Now there was a famine in the land, and Abram went down to Egypt to live there for a while because the famine was severe. [11]As he was about to enter Egypt, he said to his

[h]7 Or *seed*

°8 ק אהלו

וַיֹּאמֶר אֶל־שָׂרַי אִשְׁתּוֹ הִנֵּה־נָא יָדַעְתִּי כִּי אִשָּׁה יְפַת־מַרְאֶה
sight beautiful-of woman that I-know now! see! wife-of-him Sarai to and-he-said

אָתְּ׃ וְהָיָה כִּי־יִרְאוּ אֹתָךְ הַמִּצְרִים וְאָמְרוּ
and-they-will-say the-Egyptians you they-see when and-he-will-be (12) you

אִשְׁתּוֹ זֹאת וְהָרְגוּ אֹתִי וְאֹתָךְ יְחַיּוּ׃ אִמְרִי־נָא
now! say! (13) they-will-let-live but-you me and-they-will-kill this wife-of-him

אֲחֹתִי אָתְּ לְמַעַן יִיטַב־לִי בַעֲבוּרֵךְ
for-sake-of-you for-me he-will-be-well so-that you sister-of-me

וְחָיְתָה נַפְשִׁי בִּגְלָלֵךְ׃ וַיְהִי כְּבוֹא
as-to-come and-he-was (14) on-account-of-you life-of-me and-she-will-be-spared

אַבְרָם מִצְרָיְמָה וַיִּרְאוּ הַמִּצְרִים אֶת־הָאִשָּׁה כִּי־יָפָה הִוא
she beautiful that the-woman *** the-Egyptians and-they-saw to-Egypt Abram

מְאֹד׃ וַיִּרְאוּ אֹתָהּ שָׂרֵי פַרְעֹה וַיְהַלְלוּ אֹתָהּ אֶל־
to her and-they-praised Pharaoh officials-of her when-they-saw (15) very

פַּרְעֹה וַתֻּקַּח הָאִשָּׁה בֵּית פַּרְעֹה׃ וּלְאַבְרָם
and-for-Abram (16) Pharaoh palace-of the-woman and-she-was-taken Pharaoh

הֵיטִיב בַּעֲבוּרָהּ וַיְהִי־לוֹ צֹאן־וּבָקָר
and-cattle sheep to-him and-he-was for-sake-of-her he-treated-well

וַחֲמֹרִים וַעֲבָדִים וּשְׁפָחֹת וַאֲתֹנֹת וּגְמַלִּים׃
and-camels and-female-donkeys and-maidservants and-menservants and-donkeys

וַיְנַגַּע יְהוָה ׀ אֶת־פַּרְעֹה נְגָעִים גְּדֹלִים וְאֶת־
and serious-ones diseases Pharaoh *** Yahweh but-he-inflicted (17)

בֵּיתוֹ עַל־דְּבַר שָׂרַי אֵשֶׁת אַבְרָם׃ וַיִּקְרָא
and-he-summoned (18) Abram wife-of Sarai reason-of for household-of-him

פַרְעֹה לְאַבְרָם וַיֹּאמֶר מַה־זֹּאת עָשִׂיתָ לִּי לָמָּה לֹא־הִגַּדְתָּ
you-tell not why? to-me you-did this what? and-he-said for-Abram Pharaoh

לִּי כִּי אִשְׁתְּךָ הִוא׃ לָמָה אָמַרְתָּ אֲחֹתִי הִוא וָאֶקַּח אֹתָהּ
her so-I-took she sister-of-me you-say why? (19) she wife-of-you that to-me

לִי לְאִשָּׁה וְעַתָּה הִנֵּה אִשְׁתְּךָ קַח וָלֵךְ׃ וַיְצַו
and-he-gave-orders (20) and-go! take! wife-of-you see! and-now for-wife to-me

עָלָיו פַּרְעֹה אֲנָשִׁים וַיְשַׁלְּחוּ אֹתוֹ וְאֶת־אִשְׁתּוֹ וְאֶת־כָּל־אֲשֶׁר־
that everything and wife-of-him and him and-they-sent men Pharaoh about-him

לוֹ׃ וַיַּעַל אַבְרָם מִמִּצְרַיִם הוּא וְאִשְׁתּוֹ וְכָל־
and-everything and-wife-of-him he from-Egypt Abram so-he-went-up (13:1) to-him

אֲשֶׁר־לוֹ וְלוֹט עִמּוֹ הַנֶּגְבָּה׃ וְאַבְרָם כָּבֵד
he-became-wealthy and-Abram (2) to-the-Negev with-him and-Lot to-him that

מְאֹד בַּמִּקְנֶה בַּכֶּסֶף וּבַזָּהָב׃ וַיֵּלֶךְ
and-he-went (3) and-in-the-gold in-the-silver in-the-livestock very

wife Sarai, "I know what a beautiful woman you are. [12]When the Egyptians see you, they will say, 'This is his wife.' Then they will kill me but will let you live. [13]Say you are my sister, so that I will be treated well for your sake and my life will be spared because of you."

[14]When Abram came to Egypt, the Egyptians saw that she was a very beautiful woman. [15]And when Pharaoh's officials saw her, they praised her to Pharaoh, and she was taken into his palace. [16]He treated Abram well for her sake, and Abram acquired sheep and cattle, male and female donkeys, menservants and maidservants, and camels.

[17]But the LORD inflicted serious diseases on Pharaoh and his household because of Abram's wife Sarai. [18]So Pharaoh summoned Abram. "What have you done to me?" he said. "Why didn't you tell me she was your wife? [19]Why did you say, 'She is my sister,' so that I took her to be my wife? Now then, here is your wife. Take her and go!" [20]Then Pharaoh gave orders about Abram to his men, and they sent him on his way, with his wife and everything he had.

Abram and Lot Separate

13 So Abram went up from Egypt to the Negev, with his wife and everything he had, and Lot went with him. [2]Abram had become very wealthy in livestock and in silver and gold.

לְמַסָּעָיו מִנֶּגֶב וְעַד־בֵּית־אֵל עַד־הַמָּקוֹם אֲשֶׁר־הָיָה שָׁם
there he-was where the-place to El Beth and-to from-Negev on-journeys-of-him

אָהֳלֹה° בַּתְּחִלָּה בֵּין בֵּית־אֵל וּבֵין הָעָי׃ אֶל־מְקוֹם
place-of to (4) the-Ai and-between El Beth between at-the-first tent-of-him

הַמִּזְבֵּחַ אֲשֶׁר־עָשָׂה שָׁם בָּרִאשֹׁנָה וַיִּקְרָא שָׁם אַבְרָם
Abram there and-he-called at-the-first there he-built that the-altar

בְּשֵׁם יְהוָה׃ וְגַם־לְלוֹט הַהֹלֵךְ אֶת־אַבְרָם הָיָה צֹאן־
flock he-was Abram with the-one-moving to-Lot and-also (5) Yahweh on-name-of

וּבָקָר וְאֹהָלִים׃ וְלֹא־נָשָׂא אֹתָם הָאָרֶץ לָשֶׁבֶת
to-stay the-land them he-could-support but-not (6) and-tents and-herd

יַחְדָּו כִּי־הָיָה רְכוּשָׁם רָב וְלֹא יָכְלוּ לָשֶׁבֶת
to-stay they-were-able that-not great possession-of-them he-was for together

יַחְדָּו׃ וַיְהִי־רִיב בֵּין רֹעֵי מִקְנֵה־אַבְרָם
Abram herd-of ones-tending-of between quarrel and-he-rose (7) together

וּבֵין רֹעֵי מִקְנֵה־לוֹט וְהַכְּנַעֲנִי וְהַפְּרִזִּי
and-the-Perizzite and-the-Canaanite Lot herd-of ones-tending-of and-between

אָז יֹשֵׁב בָּאָרֶץ׃ וַיֹּאמֶר אַבְרָם אֶל־לוֹט אַל־נָא תְהִי מְרִיבָה
quarrel let-her-be now! not Lot to Abram so-he-said (8) in-the-land living then

בֵּינִי וּבֵינֶךָ וּבֵין רֹעַי וּבֵין
and-between ones-tending-of-me and-between and-between-you between-me

רֹעֶיךָ כִּי־אֲנָשִׁים אַחִים אֲנָחְנוּ׃ הֲלֹא כָל־הָאָרֶץ לְפָנֶיךָ
before-you the-land whole-of not? (9) we brothers men for ones-tending-of-you

הִפָּרֶד נָא מֵעָלָי אִם־הַשְּׂמֹאל וְאֵימִנָה וְאִם־הַיָּמִין
the-right and-if then-I-will-go-right the-left if from-me now! part-company!

וְאַשְׂמְאִילָה׃ וַיִּשָּׂא־לוֹט אֶת־עֵינָיו וַיַּרְא אֶת־
*** and-he-saw eyes-of-him *** Lot and-he-lifted (10) then-I-will-go-left

כָּל־כִּכַּר הַיַּרְדֵּן כִּי כֻלָּהּ מַשְׁקֶה לִפְנֵי ׀ שַׁחֵת
to-destroy before well-watered all-of-her that the-Jordan plain-of whole-of

יְהוָה אֶת־סְדֹם וְאֶת־עֲמֹרָה כְּגַן־יְהוָה כְּאֶרֶץ מִצְרַיִם
Egypt like-land-of Yahweh like-garden-of Gomorrah and Sodom *** Yahweh

בֹּאֲכָה צֹעַר׃ וַיִּבְחַר־לוֹ לוֹט אֵת כָּל־כִּכַּר הַיַּרְדֵּן
the-Jordan plain-of whole-of *** Lot for-him so-he-chose (11) Zoar to-go-you

וַיִּסַּע לוֹט מִקֶּדֶם וַיִּפָּרְדוּ אִישׁ מֵעַל אָחִיו׃ אַבְרָם
Abram (12) brother-of-him from each and-they-parted to-east Lot and-he-set-out

יָשַׁב בְּאֶרֶץ־כְּנָעַן וְלוֹט יָשַׁב בְּעָרֵי הַכִּכָּר
the-plain among-cities-of he-lived and-Lot Canaan in-land-of he-lived

וַיֶּאֱהַל עַד־סְדֹם׃ וְאַנְשֵׁי סְדֹם רָעִים וְחַטָּאִים
and-sinners wicked-ones Sodom now-men-of (13) Sodom near and-he-pitched-tent

[3]From the Negev he went
from place to place until he
came to Bethel, to the place between Bethel and Ai where his
tent had been earlier [4]and
where he had first built an altar. There Abram called on the
name of the LORD.
[5]Now Lot, who was moving
about with Abram, also had
flocks and herds and tents.
[6]But the land could not support them while they stayed
together, for their possessions
were so great that they were
not able to stay together. [7]And
quarreling arose between
Abram's herdsmen and the
herdsmen of Lot. The Canaanites and Perizzites were also
living in the land at that time.
[8]So Abram said to Lot, "Let's
not have any quarreling between you and me, or between
your herdsmen and mine, for
we are brothers. [9]Is not the
whole land before you? Let's
part company. If you go to the
left, I'll go to the right; if you
go to the right, I'll go to the
left."
[10]Lot looked up and saw that
the whole plain of the Jordan
was well watered, like the garden of the LORD, like the land
of Egypt, toward Zoar. (This
was before the LORD destroyed
Sodom and Gomorrah.) [11]So
Lot chose for himself the
whole plain of the Jordan and
set out toward the east. The
two men parted company:
[12]Abram lived in the land of
Canaan, while Lot lived
among the cities of the plain
and pitched his tents near
Sodom. [13]Now the men of
Sodom were wicked and were

°3 ק אהלו

לַיהוָה מְאֹד׃ וַיהוָה אָמַר אֶל־אַבְרָם אַחֲרֵי הִפָּרֶד־לוֹט
Lot he-parted after Abram to he-said and-Yahweh (14) great against-Yahweh

מֵעִמּוֹ שָׂא נָא עֵינֶיךָ וּרְאֵה מִן־הַמָּקוֹם אֲשֶׁר־אַתָּה שָׁם
there you where the-place from and-look! eyes-of-you now! lift! from-with-him

צָפֹנָה וָנֶגְבָּה וָקֵדְמָה וָיָמָּה׃ כִּי אֶת־כָּל־הָאָרֶץ
the-land all-of *** for (15) and-to-west and-to-east and-to-south to-north

אֲשֶׁר־אַתָּה רֹאֶה לְךָ אֶתְּנֶנָּה וּלְזַרְעֲךָ עַד־עוֹלָם׃
ever for and-to-offspring-of-you I-will-give-her to-you seeing you that

וְשַׂמְתִּי אֶת־זַרְעֲךָ כַּעֲפַר הָאָרֶץ אֲשֶׁר ׀ אִם־
if that the-earth like-dust-of offspring-of-you *** and-I-will-make (16)

יוּכַל אִישׁ לִמְנוֹת אֶת־עֲפַר הָאָרֶץ גַּם־זַרְעֲךָ
offspring-of-you then the-earth dust-of *** to-count anyone he-could

יִמָּנֶה׃ קוּם הִתְהַלֵּךְ בָּאָרֶץ לְאָרְכָּהּ
through-length-of-her through-the-land walk! go! (17) he-could-be-counted

וּלְרָחְבָּהּ כִּי לְךָ אֶתְּנֶנָּה׃ וַיֶּאֱהַל אַבְרָם
Abram so-he-moved-tent (18) I-give-her to-you for and-through-breadth-of-her

וַיָּבֹא וַיֵּשֶׁב בְּאֵלֹנֵי מַמְרֵא אֲשֶׁר בְּחֶבְרוֹן וַיִּבֶן־
and-he-built at-Hebron that Mamre near-trees-of and-he-lived and-he-went

שָׁם מִזְבֵּחַ לַיהוָה׃ וַיְהִי בִּימֵי אַמְרָפֶל מֶלֶךְ־שִׁנְעָר
Shinar king-of Amraphel in-days-of now-he-was (14:1) to-Yahweh altar there

אַרְיוֹךְ מֶלֶךְ אֶלָּסָר כְּדָרְלָעֹמֶר מֶלֶךְ עֵילָם וְתִדְעָל מֶלֶךְ גּוֹיִם׃
Goiim king-of and-Tidal Elam king-of Kedorlaomer Ellasar king-of Arioch

עָשׂוּ מִלְחָמָה אֶת־בֶּרַע מֶלֶךְ סְדֹם וְאֶת־בִּרְשַׁע מֶלֶךְ עֲמֹרָה
Gomorrah king-of Birsha and-with Sodom king-of Bera with war they-made (2)

שִׁנְאָב ׀ מֶלֶךְ אַדְמָה וְשֶׁמְאֵבֶר מֶלֶךְ צְבֹיִים וּמֶלֶךְ בֶּלַע הִיא־צֹעַר׃
Zoar that Bela and-king-of Zeboiim king-of and-Shemeber Admah king-of Shinab

כָּל־אֵלֶּה חָבְרוּ אֶל־עֵמֶק הַשִּׂדִּים הוּא יָם
sea-of that the-Siddim valley-of in they-joined-forces these all-of (3)

הַמֶּלַח׃ שְׁתֵּים עֶשְׂרֵה שָׁנָה עָבְדוּ אֶת־כְּדָרְלָעֹמֶר וּשְׁלֹשׁ־עֶשְׂרֵה שָׁנָה
year ten but-three Kedorlaomer *** they-served year ten two (4) the-salt

מָרָדוּ׃ וּבְאַרְבַּע עֶשְׂרֵה שָׁנָה בָּא כְדָרְלָעֹמֶר וְהַמְּלָכִים
and-the-kings Kedorlaomer he-went year ten and-in-four (5) they-rebelled

אֲשֶׁר אִתּוֹ וַיַּכּוּ אֶת־רְפָאִים בְּעַשְׁתְּרֹת קַרְנַיִם וְאֶת־
and Karnaim in-Ashteroth Rephaites *** and-they-defeated with-him that

הַזּוּזִים בְּהָם וְאֵת הָאֵימִים בְּשָׁוֵה קִרְיָתָיִם׃ וְאֶת־הַחֹרִי
the-Horite and (6) Kiriathaim in-Shaveh the-Emites and in-Ham the-Zuzites

בְּהַרְרָם שֵׂעִיר עַד אֵיל פָּארָן אֲשֶׁר עַל־הַמִּדְבָּר׃
the-desert near that Paran El as-far-as Seir on-hill-of-them

°2 ק צבוים

sinning greatly against the Lord.

[14]The Lord said to Abram after Lot had parted from him, "Lift up your eyes from where you are and look north and south, east and west. [15]All the land that you see I will give to you and your offspring[i] forever. [16]I will make your offspring like the dust of the earth, so that if anyone could count the dust, then your offspring could be counted. [17]Go, walk through the length and breadth of the land, for I am giving it to you."

[18]So Abram moved his tents and went to live near the great trees of Mamre at Hebron, where he built an altar to the Lord.

Abram Rescues Lot

14 At this time Amraphel king of Shinar,[j] Arioch king of Ellasar, Kedorlaomer king of Elam and Tidal king of Goiim [2]went to war against Bera king of Sodom, Birsha king of Gomorrah, Shinab king of Admah, Shemeber king of Zeboiim, and the king of Bela (that is, Zoar). [3]All these latter kings joined forces in the Valley of Siddim (the Salt Sea[k]). [4]For twelve years they had been subject to Kedorlaomer, but in the thirteenth year they rebelled.

[5]In the fourteenth year, Kedorlaomer and the kings allied with him went out and defeated the Rephaites in Ashteroth Karnaim, the Zuzites in Ham, the Emites in Shaveh Kiriathaim [6]and the Horites in the hill country of Seir, as far as El Paran near the desert.

i15 Or *seed;* also in verse 16
j1 That is, Babylonia; also in verse 9
k3 That is, the Dead Sea

(7) וַיָּשֻׁבוּ וַיָּבֹאוּ אֶל־עֵין מִשְׁפָּט הִוא קָדֵשׁ וַיַּכּוּ
and-they-conquered Kadesh that Mishpat En to and-they-went then-they-turned (7)

אֶת־ כָּל־ שְׂדֵה הָעֲמָלֵקִי וְגַם אֶת־ הָאֱמֹרִי
the-Amorite *** as-well-as the-Amalekite territory-of whole-of ***

הַיֹּשֵׁב בְּחַצְצֹן תָּמָר׃ (8) וַיֵּצֵא מֶלֶךְ־ סְדֹם
Sodom king-of then-he-marched-out (8) Tamar in-Hazezon the-one-living

וּמֶלֶךְ עֲמֹרָה וּמֶלֶךְ אַדְמָה וּמֶלֶךְ צְבֹיִים וּמֶלֶךְ בֶּלַע
Bela and-king-of Zeboiim and-king-of Admah and-king-of Gomorrah and-king-of

הִוא־ צֹעַר וַיַּעַרְכוּ אִתָּם מִלְחָמָה בְּעֵמֶק הַשִּׂדִּים׃ (9) אֵת
against (9) the-Siddim in-valley-of battle with-them and-they-joined Zoar that

כְּדָרְלָעֹמֶר מֶלֶךְ עֵילָם וְתִדְעָל מֶלֶךְ גּוֹיִם וְאַמְרָפֶל מֶלֶךְ שִׁנְעָר
Shinar king-of and-Amraphel Goiim king-of and-Tidal Elam king-of Kedorlaomer

וְאַרְיוֹךְ מֶלֶךְ אֶלָּסָר אַרְבָּעָה מְלָכִים אֶת־ הַחֲמִשָּׁה׃ (10) וְעֵמֶק
now-valley-of (10) the-five against kings four Ellasar king-of and-Arioch

הַשִּׂדִּים בֶּאֱרֹת בֶּאֱרֹת חֵמָר וַיָּנֻסוּ מֶלֶךְ־ סְדֹם וַעֲמֹרָה
and-Gomorrah Sodom king-of when-they-fled tar pits-of pits the-Siddim

וַיִּפְּלוּ־ שָׁמָּה וְהַנִּשְׁאָרִים הֶרָה נָּסוּ׃
they-fled to-hill and-the-ones-remaining into-there and-they-fell

(11) וַיִּקְחוּ אֶת־ כָּל־ רְכֻשׁ סְדֹם וַעֲמֹרָה וְאֶת־ כָּל־
all-of and and-Gomorrah Sodom goods-of all-of *** and-they-seized (11)

אָכְלָם וַיֵּלֵכוּ׃ (12) וַיִּקְחוּ אֶת־ לוֹט וְאֶת־
and Lot *** and-they-carried-off (12) then-they-left food-of-them

רְכֻשׁוֹ בֶּן־ אֲחִי אַבְרָם וַיֵּלֵכוּ וְהוּא יֹשֵׁב
living since-he and-they-left Abram brother-of son-of possession-of-him

בִּסְדֹם׃ (13) וַיָּבֹא הַפָּלִיט וַיַּגֵּד לְאַבְרָם הָעִבְרִי
the-Hebrew to-Abram and-he-reported the-escapee and-he-came (13) in-Sodom

וְהוּא שֹׁכֵן בְּאֵלֹנֵי מַמְרֵא הָאֱמֹרִי אֲחִי אֶשְׁכֹּל וַאֲחִי
and-brother-of Eshcol brother-of the-Amorite Mamre near-trees-of living now-he

עָנֵר וְהֵם בַּעֲלֵי בְרִית־ אַבְרָם׃ (14) וַיִּשְׁמַע אַבְרָם כִּי
that Abram when-he-heard (14) Abram covenant-of owners-of and-these Aner

נִשְׁבָּה אָחִיו וַיָּרֶק אֶת־ חֲנִיכָיו
trained-men-of-him *** and-he-called-out relative-of-him he-was-captive

יְלִידֵי בֵיתוֹ שְׁמֹנָה עָשָׂר וּשְׁלֹשׁ מֵאוֹת וַיִּרְדֹּף
and-he-pursued hundreds and-three ten eight household-of-him born-ones-of

עַד־ דָּן׃ (15) וַיֵּחָלֵק עֲלֵיהֶם ׀ לַיְלָה הוּא וַעֲבָדָיו
and-servants-of-him he night against-them and-he-divided (15) Dan as-far-as

וַיַּכֵּם וַיִּרְדְּפֵם עַד־ חוֹבָה אֲשֶׁר מִשְּׂמֹאל
to-north that Hobah as-far-as and-he-pursued-them and-he-routed-them

7Then they turned back and
went to En Mishpat (that is,
Kadesh), and they conquered
the whole territory of the
Amalekites, as well as the Amorites who were living in
Hazezon Tamar.
8Then the king of Sodom,
the king of Gomorrah, the
king of Admah, the king of Zeboiim and the king of Bela
(that is, Zoar) marched out and
drew up their battle lines in
the Valley of Siddim 9against
Kedorlaomer king of Elam, Tidal king of Goiim, Amraphel
king of Shinar and Arioch
king of Ellasar—four kings
against five. 10Now the Valley
of Siddim was full of tar pits,
and when the kings of Sodom
and Gomorrah fled, some of
the men fell into them and the
rest fled to the hills. 11The four
kings seized all the goods of
Sodom and Gomorrah and all
their food; then they went
away. 12They also carried off
Abram's nephew Lot and his
possessions, since he was living in Sodom.
13One who had escaped
came and reported this to
Abram the Hebrew. Now
Abram was living near the
great trees of Mamre the Amorite, a brother[l] of Eshcol and
Aner, all of whom were allied
with Abram. 14When Abram
heard that his relative had
been taken captive, he called
out the 318 trained men born
in his household and went in
pursuit as far as Dan. 15During
the night Abram divided his
men to attack them and he
routed them, pursuing them
as far as Hobah, north of

l13 Or *a relative*; or *an ally*

*10 Most mss have *dagesh* in the *sin* (הַשִּׂ).

°8 ק צבוים

לְדַמָּשֶׂק׃ וַיָּשֶׁב אֵת כָּל־ הָרְכֻשׁ וְגַם אֶת־ לוֹט
Lot *** and-also the-goods all-of *** and-he-recovered (16) to-Damascus

אָחִיו וּרְכֻשׁוֹ הֵשִׁיב וְגַם אֶת־ הַנָּשִׁים
the-women *** and-also he-brought-back and-possession-of-him relative-of-him

וְאֶת־ הָעָם׃ וַיֵּצֵא־ מֶלֶךְ סְדֹם לִקְרָאתוֹ אַחֲרֵי
after to-meet-him Sodom king-of and-he-came-out (17) the-people and

שׁוּבוֹ מֵהַכּוֹת אֶת־ כְּדָר־לָעֹמֶר וְאֶת־ הַמְּלָכִים אֲשֶׁר אִתּוֹ אֶל־
in with-him that the-kings and Kedorlaomer *** from-to-defeat to-return-him

עֵמֶק שָׁוֵה הוּא עֵמֶק הַמֶּלֶךְ׃ וּמַלְכִּי־צֶדֶק מֶלֶךְ
king-of then-Melchizedek (18) the-king valley-of that Shaveh valley-of

שָׁלֵם הוֹצִיא לֶחֶם וָיָיִן וְהוּא כֹהֵן לְאֵל עֶלְיוֹן׃
Most-High to-God priest now-he and-wine bread he-brought-out Salem

וַיְבָרְכֵהוּ וַיֹּאמַר בָּרוּךְ אַבְרָם לְאֵל עֶלְיוֹן
Most-High by-God Abram being-blessed and-he-said and-he-blessed-him (19)

קֹנֵה שָׁמַיִם וָאָרֶץ׃ וּבָרוּךְ אֵל עֶלְיוֹן אֲשֶׁר־
who Most-High God and-being-blessed (20) and-earth heaven creating-of

מִגֵּן צָרֶיךָ בְּיָדֶךָ וַיִּתֶּן־ לוֹ מַעֲשֵׂר
tenth to-him then-he-gave into-hand-of-you enemies-of-you he-delivered

מִכֹּל׃ וַיֹּאמֶר מֶלֶךְ־ סְדֹם אֶל־אַבְרָם תֶּן־ לִי הַנֶּפֶשׁ
the-people to-me give! Abram to Sodom king-of and-he-said (21) from-everything

וְהָרְכֻשׁ קַח־ לָךְ׃ וַיֹּאמֶר אַבְרָם אֶל־ מֶלֶךְ סְדֹם הֲרִימֹתִי
I-raised Sodom king-of to Abram but-he-said (2) for-you keep! and-the-goods

יָדִי אֶל־ יְהוָה אֵל עֶלְיוֹן קֹנֵה שָׁמַיִם וָאָרֶץ׃ אִם־
that (23) and-earth heaven creating-of Most-High God Yahweh to hand-of-me

מִחוּט וְעַד שְׂרוֹךְ־ נַעַל וְאִם־ אֶקַּח מִכָּל־ אֲשֶׁר־
that from-anything I-will-accept and-not sandal thong-of or-even even-thread

לָךְ וְלֹא תֹאמַר אֲנִי הֶעֱשַׁרְתִּי אֶת־ אַבְרָם׃ בִּלְעָדַי רַק
but nothing-to-me (24) Abram *** I-made-rich I you-will-say so-never to-you

אֲשֶׁר אָכְלוּ הַנְּעָרִים וְחֵלֶק הָאֲנָשִׁים אֲשֶׁר הָלְכוּ אִתִּי עָנֵר
Aner with-me they-went who the-men and-share-of the-men they-ate what

אֶשְׁכֹּל וּמַמְרֵא הֵם יִקְחוּ חֶלְקָם׃ אַחַר ׀ הַדְּבָרִים
the-events after (15:1) share-of-them let-them-have they and-Mamre Eshcol

הָאֵלֶּה הָיָה דְבַר־ יְהוָה אֶל־אַבְרָם בַּמַּחֲזֶה לֵאמֹר אַל־ תִּירָא
you-fear not to-say in-the-vision Abram to Yahweh word-of he-came the-these

אַבְרָם אָנֹכִי מָגֵן לָךְ שְׂכָרְךָ הַרְבֵּה מְאֹד׃ וַיֹּאמֶר אַבְרָם אֲדֹנָי
Lord Abram but-he-said (2) very to-be-great reward-of-you to-you shield I Abram

יֱהוִה מַה־ תִּתֶּן־ לִי וְאָנֹכִי הוֹלֵךְ עֲרִירִי וּבֶן־
and-son-of childless to-remain since-I to-me you-will-give what? Yahweh

Damascus. [16]He recovered all the goods and brought back his relative Lot and his possessions, together with the women and the other people.
[17]After Abram returned from defeating Kedorlaomer and the kings allied with him, the king of Sodom came out to meet him in the Valley of Shaveh (that is, the King's Valley).
[18]Then Melchizedek king of Salem[m] brought out bread and wine. He was priest of God Most High, [19]and he blessed Abram, saying,

"Blessed be Abram by God Most High,
Creator[n] of heaven and earth.
[20]And blessed be[o] God Most High,
who delivered your enemies into your hand."

Then Abram gave him a tenth of everything.
[21]The king of Sodom said to Abram, "Give me the people and keep the goods for yourself."
[22]But Abram said to the king of Sodom, "I have raised my hand to the LORD, God Most High, Creator of heaven and earth, and have taken an oath
[23]that I will accept nothing belonging to you, not even a thread or the thong of a sandal, so that you will never be able to say, 'I made Abram rich.'
[24]I will accept nothing but what my men have eaten and the share that belongs to the men who went with me—to Aner, Eshcol and Mamre. Let them have their share."

God's Covenant With Abram

15 After this, the word of the LORD came to Abram in a vision:

"Do not be afraid, Abram.
I am your shield,[p]
your very great reward.[q]"

[2]But Abram said, "O Sovereign LORD, what can you give me since I remain childless

[m]18 That is, Jerusalem
[n]19 Or *Possessor*; also in verse 22
[o]20 Or *And praise be to*
[p]1 Or *sovereign*
[q]1 Or *shield; / your reward will be very great*

מֶשֶׁק בֵּיתִי הוּא דַּמֶּשֶׂק אֱלִיעֶזֶר׃ וַיֹּאמֶר אַבְרָם הֵן

see! Abram and-he-said (3) Eliezer Damascus he estate-of-me inheritance-of

לִי לֹא נָתַתָּה זָרַע וְהִנֵּה בֶן־ בֵּיתִי יוֹרֵשׁ אֹתִי׃

me being-heir household-of-me servant-of and-see! child you-gave not to-me

(4) וְהִנֵּה דְבַר־ יְהוָה אֵלָיו לֵאמֹר לֹא יִירָשְׁךָ זֶה

this he-will-be-heir-of-you not to-say to-him Yahweh word-of and-see! (4)

כִּי־ אִם אֲשֶׁר יֵצֵא מִמֵּעֶיךָ הוּא יִירָשֶׁךָ׃

he-will-be-heir-of-you he from-body-of-you he-will-come who rather but

(5) וַיּוֹצֵא אֹתוֹ הַחוּצָה וַיֹּאמֶר הַבֶּט־ נָא הַשָּׁמַיְמָה וּסְפֹר

and-count! at-the-heavens now! look! and-he-said to-the-outside him and-he-took (5)

הַכּוֹכָבִים אִם־ תּוּכַל לִסְפֹּר אֹתָם וַיֹּאמֶר לוֹ כֹּה יִהְיֶה

he-shall-be so to-him then-he-said them to-count you-can if the-stars

זַרְעֶךָ׃ (6) וְהֶאֱמִן בַּיהוָה וַיַּחְשְׁבֶהָ לּוֹ

to-him and-he-credited-her in-Yahweh and-he-believed (6) offspring-of-you

צְדָקָה׃ (7) וַיֹּאמֶר אֵלָיו אֲנִי יְהוָה אֲשֶׁר הוֹצֵאתִיךָ מֵאוּר

from-Ur-of I-brought-you who Yahweh I to-him also-he-said (7) righteousness

כַּשְׂדִּים לָתֶת לְךָ אֶת־ הָאָרֶץ הַזֹּאת לְרִשְׁתָּהּ׃ (8) וַיֹּאמַר

but-he-said (8) to-possess-her the-this the-land *** to-you to-give Chaldeans

אֲדֹנָי יֱהוִה בַּמָּה אֵדַע כִּי אִירָשֶׁנָּה׃ (9) וַיֹּאמֶר אֵלָיו

to-him so-he-said (9) I-will-possess-her that I-can-know how? Yahweh Lord

קְחָה לִי עֶגְלָה מְשֻׁלֶּשֶׁת וְעֵז מְשֻׁלֶּשֶׁת

being-three-years-old and-goat being-three-years-old heifer to-me bring!

וְאַיִל מְשֻׁלָּשׁ וְתֹר וְגוֹזָל׃ (10) וַיִּקַּח־ לוֹ

to-him so-he-brought (10) and-pigeon and-dove being-three-years-old and-ram

אֶת־ כָּל־ אֵלֶּה וַיְבַתֵּר אֹתָם בַּתָּוֶךְ וַיִּתֵּן אִישׁ־

each and-he-arranged in-the-middle them and-he-cut-in-two these all-of ***

בִּתְרוֹ לִקְרַאת רֵעֵהוּ וְאֶת־ הַצִּפֹּר* לֹא בָתָר׃

he-cut-in-half not the-bird but other-of-him to-be-opposite half-of-him

(11) וַיֵּרֶד הָעַיִט עַל־ הַפְּגָרִים וַיַּשֵּׁב

but-he-drive-away the-carcasses on the-bird-of-prey then he came-down (11)

אֹתָם אַבְרָם׃ (12) וַיְהִי הַשֶּׁמֶשׁ לָבוֹא וְתַרְדֵּמָה נָפְלָה עַל־ אַבְרָם

Abram on she-fell and-deep-sleep to-set the-sun as-he-was (12) Abram them

וְהִנֵּה אֵימָה חֲשֵׁכָה גְדֹלָה נֹפֶלֶת עָלָיו׃ (13) וַיֹּאמֶר לְאַבְרָם

to-Abram then-he-said (13) over-him coming great darkness dreadful and-see!

יָדֹעַ תֵּדַע כִּי־ גֵר ׀ יִהְיֶה זַרְעֲךָ בְּאֶרֶץ לֹא

not in-country descendant-of-you he-will-be stranger that you-know to-know

לָהֶם וַעֲבָדוּם וְעִנּוּ אֹתָם אַרְבַּע מֵאוֹת

hundreds four them and-they-will-mistreat and-they-will-serve-them to-them

and the one who will inherit[r]
my estate is Eliezer of Damascus?" [3]And Abram said, "You
have given me no children; so
a servant in my household
will be my heir."
[4]Then the word of the LORD
came to him: "This man will
not be your heir, but a son
coming from your own body
will be your heir." [5]He took
him outside and said, "Look
up at the heavens and count
the stars—if indeed you can
count them." Then he said to
him, "So shall your offspring
be."
[6]Abram believed the LORD,
and he credited it to him as
righteousness.
[7]He also said to him, "I am
the LORD, who brought you
out of Ur of the Chaldeans to
give you this land to take
possession of it."
[8]But Abram said, "O Sovereign LORD, how can I know
that I will gain possession of
it?"
[9]So the LORD said to him,
"Bring me a heifer, a goat and
a ram, each three years old,
along with a dove and a young
pigeon."
[10]Abram brought all these to
him, cut them in two and arranged the halves opposite
each other; the birds, however, he did not cut in half.
[11]Then birds of prey came
down on the carcasses, but
Abram drove them away.
[12]As the sun was setting,
Abram fell into a deep sleep,
and a thick and dreadful darkness came over him. [13]Then
the LORD said to him, "Know
for certain that your descendants will be strangers in a
country not their own, and
they will be enslaved and mistreated four hundred years.

r2 The meaning of the Hebrew for this phrase is uncertain.

*10 Most mss have *dagesh* in the *tsade* (הַצִּ).

שָׁנָה׃ וְגַם אֶת־ הַגּוֹי אֲשֶׁר יַעֲבֹדוּ דָּן אָנֹכִי וְאַחֲרֵי־

and-after I punishing they-serve that the-nation *** but-indeed (14) year

כֵן יֵצְאוּ בִּרְכֻשׁ גָּדוֹל׃ וְאַתָּה תָּבוֹא אֶל־

to you-will-go but-you (15) great with-possession they-will-come-out that

אֲבֹתֶיךָ בְּשָׁלוֹם תִּקָּבֵר בְּשֵׂיבָה טוֹבָה׃ וְדוֹר

and-generation (16) good at-old-age you-will-be-buried in-peace fathers-of-you

רְבִיעִי יָשׁוּבוּ הֵנָּה כִּי לֹא־ שָׁלֵם עֲוֺן הָאֱמֹרִי עַד־ הֵנָּה׃

here to the-Amorite sin-of full not for here they-will-come-back fourth

וַיְהִי הַשֶּׁמֶשׁ בָּאָה וַעֲלָטָה הָיָה וְהִנֵּה תַנּוּר עָשָׁן

smoke fire-pot and-see! he-fell and-darkness he-set the-sun and-he-was (17)

וְלַפִּיד אֵשׁ אֲשֶׁר עָבַר בֵּין הַגְּזָרִים הָאֵלֶּה׃ בַּיּוֹם

on-the-day (18) the-these the-pieces between he-passed that blaze and-torch

הַהוּא כָּרַת יְהוָה אֶת־ אַבְרָם בְּרִית לֵאמֹר לְזַרְעֲךָ נָתַתִּי

I-give to-descendant-of-you to-say covenant Abram with Yahweh he-made the-that

אֶת־ הָאָרֶץ הַזֹּאת מִנְּהַר מִצְרַיִם עַד־ הַנָּהָר הַגָּדֹל נְהַר־

river-of the-great the-river to Egypt from-river-of the-this the-land ***

פְּרָת׃ אֶת־ הַקֵּינִי וְאֶת־ הַקְּנִזִּי וְאֵת הַקַּדְמֹנִי׃ וְאֶת־

and (20) the-Kadmonite and the-Kenizzite and the-Kenite *** (19) Euphrates

הַחִתִּי וְאֶת־ הַפְּרִזִּי וְאֶת־ הָרְפָאִים׃ וְאֶת־ הָאֱמֹרִי וְאֶת־

and the-Amorite and (21) the-Rephaites and the-Perizzite and the-Hittite

הַכְּנַעֲנִי וְאֶת־ הַגִּרְגָּשִׁי וְאֶת־ הַיְבוּסִי׃ וְשָׂרַי אֵשֶׁת

wife-of now-Sarai (16:1) the-Jebusite and the-Girgashite and the-Canaanite

אַבְרָם לֹא יָלְדָה לוֹ וְלָהּ שִׁפְחָה מִצְרִית וּשְׁמָהּ

and-name-of-her Egyptian maidservant but-to-her for-him she-bore not Abram

הָגָר׃ וַתֹּאמֶר שָׂרַי אֶל־ אַבְרָם הִנֵּה־ נָא עֲצָרַנִי יְהוָה מִלֶּדֶת

from-to-bear Yahweh he-kept-me now! see! Abram to Sarai so-she-said (2) Hagar

בֹּא־ נָא אֶל־ שִׁפְחָתִי אוּלַי אִבָּנֶה מִמֶּנָּה*

through-her I-can-build-family perhaps maidservant-of-me to now! go!

וַיִּשְׁמַע אַבְרָם לְקוֹל שָׂרָי׃ וַתִּקַּח שָׂרַי אֵשֶׁת־ אַבְרָם

Abram wife-of Sarai so-she-took (3) Sarai to-voice-of Abram and-he-listened

אֶת־ הָגָר הַמִּצְרִית שִׁפְחָתָהּ מִקֵּץ עֶשֶׂר שָׁנִים לְשֶׁבֶת אַבְרָם

Abram to-live years ten at-end-of maidservant-of-her the-Egyptian Hagar ***

בְּאֶרֶץ כְּנָעַן וַתִּתֵּן אֹתָהּ לְאַבְרָם אִישָׁהּ לוֹ לְאִשָּׁה׃

as-wife to-him husband-of-her to-Abram her and-she-gave Canaan in-land-of

וַיָּבֹא אֶל־ הָגָר וַתַּהַר וַתֵּרֶא כִּי הָרָתָה

she-was-pregnant that when-she-saw and-she-conceived Hagar to and-he-went (4)

וַתֵּקַל גְּבִרְתָּהּ בְּעֵינֶיהָ׃ וַתֹּאמֶר שָׂרַי אֶל־

to Sarai so-she-said (5) with-eyes-of-her mistress-of-her then-she-despised

[14]But I will punish the nation
they serve as slaves, and afterward they will come out with
great possessions. [15]You, however, will go to your fathers in
peace and be buried at a good
old age. [16]In the fourth generation your descendants will
come back here, for the sin of
the Amorites has not yet
reached its full measure."
[17]When the sun had set and
darkness had fallen, a smoking fire pot with a blazing
torch appeared and passed between the pieces. [18]On that
day the LORD made a covenant
with Abram and said, "To
your descendants I give this
land, from the river[s] of Egypt
to the great river, the Euphrates— [19]the land of the Kenites, Kenizzites, Kadmo-
nites, [20]Hittites, Perizzites,
Rephaites, [21]Amorites,
Canaanites, Girgashites and
Jebusites."

Hagar and Ishmael

16 Now Sarai, Abram's
wife, had borne him
no children. But she had an
Egyptian maidservant named
Hagar; [2]so she said to Abram,
"The LORD has kept me from
having children. Go, sleep
with my maidservant; per-
haps I can build a family
through her."
Abram agreed to what Sarai
said. [3]So after Abram had been
living in Canaan ten years,
Sarai his wife took her Egyptian maidservant Hagar and
gave her to her husband to be
his wife. [4]He slept with Hagar,
and she conceived.
When she knew she was
pregnant, she began to de-
spise her mistress. [5]Then Sarai

[s]18 Or *Wadi*

*2 Most mss have *segol* under the second *mem* (מֶּ).

אַבְרָם חֲמָסִי עָלֶיךָ אָנֹכִי נָתַתִּי שִׁפְחָתִי בְּחֵיקֶךָ וַתֵּרֶא
now-she-sees in-arm-of-you servant-of-me I-put I upon-you wrong-to-me Abram

כִּי הָרָתָה וָאֵקַל בְּעֵינֶיהָ יִשְׁפֹּט יְהוָה
Yahweh may-he-judge in-eyes-of-her and-I-am-despised she-is-pregnant that

בֵּינִי וּבֵינֶיךָ׃ (6) וַיֹּאמֶר אַבְרָם אֶל־ שָׂרַי הִנֵּה שִׁפְחָתֵךְ
servant-of-you see! Sarai to Abram so-he-said (6) and-between-you between-me

בְּיָדֵךְ עֲשִׂי־ לָהּ הַטּוֹב בְּעֵינָיִךְ וַתְּעַנֶּהָ
then-she-mistreated-her in-eyes-of-you the-good with-her do! in-hands-of-you

שָׂרַי וַתִּבְרַח מִפָּנֶיהָ׃ (7) וַיִּמְצָאָהּ מַלְאַךְ יְהוָה עַל־
near Yahweh angel-of and-he-found-her (7) from-face-of-her so-she-fled Sarai

עֵין הַמַּיִם בַּמִּדְבָּר עַל־ הָעַיִן בְּדֶרֶךְ שׁוּר׃
Shur beside-road-of the-spring near in-the-desert the-water spring-of

(8) וַיֹּאמַר הָגָר שִׁפְחַת שָׂרַי אֵי־ מִזֶּה בָאת וְאָנָה
and-where you-came from-there where? Sarai servant-of Hagar and-he-said (8)

תֵלֵכִי וַתֹּאמֶר מִפְּנֵי שָׂרַי גְּבִרְתִּי אָנֹכִי בֹּרַחַת׃
running I mistress-of-me Sarai from-face-of and-she-answered you-go

(9) וַיֹּאמֶר לָהּ מַלְאַךְ יְהוָה שׁוּבִי אֶל־ גְּבִרְתֵּךְ
mistress-of-you to go-back! Yahweh angel-of to-her then-he-told (9)

וְהִתְעַנִּי תַּחַת יָדֶיהָ׃ (10) וַיֹּאמֶר לָהּ מַלְאַךְ יְהוָה
Yahweh angel-of to-her and-he-said (10) hands-of-her under and-submit!

הַרְבָּה אַרְבֶּה אֶת־ זַרְעֵךְ וְלֹא יִסָּפֵר
he-will-be-counted so-not descendant-of-you *** I-will-increase to-increase

מֵרֹב׃ (11) וַיֹּאמֶר לָהּ מַלְאַךְ יְהוָה הִנָּךְ הָרָה
with-child see-you! Yahweh angel-of to-her also-he-said (11) because-of-size

וְיֹלַדְתְּ בֵּן וְקָרָאת שְׁמוֹ יִשְׁמָעֵאל כִּי־ שָׁמַע
he-heard for Ishmael name-of-him and-you-shall-call son and-you-will-have

יְהוָה אֶל־ עָנְיֵךְ׃ (12) וְהוּא יִהְיֶה פֶּרֶא אָדָם יָדוֹ
hand-of-him man wild-donkey-of he-will-be and-he (12) misery-of-you to Yahweh

בַכֹּל וְיַד כֹּל בּוֹ וְעַל־ פְּנֵי
faces-of and-against against-him everyone and-hand-of against-everyone

כָל־ אֶחָיו יִשְׁכֹּן׃ (13) וַתִּקְרָא שֵׁם־ יְהוָה
Yahweh name-of and-she-called (13) he-will-live brothers-of-him all-of

הַדֹּבֵר אֵלֶיהָ אַתָּה אֵל רֳאִי כִּי אָמְרָה הֲגַם הֲלֹם רָאִיתִי אַחֲרֵי
back-of I-saw here now? she-said for sight God-of you to-her the-one-speaking

רֹאִי׃ (14) עַל־ כֵּן קָרָא לַבְּאֵר בְּאֵר לַחַי רֹאִי הִנֵּה בֵין־
between see! Roi Lahai Beer to-the-well he-called this for (14) one-seeing-me

קָדֵשׁ וּבֵין בָּרֶד׃ (15) וַתֵּלֶד הָגָר לְאַבְרָם בֵּן וַיִּקְרָא
and-he-gave son to-Abram Hagar so-she-bore (15) Bered and-between Kadesh

said to Abram, "You are responsible for the wrong I am suffering. I put my servant in your arms, and now that she knows she is pregnant, she despises me. May the LORD judge between you and me."

6 "Your servant is in your hands," Abram said. "Do with her whatever you think best." Then Sarai mistreated Hagar; so she fled from her.

7 The angel of the LORD found Hagar near a spring in the desert; it was the spring that is beside the road to Shur. 8 And he said, "Hagar, servant of Sarai, where have you come from, and where are you going?"

"I'm running away from my mistress Sarai," she answered.

9 Then the angel of the LORD told her, "Go back to your mistress and submit to her." 10 The angel added, "I will so increase your descendants that they will be too numerous to count."

11 The angel of the LORD also said to her:

"You are now with child
and you will have a son.
You shall name him
Ishmael,[t]
for the LORD has heard of
your misery.
12 He will be a wild donkey
of a man;
his hand will be against
everyone
and everyone's hand
against him,
and he will live in hostility
toward[u] all his brothers."

13 She gave this name to the LORD who spoke to her: "You are the God who sees me," for she said, "I have now seen[v] the One who sees me." 14 That is why the well was called Beer Lahai Roi[w]; it is still there, between Kadesh and Bered.

15 So Hagar bore Abram a son, and Abram gave the

[t] 11 *Ishmael* means *God hears.*
[u] 12 Or *live to the east / of*
[v] 13 Or *seen the back of*
[w] 14 *Beer Lahai Roi* means *well of the Living One who sees me.*

אַבְרָם שֶׁם־ בְּנוֹ אֲשֶׁר־ יָלְדָה הָגָר יִשְׁמָעֵאל׃ וְאַבְרָם בֶּן־
son-of and-Abram (16) Ishmael Hagar she-bore whom son-of-him name-of Abram

שְׁמֹנִים שָׁנָה וְשֵׁשׁ שָׁנִים בְּלֶדֶת־ הָגָר אֶת־יִשְׁמָעֵאל לְאַבְרָם׃
for-Abram Ishmael *** Hagar when-to-bear years and-six year eighty

וַיְהִי אַבְרָם בֶּן־ תִּשְׁעִים שָׁנָה וְתֵשַׁע שָׁנִים וַיֵּרָא
and-he-appeared years and-nine year ninety son-of Abram when-he-was (17:1)

יְהוָה אֶל־אַבְרָם וַיֹּאמֶר אֵלָיו אֲנִי־אֵל שַׁדַּי הִתְהַלֵּךְ לְפָנַי וֶהְיֵה
and-be! before-me walk! Almighty God I to-him and-he-said Abram to Yahweh

תָמִים׃ וְאֶתְּנָה בְרִיתִי בֵּינִי וּבֵינֶךָ
and-between-you between-me covenant-of-me and-I-will-confirm (2) blameless

וְאַרְבֶּה אוֹתְךָ בִּמְאֹד מְאֹד׃ וַיִּפֹּל אַבְרָם עַל־ פָּנָיו
face-of-him on Abram and-he-fell (3) greatly greatly you and-I-will-increase

וַיְדַבֵּר אִתּוֹ אֱלֹהִים לֵאמֹר׃ אֲנִי הִנֵּה בְרִיתִי אִתָּךְ וְהָיִיתָ
now-you-will-be with-you covenant-of-me see! I (4) to-say God to-him and-he-said

לְאַב הֲמוֹן גּוֹיִם׃ וְלֹא־ יִקָּרֵא עוֹד אֶת־
*** longer he-will-be-called and-not (5) nations many-of as-father-of

שִׁמְךָ אַבְרָם וְהָיָה שִׁמְךָ אַבְרָהָם כִּי אַב־ הֲמוֹן
many-of father-of for Abraham name-of-you but-he-will-be Abram name-of-you

גּוֹיִם נְתַתִּיךָ׃ וְהִפְרֵתִי אֹתְךָ בִּמְאֹד מְאֹד
greatly greatly you and-I-will-make-fruitful (6) I-made-you nations

וּנְתַתִּיךָ לְגוֹיִם וּמְלָכִים מִמְּךָ יֵצֵאוּ׃
they-will-come from-you and-kings into-nations and-I-will-make-you

וַהֲקִמֹתִי אֶת־ בְּרִיתִי בֵּינִי וּבֵינֶךָ וּבֵין
and-between and-between-you between-me covenant-of-me *** and-I-will-establish (7)

זַרְעֲךָ אַחֲרֶיךָ לְדֹרֹתָם לִבְרִית עוֹלָם
everlasting as-covenant-of for-generations-of-them after-you descendant-of-you

לִהְיוֹת לְךָ לֵאלֹהִים וּלְזַרְעֲךָ אַחֲרֶיךָ׃ וְנָתַתִּי
and-I-will-give (8) after-you and-to-descendant-of-you as-God to-you to-be

לְךָ וּלְזַרְעֲךָ אַחֲרֶיךָ אֵת ׀ אֶרֶץ מְגֻרֶיךָ אֵת
*** journeys-of-you land-of *** after-you and-to-descendant-of-you to-you

כָּל־ אֶרֶץ כְּנַעַן לַאֲחֻזַּת עוֹלָם וְהָיִיתִי לָהֶם
to-them and-I-will-be everlasting as-possession-of Canaan land-of whole-of

לֵאלֹהִים׃ וַיֹּאמֶר אֱלֹהִים אֶל־אַבְרָהָם וְאַתָּה אֶת־ בְּרִיתִי תִשְׁמֹר
you-keep covenant-of-me *** now-you Abraham to God then-he-said (9) as-God

אַתָּה וְזַרְעֲךָ אַחֲרֶיךָ לְדֹרֹתָם׃ זֹאת
this (10) for-generations-of-them after-you and-descendant-of-you you

בְּרִיתִי אֲשֶׁר תִּשְׁמְרוּ בֵּינִי וּבֵינֵיכֶם וּבֵין
and-between and-between-you between-me you-must-keep that covenant-of-me

name Ishmael to the son she had borne. [16]Abram was eighty-six years old when Hagar bore him Ishmael.

The Covenant of Circumcision

17 When Abram was ninety-nine years old, the LORD appeared to him and said, "I am God Almighty[x]; walk before me and be blameless. [2]I will confirm my covenant between me and you and will greatly increase your numbers."

[3]Abram fell facedown, and God said to him, [4]"As for me, this is my covenant with you: You will be the father of many nations. [5]No longer will you be called Abram[y]; your name will be Abraham,[z] for I have made you a father of many nations. [6]I will make you very fruitful; I will make nations of you, and kings will come from you. [7]I will establish my covenant as an everlasting covenant between me and you and your descendants after you for the generations to come, to be your God and the God of your descendants after you. [8]The whole land of Canaan, where you are now an alien, I will give as an everlasting possession to you and your descendants after you; and I will be their God."

[9]Then God said to Abraham, "As for you, you must keep my covenant, you and your descendants after you for the generations to come. [10]This is my covenant with you and your descendants after you, the covenant you are to keep:

[x]1 Hebrew *El-Shaddai*
[y]5 *Abram* means *exalted father.*
[z]5 *Abraham* means *father of many.*

זַרְעֲךָ אַחֲרֶיךָ הִמּוֹל לָכֶם כָּל־ זָכָר׃
male every-of among-you to-be-circumcised after-you descendant-of-you

וּנְמַלְתֶּם אֵת בְּשַׂר עָרְלַתְכֶם וְהָיָה
and-he-will-be foreskin-of-you flesh-of *** and-you-will-be-circumcised (11)

לְאוֹת בְּרִית בֵּינִי וּבֵינֵיכֶם׃ וּבֶן־ שְׁמֹנַת יָמִים
days eight-of and-son-of (12) and-between-you between-me covenant as-sign-of

יִמּוֹל לָכֶם כָּל־ זָכָר לְדֹרֹתֵיכֶם יְלִיד
born-of for-generations-of-you male every-of among-you he-must-be-circumcised

בָּיִת וּמִקְנַת־ כֶּסֶף מִכֹּל בֶּן־ נֵכָר אֲשֶׁר לֹא
not who foreigner son-of from-every-of money or-bought-of household

מִזַּרְעֲךָ הוּא׃ הִמּוֹל ׀ יִמּוֹל יְלִיד
born-of he-must-be-circumcised to-be-circumcised (13) he from-offspring-of-you

בֵּיתְךָ וּמִקְנַת כַּסְפֶּךָ וְהָיְתָה בְרִיתִי
covenant-of-me so-she-will-be money-of-you or-bought-of household-of-you

בִּבְשַׂרְכֶם לִבְרִית עוֹלָם׃ וְעָרֵל ׀ זָכָר אֲשֶׁר
who male but-uncircumcised (14) everlasting as-covenant-of in-flesh-of-you

לֹא־ יִמּוֹל אֶת־ בְּשַׂר עָרְלָתוֹ וְנִכְרְתָה
and-she-will-be-cut-off foreskin-of-him flesh-of *** he-is-circumcised not

הַנֶּפֶשׁ הַהִוא מֵעַמֶּיהָ אֶת־ בְּרִיתִי הֵפַר׃
he-broke covenant-of-me *** from-people-of-her the-that the-person

וַיֹּאמֶר אֱלֹהִים אֶל־אַבְרָהָם שָׂרַי אִשְׁתְּךָ לֹא־ תִקְרָא אֶת־ שְׁמָהּ
name-of-her *** you-call not wife-of-you Sarai Abraham to God and-he-said (15)

שָׂרָי כִּי שָׂרָה שְׁמָהּ׃ וּבֵרַכְתִּי אֹתָהּ וְגַם נָתַתִּי
I-will-give and-surely her and-I-will-bless (16) name-of-her Sarah for Sarai

מִמֶּנָּה לְךָ בֵּן וּבֵרַכְתִּיהָ וְהָיְתָה לְגוֹיִם מַלְכֵי
kings-of as-nations so-she-will-be and-I-will-bless-her son to-you by-her

עַמִּים מִמֶּנָּה יִהְיוּ׃ וַיִּפֹּל אַבְרָהָם עַל־ פָּנָיו
face-of-him on Abraham and-he-fell (17) they-will-come from-her peoples

וַיִּצְחָק וַיֹּאמֶר בְּלִבּוֹ הַלְּבֶן מֵאָה־ שָׁנָה יִוָּלֵד
he-will-be-born year hundred to-son-of? in-heart-him and-he-said and-he-laughed

וְאִם־ שָׂרָה הֲבַת תִּשְׁעִים שָׁנָה תֵּלֵד׃ וַיֹּאמֶר אַבְרָהָם
Abraham and-he-said (18) she-will-bear year ninety daughter-of? Sarah and-if

אֶל־הָאֱלֹהִים לוּ יִשְׁמָעֵאל יִחְיֶה לְפָנֶיךָ׃ וַיֹּאמֶר אֱלֹהִים אֲבָל
yes-but God then-he-said (19) before-you he-might-live Ishmael if-only the-God to

שָׂרָה אִשְׁתְּךָ יֹלֶדֶת לְךָ בֵּן וְקָרָאתָ אֶת־ שְׁמוֹ יִצְחָק
Isaac name-of-him *** and-you-will-call son for-you bearing wife-of-you Sarah

וַהֲקִמֹתִי אֶת־ בְּרִיתִי אִתּוֹ לִבְרִית עוֹלָם
everlasting as-covenant-of with-him covenant-of-me *** and-I-will-establish

Every male among you shall
be circumcised. 11You are to
undergo circumcision, and it
will be the sign of the covenant between me and you.
12For the generations to come
every male among you who is
eight days old must be circumcised, including those born in
your household or bought
with money from a foreigner—those who are not your
offspring. 13Whether born in
your household or bought
with your money, they must
be circumcised. My covenant
in your flesh is to be an everlasting covenant. 14Any uncircumcised male, who has not
been circumcised in the flesh,
will be cut off from his people;
he has broken my covenant."
15God also said to Abraham,
"As for Sarai your wife, you
are no longer to call her Sarai;
her name will be Sarah.[a] 16I
will bless her and will surely
give you a son by her. I will
bless her so that she will be the
mother of nations; kings of
peoples will come from her."
17Abraham fell facedown; he
laughed and said to himself,
"Will a son be born to a man
a hundred years old? Will Sarah bear a child at the age of
ninety?" 18And Abraham said
to God, "If only Ishmael might
live under your blessing!"
19Then God said, "Yes, but
your wife Sarah will bear you
a son, and you will call him
Isaac.[b] I will establish my covenant with him as an everlasting covenant for his descendants after him. 20And as for

[a]15 *Sarah* means *princess.*
[b]19 *Isaac* means *he laughs.*

לְזַרְעוֹ אַחֲרָיו׃ וּלְיִשְׁמָעֵאל שְׁמַעְתִּיךָ הִנֵּה ׀
see! I-heard-you and-for-Ishmael (20) after-him for-descendant-of-him

בֵּרַכְתִּי אֹתוֹ וְהִפְרֵיתִי אֹתוֹ וְהִרְבֵּיתִי אֹתוֹ בִּמְאֹד
greatly him and-I-will-increase him and-I-will-make-fruitful him I-will-bless

מְאֹד שְׁנֵים־עָשָׂר נְשִׂיאִם יוֹלִיד וּנְתַתִּיו לְגוֹי גָּדוֹל׃
great into-nation and-I-will-make-him he-will-father rulers ten two greatly

וְאֶת־ בְּרִיתִי אָקִים אֶת־ יִצְחָק אֲשֶׁר תֵּלֵד לְךָ
to-you she-will-bear whom Isaac with I-will-establish covenant-of-me but (21)

שָׂרָה לַמּוֹעֵד הַזֶּה בַּשָּׁנָה הָאַחֶרֶת׃ וַיְכַל
when-he-finished (22) the-next in-the-year the-this by-the-time Sarah

לְדַבֵּר אִתּוֹ וַיַּעַל אֱלֹהִים מֵעַל אַבְרָהָם׃ וַיִּקַּח אַבְרָהָם
Abraham and-he-took (23) Abraham from God then-he-went-up with-him to-speak

אֶת־ יִשְׁמָעֵאל בְּנוֹ וְאֵת כָּל־ יְלִידֵי בֵיתוֹ וְאֵת כָּל־
all-of and household-of-him born-ones-of all-of and son-of-him Ishmael ***

מִקְנַת כַּסְפּוֹ כָּל־ זָכָר בְּאַנְשֵׁי בֵּית אַבְרָהָם
Abraham household-of among-men-of male every-of money-of-him bought-of

וַיָּמָל אֶת־ בְּשַׂר עָרְלָתָם בְּעֶצֶם הַיּוֹם הַזֶּה
the-that the-day on-very-of foreskin-of-them flesh-of *** and-he-circumcised

כַּאֲשֶׁר דִּבֶּר אִתּוֹ אֱלֹהִים׃ וְאַבְרָהָם בֶּן־ תִּשְׁעִים וָתֵשַׁע שָׁנָה
year and-nine ninety son-of now-Abraham (24) God him he-told just-as

בְּהִמֹּלוֹ בְּשַׂר עָרְלָתוֹ׃ וְיִשְׁמָעֵאל בְּנוֹ
son-of-him and-Ishmael (25) foreskin-of-him flesh-of when-to-be-circumcised-him

בֶּן־ שְׁלֹשׁ עֶשְׂרֵה שָׁנָה בְּהִמֹּלוֹ אֵת בְּשַׂר עָרְלָתוֹ׃
foreskin-of-him flesh-of *** when-to-be-circumcised-him year ten three son-of

בְּעֶצֶם הַיּוֹם הַזֶּה נִמּוֹל אַבְרָהָם וְיִשְׁמָעֵאל
and-Ishmael Abraham being-circumcised the-that the-day on-very-of (26)

בְּנוֹ׃ וְכָל־ אַנְשֵׁי בֵיתוֹ יְלִיד בָּיִת
household born-of household-of-him men-of and-all-of (27) son-of-him

וּמִקְנַת־ כֶּסֶף מֵאֵת בֶּן־ נֵכָר נִמֹּלוּ אִתּוֹ׃
with-him they-were-circumcised foreigner son-of from money or-bought-of

וַיֵּרָא אֵלָיו יְהוָה בְּאֵלֹנֵי מַמְרֵא וְהוּא יֹשֵׁב
sitting and-he Mamre near-trees-of Yahweh to-him and-he-appeared (18:1)

פֶּתַח־ הָאֹהֶל כְּחֹם הַיּוֹם׃ וַיִּשָּׂא עֵינָיו
eyes-of-him and-he-lifted (2) the-day in-heat-of the-tent entrance-of

וַיַּרְא וְהִנֵּה שְׁלֹשָׁה אֲנָשִׁים נִצָּבִים עָלָיו וַיַּרְא וַיָּרָץ
then-he-ran when-he-saw near-him ones-standing men three and-see! and-he-saw

לִקְרָאתָם מִפֶּתַח הָאֹהֶל וַיִּשְׁתַּחוּ אָרְצָה׃ וַיֹּאמַר
and-he-said (3) to-ground and-he-bowed the-tent from-entrance-of to-meet-them

Ishmael, I have heard you: I
will surely bless him; I will
make him fruitful and will
greatly increase his numbers.
He will be the father of twelve
rulers, and I will make him
into a great nation. [21]But my
covenant I will establish with
Isaac, whom Sarah will bear to
you by this time next year."
[22]When he had finished
speaking with Abraham, God
went up from him.

[23]On that very day Abraham
took his son Ishmael and all
those born in his household or
bought with his money, every
male in his household, and
circumcised them, as God told
him. [24]Abraham was ninety-
nine years old when he was
circumcised, [25]and his son Ishmael was thirteen; [26]Abraham
and his son Ishmael were both
circumcised on that same day.
[27]And every male in Abraham's household, including
those born in his household or
bought from a foreigner, was
circumcised with him.

The Three Visitors

18 The LORD appeared to
Abraham near the
great trees of Mamre while he
was sitting at the entrance to
his tent in the heat of the day.
[2]Abraham looked up and saw
three men standing nearby.
When he saw them, he hur-
ried from the entrance of his
tent to meet them and bowed
low to the ground.

אֲדֹנָי אִם־נָא מָצָאתִי חֵן בְּעֵינֶיךָ אַל־נָא תַעֲבֹר מֵעַל עַבְדֶּךָ׃

servant-of-you by you-pass now! not in-eyes-of-you favor I-found now! if my-lord

יֻקַּח־נָא מְעַט־מַיִם וְרַחֲצוּ רַגְלֵיכֶם וְהִשָּׁעֲנוּ

and-rest! feet-of-you then-wash! water little-of now! let-him-be-brought (4)

תַּחַת הָעֵץ׃ וְאֶקְחָה פַת־לֶחֶם וְסַעֲדוּ לִבְּכֶם אַחַר

then heart-of-you and-refresh! bread piece-of and-let-me-get (5) the-tree under

תַּעֲבֹרוּ כִּי־עַל־כֵּן עֲבַרְתֶּם עַל־עַבְדְּכֶם וַיֹּאמְרוּ כֵּן

very-well and-they-answered servant-of-you to you-came now-that you-go-away

תַּעֲשֶׂה כַּאֲשֶׁר דִּבַּרְתָּ׃ וַיְמַהֵר אַבְרָהָם הָאֹהֱלָה אֶל־שָׂרָה

Sarah to into-the-tent Abraham so-he-hurried (6) you-say just-as you-do

וַיֹּאמֶר מַהֲרִי שְׁלֹשׁ סְאִים קֶמַח סֹלֶת לוּשִׁי וַעֲשִׂי עֻגוֹת׃

loaves and-make! knead! fine flour seahs-of three-of be-quick! and-he-said

וְאֶל־הַבָּקָר רָץ אַבְרָהָם וַיִּקַּח בֶּן־בָּקָר רַךְ

tender herd calf-of and-he-selected Abraham he-ran the-herd and-to (7)

וָטוֹב וַיִּתֵּן אֶל־הַנַּעַר וַיְמַהֵר לַעֲשׂוֹת אֹתוֹ׃

him to-prepare and-he-hurried the-servant to and-he-gave and-choice

וַיִּקַּח חֶמְאָה וְחָלָב וּבֶן־הַבָּקָר אֲשֶׁר עָשָׂה

he-prepared that the-herd and-calf-of and-milk curd then-he-brought (8)

וַיִּתֵּן לִפְנֵיהֶם וְהוּא־עֹמֵד עֲלֵיהֶם תַּחַת הָעֵץ וַיֹּאכֵלוּ׃

as-they-ate the-tree under near-them standing and-he before-them and-he-set

וַיֹּאמְרוּ אֵלָיו אַיֵּה שָׂרָה אִשְׁתֶּךָ וַיֹּאמֶר הִנֵּה

see! and-he-said wife-of-you Sarah where? to-him and-they-asked (9)

בָאֹהֶל׃ וַיֹּאמֶר שׁוֹב אָשׁוּב אֵלֶיךָ כָּעֵת

about-the-time to-you I-will-return to-return then-he-said (10) in-the-tent

חַיָּה וְהִנֵּה־בֵן לְשָׂרָה אִשְׁתֶּךָ וְשָׂרָה שֹׁמַעַת פֶּתַח

entrance-of listening now-Sarah wife-of-you to-Sarah son and-see! spring

הָאֹהֶל וְהוּא אַחֲרָיו׃ וְאַבְרָהָם וְשָׂרָה זְקֵנִים בָּאִים

being-advanced old-ones and-Sarah now-Abraham (11) behind-him and-he the-tent

בַּיָּמִים חָדַל לִהְיוֹת לְשָׂרָה אֹרַח כַּנָּשִׁים׃

normal-to-the-women manner with-Sarah to-be he-was-past in-the-days

וַתִּצְחַק שָׂרָה בְּקִרְבָּהּ לֵאמֹר אַחֲרֵי בְלֹתִי הָיְתָה־

she-is to-be-worn-out-me after to-say to-self-of-her Sarah so-she-laughed (12)

לִּי עֶדְנָה וַאדֹנִי זָקֵן׃ וַיֹּאמֶר יְהוָה אֶל־אַבְרָהָם

Abraham to Yahweh then-he-said (13) he-is-old and-master-of-me pleasure to-me

לָמָּה זֶּה צָחֲקָה שָׂרָה לֵאמֹר הַאַף אֻמְנָם אֵלֵד וַאֲנִי זָקַנְתִּי׃

I-am-old yet-I I-will-bear really? now? to-say Sarah she-laughed this why?

הֲיִפָּלֵא מֵיְהוָה דָּבָר לַמּוֹעֵד אָשׁוּב אֵלֶיךָ

to-you I-will-return at-the-time anything for-Yahweh is-he-too-hard? (14)

3 He said, "If I have found favor in your eyes, my lord,[c] do
not pass your servant by. 4 Let
a little water be brought, and
then you may all wash your
feet and rest under this tree.
5 Let me get you something to
eat, so you can be refreshed
and then go on your way—
now that you have come to
your servant."
"Very well," they answered,
"do as you say."
6 So Abraham hurried into
the tent to Sarah. "Quick," he
said, "get three seahs[d] of fine
flour and knead it and bake
some bread."
7 Then he ran to the herd and
selected a choice, tender calf
and gave it to a servant, who
hurried to prepare it. 8 He then
brought some curds and milk
and the calf that had been prepared, and set these before
them. While they ate, he stood
near them under a tree.
9 "Where is your wife Sarah?" they asked him.
"There, in the tent," he said.
10 Then the LORD[e] said, "I will
surely return to you about this
time next year, and Sarah your
wife will have a son."
Now Sarah was listening at
the entrance to the tent, which
was behind him. 11 Abraham
and Sarah were already old
and well advanced in years,
and Sarah was past the age of
childbearing. 12 So Sarah
laughed to herself as she
thought, "After I am worn out
and my master[f] is old, will I
now have this pleasure?"
13 Then the LORD said to
Abraham, "Why did Sarah
laugh and say, 'Will I really
have a child, now that I am
old?' 14 Is anything too hard for
the LORD? I will return to you

c3 Or *O Lord*
d6 That is, probably about 20 quarts (about 22 liters)
e10 Hebrew *he*
f12 Or *husband*

כָּעֵת חַיָּה וּלְשָׂרָה בֵן׃ וַתְּכַחֵשׁ שָׂרָה לֵאמֹר לֹא
not to-say Sarah so-she-lied (15) son and-to-Sarah spring at-the-time

צָחַקְתִּי כִּי יָרֵאָה וַיֹּאמֶר לֹא כִּי צָחָקְתְּ׃
you-did-laugh indeed no but-he-said she-was-afraid for I-laughed

וַיָּקֻמוּ מִשָּׁם הָאֲנָשִׁים וַיַּשְׁקִפוּ עַל־פְּנֵי סְדֹם
Sodom toward-of down then-they-looked the-men from-there when-they-got-up (16)

וְאַבְרָהָם הֹלֵךְ עִמָּם לְשַׁלְּחָם׃ וַיהוָה אָמָר
he-said then-Yahweh (17) to-send-off-them with-them walking and-Abraham

הַמְכַסֶּה אֲנִי מֵאַבְרָהָם אֲשֶׁר אֲנִי עֹשֶׂה׃ וְאַבְרָהָם הָיוֹ יִהְיֶה
he-will-become to-become now-Abraham (18) doing I what from-Abraham I hiding?

לְגוֹי גָּדוֹל וְעָצוּם וְנִבְרְכוּ בוֹ כֹּל
all-of through-him and-they-will-be-blessed and-powerful great to-nation

גּוֹיֵי הָאָרֶץ׃ כִּי יְדַעְתִּיו לְמַעַן אֲשֶׁר יְצַוֶּה אֶת־
*** he-will-direct that so I-chose-him for (19) the-earth nations-of

בָּנָיו וְאֶת־ בֵּיתוֹ אַחֲרָיו וְשָׁמְרוּ דֶּרֶךְ
way-of so-they-will-keep after-him household-of-him and children-of-him

יְהוָה לַעֲשׂוֹת צְדָקָה וּמִשְׁפָּט לְמַעַן הָבִיא יְהוָה עַל־אַבְרָהָם אֵת אֲשֶׁר־
what *** Abraham for Yahweh he-will-bring so-that and-just right to-do Yahweh

דִּבֶּר עָלָיו׃ וַיֹּאמֶר יְהוָה זַעֲקַת סְדֹם וַעֲמֹרָה כִּי־
so and-Gomorrah Sodom outcry-of Yahweh then-he-said (20) to-him he-promised

רָבָּה וְחַטָּאתָם כִּי כָבְדָה מְאֹד׃ אֵרֲדָה־ נָּא
now! I-will-go-down (21) very she-is-grievous so and-sin-of-them she-is-great

וְאֶרְאֶה הַכְּצַעֲקָתָהּ הַבָּאָה אֵלַי עָשׂוּ
they-did to-me the-one-reaching if-according-to-outcry-of-her and-I-will-see

כָּלָה וְאִם־ לֹא אֵדָעָה׃ וַיִּפְנוּ מִשָּׁם הָאֲנָשִׁים
the-men from-there and-they-turned (22) I-will-know not and-if all

וַיֵּלְכוּ סְדֹמָה וְאַבְרָהָם עוֹדֶנּוּ עֹמֵד לִפְנֵי יְהוָה׃
Yahweh before standing remained-him but-Abraham toward-Sodom and-they-went

וַיִּגַּשׁ אַבְרָהָם וַיֹּאמַר הַאַף תִּסְפֶּה
you-will-sweep-away indeed? and-he-said Abraham then-he-approached (23)

צַדִּיק עִם־ רָשָׁע׃ אוּלַי יֵשׁ חֲמִשִּׁים צַדִּיקִם בְּתוֹךְ
in righteous-ones fifty there-are what-if (24) wicked with righteous

הָעִיר הַאַף תִּסְפֶּה וְלֹא־ תִשָּׂא לַמָּקוֹם
to-the-place you-will-spare and-not you-will-sweep-away indeed? the-city

לְמַעַן חֲמִשִּׁים הַצַּדִּיקִם אֲשֶׁר בְּקִרְבָּהּ׃ חָלִלָה לְּךָ
from-you far-be-it! (25) in-midst-of-her who the-righteous-ones fifty for-sake-of

מֵעֲשֹׂת כַּדָּבָר הַזֶּה לְהָמִית צַדִּיק עִם־ רָשָׁע וְהָיָה
and-he-be wicked with righteous to-kill the-this such-the-thing from-to-do

at the appointed time next year and Sarah will have a son."

15 Sarah was afraid, so she lied and said, "I did not laugh."

But he said, "Yes, you did laugh."

Abraham Pleads for Sodom

16 When the men got up to leave, they looked down toward Sodom, and Abraham walked along with them to see them on their way. 17 Then the LORD said, "Shall I hide from Abraham what I am about to do? 18 Abraham will surely become a great and powerful nation, and all nations on earth will be blessed through him. 19 For I have chosen him, so that he will direct his children and his household after him to keep the way of the LORD by doing what is right and just, so that the LORD will bring about for Abraham what he has promised him."

20 Then the LORD said, "The outcry against Sodom and Gomorrah is so great and their sin so grievous 21 that I will go down and see if what they have done is as bad as the outcry that has reached me. If not, I will know."

22 The men turned away and went toward Sodom, but Abraham remained standing before the LORD.[g] 23 Then Abraham approached him and said: "Will you sweep away the righteous with the wicked? 24 What if there are fifty righteous people in the city? Will you really sweep it away and not spare[h] the place for the sake of the fifty righteous people in it? 25 Far be it from you to do such a thing—to kill the righteous with the

g22 Masoretic Text; an ancient Hebrew scribal tradition *but the LORD remained standing before Abraham*

h24 Or *forgive*; also in verse 26

כַּצַּדִּיק כָּרָשָׁע חָלִלָה לָּךְ הֲשֹׁפֵט כָּל־
all-of one-judging-of? from-you far-be-it! as-the-wicked as-the-righteous

הָאָרֶץ לֹא יַעֲשֶׂה מִשְׁפָּט׃ וַיֹּאמֶר יְהוָה אִם־אֶמְצָא בִסְדֹם
in-Sodom I-find if Yahweh so-he-said (26) right will-he-do not the-earth

חֲמִשִּׁים צַדִּיקִם בְּתוֹךְ הָעִיר וְנָשָׂאתִי לְכָל־ הַמָּקוֹם
the-place to-whole-of then-I-will-spare the-city in righteous-ones fifty

בַּעֲבוּרָם׃ וַיַּעַן אַבְרָהָם וַיֹּאמַר הִנֵּה־ נָא הוֹאַלְתִּי
I-was-bold now! see! and-he-said Abraham then-he-answered (27) for-sake-of-them

לְדַבֵּר אֶל־אֲדֹנָי וְאָנֹכִי עָפָר וָאֵפֶר׃ אוּלַי יַחְסְרוּן חֲמִשִּׁים
the-fifty they-lacked what-if (28) and-ash dust though-I Lord to to-speak

הַצַּדִּיקִם חֲמִשָּׁה הֲתַשְׁחִית בַּחֲמִשָּׁה אֶת־ כָּל־ הָעִיר
the-city whole-of *** because-of-five will-you-destroy? five the-righteous-ones

וַיֹּאמֶר לֹא אַשְׁחִית אִם־ אֶמְצָא שָׁם אַרְבָּעִים וַחֲמִשָּׁה׃
and-five forty there I-find if I-will-destroy not and-he-said

וַיֹּסֶף עוֹד לְדַבֵּר אֵלָיו וַיֹּאמַר אוּלַי יִמָּצְאוּן
they-are-found what-if and-he-said to-him to-speak again and-he-repeated (29)

שָׁם אַרְבָּעִים וַיֹּאמֶר לֹא אֶעֱשֶׂה בַּעֲבוּר הָאַרְבָּעִים׃ וַיֹּאמֶר
and-he-said (30) the-forty for-sake-of I-will-do not and-he-said forty there

אַל־ נָא יִחַר לַאדֹנָי וַאֲדַבֵּרָה אוּלַי יִמָּצְאוּן שָׁם
there they-were-found what-if but-let-me-speak to-Lord may-he-be-angry now! not

שְׁלֹשִׁים וַיֹּאמֶר לֹא אֶעֱשֶׂה אִם־אֶמְצָא שָׁם שְׁלֹשִׁים׃ וַיֹּאמֶר
and-he-said (31) thirty there I-find if I-will-do not and-he-answered thirty

הִנֵּה־ נָא הוֹאַלְתִּי לְדַבֵּר אֶל־ אֲדֹנָי אוּלַי יִמָּצְאוּן שָׁם עֶשְׂרִים
twenty there they-were-found what-if Lord to to-speak I-was-bold now! see!

וַיֹּאמֶר לֹא אַשְׁחִית בַּעֲבוּר הָעֶשְׂרִים׃ וַיֹּאמֶר אַל־ נָא
now! not so-he-said (32) the-twenty for-sake-of I-will-destroy not and-he-said

יִחַר לַאדֹנָי וַאֲדַבְּרָה אַךְ־ הַפַּעַם אוּלַי יִמָּצְאוּן
they-are-found what-if the-once just but-let-me-speak to-Lord may-he-be-angry

שָׁם עֲשָׂרָה וַיֹּאמֶר לֹא אַשְׁחִית בַּעֲבוּר הָעֲשָׂרָה׃
the-ten for-sake-of I-will-destroy not and-he-answered ten there

וַיֵּלֶךְ יְהוָה כַּאֲשֶׁר כִּלָּה לְדַבֵּר אֶל־אַבְרָהָם וְאַבְרָהָם
and-Abraham Abraham with to-speak he-finished as-soon-as Yahweh and-he-left (33)

שָׁב לִמְקֹמוֹ׃ וַיָּבֹאוּ שְׁנֵי הַמַּלְאָכִים סְדֹמָה
at-Sodom the-angels two-of and-they-arrived (19:1) to-home-of-him he-returned

בָּעֶרֶב וְלוֹט יֹשֵׁב בְּשַׁעַר־ סְדֹם וַיַּרְא־ לוֹט
Lot when-he-saw Sodom in-gateway-of sitting and-Lot in-the-evening

וַיָּקָם לִקְרָאתָם וַיִּשְׁתַּחוּ אַפַּיִם אָרְצָה׃ וַיֹּאמֶר הִנֶּה
see! and-he-said (2) to-ground faces and-he-bowed to-meet-them then-he-got-up

wicked, treating the righteous and the wicked alike. Far be it from you! Will not the Judge of all the earth do right?"
[26]The LORD said, "If I find fifty righteous people in the city of Sodom, I will spare the whole place for their sake."
[27]Then Abraham spoke up again: "Now that I have been so bold as to speak to the Lord, though I am nothing but dust and ashes, [28]what if the number of the righteous is five less than fifty? Will you destroy the whole city because of five people?"

"If I find forty-five there," he said, "I will not destroy it."
[29]Once again he spoke to him, "What if only forty are found there?"

He said, "For the sake of forty, I will not do it."
[30]Then he said, "May the Lord not be angry, but let me speak. What if only thirty can be found there?"

He answered, "I will not do it if I find thirty there."
[31]Abraham said, "Now that I have been so bold as to speak to the Lord, what if only twenty can be found there?"

He said, "For the sake of twenty, I will not destroy it."
[32]Then he said, "May the Lord not be angry, but let me speak just once more. What if only ten can be found there?"

He answered, "For the sake of ten, I will not destroy it."
[33]When the LORD had finished speaking with Abraham, he left, and Abraham returned home.

Sodom and Gomorrah Destroyed

19 The two angels arrived at Sodom in the evening, and Lot was sitting in the gateway of the city. When he saw them, he got up to meet them and bowed down with his face to the ground. [2]"My

נָא־ אֲדֹנַי סוּרוּ נָא אֶל־ בֵּית עַבְדְּכֶם וְלִינוּ וְרַחֲצוּ
and-wash! and-spend-night! servant-of-you house-of to now! turn! lords-of-me now!

רַגְלֵיכֶם וְהִשְׁכַּמְתֶּם וַהֲלַכְתֶּם לְדַרְכְּכֶם וַיֹּאמְרוּ לֹּא
no but-they-said on-way-of-you and-you-may-go then-you-may-rise feet-of-you

כִּי בָרְחוֹב נָלִין׃ וַיִּפְצַר־ בָּם מְאֹד
strongly with-them but-he-persisted (3) we-will-spend-night in-the-square for

וַיָּסֻרוּ אֵלָיו וַיָּבֹאוּ אֶל־ בֵּיתוֹ וַיַּעַשׂ
and-he-prepared house-of-him to and-they-entered with-him and-they-went

לָהֶם מִשְׁתֶּה וּמַצּוֹת אָפָה וַיֹּאכֵלוּ׃ טֶרֶם
before (4) and-they-ate he-baked and-bread-without-yeast meal for-them

יִשְׁכָּבוּ וְאַנְשֵׁי הָעִיר אַנְשֵׁי סְדֹם נָסַבּוּ עַל־
around they-surrounded Sodom men-of the-city now-men-of they-went-to-bed

הַבַּיִת מִנַּעַר וְעַד־ זָקֵן כָּל־ הָעָם מִקָּצֶה׃
to-last-one the-people all-of old and-to from-young the-house

וַיִּקְרְאוּ אֶל־לוֹט וַיֹּאמְרוּ לוֹ אַיֵּה הָאֲנָשִׁים† אֲשֶׁר־ בָּאוּ
they-came who the-men where? to-him and-they-said Lot to and-they-called (5)

אֵלֶיךָ הַלָּיְלָה הוֹצִיאֵם אֵלֵינוּ וְנֵדְעָה אֹתָם׃ וַיֵּצֵא
but-he-went (6) with-them so-we-can-have-sex to-us bring-them! the-night to-you

אֲלֵהֶם לוֹט הַפֶּתְחָה וְהַדֶּלֶת סָגַר אַחֲרָיו׃ וַיֹּאמַר אַל־נָא
now! not and-he-said (7) after-him he-shut and-the-door to-the-outside Lot to-them

אַחַי תָּרֵעוּ׃ הִנֵּה־ נָא לִי שְׁתֵּי בָנוֹת אֲשֶׁר לֹא־ יָדְעוּ
they-slept not who daughters two-of to-me now! see! (8) you-do-evil friends-of-me

אִישׁ אוֹצִיאָה־ נָּא אֶתְהֶן אֲלֵיכֶם וַעֲשׂוּ לָהֶן כַּטּוֹב בְּעֵינֵיכֶם
in-eyes-of-you as-the-good to-them and-you-do to-you them now! let-me-bring man

רַק לָאֲנָשִׁים הָאֵל אַל־ תַּעֲשׂוּ דָבָר כִּי־עַל־ כֵּן בָּאוּ בְּצֵל
under-shelter-of they-came for anything you-do not the-these to-the-men but

קֹרָתִי׃ וַיֹּאמְרוּ׀ גֶּשׁ־ הָלְאָה וַיֹּאמְרוּ הָאֶחָד בָּא־
he-came the-one and-they-said away get! but-they-replied (9) roof-of-me

לָגוּר וַיִּשְׁפֹּט שָׁפוֹט עַתָּה נָרַע לְךָ
to-you we-will-treat-worse now to-judge and-he-would-judge to-be-alien

מֵהֶם וַיִּפְצְרוּ בָאִישׁ בְּלוֹט מְאֹד וַיִּגְּשׁוּ
and-they-moved strongly against-Lot against-the-man and-they-pressed than-them

לִשְׁבֹּר הַדָּלֶת׃ וַיִּשְׁלְחוּ הָאֲנָשִׁים אֶת־ יָדָם
hand-of-them *** the-men but-they-reached-out (10) the-door to-break-down

וַיָּבִיאוּ אֶת־ לוֹט אֲלֵיהֶם הַבַּיְתָה וְאֶת־ הַדֶּלֶת סָגָרוּ׃
they-shut the-door and into-the-house to-them Lot *** and-they-pulled

וְאֶת־ הָאֲנָשִׁים אֲשֶׁר־ פֶּתַח הַבַּיִת הִכּוּ בַּסַּנְוֵרִים
with-the-blindnesses they-struck the-house door-of who the-men and (11)

lords," he said, "please turn aside to your servant's house. You can wash your feet and spend the night and then go on your way early in the morning."

"No," they answered, "we will spend the night in the square."

[3]But he insisted so strongly that they did go with him and entered his house. He prepared a meal for them, baking bread without yeast, and they ate. [4]Before they had gone to bed, all the men from every part of the city of Sodom—both young and old—surrounded the house. [5]They called to Lot, "Where are the men who came to you tonight? Bring them out to us so that we can have sex with them."

[6]Lot went outside to meet them and shut the door behind him [7]and said, "No, my friends. Don't do this wicked thing. [8]Look, I have two daughters who have never slept with a man. Let me bring them out to you, and you can do what you like with them. But don't do anything to these men, for they have come under the protection of my roof."

[9]"Get out of our way," they replied. And they said, "This fellow came here as an alien, and now he wants to play the judge! We'll treat you worse than them." They kept bringing pressure on Lot and moved forward to break down the door.

[10]But the men inside reached out and pulled Lot back into the house and shut the door. [11]Then they struck the men who were at the door of the house, young and old, with

*2 Most mss have *bateph pathah* under the *be* (וַהֲ).

†5 Most mss have *bateph pathah* under the *aleph* (הָאֲ).

מִקָּטֹן וְעַד־ גָּדוֹל וַיִּלְאוּ לִמְצֹא הַפָּתַח׃ וַיֹּאמְרוּ
then-they-said (12) the-door to-find so-they-gave-up great and-to from-small

הָאֲנָשִׁים אֶל־ לוֹט עֹד מִי־ לְךָ פֹה חָתָן וּבָנֶיךָ
or-sons-of-you son-in-law here with-you who? else Lot to the-men

וּבְנֹתֶיךָ וְכֹל אֲשֶׁר־ לְךָ בָּעִיר הוֹצֵא מִן־הַמָּקוֹם׃
the-place from bring-out! in-the-city to-you who or-anyone or-daughters-of-you

כִּי־ מַשְׁחִתִים אֲנַחְנוּ אֶת־הַמָּקוֹם הַזֶּה כִּי־ גָדְלָה צַעֲקָתָם
cry-of-them great for the-this the-place *** we ones-destroying because (13)

אֶת־ פְּנֵי יְהוָה וַיְשַׁלְּחֵנוּ יְהוָה לְשַׁחֲתָהּ׃ וַיֵּצֵא
so-he-went-out (14) to-destroy-her Yahweh that-he-sent-us Yahweh face-of ***

לוֹט וַיְדַבֵּר ׀ אֶל־ חֲתָנָיו ׀ לֹקְחֵי בְנֹתָיו
daughters-of-him ones-being-pledged-of sons-in-law-of-him to and-he-spoke Lot

וַיֹּאמֶר קוּמוּ צְּאוּ מִן־ הַמָּקוֹם הַזֶּה כִּי־ מַשְׁחִית
destroying because the-this the-place from get-out! get-up! and-he-said

יְהוָה אֶת־ הָעִיר וַיְהִי כִמְצַחֵק בְּעֵינֵי חֲתָנָיו׃
sons-in-law-of-him in-eyes-of as-joking but-he-was the-city *** Yahweh

וּכְמוֹ הַשַּׁחַר עָלָה וַיָּאִיצוּ הַמַּלְאָכִים בְּלוֹט לֵאמֹר
to-say with-Lot the-angels then-they-urged he-came the-morning and-when (15)

קוּם קַח אֶת־ אִשְׁתְּךָ וְאֶת־ שְׁתֵּי בְנֹתֶיךָ הַנִּמְצָאֹת
the-ones-being-here daughters-of-you two-of and wife-of-you *** take! get-up!

פֶּן־ תִּסָּפֶה בַּעֲוֹן הָעִיר׃ וַיִּתְמַהְמָהּ ׀
when-he-hesitated (16) the-city in-punishment-of you-will-be-swept-away or

וַיַּחֲזִקוּ הָאֲנָשִׁים בְּיָדוֹ וּבְיַד־ אִשְׁתּוֹ
wife-of-him and-on-hand-of on-hand-of-him the-men then-they-grasped

וּבְיַד שְׁתֵּי בְנֹתָיו בְּחֶמְלַת יְהוָה עָלָיו
to-him Yahweh for-merciful-of daughters-of-him two-of and-on-hand-of

וַיֹּצִאֻהוּ וַיַּנִּחֻהוּ מִחוּץ לָעִיר׃ וַיְהִי
and-he-was (17) the-city outside and-they-set-him and-they-led-him

כְהוֹצִיאָם אֹתָם הַחוּצָה וַיֹּאמֶר הִמָּלֵט עַל־ נַפְשֶׁךָ אַל־
not life-of-you for flee! that-he-said to-the-outside them as-to-bring-them

תַּבִּיט אַחֲרֶיךָ וְאַל־ תַּעֲמֹד בְּכָל־ הַכִּכָּר הָהָרָה
to-the-hill the-plain in-anywhere-of you-stop and-not back-of-you you-look

הִמָּלֵט פֶּן־ תִּסָּפֶה׃ וַיֹּאמֶר לוֹט אֲלֵהֶם אַל־ נָא אֲדֹנָי׃
lords-of-me now! no to-them Lot but-he-said (18) you-be-swept-away or flee!

הִנֵּה־ נָא מָצָא עַבְדְּךָ חֵן בְּעֵינֶיךָ וַתַּגְדֵּל
and-you-made-great in-eyes-of-you favor servant-of-you he-found now! see! (19)

חַסְדְּךָ אֲשֶׁר עָשִׂיתָ עִמָּדִי לְהַחֲיוֹת אֶת־ נַפְשִׁי וְאָנֹכִי לֹא אוּכַל
I-can not but-I life-of-me *** to-spare to-me you-showed that kindness-of-you

blindness so that they could
not find the door.
12The two men said to Lot,
"Do you have anyone else
here—sons-in-law, sons or
daughters, or anyone else in
the city who belongs to you?
Get them out of here, 13because
we are going to destroy this
place. The outcry to the LORD
against its people is so great
that he has sent us to destroy
it."
14So Lot went out and spoke
to his sons-in-law, who were
pledged to marry[i] his daughters. He said, "Hurry and get
out of this place, because the
LORD is about to destroy the
city!" But his sons-in-law
thought he was joking.
15With the coming of dawn,
the angels urged Lot, saying,
"Hurry! Take your wife and
your two daughters who are
here, or you will be swept
away when the city is punished."
16When he hesitated, the
men grasped his hand and the
hands of his wife and of his
two daughters and led them
safely out of the city, for the
LORD was merciful to them.
17As soon as they had brought
them out, one of them said,
"Flee for your lives! Don't look
back, and don't stop any-
where in the plain! Flee to the
mountains or you will be
swept away!"
18But Lot said to them, "No,
my lords,[j] please! 19Your[k] servant has found favor in your[k]
eyes, and you[k] have shown
great kindness to me in spar-
ing my life. But I can't flee to

[i]14 Or *were married to*
[j]18 Or *No, Lord;* or *No, my lord*
[k]19 The Hebrew is singular.

לְהִמָּלֵט הָהָרָה פֶּן־ תִּדְבָּקַנִי הָרָעָה וָמַתִּי׃ הִנֵּה־ נָא
now! see! (20) and-I-die the-disaster she-overtake-me lest to-the-mountain to-flee

הָעִיר הַזֹּאת קְרֹבָה לָנוּס שָׁמָּה וְהִוא מִצְעָר אִמָּלְטָה נָּא שָׁמָּה
to-there now! let-me-flee small and-she to-there to-run near the-this the-town

הֲלֹא מִצְעָר הִוא וּתְחִי נַפְשִׁי׃ וַיֹּאמֶר אֵלָיו הִנֵּה
see! to-him and-he-said (21) life-of-me and-she-will-live she small not?

נָשָׂאתִי פָנֶיךָ גַּם לַדָּבָר הַזֶּה לְבִלְתִּי הָפְכִּי אֶת־
*** to-overthrow-me not the-this to-the-request also face-of-you I-will-grant

הָעִיר אֲשֶׁר דִּבַּרְתָּ׃ מַהֵר הִמָּלֵט שָׁמָּה כִּי לֹא אוּכַל לַעֲשׂוֹת
to-do I-can not because to-there flee! hurry! (22) you-speak-of that the-town

דָּבָר עַד־ בֹּאֲךָ שָׁמָּה עַל־ כֵּן קָרָא שֵׁם־ הָעִיר צוֹעַר׃
Zoar the-town name-of he-called this for to-there to-reach-you until anything

הַשֶּׁמֶשׁ יָצָא עַל־ הָאָרֶץ וְלוֹט בָּא צֹעֲרָה׃ וַיהוָה
and-Yahweh (24) to-Zoar he-reached when-Lot the-land over he-rose the-sun (23)

הִמְטִיר עַל־סְדֹם וְעַל־ עֲמֹרָה גָּפְרִית וָאֵשׁ מֵאֵת יְהוָה מִן־ הַשָּׁמָיִם׃
the-heavens from Yahweh from and-fire sulfur Gomorrah and-on Sodom on he-rained

וַיַּהֲפֹךְ אֶת־ הֶעָרִים הָאֵל וְאֵת כָּל־ הַכִּכָּר וְאֵת כָּל־
all-of and the-plain all-of and the-these the-cities *** so-he-overthrew (25)

יֹשְׁבֵי הֶעָרִים וְצֶמַח הָאֲדָמָה׃ וַתַּבֵּט
but-she-looked (26) the-land vegetation-of the-cities the-ones-living-of

אִשְׁתּוֹ מֵאַחֲרָיו וַתְּהִי נְצִיב מֶלַח׃ וַיַּשְׁכֵּם
and-he-got-up (27) salt pillar-of and-she-became behind-him wife-of-him

אַבְרָהָם בַּבֹּקֶר אֶל־ הַמָּקוֹם אֲשֶׁר־ עָמַד שָׁם אֶת־ פְּנֵי יְהוָה׃
Yahweh before *** there he-stood where the-place to in-the-morning Abraham

וַיַּשְׁקֵף עַל־ פְּנֵי סְדֹם וַעֲמֹרָה וְעַל־ כָּל־ פְּנֵי
surface-of all-of and-to and-Gomorrah Sodom toward down and-he-looked (28)

אֶרֶץ הַכִּכָּר וַיַּרְא וְהִנֵּה עָלָה קִיטֹר הָאָרֶץ כְּקִיטֹר
like-smoke-of the-land smoke-of he-rose and-see! and-he-saw the-plain land-of

הַכִּבְשָׁן׃ וַיְהִי בְּשַׁחֵת אֱלֹהִים אֶת־ עָרֵי הַכִּכָּר
the-plain cities-of *** God when-to-destroy so-he-was (29) the-furnace

וַיִּזְכֹּר אֱלֹהִים אֶת־ אַבְרָהָם וַיְשַׁלַּח אֶת־ לוֹט מִתּוֹךְ
from-midst-of Lot *** and-he-brougnt Abraham *** God that-he-remembered

הַהֲפֵכָה בַּהֲפֹךְ אֶת־ הֶעָרִים אֲשֶׁר־ יָשַׁב בָּהֵן לוֹט׃
Lot in-them he-lived where the-cities *** when-to-overthrow the-catastrophe

וַיַּעַל[9] לוֹט מִצּוֹעַר וַיֵּשֶׁב בָּהָר וּשְׁתֵּי
and-two-of in-the-mountain and-he-settled from-Zoar Lot and-he-left (30)

בְנֹתָיו עִמּוֹ כִּי יָרֵא לָשֶׁבֶת בְּצוֹעַר וַיֵּשֶׁב
and-he-lived in-Zoar to-stay he-was-afraid for with-him daughters-of-him

the mountains; this disaster will overtake me, and I'll die. [20]Look, here is a town near enough to run to, and it is small. Let me flee to it—it is very small, isn't it? Then my life will be spared."

[21]He said to him, "Very well, I will grant this request too; I will not overthrow the town you speak of. [22]But flee there quickly, because I cannot do anything until you reach it." (That is why the town was called Zoar.[l])

[23]By the time Lot reached Zoar, the sun had risen over the land. [24]Then the LORD rained down burning sulfur on Sodom and Gomorrah—from the LORD out of the heavens. [25]Thus he overthrew those cities and the entire plain, including all those living in the cities—and also the vegetation in the land. [26]But Lot's wife looked back and she became a pillar of salt.

[27]Early the next morning Abraham got up and returned to the place where he had stood before the LORD. [28]He looked down toward Sodom and Gomorrah, toward all the land of the plain, and he saw dense smoke rising from the land, like smoke from a furnace.

[29]So when God destroyed the cities of the plain, he remembered Abraham, and he brought Lot out of the catastrophe that overthrew the cities where Lot had lived.

Lot and His Daughters

[30]Lot and his two daughters left Zoar and settled in the mountains, for he was afraid to stay in Zoar. He and his two

[l]22 *Zoar* means *small.*

בַּמְּעָרָה הוּא וּשְׁתֵּי בְנֹתָיו׃ וַתֹּאמֶר הַבְּכִירָה אֶל־
to the-older now-said (31) daughters-of-him and-two-of he in-the-cave

הַצְּעִירָה אָבִינוּ זָקֵן וְאִישׁ אֵין בָּאָרֶץ לָבוֹא
to-lie in-the-area there-is-no and-man he-is-old father-of-us the-younger

עָלֵינוּ כְּדֶרֶךְ כָּל־ הָאָרֶץ׃ לְכָה נַשְׁקֶה אֶת־
*** let-us-make-drink come! (32) the-earth all-of as-custom-of with-us

אָבִינוּ יַיִן וְנִשְׁכְּבָה עִמּוֹ וּנְחַיֶּה מֵאָבִינוּ
by-father-of-us and-let-us-preserve with-him then-let-us-lie wine father-of-us

זָרַע׃ וַתַּשְׁקֶיןָ אֶת־ אֲבִיהֶן יַיִן בַּלַּיְלָה הוּא
that in-the-night wine father-of-them *** so-they-made-drink (33) family

וַתָּבֹא הַבְּכִירָה וַתִּשְׁכַּב אֶת־ אָבִיהָ וְלֹא־ יָדַע
he-knew and-not father-of-her with and-she-lay the-older and-she-went-in

בְּשִׁכְבָהּ וּבְקוּמָהּ׃ וַיְהִי מִמָּחֳרָת
on-next-day and-he-was (34) or-when-to-get-up-her when-to-lie-down-her

וַתֹּאמֶר הַבְּכִירָה אֶל־ הַצְּעִירָה הֵן־שָׁכַבְתִּי אֶמֶשׁ אֶת־ אָבִי
father-of-me with last-night I-lay see! the-younger to the-older that-she-said

נַשְׁקֶנּוּ יַיִן גַּם־ הַלַּיְלָה וּבֹאִי שִׁכְבִי עִמּוֹ
with-him lie! and-go! the-night also wine let-us-make-drink-him

וּנְחַיֶּה מֵאָבִינוּ זָרַע׃ וַתַּשְׁקֶיןָ גַּם
also so-they-made-drink (35) family by-father-of-us and-let-us-preserve

בַּלַּיְלָה הַהוּא אֶת־ אֲבִיהֶן יַיִן וַתָּקָם הַצְּעִירָה
the-younger and-she-went wine father-of-them *** the-that on-the-night

וַתִּשְׁכַּב עִמּוֹ וְלֹא־ יָדַע בְּשִׁכְבָהּ וּבְקֻמָהּ׃
or-when-to-get-up-her when-to-lie-down-her he-knew and-not with-him and-she-lay

וַתַּהֲרֶיןָ שְׁתֵּי בְנוֹת־ לוֹט מֵאֲבִיהֶן׃
by-father-of-them Lot daughters-of two-of so-they-became-pregnant (36)

וַתֵּלֶד הַבְּכִירָה בֵּן וַתִּקְרָא שְׁמוֹ מוֹאָב הוּא אֲבִי־
father-of he Moab name-of-him and-she-called son the-older and-she-bore (37)

מוֹאָב עַד־ הַיּוֹם׃ וְהַצְּעִירָה גַם־ הִוא יָלְדָה בֵּן וַתִּקְרָא
and-she-called son she-bore she also and-the-younger (38) the-day to Moab

שְׁמוֹ בֶּן־ עַמִּי הוּא אֲבִי בְנֵי־ עַמּוֹן עַד־ הַיּוֹם׃ וַיִּסַּע
now-he-left (20:1) the-day to Ammon sons-of father-of he Ammi Ben name-of-him

מִשָּׁם אַבְרָהָם אַרְצָה הַנֶּגֶב וַיֵּשֶׁב בֵּין־ קָדֵשׁ
Kadesh between and-he-lived the-Negev into-region Abraham from-there

וּבֵין שׁוּר וַיָּגָר בִּגְרָר׃ וַיֹּאמֶר אַבְרָהָם אֶל־ שָׂרָה
Sarah about Abraham and-he-said (2) in-Gerar and-he-stayed Shur and-between

אִשְׁתּוֹ אֲחֹתִי הִוא וַיִּשְׁלַח אֲבִימֶלֶךְ מֶלֶךְ גְּרָר וַיִּקַּח
and-he-took Gerar king-of Abimelech then-he-sent she sister-of-me wife-of-him

daughters lived in a cave.
[31]One day the older daughter
said to the younger, "Our father is old, and there is no
man around here to lie with
us, as is the custom all over the
earth. [32]Let's get our father to
drink wine and then lie with
him and preserve our family
line through our father."
[33]That night they got their
father to drink wine, and the
older daughter went in and lay
with him. He was not aware of
it when she lay down or when
she got up.
[34]The next day the older
daughter said to the younger,
"Last night I lay with my father. Let's get him to drink
wine again tonight, and you
go in and lie with him so we
can preserve our family line
through our father." [35]So they
got their father to drink wine
that night also, and the
younger daughter went and
lay with him. Again he was
not aware of it when she lay
down or when she got up.
[36]So both of Lot's daughters
became pregnant by their father. [37]The older daughter had
a son, and she named him
Moab[m]; he is the father of the
Moabites of today. [38]The
younger daughter also had a
son, and she named him Ben-
Ammi[n]; he is the father of the
Ammonites of today.

Abraham and Abimelech

20 Now Abraham moved
on from there into the
region of the Negev and lived
between Kadesh and Shur.
For a while he stayed in Gerar,
[2]and there Abraham said of
his wife Sarah, "She is my sister." Then Abimelech king of
Gerar sent for Sarah and took
her.

[m]37 *Moab* sounds like the Hebrew for *from father*
[n]38 *Ben-Ammi* means *son of my people*.

אֶת־שָׂרָה׃ וַיָּבֹא אֱלֹהִים אֶל־אֲבִימֶלֶךְ בַּחֲלוֹם הַלָּיְלָה וַיֹּאמֶר
and-he-said the-night in-dream-of Abimelech to God but-he-came (3) Sarah ***

לוֹ הִנְּךָ מֵת עַל־הָאִשָּׁה אֲשֶׁר־לָקַחְתָּ וְהִוא
now-she you-took whom the-woman because-of being-dead see-you! to-him

בְּעֻלַת בָּעַל׃ וַאֲבִימֶלֶךְ לֹא קָרַב אֵלֶיהָ וַיֹּאמַר
and-he-said to-her he-went-near not now-Abimelech (4) husband being-married-of

אֲדֹנָי הֲגוֹי גַּם־צַדִּיק תַּהֲרֹג׃ הֲלֹא הוּא אָמַר־לִי
to-me he-said he not? (5) will-you-destroy innocent indeed nation? Lord

אֲחֹתִי הִוא וְהִיא־גַם־הִוא אָמְרָה אָחִי הוּא בְּתָם־
with-clear-of he brother-of-me she-said she also and-she she sister-of-me

לְבָבִי וּבְנִקְיֹן כַּפַּי עָשִׂיתִי זֹאת׃ וַיֹּאמֶר
then-he-said (6) this I-did hands-of-me and-with-clean-of conscience-of-me

אֵלָיו הָאֱלֹהִים בַּחֲלֹם גַּם אָנֹכִי יָדַעְתִּי כִּי בְתָם־לְבָבְךָ
conscience-of-you with-clear-of that I-know I yes in-the-dream the-God to-him

עָשִׂיתָ זֹּאת וָאֶחְשֹׂךְ גַּם־אָנֹכִי אוֹתְךָ מֵחֲטוֹ־לִי עַל־כֵּן לֹא־
not this for against-me from-to-sin you I indeed so-I-kept this you-did

נְתַתִּיךָ לִנְגֹּעַ אֵלֶיהָ׃ וְעַתָּה הָשֵׁב אֵשֶׁת־הָאִישׁ כִּי־נָבִיא
prophet for the-man wife-of return! now-you (7) on-her to-touch I-let-you

הוּא וְיִתְפַּלֵּל בַּעַדְךָ וֶחְיֵה וְאִם־אֵינְךָ מֵשִׁיב דַּע כִּי־
that be-sure! returning not-you but-if and-live! for-you and-he-will-pray he

מוֹת תָּמוּת אַתָּה וְכָל־אֲשֶׁר־לָךְ׃ וַיַּשְׁכֵּם אֲבִימֶלֶךְ
Abimelech and-he-rose (8) to-you that and-all you you-will-die to-die

בַּבֹּקֶר וַיִּקְרָא לְכָל־עֲבָדָיו וַיְדַבֵּר אֶת־
*** and-he-told officials-of-him to-all-of and-he-summoned in-the-morning

כָּל־הַדְּבָרִים הָאֵלֶּה בְּאָזְנֵיהֶם וַיִּירְאוּ הָאֲנָשִׁים מְאֹד׃
very the-men and-they-were-afraid in-ears-of-them the-these the-things all-of

וַיִּקְרָא אֲבִימֶלֶךְ לְאַבְרָהָם וַיֹּאמֶר לוֹ מֶה־עָשִׂיתָ לָּנוּ
to-us you-did what? to-him and-he-said to-Abraham Abimelech and-he-called (9)

וּמֶה־חָטָאתִי לָךְ כִּי־הֵבֵאתָ עָלַי וְעַל־מַמְלַכְתִּי חֲטָאָה
guilt kingdom-of-me and-on on-me you-brought that to-you I-wronged and-how?

גְדֹלָה מַעֲשִׂים אֲשֶׁר לֹא־יֵעָשׂוּ עָשִׂיתָ עִמָּדִי׃ וַיֹּאמֶר
and-he-asked (10) to-me you-did they-should-be-done not that things great

אֲבִימֶלֶךְ אֶל־אַבְרָהָם מָה רָאִיתָ כִּי עָשִׂיתָ אֶת־הַדָּבָר הַזֶּה׃
the-this the-thing *** you-did that you-reasoned what? Abraham to Abimelech

וַיֹּאמֶר אַבְרָהָם כִּי אָמַרְתִּי רַק אֵין־יִרְאַת אֱלֹהִים
God fear-of there-is-no surely I-said because Abraham and-he-replied (11)

בַּמָּקוֹם הַזֶּה וַהֲרָגוּנִי עַל־דְּבַר אִשְׁתִּי׃
wife-of-me account-of on and-they-will-kill-me the-this in-the-place

[3]But God came to Abimelech in a dream one night and said to him, "You are as good as dead because of the woman you have taken; she is a married woman."

[4]Now Abimelech had not gone near her, so he said, "Lord, will you destroy an innocent nation? [5]Did he not say to me, 'She is my sister,' and didn't she also say, 'He is my brother'? I have done this with a clear conscience and clean hands."

[6]Then God said to him in the dream, "Yes, I know you did this with a clear conscience, and so I have kept you from sinning against me. That is why I did not let you touch her. [7]Now return the man's wife, for he is a prophet, and he will pray for you and you will live. But if you do not return her, you may be sure that you and all yours will die."

[8]Early the next morning Abimelech summoned all his officials, and when he told them all that had happened, they were very much afraid. [9]Then Abimelech called Abraham in and said, "What have you done to us? How have I wronged you that you have brought such great guilt upon me and my kingdom? You have done things to me that should not be done." [10]And Abimelech asked Abraham, "What was your reason for doing this?"

[11]Abraham replied, "I said to myself, 'There is surely no fear of God in this place, and they will kill me because of my

וְגַם־ אָמְנָה אֲחֹתִי בַת־ אָבִי הִוא אַךְ לֹא
not though she father-of-me daughter-of sister-of-me really and-besides (12)

בַת־ אִמִּי וַתְּהִי־ לִי לְאִשָּׁה׃ וַיְהִי כַּאֲשֶׁר
when and-he-was (13) for-wife to-me and-she-became mother-of-me daughter-of

הִתְעוּ אֹתִי אֱלֹהִים מִבֵּית אָבִי וָאֹמַר לָהּ זֶה
this to-her that-I-said father-of-me from-household-of God me he-make-wander

חַסְדֵּךְ אֲשֶׁר תַּעֲשִׂי עִמָּדִי אֶל כָּל־ הַמָּקוֹם אֲשֶׁר נָבוֹא
we-go where the-place every-of in to-me you-can-show that love-of-you

שָׁמָּה אִמְרִי־ לִי אָחִי הוּא׃ וַיִּקַּח אֲבִימֶלֶךְ צֹאן
sheep Abimelech then-he-brought (14) he brother-of-me of-me say! to-there

וּבָקָר וַעֲבָדִים וּשְׁפָחֹת וַיִּתֵּן לְאַבְרָהָם
to-Abraham and-he-gave and-female-slaves and-male-slaves and-cattle

וַיָּשֶׁב לוֹ אֵת שָׂרָה אִשְׁתּוֹ׃ וַיֹּאמֶר אֲבִימֶלֶךְ הִנֵּה
see! Abimelech and-he-said (15) wife-of-him Sarah *** to-him and-he-returned

אַרְצִי לְפָנֶיךָ בַּטּוֹב בְּעֵינֶיךָ שֵׁב׃ וּלְשָׂרָה
and-to-Sarah (16) live! to-eyes-of-you in-the-good before-you land-of-me

אָמַר הִנֵּה נָתַתִּי אֶלֶף כֶּסֶף לְאָחִיךְ הִנֵּה הוּא־ לָךְ
to-you he see! to-brother-of-you silver thousand-of I-give see! he-said

כְּסוּת עֵינַיִם לְכֹל אֲשֶׁר אִתָּךְ וְאֵת כֹּל וְנֹכָחַת׃
now-you-are-vindicated all and-before with-you who before-all eyes cover-of

וַיִּתְפַּלֵּל אַבְרָהָם אֶל־הָאֱלֹהִים וַיִּרְפָּא אֱלֹהִים אֶת־אֲבִימֶלֶךְ וְאֶת־
and Abimelech *** God and-he-healed the-God to Abraham then-he-prayed (17)

אִשְׁתּוֹ וְאַמְהֹתָיו וַיֵּלֵדוּ׃ כִּי־ עָצֹר עָצַר
he-closed to-close for (18) so-they-could-bear and-slave-girls-of-him wife-of-him

יְהוָה בְּעַד כָּל־ רֶחֶם לְבֵית אֲבִימֶלֶךְ עַל־ דְּבַר שָׂרָה
Sarah account-of on Abimelech in-household-of womb every-of up Yahweh

אֵשֶׁת אַבְרָהָם׃ וַיהוָה פָּקַד אֶת־ שָׂרָה כַּאֲשֶׁר אָמָר
he-said just-as Sarah *** he-was-gracious now-Yahweh (21:1) Abraham wife-of

וַיַּעַשׂ יְהוָה לְשָׂרָה כַּאֲשֶׁר דִּבֵּר׃ וַתַּהַר
and-she-became-pregnant (2) he-promised just-as for-Sarah Yahweh and-he-did

וַתֵּלֶד שָׂרָה לְאַבְרָהָם בֵּן לִזְקֻנָיו לַמּוֹעֵד אֲשֶׁר־
that at-the-time in-old-age-of-him son to-Abraham Sarah and-she-bore

דִּבֶּר אֹתוֹ אֱלֹהִים׃ וַיִּקְרָא אַבְרָהָם אֶת־ שֶׁם־ בְּנוֹ
son-of-him name-of *** Abraham and-he-gave (3) God him he-promised

הַנּוֹלַד־ לוֹ אֲשֶׁר־ יָלְדָה־ לּוֹ שָׂרָה יִצְחָק׃ וַיָּמָל
and-he-circumcised (4) Isaac Sarah to-him she-bore whom to-him the-one-being-born

אַבְרָהָם אֶת־יִצְחָק בְּנוֹ בֶּן־ שְׁמֹנַת יָמִים כַּאֲשֶׁר צִוָּה אֹתוֹ אֱלֹהִים׃
God him he-commanded just-as days eight son-of son-of-him Isaac *** Abraham

wife.' 12 Besides, she really is
my sister, the daughter of my
father though not of my
mother; and she became my
wife. 13 And when God had me
wander from my father's
household, I said to her, 'This
is how you can show your love
to me: Everywhere we go, say
of me, "He is my brother." ' "

14 Then Abimelech brought
sheep and cattle and male and
female slaves and gave them
to Abraham, and he returned
Sarah his wife to him. 15 And
Abimelech said, "My land is
before you; live wherever you
like."

16 To Sarah he said, "I am
giving your brother a thousand shekels[o] of silver. This is
to cover the offense against
you before all who are with
you; you are completely vindicated."

17 Then Abraham prayed to
God, and God healed Abimelech, his wife and his slave
girls so they could have children again, 18 for the LORD had
closed up every womb in
Abimelech's household be-
cause of Abraham's wife Sarah.

The Birth of Isaac

21 Now the LORD was gra-
cious to Sarah as he
had said, and the LORD did for
Sarah what he had promised.
2 Sarah became pregnant and
bore a son to Abraham in his
old age, at the very time God
had promised him. 3 Abraham
gave the name Isaac[p] to the
son Sarah bore him. 4 When
his son Isaac was eight days
old, Abraham circumcised
him, as God commanded him.

[o] *16* That is, about 25 pounds (about 11.5 kilograms)
[p] *3 Isaac* means *he laughs.*

וְאַבְרָהָם בֶּן־ מְאַת שָׁנָה בְּהִוָּלֶד לוֹ אֵת יִצְחָק
Isaac *** to-him when-to-be-born year hundred-of son-of now-Abraham (5)

בְּנוֹ׃ וַתֹּאמֶר שָׂרָה צְחֹק עָשָׂה לִי אֱלֹהִים כָּל־
every-of God to-me he-brought laughter Sarah and-she-said (6) son-of-him

הַשֹּׁמֵעַ יִצְחַק־ לִי׃ וַתֹּאמֶר מִי מִלֵּל
he-would-have-said who? and-she-said (7) with-me he-will-laugh the-one-hearing

לְאַבְרָהָם הֵינִיקָה בָנִים שָׂרָה כִּי־ יָלַדְתִּי בֵן לִזְקֻנָיו׃
in-old-age-of-him son I-bore yet Sarah children she-would-nurse to-Abraham

וַיִּגְדַּל הַיֶּלֶד וַיִּגָּמַל וַיַּעַשׂ אַבְרָהָם מִשְׁתֶּה גָדוֹל
great feast Abraham and-he-held and-he-was-weaned the-child and-he-grew (8)

בְּיוֹם הִגָּמֵל אֶת־ יִצְחָק׃ וַתֵּרֶא שָׂרָה אֶת־ בֶּן־ הָגָר
Hagar son-of *** Sarah but-she-was (9) Isaac *** to-be-weaned on-day-of

הַמִּצְרִית אֲשֶׁר־ יָלְדָה לְאַבְרָהָם מְצַחֵק׃ וַתֹּאמֶר לְאַבְרָהָם
to-Abraham and-she-said (10) mocking to-Abraham she-bore whom the-Egyptian

גָּרֵשׁ הָאָמָה הַזֹּאת וְאֶת־ בְּנָהּ כִּי לֹא יִירַשׁ
he-will-inherit never for son-of-her and the-that the-slave-woman get-rid-of!

בֶּן־ הָאָמָה הַזֹּאת עִם־ בְּנִי עִם־ יִצְחָק׃
Isaac with son-of-me with the-that the-slave-woman son-of

וַיֵּרַע הַדָּבָר מְאֹד בְּעֵינֵי אַבְרָהָם עַל אוֹדֹת
concerns-of for Abraham in-eyes-of greatly the-matter and-he-was-distressing (11)

בְּנוֹ׃ וַיֹּאמֶר אֱלֹהִים אֶל־ אַבְרָהָם אַל־ יֵרַע בְּעֵינֶיךָ
in-eyes-of-you he-be-distressing not Abraham to God but-he-said (12) son-of-him

עַל־ הַנַּעַר וְעַל־ אֲמָתֶךָ כֹּל אֲשֶׁר תֹּאמַר אֵלֶיךָ שָׂרָה
Sarah to-you she-tells that all maidservant-of-you and-about the-boy about

שְׁמַע בְּקֹלָהּ כִּי בְיִצְחָק יִקָּרֵא לְךָ
to-you he-will-be-reckoned through-Isaac because to-voice-of-her listen!

זָרַע׃ וְגַם אֶת־ בֶּן־ הָאָמָה לְגוֹי אֲשִׂימֶנּוּ
I-will-make-him into-nation the-maidservant son-of *** and-also (13) offspring

כִּי זַרְעֲךָ הוּא׃ וַיַּשְׁכֵּם אַבְרָהָם ׀ בַּבֹּקֶר
in-the-morning Abraham and-he-rose (14) he offspring-of-you because

וַיִּקַּח־ לֶחֶם וְחֵמַת מַיִם וַיִּתֵּן אֶל־ הָגָר שָׂם עַל־
on setting Hagar to and-he-gave waters and-skin-of food and-he-took

שִׁכְמָהּ וְאֶת־ הַיֶּלֶד וַיְשַׁלְּחֶהָ וַתֵּלֶךְ וַתֵּתַע
and-she-wandered and-she-went then-he-sent-off-her the-boy and shoulder-of-her

בְּמִדְבַּר בְּאֵר שָׁבַע׃ וַיִּכְלוּ הַמַּיִם מִן־ הַחֵמֶת
the-skin from the-waters when-they-were-gone (15) Sheba Beer in-desert-of

וַתַּשְׁלֵךְ אֶת־ הַיֶּלֶד תַּחַת אַחַד הַשִּׂיחִם׃ וַתֵּלֶךְ וַתֵּשֶׁב
and-she-sat then-she-went (16) the-bushes one-of under the-boy *** then-she-put

5Abraham was a hundred
years old when his son Isaac
was born to him.
6Sarah said, "God has brought me laughter, and everyone who hears about this will laugh with me."
7And
she added, "Who would have said to Abraham that Sarah would nurse children? Yet I have borne him a son in his old age."

Hagar and Ishmael Sent Away

8The child grew and was weaned, and on the day Isaac was weaned Abraham held a great feast.
9But Sarah saw that
the son whom Hagar the Egyptian had borne to Abraham was mocking,
10and she
said to Abraham, "Get rid of that slave woman and her son, for that slave woman's son will never share in the inheritance with my son Isaac."
11The matter distressed Abraham greatly because it concerned his son.
12But God
said to him, "Do not be so distressed about the boy and your maidservant. Listen to whatever Sarah tells you, because it is through Isaac that your offspring[q] will be reckoned.
13I
will make the son of the maidservant into a nation also, because he is your offspring."
14Early the next morning Abraham took some food and a skin of water and gave them to Hagar. He set them on her shoulders and then sent her off with the boy. She went on her way and wandered in the desert of Beersheba.
15When the water in the skin was gone, she put the boy under one of the bushes.
16Then
she went off and sat down

[q] 12 Or *seed*

לָהּ מִנֶּגֶד הַרְחֵק כִּמְטַחֲוֵי קֶשֶׁת כִּי אָמְרָה אַל־
not she-said for bow like-ones-shooting-of to-be-away by-near by-herself

אֶרְאֶה בְּמוֹת הַיָּלֶד וַתֵּשֶׁב מִנֶּגֶד וַתִּשָּׂא אֶת־
*** and-she-lifted by-near and-she-sat the-boy on-death-of I-can-look

קֹלָהּ וַתֵּבְךְּ׃ וַיִּשְׁמַע אֱלֹהִים אֶת־ קוֹל הַנַּעַר
the-boy cry-of *** God and-he-heard (17) and-she-sobbed voice-of-her

וַיִּקְרָא מַלְאַךְ אֱלֹהִים ׀ אֶל־הָגָר מִן־ הַשָּׁמַיִם וַיֹּאמֶר לָהּ מַה־
what? to-her and-he-said the-heavens from Hagar to God angel-of and-he-called

לָּךְ הָגָר אַל־ תִּירְאִי כִּי־ שָׁמַע אֱלֹהִים אֶל־קוֹל הַנַּעַר בַּאֲשֶׁר
as the-boy cry-of to God he-heard for you-be-afraid not Hagar with-you

הוּא־שָׁם׃ קוּמִי שְׂאִי אֶת־ הַנַּעַר וְהַחֲזִיקִי אֶת־ יָדֵךְ בּוֹ כִּי־
for on-him hand-of-you with and-hold! the-boy *** lift! rise! (18) there he

לְגוֹי גָּדוֹל אֲשִׂימֶנּוּ׃ וַיִּפְקַח אֱלֹהִים אֶת־ עֵינֶיהָ
eyes-of-her *** God then-he-opened (19) I-will-make-him great into-nation

וַתֵּרֶא בְּאֵר מָיִם וַתֵּלֶךְ וַתְּמַלֵּא אֶת־ הַחֵמֶת מַיִם
waters the-skin *** and-she-filled so-she-went waters well-of and-she-saw

וַתַּשְׁקְ אֶת־ הַנָּעַר׃ וַיְהִי אֱלֹהִים אֶת־ הַנַּעַר וַיִּגְדָּל
and-he-grew the-boy with God and-he-was (20) the-boy *** and-she-gave-drink

וַיֵּשֶׁב בַּמִּדְבָּר וַיְהִי רֹבֶה קַשָּׁת׃ וַיֵּשֶׁב
and-he-lived (21) bow one-shooting and-he-became in-the-desert and-he-lived

בְּמִדְבַּר פָּארָן וַתִּקַּח־ לוֹ אִמּוֹ אִשָּׁה מֵאֶרֶץ מִצְרָיִם׃
Egypt from-land-of wife mother-of-him for-him and-she-got Paran in-desert-of

וַיְהִי בָּעֵת הַהִוא וַיֹּאמֶר אֲבִימֶלֶךְ וּפִיכֹל
and-Phicol Abimelech and-he-said the-that at-the-time and-he-was (22)

שַׂר־ צְבָאוֹ אֶל־אַבְרָהָם לֵאמֹר אֱלֹהִים עִמְּךָ בְּכֹל אֲשֶׁר־אַתָּה
you that in-all with-you God to-say Abraham to force-of-him commander-of

עֹשֶׂה׃ וְעַתָּה הִשָּׁבְעָה לִּי בֵאלֹהִים הֵנָּה אִם־ תִּשְׁקֹר
you-will-deal-falsely not here before-God to-me swear! and-now (23) doing

לִי וּלְנִינִי וּלְנֶכְדִּי כַּחֶסֶד אֲשֶׁר־
that as-the kindness or-with-descendant-of-me or-with-child-of-me with-me

עָשִׂיתִי עִמְּךָ תַּעֲשֶׂה עִמָּדִי וְעִם־ הָאָרֶץ אֲשֶׁר־ גַּרְתָּה בָּהּ׃
in-her you-live that the-country and-to to-me you-show to-you I-showed

וַיֹּאמֶר אַבְרָהָם אָנֹכִי אִשָּׁבֵעַ׃ וְהוֹכִחַ אַבְרָהָם אֶת־
*** Abraham then-he-complained (25) I-swear I Abraham and-he-said (24)

אֲבִימֶלֶךְ עַל־ אֹדוֹת בְּאֵר הַמַּיִם אֲשֶׁר גָּזְלוּ עַבְדֵי
servants-of they-seized that the-water well-of accounts-of on Abimelech

אֲבִימֶלֶךְ׃ וַיֹּאמֶר אֲבִימֶלֶךְ לֹא יָדַעְתִּי מִי עָשָׂה אֶת־ הַדָּבָר
the-thing *** he-did who? I-know not Abimelech but-he-said (26) Abimelech

nearby, about a bowshot
away, for she thought, "I cannot watch the boy die." And
as she sat there nearby, she
began to sob.
[17]God heard the boy crying,
and the angel of God called to
Hagar from heaven and said
to her, "What is the matter,
Hagar? Do not be afraid; God
has heard the boy crying as he
lies there. [18]Lift the boy up and
take him by the hand, for I
will make him into a great nation."
[19]Then God opened her eyes
and she saw a well of water. So
she went and filled the skin
with water and gave the boy a
drink.
[20]God was with the boy as he
grew up. He lived in the desert
and became an archer. [21]While
he was living in the Desert of
Paran, his mother got a wife
for him from Egypt.

The Treaty at Beersheba

[22]At that time Abimelech
and Phicol the commander of
his forces said to Abraham,
"God is with you in everything you do. [23]Now swear to
me here before God that you
will not deal falsely with me or
my children or my descendants. Show to me and the
country where you are living
as an alien the same kindness
I have shown to you."
[24]Abraham said, "I swear
it."
[25]Then Abraham com-
plained to Abimelech about a
well of water that Abimelech's
servants had seized. [26]But
Abimelech said, "I don't
know who has done this. You

הַזֶּה וְגַם־אַתָּה לֹא־הִגַּדְתָּ לִּי וְגַם אָנֹכִי לֹא שָׁמַעְתִּי בִּלְתִּי הַיּוֹם׃
the-day until I-heard not I and-also to-me you-told not you and-also the-this

וַיִּקַּח אַבְרָהָם צֹאן וּבָקָר וַיִּתֵּן לַאֲבִימֶלֶךְ
to-Abimelech and-he-gave and-cattle sheep Abraham so-he-brought (27)

וַיִּכְרְתוּ שְׁנֵיהֶם בְּרִית׃ וַיַּצֵּב אַבְרָהָם אֶת־שֶׁבַע
seven *** Abraham and-he-set-apart (28) treaty two-of-them and-they-made

כִּבְשֹׂת הַצֹּאן לְבַדְּהֶן׃ וַיֹּאמֶר אֲבִימֶלֶךְ אֶל־אַבְרָהָם
Abraham to Abimelech and-he-asked (29) by-themselves the-flock ewe-lambs-of

מָה הֵנָּה שֶׁבַע כְּבָשֹׂת הָאֵלֶּה אֲשֶׁר הִצַּבְתָּ לְבַדָּנָה׃
by-themselves you-set-apart that the-these ewe-lambs seven these what?

וַיֹּאמֶר כִּי אֶת־שֶׁבַע כְּבָשֹׂת תִּקַּח מִיָּדִי
from-hand-of-me you-accept ewe-lambs seven *** indeed and-he-replied (30)

בַּעֲבוּר תִּהְיֶה־לִּי לְעֵדָה כִּי חָפַרְתִּי אֶת־הַבְּאֵר הַזֹּאת׃
the-this the-well *** I-dug that as-witness for-me you-may-be so-that

עַל־כֵּן קָרָא לַמָּקוֹם הַהוּא בְּאֵר שָׁבַע כִּי שָׁם
there because Sheba Beer the-that to-the-place he-called this for (31)

נִשְׁבְּעוּ שְׁנֵיהֶם׃ וַיִּכְרְתוּ בְרִית בִּבְאֵר שָׁבַע וַיָּקָם
then-he-rose Sheba at-Beer treaty so-they-made (32) two-of-them they-swore-oath

אֲבִימֶלֶךְ וּפִיכֹל שַׂר־צְבָאוֹ וַיָּשֻׁבוּ אֶל־אֶרֶץ
land-of to and-they-returned force-of-him commander-of and-Phicol Abimelech

פְּלִשְׁתִּים׃ וַיִּטַּע אֶשֶׁל בִּבְאֵר שָׁבַע וַיִּקְרָא־
and-he-called Sheba in-Beer tamarisk-tree and-he-planted (33) Philistines

שָׁם בְּשֵׁם יְהוָה אֵל עוֹלָם׃ וַיָּגָר אַבְרָהָם בְּאֶרֶץ
in-land-of Abraham and-he-stayed (34) Eternal God Yahweh upon-name-of there

פְּלִשְׁתִּים יָמִים רַבִּים׃ וַיְהִי אַחַר הַדְּבָרִים הָאֵלֶּה
the-these the-events after and-he-was (22:1) many days Philistines

וְהָאֱלֹהִים נִסָּה אֶת־אַבְרָהָם וַיֹּאמֶר אֵלָיו אַבְרָהָם וַיֹּאמֶר
and-he-replied Abraham to-him and-he-said Abraham *** he-tested that-the-God

הִנֵּנִי׃ וַיֹּאמֶר קַח־נָא אֶת־בִּנְךָ אֶת־יְחִידְךָ אֲשֶׁר־
whom only-of-you *** son-of-you *** now! take! then-he-said (2) here-I

אָהַבְתָּ אֶת־יִצְחָק וְלֶךְ־לְךָ אֶל־אֶרֶץ הַמֹּרִיָּה וְהַעֲלֵהוּ
and-sacrifice-him! the-Moriah region-of to yourself and-go! Isaac *** you-love

שָׁם לְעֹלָה עַל אַחַד הֶהָרִים אֲשֶׁר אֹמַר אֵלֶיךָ׃
to-you I-will-tell that the-mountains one-of on as-burnt-offering there

וַיַּשְׁכֵּם אַבְרָהָם בַּבֹּקֶר וַיַּחֲבֹשׁ אֶת־חֲמֹרוֹ
donkey-of-him *** and-he-saddled in-the-morning Abraham so-he-rose (3)

וַיִּקַּח אֶת־שְׁנֵי נְעָרָיו אִתּוֹ וְאֵת יִצְחָק בְּנוֹ
son-of-him Isaac and with-him servants-of-him two-of *** and-he-took

did not tell me, and I heard
about it only today."
27So Abraham brought sheep
and cattle and gave them to
Abimelech, and the two men
made a treaty. 28Abraham set
apart seven ewe lambs from
the flock, 29and Abimelech
asked Abraham, "What is the
meaning of these seven ewe
lambs you have set apart by
themselves?"
30He replied, "Accept these
seven lambs from my hand as
a witness that I dug this well."
31So that place was called
Beersheba,[r] because the two
men swore an oath there.
32After the treaty had been
made at Beersheba, Abime-
lech and Phicol the com-
mander of his forces returned
to the land of the Philistines.
33Abraham planted a tamarisk
tree in Beersheba, and there
he called upon the name of the
LORD, the Eternal God. 34And
Abraham stayed in the land of
the Philistines for a long time.

Abraham Tested

22 Some time later God
tested Abraham. He
said to him, "Abraham!"
"Here I am," he replied.
2Then God said, "Take your
son, your only son Isaac,
whom you love, and go to the
region of Moriah. Sacrifice
him there as a burnt offering
on one of the mountains I will
tell you about."
3Early the next morning
Abraham got up and saddled
his donkey. He took with him
two of his servants and his
son Isaac. When he had cut

r31 *Beersheba* can mean *well of seven* or *well of the oath*.

וַיְבַקַּע עֲצֵי עֹלָה וַיָּקָם וַיֵּלֶךְ אֶל־ הַמָּקוֹם
and-he-cut wood-of burnt-offering then-he-rose and-he-set-out for the-place

אֲשֶׁר־ אָמַר־ לוֹ הָאֱלֹהִים׃ בַּיּוֹם הַשְּׁלִישִׁי וַיִּשָּׂא אַבְרָהָם
that he-told to-him the-God (4) on-the-day the-third then-he-lifted Abraham

אֶת־ עֵינָיו וַיַּרְא אֶת־ הַמָּקוֹם מֵרָחֹק׃ וַיֹּאמֶר אַבְרָהָם
*** eyes-of-him and-he-saw *** the-place in-distance (5) and-he-said Abraham

אֶל־ נְעָרָיו שְׁבוּ־ לָכֶם פֹּה עִם־ הַחֲמוֹר וַאֲנִי וְהַנַּעַר
to servants-of-him stay! yourselves here with the-donkey while-I and-the-boy

נֵלְכָה עַד־ כֹּה וְנִשְׁתַּחֲוֶה וְנָשׁוּבָה אֲלֵיכֶם׃
we-go over there then-we-will-worship and-we-will-come-back to-you

וַיִּקַּח אַבְרָהָם אֶת־ עֲצֵי הָעֹלָה וַיָּשֶׂם עַל־
(6) then-he-took Abraham *** wood-of the-burnt-offering and-he-placed on

יִצְחָק בְּנוֹ וַיִּקַּח בְּיָדוֹ אֶת־ הָאֵשׁ וְאֶת־הַמַּאֲכֶלֶת
Isaac son-of-him and-he-carried in-hand-of-him *** the-fire and the-knife

וַיֵּלְכוּ שְׁנֵיהֶם יַחְדָּו׃ וַיֹּאמֶר יִצְחָק אֶל־אַבְרָהָם
and-they-went-on two-of-them together (7) and-he-spoke Isaac to Abraham

אָבִיו וַיֹּאמֶר אָבִי וַיֹּאמֶר הִנֶּנִּי בְנִי
father-of-him and-he-said father-of-me and-he-replied here-I son-of-me

וַיֹּאמֶר הִנֵּה הָאֵשׁ וְהָעֵצִים וְאַיֵּה הַשֶּׂה לְעֹלָה׃
and-he-said see! the-fire and-the-wood but-where? the-lamb for-burnt-offering

וַיֹּאמֶר אַבְרָהָם אֱלֹהִים יִרְאֶה־ לּוֹ הַשֶּׂה
(8) and-he-answered Abraham God he-will-provide himself the-lamb

לְעֹלָה בְּנִי וַיֵּלְכוּ שְׁנֵיהֶם יַחְדָּו׃
for-burnt-offering son-of-me and-they-went-on two-of-them together

וַיָּבֹאוּ אֶל־ הַמָּקוֹם אֲשֶׁר אָמַר־ לוֹ הָאֱלֹהִים וַיִּבֶן
(9) and-they-reached to the-place that he-told to-him the-God and-he-built

שָׁם אַבְרָהָם אֶת־ הַמִּזְבֵּחַ וַיַּעֲרֹךְ אֶת־ הָעֵצִים וַיַּעֲקֹד אֶת־
there Abraham *** the-altar and-he-arranged *** the-wood and-he-bound ***

יִצְחָק בְּנוֹ וַיָּשֶׂם אֹתוֹ עַל־ הַמִּזְבֵּחַ מִמַּעַל לָעֵצִים׃
Isaac son-of-him and-he-laid him on the-altar on-top on-the-woods

וַיִּשְׁלַח אַבְרָהָם אֶת־ יָדוֹ וַיִּקַּח אֶת־הַמַּאֲכֶלֶת לִשְׁחֹט אֶת־
(10) then-he-reached Abraham *** hand-of-him and-he-took *** the-knife to-slay ***

בְּנוֹ׃ וַיִּקְרָא אֵלָיו מַלְאַךְ יְהוָה מִן־ הַשָּׁמַיִם
son-of-him (11) but-he-called to-him angel-of Yahweh from the-heavens

וַיֹּאמֶר אַבְרָהָם ׀ אַבְרָהָם וַיֹּאמֶר הִנֵּנִי׃ וַיֹּאמֶר אַל־
and-he-said Abraham Abraham and-he-replied here-I (12) and-he-said not

תִּשְׁלַח יָדְךָ אֶל־הַנַּעַר וְאַל־ תַּעַשׂ לוֹ מְאוּמָּה* כִּי ׀ עַתָּה יָדַעְתִּי
you-lay hand-of-you on the-boy and-not you-do to-him anything for now I-know

enough wood for the burnt
offering, he set out for the
place God had told him about.
4On the third day Abraham
looked up and saw the place in
the distance. 5He said to his
servants, "Stay here with the
donkey while I and the boy go
over there. We will worship
and then we will come back to
you."

6Abraham took the wood for
the burnt offering and placed
it on his son Isaac, and he
himself carried the fire and the
knife. As the two of them
went on together, 7Isaac spoke
up and said to his father Abraham, "Father?"

"Yes, my son?" Abraham replied.

"The fire and wood are
here," Isaac said, "but where
is the lamb for the burnt
offering?"

8Abraham answered, "God
himself will provide the lamb
for the burnt offering, my
son." And the two of them
went on together.

9When they reached the
place God had told him about,
Abraham built an altar there
and arranged the wood on it.
He bound his son Isaac and
laid him on the altar, on top of
the wood. 10Then he reached
out his hand and took the
knife to slay his son. 11But the
angel of the LORD called out to
him from heaven, "Abraham!
Abraham!"

"Here I am," he replied.

12"Do not lay a hand on the
boy," he said. "Do not do anything to him. Now I know that

*12 Most mss have no *dagesh* in the second *mem* (וּמָה־).

כִּֽי־ יְרֵא אֱלֹהִים֙ אַתָּ֔ה וְלֹ֥א חָשַׂ֛כְתָּ אֶת־ בִּנְךָ֥ אֶת־ יְחִידְךָ֖
only-of-you *** son-of-you *** you-withheld for-not you God fearing-of that

מִמֶּֽנִּי׃ וַיִּשָּׂ֨א אַבְרָהָ֜ם אֶת־ עֵינָ֗יו וַיַּרְא֙ וְהִנֵּה־
and-see! and-he-looked eyes-of-him *** Abraham and-he-lifted (13) from-me

אַ֔יִל אַחַ֕ר נֶאֱחַ֥ז בַּסְּבַ֖ךְ בְּקַרְנָ֑יו וַיֵּ֤לֶךְ אַבְרָהָם֙
Abraham so-he-went by-horns-of-him in-the-thicket being-caught behind ram

וַיִּקַּ֣ח אֶת־ הָאַ֔יִל וַיַּעֲלֵ֥הוּ לְעֹלָ֖ה תַּ֥חַת
instead-of as-burnt-offering and-he-sacrificed-him the-ram *** and-he-took

בְּנֽוֹ׃ וַיִּקְרָ֧א אַבְרָהָ֛ם שֵֽׁם־ הַמָּק֥וֹם הַה֖וּא יְהוָ֣ה ׀
Yahweh the-that the-place name-of Abraham so-he-called (14) son-of-him

יִרְאֶ֑ה אֲשֶׁר֙ יֵאָמֵ֣ר הַיּ֔וֹם בְּהַ֥ר יְהוָ֖ה יֵרָאֶֽה׃
he-will-be-provided Yahweh on-mountain-of the-day he-is-said as he-will-provide

וַיִּקְרָ֛א מַלְאַ֥ךְ יְהוָ֖ה אֶל־ אַבְרָהָ֑ם שֵׁנִ֖ית מִן־ הַשָּׁמָֽיִם׃
the-heavens from second Abraham to Yahweh angel-of and-he-called (15)

וַיֹּ֕אמֶר בִּ֥י נִשְׁבַּ֖עְתִּי נְאֻם־ יְהוָ֑ה כִּ֗י יַ֚עַן אֲשֶׁ֤ר עָשִׂ֙יתָ֙
you-did that because that Yahweh declares I-swear by-myself and-he-said (16)

אֶת־ הַדָּבָ֣ר הַזֶּ֔ה וְלֹ֥א חָשַׂ֖כְתָּ אֶת־ בִּנְךָ֥ אֶת־ יְחִידֶֽךָ׃
only-of-you *** son-of-you *** you-withheld and-not the-this the-thing ***

כִּֽי־ בָרֵ֣ךְ אֲבָרֶכְךָ֗ וְהַרְבָּ֨ה אַרְבֶּ֤ה אֶת־
*** I-will-increase and-to-increase I-will-bless-you to-bless surely (17)

זַרְעֲךָ֙ כְּכוֹכְבֵ֣י הַשָּׁמַ֔יִם וְכַח֕וֹל אֲשֶׁ֖ר עַל־ שְׂפַ֣ת
shore-of on that and-as-the-sand the-skies as-stars-of descendant-of-you

הַיָּ֑ם וְיִרַ֣שׁ זַרְעֲךָ֔ אֵ֖ת שַׁ֥עַר אֹיְבָֽיו׃
being-enemies-of-him gate-of *** descendant-of-you and-he-will-possess the-sea

וְהִתְבָּרֲכ֣וּ בְזַרְעֲךָ֔ כֹּ֖ל גּוֹיֵ֣י הָאָ֑רֶץ
the-earth nations-of all-of through-seed-of-you and-they-will-be-blessed (18)

עֵ֕קֶב אֲשֶׁ֥ר שָׁמַ֖עְתָּ בְּקֹלִֽי׃ וַיָּ֤שָׁב אַבְרָהָם֙ אֶל־
to Abraham then-he-returned (19) to-voice-of-me you-obeyed that because

נְעָרָ֔יו וַיָּקֻ֛מוּ וַיֵּלְכ֥וּ יַחְדָּ֖ו אֶל־ בְּאֵ֣ר שָׁ֑בַע
Sheba Beer to together and-they-set-off and-they-rose servants-of-him

וַיֵּ֥שֶׁב אַבְרָהָ֖ם בִּבְאֵ֥ר שָֽׁבַע׃ וַיְהִ֗י אַחֲרֵי֙ הַדְּבָרִ֣ים הָאֵ֔לֶּה
the-these the-things after and-he-was (20) Sheba in-Beer Abraham and-he-stayed

וַיֻּגַּ֥ד לְאַבְרָהָ֖ם לֵאמֹ֑ר הִ֨נֵּ֜ה יָֽלְדָ֧ה מִלְכָּ֛ה גַּם־הִ֖וא בָּנִ֑ים לְנָח֖וֹר
to-Nahor sons she also Milcah she-bore see! to-say to-Abraham that-he-was-told

אָחִֽיךָ׃ אֶת־ע֥וּץ בְּכֹר֖וֹ וְאֶת־בּ֣וּז אָחִ֑יו וְאֶת־קְמוּאֵ֖ל
Kemuel and brother-of-him Buz and firstborn-of-him Uz *** (21) brother-of-you

אֲבִ֥י אֲרָֽם׃ וְאֶת־ כֶּ֣שֶׂד וְאֶת־ חֲז֔וֹ וְאֶת־פִּלְדָּ֖שׁ וְאֶת־ יִדְלָ֑ף וְאֵ֖ת בְּתוּאֵֽל׃
Bethuel and Jidlaph and Pildash and Hazo and Kesed and (22) Aram father-of

you fear God, because you
have not withheld from me
your son, your only son."
[13]Abraham looked up and
there in a thicket he saw a
ram[s] caught by its horns. He
went over and took the ram
and sacrificed it as a burnt
offering instead of his son.
[14]So Abraham called that place
"The LORD will provide." And
to this day it is said, "On the
mountain of the LORD it will
be provided."
[15]The angel of the LORD
called to Abraham from heav-
en a second time [16]and said, "I
swear by myself, declares the
LORD, that because you have
done this and have not withheld your son, your only son,
[17]I will surely bless you and
make your descendants as numerous as the stars in the sky
and as the sand on the seashore. Your descendants will
take possession of the cities of
their enemies, [18]and through
your offspring[t] all nations on
earth will be blessed, because
you have obeyed me."
[19]Then Abraham returned to
his servants, and they set off
together for Beersheba. And
Abraham stayed in Beersheba.

Nahor's Sons

[20]Some time later Abraham
was told, "Milcah is also a
mother; she has borne sons to
your brother Nahor: [21]Uz the
firstborn, Buz his brother,
Kemuel (the father of Aram),
[22]Kesed, Hazo, Pildash, Jidlaph and Bethuel." [23]Bethuel

[s]13 Many manuscripts of the Masoretic Text, Samaritan Pentateuch, Septuagint and Syriac; most manuscripts of the Masoretic Text *a ram behind* ⌊*him*⌋

[t]18 Or *seed*

וּבְתוּאֵל יָלַד אֶת־ רִבְקָה שְׁמֹנָה אֵלֶּה יָלְדָה מִלְכָּה לְנָחוֹר
to-Nahor Milcah she-bore these eight Rebekah *** he-fathered and-Bethuel (23)

אֲחִי אַבְרָהָם׃ וּפִילַגְשׁוֹ וּשְׁמָהּ רְאוּמָה
Reumah now-name-of-her and-concubine-of-him (24) Abraham brother-of

וַתֵּלֶד גַּם־ הִוא אֶת־ טֶבַח וְאֶת־ גַּחַם וְאֶת־ תַּחַשׁ וְאֶת־ מַעֲכָה׃
Maacah and Tahash and Gaham and Tebah *** she also and-she-bore

וַיִּהְיוּ חַיֵּי שָׂרָה מֵאָה שָׁנָה וְעֶשְׂרִים שָׁנָה וְשֶׁבַע
and-seven year and-twenty year hundred Sarah lives-of and-they-were (23:1)

שָׁנִים שְׁנֵי חַיֵּי שָׂרָה׃ וַתָּמָת שָׂרָה בְּקִרְיַת אַרְבַּע הִוא
that Arba in-Kiriath Sarah and-she-died (2) Sarah lives-of years-of years

חֶבְרוֹן בְּאֶרֶץ כְּנָעַן וַיָּבֹא אַבְרָהָם לִסְפֹּד לְשָׂרָה
for-Sarah to-mourn Abraham and-he-went Canaan in-land-of Hebron

וְלִבְכֹּתָהּ׃ וַיָּקָם אַבְרָהָם מֵעַל פְּנֵי מֵתוֹ
being-dead-of-him beside-of from Abraham then-he-rose (3) and-to-weep-over-her

וַיְדַבֵּר אֶל־ בְּנֵי־ חֵת לֵאמֹר׃ גֵּר־ וְתוֹשָׁב אָנֹכִי עִמָּכֶם
among-you I and-stranger alien (4) to-say Heth sons-of to and-he-spoke

תְּנוּ לִי אֲחֻזַּת־ קֶבֶר עִמָּכֶם וְאֶקְבְּרָה מֵתִי
being-dead-of-me so-I-can-bury among-you burial property-of to-me sell!

מִלְּפָנָי׃ וַיַּעֲנוּ בְנֵי־ חֵת אֶת־אַבְרָהָם לֵאמֹר לוֹ׃
to-him to-say Abraham to Heth sons-of and-they-replied (5) from-before-me

שְׁמָעֵנוּ ׀ אֲדֹנִי נְשִׂיא אֱלֹהִים אַתָּה בְּתוֹכֵנוּ בְּמִבְחַר קְבָרֵינוּ
tombs-of-us in-choice-of-us among-us you mighty prince-of sir-of-me listen-to-us! (6)

קְבֹר אֶת־ מֵתֶךָ אִישׁ מִמֶּנּוּ אֶת־ קִבְרוֹ לֹא־ יִכְלֶה
he-will-refuse not tomb-of-him *** from-us man being-dead-of-you *** bury!

מִמְּךָ מִקְּבֹר מֵתֶךָ׃ וַיָּקָם אַבְרָהָם וַיִּשְׁתַּחוּ
and-he-bowed Abraham then-he-rose (7) being-dead-of-you for-to-bury to-you

לְעַם־ הָאָרֶץ לִבְנֵי־ חֵת׃ וַיְדַבֵּר אִתָּם לֵאמֹר
to-say to-them and-he-said (8) Heth before-sons-of the-land before-people-of

אִם־ יֵשׁ אֶת־ נַפְשְׁכֶם לִקְבֹּר אֶת־ מֵתִי מִלְּפָנַי
from-before-me being-dead-of-me *** to-bury will-of-you in it-is if

שְׁמָעוּנִי וּפִגְעוּ־ לִי בְּעֶפְרוֹן בֶּן־ צֹחַר׃
Zohar son-of with-Ephron for-me and-intercede! listen-to-me!

וְיִתֶּן־ לִי אֶת־מְעָרַת הַמַּכְפֵּלָה אֲשֶׁר־ לוֹ אֲשֶׁר בִּקְצֵה
in-end-of which to-him which the-Machpelah cave-of *** to-me so-he-will-sell (9)

שָׂדֵהוּ בְּכֶסֶף מָלֵא יִתְּנֶנָּה לִּי בְּתוֹכְכֶם לַאֲחֻזַּת־ קָבֶר׃
burial as-site-of among-you to-me let-him-sell-her full for-price field-of-him

וְעֶפְרוֹן יֹשֵׁב בְּתוֹךְ בְּנֵי־ חֵת וַיַּעַן עֶפְרוֹן הַחִתִּי
the-Hittite Ephron and-he-replied Heth sons-of among sitting now-Ephron (10)

became the father of Rebekah.
Milcah bore these eight sons
to Abraham's brother Nahor.
24His concubine, whose name
was Reumah, also had sons:
Tebah, Gaham, Tahash and
Maacah.

The Death of Sarah

23 Sarah lived to be a
hundred and twenty-
seven years old. 2She died at
Kiriath Arba (that is, Hebron)
in the land of Canaan, and
Abraham went to mourn for
Sarah and to weep over her.
3Then Abraham rose from
beside his dead wife and
spoke to the Hittites.[u] He said,
4"I am an alien and a stranger
among you. Sell me some
property for a burial site here
so I can bury my dead."
5The Hittites replied to
Abraham, 6"Sir, listen to us.
You are a mighty prince
among us. Bury your dead in
the choicest of our tombs.
None of us will refuse you his
tomb for burying your dead."
7Then Abraham rose and
bowed down before the
people of the land, the Hittites. 8He said to them, "If you
are willing to let me bury my
dead, then listen to me and in-
tercede with Ephron son of
Zohar on my behalf 9so he will
sell me the cave of Machpelah,
which belongs to him and is
in the end of his field. Ask him
to sell it to me for the full price
as a burial site among you."
10Ephron the Hittite was sitting among his people and he

[u]3 Or *the sons of Heth;* also in verses 5, 7, 10, 16, 18 and 20

אֶת־אַבְרָהָם בְּאָזְנֵי בְנֵי־חֵת לְכֹל בָּאֵי שַׁעַר־
gate-of ones-coming-of to-all Heth sons-of in-hearing-of Abraham ***

עִירוֹ לֵאמֹר׃ לֹא־אֲדֹנִי שְׁמָעֵנִי הַשָּׂדֶה נָתַתִּי לָךְ
to-you I-give the-field listen-to-me! lord-of-me no (11) to-say city-of-him

וְהַמְּעָרָה אֲשֶׁר־בּוֹ לְךָ נְתַתִּיהָ לְעֵינֵי בְנֵי־עַמִּי
people-of-me sons-of before-eyes-of I-give-her to-you in-him that and-the-cave

נְתַתִּיהָ לָּךְ קְבֹר מֵתֶךָ׃ וַיִּשְׁתַּחוּ אַבְרָהָם לִפְנֵי
before Abraham and-he-bowed (12) being-dead-of-you bury! to-you I-give-her

עַם הָאָרֶץ׃ וַיְדַבֵּר אֶל־עֶפְרוֹן בְּאָזְנֵי עַם־הָאָרֶץ
the-land people-of in-hearing-of Ephron to and-he-said (13) the-land people-of

לֵאמֹר אַךְ אִם־אַתָּה לוּ שְׁמָעֵנִי נָתַתִּי כֶּסֶף הַשָּׂדֶה קַח
accept! the-field price-of I-will-pay listen-to-me! will you if now to-say

מִמֶּנִּי וְאֶקְבְּרָה אֶת־מֵתִי שָׁמָּה׃ וַיַּעַן עֶפְרוֹן
Ephron and-he-answered (14) at-there being-dead-of-me *** so-I-can-bury from-me

אֶת־אַבְרָהָם לֵאמֹר לוֹ׃ אֲדֹנִי שְׁמָעֵנִי אֶרֶץ אַרְבַּע מֵאֹת
hundreds-of four land listen-to-me! lord-of-me (15) to-him to-say Abraham ***

שֶׁקֶל־כֶּסֶף בֵּינִי וּבֵינְךָ מַה־הִוא וְאֶת־מֵתְךָ
being-dead-of-you now that what? and-between-you between-me silver shekel-of

קְבֹר׃ וַיִּשְׁמַע אַבְרָהָם אֶל־עֶפְרוֹן וַיִּשְׁקֹל אַבְרָהָם לְעֶפְרֹן
for-Ephron Abraham and-he-weighed Ephron with Abraham and-he-agreed (16) bury!

אֶת־הַכֶּסֶף אֲשֶׁר דִּבֶּר בְּאָזְנֵי בְנֵי־חֵת אַרְבַּע מֵאוֹת
hundreds-of four Heth sons-of in-hearing-of he-named that the-price ***

שֶׁקֶל כֶּסֶף עֹבֵר לַסֹּחֵר׃ וַיָּקָם ׀ שְׂדֵה
field-of so-he-was-deeded (17) to-the-ones-selling according silver shekel-of

עֶפְרוֹן אֲשֶׁר בַּמַּכְפֵּלָה אֲשֶׁר לִפְנֵי מַמְרֵא הַשָּׂדֶה וְהַמְּעָרָה אֲשֶׁר־
that and-the-cave the-field Mamre near that in-the-Machpelah that Ephron

בּוֹ וְכָל־הָעֵץ אֲשֶׁר בַּשָּׂדֶה אֲשֶׁר בְּכָל־גְּבֻלוֹ
border-of-him in-all-of that in-the-field that the-tree and-every-of in-him

סָבִיב׃ לְאַבְרָהָם לְמִקְנָה לְעֵינֵי בְנֵי־חֵת בְּכֹל
before-all-of Heth sons-of in-presence-of as-property to-Abraham (18) around

בָּאֵי שַׁעַר־עִירוֹ׃ וְאַחֲרֵי־כֵן קָבַר אַבְרָהָם אֶת־
*** Abraham he-buried this and-after (19) city-of-him gate-of ones-coming-of

שָׂרָה אִשְׁתּוֹ אֶל־מְעָרַת שְׂדֵה הַמַּכְפֵּלָה עַל־פְּנֵי מַמְרֵא הִוא
which Mamre near by the-Machpelah field-of cave-of in wife-of-him Sarah

חֶבְרוֹן בְּאֶרֶץ כְּנָעַן׃ וַיָּקָם הַשָּׂדֶה וְהַמְּעָרָה אֲשֶׁר־
that and-the-cave the-field so-he-was-deeded (20) Canaan in-land-of Hebron

בּוֹ לְאַבְרָהָם לַאֲחֻזַּת־קָבֶר מֵאֵת בְּנֵי־חֵת׃ וְאַבְרָהָם
now-Abraham (24:1) Heth sons-of by burial as-site-of to-Abraham in-him

replied to Abraham in the
hearing of all the Hittites who
had come to the gate of his
city. 11 "No, my lord," he said.
"Listen to me; I give[v] you the
field, and I give[v] you the cave
that is in it. I give[v] it to you in
the presence of my people.
Bury your dead."
12 Again Abraham bowed
down before the people of the
land 13 and he said to Ephron
in their hearing, "Listen to
me, if you will. I will pay the
price of the field. Accept it
from me so I can bury my dead
there."
14 Ephron answered Abra-
ham, 15 "Listen to me, my lord;
the land is worth four hundred shekels[w] of silver, but
what is that between me and
you? Bury your dead."
16 Abraham agreed to
Ephron's terms and weighed
out for him the price he had
named in the hearing of the
Hittites: four hundred shekels
of silver, according to the
weight current among the
merchants.
17 So Ephron's field in Machpelah near Mamre—both the
field and the cave in it, and all
the trees within the borders of
the field—was deeded 18 to
Abraham as his property in
the presence of all the Hittites
who had come to the gate of
the city. 19 Afterward Abraham
buried his wife Sarah in the
cave in the field of Machpelah
near Mamre (which is at Hebron) in the land of Canaan.
20 So the field and the cave in it
were deeded to Abraham by
the Hittites as a burial site.

[v] 11 Or *sell*
[w] 15 That is, about 10 pounds (about 4.5 kilograms)

זָקֵן בָּא בַּיָּמִים וַֽיהוָה בֵּרַךְ אֶת־אַבְרָהָם
he-was-old he-was-advanced in-the-days and-Yahweh he-blessed *** Abraham

בַּכֹּל׃ וַיֹּאמֶר אַבְרָהָם אֶל־עַבְדּוֹ זְקַן
in-the-every-way (2) and-he-said Abraham to servant-of-him chief-of

בֵּיתוֹ הַמֹּשֵׁל בְּכָל־אֲשֶׁר־לוֹ שִׂים־נָא
household-of-him the-one-having-charge over-all that to-him put! now!

יָדְךָ תַּחַת יְרֵכִי׃ וְאַשְׁבִּיעֲךָ בַּיהוָה אֱלֹהֵי
hand-of-you under thigh-of-me (3) and-I-want-to-swear-you by-Yahweh God-of

הַשָּׁמַיִם וֵאלֹהֵי הָאָרֶץ אֲשֶׁר לֹא־תִקַּח אִשָּׁה לִבְנִי
the-heavens and-God-of the-earth that not you-will-get wife for-son-of-me

מִבְּנוֹת הַכְּנַעֲנִי אֲשֶׁר אָנֹכִי יוֹשֵׁב בְּקִרְבּוֹ׃ כִּי אֶל־
from-daughters-of the-Canaanite whom I living in-midst-of-him (4) but to

אַרְצִי וְאֶל־מוֹלַדְתִּי תֵּלֵךְ וְלָקַחְתָּ אִשָּׁה לִבְנִי
country-of-me and-to relative-of-me you-will-go and-you-get wife for-son-of-me

לְיִצְחָק׃ וַיֹּאמֶר אֵלָיו הָעֶבֶד אוּלַי לֹא־תֹאבֶה הָאִשָּׁה
for-Isaac (5) and-he-asked to-him the-servant what-if? not she-wills the-woman

לָלֶכֶת אַחֲרַי אֶל־הָאָרֶץ הַזֹּאת הֶהָשֵׁב אָשִׁיב אֶת־
to-come after-me to the-land the-this to-take-back? shall-I-take-back ***

בִּנְךָ אֶל־הָאָרֶץ אֲשֶׁר־יָצָאתָ מִשָּׁם׃ וַיֹּאמֶר אֵלָיו
son-of-you to the-country that you-came from-there (6) and-he-said to-him

אַבְרָהָם הִשָּׁמֶר לְךָ פֶּן־תָּשִׁיב אֶת־בְּנִי שָׁמָּה׃ יְהוָה ׀
Abraham be-sure! to-you that-not you-take *** son-of-me to-there (7) Yahweh

אֱלֹהֵי הַשָּׁמַיִם אֲשֶׁר לְקָחַנִי מִבֵּית אָבִי וּמֵאֶרֶץ
God-of the-heavens who he-brought-me from-house-of father-of-me and-from-land-of

מוֹלַדְתִּי וַאֲשֶׁר דִּבֶּר־לִי וַאֲשֶׁר נִשְׁבַּע־לִי לֵאמֹר
relative-of-me and-who he-spoke to-me and-who he-swore to-me to-say

לְזַרְעֲךָ אֶתֵּן אֶת־הָאָרֶץ הַזֹּאת הוּא יִשְׁלַח
to-offspring-of-you I-will-give *** the-land the-this he he-will-send

מַלְאָכוֹ לְפָנֶיךָ וְלָקַחְתָּ אִשָּׁה לִבְנִי מִשָּׁם׃ וְאִם־
angel-of-him before-you so-you-can-get wife for-son-of-me from-there (8) but-if

לֹא תֹאבֶה הָאִשָּׁה לָלֶכֶת אַחֲרֶיךָ וְנִקִּיתָ מִשְּׁבֻעָתִי זֹאת
not she-will the-woman to-come with-you so-you-are-free from-oath-of-me this

רַק אֶת־בְּנִי לֹא תָשֵׁב שָׁמָּה׃ וַיָּשֶׂם הָעֶבֶד אֶת־יָדוֹ
only *** son-of-me not you-take to-there (9) so-he-put the-servant *** hand-of-him

תַּחַת יֶרֶךְ אַבְרָהָם אֲדֹנָיו וַיִּשָּׁבַע לוֹ עַל־הַדָּבָר
under thigh-of Abraham master-of-him and-he-swore to-him concerning the-matter

הַזֶּה׃ וַיִּקַּח הָעֶבֶד עֲשָׂרָה גְמַלִּים מִגְּמַלֵּי אֲדֹנָיו
the-this (10) then-he-took the-servant ten camels from-camels-of master-of-him

Isaac and Rebekah

24 Abraham was now old and well advanced in years, and the LORD had blessed him in every way. 2 He said to the chief[x] servant in his household, the one in charge of all that he had, "Put your hand under my thigh. 3 I want you to swear by the LORD, the God of heaven and the God of earth, that you will not get a wife for my son from the daughters of the Canaanites, among whom I am living, 4 but will go to my country and my own relatives and get a wife for my son Isaac."

5 The servant asked him, "What if the woman is unwilling to come back with me to this land? Shall I then take your son back to the country you came from?"

6 "Make sure that you do not take my son back there," Abraham said. 7 "The LORD, the God of heaven, who brought me out of my father's household and my native land and who spoke to me and promised me on oath, saying, 'To your offspring[y] I will give this land'—he will send his angel before you so that you can get a wife for my son from there. 8 If the woman is unwilling to come back with you, then you will be released from this oath of mine. Only do not take my son back there." 9 So the servant put his hand under the thigh of his master Abraham and swore an oath to him concerning this matter.

10 Then the servant took ten of his master's camels and left,

x2 Or oldest y7 Or seed

וַיֵּלֶךְ וְכָל־ טוּב אֲדֹנָיו בְּיָדוֹ וַיָּקָם
and-he-rose in-hand-of-him master-of-him good-of with-all-of and-he-left

וַיֵּלֶךְ אֶל־ אֲרַם נַהֲרַיִם אֶל־ עִיר נָחוֹר׃ וַיַּבְרֵךְ
and-he-made-kneel (11) Nahor city-of to Nahariam Aram for and-he-set-out

הַגְּמַלִּים מִחוּץ לָעִיר אֶל־ בְּאֵר הַמָּיִם לְעֵת עֶרֶב
evening at-time-of the-waters well-of near to-the-city outside the-camels

לְעֵת צֵאת הַשֹּׁאֲבֹת׃ וַיֹּאמַר ׀ יְהוָה אֱלֹהֵי
God-of Yahweh and-he-prayed (12) the-women-drawing-water to-go-out at-time-of

אֲדֹנִי אַבְרָהָם הַקְרֵה־ נָא לְפָנַי הַיּוֹם וַעֲשֵׂה־ חֶסֶד עִם
to kindness and-show! the-day to-me now! give-success! Abraham master-of-me

אֲדֹנִי אַבְרָהָם׃ הִנֵּה אָנֹכִי נִצָּב עַל־ עֵין הַמָּיִם
the-waters spring-of by standing I see! (13) Abraham master-of-me

וּבְנוֹת אַנְשֵׁי הָעִיר יֹצְאֹת לִשְׁאֹב מָיִם׃
waters to-draw ones-coming the-city people-of and-daughters-of

וְהָיָה הַנַּעֲרָ אֲשֶׁר אֹמַר אֵלֶיהָ הַטִּי־ נָא כַדֵּךְ
jar-of-you now! let-down! to-her I-say whom the-girl now-may-he-be (14)

וְאֶשְׁתֶּה וְאָמְרָה שְׁתֵה וְגַם־ גְּמַלֶּיךָ אַשְׁקֶה אֹתָהּ
her I-will-water camels-of-you and-also drink! and-she-says so-I-may-drink

הֹכַחְתָּ לְעַבְדְּךָ לְיִצְחָק וּבָהּ אֵדַע כִּי־ עָשִׂיתָ
you-showed that I-will-know and-by-her for-Isaac for-servant-of-you you-chose

חֶסֶד עִם־ אֲדֹנִי׃ וַיְהִי־ הוּא טֶרֶם כִּלָּה לְדַבֵּר
to-pray he-finished before this and-he-was (15) master-of-me to kindness

וְהִנֵּה רִבְקָה יֹצֵאת אֲשֶׁר יֻלְּדָה לִבְתוּאֵל בֶּן־ מִלְכָּה אֵשֶׁת
wife-of Milcah son-of to-Bethuel she-was-born whom coming Rebekah and-see!

נָחוֹר אֲחִי אַבְרָהָם וְכַדָּהּ עַל־ שִׁכְמָהּ׃ וְהַנַּעֲרָ
now-the-girl (16) shoulder-of-her on and-jar-of-her Abraham brother-of Nahor

טֹבַת מַרְאֶה מְאֹד בְּתוּלָה וְאִישׁ לֹא יְדָעָהּ וַתֵּרֶד
and-she-went-down he-knew-her no and-man virgin very sight beautiful-of

הָעַיְנָה וַתְּמַלֵּא כַדָּהּ וַתָּעַל׃ וַיָּרָץ
and-he-hurried (17) and-she-came-up jar-of-her and-she-filled to-the-spring

הָעֶבֶד לִקְרָאתָהּ וַיֹּאמֶר הַגְמִיאִינִי נָא מְעַט־ מַיִם
waters little-of now! give-me! and-he-said to-meet-her the-servant

מִכַּדֵּךְ׃ וַתֹּאמֶר שְׁתֵה אֲדֹנִי וַתְּמַהֵר
and-she-hurried lord-of-me drink! and-she-said (18) from-jar-of-you

וַתֹּרֶד כַּדָּהּ עַל־ יָדָהּ וַתַּשְׁקֵהוּ׃
and-she-gave-drink-him hand-of-her to jar-of-her and-she-lowered

וַתְּכַל לְהַשְׁקֹתוֹ וַתֹּאמֶר גַּם לִגְמַלֶּיךָ
for-camels-of-you also then-she-said to-give-drink-him when-she-finished (19)

taking with him all kinds of
good things from his master.
He set out for Aram Naha-
raim[z] and made his way to the
town of Nahor. 11He had the
camels kneel down near the
well outside the town; it was
toward evening, the time the
women go out to draw water.
12Then he prayed, "O LORD,
God of my master Abraham,
give me success today, and
show kindness to my master
Abraham. 13See, I am standing
beside this spring, and the
daughters of the townspeople
are coming out to draw water.
14May it be that when I say to
a girl, 'Please let down your jar
that I may have a drink,' and
she says, 'Drink, and I'll water
your camels too'—let her be
the one you have chosen for
your servant Isaac. By this I
will know that you have
shown kindness to my mas-
ter."
15Before he had finished
praying, Rebekah came out
with her jar on her shoulder.
She was the daughter of Bethuel son of Milcah, who was
the wife of Abraham's brother
Nahor. 16The girl was very
beautiful, a virgin; no man
had ever lain with her. She
went down to the spring, filled
her jar and came up again.
17The servant hurried to
meet her and said, "Please
give me a little water from
your jar."
18"Drink, my lord," she said,
and quickly lowered the jar to
her hands and gave him a
drink.
19After she had given him a
drink, she said, "I'll draw

z10 That is, Northwest Mesopotamia

אֶשְׁאָב עַד אִם־ כִּלּוּ לִשְׁתֹּת׃ וַתְּמַהֵר
and-she-hurried (20) to-drink they-finish when until I-will-draw

וַתְּעַר כַּדָּהּ אֶל־ הַשֹּׁקֶת וַתָּרָץ עוֹד אֶל־ הַבְּאֵר
the-well to back and-she-ran the-trough into jar-of-her and-she-emptied

לִשְׁאֹב וַתִּשְׁאַב לְכָל־ גְּמַלָּיו׃ וְהָאִישׁ מִשְׁתָּאֵה לָהּ
to-her watching and-the-man (21) camels-of-him for-all-of and-she-drew to-draw

מַחֲרִישׁ לָדַעַת הַהִצְלִיחַ יְהוָה דַּרְכּוֹ אִם־לֹא׃
not or journey-of-him Yahweh if-he-made-successful to-learn being-silent

וַיְהִי כַּאֲשֶׁר כִּלּוּ הַגְּמַלִּים לִשְׁתּוֹת וַיִּקַּח הָאִישׁ
the-man that-he-took to-drink the-camels they-finished just-as and-he-was (22)

נֶזֶם זָהָב בֶּקַע מִשְׁקָלוֹ וּשְׁנֵי צְמִידִים עַל־ יָדֶיהָ עֲשָׂרָה
ten arms-of-her for bracelets and-two-of weight-of-him beka gold nose-ring

זָהָב מִשְׁקָלָם׃ וַיֹּאמֶר בַּת־ מִי אַתְּ הַגִּידִי נָא לִי
to-me now! tell! you whose? daughter-of and-he-said (23) weight-of-them gold

הֲיֵשׁ בֵּית־ אָבִיךְ מָקוֹם לָנוּ לָלִין׃ וַתֹּאמֶר
so-she-said (24) to-spend-night for-us room father-of-you in-house-of is-there?

אֵלָיו בַּת־ בְּתוּאֵל אָנֹכִי בֶּן־ מִלְכָּה אֲשֶׁר יָלְדָה לְנָחוֹר׃
to-Nahor she-bore whom Milcah son-of I Bethuel daughter-of to-him

וַתֹּאמֶר אֵלָיו גַּם־ תֶּבֶן גַּם־מִסְפּוֹא רַב עִמָּנוּ גַּם־ מָקוֹם
room as-well-as with-us plenty fodder also straw also to-him and-she-said (25)

לָלוּן׃ וַיִּקֹּד הָאִישׁ וַיִּשְׁתַּחוּ לַיהוָה׃
to-Yahweh and-he-worshiped the-man then-he-bowed (26) to-spend-night

וַיֹּאמֶר בָּרוּךְ יְהוָה אֱלֹהֵי אֲדֹנִי אַבְרָהָם אֲשֶׁר לֹא־
not who Abraham master-of-me God-of Yahweh being-praised and-he-said (27)

עָזַב חַסְדּוֹ וַאֲמִתּוֹ מֵעִם אֲדֹנִי אָנֹכִי
I master-of-me to and-faithfulness-of-him kindness-of-him he-abandoned

בַּדֶּרֶךְ נָחַנִי יְהוָה בֵּית אֲחֵי אֲדֹנִי׃
master-of-me relatives-of to-house-of Yahweh he-led-me on-the-journey

וַתָּרָץ הַנַּעֲרָ וַתַּגֵּד לְבֵית אִמָּהּ
mother-of-her to-household-of and-she-told the-girl and-she-ran (28)

כַּדְּבָרִים הָאֵלֶּה׃ וּלְרִבְקָה אָח וּשְׁמוֹ לָבָן
Laban and-name-of-him brother now-to-Rebekah (29) the-these about-the-things

וַיָּרָץ לָבָן אֶל־ הָאִישׁ הַחוּצָה אֶל־ הָעָיִן׃ וַיְהִי ׀
and-he-was (30) the-spring to to-the-outside the-man to Laban and-he-hurried

כִּרְאֹת אֶת־ הַנֶּזֶם וְאֶת־ הַצְּמִדִים עַל־ יְדֵי אֲחֹתוֹ
sister-of-him arms-of on the-bracelets and the-nose-ring *** as-to-see

וּכְשָׁמְעוֹ אֶת־ דִּבְרֵי רִבְקָה אֲחֹתוֹ לֵאמֹר כֹּה־ דִבֶּר
he-said what to-say sister-of-him Rebekah words-of *** and-as-to-hear-him

water for your camels too, until they have finished drinking." 20So she quickly emptied
her jar into the trough, ran
back to the well to draw more
water, and drew enough for all
his camels. 21Without saying a
word, the man watched her
closely to learn whether or not
the LORD had made his journey successful.
22When the camels had
finished drinking, the man
took out a gold nose ring
weighing a beka[a] and two
gold bracelets weighing ten
shekels.[b] 23Then he asked,
"Whose daughter are you?
Please tell me, is there room in
your father's house for us to
spend the night?"
24She answered him, "I am
the daughter of Bethuel, the
son that Milcah bore to Nahor." 25And she added, "We
have plenty of straw and fodder, as well as room for you to
spend the night."
26Then the man bowed
down and worshiped the
LORD, 27saying, "Praise be to
the LORD, the God of my master Abraham, who has not
abandoned his kindness and
faithfulness to my master. As
for me, the LORD has led me on
the journey to the house of my
master's relatives."
28The girl ran and told her
mother's household about
these things. 29Now Rebekah
had a brother named Laban,
and he hurried out to the man
at the spring. 30As soon as he
had seen the nose ring, and
the bracelets on his sister's
arms, and had heard Rebekah
tell what the man said to her,

[a]22 That is, about 1/5 ounce (about 5.5 grams)
[b]22 That is, about 4 ounces (about 110 grams)

אֵלַי הָאִישׁ וַיָּבֹא אֶל־הָאִישׁ וְהִנֵּה עֹמֵד עַל־הַגְּמַלִּים עַל־
near the-camels by standing and-see! the-man to that-he-went the-man to-me

הָעָיִן׃ וַיֹּאמֶר בּוֹא בְּרוּךְ יְהוָה לָמָּה תַעֲמֹד
you-stand why? Yahweh being-blessed-of come! and-he-said (31) the-spring

בַּחוּץ וְאָנֹכִי פִּנִּיתִי הַבַּיִת וּמָקוֹם לַגְּמַלִּים׃ וַיָּבֹא
so-he-went (32) for-the-camels and-place the-house I-prepared now-I out-here

הָאִישׁ הַבַּיְתָה וַיְפַתַּח הַגְּמַלִּים וַיִּתֵּן תֶּבֶן
straw and-he-brought the-camels and-he-unloaded to-the-house the-man

וּמִסְפּוֹא לַגְּמַלִּים וּמַיִם לִרְחֹץ רַגְלָיו וְרַגְלֵי הָאֲנָשִׁים
the-men and-feet-of feet-of-him to-wash and-water for-the-camels and-fodder

אֲשֶׁר אִתּוֹ׃ וַיּישַׂם לְפָנָיו לֶאֱכֹל וַיֹּאמֶר לֹא אֹכַל
I-will-eat not but-he-said to-eat before-him and-he-was-set (33) with-him who

עַד אִם־דִּבַּרְתִּי דְּבָרָי וַיֹּאמֶר דַּבֵּר׃ וַיֹּאמַר עֶבֶד
servant-of so-he-said (34) tell! so-he-said words-of-me I-tell when until

אַבְרָהָם אָנֹכִי׃ וַיהוָה בֵּרַךְ אֶת־אֲדֹנִי מְאֹד וַיִּגְדָּל
and-he-is-wealthy greatly master-of-me *** he-blessed now-Yahweh (35) I Abraham

וַיִּתֶּן־לוֹ צֹאן וּבָקָר וְכֶסֶף וְזָהָב וַעֲבָדִם
and-menservants and-gold and-silver and-cattle sheep to-him and-he-gave

וּשְׁפָחֹת וּגְמַלִּים וַחֲמֹרִים׃ וַתֵּלֶד שָׂרָה אֵשֶׁת
wife-of Sarah and-she-bore (36) and-donkeys and-camels and-maidservants

אֲדֹנִי בֵן לַאדֹנִי אַחֲרֵי זִקְנָתָהּ וַיִּתֶּן־לוֹ אֶת־כָּל־
all *** to-him and-he-gave old-age-of-her in to-master-of-me son master-of-me

אֲשֶׁר־לוֹ׃ וַיַּשְׁבִּעֵנִי אֲדֹנִי לֵאמֹר לֹא־תִקַּח אִשָּׁה
wife you-must-get not to-say master-of-me and-he-made-swear-me (37) to-him that

לִבְנִי מִבְּנוֹת הַכְּנַעֲנִי אֲשֶׁר אָנֹכִי יֹשֵׁב בְּאַרְצוֹ׃
in-land-of-him living I whom the-Canaanite from-daughters-of for-son-of-me

אִם־לֹא אֶל־בֵּית־אָבִי תֵּלֵךְ וְאֶל־מִשְׁפַּחְתִּי וְלָקַחְתָּ
and-you-get clan-of-me and-to you-go father-of-me family-of to rather but (38)

אִשָּׁה לִבְנִי׃ וָאֹמַר אֶל־אֲדֹנִי אֻלַי לֹא־תֵלֵךְ
she-comes not what-if? master-of-me to then-I-asked (39) for-son-of-me wife

הָאִשָּׁה אַחֲרָי׃ וַיֹּאמֶר אֵלָי יְהוָה אֲשֶׁר־הִתְהַלַּכְתִּי לְפָנָיו
before-him I-walk whom Yahweh to-me and-he-replied (40) after-me the-woman

יִשְׁלַח מַלְאָכוֹ אִתָּךְ וְהִצְלִיחַ דַּרְכֶּךָ
journey-of-you and-he-will-make-succeed with-you angel-of-him he-will-send

וְלָקַחְתָּ אִשָּׁה לִבְנִי מִמִּשְׁפַּחְתִּי וּמִבֵּית
and-from-family-of from-clan-of-me for-son-of-me wife so-you-can-get

אָבִי׃ אָז תִּנָּקֶה מֵאָלָתִי כִּי תָבוֹא אֶל־
to you-go when from-oath-of-me you-will-be-free then (41) father-of-me

he went out to the man and
found him standing by the
camels near the spring.
31"Come, you who are blessed
by the LORD," he said. "Why
are you standing out here? I
have prepared the house and a
place for the camels."
32So the man went to the
house, and the camels were
unloaded. Straw and fodder
were brought for the camels,
and water for him and his
men to wash their feet. 33Then
food was set before him, but
he said, "I will not eat until I
have told you what I have to
say."
"Then tell us," ⌊Laban⌋ said.
34So he said, "I am Abra-
ham's servant. 35The LORD has
blessed my master abundant-
ly, and he has become
wealthy. He has given him
sheep and cattle, silver and
gold, menservants and maidservants, and camels and donkeys. 36My master's wife Sarah
has borne him a son in her[c]
old age, and he has given him
everything he owns. 37And my
master made me swear an
oath, and said, 'You must not
get a wife for my son from the
daughters of the Canaanites,
in whose land I live, 38but go to
my father's family and to my
own clan, and get a wife for
my son.'
39"Then I asked my master,
'What if the woman will not
come back with me?'
40"He replied, 'The LORD, before whom I have walked, will
send his angel with you and
make your journey a success,
so that you can get a wife for
my son from my own clan and
from my father's family.
41Then, when you go to my
clan, you will be released from

c36 Or *his*

*36 Most mss have no *dagesh* in the *lamed* (לוֹ).

°33 ק ויושם

משפחתי ואם־ לא יתנו לך והיית נקי מאלתי׃
from-oath-of-me free and-you-will-be to-you they-give not even-if clan-of-me

(42) ואבא היום אל־ העין ואמר יהוה אלהי אדני
master-of-me God-of Yahweh then-I-said the-spring to the-day when-I-came (42)

אברהם אם־ ישך־ נא מצליח דרכי אשר אנכי הלך
coming I that journey-of-me granting-success now! will-of-you if Abraham

עליה׃ (43) הנה אנכי נצב על־ עין המים והיה העלמה
the-maiden now-may-he-be the-water spring-of beside standing I see! (43) on-her

היצאת לשאב ואמרתי אליה השקיני־ נא מעט־ מים
water little-of now! give-drink-me! to-her that-I-say to-draw the-one-coming

מכדך׃ (44) ואמרה אלי גם־ אתה שתה וגם
and-also drink! you indeed to-me and-she-says (44) from-jar-of-you

לגמליך אשאב הוא האשה אשר־ הכיח יהוה לבן־
for-son-of Yahweh he-chose whom the-woman she I-will-draw for-camels-of-you

אדני׃ (45) אני טרם אכלה לדבר אל־ לבי והנה רבקה
Rebekah and-see! heart-of-me in to-pray I-finished before I (45) master-of-me

יצאת וכדה על־ שכמה ותרד העינה
to-the-spring and-she-went-down shoulder-of-her on with-jar-of-her coming

ותשאב ואמר אליה השקיני נא׃ (46) ותמהר
and-she-hurried (46) now! give-drink-me! to-her and-I-said and-she-drew

ותורד כדה מעליה ותאמר שתה וגם־
and-also drink! and-she-said from-on-her jar-of-her and-she-lowered

גמליך אשקה ואשת וגם הגמלים השקתה׃
she-watered the-camels and-also so-I-drank I-will-water camels-of-you

(47) ואשאל אתה ואמר בת־ מי את ותאמר
and-she-said you whom? daughter-of and-I-said her then-I-asked (47)

בת־ בתואל בן־ נחור אשר ילדה־ לו מלכה ואשם
then-I-put Milcah to-him she-bore whom Nahor son-of Bethuel daughter-of

הנזם על־ אפה והצמידים על־ ידיה׃ (48) ואקד
then-I-bowed (48) arms-of-her on and-the-bracelets nose-of-her in the-ring

ואשתחוה ליהוה ואברך את־ יהוה אלהי אדני
master-of-me God-of Yahweh *** and-I-praised to-Yahweh and-I-worshiped

אברהם אשר הנחני בדרך אמת לקחת את־ בת־ אחי
brother-of granddaughter-of *** to-get right on-road-of he-led-me who Abraham

אדני לבנו׃ (49) ועתה אם־ ישכם עשים חסד
kindness ones-showing will-of-you if and-now (49) for-son-of-him master-of-me

ואמת את־ אדני הגידו לי ואם־ לא הגידו לי
to-me tell! not and-if to-me tell! master-of-me to and-faithfulness

my oath even if they refuse to
give her to you—you will be
released from my oath.'
42"When I came to the
spring today, I said, 'O LORD,
God of my master Abraham, if
you will, please grant success
to the journey on which I have
come. 43See, I am standing beside this spring; if a maiden
comes out to draw water and I
say to her, "Please let me drink
a little water from your jar,"
44and if she says to me,
"Drink, and I'll draw water for
your camels too," let her be the
one the LORD has chosen for
my master's son.'
45"Before I finished praying
in my heart, Rebekah came
out, with her jar on her shoulder. She went down to the
spring and drew water, and I
said to her, 'Please give me a
drink.'
46"She quickly lowered her
jar from her shoulder and said,
'Drink, and I'll water your
camels too.' So I drank, and
she watered the camels also.
47"I asked her, 'Whose
daughter are you?'
"She said, 'The daughter of
Bethuel son of Nahor, whom
Milcah bore to him.'
"Then I put the ring in her
nose and the bracelets on her
arms, 48and I bowed down and
worshiped the LORD. I praised
the LORD, the God of my master Abraham, who had led me
on the right road to get the
granddaughter of my master's
brother for his son. 49Now if
you will show kindness and
faithfulness to my master, tell
me; and if not, tell me, so I

וְאֶפְנֶה עַל־יָמִין אוֹ עַל־שְׂמֹאל׃ וַיַּעַן לָבָן וּבְתוּאֵל
and-Bethuel Laban and-he-answered (50) left to or right to so-I-may-turn

וַיֹּאמְרוּ מֵיְהוָה יָצָא הַדָּבָר לֹא נוּכַל דַּבֵּר אֵלֶיךָ רַע
bad to-you to-say we-can not the-thing he-comes from-Yahweh and-they-said

אוֹ־טוֹב׃ הִנֵּה־רִבְקָה לְפָנֶיךָ קַח וָלֵךְ וּתְהִי אִשָּׁה
wife and-let-her-be and-go take! before-you Rebekah see! (51) good or

לְבֶן־אֲדֹנֶיךָ כַּאֲשֶׁר דִּבֶּר יְהוָה׃ וַיְהִי כַּאֲשֶׁר
when and-he-was (52) Yahweh he-directed just-as master-of-you for-son-of

שָׁמַע עֶבֶד אַבְרָהָם אֶת־דִּבְרֵיהֶם וַיִּשְׁתַּחוּ אַרְצָה
to-ground that-he-bowed words-of-them *** Abraham servant-of he-heard

לַיהוָה׃ וַיּוֹצֵא הָעֶבֶד כְּלֵי־כֶסֶף וּכְלֵי
and-jewelry-of silver jewelry-of the-servant and-he-brought-out (53) to-Yahweh

זָהָב וּבְגָדִים וַיִּתֵּן לְרִבְקָה וּמִגְדָּנֹת נָתַן לְאָחִיהָ
to-brother-of-her he-gave and-gifts to-Rebekah and-he-gave and-clothing gold

וּלְאִמָּהּ׃ וַיֹּאכְלוּ וַיִּשְׁתּוּ הוּא וְהָאֲנָשִׁים אֲשֶׁר־
who and-the-men he and-they-drank then-they-ate (54) and-to-mother-of-her

עִמּוֹ וַיָּלִינוּ וַיָּקוּמוּ בַבֹּקֶר וַיֹּאמֶר
then-he-said in-the-morning when-they-rose and-they-spent-night with-him

שַׁלְּחֻנִי לַאדֹנִי׃ וַיֹּאמֶר אָחִיהָ וְאִמָּהּ
and-mother-of-her brother-of-her but-he-replied (55) to-master-of-me send-me!

תֵּשֵׁב הַנַּעֲרָ אִתָּנוּ יָמִים אוֹ עָשׂוֹר אַחַר תֵּלֵךְ׃
you-may-go then ten about days with-us the-girl let-her-remain

וַיֹּאמֶר אֲלֵהֶם אַל־תְּאַחֲרוּ אֹתִי וַיהוָה הִצְלִיחַ דַּרְכִּי
journey-of-me he-made-succeed as-Yahweh me you-detain not to-them but-he-said (56)

שַׁלְּחוּנִי וְאֵלְכָה לַאדֹנִי׃ וַיֹּאמְרוּ נִקְרָא
let-us-call then-they-said (57) to-master-of-me so-I-may-go send-me!

לַנַּעֲרָ וְנִשְׁאֲלָה אֶת־פִּיהָ׃ וַיִּקְרְאוּ לְרִבְקָה
to-Rebekah to-they-called (58) mouth-of-her *** and-let-us-ask to-the-girl

וַיֹּאמְרוּ אֵלֶיהָ הֲתֵלְכִי עִם־הָאִישׁ הַזֶּה וַתֹּאמֶר
and-she-said the-this the-man with will-you-go? to-her and-they-asked

אֵלֵךְ׃ וַיְשַׁלְּחוּ אֶת־רִבְקָה אֲחֹתָם וְאֶת־מֵנִקְתָּהּ
one-nursing-her and sister-of-them Rebekah *** so-they-sent (59) I-will-go

וְאֶת־עֶבֶד אַבְרָהָם וְאֶת־אֲנָשָׁיו׃ וַיְבָרְכוּ אֶת־רִבְקָה
Rebekah *** and-they-blessed (60) men-of-him and Abraham servant-of and

וַיֹּאמְרוּ לָהּ אֲחֹתֵנוּ אַתְּ הֲיִי לְאַלְפֵי רְבָבָה
ten-thousand to-thousands-of increase! you sister-of-us to-her and-they-said

וְיִירַשׁ זַרְעֵךְ אֵת שַׁעַר שֹׂנְאָיו׃
ones-hating-him gate-of *** offspring-of-you and-may-he-possess

may know which way to
turn."
50Laban and Bethuel an-
swered, "This is from the
LORD; we can say nothing to
you one way or the other.
51Here is Rebekah; take her
and go, and let her become the
wife of your master's son, as
the LORD has directed."
52When Abraham's servant
heard what they said, he
bowed down to the ground
before the LORD. 53Then the
servant brought out gold and
silver jewelry and articles of
clothing and gave them to Rebekah; he also gave costly gifts
to her brother and to her
mother. 54Then he and the
men who were with him ate
and drank and spent the night
there.
When they got up the next
morning, he said, "Send me
on my way to my master."
55But her brother and her
mother replied, "Let the girl
remain with us ten days or so;
then you[d] may go."
56But he said to them, "Do
not detain me, now that the
LORD has granted success to
my journey. Send me on my
way so I may go to my master."
57Then they said, "Let's call
the girl and ask her about it."
58So they called Rebekah and
asked her, "Will you go with
this man?"
"I will go," she said.
59So they sent their sister Rebekah on her way, along with
her nurse and Abraham's servant and his men. 60And they
blessed Rebekah and said to
her,

"Our sister, may you
increase
to thousands upon
thousands;
may your offspring possess
the gates of their
enemies."

[d]55 Or *she*

וַתָּקָם רִבְקָה וְנַעֲרֹתֶיהָ וַתִּרְכַּבְנָה עַל־ הַגְּמַלִּים
the-camels on and-they-mounted and-maids-of-her Rebekah then-she-rose (61)

וַתֵּלַכְנָה אַחֲרֵי הָאִישׁ וַיִּקַּח הָעֶבֶד אֶת־ רִבְקָה וַיֵּלַךְ׃
and-he-left Rebekah *** the-servant so-he-took the-man after and-they-went

וְיִצְחָק בָּא מִבּוֹא בְּאֵר לַחַי רֹאִי וְהוּא יוֹשֵׁב בְּאֶרֶץ
in-land-of living for-he Roi Lahai Beer from-to-come he-came now-Isaac (62)

הַנֶּגֶב׃ וַיֵּצֵא יִצְחָק לָשׂוּחַ בַּשָּׂדֶה לִפְנוֹת עָרֶב
evening to-be in-the-field to-meditate Isaac and-he-went (63) the-Negev

וַיִּשָּׂא עֵינָיו וַיַּרְא וְהִנֵּה גְמַלִּים בָּאִים׃
ones-coming camels and-see! and-he-saw eyes-of-him and-he-lifted

וַתִּשָּׂא רִבְקָה אֶת־ עֵינֶיהָ וַתֵּרֶא אֶת־יִצְחָק וַתִּפֹּל
and-she-got-down Isaac *** and-she-saw eyes-of-her *** Rebekah and-she-lifted (64)

מֵעַל הַגָּמָל׃ וַתֹּאמֶר אֶל־ הָעֶבֶד מִי־ הָאִישׁ הַלָּזֶה
the-that the-man who? the-servant to and-she-asked (65) the-camel from-on

הַהֹלֵךְ בַּשָּׂדֶה לִקְרָאתֵנוּ וַיֹּאמֶר הָעֶבֶד הוּא
he the-servant and-he-answered to-meet-us in-the-field the-one-coming

אֲדֹנִי וַתִּקַּח הַצָּעִיף וַתִּתְכָּס׃ וַיְסַפֵּר
then-he-told (66) and-she-covered-herself the-veil so-she-took master-of-me

הָעֶבֶד לְיִצְחָק אֵת כָּל־ הַדְּבָרִים אֲשֶׁר עָשָׂה׃ וַיְבִאֶהָ
and-he-brought-her (67) he-did that the-things all-of *** to-Isaac the-servant

יִצְחָק הָאֹהֱלָה שָׂרָה אִמּוֹ וַיִּקַּח אֶת־ רִבְקָה
Rebekah *** and-he-married mother-of-him Sarah into-the-tent Isaac

וַתְּהִי־ לוֹ לְאִשָּׁה וַיֶּאֱהָבֶהָ וַיִּנָּחֵם יִצְחָק
Isaac and-he-was-comforted and-he-loved-her as-wife to-him so-she-became

אַחֲרֵי אִמּוֹ׃ וַיֹּסֶף אַבְרָהָם וַיִּקַּח אִשָּׁה
wife and-he-took Abraham and-he-added (25:1) mother-of-him after

וּשְׁמָהּ קְטוּרָה׃ וַתֵּלֶד לוֹ אֶת־ זִמְרָן וְאֶת־ יָקְשָׁן וְאֶת־
and Jokshan and Zimran *** to-him and-she-bore (2) Keturah and-name-of-her

מְדָן וְאֶת־ מִדְיָן וְאֶת־ יִשְׁבָּק וְאֶת־ שׁוּחַ׃ וְיָקְשָׁן יָלַד אֶת־ שְׁבָא
Sheba *** he-fathered and-Jokshan (3) Shuah and Ishbak and Midian and Medan

וְאֶת־ דְּדָן וּבְנֵי דְדָן הָיוּ אַשּׁוּרִם וּלְטוּשִׁים
and Letushites Asshurites they-were Dedan and-descendants-of Dedan and

וּלְאֻמִּים׃ וּבְנֵי מִדְיָן עֵיפָה וָעֵפֶר וַחֲנֹךְ וַאֲבִידָע
and-Abida and-Hanoch and-Epher Ephah Midian and-sons-of (4) and-Leummites

וְאֶלְדָּעָה כָּל־ אֵלֶּה בְּנֵי קְטוּרָה׃ וַיִּתֵּן אַבְרָהָם אֶת־
*** Abraham and-he-left (5) Keturah descendants-of these all-of and-Eldaah

כָּל־אֲשֶׁר־ לוֹ לְיִצְחָק׃ וְלִבְנֵי הַפִּילַגְשִׁים אֲשֶׁר לְאַבְרָהָם
to-Abraham that the-concubines and-to-sons-of (6) to-Isaac to-him that all

[61]Then Rebekah and her maids got ready and mounted their camels and went back with the man. So the servant took Rebekah and left.

[62]Now Isaac had come from Beer Lahai Roi, for he was living in the Negev. [63]He went out to the field one evening to meditate,[e] and as he looked up, he saw camels approaching. [64]Rebekah also looked up and saw Isaac. She got down from her camel [65]and asked the servant, "Who is that man in the field coming to meet us?"

"He is my master," the servant answered. So she took her veil and covered herself.

[66]Then the servant told Isaac all he had done. [67]Isaac brought her into the tent of his mother Sarah, and he married Rebekah. So she became his wife, and he loved her; and Isaac was comforted after his mother's death.

The Death of Abraham

25 Abraham took[f] another wife, whose name was Keturah. [2]She bore him Zimran, Jokshan, Medan, Midian, Ishbak and Shuah. [3]Jokshan was the father of Sheba and Dedan; the descendants of Dedan were the Asshurites, the Letushites and the Leummites. [4]The sons of Midian were Ephah, Epher, Hanoch, Abida and Eldaah. All these were descendants of Keturah.

[5]Abraham left everything he owned to Isaac. [6]But while he was still living, he gave gifts to the sons of his concubines and

[e]63 The meaning of the Hebrew for this word is uncertain.
[f]1 Or *had taken*

נָתַן אַבְרָהָם מַתָּנֹת וַיְשַׁלְּחֵם מֵעַל יִצְחָק בְּנוֹ בְּעוֹדֶנּוּ
while-he son-of-him Isaac away-from and-he-sent-them gifts Abraham he-gave

חַי קֵדְמָה אֶל־אֶרֶץ קֶדֶם׃ וְאֵלֶּה יְמֵי שְׁנֵי־חַיֵּי אַבְרָהָם
Abraham lives-of years-of days-of and-these (7) east land-of to to-east alive

אֲשֶׁר־חָי מְאַת שָׁנָה וְשִׁבְעִים שָׁנָה וְחָמֵשׁ שָׁנִים׃
years and-five year and-seventy year hundred-of alive that

וַיִּגְוַע וַיָּמָת אַבְרָהָם בְּשֵׂיבָה טוֹבָה זָקֵן וְשָׂבֵעַ
and-full old good at-old-age Abraham and-he-died and-he-breathed-last (8)

וַיֵּאָסֶף אֶל־עַמָּיו׃ וַיִּקְבְּרוּ אֹתוֹ יִצְחָק
Isaac him and-they-buried (9) people-of-him to and-he-was-gathered

וְיִשְׁמָעֵאל בָּנָיו אֶל־מְעָרַת הַמַּכְפֵּלָה אֶל־שְׂדֵה עֶפְרֹן בֶּן־
son-of Ephron field-of in the-Machpelah cave-of in sons-of-him and-Ishmael

צֹחַר הַחִתִּי אֲשֶׁר עַל־פְּנֵי מַמְרֵא׃ הַשָּׂדֶה אֲשֶׁר־קָנָה
he-bought that the-field (10) Mamre area-of near that the-Hittite Zohar

אַבְרָהָם מֵאֵת בְּנֵי־חֵת שָׁמָּה קֻבַּר אַבְרָהָם וְשָׂרָה אִשְׁתּוֹ׃
wife-of-him and-Sarah Abraham he-was-buried at-there Heth sons-of from Abraham

וַיְהִי אַחֲרֵי מוֹת אַבְרָהָם וַיְבָרֶךְ אֱלֹהִים אֶת־יִצְחָק
Isaac *** God that-he-blessed Abraham death-of after and-he-was (11)

בְּנוֹ וַיֵּשֶׁב יִצְחָק עִם־בְּאֵר לַחַי רֹאִי׃ וְאֵלֶּה תֹּלְדֹת
lines-of now-these (12) Roi Lahai Beer near Isaac and-he-lived son-of-him

יִשְׁמָעֵאל בֶּן־אַבְרָהָם אֲשֶׁר יָלְדָה הָגָר הַמִּצְרִית שִׁפְחַת שָׂרָה
Sarah maidservant-of the-Egyptian Hagar she-bore whom Abraham son-of Ishmael

לְאַבְרָהָם׃ וְאֵלֶּה שְׁמוֹת בְּנֵי יִשְׁמָעֵאל בִּשְׁמֹתָם
by-names-of-them Ishmael sons-of names-of and-these (13) to-Abraham

לְתוֹלְדֹתָם בְּכֹר יִשְׁמָעֵאל נְבָיֹת וְקֵדָר וְאַדְבְּאֵל
and-Adbeel and-Kedar Nebaioth Ishmael firstborn-of by-births-of-them

וּמִבְשָׂם׃ וּמִשְׁמָע וְדוּמָה וּמַשָּׂא׃ חֲדַד וְתֵימָא יְטוּר
Jetur and-Tema Hadad (15) and-Massa and-Dumah and-Mishma (14) and-Mibsam

נָפִישׁ וָקֵדְמָה׃ אֵלֶּה הֵם בְּנֵי יִשְׁמָעֵאל וְאֵלֶּה שְׁמֹתָם
names-of-them and-these Ishmael sons-of they these (16) and-Kedemah Naphish

בְּחַצְרֵיהֶם וּבְטִירֹתָם שְׁנֵים־עָשָׂר נְשִׂיאִם לְאֻמֹּתָם׃
by-tribes-of-them rulers ten two and-by-camps-of-them by-settlements-of-them

וְאֵלֶּה שְׁנֵי חַיֵּי יִשְׁמָעֵאל מְאַת שָׁנָה וּשְׁלֹשִׁים שָׁנָה
year and-thirty year hundred-of Ishmael lives-of years-of and-these (17)

וְשֶׁבַע שָׁנִים וַיִּגְוַע וַיָּמָת וַיֵּאָסֶף אֶל־
to and-he-was-gathered and-he-died and-he-breathed-last years and-seven

עַמָּיו׃ וַיִּשְׁכְּנוּ מֵחֲוִילָה עַד־שׁוּר אֲשֶׁר עַל־פְּנֵי
border-of near that Shur to from-Havilah and-they-settled (18) people-of-him

sent them away from his son Isaac to the land of the east. [7]Altogether, Abraham lived a hundred and seventy-five years. [8]Then Abraham breathed his last and died at a good old age, an old man and full of years; and he was gathered to his people. [9]His sons Isaac and Ishmael buried him in the cave of Machpelah near Mamre, in the field of Ephron son of Zohar the Hittite, [10]the field Abraham had bought from the Hittites.[g] There Abraham was buried with his wife Sarah. [11]After Abraham's death, God blessed his son Isaac, who then lived near Beer Lahai Roi.

Ishmael's Sons

[12]This is the account of Abraham's son Ishmael, whom Sarah's maidservant, Hagar the Egyptian, bore to Abraham.

[13]These are the names of the sons of Ishmael, listed in the order of their birth: Nebaioth the firstborn of Ishmael, Kedar, Adbeel, Mibsam, [14]Mishma, Dumah, Massa, [15]Hadad, Tema, Jetur, Naphish and Kedemah. [16]These were the sons of Ishmael, and these are the names of the twelve tribal rulers according to their settlements and camps. [17]Altogether, Ishmael lived a hundred and thirty-seven years. He breathed his last and died, and he was gathered to his people. [18]His descendants settled in the area from Havilah to Shur, near the border of

g10 Or *the sons of Heth*

מִצְרַיִם בֹּאֲכָה אַשּׁוּרָה עַל־פְּנֵי כָל־אֶחָיו נָפָל׃
he-was-hostile brothers-of-him all-of faces-of to to-Asshur to-go-you Egypt

וְאֵלֶּה תּוֹלְדֹת יִצְחָק בֶּן־אַבְרָהָם אַבְרָהָם הוֹלִיד אֶת־יִצְחָק׃
Isaac *** he-fathered Abraham Abraham son-of Isaac lines-of and-these (19)

וַיְהִי יִצְחָק בֶּן־אַרְבָּעִים שָׁנָה בְּקַחְתּוֹ אֶת־רִבְקָה
Rebekah *** when-to-take-him year forty son-of Isaac and-he-was (20)

בַּת־בְּתוּאֵל הָאֲרַמִּי מִפַּדַּן אֲרָם אֲחוֹת לָבָן הָאֲרַמִּי
the-Aramean Laban sister-of Aram from-Paddan the-Aramean Bethuel daughter-of

לוֹ לְאִשָּׁה׃ וַיֶּעְתַּר יִצְחָק לַיהוָה לְנֹכַח אִשְׁתּוֹ
wife-of-him on-behalf-of to-Yahweh Isaac and-he-prayed (21) as-wife to-him

כִּי עֲקָרָה הִוא וַיֵּעָתֶר לוֹ יְהוָה וַתַּהַר רִבְקָה
Rebekah and-she-conceived Yahweh to-him and-he-answered-prayer she barren for

אִשְׁתּוֹ׃ וַיִּתְרֹצְצוּ הַבָּנִים בְּקִרְבָּהּ וַתֹּאמֶר אִם־כֵּן
so if and-she-said within-her the-babies and-they-jostled (22) wife-of-him

לָמָּה זֶּה אָנֹכִי וַתֵּלֶךְ לִדְרֹשׁ אֶת־יְהוָה׃ וַיֹּאמֶר יְהוָה לָהּ
to-her Yahweh and-he-said (23) Yahweh *** to-inquire so-she-went me this why?

שְׁנֵי גֹיִים° בְּבִטְנֵךְ וּשְׁנֵי לְאֻמִּים מִמֵּעַיִךְ
from-within-you peoples and-two-of in-womb-of-you nations two-of

יִפָּרֵדוּ וּלְאֹם מִלְאֹם יֶאֱמָץ וְרַב
and-older he will be stronger than-people and-people they-will-be-separated

יַעֲבֹד צָעִיר׃ וַיִּמְלְאוּ יָמֶיהָ לָלֶדֶת
to-give-birth days-of-her when-they-were-fulfilled (24) younger he-will-serve

וְהִנֵּה תוֹמִם בְּבִטְנָהּ׃ וַיֵּצֵא הָרִאשׁוֹן אַדְמוֹנִי
red the-first and-he-came-out (25) in-womb-of-her twin-boys now-see!

כֻּלּוֹ כְּאַדֶּרֶת שֵׂעָר וַיִּקְרְאוּ שְׁמוֹ עֵשָׂו׃
Esau name-of-him so-they-called hair like-garment-of whole-of-him

וְאַחֲרֵי־כֵן יָצָא אָחִיו וְיָדוֹ אֹחֶזֶת
grasping with-hand-of-him brother-of-him he-came-out this and-after (26)

בַּעֲקֵב עֵשָׂו וַיִּקְרָא שְׁמוֹ יַעֲקֹב וְיִצְחָק בֶּן־שִׁשִּׁים שָׁנָה
year sixty son-of now-Isaac Jacob name-of-him so-he-called Esau on-heel-of

בְּלֶדֶת אֹתָם׃ וַיִּגְדְּלוּ הַנְּעָרִים וַיְהִי עֵשָׂו אִישׁ
man Esau and-he-became the-boys and-they-grew-up (27) them when-to-bear

יֹדֵעַ צַיִד אִישׁ שָׂדֶה וְיַעֲקֹב אִישׁ תָּם יֹשֵׁב אֹהָלִים׃
tents staying quiet man-of while-Jacob field man-of hunting being-skilled

וַיֶּאֱהַב יִצְחָק אֶת־עֵשָׂו כִּי־צַיִד בְּפִיו וְרִבְקָה אֹהֶבֶת
loving but-Rebekah in-taste-of-him game for Esau *** Isaac now-he-loved (28)

אֶת־יַעֲקֹב׃ וַיָּזֶד יַעֲקֹב נָזִיד וַיָּבֹא עֵשָׂו מִן־הַשָּׂדֶה
the-field from Esau and-he-came stew Jacob now-he-cooked (29) Jacob ***

Egypt, as you go toward
Asshur. And they lived in hostility toward all their brothers.

Jacob and Esau

19This is the account of
Abraham's son Isaac.

Abraham became the father
of Isaac, 20and Isaac was forty
years old when he married Rebekah daughter of Bethuel the
Aramean from Paddan Aram[h]
and sister of Laban the Aramean.
21Isaac prayed to the LORD on
behalf of his wife, because she
was barren. The LORD an-
swered his prayer, and his
wife Rebekah became preg-
nant. 22The babies jostled each
other within her, and she said,
"Why is this happening to
me?" So she went to inquire of
the LORD.
23The LORD said to her,

"Two nations are in your womb,
and two peoples from within you will be separated;
one people will be stronger than the other,
and the older will serve the younger."

24When the time came for
her to give birth, there were
twin boys in her womb. 25The
first to come out was red, and
his whole body was like a
hairy garment; so they named
him Esau.[i] 26After this, his
brother came out, with his
hand grasping Esau's heel; so
he was named Jacob.[j] Isaac
was sixty years old when Rebekah gave birth to them.
27The boys grew up, and
Esau became a skillful hunter,
a man of the open country,
while Jacob was a quiet man,
staying among the tents.
28Isaac, who had a taste for
wild game, loved Esau, but Rebekah loved Jacob.
29Once when Jacob was
cooking some stew, Esau came
in from the open country,

h20 That is, Northwest Mesopotamia
i25 *Esau* may mean *hairy;* he is also called Edom, which means *red.*
j26 *Jacob* means *he grasps the heel* (figuratively, *he deceives*).

°23 ק גוים

וְהוּא עָיֵף׃ וַיֹּאמֶר עֵשָׂו אֶל־יַעֲקֹב הַלְעִיטֵנִי נָא מִן־
some-of now! let-eat-me! Jacob to Esau and-he-said (30) famished and-he

הָאָדֹם הָאָדֹם הַזֶּה כִּי עָיֵף אָנֹכִי עַל־כֵּן קָרָא־
he-called this for I famished for the-that the-red-stew the-red-stew

שְׁמוֹ אֱדוֹם׃ וַיֹּאמֶר יַעֲקֹב מִכְרָה כַיּוֹם אֶת־בְּכֹרָתְךָ
birthright-of-you *** on-the-day sell! Jacob and-he-said (31) Edom name-of-him

לִי׃ וַיֹּאמֶר עֵשָׂו הִנֵּה אָנֹכִי הוֹלֵךְ לָמוּת וְלָמָּה־זֶּה לִי בְּכֹרָה׃
birthright to-me this so-what? to-die going I see! Esau and-he-said (32) to-me

וַיֹּאמֶר יַעֲקֹב הִשָּׁבְעָה לִּי כַּיּוֹם וַיִּשָּׁבַע לוֹ וַיִּמְכֹּר
so-he-sold to-him so-he-swore on-the-day to-me swear! Jacob but-he-said (33)

אֶת־בְּכֹרָתוֹ לְיַעֲקֹב׃ וְיַעֲקֹב נָתַן לְעֵשָׂו לֶחֶם
bread to-Esau he-gave then-Jacob (34) to-Jacob birthright-of-him ***

וּנְזִיד עֲדָשִׁים וַיֹּאכַל וַיֵּשְׁתְּ וַיָּקָם וַיֵּלַךְ
and-he-left then-he-got-up and-he-drank and-he-ate lentils and-stew-of

וַיִּבֶז עֵשָׂו אֶת־הַבְּכֹרָה׃ וַיְהִי רָעָב בָּאָרֶץ
in-the-land famine now-he-was (26:1) the-birthright *** Esau so-he-despised

מִלְּבַד הָרָעָב הָרִאשׁוֹן אֲשֶׁר הָיָה בִּימֵי אַבְרָהָם וַיֵּלֶךְ
so-he-went Abraham in-days-of he-was that the-earlier the-famine besides

יִצְחָק אֶל־אֲבִימֶּלֶךְ* מֶלֶךְ־פְּלִשְׁתִּים גְּרָרָה׃ וַיֵּרָא אֵלָיו
to-him and-he-appeared (2) in-Gerar Philistines king-of Abimelech to Isaac

יְהוָה וַיֹּאמֶר אַל־תֵּרֵד מִצְרָיְמָה שְׁכֹן בָּאָרֶץ אֲשֶׁר אֹמַר
I-tell where in-the-land live! to-Egypt you-go-down not and-he-said Yahweh

אֵלֶיךָ׃ גּוּר בָּאָרֶץ הַזֹּאת וְאֶהְיֶה עִמְּךָ וַאֲבָרְכֶךָּ
and-I-will-bless-you with-you and-I-will-be the-this in-the-land stay! (3) to-you

כִּי־לְךָ וּלְזַרְעֲךָ אֶתֵּן אֶת־כָּל־הָאֲרָצֹת
the-lands all-of *** I-will-give and-to-descendant-of-you to-you for

הָאֵל וַהֲקִמֹתִי אֶת־הַשְּׁבֻעָה אֲשֶׁר נִשְׁבַּעְתִּי לְאַבְרָהָם
to-Abraham I-swore that the-oath *** and-I-will-confirm the-these

אָבִיךָ׃ וְהִרְבֵּיתִי אֶת־זַרְעֲךָ כְּכוֹכְבֵי
as-stars-of descendant-of-you *** and-I-will-increase (4) father-of-you

הַשָּׁמַיִם וְנָתַתִּי לְזַרְעֲךָ אֵת כָּל־הָאֲרָצֹת הָאֵל
the-these the-lands all-of *** to-descendant-of-you and-I-will-give the-skies

וְהִתְבָּרְכוּ בְזַרְעֲךָ כֹּל גּוֹיֵי הָאָרֶץ׃
the-earth nations-of all-of through-offspring-of-you and-they-will-be-blessed

עֵקֶב אֲשֶׁר־שָׁמַע אַבְרָהָם בְּקֹלִי וַיִּשְׁמֹר מִשְׁמַרְתִּי
requirements-of-me and-he-kept to-voice-me Abraham he-obeyed that because (5)

מִצְוֹתַי חֻקּוֹתַי וְתוֹרֹתָי׃ וַיֵּשֶׁב יִצְחָק בִּגְרָר׃
in-Gerar Isaac so-he-stayed (6) and-laws-of-me decrees-of-me commands-of-me

famished. 30He said to Jacob,
"Quick, let me have some of
that red stew! I'm famished!"
(That is why he was also called
Edom.[k])
31Jacob replied, "First sell me
your birthright."
32"Look, I am about to die,"
Esau said. "What good is the
birthright to me?"
33But Jacob said, "Swear to
me first." So he swore an oath
to him, selling his birthright
to Jacob.
34Then Jacob gave Esau some
bread and some lentil stew. He
ate and drank, and then got up
and left.
So Esau despised his birthright.

Isaac and Abimelech

26 Now there was a fam-
ine in the land—
besides the earlier famine of
Abraham's time—and Isaac
went to Abimelech king of the
Philistines in Gerar. 2The LORD
appeared to Isaac and said,
"Do not go down to Egypt;
live in the land where I tell
you to live. 3Stay in this land
for a while, and I will be with
you and will bless you. For to
you and your descendants I
will give all these lands and
will confirm the oath I swore
to your father Abraham. 4I will
make your descendants as numerous as the stars in the sky
and will give them all these
lands, and through your
offspring all nations on earth
will be blessed, 5because Abraham obeyed me and kept my
requirements, my commands,
my decrees and my laws." 6So
Isaac stayed in Gerar.

[k]30 *Edom* means *red*.

*1 Most mss have no *dagesh* in the *mem* (מ).

וַיִּשְׁאֲלוּ אַנְשֵׁי הַמָּקוֹם לְאִשְׁתּוֹ וַיֹּאמֶר
then-he-said about-wife-of-him the-place men-of when-they-asked (7)

אֲחֹתִי הִוא כִּי יָרֵא לֵאמֹר אִשְׁתִּי פֶּן־ יַהַרְגֻנִי אַנְשֵׁי
men-of they-kill-me lest wife-of-me to-say he-was-afraid for she sister-of-me

הַמָּקוֹם עַל־ רִבְקָה כִּי־ טוֹבַת מַרְאֶה הִיא׃ וַיְהִי
and-he-was (8) she sight beautiful-of for Rebekah on-account-of the-place

כִּי אָרְכוּ־ לוֹ שָׁם הַיָּמִים וַיַּשְׁקֵף אֲבִימֶלֶךְ מֶלֶךְ
king-of Abimelech that-he-looked the-days there to-him they-were-long when

פְּלִשְׁתִּים בְּעַד הַחַלּוֹן וַיַּרְא וְהִנֵּה יִצְחָק מְצַחֵק אֵת
*** caressing Isaac and-see! and-he-saw the-window down-from Philistines

רִבְקָה אִשְׁתּוֹ׃ וַיִּקְרָא אֲבִימֶלֶךְ לְיִצְחָק וַיֹּאמֶר אַךְ
really and-he-said to-Isaac Abimelech and-he-summoned (9) wife-of-him Rebekah

הִנֵּה אִשְׁתְּךָ הִוא וְאֵיךְ אָמַרְתָּ אֲחֹתִי הִוא וַיֹּאמֶר אֵלָיו
to-him and-he-answered she sister-of-me you-said so-why? she wife-of-you see!

יִצְחָק כִּי אָמַרְתִּי פֶּן־ אָמוּת עָלֶיהָ׃ וַיֹּאמֶר
then-he-said (10) because-of-her I-will-die perhaps I-thought because Isaac

אֲבִימֶלֶךְ מַה־ זֹּאת עָשִׂיתָ לָּנוּ כִּמְעַט שָׁכַב אַחַד הָעָם אֶת־
with the-people one-of he-slept might-well to-us you-did this what? Abimelech

אִשְׁתֶּךָ וְהֵבֵאתָ עָלֵינוּ אָשָׁם׃ וַיְצַו אֲבִימֶלֶךְ אֶת־
*** Abimelech so-he-ordered (11) guilt upon-us and-you-brought wife-of-you

כָּל־ הָעָם לֵאמֹר הַנֹּגֵעַ בָּאִישׁ הַזֶּה
the-this on-the-man the-one-molesting to-say the-people all-of

וּבְאִשְׁתּוֹ מוֹת יוּמָת׃ וַיִּזְרַע יִצְחָק
Isaac and-he-planted-seed (12) he-will-be-killed to-kill or-on-wife-of-him

בָּאָרֶץ הַהִוא וַיִּמְצָא בַּשָּׁנָה הַהִוא מֵאָה שְׁעָרִים
times hundred the-that in-the-year and-he-reaped the-that in-the-land

וַיְבָרְכֵהוּ יְהוָה׃ וַיִּגְדַּל הָאִישׁ וַיֵּלֶךְ הָלוֹךְ
to-grow and-he-grew the-man and-he-became-rich (13) Yahweh for-he-blessed-him

וְגָדֵל עַד כִּי־ גָדַל מְאֹד׃ וַיְהִי־ לוֹ
to-him and-he-was (14) very he-became-wealthy when until more-rich

מִקְנֵה־ צֹאן וּמִקְנֵה בָקָר וַעֲבֻדָּה רַבָּה וַיְקַנְאוּ
and-they-envied many and-servant cattle and-possession-of flock possession-of

אֹתוֹ פְּלִשְׁתִּים׃ וְכָל־ הַבְּאֵרֹת אֲשֶׁר חָפְרוּ עַבְדֵי אָבִיו
father-of-him servanst-of they-dug that the-wells so-all-of (15) Philistines him

בִּימֵי אַבְרָהָם אָבִיו סִתְּמוּם פְּלִשְׁתִּים
Philistines they-stopped-up-them father-of-him Abraham in-days-of

וַיְמַלְאוּם עָפָר׃ וַיֹּאמֶר אֲבִימֶלֶךְ אֶל־ יִצְחָק לֵךְ
move-away! Isaac to Abimelech then-he-said (16) earth and-they-filled-them

7 When the men of that place
asked him about his wife, he
said, "She is my sister," because he was afraid to say,
"She is my wife." He thought,
"The men of this place might
kill me on account of Rebekah,
because she is beautiful."
8 When Isaac had been there
a long time, Abimelech king of
the Philistines looked down
from a window and saw Isaac
caressing his wife Rebekah.
9 So Abimelech summoned
Isaac and said, "She is really
your wife! Why did you say,
'She is my sister'?"
Isaac answered him, "Be-
cause I thought I might lose
my life on account of her."
10 Then Abimelech said,
"What is this you have done
to us? One of the men might
well have slept with your wife,
and you would have brought
guilt upon us."
11 So Abimelech gave orders
to all the people: "Anyone
who molests this man or his
wife shall surely be put to
death."
12 Isaac planted crops in that
land and the same year reaped
a hundredfold, because the
LORD blessed him. 13 The man
became rich, and his wealth
continued to grow until he
became very wealthy. 14 He
had so many flocks and herds
and servants that the Philistines envied him. 15 So all the
wells that his father's servants
had dug in the time of his father Abraham, the Philistines
stopped up, filling them with
earth.
16 Then Abimelech said to
Isaac, "Move away from us;

מֵעִמָּנוּ כִּֽי־ עָצַֽמְתָּ מִמֶּנּוּ מְאֹֽד׃ וַיֵּלֶךְ מִשָּׁם יִצְחָק
Isaac from-there so-he-moved (17) more than-us you-are-powerful for from-us

וַיִּחַן בְּנַֽחַל־ גְּרָר וַיֵּשֶׁב שָֽׁם׃ וַיָּשָׁב
and-he-returned (18) there and-he-settled Gerar in-valley-of and-he-camped

יִצְחָק וַיַּחְפֹּר׀ אֶת־ בְּאֵרֹת הַמַּיִם אֲשֶׁר חָֽפְרוּ בִּימֵי אַבְרָהָם
Abraham in-days-of they-dug that the-water wells-of *** and-he-reopened Isaac

אָבִיו וַיְסַתְּמוּם פְּלִשְׁתִּים אַחֲרֵי מוֹת אַבְרָהָם
Abraham death-of after Philistines and-they-stopped-up-them father-of-him

וַיִּקְרָא לָהֶן שֵׁמוֹת כַּשֵּׁמֹת אֲשֶׁר־ קָרָא לָהֶן
to-them he-called that same-as-the-names names to-them and-he-called

אָבִֽיו׃ וַיַּחְפְּרוּ עַבְדֵֽי־ יִצְחָק בַּנָּחַל וַיִּמְצְאוּ־
and-they-found in-the-valley Isaac servants-of and-they-dug (19) father-of-him

שָׁם בְּאֵר מַיִם חַיִּֽים׃ וַיָּרִיבוּ רֹעֵי גְרָר עִם־
with Gerar ones-herding-of but-they-quarreled (20) fresh water well-of there

רֹעֵי יִצְחָק לֵאמֹר לָנוּ הַמָּיִם וַיִּקְרָא שֵֽׁם־ הַבְּאֵר
the-well name-of so-he-called the-water to-us to-say Isaac ones-herding-of

עֵשֶׂק כִּי הִֽתְעַשְּׂקוּ עִמּֽוֹ׃ וַֽיַּחְפְּרוּ בְּאֵר אַחֶרֶת
another well then-they-dug (21) with-him they-disputed for Esek

וַיָּרִיבוּ גַּם־ עָלֶיהָ וַיִּקְרָא שְׁמָהּ שִׂטְנָֽה׃
Sitnah name-of-her so-he-called over-her also but-they-quarreled

וַיַּעְתֵּק מִשָּׁם וַיַּחְפֹּר בְּאֵר אַחֶרֶת וְלֹא רָבוּ
they-quarreled and-not another well and-he-dug from-there so-he-moved (22)

עָלֶיהָ וַיִּקְרָא שְׁמָהּ רְחֹבוֹת וַיֹּאמֶר כִּֽי־ עַתָּה הִרְחִיב
he-gave-room now for and-he-said Rehoboth name-of-her so-he-called over-her

יְהוָה לָנוּ וּפָרִינוּ בָאָֽרֶץ׃ וַיַּעַל מִשָּׁם בְּאֵר
Beer from-there and-he-went (23) in-the-land and-we-will-flourish to-us Yahweh

שָֽׁבַע׃ וַיֵּרָא אֵלָיו יְהוָה בַּלַּיְלָה הַהוּא וַיֹּאמֶר
and-he-said the-that in-the-night Yahweh to-him and-he-appeared (24) Sheba

אָנֹכִי אֱלֹהֵי אַבְרָהָם אָבִיךָ אַל־ תִּירָא כִּֽי־ אִתְּךָ אָנֹכִי וּבֵרַכְתִּיךָ
and-I-will-bless-you I with-you for you-fear not father-of-you Abraham God-of I

וְהִרְבֵּיתִי אֶֽת־ זַרְעֲךָ בַּעֲבוּר אַבְרָהָם עַבְדִּֽי׃
servant-of-me Abraham for-sake-of descendant-of-you *** and-I-will-increase

וַיִּבֶן שָׁם מִזְבֵּחַ וַיִּקְרָא בְּשֵׁם יְהוָה וַיֶּט־
and-he-pitched Yahweh on-name-of and-he-called altar there so-he-built (25)

שָׁם אָהֳלוֹ וַיִּכְרוּ־ שָׁם עַבְדֵֽי־ יִצְחָק בְּאֵֽר׃ וַאֲבִימֶלֶךְ
and-Abimelech (26) well Isaac servants-of there and-they-dug tent-of-him there

הָלַךְ אֵלָיו מִגְּרָר וַאֲחֻזַּת מֵֽרֵעֵהוּ וּפִיכֹל שַׂר־
commander-of and-Phicol adviser-of-him with-Ahuzzath from-Gerar to-him he-came

you have become too powerful
for us."
17 So Isaac moved away from
there and encamped in the
Valley of Gerar and settled
there. 18 Isaac reopened the
wells that had been dug in the
time of his father Abraham,
which the Philistines had
stopped up after Abraham
died, and he gave them the
same names his father had
given them.
19 Isaac's servants dug in the
valley and discovered a well of
fresh water there. 20 But the
herdsmen of Gerar quarreled
with Isaac's herdsmen and
said, "The water is ours!" So
he named the well Esek,[l] because they disputed with him.
21 Then they dug another well,
but they quarreled over that
one also; so he named it Sitnah.[m] 22 He moved on from
there and dug another well,
and no one quarreled over it.
He named it Rehoboth,[n] saying, "Now the LORD has given
us room and we will flourish
in the land."
23 From there he went up to
Beersheba. 24 That night the
LORD appeared to him and
said, "I am the God of your
father Abraham. Do not be
afraid, for I am with you; I will
bless you and will increase the
number of your descendants
for the sake of my servant
Abraham."
25 Isaac built an altar there
and called on the name of the
LORD. There he pitched his
tent, and there his servants
dug a well.
26 Meanwhile, Abimelech
had come to him from Gerar,
with Ahuzzath his personal
adviser and Phicol the commander of his forces. 27 Isaac

[l] 20 *Esek* means *dispute.*
[m] 21 *Sitnah* means *opposition.*
[n] 22 *Rehoboth* means *room.*

צְבָאֽוֹ׃ וַיֹּאמֶר אֲלֵהֶם יִצְחָק מַדּוּעַ בָּאתֶם אֵלָי וְאַתֶּם
since-you to-me you-came why? Isaac to-them and-he-asked (27) force-of-him

שְׂנֵאתֶם אֹתִי וַתְּשַׁלְּחוּנִי מֵאִתְּכֶֽם׃ וַיֹּאמְרוּ
and-they-answered (28) from-you and-you-sent-me to-me you-were-hostile

רָאוֹ רָאִינוּ כִּֽי־הָיָה יְהוָה ׀ עִמָּךְ וַנֹּאמֶר תְּהִי נָא אָלָה
oath now! let-her-be so-we-said with-you Yahweh he-was that we-saw to-see

בֵּינוֹתֵינוּ בֵּינֵינוּ וּבֵינֶךָ וְנִכְרְתָה בְרִית עִמָּֽךְ׃
with-you treaty so-let-us-make and-between-you between-us between-us

אִם־תַּעֲשֵׂה עִמָּנוּ רָעָה כַּאֲשֶׁר לֹא נְגַעֲנוּךָ וְכַאֲשֶׁר
and-just-as we-molested-you not just-as harm to-us you-will-do not (29)

עָשִׂינוּ עִמְּךָ רַק־טוֹב וַנְּשַׁלֵּחֲךָ בְּשָׁלוֹם אַתָּה עַתָּה בְּרוּךְ
being-blessed-of now you in-peace and-we-sent-you good only with-you we-did

יְהוָֽה׃ וַיַּעַשׂ לָהֶם מִשְׁתֶּה וַיֹּאכְלוּ וַיִּשְׁתּֽוּ׃
and-they-drank and-they-ate feast for-them so-he-made (30) Yahweh

וַיַּשְׁכִּימוּ בַבֹּקֶר וַיִּשָּׁבְעוּ אִישׁ לְאָחִיו
to-other-of-him man and-they-swore in-the-morning and-they-rose (31)

וַיְשַׁלְּחֵם יִצְחָק וַיֵּלְכוּ מֵאִתּוֹ בְּשָׁלֽוֹם׃ וַיְהִי ׀
and-he-was (32) in-peace from-him and-they-left Isaac and-he-sent-away-them

בַּיּוֹם הַהוּא וַיָּבֹאוּ עַבְדֵי יִצְחָק וַיַּגִּדוּ לוֹ
to-him and-they-told Isaac servants-of that-they-came the-that in-the-day

עַל־אֹדוֹת הַבְּאֵר אֲשֶׁר חָפָרוּ וַיֹּאמְרוּ לוֹ מָצָאנוּ מָֽיִם׃
water we-found to-him and-they-said they-dug that the-well matter-of about

וַיִּקְרָא אֹתָהּ שִׁבְעָה עַל־כֵּן שֵׁם־הָעִיר בְּאֵר שֶׁבַע עַד הַיּוֹם
the-day to Sheba Beer the-city name-of this for Shibah her and-he-called (33)

הַזֶּֽה׃ וַיְהִי עֵשָׂו בֶּן־אַרְבָּעִים שָׁנָה וַיִּקַּח אִשָּׁה אֶת־יְהוּדִית
Judith *** wife he-took year forty son-of Esau when-he-was (34) the-this

בַּת־בְּאֵרִי הַחִתִּי וְאֶת־בָּשְׂמַת בַּת־אֵילֹן הַחִתִּֽי׃
the-Hittite Elon daughter-of Basemath and the-Hittite Berri daughter-of

וַתִּהְיֶיןָ מֹרַת רוּחַ לְיִצְחָק וּלְרִבְקָֽה׃ וַיְהִי
and-he-was (27:1) and-to-Rebekah to-Isaac spirit grief-of and-they-were (35)

כִּֽי־זָקֵן יִצְחָק וַתִּכְהֶיןָ עֵינָיו מֵרְאֹת
than-to-see eyes-of-him and-they-were-weaker Isaac he-was-old when

וַיִּקְרָא אֶת־עֵשָׂו ׀ בְּנוֹ הַגָּדֹל וַיֹּאמֶר אֵלָיו בְּנִי
son-of-me to-him and-he-said the-older son-of-him Esau *** and-he-called

וַיֹּאמֶר אֵלָיו הִנֵּֽנִי׃ וַיֹּאמֶר הִנֵּה־נָא זָקַנְתִּי לֹא יָדַעְתִּי
I-know not I-am-old now! see! and-he-said (2) here-I to-him and-he-answered

יוֹם מוֹתִֽי׃ וְעַתָּה שָׂא־נָא כֵלֶיךָ תֶּלְיְךָ
quiver-of-you weapons-of-you now! take! and-now (3) death-of-me day-of

asked them, "Why have you
come to me, since you were
hostile to me and sent me
away?"
28They answered, "We saw
clearly that the LORD was with
you; so we said, 'There ought
to be a sworn agreement between us'–between us and
you. Let us make a treaty with
you 29that you will do us no
harm, just as we did not mo-
lest you but always treated you
well and sent you away in
peace. And now you are
blessed by the LORD."
30Isaac then made a feast for
them, and they ate and drank.
31Early the next morning the
men swore an oath to each
other. Then Isaac sent them on
their way, and they left him in
peace.
32That day Isaac's servants
came and told him about the
well they had dug. They said,
"We've found water!" 33He
called it Shibah,[o] and to this
day the name of the town has
been Beersheba.[p]
34When Esau was forty years
old, he married Judith daughter of Beeri the Hittite, and
also Basemath daughter of
Elon the Hittite. 35They were a
source of grief to Isaac and Rebekah.

Jacob Gets Isaac's Blessing

27 When Isaac was old
and his eyes were so
weak that he could no longer
see, he called for Esau his older
son and said to him, "My
son."
"Here I am," he answered.
2Isaac said, "I am now an old
man and don't know the day
of my death. 3Now then, get
your weapons–your quiver

[o]33 *Shibah* can mean *oath* or *seven.*
[p]33 *Beersheba* can mean *well of the oath* or *well of seven.*

וְקַשְׁתֶּךָ וְצֵא הַשָּׂדֶה וְצוּדָה לִי צֵידָה׃ וַעֲשֵׂה־

and-prepare! (4) game for-me and-hunt! the-country and-go-out! and-bow-of-you

לִי מַטְעַמִּים כַּאֲשֶׁר אָהַבְתִּי וְהָבִיאָה לִּי וְאֹכֵלָה בַּעֲבוּר

so-that so-I-may-eat to-me and-bring I-like just-as tasty-foods for-me

תְּבָרֶכְךָ נַפְשִׁי בְּטֶרֶם אָמוּת׃ וְרִבְקָה שֹׁמַעַת בְּדַבֵּר

as-to-speak listening now-Rebekah (5) I-die before self-of-me she-may-bless-you

יִצְחָק אֶל־ עֵשָׂו בְּנוֹ וַיֵּלֶךְ עֵשָׂו הַשָּׂדֶה לָצוּד צַיִד

game to-hunt the-country Esau and-he-left son-of-him Esau to Isaac

לְהָבִיא׃ וְרִבְקָה אָמְרָה אֶל־ יַעֲקֹב בְּנָהּ לֵאמֹר הִנֵּה

see! to-say son-of-her Jacob to she-said and-Rebekah (6) to-bring-back

שָׁמַעְתִּי אֶת־ אָבִיךָ מְדַבֵּר אֶל־עֵשָׂו אָחִיךָ לֵאמֹר׃ הָבִיאָה

bring! (7) to-say brother-of-you Esau to saying father-of-you *** I-overheard

לִי צַיִד וַעֲשֵׂה־ לִי מַטְעַמִּים וְאֹכֵלָה וַאֲבָרֶכְכָה

and-I-may-bless-you so-I-may-eat tasty-foods for-me and-prepare! game to-me

לִפְנֵי יְהוָה לִפְנֵי מוֹתִי׃ וְעַתָּה בְנִי שְׁמַע בְּקֹלִי

to-voice-of-me listen! son-of-me and-now (8) death-of-me before Yahweh before

לַאֲשֶׁר אֲנִי מְצַוָּה אֹתָךְ׃ לֶךְ־ נָא אֶל־ הַצֹּאן וְקַח־ לִי מִשָּׁם

from-there to-me and-bring! the-flock to now! go! (9) you telling I to-what

שְׁנֵי גְּדָיֵי עִזִּים טֹבִים וְאֶעֱשֶׂה אֹתָם מַטְעַמִּים

tasty-foods them so-I-can-prepare choice-ones goats kids-of two-of

לְאָבִיךָ כַּאֲשֶׁר אָהֵב׃ וְהֵבֵאתָ לְאָבִיךָ

to-father-of-you then-you-take (10) he-likes just-as for-father-of-you

וְאָכָל בַּעֲבֻר אֲשֶׁר יְבָרֶכְךָ לִפְנֵי מוֹתוֹ׃

death-of-him before he-may-bless-you then so-that so-he-can-eat

וַיֹּאמֶר יַעֲקֹב אֶל־רִבְקָה אִמּוֹ הֵן עֵשָׂו אָחִי אִישׁ שָׂעִר

hairy man brother-of-me Esau see! mother-of-him Rebekah to Jacob but-he-said (11)

וְאָנֹכִי אִישׁ חָלָק׃ אוּלַי יְמֻשֵּׁנִי אָבִי וְהָיִיתִי

and-I-appear father-of-me he-touches-me what-if? (12) smooth man but-I

בְעֵינָיו כִּמְתַעְתֵּעַ וְהֵבֵאתִי עָלַי קְלָלָה וְלֹא בְרָכָה׃

blessing and-not curse on-me then-I-would-bring as-tricking in-eyes-of-him

וַתֹּאמֶר לוֹ אִמּוֹ עָלַי קִלְלָתְךָ בְּנִי אַךְ

just son-of-me curse-of-you on-me mother-of-him to-him and-she-said (13)

שְׁמַע בְּקֹלִי וְלֵךְ קַח־ לִי׃ וַיֵּלֶךְ וַיִּקַּח

and-he-got so-he-went (14) for-me get! and-go! to-voice-of-me obey!

וַיָּבֵא לְאִמּוֹ וַתַּעַשׂ אִמּוֹ מַטְעַמִּים

tasty-foods mother-of-him and-she-prepared to-mother-of-him and-he-brought

כַּאֲשֶׁר אָהֵב אָבִיו׃ וַתִּקַּח רִבְקָה אֶת־ בִּגְדֵי עֵשָׂו

Esau clothes-of *** Rebekah then-she-took (15) father-of-him he-liked just-as

and bow—and go out to the open country to hunt some wild game for me. [4]Prepare me the kind of tasty food I like and bring it to me to eat, so that I may give you my blessing before I die."

[5]Now Rebekah was listening as Isaac spoke to his son Esau. When Esau left for the open country to hunt game and bring it back, [6]Rebekah said to her son Jacob, "Look, I overheard your father say to your brother Esau, [7]'Bring me some game and prepare me some tasty food to eat, so that I may give you my blessing in the presence of the LORD before I die.' [8]Now, my son, listen carefully and do what I tell you: [9]Go out to the flock and bring me two choice young goats, so I can prepare some tasty food for your father, just the way he likes it. [10]Then take it to your father to eat, so that he may give you his blessing before he dies."

[11]Jacob said to Rebekah his mother, "But my brother Esau is a hairy man, and I'm a man with smooth skin. [12]What if my father touches me? I would appear to be tricking him and would bring down a curse on myself rather than a blessing."

[13]His mother said to him, "My son, let the curse fall on me. Just do what I say; go and get them for me."

[14]So he went and got them and brought them to his mother, and she prepared some tasty food, just the way his father liked it. [15]Then Rebekah took the best clothes of

°3 ק ציד

בְּנָהּ הַגָּדֹל הַחֲמֻדֹת אֲשֶׁר אִתָּהּ בַּבָּיִת וַתַּלְבֵּשׁ

and-she-dressed in-the-house with-her that the-best-ones the-older son-of-her

אֶת־יַעֲקֹב בְּנָהּ הַקָּטָן׃ וְאֵת עֹרֹת גְּדָיֵי הָעִזִּים

the-goats kids-of skins-of and (16) the-younger son-of-her Jacob ***

הִלְבִּישָׁה עַל־יָדָיו וְעַל חֶלְקַת צַוָּארָיו׃

neck-of-him smooth-part-of and-over hands-of-him over and-she-covered

וַתִּתֵּן אֶת־הַמַּטְעַמִּים וְאֶת־הַלֶּחֶם אֲשֶׁר עָשָׂתָה

she-made that the-bread and the-tasty-foods *** and-she-handed (17)

בְּיַד יַעֲקֹב בְּנָהּ׃ וַיָּבֹא אֶל־אָבִיו וַיֹּאמֶר

and-he-said father-of-him to and-he-went (18) son-of-her Jacob to-hand-of

אָבִי וַיֹּאמֶר הִנֶּנִּי מִי אַתָּה בְּנִי׃ וַיֹּאמֶר

and-he-said (19) son-of-me you who? here-I and-he-answered father-of-me

יַעֲקֹב אֶל־אָבִיו אָנֹכִי עֵשָׂו בְּכֹרֶךָ עָשִׂיתִי כַּאֲשֶׁר דִּבַּרְתָּ אֵלָי

to-me you-told just-as I-did firstborn-of-you Esau I father-of-him to Jacob

קוּם־נָא שְׁבָה וְאָכְלָה מִצֵּידִי בַּעֲבוּר תְּבָרְכַנִּי

she-may-bless-me so-that from-game-of-me and-eat! sit-up! now! rise!

נַפְשֶׁךָ׃ וַיֹּאמֶר יִצְחָק אֶל־בְּנוֹ מַה־זֶּה מִהַרְתָּ

you-were-quick this how? son-of-him to Isaac but-he-asked (20) self-of-you

לִמְצֹא בְּנִי וַיֹּאמֶר כִּי הִקְרָה יְהוָה אֱלֹהֶיךָ לְפָנָי׃

to-me God-of-you Yahweh he-gave-success for and-he-replied son-of-me to-find

וַיֹּאמֶר יִצְחָק אֶל־יַעֲקֹב גְּשָׁה־נָּא וַאֲמֻשְׁךָ בְּנִי

son-of-me so-I-can-touch-you now! come-near! Jacob to Isaac then-he-said (21)

הַאַתָּה זֶה בְּנִי עֵשָׂו אִם־לֹא׃ וַיִּגַּשׁ יַעֲקֹב אֶל־יִצְחָק

Isaac to Jacob so-he-went-close (22) not or Esau son-of-me really whether-you

אָבִיו וַיְמֻשֵּׁהוּ וַיֹּאמֶר הַקֹּל קוֹל יַעֲקֹב

Jacob voice-of the-voice and-he-said and-he-touched-him father-of-him

וְהַיָּדַיִם יְדֵי עֵשָׂו׃ וְלֹא הִכִּירוֹ כִּי־הָיוּ

they-were for he-recognized-him and-not (23) Esau hands-of but-the-hands

יָדָיו כִּידֵי עֵשָׂו אָחִיו שְׂעִרֹת וַיְבָרְכֵהוּ׃

so-he-blessed-him hairy-ones brother-of-him Esau like-hands-of hands-of-him

וַיֹּאמֶר אַתָּה זֶה בְּנִי עֵשָׂו וַיֹּאמֶר אָנִי׃ וַיֹּאמֶר

so-he-said (25) I and-he-replied Esau son-of-me really you and-he-asked (24)

הַגִּשָׁה לִּי וְאֹכְלָה מִצֵּיד בְּנִי לְמַעַן תְּבָרֶכְךָ

she-may-bless-you so-that son-of-me from-game-of so-I-may-eat to-me bring!

נַפְשִׁי וַיַּגֶּשׁ־לוֹ וַיֹּאכַל וַיָּבֵא לוֹ יַיִן

wine to-him and-he-brought and-he-ate to-him so-he-brought self-of-me

וַיֵּשְׁתְּ׃ וַיֹּאמֶר אֵלָיו יִצְחָק אָבִיו גְּשָׁה־נָּא

now! come-here! father-of-him Isaac to-him then-he-said (26) and-he-drank

Esau her older son, which she
had in the house, and put
them on her younger son
Jacob. [16]She also covered his
hands and the smooth part of
his neck with the goatskins.
[17]Then she handed to her son
Jacob the tasty food and the
bread she had made.
[18]He went to his father and
said, "My father."
"Yes, my son," he answered. "Who is it?"
[19]Jacob said to his father, "I
am Esau your firstborn. I have
done as you told me. Please sit
up and eat some of my game
so that you may give me your
blessing."
[20]Isaac asked his son, "How
did you find it so quickly, my
son?"
"The LORD your God gave
me success," he replied.
[21]Then Isaac said to Jacob,
"Come near so I can touch
you, my son, to know whether
you really are my son Esau or
not."
[22]Jacob went close to his father Isaac, who touched him
and said, "The voice is the
voice of Jacob, but the hands
are the hands of Esau." [23]He
did not recognize him, for his
hands were hairy like those of
his brother Esau; so he blessed
him. [24]"Are you really my son
Esau?" he asked.
"I am," he replied.
[25]Then he said, "My son,
bring me some of your game
to eat, so that I may give you
my blessing."
Jacob brought it to him and
he ate; and he brought some
wine and he drank. [26]Then his
father Isaac said to him,

וּשְׁקָה־ לִּי בְּנִי׃ וַיִּגַּשׁ וַיִּשַּׁק־ לוֹ וַיָּרַח
and-he-smelled on-him and-he-kissed so-he-went (27) son-of-me on-me and-kiss!

אֶת־ רֵיחַ בְּגָדָיו וַיְבָרְכֵהוּ וַיֹּאמֶר רְאֵה רֵיחַ
smell-of see! and-he-said and-he-blessed-him clothes-of-him smell-of ***

בְּנִי כְּרֵיחַ שָׂדֶה אֲשֶׁר בֵּרֲכוֹ יְהוָה׃ וְיִתֶּן־
now-may-he-give (28) Yahweh he-blessed-him that field like-smell-of son-of-me

לְךָ הָאֱלֹהִים מִטַּל הַשָּׁמַיִם וּמִשְׁמַנֵּי הָאָרֶץ
the-earth and-from-riches-of the-heavens from-dew-of the-God to-you

וְרֹב דָּגָן וְתִירֹשׁ׃ יַעַבְדוּךָ עַמִּים
nations may-they-serve-you (29) and-new-wine grain and-abundance-of

וְיִשְׁתַּחֲוֻ לְךָ לְאֻמִּים הֱוֵה גְבִיר לְאַחֶיךָ
over-brothers-of-you lord be! peoples to-you and-may-they-bow-down

°וְיִשְׁתַּחֲוּוּ* לְךָ בְּנֵי אִמֶּךָ אֹרְרֶיךָ
ones-cursing-you mother-of-you sons-of to-you and-may-they-bow-down

אָרוּר וּמְבָרֲכֶיךָ בָּרוּךְ׃ וַיְהִי כַּאֲשֶׁר
just-as and-he-was (30) being-blessed and-ones-blessing-you being-cursed

כִּלָּה יִצְחָק לְבָרֵךְ אֶת־יַעֲקֹב וַיְהִי אַךְ יָצֹא יָצָא
he-left to-leave scarcely and-he-was Jacob *** to-bless Isaac he-finished

יַעֲקֹב מֵאֵת פְּנֵי יִצְחָק אָבִיו וְעֵשָׂו אָחִיו בָּא
he-came brother-of-him that-Esau father-of-him Isaac presence-of from Jacob

מִצֵּידוֹ׃ וַיַּעַשׂ גַּם־ הוּא מַטְעַמִּים וַיָּבֵא
and-he-brought tasty-foods he also and-he-prepared (31) from-hunt-of-him

לְאָבִיו וַיֹּאמֶר לְאָבִיו יָקֻם אָבִי
father-of-me let-him-sit-up to-father-of-him and-he-said to-father-of-him

וְיֹאכַל מִצֵּיד בְּנוֹ בַּעֲבוּר תְּבָרְכַנִּי נַפְשֶׁךָ׃
self-of-you she-may-bless-me so-that son-of-him from-game-of and-let-him-eat

וַיֹּאמֶר לוֹ יִצְחָק אָבִיו מִי־ אָתָּה וַיֹּאמֶר אֲנִי
I and-he-answered you who? father-of-him Isaac to-him and-he-asked (32)

בִּנְךָ בְּכֹרְךָ עֵשָׂו׃ וַיֶּחֱרַד יִצְחָק חֲרָדָה גְּדֹלָה
great tremble Isaac and-he-trembled (33) Esau firstborn-of-you son-of-you

עַד־ מְאֹד וַיֹּאמֶר מִי־ אֵפוֹא הוּא הַצָּד־ צַיִד וַיָּבֵא
and-he-brought game the-one-hunting he then who? and-he-said violence to

לִי וָאֹכַל מִכֹּל בְּטֶרֶם תָּבוֹא וָאֲבָרְכֵהוּ גַּם־
indeed and-I-blessed-him you-came just-before from-all and-I-ate to-me

בָּרוּךְ יִהְיֶה׃ כִּשְׁמֹעַ עֵשָׂו אֶת־ דִּבְרֵי אָבִיו
father-of-him words-of *** Esau when-to-hear (34) he-will-be being-blessed

וַיִּצְעַק צְעָקָה גְּדֹלָה וּמָרָה עַד־ מְאֹד וַיֹּאמֶר לְאָבִיו
to-father-of-him and-he-said very to and-bitter loud cry then-he-cried

"Come here, my son, and kiss
me."
27 So he went to him and
kissed him. When Isaac
caught the smell of his clothes,
he blessed him and said,

"Ah, the smell of my son
is like the smell of a field
that the LORD has
blessed.
28 May God give you of
heaven's dew
and of earth's richness—
an abundance of grain
and new wine.
29 May nations serve you
and peoples bow down
to you.
Be lord over your brothers,
and may the sons of
your mother bow
down to you.
May those who curse you
be cursed
and those who bless you
be blessed."

30 After Isaac finished
blessing him and Jacob had
scarcely left his father's presence, his brother Esau came in
from hunting. 31 He too prepared some tasty food and
brought it to his father. Then
he said to him, "My father, sit
up and eat some of my game,
so that you may give me your
blessing."
32 His father Isaac asked him,
"Who are you?"
"I am your son," he an-
swered, "your firstborn,
Esau."
33 Isaac trembled violently
and said, "Who was it, then,
that hunted game and brought
it to me? I ate it just before you
came and I blessed him—and
indeed he will be blessed!"
34 When Esau heard his father's words, he burst out with
a loud and bitter cry and said

*29 Most mss have no *dagesh* in the first *vav* (וּ־).

°29 ק וישתחוו

בָּרְכֵנִי גַם־ אָנִי אָבִי׃ וַיֹּאמֶר בָּא אָחִיךָ

brother-of-you he-came but-he-said (35) father-of-me me also bless-me!

בְּמִרְמָה וַיִּקַּח בִּרְכָתֶךָ׃ וַיֹּאמֶר הֲכִי קָרָא

he-called rightly? and-he-said (36) blessing-of-you and-he-took in-deceit

שְׁמוֹ יַעֲקֹב וַיַּעְקְבֵנִי זֶה פַעֲמַיִם אֶת־ בְּכֹרָתִי

birthright-of-me *** two-times this now-he-deceived-me Jacob name-of-him

לָקָח וְהִנֵּה עַתָּה לָקַח בִּרְכָתִי וַיֹּאמַר הֲלֹא־ אָצַלְתָּ

you-reserved not? then-he-asked blessing-of-me he-took now and-see! he-took

לִּי בְּרָכָה׃ וַיַּעַן יִצְחָק וַיֹּאמֶר לְעֵשָׂו הֵן גְּבִיר

lord see! to-Esau and-he-said Isaac and-he-answered (37) blessing for-me

שַׂמְתִּיו לָךְ וְאֶת־ כָּל־ אֶחָיו נָתַתִּי לוֹ לַעֲבָדִים

as-servants to-him I-made brothers-of-him all-of and over-you I-made-him

וְדָגָן וְתִירֹשׁ סְמַכְתִּיו וּלְכָה אֵפוֹא מָה אֶעֱשֶׂה בְּנִי׃

son-of-me can-I-do what? then so-for-you I-sustained-him and-new-wine and-grain

וַיֹּאמֶר עֵשָׂו אֶל־ אָבִיו הַבְרָכָה אַחַת הִוא־ לְךָ אָבִי

father-of-me to-you she one blessing? father-of-him to Esau and-he-said (38)

בָּרְכֵנִי גַם־ אָנִי אָבִי וַיִּשָּׂא עֵשָׂו קֹלוֹ וַיֵּבְךְּ׃

and-he-wept voice-of-him Esau then-he-lifted father-of-me me also bless-me!

וַיַּעַן יִצְחָק אָבִיו וַיֹּאמֶר אֵלָיו הִנֵּה מִשְׁמַנֵּי

from-riches-of see! to-him and-he-said father-of-him Isaac and-he-answered (39)

הָאָרֶץ יִהְיֶה מוֹשָׁבֶךָ וּמִטַּל הַשָּׁמַיִם מֵעָל׃

above the-heavens and-from-dew-of dwelling-of-you he-will-be the-earth

וְעַל־ חַרְבְּךָ תִחְיֶה וְאֶת־ אָחִיךָ תַּעֲבֹד

you-will-serve brother-of-you and you-will-live sword-of-you and-by (40)

וְהָיָה כַּאֲשֶׁר תָּרִיד וּפָרַקְתָּ עֻלּוֹ

yoke-of-him then-you-will-throw you-grow-restless when but-he-will-be

מֵעַל צַוָּארֶךָ׃ וַיִּשְׂטֹם עֵשָׂו אֶת־ יַעֲקֹב עַל־

because-of Jacob *** Esau and-he-held-grudge (41) neck-of-you from-off

הַבְּרָכָה אֲשֶׁר בֵּרֲכוֹ אָבִיו וַיֹּאמֶר עֵשָׂו בְּלִבּוֹ

to-himself Esau and-he-said father-of-him he-blessed-him that the-blessing

יִקְרְבוּ יְמֵי אֵבֶל אָבִי וְאַהַרְגָה אֶת־ יַעֲקֹב

Jacob *** then-I-will-kill father-of-me mourning-of days-of they-are-near

אָחִי׃ וַיֻּגַּד לְרִבְקָה אֶת־ דִּבְרֵי עֵשָׂו בְּנָהּ

son-of-her Esau words-of *** to-Rebekah but-he-was-told (42) brother-of-me

הַגָּדֹל וַתִּשְׁלַח וַתִּקְרָא לְיַעֲקֹב בְּנָהּ הַקָּטָן

the-younger son-of-her for-Jacob and-she-called so-she-sent the-older

וַתֹּאמֶר אֵלָיו הִנֵּה עֵשָׂו אָחִיךָ מִתְנַחֵם לְךָ

about-you consoling-self brother-of you Esau see! to-him and-she-said

to his father, "Bless me—me too, my father!"

35But he said, "Your brother came deceitfully and took your blessing."

36Esau said, "Isn't he rightly named Jacob[q]? He has deceived me these two times: He took my birthright, and now he's taken my blessing!" Then he asked, "Haven't you reserved any blessing for me?"

37Isaac answered Esau, "I have made him lord over you and have made all his relatives his servants, and I have sustained him with grain and new wine. So what can I possibly do for you, my son?"

38Esau said to his father, "Do you have only one blessing, my father? Bless me too, my father!" Then Esau wept aloud.

39His father Isaac answered him,

"Your dwelling will be
away from the earth's
richness,
away from the dew of
heaven above.
40You will live by the sword
and you will serve your
brother.
But when you grow
restless,
you will throw his yoke
from off your neck."

Jacob Flees to Laban

41Esau held a grudge against Jacob because of the blessing his father had given him. He said to himself, "The days of mourning for my father are near; then I will kill my brother Jacob."

42When Rebekah was told what her older son Esau had said, she sent for her younger son Jacob and said to him, "Your brother Esau is consoling himself with the thought

q36 *Jacob* means *he grasps the heel* (figuratively, *he deceives*).

לְהָרְגֶךָ׃ וְעַתָּה בְנִי שְׁמַע בְּקֹלִי וְקוּם בְּרַח־
and-flee! and-rise! to-voice-of-me obey! son-of-me so-now (43) to-kill-you

לְךָ אֶל־ לָבָן אָחִי חָרָנָה׃ וְיָשַׁבְתָּ עִמּוֹ יָמִים
days with-him and-you-stay (44) in-Haran brother-of-me Laban to for-yourself

אֲחָדִים עַד אֲשֶׁר־ תָּשׁוּב חֲמַת אָחִיךָ׃ עַד־ שׁוּב
he-subsides when (45) brother-of-you fury-of she-subsides when until few-ones

אַף־ אָחִיךָ מִמְּךָ וְשָׁכַח אֵת אֲשֶׁר־ עָשִׂיתָ לּוֹ
to-him you-did what *** and-he-forgets from-you brother-of-you anger-of

וְשָׁלַחְתִּי וּלְקַחְתִּיךָ מִשָּׁם לָמָה אֶשְׁכַּל גַּם־
also should-I-lose why? from-there and-I-will-get-you then-I-will-send

שְׁנֵיכֶם יוֹם אֶחָד׃ וַתֹּאמֶר רִבְקָה אֶל־ יִצְחָק קַצְתִּי
I-am-disgusted Isaac to Rebekah then-she-said (46) one day both-of-you

בְחַיַּי מִפְּנֵי בְּנוֹת חֵת אִם־ לֹקֵחַ יַעֲקֹב אִשָּׁה
wife Jacob taking if Heth daughters-of because-of with-life-of-me

מִבְּנוֹת־ חֵת כָּאֵלֶּה מִבְּנוֹת הָאָרֶץ לָמָּה לִּי חַיִּים׃
lives to-me what? the-land from-women-of like-these Heth from-daughters-of

וַיִּקְרָא יִצְחָק אֶל־ יַעֲקֹב וַיְבָרֶךְ אֹתוֹ וַיְצַוֵּהוּ
and-he-commanded-him him and-he-blessed Jacob for Isaac so-he-called (28:1)

וַיֹּאמֶר לוֹ לֹא־ תִקַּח אִשָּׁה מִבְּנוֹת כְּנָעַן׃ קוּם לֵךְ
go! rise! (2) Canaan from-women-of wife you-take not to-him and-he-said

פַּדֶּנָה אֲרָם בֵּיתָה בְתוּאֵל אֲבִי אִמֶּךָ וְקַח־
and-take! mother-of-you father-of Bethuel to-house-of Aram to-Paddan

לְךָ מִשָּׁם אִשָּׁה מִבְּנוֹת לָבָן אֲחִי אִמֶּךָ׃
mother-of-you brother-of Laban from-daughters-of wife from-there for-yourself

וְאֵל שַׁדַּי יְבָרֵךְ אֹתְךָ וְיַפְרְךָ
and-may-he-make-fruitful-you you may-he-bless Almighty now-God (3)

וְיַרְבֶּךָ וְהָיִיתָ לִקְהַל עַמִּים׃
peoples as-community-of so-you-become and-may-he-increase-you

וְיִתֶּן־ לְךָ אֶת־ בִּרְכַּת אַבְרָהָם לְךָ וּלְזַרְעֲךָ
and-to-seed-of-you to-you Abraham blessing-of *** to-you and-may-he-give (4)

אִתָּךְ לְרִשְׁתְּךָ אֶת־ אֶרֶץ מְגֻרֶיךָ אֲשֶׁר־ נָתַן אֱלֹהִים
God he-gave that journeys-of-you land-of *** to-possess-you with-you

לְאַבְרָהָם׃ וַיִּשְׁלַח יִצְחָק אֶת־יַעֲקֹב וַיֵּלֶךְ פַּדֶּנָה אֲרָם
Aram to-Paddan and-he-went Jacob *** Isaac then-he-sent-off (5) to-Abraham

אֶל־ לָבָן בֶּן־ בְּתוּאֵל הָאֲרַמִּי אֲחִי רִבְקָה אֵם יַעֲקֹב
Jacob mother-of Rebekah brother-of the-Aramean Bethuel son-of Laban to

וְעֵשָׂו׃ וַיַּרְא עֵשָׂו כִּי־ בֵרַךְ יִצְחָק אֶת־יַעֲקֹב וְשִׁלַּח
and-he-sent Jacob *** Isaac he-blessed that Esau now-he-learned (6) and-Esau

of killing you. [43]Now then, my
son, do what I say: Flee at once
to my brother Laban in Haran.
[44]Stay with him for a while
until your brother's fury sub-
sides. [45]When your brother is
no longer angry with you and
forgets what you did to him,
I'll send word for you to come
back from there. Why should I
lose both of you in one day?"
[46]Then Rebekah said to
Isaac, "I'm disgusted with living because of these Hittite
women. If Jacob takes a wife
from among the women of
this land, from Hittite women
like these, my life will not be
worth living."

28 So Isaac called for Jacob
and blessed[r] him and
commanded him: "Do not
marry a Canaanite woman.
[2]Go at once to Paddan Aram,[s]
to the house of your mother's
father Bethuel. Take a wife for
yourself there, from among
the daughters of Laban, your
mother's brother. [3]May God
Almighty[t] bless you and make
you fruitful and increase your
numbers until you become a
community of peoples. [4]May
he give you and your descendants the blessing of Abraham,
so that you may take possession of the land where you
now live as an alien, the land
God gave to Abraham." [5]Then
Isaac sent Jacob on his way,
and he went to Paddan Aram,
to Laban son of Bethuel the
Aramean, the brother of Rebekah, who was the mother of
Jacob and Esau.
[6]Now Esau learned that
Isaac had blessed Jacob and

[r]1 Or *greeted*
[s]2 That is, Northwest Mesopotamia
[t]3 Hebrew *El-Shaddai*

אֹתוֹ פַּדֶּנָה אֲרָם לָקַחַת־ לוֹ מִשָּׁם אִשָּׁה בְּבָרֲכוֹ אֹתוֹ
him when-to-bless-him wife from-there for-him to-take Aram to-Paddan him

וַיְצַו עָלָיו לֵאמֹר לֹא־ תִקַּח אִשָּׁה מִבְּנוֹת כְּנָעַן׃
Canaan from-women-of wife you-take not to-say to-him and-he-commanded

וַיִּשְׁמַע יַעֲקֹב אֶל־ אָבִיו וְאֶל־ אִמּוֹ וַיֵּלֶךְ
and-he-went mother-of-him and-to father-of-him to Jacob and-he-obeyed (7)

פַּדֶּנָה אֲרָם׃ וַיַּרְא עֵשָׂו כִּי רָעוֹת בְּנוֹת כְּנָעַן
Canaan women-of displeasing-ones how Esau then-he-realized (8) Aram to-Paddan

בְּעֵינֵי יִצְחָק אָבִיו׃ וַיֵּלֶךְ עֵשָׂו אֶל־יִשְׁמָעֵאל וַיִּקַּח
and-he-married Ishmael to Esau so-he-went (9) father-of-him Isaac to-eyes-of

אֶת־ מָחֲלַת ׀ בַּת־ יִשְׁמָעֵאל בֶּן־ אַבְרָהָם אֲחוֹת נְבָיוֹת עַל־
besides Nebaioth sister-of Abraham son-of Ishmael daughter-of Mahalath ***

נָשָׁיו לוֹ לְאִשָּׁה׃ וַיֵּצֵא יַעֲקֹב מִבְּאֵר שָׁבַע
Sheba from-Beer Jacob and-he-left (10) as-wife to-him wives-of-him

וַיֵּלֶךְ חָרָנָה׃ וַיִּפְגַּע בַּמָּקוֹם וַיָּלֶן
then-he-stopped to-the-place when-he-reached (11) for-Haran and-he-set-out

שָׁם כִּי־בָא הַשֶּׁמֶשׁ וַיִּקַּח מֵאַבְנֵי הַמָּקוֹם וַיָּשֶׂם
and-he-put the-place from-stones-of and-he-took the-sun he-set for there

מְרַאֲשֹׁתָיו וַיִּשְׁכַּב בַּמָּקוֹם הַהוּא׃ וַיַּחֲלֹם
and-he-dreamed (12) the-that in-the-place and he-slept under-head-of-him

וְהִנֵּה סֻלָּם מֻצָּב אַרְצָה וְרֹאשׁוֹ מַגִּיעַ הַשָּׁמָיְמָה
to-the-heavens reaching and-top-of-him on-earth resting stairway and-see!

וְהִנֵּה מַלְאֲכֵי אֱלֹהִים עֹלִים וְיֹרְדִים בּוֹ׃ וְהִנֵּה
and-see! (13) on-him and-descending-ones ascending-ones God angels-of and-see!

יְהוָה נִצָּב עָלָיו וַיֹּאמַר אֲנִי יְהוָה אֱלֹהֵי אַבְרָהָם אָבִיךָ
father-of-you Abraham God-of Yahweh I and-he-said above-him standing Yahweh

וֵאלֹהֵי יִצְחָק הָאָרֶץ אֲשֶׁר אַתָּה שֹׁכֵב עָלֶיהָ לְךָ אֶתְּנֶנָּה
I-will-give-her to-you on-her lying you which the-land Isaac and-God-of

וּלְזַרְעֶךָ׃ וְהָיָה זַרְעֲךָ כַּעֲפַר
like-dust-of descendant-of-you and-he-will be (14) and-to-descendant-of-you

הָאָרֶץ וּפָרַצְתָּ יָמָּה וָקֵדְמָה וְצָפֹנָה וָנֶגְבָּה
and-to-south and-to-north and-to-east to west and-you-will-spread the-earth

וְנִבְרְכוּ בְךָ כָּל־ מִשְׁפְּחֹת הָאֲדָמָה
the-earth peoples-of all-of through-you and-they-will-be-blessed

וּבְזַרְעֶךָ׃ וְהִנֵּה אָנֹכִי עִמָּךְ וּשְׁמַרְתִּיךָ
and-I-will-watch-over-you with-you I and-see! (15) and-through-offspring-of-you

בְּכֹל אֲשֶׁר־ תֵּלֵךְ וַהֲשִׁבֹתִיךָ אֶל־הָאֲדָמָה הַזֹּאת כִּי
indeed the-this the-land to and-I-will-bring-back-you you-go where in-any-of

had sent him to Paddan Aram
to take a wife from there, and
that when he blessed him he
commanded him, "Do not
marry a Canaanite woman,"
7and that Jacob had obeyed his
father and mother and had
gone to Paddan Aram. 8Esau
then realized how displeasing
the Canaanite women were to
his father Isaac; 9so he went to
Ishmael and married Maha-
lath, the sister of Nebaioth
and daughter of Ishmael son
of Abraham, in addition to the
wives he already had.

Jacob's Dream at Bethel

10Jacob left Beersheba and
set out for Haran. 11When he
reached a certain place, he
stopped for the night because
the sun had set. Taking one of
the stones there, he put it under his head and lay down to
sleep. 12He had a dream in
which he saw a stairway[u] resting on the earth, with its top
reaching to heaven, and the
angels of God were ascending
and descending on it. 13There
above it[v] stood the LORD, and
he said: "I am the LORD, the
God of your father Abraham
and the God of Isaac. I will
give you and your descendants the land on which you
are lying. 14Your descendants
will be like the dust of the
earth, and you will spread out
to the west and to the east, to
the north and to the south. All
peoples on earth will be
blessed through you and your
offspring. 15I am with you and
will watch over you wherever
you go, and I will bring you
back to this land. I will not

[u]12 Or *ladder* [v]13 Or *There beside him*

לֹא אֶעֱזָבְךָ עַד אֲשֶׁר אִם־ עָשִׂיתִי אֵת אֲשֶׁר־ דִּבַּרְתִּי לָךְ׃
to-you I-promised what *** I-do when *** until I-will-leave-you not

וַיִּיקַץ יַעֲקֹב מִשְּׁנָתוֹ וַיֹּאמֶר אָכֵן יֵשׁ יְהוָה
Yahweh he-is surely then-he-thought from-sleep-of-him Jacob when-he-woke (16)

בַּמָּקוֹם הַזֶּה וְאָנֹכִי לֹא יָדָעְתִּי׃ וַיִּירָא וַיֹּאמַר
and-he-said and-he-was-afraid (17) I-was-aware not and-I the-this in-the-place

מַה־ נּוֹרָא הַמָּקוֹם הַזֶּה אֵין זֶה כִּי אִם־ בֵּית אֱלֹהִים
God house-of than other this not the-this the-place being-awesome how!

וְזֶה שַׁעַר הַשָּׁמָיִם׃ וַיַּשְׁכֵּם יַעֲקֹב בַּבֹּקֶר וַיִּקַּח
and-he-took in-the-morning Jacob and-he-rose (18) the-heavens gate-of yes-this

אֶת־ הָאֶבֶן אֲשֶׁר־ שָׂם מְרַאֲשֹׁתָיו וַיָּשֶׂם אֹתָהּ מַצֵּבָה
pillar her and-he-set-up under-head-of-him he-placed that the-stone ***

וַיִּצֹק שֶׁמֶן עַל־ רֹאשָׁהּ׃ וַיִּקְרָא אֶת־ שֵׁם־ הַמָּקוֹם
the-place name-of *** and-he-called (19) top-of-her on oil and-he-poured

הַהוּא בֵּית־אֵל וְאוּלָם לוּז שֵׁם־ הָעִיר לָרִאשֹׁנָה׃ וַיִּדַּר
and-he-made (20) at-the-first the-city name-of Luz even-though El Beth the-that

יַעֲקֹב נֶדֶר לֵאמֹר אִם־ יִהְיֶה אֱלֹהִים עִמָּדִי וּשְׁמָרַנִי בַּדֶּרֶךְ
on-the-journey and-he-watches-over-me with-me God he-is if to-say vow Jacob

הַזֶּה אֲשֶׁר אָנֹכִי הוֹלֵךְ וְנָתַן־ לִי לֶחֶם לֶאֱכֹל וּבֶגֶד לִלְבֹּשׁ׃
to-wear and-clothes to-eat food to-me and-he-gives taking I that the-this

וְשַׁבְתִּי בְשָׁלוֹם אֶל־ בֵּית אָבִי וְהָיָה יְהוָה
Yahweh then-he-will-be father-of-me house-of to in-safety so-I-return (21)

לִי לֵאלֹהִים׃ וְהָאֶבֶן הַזֹּאת אֲשֶׁר־ שַׂמְתִּי מַצֵּבָה יִהְיֶה
he-will-be pillar I-set-up that the-this and-the-stone (22) as-God to-me

בֵּית אֱלֹהִים וְכֹל אֲשֶׁר תִּתֶּן־ לִי עַשֵּׂר אֲעַשְּׂרֶנּוּ לָךְ׃
to-you I-will-give-him to-be-tenth to-me you-give that and-all God house-of

וַיִּשָּׂא יַעֲקֹב רַגְלָיו וַיֵּלֶךְ אַרְצָה בְנֵי־
peoples-of to-land-of and-he-continued feet-of-him Jacob and-he-lifted (29:1)

קֶדֶם׃ וַיַּרְא וְהִנֵּה בְאֵר בַּשָּׂדֶה וְהִנֵּה־ שָׁם שְׁלֹשָׁה עֶדְרֵי־
flocks-of three there and-see! in-the-field well and-see! and-he-saw (2) east

צֹאן רֹבְצִים עָלֶיהָ כִּי מִן־ הַבְּאֵר הַהִוא יַשְׁקוּ
they-were-watered the-that the-well from for near-her ones-lying sheep

הָעֲדָרִים וְהָאֶבֶן גְּדֹלָה עַל־ פִּי הַבְּאֵר׃ וְנֶאֶסְפוּ־
as-they-were-gathered (3) the-well mouth-of over large and-the-stone the-flocks

שָׁמָּה כָל־ הָעֲדָרִים וְגָלֲלוּ אֶת־ הָאֶבֶן מֵעַל פִּי
mouth-of away-from the-stone *** then-they-rolled the-flocks all-of to-there

הַבְּאֵר וְהִשְׁקוּ אֶת־ הַצֹּאן וְהֵשִׁיבוּ אֶת־ הָאֶבֶן
the-stone *** then-they-returned the-sheep *** and-they-watered the-well

leave you until I have done
what I have promised you."
16When Jacob awoke from
his sleep, he thought, "Surely
the LORD is in this place, and I
was not aware of it." 17He was
afraid and said, "How awesome is this place! This is none
other than the house of God;
this is the gate of heaven."
18Early the next morning
Jacob took the stone he had
placed under his head and set
it up as a pillar and poured oil
on top of it. 19He called that
place Bethel,[w] though the city
used to be called Luz.
20Then Jacob made a vow,
saying, "If God will be with
me and will watch over me on
this journey I am taking and
will give me food to eat and
clothes to wear 21so that I return safely to my father's
house, then the LORD[x] will be
my God. 22This stone that I
have set up as a pillar will be
God's house, and of all that
you give me I will give you a
tenth."

Jacob Arrives in Paddan Aram

29 Then Jacob continued
on his journey and
came to the land of the eastern
peoples. 2There he saw a well
in the field, with three flocks
of sheep lying near it because
the flocks were watered from
that well. The stone over the
mouth of the well was large.
3When all the flocks were
gathered there, the shepherds
would roll the stone away
from the well's mouth and
water the sheep. Then they
would return the stone to its

w19 *Bethel* means *house of God.*
x20,21 Or *Since God . . . father's house, the* LORD

עַל־ פִּי הַבְּאֵר לִמְקֹמָהּ׃ וַיֹּאמֶר לָהֶם יַעֲקֹב
Jacob to-them and-he-asked (4) to-place-of-her the-well mouth-of over

אַחַי מֵאַיִן אַתֶּם וַיֹּאמְרוּ מֵחָרָן אֲנָחְנוּ׃ וַיֹּאמֶר
and-he-said (5) we from-Haran and-they-replied you from-where? brothers-of-me

לָהֶם הַיְדַעְתֶּם אֶת־ לָבָן בֶּן־ נָחוֹר וַיֹּאמְרוּ יָדָעְנוּ׃
we-know and-they-answered Nahor son-of Laban *** you-know? to-them

וַיֹּאמֶר לָהֶם הֲשָׁלוֹם לוֹ וַיֹּאמְרוּ שָׁלוֹם וְהִנֵּה רָחֵל
Rachel now-see! well and-they-said with-him well? to-them then-he-asked (6)

בִּתּוֹ בָּאָה עִם־ הַצֹּאן׃ וַיֹּאמֶר הֵן עוֹד הַיּוֹם
the-day still see! and-he-said (7) the-sheep with coming daughter-of-him

גָּדוֹל לֹא־ עֵת הֵאָסֵף הַמִּקְנֶה הַשְׁקוּ הַצֹּאן וּלְכוּ רְעוּ׃
pasture! and-go! the-sheep water! the-flock to-be-gathered time-of not high

וַיֹּאמְרוּ לֹא נוּכַל עַד אֲשֶׁר יֵאָסְפוּ כָּל־ הָעֲדָרִים
the-flocks all-of they-are-gathered when until we-can not but-they-replied (8)

וְגָלְלוּ אֶת־ הָאֶבֶן מֵעַל פִּי הַבְּאֵר וְהִשְׁקִינוּ
then-we-will-water the-well mouth-of away-from the-stone *** and-they-roll

הַצֹּאן׃ עוֹדֶנּוּ מְדַבֵּר עִמָּם וְרָחֵל בָּאָה עִם־ הַצֹּאן
the-sheep with she-came then-Rachel with-them talking while-he (9) the-sheep

אֲשֶׁר לְאָבִיהָ כִּי רֹעָה הִוא׃ וַיְהִי כַּאֲשֶׁר רָאָה
he-saw when and-he-was (10) she being-shepherdess for to-father-of-her that

יַעֲקֹב אֶת־ רָחֵל בַּת־ לָבָן אֲחִי אִמּוֹ וְאֶת־ צֹאן
sheep-of and mother-of-him brother-of Laban daughter-of Rachel *** Jacob

לָבָן אֲחִי אִמּוֹ וַיִּגַּשׁ יַעֲקֹב וַיָּגֶל אֶת־
*** and-he-rolled Jacob then-he-went-over mother-of-him brother-of Laban

הָאֶבֶן מֵעַל פִּי הַבְּאֵר וַיַּשְׁקְ אֶת־ צֹאן לָבָן
Laban sheep-of *** and-he-watered the-well mouth-of away-from the-stone

אֲחִי אִמּוֹ׃ וַיִּשַּׁק יַעֲקֹב לְרָחֵל וַיִּשָּׂא
and-he-lifted on-Rachel Jacob then-he-kissed (11) mother-of-him brother-of

אֶת־ קֹלוֹ וַיֵּבְךְּ׃ וַיַּגֵּד יַעֲקֹב לְרָחֵל כִּי אֲחִי
relative-of that to-Rachel Jacob and-he-told (12) and-he-wept voice-of-him ***

אָבִיהָ הוּא וְכִי בֶן־ רִבְקָה הוּא וַתָּרָץ וַתַּגֵּד
and-she-told so-she-ran he Rebekah son-of and-that he father-of-her

לְאָבִיהָ׃ וַיְהִי כִשְׁמֹעַ לָבָן אֶת־ שֵׁמַע יַעֲקֹב
Jacob news-of *** Laban as-soon-as-to-hear and-he-was (13) to-father-of-her

בֶּן־ אֲחֹתוֹ וַיָּרָץ לִקְרָאתוֹ וַיְחַבֶּק־ לוֹ
on-him and-he-embraced to-meet-him that-he-ran sister-of-him son-of

וַיְנַשֶּׁק־ לוֹ וַיְבִיאֵהוּ אֶל־ בֵּיתוֹ וַיְסַפֵּר לְלָבָן
to-Laban and-he-told home-of-him to and-he-brought-him on-him and-he-kissed

place over the mouth of the well.

4Jacob asked the shepherds, "My brothers, where are you from?"

"We're from Haran," they replied.

5He said to them, "Do you know Laban, Nahor's grandson?"

"Yes, we know him," they answered.

6Then Jacob asked them, "Is he well?"

"Yes, he is," they said, "and here comes his daughter Rachel with the sheep."

7"Look," he said, "the sun is still high; it is not time for the flocks to be gathered. Water the sheep and take them back to pasture."

8"We can't," they replied, "until all the flocks are gathered and the stone has been rolled away from the mouth of the well. Then we will water the sheep."

9While he was still talking with them, Rachel came with her father's sheep, for she was a shepherdess. 10When Jacob saw Rachel daughter of Laban, his mother's brother, and Laban's sheep, he went over and rolled the stone away from the mouth of the well and watered his uncle's sheep. 11Then Jacob kissed Rachel and began to weep aloud. 12He had told Rachel that he was a relative of her father and a son of Rebekah. So she ran and told her father.

13As soon as Laban heard the news about Jacob, his sister's son, he hurried to meet him. He embraced him and kissed him and brought him to his home, and there Jacob told

אֵת כָּל־ הַדְּבָרִים הָאֵלֶּה׃ וַיֹּאמֶר לוֹ לָבָן אַךְ
indeed Laban to-him then-he-said (14) the-these the-things all-of ***

עַצְמִי וּבְשָׂרִי אָתָּה וַיֵּשֶׁב עִמּוֹ חֹדֶשׁ יָמִים׃
days month-of with-him and-he-stayed you and-flesh-of-me bone-of-me

וַיֹּאמֶר לָבָן לְיַעֲקֹב הֲכִי־ אָחִי אַתָּה וַעֲבַדְתַּנִי
should-you-serve-me you relative-of-me because? to-Jacob Laban then-he-said (15)

חִנָּם הַגִּידָה לִּי מַה־ מַּשְׂכֻּרְתֶּךָ׃ וּלְלָבָן שְׁתֵּי בָנוֹת
daughters two-of now-to-Laban (16) wage-of-you what? to-me tell! for-nothing

שֵׁם הַגְּדֹלָה לֵאָה וְשֵׁם הַקְּטַנָּה רָחֵל׃ וְעֵינֵי לֵאָה
Leah now-eyes-of (17) Rachel the-younger and-name-of Leah the-older name-of

רַכּוֹת וְרָחֵל הָיְתָה יְפַת־ תֹּאַר וִיפַת מַרְאֶה׃
appearance and-beautiful-of form lovely-of she-was but-Rachel weak-ones

וַיֶּאֱהַב יַעֲקֹב אֶת־ רָחֵל וַיֹּאמֶר אֶעֱבָדְךָ שֶׁבַע שָׁנִים
years seven I-will-serve-you and-he-said Rachel *** Jacob now-he-loved (18)

בְּרָחֵל בִּתְּךָ הַקְּטַנָּה׃ וַיֹּאמֶר לָבָן טוֹב תִּתִּי
to-give-me better Laban so-he-said (19) the-younger daughter-of-you for-Rachel

אֹתָהּ לָךְ מִתִּתִּי אֹתָהּ לְאִישׁ אַחֵר שְׁבָה עִמָּדִי׃ וַיַּעֲבֹד
so-he-served (20) with-me stay! other to-man her than-to-give-me to-you her

יַעֲקֹב בְּרָחֵל שֶׁבַע שָׁנִים וַיִּהְיוּ בְעֵינָיו כְּיָמִים אֲחָדִים
few-ones like-days in-eyes-of-him but-they-seemed years seven for-Rachel Jacob

בְּאַהֲבָתוֹ אֹתָהּ׃ וַיֹּאמֶר יַעֲקֹב אֶל־ לָבָן הָבָה אֶת־ אִשְׁתִּי
wife-of-me *** give! Laban to Jacob then-he-said (21) her because-to-love-him

כִּי מָלְאוּ יָמָי וְאָבוֹאָה אֵלֶיהָ׃ וַיֶּאֱסֹף
so-he-gathered (22) with-her and-I-would-lie days-of-me they-are-completed for

לָבָן אֶת־ כָּל־ אַנְשֵׁי הַמָּקוֹם וַיַּעַשׂ מִשְׁתֶּה׃ וַיְהִי
but-he-was (23) feast and-he-gave the-place people-of all-of *** Laban

בָעֶרֶב וַיִּקַּח אֶת־ לֵאָה בִתּוֹ וַיָּבֵא אֹתָהּ אֵלָיו
to-him her and-he-gave daughter-of-him Leah *** that-he-took in-the-evening

וַיָּבֹא אֵלֶיהָ׃ וַיִּתֵּן לָבָן לָהּ אֶת־ זִלְפָּה שִׁפְחָתוֹ
servant-of-him Zilpah *** to-her Laban and-he-gave (24) with-her and-he-lay

לְלֵאָה בִתּוֹ שִׁפְחָה׃ וַיְהִי בַבֹּקֶר וְהִנֵּה־
and-see! in-the-morning and-he-was (25) maidservant daughter-of-him to-Leah

הִוא לֵאָה וַיֹּאמֶר אֶל־ לָבָן מַה־ זֹּאת עָשִׂיתָ לִּי הֲלֹא בְרָחֵל
for-Rachel not? to-me you-did this what? Laban to so-he-said Leah she

עָבַדְתִּי עִמָּךְ וְלָמָּה רִמִּיתָנִי׃ וַיֹּאמֶר לָבָן לֹא־
not Laban and-he-replied (26) you-deceived-me so-why? for-you I-served

יֵעָשֶׂה כֵן בִּמְקוֹמֵנוּ לָתֵת הַצְּעִירָה לִפְנֵי הַבְּכִירָה׃
the-firstborn before the-younger to-give in-land-of-us so he-is-done

him all these things. [14]Then
Laban said to him, "You are
my own flesh and blood."

Jacob Marries Leah and Rachel

After Jacob had stayed with
him for a whole month, [15]La-
ban said to him, "Just because
you are a relative of mine,
should you work for me for
nothing? Tell me what your
wages should be."
[16]Now Laban had two
daughters; the name of the
older was Leah, and the name
of the younger was Rachel.
[17]Leah had weak[y] eyes, but Rachel was lovely in form, and
beautiful. [18]Jacob was in love
with Rachel and said, "I'll
work for you seven years in
return for your younger
daughter Rachel."
[19]Laban said, "It's better to
give her to you than to some
other man. Stay here with
me." [20]So Jacob served seven
years to get Rachel, but they
seemed like only a few days to
him because of his love for
her.
[21]Then Jacob said to Laban,
"Give me my wife. My time is
completed, and I want to lie
with her."
[22]So Laban brought together
all the people of the place and
gave a feast. [23]But when evening came, he took his daughter Leah and gave her to Jacob,
and Jacob lay with her. [24]And
Laban gave his servant girl
Zilpah to his daughter as her
maidservant.
[25]When morning came,
there was Leah! So Jacob said
to Laban, "What is this you
have done to me? I served you
for Rachel, didn't I? Why have
you deceived me?"
[26]Laban replied, "It is not
our custom here to give the
younger daughter in marriage
before the older one. [27]Finish

[y]17 Or *delicate*

מַלֵּא שְׁבֻעַ זֹאת וְנִתְּנָה לְךָ גַּם־אֶת־זֹאת בַּעֲבֹדָה אֲשֶׁר
that for-work other *** also to-you and-we-will-give this week-of finish! (27)

תַּעֲבֹד עִמָּדִי עוֹד שֶׁבַע־שָׁנִים אֲחֵרוֹת׃ וַיַּעַשׂ יַעֲקֹב כֵּן
so Jacob and-he-did (28) other-ones years seven for for-me you-will-do

וַיְמַלֵּא שְׁבֻעַ זֹאת וַיִּתֶּן־לוֹ אֶת־רָחֵל בִּתּוֹ
daughter-of-him Rachel *** to-him then-he-gave this week-of and-he-finished

לוֹ לְאִשָּׁה׃ וַיִּתֵּן לָבָן לְרָחֵל בִּתּוֹ אֶת־בִּלְהָה
Bilhah *** daughter-of-him to-Rachel Laban and-he-gave (29) for-wife to-him

שִׁפְחָתוֹ לָהּ לְשִׁפְחָה׃ וַיָּבֹא גַּם אֶל־רָחֵל
Rachel with also and-he-lay (30) as-maidservant to-her servant-of-him

וַיֶּאֱהַב גַּם־אֶת־רָחֵל מִלֵּאָה וַיַּעֲבֹד עִמּוֹ עוֹד שֶׁבַע־שָׁנִים
years seven for for-him and-he-worked than-Leah Rachel *** more and-he-loved

אֲחֵרוֹת׃ וַיַּרְא יְהוָה כִּי־שְׂנוּאָה לֵאָה וַיִּפְתַּח
then-he-opened Leah being-unloved that Yahweh when-he-saw (31) other-ones

אֶת־רַחְמָהּ וְרָחֵל עֲקָרָה׃ וַתַּהַר לֵאָה וַתֵּלֶד
and-she-bore Leah and-she-conceived (32) barren but-Rachel womb-of-her ***

בֵּן וַתִּקְרָא שְׁמוֹ רְאוּבֵן כִּי אָמְרָה כִּי־רָאָה יְהוָה
Yahweh he-looked because she-said for Reuben name-of-him and-she-called son

בְּעָנְיִי כִּי עַתָּה יֶאֱהָבַנִי אִישִׁי׃ וַתַּהַר
and-she-conceived (33) husband-of-me he-will-love-me now surely on-misery-of-me

עוֹד וַתֵּלֶד בֵּן וַתֹּאמֶר כִּי־שָׁמַע יְהוָה כִּי־שְׂנוּאָה
being-unloved that Yahweh he-heard because and-she-said son and-she-bore again

אָנֹכִי וַיִּתֶּן־לִי גַּם־אֶת־זֶה וַתִּקְרָא שְׁמוֹ שִׁמְעוֹן׃
Simeon name-of-him so-she-called this *** also to-me now-he-gave I

וַתַּהַר עוֹד וַתֵּלֶד בֵּן וַתֹּאמֶר עַתָּה הַפַּעַם
the-time now and-she-said son and-she-bore again and-she-conceived (34)

יִלָּוֶה אִישִׁי אֵלַי כִּי־יָלַדְתִּי לוֹ שְׁלֹשָׁה בָנִים עַל־
for sons three to-him I-bore for to-me husband-of-me he-will-become-attached

כֵּן קָרָא־שְׁמוֹ לֵוִי׃ וַתַּהַר עוֹד וַתֵּלֶד
and-she-bore again and-she-conceived (35) Levi name-of-him he-called this

בֵּן וַתֹּאמֶר הַפַּעַם אוֹדֶה אֶת־יְהוָה עַל־כֵּן קָרְאָה
she-called this for Yahweh *** I-will-praise the-time and-she-said son

שְׁמוֹ יְהוּדָה וַתַּעֲמֹד מִלֶּדֶת׃ וַתֵּרֶא רָחֵל
Rachel when-she-saw (30:1) from-to-bear then-she-stopped Judah name-of-him

כִּי לֹא יָלְדָה לְיַעֲקֹב וַתְּקַנֵּא רָחֵל בַּאֲחֹתָהּ
of-sister-of-her Rachel then-she-was-jealous to-Jacob she-bore not that

וַתֹּאמֶר אֶל־יַעֲקֹב הָבָה־לִּי בָנִים וְאִם־אַיִן מֵתָה אָנֹכִי׃ וַיִּחַר־
and-he-burned (2) I dying not and-if children to-me give! Jacob to so-she-said

out this daughter's bridal
week; then we will give you
the younger one also, in return for another seven years of
work."
28And Jacob did so. He
finished out the week with
Leah, and then Laban gave
him his daughter Rachel to be
his wife. 29Laban gave his servant girl Bilhah to his daughter Rachel as her maidservant.
30Jacob lay with Rachel also,
and he loved Rachel more
than Leah. And he worked for
Laban another seven years.

Jacob's Children

31When the LORD saw that
Leah was not loved, he opened
her womb, but Rachel was
barren. 32Leah became pregnant and gave birth to a son.
She named him Reuben,[a] for
she said, "It is because the
LORD has seen my misery.
Surely my husband will love
me now."
33She conceived again, and
when she gave birth to a son
she said, "Because the LORD
heard that I am not loved, he
gave me this one too." So she
named him Simeon.[b]
34Again she conceived, and
when she gave birth to a son
she said, "Now at last my husband will become attached to
me, because I have borne him
three sons." So he was named
Levi.[c]
35She conceived again, and
when she gave birth to a son
she said, "This time I will
praise the LORD." So she
named him Judah.[d] Then she
stopped having children.

30 When Rachel saw that
she was not bearing
Jacob any children, she
became jealous of her sister. So
she said to Jacob, "Give me
children, or I'll die!"

[a]32 *Reuben* sounds like the Hebrew for *he has seen my misery;* the name means *see, a son*
[b]33 *Simeon* probably means *one who hears*
[c]34 *Levi* sounds like and may be derived from the Hebrew for *attached.*
[d]35 *Judah* sounds like and may be derived from the Hebrew for *praise*

אַף יַעֲקֹב בְּרָחֵל וַיֹּאמֶר הֲתַחַת אֱלֹהִים אָנֹכִי אֲשֶׁר־מָנַע מִמֵּךְ
from-you he-kept who I God in-place-of? and-he-said at-Rachel Jacob anger-of

פְּרִי־בָטֶן׃ וַתֹּאמֶר הִנֵּה אֲמָתִי בִלְהָה בֹּא אֵלֶיהָ
with-her sleep! Bilhah maidservant-of-me see! then-she-said (3) womb fruit-of

וְתֵלֵד עַל־בִּרְכַּי וְאִבָּנֶה גַם־אָנֹכִי מִמֶּנָּה׃
through-her I also so-I-can-build knees-of-me at so-she-can-bear

וַתִּתֶּן־לוֹ אֶת־בִּלְהָה שִׁפְחָתָהּ לְאִשָּׁה וַיָּבֹא אֵלֶיהָ
with-her and-he-slept as-wife servant-of-her Bilhah *** to-him so-she-gave (4)

יַעֲקֹב׃ וַתַּהַר בִּלְהָה וַתֵּלֶד לְיַעֲקֹב בֵּן׃ וַתֹּאמֶר
and-she-said (6) son to-Jacob and-she-bore Bilhah and-she-conceived (5) Jacob

רָחֵל דָּנַנִּי אֱלֹהִים וְגַם שָׁמַע בְּקֹלִי וַיִּתֶּן־
and-he-gave to-plea-of-me he-listened and-also God he-vindicated-me Rachel

לִי בֵּן עַל־כֵּן קָרְאָה שְׁמוֹ דָּן׃ וַתַּהַר עוֹד
again and-she-conceived (7) Dan name-of-him she-called this for son to-me

וַתֵּלֶד בִּלְהָה שִׁפְחַת רָחֵל בֵּן שֵׁנִי לְיַעֲקֹב׃ וַתֹּאמֶר
and-she-said (8) to-Jacob second son Rachel servant-of Bilhah and-she-bore

רָחֵל נַפְתּוּלֵי אֱלֹהִים ׀ נִפְתַּלְתִּי עִם־אֲחֹתִי גַּם־יָכֹלְתִּי
I-won indeed sister-of-me with I-struggled great-ones struggles-of Rachel

וַתִּקְרָא שְׁמוֹ נַפְתָּלִי׃ וַתֵּרֶא לֵאָה כִּי עָמְדָה
she-stopped that Leah when-she-saw (9) Naphtali name-of-him so-she-called

מִלֶּדֶת וַתִּקַּח אֶת־זִלְפָּה שִׁפְחָתָהּ וַתִּתֵּן אֹתָהּ
her and-she-gave maidservant-of-her Zilpah *** then-she-took from-to-bear

לְיַעֲקֹב לְאִשָּׁה׃ וַתֵּלֶד זִלְפָּה שִׁפְחַת לֵאָה לְיַעֲקֹב בֵּן׃
son to-Jacob Leah servant-of Zilpah and-she-bore (10) as-wife to-Jacob

וַתֹּאמֶר לֵאָה בָּגָד וַתִּקְרָא אֶת־שְׁמוֹ גָּד׃
Gad name-of-him *** so-she-called *what-good-fortune Leah then-she-said (11)

וַתֵּלֶד זִלְפָּה שִׁפְחַת לֵאָה בֵּן שֵׁנִי לְיַעֲקֹב׃ וַתֹּאמֶר
and-she-said (13) to-Jacob second son Leah servant-of Zilpah and-she-bore (12)

לֵאָה בְּאָשְׁרִי כִּי אִשְּׁרוּנִי בָּנוֹת וַתִּקְרָא אֶת־
*** so-she-called women they-will-call-happy-me now how-happy-I Leah

שְׁמוֹ אָשֵׁר׃ וַיֵּלֶךְ רְאוּבֵן בִּימֵי קְצִיר־חִטִּים
wheat harvest-of in-days-of Reuben and-he-went-out (14) Asher name-of-him

וַיִּמְצָא דוּדָאִים בַּשָּׂדֶה וַיָּבֵא אֹתָם אֶל־לֵאָה אִמּוֹ
mother-of-him Leah to them and-he-brought in-the-field mandrakes and-he-found

וַתֹּאמֶר רָחֵל אֶל־לֵאָה תְּנִי־נָא לִי מִדּוּדָאֵי בְּנֵךְ׃
son-of-you from-mandrakes-of to-me now! give! Leah to Rachel and-she-said

וַתֹּאמֶר לָהּ הַמְעַט קַחְתֵּךְ אֶת־אִישִׁי וְלָקַחַת
now-you-take husband-of-me *** to-take-you enough? to-her but-she-said (15)

[2]Jacob became angry with
her and said, "Am I in the
place of God, who has kept
you from having children?"
[3]Then she said, "Here is Bilhah, my maidservant. Sleep
with her so that she can bear
children for me and that
through her I too can build a
family."
[4]So she gave him her servant
Bilhah as a wife. Jacob slept
with her, [5]and she became
pregnant and bore him a son.
[6]Then Rachel said, "God has
vindicated me; he has listened
to my plea and given me a
son." Because of this she
named him Dan.[g]
[7]Rachel's servant Bilhah
conceived again and bore
Jacob a second son. [8]Then Rachel said, "I have had a great
struggle with my sister, and I
have won." So she named him
Naphtali.[h]
[9]When Leah saw that she
had stopped having children,
she took her maidservant Zilpah and gave her to Jacob as a
wife. [10]Leah's servant Zilpah
bore Jacob a son. [11]Then Leah
said, "What good fortune!"[i]
So she named him Gad.[j]
[12]Leah's servant Zilpah bore
Jacob a second son. [13]Then
Leah said, "How happy I am!
The women will call me happy." So she named him Asher.[k]
[14]During wheat harvest,
Reuben went out into the
fields and found some man-
drake plants, which he
brought to his mother Leah.
Rachel said to Leah, "Please
give me some of your son's
mandrakes."
[15]But she said to her,
"Wasn't it enough that you
took away my husband? Will

[g]6 *Dan* here means *he has vindicated*
[h]8 *Naphtali* means *my struggle*
[i]11 Or *"A troop is coming!"*
[j]11 *Gad* can mean *good fortune* or *a troop.*
[k]13 *Asher* means *happy.*

°11 ק בא גד
*11 *good-fortune he-came* (*Qere* translation)

גַּם אֶת־ דּוּדָאֵי בְּנִי וַתֹּאמֶר רָחֵל לָכֵן יִשְׁכַּב

he-can-sleep very-well Rachel and-she-said son-of-me mandrakes-of *** also

עִמָּךְ הַלַּיְלָה תַּחַת דּוּדָאֵי בְנֵךְ׃ וַיָּבֹא יַעֲקֹב

Jacob when-he-came-in (16) son-of-you mandrakes-of for the-night with-you

מִן־ הַשָּׂדֶה בָּעֶרֶב וַתֵּצֵא לֵאָה לִקְרָאתוֹ וַתֹּאמֶר

and-she-said to-meet-him Leah then-she-went-out in-the-evening the-field from

אֵלַי תָּבוֹא כִּי שָׂכֹר שְׂכַרְתִּיךָ בְּדוּדָאֵי בְּנִי

son-of-me with-mandrakes-of I-hired-you to-hire for you-must-sleep with-me

וַיִּשְׁכַּב עִמָּהּ בַּלַּיְלָה הוּא׃ וַיִּשְׁמַע אֱלֹהִים אֶל־לֵאָה

Leah to God and-he-listened (17) that in-the-night with-her so-he-slept

וַתַּהַר וַתֵּלֶד לְיַעֲקֹב בֵּן חֲמִישִׁי׃ וַתֹּאמֶר לֵאָה

Leah then-she-said (18) fifth son to-Jacob and-she-bore and-she-conceived

נָתַן אֱלֹהִים שְׂכָרִי אֲשֶׁר־ נָתַתִּי שִׁפְחָתִי לְאִישִׁי

to-husband-of-me maidservant-of-me I-gave for reward-of-me God he-gave

וַתִּקְרָא שְׁמוֹ יִשָּׂשכָר׃ וַתַּהַר עוֹד לֵאָה

Leah again and-she-conceived (19) Issachar name-of-him so-she-called

וַתֵּלֶד בֵּן־ שִׁשִּׁי לְיַעֲקֹב*׃ וַתֹּאמֶר לֵאָה זְבָדַנִי אֱלֹהִים׀

God he-presented-me Leah and-she-said (20) to-Jacob sixth son and-she-bore

אֹתִי זֵבֶד טוֹב הַפַּעַם יִזְבְּלֵנִי אִישִׁי כִּי־ יָלַדְתִּי לוֹ

to-him I-bore for husband-of-me he-will-honor-me the-time precious gift me

שִׁשָּׁה בָנִים וַתִּקְרָא אֶת־ שְׁמוֹ זְבֻלוּן׃ וְאַחַר יָלְדָה

she-bore and-later (21) Zebulun name-of-him *** so-she-called sons six

בַּת וַתִּקְרָא אֶת־ שְׁמָהּ דִּינָה׃ וַיִּזְכֹּר אֱלֹהִים

God then-he-remembered (22) Dinah name-of-her *** and-she-called daughter

אֶת־ רָחֵל וַיִּשְׁמַע אֵלֶיהָ אֱלֹהִים וַיִּפְתַּח אֶת־ רַחְמָהּ׃

womb-of-her *** and-he-opened God to-her and-he-listened Rachel ***

וַתַּהַר וַתֵּלֶד בֵּן וַתֹּאמֶר אָסַף אֱלֹהִים אֶת־

*** God he-took-away and-she-said son and-she-bore so-she-conceived (23)

חֶרְפָּתִי׃ וַתִּקְרָא אֶת־ שְׁמוֹ יוֹסֵף לֵאמֹר יֹסֵף

may-he-add to-say Joseph name-of-him *** so-she-called (24) disgrace-of-me

יְהוָה לִי בֵּן אַחֵר׃ וַיְהִי כַּאֲשֶׁר יָלְדָה רָחֵל אֶת־ יוֹסֵף

Joseph *** Rachel she-bore after and-he-was (25) another son to-me Yahweh

וַיֹּאמֶר יַעֲקֹב אֶל־ לָבָן שַׁלְּחֵנִי וְאֵלְכָה אֶל־ מְקוֹמִי

home-of-me to so-I-can-go sent-away-me! Laban to Jacob that-he-said

וּלְאַרְצִי׃ תְּנָה אֶת־ נָשַׁי וְאֶת־ יְלָדַי אֲשֶׁר

for-whom children-of-me and wives-of-me *** give! (26) and-to-land-of-me

עָבַדְתִּי אֹתְךָ בָּהֵן וְאֵלֵכָה כִּי אַתָּה יָדַעְתָּ אֶת־ עֲבֹדָתִי אֲשֶׁר

that work-of-me *** you-know you for and-I-will-go for-them you I-served

you take my son's mandrakes
too?"
"Very well," Rachel said,
"he can sleep with you tonight
in return for your son's mandrakes."
16So when Jacob came in
from the fields that evening,
Leah went out to meet him.
"You must sleep with me,"
she said. "I have hired you
with my son's mandrakes." So
he slept with her that night.
17God listened to Leah, and
she became pregnant and bore
Jacob a fifth son. 18Then Leah
said, "God has rewarded me
for giving my maidservant to
my husband." So she named
him Issachar.[m]
19Leah conceived again and
bore Jacob a sixth son. 20Then
Leah said, "God has presented
me with a precious gift. This
time my husband will treat me
with honor, because I have
borne him six sons." So she
named him Zebulun.[n]
21Some time later she gave
birth to a daughter and named
her Dinah.
22Then God remembered Ra-
chel; he listened to her and
opened her womb. 23She
became pregnant and gave
birth to a son and said, "God
has taken away my disgrace."
24She named him Joseph,[o] and
said, "May the LORD add to me
another son."

Jacob's Flocks Increase

25After Rachel gave birth to
Joseph, Jacob said to Laban,
"Send me on my way so I can
go back to my own homeland.
26Give me my wives and children, for whom I have served
you, and I will be on my way.
You know how much work

[m]18 *Issachar* sounds like the Hebrew for *reward*
[n]20 *Zebulun* probably means *honor*.
[o]24 *Joseph* means *may he add*.

*19 Most mss have no *dagesh* in the *lamed* (לְ).

עֲבַדְתִּיךָ׃ וַיֹּאמֶר אֵלָיו לָבָן אִם־נָא מָצָאתִי חֵן
favor I-found now! if Laban to-him but-he-said (27) I-did-for-you

בְּעֵינֶיךָ נִחַשְׁתִּי וַיְבָרְכֵנִי יְהוָה בִּגְלָלֶךָ׃
because-of-you Yahweh that-he-blessed-me I-learned-by-divination in-eyes-of-you

וַיֹּאמַר נָקְבָה שְׂכָרְךָ עָלַי וְאֶתֵּנָה׃ וַיֹּאמֶר
and-he-said (29) and-I-will-pay to-me wage-of-you name! and-he-said (28)

אֵלָיו אַתָּה יָדַעְתָּ אֵת אֲשֶׁר עֲבַדְתִּיךָ וְאֵת אֲשֶׁר־הָיָה מִקְנְךָ
stock-of-you he-fared how and I-worked-for-you how *** you-know you to-him

אִתִּי׃ כִּי מְעַט אֲשֶׁר־הָיָה לְךָ לְפָנַי וַיִּפְרֹץ
now-he-increased before-me to-you he-was that little indeed (30) with-me

לָרֹב וַיְבָרֶךְ יְהוָה אֹתְךָ לְרַגְלִי וְעַתָּה מָתַי אֶעֱשֶׂה
can-I-do when? but-now at-feet-of-me you Yahweh and-he-blessed to-be-great

גַם־אָנֹכִי לְבֵיתִי׃ וַיֹּאמֶר מָה אֶתֶּן־לָךְ
to-you shall-I-give what? and-he-asked (31) for-household-of-me I also

וַיֹּאמֶר יַעֲקֹב לֹא־תִתֶּן־לִי מְאוּמָה אִם־תַּעֲשֶׂה־לִּי
for-me you-do but-if anything to-me you-give not Jacob and-he-replied

הַדָּבָר הַזֶּה אָשׁוּבָה אֶרְעֶה צֹאנְךָ אֶשְׁמֹר׃
I-will-watch flock-of-you I-will-tend I-will-go-on the-this the-thing

אֶעֱבֹר בְּכָל־צֹאנְךָ הַיּוֹם הָסֵר מִשָּׁם
from-there to-remove the-day flock-of-you through-all-of let-me-go (32)

כָּל־שֶׂה נָקֹד וְטָלוּא וְכָל־שֶׂה־חוּם בַּכְּשָׂבִים
from-the-lambs dark sheep and-every-of or-being-spotted specked sheep every-of

וְטָלוּא וְנָקֹד בָּעִזִּים וְהָיָה שְׂכָרִי׃
wage-of-me and-he-will-be from-the-goats or-speckled and-being-spotted

וְעָנְתָה־בִּי צִדְקָתִי בְּיוֹם מָחָר כִּי־תָבוֹא
you-check when future in-day honesty-of-me for-me and-she-will-testify (33)

עַל־שְׂכָרִי לְפָנֶיךָ כֹּל אֲשֶׁר־אֵינֶנּוּ נָקֹד וְטָלוּא
or-being-spotted speckled not-he that all before-you wage-of-me on

בָּעִזִּים וְחוּם בַּכְּשָׂבִים גָּנוּב הוּא אִתִּי׃
with-me he being-stolen from-the-lambs or-dark from-the-goats

וַיֹּאמֶר לָבָן הֵן לוּ יְהִי כִדְבָרֶךָ׃ וַיָּסַר
so-he-removed (35) as-word-of-you let-him-be now! agreed Laban so-he-said (34)

בַּיּוֹם הַהוּא אֶת־הַתְּיָשִׁים הָעֲקֻדִּים וְהַטְּלֻאִים
or-the-being-spotted-ones the-streaked-ones the-male-goats *** the-that on-the-day

וְאֵת כָּל־הָעִזִּים הַנְּקֻדּוֹת וְהַטְּלֻאֹת כֹּל
all or-the-being-spotted-ones the-speckled-ones the-female-goats all-of and

אֲשֶׁר־לָבָן בּוֹ וְכָל־חוּם בַּכְּשָׂבִים וַיִּתֵּן בְּיַד־
in-hand-of and-he-placed from-the-lambs dark and-every-of on-him white that

I've done for you."
[27]But Laban said to him, "If
I have found favor in your
eyes, please stay. I have
learned by divination that[p]
the LORD has blessed me because of you." [28]He added,
"Name your wages, and I will
pay them."
[29]Jacob said to him, "You
know how I have worked for
you and how your livestock
has fared under my care. [30]The
little you had before I came
has increased greatly, and the
LORD has blessed you
wherever I have been. But
now, when may I do some-
thing for my own
household?"
[31]"What shall I give you?" he
asked.
"Don't give me anything,"
Jacob replied. "But if you will
do this one thing for me, I will
go on tending your flocks and
watching over them: [32]Let me
go through all your flocks today and remove from them
every speckled or spotted
sheep, every dark-colored
lamb and every spotted or
speckled goat. They will be my
wages. [33]And my honesty will
testify for me in the future,
whenever you check on the
wages you have paid me. Any
goat in my possession that is
not speckled or spotted, or any
lamb that is not dark-colored
will be considered stolen."
[34]"Agreed," said Laban. "Let
it be as you have said." [35]That
same day he removed all the
male goats that were streaked
or spotted, and all the speckled
or spotted female goats (all
that had white on them) and
all the dark-colored lambs, and
he placed them in the care of

[p]27 Or possibly *have become rich and*

בָּנָיו׃ וַיָּשֶׂם דֶּרֶךְ שְׁלֹשֶׁת יָמִים בֵּינוֹ וּבֵין
and-between between-him days three-of journey-of then-he-put (36) sons-of-him

יַעֲקֹב וְיַעֲקֹב רֹעֶה אֶת־ צֹאן לָבָן הַנּוֹתָרֹת׃ וַיִּקַּח־
and-he-took (37) the-ones-being-left Laban flock-of *** tending and-Jacob Jacob

לוֹ יַעֲקֹב מַקַּל לִבְנֶה לַח וְלוּז וְעַרְמוֹן וַיְפַצֵּל
and-he-peeled and-plane and-almond fresh-cut poplar from-branch-of Jacob to-him

בָּהֵן פְּצָלוֹת לְבָנוֹת מַחְשֹׂף הַלָּבָן אֲשֶׁר עַל־ הַמַּקְלוֹת׃
the-branches in that the-white exposed white-ones stripes in-them

וַיַּצֵּג אֶת־ הַמַּקְלוֹת אֲשֶׁר פִּצֵּל בָּרְהָטִים בְּשִׁקְתוֹת
in-troughs-of in-the-troughs he-peeled that the-branches *** then-he-placed (38)

הַמַּיִם אֲשֶׁר תָּבֹאןָ הַצֹּאן לִשְׁתּוֹת לְנֹכַח הַצֹּאן
the-flock in-front-of to-drink the-flock they-came where the-water

וַיֵּחַמְנָה בְּבֹאָן לִשְׁתּוֹת׃ וַיֶּחֱמוּ הַצֹּאן
the-flock and-they-mated (39) to-drink when-to-come-them as-they-were-in-heat

אֶל־ הַמַּקְלוֹת וַתֵּלַדְןָ הַצֹּאן עֲקֻדִּים נְקֻדִּים
speckled-ones streaked-ones the-flock and-they-bore the-branches by

וּטְלֻאִים׃ וְהַכְּשָׂבִים הִפְרִיד יַעֲקֹב וַיִּתֵּן
but-he-made Jacob he-set-apart and-the-young-ones (40) and-being-spotted-ones

פְּנֵי הַצֹּאן אֶל־ עָקֹד וְכָל־ חוּם בְּצֹאן לָבָן וַיָּשֶׁת־
thus-he-made Laban in-flock-of dark and-all-of streaked to the-flock faces-of

לוֹ עֲדָרִים לְבַדּוֹ וְלֹא שָׁתָם עַל־ צֹאן לָבָן׃
Laban flock-of with he-put-them and-not for-himself flocks for-him

וְהָיָה בְּכָל־ יַחֵם הַצֹּאן הַמְקֻשָּׁרוֹת
the-ones-being-stronger the-female to-be-in-heat when-ever and-he-was (41)

וְשָׂם יַעֲקֹב אֶת־ הַמַּקְלוֹת לְעֵינֵי הַצֹּאן בָּרְהָטִים
in-the-troughs the-animal in-front-of the-branches *** Jacob that-he-placed

לְיַחְמֵנָּה בַּמַּקְלוֹת׃ וּבְהַעֲטִיף הַצֹּאן לֹא
not the-animal but-if-to-be-weak (42) near-the-branches to-mate-them

יָשִׂים וְהָיָה הָעֲטֻפִים לְלָבָן וְהַקְּשֻׁרִים
and-the-ones-being-strong to-Laban the-ones-being-weak so-he-was he-placed

לְיַעֲקֹב׃ וַיִּפְרֹץ הָאִישׁ מְאֹד מְאֹד וַיְהִי־ לוֹ
to-him and-he-was greatly greatly the-man so-he-prospered (43) to-Jacob

צֹאן רַבּוֹת וּשְׁפָחוֹת וַעֲבָדִים וּגְמַלִּים וַחֲמֹרִים׃
and-donkeys and-camels and-menservants and-maidservants large-ones flock

וַיִּשְׁמַע אֶת־ דִּבְרֵי בְנֵי־ לָבָן לֵאמֹר לָקַח יַעֲקֹב אֵת
*** Jacob he-took to-say Laban sons-of words-of *** now-he-heard (31:1)

כָּל־ אֲשֶׁר לְאָבִינוּ וּמֵאֲשֶׁר לְאָבִינוּ עָשָׂה אֵת כָּל־
all-of *** he-gained to-father-of-us and-from-what to-father-of-us that all

his sons. [36]Then he put a three-day journey between himself and Jacob, while Jacob continued to tend the rest of Laban's flocks.

[37]Jacob, however, took fresh-cut branches from poplar, almond and plane trees and made white stripes on them by peeling the bark and exposing the white inner wood of the branches. [38]Then he placed the peeled branches in all the watering troughs, so that they would be directly in front of the flocks when they came to drink. When the flocks were in heat and came to drink, [39]they mated in front of the branches. And they bore young that were streaked or speckled or spotted. [40]Jacob set apart the young of the flock by themselves, but made the rest face the streaked and dark-colored animals that belonged to Laban. Thus he made separate flocks for himself and did not put them with Laban's animals. [41]Whenever the stronger females were in heat, Jacob would place the branches in the troughs in front of the animals so they would mate near the branches, [42]but if the animals were weak, he would not place them there. So the weak animals went to Laban and the strong ones to Jacob. [43]In this way the man grew exceedingly prosperous and came to own large flocks, and maidservants and menservants, and camels and donkeys.

Jacob Flees From Laban

31 Jacob heard that Laban's sons were saying, "Jacob has taken everything our father owned and has gained all this wealth

הַכָּבֹד הַזֶּה׃ וַיַּרְא יַעֲקֹב אֶת־ פְּנֵי לָבָן וְהִנֵּה
and-see! Laban attitudes-of *** Jacob and-he-noticed (2) the-this the-wealth

אֵינֶנּוּ עִמּוֹ כִּתְמוֹל שִׁלְשׁוֹם׃ וַיֹּאמֶר יְהוָה אֶל־ יַעֲקֹב שׁוּב
go-back! Jacob to Yahweh then-he-said (3) formerly as-before with-him not-he

אֶל־ אֶרֶץ אֲבוֹתֶיךָ וּלְמוֹלַדְתֶּךָ וְאֶהְיֶה עִמָּךְ׃
with-you and-I-will-be and-to-relative-of-you fathers-of-you land-of to

וַיִּשְׁלַח יַעֲקֹב וַיִּקְרָא לְרָחֵל וּלְלֵאָה הַשָּׂדֶה אֶל־
to the-field and-to-Leah to-Rachel and-he-called Jacob so-he-sent (4)

צֹאנוֹ׃ וַיֹּאמֶר לָהֶן רֹאֶה אָנֹכִי אֶת־ פְּנֵי אֲבִיכֶן
father-of-you attitudes-of *** I seeing to-them and-he-said (5) flock-of-him

כִּי־ אֵינֶנּוּ אֵלַי כִּתְמֹל שִׁלְשֹׁם וֵאלֹהֵי אָבִי הָיָה עִמָּדִי׃
with-me he-is father-of-me but-God-of formerly as-before to-me not-he that

וְאַתֵּנָה יְדַעְתֶּן כִּי בְּכָל־ כֹּחִי עָבַדְתִּי אֶת־ אֲבִיכֶן׃
father-of-you *** I-served strength-of-me with-all-of that you-know now-you (6)

וַאֲבִיכֶן הֵתֶל בִּי וְהֶחֱלִף אֶת־ מַשְׂכֻּרְתִּי
wage-of-me *** and-he-changed with-me he-cheated yet-father-of-you (7)

עֲשֶׂרֶת מֹנִים וְלֹא־ נְתָנוֹ אֱלֹהִים לְהָרַע עִמָּדִי׃ אִם־ כֹּה יֹאמַר
he-said thus if (8) to-me to-do-harm God he-allowed-him but-not times ten-of

נְקֻדִּים יִהְיֶה שְׂכָרֶךָ וְיָלְדוּ כָל־ הַצֹּאן
the-flock all-of then-they-bore wage-of-you he-will-be speckled-ones

נְקֻדִּים וְאִם־ כֹּה יֹאמַר עֲקֻדִּים יִהְיֶה שְׂכָרֶךָ
wage-of-you he-will-be streaked-ones he-said thus and-if speckled-ones

וְיָלְדוּ כָל־ הַצֹּאן עֲקֻדִּים׃ וַיַּצֵּל אֱלֹהִים אֶת־ מִקְנֵה
stock-of *** God so-he-took (9) streaked-ones the-flock all-of then-they-bore

אֲבִיכֶם וַיִּתֶּן־ לִי׃ וַיְהִי בְּעֵת יַחֵם
to-breed in-season-of now-he-was (10) to-me and-he-gave father-of-you

הַצֹּאן וָאֶשָּׂא עֵינַי וָאֵרֶא בַּחֲלוֹם וְהִנֵּה הָעַתֻּדִים
the-male-goats and-see! in-dream and-I-saw eyes-of-me that-I-lifted the-flock

הָעֹלִים עַל־ הַצֹּאן עֲקֻדִּים נְקֻדִּים וּבְרֻדִּים׃
or-spotted-ones speckled-ones streaked-ones the-flock with the-ones-mating

וַיֹּאמֶר אֵלַי מַלְאַךְ הָאֱלֹהִים בַּחֲלוֹם יַעֲקֹב וָאֹמַר הִנֵּנִי׃
here-I and-I-answered Jacob in-dream the-God angel-of to-me and-he-said (11)

וַיֹּאמֶר שָׂא־ נָא עֵינֶיךָ וּרְאֵה כָּל־ הָעַתֻּדִים
the-male-goats all-of and-see! eyes-of-you now! lift! and-he-said (12)

הָעֹלִים עַל־ הַצֹּאן עֲקֻדִּים נְקֻדִּים וּבְרֻדִּים
or-spotted-ones speckled-ones streaked-ones the-flock with the-ones-mating

כִּי רָאִיתִי אֵת כָּל־אֲשֶׁר לָבָן עֹשֶׂה לָּךְ׃ אָנֹכִי הָאֵל בֵּית־אֵל אֲשֶׁר
where El Beth the-God I (13) to-you he-did Laban that all *** I-saw for

from what belonged to our father." 2And Jacob noticed that
Laban's attitude toward him was not what it had been.
3Then the LORD said to Jacob, "Go back to the land of your fathers and to your relatives, and I will be with you."
4So Jacob sent word to Rachel and Leah to come out to the fields where his flocks
were. 5He said to them, "I see that your father's attitude toward me is not what it was before, but the God of my father has been with me. 6You
know that I've worked for your father with all my
strength, 7yet your father has cheated me by changing my wages ten times. However, God has not allowed him to
harm me. 8If he said, 'The speckled ones will be your wages,' then all the flocks gave birth to speckled young; and if he said, 'The streaked ones will be your wages,' then all the flocks bore streaked
young. 9So God has taken away your father's livestock and has given them to me.
10"In breeding season I once had a dream in which I looked up and saw that the male goats mating with the flock were streaked, speckled or spotted.
11The angel of God said to me in the dream, 'Jacob.' I answered, 'Here I am.' 12And he
said, 'Look up and see that all the male goats mating with the flock are streaked, speckled or spotted, for I have seen all that Laban has been doing to
you. 13I am the God of Bethel,

מָשַׁחְתָּ שָּׁם מַצֵּבָה אֲשֶׁר נָדַרְתָּ לִּי שָׁם נֶדֶר עַתָּה קוּם צֵא
leave! rise! now! vow there to-me you-vowed where pillar there you-anointed

מִן־הָאָרֶץ הַזֹּאת וְשׁוּב אֶל־אֶרֶץ מוֹלַדְתֶּךָ׃ וַתַּעַן
so-she-replied (14) birth-of-you land-of to and-go-back! the-this the-land from

רָחֵל וְלֵאָה וַתֹּאמַרְנָה לוֹ הַעוֹד לָנוּ חֵלֶק וְנַחֲלָה
and-inheritance share to-us still? to-him and-they-said and-Leah Rachel

בְּבֵית אָבִינוּ׃ הֲלוֹא נָכְרִיּוֹת נֶחְשַׁבְנוּ לוֹ כִּי
for by-him we-are-regarded foreigners not? (15) father-of-us in-estate-of

מְכָרָנוּ וַיֹּאכַל גַּם־אָכוֹל אֶת־כַּסְפֵּנוּ׃ כִּי כָל־
all-of surely (16) pay-of-us *** to-use indeed and-he-used he-sold-us

הָעֹשֶׁר אֲשֶׁר הִצִּיל אֱלֹהִים מֵאָבִינוּ לָנוּ הוּא וּלְבָנֵינוּ
and-to-children-of-us that to-us from-father-of-us God he-took that the-wealth

וְעַתָּה כֹּל אֲשֶׁר אָמַר אֱלֹהִים אֵלֶיךָ עֲשֵׂה׃ וַיָּקָם יַעֲקֹב וַיִּשָּׂא אֶת־
*** and-he-put Jacob so-he-rose (17) do! to-you god he-told that all and-now

בָּנָיו וְאֶת־נָשָׁיו עַל־הַגְּמַלִּים׃ וַיִּנְהַג אֶת־כָּל־
all-of *** and-he-drove (18) the-camels on wives-of-him and children-of-him

מִקְנֵהוּ וְאֶת־כָּל־רְכֻשׁוֹ אֲשֶׁר רָכָשׁ מִקְנֵה
livestock-of he-accumulated that good-of-him all-of and stock-of-him

קִנְיָנוֹ אֲשֶׁר רָכַשׁ בְּפַדַּן אֲרָם לָבוֹא אֶל־יִצְחָק
Isaac to to-go Aram in-Paddan he-accumulated that possession-of-him

אָבִיו אַרְצָה כְּנָעַן׃ וְלָבָן הָלַךְ לִגְזֹז אֶת־
*** to-shear he-went when-Laban (19) Canaan to-land-of father-of-him

צֹאנוֹ וַתִּגְנֹב רָחֵל אֶת־הַתְּרָפִים אֲשֶׁר לְאָבִיהָ׃
to-father-of-her that the-gods *** Rachel then-she-stole sheep-of-him

וַיִּגְנֹב יַעֲקֹב אֶת־לֵב לָבָן הָאֲרַמִּי עַל־בְּלִי הִגִּיד
to-tell not by the-Aramean Laban heart-of *** Jacob and-he-deceived (20)

לוֹ כִּי בֹרֵחַ הוּא׃ וַיִּבְרַח הוּא וְכָל־אֲשֶׁר־לוֹ
to-him that with-all he so-he-fled (21) he running-away that to-him

וַיָּקָם וַיַּעֲבֹר אֶת־הַנָּהָר וַיָּשֶׂם אֶת־פָּנָיו
face-of-him *** and-he-headed the-river *** and-he-crossed and-he-rose

הַר הַגִּלְעָד׃ וַיֻּגַּד לְלָבָן בַּיּוֹם הַשְּׁלִישִׁי
the-third on-the-day to-Laban and-he-was-told (22) the-Gilead hill-country-of

כִּי בָרַח יַעֲקֹב׃ וַיִּקַּח אֶת־אֶחָיו עִמּוֹ וַיִּרְדֹּף
and-he-pursued with-him relatives-of-him *** so-he-took (23) Jacob he-fled that

אַחֲרָיו דֶּרֶךְ שִׁבְעַת יָמִים וַיַּדְבֵּק אֹתוֹ בְּהַר הַגִּלְעָד׃
the-Gilead in-hill-of him and-he-caught days seven-of journey-of after-him

וַיָּבֹא אֱלֹהִים אֶל־לָבָן הָאֲרַמִּי בַּחֲלֹם הַלָּיְלָה וַיֹּאמֶר
and-he-said the-night in-dream-of the-Aramean Laban to God then-he-came (24)

where you anointed a pillar and where you made a vow to me. Now leave this land at once and go back to your native land.' "

[14]Then Rachel and Leah replied, "Do we still have any share in the inheritance of our father's estate? [15]Does he not regard us as foreigners? Not only has he sold us, but he has used up what was paid for us. [16]Surely all the wealth that God took away from our father belongs to us and our children. So do whatever God has told you."

[17]Then Jacob put his children and his wives on camels, [18]and he drove all his livestock ahead of him, along with all the goods he had accumulated in Paddan Aram,[q] to go to his father Isaac in the land of Canaan.

[19]When Laban had gone to shear his sheep, Rachel stole her father's household gods. [20]Moreover, Jacob deceived Laban the Aramean by not telling him he was running away. [21]So he fled with all he had, and crossing the River,[r] he headed for the hill country of Gilead.

Laban Pursues Jacob

[22]On the third day Laban was told that Jacob had fled. [23]Taking his relatives with him, he pursued Jacob for seven days and caught up with him in the hill country of Gilead. [24]Then God came to Laban the Aramean in a dream at night and said to him, "Be

[q]*18* That is, Northwest Mesopotamia
[r]*21* That is, the Euphrates

לוֹ הִשָּׁמֶר לְךָ פֶּן־תְּדַבֵּר עִם־יַעֲקֹב מִטּוֹב עַד־רָע׃
bad or either-good Jacob to you-say that-not yourself be-careful! to-him

(25) וַיַּשֵּׂג לָבָן אֶת־יַעֲקֹב וְיַעֲקֹב תָּקַע אֶת־אָהֳלוֹ
tent-of-him *** he-pitched now-Jacob Jacob *** Laban when-he-overtook (25)

בָּהָר וְלָבָן תָּקַע אֶת־אֶחָיו בְּהַר
in-hill-country-of relatives-of-him with he-camped so-Laban on-the-hill

הַגִּלְעָד׃ (26) וַיֹּאמֶר לָבָן לְיַעֲקֹב מֶה עָשִׂיתָ וַתִּגְנֹב
now-you-deceived you-did what? to-Jacob Laban then-he-said (26) the-Gilead

אֶת־לְבָבִי וַתְּנַהֵג אֶת־בְּנֹתַי כִּשְׁבֻיוֹת
like-being-captives-of daughters-of-me *** and-you-carried-off heart-of-me ***

חָרֶב׃ (27) לָמָּה נַחְבֵּאתָ לִבְרֹחַ וַתִּגְנֹב אֹתִי וְלֹא־הִגַּדְתָּ
you-tell and-not me and-you-deceive to-run-off you-were-secret why? (27) sword

לִּי וָאֲשַׁלֵּחֲךָ בְּשִׂמְחָה וּבְשִׁרִים בְּתֹף
with-tambourine and-with-songs with-joy so-I-could-send-away-you to-me

וּבְכִנּוֹר׃ (28) וְלֹא נְטַשְׁתַּנִי לְנַשֵּׁק לְבָנַי
on-grandchildren-of-me to-kiss you-let-me and-not (28) and-with-harp

וְלִבְנֹתָי עַתָּה הִסְכַּלְתָּ עֲשׂוֹ׃ (29) יֶשׁ־לְאֵל יָדִי
power-of-me in it-is (29) to-do you-were-foolish now or-on-daughters-of-me

לַעֲשׂוֹת עִמָּכֶם רָע וֵאלֹהֵי אֲבִיכֶם אֶמֶשׁ׀ אָמַר אֵלַי לֵאמֹר
to-say to-me he-spoke last-night father-of-you but-God-of harm to-you to-do

הִשָּׁמֶר לְךָ מִדַּבֵּר עִם־יַעֲקֹב מִטּוֹב עַד־רָע׃ (30) וְעַתָּה
and-now (30) bad nor neither-good Jacob to that-to-say yourself be-careful!

הָלֹךְ הָלַכְתָּ כִּי־נִכְסֹף נִכְסַפְתָּה לְבֵית אָבִיךָ לָמָּה
why? father-of-you for-house-of you-longed to-long because you-went to-go

גָנַבְתָּ אֶת־אֱלֹהָי׃ (31) וַיַּעַן יַעֲקֹב וַיֹּאמֶר לְלָבָן
to-Laban and-he-said Jacob and-he-answered (31) gods-of-me *** you-stole

כִּי יָרֵאתִי כִּי אָמַרְתִּי פֶּן־תִּגְזֹל אֶת־
*** you-would-take-by-force that I-thought for I-was-afraid indeed

בְּנוֹתֶיךָ מֵעִמִּי׃ (32) עִם אֲשֶׁר תִּמְצָא אֶת־אֱלֹהֶיךָ לֹא
not gods-of-you *** you-find whom with (32) from-me daughters-of-you

יִחְיֶה נֶגֶד אַחֵינוּ הַכֶּר־לְךָ מָה עִמָּדִי וְקַח־
and-take! with-me what for-yourself see! relatives-of-us before he-shall-live

לָךְ וְלֹא־יָדַע יַעֲקֹב כִּי רָחֵל גְּנָבָתַם׃ (33) וַיָּבֹא
so-he-went (33) she-stole-them Rachel that Jacob he-knew now-not if-yours

לָבָן בְּאֹהֶל יַעֲקֹב׀ וּבְאֹהֶל לֵאָה וּבְאֹהֶל שְׁתֵּי
two-of and-into-tent-of Leah and-into-tent-of Jacob into-tent-of Laban

הָאֲמָהֹת וְלֹא מָצָא וַיֵּצֵא מֵאֹהֶל לֵאָה וַיָּבֹא
and-he-went Leah from-tent-of so-he-came-out he-found but-not the-maidservants

careful not to say anything to
Jacob, either good or bad."
25 Jacob had pitched his tent
in the hill country of Gilead
when Laban overtook him,
and Laban and his relatives
camped there too. 26 Then Laban said to Jacob, "What have
you done? You've deceived
me, and you've carried off my
daughters like captives in war.
27 Why did you run off secretly
and deceive me? Why didn't
you tell me, so I could send
you away with joy and singing to the music of tambourines and harps? 28 You didn't
even let me kiss my grandchildren and my daughters good-
by. You have done a foolish
thing. 29 I have the power to
harm you; but last night the
God of your father said to me,
'Be careful not to say anything
to Jacob, either good or bad.'
30 Now you have gone off because you longed to return to
your father's house. But why
did you steal my gods?"
31 Jacob answered Laban, "I
was afraid, because I thought
you would take your daughters away from me by force.
32 But if you find anyone who
has your gods, he shall not
live. In the presence of our
relatives, see for yourself
whether there is anything of
yours here with me; and if so,
take it." Now Jacob did not
know that Rachel had stolen
the gods.
33 So Laban went into Jacob's
tent and into Leah's tent and
into the tent of the two maidservants, but he found nothing. After he came out of

בְּאֹהֶל רָחֵל׃ (34) וְרָחֵל לָקְחָה אֶת־הַתְּרָפִים וַתְּשִׂמֵם
and-she-put-them the-gods *** she-took now-Rachel (34) Rachel into-tent-of

בְּכַר הַגָּמָל וַתֵּשֶׁב עֲלֵיהֶם וַיְמַשֵּׁשׁ לָבָן אֶת־כָּל־
all-of *** Laban and-he-searched on-them and-she-sat the-camel in-saddle-of

הָאֹהֶל וְלֹא מָצָא׃ (35) וַתֹּאמֶר אֶל־אָבִיהָ אַל־
not father-of-her to and-she-said (35) he-found but-not the-tent

יִחַר בְּעֵינֵי אֲדֹנִי כִּי לוֹא אוּכַל לָקוּם מִפָּנֶיךָ
in-presence-of-you to-stand I-can not but lord-of-me in-eyes-of may-he-be-angry

כִּי־דֶרֶךְ נָשִׁים לִי וַיְחַפֵּשׂ וְלֹא מָצָא אֶת־הַתְּרָפִים׃
the-gods *** he-found but-not so-he-searched to-me women way-of for

(36) וַיִּחַר לְיַעֲקֹב וַיָּרֶב בְּלָבָן וַיַּעַן יַעֲקֹב
Jacob and-he-asked at-Laban and-he-scolded to-Jacob and-he-angered (36)

וַיֹּאמֶר לְלָבָן מַה־פִּשְׁעִי מַה חַטָּאתִי כִּי דָלַקְתָּ
you-hunted that sin-of-me what? crime-of-me what? to-Laban and-he-said

אַחֲרָי׃ (37) כִּי־מִשַּׁשְׁתָּ אֶת־כָּל־כֵּלַי מַה־מָּצָאתָ
you-found what? goods-of-me all-of *** you-searched now (37) after-me

מִכֹּל כְּלֵי־בֵיתֶךָ שִׂים כֹּה נֶגֶד אַחַי
relatives-of-me in-front-of here put! household-of-you goods-of from-any-of

וְאַחֶיךָ וְיוֹכִיחוּ בֵּין שְׁנֵינוּ׃ (38) זֶה עֶשְׂרִים
twenty now (38) two-of-us between and-let-them-judge and-relatives-of-you

שָׁנָה אָנֹכִי עִמָּךְ רְחֵלֶיךָ וְעִזֶּיךָ לֹא שִׁכֵּלוּ וְאֵילֵי
and-rams-of they-miscarried not and-goats-of-you sheep-of-you with-you I year

צֹאנְךָ לֹא אָכָלְתִּי׃ (39) טְרֵפָה לֹא־הֵבֵאתִי אֵלֶיךָ אָנֹכִי אֲחַטֶּנָּה
I-bore-loss-of-her I to-you I-brought not torn-animal (39) I-ate not flock-of-you

מִיָּדִי תְּבַקְשֶׁנָּה גְּנֻבְתִי יוֹם וּגְנֻבְתִי לָיְלָה׃
night or-being-stolen-of day being-stolen-of you-required-her from-hand-of-me

(40) הָיִיתִי בַיּוֹם אֲכָלַנִי חֹרֶב וְקֶרַח בַּלָּיְלָה וַתִּדַּד
and-he-fled in-the-night and-cold heat he-consumed-me in-the-day I-was (40)

שְׁנָתִי מֵעֵינָי׃ (41) זֶה־לִּי עֶשְׂרִים שָׁנָה בְּבֵיתֶךָ
in-household-of-you year twenty to-me this (41) from-eyes-of-me sleep-of-me

עֲבַדְתִּיךָ אַרְבַּע־עֶשְׂרֵה שָׁנָה בִּשְׁתֵּי בְנֹתֶיךָ וְשֵׁשׁ שָׁנִים
years and-six daughters-of-you for-two-of year ten four I-served-you

בְּצֹאנֶךָ וַתַּחֲלֵף אֶת־מַשְׂכֻּרְתִּי עֲשֶׂרֶת מֹנִים׃ (42) לוּלֵי אֱלֹהֵי
God-of if-not (42) times ten wage-of-me *** and-you-changed for-flock-of-you

אָבִי אֱלֹהֵי אַבְרָהָם וּפַחַד יִצְחָק הָיָה לִי כִּי עַתָּה
now surely with-me he-was Isaac and-Fear-of Abraham God-of father-of-me

רֵיקָם שִׁלַּחְתָּנִי אֶת־עָנְיִי וְאֶת־יְגִיעַ
toil-of and hardship-of-me *** you-would-have-sent-me empty-handed

Leah's tent, he entered Rachel's tent. [34]Now Rachel had
taken the household gods and
put them inside her camel's
saddle and was sitting on
them. Laban searched through
everything in the tent but
found nothing.

[35]Rachel said to her father,
"Don't be angry, my lord, that
I cannot stand up in your pres-
ence; I'm having my period."
So he searched but could not
find the household gods.

[36]Jacob was angry and took
Laban to task. "What is my
crime?" he asked Laban.
"What sin have I committed
that you hunt me down?
[37]Now that you have searched
through all my goods, what
have you found that belongs
to your household? Put it here
in front of your relatives and
mine, and let them judge between the two of us.

[38]"I have been with you for
twenty years now. Your sheep
and goats have not miscarried,
nor have I eaten rams from
your flocks. [39]I did not bring
you animals torn by wild
beasts; I bore the loss myself.
And you demanded payment
from me for whatever was stolen by day or night. [40]This was
my situation: The heat consumed me in the daytime and
the cold at night, and sleep
fled from my eyes. [41]It was like
this for the twenty years I was
in your household. I worked
for you fourteen years for your
two daughters and six years
for your flocks, and you
changed my wages ten times.
[42]If the God of my father, the
God of Abraham and the Fear
of Isaac, had not been with
me, you would surely have
sent me away empty-handed.

כַּפַּי רָאָה אֱלֹהִים וַיּוֹכַח אָמֶשׁ׃ וַיַּעַן לָבָן
Laban and-he-answered (43) last-night and-he-rebuked God he-saw hands-of-me

וַיֹּאמֶר אֶל־ יַעֲקֹב הַבָּנוֹת בְּנֹתַי וְהַבָּנִים
and-the-children daughters-of-me the-women Jacob to and-he-said

בָּנַי וְהַצֹּאן צֹאנִי וְכֹל אֲשֶׁר־ אַתָּה רֹאֶה לִי־ הוּא
he to-me seeing you that and-all flock-of-me and-the-flock children-of-me

וְלִבְנֹתַי מָה־ אֶעֱשֶׂה לָאֵלֶּה הַיּוֹם אוֹ
or the-day about-these can-I-do what? yet-about-daughters-of-me

לִבְנֵיהֶן אֲשֶׁר יָלָדוּ׃ וְעַתָּה לְכָה נִכְרְתָה בְרִית
covenant let-us-make come! so-now (44) they-bore that about-children-of-them

אֲנִי וָאָתָּה וְהָיָה לְעֵד בֵּינִי וּבֵינֶךָ׃ וַיִּקַּח
so-he-took (45) and-between-you between-me as-witness and-he-will-be and-you I

יַעֲקֹב אָבֶן וַיְרִימֶהָ מַצֵּבָה׃ וַיֹּאמֶר יַעֲקֹב לְאֶחָיו
to-relatives-of-him Jacob and-he-said (46) pillar and-he-set-up-her stone Jacob

לִקְטוּ אֲבָנִים וַיִּקְחוּ אֲבָנִים וַיַּעֲשׂוּ־ גָל וַיֹּאכְלוּ שָׁם
there and-they-ate heap and-they-made stones so-they-took stones gather!

עַל־ הַגָּל׃ וַיִּקְרָא־ לוֹ לָבָן יְגַר שָׂהֲדוּתָא וְיַעֲקֹב
and-Jacob Sahadutha Jegar Laban to-him and-he-called (47) the-heap near

קָרָא לוֹ גַּלְעֵד׃ וַיֹּאמֶר לָבָן הַגַּל הַזֶּה עֵד
witness the-this the-heap Laban and-he-said (48) Galeed to-him he-called

בֵּינִי וּבֵינְךָ הַיּוֹם עַל־ כֵּן קָרָא־ שְׁמוֹ גַּלְעֵד׃
Galeed name-of-him he-called this for the-day and-between-you between-me

וְהַמִּצְפָּה אֲשֶׁר אָמַר יִצֶף יְהוָה בֵּינִי וּבֵינֶךָ
and-between-you between-me Yahweh may-he-watch he-said for also-the-Mizpah (49)

כִּי נִסָּתֵר אִישׁ מֵרֵעֵהוּ׃ אִם־ תְּעַנֶּה אֶת־
*** you-mistreat if (50) from-other-of-him one we-are-away when

בְּנֹתַי וְאִם־ תִּקַּח נָשִׁים עַל־ בְּנֹתַי אֵין אִישׁ עִמָּנוּ
with-us man not daughters-of-me besides wives you-take or-if daughters-of-me

רְאֵה אֱלֹהִים עֵד בֵּינִי וּבֵינֶךָ׃ וַיֹּאמֶר לָבָן
Laban and-he-said (51) and-between-you between-me witness God remember!

לְיַעֲקֹב הִנֵּה ׀ הַגַּל הַזֶּה וְהִנֵּה הַמַּצֵּבָה אֲשֶׁר יָרִיתִי בֵּינִי
between-me I-set-up that the-pillar and-see! the-this the-heap see! to-Jacob

וּבֵינֶךָ׃ עֵד הַגַּל הַזֶּה וְעֵדָה הַמַּצֵּבָה אִם־
that the-pillar and-witness the-this the-heap witness (52) and-between-you

אָנִי לֹא־ אֶעֱבֹר אֵלֶיךָ אֶת־ הַגַּל הַזֶּה וְאִם־ אַתָּה לֹא־
not you and-that the-this the-heap *** to-you I-will-go-past not I

תַעֲבֹר אֵלַי אֶת־ הַגַּל הַזֶּה וְאֶת־ הַמַּצֵּבָה הַזֹּאת לְרָעָה׃
for-harm the-this the-pillar and the-this the-heap *** to-me you-will-go-past

But God has seen my hardship and the toil of my hands, and last night he rebuked you."

43 Laban answered Jacob, "The women are my daughters, the children are my children, and the flocks are my flocks. All you see is mine. Yet what can I do today about these daughters of mine, or about the children they have borne? 44 Come now, let's make a covenant, you and I, and let it serve as a witness between us."

45 So Jacob took a stone and set it up as a pillar. 46 He said to his relatives, "Gather some stones." So they took stones and piled them in a heap, and they ate there by the heap. 47 Laban called it Jegar Sahadutha,[s] and Jacob called it Galeed.[t]

48 Laban said, "This heap is a witness between you and me today." That is why it was called Galeed. 49 It was also called Mizpah,[u] because he said, "May the LORD keep watch between you and me when we are away from each other. 50 If you mistreat my daughters or if you take any wives besides my daughters, even though no one is with us, remember that God is a witness between you and me."

51 Laban also said to Jacob, "Here is this heap, and here is this pillar I have set up between you and me. 52 This heap is a witness, and this pillar is a witness, that I will not go past this heap to your side to harm you and that you will not go past this heap and pillar to my side to harm me. 53 May

[s]47 The Aramaic *Jegar Sahadutha* means *witness heap.*
[t]47 The Hebrew *Galeed* means *witness heap.*
[u]49 *Mizpah* means *watchtower.*

*51 Most mss have *dagesh* in the *mem* (הַמּ׳).

אֱלֹהֵי אַבְרָהָם וֵאלֹהֵי נָחוֹר יִשְׁפְּטוּ בֵינֵינוּ אֱלֹהֵי
God-of between-us may-they-judge Nahor and-God-of Abraham God-of (53)

אֲבִיהֶם וַיִּשָּׁבַע יַעֲקֹב בְּפַחַד אָבִיו יִצְחָק׃
Isaac father-of-him by-Fear-of Jacob so-he-swore father-of-them

וַיִּזְבַּח יַעֲקֹב זֶבַח בָּהָר וַיִּקְרָא
and-he-invited in-the-hill-country sacrifice Jacob and-he-offered (54)

לְאֶחָיו לֶאֱכָל־לָחֶם וַיֹּאכְלוּ לֶחֶם וַיָּלִינוּ בָּהָר׃
on-the-hill so-they-spent-night meal so-they-ate meal to-eat to-relatives-of-him

וַיַּשְׁכֵּם לָבָן בַּבֹּקֶר וַיְנַשֵּׁק לְבָנָיו
on-grandchildren-of-him and-he-kissed in-the-morning Laban and-he-rose (32:1)*

וְלִבְנוֹתָיו וַיְבָרֶךְ אֶתְהֶם וַיֵּלֶךְ וַיָּשָׁב
and-he-returned then-he-left them and-he-blessed and-on-daughters-of-him

לָבָן לִמְקֹמוֹ׃ וְיַעֲקֹב הָלַךְ לְדַרְכּוֹ וַיִּפְגְּעוּ־בוֹ
with-him and-they-met on-way-of-him he-went and-Jacob (2) to-home-of-him Laban

מַלְאֲכֵי אֱלֹהִים׃ וַיֹּאמֶר יַעֲקֹב כַּאֲשֶׁר רָאָם מַחֲנֵה אֱלֹהִים זֶה
this God camp-of he-saw-them when Jacob and-he-said (3) God angels-of

וַיִּקְרָא שֵׁם־הַמָּקוֹם הַהוּא מַחֲנָיִם׃ וַיִּשְׁלַח יַעֲקֹב
Jacob and-he-sent (4) Mahanaim the-that the-place name-of so-he-called

מַלְאָכִים לְפָנָיו אֶל־עֵשָׂו אָחִיו אַרְצָה שֵׂעִיר שְׂדֵה אֱדוֹם׃
Edom country-of Seir to-land-of brother-of-him Esau to ahead-of-him messengers

וַיְצַו אֹתָם לֵאמֹר כֹּה תֹאמְרוּן לַאדֹנִי לְעֵשָׂו
to-Esau to-master-of-me you-will-say this to-say them and-he-instructed (5)

כֹּה אָמַר עַבְדְּךָ† יַעֲקֹב עִם־לָבָן גַּרְתִּי וָאֵחַר עַד־
till and-I-remained I-stayed Laban with Jacob servant-of-you he-says this

עָתָּה׃ וַיְהִי־לִי שׁוֹר וַחֲמוֹר צֹאן וְעֶבֶד
and-menservant flock and-donkey cattle to-me and-he-is (6) now

וְשִׁפְחָה וָאֶשְׁלְחָה לְהַגִּיד לַאדֹנִי לִמְצֹא־חֵן בְּעֵינֶיךָ׃
in-eyes-of-you favor to-find to-lord-of-me to-tell and-I-sent and-maidservant

וַיָּשֻׁבוּ הַמַּלְאָכִים אֶל־יַעֲקֹב לֵאמֹר בָּאנוּ אֶל־אָחִיךָ
brother-of-you to we-went to-say Jacob to the-messengers when they-returned (7)

אֶל־עֵשָׂו וְגַם הֹלֵךְ לִקְרָאתְךָ וְאַרְבַּע־מֵאוֹת אִישׁ עִמּוֹ׃
with-him man hundreds and-four to-meet-you coming and now Esau to

וַיִּירָא יַעֲקֹב מְאֹד וַיֵּצֶר לוֹ וַיַּחַץ
so-he-divided himself and-he-distressed greatly Jacob and-he-was-afraid (8)

אֶת־הָעָם אֲשֶׁר־אִתּוֹ וְאֶת־הַצֹּאן וְאֶת־הַבָּקָר וְהַגְּמַלִּים
and-the-camels the-herd and the-flock and with-him that the-people ***

לִשְׁנֵי מַחֲנוֹת׃ וַיֹּאמֶר אִם־יָבוֹא עֵשָׂו אֶל־הַמַּחֲנֶה הָאַחַת
the-one the-group to Esau he-comes if and-he-thought (9) groups into-two-of

the God of Abraham and the
God of Nahor, the God of their
father, judge between us."
So Jacob took an oath in the
name of the Fear of his father
Isaac. [54]He offered a sacrifice
there in the hill country and
invited his relatives to a meal.
After they had eaten, they
spent the night there.
[55]Early the next morning Laban kissed his grandchildren
and his daughters and blessed
them. Then he left and returned home.

Jacob Prepares to Meet Esau

32 Jacob also went on his
way, and the angels of
God met him. [2]When Jacob
saw them, he said, "This is the
camp of God!" So he named
that place Mahanaim.[v]
[3]Jacob sent messengers
ahead of him to his brother
Esau in the land of Seir, the
country of Edom. [4]He instructed them: "This is what you are
to say to my master Esau:
'Your servant Jacob says, I
have been staying with Laban
and have remained there till
now. [5]I have cattle and donkeys, sheep and goats, menservants and maidservants.
Now I am sending this message to my lord, that I may
find favor in your eyes.' "
[6]When the messengers returned to Jacob, they said,
"We went to your brother
Esau, and now he is coming to
meet you, and four hundred
men are with him."
[7]In great fear and distress
Jacob divided the people who
were with him into two
groups, and the flocks and
herds and camels as well. [8]He
thought, "If Esau comes and

[v]2 *Mahanaim* means *two camps.*

*The Hebrew numeration of chapter 32 begins with verse 55 of chapter 31 in English; thus, there is a one- verse discrepancy throughout chapter 32.

†5 Most mss have *dagesh* in the *daleth* (־דְּךָ).

וְהִכָּהוּ וְהָיָה הַמַּחֲנֶה הַנִּשְׁאָר לִפְלֵיטָה׃
to-escape the-one-being-left the-group then-he-may-be and-he-attacks-him

וַיֹּאמֶר יַעֲקֹב אֱלֹהֵי אָבִי אַבְרָהָם וֵאלֹהֵי אָבִי
father-of-me and-God-of Abraham father-of-me God-of Jacob then-he-prayed (10)

יִצְחָק יְהוָה הָאֹמֵר אֵלַי שׁוּב לְאַרְצְךָ וּלְמוֹלַדְתְּךָ
to-relative-of-you to-land-of-you go-back! to-me the-one-saying Yahweh Isaac

וְאֵיטִיבָה עִמָּךְ׃ קָטֹנְתִּי מִכֹּל הַחֲסָדִים
the-kindnesses of-all-of I-am-unworthy (11) with-you and-I-will-make-prosper

וּמִכָּל־ הָאֱמֶת אֲשֶׁר עָשִׂיתָ אֶת־ עַבְדֶּךָ כִּי
only servant-of-you *** you-showed that the-faithfulness and-of-all-of

בְמַקְלִי עָבַרְתִּי אֶת־ הַיַּרְדֵּן הַזֶּה וְעַתָּה הָיִיתִי לִשְׁנֵי
as-two-of I-became but-now the-this the-Jordan *** I-crossed with-staff-of-me

מַחֲנוֹת׃ הַצִּילֵנִי נָא מִיַּד אָחִי מִיַּד עֵשָׂו כִּי־
for Esau from-hand-of brother-of-me from-hand-of now! save-me! (12) groups

יָרֵא אָנֹכִי אֹתוֹ פֶּן־ יָבוֹא וְהִכַּנִי אֵם עַל־ בָּנִים׃
children with mother and-he-will-attack-me he-will-come that him I fearing

וְאַתָּה אָמַרְתָּ הֵיטֵב אֵיטִיב עִמָּךְ וְשַׂמְתִּי
and-I-will-make with-you I-will-make-prosper to-prosper you-said but-you (13)

אֶת־ זַרְעֲךָ כְּחוֹל הַיָּם אֲשֶׁר לֹא־ יִסָּפֵר
he-can-be-counted not that the-sea like-sand-of descendant-of-you ***

מֵרֹב׃ וַיָּלֶן שָׁם בַּלַּיְלָה הַהוּא וַיִּקַּח
and-he-took the-that during-the-night there so-he-stayed (14) because-of-size

מִן־ הַבָּא בְיָדוֹ מִנְחָה לְעֵשָׂו אָחִיו׃
brother-of-him for-Esau gift in-hand-of-him the-one-being from

עִזִּים מָאתַיִם וּתְיָשִׁים עֶשְׂרִים רְחֵלִים מָאתַיִם וְאֵילִים
and-rams two-hundreds ewes twenty and-male-goats two-hundreds female-goats (15)

עֶשְׂרִים׃ גְּמַלִּים מֵינִיקוֹת וּבְנֵיהֶם שְׁלֹשִׁים פָּרוֹת אַרְבָּעִים
forty cows thirty with-young-ones-of-them being-females camels (16) twenty

וּפָרִים עֲשָׂרָה אֲתֹנֹת עֶשְׂרִים וַעְיָרִם עֲשָׂרָה׃ וַיִּתֵּן
and-he-put (17) ten and-male-donkeys twenty female-donkeys ten and-bulls

בְּיַד־ עֲבָדָיו עֵדֶר עֵדֶר לְבַדּוֹ וַיֹּאמֶר אֶל־ עֲבָדָיו
servants-of-him to and-he-said by-himself herd herd servants-of-him in-care-of

עִבְרוּ לְפָנַי וְרֶוַח תָּשִׂימוּ בֵּין עֵדֶר וּבֵין עֵדֶר׃
herd and-between herd between you-keep and-space ahead-of-me go!

וַיְצַו אֶת־ הָרִאשׁוֹן לֵאמֹר כִּי יִפְגָּשְׁךָ עֵשָׂו אָחִי
brother-of-me Esau he-meets-you when to-say the-leader *** and-he-instructed (18)

וִשְׁאֵלְךָ† לֵאמֹר לְמִי־ אַתָּה וְאָנָה תֵלֵךְ וּלְמִי אֵלֶּה
these and-to-whom? you-go and-where? you to-whom? to-say and-he-asks-you

attacks one group, the group
that is left may escape."
9Then Jacob prayed, "O God
of my father Abraham, God of
my father Isaac, O LORD, who
said to me, 'Go back to your
country and your relatives,
and I will make you prosper,'
10I am unworthy of all the
kindness and faithfulness you
have shown your servant. I
had only my staff when I
crossed this Jordan, but now I
have become two groups.[w]
11Save me, I pray, from the
hand of my brother Esau, for I
am afraid he will come and attack me, and also the mothers
with their children. 12But you
have said, 'I will surely make
you prosper and will make
your descendants like the
sand of the sea, which cannot
be counted.' "
13He spent the night there,
and from what he had with
him he selected a gift for his
brother Esau: 14two hundred
female goats and twenty male
goats, two hundred ewes and
twenty rams, 15thirty female
camels with their young, forty
cows and ten bulls, and
twenty female donkeys and
ten male donkeys. 16He put
them in the care of his servants, each herd by itself, and
said to his servants, "Go
ahead of me, and keep some
space between the herds."
17He instructed the one in
the lead: "When my brother
Esau meets you and asks, 'To
whom do you belong, and
where are you going, and who
owns all these animals in

w10 Or *camps*

*See the note on page 87.

†18 Most mss have *shureq* instead of *vav* with *hireq* (וִשְׁ).

לְפָנֶיךָ׃ וְאָמַרְתָּ לְעַבְדְּךָ לְיַעֲקֹב מִנְחָה הִוא
this gift to-Jacob to-servant-of-you then-you-say (19) ahead-of-you

שְׁלוּחָה לַאדֹנִי לְעֵשָׂו וְהִנֵּה גַם־ הוּא אַחֲרֵינוּ׃
behind-us he also and-see! to-Esau to-lord-of-me being-sent

וַיְצַו גַּם אֶת־ הַשֵּׁנִי גַּם אֶת־ הַשְּׁלִישִׁי גַּם אֶת־ כָּל־
all-of *** also the-third *** also the-second *** also and-he-instructed (20)

הַהֹלְכִים אַחֲרֵי הָעֲדָרִים לֵאמֹר כַּדָּבָר הַזֶּה תְּדַבְּרוּן
you-say the-this same-the-thing to-say the-herds after the-ones-following

אֶל־עֵשָׂו בְּמֹצַאֲכֶם אֹתוֹ׃ וַאֲמַרְתֶּם גַּם הִנֵּה עַבְדְּךָ יַעֲקֹב
Jacob servant-of-you see! also then-you-say (21) him when-meeting-you Esau to

אַחֲרֵינוּ כִּי־ אָמַר אֲכַפְּרָה פָנָיו בַּמִּנְחָה
with-the-gift face-of-him I-will-pacify he-thought for behind-us

הַהֹלֶכֶת לְפָנָי וְאַחֲרֵי־ כֵן אֶרְאֶה פָנָיו אוּלַי
perhaps face-of-him I-will-see that and-after ahead-of-me the-one-coming

יִשָּׂא פָנָי׃ וַתַּעֲבֹר הַמִּנְחָה עַל־ פָּנָיו וְהוּא
but-he face-of-him ahead the-gift so-she-went (22) face-of-me he-will-receive

לָן† בַּלַּיְלָה־ הַהוּא בַּמַּחֲנֶה׃ וַיָּקָם ׀
now-he-got-up (23) in-the-camp the-that through-the-night he-stayed

בַּלַּיְלָה הוּא וַיִּקַּח אֶת־ שְׁתֵּי נָשָׁיו וְאֶת־ שְׁתֵּי
two-of and wives-of-him two-of *** and-he-took that in-the-night

שִׁפְחֹתָיו וְאֶת־אַחַד עָשָׂר יְלָדָיו וַיַּעֲבֹר אֵת מַעֲבַר יַבֹּק׃
Jabbok ford-of *** and-he-crossed sons-of-him ten one and maidservants-of-him

וַיִּקָּחֵם וַיַּעֲבִרֵם אֶת־ הַנָּחַל וַיַּעֲבֵר
and-he-sent-over the-stream *** and-he-sent-across-them and-he-took-them (24)

אֶת־אֲשֶׁר־ לוֹ׃ וַיִּוָּתֵר יַעֲקֹב לְבַדּוֹ וַיֵּאָבֵק אִישׁ
man and-he-wrestled by-himself Jacob so-he-was-alone (25) to-him that ***

עִמּוֹ עַד עֲלוֹת הַשָּׁחַר׃ וַיַּרְא כִּי לֹא יָכֹל
he-could-overpower not that when-he-saw (26) the-dawn to-come until with-him

לוֹ וַיִּגַּע בְּכַף־ יְרֵכוֹ וַתֵּקַע כַּף־
socket-of so-she-was-wrenched hip-of-him on-socket-of then-he-touched over-him

יֶרֶךְ יַעֲקֹב בְּהֵאָבְקוֹ עִמּוֹ׃ וַיֹּאמֶר שַׁלְּחֵנִי כִּי
for let-go-me! then-he-said (27) with him as-to-wrestle-him Jacob hip-of

עָלָה הַשָּׁחַר וַיֹּאמֶר לֹא אֲשַׁלֵּחֲךָ כִּי אִם־ בֵּרַכְתָּנִי׃
you-bless-me if unless I-will-let-go-you not but-he-replied the-dawn he-came

וַיֹּאמֶר אֵלָיו מַה־ שְּׁמֶךָ וַיֹּאמֶר יַעֲקֹב׃
Jacob and-he-answered name-of-you what? to-him so-he-asked (28)

וַיֹּאמֶר לֹא יַעֲקֹב יֵאָמֵר עוֹד שִׁמְךָ כִּי אִם־יִשְׂרָאֵל
Israel now but name-of-you longer he-will-be-called Jacob not then-he-said (29)

front of you?' [18]then you are to
say, 'They belong to your servant Jacob. They are a gift sent
to my lord Esau, and he is
coming behind us.' "
[19]He also instructed the second, the third and all the
others who followed the
herds: "You are to say the
same thing to Esau when you
meet him. [20]And be sure to
say, 'Your servant Jacob is
coming behind us.' " For he
thought, "I will pacify him
with these gifts I am sending
on ahead; later, when I see
him, perhaps he will receive
me." [21]So Jacob's gifts went on
ahead of him, but he himself
spent the night in the camp.

Jacob Wrestles With God

[22]That night Jacob got up
and took his two wives, his
two maidservants and his
eleven sons and crossed the
ford of the Jabbok. [23]After he
had sent them across the
stream, he sent over all his
possessions. [24]So Jacob was
left alone, and a man wrestled
with him till daybreak.
[25]When the man saw that he
could not overpower him, he
touched the socket of Jacob's
hip so that his hip was
wrenched as he wrestled with
the man. [26]Then the man said,
"Let me go, for it is daybreak."
But Jacob replied, "I will not
let you go unless you bless
me."
[27]The man asked him,
"What is your name?"
"Jacob," he answered.
[28]Then the man said, "Your
name will no longer be Jacob,
but Israel,[x] because you have

[x]28 *Israel* means *he struggles with God.*

*See the note on page 87.

†24 Most mss have *silluq* under the final word. (לוֹ).

כִּי־ שָׂרִיתָ עִם־אֱלֹהִים וְעִם־ אֲנָשִׁים וַתּוּכָל׃ וַיִּשְׁאַל

then-he-asked (30) and-you-overcame men and-with God with you-struggled for

יַעֲקֹב וַיֹּאמֶר הַגִּידָה־ נָּא שְׁמֶךָ וַיֹּאמֶר לָמָּה זֶּה תִּשְׁאַל

you-ask this why? but-he-replied name-of-you now! tell! and-he-said Jacob

לִשְׁמִי וַיְבָרֶךְ אֹתוֹ שָׁם׃ וַיִּקְרָא יַעֲקֹב שֵׁם

name-of Jacob so-he-called (31) there him then-he-blessed for-name-of-me

הַמָּקוֹם פְּנִיאֵל כִּי־ רָאִיתִי אֱלֹהִים פָּנִים אֶל־ פָּנִים וַתִּנָּצֵל נַפְשִׁי׃

life-of-me yet-she-was-spared face to face God I-saw for Peniel the-place

וַיִּזְרַח־ לוֹ הַשֶּׁמֶשׁ כַּאֲשֶׁר עָבַר אֶת־ פְּנוּאֵל וְהוּא צֹלֵעַ

limping and-he Penuel *** he-passed just-as the-sun above-him and-he-rose (32)

עַל־ יְרֵכוֹ׃ עַל־ כֵּן לֹא־ יֹאכְלוּ בְנֵי־ יִשְׂרָאֵל אֶת־ גִּיד

sinew-of *** Israel sons-of they-eat not this for (33) hip-of-him because-of

הַנָּשֶׁה אֲשֶׁר עַל־ כַּף הַיָּרֵךְ עַד הַיּוֹם הַזֶּה כִּי נָגַע

he-touched for the-this the-day to the-hip socket-of on that the-tendon

בְּכַף־ יֶרֶךְ יַעֲקֹב בְּגִיד הַנָּשֶׁה׃ וַיִּשָּׂא יַעֲקֹב

Jacob and-he-lifted (33:1) the-tendon on-sinew-of Jacob hip-of on-socket-of

עֵינָיו וַיַּרְא וְהִנֵּה עֵשָׂו בָּא וְעִמּוֹ אַרְבַּע מֵאוֹת אִישׁ

man hundreds four and-with-him coming Esau and-see! and-he-saw eyes-of-him

וַיַּחַץ אֶת־ הַיְלָדִים עַל־ לֵאָה וְעַל־ רָחֵל וְעַל שְׁתֵּי

two-of and-to Rachel and-to Leah to the-children *** so-he-divided

הַשְּׁפָחוֹת׃ וַיָּשֶׂם אֶת־ הַשְּׁפָחוֹת וְאֶת־ יַלְדֵיהֶן

children-of-them and the-maidservants *** and-he-put (2) the-maidservants

רִאשֹׁנָה וְאֶת־לֵאָה וִילָדֶיהָ אַחֲרֹנִים וְאֶת־ רָחֵל וְאֶת־ יוֹסֵף אַחֲרֹנִים׃

rear-ones Joseph and Rachel and next-ones and-children-of-her Leah and front

וְהוּא עָבַר לִפְנֵיהֶם וַיִּשְׁתַּחוּ אַרְצָה שֶׁבַע פְּעָמִים עַד־

as times seven to-ground and-he-bowed ahead-of-them he-went and-he (3)

גִּשְׁתּוֹ עַד־ אָחִיו׃ וַיָּרָץ עֵשָׂו לִקְרָאתוֹ

to-meet-him Esau but-he-ran (4) brother-of-him to to-approach-him

וַיְחַבְּקֵהוּ וַיִּפֹּל עַל־ צַוָּארָו וַיִּשָּׁקֵהוּ

and-he-kissed-him neck-of-him around and-he-hugged and-he-embraced-him

וַיִּבְכּוּ׃ וַיִּשָּׂא אֶת־ עֵינָיו וַיַּרְא אֶת־ הַנָּשִׁים

the-women *** and-he-saw eyes-of-him *** and-he-lifted (5) and-they-wept

וְאֶת־ הַיְלָדִים וַיֹּאמֶר מִי־ אֵלֶּה לָּךְ וַיֹּאמַר הַיְלָדִים

the-children and-he-answered with-you these who? and-he-asked the-children and

אֲשֶׁר־ חָנַן אֱלֹהִים אֶת־ עַבְדֶּךָ׃ וַתִּגַּשְׁןָ

then-they-approached (6) servant-of-you to God he-graciously-gave whom

הַשְּׁפָחוֹת הֵנָּה וְיַלְדֵיהֶן וַתִּשְׁתַּחֲוֶיןָ׃ וַתִּגַּשׁ

next-she-came (7) and-they-bowed and-children-of-them they the-maidservants

struggled with God and with
men and have overcome."
[29]Jacob said, "Please tell me
your name."
But he replied, "Why do you
ask my name?" Then he
blessed him there.
[30]So Jacob called the place
Peniel,[y] saying, "It is because
I saw God face to face, and yet
my life was spared."
[31]The sun rose above him as
he passed Peniel,[z] and he was
limping because of his hip.
[32]Therefore to this day the Israelites do not eat the tendon
attached to the socket of the
hip, because the socket of
Jacob's hip was touched near
the tendon.

Jacob Meets Esau

33 Jacob looked up and
there was Esau, com-
ing with his four hundred
men; so he divided the children among Leah, Rachel and
the two maidservants. [2]He put
the maidservants and their
children in front, Leah and
her children next, and Rachel
and Joseph in the rear. [3]He
himself went on ahead and
bowed down to the ground
seven times as he approached
his brother.
[4]But Esau ran to meet Jacob
and embraced him; he threw
his arms around his neck and
kissed him. And they wept.
[5]Then Esau looked up and saw
the women and children.
"Who are these with you?" he
asked.
Jacob answered, "They are
the children God has gracious-
ly given your servant."
[6]Then the maidservants and
their children approached and
bowed down. [7]Next, Leah and

y30 *Peniel* means *face of God.*
z31 Hebrew *Penuel,* a variant of *Peniel*

*See the note on page 87.

°4 ק צואריו

גַּם־ לֵאָה וִילָדֶיהָ וַיִּשְׁתַּחֲווּ וְאַחַר נִגַּשׁ יוֹסֵף
Joseph he-approached and-last and-they-bowed and-children-of-her Leah also

וְרָחֵל וַיִּשְׁתַּחֲווּ׃ וַיֹּאמֶר מִי לְךָ כָּל־ הַמַּחֲנֶה
the-drove all-of to-you what? and-he-asked (8) and-they-bowed and-Rachel

הַזֶּה אֲשֶׁר פָּגָשְׁתִּי וַיֹּאמֶר לִמְצֹא־ חֵן בְּעֵינֵי אֲדֹנִי׃
lord-of-me in-eyes-of-you favor to-find and-he-said I-met that the-this

וַיֹּאמֶר עֵשָׂו יֶשׁ־ לִי רָב אָחִי יְהִי לְךָ
to-you let-him-stay brother-of-me plenty to-me there-is Esau but-he-said (9)

אֲשֶׁר־ לָךְ׃ וַיֹּאמֶר יַעֲקֹב אַל־ נָא אִם־ נָא מָצָאתִי חֵן
favor I-found now! if now! no Jacob but-he-said (10) to-you what

בְּעֵינֶיךָ וְלָקַחְתָּ מִנְחָתִי מִיָּדִי כִּי עַל־ כֵּן
this for indeed from-hand-of-me gift-of-me now-you-accept in-eyes-of-you

רָאִיתִי פָנֶיךָ כִּרְאֹת פְּנֵי אֱלֹהִים וַתִּרְצֵנִי׃ קַח־
accept! (11) as-you-received-me God face-of like-to-see face-of-you I-see

נָא אֶת־ בִּרְכָתִי אֲשֶׁר הֻבָאת לָךְ כִּי־ חַנַּנִי
he-is-gracious-to-me for to-you she-was-brought that present-of-me *** now!

אֱלֹהִים וְכִי יֶשׁ־ לִי־ כֹל וַיִּפְצַר־ בּוֹ וַיִּקָּח׃
so-he-accepted with-him and-he-insisted all to-me there-is and-because God

וַיֹּאמֶר נִסְעָה וְנֵלֵכָה וְאֵלְכָה לְנֶגְדֶּךָ׃
next-to-you and-I-will-go and-let-us-go let-us-travel then-he-said (12)

וַיֹּאמֶר אֵלָיו אֲדֹנִי יֹדֵעַ כִּי־ הַיְלָדִים רַכִּים
tender-ones the-children that knowing lord-of-me to-him but-he-said (13)

וְהַצֹּאן וְהַבָּקָר עָלוֹת עָלָי וּדְפָקוּם
if-they-drive-hard-them care-of-me nursing-ones and-the-cattle and-the-flock

יוֹם אֶחָד וָמֵתוּ כָּל־ הַצֹּאן׃ יַעֲבָר־ נָא
now! let-him-go-ahead (14) the-flock all-of then-they-will-die one day

אֲדֹנִי לִפְנֵי עַבְדּוֹ וַאֲנִי אֶתְנָהֲלָה לְאִטִּי לְרֶגֶל
at-pace-of with-slowness-me I-move while-I servant-of-him before lord-of-me

הַמְּלָאכָה אֲשֶׁר־ לְפָנַי וּלְרֶגֶל הַיְלָדִים עַד אֲשֶׁר־ אָבֹא אֶל־
to I-come when until the-children and-at-pace-of before-me that the-drove

אֲדֹנִי שֵׂעִירָה׃ וַיֹּאמֶר עֵשָׂו אַצִּיגָה־ נָּא עִמְּךָ מִן־
from with-you now! let-me-leave Esau so-he-said (15) at-Seir lord-of-me

הָעָם אֲשֶׁר אִתִּי וַיֹּאמֶר לָמָּה זֶּה אֶמְצָא־ חֵן בְּעֵינֵי
in-eyes-of favor let-me-find that why? but-he-asked with-me that the-people

אֲדֹנִי׃ וַיָּשָׁב בַּיּוֹם הַהוּא עֵשָׂו לְדַרְכּוֹ
on-way-of-him Esau the-that on-the-day so-he-went-back (16) lord-of-me

שֵׂעִירָה׃ וְיַעֲקֹב נָסַע סֻכֹּתָה וַיִּבֶן לוֹ בָּיִת
place for-him and-he-built to-Succoth he-went but-Jacob (17) to-Seir

her children came and bowed
down. Last of all came Joseph
and Rachel, and they too
bowed down.
8 Esau asked, "What do you
mean by all these droves I
met?"
"To find favor in your eyes,
my lord," he said.
9 But Esau said, "I already
have plenty, my brother. Keep
what you have for yourself."
10 "No, please!" said Jacob.
"If I have found favor in your
eyes, accept this gift from me.
For to see your face is like seeing the face of God, now that
you have received me favorably. 11 Please accept the
present that was brought to
you, for God has been gracious
to me and I have all I need."
And because Jacob insisted,
Esau accepted it.
12 Then Esau said, "Let us be
on our way; I'll accompany
you."
13 But Jacob said to him, "My
lord knows that the children
are tender and that I must care
for the ewes and cows that are
nursing their young. If they
are driven hard just one day,
all the animals will die. 14 So let
my lord go on ahead of his servant, while I move along
slowly at the pace of the
droves before me and that of
the children, until I come to
my lord in Seir."
15 Esau said, "Then let me
leave some of my men with
you."
"But why do that?" Jacob
asked. "Just let me find favor
in the eyes of my lord."
16 So that day Esau started on
his way back to Seir. 17 Jacob,
however, went to Succoth,
where he built a place for himself and made shelters for his

וּלְמִקְנֵהוּ עָשָׂה סֻכֹּת עַל־כֵּן קָרָא שֵׁם־הַמָּקוֹם
the-place name-of he-called this for shelters he-made and-for-stock-of-him

סֻכּוֹת׃ וַיָּבֹא יַעֲקֹב שָׁלֵם עִיר שְׁכֶם אֲשֶׁר בְּאֶרֶץ
in-land-of that Shechem city-of safely Jacob and-he-arrived (18) Succoth

כְּנַעַן בְּבֹאוֹ מִפַּדַּן אֲרָם וַיִּחַן אֶת־פְּנֵי הָעִיר׃
the-city sight-of *** and-he-camped Aram from-Paddan after-to-come-him Canaan

וַיִּקֶן אֶת־חֶלְקַת הַשָּׂדֶה אֲשֶׁר נָטָה־שָׁם אָהֳלוֹ
tent-of-him there he-pitched where the-ground plot-of *** and-he-bought (19)

מִיַּד בְּנֵי־חֲמוֹר אֲבִי שְׁכֶם בְּמֵאָה קְשִׂיטָה׃
money for-hundred Shechem father-of Hamor sons-of from-hand-of

וַיַּצֶּב־שָׁם מִזְבֵּחַ וַיִּקְרָא־לוֹ אֵל אֱלֹהֵי יִשְׂרָאֵל׃
Israel Elohe El to-him and-he-called altar there and-he-set-up (20)

וַתֵּצֵא דִינָה בַּת־לֵאָה אֲשֶׁר יָלְדָה לְיַעֲקֹב
to-Jacob she-bore whom Leah daughter-of Dinah now-she-went-out (34:1)

לִרְאוֹת בִּבְנוֹת הָאָרֶץ׃ וַיַּרְא אֹתָהּ שְׁכֶם בֶּן־חֲמוֹר
Hamor son-of Shechem her and-he-saw (2) the-land with-women-of to-visit

הַחִוִּי נְשִׂיא הָאָרֶץ וַיִּקַּח אֹתָהּ וַיִּשְׁכַּב אֹתָהּ
with-her and-he-lay her and-he-took the-area ruler-of the-Hivite

וַיְעַנֶּהָ׃ וַתִּדְבַּק נַפְשׁוֹ בְּדִינָה בַּת־
daughter-of to-Dinah heart-of-him and-she-was-drawn (3) and-he-violated-her

יַעֲקֹב וַיֶּאֱהַב אֶת־הַנַּעֲרָ וַיְדַבֵּר עַל־לֵב הַנַּעֲרָ׃
the-girl heart-of to and-he-spoke the-girl *** and-he-loved Jacob

וַיֹּאמֶר שְׁכֶם אֶל־חֲמוֹר אָבִיו לֵאמֹר קַח־לִי אֶת־הַיַּלְדָּה
the-girl *** for-me get! to-say father-of-him Hamor to Shechem and-he-said (4)

הַזֹּאת לְאִשָּׁה׃ וְיַעֲקֹב שָׁמַע כִּי טִמֵּא אֶת־דִּינָה
Dinah *** he-defiled that he-heard when-Jacob (5) as-wife the-this

בִתּוֹ וּבָנָיו הָיוּ אֶת־מִקְנֵהוּ בַּשָּׂדֶה
in-the-field stock-of-him with they-were then-sons-of-him daughter-of-him

וְהֶחֱרִשׁ יַעֲקֹב עַד־בֹּאָם׃ וַיֵּצֵא חֲמוֹר
Hamor then-he-went-out (6) to-come-them until Jacob so-he-kept-quiet

אֲבִי־שְׁכֶם אֶל־יַעֲקֹב לְדַבֵּר אִתּוֹ׃ וּבְנֵי יַעֲקֹב בָּאוּ
they-came Jacob now-sons-of (7) with-him to-talk Jacob to Shechem father-of

מִן־הַשָּׂדֶה כְּשָׁמְעָם וַיִּתְעַצְּבוּ הָאֲנָשִׁים
the-men and-they-were-grieved as-soon-as-to-hear-them the-field from

וַיִּחַר לָהֶם מְאֹד כִּי־נְבָלָה עָשָׂה בְיִשְׂרָאֵל לִשְׁכַּב אֶת־
with to-lie against-Israel he-did disgrace for greatly to-them and-he-angered

בַּת־יַעֲקֹב וְכֵן לֹא יֵעָשֶׂה׃ וַיְדַבֵּר חֲמוֹר
Hamor but-he-said (8) he-should-be-done not for-this Jacob daughter-of

livestock. That is why the
place is called Succoth.[a]
18 After Jacob came from Paddan Aram,[b] he arrived safely
at the[c] city of Shechem in Canaan and camped within
sight of the city. 19 For a hundred pieces of silver,[d] he
bought from the sons of Hamor, the father of Shechem,
the plot of ground where he
pitched his tent. 20 There he set
up an altar and called it El
Elohe Israel.[e]

Dinah and the Shechemites

34 Now Dinah, the
daughter Leah had
borne to Jacob, went out to
visit the women of the land.
2 When Shechem son of Hamor
the Hivite, the ruler of that
area, saw her, he took her and
violated her. 3 His heart was
drawn to Dinah daughter of
Jacob, and he loved the girl
and spoke tenderly to her.
4 And Shechem said to his father Hamor, "Get me this girl
as my wife."
5 When Jacob heard that his
daughter Dinah had been
defiled, his sons were in the
fields with his livestock; so he
kept quiet about it until they
came home.
6 Then Shechem's father Hamor went out to talk with
Jacob. 7 Now Jacob's sons had
come in from the fields as soon
as they heard what had happened. They were filled with
grief and fury, because Shechem had done a disgraceful
thing in[f] Israel by lying with
Jacob's daughter—a thing that
should not be done.
8 But Hamor said to them,

[a]17 *Succoth* means *shelters.*
[b]18 That is, Northwest Mesopotamia
[c]18 Or *arrived at Shalem, a*
[d]19 Hebrew *hundred kesitahs;* a kesitah was a unit of money of unknown weight and value.
[e]20 *El Elohe Israel* can mean *God, the God of Israel* or *mighty is the God of Israel.*
[f]7 Or *against*

בְּבִתְּכֶם נַפְשׁוֹ חָשְׁקָה בְּנִי שְׁכֶם לֵאמֹר אִתָּם
on-daughter-of-you heart-of-him she-is-set son-of-me Shechem to-say to-them

תְּנוּ נָא אֹתָהּ לוֹ לְאִשָּׁה׃ וְהִתְחַתְּנוּ אֹתָנוּ בְּנֹתֵיכֶם תִּתְּנוּ־
give! daughters-of-you with-us intermarry! (9) as-wife to-him her now! give!

לָנוּ וְאֶת־ בְּנֹתֵינוּ תִּקְחוּ לָכֶם׃ וְאִתָּנוּ תֵּשֵׁבוּ
you-settle and-among-us (10) for-you you-take daughters-of-us and to-us

וְהָאָרֶץ תִּהְיֶה לִפְנֵיכֶם שְׁבוּ וּסְחָרוּהָ וְהֵאָחֲזוּ בָּהּ׃
in-her and-acquire! and-trade-in-her! live! before-you she-is now-the-land

וַיֹּאמֶר שְׁכֶם אֶל־ אָבִיהָ* וְאֶל־ אַחֶיהָ אֶמְצָא־
let-me-find brothers-of-her and-to father-of-her to Shechem then-he-said (11)

חֵן בְּעֵינֵיכֶם וַאֲשֶׁר תֹּאמְרוּ אֵלַי אֶתֵּן׃ הַרְבּוּ
make-great! (12) I-will-give of-me you-ask and-whatever in-eyes-of-you favor

עָלַי מְאֹד מֹהַר וּמַתָּן וְאֶתְּנָה כַּאֲשֶׁר תֹּאמְרוּ אֵלָי וּתְנוּ־
but-give! of-me you-ask what and-I-will-pay and-gift bride-price very for-me

לִי אֶת־ הַנַּעֲרָ לְאִשָּׁה׃ וַיַּעֲנוּ בְנֵי־ יַעֲקֹב אֶת־ שְׁכֶם
Shechem *** Jacob sons-of but-they-replied (13) as-wife the-girl *** to-me

וְאֶת־חֲמוֹר אָבִיו בְּמִרְמָה וַיְדַבֵּרוּ אֲשֶׁר טִמֵּא אֵת דִּינָה
Dinah *** he-defiled because as-they-spoke in-deceit father-of-him Hamor and

אֲחֹתָם׃ וַיֹּאמְרוּ אֲלֵיהֶם לֹא נוּכַל לַעֲשׂוֹת הַדָּבָר הַזֶּה
the-this the-thing to-do we-can not to-them and-they-said (14) sister-of-them

לָתֵת אֶת־ אֲחֹתֵנוּ לְאִישׁ אֲשֶׁר־ לוֹ עָרְלָה כִּי־ חֶרְפָּה הִוא לָנוּ׃
to-us that disgrace for foreskin to-him who to-man sister-of-us *** to-give

אַךְ־ בְּזֹאת נֵאוֹת לָכֶם אִם תִּהְיוּ כָמֹנוּ לְהִמֹּל
to-be-circumcised like-us you-become if to-you we-will-consent on-this only (15)

לָכֶם כָּל־ זָכָר׃ וְנָתַנּוּ אֶת־ בְּנֹתֵינוּ לָכֶם וְאֶת־
and to-you daughters-of-us *** then-we-will-give (16) male every-of to-you

בְּנֹתֵיכֶם נִקַּח־ לָנוּ וְיָשַׁבְנוּ אִתְּכֶם
among-you and-we-will-settle for-us we-will-take daughters-of-you

וְהָיִינוּ לְעַם אֶחָד׃ וְאִם־ לֹא תִשְׁמְעוּ אֵלֵינוּ
with-us you-will-agree not but-if (17) one as-people and-we-will-become

לְהִמּוֹל וְלָקַחְנוּ אֶת־ בִּתֵּנוּ וְהָלָכְנוּ׃
and-we-will-go daughter-of-us *** then-we-will-take to-be-circumcised

וַיִּיטְבוּ דִבְרֵיהֶם בְּעֵינֵי חֲמוֹר וּבְעֵינֵי
and-in-eyes-of Hamor in-eyes-of words-of-them and-they-seemed-good (18)

שְׁכֶם בֶּן־ חֲמוֹר׃ וְלֹא־ אֵחַר הַנַּעַר לַעֲשׂוֹת הַדָּבָר
the-thing to-do the-young-man he-delayed and-not (19) Hamor son-of Shechem

כִּי חָפֵץ בְּבַת־ יַעֲקֹב וְהוּא נִכְבָּד מִכֹּל
over-all-of being-honored now-he Jacob with-daughter-of he-was-delighted for

"My son Shechem has his heart set on your daughter. Please give her to him as his wife. 9Intermarry with us; give us your daughters and take our daughters for yourselves. 10You can settle among us; the land is open to you. Live in it, trade[h] in it, and acquire property in it."

11Then Shechem said to Dinah's father and brothers, "Let me find favor in your eyes, and I will give you whatever you ask. 12Make the price for the bride and the gift I am to bring as great as you like, and I'll pay whatever you ask me. Only give me the girl as my wife."

13Because their sister Dinah had been defiled, Jacob's sons replied deceitfully as they spoke to Shechem and his father Hamor. 14They said to them, "We can't do such a thing; we can't give our sister to a man who is not circumcised. That would be a disgrace to us. 15We will give our consent to you on one condition only: that you become like us by circumcising all your males. 16Then we will give you our daughters and take your daughters for ourselves. We'll settle among you and become one people with you. 17But if you will not agree to be circumcised, we'll take our sister[i] and go."

18Their proposal seemed good to Hamor and his son Shechem. 19The young man, who was the most honored of all his father's household, lost no time in doing what they said, because he was delighted with Jacob's daughter. 20So

[h]10 Or *move about freely*; also in verse 21
[i]17 Hebrew *daughter*

*11 Most mss have *qamets* under the *he* (הָ־).

בֵּית אָבִיו׃ (20) וַיָּבֹא חֲמוֹר וּשְׁכֶם בְּנוֹ
son-of-him and-Shechem Hamor so-they-went (20) father-of-him household-of

אֶל־ שַׁעַר עִירָם וַיְדַבְּרוּ אֶל־ אַנְשֵׁי עִירָם לֵאמֹר׃
to-say city-of-them men-of to and-they-spoke city-of-them gate-of to

(21) הָאֲנָשִׁים הָאֵלֶּה שְׁלֵמִים הֵם אִתָּנוּ וְיֵשְׁבוּ
so-let-them-settle with-us they friendly-ones the-these the-men (21)

בָאָרֶץ וְיִסְחֲרוּ אֹתָהּ וְהָאָרֶץ הִנֵּה רַחֲבַת־ יָדַיִם
measures large-of see! now-the-land in-her and-let-them-trade in-the-land

לִפְנֵיהֶם אֶת־ בְּנֹתָם נִקַּח־ לָנוּ לְנָשִׁים וְאֶת־
and as-wives for-us we-can-take daughters-of-them *** before-them

בְּנֹתֵינוּ נִתֵּן לָהֶם׃ (22) אַךְ־ בְּזֹאת יֵאֹתוּ לָנוּ
to-us will-they-consent on-this only (22) to-them we-can-give daughters-of-us

הָאֲנָשִׁים לָשֶׁבֶת אִתָּנוּ לִהְיוֹת לְעַם אֶחָד בְּהִמּוֹל לָנוּ
to-us that-to-be-circumcised one as-people to-be with-us to-live the-men

כָּל־ זָכָר כַּאֲשֶׁר הֵם נִמֹּלִים׃ (23) מִקְנֵהֶם
livestock-of-them (23) ones-being-circumcised they just-as male every-of

וְקִנְיָנָם וְכָל־ בְּהֶמְתָּם הֲלוֹא לָנוּ הֵם אַךְ
so they to-us not? animal-of-them and-every-of and-property-of-them

נֵאוֹתָה לָהֶם וְיֵשְׁבוּ אִתָּנוּ׃ (24) וַיִּשְׁמְעוּ אֶל־
with so-they-agreed (24) with-us and-they-will-settle to-them let-us-consent

חֲמוֹר וְאֶל־ שְׁכֶם בְּנוֹ כָּל־ יֹצְאֵי שַׁעַר
gate-of ones-going-out-of every-of son-of-him Shechem and-with Hamor

עִירוֹ וַיִּמֹּלוּ כָּל־ זָכָר כָּל־ יֹצְאֵי
ones-going-out-of every-of male every-of and-they-were-circumcised city-of-him

שַׁעַר עִירוֹ׃ (25) וַיְהִי בַיּוֹם הַשְּׁלִישִׁי בִּהְיוֹתָם
when-to-be-them the-third on-the-day and-he-was (25) city-of-him gate-of

כֹּאֲבִים וַיִּקְחוּ שְׁנֵי־ בְנֵי־ יַעֲקֹב שִׁמְעוֹן וְלֵוִי
and-Levi Simeon Jacob sons-of two-of then-they-took ones-being-in-pain

אֲחֵי דִינָה אִישׁ חַרְבּוֹ וַיָּבֹאוּ עַל־ הָעִיר בֶּטַח
unsuspected the-city into and-they-came sword-of-him each Dinah brothers-of

וַיַּהַרְגוּ כָּל־ זָכָר׃ (26) וְאֶת־ חֲמוֹר וְאֶת־ שְׁכֶם בְּנוֹ
son-of-him Shechem and Hamor and (26) male every-of and-they-killed

הָרְגוּ לְפִי־ חָרֶב וַיִּקְחוּ אֶת־ דִּינָה מִבֵּית שְׁכֶם
Shechem from-house-of Dinah *** and-they-took sword with-edge-of they-killed

וַיֵּצֵאוּ׃ (27) בְּנֵי יַעֲקֹב בָּאוּ עַל־ הַחֲלָלִים וַיָּבֹזּוּ
and-they-looted the-dead-ones upon they-came Jacob sons-of (27) and-they-left

הָעִיר אֲשֶׁר טִמְּאוּ אֲחוֹתָם׃ (28) אֶת־ צֹאנָם וְאֶת־
and flock-of-them *** (28) sister-of-them they-defiled where the-city

Hamor and his son Shechem
went to the gate of their city to
speak to their fellow towns-
men. 21"These men are friend-
ly toward us," they said. "Let
them live in our land and
trade in it; the land has plenty
of room for them. We can marry their daughters and they
can marry ours. 22But the men
will consent to live with us as
one people only on the condition that our males be circumcised, as they themselves are.
23Won't their livestock, their
property and all their other
animals become ours? So let us
give our consent to them, and
they will settle among us."
24All the men who went out
of the city gate agreed with
Hamor and his son Shechem,
and every male in the city was
circumcised.
25Three days later, while all
of them were still in pain, two
of Jacob's sons, Simeon and
Levi, Dinah's brothers, took
their swords and attacked the
unsuspecting city, killing
every male. 26They put Hamor
and his son Shechem to the
sword and took Dinah from
Shechem's house and left.
27The sons of Jacob came upon
the dead bodies and looted the
city where[j] their sister had
been defiled. 28They seized
their flocks and herds and

j27 Or *because*

בְּקָרָם וְאֶת־ חֲמֹרֵיהֶם* וְאֵת אֲשֶׁר־ בָּעִיר וְאֶת־אֲשֶׁר בַּשָּׂדֶה

in-the-field what and in-the-city what and donkeys-of-them and herd-of-them

לָקָחוּ׃ וְאֶת־ כָּל־ חֵילָם וְאֶת־ כָּל־ טַפָּם וְאֶת־

and child-of-them every-of and wealth-of-them all-of and (29) they-seized

נְשֵׁיהֶם שָׁבוּ וַיָּבֹזּוּ וְאֵת כָּל־ אֲשֶׁר בַּבָּיִת׃

in-the-house that all also and-they-plundered they-carried-off women-of-them

וַיֹּאמֶר יַעֲקֹב אֶל־ שִׁמְעוֹן וְאֶל־ לֵוִי עֲכַרְתֶּם אֹתִי

on-me you-brought-trouble Levi and-to Simeon to Jacob then-he-said (30)

לְהַבְאִישֵׁנִי בְּיֹשֵׁב הָאָרֶץ בַּכְּנַעֲנִי

to-the-Canaanite the-land to-one-living by-to-make-stench-of-me

וּבַפְּרִזִּי וַאֲנִי מְתֵי מִסְפָּר וְנֶאֶסְפוּ עָלַי

against-me if-they-join number men-of now-I and-to-the-Perizzite

וְהִכּוּנִי וְנִשְׁמַדְתִּי אֲנִי וּבֵיתִי׃

and-household-of-me I then-I-will-be-destroyed and-they-attack-me

וַיֹּאמְרוּ הַכְזוֹנָה יַעֲשֶׂה אֶת־ אֲחוֹתֵנוּ׃

sister-of-us *** should-he-treat as-being-prostitute? but-they-replied (31)

וַיֹּאמֶר אֱלֹהִים אֶל־יַעֲקֹב קוּם עֲלֵה בֵית־ אֵל וְשֶׁב־ שָׁם

there and-settle! El Beth go-up! rise! Jacob to God then-he-said (35:1)

וַעֲשֵׂה־ שָׁם מִזְבֵּחַ לָאֵל הַנִּרְאֶה אֵלֶיךָ בְּבָרְחֲךָ†

when-to-flee-you to-you the-one-appearing to-God altar there and-build!

מִפְּנֵי עֵשָׂו אָחִיךָ׃ וַיֹּאמֶר יַעֲקֹב אֶל־ בֵּיתוֹ

household-of-him to Jacob so-he-said (2) brother-of-you Esau from-face-of

וְאֶל כָּל־ אֲשֶׁר עִמּוֹ הָסִרוּ אֶת־ אֱלֹהֵי הַנֵּכָר אֲשֶׁר בְּתֹכְכֶם

with-you that the-foreign gods-of *** get-rid-of! with-him who all and-to

וְהִטַּהֲרוּ וְהַחֲלִיפוּ שִׂמְלֹתֵיכֶם׃ וְנָקוּמָה

then-let-us-rise (3) clothes-of-you and-change! and-purify-yourselves!

וְנַעֲלֶה בֵּית־ אֵל וְאֶעֱשֶׂה־ שָּׁם מִזְבֵּחַ לָאֵל הָעֹנֶה

the-one-answering to-God altar there and-I-will-build El Beth and-let-us-go-up

אֹתִי בְּיוֹם צָרָתִי וַיְהִי עִמָּדִי בַּדֶּרֶךְ אֲשֶׁר הָלָכְתִּי׃

I-go that in-the-way with-me and-he-is distress-of-me in-day-of me

וַיִּתְּנוּ אֶל־יַעֲקֹב אֵת כָּל־ אֱלֹהֵי הַנֵּכָר אֲשֶׁר בְּיָדָם

in-hand-of-them that the-foreign gods-of all-of *** Jacob to so-they-gave (4)

וְאֶת־ הַנְּזָמִים אֲשֶׁר בְּאָזְנֵיהֶם וַיִּטְמֹן אֹתָם יַעֲקֹב תַּחַת הָאֵלָה

the-oak under Jacob them and-he-buried in-ears-of-them that the-rings and

אֲשֶׁר עִם־ שְׁכֶם׃ וַיִּסָּעוּ וַיְהִי חִתַּת אֱלֹהִים עַל־ הֶעָרִים

the-cities on God terror-of and-he-was then-they-set-out (5) Shechem at that

אֲשֶׁר סְבִיבֹתֵיהֶם וְלֹא רָדְפוּ אַחֲרֵי בְּנֵי יַעֲקֹב׃ וַיָּבֹא

and-he-came (6) Jacob sons-of after they-pursued and-not around-them that

donkeys and everything else of theirs in the city and out in the fields. [29]They carried off all their wealth and all their women and children, taking as plunder everything in the houses.

[30]Then Jacob said to Simeon and Levi, "You have brought trouble on me by making me a stench to the Canaanites and Perizzites, the people living in this land. We are few in number, and if they join forces against me and attack me, I and my household will be destroyed."

[31]But they replied, "Should he have treated our sister like a prostitute?"

Jacob Returns to Bethel

35 Then God said to Jacob, "Go up to Bethel and settle there, and build an altar there to God, who appeared to you when you were fleeing from your brother Esau."

[2]So Jacob said to his household and to all who were with him, "Get rid of the foreign gods you have with you, and purify yourselves and change your clothes. [3]Then come, let us go up to Bethel, where I will build an altar to God, who answered me in the day of my distress and who has been with me wherever I have gone." [4]So they gave Jacob all the foreign gods they had and the rings in their ears, and Jacob buried them under the oak at Shechem. [5]Then they set out, and the terror of God fell upon the towns all around them so that no one pursued them.

*28 Most mss have no *dagesh* in the *he* (הֶם־).

†1 Most mss have additional accentuation (בְּבָרְחֲךָ).

יַעֲקֹב לוּזָה אֲשֶׁר בְּאֶרֶץ כְּנַעַן הִוא בֵּית־אֵל הוּא וְכָל־ הָעָם
the-people and-all-of he El Beth that Canaan in-land-of that to-Luz Jacob

אֲשֶׁר־ עִמּוֹ׃ וַיִּבֶן שָׁם מִזְבֵּחַ וַיִּקְרָא לַמָּקוֹם אֵל בֵּית־
Beth El to-the-place and-he-called altar there and-he-built (7) with-him who

אֵל כִּי שָׁם נִגְלוּ אֵלָיו הָאֱלֹהִים בְּבָרְחוֹ מִפְּנֵי
from-face-of when-to-flee-him the-God to-him they-were-revealed there for El

אָחִיו׃ וַתָּמָת דְּבֹרָה מֵינֶקֶת רִבְקָה
Rebekah one-nursing-of Deborah now-she-died (8) brother-of-him

וַתִּקָּבֵר מִתַּחַת לְבֵית־ אֵל תַּחַת הָאַלּוֹן וַיִּקְרָא שְׁמוֹ
name-of-him so-he-called the-oak under El to-Beth below and-she-was-buried

אַלּוֹן בָּכוּת׃ וַיֵּרָא אֱלֹהִים אֶל־ יַעֲקֹב עוֹד בְּבֹאוֹ
when-to-return-him again Jacob to God and-he-appeared (9) Bacuth Allon

מִפַּדַּן אֲרָם וַיְבָרֶךְ אֹתוֹ׃ וַיֹּאמֶר־ לוֹ אֱלֹהִים שִׁמְךָ
name-of-you God to-him and-he-said (10) him and-he-blessed Aram from-Paddan

יַעֲקֹב לֹא־ יִקָּרֵא שִׁמְךָ עוֹד יַעֲקֹב כִּי אִם־יִשְׂרָאֵל יִהְיֶה
he-will-be Israel now for Jacob longer name-of-you he-will-be-called not Jacob

שְׁמֶךָ וַיִּקְרָא אֶת־ שְׁמוֹ יִשְׂרָאֵל׃ וַיֹּאמֶר לוֹ אֱלֹהִים
God to-him and-he-said (11) Israel name-of-him *** so-he-called name-of-you

אֲנִי אֵל שַׁדַּי פְּרֵה וּרְבֵה גּוֹי וּקְהַל גּוֹיִם
nations and-company-of nation and-increase! be-fruitful! Almighty God I

יִהְיֶה מִמֶּךָּ וּמְלָכִים מֵחֲלָצֶיךָ יֵצֵאוּ׃ וְאֶת־
and (12) they-will-come from-loins-of-you and-kings from-you he-will-come

הָאָרֶץ אֲשֶׁר נָתַתִּי לְאַבְרָהָם וּלְיִצְחָק לְךָ אֶתְּנֶנָּה
I-will-give-her to-you and-to-Isaac to-Abraham I-gave that the-land

וּלְזַרְעֲךָ אַחֲרֶיךָ אֶתֵּן אֶת־ הָאָרֶץ׃ וַיַּעַל
then-he-went-up (13) the-land *** I-will-give after-you and-to-descendant-of-you

מֵעָלָיו אֱלֹהִים בַּמָּקוֹם אֲשֶׁר־ דִּבֶּר אִתּוֹ׃ וַיַּצֵּב יַעֲקֹב
Jacob and-he-set-up (14) with-him he-talked where at-the-place God from-him

מַצֵּבָה בַּמָּקוֹם אֲשֶׁר־ דִּבֶּר אִתּוֹ מַצֶּבֶת אָבֶן וַיַּסֵּךְ
and-he-poured stone pillar-of with-him he-talked where at-the-place pillar

עָלֶיהָ נֶסֶךְ וַיִּצֹק עָלֶיהָ שָׁמֶן׃ וַיִּקְרָא יַעֲקֹב אֶת־
*** Jacob and-he-called (15) oil on-her and-he-poured drink-offering on-her

שֵׁם הַמָּקוֹם אֲשֶׁר דִּבֶּר אִתּוֹ שָׁם אֱלֹהִים בֵּית־אֵל׃ וַיִּסְעוּ
and-they-left (16) El Beth God there with-him he-talked where the-place name-of

מִבֵּית אֵל וַיְהִי־ עוֹד כִּבְרַת־ הָאָרֶץ לָבוֹא אֶפְרָתָה
to-Ephrath to-go the-land distance-of still and-he-was El from-Beth

וַתֵּלֶד רָחֵל וַתְּקַשׁ בְּלִדְתָּהּ׃ וַיְהִי
and-he-was (17) while-to-bear-her and-she-had-difficulty Rachel then-she-bore

6Jacob and all the people
with him came to Luz (that is,
Bethel) in the land of Canaan.
7There he built an altar, and he
called the place El Bethel,[k] because it was there that God revealed himself to him when
he was fleeing from his brother.

8Now Deborah, Rebekah's
nurse, died and was buried
under the oak below Bethel. So
it was named Allon Bacuth.[l]

9After Jacob returned from
Paddan Aram,[m] God appeared
to him again and blessed him.
10God said to him, "Your name
is Jacob,[n] but you will no longer be called Jacob; your name
will be Israel.[o]" So he named
him Israel.

11And God said to him, "I
am God Almighty[p]; be fruitful
and increase in number. A nation and a community of nations will come from you, and
kings will come from your
body. 12The land I gave to
Abraham and Isaac I also give
to you, and I will give this
land to your descendants after
you." 13Then God went up
from him at the place where
he had talked with him.

14Jacob set up a stone pillar at
the place where God had
talked with him, and he
poured out a drink offering on
it; he also poured oil on it.
15Jacob named the place where
God had talked with him
Bethel.[q]

The Deaths of Rachel and Isaac

16Then they moved on from
Bethel. While they were still
some distance from Ephrath,
Rachel began to give birth and
had great difficulty. 17And as

[k] 7 *El Bethel* means *God of Bethel.*
[l] 8 *Allon Bacuth* means *oak of weeping.*
[m] 9 That is, Northwest Mesopotamia; also in verse 26
[n] 10 *Jacob* means *he grasps the heel* (figuratively, *he deceives*).
[o] 10 *Israel* means *he struggles with God.*
[p] 11 Hebrew *El-Shaddai*
[q] 15 *Bethel* means *house of God.*

בְהַקְשֹׁתָהּ בְּלִדְתָּהּ וַתֹּאמֶר לָהּ הַמְיַלֶּדֶת
the-being-midwife to-her that-she-said as-to-bear-her as-to-have-difficulty-her

אַל־ תִּירְאִי כִּי־ גַם־ זֶה לָךְ בֵּן׃ וַיְהִי בְּצֵאת
as-to-go and-he-was (18) son to-you this another for you-be-afraid not

נַפְשָׁהּ כִּי מֵתָה וַתִּקְרָא שְׁמוֹ בֶּן־ אוֹנִי וְאָבִיו
but-father-of-him Oni Ben name-of-him that-she-called she-died for life-of-her

קָרָא־ לוֹ בִנְיָמִין׃ וַתָּמָת רָחֵל וַתִּקָּבֵר בְּדֶרֶךְ
on-way-of and-she-was-buried Rachel so-she-died (19) Benjamin to-him he-named

אֶפְרָתָה הוּא בֵּית לָחֶם׃ וַיַּצֵּב יַעֲקֹב מַצֵּבָה עַל־ קְבֻרָתָהּ
tomb-of-her over pillar Jacob and-he-set-up (20) Lehem Beth that to-Ephrath

הִוא מַצֶּבֶת קְבֻרַת־ רָחֵל עַד־ הַיּוֹם׃ וַיִּסַּע יִשְׂרָאֵל
Israel so-he-moved-on (21) the-day to Rachel tomb-of pillar-of that

וַיֵּט אָהֳלֹה מֵהָלְאָה לְמִגְדַּל־ עֵדֶר׃ וַיְהִי בִּשְׁכֹּן
as-to-live and-he-was (22) Eder to-Migdal beyond tent-of-him and-he-pitched

יִשְׂרָאֵל בָּאָרֶץ הַהִוא וַיֵּלֶךְ רְאוּבֵן וַיִּשְׁכַּב אֶת־ בִּלְהָה
Bilhah with and-he-slept Reuben that-he-went the-that in-the-region Israel

פִּילֶגֶשׁ אָבִיו וַיִּשְׁמַע יִשְׂרָאֵל וַיִּהְיוּ בְנֵי־ יַעֲקֹב
Jacob sons-of now-they-were Israel and-he-heard father-of-him concubine-of

שְׁנֵים עָשָׂר׃ בְּנֵי לֵאָה בְּכוֹר יַעֲקֹב רְאוּבֵן וְשִׁמְעוֹן וְלֵוִי
and-Levi and-Simeon Reuben Jacob firstborn-of Leah sons-of (23) ten two

וִיהוּדָה וְיִשָּׂשכָר וּזְבוּלֻן׃ בְּנֵי רָחֵל יוֹסֵף וּבִנְיָמִן׃
and-Benjamin Joseph Rachel sons-of (24) and-Zebulun and-Issachar and-Judah

וּבְנֵי בִלְהָה שִׁפְחַת רָחֵל דָּן וְנַפְתָּלִי׃
and-Naphtali Dan Rachel maidservant-of Bilhah and-sons-of (25)

וּבְנֵי זִלְפָּה שִׁפְחַת לֵאָה גָּד וְאָשֵׁר אֵלֶּה בְּנֵי יַעֲקֹב
Jacob sons-of these and-Asher Gad Leah maidservant-of Zilpah and-sons-of (26)

אֲשֶׁר יֻלַּד־ לוֹ בְּפַדַּן אֲרָם׃ וַיָּבֹא יַעֲקֹב אֶל־יִצְחָק
Isaac to Jacob and-he-came (27) Aram in-Paddan to-him he-was-born who

אָבִיו מַמְרֵא קִרְיַת הָאַרְבַּע הִוא חֶבְרוֹן אֲשֶׁר־ גָּר־ שָׁם
there he-stayed where Hebron that the-Arba Kiriath Mamre father-of-him

אַבְרָהָם וְיִצְחָק׃ וַיִּהְיוּ יְמֵי יִצְחָק מְאַת שָׁנָה וּשְׁמֹנִים
and-eighty year hundred-of Isaac days-of and-they-were (28) and-Isaac Abraham

שָׁנָה׃ וַיִּגְוַע יִצְחָק וַיָּמָת וַיֵּאָסֶף אֶל־
to and-he-was-gathered and-he-died Isaac and-he-breathed-last (29) year

עַמָּיו זָקֵן וּשְׂבַע יָמִים וַיִּקְבְּרוּ אֹתוֹ עֵשָׂו וְיַעֲקֹב
and-Jacob Esau him and-they-buried days and-full-of old people-of-him

בָּנָיו׃ וְאֵלֶּה תֹּלְדוֹת עֵשָׂו הוּא אֱדוֹם׃ עֵשָׂו לָקַח אֶת־
*** he-took Esau (2) Edom that Esau lines-of now-these (36:1) sons-of-him

°21 ק אהלו

she was having great difficulty
in childbirth, the midwife
said to her, "Don't be afraid,
for you have another son."
[18]As she breathed her last—for
she was dying—she named
her son Ben-Oni.[r] But his father named him Benjamin.[s]
[19]So Rachel died and was
buried on the way to Ephrath
(that is, Bethlehem). [20]Over
her tomb Jacob set up a pillar,
and to this day that pillar
marks Rachel's tomb.
[21]Israel moved on again and
pitched his tent beyond Mig-
dal Eder. [22]While Israel was
living in that region, Reuben
went in and slept with his father's concubine Bilhah, and
Israel heard of it.

Jacob had twelve sons:
[23]The sons of Leah:
Reuben the firstborn of Jacob,
Simeon, Levi, Judah, Issachar and Zebulun.
[24]The sons of Rachel:
Joseph and Benjamin.
[25]The sons of Rachel's maidservant Bilhah:
Dan and Naphtali.
[26]The sons of Leah's maidservant Zilpah:
Gad and Asher.
These were the sons of
Jacob, who were born to him
in Paddan Aram.

[27]Jacob came home to his father Isaac in Mamre, near
Kiriath Arba (that is, Hebron),
where Abraham and Isaac had
stayed. [28]Isaac lived a hundred
and eighty years. [29]Then he
breathed his last and died and
was gathered to his people, old
and full of years. And his sons
Esau and Jacob buried him.

Esau's Descendants

36 This is the account of
Esau (that is, Edom).

[2]Esau took his wives from

[r]18 Ben-Oni means *son of my trouble.*
[s]18 Benjamin means *son of my right hand.*

נָשָׁיו מִבְּנוֹת כְּנָעַן אֶת־עָדָה בַּת־אֵילוֹן הַחִתִּי וְאֶת־
and the-Hittite Elon daughter-of Adah *** Canaan from-women-of wives-of-him

אָהֳלִיבָמָה בַּת־עֲנָה בַּת־צִבְעוֹן הַחִוִּי׃ וְאֶת־
and (3) the-Hittite Zibeon granddaughter-of Anah daughter-of Oholibamah

בָּשְׂמַת בַּת־יִשְׁמָעֵאל אֲחוֹת נְבָיוֹת׃ וַתֵּלֶד עָדָה לְעֵשָׂו
to-Esau Adah and-she-bore (4) Nebaioth sister-of Ishmael daughter-of Basemath

אֶת־אֱלִיפָז וּבָשְׂמַת יָלְדָה אֶת־רְעוּאֵל׃ וְאָהֳלִיבָמָה יָלְדָה אֶת־
*** she-bore and-Oholibamah (5) Reuel *** she-bore and-Basemath Eliphaz ***

יְעִישׁ° וְאֶת־יַעְלָם וְאֶת־קֹרַח אֵלֶּה בְּנֵי עֵשָׂו אֲשֶׁר יֻלְּדוּ־לוֹ
to-him they-were-born who Esau sons-of these Korah and Jalam and Jeush

בְּאֶרֶץ כְּנָעַן׃ וַיִּקַּח עֵשָׂו אֶת־נָשָׁיו וְאֶת־בָּנָיו וְאֶת־
and sons-of-him and wives-of-him *** Esau and-he-took (6) Canaan in-land-of

בְּנֹתָיו וְאֶת־כָּל־נַפְשׁוֹת בֵּיתוֹ וְאֶת־מִקְנֵהוּ וְאֶת־כָּל־
every-of and stock-of-him and house-of-him members-of all-of and daughters-of-him

בְּהֶמְתּוֹ וְאֵת כָּל־קִנְיָנוֹ אֲשֶׁר רָכַשׁ בְּאֶרֶץ כְּנָעַן
Canaan in-land-of he-acquired that good-of-him all-of and animal-of-him

וַיֵּלֶךְ אֶל־אֶרֶץ מִפְּנֵי יַעֲקֹב אָחִיו׃ כִּי־הָיָה
he-was for (7) brother-of-him Jacob from-face-of land to and-he-moved

רְכוּשָׁם רָב מִשֶּׁבֶת יַחְדָּו וְלֹא יָכְלָה אֶרֶץ
land-of he-could and-not together than-to-remain greater possession-of-them

מְגוּרֵיהֶם לָשֵׂאת אֹתָם מִפְּנֵי מִקְנֵיהֶם׃ וַיֵּשֶׁב
so-he-settled (8) stock-of-them because-of them to-support journeys-of-them

עֵשָׂו בְּהַר שֵׂעִיר עֵשָׂו הוּא אֱדוֹם׃ וְאֵלֶּה תֹּלְדוֹת עֵשָׂו
Esau lines-of now-these (9) Edom he Esau Seir in-hill-country-of Esau

אֲבִי אֱדוֹם בְּהַר שֵׂעִיר׃ אֵלֶּה שְׁמוֹת בְּנֵי־עֵשָׂו
Esau sons-of names-of these (10) Seir in-hill-country-of Edom father-of

אֱלִיפַז בֶּן־עָדָה אֵשֶׁת עֵשָׂו רְעוּאֵל בֶּן־בָּשְׂמַת אֵשֶׁת עֵשָׂו׃
Esau wife-of Basemath son-of Reuel Esau wife-of Adah son-of Eliphaz

וַיִּהְיוּ בְּנֵי אֱלִיפָז תֵּימָן אוֹמָר צְפוֹ וְגַעְתָּם וּקְנַז׃
and-Kenaz and-Gatam Zepho Omar Teman Eliphaz sons-of and-they-were (11)

וְתִמְנַע ׀ הָיְתָה פִילֶגֶשׁ לֶאֱלִיפַז בֶּן־עֵשָׂו וַתֵּלֶד
and-she-bore Esau son-of to-Eliphaz concubine she-was now-Timna (12)

לֶאֱלִיפַז אֶת־עֲמָלֵק אֵלֶּה בְּנֵי עָדָה אֵשֶׁת עֵשָׂו׃ וְאֵלֶּה
and-these (13) Esau wife-of Adah grandsons-of these Amalek *** to-Eliphaz

בְּנֵי רְעוּאֵל נַחַת וָזֶרַח שַׁמָּה וּמִזָּה אֵלֶּה* הָיוּ בְּנֵי
grandsons-of they-were these and-Mizzah Shammah and-Zerah Nahath Reuel sons-of

בָשְׂמַת אֵשֶׁת עֵשָׂו׃ וְאֵלֶּה הָיוּ בְּנֵי אָהֳלִיבָמָה בַת־
daughter-of Oholibamah sons-of they-were and-these (14) Esau wife-of Basemath

the women of Canaan: Adah daughter of Elon the Hittite, and Oholibamah daughter of Anah and granddaughter of Zibeon the Hivite— [3]also Basemath daughter of Ishmael and sister of Nebaioth.

[4]Adah bore Eliphaz to Esau, Basemath bore Reuel, [5]and Oholibamah bore Jeush, Jalam and Korah. These were the sons of Esau, who were born to him in Canaan.

[6]Esau took his wives and sons and daughters and all the members of his household, as well as his livestock and all his other animals and all the goods he had acquired in Canaan, and moved to a land some distance from his brother Jacob. [7]Their possessions were too great for them to remain together; the land where they were staying could not support them both because of their livestock. [8]So Esau (that is, Edom) settled in the hill country of Seir.

[9]This is the account of Esau the father of the Edomites in the hill country of Seir.

[10]These are the names of Esau's sons:
Eliphaz, the son of Esau's wife Adah, and Reuel, the son of Esau's wife Basemath.

[11]The sons of Eliphaz:
Teman, Omar, Zepho, Gatam and Kenaz.
[12]Esau's son Eliphaz also had a concubine named Timna, who bore him Amalek. These were grandsons of Esau's wife Adah.

[13]The sons of Reuel:
Nahath, Zerah, Shammah and Mizzah. These were grandsons of Esau's wife Basemath.

[14]The sons of Esau's wife Oholibamah daughter of

*13 Most mss have no *munah* after the *segol* (אֵלֶּה).

°5 ק יעוש

עֲנָה בַּת־ צִבְעוֹן אֵשֶׁת עֵשָׂו וַתֵּלֶד לְעֵשָׂו אֶת־ יְעִישׁ° וְאֶת־
and Jeush *** to-Esau and-she-bore Esau wife-of Zibeon granddaughter-of Anah

יַעְלָם וְאֶת־ קֹרַח׃ אֵלֶּה אַלּוּפֵי בְנֵי־ עֵשָׂו בְּנֵי אֱלִיפַז
Eliphaz sons-of Esau descendants-of chiefs-of these (15) Korah and Jalam

בְּכוֹר עֵשָׂו אַלּוּף תֵּימָן אַלּוּף אוֹמָר אַלּוּף צְפוֹ אַלּוּף קְנַז׃ אַלּוּף
Chief (16) Kenaz Chief Zepho Chief Omar Chief Teman Chief Esau firstborn-of

קֹרַח אַלּוּף גַּעְתָּם אַלּוּף עֲמָלֵק אֵלֶּה אַלּוּפֵי אֱלִיפַז בְּאֶרֶץ אֱדוֹם אֵלֶּה
these Edom in-land-of Eliphaz chiefs-of these Amalek Chief Gatam Chief Korah

בְּנֵי עָדָה׃ וְאֵלֶּה בְּנֵי רְעוּאֵל בֶּן־ עֵשָׂו אַלּוּף נַחַת אַלּוּף
Chief Nahath Chief Esau son-of Reuel sons-of and-these (17) Adah grandsons-of

זֶרַח אַלּוּף שַׁמָּה אַלּוּף מִזָּה אֵלֶּה אַלּוּפֵי רְעוּאֵל בְּאֶרֶץ אֱדוֹם אֵלֶּה
these Edom in-land-of Reuel chiefs-of these Mizzah Chief Shammah Chief Zerah

בְּנֵי בָשְׂמַת אֵשֶׁת עֵשָׂו׃ וְאֵלֶּה בְּנֵי אָהֳלִיבָמָה אֵשֶׁת
wife-of Oholibamah sons-of and-these (18) Esau wife-of Basemath grandsons-of

עֵשָׂו אַלּוּף יְעוּשׁ אַלּוּף יַעְלָם אַלּוּף קֹרַח אֵלֶּה אַלּוּפֵי אָהֳלִיבָמָה
Oholibamah chiefs-of these Korah Chief Jalam Chief Jeush Chief Esau

בַּת־ עֲנָה אֵשֶׁת עֵשָׂו׃ אֵלֶּה בְנֵי־ עֵשָׂו וְאֵלֶּה אַלּוּפֵיהֶם
chiefs-of-them and-these Esau sons-of these (19) Esau wife-of Anah daughter-of

הוּא אֱדוֹם׃ אֵלֶּה בְנֵי־ שֵׂעִיר הַחֹרִי יֹשְׁבֵי הָאָרֶץ
the-region ones-living-of the-Horite Seir sons-of these (20) Edom that

לוֹטָן וְשׁוֹבָל וְצִבְעוֹן וַעֲנָה׃ וְדִשׁוֹן וְאֵצֶר וְדִישָׁן
and-Dishan and-Ezer and-Dishon (21) and-Anah and-Zibeon and-Shobal Lotan

אֵלֶּה אַלּוּפֵי הַחֹרִי בְּנֵי שֵׂעִיר בְּאֶרֶץ אֱדוֹם׃ וַיִּהְיוּ
and-they-were (22) Edom in-land-of Seir sons-of the-Horite chiefs-of these

בְנֵי־ לוֹטָן חֹרִי וְהֵימָם וַאֲחוֹת לוֹטָן תִּמְנָע׃ וְאֵלֶּה בְּנֵי
sons-of and-these (23) Timna Lotan now-sister-of and-Hemam Hori Lotan sons-of

שׁוֹבָל עַלְוָן וּמָנַחַת וְעֵיבָל שְׁפוֹ וְאוֹנָם׃ וְאֵלֶּה בְנֵי־
sons-of and-these (24) and-Onam Shepho and-Ebal and-Manahath Alvan Shobal

צִבְעוֹן וְאַיָּה וַעֲנָה הוּא עֲנָה אֲשֶׁר מָצָא אֶת־ הַיֵּמִם
the-hot-springs *** he-discovered who Anah this and-Anah even-Aiah Zibeon

בַּמִּדְבָּר בִּרְעֹתוֹ אֶת־ הַחֲמֹרִים לְצִבְעוֹן אָבִיו׃
father-of-him to-Zibeon the-donkeys *** while-to-graze-him in-the-desert

וְאֵלֶּה בְנֵי־ עֲנָה דִּשֹׁן וְאָהֳלִיבָמָה בַּת־ עֲנָה׃
Anah daughter-of and-Oholibamah Dishon Anah children-of and-these (25)

וְאֵלֶּה בְּנֵי דִישָׁן חֶמְדָּן וְאֶשְׁבָּן וְיִתְרָן וּכְרָן׃
and-Keran and-Ithran and-Eshban Hemdan Dishon sons-of and-these (26)

אֵלֶּה בְּנֵי־ אֵצֶר בִּלְהָן וְזַעֲוָן וַעֲקָן׃ אֵלֶּה בְנֵי־ דִישָׁן
Dishan sons-of these (28) and-Akan and-Zaavan Bilhan Ezer sons-of these (27)

°14 ק יעוש

Anah and granddaughter of Zibeon, whom she bore to Esau:
Jeush, Jalam and Korah.

15 These were the chiefs among Esau's descendants:
The sons of Eliphaz the firstborn of Esau:
Chiefs Teman, Omar, Zepho, Kenaz, 16 Korah,[t] Gatam and Amalek. These were the chiefs descended from Eliphaz in Edom; they were grandsons of Adah.

17 The sons of Esau's son Reuel:
Chiefs Nahath, Zerah, Shammah and Mizzah. These were the chiefs descended from Reuel in Edom; they were grandsons of Esau's wife Basemath.

18 The sons of Esau's wife Oholibamah:
Chiefs Jeush, Jalam and Korah. These were the chiefs descended from Esau's wife Oholibamah daughter of Anah.

19 These were the sons of Esau (that is, Edom), and these were their chiefs.

20 These were the sons of Seir the Horite, who were living in the region:
Lotan, Shobal, Zibeon, Anah, 21 Dishon, Ezer and Dishan. These sons of Seir in Edom were Horite chiefs.

22 The sons of Lotan:
Hori and Homam.[u] Timna was Lotan's sister.

23 The sons of Shobal:
Alvan, Manahath, Ebal, Shepho and Onam.

24 The sons of Zibeon:
Aiah and Anah. This is the Anah who discovered the hot springs[v] in the desert while he was grazing the donkeys of his father Zibeon.

25 The children of Anah:
Dishon and Oholibamah daughter of Anah.

26 The sons of Dishon[w]:
Hemdan, Eshban, Ithran and Keran.

27 The sons of Ezer:
Bilhan, Zaavan and Akan.

28 The sons of Dishan:

[t] 16 Masoretic Text; Samaritan Pentateuch (see also Gen. 36:11 and 1 Chron. 1:36) does not have *Korah*.
[u] 22 Hebrew *Hemam*, a variant of *Homam*
[v] 24 Vulgate; Syriac *discovered water*; the meaning of the Hebrew for this word is uncertain.
[w] 26 Hebrew *Dishan*, a variant of *Dishon*

עוּץ וַאֲרָן׃ אֵלֶּה אַלּוּפֵי הַחֹרִי אַלּוּף לוֹטָן אַלּוּף שׁוֹבָל אַלּוּף
Chief Shobal Chief Lotan Chief the-Horite chiefs-of these (29) and-Aran Uz

צִבְעוֹן אַלּוּף עֲנָה׃ אַלּוּף דִּשֹׁן אַלּוּף אֵצֶר אַלּוּף דִּישָׁן אֵלֶּה אַלּוּפֵי
chiefs-of these Dishan Chief Ezer Chief Dishon Chief (30) Anah Chief Zibeon

הַחֹרִי לְאַלֻּפֵיהֶם בְּאֶרֶץ שֵׂעִיר׃ וְאֵלֶּה הַמְּלָכִים אֲשֶׁר
who the-kings and-these (31) Seir in-land-of by-divisions-of-them the-Horite

מָלְכוּ בְּאֶרֶץ אֱדוֹם לִפְנֵי מְלָךְ־ מֶלֶךְ לִבְנֵי יִשְׂרָאֵל׃
Israel from-sons-of king to-reign before Edom in-land-of they-reigned

וַיִּמְלֹךְ בֶּאֱדוֹם בֶּלַע בֶּן־ בְּעוֹר וְשֵׁם עִירוֹ דִּנְהָבָה׃
Dinhabah city-of-him and-name-of Beor son-of Bela in-Edom now-he-reigned (32)

וַיָּמָת בָּלַע וַיִּמְלֹךְ תַּחְתָּיו יוֹבָב בֶּן־ זֶרַח
Zerah son-of Jobab after-him then-he-reigned Bela when-he-died (33)

מִבָּצְרָה׃ וַיָּמָת יוֹבָב וַיִּמְלֹךְ תַּחְתָּיו חֻשָׁם
Husham after-him then-he-reigned Jobab when-he-died (34) from-Bozrah

מֵאֶרֶץ הַתֵּימָנִי׃ וַיָּמָת חֻשָׁם וַיִּמְלֹךְ תַּחְתָּיו
after-him then-he-reigned Husham when-he-died (35) the-Temanite from-land-of

הֲדַד בֶּן־ בְּדַד הַמַּכֶּה אֶת־ מִדְיָן בִּשְׂדֵה מוֹאָב וְשֵׁם
and-name-of Moab in-country-of Midian *** the-one-defeating Bedad son-of Hadad

עִירוֹ עֲוִית׃ וַיָּמָת הֲדָד וַיִּמְלֹךְ תַּחְתָּיו שַׂמְלָה
Samlah after-him then-he-reigned Hadad when-he-died (36) Avith city-of-him

מִמַּשְׂרֵקָה׃ וַיָּמָת שַׂמְלָה וַיִּמְלֹךְ תַּחְתָּיו שָׁאוּל
Shaul after-him then-he-reigned Samlah when-he-died (37) from-Masrekah

מֵרְחֹבוֹת הַנָּהָר׃ וַיָּמָת שָׁאוּל וַיִּמְלֹךְ תַּחְתָּיו
after-him then-he-reigned Shaul when-he-died (38) the-river from-Rehoboth-of

בַּעַל חָנָן בֶּן־ עַכְבּוֹר׃ וַיָּמָת בַּעַל חָנָן בֶּן־ עַכְבּוֹר
Acbor son-of Hanan Baal when-he-died (39) Acbor son-of Hanan Baal

וַיִּמְלֹךְ תַּחְתָּיו הֲדַר וְשֵׁם עִירוֹ פָּעוּ וְשֵׁם
and-name-of Pau city-of-him and-name-of Hadar after-him then-he-reigned

אִשְׁתּוֹ מְהֵיטַבְאֵל בַּת־ מַטְרֵד בַּת מֵי זָהָב׃ וְאֵלֶּה
and-these (40) Zahab Me daughter-of Matred daughter-of Mehetebel wife-of-him

שְׁמוֹת אַלּוּפֵי עֵשָׂו לְמִשְׁפְּחֹתָם לִמְקֹמֹתָם בִּשְׁמֹתָם
by-names-of-them by-regions-of-them by-clans-of-them Esau chiefs-of names-of

אַלּוּף תִּמְנָע אַלּוּף עַלְוָה אַלּוּף יְתֵת׃ אַלּוּף אָהֳלִיבָמָה אַלּוּף אֵלָה אַלּוּף
Chief Elah Chief Oholibamah Chief (41) Jetheth Chief Alvah Chief Timna Chief

פִּינֹן׃ אַלּוּף קְנַז אַלּוּף תֵּימָן אַלּוּף מִבְצָר׃ אַלּוּף מַגְדִּיאֵל אַלּוּף עִירָם
Iram Chief Magdiel Chief (43) Mibzar Chief Teman Chief Kenaz Chief (42) Pinon

אֵלֶּה׀ אַלּוּפֵי אֱדוֹם לְמֹשְׁבֹתָם בְּאֶרֶץ אֲחֻזָּתָם הוּא
this occupation-of-them in-land-of by-settlements-of-them Edom chiefs-of these

Uz and Aran.
29These were the Horite
chiefs:
Lotan, Shobal, Zibeon,
Anah, 30Dishon, Ezer and
Dishan. These were the
Horite chiefs, according
to their divisions, in the
land of Seir.

The Rulers of Edom

31These were the kings who
reigned in Edom before any
Israelite king reigned[x]:
32Bela son of Beor became
king of Edom. His city
was named Dinhabah.
33When Bela died, Jobab son
of Zerah from Bozrah
succeeded him as king.
34When Jobab died, Husham
from the land of the
Temanites succeeded
him as king.
35When Husham died,
Hadad son of Bedad, who
defeated Midian in the
country of Moab, succeeded him as king. His
city was named Avith.
36When Hadad died, Samlah
from Masrekah succeeded him as king.
37When Samlah died, Shaul
from Rehoboth on the
river[y] succeeded him as
king.
38When Shaul died, Baal-Hanan son of Acbor succeeded him as king.
39When Baal-Hanan son of
Acbor died, Hadad[z] succeeded him as king. His
city was named Pau, and
his wife's name was
Mehetabel daughter of
Matred, the daughter of
Me-Zahab.

40These were the chiefs descended from Esau, by name,
according to their clans and
regions:
Timna, Alvah, Jetheth,
41Oholibamah, Elah, Pinon,
42Kenaz, Teman,
Mibzar, 43Magdiel and
Iram. These were the
chiefs of Edom, according to their settlements
in the land they occupied.

x31 Or *before an Israelite king reigned over them*
y37 Or *River*
z39 Many manuscripts of the Masoretic Text, Samaritan Pentateuch and Syriac (see also 1 Chron. 1:50); most manuscripts of the Masoretic Text *Hadar*

עֵשָׂו אֲבִי אֱדוֹם׃ וַיֵּשֶׁב יַעֲקֹב בְּאֶרֶץ מְגוּרֵי
journeys-of in-land-of Jacob now-he-lived (37:1) Edom father-of Esau

אָבִיו בְּאֶרֶץ כְּנָעַן׃ אֵלֶּה ׀ תֹּלְדוֹת יַעֲקֹב יוֹסֵף בֶּן־ שְׁבַע־
seven son-of Joseph Jacob lines-of these (2) Canaan in-land-of father-of-him

עֶשְׂרֵה שָׁנָה הָיָה רֹעֶה אֶת־ אֶחָיו בַּצֹּאן וְהוּא נַעַר
young-man now-he to-the-flock brothers-of-him with tending he-was year ten

אֶת־ בְּנֵי בִלְהָה וְאֶת־בְּנֵי זִלְפָּה נְשֵׁי אָבִיו וַיָּבֵא
and-he-brought father-of-him wives-of Zilpah sons-of and Bilhah sons-of with

יוֹסֵף אֶת־ דִּבָּתָם רָעָה אֶל־ אֲבִיהֶם׃ וְיִשְׂרָאֵל אָהַב אֶת־
*** he-loved now-Israel (3) father-of-them to bad report-of-them *** Joseph

יוֹסֵף מִכָּל־ בָּנָיו כִּי־ בֶן־ זְקֻנִים הוּא לוֹ וְעָשָׂה
and-he-made to-him he old-ages son-of for sons-of-him more-than-all-of Joseph

לוֹ כְּתֹנֶת פַּסִּים׃ וַיִּרְאוּ אֶחָיו כִּי־ אֹתוֹ אָהַב
he-loved him that brothers-of-him when-they-saw (4) ornaments robe-of for-him

אֲבִיהֶם מִכָּל־ אֶחָיו וַיִּשְׂנְאוּ אֹתוֹ וְלֹא
and-not him then-they-hated brothers-of-him more-than-any-of father-of-them

יָכְלוּ דַּבְּרוֹ לְשָׁלֹם׃ וַיַּחֲלֹם יוֹסֵף חֲלוֹם
dream Joseph and-he-dreamed (5) with-kindness to-speak-to-him they-could

וַיַּגֵּד לְאֶחָיו וַיּוֹסִפוּ עוֹד שְׂנֹא אֹתוֹ׃
him to-hate more but-they-increased to-brothers-of-him and-he-told

וַיֹּאמֶר אֲלֵיהֶם שִׁמְעוּ־נָא הַחֲלוֹם הַזֶּה אֲשֶׁר חָלָמְתִּי׃
I-dreamed that the-this the-dream now! listen! to-them and-he-said (6)

וְהִנֵּה אֲנַחְנוּ מְאַלְּמִים אֲלֻמִּים בְּתוֹךְ הַשָּׂדֶה וְהִנֵּה קָמָה
she-rose and-see! the-field out-in sheaves ones-binding we now-see! (7)

אֲלֻמָּתִי וְגַם־ נִצָּבָה וְהִנֵּה תְסֻבֶּינָה אֲלֻמֹּתֵיכֶם
sheaves-of-you they-gathered-around and-see! she-stood and-also sheaf-of-me

וַתִּשְׁתַּחֲוֶיןָ לַאֲלֻמָּתִי׃ וַיֹּאמְרוּ לוֹ אֶחָיו
brothers-of-him to-him and-they-said (8) to-sheaf-of-me and-they-bowed

הֲמָלֹךְ תִּמְלֹךְ עָלֵינוּ אִם־ מָשׁוֹל תִּמְשֹׁל בָּנוּ
over-us will-you-rule to-rule really over-us will-you-reign to-reign?

וַיּוֹסִפוּ עוֹד שְׂנֹא אֹתוֹ עַל־ חֲלֹמֹתָיו וְעַל־
and-because-of dreams-of-him because-of him to-hate more and-they-increased

דְּבָרָיו׃ וַיַּחֲלֹם עוֹד חֲלוֹם אַחֵר וַיְסַפֵּר אֹתוֹ
him and-he-told another dream again then-he-dreamed (9) words-of-him

לְאֶחָיו וַיֹּאמֶר הִנֵּה חָלַמְתִּי חֲלוֹם עוֹד וְהִנֵּה הַשֶּׁמֶשׁ
the-sun and-see! again dream I-dreamed see! and-he-said to-brothers-of-him

וְהַיָּרֵחַ וְאַחַד עָשָׂר כּוֹכָבִים מִשְׁתַּחֲוִים לִי׃ וַיְסַפֵּר אֶל־
to when-he-told (10) to-me ones-bowing stars ten and-one and-the-moon

This was Esau, the father of
the Edomites.

Joseph's Dreams

37 Jacob lived in the land
where his father had
stayed, the land of Canaan.

2 This is the account of Jacob.

Joseph, a young man of
seventeen, was tending the
flocks with his brothers, the
sons of Bilhah and the sons of
Zilpah, his father's wives, and
he brought their father a bad
report about them.
3 Now Israel loved Joseph
more than any of his other
sons, because he had been
born to him in his old age; and
he made a richly ornamented[a]
robe for him. 4 When his
brothers saw that their father
loved him more than any of
them, they hated him and
could not speak a kind word to
him.
5 Joseph had a dream, and
when he told it to his brothers,
they hated him all the more.
6 He said to them, "Listen to
this dream I had: 7 We were
binding sheaves of grain out
in the field when suddenly my
sheaf rose and stood upright,
while your sheaves gathered
around mine and bowed
down to it."
8 His brothers said to him,
"Do you intend to reign over
us? Will you actually rule us?"
And they hated him all the
more because of his dream
and what he had said.
9 Then he had another
dream, and he told it to his
brothers. "Listen," he said, "I
had another dream, and this
time the sun and moon and
eleven stars were bowing
down to me."
10 When he told his father as

[a] 3 The meaning of the Hebrew for this word is uncertain; also in verses 23 and 32.

אָבִיו וְאֶל־ אֶחָיו וַיִּגְעַר־ בּוֹ אָבִיו
father-of-him to-him then-he-rebuked brothers-of-him and-to father-of-him

וַיֹּאמֶר לוֹ מָה הַחֲלוֹם הַזֶּה אֲשֶׁר חָלָמְתָּ הֲבוֹא
to-come? you-dreamed that the-this the-dream what? to-him and-he-said

נָבוֹא אֲנִי וְאִמְּךָ וְאַחֶיךָ לְהִשְׁתַּחֲוֺת לְךָ
before-you to-bow and-brothers-of-you and-mother-of-you I will-we-come

אָרְצָה׃ וַיְקַנְאוּ־ בוֹ אֶחָיו וְאָבִיו
but-father-of-him brothers-of-him of-him and-they-were-jealous (11) to-ground

שָׁמַר אֶת־ הַדָּבָר׃ וַיֵּלְכוּ אֶחָיו לִרְעוֹת
to-graze brothers-of-him now-they-went (12) the-matter *** he-kept-in-mind

אֶת־ צֹאן אֲבִיהֶם בִּשְׁכֶם׃ וַיֹּאמֶר יִשְׂרָאֵל אֶל־ יוֹסֵף
Joseph to Israel and-he-said (13) near-Shechem father-of-them flock-of ***

הֲלוֹא אַחֶיךָ רֹעִים בִּשְׁכֶם לְכָה וְאֶשְׁלָחֲךָ
and-I-will-send-you come! near-Shechem ones-grazing brothers-of-you not?

אֲלֵיהֶם וַיֹּאמֶר לוֹ הִנֵּנִי׃ וַיֹּאמֶר לוֹ לֶךְ־ נָא רְאֵה אֶת־
*** see! now! go! to-him so-he-said (14) here-I to-him and-he-replied to-them

שְׁלוֹם אַחֶיךָ וְאֶת־ שְׁלוֹם הַצֹּאן וַהֲשִׁבֵנִי דָּבָר
word and-bring-me! the-flock welfare-of and brothers-of-you welfare-of

וַיִּשְׁלָחֵהוּ מֵעֵמֶק חֶבְרוֹן וַיָּבֹא שְׁכֶמָה׃
to-Shechem and-he-went Hebron from-valley-of so-he-sent-him

וַיִּמְצָאֵהוּ אִישׁ וְהִנֵּה תֹעֶה בַּשָּׂדֶה וַיִּשְׁאָלֵהוּ הָאִישׁ
the-man and-he-asked-him in-the-field wandering and-see! man and-he-found-him (15)

לֵאמֹר מַה־ תְּבַקֵּשׁ׃ וַיֹּאמֶר אֶת־ אַחַי אָנֹכִי מְבַקֵּשׁ
looking I brothers-of-me *** and-he-replied (16) you-look-for what? to-say

הַגִּידָה־נָּא לִי אֵיפֹה הֵם רֹעִים׃ וַיֹּאמֶר הָאִישׁ נָסְעוּ
they-moved the-man and-he-answered (17) grazing they where to-me now! tell!

מִזֶּה כִּי שָׁמַעְתִּי אֹמְרִים נֵלְכָה דֹּתָיְנָה וַיֵּלֶךְ יוֹסֵף אַחַר
after Joseph so-he-went to-Dothan let-us-go ones-saying I-heard for from-here

אֶחָיו וַיִּמְצָאֵם בְּדֹתָן׃ וַיִּרְאוּ אֹתוֹ
him but-they-saw (18) near-Dothan and-he-found-them brothers-of-him

מֵרָחֹק וּבְטֶרֶם יִקְרַב אֲלֵיהֶם וַיִּתְנַכְּלוּ אֹתוֹ לַהֲמִיתוֹ׃
to-kill-him him then-they-plotted to-them he-reached and-before in-distance

וַיֹּאמְרוּ אִישׁ אֶל־ אָחִיו הִנֵּה בַּעַל הַחֲלֹמוֹת הַלָּזֶה
the-this the-dreams lord-of see! brother-of-him to each and-they-said (19)

בָּא׃ וְעַתָּה ׀ לְכוּ וְנַהַרְגֵהוּ וְנַשְׁלִכֵהוּ
and-let-us-throw-him and-let-us-kill-him come! so-now (20) he-comes

בְּאַחַד הַבֹּרוֹת וְאָמַרְנוּ חַיָּה רָעָה אֲכָלָתְהוּ
she-devoured-him ferocious animal then-we-will-say the-cisterns into-one-of

well as his brothers, his father rebuked him and said, "What is this dream you had? Will your mother and I and your brothers actually come and bow down to the ground before you?" [11]His brothers were jealous of him, but his father kept the matter in mind.

Joseph Sold by His Brothers

[12]Now his brothers had gone to graze their father's flocks near Shechem, [13]and Israel said to Joseph, "As you know, your brothers are grazing the flocks near Shechem. Come, I am going to send you to them."

"Very well," he replied.

[14]So he said to him, "Go and see if all is well with your brothers and with the flocks, and bring word back to me." So he sent him off from the Valley of Hebron.

When Joseph arrived at Shechem, [15]a man found him wandering around in the fields and asked him, "What are you looking for?"

[16]He replied, "I'm looking for my brothers. Can you tell me where they are grazing their flocks?"

[17]"They have moved on from here," the man answered. "I heard them say, 'Let's go to Dothan.' "

So Joseph went after his brothers and found them near Dothan. [18]But they saw him in the distance, and before he reached them, they plotted to kill him.

[19]"Here comes that dreamer!" they said to each other. [20]"Come now, let's kill him and throw him into one of these cisterns and say that a ferocious animal devoured

וְנִרְאֶה מַה־ יִּהְיוּ חֲלֹמֹתָיו׃ וַיִּשְׁמַע רְאוּבֵן
Reuben when-he-heard (21) dreams-of-him they-become what then-we-will-see

וַיַּצִּלֵהוּ מִיָּדָם וַיֹּאמֶר לֹא נַכֶּנּוּ נָפֶשׁ׃
life let-us-take not and-he-said from-hand-of-them then-he-rescued-him

וַיֹּאמֶר אֲלֵהֶם ׀ רְאוּבֵן אַל־ תִּשְׁפְּכוּ־ דָם הַשְׁלִיכוּ אֹתוֹ אֶל־ הַבּוֹר
the-cistern into him throw! blood you-shed not Reuben to-them and-he-said (22)

הַזֶּה אֲשֶׁר בַּמִּדְבָּר וְיָד אַל־ תִּשְׁלְחוּ־ בוֹ לְמַעַן הַצִּיל
to-rescue in-order on-him you-lay not but-hand in-the-desert that the-this

אֹתוֹ מִיָּדָם לַהֲשִׁיבוֹ אֶל־ אָבִיו׃ וַיְהִי
and-he-was (23) father-of-him to to-take-back-him from-hand-of-them him

כַּאֲשֶׁר־ בָּא יוֹסֵף אֶל־ אֶחָיו וַיַּפְשִׁיטוּ אֶת־ יוֹסֵף אֶת־
*** Joseph *** that-they-stripped brothers-of-him to Joseph he-came when

כֻּתָּנְתּוֹ אֶת־ כְּתֹנֶת הַפַּסִּים אֲשֶׁר עָלָיו׃ וַיִּקָּחֻהוּ
and-they-took-him (24) on-him that the-ornaments robe-of *** robe-of-him

וַיַּשְׁלִכוּ אֹתוֹ הַבֹּרָה וְהַבּוֹר רֵק אֵין בּוֹ מָיִם׃
water in-him not empty now-the-cistern into-the-cistern him and-they-threw

וַיֵּשְׁבוּ לֶאֱכָל־ לֶחֶם וַיִּשְׂאוּ עֵינֵיהֶם וַיִּרְאוּ
and-they-saw eyes-of-them then-they-lifted meal to-eat as-they-sat-down (25)

וְהִנֵּה אֹרְחַת יִשְׁמְעֵאלִים בָּאָה מִגִּלְעָד וּגְמַלֵּיהֶם
and-camels-of-them from-Gilead coming Ishmaelites caravan-of and-see!

נֹשְׂאִים נְכֹאת וּצְרִי וָלֹט הוֹלְכִים לְהוֹרִיד מִצְרָיְמָה׃
to-Egypt to-take-down ones-going and-myrrh and-balm spice ones-being-loaded

וַיֹּאמֶר יְהוּדָה אֶל־ אֶחָיו מַה־ בֶּצַע כִּי נַהֲרֹג אֶת־
*** we-kill if gain what? brothers-of-him to Judah and-he-said (26)

אָחִינוּ וְכִסִּינוּ אֶת־ דָּמוֹ׃ לְכוּ וְנִמְכְּרֶנּוּ
let-us-sell-him come! (27) blood-of-him *** and-we-cover brother-of-us

לַיִּשְׁמְעֵאלִים וְיָדֵנוּ אַל־ תְּהִי־ בוֹ כִּי־ אָחִינוּ
brother-of-us for on-him she-will-be not and-hand-of-us to-the-Ishmaelites

בְשָׂרֵנוּ הוּא וַיִּשְׁמְעוּ אֶחָיו׃ וַיַּעַבְרוּ אֲנָשִׁים
men when-they-came-by (28) brothers-of-him and-they-agreed he flesh-of-us

מִדְיָנִים סֹחֲרִים וַיִּמְשְׁכוּ וַיַּעֲלוּ אֶת־ יוֹסֵף מִן־
from Joseph *** and-they-lifted then-they-drew-up ones-trading Midianites

הַבּוֹר וַיִּמְכְּרוּ אֶת־ יוֹסֵף לַיִּשְׁמְעֵאלִים בְּעֶשְׂרִים כָּסֶף
silver for-twenty to-the-Ishmaelites Joseph *** and-they-sold the-cistern

וַיָּבִיאוּ אֶת־ יוֹסֵף מִצְרָיְמָה׃ וַיָּשָׁב רְאוּבֵן אֶל־ הַבּוֹר
the-cistern to Reuben when-he-returned (29) to-Egypt Joseph *** and-they-took

וְהִנֵּה אֵין־ יוֹסֵף בַּבּוֹר וַיִּקְרַע אֶת־ בְּגָדָיו׃
clothes-of-him *** then-he-tore in-the-cistern Joseph he-is-not and-see!

him. Then we'll see what comes of his dreams."

[21]When Reuben heard this, he tried to rescue him from their hands. "Let's not take his life," he said. [22]"Don't shed any blood. Throw him into this cistern here in the desert, but don't lay a hand on him." Reuben said this to rescue him from them and take him back to his father.

[23]So when Joseph came to his brothers, they stripped him of his robe—the richly ornamented robe he was wearing— [24]and they took him and threw him into the cistern. Now the cistern was empty; there was no water in it.

[25]As they sat down to eat their meal, they looked up and saw a caravan of Ishmaelites coming from Gilead. Their camels were loaded with spices, balm and myrrh, and they were on their way to take them down to Egypt.

[26]Judah said to his brothers, "What will we gain if we kill our brother and cover up his blood? [27]Come, let's sell him to the Ishmaelites and not lay our hands on him; after all, he is our brother, our own flesh and blood." His brothers agreed.

[28]So when the Midianite merchants came by, his brothers pulled Joseph up out of the cistern and sold him for twenty shekels[b] of silver to the Ishmaelites, who took him to Egypt.

[29]When Reuben returned to the cistern and saw that Joseph was not there, he tore his

[b]28 That is, about 8 ounces (about 0.2 kilogram)

וַיָּשָׁב אֶל־ אֶחָיו וַיֹּאמַר הַיֶּלֶד אֵינֶנּוּ וַאֲנִי אָנָה
where? and-I not-he the-boy and-he-said brothers-of-him to so-he-went (30)

אֲנִי־בָא׃ וַיִּקְחוּ אֶת־ כְּתֹנֶת יוֹסֵף וַיִּשְׁחֲטוּ שְׂעִיר
male-of and-they-slaughtered Joseph robe-of *** then-they-got (31) turning I

עִזִּים וַיִּטְבְּלוּ אֶת־הַכֻּתֹּנֶת בַּדָּם׃ וַיְשַׁלְּחוּ אֶת־ כְּתֹנֶת
robe-of *** then-they-took (32) in-the-blood robe *** and-they-dipped goats

הַפַּסִּים וַיָּבִיאוּ אֶל־ אֲבִיהֶם וַיֹּאמְרוּ זֹאת מָצָאנוּ
we-found this and-they-said father-of-them to and-they-brought the-ornaments

הַכֶּר־ נָא הַכְּתֹנֶת בִּנְךָ הִוא אִם־לֹא׃ וַיַּכִּירָהּ
and-he-recognized-her (33) not or he son-of-you the-robe now! examine!

וַיֹּאמֶר כְּתֹנֶת בְּנִי חַיָּה רָעָה אֲכָלָתְהוּ טָרֹף
to-be-torn she-devoured-him ferocious animal son-of-me robe-of and-he-said

טֹרַף יוֹסֵף׃ וַיִּקְרַע יַעֲקֹב שִׂמְלֹתָיו וַיָּשֶׂם
and-he-put-on clothes-of-him Jacob then-he-tore (34) Joseph he-was-torn

שַׂק בְּמָתְנָיו וַיִּתְאַבֵּל עַל־ בְּנוֹ יָמִים רַבִּים׃
many days son-of-him for and-he-mourned on-loins-of-him sackcloth

וַיָּקֻמוּ כָל־ בָּנָיו וְכָל־ בְּנֹתָיו
daughters-of-him and-all-of sons-of-him all-of and-they-came (35)

לְנַחֲמוֹ וַיְמָאֵן לְהִתְנַחֵם וַיֹּאמֶר כִּי־ אֵרֵד
I-will-go-down for and-he-said to-be-comforted but-he-refused to-comfort-him

אֶל־ בְּנִי אָבֵל שְׁאֹלָה וַיֵּבְךְּ אֹתוֹ אָבִיו׃
father-of-him for-him so-he-wept to-Sheol mourning son-of-me to

וְהַמְּדָנִים מָכְרוּ אֹתוֹ אֶל־מִצְרָיִם לְפוֹטִיפַר סְרִיס פַּרְעֹה
Pharaoh official-of to-Potiphar Egypt in him they-sold now-the-Medanites (36)

שַׂר הַטַּבָּחִים׃ וַיְהִי בָּעֵת הַהִוא וַיֵּרֶד
that-he-went-down the-that at-the-time and-he-was (38:1) the-guards captain-of

יְהוּדָה מֵאֵת אֶחָיו וַיֵּט עַד־ אִישׁ עֲדֻלָּמִי
Adullamite man with and-he-stayed brothers-of-him from-with Judah

וּשְׁמוֹ חִירָה׃ וַיַּרְא־ שָׁם יְהוּדָה בַּת־ אִישׁ כְּנַעֲנִי
Canaanite man daughter-of Judah there and-he-met (2) Hirah and-name-of-him

וּשְׁמוֹ שׁוּעַ וַיִּקָּחֶהָ וַיָּבֹא אֵלֶיהָ׃
with-her and-he-lay and-he-married-her Shua and-name-of-her

וַתַּהַר וַתֵּלֶד בֵּן וַיִּקְרָא אֶת־ שְׁמוֹ עֵר׃
Er name-of-him *** and-he-called son and-she-bore and-she-conceived (3)

וַתַּהַר עוֹד וַתֵּלֶד בֵּן וַתִּקְרָא אֶת־ שְׁמוֹ
name-of-him *** and-she-called son and-she-bore again and-she-conceived (4)

אוֹנָן׃ וַתֹּסֶף עוֹד וַתֵּלֶד בֵּן וַתִּקְרָא אֶת־
*** and-she-called son and-she-bore still and-she-continued (5) Onan

clothes. 30He went back to his brothers and said, "The boy isn't there! Where can I turn now?"

31Then they got Joseph's robe, slaughtered a goat and dipped the robe in the blood. 32They took the ornamented robe back to their father and said, "We found this. Examine it to see whether it is your son's robe."

33He recognized it and said, "It is my son's robe! Some ferocious animal has devoured him. Joseph has surely been torn to pieces."

34Then Jacob tore his clothes, put on sackcloth and mourned for his son many days. 35All his sons and daughters came to comfort him, but he refused to be comforted. "No," he said, "in mourning will I go down to the grave[c] to my son." So his father wept for him.

36Meanwhile, the Midianites[d] sold Joseph in Egypt to Potiphar, one of Pharaoh's officials, the captain of the guard.

Judah and Tamar

38 At that time, Judah left his brothers and went down to stay with a man of Adullam named Hirah. 2There Judah met the daughter of a Canaanite man named Shua. He married her and lay with her; 3she became pregnant and gave birth to a son, who was named Er. 4She conceived again and gave birth to a son and named him Onan. 5She gave birth to still another son

[c]35 Hebrew *Sheol*
[d]36 Samaritan Pentateuch, Septuagint, Vulgate and Syriac (see also verse 28); Masoretic Text *Medanites*

שְׁמוֹ שֵׁלָה וְהָיָה בִכְזִיב בְּלִדְתָּהּ אֹתוֹ׃ וַיִּקַּח
and-he-got (6) him that-to-bear-her at-Kezib now-he-was Shelah name-of-him

יְהוּדָה אִשָּׁה לְעֵר בְּכוֹרוֹ וּשְׁמָהּ תָּמָר׃ וַיְהִי עֵר
Er but-he-was (7) Tamar and-name-of-her firstborn-of-him for-Er wife Judah

בְּכוֹר יְהוּדָה רַע בְּעֵינֵי יְהוָה וַיְמִתֵהוּ יְהוָה׃
Yahweh so-he-killed-him Yahweh in-eyes-of wicked Judah firstborn-of

וַיֹּאמֶר יְהוּדָה לְאוֹנָן בֹּא אֶל־ אֵשֶׁת אָחִיךָ
brother-of-you wife-of with lie! to-Onan Judah then-he-said (8)

וְיַבֵּם אֹתָהּ וְהָקֵם זֶרַע לְאָחִיךָ׃
for-brother-of-you offspring and-produce! to-her and-fulfill-duty!

וַיֵּדַע אוֹנָן כִּי לֹּא* לוֹ יִהְיֶה הַזָּרַע וְהָיָה אִם־
when so-he-was the-offspring he-would-be to-him not that Onan but-he-knew (9)

בָּא אֶל־ אֵשֶׁת אָחִיו וְשִׁחֵת אַרְצָה לְבִלְתִּי
so-not on-the-ground and-he-spilled brother-of-him wife-of with he-lay

נְתָן־ זֶרַע לְאָחִיו׃ וַיֵּרַע בְּעֵינֵי
in-eyes-of so-he-was-wicked (10) for-brother-of-him offspring to-produce

יְהוָה אֲשֶׁר עָשָׂה וַיָּמֶת גַּם־ אֹתוֹ׃ וַיֹּאמֶר יְהוּדָה לְתָמָר
to-Tamar Judah then-he-said (11) him also so-he-killed he-did what Yahweh

כַּלָּתוֹ שְׁבִי אַלְמָנָה בֵית־ אָבִיךְ עַד־ יִגְדַּל
he-grows-up until father-of-you house-of widow live! daughter-in-law-of-him

שֵׁלָה בְנִי כִּי אָמַר פֶּן־ יָמוּת גַּם־הוּא כְּאֶחָיו
as-brothers-of-him he also he-will-die perhaps he-thought for son-of-me Shelah

וַתֵּלֶךְ תָּמָר וַתֵּשֶׁב בֵּית אָבִיהָ׃ וַיִּרְבּוּ
and-they-were-many (12) father-of-her house-of and-she-lived Tamar so-she-went

הַיָּמִים וַתָּמָת בַּת־ שׁוּעַ אֵשֶׁת־ יְהוּדָה וַיִּנָּחֶם
when-he-was-comforted Judah wife-of Shua daughter-of and-she-died the-days

יְהוּדָה וַיַּעַל עַל־ גֹּזְזֵי צֹאנוֹ הוּא וְחִירָה
and-Hirah he sheep-of-him ones-shearing-of to then-he-went-up Judah

רֵעֵהוּ הָעֲדֻלָּמִי תִּמְנָתָה׃ וַיֻּגַּד לְתָמָר לֵאמֹר
to-say to-Tamar and-he-was-told (13) to-Timnah the-Adullamite friend-of-him

הִנֵּה חָמִיךְ עֹלֶה תִמְנָתָה לָגֹז צֹאנוֹ׃
sheep-of-him to-shear to-Timnah going-up father-in-law-of-you see!

וַתָּסַר בִּגְדֵי אַלְמְנוּתָהּ מֵעָלֶיהָ וַתְּכַס
and-she-covered-self from-on-her widow-of-her clothes-of then-she-took-off (14)

בַּצָּעִיף וַתִּתְעַלָּף וַתֵּשֶׁב בְּפֶתַח עֵינַיִם אֲשֶׁר
which Enaim at-entrance-of then-she-sat and-she-disguised-self with-the-veil

עַל־ דֶּרֶךְ תִּמְנָתָה כִּי רָאֲתָה כִּי־ גָדַל שֵׁלָה וְהִוא לֹא־
not yet-she Shelah he-was-grown that she-saw for to-Timnah road on

and named him Shelah. It was at Kezib that she gave birth to him.

[6]Judah got a wife for Er, his firstborn, and her name was Tamar. [7]But Er, Judah's firstborn, was wicked in the LORD's sight; so the LORD put him to death.

[8]Then Judah said to Onan, "Lie with your brother's wife and fulfill your duty to her as a brother-in-law to produce offspring for your brother." [9]But Onan knew that the offspring would not be his; so whenever he lay with his brother's wife, he spilled his seed on the ground to keep from producing offspring for his brother. [10]What he did was wicked in the LORD's sight; so he put him to death also.

[11]Judah then said to his daughter-in-law Tamar, "Live as a widow in your father's house until my son Shelah grows up." For he thought, "He may die too, just like his brothers." So Tamar went to live in her father's house.

[12]After a long time Judah's wife, the daughter of Shua, died. When Judah had recovered from his grief, he went up to Timnah, to the men who were shearing his sheep, and his friend Hirah the Adullamite went with him.

[13]When Tamar was told, "Your father-in-law is on his way to Timnah to shear his sheep," [14]she took off her widow's clothes, covered herself with a veil to disguise herself, and then sat down at the entrance to Enaim, which is on the road to Timnah. For she saw that, though Shelah had now grown up, she had not

*9 Most mss have no *dagesh* in the *lamed* (לֹא).

נִתְּנָה לוֹ לְאִשָּׁה׃ (15) וַיִּרְאֶהָ יְהוּדָה וַיַּחְשְׁבֶהָ
then-he-thought-her Judah when-he-saw-her (15) as-wife to-him she-was-given

לְזוֹנָה כִּי כִסְּתָה פָּנֶיהָ׃ (16) וַיֵּט אֵלֶיהָ אֶל־
by to-her so-he-went (16) face-of-her she-covered for to-being-prostitute

הַדֶּרֶךְ וַיֹּאמֶר הָבָה־ נָּא אָבוֹא אֵלַיִךְ כִּי לֹא יָדַע
he-realized not for with-you let-me-lie now! come! and-he-said the-roadside

כִּי כַלָּתוֹ הִוא וַתֹּאמֶר מַה־ תִּתֶּן־ לִּי* כִּי
that to-me will-you-give what? and-she-asked she daughter-in-law-of-him that

תָבוֹא אֵלָי׃ (17) וַיֹּאמֶר אָנֹכִי אֲשַׁלַּח גְּדִי־ עִזִּים מִן־ הַצֹּאן
the-flock from goats kid-of I-will-send I and-he-said (17) with-me you-may-lie

וַתֹּאמֶר אִם־ תִּתֵּן עֵרָבוֹן עַד שָׁלְחֶךָ׃ (18) וַיֹּאמֶר
and-he-said (18) to-send-you until pledge will-you-give now and-she-asked

מָה הָעֵרָבוֹן אֲשֶׁר אֶתֶּן־ לָּךְ וַתֹּאמֶר חֹתָמְךָ
seal-of-you and-she-answered to-you I-should-give that the-pledge what?

וּפְתִילֶךָ וּמַטְּךָ אֲשֶׁר בְּיָדֶךָ וַיִּתֶּן־ לָהּ
to-her so-he-gave in-hand-of-you that and-staff-of-you and-belt-of-you

וַיָּבֹא אֵלֶיהָ וַתַּהַר לוֹ׃ (19) וַתָּקָם וַתֵּלֶךְ
and-she-left then-she-rose (19) by-him and-she-conceived with-her and-he-lay

וַתָּסַר צְעִיפָהּ מֵעָלֶיהָ וַתִּלְבַּשׁ בִּגְדֵי
clothes-of and-she-put-on from-on-her veil-of-her and-she-took-off

אַלְמְנוּתָהּ׃ (20) וַיִּשְׁלַח יְהוּדָה אֶת־ גְּדִי הָעִזִּים בְּיַד
by-hand-of the-goats kid-of *** Judah then-he-sent (20) widow-of-her

רֵעֵהוּ הָעֲדֻלָּמִי לָקַחַת הָעֵרָבוֹן מִיַּד הָאִשָּׁה
the-woman from-hand-of the-pledge to-get-back the-Adullamite friend-of-him

וְלֹא מְצָאָהּ׃ (21) וַיִּשְׁאַל אֶת־ אַנְשֵׁי מְקֹמָהּ לֵאמֹר אַיֵּה
where? to-say area-of-her men-of *** so-he-asked (21) he-found-her but-not

הַקְּדֵשָׁה הִוא בָעֵינַיִם עַל־ הַדָּרֶךְ וַיֹּאמְרוּ לֹא־ הָיְתָה
she-was not but-they-said the-road by at-the-Enaim who the-shrine-prostitute

בָזֶה קְדֵשָׁה׃ (22) וַיָּשָׁב אֶל־ יְהוּדָה וַיֹּאמֶר לֹא
not and-he-said Judah to so-he-went-back (22) shrine-prostitute at-here

מְצָאתִיהָ וְגַם אַנְשֵׁי הַמָּקוֹם אָמְרוּ לֹא־ הָיְתָה בָזֶה
at-here she-was not they-said the-area men-of and-besides I-found-her

קְדֵשָׁה׃ (23) וַיֹּאמֶר יְהוּדָה תִּקַּח־ לָהּ פֶּן נִהְיֶה
we-will-be or for-her let-her-keep Judah then-he-said (23) shrine-prostitute

לָבוּז הִנֵּה שָׁלַחְתִּי הַגְּדִי הַזֶּה וְאַתָּה לֹא מְצָאתָהּ׃
you-found-her not but-you the-this the-goat I-sent see! as-laughingstock

(24) וַיְהִי ׀ כְּמִשְׁלֹשׁ חֳדָשִׁים וַיֻּגַּד לִיהוּדָה לֵאמֹר
to-say to-Judah that-he-was-told months about-three-of and-he-was (24)

been given to him as his wife.
15 When Judah saw her, he
thought she was a prostitute,
for she had covered her face.
16 Not realizing that she was
his daughter-in-law, he went
over to her by the roadside
and said, "Come now, let me
sleep with you."
"And what will you give me
to sleep with you?" she asked.
17 "I'll send you a young goat
from my flock," he said.
"Will you give me some-
thing as a pledge until you
send it?" she asked.
18 He said, "What pledge
should I give you?"
"Your seal and its cord, and
the staff in your hand," she
answered. So he gave them to
her and slept with her, and
she became pregnant by him.
19 After she left, she took off her
veil and put on her widow's
clothes again.
20 Meanwhile Judah sent the
young goat by his friend the
Adullamite in order to get his
pledge back from the woman,
but he did not find her. 21 He
asked the men who lived
there, "Where is the shrine
prostitute who was beside the
road at Enaim?"
"There hasn't been any
shrine prostitute here," they
said.
22 So he went back to Judah
and said, "I didn't find her.
Besides, the men who lived
there said, 'There hasn't been
any shrine prostitute here.' "
23 Then Judah said, "Let her
keep what she has, or we will
become a laughingstock. After
all, I did send her this young
goat, but you didn't find her."
24 About three months later

**16* Most mss have no *dagesh* in the *lamed* (ל).

זָנְתָה תָּמָר כַּלָּתֶךָ וְגַם הִנֵּה הָרָה

pregnant see! and-also daughter-in-law-of-you Tamar she-played-harlot

לִזְנוּנִים וַיֹּאמֶר יְהוּדָה הוֹצִיאוּהָ וְתִשָּׂרֵף׃

and-let-her-be-burned bring-out-her! Judah so-he-said by-prostitutions

הִוא מוּצֵאת וְהִיא שָׁלְחָה אֶל־ חָמִיהָ לֵאמֹר

to-say father-in-law-of-her to she-sent then-she being-brought-out she (25)

לְאִישׁ אֲשֶׁר־ אֵלֶּה לּוֹ אָנֹכִי הָרָה וַתֹּאמֶר הַכֶּר־ נָא לְמִי הַחֹתֶמֶת

the-seal to-whom now! see! also-she-said pregnant I to-him these who by-man

וְהַפְּתִילִים וְהַמַּטֶּה הָאֵלֶּה׃ וַיַּכֵּר יְהוּדָה וַיֹּאמֶר

and-he-said Judah and-he-recognized (26) the-these and-the-staff and-the-belts

צָדְקָה מִמֶּנִּי כִּי־עַל־כֵּן לֹא־ נְתַתִּיהָ לְשֵׁלָה בְנִי וְלֹא־

so-not son-of-me to-Shelah I-gave-her not because more-than-I she-is-righteous

יָסַף עוֹד לְדַעְתָּה[a]׃ וַיְהִי בְּעֵת לִדְתָּהּ

to-bear-her at-time-of and-he-was (27) to-lie-with-her again he-repeated

וְהִנֵּה תְאוֹמִים בְּבִטְנָהּ׃ וַיְהִי בְלִדְתָּהּ וַיִּתֶּן־

that-he-put-out as-to-bear-her and-he-was (28) in-womb-of-her twin-boys and-see!

יָד וַתִּקַּח הַמְיַלֶּדֶת וַתִּקְשֹׁר עַל־ יָדוֹ

wrist-of-him on and-she-tied the-one-being-midwife so-she-took hand

שָׁנִי לֵאמֹר זֶה יָצָא רִאשֹׁנָה׃ וַיְהִי׀ כְּמֵשִׁיב

as-to-draw-back but-he-was (29) first he-came-out this to-say scarlet-thread

יָדוֹ וְהִנֵּה יָצָא אָחִיו וַתֹּאמֶר מַה־

this-how and-she-said brother-of-him he-came-out that-see! hand-of-him

פָּרַצְתָּ עָלֶיךָ פָּרֶץ וַיִּקְרָא שְׁמוֹ פָּרֶץ׃ וְאַחַר

and-then (30) Perez name-of-him so-he-called break for-you you-broke-out

יָצָא אָחִיו אֲשֶׁר עַל־ יָדוֹ הַשָּׁנִי וַיִּקְרָא

and-he-called the-scarlet-thread wrist-of-him on who brother-of-him he-came-out

שְׁמוֹ זָרַח׃ וְיוֹסֵף הוּרַד מִצְרָיְמָה וַיִּקְנֵהוּ

and-he-bought-him to-Egypt he-was-taken now-Joseph (39:1) Zerah name-of-him

פּוֹטִיפַר סְרִיס פַּרְעֹה שַׂר הַטַּבָּחִים אִישׁ מִצְרִי מִיַּד

from-hand-of Egyptian man the-guards captain-of Pharaoh official-of Potiphar

הַיִּשְׁמְעֵאלִים אֲשֶׁר הוֹרִדֻהוּ שָׁמָּה׃ וַיְהִי יְהוָה אֶת־ יוֹסֵף

Joseph with Yahweh and-he-was (2) to-there they-took-him who the-Ishmaelites

וַיְהִי אִישׁ מַצְלִיחַ וַיְהִי בְּבֵית אֲדֹנָיו הַמִּצְרִי׃

the-Egyptian master-of-him in-house-of and-he-was prospering man and-he-was

וַיַּרְא אֲדֹנָיו כִּי יְהוָה אִתּוֹ וְכֹל אֲשֶׁר־ הוּא עֹשֶׂה

doing he that and-all with-him Yahweh that master-of-him and-he-saw (3)

יְהוָה מַצְלִיחַ בְּיָדוֹ׃ וַיִּמְצָא יוֹסֵף חֵן

favor Joseph so-he-found (4) in-hand-of-him giving-success Yahweh

Judah was told, "Your daughter-in-law Tamar is guilty of prostitution, and as a result she is now pregnant."

Judah said, "Bring her out and have her burned to death!"

25 As she was being brought out, she sent a message to her father-in-law. "I am pregnant by the man who owns these," she said. And she added, "See if you recognize whose seal and cord and staff these are."

26 Judah recognized them and said, "She is more righteous than I, since I wouldn't give her to my son Shelah." And he did not sleep with her again.

27 When the time came for her to give birth, there were twin boys in her womb. 28 As she was giving birth, one of them put out his hand; so the midwife took a scarlet thread and tied it on his wrist and said, "This one came out first." 29 But when he drew back his hand, his brother came out, and she said, "So this is how you have broken out!" And he was named Perez.[e] 30 Then his brother, who had the scarlet thread on his wrist, came out and he was given the name Zerah.[f]

Joseph and Potiphar's Wife

39 Now Joseph had been taken down to Egypt. Potiphar, an Egyptian who was one of Pharaoh's officials, the captain of the guard, bought him from the Ishmaelites who had taken him there.

2 The LORD was with Joseph and he prospered, and he lived in the house of his Egyptian master. 3 When his master saw that the LORD was with him and that the LORD gave him success in everything he did, 4 Joseph found favor in his

e29 *Perez* means *breaking out.*
f30 *Zerah* can mean *scarlet* or *brightness.*

a26 Most mss have *mappiq* in the *he* (הּ).

בְּעֵינָיו וַיְשָׁרֶת אֹתוֹ וַיַּפְקִדֵהוּ עַל־ בֵּיתוֹ
house-of-him over and-he-put-in-charge-him him so-he-attended in-eyes-of-him

וְכָל־ יֶשׁ־ לוֹ נָתַן בְּיָדוֹ׃ וַיְהִי מֵאָז
from-time and-he-was (5) to-care-of-him he-entrusted to-him that-is and-all

הִפְקִיד אֹתוֹ בְּבֵיתוֹ וְעַל כָּל־ אֲשֶׁר יֶשׁ־ לוֹ
to-him he-is that all and-over of-house-of-him him he-put-in-charge

וַיְבָרֶךְ יְהוָה אֶת־ בֵּית הַמִּצְרִי בִּגְלַל יוֹסֵף
Joseph because-of the-Egyptian household-of *** Yahweh that-he-blessed

וַיְהִי בִּרְכַּת יְהוָה בְּכָל־ אֲשֶׁר יֶשׁ־ לוֹ בַּבַּיִת
in-the-house to-him he-is that on-all Yahweh blessing-of and-he-was

וּבַשָּׂדֶה׃ וַיַּעֲזֹב כָּל־ אֲשֶׁר־ לוֹ בְּיַד־ יוֹסֵף וְלֹא־
and-not Joseph in-care-of to-him that all so-he-left (6) and-in-the-field

יָדַע אִתּוֹ מְאוּמָה כִּי אִם־ הַלֶּחֶם אֲשֶׁר־הוּא אוֹכֵל וַיְהִי
now-he-was eating he that the-food only except anything to-him he-concerned

יוֹסֵף יְפֵה־ תֹאַר וִיפֵה מַרְאֶה׃ וַיְהִי אַחַר הַדְּבָרִים
the-things after and-he-was (7) sight and-good-of build good-of Joseph

הָאֵלֶּה וַתִּשָּׂא אֵשֶׁת־ אֲדֹנָיו אֶת־ עֵינֶיהָ אֶל־ יוֹסֵף
Joseph to eyes-of-her *** master-of-him wife-of that-she-lifted the-these

וַתֹּאמֶר שִׁכְבָה עִמִּי׃ וַיְמָאֵן ׀ וַיֹּאמֶר אֶל־ אֵשֶׁת
wife-of to and-he-said but-he-refused (8) with-me lie! and-she-said

אֲדֹנָיו הֵן אֲדֹנִי לֹא־ יָדַע אִתִּי מַה־ בַּבָּיִת
in-the-house what to-him he-concerns not master-of-me see! master-of-him

וְכֹל אֲשֶׁר־ יֶשׁ־ לוֹ נָתַן בְּיָדִי׃ אֵינֶנּוּ גָּדוֹל
greater not-he (9) to-care-of-me he-entrusted to-him he-is that and-all

בַּבַּיִת הַזֶּה מִמֶּנִּי וְלֹא־ חָשַׂךְ מִמֶּנִּי מְאוּמָה כִּי
except anything from-me he-withheld and-not than-me the-this in-the-house

אִם־ אוֹתָךְ בַּאֲשֶׁר אַתְּ־ אִשְׁתּוֹ וְאֵיךְ אֶעֱשֶׂה הָרָעָה
the-wicked-thing could-I-do then-how? wife-of-him you because you only

הַגְּדֹלָה הַזֹּאת וְחָטָאתִי לֵאלֹהִים׃ וַיְהִי כְּדַבְּרָהּ
though-to-speak-her and-he-was (10) against-God and-I-sin the-this the-great

אֶל־ יוֹסֵף יוֹם ׀ יוֹם וְלֹא־ שָׁמַע אֵלֶיהָ לִשְׁכַּב אֶצְלָהּ לִהְיוֹת עִמָּהּ׃
with-her to-be with-her to-lie to-her he-listened yet-not day day Joseph to

וַיְהִי כְּהַיּוֹם הַזֶּה וַיָּבֹא הַבַּיְתָה לַעֲשׂוֹת
to-attend into-the-house that-he-went the-this on-the-day now-he-was (11)

מְלַאכְתּוֹ וְאֵין אִישׁ מֵאַנְשֵׁי הַבַּיִת שָׁם בַּבָּיִת׃
in-the-house there the-house from-men-of man and-there-is-no duty-of-him

וַתִּתְפְּשֵׂהוּ בְּבִגְדוֹ לֵאמֹר שִׁכְבָה עִמִּי וַיַּעֲזֹב
but-he-left with-me lie! to-say by-cloak-of-him and-she-caught-him (12)

eyes and became his atten-
dant. Potiphar put him in
charge of his household, and
he entrusted to his care everything he owned. 5From the
time he put him in charge of
his household and of all that
he owned, the LORD blessed
the household of the Egyptian
because of Joseph. The
blessing of the LORD was on
everything Potiphar had, both
in the house and in the field.
6So he left in Joseph's care
everything he had; with Joseph in charge, he did not
concern himself with any-
thing except the food he ate.
Now Joseph was well-built
and handsome, 7and after a
while his master's wife took
notice of Joseph and said,
"Come to bed with me!"
8But he refused. "With me in
charge," he told her, "my master does not concern himself
with anything in the house;
everything he owns he has
entrusted to my care. 9No one
is greater in this house than I
am. My master has withheld
nothing from me except you,
because you are his wife. How
then could I do such a wicked
thing and sin against God?"
10And though she spoke to Joseph day after day, he refused
to go to bed with her or even
be with her.
11One day he went into the
house to attend to his duties,
and none of the household
servants was inside. 12She
caught him by his cloak and
said, "Come to bed with me!"

בְּגָדוֹ בְּיָדָהּ וַיָּנָס וַיֵּצֵא הַחוּצָה׃
to-the-outside and-he-went and-he-ran in-hand-of-her cloak-of-him

וַיְהִי כִּרְאוֹתָהּ כִּי־ עָזַב בִּגְדוֹ בְּיָדָהּ
in-hand-of-her cloak-of-him he-left that when-to-see-her and-he-was (13)

וַיָּנָס הַחוּצָה׃ וַתִּקְרָא לְאַנְשֵׁי בֵיתָהּ
household-of-her to-men-of that-she-called (14) to-the-outside and-he-ran

וַתֹּאמֶר לָהֶם לֵאמֹר רְאוּ הֵבִיא לָנוּ אִישׁ עִבְרִי לְצַחֶק
to-make-sport Hebrew man to-us he-brought look! to-say to-them and-she-said

בָּנוּ בָּא אֵלַי לִשְׁכַּב עִמִּי וָאֶקְרָא בְּקוֹל גָּדוֹל׃
loud with-voice but-I-screamed with-me to-sleep to-me he-came of-us

וַיְהִי כְשָׁמְעוֹ כִּי־ הֲרִימֹתִי קוֹלִי וָאֶקְרָא
and-I-screamed voice-of-me I-lifted that when-to-hear-him and-he-was (15)

וַיַּעֲזֹב בִּגְדוֹ אֶצְלִי וַיָּנָס וַיֵּצֵא הַחוּצָה׃
to-the-outside and-he-went and-he-ran with-me cloak-of-him then-he-left

וַתַּנַּח בִּגְדוֹ אֶצְלָהּ עַד־ בּוֹא אֲדֹנָיו אֶל־
to masters-of-him to-come until beside-her cloak-of-him so-she-kept (16)

בֵּיתוֹ׃ וַתְּדַבֵּר אֵלָיו כַּדְּבָרִים הָאֵלֶּה לֵאמֹר
to-say the-these according-to-the-words to-him then-she-told (17) home-of-him

בָּא־ אֵלַי הָעֶבֶד הָעִבְרִי אֲשֶׁר־ הֵבֵאתָ לָּנוּ לְצַחֶק בִּי׃
of-me to-make-sport to-us you-brought whom the-Hebrew the-slave to-me he-came

וַיְהִי כַּהֲרִימִי קוֹלִי וָאֶקְרָא וַיַּעֲזֹב
that-he-left and-I-screamed voice-of-me as-to-raise-me and-he-was (18)

בִּגְדוֹ אֶצְלִי וַיָּנָס הַחוּצָה׃ וַיְהִי כִשְׁמֹעַ
when-to-hear and-he-was (19) to-the-outside and-he-ran beside-me cloak-of-him

אֲדֹנָיו אֶת־ דִּבְרֵי אִשְׁתּוֹ אֲשֶׁר דִּבְּרָה אֵלָיו לֵאמֹר
to-say to-him she-told that wife-of-him words-of *** masters-of-him

כַּדְּבָרִים הָאֵלֶּה עָשָׂה* לִי עַבְדֶּךָ וַיִּחַר אַפּוֹ׃
anger-of-him that-he-burned slave-of-you to-me he-did the-these as-the-things

וַיִּקַּח אֲדֹנֵי יוֹסֵף אֹתוֹ וַיִּתְּנֵהוּ אֶל־ בֵּית הַסֹּהַר
the-prison house-of in and-he-put-him him Joseph masters-of and-he-took (20)

מְקוֹם אֲשֶׁר־ אֲסוּרֵי° הַמֶּלֶךְ אֲסוּרִים וַיְהִי־ שָׁם
there and-he-was ones-being-confined the-king prisoners-of where place-of

בְּבֵית הַסֹּהַר׃ וַיְהִי יְהוָה אֶת־ יוֹסֵף וַיֵּט
and-he-showed Joseph with Yahweh but-he-was (21) the-prison in-house-of

אֵלָיו חָסֶד וַיִּתֵּן חִנּוֹ בְּעֵינֵי שַׂר בֵּית־
house-of warden-of in-eyes-of favor-of-him and-he-granted kindness to-him

הַסֹּהַר׃ וַיִּתֵּן שַׂר בֵּית־ הַסֹּהַר בְּיַד־ יוֹסֵף
Joseph in-care-of the-prison house-of warden-of so-he-put (22) the-prison

But he left his cloak in her hand and ran out of the house.

[13]When she saw that he had left his cloak in her hand and had run out of the house, [14]she called her household servants. "Look," she said to them, "this Hebrew has been brought to us to make sport of us! He came in here to sleep with me, but I screamed. [15]When he heard me scream for help, he left his cloak beside me and ran out of the house."

[16]She kept his cloak beside her until his master came home. [17]Then she told him this story: "That Hebrew slave you brought us came to me to make sport of me. [18]But as soon as I screamed for help, he left his cloak beside me and ran out of the house."

[19]When his master heard the story his wife told him, saying, "This is how your slave treated me," he burned with anger. [20]Joseph's master took him and put him in prison, the place where the king's prisoners were confined.

But while Joseph was there in the prison, [21]the LORD was with him; he showed him kindness and granted him favor in the eyes of the prison warden. [22]So the warden put Joseph in charge of all those

**19* Most mss have no *mappiq* in the *he* (ָה).

°*20* ק אסירי

אֵת כָּל־ הָאֲסִירִם אֲשֶׁר בְּבֵית הַסֹּהַר וְאֵת כָּל־אֲשֶׁר עֹשִׂים
ones-doing that all and the-prison in-house-of who the-prisoners all-of ***

שָׁם הוּא הָיָה עֹשֶׂה׃ (23) אֵין ׀ שַׂר בֵּית־ הַסֹּהַר רֹאֶה
attending the-prison house-of warden-of he-is-not (23) doing he-was he there

אֶת־ כָּל־ מְאוּמָה בְּיָדוֹ בַּאֲשֶׁר יְהוָה אִתּוֹ וַאֲשֶׁר־הוּא
he and-what with-him Yahweh because under-care-of-him anything any-of ***

עֹשֶׂה יְהוָה מַצְלִיחַ׃ (40:1) וַיְהִי אַחַר הַדְּבָרִים הָאֵלֶּה
the-these the-things after and-he-was (40:1) giving-success Yahweh doing

חָטְאוּ מַשְׁקֵה מֶלֶךְ־ מִצְרַיִם וְהָאֹפֶה לַאֲדֹנֵיהֶם
to-masters-of-them and-the-one-baking Egypt king-of cupbearer-of they-offended

לְמֶלֶךְ מִצְרָיִם׃ (2) וַיִּקְצֹף פַּרְעֹה עַל שְׁנֵי סָרִיסָיו
officials-of-him two-of with Pharaoh and-he-was-angry (2) Egypt to-king-of

עַל שַׂר הַמַּשְׁקִים וְעַל שַׂר הָאוֹפִים׃ (3) וַיִּתֵּן
so-he-put (3) the-ones-baking chief-of and-with the-cupbearers chief-of with

אֹתָם בְּמִשְׁמַר בֵּית שַׂר הַטַבָּחִים* אֶל־ בֵּית הַסֹּהַר
the-prison house-of in the-guards captain-of house-of in-custody-of them

מְקוֹם אֲשֶׁר יוֹסֵף אָסוּר שָׁם׃ (4) וַיִּפְקֹד שַׂר
captain-of and-he-assigned (4) there being-confined Joseph where place-of

הַטַּבָּחִים אֶת־ יוֹסֵף אִתָּם וַיְשָׁרֶת אֹתָם וַיִּהְיוּ יָמִים
days and-they-were them and-he-attended with-them Joseph *** the-guards

בְּמִשְׁמָר׃ (5) וַיַּחַלְמוּ חֲלוֹם שְׁנֵיהֶם אִישׁ חֲלֹמוֹ בְּלַיְלָה
in-night dream-of-him each two-of-them dream and-they-dreamed (5) in-custody

אֶחָד אִישׁ כְּפִתְרוֹן חֲלֹמוֹ הַמַּשְׁקֶה וְהָאֹפֶה אֲשֶׁר
who and-the-one-baking the-cupbearer dream-of-him own-meaning-of each same

לְמֶלֶךְ מִצְרַיִם אֲשֶׁר אֲסוּרִים בְּבֵית הַסֹּהַר׃ (6) וַיָּבֹא
when-he-came (6) the-prison in-house-of ones-being-held who Egypt to-king-of

אֲלֵיהֶם יוֹסֵף בַּבֹּקֶר וַיַּרְא אֹתָם וְהִנָּם זֹעֲפִים׃
being-dejected-ones and-see-them! them then-he-saw in-the-morning Joseph to-them

(7) וַיִּשְׁאַל אֶת־ סְרִיסֵי פַרְעֹה אֲשֶׁר אִתּוֹ בְמִשְׁמַר בֵּית
house-of in-custody-of with-him who Pharaoh officials-of *** so-he-asked (7)

אֲדֹנָיו לֵאמֹר מַדּוּעַ פְּנֵיכֶם רָעִים הַיּוֹם׃ (8) וַיֹּאמְרוּ
so-they-answered (8) the-day sad-ones faces-of-you why? to-say masters-of-him

אֵלָיו חֲלוֹם חָלַמְנוּ וּפֹתֵר אֵין אֹתוֹ וַיֹּאמֶר
and-he-said for-him there-is-not but-one-interpreting we-dreamed dream to-him

אֲלֵהֶם יוֹסֵף הֲלוֹא לֵאלֹהִים פִּתְרֹנִים סַפְּרוּ־ נָא לִי׃ (9) וַיְסַפֵּר
so-he-told (9) to-me now! tell! interpretations to-God not? Joseph to-them

שַׂר־ הַמַּשְׁקִים אֶת־ חֲלֹמוֹ לְיוֹסֵף וַיֹּאמֶר לוֹ
to-him and-he-said to-Joseph dream-of-him *** the-cupbearers chief-of

held in the prison, and he was
made responsible for all that
was done there. [23]The warden
paid no attention to anything
under Joseph's care, because
the LORD was with Joseph and
gave him success in whatever
he did.

The Cupbearer and the Baker

40 Some time later, the
cupbearer and the
baker of the king of Egypt
offended their master, the
king of Egypt. [2]Pharaoh was
angry with his two officials,
the chief cupbearer and the
chief baker, [3]and put them in
custody in the house of the
captain of the guard, in the
same prison where Joseph was
confined. [4]The captain of the
guard assigned them to Joseph, and he attended them.
After they had been in custody for some time, [5]each of
the two men—the cupbearer
and the baker of the king of
Egypt, who were being held in
prison—had a dream the same
night, and each dream had a
meaning of its own.
[6]When Joseph came to them
the next morning, he saw that
they were dejected. [7]So he
asked Pharaoh's officials who
were in custody with him in
his master's house, "Why are
your faces so sad today?"
[8]"We both had dreams,"
they answered, "but there is
no one to interpret them."
Then Joseph said to them,
"Do not interpretations belong to God? Tell me your
dreams."
[9]So the chief cupbearer told
Joseph his dream. He said to

*3 Most mss have *dagesh* in the *teth* (הט׳).

בַּחֲלוֹמִי וְהִנֵּה־ גֶפֶן לְפָנָי׃ וּבַגֶּפֶן שְׁלֹשָׁה
three and-on-the-vine (10) in-front-of-me vine now-see! in-dream-of-me

שָׂרִיגִם וְהִוא כְפֹרַחַת עָלְתָה נִצָּהּ הִבְשִׁילוּ
and-they-ripened blossom-of-her she-came budding when-she branches

אַשְׁכְּלֹתֶיהָ עֲנָבִים׃ וְכוֹס פַּרְעֹה בְּיָדִי וָאֶקַּח אֶת־
*** and-I-took in-hand-of-me Pharaoh now-cup-of (11) grapes clusters-of-her

הָעֲנָבִים וָאֶשְׂחַט אֹתָם אֶל־ כּוֹס פַּרְעֹה וָאֶתֵּן אֶת־ הַכּוֹס
the-cup *** and-I-put Pharaoh cup-of into them and-I-squeezed the-grapes

עַל־ כַּף פַּרְעֹה׃ וַיֹּאמֶר לוֹ יוֹסֵף זֶה פִּתְרֹנוֹ
meaning-of-him this Joseph to-him and-he-said (12) Pharaoh hand-of into

שְׁלֹשֶׁת הַשָּׂרִגִים שְׁלֹשֶׁת יָמִים הֵם׃ בְּעוֹד שְׁלֹשֶׁת יָמִים יִשָּׂא
he-will-lift days three-of within (13) they days three-of branches three-of

פַרְעֹה אֶת־ רֹאשֶׁךָ וַהֲשִׁיבְךָ עַל־ כַּנֶּךָ
position-of-you to and-he-will-restore-you head-of-you *** Pharaoh

וְנָתַתָּ כוֹס־ פַּרְעֹה בְּיָדוֹ כַּמִּשְׁפָּט הָרִאשׁוֹן אֲשֶׁר
when the-former as-the-custom in-hand-of-him Pharaoh cup-of and-you-will-put

הָיִיתָ מַשְׁקֵהוּ׃ כִּי אִם־ זְכַרְתַּנִי אִתְּךָ כַּאֲשֶׁר
when with-you you-remember-me now indeed (14) cupbearer-of-him you-were

יִיטַב לָךְ וְעָשִׂיתָ־ נָּא עִמָּדִי חָסֶד וְהִזְכַּרְתַּנִי
and-you-mention-me kindness with-me now! and-you-show with-you he-goes-well

אֶל־פַּרְעֹה וְהוֹצֵאתַנִי מִן־ הַבַּיִת הַזֶּה׃ כִּי־ גֻנֹּב
to-be-forced for (15) the-this the-prison from so-you-get-out-me Pharaoh to

גֻּנַּבְתִּי מֵאֶרֶץ הָעִבְרִים וְגַם־ פֹּה לֹא־עָשִׂיתִי מְאוּמָה כִּי־
that anything I-did not here and-even the-Hebrews from-land-of I-was-forced

שָׂמוּ אֹתִי בַּבּוֹר׃ וַיַּרְא שַׂר־ הָאֹפִים
the-ones-baking chief-of when-he-saw (16) in-the-dungeon me they-should-put

כִּי טוֹב פָּתָר וַיֹּאמֶר אֶל־ יוֹסֵף אַף־אֲנִי בַּחֲלוֹמִי
in-dream-of-me I also Joseph to then-he-said he-interpreted favorably that

וְהִנֵּה שְׁלֹשָׁה סַלֵּי חֹרִי עַל־ רֹאשִׁי׃ וּבַסַּל
and-in-the-basket (17) head-of-me on bread baskets-of three-of and-see!

הָעֶלְיוֹן מִכֹּל מַאֲכַל פַּרְעֹה מַעֲשֵׂה אֹפֶה וְהָעוֹף אֹכֵל
eating but-the-bird one-baking work-of Pharaoh food-of from-all-of the-top

אֹתָם מִן־ הַסַּל מֵעַל רֹאשִׁי׃ וַיַּעַן יוֹסֵף וַיֹּאמֶר
and-he-said Joseph and-he-replied (18) head-of-me upon the-basket from them

זֶה פִּתְרֹנוֹ שְׁלֹשֶׁת הַסַּלִּים שְׁלֹשֶׁת יָמִים הֵם׃ בְּעוֹד
within (19) they days three-of the-baskets three-of meaning-of-him this

שְׁלֹשֶׁת יָמִים יִשָּׂא פַרְעֹה אֶת־ רֹאשְׁךָ מֵעָלֶיךָ
from-on-you head-of-you *** Pharaoh he-will-lift-off days three-of

him, "In my dream I saw a vine in front of me,
10and on
the vine were three branches. As soon as it budded, it blossomed, and its clusters ripened into grapes.
11Pharaoh's
cup was in my hand, and I took the grapes, squeezed them into Pharaoh's cup and put the cup in his hand."
12"This is what it means," Joseph said to him. "The three branches are three days.
13Within three days Pharaoh will lift up your head and restore you to your position, and you will put Pharaoh's cup in his hand, just as you used to do when you were his cupbearer.
14But when all goes
well with you, remember me and show me kindness; mention me to Pharaoh and get me out of this prison.
15For I was
forcibly carried off from the land of the Hebrews, and even here I have done nothing to deserve being put in a dungeon."
16When the chief baker saw that Joseph had given a favorable interpretation, he said to Joseph, "I too had a dream: On my head were three baskets of bread.[g]
17In the top basket
were all kinds of baked goods for Pharaoh, but the birds were eating them out of the basket on my head."
18"This is what it means," Joseph said. "The three baskets are three days.
19Within
three days Pharaoh will lift off

g16 Or *three wicker baskets*

וְתָלָה אוֹתְךָ עַל־ עֵץ וְאָכַל הָעוֹף אֶת־ בְּשָׂרְךָ
flesh-of-you *** the-bird and-he-will-eat tree on you and-he-will-hang

מֵעָלֶיךָ׃ וַיְהִי ׀ בַּיּוֹם הַשְּׁלִישִׁי יוֹם הֻלֶּדֶת אֶת־ פַּרְעֹה
Pharaoh *** to-be-born day-of the-third on-the-day and-he-was (20) from-you

וַיַּעַשׂ מִשְׁתֶּה לְכָל־ עֲבָדָיו וַיִּשָּׂא אֶת־ רֹאשׁ ׀
head-of *** and-he-lifted officials-of-him for-all-of feast and-he-gave

שַׂר הַמַּשְׁקִים וְאֶת־ רֹאשׁ שַׂר הָאֹפִים בְּתוֹךְ
in-presence-of the-ones-baking chief-of head-of and the-cupbearers chief-of

עֲבָדָיו׃ וַיָּשֶׁב אֶת־ שַׂר הַמַּשְׁקִים עַל־
to the-cupbearers chief-of *** and-he-restored (21) officials-of-him

מַשְׁקֵהוּ וַיִּתֵּן הַכּוֹס עַל־ כַּף פַּרְעֹה׃ וְאֵת שַׂר
chief-of but (22) Pharaoh hand-of into the-cup again-he-put position-of-him

הָאֹפִים תָּלָה כַּאֲשֶׁר פָּתַר לָהֶם יוֹסֵף׃ וְלֹא־
yet-not (23) Joseph to-them he-interpreted just-as he-hanged the-ones-baking

זָכַר שַׂר־ הַמַּשְׁקִים אֶת־ יוֹסֵף וַיִּשְׁכָּחֵהוּ׃
but-he-forgot-him Joseph *** the-cupbearers chief-of he-remembered

וַיְהִי מִקֵּץ שְׁנָתַיִם יָמִים וּפַרְעֹה חֹלֵם וְהִנֵּה
and-see! dreaming that-Pharaoh full-ones two-years at-end-of and-he-was (41:1)

עֹמֵד עַל־ הַיְאֹר׃ וְהִנֵּה מִן־ הַיְאֹר עֹלֹת שֶׁבַע פָּרוֹת
cows seven ones-coming the-Nile from and-see! (2) the-Nile by standing

יְפוֹת מַרְאֶה וּבְרִיאֹת בָּשָׂר וַתִּרְעֶינָה בָּאָחוּ׃
among-the-reed and-they-grazed body and-fat-of appearance ones-sleek-of

וְהִנֵּה שֶׁבַע פָּרוֹת אֲחֵרוֹת עֹלוֹת אַחֲרֵיהֶן מִן־ הַיְאֹר
the-Nile from after-them ones-coming other-ones cows seven and-see! (3)

רָעוֹת מַרְאֶה וְדַקּוֹת בָּשָׂר וַתַּעֲמֹדְנָה אֵצֶל הַפָּרוֹת
the-cows beside and-they-stood body and-ones-gaunt-of appearance ones-ugly-of

עַל־ שְׂפַת הַיְאֹר׃ וַתֹּאכַלְנָה הַפָּרוֹת רָעוֹת הַמַּרְאֶה
the-appearance ones-ugly-of the-cows and-they-ate (4) the-Nile bank-of on

וְדַקֹּת הַבָּשָׂר אֵת שֶׁבַע הַפָּרוֹת יְפֹת הַמַּרְאֶה
the-appearance ones-sleek-of the-cows seven *** the-body and-ones-gaunt-of

וְהַבְּרִיאֹת וַיִּיקַץ פַּרְעֹה׃ וַיִּישָׁן וַיַּחֲלֹם שֵׁנִית
second and-he-dreamed and-he-slept (5) Pharaoh then-he-woke and-the-fat-ones

וְהִנֵּה ׀ שֶׁבַע שִׁבֳּלִים עֹלוֹת בְּקָנֶה אֶחָד בְּרִיאוֹת וְטֹבוֹת׃
and-good-ones fat-ones one on-stalk ones-growing heads-of-grain seven and-see!

וְהִנֵּה שֶׁבַע שִׁבֳּלִים דַּקּוֹת וּשְׁדוּפֹת
and-ones-being-scorched-of thin-ones heads-of-grain seven and-see! (6)

קָדִים צֹמְחוֹת אַחֲרֵיהֶן׃ וַתִּבְלַעְנָה הַשִּׁבֳּלִים
the-heads-of-grain and-they-swallowed (7) after-them sprouting east-winds

your head and hang you on a
tree.[h] And the birds will eat
away your flesh."
[20]Now the third day was
Pharaoh's birthday, and he
gave a feast for all his officials.
He lifted up the heads of the
chief cupbearer and the chief
baker in the presence of his
officials: [21]He restored the
chief cupbearer to his position, so that he once again put
the cup into Pharaoh's hand,
[22]but he hanged[i] the chief
baker, just as Joseph had said
to them in his interpretation.
[23]The chief cupbearer, however, did not remember Joseph; he forgot him.

Pharaoh's Dreams

41 When two full years
had passed, Pharaoh
had a dream: He was standing
by the Nile, [2]when out of the
river there came up seven
cows, sleek and fat, and they
grazed among the reeds. [3]After
them, seven other cows, ugly
and gaunt, came up out of the
Nile and stood beside those on
the riverbank. [4]And the cows
that were ugly and gaunt ate
up the seven sleek, fat cows.
Then Pharaoh woke up.
[5]He fell asleep again and had
a second dream: Seven heads
of grain, healthy and good,
were growing on a single
stalk. [6]After them, seven other
heads of grain sprouted—thin
and scorched by the east
wind. [7]The thin heads of grain
swallowed up the seven

[h]19 Or *and impale you on a pole*
[i]22 Or *impaled*

הַדַּקּוֹת אֵת שֶׁבַע הַשִּׁבֳּלִים הַבְּרִיאוֹת וְהַמְּלֵאוֹת
and-the-full-ones the-fat-ones the-heads-of-grain seven *** the-thin-ones

וַיִּיקַץ פַּרְעֹה וְהִנֵּה חֲלוֹם׃ וַיְהִי בַבֹּקֶר
in-the-morning and-he-was (8) dream and-see! Pharaoh then-he-woke

וַתִּפָּעֶם רוּחוֹ וַיִּשְׁלַח וַיִּקְרָא אֶת־ כָּל־
all-of *** and-he-called so-he-sent mind-of-him that-she-was-troubled

חַרְטֻמֵּי מִצְרַיִם וְאֶת־ כָּל־ חֲכָמֶיהָ וַיְסַפֵּר פַּרְעֹה לָהֶם
to-them Pharaoh then-he-told wise-men-of-her all-of and Egypt magicians-of

אֶת־ חֲלֹמוֹ וְאֵין־ פּוֹתֵר אוֹתָם לְפַרְעֹה׃
for-Pharaoh them one-interpreting but-there-is-no dream-of-him ***

וַיְדַבֵּר שַׂר הַמַּשְׁקִים אֶת־ פַּרְעֹה לֵאמֹר אֶת־ חֲטָאַי
faults-of-me *** to-say Pharaoh to the-cupbearers chief-of then-he-spoke (9)

אֲנִי מַזְכִּיר הַיּוֹם׃ פַּרְעֹה קָצַף עַל־ עֲבָדָיו
servants-of-him with he-was-angry Pharaoh (10) the-day remembering I

וַיִּתֵּן אֹתִי בְּמִשְׁמַר בֵּית שַׂר הַטַּבָּחִים אֹתִי וְאֵת שַׂר
chief-of and me the-guards captain-of house-of in-custody-of me and-he-put

הָאֹפִים׃ וַנַּחַלְמָה חֲלוֹם בְּלַיְלָה אֶחָד אֲנִי וָהוּא אִישׁ
each and-he I same in-night dream and-we-dreamed (11) the-ones-baking

כְּפִתְרוֹן חֲלֹמוֹ חָלָמְנוּ׃ וְשָׁם אִתָּנוּ נַעַר
young-man with-us now-there (12) we-dreamed dream-of-him own-meaning-of

עִבְרִי עֶבֶד לְשַׂר הַטַּבָּחִים וַנְּסַפֶּר־ לוֹ וַיִּפְתָּר־
and-he-interpreted to-him and-we-told the-guards to-captain-of servant Hebrew

לָנוּ אֶת־ חֲלֹמֹתֵינוּ אִישׁ כַּחֲלֹמוֹ פָּתָר׃ וַיְהִי
and-he-was (13) he-interpreted own-dream-of-him each dreams-of-us *** for-us

כַּאֲשֶׁר פָּתַר־ לָנוּ כֵּן הָיָה אֹתִי הֵשִׁיב עַל־ כַּנִּי
position-of-me to he-restored me he-happened so to-us he-interpreted just-as

וְאֹתוֹ תָלָה׃ וַיִּשְׁלַח פַּרְעֹה וַיִּקְרָא אֶת־ יוֹסֵף
Joseph *** and-he-called Pharaoh so-he-sent (14) he-hanged and-him

וַיְרִיצֻהוּ מִן־ הַבּוֹר וַיְגַלַּח וַיְחַלֵּף
and-he-changed when-he-shaved the-dungeon from and-they-brought-him

שִׂמְלֹתָיו וַיָּבֹא אֶל־ פַּרְעֹה׃ וַיֹּאמֶר פַּרְעֹה אֶל־ יוֹסֵף
Joseph to Pharaoh and-he-said (15) Pharaoh before then-he-came clothes-of-him

חֲלוֹם חָלַמְתִּי וּפֹתֵר אֵין אֹתוֹ וַאֲנִי שָׁמַעְתִּי
I-heard but-I for-him there-is-not but-one-interpreting I-dreamed dream

עָלֶיךָ לֵאמֹר תִּשְׁמַע חֲלוֹם לִפְתֹּר אֹתוֹ׃ וַיַּעַן יוֹסֵף אֶת־
to Joseph and-he-replied (16) him to-interpret dream you-hear to-say of-you

פַּרְעֹה לֵאמֹר בִּלְעָדָי אֱלֹהִים יַעֲנֶה אֶת־ שְׁלוֹם פַּרְעֹה׃
Pharaoh favorably *** he-will-answer God not-in-me to-say Pharaoh

healthy, full heads. Then Pharaoh woke up; it had been a
dream.
8 In the morning his mind
was troubled, so he sent for all
the magicians and wise men
of Egypt. Pharaoh told them
his dreams, but no one could
interpret them for him.
9 Then the chief cupbearer
said to Pharaoh, "Today I am
reminded of my shortcom-
ings. 10 Pharaoh was once angry with his servants, and he
imprisoned me and the chief
baker in the house of the captain of the guard. 11 Each of us
had a dream the same night,
and each dream had a meaning of its own. 12 Now a young
Hebrew was there with us, a
servant of the captain of the
guard. We told him our
dreams, and he interpreted
them for us, giving each man
the interpretation of his
dream. 13 And things turned
out exactly as he interpreted
them to us: I was restored to
my position, and the other
man was hanged.[j]"
14 So Pharaoh sent for Joseph,
and he was quickly brought
from the dungeon. When he
had shaved and changed his
clothes, he came before Pharaoh.
15 Pharaoh said to Joseph, "I
had a dream, and no one can
interpret it. But I have heard it
said of you that when you
hear a dream you can interpret
it."
16 "I cannot do it," Joseph replied to Pharaoh, "but God
will give Pharaoh the answer
he desires."

[j]13 Or *impaled*

וַיְדַבֵּר פַּרְעֹה אֶל־יוֹסֵף בַּחֲלֹמִי הִנְנִי עֹמֵד עַל־שְׂפַת
bank-of on standing see-I! in-dream-of-me Joseph to Pharaoh then-he-said (17)

הַיְאֹר׃ וְהִנֵּה מִן־הַיְאֹר עֹלֹת שֶׁבַע פָּרוֹת בְּרִיאוֹת
ones-fat-of cows seven ones-coming-up the-Nile from and-see! (18) the-Nile

בָּשָׂר וִיפֹת תֹּאַר וַתִּרְעֶינָה בָּאָחוּ׃ וְהִנֵּה
then-see! (19) among-the-reed and-they-grazed form and-ones-sleek-of body

שֶׁבַע־פָּרוֹת אֲחֵרוֹת עֹלוֹת אַחֲרֵיהֶן דַּלּוֹת וְרָעוֹת
and-ones-ugly-of ones-scrawny-of after-them ones-coming-up other-ones cows seven

תֹּאַר מְאֹד וְרַקּוֹת בָּשָׂר לֹא־רָאִיתִי כָהֵנָּה בְּכָל־אֶרֶץ
land-of in-all-of such-as-these I-saw never body and-ones-lean-of very form

מִצְרַיִם לָרֹעַ׃ וַתֹּאכַלְנָה הַפָּרוֹת הָרַקּוֹת וְהָרָעוֹת אֵת
*** and-the-ugly-ones the-lean-ones the-cows and-they-ate (20) so-ugly Egypt

שֶׁבַע הַפָּרוֹת הָרִאשֹׁנוֹת הַבְּרִיאֹת׃ וַתָּבֹאנָה אֶל־קִרְבֶּנָה
midst-of-them to and-they-went (21) the-fat-ones the-first-ones the-cows seven

וְלֹא נוֹדַע כִּי־בָאוּ אֶל־קִרְבֶּנָה וּמַרְאֵיהֶן
for-appearance-of-them midst-of-them into they-went that he-could-tell but-not

רַע כַּאֲשֶׁר בַּתְּחִלָּה וָאִיקָץ׃ וָאֵרֶא בַּחֲלֹמִי וְהִנֵּה׀
and-see! in-dream-of-me then-I-saw (22) then-I-woke at-the-start just-as ugly

שֶׁבַע שִׁבֳּלִים עֹלֹת בְּקָנֶה אֶחָד מְלֵאֹת וְטֹבוֹת׃
and-good-ones full-ones single on-stalk ones-growing heads-of-grain seven

וְהִנֵּה שֶׁבַע שִׁבֳּלִים צְנֻמוֹת דַּקּוֹת
and-ones-thin ones-being-withered heads-of-grain seven then-see! (23)

שְׁדֻפוֹת קָדִים צֹמְחוֹת אַחֲרֵיהֶם׃
after-them ones-sprouting east-winds and-ones-being-scorched-of

וַתִּבְלַעְןָ הַשִּׁבֳּלִים הַדַּקֹּת אֵת שֶׁבַע הַשִּׁבֳּלִים*
the-heads-of-grain seven *** the-thin-ones the-heads-of-grain and-they-swallowed (24)

הַטֹּבוֹת וָאֹמַר אֶל־הַחַרְטֻמִּים וְאֵין מַגִּיד לִי׃
to-me explaining but-there-is-no the-magicians to and-I-told the-good-ones

וַיֹּאמֶר יוֹסֵף אֶל־פַּרְעֹה חֲלוֹם פַּרְעֹה אֶחָד הוּא אֵת אֲשֶׁר
what *** he one Pharoah dream-of Pharoah to Joseph then-he-said (25)

הָאֱלֹהִים עֹשֶׂה הִגִּיד לְפַרְעֹה׃ שֶׁבַע פָּרֹת הַטֹּבֹת שֶׁבַע שָׁנִים
years seven the-good-ones cows seven (26) to-Pharaoh he-revealed doing the-God

הֵנָּה וְשֶׁבַע הַשִּׁבֳּלִים† הַטֹּבֹת שֶׁבַע שָׁנִים הֵנָּה חֲלוֹם אֶחָד
one dream they years seven the-good-ones the-heads-of-grain and-seven they

הוּא׃ וְשֶׁבַע הַפָּרוֹת הָרַקּוֹת וְהָרָעֹת הָעֹלֹת
the-ones-coming-up and-the-ugly-ones the-lean-ones the-cows and-seven (27) he

אַחֲרֵיהֶן שֶׁבַע שָׁנִים הֵנָּה וְשֶׁבַע הַשִּׁבֳּלִים הָרֵקוֹת
the-worthless-ones the-heads-of-grain and-seven they years seven after-them

17 Then Pharaoh said to Joseph, "In my dream I was
standing on the bank of the
Nile, 18 when out of the river
there came up seven cows, fat
and sleek, and they grazed
among the reeds. 19 After them,
seven other cows came up—
scrawny and very ugly and
lean. I had never seen such
ugly cows in all the land of
Egypt. 20 The lean, ugly cows
ate up the seven fat cows that
came up first. 21 But even after
they ate them, no one could
tell that they had done so; they
looked just as ugly as before.
Then I woke up.

22 "In my dreams I also saw
seven heads of grain, full and
good, growing on a single
stalk. 23 After them, seven other heads sprouted—withered
and thin and scorched by the
east wind. 24 The thin heads of
grain swallowed up the seven
good heads. I told this to the
magicians, but none could explain it to me."

25 Then Joseph said to Pharaoh, "The dreams of Pharaoh
are one and the same. God has
revealed to Pharaoh what he is
about to do. 26 The seven good
cows are seven years, and the
seven good heads of grain are
seven years; it is one and the
same dream. 27 The seven lean,
ugly cows that came up after
they did are seven years, and
so are the seven worthless
heads of grain scorched by the

*24 Most mss have *pathah* under the *he* and *dagesh* in the *shin* (הַשּׁ).

†26 Most mss have *hateph qamets* under the *beth* (בֳּ).

שְׁדֻפוֹת הַקָּדִים יִהְיוּ שֶׁבַע שְׁנֵי רָעָב׃
famine years-of seven they-are the-east-winds and-ones-being-scorched-of

הוּא הַדָּבָר אֲשֶׁר דִּבַּרְתִּי אֶל־פַּרְעֹה אֲשֶׁר הָאֱלֹהִים עֹשֶׂה הֶרְאָה אֶת־
*** he-showed doing the-God what Pharaoh to I-said as the-thing this (28)

פַּרְעֹה׃ הִנֵּה שֶׁבַע שָׁנִים בָּאוֹת שָׂבָע גָּדוֹל בְּכָל־
through-all-of great abundance ones-coming years seven see! (29) Pharaoh

אֶרֶץ מִצְרָיִם׃ וְקָמוּ שֶׁבַע שְׁנֵי רָעָב אַחֲרֵיהֶן
after-them famine years-of seven but-they-will-come (30) Egypt land-of

וְנִשְׁכַּח כָּל־ הַשָּׂבָע בְּאֶרֶץ מִצְרָיִם
Egypt in-land-of the-abundance all-of and-he-will-be-forgotten

וְכִלָּה הָרָעָב אֶת־ הָאָרֶץ׃ וְלֹא־ יִוָּדַע
he-will-be-remembered and-not (31) the-land *** the-famine and-he-will-ravage

הַשָּׂבָע בָּאָרֶץ מִפְּנֵי הָרָעָב הַהוּא אַחֲרֵי־ כֵן כִּי־
for this after the-that the-famine because-of in-the-land the-abundance

כָבֵד הוּא מְאֹד׃ וְעַל הִשָּׁנוֹת הַחֲלוֹם אֶל־ פַּרְעֹה פַּעֲמָיִם כִּי־
because two-times Pharaoh to the-dream to-repeat and-so (32) very he severe

נָכוֹן הַדָּבָר מֵעִם הָאֱלֹהִים וּמְמַהֵר הָאֱלֹהִים לַעֲשֹׂתוֹ׃
to-do-him the-God and-being-soon the-God by the-matter being-decided

וְעַתָּה יֵרֶא פַרְעֹה אִישׁ נָבוֹן וְחָכָם וִישִׁיתֵהוּ
and-let-him-set-him and-wise discerning man Pharaoh let-him-seek and-now (33)

עַל־ אֶרֶץ מִצְרָיִם׃ יַעֲשֶׂה פַרְעֹה וְיַפְקֵד
and-let-him-appoint Pharaoh and-let-him-make (34) Egypt land-of over

פְּקִדִים עַל־ הָאָרֶץ וְחִמֵּשׁ אֶת־ אֶרֶץ מִצְרַיִם בְּשֶׁבַע
in-seven Egypt land-of *** and-let-him-take-fifth the-land over commissioners

שְׁנֵי הַשָּׂבָע׃ וְיִקְבְּצוּ אֶת־ כָּל־ אֹכֶל הַשָּׁנִים
the-years food-of all-of *** and-they-will-collect (35) the-abundance years-of

הַטֹּבֹת הַבָּאֹת הָאֵלֶּה וְיִצְבְּרוּ־ בָר תַּחַת
under grain and-they-will-store the-these the-ones-coming the-good-ones

יַד־ פַּרְעֹה אֹכֶל בֶּעָרִים וְשָׁמָרוּ׃ וְהָיָה
and-he-will-be (36) they-will-keep in-the-cities food Pharaoh authority-of

הָאֹכֶל לְפִקָּדוֹן לָאָרֶץ לְשֶׁבַע שְׁנֵי הָרָעָב אֲשֶׁר
that the-faime years-of for-seven for-the-country in-reserve the-food

תִּהְיֶיןָ בְּאֶרֶץ מִצְרָיִם וְלֹא־ תִכָּרֵת הָאָרֶץ
the-country she-will-be-ruined so-not Egypt on-land-of they-will-come

בָּרָעָב׃ וַיִּיטַב הַדָּבָר בְּעֵינֵי פַרְעֹה
Pharaoh in-eyes-of the-plan and-he-seemed-good (37) by-the-famine

וּבְעֵינֵי כָּל־ עֲבָדָיו׃ וַיֹּאמֶר פַּרְעֹה אֶל־
to Pharaoh then-he-asked (38) officials-of-him all-of and-in-eyes-of

east wind: They are seven
years of famine.
28"It is just as I said to Pharaoh: God has shown Pharaoh
what he is about to do. 29Seven
years of great abundance are
coming throughout the land of
Egypt, 30but seven years of
famine will follow them. Then
all the abundance in Egypt
will be forgotten, and the famine will ravage the land. 31The
abundance in the land will not
be remembered, because the
famine that follows it will be
so severe. 32The reason the
dream was given to Pharaoh
in two forms is that the matter
has been firmly decided by
God, and God will do it soon.
33"And now let Pharaoh look
for a discerning and wise man
and put him in charge of the
land of Egypt. 34Let Pharaoh
appoint commissioners over
the land to take a fifth of the
harvest of Egypt during the
seven years of abundance.
35They should collect all the
food of these good years that
are coming and store up the
grain under the authority of
Pharaoh, to be kept in the cities for food. 36This food should
be held in reserve for the
country, to be used during the
seven years of famine that will
come upon Egypt, so that the
country may not be ruined by
the famine."
37The plan seemed good to
Pharaoh and to all his officials.
38So Pharaoh asked them,

עֲבָדָיו הֲנִמְצָא כָזֶה אִישׁ אֲשֶׁר רוּחַ אֱלֹהִים בּוֹ׃
in-him God spirit-of whom man like-this can-we-find? officials-of-him

וַיֹּאמֶר פַּרְעֹה אֶל־יוֹסֵף אַחֲרֵי הוֹדִיעַ אֱלֹהִים אוֹתְךָ אֶת־כָּל־
all-of *** to-you God to-show since Joseph to Pharaoh then-he-said (39)

זֹאת אֵין־נָבוֹן וְחָכָם כָּמוֹךָ׃ אַתָּה תִּהְיֶה עַל־
over you-shall-be you (40) as-you and-wise discerning there-is-none this

בֵּיתִי וְעַל־פִּיךָ יִשַּׁק כָּל־עַמִּי רַק
only people-of-me all-of he-will-submit order-of-you and-to palace-of-me

הַכִּסֵּא אֶגְדַּל מִמֶּךָּ׃ וַיֹּאמֶר פַּרְעֹה אֶל־יוֹסֵף
Joseph to Pharaoh so-he-said (41) than-you I-will-be-greater the-throne

רְאֵה נָתַתִּי אֹתְךָ עַל כָּל־אֶרֶץ מִצְרָיִם׃ וַיָּסַר פַּרְעֹה
Pharaoh then-he-took (42) Egypt land-of all-of over you I-put-in-charge see!

אֶת־טַבַּעְתּוֹ מֵעַל יָדוֹ וַיִּתֵּן אֹתָהּ עַל־יַד
finger-of on her and-he-put finger-of-him from-on signet-ring-of-him ***

יוֹסֵף וַיַּלְבֵּשׁ אֹתוֹ בִּגְדֵי־שֵׁשׁ וַיָּשֶׂם רְבִד הַזָּהָב
the-gold chain-of and-he-put linen robes-of him and-he-dressed Joseph

עַל־צַוָּארוֹ׃ וַיַּרְכֵּב אֹתוֹ בְּמִרְכֶּבֶת הַמִּשְׁנֶה אֲשֶׁר־
that the-second in-chariot-of him then-he-had-ride (43) neck-of-him around

לוֹ וַיִּקְרְאוּ לְפָנָיו אַבְרֵךְ וְנָתוֹן אֹתוֹ עַל כָּל־
all-of over him so-to-put make-way! before-him and-they-shouted to-him

אֶרֶץ מִצְרָיִם׃ וַיֹּאמֶר פַּרְעֹה אֶל־יוֹסֵף אֲנִי פַרְעֹה וּבִלְעָדֶיךָ
and-without-you Pharaoh I Joseph to Pharaoh then-he-said (44) Egypt land-of

לֹא־יָרִים אִישׁ אֶת־יָדוֹ וְאֶת־רַגְלוֹ בְּכָל־אֶרֶץ מִצְרָיִם׃
Egypt land-of in-all-of foot-of-him or hand-of-him *** man he-will-lift not

וַיִּקְרָא פַרְעֹה שֵׁם־יוֹסֵף צָפְנַת פַּעְנֵחַ וַיִּתֶּן־לוֹ
to-him and-he-gave Paneah Zaphenath Joseph name-of Pharaoh and-he-called (45)

אֶת־אָסְנַת בַּת־פּוֹטִי פֶרַע כֹּהֵן אֹן לְאִשָּׁה וַיֵּצֵא יוֹסֵף
Joseph he-went as-wife On priest-of Phera Poti daughter-of Asenath ***

עַל־אֶרֶץ מִצְרָיִם׃ וְיוֹסֵף בֶּן־שְׁלֹשִׁים שָׁנָה בְּעָמְדוֹ
when-to-serve-him year thirty son-of now-Joseph (46) Egypt land-of throughout

לִפְנֵי פַּרְעֹה מֶלֶךְ־מִצְרָיִם וַיֵּצֵא יוֹסֵף מִלִּפְנֵי פַרְעֹה
Pharaoh from-presence-of Joseph and-he-went-out Egypt king-of Pharaoh before

וַיַּעְבֹר* בְּכָל־אֶרֶץ מִצְרָיִם׃ וַתַּעַשׂ הָאָרֶץ
the-land and-she-produced (47) Egypt land-of through-all-of and-he-traveled

בְּשֶׁבַע שְׁנֵי הַשָּׂבָע לִקְמָצִים׃ וַיִּקְבֹּץ אֶת־
*** and-he-collected (48) by-great-amounts the-abundance years-of in-seven

כָּל־אֹכֶל ׀ שֶׁבַע שָׁנִים אֲשֶׁר הָיוּ בְּאֶרֶץ מִצְרַיִם וַיִּתֶּן־
and-he-put Egypt in-land-of they-produced that years seven food-of all-of

"Can we find anyone like this
man, one in whom is the spirit
of God[k]?"
39Then Pharaoh said to Joseph, "Since God has made all
this known to you, there is no
one so discerning and wise as
you. 40You shall be in charge of
my palace, and all my people
are to submit to your orders.
Only with respect to the
throne will I be greater than
you."

Joseph in Charge of Egypt

41So Pharaoh said to Joseph,
"I hereby put you in charge of
the whole land of Egypt."
42Then Pharaoh took his signet
ring from his finger and put it
on Joseph's finger. He dressed
him in robes of fine linen and
put a gold chain around his
neck. 43He had him ride in a
chariot as his second-in-command,[l] and men shouted before him, "Make way[m]!" Thus
he put him in charge of the
whole land of Egypt.
44Then Pharaoh said to Joseph, "I am Pharaoh, but
without your word no one will
lift hand or foot in all Egypt."
45Pharaoh gave Joseph the
name Zaphenath-Paneah and
gave him Asenath daughter of
Potiphera, priest of On,[n] to be
his wife. And Joseph went
throughout the land of Egypt.
46Joseph was thirty years old
when he entered the service of
Pharaoh king of Egypt. And
Joseph went out from Pharaoh's presence and traveled
throughout Egypt. 47During
the seven years of abundance
the land produced plentifully.
48Joseph collected all the food
produced in those seven years
of abundance in Egypt and

[k]38 *Or of the gods*
[l]43 *Or in the chariot of his second-in-command; or in his second chariot*
[m]43 *Or Bow down*
[n]45 *That is, Heliopolis; also in verse 50*

*46 **Most mss have *hateph pathah* under the *ayin* (וַיַּעֲבֹר).**

אֹכֶל בֶּעָרִים אֹכֶל שְׂדֵה־ הָעִיר אֲשֶׁר סְבִיבֹתֶיהָ נָתַן
he-put surround-her that the-city field-of food-of in-the-cities food

בְּתוֹכָהּ׃ וַיִּצְבֹּר יוֹסֵף בָּר כְּחוֹל הַיָּם הַרְבֵּה
to-be-great the-sea like-sand-of grain Joseph and-he-stored (49) within-her

מְאֹד עַד כִּי־ חָדַל לִסְפֹּר כִּי־ אֵין מִסְפָּר׃
measurable he-is-not for to-keep-record he-stopped when until very

וּלְיוֹסֵף יֻלַּד שְׁנֵי בָנִים בְּטֶרֶם תָּבוֹא שְׁנַת הָרָעָב
the-famine year-of she-came before sons two-of he-was-born and-to-Joseph (50)

אֲשֶׁר יָלְדָה־ לּוֹ אָסְנַת בַּת־ פּוֹטִי פֶרַע כֹּהֵן אוֹן׃
On priest-of Phera Poti daughter-of Asenath to-him she-bore when

וַיִּקְרָא יוֹסֵף אֶת־ שֵׁם הַבְּכוֹר מְנַשֶּׁה כִּי־ נַשַּׁנִי
he-made-forget-me for Manasseh the-firstborn name-of *** Joseph and-he-called (51)

אֱלֹהִים אֶת־כָּל־ עֲמָלִי וְאֵת כָּל־ בֵּית אָבִי׃ וְאֵת
and (52) father-of-me household-of all-of and trouble-of-me all-of *** God

שֵׁם הַשֵּׁנִי קָרָא אֶפְרָיִם כִּי־ הִפְרַנִי אֱלֹהִים בְּאֶרֶץ
in-land-of God he-made-fruitful-me for Ephraim he-called the-second name-of

עָנְיִי׃ וַתִּכְלֶינָה שֶׁבַע שְׁנֵי הַשָּׂבָע אֲשֶׁר הָיָה
he-was that the-abundance years-of seven then-they-ended (53) suffering-of-me

בְּאֶרֶץ מִצְרָיִם׃ וַתְּחִלֶּינָה שֶׁבַע שְׁנֵי הָרָעָב לָבוֹא
to-come the-famine years-of seven and-they-began (54) Egypt in-land-of

כַּאֲשֶׁר אָמַר יוֹסֵף וַיְהִי רָעָב בְּכָל־ הָאֲרָצוֹת וּבְכָל־
but-in-whole-of the-lands in-all-of famine and-he-was Joseph he-said just-as

אֶרֶץ מִצְרַיִם הָיָה לָחֶם׃ וַתִּרְעַב כָּל־ אֶרֶץ מִצְרַיִם
Egypt land-of all-of and-she-felt-famine (55) food he-was Egypt land-of

וַיִּצְעַק הָעָם אֶל־ פַּרְעֹה לַלָּחֶם וַיֹּאמֶר פַּרְעֹה לְכָל־
to-all-of Pharaoh then-he-told for-the-food Pharaoh to the-people and-he-cried

מִצְרַיִם לְכוּ אֶל־יוֹסֵף אֲשֶׁר־ יֹאמַר לָכֶם תַּעֲשׂוּ׃ וְהָרָעָב הָיָה
he-was when-the-famine (56) you-do to-you he-tells what Joseph to go! Egypt

עַל כָּל־ פְּנֵי הָאָרֶץ וַיִּפְתַּח יוֹסֵף אֶת־ כָּל־ אֲשֶׁר
what all-of *** Joseph then-he-opened the-country surface-of all-of over

בָּהֶם וַיִּשְׁבֹּר לְמִצְרַיִם וַיֶּחֱזַק הָרָעָב בְּאֶרֶץ
in-land-of the-famine for-he-was-severe to-Egyptians and-he-sold in-them

מִצְרָיִם׃ וְכָל־ הָאָרֶץ בָּאוּ מִצְרַיְמָה לִשְׁבֹּר אֶל־ יוֹסֵף כִּי־
for Joseph from to-buy to-Egypt they-came the-world and-all-of (57) Egypt

חָזַק הָרָעָב בְּכָל־ הָאָרֶץ׃ וַיַּרְא יַעֲקֹב
Jacob when-he-learned (42:1) the-world in-all-of the-famine he-was-severe

כִּי יֶשׁ־ שֶׁבֶר בְּמִצְרָיִם וַיֹּאמֶר יַעֲקֹב לְבָנָיו לָמָּה
why? to-sons-of-him Jacob then-he-said in-Egypt grain there-is that

stored it in the cities. In each city he put the food grown in the fields surrounding it.
49Joseph stored up huge quantities of grain, like the sand of the sea; it was so much that he stopped keeping records because it was beyond measure.
50Before the years of famine came, two sons were born to Joseph by Asenath daughter of Potiphera, priest of On.
51Joseph named his firstborn Manasseh[p] and said, "It is because God has made me forget all my trouble and all my father's household."
52The second son he named Ephraim[q] and said, "It is because God has made me fruitful in the land of my suffering."
53The seven years of abundance in Egypt came to an end,
54and the seven years of famine began, just as Joseph had said. There was famine in all the other lands, but in the whole land of Egypt there was food.
55When all Egypt began to feel the famine, the people cried to Pharaoh for food. Then Pharaoh told all the Egyptians, "Go to Joseph and do what he tells you."
56When the famine had spread over the whole country, Joseph opened the storehouses and sold grain to the Egyptians, for the famine was severe throughout Egypt.
57And all the countries came to Egypt to buy grain from Joseph, because the famine was severe in all the world.

Joseph's Brothers Go to Egypt

42 When Jacob learned that there was grain in Egypt, he said to his sons,

p51 *Manasseh* sounds like and may be derived from the Hebrew for *forget.*
q52 *Ephraim* sounds like the Hebrew for *twice fruitful.*

תִּתְרָאוּ׃ וַיֹּאמֶר הִנֵּה שָׁמַעְתִּי כִּי יֶשׁ־שֶׁבֶר

grain there-is that I-heard see! and-he-said (2) you-look-at-each-other

בְּמִצְרָיִם רְדוּ־שָׁמָּה וְשִׁבְרוּ־לָנוּ מִשָּׁם וְנִחְיֶה וְלֹא

and-not so-we-may-live from-there for-us and-buy! to-there go-down! in-Egypt

נָמוּת׃ וַיֵּרְדוּ אֲחֵי־יוֹסֵף עֲשָׂרָה לִשְׁבֹּר בָּר מִמִּצְרָיִם׃

from-Egypt grain to-buy ten Joseph brothers-of then-they-went-down (3) we-die

וְאֶת־בִּנְיָמִין אֲחִי יוֹסֵף לֹא־שָׁלַח יַעֲקֹב אֶת־אֶחָיו

brothers-of-him with Jacob he-sent not Joseph brother-of Benjamin but (4)

כִּי אָמַר פֶּן־יִקְרָאֶנּוּ אָסוֹן׃ וַיָּבֹאוּ בְּנֵי

sons-of so-they-went (5) harm he-might-come-to-him perhaps he-thought for

יִשְׂרָאֵל לִשְׁבֹּר בְּתוֹךְ הַבָּאִים כִּי־הָיָה הָרָעָב בְּאֶרֶץ כְּנָעַן׃

Canaan in-land-of the-famine he-was for the-ones-going among to-buy Israel

וְיוֹסֵף הוּא הַשַּׁלִּיט עַל־הָאָרֶץ הוּא הַמַּשְׁבִּיר לְכָל־

to-all-of the-one-selling he the-land over the-governor he now-Joseph (6)

עַם הָאָרֶץ וַיָּבֹאוּ אֲחֵי יוֹסֵף וַיִּשְׁתַּחֲווּ־לוֹ

to-him and-they-bowed Joseph brothers-of and-they-came the-world people-of

אַפַּיִם אָרְצָה׃ וַיַּרְא יוֹסֵף אֶת־אֶחָיו וַיַּכִּרֵם

and-he-recognized-them brothers-of-him *** Joseph and-he-saw (7) to-ground faces

וַיִּתְנַכֵּר אֲלֵיהֶם וַיְדַבֵּר אִתָּם קָשׁוֹת וַיֹּאמֶר

and-he-asked harshly to-them and-he-spoke to-them but-he-was-as-stranger

אֲלֵהֶם מֵאַיִן בָּאתֶם וַיֹּאמְרוּ מֵאֶרֶץ כְּנַעַן לִשְׁבָּר־

to-buy Canaan from-land-of and-they-replied you-come from-where? to-them

אֹכֶל׃ וַיַּכֵּר יוֹסֵף אֶת־אֶחָיו וְהֵם לֹא

not but-they brothers-of-him *** Joseph so-he-recognized (8) food

הִכִּרֻהוּ׃ וַיִּזְכֹּר יוֹסֵף אֵת הַחֲלֹמוֹת אֲשֶׁר

that the-dreams *** Joseph then-he-remembered (9) they-recognized-him

חָלַם לָהֶם וַיֹּאמֶר אֲלֵהֶם מְרַגְּלִים אַתֶּם לִרְאוֹת אֶת־

*** to-see you ones-spying to-them and-he-said about-them he-dreamed

עֶרְוַת הָאָרֶץ בָּאתֶם׃ וַיֹּאמְרוּ אֵלָיו לֹא אֲדֹנִי

lord-of-me no to-him but-they-said (10) you-came the-land weakness-of

וַעֲבָדֶיךָ בָּאוּ לִשְׁבָּר־אֹכֶל׃ כֻּלָּנוּ בְּנֵי אִישׁ־אֶחָד נָחְנוּ

we one man sons-of all-of-us (11) food to-buy they-came but-servants-of-you

כֵּנִים אֲנַחְנוּ לֹא־הָיוּ עֲבָדֶיךָ מְרַגְּלִים׃ וַיֹּאמֶר

but-he-said (12) ones-spying servants-of-you they-are not we honest-ones

אֲלֵהֶם לֹא כִּי־עֶרְוַת הָאָרֶץ בָּאתֶם לִרְאוֹת׃ וַיֹּאמְרוּ

but-they-replied (13) to-see you-came the-land weakness-of for no to-them

שְׁנֵים עָשָׂר עֲבָדֶיךָ אַחִים ׀ אֲנַחְנוּ בְּנֵי אִישׁ־אֶחָד בְּאֶרֶץ כְּנָעַן

Canaan in-land-of one man sons-of we brothers servants-of-you ten two

"Why do you just keep looking at each other?" [2]He continued, "I have heard that there is grain in Egypt. Go down there and buy some for us, so that we may live and not die."

[3]Then ten of Joseph's brothers went down to buy grain from Egypt. [4]But Jacob did not send Benjamin, Joseph's brother, with the others, because he was afraid that harm might come to him. [5]So Israel's sons were among those who went to buy grain, for the famine was in the land of Canaan also.

[6]Now Joseph was the governor of the land, the one who sold grain to all its people. So when Joseph's brothers arrived, they bowed down to him with their faces to the ground. [7]As soon as Joseph saw his brothers, he recognized them, but he pretended to be a stranger and spoke harshly to them. "Where do you come from?" he asked.

"From the land of Canaan," they replied, "to buy food."

[8]Although Joseph recognized his brothers, they did not recognize him. [9]Then he remembered his dreams about them and said to them, "You are spies! You have come to see where our land is unprotected."

[10]"No, my lord," they answered. "Your servants have come to buy food. [11]We are all the sons of one man. Your servants are honest men, not spies."

[12]"No!" he said to them. "You have come to see where our land is unprotected."

[13]But they replied, "Your servants were twelve brothers, the sons of one man, who lives in the land of Canaan. The

וְהִנֵּה הַקָּטֹן אֶת־ אָבִינוּ הַיּוֹם וְהָאֶחָד אֵינֶנּוּ׃
not-is-he and-the-one the-day father-of-us with the-young and-see!

וַיֹּאמֶר אֲלֵהֶם יוֹסֵף הוּא אֲשֶׁר דִּבַּרְתִּי אֲלֵכֶם לֵאמֹר מְרַגְּלִים
ones-spying to-say to-you I-told as he Joseph to-them but-he-said (14)

אַתֶּם׃ בְּזֹאת תִּבָּחֵנוּ חֵי פַרְעֹה אִם־ תֵּצְאוּ
you-will-leave not Pharaoh life-of you-will-be-tested by-this (15) you

מִזֶּה כִּי אִם־ בְּבוֹא אֲחִיכֶם הַקָּטֹן הֵנָּה׃ שִׁלְחוּ מִכֶּם
from-you send! (16) here the-young brother-of-you to-come if unless from-this

אֶחָד וְיִקַּח אֶת־ אֲחִיכֶם וְאַתֶּם הֵאָסְרוּ וְיִבָּחֲנוּ
so-they-be-tested be-in-prison! and-you brother-of-you *** and-let-him-get one

דִּבְרֵיכֶם הַאֱמֶת אִתְּכֶם וְאִם־ לֹא חֵי פַרְעֹה כִּי מְרַגְּלִים
ones-spying then Pharaoh life-of not but-if in-you whether-truth words-of-you

אַתֶּם׃ וַיֶּאֱסֹף אֹתָם אֶל־ מִשְׁמָר שְׁלֹשֶׁת יָמִים׃ וַיֹּאמֶר אֲלֵהֶם
to-them and-he-said (18) days three-of custody in them and-he-put (17) you

יוֹסֵף בַּיּוֹם הַשְּׁלִישִׁי זֹאת עֲשׂוּ וִחְיוּ אֶת־ הָאֱלֹהִים אֲנִי יָרֵא׃
fearing I the-God *** and-live! do! this the-third on-the-day Joseph

אִם־ כֵּנִים אַתֶּם אֲחִיכֶם אֶחָד יֵאָסֵר בְּבֵית
in-house-of let-him-stay one brother-of-you you honest-men if (19)

מִשְׁמַרְכֶם וְאַתֶּם לְכוּ הָבִיאוּ שֶׁבֶר רַעֲבוֹן בָּתֵּיכֶם׃
households-of-you famine-of grain take-back! go! and-you prison-of-you

וְאֶת־ אֲחִיכֶם הַקָּטֹן תָּבִיאוּ אֵלַי וְיֵאָמְנוּ
so-they-may-be-verified to-me you-bring the-young brother-of-you but (20)

דִּבְרֵיכֶם וְלֹא תָמוּתוּ וַיַּעֲשׂוּ־ כֵן׃ וַיֹּאמְרוּ אִישׁ אֶל־
to each and-they-said (21) this so-they-did you-die so-not words-of-you

אָחִיו אֲבָל אֲשֵׁמִים ׀ אֲנַחְנוּ עַל־ אָחִינוּ אֲשֶׁר רָאִינוּ
we-saw whom brother-of-us because-of we punished-ones surely brother-of-him

צָרַת נַפְשׁוֹ בְּהִתְחַנְנוֹ אֵלֵינוּ וְלֹא שָׁמַעְנוּ עַל־
for we-listened but-not with-us when-to-plead-him life-of-him distress-of

כֵּן בָּאָה אֵלֵינוּ הַצָּרָה הַזֹּאת׃ וַיַּעַן רְאוּבֵן אֹתָם
to-them Reuben and-he-replied (22) the-this the-distress on-us she-came this

לֵאמֹר הֲלוֹא אָמַרְתִּי אֲלֵיכֶם ׀ לֵאמֹר אַל־ תֶּחֶטְאוּ בַיֶּלֶד וְלֹא
but-not against-the-boy you-sin not to-say to-you I-told not? to-say

שְׁמַעְתֶּם וְגַם־ דָּמוֹ הִנֵּה נִדְרָשׁ׃ וְהֵם לֹא יָדְעוּ
they-knew not now-they (23) accounting see! blood-of-him so-now you-listened

כִּי שֹׁמֵעַ יוֹסֵף כִּי הַמֵּלִיץ בֵּינֹתָם׃
between-them the-one-interpreting for Joseph understanding that

וַיִּסֹּב מֵעֲלֵיהֶם וַיֵּבְךְּ וַיָּשָׁב אֲלֵהֶם וַיְדַבֵּר
and-he-spoke to-them but-he-returned and-he-wept from-them then-he-turned (24)

youngest is now with our father, and one is no more."
[14]Joseph said to them, "It is
just as I told you: You are
spies! [15]And this is how you
will be tested: As surely as
Pharaoh lives, you will not
leave this place unless your
youngest brother comes here.
[16]Send one of your number to
get your brother; the rest of
you will be kept in prison, so
that your words may be tested
to see if you are telling the
truth. If you are not, then as
surely as Pharaoh lives, you
are spies!" [17]And he put them
all in custody for three days.
[18]On the third day, Joseph
said to them, "Do this and you
will live, for I fear God: [19]If you
are honest men, let one of
your brothers stay here in
prison, while the rest of you
go and take grain back for
your starving households.
[20]But you must bring your
youngest brother to me, so
that your words may be
verified and that you may not
die." This they proceeded to
do.
[21]They said to one another,
"Surely we are being punished because of our brother.
We saw how distressed he was
when he pleaded with us for
his life, but we would not listen; that's why this distress
has come upon us."
[22]Reuben replied, "Didn't I
tell you not to sin against the
boy? But you wouldn't listen!
Now we must give an accounting for his blood."
[23]They did not realize that Joseph could understand them,
since he was using an interpreter.
[24]He turned away from them
and began to weep, but then
turned back and spoke to them

אֲלֵהֶם וַיִּקַּח מֵאִתָּם אֶת־שִׁמְעוֹן וַיֶּאֱסֹר אֹתוֹ לְעֵינֵיהֶם׃
before-eyes-of-them him and-he-bound Simeon *** from-them and-he-took to-them

וַיְצַו יוֹסֵף וַיְמַלְאוּ אֶת־כְּלֵיהֶם בָּר וּלְהָשִׁיב
and-to-put grain bags-of-them *** and-they-filled Joseph and-he-ordered (25)

כַּסְפֵּיהֶם אִישׁ אֶל־שַׂקּוֹ וְלָתֵת לָהֶם צֵדָה לַדָּרֶךְ
for-journey provision to-them and-to-give sack-of-him in each silvers-of-them

וַיַּעַשׂ לָהֶם כֵּן׃ וַיִּשְׂאוּ אֶת־שִׁבְרָם עַל־
on grain-of-them *** so-they-loaded (26) this for-them and-he-did

חֲמֹרֵיהֶם וַיֵּלְכוּ מִשָּׁם׃ וַיִּפְתַּח הָאֶחָד אֶת־
*** the-one now-he-opened (27) from-there and-they-left donkeys-of-them

שַׂקּוֹ לָתֵת מִסְפּוֹא לַחֲמֹרוֹ בַּמָּלוֹן וַיַּרְא אֶת־
*** and-he-saw at-the-place for-donkey-of-him feed to-get sack-of-him

כַּסְפּוֹ וְהִנֵּה־הוּא בְּפִי אַמְתַּחְתּוֹ׃ וַיֹּאמֶר אֶל־
to so-he-said (28) sack-of-him in-mouth-of he now-see! silver-of-him

אֶחָיו הוּשַׁב כַּסְפִּי וְגַם הִנֵּה בְאַמְתַּחְתִּי
in-sack-of-me see! now-indeed silver-of-me he-was-returned brothers-of-him

וַיֵּצֵא לִבָּם וַיֶּחֶרְדוּ אִישׁ אֶל־אָחִיו לֵאמֹר
to-say brother-of-him with each and-they-trembled heart-of-them and-he-sank

מַה־זֹּאת עָשָׂה אֱלֹהִים לָנוּ׃ וַיָּבֹאוּ אֶל־יַעֲקֹב אֲבִיהֶם
father-of-them Jacob to when-they-came (29) to-us God he-did this what?

אַרְצָה כְּנָעַן וַיַּגִּידוּ לוֹ אֵת כָּל־הַקֹּרֹת אֹתָם
to-them the-ones-happening all-of *** to-him then-they-told Canaan in-land-of

לֵאמֹר׃ דִּבֶּר הָאִישׁ אֲדֹנֵי הָאָרֶץ אִתָּנוּ קָשׁוֹת וַיִּתֵּן
and-he-treated harshly to-us the-land lords-of the-man he-spoke (30) to-say

אֹתָנוּ כִּמְרַגְּלִים אֶת־הָאָרֶץ׃ וַנֹּאמֶר אֵלָיו כֵּנִים אֲנַחְנוּ לֹא
not we honest-men to-him but-we-said (31) the-land *** as-ones-spying us

הָיִינוּ מְרַגְּלִים׃ שְׁנֵים־עָשָׂר אֲנַחְנוּ אַחִים בְּנֵי אָבִינוּ הָאֶחָד
the-one father-of-us sons-of brothers we ten two (32) ones-spying we-are

אֵינֶנּוּ וְהַקָּטֹן הַיּוֹם אֶת־אָבִינוּ בְּאֶרֶץ כְּנָעַן׃
Canaan in-land-of father-of-us with the-day and-the-young not-is-he

וַיֹּאמֶר אֵלֵינוּ הָאִישׁ אֲדֹנֵי הָאָרֶץ בְּזֹאת אֵדַע כִּי
that I-will-know by-this the-land lords-of the-man to-us then-he-said (33)

כֵנִים אַתֶּם אֲחִיכֶם הָאֶחָד הַנִּיחוּ אִתִּי וְאֶת־רַעֲבוֹן
famine-of and with-me leave! the-one brother-of-you you honest-men

בָּתֵּיכֶם קְחוּ וָלֵכוּ׃ וְהָבִיאוּ אֶת־אֲחִיכֶם הַקָּטֹן
the-young brother-of-you *** but-bring! (34) and-go! take! houses-of-you

אֵלַי וְאֵדְעָה כִּי לֹא מְרַגְּלִים אַתֶּם כִּי כֵנִים אַתֶּם אֶת־אֲחִיכֶם
brother-of-you *** you honest-men but you ones-spying not that so-I-know to-me

again. He had Simeon taken from them and bound before their eyes.

25Joseph gave orders to fill their bags with grain, to put each man's silver back in his sack, and to give them provisions for their journey. After this was done for them, 26they loaded their grain on their donkeys and left.

27At the place where they stopped for the night one of them opened his sack to get feed for his donkey, and he saw his silver in the mouth of his sack. 28"My silver has been returned," he said to his brothers. "Here it is in my sack."

Their hearts sank and they turned to each other trembling and said, "What is this that God has done to us?"

29When they came to their father Jacob in the land of Canaan, they told him all that had happened to them. They said, 30"The man who is lord over the land spoke harshly to us and treated us as though we were spying on the land. 31But we said to him, 'We are honest men; we are not spies. 32We were twelve brothers, sons of one father. One is no more, and the youngest is now with our father in Canaan.'

33"Then the man who is lord over the land said to us, 'This is how I will know whether you are honest men: Leave one of your brothers here with me, and take food for your starving households and go. 34But bring your youngest brother to me so I will know that you are not spies but honest men. Then I will give your

אֶתֵּן לָכֶם וְאֶת־ הָאָרֶץ תִּסְחָרוּ׃ וַיְהִי הֵם

they and-he-was (35) you-can-trade the-land and to-you I-will-return

מְרִיקִים שַׂקֵּיהֶם וְהִנֵּה־ אִישׁ צְרוֹר־ כַּסְפּוֹ בְּשַׂקּוֹ

in-sack-of-him silver-of-him pouch-of each and-see! sacks-of-them ones-emptying

וַיִּרְאוּ אֶת־ צְרֹרוֹת כַּסְפֵּיהֶם הֵמָּה וַאֲבִיהֶם

and-father-of-them they silvers-of-them pouches-of *** when-they-saw

וַיִּירָאוּ׃ וַיֹּאמֶר אֲלֵהֶם יַעֲקֹב אֲבִיהֶם אֹתִי

me father-of-them Jacob to-them and-he-said (36) then-they-were-afraid

שִׁכַּלְתֶּם יוֹסֵף אֵינֶנּוּ וְשִׁמְעוֹן אֵינֶנּוּ וְאֶת־ בִּנְיָמִן תִּקָּחוּ

you-would-take Benjamin and not-is-he and-Simeon not-is-he Joseph you-deprived

עָלַי הָיוּ כֻלָּנָה׃ וַיֹּאמֶר רְאוּבֵן אֶל־ אָבִיו

father-of-him to Reuben then-he-said (37) all-things they-are against-me

לֵאמֹר אֶת־ שְׁנֵי בָנַי תָּמִית אִם־לֹא אֲבִיאֶנּוּ אֵלֶיךָ תְּנָה

entrust! to-you I-bring-him not if you-may-kill sons-of-me two-of *** to-say

אֹתוֹ עַל־ יָדִי וַאֲנִי אֲשִׁיבֶנּוּ אֵלֶיךָ׃ וַיֹּאמֶר לֹא־

not but-he-said (38) to-you I-will-bring-back-him and-I care-of-me to him

יֵרֵד בְּנִי עִמָּכֶם כִּי־ אָחִיו מֵת וְהוּא

and-he he-is-dead brother-of-him for with-you son-of-me he-will-go-down

לְבַדּוֹ נִשְׁאָר וּקְרָאָהוּ אָסוֹן בַּדֶּרֶךְ אֲשֶׁר תֵּלְכוּ־ בָהּ

on-her you-go that on-the-journey harm if-he-comes-to-him being-left only-he

וְהוֹרַדְתֶּם אֶת־ שֵׂיבָתִי בְּיָגוֹן שְׁאוֹלָה׃

to-Sheol in-sorrow gray-head-of-me *** then-you-will-bring-down

וְהָרָעָב כָּבֵד בָּאָרֶץ׃ וַיְהִי כַּאֲשֶׁר כִּלּוּ

they-finished when so-he-was (2) in-the-land severe now-the-famine (43:1)

לֶאֱכֹל אֶת־ הַשֶּׁבֶר אֲשֶׁר הֵבִיאוּ מִמִּצְרָיִם וַיֹּאמֶר אֲלֵיהֶם

to-them then-he-said from-Egypt they-brought that the-grain *** to-eat

אֲבִיהֶם שֻׁבוּ שִׁבְרוּ־ לָנוּ מְעַט־ אֹכֶל׃ וַיֹּאמֶר אֵלָיו

to-him but-he-said (3) food little-of for-us buy! go-back! father-of-them

יְהוּדָה לֵאמֹר הָעֵד הֵעִד בָּנוּ הָאִישׁ לֵאמֹר לֹא־ תִרְאוּ פָנַי

face-of-me you-will-see not to-say the-man to-us he-warned to-warn to-say Judah

בִּלְתִּי אֲחִיכֶם אִתְּכֶם׃ אִם־ יֶשְׁךָ מְשַׁלֵּחַ אֶת־ אָחִינוּ

brother-of-us *** sending will-of-you if (4) with-you brother-of-you unless

אִתָּנוּ נֵרְדָה וְנִשְׁבְּרָה לְךָ אֹכֶל׃ וְאִם־ אֵינְךָ

not-you but-if (5) food for-you and-we-will-buy we-will-go-down with-us

מְשַׁלֵּחַ לֹא נֵרֵד כִּי־ הָאִישׁ אָמַר אֵלֵינוּ לֹא־ תִרְאוּ

you-will-see not to-us he-said the-man for we-will-go-down not sending

פָנַי בִּלְתִּי אֲחִיכֶם אִתְּכֶם׃ וַיֹּאמֶר יִשְׂרָאֵל לָמָה

why? Israel and-he-asked (6) with-you brother-of-you unless face-of-me

brother back to you, and you
can trade[r] in the land.' "
[35]As they were emptying
their sacks, there in each
man's sack was his pouch of
silver! When they and their father saw the money pouches,
they were frightened. [36]Their
father Jacob said to them,
"You have deprived me of my
children. Joseph is no more
and Simeon is no more, and
now you want to take Benjamin. Everything is against
me!"
[37]Then Reuben said to his father, "You may put both of my
sons to death if I do not bring
him back to you. Entrust him
to my care, and I will bring
him back."
[38]But Jacob said, "My son
will not go down there with
you; his brother is dead and he
is the only one left. If harm
comes to him on the journey
you are taking, you will bring
my gray head down to the
grave[s] in sorrow."

The Second Journey to Egypt

43 Now the famine was
still severe in the land.
[2]So when they had eaten all
the grain they had brought
from Egypt, their father said to
them, "Go back and buy us a
little more food."
[3]But Judah said to him, "The
man warned us solemnly,
'You will not see my face
again unless your brother is
with you.' [4]If you will send our
brother along with us, we will
go down and buy food for you.
[5]But if you will not send him,
we will not go down, because
the man said to us, 'You will
not see my face again unless
your brother is with you.' "
[6]Israel asked, "Why did you

r34 Or *move about freely*
s38 Hebrew *Sheol*

הֲרֵעֹתֶם לִי לְהַגִּיד לָאִישׁ הַעוֹד לָכֶם אָח׃
brother to-you another? to-the-man to-tell to-me you-bring-trouble

וַיֹּאמְרוּ שָׁאוֹל שָׁאַל־הָאִישׁ לָנוּ וּלְמוֹלַדְתֵּנוּ
and-about-family-of-us about-us the-man he-asked to-ask and-they-replied (7)

לֵאמֹר הַעוֹד אֲבִיכֶם חַי הֲיֵשׁ לָכֶם אָח וַנַּגֶּד־*
so-we-answered brother to-you is-there? alive father-of-you still? to-say

לוֹ עַל־פִּי הַדְּבָרִים הָאֵלֶּה הֲיָדוֹעַ נֵדַע כִּי יֹאמַר
he-would-say that could-we-know to-know? the-these the-words mouth-of on to-him

הוֹרִידוּ אֶת־אֲחִיכֶם׃ וַיֹּאמֶר יְהוּדָה אֶל־יִשְׂרָאֵל אָבִיו
father-of-him Israel to Judah then-he-said (8) brother-of-you *** bring-down!

שִׁלְחָה הַנַּעַר אִתִּי וְנָקוּמָה וְנֵלֵכָה וְנִחְיֶה וְלֹא
and-not so-we-may-live and-we-will-go and-we-will-rise with-me the-boy send!

נָמוּת גַּם־אֲנַחְנוּ גַם־אַתָּה גַּם־טַפֵּנוּ׃ אָנֹכִי אֶעֶרְבֶנּוּ
I-guarantee-him I (9) children-of-us also you also we indeed we-die

מִיָּדִי תְּבַקְשֶׁנּוּ אִם־לֹא הֲבִיאֹתִיו אֵלֶיךָ
to-you I-bring-back-him not if you-can-require-him from-hand-of-me

וְהִצַּגְתִּיו לְפָנֶיךָ וְחָטָאתִי לְךָ כָּל־הַיָּמִים׃
the-days all-of before-you I-will-bear-blame before-you and-I-set-him

כִּי לוּלֵא הִתְמַהְמָהְנוּ כִּי־עַתָּה שַׁבְנוּ זֶה פַעֲמָיִם׃
twice here we-could-have-returned now then we-had-delayed if-not for (10)

וַיֹּאמֶר אֲלֵהֶם יִשְׂרָאֵל אֲבִיהֶם אִם־כֵּן ׀ אֵפוֹא זֹאת עֲשׂוּ קְחוּ
put! do! this then so if father-of-them Israel to-them then-he-said (11)

מִזִּמְרַת הָאָרֶץ בִּכְלֵיכֶם וְהוֹרִידוּ לָאִישׁ מִנְחָה
gift to-the-man and-take-down! in-bags-of-you the-land from-best-produce-of

מְעַט צֳרִי וּמְעַט דְּבַשׁ נְכֹאת וָלֹט בָּטְנִים וּשְׁקֵדִים׃
and-almonds pistachio-nuts and-myrrh spice honey and-little-of balm little-of

וְכֶסֶף מִשְׁנֶה קְחוּ בְיֶדְכֶם וְאֶת־הַכֶּסֶף הַמּוּשָׁב
the-being-returned the-silver and in-hand-of-you take! twice and-silver (12)

בְּפִי אַמְתְּחֹתֵיכֶם תָּשִׁיבוּ בְיֶדְכֶם אוּלַי מִשְׁגֶּה הוּא׃
he mistake perhaps in-hand-of-you you-must-take-back sacks-of-you in-mouth-of

וְאֶת־אֲחִיכֶם קָחוּ וְקוּמוּ שׁוּבוּ אֶל־הָאִישׁ׃ וְאֵל
and-God (14) the-man to go-back! and-rise! take! brother-of-you and (13)

שַׁדַּי יִתֵּן לָכֶם רַחֲמִים לִפְנֵי הָאִישׁ וְשִׁלַּח לָכֶם
with-you so-he-will-send the-man before mercies to-you may-he-grant Almighty

אֶת־אֲחִיכֶם אַחֵר וְאֶת־בִּנְיָמִין וַאֲנִי כַּאֲשֶׁר שָׁכֹלְתִּי שָׁכָלְתִּי׃
I-am-bereaved I-am-bereaved if but-I Benjamin and other brother-of-you ***

וַיִּקְחוּ הָאֲנָשִׁים אֶת־הַמִּנְחָה הַזֹּאת וּמִשְׁנֶה־כֶּסֶף לָקְחוּ
they-took silver and-double the-this the-gift *** the-men so-they-took (15)

bring this trouble on me by
telling the man you had another brother?"
[7]They replied, "The man
questioned us closely about
ourselves and our family. 'Is
your father still living?' he
asked us. 'Do you have another brother?' We simply answered his questions. How
were we to know he would
say, 'Bring your brother down
here'?"
[8]Then Judah said to Israel
his father, "Send the boy
along with me and we will go
at once, so that we and you
and our children may live and
not die. [9]I myself will guaran-
tee his safety; you can hold me
personally responsible for
him. If I do not bring him back
to you and set him here before
you, I will bear the blame before you all my life. [10]As it is, if
we had not delayed, we could
have gone and returned
twice."
[11]Then their father Israel
said to them, "If it must be,
then do this: Put some of the
best products of the land in
your bags and take them
down to the man as a gift—a
little balm and a little honey,
some spices and myrrh, some
pistachio nuts and almonds.
[12]Take double the amount of
silver with you, for you must
return the silver that was put
back into the mouths of your
sacks. Perhaps it was a mistake. [13]Take your brother also
and go back to the man at
once. [14]And may God Al-
mighty[t] grant you mercy before the man so that he will let
your other brother and Benjamin come back with you. As
for me, if I am bereaved, I am
bereaved."
[15]So the men took the gifts

[t]14 Hebrew *El-Shaddai*

*7 Most mss have *dagesh* in the *nun* (נַּ).

בְּיָדָם וְאֶת־ בִּנְיָמִן וַיָּקֻמוּ וַיֵּרְדוּ מִצְרַיִם
Egypt and-they-went-down then-they-rose Benjamin and in-hand-of-them

וַיַּעַמְדוּ לִפְנֵי יוֹסֵף׃ וַיַּרְא יוֹסֵף אִתָּם אֶת־ בִּנְיָמִין
Benjamin *** with-them Joseph when-he-saw (16) Joseph before and-they-stood

וַיֹּאמֶר לַאֲשֶׁר עַל־ בֵּיתוֹ הָבֵא אֶת־ הָאֲנָשִׁים הַבָּיְתָה
to-the-house the-men *** take! house-of-him over to-whom then-he-said

וּטְבֹחַ טֶבַח וְהָכֵן כִּי אִתִּי יֹאכְלוּ הָאֲנָשִׁים
the-men they-will-eat with-me for and-prepare! animal and-slaughter!

בַּצָּהֳרָיִם׃ וַיַּעַשׂ הָאִישׁ כַּאֲשֶׁר אָמַר יוֹסֵף וַיָּבֵא הָאִישׁ
the-man and-he-took Joseph he-said just-as the-man so-he-did (17) at-the-noon

אֶת־הָאֲנָשִׁים בֵּיתָה יוֹסֵף׃ וַיִּירְאוּ הָאֲנָשִׁים כִּי
when the-men now-they-were-afraid (18) Joseph to-house-of the-men ***

הוּבְאוּ בֵּית יוֹסֵף וַיֹּאמְרוּ עַל־ דְּבַר
matter-of because-of and-they-thought Joseph house-of they-were-taken

הַכֶּסֶף הַשָּׁב בְּאַמְתְּחֹתֵינוּ בַּתְּחִלָּה אֲנַחְנוּ
we on-the-first-time into-sacks-of-us the-being-put-back the-silver

מוּבָאִים לְהִתְגֹּלֵל עָלֵינוּ וּלְהִתְנַפֵּל עָלֵינוּ וְלָקַחַת
and-to-seize over-us and-to-overpower against-us to-attack ones-being-brought

אֹתָנוּ לַעֲבָדִים וְאֶת־ חֲמֹרֵינוּ׃ וַיִּגְּשׁוּ אֶל־ הָאִישׁ אֲשֶׁר עַל־
over who the-man to so-they-went-up (19) donkeys-of-us and as-slaves us

בֵּית יוֹסֵף וַיְדַבְּרוּ אֵלָיו פֶּתַח הַבָּיִת׃ וַיֹּאמְרוּ
and-they-said (20) the-house entrance-of to-him and-they-spoke Joseph house-of

בִּי אֲדֹנִי יָרֹד יָרַדְנוּ בַּתְּחִלָּה לִשְׁבָּר־אֹכֶל׃
food to-buy on-the-first-time we-came-down to-come-down sir-of-me Oh

וַיְהִי כִּי־ בָאנוּ אֶל־ הַמָּלוֹן וַנִּפְתְּחָה אֶת־ אַמְתְּחֹתֵינוּ
sacks-of-us *** and-we-opened the-place to we-came when and-he-was (21)

וְהִנֵּה כֶסֶף־ אִישׁ בְּפִי אַמְתַּחְתּוֹ כַּסְפֵּנוּ
silver-of-us sack-of-him in-mouth-of each silver-of and-see!

בְּמִשְׁקָלוֹ וַנָּשֶׁב אֹתוֹ בְּיָדֵנוּ׃ וְכֶסֶף
and-silver (22) in-hand-of-us him so-we-brought-back in-exact-weight-of-him

אַחֵר הוֹרַדְנוּ בְיָדֵנוּ לִשְׁבָּר־אֹכֶל לֹא יָדַעְנוּ מִי־ שָׂם
he-put who we-know not food to-buy in-hand-of-us we-brought-down additional

כַּסְפֵּנוּ בְּאַמְתְּחֹתֵינוּ׃ וַיֹּאמֶר שָׁלוֹם לָכֶם אַל־ תִּירָאוּ
you-be-afraid not to-you all-right but-he-said (23) in-sacks-of-us silver-of-us

אֱלֹהֵיכֶם וֵאלֹהֵי אֲבִיכֶם נָתַן לָכֶם מַטְמוֹן בְּאַמְתְּחֹתֵיכֶם
in-sacks-of-you treasure to-you he-gave father-of-you and-God-of God-of-you

כַּסְפְּכֶם בָּא אֵלָי וַיּוֹצֵא אֲלֵהֶם אֶת־ שִׁמְעוֹן׃
Simeon *** to-them then-he-brought-out to-me he-came silver-of-you

and double the amount of silver, and Benjamin also. They hurried down to Egypt and presented themselves to Joseph. [16]When Joseph saw Benjamin with them, he said to the steward of his house, "Take these men to my house, slaughter an animal and prepare dinner; they are to eat with me at noon."

[17]The man did as Joseph told him and took the men to Joseph's house. [18]Now the men were frightened when they were taken to his house. They thought, "We were brought here because of the silver that was put back into our sacks the first time. He wants to attack us and overpower us and seize us as slaves and take our donkeys."

[19]So they went up to Joseph's steward and spoke to him at the entrance to the house. [20]"Please, sir," they said, "we came down here the first time to buy food. [21]But at the place where we stopped for the night we opened our sacks and each of us found his silver—the exact weight—in the mouth of his sack. So we have brought it back with us. [22]We have also brought additional silver with us to buy food. We don't know who put our silver in our sacks."

[23]"It's all right," he said. "Don't be afraid. Your God and the God of your father has given you treasure in your sacks; I received your silver." Then he brought Simeon out to them.

וַיָּבֵא הָאִישׁ אֶת־הָאֲנָשִׁים בֵּיתָה יוֹסֵף וַיִּתֶּן־מַיִם

water and-he-gave Joseph into-house-of the-men *** the-man then-he-took (24)

וַיִּרְחֲצוּ רַגְלֵיהֶם וַיִּתֵּן מִסְפּוֹא לַחֲמֹרֵיהֶם׃

for-donkeys-of-them fodder and-he-provided feet-of-them and-they-washed

וַיָּכִינוּ אֶת־הַמִּנְחָה עַד־בּוֹא יוֹסֵף בַּצָּהֳרָיִם כִּי

for at-the-noon Joseph to-come for the-gift *** then-they-prepared (25)

שָׁמְעוּ כִּי־שָׁם יֹאכְלוּ לָחֶם׃ וַיָּבֹא יוֹסֵף הַבַּיְתָה

to-the-home Joseph when-he-came (26) meal they-would-eat there that they-heard

וַיָּבִיאוּ לוֹ אֶת־הַמִּנְחָה אֲשֶׁר־בְּיָדָם הַבָּיְתָה

into-the-house in-hand-of-them that the-gift *** to-him then-they-presented

וַיִּשְׁתַּחֲווּ־לוֹ אָרְצָה׃ וַיִּשְׁאַל לָהֶם לְשָׁלוֹם

about-welfare to-them and-he-asked (27) to-ground before-him and-they-bowed

וַיֹּאמֶר הֲשָׁלוֹם אֲבִיכֶם הַזָּקֵן אֲשֶׁר אֲמַרְתֶּם הַעוֹדֶנּוּ חָי׃

alive still-he? you-spoke whom the-aged father-of-you well? then-he-said

וַיֹּאמְרוּ שָׁלוֹם לְעַבְדְּךָ לְאָבִינוּ עוֹדֶנּוּ חָי

alive still-he with-father-of-us with-servant-of-you well and-they-replied (28)

וַיִּקְּדוּ וַיִּשְׁתַּחֲוֻ׃ וַיִּשָּׂא עֵינָיו

eyes-of-him and-he-lifted (29) and-they-bowed-low then-they-bowed-head

וַיַּרְא אֶת־בִּנְיָמִין אָחִיו בֶּן־אִמּוֹ וַיֹּאמֶר

and-he-asked mother-of-him son-of brother-of-him Benjamin *** and-he-saw

הֲזֶה אֲחִיכֶם הַקָּטֹן אֲשֶׁר אֲמַרְתֶּם אֵלָי וַיֹּאמַר אֱלֹהִים

God and-he-said to-me you-told whom the-young brother-of-you this?

יָחְנְךָ בְּנִי׃ וַיְמַהֵר יוֹסֵף כִּי־

for Joseph then-he-hurried (30) son-of-me may-he-be-gracious-to-you

נִכְמְרוּ רַחֲמָיו אֶל־אָחִיו וַיְבַקֵּשׁ לִבְכּוֹת

to-weep and-he-looked brother-of-him at compassions-of-him they-were-moved

וַיָּבֹא הַחַדְרָה וַיֵּבְךְּ שָׁמָּה׃ וַיִּרְחַץ

then-he-washed (31) at-there and-he-wept to-the-private-room so-he-went

פָּנָיו וַיֵּצֵא וַיִּתְאַפַּק וַיֹּאמֶר שִׂימוּ לָחֶם׃

food serve! and-he-said and-he-controlled-self and-he-came-out face-of-him

וַיָּשִׂימוּ לוֹ לְבַדּוֹ וְלָהֶם לְבַדָּם

by-themselves and-to-them by-himself to-him so-they-served (32)

וְלַמִּצְרִים הָאֹכְלִים אִתּוֹ לְבַדָּם כִּי לֹא יוּכְלוּן

they-could not for by-themselves with-him the-ones-eating and-to-the-Egyptians

הַמִּצְרִים לֶאֱכֹל אֶת־הָעִבְרִים לֶחֶם כִּי־תוֹעֵבָה הִוא לְמִצְרָיִם׃

to-Egyptians that destestable for food the-Hebrews with to-eat the-Egyptians

וַיֵּשְׁבוּ לְפָנָיו הַבְּכֹר כִּבְכֹרָתוֹ

according-to-age-of-him the-firstborn before-him now-they-sat (33)

24 The steward took the men
into Joseph's house, gave
them water to wash their feet
and provided fodder for their
donkeys. 25 They prepared
their gifts for Joseph's arrival
at noon, because they had
heard that they were to eat
there.
26 When Joseph came home,
they presented to him the gifts
they had brought into the
house, and they bowed down
before him to the ground. 27 He
asked them how they were,
and then he said, "How is
your aged father you told me
about? Is he still living?"
28 They replied, "Your servant our father is still alive
and well." And they bowed
low to pay him honor.
29 As he looked about and
saw his brother Benjamin, his
own mother's son, he asked,
"Is this your youngest brother, the one you told me
about?" And he said, "God be
gracious to you, my son."
30 Deeply moved at the sight of
his brother, Joseph hurried out
and looked for a place to weep.
He went into his private room
and wept there.
31 After he had washed his
face, he came out and, control-
ling himself, said, "Serve the
food."
32 They served him by himself, the brothers by themselves, and the Egyptians who
ate with him by themselves,
because Egyptians could not
eat with Hebrews, for that is
detestable to Egyptians. 33 The
men had been seated before
him in the order of their ages,
from the firstborn to the

*28 Most mss have the *Qere* form in the text (חוו-).

°28 ק וישתחוו

וְהַצָּעִיר כִּצְעִרָתוֹ וַיִּתְמְהוּ הָאֲנָשִׁים

the-men and-they-were-astonished according-to-youth-of-him and-the-young

אִישׁ אֶל־ רֵעֵהוּ׃ וַיִּשָּׂא מַשְׂאֹת מֵאֵת פָּנָיו אֲלֵהֶם

to-them before-him from portions and-he-served (34) other-of-him with each

וַתֵּרֶב מַשְׂאַת בִּנְיָמִן מִמַּשְׂאֹת כֻּלָּם חָמֵשׁ

five all-of-them than-portions-of Benjamin portion-of and-she-was-greater

יָדוֹת וַיִּשְׁתּוּ וַיִּשְׁכְּרוּ עִמּוֹ׃ וַיְצַו אֶת־

*** then-he-instructed (44:1) with-him and-they-feasted so-they-drank times

אֲשֶׁר עַל־ בֵּיתוֹ לֵאמֹר מַלֵּא אֶת־אַמְתְּחֹת הָאֲנָשִׁים אֹכֶל כַּאֲשֶׁר

as-much-as food the-men sacks-of *** fill! to-say house-of-him over whom

יוּכְלוּן שְׂאֵת וְשִׂים כֶּסֶף־ אִישׁ בְּפִי אַמְתַּחְתּוֹ׃ וְאֶת־

and (2) sack-of-him in-mouth-of each silver-of and-put! to-carry they-can

גְּבִיעִי גְּבִיעַ הַכֶּסֶף תָּשִׂים בְּפִי אַמְתַּחַת הַקָּטֹן וְאֵת

and the-young sack-of in-mouth-of you-put the-silver cup-of cup-of-me

כֶּסֶף שִׁבְרוֹ וַיַּעַשׂ כִּדְבַר יוֹסֵף אֲשֶׁר דִּבֵּר׃

he-spoke that Joseph as-word-of and-he-did grain-of-him silver-of

הַבֹּקֶר אוֹר וְהָאֲנָשִׁים שֻׁלְּחוּ הֵמָּה וַחֲמֹרֵיהֶם׃

and-donkeys-of-them they they-were-sent and-the-men light the-morning (3)

הֵם יָצְאוּ אֶת־ הָעִיר לֹא הִרְחִיקוּ וְיוֹסֵף אָמַר

he-said when-Joseph they-went-far not the-city *** they-went they (4)

לַאֲשֶׁר עַל־ בֵּיתוֹ קוּם רְדֹף אַחֲרֵי הָאֲנָשִׁים וְהִשַּׂגְתָּם

when-you-catch-them the-men after go! rise! house-of-him over to-whom

וְאָמַרְתָּ אֲלֵהֶם לָמָּה שִׁלַּמְתֶּם רָעָה תַּחַת טוֹבָה׃ הֲלוֹא זֶה אֲשֶׁר

which this not? (5) good for evil you-repaid why? to-them then-you-say

יִשְׁתֶּה אֲדֹנִי בּוֹ וְהוּא נַחֵשׁ יְנַחֵשׁ בּוֹ

with-him he-divines to-divine also-he from-him master-of-me he-drinks

הֲרֵעֹתֶם אֲשֶׁר עֲשִׂיתֶם׃ וַיַּשִּׂגֵם וַיְדַבֵּר אֲלֵהֶם

to-them then-he-said when-he-caught-them (6) you-did what you-were-wicked

אֶת־ הַדְּבָרִים הָאֵלֶּה׃ וַיֹּאמְרוּ אֵלָיו לָמָּה יְדַבֵּר אֲדֹנִי

master-of-me he-says why? to-him but-they-said (7) the-these the words ***

כַּדְּבָרִים הָאֵלֶּה חָלִילָה לַעֲבָדֶיךָ מֵעֲשׂוֹת

from-to-do from-servants-of-you far-be-it! the-these such-the-things

כַּדָּבָר הַזֶּה׃ הֵן כֶּסֶף אֲשֶׁר מָצָאנוּ בְּפִי אַמְתְּחֹתֵינוּ

sacks-of-us in-mouth-of we-found that silver see! (8) the-that such-the-thing

הֱשִׁיבֹנוּ אֵלֶיךָ מֵאֶרֶץ כְּנָעַן וְאֵיךְ נִגְנֹב

would-we-steal so-why? Canaan from-land-of to-you we-brought-back

מִבֵּית אֲדֹנֶיךָ כֶּסֶף אוֹ זָהָב׃ אֲשֶׁר יִמָּצֵא אִתּוֹ

with-him he-is-found whom (9) gold or silver masters-of-you from-house-of

youngest; and they looked at
each other in astonishment.
34When portions were served
to them from Joseph's table,
Benjamin's portion was five
times as much as anyone
else's. So they feasted and
drank freely with him.

A Silver Cup in a Sack

44 Now Joseph gave these
instructions to the
steward of his house: "Fill the
men's sacks with as much
food as they can carry, and put
each man's silver in the
mouth of his sack. 2Then put
my cup, the silver one, in the
mouth of the youngest one's
sack, along with the silver for
his grain." And he did as Joseph said.
3As morning dawned, the
men were sent on their way
with their donkeys. 4They had
not gone far from the city
when Joseph said to his steward, "Go after those men at
once, and when you catch up
with them, say to them, 'Why
have you repaid good with
evil? 5Isn't this the cup my
master drinks from and also
uses for divination? This is a
wicked thing you have
done.' "
6When he caught up with
them, he repeated these words
to them. 7But they said to him,
"Why does my lord say such
things? Far be it from your servants to do anything like that!
8We even brought back to you
from the land of Canaan the
silver we found inside the
mouths of our sacks. So why
would we steal silver or gold
from your master's house? 9If
any of your servants is found

מֵעֲבָדֶ֛יךָ וָמֵ֑ת וְגַם־אֲנַ֕חְנוּ נִהְיֶ֥ה לַֽאדֹנִ֖י
to-master-of-me we-will-become we and-also now-he-will-die from-servants-of-you

לַעֲבָדִֽים׃ וַיֹּ֕אמֶר גַּם־עַתָּ֥ה כְדִבְרֵיכֶ֖ם כֶּן־ה֑וּא אֲשֶׁ֨ר
whom he thus as-words-of-you then very-well so-he-said (10) as-slaves

יִמָּצֵ֤א אִתּוֹ֙ יִֽהְיֶה־לִּ֣י עָ֔בֶד וְאַתֶּ֖ם תִּהְי֥וּ נְקִיִּֽם׃
blameless-ones you-will-be but-you slave to-me he-will-be with-him he-is-found

וַֽיְמַהֲר֔וּ וַיּוֹרִ֛דוּ אִ֥ישׁ אֶת־אַמְתַּחְתּ֖וֹ אָ֑רְצָה
to-ground sack-of-him *** each and-they-lowered so-they-hurried (11)

וַֽיִּפְתְּח֖וּ אִ֥ישׁ אַמְתַּחְתּֽוֹ׃ וַיְחַפֵּ֕שׂ בַּגָּד֣וֹל
with-the-oldest then-he-searched (12) sack-of-him each and-they-opened

הֵחֵ֔ל וּבַקָּטֹ֖ן כִּלָּ֑ה וַיִּמָּצֵא֙ הַגָּבִ֔יעַ בְּאַמְתַּ֖חַת
in-sack-of the-cup and-he-was-found he-ended and-with-the-youngest he-began

בִּנְיָמִֽן׃ וַֽיִּקְרְע֖וּ שִׂמְלֹתָ֑ם וַֽיַּעֲמֹס֙ אִ֣ישׁ עַל־
on each and-they-loaded clothes-of-them then-they-tore (13) Benjamin

חֲמֹר֔וֹ וַיָּשֻׁ֖בוּ הָעִֽירָה׃ וַיָּבֹ֨א יְהוּדָ֤ה
Judah when-he-came (14) to-the-city and-they-returned donkey-of-him

וְאֶחָיו֙ בֵּ֣יתָה יוֹסֵ֔ף וְה֖וּא עוֹדֶ֣נּוּ שָׁ֑ם וַיִּפְּל֥וּ
and-they-fell there still-he now-he Joseph into-house-of and-brothers-of-him

לְפָנָ֖יו אָֽרְצָה׃ וַיֹּ֤אמֶר לָהֶם֙ יוֹסֵ֔ף מָֽה־הַמַּעֲשֶׂ֥ה הַזֶּ֖ה
the-this the-deed what? Joseph to-them and-he-said (15) to-ground before-him

אֲשֶׁ֣ר עֲשִׂיתֶ֑ם הֲל֣וֹא יְדַעְתֶּ֔ם כִּֽי־נַחֵ֧שׁ יְנַחֵ֛שׁ אִ֖ישׁ אֲשֶׁ֥ר כָּמֹֽנִי׃
like-me who man he-divines to-divine that you-know not? you-did that

וַיֹּ֣אמֶר יְהוּדָ֗ה מַה־נֹּאמַר֙ לַֽאדֹנִ֔י מַה־נְּדַבֵּ֖ר
can-we-speak what? to-lord-of-me can-we-say what? Judah and-he-replied (16)

וּמַה־נִּצְטַדָּ֑ק הָאֱלֹהִ֗ים מָצָא֙ אֶת־עֲוֹ֣ן
guilt-of *** he-uncovered the-God can-we-show-innocence and-how?

עֲבָדֶ֔יךָ הִנֶּ֤נּוּ עֲבָדִים֙ לַֽאדֹנִ֔י גַּם־אֲנַ֕חְנוּ גַּ֛ם אֲשֶׁר־נִמְצָ֥א
he-was-found whom also we indeed to-lord-of-me slaves see-us! servants-of-you

הַגָּבִ֖יעַ בְּיָדֽוֹ׃ וַיֹּ֕אמֶר חָלִ֣ילָה לִּ֔י מֵעֲשׂ֖וֹת זֹ֑את
this from-to-do from-me far-be-it! but-he-said (17) in-hand-of-him the-cup

הָאִ֡ישׁ אֲשֶׁר֩ נִמְצָ֨א הַגָּבִ֜יעַ בְּיָד֗וֹ ה֚וּא יִהְיֶה־לִּ֣י
to-me he-will-become he in-hand-of-him the-cup he-was-found whom the-man

עָ֔בֶד וְאַתֶּ֕ם עֲל֥וּ לְשָׁל֖וֹם אֶל־אֲבִיכֶֽם׃ וַיִּגַּ֨שׁ אֵלָ֜יו
to-him then-he-went-up (18) father-of-you to in-peace go-back! but-you slave

יְהוּדָ֗ה וַיֹּאמֶר֮ בִּ֣י אֲדֹנִי֒ יְדַבֶּר־נָ֨א עַבְדְּךָ֤ דָבָר֙
word servant-of-you now! let-him-speak lord-of-me Oh and-he-said Judah

בְּאָזְנֵ֣י אֲדֹנִ֔י וְאַל־יִ֥חַר אַפְּךָ֖ בְּעַבְדֶּ֑ךָ
against-servant-of-you anger-of-you let-him-burn and-not lord-of-me in-ears-of

to have it, he will die; and the
rest of us will become my
lord's slaves."
10 "Very well, then," he said,
"let it be as you say. Whoever
is found to have it will become
my slave; the rest of you will
be free from blame."
11 Each of them quickly lowered his sack to the ground
and opened it.
12 Then the
steward proceeded to search,
beginning with the oldest and
ending with the youngest.
And the cup was found in
Benjamin's sack.
13 At this,
they tore their clothes. Then
they all loaded their donkeys
and returned to the city.
14 Joseph was still in the
house when Judah and his
brothers came in, and they
threw themselves to the
ground before him.
15 Joseph
said to them, "What is this
you have done? Don't you
know that a man like me can
find things out by divination?"
16 "What can we say to my
lord?" Judah replied. "What
can we say? How can we
prove our innocence? God has
uncovered your servants'
guilt. We are now my lord's
slaves—we ourselves and the
one who was found to have
the cup."
17 But Joseph said, "Far be it
from me to do such a thing!
Only the man who was found
to have the cup will become
my slave. The rest of you, go
back to your father in peace."
18 Then Judah went up to him
and said: "Please, my lord, let
your servant speak a word to
my lord. Do not be angry with

כִּי כָמוֹךָ כְּפַרְעֹה׃ אֲדֹנִי שָׁאַל אֶת־ עֲבָדָיו
servants-of-him *** he-asked lord-of-me (19) to-Pharaoh equal-you though

לֵאמֹר הֲיֵשׁ־ לָכֶם אָב אוֹ־ אָח׃ וַנֹּאמֶר אֶל־ אֲדֹנִי
lord-of-me to and-we-answered (20) brother or father to-you is-there? to-say

יֶשׁ־ לָנוּ אָב זָקֵן וְיֶלֶד זְקֻנִים קָטָן וְאָחִיו
and-brother-of-him young old-ages and-son-of old father to-us there-is

מֵת וַיִּוָּתֵר הוּא לְבַדּוֹ לְאִמּוֹ וְאָבִיו
and-father-of-him from-mother-of-him by-himself he and-he-is-left he-is-dead

אֲהֵבוֹ׃ וַתֹּאמֶר אֶל־ עֲבָדֶיךָ הוֹרִדֻהוּ אֵלָי
to-me bring-down-him! servants-of-you to then-you-said (21) he-loves-him

וְאָשִׂימָה עֵינִי עָלָיו׃ וַנֹּאמֶר אֶל־ אֲדֹנִי לֹא־ יוּכַל
he-can not lord-of-me to and-we-said (22) on-him eye-of-me so-I-can-set

הַנַּעַר לַעֲזֹב אֶת־ אָבִיו וְעָזַב אֶת־ אָבִיו וָמֵת׃
he-will-die father-of-him *** if-he-leaves father-of-him *** to-leave the-boy

וַתֹּאמֶר אֶל־ עֲבָדֶיךָ אִם־ לֹא יֵרֵד אֲחִיכֶם
brother-of-you he-comes-down not if servants-of-you to but-you-told (23)

הַקָּטֹן אִתְּכֶם לֹא תֹסִפוּן לִרְאוֹת פָּנָי׃ וַיְהִי כִּי
when and-he-was (24) face-of-me to-see you-will-again not with-you the-young

עָלִינוּ אֶל־ עַבְדְּךָ אָבִי וַנַּגֶּד־ לוֹ אֵת דִּבְרֵי
words-of *** to-him then-we-told father-of-me servant-of-you to we-went-back

אֲדֹנִי׃ וַיֹּאמֶר אָבִינוּ שֻׁבוּ שִׁבְרוּ־ לָנוּ מְעַט־ אֹכֶל׃
food little-of for-us buy! go-back! father-of-us then-he-said (25) lord-of-me

וַנֹּאמֶר לֹא נוּכַל לָרֶדֶת אִם־ יֵשׁ אָחִינוּ הַקָּטֹן
the-young brother-of-us he-is if to-go-down we-can not but-we-said (26)

אִתָּנוּ וְיָרַדְנוּ כִּי־ לֹא נוּכַל לִרְאוֹת פְּנֵי הָאִישׁ וְאָחִינוּ
if-brother-of-us the-man face-of to-see we-can not for then-we-will-go with-us

הַקָּטֹן אֵינֶנּוּ אִתָּנוּ׃ וַיֹּאמֶר עַבְדְּךָ אָבִי אֵלֵינוּ
to-us father-of-me servant-of-you then-he-said (27) with-us not-he the-young

אַתֶּם יְדַעְתֶּם כִּי שְׁנַיִם יָלְדָה־ לִּי אִשְׁתִּי׃ וַיֵּצֵא הָאֶחָד
the-one and-he-went-away (28) wife-of-me to-me she-bore two that you-know you

מֵאִתִּי וָאֹמַר אַךְ טָרֹף טֹרָף וְלֹא רְאִיתִיו עַד־ הֵנָּה׃
now until I-saw-him and-not he-was-torn to-be-torn surely and-I-said from-me

וּלְקַחְתֶּם גַּם־ אֶת־ זֶה מֵעִם פָּנַי וְקָרָהוּ אָסוֹן
harm and-he-comes-to-him presence-of-me from this *** also if-you-take (29)

וְהוֹרַדְתֶּם אֶת־ שֵׂיבָתִי בְּרָעָה שְׁאֹלָה׃ וְעַתָּה
so-now (30) to-Sheol in-misery gray-head-of-me *** then-you-will-bring-down

כְּבֹאִי אֶל־ עַבְדְּךָ אָבִי וְהַנַּעַר אֵינֶנּוּ אִתָּנוּ
with-us not-he and the-boy father-of-me servant-of-you to when-to-go-me

your servant, though you are equal to Pharaoh himself. [19]My lord asked his servants, 'Do you have a father or a brother?' [20]And we answered, 'We have an aged father, and there is a young son born to him in his old age. His brother is dead, and he is the only one of his mother's sons left, and his father loves him.'

[21]"Then you said to your servants, 'Bring him down to me so I can see him for myself.' [22]And we said to my lord, 'The boy cannot leave his father; if he leaves him, his father will die.' [23]But you told your servants, 'Unless your youngest brother comes down with you, you will not see my face again.' [24]When we went back to your servant my father, we told him what my lord had said.

[25]"Then our father said, 'Go back and buy a little more food.' [26]But we said, 'We cannot go down. Only if our youngest brother is with us will we go. We cannot see the man's face unless our youngest brother is with us.'

[27]"Your servant my father said to us, 'You know that my wife bore me two sons. [28]One of them went away from me, and I said, "He has surely been torn to pieces." And I have not seen him since. [29]If you take this one from me too and harm comes to him, you will bring my gray head down to the grave[u] in misery.'

[30]"So now, if the boy is not with us when I go back to your servant my father and if my

[u]29 Hebrew *Sheol*; also in verse 31

וְנַפְשׁוֹ קְשׁוּרָה בְנַפְשׁוֹ׃ וְהָיָה כִּרְאוֹתוֹ
as-to-see-him then-he-will-be (31) with-life-of-him being-bound and-life-of-him

כִּי־ אֵין הַנַּעַר וָמֵת וְהוֹרִידוּ עֲבָדֶיךָ
servants-of-you and-they-will-bring then-he-will-die the-boy he-is-not that

אֶת־ שֵׂיבַת עַבְדְּךָ אָבִינוּ בְּיָגוֹן שְׁאֹלָה׃ כִּי
now (32) to-Sheol in-sorrow father-of-us servant-of-you gray-head-of ***

עַבְדְּךָ עָרַב אֶת־ הַנַּעַר מֵעִם אָבִי לֵאמֹר אִם־ לֹא
not if to-say father-of-me to the-boy *** he-guaranteed servant-of-you

אֲבִיאֶנּוּ אֵלֶיךָ וְחָטָאתִי לְאָבִי כָּל־ הַיָּמִים׃
the-days all-of before-father-of-me then-I-will-bear-blame to-you I-bring-him

וְעַתָּה יֵשֶׁב־ נָא עַבְדְּךָ תַּחַת הַנַּעַר עֶבֶד
slave the-boy in-place-of servant-of-you now! let-him-remain so-now (33)

לַאדֹנִי וְהַנַּעַר יַעַל עִם־ אֶחָיו׃ כִּי־ אֵיךְ
how? for (34) brothers-of-him with let-him-return and-the-boy to-lord-of-me

אֶעֱלֶה אֶל־ אָבִי וְהַנַּעַר אֵינֶנּוּ אִתִּי פֶּן אֶרְאֶה
I-look lest with-me not-he if-the-boy father-of-me to can-I-go-back

בָרָע אֲשֶׁר יִמְצָא אֶת־ אָבִי׃ וְלֹא־ יָכֹל
he-could then-not (45:1) father-of-me to he-would-come that on-the-misery

יוֹסֵף לְהִתְאַפֵּק לְכֹל הַנִּצָּבִים עָלָיו
to-him the-ones-attending before-all-of to-control-himself Joseph

וַיִּקְרָא הוֹצִיאוּ כָל־ אִישׁ מֵעָלָי וְלֹא־ עָמַד אִישׁ אִתּוֹ
with-him man he-stood so-not from-me man every-of make-leave! and-he-cried

בְּהִתְוַדַּע יוֹסֵף אֶל־ אֶחָיו׃ וַיִּתֵּן אֶת־
*** and-he-raised (2) brothers-of-him to Joseph when-to-make-self-known

קֹלוֹ בִּבְכִי וַיִּשְׁמְעוּ מִצְרַיִם וַיִּשְׁמַע בֵּית
house-of and-he-heard Egyptians and-they-heard in-weeping voice-of-him

פַּרְעֹה׃ וַיֹּאמֶר יוֹסֵף אֶל־ אֶחָיו אֲנִי יוֹסֵף הַעוֹד אָבִי
father-of-me still? Joseph I brothers-of-him to Joseph and-he-said (3) Pharaoh

חָי וְלֹא־ יָכְלוּ אֶחָיו לַעֲנוֹת אֹתוֹ כִּי נִבְהֲלוּ
they-were-terrified for him to-answer brothers-of-him they-could but-not alive

מִפָּנָיו׃ וַיֹּאמֶר יוֹסֵף אֶל־ אֶחָיו גְּשׁוּ־
come-close! brothers-of-him to Joseph then-he-said (4) at-presence-of-him

נָא אֵלַי וַיִּגָּשׁוּ וַיֹּאמֶר אֲנִי יוֹסֵף אֲחִיכֶם אֲשֶׁר־
whom brother-of-you Joseph I and-he-said so-they-came-close to-me now!

מְכַרְתֶּם אֹתִי מִצְרָיְמָה׃ וְעַתָּה ׀ אַל־ תֵּעָצְבוּ וְאַל־
and-not you-be-distressed not and-now (5) into-Egypt me you-sold

יִחַר בְּעֵינֵיכֶם כִּי־ מְכַרְתֶּם אֹתִי הֵנָּה כִּי לְמִחְיָה
to-save-life for here me you-sold because in-eyes-of-you let-him-be-angry

father, whose life is closely
bound up with the boy's life,
31 sees that the boy isn't there,
he will die. Your servants will
bring the gray head of our father down to the grave in sorrow.
32 Your servant guaranteed the boy's safety to my father. I said, 'If I do not bring
him back to you, I will bear the
blame before you, my father,
all my life!'
33 "Now then, please let your
servant remain here as my
lord's slave in place of the boy,
and let the boy return with his
brothers. 34 How can I go back
to my father if the boy is not
with me? No! Do not let me see
the misery that would come
upon my father."

Joseph Makes Himself Known

45 Then Joseph could no
longer control himself
before all his attendants, and
he cried out, "Have everyone
leave my presence!" So there
was no one with Joseph when
he made himself known to his
brothers. 2 And he wept so
loudly that the Egyptians
heard him, and Pharaoh's
household heard about it.
3 Joseph said to his brothers,
"I am Joseph! Is my father still
living?" But his brothers were
not able to answer him, because they were terrified at his
presence.
4 Then Joseph said to his
brothers, "Come close to me."
When they had done so, he
said, "I am your brother Joseph, the one you sold into
Egypt! 5 And now, do not be
distressed and do not be angry
with yourselves for selling me
here, because it was to save

שְׁלָחַנִי אֱלֹהִים לִפְנֵיכֶם׃ כִּי־ זֶה שְׁנָתַיִם הָרָעָב בְּקֶרֶב
in-midst-of the-famine two-years now for (6) ahead-of-you God he-sent-me

הָאָרֶץ וְעוֹד חָמֵשׁ שָׁנִים אֲשֶׁר אֵין־ חָרִישׁ וְקָצִּיר*׃ וַיִּשְׁלָחֵנִי אֱלֹהִים
God but-he-sent-me (7) or-harvest plowing not that years five and-next the-land

לִפְנֵיכֶם לָשׂוּם לָכֶם שְׁאֵרִית בָּאָרֶץ וּלְהַחֲיוֹת
and-to-save-life on-the-earth remnant for-you to-preserve ahead-of-you

לָכֶם לִפְלֵיטָה גְּדֹלָה׃ וְעַתָּה לֹא־ אַתֶּם שְׁלַחְתֶּם אֹתִי הֵנָּה כִּי
but here me you-sent you not so-then (8) great by-deliverance for-you

הָאֱלֹהִים וַיְשִׂימֵנִי לְאָב לְפַרְעֹה וּלְאָדוֹן לְכָל־
over-all-of and-as-lord to-Pharaoh as-father and-he-made-me the-God

בֵּיתוֹ וּמֹשֵׁל בְּכָל־ אֶרֶץ מִצְרָיִם׃ מַהֲרוּ וַעֲלוּ
and-go-back! hurry! (9) Egypt land-of over-all-of and-one-ruling house-of-him

אֶל־ אָבִי וַאֲמַרְתֶּם אֵלָיו כֹּה אָמַר בִּנְךָ יוֹסֵף שָׂמַנִי
he-made-me Joseph son-of-you he-says this to-him and-you-say father-of-me to

אֱלֹהִים לְאָדוֹן לְכָל־ מִצְרָיִם רְדָה אֵלַי אַל־ תַּעֲמֹד׃ וְיָשַׁבְתָּ
and-you-live (10) you-delay not to-me come-down! Egypt over-all-of as-lord God

בְאֶרֶץ־ גֹּשֶׁן וְהָיִיתָ קָרוֹב אֵלַי אַתָּה וּבָנֶיךָ
and-children-of-you you to-me near and-you-be Goshen in-region-of

וּבְנֵי בָנֶיךָ וְצֹאנְךָ וּבְקָרְךָ וְכָל־ אֲשֶׁר־
that and-all and-herd-of-you and-flock-of-you children-of-you and-children-of

לָךְ׃ וְכִלְכַּלְתִּי אֹתְךָ שָׁם כִּי־ עוֹד חָמֵשׁ שָׁנִים רָעָב
famine years five still for there for-you and-I-will-provide (11) to-you

פֶּן־ תִּוָּרֵשׁ אַתָּה וּבֵיתְךָ וְכָל־ אֲשֶׁר־ לָךְ׃
to-you that and-all and-house-of-you you you-will-be-destitute otherwise

וְהִנֵּה עֵינֵיכֶם רֹאוֹת וְעֵינֵי אָחִי בִנְיָמִין
Benjamin brother-of-me and-eyes-of ones-seeing eyes-of-you now-see! (12)

כִּי־ פִי הַמְדַבֵּר אֲלֵיכֶם׃ וְהִגַּדְתֶּם לְאָבִי
to-father-of-me so-you-tell (13) to-you the-one-speaking mouth-of-me really

אֶת־ כָּל־ כְּבוֹדִי בְּמִצְרַיִם וְאֵת כָּל־ אֲשֶׁר רְאִיתֶם וּמִהַרְתֶּם
then-you-hurry you-saw that all and in-Egypt honor-of-me all-of ***

וְהוֹרַדְתֶּם אֶת־ אָבִי הֵנָּה׃ וַיִּפֹּל עַל־ צַוְּארֵי
neck-of around then-he-hugged (14) here father-of-me *** and-you-bring-down

בִנְיָמִן־ אָחִיו וַיֵּבְךְּ וּבִנְיָמִן בָּכָה עַל־ צַוָּארָיו׃
neck-of-him on he-wept and-Benjamin and-he-wept brother-of-him Benjamin

וַיְנַשֵּׁק לְכָל־ אֶחָיו וַיֵּבְךְּ עֲלֵיהֶם וְאַחֲרֵי
and-after over-them and-he-wept brothers-of-him on-all-of and-he-kissed (15)

כֵן דִּבְּרוּ אֶחָיו אִתּוֹ׃ וְהַקֹּל נִשְׁמַע
he-was-heard when-the-news (16) with-him brothers-of-him they-talked this

lives that God sent me ahead
of you. [6]For two years now
there has been famine in the
land, and for the next five
years there will not be plowing and reaping. [7]But God sent
me ahead of you to preserve
for you a remnant on earth
and to save your lives by a
great deliverance.[v]
[8]"So then, it was not you
who sent me here, but God.
He made me father to Pharaoh, lord of his entire
household and ruler of all
Egypt. [9]Now hurry back to my
father and say to him, 'This is
what your son Joseph says:
God has made me lord of all
Egypt. Come down to me;
don't delay. [10]You shall live in
the region of Goshen and be
near me—you, your children
and grandchildren, your
flocks and herds, and all you
have. [11]I will provide for you
there, because five years of
famine are still to come. Otherwise you and your
household and all who belong
to you will become destitute.'
[12]"You can see for yourselves, and so can my brother
Benjamin, that it is really I
who am speaking to you. [13]Tell
my father about all the honor
accorded me in Egypt and
about everything you have
seen. And bring my father
down here quickly."
[14]Then he threw his arms
around his brother Benjamin
and wept, and Benjamin embraced him, weeping. [15]And
he kissed all his brothers and
wept over them. Afterward his
brothers talked with him.
[16]When the news reached

[v]7 Or *save you as a great band of survivors*

*6 Most mss have no *dagesh* in the *tsade* (צּ־).

בֵּית פַּרְעֹה לֵאמֹר בָּאוּ אֲחֵי יוֹסֵף וַיִּיטַב
then-he-pleased Joseph brothers-of they-came to-say Pharaoh palace-of

בְּעֵינֵי פַרְעֹה וּבְעֵינֵי עֲבָדָיו׃ וַיֹּאמֶר פַּרְעֹה
Pharaoh and-he-said (17) officials-of-him and-in-eyes-of Pharaoh in-eyes-of

אֶל־יוֹסֵף אֱמֹר אֶל־אַחֶיךָ זֹאת עֲשׂוּ טַעֲנוּ אֶת־בְּעִירְכֶם וּלְכוּ־
and-go! animal-of-you *** load! do! this brothers-of-you to tell! Joseph to

בֹאוּ אַרְצָה כְּנָעַן׃ וּקְחוּ אֶת־אֲבִיכֶם וְאֶת־
and father-of-you *** and-get! (18) Canaan to-land-of return!

בָּתֵּיכֶם וּבֹאוּ אֵלָי וְאֶתְּנָה לָכֶם אֶת־טוּב אֶרֶץ
land-of best-of *** to-you and-I-will-give to-me and-come! families-of-you

מִצְרַיִם וְאִכְלוּ אֶת־חֵלֶב הָאָרֶץ׃ וְאַתָּה צֻוֵּיתָה זֹאת עֲשׂוּ
do! this you-are-directed and-you (19) the-land fat-of *** and-eat! Egypt

קְחוּ־לָכֶם מֵאֶרֶץ מִצְרַיִם עֲגָלוֹת לְטַפְּכֶם וְלִנְשֵׁיכֶם
and-for-wives-of-you for-children-of-you carts Egypt from-land-of with-you take!

וּנְשָׂאתֶם אֶת־אֲבִיכֶם וּבָאתֶם׃ וְעֵינְכֶם אַל־תָּחֹס
you-think not and-eye-of-you (20) and-you-come father-of-you *** then-you-get

עַל־כְּלֵיכֶם כִּי־טוּב כָּל־אֶרֶץ מִצְרַיִם לָכֶם הוּא׃
he to-you Egypt land-of all-of best-of for belongings-of-you about

וַיַּעֲשׂוּ־כֵן בְּנֵי יִשְׂרָאֵל וַיִּתֵּן לָהֶם יוֹסֵף עֲגָלוֹת עַל־
as carts Joseph to-them and-he-gave Israel sons-of this so-they-did (21)

פִּי פַרְעֹה וַיִּתֵּן לָהֶם צֵדָה לַדָּרֶךְ׃
for-the-journey provision to-them and-he-gave Pharaoh command-of

לְכֻלָּם נָתַן לָאִישׁ חֲלִפוֹת שְׂמָלֹת וּלְבִנְיָמִן
but-to-Benjamin clothing changes-of to-each he-gave to-each-of-them (22)

נָתַן שְׁלֹשׁ מֵאוֹת כֶּסֶף וְחָמֵשׁ חֲלִפֹת שְׂמָלֹת׃
clothes sets-of and-five silver hundreds three-of he-gave

וּלְאָבִיו שָׁלַח כְּזֹאת עֲשָׂרָה חֲמֹרִים נֹשְׂאִים מִטּוּב
with-best-of ones-being-loaded donkeys ten as-this he-sent and-to-father-of-him (23)

מִצְרַיִם וְעֶשֶׂר אֲתֹנֹת נֹשְׂאֹת בָּר וָלֶחֶם וּמָזוֹן
and-provision and-bread grain ones-being-loaded female-donkeys and-ten Egypt

לְאָבִיו לַדָּרֶךְ׃ וַיְשַׁלַּח אֶת־אֶחָיו
brothers-of-him *** then-he-sent (24) for-the-journey for-father-of-him

וַיֵּלֵכוּ וַיֹּאמֶר אֲלֵהֶם אַל־תִּרְגְּזוּ בַּדָּרֶךְ׃ וַיַּעֲלוּ
so-they-left (25) on-the-way you-quarrel not to-them and-he-said and-they-left

מִמִּצְרָיִם וַיָּבֹאוּ אֶרֶץ כְּנַעַן אֶל־יַעֲקֹב אֲבִיהֶם׃
father-of-them Jacob to Canaan land-of and-they-came from-Egypt

וַיַּגִּדוּ לוֹ לֵאמֹר עוֹד יוֹסֵף חַי וְכִי־הוּא מֹשֵׁל
one-ruling he and-in-fact alive Joseph still to-say to-him then-they-told (26)

Pharaoh's palace that Joseph's brothers had come, Pharaoh and all his officials were pleased. [17]Pharaoh said to Joseph, "Tell your brothers, 'Do this: Load your animals and return to the land of Canaan, [18]and bring your father and your families back to me. I will give you the best of the land of Egypt and you can enjoy the fat of the land.'

[19]"You are also directed to tell them, 'Do this: Take some carts from Egypt for your children and your wives, and get your father and come. [20]Never mind about your belongings, because the best of all Egypt will be yours.' "

[21]So the sons of Israel did this. Joseph gave them carts, as Pharaoh had commanded, and he also gave them provisions for their journey. [22]To each of them he gave new clothing, but to Benjamin he gave three hundred shekels[w] of silver and five sets of clothes. [23]And this is what he sent to his father: ten donkeys loaded with the best things of Egypt, and ten female donkeys loaded with grain and bread and other provisions for his journey. [24]Then he sent his brothers away, and as they were leaving he said to them, "Don't quarrel on the way!"

[25]So they went up out of Egypt and came to their father Jacob in the land of Canaan. [26]They told him, "Joseph is still alive! In fact, he is ruler of

[w]22 That is, about 7 1/2 pounds (about 3.5 kilograms)

בְּכָל־ אֶרֶץ מִצְרָיִם וַיָּפָג לִבּוֹ כִּי לֹא־ הֶאֱמִין
he-believed not for heart-of-him but-he-was-stunned Egypt land-of over-all-of

לָהֶם׃ (27) וַיְדַבְּרוּ אֵלָיו אֵת כָּל־ דִּבְרֵי יוֹסֵף אֲשֶׁר דִּבֶּר
he-said that Joseph words-of all-of *** to-him but-they-told (27) to-them

אֲלֵהֶם וַיַּרְא אֶת־ הָעֲגָלוֹת אֲשֶׁר־ שָׁלַח יוֹסֵף לָשֵׂאת אֹתוֹ
him to-carry Joseph he-sent that the-carts *** and-he-saw to-them

וַתְּחִי רוּחַ יַעֲקֹב אֲבִיהֶם׃ (28) וַיֹּאמֶר יִשְׂרָאֵל רַב
enough! Israel and-he-said (28) father-of-them Jacob spirit-of and-she-revived

עוֹד־ יוֹסֵף בְּנִי חָי אֵלְכָה וְאֶרְאֶנּוּ בְּטֶרֶם אָמוּת׃
I-die before and-I-will-see-him I-will-go alive son-of-me Joseph still

(46:1) וַיִּסַּע יִשְׂרָאֵל וְכָל־ אֲשֶׁר־ לוֹ וַיָּבֹא בְּאֵרָה שָּׁבַע
Sheba to-Beer and-he-went to-him that with-all Israel so-he-set-out (46:1)

וַיִּזְבַּח זְבָחִים לֵאלֹהֵי אָבִיו יִצְחָק׃ (2) וַיֹּאמֶר
and-he-spoke (2) Isaac father-of-him to-God-of sacrifices and-he-offered

אֱלֹהִים ׀ לְיִשְׂרָאֵל בְּמַרְאֹת הַלַּיְלָה וַיֹּאמֶר יַעֲקֹב ׀ יַעֲקֹב וַיֹּאמֶר
and-he-replied Jacob Jacob and-he-said the-night in-visions-of to-Israel God

הִנֵּנִי׃ (3) וַיֹּאמֶר אָנֹכִי הָאֵל אֱלֹהֵי אָבִיךָ אַל־ תִּירָא
you-be-afraid not father-of-you God-of the-God I and-he-said (3) here-I

מֵרְדָה מִצְרַיְמָה כִּי־ לְגוֹי גָּדוֹל אֲשִׂימְךָ שָׁם׃
there I-will-make-you great into-nation for to-Egypt from-to-go-down

(4) אָנֹכִי אֵרֵד עִמְּךָ מִצְרַיְמָה וְאָנֹכִי אַעַלְךָ גַם־
surely I-will-bring-up-you and-I to-Egypt with-you I-will-go-down I (4)

עָלֹה וְיוֹסֵף יָשִׁית יָדוֹ עַל־ עֵינֶיךָ׃ (5) וַיָּקָם
then-he-left (5) eyes-of-you on hand-of-him he-will-set and-Joseph to-go-up

יַעֲקֹב מִבְּאֵר שָׁבַע וַיִּשְׂאוּ בְנֵי־ יִשְׂרָאֵל אֶת־יַעֲקֹב אֲבִיהֶם
father-of-them Jacob *** Israel sons-of and-they-took Sheba from-Beer Jacob

וְאֶת־ טַפָּם וְאֶת־ נְשֵׁיהֶם בָּעֲגָלוֹת אֲשֶׁר־ שָׁלַח פַּרְעֹה
Pharaoh he-sent that in-the-carts wives-of-them and children-of-them and

לָשֵׂאת אֹתוֹ׃ (6) וַיִּקְחוּ אֶת־ מִקְנֵיהֶם וְאֶת־ רְכוּשָׁם
possession-of-them and stock-of-them *** and-they-took (6) him to-transport

אֲשֶׁר רָכְשׁוּ בְּאֶרֶץ כְּנַעַן וַיָּבֹאוּ מִצְרָיְמָה יַעֲקֹב וְכָל־
and-all-of Jacob to-Egypt and-they-went Canaan in-land-of they-acquired that

זַרְעוֹ אִתּוֹ׃ (7) בָּנָיו וּבְנֵי בָנָיו אִתּוֹ
with-him sons-of-him and-sons-of sons-of-him (7) with-him offspring-of-him

בְּנֹתָיו וּבְנוֹת בָּנָיו וְכָל־ זַרְעוֹ
offspring-of-him and-all-of sons-of-him and-daughters-of daughters-of-him

הֵבִיא אִתּוֹ מִצְרָיְמָה׃ (8) וְאֵלֶּה שְׁמוֹת בְּנֵי־ יִשְׂרָאֵל הַבָּאִים
the-ones-going Israel sons-of names-of now-these (8) to-Egypt with-him he-took

all Egypt." Jacob was stunned; he did not believe them. [27]But when they told him everything Joseph had said to them, and when he saw the carts Joseph had sent to carry him back, the spirit of their father Jacob revived. [28]And Israel said, "I'm convinced! My son Joseph is still alive. I will go and see him before I die."

Jacob Goes to Egypt

46 So Israel set out with all that was his, and when he reached Beersheba, he offered sacrifices to the God of his father Isaac.

[2]And God spoke to Israel in a vision at night and said, "Jacob! Jacob!"

"Here I am," he replied.

[3]"I am God, the God of your father," he said. "Do not be afraid to go down to Egypt, for I will make you into a great nation there. [4]I will go down to Egypt with you, and I will surely bring you back again. And Joseph's own hand will close your eyes."

[5]Then Jacob left Beersheba, and Israel's sons took their father Jacob and their children and their wives in the carts that Pharaoh had sent to transport him. [6]They also took with them their livestock and the possessions they had acquired in Canaan, and Jacob and all his offspring went to Egypt. [7]He took with him to Egypt his sons and grandsons and his daughters and granddaughters—all his offspring.

[8]These are the names of the

מִצְרַיְמָה יַעֲקֹב וּבָנָיו בְּכֹר יַעֲקֹב רְאוּבֵן׃ וּבְנֵי
and-sons-of (9) Reuben Jacob firstborn-of and-children-of-him Jacob to-Egypt

רְאוּבֵן חֲנוֹךְ וּפַלּוּא וְחֶצְרֹן וְכַרְמִי׃ וּבְנֵי שִׁמְעוֹן יְמוּאֵל
Jemuel Simeon and-sons-of (10) and-Carmi and-Hezron and-Pallu Hanoch Reuben

וְיָמִין וְאֹהַד וְיָכִין וְצֹחַר וְשָׁאוּל בֶּן־ הַכְּנַעֲנִית׃
the-Canaanite-woman son-of and-Shaul and-Zohar and-Jakin and-Ohad and-Jamin

וּבְנֵי לֵוִי גֵּרְשׁוֹן קְהָת וּמְרָרִי׃ וּבְנֵי יְהוּדָה עֵר
Er Judah and-sons-of (12) and-Merari Kohath Gershon Levi and-sons-of (11)

וְאוֹנָן וְשֵׁלָה וָפֶרֶץ וָזָרַח וַיָּמָת עֵר וְאוֹנָן בְּאֶרֶץ
in-land-of and-Onan Er but-he-died and-Zerah and-Perez and-Shelah and-Onan

כְּנַעַן וַיִּהְיוּ בְנֵי־ פֶרֶץ חֶצְרֹן וְחָמוּל׃ וּבְנֵי יִשָּׂשכָר
Issachar and-sons-of (13) and-Hamul Hezron Perez sons-of and-they-were Canaan

תּוֹלָע וּפֻוָּה וְיוֹב וְשִׁמְרֹן׃ וּבְנֵי זְבֻלוּן סֶרֶד וְאֵלוֹן
and-Elon Sered Zebulun and-sons-of (14) and-Shimron and-Job and-Puvah Tola

וְיַחְלְאֵל׃ אֵלֶּה ׀ בְּנֵי לֵאָה אֲשֶׁר יָלְדָה לְיַעֲקֹב בְּפַדַּן אֲרָם
Aram in-Paddan to-Jacob she-bore whom Leah sons-of these (15) and-Jahleel

וְאֵת דִּינָה בִתּוֹ כָּל־ נֶפֶשׁ בָּנָיו וּבְנוֹתָיו
and-daughters-of-him sons-of-him person all-of daughter-of-him Dinah and

שְׁלֹשִׁים וְשָׁלֹשׁ׃ וּבְנֵי גָד צִפְיוֹן וְחַגִּי שׁוּנִי וְאֶצְבֹּן עֵרִי
Eri and-Ezbon Shuni and-Haggi Ziphion Gad and-sons-of (16) and-three thirty

וַאֲרוֹדִי וְאַרְאֵלִי׃ וּבְנֵי אָשֵׁר יִמְנָה וְיִשְׁוָה וְיִשְׁוִי
and-Ishvi and-Ishvah Imnah Asher and-sons-of (17) and-Areli and-Arodi

וּבְרִיעָה וְשֶׂרַח אֲחֹתָם וּבְנֵי בְרִיעָה חֶבֶר וּמַלְכִּיאֵל׃
and-Malkiel Heber Beriah and-sons-of sister-of-them and-Serah and-Beriah

אֵלֶּה בְּנֵי זִלְפָּה אֲשֶׁר־ נָתַן לָבָן לְלֵאָה בִתּוֹ
daughter-of-him to-Leah Laban he-gave whom Zilpah sons-of these (18)

וַתֵּלֶד אֶת־ אֵלֶּה לְיַעֲקֹב שֵׁשׁ עֶשְׂרֵה נָפֶשׁ׃ בְּנֵי רָחֵל אֵשֶׁת
wife-of Rachel sons-of (19) person ten six to-Jacob these *** and-she-bore

יַעֲקֹב יוֹסֵף וּבִנְיָמִן׃ וַיִּוָּלֵד לְיוֹסֵף בְּאֶרֶץ מִצְרַיִם
Egypt in-land-of to-Joseph and-he-was-born (20) and-Benjamin Joseph Jacob

אֲשֶׁר יָלְדָה־ לּוֹ אָסְנַת בַּת־ פּוֹטִי פֶרַע כֹּהֵן אֹן אֶת־ מְנַשֶּׁה
Manasseh *** On priest-of Phera Poti daughter-of Asenath to-him she-bore whom

וְאֶת־ אֶפְרָיִם׃ וּבְנֵי בִנְיָמִן בֶּלַע וָבֶכֶר וְאַשְׁבֵּל גֵּרָא
Gera and-Ashbel and-Beker Bela Benjamin and-sons-of (21) Ephraim and

וְנַעֲמָן אֵחִי וָרֹאשׁ מֻפִּים וְחֻפִּים וָאָרְדְּ׃ אֵלֶּה בְּנֵי רָחֵל
Rachel sons-of these (22) and-Ard and-Huppim Muppim and-Rosh Ehi and-Naaman

אֲשֶׁר יֻלַּד לְיַעֲקֹב כָּל־ נֶפֶשׁ אַרְבָּעָה עָשָׂר׃ וּבְנֵי־ דָן חֻשִׁים׃
Hushim Dan and-sons-of (23) ten four person all-of to-Jacob she-bore whom

Israelites (Jacob and his descendants) who went to Egypt:

Reuben the firstborn of Jacob.
9 The sons of Reuben:
Hanoch, Pallu, Hezron and Carmi.
10 The sons of Simeon:
Jemuel, Jamin, Ohad, Jakin, Zohar and Shaul the son of a Canaanite woman.
11 The sons of Levi:
Gershon, Kohath and Merari.
12 The sons of Judah:
Er, Onan, Shelah, Perez and Zerah (but Er and Onan had died in the land of Canaan).
The sons of Perez:
Hezron and Hamul.
13 The sons of Issachar:
Tola, Puah,[x] Jashub[y] and Shimron.
14 The sons of Zebulun:
Sered, Elon and Jahleel.
15 These were the sons Leah bore to Jacob in Paddan Aram,[z] besides his daughter Dinah. These sons and daughters of his were thirty-three in all.

16 The sons of Gad:
Zephon,[a] Haggi, Shuni, Ezbon, Eri, Arodi and Areli.
17 The sons of Asher:
Imnah, Ishvah, Ishvi and Beriah.
Their sister was Serah.
The sons of Beriah:
Heber and Malkiel.
18 These were the children born to Jacob by Zilpah, whom Laban had given to his daughter Leah—sixteen in all.

19 The sons of Jacob's wife Rachel:
Joseph and Benjamin.
20 In Egypt, Manasseh and Ephraim were born to Joseph by Asenath daughter of Potiphera, priest of On.[b]
21 The sons of Benjamin:
Bela, Beker, Ashbel, Gera, Naaman, Ehi, Rosh, Muppim, Huppim and Ard.
22 These were the sons of Rachel who were born to Jacob—fourteen in all.

23 The son of Dan:
Hushim.

x13 Samaritan Pentateuch and Syriac (see also 1 Chron. 7:1); Masoretic Text *Puvah*
y13 Samaritan Pentateuch and some Septuagint manuscripts (see also Num. 26:24 and 1 Chron. 7:1); Masoretic Text *Iob*
z15 That is, Northwest Mesopotamia
a16 Samaritan Pentateuch and Septuagint (see also Num. 26:15); Masoretic Text *Ziphion*
b20 That is, Heliopolis

וּבְנֵי נַפְתָּלִי יַחְצְאֵל וְגוּנִי וְיֵצֶר וְשִׁלֵּם׃ אֵלֶּה
these (25) and-Shillem and-Jezer and-Guni Jahziel Naphtali and-sons-of (24)

בְּנֵי בִלְהָה אֲשֶׁר־ נָתַן לָבָן לְרָחֵל בִּתּוֹ וַתֵּלֶד אֶת־
*** and-she-bore daughter-of-him to-Rachel Laban he-gave whom Bilhah sons-of

אֵלֶּה לְיַעֲקֹב כָּל־ נֶפֶשׁ שִׁבְעָה׃ כָּל־ הַנֶּפֶשׁ הַבָּאָה
the-one-going the-person all-of (26) seven person all-of to-Jacob these

לְיַעֲקֹב מִצְרַיְמָה יֹצְאֵי יְרֵכוֹ מִלְּבַד נְשֵׁי בְנֵי־
sons-of wives-of apart-from body-of-him ones-coming-out-of to-Egypt with-Jacob

יַעֲקֹב כָּל־ נֶפֶשׁ שִׁשִּׁים וָשֵׁשׁ׃ וּבְנֵי יוֹסֵף אֲשֶׁר־ יֻלַּד־
he-was-born who Joseph with-sons-of (27) and-six sixty person all-of Jacob

לוֹ בְמִצְרַיִם נֶפֶשׁ שְׁנָיִם כָּל־ הַנֶּפֶשׁ לְבֵית־ יַעֲקֹב הַבָּאָה
the-one-going Jacob to-family-of the-person all-of two person in-Egypt to-him

מִצְרַיְמָה שִׁבְעִים׃ וְאֶת־ יְהוּדָה שָׁלַח לְפָנָיו אֶל־ יוֹסֵף לְהוֹרֹת
to-direct Joseph to ahead-of-him he-sent Judah and (28) seventy to-Egypt

לְפָנָיו גֹּשְׁנָה וַיָּבֹאוּ אַרְצָה גֹּשֶׁן׃
Goshen in-region-of and-they-arrived to-Goshen ahead-of-him

וַיֶּאְסֹר יוֹסֵף מֶרְכַּבְתּוֹ וַיַּעַל לִקְרַאת־יִשְׂרָאֵל
Israel to-meet and-he-went chariot-of-him Joseph and-he-made-ready (29)

אָבִיו גֹּשְׁנָה וַיֵּרָא אֵלָיו וַיִּפֹּל עַל־
around then-he-hugged to-him when-he-appeared in-Goshen father-of-him

צַוָּארָיו וַיֵּבְךְּ עַל־ צַוָּארָיו עוֹד׃ וַיֹּאמֶר יִשְׂרָאֵל אֶל־
to Israel and-he-said (30) long-time neck-of-him on and-he-wept neck-of-him

יוֹסֵף אָמוּתָה הַפָּעַם אַחֲרֵי רְאוֹתִי אֶת־ פָּנֶיךָ כִּי עוֹדְךָ חָי׃
alive still-you that face-of-you *** I-saw since the-now I-can-die Joseph

וַיֹּאמֶר יוֹסֵף אֶל־ אֶחָיו וְאֶל־ בֵּית אָבִיו
father-of-him household-of and-to brothers-of-him to Joseph then-he-said (31)

אֶעֱלֶה וְאַגִּידָה לְפַרְעֹה וְאֹמְרָה אֵלָיו אַחַי
brothers-of-me to-him and-I-will-say to-Pharaoh and-I-will-speak I-will-go-up

וּבֵית־ אָבִי אֲשֶׁר בְּאֶרֶץ־ כְּנַעַן בָּאוּ אֵלָי׃
to-me they-came Canaan in-land-of who father-of-me and-house-of

וְהָאֲנָשִׁים רֹעֵי צֹאן כִּי־ אַנְשֵׁי מִקְנֶה הָיוּ
they-are livestock tenders-of for sheep ones-herding-of now-the-men (32)

וְצֹאנָם וּבְקָרָם וְכָל־ אֲשֶׁר לָהֶם הֵבִיאוּ׃
they-brought to-them that and-all and-herd-of-them and-flock-of-them

וְהָיָה כִּי־ יִקְרָא לָכֶם פַּרְעֹה וְאָמַר מַה־
what? and-he-asks Pharaoh for-you he-calls when and-he-will-be (33)

מַעֲשֵׂיכֶם׃ וַאֲמַרְתֶּם אַנְשֵׁי מִקְנֶה הָיוּ
they-are stock tenders-of then-you-answer (34) occupations-of-you

24 The sons of Naphtali:
Jahziel, Guni, Jezer and
Shillem.
25 These were the sons born
to Jacob by Bilhah, whom Laban had given to his daughter
Rachel—seven in all.

26 All those who went to
Egypt with Jacob—those who
were his direct descendants,
not counting his sons' wives—
numbered sixty-six persons.
27 With the two sons who had
been born to Joseph in Egypt,
the members of Jacob's family,
which went to Egypt, were
seventy in all.

28 Now Jacob sent Judah
ahead of him to Joseph to get
directions to Goshen. When
they arrived in the region of
Goshen, 29 Joseph had his chariot made ready and went to
Goshen to meet his father Israel. As soon as Joseph appeared before him, he threw
his arms around his father[c]
and wept for a long time.
30 Israel said to Joseph, "Now
I am ready to die, since I have
seen for myself that you are
still alive."
31 Then Joseph said to his
brothers and to his father's
household, "I will go up and
speak to Pharaoh and will say
to him, 'My brothers and my
father's household, who were
living in the land of Canaan,
have come to me. 32 The men
are shepherds; they tend livestock, and they have brought
along their flocks and herds
and everything they own.'
33 When Pharaoh calls you in
and asks, 'What is your occupation?' 34 you should answer,
'Your servants have tended

[c]29 Hebrew *around him*

עֲבָדֶיךָ מִנְּעוּרֵינוּ וְעַד־ עַתָּה גַּם־ אֲנַחְנוּ גַּם־ אֲבֹתֵינוּ
fathers-of-us also we also now even-until from-youths-of-us servants-of-you

בַּעֲבוּר תֵּשְׁבוּ בְּאֶרֶץ גֹּשֶׁן כִּי־ תוֹעֲבַת מִצְרַיִם כָּל־
all-of Egyptians detestable-of for Goshen in-region-of you-may-settle so-that

רֹעֵה צֹאן׃ וַיָּבֹא יוֹסֵף וַיַּגֵּד לְפַרְעֹה וַיֹּאמֶר
and-he-said to-Pharaoh and-he-told Joseph so-he-went (47:1) sheep herding-of

אָבִי וְאַחַי וְצֹאנָם וּבְקָרָם וְכָל־
and-all and-herd-of-them and-flock-of-them and-brothers-of-me father-of-me

אֲשֶׁר לָהֶם בָּאוּ מֵאֶרֶץ כְּנָעַן וְהִנָּם בְּאֶרֶץ גֹּשֶׁן׃
Goshen in-region-of and-now-they Canaan from-land-of they-came to-them that

וּמִקְצֵה אֶחָיו לָקַח חֲמִשָּׁה אֲנָשִׁים וַיַּצִּגֵם
and-he-presented-them men five he-chose brothers-of-him and-from-midst-of (2)

לִפְנֵי פַרְעֹה׃ וַיֹּאמֶר פַּרְעֹה אֶל־ אֶחָיו מַה־
what? brothers-of-him to Pharaoh and-he-asked (3) Pharaoh before

מַּעֲשֵׂיכֶם וַיֹּאמְרוּ אֶל־ פַּרְעֹה רֹעֵה צֹאן עֲבָדֶיךָ
servants-of-you sheep herding-of Pharaoh to and-they-said occupations-of-you

גַּם־ אֲנַחְנוּ גַּם־ אֲבוֹתֵינוּ׃ וַיֹּאמְרוּ אֶל־ פַּרְעֹה לָגוּר
to-live-awhile Pharaoh to and-they-said (4) fathers-of-us also we also

בָּאָרֶץ בָּאנוּ כִּי־ אֵין מִרְעֶה לַצֹּאן אֲשֶׁר
that for-the-flock pasture there-is-no for we-came in-the-land

לַעֲבָדֶיךָ כִּי־ כָבֵד הָרָעָב בְּאֶרֶץ כְּנַעַן וְעַתָּה
so-now Canaan in-land-of the-famine severe for to-servants-of-you

יֵשְׁבוּ־ נָא עֲבָדֶיךָ בְּאֶרֶץ גֹּשֶׁן׃ וַיֹּאמֶר
then-he-said (5) Goshen in-region-of servants-of-you now! let-them-settle

פַּרְעֹה אֶל־ יוֹסֵף לֵאמֹר אָבִיךָ וְאַחֶיךָ בָּאוּ אֵלֶיךָ׃
to-you they-came and-brothers-of-you father-of-you to-say Joseph to Pharaoh

אֶרֶץ מִצְרַיִם לְפָנֶיךָ הִוא בְּמֵיטַב הָאָרֶץ הוֹשֵׁב אֶת־ אָבִיךָ
father-of-you *** settle! the-land in-best-of he before-you Egypt land-of (6)

וְאֶת־ אַחֶיךָ יֵשְׁבוּ בְּאֶרֶץ גֹּשֶׁן וְאִם־ יָדַעְתָּ
you-know and-if Goshen in-region-of let-them-live brothers-of-you and

וְיֶשׁ־ בָּם אַנְשֵׁי־ חַיִל וְשַׂמְתָּם
them-you-put-them special-ability men-of among-them that-there-is

שָׂרֵי מִקְנֶה עַל־ אֲשֶׁר־ לִי׃ וַיָּבֵא יוֹסֵף אֶת־יַעֲקֹב
Jacob *** Joseph then-he-brought (7) to-me what over stock ones-in-charge-of

אָבִיו וַיַּעֲמִדֵהוּ לִפְנֵי פַרְעֹה וַיְבָרֶךְ יַעֲקֹב אֶת־
*** Jacob and-he-blessed Pharaoh before and-he-presented-him father-of-him

פַּרְעֹה׃ וַיֹּאמֶר פַּרְעֹה אֶל־יַעֲקֹב כַּמָּה יְמֵי שְׁנֵי
years-of days-of how-many? Jacob to Pharaoh and-he-asked (8) Pharaoh

livestock from our boyhood
on, just as our fathers did.'
Then you will be allowed to
settle in the region of Goshen,
for all shepherds are detestable
to the Egyptians."

47 Joseph went and told
Pharaoh, "My father
and brothers, with their flocks
and herds and everything
they own, have come from the
land of Canaan and are now
in Goshen." 2He chose five of
his brothers and presented
them before Pharaoh.
3Pharaoh asked the brothers,
"What is your occupation?"
"Your servants are shep-
herds," they replied to Pharaoh, "just as our fathers
were." 4They also said to him,
"We have come to live here
awhile, because the famine is
severe in Canaan and your
servants' flocks have no pasture. So now, please let your
servants settle in Goshen."
5Pharaoh said to Joseph,
"Your father and your brothers have come to you, 6and the
land of Egypt is before you;
settle your father and your
brothers in the best part of the
land. Let them live in Goshen.
And if you know of any
among them with special ability, put them in charge of my
own livestock."
7Then Joseph brought his father Jacob in and presented
him before Pharaoh. After
Jacob blessed[d] Pharaoh, 8Phar-
aoh asked him, "How old are
you?"

[d]7 Or *greeted*

חַיֶּיךָ׃ וַיֹּאמֶר יַעֲקֹב אֶל־פַּרְעֹה יְמֵי שְׁנֵי מְגוּרַי
journeys-of-me years-of days-of Pharaoh to Jacob and-he-said (9) lives-of-you

שְׁלֹשִׁים וּמְאַת שָׁנָה מְעַט וְרָעִים הָיוּ יְמֵי שְׁנֵי
years-of days-of they-are difficult-ones few year and-hundred-of thirty

חַיַּי וְלֹא הִשִּׂיגוּ אֶת־ יְמֵי שְׁנֵי חַיֵּי אֲבֹתַי
fathers-of-me lives-of years-of days-of *** they-equal and-not lives-of-me

בִּימֵי מְגוּרֵיהֶם׃ וַיְבָרֶךְ יַעֲקֹב אֶת־ פַּרְעֹה וַיֵּצֵא
and-he-left Pharaoh *** Jacob then-he-blessed (10) journeys-of-them in-days-of

מִלִּפְנֵי פַרְעֹה׃ וַיּוֹשֵׁב יוֹסֵף אֶת־ אָבִיו וְאֶת־
and father-of-him *** Joseph so-he-settled (11) Pharaoh from-presence-of

אֶחָיו וַיִּתֵּן לָהֶם אֲחֻזָּה בְּאֶרֶץ מִצְרַיִם בְּמֵיטַב
in-best-of Egypt in-land-of property to-them and-he-gave brothers-of-him

הָאָרֶץ בְּאֶרֶץ רַעְמְסֵס כַּאֲשֶׁר צִוָּה פַּרְעֹה׃
Pharaoh he-directed just-as Rameses in-district-of the-land

וַיְכַלְכֵּל יוֹסֵף אֶת־ אָבִיו וְאֶת־ אֶחָיו וְאֵת כָּל־
all-of and brothers-of-him and father-of-him *** Joseph and-he-provided (12)

בֵּית אָבִיו לֶחֶם לְפִי הַטָּף׃
the-children according-to-number-of food father-of-him household-of

וְלֶחֶם אֵין בְּכָל־ הָאָרֶץ כִּי־ כָבֵד הָרָעָב מְאֹד
very the-famine severe for the-region in-all-of there-is-no but-food (13)

וַתֵּלַהּ אֶרֶץ מִצְרַיִם וְאֶרֶץ כְּנַעַן מִפְּנֵי הָרָעָב׃
the-famine because-of Canaan and-land-of Egypt land-of and-she-wasted-away

וַיְלַקֵּט יוֹסֵף אֶת־ כָּל־ הַכֶּסֶף הַנִּמְצָא בְאֶרֶץ־
in-land-of the-being-found the-money all-of *** Joseph and-he-collected (14)

מִצְרַיִם וּבְאֶרֶץ כְּנַעַן בַּשֶּׁבֶר אֲשֶׁר־ הֵם שֹׁבְרִים וַיָּבֵא
and-he-brought ones-buying they that for-the-grain Canaan and-in-land-of Egypt

יוֹסֵף אֶת־ הַכֶּסֶף בֵּיתָה פַּרְעֹה׃ וַיִּתֹּם הַכֶּסֶף
the-money when-he-was-gone (15) Pharaoh to-palace-of the-money *** Joseph

מֵאֶרֶץ מִצְרַיִם וּמֵאֶרֶץ כְּנַעַן וַיָּבֹאוּ כָל־מִצְרַיִם אֶל־
to Egypt all-of then-they-came Canaan and-from-land-of Egypt from-land-of

יוֹסֵף לֵאמֹר הָבָה־ לָּנוּ לֶחֶם וְלָמָּה נָמוּת נֶגְדֶּךָ כִּי
because before-you should-we-die now-why? food to-us give! to say Joseph

אָפֵס כָּסֶף׃ וַיֹּאמֶר יוֹסֵף הָבוּ מִקְנֵיכֶם
cattle-of-you bring! Joseph and-he-said (16) money he-is-used-up

וְאֶתְּנָה לָכֶם בְּמִקְנֵיכֶם אִם־ אָפֵס כָּסֶף׃
money he-is-gone since for-cattle-of-you to-you and-I-will-sell

וַיָּבִיאוּ אֶת־ מִקְנֵיהֶם אֶל־יוֹסֵף וַיִּתֵּן לָהֶם יוֹסֵף לֶחֶם
food Joseph to-them and-he-gave Joseph to stock-of-them *** so-they-brought (17)

9 And Jacob said to Pharaoh, "The years of my pilgrimage are a hundred and thirty. My years have been few and difficult, and they do not equal the years of the pilgrimage of my fathers." 10 Then Jacob blessed[c] Pharaoh and went out from his presence.

11 So Joseph settled his father and his brothers in Egypt and gave them property in the best part of the land, the district of Rameses, as Pharaoh directed. 12 Joseph also provided his father and his brothers and all his father's household with food, according to the number of their children.

Joseph and the Famine

13 There was no food, however, in the whole region because the famine was severe; both Egypt and Canaan wasted away because of the famine. 14 Joseph collected all the money that was to be found in Egypt and Canaan in payment for the grain they were buying, and he brought it to Pharaoh's palace. 15 When the money of the people of Egypt and Canaan was gone, all Egypt came to Joseph and said, "Give us food. Why should we die before your eyes? Our money is used up."

16 "Then bring your livestock," said Joseph. "I will sell you food in exchange for your livestock, since your money is gone." 17 So they brought their livestock to Joseph, and he gave them food in exchange

c10 Or *said farewell to*

בַּסּוּסִים וּבְמִקְנֵה הַצֹּאן וּבְמִקְנֵה הַבָּקָר
the-herd and-for-stock-of the-flock and-for-stock-of for-the-horses

וּבַחֲמֹרִים וַיְנַהֲלֵם בַּלֶּחֶם בְּכָל־ מִקְנֵהֶם
stock-of-them for-all-of with-the-food and-he-provided-them and-for-the-donkeys

בַּשָּׁנָה הַהִוא׃ (18) וַתִּתֹּם הַשָּׁנָה הַהִוא וַיָּבֹאוּ
then-they-came the-that the-year when-she-ended (18) the-that in-the-year

אֵלָיו בַּשָּׁנָה הַשֵּׁנִית וַיֹּאמְרוּ לוֹ לֹא־ נְכַחֵד
we-can-hide not to-him and-they-said the-second in-the-year to-him

מֵאֲדֹנִי כִּי אִם־ תַּם הַכֶּסֶף וּמִקְנֵה הַבְּהֵמָה אֶל־
to the-livestock and-herd-of the-money he-is-gone since that from-lord-of-me

אֲדֹנִי לֹא נִשְׁאַר לִפְנֵי אֲדֹנִי בִּלְתִּי אִם־ גְּוִיָּתֵנוּ
body-of-us but nothing lord-of-me before he-is-left not lord-of-me

וְאַדְמָתֵנוּ׃ (19) לָמָּה נָמוּת לְעֵינֶיךָ גַּם־ אֲנַחְנוּ גַּם
also we indeed before-eyes-of-you should-we-perish why? (19) and-land-of-us

אַדְמָתֵנוּ קְנֵה־ אֹתָנוּ וְאֶת־ אַדְמָתֵנוּ בַּלָּחֶם וְנִהְיֶה אֲנַחְנוּ
we and-we-will-be for-the-food land-of-us and us buy! land-of-us

וְאַדְמָתֵנוּ עֲבָדִים לְפַרְעֹה וְתֶן־ זֶרַע וְנִחְיֶה וְלֹא נָמוּת
we-die and-not so-we-may-live seed so-give! to-Pharaoh slaves and-land-of-us

וְהָאֲדָמָה לֹא תֵשָׁם׃ (20) וַיִּקֶן יוֹסֵף אֶת־ כָּל־ אַדְמַת
land-of all-of *** Joseph so-he-bought (20) she-be-desolate not and-the-land

מִצְרַיִם לְפַרְעֹה כִּי־ מָכְרוּ מִצְרַיִם אִישׁ שָׂדֵהוּ כִּי־ חָזַק
he-was-severe for field-of-him each Egyptians they-sold for for-Pharaoh Egypt

עֲלֵהֶם הָרָעָב וַתְּהִי הָאָרֶץ לְפַרְעֹה׃ (21) וְאֶת־ הָעָם
the-people and (21) to-Pharaoh the-land so-she-became the-famine for-them

הֶעֱבִיר אֹתוֹ לֶעָרִים מִקְצֵה גְבוּל־ מִצְרַיִם וְעַד־ קָצֵהוּ׃
other-of-him and-to Egypt border-of from-end-of *into-the-cities him he-moved*

(22) רַק אַדְמַת הַכֹּהֲנִים לֹא קָנָה כִּי חֹק לַכֹּהֲנִים
to-the-priests allotment for he-bought not the-priests land-of however (22)

מֵאֵת פַּרְעֹה וְאָכְלוּ אֶת־ חֻקָּם אֲשֶׁר נָתַן לָהֶם פַּרְעֹה
Pharaoh to-them he-gave that allotment-of-them *** and-they-ate Pharaoh from

עַל־ כֵּן לֹא מָכְרוּ אֶת־ אַדְמָתָם׃ (23) וַיֹּאמֶר יוֹסֵף אֶל־ הָעָם
the-people to Joseph then-he-said (23) land-of-them *** they-sold not this for

הֵן קָנִיתִי אֶתְכֶם הַיּוֹם וְאֶת־ אַדְמַתְכֶם לְפַרְעֹה הֵא־ לָכֶם זֶרַע
seed for-you here! for-Pharaoh land-of-you and the-day you I-bought see!

וּזְרַעְתֶּם אֶת־ הָאֲדָמָה׃ (24) וְהָיָה בַּתְּבוּאֹת
at-the-harvests but-he-will-be (24) the-ground *** so-you-can-plant

וּנְתַתֶּם חֲמִישִׁית לְפַרְעֹה וְאַרְבַּע הַיָּדֹת יִהְיֶה לָכֶם לְזֶרַע
as-seed-of for-you he-will-be the-parts and-four to-Pharaoh fifth that-you-give

for their horses, their sheep and goats, their cattle and donkeys. And he brought them through that year with food in exchange for all their livestock.

18When that year was over, they came to him the following year and said, "We cannot hide from our lord the fact that since our money is gone and our livestock belongs to you, there is nothing left for our lord except our bodies and our
land. 19Why should we perish before your eyes—we and our land as well? Buy us and our land in exchange for food, and we with our land will be in bondage to Pharaoh. Give us seed so that we may live and not die, and that the land may not become desolate."

20So Joseph bought all the land in Egypt for Pharaoh. The Egyptians, one and all, sold their fields, because the famine was too severe for them. The land became Pharaoh's,
21and Joseph reduced the people to servitude,[f] from one end of Egypt to the other.
22However, he did not buy the land of the priests, because they received a regular allotment from Pharaoh and had food enough from the allotment Pharaoh gave them. That is why they did not sell their land.

23Joseph said to the people, "Now that I have bought you and your land today for Pharaoh, here is seed for you so you can plant the ground.
24But when the crop comes in, give a fifth of it to Pharaoh. The other four-fifths you may keep as seed for the fields and

f21 Samaritan Pentateuch and Septuagint (see also Vulgate); Masoretic Text *and he moved the people into the cities*

*21 הֶעֱבִיד אתו לַעֲבָדִים
to-slaves him be-reduced
This Hebrew text and translation is conjectured on the basis of the early versions listed above in footnote *f*.

הַשָּׂדֶה וּלְאָכְלְכֶם וְלַאֲשֶׁר בְּבָתֵּיכֶם וְלֶאֱכֹל
and-to-eat in-houses-of-you and-for-whom and-as-food-of-you the-field

לְטַפְּכֶם׃ וַיֹּאמְרוּ הֶחֱיִתָנוּ נִמְצָא־ חֵן
favor may-we-find you-saved-lives-of-us and-they-said (25) for-children-of-you

בְּעֵינֵי אֲדֹנִי וְהָיִינוּ עֲבָדִים לְפַרְעֹה׃ וַיָּשֶׂם
so-he-established (26) to-Pharaoh slaves now-we-will-be lord-of-me in-eyes-of

אֹתָהּ יוֹסֵף לְחֹק עַד־ הַיּוֹם הַזֶּה עַל־ אַדְמַת מִצְרַיִם לְפַרְעֹה
to-Pharaoh Egypt land-of concerning the-this the-day to as-law Joseph her

לַחֹמֶשׁ רַק אַדְמַת הַכֹּהֲנִים לְבַדָּם לֹא הָיְתָה לְפַרְעֹה׃
to-Pharaoh she-became not by-themselves the-priests land-of only the-fifth

וַיֵּשֶׁב יִשְׂרָאֵל בְּאֶרֶץ מִצְרַיִם בְּאֶרֶץ גֹּשֶׁן
Goshen in-region-of Egypt in-land-of Israel now-he-settled (27)

וַיֵּאָחֲזוּ בָהּ וַיִּפְרוּ וַיִּרְבּוּ
and-they-increased and-they-were-fruitful in-her and-they-acquired-property

מְאֹד׃ וַיְחִי יַעֲקֹב בְּאֶרֶץ מִצְרַיִם שְׁבַע עֶשְׂרֵה שָׁנָה וַיְהִי
and-he-was year ten seven Egypt in-land-of Jacob and-he-lived (28) greatly

יְמֵי־ יַעֲקֹב שְׁנֵי חַיָּיו שֶׁבַע שָׁנִים וְאַרְבָּעִים וּמְאַת שָׁנָה׃
year and-hundred-of and-forty years seven lives-of-him years-of Jacob days-of

וַיִּקְרְבוּ יְמֵי־ יִשְׂרָאֵל לָמוּת וַיִּקְרָא ׀ לִבְנוֹ
for-son-of-him then-he-called to-die Israel days-of when-they-drew-near (29)

לְיוֹסֵף וַיֹּאמֶר לוֹ אִם־ נָא מָצָאתִי חֵן בְּעֵינֶיךָ שִׂים־ נָא
now! put! in-eyes-of-you favor I-found now! if to-him and-he-said for-Joseph

יָדְךָ תַּחַת יְרֵכִי וְעָשִׂיתָ עִמָּדִי חֶסֶד וֶאֱמֶת
and-faithfulness kindness to-me and-you-show thigh-of-me under hand-of-you

אַל־ נָא תִקְבְּרֵנִי בְּמִצְרָיִם׃ וְשָׁכַבְתִּי עִם־ אֲבֹתַי
fathers-of-me with when-I-rest (30) in-Egypt you-bury-me now! not

וּנְשָׂאתַנִי מִמִּצְרַיִם וּקְבַרְתַּנִי בִּקְבֻרָתָם וַיֹּאמַר אָנֹכִי
I and-he-said in-tomb-of-them and-you-bury-me from-Egypt then-you-carry-me

אֶעֱשֶׂה כִדְבָרֶךָ׃ וַיֹּאמֶר הִשָּׁבְעָה לִי וַיִּשָּׁבַע לוֹ
to-him and-he-swore to-me swear! then-he-said (31) as-word-of-you I-will-do

וַיִּשְׁתַּחוּ יִשְׂרָאֵל עַל־ רֹאשׁ הַמִּטָּה׃ וַיְהִי אַחֲרֵי הַדְּבָרִים
the-things after and-he-was (48:1) the-bed head-of at Israel then-he-bowed

הָאֵלֶּה וַיֹּאמֶר לְיוֹסֵף הִנֵּה אָבִיךָ חֹלֶה וַיִּקַּח אֶת־
*** so-he-took being-ill father-of-you see! to-Joseph that-he-said the-these

שְׁנֵי בָנָיו עִמּוֹ אֶת־ מְנַשֶּׁה וְאֶת־ אֶפְרָיִם׃ וַיַּגֵּד לְיַעֲקֹב
to-Jacob and-he-told (2) Ephraim and Manasseh *** with-him sons-of-him two-of

וַיֹּאמֶר הִנֵּה בִּנְךָ יוֹסֵף בָּא אֵלֶיךָ וַיִּתְחַזֵּק יִשְׂרָאֵל
Israel and-he-strengthened to-you he-came Joseph son-of-you see! and-he-said

as food for yourselves and your households and your children."
25"You have saved our lives," they said. "May we find favor in the eyes of our lord; we will be in bondage to Pharaoh."
26So Joseph established it as a law concerning land in Egypt—still in force today—that a fifth of the produce belongs to Pharaoh. It was only the land of the priests that did not become Pharaoh's.
27Now the Israelites settled in Egypt in the region of Goshen. They acquired property there and were fruitful and increased greatly in number.
28Jacob lived in Egypt seventeen years, and the years of his life were a hundred and forty-
seven. 29When the time drew near for Israel to die, he called for his son Joseph and said to him, "If I have found favor in your eyes, put your hand under my thigh and promise that you will show me kindness and faithfulness. Do not bury
me in Egypt, 30but when I rest with my fathers, carry me out of Egypt and bury me where they are buried."

"I will do as you say," he said.
31"Swear to me," he said. Then Joseph swore to him, and Israel worshiped as he leaned on the top of his staff.[g]

Manasseh and Ephraim

48 Some time later Joseph was told, "Your father is ill." So he took his two sons Manasseh and Ephraim along
with him. 2When Jacob was told, "Your son Joseph has come to you," Israel rallied his

g31 *Or Israel bowed down at the head of his bed*

וַיֵּשֶׁב עַל־ הַמִּטָּה׃ וַיֹּאמֶר יַעֲקֹב אֶל־ יוֹסֵף אֵל שַׁדַּי
Almighty God Joseph to Jacob and-he-said (3) the-bed on and-he-sat-up

נִרְאָה־ אֵלַי בְּלוּז בְּאֶרֶץ כְּנַעַן וַיְבָרֶךְ אֹתִי׃ וַיֹּאמֶר
and-he-said (4) me and-he-blessed Canaan in-land-of at-Luz to-me he-appeared

אֵלַי הִנְנִי מַפְרְךָ וְהִרְבִּיתִךָ וּנְתַתִּיךָ
and-I-will-make-you and-I-will-increase-you making-fruitful-you see-I! to-me

לִקְהַל עַמִּים וְנָתַתִּי אֶת־ הָאָרֶץ הַזֹּאת
the-this the-land *** and-I-will-give peoples into-community-of

לְזַרְעֲךָ אַחֲרֶיךָ אֲחֻזַּת עוֹלָם׃ וְעַתָּה שְׁנֵי־
two-of and-now (5) everlasting possession-of after-you to-descendant-of-you

בָנֶיךָ הַנּוֹלָדִים לְךָ בְּאֶרֶץ מִצְרַיִם עַד־ בֹּאִי
to-come-me before Egypt in-land-of to-you the-ones-being-born sons-of-you

אֵלֶיךָ מִצְרַיְמָה לִי־ הֵם אֶפְרַיִם וּמְנַשֶּׁה כִּרְאוּבֵן וְשִׁמְעוֹן
and-Simeon as-Reuben and-Manasseh Ephraim they to-me to-Egypt to-you

יִהְיוּ־ לִי׃ וּמוֹלַדְתְּךָ אֲשֶׁר־ הוֹלַדְתָּ אַחֲרֵיהֶם לְךָ
to-you after-them you-father whom but-children-of-you (6) to-me they-are

יִהְיוּ עַל שֵׁם אֲחֵיהֶם יִקָּרְאוּ
they-will-be-reckoned brothers-of-them name-of under they-are

בְּנַחֲלָתָם׃ וַאֲנִי ׀ בְּבֹאִי מִפַּדָּן מֵתָה עָלַי
by-me she-died from-Paddan as-to-return-me now-I (7) in-inheritance-of-them

רָחֵל בְּאֶרֶץ כְּנַעַן בַּדֶּרֶךְ בְּעוֹד כִּבְרַת־ אֶרֶץ לָבֹא
to-go land distance-of while-still on-the-way Canaan in-land-of Rachel

אֶפְרָתָה וָאֶקְבְּרֶהָ שָּׁם בְּדֶרֶךְ אֶפְרָת הִוא בֵּית לָחֶם׃
Lehem Beth that Ephrath by-road-of there so-I-buried-her to-Ephrath

וַיַּרְא יִשְׂרָאֵל אֶת־ בְּנֵי יוֹסֵף וַיֹּאמֶר מִי־ אֵלֶּה׃
these who? then-he-asked Joseph sons-of *** Israel when-he-saw (8)

וַיֹּאמֶר יוֹסֵף אֶל־ אָבִיו בָּנַי הֵם אֲשֶׁר־ נָתַן־ לִי אֱלֹהִים
God to-me he-gave whom they sons-of-me father-of-him to Joseph and-he-said (9)

בָּזֶה וַיֹּאמַר קָחֶם־ נָא אֵלַי וַאֲבָרְכֵם׃ וְעֵינֵי
now-eyes-of (10) so-I-may-bless-them to-me now! bring-them! then-he-said at-here

יִשְׂרָאֵל כָּבְדוּ מִזֹּקֶן לֹא יוּכַל לִרְאוֹת וַיַּגֵּשׁ אֹתָם
them so-he-brought to-see he-could not from-age they-were-failing Israel

אֵלָיו וַיִּשַּׁק לָהֶם וַיְחַבֵּק לָהֶם׃ וַיֹּאמֶר
and-he-said (11) on-them and-he-embraced on-them and-he-kissed to-him

יִשְׂרָאֵל אֶל־יוֹסֵף רְאֹה פָנֶיךָ לֹא פִלָּלְתִּי וְהִנֵּה הֶרְאָה אֹתִי
me he-let-see but-see! I-expected not face-of-you to-see Joseph to Israel

אֱלֹהִים גַּם אֶת־ זַרְעֶךָ׃ וַיּוֹצֵא יוֹסֵף אֹתָם מֵעִם
from-on them Joseph then-he-removed (12) children-of-you *** also God

strength and sat up on the bed.

3 Jacob said to Joseph, "God Almighty[h] appeared to me at Luz in the land of Canaan, and there he blessed me 4 and said to me, 'I am going to make you fruitful and will increase your numbers. I will make you a community of peoples, and I will give this land as an everlasting possession to your descendants after you.'

5 "Now then, your two sons born to you in Egypt before I came to you here will be reckoned as mine; Ephraim and Manasseh will be mine, just as Reuben and Simeon are mine. 6 Any children born to you after them will be yours; in the territory they inherit they will be reckoned under the names of their brothers. 7 As I was returning from Paddan,[i] to my sorrow Rachel died in the land of Canaan while we were still on the way, a little distance from Ephrath. So I buried her there beside the road to Ephrath" (that is, Bethlehem).

8 When Israel saw the sons of Joseph, he asked, "Who are these?"

9 "They are the sons God has given me here," Joseph said to his father.

Then Israel said, "Bring them to me so I may bless them."

10 Now Israel's eyes were failing because of old age, and he could hardly see. So Joseph brought his sons close to him, and his father kissed them and embraced them.

11 Israel said to Joseph, "I never expected to see your face again, and now God has allowed me to see your children too."

12 Then Joseph removed

[h]3 Hebrew *El-Shaddai*
[i]7 That is, Northwest Mesopotamia

בִּרְכָּיו וַיִּשְׁתַּחוּ לְאַפָּיו אָֽרְצָה׃ וַיִּקַּח יוֹסֵף
Joseph and-he-took (13) to-ground with-face-of-him and-he-bowed knees-of-him

אֶת־שְׁנֵיהֶם אֶת־אֶפְרַיִם בִּימִינוֹ מִשְּׂמֹאל יִשְׂרָאֵל וְאֶת־
and Israel toward-left-of on-right-of-him Ephraim *** both-of-them ***

מְנַשֶּׁה בִשְׂמֹאלוֹ מִימִין יִשְׂרָאֵל וַיַּגֵּשׁ אֵלָיו׃
to-him and-he-brought Israel toward-right-of on-left-of-him Manasseh

וַיִּשְׁלַח יִשְׂרָאֵל אֶת־יְמִינוֹ וַיָּשֶׁת עַל־רֹאשׁ
head-of on and-he-put right-hand-of-him *** Israel but-he-reached (14)

אֶפְרַיִם וְהוּא הַצָּעִיר וְאֶת־שְׂמֹאלוֹ עַל־רֹאשׁ מְנַשֶּׁה
Manasseh head-of on left-hand-of-him and the-younger though-he Ephraim

שִׂכֵּל אֶת־יָדָיו כִּי מְנַשֶּׁה הַבְּכוֹר׃ וַיְבָרֶךְ
and-he-blessed (15) the-firstborn Manasseh though arms-of-him *** he-crossed

אֶת־יוֹסֵף וַיֹּאמַר הָאֱלֹהִים אֲשֶׁר הִתְהַלְּכוּ אֲבֹתַי לְפָנָיו
before-him fathers-of-me they-walked whom the-God and-he-said Joseph ***

אַבְרָהָם וְיִצְחָק הָאֱלֹהִים הָרֹעֶה אֹתִי מֵעוֹדִי עַד־הַיּוֹם
the-day to all-life-of-me me the-one-shepherding the-God and-Isaac Abraham

הַזֶּה׃ הַמַּלְאָךְ הַגֹּאֵל אֹתִי מִכָּל־רָע יְבָרֵךְ
may-he-bless harm from-all-of me the-one-delivering the-angel (16) the-this

אֶת־הַנְּעָרִים וְיִקָּרֵא בָהֶם שְׁמִי וְשֵׁם אֲבֹתַי
fathers-of-me and-name-of and-name-of-me on-them and-may-he-be-called the-boys ***

אַבְרָהָם וְיִצְחָק וְיִדְגּוּ לָרֹב בְּקֶרֶב הָאָרֶץ׃
the-earth in-midst-of greatly and-may-they-increase and-Isaac Abraham

וַיַּרְא יוֹסֵף כִּי־יָשִׁית אָבִיו יַד־יְמִינוֹ
right-of-him hand-of father-of-him he-placed that Joseph when-he-saw (17)

עַל־רֹאשׁ אֶפְרַיִם וַיֵּרַע בְּעֵינָיו וַיִּתְמֹךְ
then-he-took-hold in-eyes-of-him and-he-was-displeasing Ephraim head-of on

יַד־אָבִיו לְהָסִיר אֹתָהּ מֵעַל רֹאשׁ־אֶפְרַיִם עַל־רֹאשׁ מְנַשֶּׁה׃
Manasseh head-of to Ephraim head-of from-on her to-move father-of-him hand-of

וַיֹּאמֶר יוֹסֵף אֶל־אָבִיו לֹא־כֵן אָבִי כִּי־זֶה
this for father-of-me so not father-of-him to Joseph and-he-said (18)

הַבְּכֹר שִׂים יְמִינְךָ עַל־רֹאשׁוֹ׃ וַיְמָאֵן
but-he-refused (19) head-of-him on right-hand-of-you put! the-firstborn

אָבִיו וַיֹּאמֶר יָדַעְתִּי בְנִי יָדַעְתִּי גַּם־הוּא יִהְיֶה־
he-will-become he indeed I-know son-of-me I-know and-he-said father-of-him

לְעָם וְגַם־הוּא יִגְדָּל וְאוּלָם אָחִיו הַקָּטֹן
the-young brother-of-him nevertheless he-will-be-great he and-also as-people

יִגְדַּל מִמֶּנּוּ וְזַרְעוֹ יִהְיֶה מְלֹא־
group-of he-will-become and-descendant-of-him than-he he-will-be-greater

them from Israel's knees and bowed down with his face to the ground. 13And Joseph took both of them, Ephraim on his right toward Israel's left hand and Manasseh on his left toward Israel's right hand, and brought them close to him. 14But Israel reached out his right hand and put it on Ephraim's head, though he was the younger, and crossing his arms, he put his left hand on Manasseh's head, even though Manasseh was the firstborn.

15Then he blessed Joseph and said,

"May the God before whom my fathers
Abraham and Isaac walked,
the God who has been my Shepherd
all my life to this day,
16the Angel who has delivered me from all harm
—may he bless these boys.
May they be called by my name
and the names of my fathers Abraham and Isaac,
and may they increase greatly
upon the earth."

17When Joseph saw his father placing his right hand on Ephraim's head he was displeased; so he took hold of his father's hand to move it from Ephraim's head to Manasseh's head. 18Joseph said to him, "No, my father, this one is the firstborn; put your right hand on his head."

19But his father refused and said, "I know, my son, I know. He too will become a people, and he too will become great. Nevertheless, his younger brother will be greater than he, and his descendants will become a group of nations."

הַגּוֹיִם׃ (20) וַיְבָרְכֵם בַּיּוֹם הַהוּא לֵאמוֹר בְּךָ
by-you to-say the-that on-the-day and-he-blessed-them (20) the-nations

יְבָרֵךְ יִשְׂרָאֵל לֵאמֹר יְשִׂמְךָ אֱלֹהִים כְּאֶפְרַיִם וְכִמְנַשֶּׁה
and-like-Manasseh like-Ephraim God may-he-make-you to-say Israel he-will-bless

וַיָּשֶׂם אֶת־אֶפְרַיִם לִפְנֵי מְנַשֶּׁה׃ (21) וַיֹּאמֶר יִשְׂרָאֵל אֶל־יוֹסֵף
Joseph to Israel then-he-said (21) Manasseh ahead-of Ephraim *** so-he-put

הִנֵּה אָנֹכִי מֵת וְהָיָה אֱלֹהִים עִמָּכֶם וְהֵשִׁיב אֶתְכֶם אֶל־אֶרֶץ
land-of to you and-he-will-take-back with-you God but-he-will-be dying I see!

אֲבֹתֵיכֶם׃ (22) וַאֲנִי נָתַתִּי לְךָ שְׁכֶם אַחַד עַל־אַחֶיךָ
brothers-of-you over one portion to-you I-give and-I (22) fathers-of-you

אֲשֶׁר לָקַחְתִּי מִיַּד הָאֱמֹרִי בְּחַרְבִּי וּבְקַשְׁתִּי׃
and-with-bow-of-me with-sword-of-me the-Amorite from-hand-of I-took which

(49:1) וַיִּקְרָא יַעֲקֹב אֶל־בָּנָיו וַיֹּאמֶר הֵאָסְפוּ וְאַגִּידָה
so-I-can-tell gather! and-he-said sons-of-him for Jacob then-he-called (49:1)

לָכֶם אֵת אֲשֶׁר־יִקְרָא אֶתְכֶם בְּאַחֲרִית הַיָּמִים׃ (2) הִקָּבְצוּ
assemble! (2) the-days in-coming-of to-you he-will-happen what *** to-you

וְשִׁמְעוּ בְּנֵי יַעֲקֹב וְשִׁמְעוּ אֶל־יִשְׂרָאֵל אֲבִיכֶם׃ (3) רְאוּבֵן
Reuben (3) father-of-you Israel to and-listen! Jacob sons-of and-listen!

בְּכֹרִי אַתָּה כֹּחִי וְרֵאשִׁית אוֹנִי יֶתֶר
excelling-of strength-of-me and-first-of might-of-me you firstborn-of-me

שְׂאֵת וְיֶתֶר עָז׃ (4) פַּחַז כַּמַּיִם אַל־תּוֹתַר
you-will-excel not as-the-waters turbulent (4) power and-excelling-of honor

כִּי עָלִיתָ מִשְׁכְּבֵי אָבִיךָ אָז חִלַּלְתָּ יְצוּעִי עָלָה׃
he-went-up couch-of-me you-defiled then father-of-you beds-of you-went-up for

(5) שִׁמְעוֹן וְלֵוִי אַחִים כְּלֵי חָמָס מְכֵרֹתֵיהֶם׃
swords-of-them violence weapons-of brothers and-Levi Simeon (5)

(6) בְּסֹדָם אַל־תָּבֹא נַפְשִׁי בִּקְהָלָם אַל־
not to-assembly-of-them self-of-me let-her-enter not in-council-of-them (6)

תֵּחַד כְּבֹדִי כִּי בְאַפָּם הָרְגוּ אִישׁ
man they-killed in-anger-of-them for glory-of-me let-her-join

וּבִרְצֹנָם עִקְּרוּ־שׁוֹר׃ (7) אָרוּר אַפָּם כִּי
so anger-of-them being-cursed (7) ox they-hamstrung and-in-pleasure-of-them

עָז וְעֶבְרָתָם כִּי קָשָׁתָה אֲחַלְּקֵם בְּיַעֲקֹב
in-Jacob I-will-scatter-them cruel so and-fury-of-them fierce

וַאֲפִיצֵם בְּיִשְׂרָאֵל׃ (8) יְהוּדָה אַתָּה יוֹדוּךָ
they-will-praise-you you Judah (8) in-Israel and-I-will-disperse-them

אַחֶיךָ יָדְךָ בְּעֹרֶף אֹיְבֶיךָ יִשְׁתַּחֲווּ לְךָ
to-you they-will-bow ones-opposing-you on-neck-of hand-of-you brothers-of-you

---

20 He blessed them that day and said,

"In your[j] name will Israel
pronounce this blessing:
'May God make you like
Ephraim and Manasseh.' "

So he put Ephraim ahead of Manasseh.
21 Then Israel said to Joseph, "I am about to die, but God will be with you[k] and take you[k] back to the land of your[k] fathers. 22 And to you, as one who is over your brothers, I give the ridge of land[l] I took from the Amorites with my sword and my bow."

Jacob Blesses His Sons

49 Then Jacob called for his sons and said: "Gather around so I can tell you what will happen to you in days to come.

2 "Assemble and listen, sons of Jacob;
listen to your father Israel.

3 "Reuben, you are my firstborn,
my might, the first sign of my strength,
excelling in honor, excelling in power.
4 Turbulent as the waters, you will no longer excel,
for you went up onto your father's bed,
onto my couch and defiled it.

5 "Simeon and Levi are brothers—
their swords[m] are weapons of violence.
6 Let me not enter their council,
let me not join their assembly,
for they have killed men in their anger
and hamstrung oxen as they pleased.
7 Cursed be their anger, so fierce,
and their fury, so cruel!
I will scatter them in Jacob
and disperse them in Israel.

8 "Judah,[n] your brothers will praise you;
your hand will be on the neck of your enemies;
your father's sons will bow down to you.

j20 The Hebrew is singular.
k21 The Hebrew is plural.
l22 Or *And to you I give one portion more than to your brothers—the portion*
m5 The meaning of the Hebrew for this word is uncertain.
n8 *Judah* sounds like and may be derived from the Hebrew for *praise*.

*8 Most mss have no *dagesh* in the first *vav* (יו־).

בְּנֵי אָבִיךָ׃ (9) גּוּר אַרְיֵה יְהוּדָה מִטֶּרֶף בְּנִי עָלִיתָ
you-return son-of-me from-prey Judah lion cub-of (9) father-of-you sons-of

כָּרַע רָבַץ כְּאַרְיֵה וּכְלָבִיא מִי יְקִימֶנּוּ׃ (10) לֹא־
not (10) he-rouses-him who? and-like-lioness like-lion he-lies he-crouches

יָסוּר שֵׁבֶט מִיהוּדָה וּמְחֹקֵק מִבֵּין רַגְלָיו
feet-of-him from-between nor-ruling-staff from-Judah scepter he-will-depart

עַד כִּי־ יָבֹא שִׁילֹּה וְלוֹ יִקְּהַת עַמִּים׃
peoples obedience-of and-to-him whose-he he-comes when until

(11) אֹסְרִי לַגֶּפֶן עִירֹה וְלַשֹּׂרֵקָה בְּנִי
colt-of and-to-choicest-branch donkey-of-him to-the-vine tethering-of (11)

אֲתֹנוֹ כִּבֵּס בַּיַּיִן לְבֻשׁוֹ וּבְדַם־ עֲנָבִים
grapes and-in-blood-of garment-of-him in-the-wine he-will-wash donkey-of-him

סוּתֹה׃ (12) חַכְלִילִי עֵינַיִם מִיָּיִן וּלְבֶן־ שִׁנַּיִם מֵחָלָב׃ (13) זְבוּלֻן
Zebulun (13) than-milk teeth and-whiter than-wine eyes darker (12) robe-of-him

לְחוֹף יַמִּים יִשְׁכֹּן וְהוּא לְחוֹף אֳנִיֹּת וְיַרְכָתוֹ
and-border-of-him ships as-haven-of and-he he-will-live seas by-shore-of

עַל־ צִידֹן׃ (14) יִשָּׂשכָר חֲמֹר גָּרֶם רֹבֵץ בֵּין הַמִּשְׁפְּתָיִם׃
the-two-saddlebags between lying-down strong donkey Issachar (14) Sidon up-to

(15) וַיַּרְא מְנֻחָה כִּי טוֹב וְאֶת־ הָאָרֶץ כִּי נָעֵמָה
she-is-pleasant how the-land and good how resting-place when-he-sees (15)

וַיֵּט שִׁכְמוֹ לִסְבֹּל וַיְהִי לְמַס־
to-forced-labor and-he-will-be to-bear shoulder-of-him then-he-will-bend

עֹבֵד׃ (16) דָּן יָדִין עַמּוֹ כְּאַחַד שִׁבְטֵי
tribes-of as-one-of people-of-him he-will-provide-justice Dan (16) submitting

יִשְׂרָאֵל׃ (17) יְהִי־ דָן נָחָשׁ עֲלֵי־ דֶרֶךְ שְׁפִיפֹן עֲלֵי־ אֹרַח הַנֹּשֵׁךְ
the-one-biting path along viper road beside serpent Dan he-will-be (17) Israel

עִקְּבֵי־ סוּס וַיִּפֹּל רֹכְבוֹ אָחוֹר׃ (18) לִישׁוּעָתְךָ
for-deliverance-of-you (18) backward one-riding-him so-he-tumbles horse heels-of

קִוִּיתִי יְהוָה׃ (19) גָּד גְּדוּד יְגוּדֶנּוּ וְהוּא יָגֻד עָקֵב׃
heel he-will-attack but-he he-will-attach-him raider Gad (19) Yahweh I-look

(20) מֵאָשֵׁר שְׁמֵנָה לַחְמוֹ וְהוּא יִתֵּן מַעֲדַנֵּי־ מֶלֶךְ׃
king delicacies-of he-will-provide and-he food-of-him rich for-Asher (20)

(21) נַפְתָּלִי אַיָּלָה שְׁלֻחָה הַנֹּתֵן אִמְרֵי־ שָׁפֶר׃ (22) בֵּן
son-of (22) beauty fawns-of the-one-bearing being-set-free doe Naphtali (21)

פֹּרָת יוֹסֵף בֵּן פֹּרָת עֲלֵי־ עָיִן בָּנוֹת צָעֲדָה
climbing branches spring near being-fruitful son-of Joseph being-fruitful

עֲלֵי־ שׁוּר׃ (23) וַיְמָרֲרֻהוּ וָרֹבּוּ וַיִּשְׂטְמֻהוּ
and-they-harassed-him and-they-shot and-they-attached-him (23) wall over

9You are a lion's cub, O Judah;
you return from the prey, my son.
Like a lion he crouches and lies down,
like a lioness—who dares to rouse him?
10The scepter will not depart from Judah,
nor the ruler's staff from between his feet,
until he comes to whom it belongs[o]
and the obedience of the nations is his.
11He will tether his donkey to a vine,
his colt to the choicest branch;
he will wash his garments in wine,
his robes in the blood of grapes.
12His eyes will be darker than wine,
his teeth whiter than milk.[p]

13"Zebulun will live by the seashore
and become a haven for ships;
his border will extend toward Sidon.

14"Issachar is a rawboned[q] donkey
lying down between two saddlebags.[r]
15When he sees how good is his resting place
and how pleasant is his land,
he will bend his shoulder to the burden
and submit to forced labor.

16"Dan[s] will provide justice for his people
as one of the tribes of Israel.
17Dan will be a serpent by the roadside,
a viper along the path,
that bites the horse's heels
so that its rider tumbles backward.

18"I look for your deliverance, O LORD.

19"Gad[t] will be attacked by a band of raiders,
but he will attack them at their heels.

20"Asher's food will be rich;
he will provide delicacies fit for a king.

21"Naphtali is a doe set free
that bears beautiful fawns.[u]

[o]10 Or *until Shiloh comes;* or *until he comes to whom tribute belongs*
[p]12 Or *will be dull from wine, / his teeth white from milk* [q]14 Or *strong* [r]14 Or *campfires*
[s]16 *Dan* here means *he provides justice.*
[t]19 *Gad* can mean *attack* and *band of raiders.*
[u]21 Or *free; / he utters beautiful words*

°10 שילו, °11a עירו, °11b סותו ק

בַּעֲלֵ֥י חִצִּֽים׃ וַתֵּ֤שֶׁב בְּאֵיתָן֙ קַשְׁתּ֔וֹ וַיָּפֹ֖זּוּ
and-they-were-limber bow-of-him steady but-she-remained (24) arrows masters-of

זְרֹעֵ֣י יָדָ֑יו מִידֵי֙ אֲבִ֣יר יַעֲקֹ֔ב מִשָּׁ֥ם
because-of Jacob Mighty-One-of because-of-hands-of arms-of-him strong-ones-of

רֹעֶ֖ה אֶ֥בֶן יִשְׂרָאֵֽל׃ מֵאֵ֨ל אָבִ֜יךָ
father-of-you because-of-God-of (25) Israel Rock-of Shepherding-One

וְיַעְזְרֶ֗ךָּ וְאֵ֤ת שַׁדַּי֙ וִיבָ֣רְכֶ֔ךָּ בִּרְכֹ֤ת שָׁמַ֙יִם֙ מֵעָ֔ל
above heavens blessings-of for-he-blesses-you Almighty and for-he-helps-you

בִּרְכֹ֥ת תְּה֖וֹם רֹבֶ֣צֶת תָּ֑חַת בִּרְכֹ֥ת שָׁדַ֖יִם וָרָֽחַם׃ בִּרְכֹ֣ת
blessings-of (26) and-womb breasts blessings-of below lying deep blessings-of

אָבִ֗יךָ גָּֽבְרוּ֙ עַל־ בִּרְכֹ֣ת הוֹרַ֔י עַד־
ancient mountains-of blessing-of than they-are-greater father-of-you

תַּאֲוַ֖ת גִּבְעֹ֣ת עוֹלָ֑ם תִּֽהְיֶ֙יןָ֙ לְרֹ֣אשׁ יוֹסֵ֔ף וּלְקָדְקֹ֖ד
and-on-brow-of Joseph on-head-of let-them-rest age-old hills-of bounty-of

נְזִ֥יר אֶחָֽיו׃ בִּנְיָמִין֙ זְאֵ֣ב יִטְרָ֔ף בַּבֹּ֖קֶר
in-the-morning he-is-ravenous wolf Benjamin (27) brothers-of-him prince-of

יֹ֣אכַל עַ֑ד וְלָעֶ֖רֶב יְחַלֵּ֥ק שָׁלָֽל׃ כָּל־ אֵ֛לֶּה
these all-of (28) plunder he-divides and-in-the-evening prey he-devours

שִׁבְטֵ֥י יִשְׂרָאֵ֖ל שְׁנֵ֣ים עָשָׂ֑ר וְ֠זֹאת אֲשֶׁר־ דִּבֶּ֨ר לָהֶ֤ם אֲבִיהֶם֙
father-of-them to-them he-said what and-this ten two Israel tribes-of

וַיְבָ֣רֶךְ אוֹתָ֔ם אִ֛ישׁ אֲשֶׁ֥ר כְּבִרְכָת֖וֹ בֵּרַ֥ךְ אֹתָֽם׃
them he-blessed blessing-of-him whose each them when-he-blessed

וַיְצַ֣ו אוֹתָ֗ם וַיֹּ֤אמֶר אֲלֵהֶם֙ אֲנִי֙ נֶאֱסָ֣ף אֶל־ עַמִּ֔י
people-of-me to being-gathered I to-them and-he-said them and-he-instructed (29)

קִבְר֥וּ אֹתִ֖י אֶל־ אֲבֹתָ֑י אֶל־הַ֨מְּעָרָ֔ה אֲשֶׁ֥ר בִּשְׂדֵ֖ה עֶפְר֥וֹן הַחִתִּֽי׃
the-Hittite Ephron in-field-of that the-cave in fathers-of-me with me bury!

בַּמְּעָרָ֞ה אֲשֶׁ֨ר בִּשְׂדֵ֧ה הַמַּכְפֵּלָ֛ה אֲשֶׁר־ עַל־ פְּנֵֽי־ מַמְרֵ֖א
Mamre area-of near that the-Machpelah in-field-of which in-the-cave (30)

בְּאֶ֣רֶץ כְּנָ֑עַן אֲשֶׁ֨ר קָנָ֜ה אַבְרָהָ֣ם אֶת־ הַשָּׂדֶ֗ה מֵאֵ֛ת עֶפְרֹ֥ן
Ephron from the-field *** Abraham he-bought which Canaan in-land-of

הַחִתִּ֖י לַאֲחֻזַּת־ קָֽבֶר׃ שָׁ֣מָּה קָֽבְר֞וּ אֶת־ אַבְרָהָ֗ם וְאֵת֙
and Abraham *** they-buried at-there (31) burial as-place-of the-Hittite

שָׂרָ֣ה אִשְׁתּ֔וֹ שָׁ֚מָּה קָבְר֣וּ אֶת־ יִצְחָ֔ק וְאֵ֖ת רִבְקָ֣ה אִשְׁתּ֑וֹ
wife-of-him Rebekah and Isaac *** they-buried at-there wife-of-him Sarah

וְשָׁ֥מָּה קָבַ֖רְתִּי אֶת־ לֵאָֽה׃ מִקְנֵ֧ה הַשָּׂדֶ֛ה וְהַמְּעָרָ֥ה אֲשֶׁר־
that and-the-cave the-field purchase-of (32) Leah *** I-buried and-at-there

בּ֖וֹ מֵאֵ֥ת בְּנֵי־ חֵֽת׃ וַיְכַ֤ל יַעֲקֹב֙ לְצַוֹּ֣ת אֶת־
*** to-instruct Jacob when-he-finished (33) Heth sons-of from in-him

22"Joseph is a fruitful vine,
a fruitful vine near a spring,
whose branches climb over a wall.[w]
23With bitterness archers attacked him;
they shot at him with hostility.
24But his bow remained steady,
his strong arms stayed[x] limber,
because of the hand of the Mighty One of Jacob,
because of the Shepherd, the Rock of Israel,
25because of your father's God, who helps you,
because of the Almighty,[y] who blesses you
with blessings of the heavens above,
blessings of the deep that lies below,
blessings of the breast and womb.
26Your father's blessings are greater
than the blessings of the ancient mountains,
than[z] the bounty of the age-old hills.
Let all these rest on the head of Joseph,
on the brow of the prince among[a] his brothers.

27"Benjamin is a ravenous wolf;
in the morning he devours the prey,
in the evening he divides the plunder."

28All these are the twelve
tribes of Israel, and this is
what their father said to them
when he blessed them, giving
each the blessing appropriate
to him.

The Death of Jacob

29Then he gave them these
instructions: "I am about to be
gathered to my people. Bury
me with my fathers in the
cave in the field of Ephron the
Hittite, 30the cave in the field
of Machpelah, near Mamre in
Canaan, which Abraham
bought as a burial place from
Ephron the Hittite, along with
the field. 31There Abraham
and his wife Sarah were buried, there Isaac and his wife
Rebekah were buried, and
there I buried Leah. 32The field
and the cave in it were bought
from the Hittites.[b]"
33When Jacob had finished
giving instructions to his

[w]22 *Joseph is a wild colt, / a wild colt near a spring, / a wild donkey on a terraced hill*
[x]23,24 Or *archers will attack ... will shoot ... will remain ... will stay* [y]25 Hebrew *Shaddai*
[z]26 Or *of my progenitors, / as great as*
[a]26 Or *the one separated from*
[b]32 Or *the sons of Heth*

בָּנָיו וַיֶּאֱסֹף רַגְלָיו אֶל־ הַמִּטָּה וַיִּגְוַע
and-he-breathed-last the-bed into feet-of-him then-he-drew sons-of-him

וַיֵּאָסֶף אֶל־ עַמָּיו׃ וַיִּפֹּל יוֹסֵף עַל־ פְּנֵי
face-of on Joseph and-he-fell (50:1) people-of-him to and-he-was-gathered

אָבִיו וַיֵּבְךְּ עָלָיו וַיִּשַּׁק־ לוֹ׃ וַיְצַו
then-he-directed (2) on-him and-he-kissed over-him and-he-wept father-of-him

יוֹסֵף אֶת־ עֲבָדָיו אֶת־ הָרֹפְאִים לַחֲנֹט אֶת־ אָבִיו
father-of-him *** to-embalm the-ones-healing *** servants-of-him *** Joseph

וַיַּחַנְטוּ הָרֹפְאִים אֶת־ יִשְׂרָאֵל׃ וַיִּמְלְאוּ־ לוֹ אַרְבָּעִים
forty for-him and-they-took (3) Israel *** the-ones-healing so-they-embalmed

יוֹם כִּי כֵּן יִמְלְאוּ יְמֵי הַחֲנֻטִים וַיִּבְכּוּ אֹתוֹ
for-him and-they-mourned the-embalmings days-of they-required that for day

מִצְרַיִם שִׁבְעִים יוֹם׃ וַיַּעַבְרוּ יְמֵי בְכִיתוֹ וַיְדַבֵּר
then-he-said mourning-of-him days-of when-they-passed (4) day seventy Egyptians

יוֹסֵף אֶל־ בֵּית פַּרְעֹה לֵאמֹר אִם־ נָא מָצָאתִי חֵן בְּעֵינֵיכֶם
in-eyes-of-you favor I-found now! if to-say Pharaoh court-of to Joseph

דַּבְּרוּ־נָא בְּאָזְנֵי פַרְעֹה לֵאמֹר׃ אָבִי הִשְׁבִּיעַנִי
he-made-swear-me father-of-me (5) to-say Pharaoh in-ears-of now! speak!

לֵאמֹר הִנֵּה אָנֹכִי מֵת בְּקִבְרִי אֲשֶׁר כָּרִיתִי לִי בְּאֶרֶץ כְּנַעַן
Canaan in-land-of for-myself I-dug that in-tomb-of-me dying I see! to-say

שָׁמָּה תִּקְבְּרֵנִי וְעַתָּה אֶעֱלֶה־ נָּא וְאֶקְבְּרָה אֶת־ אָבִי
father-of-me *** and-let-me-bury now! let-me-go-up so-now you-bury-me at-there

וְאָשׁוּבָה׃ וַיֹּאמֶר פַּרְעֹה עֲלֵה וּקְבֹר אֶת־ אָבִיךָ
father-of-you *** and-bury! go-up! Pharaoh and-he-said (6) then-I-will-return

כַּאֲשֶׁר הִשְׁבִּיעֶךָ׃ וַיַּעַל יוֹסֵף לִקְבֹּר אֶת־ אָבִיו
father-of-him *** to-bury Joseph so-he-went-up (7) he-made-swear-you just-as

וַיַּעֲלוּ אִתּוֹ כָּל־ עַבְדֵי פַרְעֹה זִקְנֵי
dignitaries-of Pharaoh officials-of all-of with-him and-they-went-up

בֵיתוֹ וְכֹל זִקְנֵי אֶרֶץ־ מִצְרָיִם׃ וְכֹל בֵּית
house-of and-all-of (8) Egypt land-of dignitaries-of and-all-of court-of-him

יוֹסֵף וְאֶחָיו וּבֵית אָבִיו רַק טַפָּם
children-of-them only father-of-him and-house-of and-brothers-of-him Joseph

וְצֹאנָם וּבְקָרָם עָזְבוּ בְּאֶרֶץ גֹּשֶׁן׃
Goshen in-region-of they-left and-herd-of-them and-flock-of-them

וַיַּעַל עִמּוֹ גַּם־ רֶכֶב גַּם־ פָּרָשִׁים וַיְהִי הַמַּחֲנֶה
the-company so-he-was horsemen also chariot also with-him and-he-went-up (9)

כָּבֵד מְאֹד׃ וַיָּבֹאוּ עַד־ גֹּרֶן הָאָטָד אֲשֶׁר בְּעֵבֶר
near-to that the-Atad threshing-floor-of to when-they-came (10) very large

sons, he drew his feet up into
the bed, breathed his last and
was gathered to his people.

50 Joseph threw himself
upon his father and
wept over him and kissed
him. [2]Then Joseph directed the
physicians in his service to
embalm his father Israel. So
the physicians embalmed
him, [3]taking a full forty days,
for that was the time required
for embalming. And the Egyptians mourned for him seventy days.
[4]When the days of mourning had passed, Joseph said to
Pharaoh's court, "If I have
found favor in your eyes,
speak to Pharaoh for me. Tell
him, [5]'My father made me
swear an oath and said, "I am
about to die; bury me in the
tomb I dug for myself in the
land of Canaan." Now let me
go up and bury my father;
then I will return.' "
[6]Pharaoh said, "Go up and
bury your father, as he made
you swear to do."
[7]So Joseph went up to bury
his father. All Pharaoh's
officials accompanied him—
the dignitaries of his court and
all the dignitaries of Egypt—
[8]besides all the members of Joseph's household and his
brothers and those belonging
to his father's household.
Only their children and their
flocks and herds were left in
Goshen. [9]Chariots and horsemen[d] also went up with him.
It was a very large company.
[10]When they reached the
threshing floor of Atad, near

[d]9 Or *charioteers*

הַיַּרְדֵּן וַיִּסְפְּדוּ־ שָׁם מִסְפֵּד גָּדוֹל וְכָבֵד מְאֹד
very and-bitter loud with-lamentation there then-they-lamented the-Jordan

וַיַּעַשׂ לְאָבִיו אֵבֶל שִׁבְעַת יָמִים׃ וַיַּרְא
when-they-saw (11) days seven-of mourning for-father-of-him and-he-observed

יוֹשֵׁב הָאָרֶץ הַכְּנַעֲנִי אֶת־ הָאֵבֶל בְּגֹרֶן
at-threshing-floor-of the-mourning *** the-Canaanite the-land one-living-of

הָאָטָד וַיֹּאמְרוּ אֵבֶל־ כָּבֵד זֶה לְמִצְרָיִם עַל־ כֵּן קָרָא
he-called this for by-Egyptians this solemn mourning then-they-said the-Atad

שְׁמָהּ אָבֵל מִצְרַיִם אֲשֶׁר בְּעֵבֶר הַיַּרְדֵּן׃ וַיַּעֲשׂוּ בָנָיו
sons-of-him so-they-did (12) the-Jordan near-to that Mizraim Abel name-of-her

לוֹ כֵּן כַּאֲשֶׁר צִוָּם׃ וַיִּשְׂאוּ אֹתוֹ בָנָיו
sons-of-him him and-they-carried (13) he-commanded-them just-as this for-him

אַרְצָה כְּנַעַן וַיִּקְבְּרוּ אֹתוֹ בִּמְעָרַת שְׂדֵה הַמַּכְפֵּלָה אֲשֶׁר
that the-Machpelah field-of in-cave-of him and-they-buried Canaan to-land-of

קָנָה אַבְרָהָם אֶת־ הַשָּׂדֶה לַאֲחֻזַּת־ קֶבֶר מֵאֵת עֶפְרֹן הַחִתִּי
the-Hittite Ephron from burial as-place-of the-field *** Abraham he-bought

עַל־ פְּנֵי מַמְרֵא׃ וַיָּשָׁב יוֹסֵף מִצְרַיְמָה הוּא וְאֶחָיו
and-brothers-of-him he to-Egypt Joseph then-he-returned (14) Mamre area-of near

וְכָל־ הָעֹלִים אִתּוֹ לִקְבֹּר אֶת־ אָבִיו אַחֲרֵי
after father-of-him *** to-bury with-him the-ones-going and-all-of

קָבְרוֹ אֶת־ אָבִיו׃ וַיִּרְאוּ אֲחֵי־ יוֹסֵף כִּי־
that Joseph brothers-of when-they-saw (15) father-of-him *** to-bury-him

מֵת אֲבִיהֶם וַיֹּאמְרוּ לוּ יִשְׂטְמֵנוּ
he-holds-grudge-against-us what-if then-they-said father-of-them he-was-dead

יוֹסֵף וְהָשֵׁב יָשִׁיב לָנוּ אֵת כָּל־ הָרָעָה אֲשֶׁר גָּמַלְנוּ אֹתוֹ׃
to-him we-did that the-wrong all-of *** to-us he-repays and-to-repay Joseph

וַיְצַוּוּ אֶל־ יוֹסֵף לֵאמֹר אָבִיךָ צִוָּה לִפְנֵי
before he-instructed father-of-you to-say Joseph to so-they-sent-word (16)

מוֹתוֹ לֵאמֹר׃ כֹּה־ תֹאמְרוּ לְיוֹסֵף אָנָּא שָׂא נָא פֶּשַׁע
sin-of now! forgive! please! to-Joseph you-say this (17) to-say to-die-him

אַחֶיךָ וְחַטָּאתָם כִּי־ רָעָה גְמָלוּךָ וְעַתָּה שָׂא
forgive! so-now they-treated-you badly so and-wrong-of-them brothers-of-you

נָא לְפֶשַׁע עַבְדֵי אֱלֹהֵי אָבִיךָ וַיֵּבְךְּ יוֹסֵף
Joseph and-he-wept father-of-you God-of servants-of to-sin-of now!

בְּדַבְּרָם אֵלָיו׃ וַיֵּלְכוּ גַּם־ אֶחָיו
brothers-of-him also then-they-came (18) to-him when-to-speak-them

וַיִּפְּלוּ לְפָנָיו וַיֹּאמְרוּ הִנֶּנּוּ לְךָ לַעֲבָדִים׃
as-slaves to-you see-us! and-they-said before-him and-they-fell

the Jordan, they lamented loudly and bitterly; and there Joseph observed a seven-day period of mourning for his father. [11]When the Canaanites who lived there saw the mourning at the threshing floor of Atad, they said, "The Egyptians are holding a solemn ceremony of mourning." That is why that place near the Jordan is called Abel Mizraim.[c]

[12]So Jacob's sons did as he had commanded them: [13]They carried him to the land of Canaan and buried him in the cave in the field of Machpelah, near Mamre, which Abraham had bought as a burial place from Ephron the Hittite, along with the field. [14]After burying his father, Joseph returned to Egypt, together with his brothers and all the others who had gone with him to bury his father.

Joseph Reassures His Brothers

[15]When Joseph's brothers saw that their father was dead, they said, "What if Joseph holds a grudge against us and pays us back for all the wrongs we did to him?" [16]So they sent word to Joseph, saying, "Your father left these instructions before he died: [17]'This is what you are to say to Joseph: I ask you to forgive your brothers the sins and the wrongs they committed in treating you so badly.' Now please forgive the sins of the servants of the God of your father." When their message came to him, Joseph wept.

[18]His brothers then came and threw themselves down before him. "We are your slaves," they said.

[c]11 *Abel Mizraim* means *mourning of the Egyptians.*

וַיֹּאמֶר אֲלֵהֶם יוֹסֵף אַל־תִּירָאוּ כִּי הֲתַחַת אֱלֹהִים אָנִי׃

I God in-place-of? for you-be-afraid not Joseph to-them but-he-said (19)

וְאַתֶּם חֲשַׁבְתֶּם עָלַי רָעָה אֱלֹהִים חֲשָׁבָהּ לְטֹבָה

for-good he-intended-her God harm against-me you-intended now-you (20)

לְמַעַן עֲשֹׂה כַּיּוֹם הַזֶּה לְהַחֲיֹת עַם־רָב׃

many people to-keep-alive the-this as-the-day to-accomplish in-order

וְעַתָּה אַל־תִּירָאוּ אָנֹכִי אֲכַלְכֵּל אֶתְכֶם וְאֶת־טַפְּכֶם

children-of-you and for-you I-will-provide I you-be-afraid not so-then (21)

וַיְנַחֵם אוֹתָם וַיְדַבֵּר עַל־לִבָּם׃ וַיֵּשֶׁב יוֹסֵף

Joseph so-he-stayed (22) heart-of-them to and-he-spoke them and-he-reassured

בְּמִצְרַיִם הוּא וּבֵית אָבִיו וַיְחִי יוֹסֵף מֵאָה וָעֶשֶׂר

and-ten hundred Joseph and-he-lived father-of-him and-family-of he in-Egypt

שָׁנִים׃ וַיַּרְא יוֹסֵף לְאֶפְרַיִם בְּנֵי שִׁלֵּשִׁים גַּם

also third-generations children-of to-Ephraim Joseph and-he-saw (23) years

בְּנֵי מָכִיר בֶּן־מְנַשֶּׁה יֻלְּדוּ עַל־בִּרְכֵּי יוֹסֵף׃

Joseph knees-of on they-were-born Manasseh son-of Makir children-of

וַיֹּאמֶר יוֹסֵף אֶל־אֶחָיו אָנֹכִי מֵת וֵאלֹהִים פָּקֹד

to-aid but-God dying I brothers-of-him to Joseph then-he-said (24)

יִפְקֹד אֶתְכֶם וְהֶעֱלָה אֶתְכֶם מִן־הָאָרֶץ הַזֹּאת אֶל־הָאָרֶץ

the-land to the-this the-land from you and-he-will-take-up you he-will-aid

אֲשֶׁר נִשְׁבַּע לְאַבְרָהָם לְיִצְחָק וּלְיַעֲקֹב׃ וַיַּשְׁבַּע

and-he-made-swear (25) and-to-Jacob to-Isaac to-Abraham he-promised that

יוֹסֵף אֶת־בְּנֵי יִשְׂרָאֵל לֵאמֹר פָּקֹד יִפְקֹד אֱלֹהִים אֶתְכֶם וְהַעֲלִתֶם

then-you-carry you God he-will-aid to-aid to-say Israel sons-of *** Joseph

אֶת־עַצְמֹתַי מִזֶּה׃ וַיָּמָת יוֹסֵף בֶּן־מֵאָה וָעֶשֶׂר

and-ten hundred son-of Joseph so-he-died (26) from-this bones-of-me ***

שָׁנִים וַיַּחַנְטוּ אֹתוֹ וַיִּישֶׂם בָּאָרוֹן בְּמִצְרָיִם׃

in-Egypt in-the-coffin and-he-was-placed him and-they-embalmed years

19But Joseph said to them,
"Don't be afraid. Am I in the
place of God? 20You intended
to harm me, but God intended
it for good to accomplish what
is now being done, the saving
of many lives. 21So then, don't
be afraid. I will provide for
you and your children." And
he reassured them and spoke
kindly to them.

The Death of Joseph

22Joseph stayed in Egypt,
along with all his father's
family. He lived a hundred
and ten years 23and saw the
third generation of Ephraim's
children. Also the children of
Makir son of Manasseh were
placed at birth on Joseph's
knees.[f]
24Then Joseph said to his
brothers, "I am about to die.
But God will surely come to
your aid and take you up out
of this land to the land he
promised on oath to Abraham,
Isaac and Jacob." 25And Joseph
made the sons of Israel swear
an oath and said, "God will
surely come to your aid, and
then you must carry my bones
up from this place."
26So Joseph died at the age of
a hundred and ten. And after
they embalmed him, he was
placed in a coffin in Egypt.

[f] 23 That is, were counted as his

וְאֵלֶּה שְׁמוֹת בְּנֵי יִשְׂרָאֵל הַבָּאִים מִצְרָיְמָה אֵת
with to-Egypt the-ones-entering Israel sons-of names-of now-these (1:1)

יַעֲקֹב אִישׁ וּבֵיתוֹ בָּאוּ׃ רְאוּבֵן שִׁמְעוֹן לֵוִי וִיהוּדָה׃
and-Judah Levi Simeon Reuben (2) they-came with-family-of-him each Jacob

יִשָּׂשכָר זְבוּלֻן וּבִנְיָמִן׃ דָּן וְנַפְתָּלִי גָּד וְאָשֵׁר׃
and-Asher Gad and-Naphtali Dan (4) and-Benjamin Zebulun Issachar (3)

וַיְהִי כָּל־ נֶפֶשׁ יֹצְאֵי יֶרֶךְ־ יַעֲקֹב שִׁבְעִים נָפֶשׁ
person seventy Jacob body-of ones-coming-out-of person all-of and-he-was (5)

וְיוֹסֵף הָיָה בְמִצְרָיִם׃ וַיָּמָת יוֹסֵף וְכָל־ אֶחָיו
brothers-of-him and-all-of Joseph now-he-died (6) in-Egypt he-was now-Joseph

וְכֹל הַדּוֹר הַהוּא׃ וּבְנֵי יִשְׂרָאֵל פָּרוּ
they-were-fruitful Israel but-sons-of (7) the-that the-generation and-all-of

וַיִּשְׁרְצוּ וַיִּרְבּוּ וַיַּעַצְמוּ בִּמְאֹד מְאֹד
greatly so-greatly and-they-grew and-they-increased and-they-multiplied

וַתִּמָּלֵא הָאָרֶץ אֹתָם׃ וַיָּקָם מֶלֶךְ־ חָדָשׁ
new king then-he-came-to-power (8) with-them the-land that-she-was-filled

עַל־ מִצְרָיִם אֲשֶׁר לֹא־ יָדַע אֶת־ יוֹסֵף׃ וַיֹּאמֶר אֶל־ עַמּוֹ הִנֵּה
see! people-of-him to and-he-said (9) Joseph *** he-knew not who Egypt over

עַם בְּנֵי יִשְׂרָאֵל רַב וְעָצוּם מִמֶּנּוּ׃ הָבָה
come! (10) than-us and-powerful numerous Israel sons-of people-of

נִתְחַכְּמָה לוֹ פֶּן־ יִרְבֶּה וְהָיָה כִּי־
if and-he-will-be he-will-increase or with-him we-must-deal-shrewdly

תִקְרֶאנָה מִלְחָמָה וְנוֹסַף גַּם־ הוּא עַל־ שֹׂנְאֵינוּ
ones-opposing-us with he indeed then-he-will-join war they-break-out

וְנִלְחַם־ בָּנוּ וְעָלָה מִן־ הָאָרֶץ׃
the-country from and-he-will-leave against-us and-he-will-fight

וַיָּשִׂימוּ עָלָיו שָׂרֵי מִסִּים לְמַעַן עַנֹּתוֹ
to-afflict-him in-order slaves masters-of over-him so-they-put (11)

בְּסִבְלֹתָם וַיִּבֶן עָרֵי מִסְכְּנוֹת לְפַרְעֹה אֶת־ פִּתֹם
Pithom *** for-Pharaoh storages cities-of and-he-built with-labors-of-them

וְאֶת־ רַעַמְסֵס׃ וְכַאֲשֶׁר יְעַנּוּ אֹתוֹ כֵּן יִרְבֶּה וְכֵן
and-more he-multiplied more him they-oppressed but-more (12) Rameses and

יִפְרֹץ וַיָּקֻצוּ מִפְּנֵי בְּנֵי יִשְׂרָאֵל׃ וַיַּעֲבִדוּ
so-they-made-work (13) Israel sons-of presence-of so-they-dreaded he-spread

מִצְרַיִם אֶת־ בְּנֵי יִשְׂרָאֵל בְּפָרֶךְ׃ וַיְמָרְרוּ אֶת־
*** and-they-made-bitter (14) ruthlessly Israel sons-of *** Egyptians

חַיֵּיהֶם בַּעֲבֹדָה קָשָׁה בְּחֹמֶר וּבִלְבֵנִים וּבְכָל־ עֲבֹדָה
labor and-with-all-of and-in-bricks in-mortar hard with-labor lives-of-them

The Israelites Oppressed

1 These are the names of the sons of Israel who entered Egypt with Jacob, each with his family: [2]Reuben, Simeon, Levi and Judah; [3]Issachar, Zebulun and Benjamin; [4]Dan and Naphtali; Gad and Asher. [5]The descendants of Jacob numbered seventy[a] in all; Joseph was already in Egypt.

[6]Now Joseph and all his brothers and all that generation died, [7]but the Israelites were fruitful and multiplied greatly and became exceedingly numerous, so that the land was filled with them.

[8]Then a new king, who did not know about Joseph, came to power in Egypt. [9]"Look," he said to his people, "the Israelites have become much too numerous for us. [10]Come, we must deal shrewdly with them or they will become even more numerous and, if war breaks out, will join our enemies, fight against us and leave the country."

[11]So they put slave masters over them to oppress them with forced labor, and they built Pithom and Rameses as store cities for Pharaoh. [12]But the more they were oppressed, the more they multiplied and spread; so the Egyptians came to dread the Israelites [13]and worked them ruthlessly. [14]They made their lives bitter with hard labor in brick and mortar and with all kinds of work in the fields; in all their

[a]5 Masoretic Text (see also Gen. 46:27); Dead Sea Scrolls and Septuagint (see also Acts 7:14) *seventy-five*

בַּשָּׂדֶה אֵת כָּל־ עֲבֹדָתָם אֲשֶׁר־ עָבְדוּ בָהֶם בְּפָרֶךְ׃
ruthlessly with-them they-used that labor-of-them all-of *** in-the-field

וַיֹּאמֶר מֶלֶךְ מִצְרַיִם לַמְיַלְּדֹת הָעִבְרִיֹּת אֲשֶׁר
whose the-Hebrews to-the-being-midwives Egypt king-of then-he-said (15)

שֵׁם הָאַחַת שִׁפְרָה וְשֵׁם הַשֵּׁנִית פּוּעָה׃ וַיֹּאמֶר
and-he-said (16) Puah the-second and-name-of Shiphrah the-first name-of

בְּיַלֶּדְכֶן אֶת־ הָעִבְרִיּוֹת וּרְאִיתֶן עַל־
on and-you-observe the-Hebrew-women *** when-to-help-in-childbirth-you

הָאָבְנָיִם אִם־ בֵּן הוּא וַהֲמִתֶּן אֹתוֹ וְאִם־ בַּת הִיא וָחָיָה׃
then-let-him-live she girl but-if him then-you-kill he boy if the-delivery-stool

וַתִּירֶאןָ הַמְיַלְּדֹת אֶת־ הָאֱלֹהִים וְלֹא עָשׂוּ כַּאֲשֶׁר
as-what they-did and-not the-God *** the-being-midwives but-they-feared (17)

דִּבֶּר אֲלֵיהֶן מֶלֶךְ מִצְרָיִם וַתְּחַיֶּיןָ אֶת־ הַיְלָדִים׃ וַיִּקְרָא
so-he-called (18) the-boys *** but-they-let-live Egypt king-of to-them he-told

מֶלֶךְ־ מִצְרַיִם לַמְיַלְּדֹת וַיֹּאמֶר לָהֶן מַדּוּעַ עֲשִׂיתֶן
you-did why? to-them and-he-asked for-the-being-midwives Egypt king-of

הַדָּבָר הַזֶּה וַתְּחַיֶּיןָ אֶת־ הַיְלָדִים׃ וַתֹּאמַרְןָ
and-they-answered (19) the-boys *** that-you-let-live the-this the-thing

הַמְיַלְּדֹת אֶל־ פַּרְעֹה כִּי לֹא כַנָּשִׁים הַמִּצְרִיֹּת הָעִבְרִיֹּת
the-Hebrews the-Egyptians like-the-woman not now Pharaoh to the-being-midwives

כִּי־ חָיוֹת הֵנָּה בְּטֶרֶם תָּבוֹא אֲלֵהֶן הַמְיַלֶּדֶת
the-one-being-midwife to-them she-arrives before they vigorous-ones for

וְיָלָדוּ׃ וַיֵּיטֶב אֱלֹהִים לַמְיַלְּדֹת
to-the-ones-being-midwives God so-he-was-kind (20) then-they-give-birth

וַיִּרֶב הָעָם וַיַּעַצְמוּ מְאֹד׃ וַיְהִי
and-he-was (21) more and-they-became-numerous the-people and-he-increased

כִּי־ יָרְאוּ הַמְיַלְּדֹת אֶת־ הָאֱלֹהִים וַיַּעַשׂ לָהֶם
to-them that-he-gave the-God *** the-being-midwives they-feared because

בָּתִּים׃ וַיְצַו פַּרְעֹה לְכָל־ עַמּוֹ לֵאמֹר כָּל־
every-of to-say people-of-him to all of Pharaoh then-he-ordered (22) families

הַבֵּן הַיִּלּוֹד הַיְאֹרָה תַּשְׁלִיכֻהוּ וְכָל־ הַבַּת
the-girl but-every-of you-must-throw him into-the-Nile the-born the-boy

תְּחַיּוּן׃ וַיֵּלֶךְ אִישׁ מִבֵּית לֵוִי וַיִּקַּח אֶת־
*** and-he-married Levi from-house-of man now-he-went (2:1) you-let-live

בַּת־ לֵוִי׃ וַתַּהַר הָאִשָּׁה וַתֵּלֶד בֵּן וַתֵּרֶא
when-she-saw son and-she-bore the-woman and-she-conceived (2) Levi daughter-of

אֹתוֹ כִּי־ טוֹב הוּא וַתִּצְפְּנֵהוּ שְׁלֹשָׁה יְרָחִים׃ וְלֹא־ יָכְלָה עוֹד
longer she-could when-not (3) months three then-she-hid-him he fine that him

hard labor the Egyptians used
them ruthlessly.
15The king of Egypt said to
the Hebrew midwives, whose
names were Shiphrah and
Puah, 16"When you help the
Hebrew women in childbirth
and observe them on the de-
livery stool, if it is a boy, kill
him; but if it is a girl, let her
live." 17The midwives, however, feared God and did not
do what the king of Egypt had
told them to do; they let the
boys live. 18Then the king of
Egypt summoned the mid-
wives and asked them, "Why
have you done this? Why have
you let the boys live?"
19The midwives answered
Pharaoh, "Hebrew women are
not like Egyptian women;
they are vigorous and give
birth before the midwives ar-
rive."
20So God was kind to the
midwives and the people increased and became even
more numerous. 21And be-
cause the midwives feared
God, he gave them families of
their own.
22Then Pharaoh gave this order to all his people: "Every
boy that is born you must
throw into the river, but let
every girl live."

The Birth of Moses

2 Now a man of the house
of Levi married a Levite
woman, 2and she became
pregnant and gave birth to a
son. When she saw that he
was a fine child, she hid him
for three months. 3But when
she could hide him no longer,

הַצְפִּנוֹ וַתִּקַּח־ לוֹ תֵּבַת גֹּמֶא וַתַּחְמְרָה

and-she-coated-her papyrus basket-of for-him then-she-got to-hide-him

בַחֵמָר וּבַזָּפֶת וַתָּשֶׂם בָּהּ אֶת־ הַיֶּלֶד

the-child *** in-her then-she-placed and-with-the-pitch with-the-tar

וַתָּשֶׂם בַּסּוּף עַל־ שְׂפַת הַיְאֹר׃ (4) וַתֵּתַצַּב

and-she-stood (4) the-Nile bank-of along among-the-reed and-she-put

אֲחֹתוֹ מֵרָחֹק לְדֵעָה מַה־ יֵּעָשֶׂה לוֹ׃

to-him he-would-happen what to-see at-distance sister-of-him

(5) וַתֵּרֶד בַּת־ פַּרְעֹה לִרְחֹץ עַל־הַיְאֹר וְנַעֲרֹתֶיהָ

and-maidens-of-her the-Nile in to-bathe Pharaoh daughter-of then-she-went-down (5)

הֹלְכֹת עַל־ יַד הַיְאֹר וַתֵּרֶא אֶת־ הַתֵּבָה בְּתוֹךְ הַסּוּף

the-reed among the-basket *** and-she-saw the-Nile bank-of along ones-walking

וַתִּשְׁלַח אֶת־ אֲמָתָהּ וַתִּקָּחֶהָ (6) וַתִּפְתַּח

then-she-opened (6) and-she-got-her slave-girl-of-her *** and-she-sent

וַתִּרְאֵהוּ אֶת־ הַיֶּלֶד וְהִנֵּה־ נַעַר בֹּכֶה וַתַּחְמֹל עָלָיו

for-him and-she-felt-sorry crying child and-see! the-baby *** and-she-saw-him

וַתֹּאמֶר מִיַּלְדֵי הָעִבְרִים זֶה׃ (7) וַתֹּאמֶר אֲחֹתוֹ

sister-of-him then-she-asked (7) this the-Hebrews from-babies-of and-she-said

אֶל־ בַּת־ פַּרְעֹה הַאֵלֵךְ וְקָרָאתִי לָךְ אִשָּׁה מֵינֶקֶת מִן

from nursing woman for-you and-I-get shall-I-go? Pharaoh daughter-of to

הָעִבְרִיֹּת וְתֵינִק לָךְ אֶת־ הַיָּלֶד׃ (8) וַתֹּאמֶר־ לָהּ

to-her and-she-answered (8) the-baby *** for-you so-she-can-nurse the-Hebrews

בַּת־ פַּרְעֹה לֵכִי וַתֵּלֶךְ הָעַלְמָה וַתִּקְרָא אֶת־ אֵם

mother-of *** and-she-got the-girl and-she-went go! Pharaoh daughter-of

הַיָּלֶד׃ (9) וַתֹּאמֶר לָהּ בַּת־ פַּרְעֹה הֵילִיכִי אֶת־ הַיֶּלֶד

the-baby *** take! Pharaoh daughter-of to-her and-she-said (9) the-baby

הַזֶּה וְהֵינִקִהוּ לִי וַאֲנִי אֶתֵּן אֶת־ שְׂכָרֵךְ וַתִּקַּח

so-she-took wage-of-you *** I-will-pay and-I for-me and-nurse-him! the-this

הָאִשָּׁה הַיֶּלֶד וַתְּנִיקֵהוּ׃ (10) וַיִגְדַּל* הַיֶּלֶד

the-child when-he-grew (10) and-she-nursed-him the-baby the-woman

וַתְּבִאֵהוּ לְבַת־ פַּרְעֹה וַיְהִי־ לָהּ לְבֵן

as-son to-her and-he-became Pharaoh to-daughter-of then-she-took-him

וַתִּקְרָא שְׁמוֹ מֹשֶׁה וַתֹּאמֶר כִּי מִן־ הַמַּיִם מְשִׁיתִהוּ׃

I-drew-him the-waters from for and-she-said Moses name-of-him and-she-called

(11) וַיְהִי ׀ בַּיָּמִים הָהֵם וַיִּגְדַּל מֹשֶׁה וַיֵּצֵא

that-he-went-out Moses when-he-grew the-these in-the-days and-he-was (11)

אֶל־ אֶחָיו וַיַּרְא בְּסִבְלֹתָם וַיַּרְא אִישׁ מִצְרִי

Egyptian man and-he-saw at-labors-of-them and-he-watched brothers-of-him among

she got a papyrus basket for him and coated it with tar and pitch. Then she placed the child in it and put it among the reeds along the bank of the Nile. 4 His sister stood at a distance to see what would happen to him.

5 Then Pharaoh's daughter went down to the Nile to bathe, and her attendants were walking along the river bank. She saw the basket among the reeds and sent her slave girl to get it. 6 She opened it and saw the baby. He was crying, and she felt sorry for him. "This is one of the Hebrew babies," she said.

7 Then his sister asked Pharaoh's daughter, "Shall I go and get one of the Hebrew women to nurse the baby for you?"

8 "Yes, go," she answered. And the girl went and got the baby's mother. 9 Pharaoh's daughter said to her, "Take this baby and nurse him for me, and I will pay you." So the woman took the baby and nursed him. 10 When the child grew older, she took him to Pharaoh's daughter and he became her son. She named him Moses,[b] saying, "I drew him out of the water."

Moses Flees to Midian

11 One day, after Moses had grown up, he went out to where his own people were and watched them at their hard labor. He saw an Egyptian beating a Hebrew, one of

[b]10 *Moses* sounds like the Hebrew for *draw out.*

*10 Most mss have *dagesh* in the *yod* (וַיִּגְ).

מַכֶּה אִישׁ־ עִבְרִי מֵאֶחָיו׃ וַיִּפֶן כֹּה וָכֹה
and-that this and-he-glanced (12) from-brothers-of-him Hebrew man beating

וַיַּרְא כִּי אֵין אִישׁ וַיַּךְ אֶת־ הַמִּצְרִי וַיִּטְמְנֵהוּ
and-he-hid-him the-Egyptian *** and-he-killed man there-is-no that and-he-saw

בַּחוֹל׃ וַיֵּצֵא בַּיּוֹם הַשֵּׁנִי וְהִנֵּה שְׁנֵי־ אֲנָשִׁים
men two-of and-see! the-next on-the-day and-he-went-out (13) in-the-sand

עִבְרִים נִצִּים וַיֹּאמֶר לָרָשָׁע לָמָּה תַכֶּה
you-hit why? to-the-one-in-wrong and-he-asked ones-fighting Hebrews

רֵעֶךָ׃ וַיֹּאמֶר מִי שָׂמְךָ לְאִישׁ שַׂר וְשֹׁפֵט
and-judging ruler as-one he-made-you who? and-he-said (14) fellow-of-you

עָלֵינוּ הַלְהָרְגֵנִי אַתָּה אֹמֵר כַּאֲשֶׁר הָרַגְתָּ אֶת־ הַמִּצְרִי
the-Egyptian *** you-killed just-as thinking you to-kill-me? over-us

וַיִּירָא מֹשֶׁה וַיֹּאמַר אָכֵן נוֹדַע הַדָּבָר׃
the-thing he-is-known surely and-he-thought Moses and-he-was-afraid

וַיִּשְׁמַע פַּרְעֹה אֶת־ הַדָּבָר הַזֶּה וַיְבַקֵּשׁ לַהֲרֹג אֶת־
*** to-kill then-he-tried the-this the-thing *** Pharaoh when-he-heard (15)

מֹשֶׁה וַיִּבְרַח מֹשֶׁה מִפְּנֵי פַרְעֹה וַיֵּשֶׁב בְּאֶרֶץ־ מִדְיָן
Midian to-land-of and-he-went Pharaoh from-face-of Moses but-he-fled Moses

וַיֵּשֶׁב עַל־ הַבְּאֵר׃ וּלְכֹהֵן מִדְיָן שֶׁבַע בָּנוֹת
daughters seven Midian now-to-priest-of (16) the-well by and-he-sat

וַתָּבֹאנָה וַתִּדְלֶנָה וַתְּמַלֶּאנָה אֶת־ הָרְהָטִים לְהַשְׁקוֹת
to-water the-troughs *** and-they-filled and-they-drew and-they-came

צֹאן אֲבִיהֶן׃ וַיָּבֹאוּ הָרֹעִים וַיְגָרְשׁוּם
and-they-drove-them the-ones-herding but-they-came (17) father-of-them flock-of

וַיָּקָם מֹשֶׁה וַיּוֹשִׁעָן וַיַּשְׁקְ אֶת־ צֹאנָם׃
flock-of-them *** and-he-watered and-he-rescued-them Moses but-he-got-up

וַתָּבֹאנָה אֶל־ רְעוּאֵל אֲבִיהֶן וַיֹּאמֶר מַדּוּעַ מִהַרְתֶּן
you-are-early why? and-he-asked father-of-them Reuel to when-they-returned (18)

בֹּא הַיּוֹם׃ וַתֹּאמַרְןָ אִישׁ מִצְרִי הִצִּילָנוּ
he-rescued-us Egyptian man and-they-answered (19) the-day to return

מִיַּד הָרֹעִים וְגַם־ דָּלֹה דָלָה לָנוּ וַיַּשְׁקְ
and-he-watered for-us he-drew to-draw and-even the-ones-herding from-hand-of

אֶת־ הַצֹּאן׃ וַיֹּאמֶר אֶל־ בְּנֹתָיו וְאַיּוֹ לָמָּה זֶּה
this why? and-where-he? daughters-of-him to and-he-asked (20) the-flock ***

עֲזַבְתֶּן אֶת־ הָאִישׁ קִרְאֶן לוֹ וְיֹאכַל לָחֶם׃ וַיּוֹאֶל
so-he-agreed (21) meal so-he-can-eat to-him invite! the-man *** you-left

מֹשֶׁה לָשֶׁבֶת אֶת־ הָאִישׁ וַיִּתֵּן אֶת־ צִפֹּרָה בִתּוֹ לְמֹשֶׁה׃
to-Moses daughter-of-him Zipporah *** and-he-gave the-man with to-stay Moses

his own people. [12]Glancing
this way and that and seeing
no one, he killed the Egyptian
and hid him in the sand. [13]The
next day he went out and saw
two Hebrews fighting. He
asked the one in the wrong,
"Why are you hitting your fellow Hebrew?"
[14]The man said, "Who made
you ruler and judge over us?
Are you thinking of killing me
as you killed the Egyptian?"
Then Moses was afraid and
thought, "What I did must
have become known."
[15]When Pharaoh heard of
this, he tried to kill Moses, but
Moses fled from Pharaoh and
went to live in Midian, where
he sat down by a well. [16]Now
a priest of Midian had seven
daughters, and they came to
draw water and fill the troughs
to water their father's flock.
[17]Some shepherds came along
and drove them away, but
Moses got up and came to
their rescue and watered their
flock.
[18]When the girls returned to
Reuel their father, he asked
them, "Why have you re-
turned so early today?"
[19]They answered, "An Egyptian rescued us from the shepherds. He even drew water for
us and watered the flock."
[20]"And where is he?" he
asked his daughters. "Why
did you leave him? Invite him
to have something to eat."
[21]Moses agreed to stay with
the man, who gave his daughter Zipporah to Moses in marriage. [22]Zipporah gave birth to

וַתֵּלֶד בֵּן וַיִּקְרָא אֶת־שְׁמוֹ גֵּרְשֹׁם כִּי אָמַר גֵּר
alien he-said for Gershom name-of-him *** and-he-called son and-she-bore (22)

הָיִיתִי בְּאֶרֶץ נָכְרִיָּה׃ וַיְהִי בַיָּמִים הָרַבִּים הָהֵם
the-those the-many during-the-days and-he-was (23) foreign in-land I-became

וַיָּמָת מֶלֶךְ מִצְרַיִם וַיֵּאָנְחוּ בְנֵי־יִשְׂרָאֵל מִן־הָעֲבֹדָה
the-slavery from Israel sons-of and-they-groaned Egypt king-of that-he-died

וַיִּזְעָקוּ וַתַּעַל שַׁוְעָתָם אֶל־הָאֱלֹהִים מִן־הָעֲבֹדָה׃
the-slavery from the-God to cry-of-them and-she-went-up and-they-cried-out

וַיִּשְׁמַע אֱלֹהִים אֶת־נַאֲקָתָם וַיִּזְכֹּר אֱלֹהִים אֶת־
*** God and-he-remembered groan-of-them *** God and-he-heard (24)

בְּרִיתוֹ אֶת־אַבְרָהָם אֶת־יִצְחָק וְאֶת־יַעֲקֹב׃ וַיַּרְא
so-he-looked (25) Jacob and-with Isaac with Abraham with covenant-of-him

אֱלֹהִים אֶת־בְּנֵי יִשְׂרָאֵל וַיֵּדַע אֱלֹהִים׃ וּמֹשֶׁה הָיָה
he-was now-Moses (3:1) God and-he-was-concerned Israel sons-of *** God

רֹעֶה אֶת־צֹאן יִתְרוֹ חֹתְנוֹ כֹּהֵן מִדְיָן וַיִּנְהַג
and-he-led Midian priest-of father-in-law-of-him Jethro flock-of *** tending

אֶת־הַצֹּאן אַחַר הַמִּדְבָּר וַיָּבֹא אֶל־הַר הָאֱלֹהִים חֹרֵבָה׃
to-Horeb the-God mountain-of to and-he-came the-desert far-side the-flock ***

וַיֵּרָא מַלְאַךְ יְהוָה אֵלָיו בְּלַבַּת־אֵשׁ מִתּוֹךְ
from-within fire in-flame-of to-him Yahweh angel-of and-he-appeared (2)

הַסְּנֶה וַיַּרְא וְהִנֵּה הַסְּנֶה בֹּעֵר בָּאֵשׁ וְהַסְּנֶה
yet-the-bush with-the-fire burning the-bush and-see! and-he-saw the-bush

אֵינֶנּוּ אֻכָּל׃ וַיֹּאמֶר מֹשֶׁה אָסֻרָה־נָּא
now! I-will-go-over Moses so-he-thought (3) being-consumed not-he

וְאֶרְאֶה אֶת־הַמַּרְאֶה הַגָּדֹל הַזֶּה מַדּוּעַ לֹא־יִבְעַר הַסְּנֶה׃
the-bush he-burns-up not why the-this the-strange the-sight *** and-I-will-see

וַיַּרְא יְהוָה כִּי סָר לִרְאוֹת וַיִּקְרָא אֵלָיו
to-him then-he-called to-look he-went-over that Yahweh when-he-saw (4)

אֱלֹהִים מִתּוֹךְ הַסְּנֶה וַיֹּאמֶר מֹשֶׁה מֹשֶׁה וַיֹּאמֶר הִנֵּנִי׃
here-I and-he-said Moses Moses and-he-said the-bush from-within God

וַיֹּאמֶר אַל־תִּקְרַב הֲלֹם שַׁל־נְעָלֶיךָ מֵעַל
from-on sandals-of-you take-off! closer you-come not and-he-said (5)

רַגְלֶיךָ כִּי הַמָּקוֹם אֲשֶׁר אַתָּה עוֹמֵד עָלָיו אַדְמַת־קֹדֶשׁ הוּא׃
he holy ground-of on-him standing you where the-place for feet-of-you

וַיֹּאמֶר אָנֹכִי אֱלֹהֵי אָבִיךָ אֱלֹהֵי אַבְרָהָם אֱלֹהֵי יִצְחָק וֵאלֹהֵי
and-God-of Isaac God-of Abraham God-of father-of-you God-of I then-he-said (6)

יַעֲקֹב וַיַּסְתֵּר מֹשֶׁה פָּנָיו כִּי יָרֵא מֵהַבִּיט אֶל־הָאֱלֹהִים׃
the-God at from-to-look he-was-afraid for face-of-him Moses and-he-hid Jacob

a son, and Moses named him
Gershom,[c] saying, "I have
become an alien in a foreign
land."
23During that long period,
the king of Egypt died. The Israelites groaned in their slavery and cried out, and their cry
for help because of their slavery went up to God. 24God
heard their groaning and he
remembered his covenant
with Abraham, with Isaac and
with Jacob. 25So God looked on
the Israelites and was concerned about them.

Moses and the Burning Bush

3 Now Moses was tending
the flock of Jethro his father-in-law, the priest of
Midian, and he led the flock to
the far side of the desert and
came to Horeb, the mountain
of God. 2There the angel of the
LORD appeared to him in
flames of fire from within a
bush. Moses saw that though
the bush was on fire it did not
burn up. 3So Moses thought, "I
will go over and see this
strange sight—why the bush
does not burn up."
4When the LORD saw that he
had gone over to look, God
called to him from within the
bush, "Moses, Moses!"
And Moses said, "Here I
am."
5"Do not come any closer,"
God said. "Take off your sandals, for the place where you
are standing is holy ground."
6Then he said, "I am the God
of your father, the God of
Abraham, the God of Isaac
and the God of Jacob." At this,
Moses hid his face, because he
was afraid to look at God.

[c]22 *Gershom* sounds like the Hebrew for *an alien there.*

וַיֹּאמֶר יְהוָה רָאֹה רָאִיתִי אֶת־ עֳנִי עַמִּי אֲשֶׁר בְּמִצְרָיִם
in-Egypt who people-of-me misery-of *** I-saw to-see Yahweh and-he-said (7)

וְאֶת־ צַעֲקָתָם שָׁמַעְתִּי מִפְּנֵי נֹגְשָׂיו כִּי יָדַעְתִּי
I-am-concerned indeed ones-driving-him because-of I-heard cry-of-them and

אֶת־ מַכְאֹבָיו׃ וָאֵרֵד לְהַצִּילוֹ ׀ מִיַּד מִצְרַיִם
Egyptians from-hand-of to-rescue-him so-I-came-down (8) sufferings-of-him ***

וּלְהַעֲלֹתוֹ מִן־ הָאָרֶץ הַהִוא אֶל־ אֶרֶץ טוֹבָה וּרְחָבָה אֶל־
into and-spacious good land into the-that the-land from and-to-bring-him

אֶרֶץ זָבַת חָלָב וּדְבָשׁ אֶל־ מְקוֹם הַכְּנַעֲנִי וְהַחִתִּי
and-the-Hittite the-Canaanite home-of into and-honey milk flowing-of land

וְהָאֱמֹרִי וְהַפְּרִזִּי וְהַחִוִּי וְהַיְבוּסִי׃ וְעַתָּה
and-now (9) and-the-Jebusite and-the-Hivite and-the-Perizzite and-the-Amorite

הִנֵּה צַעֲקַת בְּנֵי־ יִשְׂרָאֵל בָּאָה אֵלָי וְגַם־ רָאִיתִי אֶת־ הַלַּחַץ
the-oppression *** I-saw and-also to-me she-reached Israel sons-of cry-of see!

אֲשֶׁר מִצְרַיִם לֹחֲצִים אֹתָם׃ וְעַתָּה לְכָה וְאֶשְׁלָחֲךָ אֶל־
to for-I-send-you go! so-now (10) them ones-oppressing Egyptians that

פַּרְעֹה וְהוֹצֵא אֶת־ עַמִּי בְנֵי־ יִשְׂרָאֵל מִמִּצְרָיִם׃ וַיֹּאמֶר
but-he-said (11) from-Egypt Israel sons-of people-of-me *** and-bring! Pharaoh

מֹשֶׁה אֶל־הָאֱלֹהִים מִי אָנֹכִי כִּי אֵלֵךְ אֶל־פַּרְעֹה וְכִי אוֹצִיא
I-should-bring and-that Pharaoh to I-should-go that I who? the-God to Moses

אֶת־ בְּנֵי יִשְׂרָאֵל מִמִּצְרָיִם׃ וַיֹּאמֶר כִּי־ אֶהְיֶה עִמָּךְ
with-you I-will-be indeed and-he-said (12) from-Egypt Israel sons-of ***

וְזֶה־ לְּךָ הָאוֹת כִּי אָנֹכִי שְׁלַחְתִּיךָ בְּהוֹצִיאֲךָ אֶת־ הָעָם
the-people *** when-to-bring-you I-sent-you I that the-sign to-you and-this

מִמִּצְרַיִם תַּעַבְדוּן אֶת־ הָאֱלֹהִים עַל הָהָר הַזֶּה׃
the-this the-mountain on the-God *** you-will-worship from-Egypt

וַיֹּאמֶר מֹשֶׁה אֶל־הָאֱלֹהִים הִנֵּה אָנֹכִי בָא אֶל־ בְּנֵי יִשְׂרָאֵל וְאָמַרְתִּי
and-I-say Israel sons-of to going I suppose the-God to Moses but-he-said (13)

לָהֶם אֱלֹהֵי אֲבוֹתֵיכֶם שְׁלָחַנִי אֲלֵיכֶם וְאָמְרוּ־ לִי מַה־
what? to-me and-they-ask to-you he-sent-me fathers-of-you God-of to-them

שְּׁמוֹ מָה אֹמַר אֲלֵהֶם׃ וַיֹּאמֶר אֱלֹהִים אֶל־מֹשֶׁה אֶהְיֶה
I-am Moses to God and-he-said (14) to-them shall-I-tell what? name-of-him

אֲשֶׁר אֶהְיֶה וַיֹּאמֶר כֹּה תֹאמַר לִבְנֵי יִשְׂרָאֵל אֶהְיֶה שְׁלָחַנִי
he-sent-me I-am Israel to-sons-of you-shall-say this and-he-said I-am who

אֲלֵיכֶם׃ וַיֹּאמֶר עוֹד אֱלֹהִים אֶל־מֹשֶׁה כֹּה־ תֹאמַר אֶל־ בְּנֵי
sons-of to you-shall-say this Moses to God also and-he-said (15) to-you

יִשְׂרָאֵל יְהוָה אֱלֹהֵי אֲבֹתֵיכֶם אֱלֹהֵי אַבְרָהָם אֱלֹהֵי יִצְחָק וֵאלֹהֵי
and-God-of Isaac God-of Abraham God-of fathers-of-you God-of Yahweh Israel

7 The LORD said, "I have indeed seen the misery of my
people in Egypt. I have heard
them crying out because of
their slave drivers, and I am
concerned about their
suffering. 8 So I have come
down to rescue them from the
hand of the Egyptians and to
bring them up out of that land
into a good and spacious land,
a land flowing with milk and
honey—the home of the Ca-
naanites, Hittites, Amorites,
Perizzites, Hivites and Jebusites. 9 And now the cry of the
Israelites has reached me, and
I have seen the way the Egyptians are oppressing them.
10 So now, go. I am sending you
to Pharaoh to bring my people
the Israelites out of Egypt."
11 But Moses said to God,
"Who am I, that I should go to
Pharaoh and bring the Israelites out of Egypt?"
12 And God said, "I will be
with you. And this will be the
sign to you that it is I who
have sent you: When you have
brought the people out of
Egypt, you[d] will worship God
on this mountain."
13 Moses said to God, "Suppose I go to the Israelites and
say to them, 'The God of your
fathers has sent me to you,'
and they ask me, 'What is his
name?' Then what shall I tell
them?"
14 God said to Moses, "I am
who I am.[e] This is what you
are to say to the Israelites: 'I
AM has sent me to you.'"
15 God also said to Moses,
"Say to the Israelites, 'The
LORD,[f] the God of your fathers—the God of Abraham,
the God of Isaac and the God

[d] 12 The Hebrew is plural.
[e] 14 Or *I will be what I will be*
[f] 15 The Hebrew for LORD sounds like and may be derived from the Hebrew for *I AM* in verse 14.

יַעֲקֹב שְׁלָחַנִי אֲלֵיכֶם זֶה־ שְּׁמִי לְעֹלָם וְזֶה זִכְרִי
memorial-of-me and-this for-ever name-of-me this to-you he-sent-me Jacob

לְדֹר דֹּר׃ לֵךְ וְאָסַפְתָּ אֶת־ זִקְנֵי יִשְׂרָאֵל
Israel elders-of *** and-you-assemble go! (16) generation for-generation

וְאָמַרְתָּ אֲלֵהֶם יְהוָה אֱלֹהֵי אֲבֹתֵיכֶם נִרְאָה אֵלַי אֱלֹהֵי
God-of to-me he-appeared fathers-of-you God-of Yahweh to-them and-you-say

אַבְרָהָם יִצְחָק וְיַעֲקֹב לֵאמֹר פָּקֹד פָּקַדְתִּי אֶתְכֶם וְאֶת־ הֶעָשׂוּי
the-being-done and over-you I-watched to-watch to-say and-Jacob Isaac Abraham

לָכֶם בְּמִצְרָיִם׃ וָאֹמַר אַעֲלֶה אֶתְכֶם מֵעֳנִי מִצְרַיִם
Egypt from-misery-of you I-will-bring-up and-I-promised (17) in-Egypt to-you

אֶל־ אֶרֶץ הַכְּנַעֲנִי וְהַחִתִּי וְהָאֱמֹרִי וְהַפְּרִזִּי
and-the-Perizzite and-the-Amorite and-the-Hittite the-Canaanite land-of into

וְהַחִוִּי וְהַיְבוּסִי אֶל־ אֶרֶץ זָבַת חָלָב וּדְבָשׁ׃
and-honey milk flowing-of land into and-the-Jebusite and-the-Hivite

וְשָׁמְעוּ לְקֹלֶךָ וּבָאתָ אַתָּה וְזִקְנֵי
and-elders-of you than-you-will-go to-voice-of-you and-they-will-listen (18)

יִשְׂרָאֵל אֶל־מֶלֶךְ מִצְרַיִם וַאֲמַרְתֶּם אֵלָיו יְהוָה אֱלֹהֵי הָעִבְרִיִּים
the-Hebrews God-of Yahweh to-him and-you-will-say Egypt king-of to Israel

נִקְרָה עָלֵינוּ וְעַתָּה נֵלֲכָה־ נָּא דֶּרֶךְ שְׁלֹשֶׁת יָמִים
days three-of journey-of now! let-us-take and-now with-us he-met

בַּמִּדְבָּר וְנִזְבְּחָה לַיהוָה אֱלֹהֵינוּ׃ וַאֲנִי יָדַעְתִּי
I-know but-I (19) God-of-us to-Yahweh and-let-us-sacrifice into-the-desert

כִּי לֹא־ יִתֵּן אֶתְכֶם מֶלֶךְ מִצְרַיִם לַהֲלֹךְ וְלֹא בְּיָד חֲזָקָה׃
mighty by-hand if-not to-go Egypt king-of you he-will-let not that

וְשָׁלַחְתִּי אֶת־ יָדִי וְהִכֵּיתִי אֶת־ מִצְרַיִם
Egyptians *** and-I-will-strike hand-of-me *** so-I-will-stretch-out (20)

בְּכֹל נִפְלְאֹתַי אֲשֶׁר אֶעֱשֶׂה בְּקִרְבּוֹ וְאַחֲרֵי־
and-after in-midst-of-him I-will-perform that being-wonders-of-me with-all-of

כֵן יְשַׁלַּח אֶתְכֶם׃ וְנָתַתִּי אֶת־ חֵן הָעָם־
the-people favorable *** and-I-will-make (21) you he-will-let-go that

הַזֶּה בְּעֵינֵי מִצְרָיִם וְהָיָה כִּי תֵלֵכוּן לֹא תֵלְכוּ
you-will-go not you-leave when so-he-will-be Egyptians in-eyes-of the-this

רֵיקָם׃ וְשָׁאֲלָה אִשָּׁה מִשְּׁכֶנְתָּהּ
from-neighbor-of-her woman so-she-shall-ask (22) empty-handed

וּמִגָּרַת בֵּיתָהּ כְּלֵי־ כֶסֶף וּכְלֵי זָהָב
gold and-articles-of silver articles-of house-of-her and-from-one-living-of

וּשְׂמָלֹת וְשַׂמְתֶּם עַל־ בְּנֵיכֶם וְעַל־ בְּנֹתֵיכֶם
daughters-of-you and-on sons-of-you on and-you-shall-put and-clothing

of Jacob—has sent me to you.' This is my name forever, the name by which I am to be remembered from generation to generation.

[16]"Go, assemble the elders of Israel and say to them, 'The LORD, the God of your fathers, the God of Abraham, Isaac and Jacob, appeared to me and said: I have watched over you and have seen what has been done to you in Egypt. [17]And I have promised to bring you up out of your misery in Egypt into the land of the Canaanites, Hittites, Amorites, Perizzites, Hivites and Jebusites—a land flowing with milk and honey.'

[18]"The elders of Israel will listen to you. Then you and the elders are to go to the king of Egypt and say to him, 'The LORD, the God of the Hebrews, has met with us. Let us take a three-day journey into the desert to offer sacrifices to the LORD our God.' [19]But I know that the king of Egypt will not let you go unless a mighty hand compels him. [20]So I will stretch out my hand and strike the Egyptians with all the wonders that I will perform among them. After that, he will let you go.

[21]"And I will make the Egyptians favorably disposed toward this people, so that when you leave you will not go empty-handed. [22]Every woman is to ask her neighbor and any woman living in her house for articles of silver and gold and for clothing, which you will put on your sons and

וְנִצַּלְתֶּם אֶת־ מִצְרָיִם׃ (4:1) וַיַּעַן מֹשֶׁה וַיֹּאמֶר
and-he-said Moses but-he-answered (4:1) Egyptians *** so-you-will-plunder

וְהֵן לֹא־ יַאֲמִינוּ לִי וְלֹא יִשְׁמְעוּ בְּקֹלִי כִּי
but to-voice-of-me they-listen and-not in-me they-believe not but-what-if

יֹאמְרוּ לֹא־ נִרְאָה אֵלֶיךָ יְהוָה׃ (2) וַיֹּאמֶר אֵלָיו יְהוָה
Yahweh to-him then-he-said (2) Yahweh to-you he-appeared not they-say

מַזֶּה בְיָדֶךָ וַיֹּאמֶר מַטֶּה׃ (3) וַיֹּאמֶר הַשְׁלִיכֵהוּ
throw-him! so-he-said (3) staff and-he-replied in-hand-of-you what-that?

אַרְצָה וַיַּשְׁלִיכֵהוּ אַרְצָה וַיְהִי לְנָחָשׁ וַיָּנָס מֹשֶׁה
Moses and-he-ran into-snake and-he-became on-ground so-he-threw-him on-ground

מִפָּנָיו׃ (4) וַיֹּאמֶר יְהוָה אֶל־ מֹשֶׁה שְׁלַח יָדְךָ
hand-of-you reach-out! Moses to Yahweh then-he-said (4) from-before-him

וֶאֱחֹז בִּזְנָבוֹ וַיִּשְׁלַח יָדוֹ וַיַּחֲזֶק בּוֹ
onto-him and-he-held hand-of-him so-he-reached by-tail-of-him and-take!

וַיְהִי לְמַטֶּה בְּכַפּוֹ׃ (5) לְמַעַן יַאֲמִינוּ כִּי־
that they-will-believe so-that (5) in-hand-of-him into-staff and-he-turned

נִרְאָה אֵלֶיךָ יְהוָה אֱלֹהֵי אֲבֹתָם אֱלֹהֵי אַבְרָהָם אֱלֹהֵי יִצְחָק
Isaac God-of Abraham God-of fathers-of-them God-of Yahweh to-you he-appeared

וֵאלֹהֵי יַעֲקֹב׃ (6) וַיֹּאמֶר יְהוָה לוֹ עוֹד הָבֵא־נָא יָדְךָ
hand-of-you now! put! also to-him Yahweh then-he-said (6) Jacob and-God-of

בְּחֵיקֶךָ וַיָּבֵא יָדוֹ בְּחֵיקוֹ וַיּוֹצִאָהּ
when-he-took-out-her into-cloak-of-him hand-of-him so-he-put into-cloak-of-you

וְהִנֵּה יָדוֹ מְצֹרַעַת כַּשָּׁלֶג׃ (7) וַיֹּאמֶר הָשֵׁב
put-back! than-he-said (7) like-the-snow being-leprous hand-of-him now-see!

יָדְךָ אֶל־ חֵיקֶךָ וַיָּשֶׁב יָדוֹ אֶל־ חֵיקוֹ
cloak-of-him into hand-of-him so-he-put-back cloak-of-you into hand-of-you

וַיּוֹצִאָהּ מֵחֵיקוֹ וְהִנֵּה־ שָׁבָה
she-was-restored now-see! from-cloak-of-him when-he-took-out-her

כִּבְשָׂרוֹ׃ (8) וְהָיָה אִם־ לֹא יַאֲמִינוּ לָךְ וְלֹא
or-not in-you they-believe not if and-he-will-be (8) like-flesh-of-him

יִשְׁמְעוּ לְקֹל הָאֹת הָרִאשׁוֹן וְהֶאֱמִינוּ
then-they-may-believe the-first the-sign to-voice-of they-pay-attention

לְקֹל הָאֹת הָאַחֲרוֹן׃ (9) וְהָיָה אִם־ לֹא יַאֲמִינוּ
they-believe not if but-he-will-be (9) the-second the-sign in-voice-of

גַּם לִשְׁנֵי הָאֹתוֹת הָאֵלֶּה וְלֹא יִשְׁמְעוּן לְקֹלֶךָ
to-voice-of-you they-listen or-not the-these the-signs in-two-of either

וְלָקַחְתָּ מִמֵּימֵי הַיְאֹר וְשָׁפַכְתָּ הַיַּבָּשָׁה
the-dry-ground and you pour the-Nile from-waters-of then-you-take

°2 ק מה זה

daughters. And so you will plunder the Egyptians."

Signs for Moses

4 Moses answered, "What if
they do not believe me or
listen to me and say, 'The
LORD did not appear to you'?"
2Then the LORD said to him,
"What is that in your hand?"
"A staff," he replied.
3The LORD said, "Throw it on
the ground."
Moses threw it on the ground and it became a snake, and he ran from it.
4Then the
LORD said to him, "Reach out your hand and take it by the tail." So Moses reached out and took hold of the snake and it turned back into a staff in his hand.
5"This," said the
LORD, "is so that they may believe that the LORD, the God of their fathers—the God of Abraham, the God of Isaac and the God of Jacob—has appeared to you."
6Then the LORD said, "Put
your hand inside your cloak." So Moses put his hand into his cloak, and when he took it out, it was leprous,[g] like snow.
7"Now put it back into your
cloak," he said. So Moses put his hand back into his cloak, and when he took it out, it was restored, like the rest of his flesh.
8Then the LORD said, "If they
do not believe you or pay attention to the first miraculous sign, they may believe the second.
9But if they do not believe
these two signs or listen to you, take some water from the Nile and pour it on the dry

g6 The Hebrew word was used for various diseases affecting the skin—not necessarily leprosy.

וְהָיוּ הַמַּיִם אֲשֶׁר תִּקַּח מִן־הַיְאֹר וְהָיוּ
and-they-will-become the-Nile from you-take that the-waters and-they-will-become

לְדָם בַּיַּבָּשֶׁת׃ וַיֹּאמֶר מֹשֶׁה אֶל־יְהוָה בִּי אֲדֹנָי
Lord oh! Yahweh to Moses then-he-said (10) on-the-dry-ground into-blood

לֹא אִישׁ דְּבָרִים אָנֹכִי גַּם מִתְּמוֹל גַּם מִשִּׁלְשֹׁם גַּם מֵאָז דַּבֶּרְךָ*
to-speak-you from-since nor in-past nor in-yesterday neither I words man-of not

אֶל־עַבְדֶּךָ כִּי כְבַד־פֶּה וּכְבַד לָשׁוֹן אָנֹכִי׃
I tongue and-slow-of speech slow-of but servant-of-you to

וַיֹּאמֶר יְהוָה אֵלָיו מִי שָׂם פֶּה לָאָדָם אוֹ מִי־יָשׂוּם אִלֵּם
dumb he-makes who? or to-man mouth he-gave who? to-him Yahweh and-he-said (11)

אוֹ חֵרֵשׁ אוֹ פִקֵּחַ אוֹ עִוֵּר הֲלֹא אָנֹכִי יְהוָה׃ וְעַתָּה לֵךְ וְאָנֹכִי אֶהְיֶה
I-will-be and-I go! so-now (12) Yahweh I not? blind or sight or deaf or

עִם־פִּיךָ וְהוֹרֵיתִיךָ אֲשֶׁר תְּדַבֵּר׃ וַיֹּאמֶר
but-he-said (13) you-will-say what and-I-will-teach-you mouth-of-you with

בִּי אֲדֹנָי שְׁלַח־נָא בְּיַד־תִּשְׁלָח׃ וַיִּחַר־אַף יְהוָה
Yahweh anger-of then-he-burned (14) you-send by-another now! send! Lord oh!

בְּמֹשֶׁה וַיֹּאמֶר הֲלֹא אַהֲרֹן אָחִיךָ הַלֵּוִי יָדַעְתִּי כִּי־
that I-know the-Levite brother-of-you Aaron not? and-he-said against-Moses

דַבֵּר יְדַבֵּר הוּא וְגַם הִנֵּה־הוּא יֹצֵא לִקְרָאתֶךָ וְרָאֲךָ
when-he-sees-you to-meet-you going-out he see! and-also he he-speaks to-speak

וְשָׂמַח בְּלִבּוֹ׃ וְדִבַּרְתָּ אֵלָיו וְשַׂמְתָּ
and-you-put to-him so-you-speak (15) in-heart-of-him then-he-will-be-glad

אֶת־הַדְּבָרִים בְּפִיו וְאָנֹכִי אֶהְיֶה עִם־פִּיךָ וְעִם־
and-with mouth-of-you with I-will-be and-I in-mouth-of-him the-words ***

פִּיהוּ וְהוֹרֵיתִי אֶתְכֶם אֵת אֲשֶׁר תַּעֲשׂוּן׃ וְדִבֶּר־
and-he-will-speak (16) you-will-do what *** you and-I-will-teach mouth-of-him

הוּא לְךָ אֶל־הָעָם וְהָיָה הוּא יִהְיֶה־לְּךָ לְפֶה
as-mouth to-you he-will-be he and-he-will-be the-people to for-you he

וְאַתָּה תִּהְיֶה־לּוֹ לֵאלֹהִים׃ וְאֶת־הַמַּטֶּה הַזֶּה תִּקַּח
you-take the-this the-staff but (17) as-God to-him you-will-be and-you

בְּיָדֶךָ אֲשֶׁר תַּעֲשֶׂה־בּוֹ אֶת־הָאֹתֹת׃ וַיֵּלֶךְ
then-he-went (18) the-signs *** with-him you-can-perform that in-hand-of-you

מֹשֶׁה וַיָּשָׁב ׀ אֶל־יֶתֶר חֹתְנוֹ וַיֹּאמֶר לוֹ
to-him and-he-said father-in-law-of-him Jethro to and-he-returned Moses

אֵלְכָה נָּא וְאָשׁוּבָה אֶל־אַחַי אֲשֶׁר־בְּמִצְרַיִם וְאֶרְאֶה
and-let-me-see in-Egypt who people-of-me to and-let-me-return now! let-me-go

הַעוֹדָם חַיִּים וַיֹּאמֶר יִתְרוֹ לְמֹשֶׁה לֵךְ לְשָׁלוֹם׃
in-peace go! to-Moses Jethro and-he-said alive-ones if-still-them

ground. The water you take from the river will become blood on the ground."

[10]Moses said to the LORD, "O Lord, I have never been eloquent, neither in the past nor since you have spoken to your servant. I am slow of speech and tongue."

[11]The LORD said to him, "Who gave man his mouth? Who makes him deaf or dumb? Who gives him sight or makes him blind? Is it not I, the LORD? [12]Now go; I will help you speak and will teach you what to say."

[13]But Moses said, "O Lord, please send someone else to do it."

[14]Then the LORD's anger burned against Moses and he said, "What about your brother, Aaron the Levite? I know he can speak well. He is already on his way to meet you, and his heart will be glad when he sees you. [15]You shall speak to him and put words in his mouth; I will help both of you speak and will teach you what to do. [16]He will speak to the people for you, and it will be as if he were your mouth and as if you were God to him. [17]But take this staff in your hand so you can perform miraculous signs with it."

Moses Returns to Egypt

[18]Then Moses went back to Jethro his father-in-law and said to him, "Let me go back to my own people in Egypt to see if any of them are still alive."

Jethro said, "Go, and I wish you well."

**10* Most mss have the accent *tiphha* (ךָ֖-).

וַיֹּאמֶר יְהוָה אֶל־מֹשֶׁה בְּמִדְיָן לֵךְ שֻׁב מִצְרָיִם כִּי־מֵתוּ
they-died for Egypt return! go! in-Midian Moses to Yahweh now-he-said (19)

כָּל־הָאֲנָשִׁים הַמְבַקְשִׁים אֶת־נַפְשֶׁךָ׃ וַיִּקַּח מֹשֶׁה אֶת־
*** Moses so-he-took (20) life-of-you *** the-ones-wanting the-men all-of

אִשְׁתּוֹ וְאֶת־בָּנָיו וַיַּרְכִּבֵם עַל־הַחֲמֹר וַיָּשָׁב
and-he-went-back the-donkey on and-he-put-them sons-of-him and wife-of-him

אַרְצָה מִצְרַיִם וַיִּקַּח מֹשֶׁה אֶת־מַטֵּה הָאֱלֹהִים בְּיָדוֹ׃
in-hand-of-him the-God staff-of *** Moses and-he-took Egypt to-land-of

וַיֹּאמֶר יְהוָה אֶל־מֹשֶׁה בְּלֶכְתְּךָ לָשׁוּב מִצְרַיְמָה רְאֵה
see! to-Egypt to-return when-to-go-you Moses to Yahweh and-he-said (21)

כָּל־הַמֹּפְתִים אֲשֶׁר־שַׂמְתִּי בְיָדֶךָ וַעֲשִׂיתָם לִפְנֵי
before that-you-perform-them in-hand-of-you I-gave that the-wonders all-of

פַרְעֹה וַאֲנִי אֲחַזֵּק אֶת־לִבּוֹ וְלֹא יְשַׁלַּח אֶת־
*** he-will-let-go so-not heart-of-him *** I-will-harden but-I Pharaoh

הָעָם׃ וְאָמַרְתָּ אֶל־פַּרְעֹה כֹּה אָמַר יְהוָה בְּנִי
son-of-me Yahweh he-says this Pharaoh to then-you-say (22) the-people

בְכֹרִי יִשְׂרָאֵל׃ וָאֹמַר אֵלֶיךָ שַׁלַּח אֶת־בְּנִי
son-of-me *** let-go! to-you and-I-told (23) Israel firstborn-of-me

וְיַעַבְדֵנִי וַתְּמָאֵן לְשַׁלְּחוֹ הִנֵּה אָנֹכִי הֹרֵג אֶת־
*** killing I see! to-let-go-him but-you-refused so-he-may-worship-me

בִּנְךָ בְּכֹרֶךָ׃ וַיְהִי בַדֶּרֶךְ בַּמָּלוֹן
at-the-lodging-place on-the-way and-he-was (24) firstborn-of-you son-of-you

וַיִּפְגְּשֵׁהוּ יְהוָה וַיְבַקֵּשׁ הֲמִיתוֹ׃ וַתִּקַּח צִפֹּרָה
Zipporah but-she-took (25) to-kill-him and-he-wanted Yahweh that-he-met-him

צֹר וַתִּכְרֹת אֶת־עָרְלַת בְּנָהּ וַתַּגַּע
and-she-touched son-of-her foreskin-of *** and-she-cut-off flint-knife

לְרַגְלָיו וַתֹּאמֶר כִּי חֲתַן־דָּמִים אַתָּה לִי׃
to-me you bloods bridegroom-of surely and-she-said on-feet-of-him

וַיִּרֶף מִמֶּנּוּ אָז אָמְרָה חֲתַן דָּמִים לַמּוּלֹת׃
about-the-circumcision bloods bridegroom-of she-said then from-him so-he-left (26)

וַיֹּאמֶר יְהוָה אֶל־אַהֲרֹן לֵךְ לִקְרַאת מֹשֶׁה הַמִּדְבָּרָה וַיֵּלֶךְ
so-he-went in-the-desert Moses to-meet go! Aaron to Yahweh and-he-said (27)

וַיִּפְגְּשֵׁהוּ בְּהַר הָאֱלֹהִים וַיִּשַּׁק־לוֹ׃ וַיַּגֵּד
then-he-told (28) on-him and-he-kissed the-God at-mountain-of and-he-met-him

מֹשֶׁה לְאַהֲרֹן אֵת כָּל־דִּבְרֵי יְהוָה אֲשֶׁר שְׁלָחוֹ וְאֵת כָּל־
all-of and he-sent-him that Yahweh words-of all-of *** to-Aaron Moses

הָאֹתֹת אֲשֶׁר צִוָּהוּ׃ וַיֵּלֶךְ מֹשֶׁה וְאַהֲרֹן
and-Aaron Moses so-he-went (29) he-commanded-him that the-signs

[19]Now the LORD had said to
Moses in Midian, "Go back to
Egypt, for all the men who
wanted to kill you are dead."
[20]So Moses took his wife and
sons, put them on a donkey
and started back to Egypt. And
he took the staff of God in his
hand.
[21]The LORD said to Moses,
"When you return to Egypt,
see that you perform before
Pharaoh all the wonders I
have given you the power to
do. But I will harden his heart
so that he will not let the
people go. [22]Then say to Pharaoh, 'This is what the LORD
says: Israel is my firstborn
son, [23]and I told you, "Let my
son go, so he may worship
me." But you refused to let
him go; so I will kill your
firstborn son.' "
[24]At a lodging place on the
way, the LORD met Moses and
was about to kill him. [25]But
Zipporah took a flint knife, cut
off her son's foreskin and
touched ⌞Moses'⌟ feet with it.[h]
"Surely you are a bridegroom
of blood to me," she said. [26]So
the LORD let him alone. (At
that time she said "bridegroom of blood," referring to
circumcision.)
[27]The LORD said to Aaron,
"Go into the desert to meet
Moses." So he met Moses at
the mountain of God and
kissed him. [28]Then Moses told
Aaron everything the LORD
had sent him to say, and also
about all the miraculous signs
he had commanded him to
perform.
[29]Moses and Aaron brought

[h]25 Or *and drew near ⌞Moses'⌟ feet*

וַיַּאַסְפוּ אֶת־ כָּל־ זִקְנֵי בְּנֵי יִשְׂרָאֵל׃ וַיְדַבֵּר
and-he-told (30) Israel sons-of elders-of all-of *** and-they-assembled

אַהֲרֹן אֵת כָּל־ הַדְּבָרִים אֲשֶׁר־ דִּבֶּר יְהוָה אֶל־מֹשֶׁה וַיַּעַשׂ
and-he-performed Moses to Yahweh he-said that the-words all-of *** Aaron

הָאֹתֹת לְעֵינֵי הָעָם׃ וַיַּאֲמֵן הָעָם
the-people and-he-believed (31) the-people before-eyes-of the-signs

וַיִּשְׁמְעוּ כִּי־ פָקַד יְהוָה אֶת־ בְּנֵי יִשְׂרָאֵל וְכִי
and-that Israel sons-of *** Yahweh he-was-concerned that when-they-heard

רָאָה אֶת־ עָנְיָם וַיִּקְּדוּ וַיִּשְׁתַּחֲוּוּ*׃ וְאַחַר
and-afterwards (5:1) and-they-worshiped then-they-bowed misery-of-them *** he-saw

בָּאוּ מֹשֶׁה וְאַהֲרֹן וַיֹּאמְרוּ אֶל־ פַּרְעֹה כֹּה־ אָמַר יְהוָה
Yahweh he-says this Pharaoh to and-they-said and-Aaron Moses they-went

אֱלֹהֵי יִשְׂרָאֵל שַׁלַּח אֶת־ עַמִּי וְיָחֹגּוּ לִי
to-me so-they-may-hold-festival people-of-me *** let-go! Israel God-of

בַּמִּדְבָּר׃ וַיֹּאמֶר פַּרְעֹה מִי יְהוָה אֲשֶׁר אֶשְׁמַע
I-should-obey that Yahweh who? Pharaoh but-he-said (2) in-the-desert

בְּקֹלוֹ לְשַׁלַּח אֶת־יִשְׂרָאֵל לֹא יָדַעְתִּי אֶת־ יְהוָה וְגַם אֶת־יִשְׂרָאֵל
Israel *** and-so Yahweh *** I-know not Israel *** to-let-go to-voice-of-him

לֹא אֲשַׁלֵּחַ׃ וַיֹּאמְרוּ אֱלֹהֵי הָעִבְרִים נִקְרָא עָלֵינוּ
with-us he-met the-Hebrews God-of then-they-said (3) I-will-let-go not

נֵלֲכָה נָּא דֶּרֶךְ שְׁלֹשֶׁת יָמִים בַּמִּדְבָּר וְנִזְבְּחָה
and-let-us-sacrifice into-the-desert days three-of journey-of now! let-us-take

לַיהוָה אֱלֹהֵינוּ פֶּן־ יִפְגָּעֵנוּ בַּדֶּבֶר אוֹ בֶחָרֶב׃
with-the-sword or with-the-plague he-may-strike-us or God-of-us to-Yahweh

וַיֹּאמֶר אֲלֵהֶם מֶלֶךְ מִצְרַיִם לָמָּה מֹשֶׁה וְאַהֲרֹן תַּפְרִיעוּ אֶת־
*** you-take and-Aaron Moses why? Egypt king-of to-them but-he-said (4)

הָעָם מִמַּעֲשָׂיו לְכוּ לְסִבְלֹתֵיכֶם׃ וַיֹּאמֶר
then-he-said (5) to-burdens-of-you get-back! from-labors-of-him the-people

פַּרְעֹה הֵן־ רַבִּים עַתָּה עַם הָאָרֶץ וְהִשְׁבַּתֶּם אֹתָם
them and-you-stop the-land people-of now numerous-ones see! Pharaoh

מִסִּבְלֹתָם׃ וַיְצַו פַּרְעֹה בַּיּוֹם הַהוּא אֶת־
*** the-same on-the-day Pharaoh and-he-ordered (6) from-burdens-of-them

הַנֹּגְשִׂים בָּעָם וְאֶת־ שֹׁטְרָיו לֵאמֹר׃ לֹא
not (7) to-say foremen-of-him and over-the-people the-ones-driving

תֹאסִפוּן לָתֵת תֶּבֶן לָעָם לִלְבֹּן הַלְּבֵנִים כִּתְמוֹל
as-yesterday the-bricks to-make to-the-people straw to-supply you-continue

שִׁלְשֹׁם הֵם יֵלְכוּ וְקֹשְׁשׁוּ לָהֶם תֶּבֶן׃ וְאֶת־
but (8) straw for-themselves and-let-them-gather let-them-go they before

together all the elders of the Israelites, [30]and Aaron told them everything the LORD had said to Moses. He also performed the signs before the people, [31]and they believed. And when they heard that the LORD was concerned about them and had seen their misery, they bowed down and worshiped.

Bricks Without Straw

5 Afterward Moses and Aaron went to Pharaoh and said, "This is what the LORD, the God of Israel, says: 'Let my people go, so that they may hold a festival to me in the desert.' "

[2]Pharaoh said, "Who is the LORD, that I should obey him and let Israel go? I do not know the LORD and I will not let Israel go."

[3]Then they said, "The God of the Hebrews has met with us. Now let us take a three-day journey into the desert to offer sacrifices to the LORD our God, or he may strike us with plagues or with the sword."

[4]But the king of Egypt said, "Moses and Aaron, why are you taking the people away from their labor? Get back to your work!" [5]Then Pharaoh said, "Look, the people of the land are now numerous, and you are stopping them from working."

[6]That same day Pharaoh gave this order to the slave drivers and foremen in charge of the people: [7]"You are no longer to supply the people with straw for making bricks; let them go and gather their

**31* Most mss have no *dagesh* in the first *vav* (וּו–).

מַתְכֹּנֶת הַלְּבֵנִים אֲשֶׁר הֵם עֹשִׂים תְּמוֹל שִׁלְשֹׁם תָּשִׂימוּ עֲלֵיהֶם
from-them you-require before yesterday ones-making they that the-bricks number-of

לֹא תִגְרְעוּ מִמֶּנּוּ כִּי־ נִרְפִּים הֵם עַל־ כֵּן הֵם צֹעֲקִים
ones-crying they this for they being-lazy-ones for from-him you-reduce not

לֵאמֹר נֵלְכָה נִזְבְּחָה לֵאלֹהֵינוּ׃ תִּכְבַּד הָעֲבֹדָה
the-work let-her-be-hard (9) to-God-of-us let-us-sacrifice let-us-go to-say

עַל־ הָאֲנָשִׁים וְיַעֲשׂוּ־ בָהּ וְאַל־ יִשְׁעוּ בְּדִבְרֵי־
to-words-of they-will-attend and-not at-her so-they-will-work the-men for

שָׁקֶר׃ וַיֵּצְאוּ נֹגְשֵׂי הָעָם וְשֹׁטְרָיו
and-foremen-of-him the-people ones-driving-of then-they-went-out (10) lie

וַיֹּאמְרוּ אֶל־ הָעָם לֵאמֹר כֹּה אָמַר פַּרְעֹה אֵינֶנִּי נֹתֵן לָכֶם
to-you giving not-I Pharaoh he-says this to-say the-people to and-they-said

תֶּבֶן׃ אַתֶּם לְכוּ קְחוּ לָכֶם תֶּבֶן מֵאֲשֶׁר תִּמְצָאוּ כִּי אֵין
not but you-find from-where straw for-yourselves get! go! you (11) straw

נִגְרָע מֵעֲבֹדַתְכֶם דָּבָר׃ וַיָּפֶץ הָעָם
the-people so-he-scattered (12) at-all from-work-of-you being-reduced

בְּכָל־ אֶרֶץ מִצְרָיִם לְקֹשֵׁשׁ קַשׁ לַתֶּבֶן׃
for-the-straw stubble to-gather Egypt land-of over-all-of

וְהַנֹּגְשִׂים אָצִים לֵאמֹר כַּלּוּ מַעֲשֵׂיכֶם דְּבַר־
required-of work-of-you complete! to-say ones-pressing and-the-ones-driving (13)

יוֹם בְּיוֹמוֹ כַּאֲשֶׁר בִּהְיוֹת הַתֶּבֶן׃ וַיֻּכּוּ
and-they-were-beaten (14) the-straw when-to-have just-as in-day-of-him day

שֹׁטְרֵי בְּנֵי יִשְׂרָאֵל אֲשֶׁר־ שָׂמוּ עֲלֵהֶם נֹגְשֵׂי
ones-driving-of over-them they-appointed whom Israel sons-of foremen-of

פַרְעֹה לֵאמֹר מַדּוּעַ לֹא כִלִּיתֶם חָקְכֶם לִלְבֹּן כִּתְמוֹל
as-yesterday to-make-brick quota-of-you you-met not why? to-say Pharaoh

שִׁלְשֹׁם גַּם־ תְּמוֹל גַּם־ הַיּוֹם׃ וַיָּבֹאוּ שֹׁטְרֵי בְּנֵי
sons-of foremen-of then-they-went (15) the-day or yesterday either before

יִשְׂרָאֵל וַיִּצְעֲקוּ אֶל־ פַּרְעֹה לֵאמֹר לָמָּה תַעֲשֶׂה כֹה לַעֲבָדֶיךָ׃
to-servants-of-you this you-do why? to-say Pharaoh to and-they-appealed Israel

תֶּבֶן אֵין נִתָּן לַעֲבָדֶיךָ וּלְבֵנִים אֹמְרִים לָנוּ
to-us ones-telling yet-bricks to-servants-of-you being-given no straw (16)

עֲשׂוּ וְהִנֵּה עֲבָדֶיךָ מֻכִּים וְחָטָאת
but-he-is-at-fault ones-being-beaten servants-of-you and-see! make!

עַמֶּךָ׃ וַיֹּאמֶר נִרְפִּים אַתֶּם נִרְפִּים עַל־ כֵּן
this for ones-being-lazy you ones-being-lazy but-he-said (17) people-of-you

אַתֶּם אֹמְרִים נֵלְכָה נִזְבְּחָה לַיהוָה׃ וְעַתָּה לְכוּ עִבְדוּ
work! go! so-now (18) to-Yahweh let-us-sacrifice let-us-go ones-saying you

own straw. 8 But require them
to make the same number of
bricks as before; don't reduce
the quota. They are lazy; that
is why they are crying out,
'Let us go and sacrifice to our
God.' 9 Make the work harder
for the men so that they keep
working and pay no attention
to lies."
10 Then the slave drivers and
the foremen went out and said
to the people, "This is what
Pharaoh says: 'I will not give
you any more straw. 11 Go and
get your own straw wherever
you can find it, but your work
will not be reduced at all.'"
12 So the people scattered all
over Egypt to gather stubble to
use for straw. 13 The slave
drivers kept pressing them,
saying, "Complete the work
required of you for each day,
just as when you had straw."
14 The Israelite foremen appointed by Pharaoh's slave
drivers were beaten and were
asked, "Why haven't you met
your quota of bricks yesterday
or today, as before?"
15 Then the Israelite foremen
went and appealed to Pharaoh: "Why have you treated
your servants this way? 16 Your
servants are given no straw,
yet we are told, 'Make bricks!'
Your servants are being beat-
en, but the fault is with your
own people."
17 Pharaoh said, "Lazy, that's
what you are—lazy! That is
why you keep saying, 'Let us
go and sacrifice to the LORD.'
18 Now get to work. You will

וְתֶבֶן לֹא־ יִנָּתֵן לָכֶם וְתֹכֶן לְבֵנִים תִּתֵּנּוּ*׃
you-must-produce bricks yet-quota-of to-you he-will-be-given not but-straw

וַיִּרְאוּ שֹׁטְרֵי בְנֵי־ יִשְׂרָאֵל אֹתָם בְּרָע לֵאמֹר
to-say in-trouble they Israel sons-of foremen-of and-they-realized (19)

לֹא־ תִגְרְעוּ מִלִּבְנֵיכֶם דְּבַר־ יוֹם בְּיוֹמוֹ׃
in-day-of-him day required-of from-bricks-of-you you-can-reduce not

וַיִּפְגְּעוּ אֶת־ מֹשֶׁה וְאֶת־ אַהֲרֹן נִצָּבִים לִקְרָאתָם
to-meet-them ones-waiting Aaron and Moses *** and-they-found (20)

בְּצֵאתָם מֵאֵת פַּרְעֹה׃ וַיֹּאמְרוּ אֲלֵהֶם יֵרֶא
may-he-look to-them and-they-said (21) Pharaoh from when-to-leave-them

יְהוָה עֲלֵיכֶם וְיִשְׁפֹּט אֲשֶׁר הִבְאַשְׁתֶּם אֶת־ רֵיחֵנוּ
stench-of-us *** you-made-stink for and-may-he-judge on-you Yahweh

בְּעֵינֵי פַרְעֹה וּבְעֵינֵי עֲבָדָיו לָתֶת־ חֶרֶב בְּיָדָם
in-hand-of-them sword to-put servants-of-him and-in-eyes-of Pharaoh in-eyes-of

לְהָרְגֵנוּ׃ וַיָּשָׁב מֹשֶׁה אֶל־ יְהוָה וַיֹּאמַר אֲדֹנָי לָמָה
why? Lord and-he-said Yahweh to Moses so-he-returned (22) to-kill-us

הֲרֵעֹתָה לָעָם הַזֶּה לָמָּה זֶּה שְׁלַחְתָּנִי׃
you-sent-me this why? the-this on-the-people you-brought-trouble

וּמֵאָז בָּאתִי אֶל־פַּרְעֹה לְדַבֵּר בִּשְׁמֶךָ הֵרַע
he-brought-trouble in-name-of-you to-speak Pharaoh to I-went for-ever-since (23)

לָעָם הַזֶּה וְהַצֵּל לֹא־ הִצַּלְתָּ אֶת־ עַמֶּךָ׃
people-of-you *** you-rescued not and-to-rescue the-this on-the-people

וַיֹּאמֶר יְהוָה אֶל־ מֹשֶׁה עַתָּה תִרְאֶה אֲשֶׁר אֶעֱשֶׂה לְפַרְעֹה
to-Pharaoh I-will-do what you-will-see now Moses to Yahweh then-he-said (6:1)

כִּי בְיָד חֲזָקָה יְשַׁלְּחֵם וּבְיָד חֲזָקָה
mighty and-because-of-hand he-will-let-go-them mighty because-of-hand for

יְגָרְשֵׁם מֵאַרְצוֹ׃ וַיְדַבֵּר אֱלֹהִים אֶל־ מֹשֶׁה
Moses to God and-he-spoke (2) from-country-of-him he-will-drive-them

וַיֹּאמֶר אֵלָיו אֲנִי יְהוָה׃ וָאֵרָא אֶל־ אַבְרָהָם אֶל־יִצְחָק וְאֶל־
and-to Isaac to Abraham to and-I-appeared (3) Yahweh I to-him and-he-said

יַעֲקֹב בְּאֵל שַׁדָּי וּשְׁמִי יְהוָה לֹא נוֹדַעְתִּי לָהֶם׃
to-them I-made-myself-known not Yahweh but-name-of-me Almighty as-God Jacob

וְגַם הֲקִמֹתִי אֶת־ בְּרִיתִי אִתָּם לָתֵת לָהֶם אֶת־
*** to-them to-give with-them covenant-of-me *** I-established and-also (4)

אֶרֶץ כְּנָעַן אֵת אֶרֶץ מְגֻרֵיהֶם אֲשֶׁר־ גָּרוּ בָהּ׃
in-her they-lived where journeys-of-them land-of *** Canaan land-of

וְגַם ׀ אֲנִי שָׁמַעְתִּי אֶת־ נַאֲקַת בְּנֵי יִשְׂרָאֵל אֲשֶׁר מִצְרַיִם
Egyptians whom Israel sons-of groan-of *** I-heard I and-also (5)

not be given any straw, yet you must produce your full quota of bricks."

19 The Israelite foremen realized they were in trouble when they were told, "You are not to reduce the number of bricks required of you for each day." 20 When they left Pharaoh, they found Moses and Aaron waiting to meet them, 21 and they said, "May the LORD look upon you and judge you! You have made us a stench to Pharaoh and his servants and have put a sword in their hand to kill us."

God Promises Deliverance

22 Moses returned to the LORD and said, "O Lord, why have you brought trouble upon this people? Is this why you sent me? 23 Ever since I went to Pharaoh to speak in your name, he has brought trouble upon this people, and you have not rescued your people at all."

6 Then the LORD said to Moses, "Now you will see what I will do to Pharaoh: Because of my mighty hand he will let them go; because of my mighty hand he will drive them out of his country."

2 God also said to Moses, "I am the LORD. 3 I appeared to Abraham, to Isaac and to Jacob as God Almighty,[i] but by my name the LORD[j] I did not make myself known to them.[k] 4 I also established my covenant with them to give them the land of Canaan, where they lived as aliens. 5 Moreover, I have heard the groaning of the Israelites,

[i] 3 Hebrew *El-Shaddai*
[j] 3 See note at Exodus 3:15.
[k] 3 Or *Almighty, and by my name the LORD did I not let myself be known to them?*

*18 Most mss have no *dagesh* in the *nun* (תתנו).

מַעֲבִדִים אֹתָם וָאֶזְכֹּר אֶת־ בְּרִיתִי׃ לָכֵן אֱמֹר
say! therefore (6) covenant-of-me *** and-I-remembered them ones-enslaving

לִבְנֵי־ יִשְׂרָאֵל אֲנִי יְהוָה וְהוֹצֵאתִי אֶתְכֶם מִתַּחַת סִבְלֹת
yokes-of from-under you and-I-will-bring Yahweh I Israel to-sons-of

מִצְרַיִם וְהִצַּלְתִּי אֶתְכֶם מֵעֲבֹדָתָם וְגָאַלְתִּי אֶתְכֶם
you and-I-will-redeem from-service-of-them you and-I-will-free Egyptians

בִּזְרוֹעַ נְטוּיָה וּבִשְׁפָטִים גְּדֹלִים׃
mighty-ones and-with-acts-of-judgment being-outstretched with-arm

וְלָקַחְתִּי אֶתְכֶם לִי לְעָם וְהָיִיתִי לָכֶם לֵאלֹהִים
as-God to-you and-I-will-be as-people to-me you and-I-will-take (7)

וִידַעְתֶּם כִּי אֲנִי יְהוָה אֱלֹהֵיכֶם הַמּוֹצִיא אֶתְכֶם מִתַּחַת
from-under you the-one-bringing God-of-you Yahweh I that then-you-will-know

סִבְלוֹת מִצְרָיִם׃ וְהֵבֵאתִי אֶתְכֶם אֶל־הָאָרֶץ אֲשֶׁר נָשָׂאתִי אֶת־
*** I-lifted that the-land to you and-I-will-bring (8) Egyptians yokes-of

יָדִי לָתֵת אֹתָהּ לְאַבְרָהָם לְיִצְחָק וּלְיַעֲקֹב וְנָתַתִּי אֹתָהּ
her and-I-will-give and-to-Jacob to-Isaac to-Abraham her to-give hand-of-me

לָכֶם מוֹרָשָׁה אֲנִי יְהוָה׃ וַיְדַבֵּר מֹשֶׁה כֵּן אֶל־ בְּנֵי יִשְׂרָאֵל
Israel sons-of to this Moses and-he-reported (9) Yahweh I possession to-you

וְלֹא שָׁמְעוּ אֶל־ מֹשֶׁה מִקֹּצֶר רוּחַ וּמֵעֲבֹדָה קָשָׁה׃
cruel and-for-bondage spirit for-shortness-of Moses to they-listened but-not

וַיְדַבֵּר יְהוָה אֶל־מֹשֶׁה לֵּאמֹר׃ בֹּא דַבֵּר אֶל־פַּרְעֹה מֶלֶךְ
king-of Pharaoh to tell! go! (11) to-say Moses to Yahweh then-he-said (10)

מִצְרָיִם וִישַׁלַּח אֶת־ בְּנֵי־ יִשְׂרָאֵל מֵאַרְצוֹ׃ וַיְדַבֵּר
but-he-said (12) from-country-of-him Israel sons-of *** so-he-will-let-go Egypt

מֹשֶׁה לִפְנֵי יְהוָה לֵאמֹר הֵן בְּנֵי־ יִשְׂרָאֵל לֹא־ שָׁמְעוּ אֵלַי וְאֵיךְ
so-why? to-me they-listen not Israel sons-of see! to-say Yahweh to Moses

יִשְׁמָעֵנִי פַרְעֹה וַאֲנִי עֲרַל שְׂפָתָיִם׃ וַיְדַבֵּר
now-he-spoke (13) lips uncircumcised-of since-I Pharaoh would-he-listen-to-me

יְהוָה אֶל־ מֹשֶׁה וְאֶל־ אַהֲרֹן וַיְצַוֵּם אֶל־ בְּנֵי יִשְׂרָאֵל
Israel sons-of about and-he-commanded-them Aaron and-to Moses to Yahweh

וְאֶל־ פַּרְעֹה מֶלֶךְ מִצְרַיִם לְהוֹצִיא אֶת־ בְּנֵי־ יִשְׂרָאֵל מֵאֶרֶץ
from-land-of Israel sons-of *** to-bring Egypt king-of Pharaoh and-about

מִצְרָיִם׃ אֵלֶּה רָאשֵׁי בֵית־ אֲבֹתָם בְּנֵי רְאוּבֵן בְּכֹר
firstborn-of Reuben sons-of fathers-of-them house-of heads-of these (14) Egypt

יִשְׂרָאֵל חֲנוֹךְ וּפַלּוּא חֶצְרוֹן וְכַרְמִי אֵלֶּה מִשְׁפְּחֹת רְאוּבֵן׃ וּבְנֵי
and-sons-of (15) Reuben clans-of these and-Carmi Hezron and-Pallu Hanoch Israel

שִׁמְעוֹן יְמוּאֵל וְיָמִין וְאֹהַד וְיָכִין וְצֹחַר וְשָׁאוּל בֶּן־
son-of and-Shaul and-Zohar and-Jakin and-Ohad and-Jamin Jemuel Simeon

whom the Egyptians are enslaving, and I have remembered my covenant.

6"Therefore, say to the Israelites: 'I am the LORD and I will bring you out from under the yoke of the Egyptians. I will free you from being slaves to them and will redeem you with an outstretched arm and with mighty acts of judgment.
7I will take you as my own people, and I will be your God. Then you will know that I am the LORD your God, who brought you out from under the yoke of the Egyptians.
8And I will bring you to the land I swore with uplifted hand to give to Abraham, to Isaac and to Jacob. I will give it to you as a possession. I am the LORD.'"

9Moses reported this to the Israelites, but they did not listen to him because of their discouragement and cruel bondage.

10Then the LORD said to Moses, 11"Go, tell Pharaoh king of Egypt to let the Israelites go out of his country."

12But Moses said to the LORD, "If the Israelites will not listen to me, why would Pharaoh listen to me, since I speak with faltering lips[m]?"

Family Record of Moses and Aaron

13Now the LORD spoke to Moses and Aaron about the Israelites and Pharaoh king of Egypt, and he commanded them to bring the Israelites out of Egypt.

14These were the heads of their families[n]:

The sons of Reuben the firstborn son of Israel were Hanoch and Pallu, Hezron and Carmi. These were the clans of Reuben.

15The sons of Simeon were Jemuel, Jamin, Ohad, Jakin, Zohar and Shaul the

[m]12 Hebrew *I am uncircumcised of lips*; also in verse 30

[n]14 The Hebrew for *families* here and in verse 25 refers to units larger than clans.

הַכְּנַעֲנִית אֵלֶּה מִשְׁפְּחֹת שִׁמְעוֹן׃ וְאֵלֶּה שְׁמוֹת בְּנֵי־
sons-of names-of and-these (16) Simeon clans-of these the-Canaanite-woman

לֵוִי לְתֹלְדֹתָם גֵּרְשׁוֹן וּקְהָת וּמְרָרִי וּשְׁנֵי חַיֵּי
lives-of and-years-of and-Merari and-Kohath Gershon by-records-of-them Levi

לֵוִי שֶׁבַע וּשְׁלֹשִׁים וּמְאַת שָׁנָה׃ בְּנֵי גֵרְשׁוֹן לִבְנִי
Libni Gershon sons-of (17) year and-hundred-of and-thirty seven Levi

וְשִׁמְעִי לְמִשְׁפְּחֹתָם׃ וּבְנֵי קְהָת עַמְרָם וְיִצְהָר
and-Izhar Amram Kohath and-sons-of (18) by-clans-of-them and-Shimei

וְחֶבְרוֹן וְעֻזִּיאֵל וּשְׁנֵי חַיֵּי קְהָת שָׁלֹשׁ וּשְׁלֹשִׁים
and-thirty three Kohath lives-of and-years-of and-Uzziel and-Hebron

וּמְאַת שָׁנָה׃ וּבְנֵי מְרָרִי מַחְלִי וּמוּשִׁי אֵלֶּה מִשְׁפְּחֹת
clans-of these and-Mushi Mahli Merari and-sons-of (19) year and-hundred-of

הַלֵּוִי לְתֹלְדֹתָם׃ וַיִּקַּח עַמְרָם אֶת־ יוֹכֶבֶד
Jochebed *** Amram and-he-took (20) by-records-of-them the-Levi

דֹּדָתוֹ לוֹ לְאִשָּׁה וַתֵּלֶד לוֹ אֶת־ אַהֲרֹן וְאֶת־
and Aaron *** to-him and-she-bore for-wife to-him sister-of-father-of-him

מֹשֶׁה וּשְׁנֵי חַיֵּי עַמְרָם שֶׁבַע וּשְׁלֹשִׁים וּמְאַת שָׁנָה׃
year and-hundred-of and-thirty seven Amram lives-of and-years-of Moses

וּבְנֵי יִצְהָר קֹרַח וָנֶפֶג וְזִכְרִי׃ וּבְנֵי עֻזִּיאֵל
Uzziel and-sons-of (22) and-Zicri and-Nepheg Korah Izhar and-sons-of (21)

מִישָׁאֵל וְאֶלְצָפָן וְסִתְרִי׃ וַיִּקַּח אַהֲרֹן אֶת־אֱלִישֶׁבַע
Elisheba *** Aaron and-he-took (23) and-Sithri and-Elzaphan Mishael

בַּת־ עַמִּינָדָב אֲחוֹת נַחְשׁוֹן לוֹ לְאִשָּׁה וַתֵּלֶד לוֹ
to-him and-she-bore for-wife to-him Nahshon sister-of Amminadab daughter-of

אֶת־ נָדָב וְאֶת־אֲבִיהוּא אֶת־ אֶלְעָזָר וְאֶת־אִיתָמָר׃ וּבְנֵי קֹרַח אַסִּיר
Assir Korah and-sons-of (24) Ithamar and Eleazar *** Abihu and Nadab ***

וְאֶלְקָנָה וַאֲבִיאָסָף אֵלֶּה מִשְׁפְּחֹת הַקָּרְחִי׃ וְאֶלְעָזָר בֶּן־
son-of and-Eleazar (25) the-Korahite clans-of these and-Abiasaph and-Elkanah

אַהֲרֹן לָקַח־ לוֹ מִבְּנוֹת פּוּטִיאֵל לוֹ לְאִשָּׁה וַתֵּלֶד
and-she-bore for-wife to-him Putiel from-daughters-of to-him he-took Aaron

לוֹ אֶת־ פִּינְחָס אֵלֶּה רָאשֵׁי אֲבוֹת הַלְוִיִּם לְמִשְׁפְּחֹתָם׃
by-clans-of-them the-Levites fathers-of heads-of these Phinehas *** to-him

הוּא אַהֲרֹן וּמֹשֶׁה אֲשֶׁר אָמַר יְהוָה לָהֶם הוֹצִיאוּ אֶת־ בְּנֵי
sons-of *** bring! to-them Yahweh he-said whom and-Moses Aaron this (26)

יִשְׂרָאֵל מֵאֶרֶץ מִצְרַיִם עַל־ צִבְאֹתָם׃ הֵם הַמְדַבְּרִים
the-ones-speaking they (27) divisions-of-them by Egypt from-land-of Israel

אֶל־פַּרְעֹה מֶלֶךְ־ מִצְרַיִם לְהוֹצִיא אֶת־ בְּנֵי־ יִשְׂרָאֵל מִמִּצְרָיִם הוּא מֹשֶׁה
Moses this from-Egypt Israel sons-of *** to-bring Egypt king-of Pharaoh to

son of a Canaanite woman. These were the clans of Simeon.

[16]These were the names of the sons of Levi according to their records: Gershon, Kohath and Merari. Levi lived 137 years.

[17]The sons of Gershon, by clans, were Libni and Shimei.

[18]The sons of Kohath were Amram, Izhar, Hebron and Uzziel. Kohath lived 133 years.

[19]The sons of Merari were Mahli and Mushi.

These were the clans of Levi according to their records.

[20]Amram married his father's sister Jochebed, who bore him Aaron and Moses. Amram lived 137 years.

[21]The sons of Izhar were Korah, Nepheg and Zicri.

[22]The sons of Uzziel were Mishael, Elzaphan and Sithri.

[23]Aaron married Elisheba, daughter of Amminadab and sister of Nahshon, and she bore him Nadab and Abihu, Eleazar and Ithamar.

[24]The sons of Korah were Assir, Elkanah and Abiasaph. These were the Korahite clans.

[25]Eleazar son of Aaron married one of the daughters of Putiel, and she bore him Phinehas.

These were the heads of the Levite families, clan by clan.

[26]It was this same Aaron and Moses to whom the LORD said, "Bring the Israelites out of Egypt by their divisions."
[27]They were the ones who spoke to Pharaoh king of Egypt about bringing the Israelites out of Egypt. It was the same Moses and Aaron.

וְאַהֲרֹן׃ וַיְהִי בְּיוֹם דִּבֶּר יְהוָה אֶל־מֹשֶׁה בְּאֶרֶץ מִצְרָיִם׃
Egypt in-land-of Moses to Yahweh he-spoke on-day and-he-was (28) and-Aaron

וַיְדַבֵּר יְהוָה אֶל־מֹשֶׁה לֵּאמֹר אֲנִי יְהוָה דַּבֵּר אֶל־פַּרְעֹה מֶלֶךְ
king-of Pharaoh to tell! Yahweh I to-say Moses to Yahweh that-he-said (29)

מִצְרַיִם אֵת כָּל־אֲשֶׁר אֲנִי דֹּבֵר אֵלֶיךָ׃ וַיֹּאמֶר מֹשֶׁה לִפְנֵי יְהוָה הֵן
see! Yahweh to Moses but-he-said (30) to-you telling I that all *** Egypt

אֲנִי עֲרַל שְׂפָתַיִם וְאֵיךְ יִשְׁמַע אֵלַי פַּרְעֹה׃ וַיֹּאמֶר
so-he-said (7:1) Pharaoh to-me would-he-listen so-why? lips uncircumcised-of I

יְהוָה אֶל־מֹשֶׁה רְאֵה נְתַתִּיךָ אֱלֹהִים לְפַרְעֹה וְאַהֲרֹן אָחִיךָ
brother-of-you and-Aaron to-Pharaoh God I-made-you see! Moses to Yahweh

יִהְיֶה נְבִיאֶךָ׃ אַתָּה תְדַבֵּר אֵת כָּל־אֲשֶׁר אֲצַוֶּךָּ וְאַהֲרֹן
and-Aaron I-command-you that all *** you-say you (2) prophet-of-you he-is

אָחִיךָ יְדַבֵּר אֶל־פַּרְעֹה וְשִׁלַּח אֶת־בְּנֵי־יִשְׂרָאֵל
Israel sons-of *** so-he-will-let-go Pharaoh to he-will-tell brother-of-you

מֵאַרְצוֹ׃ וַאֲנִי אַקְשֶׁה אֶת־לֵב פַּרְעֹה
Pharaoh heart-of *** I-will-harden but-I (3) from-land-of-him

וְהִרְבֵּיתִי אֶת־אֹתֹתַי וְאֶת־מוֹפְתַי בְּאֶרֶץ מִצְרָיִם׃
Egypt in-land-of wonders-of-me and signs-of-me *** and-I-will-multiply

וְלֹא־יִשְׁמַע אֲלֵכֶם פַּרְעֹה וְנָתַתִּי אֶת־יָדִי
hand-of-me *** then-I-will-lay Pharaoh to-you he-will-listen but-not (4)

בְּמִצְרָיִם וְהוֹצֵאתִי אֶת־צִבְאֹתַי אֶת־עַמִּי בְנֵי־
sons-of people-of-me *** divisions-of-me *** and-I-will-bring on-Egypt

יִשְׂרָאֵל מֵאֶרֶץ מִצְרַיִם בִּשְׁפָטִים גְּדֹלִים׃
mighty-ones by-acts-of-judgment Egypt from-land-of Israel

וְיָדְעוּ מִצְרַיִם כִּי־אֲנִי יְהוָה בִּנְטֹתִי אֶת־
*** when-to-stretch-out-me Yahweh I that Egyptians and-they-will-know (5)

יָדִי עַל־מִצְרָיִם וְהוֹצֵאתִי אֶת־בְּנֵי־יִשְׂרָאֵל מִתּוֹכָם׃
from-midst-of-them Israel sons-of *** and-I-bring Egypt against hand-of-me

וַיַּעַשׂ מֹשֶׁה וְאַהֲרֹן כַּאֲשֶׁר צִוָּה יְהוָה אֹתָם כֵּן
this them Yahweh he-commanded just-as and-Aaron Moses and-he-did (6)

עָשׂוּ׃ וּמֹשֶׁה בֶּן־שְׁמֹנִים שָׁנָה וְאַהֲרֹן בֶּן־שָׁלֹשׁ וּשְׁמֹנִים
and-eighty three son-of and-Aaron year eighty son-of now-Moses (7) they-did

שָׁנָה בְּדַבְּרָם אֶל־פַּרְעֹה׃ וַיֹּאמֶר יְהוָה אֶל־מֹשֶׁה וְאֶל־
and-to Moses to Yahweh and-he-said (8) Pharaoh to when-to-speak-them year

אַהֲרֹן לֵאמֹר׃ כִּי יְדַבֵּר אֲלֵכֶם פַּרְעֹה לֵאמֹר תְּנוּ לָכֶם מוֹפֵת
miracle to-you perform! to-say Pharaoh to-you he-says when (9) to-say Aaron

וְאָמַרְתָּ אֶל־אַהֲרֹן קַח אֶת־מַטְּךָ וְהַשְׁלֵךְ לִפְנֵי־פַרְעֹה
Pharaoh before and-throw-down! staff-of-you *** take! Aaron to then-you-say

Aaron to Speak for Moses

28Now when the LORD spoke
to Moses in Egypt, 29he said to
him, "I am the LORD. Tell Pharaoh king of Egypt everything I
tell you."
30But Moses said to the LORD,
"Since I speak with faltering
lips, why would Pharaoh listen to me?"

7 Then the LORD said to
Moses, "See, I have made
you like God to Pharaoh, and
your brother Aaron will be
your prophet. 2You are to say
everything I command you,
and your brother Aaron is to
tell Pharaoh to let the Israelites
go out of his country. 3But I
will harden Pharaoh's heart,
and though I multiply my
miraculous signs and wonders
in Egypt, 4he will not listen to
you. Then I will lay my hand
on Egypt and with mighty acts
of judgment I will bring out
my divisions, my people the
Israelites. 5And the Egyptians
will know that I am the LORD
when I stretch out my hand
against Egypt and bring the
Israelites out of it."

Moses' Staff Becomes a Snake

6Moses and Aaron did just as
the LORD commanded them.
7Moses was eighty years old
and Aaron eighty-three when
they spoke to Pharaoh.
8The LORD said to Moses and
Aaron, 9"When Pharaoh says
to you, 'Perform a miracle,'
then say to Aaron, 'Take your
staff and throw it down before

יְהִי לְתַנִּין׃ וַיָּבֹא מֹשֶׁה וְאַהֲרֹן אֶל־פַּרְעֹה
Pharaoh to and-Aaron Moses so-he-went (10) into-snake he-will-become

וַיַּעַשׂוּ* כֵן כַּאֲשֶׁר צִוָּה יְהוָה וַיַּשְׁלֵךְ אַהֲרֹן אֶת־
*** Aaron and-he-threw-down Yahweh he-commanded just-as this and-they-did

מַטֵּהוּ לִפְנֵי פַרְעֹה וְלִפְנֵי עֲבָדָיו וַיְהִי
and-he-became officials-of-him and-before Pharaoh before staff-of-him

לְתַנִּין׃ וַיִּקְרָא גַּם־פַּרְעֹה לַחֲכָמִים
to-the-wise-men Pharaoh also then-he-summoned (11) into-snake

וְלַמְכַשְּׁפִים וַיַּעֲשׂוּ גַם־הֵם חַרְטֻמֵּי מִצְרַיִם
Egypt magicians-of they also and-they-did and-to-the-ones-being-sorcerors

בְּלַהֲטֵיהֶם כֵּן׃ וַיַּשְׁלִיכוּ אִישׁ מַטֵּהוּ
staff-of-him each and-they-threw-down (12) same by-secret-arts-of-them

וַיִּהְיוּ לְתַנִּינִם וַיִּבְלַע מַטֵּה־אַהֲרֹן אֶת־מַטֹּתָם׃
staffs-of-them *** Aaron staff-of but-he-swallowed into-snakes and-they-became

וַיֶּחֱזַק לֵב פַּרְעֹה וְלֹא שָׁמַע אֲלֵהֶם כַּאֲשֶׁר
just-as to-them he-listened and-not Pharaoh heart-of yet-he-was-hard (13)

דִּבֶּר יְהוָה׃ וַיֹּאמֶר יְהוָה אֶל־מֹשֶׁה כָּבֵד לֵב
heart-of he-is-unyielding Moses to Yahweh then-he-said (14) Yahweh he-said

פַּרְעֹה מֵאֵן לְשַׁלַּח הָעָם׃ לֵךְ אֶל־פַּרְעֹה בַּבֹּקֶר
in-the-morning Pharaoh to go! (15) the-people to-let-go he-refuses Pharaoh

הִנֵּה יֹצֵא הַמַּיְמָה וְנִצַּבְתָּ לִקְרָאתוֹ עַל־שְׂפַת הַיְאֹר
the-Nile bank-of on to-meet-him and-you-wait to-the-waters going-out see!

וְהַמַּטֶּה אֲשֶׁר־נֶהְפַּךְ לְנָחָשׁ תִּקַּח בְּיָדֶךָ׃
in-hand-of-you you-take into-snake he-was-changed that and-the-staff

וְאָמַרְתָּ אֵלָיו יְהוָה אֱלֹהֵי הָעִבְרִים שְׁלָחַנִי אֵלֶיךָ לֵאמֹר
to-say to-you he-sent-me the-Hebrews God-of Yahweh to-him then-you-say (16)

שַׁלַּח אֶת־עַמִּי וְיַעַבְדֻנִי בַּמִּדְבָּר וְהִנֵּה לֹא־
not but-see! in-the-desert so-they-may-worship-me people-of-me *** let-go!

שָׁמַעְתָּ עַד־כֹּה׃ כֹּה אָמַר יְהוָה בְּזֹאת תֵּדַע כִּי
that you-will-know by-this Yahweh he-says this (17) now until you-listened

אֲנִי יְהוָה הִנֵּה אָנֹכִי מַכֶּה ׀ בַּמַּטֶּה אֲשֶׁר־בְּיָדִי עַל־הַמַּיִם
the-waters on in-hand-of-me that with-the-staff striking I see! Yahweh I

אֲשֶׁר בַּיְאֹר וְנֶהֶפְכוּ לְדָם׃ וְהַדָּגָה אֲשֶׁר־
that and-the-fish (18) into-blood and-they-will-be-changed in-the-Nile that

בַּיְאֹר תָּמוּת וּבָאַשׁ הַיְאֹר וְנִלְאוּ
and-they-will-be-unable the-Nile and-he-will-stink she-will-die in-the-Nile

מִצְרַיִם לִשְׁתּוֹת מַיִם מִן־הַיְאֹר׃ וַיֹּאמֶר יְהוָה אֶל־מֹשֶׁה
Moses to Yahweh and-he-said (19) the-Nile from waters to-drink Egyptians

Pharaoh,' and it will become a
snake."
10Then Moses and Aaron
went to Pharaoh and did just
as the LORD commanded.
Aaron threw his staff down in
front of Pharaoh and his
officials, and it became a
snake. 11Pharaoh then summoned wise men and sorcer-
ers, and the Egyptian magicians also did the same things
by their secret arts: 12Each one
threw down his staff and it
became a snake. But Aaron's
staff swallowed up their staffs.
13Yet Pharaoh's heart became
hard and he would not listen
to them, just as the LORD had
said.

The Plague of Blood

14Then the LORD said to
Moses, "Pharaoh's heart is
unyielding; he refuses to let
the people go. 15Go to Pharaoh
in the morning as he goes out
to the water. Wait on the bank
of the Nile to meet him, and
take in your hand the staff that
was changed into a snake.
16Then say to him, 'The LORD,
the God of the Hebrews, has
sent me to say to you: Let my
people go, so that they may
worship me in the desert. But
until now you have not listened. 17This is what the LORD
says: By this you will know
that I am the LORD: With the
staff that is in my hand I will
strike the water of the Nile,
and it will be changed into
blood. 18The fish in the Nile
will die, and the river will
stink; the Egyptians will not
be able to drink its water.' "
19The LORD said to Moses,

**10* Most mss have *hateph pathah* under the *ayin* (וַיַּעֲשׂוּ).

אֱמֹר אֶל־אַהֲרֹן קַח מַטְּךָ וּנְטֵה־יָדְךָ עַל־מֵימֵי
waters-of over hand-of-you and-stretch! staff-of-you take! Aaron to tell!

מִצְרַיִם עַל נַהֲרֹתָם ׀ עַל־יְאֹרֵיהֶם וְעַל־אַגְמֵיהֶם
ponds-of-them and-over canals-of-them over streams-of-them over Egypt

וְעַל כָּל־מִקְוֵה מֵימֵיהֶם וְיִהְיוּ־דָם
blood and-they-will-become waters-of-them reservoir-of every-of and-over

וְהָיָה דָם בְּכָל־אֶרֶץ מִצְרַיִם וּבָעֵצִים
even-in-the-wood-buckets Egypt land-of in-all-of blood and-he-will-be

וּבָאֲבָנִים׃ וַיַּעֲשׂוּ־כֵן מֹשֶׁה וְאַהֲרֹן כַּאֲשֶׁר ׀ צִוָּה
he-commanded just-as and-Aaron Moses this and-they-did (20) and-in-the-stone-jars

יְהוָה וַיָּרֶם בַּמַּטֶּה וַיַּךְ אֶת־הַמַּיִם אֲשֶׁר
that the-waters *** and-he-struck with-the-staff and-he-raised Yahweh

בַּיְאֹר לְעֵינֵי פַרְעֹה וּלְעֵינֵי עֲבָדָיו
officials-of-him and-before-eyes-of Pharaoh before-eyes-of in-the-Nile

וַיֵּהָפְכוּ כָּל־הַמַּיִם אֲשֶׁר־בַּיְאֹר לְדָם׃
into-blood in-the-Nile that the-waters all-of and-they-were-changed

וְהַדָּגָה אֲשֶׁר־בַּיְאֹר מֵתָה וַיִּבְאַשׁ הַיְאֹר וְלֹא־
so-not the-Nile and-he-stunk she-died in-the-Nile that and-the-fish (21)

יָכְלוּ מִצְרַיִם לִשְׁתּוֹת מַיִם מִן־הַיְאֹר וַיְהִי הַדָּם
the-blood and-he-was the-Nile from waters to-drink Egyptians they-could

בְּכָל־אֶרֶץ מִצְרָיִם׃ וַיַּעֲשׂוּ־כֵן חַרְטֻמֵּי מִצְרַיִם
Egypt magicians-of same but-they-did (22) Egypt land-of in-all-of

בְּלָטֵיהֶם וַיֶּחֱזַק לֵב־פַּרְעֹה וְלֹא־שָׁמַע אֲלֵהֶם
to-them he-listened and-not Pharaoh heart-of so-he-was-hard by-arts-of-them

כַּאֲשֶׁר דִּבֶּר יְהוָה׃ וַיִּפֶן פַּרְעֹה וַיָּבֹא אֶל־בֵּיתוֹ
palace-of-him into and-he-went Pharaoh so-he-turned (23) Yahweh he-said just-as

וְלֹא־שָׁת לִבּוֹ גַּם־לָזֹאת׃ וַיַּחְפְּרוּ כָל־מִצְרַיִם
Egyptians all-of and-they-dug (24) to-this even heart-of-him he-took and-not

סְבִיבֹת הַיְאֹר מַיִם לִשְׁתּוֹת כִּי לֹא יָכְלוּ לִשְׁתֹּת מִמֵּימֵי
from-waters-of to-drink they-could not for to-drink waters the-Nile along

הַיְאֹר׃ וַיִּמָּלֵא שִׁבְעַת יָמִים אַחֲרֵי הַכּוֹת־יְהוָה אֶת־הַיְאֹר׃
the-Nile *** Yahweh to-strike after days seven-of and-he-passed (25) the-Nile

וַיֹּאמֶר יְהוָה אֶל־מֹשֶׁה בֹּא אֶל־פַּרְעֹה וְאָמַרְתָּ אֵלָיו כֹּה
this to-him and-you-say Pharaoh to go! Moses to Yahweh then-he-said *(26[1])

אָמַר יְהוָה שַׁלַּח אֶת־עַמִּי וְיַעַבְדֻנִי׃ וְאִם־
but-if (27[2]) so-they-may-worship-me people-of-me *** let-go! Yahweh he-says

מָאֵן אַתָּה לְשַׁלֵּחַ הִנֵּה אָנֹכִי נֹגֵף אֶת־כָּל־גְּבוּלְךָ בַּצְפַרְדְּעִים׃
with-the-frogs country-of-you all-of *** plaguing I see! to-let-go you to-refuse

"Tell Aaron, 'Take your staff
and stretch out your hand over
the waters of Egypt—over the
streams and canals, over the
ponds and all the reser-
voirs'—and they will turn to
blood. Blood will be everywhere in Egypt, even in the
wooden buckets and stone
jars."
[20]Moses and Aaron did just
as the LORD had commanded.
He raised his staff in the presence of Pharaoh and his
officials and struck the water
of the Nile, and all the water
was changed into blood. [21]The
fish in the Nile died, and the
river smelled so bad that the
Egyptians could not drink its
water. Blood was everywhere
in Egypt.
[22]But the Egyptian magicians did the same things by
their secret arts, and Pharaoh's
heart became hard; he would
not listen to Moses and Aaron,
just as the LORD had said. [23]In-
stead, he turned and went into
his palace, and did not take
even this to heart. [24]And all the
Egyptians dug along the Nile
to get drinking water, because
they could not drink the water
of the river.

The Plague of Frogs

[25]Seven days passed after the
8 LORD struck the Nile.
[1]Then the LORD said to
Moses, "Go to Pharaoh and
say to him, 'This is what the
LORD says: Let my people go,
so that they may worship me.
[2]If you refuse to let them go, I
will plague your whole country with frogs. [3]The Nile will

*The Hebrew numeration of chapter 8 begins with verse 5 in English. The number in brackets indicates the English numeration.

וְשָׁרַ֣ץ הַיְאֹר֮ צְפַרְדְּעִים֒ וְעָלוּ֙ וּבָ֣אוּ
and-they-will-go and-they-will-come-up frogs the-Nile and-he-will-teem (28[3])

בְּבֵיתֶ֔ךָ וּבַחֲדַ֥ר מִשְׁכָּבְךָ֖ וְעַל־ מִטָּתֶ֑ךָ
bed-of-you and-onto sleep-of-you and-into-room-of into-palace-of-you

וּבְבֵ֤ית עֲבָדֶ֙יךָ֙ וּבְעַמֶּ֔ךָ וּבְתַנּוּרֶ֖יךָ
and-into-ovens-of-you and-on-people-of-you officials-of-you and-into-house-of

וּבְמִשְׁאֲרוֹתֶֽיךָ׃ וּבְכָ֥ה וּֽבְעַמְּךָ֖
and-on-people-of-you and-on-you (29[4]) and-into-kneading-troughs-of-you

וּבְכָל־ עֲבָדֶ֑יךָ יַעֲל֖וּ הַֽצְפַרְדְּעִֽים׃ וַיֹּ֣אמֶר
then-he-said (8:1[5]) the-frogs they-will-go-up officials-of-you and-on-all-of

יְהוָה֮ אֶל־מֹשֶׁה֒ אֱמֹ֣ר אֶֽל־אַהֲרֹ֗ן נְטֵ֤ה אֶת־ יָֽדְךָ֙ בְּמַטֶּ֔ךָ
with-staff-of-you hand-of-you *** stretch-out! Aaron to tell! Moses to Yahweh

עַל־ הַנְּהָרֹ֔ת עַל־ הַיְאֹרִ֖ים וְעַל־ הָאֲגַמִּ֑ים וְהַ֥עַל אֶת־
*** and-make-come-up! the-ponds and-over the-canals over the-streams over

הַֽצְפַרְדְּעִ֖ים עַל־אֶ֥רֶץ מִצְרָֽיִם׃ וַיֵּ֤ט אַהֲרֹן֙ אֶת־ יָד֔וֹ עַ֖ל
over hand-of-him *** Aaron so-he-stretched (2[6]) Egypt land-of on the-frogs

מֵימֵ֣י מִצְרָ֑יִם וַתַּ֙עַל֙ הַֽצְפַרְדֵּ֔עַ וַתְּכַ֖ס אֶת־ אֶ֥רֶץ מִצְרָֽיִם׃
Egypt land-of *** and-she-covered the-frog and-she-came-up Egypt waters-of

וַיַּעֲשׂוּ־ כֵ֥ן הַֽחַרְטֻמִּ֖ים† בְּלָטֵיהֶ֑ם וַיַּעֲל֥וּ
and-they-brought-up by-arts-of-them the-magicians same but-they-did (3[7])

אֶת־הַֽצְפַרְדְּעִ֖ים עַל־אֶ֥רֶץ מִצְרָֽיִם׃ וַיִּקְרָ֨א פַרְעֹ֜ה לְמֹשֶׁ֣ה
to-Moses Pharaoh then-he-summoned (4[8]) Egypt land-of on the-frogs ***

וּֽלְאַהֲרֹ֗ן וַיֹּ֙אמֶר֙ הַעְתִּ֣ירוּ אֶל־יְהוָ֔ה וְיָסֵר֙ הַֽצְפַרְדְּעִ֔ים מִמֶּ֖נִּי
from-me the-frogs so-he-will-take-away Yahweh to pray! and-he-said and-to-Aaron

וּמֵֽעַמִּ֑י וַאֲשַׁלְּחָה֙ אֶת־ הָעָ֔ם וְיִזְבְּח֖וּ
so-they-may-sacrifice the-people *** and-I-will-let-go and-from-people-of-me

לַיהוָֽה׃ וַיֹּ֨אמֶר מֹשֶׁ֣ה לְפַרְעֹה֮ הִתְפָּאֵ֣ר עָלַי֒ לְמָתַ֣י ׀
as-when? for-me declare! to-Pharaoh Moses and-he-said (5[9]) to-Yahweh

אַעְתִּ֣יר לְךָ֗ וְלַעֲבָדֶ֙יךָ֙ וּֽלְעַמְּךָ֔ לְהַכְרִית֙
to-remove and-for-people-of-you and-for-officials-of-you for-you I-pray

הַֽצְפַרְדְּעִ֔ים†† מִמְּךָ֖ וּמִבָּתֶּ֑יךָ רַ֥ק בַּיְאֹ֖ר תִּשָּׁאַֽרְנָה׃
they-remain in-the-Nile except and-from-houses-of-you from-you the-frogs

וַיֹּ֖אמֶר לְמָחָ֑ר וַיֹּ֙אמֶר֙ כִּדְבָ֣רְךָ֔ לְמַ֣עַן
so-that as-word-of-you and-he-replied on-tomorrow and-he-said (6[10])

תֵּדַ֔ע כִּי־ אֵ֖ין כַּיהוָ֥ה אֱלֹהֵֽינוּ׃
God-of-us like-Yahweh there-is-no-one that you-may-know

וְסָר֣וּ הַֽצְפַרְדְּעִ֗ים מִמְּךָ֙ וּמִבָּ֣תֶּ֔יךָ
and-from-houses-of-you from-you the-frogs and-they-will-leave (7[11])

teem with frogs. They will come up into your palace and your bedroom and onto your bed, into the houses of your officials and on your people, and into your ovens and
kneading troughs. [4]The frogs will go up on you and your people and all your officials.' "
[5]Then the LORD said to Moses, "Tell Aaron, 'Stretch out your hand with your staff over the streams and canals and ponds, and make frogs come up on the land of Egypt.' "
[6]So Aaron stretched out his hand over the waters of Egypt, and the frogs came up and covered the land.
[7]But the magicians did the same things by their secret arts; they also made frogs come up on the land of Egypt.
[8]Pharaoh summoned Moses and Aaron and said, "Pray to the LORD to take the frogs away from me and my people, and I will let your people go to offer sacrifices to the LORD."
[9]Moses said to Pharaoh, "I leave to you the honor of setting the time for me to pray for you and your officials and your people that you and your houses may be rid of the frogs, except for those that remain in the Nile."
[10]"Tomorrow," Pharaoh said.
Moses replied, "It will be as you say, so that you may know there is no one like the LORD our God.
[11]The frogs will leave you and your houses, your

*See the note on page 163.

†3 Most mss have *pathah* under the *beth* ('הַחַר).

††5 Most mss have *sheva* under the *tsade* ('הַצְ).

וּמֵעֲבָדֶיךָ וּמֵעַמֶּךָ רַק בַּיְאֹר תִּשָּׁאַרְנָה׃

they-remain in-the-Nile except and-from-people-of-you and-from-officials-of-you

וַיֵּצֵא מֹשֶׁה וְאַהֲרֹן מֵעִם פַּרְעֹה וַיִּצְעַק מֹשֶׁה

Moses and-he-cried-out Pharaoh from-with and-Aaron Moses and-he-left (8[12])

אֶל־ יְהוָה עַל־ דְּבַר הַצְפַרְדְּעִים אֲשֶׁר־ שָׂם לְפַרְעֹה׃

on-Pharaoh he-brought that the-frogs matter-of about Yahweh to

וַיַּעַשׂ יְהוָה כִּדְבַר מֹשֶׁה וַיָּמֻתוּ הַצְפַרְדְּעִים מִן־הַבָּתִּים

the-houses in the-frogs and-they-died Moses as-request-of Yahweh and-he-did (9[13])

מִן־ הַחֲצֵרֹת וּמִן־ הַשָּׂדֹת׃ וַיִּצְבְּרוּ אֹתָם חֳמָרִם חֳמָרִם

heaps heaps them and-they-piled (10[14]) the-fields and-in the-courtyards in

וַתִּבְאַשׁ הָאָרֶץ׃ וַיַּרְא פַּרְעֹה כִּי הָיְתָה הָרְוָחָה

the-relief she-was that Pharaoh when-he-saw (11[15]) the-land and-she-reeked

וְהַכְבֵּד אֶת־ לִבּוֹ וְלֹא שָׁמַע אֲלֵהֶם כַּאֲשֶׁר

just-as to-them he-listened and-not heart-of-him *** then-he-hardened

דִּבֶּר יְהוָה׃ וַיֹּאמֶר יְהוָה אֶל־ מֹשֶׁה אֱמֹר אֶל־ אַהֲרֹן

Aaron to tell! Moses to Yahweh then-he-said (12[16]) Yahweh he-said

נְטֵה אֶת־ מַטְּךָ וְהַךְ אֶת־ עֲפַר הָאָרֶץ

the-ground dust-of *** and-strike! staff-of-you *** stretch-out!

וְהָיָה לְכִנִּם בְּכָל־ אֶרֶץ מִצְרָיִם׃ וַיַּעֲשׂוּ־

so-they-did (13[17]) Egypt land-of in-all-of into-gnats and-he-will-become

כֵן וַיֵּט אַהֲרֹן אֶת־ יָדוֹ בְמַטֵּהוּ וַיַּךְ

and-he-struck with-staff-of-him hand-of-him *** Aaron and-he-stretched this

אֶת־ עֲפַר הָאָרֶץ וַתְּהִי הַכִּנָּם בָּאָדָם וּבַבְּהֵמָה

and-upon-the-animal upon-the-man the-gnat and-she-came the-ground dust-of ***

כָּל־ עֲפַר הָאָרֶץ הָיָה כִנִּים בְּכָל־ אֶרֶץ מִצְרָיִם׃

Egypt land-of in-all-of gnats he-became the-ground dust-of all-of

וַיַּעֲשׂוּ־ כֵן הַחַרְטֻמִּים בְּלָטֵיהֶם לְהוֹצִיא אֶת־ הַכִּנִּים

the-gnats *** to-produce by-arts-of-them the-magicians same and-they-tried (14[18])

וְלֹא יָכֹלוּ וַתְּהִי הַכִּנָּם בָּאָדָם וּבַבְּהֵמָה׃

and-on-the-animal on-the-man the-gnat and-she-was they-could but-not

וַיֹּאמְרוּ הַחַרְטֻמִּם אֶל־ פַּרְעֹה אֶצְבַּע אֱלֹהִים הִוא

this God finger-of Pharaoh to the-magicians so-they-said (15[19])

וַיֶּחֱזַק לֵב־ פַּרְעֹה וְלֹא־ שָׁמַע אֲלֵהֶם כַּאֲשֶׁר דִּבֶּר

he-said just-as to-them he-listened and-not Pharaoh heart-of but-he-was-hard

יְהוָה׃ וַיֹּאמֶר יְהוָה אֶל־ מֹשֶׁה הַשְׁכֵּם בַּבֹּקֶר

in-the-morning rise-early! Moses to Yahweh then-he-said (16[20]) Yahweh

וְהִתְיַצֵּב לִפְנֵי פַרְעֹה הִנֵּה יוֹצֵא הַמָּיְמָה וְאָמַרְתָּ אֵלָיו

to-him and-you-say to-the-waters going see! Pharaoh before and-confront!

officials and your people; they will remain only in the Nile."

[12]After Moses and Aaron left Pharaoh, Moses cried out to the LORD about the frogs he had brought on Pharaoh. [13]And the LORD did what Moses asked. The frogs died in the houses, in the courtyards and in the fields. [14]They were piled into heaps, and the land reeked of them. [15]But when Pharaoh saw that there was relief, he hardened his heart and would not listen to Moses and Aaron, just as the LORD had said.

The Plague of Gnats

[16]Then the LORD said to Moses, "Tell Aaron, 'Stretch out your staff and strike the dust of the ground,' and throughout the land of Egypt the dust will become gnats." [17]They did this, and when Aaron stretched out his hand with the staff and struck the dust of the ground, gnats came upon men and animals. All the dust throughout the land of Egypt became gnats. [18]But when the magicians tried to produce gnats by their secret arts, they could not. And the gnats were on men and animals.

[19]The magicians said to Pharaoh, "This is the finger of God." But Pharaoh's heart was hard and he would not listen, just as the LORD had said.

The Plague of Flies

[20]Then the LORD said to Moses, "Get up early in the morning and confront Pharaoh as he goes to the water and say to him, 'This is what

*See the note on page 163.

כֹּה אָמַר יְהוָה שַׁלַּח עַמִּי וְיַעַבְדֻנִי׃ כִּי
but (17[21]) so-they-may-worship-me people-of-me let-go! Yahweh he-says this

אִם־ אֵינְךָ מְשַׁלֵּחַ אֶת־ עַמִּי הִנְנִי מַשְׁלִיחַ בְּךָ
on-you sending see-I! people-of-me *** letting-go not-you if

וּבַעֲבָדֶיךָ וּבְעַמְּךָ וּבְבָתֶּיךָ אֶת־
*** and-into-houses-of-you and-on-people-of-you and-on-officials-of-you

הֶעָרֹב וּמָלְאוּ בָּתֵּי מִצְרַיִם אֶת־הֶעָרֹב וְגַם הָאֲדָמָה
the-ground and-even the-fly *** Egypt houses-of and-they-will-be-full the-fly

אֲשֶׁר־ הֵם עָלֶיהָ׃ וְהִפְלֵיתִי בַיּוֹם הַהוּא
the-that on-the-day but-I-will-deal-differently (18[22]) on-her they where

אֶת־ אֶרֶץ גֹּשֶׁן אֲשֶׁר עַמִּי עֹמֵד עָלֶיהָ לְבִלְתִּי הֱיוֹת־שָׁם עָרֹב
fly there to-be not in-her living people-of-me where Goshen land-of ***

לְמַעַן תֵּדַע כִּי אֲנִי יְהוָה בְּקֶרֶב הָאָרֶץ׃
the-land in-midst-of Yahweh I that you-will-know so-that

וְשַׂמְתִּי פְדֻת בֵּין עַמִּי וּבֵין עַמֶּךָ
people-of-you and-between people-of-me between †distinction and-I-will-make (19[23])

לְמָחָר יִהְיֶה הָאֹת הַזֶּה׃ וַיַּעַשׂ יְהוָה כֵּן
this Yahweh and-he-did (20[24]) the-this the-sign he-will-occur on-tomorrow

וַיָּבֹא עָרֹב כָּבֵד בֵּיתָה פַרְעֹה וּבֵית עֲבָדָיו
officials-of-him and-house-of Pharaoh into-palace-of many fly and-he-came

וּבְכָל־ אֶרֶץ מִצְרַיִם תִּשָּׁחֵת הָאָרֶץ מִפְּנֵי הֶעָרֹב׃
the-fly because-of the-land she-was-ruined Egypt land-of and-in-all-of

וַיִּקְרָא פַרְעֹה אֶל־ מֹשֶׁה וּלְאַהֲרֹן וַיֹּאמֶר לְכוּ
go! and-he-said and-to-Aaron Moses to Pharaoh then-he-summoned (21[25])

זִבְחוּ לֵאלֹהֵיכֶם בָּאָרֶץ׃ וַיֹּאמֶר מֹשֶׁה לֹא
not Moses but-he-said (22[26]) in-the-land to-God-of-you sacrifice!

נָכוֹן לַעֲשׂוֹת כֵּן כִּי תּוֹעֲבַת מִצְרַיִם נִזְבַּח
we-would-sacrifice Egyptians detestable-of for this to-do he-would-be-right

לַיהוָה אֱלֹהֵינוּ הֵן נִזְבַּח אֶת־ תּוֹעֲבַת מִצְרַיִם לְעֵינֵיהֶם
in-eyes-of-them Egyptians detestable-of *** we-sacrifice if God-of-us to-Yahweh

וְלֹא יִסְקְלֻנוּ׃ דֶּרֶךְ שְׁלֹשֶׁת יָמִים נֵלֵךְ
we-must-take days three-of journey-of (23[27]) they-stone-us now-not

בַּמִּדְבָּר וְזָבַחְנוּ לַיהוָה אֱלֹהֵינוּ כַּאֲשֶׁר יֹאמַר
he-tells just-as God-of-us to-Yahweh and-we-must-sacrifice into-the-desert

אֵלֵינוּ׃ וַיֹּאמֶר פַּרְעֹה אָנֹכִי אֲשַׁלַּח אֶתְכֶם וּזְבַחְתֶּם
so-you-can-sacrifice you I-will-let-go I Pharaoh so-he-said (24[28]) to-us

לַיהוָה אֱלֹהֵיכֶם בַּמִּדְבָּר רַק הַרְחֵק לֹא־ תַרְחִיקוּ לָלֶכֶת
to-go you-must-go-far not to-go-far but in-the-desert God-of-you to-Yahweh

the LORD says: Let my people
go, so that they may worship
me. [21]If you do not let my
people go, I will send swarms
of flies on you and your
officials, on your people and
into your houses. The houses
of the Egyptians will be full of
flies, and even the ground
where they are.
[22]" 'But on that day I will
deal differently with the land
of Goshen, where my people
live; no swarms of flies will be
there, so that you will know
that I, the LORD, am in this
land. [23]I will make a dis-
tinction° between my people
and your people. This miraculous sign will occur tomorrow.' "
[24]And the LORD did this.
Dense swarms of flies poured
into Pharaoh's palace and into
the houses of his officials, and
throughout Egypt the land
was ruined by the flies.
[25]Then Pharaoh summoned
Moses and Aaron and said,
"Go, sacrifice to your God here
in the land."
[26]But Moses said, "That
would not be right. The sacrifices we offer the LORD our
God would be detestable to the
Egyptians. And if we offer sacrifices that are detestable in
their eyes, will they not stone
us? [27]We must take a three-day
journey into the desert to offer
sacrifices to the LORD our God,
as he commands us."
[28]Pharaoh said, "I will let
you go to offer sacrifices to the
LORD your God in the desert,
but you must not go very far.

°23 Septuagint and Vulgate; Hebrew *will put a deliverance*

*See the note on page 163.

†19 The normal definition of this Hebrew word is *deliverance*. The word translated by *distinction* suggested by the versions may be פְּלֻת.

הַעְתִּירוּ בַּעֲדִי׃ וַיֹּאמֶר מֹשֶׁה הִנֵּה אָנֹכִי יוֹצֵא מֵעִמָּךְ

from-with-you leaving I see! Moses and-he-answered (25[29]) for-me pray!

וְהַעְתַּרְתִּי אֶל־יְהוָה וְסָר הֶעָרֹב מִפַּרְעֹה

from-Pharaoh the-fly and-he-will-leave Yahweh to and-I-will-pray

מֵעֲבָדָיו וּמֵעַמּוֹ מָחָר רַק אַל־יֹסֵף

may-he-repeat not only tomorrow and-from-people-of-him from-officials-of-him

פַּרְעֹה הָתֵל לְבִלְתִּי שַׁלַּח אֶת־הָעָם לִזְבֹּחַ לַיהוָה׃

to-Yahweh to-sacrifice the-people *** to-let-go not to-deceive Pharaoh

וַיֵּצֵא מֹשֶׁה מֵעִם פַּרְעֹה וַיֶּעְתַּר אֶל־יְהוָה׃

Yahweh to and-he-prayed Pharaoh from-with Moses then-he-left (26[30])

וַיַּעַשׂ יְהוָה כִּדְבַר מֹשֶׁה וַיָּסַר הֶעָרֹב

the-fly and-he-left Moses as-request-of Yahweh and-he-did (27[31])

מִפַּרְעֹה מֵעֲבָדָיו וּמֵעַמּוֹ לֹא נִשְׁאַר

he-remained not and-from-people-of-him and-from-officials-of-him from-Pharaoh

אֶחָד׃ וַיַּכְבֵּד פַּרְעֹה אֶת־לִבּוֹ גַּם בַּפַּעַם

on-the-time also heart-of-him *** Pharaoh but-he-hardened (28[32]) one

הַזֹּאת וְלֹא שִׁלַּח אֶת־הָעָם׃ וַיֹּאמֶר יְהוָה אֶל־מֹשֶׁה

Moses to Yahweh then-he-said (9:1) the-people *** he-let-go and-not the-this

בֹּא אֶל־פַּרְעֹה וְדִבַּרְתָּ אֵלָיו כֹּה־אָמַר יְהוָה אֱלֹהֵי הָעִבְרִים

the-Hebrews God-of Yahweh he-says this to-him and-you-say Pharaoh to go!

שַׁלַּח אֶת־עַמִּי וְיַעַבְדֻנִי׃ כִּי אִם־מָאֵן אַתָּה

you to-refuse if but (2) so-they-may-worship-me people-of-me *** let-go!

לְשַׁלֵּחַ וְעוֹדְךָ מַחֲזִיק בָּם׃ הִנֵּה יַד־יְהוָה הוֹיָה

bringing Yahweh hand-of see! (3) on-them holding-back and-still-you to-let-go

בְּמִקְנְךָ אֲשֶׁר בַּשָּׂדֶה בַּסּוּסִים בַּחֲמֹרִים בַּגְּמַלִּים

on-the-camels on-the-donkeys on-the-horses in-the-field that on-stock-of-you

בַּבָּקָר וּבַצֹּאן דֶּבֶר כָּבֵד מְאֹד׃ וְהִפְלָה

but-he-will-separate (4) very terrible plague and-on-the-flock on-the-cattle

יְהוָה בֵּין מִקְנֵה יִשְׂרָאֵל וּבֵין מִקְנֵה מִצְרָיִם וְלֹא יָמוּת

he-will-die so-not Egypt stock-of and-between Israel stock-of between Yahweh

מִכָּל־לִבְנֵי יִשְׂרָאֵל דָּבָר׃ וַיָּשֶׂם יְהוָה מוֹעֵד לֵאמֹר

to-say time Yahweh and-he-set (5) animal Israel to-sons-of from-any-of

מָחָר יַעֲשֶׂה יְהוָה הַדָּבָר הַזֶּה בָּאָרֶץ׃ וַיַּעַשׂ

and-he-did (6) in-the-land the-this the-thing Yahweh he-will-do tomorrow

יְהוָה אֶת־הַדָּבָר הַזֶּה מִמָּחֳרָת וַיָּמָת כֹּל מִקְנֵה

stock-of all-of and-he-died on-next-day the-this the-thing *** Yahweh

מִצְרָיִם וּמִמִּקְנֵה בְנֵי־יִשְׂרָאֵל לֹא־מֵת אֶחָד׃ וַיִּשְׁלַח

and-he-sent (7) one he-died not Israel sons-of but-from-stock-of Egyptians

Now pray for me."
[29]Moses answered, "As soon
as I leave you, I will pray to the
LORD, and tomorrow the flies
will leave Pharaoh and his
officials and his people. Only
be sure that Pharaoh does not
act deceitfully again by not let-
ting the people go to offer sacrifices to the LORD."
[30]Then Moses left Pharaoh
and prayed to the LORD, [31]and
the LORD did what Moses
asked: The flies left Pharaoh
and his officials and his
people; not a fly remained.
[32]But this time also Pharaoh
hardened his heart and would
not let the people go.

The Plague on Livestock

9 Then the LORD said to
Moses, "Go to Pharaoh
and say to him, 'This is what
the LORD, the God of the Hebrews, says: "Let my people
go, so that they may worship
me." [2]If you refuse to let them
go and continue to hold them
back, [3]the hand of the LORD
will bring a terrible plague on
your livestock in the field—on
your horses and donkeys and
camels and on your cattle and
sheep and goats. [4]But the LORD
will make a distinction between the livestock of Israel
and that of Egypt, so that no
animal belonging to the Israelites will die.' "
[5]The LORD set a time and
said, "Tomorrow the LORD will
do this in the land." [6]And the
next day the LORD did it: All
the livestock of the Egyptians
died, but not one animal belonging to the Israelites died.

*See the note on page 163.

פַּרְעֹה וְהִנֵּה לֹא־מֵת מִמִּקְנֵה יִשְׂרָאֵל עַד־אֶחָד וַיִּכְבַּד
but-he-was-hard one even Israel from-stock-of he-died not and-see! Pharaoh

לֵב פַּרְעֹה וְלֹא שִׁלַּח אֶת־הָעָם׃ וַיֹּאמֶר יְהוָה
Yahweh then-he-said (8) the-people *** he-let-go and-not Pharaoh heart-of

אֶל־מֹשֶׁה וְאֶל־אַהֲרֹן קְחוּ לָכֶם מְלֹא חָפְנֵיכֶם פִּיחַ כִּבְשָׁן
furnace soot-of hands-of-you full-of to-you take! Aaron and-to Moses to

וּזְרָקוֹ מֹשֶׁה הַשָּׁמַיְמָה לְעֵינֵי פַרְעֹה׃
Pharaoh before-eyes-of into-the-air Moses and-let-him-toss-him

וְהָיָה לְאָבָק עַל כָּל־אֶרֶץ מִצְרָיִם וְהָיָה
and-he-will-be Egypt land-of all-of over into-fine-dust and-he-will-become (9)

עַל־הָאָדָם וְעַל־הַבְּהֵמָה לִשְׁחִין פֹּרֵחַ אֲבַעְבֻּעֹת בְּכָל־אֶרֶץ
land-of in-all-of festers breaking-out into-boil the-animal and-on the-man on

מִצְרָיִם׃ וַיִּקְחוּ אֶת־פִּיחַ הַכִּבְשָׁן וַיַּעַמְדוּ לִפְנֵי
before and-they-stood the-furnace soot-of *** so-they-took (10) Egypt

פַרְעֹה וַיִּזְרֹק אֹתוֹ מֹשֶׁה הַשָּׁמָיְמָה וַיְהִי שְׁחִין אֲבַעְבֻּעֹת
festers boil and-he-became into-the-air Moses him and-he-tossed Pharaoh

פֹּרֵחַ בָּאָדָם וּבַבְּהֵמָה׃ וְלֹא־יָכְלוּ
they-could and-not (11) and-on-the-animal on-the-man breaking-out

הַחַרְטֻמִּים לַעֲמֹד לִפְנֵי מֹשֶׁה מִפְּנֵי הַשְּׁחִין כִּי־הָיָה הַשְּׁחִין
the-boil he-was for the-boil because-of Moses before to-stand the-magicians

בְּחַרְטֻמִּם* וּבְכָל־מִצְרָיִם׃ וַיְחַזֵּק יְהוָה אֶת־
*** Yahweh but-he-hardened (12) Egyptians and-on-all-of on-the-magicians

לֵב פַּרְעֹה וְלֹא שָׁמַע אֲלֵהֶם כַּאֲשֶׁר דִּבֶּר יְהוָה אֶל־מֹשֶׁה׃
Moses to Yahweh he-said just-as to-them he-listened and-not Pharaoh heart-of

וַיֹּאמֶר יְהוָה אֶל־מֹשֶׁה הַשְׁכֵּם בַּבֹּקֶר וְהִתְיַצֵּב
and-confront! in-the-morning get-up-early! Moses to Yahweh then-he-said (13)

לִפְנֵי פַרְעֹה וְאָמַרְתָּ אֵלָיו כֹּה־אָמַר יְהוָה אֱלֹהֵי הָעִבְרִים
the-Hebrews God-of Yahweh he-says this to-him and-you-say Pharaoh before

שַׁלַּח אֶת־עַמִּי וְיַעַבְדֻנִי׃ כִּי ׀ בַּפַּעַם
on-the-time or (14) so-they-may-worship-me people-of-me *** let-go!

הַזֹּאת אֲנִי שֹׁלֵחַ אֶת־כָּל־מַגֵּפֹתַי אֶל־לִבְּךָ
heart-of-you against plagues-of-me full-force-of *** sending I the-this

וּבַעֲבָדֶיךָ וּבְעַמֶּךָ בַּעֲבוּר תֵּדַע
you-may-know so-that and-against-people-of-you and-against-officials-of-you

כִּי אֵין כָּמֹנִי בְּכָל־הָאָרֶץ׃ כִּי עַתָּה שָׁלַחְתִּי
I-could-stretch now for (15) the-earth in-all-of like-me there-is-no-one that

אֶת־יָדִי וָאַךְ אוֹתְךָ וְאֶת־עַמְּךָ בַּדָּבֶר
with-the-plague people-of-you and you and-I-could-strike hand-of-me ***

7Pharaoh sent men to investigate and found that not even
one of the animals of the Israelites had died. Yet his heart
was unyielding and he would
not let the people go.

The Plague of Boils

8Then the LORD said to
Moses and Aaron, "Take
handfuls of soot from a furnace and have Moses toss it
into the air in the presence of
Pharaoh. 9It will become fine
dust over the whole land of
Egypt, and festering boils will
break out on men and animals
throughout the land."
10So they took soot from a
furnace and stood before
Pharaoh. Moses tossed it into
the air, and festering boils
broke out on men and ani-
mals. 11The magicians could
not stand before Moses because of the boils that were on
them and on all the Egyptians.
12But the LORD hardened Pharaoh's heart and he would not
listen to Moses and Aaron,
just as the LORD had said to
Moses.

The Plague of Hail

13Then the LORD said to
Moses, "Get up early in the
morning, confront Pharaoh
and say to him, 'This is what
the LORD, the God of the Hebrews, says: Let my people go,
so that they may worship me,
14or this time I will send the
full force of my plagues
against you and against your
officials and your people, so
you may know that there is no
one like me in all the earth.
15For by now I could have
stretched out my hand and
struck you and your people
with a plague that would have

**11* Most mss have *pathah* under the *beth* (בַּחַ).

וַתִּכָּחֵד מִן־הָאָרֶץ׃ וְאוּלָם בַּעֲבוּר זֹאת
this for-purpose but-however (16) the-earth off and-you-would-be-wiped

הֶעֱמַדְתִּיךָ בַּעֲבוּר הַרְאֹתְךָ אֶת־כֹּחִי וּלְמַעַן סַפֵּר
to-proclaim and-so-that power-of-me *** to-show-you so-that I-raised-you

שְׁמִי בְּכָל־הָאָרֶץ׃ עוֹדְךָ מִסְתּוֹלֵל
setting-yourself still-you (17) the-earth in-all-of name-of-me

בְּעַמִּי לְבִלְתִּי שַׁלְּחָם׃ הִנְנִי מַמְטִיר כָּעֵת
at-the-time sending see-I! (18) to-let-go-them not against-people-of-me

מָחָר בָּרָד כָּבֵד מְאֹד אֲשֶׁר לֹא־הָיָה כָמֹהוּ בְּמִצְרַיִם לְמִן־
from in-Egypt like-him he-was never that very severe hailstorm tomorrow

הַיּוֹם הִוָּסְדָה וְעַד־עָתָּה׃ וְעַתָּה שְׁלַח הָעֵז אֶת־
*** shelter! give-order! so-now (19) now even-till to-be-founded-her the-day

מִקְנְךָ וְאֵת כָּל־אֲשֶׁר לְךָ בַּשָּׂדֶה כָּל־הָאָדָם וְהַבְּהֵמָה
and-the-animal the-man every-of in-the-field to-you that all and stock-of-you

אֲשֶׁר־יִמָּצֵא בַשָּׂדֶה וְלֹא יֵאָסֵף הַבַּיְתָה
into-the-shelter he-was-brought and-not in-the-field he-is-found that

וְיָרַד עֲלֵהֶם הַבָּרָד וָמֵתוּ׃ הַיָּרֵא
the-one-fearing (20) and-they-will-die the-hail on-them then-he-will-fall

אֶת־דְּבַר יְהוָה מֵעַבְדֵי פַּרְעֹה הֵנִיס אֶת־עֲבָדָיו
slaves-of-him *** he-brought Pharaoh from-officials-of Yahweh word-of ***

וְאֶת־מִקְנֵהוּ אֶל־הַבָּתִּים׃ וַאֲשֶׁר לֹא־שָׂם לִבּוֹ
heart-of-him he-took not but-who (21) the-shelters into stock-of-him and

אֶל־דְּבַר יְהוָה וַיַּעֲזֹב אֶת־עֲבָדָיו וְאֶת־מִקְנֵהוּ
stock-of-him and slaves-of-him *** then-he-left Yahweh word-of about

בַּשָּׂדֶה׃ וַיֹּאמֶר יְהוָה אֶל־מֹשֶׁה* נְטֵה אֶת־יָדְךָ
hand-of-you *** stretch-out! Moses to Yahweh then-he-said (22) in-the-field

עַל־הַשָּׁמַיִם וִיהִי בָרָד בְּכָל־אֶרֶץ מִצְרַיִם עַל־הָאָדָם
the-man on Egypt land-of over-all-of hail so-he-will-fall the-heavens to

וְעַל־הַבְּהֵמָה וְעַל כָּל־עֵשֶׂב הַשָּׂדֶה בְּאֶרֶץ מִצְרָיִם׃
Egypt in-land-of the-field plant-of every-of and-on the-animal and-on

וַיֵּט מֹשֶׁה אֶת־מַטֵּהוּ עַל־הַשָּׁמַיִם וַיהוָה נָתַן
he-sent and-Yahweh the-heavens to staff-of-him *** Moses so-he-stretched (23)

קֹלֹת וּבָרָד וַתִּהֲלַךְ אֵשׁ אַרְצָה וַיַּמְטֵר
so-he-rained to-ground lightning and-she-flashed-down and-hail thunders

יְהוָה בָּרָד עַל־אֶרֶץ מִצְרָיִם׃ וַיְהִי בָרָד וְאֵשׁ מִתְלַקַּחַת
flashing and-lightning hail and-he-fell (24) Egypt land-of on hail Yahweh

בְּתוֹךְ הַבָּרָד כָּבֵד מְאֹד אֲשֶׁר לֹא־הָיָה כָמֹהוּ בְּכָל־אֶרֶץ
land-of in-all-of like-him he-was never that very severe the-hail in-midst-of

wiped you off the earth. 16But I
have raised you up[p] for this
very purpose, that I might
show you my power and that
my name might be proclaimed
in all the earth. 17You still set
yourself against my people
and will not let them go.
18Therefore, at this time tomorrow I will send the worst
hailstorm that has ever fallen
on Egypt, from the day it was
founded till now. 19Give an order now to bring your livestock and everything you have
in the field to a place of shelter,
because the hail will fall on
every man and animal that
has not been brought in and is
still out in the field, and they
will die.' "

20Those officials of Pharaoh
who feared the word of the
LORD hurried to bring their
slaves and their livestock inside. 21But those who ignored
the word of the LORD left their
slaves and livestock in the
field.

22Then the LORD said to
Moses, "Stretch out your hand
toward the sky so that hail will
fall all over Egypt—on men
and animals and on every-
thing growing in the fields of
Egypt." 23When Moses
stretched out his staff toward
the sky, the LORD sent thunder
and hail, and lightning
flashed down to the ground.
So the LORD rained hail on the
land of Egypt; 24hail fell and
lightning flashed back and
forth. It was the worst storm

p16 *Or have spared you*

*22 Most mss have the accent *rebia* (מֹשֶׁה).

מִצְרַיִם מֵאָז הָיְתָה לְגוֹי׃ וַיַּךְ הַבָּרָד
the-hail and-he-struck (25) into-nation she-became since-when Egypt

בְּכָל־ אֶרֶץ מִצְרַיִם אֵת כָּל־ אֲשֶׁר בַּשָּׂדֶה מֵאָדָם וְעַד־
and-to from-man in-the-field that everything *** Egypt land-of through-all-of

בְּהֵמָה וְאֵת כָּל־ עֵשֶׂב הַשָּׂדֶה הִכָּה הַבָּרָד וְאֶת־ כָּל־
every-of and the-hail he-beat-down the-field plant-of every-of and animal

עֵץ הַשָּׂדֶה שִׁבֵּר׃ רַק בְּאֶרֶץ גֹּשֶׁן אֲשֶׁר־ שָׁם בְּנֵי
sons-of there where Goshen in-land-of only (26) he-stripped the-field tree-of

יִשְׂרָאֵל לֹא הָיָה בָּרָד׃ וַיִּשְׁלַח פַּרְעֹה וַיִּקְרָא לְמֹשֶׁה
to-Moses and-he-called Pharaoh then-he-summoned (27) hail he-was not Israel

וּלְאַהֲרֹן וַיֹּאמֶר אֲלֵהֶם חָטָאתִי הַפָּעַם יְהוָה הַצַּדִּיק וַאֲנִי
and-I the-right Yahweh the-time I-sinned to-them and-he-said and-to-Aaron

וְעַמִּי הָרְשָׁעִים׃ הַעְתִּירוּ אֶל־ יְהוָה וְרַב מִהְיֹת
from-to-be for-enough Yahweh to pray! (28) the-wrong-ones and-people-of-me

קֹלֹת אֱלֹהִים וּבָרָד וַאֲשַׁלְּחָה אֶתְכֶם וְלֹא
and-not you and-I-will-let-go and-hail mighty-ones thunders-of

תֹסִפוּן לַעֲמֹד׃ וַיֹּאמֶר אֵלָיו מֹשֶׁה כְּצֵאתִי
when-to-leave-me Moses to-him and-he-replied (29) to-stay you-will-continue

אֶת־ הָעִיר אֶפְרֹשׂ אֶת־ כַּפַּי אֶל־ יְהוָה הַקֹּלוֹת
the-thunders Yahweh to hands-of-me *** I-will-spread the-city ***

יֶחְדָּלוּן וְהַבָּרָד לֹא יִהְיֶה־ עוֹד לְמַעַן תֵּדַע
you-may-know so-that any-more he-will-be not and-the-hail they-will-stop

כִּי לַיהוָה הָאָרֶץ׃ וְאַתָּה וַעֲבָדֶיךָ יָדַעְתִּי כִּי
that I-know and-officials-of-you but-you (30) the-earth to-Yahweh that

טֶרֶם תִּירְאוּן מִפְּנֵי יְהוָה אֱלֹהִים׃ וְהַפִּשְׁתָּה וְהַשְּׂעֹרָה
and-the-barley now-the-flax (31) God Yahweh before you-fear not-yet

נֻכָּתָה כִּי הַשְּׂעֹרָה אָבִיב וְהַפִּשְׁתָּה גִּבְעֹל׃ וְהַחִטָּה
but-the-wheat (32) bloom and-the-flax head the-barley for she-was-destroyed

וְהַכֻּסֶּמֶת לֹא נֻכּוּ כִּי אֲפִילֹת הֵנָּה׃ וַיֵּצֵא
then-he-left (33) they later-ripen for they-were-destroyed not and-the-spelt

מֹשֶׁה מֵעִם פַּרְעֹה אֶת־ הָעִיר וַיִּפְרֹשׂ כַּפָּיו אֶל־ יְהוָה
Yahweh to hands-of-him and-he-spread the-city *** Pharaoh from-with Moses

וַיַּחְדְּלוּ הַקֹּלוֹת וְהַבָּרָד וּמָטָר לֹא־ נִתַּךְ אָרְצָה׃
on-land he-poured not and-rain and-the-hail the-thunders and-they-stopped

וַיַּרְא פַּרְעֹה כִּי־ חָדַל הַמָּטָר וְהַבָּרָד
and-the-hail the-rain he-stopped that Pharaoh when-he-saw (34)

וְהַקֹּלֹת וַיֹּסֶף לַחֲטֹא וַיַּכְבֵּד לִבּוֹ הוּא
he heart-of-him and-he-hardened to-sin then-he-repeated and-the-thunders

in all the land of Egypt since it
had become a nation.
25 Throughout Egypt hail
struck everything in the
fields—both men and animals;
it beat down everything growing in the fields and stripped
every tree. 26 The only place it
did not hail was the land of
Goshen, where the Israelites
were.

27 Then Pharaoh summoned
Moses and Aaron. "This time
I have sinned," he said to
them. "The LORD is in the
right, and I and my people are
in the wrong. 28 Pray to the
LORD, for we have had enough
thunder and hail. I will let you
go; you don't have to stay any
longer."

29 Moses replied, "When I
have gone out of the city, I will
spread out my hands in prayer
to the LORD. The thunder will
stop and there will be no more
hail, so you may know that the
earth is the LORD's. 30 But I
know that you and your
officials still do not fear the
LORD God."

31 (The flax and barley were
destroyed, since the barley
had headed and the flax was
in bloom. 32 The wheat and
spelt, however, were not destroyed, because they ripen
later.)

33 Then Moses left Pharaoh
and went out of the city. He
spread out his hands toward
the LORD; the thunder and hail
stopped, and the rain no longer poured down on the land.
34 When Pharaoh saw that the
rain and hail and thunder had
stopped, he sinned again: He
and his officials hardened

וַעֲבָדָיו׃ וַיֶּחֱזַק לֵב פַּרְעֹה וְלֹא שִׁלַּח
he-let-go and-not Pharaoh heart-of so-he-was-hard (35) and-officials-of-him

אֶת־בְּנֵי יִשְׂרָאֵל כַּאֲשֶׁר דִּבֶּר יְהוָה בְּיַד־מֹשֶׁה׃ וַיֹּאמֶר
then-he-said (10:1) Moses by-hand-of Yahweh he-said just-as Israel sons-of ***

יְהוָה אֶל־מֹשֶׁה בֹּא אֶל־פַּרְעֹה כִּי־אֲנִי הִכְבַּדְתִּי אֶת־לִבּוֹ וְאֶת־
and heart-of-him *** I-hardened I for Pharaoh to go! Moses to Yahweh

לֵב עֲבָדָיו לְמַעַן שִׁתִי אֹתֹתַי אֵלֶּה בְּקִרְבּוֹ׃
among-him these signs-of-me performing-me so-that officials-of-him heart-of

וּלְמַעַן תְּסַפֵּר בְּאָזְנֵי בִנְךָ וּבֶן־בִּנְךָ
child-of-you and-child-of child-of-you in-ears-of you-may-tell and-that (2)

אֵת אֲשֶׁר הִתְעַלַּלְתִּי בְּמִצְרַיִם וְאֶת־אֹתֹתַי אֲשֶׁר־שַׂמְתִּי
I-performed how signs-of-me and with-Egyptians I-dealt-harshly how ***

בָם וִידַעְתֶּם כִּי־אֲנִי יְהוָה׃ וַיָּבֹא מֹשֶׁה וְאַהֲרֹן
and-Aaron Moses so-he-went (3) Yahweh I that that-you-may-know among-them

אֶל־פַּרְעֹה וַיֹּאמְרוּ אֵלָיו כֹּה־אָמַר יְהוָה אֱלֹהֵי הָעִבְרִים עַד־
how the-Hebrews God-of Yahweh he-says this to-him and-they-said Pharaoh to

מָתַי מֵאַנְתָּ לֵעָנֹת מִפָּנָי שַׁלַּח עַמִּי
people-of-me to-let-go before-me to-humble-yourself will-you-refuse long

וְיַעַבְדֻנִי׃ כִּי אִם־מָאֵן אַתָּה לְשַׁלֵּחַ אֶת־עַמִּי
people-of-me *** to-let-go you to-refuse if but (4) so-they-may-worship-me

הִנְנִי מֵבִיא מָחָר אַרְבֶּה בִּגְבֻלֶךָ׃ וְכִסָּה
and-he-will-cover (5) into-country-of-you locust tomorrow bringing see-I!

אֶת־עֵין הָאָרֶץ וְלֹא יוּכַל לִרְאֹת אֶת־הָאָרֶץ וְאָכַל
and-he-will-devour the-ground *** to-see he-can so-not the-ground face-of ***

אֶת־יֶתֶר הַפְּלֵטָה הַנִּשְׁאֶרֶת לָכֶם מִן־הַבָּרָד וְאָכַל
and-he-will-devour the-hail after to-you the-remaining the-remnant left-of ***

אֶת־כָּל־הָעֵץ הַצֹּמֵחַ לָכֶם מִן־הַשָּׂדֶה׃ וּמָלְאוּ
and-they-will-fill (6) the-field in to-you the-one-growing the-tree every-of ***

בָתֶּיךָ וּבָתֵּי כָל־עֲבָדֶיךָ וּבָתֵּי כָל־
all-of and-houses-of officials-of-you all-of and-houses-of houses-of-you

מִצְרַיִם אֲשֶׁר לֹא־רָאוּ אֲבֹתֶיךָ וַאֲבוֹת אֲבֹתֶיךָ
fathers-of-you nor-fathers-of fathers-of-you they-saw not that Egyptians

מִיּוֹם הֱיוֹתָם עַל־הָאֲדָמָה עַד הַיּוֹם הַזֶּה וַיִּפֶן
then-he-turned the-this the-day until the-land in to-settle-them from-day

וַיֵּצֵא מֵעִם פַּרְעֹה׃ וַיֹּאמְרוּ עַבְדֵי פַרְעֹה אֵלָיו
to-him Pharaoh officials-of and-they-said (7) Pharaoh from-with and-he-left

עַד־מָתַי יִהְיֶה זֶה לָנוּ לְמוֹקֵשׁ שַׁלַּח אֶת־הָאֲנָשִׁים
the-people *** let-go! as-snare to-us this will-he-be long how

their hearts.
35So Pharaoh's heart was hard and he would not let the Israelites go, just as the LORD had said through Moses.

The Plague of Locusts

10 Then the LORD said to Moses, "Go to Pharaoh, for I have hardened his heart and the hearts of his officials so that I may perform these miraculous signs of mine among them
2that you may tell your children and grandchildren how I dealt harshly with the Egyptians and how I performed my signs among them, and that you may know that I am the LORD."
3So Moses and Aaron went to Pharaoh and said to him, "This is what the LORD, the God of the Hebrews, says: 'How long will you refuse to humble yourself before me? Let my people go, so that they may worship me.
4If you refuse to let them go, I will bring locusts into your country tomorrow.
5They will cover the face of the ground so that it cannot be seen. They will devour what little you have left after the hail, including every tree that is growing in your fields.
6They will fill your houses and those of all your officials and all the Egyptians—something neither your fathers nor your forefathers have ever seen from the day they settled in this land till now.' " Then Moses turned and left Pharaoh.
7Pharaoh's officials said to him, "How long will this man be a snare to us? Let the people

וְיַֽעַבְדוּ אֶת־ יְהוָה אֱלֹהֵיהֶם הֲטֶרֶם תֵּדַע כִּי
that you-realize not-yet? God-of-them Yahweh *** so-they-may-worship

אָבְדָה מִצְרָיִם׃ וַיּוּשַׁב אֶת־ מֹשֶׁה וְאֶת־ אַהֲרֹן אֶל־
to Aaron and Moses *** so-he-was-brought-back (8) Egypt she-is-ruined

פַּרְעֹה וַיֹּאמֶר אֲלֵהֶם לְכוּ עִבְדוּ אֶת־ יְהוָה אֱלֹהֵיכֶם מִי וָמִי
and-who? who? God-of-you Yahweh *** worship! go! to-them and-he-said Pharaoh

הַהֹלְכִים׃ וַיֹּאמֶר מֹשֶׁה בִּנְעָרֵינוּ
with-young-ones-of-us Moses and-he-answered (9) the-ones-going

וּבִזְקֵנֵינוּ נֵלֵךְ בְּבָנֵינוּ וּבִבְנוֹתֵנוּ
and-with-daughters-of-us with-sons-of-us we-will-go and-with-ones-of-us

בְּצֹאנֵנוּ וּבִבְקָרֵנוּ נֵלֵךְ כִּי חַג־ יְהוָה לָנוּ׃
to-us Yahweh festival-of for we-will-go and-with-herd-of-us with-flock-of-us

וַיֹּאמֶר אֲלֵהֶם יְהִי כֵן יְהוָה עִמָּכֶם כַּאֲשֶׁר אֲשַׁלַּח אֶתְכֶם
you I-let-go if-ever with-you Yahweh so may-he-be to-them but-he-said (10)

וְאֶת־ טַפְּכֶם רְאוּ כִּי רָעָה נֶגֶד פְּנֵיכֶם׃ לֹא כֵן לְכוּ־
go! so not (11) faces-of-you before evil clearly see! children-of-you and

נָא הַגְּבָרִים וְעִבְדוּ אֶת־ יְהוָה כִּי אֹתָהּ אַתֶּם מְבַקְשִׁים
ones-requesting you she since Yahweh *** and-worship! the-men now!

וַיְגָרֶשׁ אֹתָם מֵאֵת פְּנֵי פַרְעֹה׃ וַיֹּאמֶר יְהוָה אֶל־
to Yahweh and-he-said (12) Pharaoh presence-of from them then-he-drove-out

מֹשֶׁה נְטֵה יָדְךָ עַל־ אֶרֶץ מִצְרַיִם בָּאַרְבֶּה
for-the-locust Egypt land-of over hand-of-you stretch-out! Moses

וְיַעַל עַל־ אֶרֶץ מִצְרָיִם וְיֹאכַל אֶת־ כָּל־ עֵשֶׂב
plant-of every-of *** and-he-will-devour Egypt land-of over so-he-will-swarm

הָאָרֶץ אֵת כָּל־ אֲשֶׁר הִשְׁאִיר הַבָּרָד׃ וַיֵּט מֹשֶׁה אֶת־
*** Moses so-he-stretched (13) the-hail he-left that all *** the-land

מַטֵּהוּ עַל־ אֶרֶץ מִצְרַיִם וַיהוָה נִהַג רוּחַ קָדִים
east wind-of he-made-blow and-Yahweh Egypt land-of over staff-of-him

בָּאָרֶץ כָּל־ הַיּוֹם הַהוּא וְכָל־ הַלַּיְלָה הַבֹּקֶר
the-morning the-night and-all-of the-that the-day all-of across-the-land

הָיָה וְרוּחַ הַקָּדִים נָשָׂא אֶת־ הָאַרְבֶּה׃ וַיַּעַל
and-he-invaded (14) the-locust *** he-brought the-east and-wind-of he-was

הָאַרְבֶּה עַל כָּל־ אֶרֶץ מִצְרַיִם וַיָּנַח בְּכֹל גְּבוּל מִצְרָיִם
Egypt area-of in-every-of and-he-settled Egypt land-of all-of on the-locust

כָּבֵד מְאֹד לְפָנָיו לֹא־ הָיָה כֵן אַרְבֶּה כָּמֹהוּ וְאַחֲרָיו לֹא
not and-after-him like-him locust such he-was never before-him very many

יִהְיֶה־ כֵּן׃ וַיְכַס אֶת־ עֵין כָּל־ הָאָרֶץ
the-ground all-of face-of *** and-he-covered (15) again he-will-be

go, so that they may worship
the LORD their God. Do you
not yet realize that Egypt is
ruined?"
8Then Moses and Aaron
were brought back to Pharaoh.
"Go, worship the LORD your
God," he said. "But just who
will be going?"
9Moses answered, "We will
go with our young and old,
with our sons and daughters,
and with our flocks and herds,
because we are to celebrate a
festival to the LORD."
10Pharaoh said, "The LORD
be with you—if I let you go,
along with your women and
children! Clearly you are bent
on evil.[p] 11No! Have only the
men go; and worship the
LORD, since that's what you
have been asking for." Then
Moses and Aaron were driven
out of Pharaoh's presence.
12And the LORD said to
Moses, "Stretch out your hand
over Egypt so that locusts will
swarm over the land and devour everything growing in
the fields, everything left by
the hail."
13So Moses stretched out his
staff over Egypt, and the LORD
made an east wind blow
across the land all that day and
all that night. By morning the
wind had brought the locusts;
14they invaded all Egypt and
settled down in every area of
the country in great numbers.
Never before had there been
such a plague of locusts, nor
will there ever be again.
15They covered all the ground

p10 Or *Be careful, trouble is in store for you!*

וַתֶּחְשַׁךְ הָאָרֶץ וַיֹּאכַל אֶת־ כָּל־ עֵשֶׂב הָאָרֶץ
the-land plant-of every-of *** and-he-devoured the-ground so-she-was-black

וְאֵת כָּל־ פְּרִי הָעֵץ אֲשֶׁר הוֹתִיר הַבָּרָד וְלֹא־ נוֹתַר
he-remained and-not the-hail he-left that the-tree fruit-of all-of and

כָּל־ יֶרֶק בָּעֵץ וּבְעֵשֶׂב הַשָּׂדֶה בְּכָל־ אֶרֶץ מִצְרָיִם׃
Egypt land-of in-all-of the-field or-on-plant-of on-the-tree green any-of

וַיְמַהֵר פַּרְעֹה לִקְרֹא לְמֹשֶׁה וּלְאַהֲרֹן וַיֹּאמֶר
and-he-said and-to-Aaron to-Moses to-summon Pharaoh and-he-hurried (16)

חָטָאתִי לַיהוָה אֱלֹהֵיכֶם וְלָכֶם׃ וְעַתָּה שָׂא נָא
now! forgive! and-now (17) and-against-you God-of-you against-Yahweh I-sinned

חַטָּאתִי אַךְ הַפַּעַם וְהַעְתִּירוּ לַיהוָה אֱלֹהֵיכֶם וְיָסֵר
so-he-will-take God-of-you to-Yahweh and-pray! the-time again sin-of-me

מֵעָלַי רַק אֶת־ הַמָּוֶת הַזֶּה׃ וַיֵּצֵא מֵעִם
from-with then-he-left (18) the-this the-deadly-plague *** also away-from-me

פַּרְעֹה וַיֶּעְתַּר אֶל־ יְהוָה׃ וַיַּהֲפֹךְ יְהוָה רוּחַ־ יָם
west wind-of Yahweh and-he-changed (19) Yahweh to and-he-prayed Pharaoh

חָזָק מְאֹד וַיִּשָּׂא אֶת־ הָאַרְבֶּה וַיִּתְקָעֵהוּ יָמָּה סּוּף
Reed into-Sea-of and-he-carried-him the-locust *** and-he-caught very strong

לֹא נִשְׁאַר אַרְבֶּה אֶחָד בְּכֹל גְּבוּל מִצְרָיִם׃ וַיְחַזֵּק
but-he-hardened (20) Egypt area-of in-any-of one locust he-was-left not

יְהוָה אֶת לֵב פַּרְעֹה וְלֹא שִׁלַּח אֶת־ בְּנֵי יִשְׂרָאֵל׃
Israel sons-of *** he-let-go and-not Pharaoh heart-of *** Yahweh

וַיֹּאמֶר יְהוָה אֶל־ מֹשֶׁה נְטֵה יָדְךָ עַל־ הַשָּׁמַיִם
the-heavens to hand-of-you stretch-out! Moses to Yahweh then-he-said (21)

וִיהִי חֹשֶׁךְ עַל־ אֶרֶץ מִצְרָיִם וְיָמֵשׁ חֹשֶׁךְ׃
darkness and-he-can-feel Egypt land-of over darkness so-he-will-spread

וַיֵּט מֹשֶׁה אֶת־ יָדוֹ עַל־ הַשָּׁמָיִם וַיְהִי
and-he-covered the-heavens to hand-of-him *** Moses so-he-stretched (22)

חֹשֶׁךְ־ אֲפֵלָה בְּכָל־ אֶרֶץ מִצְרַיִם שְׁלֹשֶׁת יָמִים׃ לֹא־ רָאוּ
they-saw not (23) days three-of Egypt land-of over-all-of thick darkness

אִישׁ אֶת־ אָחִיו וְלֹא־ קָמוּ אִישׁ מִתַּחְתָּיו שְׁלֹשֶׁת יָמִים
days three-of from-place-of-him any they-left and-not fellow-of-him *** any

וּלְכָל־ בְּנֵי יִשְׂרָאֵל הָיָה אוֹר בְּמוֹשְׁבֹתָם׃
in-dwellings-of-them light he-was Israel sons-of yet-to-all-of

וַיִּקְרָא פַּרְעֹה אֶל־מֹשֶׁה וַיֹּאמֶר לְכוּ עִבְדוּ אֶת־ יְהוָה רַק
only Yahweh *** worship! go! and-he-said Moses to Pharaoh and-he-summoned (24)

צֹאנְכֶם וּבְקַרְכֶם יֻצָּג גַּם־ טַפְּכֶם יֵלֵךְ
he-may-go child-of-you even he-will-be-left and-herd-of-you flock-of-you

until it was black. They devoured all that was left after the hail—everything growing in the fields and the fruit on the trees. Nothing green remained on tree or plant in all the land of Egypt.

16 Pharaoh quickly summoned Moses and Aaron and said, "I have sinned against the LORD your God and against you. 17 Now forgive my sin once more and pray to the LORD your God to take this deadly plague away from me."

18 Moses then left Pharaoh and prayed to the LORD. 19 And the LORD changed the wind to a very strong west wind, which caught up the locusts and carried them into the Red Sea.[q] Not a locust was left anywhere in Egypt. 20 But the LORD hardened Pharaoh's heart, and he would not let the Israelites go.

The Plague of Darkness

21 Then the LORD said to Moses, "Stretch out your hand toward the sky so that darkness will spread over Egypt—darkness that can be felt." 22 So Moses stretched out his hand toward the sky, and total darkness covered all Egypt for three days. 23 No one could see anyone else or leave his place for three days. Yet all the Israelites had light in the places where they lived.

24 Then Pharaoh summoned Moses and said, "Go, worship the LORD. Even your women and children may go with you; only leave your flocks and herds behind."

[q] 19 Hebrew *Yam Suph*, that is, Sea of Reeds

עִמָּכֶם׃ וַיֹּאמֶר מֹשֶׁה גַּם־אַתָּה תִּתֵּן בְּיָדֵנוּ

in-hand-of-us you-must-allow you also Moses but-he-said (25) with-you

זְבָחִים וְעֹלוֹת וְעָשִׂינוּ לַיהוָה אֱלֹהֵינוּ׃ וְגַם־

so-also (26) God-of-us to-Yahweh so-we-may-present and-burnt-offerings sacrifices

מִקְנֵנוּ יֵלֵךְ עִמָּנוּ לֹא תִשָּׁאֵר פַּרְסָה כִּי מִמֶּנּוּ

from-him for hoof she-may-be-left not with-us he-must-go cattle-of-us

נִקַּח לַעֲבֹד אֶת־ יְהוָה אֱלֹהֵינוּ וַאֲנַחְנוּ לֹא־ נֵדַע מַה־

what we-know not and-we God-of-us Yahweh *** to-worship we-must-use

נַּעֲבֹד אֶת־ יְהוָה עַד־ בֹּאֵנוּ שָׁמָּה׃ וַיְחַזֵּק

but-he-hardened (27) to-there to-get-us until Yahweh *** we-must-offer

יְהוָה אֶת־ לֵב פַּרְעֹה וְלֹא אָבָה לְשַׁלְּחָם׃

to-let-go-them he-was-willing and-not Pharaoh heart-of *** Yahweh

וַיֹּאמֶר־ לוֹ פַרְעֹה לֵךְ מֵעָלָי הִשָּׁמֶר לְךָ אֶל*־

not to-you make-sure! from-me go! Pharaoh to-him then-he-said (28)

תֹּסֶף רְאוֹת פָּנַי כִּי בְּיוֹם רְאֹתְךָ פָנַי תָּמוּת׃

you-will-die face-of-me to-see-you on-day for face-of-me to-see you-repeat

וַיֹּאמֶר מֹשֶׁה כֵּן דִּבַּרְתָּ לֹא־ אֹסִף עוֹד רְאוֹת פָּנֶיךָ׃

face-of-you to-see again I-will-repeat not you-say as Moses and-he-replied (29)

וַיֹּאמֶר יְהוָה אֶל־ מֹשֶׁה עוֹד נֶגַע אֶחָד אָבִיא עַל־ פַּרְעֹה

Pharaoh on I-will-bring one plague again Moses to Yahweh now-he-said (11:1)

וְעַל־ מִצְרַיִם אַחֲרֵי־ כֵן יְשַׁלַּח אֶתְכֶם מִזֶּה כְּשַׁלְּחוֹ

when-to-let-go-him from-here you he-will-let-go that after Egypt and-on

כָּלָה גָּרֵשׁ יְגָרֵשׁ אֶתְכֶם מִזֶּה׃ דַּבֶּר־ נָא

now! tell! (2) from-here you he-will-drive-out to-drive-out completely

בְּאָזְנֵי הָעָם וְיִשְׁאֲלוּ אִישׁ ׀ מֵאֵת רֵעֵהוּ וְאִשָּׁה

and-woman neighbor-of-him from man so-they-may-ask the-people in-ears-of

מֵאֵת רְעוּתָהּ כְּלֵי־ כֶסֶף וּכְלֵי זָהָב׃ וַיִּתֵּן

and-he-made (3) gold and-articles-of silver articles-of neighbor-of-her from

יְהוָה אֶת־ חֵן הָעָם בְּעֵינֵי מִצְרָיִם גַּם ׀ הָאִישׁ מֹשֶׁה

Moses the-man also Egyptians in-eyes-of the-people favorable *** Yahweh

גָּדוֹל מְאֹד בְּאֶרֶץ מִצְרַיִם בְּעֵינֵי עַבְדֵי־ פַרְעֹה

Pharaoh officials-of in-eyes-of Egypt in-land-of highly regarded

וּבְעֵינֵי הָעָם׃ וַיֹּאמֶר מֹשֶׁה כֹּה אָמַר יְהוָה

Yahweh he-says this Moses so-he-said (4) the-people and-in-eyes-of

כַּחֲצֹת הַלַּיְלָה אֲנִי יוֹצֵא בְּתוֹךְ מִצְרָיִם׃ וּמֵת כָּל־

every-of and-he-will-die (5) Egypt throughout going I the-night about-mid-of

בְּכוֹר בְּאֶרֶץ מִצְרַיִם מִבְּכוֹר פַּרְעֹה הַיֹּשֵׁב עַל־

on the-one-sitting Pharaoh from-firstborn-of Egypt in-land-of firstborn

[25]But Moses said, "You must allow us to have sacrifices and burnt offerings to present to the LORD our God. [26]Our livestock too must go with us; not a hoof is to be left behind. We have to use some of them in worshiping the LORD our God, and until we get there we will not know what we are to use to worship the LORD."

[27]But the LORD hardened Pharaoh's heart, and he was not willing to let them go. [28]Pharaoh said to Moses, "Get out of my sight! Make sure you do not appear before me again! The day you see my face you will die."

[29]"Just as you say," Moses replied, "I will never appear before you again."

The Plague on the Firstborn

11 Now the LORD had said to Moses, "I will bring one more plague on Pharaoh and on Egypt. After that, he will let you go from here, and when he does, he will drive you out completely. [2]Tell the people that men and women alike are to ask their neighbors for articles of silver and gold." [3](The LORD made the Egyptians favorably disposed toward the people, and Moses himself was highly regarded in Egypt by Pharaoh's officials and by the people.)

[4]So Moses said, "This is what the LORD says: 'About midnight I will go throughout Egypt. [5]Every firstborn son in Egypt will die, from the firstborn son of Pharaoh, who

*28 Most mss have *pathah* under the *aleph* (אַל).

כִּסְאוֹ עַד בְּכוֹר הַשִּׁפְחָה אֲשֶׁר אַחַר הָרֵחָיִם וְכֹל
and-all-of the-handmill at who the-slave-girl firstborn-of to throne-of-him

בְּכוֹר בְּהֵמָה׃ וְהָיְתָה צְעָקָה גְדֹלָה בְּכָל־ אֶרֶץ
land-of through-all-of loud wail and-she-will-be (6) cattle firstborn-of

מִצְרָיִם אֲשֶׁר כָּמֹהוּ לֹא נִהְיָתָה וְכָמֹהוּ לֹא תֹסִף׃
she-will-be-again never and-like-him she-was never like-him that Egypt

וּלְכֹל ׀ בְּנֵי יִשְׂרָאֵל לֹא יֶחֱרַץ־ כֶּלֶב לְשֹׁנוֹ
tongue-of-him dog he-will-bark not Israel sons-of but-among-all-of (7)

לְמֵאִישׁ וְעַד־ בְּהֵמָה לְמַעַן תֵּדְעוּן אֲשֶׁר יַפְלֶה
he-distinguishes that you-will-know so-that animal or-at either-at-man

יְהוָה בֵּין מִצְרַיִם וּבֵין יִשְׂרָאֵל׃ וְיָרְדוּ כָל־
all-of and-they-will-come-down (8) Israel and-between Egypt between Yahweh

עֲבָדֶיךָ אֵלֶּה אֵלַי וְהִשְׁתַּחֲווּ־ לִי לֵאמֹר צֵא אַתָּה
you go! to-say to-me and-they-will-bow to-me these officials-of-you

וְכָל־ הָעָם אֲשֶׁר־ בְּרַגְלֶיךָ וְאַחֲרֵי־ כֵן אֵצֵא
I-will-leave that and-after at-feet-of-you who the-people and-all-of

וַיֵּצֵא מֵעִם־ פַּרְעֹה בָּחֳרִי־ אָף׃ וַיֹּאמֶר יְהוָה אֶל־
to Yahweh now-he-said (9) anger in-heat-of Pharaoh from-with then-he-left

מֹשֶׁה לֹא־ יִשְׁמַע אֲלֵיכֶם פַּרְעֹה לְמַעַן רְבוֹת מוֹפְתַי
wonders-of-me to-be-multiplied so-that Pharaoh to-you he-will-listen not Moses

בְּאֶרֶץ מִצְרָיִם׃ וּמֹשֶׁה וְאַהֲרֹן עָשׂוּ אֶת־ כָּל־ הַמֹּפְתִים
the-wonders all-of *** they-performed and-Aaron so-Moses (10) Egypt in-land-of

הָאֵלֶּה לִפְנֵי פַרְעֹה וַיְחַזֵּק יְהוָה אֶת־ לֵב פַּרְעֹה וְלֹא־
and-not Pharaoh heart-of *** Yahweh but-he-hardened Pharaoh before the-these

שִׁלַּח אֶת־ בְּנֵי־ יִשְׂרָאֵל מֵאַרְצוֹ׃ וַיֹּאמֶר יְהוָה
Yahweh and-he-said (12:1) from-country-of-him Israel sons-of *** he-let-go

אֶל־מֹשֶׁה וְאֶל־ אַהֲרֹן בְּאֶרֶץ מִצְרַיִם לֵאמֹר׃ הַחֹדֶשׁ הַזֶּה לָכֶם
for-you the-this the-month (2) to-say Egypt in-land-of Aaron and-to Moses to

רֹאשׁ חֳדָשִׁים רִאשׁוֹן הוּא לָכֶם לְחָדְשֵׁי הַשָּׁנָה׃ דַּבְּרוּ אֶל־
to tell! (3) the-year among-months-of for-you he first months first-of

כָּל־ עֲדַת יִשְׂרָאֵל לֵאמֹר בֶּעָשֹׂר לַחֹדֶשׁ הַזֶּה
the-this of-the-month on-the-tenth to-say Israel community-of whole-of

וְיִקְחוּ לָהֶם אִישׁ שֶׂה לְבֵית־ אָבֹת שֶׂה לַבָּיִת׃
for-the-household lamb fathers for-house-of lamb each to-them that-they-take

וְאִם־ יִמְעַט הַבַּיִת מִהְיֹת מִשֶּׂה
whole-lamb than-to-have the-household he-is-too-small and-if (4)

וְלָקַח הוּא וּשְׁכֵנוֹ הַקָּרֹב אֶל־ בֵּיתוֹ
household-of-him with the-nearest with-neighbor-of-him he then-he-must-share

sits on the throne, to the
firstborn son of the slave girl,
who is at her hand mill, and
all the firstborn of the cattle as
well. [6]There will be loud wailing throughout Egypt—worse
than there has ever been or
ever will be again. [7]But among
the Israelites not a dog will
bark at any man or animal.'
Then you will know that the
LORD makes a distinction between Egypt and Israel. [8]All
these officials of yours will
come to me, bowing down before me and saying, 'Go, you
and all the people who follow
you!' After that I will leave."
Then Moses, hot with anger,
left Pharaoh.
[9]The LORD had said to
Moses, "Pharaoh will refuse to
listen to you—so that my wonders may be multiplied in
Egypt." [10]Moses and Aaron
performed all these wonders
before Pharaoh, but the LORD
hardened Pharaoh's heart,
and he would not let the Israelites go out of his country.

The Passover

12 The LORD said to Moses
and Aaron in Egypt,
[2]"This month is to be for you
the first month, the first
month of your year. [3]Tell the
whole community of Israel
that on the tenth day of this
month each man is to take a
lamb[r] for his family, one for
each household. [4]If any
household is too small for a
whole lamb, they must share
one with their nearest neighbor, having taken into account

[r]3 The Hebrew word can mean both *lamb* or *kid*; also in verse 4.

*8 Most mss have no *dagesh* in the first *vav* (וּו־).

בְּמִכְסַת נְפָשֹׁת אִישׁ לְפִי אָכְלוֹ תָּכֹסּוּ עַל־

about you-will-determine to-eat-him by-amount-of each people by-number-of

הַשֶּׂה׃ שֶׂה תָמִים זָכָר בֶּן־ שָׁנָה יִהְיֶה לָכֶם מִן־

from to-you he-must-be year son-of male without-defect lamb (5) the-lamb

הַכְּבָשִׂים וּמִן־ הָעִזִּים תִּקָּחוּ׃ וְהָיָה לָכֶם

with-you and-he-will-be (6) you-may-take the-goats or-from the-sheep

לְמִשְׁמֶרֶת עַד אַרְבָּעָה עָשָׂר יוֹם לַחֹדֶשׁ הַזֶּה וְשָׁחֲטוּ

and-they-must-slaughter the-this of-the-month day ten four until for-care

אֹתוֹ כֹּל קְהַל עֲדַת־ יִשְׂרָאֵל בֵּין הָעַרְבָּיִם׃ וְלָקְחוּ

then-they-take (7) the-twilight at Israel community-of people-of all-of him

מִן־ הַדָּם וְנָתְנוּ עַל־ שְׁתֵּי הַמְּזוּזֹת וְעַל־

and-on the-doorposts the-two-sides-of on and-they-must-put the-blood from

הַמַּשְׁקוֹף עַל הַבָּתִּים אֲשֶׁר־ יֹאכְלוּ אֹתוֹ בָּהֶם׃ וְאָכְלוּ

then-they-must-eat (8) in-them him they-eat where the-houses on the-top-post

אֶת־ הַבָּשָׂר בַּלַּיְלָה הַזֶּה צְלִי־ אֵשׁ וּמַצּוֹת

and-breads-without-yeast fire roasted-of the-that in-the-night the-meat ***

עַל־ מְרֹרִים יֹאכְלֻהוּ׃ אַל־ תֹּאכְלוּ מִמֶּנּוּ נָא וּבָשֵׁל

or-boiled raw from-him you-eat not (9) they-must-eat-him bitter-herbs with

מְבֻשָּׁל בַּמָּיִם כִּי אִם־ צְלִי־ אֵשׁ רֹאשׁוֹ עַל־

with head-of-him fire roasted-of only but in-the-water being-cooked

כְּרָעָיו וְעַל־ קִרְבּוֹ׃ וְלֹא־ תוֹתִירוּ מִמֶּנּוּ עַד־

till from-him you-leave and-not (10) inner-part-of-him and-with legs-of-him

בֹּקֶר וְהַנֹּתָר מִמֶּנּוּ עַד־ בֹּקֶר בָּאֵשׁ תִּשְׂרֹפוּ׃

you-must-burn in-the-fire morning until from-him and-the-being-left morning

וְכָכָה תֹּאכְלוּ אֹתוֹ מָתְנֵיכֶם חֲגֻרִים

being-tucked-in-ones loins-of-you him you-must-eat and-this-way (11)

נַעֲלֵיכֶם בְּרַגְלֵיכֶם וּמַקֶּלְכֶם בְּיֶדְכֶם וַאֲכַלְתֶּם

and-you-eat in-hand-of-you and-staff-of-you on-feet-of-you sandals-of-you

אֹתוֹ בְּחִפָּזוֹן פֶּסַח הוּא לַיהוָה׃ וְעָבַרְתִּי בְאֶרֶץ־

through-land-of and-I-will-pass (12) to-Yahweh he Passover in-haste him

מִצְרַיִם בַּלַּיְלָה הַזֶּה וְהִכֵּיתִי כָל־ בְּכוֹר בְּאֶרֶץ

in-land-of firstborn every-of and-I-will-strike the-that on-the-night Egypt

מִצְרַיִם מֵאָדָם וְעַד־ בְּהֵמָה וּבְכָל־ אֱלֹהֵי מִצְרַיִם אֶעֱשֶׂה

I-will-bring Egypt gods-of and-on-all-of animal even-to from-man Egypt

שְׁפָטִים אֲנִי יְהוָה׃ וְהָיָה הַדָּם לָכֶם לְאֹת עַל

on as-sign for-you the-blood and-he-will-be (13) Yahweh I judgments

הַבָּתִּים אֲשֶׁר אַתֶּם שָׁם וְרָאִיתִי אֶת־ הַדָּם וּפָסַחְתִּי עֲלֵכֶם

over-you then-I-will-pass the-blood *** when-I-see there you where the-houses

the number of people there are. You are to determine the amount of lamb needed in accordance with what each person will eat.
5The animals you choose must be year-old males without defect, and you may take them from the sheep or
the goats.
6Take care of them until the fourteenth day of the month, when all the people of the community of Israel must slaughter them at twilight.
7Then they are to take some of the blood and put it on the sides and tops of the doorframes of the houses where they eat the lambs.
8That same night they are to eat the meat roasted over the fire, along with bitter herbs, and bread made without yeast.
9Do not eat the meat raw or cooked in water, but roast it over the fire—head, legs and inner parts.
10Do not leave any of it till morning; if some is left till morning, you must burn it.
11This is how you are to eat it: with your cloak tucked into your belt, your sandals on your feet and your staff in your hand. Eat it in haste; it is the LORD's Passover.
12"On that same night I will pass through Egypt and strike down every firstborn—both men and animals—and I will bring judgment on all the gods of Egypt. I am the LORD.
13The blood will be a sign for you on the houses where you are; and when I see the blood, I will pass over you. No destructive

וְלֹא־ יִהְיֶה בָכֶם נֶגֶף לְמַשְׁחִית בְּהַכֹּתִי בְּאֶרֶץ
on-land-of when-to-strike-me to-destroy plague among-you he-will-be and-not

מִצְרָיִם׃ (14) וְהָיָה הַיּוֹם הַזֶּה לָכֶם לְזִכָּרוֹן וְחַגֹּתֶם
and-you-celebrate to-commemorate to-you the-this the-day and-he-is (14) Egypt

אֹתוֹ חַג לַיהוָה לְדֹרֹתֵיכֶם חֻקַּת עוֹלָם
lasting ordinance-of for-generations-of-you to-Yahweh festival him

תְּחָגֻּהוּ׃ (15) שִׁבְעַת יָמִים מַצּוֹת תֹּאכֵלוּ אַךְ
indeed you-must-eat breads-without-yeast days seven-of (15) you-celebrate-him

בַּיּוֹם הָרִאשׁוֹן תַּשְׁבִּיתוּ שְּׂאֹר* מִבָּתֵּיכֶם כִּי ׀ כָּל־ אֹכֵל
eating any-of for from-houses-of-you yeast you-remove the-first on-the-day

חָמֵץ וְנִכְרְתָה הַנֶּפֶשׁ הַהִוא מִיִּשְׂרָאֵל מִיּוֹם
from-day from-Israel the-that the-person now-she-must-be-cut-off leavened

הָרִאשֹׁן עַד־ יוֹם הַשְּׁבִעִי׃ (16) וּבַיּוֹם הָרִאשׁוֹן מִקְרָא־
assembly the-first and-on-the-day (16) the-seventh day through the-first

קֹדֶשׁ וּבַיּוֹם הַשְּׁבִיעִי מִקְרָא־ קֹדֶשׁ יִהְיֶה לָכֶם כָּל־
any-of to-you he-will-be holy assembly the-seventh and-on-the-day holy

מְלָאכָה לֹא־ יֵעָשֶׂה בָהֶם אַךְ אֲשֶׁר יֵאָכֵל לְכָל־ נֶפֶשׁ
person by-every-of he-is-eaten what except on-them he-may-be-done not work

הוּא לְבַדּוֹ יֵעָשֶׂה לָכֶם׃ (17) וּשְׁמַרְתֶּם אֶת־
*** and-you-celebrate (17) by-you he-may-be-done by-himself that

הַמַּצּוֹת כִּי בְּעֶצֶם הַיּוֹם הַזֶּה הוֹצֵאתִי
I-brought-out the-this the-day on-very for the-Feast-of-Unleavened-Breads

אֶת־ צִבְאוֹתֵיכֶם מֵאֶרֶץ מִצְרָיִם וּשְׁמַרְתֶּם אֶת־ הַיּוֹם הַזֶּה
the-this the-day *** so-you-celebrate Egypt from-land-of divisions-of-you ***

לְדֹרֹתֵיכֶם חֻקַּת עוֹלָם׃ (18) בָּרִאשֹׁן בְּאַרְבָּעָה עָשָׂר
ten on-four in-the-first (18) lasting ordinance-of for-generations-of-you

יוֹם לַחֹדֶשׁ בָּעֶרֶב תֹּאכְלוּ מַצֹּת עַד יוֹם
day until breads-without-yeast you-must-eat in-the-evening of-the-month day

הָאֶחָד וְעֶשְׂרִים לַחֹדֶשׁ בָּעָרֶב׃ (19) שִׁבְעַת יָמִים שְׂאֹר לֹא
not yeast days seven-of (19) the-evening of-the-month and-twenty the-one

יִמָּצֵא בְּבָתֵּיכֶם כִּי ׀ כָּל־ אֹכֵל מַחְמֶצֶת
leavened eating any-of for in-houses-of-you he-may-be-found

וְנִכְרְתָה הַנֶּפֶשׁ הַהִוא מֵעֲדַת יִשְׂרָאֵל
Israel from-community-of the-that the-person now-she-must-be-cut-off

בַּגֵּר וּבְאֶזְרַח הָאָרֶץ׃ (20) כָּל־ מַחְמֶצֶת לֹא
not leavened any-of (20) the-land or-whether-born-of whether-the-alien

תֹאכֵלוּ בְּכָל מוֹשְׁבֹתֵיכֶם תֹּאכְלוּ מַצּוֹת׃
breads-without-yeast you-must-eat dwellings-of-you in-all-of you-may-eat

plague will touch you when I strike Egypt.

14"This is a day you are to commemorate; for the generations to come you shall celebrate it as a festival to the LORD—a lasting ordinance. 15For seven days you are to eat bread made without yeast. On the first day remove the yeast from your houses, for whoever eats anything with yeast in it from the first day through the seventh must be cut off from Israel. 16On the first day hold a sacred assembly, and another one on the seventh day. Do no work at all on these days, except to prepare food for everyone to eat—that is all you may do.

17"Celebrate the Feast of Unleavened Bread, because it was on this very day that I brought your divisions out of Egypt. Celebrate this day as a lasting ordinance for the generations to come. 18In the first month you are to eat bread made without yeast, from the evening of the fourteenth day until the evening of the twenty-first day. 19For seven days no yeast is to be found in your houses. And whoever eats anything with yeast in it must be cut off from the community of Israel, whether he is an alien or native-born. 20Eat nothing made with yeast. Wherever you live, you must eat unleavened bread."

**15* Most mss have no *dagesh* in the *sin* (שׂאר).

וַיִּקְרָא מֹשֶׁה לְכָל־ זִקְנֵי יִשְׂרָאֵל וַיֹּאמֶר אֲלֵהֶם
to-them and-he-said Israel elders-of to-all-of Moses then-he-summoned (21)

מִשְׁכוּ וּקְחוּ לָכֶם צֹאן לְמִשְׁפְּחֹתֵיכֶם וְשַׁחֲטוּ
and-slaughter! for-families-of-you animal for-you and-take! select!

הַפָּסַח׃ וּלְקַחְתֶּם אֲגֻדַּת אֵזוֹב וּטְבַלְתֶּם בַּדָּם
in-the-blood and-you-dip hyssop bunch-of and-you-take (22) the-Passover-lamb

אֲשֶׁר־ בַּסַּף וְהִגַּעְתֶּם אֶל־ הַמַּשְׁקוֹף וְאֶל־ שְׁתֵּי
two-sides-of and-on the-top-post on and-you-put in-the-basin that

הַמְּזוּזֹת מִן־ הַדָּם אֲשֶׁר בַּסָּף וְאַתֶּם לֹא תֵצְאוּ אִישׁ
any you-must-go not and-you in-the-basin that the-blood from the-doorposts

מִפֶּתַח־ בֵּיתוֹ עַד־ בֹּקֶר׃ וְעָבַר יְהוָה לִנְגֹּף
to-strike Yahweh when-he-passes (23) morning until house-of-him from-door-of

אֶת־ מִצְרַיִם וְרָאָה אֶת־ הַדָּם עַל־ הַמַּשְׁקוֹף וְעַל
and-on the-top-post on the-blood *** then-he-will-see Egyptians ***

שְׁתֵּי הַמְּזוּזֹת וּפָסַח יְהוָה עַל־ הַפֶּתַח וְלֹא
and-not the-doorway over Yahweh and-he-will-pass the-doorposts two-sides-of

יִתֵּן הַמַּשְׁחִית לָבֹא אֶל־ בָּתֵּיכֶם לִנְגֹּף׃
to-strike houses-of-you into to-enter the-one-destroying he-will-permit

וּשְׁמַרְתֶּם אֶת־ הַדָּבָר הַזֶּה לְחָק־ לְךָ
for-you as-ordinance the-this the-instruction *** now-you-obey (24)

וּלְבָנֶיךָ עַד־ עוֹלָם׃ וְהָיָה כִּי־ תָבֹאוּ אֶל־
to you-come when and-he-will-be (25) ever for and-for-descendants-of-you

הָאָרֶץ אֲשֶׁר יִתֵּן יְהוָה לָכֶם כַּאֲשֶׁר דִּבֵּר וּשְׁמַרְתֶּם
then-you-observe he-promised just-as to-you Yahweh he-will-give that the-land

אֶת־ הָעֲבֹדָה הַזֹּאת׃ וְהָיָה כִּי־ יֹאמְרוּ אֲלֵיכֶם
to-you they-say when and-he-will-be (26) the-this the-ceremony ***

בְּנֵיכֶם מָה הָעֲבֹדָה הַזֹּאת לָכֶם׃ וַאֲמַרְתֶּם
then-you-tell (27) to-you the-this the-ceremony what? children-of-you

זֶבַח־ פֶּסַח הוּא לַיהוָה אֲשֶׁר פָּסַח עַל־ בָּתֵּי בְנֵי־
sons-of houses-of over he-passed who to-Yahweh this Passover sacrifice-of

יִשְׂרָאֵל בְּמִצְרַיִם בְּנָגְפּוֹ אֶת־ מִצְרַיִם וְאֶת־ בָּתֵּינוּ הִצִּיל
he-spared homes-of-us and Egyptians *** when-to-strike-him in-Egypt Israel

וַיִּקֹּד הָעָם וַיִּשְׁתַּחֲווּ׃* וַיֵּלְכוּ וַיַּעֲשׂוּ
and-they-did and-they-went (28) and-they-worshiped the-people and-he-bowed

בְּנֵי יִשְׂרָאֵל כַּאֲשֶׁר צִוָּה יְהוָה אֶת־ מֹשֶׁה וְאַהֲרֹן כֵּן עָשׂוּ׃
they-did this and-Aaron Moses *** Yahweh he-commanded just-as Israel sons-of

וַיְהִי ׀ בַּחֲצִי הַלַּיְלָה וַיהוָה הִכָּה כָל־ בְּכוֹר
firstborn every-of he-struck that-Yahweh the-night at-mid-of and-he-was (29)

21Then Moses summoned all
the elders of Israel and said to
them, "Go at once and select
the animals for your families
and slaughter the Passover
lamb. 22Take a bunch of hyssop, dip it into the blood in the
basin and put some of the
blood on the top and on both
sides of the doorframe. Not
one of you shall go out the
door of his house until morning. 23When the LORD goes
through the land to strike
down the Egyptians, he will
see the blood on the top and
sides of the doorframe and
will pass over that doorway,
and he will not permit the de-
stroyer to enter your houses
and strike you down.
24"Obey these instructions
as a lasting ordinance for you
and your descendants. 25When
you enter the land that the
LORD will give you as he promised, observe this ceremony.
26And when your children ask
you, 'What does this ceremony mean to you?' 27then tell
them, 'It is the Passover sacrifice to the LORD, who passed
over the houses of the Israelites in Egypt and spared our
homes when he struck down
the Egyptians.'" Then the
people bowed down and worshiped. 28The Israelites did just
what the LORD commanded
Moses and Aaron.
29At midnight the LORD
struck down all the firstborn

*27 Most mss have no *dagesh* in the first *vav* (וו–).

בְּאֶרֶץ מִצְרַיִם מִבְּכֹר פַּרְעֹה הַיֹּשֵׁב עַל־ כִּסְאוֹ
throne-of-him on the-one-sitting Pharaoh from-firstborn-of Egypt in-land-of

עַד בְּכוֹר הַשְּׁבִי אֲשֶׁר בְּבֵית הַבּוֹר וְכֹל
and-every-of the-dungeon in-house-of who the-prisoner firstborn-of to

בְּכוֹר בְּהֵמָה׃ (30) וַיָּקָם פַּרְעֹה לַיְלָה הוּא וְכָל־
and-all-of he night Pharaoh and-he-got-up (30) animal firstborn-of

עֲבָדָיו וְכָל־ מִצְרַיִם וַתְּהִי צְעָקָה גְדֹלָה בְּמִצְרָיִם כִּי־
for in-Egypt loud wail and-she-was Egyptians and-all-of officials-of-him

אֵין בַּיִת אֲשֶׁר אֵין־ שָׁם מֵת׃ (31) וַיִּקְרָא לְמֹשֶׁה
to-Moses so-he-summoned (31) being-dead there not where house not

וּלְאַהֲרֹן לַיְלָה וַיֹּאמֶר קוּמוּ צְּאוּ מִתּוֹךְ עַמִּי גַּם־
indeed people-of-me from-among leave! get-up! and-he-said night and-to-Aaron

אַתֶּם גַּם־ בְּנֵי יִשְׂרָאֵל וּלְכוּ עִבְדוּ אֶת־ יְהוָה כְּדַבֶּרְכֶם׃
as-to-request-you Yahweh *** worship! and-go! Israel sons-of also you

(32) גַּם־ צֹאנְכֶם גַּם־ בְּקַרְכֶם קְחוּ כַּאֲשֶׁר דִּבַּרְתֶּם וָלֵכוּ
and-go! you-said just-as take! herd-of-you also flock-of-you also (32)

וּבֵרַכְתֶּם גַּם־ אֹתִי׃ (33) וַתֶּחֱזַק מִצְרַיִם עַל־ הָעָם לְמַהֵר
to-hurry the-people with Egyptians and-she-urged (33) me also and-you-bless

לְשַׁלְּחָם מִן־ הָאָרֶץ כִּי אָמְרוּ כֻּלָּנוּ מֵתִים׃
being-dead-ones all-of-us they-said for the-country from to-leave-them

(34) וַיִּשָּׂא הָעָם אֶת־ בְּצֵקוֹ טֶרֶם יֶחְמָץ
he-was-leavened before dough-of-him *** the-people so-he-took (34)

מִשְׁאֲרֹתָם צְרֻרֹת בְּשִׂמְלֹתָם עַל־
on in-clothing-of-them ones-being-wrapped kneading-troughs-of-them

שִׁכְמָם׃ (35) וּבְנֵי־ יִשְׂרָאֵל עָשׂוּ כִּדְבַר מֹשֶׁה
Moses as-instruction-of they-did Israel and-sons-of (35) shoulder-of-them

וַיִּשְׁאֲלוּ מִמִּצְרַיִם כְּלֵי־ כֶסֶף וּכְלֵי זָהָב
gold and-articles-of silver articles-of from-Egyptians and-they-asked

וּשְׂמָלֹת׃ (36) וַיהוָה נָתַן אֶת־ חֵן הָעָם בְּעֵינֵי
in-eyes-of the-people favorable *** he-made now-Yahweh (36) and-clothing

מִצְרַיִם וַיַּשְׁאִלוּם וַיְנַצְּלוּ אֶת־ מִצְרָיִם׃
Egyptians *** so-they-plundered and-they-granted-request-of-them Egyptians

(37) וַיִּסְעוּ בְנֵי־ יִשְׂרָאֵל מֵרַעְמְסֵס סֻכֹּתָה כְּשֵׁשׁ־
about-six to-Succoth from-Rameses Israel sons-of and-they-journeyed (37)

מֵאוֹת אֶלֶף רַגְלִי הַגְּבָרִים לְבַד מִטָּף׃ (38) וְגַם־
and-also (38) from-children beside the-men on-foot thousand hundreds

עֵרֶב רַב עָלָה אִתָּם וְצֹאן וּבָקָר מִקְנֶה כָּבֵד מְאֹד׃
very many stock and-herd and-flock with-them he-went-up many other-people

in Egypt, from the firstborn of
Pharaoh, who sat on the
throne, to the firstborn of the
prisoner, who was in the dungeon, and the firstborn of all
the livestock as well. [30]Pharaoh
and all his officials and all the
Egyptians got up during the
night, and there was loud
wailing in Egypt, for there
was not a house without
someone dead.

The Exodus

[31]During the night Pharaoh
summoned Moses and Aaron
and said, "Up! Leave my
people, you and the Israelites!
Go, worship the LORD as you
have requested. [32]Take your
flocks and herds, as you have
said, and go. And also bless
me."

[33]The Egyptians urged the
people to hurry and leave the
country. "For otherwise,"
they said, "we will all die!"
[34]So the people took their
dough before the yeast was
added, and carried it on their
shoulders in kneading troughs
wrapped in clothing. [35]The Israelites did as Moses instructed and asked the Egyptians for
articles of silver and gold and
for clothing. [36]The LORD had
made the Egyptians favorably
disposed toward the people,
and they gave them what they
asked for; so they plundered
the Egyptians.

[37]The Israelites journeyed
from Rameses to Succoth.
There were about six hundred
thousand men on foot, besides
women and children. [38]Many
other people went up with
them, as well as large droves of
livestock, both flocks and

וַיֹּאפוּ אֶת־ הַבָּצֵק אֲשֶׁר הוֹצִיאוּ מִמִּצְרַיִם עֻגֹת
cakes-of from-Egypt they-brought that the-dough *** and-they-baked (39)

מַצּוֹת כִּי לֹא חָמֵץ כִּי־ גֹרְשׁוּ מִמִּצְרַיִם
from-Egypt they-were-driven for he-had-yeast not for unleavened-breads

וְלֹא יָכְלוּ לְהִתְמַהְמֵהַּ וְגַם־ צֵדָה לֹא־ עָשׂוּ לָהֶם׃
for-themselves they-made not food and-also to-take-time they-could and-not

וּמוֹשַׁב בְּנֵי יִשְׂרָאֵל אֲשֶׁר יָשְׁבוּ בְּמִצְרָיִם שְׁלֹשִׁים שָׁנָה וְאַרְבַּע
and-four year thirty in-Egypt they-lived that Israel sons-of now-time-of (40)

מֵאוֹת שָׁנָה׃ וַיְהִי מִקֵּץ שְׁלֹשִׁים שָׁנָה וְאַרְבַּע מֵאוֹת שָׁנָה
year hundreds and-four year thirty at-end-of and-he-was (41) year hundreds

וַיְהִי בְּעֶצֶם הַיּוֹם הַזֶּה יָצְאוּ כָּל־ צִבְאוֹת יְהוָה
Yahweh divisions-of all-of they-left the-this the-day to-very and-he-was

מֵאֶרֶץ מִצְרָיִם׃ לֵיל שִׁמֻּרִים הוּא לַיהוָה לְהוֹצִיאָם
to-bring-out-them by-Yahweh that vigils night-of (42) Egypt from-land-of

מֵאֶרֶץ מִצְרָיִם הוּא־ הַלַּיְלָה הַזֶּה לַיהוָה שִׁמֻּרִים לְכָל־
by-all-of vigils to-Yahweh the-this the-night this Egypt from-land-of

בְּנֵי יִשְׂרָאֵל לְדֹרֹתָם׃ וַיֹּאמֶר יְהוָה אֶל־ מֹשֶׁה
Moses to Yahweh then-he-said (43) for-generations-of-them Israel sons-of

וְאַהֲרֹן זֹאת חֻקַּת הַפָּסַח כָּל־ בֶּן־ נֵכָר לֹא־
not foreigner son-of any-of the-Passover regulation-of this and-Aaron

יֹאכַל בּוֹ׃ וְכָל־ עֶבֶד אִישׁ מִקְנַת־ כָּסֶף
money bought-of man slave but-any-of (44) from-it he-may-eat

וּמַלְתָּה אֹתוֹ אָז יֹאכַל בּוֹ׃ תּוֹשָׁב
temporary-resident (45) from-him he-may-eat then him and-you-circumcised

וְשָׂכִיר לֹא־ יֹאכַל־ בּוֹ׃ בְּבַיִת אֶחָד יֵאָכֵל
he-must-be-eaten one in-house (46) from-him he-may-eat not or-hired-worker

לֹא־ תוֹצִיא מִן־ הַבַּיִת מִן־ הַבָּשָׂר חוּצָה וְעֶצֶם לֹא תִשְׁבְּרוּ־
you-break not and-bone to-outside the-meat from the-house from you-take not

בוֹ׃ כָּל־ עֲדַת יִשְׂרָאֵל יַעֲשׂוּ אֹתוֹ׃ וְכִי־
and-if (48) him he-must-celebrate Israel community-of whole-of (47) in-him

יָגוּר אִתְּךָ גֵּר וְעָשָׂה פֶסַח לַיהוָה הִמּוֹל
circumcise! to-Yahweh Passover and-he-would-celebrate alien with-you he-lives

לוֹ כָל־ זָכָר וְאָז יִקְרַב לַעֲשֹׂתוֹ וְהָיָה
and-he-will-be to-celebrate-him he-may-take-part and-then male every-of to-him

כְּאֶזְרַח הָאָרֶץ וְכָל־ עָרֵל לֹא־ יֹאכַל בּוֹ׃
from-him he-may-eat not uncircumcised but-any-of the-land like-born-of

תּוֹרָה אַחַת יִהְיֶה לָאֶזְרָח וְלַגֵּר הַגָּר
the-one-living and-to-the-alien to-the-native-born he-applies same law (49)

herds. [39]With the dough they had brought from Egypt, they baked cakes of unleavened bread. The dough was without yeast because they had been driven out of Egypt and did not have time to prepare food for themselves.

[40]Now the length of time the Israelite people lived in Egypt[s] was 430 years. [41]At the end of the 430 years, to the very day, all the LORD's divisions left Egypt. [42]Because the LORD kept vigil that night to bring them out of Egypt, on this night all the Israelites are to keep vigil to honor the LORD for the generations to come.

Passover Restrictions

[43]The LORD said to Moses and Aaron, "These are the regulations for the Passover:

"No foreigner is to eat of it. [44]Any slave you have bought may eat of it after you have circumcised him, [45]but a temporary resident and a hired worker may not eat of it.

[46]"It must be eaten inside one house; take none of the meat outside the house. Do not break any of the bones. [47]The whole community of Israel must celebrate it.

[48]"An alien living among you who wants to celebrate the LORD's Passover must have all the males in his household circumcised; then he may take part like one born in the land. No uncircumcised male may eat of it. [49]The same law applies to the native-born and to the alien living among you."

[s]40 Masoretic Text; Samaritan Pentateuch and Septuagint *Egypt and Canaan*

בְּתוֹכְכֶם׃ וַיַּעֲשׂוּ כָּל־ בְּנֵי יִשְׂרָאֵל כַּאֲשֶׁר צִוָּה יְהוָה
Yahweh he-commanded just-as Israel sons-of all-of so-they-did (50) among-you

אֶת־ מֹשֶׁה וְאֶת־ אַהֲרֹן כֵּן עָשׂוּ׃ וַיְהִי בְּעֶצֶם הַיּוֹם הַזֶּה
the-that the-day on-very and-he-was (51) they-did this Aaron and Moses ***

הוֹצִיא יְהוָה אֶת־ בְּנֵי יִשְׂרָאֵל מֵאֶרֶץ מִצְרַיִם עַל־ צִבְאֹתָם׃
divisions-of-them by Egypt from-land-of Israel sons-of *** Yahweh he-brought

וַיְדַבֵּר יְהוָה אֶל־ מֹשֶׁה לֵּאמֹר׃ קַדֶּשׁ־ לִי כָל־
every-of to-me consecrate! (2) to-say Moses to Yahweh then-he-said (13:1)

בְּכוֹר פֶּטֶר כָּל־ רֶחֶם בִּבְנֵי יִשְׂרָאֵל בָּאָדָם
whether-the-man Israel among-sons-of womb every-of first-of firstborn

וּבַבְּהֵמָה לִי הוּא׃ וַיֹּאמֶר מֹשֶׁה אֶל־ הָעָם
the-people to Moses then-he-said (3) he to-me or-whether-the-animal

זָכוֹר אֶת־ הַיּוֹם הַזֶּה אֲשֶׁר יְצָאתֶם מִמִּצְרַיִם מִבֵּית
from-house-of from-Egypt you-came-out that the-this the-day *** to-commemorate

עֲבָדִים כִּי בְּחֹזֶק יָד הוֹצִיא יְהוָה אֶתְכֶם מִזֶּה וְלֹא
so-not from-this you Yahweh he-brought-out hand with-mighty-of for slaveries

יֵאָכֵל חָמֵץ׃ הַיּוֹם אַתֶּם יֹצְאִים בְּחֹדֶשׁ הָאָבִיב׃
the-Abib in-month-of ones-leaving you the-day (4) leavened he-may-be-eaten

וְהָיָה כִי־ יְבִיאֲךָ יְהוָה אֶל־ אֶרֶץ הַכְּנַעֲנִי
the-Canaanite land-of into Yahweh he-brings-you when and-he-will-be (5)

וְהַחִתִּי וְהָאֱמֹרִי וְהַחִוִּי וְהַיְבוּסִי אֲשֶׁר
that and-the-Jebusite and-the-Hivite and-the-Amorite and-the-Hittite

נִשְׁבַּע לַאֲבֹתֶיךָ לָתֶת לָךְ אֶרֶץ זָבַת חָלָב וּדְבָשׁ
and-honey milk flowing-of land to-you to-give to-fathers-of-you he-swore

וְעָבַדְתָּ אֶת־ הָעֲבֹדָה הַזֹּאת בַּחֹדֶשׁ הַזֶּה׃ שִׁבְעַת
seven-of (6) the-this in-the-month the-this the-ceremony *** then-you-observe

יָמִים תֹּאכַל מַצֹּת וּבַיּוֹם הַשְּׁבִיעִי חַג
festival the-seventh and-on-the-day breads-without-yeast you-eat days

לַיהוָה׃ מַצּוֹת יֵאָכֵל אֵת שִׁבְעַת הַיָּמִים וְלֹא־
and-not the-days seven-of *** he-must-be-eaten unleavened-breads (7) to-Yahweh

יֵרָאֶה לְךָ חָמֵץ וְלֹא־ יֵרָאֶה לְךָ שְׂאֹר
yeast among-you he-may-be-seen and-not leavened among-you he-may-be-seen

בְּכָל־ גְּבֻלֶךָ׃ וְהִגַּדְתָּ לְבִנְךָ בַּיּוֹם
on-the-day to-son-of-you and-you-tell (8) border-of-you within-all-of

הַהוּא לֵאמֹר בַּעֲבוּר זֶה עָשָׂה יְהוָה לִי בְּצֵאתִי
when-to-come-me for-me Yahweh he-did what because-of to-say the-that

מִמִּצְרָיִם׃ וְהָיָה לְךָ לְאוֹת עַל־ יָדְךָ וּלְזִכָּרוֹן
and-as-reminder hand-of-you on as-sign for-you and-he-will-be (9) from-Egypt

50All the Israelites did just
what the LORD had com-
manded Moses and Aaron.
51And on that very day the
LORD brought the Israelites out
of Egypt by their divisions.

Consecration of the Firstborn

13 The LORD said to
Moses, 2"Consecrate to
me every firstborn male. The
first offspring of every womb
among the Israelites belongs
to me, whether man or animal."
3Then Moses said to the
people, "Commemorate this
day, the day you came out of
Egypt, out of the land of slavery, because the LORD brought
you out of it with a mighty
hand. Eat nothing containing
yeast. 4Today, in the month of
Abib, you are leaving. 5When
the LORD brings you into the
land of the Canaanites, Hittites, Amorites, Hivites and
Jebusites—the land he swore
to your forefathers to give you,
a land flowing with milk and
honey—you are to observe this
ceremony in this month: 6For
seven days eat bread made
without yeast and on the seventh day hold a festival to the
LORD. 7Eat unleavened bread
during those seven days;
nothing with yeast in it is to
be seen among you, nor shall
any yeast be seen anywhere
within your borders. 8On that
day tell your son, 'I do this because of what the LORD did for
me when I came out of Egypt.'
9This observance will be for
you like a sign on your hand

בֵּין עֵינֶיךָ לְמַעַן תִּהְיֶה תּוֹרַת יְהוָה בְּפִיךָ כִּי
for in-mouth-of-you Yahweh law-of she-must-be that eyes-of-you between

בְּיָד חֲזָקָה הוֹצִאֲךָ יְהוָה מִמִּצְרָיִם׃ וְשָׁמַרְתָּ אֶת־
*** so-you-must-keep (10) from-Egypt Yahweh he-brought-you mighty with-hand

הַחֻקָּה הַזֹּאת לְמוֹעֲדָהּ מִיָּמִים יָמִימָה׃ וְהָיָה
and-he-will-be (11) to-days from-days at-time-of-her the-this the-ordinance

כִּי־ יְבִאֲךָ יְהוָה אֶל־ אֶרֶץ הַכְּנַעֲנִי כַּאֲשֶׁר נִשְׁבַּע לְךָ
to-you he-swore just-as the-Canaanite land-of to Yahweh he-brings-you after

וְלַאֲבֹתֶיךָ וּנְתָנָהּ לָךְ׃ וְהַעֲבַרְתָּ
then-you-must-give (12) to-you and-he-gives-her and-to-fathers-of-you

כָל־ פֶּטֶר־ רֶחֶם לַיהוָה וְכָל־ פֶּטֶר ׀ שֶׁגֶר בְּהֵמָה אֲשֶׁר
that animal born-of first-of and-every-of to-Yahweh womb first-of every-of

יִהְיֶה לְךָ הַזְּכָרִים לַיהוָה׃ וְכָל־ פֶּטֶר חֲמֹר
donkey firstborn-of but-every-of (13) to-Yahweh the-males to-you he-is

תִּפְדֶּה בְשֶׂה וְאִם־ לֹא תִפְדֶּה וַעֲרַפְתּוֹ
then-you-break-neck-of-him you-redeem not but-if with-lamb you-redeem

וְכֹל בְּכוֹר אָדָם בְּבָנֶיךָ תִּפְדֶּה׃ וְהָיָה
and-he-will-be (14) you-redeem among-sons-of-you man firstborn-of and-every-of

כִּי־ יִשְׁאָלְךָ בִנְךָ מָחָר לֵאמֹר מַה־ זֹּאת וְאָמַרְתָּ אֵלָיו
to-him then-you-say this what? to-say day-to-come son-of-you he-asks-you when

בְּחֹזֶק יָד הוֹצִיאָנוּ יְהוָה מִמִּצְרַיִם מִבֵּית עֲבָדִים׃
slaveries from-house-of from-Egypt Yahweh he-brought-us hand with-mighty-of

וַיְהִי כִּי־ הִקְשָׁה פַרְעֹה לְשַׁלְּחֵנוּ וַיַּהֲרֹג יְהוָה
Yahweh then-he-killed to-let-go-us Pharaoh he-refused when and-he-was (15)

כָּל־ בְּכוֹר בְּאֶרֶץ מִצְרַיִם מִבְּכֹר אָדָם וְעַד־ בְּכוֹר
firstborn-of even-to man from-firstborn-of Egypt in-land-of firstborn every-of

בְּהֵמָה עַל־ כֵּן אֲנִי זֹבֵחַ לַיהוָה כָּל־ פֶּטֶר רֶחֶם הַזְּכָרִים
the-males womb first-of every-of to-Yahweh sacrificing I this for animal

וְכָל־ בְּכוֹר בָּנַי אֶפְדֶּה׃ וְהָיָה לְאוֹת
like-sign and-he-will-be (16) I-redeem sons-of-me firstborn-of and-every-of

עַל־ יָדְכָה וּלְטוֹטָפֹת בֵּין עֵינֶיךָ כִּי בְּחֹזֶק יָד
hand with-mighty-of for eyes-of-you between and-like-symbols hand-of-you on

הוֹצִיאָנוּ יְהוָה מִמִּצְרָיִם׃ וַיְהִי בְּשַׁלַּח פַּרְעֹה אֶת־
*** Pharaoh when-to-let-go and-he-was (17) from-Egypt Yahweh he-brought-us

הָעָם וְלֹא־ נָחָם אֱלֹהִים דֶּרֶךְ אֶרֶץ פְּלִשְׁתִּים כִּי
though Philistines country-of road-of God he-led-them and-not the-people

קָרוֹב הוּא כִּי ׀ אָמַר אֱלֹהִים פֶּן־ יִנָּחֵם הָעָם בִּרְאֹתָם
if-to-face-them the-people he-change-mind might God he-said for that short

and a reminder on your forehead that the law of the LORD
is to be on your lips. For the
LORD brought you out of Egypt
with his mighty hand. 10 You
must keep this ordinance at
the appointed time year after
year.
11 "After the LORD brings you
into the land of the Canaanites and gives it to you, as he
promised on oath to you and
your forefathers, 12 you are to
give over to the LORD the first
offspring of every womb. All
the firstborn males of your
livestock belong to the LORD.
13 Redeem with a lamb every
firstborn donkey, but if you do
not redeem it, break its neck.
Redeem every firstborn
among your sons.
14 "In days to come, when
your son asks you, 'What does
this mean?' say to him, 'With
a mighty hand the LORD
brought us out of Egypt, out of
the land of slavery. 15 When
Pharaoh stubbornly refused to
let us go, the LORD killed every
firstborn in Egypt, both man
and animal. This is why I sacrifice to the LORD the first male
offspring of every womb and
redeem each of my firstborn
sons.' 16 And it will be like a
sign on your hand and a symbol on your forehead that the
LORD brought us out of Egypt
with his mighty hand."

Crossing the Sea

17 When Pharaoh let the
people go, God did not lead
them on the road through the
Philistine country, though
that was shorter. For God said,
"If they face war, they might
change their minds and return

מִלְחָמָה וְשָׁבוּ מִצְרָיְמָה׃ וַיַּסֵּב אֱלֹהִים ׀ אֶת־ הָעָם
the-people *** God so-he-led-around (18) to-Egypt and-they-return war

דֶּרֶךְ הַמִּדְבָּר יַם־ סוּף וַחֲמֻשִׁים עָלוּ בְנֵי־ יִשְׂרָאֵל
Israel sons-of they-went-up and-ones-armed Reed Sea-of the-desert road-of

מֵאֶרֶץ מִצְרָיִם׃ וַיִּקַּח מֹשֶׁה אֶת־ עַצְמוֹת יוֹסֵף עִמּוֹ כִּי
for with-him Joseph bones-of *** Moses and-he-took (19) Egypt from-land-of

הַשְׁבֵּעַ הִשְׁבִּיעַ אֶת־ בְּנֵי יִשְׂרָאֵל לֵאמֹר פָּקֹד יִפְקֹד
he-will-aid to-aid to-say Israel sons-of *** he-made-swear to-make-swear

אֱלֹהִים אֶתְכֶם וְהַעֲלִיתֶם אֶת־ עַצְמֹתַי מִזֶּה אִתְּכֶם׃
with-you from-this bones-of-me *** then-you-must-carry you God

וַיִּסְעוּ מִסֻּכֹּת וַיַּחֲנוּ בְאֵתָם בִּקְצֵה הַמִּדְבָּר׃
the-desert on-edge-of at-Etham and-they-camped from-Succoth so-they-left (20)

וַיהוָה הֹלֵךְ לִפְנֵיהֶם יוֹמָם בְּעַמּוּד עָנָן לַנְחֹתָם
to-guide-them cloud in-pillar-of by-day ahead-of-them going now-Yahweh (21)

הַדֶּרֶךְ וְלַיְלָה בְּעַמּוּד אֵשׁ לְהָאִיר לָהֶם לָלֶכֶת יוֹמָם
by-day to-travel to-them to-give-light fire in-pillar-of and-night the-way

וָלָיְלָה׃ לֹא־ יָמִישׁ עַמּוּד הֶעָנָן יוֹמָם וְעַמּוּד הָאֵשׁ
the-fire nor-pillar-of by-day the-cloud pillar-of he-left not (22) or-night

לָיְלָה לִפְנֵי הָעָם׃ וַיְדַבֵּר יְהוָה אֶל־ מֹשֶׁה לֵּאמֹר׃
to-say Moses to Yahweh then-he-said (14:1) the-people in-front-of night

דַּבֵּר אֶל־ בְּנֵי יִשְׂרָאֵל וְיָשֻׁבוּ וְיַחֲנוּ לִפְנֵי פִּי
Pi near and-they-encamp so-they-turn-back Israel sons-of to tell! (2)

הַחִירֹת בֵּין מִגְדֹּל וּבֵין הַיָּם לִפְנֵי בַּעַל צְפֹן נִכְחוֹ
opposite-him Zephon Baal near the-sea and-between Migdol between Hahiroth

תַּחֲנוּ עַל־ הַיָּם׃ וְאָמַר פַּרְעֹה לִבְנֵי
about-sons-of Pharaoh and-he-will-think (3) the-sea by you-shall-encamp

יִשְׂרָאֵל נְבֻכִים הֵם בָּאָרֶץ סָגַר עֲלֵיהֶם הַמִּדְבָּר׃
the-desert on-them he-hemmed-in around-the-land they ones-wandering Israel

וְחִזַּקְתִּי אֶת־ לֵב־ פַּרְעֹה וְרָדַף אַחֲרֵיהֶם
after-them and-he-will-pursue Pharaoh heart-of *** and-I-will-harden (4)

וְאִכָּבְדָה בְּפַרְעֹה וּבְכָל־ חֵילוֹ
army-of-him and-through-all-of through-Pharaoh but-I-will-glorify-myself

וְיָדְעוּ מִצְרַיִם כִּי־ אֲנִי יְהוָה וַיַּעֲשׂוּ־ כֵן׃ וַיֻּגַּד
and-he-was-told (5) this so-they-did Yahweh I that Egyptians and-they-will-know

לְמֶלֶךְ מִצְרַיִם כִּי בָרַח הָעָם וַיֵּהָפֵךְ לְבַב פַּרְעֹה
Pharaoh mind-of and-he-was-changed the-people he-fled that Egypt to-king-of

וַעֲבָדָיו אֶל־ הָעָם וַיֹּאמְרוּ מַה־ זֹּאת עָשִׂינוּ כִּי־
for we-did this what? and-they-said the-people about and-officials-of-him

to Egypt." [18]So God led the
people around by the desert
road toward the Red Sea.[t] The
Israelites went up out of Egypt
armed for battle.
[19]Moses took the bones of Joseph with him because Joseph
had made the sons of Israel
swear an oath. He had said,
"God will surely come to your
aid, and then you must carry
my bones up with you from
this place."[u]
[20]After leaving Succoth they
camped at Etham on the edge
of the desert. [21]By day the LORD
went ahead of them in a pillar
of cloud to guide them on their
way and by night in a pillar of
fire to give them light, so that
they could travel by day or
night. [22]Neither the pillar of
cloud by day nor the pillar of
fire by night left its place in
front of the people.
14 Then the LORD said to
Moses, [2]"Tell the Isra-
elites to turn back and encamp
near Pi Hahiroth, between
Migdol and the sea. They are
to encamp by the sea, directly
opposite Baal Zephon. [3]Phar-
aoh will think, 'The Israelites
are wandering around the
land in confusion, hemmed in
by the desert.' [4]And I will
harden Pharaoh's heart, and
he will pursue them. But I will
gain glory for myself through
Pharaoh and all his army, and
the Egyptians will know that I
am the LORD." So the Israelites
did this.
[5]When the king of Egypt
was told that the people had
fled, Pharaoh and his officials
changed their minds about
them and said, "What have

[t]18 Hebrew *Yam Suph*; that is, Sea of Reeds
[u]19 See Genesis 50:25.

שִׁלַּחְנוּ אֶת־ יִשְׂרָאֵל מֵעָבְדֵנוּ׃ וַיֶּאְסֹר אֶת־ רִכְבּוֹ
chariot-of-him *** so-he-readied (6) from-to-serve-us Israel *** we-let-go

וְאֶת־ עַמּוֹ לָקַח עִמּוֹ׃ וַיִּקַּח שֵׁשׁ־ מֵאוֹת רֶכֶב
chariot hundreds six and-he-took (7) with-him he-took army-of-him and

בָּחוּר וְכֹל רֶכֶב מִצְרָיִם וְשָׁלִשִׁם עַל־ כֻּלּוֹ׃
each-of-him over with-officers Egypt chariot-of with-all-of being-best

וַיְחַזֵּק יְהוָה אֶת־ לֵב פַּרְעֹה מֶלֶךְ מִצְרַיִם וַיִּרְדֹּף
so-he-pursued Egypt king-of Pharaoh heart-of *** Yahweh and-he-hardened (8)

אַחֲרֵי בְּנֵי יִשְׂרָאֵל וּבְנֵי יִשְׂרָאֵל יֹצְאִים בְּיָד
with-hand ones-marching-out Israel now-sons-of Israel sons-of after

רָמָה׃ וַיִּרְדְּפוּ מִצְרַיִם אַחֲרֵיהֶם וַיַּשִּׂיגוּ
and-they-overtook after-them Egyptians so-they-pursued (9) being-boldly-lifted

אוֹתָם חֹנִים עַל־ הַיָּם כָּל־ סוּס רֶכֶב פַּרְעֹה
Pharaoh chariot-of horse-of every-of the-sea by ones-camping them

וּפָרָשָׁיו וְחֵילוֹ עַל־ פִּי הַחִירֹת לִפְנֵי בַּעַל צְפֹן׃
Zephon Baal opposite-of Hahiroth Pi near and-army-of-him and-horsemen-of-him

וּפַרְעֹה הִקְרִיב וַיִּשְׂאוּ בְנֵי־ יִשְׂרָאֵל אֶת־ עֵינֵיהֶם
eyes-of-them *** Israel sons-of then-they-lifted he-approached as-Pharaoh (10)

וְהִנֵּה מִצְרַיִם ׀ נֹסֵעַ אַחֲרֵיהֶם וַיִּירְאוּ מְאֹד
very and-they-were-terrified after-them marching Egyptians and-see!

וַיִּצְעֲקוּ בְנֵי־ יִשְׂרָאֵל אֶל־ יְהוָה׃ וַיֹּאמְרוּ אֶל־ מֹשֶׁה הֲמִבְּלִי
because? Moses to and-they-said (11) Yahweh to Israel sons-of and-they-cried

אֵין־ קְבָרִים בְּמִצְרַיִם לְקַחְתָּנוּ לָמוּת בַּמִּדְבָּר מַה־ זֹּאת עָשִׂיתָ
you-did this what? in-the-desert to-die you-brought-us in-Egypt graves no

לָּנוּ לְהוֹצִיאָנוּ מִמִּצְרָיִם׃ הֲלֹא־ זֶה הַדָּבָר אֲשֶׁר דִּבַּרְנוּ אֵלֶיךָ
to-you we-said that the-word this not? (12) from-Egypt to-bring-us to-us

בְמִצְרַיִם לֵאמֹר חֲדַל מִמֶּנּוּ וְנַעַבְדָה אֶת־ מִצְרָיִם כִּי
for Egyptians *** and-let-us-serve from-us leave-alone! to-say in-Egypt

טוֹב לָנוּ עֲבֹד אֶת־ מִצְרַיִם מִמֻּתֵנוּ בַּמִּדְבָּר׃
in-the-desert than-to-die-us Egyptians *** to-serve for-us better

וַיֹּאמֶר מֹשֶׁה אֶל־ הָעָם אַל־ תִּירָאוּ הִתְיַצְבוּ* וּרְאוּ
and-see! stand-firm! you-fear not the-people to Moses and-he-answered (13)

אֶת־ יְשׁוּעַת יְהוָה אֲשֶׁר־ יַעֲשֶׂה לָכֶם הַיּוֹם כִּי אֲשֶׁר רְאִיתֶם
you-see whom for the-day to-you he-will-bring that Yahweh deliverance-of ***

אֶת־ מִצְרַיִם הַיּוֹם לֹא תֹסִפוּ לִרְאֹתָם עוֹד עַד־ עוֹלָם׃
forever to again to-see you-will-repeat not the-day Egyptians ***

יְהוָה יִלָּחֵם לָכֶם וְאַתֶּם תַּחֲרִשׁוּן׃ וַיֹּאמֶר
then-he-said (15) you-be-still and-you for-you he-will-fight Yahweh (14)

we done? We have let the Israelites go and have lost their services!" [6]So he had his chariot made ready and took his army with him. [7]He took six hundred of the best chariots, along with all the other chariots of Egypt, with officers over all of them. [8]The LORD hardened the heart of Pharaoh king of Egypt, so that he pursued the Israelites, who were marching out boldly. [9]The Egyptians—all Pharaoh's horses and chariots, horsemen[v] and troops—pursued the Israelites and overtook them as they camped by the sea near Pi Hahiroth, opposite Baal Zephon.

[10]As Pharaoh approached, the Israelites looked up, and there were the Egyptians, marching after them. They were terrified and cried out to the LORD. [11]They said to Moses, "Was it because there were no graves in Egypt that you brought us to the desert to die? What have you done to us by bringing us out of Egypt? [12]Didn't we say to you in Egypt, 'Leave us alone; let us serve the Egyptians'? It would have been better for us to serve the Egyptians than to die in the desert!"

[13]Moses answered the people, "Do not be afraid. Stand firm and you will see the deliverance the LORD will bring you today. The Egyptians you see today you will never see again. [14]The LORD will fight for you; you need only to be still."

[v]9 Or *charioteers;* also in verses 17, 18, 23, 26 and 28

**13* Most mss have *dagesh* in the *tsade* ('צּ־).

יְהוָה֙ אֶל־ מֹשֶׁ֔ה מַה־ תִּצְעַ֖ק אֵלָ֑י דַּבֵּ֛ר אֶל־ בְּנֵֽי־ יִשְׂרָאֵ֖ל וְיִסָּֽעוּ׃
so-they-move-on Israel sons-of to tell! to-me you-cry why? Moses to Yahweh

וְאַתָּ֞ה הָרֵ֣ם אֶת־ מַטְּךָ֗ וּנְטֵ֥ה אֶת־ יָדְךָ֛ עַל־
over hand-of-you *** and-stretch! staff-of-you *** raise! now-you (16)

הַיָּ֖ם וּבְקָעֵ֑הוּ וְיָבֹ֧אוּ בְנֵֽי־ יִשְׂרָאֵ֛ל בְּת֥וֹךְ הַיָּ֖ם
the-sea through Israel sons-of so-they-can-go and-divide-him! the-sea

בַּיַּבָּשָֽׁה׃ וַאֲנִ֗י הִנְנִ֤י מְחַזֵּק֙ אֶת־ לֵ֣ב מִצְרַ֔יִם
Egyptians heart-of *** hardening see-I! and-I (17) on-the-dry-ground

וְיָבֹ֖אוּ אַחֲרֵיהֶ֑ם וְאִכָּבְדָ֤ה בְּפַרְעֹה֙
through-Pharaoh and-I-will-glorify-myself after-them so-they-will-go

וּבְכָל־ חֵיל֔וֹ בְּרִכְבּ֖וֹ וּבְפָרָשָֽׁיו׃
and-through-horsemen-of-him through-chariot-of-him army-of-him and-through-all-of

וְיָדְע֥וּ מִצְרַ֖יִם כִּֽי־ אֲנִ֣י יְהוָ֑ה בְּהִכָּבְדִ֣י
when-to-be-glorified-me Yahweh I that Egyptians then-they-will-know (18)

בְּפַרְעֹ֔ה בְּרִכְבּ֖וֹ וּבְפָרָשָֽׁיו׃
and-through-horsemen-of-him through-chariot-of-him through-Pharaoh

וַיִּסַּ֞ע מַלְאַ֣ךְ הָאֱלֹהִ֗ים הַהֹלֵךְ֙ לִפְנֵי֙ מַחֲנֵ֣ה
army-of in-front-of the-one-traveling the-God angel-of then-he-withdrew (19)

יִשְׂרָאֵ֔ל וַיֵּ֖לֶךְ מֵאַחֲרֵיהֶ֑ם וַיִּסַּ֞ע עַמּ֤וּד הֶֽעָנָן֙
the-cloud pillar-of and-he-moved to-behind-them and-he-went Israel

מִפְּנֵיהֶ֔ם וַיַּֽעֲמֹ֖ד מֵאַחֲרֵיהֶֽם׃ וַיָּבֹ֞א בֵּ֣ין ׀
between and-he-came (20) at-behind-them and-he-stood from-in-front-of-them

מַחֲנֵ֣ה מִצְרַ֗יִם וּבֵין֙ מַחֲנֵ֣ה יִשְׂרָאֵ֔ל וַיְהִ֤י הֶֽעָנָן֙
the-cloud and-he-brought Israel army-of and-between Egypt army-of

וְהַחֹ֔שֶׁךְ וַיָּ֖אֶר אֶת־ הַלָּ֑יְלָה וְלֹא־ קָרַ֥ב
he-went-near so-not the-night *** and-he-brought-light both-the-darkness

זֶ֛ה אֶל־ זֶ֖ה כָּל־ הַלָּֽיְלָה׃ וַיֵּ֨ט מֹשֶׁ֣ה אֶת־ יָדוֹ֮
hand-of-him *** Moses then-he-stretched (21) the-night all-of other to this

עַל־ הַיָּם֒ וַיּ֣וֹלֶךְ יְהוָ֣ה ׀ אֶת־ הַ֠יָּם בְּר֨וּחַ קָדִ֤ים עַזָּה֙
strong east with-wind-of the-sea *** Yahweh and-he-drove-back the-sea over

כָּל־ הַלַּ֔יְלָה וַיָּ֥שֶׂם אֶת־ הַיָּ֖ם לֶחָרָבָ֑ה
into-the-dry-land the-sea *** and-he-turned the-night all-of

וַיִּבָּקְע֖וּ הַמָּֽיִם׃ וַיָּבֹ֧אוּ בְנֵֽי־ יִשְׂרָאֵ֛ל בְּת֥וֹךְ
through Israel sons-of and-they-went (22) the-waters and-they-were-divided

הַיָּ֖ם בַּיַּבָּשָׁ֑ה וְהַמַּ֤יִם לָהֶם֙ חֹמָ֔ה מִֽימִינָ֖ם
on-right-of-them wall to-them and-the-waters on-the-dry-ground the-sea

וּמִשְּׂמֹאלָֽם׃ וַיִּרְדְּפ֤וּ מִצְרַ֙יִם֙ וַיָּבֹ֣אוּ אַחֲרֵיהֶ֔ם
after-them and-they-went Egyptians and-they-pursued (23) and-on-left-of-them

15 Then the LORD said to
Moses, "Why are you crying
out to me? Tell the Israelites to
move on. 16 Raise your staff
and stretch out your hand over
the sea to divide the water so
that the Israelites can go
through the sea on dry
ground. 17 I will harden the
hearts of the Egyptians so that
they will go in after them. And
I will gain glory through Pharaoh and all his army, through
his chariots and his horsemen.
18 The Egyptians will know
that I am the LORD when I gain
glory through Pharaoh, his
chariots and his horsemen."
19 Then the angel of God,
who had been traveling in
front of Israel's army, withdrew and went behind them.
The pillar of cloud also moved
from in front and stood behind them, 20 coming between
the armies of Egypt and Israel.
Throughout the night the
cloud brought darkness to the
one side and light to the other
side; so neither went near the
other all night long.
21 Then Moses stretched out
his hand over the sea, and all
that night the LORD drove the
sea back with a strong east
wind and turned it into dry
land. The waters were divided, 22 and the Israelites went
through the sea on dry
ground, with a wall of water
on their right and on their left.
23 The Egyptians pursued

כֹּל סוּס פַּרְעֹה רִכְבּוֹ וּפָרָשָׁיו אֶל־ תּוֹךְ
midst-of into and-horsemen-of-him chariot-of-him Pharaoh horse-of every-of

הַיָּם׃ וַיְהִי בְּאַשְׁמֹרֶת הַבֹּקֶר וַיַּשְׁקֵף יְהוָה
Yahweh that-he-looked-down the-morning in-watch-of and-he-was (24) the-sea

אֶל־ מַחֲנֵה מִצְרַיִם בְּעַמּוּד אֵשׁ וְעָנָן וַיָּהָם אֵת מַחֲנֵה
army-of *** and-he-confused and-cloud fire from-pillar-of Egypt army-of at

מִצְרָיִם׃ וַיָּסַר* אֵת אֹפַן מַרְכְּבֹתָיו וַיְנַהֲגֵהוּ
so-he-drove-him chariots-of-him wheel-of *** *and-he-made-come-off (25) Egypt

בִּכְבֵדֻת וַיֹּאמֶר מִצְרַיִם אָנוּסָה מִפְּנֵי יִשְׂרָאֵל כִּי
for Israel from-before let-me-get-away Egyptians and-he-said with-difficulty

יְהוָה נִלְחָם לָהֶם בְּמִצְרָיִם† וַיֹּאמֶר יְהוָה אֶל־ מֹשֶׁה
Moses to Yahweh then-he-said (26) against-Egypt for-them fighting Yahweh

נְטֵה אֶת־ יָדְךָ עַל־ הַיָּם וְיָשֻׁבוּ הַמַּיִם עַל־
over the-waters so-they-may-flow-back the-sea over hand-of-you *** stretch!

מִצְרַיִם עַל־ רִכְבּוֹ וְעַל־ פָּרָשָׁיו׃ וַיֵּט
so-he-stretched (27) horsemen-of-him and-over chariot-of-him over Egyptians

מֹשֶׁה אֶת־ יָדוֹ עַל־ הַיָּם וַיָּשָׁב הַיָּם לִפְנוֹת
at-to-dawn the-sea and-he-went-back the-sea over hand-of-him *** Moses

בֹּקֶר לְאֵיתָנוֹ וּמִצְרַיִם נָסִים לִקְרָאתוֹ וַיְנַעֵר
and-he-swept to-meet-him ones-fleeing and-Egyptians to-place-of-him morning

יְהוָה אֶת־ מִצְרַיִם בְּתוֹךְ הַיָּם׃ וַיָּשֻׁבוּ הַמַּיִם
the-waters and-they-flowed-back (28) the-sea into Egyptians *** Yahweh

וַיְכַסּוּ אֶת־ הָרֶכֶב וְאֶת־ הַפָּרָשִׁים לְכֹל חֵיל פַּרְעֹה
Pharaoh army-of over-all-of the-horsemen and the-chariot *** and-they-covered

הַבָּאִים אַחֲרֵיהֶם בַּיָּם לֹא־ נִשְׁאַר בָּהֶם עַד־אֶחָד׃
one even of-them he-survived not into-the-sea after-them the-ones-following

וּבְנֵי יִשְׂרָאֵל הָלְכוּ בַיַּבָּשָׁה בְּתוֹךְ הַיָּם
the-sea through on-the-dry-ground they-went Israel but-sons-of (29)

וְהַמַּיִם לָהֶם חֹמָה מִימִינָם וּמִשְּׂמֹאלָם†
and-on-left-of-them on-right-of-them wall to-them and-the-waters

וַיּוֹשַׁע יְהוָה בַּיּוֹם הַהוּא אֶת־ יִשְׂרָאֵל מִיַּד מִצְרָיִם
Egyptians from-hand-of Israel *** the-that on-the-day Yahweh so-he-saved (30)

וַיַּרְא יִשְׂרָאֵל אֶת־ מִצְרַיִם מֵת עַל־ שְׂפַת הַיָּם׃
the-sea shore-of on being-dead Egyptians *** Israel and-he-saw

וַיַּרְא יִשְׂרָאֵל אֶת־ הַיָּד הַגְּדֹלָה אֲשֶׁר עָשָׂה יְהוָה
Yahweh he-displayed that the-great the-power *** Israel when-he-saw (31)

בְּמִצְרַיִם וַיִּירְאוּ הָעָם אֶת־ יְהוָה וַיַּאֲמִינוּ
and-they-trusted Yahweh *** the-people then-they-feared against-Egyptians

them, and all Pharaoh's horses
and chariots and horsemen
followed them into the sea.
[24]In the morning watch the
LORD looked down from the
pillar of fire and cloud at the
Egyptian army and threw it
into confusion. [25]He made the
wheels of their chariots
come off[w] so that they had
difficulty driving. And the
Egyptians said, "Let's get
away from the Israelites! The
LORD is fighting for them
against Egypt."
[26]Then the LORD said to
Moses, "Stretch out your hand
over the sea so that the waters
may flow back over the Egyptians and their chariots and
horsemen." [27]Moses stretched
out his hand over the sea, and
at daybreak the sea went back
to its place. The Egyptians
were fleeing toward[x] it, and
the LORD swept them into the
sea. [28]The water flowed back
and covered the chariots and
horsemen—the entire army of
Pharaoh that had followed the
Israelites into the sea. Not one
of them survived.
[29]But the Israelites went
through the sea on dry
ground, with a wall of water
on their right and on their left.
[30]That day the LORD saved Israel from the hands of the Egyptians, and Israel saw the Egyptians lying dead on the shore.
[31]And when the Israelites saw
the great power the LORD displayed against the Egyptians,
the people feared the LORD and

[w]25 Or *He jammed the wheels of their chariots* (see Samaritan Pentateuch, Septuagint and Syriac)

*25 וַיֶּאְסֹר, *and-he-jammed*
This Hebrew reading and translation is conjectured on the basis of the early versions listed above in note w.

†25, 29 Most mss end verses 25 and 29 with *soph pasuq* (׃).

בַּיהוָה וּבְמֹשֶׁה עַבְדּוֹ׃ אָז יָשִׁיר־מֹשֶׁה וּבְנֵי

and-sons-of Moses he-sang then (15:1) servant-of-him and-in-Moses in-Yahweh

יִשְׂרָאֵל אֶת־הַשִּׁירָה הַזֹּאת לַיהוָה וַיֹּאמְרוּ לֵאמֹר אָשִׁירָה

I-will-sing to-say and-they-said to-Yahweh the-this the-song *** Israel

לַיהוָה כִּי־גָאֹה גָּאָה סוּס וְרֹכְבוֹ רָמָה

he-hurled and-one-riding-him horse he-is-exalted to-be-exalted for to-Yahweh

בַיָּם׃ עָזִּי וְזִמְרָת יָהּ וַיְהִי־לִי לִישׁוּעָה

as-salvation to-me and-he-became Yah and-song strength-of-me (2) into-the-sea

זֶה אֵלִי וְאַנְוֵהוּ אֱלֹהֵי אָבִי וַאֲרֹמְמֶנְהוּ׃

and-I-will-exalt-him father-of-me God-of and-I-will-praise-him God-of-me this

יְהוָה אִישׁ מִלְחָמָה יְהוָה שְׁמוֹ׃ מַרְכְּבֹת פַּרְעֹה

Pharaoh chariots-of (4) name-of-him Yahweh war man-of Yahweh (3)

וְחֵילוֹ יָרָה בַיָּם וּמִבְחַר שָׁלִשָׁיו

officers-of-him and-best-of into-the-sea he-hurled and-army-of-him

טֻבְּעוּ בְיַם־סוּף׃ תְּהֹמֹת יְכַסְיֻמוּ יָרְדוּ

they-sank they-covered-them deep-waters (5) Reed in-Sea-of they-drowned

בִמְצוֹלֹת כְּמוֹ־אָבֶן׃ יְמִינְךָ יְהוָה נֶאְדָּרִי

being-majestic-of Yahweh right-hand-of-you (6) stone like to-depths

בַּכֹּחַ יְמִינְךָ יְהוָה תִּרְעַץ אוֹיֵב׃

being-enemy she-shattered Yahweh right-hand-of-you in-the-power

וּבְרֹב גְּאוֹנְךָ תַּהֲרֹס קָמֶיךָ

ones-opposing-you you-threw-down majesty-of-you and-in-greatness-of (7)

תְּשַׁלַּח חֲרֹנְךָ יֹאכְלֵמוֹ כַּקַּשׁ׃ וּבְרוּחַ

and-by-blast-of (8) like-the-stubble he-consumed-them anger-of-you you-unleased

אַפֶּיךָ נֶעֶרְמוּ מַיִם נִצְּבוּ כְמוֹ־נֵד נֹזְלִים

ones-raging wall like they-stood-firm waters they-piled-up nostrils-of-you

קָפְאוּ תְהֹמֹת בְּלֶב־יָם׃ אָמַר אוֹיֵב

being-enemy he-boasted (9) sea in-heart-of deep-waters they-congealed

אֶרְדֹּף אַשִּׂיג אֲחַלֵּק שָׁלָל תִּמְלָאֵמוֹ

she-will-gorge-on-them spoil I-will-divide I-will-overtake I-will-pursue

נַפְשִׁי אָרִיק חַרְבִּי תּוֹרִישֵׁמוֹ יָדִי׃

hand-of-me she-will-destroy them sword-of-me I-will-draw self-of-me

נָשַׁפְתָּ בְרוּחֲךָ כִּסָּמוֹ יָם צָלְלוּ כַּעוֹפֶרֶת

like-the-lead they-sank sea he-covered-them with-breath-of-you you-blew (10)

בְּמַיִם אַדִּירִים׃ מִי־כָמֹכָה בָּאֵלִם יְהוָה מִי כָּמֹכָה

like-you who? Yahweh among-the-gods like-you who? (11) mighty-ones in-waters

נֶאְדָּר בַּקֹּדֶשׁ נוֹרָא תְהִלֹּת עֹשֵׂה פֶלֶא׃

wonder working glories being-awesome in-the-holiness being-majestic

put their trust in him and in Moses his servant.

The Song of Moses

15 Then Moses and the Israelites sang this song to the LORD:

"I will sing to the LORD,
for he is highly exalted.
The horse and its rider
he has hurled into the sea.
2The LORD is my strength and my song;
he has become my salvation.
He is my God, and I will praise him,
my father's God, and I will exalt him.
3The LORD is a warrior;
the LORD is his name.
4Pharaoh's chariots and his army
he has hurled into the sea.
The best of Pharaoh's officers
are drowned in the Red Sea.[y]
5The deep waters have covered them;
they sank to the depths like a stone.

6"Your right hand, O LORD,
was majestic in power.
Your right hand, O LORD,
shattered the enemy.
7In the greatness of your majesty
you threw down those who opposed you.
You unleashed your burning anger;
it consumed them like stubble.
8By the blast of your nostrils
the waters piled up.
The surging waters stood firm like a wall;
the deep waters congealed in the heart of the sea.

9"The enemy boasted,
'I will pursue, I will overtake them.
I will divide the spoils;
I will gorge myself on them.
I will draw my sword
and my hand will destroy them.'
10But you blew with your breath,
and the sea covered them.
They sank like lead
in the mighty waters.

11"Who among the gods is like you, O LORD?
Who is like you—
majestic in holiness,
awesome in glory,

x27 Or *from*
y4 Hebrew *Yam Suph*; that is, Sea of Reeds; also in verse 22

נָטִיתָ יְמִינְךָ תִּבְלָעֵמוֹ אָרֶץ׃ נָחִיתָ
you-will-lead (13) earth she-swallowed-them right-hand-of-you you-stretched (12)

בְחַסְדְּךָ עַם־ זוּ גָּאָלְתָּ נֵהַלְתָּ בְעָזְּךָ
in-strength-of-you you-will-guide you-redeemed whom people in-love-of-you

אֶל־ נְוֵה קָדְשֶׁךָ׃ שָׁמְעוּ עַמִּים יִרְגָּזוּן
they-will-tremble nations they-will-hear (14) holy-of-you dwelling-of to

חִיל אָחַז יֹשְׁבֵי פְּלָשֶׁת׃ אָז נִבְהֲלוּ
they-will-be-terrified then (15) Philistia ones-living-of he-will-grip anguish

אַלּוּפֵי אֱדוֹם אֵילֵי מוֹאָב יֹאחֲזֵמוֹ רָעַד נָמֹגוּ
they-will-melt trembling he-will-seize-them Moab leaders-of Edom chiefs-of

כֹּל יֹשְׁבֵי כְנָעַן׃ תִּפֹּל עֲלֵיהֶם אֵימָתָה וָפַחַד
and-dread terror on-them she-will-fall (16) Canaan ones-living-of all-of

בִּגְדֹל זְרוֹעֲךָ יִדְּמוּ כָּאָבֶן עַד־ יַעֲבֹר
he-passes-by until as-the-stone they-will-be-still arm-of-you by-power-of

עַמְּךָ יְהוָה עַד־ יַעֲבֹר עַם־ זוּ קָנִיתָ׃
you-bought whom people he-passes-by until Yahweh people-of-you

תְּבִאֵמוֹ וְתִטָּעֵמוֹ בְּהַר
on-mountain-of and-you-will-plant-them you-will-bring-in-them (17)

נַחֲלָתְךָ מָכוֹן לְשִׁבְתְּךָ פָּעַלְתָּ יְהוָה מִקְּדָשׁ אֲדֹנָי
Lord sanctuary Yahweh you-made to-dwell-you place inheritance-of-you

כּוֹנְנוּ יָדֶיךָ׃ יְהוָה׀ יִמְלֹךְ לְעֹלָם וָעֶד׃
and-ever for-ever he-will-reign Yahweh (18) hands-of-you they-established

כִּי בָא סוּס פַּרְעֹה בְּרִכְבּוֹ וּבְפָרָשָׁיו
and-with-horsemen-of-him with-chariot-of-him Pharaoh horse-of he-went when (19)

בַּיָּם וַיָּשֶׁב יְהוָה עֲלֵהֶם אֶת־ מֵי הַיָּם
the-sea waters-of *** over-them Yahweh then-he-brought into-the-sea

וּבְנֵי יִשְׂרָאֵל הָלְכוּ בַיַּבָּשָׁה בְּתוֹךְ הַיָּם׃
the-sea through on-the-dry-ground they-walked Israel but-sons-of

וַתִּקַּח מִרְיָם הַנְּבִיאָה אֲחוֹת אַהֲרֹן אֶת־ הַתֹּף
the-tambourine *** Aaron sister-of the-prophetess Miriam then-she-took (20)

בְּיָדָהּ וַתֵּצֶאןָ כָל־ הַנָּשִׁים אַחֲרֶיהָ בְּתֻפִּים
with-tambourines after-her the-women all-of and-they-followed in-hand-of-her

וּבִמְחֹלֹת׃ וַתַּעַן לָהֶם מִרְיָם שִׁירוּ לַיהוָה כִּי־
for to-Yahweh sing! Miriam to-them and-she-sang (21) and-with-dances

גָאֹה גָּאָה סוּס וְרֹכְבוֹ רָמָה בַיָּם׃
into-the-sea he-hurled and-one-riding-him horse he-is-exalted to-be-exalted

וַיַּסַּע מֹשֶׁה אֶת־ יִשְׂרָאֵל מִיַּם־ סוּף וַיֵּצְאוּ אֶל־
into and-they-went Reed from-Sea-of Israel *** Moses then-he-led (22)

working wonders?
12You stretched out your right hand
and the earth swallowed them.

13"In your unfailing love you will lead
the people you have redeemed.
In your strength you will guide them
to your holy dwelling.
14The nations will hear and tremble;
anguish will grip the people of Philistia.
15The chiefs of Edom will be terrified,
the leaders of Moab will be seized with trembling,
the people[z] of Canaan will melt away;
16 terror and dread will fall upon them.
By the power of your arm they will be as still as a stone—
until your people pass by, O LORD,
until the people you bought pass by.
17You will bring them in and plant them
on the mountain of your inheritance—
the place, O LORD, you made for your dwelling,
the sanctuary, O Lord, your hands established.
18The LORD will reign for ever and ever."

19When Pharaoh's horses,
chariots and horsemen[a] went
into the sea, the LORD brought
the waters of the sea back over
them, but the Israelites walked
through the sea on dry
ground. 20Then Miriam the
prophetess, Aaron's sister,
took a tambourine in her
hand, and all the women followed her, with tambourines
and dancing. 21Miriam sang to
them:

"Sing to the LORD,
for he is highly exalted.
The horse and its rider
he has hurled into the sea."

The Waters of Marah and Elim

22Then Moses led Israel from
the Red Sea and they went

z15 Or *rulers* a19 Or *charioteers*

מִדְבַּר־ שׁוּר וַיֵּלְכוּ שְׁלֹשֶׁת־ יָמִים בַּמִּדְבָּר וְלֹא־
and-not in-the-desert days three-of and-they-traveled Shur Desert-of

מָצְאוּ מָיִם׃ וַיָּבֹאוּ מָרָתָה וְלֹא יָכְלוּ לִשְׁתֹּת
to-drink they-could but-not to-Marah and-they-came (23) waters they-found

מַיִם מִמָּרָה כִּי מָרִים הֵם עַל־ כֵּן קָרָא־ שְׁמָהּ מָרָה׃
Marah name-of-her he-called this for they bitter-ones for from-Marah waters

וַיִּלֹּנוּ הָעָם עַל־ מֹשֶׁה לֵּאמֹר מַה־ נִּשְׁתֶּה׃
will-we-drink what? to-say Moses against the-people so-they-grumbled (24)

וַיִּצְעַק אֶל־ יְהוָה וַיּוֹרֵהוּ יְהוָה עֵץ וַיַּשְׁלֵךְ אֶל־
into and-he-threw wood Yahweh and-he-showed-him Yahweh to then-he-cried (25)

הַמַּיִם וַיִּמְתְּקוּ הַמָּיִם שָׁם שָׂם לוֹ חֹק
decree for-him he-made there the-waters and-they-became-sweet the-waters

וּמִשְׁפָּט וְשָׁם נִסָּהוּ׃ וַיֹּאמֶר אִם־ שָׁמוֹעַ תִּשְׁמַע
you-listen to-listen if and-he-said (26) he-tested-him and-there and-law

לְקוֹל יְהוָה אֱלֹהֶיךָ וְהַיָּשָׁר בְּעֵינָיו תַּעֲשֶׂה
you-do in-eyes-of-him and-the-right God-of-you Yahweh to-voice-of

וְהַאֲזַנְתָּ לְמִצְוֹתָיו וְשָׁמַרְתָּ כָּל־ חֻקָּיו כָּל־
all-of decrees-of-him all-of and-you-keep to-commands-of-him and-you-attend

הַמַּחֲלָה אֲשֶׁר־ שַׂמְתִּי בְמִצְרַיִם לֹא־ אָשִׂים עָלֶיךָ כִּי אֲנִי
I for on-you I-will-bring not on-Egyptians I-brought that the-disease

יְהוָה רֹפְאֶךָ׃ וַיָּבֹאוּ אֵילִמָה וְשָׁם שְׁתֵּים עֶשְׂרֵה
ten two and-there to-Elim then-they-came (27) one-healing-you Yahweh

עֵינֹת מַיִם וְשִׁבְעִים תְּמָרִים וַיַּחֲנוּ־ שָׁם עַל־ הַמָּיִם׃
the-waters by there and-they-camped palm-trees and-seventy waters springs-of

וַיִּסְעוּ מֵאֵילִם וַיָּבֹאוּ כָּל־ עֲדַת
community-of whole-of and-they-came from-Elim then-they-set-out (16:1)

בְּנֵי־ יִשְׂרָאֵל אֶל־ מִדְבַּר־ סִין אֲשֶׁר בֵּין־ אֵילִם וּבֵין סִינָי בַּחֲמִשָּׁה
on-five Sinai and-between Elim between which Sin Desert-of to Israel sons-of

עָשָׂר יוֹם לַחֹדֶשׁ הַשֵּׁנִי לְצֵאתָם מֵאֶרֶץ מִצְרָיִם׃
Egypt from-land-of after-to-come-out-them the-second of-the-month day ten

וַיִּלּוֹנוּ כָּל־ עֲדַת בְּנֵי־ יִשְׂרָאֵל עַל־ מֹשֶׁה
Moses against Israel sons-of community-of whole-of and-they-grumbled (2)

וְעַל־ אַהֲרֹן בַּמִּדְבָּר׃ וַיֹּאמְרוּ אֲלֵהֶם בְּנֵי יִשְׂרָאֵל
Israel sons-of to-them and-they-said (3) in-the-desert Aaron and-against

מִי־ יִתֵּן מוּתֵנוּ בְיַד־ יְהוָה בְּאֶרֶץ מִצְרַיִם בְּשִׁבְתֵּנוּ
when-to-sit-us Egypt in-land-of Yahweh by-hand-of to-die-us he-let if-only

עַל־ סִיר הַבָּשָׂר בְּאָכְלֵנוּ לֶחֶם לָשֹׂבַע כִּי־ הוֹצֵאתֶם אֹתָנוּ
us you-brought but to-fullness food when-to-eat-us the-meat pot-of around

ק וילונו °2

into the Desert of Shur. For
three days they traveled in the
desert without finding water.
23When they came to Marah,
they could not drink its water
because it was bitter. (That is
why the place is called Marah.[b]) 24So the people grumbled
against Moses, saying, "What
are we to drink?"
25Then Moses cried out to
the LORD, and the LORD
showed him a piece of wood.
He threw it into the water,
and the water became sweet.
There the LORD made a de-
cree and a law for them, and
there he tested them. 26He
said, "If you listen carefully to
the voice of the LORD your God
and do what is right in his
eyes, if you pay attention to
his commands and keep all his
decrees, I will not bring on
you any of the diseases I
brought on the Egyptians, for
I am the LORD who heals you."
27Then they came to Elim,
where there were twelve
springs and seventy palm
trees, and they camped there
near the water.

Manna and Quail

16 The whole Israelite
community set out
from Elim and came to the
Desert of Sin, which is between Elim and Sinai, on the
fifteenth day of the second
month after they had come out
of Egypt. 2In the desert the
whole community grumbled
against Moses and Aaron.
3The Israelites said to them, "If
only we had died by the
LORD's hand in Egypt! There
we sat around pots of meat
and ate all the food we wanted, but you have brought us

b23 *Marah* means *bitter*.

אֶל־ הַמִּדְבָּר הַזֶּה לְהָמִית אֶת־ כָּל־ הַקָּהָל הַזֶּה
the-this the-assembly whole-of *** to-kill the-this the-desert into

בָּרָעָב׃ וַיֹּאמֶר יְהוָה אֶל־מֹשֶׁה הִנְנִי מַמְטִיר לָכֶם לֶחֶם
bread for-you raining see-I! Moses to Yahweh then-he-said (4) with-the-hunger

מִן־ הַשָּׁמָיִם וְיָצָא הָעָם וְלָקְטוּ דְּבַר־
amount-of and-they-will-gather the-people and-he-will-go-out the-heavens from

יוֹם בְּיוֹמוֹ לְמַעַן אֲנַסֶּנּוּ הֲיֵלֵךְ בְּתוֹרָתִי
by-instruction-of-me whether-he-follows I-will-test-him in-this in-day-of-him day

אִם־לֹא׃ וְהָיָה בַּיּוֹם הַשִּׁשִּׁי וְהֵכִינוּ אֵת
*** that-they-will-prepare the-sixth on-the-day and-he-will-be (5) not or

אֲשֶׁר־ יָבִיאוּ וְהָיָה מִשְׁנֶה עַל אֲשֶׁר־ יִלְקְטוּ יוֹם ׀ יוֹם׃
day day they-gather what than twice and-he-will-be they-bring-in what

וַיֹּאמֶר מֹשֶׁה וְאַהֲרֹן אֶל־כָּל־ בְּנֵי יִשְׂרָאֵל עֶרֶב וִידַעְתֶּם
then-you-will-know evening Israel sons-of all-of to and-Aaron Moses so-he-said (6)

כִּי יְהוָה הוֹצִיא אֶתְכֶם מֵאֶרֶץ מִצְרָיִם׃ וּבֹקֶר וּרְאִיתֶם
also-you-will-see and-morning (7) Egypt from-land-of you he-brought Yahweh that

אֶת־ כְּבוֹד יְהוָה בְּשָׁמְעוֹ אֶת־ תְּלֻנֹּתֵיכֶם עַל־ יְהוָה
Yahweh against grumblings-of-you *** because-to-hear-him Yahweh glory-of ***

וְנַחְנוּ מָה כִּי תַלּוֹנוּ° עָלֵינוּ׃ וַיֹּאמֶר מֹשֶׁה בְּתֵת
when-to-give Moses and-he-said (8) against-us you-grumble that who? and-we

יְהוָה לָכֶם בָּעֶרֶב בָּשָׂר לֶאֱכֹל וְלֶחֶם בַּבֹּקֶר לִשְׂבֹּעַ
to-satisfy in-the-morning and-bread to-eat meat in-the-evening to-you Yahweh

בִּשְׁמֹעַ יְהוָה אֶת־ תְּלֻנֹּתֵיכֶם אֲשֶׁר־ אַתֶּם מַלִּינִם
ones-grumbling you that grumblings-of-you *** Yahweh because-to-hear

עָלָיו וְנַחְנוּ מָה לֹא־ עָלֵינוּ תְלֻנֹּתֵיכֶם כִּי עַל־ יְהוָה׃
Yahweh against but grumblings-of-you against-us not who? and-we against-him

וַיֹּאמֶר מֹשֶׁה אֶל־אַהֲרֹן אֱמֹר אֶל־כָּל־ עֲדַת בְּנֵי יִשְׂרָאֵל
Israel sons-of community-of whole-of to say! Aaron to Moses then-he-told (9)

קִרְבוּ לִפְנֵי יְהוָה כִּי שָׁמַע אֵת תְּלֻנֹּתֵיכֶם׃ וַיְהִי
and-he-was (10) grumblings-of-you *** he-heard for Yahweh before come!

כְּדַבֵּר אַהֲרֹן אֶל־ כָּל־ עֲדַת בְּנֵי־ יִשְׂרָאֵל וַיִּפְנוּ
that-they-looked Israel sons-of community-of whole-of to Aaron while-to-speak

אֶל־ הַמִּדְבָּר וְהִנֵּה כְּבוֹד יְהוָה נִרְאָה בֶּעָנָן׃
in-the-cloud appearing Yahweh glory-of and-see! the-desert toward

וַיְדַבֵּר יְהוָה אֶל־ מֹשֶׁה לֵּאמֹר׃ שָׁמַעְתִּי אֶת־ תְּלוּנֹּת
grumblings-of *** I-heard (12) to-say Moses to Yahweh and-he-spoke (11)

בְּנֵי יִשְׂרָאֵל דַּבֵּר אֲלֵהֶם לֵאמֹר בֵּין הָעַרְבַּיִם תֹּאכְלוּ בָשָׂר
meat you-will-eat the-twilight at to-say to-them tell! Israel sons-of

out into this desert to starve
this entire assembly to death."
4 Then the LORD said to
Moses, "I will rain down
bread from heaven for you.
The people are to go out each
day and gather enough for
that day. In this way I will test
them and see whether they
will follow my instructions.
5 On the sixth day they are to
prepare what they bring in,
and that is to be twice as much
as they gather on the other
days."
6 So Moses and Aaron said to
all the Israelites, "In the evening you will know that it was
the LORD who brought you out
of Egypt, 7 and in the morning
you will see the glory of the
LORD, because he has heard
your grumbling against him.
Who are we, that you should
grumble against us?" 8 Moses
also said, "You will know that
it was the LORD when he gives
you meat to eat in the evening
and all the bread you want in
the morning, because he has
heard your grumbling against
him. Who are we? You are not
grumbling against us, but
against the LORD."
9 Then Moses told Aaron,
"Say to the entire Israelite
community, 'Come before the
LORD, for he has heard your
grumbling.'"
10 While Aaron was speaking
to the whole Israelite community, they looked toward the
desert, and there was the glory
of the LORD appearing in the
cloud.
11 The LORD said to Moses,
12 "I have heard the grumbling
of the Israelites. Tell them, 'At
twilight you will eat meat, and

°7 ק תלינו

וּבַבֹּקֶר תִּשְׂבְּעוּ־ לָחֶם וִידַעְתֶּם כִּי אֲנִי יְהוָה
Yahweh I that then-you-will-know bread you-will-be-filled and-in-the-morning

אֱלֹהֵיכֶם׃ וַיְהִי בָעֶרֶב וַתַּעַל הַשְּׂלָו
the-quail that-she-came in-the-evening and-he-was (13) God-of-you

וַתְּכַס אֶת־ הַמַּחֲנֶה וּבַבֹּקֶר הָיְתָה שִׁכְבַת הַטַּל
the-dew layer-of she-was and-in-the-morning the-camp *** and-she-covered

סָבִיב לַמַּחֲנֶה׃ וַתַּעַל שִׁכְבַת הַטָּל וְהִנֵּה עַל־ פְּנֵי
floor-of on then-see! the-dew layer-of when-she-went (14) to-the-camp around

הַמִּדְבָּר דַּק מְחֻסְפָּס דַּק כַּכְּפֹר עַל־ הָאָרֶץ׃ וַיִּרְאוּ
when-they-saw (15) the-ground on like-the-frost thin flaking thin the-desert

בְנֵי־ יִשְׂרָאֵל וַיֹּאמְרוּ אִישׁ אֶל־ אָחִיו מָן הוּא כִּי לֹא
not for this what? other-of-him to each then-they-said Israel sons-of

יָדְעוּ מַה־ הוּא וַיֹּאמֶר מֹשֶׁה אֲלֵהֶם הוּא הַלֶּחֶם אֲשֶׁר נָתַן
he-gave that the-bread this to-them Moses so-he-said this what they-knew

יְהוָה לָכֶם לְאָכְלָה׃ זֶה הַדָּבָר אֲשֶׁר צִוָּה יְהוָה לִקְטוּ
gather! Yahweh he-commanded that the-thing this (16) for-food to-you Yahweh

מִמֶּנּוּ אִישׁ לְפִי אָכְלוֹ עֹמֶר לַגֻּלְגֹּלֶת מִסְפַּר
number-of for-the-each omer to-eat-him by-need-of each from-him

נַפְשֹׁתֵיכֶם אִישׁ לַאֲשֶׁר בְּאָהֳלוֹ תִּקָּחוּ׃ וַיַּעֲשׂוּ־ כֵן
this so-they-did (17) you-take in-tent-of-him for-whom each persons-of-you

בְּנֵי יִשְׂרָאֵל וַיִּלְקְטוּ הַמַּרְבֶּה וְהַמַּמְעִיט׃
and-the-being-little the-being-much and-they-gathered Israel sons-of

וַיָּמֹדּוּ בָעֹמֶר וְלֹא הֶעְדִּיף הַמַּרְבֶּה
the-being-much he-had-too-much and-not by-the-omer and-they-measured (18)

וְהַמַּמְעִיט לֹא הֶחְסִיר אִישׁ לְפִי־ אָכְלוֹ
to-eat-him by-need-of each he-had-too-little not and-the-being-little

לָקָטוּ׃ וַיֹּאמֶר מֹשֶׁה אֲלֵהֶם אִישׁ אַל־ יוֹתֵר מִמֶּנּוּ
from-him he-may-keep not anyone to-them Moses then-he-said (19) they-gathered

עַד־ בֹּקֶר׃ וְלֹא־ שָׁמְעוּ אֶל־ מֹשֶׁה וַיּוֹתִרוּ אֲנָשִׁים מִמֶּנּוּ
from-him men and-they-kept Moses to they-listened but-not (20) morning until

עַד־ בֹּקֶר וַיָּרֻם תּוֹלָעִים וַיִּבְאַשׁ וַיִּקְצֹף עֲלֵהֶם
with-them so-he-was-angry and-he-smelled maggots he-became-full morning until

מֹשֶׁה׃ וַיִּלְקְטוּ אֹתוֹ בַּבֹּקֶר בַּבֹּקֶר אִישׁ
each in-the-morning in-the-morning him so-they-gathered (21) Moses

כְּפִי אָכְלוֹ וְחַם הַשֶּׁמֶשׁ וְנָמָס׃ וַיְהִי ׀
and-he-was (22) then-he-melted the-sun when-he-grew-hot to-eat-him by-need-of

בַּיּוֹם הַשִּׁשִּׁי לָקְטוּ לֶחֶם מִשְׁנֶה שְׁנֵי הָעֹמֶר לָאֶחָד
for-the-each the-omer two-of twice bread they-gathered the-sixth on-the-day

in the morning you will be
filled with bread. Then you
will know that I am the LORD
your God.' "
13 That evening quail came
and covered the camp, and in
the morning there was a layer
of dew around the camp.
14 When the dew was gone,
thin flakes like frost on the
ground appeared on the desert
floor. 15 When the Israelites
saw it, they said to each other,
"What is it?" For they did not
know what it was.
Moses said to them, "It is
the bread the LORD has given
you to eat. 16 This is what the
LORD has commanded: 'Each
one is to gather as much as he
needs. Take an omer[c] for each
person you have in your
tent.' "
17 The Israelites did as they
were told; some gathered
much, some little. 18 And when
they measured it by the omer,
he who gathered much did not
have too much, and he who
gathered little did not have too
little. Each one gathered as
much as he needed.
19 Then Moses said to them,
"No one is to keep any of it
until morning."
20 However, some of them
paid no attention to Moses;
they kept part of it until morning, but it was full of maggots
and began to smell. So Moses
was angry with them.
21 Each morning everyone
gathered as much as he needed, and when the sun grew
hot, it melted away. 22 On the
sixth day, they gathered twice
as much—two omers[d] for each

[c] 16 That is, probably about 2 quarts (about 2 liters); also in verses 18, 32, 33 and 36
[d] 22 That is, probably about 4 quarts (about 4.5 liters)

וַיָּבֹאוּ כָּל־ נְשִׂיאֵי הָעֵדָה וַיַּגִּידוּ לְמֹשֶׁה׃
to-Moses and-they-reported the-community leaders-of all-of and-they-came

(23) וַיֹּאמֶר אֲלֵהֶם הוּא אֲשֶׁר דִּבֶּר יְהוָה שַׁבָּתוֹן שַׁבַּת־
Sabbath-of day-of-rest Yahweh he-commanded what this to-them and-he-said (23)

קֹדֶשׁ לַיהוָה מָחָר אֵת אֲשֶׁר־ תֹּאפוּ אֵפוּ וְאֵת אֲשֶׁר־ תְּבַשְּׁלוּ
you-will-boil what and bake! you-will-bake what *** tomorrow to-Yahweh holy

בַּשֵּׁלוּ וְאֵת כָּל־ הָעֹדֵף הַנִּיחוּ לָכֶם לְמִשְׁמֶרֶת עַד־ הַבֹּקֶר׃
the-morning until for-keeping for-you save! the-being-left all-of and boil!

(24) וַיַּנִּיחוּ אֹתוֹ עַד־ הַבֹּקֶר כַּאֲשֶׁר צִוָּה מֹשֶׁה וְלֹא
and-not Moses he-commanded just-as the-morning until him so-they-saved (24)

הִבְאִישׁ וְרִמָּה לֹא־ הָיְתָה בּוֹ׃ (25) וַיֹּאמֶר מֹשֶׁה אִכְלֻהוּ
eat-him! Moses and-he-said (25) in-him she-was not and-maggot he-stank

הַיּוֹם כִּי־ שַׁבָּת הַיּוֹם לַיהוָה הַיּוֹם לֹא תִמְצָאֻהוּ
you-will-find-him not the-day to-Yahweh the-day Sabbath for the-day

בַּשָּׂדֶה׃ (26) שֵׁשֶׁת יָמִים תִּלְקְטֻהוּ וּבַיּוֹם הַשְּׁבִיעִי
the-seventh but-on-the-day you-will-gather-him days six-of (26) on-the-ground

שַׁבָּת לֹא יִהְיֶה־ בּוֹ׃ (27) וַיְהִי בַּיּוֹם הַשְּׁבִיעִי
the-seventh on-the-day but-he-was (27) on-him he-will-be not Sabbath

יָצְאוּ מִן־ הָעָם לִלְקֹט וְלֹא מָצָאוּ׃ (28) וַיֹּאמֶר
then-he-said (28) they-found but-not to-gather the-people from they-went-out

יְהוָה אֶל־ מֹשֶׁה עַד־ אָנָה מֵאַנְתֶּם לִשְׁמֹר מִצְוֺתַי
commands-of-me to-keep will-you-refuse long how Moses to Yahweh

וְתוֹרֹתָי׃ (29) רְאוּ כִּי־ יְהוָה נָתַן לָכֶם
to-you he-gave Yahweh that bear-in-mind! (29) and-instructions-of-me

הַשַּׁבָּת עַל־ כֵּן הוּא נֹתֵן לָכֶם בַּיּוֹם הַשִּׁשִּׁי לֶחֶם יוֹמָיִם
two-days bread the-sixth on-the-day to-you giving he this for the-Sabbath

שְׁבוּ ׀ אִישׁ תַּחְתָּיו אַל־ יֵצֵא אִישׁ מִמְּקֹמוֹ בַּיּוֹם
on-the-day from-place-of-him anyone he-may-go-out not place-of-him each stay!

הַשְּׁבִיעִי׃ (30) וַיִּשְׁבְּתוּ הָעָם בַּיּוֹם הַשְּׁבִעִי׃
the-seventh on-the-day the-people so-he-rested (30) the-seventh

(31) וַיִּקְרְאוּ בֵית־ יִשְׂרָאֵל אֶת־ שְׁמוֹ מָן וְהוּא כְּזֶרַע
like-seed-of now-he manna name-of-him *** Israel house-of and-they-called (31)

גַּד לָבָן וְטַעְמוֹ כְּצַפִּיחִת בִּדְבָשׁ׃ (32) וַיֹּאמֶר מֹשֶׁה
Moses and-he-said (32) with-honey like-wafer and-taste-of-him white coriander

זֶה הַדָּבָר אֲשֶׁר צִוָּה יְהוָה מְלֹא הָעֹמֶר מִמֶּנּוּ לְמִשְׁמֶרֶת
to-keep from-him the-omer fullness-of Yahweh he-commanded that the-thing this

לְדֹרֹתֵיכֶם לְמַעַן ׀ יִרְאוּ אֶת־ הַלֶּחֶם אֲשֶׁר הֶאֱכַלְתִּי אֶתְכֶם
you I-fed that the-bread *** they-can-see so-that for-generations-of-you

person—and the leaders of the
community came and re-
ported this to Moses. 23 He said
to them, "This is what the
LORD commanded: 'Tomorrow
is to be a day of rest, a holy
Sabbath to the LORD. So bake
what you want to bake and
boil what you want to boil.
Save whatever is left and keep
it until morning.'"
24 So they saved it until
morning, as Moses com-
manded, and it did not stink
or get maggots in it. 25 "Eat it
today," Moses said, "because
today is a Sabbath to the LORD.
You will not find any of it on
the ground today. 26 Six days
you are to gather it, but on the
seventh day, the Sabbath,
there will not be any."
27 Nevertheless, some of the
people went out on the seventh day to gather it, but they
found none. 28 Then the LORD
said to Moses, "How long will
you[e] refuse to keep my commands and my instructions?
29 Bear in mind that the LORD
has given you the Sabbath;
that is why on the sixth day he
gives you bread for two days.
Everyone is to stay where he is
on the seventh day; no one is
to go out." 30 So the people rested on the seventh day.
31 The people of Israel called
the bread manna.[f] It was
white like coriander seed and
tasted like wafers made with
honey. 32 Moses said, "This is
what the LORD has com-
manded: 'Take an omer of
manna and keep it for the generations to come, so they can
see the bread I gave you to eat

[e] 28 The Hebrew is plural.
[f] 31 *Manna* means *What is it?* (see verse 15).

בַּמִּדְבָּר בְּהוֹצִיאִי אֶתְכֶם מֵאֶרֶץ מִצְרָיִם׃ וַיֹּאמֶר מֹשֶׁה

Moses so-he-said (33) Egypt from-land-of you when-to-bring-me in-the-desert

אֶל־ אַהֲרֹן קַח צִנְצֶנֶת אַחַת וְתֶן־ שָׁמָּה מְלֹא־ הָעֹמֶר מָן

manna the-omer fullness-of in-there and-put! one jar take! Aaron to

וְהַנַּח אֹתוֹ לִפְנֵי יְהוָה לְמִשְׁמֶרֶת לְדֹרֹתֵיכֶם׃ כַּאֲשֶׁר

just-as (34) for-generations-of-you to-keep Yahweh before him then-place!

צִוָּה יְהוָה אֶל־ מֹשֶׁה וַיַּנִּיחֵהוּ אַהֲרֹן לִפְנֵי הָעֵדֻת

the-Testimony before Aaron so-he-put-him Moses to Yahweh he-commanded

לְמִשְׁמָרֶת׃ וּבְנֵי יִשְׂרָאֵל אָכְלוּ אֶת־ הַמָּן אַרְבָּעִים שָׁנָה עַד־

until year forty the-manna *** they-ate Israel so-sons-of (35) to-keep

בֹּאָם אֶל־ אֶרֶץ נוֹשָׁבֶת אֶת־ הַמָּן אָכְלוּ עַד־

until they-ate the-manna *** being-settled land-of to to-come-them

בֹּאָם אֶל־ קְצֵה אֶרֶץ כְּנָעַן׃ וְהָעֹמֶר עֲשִׂרִית הָאֵיפָה

the-ephah tenth-of now-the-omer (36) Canaan land-of border-of to to-come-them

הוּא׃ וַיִּסְעוּ כָּל־ עֲדַת בְּנֵי־ יִשְׂרָאֵל מִמִּדְבַּר־

from-Desert-of Israel sons-of community-of whole-of and-they-set-out (17:1) he

סִין לְמַסְעֵיהֶם עַל־ פִּי יְהוָה וַיַּחֲנוּ בִּרְפִידִים

at-Rephidim and-they-camped Yahweh command-of as by-travels-of-them Sin

וְאֵין מַיִם לִשְׁתֹּת הָעָם׃ וַיָּרֶב הָעָם עִם־

with the-people so-they-quarreled (2) the-people for-to-drink waters but-no

מֹשֶׁה וַיֹּאמְרוּ תְּנוּ־ לָנוּ מַיִם וְנִשְׁתֶּה וַיֹּאמֶר

but-he-replied so-we-may-drink waters to-us give! and-they-said Moses

לָהֶם מֹשֶׁה מַה־ תְּרִיבוּן עִמָּדִי מַה־ תְּנַסּוּן אֶת־ יְהוָה׃

Yahweh *** you-test why? with-me you-quarrel why? Moses to-them

וַיִּצְמָא שָׁם הָעָם לַמַּיִם וַיָּלֶן הָעָם

the-people so-he-grumbled for-the-waters the-people there but-he-was-thirsty (3)

עַל־ מֹשֶׁה וַיֹּאמֶר לָמָּה זֶּה הֶעֱלִיתָנוּ מִמִּצְרַיִם לְהָמִית אֹתִי

me to-kill from-Egypt you-brought-us this why? and-he-said Moses against

וְאֶת־ בָּנַי וְאֶת־ מִקְנַי בַּצָּמָא׃ וַיִּצְעַק מֹשֶׁה

Moses then-he-cried (4) with-the-thirst stocks-of-me and children-of-me and

אֶל־ יְהוָה לֵאמֹר מָה אֶעֱשֶׂה לָעָם הַזֶּה עוֹד מְעַט

little longer the-this with-the-people can-I-do what? to-say Yahweh to

וּסְקָלֻנִי׃ וַיֹּאמֶר יְהוָה אֶל־ מֹשֶׁה עֲבֹר לִפְנֵי

ahead-of walk-on! Moses to Yahweh and-he-answered (5) and-they-will-stone-me

הָעָם וְקַח אִתְּךָ מִזִּקְנֵי יִשְׂרָאֵל וּמַטְּךָ אֲשֶׁר

that and-staff-of-you Israel from-elders-of with-you and-take! the-people

הִכִּיתָ בּוֹ אֶת־ הַיְאֹר קַח בְּיָדְךָ וְהָלָכְתָּ׃ הִנְנִי

see-I! (6) and-you-go in-hand-of-you take! the-Nile *** with-him you-struck

in the desert when I brought you out of Egypt.' "

33 So Moses said to Aaron, "Take a jar and put an omer of manna in it. Then place it before the LORD to be kept for the generations to come."

34 As the LORD commanded Moses, Aaron put the manna in front of the Testimony, that it might be kept. 35 The Israelites ate manna forty years, until they came to a land that was settled; they ate manna until they reached the border of Canaan.

36 (An omer is one tenth of an ephah.)

Water From the Rock

17 The whole Israelite community set out from the Desert of Sin, traveling from place to place as the LORD commanded. They camped at Rephidim, but there was no water for the people to drink. 2 So they quarreled with Moses and said, "Give us water to drink."

Moses replied, "Why do you quarrel with me? Why do you put the LORD to the test?"

3 But the people were thirsty for water there, and they grumbled against Moses. They said, "Why did you bring us up out of Egypt to make us and our children and livestock die of thirst?"

4 Then Moses cried out to the LORD, "What am I to do with these people? They are almost ready to stone me."

5 The LORD answered Moses, "Walk on ahead of the people. Take with you some of the elders of Israel and take in your hand the staff with which you struck the Nile, and go. 6 I will

עֹמֵד לְפָנֶיךָ שָּׁם ׀ עַל־ הַצּוּר בְּחֹרֵב וְהִכִּיתָ בַצּוּר
on-the-rock and-you-strike at-Horeb the-rock by there before-you standing

וְיָצְאוּ מִמֶּנּוּ מַיִם וְשָׁתָה הָעָם וַיַּעַשׂ
so-he-did the-people so-he-may-drink waters from-him and-they-will-come

כֵּן מֹשֶׁה לְעֵינֵי זִקְנֵי יִשְׂרָאֵל׃ וַיִּקְרָא שֵׁם
name-of and-he-called (7) Israel elders-of before-eyes-of Moses this

הַמָּקוֹם מַסָּה וּמְרִיבָה עַל־ רִיב ׀ בְּנֵי יִשְׂרָאֵל וְעַל
and-because Israel sons-of to-quarrel because and-Meribah Massah the-place

נַסֹּתָם אֶת־ יְהוָה לֵאמֹר הֲיֵשׁ יְהוָה בְּקִרְבֵּנוּ אִם־ אָיִן׃ וַיָּבֹא
and-he-came (8) not or among-us Yahweh is-he? to-say Yahweh *** to-test-them

עֲמָלֵק וַיִּלָּחֶם עִם־ יִשְׂרָאֵל בִּרְפִידִם׃ וַיֹּאמֶר מֹשֶׁה אֶל־
to Moses and-he-said (9) at-Rephidim Israel against and-he-attacked Amalek

יְהוֹשֻׁעַ בְּחַר־ לָנוּ אֲנָשִׁים וְצֵא הִלָּחֵם בַּעֲמָלֵק מָחָר אָנֹכִי נִצָּב
standing I tomorrow with-Amalek fight! and-go-out! men for-us choose! Joshua

עַל־ רֹאשׁ הַגִּבְעָה וּמַטֵּה הָאֱלֹהִים בְּיָדִי׃ וַיַּעַשׂ יְהוֹשֻׁעַ
Joshua so-he-did (10) in-hand-of-me the-God and-staff-of the-hill top-of on

כַּאֲשֶׁר אָמַר־ לוֹ מֹשֶׁה לְהִלָּחֵם בַּעֲמָלֵק וּמֹשֶׁה אַהֲרֹן וְחוּר
and-Hur Aaron and-Moses with-Amalek to-fight Moses to-him he-ordered just-as

עָלוּ רֹאשׁ הַגִּבְעָה׃ וְהָיָה כַּאֲשֶׁר יָרִים מֹשֶׁה
Moses he-held-up as-long-as and-he-was (11) the-hill top-of they-went

יָדוֹ וְגָבַר יִשְׂרָאֵל וְכַאֲשֶׁר יָנִיחַ יָדוֹ
hand-of-him he-lowered but-when-ever Israel then-he-won hand-of-him

וְגָבַר עֲמָלֵק׃ וִידֵי מֹשֶׁה כְּבֵדִים וַיִּקְחוּ־ אֶבֶן
stone then-they-took tired-ones Moses when-hands-of (12) Amalek then-he-won

וַיָּשִׂימוּ תַחְתָּיו וַיֵּשֶׁב עָלֶיהָ וְאַהֲרֹן וְחוּר תָּמְכוּ
they-held-up and-Hur and-Aaron on-her and-he-sat under-him and-they-put

בְיָדָיו מִזֶּה אֶחָד וּמִזֶּה אֶחָד וַיְהִי יָדָיו
hands-of-him and-he-was one and-on-that-side one on-this-side on-hands-of-him

אֱמוּנָה עַד־ בֹּא הַשָּׁמֶשׁ׃ וַיַּחֲלֹשׁ יְהוֹשֻׁעַ אֶת־עֲמָלֵק וְאֶת־
and Amalek *** Joshua so-he-overcame (13) the-sun to-set until being-steady

עַמּוֹ לְפִי־ חָרֶב׃ וַיֹּאמֶר יְהוָה אֶל־ מֹשֶׁה כְּתֹב
write! Moses to Yahweh then-he-said (14) sword with-edge-of army-of-him

זֹאת זִכָּרוֹן בַּסֵּפֶר וְשִׂים בְּאָזְנֵי יְהוֹשֻׁעַ כִּי־ מָחֹה
to-erase for Joshua in-ears-of and-tell! on-the-scroll memorial this

אֶמְחֶה אֶת־ זֵכֶר עֲמָלֵק מִתַּחַת הַשָּׁמָיִם׃ וַיִּבֶן
so-he-built (15) the-heavens from-under Amalek memory-of *** I-will-erase

מֹשֶׁה מִזְבֵּחַ וַיִּקְרָא שְׁמוֹ יְהוָה ׀ נִסִּי׃ וַיֹּאמֶר
and-he-said (16) Banner-of-me Yahweh name-of-him and-he-called altar Moses

stand there before you by the rock at Horeb. Strike the rock, and water will come out of it for the people to drink." So Moses did this in the sight of the elders of Israel. 7And he called the place Massah[g] and Meribah[h] because the Israelites quarreled and because they tested the LORD saying, "Is the LORD among us or not?"

The Amalekites Defeated

8The Amalekites came and attacked the Israelites at Rephidim. 9Moses said to Joshua, "Choose some of our men and go out to fight the Amalekites. Tomorrow I will stand on top of the hill with the staff of God in my hands."

10So Joshua fought the Amalekites as Moses had ordered, and Moses, Aaron and Hur went to the top of the hill. 11As long as Moses held up his hands, the Israelites were winning, but whenever he lowered his hands, the Amalekites were winning. 12When Moses' hands grew tired, they took a stone and put it under him and he sat on it. Aaron and Hur held his hands up—one on one side, one on the other—so that his hands remained steady till sunset. 13So Joshua overcame the Amalekite army with the sword.

14Then the LORD said to Moses, "Write this on a scroll as something to be remembered and make sure that Joshua hears it, because I will completely erase the memory of the Amalekites from under heaven."

15Moses built an altar and called it The LORD is my Banner. 16He said, "For hands

g7 *Massah* means *testing*.
h7 *Meribah* means *quarreling*.

כִּי־ יָד עַל־ כֵּס יָהּ מִלְחָמָה לַיהוָה בַּעֲמָלֵק מִדֹּר
from-generation against-Amalek with-Yahweh war Yah throne-of up-to hand for

דֹּר׃ וַיִּשְׁמַע יִתְרוֹ כֹהֵן מִדְיָן חֹתֵן מֹשֶׁה
Moses father-in-law-of Midian priest-of Jethro now-he-heard (18:1) generation

אֵת כָּל־ אֲשֶׁר עָשָׂה אֱלֹהִים לְמֹשֶׁה וּלְיִשְׂרָאֵל עַמּוֹ כִּי־ הוֹצִיא
he-brought how people-of-him and-for-Israel for-Moses God he-did that all ***

יְהוָה אֶת־ יִשְׂרָאֵל מִמִּצְרָיִם׃ וַיִּקַּח יִתְרוֹ חֹתֵן
father-in-law-of Jethro and-he-received (2) from-Egypt Israel *** Yahweh

מֹשֶׁה אֶת־ צִפֹּרָה אֵשֶׁת מֹשֶׁה אַחַר שִׁלּוּחֶיהָ׃ וְאֵת שְׁנֵי
two-of and (3) departures-of-her after Moses wife-of Zipporah *** Moses

בָנֶיהָ אֲשֶׁר שֵׁם הָאֶחָד גֵּרְשֹׁם כִּי אָמַר גֵּר הָיִיתִי בְּאֶרֶץ
in-land I-became alien he-said for Gershom the-one name-of whose sons-of-her

נָכְרִיָּה׃ וְשֵׁם הָאֶחָד אֱלִיעֶזֶר כִּי־ אֱלֹהֵי אָבִי
father-of-me God-of for Eliezer the-other and-name-of (4) foreign

בְּעֶזְרִי וַיַּצִּלֵנִי מֵחֶרֶב פַּרְעֹה׃ וַיָּבֹא יִתְרוֹ
Jethro and-he-came (5) Pharaoh from-sword-of and-he-saved-me as-helper-of-me

חֹתֵן מֹשֶׁה וּבָנָיו וְאִשְׁתּוֹ אֶל־ מֹשֶׁה אֶל־ הַמִּדְבָּר
the-desert in Moses to and-wife-of-him with-sons-of-him Moses father-in-law-of

אֲשֶׁר־ הוּא חֹנֶה שָׁם הַר הָאֱלֹהִים׃ וַיֹּאמֶר אֶל־ מֹשֶׁה אֲנִי
I Moses to and-he-said (6) the-God mountain-of there camping he where

חֹתֶנְךָ יִתְרוֹ בָּא אֵלֶיךָ וְאִשְׁתְּךָ וּשְׁנֵי
and-two-of with-wife-of-you to-you coming Jethro father-in-law-of-you

בָנֶיהָ עִמָּהּ׃ וַיֵּצֵא מֹשֶׁה לִקְרַאת חֹתְנוֹ
father-in-law-of-him to-meet Moses so-he-went-out (7) with-her sons-of-her

וַיִּשְׁתַּחוּ וַיִּשַּׁק־ לוֹ וַיִּשְׁאֲלוּ אִישׁ־ לְרֵעֵהוּ
to-other-of-him each and-they-asked on-him and-he-kissed and-he-bowed

לְשָׁלוֹם וַיָּבֹאוּ הָאֹהֱלָה׃ וַיְסַפֵּר מֹשֶׁה
Moses and-he-told (8) into-the-tent then-they-went about-welfare

לְחֹתְנוֹ אֵת כָּל־ אֲשֶׁר עָשָׂה יְהוָה לְפַרְעֹה וּלְמִצְרַיִם
and-to-Egypt to-Pharaoh Yahweh he-did that all *** to-father-in-law-of-him

עַל אוֹדֹת יִשְׂרָאֵל אֵת כָּל־ הַתְּלָאָה אֲשֶׁר מְצָאָתַם בַּדֶּרֶךְ
along-the-way she-met-them that the-hardship all-of *** Israel sakes-of for

וַיַּצִּלֵם יְהוָה׃ וַיִּחַדְּ יִתְרוֹ עַל כָּל־
all-of about Jethro and-he-was-delighted (9) Yahweh and-he-saved-them

הַטּוֹבָה אֲשֶׁר־ עָשָׂה יְהוָה לְיִשְׂרָאֵל אֲשֶׁר הִצִּילוֹ מִיַּד
from-hand-of he-rescued-him when for-Israel Yahweh he-did that the-good

מִצְרָיִם׃ וַיֹּאמֶר יִתְרוֹ בָּרוּךְ יְהוָה אֲשֶׁר הִצִּיל אֶתְכֶם
you he-rescued who Yahweh being-praised Jethro and-he-said (10) Egyptians

were lifted up to the throne of
the LORD. The[i] LORD will be at
war against the Amalekites
from generation to generation."

Jethro Visits Moses

18 Now Jethro, the priest
of Midian and father-
in-law of Moses, heard of
everything God had done for
Moses and for his people Israel, and how the LORD had
brought Israel out of Egypt.
[2]After Moses had sent away
his wife Zipporah, his father-
in-law Jethro received her
[3]and her two sons. One son
was named Gershom,[j] for
Moses said, "I have become an
alien in a foreign land"; [4]and
the other was named Eliezer,[k]
for he said, "My father's God
was my helper; he saved me
from the sword of Pharaoh."
[5]Jethro, Moses' father-in-
law, together with Moses'
sons and wife, came to him in
the desert, where he was
camped near the mountain of
God. [6]Jethro had sent word to
him, "I, your father-in-law
Jethro, am coming to you with
your wife and her two sons."
[7]So Moses went out to meet
his father-in-law and bowed
down and kissed him. They
greeted each other and then
went into the tent. [8]Moses told
his father-in-law about everything the LORD had done to
Pharaoh and the Egyptians for
Israel's sake and about all the
hardships they had met along
the way and how the LORD
had saved them.
[9]Jethro was delighted to hear
about all the good things the
LORD had done for Israel in re-
scuing them from the hand of
the Egyptians. [10]He said,
"Praise be to the LORD, who
rescued you from the hand of

[i]16 Or *"Because a hand was against the throne of the* LORD, *the*
[j]3 *Gershom* sounds like the Hebrew for *an alien there.*
[k]4 *Eliezer* means *my God is helper.*

מִיַּד מִצְרַיִם וּמִיַּד פַּרְעֹה אֲשֶׁר הִצִּיל אֶת־ הָעָם
the-people *** he-rescued who Pharaoh and-from-hand-of Egyptians from-hand-of

מִתַּחַת יַד־ מִצְרָיִם׃ עַתָּה יָדַעְתִּי כִּי־ גָדוֹל יְהוָה מִכָּל־
than-all-of Yahweh greater that I-know now (11) Egyptians hand-of from-under

הָאֱלֹהִים כִּי בַדָּבָר אֲשֶׁר זָדוּ עֲלֵיהֶם׃
to-them they-were-arrogant when of-the-matter because the-gods

וַיִּקַּח יִתְרוֹ חֹתֵן מֹשֶׁה עֹלָה וּזְבָחִים
and-sacrifices burnt-offering Moses father-in-law-of Jethro then-he-brought (12)

לֵאלֹהִים וַיָּבֹא אַהֲרֹן וְכֹל ׀ זִקְנֵי יִשְׂרָאֵל לֶאֱכָל־ לֶחֶם עִם־
with bread to-eat Israel elders-of and-all-of Aaron and-he-came to-God

חֹתֵן מֹשֶׁה לִפְנֵי הָאֱלֹהִים׃ וַיְהִי מִמָּחֳרָת
on-next-day and-he-was (13) the-God in-presence-of Moses father-in-law-of

וַיֵּשֶׁב מֹשֶׁה לִשְׁפֹּט אֶת־ הָעָם וַיַּעֲמֹד הָעָם עַל־
around the-people and-they-stood the-people *** to-judge Moses that-he-sat

מֹשֶׁה מִן־ הַבֹּקֶר עַד־ הָעָרֶב׃ וַיַּרְא חֹתֵן
father-in-law-of when-he-saw (14) the-evening till the-morning from Moses

מֹשֶׁה אֵת כָּל־ אֲשֶׁר־ הוּא עֹשֶׂה לָעָם וַיֹּאמֶר מָה־ הַדָּבָר
the-thing what? then-he-said for-the-people doing he that all *** Moses

הַזֶּה אֲשֶׁר אַתָּה עֹשֶׂה לָעָם מַדּוּעַ אַתָּה יוֹשֵׁב לְבַדֶּךָ
by-yourself sitting you why? for-the-people doing you that the-this

וְכָל־ הָעָם נִצָּב עָלֶיךָ מִן־ בֹּקֶר עַד־ עָרֶב׃
evening till morning from around-you standing the-people while-all-of

וַיֹּאמֶר מֹשֶׁה לְחֹתְנוֹ כִּי־ יָבֹא אֵלַי
to-me he-comes because to-father-in-law-of-him Moses then-he-answered (15)

הָעָם לִדְרֹשׁ אֱלֹהִים׃ כִּי־ יִהְיֶה לָהֶם דָּבָר בָּא אֵלַי
to-me he-comes dispute with-them he-is when (16) God to-seek the-people

וְשָׁפַטְתִּי בֵּין אִישׁ וּבֵין רֵעֵהוּ וְהוֹדַעְתִּי אֶת־
*** and-I-inform fellow-of-him and-between man between and-I-decide

חֻקֵּי הָאֱלֹהִים וְאֶת־ תּוֹרֹתָיו׃ וַיֹּאמֶר חֹתֵן מֹשֶׁה
Moses father-in-law-of and-he-replied (17) laws-of-him and the-God decrees-of

אֵלָיו לֹא־ טוֹב הַדָּבָר אֲשֶׁר אַתָּה עֹשֶׂה׃ נָבֹל תִּבֹּל
you-will-wear-out to-wear-out (18) doing you that the-thing good not to-him

גַּם־ אַתָּה גַּם־ הָעָם הַזֶּה אֲשֶׁר עִמָּךְ כִּי־ כָבֵד מִמְּךָ הַדָּבָר
the-work for-you too-heavy for with-you who the-this the-people and you both

לֹא־ תוּכַל עֲשֹׂהוּ לְבַדֶּךָ׃ עַתָּה שְׁמַע בְּקֹלִי
to-voice-of-me listen! now (19) by-yourself to-handle-him you-can not

אִיעָצְךָ וִיהִי אֱלֹהִים עִמָּךְ הֱיֵה אַתָּה לָעָם מוּל
before for-the-people you be! with-you God and-may-he-be I-will-advise-you

the Egyptians and of Pharaoh,
and who rescued the people
from the hand of the Egyptians. [11]Now I know that the
LORD is greater than all other
gods, for he did this to those
who had treated Israel arro-
gantly." [12]Then Jethro, Moses'
father-in-law, brought a burnt
offering and other sacrifices to
God, and Aaron came with all
the elders of Israel to eat bread
with Moses' father-in-law in
the presence of God.

[13]The next day Moses took
his seat to serve as judge for
the people, and they stood
around him from morning till
evening. [14]When his father-
in-law saw all that Moses was
doing for the people, he said,
"What is this you are doing for
the people? Why do you alone
sit as judge, while all these
people stand around you from
morning till evening?"

[15]Moses answered him, "Because the people come to me to
seek God's will. [16]Whenever
they have a dispute, it is
brought to me, and I decide
between the parties and in-
form them of God's decrees
and laws."

[17]Moses' father-in-law replied, "What you are doing is
not good. [18]You and these
people who come to you will
only wear yourselves out. The
work is too heavy for you; you
cannot handle it alone. [19]Lis-
ten now to me and I will give
you some advice, and may
God be with you. You must be

הָאֱלֹהִים וְהֵבֵאתָ אַתָּה אֶת־ הַדְּבָרִים אֶל־ הָאֱלֹהִים׃ וְהִזְהַרְתָּה
and-you-teach (20) the-God to the-disputes *** you and-you-bring the-God

אֶתְהֶם אֶת־ הַחֻקִּים וְאֶת־ הַתּוֹרֹת וְהוֹדַעְתָּ לָהֶם אֶת־ הַדֶּרֶךְ
the-way *** to-them and-you-show the-laws and the-decrees *** them

יֵלְכוּ בָהּ וְאֶת־ הַמַּעֲשֶׂה אֲשֶׁר יַעֲשׂוּן׃ וְאַתָּה
but-you (21) they-should-perform that the-duty and in-her they-should-live

תֶחֱזֶה מִכָּל־ הָעָם אַנְשֵׁי־ חַיִל יִרְאֵי אֱלֹהִים
God ones-fearing-of capable men-of the-people from-all-of you-select

אַנְשֵׁי אֱמֶת שֹׂנְאֵי בָצַע וְשַׂמְתָּ עֲלֵהֶם שָׂרֵי
officials-of over-them and-you-appoint bribe ones-hating-of trust men-of

אֲלָפִים שָׂרֵי מֵאוֹת שָׂרֵי חֲמִשִּׁים וְשָׂרֵי עֲשָׂרֹת׃
tens and-officials-of fifties officials-of hundreds officials-of thousands

וְשָׁפְטוּ אֶת־ הָעָם בְּכָל־ עֵת וְהָיָה
and-he-will-be time at-all-of the-people *** and-let-them-judge (22)

כָּל־ הַדָּבָר הַגָּדֹל יָבִיאוּ אֵלֶיךָ וְכָל־ הַדָּבָר
the-case but-every-of to-you they-will-bring the-difficult the-case every-of

הַקָּטֹן יִשְׁפְּטוּ־ הֵם וְהָקֵל מֵעָלֶיךָ
from-on-you so-he-will-be-lighter they they-will-decide the-simple

וְנָשְׂאוּ אִתָּךְ׃ אִם אֶת־ הַדָּבָר הַזֶּה תַּעֲשֶׂה
you-do the-this the-thing *** if (23) with-you and-they-will-share

וְצִוְּךָ אֱלֹהִים וְיָכָלְתָּ עֲמֹד וְגַם כָּל־
all-of and-also to-stand then-you-will-be-able God and-he-commands-you

הָעָם הַזֶּה עַל־ מְקֹמוֹ יָבֹא בְשָׁלוֹם׃
in-satisfaction he-will-go home-of-him to the-this the-people

וַיִּשְׁמַע מֹשֶׁה לְקוֹל חֹתְנוֹ וַיַּעַשׂ כֹּל אֲשֶׁר
that all and-he-did father-in-law-of-him to-voice-of Moses and-he-listened (24)

אָמָר׃ וַיִּבְחַר מֹשֶׁה אַנְשֵׁי־ חַיִל מִכָּל־ יִשְׂרָאֵל וַיִּתֵּן
and-he-made Israel from-all-of capable men-of Moses and-he-chose (25) he-said

אֹתָם רָאשִׁים עַל־ הָעָם שָׂרֵי אֲלָפִים שָׂרֵי מֵאוֹת
hundreds officials-of thousands officials-of the-people over leaders them

שָׂרֵי חֲמִשִּׁים וְשָׂרֵי עֲשָׂרֹת׃ וְשָׁפְטוּ אֶת־ הָעָם
the-people *** and-they-judged (26) tens and-officials-of fifties officials-of

בְּכָל־ עֵת אֶת־ הַדָּבָר הַקָּשֶׁה יְבִיאוּן אֶל־ מֹשֶׁה וְכָל־
but-every-of Moses to they-brought the-difficult the-case *** time at-all-of

הַדָּבָר הַקָּטֹן יִשְׁפּוּטוּ הֵם׃ וַיְשַׁלַּח מֹשֶׁה אֶת־
*** Moses then-he-sent (27) they they-decided the-simple the-case

חֹתְנוֹ וַיֵּלֶךְ לוֹ אֶל־ אַרְצוֹ׃ בַּחֹדֶשׁ
in-the-month (19:1) country-of-him to to-him and-he-went father-in-law-of-him

the people's representative before God and bring their disputes to him. [20]Teach them the decrees and laws, and show them the way to live and the duties they are to perform. [21]But select capable men from all the people—men who fear God, trustworthy men who hate dishonest gain—and appoint them as officials over thousands, hundreds, fifties and tens. [22]Have them serve as judges for the people at all times, but have them bring every difficult case to you; the simple cases they can decide themselves. That will make your load lighter, because they will share it with you. [23]If you do this and God so commands, you will be able to stand the strain, and all these people will go home satisfied."

[24]Moses listened to his father-in-law and did everything he said. [25]He chose capable men from all Israel and made them leaders of the people, officials over thousands, hundreds, fifties and tens. [26]They served as judges for the people at all times. The difficult cases they brought to Moses, but the simple ones they decided themselves.

[27]Then Moses sent his father-in-law on his way, and he returned to his own country.

הַשְּׁלִישִׁי לְצֵאת בְּנֵי־ יִשְׂרָאֵל מֵאֶרֶץ מִצְרַיִם בַּיּוֹם
on-the-day Egypt from-land-of Israel sons-of after-to-leave the-third

הַזֶּה בָּאוּ מִדְבַּר סִינָי׃ (2) וַיִּסְעוּ מֵרְפִידִים
from-Rephidim and-they-set-out (2) Sinai Desert-of they-came the-that

וַיָּבֹאוּ מִדְבַּר סִינַי וַיַּחֲנוּ בַּמִּדְבָּר וַיִּחַן־
and-he-camped in-the-desert and-they-camped Sinai Desert-of and-they-entered

שָׁם יִשְׂרָאֵל נֶגֶד הָהָר׃ (3) וּמֹשֶׁה עָלָה אֶל־הָאֱלֹהִים
the-God to he-went-up then-Moses (3) the-mountain in-front-of Israel there

וַיִּקְרָא אֵלָיו יְהוָה מִן־ הָהָר לֵאמֹר כֹּה תֹאמַר לְבֵית
to-house-of you-say this to-say the-mountain from Yahweh to-him and-he-called

יַעֲקֹב וְתַגֵּיד לִבְנֵי יִשְׂרָאֵל׃ (4) אַתֶּם רְאִיתֶם אֲשֶׁר עָשִׂיתִי לְמִצְרָיִם
to-Egypt I-did what you-saw you (4) Israel to-sons-of and-you-tell Jacob

וָאֶשָּׂא אֶתְכֶם עַל־ כַּנְפֵי נְשָׁרִים וָאָבִא אֶתְכֶם אֵלָי׃ (5) וְעַתָּה
and-now (5) to-myself you and-I-brought eagles wings-of on you and-I-carried

אִם־ שָׁמוֹעַ תִּשְׁמְעוּ בְּקֹלִי וּשְׁמַרְתֶּם אֶת־ בְּרִיתִי
covenant-of-me *** and-you-keep to-voice-of-me you-obey to-obey if

וִהְיִיתֶם לִי סְגֻלָּה מִכָּל־ הָעַמִּים כִּי־ לִי
to-me although the-nations from-all-of possession to-me then-you-will-be

כָּל־ הָאָרֶץ׃ (6) וְאַתֶּם תִּהְיוּ־ לִי מַמְלֶכֶת כֹּהֲנִים וְגוֹי
and-nation priests kingdom-of for-me you-will-be and-you (6) the-earth all-of

קָדוֹשׁ אֵלֶּה הַדְּבָרִים אֲשֶׁר תְּדַבֵּר אֶל־ בְּנֵי יִשְׂרָאֵל׃ (7) וַיָּבֹא
so-he-went-back (7) Israel sons-of to you-speak that the-words these holy

מֹשֶׁה וַיִּקְרָא לְזִקְנֵי הָעָם וַיָּשֶׂם לִפְנֵיהֶם אֵת
*** before-them and-he-set the-people to-elders-of and-he-summoned Moses

כָּל־ הַדְּבָרִים הָאֵלֶּה אֲשֶׁר צִוָּהוּ יְהוָה׃ (8) וַיַּעֲנוּ
and-they-responded (8) Yahweh he-commanded-him that the-these the-words all-of

כָל־ הָעָם יַחְדָּו וַיֹּאמְרוּ כֹּל אֲשֶׁר־ דִּבֶּר יְהוָה נַעֲשֶׂה
we-will-do Yahweh he-said that all and-they-said together the-people all-of

וַיָּשֶׁב מֹשֶׁה אֶת־ דִּבְרֵי הָעָם אֶל־ יְהוָה׃ (9) וַיֹּאמֶר
and-he-said (9) Yahweh to the-people answers-of *** Moses and-he-brought-back

יְהוָה אֶל־ מֹשֶׁה הִנֵּה אָנֹכִי בָּא אֵלֶיךָ בְּעַב הֶעָנָן בַּעֲבוּר
so-that the-cloud in-dense-of to-you coming I see! Moses to Yahweh

יִשְׁמַע הָעָם בְּדַבְּרִי עִמָּךְ וְגַם־ בְּךָ
in-you and-also with-you when-to-speak-me the-people he-will-hear

יַאֲמִינוּ לְעוֹלָם וַיַּגֵּד מֹשֶׁה אֶת־ דִּבְרֵי הָעָם אֶל־
to the-people words-of *** Moses then-he-told for-always they-will-trust

יְהוָה׃ (10) וַיֹּאמֶר יְהוָה אֶל־ מֹשֶׁה לֵךְ אֶל־ הָעָם
the-people to go! Moses to Yahweh and-he-said (10) Yahweh

At Mount Sinai

19 In the third month after the Israelites left
Egypt—on the very day—they
came to the Desert of Sinai.
[2]After they set out from Rephidim, they entered the Desert
of Sinai, and Israel camped
there in the desert in front of
the mountain.
[3]Then Moses went up to
God, and the LORD called to
him from the mountain and
said, "This is what you are to
say to the house of Jacob and
what you are to tell the people
of Israel: [4]'You yourselves
have seen what I did to Egypt,
and how I carried you on eagles' wings and brought you to
myself. [5]Now if you obey me
fully and keep my covenant,
then out of all nations you will
be my treasured possession.
Although the whole earth is
mine, [6]you will be for me a
kingdom of priests and a holy
nation.' These are the words
you are to speak to the Israelites."
[7]So Moses went back and
summoned the elders of the
people and set before them all
the words the LORD had commanded him to speak. [8]The
people all responded together,
"We will do everything the
LORD has said." So Moses
brought their answer back to
the LORD.
[9]The LORD said to Moses, "I
am going to come to you in a
dense cloud, so that the people
will hear me speaking with
you and will always put their
trust in you." Then Moses told
the LORD what the people had
said.
[10]And the LORD said to
Moses, "Go to the people and

וְקִדַּשְׁתָּם הַיּוֹם וּמָחָר וְכִבְּסוּ שִׂמְלֹתָם׃
clothes-of-them and-let-them-wash and-tommorow the-day and-you-consecrate-them

וְהָיוּ נְכֹנִים לַיּוֹם הַשְּׁלִישִׁי כִּי ׀ בַּיּוֹם
on-the-day for the-third by-the-day ones-being-ready and-they-will-be (11)

הַשְּׁלִשִׁי יֵרֵד יְהוָה לְעֵינֵי כָל־ הָעָם עַל־
onto the-people all-of before-eyes-of Yahweh he-will-come-down the-third

הַר סִינָי׃ וְהִגְבַּלְתָּ אֶת־ הָעָם סָבִיב לֵאמֹר הִשָּׁמְרוּ
be-careful! to-say around the-people *** and-you-limit (12) Sinai Mount-of

לָכֶם עֲלוֹת בָּהָר וּנְגֹעַ בְּקָצֵהוּ כָּל־
every-of on-border-of-him or-to-touch on-the-mountain to-go-up to-you

הַנֹּגֵעַ בָּהָר מוֹת יוּמָת׃ לֹא־ תִגַּע בּוֹ
on-him you-lay not (13) he-will-die to-die on-the-mountain the-one-touching

יָד כִּי־ סָקוֹל יִסָּקֵל אוֹ־ יָרֹה יִיָּרֶה
he-will-be-shot to-he-shot or he-will-be-stoned to-be-stoned for hand

אִם־ בְּהֵמָה אִם־ אִישׁ לֹא יִחְיֶה בִּמְשֹׁךְ הַיֹּבֵל הֵמָּה
they the-trumpet when-to-blast he-shall-live not man or animal whether

יַעֲלוּ בָהָר׃ וַיֵּרֶד מֹשֶׁה מִן־ הָהָר
the-mountain from Moses and-he-came-down (14) to-the-mountain they-may-go-up

אֶל־ הָעָם וַיְקַדֵּשׁ אֶת־ הָעָם וַיְכַבְּסוּ
and-they-washed the-people *** and-he-consecrated the-people to

שִׂמְלֹתָם׃ וַיֹּאמֶר אֶל־ הָעָם הֱיוּ נְכֹנִים
ones-being-prepared be! the-people to and-he-said (15) clothes-of-them

לִשְׁלֹשֶׁת יָמִים אַל־ תִּגְּשׁוּ אֶל־ אִשָּׁה׃ וַיְהִי
and-he-was (16) woman with you-may-have-relations not days by-third-of

בַיּוֹם הַשְּׁלִישִׁי בִּהְיֹת הַבֹּקֶר וַיְהִי קֹלֹת
thunders and-he-was the-morning when-to-come the-third on-the-day

וּבְרָקִים וְעָנָן כָּבֵד עַל־ הָהָר וְקֹל שֹׁפָר חָזָק
loud trumpet and-blast-of the-mountain over thick with-cloud and-lightnings

מְאֹד וַיֶּחֱרַד כָּל־ הָעָם אֲשֶׁר בַּמַּחֲנֶה׃ וַיּוֹצֵא
and-he-led-out (17) in-the-camp that the-people all-of and-he-trembled very

מֹשֶׁה אֶת־ הָעָם לִקְרַאת הָאֱלֹהִים מִן־ הַמַּחֲנֶה וַיִּתְיַצְּבוּ בְּתַחְתִּית
at-foot-of and-they-stood the-camp from the-God to-meet the-people *** Moses

הָהָר׃ וְהַר סִינַי עָשַׁן כֻּלּוֹ מִפְּנֵי אֲשֶׁר
when because-of around-him he-had-smoke Sinai and-Mount-of (18) the-mountain

יָרַד עָלָיו יְהוָה בָּאֵשׁ וַיַּעַל עֲשָׁנוֹ
smoke-of-him and-he-billowed-up in-the-fire Yahweh on-him he-descended

כְּעֶשֶׁן הַכִּבְשָׁן וַיֶּחֱרַד כָּל־ הָהָר מְאֹד׃
violently the-mountain whole-of and-he-trembled the-furnace like-smoke-of

consecrate them today and tomorrow. Have them wash
their clothes [11]and be ready by
the third day, because on that
day the LORD will come down
on Mount Sinai in the sight of
all the people. [12]Put limits for
the people around the mountain and tell them, 'Be careful
that you do not go up the
mountain or touch the foot of
it. Whoever touches the
mountain shall surely be put
to death. [13]He shall surely be
stoned or shot with arrows;
not a hand is to be laid on him.
Whether man or animal, he
shall not be permitted to live.'
Only when the ram's horn
sounds a long blast may they
go up to the mountain."
[14]After Moses had gone
down the mountain to the
people, he consecrated them,
and they washed their clothes.
[15]Then he said to the people,
"Prepare yourselves for the
third day. Abstain from sexual
relations."
[16]On the morning of the
third day there was thunder
and lightning, with a thick
cloud over the mountain, and
a very loud trumpet blast.
Everyone in the camp trembled. [17]Then Moses led the
people out of the camp to meet
with God, and they stood at
the foot of the mountain.
[18]Mount Sinai was covered
with smoke, because the LORD
descended on it in fire. The
smoke billowed up from it like
smoke from a furnace, the
whole mountain[l] trembled violently, [19]and the sound of the

[l]18 Most Hebrew manuscripts; a few Hebrew manuscripts and Septuagint *all the people*

וַיְהִי קוֹל הַשּׁוֹפָר הוֹלֵךְ וְחָזֵק מְאֹד מֹשֶׁה
Moses very and-being-loud growing the-trumpet sound-of and-he-was (19)

יְדַבֵּר וְהָאֱלֹהִים יַעֲנֶנּוּ בְקוֹל׃ וַיֵּרֶד
and-he-descended (20) with-thunder he-answered-him and-the-God he-spoke

יְהוָה עַל־ הַר סִינַי אֶל־ רֹאשׁ הָהָר וַיִּקְרָא יְהוָה לְמֹשֶׁה
to-Moses Yahweh and-he-called the-mountain top-of to Sinai Mount-of on Yahweh

אֶל־רֹאשׁ הָהָר וַיַּעַל מֹשֶׁה׃ וַיֹּאמֶר יְהוָה אֶל־ מֹשֶׁה
Moses to Yahweh and-he-said (21) Moses so-he-went-up the-mountain top-of to

רֵד הָעֵד בָּעָם פֶּן־ יֶהֶרְסוּ אֶל־ יְהוָה לִרְאוֹת
to-see Yahweh to they-force-through so-not to-the-people warn! go-down!

וְנָפַל מִמֶּנּוּ רָב׃ וְגַם הַכֹּהֲנִים הַנִּגָּשִׁים
the-ones-approaching the-priests and-even (22) many from-him and-he-perish

אֶל־ יְהוָה יִתְקַדָּשׁוּ פֶּן־ יִפְרֹץ בָּהֶם
against-them he-will-break-out or they-must-consecrate-themselves Yahweh to

יְהוָה׃ וַיֹּאמֶר מֹשֶׁה אֶל־ יְהוָה לֹא־ יוּכַל הָעָם לַעֲלֹת
to-come-up the-people he-can not Yahweh to Moses and-he-said (23) Yahweh

אֶל־ הַר סִינָי כִּי־ אַתָּה הַעֵדֹתָה בָּנוּ לֵאמֹר הַגְבֵּל אֶת־
*** put-limit! to-say to-us you-warned you for Sinai Mount-of onto

הָהָר וְקִדַּשְׁתּוֹ׃ וַיֹּאמֶר אֵלָיו יְהוָה לֶךְ־
go! Yahweh to-him then-he-said (24) and-you-make-holy-him the-mountain

רֵד וְעָלִיתָ אַתָּה וְאַהֲרֹן עִמָּךְ וְהַכֹּהֲנִים וְהָעָם
and-the-people but-the-priests with-you and-Aaron you and-you-bring-up go-down!

אַל־ יֶהֶרְסוּ לַעֲלֹת אֶל־ יְהוָה פֶּן־ יִפְרָץ־
he-will-break-out or Yahweh to to-come-up they-may-force-through not

בָּם׃ וַיֵּרֶד מֹשֶׁה אֶל־ הָעָם וַיֹּאמֶר אֲלֵהֶם׃
to-them and-he-told the-people to Moses so-he-went-down (25) against-them

וַיְדַבֵּר אֱלֹהִים אֵת כָּל־ הַדְּבָרִים הָאֵלֶּה לֵאמֹר׃ אָנֹכִי יְהוָה
Yahweh I (2) to-say the-these the-words all-of *** God and-he-spoke (20:1)

אֱלֹהֶיךָ אֲשֶׁר הוֹצֵאתִיךָ מֵאֶרֶץ מִצְרַיִם מִבֵּית עֲבָדִים׃
slaveries from-house-of Egypt from-land-of I-brought-you who God-of-you

לֹא יִהְיֶה־ לְךָ אֱלֹהִים אֲחֵרִים עַל־ פָּנָיַ* לֹא
not (4) face-of-me before other-ones gods to-you he-shall-be not (3)

תַעֲשֶׂה־ לְךָ פֶסֶל | וְכָל־ תְּמוּנָה אֲשֶׁר בַּשָּׁמַיִם |
in-the-heavens that image or-any-of idol for-yourself you-shall-make

מִמַּעַל וַאֲשֶׁר בָּאָרֶץ מִתָּחַת וַאֲשֶׁר בַּמַּיִם |
in-the-waters or-that from-beneath on-the-earth or-that from-above

מִתַּחַת לָאָרֶץ לֹא־ תִשְׁתַּחֲוֶה לָהֶם וְלֹא
and-not to-them you-shall-bow not (5) to-the-earth from-below

trumpet grew louder and louder. Then Moses spoke and the
voice of God answered him.[m]
20The LORD descended to the
top of Mount Sinai and called
Moses to the top of the mountain. So Moses went up 21and
the LORD said to him, "Go
down and warn the people so
they do not force their way
through to see the LORD and
many of them perish. 22Even
the priests, who approach the
LORD, must consecrate themselves, or the LORD will break
out against them."
23Moses said to the LORD,
"The people cannot come up
Mount Sinai, because you
yourself warned us, 'Put limits
around the mountain and set
it apart as holy.'"
24The LORD replied, "Go
down and bring Aaron up
with you. But the priests and
the people must not force their
way through to come up to the
LORD, or he will break out
against them."
25So Moses went down to the
people and told them.

The Ten Commandments

20 And God spoke all these words:

2"I am the LORD your God,
who brought you out of
Egypt, out of the land of
slavery.
3"You shall have no other
gods before[n] me.
4"You shall not make for
yourself an idol in the
form of anything in
heaven above or on the
earth beneath or in the
waters below. 5You shall
not bow down to them or

m19 Or *and God answered him with thunder*
n3 Or *besides*

*3 Most mss end verse 3 with *soph pasuq* (:).

תַעָבְדֵם כִּי אָנֹכִי יְהוָה אֱלֹהֶיךָ אֵל קַנָּא פֹּקֵד עֲוֹן

sin-of punishing jealous God God-of-you Yahweh I for you-shall-worship-them

אָבֹת עַל־ בָּנִים עַל־ שִׁלֵּשִׁים וְעַל־ רִבֵּעִים לְשֹׂנְאָי׃

to-ones-hating-me fourth-ones and-to third-ones to children on fathers

וְעֹשֶׂה חֶסֶד לַאֲלָפִים לְאֹהֲבַי וּלְשֹׁמְרֵי

and-to-ones-keeping-of to-ones-loving-me to-thousands love but-showing (6)

מִצְוֹתָי׃ לֹא תִשָּׂא אֶת־ שֵׁם־ יְהוָה אֱלֹהֶיךָ

God-of-you Yahweh name-of *** you-shall-take not (7) commandments-of-me

לַשָּׁוְא כִּי לֹא יְנַקֶּה יְהוָה אֵת אֲשֶׁר־ יִשָּׂא אֶת־

*** he-takes who *** Yahweh he-will-hold-guiltless not for for-the-misuse

שְׁמוֹ לַשָּׁוְא׃ זָכוֹר אֶת־ יוֹם הַשַּׁבָּת

the-Sabbath day-of *** to-remember (8) for-the-misuse name-of-him

לְקַדְּשׁוֹ שֵׁשֶׁת יָמִים תַּעֲבֹד וְעָשִׂיתָ כָּל־

all-of and-you-shall-do you-shall-labor days six-of (9) to-keep-holy-him

מְלַאכְתֶּךָ וְיוֹם הַשְּׁבִיעִי שַׁבָּת ׀ לַיהוָה אֱלֹהֶיךָ לֹא־

not God-of-you to-Yahweh Sabbath the-seventh but-day-of (10) work-of-you

תַעֲשֶׂה כָל־ מְלָאכָה אַתָּה ׀ וּבִנְךָ־ וּבִתֶּךָ

or-daughter-of-you or-son-of-you you work any-of you-shall-do

עַבְדְּךָ וַאֲמָתְךָ וּבְהֶמְתֶּךָ וְגֵרְךָ אֲשֶׁר

who or-alien-of-you or-animal-of-you or-maidservant-of-you manservant-of-you

בִּשְׁעָרֶיךָ כִּי שֵׁשֶׁת־ יָמִים עָשָׂה יְהוָה אֶת־ הַשָּׁמַיִם וְאֶת־

and the-heavens *** Yahweh he-made days six-of for (11) within-gates-of-you

הָאָרֶץ אֶת־ הַיָּם וְאֶת־ כָּל־ אֲשֶׁר־ בָּם וַיָּנַח בַּיּוֹם

on-the-day but-he-rested in-them that all and the-sea *** the-earth

הַשְּׁבִיעִי עַל־ כֵּן בֵּרַךְ יְהוָה אֶת־ יוֹם הַשַּׁבָּת

the-Sabbath day-of *** Yahweh he-blessed this for the-seventh

וַיְקַדְּשֵׁהוּ׃ כַּבֵּד אֶת־ אָבִיךָ וְאֶת־ אִמֶּךָ לְמַעַן

that mother-of-you and father-of-you *** honor! (12) and-he-made-holy-him

יַאֲרִכוּן יָמֶיךָ עַל הָאֲדָמָה אֲשֶׁר־ יְהוָה אֱלֹהֶיךָ נֹתֵן

giving God-of-you Yahweh that the-land in days-of-you they-may-be-long

לָךְ׃ לֹא תִּרְצָח׃ לֹא תִּנְאָף׃ לֹא

not (15) you-shall-commit-adultery not (14) you-shall-murder not (13) to-you

תִּגְנֹב׃ לֹא־ תַעֲנֶה בְרֵעֲךָ עֵד

testimony-of against-neighbor-of-you you-shall-give not (16) you-shall-steal

שָׁקֶר׃ לֹא תַחְמֹד בֵּית רֵעֶךָ לֹא־ תַחְמֹד

you-shall-covet not neighbor-of-you house-of you-shall-covet not (17) false

אֵשֶׁת רֵעֶךָ וְעַבְדּוֹ וַאֲמָתוֹ

or-maidservant-of-him or-manservant-of-him neighbor-of-you wife-of

worship them; for I, the
LORD your God, am a jeal-
ous God, punishing the
children for the sin of the
fathers to the third and
fourth generation of
those who hate me, 6but
showing love to thou-
sands who love me and
keep my command-
ments.
7"You shall not misuse the
name of the LORD your
God, for the LORD will not
hold anyone guiltless
who misuses his name.
8"Remember the Sabbath
day by keeping it holy.
9Six days you shall labor
and do all your work,
10but the seventh day is a
Sabbath to the LORD your
God. On it you shall not
do any work, neither
you, nor your son or
daughter, nor your man-
servant or maidservant,
nor your animals, nor the
alien within your gates.
11For in six days the LORD
made the heavens and
the earth, the sea, and all
that is in them, but he
rested on the seventh
day. Therefore the LORD
blessed the Sabbath day
and made it holy.
12"Honor your father and
your mother, so that you
may live long in the land
the LORD your God is giv-
ing you.
13"You shall not murder.
14"You shall not commit
adultery.
15"You shall not steal.
16"You shall not give false
testimony against your
neighbor.
17"You shall not covet your
neighbor's house. You
shall not covet your
neighbor's wife, or his

וְשׁוֹרוֹ וַחֲמֹרוֹ וְכֹל אֲשֶׁר לְרֵעֶךָ׃

to-neighbor-of-you that or-anything or-donkey-of-him or-ox-of-him

וְכָל־ הָעָם רֹאִים אֶת־ הַקּוֹלֹת וְאֶת־ הַלַּפִּידִם וְאֵת

and the-lightnings and the-thunders *** ones-seeing the-people and-all-of (18)

קוֹל הַשֹּׁפָר וְאֶת־ הָהָר עָשֵׁן וַיִּרָא* הָעָם

the-people *then-they-saw smoking the-mountain and the-trumpet sound-of

וַיָּנֻעוּ וַיַּעַמְדוּ מֵרָחֹק׃ וַיֹּאמְרוּ אֶל־ מֹשֶׁה

Moses to and-they-said (19) at-distance and-they-stayed and-they-trembled

דַּבֵּר־ אַתָּה עִמָּנוּ וְנִשְׁמָעָה וְאַל־ יְדַבֵּר עִמָּנוּ אֱלֹהִים

God to-us have-him-speak but-not and-we-will-listen to-us you speak!

פֶּן־ נָמוּת׃ וַיֹּאמֶר מֹשֶׁה אֶל־ הָעָם אַל־ תִּירָאוּ כִּי

for you-be-afraid not the-people to Moses so-he-said (20) we-will-die or

לְבַעֲבוּר נַסּוֹת אֶתְכֶם בָּא הָאֱלֹהִים וּבַעֲבוּר תִּהְיֶה יִרְאָתוֹ

fear-of-him she-will-be and-so-that the-God he-became you to-test in-order-to

עַל־ פְּנֵיכֶם לְבִלְתִּי תֶחֱטָאוּ׃ וַיַּעֲמֹד הָעָם

the-people but-they-remained (21) you-will-sin so-not faces-of-you before

מֵרָחֹק וּמֹשֶׁה נִגַּשׁ אֶל־ הָעֲרָפֶל אֲשֶׁר־ שָׁם הָאֱלֹהִים׃

the-God there where the-darkness to he-approached while-Moses at-distance

וַיֹּאמֶר יְהוָה אֶל־מֹשֶׁה כֹּה תֹאמַר אֶל־ בְּנֵי יִשְׂרָאֵל אַתֶּם רְאִיתֶם

you-saw you Israel sons-of to you-say this Moses to Yahweh then-he-said (22)

כִּי מִן־ הַשָּׁמַיִם דִּבַּרְתִּי עִמָּכֶם׃ לֹא תַעֲשׂוּן אִתִּי אֱלֹהֵי

gods-of alongside-me you-make not (23) to-you I-spoke the-heavens from that

כֶסֶף וֵאלֹהֵי זָהָב לֹא תַעֲשׂוּ לָכֶם׃ מִזְבַּח אֲדָמָה תַּעֲשֶׂה־

you-make earth altar-of (24) for-you you-make not gold or-gods-of silver

לִּי וְזָבַחְתָּ עָלָיו אֶת־ עֹלֹתֶיךָ וְאֶת־

and burnt-offerings-of-you *** on-him and-you-sacrifice for-me

שְׁלָמֶיךָ אֶת־ צֹאנְךָ וְאֶת־ בְּקָרֶךָ בְּכָל־

in-every-of cattle-of-you and sheep-of-you *** fellowship-offerings-of-you

הַמָּקוֹם אֲשֶׁר אַזְכִּיר אֶת־ שְׁמִי אָבוֹא אֵלֶיךָ

to-you I-will-come name-of-me *** I-cause-honor where the-place

וּבֵרַכְתִּיךָ׃ וְאִם־ מִזְבַּח אֲבָנִים תַּעֲשֶׂה־ לִּי לֹא־

not for-me you-make stones altar-of and-if (25) and-I-will-bless-you

תִבְנֶה אֶתְהֶן גָּזִית כִּי חַרְבְּךָ הֵנַפְתָּ עָלֶיהָ

on-her you-use tool-of-you if dressed-stone them you-build

וַתְּחַלְלֶהָ׃ וְלֹא־ תַעֲלֶה בְמַעֲלֹת עַל־ מִזְבְּחִי אֲשֶׁר לֹא־

not so altar-of-me to on-steps you-go-up and-not (26) then-you-defile-her

תִגָּלֶה עֶרְוָתְךָ עָלָיו׃ וְאֵלֶּה הַמִּשְׁפָּטִים אֲשֶׁר

that the-laws now-these (21:1) on-him nakedness-of-you she-be-exposed

manservant or maid-servant, his ox or donkey, or anything that belongs to your neighbor."

[18]When the people saw the thunder and lightning and heard the trumpet and saw the mountain in smoke, they trembled with fear. They stayed at a distance [19]and said to Moses, "Speak to us yourself and we will listen. But do not have God speak to us or we will die."

[20]Moses said to the people, "Do not be afraid. God has come to test you, so that the fear of God will be with you to keep you from sinning."

[21]The people remained at a distance, while Moses approached the thick darkness where God was.

Idols and Altars

[22]Then the LORD said to Moses, "Tell the Israelites this: 'You have seen for yourselves that I have spoken to you from heaven: [23]Do not make any gods to be alongside me; do not make for yourselves gods of silver or gods of gold.

[24]" 'Make an altar of earth for me and sacrifice on it your burnt offerings and fellowship offerings,[°] your sheep and goats and your cattle. Wherever I cause my name to be honored, I will come to you and bless you. [25]If you make an altar of stones for me, do not build it with dressed stones, for you will defile it if you use a tool on it. [26]And do not go up to my altar on steps, lest your nakedness be exposed on it.'

21 "These are the laws you are to set before them:

°24 Traditionally *peace offerings*

*18 וַיִּרְאוּ, *then-they-were-afraid*
This reading is conjectured by repointing the Hebrew word on the basis of the major ancient versions.

תָּשִׂים לִפְנֵיהֶם׃ (2) כִּי תִקְנֶה עֶבֶד עִבְרִי שֵׁשׁ שָׁנִים יַעֲבֹד
he-may-serve years six Hebrew slave you-buy if (2) before-them you-set

וּבַשְּׁבִעִת יֵצֵא לַחָפְשִׁי חִנָּם׃ (3) אִם־
if (3) without-pay to-the-freedom he-shall-go-out but-in-the-seventh

בְּגַפּוֹ יָבֹא בְּגַפּוֹ יֵצֵא אִם־ בַּעַל אִשָּׁה הוּא וְיָצְאָה
then-she-goes he wife husband-of if he-goes-free by-himself he-comes by-himself

אִשְׁתּוֹ עִמּוֹ׃ (4) אִם־ אֲדֹנָיו יִתֶּן־ לוֹ אִשָּׁה וְיָלְדָה־
and-she-bears wife to-him he-gives masters-of-him if (4) with-him wife-of-him

לוֹ בָנִים אוֹ בָנוֹת הָאִשָּׁה וִילָדֶיהָ תִּהְיֶה לַאדֹנֶיהָ
to-masters-of-her she-is and-children-of-her the-woman daughters or sons to-him

וְהוּא יֵצֵא בְגַפּוֹ׃ (5) וְאִם־ אָמֹר יֹאמַר הָעֶבֶד
the-servant he-declares to-declare but-if (5) by-himself he-goes-free only-he

אָהַבְתִּי אֶת־ אֲדֹנִי אֶת־ אִשְׁתִּי וְאֶת־ בָּנָי לֹא אֵצֵא
I-would-go not children-of-me and wife-of-me *** master-of-me *** I-love

חָפְשִׁי׃ (6) וְהִגִּישׁוֹ אֲדֹנָיו אֶל־ הָאֱלֹהִים
the-judges before masters-of-him then-he-must-take-him (6) free

וְהִגִּישׁוֹ אֶל־ הַדֶּלֶת אוֹ אֶל־ הַמְּזוּזָה וְרָצַע
and-he-shall-pierce the-doorpost to or the-door to then-he-shall-take-him

אֲדֹנָיו אֶת־ אָזְנוֹ בַּמַּרְצֵעַ וַעֲבָדוֹ לְעֹלָם׃
for-life then-he-shall-serve-him with-the-awl ear-of-him *** masters-of-him

(7) וְכִי־ יִמְכֹּר אִישׁ אֶת־ בִּתּוֹ לְאָמָה לֹא תֵצֵא
she-may-go-free not as-servant daughter-of-him *** man he-sells and-if (7)

כְּצֵאת הָעֲבָדִים׃ (8) אִם־ רָעָה בְּעֵינֵי אֲדֹנֶיהָ
masters-of-her in-eyes-of she-displeases if (8) the-menservants as-to-go-free

אֲשֶׁר־ לֹא° יְעָדָהּ וְהֶפְדָּהּ לְעַם נָכְרִי לֹא־
not foreign to-people then-he-must-let-be-redeemed-her he-selected-her for-him who

יִמְשֹׁל לְמָכְרָהּ בְּבִגְדוֹ־ בָהּ׃ (9) וְאִם־
and-if (9) with-her for-to-break-faith-him to-sell-her he-has-right

לִבְנוֹ יִיעָדֶנָּה כְּמִשְׁפַּט הַבָּנוֹת יַעֲשֶׂה־ לָּהּ׃
to-her he-must-grant the-daughters as-right-of he-selects-her for-son-of-him

(10) אִם־ אַחֶרֶת יִקַּח־ לוֹ שְׁאֵרָהּ כְּסוּתָהּ
clothing-of-her food-of-her for-him he-takes another-woman if (10)

וְעֹנָתָהּ לֹא יִגְרָע׃ (11) וְאִם־ שְׁלָשׁ־ אֵלֶּה לֹא
not these three and-if (11) he-must-deprive not and-marital-right-of-her

יַעֲשֶׂה לָהּ וְיָצְאָה חִנָּם אֵין כָּסֶף׃ (12) מַכֵּה אִישׁ
man one-striking (12) money without free then-she-may-go to-her he-provides

וָמֵת מוֹת יוּמָת׃ (13) וַאֲשֶׁר לֹא צָדָה וְהָאֱלֹהִים
but-the-God he-is-intentional not but-who (13) he-must-die to-die so-he-dies

°8 ק לו

Hebrew Servants

2"If you buy a Hebrew servant, he is to serve you for six years. But in the seventh year, he shall go free, without paying anything. 3If he comes alone, he is to go free alone; but if he has a wife when he comes, she is to go with him. 4If his master gives him a wife and she bears him sons or daughters, the woman and her children shall belong to her master, and only the man shall go free.

5"But if the servant declares, 'I love my master and my wife and children and do not want to go free,' 6then his master must take him before the judges.[p] He shall take him to the door or the doorpost and pierce his ear with an awl. Then he will be his servant for life.

7"If a man sells his daughter as a servant, she is not to go free as menservants do. 8If she does not please the master who has selected her for himself,[q] he must let her be redeemed. He has no right to sell her to foreigners, because he has broken faith with her. 9If he selects her for his son, he must grant her the rights of a daughter. 10If he marries another woman, he must not deprive the first one of her food, clothing and marital rights. 11If he does not provide her with these three things, she is to go free, without any payment of money.

Personal Injuries

12"Anyone who strikes a man and kills him shall surely be put to death. 13However, if he does not do it intentionally,

p6 Or *before God*
q8 Or *master so that he does not choose her*

אִנָּה לְיָדוֹ וְשַׂמְתִּי לְךָ מָקוֹם אֲשֶׁר
where place for-you then-I-will-designate into-hand-of-him he-allows

יָנוּס שָׁמָּה׃ וְכִי־ יָזִד אִישׁ עַל־ רֵעֵהוּ
fellow-of-him about man he-deliberates but-if (14) to-there he-may-flee

לְהָרְגוֹ בְעָרְמָה מֵעִם מִזְבְּחִי תִּקָּחֶנּוּ לָמוּת׃
to-kill you-take-him altar-of-me from-on by-scheme to-kill-him

וּמַכֵּה אָבִיו וְאִמּוֹ מוֹת יוּמָת׃
he-must-die to-die or-mother-of-him father-of-him and-one-attacking (15)

וְגֹנֵב אִישׁ וּמְכָרוֹ וְנִמְצָא
or-he-is-caught whether-he-sells-him another and-one-kidnapping (16)

בְיָדוֹ מוֹת יוּמָת׃ וּמְקַלֵּל אָבִיו
father-of-him and-one-cursing (17) he-must-die to-die in-hand-of-him

וְאִמּוֹ מוֹת יוּמָת׃ וְכִי־ יְרִיבֻן אֲנָשִׁים וְהִכָּה־
and-he-hits men they-quarrel and-if (18) he-must-die to-die or-mother-of-him

אִישׁ אֶת־ רֵעֵהוּ בְּאֶבֶן אוֹ בְאֶגְרֹף וְלֹא יָמוּת וְנָפַל
but-he-stays he-dies and-not with-fist or with-stone fellow-of-him *** one

לְמִשְׁכָּב׃ אִם־ יָקוּם וְהִתְהַלֵּךְ בַּחוּץ עַל־ מִשְׁעַנְתּוֹ
staff-of-him with in-the-outside and-he-walks-around he-gets-up if (19) in-bed

וְנִקָּה הַמַּכֶּה רַק שִׁבְתּוֹ יִתֵּן
he-must-pay lost-time-of-him however the-one-striking then-he-is-cleared

וְרַפֹּא יְרַפֵּא׃ וְכִי־ יַכֶּה אִישׁ אֶת־
*** man he-beats and-if (20) he-must-see-healed and-to-see-healed

עַבְדּוֹ אוֹ אֶת־ אֲמָתוֹ בַּשֵּׁבֶט וּמֵת תַּחַת
under and-he-dies with-the-rod female-slave-of-him *** or male-slave-of-him

יָדוֹ נָקֹם יִנָּקֵם׃ אַךְ אִם־ יוֹם אוֹ יוֹמַיִם
two-days or day if but (21) he-must-be-punished to-be-punished hand-of-him

יַעֲמֹד לֹא יֻקַּם כִּי כַסְפּוֹ הוּא׃ וְכִי־
and-if (22) he property-of-him since he-may-be-punished not he-gets-up

יִנָּצוּ אֲנָשִׁים וְנָגְפוּ אִשָּׁה הָרָה וְיָצְאוּ יְלָדֶיהָ
children-of-her so-they-come-out pregnant woman and-they-hit men they-fight

וְלֹא יִהְיֶה אָסוֹן עָנוֹשׁ יֵעָנֵשׁ כַּאֲשֶׁר יָשִׁית עָלָיו
from-him he-demands as-what he-must-be-fined to-be-fined injury he-is but-not

בַּעַל הָאִשָּׁה וְנָתַן בִּפְלִלִים׃ וְאִם־ אָסוֹן יִהְיֶה
he-is injury but-if (23) by-judges and-he-allows the-woman husband-of

וְנָתַתָּה נֶפֶשׁ תַּחַת נָפֶשׁ׃ עַיִן תַּחַת עַיִן שֵׁן תַּחַת שֵׁן יָד
hand tooth for tooth eye for eye (24) life for life then-you-must-take

תַּחַת יָד רֶגֶל תַּחַת רָגֶל׃ כְּוִיָּה תַּחַת כְּוִיָּה פֶּצַע תַּחַת פָּצַע חַבּוּרָה תַּחַת חַבּוּרָה׃
bruise for bruise wound for wound burn for burn (25) foot for foot hand for

but God lets it happen, he is to
flee to a place I will designate.
14But if a man schemes and
kills another man deliberately,
take him away from my altar
and put him to death.
15"Anyone who attacks[r] his
father or his mother must be
put to death.
16"Anyone who kidnaps an-
other and either sells him or
still has him when he is
caught must be put to death.
17"Anyone who curses his
father or mother must be put
to death.
18"If men quarrel and one
hits the other with a stone or
with his fist[s] and he does not
die but is confined to bed,
19the one who struck the blow
will not be held responsible if
the other gets up and walks
around outside with his staff;
however, he must pay the injured man for the loss of his
time and see that he is completely healed.
20"If a man beats his male or
female slave with a rod and
the slave dies as a direct result,
he must be punished, 21but he
is not to be punished if the
slave gets up after a day or
two, since the slave is his
property.
22"If men who are fighting
hit a pregnant woman and she
gives birth prematurely[t] but
there is no serious injury, the
offender must be fined whatever the woman's husband
demands and the court allows.
23But if there is serious injury,
you are to take life for life,
24eye for eye, tooth for tooth,
hand for hand, foot for foot,
25burn for burn, wound for
wound, bruise for bruise.

r15 Or *kills* s18 Or *with a tool*
t22 Or *she has a miscarriage*

וְכִֽי־ יַכֶּה אִישׁ אֶת־ עֵין עַבְדּוֹ אֽוֹ־ אֶת־ עֵין
eye-of *** or manservant-of-him eye-of *** man he-hits and-if (26)

אֲמָתוֹ וְשִׁחֲתָהּ לַחָפְשִׁי יְשַׁלְּחֶנּוּ
he-must-let-go-him to-the-freedom and-he-destroys-her maidservant-of-him

תַּחַת עֵינֽוֹ׃ וְאִם־ שֵׁן עַבְדּוֹ אֽוֹ־ שֵׁן
tooth-of or manservant-of-him tooth-of and-if (27) eye-of-him because-of

אֲמָתוֹ יַפִּיל לַחָפְשִׁי יְשַׁלְּחֶנּוּ
he-must-let-go-him to-the-freedom he-knocks-out maidservant-of-him

תַּחַת שִׁנּֽוֹ׃ וְכִֽי־ יִגַּח שׁוֹר אֶת־ אִישׁ אוֹ אֶת־ אִשָּׁה
woman *** or man *** bull he-gores and-if (28) tooth-of-him because-of

וָמֵת סָקוֹל יִסָּקֵל הַשּׁוֹר וְלֹא יֵאָכֵל
he-may-be-eaten and-not the-bull he-must-be-stoned to-be-stoned so-he-dies

אֶת־ בְּשָׂרוֹ וּבַעַל הַשּׁוֹר נָקִֽי׃ וְאִם שׁוֹר נַגָּח
he-gored bull but-if (29) not-liable the-bull but-owner-of meat-of-him ***

הוּא מִתְּמֹל שִׁלְשֹׁם וְהוּעַד בִּבְעָלָיו וְלֹא יִשְׁמְרֶנּוּ
he-penned-him but-not to-owner-of-him and-he-was-warned past on-yesterday he

וְהֵמִית אִישׁ אוֹ אִשָּׁה הַשּׁוֹר יִסָּקֵל וְגַם־ בְּעָלָיו
owner-of-him and-also he-must-be-stoned the-bull woman or man and-he-kills

יוּמָֽת׃ אִם־ כֹּפֶר יוּשַׁת עָלָיו וְנָתַן
then-he-may-pay from-him he-is-demanded payment if (30) he-must-die

פִּדְיֹן נַפְשׁוֹ כְּכֹל אֲשֶׁר־ יוּשַׁת עָלָֽיו׃ אוֹ־ בֵן
son if (31) from-him he-is-demanded that by-all life-of-him redemption-of

יִגָּח אוֹ־ בַת יִגָּח כַּמִּשְׁפָּט הַזֶּה יֵעָשֶׂה לּֽוֹ׃
to-him he-applies the-this also-the-law he-gores daughter or he-gores

אִם־ עֶבֶד יִגַּח הַשּׁוֹר אוֹ אָמָה כֶּסֶף ׀ שְׁלֹשִׁים
thirty silver-of female-slave or the-bull he-gores male-slave if (32)

שְׁקָלִים יִתֵּן לַֽאדֹנָיו וְהַשּׁוֹר יִסָּקֵֽל׃
he-must-be-stoned and-the-bull to-masters-of-him he-must-pay shekels

וְכִֽי־ יִפְתַּח אִישׁ בּוֹר אוֹ כִּֽי־ יִכְרֶה אִישׁ בֹּר וְלֹא
and-not pit man he-digs if or pit man he-uncovers and-if (33)

יְכַסֶּנּוּ וְנָֽפַל־ שָׁמָּה שׁוֹר אוֹ חֲמוֹר׃ בַּעַל הַבּוֹר
the-pit owner-of (34) donkey or ox into-there and-he-falls he-covers-him

יְשַׁלֵּם כֶּסֶף יָשִׁיב לִבְעָלָיו וְהַמֵּת
and-the-one-being-dead to-owners-of-him he-must-pay money he-must-pay-for-loss

יִֽהְיֶה־ לּֽוֹ׃ וְכִֽי־ יִגֹּף שֽׁוֹר־ אִישׁ אֶת־ שׁוֹר רֵעֵהוּ
fellow-of-him bull-of *** man bull-of he-injures and-if (35) to-him he-will-be

וָמֵת וּמָכְרוּ אֶת־ הַשּׁוֹר הַחַי וְחָצוּ
and-they-must-divide the-live the-bull *** then-they-must-sell so-he-dies

[26]"If a man hits a manservant or maidservant in the eye and destroys it, he must let the servant go free to compensate for the eye. [27]And if he knocks out the tooth of a manservant or maidservant, he must let the servant go free to compensate for the tooth.

[28]"If a bull gores a man or a woman to death, the bull must be stoned to death, and its meat must not be eaten. But the owner of the bull will not be held responsible. [29]If, however, the bull has had the habit of goring and the owner has been warned but has not kept it penned up and it kills a man or woman, the bull must be stoned and the owner also must be put to death. [30]However, if payment is demanded of him, he may redeem his life by paying whatever is demanded. [31]This law also applies if the bull gores a son or daughter. [32]If the bull gores a male or female slave, the owner must pay thirty shekels[u] of silver to the master of the slave, and the bull must be stoned.

[33]"If a man uncovers a pit or digs one and fails to cover it and an ox or a donkey falls into it, [34]the owner of the pit must pay for the loss; he must pay its owner, and the dead animal will be his.

[35]"If a man's bull injures the bull of another and it dies, they are to sell the live one and

[u]32 That is, about 12 ounces (about 0.3 kilogram)

אֶת־כַּסְפּוֹ וְגַם אֶת־הַמֵּת יֶחֱצוּן׃ אוֹ
however (36) they-must-divide the-being-dead *** and-also money-of-him ***

נוֹדַע כִּי שׁוֹר נַגָּח הוּא מִתְּמוֹל שִׁלְשֹׁם וְלֹא יִשְׁמְרֶנּוּ
he-penned-him but-not past on-yesterday he he-gored bull that being-known

בְּעָלָיו שַׁלֵּם יְשַׁלֵּם שׁוֹר תַּחַת הַשּׁוֹר וְהַמֵּת יִהְיֶה־
he-will-be and-the-being-dead the-bull for bull he-must-pay to-pay owners-of-him

לּוֹ׃ כִּי יִגְנֹב־אִישׁ שׁוֹר אוֹ־שֶׂה וּטְבָחוֹ אוֹ
or and-he-slaughters-him sheep or bull man he-steals if (37)* to-him

מְכָרוֹ חֲמִשָּׁה בָקָר יְשַׁלֵּם תַּחַת הַשּׁוֹר וְאַרְבַּע־צֹאן תַּחַת
for sheep and-four the-bull for he-must-pay-back cattle five he-sells-him

הַשֶּׂה׃ אִם־בַּמַּחְתֶּרֶת יִמָּצֵא הַגַּנָּב וְהֻכָּה
and-he-is-struck the-thief he-is-caught in-the-break-in if (22:1)* the-sheep

וָמֵת אֵין לוֹ דָּמִים׃ אִם־זָרְחָה הַשֶּׁמֶשׁ עָלָיו דָּמִים
bloodsheds on-him the-sun he-rose if (2) bloodsheds to-him not so-he-dies

לוֹ שַׁלֵּם יְשַׁלֵּם אִם־אֵין לוֹ וְנִמְכַּר
then-he-must-be-sold to-him nothing if he-must-restitute to-restitute to-him

בִּגְנֵבָתוֹ׃ אִם־הִמָּצֵא תִמָּצֵא בְיָדוֹ הַגְּנֵבָה
the-stolen in-hand-of-him she-is-found to-be-found if (3) for-theft-of-him

מִשּׁוֹר עַד־חֲמוֹר עַד־שֶׂה חַיִּים שְׁנַיִם יְשַׁלֵּם׃ כִּי
if (4) he-must-pay-back double alive-ones sheep or donkey or whether-ox

יַבְעֶר־אִישׁ שָׂדֶה אוֹ־כֶרֶם וְשִׁלַּח אֶת־בְּעִירֹה
livestock-of-him *** and-he-lets-stray vineyard or field man he-grazes

וּבִעֵר בִּשְׂדֵה אַחֵר מֵיטַב שָׂדֵהוּ וּמֵיטַב
or-from-best-of field-of-him from-best-of another in-field-of and-he-grazes

כַּרְמוֹ יְשַׁלֵּם׃ כִּי־תֵצֵא אֵשׁ וּמָצְאָה
and-she-spreads fire she-breaks-out if (5) he-must-restitute vineyard-of-him

קֹצִים וְנֶאֱכַל גָּדִישׁ אוֹ הַקָּמָה אוֹ הַשָּׂדֶה
the-field or the-standing-grain or shock-of-grain so-he-is-burned thorns

שַׁלֵּם יְשַׁלֵּם הַמַּבְעִר אֶת־הַבְּעֵרָה׃ כִּי־יִתֵּן
he-gives if (6) the-fire *** the-one-starting he-must-restitute to-restitute

אִישׁ אֶל־רֵעֵהוּ כֶּסֶף אוֹ־כֵלִים לִשְׁמֹר וְגֻנַּב
and-he-is-stolen to-safekeep goods or money neighbor-of-him to man

מִבֵּית הָאִישׁ אִם־יִמָּצֵא הַגַּנָּב יְשַׁלֵּם שְׁנָיִם׃
double he-must-pay-back the-thief he-is-caught if the-man from-house-of

אִם־לֹא יִמָּצֵא הַגַּנָּב וְנִקְרַב בַּעַל־הַבַּיִת
the-house owner-of then-he-must-appear the-thief he-is-found not if (7)

אֶל־הָאֱלֹהִים אִם־לֹא שָׁלַח יָדוֹ בִּמְלֶאכֶת רֵעֵהוּ׃
neighbor-of-him on-property-of hand-of-him he-laid not whether the-judges before

divide both the money and
the dead animal equally.
36However, if it was known
that the bull had the habit of
goring, yet the owner did not
keep it penned up, the owner
must pay, animal for animal,
and the dead animal will be
his.

Protection of Property

22 "If a man steals an ox
or a sheep and slaugh-
ters it or sells it, he must pay
back five head of cattle for the
ox and four sheep for the
sheep.
2"If a thief is caught breaking in and is struck so that he
dies, the defender is not guilty
of bloodshed; 3but if it happens[v] after sunrise, he is guilty
of bloodshed.
"A thief must certainly
make restitution, but if he has
nothing, he must be sold to
pay for his theft.
4"If the stolen animal is
found alive in his possession—whether ox or donkey or
sheep—he must pay back double.
5"If a man grazes his livestock in a field or vineyard
and lets them stray and they
graze in another man's field,
he must make restitution from
the best of his own field or
vineyard.
6"If a fire breaks out and
spreads into thornbushes so
that it burns shocks of grain or
standing grain or the whole
field, the one who started the
fire must make restitution.
7"If a man gives his neighbor silver or goods for safekeeping and they are stolen
from the neighbor's house, the
thief, if he is caught, must pay
back double. 8But if the thief is
not found, the owner of the
house must appear before the
judges[w] to determine whether
he has laid his hands on the
other man's property. 9In all

[v]3 Or *if he strikes him*
[w]8 Or *before God;* also in verse 9

*The Hebrew numeration of chapter 22 begins with verse 2 of the English numeration; thus, there is a one-verse discrepancy throughout the chapter.

°4 ק בעירו

עַל־ כָּל־ דְּבַר־ פֶּשַׁע עַל־ שׁוֹר עַל־ חֲמוֹר עַל־ שֶׂה
sheep or donkey or ox whether illegal-possession case-of every-of in (8)

עַל־שַׂלְמָה עַל־ כָּל־ אֲבֵדָה אֲשֶׁר יֹאמַר כִּי־ הוּא זֶה עַד
before this he that he-says of-which lost-property any-of or clothing or

הָאֱלֹהִים יָבֹא דְּבַר־ שְׁנֵיהֶם אֲשֶׁר יַרְשִׁיעֻן
they-declare-guilty whom both-of-them case-of he-must-bring the-judges

אֱלֹהִים יְשַׁלֵּם שְׁנַיִם לְרֵעֵהוּ׃ כִּי־ יִתֵּן אִישׁ אֶל־
to man he-gives if (9) to-neighbor-of-him double he-must-pay-back judges

רֵעֵהוּ חֲמוֹר אוֹ־ שׁוֹר אוֹ־ שֶׂה וְכָל־ בְּהֵמָה לִשְׁמֹר
to-safekeep animal or-any-of sheep or ox or donkey neighbor-of-him

וּמֵת אוֹ־ נִשְׁבַּר אוֹ־ נִשְׁבָּה אֵין רֹאֶה׃ שְׁבֻעַת
oath-of (10) looking no-one he-is-taken-away or he-is-injured or and-he-dies

יְהוָה תִּהְיֶה בֵּין שְׁנֵיהֶם אִם־ לֹא שָׁלַח יָדוֹ
hand-of-him he-laid not that two-of-them between she-must-be Yahweh

בִּמְלֶאכֶת רֵעֵהוּ וְלָקַח בְּעָלָיו וְלֹא
and-not owners-of-him then-he-will-accept neighbor-of-him on-property-of

יְשַׁלֵּם׃ וְאִם־ גָּנֹב יִגָּנֵב מֵעִמּוֹ
from-with-him he-was-stolen to-be-stolen but-if (11) he-must-restitute

יְשַׁלֵּם לִבְעָלָיו׃ אִם־ טָרֹף יִטָּרֵף
he-was-torn to-be-torn if (12) to-owners-of-him he-must-restitute

יְבִאֵהוּ עֵד הַטְּרֵפָה לֹא יְשַׁלֵּם׃ וְכִי־
and-if (13) he-must-repay not the-torn-animal evidence he-shall-bring-him

יִשְׁאַל אִישׁ מֵעִם רֵעֵהוּ וְנִשְׁבַּר אוֹ־ מֵת
he-dies or and-he-is-injured neighbor-of-him from-with man he-borrows

בְּעָלָיו אֵין־ עִמּוֹ שַׁלֵּם יְשַׁלֵּם׃ אִם־ בְּעָלָיו
owners-of-him if (14) he-must-restitute to-restitute with-him not owners-of-him

עִמּוֹ לֹא יְשַׁלֵּם אִם־שָׂכִיר הוּא בָּא בִּשְׂכָרוֹ׃ וְכִי־
and-if (15) by-hire-of-him he-covers he hired if he-must-repay not with-him

יְפַתֶּה אִישׁ בְּתוּלָה אֲשֶׁר לֹא־ אֹרָשָׂה וְשָׁכַב עִמָּהּ מָהֹר
to-pay with-her and-he-sleeps she-is-pledged not who virgin man he-seduces

יִמְהָרֶנָּה לּוֹ לְאִשָּׁה׃ אִם־ מָאֵן יְמָאֵן
he-refuses to-refuse if (16) as-wife for-him he-must-pay-price-of-her

אָבִיהָ לְתִתָּהּ לוֹ כֶּסֶף יִשְׁקֹל כְּמֹהַר
for-bride-price-of he-must-pay money to-him to-give-her father-of-her

הַבְּתוּלֹת׃ מְכַשֵּׁפָה לֹא תְחַיֶּה׃ כָּל־
every-of (18) you-let-live not one-being-sorceress (17) the-virgins

שֹׁכֵב עִם־ בְּהֵמָה מוֹת יוּמָת׃ זֹבֵחַ
sacrificing (19) he-must-die to-die animal with having-sexual-relation

cases of illegal possession of
an ox, a donkey, a sheep, a
garment, or any other lost
property about which some-
body says, 'This is mine,' both
parties are to bring their cases
before the judges. The one
whom the judges declare[x]
guilty must pay back double to
his neighbor.
10"If a man gives a donkey,
an ox, a sheep or any other
animal to his neighbor for
safekeeping and it dies or is
injured or is taken away while
no one is looking, 11the issue
between them will be settled
by the taking of an oath before
the LORD that the neighbor did
not lay hands on the other
person's property. The owner
is to accept this, and no restitution is required. 12But if the
animal was stolen from the
neighbor, he must make restitution to the owner. 13If it was
torn to pieces by a wild animal, he shall bring in the remains as evidence and he will
not be required to pay for the
torn animal.
14"If a man borrows an animal from his neighbor and it
is injured or dies while the
owner is not present, he must
make restitution. 15But if the
owner is with the animal, the
borrower will not have to pay.
If the animal was hired, the
money paid for the hire covers
the loss.

Social Responsibility

16"If a man seduces a virgin
who is not pledged to be married and sleeps with her, he
must pay the bride-price, and
she shall be his wife. 17If her
father absolutely refuses to
give her to him, he must still
pay the bride-price for virgins.
18"Do not allow a sorceress
to live.
19"Anyone who has sexual
relations with an animal must
be put to death.

x9 Or *whom God declares*

*See the note on page 206.

לָאֱלֹהִים יָחֳרָם בִּלְתִּי לַיהוָה לְבַדּוֹ׃ וְגֵר
and-alien (20) by-himself to-Yahweh other-than he-must-be-destroyed to-the-gods

לֹא־ תוֹנֶה וְלֹא תִלְחָצֶנּוּ כִּי־ גֵרִים הֱיִיתֶם בְּאֶרֶץ
in-land-of you-were aliens for you-oppress-him and-not you-mistreat not

מִצְרָיִם׃ כָּל־ אַלְמָנָה וְיָתוֹם לֹא תְעַנּוּן׃ אִם־
if (22) you-take-advantage not or-orphan widow any-of (21) Egypt

עַנֵּה תְעַנֶּה אֹתוֹ כִּי אִם־ צָעֹק יִצְעַק אֵלַי
to-me he-cries to-cry if then him you-take-advantage to-take-advantage

שָׁמֹעַ אֶשְׁמַע צַעֲקָתוֹ׃ וְחָרָה אַפִּי
anger-of-me and-he-will-be-aroused (23) cry-of-him I-will-hear to-hear

וְהָרַגְתִּי אֶתְכֶם בֶּחָרֶב וְהָיוּ נְשֵׁיכֶם אַלְמָנוֹת
widows wives-of-you and-they-will-become with-the-sword you and-I-will-kill

וּבְנֵיכֶם יְתֹמִים׃ אִם־ כֶּסֶף ׀ תַּלְוֶה אֶת־ עַמִּי
people-of-me *** you-lend money if (24) fatherless-ones and-children-of-you

אֶת־ הֶעָנִי עִמָּךְ לֹא־ תִהְיֶה לוֹ כְּנֹשֶׁה לֹא־
not like-one-lending-money to-him you-shall-be not among-you the-needy ***

תְשִׂימוּן עָלָיו נֶשֶׁךְ׃ אִם־ חָבֹל תַּחְבֹּל
you-take-pledge to-take-pledge if (25) interest to-him you-shall-charge

שַׂלְמַת רֵעֶךָ עַד־ בֹּא הַשֶּׁמֶשׁ תְּשִׁיבֶנּוּ לוֹ׃ כִּי
for (26) to-him you-return-him the-sun to-set when neighbor-of-you cloak-of

הִוא כְסוּתֹה° לְבַדָּהּ הִוא שִׂמְלָתוֹ לְעֹרוֹ בַּמֶּה
with-the-what? for-body-of-him cloak-of-him she only-her covering-of-him she

יִשְׁכָּב וְהָיָה כִּי־ יִצְעַק אֵלַי וְשָׁמַעְתִּי כִּי־
for then-I-will-hear to-me he-cries when and-he-will-be will-he-sleep

חַנּוּן אָנִי׃ אֱלֹהִים לֹא תְקַלֵּל וְנָשִׂיא בְעַמְּךָ לֹא
not over-people-of-you and-ruler you-blaspheme not God (27) I compassionate

תָאֹר׃ מְלֵאָתְךָ וְדִמְעֲךָ לֹא תְאַחֵר
you-hold-back not and-outflow-of-you fullness-of-you (28) you-curse

בְּכוֹר בָּנֶיךָ תִּתֶּן־ לִי׃ כֵּן־ תַּעֲשֶׂה
you-shall-do same (29) to-me you-must-give sons-of-you firstborn-of

לְשֹׁרְךָ לְצֹאנֶךָ שִׁבְעַת יָמִים יִהְיֶה עִם־
with let-him-stay days seven-of with-sheep-of-you with-cattle-of-you

אִמּוֹ בַּיּוֹם הַשְּׁמִינִי תִּתְּנוֹ־ לִי׃ וְאַנְשֵׁי־
now-men-of (30) to-me you-give-him the-eighth but-on-the-day mother-of-him

קֹדֶשׁ תִּהְיוּן לִי וּבָשָׂר בַּשָּׂדֶה טְרֵפָה לֹא תֹאכֵלוּ
you-shall-eat not torn in-the-field and-meat to-me you-must-be holy

לַכֶּלֶב תַּשְׁלִכוּן אֹתוֹ׃ לֹא תִשָּׂא שֵׁמַע שָׁוְא אַל־
not false report-of you-spread not (23:1) him you-shall-throw to-the-dog

20"Whoever sacrifices to any
god other than the LORD must
be destroyed.[y]
21"Do not mistreat an alien
or oppress him, for you were
aliens in Egypt.
22"Do not take advantage of
a widow or an orphan. 23If you
do and they cry out to me, I
will certainly hear their cry.
24My anger will be aroused,
and I will kill you with the
sword; your wives will
become widows and your
children fatherless.
25"If you lend money to one
of my people among you who
is needy, do not be like a
moneylender; charge him no
interest.[z] 26If you take your
neighbor's cloak as a pledge,
return it to him by sunset,
27because his cloak is the only
covering he has for his body.
What else will he sleep in?
When he cries out to me, I will
hear, for I am compassionate.
28"Do not blaspheme God[a]
or curse the ruler of your
people.
29"Do not hold back
offerings from your granaries
or your vats.[b]
"You must give me the
firstborn of your sons. 30Do the
same with your cattle and
your sheep. Let them stay with
their mothers for seven days,
but give them to me on the
eighth day.
31"You are to be my holy
people. So do not eat the meat
of an animal torn by wild
beasts; throw it to the dogs.

Laws of Justice and Mercy

23 "Do not spread false reports. Do not help a

[y]20 The Hebrew term refers to the irrevocable giving over of things or persons to the LORD, often by totally destroying them.
[z]25 Or *excessive interest*
[a]28 Or *Do not revile the judges*
[b]29 The meaning of the Hebrew for this phrase is uncertain.

*See the note on page 206.

°26 ק כסותו

תָּשֶׁת יָדְךָ עִם־ רָשָׁע לִהְיֹת עֵד חָמָס׃ לֹא־
not (2) malicious witness-of to-be wicked-man with hand-of-you you-join

תִהְיֶה אַחֲרֵי־ רַבִּים לְרָעֹת וְלֹא־ תַעֲנֶה עַל־ רִב לִנְטֹת אַחֲרֵי
with to-side court in you-testify and-not in-wrong crowds after you-go

רַבִּים לְהַטֹּת׃ וְדָל לֹא תֶהְדַּר בְּרִיבוֹ׃
in-lawsuit-of-him you-favor not and-poor (3) to-pervert-justice crowds

כִּי תִפְגַּע שׁוֹר אֹיִבְךָ אוֹ חֲמֹרוֹ תֹּעֶה
wandering donkey-of-him or being-enemy-of-you ox-of you-find if (4)

הָשֵׁב תְּשִׁיבֶנּוּ לוֹ׃ כִּי־ תִרְאֶה חֲמוֹר שֹׂנַאֲךָ
one-hating-you donkey-of you-see if (5) to-him you-take-back-him to-take-back

רֹבֵץ תַּחַת מַשָּׂאוֹ וְחָדַלְתָּ מֵעֲזֹב לוֹ עָזֹב
to-help to-him from-to-leave then-you-refrain load-of-him under lying

תַּעֲזֹב עִמּוֹ׃ לֹא תַטֶּה מִשְׁפַּט אֶבְיֹנְךָ בְּרִיבוֹ׃
in-lawsuit-of-him poor-of-you justice-of you-deny not (6) with-him you-help

מִדְּבַר־ שֶׁקֶר תִּרְחָק וְנָקִי וְצַדִּיק אַל־ תַּהֲרֹג
you-kill not or-honest and-innocent you-stay-far false from-charge-of (7)

כִּי לֹא־ אַצְדִּיק רָשָׁע׃ וְשֹׁחַד לֹא תִקָּח כִּי הַשֹּׁחַד
the-bribe for you-accept not and-bribe (8) guilty I-will-acquit not for

יְעַוֵּר פִּקְחִים וִיסַלֵּף דִּבְרֵי צַדִּיקִים׃ וְגֵר
and-alien (9) righteous-ones words-of and-he-twists those-who-see he-blinds

לֹא תִלְחָץ וְאַתֶּם יְדַעְתֶּם אֶת־ נֶפֶשׁ הַגֵּר כִּי־ גֵרִים הֱיִיתֶם
you-were aliens for the-alien feeling-of *** you-know for-you you-oppress not

בְּאֶרֶץ מִצְרָיִם׃ וְשֵׁשׁ שָׁנִים תִּזְרַע אֶת־ אַרְצֶךָ וְאָסַפְתָּ
and-you-harvest field-of-you *** you-sow years and-six (10) Egypt in-land-of

אֶת־ תְּבוּאָתָהּ׃ וְהַשְּׁבִיעִת תִּשְׁמְטֶנָּה
you-let-lie-unplowed-her but-the-seventh (11) the-crop-of-her ***

וּנְטַשְׁתָּהּ וְאָכְלוּ אֶבְיֹנֵי עַמֶּךָ
people-of-you poor-ones-of then-they-may-eat and-you-let-lie-unused-her

וְיִתְרָם תֹּאכַל חַיַּת הַשָּׂדֶה כֵּן־ תַּעֲשֶׂה
you-do same the-field animal-of she-may-eat and-leftover-of-them

לְכַרְמְךָ לְזֵיתֶךָ׃ שֵׁשֶׁת יָמִים תַּעֲשֶׂה מַעֲשֶׂיךָ
works-of-you you-do days six (12) with-olive-grove-of-you with-vineyard-of-you

וּבַיּוֹם הַשְּׁבִיעִי תִּשְׁבֹּת לְמַעַן יָנוּחַ שׁוֹרְךָ
ox-of-you he-may-rest so-that you-rest the-seventh but-on-the-day

וַחֲמֹרֶךָ וְיִנָּפֵשׁ בֶּן־ אֲמָתְךָ וְהַגֵּר׃
and-the-alien servant-of-you son-of and-he-may-be-refreshed and-donkey-of-you

וּבְכֹל אֲשֶׁר־ אָמַרְתִּי אֲלֵיכֶם תִּשָּׁמֵרוּ וְשֵׁם אֱלֹהִים
gods and-name-of you-take-care-to-do to-you I-said that and-to-all (13)

wicked man by being a malicious witness.
2"Do not follow the crowd in doing wrong. When you give testimony in a lawsuit, do not pervert justice by siding with the crowd,
3and do not show favoritism to a poor man in his lawsuit.
4"If you come across your enemy's ox or donkey wandering off, be sure to take it back to him.
5If you see the donkey of someone who hates you fallen down under its load, do not leave it there; be sure you help him with it.
6"Do not deny justice to your poor people in their lawsuits.
7Have nothing to do with a false charge and do not put an innocent or honest person to death, for I will not acquit the guilty.
8"Do not accept a bribe, for a bribe blinds those who see and twists the words of the righteous.
9"Do not oppress an alien; you yourselves know how it feels to be aliens, because you were aliens in Egypt.

Sabbath Laws

10"For six years you are to sow your fields and harvest the crops,
11but during the seventh year let the land lie unplowed and unused. Then the poor among your people may get food from it, and the wild animals may eat what they leave. Do the same with your vineyard and your olive grove.
12"Six days do your work, but on the seventh day do not work, so that your ox and your donkey may rest and the slave born in your household, and the alien as well, may be refreshed.
13"Be careful to do everything I have said to you. Do

אֲחֵרִים לֹא תַזְכִּירוּ לֹא יִשָּׁמַע עַל־פִּיךָ׃
mouth-of-you in you-let-him-be-heard not you-invoke not other-ones

שָׁלֹשׁ רְגָלִים תָּחֹג לִי בַּשָּׁנָה׃ אֶת־חַג
Feast-of *** (15) in-the-year to-me you-celebrate-festival times three (14)

הַמַּצּוֹת תִּשְׁמֹר שִׁבְעַת יָמִים תֹּאכַל מַצּוֹת
breads-without-yeast you-eat days seven-of you-celebrate the-Unleavened-Breads

כַּאֲשֶׁר צִוִּיתִךָ לְמוֹעֵד חֹדֶשׁ הָאָבִיב כִּי־בוֹ
in-him for the-Abib month-of at-appointed-time I-commanded-you just-as

יָצָאתָ מִמִּצְרָיִם וְלֹא־יֵרָאוּ פָנַי רֵיקָם׃
empty-handed before-me he-may-appear and-none from-Egypt you-came-out

וְחַג הַקָּצִיר בִּכּוּרֵי מַעֲשֶׂיךָ אֲשֶׁר תִּזְרַע
you-sow that crops-of-you firstfruits-of the-Harvest and-Feast-of (16)

בַּשָּׂדֶה וְחַג הָאָסִף בְּצֵאת הַשָּׁנָה
the-year when-to-end the-Ingathering and-Feast-of in-the-field

בְּאָסְפְּךָ אֶת־מַעֲשֶׂיךָ מִן־הַשָּׂדֶה׃ שָׁלֹשׁ פְּעָמִים
times three (17) the-field from crops-of-you *** when-to-gather-you

בַּשָּׁנָה יֵרָאֶה כָּל־זְכוּרְךָ אֶל־פְּנֵי הָאָדֹן ׀
the-Sovereign face-of before male-of-you every-of he-must-appear in-the-year

יְהוָה׃ לֹא־תִזְבַּח עַל־חָמֵץ דַּם־זִבְחִי וְלֹא־
and-not sacrifice-of-me blood-of yeast with you-offer not (18) Yahweh

יָלִין חֵלֶב־חַגִּי עַד־בֹּקֶר׃ רֵאשִׁית בִּכּוּרֵי
firstfruits-of best-of (19) morning until offering-of-me fat-of he-may-remain

אַדְמָתְךָ תָּבִיא בֵּית יְהוָה אֱלֹהֶיךָ לֹא־תְבַשֵּׁל גְּדִי
young-goat you-cook not God-of-you Yahweh house-of you-bring soil-of-you

בַּחֲלֵב אִמּוֹ׃ הִנֵּה אָנֹכִי שֹׁלֵחַ מַלְאָךְ לְפָנֶיךָ לִשְׁמָרְךָ
to-guard-you ahead-of-you angel sending I see! (20) mother-of-him in-milk-of

בַּדָּרֶךְ וְלַהֲבִיאֲךָ אֶל־הַמָּקוֹם אֲשֶׁר הֲכִנֹתִי׃ הִשָּׁמֶר
attend! (21) I-prepared that the-place to and-to-bring-you along-the-way

מִפָּנָיו וּשְׁמַע בְּקֹלוֹ אַל־תַּמֵּר בּוֹ כִּי לֹא
not for against-him you-rebel not to-voice-of-him and-listen! to-him

יִשָּׂא לְפִשְׁעֲכֶם כִּי שְׁמִי בְּקִרְבּוֹ׃ כִּי אִם־
if now (22) in-him Name-of-me since to-rebellion-of-you he-will-forgive

שָׁמוֹעַ תִּשְׁמַע בְּקֹלוֹ וְעָשִׂיתָ כֹּל אֲשֶׁר אֲדַבֵּר
I-say that all and-you-do to-voice-of-him you-listen to-listen

וְאָיַבְתִּי אֶת־אֹיְבֶיךָ וְצַרְתִּי אֶת־
*** and-I-will-oppose being-enemies-of-you *** then-I-will-be-enemy

צֹרְרֶיךָ׃ כִּי־יֵלֵךְ מַלְאָכִי לְפָנֶיךָ וֶהֱבִיאֲךָ
and-he-brings-you ahead-of-you angel-of-me he-goes when (23) ones-opposing-you

not invoke the names of other
gods; do not let them be heard
on your lips.

The Three Annual Festivals

14 "Three times a year you are
to celebrate a festival to me.
15 "Celebrate the Feast of Unleavened Bread; for seven days
eat bread made without yeast,
as I commanded you. Do this
at the appointed time in the
month of Abib, for in that
month you came out of Egypt.
"No one is to appear before
me empty-handed.
16 "Celebrate the Feast of
Harvest with the firstfruits of
the crops you sow in your
field.
"Celebrate the Feast of Ingathering at the end of the
year, when you gather in your
crops from the field.
17 "Three times a year all the
men are to appear before the
Sovereign LORD.
18 "Do not offer the blood of a
sacrifice to me along with anything containing yeast.
"The fat of my festival
offerings must not be kept until morning.
19 "Bring the best of the
firstfruits of your soil to the
house of the LORD your God.
"Do not cook a young goat
in its mother's milk.

God's Angel to Prepare the Way

20 "See, I am sending an angel ahead of you to guard you
along the way and to bring
you to the place I have prepared.
21 Pay attention to him
and listen to what he says. Do
not rebel against him; he will
not forgive your rebellion,
since my Name is in him.
22 If
you listen carefully to what he
says and do all that I say, I will
be an enemy to your enemies
and will oppose those who oppose you.
23 My angel will go
ahead of you and bring you

אֶל־ הָאֱמֹרִי וְהַחִתִּי וְהַפְּרִזִּי וְהַכְּנַעֲנִי
and-the-Canaanite and-the-Perizzite and-the-Hittite the-Amorite into

הַחִוִּי וְהַיְבוּסִי וְהִכְחַדְתִּיו׃ לֹא־ תִשְׁתַּחֲוֶה
you-bow not (24) then-I-will-wipe-out-him and-the-Jebusite the-Hivite

לֵאלֹהֵיהֶם וְלֹא תָעָבְדֵם וְלֹא תַעֲשֶׂה
you-follow and-not you-worship-them and-not before-gods-of-them

כְּמַעֲשֵׂיהֶם כִּי הָרֵס תְּהָרְסֵם וְשַׁבֵּר תְּשַׁבֵּר
you-break and-to-break you-demolish-them to-demolish but after-practices-of-them

מַצֵּבֹתֵיהֶם׃ וַעֲבַדְתֶּם אֵת יְהוָה אֱלֹהֵיכֶם וּבֵרַךְ
and-he-will-bless God-of-you Yahweh *** but-you-worship (25) pillars-of-them

אֶת־ לַחְמְךָ וְאֶת־ מֵימֶיךָ וַהֲסִרֹתִי מַחֲלָה מִקִּרְבֶּךָ׃
from-among-you sickness and-I-will-take-away waters-of-you and food-of-you ***

לֹא תִהְיֶה מְשַׁכֵּלָה וַעֲקָרָה בְּאַרְצֶךָ אֶת־ מִסְפַּר
and-span-of *** in-land-of-you or-barren miscarrying she-will-be not (26)

יָמֶיךָ אֲמַלֵּא׃ אֶת־ אֵימָתִי אֲשַׁלַּח לְפָנֶיךָ
ahead-of-you I-will-send terror-of-me *** (27) I-will-lengthen days-of-you

וְהַמֹּתִי אֶת־ כָּל־ הָעָם אֲשֶׁר תָּבֹא בָּהֶם
against-them you-encounter that the-nation every-of *** and-I-will-confuse

וְנָתַתִּי אֶת־ כָּל־ אֹיְבֶיךָ אֵלֶיךָ עֹרֶף׃
back toward-you being-enemies-of-you all-of *** and-I-will-make

וְשָׁלַחְתִּי אֶת־ הַצִּרְעָה לְפָנֶיךָ וְגֵרְשָׁה אֶת־
*** and-she-will-drive-out ahead-of-you the-hornet *** and-I-will-send (28)

הַחִוִּי אֶת־ הַכְּנַעֲנִי וְאֶת־ הַחִתִּי מִלְּפָנֶיךָ׃ לֹא
not (29) from-before-you the-Hittite and the-Canaanite *** the-Hivite

אֲגָרְשֶׁנּוּ מִפָּנֶיךָ בְּשָׁנָה אֶחָת פֶּן־ תִּהְיֶה
she-would-become or single in-year from-before-you I-will-drive-out-him

הָאָרֶץ שְׁמָמָה וְרַבָּה עָלֶיךָ חַיַּת הַשָּׂדֶה׃ מְעַט
little (30) the-field animal-of for-you and-too-numerous desolate the-land

מְעַט אֲגָרְשֶׁנּוּ מִפָּנֶיךָ עַד אֲשֶׁר תִּפְרֶה
you-increase when until from-before-you I-will-drive-out-him little

וְנָחַלְתָּ אֶת־ הָאָרֶץ׃ וְשַׁתִּי אֶת־ גְּבֻלְךָ
border-of-you *** and-I-will-establish (31) the-land *** so-you-possess

מִיַּם־ סוּף וְעַד־ יָם פְּלִשְׁתִּים וּמִמִּדְבָּר עַד־ הַנָּהָר
the-River to and-from-desert Philistines Sea-of even-to Reed from-Sea-of

כִּי׀ אֶתֵּן בְּיֶדְכֶם אֵת יֹשְׁבֵי הָאָרֶץ
the-land ones-living-of *** into-hand-of-you I-will-give for

וְגֵרַשְׁתָּמוֹ מִפָּנֶיךָ׃ לֹא־ תִכְרֹת לָהֶם
with-them you-make not (32) from-before-you and-you-will-drive-out-them

into the land of the Amorites,
Hittites, Perizzites, Canaanites, Hivites and Jebusites,
and I will wipe them out. 24Do
not bow down before their
gods or worship them or follow their practices. You must
demolish them and break
their sacred stones to pieces.
25Worship the LORD your God,
and his blessing will be on
your food and water. I will
take away sickness from
among you, 26and none will
miscarry or be barren in your
land. I will give you a full life
span.
27"I will send my terror
ahead of you and throw into
confusion every nation you
encounter. I will make all your
enemies turn their backs and
run. 28I will send the hornet
ahead of you to drive the Hivites, Canaanites and Hittites
out of your way. 29But I will
not drive them out in a single
year, because the land would
become desolate and the wild
animals too numerous for you.
30Little by little I will drive
them out before you, until you
have increased enough to take
possession of the land.
31"I will establish your borders from the Red Sea[b] to the
Sea of the Philistines,[c] and
from the desert to the River.[d] I
will hand over to you the
people who live in the land
and you will drive them out
before you. 32Do not make a

[b]31 Hebrew *Yam Suph;* that is, Sea of Reeds
[c]31 That is, the Mediterranean
[d]31 That is, the Euphrates

וְלֵאלֹהֵיהֶם בְּרִית׃ לֹא יֵשְׁבוּ בְּאַרְצְךָ פֶּן־
or in-land-of-you let-them-live not (33) covenant or-with-gods-of-them

יַחֲטִיאוּ אֹתְךָ לִי כִּי תַעֲבֹד אֶת־ אֱלֹהֵיהֶם כִּי־
surely gods-of-them *** you-worship if against-me you they-will-cause-to-sin

יִהְיֶה לְךָ לְמוֹקֵשׁ׃ וְאֶל־ מֹשֶׁה אָמַר עֲלֵה אֶל־ יְהוָה
Yahweh to come-up! he-said Moses then-to (24:1) as-snare to-you he-will-be

אַתָּה וְאַהֲרֹן נָדָב וַאֲבִיהוּא וְשִׁבְעִים מִזִּקְנֵי יִשְׂרָאֵל
Israel from-elders-of and-seventy and-Abihu Nadab and-Aaron you

וְהִשְׁתַּחֲוִיתֶם מֵרָחֹק׃ וְנִגַּשׁ מֹשֶׁה לְבַדּוֹ אֶל־
to by-himself Moses but-he-shall-approach (2) at-distance and-you-worship

יְהוָה וְהֵם לֹא יִגָּשׁוּ וְהָעָם לֹא יַעֲלוּ
they-may-come-up not and-the-people they-may-approach not and-they Yahweh

עִמּוֹ׃ וַיָּבֹא מֹשֶׁה וַיְסַפֵּר לָעָם אֵת כָּל־ דִּבְרֵי
words-of all-of *** to-the-people and-he-told Moses when-he-went (3) with-him

יְהוָה וְאֵת כָּל־ הַמִּשְׁפָּטִים וַיַּעַן כָּל־ הָעָם קוֹל אֶחָד
one voice the-people all-of then-he-responded the-laws all-of and Yahweh

וַיֹּאמְרוּ כָּל־ הַדְּבָרִים אֲשֶׁר־ דִּבֶּר יְהוָה נַעֲשֶׂה׃ וַיִּכְתֹּב
and-he-wrote (4) we-will-do Yahweh he-said that the-things all-of and-they-said

מֹשֶׁה אֵת כָּל־ דִּבְרֵי יְהוָה וַיַּשְׁכֵּם בַּבֹּקֶר וַיִּבֶן
and-he-built in-the-morning and-he-got-up Yahweh words-of all-of *** Moses

מִזְבֵּחַ תַּחַת הָהָר וּשְׁתֵּים עֶשְׂרֵה מַצֵּבָה לִשְׁנֵים עָשָׂר שִׁבְטֵי
tribes-of ten for-two stone-pillar ten and-two the-mountain foot-of altar

יִשְׂרָאֵל׃ וַיִּשְׁלַח אֶת־ נַעֲרֵי בְּנֵי יִשְׂרָאֵל וַיַּעֲלוּ
and-they-offered Israel sons-of young-men-of *** and-he-sent (5) Israel

עֹלֹת וַיִּזְבְּחוּ זְבָחִים שְׁלָמִים לַיהוָה
to-Yahweh fellowship-offerings sacrifices and-they-sacrificed burnt-offerings

פָּרִים׃ וַיִּקַּח מֹשֶׁה חֲצִי הַדָּם וַיָּשֶׂם בָּאַגָּנֹת
in-the-bowls and-he-put the-blood half-of Moses and-he-took (6) bulls

וַחֲצִי הַדָּם זָרַק עַל־ הַמִּזְבֵּחַ׃ וַיִּקַּח סֵפֶר
Book-of then-he-took (7) the-altar against he-sprinkled the-blood and-half-of

הַבְּרִית וַיִּקְרָא בְּאָזְנֵי הָעָם וַיֹּאמְרוּ כֹּל אֲשֶׁר־
that all and-they-responded the-people in-ears-of and-he-read the-Covenant

דִּבֶּר יְהוָה נַעֲשֶׂה וְנִשְׁמָע׃ וַיִּקַּח מֹשֶׁה אֶת־ הַדָּם
the-blood *** Moses then-he-took (8) and-we-will-obey we-will-do Yahweh he-said

וַיִּזְרֹק עַל־ הָעָם וַיֹּאמֶר הִנֵּה דַם־ הַבְּרִית אֲשֶׁר
that the-covenant blood-of see! and-he-said the-people on and-he-sprinkled

כָּרַת יְהוָה עִמָּכֶם עַל כָּל־ הַדְּבָרִים הָאֵלֶּה׃
the-these the-words all-of according-to with-you Yahweh he-made

covenant with them or with
their gods. 33Do not let them
live in your land, or they will
cause you to sin against me,
because the worship of their
gods will certainly be a snare
to you."

The Covenant Confirmed

24 Then he said to Moses, "Come up to the LORD, you and Aaron, Nadab and Abihu, and seventy of the elders of Israel. You are to worship at a distance,
2but Moses alone is to approach the LORD; the others must not come near. And the people may not come up with him."
3When Moses went and told the people all the LORD's words and laws, they responded with one voice, "Everything the LORD has said we will do."
4Moses then wrote down everything the LORD had said.
He got up early the next morning and built an altar at the foot of the mountain and set up twelve stone pillars representing the twelve tribes of Israel.
5Then he sent young Israelite men, and they offered burnt offerings and sacrificed young bulls as fellowship offerings[c] to the LORD.
6Moses took half of the blood and put it in bowls, and the other half he sprinkled on the altar.
7Then he took the Book of the Covenant and read it to the people. They responded, "We will do everything the LORD has said; we will obey."
8Moses then took the blood, sprinkled it on the people and said, "This is the blood of the covenant that the LORD has made with you in accordance with all these words."

[c]5 Traditionally *peace offerings*

וַיַּעַל מֹשֶׁה וְאַהֲרֹן נָדָב וַאֲבִיהוּא וְשִׁבְעִים מִזִּקְנֵי

from-elders-of and-seventy and-Abihu Nadab and-Aaron Moses then-he-went-up (9)

יִשְׂרָאֵל׃ וַיִּרְאוּ אֵת אֱלֹהֵי יִשְׂרָאֵל וְתַחַת רַגְלָיו

feet-of-him and-under Israel God-of *** and-they-saw (10) Israel

כְּמַעֲשֵׂה לִבְנַת הַסַּפִּיר וּכְעֶצֶם הַשָּׁמַיִם לָטֹהַר׃

for-clearness the-skies and-like-very-of the-sapphire stone-of like-pavement-of

וְאֶל־ אֲצִילֵי בְּנֵי יִשְׂרָאֵל לֹא שָׁלַח יָדוֹ

hand-of-him he-raised not Israel sons-of leaders-of but-against (11)

וַיֶּחֱזוּ אֶת־ הָאֱלֹהִים וַיֹּאכְלוּ וַיִּשְׁתּוּ׃ וַיֹּאמֶר יְהוָה

Yahweh then-he-said (12) and-they-drank and-they-ate the-God *** so-they-saw

אֶל־ מֹשֶׁה עֲלֵה אֵלַי הָהָרָה וֶהְיֵה־ שָׁם וְאֶתְּנָה

and-I-will-give here and-stay! on-the-mountain to-me come-up! Moses to

לְךָ אֶת־ לֻחֹת הָאֶבֶן וְהַתּוֹרָה וְהַמִּצְוָה אֲשֶׁר כָּתַבְתִּי

I-wrote that and-the-command with-the-law the-stone tablets-of *** to-you

לְהוֹרֹתָם׃ וַיָּקָם מֹשֶׁה וִיהוֹשֻׁעַ מְשָׁרְתוֹ

one-aiding-him with-Joshua Moses so-he-set-out (13) to-instruct-them

וַיַּעַל מֹשֶׁה אֶל־ הַר הָאֱלֹהִים׃ וְאֶל־ הַזְּקֵנִים אָמַר

he-said the-elders and-to (14) the-God mountain-of on Moses and-he-went-up

שְׁבוּ־ לָנוּ בָזֶה עַד אֲשֶׁר־ נָשׁוּב אֲלֵיכֶם וְהִנֵּה אַהֲרֹן וְחוּר

and-Hur Aaron now-see! to-you we-come-back when until at-here for-us wait!

עִמָּכֶם מִי־ בַעַל דְּבָרִים יִגַּשׁ אֲלֵהֶם׃ וַיַּעַל

when-he-went-up (15) to-them he-can-go disputes involved-of whoever with-you

מֹשֶׁה אֶל־ הָהָר וַיְכַס הֶעָנָן אֶת־ הָהָר׃

the-mountain *** the-cloud then-he-covered the-mountain on Moses

וַיִּשְׁכֹּן כְּבוֹד־ יְהוָה עַל־ הַר סִינַי וַיְכַסֵּהוּ הֶעָנָן

the-cloud and-he-covered-him Sinai Mount-of on Yahweh glory-of and-he-settled (16)

שֵׁשֶׁת יָמִים וַיִּקְרָא אֶל־ מֹשֶׁה בַּיּוֹם הַשְּׁבִיעִי מִתּוֹךְ

from-within the-seventh on-the-day Moses to then-he-called days six-of

הֶעָנָן׃ וּמַרְאֵה כְּבוֹד יְהוָה כְּאֵשׁ אֹכֶלֶת

consuming like-fire Yahweh glory-of and-appearance-of (17) the-cloud

בְּרֹאשׁ הָהָר לְעֵינֵי בְּנֵי יִשְׂרָאֵל׃ וַיָּבֹא מֹשֶׁה

Moses then-he-entered (18) Israel sons-of to-eyes-of the-mountain on-top-of

בְּתוֹךְ הֶעָנָן וַיַּעַל אֶל־ הָהָר וַיְהִי מֹשֶׁה בָּהָר

on-the-mountain Moses and-he-was the-mountain on and-he-went-up the-cloud into

אַרְבָּעִים יוֹם וְאַרְבָּעִים לָיְלָה׃ וַיְדַבֵּר יְהוָה אֶל־ מֹשֶׁה לֵּאמֹר׃

to-say Moses to Yahweh and-he-spoke (25:1) night and-forty day forty

דַּבֵּר אֶל־ בְּנֵי יִשְׂרָאֵל וְיִקְחוּ־ לִי תְּרוּמָה מֵאֵת כָּל־ אִישׁ

man every-of from offering to-me so-they-bring Israel sons-of to tell! (2)

9 Moses and Aaron, Nadab
and Abihu, and the seventy
elders of Israel went up 10 and
saw the God of Israel. Under
his feet was something like a
pavement made of sapphire,[f]
clear as the sky itself. 11 But
God did not raise his hand
against these leaders of the Israelites;
they saw God, and
they ate and drank.

12 The LORD said to Moses,
"Come up to me on the mountain
and stay here, and I will
give you the tablets of stone,
with the law and commands I
have written for their instruction."

13 Then Moses set out with
Joshua his aide, and Moses
went up on the mountain of
God. 14 He said to the elders,
"Wait here for us until we
come back to you. Aaron and
Hur are with you, and anyone
involved in a dispute can go to
them."

15 When Moses went up on
the mountain, the cloud
covered it, 16 and the glory of
the LORD settled on Mount
Sinai. For six days the cloud
covered the mountain, and on
the seventh day the LORD
called to Moses from within
the cloud. 17 To the Israelites
the glory of the LORD looked
like a consuming fire on top of
the mountain. 18 Then Moses
entered the cloud as he went
on up the mountain. And he
stayed on the mountain forty
days and forty nights.

Offerings for the Tabernacle

25 The LORD said to
Moses, 2 "Tell the Israelites
to bring me an offering.

[f] 10 Or *lapis lazuli*

אֲשֶׁר יִדְּבֶנּוּ לִבּוֹ תִּקְחוּ אֶת־ תְּרוּמָתִי׃ וְזֹאת
and-this (3) offering-of-me *** you-receive heart-of-him he-prompts-him who

הַתְּרוּמָה אֲשֶׁר תִּקְחוּ מֵאִתָּם זָהָב וָכֶסֶף וּנְחֹשֶׁת׃
and-bronze and-silver gold from-them you-receive that the-offering

וּתְכֵלֶת וְאַרְגָּמָן וְתוֹלַעַת שָׁנִי וְשֵׁשׁ וְעִזִּים׃
and-goat-hairs and-fine-linen yarn and-scarlet-of and-purple and-blue (4)

וְעֹרֹת אֵילִם מְאָדָּמִים וְעֹרֹת תְּחָשִׁים וַעֲצֵי
and-woods-of sea-cows and-hides-of being-dyed-red rams and-skins-of (5)

שִׁטִּים׃ שֶׁמֶן לַמָּאֹר בְּשָׂמִים לְשֶׁמֶן הַמִּשְׁחָה
the-annointing for-oil-of spices for-the-light olive-oil (6) acacias

וְלִקְטֹרֶת הַסַּמִּים׃ אַבְנֵי־ שֹׁהַם וְאַבְנֵי
and-stones-of onyx stones-of (7) the-fragrances and-for-incense-of

מִלֻּאִים לָאֵפֹד וְלַחֹשֶׁן׃ וְעָשׂוּ
then-they-shall-make (8) and-for-the-breastpiece for-the-ephod mounted-ones

לִי מִקְדָּשׁ וְשָׁכַנְתִּי בְּתוֹכָם׃ כְּכֹל אֲשֶׁר אֲנִי מַרְאֶה
showing I that like-all (9) among-them and-I-will-dwell sanctuary for-me

אוֹתְךָ אֵת תַּבְנִית הַמִּשְׁכָּן וְאֵת תַּבְנִית כָּל־ כֵּלָיו
furnishings-of-him all-of pattern-of and the-tabernacle pattern-of *** you

וְכֵן תַּעֲשׂוּ׃ וְעָשׂוּ אֲרוֹן עֲצֵי שִׁטִּים
acacias woods-of chest-of now-they-shall-make (10) you-shall-make and-so

אַמָּתַיִם וָחֵצִי אָרְכּוֹ וְאַמָּה וָחֵצִי רָחְבּוֹ וְאַמָּה
and-cubit width-of-him and-half and-cubit length-of-him and-half two-cubits

וָחֵצִי קֹמָתוֹ׃ וְצִפִּיתָ אֹתוֹ זָהָב טָהוֹר מִבַּיִת
on-inside pure gold him then-you-overlay (11) height-of-him and-half

וּמִחוּץ תְּצַפֶּנּוּ וְעָשִׂיתָ עָלָיו זֵר זָהָב סָבִיב׃
around gold molding on-him and-you-make you-overlay-him and-on-outside

וְיָצַקְתָּ לּוֹ אַרְבַּע טַבְּעֹת זָהָב וְנָתַתָּה עַל אַרְבַּע פַּעֲמֹתָיו
feet-of-him four to and-you-fasten gold rings four for-him and-you-cast (12)

וּשְׁתֵּי טַבָּעֹת עַל־ צַלְעוֹ הָאֶחָת וּשְׁתֵּי טַבָּעֹת עַל־ צַלְעוֹ
side-of-him on rings and-two-of the-one side-of-him on rings with-two-of

הַשֵּׁנִית׃ וְעָשִׂיתָ בַדֵּי עֲצֵי שִׁטִּים וְצִפִּיתָ אֹתָם
them and-you-overlay acacias woods-of poles-of then-you-make (13) the-other

זָהָב׃ וְהֵבֵאתָ אֶת־ הַבַּדִּים בַּטַּבָּעֹת עַל צַלְעֹת הָאָרֹן
the-chest sides-of on into-the-rings the-poles *** and-you-insert (14) gold

לָשֵׂאת אֶת־ הָאָרֹן בָּהֶם׃ בְּטַבְּעֹת הָאָרֹן יִהְיוּ
they-will-remain the-chest in-rings-of (15) with-them the-chest *** to-carry

הַבַּדִּים לֹא יָסֻרוּ מִמֶּנּוּ׃ וְנָתַתָּ אֶל־ הָאָרֹן
the-chest in then-you-put (16) from-him they-may-be-removed not the-poles

You are to receive the offering
for me from each man whose
heart prompts him to give.
3These are the offerings you
are to receive from them: gold,
silver and bronze; 4blue, purple and scarlet yarn and fine
linen; goat hair; 5ram skins
dyed red and hides of sea
cows; acacia wood; 6olive oil
for the light; spices for the
anointing oil and for the fragrant incense; 7and onyx
stones and other gems to be
mounted on the ephod and
breastpiece.

8"Then have them make a
sanctuary for me, and I will
dwell among them. 9Make this
tabernacle and all its furnishings exactly like the pattern I will show you.

The Ark

10"Have them make a chest
of acacia wood—two and a
half cubits long, a cubit and a
half wide, and a cubit and a
half high.[g] 11Overlay it with
pure gold, both inside and out,
and make a gold molding
around it. 12Cast four gold
rings for it and fasten them to
its four feet, with two rings on
one side and two rings on the
other. 13Then make poles of
acacia wood and overlay them
with gold. 14Insert the poles
into the rings on the sides of
the chest to carry it. 15The
poles are to remain in the
rings of this ark; they are not
to be removed. 16Then put in

g10 That is, about 3 3/4 feet (about 1.1 meters) long and 2 1/4 feet (about 0.7 meter) wide and high

אֶת הָעֵדֻת אֲשֶׁר אֶתֵּן אֵלֶיךָ׃ וְעָשִׂיתָ כַפֹּרֶת
atonement-cover then-you-make (17) to-you I-will-give which the-Testimony ***

זָהָב טָהוֹר אַמָּתַיִם וָחֵצִי אָרְכָּהּ וְאַמָּה וָחֵצִי רָחְבָּהּ׃
width-of-her and-half and-cubit length-of-her and-half two-cubits pure gold

וְעָשִׂיתָ שְׁנַיִם כְּרֻבִים זָהָב מִקְשָׁה תַּעֲשֶׂה אֹתָם מִשְּׁנֵי קְצוֹת
ends-of at-two-of them you-make hammered gold cherubim two and-you-make (18)

הַכַּפֹּרֶת׃ וַעֲשֵׂה כְּרוּב אֶחָד מִקָּצָה מִזֶּה וּכְרוּב־אֶחָד מִקָּצָה
at-end one and-cherub at-this at-end one cherub and-make! (19) the-cover

מִזֶּה מִן־הַכַּפֹּרֶת תַּעֲשׂוּ אֶת־הַכְּרֻבִים עַל־שְׁנֵי קְצוֹתָיו׃
ends-of-him two-of at the-cherubim *** you-make the-cover with at-other

וְהָיוּ הַכְּרֻבִים פֹּרְשֵׂי כְנָפַיִם לְמַעְלָה
to-upward wings ones-spreading-of the-cherubim and-they-shall-be (20)

סֹכְכִים בְּכַנְפֵיהֶם עַל־הַכַּפֹּרֶת וּפְנֵיהֶם
and-faces-of-them the-cover over with-wings-of-them ones-overshadowing

אִישׁ אֶל־אָחִיו אֶל־הַכַּפֹּרֶת יִהְיוּ פְּנֵי
faces-of they-shall-be the-cover toward other-of-him toward each

הַכְּרֻבִים׃ וְנָתַתָּ אֶת־הַכַּפֹּרֶת עַל־הָאָרֹן מִלְמָעְלָה וְאֶל־
and-into onto-top the-ark on the-cover *** then-you-place (21) the-cherubim

הָאָרֹן תִּתֵּן אֶת־הָעֵדֻת אֲשֶׁר אֶתֵּן אֵלֶיךָ׃
to-you I-will-give which the-Testimony *** you-put the-ark

וְנוֹעַדְתִּי לְךָ שָׁם וְדִבַּרְתִּי אִתְּךָ מֵעַל הַכַּפֹּרֶת
the-cover from-above to-you and-I-will-tell there with-you and-I-will-meet (22)

מִבֵּין שְׁנֵי הַכְּרֻבִים אֲשֶׁר עַל־אֲרֹן הָעֵדֻת אֵת כָּל־
all *** the-Testimony ark-of over that the-cherubim two-of from-between

אֲשֶׁר אֲצַוֶּה אוֹתְךָ אֶל־בְּנֵי יִשְׂרָאֵל׃ וְעָשִׂיתָ שֻׁלְחָן עֲצֵי
woods-of table and-you-make (23) Israel sons-of for you I-command that

שִׁטִּים אַמָּתַיִם אָרְכּוֹ וְאַמָּה רָחְבּוֹ וְאַמָּה וָחֵצִי
and-half and-cubit width-of-him and-cubit length-of-him two-cubits acacias

קֹמָתוֹ׃ וְצִפִּיתָ אֹתוֹ זָהָב טָהוֹר וְעָשִׂיתָ לּוֹ
for-him and-you-make pure gold him and-you-overlay (24) height-of-him

זֵר זָהָב סָבִיב׃ וְעָשִׂיתָ לּוֹ מִסְגֶּרֶת טֹפַח סָבִיב
around handbreadth rim-of for-him also-you-make (25) around gold molding

וְעָשִׂיתָ זֵר־זָהָב לְמִסְגַּרְתּוֹ סָבִיב׃ וְעָשִׂיתָ לּוֹ
for-him and-you-make (26) around on-rim-of-him gold molding and-you-put

אַרְבַּע טַבְּעֹת זָהָב וְנָתַתָּ אֶת־הַטַּבָּעֹת עַל אַרְבַּע הַפֵּאֹת אֲשֶׁר
which the-corners four to the-rings *** and-you-fasten gold rings four

לְאַרְבַּע רַגְלָיו׃ לְעֻמַּת הַמִּסְגֶּרֶת תִּהְיֶיןָ הַטַּבָּעֹת לְבָתִּים
as-holders the-rings they-shall-be the-rim close-to (27) legs-of-him at-four

the ark the Testimony, which I will give you.

17 "Make an atonement cover of pure gold—two and a half cubits long and a cubit and a half wide.[i] 18 And make two cherubim out of hammered gold at the ends of the cover. 19 Make one cherub on one end and the second cherub on the other; make the cherubim of one piece with the cover, at the two ends. 20 The cherubim are to have their wings spread upward, overshadowing the cover with them. The cherubim are to face each other, looking toward the cover. 21 Place the cover on top of the ark and put in the ark the Testimony, which I will give you. 22 There, above the cover between the two cherubim that are over the ark of the Testimony, I will meet with you and give you all my commands for the Israelites.

The Table

23 "Make a table of acacia wood—two cubits long, a cubit wide and a cubit and a half high.[j] 24 Overlay it with pure gold and make a gold molding around it. 25 Also make around it a rim a handbreadth wide and put a gold molding on the rim. 26 Make four gold rings for the table and fasten them to the four corners, where the four legs are. 27 The rings are to be close to the rim to hold the

i 17 That is, about 3 3/4 feet (about 1.1 meters) long and 2 1/4 feet (about 0.7 meter) wide

j 23 That is, about 3 feet (about 0.9 meter) long and 1 1/2 feet (about 0.5 meter) wide and 2 1/4 feet (about 0.7 meter) high

לְבַדִּים לָשֵׂאת אֶת־ הַשֻּׁלְחָן׃ וְעָשִׂיתָ אֶת־ הַבַּדִּים עֲצֵי
woods-of the-poles *** and-you-make (28) the-table *** to-carry for-poles

שִׁטִּים וְצִפִּיתָ אֹתָם זָהָב וְנִשָּׂא־ בָם אֶת־
*** with-them and-he-shall-be-carried gold them and-you-overlay acacias

הַשֻּׁלְחָן׃ וְעָשִׂיתָ קְּעָרֹתָיו וְכַפֹּתָיו וּקְשׂוֹתָיו
and-pitchers-of-him and-ladles-of-him plates-of-him and-you-make (29) the-table

וּמְנַקִּיֹּתָיו אֲשֶׁר יֻסַּךְ בָּהֵן זָהָב טָהוֹר תַּעֲשֶׂה אֹתָם׃
them you-make pure gold with-them he-pours-offering that and-bowls-of-him

וְנָתַתָּ עַל־ הַשֻּׁלְחָן לֶחֶם פָּנִים לְפָנַי תָּמִיד׃
always before-me Presences bread-of the-table on and-you-put (30)

וְעָשִׂיתָ מְנֹרַת זָהָב טָהוֹר מִקְשָׁה תֵּעָשֶׂה
she-shall-be-made hammered pure gold lampstand-of and-you-make (31)

הַמְּנוֹרָה יְרֵכָהּ וְקָנָהּ גְּבִיעֶיהָ כַּפְתֹּרֶיהָ
buds-of-her flower-cups-of-her and-shaft-of-her base-of-her the-lampstand

וּפְרָחֶיהָ מִמֶּנָּה יִהְיוּ׃ וְשִׁשָּׁה קָנִים
branches and-six (32) they-shall-be from-her and-blossoms-of-her

יֹצְאִים מִצִּדֶּיהָ שְׁלֹשָׁה ׀ קְנֵי מְנֹרָה מִצִּדָּהּ
from-side-of-her lampstand branches-of three from-sides-of-her ones-extending

הָאֶחָד וּשְׁלֹשָׁה קְנֵי מְנֹרָה מִצִּדָּהּ הַשֵּׁנִי׃ שְׁלֹשָׁה
three (33) the-other from-side-of-her lampstand branches-of and-three the-one

גְבִעִים מְשֻׁקָּדִים בַּקָּנֶה הָאֶחָד כַּפְתֹּר וָפֶרַח וּשְׁלֹשָׁה גְבִעִים
cups and-three and-blossom bud the-one on-the-branch being-like-almonds cups

מְשֻׁקָּדִים בַּקָּנֶה הָאֶחָד כַּפְתֹּר וָפָרַח כֵּן לְשֵׁשֶׁת
for-six-of same and-blossom bud the-next on-the-branch being-like-almonds

הַקָּנִים הַיֹּצְאִים מִן־ הַמְּנֹרָה׃ וּבַמְּנֹרָה
and-on-the-lampstand (34) the-lampstand from the-ones-extending the-branches

אַרְבָּעָה גְבִעִים מְשֻׁקָּדִים כַּפְתֹּרֶיהָ וּפְרָחֶיהָ׃ וְכַפְתֹּר
and-bud (35) and-blossoms-of-her buds-of-her being-like-almonds cups four

תַּחַת שְׁנֵי הַקָּנִים מִמֶּנָּה וְכַפְתֹּר תַּחַת שְׁנֵי הַקָּנִים
the-branches pair-of under and-bud from-her the-branches pair-of under

מִמֶּנָּה וְכַפְתֹּר תַּחַת־ שְׁנֵי הַקָּנִים מִמֶּנָּה לְשֵׁשֶׁת הַקָּנִים
the-branches for-six-of from-her the-branches pair-of under and-bud from-her

הַיֹּצְאִים מִן־ הַמְּנֹרָה׃ כַּפְתֹּרֵיהֶם וּקְנֹתָם
and-branches-of-them buds-of-them (36) the-lampstand from the-ones-extending

מִמֶּנָּה יִהְיוּ כֻּלָּהּ מִקְשָׁה אַחַת זָהָב טָהוֹר׃
pure gold one-piece hammered-out all-of-her they-shall-be from-her

וְעָשִׂיתָ אֶת־ נֵרֹתֶיהָ שִׁבְעָה וְהֶעֱלָה אֶת־
*** and-he-will-be-set-up seven lamps-of-her *** then-you-make (37)

poles used in carrying the table. [28]Make the poles of acacia
wood, overlay them with gold
and carry the table with them.
[29]And make its plates and ladles of pure gold, as well as its
pitchers and bowls for the
pouring out of offerings. [30]Put
the bread of the Presence on
this table to be before me at all
times.

The Lampstand

[31]"Make a lampstand of pure
gold and hammer it out, base
and shaft; its flowerlike cups,
buds and blossoms shall be of
one piece with it. [32]Six branches are to extend from the sides
of the lampstand—three on
one side and three on the other. [33]Three cups shaped like almond flowers with buds and
blossoms are to be on one
branch, three on the next
branch, and the same for all
six branches extending from
the lampstand. [34]And on the
lampstand there are to be four
cups shaped like almond flowers with buds and blossoms.
[35]One bud shall be under the
first pair of branches extending from the lampstand, a
second bud under the second
pair, and a third bud under the
third pair—six branches in all.
[36]The buds and branches shall
all be of one piece with the
lampstand, hammered out of
pure gold.

[37]"Then make its seven
lamps and set them up on it so

נֵרֹתֶיהָ וְהֵאִיר עַל־ עֵבֶר פָּנֶיהָ׃ וּמַלְקָחֶיהָ
and-trimmers-of-her (38) in-front-of-her space on so-he-will-light lamps-of-her

וּמַחְתֹּתֶיהָ זָהָב טָהוֹר׃ כִּכָּר זָהָב טָהוֹר יַעֲשֶׂה אֹתָהּ אֵת
*** her he-shall-make pure gold talent (39) pure gold and-trays-of-her

כָּל־ הַכֵּלִים הָאֵלֶּה׃ וּרְאֵה וַעֲשֵׂה בְּתַבְנִיתָם
as-pattern-of-them and-make! now-see! (40) the-these the-accessories all-of

אֲשֶׁר־אַתָּה מָרְאֶה בָּהָר׃ וְאֶת־ הַמִּשְׁכָּן תַּעֲשֶׂה עֶשֶׂר
ten you-make the-tabernacle and (26:1) on-the-mountain being-shown you that

יְרִיעֹת שֵׁשׁ מָשְׁזָר וּתְכֵלֶת וְאַרְגָּמָן וְתֹלַעַת שָׁנִי
yarn and-scarlet and-purple and-blue being-twisted fine-linen curtains

כְּרֻבִים מַעֲשֵׂה חֹשֵׁב תַּעֲשֶׂה אֹתָם׃ אֹרֶךְ ׀ הַיְרִיעָה הָאַחַת
the-each the-curtain length-of (2) them you-make being-skillful work-of cherubim

שְׁמֹנֶה וְעֶשְׂרִים בָּאַמָּה וְרֹחַב אַרְבַּע בָּאַמָּה הַיְרִיעָה
the-curtain by-the-cubit four and-width by-the-cubit and-twenty eight

הָאֶחָת מִדָּה אַחַת לְכָל־ הַיְרִיעֹת׃ חֲמֵשׁ הַיְרִיעֹת
the-curtains five-of (3) the-curtains for-all-of same size the-each

תִּהְיֶיןָ חֹבְרֹת אִשָּׁה אֶל־ אֲחֹתָהּ וְחָמֵשׁ יְרִיעֹת
curtains and-five other-of-her with each ones-being-joined they-shall-be

חֹבְרֹת אִשָּׁה אֶל־ אֲחֹתָהּ׃ וְעָשִׂיתָ לֻלְאֹת תְּכֵלֶת
blue loops-of and-you-make (4) other-of-her with each ones-being-joined

עַל שְׂפַת הַיְרִיעָה הָאֶחָת מִקָּצָה בַּחֹבָרֶת וְכֵן תַּעֲשֶׂה
you-do and-same of-the-set at-end the-one the-curtain edge-of along

בִּשְׂפַת הַיְרִיעָה הַקִּיצוֹנָה בַּמַּחְבֶּרֶת הַשֵּׁנִית׃ חֲמִשִּׁים לֻלָאֹת
loops fifty (5) the-other of-the-set the-end-one the-curtain on-edge-of

תַּעֲשֶׂה בַּיְרִיעָה הָאֶחָת וַחֲמִשִּׁים לֻלָאֹת תַּעֲשֶׂה בִּקְצֵה הַיְרִיעָה
the-curtain on-end-of you-make loops and-fity the-one on-the-curtain you-make

אֲשֶׁר בַּמַּחְבֶּרֶת הַשֵּׁנִית מַקְבִּילֹת הַלֻּלָאֹת אִשָּׁה אֶל־ אֲחֹתָהּ׃
other-of-her to each the-loops opposing the-other of-the-set that

וְעָשִׂיתָ חֲמִשִּׁים קַרְסֵי זָהָב וְחִבַּרְתָּ אֶת־ הַיְרִיעֹת אִשָּׁה
each the-curtains *** and-you-fasten gold clasps-of fifty and-you-make (6)

אֶל־ אֲחֹתָהּ בַּקְּרָסִים וְהָיָה הַמִּשְׁכָּן אֶחָד׃ וְעָשִׂיתָ
and-you-make (7) unit the-tabernacle so-he-is with-the-clasps other-of-her to

יְרִיעֹת עִזִּים לְאֹהֶל עַל־ הַמִּשְׁכָּן עַשְׁתֵּי־ עֶשְׂרֵה יְרִיעֹת
curtains ten one the-tabernacle over for-tent goat-hairs curtains-of

תַּעֲשֶׂה אֹתָם׃ אֹרֶךְ ׀ הַיְרִיעָה הָאַחַת שְׁלֹשִׁים בָּאַמָּה
by-the-cubit thirty the-each the-curtain length-of (8) them you-make

וְרֹחַב אַרְבַּע בָּאַמָּה הַיְרִיעָה הָאֶחָת מִדָּה אַחַת לְעַשְׁתֵּי עֶשְׂרֵה
ten for-one same size the-each the-curtain by-the-cubit four and-width

that they light the space in
front of it. 38Its wick trimmers
and trays are to be of pure
gold. 39A talent[k] of pure gold is
to be used for the lampstand
and all these accessories. 40See
that you make them according
to the pattern shown you on
the mountain.

The Tabernacle

26 "Make the tabernacle
with ten curtains of
finely twisted linen and blue,
purple and scarlet yarn, with
cherubim worked into them
by a skilled craftsman. 2All the
curtains are to be the same
size—twenty-eight cubits long
and four cubits wide.[l] 3Join
five of the curtains together,
and do the same with the other five. 4Make loops of blue
material along the edge of the
end curtain in one set, and do
the same with the end curtain
in the other set. 5Make fifty
loops on one curtain and fifty
loops on the end curtain of the
other set, with the loops opposite each other. 6Then make
fifty gold clasps and use them
to fasten the curtains together
so that the tabernacle is a unit.
7"Make curtains of goat hair
for the tent over the tabernacle—eleven altogether. 8All
eleven curtains are to be the
same size—thirty cubits long
and four cubits wide.[m] 9Join

[k]39 That is, about 75 pounds (about 34 kilograms)
[l]2 That is, about 42 feet (about 12.5 meters) long and 6 feet (about 1.8 meters) wide
[m]8 That is, about 45 feet (about 13.5 meters) long and 6 feet (about 1.8 meters) wide

יְרִיעֹת׃ וְחִבַּרְתָּ אֶת־ חֲמֵשׁ הַיְרִיעֹת לְבָד וְאֶת־ שֵׁשׁ

six-of and into-one the-curtains five-of *** then-you-join (9) curtains

הַיְרִיעֹת לְבָד וְכָפַלְתָּ אֶת־ הַיְרִיעָה הַשִּׁשִּׁית אֶל־ מוּל

front at the-sixth the-curtain *** then-you-fold into-one the-curtains

פְּנֵי הָאֹהֶל׃ וְעָשִׂיתָ חֲמִשִּׁים לֻלָאֹת עַל שְׂפַת הַיְרִיעָה

the-curtain edge-of along loops fifty and-you-make (10) the-tent face-of

הָאֶחָת הַקִּיצֹנָה בַּחֹבָרֶת וַחֲמִשִּׁים לֻלָאֹת עַל שְׂפַת הַיְרִיעָה

the-curtain edge-of along loops and-fifty of-the-set the-end-one the-one

הַחֹבֶרֶת הַשֵּׁנִית׃ וְעָשִׂיתָ קַרְסֵי נְחֹשֶׁת חֲמִשִּׁים וְהֵבֵאתָ אֶת־

*** and-you-put fifty bronze clasps-of and-you-make (11) the-other the-set

הַקְּרָסִים בַּלֻּלָאֹת וְחִבַּרְתָּ אֶת־ הָאֹהֶל וְהָיָה אֶחָד׃

unit so-he-is the-tent *** so-you-fasten in-the-loops the-clasps

וְסֶרַח הָעֹדֵף בִּירִיעֹת הָאֹהֶל חֲצִי הַיְרִיעָה

the-curtain half-of the-tent on-curtains-of the-being-additional and-length-of (12)

הָעֹדֶפֶת תִּסְרַח עַל אֲחֹרֵי הַמִּשְׁכָּן׃

the-tabernacle rear-of at she-will-hang-down the-being-left-over

וְהָאַמָּה מִזֶּה וְהָאַמָּה מִזֶּה בָּעֹדֵף

on-the-being-left-over on-that-side and-the-cubit on-this-side and-the-cubit (13)

בְּאֹרֶךְ יְרִיעֹת הָאֹהֶל יִהְיֶה סָרוּחַ עַל־ צִדֵּי

sides-of over hanging he-will-be the-tent curtains-of in-length-of

הַמִּשְׁכָּן מִזֶּה וּמִזֶּה לְכַסֹּתוֹ׃ וְעָשִׂיתָ

and-you-make (14) to-cover-him and-on-that-side on-this-side the-tabernacle

מִכְסֶה לָאֹהֶל עֹרֹת אֵילִם מְאָדָּמִים וּמִכְסֵה עֹרֹת

hides-of and-cover-of being-dyed-red rams skins-of for-the-tent cover

תְּחָשִׁים מִלְמָעְלָה׃ וְעָשִׂיתָ אֶת־ הַקְּרָשִׁים לַמִּשְׁכָּן עֲצֵי

woods-of for-the-tabernacle the-frames *** and-you-make (15) for-above sea-cows

שִׁטִּים עֹמְדִים׃ עֶשֶׂר אַמּוֹת אֹרֶךְ הַקָּרֶשׁ וְאַמָּה

and-cubit the-frame length-of cubits ten (16) ones-being-upright acacias

וַחֲצִי הָאַמָּה רֹחַב הַקֶּרֶשׁ הָאֶחָד׃ שְׁתֵּי יָדוֹת

projections two-of (17) the-each the-frame width-of the-cubit and-half-of

לַקֶּרֶשׁ הָאֶחָד מְשֻׁלָּבֹת אִשָּׁה אֶל־ אֲחֹתָהּ כֵּן תַּעֲשֶׂה לְכֹל

to-all-of you-do same other-of-her to each paralleling the-each in-the-frame

קַרְשֵׁי הַמִּשְׁכָּן׃ וְעָשִׂיתָ אֶת־ הַקְּרָשִׁים לַמִּשְׁכָּן

for-the-tabernacle the-frames *** and-you-make (18) the-tabernacle frames-of

עֶשְׂרִים קֶרֶשׁ לִפְאַת נֶגְבָּה תֵימָנָה׃ וְאַרְבָּעִים אַדְנֵי־ כֶסֶף תַּעֲשֶׂה

you-make silver bases-of and-forty (19) south to-south for-side-of frame twenty

תַּחַת עֶשְׂרִים הַקָּרֶשׁ שְׁנֵי אֲדָנִים תַּחַת־ הַקֶּרֶשׁ הָאֶחָד לִשְׁתֵּי

for-two-of the-each the-frame under bases two-of the-frame twenty under

five of the curtains together into one set and the other six into another set. Fold the sixth curtain double at the front of the tent. [10]Make fifty loops along the edge of the end curtain in one set and also along the edge of the end curtain in the other set. [11]Then make fifty bronze clasps and put them in the loops to fasten the tent together as a unit. [12]As for the additional length of the tent curtains, the half curtain that is left over is to hang down at the rear of the tabernacle. [13]The tent curtains will be a cubit[n] longer on both sides; what is left will hang over the sides of the tabernacle so as to cover it. [14]Make for the tent a covering of ram skins dyed red, and over that a covering of hides of sea cows.

[15]"Make upright frames of acacia wood for the tabernacle. [16]Each frame is to be ten cubits long and a cubit and a half wide,[o] [17]with two projections set parallel to each other. Make all the frames of the tabernacle in this way. [18]Make twenty frames for the south side of the tabernacle [19]and make forty silver bases to go under them—two bases for each frame, one under

[n]*13* That is, about 1 1/2 feet (about 0.5 meter)

[o]*16* That is, about 15 feet (about 4.5 meters) long and 2 1/4 feet (about 0.7 meter) wide

יְדֹתָיו וּשְׁנֵי אֲדָנִים תַּחַת־ הַקֶּרֶשׁ הָאֶחָד לִשְׁתֵּי
for-two-of the-each the-frame under bases and-two-of projections-of-him

יְדֹתָיו׃ וּלְצֶלַע הַמִּשְׁכָּן הַשֵּׁנִית לִפְאַת
for side-of the-other the-tabernacle and-for-side-of (20) projections-of-him

צָפוֹן עֶשְׂרִים קָרֶשׁ׃ וְאַרְבָּעִים אַדְנֵיהֶם כֶּסֶף שְׁנֵי אֲדָנִים תַּחַת
under bases two-of silver bases-of-them and-forty (21) frame twenty north

הַקֶּרֶשׁ הָאֶחָד וּשְׁנֵי אֲדָנִים תַּחַת הַקֶּרֶשׁ הָאֶחָד׃
the-each the-frame under bases and-two-of the-each the-frame

וּלְיַרְכְּתֵי הַמִּשְׁכָּן יָמָּה תַּעֲשֶׂה שִׁשָּׁה קְרָשִׁים׃
frames six you-make west-end the-tabernacle and-for-far-ends-of (22)

וּשְׁנֵי קְרָשִׁים תַּעֲשֶׂה לִמְקֻצְעֹת הַמִּשְׁכָּן בַּיַּרְכָתָיִם׃
at-the-far-ends the-tabernacle for-corners-of you-make frames and-two-of (23)

וְיִהְיוּ תֹאֲמִם מִלְּמַטָּה וְיַחְדָּו יִהְיוּ
they-must-be and-fitted from-bottom ones-being-double and-they-must-be (24)

תַמִּים עַל־ רֹאשׁוֹ אֶל־ הַטַּבַּעַת הָאֶחָת כֵּן יִהְיֶה
he-shall-be same the-single the-ring into top-of-him at being-double

לִשְׁנֵיהֶם לִשְׁנֵי הַמִּקְצֹעֹת יִהְיוּ׃ וְהָיוּ
so-they-will-be (25) they-shall-be the-corners for-both-of for-both-of-them

שְׁמֹנָה קְרָשִׁים וְאַדְנֵיהֶם כֶּסֶף שִׁשָּׁה עָשָׂר אֲדָנִים שְׁנֵי אֲדָנִים תַּחַת
under bases two-of bases ten six silver and-bases-of-them frames eight

הַקֶּרֶשׁ הָאֶחָד וּשְׁנֵי אֲדָנִים תַּחַת הַקֶּרֶשׁ הָאֶחָד׃ וְעָשִׂיתָ
and-you-make (26) the-each the-frame under bases and-two-of the-each the-frame

בְרִיחִם עֲצֵי שִׁטִּים חֲמִשָּׁה לְקַרְשֵׁי צֶלַע־ הַמִּשְׁכָּן הָאֶחָד׃
the-one the-tabernacle side-of for-frames-of five acacias woods-of crossbars

וַחֲמִשָּׁה בְרִיחִם לְקַרְשֵׁי צֶלַע־ הַמִּשְׁכָּן הַשֵּׁנִית
the-other the-tabernacle side-of for-frames-of crossbars and-five (27)

וַחֲמִשָּׁה בְרִיחִם לְקַרְשֵׁי צֶלַע הַמִּשְׁכָּן לַיַּרְכָתַיִם
at-the-far-ends the-tabernacle side-of for-frames-of crossbars and-five

יָמָּה׃ וְהַבְּרִיחַ הַתִּיכֹן בְּתוֹךְ הַקְּרָשִׁים מַבְרִחַ מִן־
from extending the-frames middle-of the-center and-the-crossbar (28) on-west

הַקָּצֶה אֶל־ הַקָּצֶה׃ וְאֶת־ הַקְּרָשִׁים תְּצַפֶּה זָהָב וְאֶת־ טַבְּעֹתֵיהֶם
rings-of-them and gold you-overlay the-frames and (29) the-end to the-end

תַּעֲשֶׂה זָהָב בָּתִּים לַבְּרִיחִם וְצִפִּיתָ אֶת־ הַבְּרִיחִם
the-crossbars *** also-you-overlay for-the-crossbars holders gold you-make

זָהָב׃ וַהֲקֵמֹתָ אֶת־ הַמִּשְׁכָּן כְּמִשְׁפָּטוֹ אֲשֶׁר הָרְאֵיתָ
you-were-shown that as-plan-of-him the-tabernacle *** now-you-set-up (30) gold

בָּהָר׃ וְעָשִׂיתָ פָרֹכֶת תְּכֵלֶת וְאַרְגָּמָן וְתוֹלַעַת שָׁנִי
yarn and-scarlet-of and-purple blue curtain and-you-make (31) on-the-mountain

each projection. [20]For the other side, the north side of the tabernacle, make twenty frames [21]and forty silver bases—two under each frame. [22]Make six frames for the far end, that is, the west end of the tabernacle, [23]and make two frames for the corners at the far end. [24]At these two corners they must be double from the bottom all the way to the top, and fitted into a single ring; both shall be like that. [25]So there will be eight frames and sixteen silver bases—two under each frame.

[26]"Also make crossbars of acacia wood: five for the frames on one side of the tabernacle, [27]five for those on the other side, and five for the frames on the west, at the far end of the tabernacle. [28]The center crossbar is to extend from end to end at the middle of the frames. [29]Overlay the frames with gold and make gold rings to hold the crossbars. Also overlay the crossbars with gold.

[30]"Set up the tabernacle according to the plan shown you on the mountain.

[31]"Make a curtain of blue, purple and scarlet yarn and

וְשֵׁשׁ מָשְׁזָר מַעֲשֵׂה חֹשֵׁב יַעֲשֶׂה אֹתָהּ כְּרֻבִים׃
cherubim her he-shall-make being-skilled work-of being-twisted and-fine-linen

וְנָתַתָּה אֹתָהּ עַל־אַרְבָּעָה עַמּוּדֵי שִׁטִּים מְצֻפִּים זָהָב
gold ones-being-overlaid acacias posts-of four on her and-you-hang (32)

וָוֵיהֶם זָהָב עַל־אַרְבָּעָה אַדְנֵי־כָסֶף׃ וְנָתַתָּה אֶת־הַפָּרֹכֶת
the-curtain *** and-you-hang (33) silver bases-of four on gold hooks-of-them

תַּחַת הַקְּרָסִים וְהֵבֵאתָ שָׁמָּה מִבֵּית לַפָּרֹכֶת אֵת אֲרוֹן
ark-of *** of-the-curtain at-behind there and-you-place the-clasps from

הָעֵדוּת וְהִבְדִּילָה הַפָּרֹכֶת לָכֶם בֵּין
between for-you the-curtain and-she-will-separate the-Testimony

הַקֹּדֶשׁ וּבֵין קֹדֶשׁ הַקֳּדָשִׁים׃ וְנָתַתָּ אֶת־
*** and-you-put (34) the-Holy-Places Holiest-of and-between the-Holy-Place

הַכַּפֹּרֶת עַל אֲרוֹן הָעֵדֻת בְּקֹדֶשׁ הַקֳּדָשִׁים׃
the-Holy-Places in-Holiest-of the-Testimony ark-of on the-atonement-cover

וְשַׂמְתָּ אֶת־הַשֻּׁלְחָן מִחוּץ לַפָּרֹכֶת וְאֶת־הַמְּנֹרָה
the-lampstand and of-the-curtain outside the-table *** and-you-place (35)

נֹכַח הַשֻּׁלְחָן עַל צֶלַע הַמִּשְׁכָּן תֵּימָנָה וְהַשֻּׁלְחָן תִּתֵּן
you-put and-the-table to-south the-tabernacle side-of on the-table opposite

עַל־צֶלַע צָפוֹן׃ וְעָשִׂיתָ מָסָךְ לְפֶתַח הָאֹהֶל תְּכֵלֶת
blue the-tent for-door-of curtain and-you-make (36) north side-of on

וְאַרְגָּמָן וְתוֹלַעַת שָׁנִי וְשֵׁשׁ מָשְׁזָר מַעֲשֵׂה
work-of being-twisted and-fine-linen yarn and-scarlet-of and-purple

רֹקֵם׃ וְעָשִׂיתָ לַמָּסָךְ חֲמִשָּׁה עַמּוּדֵי שִׁטִּים
acacias posts-of five for-the-curtain and-you-make (37) embroidering

וְצִפִּיתָ אֹתָם זָהָב וָוֵיהֶם זָהָב וְיָצַקְתָּ לָהֶם חֲמִשָּׁה
five for-them and-you-cast gold hooks-of-them gold them and-you-overlay

אַדְנֵי נְחֹשֶׁת׃ וְעָשִׂיתָ אֶת־הַמִּזְבֵּחַ עֲצֵי שִׁטִּים חָמֵשׁ
five acacias woods-of the-altar *** and-you-build (27:1) bronze bases-of

אַמּוֹת אֹרֶךְ וְחָמֵשׁ אַמּוֹת רֹחַב רָבוּעַ יִהְיֶה הַמִּזְבֵּחַ וְשָׁלֹשׁ
and-three the-altar he-shall-be being-square wide cubits and-five long cubits

אַמּוֹת קֹמָתוֹ׃ וְעָשִׂיתָ קַרְנֹתָיו עַל אַרְבַּע פִּנֹּתָיו
corners-of-him four at horns-of-him and-you-make (3) height-of-him cubits

מִמֶּנּוּ תִּהְיֶיןָ קַרְנֹתָיו וְצִפִּיתָ אֹתוֹ נְחֹשֶׁת׃
bronze him and-you-overlay horns-of-him they-shall-be from-him

וְעָשִׂיתָ סִּירֹתָיו לְדַשְּׁנוֹ וְיָעָיו
and-shovels-of-him to-remove-ash-of-him pots-of-him and-you-make (3)

וּמִזְרְקֹתָיו וּמִזְלְגֹתָיו וּמַחְתֹּתָיו
and-firepans-of-him and-meat-forks-of-him and-sprinkling-bowls-of-him

finely twisted linen, with cherubim worked into it by a skilled craftsman. 32 Hang it with gold hooks on four posts of acacia wood overlaid with gold and standing on four silver bases. 33 Hang the curtain from the clasps and place the ark of the Testimony behind the curtain. The curtain will separate the Holy Place from the Most Holy Place. 34 Put the atonement cover on the ark of the Testimony in the Most Holy Place. 35 Place the table outside the curtain on the north side of the tabernacle and put the lampstand opposite it on the south side.

36 "For the entrance to the tent make a curtain of blue, purple and scarlet yarn and finely twisted linen—the work of an embroiderer. 37 Make gold hooks for this curtain and five posts of acacia wood overlaid with gold. And cast five bronze bases for them.

The Altar of Burnt Offering

27 "Build an altar of acacia wood, three cubits[p] high; it is to be square, five cubits long and five cubits wide.[q] 2 Make a horn at each of the four corners, so that the horns and the altar are of one piece, and overlay the altar with bronze. 3 Make all its utensils of bronze—its pots to remove the ashes, and its shovels, sprinkling bowls, meat forks and firepans.

p1 That is, about 4 1/2 feet (about 1.3 meters)
q1 That is, about 7 1/2 feet (about 2.3 meters) long and wide

לְכָל־ כֵּלָיו תַּעֲשֶׂה נְחֹשֶׁת׃ וְעָשִׂיתָ לּוֹ מִכְבָּר
grate for-him and-you-make (4) bronze you-make utensils-of-him now-all-of

מַעֲשֵׂה רֶשֶׁת נְחֹשֶׁת וְעָשִׂיתָ עַל־ הָרֶשֶׁת אַרְבַּע טַבְּעֹת נְחֹשֶׁת עַל אַרְבַּע
four at bronze rings-of four the-net on and-you-make bronze net-of work-of

קְצוֹתָיו׃ וְנָתַתָּה אֹתָהּ תַּחַת כַּרְכֹּב הַמִּזְבֵּחַ מִלְּמָטָּה וְהָיְתָה
so-she-is beneath the-altar ledge-of under her and-you-put (5) corners-of-him

הָרֶשֶׁת עַד חֲצִי הַמִּזְבֵּחַ׃ וְעָשִׂיתָ בַדִּים לַמִּזְבֵּחַ בַּדֵּי
poles-of for-the-altar poles then-you-make (6) the-altar halfway up the-net

עֲצֵי שִׁטִּים וְצִפִּיתָ אֹתָם נְחֹשֶׁת׃ וְהוּבָא
and-he-shall-be-inserted (7) bronze them and-you-overlay acacias woods-of

אֶת־ בַּדָּיו בַּטַּבָּעֹת וְהָיוּ הַבַּדִּים עַל־ שְׁתֵּי צַלְעֹת
sides-of two-of on the-poles so-they-will-be into-the-rings poles-of-him ***

הַמִּזְבֵּחַ בִּשְׂאֵת אֹתוֹ׃ נְבוּב לֻחֹת תַּעֲשֶׂה אֹתוֹ כַּאֲשֶׁר
just-as him you-make boards being-hollow-of (8) him when-to-carry the-altar

הֶרְאָה אֹתְךָ בָּהָר כֵּן יַעֲשׂוּ׃ וְעָשִׂיתָ אֵת
*** and-you-make (9) they-shall-make so on-the-mountain you he-showed

חֲצַר הַמִּשְׁכָּן לִפְאַת נֶגֶב־ תֵּימָנָה קְלָעִים לֶחָצֵר
for-the-courtyard curtains south south at-side-of the-tabernacle courtyard-of

שֵׁשׁ מָשְׁזָר מֵאָה בָאַמָּה אֹרֶךְ לַפֵּאָה הָאֶחָת׃
the-one for-the-side long by-the-cubit hundred being-twisted fine-linen

וְעַמֻּדָיו עֶשְׂרִים וְאַדְנֵיהֶם עֶשְׂרִים נְחֹשֶׁת וָוֵי
hooks-of bronze twenty and-bases-of-them twenty and-posts-of-him (10)

הָעַמֻּדִים וַחֲשֻׁקֵיהֶם כָּסֶף׃ וְכֵן לִפְאַת צָפוֹן
north for-side-of and-same (11) silver and-bands-of-them the-posts

בָּאֹרֶךְ קְלָעִים מֵאָה אֹרֶךְ וְעַמֻּדָו עֶשְׂרִים וְאַדְנֵיהֶם
and-bases-of-them twenty and-posts-of-him long hundred curtains for-the-length

עֶשְׂרִים נְחֹשֶׁת וָוֵי הָעַמֻּדִים וַחֲשֻׁקֵיהֶם כָּסֶף׃ וְרֹחַב
and-width-of (12) silver and-bands-of-them the-posts hooks-of bronze twenty

הֶחָצֵר לִפְאַת־ יָם קְלָעִים חֲמִשִּׁים אַמָּה עַמֻּדֵיהֶם עֲשָׂרָה
ten posts-of-them cubit fifty curtains west at-end-of the-courtyard

וְאַדְנֵיהֶם עֲשָׂרָה׃ וְרֹחַב הֶחָצֵר לִפְאַת קֵדְמָה
east at-end-of the-courtyard and-width-of (13) ten and-bases-of-them

מִזְרָחָה חֲמִשִּׁים אַמָּה׃ וַחֲמֵשׁ עֶשְׂרֵה אַמָּה קְלָעִים לַכָּתֵף
on-the-side curtains cubit ten and-five (14) cubit fifty toward-sunrise

עַמֻּדֵיהֶם שְׁלֹשָׁה וְאַדְנֵיהֶם שְׁלֹשָׁה׃ וְלַכָּתֵף הַשֵּׁנִית
the-other and-on-the-side (15) three and-bases-of-them three posts-of-them

חֲמֵשׁ* עֶשְׂרֵה קְלָעִים עַמֻּדֵיהֶם שְׁלֹשָׁה וְאַדְנֵיהֶם שְׁלֹשָׁה׃
three and-bases-of-them three posts-of-them curtains ten five-of

4 Make a grating for it, a bronze network, and make a bronze ring at each of the four corners of the network.
5 Put it under the ledge of the altar so that it is halfway up the altar.
6 Make poles of acacia wood for the altar and overlay them with bronze.
7 The poles are to be inserted into the rings so they will be on two sides of the altar when it is carried.
8 Make the altar hollow, out of boards. It is to be made just as you were shown on the mountain.

The Courtyard

9 "Make a courtyard for the tabernacle. The south side shall be a hundred cubits[r] long and is to have curtains of finely twisted linen,
10 with twenty posts and twenty bronze bases and with silver hooks and bands on the posts.
11 The north side shall also be a hundred cubits long and is to have curtains, with twenty posts and twenty bronze bases and with silver hooks and bands on the posts.

12 "The west end of the courtyard shall be fifty cubits[s] wide and have curtains, with ten posts and ten bases.
13 On the east end, toward the sunrise, the courtyard shall also be fifty cubits wide.
14 Curtains fifteen cubits[t] long are to be on one side of the entrance, with three posts and three bases,
15 and curtains fifteen cubits long are to be on the other side, with three posts and three bases.

[r] 9 That is, about 150 feet (about 46 meters); also in verse 11
[s] 12 That is, about 75 feet (about 23 meters); also in verse 13
[t] 14 That is, about 22 1/2 feet (about 6.9 meters); also in verse 15

*15 Most mss have *hateph pathah* under the *beth* (חֲמֵשׁ).

°11 ק ועמודיו

וּלְשַׁעַר הֶחָצֵר מָסָךְ ׀ עֶשְׂרִים אַמָּה תְּכֵלֶת וְאַרְגָּמָן
and-purple blue cubit twenty curtain the-courtyard and-for-entrance-of (16)

וְתוֹלַעַת שָׁנִי וְשֵׁשׁ מָשְׁזָר מַעֲשֵׂה רֹקֵם
embroidering work-of being-twisted and-fine-linen yarn and-scarlet-of

עַמֻּדֵיהֶם אַרְבָּעָה וְאַדְנֵיהֶם אַרְבָּעָה׃ כָּל־ עַמּוּדֵי הֶחָצֵר
the-courtyard posts-of all-of (17) four and-bases-of-them four posts-of-them

סָבִיב מְחֻשָּׁקִים כֶּסֶף וָוֵיהֶם כָּסֶף וְאַדְנֵיהֶם נְחֹשֶׁת׃
bronze and-bases-of-them silver hooks-of-them silver ones-having-bands around

אֹרֶךְ הֶחָצֵר מֵאָה בָאַמָּה וְרֹחַב ׀ חֲמִשִּׁים בַּחֲמִשִּׁים
by-the-fifty fifty and-width by-the-cubit hundred the-courtyard length-of (18)

וְקֹמָה חָמֵשׁ אַמּוֹת שֵׁשׁ מָשְׁזָר וְאַדְנֵיהֶם נְחֹשֶׁת׃
bronze with-bases-of-them being-twisted fine-linen cubits five and-height

לְכֹל כְּלֵי הַמִּשְׁכָּן בְּכֹל עֲבֹדָתוֹ
service-of-him in-every-of the-tabernacle utensils-of now-all-of (19)

וְכָל־ יְתֵדֹתָיו וְכָל־ יִתְדֹת הֶחָצֵר נְחֹשֶׁת׃
bronze the-courtyard pegs-of and-all-of tent-pegs-of-him even-all-of

וְאַתָּה תְּצַוֶּה ׀ אֶת־ בְּנֵי יִשְׂרָאֵל וְיִקְחוּ אֵלֶיךָ שֶׁמֶן
oil-of to-you so-they-bring Israel sons-of *** you-command now-you (20)

זַיִת זָךְ כָּתִית לַמָּאוֹר לְהַעֲלֹת נֵר תָּמִיד׃ בְּאֹהֶל
in-Tent-of (21) continually lamp to-burn for-the-light pressed clear olive

מוֹעֵד מִחוּץ לַפָּרֹכֶת אֲשֶׁר עַל־ הָעֵדֻת יַעֲרֹךְ אֹתוֹ
him he-shall-keep the-Testimony before that of-the-curtain outside Meeting

אַהֲרֹן וּבָנָיו מֵעֶרֶב עַד־ בֹּקֶר לִפְנֵי יְהוָה חֻקַּת
ordinance-of Yahweh before morning till from-evening and-sons-of-him Aaron

עוֹלָם לְדֹרֹתָם מֵאֵת בְּנֵי יִשְׂרָאֵל׃ וְאַתָּה הַקְרֵב
bring! now-you (28:1) Israel sons-of among for-generations-of-them lasting

אֵלֶיךָ אֶת־ אַהֲרֹן אָחִיךָ וְאֶת־ בָּנָיו אִתּוֹ מִתּוֹךְ בְּנֵי
sons-of from-among with-him sons-of-him and brother-of-you Aaron *** to-you

יִשְׂרָאֵל לְכַהֲנוֹ־ לִי אַהֲרֹן נָדָב וַאֲבִיהוּא אֶלְעָזָר וְאִיתָמָר
and-Ithamar Eleazar and-Abihu Nadab Aaron to-me to-serve-as-priest-him Israel

בְּנֵי אַהֲרֹן׃ וְעָשִׂיתָ בִגְדֵי־ קֹדֶשׁ לְאַהֲרֹן אָחִיךָ
brother-of-you for-Aaron sacred garments-of and-you-make (2) Aaron sons-of

לְכָבוֹד וּלְתִפְאָרֶת׃ וְאַתָּה תְּדַבֵּר אֶל־ כָּל־ חַכְמֵי־
ones-skilled-of all-of to you-tell and-you (3) and-for-honor for-dignity

לֵב אֲשֶׁר מִלֵּאתִיו רוּחַ חָכְמָה וְעָשׂוּ אֶת־ בִּגְדֵי אַהֲרֹן
Aaron garments-of *** that-they-make wisdom spirit-of I-gave-him whom heart

לְקַדְּשׁוֹ לְכַהֲנוֹ־ לִי׃ וְאֵלֶּה הַבְּגָדִים
the-garments and-these (4) to-me to-serve-as-priest-him to-consecrate-him

16"For the entrance to the
courtyard, provide a curtain
twenty cubits[v] long, of blue,
purple and scarlet yarn and
finely twisted linen—the work
of an embroiderer—with four
posts and four bases. 17All the
posts around the courtyard are
to have silver bands and
hooks, and bronze bases. 18The
courtyard shall be a hundred
cubits long and fifty cubits
wide,[w] with curtains of finely
twisted linen five cubits[x] high,
and with bronze bases. 19All
the other articles used in the
service of the tabernacle,
whatever their function, including all the tent pegs for it
and those for the courtyard,
are to be of bronze.

Oil for the Lampstand

20"Command the Israelites
to bring you clear oil of
pressed olives for the light so
that the lamps may be kept
burning. 21In the Tent of Meeting, outside the curtain that is
in front of the Testimony,
Aaron and his sons are to keep
the lamps burning before the
LORD from evening till morning. This is to be a lasting ordinance among the Israelites for
the generations to come.

The Priestly Garments

28 "Have Aaron your
brother brought to you
from among the Israelites,
along with his sons Nadab
and Abihu, Eleazar and Ithamar, so they may serve me as
priests. 2Make sacred gar-
ments for your brother Aaron,
to give him dignity and honor. 3Tell all the skilled men to
whom I have given wisdom in
such matters that they are to
make garments for Aaron, for
his consecration, so he may
serve me as priest. 4These are

v16 That is, about 30 feet (about 9 meters)
w18 That is, about 150 feet (about 46 meters) long and 75 feet (about 23 meters) wide
x18 That is, about 7 1/2 feet (about 2.3 meters)

אֲשֶׁר יַעֲשׂוּ חֹשֶׁן וְאֵפוֹד וּמְעִיל וּכְתֹנֶת תַּשְׁבֵּץ מִצְנֶפֶת
turban woven and-tunic-of and-robe and-ephod breastpiece they-make that

וְאַבְנֵט וְעָשׂוּ בִגְדֵי־ קֹדֶשׁ לְאַהֲרֹן אָחִיךָ
brother-of-you for-Aaron sacred garments-of so-they-shall-make and-sash

וּלְבָנָיו לְכַהֲנוֹ־ לִי׃ וְהֵם יִקְחוּ
they-shall-use now-they (5) to-me to-serve-as-priest-him and-for-sons-of-him

אֶת־ הַזָּהָב וְאֶת־ הַתְּכֵלֶת וְאֶת־ הָאַרְגָּמָן וְאֶת־ תּוֹלַעַת הַשָּׁנִי וְאֶת־
and the-yarn scarlet-of and the-purple and the-blue and the-gold ***

הַשֵּׁשׁ׃ וְעָשׂוּ אֶת־ הָאֵפֹד זָהָב תְּכֵלֶת וְאַרְגָּמָן
and-purple blue gold the-ephod *** and-they-shall-make (6) the-fine-linen

תּוֹלַעַת שָׁנִי וְשֵׁשׁ מָשְׁזָר מַעֲשֵׂה חֹשֵׁב׃ שְׁתֵּי
two-of (7) being-skilled work-of being-twisted and-fine-linen yarn scarlet-of

כְתֵפֹת חֹבְרֹת יִהְיֶה־ לּוֹ אֶל־ שְׁנֵי
two-of on on-him he-shall-have ones-being-attached shoulder-pieces

קְצוֹתָיו וְחֻבָּר׃ וְחֵשֶׁב אֲפֻדָּתוֹ אֲשֶׁר
that ephod-of-him and-woven-part-of (8) so-being-fastened corners-of-him

עָלָיו כְּמַעֲשֵׂהוּ מִמֶּנּוּ יִהְיֶה זָהָב תְּכֵלֶת וְאַרְגָּמָן
and-purple blue gold he-shall-be from-him like-work-of-him on-him

וְתוֹלַעַת שָׁנִי וְשֵׁשׁ מָשְׁזָר׃ וְלָקַחְתָּ אֶת־
*** then-you-take (9) being-twisted and-fine-linen yarn and-scarlet-of

שְׁתֵּי אַבְנֵי־ שֹׁהַם וּפִתַּחְתָּ עֲלֵיהֶם שְׁמוֹת בְּנֵי יִשְׂרָאֵל׃
Israel sons-of names-of on-them and-you-engrave onyx stones-of two-of

שִׁשָּׁה מִשְּׁמֹתָם עַל הָאֶבֶן הָאֶחָת וְאֶת־ שְׁמוֹת הַשִּׁשָּׁה
the-six names-of and the-one the-stone on from-names-of-them six (10)

הַנּוֹתָרִים עַל־ הָאֶבֶן הַשֵּׁנִית כְּתוֹלְדֹתָם׃ מַעֲשֵׂה
work-of (11) by-births-of-them the-other the-stone on the-ones-remaining

חָרַשׁ אֶבֶן פִּתּוּחֵי חֹתָם תְּפַתַּח אֶת־ שְׁתֵּי הָאֲבָנִים עַל־
with the-stones two-of *** you-engrave seal engraves-of gem cutter-of

שְׁמֹת בְּנֵי יִשְׂרָאֵל מֻסַבֹּת מִשְׁבְּצוֹת זָהָב תַּעֲשֶׂה אֹתָם׃
them you-mount gold filigrees-of settings-of Israel sons-of names-of

וְשַׂמְתָּ אֶת־ שְׁתֵּי הָאֲבָנִים עַל כִּתְפֹת הָאֵפֹד
the-ephod shoulder-pieces-of on the-stones two-of *** and-you-fasten (12)

אַבְנֵי זִכָּרֹן לִבְנֵי יִשְׂרָאֵל וְנָשָׂא אַהֲרֹן אֶת־
*** Aaron and-he-shall-bear Israel for-sons-of memorial stones-of

שְׁמוֹתָם לִפְנֵי יְהוָה עַל־ שְׁתֵּי כְתֵפָיו לְזִכָּרֹן׃
as-memorial shoulders-of-him two-of on Yahweh before names-of-them

וְעָשִׂיתָ מִשְׁבְּצֹת זָהָב׃ וּשְׁתֵּי שַׁרְשְׁרֹת זָהָב טָהוֹר
pure gold chains-of and-two-of (14) gold filigrees-of and-you-make (13)

the garments they are to make:
a breastpiece, an ephod, a
robe, a woven tunic, a turban
and a sash. They are to make
these sacred garments for your
brother Aaron and his sons, so
they may serve me as priests.
[5]Have them use gold, and
blue, purple and scarlet yarn,
and fine linen.

The Ephod

[6]"Make the ephod of gold,
and of blue, purple and scarlet
yarn, and of finely twisted lin-
en—the work of a skilled
craftsman. [7]It is to have two
shoulder pieces attached to
two of its corners, so it can be
fastened. [8]Its skillfully woven
waistband is to be like it—of
one piece with the ephod and
made with gold, and with
blue, purple and scarlet yarn,
and with finely twisted linen.
[9]"Take two onyx stones and
engrave on them the names of
the sons of Israel [10]in the order
of their birth—six names on
one stone and the remaining
six on the other. [11]Engrave the
names of the sons of Israel on
the two stones the way a gem
cutter engraves a seal. Then
mount the stones in gold filigree settings [12]and fasten them
on the shoulder pieces of the
ephod as memorial stones for
the sons of Israel. Aaron is to
bear the names on his shoulders as a memorial before the
LORD. [13]Make gold filigree settings [14]and two braided chains

מִגְבָּלֹת תַּעֲשֶׂה אֹתָם מַעֲשֵׂה עֲבֹת וְנָתַתָּה אֶת־ שַׁרְשְׁרֹת

chains-of *** and-you-attach ropes work-of them you-make braided-ones

הָעֲבֹתֹת עַל־ הַמִּשְׁבְּצֹת׃ וְעָשִׂיתָ חֹשֶׁן מִשְׁפָּט

decision breastpiece-of and-you-fashion (15) the-settings to the-ropes

מַעֲשֵׂה חֹשֵׁב כְּמַעֲשֵׂה אֵפֹד תַּעֲשֶׂנּוּ זָהָב תְּכֵלֶת וְאַרְגָּמָן

and-purple blue gold you-make-him ephod like-work-of being-skilled work-of

וְתוֹלַעַת שָׁנִי וְשֵׁשׁ מָשְׁזָר תַּעֲשֶׂה אֹתוֹ׃

him you-make being-twisted and-fine-linen yarn and-scarlet-of

רָבוּעַ יִהְיֶה כָּפוּל זֶרֶת אָרְכּוֹ וְזֶרֶת

and-span length-of-him span being-doubled he-shall-be being-square (16)

רָחְבּוֹ׃ וּמִלֵּאתָ בוֹ מִלֻּאַת אֶבֶן אַרְבָּעָה טוּרִים אָבֶן

stone rows four stone setting-of on-him then-you-mount (17) width-of-him

טוּר אֹדֶם פִּטְדָה וּבָרֶקֶת הַטּוּר הָאֶחָד׃ וְהַטּוּר הַשֵּׁנִי

the-second and-the-row (18) the-first the-row and-beryl topaz ruby row-of

נֹפֶךְ סַפִּיר וְיָהֲלֹם׃ וְהַטּוּר הַשְּׁלִישִׁי לֶשֶׁם שְׁבוֹ

agate jacinth the-third and-the-row (19) and-emerald sapphire turquoise

וְאַחְלָמָה׃ וְהַטּוּר הָרְבִיעִי תַּרְשִׁישׁ וְשֹׁהַם וְיָשְׁפֵה

and-jasper and-onyx chrysolite the-fourth and-the-row (20) and-amethyst

מְשֻׁבָּצִים זָהָב יִהְיוּ בְּמִלּוּאֹתָם׃ וְהָאֲבָנִים

and-the-stones (21) in-settings-of-them they-shall-be gold ones-being-mounted

תִּהְיֶיןָ עַל־ שְׁמֹת בְּנֵי־ יִשְׂרָאֵל שְׁתֵּים עֶשְׂרֵה עַל־ שְׁמֹתָם

names-of-them for ten two Israel sons-of names-of for they-shall-be

פִּתּוּחֵי חוֹתָם אִישׁ עַל־ שְׁמוֹ תִּהְיֶיןָ לִשְׁנֵי עָשָׂר שָׁבֶט׃

tribe ten for-two they-shall-be name-of-him with each seal ones-engraved-of

וְעָשִׂיתָ עַל־ הַחֹשֶׁן שַׁרְשֹׁת גַּבְלֻת מַעֲשֵׂה עֲבֹת זָהָב

gold ropes work-of braid chains-of the-breastpiece for and-you-make (22)

טָהוֹר׃ וְעָשִׂיתָ עַל־ הַחֹשֶׁן שְׁתֵּי טַבְּעוֹת זָהָב וְנָתַתָּ

and-you-fasten gold rings-of two-of the-breastpiece for and-you-make (23) pure

אֶת־ שְׁתֵּי הַטַּבָּעוֹת עַל־ שְׁנֵי קְצוֹת הַחֹשֶׁן׃ וְנָתַתָּה

and-you-fasten (24) the-breastpiece corners-of two-of to the-rings two-of ***

אֶת־ שְׁתֵּי עֲבֹתֹת הַזָּהָב עַל־ שְׁתֵּי הַטַּבָּעֹת אֶל־ קְצוֹת הַחֹשֶׁן׃

the-breastpiece corners-of at the-rings two-of to the-gold chains-of two-of ***

וְאֵת שְׁתֵּי קְצוֹת שְׁתֵּי הָעֲבֹתֹת תִּתֵּן עַל־ שְׁתֵּי הַמִּשְׁבְּצוֹת

the-settings two-of to you-fasten the-chains two-of ends-of two-of and (25)

וְנָתַתָּה עַל־ כִּתְפוֹת הָאֵפֹד אֶל־ מוּל פָּנָיו׃

face-of-him front at the-ephod shoulder-pieces-of to and-you-attach

וְעָשִׂיתָ שְׁתֵּי טַבְּעוֹת זָהָב וְשַׂמְתָּ אֹתָם עַל־ שְׁנֵי

two-of to them and-you-attach gold rings-of two-of and-you-make (26)

of pure gold, like a rope, and attach the chains to the settings.

The Breastpiece

15 "Fashion a breastpiece for making decisions—the work of a skilled craftsman. Make it like the ephod: of gold, and of blue, purple and scarlet yarn, and of finely twisted linen.
16 It is to be square—a span[y] long and a span wide—and folded double.
17 Then mount four rows of precious stones on it. In the first row there shall be a ruby, a topaz and a beryl;
18 in the second row a turquoise, a sapphire[z] and an emerald;
19 in the third row a jacinth, an agate and an amethyst;
20 in the fourth row a chrysolite, an onyx and a jasper.[a] Mount them in gold filigree settings.
21 There are to be twelve stones, one for each of the names of the sons of Israel, each engraved like a seal with the name of one of the twelve tribes.
22 "For the breastpiece make braided chains of pure gold, like a rope.
23 Make two gold rings for it and fasten them to two corners of the breastpiece.
24 Fasten the two gold chains to the rings at the corners of the breastpiece,
25 and the other ends of the chains to the two settings, attaching them to the shoulder pieces of the ephod at the front.
26 Make two gold rings and attach them to the

[y]16 That is, about 9 inches (about 22 centimeters)
[z]18 Or *lapis lazuli*
[a]20 The precise identification of some of these precious stones is uncertain.

קְצוֹת הַחֹשֶׁן עַל־ שְׂפָתוֹ אֲשֶׁר אֶל־ עֵבֶר הָאֵפֹד בָּיְתָה׃

on-inside the-ephod side-of on that edge-of-him on the-breastpiece corners-of

וְעָשִׂיתָ שְׁתֵּי טַבְּעוֹת זָהָב וְנָתַתָּה אֹתָם עַל־ שְׁתֵּי

two-of to them and-you-attach gold rings-of two-of and-you-make (27)

כִתְפוֹת הָאֵפוֹד מִלְּמַטָּה מִמּוּל פָּנָיו לְעֻמַּת

by-close-of face-of-him on-front at-bottom the-ephod shoulder-pieces-of

מֶחְבַּרְתּוֹ מִמַּעַל לְחֵשֶׁב הָאֵפוֹד׃ וְיִרְכְּסוּ אֶת־

*** and-they-shall-tie (28) the-ephod to-waistband-of just-above seam-of-him

הַחֹשֶׁן מִטַּבְּעֹתָו° אֶל־ טַבְּעֹת הָאֵפֹד בִּפְתִיל תְּכֵלֶת

blue with-cord-of the-ephod rings-of to by-rings-of-him the-breastpiece

לִהְיוֹת עַל־ חֵשֶׁב הָאֵפוֹד וְלֹא־ יִזַּח הַחֹשֶׁן

the-breastpiece he-will-swing so-not the-ephod waistband-of to to-connect

מֵעַל הָאֵפוֹד׃ וְנָשָׂא אַהֲרֹן אֶת־ שְׁמוֹת בְּנֵי־ יִשְׂרָאֵל

Israel sons-of names-of *** Aaron and-he-will-bear (29) the-ephod out-from

בְּחֹשֶׁן הַמִּשְׁפָּט עַל־ לִבּוֹ בְּבֹאוֹ אֶל־

into when-to-enter-him heart-of-him over the-decision on-breastpiece-of

הַקֹּדֶשׁ לְזִכָּרֹן לִפְנֵי־ יְהוָה תָּמִיד׃ וְנָתַתָּ אֶל־

in also-you-put (30) continual Yahweh before as-memorial the-Holy-Place

חֹשֶׁן הַמִּשְׁפָּט אֶת־ הָאוּרִים וְאֶת־ הַתֻּמִּים וְהָיוּ עַל־

over so-they-may-be the-Thummim and the-Urim *** the-decision breastpiece-of

לֵב אַהֲרֹן בְּבֹאוֹ לִפְנֵי יְהוָה וְנָשָׂא אַהֲרֹן

Aaron thus-he-will-bear Yahweh presence-of when-to-enter-him Aaron heart-of

אֶת־ מִשְׁפַּט בְּנֵי־ יִשְׂרָאֵל עַל־ לִבּוֹ לִפְנֵי יְהוָה תָּמִיד׃

always Yahweh before heart-of-him over Israel sons-of decision-maker-of ***

וְעָשִׂיתָ אֶת־ מְעִיל הָאֵפוֹד כְּלִיל תְּכֵלֶת׃

blue-cloth entirely-of the-ephod robe-of *** now-you-make (31)

וְהָיָה פִי־ רֹאשׁוֹ בְּתוֹכוֹ שָׂפָה יִהְיֶה

he-shall-be edge in-center-of-him head-of-him opening-of and-he-shall-be (32)

לְפִיו סָבִיב מַעֲשֵׂה אֹרֵג כְּפִי תַחְרָא

collar like-opening-of weaving work-of around for-opening-of-him

יִהְיֶה־ לּוֹ לֹא יִקָּרֵעַ׃ וְעָשִׂיתָ עַל־ שׁוּלָיו

hems-of-him for and-you-make (33) he-will-tear not for-him he-will-be

רִמֹּנֵי תְּכֵלֶת וְאַרְגָּמָן וְתוֹלַעַת שָׁנִי עַל־ שׁוּלָיו סָבִיב

around hems-of-him for yarn and-scarlet-of and-purple blue pomegranates-of

וּפַעֲמֹנֵי זָהָב בְּתוֹכָם סָבִיב׃ פַּעֲמֹן זָהָב וְרִמּוֹן

and-pomegranate gold bell-of (34) around between-them gold with-bells-of

פַּעֲמֹן זָהָב וְרִמּוֹן עַל־ שׁוּלֵי הַמְּעִיל סָבִיב׃ וְהָיָה

and-he-must-be (35) around the-robe hems-of on and-pomegranate gold bell-of

other two corners of the
breastpiece on the inside edge
next to the ephod. 27Make two
more gold rings and attach
them to the bottom of the
shoulder pieces on the front of
the ephod, close to the seam
just above the waistband of
the ephod. 28The rings of the
breastpiece are to be tied to the
rings of the ephod with blue
cord, connecting it to the
waistband, so that the breastpiece will not swing out from
the ephod.

29"Whenever Aaron enters
the Holy Place, he will bear the
names of the sons of Israel
over his heart on the breastpiece of decision as a continuing memorial before the LORD.
30Also put the Urim and the
Thummim in the breastpiece,
so they may be over Aaron's
heart whenever he enters the
presence of the LORD. Thus
Aaron will always bear the
means of making decisions for
the Israelites over his heart before the LORD.

Other Priestly Garments

31"Make the robe of the
ephod entirely of blue cloth,
32with an opening for the head
in its center. There shall be a
woven edge like a collar[b]
around this opening, so that it
will not tear. 33Make pomegranates of blue, purple and
scarlet yarn around the hem of
the robe, with gold bells between them. 34The gold bells
and the pomegranates are to
alternate around the hem of
the robe. 35Aaron must wear it

[b]32 The meaning of the Hebrew for this word is uncertain.

°28 ק מטבעתיו

עַל־אַהֲרֹן לְשָׁרֵת וְנִשְׁמַע קוֹלוֹ בְּבֹאוֹ אֶל־
into when-to-enter-him sound-of-him and-he-will-be-heard to-minister Aaron on

הַקֹּדֶשׁ לִפְנֵי יְהוָה וּבְצֵאתוֹ וְלֹא יָמוּת׃
he-will-die so-not and-when-to-come-out-him Yahweh before the-Holy-Place

וְעָשִׂיתָ צִּיץ זָהָב טָהוֹר וּפִתַּחְתָּ עָלָיו פִּתּוּחֵי
engravings-of on-him and-you-engrave pure gold plate-of and-you-make (36)

חֹתָם קֹדֶשׁ לַיהוָה׃ וְשַׂמְתָּ אֹתוֹ עַל־ פְּתִיל תְּכֵלֶת וְהָיָה
and-he-will-be blue cord-of on him and-you-fasten (37) to-Yahweh holy seal

עַל־ הַמִּצְנֶפֶת אֶל־ מוּל פְּנֵי־ הַמִּצְנֶפֶת יִהְיֶה׃ וְהָיָה
and-he-will-be (38) he-shall-be the-turban face-of front on the-turban on

עַל־ מֵצַח אַהֲרֹן וְנָשָׂא אַהֲרֹן אֶת־ עֲוֹן הַקֳּדָשִׁים
the-sacred-gifts guilt-of *** Aaron and-he-will-bear Aaron forehead-of on

אֲשֶׁר יַקְדִּישׁוּ בְּנֵי יִשְׂרָאֵל לְכָל־ מַתְּנֹת קָדְשֵׁיהֶם
sacred-ones-of-them gifts-of among-all-of Israel sons-of they-consecrate that

וְהָיָה עַל־ מִצְחוֹ תָּמִיד לְרָצוֹן לָהֶם
for-them to-make-acceptable continually forehead-of-him on and-he-will-be

לִפְנֵי יְהוָה׃ וְשִׁבַּצְתָּ הַכְּתֹנֶת שֵׁשׁ וְעָשִׂיתָ מִצְנֶפֶת
turban and-you-make fine-linen the-tunic and-you-weave (39) Yahweh before

שֵׁשׁ וְאַבְנֵט תַּעֲשֶׂה מַעֲשֵׂה רֹקֵם׃ וְלִבְנֵי אַהֲרֹן
Aaron and-for-sons-of (40) embroidering work-of you-make and-sash fine-linen

תַּעֲשֶׂה כֻתֳּנֹת וְעָשִׂיתָ לָהֶם אַבְנֵטִים וּמִגְבָּעוֹת תַּעֲשֶׂה לָהֶם
for-them you-make and-headbands sashes for-them and-you-make tunics you-make

לְכָבוֹד וּלְתִפְאָרֶת׃ וְהִלְבַּשְׁתָּ אֹתָם אֶת־ אַהֲרֹן אָחִיךָ
brother-of-you Aaron *** them and-you-clothe (41) and-for-honor for-dignity

וְאֶת־ בָּנָיו אִתּוֹ וּמָשַׁחְתָּ אֹתָם וּמִלֵּאתָ אֶת־ יָדָם
hand-of-them *** and-you-ordain them and-you-anoint with-him sons-of-him and

וְקִדַּשְׁתָּ אֹתָם וְכִהֲנוּ לִי׃ וַעֲשֵׂה
and-make! (42) to-me so-they-may-serve-as-priests them and-you-consecrate

לָהֶם מִכְנְסֵי־ בָד לְכַסּוֹת בְּשַׂר עֶרְוָה מִמָּתְנַיִם וְעַד־
even-to from-waists naked body-of to-cover linen undergarments-of for-them

יְרֵכַיִם יִהְיוּ׃ וְהָיוּ עַל־ אַהֲרֹן וְעַל־ בָּנָיו
sons-of-him and-on Aaron on and-they-must-be (43) they-shall-reach thighs

בְּבֹאָם ׀ אֶל־ אֹהֶל מוֹעֵד אוֹ בְגִשְׁתָּם אֶל־הַמִּזְבֵּחַ
the-altar to when-to-approach-them or Meeting Tent-of into when-to-enter-them

לְשָׁרֵת בַּקֹּדֶשׁ וְלֹא־ יִשְׂאוּ עָוֹן וָמֵתוּ
and-they-die guilt they-will-incur so-not in-the-Holy-Place to-minister

חֻקַּת עוֹלָם לוֹ וּלְזַרְעוֹ אַחֲרָיו׃
after-him and-for-descendant-of-him for-him lasting ordinance-of

when he ministers. The sound
of the bells will be heard when
he enters the Holy Place before
the LORD and when he comes
out, so that he will not die.
[36]"Make a plate of pure gold
and engrave on it as on a seal:
HOLY TO THE LORD. [37]Fasten a
blue cord to it to attach it to the
turban; it is to be on the front
of the turban. [38]It will be on
Aaron's forehead, and he will
bear the guilt involved in the
sacred gifts the Israelites
consecrate, whatever their
gifts may be. It will be on
Aaron's forehead continually
so that they will be acceptable
to the LORD.
[39]"Weave the tunic of fine
linen and make the turban of
fine linen. The sash is to be the
work of an embroiderer.
[40]Make tunics, sashes and
headbands for Aaron's sons,
to give them dignity and hon-
or. [41]After you put these
clothes on your brother Aaron
and his sons, anoint and ordain them. Consecrate them
so they may serve me as
priests.
[42]"Make linen undergar-
ments as a covering for the
body, reaching from the waist
to the thigh. [43]Aaron and his
sons must wear them when-
ever they enter the Tent of
Meeting or approach the altar
to minister in the Holy Place,
so that they will not incur guilt
and die.
"This is to be a lasting ordinance for Aaron and his descendants.

וְזֶה הַדָּבָר אֲשֶׁר־ תַּעֲשֶׂה לָהֶם לְקַדֵּשׁ אֹתָם לְכַהֵן
to-be-priest them to-consecrate to-them you-do that the-thing now-this (29:1)

לִי לְקַח פַּר אֶחָד בֶּן־ בָּקָר וְאֵילִם שְׁנַיִם תְּמִימִם׃
ones-without-defect two and-rams herd young-of one bull take! to-me

וְלֶחֶם מַצּוֹת וְחַלֹּת מַצֹּת בְּלוּלֹת
ones-being-mixed without-yeasts and-cakes-of without-yeasts and-bread-of (2)

בַּשֶּׁמֶן וּרְקִיקֵי מַצּוֹת מְשֻׁחִים בַּשָּׁמֶן
with-the-oil ones-being-spread without-yeasts and-wafers-of with-the-oil

סֹלֶת חִטִּים תַּעֲשֶׂה אֹתָם׃ וְנָתַתָּ אוֹתָם עַל־ סַל אֶחָד
one basket in them and-you-put (3) them you-make fine-ones flour-of

וְהִקְרַבְתָּ אֹתָם בַּסָּל וְאֶת־ הַפָּר וְאֵת שְׁנֵי הָאֵילִם׃
the-rams two-of and the-bull with in-the-basket them and-you-present

וְאֶת־ אַהֲרֹן וְאֶת־ בָּנָיו תַּקְרִיב אֶל־ פֶּתַח אֹהֶל מוֹעֵד
Meeting Tent-of entrance-of to you-bring sons-of-him and Aaron and (4)

וְרָחַצְתָּ אֹתָם בַּמָּיִם׃ וְלָקַחְתָּ אֶת־ הַבְּגָדִים
the-garments *** then-you-take (5) with-the-waters them and-you-wash

וְהִלְבַּשְׁתָּ אֶת־ אַהֲרֹן אֶת־הַכֻּתֹּנֶת וְאֵת מְעִיל הָאֵפֹד וְאֶת־ הָאֵפֹד
the-ephod and the-ephod robe-of and the-tunic *** Aaron *** and-you-dress

וְאֶת־ הַחֹשֶׁן וְאָפַדְתָּ לוֹ בְּחֵשֶׁב הָאֵפֹד׃
the-ephod by-waistband-of on-him and-you-fasten-ephod the-breastpiece and

וְשַׂמְתָּ הַמִּצְנֶפֶת עַל־ רֹאשׁוֹ וְנָתַתָּ אֶת־ נֵזֶר
diadem-of *** and-you-attach head-of-him on the-turban and-you-put (6)

הַקֹּדֶשׁ עַל־ הַמִּצְנָפֶת׃ וְלָקַחְתָּ אֶת־ שֶׁמֶן הַמִּשְׁחָה
the-anointing oil-of *** then-you-take (7) the-turban to the-sacred

וְיָצַקְתָּ עַל־ רֹאשׁוֹ וּמָשַׁחְתָּ אֹתוֹ׃ וְאֶת־ בָּנָיו תַּקְרִיב
you-bring sons-of-him and (8) him and-you-anoint head-of-him on and-you-pour

וְהִלְבַּשְׁתָּם כֻּתֳּנֹת׃ וְחָגַרְתָּ אֹתָם אַבְנֵט אַהֲרֹן וּבָנָיו
and-sons-of-him Aaron sash them then-you-tie (9) tunics and-you-dress-them

וְחָבַשְׁתָּ לָהֶם מִגְבָּעֹת וְהָיְתָה לָהֶם כְּהֻנָּה
priesthood for-them and-she-will-be headbands on-them and-you-put

לְחֻקַּת עוֹלָם וּמִלֵּאתָ יַד־ אַהֲרֹן וְיַד־
and-hand-of Aaron hand-of so-you-shall-ordain lasting as-ordinance-of

בָּנָיו׃ וְהִקְרַבְתָּ אֶת־ הַפָּר לִפְנֵי אֹהֶל מוֹעֵד
Meeting Tent-of to-front-of the-bull *** and-you-bring (10) sons-of-him

וְסָמַךְ אַהֲרֹן וּבָנָיו אֶת־ יְדֵיהֶם עַל־ רֹאשׁ הַפָּר׃
the-bull head-of on hands-of-them *** and-sons-of-him Aaron and-he-shall-lay

וְשָׁחַטְתָּ אֶת־ הַפָּר לִפְנֵי יְהוָה פֶּתַח אֹהֶל
Tent-of entrance-of Yahweh in-presence-of the-bull *** then-you-slaughter (11)

Consecration of the Priests

29 "This is what you are to do to consecrate them, so they may serve me as priests: Take a young bull and two rams without defect.
2And from fine wheat flour, without yeast, make bread, and cakes mixed with oil, and wafers spread with oil.
3Put them in a basket and present them in it—along with the bull and the two rams.
4Then bring Aaron and his sons to the entrance to the Tent of Meeting and wash them with water.
5Take the garments and dress Aaron with the tunic, the robe of the ephod, the ephod itself and the breastpiece. Fasten the ephod on him by its skillfully woven waistband.
6Put the turban on his head and attach the sacred diadem to the turban.
7Take the anointing oil and anoint him by pouring it on his head.
8Bring his sons and dress them in tunics
9and put headbands on them. Then tie sashes on Aaron and his sons.[c] The priesthood is theirs by a lasting ordinance. In this way you shall ordain Aaron and his sons.

10"Bring the bull to the front of the Tent of Meeting, and Aaron and his sons shall lay their hands on its head.
11Slaughter it in the LORD's presence at the entrance to the

[c]9 Hebrew; Septuagint *on them*

מוֹעֵד׃ וְלָקַחְתָּ֙ מִדַּ֣ם הַפָּ֔ר וְנָתַתָּ֥ה עַל־ קַרְנֹ֥ת
horns-of on and-you-put the-bull from-blood-of and-you-take (12) Meeting

הַמִּזְבֵּ֖חַ בְּאֶצְבָּעֶ֑ךָ וְאֶת־ כָּל־ הַדָּ֣ם תִּשְׁפֹּ֔ךְ אֶל־ יְס֖וֹד
base-of at you-pour-out the-blood rest-of and with-finger-of-you the-altar

הַמִּזְבֵּֽחַ׃ וְלָקַחְתָּ֗ אֶֽת־ כָּל־ הַחֵ֘לֶב֮ הַֽמְכַסֶּ֣ה אֶת־
*** the-covering the-fat all-of *** then-you-take (13) the-altar

הַקֶּ֒רֶב֒ וְאֵ֗ת הַיֹּתֶ֙רֶת֙ עַל־ הַכָּבֵ֔ד וְאֵת֙ שְׁתֵּ֣י הַכְּלָיֹ֔ת וְאֶת־
and the-kidneys both-of and the-liver on the-cover and the-inner-part

הַחֵ֖לֶב אֲשֶׁ֣ר עֲלֵיהֶ֑ן וְהִקְטַרְתָּ֖ הַמִּזְבֵּֽחָה׃ וְאֶת־ בְּשַׂ֤ר
flesh-of but (14) on-the-altar and-you-burn around-them that the-fat

הַפָּר֙ וְאֶת־ עֹר֣וֹ וְאֶת־ פִּרְשׁ֔וֹ תִּשְׂרֹ֥ף בָּאֵ֖שׁ מִח֣וּץ
outside with-the-fire you-burn offal-of-him and hide-of-him and the-bull

לַֽמַּחֲנֶ֑ה חַטָּ֖את הֽוּא׃ וְאֶת־ הָאַ֥יִל הָאֶחָ֖ד תִּקָּ֑ח
you-take the-one the-ram and (15) he sin-offering of-the-camp

וְ֠סָמְכוּ אַהֲרֹ֧ן וּבָנָ֛יו אֶת־ יְדֵיהֶ֖ם עַל־ רֹ֥אשׁ הָאָֽיִל׃
the-ram head-of on hands-of-them *** and-sons-of-him Aaron and-they-shall-lay

וְשָׁחַטְתָּ֖ אֶת־ הָאָ֑יִל וְלָקַחְתָּ֙ אֶת־ דָּמ֔וֹ
blood-of-him *** and-you-take the-ram *** then-you-slaughter (16)

וְזָרַקְתָּ֥ עַל־ הַמִּזְבֵּ֖חַ סָבִֽיב׃ וְאֶת־ הָאַ֕יִל תְּנַתֵּ֖חַ
you-cut the-ram and (17) around the-altar on and-you-sprinkle

לִנְתָחָ֑יו וְרָחַצְתָּ֤ קִרְבּוֹ֙ וּכְרָעָ֔יו וְנָתַתָּ֥
and-you-put and-legs-of-him inner-part-of-him and-you-wash into-pieces-of-him

עַל־ נְתָחָ֖יו וְעַל־ רֹאשֽׁוֹ׃ וְהִקְטַרְתָּ֣ אֶת־ כָּל־
entire-of *** then-you-burn (18) head-of-him and-with pieces-of-him with

הָאַ֙יִל֙ הַמִּזְבֵּ֔חָה עֹלָ֥ה ה֖וּא לַֽיהוָ֑ה רֵ֣יחַ נִיח֔וֹחַ אִשֶּׁ֥ה
by-fire pleasant aroma-of to-Yahweh he burnt-offering on-the-altar the-ram

לַיהוָ֖ה הֽוּא׃ וְלָקַחְתָּ֖ אֵ֣ת הָאַ֣יִל הַשֵּׁנִ֑י וְסָמַ֨ךְ אַהֲרֹ֧ן
Aaron and-he-shall-lay the-other the-ram *** then-you-take (19) he to-Yahweh

וּבָנָ֛יו אֶת־ יְדֵיהֶ֖ם עַל־ רֹ֥אשׁ הָאָֽיִל׃ וְשָׁחַטְתָּ֣
and-you-slaughter (20) the-ram head-of on hands-of-them *** and-sons-of-him

אֶת־ הָאַ֗יִל וְלָקַחְתָּ֣ מִדָּמוֹ֒ וְנָתַתָּ֡ה עַל־ תְּנוּךְ֩ אֹ֨זֶן
ear-of lobe-of on and-you-put from-blood-of-him and-you-take the-ram ***

אַהֲרֹ֜ן וְעַל־ תְּנ֨וּךְ אֹ֤זֶן בָּנָיו֙ הַיְמָנִ֔ית וְעַל־ בֹּ֤הֶן
thumb-of and-on the-right sons-of-him ear-of lobe-of and-on Aaron

יָדָם֙ הַיְמָנִ֔ית וְעַל־ בֹּ֥הֶן רַגְלָ֖ם הַיְמָנִ֑ית
the-right foot-of-them big-toe-of and-on the-right hand-of-them

וְזָרַקְתָּ֧ אֶת־ הַדָּ֛ם עַל־ הַמִּזְבֵּ֖חַ סָבִֽיב׃ וְלָקַחְתָּ֞
and-you-take (21) around the-altar against the-blood *** then-you-sprinkle

Tent of Meeting. 12Take some
of the bull's blood and put it
on the horns of the altar with
your finger, and pour out the
rest of it at the base of the altar.
13Then take all the fat around
the inner parts, the covering
of the liver, and both kidneys
with the fat around them, and
burn them on the altar. 14But
burn the bull's flesh and its
hide and its offal outside the
camp. It is a sin offering.

15"Take one of the rams, and
Aaron and his sons shall lay
their hands on its head.
16Slaughter it and take the
blood and sprinkle it against
the altar on all sides. 17Cut the
ram into pieces and wash the
inner parts and the legs, putting them with the head and
the other pieces. 18Then burn
the entire ram on the altar. It is
a burnt offering to the LORD, a
pleasing aroma, an offering
made to the LORD by fire.

19"Take the other ram, and
Aaron and his sons shall lay
their hands on its head.
20Slaughter it, take some of its
blood and put it on the lobes of
the right ears of Aaron and his
sons, on the thumbs of their
right hands, and on the big
toes of their right feet. Then
sprinkle blood against the altar on all sides. 21And take

מִן־ הַדָּם אֲשֶׁר עַל־הַמִּזְבֵּחַ וּמִשֶּׁמֶן הַמִּשְׁחָה וְהִזֵּיתָ
and-you-sprinkle the-anointing and-from-oil-of the-altar on that the-blood from

עַל־ אַהֲרֹן וְעַל־ בְּגָדָיו וְעַל־ בָּנָיו וְעַל־ בִּגְדֵי
garments-of and-on sons-of-him and-on garments-of-him and-on Aaron on

בָנָיו אִתּוֹ וְקָדַשׁ הוּא וּבְגָדָיו
and-garments-of-him he then-he-will-be-consecrated with-him sons-of-him

וּבָנָיו וּבִגְדֵי בָנָיו אִתּוֹ׃ וְלָקַחְתָּ מִן־
from then-you-take (22) with-him sons-of-him and-garments-of and-sons-of-him

הָאַיִל הַחֵלֶב וְהָאַלְיָה וְאֶת־ הַחֵלֶב ׀ הַמְכַסֶּה אֶת־ הַקֶּרֶב
the-inner-part *** the-covering the-fat and and-the-fat-tail the-fat the-ram

וְאֵת יֹתֶרֶת הַכָּבֵד וְאֵת ׀ שְׁתֵּי הַכְּלָיֹת וְאֶת־ הַחֵלֶב אֲשֶׁר עֲלֵהֶן
around-them that the-fat with the-kidneys both-of and the-liver cover-of and

וְאֵת שׁוֹק הַיָּמִין כִּי אֵיל מִלֻּאִים הוּא׃ וְכִכַּר לֶחֶם
bread and-loaf-of (23) this ordinations ram-of now the-right thigh-of and

אַחַת וְחַלַּת לֶחֶם שֶׁמֶן אַחַת וְרָקִיק אֶחָד מִסַּל־ הַמַּצּוֹת
the-unleavened-breads from-basket-of one and-wafer one oil bread and-cake-of one

אֲשֶׁר לִפְנֵי יְהוָה׃ וְשַׂמְתָּ הַכֹּל עַל כַּפֵּי אַהֲרֹן וְעַל כַּפֵּי
hands-of and-in Aaron hands-of in the-all and-you-put (24) Yahweh before that

בָנָיו וְהֵנַפְתָּ אֹתָם תְּנוּפָה לִפְנֵי יְהוָה׃ וְלָקַחְתָּ
then-you-take (25) Yahweh before wave-offering them and-you-wave sons-of-him

אֹתָם מִיָּדָם וְהִקְטַרְתָּ הַמִּזְבֵּחָה עַל־ הָעֹלָה
the-burnt-offering with on-the-altar and-you-burn from-hand-of-them them

לְרֵיחַ נִיחוֹחַ לִפְנֵי יְהוָה אִשֶּׁה הוּא לַיהוָה׃ וְלָקַחְתָּ
then-you-take (26) to-Yahweh he by-fire Yahweh before pleasant for-aroma-of

אֶת־ הֶחָזֶה מֵאֵיל הַמִּלֻּאִים אֲשֶׁר לְאַהֲרֹן וְהֵנַפְתָּ אֹתוֹ
him and-you-wave for-Aaron that the-ordinations from-ram-of the-breast ***

תְּנוּפָה לִפְנֵי יְהוָה וְהָיָה לְךָ לְמָנָה׃
for-share for-you and-he-will-be Yahweh before wave-offering

וְקִדַּשְׁתָּ אֵת ׀ חֲזֵה הַתְּנוּפָה וְאֵת שׁוֹק
thigh-of and the-wave-offering breast-of *** and-you consecrate (27)

הַתְּרוּמָה אֲשֶׁר הוּנַף וַאֲשֶׁר הוּרָם מֵאֵיל
from-ram-of he-was-presented and-that he-was-waved that the-presentation

הַמִּלֻּאִים מֵאֲשֶׁר לְאַהֲרֹן וּמֵאֲשֶׁר לְבָנָיו׃
to-sons-of-him and-from-that to-Aaron from-that the-ordinations

וְהָיָה לְאַהֲרֹן וּלְבָנָיו לְחָק־ עוֹלָם מֵאֵת בְּנֵי
sons-of from perpetual share-of and-for-sons-of-him for-Aaron and-he-will-be (28)

יִשְׂרָאֵל כִּי תְרוּמָה הוּא וּתְרוּמָה יִהְיֶה מֵאֵת בְּנֵי־יִשְׂרָאֵל
Israel sons-of from he-shall-be and-contribution he contribution for Israel

some of the blood on the altar
and some of the anointing oil
and sprinkle it on Aaron and
his garments and on his sons
and their garments. Then he
and his sons and their garments will be consecrated.
22"Take from this ram the
fat, the fat tail, the fat around
the inner parts, the covering
of the liver, both kidneys with
the fat around them, and the
right thigh. (This is the ram for
the ordination.) 23From the
basket of bread made without
yeast, which is before the
LORD, take a loaf, and a cake
made with oil, and a wafer.
24Put all these in the hands of
Aaron and his sons and wave
them before the LORD as a
wave offering. 25Then take
them from their hands and
burn them on the altar along
with the burnt offering for a
pleasing aroma to the LORD, an
offering made to the LORD by
fire. 26After you take the breast
of the ram for Aaron's ordination, wave it before the LORD
as a wave offering, and it will
be your share.
27"Consecrate those parts of
the ordination ram that belong to Aaron and his sons:
the breast that was waved and
the thigh that was presented.
28This is always to be the regular share from the Israelites for
Aaron and his sons. It is the
contribution the Israelites are

מִזִּבְחֵי שַׁלְמֵיהֶם תְּרוּמָתָם לַיהוָה׃
to-Yahweh contribution-of-them fellowship-ones-of-them from-offerings-of

(29) וּבִגְדֵי הַקֹּדֶשׁ אֲשֶׁר לְאַהֲרֹן יִהְיוּ לְבָנָיו
to-sons-of-him they-will-belong to-Aaron that the-sacred and-garments-of (29)

אַחֲרָיו לְמָשְׁחָה בָהֶם וּלְמַלֵּא־ בָם אֶת־ יָדָם׃
hand-of-them *** in-them and-to-be-ordained in-them to-be-anointed after-him

(30) שִׁבְעַת יָמִים יִלְבָּשָׁם הַכֹּהֵן תַּחְתָּיו מִבָּנָיו
from-sons-of-him succeeding-him the-priest he-shall-wear-them days seven-of (30)

אֲשֶׁר יָבֹא אֶל־ אֹהֶל מוֹעֵד לְשָׁרֵת בַּקֹּדֶשׁ׃ (31) וְאֵת
and (31) in-the-Holy-Place to-minister Meeting Tent-of into he-comes when

אֵיל הַמִּלֻּאִים תִּקָּח וּבִשַּׁלְתָּ אֶת־ בְּשָׂרוֹ בְּמָקֹם
in-place meat-of-him *** and-you-cook you-take the-ordinations ram-of

קָדֹשׁ׃ (32) וְאָכַל אַהֲרֹן וּבָנָיו אֶת־ בְּשַׂר הָאַיִל וְאֶת־
and the-ram meat-of *** and-sons-of-him Aaron and-he-shall-eat (32) sacred

הַלֶּחֶם אֲשֶׁר בַּסָּל פֶּתַח אֹהֶל מוֹעֵד׃ (33) וְאָכְלוּ
and-they-shall-eat (33) Meeting Tent-of entrance-of in-the-basket that the-bread

אֹתָם אֲשֶׁר כֻּפַּר בָּהֶם לְמַלֵּא אֶת־ יָדָם לְקַדֵּשׁ
to-consecrate hand-of-them *** to-ordain by-them he-was-atoned that them

אֹתָם וְזָר לֹא־ יֹאכַל כִּי־ קֹדֶשׁ הֵם׃ (34) וְאִם־ יִוָּתֵר
he-is-left and-if (34) they sacred for he-may-eat not but-being-other them

מִבְּשַׂר הַמִּלֻּאִים וּמִן־ הַלֶּחֶם עַד־ הַבֹּקֶר וְשָׂרַפְתָּ
then-you-burn the-morning till the-bread or-from the-ordinations from-meat-of

אֶת־ הַנּוֹתָר בָּאֵשׁ לֹא יֵאָכֵל כִּי־ קֹדֶשׁ הוּא׃
he sacred for he-may-be-eaten not with-the-fire the-remaining ***

(35) וְעָשִׂיתָ לְאַהֲרֹן וּלְבָנָיו כָּכָה כְּכֹל אֲשֶׁר־
that as-everything thus and-for-sons-of-him for-Aaron so-you-do (35)

צִוִּיתִי אֹתָכָה שִׁבְעַת יָמִים תְּמַלֵּא יָדָם׃ (36) וּפַר
and-bull-of (36) hand-of-them you-ordain days seven-of you I-commanded

חַטָּאת תַּעֲשֶׂה לַיּוֹם עַל־ הַכִּפֻּרִים וְחִטֵּאתָ
and-you-purify the-atonement for each-the-day you-sacrifice the-sin-offering

עַל־ הַמִּזְבֵּחַ בְּכַפֶּרְךָ עָלָיו וּמָשַׁחְתָּ אֹתוֹ לְקַדְּשׁוֹ׃
to-consecrate-him him and-you-anoint for-him by-to-atone-you the-altar on

(37) שִׁבְעַת יָמִים תְּכַפֵּר עַל־ הַמִּזְבֵּחַ וְקִדַּשְׁתָּ אֹתוֹ
him and-you-consecrate the-altar for you-atone days seven-of (37)

וְהָיָה הַמִּזְבֵּחַ קֹדֶשׁ קָדָשִׁים כָּל־ הַנֹּגֵעַ
the-one-touching every-of the-holy-ones holiest-of the-altar then-he-will-be

בַּמִּזְבֵּחַ יִקְדָּשׁ׃ (38) וְזֶה אֲשֶׁר תַּעֲשֶׂה עַל־ הַמִּזְבֵּחַ כְּבָשִׂים
lambs the-altar on you-offer what now-this (38) he-will-be-holy on-the-altar

to make to the LORD from their fellowship offerings.[d]
29"Aaron's sacred garments will belong to his descendants so that they can be anointed and ordained in them.
30The son who succeeds him as priest and comes to the Tent of Meeting to minister in the Holy Place is to wear them seven days.
31"Take the ram for the ordination and cook the meat in a sacred place.
32At the entrance to the Tent of Meeting, Aaron and his sons are to eat the meat of the ram and the bread that is in the basket.
33They are to eat these offerings by which atonement was made for their ordination and consecration. But no one else may eat them, because they are sacred.
34And if any of the meat of the ordination ram or any bread is left over till morning, burn it up. It must not be eaten, because it is sacred.
35"Do for Aaron and his sons everything I have commanded you, taking seven days to ordain them.
36Sacrifice a bull each day as a sin offering to make atonement. Purify the altar by making atonement for it, and anoint it to consecrate it.
37For seven days make atonement for the altar and consecrate it. Then the altar will be most holy, and whatever touches it will be holy.
38"This is what you are to offer on the altar regularly

[d]28 Traditionally *peace offerings*

בְּנֵי־ שָׁנָה שְׁנַיִם לַיּוֹם תָּמִיד׃ אֶת־ הַכֶּבֶשׂ הָאֶחָד

the-one the-lamb *** (39) regularly each-the-day two one-year sons-of

תַּעֲשֶׂה בַבֹּקֶר וְאֵת הַכֶּבֶשׂ הַשֵּׁנִי תַּעֲשֶׂה בֵּין הָעַרְבָּיִם׃

the-twilight at you-offer the-other the-lamb and in-the-morning you-offer

וְעִשָּׂרֹן סֹלֶת בָּלוּל בְּשֶׁמֶן כָּתִית רֶבַע הַהִין

the-hin fourth-of pressed with-oil being-mixed fine-flour and-tenth (40)

וְנֶסֶךְ רְבִיעִת הַהִין יָיִן לַכֶּבֶשׂ הָאֶחָד׃ וְאֵת

and (41) the-first with-the-lamb wine the-hin fourth-of and-drink-offering

הַכֶּבֶשׂ הַשֵּׁנִי תַּעֲשֶׂה בֵּין הָעַרְבָּיִם כְּמִנְחַת הַבֹּקֶר

the-morning as-offering-of the-twilight at you-offer the-other the-lamb

וּכְנִסְכָּהּ תַּעֲשֶׂה־ לָּהּ לְרֵיחַ נִיחֹחַ אִשֶּׁה

by-fire pleasant for-aroma-of with-her you-offer and-as-drink-offering-of-her

לַיהוָה׃ עֹלַת תָּמִיד לְדֹרֹתֵיכֶם פֶּתַח

entrance-of for-generations-of-you continual burnt-offering-of (42) to-Yahweh

אֹהֶל־ מוֹעֵד לִפְנֵי יְהוָה אֲשֶׁר אִוָּעֵד לָכֶם שָׁמָּה לְדַבֵּר

to-speak at-there with-you I-will-meet where Yahweh before Meeting Tent-of

אֵלֶיךָ שָׁם׃ וְנֹעַדְתִּי שָׁמָּה לִבְנֵי יִשְׂרָאֵל

Israel with-sons-of at-there also-I-will-meet (43) there to-you

וְנִקְדַּשׁ בִּכְבֹדִי׃ וְקִדַּשְׁתִּי אֶת־

*** so-I-will-consecrate (44) by-glory-of-me and-he-will-be-consecrated

אֹהֶל מוֹעֵד וְאֶת־ הַמִּזְבֵּחַ וְאֶת־ אַהֲרֹן וְאֶת־ בָּנָיו אֲקַדֵּשׁ

I-will-consecrate sons-of-him and Aaron and the-altar and Meeting Tent-of

לְכַהֵן לִי׃ וְשָׁכַנְתִּי בְּתוֹךְ בְּנֵי יִשְׂרָאֵל וְהָיִיתִי

and-I-will-be Israel sons-of among then-I-will-dwell (45) to-me to-be-priest

לָהֶם לֵאלֹהִים׃ וְיָדְעוּ כִּי אֲנִי יְהוָה אֱלֹהֵיהֶם אֲשֶׁר

who God-of-them Yahweh I that then-they-will-know (46) as-God to-them

הוֹצֵאתִי אֹתָם מֵאֶרֶץ מִצְרַיִם לְשָׁכְנִי בְתוֹכָם אֲנִי יְהוָה

Yahweh I among-them so-to-dwell-me Egypt from-land-of them I-brought

אֱלֹהֵיהֶם׃ וְעָשִׂיתָ מִזְבֵּחַ מִקְטַר קְטֹרֶת עֲצֵי שִׁטִּים

acacias woods-of incense burner-of altar and-you-make (30:1) God-of-them

תַּעֲשֶׂה אֹתוֹ׃ אַמָּה אָרְכּוֹ וְאַמָּה רָחְבּוֹ רָבוּעַ

being-square width-of-him and-cubit length-of-him cubit (2) him you-make

יִהְיֶה וְאַמָּתַיִם קֹמָתוֹ מִמֶּנּוּ קַרְנֹתָיו׃

horns-of-him from-him height-of-him and-two-cubits he-shall-be

וְצִפִּיתָ אֹתוֹ זָהָב טָהוֹר אֶת־ גַּגּוֹ וְאֶת־ קִירֹתָיו סָבִיב וְאֶת־

and around sides-of-him and top-of-him *** pure gold him and-you-overlay (3)

קַרְנֹתָיו וְעָשִׂיתָ לּוֹ זֵר זָהָב סָבִיב׃ וּשְׁתֵּי

and-two-of (4) around gold molding-of for him and-you-make horns-of-him

each day: two lambs a year
old. 39Offer one in the morning and the other at twilight.
40With the first lamb offer a
tenth of an ephah[f] of fine flour
mixed with a fourth of a hin[g]
of oil from pressed olives, and
a fourth of a hin of wine as a
drink offering. 41Sacrifice the
other lamb at twilight with the
same grain offering and its
drink offering as in the morning—a pleasing aroma, an
offering made to the LORD by
fire.

42"For the generations to
come this burnt offering is to
be made regularly at the entrance to the Tent of Meeting
before the LORD. There I will
meet you and speak to you;
43there also I will meet with
the Israelites, and the place
will be consecrated by my glory.

44"So I will consecrate the
Tent of Meeting and the altar
and will consecrate Aaron and
his sons to serve me as priests.
45Then I will dwell among the
Israelites and be their God.
46They will know that I am the
LORD their God, who brought
them out of Egypt so that I
might dwell among them. I am
the LORD their God.

The Altar of Incense

30 "Make an altar of
acacia wood for burn-
ing incense. 2It is to be square,
a cubit long and a cubit wide,
and two cubits high[h]—its
horns of one piece with it.
3Overlay the top and all the
sides and the horns with pure
gold, and make a gold molding

[f]40 That is, probably about 2 quarts (about 2 liters)
[g]40 That is, probably about 1 quart (about 1 liter)
[h]2 That is, about 1 1/2 feet (about 0.5 meter) long and wide and about 3 feet (about 0.9 meter) high

טַבְּעֹת זָהָב תַּעֲשֶׂה־ לּוֹ ׀ מִתַּחַת לְזֵרוֹ עַל שְׁתֵּי
two-of on to-molding-of-him for-below for-him you-make gold rings-of

צַלְעֹתָיו תַּעֲשֶׂה עַל־ שְׁנֵי צִדָּיו וְהָיָה לְבָתִּים
as-holders and-he-shall-be sides-of-him two-of on you-make sides-of-him

לְבַדִּים לָשֵׂאת אֹתוֹ בָּהֵמָּה׃ וְעָשִׂיתָ אֶת־ הַבַּדִּים עֲצֵי
woods-of the-poles *** and-you-make (5) with-them him to-carry for-poles

שִׁטִּים וְצִפִּיתָ אֹתָם זָהָב׃ וְנָתַתָּה אֹתוֹ לִפְנֵי הַפָּרֹכֶת
the-curtain in-front-of him and-you-put (6) gold them and-you-overlay acacias

אֲשֶׁר עַל־ אֲרֹן הָעֵדֻת לִפְנֵי הַכַּפֹּרֶת אֲשֶׁר עַל־
over that the-atonement-cover before the-Testimony ark-of before that

הָעֵדֻת אֲשֶׁר אִוָּעֵד לְךָ שָׁמָּה׃ וְהִקְטִיר עָלָיו
on-him and-he-must-burn (7) at-there with-you I-will-meet where the-Testimony

אַהֲרֹן קְטֹרֶת סַמִּים בַּבֹּקֶר בַּבֹּקֶר בְּהֵיטִיבוֹ
when-to-tend-him in-the-morning in-the-morning fragrances incense-of Aaron

אֶת־ הַנֵּרֹת יַקְטִירֶנָּה׃ וּבְהַעֲלֹת אַהֲרֹן אֶת־ הַנֵּרֹת
the-lamps *** Aaron and-when-to-light (8) he-must-burn-her the-lamps ***

בֵּין הָעַרְבַּיִם* יַקְטִירֶנָּה קְטֹרֶת תָּמִיד לִפְנֵי יְהוָה
Yahweh before regularly incense he-must-burn-her the-twilight at

לְדֹרֹתֵיכֶם׃ לֹא־ תַעֲלוּ עָלָיו קְטֹרֶת זָרָה
other incense-of on-him you-offer not (9) for-generations-of-you

וְעֹלָה וּמִנְחָה וְנֵסֶךְ לֹא תִסְּכוּ עָלָיו׃
on-him you-pour not and-drink-offering or-grain-offering or-burnt-offering

וְכִפֶּר אַהֲרֹן עַל־ קַרְנֹתָיו אַחַת בַּשָּׁנָה מִדַּם
from-blood-of in-the-year once horns-of-him on Aaron and-he-shall-atone (10)

חַטַּאת הַכִּפֻּרִים אַחַת בַּשָּׁנָה יְכַפֵּר עָלָיו
with-him he-shall-atone in-the-year once the-atonements sin-offering-of

לְדֹרֹתֵיכֶם קֹדֶשׁ־ קָדָשִׁים הוּא לַיהוָה׃ וַיְדַבֵּר
then-he-spoke (11) to-Yahweh this holy-ones holiest-of for-generations-of-you

יְהוָה אֶל־ מֹשֶׁה לֵּאמֹר׃ כִּי תִשָּׂא אֶת־ רֹאשׁ בְּנֵי־ יִשְׂרָאֵל
Israel sons-of census-of *** you-take when (12) to-say Moses to Yahweh

לִפְקֻדֵיהֶם וְנָתְנוּ אִישׁ כֹּפֶר נַפְשׁוֹ לַיהוָה
to-Yahweh life-of-him ransom-of each then-they-must-pay in-countings-of-them

בִּפְקֹד אֹתָם וְלֹא־ יִהְיֶה בָהֶם נֶגֶף בִּפְקֹד אֹתָם׃
them when-to-count plague on-them he-will-come then-not them when-to-count

זֶה ׀ יִתְּנוּ כָּל־ הָעֹבֵר עַל־ הַפְּקֻדִים
the-ones-being-counted to the-one-crossing every-of they-shall-give this (13)

מַחֲצִית הַשֶּׁקֶל בְּשֶׁקֶל הַקֹּדֶשׁ עֶשְׂרִים גֵּרָה הַשֶּׁקֶל
the-shekel gerah twenty the-sanctuary by-shekel-of the-shekel half-of

around it. [4]Make two gold
rings for the altar below the
molding—two on opposite
sides—to hold the poles used
to carry it. [5]Make the poles of
acacia wood and overlay them
with gold. [6]Put the altar in
front of the curtain that is before the ark of the Testimony—
before the atonement cover
that is over the Testimony—
where I will meet with you.

[7]"Aaron must burn fragrant
incense on the altar every
morning when he tends the
lamps. [8]He must burn incense
again when he lights the
lamps at twilight so incense
will burn regularly before the
LORD for the generations to
come. [9]Do not offer on this altar any other incense or any
burnt offering or grain
offering, and do not pour a
drink offering on it. [10]Once a
year Aaron shall make atonement on its horns. This annual
atonement must be made with
the blood of the atoning sin
offering for the generations to
come. It is most holy to the
LORD."

Atonement Money

[11]Then the LORD said to
Moses, [12]"When you take a
census of the Israelites to
count them, each one must
pay the LORD a ransom for his
life at the time he is counted.
Then no plague will come on
them when you number them.
[13]Each one who crosses over to
those already counted is to
give a half shekel,[i] according
to the sanctuary shekel, which
weighs twenty gerahs. This

[i]*13* That is, about 1/5 ounce (about 6 grams); also in verse 15

*8 Most mss have *pathah* under the *ayin* (הָעַרְ').

מַחֲצִית הַשֶּׁקֶל תְּרוּמָה לַיהוָה׃ כֹּל הָעֹבֵר עַל־
to the-one-crossing every-of (14) to-Yahweh offering the-shekel half-of

הַפְּקֻדִים מִבֶּן עֶשְׂרִים שָׁנָה וָמָעְלָה יִתֵּן
he-shall-give and-upward year twenty from-son-of the-ones-being-counted

תְּרוּמַת יְהוָה׃ הֶעָשִׁיר לֹא־ יַרְבֶּה וְהַדַּל לֹא
not and-the-poor he-may-give-more not the-rich (15) Yahweh offering-of

יַמְעִיט מִמַּחֲצִית הַשָּׁקֶל לָתֵת אֶת־ תְּרוּמַת יְהוָה לְכַפֵּר
to-atone Yahweh offering-of *** to-make the-shekel than-half-of he-may-give-less

עַל־ נַפְשֹׁתֵיכֶם׃ וְלָקַחְתָּ אֶת־ כֶּסֶף הַכִּפֻּרִים מֵאֵת
from the-atonements money-of *** and-you-receive (16) lives-of-you for

בְּנֵי יִשְׂרָאֵל וְנָתַתָּ אֹתוֹ עַל־ עֲבֹדַת אֹהֶל מוֹעֵד וְהָיָה
and-he-will-be Meeting Tent-of service-of for him and-you-use Israel sons-of

לִבְנֵי יִשְׂרָאֵל לְזִכָּרוֹן לִפְנֵי יְהוָה לְכַפֵּר עַל־ נַפְשֹׁתֵיכֶם׃
lives-of-you for to-atone Yahweh before as-memorial Israel for-sons-of

וַיְדַבֵּר יְהוָה אֶל־ מֹשֶׁה לֵּאמֹר׃ וְעָשִׂיתָ כִּיּוֹר נְחֹשֶׁת
bronze basin-of now-you-make (18) to-say Moses to Yahweh then-he-spoke (17)

וְכַנּוֹ נְחֹשֶׁת לְרָחְצָה וְנָתַתָּ אֹתוֹ בֵּין־ אֹהֶל מוֹעֵד
Meeting Tent-of between him and-you-place for-to-wash bronze and-stand-of-him

וּבֵין הַמִּזְבֵּחַ וְנָתַתָּ שָׁמָּה מָיִם׃ וְרָחֲצוּ
and-they-shall-wash (19) waters in-there and-you-put the-altar and-between

אַהֲרֹן וּבָנָיו מִמֶּנּוּ אֶת־ יְדֵיהֶם וְאֶת־ רַגְלֵיהֶם׃
feet-of-them and hands-of-them *** from-him and-sons-of-him Aaron

בְּבֹאָם אֶל־ אֹהֶל מוֹעֵד יִרְחֲצוּ־ מַיִם וְלֹא
so-not waters they-shall-wash Meeting Tent-of into when-to-enter-them (20)

יָמֻתוּ אוֹ בְגִשְׁתָּם אֶל־ הַמִּזְבֵּחַ לְשָׁרֵת לְהַקְטִיר
to-present to-minister the-altar to when-to-approach-them also they-will-die

אִשֶּׁה לַיהוָה׃ וְרָחֲצוּ יְדֵיהֶם
hands-of-them and-they-shall-wash (21) to-Yahweh fire-offering

וְרַגְלֵיהֶם וְלֹא יָמֻתוּ וְהָיְתָה לָהֶם חָק־
ordinance-of for-them and-she-will-be they-will-die so-not and-feet-of-them

עוֹלָם לוֹ וּלְזַרְעוֹ לְדֹרֹתָם׃
for-generations-of-them and-for-descendant-of-him for-him lasting

וַיְדַבֵּר יְהוָה אֶל־מֹשֶׁה לֵּאמֹר׃ וְאַתָּה קַח־ לְךָ בְּשָׂמִים רֹאשׁ
fine spices to-you take! now-you (23) to-say Moses to Yahweh then-he-spoke (22)

מָר־ דְּרוֹר חֲמֵשׁ מֵאוֹת וְקִנְּמָן־ בֶּשֶׂם מַחֲצִיתוֹ חֲמִשִּׁים
fifty half-of-him fragrant and-cinnamon-of hundreds five-of liquid myrrh-of

וּמָאתָיִם וּקְנֵה־ בֹשֶׂם חֲמִשִּׁים וּמָאתָיִם׃ וְקִדָּה
and-cassia (24) and-two-hundred fifty fragrant and-cane-of and-two-hundred

half shekel is an offering to the
LORD. [14]All who cross over,
those twenty years old or
more, are to give an offering to
the LORD. [15]The rich are not to
give more than a half shekel
and the poor are not to give
less when you make the
offering to the LORD to atone
for your lives. [16]Receive the
atonement money from the Israelites and use it for the service of the Tent of Meeting. It
will be a memorial for the Israelites before the LORD, making
atonement for your lives."

Basin for Washing

[17]Then the LORD said to
Moses, [18]"Make a bronze basin, with its bronze stand, for
washing. Place it between the
Tent of Meeting and the altar,
and put water in it. [19]Aaron
and his sons are to wash their
hands and feet with water
from it. [20]Whenever they enter
the Tent of Meeting, they shall
wash with water so that they
will not die. Also, when they
approach the altar to minister
by presenting an offering
made to the LORD by fire,
[21]they shall wash their hands
and feet so that they will not
die. This is to be a lasting ordinance for Aaron and his descendants for the generations
to come."

Anointing Oil

[22]Then the LORD said to
Moses, [23]"Take the following
fine spices: 500 shekels[j] of liquid myrrh, half as much (that
is, 250 shekels) of fragrant cin-
namon, 250 shekels of fragrant cane, [24]500 shekels of

j23 That is, about 12 1/2 pounds (about 6 kilograms)

חֲמֵשׁ מֵאוֹת בְּשֶׁקֶל הַקֹּדֶשׁ וְשֶׁמֶן זַיִת הִין׃

hin olive and-oil-of the-sanctuary by-shekel-of hundreds five-of

וְעָשִׂיתָ אֹתוֹ שֶׁמֶן מִשְׁחַת־ קֹדֶשׁ רֹקַח מִרְקַחַת מַעֲשֵׂה

work-of fragrant blend-of sacred anointing-of oil-of him and-you-make (25)

רֹקֵחַ שֶׁמֶן מִשְׁחַת־ קֹדֶשׁ יִהְיֶה׃ וּמָשַׁחְתָּ

then-you-anoint (26) he-will-be sacred anointing-of oil-of one-perfuming

בוֹ אֶת־ אֹהֶל מוֹעֵד וְאֵת אֲרוֹן הָעֵדֻת׃ וְאֶת־ הַשֻּׁלְחָן וְאֶת־

and the-table and (27) the-Testimony ark-of and Meeting Tent-of *** with-him

כָּל־ כֵּלָיו וְאֶת־ הַמְּנֹרָה וְאֶת־ כֵּלֶיהָ וְאֵת מִזְבַּח

altar-of and accessories-of-her and the-lampstand and articles-of-him all-of

הַקְּטֹרֶת׃ וְאֶת־ מִזְבַּח הָעֹלָה וְאֶת־ כָּל־ כֵּלָיו

utensils-of-him all-of and the-burnt-offering altar-of and (28) the-incense

וְאֶת־ הַכִּיֹּר וְאֶת־ כַּנּוֹ׃ וְקִדַּשְׁתָּ אֹתָם

them so-you-shall-consecrate (29) stand-of-him and the-basin and

וְהָיוּ קֹדֶשׁ קָדָשִׁים כָּל־ הַנֹּגֵעַ בָּהֶם

on-them the-one-touching every-of holy-ones holiest-of so-they-will-be

יִקְדָּשׁ׃ וְאֶת־ אַהֲרֹן וְאֶת־ בָּנָיו תִּמְשָׁח וְקִדַּשְׁתָּ

and-you-consecrate you-anoint sons-of-him and Aaron and (30) he-will-be-holy

אֹתָם לְכַהֵן לִי׃ וְאֶל־ בְּנֵי יִשְׂרָאֵל תְּדַבֵּר לֵאמֹר שֶׁמֶן

oil-of to-say you-speak Israel sons-of and-to (31) to-me to-be-priest them

מִשְׁחַת־ קֹדֶשׁ יִהְיֶה זֶה לִי לְדֹרֹתֵיכֶם׃ עַל־ בְּשַׂר

body-of on (32) for-generations-of-you to-me this he-is sacred anointing-of

אָדָם לֹא יִיסָךְ וּבְמַתְכֻּנְתּוֹ לֹא תַעֲשׂוּ כָּמֹהוּ קֹדֶשׁ

sacred like-him you-make not and-with-formula-of-him he-shall-pour not man

הוּא קֹדֶשׁ יִהְיֶה לָכֶם׃ אִישׁ אֲשֶׁר יִרְקַח כָּמֹהוּ וַאֲשֶׁר

or-who like-him he-mixes who anyone (33) to-you he-shall-be sacred he

יִתֵּן מִמֶּנּוּ עַל־ זָר וְנִכְרַת מֵעַמָּיו׃

from-people-of-him now-he-must-be-cut-off being-outsider on from-him he-puts

וַיֹּאמֶר יְהוָה אֶל־ מֹשֶׁה קַח־ לְךָ סַמִּים נָטָף ׀ וּשְׁחֵלֶת

and-onycha gum-resin spices to-you take! Moses to Yahweh then-he-said (34)

וְחֶלְבְּנָה סַמִּים וּלְבֹנָה זַכָּה בַּד בְּבַד יִהְיֶה׃

he-shall-be for-amount amount pure and-frankincense spices and-galbanum

וְעָשִׂיתָ אֹתָהּ קְטֹרֶת רֹקַח מַעֲשֵׂה רוֹקֵחַ מְמֻלָּח טָהוֹר

pure being-salted one-perfuming work-of blend incense her and-you-make (35)

קֹדֶשׁ׃ וְשָׁחַקְתָּ מִמֶּנָּה הָדֵק וְנָתַתָּה מִמֶּנָּה

from-her and-you-place to-be-powder from-her then-you-beat (36) sacred

לִפְנֵי הָעֵדֻת בְּאֹהֶל מוֹעֵד אֲשֶׁר אִוָּעֵד לְךָ

with-you I-will-meet where Meeting in-Tent-of the-Testimony in-front-of

cassia—all according to the sanctuary shekel—and a hin[k]
of olive oil. 25Make these into a
sacred anointing oil, a fragrant blend, the work of a perfumer. It will be the sacred anointing oil. 26Then use it to
anoint the Tent of Meeting, the ark of the Testimony, 27the
table and all its articles, the lampstand and its accessories, the altar of incense, 28the altar
of burnt offering and all its utensils, and the basin with its
stand. 29You shall consecrate
them so they will be most holy, and whatever touches them will be holy.
30"Anoint Aaron and his sons and consecrate them so they may serve me as priests.
31Say to the Israelites, 'This is to be my sacred anointing oil for the generations to come.
32Do not pour it on men's bodies and do not make any oil with the same formula. It is sacred, and you are to consider it sacred.
33Whoever makes perfume like it and whoever puts it on anyone other than a priest must be cut off from his people.' "

Incense

34Then the LORD said to Moses, "Take fragrant spices—gum resin, onycha and galbanum—and pure frankincense, all in equal amounts,
35and make a fragrant blend of incense, the work of a perfumer. It is to be salted and pure and sacred.
36Grind some of it to powder and place it in front of the Testimony in the Tent of Meeting, where I will meet

[k]24 That is, probably about 4 quarts (about 4 liters)

שָׁמָּה קֹדֶשׁ קָדָשִׁים תִּהְיֶה לָכֶם׃ וְהַקְּטֹרֶת אֲשֶׁר

that and-the-incense (37) to-you she-shall-be holy-ones holiest-of at-there

תַּעֲשֶׂה בְּמַתְכֻּנְתָּהּ לֹא תַעֲשׂוּ לָכֶם קֹדֶשׁ תִּהְיֶה לְךָ

to-you she-is holy for-yourselves you-make not with-formula-of-her you-make

לַיהוָה׃ אִישׁ אֲשֶׁר־יַעֲשֶׂה כָמוֹהָ לְהָרִיחַ בָּהּ

from-her to-enjoy-fragrance like-her he-makes who anyone (38) to-Yahweh

וְנִכְרַת מֵעַמָּיו׃ וַיְדַבֵּר יְהוָה אֶל־

to Yahweh then-he-spoke (31:1) from-people-of-him now-he-must-be-cut-off

מֹשֶׁה לֵּאמֹר׃ רְאֵה קָרָאתִי בְשֵׁם בְּצַלְאֵל בֶּן־אוּרִי בֶן־חוּר

Hur son-of Uri son-of Bezalel by-name I-chose see! (2) to-say Moses

לְמַטֵּה יְהוּדָה׃ וָאֲמַלֵּא אֹתוֹ רוּחַ אֱלֹהִים בְּחָכְמָה

with-skill God Spirit-of him and-I-filled (3) Judah from-tribe-of

וּבִתְבוּנָה וּבְדַעַת וּבְכָל־מְלָאכָה׃ לַחְשֹׁב

to-make (4) craft and-with-all-of and-with-knowledge and-with-ability

מַחֲשָׁבֹת לַעֲשׂוֹת בַּזָּהָב וּבַכֶּסֶף וּבַנְּחֹשֶׁת׃

and-in-the-bronze and-in-the-silver in-the-gold to-work artistic-designs

וּבַחֲרֹשֶׁת אֶבֶן לְמַלֹּאת וּבַחֲרֹשֶׁת עֵץ לַעֲשׂוֹת בְּכָל־

in-all-of to-engage wood and-in-cutting-of to-set stone and-in-cutting-of (5)

מְלָאכָה׃ וַאֲנִי הִנֵּה נָתַתִּי אִתּוֹ אֵת אָהֳלִיאָב בֶּן־

son-of Oholiab *** with-him I-appointed see! and-I (6) craftsmanship

אֲחִיסָמָךְ לְמַטֵּה־דָן וּבְלֵב כָּל־חֲכַם־לֵב נָתַתִּי

I-gave heart skilled-of every-of and-in-heart-of Dan from-tribe-of Ahisamach

חָכְמָה וְעָשׂוּ אֵת כָּל־אֲשֶׁר צִוִּיתִךָ׃ אֵת ׀ אֹהֶל מוֹעֵד

Meeting Tent-of *** (7) I-commanded-you that all *** so-they-can-make skill

וְאֶת־הָאָרֹן לָעֵדֻת וְאֶת־הַכַּפֹּרֶת אֲשֶׁר עָלָיו וְאֵת כָּל־

all-of and on-him that the-atonement-cover and of-the-Testimony the-ark and

כְּלֵי הָאֹהֶל׃ וְאֶת־הַשֻּׁלְחָן וְאֶת־כֵּלָיו וְאֶת־הַמְּנֹרָה

the-lampstand and articles-of-him and the-table and (8) the-Tent furnishings-of

הַטְּהֹרָה וְאֶת־כָּל־כֵּלֶיהָ וְאֵת מִזְבַּח הַקְּטֹרֶת׃ וְאֶת־

and (9) the-incense altar-of and accessories-of-her all-of and the pure

מִזְבַּח הָעֹלָה וְאֶת־כָּל־כֵּלָיו וְאֶת־הַכִּיֹּר וְאֶת־

and the-basin and utensils-of-him all-of and the-burnt-offering altar-of

כַּנּוֹ׃ וְאֵת בִּגְדֵי הַשְּׂרָד וְאֶת־בִּגְדֵי הַקֹּדֶשׁ

the-sacred garments-of and the-woven garments-of and (10) stand-of-him

לְאַהֲרֹן הַכֹּהֵן וְאֶת־בִּגְדֵי בָנָיו לְכַהֵן׃ וְאֵת

and (11) for-to-be-priest sons-of-him garments-of and the-priest for-Aaron

שֶׁמֶן הַמִּשְׁחָה וְאֶת־קְטֹרֶת הַסַּמִּים לַקֹּדֶשׁ כְּכֹל

as-all for-the-Holy-Place the-fragrances incense-of and the-anointing oil-of

with you. It shall be most holy
to you. 37Do not make any incense with this formula for
yourselves; consider it holy to
the LORD. 38Whoever makes
any like it to enjoy its fra-
grance must be cut off from his
people."

Bezalel and Oholiab

31 Then the LORD said to
Moses, 2"See, I have
chosen Bezalel son of Uri, the
son of Hur, of the tribe of
Judah, 3and I have filled him
with the Spirit of God, with
skill, ability and knowledge in
all kinds of crafts— 4to make
artistic designs for work in
gold, silver and bronze, 5to cut
and set stones, to work in
wood, and to engage in all
kinds of craftsmanship.
6Moreover, I have appointed
Oholiab son of Ahisamach, of
the tribe of Dan, to help him.
Also I have given skill to all
the craftsmen to make everything I have commanded you:
7the Tent of Meeting, the ark
of the Testimony with the
atonement cover on it, and all
the other furnishings of the
tent— 8the table and its articles, the pure gold lampstand
and all its accessories, the altar
of incense, 9the altar of burnt
offering and all its utensils, the
basin with its stand— 10and
also the woven garments, both
the sacred garments for Aaron
the priest and the garments for
his sons when they serve as
priests, 11and the anointing oil
and fragrant incense for the
Holy Place. They are to make

אֲשֶׁר־ צִוִּיתִךָ יַעֲשׂוּ׃ וַיֹּאמֶר יְהוָה אֶל־ מֹשֶׁה

Moses to Yahweh then-he-said (12) they-will-make I-commanded-you that

לֵּאמֹר׃ וְאַתָּה דַּבֵּר אֶל־ בְּנֵי יִשְׂרָאֵל לֵאמֹר אַךְ אֶת־ שַׁבְּתֹתַי

Sabbaths-of-me *** surely to-say Israel sons-of to speak! now-you (13) to-say

תִּשְׁמֹרוּ כִּי אוֹת הִוא בֵּינִי וּבֵינֵיכֶם

and-between-you between-me this sign for you-must-observe

לְדֹרֹתֵיכֶם לָדַעַת כִּי אֲנִי יְהוָה מְקַדִּשְׁכֶם׃

one-making-holy-you Yahweh I that to-know for-generations-of-you

וּשְׁמַרְתֶּם אֶת־ הַשַּׁבָּת כִּי קֹדֶשׁ הִוא לָכֶם מְחַלְלֶיהָ

one-desecrating-her to-you she holy for the-Sabbath *** so-you-observe (14)

מוֹת יוּמָת כִּי כָּל־ הָעֹשֶׂה בָהּ מְלָאכָה וְנִכְרְתָה

now-she-must-be-cut work on-her the-one-doing every-of also he-must-die to-die

הַנֶּפֶשׁ הַהִוא מִקֶּרֶב עַמֶּיהָ׃ שֵׁשֶׁת יָמִים יֵעָשֶׂה

he-may-be-done days six-of (15) people-of-her from-among the-that the-person

מְלָאכָה וּבַיּוֹם הַשְּׁבִיעִי שַׁבַּת שַׁבָּתוֹן קֹדֶשׁ לַיהוָה כָּל־

every-of to-Yahweh holy rest Sabbath-of the-seventh but-on-the-day work

הָעֹשֶׂה מְלָאכָה בְּיוֹם הַשַּׁבָּת מוֹת יוּמָת׃

he-must-die to-die the-Sabbath on-day-of work the-one-doing

וְשָׁמְרוּ בְנֵי־ יִשְׂרָאֵל אֶת־ הַשַּׁבָּת לַעֲשׂוֹת אֶת־

*** to-celebrate the-Sabbath *** Israel sons-of so-they-must-observe (16)

הַשַּׁבָּת לְדֹרֹתָם בְּרִית עוֹלָם׃ בֵּינִי

between-me (17) lasting covenant-of for-generations-of-them the-Sabbath

וּבֵין בְּנֵי יִשְׂרָאֵל אוֹת הִוא לְעֹלָם כִּי־ שֵׁשֶׁת יָמִים עָשָׂה יְהוָה

Yahweh he-made days six-of for for-ever she sign Israel sons-of and-between

אֶת־ הַשָּׁמַיִם וְאֶת־ הָאָרֶץ וּבַיּוֹם הַשְּׁבִיעִי שָׁבַת

he-stopped-work the-seventh and-on-the-day the-earth and the-heavens ***

וַיִּנָּפַשׁ׃ וַיִּתֵּן אֶל־ מֹשֶׁה כְּכַלֹּתוֹ לְדַבֵּר אִתּוֹ

to-him to-speak when-to-finish-him Moses to and-he-gave (18) and-he-rested

בְּהַר סִינַי שְׁנֵי לֻחֹת הָעֵדֻת לֻחֹת אֶבֶן

stone tablets-of the-Testimony tablets-of two-of Sinai on-Mount-of

כְּתֻבִים בְּאֶצְבַּע אֱלֹהִים׃ וַיַּרְא הָעָם כִּי־

that the-people when-he-saw (32:1) God by-finger-of being-inscribed

בֹשֵׁשׁ מֹשֶׁה לָרֶדֶת מִן־ הָהָר וַיִּקָּהֵל הָעָם

the-people then-he-gathered the-mountain from to-come-down Moses he-took-long

עַל־ אַהֲרֹן וַיֹּאמְרוּ אֵלָיו קוּם | עֲשֵׂה־ לָנוּ אֱלֹהִים אֲשֶׁר יֵלְכוּ

they-will-go who gods for-us make! come! to-him and-they-said Aaron around

לְפָנֵינוּ כִּי־ זֶה | מֹשֶׁה הָאִישׁ אֲשֶׁר הֶעֱלָנוּ מֵאֶרֶץ מִצְרָיִם

Egypt from-land-of he-brought-us who the-fellow Moses this for before-us

them just as I commanded you."

The Sabbath

[12]Then the LORD said to Moses, [13]"Say to the Israelites, 'You must observe my Sabbaths. This will be a sign between me and you for the generations to come, so you may know that I am the LORD, who makes you holy.[l]

[14]" 'Observe the Sabbath, because it is holy to you. Anyone who desecrates it must be put to death; whoever does any work on that day must be cut off from his people. [15]For six days work is to be done, but the seventh day is a Sabbath of rest, holy to the LORD. Whoever does any work on the Sabbath day must be put to death. [16]The Israelites are to observe the Sabbath, celebrating it for the generations to come as a lasting covenant. [17]It will be a sign between me and the Israelites forever, for in six days the LORD made the heavens and the earth, and on the seventh day he abstained from work and rested.' "

[18]When the LORD finished speaking to Moses on Mount Sinai, he gave him the two tablets of the Testimony, the tablets of stone inscribed by the finger of God.

The Golden Calf

32 When the people saw that Moses was so long in coming down from the mountain, they gathered around Aaron and said, "Come, make us gods[m] who will go before us. As for this fellow Moses who brought us up out of Egypt, we don't

[l]13 Or *who sanctifies you*; or *who sets you apart as holy*
[m]1 Or *a god*; also in verses 23 and 31

לֹא יָדַעְנוּ מֶה־ הָיָה לוֹ׃ וַיֹּאמֶר אֲלֵהֶם אַהֲרֹן פָּרְקוּ
take-off! Aaron to-them and-he-said (2) to-him he-happened what we-know not

נִזְמֵי הַזָּהָב אֲשֶׁר בְּאָזְנֵי נְשֵׁיכֶם בְּנֵיכֶם
sons-of-you wives-of-you in-ears-of that the-gold earrings-of

וּבְנֹתֵיכֶם וְהָבִיאוּ אֵלָי׃ וַיִּתְפָּרְקוּ כָּל־ הָעָם
the-people all-of so-they-took-off (3) to-me and-bring! and-daughters-of-you

אֶת־ נִזְמֵי הַזָּהָב אֲשֶׁר בְּאָזְנֵיהֶם וַיָּבִיאוּ אֶל־ אַהֲרֹן׃
Aaron to and-they-brought in-ears-of-them that the-gold earrings-of ***

וַיִּקַּח מִיָּדָם וַיָּצַר אֹתוֹ בַּחֶרֶט
with-the-tool him and-he-fashioned from-hand-of-them and-he-took (4)

וַיַּעֲשֵׂהוּ עֵגֶל מַסֵּכָה וַיֹּאמְרוּ אֵלֶּה אֱלֹהֶיךָ יִשְׂרָאֵל אֲשֶׁר
who Israel gods-of-you these then-they-said cast calf-of and-he-make-him

הֶעֱלוּךָ מֵאֶרֶץ מִצְרָיִם׃ וַיַּרְא אַהֲרֹן וַיִּבֶן
then-he-built Aaron when-he-saw (5) Egypt from-land-of they-brought-you

מִזְבֵּחַ לְפָנָיו וַיִּקְרָא אַהֲרֹן וַיֹּאמַר חַג לַיהוָה
to-Yahweh festival and-he-said Aaron and-he-announced in-front-of-him altar

מָחָר׃ וַיַּשְׁכִּימוּ מִמָּחֳרָת וַיַּעֲלוּ עֹלֹת
burnt-offerings and-they-sacrificed on-next-day so-they-rose-early (6) tomorrow

וַיַּגִּשׁוּ שְׁלָמִים וַיֵּשֶׁב הָעָם לֶאֱכֹל
to-eat the-people and-he-sat fellowship-offerings and-they-presented

וְשָׁתוֹ וַיָּקֻמוּ לְצַחֵק׃ וַיְדַבֵּר יְהוָה אֶל־ מֹשֶׁה לֶךְ־
go! Moses to Yahweh then-he-said (7) to-revel and-they-got-up and-to-drink

רֵד כִּי שִׁחֵת עַמְּךָ אֲשֶׁר הֶעֱלֵיתָ מֵאֶרֶץ
from-land-of you-brought whom people-of-you he-became-corrupt for descend!

מִצְרָיִם׃ סָרוּ מַהֵר מִן־ הַדֶּרֶךְ אֲשֶׁר צִוִּיתִם עָשׂוּ
they-made I-commanded-them that the-way from quickly they-turned (8) Egypt

לָהֶם עֵגֶל מַסֵּכָה וַיִּשְׁתַּחֲווּ־ לוֹ וַיִּזְבְּחוּ־ לוֹ
to-him and-they-sacrificed to-him and-they-bowed cast calf-of for-themselves

וַיֹּאמְרוּ אֵלֶּה אֱלֹהֶיךָ יִשְׂרָאֵל אֲשֶׁר הֶעֱלוּךָ מֵאֶרֶץ
from-land-of they-brought-you who Israel gods-of-you these and-they-said

מִצְרָיִם׃ וַיֹּאמֶר יְהוָה אֶל־ מֹשֶׁה רָאִיתִי אֶת־ הָעָם הַזֶּה וְהִנֵּה
and-see! the-this the-people *** I-saw Moses to Yahweh and-he-said (9) Egypt

עַם־ קְשֵׁה־ עֹרֶף הוּא׃ וְעַתָּה הַנִּיחָה לִּי וְיִחַר־
so-he-may-burn to-me leave-alone! and-now (10) he neck stiff-of people-of

אַפִּי בָהֶם וַאֲכַלֵּם וְאֶעֱשֶׂה אוֹתְךָ
you then-I-will-make so-I-may-destroy-them against-them anger-of-me

לְגוֹי גָּדוֹל׃ וַיְחַל מֹשֶׁה אֶת־ פְּנֵי יְהוָה אֱלֹהָיו
God-of-him Yahweh face-of *** Moses then-he-sought (11) great into-nation

know what has happened to
him."
2Aaron answered them,
"Take off the gold earrings
that your wives, your sons and
your daughters are wearing,
and bring them to me." 3So all
the people took off their earrings and brought them to
Aaron. 4He took what they
handed him and made it into
an idol cast in the shape of a
calf, fashioning it with a tool.
Then they said, "These are
your gods,[n] O Israel, who
brought you up out of Egypt."
5When Aaron saw this, he
built an altar in front of the
calf and announced, "Tomorrow there will be a festival to
the LORD." 6So the next day the
people rose early and sacrificed burnt offerings and
presented fellowship of-
ferings.[o] Afterward they sat
down to eat and drink and got
up to indulge in revelry.
7Then the LORD said to
Moses, "Go down, because
your people, whom you
brought up out of Egypt, have
become corrupt. 8They have
been quick to turn away from
what I commanded them and
have made themselves an idol
cast in the shape of a calf. They
have bowed down to it and
sacrificed to it and have said,
'These are your gods, O Israel,
who brought you up out of
Egypt.'
9"I have seen these people,"
the LORD said to Moses, "and
they are a stiff-necked people.
10Now leave me alone so that
my anger may burn against
them and that I may destroy
them. Then I will make you
into a great nation."
11But Moses sought the favor
of the LORD his God. "O

[n]4 Or *This is your god*; also in verse 8
[o]6 Traditionally *peace offerings*

וַיֹּאמֶר לָמָה יְהוָה יֶחֱרֶה אַפְּךָ בְּעַמֶּךָ
against-people-of-you anger-of-you should-he-burn Yahweh why? and-he-said

אֲשֶׁר הוֹצֵאתָ מֵאֶרֶץ מִצְרַיִם בְּכֹחַ גָּדוֹל וּבְיָד חֲזָקָה׃
mighty and-with-hand great with-power Egypt from-land-of you-brought whom

(12) לָמָּה יֹאמְרוּ מִצְרַיִם לֵאמֹר בְּרָעָה הוֹצִיאָם
he-brought-them with-evil-intent to-say Egyptians should-they-say why? (12)

לַהֲרֹג אֹתָם בֶּהָרִים וּלְכַלֹּתָם מֵעַל פְּנֵי הָאֲדָמָה
the-earth face-of from-on and-to-wipe-them in-the-mountains them to-kill

שׁוּב מֵחֲרוֹן אַפֶּךָ וְהִנָּחֵם עַל־ הָרָעָה
the-disaster from and-relent! anger-of-you from-fierceness-of turn!

לְעַמֶּךָ׃ (13) זְכֹר לְאַבְרָהָם לְיִצְחָק וּלְיִשְׂרָאֵל
and-to-Israel to-Isaac to-Abraham remember! (13) on-people-of-you

עֲבָדֶיךָ אֲשֶׁר נִשְׁבַּעְתָּ לָהֶם בָּךְ וַתְּדַבֵּר אֲלֵהֶם
to-them and-you-said by-yourself to-them you-swore whom servants-of-you

אַרְבֶּה אֶת־ זַרְעֲכֶם כְּכוֹכְבֵי הַשָּׁמָיִם וְכָל־ הָאָרֶץ
the-land and-all-of the-skies as-stars-of descendant-of-you *** I-will-increase

הַזֹּאת אֲשֶׁר אָמַרְתִּי אֶתֵּן לְזַרְעֲכֶם וְנָחֲלוּ
and-they-will-inherit to-descendant-of-you I-will-give I-promised that the-this

לְעֹלָם׃ (14) וַיִּנָּחֶם יְהוָה עַל־ הָרָעָה אֲשֶׁר דִּבֶּר
he-threatened that the-disaster from Yahweh then-he-relented (14) for-ever

לַעֲשׂוֹת לְעַמּוֹ׃ (15) וַיִּפֶן וַיֵּרֶד מֹשֶׁה מִן־
from Moses and-he-went-down then-he-turned (15) on-people-of-him to-bring

הָהָר וּשְׁנֵי לֻחֹת הָעֵדֻת בְּיָדוֹ לֻחֹת
tablets in-hand-of-him the-Testimony tablets-of with-two-of the-mountain

כְּתֻבִים מִשְּׁנֵי עֶבְרֵיהֶם מִזֶּה וּמִזֶּה הֵם
they and-on-that on-this sides-of-them on-both-of ones-being-inscribed

כְּתֻבִים׃ (16) וְהַלֻּחֹת מַעֲשֵׂה אֱלֹהִים הֵמָּה וְהַמִּכְתָּב
and-the-writing they God work-of now-the-tablets (16) ones-being-inscribed

מִכְתַּב אֱלֹהִים הוּא חָרוּת עַל־ הַלֻּחֹת׃ (17) וַיִּשְׁמַע יְהוֹשֻׁעַ
Joshua when-he-heard (17) the-tablets on being-engraved he God writing-of

אֶת־ קוֹל הָעָם בְּרֵעֹה° וַיֹּאמֶר אֶל־ מֹשֶׁה קוֹל
sound-of Moses to then-he-said in-shout-of-him the-people sound-of ***

מִלְחָמָה בַּמַּחֲנֶה׃* (18) וַיֹּאמֶר אֵין קוֹל עֲנוֹת גְּבוּרָה
victory to-shout sound-of he-is-not but-he-replied (18) in-the-camp war

וְאֵין קוֹל עֲנוֹת חֲלוּשָׁה קוֹל עַנּוֹת אָנֹכִי שֹׁמֵעַ׃
hearing I to-sing sound-of defeat to-shout sound-of and-he-is-not

(19) וַיְהִי כַּאֲשֶׁר קָרַב אֶל־ הַמַּחֲנֶה וַיַּרְא אֶת־ הָעֵגֶל
the-calf *** and-he-saw the-camp to he-approached when and-he-was (19)

LORD," he said, "why should
your anger burn against your
people, whom you brought
out of Egypt with great power
and a mighty hand? 12Why
should the Egyptians say, 'It
was with evil intent that he
brought them out, to kill them
in the mountains and to wipe
them off the face of the earth'?
Turn from your fierce anger;
relent and do not bring disaster on your people. 13Remem-
ber your servants Abraham,
Isaac and Israel, to whom you
swore by your own self: 'I will
make your descendants as numerous as the stars in the sky
and I will give your descendants all this land I promised
them, and it will be their inheritance forever.'" 14Then
the LORD relented and did not
bring on his people the disaster he had threatened.
15Moses turned and went
down the mountain with the
two tablets of the Testimony
in his hands. They were inscribed on both sides, front
and back. 16The tablets were
the work of God; the writing
was the writing of God, engraved on the tablets.
17When Joshua heard the
noise of the people shouting,
he said to Moses, "There is the
sound of war in the camp."
18Moses replied:

"It is not the sound of
victory,
it is not the sound of
defeat;
it is the sound of singing
that I hear."

19When Moses approached
the camp and saw the calf and

**17 Most mss have the accent *silluq* at the end of the final word (נֶה–).*

°*17* ברעו ק

וּמְחֹלֹת וַיִּחַר־ אַף מֹשֶׁה וַיַּשְׁלֵךְ מִיָּדוֹ אֶת־
*** from-hand-of-him and-he-threw Moses anger-of then-he-burned and-dances

הַלֻּחֹת וַיְשַׁבֵּר אֹתָם תַּחַת הָהָר׃ וַיִּקַּח אֶת־
*** and-he-took (20) the-mountain at-foot-of them and-he-broke the-tablets

הָעֵגֶל אֲשֶׁר עָשׂוּ וַיִּשְׂרֹף בָּאֵשׁ וַיִּטְחַן עַד אֲשֶׁר־
*** to and-he-ground in-the-fire and-he-burned they-made that the-calf

דָּק וַיִּזֶר עַל־ פְּנֵי הַמַּיִם וַיַּשְׁק אֶת־
*** and-he-made-drink the-waters surface-of on and-he-scattered powder

בְּנֵי יִשְׂרָאֵל׃ וַיֹּאמֶר מֹשֶׁה אֶל־ אַהֲרֹן מֶה־ עָשָׂה לְךָ
to-you he-did what? Aaron to Moses then-he-said (21) Israel sons-of

הָעָם הַזֶּה כִּי־ הֵבֵאתָ עָלָיו חֲטָאָה גְדֹלָה׃ וַיֹּאמֶר
and-he-answered (22) great sin into-him you-led that the-this the-people

אַהֲרֹן אַל־ יִחַר אַף אֲדֹנִי אַתָּה יָדַעְתָּ אֶת־ הָעָם כִּי
how the-people *** you-know you lord-of-me anger-of may-he-burn not Aaron

בְרָע הוּא׃ וַיֹּאמְרוּ לִי עֲשֵׂה־ לָנוּ אֱלֹהִים אֲשֶׁר יֵלְכוּ
they-will-go who gods for-us make! to-me and-they-said (23) he prone-to-evil

לְפָנֵינוּ כִּי־ זֶה ׀ מֹשֶׁה הָאִישׁ אֲשֶׁר הֶעֱלָנוּ מֵאֶרֶץ מִצְרַיִם
Egypt from-land-of he-brought-us who the-fellow Moses this for before-us

לֹא יָדַעְנוּ מֶה־ הָיָה לוֹ׃ וָאֹמַר לָהֶם לְמִי זָהָב
gold to-whom to-them so-I-told (24) to him he-happened what we-know not

הִתְפָּרָקוּ וַיִּתְּנוּ־ לִי וָאַשְׁלִכֵהוּ בָאֵשׁ וַיֵּצֵא
and-he-came-out into-the-fire and-I-threw-him to-me then-they-gave take-off!

הָעֵגֶל הַזֶּה׃ וַיַּרְא מֹשֶׁה אֶת־ הָעָם כִּי פָרֻעַ הוּא
he running-wild that the-people *** Moses and-he-saw (25) the-this the-calf

כִּי־ פְרָעֹה אַהֲרֹן לְשִׁמְצָה בְּקָמֵיהֶם׃
to-ones-opposing-them into-laughingstock Aaron he-let-run-wild-him for

וַיַּעֲמֹד מֹשֶׁה בְּשַׁעַר הַמַּחֲנֶה וַיֹּאמֶר מִי לַיהוָה
for-Yahweh whoever and-he-said the-camp at-entrance-of Moses so-he-stood (26)

אֵלָי וַיֵּאָסְפוּ אֵלָיו כָּל־ בְּנֵי לֵוִי׃ וַיֹּאמֶר לָהֶם
to-them then-he-said (27) Levi sons-of all-of to-him and-they-rallied to-me

כֹּה־ אָמַר יְהוָה אֱלֹהֵי יִשְׂרָאֵל שִׂימוּ אִישׁ־ חַרְבּוֹ עַל־ יְרֵכוֹ
side-of-him to sword-of-him each strap! Israel God-of Yahweh he-says this

עִבְרוּ וָשׁוּבוּ מִשַּׁעַר לָשַׁעַר בַּמַּחֲנֶה וְהִרְגוּ אִישׁ־אֶת־
*** each and-kill! through-the-camp to-end from-end and-go-forth! go-back!

אָחִיו וְאִישׁ אֶת־ רֵעֵהוּ וְאִישׁ אֶת־ קְרֹבוֹ׃
neighbor-of-him *** and-each friend-of-him *** and-each brother-of-him

וַיַּעֲשׂוּ בְנֵי־ לֵוִי כִּדְבַר מֹשֶׁה וַיִּפֹּל מִן־ הָעָם
the-people from and-he-died Moses as-command-of Levi sons-of and-they-did (28)

the dancing, his anger burned
and he threw the tablets out of
his hands, breaking them to
pieces at the foot of the mountain. [20]And he took the calf
they had made and burned it
in the fire; then he ground it to
powder, scattered it on the
water and made the Israelites
drink it.
[21]He said to Aaron, "What
did these people do to you,
that you led them into such
great sin?"
[22]"Do not be angry, my
lord," Aaron answered. "You
know how prone these people
are to evil. [23]They said to me,
'Make us gods who will go before us. As for this fellow
Moses who brought us up out
of Egypt, we don't know what
has happened to him.' [24]So I
told them, 'Whoever has any
gold jewelry, take it off.' Then
they gave me the gold, and I
threw it into the fire, and out
came this calf!"
[25]Moses saw that the people
were running wild and that
Aaron had let them get out of
control and so become a
laughingstock to their enemies. [26]So he stood at the entrance to the camp and said,
"Whoever is for the LORD,
come to me." And all the Levites rallied to him.
[27]Then he said to them,
"This is what the LORD, the
God of Israel, says: 'Each man
strap a sword to his side. Go
back and forth through the
camp from one end to the other, each killing his brother and
friend and neighbor.' " [28]The
Levites did as Moses com-
manded, and that day about

°19 ק מידיו

בַּיּוֹם הַהוּא כִּשְׁלֹשֶׁת אַלְפֵי אִישׁ׃ וַיֹּאמֶר
then-he-said (29) people thousands-of about-three-of the-that on-the-day

מֹשֶׁה מִלְאוּ יֶדְכֶם הַיּוֹם לַיהוָה כִּי אִישׁ בִּבְנוֹ
against-son-of-him each for to-Yahweh the-day hand-of-you they-set-apart Moses

וּבְאָחִיו וְלָתֵת עֲלֵיכֶם הַיּוֹם בְּרָכָה׃ וַיְהִי
and-he-was (30) blessing the-day to-you to-give and-against-brother-of-him

מִמָּחֳרָת וַיֹּאמֶר מֹשֶׁה אֶל־ הָעָם אַתֶּם חֲטָאתֶם חֲטָאָה גְדֹלָה
great sin you-sinned you the-people to Moses that-he-said on-next-day

וְעַתָּה אֶעֱלֶה אֶל־ יְהוָה אוּלַי אֲכַפְּרָה בְּעַד חַטַּאתְכֶם׃
sin-of-you for I-can-atone perhaps Yahweh to I-will-go-up but-now

וַיָּשָׁב מֹשֶׁה אֶל־ יְהוָה וַיֹּאמַר אָנָּא חָטָא הָעָם
the-people he-sinned oh! and-he-said Yahweh to Moses so-he-went-back (31)

הַזֶּה חֲטָאָה גְדֹלָה וַיַּעֲשׂוּ לָהֶם אֱלֹהֵי זָהָב׃ וְעַתָּה
but-now (32) gold gods-of for-themselves for-they-made great sin the-this

אִם־ תִּשָּׂא חַטָּאתָם וְאִם־ אַיִן מְחֵנִי נָא מִסִּפְרְךָ
from-book-of-you now! blot-out-me! not but-if sin-of-them you-forgive please

אֲשֶׁר כָּתָבְתָּ׃ וַיֹּאמֶר יְהוָה אֶל־ מֹשֶׁה מִי אֲשֶׁר חָטָא־
he-sinned ever who Moses to Yahweh and-he-replied (33) you-wrote that

לִי אֶמְחֶנּוּ מִסִּפְרִי׃ וְעַתָּה לֵךְ ׀ נְחֵה אֶת־
*** lead! go! and-now (34) from-book-of-me I-will-blot-out-him against-me

הָעָם אֶל אֲשֶׁר־ דִּבַּרְתִּי לָךְ הִנֵּה מַלְאָכִי יֵלֵךְ לְפָנֶיךָ
before-you he-will-go angel-of-me see! to-you I-spoke where to the-people

וּבְיוֹם פָּקְדִי וּפָקַדְתִּי עֲלֵיהֶם חַטָּאתָם׃
sin-of-them on-them then-I-will-punish to-punish-me but-in-day-of

וַיִּגֹּף יְהוָה אֶת־ הָעָם עַל אֲשֶׁר עָשׂוּ אֶת־ הָעֵגֶל אֲשֶׁר
that the-calf with they-did what for the-people *** Yahweh then-he-plagued (35)

עָשָׂה אַהֲרֹן׃ וַיְדַבֵּר יְהוָה אֶל־ מֹשֶׁה לֵךְ עֲלֵה מִזֶּה אַתָּה
you from-here leave! go! Moses to Yahweh then-he-said (33:1) Aaron he-made

וְהָעָם אֲשֶׁר הֶעֱלִיתָ מֵאֶרֶץ מִצְרָיִם אֶל־הָאָרֶץ אֲשֶׁר נִשְׁבַּעְתִּי
I-swore that the-land to Egypt from-land-of you-brought whom and-the-people

לְאַבְרָהָם לְיִצְחָק וּלְיַעֲקֹב לֵאמֹר לְזַרְעֲךָ אֶתְּנֶנָּה׃
I-will-give-her to-descendant-of-you to-say and-to-Jacob to-Isaac to-Abraham

וְשָׁלַחְתִּי לְפָנֶיךָ מַלְאָךְ וְגֵרַשְׁתִּי אֶת־ הַכְּנַעֲנִי
the-Canaanite *** and-I-will-drive-out angel before-you and-I-will-send (2)

הָאֱמֹרִי וְהַחִתִּי וְהַפְּרִזִּי הַחִוִּי וְהַיְבוּסִי׃
and-the-Jebusite the-Hivite and-the-Perizzite and-the-Hittite the-Amorite

אֶל־ אֶרֶץ זָבַת חָלָב וּדְבָשׁ כִּי לֹא אֶעֱלֶה בְּקִרְבְּךָ כִּי
for among-you I-will-go-up not but and-honey milk flowing-of land to (3)

three thousand of the people
died. 29 Then Moses said, "You
have been set apart to the
LORD today, for you were
against your own sons and
brothers, and he has blessed
you this day."
30 The next day Moses said to
the people, "You have committed a great sin. But now I
will go up to the LORD; perhaps
I can make atonement for your
sin."
31 So Moses went back to the
LORD and said, "Oh, what a
great sin these people have
committed! They have made
themselves gods of gold. 32 But
now, please forgive their sin—
but if not, then blot me out of
the book you have written."
33 The LORD replied to Moses,
"Whoever has sinned against
me I will blot out of my book.
34 Now go, lead the people to
the place I spoke of, and my
angel will go before you. However, when the time comes for
me to punish, I will punish
them for their sin."
35 And the LORD struck the
people with a plague because
of what they did with the calf
Aaron had made.
33 Then the LORD said to
Moses, "Leave this
place, you and the people you
brought up out of Egypt, and
go up to the land I promised
on oath to Abraham, Isaac and
Jacob, saying, 'I will give it to
your descendants.' 2 I will send
an angel before you and drive
out the Canaanites, Amorites,
Hittites, Perizzites, Hivites
and Jebusites. 3 Go up to the
land flowing with milk and
honey. But I will not go with

עַם־ קְשֵׁה־ עֹ֔רֶף אַ֖תָּה פֶּן־ אֲכֶלְךָ֖ בַּדָּֽרֶךְ׃ וַיִּשְׁמַ֣ע
when-he-heard (4) on-the-way I-destroy-you lest you neck stiff-of people-of

הָעָ֗ם אֶת־ הַדָּבָ֥ר הָרָ֛ע הַזֶּ֖ה וַיִּתְאַבָּ֑לוּ וְלֹא־
and-not then-they-mourned the-this the-distressing the-word *** the-people

שָׁ֛תוּ אִ֥ישׁ עֶדְי֖וֹ עָלָֽיו׃ וַיֹּ֨אמֶר יְהוָ֜ה אֶל־מֹשֶׁ֗ה אֱמֹ֤ר
tell! Moses to Yahweh for-he-said (5) on-him ornament-of-him anyone they-put

אֶל־בְּנֵֽי־יִשְׂרָאֵל֙ אַתֶּ֣ם עַם־ קְשֵׁה־ עֹ֔רֶף רֶ֧גַע אֶחָ֛ד אֶֽעֱלֶ֥ה בְקִרְבְּךָ֖
among-you if-I-went one moment neck stiff-of people-of you Israel sons-of to

וְכִלִּיתִ֑יךָ וְעַתָּ֗ה הוֹרֵ֤ד עֶדְיְךָ֙ מֵעָלֶ֔יךָ
from-on-you ornament-of-you take-off! and-now then-I-might-destroy-you

וְאֵדְעָ֖ה מָ֥ה אֶֽעֱשֶׂה־ לָּֽךְ׃ וַיִּֽתְנַצְּל֧וּ בְנֵֽי־
sons-of so-they-stripped-off (6) with-you I-will-do what and-I-will-decide

יִשְׂרָאֵ֛ל אֶת־ עֶדְיָ֖ם מֵהַ֥ר חוֹרֵֽב׃ וּמֹשֶׁה֩ יִקַּ֨ח אֶת־
*** he-took now-Moses (7) Horeb at-Mount-of ornament-of-them *** Israel

הָאֹ֜הֶל וְנָֽטָה־ ל֣וֹ ׀ מִח֣וּץ לַֽמַּחֲנֶ֗ה הַרְחֵק֙ מִן־
from to-be-distant of-the-camp outside for-him and-he-pitched the-tent

הַֽמַּחֲנֶ֔ה וְקָ֥רָא ל֖וֹ אֹ֣הֶל מוֹעֵ֑ד וְהָיָה֙ כָּל־ מְבַקֵּ֣שׁ
inquiring every-of and-he-was meeting tent-of to-him and-he-called the-camp

יְהוָ֔ה יֵצֵא֙ אֶל־ אֹ֣הֶל מוֹעֵ֔ד אֲשֶׁ֖ר מִח֥וּץ לַֽמַּחֲנֶֽה׃ וְהָיָ֗ה
and-he-was (8) of-the-camp outside that meeting tent-of to he-went Yahweh

כְּצֵ֤את מֹשֶׁה֙ אֶל־ הָאֹ֔הֶל יָק֙וּמוּ֙ כָּל־ הָעָ֔ם וְנִ֨צְּב֔וּ
and-they-stood the-people all-of that-they-rose the-tent to Moses when-to-go

אִ֖ישׁ פֶּ֣תַח אָהֳל֑וֹ וְהִבִּ֙יטוּ֙ אַחֲרֵ֣י מֹשֶׁ֔ה עַד־ בֹּא֖וֹ
to-enter-him until Moses after and-they-watched tent-of-him entrance-of each

הָאֹֽהֱלָה׃ וְהָיָ֗ה כְּבֹ֤א מֹשֶׁה֙ הָאֹ֔הֱלָה יֵרֵד֙
he-came-down into-the-tent Moses as-to-go and-he-was (9) into-the-tent

עַמּ֣וּד הֶֽעָנָ֔ן וְעָמַ֖ד פֶּ֣תַח הָאֹ֑הֶל וְדִבֶּ֖ר עִם־
with and-he-spoke the-tent entrance-of and-he-stayed the-cloud pillar-of

מֹשֶֽׁה׃ וְרָאָ֤ה כָל־ הָעָם֙ אֶת־ עַמּ֣וּד הֶֽעָנָ֔ן עֹמֵ֖ד
standing the-cloud pillar-of *** the-people all-of when-he-saw (10) Moses

פֶּ֣תַח הָאֹ֑הֶל וְקָ֤ם כָּל־ הָעָם֙ וְהִֽשְׁתַּחֲוּ֔וּ* אִ֖ישׁ
each and-they-worshiped the-people all-of then-he-stood the-tent entrance-of

פֶּ֥תַח אָהֳלֽוֹ׃ וְדִבֶּ֨ר יְהוָ֤ה אֶל־ מֹשֶׁה֙ פָּנִ֣ים אֶל־פָּנִ֔ים
faces to faces Moses to Yahweh and-he-spoke (11) tent-of-him entrance-of

כַּאֲשֶׁ֛ר יְדַבֵּ֥ר אִ֖ישׁ אֶל־ רֵעֵ֑הוּ וְשָׁב֙ אֶל־ הַֽמַּחֲנֶ֔ה
the-camp to then-he-returned friend-of-him with man he-speaks just-as

וּמְשָׁרְת֗וֹ יְהוֹשֻׁ֤עַ בִּן־ נוּן֙ נַ֔עַר לֹ֥א יָמִ֖ישׁ מִתּ֥וֹךְ הָאֹֽהֶל׃
the-tent from he-left not young Nun son-of Joshua but-being-aide-of-him

you, because you are a
stiff-necked people and I
might destroy you on the
way."
4When the people heard
these distressing words, they
began to mourn and no one
put on any ornaments. 5For
the LORD had said to Moses,
"Tell the Israelites, 'You are a
stiff-necked people. If I were
to go with you even for a moment, I might destroy you.
Now take off your ornaments
and I will decide what to do
with you.' " 6So the Israelites
stripped off their ornaments at
Mount Horeb.

The Tent of Meeting

7Now Moses used to take a
tent and pitch it outside the
camp some distance away,
calling it the "tent of meeting." Anyone inquiring of the
LORD would go to the tent of
meeting outside the camp.
8And whenever Moses went
out to the tent, all the people
rose and stood at the entrances
to their tents, watching Moses
until he entered the tent. 9As
Moses went into the tent, the
pillar of cloud would come
down and stay at the entrance,
while the LORD spoke with
Moses. 10Whenever the people
saw the pillar of cloud standing at the entrance to the tent,
they all stood and worshiped,
each at the entrance to his
tent. 11The LORD would speak
to Moses face to face, as a man
speaks with his friend. Then
Moses would return to the
camp, but his young aide
Joshua son of Nun did not
leave the tent.

*10 Most mss have no *dagesh* in the first *vav* (וּו־).

וַיֹּאמֶר מֹשֶׁה אֶל־יְהוָה רְאֵה אַתָּה אֹמֵר אֵלַי הַעַל אֶת־הָעָם
the-people *** lead! to-me telling you see! Yahweh to Moses and-he-said (12)

הַזֶּה וְאַתָּה לֹא הוֹדַעְתַּנִי אֵת אֲשֶׁר־תִּשְׁלַח עִמִּי וְאַתָּה
and-you with-me you-will-send whom *** you-let-know-me not but-you the-this

אָמַרְתָּ יְדַעְתִּיךָ בְשֵׁם וְגַם־מָצָאתָ חֵן בְּעֵינָי׃
in-eyes-of-me favor you-found and-also by-name I-know-you you-said

וְעַתָּה אִם־נָא מָצָאתִי חֵן בְּעֵינֶיךָ הוֹדִעֵנִי נָא אֶת־דְּרָכֶךָ
way-of-you *** now! teach-me! in-eyes-of-you favor I-found now! if so-now (13)

וְאֵדָעֲךָ לְמַעַן אֶמְצָא־חֵן בְּעֵינֶיךָ וּרְאֵה כִּי
that and-remember! in-eyes-of-you favor I-may-find so-that so-I-may-know-you

עַמְּךָ הַגּוֹי הַזֶּה׃ וַיֹּאמַר פָּנַי
Presences-of-me and-he-replied (14) the-this the-nation people-of-you

יֵלֵכוּ וַהֲנִחֹתִי לָךְ׃ וַיֹּאמֶר אֵלָיו אִם־אֵין
not if to-him then-he-said (15) to-you and-I-will-give-rest they-will-go

פָּנֶיךָ הֹלְכִים אַל־תַּעֲלֵנוּ מִזֶּה׃ וּבַמֶּה ׀
and-by-the-what? (16) from-here you-send-up-us not ones-going Presences-of-you

יִוָּדַע אֵפוֹא כִּי־מָצָאתִי חֵן בְּעֵינֶיךָ אֲנִי וְעַמֶּךָ
and-people-of-you I in-eyes-of-you favor I-found that then will-he-be-known

הֲלוֹא בְּלֶכְתְּךָ עִמָּנוּ וְנִפְלֵינוּ אֲנִי וְעַמְּךָ מִכָּל־
from-all-of and-people-of-you I so-we-are-distinct with-us by-to-go-you if-not

הָעָם אֲשֶׁר עַל־פְּנֵי הָאֲדָמָה׃ וַיֹּאמֶר יְהוָה אֶל־מֹשֶׁה גַּם
indeed Moses to Yahweh and-he-said (17) the-earth face-of on that the-people

אֶת־הַדָּבָר הַזֶּה אֲשֶׁר דִּבַּרְתָּ אֶעֱשֶׂה כִּי־מָצָאתָ חֵן
favor you-found for I-will-do you-asked that the-this the-thing ***

בְּעֵינַי וָאֵדָעֲךָ בְּשֵׁם׃ וַיֹּאמַר הַרְאֵנִי נָא אֶת־
*** now! show-me! then-he-said (18) by-name and-I-know-you in-eyes-of-me

כְּבֹדֶךָ׃ וַיֹּאמֶר אֲנִי אַעֲבִיר כָּל־טוּבִי עַל־
in goodness-of-me all-of I-will-make-pass I and-he-said (19) glory-of-you

פָּנֶיךָ וְקָרָאתִי בְשֵׁם יְהוָה לְפָנֶיךָ
in-presence-of-you Yahweh by-name and-I-will-proclaim front-of-you

וְחַנֹּתִי אֶת־אֲשֶׁר אָחֹן וְרִחַמְתִּי
and-I-will-have-compassion I-will-have-mercy whom *** and-I-will-have-mercy

אֶת־אֲשֶׁר אֲרַחֵם׃ וַיֹּאמֶר לֹא תוּכַל לִרְאֹת אֶת־
*** to-see you-can not and-he-said (20) I-will-have-compassion whom ***

פָּנָי כִּי לֹא־יִרְאַנִי הָאָדָם וָחָי׃ וַיֹּאמֶר
then-he-said (21) and-he-lives the-man he-may-see-me not for face-of-me

יְהוָה הִנֵּה מָקוֹם אִתִּי וְנִצַּבְתָּ עַל־הַצּוּר׃ וְהָיָה
and-he-will-be (22) the-rock on and-you-may-stand near-me place see! Yahweh

Moses and the Glory of the LORD

12 Moses said to the LORD,
"You have been telling me,
'Lead these people,' but you
have not let me know whom
you will send with me. You
have said, 'I know you by
name and you have found favor with me.' 13 If I have found
favor in your eyes, teach me
your ways so I may know you
and continue to find favor
with you. Remember that this
nation is your people."
14 The LORD replied, "My
Presence will go with you, and
I will give you rest."
15 Then Moses said to him,
"If your Presence does not go
with us, do not send us up
from here. 16 How will anyone
know that you are pleased
with me and with your people
unless you go with us? What
else will distinguish me and
your people from all the other
people on the face of the
earth?"
17 And the LORD said to
Moses, "I will do the very
thing you have asked, because
I am pleased with you and I
know you by name."
18 Then Moses said, "Now
show me your glory."
19 And the LORD said, "I will
cause all my goodness to pass
in front of you, and I will proclaim my name, the LORD, in
your presence. I will have
mercy on whom I will have
mercy, and I will have compassion on whom I will have
compassion. 20 But," he said,
"you cannot see my face, for
no one may see me and live."
21 Then the LORD said, "There
is a place near me where you
may stand on a rock. 22 When

בַּעֲבֹר כְּבֹדִי וְשַׂמְתִּיךָ בְּנִקְרַת הַצּוּר
the-rock in-cleft-of then-I-will-put-you glory-of-me when-to-pass-by

וְשַׂכֹּתִי כַפִּי עָלֶיךָ עַד־ עָבְרִי׃ (23) וַהֲסִרֹתִי
then-I-will-remove (23) to-pass-by-me until over-you hand-of-me and-I-will-put

אֶת־ כַּפִּי וְרָאִיתָ אֶת־ אֲחֹרָי וּפָנַי לֹא
not but-faces-of-me back-of-me *** and-you-will-see hand-of-me ***

יֵרָאוּ׃ (34:1) וַיֹּאמֶר יְהוָה אֶל־ מֹשֶׁה פְּסָל־ לְךָ שְׁנֵי־
two-of for-you chisel! Moses to Yahweh then-he-said (34:1) they-may-be-seen

לֻחֹת אֲבָנִים כָּרִאשֹׁנִים וְכָתַבְתִּי עַל־ הַלֻּחֹת אֶת־
*** the-tablets on and-I-will-write like-the-first-ones stones tablets-of

הַדְּבָרִים אֲשֶׁר הָיוּ עַל־ הַלֻּחֹת הָרִאשֹׁנִים אֲשֶׁר שִׁבַּרְתָּ׃
you-broke which the-first-ones the-tablets on they-were that the-words

(2) וֶהְיֵה נָכוֹן לַבֹּקֶר וְעָלִיתָ בַבֹּקֶר אֶל־
on in-the-morning then-you-come-up in-the-morning being-ready and-be! (2)

הַר סִינַי וְנִצַּבְתָּ לִי שָׁם עַל־ רֹאשׁ הָהָר׃ (3) וְאִישׁ
but-man (3) the-mountain top-of on there to-me and-you-present Sinai Mount-of

לֹא־ יַעֲלֶה עִמָּךְ וְגַם־ אִישׁ אַל־ יֵרָא בְּכָל־
on-any-part-of he-may-be-seen not man or-even with-you he-may-come not

הָהָר גַּם־ הַצֹּאן וְהַבָּקָר אַל־ יִרְעוּ אֶל־ מוּל
front in they-may-graze not and-the-herd the-flock even the-mountain

הָהָר הַהוּא׃ (4) וַיִּפְסֹל שְׁנֵי־ לֻחֹת אֲבָנִים
stones tablets-of two-of so-he-chiseled (4) the-this the-mountain

כָּרִאשֹׁנִים וַיַּשְׁכֵּם מֹשֶׁה בַבֹּקֶר וַיַּעַל אֶל־
on and-he-went-up in-the-morning Moses and-he-got-up like-the-first-ones

הַר סִינַי כַּאֲשֶׁר צִוָּה יְהוָה אֹתוֹ וַיִּקַּח בְּיָדוֹ
in-hand-of-him and-he-carried him Yahweh he-commanded just-as Sinai Mount-of

שְׁנֵי לֻחֹת אֲבָנִים׃ (5) וַיֵּרֶד יְהוָה בֶּעָנָן וַיִּתְיַצֵּב
and-he-stood in-the-cloud Yahweh then-he-came-down (5) stones tablets-of two-of

עִמּוֹ שָׁם וַיִּקְרָא בְשֵׁם יְהוָה׃ (6) וַיַּעֲבֹר יְהוָה ׀
Yahweh and-he-passed (6) Yahweh in-name-of and-he-proclaimed there with-him

עַל־ פָּנָיו וַיִּקְרָא יְהוָה ׀ יְהוָה אֵל רַחוּם וְחַנּוּן
and-gracious compassionate God Yahweh Yahweh and-he-proclaimed front-of-him by

אֶרֶךְ אַפַּיִם וְרַב־ חֶסֶד וֶאֱמֶת׃ (7) נֹצֵר חֶסֶד
love maintaining (7) and-faithfulness love and-abundant-of angers slow-of

לָאֲלָפִים נֹשֵׂא עָוֹן וָפֶשַׁע וְחַטָּאָה
and-sin and-rebellion wickedness forgiving to-the-thousands

וְנַקֵּה לֹא יְנַקֶּה פֹּקֵד ׀ עֲוֹן אָבוֹת
fathers sin-of punishing he-will-leave-unpunished not yet-to-leave-unpunished

my glory passes by, I will put
you in a cleft in the rock and
cover you with my hand until
I have passed by. 23Then I will
remove my hand and you will
see my back; but my face must
not be seen."

The New Stone Tablets

34 The LORD said to
Moses, "Chisel out two
stone tablets like the first ones,
and I will write on them the
words that were on the first
tablets, which you broke. 2Be
ready in the morning, and
then come up on Mount Sinai.
Present yourself to me there
on top of the mountain. 3No
one is to come with you or be
seen anywhere on the mountain; not even the flocks and
herds may graze in front of the
mountain."

4So Moses chiseled out two
stone tablets like the first ones
and went up Mount Sinai early in the morning, as the LORD
had commanded him; and he
carried the two stone tablets in
his hands. 5Then the LORD
came down in the cloud and
stood there with him and proclaimed his name, the LORD.
6And he passed in front of
Moses, proclaiming, "The
LORD, the LORD, the compassionate and gracious God,
slow to anger, abounding in
love and faithfulness, 7main-
taining love to thousands, and
forgiving wickedness, rebellion and sin. Yet he does not
leave the guilty unpunished;

עַל־ בָּנִים֙ וְעַל־ בְּנֵ֣י בָנִ֔ים עַל־ שִׁלֵּשִׁ֖ים וְעַל־ רִבֵּעִֽים׃
fourth-ones and-to third-ones to children children-of and-on children on

(8) וַיְמַהֵ֖ר מֹשֶׁ֑ה וַיִּקֹּ֥ד אַ֖רְצָה וַיִּשְׁתָּֽחוּ׃
and-he-worshiped to-ground and-he-bowed Moses and-he-hurried (8)

(9) וַיֹּ֡אמֶר אִם־ נָא֩ מָצָ֨אתִי חֵ֤ן בְּעֵינֶ֙יךָ֙ אֲדֹנָ֔י יֵֽלֶךְ־ נָ֥א
now! let-him-go Lord in-eyes-of-you favor I-found now! if and-he-said (9)

אֲדֹנָ֖י בְּקִרְבֵּ֑נוּ כִּ֤י עַם־ קְשֵׁה־ עֹ֙רֶף֙ ה֔וּא וְסָלַחְתָּ֛
and-you-forgive this neck stiff-of people-of although with-us Lord

לַעֲוֺנֵ֥נוּ וּלְחַטָּאתֵ֖נוּ וּנְחַלְתָּֽנוּ׃
and-you-take-as-inheritance-us and-to-sin-of-us to-wickedness-of-us

(10) וַיֹּ֗אמֶר הִנֵּ֣ה אָנֹכִי֮ כֹּרֵ֣ת בְּרִית֒ נֶ֤גֶד כָּֽל־ עַמְּךָ֙
people-of-you all-of before covenant making I see! then-he-said (10)

אֶעֱשֶׂ֣ה נִפְלָאֹ֔ת אֲשֶׁ֛ר לֹא־ נִבְרְא֥וּ בְכָל־ הָאָ֖רֶץ
the-world in-all-of they-were-done never that being-wonders I-will-do

וּבְכָל־ הַגּוֹיִ֑ם וְרָאָ֣ה כָל־ הָ֠עָם אֲשֶׁר־ אַתָּ֨ה
you whom the-people all-of then-he-will-see the-nations or-in-any-of

בְקִרְבּ֜וֹ אֶת־ מַעֲשֵׂ֤ה יְהוָה֙ כִּֽי־ נוֹרָ֣א ה֔וּא אֲשֶׁ֥ר אֲנִ֖י עֹשֶׂ֥ה עִמָּֽךְ׃
for-you doing I that he being-awesome that Yahweh work-of *** among-him

(11) שְׁמָ֨ר־ לְךָ֔ אֵ֛ת אֲשֶׁ֥ר אָנֹכִ֖י מְצַוְּךָ֣ הַיּ֑וֹם הִנְנִ֧י גֹרֵ֣שׁ
driving-out see-I! the-day commanding-you I what *** for-you obey! (11)

מִפָּנֶ֗יךָ אֶת־ הָֽאֱמֹרִי֙ וְהַֽכְּנַעֲנִ֔י וְהַֽחִתִּי֙
and-the-Hittite and-the-Canaanite the-Amorite *** from-before-you

וְהַפְּרִזִּ֔י וְהַחִוִּ֖י וְהַיְבוּסִֽי׃ (12) הִשָּׁ֣מֶר לְךָ֗
for-you be-careful! (12) and-the-Jebusite and-the-Hivite and-the-Perizzite

פֶּן־ תִּכְרֹ֤ת בְּרִית֙ לְיוֹשֵׁ֣ב הָאָ֔רֶץ אֲשֶׁ֥ר אַתָּ֖ה בָּ֣א עָלֶ֑יהָ
into-her going you where the-land with-one-living-of treaty you-make not

פֶּן־ יִהְיֶ֥ה לְמוֹקֵ֖שׁ בְּקִרְבֶּֽךָ׃ (13) כִּ֤י אֶת־ מִזְבְּחֹתָם֙ תִּתֹּצ֔וּן
you-break-down altars-of-them *** but (13) among-you as-snare he-will-be or

וְאֶת־ מַצֵּבֹתָ֖ם תְּשַׁבֵּר֑וּן וְאֶת־ אֲשֵׁרָ֖יו תִּכְרֹתֽוּן׃
you-cut-down Asherah-poles-of-him and you-smash sacred-stones-of-them and

(14) כִּ֛י לֹ֥א תִֽשְׁתַּחֲוֶ֖ה לְאֵ֣ל אַחֵ֑ר כִּ֤י יְהוָה֙ קַנָּ֣א שְׁמ֔וֹ אֵ֥ל
God name-of-him Jealous Yahweh for other to-god you-worship not but (14)

קַנָּ֖א הֽוּא׃ (15) פֶּן־ תִּכְרֹ֥ת בְּרִ֖ית לְיוֹשֵׁ֣ב הָאָ֑רֶץ
the-land with-one-living-of treaty you-make not (15) he jealous

וְזָנ֣וּ ׀ אַחֲרֵ֣י אֱלֹֽהֵיהֶ֗ם וְזָבְחוּ֙ לֵאלֹ֣הֵיהֶ֔ם
to-gods-of-them and-they-sacrifice gods-of-them to for-they-prostitute

וְקָרָ֣א לְךָ֔ וְאָכַלְתָּ֖ מִזִּבְחֽוֹ׃
from-sacrifice-of-him and-you-will-eat to-you and-he-will-invite

he punishes the children and
their children for the sin of the
fathers to the third and fourth
generation."
8 Moses bowed to the ground
at once and worshiped. 9 "O
Lord, if I have found favor in
your eyes," he said, "then let
the Lord go with us. Although
this is a stiff-necked people,
forgive our wickedness and
our sin, and take us as your
inheritance."
10 Then the LORD said: "I am
making a covenant with you.
Before all your people I will do
wonders never before done in
any nation in all the world.
The people you live among
will see how awesome is the
work that I, the LORD, will do
for you. 11 Obey what I command you today. I will drive
out before you the Amorites,
Canaanites, Hittites, Perizzites, Hivites and Jebusites.
12 Be careful not to make a
treaty with those who live in
the land where you are going,
or they will be a snare among
you. 13 Break down their altars,
smash their sacred stones and
cut down their Asherah
poles.[p] 14 Do not worship any
other god, for the LORD, whose
name is Jealous, is a jealous
God.
15 "Be careful not to make a
treaty with those who live in
the land; for when they prostitute themselves to their gods
and sacrifice to them, they will
invite you and you will eat
their sacrifices. 16 And when

[p]13 That is, symbols of the goddess Asherah

וְלָקַחְתָּ מִבְּנֹתָיו לְבָנֶיךָ וְזָנוּ
and-they-prostitute for-sons-of-you from-daughters-of-him when-you-choose (16)

בְנֹתָיו אַחֲרֵי אֱלֹהֵיהֶן וְהִזְנוּ אֶת־
*** then-they-will-lead-to-prostitute gods-of-them to daughters-of-him

בָּנֶיךָ אַחֲרֵי אֱלֹהֵיהֶן׃ אֱלֹהֵי מַסֵּכָה לֹא תַעֲשֶׂה־ לָּךְ׃ אֶת־
*** (18) for-you you-make not cast idols-of (17) gods-of-them to sons-of-you

חַג הַמַּצּוֹת תִּשְׁמֹר שִׁבְעַת יָמִים תֹּאכַל
you-eat days seven-of you-celebrate the-Unleavened-Breads Feast-of

מַצּוֹת אֲשֶׁר צִוִּיתִךָ לְמוֹעֵד חֹדֶשׁ הָאָבִיב
the-Abib month-of at-appointed-time I-commanded-you as breads-without-yeast

כִּי בְּחֹדֶשׁ הָאָבִיב יָצָאתָ מִמִּצְרָיִם׃ כָּל־ פֶּטֶר
firstborn-of every-of (19) from-Egypt you-came-out the-Abib in-month-of for

רֶחֶם לִי וְכָל־ מִקְנְךָ תִּזָּכָר* פֶּטֶר שׁוֹר וָשֶׂה׃
or-flock herd firstborn-of male stock-of-you and-all-of to-me womb

וּפֶטֶר חֲמוֹר תִּפְדֶּה בְשֶׂה וְאִם־ לֹא תִפְדֶּה
you-redeem not but-if with-lamb you-redeem donkey but-firstborn-of (20)

וַעֲרַפְתּוֹ כֹּל בְּכוֹר בָּנֶיךָ תִּפְדֶּה וְלֹא־
and-not you-redeem sons-of-you firstborn-of all-of then-you-break-neck-of-him

יֵרָאוּ פָנַי רֵיקָם׃ שֵׁשֶׁת יָמִים תַּעֲבֹד
you-shall-labor days six-of (21) empty-handed before-me they-shall-appear

וּבַיּוֹם הַשְּׁבִיעִי תִּשְׁבֹּת בֶּחָרִישׁ
in-the-plowing-season you-shall-rest the-seventh but-on-the-day

וּבַקָּצִיר תִּשְׁבֹּת׃ וְחַג שָׁבֻעֹת תַּעֲשֶׂה לְךָ
for-you you-celebrate Weeks and-Feast-of (22) you-must-rest and-in-the-harvest

בִּכּוּרֵי קְצִיר חִטִּים וְחַג הָאָסִיף תְּקוּפַת
turn-of the-Ingathering and-Feast-of wheats harvest-of firstfruits-of

הַשָּׁנָה׃ שָׁלֹשׁ פְּעָמִים בַּשָּׁנָה יֵרָאֶה כָּל־ זְכוּרְךָ אֶת־
*** male-of-you every-of he-must-appear in-the-year times three (23) the-year

פְּנֵי הָאָדֹן ׀ יְהוָה אֱלֹהֵי יִשְׂרָאֵל׃ כִּי־ אוֹרִישׁ גּוֹיִם
nations I-will-drive-out for (24) Israel God-of Yahweh the-Sovereign before

מִפָּנֶיךָ וְהִרְחַבְתִּי אֶת־ גְּבוּלֶךָ וְלֹא־ יַחְמֹד
he-will-covet and-not territory-of-you *** and-I-will-enlarge from-before-you

אִישׁ אֶת־ אַרְצְךָ בַּעֲלֹתְךָ לֵרָאוֹת אֶת־ פְּנֵי יְהוָה
Yahweh before *** to-appear when-to-go-up-you land-of-you *** anyone

אֱלֹהֶיךָ שָׁלֹשׁ פְּעָמִים בַּשָּׁנָה׃ לֹא־ תִשְׁחַט עַל־ חָמֵץ דַּם־
blood-of yeast with you-offer not (25) in-the-year times three God-of-you

זִבְחִי וְלֹא־ יָלִין לַבֹּקֶר זֶבַח
sacrifice-of until-the-morning he-may-remain and-not sacrifice-of-me

you choose some of their
daughters as wives for your
sons and those daughters
prostitute themselves to their
gods, they will lead your sons
to do the same.
17"Do not make cast idols.
18"Celebrate the Feast of Unleavened Bread. For seven
days eat bread made without
yeast, as I commanded you.
Do this at the appointed time
in the month of Abib, for in
that month you came out of
Egypt.
19"The first offspring of
every womb belongs to me,
including all the firstborn
males of your livestock,
whether from herd or flock.
20Redeem the firstborn donkey
with a lamb, but if you do not
redeem it, break its neck. Redeem all your firstborn sons.
"No one is to appear before
me empty-handed.
21"Six days you shall labor,
but on the seventh day you
shall rest; even during the
plowing season and harvest
you must rest.
22"Celebrate the Feast of
Weeks with the firstfruits of
the wheat harvest, and the
Feast of Ingathering at the
turn of the year.[q] 23Three times
a year all your men are to appear before the Sovereign
LORD, the God of Israel. 24I will
drive out nations before you
and enlarge your territory,
and no one will covet your
land when you go up three
times each year to appear before the LORD your God.
25"Do not offer the blood of a
sacrifice to me along with anything containing yeast, and do
not let any of the sacrifice

[q]22 That is, in the fall

*19 It is suggested that the first letter of the Hebrew word be dropped or replaced with the definite article.

חַג הַפָּסַח׃ רֵאשִׁית בִּכּוּרֵי אַדְמָתְךָ תָּבִיא
you-bring soil-of-you firstfruits-of best-of (26) the-Passover Feast-of

בֵּית יְהוָה אֱלֹהֶיךָ לֹא־תְבַשֵּׁל גְּדִי בַּחֲלֵב אִמּוֹ׃
mother-of-him in-milk-of young-goat you-cook not God-of-you Yahweh house-of

וַיֹּאמֶר יְהוָה אֶל־מֹשֶׁה כְּתָב־לְךָ אֶת־הַדְּבָרִים הָאֵלֶּה
the-these the-words *** for-you write! Moses to Yahweh then-he-said (27)

כִּי עַל־פִּי ׀ הַדְּבָרִים הָאֵלֶּה כָּרַתִּי אִתְּךָ בְּרִית וְאֶת־
and-with covenant with-you I-made the-these the-words accord-of in for

יִשְׂרָאֵל׃ וַיְהִי־שָׁם עִם־יְהוָה אַרְבָּעִים יוֹם וְאַרְבָּעִים לַיְלָה לֶחֶם
bread night and-forty day forty Yahweh with there and-he-was (28) Israel

לֹא אָכַל וּמַיִם לֹא שָׁתָה וַיִּכְתֹּב עַל־הַלֻּחֹת אֵת דִּבְרֵי
words-of *** the-tablets on and-he-wrote he-drank not and-waters he-ate not

הַבְּרִית עֲשֶׂרֶת הַדְּבָרִים׃ וַיְהִי בְּרֶדֶת מֹשֶׁה
Moses when-to-come-down and-he-was (29) the-Commandments Ten-of the-covenant

מֵהַר סִינַי וּשְׁנֵי לֻחֹת הָעֵדֻת בְּיַד־מֹשֶׁה
Moses in-hand-of the-Testimony tablets-of with-two-of Sinai from-Mount-of

בְּרִדְתּוֹ מִן־הָהָר וּמֹשֶׁה לֹא־יָדַע כִּי
that he-was-aware not and-Moses the-mountain from when-to-come-down-him

קָרַן עוֹר פָּנָיו בְּדַבְּרוֹ אִתּוֹ׃
with-him because-to-speak-him face-of-him skin-of he-was-radiant

וַיַּרְא אַהֲרֹן וְכָל־בְּנֵי יִשְׂרָאֵל אֶת־מֹשֶׁה וְהִנֵּה
and-see! Moses *** Israel sons-of and-all-of Aaron when-he-saw (30)

קָרַן עוֹר פָּנָיו וַיִּירְאוּ מִגֶּשֶׁת
from-to-come-near then-they-were-afraid face-of-him skin-of he-was-radiant

אֵלָיו׃ וַיִּקְרָא אֲלֵהֶם מֹשֶׁה וַיָּשֻׁבוּ אֵלָיו אַהֲרֹן
Aaron to-him and-they-came-back Moses to-them but-he-called (31) to-him

וְכָל־הַנְּשִׂאִים בָּעֵדָה וַיְדַבֵּר מֹשֶׁה אֲלֵהֶם׃
to-them Moses and-he-spoke of-the-community the-leaders and-all-of

וְאַחֲרֵי־כֵן נִגְּשׁוּ כָּל־בְּנֵי יִשְׂרָאֵל וַיְצַוֵּם
and-he-commanded-them Israel sons-of all-of they-came-near this and-after (32)

אֵת כָּל־אֲשֶׁר דִּבֶּר יְהוָה אִתּוֹ בְּהַר סִינָי׃ וַיְכַל
when-he-finished (33) Sinai on-Mount-of to-him Yahweh he-said that all ***

מֹשֶׁה מִדַּבֵּר אִתָּם וַיִּתֵּן עַל־פָּנָיו מַסְוֶה׃
veil face-of-him over then-he-put with-them from-to-speak Moses

וּבְבֹא מֹשֶׁה לִפְנֵי יְהוָה לְדַבֵּר אִתּוֹ יָסִיר
he-removed with-him to-speak Yahweh to-presences-of Moses but-when-to-enter (34)

אֶת־הַמַּסְוֶה עַד־צֵאתוֹ וְיָצָא וְדִבֶּר אֶל־בְּנֵי
sons-of to then-he-told when-he-came-out to-come-out-him until the-veil ***

from the Passover Feast remain until morning.
26"Bring the best of the firstfruits of your soil to the house of the LORD your God.
"Do not cook a young goat in its mother's milk."
27Then the LORD said to Moses, "Write down these words, for in accordance with these words I have made a covenant with you and with
Israel." 28Moses was there with the LORD forty days and forty nights without eating bread or drinking water. And he wrote on the tablets the words of the covenant—the Ten Commandments.

The Radiant Face of Moses

29When Moses came down from Mount Sinai with the two tablets of the Testimony in his hands, he was not aware that his face was radiant because he had spoken
with the LORD. 30When Aaron and all the Israelites saw Moses, his face was radiant, and they were afraid to come
near him. 31But Moses called to them; so Aaron and all the leaders of the community came back to him, and he
spoke to them. 32Afterward all the Israelites came near him, and he gave them all the commands the LORD had given him on Mount Sinai.
33When Moses finished speaking to them, he put a veil
over his face. 34But whenever he entered the LORD's presence to speak with him, he removed the veil until he came out. And when he came out and told the Israelites what he

יִשְׂרָאֵל אֵת אֲשֶׁר יְצֻוֶּה׃ וְרָאוּ בְנֵי־ יִשְׂרָאֵל אֶת־ פְּנֵי
face-of *** Israel sons-of and-they-saw (35) he-was-commanded what *** Israel

מֹשֶׁה כִּי קָרַן עוֹר פְּנֵי מֹשֶׁה וְהֵשִׁיב מֹשֶׁה אֶת־
*** Moses then-he-put-back Moses face-of skin-of he-was-radiant that Moses

הַמַּסְוֶה עַל־ פָּנָיו עַד־ בֹּאוֹ לְדַבֵּר אִתּוֹ׃
with-him to-speak to-go-him until face-of-him over the-veil

וַיַּקְהֵל מֹשֶׁה אֶת־ כָּל־ עֲדַת בְּנֵי־יִשְׂרָאֵל וַיֹּאמֶר
and-he-said Israel sons-of community-of whole-of *** Moses and-he-assembled (35:1)

אֲלֵהֶם אֵלֶּה הַדְּבָרִים אֲשֶׁר־ צִוָּה יְהוָה לַעֲשֹׂת אֹתָם׃ שֵׁשֶׁת
six-of (2) them to-do Yahweh he-commanded that the-things these to-them

יָמִים תֵּעָשֶׂה מְלָאכָה וּבַיּוֹם הַשְּׁבִיעִי יִהְיֶה לָכֶם
for-you he-shall-be the-seventh but-on-the-day work she-may-be-done days

קֹדֶשׁ שַׁבַּת שַׁבָּתוֹן לַיהוָה כָּל־ הָעֹשֶׂה בוֹ מְלָאכָה יוּמָת׃
he-must-die work on-him the-one-doing every-of to-Yahweh rest Sabbath-of holy

לֹא־ תְבַעֲרוּ אֵשׁ בְּכֹל מֹשְׁבֹתֵיכֶם בְּיוֹם הַשַּׁבָּת׃
the-Sabbath on-day-of dwellings-of-you in-any-of fire you-light not (3)

וַיֹּאמֶר מֹשֶׁה אֶל־ כָּל־ עֲדַת בְּנֵי־ יִשְׂרָאֵל לֵאמֹר זֶה
this to-say Israel sons-of community-of all-of to Moses and-he-said (4)

הַדָּבָר אֲשֶׁר־ צִוָּה יְהוָה לֵאמֹר׃ קְחוּ מֵאִתְּכֶם תְּרוּמָה
offering from-among-you take! (5) to-say Yahweh he-commanded that the-thing

לַיהוָה כֹּל נְדִיב לִבּוֹ יְבִיאֶהָ אֵת תְּרוּמַת
offering-of *** let-him-bring-her heart-of-him generous-of every-of to-Yahweh

יְהוָה זָהָב וָכֶסֶף וּנְחֹשֶׁת׃ וּתְכֵלֶת וְאַרְגָּמָן וְתוֹלַעַת
and-scarlet-of and-purple and-blue (6) and-bronze and-silver gold Yahweh

שָׁנִי וְשֵׁשׁ וְעִזִּים׃ וְעֹרֹת אֵילִם מְאָדָּמִים
ones-being-dyed-red rams and-skins-of (7) and-goat-hairs and-fine-linen yarn

וְעֹרֹת תְּחָשִׁים וַעֲצֵי שִׁטִּים*׃ וְשֶׁמֶן לַמָּאוֹר
for-the-light and-oil (8) acacias and-woods-of sea-cows and-hides-of

וּבְשָׂמִים לְשֶׁמֶן הַמִּשְׁחָה וְלִקְטֹרֶת הַסַּמִּים׃
the-fragrances and-for-incense-of the-anointing for-oil-of and-spices

וְאַבְנֵי־ שֹׁהַם וְאַבְנֵי מִלֻּאִים לָאֵפוֹד
for-the-ephod settings and-stones-of onyx and-stones-of (9)

וְלַחֹשֶׁן׃ וְכָל־ חֲכַם־ לֵב בָּכֶם
among-you heart skilled-of and-all-of (10) and-for-the-breastpiece

יָבֹאוּ וְיַעֲשׂוּ אֵת כָּל־ אֲשֶׁר צִוָּה יְהוָה׃ אֶת־
*** (11) Yahweh he-commanded that all *** and-let-them-make let-them-come

הַמִּשְׁכָּן אֶת־ אָהֳלוֹ וְאֶת־ מִכְסֵהוּ אֶת־ קְרָסָיו וְאֶת־
and clasps-of-him *** cover-of-him and tent-of-him *** the-tabernacle

had been commanded, 35they
saw that his face was radiant.
Then Moses would put the veil
back over his face until he
went in to speak with the
LORD.

Sabbath Regulations

35 Moses assembled the
whole Israelite com-
munity and said to them,
"These are the things the LORD
has commanded you to do:
2For six days, work is to be
done, but the seventh day
shall be your holy day, a Sabbath of rest to the LORD. Whoever does any work on it must
be put to death. 3Do not light a
fire in any of your dwellings
on the Sabbath day."

Materials for the Tabernacle

4Moses said to the whole Israelite community, "This is
what the LORD has com-
manded: 5From what you
have, take an offering for the
LORD. Everyone who is willing
is to bring to the LORD an offering of gold, silver and
bronze; 6blue, purple and scarlet yarn and fine linen; goat
hair; 7ram skins dyed red and
hides of sea cows; acacia
wood; 8olive oil for the light;
spices for the anointing oil
and for the fragrant incense;
9and onyx stones and other
gems to be mounted on the
ephod and breastpiece.
10"All who are skilled among
you are to come and make
everything the LORD has commanded: 11the tabernacle with
its tent and its covering,

*7 Most mss have *shin* instead of *sin* (שׁטים).

קְרָשָׁיו אֶת־ בְּרִיחָו אֶת־ עַמֻּדָיו וְאֶת־ אֲדָנָיו׃
bases-of-him and posts-of-him *** crossbars-of-him *** frames-of-him

(12) אֶת־ הָאָרֹן וְאֶת־ בַּדָּיו אֶת־ הַכַּפֹּרֶת וְאֵת פָּרֹכֶת
curtain-of and the-atonement-cover *** poles-of-him and the-ark *** (12)

הַמָּסָךְ׃ (13) אֶת־ הַשֻּׁלְחָן וְאֶת־ בַּדָּיו וְאֶת־ כָּל־ כֵּלָיו
articles-of-him all-of and poles-of-him and the-table *** (13) the-shield

וְאֵת לֶחֶם הַפָּנִים׃ (14) וְאֶת־ מְנֹרַת הַמָּאוֹר וְאֶת־
and the-light lampstand-of and (14) the-Presences bread-of and

כֵּלֶיהָ וְאֶת־ נֵרֹתֶיהָ וְאֵת שֶׁמֶן הַמָּאוֹר׃ (15) וְאֶת־ מִזְבַּח
altar-of and (15) the-light oil-of and lamps-of-her and accessories-of-her

הַקְּטֹרֶת וְאֶת־ בַּדָּיו וְאֵת שֶׁמֶן הַמִּשְׁחָה וְאֵת קְטֹרֶת
incense-of and the-anointing oil-of and poles-of-him and the-incense

הַסַּמִּים וְאֶת־ מָסַךְ הַפֶּתַח לְפֶתַח הַמִּשְׁכָּן׃
the-tabernacle at-entrance-of the-doorway curtain-of and the-fragrances

(16) אֵת ׀ מִזְבַּח הָעֹלָה וְאֶת־ מִכְבַּר הַנְּחֹשֶׁת אֲשֶׁר־ לוֹ
for-him that the-bronze grate-of and the-burnt-offering altar-of *** (16)

אֶת־ בַּדָּיו וְאֶת־ כָּל־ כֵּלָיו אֶת־ הַכִּיֹּר וְאֶת־ כַּנּוֹ׃
stand-of-him and the-basin *** utensils-of-him all-of and poles-of-him ***

(17) אֵת קַלְעֵי הֶחָצֵר אֶת־ עַמֻּדָיו וְאֶת־ אֲדָנֶיהָ וְאֵת
and bases-of-her and posts-of-him *** the-courtyard curtains-of *** (17)

מָסַךְ שַׁעַר הֶחָצֵר׃ (18) אֶת־ יִתְדֹת הַמִּשְׁכָּן
the-tabernacle tent-pegs-of *** (18) the-courtyard entrance-of curtain-of

וְאֶת־ יִתְדֹת הֶחָצֵר וְאֶת־ מֵיתְרֵיהֶם׃ (19) אֶת־ בִּגְדֵי הַשְּׂרָד
the-woven garments-of *** (19) ropes-of-them and the-courtyard pegs-of and

לְשָׁרֵת בַּקֹּדֶשׁ אֶת־ בִּגְדֵי הַקֹּדֶשׁ לְאַהֲרֹן
for-Aaron the-sacred garments-of *** in-the-sanctuary for-to-minister

הַכֹּהֵן וְאֶת־ בִּגְדֵי בָנָיו לְכַהֵן׃ (20) וַיֵּצְאוּ
then-they-left (20) for-to-be-priest sons-of-him garments-of and the-priest

כָּל־ עֲדַת בְּנֵי־ יִשְׂרָאֵל מִלִּפְנֵי מֹשֶׁה׃ (21) וַיָּבֹאוּ
and-they-came (21) Moses from-presence-of Israel sons-of community-of whole-of

כָּל־ אִישׁ אֲשֶׁר־ נְשָׂאוֹ לִבּוֹ וְכֹל אֲשֶׁר נָדְבָה
she-moved whom and-everyone heart-of-him he-moved-him whom one every-of

רוּחוֹ אֹתוֹ הֵבִיאוּ אֶת־ תְּרוּמַת יְהוָה לִמְלֶאכֶת אֹהֶל
Tent-of for-work-of Yahweh offering-of *** they-brought him spirit-of-him

מוֹעֵד וּלְכָל־ עֲבֹדָתוֹ וּלְבִגְדֵי הַקֹּדֶשׁ׃
the-sacred and-for-garments-of service-of-him and-for-all-of Meeting

(22) וַיָּבֹאוּ הָאֲנָשִׁים עַל־ הַנָּשִׁים כֹּל ׀ נְדִיב לֵב הֵבִיאוּ
they-brought heart willing-of all-of the-women with the-men and-they-came (22)

clasps, frames, crossbars, posts
and bases; [12]the ark with its
poles and the atonement cover
and the curtain that shields it;
[13]the table with its poles and
all its articles and the bread of
the Presence; [14]the lampstand
that is for light with its accessories, lamps and oil for the
light; [15]the altar of incense
with its poles, the anointing
oil and the fragrant incense;
the curtain for the doorway at
the entrance to the tabernacle;
[16]the altar of burnt offering
with its bronze grating, its
poles and all its utensils; the
bronze basin with its stand;
[17]the curtains of the courtyard
with its posts and bases, and
the curtain for the entrance to
the courtyard; [18]the tent pegs
for the tabernacle and for the
courtyard, and their ropes;
[19]the woven garments worn
for ministering in the sanctuary—both the sacred garments
for Aaron the priest and the
garments for his sons when
they serve as priests."
[20]Then the whole Israelite
community withdrew from
Moses' presence, [21]and everyone who was willing and
whose heart moved him came
and brought an offering to the
LORD for the work on the Tent
of Meeting, for all its service,
and for the sacred garments.
[22]All who were willing, men
and women alike, came and

ק בריחיו 11°

חָח וָנֶזֶם וְטַבַּעַת וְכוּמָז כָּל־ כְּלִי זָהָב וְכָל־

and-every-of gold jewelry-of every-of and-ornament and-ring and-earring brooch

אִישׁ אֲשֶׁר הֵנִיף תְּנוּפַת זָהָב לַיהוָה׃ וְכָל־ אִישׁ

one and-every-of (23) to-Yahweh gold wave-offering-of he-presented who one

אֲשֶׁר־ נִמְצָא אִתּוֹ תְּכֵלֶת וְאַרְגָּמָן וְתוֹלַעַת שָׁנִי וְשֵׁשׁ

or-fine-linen yarn or-scarlet-of or-purple blue with-him he-was-found who

וְעִזִּים וְעֹרֹת אֵילִם מְאָדָּמִים וְעֹרֹת תְּחָשִׁים

sea-cows or-hides-of ones-being-dyed-red rams or-skins-of or-goat-hairs

הֵבִיאוּ׃ כָּל־ מֵרִים תְּרוּמַת כֶּסֶף וּנְחֹשֶׁת

or-bronze silver offering-of ones-presenting all-of (24) they-brought

הֵבִיאוּ אֵת תְּרוּמַת יְהוָה וְכֹל אֲשֶׁר נִמְצָא אִתּוֹ

with-him he-was-found who and-everyone Yahweh offering-of *** they-brought

עֲצֵי שִׁטִּים לְכָל־ מְלֶאכֶת הָעֲבֹדָה הֵבִיאוּ׃ וְכָל־

and-every-of (25) they-brought the-work part-of for-any-of acacias woods-of

אִשָּׁה חַכְמַת־ לֵב בְּיָדֶיהָ טָווּ וַיָּבִיאוּ מַטְוֶה

product and-they-brought they-spun with-hands-of-her heart skilled-of woman

אֶת־ הַתְּכֵלֶת וְאֶת־ הָאַרְגָּמָן אֶת־ תּוֹלַעַת הַשָּׁנִי וְאֶת־ הַשֵּׁשׁ׃

the-fine-linen and the-yarn scarlet-of *** the-purple and the-blue ***

וְכָל־ הַנָּשִׁים אֲשֶׁר נָשָׂא לִבָּן אֹתָנָה בְּחָכְמָה

with-skill them heart-of-them he-moved whom the-women and-all-of (26)

טָווּ אֶת־ הָעִזִּים׃ וְהַנְּשִׂאִם הֵבִיאוּ אֵת אַבְנֵי

stones-of *** they-brought and-the-leaders (27) the-goat-hairs *** they-spun

הַשֹּׁהַם וְאֵת אַבְנֵי הַמִּלֻּאִים לָאֵפוֹד וְלַחֹשֶׁן׃

and-for-the-breastpiece for-the-ephod the-mountings stones-of and the-onyx

וְאֶת־ הַבֹּשֶׂם וְאֶת־ הַשֶּׁמֶן לְמָאוֹר וּלְשֶׁמֶן הַמִּשְׁחָה

the-anointing and-for-oil-of for-light the-oil and the-spice and (28)

וְלִקְטֹרֶת הַסַּמִּים׃ כָּל־ אִישׁ וְאִשָּׁה אֲשֶׁר נָדַב

he-moved whom and-woman man every-of (29) the-fragrances and-for-incense-of

לִבָּם אֹתָם לְהָבִיא לְכָל־ הַמְּלָאכָה אֲשֶׁר צִוָּה יְהוָה

Yahweh he-commanded that the-work for-all-of to-bring them heart-of them

לַעֲשׂוֹת בְּיַד־ מֹשֶׁה הֵבִיאוּ בְנֵי־ יִשְׂרָאֵל נְדָבָה

freewill-offering Israel sons-of they-brought Moses through-hand-of to do

לַיהוָה׃ וַיֹּאמֶר מֹשֶׁה אֶל־ בְּנֵי יִשְׂרָאֵל רְאוּ קָרָא יְהוָה

Yahweh he-chose see! Israel sons-of to Moses then-he-said (30) to-Yahweh

בְשֵׁם בְּצַלְאֵל בֶּן־ אוּרִי בֶן־ חוּר לְמַטֵּה יְהוּדָה׃ וַיְמַלֵּא

and-he-filled (31) Judah from-tribe-of Hur son-of Uri son-of Bezalel by-name

אֹתוֹ רוּחַ אֱלֹהִים בְּחָכְמָה בִּתְבוּנָה וּבְדַעַת וּבְכָל־מְלָאכָה׃

craft in-all-of and-with-knowledge with-ability with-skill God Spirit-of him

brought gold jewelry of all
kinds: brooches, earrings,
rings and ornaments. They all
presented their gold as a wave
offering to the LORD. 23Every-
one who had blue, purple or
scarlet yarn or fine linen, or
goat hair, ram skins dyed red
or hides of sea cows brought
them. 24Those presenting an
offering of silver or bronze
brought it as an offering to the
LORD, and everyone who had
acacia wood for any part of the
work brought it. 25Every
skilled woman spun with her
hands and brought what she
had spun—blue, purple or
scarlet yarn or fine linen.
26And all the women who
were willing and had the skill
spun the goat hair. 27The leaders brought onyx stones and
other gems to be mounted on
the ephod and breastpiece.
28They also brought spices and
olive oil for the light and for
the anointing oil and for the
fragrant incense. 29All the Israelite men and women who
were willing brought to the
LORD freewill offerings for all
the work the LORD through
Moses had commanded them
to do.

Bezalel and Oholiab

30Then Moses said to the Israelites, "See, the LORD has
chosen Bezalel son of Uri, the
son of Hur, of the tribe of
Judah, 31and he has filled him
with the Spirit of God, with
skill, ability and knowledge in
all kinds of crafts— 32to make

וְלַחְשֹׁב מַחֲשָׁבֹת* לַעֲשֹׂת בַּזָּהָב וּבַכֶּסֶף
and-in-the-silver in-the-gold to-work artistic-designs and-to-make (32)

וּבַנְּחֹשֶׁת׃ וּבַחֲרֹשֶׁת אֶבֶן לְמַלֹּאת וּבַחֲרֹשֶׁת
and-for-cutting-of to-set stone and-for-cutting-of (33) and-in-the-bronze

עֵץ לַעֲשׂוֹת בְּכָל־ מְלֶאכֶת מַחֲשָׁבֶת׃ וּלְהוֹרֹת נָתַן
he-put and-to-teach (34) craftsmanship kind-of in-all-of to-engage wood

בְּלִבּוֹ הוּא וְאָהֳלִיאָב בֶּן־ אֲחִיסָמָךְ לְמַטֵּה־ דָן׃
Dan from-tribe-of Ahisamach son-of and-Oholiab he in-heart-of-him

מִלֵּא אֹתָם חָכְמַת־ לֵב לַעֲשׂוֹת כָּל־ מְלֶאכֶת חָרָשׁ ׀
craftsman work-of all-of to-do heart skill-of them he-filled (35)

וְחֹשֵׁב וְרֹקֵם בַּתְּכֵלֶת וּבָאַרְגָּמָן בְּתוֹלַעַת
and-in-scarlet-of and-in-the-purple in-the-blue and-embroidering and-designing

הַשָּׁנִי וּבַשֵּׁשׁ וְאֹרֵג עֹשֵׂי כָּל־מְלָאכָה
craft all-of ones-doing-of and-weaving and-in-the-fine-linen the-yarn

וְחֹשְׁבֵי מַחֲשָׁבֹת׃ וְעָשָׂה בְצַלְאֵל וְאָהֳלִיאָב
and-Oholiab Bezalel so-he-shall-do (36:1) designs and-ones-designing-of

וְכֹל ׀ אִישׁ חֲכַם־ לֵב אֲשֶׁר נָתַן יְהוָה חָכְמָה וּתְבוּנָה
and-ability skill Yahweh he-gave whom heart skilled-of person and-every-of

בָּהֵמָּה לָדַעַת לַעֲשֹׂת אֶת־ כָּל־ מְלֶאכֶת עֲבֹדַת הַקֹּדֶשׁ
the-sanctuary construction-of work-of all-of *** to-do to-know in-them

לְכֹל אֲשֶׁר־ צִוָּה יְהוָה׃ וַיִּקְרָא מֹשֶׁה אֶל־בְּצַלְאֵל
Bezalel to Moses then-he-summoned (2) Yahweh he-commanded that as-all

וְאֶל־ אָהֳלִיאָב וְאֶל כָּל־ אִישׁ חֲכַם־ לֵב אֲשֶׁר נָתַן יְהוָה
Yahweh he-gave whom heart skilled-of person every-of and-to Oholiab and-to

חָכְמָה בְּלִבּוֹ כֹּל אֲשֶׁר נְשָׂאוֹ לִבּוֹ לְקָרְבָה
to-come heart-of-him he-moved-him whom everyone in-heart-of-him ability

אֶל־הַמְּלָאכָה לַעֲשֹׂת אֹתָהּ׃ וַיִּקְחוּ מִלִּפְנֵי מֹשֶׁה אֵת כָּל־
all-of *** Moses from and-they-received (3) her to-do the-work to

הַתְּרוּמָה אֲשֶׁר הֵבִיאוּ בְּנֵי יִשְׂרָאֵל לִמְלֶאכֶת עֲבֹדַת
construction-of for-work-of Israel sons-of they-brought that the-offering

הַקֹּדֶשׁ לַעֲשֹׂת אֹתָהּ וְהֵם הֵבִיאוּ אֵלָיו עוֹד נְדָבָה
freewill-offering still to-him they-brought and-they her to-do the-sanctuary

בַּבֹּקֶר בַּבֹּקֶר׃ וַיָּבֹאוּ כָּל־ הַחֲכָמִים
the-craftsmen all-of so-they-left (4) in-the-morning in-the-morning

הָעֹשִׂים אֵת כָּל־ מְלֶאכֶת הַקֹּדֶשׁ אִישׁ־ אִישׁ מִמְּלַאכְתּוֹ
from-work-of-him each each the-sanctuary work-of all-of *** the-ones-doing

אֲשֶׁר־הֵמָּה עֹשִׂים׃ וַיֹּאמְרוּ אֶל־ מֹשֶׁה לֵּאמֹר מַרְבִּים
amounts-being-more to-say Moses to and-they-said (5) ones-doing they that

artistic designs for work in
gold, silver and bronze, 33to cut
and set stones, to work in
wood and to engage in all
kinds of artistic craftsmanship. 34And he has given both
him and Oholiab son of
Ahisamach, of the tribe of
Dan, the ability to teach
others. 35He has filled them
with skill to do all kinds of
work as craftsmen, designers,
embroiderers in blue, purple
and scarlet yarn and fine lin-
en, and weavers—all of them
master craftsmen and design-
36 ers. 1So Bezalel, Oho-
liab and every skilled
person to whom the LORD has
given skill and ability to know
how to carry out all the work
of constructing the sanctuary
are to do the work just as the
LORD has commanded."
2Then Moses summoned
Bezalel and Oholiab and every
skilled person to whom the
LORD had given ability and
who was willing to come and
do the work. 3They received
from Moses all the offerings
the Israelites had brought to
carry out the work of constructing the sanctuary. And
the people continued to bring
freewill offerings morning after morning. 4So all the skilled
craftsmen who were doing all
the work on the sanctuary left
their work 5and said to Moses,

*32 Most mss have *hateph pathah* under the *beth* (מַחֲ׳).

הָעָם לְהָבִיא מִדֵּי הָעֲבֹדָה לַמְּלָאכָה אֲשֶׁר־צִוָּה
he-commanded that for-the-labor the-work than-need-of to-bring the-people

יְהוָה לַעֲשֹׂת אֹתָהּ׃ וַיְצַו מֹשֶׁה וַיַּעֲבִירוּ קוֹל
word and-they-sent Moses then-he-gave-order (6) her to-do Yahweh

בַּמַּחֲנֶה לֵאמֹר אִישׁ וְאִשָּׁה אַל־יַעֲשׂוּ־עוֹד מְלָאכָה
anything else they-shall-make not or-woman man to-say through-the-camp

לִתְרוּמַת הַקֹּדֶשׁ וַיִּכָּלֵא הָעָם מֵהָבִיא׃
from-to-bring the-people so-they-were-restrained the-sanctuary as-offering-of

וְהַמְּלָאכָה הָיְתָה דַיָּם לְכָל־הַמְּלָאכָה לַעֲשׂוֹת אֹתָהּ
her to-do the-work for-all-of enough-for-them she-was for-the-material (7)

וְהוֹתֵר׃ וַיַּעֲשׂוּ כָל־חֲכַם־לֵב בְּעֹשֵׂי
among-ones-doing-of heart skilled-of all-of and-they-made (8) and-to-be-more

הַמְּלָאכָה אֶת־הַמִּשְׁכָּן עֶשֶׂר יְרִיעֹת שֵׁשׁ מָשְׁזָר וּתְכֵלֶת
and-blue being-twisted fine-linen curtains ten the-tabernacle *** the-work

וְאַרְגָּמָן וְתוֹלַעַת שָׁנִי כְּרֻבִים מַעֲשֵׂה חֹשֵׁב עָשָׂה אֹתָם׃
them he-made being-skilled work-of cherubim yarn and-scarlet-of and-purple

אֹרֶךְ הַיְרִיעָה הָאַחַת שְׁמֹנֶה וְעֶשְׂרִים בָּאַמָּה וְרֹחַב
and-width by-the-cubit and-twenty eight the-each the-curtain length-of (9)

אַרְבַּע בָּאַמָּה הַיְרִיעָה הָאֶחָת מִדָּה אַחַת לְכָל־הַיְרִיעֹת׃
the-curtains for-all-of same size the-each the-curtain by-the-cubit four

וַיְחַבֵּר אֶת־חֲמֵשׁ הַיְרִיעֹת אַחַת אֶל־אֶחָת וְחָמֵשׁ יְרִיעֹת
curtains and-five other to each the-curtains five-of *** and-he-joined (10)

חִבַּר אַחַת אֶל־אֶחָת׃ וַיַּעַשׂ לֻלְאֹת תְּכֵלֶת עַל שְׂפַת
edge-of along blue loops-of then-he-made (11) other to each he-joined

הַיְרִיעָה הָאֶחָת מִקָּצָה בַּמַּחְבָּרֶת כֵּן עָשָׂה בִּשְׂפַת הַיְרִיעָה
the-curtain on-edge-of he-did same of-the-set at-end the-one the-curtain

הַקִּיצוֹנָה בַּמַּחְבֶּרֶת הַשֵּׁנִית׃ חֲמִשִּׁים לֻלָאֹת עָשָׂה בַּיְרִיעָה הָאֶחָת
the-one on-the-curtain he-made loops fifty (12) the-other in-the-set the-end

וַחֲמִשִּׁים לֻלָאֹת עָשָׂה בִּקְצֵה הַיְרִיעָה אֲשֶׁר בַּמַּחְבֶּרֶת הַשֵּׁנִית
the-other in-the-set that the-curtain on-end-of he-made loops and-fifty

מַקְבִּילֹת הַלֻּלָאֹת אַחַת אֶל־אֶחָת׃ וַיַּעַשׂ חֲמִשִּׁים קַרְסֵי
clasps-of fifty then-he-made (13) other to each the-loops ones-opposing

זָהָב וַיְחַבֵּר אֶת־הַיְרִיעֹת אַחַת אֶל־אַחַת בַּקְּרָסִים
with-the-clasps other to each the-curtains *** and-he-fastened gold

וַיְהִי הַמִּשְׁכָּן אֶחָד׃ וַיַּעַשׂ יְרִיעֹת עִזִּים לְאֹהֶל
for-tent goat-hairs curtains-of and-he-made (14) unit the-tabernacle so-he-was

עַל־הַמִּשְׁכָּן עַשְׁתֵּי־עֶשְׂרֵה יְרִיעֹת עָשָׂה אֹתָם׃ אֹרֶךְ הַיְרִיעָה
the-curtain length-of (15) them he-made curtains ten one the-tabernacle over

"The people are bringing more than enough for doing the work the LORD commanded to be done."
[6]Then Moses gave an order and they sent this word throughout the camp: "No man or woman is to make anything else as an offering for the sanctuary." And so the people were restrained from bringing more,
[7]because what they already had was more than enough to do all the work.

The Tabernacle

[8]All the skilled men among the workmen made the tabernacle with ten curtains of finely twisted linen and blue, purple and scarlet yarn, with cherubim worked into them by a skilled craftsman.
[9]All the curtains were the same size—twenty-eight cubits long and four cubits wide.[r]
[10]They joined five of the curtains together and did the same with the other five.
[11]Then they made loops of blue material along the edge of the end curtain in one set, and the same was done with the end curtain in the other set.
[12]They also made fifty loops on one curtain and fifty loops on the end curtain of the other set, with the loops opposite each other.
[13]Then they made fifty gold clasps and used them to fasten the two sets of curtains together so that the tabernacle was a unit.
[14]They made curtains of goat hair for the tent over the tabernacle—eleven all together.

[r]9 That is, about 42 feet (about 12.5 meters) long and 6 feet (about 1.8 meters) wide

הָאַחַת שְׁלֹשִׁים בָּאַמָּה וְאַרְבַּע אַמּוֹת רֹחַב הַיְרִיעָה הָאֶחָת
the-each the-curtain width-of cubits and-four by-the-cubit thirty the-each

מִדָּה אַחַת לְעַשְׁתֵּי עֶשְׂרֵה יְרִיעֹת׃ (16) וַיְחַבֵּר אֶת־ חֲמֵשׁ הַיְרִיעֹת
the-curtains five-of *** and-he-joined (16) curtains ten for-one same size

לְבָד וְאֶת־ שֵׁשׁ הַיְרִיעֹת לְבָד׃ (17) וַיַּעַשׂ לֻלָאֹת חֲמִשִּׁים עַל
along fifty loops and-he-made (17) into-set the-curtains six-of and into-set

שְׂפַת הַיְרִיעָה הַקִּיצֹנָה בַּמַּחְבָּרֶת וַחֲמִשִּׁים לֻלָאֹת עָשָׂה עַל־ שְׂפַת
edge-of along he-made loops and-fifty of-the-set the-end the-curtain edge-of

הַיְרִיעָה הַחֹבֶרֶת הַשֵּׁנִית׃ (18) וַיַּעַשׂ קַרְסֵי נְחֹשֶׁת חֲמִשִּׁים
fifty bronze clasps-of and-he-made (18) the-other the-set the-curtain

לְחַבֵּר אֶת־ הָאֹהֶל לִהְיֹת אֶחָד׃ (19) וַיַּעַשׂ מִכְסֶה לָאֹהֶל
for-the-tent cover then-he-made (19) unit to-be the-tent *** to-fasten

עֹרֹת אֵילִם מְאָדָּמִים וּמִכְסֵה עֹרֹת תְּחָשִׁים מִלְמָעְלָה׃
for-above sea-cows hides-of and-cover-of ones-being-dyed-red rams skins-of

(20) וַיַּעַשׂ אֶת־ הַקְּרָשִׁים לַמִּשְׁכָּן עֲצֵי שִׁטִּים
acacias woods-of for-the-tabernacle the-frames *** and-he-made (20)

עֹמְדִים׃ (21) עֶשֶׂר אַמֹּת אֹרֶךְ הַקָּרֶשׁ וְאַמָּה וַחֲצִי
and-half-of and-cubit the-frame length-of cubits ten (21) ones-being-upright

הָאַמָּה רֹחַב הַקֶּרֶשׁ הָאֶחָד׃ (22) שְׁתֵּי יָדֹת לַקֶּרֶשׁ
for-the-frame projections two-of (22) the-each the-frame width-of the-cubit

הָאֶחָד מְשֻׁלָּבֹת אַחַת אֶל־ אֶחָת כֵּן עָשָׂה לְכֹל קַרְשֵׁי
frames-of for-all-of he-did same other to each ones-paralleling the-each

הַמִּשְׁכָּן׃ (23) וַיַּעַשׂ אֶת־ הַקְּרָשִׁים לַמִּשְׁכָּן עֶשְׂרִים קְרָשִׁים
frames twenty for-the-tabernacle the-frames *** and-he-made (23) the-tabernacle

לִפְאַת נֶגֶב תֵּימָנָה׃ (24) וְאַרְבָּעִים אַדְנֵי־ כֶסֶף עָשָׂה תַּחַת עֶשְׂרִים
twenty under he-made silver bases-of and-forty (24) to-south south for-side-of

הַקְּרָשִׁים שְׁנֵי אֲדָנִים תַּחַת־ הַקֶּרֶשׁ הָאֶחָד לִשְׁתֵּי יְדֹתָיו
projections-of-him for-two-of the-one the-frame under bases two-of the-frames

וּשְׁנֵי אֲדָנִים תַּחַת־ הַקֶּרֶשׁ הָאֶחָד לִשְׁתֵּי יְדֹתָיו׃
projections-of-him for-two-of the-other the-frame under bases and-two-of

(25) וּלְצֶלַע הַמִּשְׁכָּן הַשֵּׁנִית לִפְאַת צָפוֹן עָשָׂה
he-made north for-side-of the-other the-tabernacle and-for-side-of (25)

עֶשְׂרִים קְרָשִׁים׃ (26) וְאַרְבָּעִים אַדְנֵיהֶם כָּסֶף שְׁנֵי אֲדָנִים תַּחַת
under bases two-of silver bases-of-them and-forty (26) frames twenty

הַקֶּרֶשׁ הָאֶחָד וּשְׁנֵי אֲדָנִים תַּחַת הַקֶּרֶשׁ הָאֶחָד׃
the-other the-frame under bases and-two-of the-one the-frame

(27) וּלְיַרְכְּתֵי הַמִּשְׁכָּן יָמָּה עָשָׂה שִׁשָּׁה קְרָשִׁים׃ (28) וּשְׁנֵי
and-two-of (28) frames six he-made to-west the-tabernacle and-for-far-ends-of (27)

15All eleven curtains were the
same size—thirty cubits long
and four cubits wide.[t] 16They
joined five of the curtains into
one set and the other six into
another set. 17Then they made
fifty loops along the edge of
the end curtain in one set and
also along the edge of the end
curtain in the other set. 18They
made fifty bronze clasps to fasten the tent together as a unit.
19Then they made for the tent
a covering of ram skins dyed
red, and over that a covering
of hides of sea cows.

20They made upright frames
of acacia wood for the tabernacle. 21Each frame was ten
cubits long and a cubit and a
half wide,[u] 22with two
projections set parallel to each
other. They made all the
frames of the tabernacle in
this way. 23They made twenty
frames for the south side of the
tabernacle 24and made forty
silver bases to go under
them—two bases for each
frame, one under each
projection. 25For the other
side, the north side of the tabernacle, they made twenty
frames 26and forty silver
bases—two under each frame.
27They made six frames for the
far end, that is, the west end of
the tabernacle, 28and two

[t] *15* That is, about 45 feet (about 13.5 meters) long and 6 feet (about 1.8 meters) wide

[u] *21* That is, about 15 feet (about 4.5 meters) long and 2 1/4 feet (about 0.7 meter) wide

קְרָשִׁים עָשָׂה לִמְקֻצְעֹת הַמִּשְׁכָּן בַּיַּרְכָתָיִם׃ וְהָיוּ
and-they-were (29) at-the-far-ends the-tabernacle for-corners-of he-made frames

תוֹאֲמִם מִלְּמַטָּה וְיַחְדָּו יִהְיוּ תַמִּים אֶל־
at being-fitted they-were and-together from-bottom ones-being-double

רֹאשׁוֹ אֶל־ הַטַּבַּעַת הָאֶחָת כֵּן עָשָׂה לִשְׁנֵיהֶם
for-both-of-them he-made alike the-single the-ring into top-of-him

לִשְׁנֵי הַמִּקְצֹעֹת׃ וְהָיוּ שְׁמֹנָה קְרָשִׁים וְאַדְנֵיהֶם
and-bases-of-them frames eight so-they-were (30) the-corners for-both-of

כֶּסֶף שִׁשָּׁה עָשָׂר אֲדָנִים שְׁנֵי אֲדָנִים שְׁנֵי אֲדָנִים תַּחַת הַקֶּרֶשׁ הָאֶחָד׃
the-each the-frame under bases two-of bases two-of bases ten six silver

וַיַּעַשׂ בְּרִיחֵי עֲצֵי שִׁטִּים חֲמִשָּׁה לְקַרְשֵׁי צֶלַע־
side-of for-frames-of five acacias woods-of crossbars-of and-he-made (31)

הַמִּשְׁכָּן הָאֶחָת׃ וַחֲמִשָּׁה בְּרִיחִם לְקַרְשֵׁי צֶלַע־
side-of for-frames-of crossbars and-five (32) the-one the-tabernacle

הַמִּשְׁכָּן הַשֵּׁנִית וַחֲמִשָּׁה בְּרִיחִם לְקַרְשֵׁי הַמִּשְׁכָּן
the-tabernacle for-frames-of crossbars and-five the-other the-tabernacle

לַיַּרְכָתַיִם יָמָּה׃ וַיַּעַשׂ אֶת־ הַבְּרִיחַ הַתִּיכֹן
the-center the-crossbar *** and-he-made (33) to-west at-the-far-ends

לִבְרֹחַ בְּתוֹךְ הַקְּרָשִׁים מִן־ הַקָּצֶה אֶל־ הַקָּצֶה׃ וְאֶת־ הַקְּרָשִׁים
the-frames and (34) the-end to the-end from the-frames at-middle-of to-extend

צִפָּה זָהָב וְאֶת־ טַבְּעֹתָם עָשָׂה זָהָב בָּתִּים לַבְּרִיחִם
for-the-crossbars holders gold he-made rings-of-them and gold he-overlaid

וַיְצַף אֶת־ הַבְּרִיחִם זָהָב׃ וַיַּעַשׂ אֶת־ הַפָּרֹכֶת
the-curtain *** and-he-made (35) gold the-crossbars *** and-he-overlaid

תְּכֵלֶת וְאַרְגָּמָן וְתוֹלַעַת שָׁנִי וְשֵׁשׁ מָשְׁזָר מַעֲשֵׂה
work-of being-twisted and-fine-linen yarn and-scarlet-of and-purple blue

חֹשֵׁב עָשָׂה אֹתָהּ כְּרֻבִים׃ וַיַּעַשׂ לָהּ אַרְבָּעָה עַמּוּדֵי
posts-of four for-her and-he-made (36) cherubim her he-made being-skilled

שִׁטִּים וַיְצַפֵּם זָהָב וָוֵיהֶם זָהָב וַיִּצֹק לָהֶם
for-them and-he-cast gold hooks-of-them gold and-he-overlaid-them acacias

אַרְבָּעָה אַדְנֵי־ כָסֶף׃ וַיַּעַשׂ מָסָךְ לְפֶתַח הָאֹהֶל תְּכֵלֶת
blue the-tent for-entrance-of curtain and-he-made (37) silver bases-of four

וְאַרְגָּמָן וְתוֹלַעַת שָׁנִי וְשֵׁשׁ מָשְׁזָר מַעֲשֵׂה
work-of being-twisted and-fine-linen yarn and-scarlet-of and-purple

רֹקֵם׃ וְאֶת־ עַמּוּדָיו חֲמִשָּׁה וְאֶת־ וָוֵיהֶם וְצִפָּה
and-he-overlaid hooks-of-them and five posts-of-him and (38) embroidering

רָאשֵׁיהֶם וַחֲשֻׁקֵיהֶם זָהָב וְאַדְנֵיהֶם חֲמִשָּׁה נְחֹשֶׁת׃
bronze five and-bases-of-them gold and-bands-of-them tops-of-them

frames were made for the corners of the tabernacle at the far
end. [29]At these two corners the
frames were double from the
bottom all the way to the top
and fitted into a single ring;
both were made alike. [30]So
there were eight frames and
sixteen silver bases—two under each frame.

[31]They also made crossbars
of acacia wood: five for the
frames on one side of the tabernacle, [32]five for those on the
other side, and five for the
frames on the west, at the far
end of the tabernacle. [33]They
made the center crossbar so
that it extended from end to
end at the middle of the
frames. [34]They overlaid the
frames with gold and made
gold rings to hold the crossbars. They also overlaid the
crossbars with gold.

[35]They made the curtain of
blue, purple and scarlet yarn
and finely twisted linen, with
cherubim worked into it by a
skilled craftsman. [36]They made
four posts of acacia wood for it
and overlaid them with gold.
They made gold hooks for
them and cast their four silver
bases. [37]For the entrance to the
tent they made a curtain of
blue, purple and scarlet yarn
and finely twisted linen—the
work of an embroiderer; [38]and
they made five posts with
hooks for them. They overlaid
the tops of the posts and their
bands with gold and made
their five bases of bronze.

וַיַּעַשׂ בְּצַלְאֵל אֶת־ הָאָרֹן עֲצֵי שִׁטִּים אַמָּתַיִם וָחֵצִי
and-half two-cubits acacias woods-of the-ark *** Bezalel and-he-made (37:1)

אָרְכּוֹ וְאַמָּה וָחֵצִי רָחְבּוֹ וְאַמָּה וָחֵצִי
and-half and-cubit width-of-him and-half and-cubit length-of-him

קֹמָתוֹ: וַיְצַפֵּהוּ זָהָב טָהוֹר מִבַּיִת וּמִחוּץ
and-on-outside on-inside pure gold and-he-overlaid-him (2) height-of-him

וַיַּעַשׂ לוֹ זֵר זָהָב סָבִיב: וַיִּצֹק לוֹ אַרְבַּע
four for-him and-he-cast (3) around gold molding-of for-him and-he-made

טַבְּעֹת זָהָב עַל אַרְבַּע פַּעֲמֹתָיו וּשְׁתֵּי טַבָּעֹת עַל־ צַלְעוֹ הָאֶחָת
the-one side-of-him on rings and-two-of feet-of-him four for gold rings-of

וּשְׁתֵּי טַבָּעוֹת עַל־ צַלְעוֹ הַשֵּׁנִית: וַיַּעַשׂ בַּדֵּי עֲצֵי
woods-of poles-of then-he-made (4) the-other side-of-him on rings and-two-of

שִׁטִּים וַיְצַף אֹתָם זָהָב: וַיָּבֵא אֶת־ הַבַּדִּים
the-poles *** and-he-inserted (5) gold them and-he-overlaid acacias

בַּטַּבָּעֹת עַל צַלְעֹת הָאָרֹן לָשֵׂאת אֶת־ הָאָרֹן: וַיַּעַשׂ
and-he-made (6) the-ark *** to-carry the-ark sides-of on into-the-rings

כַּפֹּרֶת זָהָב טָהוֹר אַמָּתַיִם וָחֵצִי אָרְכָּהּ וְאַמָּה וָחֵצִי
and-half and-cubit length-of-her and-half two-cubits pure gold atonement-cover

רָחְבָּהּ: וַיַּעַשׂ שְׁנֵי כְרֻבִים זָהָב מִקְשָׁה עָשָׂה אֹתָם
them he-made hammered gold cherubim two-of then-he-made (7) width-of-her

מִשְּׁנֵי קְצוֹת הַכַּפֹּרֶת: כְּרוּב־ אֶחָד מִקָּצָה מִזֶּה וּכְרוּב־ אֶחָד
one and-cherub on-one on-end one cherub (8) the-cover ends-of at-two-of

מִקָּצָה מִזֶּה מִן־ הַכַּפֹּרֶת עָשָׂה אֶת־ הַכְּרֻבִים מִשְּׁנֵי קְצוֹוֹתָו:
ends-of-him at-two-of the-cherubim *** he-made the-cover from on-other on-end

וַיִּהְיוּ הַכְּרֻבִים פֹּרְשֵׂי כְנָפַיִם לְמַעְלָה
upward wings ones-spreading-of the-cherubim and-they-were (9)

סֹכְכִים בְּכַנְפֵיהֶם עַל־ הַכַּפֹּרֶת וּפְנֵיהֶם אִישׁ
each and-faces-of-them the-cover over with-wings-of-them ones-overshadowing

אֶל־ אָחִיו אֶל־ הַכַּפֹּרֶת הָיוּ פְּנֵי הַכְּרֻבִים:
the-cherubim faces-of they-were the-cover toward other-of-him toward

וַיַּעַשׂ אֶת־ הַשֻּׁלְחָן עֲצֵי שִׁטִּים אַמָּתַיִם אָרְכּוֹ
length-of-him two-cubits acacias woods-of the-table *** and-he-made (10)

וְאַמָּה רָחְבּוֹ וְאַמָּה וָחֵצִי קֹמָתוֹ: וַיְצַף
and-he-overlaid (11) height-of-him and-half and-cubit width-of-him and-cubit

אֹתוֹ זָהָב טָהוֹר וַיַּעַשׂ לוֹ זֵר זָהָב סָבִיב: וַיַּעַשׂ
and-he-made (12) around gold molding-of for-him and-he-made pure gold him

לוֹ מִסְגֶּרֶת טֹפַח סָבִיב וַיַּעַשׂ זֵר־ זָהָב לְמִסְגַּרְתּוֹ
on-rim-of-him gold molding-of and-he-put around handbreadth rim-of for-him

°8 ק קצותיו

The Ark

37 Bezalel made the ark of acacia wood—two and a half cubits long, a cubit and a half wide, and a cubit and a half high.[v] [2]He overlaid it with pure gold, both inside and out, and made a gold molding around it. [3]He cast four gold rings for it and fastened them to its four feet, with two rings on one side and two rings on the other. [4]Then he made poles of acacia wood and overlaid them with gold. [5]And he inserted the poles into the rings on the sides of the ark to carry it.

[6]He made the atonement cover of pure gold—two and a half cubits long and a cubit and a half wide.[w] [7]Then he made two cherubim out of hammered gold at the ends of the cover. [8]He made one cherub on one end and the second cherub on the other; at the two ends he made them of one piece with the cover. [9]The cherubim had their wings spread upward, overshadowing the cover with them. The cherubim faced each other, looking toward the cover.

The Table

[10]They[x] made the table of acacia wood—two cubits long, a cubit wide, and a cubit and a half high.[y] [11]Then they overlaid it with pure gold and made a gold molding around it. [12]They also made around it a rim a handbreadth wide and put a gold molding on the rim.

v1 That is, about 3 3/4 feet (about 1.1 meters) long and 2 1/4 feet (about 0.7 meter) wide and high
w6 That is, about 3 3/4 feet (about 1.1 meters) long and 2 1/4 feet (about 0.7 meter) wide
x10 Or *He;* also in verses 11-29
y10 That is, about 3 feet (about 0.9 meter) long, 1 1/2 feet (about 0.5 meter) wide, and 2 1/4 feet (about 0.7 meter) high

סָבִיב׃ וַיִּצֹק לוֹ אַרְבַּע טַבְּעֹת זָהָב וַיִּתֵּן אֶת־
*** and-he-fastened gold rings-of four for-him and-he-cast (13) around

הַטַּבָּעֹת עַל אַרְבַּע הַפֵּאֹת אֲשֶׁר לְאַרְבַּע רַגְלָיו׃ לְעֻמַּת
close-of (14) legs-of-him to-four-of where the-corners four-of to the-rings

הַמִּסְגֶּרֶת הָיוּ הַטַּבָּעֹת בָּתִּים לַבַּדִּים לָשֵׂאת אֶת־הַשֻּׁלְחָן׃
the-table *** to-carry for-the-poles holders the-rings they-were the-rim

וַיַּעַשׂ אֶת־הַבַּדִּים עֲצֵי שִׁטִּים וַיְצַף אֹתָם זָהָב
gold them and-he-overlaid acacias woods-of the-poles *** and-he-made (15)

לָשֵׂאת אֶת־הַשֻּׁלְחָן׃ וַיַּעַשׂ אֶת־הַכֵּלִים ׀ אֲשֶׁר עַל־הַשֻּׁלְחָן
the-table for that the-articles *** and-he-made (16) the-table *** to-carry

אֶת־קְעָרֹתָיו וְאֶת־כַּפֹּתָיו וְאֵת מְנַקִּיֹּתָיו וְאֶת־הַקְּשָׂוֺת אֲשֶׁר
that the-pitchers and bowls-of-him and ladles-of-him and plates-of-him ***

יֻסַּךְ בָּהֵן זָהָב טָהוֹר׃ וַיַּעַשׂ אֶת־הַמְּנֹרָה
the-lampstand *** and-he-made (17) pure gold from-them he-poured-offering

זָהָב טָהוֹר מִקְשָׁה עָשָׂה אֶת־הַמְּנֹרָה יְרֵכָהּ וְקָנָהּ
and-shaft-of-her base-of-her the-lampstand *** he-made hammered pure gold

גְּבִיעֶיהָ כַּפְתֹּרֶיהָ וּפְרָחֶיהָ מִמֶּנָּה הָיוּ׃ וְשִׁשָּׁה
and-six (18) they-were from-her and-blossoms-of-her buds-of-her cups-of-her

קָנִים יֹצְאִים מִצִּדֶּיהָ שְׁלֹשָׁה ׀ קְנֵי מְנֹרָה
lampstand branches-of three from-sides-of-her ones-extending branches

מִצִּדָּהּ הָאֶחָד וּשְׁלֹשָׁה קְנֵי מְנֹרָה מִצִּדָּהּ
from-side-of-her lampstand branches-of and-three the-one from-side-of-her

הַשֵּׁנִי׃ שְׁלֹשָׁה גְבִעִים מְשֻׁקָּדִים בַּקָּנֶה הָאֶחָד כַּפְתֹּר
bud the-one on-the-branch being-like-almonds cups three (19) the-other

וָפֶרַח וּשְׁלֹשָׁה גְבִעִים מְשֻׁקָּדִים בְּקָנֶה אֶחָד כַּפְתֹּר וָפָרַח
and-blossom bud next on-branch being-like-almonds cups and-three and-blossom

כֵּן לְשֵׁשֶׁת הַקָּנִים הַיֹּצְאִים מִן־הַמְּנֹרָה׃
the-lampstand from the-ones-extending the-branches for-six-of same

וּבַמְּנֹרָה אַרְבָּעָה גְבִעִים מְשֻׁקָּדִים כַּפְתֹּרֶיהָ
buds-of-her being-like-almonds cups four and-on-the-lampstand (20)

וּפְרָחֶיהָ׃ וְכַפְתֹּר תַּחַת שְׁנֵי הַקָּנִים מִמֶּנָּה וְכַפְתֹּר
and-bud from-her the-branches pair-of under and-bud (21) and-blossoms-of-her

תַּחַת שְׁנֵי הַקָּנִים מִמֶּנָּה וְכַפְתֹּר תַּחַת־שְׁנֵי הַקָּנִים
the-branches pair-of under and-bud from-her the-branches pair-of under

מִמֶּנָּה לְשֵׁשֶׁת הַקָּנִים הַיֹּצְאִים מִמֶּנָּה׃ כַּפְתֹּרֵיהֶם
buds-of-them (22) from-her the-ones-extending the-branches for-six-of from-her

וּקְנֹתָם מִמֶּנָּה הָיוּ כֻּלָּהּ מִקְשָׁה אַחַת זָהָב
gold one-piece hammered all-of-her they-were from-her and-branches-of-them

[13]They cast four gold rings for the table and fastened them to the four corners, where the four legs were. [14]The rings were put close to the rim to hold the poles used in carrying the table. [15]The poles for carrying the table were made of acacia wood and were overlaid with gold. [16]And they made from pure gold the articles for the table—its plates and ladles and bowls and its pitchers for the pouring out of drink offerings.

The Lampstand

[17]They made the lampstand of pure gold and hammered it out, base and shaft; its flowerlike cups, buds and blossoms were of one piece with it. [18]Six branches extended from the sides of the lampstand—three on one side and three on the other. [19]Three cups shaped like almond flowers with buds and blossoms were on one branch, three on the next branch and the same for all six branches extending from the lampstand. [20]And on the lampstand were four cups shaped like almond flowers with buds and blossoms. [21]One bud was under the first pair of branches extending from the lampstand, a second bud under the second pair, and a third bud under the third pair—six branches in all. [22]The buds and the branches were all of one piece with the lampstand, hammered out of pure gold.

טָהוֹר׃ וַיַּעַשׂ אֶת־ נֵרֹתֶיהָ שִׁבְעָה וּמַלְקָחֶיהָ
and-trimmers-of-her seven lamps-of-her *** and-he-made (23) pure

וּמַחְתֹּתֶיהָ זָהָב טָהוֹר׃ כִּכָּר זָהָב טָהוֹר עָשָׂה אֹתָהּ וְאֵת כָּל־
all-of and her he-made pure gold talent (24) pure gold and-trays-of-her

כֵּלֶיהָ׃ וַיַּעַשׂ אֶת־ מִזְבַּח הַקְּטֹרֶת עֲצֵי
woods-of the-incense altar-of *** and-he-made (25) accessories-of-her

שִׁטִּים אַמָּה אָרְכּוֹ וְאַמָּה רָחְבּוֹ רָבוּעַ וְאַמָּתַיִם
and-two-cubits being-square width-of-him and-cubit length-of-him cubit acacias

קֹמָתוֹ מִמֶּנּוּ הָיוּ קַרְנֹתָיו׃ וַיְצַף אֹתוֹ זָהָב
gold him and-he-overlaid (26) horns-of-him they-were from-him height-of-him

טָהוֹר אֶת־ גַּגּוֹ וְאֶת־ קִירֹתָיו סָבִיב וְאֶת־ קַרְנֹתָיו וַיַּעַשׂ
and-he-made horns-of-him and around sides-of-him and top-of-him *** pure

לוֹ זֵר זָהָב סָבִיב׃ וּשְׁתֵּי טַבְּעֹת זָהָב עָשָׂה־ לוֹ
for-him he-made gold rings-of and-two-of (27) around gold molding-of for-him

מִתַּחַת לְזֵרוֹ עַל שְׁתֵּי צַלְעֹתָיו עַל שְׁנֵי צִדָּיו
sides-of-him two-of on sides-of-him two-of on to-molding-of-him for-below

לְבָתִּים לְבַדִּים לָשֵׂאת אֹתוֹ בָּהֶם׃ וַיַּעַשׂ אֶת־ הַבַּדִּים
the-poles *** and-he-made (28) with-them him to-carry for-poles as-holders

עֲצֵי שִׁטִּים וַיְצַף אֹתָם זָהָב׃ וַיַּעַשׂ אֶת־ שֶׁמֶן
oil-of *** and-he-made (29) gold them and-he-overlaid acacias woods-of

הַמִּשְׁחָה קֹדֶשׁ וְאֶת־ קְטֹרֶת הַסַּמִּים טָהוֹר מַעֲשֵׂה רֹקֵחַ׃
one-perfuming work-of pure the-fragrances incense-of and sacred the-anointing

וַיַּעַשׂ אֶת־ מִזְבַּח הָעֹלָה עֲצֵי שִׁטִּים חָמֵשׁ
five acacias woods-of the-burnt-offering altar-of *** and-he-made (38:1)

אַמּוֹת אָרְכּוֹ וְחָמֵשׁ־ אַמּוֹת רָחְבּוֹ רָבוּעַ וְשָׁלֹשׁ
and-three being-square width-of-him cubits and-five length-of-him cubits

אַמּוֹת קֹמָתוֹ׃ וַיַּעַשׂ קַרְנֹתָיו עַל אַרְבַּע פִּנֹּתָיו
corners-of-him four at horns-of-him and-he-made (2) height-of-him cubits

מִמֶּנּוּ הָיוּ קַרְנֹתָיו וַיְצַף אֹתוֹ נְחֹשֶׁת׃ וַיַּעַשׂ
and-he-made (3) bronze him and-he-overlaid horns-of-him they-were from-him

אֶת־ כָּל־ כְּלֵי הַמִּזְבֵּחַ אֶת־ הַסִּירֹת וְאֶת־ הַיָּעִים וְאֶת־
and the-shovels and the-pots *** the-altar utensils-of all-of ***

הַמִּזְרָקֹת אֶת־ הַמִּזְלָגֹת וְאֶת־ הַמַּחְתֹּת כָּל־ כֵּלָיו
utensils-of-him all-of the-firepans and the-meat-forks *** the-sprinkling-bowls

עָשָׂה נְחֹשֶׁת׃ וַיַּעַשׂ לַמִּזְבֵּחַ מִכְבָּר מַעֲשֵׂה רֶשֶׁת נְחֹשֶׁת
bronze net-of work-of grate for-the-altar and-he-made (4) bronze he-made

תַּחַת כַּרְכֻּבּוֹ מִלְּמַטָּה עַד־ חֶצְיוֹ׃ וַיִּצֹק אַרְבַּע טַבָּעֹת
rings four and-he-cast (5) halfway-of-him to downward ledge-of-him under

[23]They made its seven lamps, as well as its wick trimmers and trays, of pure gold. [24]They made the lampstand and all its accessories from one talent[z] of pure gold.

The Altar of Incense

[25]They made the altar of incense out of acacia wood. It was square, a cubit long and a cubit wide, and two cubits high[a]—its horns of one piece with it. [26]They overlaid the top and all the sides and the horns with pure gold, and made a gold molding around it. [27]They made two gold rings below the molding—two on opposite sides—to hold the poles used to carry it. [28]They made the poles of acacia wood and overlaid them with gold.

[29]They also made the sacred anointing oil and the pure, fragrant incense—the work of a perfumer.

The Altar of Burnt Offering

38 They[b] built the altar of burnt offering of acacia wood, three cubits[c] high; it was square, five cubits long and five cubits wide.[d] [2]They made a horn at each of the four corners, so that the horns and the altar were of one piece, and they overlaid the altar with bronze. [3]They made all its utensils of bronze—its pots, shovels, sprinkling bowls, meat forks and firepans. [4]They made a grating for the altar, a bronze network, to be under its ledge, halfway up the altar. [5]They cast bronze

[z]24 That is, about 75 pounds (about 34 kilograms)
[a]25 That is, about 1 1/2 feet (about 0.5 meter) long and wide, and about 3 feet (about 0.9 meter) high
[b]1 Or *He;* also in verses 2-9
[c]1 That is, about 4 1/2 feet (about 1.3 meters)
[d]1 That is, about 7 1/2 feet (about 2.3 meters) long and wide

בְּאַרְבַּע הַקְּצָוֺת לְמִכְבַּר הַנְּחֹשֶׁת בָּתִּים לַבַּדִּים׃
for-the-poles holders the-bronze for-grate-of the-corners for-four-of

וַיַּעַשׂ אֶת־ הַבַּדִּים עֲצֵי שִׁטִּים וַיְצַף אֹתָם נְחֹשֶׁת׃
bronze them and-he-overlaid acacias woods-of the-poles *** and-he-made (6)

וַיָּבֵא אֶת־ הַבַּדִּים בַּטַּבָּעֹת עַל צַלְעֹת הַמִּזְבֵּחַ
the-altar sides-of on into-the-rings the-poles *** and-he-inserted (7)

לָשֵׂאת אֹתוֹ בָּהֶם נְבוּב לֻחֹת עָשָׂה אֹתוֹ׃ וַיַּעַשׂ
and-he-made (8) him he-made boards being-hollow-of with-them him to-carry

אֵת הַכִּיּוֹר נְחֹשֶׁת וְאֵת כַּנּוֹ נְחֹשֶׁת בְּמַרְאֹת הַצֹּבְאֹת
the-woman-serving from-mirrors-of bronze stand-of-him and bronze the-basin ***

אֲשֶׁר צָבְאוּ פֶּתַח אֹהֶל מוֹעֵד׃ וַיַּעַשׂ אֶת־
*** next-he-made (9) Meeting Tent-of entrance-of they-served who

הֶחָצֵר לִפְאַת ׀ נֶגֶב תֵּימָנָה קַלְעֵי הֶחָצֵר שֵׁשׁ
fine-linen the-courtyard curtains-of to-south south for-side-of the-courtyard

מָשְׁזָר מֵאָה בָּאַמָּה׃ עַמּוּדֵיהֶם עֶשְׂרִים וְאַדְנֵיהֶם
and-bases-of-them twenty posts-of-them (10) by-the-cubit hundred being-twisted

עֶשְׂרִים נְחֹשֶׁת וָוֵי הָעַמֻּדִים וַחֲשֻׁקֵיהֶם כָּסֶף׃ וְלִפְאַת
and-for-side-of (11) silver and-bands-of-them the-posts hooks-of bronze twenty

צָפוֹן מֵאָה בָאַמָּה עַמּוּדֵיהֶם עֶשְׂרִים וְאַדְנֵיהֶם עֶשְׂרִים
twenty and-bases-of-them twenty posts-of-them by-the-cubit hundred north

נְחֹשֶׁת וָוֵי הָעַמּוּדִים וַחֲשֻׁקֵיהֶם כָּסֶף׃ וְלִפְאַת־ יָם
west and-for-side-of (12) silver and-bands-of-them the-posts hooks-of bronze

קְלָעִים חֲמִשִּׁים בָּאַמָּה עַמּוּדֵיהֶם עֲשָׂרָה וְאַדְנֵיהֶם עֲשָׂרָה וָוֵי
hooks-of ten and-bases-of-them ten posts-of-them by-the-cubit fifty curtains

הָעַמֻּדִים וַחֲשׁוּקֵיהֶם כָּסֶף׃ וְלִפְאַת קֵדְמָה מִזְרָחָה
to-east to-east and-for-side-of (13) silver and-bands-of-them the-posts

חֲמִשִּׁים אַמָּה׃ קְלָעִים חֲמֵשׁ־ עֶשְׂרֵה אַמָּה אֶל־ הַכָּתֵף עַמּוּדֵיהֶם
posts-of-them the-one-side on cubit ten five-of curtains (14) cubit fifty

שְׁלֹשָׁה וְאַדְנֵיהֶם שְׁלֹשָׁה׃ וְלַכָּתֵף הַשֵּׁנִית מִזֶּה
on-this the-other and-for-the-side (15) three and-bases-of-them three

וּמִזֶּה לְשַׁעַר הֶחָצֵר קְלָעִים חֲמֵשׁ עֶשְׂרֵה אַמָּה
cubit ten five-of curtains the-courtyard at-entrance-of and-on-that

עַמֻּדֵיהֶם שְׁלֹשָׁה וְאַדְנֵיהֶם שְׁלֹשָׁה׃ כָּל־ קַלְעֵי
curtains-of all-of (16) three and-bases-of-them three posts-of-them

הֶחָצֵר סָבִיב שֵׁשׁ מָשְׁזָר׃ וְהָאֲדָנִים לָעַמֻּדִים
for-the-posts and-the-bases (17) being-twisted fine-linen around the-courtyard

נְחֹשֶׁת וָוֵי הָעַמּוּדִים וַחֲשׁוּקֵיהֶם כֶּסֶף וְצִפּוּי
and-overlay-of silver and-bands-of-them the-posts hooks-of bronze

rings to hold the poles for the four corners of the bronze
grating. 6 They made the poles
of acacia wood and overlaid
them with bronze. 7 They inserted the poles into the rings so they would be on the sides of the altar for carrying it. They made it hollow, out of boards.

8 They made the bronze basin and its bronze stand from the mirrors of the women who served at the entrance to the Tent of Meeting.

The Courtyard

9 Next they made the courtyard. The south side was a hundred cubits[e] long and had curtains of finely twisted linen,
10 with twenty posts and twenty bronze bases, and with silver hooks and bands on the posts.
11 The north side was also a hundred cubits long and had twenty posts and twenty bronze bases, with silver hooks and bands on the posts.

12 The west end was fifty cubits[f] wide and had curtains, with ten posts and ten bases, with silver hooks and bands on the posts.
13 The east end, toward the sunrise, was also fifty cubits wide.
14 Curtains fifteen cubits[g] long were on one side of the entrance, with three posts and three bases,
15 and curtains fifteen cubits long were on the other side of the entrance to the courtyard, with three posts and three bases.
16 All the curtains around the courtyard were of finely twisted linen.
17 The bases for the posts were bronze. The hooks and bands on the posts were silver, and their tops were overlaid with

[e] 9 That is, about 150 feet (about 46 meters)
[f] 12 That is, about 75 feet (about 23 meters)
[g] 14 That is, about 22 1/2 feet (about 6.9 meters)

רָאשֵׁיהֶם כָּסֶף וְהֵם מְחֻשָּׁקִים כֶּסֶף כֹּל עַמֻּדֵי
posts-of all-of silver ones-being-banded and-they silver tops-of-them

הֶחָצֵר׃ וּמָסַךְ שַׁעַר הֶחָצֵר מַעֲשֵׂה
work-of the-courtyard entrance-of and-curtain-of (18) the-courtyard

רֹקֵם תְּכֵלֶת וְאַרְגָּמָן וְתוֹלַעַת שָׁנִי וְשֵׁשׁ מָשְׁזָר
being-twisted and-fine-linen yarn and-scarlet-of and-purple blue embroidering

וְעֶשְׂרִים אַמָּה אֹרֶךְ וְקוֹמָה בְרֹחַב חָמֵשׁ אַמּוֹת לְעֻמַּת קַלְעֵי
curtains-of just-like cubits five in-width and-high long cubit and-twenty

הֶחָצֵר׃ וְעַמֻּדֵיהֶם אַרְבָּעָה וְאַדְנֵיהֶם אַרְבָּעָה נְחֹשֶׁת
bronze four bases-of-them four and-posts-of-them (19) the-courtyard

וָוֵיהֶם כֶּסֶף וְצִפּוּי רָאשֵׁיהֶם וַחֲשֻׁקֵיהֶם כָּסֶף׃
silver and-bands-of-them tops-of-them and-overlay-of silver hooks-of-them

וְכָל־ הַיְתֵדֹת לַמִּשְׁכָּן וְלֶחָצֵר סָבִיב
around and-for-the-courtyard for-the-tabernacle the-tent-pegs and-all-of (20)

נְחֹשֶׁת׃ אֵלֶּה פְקוּדֵי הַמִּשְׁכָּן מִשְׁכַּן הָעֵדֻת אֲשֶׁר
which the-Testimony tabernacle-of the-tabernacle amounts-of these (21) bronze

פֻּקַּד עַל־ פִּי מֹשֶׁה עֲבֹדַת הַלְוִיִּם בְּיַד
under-direction-of the-Levites work-of Moses command-of at he-was-recorded

אִיתָמָר בֶּן־ אַהֲרֹן הַכֹּהֵן׃ וּבְצַלְאֵל בֶּן־ אוּרִי בֶן־ חוּר
Hur son-of Uri son-of and-Bezalel (22) the-priest Aaron son-of Ithamar

לְמַטֵּה יְהוּדָה עָשָׂה אֵת כָּל־ אֲשֶׁר־ צִוָּה יְהוָה אֶת־
*** Yahweh he-commanded that everything *** he-made Judah from-tribe-of

מֹשֶׁה׃ וְאִתּוֹ אָהֳלִיאָב בֶּן־ אֲחִיסָמָךְ לְמַטֵּה־ דָן חָרָשׁ
craftsman Dan from-tribe-of Ahisamach son-of Oholiab and-with-him (23) Moses

וְחֹשֵׁב וְרֹקֵם בַּתְּכֵלֶת וּבָאַרְגָּמָן
and-in-the-purple in-the-blue and-embroidering and-one-designing

וּבְתוֹלַעַת הַשָּׁנִי וּבַשֵּׁשׁ׃ כָּל־ הַזָּהָב
the-gold all-of (24) and-in-the-fine-linen the-yarn and-in-scarlet-of

הֶעָשׂוּי לַמְּלָאכָה בְּכֹל מְלֶאכֶת הַקֹּדֶשׁ וַיְהִי
now-he-was the-sanctuary work-of in-all-of for-the-work the-being-used

זְהַב הַתְּנוּפָה תֵּשַׁע וְעֶשְׂרִים כִּכָּר וּשְׁבַע מֵאוֹת
hundreds and-seven-of talent and-twenty nine the-wave-offering gold-of

וּשְׁלֹשִׁים שֶׁקֶל בְּשֶׁקֶל הַקֹּדֶשׁ׃ וְכֶסֶף פְּקוּדֵי
countings-of and-silver-of (25) the-sanctuary by-shekel-of shekel and-thirty

הָעֵדָה מְאַת כִּכָּר וְאֶלֶף וּשְׁבַע מֵאוֹת וַחֲמִשָּׁה
and-five hundreds and-seven-of and-thousand talent hundred-of the-community

וְשִׁבְעִים שֶׁקֶל בְּשֶׁקֶל הַקֹּדֶשׁ׃ בֶּקַע לַגֻּלְגֹּלֶת
per-the-person beka (26) the-sanctuary by-shekel-of shekel and-seventy

silver; so all the posts of the courtyard had silver bands.

18 The curtain for the entrance to the courtyard was of blue, purple and scarlet yarn and finely twisted linen—the work of an embroiderer. It was twenty cubits[h] long and, like the curtains of the courtyard, five cubits[i] high, 19 with four posts and four bronze bases. Their hooks and bands were silver, and their tops were overlaid with silver. 20 All the tent pegs of the tabernacle and of the surrounding courtyard were bronze.

The Materials Used

21 These are the amounts of the materials used for the tabernacle, the tabernacle of the Testimony, which were recorded at Moses' command by the Levites under the direction of Ithamar son of Aaron, the priest. 22 (Bezalel son of Uri, the son of Hur, of the tribe of Judah, made everything the LORD commanded Moses; 23 with him was Oholiab son of Ahisamach, of the tribe of Dan—a craftsman and designer, and an embroiderer in blue, purple and scarlet yarn and fine linen.) 24 The total amount of the gold from the wave offering used for all the work on the sanctuary was 29 talents and 730 shekels,[j] according to the sanctuary shekel.

25 The silver obtained from those of the community who were counted in the census was 100 talents and 1,775 shekels,[k] according to the sanctuary shekel— 26 one beka

[h] 18 That is, about 30 feet (about 9 meters)
[i] 18 That is, about 7 1/2 feet (about 2.3 meters)
[j] 24 The weight of the gold was a little over one ton (about 1 metric ton).
[k] 25 The weight of the silver was a little over 3 3/4 tons (about 3.4 metric tons).

מַחֲצִית הַשֶּׁקֶל בְּשֶׁקֶל הַקֹּדֶשׁ לְכֹל הָעֹבֵר
the-ones-crossing from-every-of the-sanctuary by-shekel-of the-shekel half-of

עַל־ הַפְּקֻדִים מִבֶּן עֶשְׂרִים שָׁנָה וָמַעְלָה לְשֵׁשׁ־
for-six and-upward year twenty from-son-of the-ones-being-counted to

מֵאוֹת אֶלֶף וּשְׁלֹשֶׁת אֲלָפִים וַחֲמֵשׁ מֵאוֹת וַחֲמִשִּׁים׃
and-fifty hundreds and-five-of thousands and-three thousand hundreds

וַיְהִי מְאַת כִּכַּר הַכֶּסֶף לָצֶקֶת אֵת אַדְנֵי
bases-of *** to-cast the-silver talent-of hundred-of and-he-used (27)

הַקֹּדֶשׁ וְאֵת אַדְנֵי הַפָּרֹכֶת מְאַת אֲדָנִים לִמְאַת
from-hundred-of bases hundred-of the-curtain bases-of and the-sanctuary

הַכִּכָּר כִּכָּר לָאָדֶן׃ וְאֶת־ הָאֶלֶף וּשְׁבַע הַמֵּאוֹת
the-hundreds and-seven-of the-thousand and (28) for-the-base talent the-talent

וַחֲמִשָּׁה וְשִׁבְעִים עָשָׂה וָוִים לָעַמּוּדִים וְצִפָּה רָאשֵׁיהֶם
tops-of-them and-he-overlaid for-the-posts hooks he-made and-seventy and-five

וְחִשַּׁק אֹתָם׃ וּנְחֹשֶׁת הַתְּנוּפָה שִׁבְעִים כִּכָּר
talent seventy the-wave-offering and-bronze-of (29) them and-he-made-bands

וְאַלְפַּיִם וְאַרְבַּע־ מֵאוֹת שָׁקֶל׃ וַיַּעַשׂ בָּהּ אֶת־
*** with-her and-he-made (30) shekel hundreds and-four and-two-thousand

אַדְנֵי פֶּתַח אֹהֶל מוֹעֵד וְאֵת מִזְבַּח הַנְּחֹשֶׁת וְאֶת־ מִכְבַּר
grate-of and the-bronze altar-of and Meeting Tent-of entrance-of bases-of

הַנְּחֹשֶׁת אֲשֶׁר־ לוֹ וְאֵת כָּל־ כְּלֵי הַמִּזְבֵּחַ׃ וְאֶת־ אַדְנֵי
bases-of and (31) the-altar utensils-of all-of and for-him that the-bronze

הֶחָצֵר סָבִיב וְאֶת־ אַדְנֵי שַׁעַר הֶחָצֵר וְאֵת כָּל־
all-of and the-courtyard entrance-of bases-of and around the-courtyard

יִתְדֹת הַמִּשְׁכָּן וְאֶת־ כָּל־ יִתְדֹת הֶחָצֵר סָבִיב׃
around the-courtyard pegs-of all-of and the-tabernacle tent-pegs-of

וּמִן־ הַתְּכֵלֶת וְהָאַרְגָּמָן וְתוֹלַעַת הַשָּׁנִי עָשׂוּ
they-made the-yarn and-scarlet-of and-the-purple the-blue and-from (39:1)

בִגְדֵי־ שְׂרָד לְשָׁרֵת בַּקֹּדֶשׁ וַיַּעֲשׂוּ אֶת־ בִּגְדֵי
garments-of *** and-they-made in-the-sanctuary to-minister woven garments-of

הַקֹּדֶשׁ אֲשֶׁר לְאַהֲרֹן כַּאֲשֶׁר צִוָּה יְהוָה אֶת־ מֹשֶׁה׃
Moses *** Yahweh he-commanded just-as for-Aaron that the-sacred

וַיַּעַשׂ אֶת־ הָאֵפֹד זָהָב תְּכֵלֶת וְאַרְגָּמָן וְתוֹלַעַת שָׁנִי
yarn and-scarlet-of and-purple blue gold the-ephod *** and-he-made (2)

וְשֵׁשׁ מָשְׁזָר׃ וַיְרַקְּעוּ אֶת־ פַּחֵי הַזָּהָב
the-gold sheets-of *** and-they-hammered (3) being-twisted and-fine-linen

וְקִצֵּץ פְּתִילִם לַעֲשׂוֹת בְּתוֹךְ הַתְּכֵלֶת וּבְתוֹךְ הָאַרְגָּמָן וּבְתוֹךְ
and-into the-purple and-into the-blue into to-work strands and-he-cut

per person, that is, half a
shekel,[l] according to the sanctuary shekel, from everyone
who had crossed over to those
counted, twenty years old or
more, a total of 603,550 men.
27The 100 talents[m] of silver
were used to cast the bases for
the sanctuary and for the curtain—100 bases from the 100
talents, one talent for each
base. 28They used the 1,775
shekels[n] to make the hooks for
the posts, to overlay the tops of
the posts, and to make their
bands.
29The bronze from the wave
offering was 70 talents and 2,-
400 shekels.[o] 30They used it to
make the bases for the entrance to the Tent of Meeting,
the bronze altar with its
bronze grating and all its utensils, 31the bases for the surrounding courtyard and those
for its entrance and all the tent
pegs for the tabernacle and
those for the surrounding
courtyard.

The Priestly Garments

39 From the blue, purple
and scarlet yarn they
made woven garments for
ministering in the sanctuary.
They also made sacred garments for Aaron, as the LORD
commanded Moses.

The Ephod

2They[p] made the ephod of
gold, and of blue, purple and
scarlet yarn, and of finely
twisted linen. 3They ham-
mered out thin sheets of gold
and cut strands to be worked
into the blue, purple and scarlet yarn and fine linen—the

[l]26 That is, about 1/5 ounce (about 6 grams)
[m]27 That is, about 3 3/4 tons (about 3.4 metric tons)
[n]28 That is, about 45 pounds (about 20 kilograms)
[o]29 The weight of the bronze was about 2 1/2 tons (about 2.4 metric tons).
[p]2 Or *He;* also in verses 7, 8 and 22

תּוֹלַעַת הַשָּׁנִי וּבְתוֹךְ הַשֵּׁשׁ מַעֲשֵׂה חֹשֵׁב׃
one-being-skilled work-of the-fine-linen and-into the-yarn scarlet-of

כְּתֵפֹת עָשׂוּ־ לוֹ חֹבְרֹת עַל־ שְׁנֵי קְצוֹתָו°
corners-of-him two-of to ones-attaching for-him they-made shoulder-pieces (4)

חֻבָּר׃ וְחֵשֶׁב אֲפֻדָּתוֹ אֲשֶׁר עָלָיו מִמֶּנּוּ
from-him on-him that ephod-of-him and-woven-band-of (5) he-was-fastened

הוּא כְּמַעֲשֵׂהוּ זָהָב תְּכֵלֶת וְאַרְגָּמָן וְתוֹלַעַת שָׁנִי וְשֵׁשׁ
and-fine-linen yarn and-scarlet-of and-purple blue gold like-work-of-him he

מָשְׁזָר כַּאֲשֶׁר צִוָּה יְהוָה אֶת־ מֹשֶׁה׃ וַיַּעֲשׂוּ אֶת־
*** and-they-mounted (6) Moses *** Yahweh he-commanded just-as being-twisted

אַבְנֵי הַשֹּׁהַם מֻסַבֹּת מִשְׁבְּצֹת זָהָב מְפֻתָּחֹת
ones-being-engraved gold filigrees-of ones-being-set-of the-onyx stones-of

פִּתּוּחֵי חוֹתָם עַל־ שְׁמוֹת בְּנֵי יִשְׂרָאֵל׃ וַיָּשֶׂם אֹתָם
them and-he-fastened (7) Israel sons-of names-of with seal engravings-of

עַל כִּתְפֹת הָאֵפֹד אַבְנֵי זִכָּרוֹן לִבְנֵי יִשְׂרָאֵל כַּאֲשֶׁר
just-as Israel for-sons-of memorial stones-of the-ephod shoulder-pieces-of on

צִוָּה יְהוָה אֶת־ מֹשֶׁה׃ וַיַּעַשׂ אֶת־ הַחֹשֶׁן מַעֲשֵׂה
work-of the-breastpiece *** and-he-made (8) Moses *** Yahweh he-commanded

חֹשֵׁב כְּמַעֲשֵׂה אֵפֹד זָהָב תְּכֵלֶת וְאַרְגָּמָן וְתוֹלַעַת
and-scarlet-of and-purple blue gold ephod like-work-of one-being-skilled

שָׁנִי וְשֵׁשׁ מָשְׁזָר׃ רָבוּעַ הָיָה כָּפוּל
being-doubled he-was being-square (9) being-twisted and-fine-linen yarn

עָשׂוּ אֶת־ הַחֹשֶׁן זֶרֶת אָרְכּוֹ וְזֶרֶת רָחְבּוֹ
width-of-him and-span length-of-him span the-breastpiece *** they-made

כָּפוּל׃ וַיְמַלְאוּ־ בוֹ אַרְבָּעָה טוּרֵי אָבֶן טוּר אֹדֶם
ruby row stone rows-of four on-him and-they-mounted (10) being-doubled

פִּטְדָה וּבָרֶקֶת הַטּוּר הָאֶחָד׃ וְהַטּוּר הַשֵּׁנִי נֹפֶךְ
turquoise the-second and-the-row (11) the-first the-row and-beryl topaz

סַפִּיר וְיָהֲלֹם*׃ וְהַטּוּר הַשְּׁלִישִׁי לֶשֶׁם שְׁבוֹ וְאַחְלָמָה׃
and-amethyst agate jacinth the-third and-the-row (12) and-emerald sapphire

וְהַטּוּר הָרְבִיעִי תַּרְשִׁישׁ שֹׁהַם וְיָשְׁפֵה מוּסַבֹּת
ones-being-mounted-of and-jasper onyx chrysolite the-fourth and-the-row (13)

מִשְׁבְּצוֹת זָהָב בְּמִלֻּאֹתָם׃ וְהָאֲבָנִים עַל־ שְׁמֹת
names-of with and-the-stones (14) in-settings-of-them gold filigrees-of

בְּנֵי־ יִשְׂרָאֵל הֵנָּה שְׁתֵּים עֶשְׂרֵה עַל־ שְׁמֹתָם פִּתּוּחֵי חֹתָם אִישׁ
each seal engravings-of names-of-them with ten two they Israel sons-of

עַל־ שְׁמוֹ לִשְׁנֵים עָשָׂר שָׁבֶט׃ וַיַּעֲשׂוּ עַל־ הַחֹשֶׁן
the-breastpiece for and-they-made (15) tribe ten for-two name-of-him with

work of a skilled craftsman.
[4]They made shoulder pieces
for the ephod, which were attached to two of its corners, so
it could be fastened. [5]Its skillfully woven waistband was
like it—of one piece with the ephod and made with gold,
and with blue, purple and scarlet yarn, and with finely
twisted linen, as the LORD commanded Moses.

[6]They mounted the onyx stones in gold filigree settings
and engraved them like a seal with the names of the sons of
Israel. [7]Then they fastened
them on the shoulder pieces of the ephod as memorial stones
for the sons of Israel, as the LORD commanded Moses.

The Breastpiece

[8]They fashioned the breastpiece—the work of a skilled
craftsman. They made it like the ephod: of gold, and of blue,
purple and scarlet yarn, and of finely twisted linen. [9]It was
square—a span[q] long and a span wide—and folded double. [10]Then they mounted four
rows of precious stones on it. In the first row there was a
ruby, a topaz and a beryl; [11]in
the second row a turquoise, a sapphire[r] and an emerald; [12]in
the third row a jacinth, an agate and an amethyst; [13]in
the fourth row a chrysolite, an onyx and a jasper.[s] They were
mounted in gold filigree settings. [14]There were twelve
stones, one for each of the names of the sons of Israel,
each engraved like a seal with the name of one of the twelve tribes.
[15]For the breastpiece they

q9 That is, about 9 inches (about 22 centimeters)
r11 Or *lapis lazuli*
s13 The precise identification of some of these precious stones is uncertain.

*11 Most mss have *pathah* under the *yod* (וַיַּהֲ).

°4 ק קצותיו

שַׁרְשְׁרֹת גַּבְלֻת מַעֲשֵׂה עֲבֹת זָהָב טָהוֹר׃ וַיַּעֲשׂוּ שְׁתֵּי מִשְׁבְּצֹת

settings-of two-of and-they-made (16) pure gold rope work-of braid chains-of

זָהָב וּשְׁתֵּי טַבְּעֹת זָהָב וַיִּתְּנוּ אֶת־ שְׁתֵּי הַטַּבָּעֹת עַל־

to the-rings two-of *** and-they-fastened gold rings-of and-two-of gold

שְׁנֵי קְצוֹת הַחֹשֶׁן׃ וַיִּתְּנוּ שְׁתֵּי הָעֲבֹתֹת

the-chains two-of and-they-fastened (17) the-breastpiece corners-of two-of

הַזָּהָב עַל־ שְׁתֵּי הַטַּבָּעֹת עַל־ קְצוֹת הַחֹשֶׁן׃ וְאֵת שְׁתֵּי

two-of and (18) the-breastpiece corners-of at the-rings two-of to the-gold

קְצוֹת שְׁתֵּי הָעֲבֹתֹת נָתְנוּ עַל־ שְׁתֵּי הַמִּשְׁבְּצֹת

the-settings two-of to they-fastened the-chains two-of ends-of

וַיִּתְּנֻם עַל־ כִּתְפֹת הָאֵפֹד אֶל־ מוּל פָּנָיו׃

face-of-him front at the-ephod shoulder-pieces-of to and-they-attached-them

וַיַּעֲשׂוּ שְׁתֵּי טַבְּעֹת זָהָב וַיָּשִׂימוּ עַל־ שְׁנֵי

two-of to and-they-attached gold rings-of two-of and-they-made (19)

קְצוֹת הַחֹשֶׁן עַל־ שְׂפָתוֹ אֲשֶׁר אֶל־ עֵבֶר הָאֵפֹד בָּיְתָה׃

inside the-ephod side-of on that edge-of-him on the-breastpiece corners-of

וַיַּעֲשׂוּ שְׁתֵּי טַבְּעֹת זָהָב וַיִּתְּנֻם עַל־ שְׁתֵּי

two-of to and-they-attached-them gold rings-of two-of then-they-made (20)

כִתְפֹת הָאֵפֹד מִלְּמַטָּה מִמּוּל פָּנָיו לְעֻמַּת

to-close-of face-of-him on-front at-bottom the-ephod shoulder-pieces-of

מֶחְבַּרְתּוֹ מִמַּעַל לְחֵשֶׁב הָאֵפֹד׃ וַיִּרְכְּסוּ אֶת־

*** and-they-tied (21) the-ephod to-waistband-of just-above seams-of-him

הַחֹשֶׁן מִטַּבְּעֹתָיו אֶל־ טַבְּעֹת הָאֵפֹד בִּפְתִיל תְּכֵלֶת

blue with-cord-of the-ephod rings-of to by-rings-of-him the-breastpiece

לִהְיֹת עַל־ חֵשֶׁב הָאֵפֹד וְלֹא־ יִזַּח הַחֹשֶׁן

the-breastpiece he-would-swing so-not the-ephod waistband-of to to-connect

מֵעַל הָאֵפֹד כַּאֲשֶׁר צִוָּה יְהוָה אֶת־ מֹשֶׁה׃ וַיַּעַשׂ

and-he-made (22) Moses *** Yahweh he-commanded just-as the-ephod from-on

אֶת־מְעִיל הָאֵפֹד מַעֲשֵׂה אֹרֵג כְּלִיל תְּכֵלֶת׃ וּפִי־

and-opening-of (23) blue entirely-of weaving work-of the-ephod robe-of ***

הַמְּעִיל בְּתוֹכוֹ כְּפִי תַחְרָא שָׂפָה לְפִיו

for-opening-of-him and-band collar like-opening-of in-center-of-him the-robe

סָבִיב לֹא יִקָּרֵעַ׃ וַיַּעֲשׂוּ עַל־ שׁוּלֵי הַמְּעִיל

the-robe hems-of around and-they-made (24) he-would-tear not around

רִמּוֹנֵי תְּכֵלֶת וְאַרְגָּמָן וְתוֹלַעַת שָׁנִי מָשְׁזָר׃

being-twisted yarn and-scarlet-of and-purple blue pomegranates-of

וַיַּעֲשׂוּ פַּעֲמֹנֵי זָהָב טָהוֹר וַיִּתְּנוּ אֶת־הַפַּעֲמֹנִים בְּתוֹךְ

between the-bells *** and-they-attached pure gold bells-of and-they-made (25)

made braided chains of pure
gold, like a rope. 16They made
two gold filigree settings and
two gold rings, and fastened
the rings to two of the corners
of the breastpiece. 17They fastened the two gold chains to
the rings at the corners of the
breastpiece, 18and the other
ends of the chains to the two
settings, attaching them to the
shoulder pieces of the ephod
at the front. 19They made two
gold rings and attached them
to the other two corners of the
breastpiece on the inside edge
next to the ephod. 20Then they
made two more gold rings and
attached them to the bottom of
the shoulder pieces on the
front of the ephod, close to the
seam just above the waistband
of the ephod. 21They tied the
rings of the breastpiece to the
rings of the ephod with blue
cord, connecting it to the
waistband so that the breastpiece would not swing out
from the ephod—as the LORD
commanded Moses.

Other Priestly Garments

22They made the robe of the
ephod entirely of blue cloth—
the work of a weaver— 23with
an opening in the center of the
robe like the opening of a collar,[t] and a band around this
opening, so that it would not
tear. 24They made pomegranates of blue, purple and scarlet
yarn and finely twisted linen
around the hem of the robe.
25And they made bells of pure
gold and attached them

[t]23 The meaning of the Hebrew for this word is uncertain.

הָרִמֹּנִים עַל־ שׁוּלֵי הַמְּעִיל סָבִיב בְּתוֹךְ הָרִמֹּנִים׃
the-pomegranates between around the-robe hems-of on the-pomegranates

פַּעֲמֹן וְרִמֹּן פַּעֲמֹן וְרִמֹּן עַל־ שׁוּלֵי הַמְּעִיל סָבִיב
around the-robe hems-of on and-pomegranate bell and-pomegranate bell (26)

לְשָׁרֵת כַּאֲשֶׁר צִוָּה יְהוָה אֶת־ מֹשֶׁה׃ וַיַּעֲשׂוּ אֶת־
*** and-they-made (27) Moses *** Yahweh he-commanded just-as to-minister

הַכָּתְנֹת שֵׁשׁ מַעֲשֵׂה אֹרֵג לְאַהֲרֹן וּלְבָנָיו׃
and-for-sons-of-him for-Aaron weaving work-of fine-linen the-tunics

וְאֵת הַמִּצְנֶפֶת שֵׁשׁ וְאֶת־ פַּאֲרֵי הַמִּגְבָּעֹת שֵׁשׁ וְאֶת־
and fine-linen the-headbands hats-of and fine-linen the-turban and (28)

מִכְנְסֵי הַבָּד שֵׁשׁ מָשְׁזָר׃ וְאֶת־ הָאַבְנֵט
the-sash and (29) being-twisted fine-linen the-underwear garments-of

שֵׁשׁ מָשְׁזָר וּתְכֵלֶת וְאַרְגָּמָן וְתוֹלַעַת שָׁנִי מַעֲשֵׂה
work-of yarn and-scarlet-of and-purple and-blue being-twisted fine-linen

רֹקֵם כַּאֲשֶׁר צִוָּה יְהוָה אֶת־ מֹשֶׁה׃ וַיַּעֲשׂוּ אֶת־
*** and-they-made (30) Moses *** Yahweh he-commanded just-as embroidering

צִיץ נֵזֶר־ הַקֹּדֶשׁ זָהָב טָהוֹר וַיִּכְתְּבוּ עָלָיו מִכְתַּב
inscription-of on-him and-they-engraved pure gold the-holy diadem-of plate

פִּתּוּחֵי חוֹתָם קֹדֶשׁ לַיהוָה׃ וַיִּתְּנוּ עָלָיו פְּתִיל
cord-of to-him and-they-fastened (31) to-Yahweh holy seal engravings-of

תְּכֵלֶת לָתֵת עַל־ הַמִּצְנֶפֶת מִלְמָעְלָה כַּאֲשֶׁר צִוָּה יְהוָה אֶת־מֹשֶׁה׃
Moses *** Yahweh he-commanded just-as on-top the-turban to to-attach blue

וַתֵּכֶל כָּל־ עֲבֹדַת מִשְׁכַּן אֹהֶל מוֹעֵד וַיַּעֲשׂוּ
and-they-did Meeting Tent-of tabernacle work-of all-of so-he-completed (32)

בְּנֵי יִשְׂרָאֵל כְּכֹל אֲשֶׁר צִוָּה יְהוָה אֶת־ מֹשֶׁה כֵּן עָשׂוּ׃
they-did so Moses *** Yahweh he-commanded that as-all Israel sons-of

וַיָּבִיאוּ אֶת־ הַמִּשְׁכָּן אֶל־ מֹשֶׁה אֶת־ הָאֹהֶל וְאֶת־ כָּל־
all-of and the-tent *** Moses to the-tabernacle *** then-they-brought (33)

כֵּלָיו קְרָסָיו קְרָשָׁיו בְּרִיחָו°
crossbars-of-him frames-of-him clasps-of-him furnishings-of-him

וְעַמֻּדָיו וַאֲדָנָיו׃ וְאֶת־ מִכְסֵה עוֹרֹת הָאֵילִם
the-rams skins-of cover-of and (34) and-bases-of-him and-posts-of-him

הַמְאָדָּמִים וְאֶת־ מִכְסֵה עֹרֹת הַתְּחָשִׁים וְאֵת פָּרֹכֶת
curtain-of and the-sea-cows hides-of cover-of and the-ones-being-dyed-red

הַמָּסָךְ׃ אֶת־ אֲרֹן הָעֵדֻת וְאֶת־ בַּדָּיו וְאֵת
and poles-of-him and the-Testimony ark-of *** (35) the-shield

הַכַּפֹּרֶת׃ אֶת־ הַשֻּׁלְחָן אֶת־ כָּל־ כֵּלָיו וְאֵת
and articles-of-him all-of *** the-table *** (36) the-atonement-cover

around the hem between the
pomegranates. [26]The bells and
pomegranates alternated
around the hem of the robe to
be worn for ministering, as
the LORD commanded Moses.
[27]For Aaron and his sons,
they made tunics of fine lin-
en—the work of a weaver—
[28]and the turban of fine linen,
the linen headbands and the
undergarments of finely twisted linen. [29]The sash was of
finely twisted linen and blue,
purple and scarlet yarn—the
work of an embroiderer—as
the LORD commanded Moses.
[30]They made the plate, the
sacred diadem, out of pure
gold and engraved on it, like
an inscription on a seal: HOLY
TO THE LORD. [31]Then they fastened a blue cord to it to attach
it to the turban, as the LORD
commanded Moses.

Moses Inspects the Tabernacle

[32]So all the work on the tabernacle, the Tent of Meeting,
was completed. The Israelites
did everything just as the
LORD commanded Moses.
[33]Then they brought the tabernacle to Moses: the tent and all
its furnishings, its clasps,
frames, crossbars, posts and
bases; [34]the covering of ram
skins dyed red, the covering of
hides of sea cows and the
shielding curtain; [35]the ark of
the Testimony with its poles
and the atonement cover; [36]the
table with all its articles and

°33 ק בריחיו

לֶחֶם הַפָּנִים׃ אֶת־הַמְּנֹרָה הַטְּהֹרָה אֶת־נֵרֹתֶיהָ
lamps-of-her *** the-pure the-lampstand *** (37) the-Presences bread-of

נֵרֹת הַמַּעֲרָכָה וְאֶת־כָּל־כֵּלֶיהָ וְאֵת שֶׁמֶן הַמָּאוֹר׃
the-light oil-of and accessories-of-her all-of and the-row lamps-of

וְאֵת מִזְבַּח הַזָּהָב וְאֵת שֶׁמֶן הַמִּשְׁחָה וְאֵת קְטֹרֶת
incense-of and the-anointing oil-of and the-gold altar-of and (38)

הַסַּמִּים וְאֵת מָסַךְ פֶּתַח הָאֹהֶל׃ אֵת ׀ מִזְבַּח
altar-of *** (39) the-tent entrance-of curtain-of and the-fragrances

הַנְּחֹשֶׁת וְאֶת־מִכְבַּר הַנְּחֹשֶׁת אֲשֶׁר־לוֹ אֶת־בַּדָּיו וְאֶת־כָּל־
all-of and poles-of-him *** for-him that the-bronze grate-of and the-bronze

כֵּלָיו אֶת־הַכִּיֹּר וְאֶת־כַּנּוֹ׃ אֵת קַלְעֵי
curtains-of *** (40) stand-of-him and the-basin *** utensils-of-him

הֶחָצֵר אֶת־עַמֻּדֶיהָ וְאֶת־אֲדָנֶיהָ וְאֶת־הַמָּסָךְ
the-curtain and bases-of-her and posts-of-her *** the-courtyard

לְשַׁעַר הֶחָצֵר אֶת־מֵיתָרָיו וִיתֵדֹתֶיהָ וְאֵת
and and-tent-pegs-of-her ropes-of-him *** the-courtyard for-entrance-of

כָּל־כְּלֵי עֲבֹדַת הַמִּשְׁכָּן לְאֹהֶל מוֹעֵד׃ אֶת־
*** (41) Meeting for-Tent-of the-tabernacle service-of furnishings-of all-of

בִּגְדֵי הַשְּׂרָד לְשָׁרֵת בַּקֹּדֶשׁ אֶת־בִּגְדֵי הַקֹּדֶשׁ
the-sacred garments-of *** in-the-sanctuary to-minister the-woven garments-of

לְאַהֲרֹן הַכֹּהֵן וְאֶת־בִּגְדֵי בָנָיו לְכַהֵן׃ כְּכֹל
as-all (42) to-be-priest sons-of-him garments-of and the-priest for-Aaron

אֲשֶׁר־צִוָּה יְהוָה אֶת־מֹשֶׁה כֵּן עָשׂוּ בְּנֵי יִשְׂרָאֵל אֵת כָּל־
all-of *** Israel sons-of they-did thus Moses *** Yahweh he-commanded that

הָעֲבֹדָה׃ וַיַּרְא מֹשֶׁה אֶת־כָּל־הַמְּלָאכָה וְהִנֵּה עָשׂוּ
they-did and-see! the-work all-of *** Moses and-he-inspected (43) the-work

אֹתָהּ כַּאֲשֶׁר צִוָּה יְהוָה כֵּן עָשׂוּ וַיְבָרֶךְ אֹתָם מֹשֶׁה׃
Moses them so-he-blessed they-did thus Yahweh he-commanded just-as her

וַיְדַבֵּר יְהוָה אֶל־מֹשֶׁה לֵּאמֹר׃ בְּיוֹם־הַחֹדֶשׁ הָרִאשׁוֹן
the-first the-month on-day-of (2) to-say Moses to Yahweh then-he-spoke (40:1)

בְּאֶחָד לַחֹדֶשׁ תָּקִים אֶת־מִשְׁכַּן אֹהֶל מוֹעֵד׃
Meeting Tent-of tabernacle *** you-set-up of-the-month on-first

וְשַׂמְתָּ שָׁם אֵת אֲרוֹן הָעֵדוּת וְסַכֹּתָ עַל־הָאָרֹן
the-ark over and-you-shield the-Testimony ark-of *** there and-you-place (3)

אֶת־הַפָּרֹכֶת׃ וְהֵבֵאתָ אֶת־הַשֻּׁלְחָן וְעָרַכְתָּ אֶת־
*** and-you-set-out the-table *** and-you-bring-in (4) the-curtain with

עֶרְכּוֹ וְהֵבֵאתָ אֶת־הַמְּנֹרָה וְהַעֲלֵיתָ אֶת־
*** and-you-set-up the-lampstand *** then-you-bring-in material-of-him

the bread of the Presence; [37]the
pure gold lampstand with its
row of lamps and all its accessories, and the oil for the light;
[38]the gold altar, the anointing
oil, the fragrant incense, and
the curtain for the entrance to
the tent; [39]the bronze altar
with its bronze grating, its
poles and all its utensils; the
basin with its stand; [40]the curtains of the courtyard with its
posts and bases, and the curtain for the entrance to the
courtyard; the ropes and tent
pegs for the courtyard; all the
furnishings for the tabernacle,
the Tent of Meeting; [41]and the
woven garments worn for
ministering in the sanctuary,
both the sacred garments for
Aaron the priest and the garments for his sons when serving as priests.
[42]The Israelites had done all
the work just as the LORD had
commanded Moses. [43]Moses
inspected the work and saw
that they had done it just as
the LORD had commanded. So
Moses blessed them.

Setting Up the Tabernacle

40 Then the LORD said to
Moses: [2]"Set up the
tabernacle, the Tent of Meeting, on the first day of the first
month. [3]Place the ark of the
Testimony in it and shield the
ark with the curtain. [4]Bring in
the table and set out what belongs on it. Then bring in the
lampstand and set up its

נֵרֹתֶיהָ׃ וְנָתַתָּה אֶת־ מִזְבַּח הַזָּהָב לִקְטֹרֶת לִפְנֵי
in-front-of of-incense the-gold altar-of *** then-you-place (5) lamps-of-her

אֲרוֹן הָעֵדֻת וְשַׂמְתָּ אֶת־ מָסַךְ הַפֶּתַח לַמִּשְׁכָּן׃
to-the-tabernacle the-entrance curtain-of *** and-you-put the-Testimony ark-of

וְנָתַתָּה אֵת מִזְבַּח הָעֹלָה לִפְנֵי פֶּתַח
entrance-of in-front-of the-burnt-offering altar-of *** then-you-place (6)

מִשְׁכַּן אֹהֶל־ מוֹעֵד׃ וְנָתַתָּ אֶת־ הַכִּיֹּר בֵּין־ אֹהֶל
Tent-of between the-basin *** and-you-place (7) Meeting Tent-of tabernacle

מוֹעֵד וּבֵין הַמִּזְבֵּחַ וְנָתַתָּ שָׁם מָיִם׃ וְשַׂמְתָּ
and-you-set-up (8) water there and-you-put the-altar and-between Meeting

אֶת־ הֶחָצֵר סָבִיב וְנָתַתָּ אֶת־ מָסַךְ שַׁעַר הֶחָצֵר׃
the-courtyard entrance-of curtain-of *** and-you-put around the-courtyard ***

וְלָקַחְתָּ אֶת־ שֶׁמֶן הַמִּשְׁחָה וּמָשַׁחְתָּ אֶת־ הַמִּשְׁכָּן
the-tabernacle *** and-you-anoint the-anointing oil-of *** then-you-take (9)

וְאֶת־ כָּל־ אֲשֶׁר־ בּוֹ וְקִדַּשְׁתָּ אֹתוֹ וְאֶת־ כָּל־ כֵּלָיו
furnishings-of-him all-of and him and-you-consecrate in-him that all and

וְהָיָה קֹדֶשׁ׃ וּמָשַׁחְתָּ אֶת־ מִזְבַּח הָעֹלָה וְאֶת־
and the-burnt-offering altar-of *** then-you-anoint (10) holy and-he-will-be

כָּל־ כֵּלָיו וְקִדַּשְׁתָּ אֶת־ הַמִּזְבֵּחַ וְהָיָה
and-he-will-be the-altar *** and-you-consecrate utensils-of-him all-of

הַמִּזְבֵּחַ קֹדֶשׁ קָדָשִׁים׃ וּמָשַׁחְתָּ אֶת־ הַכִּיֹּר וְאֶת־
and the-basin *** then-you-anoint (11) holy-ones holiest-of the-altar

כַּנּוֹ וְקִדַּשְׁתָּ אֹתוֹ׃ וְהִקְרַבְתָּ אֶת־ אַהֲרֹן וְאֶת־
and Aaron *** and-you-bring (12) him and-you-consecrate stand-of-him

בָּנָיו אֶל־ פֶּתַח אֹהֶל מוֹעֵד וְרָחַצְתָּ אֹתָם בַּמָּיִם׃
with-the-waters them and-you-wash Meeting Tent-of entrance-of to sons-of-him

וְהִלְבַּשְׁתָּ אֶת־ אַהֲרֹן אֵת בִּגְדֵי הַקֹּדֶשׁ וּמָשַׁחְתָּ אֹתוֹ
him and-you-anoint the-sacred garments-of *** Aaron *** then-you-dress (13)

וְקִדַּשְׁתָּ אֹתוֹ וְכִהֵן לִי׃ וְאֶת־ בָּנָיו
sons-of-him and (14) to-me so-he-may-be-priest him and-you-consecrate

תַּקְרִיב וְהִלְבַּשְׁתָּ אֹתָם כֻּתֳּנֹת׃ וּמָשַׁחְתָּ אֹתָם כַּאֲשֶׁר
just-as them and-you-anoint (15) tunics them and-you-dress you-bring

מָשַׁחְתָּ אֶת־ אֲבִיהֶם וְכִהֲנוּ לִי וְהָיְתָה
and-she-will-be to-me so-they-may-be-priests father-of-them *** you-anointed

לִהְיֹת לָהֶם מָשְׁחָתָם לִכְהֻנַּת עוֹלָם לְדֹרֹתָם׃
for-generations-of-them continual to-priesthood-of to-anoint-them for-them to-be

וַיַּעַשׂ מֹשֶׁה כְּכֹל אֲשֶׁר צִוָּה יְהוָה אֹתוֹ כֵּן עָשָׂה׃
he-did so him Yahweh he-commanded that as-all Moses and-he-did (16)

lamps. 5Place the gold altar of
incense in front of the ark of
the Testimony and put the
curtain at the entrance to the
tabernacle.
6"Place the altar of burnt
offering in front of the entrance to the tabernacle, the
Tent of Meeting; 7place the basin between the Tent of Meeting and the altar and put water
in it. 8Set up the courtyard
around it and put the curtain
at the entrance to the courtyard.
9"Take the anointing oil and
anoint the tabernacle and
everything in it; consecrate it
and all its furnishings, and it
will be holy. 10Then anoint the
altar of burnt offering and all
its utensils; consecrate the altar, and it will be most holy.
11Anoint the basin and its
stand and consecrate them.
12"Bring Aaron and his sons
to the entrance to the Tent of
Meeting and wash them with
water. 13Then dress Aaron in
the sacred garments, anoint
him and consecrate him so he
may serve me as priest. 14Bring
his sons and dress them in
tunics. 15Anoint them just as
you anointed their father, so
they may serve me as priests.
Their anointing will be to a
priesthood that will continue
for all generations to come."
16Moses did everything just as
the LORD commanded him.

וַיְהִי בַּחֹדֶשׁ הָרִאשׁוֹן בַּשָּׁנָה הַשֵּׁנִית בְּאֶחָד
on-first the-second in-the-year the-first on-the-month so-he-was (17)

לַחֹדֶשׁ הוּקַם הַמִּשְׁכָּן׃ וַיָּקֶם מֹשֶׁה אֶת־
*** Moses when-he-set-up (18) the-tabernacle he-was-set-up of-the-month

הַמִּשְׁכָּן וַיִּתֵּן אֶת־ אֲדָנָיו וַיָּשֶׂם אֶת־ קְרָשָׁיו
frames-of-him *** and-he-erected bases-of-him *** then-he-put the-tabernacle

וַיִּתֵּן אֶת־ בְּרִיחָיו וַיָּקֶם אֶת־ עַמּוּדָיו׃
posts-of-him *** and-he-set-up crossbars-of-him *** and-he-inserted

וַיִּפְרֹשׂ אֶת־ הָאֹהֶל עַל־ הַמִּשְׁכָּן וַיָּשֶׂם אֶת־ מִכְסֵה
cover-of *** and-he-put the-tabernacle over the-tent *** then-he-spread (19)

הָאֹהֶל עָלָיו מִלְמָעְלָה כַּאֲשֶׁר צִוָּה יְהוָה אֶת־ מֹשֶׁה׃
Moses *** Yahweh he-commanded just-as on-top over-him the-tent

וַיִּקַּח וַיִּתֵּן אֶת־ הָעֵדֻת אֶל־ הָאָרֹן וַיָּשֶׂם אֶת־
*** and-he-attached the-ark in the-Testimony *** and-he-placed and-he-took (20)

הַבַּדִּים עַל־ הָאָרֹן וַיִּתֵּן אֶת־ הַכַּפֹּרֶת עַל־ הָאָרֹן מִלְמָעְלָה׃
on-top the-ark over the-cover *** and-he-put the-ark to the-poles

וַיָּבֵא אֶת־ הָאָרֹן אֶל־ הַמִּשְׁכָּן וַיָּשֶׂם אֵת פָּרֹכֶת
curtain-of *** and-he-hung the-tabernacle into the-ark *** then-he-brought (21)

הַמָּסָךְ וַיָּסֶךְ עַל אֲרוֹן הָעֵדוּת כַּאֲשֶׁר צִוָּה
he-commanded just-as the-Testimony ark-of over and-he-shielded the-shield

יְהוָה אֶת־ מֹשֶׁה׃ וַיִּתֵּן אֶת־ הַשֻּׁלְחָן בְּאֹהֶל מוֹעֵד עַל
on Meeting in-Tent-of the-table *** and-he-placed (22) Moses *** Yahweh

יֶרֶךְ הַמִּשְׁכָּן צָפֹנָה מִחוּץ לַפָּרֹכֶת׃ וַיַּעֲרֹךְ
and-he-set-out (23) of-the-curtain outside to-north the-tabernacle side-of

עָלָיו עֵרֶךְ לֶחֶם לִפְנֵי יְהוָה כַּאֲשֶׁר צִוָּה יְהוָה אֶת־ מֹשֶׁה׃
Moses *** Yahweh he-commanded just-as Yahweh before bread set-of on-him

וַיָּשֶׂם אֶת־ הַמְּנֹרָה בְּאֹהֶל מוֹעֵד נֹכַח הַשֻּׁלְחָן
the-table opposite Meeting in-Tent-of the-lampstand *** and-he-placed (24)

עַל יֶרֶךְ הַמִּשְׁכָּן נֶגְבָּה׃ וַיַּעַל הַנֵּרֹת לִפְנֵי יְהוָה
Yahweh before the-lamps and-he-set-up (25) to-south the-tabernacle side-of on

כַּאֲשֶׁר צִוָּה יְהוָה אֶת־ מֹשֶׁה׃ וַיָּשֶׂם אֶת־ מִזְבַּח הַזָּהָב
the-gold altar-of *** and-he-placed (26) Moses *** Yahweh he-commanded just-as

בְּאֹהֶל מוֹעֵד לִפְנֵי הַפָּרֹכֶת׃ וַיַּקְטֵר עָלָיו
on-him and-he-burned (27) the-curtain in-front-of Meeting in-Tent-of

קְטֹרֶת סַמִּים כַּאֲשֶׁר צִוָּה יְהוָה אֶת־ מֹשֶׁה׃ וַיָּשֶׂם
then-he-put (28) Moses *** Yahweh he-commanded just-as fragrances incense-of

אֶת־ מָסַךְ הַפֶּתַח לַמִּשְׁכָּן׃ וְאֵת מִזְבַּח הָעֹלָה
the-offering altar-of and (29) to-the-tabernacle the-entrance curtain-of ***

17So the tabernacle was set
up on the first day of the first
month in the second year.
18When Moses set up the tabernacle, he put the bases in
place, erected the frames, inserted the crossbars and set up
the posts. 19Then he spread the
tent over the tabernacle and
put the covering over the tent,
as the LORD commanded him.
20He took the Testimony and
placed it in the ark, attached
the poles to the ark and put the
atonement cover over it.
21Then he brought the ark into
the tabernacle and hung the
shielding curtain and shielded
the ark of the Testimony, as
the LORD commanded him.
22Moses placed the table in
the Tent of Meeting on the
north side of the tabernacle
outside the curtain 23and set
out the bread on it before the
LORD, as the LORD commanded
him.
24He placed the lampstand in
the Tent of Meeting opposite
the table on the south side of
the tabernacle 25and set up the
lamps before the LORD, as the
LORD commanded him.
26Moses placed the gold altar
in the Tent of Meeting in front
of the curtain 27and burned
fragrant incense on it, as the
LORD commanded him. 28Then
he put up the curtain at the
entrance to the tabernacle.
29He set the altar of burnt

שָׂם פֶּתַח מִשְׁכַּן אֹהֶל־מוֹעֵד וַיַּעַל עָלָיו אֶת־
*** on-him and-he-offered Meeting Tent-of tabernacle entrance-of he-set

הָעֹלָה וְאֶת־הַמִּנְחָה כַּאֲשֶׁר צִוָּה יְהוָה אֶת־מֹשֶׁה׃
Moses *** Yahweh he-commanded just-as the-grain-offering and the-burnt-offering

וַיָּשֶׂם אֶת־הַכִּיֹּר בֵּין־אֹהֶל מוֹעֵד וּבֵין הַמִּזְבֵּחַ
the-altar and-between Meeting Tent-of between the-basin *** and-he-placed (30)

וַיִּתֵּן שָׁמָּה מַיִם לְרָחְצָה׃ וְרָחֲצוּ מִמֶּנּוּ מֹשֶׁה וְאַהֲרֹן
and-Aaron Moses in-him and-they-washed (31) to-wash waters in-there and-he-put

וּבָנָיו אֶת־יְדֵיהֶם וְאֶת־רַגְלֵיהֶם׃ בְּבֹאָם
when-to-enter-them (32) feet-of-them and hands-of-them *** and-sons-of-him

אֶל־אֹהֶל מוֹעֵד וּבְקָרְבָתָם אֶל־הַמִּזְבֵּחַ יִרְחָצוּ כַּאֲשֶׁר
just-as they-washed the-altar to or-when-to-approach-them Meeting Tent-of into

צִוָּה יְהוָה אֶת־מֹשֶׁה׃ וַיָּקֶם אֶת־הֶחָצֵר סָבִיב
around the-courtyard *** then-he-set-up (33) Moses *** Yahweh he-commanded

לַמִּשְׁכָּן וְלַמִּזְבֵּחַ וַיִּתֵּן אֶת־מָסַךְ שַׁעַר
entrance-of curtain-of *** and-he-put-up and-to-the-altar to-the-tabernacle

הֶחָצֵר וַיְכַל מֹשֶׁה אֶת־הַמְּלָאכָה׃ וַיְכַס
then-he-covered (34) the-work *** Moses so-he-finished the-courtyard

הֶעָנָן אֶת־אֹהֶל מוֹעֵד וּכְבוֹד יְהוָה מָלֵא אֶת־
*** he-filled Yahweh and-glory-of Meeting Tent-of *** the-cloud

הַמִּשְׁכָּן׃ וְלֹא־יָכֹל מֹשֶׁה לָבוֹא אֶל־אֹהֶל מוֹעֵד כִּי־
for Meeting Tent-of into to-enter Moses he-could and-not (35) the-tabernacle

שָׁכַן עָלָיו הֶעָנָן וּכְבוֹד יְהוָה מָלֵא אֶת־הַמִּשְׁכָּן׃
the-tabernacle *** he-filled Yahweh and-glory-of the-cloud on-him he-settled

וּבְהֵעָלוֹת הֶעָנָן מֵעַל הַמִּשְׁכָּן יִסְעוּ בְּנֵי
sons-of they-set-out the-tabernacle from-on the-cloud and-when-to-lift (36)

יִשְׂרָאֵל בְּכֹל מַסְעֵיהֶם׃ וְאִם־לֹא יֵעָלֶה הֶעָנָן
the-cloud he-lifted not but-if (37) travels-of-them in-all-of Israel

וְלֹא יִסְעוּ עַד־יוֹם הֵעָלֹתוֹ׃ כִּי עֲנַן יְהוָה עַל־
over Yahweh cloud-of so (38) to-lift-him day until they-set-out then-not

הַמִּשְׁכָּן יוֹמָם וְאֵשׁ תִּהְיֶה לַיְלָה בּוֹ לְעֵינֵי כָל־
all-of before-eyes-of in-him night she-was and-fire by-day the-tabernacle

בֵּית־יִשְׂרָאֵל בְּכָל־מַסְעֵיהֶם׃
travels-of-them in-all-of Israel house-of

offering near the entrance to
the tabernacle, the Tent of
Meeting, and offered on it
burnt offerings and grain offerings, as the LORD com-
manded him.
30He placed the basin be-
tween the Tent of Meeting
and the altar and put water in
it for washing, 31and Moses
and Aaron and his sons used
it to wash their hands and
feet. 32They washed whenever
they entered the Tent of Meeting or approached the altar, as
the LORD commanded Moses.
33Then Moses set up the
courtyard around the tabernacle and altar and put up the
curtain at the entrance to the
courtyard. And so Moses
finished the work.

The Glory of the LORD

34Then the cloud covered the
Tent of Meeting, and the glory
of the LORD filled the tabernacle. 35Moses could not enter
the Tent of Meeting because
the cloud had settled upon it,
and the glory of the LORD filled
the tabernacle.
36In all the travels of the Israelites, whenever the cloud lifted from above the tabernacle,
they would set out; 37but if the
cloud did not lift, they did not
set out—until the day it lifted.
38So the cloud of the LORD was
over the tabernacle by day,
and fire was in the cloud by
night, in the sight of all the
house of Israel during all their
travels.

וַיִּקְרָא אֶל־מֹשֶׁה וַיְדַבֵּר יְהוָה אֵלָיו מֵאֹהֶל מוֹעֵד
Meeting from-Tent-of to-him Yahweh and-he-spoke Moses to and-he-called (1:1)

לֵאמֹר׃ דַּבֵּר אֶל־בְּנֵי יִשְׂרָאֵל וְאָמַרְתָּ אֲלֵהֶם אָדָם כִּי־יַקְרִיב
he-brings when anyone to-them and-you-say Israel sons-of to speak! (2) to-say

מִכֶּם קָרְבָּן לַיהוָה מִן־הַבְּהֵמָה מִן־הַבָּקָר וּמִן־הַצֹּאן
the-flock or-from the-herd from the-animal from to-Yahweh offering from-you

תַּקְרִיבוּ אֶת־קָרְבַּנְכֶם׃ אִם־עֹלָה קָרְבָּנוֹ מִן־
from offering-of-him burnt-offering if (3) offering-of-you *** you-bring

הַבָּקָר זָכָר תָּמִים יַקְרִיבֶנּוּ אֶל־פֶּתַח אֹהֶל מוֹעֵד
Meeting Tent-of entrance-of at he-must-offer-him without-defect male the-herd

יַקְרִיב אֹתוֹ לִרְצֹנוֹ לִפְנֵי יְהוָה׃ וְסָמַךְ
and-he-must-lay (4) Yahweh before for-acceptance-of-him him he-must-present

יָדוֹ עַל רֹאשׁ הָעֹלָה וְנִרְצָה לוֹ
for-him and-he-will-be-accepted the-burnt-offering head-of on hand-of-him

לְכַפֵּר עָלָיו׃ וְשָׁחַט אֶת־בֶּן הַבָּקָר לִפְנֵי
before the-herd son-of *** then-he-must-slaughter (5) for-him to-atone

יְהוָה וְהִקְרִיבוּ בְּנֵי אַהֲרֹן הַכֹּהֲנִים אֶת־הַדָּם
the-blood *** the-priests Aaron sons-of and-they-will-bring Yahweh

וְזָרְקוּ אֶת־הַדָּם עַל־הַמִּזְבֵּחַ סָבִיב אֲשֶׁר־פֶּתַח
entrance-of at around the-altar against the-blood *** and-they-will-sprinkle

אֹהֶל מוֹעֵד׃ וְהִפְשִׁיט אֶת־הָעֹלָה וְנִתַּח
and-he-must-cut the-burnt-offering *** and-he-must-skin (6) Meeting Tent-of

אֹתָהּ לִנְתָחֶיהָ׃ וְנָתְנוּ בְּנֵי אַהֲרֹן הַכֹּהֵן אֵשׁ
fire the-priest Aaron sons-of and-they-must-put (7) into-pieces-of-her her

עַל־הַמִּזְבֵּחַ וְעָרְכוּ עֵצִים עַל־הָאֵשׁ׃ וְעָרְכוּ
and-they-shall-arrange (8) the-fire on woods and-they-must-arrange the-altar on

בְּנֵי אַהֲרֹן הַכֹּהֲנִים אֵת הַנְּתָחִים אֶת־הָרֹאשׁ וְאֶת־הַפָּדֶר עַל־
on the-fat and the-head *** the-pieces *** the-priests Aaron sons-of

הָעֵצִים אֲשֶׁר עַל־הָאֵשׁ אֲשֶׁר עַל־הַמִּזְבֵּחַ׃ וְקִרְבּוֹ
and-inner-part-of-him (9) the-altar on that the-fire on that the-woods

וּכְרָעָיו יִרְחַץ בַּמָּיִם וְהִקְטִיר הַכֹּהֵן אֶת־
*** the-priest and-he-must-burn with-the-waters he-must-wash and-legs-of-him

הַכֹּל הַמִּזְבֵּחָה עֹלָה אִשֵּׁה רֵיחַ־נִיחוֹחַ לַיהוָה׃
to-Yahweh pleasant aroma-of by-fire burnt-offering on-the-altar the-whole

וְאִם־מִן־הַצֹּאן קָרְבָּנוֹ מִן־הַכְּשָׂבִים אוֹ מִן־
from or the-sheep from offering-of-him the-flock from and-if (10)

הָעִזִּים לְעֹלָה זָכָר תָּמִים יַקְרִיבֶנּוּ׃
he-must-offer-him without-defect male for-burnt-offering the-goats

The Burnt Offering

1 The LORD called to Moses
and spoke to him from the
Tent of Meeting. He said,
2"Speak to the Israelites and
say to them: 'When any of you
brings an offering to the LORD,
bring as your offering an animal from either the herd or the
flock.
3" 'If the offering is a burnt
offering from the herd, he is to
offer a male without defect. He
must present it at the entrance
to the Tent of Meeting so that
it[a] will be acceptable to the
LORD. 4He is to lay his hand on
the head of the burnt offering,
and it will be accepted on his
behalf to make atonement for
him. 5He is to slaughter the
young bull before the LORD,
and then Aaron's sons the
priests shall bring the blood
and sprinkle it against the altar on all sides at the entrance
to the Tent of Meeting. 6He is
to skin the burnt offering and
cut it into pieces. 7The sons of
Aaron the priest are to put fire
on the altar and arrange wood
on the fire. 8Then Aaron's sons
the priests shall arrange the
pieces, including the head and
the fat, on the burning wood
that is on the altar. 9He is to
wash the inner parts and the
legs with water, and the priest
is to burn all of it on the altar.
It is a burnt offering, an
offering made by fire, an
aroma pleasing to the LORD.
10" 'If the offering is a burnt
offering from the flock, from
either the sheep or the goats,
he is to offer a male without

[a]3 Or *he*

וְשָׁחַט אֹתוֹ עַל יֶרֶךְ הַמִּזְבֵּחַ צָפֹנָה לִפְנֵי יְהוָה
Yahweh before to-north the-altar side-of on him and-he-must-slaughter (11)

וְזָרְקוּ בְּנֵי אַהֲרֹן הַכֹּהֲנִים אֶת־ דָּמוֹ עַל־
against blood-of-him *** the-priests Aaron sons-of and-they-shall-sprinkle

הַמִּזְבֵּחַ סָבִיב׃ וְנִתַּח אֹתוֹ לִנְתָחָיו וְאֶת־ רֹאשׁוֹ
head-of-him and into-pieces-of-him him and-he-must-cut (12) around the-altar

וְאֶת־ פִּדְרוֹ וְעָרַךְ הַכֹּהֵן אֹתָם עַל־ הָעֵצִים אֲשֶׁר עַל־
on that the-woods on them the-priest and-he-shall-arrange fat-of-him and

הָאֵשׁ אֲשֶׁר עַל־ הַמִּזְבֵּחַ׃ וְהַקֶּרֶב וְהַכְּרָעַיִם יִרְחַץ
he-must-wash and-the-legs and-the-inner-part (13) the-altar on that the-fire

בַּמָּיִם וְהִקְרִיב הַכֹּהֵן אֶת־ הַכֹּל וְהִקְטִיר
and-he-must-burn the-whole *** the-priest then-he-must-bring with-the-waters

הַמִּזְבֵּחָה עֹלָה הוּא אִשֵּׁה רֵיחַ נִיחֹחַ לַיהוָה׃
to-Yahweh pleasant aroma-of by-fire he burnt-offering on-the-altar

וְאִם מִן־ הָעוֹף עֹלָה קָרְבָּנוֹ לַיהוָה
to-Yahweh offering-of-him burnt-offering the-bird from and-if (14)

וְהִקְרִיב מִן־ הַתֹּרִים אוֹ מִן־ בְּנֵי הַיּוֹנָה אֶת־
*** the-pigeon young-ones-of from or the-doves from then-he-must-offer

קָרְבָּנוֹ׃ וְהִקְרִיבוֹ הַכֹּהֵן אֶל־ הַמִּזְבֵּחַ
the-altar to the-priest and-he-shall-bring-him (15) offering-of-him

וּמָלַק אֶת־ רֹאשׁוֹ וְהִקְטִיר הַמִּזְבֵּחָה
on-the-altar and-he-shall-burn head-of-him *** and-he-shall-wring-off

וְנִמְצָה דָמוֹ עַל קִיר הַמִּזְבֵּחַ׃
the-altar side-of on blood-of-him and-he-shall-be-drained

וְהֵסִיר אֶת־ מֻרְאָתוֹ בְּנֹצָתָהּ וְהִשְׁלִיךְ
and-he-shall-throw with-content-of-her crop-of-him *** and-he-shall-remove (16)

אֹתָהּ אֵצֶל הַמִּזְבֵּחַ קֵדְמָה אֶל־ מְקוֹם הַדָּשֶׁן׃ וְשִׁסַּע
and-he-shall-tear-open (17) the-ash place-of at to-east the-altar side-of her

אֹתוֹ בִכְנָפָיו לֹא יַבְדִּיל וְהִקְטִיר אֹתוֹ הַכֹּהֵן
the-priest him and-he-shall-burn he-shall-sever not by-wings-of-him him

הַמִּזְבֵּחָה עַל־ הָעֵצִים אֲשֶׁר עַל־ הָאֵשׁ עֹלָה הוּא אִשֵּׁה רֵיחַ
aroma-of by-fire he burnt-offering the-fire on that the-woods on on-the-altar

נִיחֹחַ לַיהוָה׃ וְנֶפֶשׁ כִּי־ תַקְרִיב קָרְבַּן מִנְחָה
grain offering-of she-brings when and-someone (2:1) to-Yahweh pleasant

לַיהוָה סֹלֶת יִהְיֶה קָרְבָּנוֹ וְיָצַק עָלֶיהָ שֶׁמֶן
oil on-her and-he-must-pour offering-of-him he-must-be fine-flour to-Yahweh

וְנָתַן עָלֶיהָ לְבֹנָה׃ וֶהֱבִיאָהּ אֶל־ בְּנֵי אַהֲרֹן
Aaron sons-of to then-he-must-take-her (2) incense on-her and-he-must-put

defect. [11]He is to slaughter it at the north side of the altar before the LORD, and Aaron's sons the priests shall sprinkle its blood against the altar on all sides. [12]He is to cut it into pieces, and the priest shall arrange them, including the head and the fat, on the burning wood that is on the altar. [13]He is to wash the inner parts and the legs with water, and the priest is to bring all of it and burn it on the altar. It is a burnt offering, an offering made by fire, an aroma pleasing to the LORD.

[14]" 'If the offering to the LORD is a burnt offering of birds, he is to offer a dove or a young pigeon. [15]The priest shall bring it to the altar, wring off the head and burn it on the altar; its blood shall be drained out on the side of the altar. [16]He is to remove the crop with its contents[b] and throw it to the east side of the altar, where the ashes are. [17]He shall tear it open by the wings, not severing it completely, and then the priest shall burn it on the wood that is on the fire on the altar. It is a burnt offering, an offering made by fire, an aroma pleasing to the LORD.

The Grain Offering

2 " 'When someone brings a grain offering to the LORD, his offering is to be of fine flour. He is to pour oil on it, put incense on it [2]and take it to Aaron's sons the priests. The

[b]16 Or *crop and the feathers;* the meaning of the Hebrew for this word is uncertain.

הַכֹּהֲנִים וְקָמַץ מִשָּׁם מְלֹא קֻמְצוֹ מִסָּלְתָּהּ
from-flour-of-her handful-of-him full-of from-there and-he-shall-take the-priests

וּמִשַּׁמְנָהּ עַל כָּל־ לְבֹנָתָהּ וְהִקְטִיר הַכֹּהֵן
the-priest and-he-shall-burn incense-of-her all-of with and-from-oil-of-her

אֶת־ אַזְכָּרָתָהּ הַמִּזְבֵּחָה אִשֵּׁה רֵיחַ נִיחֹחַ לַיהוָה׃
to-Yahweh pleasant aroma-of by-fire on-the-altar memorial-portion-of-her ***

וְהַנּוֹתֶרֶת מִן־ הַמִּנְחָה לְאַהֲרֹן וּלְבָנָיו
and-for-sons-of-him for-Aaron the-grain-offering from and-the-being-left (3)

קֹדֶשׁ קָדָשִׁים מֵאִשֵּׁי יְהוָה׃ וְכִי תַקְרִב
you-bring and-if (4) Yahweh from-fire-offerings-of holy-ones holiest-of

קָרְבַּן מִנְחָה מַאֲפֵה תַנּוּר סֹלֶת חַלּוֹת מַצֹּת
without-yeast cakes-of fine-flour oven baked-of grain offering-of

בְּלוּלֹת בַּשֶּׁמֶן וּרְקִיקֵי מַצּוֹת מְשֻׁחִים
ones-being-spread without-yeast or-wafers-of with-the-oil ones-being-mixed

בַּשָּׁמֶן׃ וְאִם־ מִנְחָה עַל־ הַמַּחֲבַת קָרְבָּנֶךָ
offering-of-you the-griddle on grain-offering and-if (5) with-the-oil

סֹלֶת בְּלוּלָה בַשֶּׁמֶן מַצָּה תִהְיֶה׃ פָּתוֹת
to-crumble (6) she-must-be without-yeast with-the-oil being-mixed fine-flour

אֹתָהּ פִּתִּים וְיָצַקְתָּ עָלֶיהָ שָׁמֶן מִנְחָה הִוא׃ וְאִם־
and-if (7) he grain-offering oil on-her and-you pour crumbs her

מִנְחַת מַרְחֶשֶׁת קָרְבָּנֶךָ סֹלֶת בַּשֶּׁמֶן תֵּעָשֶׂה׃
she-must-be-made with-the-oil fine-flour offering-of-you pan-cooked grain-offering-of

וְהֵבֵאתָ אֶת־ הַמִּנְחָה אֲשֶׁר יֵעָשֶׂה מֵאֵלֶּה
from-these he-was-made that the-grain-offering *** then-you-bring (8)

לַיהוָה וְהִקְרִיבָהּ אֶל־ הַכֹּהֵן וְהִגִּישָׁהּ אֶל־
to and-he-shall-take-her the-priest to and-he-will-present-her to-Yahweh

הַמִּזְבֵּחַ׃ וְהֵרִים הַכֹּהֵן מִן־ הַמִּנְחָה אֶת־
*** grain-offering from the-priest and-he-shall-take (9) the-altar

אַזְכָּרָתָהּ וְהִקְטִיר הַמִּזְבֵּחָה אִשֵּׁה רֵיחַ
aroma-of fire-offering on-the-altar and-he-shall-burn memorial-portion-of-her

נִיחֹחַ לַיהוָה׃ וְהַנּוֹתֶרֶת מִן־ הַמִּנְחָה לְאַהֲרֹן
for-Aaron the-grain-offering from and-the-being-left (10) to-Yahweh pleasant

וּלְבָנָיו קֹדֶשׁ קָדָשִׁים מֵאִשֵּׁי יְהוָה׃
Yahweh from-fire-offerings-of holy-ones holiest-of and-for-sons-of-him

כָּל־ הַמִּנְחָה אֲשֶׁר תַּקְרִיבוּ לַיהוָה לֹא תֵעָשֶׂה
she-may-be-made not to-Yahweh you-bring that the-grain-offering every-of (11)

חָמֵץ כִּי כָל־ שְׂאֹר וְכָל־ דְּבַשׁ לֹא־ תַקְטִירוּ מִמֶּנּוּ אִשֶּׁה
fire-offering from-him you-may-burn not honey or-any-of yeast any-of for yeast

priest shall take a handful of
the fine flour and oil, together
with all the incense, and burn
this as a memorial portion on
the altar, an offering made by
fire, an aroma pleasing to the
LORD. 3The rest of the grain
offering belongs to Aaron and
his sons; it is a most holy part
of the offerings made to the
LORD by fire.
4" 'If you bring a grain
offering baked in an oven, it is
to consist of fine flour: cakes
made without yeast and
mixed with oil, or[c] wafers
made without yeast and
spread with oil. 5If your grain
offering is prepared on a griddle, it is to be made of fine
flour mixed with oil, and
without yeast. 6Crumble it and
pour oil on it; it is a grain
offering. 7If your grain
offering is cooked in a pan, it
is to be made of fine flour and
oil. 8Bring the grain offering
made of these things to the
LORD; present it to the priest,
who shall take it to the altar.
9He shall take out the memorial portion from the grain
offering and burn it on the altar as an offering made by fire,
an aroma pleasing to the LORD.
10The rest of the grain offering
belongs to Aaron and his sons;
it is a most holy part of the
offerings made to the LORD by
fire.
11" 'Every grain offering you
bring to the LORD must be
made without yeast, for you
are not to burn any yeast or
honey in an offering made to

c4 Or *and*

לַֽיהוָֽה׃ קָרְבַּ֥ן רֵאשִׁ֛ית תַּקְרִ֥יבוּ אֹתָ֖ם לַֽיהוָ֑ה וְאֶל־
but-on to-Yahweh them you-may-bring firstfruit offering-of (12) to-Yahweh

הַמִּזְבֵּ֥חַ לֹא־יַעֲל֖וּ לְרֵ֥יחַ נִיחֹֽחַ׃ וְכָל־
and-every-of (13) pleasant as-aroma-of they-may-be-offered not the-altar

קָרְבַּ֣ן מִנְחָתְךָ֮ בַּמֶּ֣לַח תִּמְלָח֒ וְלֹ֣א תַשְׁבִּ֗ית
you-leave-out and-not you-season with-the-salt grain-of-you offering-of

מֶ֚לַח בְּרִ֣ית אֱלֹהֶ֔יךָ מֵעַ֖ל מִנְחָתֶ֑ךָ עַ֥ל כָּל־
every-of to grain-offering-of-you from-in God-of-you covenant-of salt-of

קָרְבָּנְךָ֖ תַּקְרִ֥יב מֶֽלַח׃ וְאִם־תַּקְרִ֛יב מִנְחַ֥ת בִּכּוּרִ֖ים
firstfruits offering-of you-bring and-if (14) salt you-add offering-of-you

לַֽיהוָ֑ה אָבִ֞יב קָל֣וּי בָּאֵ֗שׁ גֶּ֚רֶשׂ כַּרְמֶ֔ל תַּקְרִ֕יב אֵ֖ת
*** you-offer new-grain crushed in-the-fire being-roasted head to-Yahweh

מִנְחַ֥ת בִּכּוּרֶֽיךָ׃ וְנָתַתָּ֤ עָלֶ֙יהָ֙ שֶׁ֔מֶן וְשַׂמְתָּ֥ עָלֶ֖יהָ
on-her and-you-put oil on-her and-you-put (15) firstfruits-of-you offering-of

לְבֹנָ֑ה מִנְחָ֖ה הִֽוא׃ וְהִקְטִ֨יר הַכֹּהֵ֜ן אֶת־
*** the-priest and-he-shall-burn (16) she grain-offering incense

אַזְכָּרָתָ֗הּ מִגִּרְשָׂהּ֙ וּמִשַּׁמְנָ֔הּ עַ֖ל כָּל־
all-of with and-from-oil-of-her from-grain-of-her memorial-portion-of-her

לְבֹנָתָ֑הּ אִשֶּׁ֖ה לַֽיהוָֽה׃ וְאִם־זֶ֥בַח שְׁלָמִ֖ים
fellowships offering-of and-if (3:1) to-Yahweh fire-offering incense-of-her

קָרְבָּנ֑וֹ אִ֤ם מִן־הַבָּקָר֙ ה֣וּא מַקְרִ֔יב אִם־זָכָר֙ אִם־נְקֵבָ֔ה
female or male whether one-offering he the-herd from if offering-of-him

תָּמִ֥ים יַקְרִיבֶ֖נּוּ לִפְנֵ֥י יְהוָֽה׃ וְסָמַ֤ךְ
and-he-must-lay (2) Yahweh before he-must-present-him without-defect

יָדוֹ֙ עַל־רֹ֣אשׁ קָרְבָּנ֔וֹ וּשְׁחָט֕וֹ פֶּ֖תַח
entrance-of and-he-must-slaughter-him offering-of-him head-of on hand-of-him

אֹ֣הֶל מוֹעֵ֑ד וְזָרְק֡וּ בְּנֵי֩ אַהֲרֹ֨ן הַכֹּהֲנִ֧ים אֶת־
*** the-priests Aaron sons-of and-they-shall-sprinkle Meeting Tent-of

הַדָּ֛ם עַל־הַמִּזְבֵּ֖חַ סָבִֽיב׃ וְהִקְרִיב֙ מִזֶּ֣בַח
from-offering-of then-he-must-bring (3) around the-altar against the-blood

הַשְּׁלָמִ֔ים אִשֶּׁ֖ה לַֽיהוָ֑ה אֶת־הַחֵ֙לֶב֙ הַֽמְכַסֶּ֣ה אֶת־
*** the-covering the-fat *** to-Yahweh fire-offering the-fellowships

הַקֶּ֔רֶב וְאֵת֙ כָּל־הַחֵ֔לֶב אֲשֶׁ֖ר עַל־הַקֶּֽרֶב׃ וְאֵת֙ שְׁתֵּ֣י
both-of and (4) the-inner-part on that the-fat all-of and the-inner-part

הַכְּלָיֹ֔ת וְאֶת־הַחֵ֙לֶב֙ אֲשֶׁ֣ר עֲלֵהֶ֔ן אֲשֶׁ֖ר עַל־הַכְּסָלִ֑ים וְאֶת־הַיֹּתֶ֙רֶת֙
the-cover and the-loins near that around-them that the-fat and the-kidneys

עַל־הַכָּבֵ֔ד עַל־הַכְּלָי֖וֹת יְסִירֶֽנָּה׃ וְהִקְטִ֨ירוּ אֹת֤וֹ
him and-they-shall-burn (5) he-will-remove-her the-kidneys with the-liver on

the LORD by fire. 12You may
bring them to the LORD as an
offering of the firstfruits, but
they are not to be offered on
the altar as a pleasing aroma.
13Season all your grain
offerings with salt. Do not
leave the salt of the covenant
of your God out of your grain
offerings; add salt to all your
offerings.
14" 'If you bring a grain
offering of firstfruits to the
LORD, offer crushed heads of
new grain roasted in the fire.
15Put oil and incense on it; it is
a grain offering. 16The priest
shall burn the memorial portion of the crushed grain and
the oil, together with all the
incense, as an offering made
to the LORD by fire.

The Fellowship Offering

3 " 'If someone's offering is
a fellowship offering,[d] and
he offers an animal from the
herd, whether male or female,
he is to present before the
LORD an animal without defect. 2He is to lay his hand on
the head of his offering and
slaughter it at the entrance to
the Tent of Meeting. Then
Aaron's sons the priests shall
sprinkle the blood against the
altar on all sides. 3From the fellowship offering he is to bring
a sacrifice made to the LORD by
fire: all the fat that covers the
inner parts or is connected to
them, 4both kidneys with the
fat around them near the
loins, and the covering of the
liver, which he will remove
with the kidneys. 5Then
Aaron's sons are to burn it on

[d]1 Traditionally *peace offering;* also in verses 3, 6 and 9

בְנֵי־ אַהֲרֹן הַמִּזְבֵּחָה עַל־ הָעֹלָה אֲשֶׁר עַל־ הָעֵצִים אֲשֶׁר
that the-woods on that the-burnt-offering upon on-the-altar Aaron sons-of

עַל־ הָאֵשׁ אִשֵּׁה רֵיחַ נִיחֹחַ לַיהוָה׃ וְאִם־ מִן־
from and-if (6) to-Yahweh pleasant aroma-of fire-offering-of the-fire on

הַצֹּאן קָרְבָּנוֹ לְזֶבַח שְׁלָמִים לַיהוָה זָכָר אוֹ
or male to-Yahweh fellowships as-offering-of offering-of-him the-flock

נְקֵבָה תָּמִים יַקְרִיבֶנּוּ׃ אִם־ כֶּשֶׂב הוּא־ מַקְרִיב אֶת־
*** one-offering he lamb if (7) he-must-offer-him without-defect female

קָרְבָּנוֹ וְהִקְרִיב אֹתוֹ לִפְנֵי יְהוָה׃ וְסָמַךְ
and-he-must-lay (8) Yahweh before him then-he-must-present offering-of-him

אֶת־ יָדוֹ עַל־ רֹאשׁ קָרְבָּנוֹ וְשָׁחַט אֹתוֹ לִפְנֵי
in-front-of him and-he-must-slaughter offering-of-him head-of on hand-of-him ***

אֹהֶל מוֹעֵד וְזָרְקוּ בְּנֵי אַהֲרֹן אֶת־ דָּמוֹ
blood-of-him *** Aaron sons-of then-they-shall-sprinkle Meeting Tent-of

עַל־ הַמִּזְבֵּחַ סָבִיב׃ וְהִקְרִיב מִזֶּבַח
from-offering-of then-he-must-bring (9) around the-altar against

הַשְּׁלָמִים אִשֶּׁה לַיהוָה חֶלְבּוֹ הָאַלְיָה תְמִימָה
entire the-fat-tail fat-of-him to-Yahweh fire-offering the-fellowships

לְעֻמַּת הֶעָצֶה יְסִירֶנָּה וְאֶת־ הַחֵלֶב הַמְכַסֶּה אֶת־
*** the-covering the-fat and he-must-cut-off-her the-backbone close-to

הַקֶּרֶב וְאֵת כָּל־ הַחֵלֶב אֲשֶׁר עַל־ הַקֶּרֶב׃ וְאֵת שְׁתֵּי
both-of and (10) the-inner-part on that the-fat all-of and the-inner-part

הַכְּלָיֹת וְאֶת־ הַחֵלֶב אֲשֶׁר עֲלֵהֶן אֲשֶׁר עַל־ הַכְּסָלִים וְאֶת־הַיֹּתֶרֶת
the-cover and the-loins near that around-them that the-fat and the-kidneys

עַל־ הַכָּבֵד עַל־ הַכְּלָיוֹת יְסִירֶנָּה׃ וְהִקְטִירוֹ
and-he-shall-burn-him (11) he-will-remove-her the-kidneys with the-liver on

הַכֹּהֵן הַמִּזְבֵּחָה לֶחֶם אִשֶּׁה לַיהוָה׃ וְאִם־ עֵז
goat and-if (12) to-Yahweh fire-offering food on-the-altar the-priest

קָרְבָּנוֹ וְהִקְרִיבוֹ לִפְנֵי יְהוָה׃ וְסָמַךְ
and-he-must-lay (13) Yahweh before then-he-must-present-him offering-of-him

אֶת־ יָדוֹ עַל־ רֹאשׁוֹ וְשָׁחַט אֹתוֹ לִפְנֵי אֹהֶל
Tent-of in-front-of him and-he-must-slaughter head-of-him on hand-of-him ***

מוֹעֵד וְזָרְקוּ בְּנֵי אַהֲרֹן אֶת־ דָּמוֹ עַל־
against blood-of-him *** Aaron sons-of then-they-shall-sprinkle Meeting

הַמִּזְבֵּחַ סָבִיב׃ וְהִקְרִיב מִמֶּנּוּ קָרְבָּנוֹ אִשֶּׁה
by-fire offering-of-him from-him then-he-must-offer (14) around the-altar

לַיהוָה אֶת־ הַחֵלֶב הַמְכַסֶּה אֶת־ הַקֶּרֶב וְאֵת כָּל־ הַחֵלֶב
the fat all-of and the-inner-part *** the-covering the-fat *** to-Yahweh

the altar on top of the burnt
offering that is on the burning
wood, as an offering made by
fire, an aroma pleasing to the
LORD.
6" 'If he offers an animal
from the flock as a fellowship
offering to the LORD, he is to
offer a male or female without
defect. 7If he offers a lamb, he
is to present it before the LORD.
8He is to lay his hand on the
head of his offering and
slaughter it in front of the Tent
of Meeting. Then Aaron's sons
shall sprinkle its blood against
the altar on all sides. 9From the
fellowship offering he is to
bring a sacrifice made to the
LORD by fire: its fat, the entire
fat tail cut off close to the back-
bone, all the fat that covers the
inner parts or is connected to
them, 10both kidneys with the
fat around them near the
loins, and the covering of the
liver, which he will remove
with the kidneys. 11The priest
shall burn them on the altar as
food, an offering made to the
LORD by fire.
12" 'If his offering is a goat,
he is to present it before the
LORD. 13He is to lay his hand
on its head and slaughter it in
front of the Tent of Meeting.
Then Aaron's sons shall sprinkle its blood against the altar
on all sides. 14From what he
offers he is to make this
offering to the LORD by fire: all
the fat that covers the inner

אֲשֶׁר עַל־ הַקֶּרֶב׃ וְאֵת שְׁתֵּי הַכְּלָיֹת וְאֶת־ הַחֵלֶב אֲשֶׁר
that the-fat and the-kidneys both-of and (15) the-inner-part on that

עֲלֵהֶן אֲשֶׁר עַל־הַכְּסָלִים וְאֶת־ הַיֹּתֶרֶת עַל־ הַכָּבֵד עַל־ הַכְּלָיֹת
the-kidneys with the-liver on the-cover and the-loins near that on-them

יְסִירֶנָּה׃ וְהִקְטִירָם הַכֹּהֵן הַמִּזְבֵּחָה לֶחֶם
food on-the-altar the-priest and-he-shall-burn-them (16) he-will-remove-her

אִשֶּׁה לְרֵיחַ נִיחֹחַ כָּל־ חֵלֶב לַיהוָה׃ חֻקַּת
ordinance-of (17) to-Yahweh fat all-of pleasant for-aroma-of fire-offering

עוֹלָם לְדֹרֹתֵיכֶם בְּכֹל מוֹשְׁבֹתֵיכֶם כָּל־ חֵלֶב וְכָל־
or-any-of fat any-of dwellings-of-you in-all-of for-generations-of-you lasting

דָּם לֹא תֹאכֵלוּ׃ וַיְדַבֵּר יְהוָה אֶל־מֹשֶׁה לֵּאמֹר׃ דַּבֵּר
say! (2) to-say Moses to Yahweh and-he-spoke (4:1) you-must-eat not blood

אֶל־ בְּנֵי יִשְׂרָאֵל לֵאמֹר נֶפֶשׁ כִּי־ תֶחֱטָא בִשְׁגָגָה מִכֹּל
against-any-of with-no-intention she-sins when anyone to-say Israel sons-of to

מִצְוֹת יְהוָה אֲשֶׁר לֹא תֵעָשֶׂינָה וְעָשָׂה מֵאַחַת
against-one and-he-does they-may-be-done not that Yahweh commands-of

מֵהֵנָּה׃ אִם הַכֹּהֵן הַמָּשִׁיחַ יֶחֱטָא לְאַשְׁמַת הָעָם
the-people to-guilt-of he-sins the-anointed the-priest if (3) from-them

וְהִקְרִיב עַל חַטָּאתוֹ אֲשֶׁר חָטָא פַּר בֶּן־ בָּקָר
herd young-of bull he-sinned that sin-of-him for then-he-must-bring

תָּמִים לַיהוָה לְחַטָּאת׃ וְהֵבִיא אֶת־ הַפָּר
the-bull *** and-he-must-present (4) as-sin-offering to-Yahweh without-defect

אֶל־ פֶּתַח אֹהֶל מוֹעֵד לִפְנֵי יְהוָה וְסָמַךְ אֶת־ יָדוֹ
hand-of-him *** and-he-must-lay Yahweh before Meeting Tent-of entrance-of at

עַל־ רֹאשׁ הַפָּר וְשָׁחַט אֶת־ הַפָּר לִפְנֵי יְהוָה׃
Yahweh before the-bull *** and-he-must-slaughter the-bull head-of on

וְלָקַח הַכֹּהֵן הַמָּשִׁיחַ מִדַּם הַפָּר
the-bull from-blood-of the-anointed the-priest then-he-shall-take (5)

וְהֵבִיא אֹתוֹ אֶל־ אֹהֶל מוֹעֵד׃ וְטָבַל הַכֹּהֵן
the-priest and-he-must-dip (6) Meeting Tent-of into him and-he-shall-carry

אֶת־ אֶצְבָּעוֹ בַּדָּם וְהִזָּה מִן־ הַדָּם שֶׁבַע
seven the-blood from and-he-must-sprinkle into-the-blood finger-of-him ***

פְּעָמִים לִפְנֵי יְהוָה אֶת־ פְּנֵי פָּרֹכֶת הַקֹּדֶשׁ׃ וְנָתַן
then-he-shall-put (7) the-sanctuary curtain-of front-of *** Yahweh before times

הַכֹּהֵן מִן־ הַדָּם עַל־ קַרְנוֹת מִזְבַּח קְטֹרֶת הַסַּמִּים
the-fragrances incense-of altar-of horns-of on the-blood from the-priest

לִפְנֵי יְהוָה אֲשֶׁר בְּאֹהֶל מוֹעֵד וְאֵת׀ כָּל־ דַּם הַפָּר
the-bull blood-of rest-of and Meeting in-Tent-of that Yahweh before

parts or is connected to them,
15both kidneys with the fat on
them near the loins, and the
covering of the liver, which he
will remove with the kidneys.
16The priest shall burn them
on the altar as food, an
offering made by fire, a pleasing aroma. All the fat is the
LORD's.
17" 'This is a lasting ordinance for the generations to
come, wherever you live: You
must not eat any fat or any
blood.' "

The Sin Offering

4 The LORD said to Moses,
2"Say to the Israelites:
'When anyone sins unintentionally and does what is forbidden in any of the LORD's
commands—
3" 'If the anointed priest
sins, bringing guilt on the
people, he must bring to the
LORD a young bull without defect as a sin offering for the sin
he has committed. 4He is to
present the bull at the entrance to the Tent of Meeting
before the LORD. He is to lay
his hand on its head and
slaughter it before the LORD.
5Then the anointed priest shall
take some of the bull's blood
and carry it into the Tent of
Meeting. 6He is to dip his
finger into the blood and
sprinkle some of it seven
times before the LORD, in front
of the curtain of the sanctuary.
7The priest shall then put some
of the blood on the horns of
the altar of fragrant incense
that is before the LORD in the
Tent of Meeting. The rest of

יִשְׁפֹּךְ אֶל־ יְסוֹד מִזְבַּח הָעֹלָה אֲשֶׁר־ פֶּתַח
entrance-of that the-burnt-offering altar-of base-of at he-shall-pour-out

אֹהֶל מוֹעֵד׃ וְאֶת־ כָּל־ חֵלֶב פַּר הַחַטָּאת יָרִים
he-shall-remove the-sin-offering bull-of fat-of all-of and (8) Meeting Tent-of

מִמֶּנּוּ אֶת־ הַחֵלֶב הַמְכַסֶּה עַל־ הַקֶּרֶב וְאֵת כָּל־ הַחֵלֶב אֲשֶׁר
that the-fat all-of and the-inner-part over the-cover the-fat *** from-him

עַל־ הַקֶּרֶב׃ וְאֵת שְׁתֵּי הַכְּלָיֹת וְאֶת־הַחֵלֶב אֲשֶׁר עֲלֵיהֶן אֲשֶׁר
that on-them that the-fat and the-kidneys both-of and (9) the-inner-part onto

עַל־הַכְּסָלִים וְאֶת־הַיֹּתֶרֶת עַל־ הַכָּבֵד עַל־ הַכְּלָיוֹת יְסִירֶנָּה׃
he-will-remove-her the-kidneys with the-liver over the-cover and the-loins near

כַּאֲשֶׁר יוּרַם מִשּׁוֹר זֶבַח הַשְּׁלָמִים
the-fellowship-offerings sacrifice-of from-cow-of he-is-removed just-as (10)

וְהִקְטִירָם הַכֹּהֵן עַל מִזְבַּח הָעֹלָה׃ וְאֶת־
but (11) the-burnt-offering altar-of on the-priest and-he-shall-burn-them

עוֹר הַפָּר וְאֶת־כָּל־ בְּשָׂרוֹ עַל־ רֹאשׁוֹ וְעַל־ כְּרָעָיו
legs-of-him and-with head-of-him with flesh-of-him all-of and the-bull hide-of

וְקִרְבּוֹ וּפִרְשׁוֹ׃ וְהוֹצִיא אֶת־ כָּל־
rest-of *** now-he-must-take (12) and-offal-of-him and-inner-part-of-him

הַפָּר אֶל־ מִחוּץ לַמַּחֲנֶה אֶל־ מָקוֹם טָהוֹר אֶל־ שֶׁפֶךְ הַדֶּשֶׁן
the-ash dump-of to clean place to of-the-camp outside to the-bull

וְשָׂרַף אֹתוֹ עַל־עֵצִים בָּאֵשׁ עַל־ שֶׁפֶךְ הַדֶּשֶׁן יִשָּׂרֵף׃
he-must-be-burned the-ash dump-of at in-the-fire woods on him and-he-must-burn

וְאִם כָּל־ עֲדַת יִשְׂרָאֵל יִשְׁגּוּ
they-sin-unintentionally Israel community-of whole-of and-if (13)

וְנֶעְלַם דָּבָר מֵעֵינֵי הַקָּהָל וְעָשׂוּ אַחַת
one and-they-do the-community from-eyes-of matter but-he-is-hidden

מִכָּל־ מִצְוֺת יְהוָה אֲשֶׁר לֹא־ תֵעָשֶׂינָה וְאָשֵׁמוּ׃
then-they-are-guilty they-may-be-done not that Yahweh commands-of from-any-of

וְנוֹדְעָה הַחַטָּאת אֲשֶׁר חָטְאוּ עָלֶיהָ וְהִקְרִיבוּ
then-they-must-bring by-her they-sinned that the-sin when-she-becomes-known (14)

הַקָּהָל פַּר בֶּן־ בָּקָר לְחַטָּאת וְהֵבִיאוּ אֹתוֹ
him and-they-must-present as-sin-offering herd young-of bull-of the-assembly

לִפְנֵי אֹהֶל מוֹעֵד׃ וְסָמְכוּ זִקְנֵי הָעֵדָה אֶת־
*** the-community elders-of and-they-must-lay (15) Meeting Tent-of before

יְדֵיהֶם עַל־ רֹאשׁ הַפָּר לִפְנֵי יְהוָה וְשָׁחַט אֶת־
*** and-he-must-slaughter Yahweh before the-bull head-of on hands-of-them

הַפָּר לִפְנֵי יְהוָה׃ וְהֵבִיא הַכֹּהֵן הַמָּשִׁיחַ
the-anointed the-priest then-he-must-take (16) Yahweh before the-bull

the bull's blood he shall pour
out at the base of the altar of
burnt offering at the entrance
to the Tent of Meeting. 8He
shall remove all the fat from
the bull of the sin
offering—the fat that covers
the inner parts or is connected
to them, 9both kidneys with
the fat on them near the loins,
and the covering of the liver,
which he will remove with the
kidneys— 10just as the fat is
removed from the cow[e] sacrificed
as a fellowship
offering.[f] Then the priest shall
burn them on the altar of
burnt offering. 11But the hide
of the bull and all its flesh, as
well as the head and legs, the
inner parts and offal— 12that
is, all the rest of the bull—he
must take outside the camp to
a place ceremonially clean,
where the ashes are thrown,
and burn it in a wood fire on
the ash heap.

13" 'If the whole Israelite
community sins unintentionally
and does what is forbidden
in any of the LORD's
commands, even though the
community is unaware of the
matter, they are guilty. 14When
they become aware of the sin
they committed, the assembly
must bring a young bull as a
sin offering and present it before
the Tent of Meeting. 15The
elders of the community are to
lay their hands on the bull's
head before the LORD, and the
bull shall be slaughtered before
the LORD. 16Then the
anointed priest is to take some

[e]10 The Hebrew word can include both male and female.
[f]10 Traditionally *peace offering*; also in verses 26, 31 and 35

מִדַּם הַפָּר אֶל־ אֹהֶל מוֹעֵד׃ וְטָבַל הַכֹּהֵן
the-priest and-he-shall-dip (17) Meeting Tent-of into the-bull from-blood-of

אֶצְבָּעוֹ מִן־ הַדָּם וְהִזָּה שֶׁבַע פְּעָמִים לִפְנֵי יְהוָה
Yahweh before times seven and-he-shall-sprinkle the-blood into finger-of-him

אֶת פְּנֵי הַפָּרֹכֶת׃ וּמִן־ הַדָּם יִתֵּן ׀ עַל־ קַרְנֹת
horns-of on he-must-put the-blood and-from (18) the-curtain front-of ***

הַמִּזְבֵּחַ אֲשֶׁר לִפְנֵי יְהוָה אֲשֶׁר בְּאֹהֶל מוֹעֵד וְאֵת כָּל־ הַדָּם
the-blood rest-of and Meeting in-Tent-of that Yahweh before that the-altar

יִשְׁפֹּךְ אֶל־ יְסוֹד מִזְבַּח הָעֹלָה אֲשֶׁר־ פֶּתַח
entrance-of that the-burnt-offering altar-of base-of at he-shall-pour-out

אֹהֶל מוֹעֵד׃ וְאֵת כָּל־ חֶלְבּוֹ יָרִים מִמֶּנּוּ
from-him he-shall-remove fat-of-him all-of and (19) Meeting Tent-of

וְהִקְטִיר הַמִּזְבֵּחָה׃ וְעָשָׂה לַפָּר כַּאֲשֶׁר
just-as with-the-bull and-he-must-do (20) on-the-altar and-he-shall-burn

עָשָׂה לְפַר הַחַטָּאת כֵּן יַעֲשֶׂה־ לּוֹ
with-him he-shall-do same the-sin-offering with-bull-of he-did

וְכִפֶּר עֲלֵהֶם הַכֹּהֵן וְנִסְלַח לָהֶם׃
to-them and-he-will-be-forgiven the-priest for-them so-he-will-atone

וְהוֹצִיא אֶת־ הַפָּר אֶל־ מִחוּץ לַמַּחֲנֶה וְשָׂרַף
and-he-shall-burn of-the-camp outside to the-bull *** then-he-shall-take (21)

אֹתוֹ כַּאֲשֶׁר שָׂרַף אֵת הַפָּר הָרִאשׁוֹן חַטַּאת הַקָּהָל
the-community sin-offering-of the-first the-bull *** he-burned just-as him

הוּא׃ אֲשֶׁר נָשִׂיא יֶחֱטָא וְעָשָׂה אַחַת מִכָּל־ מִצְוֹת יְהוָה
Yahweh commands-of from-any-of one and-he-does he-sins leader when (22) this

אֱלֹהָיו אֲשֶׁר לֹא־ תֵעָשֶׂינָה בִּשְׁגָגָה וְאָשֵׁם׃
then-he-is-guilty with-no-intention they-may-be-done not that God-of-him

אוֹ־ הוֹדַע אֵלָיו חַטָּאתוֹ אֲשֶׁר חָטָא בָּהּ
by-her he-sinned that sin-of-him to-him he-is-made-aware when (23)

וְהֵבִיא אֶת־ קָרְבָּנוֹ שְׂעִיר עִזִּים זָכָר תָּמִים׃
without-defect male goats male-goat-of offering-of-him *** then-he-must-bring

וְסָמַךְ יָדוֹ עַל־ רֹאשׁ הַשָּׂעִיר וְשָׁחַט
and-he-must-slaughter the-goat head-of on hand-of-him and-he-must-lay (24)

אֹתוֹ בִּמְקוֹם אֲשֶׁר־ יִשְׁחַט אֶת־ הָעֹלָה לִפְנֵי יְהוָה
Yahweh before the-burnt-offering *** he-slaughtered where at-place him

חַטָּאת הוּא׃ וְלָקַח הַכֹּהֵן מִדַּם
from-blood-of the-priest then-he-shall-take (25) he sin-offering

הַחַטָּאת בְּאֶצְבָּעוֹ וְנָתַן עַל־ קַרְנֹת מִזְבַּח
altar-of horns-of on and-he-shall-put with-finger-of-him the-sin-offering

of the bull's blood into the
Tent of Meeting. [17]He shall dip
his finger into the blood and
sprinkle it before the LORD
seven times in front of the curtain. [18]He is to put some of the
blood on the horns of the altar
that is before the LORD in the
Tent of Meeting. The rest of
the blood he shall pour out at
the base of the altar of burnt
offering at the entrance to the
Tent of Meeting. [19]He shall
remove all the fat from it and
burn it on the altar, [20]and do
with this bull just as he did
with the bull for the sin
offering. In this way the priest
will make atonement for
them, and they will be forgiven. [21]Then he shall take the
bull outside the camp and
burn it as he burned the first
bull. This is the sin offering for
the community.

[22]" 'When a leader sins
unintentionally and does
what is forbidden in any of
the commands of the LORD his
God, he is guilty. [23]When he is
made aware of the sin he committed, he must bring as his
offering a male goat without
defect. [24]He is to lay his hand
on the goat's head and slaughter it at the place where the
burnt offering is slaughtered
before the LORD. It is a sin
offering. [25]Then the priest
shall take some of the blood of
the sin offering with his finger
and put it on the horns of the

הָעֹלָה וְאֶת־ דָּמוֹ יִשְׁפֹּךְ אֶל־ יְסוֹד מִזְבַּח
altar-of base-of at he-shall-pour-out blood-of-him and the-burnt-offering

הָעֹלָה׃ (26) וְאֶת־ כָּל־ חֶלְבּוֹ יַקְטִיר הַמִּזְבֵּחָה
on-the-altar he-shall-burn fat-of-him all-of and (26) the-burnt-offering

כְּחֵלֶב זֶבַח הַשְּׁלָמִים וְכִפֶּר עָלָיו הַכֹּהֵן
the-priest for-him so-he-will-atone the-fellowships offering-of as-fat-of

מֵחַטָּאתוֹ וְנִסְלַח לוֹ׃ (27) וְאִם־ נֶפֶשׁ אַחַת
one member and-if (27) to-him and-he-will-be-forgiven for-sin-of-him

תֶּחֱטָא בִשְׁגָגָה מֵעַם הָאָרֶץ בַּעֲשֹׂתָהּ אַחַת
one by-to-do-her the-land from-people-of without-intention she-sins

מִמִּצְוֺת יְהוָה אֲשֶׁר לֹא־ תֵעָשֶׂינָה וְאָשֵׁם׃ (28) אוֹ
when (28) then-he-is-guilty they-may-be-done not that Yahweh from-commands-of

הוֹדַע אֵלָיו חַטָּאתוֹ אֲשֶׁר חָטָא וְהֵבִיא
then-he-must-bring he-sinned that sin-of-him to-him he-is-made-aware

קָרְבָּנוֹ שְׂעִירַת עִזִּים תְּמִימָה נְקֵבָה עַל־ חַטָּאתוֹ
sin-of-him for female without-defect goats female-goat-of offering-of-him

אֲשֶׁר חָטָא׃ (29) וְסָמַךְ אֶת־ יָדוֹ עַל רֹאשׁ
head-of on hand-of-him *** and-he-must-lay (29) he-sinned that

הַחַטָּאת וְשָׁחַט אֶת־ הַחַטָּאת בִּמְקוֹם
at-place-of the-sin-offering *** and-he-must-slaughter the-sin-offering

הָעֹלָה׃ (30) וְלָקַח הַכֹּהֵן מִדָּמָהּ
from-blood-of-her the-priest then-he-must-take (30) the-burnt-offering

בְּאֶצְבָּעוֹ וְנָתַן עַל־ קַרְנֹת מִזְבַּח הָעֹלָה
the-burnt-offering altar-of horns-of on and-he-must-put with-finger-of-him

וְאֶת־ כָּל־ דָּמָהּ יִשְׁפֹּךְ אֶל־ יְסוֹד הַמִּזְבֵּחַ׃ (31) וְאֶת־
and (31) the-altar base-of at he-must-pour-out blood-of-her rest-of and

כָּל־ חֶלְבָּהּ יָסִיר כַּאֲשֶׁר הוּסַר חֵלֶב מֵעַל
from-on fat he-is-removed just-as he-shall-remove fat-of-her all-of

זֶבַח הַשְּׁלָמִים וְהִקְטִיר הַכֹּהֵן הַמִּזְבֵּחָה
on-the-altar the-priest and-he-shall-burn the-fellowships offering-of

לְרֵיחַ נִיחֹחַ לַיהוָה וְכִפֶּר עָלָיו הַכֹּהֵן
the-priest for-him so-he-will-atone to-Yahweh pleasant as-aroma-of

וְנִסְלַח לוֹ׃ (32) וְאִם־ כֶּבֶשׂ יָבִיא קָרְבָּנוֹ
offering-of-him he-brings lamb and-if (32) to-him and-he-will-be-forgiven

לְחַטָּאת נְקֵבָה תְמִימָה יְבִיאֶנָּה׃ (33) וְסָמַךְ
and-he-must-lay (33) he-must-bring-her without-defect female as-sin-offering

אֶת־ יָדוֹ עַל רֹאשׁ הַחַטָּאת וְשָׁחַט אֹתָהּ
her and-he-must-slaughter the-sin-offering head-of on hand-of-him ***

altar of burnt offering and pour out the rest of the blood at the base of the altar. [26]He shall burn all the fat on the altar as he burned the fat of the fellowship offering. In this way the priest will make atonement for the man's sin, and he will be forgiven.

[27]" 'If a member of the community sins unintentionally and does what is forbidden in any of the LORD's commands, he is guilty. [28]When he is made aware of the sin he committed, he must bring as his offering for the sin he committed a female goat without defect. [29]He is to lay his hand on the head of the sin offering and slaughter it at the place of the burnt offering. [30]Then the priest is to take some of the blood with his finger and put it on the horns of the altar of burnt offering and pour out the rest of the blood at the base of the altar. [31]He shall remove all the fat, just as the fat is removed from the fellowship offering, and the priest shall burn it on the altar as an aroma pleasing to the LORD. In this way the priest will make atonement for him, and he will be forgiven.

[32]" 'If he brings a lamb as his sin offering, he is to bring a female without defect. [33]He is to lay his hand on its head and

לְחַטָּאת בִּמְקוֹם אֲשֶׁר יִשְׁחַט אֶת־ הָעֹלָה׃
the-burnt-offering *** he-slaughters where at-place as-sin-offering

(34) וְלָקַח הַכֹּהֵן מִדַּם הַחַטָּאת
the-sin-offering from-blood-of the-priest then-he-shall-take (34)

בְּאֶצְבָּעוֹ וְנָתַן עַל־ קַרְנֹת מִזְבַּח הָעֹלָה
the-burnt-offering altar-of horns-of on and-he-shall-put with-finger-of-him

וְאֶת־ כָּל־ דָּמָהּ יִשְׁפֹּךְ אֶל־ יְסוֹד הַמִּזְבֵּחַ׃ (35) וְאֶת־
and (35) the-altar base-of at he-shall-pour-out blood-of-her rest-of and

כָּל־ חֶלְבָּה* יָסִיר כַּאֲשֶׁר יוּסַר חֵלֶב־ הַכֶּשֶׂב
the-lamb fat-of he-is-removed just-as he-shall-remove fat-of-her all-of

מִזֶּבַח הַשְּׁלָמִים וְהִקְטִיר הַכֹּהֵן אֹתָם
them the-priest and-he-shall-burn the-fellowships from-sacrifice-of

הַמִּזְבֵּחָה עַל אִשֵּׁי יְהוָה וְכִפֶּר עָלָיו
for-him so-he-will-atone Yahweh fire-offerings-of upon on-the-altar

הַכֹּהֵן עַל־ חַטָּאתוֹ אֲשֶׁר־ חָטָא וְנִסְלַח לוֹ׃
to-him and-he-will-be-forgiven he-sinned that sin-of-him for the-priest

(5:1) וְנֶפֶשׁ כִּי־ תֶחֱטָא וְשָׁמְעָה קוֹל אָלָה וְהוּא
and-he public-charge report-of when-she-hears she-sins if and-person (5:1)

עֵד אוֹ רָאָה אוֹ יָדָע אִם־ לוֹא יַגִּיד וְנָשָׂא
then-he-will-bear he-speaks-up not but he-knows or he-was or witness

עֲוֹנוֹ׃ (2) אוֹ נֶפֶשׁ אֲשֶׁר תִּגַּע בְּכָל־ דָּבָר טָמֵא
unclean thing on-any-of she-touches who person or (2) responsibility-of-him

אוֹ בְנִבְלַת חַיָּה טְמֵאָה אוֹ בְּנִבְלַת בְּהֵמָה טְמֵאָה אוֹ
or unclean livestock on-carcass-of or unclean animal on-carcass-of whether

בְּנִבְלַת שֶׁרֶץ טָמֵא וְנֶעְלַם מִמֶּנּוּ וְהוּא טָמֵא
unclean then-he of-him and-he-is-unaware unclean creeper on-carcass-of

וְאָשֵׁם׃ (3) אוֹ כִי יִגַּע בְּטֻמְאַת אָדָם לְכֹל
on-any-of human on-uncleanness-of he-touches if or (3) and-he-is-guilty

טֻמְאָתוֹ אֲשֶׁר יִטְמָא בָּהּ וְנֶעְלַם מִמֶּנּוּ
of-him and-he-is-unaware by-her he-would-be-unclean that uncleanness-of-him

וְהוּא יָדַע וְאָשֵׁם׃ (4) אוֹ נֶפֶשׁ כִּי תִשָּׁבַע
she-takes-oath if person or (4) then-he-will-be-guilty he-learns when-he

לְבַטֵּא בִשְׂפָתַיִם לְהָרַע ׀ אוֹ לְהֵיטִיב לְכֹל אֲשֶׁר יְבַטֵּא
he-is-careless that in-any to-do-good or to-do-evil with-lips to-be-careless

הָאָדָם בִּשְׁבֻעָה וְנֶעְלַם מִמֶּנּוּ וְהוּא־ יָדַע
he-learns when-he of-him and-he-is-unaware with-oath the-man

וְאָשֵׁם לְאַחַת מֵאֵלֶּה׃ (5) וְהָיָה כִי־ יֶאְשַׁם
he-is-guilty when and-he-will-be (5) of-these in-any then-he-will-be-guilty

slaughter it for a sin offering at
the place where the burnt
offering is slaughtered. 34Then
the priest shall take some of
the blood of the sin offering
with his finger and put it on
the horns of the altar of burnt
offering and pour out the rest
of the blood at the base of the
altar. 35He shall remove all the
fat, just as the fat is removed
from the lamb of the fellowship offering, and the priest
shall burn it on the altar on top
of the offerings made to the
LORD by fire. In this way the
priest will make atonement for
him for the sin he has committed, and he will be forgiven.

5 " 'If a person sins because
he does not speak up
when he hears a public charge
to testify regarding something
he has seen or learned about,
he will be held responsible.
2" 'Or if a person touches
anything ceremonially un-
clean—whether the carcasses
of unclean wild animals or of
unclean livestock or of unclean creatures that move
along the ground—even
though he is unaware of it, he
has become unclean and is
guilty.
3" 'Or if he touches human
uncleanness—anything that
would make him unclean—
even though he is unaware of
it, when he learns of it he will
be guilty.
4" 'Or if a person thought-
lessly takes an oath to do anything, whether good or evil—
in any matter one might care-
lessly swear about—even
though he is unaware of it, in
any case when he learns of it
he will be guilty.
5" 'When anyone is guilty in

*35 Most mss have *mappiq* in the *he* (בָּהּ-).

לְאַחַת מֵאֵלֶּה וְהִתְוַדָּה אֲשֶׁר חָטָא עָלֶיהָ׃
by-her he-sinned what-way then-he-must-confess of-these in-any

וְהֵבִיא אֶת־ אֲשָׁמוֹ לַיהוָה עַל חַטָּאתוֹ אֲשֶׁר חָטָא
he-sinned that sin-of-him for to-Yahweh penalty-of-him *** and-he-must-bring (6)

נְקֵבָה מִן־ הַצֹּאן כִּשְׂבָּה אוֹ־ שְׂעִירַת עִזִּים לְחַטָּאת
as-sin-offering goats female-goat-of or lamb the-flock from female

וְכִפֶּר עָלָיו הַכֹּהֵן מֵחַטָּאתוֹ׃ וְאִם־ לֹא
not and-if (7) for-sin-of-him the-priest for-him and-he-shall-atone

תַגִּיע* יָדוֹ דֵּי שֶׂה וְהֵבִיא אֶת־ אֲשָׁמוֹ
penalty-of-him *** then-he-must-bring lamb amount-of hand-of-him she-can-afford

אֲשֶׁר חָטָא שְׁתֵּי תֹרִים אוֹ־ שְׁנֵי בְנֵי־ יוֹנָה לַיהוָה אֶחָד
one to-Yahweh pigeon young-ones-of two-of or doves two-of he-sinned that

לְחַטָּאת וְאֶחָד לְעֹלָה׃ וְהֵבִיא אֹתָם אֶל־
to them and-he-must-bring (8) for-burnt-offering and-other for-sin-offering

הַכֹּהֵן וְהִקְרִיב אֶת־ אֲשֶׁר לַחַטָּאת רִאשׁוֹנָה
first for-the-sin-offering one *** and-he-shall-offer the-priest

וּמָלַק אֶת־ רֹאשׁוֹ מִמּוּל עָרְפּוֹ וְלֹא יַבְדִּיל׃
he-shall-sever but-not neck-of-him from-on head-of-him *** and-he-shall-wring

וְהִזָּה מִדַּם הַחַטָּאת עַל־ קִיר הַמִּזְבֵּחַ
the-altar side-of on the-sin-offering from-blood-of and-he-shall-sprinkle (9)

וְהַנִּשְׁאָר בַּדָּם יִמָּצֵה אֶל־ יְסוֹד הַמִּזְבֵּחַ
the-altar base-of at he-must-be-drained of-the-blood and-the-being-left

חַטָּאת הוּא׃ וְאֶת־ הַשֵּׁנִי יַעֲשֶׂה עֹלָה
burnt-offering he-shall-offer the-other and (10) he sin-offering

כַּמִּשְׁפָּט וְכִפֶּר עָלָיו הַכֹּהֵן מֵחַטָּאתוֹ אֲשֶׁר־
that for-sin-of-him the-priest for-him and-he-shall-atone as-the-direction

חָטָא וְנִסְלַח לוֹ׃ וְאִם־ לֹא תַשִּׂיג
she-can-afford not and-if (11) to-him and-he-will-be-forgiven he-sinned

יָדוֹ לִשְׁתֵּי תֹרִים אוֹ לִשְׁנֵי בְנֵי־ יוֹנָה
pigeon young-ones-of for-two-of or doves for-two-of hand-of-him

וְהֵבִיא אֶת־ קָרְבָּנוֹ אֲשֶׁר חָטָא עֲשִׂירִת הָאֵפָה
the-ephah tenth-of he-sinned that offering-of-him *** then-he-must-bring

סֹלֶת לְחַטָּאת לֹא־ יָשִׂים עָלֶיהָ שֶׁמֶן וְלֹא־ יִתֵּן עָלֶיהָ
on-her he-must-put and-not oil on-her he-must-put not for-sin-offering flour

לְבֹנָה כִּי חַטָּאת הִיא׃ וֶהֱבִיאָה† אֶל־ הַכֹּהֵן
the-priest to and-he-must-bring-her (12) she sin-offering for incense

וְקָמַץ הַכֹּהֵן | מִמֶּנָּה מְלוֹא קֻמְצוֹ אֶת־ אַזְכָּרָתָהּ
memorial-portion-of-her *** hand-of-him full-of from-her the-priest and-he-shall-take

any of these ways, he must
confess in what way he has
sinned 6 and, as a penalty for
the sin he has committed, he
must bring to the LORD a
female lamb or goat from the
flock as a sin offering; and the
priest shall make atonement
for him for his sin.
7 "'If he cannot afford a
lamb, he is to bring two doves
or two young pigeons to the
LORD as a penalty for his sin—
one for a sin offering and the
other for a burnt offering. 8 He
is to bring them to the priest,
who shall first offer the one for
the sin offering. He is to wring
its head from its neck, not severing it completely, 9 and is to
sprinkle some of the blood of
the sin offering against the
side of the altar; the rest of the
blood must be drained out at
the base of the altar. It is a sin
offering. 10 The priest shall
then offer the other as a burnt
offering in the prescribed way
and make atonement for him
for the sin he has committed,
and he will be forgiven.
11 "'If, however, he cannot
afford two doves or two young
pigeons, he is to bring as an
offering for his sin a tenth of
an ephah[g] of fine flour for a
sin offering. He must not put
oil or incense on it, because it
is a sin offering. 12 He is to
bring it to the priest, who shall
take a handful of it as a
memorial portion and burn it

g11 That is, probably about 2 quarts (about 2 liters)

*7 Most mss have furtive *pathah* under the *ayin* (עַ–).

†12 Most mss have *mappiq* in the *he* (הּ–).

וְהִקְטִיר הַמִּזְבֵּחָה עַל אִשֵּׁי יְהוָה חַטָּאת הִוא׃
she sin-offering Yahweh fire-offerings-of upon on-the-altar and-he-shall-burn

(13) וְכִפֶּר עָלָיו הַכֹּהֵן עַל־ חַטָּאתוֹ אֲשֶׁר־ חָטָא
he-sinned that sin-of-him for the-priest for-him so-he-shall-atone (13)

מֵאַחַת מֵאֵלֶּה וְנִסְלַח לוֹ וְהָיְתָה לַכֹּהֵן
for-the-priest and-she-will-be to-him and-he-will-be-forgiven of-these for-any

כַּמִּנְחָה׃ (14) וַיְדַבֵּר יְהוָה אֶל־מֹשֶׁה לֵּאמֹר׃ (15) נֶפֶשׁ
person (15) to-say Moses to Yahweh and-he-spoke (14) as-the-grain-offering

כִּי־ תִמְעֹל מַעַל וְחָטְאָה בִּשְׁגָגָה מִקָּדְשֵׁי
at-holy-things-of without-intention and-she-sins violation she-commits when

יְהוָה וְהֵבִיא אֶת־ אֲשָׁמוֹ לַיהוָה אַיִל תָּמִים
without-defect ram to-Yahweh penalty-of-him *** then-he-must-bring Yahweh

מִן־ הַצֹּאן בְּעֶרְכְּךָ כֶּסֶף־ שְׁקָלִים בְּשֶׁקֶל־ הַקֹּדֶשׁ
the-sanctuary as-shekel-of shekels silver of-value-of-you the-flock from

לְאָשָׁם׃ (16) וְאֵת אֲשֶׁר חָטָא מִן־ הַקֹּדֶשׁ
the-holy-things from he-neglected what and (16) for-guilt-offering

יְשַׁלֵּם וְאֶת־ חֲמִישִׁתוֹ יוֹסֵף עָלָיו וְנָתַן אֹתוֹ
him and-he-must-give to-him he-must-add fifth-of-him and he-must-restitute

לַכֹּהֵן וְהַכֹּהֵן יְכַפֵּר עָלָיו בְּאֵיל
with-ram-of for-him he-will-atone and-the-priest to-the-priest

הָאָשָׁם וְנִסְלַח לוֹ׃ (17) וְאִם־ נֶפֶשׁ כִּי
when person and-if (17) to-him and-he-will-be-forgiven the-guilt-offering

תֶחֱטָא וְעָשְׂתָה אַחַת מִכָּל־ מִצְוֹת יְהוָה אֲשֶׁר לֹא
not that Yahweh commands-of from-any-of one and-she-does she-sins

תֵעָשֶׂינָה וְלֹא־ יָדַע וְאָשֵׁם וְנָשָׂא
and-he-bears then-he-is-guilty he-knows and-not they-may-be-done

עֲוֹנוֹ׃ (18) וְהֵבִיא אַיִל תָּמִים מִן־
from without-defect ram then-he-must-bring (18) responsibility-of-him

הַצֹּאן בְּעֶרְכְּךָ לְאָשָׁם אֶל־ הַכֹּהֵן וְכִפֶּר
so-he-will-atone the-priest to as-guilt-offering of-value-of-you the-flock

עָלָיו הַכֹּהֵן עַל שִׁגְגָתוֹ אֲשֶׁר־ שָׁגָג וְהוּא לֹא־ יָדַע
he-knew not but-he he-committed that wrong-of-him for the-priest for-him

וְנִסְלַח לוֹ׃ (19) אָשָׁם הוּא אָשֹׁם
to-do-wrong he guilt-offering (19) to-him and-he-will-be-forgiven

אָשַׁם לַיהוָה׃ *(20[1]) וַיְדַבֵּר יְהוָה אֶל־ מֹשֶׁה לֵּאמֹר׃
to-say Moses to Yahweh and-he-spoke *(20[1]) against-Yahweh he-did-wrong

(21[2]) נֶפֶשׁ כִּי תֶחֱטָא וּמָעֲלָה מַעַל בַּיהוָה
against-Yahweh violation and-she-commits she-sins if person (21[2])

on the altar on top of the offerings made to the LORD by fire. It is a sin offering.
13In this way the priest will make atonement for him for any of these sins he has committed, and he will be forgiven. The rest of the offering will belong to the priest, as in the case of the grain offering.' "

The Guilt Offering

14The LORD said to Moses:
15"When a person commits a violation and sins unintentionally in regard to any of the LORD's holy things, he is to bring to the LORD as a penalty a ram from the flock, one without defect and of the proper value in silver, according to the sanctuary shekel.[h] It is a guilt offering.
16He must make restitution for what he has failed to do in regard to the holy things, add a fifth of the value to that and give it all to the priest, who will make atonement for him with the ram as a guilt offering, and he will be forgiven.
17"If a person sins and does what is forbidden in any of the LORD's commands, even though he does not know it, he is guilty and will be held responsible.
18He is to bring to the priest as a guilt offering a ram from the flock, one without defect and of the proper value. In this way the priest will make atonement for him for the wrong he has committed unintentionally, and he will be forgiven.
19It is a guilt offering; he has been guilty of[i] wrongdoing against the LORD."

6 The LORD said to Moses:
2"If anyone sins and is

[h]15 That is, about 2/5 ounce (about 11.5 grams)
[i]19 Or *has made full expiation for his*

*The Hebrew numeration of chapter 6 begins with verse 8 in English. The number in brackets indicates the English numeration.

וְכִחֵשׁ בַּעֲמִיתוֹ בְּפִקָּדוֹן אוֹ־ בִתְשׂוּמֶת
about-something-left-of or about-trust against-neighbor-of-him and-he-deceives

יָד אוֹ בְגָזֵל אוֹ עָשַׁק אֶת־ עֲמִיתוֹ׃ אוֹ־ מָצָא
he-finds or (22[3]) neighbor-of-him *** he-cheats or about-stolen or care

אֲבֵדָה וְכִחֶשׁ בָּהּ וְנִשְׁבַּע עַל־ שָׁקֶר עַל־ אַחַת
one about falsehood with or-he-swears about-her and-he-lies lost-property

מִכֹּל אֲשֶׁר־ יַעֲשֶׂה הָאָדָם לַחֲטֹא בָהֵנָּה׃ וְהָיָה כִּי־
when and-he-will-be (23[4]) by-them to-sin the-man he-does that of-any

יֶחֱטָא וְאָשֵׁם וְהֵשִׁיב אֶת־ הַגְּזֵלָה אֲשֶׁר
that the-stolen-thing *** that-he-must-return and-he-becomes-guilty he-sins

גָּזָל אוֹ אֶת־ הָעֹשֶׁק אֲשֶׁר עָשָׁק אוֹ אֶת־ הַפִּקָּדוֹן אֲשֶׁר הָפְקַד
he-was-left that the-trust *** or he-extorted that the-thing *** or he-stole

אִתּוֹ אוֹ אֶת־ הָאֲבֵדָה אֲשֶׁר מָצָא׃ אוֹ מִכֹּל אֲשֶׁר־
that what-ever or (24[5]) he-found that the-lost-property *** or with-him

יִשָּׁבַע עָלָיו לַשֶּׁקֶר וְשִׁלַּם אֹתוֹ בְּרֹאשׁוֹ
in-full-of-him him and-he-must-restitute with-the-falsehood about-him he-swore

וַחֲמִשִׁתָיו יֹסֵף עָלָיו לַאֲשֶׁר הוּא לוֹ יִתְּנֶנּוּ
he-must-give-him to-him he to-whom to-him he-must-add and-fifth-of-him

בְּיוֹם אַשְׁמָתוֹ׃ וְאֶת־ אֲשָׁמוֹ יָבִיא
he-must-bring penalty-of-him and (25[6]) guilt-offering-of-him on-day-of

לַיהוָה אַיִל תָּמִים מִן־ הַצֹּאן בְּעֶרְכְּךָ לְאָשָׁם
as-guilt-offering of-value-of-you the-flock from without-defect ram to-Yahweh

אֶל־ הַכֹּהֵן׃ וְכִפֶּר עָלָיו הַכֹּהֵן לִפְנֵי יְהוָה
Yahweh before the-priest for-him so-he-will-atone (26[7]) the-priest to

וְנִסְלַח לוֹ עַל־ אַחַת מִכֹּל אֲשֶׁר־ יַעֲשֶׂה לְאַשְׁמָה בָהּ׃
by-her for-guilt he-did that from-all any for to-him and-he-will-be-forgiven

וַיְדַבֵּר יְהוָה אֶל־ מֹשֶׁה לֵּאמֹר׃ צַו אֶת־ אַהֲרֹן
Aaron *** command! (2[9]) to-say Moses to Yahweh and-he-spoke (6:1[8])

וְאֶת־ בָּנָיו לֵאמֹר זֹאת תּוֹרַת הָעֹלָה הִוא
she the-burnt-offering regulation-of this to-say sons-of-him and

הָעֹלָה עַל[9] מוֹקְדָה עַל־ הַמִּזְבֵּחַ כָּל־ הַלַּיְלָה עַד־ הַבֹּקֶר
the-morning till the-night all-of the-altar on hearth on the-burnt-offering

וְאֵשׁ הַמִּזְבֵּחַ תּוּקַד בּוֹ׃ וְלָבַשׁ
and-he-shall-put-on (3[10]) on-him she-must-burn the-altar and-fire-of

הַכֹּהֵן מִדּוֹ בַד וּמִכְנְסֵי־ בַד יִלְבַּשׁ עַל־
on he-shall-put linen and-undergarments-of linen garment-of-him the-priest

בְּשָׂרוֹ וְהֵרִים אֶת־ הַדֶּשֶׁן אֲשֶׁר תֹּאכַל הָאֵשׁ
the-fire she-consumed that the-ash *** and-he-shall-remove body-of-him

unfaithful to the LORD by de-
ceiving his neighbor about
something entrusted to him or
left in his care or stolen, or if
he cheats him, 3or if he finds
lost property and lies about it,
or if he swears falsely, or if he
commits any such sin that
people may do— 4when he
thus sins and becomes guilty,
he must return what he has
stolen or taken by extortion, or
what was entrusted to him, or
the lost property he found, 5or
whatever it was he swore
falsely about. He must make
restitution in full, add a fifth of
the value to it and give it all to
the owner on the day he
presents his guilt offering.
6And as a penalty he must
bring to the priest, that is, to
the LORD, his guilt offering, a
ram from the flock, one without defect and of the proper
value. 7In this way the priest
will make atonement for him
before the LORD, and he will be
forgiven for any of these
things he did that made him
guilty."

The Burnt Offering

8The LORD said to Moses:
9"Give Aaron and his sons
this command: 'These are the
regulations for the burnt
offering: The burnt offering is
to remain on the altar hearth
throughout the night, till
morning, and the fire must be
kept burning on the altar.
10The priest shall then put on
his linen clothes, with linen
undergarments next to his
body, and shall remove the
ashes of the burnt offering
that the fire has consumed on

*See the note on page 278.

אֶת־ הָעֹלָה עַל־ הַמִּזְבֵּחַ וְשָׂמוֹ אֵצֶל הַמִּזְבֵּחַ׃
the-altar beside and-he-shall-place-him the-altar on the-burnt-offering ***

וּפָשַׁט אֶת־ בְּגָדָיו וְלָבַשׁ בְּגָדִים
clothes and-he-shall-put-on clothes-of-him *** then-he-shall-take-off (4[11])

אֲחֵרִים וְהוֹצִיא אֶת־ הַדֶּשֶׁן אֶל־ מִחוּץ לַמַּחֲנֶה אֶל־ מָקוֹם
place to of-the-camp outside to the-ash *** and-he-shall-carry other-ones

טָהוֹר׃ וְהָאֵשׁ עַל־ הַמִּזְבֵּחַ תּוּקַד־ בּוֹ לֹא
not on-him she-must-burn the-altar on and-the-fire (5[12]) clean

תִכְבֶּה וּבִעֵר עָלֶיהָ הַכֹּהֵן עֵצִים בַּבֹּקֶר
in-the-morning woods the-priest on-her and-he-must-burn she-must-go-out

בַּבֹּקֶר וְעָרַךְ עָלֶיהָ הָעֹלָה וְהִקְטִיר
and-he-must-burn the-burnt-offering on-her and-he-must-arrange in-the-morning

עָלֶיהָ חֶלְבֵי הַשְּׁלָמִים׃ אֵשׁ תָּמִיד
continuously fire (6[13]) the-fellowship-offerings fats-of on-her

תּוּקַד עַל־ הַמִּזְבֵּחַ לֹא תִכְבֶּה׃† וְזֹאת תּוֹרַת
regulation-of and-this (7[14]) she-must-go-out not the-altar on she-must-burn

הַמִּנְחָה הַקְרֵב אֹתָהּ בְּנֵי־ אַהֲרֹן לִפְנֵי יְהוָה אֶל־ פְּנֵי
front-of to Yahweh before Aaron sons-of her he-must-bring the-grain-offering

הַמִּזְבֵּחַ׃ וְהֵרִים מִמֶּנּוּ בְּקֻמְצוֹ מִסֹּלֶת
from-flour-of with-handful-of-him from-him and-he-must-take (8[15]) the-altar

הַמִּנְחָה וּמִשַּׁמְנָהּ וְאֵת כָּל־ הַלְּבֹנָה אֲשֶׁר עַל־
on that the-incense all-of and and-from-oil-of-her the-grain-offering

הַמִּנְחָה וְהִקְטִיר הַמִּזְבֵּחַ רֵיחַ נִיחֹחַ
pleasant aroma-of the-altar and-he-must-burn the-grain-offering

אַזְכָּרָתָהּ לַיהוָה׃ וְהַנּוֹתֶרֶת מִמֶּנָּה
from-her and-the-being-left (9[16]) to-Yahweh memorial-portion-of-her

יֹאכְלוּ אַהֲרֹן וּבָנָיו מַצּוֹת תֵּאָכֵל בְּמָקוֹם
in-place she-must-be-eaten without-yeast and-sons-of-him Aaron they-shall-eat

קָדֹשׁ בַּחֲצַר אֹהֶל־ מוֹעֵד יֹאכְלוּהָ׃ לֹא
not (10[17]) they-shall-eat-her Meeting Tent-of in-courtyard-of holy

תֵאָפֶה חָמֵץ חֶלְקָם נָתַתִּי אֹתָהּ מֵאִשָּׁי
from-fire-offerings-of-me her I-gave share-of-them yeast she-must-be-baked

קֹדֶשׁ קָדָשִׁים הִוא כַּחַטָּאת וְכָאָשָׁם׃
and-like-the-guilt-offering like-the-sin-offering she holy-ones holiest-of

כָּל־ זָכָר בִּבְנֵי אַהֲרֹן יֹאכְלֶנָּה חָק־ עוֹלָם
regular share-of he-may-eat-her Aaron among-sons-of male any-of (11[18])

לְדֹרֹתֵיכֶם מֵאִשֵּׁי יְהוָה כֹּל אֲשֶׁר־ יִגַּע
he-touches that anything Yahweh from-fire-offerings-of for-generations-of-you

the altar and place them beside the altar. [11]Then he is to take off these clothes and put on others, and carry the ashes outside the camp to a place that is ceremonially clean. [12]The fire on the altar must be kept burning; it must not go out. Every morning the priest is to add firewood and arrange the burnt offering on the fire and burn the fat of the fellowship offerings[j] on it. [13]The fire must be kept burning on the altar continuously; it must not go out.

The Grain Offering

[14]" 'These are the regulations for the grain offering: Aaron's sons are to bring it before the LORD, in front of the altar. [15]The priest is to take a handful of fine flour and oil, together with all the incense on the grain offering, and burn the memorial portion on the altar as an aroma pleasing to the LORD. [16]Aaron and his sons shall eat the rest of it, but it is to be eaten without yeast in a holy place; they are to eat it in the courtyard of the Tent of Meeting. [17]It must not be baked with yeast; I have given it as their share of the offerings made to me by fire. Like the sin offering and the guilt offering, it is most holy. [18]Any male descendant of Aaron may eat it. It is his regular share of the offerings made to the LORD by fire for the generations to come. Whatever[k]

j12 Traditionally *peace offerings*
k18 Or *Whoever*; also in verse 27

*See the note on page 278.

†6 Most mss have *dagesh* in the *beth* (בּה–).

בָּהֶם יִקְדָּשׁ׃ (12[19]) וַיְדַבֵּר יְהוָה אֶל־ מֹשֶׁה לֵּאמֹר׃
to-say Moses to Yahweh and-he-spoke (12[19]) he-will-become-holy on-them

(13[20]) זֶה קָרְבַּן אַהֲרֹן וּבָנָיו אֲשֶׁר־ יַקְרִיבוּ
they-must-bring that and-sons-of-him Aaron offering-of this (13[20])

לַיהוָה בְּיוֹם הִמָּשַׁח אֹתוֹ עֲשִׂירִת הָאֵפָה סֹלֶת
fine-flour the-ephah tenth-of him to-be-anointed on-day to-Yahweh

מִנְחָה תָּמִיד מַחֲצִיתָהּ בַּבֹּקֶר וּמַחֲצִיתָהּ
and-half-of-her in-the-morning half-of-her regular grain-offering

בָּעָרֶב׃ (14[21]) עַל־ מַחֲבַת בַּשֶּׁמֶן תֵּעָשֶׂה
she-must-be-prepared with-the-oil griddle on (14[21]) in-the-evening

מֻרְבֶּכֶת תְּבִיאֶנָּה תֻּפִינֵי מִנְחַת פִּתִּים תַּקְרִיב
you-present pieces grain-offering-of ones-broken-of you-bring-her being-mixed

רֵיחַ־ נִיחֹחַ לַיהוָה׃ (15[22]) וְהַכֹּהֵן הַמָּשִׁיחַ תַּחְתָּיו
after-him the-anointed and-the-priest (15[22]) to-Yahweh pleasant aroma-of

מִבָּנָיו יַעֲשֶׂה אֹתָהּ חָק־ עוֹלָם לַיהוָה כָּלִיל
completely for-Yahweh regular share-of her he-shall-prepare from-sons-of-him

תָּקְטָר׃ (16[23]) וְכָל־ מִנְחַת כֹּהֵן כָּלִיל
completely priest grain-offering-of and-every-of (16[23]) she-must-be-burned

תִּהְיֶה לֹא תֵאָכֵל׃ (17[24]) וַיְדַבֵּר יְהוָה אֶל־ מֹשֶׁה
Moses to Yahweh and-he-spoke (17[24]) she-must-be-eaten not she-must-be

לֵּאמֹר׃ (18[25]) דַּבֵּר אֶל־ אַהֲרֹן וְאֶל־ בָּנָיו לֵאמֹר זֹאת תּוֹרַת
regulation-of this to-say sons-of-him and-to Aaron to say! (18[25]) to-say

הַחַטָּאת בִּמְקוֹם אֲשֶׁר תִּשָּׁחֵט הָעֹלָה
the-burnt-offering she-is-slaughtered where in-place the-sin-offering

תִּשָּׁחֵט הַחַטָּאת לִפְנֵי יְהוָה קֹדֶשׁ קָדָשִׁים הִוא׃
she holy-ones most-holy-of Yahweh before the-sin-offering she-is-slaughtered

(19[26]) הַכֹּהֵן הַמְחַטֵּא אֹתָהּ יֹאכְלֶנָּה בְּמָקוֹם קָדֹשׁ
holy in-place he-shall-eat-her her the-one-offering the-priest (19[26])

תֵּאָכֵל בַּחֲצַר אֹהֶל מוֹעֵד׃ (20[27]) כֹּל אֲשֶׁר־
that anything (20[27]) Meeting Tent-of in-courtyard-of she-must-be-eaten

יִגַּע בִּבְשָׂרָהּ יִקְדָּשׁ וַאֲשֶׁר יִזֶּה
he-is-spattered and-if he-will-become-holy on-flesh-of-her he-touches

מִדָּמָהּ עַל־ הַבֶּגֶד אֲשֶׁר יִזֶּה עָלֶיהָ תְּכַבֵּס
you-wash with-her he-is-spattered whatever the-garment on from-blood-of-her

בְּמָקוֹם קָדֹשׁ׃ (21[28]) וּכְלִי־ חֶרֶשׂ אֲשֶׁר תְּבֻשַּׁל־ בּוֹ
in-him she-is-cooked that clay and-pot-of (21[28]) holy in-place

יִשָּׁבֵר וְאִם־ בִּכְלִי נְחֹשֶׁת בֻּשָּׁלָה וּמֹרַק
he-must-be-scoured she-is-cooked bronze in-pot-of but-if he-must-be-broken

touches it will become holy.' "
19The LORD also said to
Moses, 20"This is the offering
Aaron and his sons are to
bring to the LORD on the day
he[l] is anointed: a tenth of an
ephah[m] of fine flour as a regular grain offering, half of it in
the morning and half in the
evening. 21Prepare it with oil
on a griddle; bring it well-mix-
ed and present the grain
offering broken[n] in pieces as
an aroma pleasing to the LORD.
22The son who is to succeed
him as anointed priest shall
prepare it. It is the LORD's regular share and is to be burned
completely. 23Every grain
offering of a priest shall be
burned completely; it must not
be eaten."

The Sin Offering

24The LORD said to Moses,
25"Say to Aaron and his sons:
'These are the regulations for
the sin offering: The sin
offering is to be slaughtered
before the LORD in the place
the burnt offering is slaughtered; it is most holy. 26The
priest who offers it shall eat it;
it is to be eaten in a holy place,
in the courtyard of the Tent of
Meeting. 27Whatever touches
any of the flesh will become
holy, and if any of the blood is
spattered on a garment, you
must wash it in a holy place.
28The clay pot the meat is
cooked in must be broken; but
if it is cooked in a bronze pot,
the pot is to be scoured and

[l]20 Or *each*
[m]20 That is, probably about 2 quarts (about 2 liters)
[n]21 The meaning of the Hebrew for this word is uncertain.

*See the note on page 278.

וְשֻׁטַּף בַּמָּיִם׃ כָּל־ זָכָר בַּכֹּהֲנִים
from-the-priests male any-of (22[29]) with-the-waters and-he-must-be-rinsed

יֹאכַל אֹתָהּ קֹדֶשׁ קָדָשִׁים הִוא׃ וְכָל־ חַטָּאת
sin-offering but-any-of (23[30]) she holy-ones most-holy-of her he-may-eat

אֲשֶׁר יוּבָא מִדָּמָהּ אֶל־ אֹהֶל מוֹעֵד לְכַפֵּר
to-make-atonement Meeting Tent-of into from-blood-of-her he-is-brought that

בַּקֹּדֶשׁ לֹא תֵאָכֵל בָּאֵשׁ תִּשָּׂרֵף׃
she-must-be-burned in-the-fire she-must-be-eaten not in-the-holy-place

וְזֹאת תּוֹרַת הָאָשָׁם קֹדֶשׁ קָדָשִׁים הוּא׃
he holy-ones most-holy-of the-guilt-offering regulation-of and-this (7:1)

בִּמְקוֹם אֲשֶׁר יִשְׁחֲטוּ אֶת־ הָעֹלָה יִשְׁחֲטוּ
they-must-slaughter the-burnt-offering *** they-slaughter where in-place (2)

אֶת־ הָאָשָׁם וְאֶת־ דָּמוֹ יִזְרֹק עַל־ הַמִּזְבֵּחַ
the-altar against he-must-sprinkle blood-of-him and the-guilt-offering ***

סָבִיב׃ וְאֵת כָּל־ חֶלְבּוֹ יַקְרִיב מִמֶּנּוּ אֵת הָאַלְיָה
the-fat-tail *** from-him he-shall-offer fat-of-him all-of and (3) around

וְאֶת־ הַחֵלֶב הַמְכַסֶּה אֶת־ הַקֶּרֶב׃ וְאֵת שְׁתֵּי הַכְּלָיֹת וְאֶת־
and the-kidneys both-of and (4) the-inner-part *** the-cover the-fat and

הַחֵלֶב אֲשֶׁר עֲלֵיהֶן אֲשֶׁר עַל־ הַכְּסָלִים וְאֶת־ הַיֹּתֶרֶת עַל־ הַכָּבֵד
the-liver on the-cover and the-loins near that around-them that the-fat

עַל־ הַכְּלָיֹת יְסִירֶנָּה׃ וְהִקְטִיר אֹתָם הַכֹּהֵן
the-priest them and-he-shall-burn (5) he-must-remove-her the-kidneys with

הַמִּזְבֵּחָה אִשֶּׁה לַיהוָה אָשָׁם הוּא׃ כָּל־ זָכָר
male any-of (6) he guilt-offering to-Yahweh fire-offering on-the-altar

בַּכֹּהֲנִים יֹאכְלֶנּוּ בְּמָקוֹם קָדוֹשׁ יֵאָכֵל קֹדֶשׁ
most-holy-of he-must-be-eaten holy in-place he-may-eat-him from-the-priests

קָדָשִׁים הוּא׃ כַּחַטָּאת כָּאָשָׁם תּוֹרָה אַחַת
same regulation so-the-guilt-offering as-the-sin-offering (7) he holy-ones

לָהֶם הַכֹּהֵן אֲשֶׁר יְכַפֶּר־ בּוֹ לוֹ יִהְיֶה׃ וְהַכֹּהֵן
and-the-priest (8) he-is for-him with-him he-atones who the-priest for-them

הַמַּקְרִיב אֶת־ עֹלַת אִישׁ עוֹר הָעֹלָה
the-burnt-offering hide-of anyone burnt-offering-of *** the-one-offering

אֲשֶׁר הִקְרִיב לַכֹּהֵן לוֹ יִהְיֶה׃ וְכָל־ מִנְחָה
grain-offering and-every-of (9) he-is for-him for-the-priest he-offers that

אֲשֶׁר תֵּאָפֶה בַּתַּנּוּר וְכָל־ נַעֲשָׂה בַמַּרְחֶשֶׁת וְעַל־ מַחֲבַת
griddle or-on in-the-pan being-cooked or-every-of in-the-oven she-is-baked that

לַכֹּהֵן הַמַּקְרִיב אֹתָהּ לוֹ תִהְיֶה׃ וְכָל־
and-every-of (10) she-is for-him her the-one-offering for-the-priest

rinsed with water. [29]Any male in a priest's family may eat it; it is most holy. [30]But any sin offering whose blood is brought into the Tent of Meeting to make atonement in the Holy Place must not be eaten; it must be burned.

The Guilt Offering

7 " 'These are the regulations for the guilt offering, which is most holy: [2]The guilt offering is to be slaughtered in the place where the burnt offering is slaughtered, and its blood is to be sprinkled against the altar on all sides. [3]All its fat shall be offered: the fat tail and the fat that covers the inner parts, [4]both kidneys with the fat around them near the loins, and the covering of the liver, which is to be removed with the kidneys. [5]The priest shall burn them on the altar as an offering made to the LORD by fire. It is a guilt offering. [6]Any male in a priest's family may eat it, but it must be eaten in a holy place; it is most holy.

[7]" 'The same law applies to both the sin offering and the guilt offering: They belong to the priest who makes atonement with them. [8]The priest who offers a burnt offering for anyone may keep its hide for himself. [9]Every grain offering baked in an oven or cooked in a pan or on a griddle belongs to the priest who offers it,

*See the note on page 278.

מִנְחָה בְּלוּלָה־ בַשֶּׁמֶן וַחֲרֵבָה לְכָל־ בְּנֵי אַהֲרֹן
Aaron sons-of for-all-of or-dry with-the-oil being-mixed grain-offering

תִּהְיֶה אִישׁ כְּאָחִיו׃ (11) וְזֹאת תּוֹרַת זֶבַח
offering-of regulation-of and-this (11) equal-with-brother-of-him each she-is

הַשְּׁלָמִים אֲשֶׁר יַקְרִיב לַיהוָה׃ (12) אִם עַל־ תּוֹדָה
thankfulness for if (12) to-Yahweh he-may-present that the-fellowships

יַקְרִיבֶנּוּ וְהִקְרִיב | עַל־ זֶבַח הַתּוֹדָה חַלּוֹת
cakes-of the-thanksgiving sacrifice-of with then-he-must-offer he-offers-him

מַצּוֹת בְּלוּלֹת בַּשֶּׁמֶן וּרְקִיקֵי
and-wafers-of with-the-oil ones-being-mixed breads-without-yeast

מַצּוֹת מְשֻׁחִים בַּשָּׁמֶן וְסֹלֶת מֻרְבֶּכֶת
being-kneaded and-fine-flour with-the-oil ones-being-spread without-yeast

חַלֹּת בְּלוּלֹת בַּשָּׁמֶן׃ (13) עַל־ חַלֹּת לֶחֶם חָמֵץ
without-yeast bread cakes-of with (13) with-the-oil ones-being-mixed cakes

יַקְרִיב קָרְבָּנוֹ עַל־ זֶבַח תּוֹדַת
thanksgiving-of offering-of with offering-of-him he-must-present

שְׁלָמָיו׃ (14) וְהִקְרִיב מִמֶּנּוּ אֶחָד מִכָּל־ קָרְבָּן
offering from-every-of one from-him and-he-must-bring (14) fellowships-of-him

תְּרוּמָה לַיהוָה לַכֹּהֵן הַזֹּרֵק אֶת־ דַּם
blood-of *** the-one-sprinkling for-the-priest to-Yahweh contribution

הַשְּׁלָמִים לוֹ יִהְיֶה׃ (15) וּבְשַׂר זֶבַח
offering-of and-meat-of (15) he-is for-him the-fellowship-offerings

תּוֹדַת שְׁלָמָיו בְּיוֹם קָרְבָּנוֹ יֵאָכֵל
he-must-be-eaten offering-of-him on-day-of fellowships-of-him thanksgiving-of

לֹא־ יַנִּיחַ מִמֶּנּוּ עַד־ בֹּקֶר׃ (16) וְאִם־ נֶדֶר | אוֹ נְדָבָה
freewill or vow but-if (16) morning till from-him he-must-leave not

זֶבַח קָרְבָּנוֹ בְּיוֹם הַקְרִיבוֹ אֶת־ זִבְחוֹ
sacrifice-of-him *** to-offer-him on-day offering-of-him sacrifice-of

יֵאָכֵל וּמִמָּחֳרָת וְהַנּוֹתָר מִמֶּנּוּ
from-him also-the-being-left but-on-next-day he-shall-be-eaten

יֵאָכֵל׃ (17) וְהַנּוֹתָר מִבְּשַׂר הַזָּבַח בַּיּוֹם
on-the-day the-sacrifice from-meat-of and-the-being-left (17) he-may-be-eaten

הַשְּׁלִישִׁי בָּאֵשׁ יִשָּׂרֵף׃ (18) וְאִם הֵאָכֹל יֵאָכֵל
he-is-eaten to-be-eaten and-if (18) he-must-be-burned in-the-fire the-third

מִבְּשַׂר־ זֶבַח שְׁלָמָיו בַּיּוֹם הַשְּׁלִישִׁי לֹא
not the-third on-the-day fellowships-of-him offering-of from-meat-of

יֵרָצֶה הַמַּקְרִיב אֹתוֹ לֹא יֵחָשֵׁב לוֹ
to-him he-will-be-credited not him the-one-offering he-will-be-accepted

10and every grain offering,
whether mixed with oil or dry,
belongs equally to all the sons
of Aaron.

The Fellowship Offering

11" 'These are the regulations
for the fellowship offering° a
person may present to the
LORD:
12" 'If he offers it as an expression of thankfulness, then
along with this sacrifice of
thanksgiving he is to offer
cakes of bread made without
yeast and mixed with oil, wafers made without yeast and
spread with oil, and cakes of
fine flour well-kneaded and
mixed with oil. 13Along with
his fellowship offering of
thanksgiving he is to present
an offering with cakes of
bread made with yeast. 14He is
to bring one of each kind as an
offering, a contribution to the
LORD; it belongs to the priest
who sprinkles the blood of the
fellowship offerings. 15The
meat of his fellowship offering
of thanksgiving must be eaten
on the day it is offered; he
must leave none of it till
morning.
16" 'If, however, his offering
is the result of a vow or is a
freewill offering, the sacrifice
shall be eaten on the day he
offers it, but anything left over
may be eaten on the next day.
17Any meat of the sacrifice left
over till the third day must be
burned up. 18If any meat of the
fellowship offering is eaten on
the third day, it will not be accepted. It will not be credited
to the one who offered it, for it

°11 Traditionally *peace offering;* also in verses 13-37

פִּגּוּל יִהְיֶה וְהַנֶּפֶשׁ הָאֹכֶלֶת מִמֶּנּוּ עֲוֺנָהּ
responsibility-of-her from-him the-one-eating and-the-person he-is impure

תִּשָּׂא׃ וְהַבָּשָׂר אֲשֶׁר־ יִגַּע בְּכָל־ טָמֵא לֹא
not unclean on-any-of he-touches that and-the-meat (19) she-will-bear

יֵאָכֵל בָּאֵשׁ יִשָּׂרֵף וְהַבָּשָׂר כָּל־ טָהוֹר
clean anyone-of and-the-meat he-must-be-burned in-the-fire he-must-be-eaten

יֹאכַל בָּשָׂר׃ וְהַנֶּפֶשׁ אֲשֶׁר־ תֹּאכַל בָּשָׂר מִזֶּבַח
from-offering-of meat she-eats who but-the-person (20) meat he-may-eat

הַשְּׁלָמִים אֲשֶׁר לַיהוָה וְטֻמְאָתוֹ עָלָיו
on-him and-uncleanness-of-him to-Yahweh that the-fellowships

וְנִכְרְתָה הַנֶּפֶשׁ הַהִוא מֵעַמֶּיהָ׃ וְנֶפֶשׁ
and-one (21) from-people-of-her the-that the-person then-she-must-be-cut-off

כִּי־ תִגַּע בְּכָל־ טָמֵא בְּטֻמְאַת אָדָם אוֹ בִּבְהֵמָה טְמֵאָה
unclean on-animal or human on-uncleanness-of unclean on-any-of she-touches if

אוֹ בְּכָל־ שֶׁקֶץ טָמֵא וְאָכַל מִבְּשַׂר־ זֶבַח
offering-of from-meat-of and-he-eats unclean detestable on-any-of or

הַשְּׁלָמִים אֲשֶׁר לַיהוָה וְנִכְרְתָה הַנֶּפֶשׁ הַהִוא
the-that the-person then-she-must-be-off to-Yahweh that the-fellowships

מֵעַמֶּיהָ׃ וַיְדַבֵּר יְהוָה אֶל־ מֹשֶׁה לֵּאמֹר׃ דַּבֵּר אֶל־
to say! (23) to-say Moses to Yahweh and-he-spoke (22) from-people-of-her

בְּנֵי יִשְׂרָאֵל לֵאמֹר כָּל־ חֵלֶב שׁוֹר וְכֶשֶׂב וָעֵז לֹא תֹאכֵלוּ׃
you-eat not or-goat or-sheep cattle fat-of any-of to-say Israel sons-of

וְחֵלֶב נְבֵלָה וְחֵלֶב טְרֵפָה יֵעָשֶׂה לְכָל־
for-any-of he-may-be-used torn-animal and-fat-of dead-animal and-fat-of (24)

מְלָאכָה וְאָכֹל לֹא תֹאכְלֻהוּ׃ כִּי כָּל־ אֹכֵל חֵלֶב מִן־
from fat eating any-of if (25) you-must-eat-him not but-to-eat purpose

הַבְּהֵמָה אֲשֶׁר יַקְרִיב מִמֶּנָּה אִשֶּׁה לַיהוָה וְנִכְרְתָה
then-she-must-be-cut to-Yahweh fire-offering from-her he-makes that the-animal

הַנֶּפֶשׁ הָאֹכֶלֶת מֵעַמֶּיהָ׃ וְכָל־ דָּם לֹא
not blood and-any-of (26) from-people-of-her the-one-eating the-person

תֹאכְלוּ בְּכֹל מוֹשְׁבֹתֵיכֶם לָעוֹף וְלַבְּהֵמָה׃
or-from-the-animal from-the-bird dwellings-of-you in-any-of you-must-eat

כָּל־ נֶפֶשׁ אֲשֶׁר־ תֹּאכַל כָּל־ דָּם וְנִכְרְתָה
then-she-must-be-cut-off blood any-of she-eats who person any-of (27)

הַנֶּפֶשׁ הַהִוא מֵעַמֶּיהָ׃ וַיְדַבֵּר יְהוָה אֶל־ מֹשֶׁה
Moses to Yahweh and-he-spoke (28) from-people-of-her the-that the-person

לֵּאמֹר׃ דַּבֵּר אֶל־ בְּנֵי יִשְׂרָאֵל לֵאמֹר הַמַּקְרִיב אֶת־ זֶבַח
offering-of *** the-one-bringing to-say Israel sons-of to say! (29) to-say

is impure; the person who eats
any of it will be held responsible.
19" 'Meat that touches anything ceremonially unclean
must not be eaten; it must be
burned up. As for other meat,
anyone ceremonially clean
may eat it. 20But if anyone who
is unclean eats any meat of the
fellowship offering belonging
to the LORD, that person must
be cut off from his people. 21If
anyone touches something
unclean—whether human un-
cleanness or an unclean animal or any unclean, detestable
thing—and then eats any of
the meat of the fellowship
offering belonging to the
LORD, that person must be cut
off from his people.' "

Eating Fat and Blood Forbidden

22The LORD said to Moses,
23"Say to the Israelites: 'Do not
eat any of the fat of cattle,
sheep or goats. 24The fat of an
animal found dead or torn by
wild animals may be used for
any other purpose, but you
must not eat it. 25Anyone who
eats the fat of an animal from
which an offering by fire may
be[p] made to the LORD must be
cut off from his people. 26And
wherever you live, you must
not eat the blood of any bird or
animal. 27If anyone eats blood,
that person must be cut off
from his people.' "

The Priests' Share

28The LORD said to Moses,
29"Say to the Israelites: 'Anyone who brings a fellowship

[p]25 Or *fire is*

שְׁלָמָיו לַיהוָה יָבִיא אֶת־ קָרְבָּנוֹ לַיהוָה
to-Yahweh presentation-of-him *** he-must-bring to-Yahweh fellowships-of-him

מִזֶּבַח שְׁלָמָיו׃ יָדָיו תְּבִיאֶינָה אֵת
*** they-must-bring hands-of-him (30) fellowships-of-him from-offering-of

אִשֵּׁי יְהוָה אֶת־ הַחֵלֶב עַל־ הֶחָזֶה יְבִיאֶנּוּ אֵת
*** he-must-bring-him the-breast with the-fat *** Yahweh fire-offerings-of

הֶחָזֶה לְהָנִיף אֹתוֹ תְּנוּפָה לִפְנֵי יְהוָה׃ וְהִקְטִיר
and-he-shall-burn (31) Yahweh before wave-offering him to-wave the-breast

הַכֹּהֵן אֶת־ הַחֵלֶב הַמִּזְבֵּחָה וְהָיָה הֶחָזֶה לְאַהֲרֹן
for-Aaron the-breast but-he-is on-the-altar the-fat *** the-priest

וּלְבָנָיו׃ וְאֵת שׁוֹק הַיָּמִין תִּתְּנוּ תְרוּמָה
contribution you-give the-right thigh-of and (32) and-for-sons-of-him

לַכֹּהֵן מִזִּבְחֵי שַׁלְמֵיכֶם׃ הַמַּקְרִיב אֶת־
*** the-one-offering (33) fellowships-of-you from-offerings-of to-the-priest

דַּם הַשְּׁלָמִים וְאֶת־ הַחֵלֶב מִבְּנֵי אַהֲרֹן לוֹ
for-him Aaron from-sons-of the-fat and the-fellowship-offerings blood-of

תִהְיֶה שׁוֹק הַיָּמִין לְמָנָה׃ כִּי אֶת־ חֲזֵה הַתְּנוּפָה וְאֵת
and the-one-waved breast-of *** for (34) as-share the-right thigh-of she-is

שׁוֹק הַתְּרוּמָה לָקַחְתִּי מֵאֵת בְּנֵי־ יִשְׂרָאֵל מִזִּבְחֵי
from-offerings-of Israel sons-of from I-took the-presentation thigh-of

שַׁלְמֵיהֶם וָאֶתֵּן אֹתָם לְאַהֲרֹן הַכֹּהֵן וּלְבָנָיו
and-to-sons-of-him the-priest to-Aaron them and-I-gave fellowships-of-them

לְחָק־ עוֹלָם מֵאֵת בְּנֵי יִשְׂרָאֵל׃ זֹאת מִשְׁחַת אַהֲרֹן
Aaron portion-of this (35) Israel sons-of from regular as-share-of

וּמִשְׁחַת בָּנָיו מֵאִשֵּׁי יְהוָה בְּיוֹם הִקְרִיב
he-presented on-day Yahweh from-fire-offerings-of sons-of-him and-portion-of

אֹתָם לְכַהֵן לַיהוָה׃ אֲשֶׁר צִוָּה יְהוָה לָתֵת לָהֶם
to-them to-give Yahweh he-commanded that (36) to-Yahweh to-be-priest them

בְּיוֹם מָשְׁחוֹ אֹתָם מֵאֵת בְּנֵי יִשְׂרָאֵל חֻקַּת עוֹלָם
regular share-of Israel sons-of from them to-anoint-him on-day

לְדֹרֹתָם׃ זֹאת הַתּוֹרָה לָעֹלָה
for-the-burnt-offering the-regulation this (37) for-generations-of-them

לַמִּנְחָה וְלַחַטָּאת וְלָאָשָׁם
and-for-the-guilt-offering and-for-the-sin-offering for-the-grain-offering

וְלַמִּלּוּאִים וּלְזֶבַח הַשְּׁלָמִים׃ אֲשֶׁר
that (38) the-fellowships and-for-offering-of and-for-the-ordination-offerings

צִוָּה יְהוָה אֶת־ מֹשֶׁה בְּהַר סִינָי בְּיוֹם צַוֺּתוֹ אֶת־
*** to-command-him on-day Sinai on-Mount-of Moses *** Yahweh he-commanded

offering to the LORD is to bring part of it as his sacrifice to the LORD. [30]With his own hands he is to bring the offering made to the LORD by fire; he is to bring the fat, together with the breast, and wave the breast before the LORD as a wave offering. [31]The priest shall burn the fat on the altar, but the breast belongs to Aaron and his sons. [32]You are to give the right thigh of your fellowship offerings to the priest as a contribution. [33]The son of Aaron who offers the blood and the fat of the fellowship offering shall have the right thigh as his share. [34]From the fellowship offerings of the Israelites, I have taken the breast that is waved and the thigh that is presented and have given them to Aaron the priest and his sons as their regular share from the Israelites.' "

[35]This is the portion of the offerings made to the LORD by fire that were allotted to Aaron and his sons on the day they were presented to serve the LORD as priests. [36]On the day they were anointed, the LORD commanded that the Israelites give this to them as their regular share for the generations to come.

[37]These, then, are the regulations for the burnt offering, the grain offering, the sin offering, the guilt offering, the ordination offering and the fellowship offering, [38]which the LORD gave Moses on Mount Sinai on the day he commanded the Israelites to

בְּנֵי יִשְׂרָאֵל לְהַקְרִיב אֶת־ קָרְבְּנֵיהֶם לַיהוָה בְּמִדְבַּר סִינָי׃
Sinai in-Desert-of to-Yahweh offerings-of-them *** to-bring Israel sons-of

וַיְדַבֵּר יְהוָה אֶל־ מֹשֶׁה לֵּאמֹר׃ קַח אֶת־ אַהֲרֹן וְאֶת־
and Aaron *** bring! (2) to-say Moses to Yahweh and-he-spoke (8:1)

בָּנָיו אִתּוֹ וְאֵת הַבְּגָדִים וְאֵת שֶׁמֶן הַמִּשְׁחָה וְאֵת ׀ פַּר
bull-of and the-anointing oil-of and the-garments and with-him sons-of-him

הַחַטָּאת וְאֵת שְׁנֵי הָאֵילִים וְאֵת סַל הַמַּצּוֹת׃
the-breads-without-yeast basket-of and the-rams two-of and the-sin-offering

וְאֵת כָּל־ הָעֵדָה הַקְהֵל אֶל־ פֶּתַח אֹהֶל מוֹעֵד׃
Meeting Tent-of entrance-of at gather! the-assembly all-of and (3)

וַיַּעַשׂ מֹשֶׁה כַּאֲשֶׁר צִוָּה יְהוָה אֹתוֹ וַתִּקָּהֵל
and-she-gathered him Yahweh he-commanded just-as Moses and-he-did (4)

הָעֵדָה אֶל־ פֶּתַח אֹהֶל מוֹעֵד׃ וַיֹּאמֶר מֹשֶׁה אֶל־
to Moses and-he-said (5) Meeting Tent-of entrance-of at the-assembly

הָעֵדָה זֶה הַדָּבָר אֲשֶׁר־ צִוָּה יְהוָה לַעֲשׂוֹת׃ וַיַּקְרֵב
then-he-brought (6) to-do Yahweh he-commanded that the-thing this the-assembly

מֹשֶׁה אֶת־ אַהֲרֹן וְאֶת־ בָּנָיו וַיִּרְחַץ אֹתָם בַּמָּיִם׃
with-the-waters them and-he-washed sons-of-him and Aaron *** Moses

וַיִּתֵּן עָלָיו אֶת־ הַכֻּתֹּנֶת וַיַּחְגֹּר אֹתוֹ בָּאַבְנֵט
with-the-sash him and-he-tied the-tunic *** on-him and-he-put (7)

וַיַּלְבֵּשׁ אֹתוֹ אֶת־ הַמְּעִיל וַיִּתֵּן עָלָיו אֶת־ הָאֵפֹד וַיַּחְגֹּר
and-he-tied the-ephod *** on-him and-he-put the-robe *** him and-he-clothed

אֹתוֹ בְּחֵשֶׁב הָאֵפֹד וַיֶּאְפֹּד לוֹ בּוֹ׃ וַיָּשֶׂם
and-he-put (8) by-him on-him so-he-was-fastened the-ephod by-waistband-of him

עָלָיו אֶת־ הַחֹשֶׁן וַיִּתֵּן אֶל־ הַחֹשֶׁן אֶת־ הָאוּרִים וְאֶת־
and the-Urim *** the-breastpiece in and-he-put the-breastpiece *** on-him

הַתֻּמִּים׃ וַיָּשֶׂם אֶת־ הַמִּצְנֶפֶת עַל־ רֹאשׁוֹ וַיָּשֶׂם עַל־
on and-he-set head-of-him on the-turban *** then-he-placed (9) the-Thummim

הַמִּצְנֶפֶת אֶל־ מוּל פָּנָיו אֵת צִיץ הַזָּהָב נֵזֶר הַקֹּדֶשׁ
the-sacred diadem-of the-gold plate-of *** face-of-him front-of on the-turban

כַּאֲשֶׁר צִוָּה יְהוָה אֶת־ מֹשֶׁה׃ וַיִּקַּח מֹשֶׁה אֶת־ שֶׁמֶן
oil-of *** Moses then-he-took (10) Moses *** Yahweh he-commanded just-as

הַמִּשְׁחָה וַיִּמְשַׁח אֶת־ הַמִּשְׁכָּן וְאֶת־ כָּל־ אֲשֶׁר־ בּוֹ
in-him that everything and the-tabernacle *** and-he-anointed the-anointing

וַיְקַדֵּשׁ אֹתָם׃ וַיַּז מִמֶּנּוּ עַל־ הַמִּזְבֵּחַ שֶׁבַע פְּעָמִים
times seven the-altar on from-him and-he-sprinkled (11) them so-he-consecrated

וַיִּמְשַׁח אֶת־ הַמִּזְבֵּחַ וְאֶת־ כָּל־ כֵּלָיו וְאֶת־ הַכִּיֹּר וְאֶת־
and the-basin and utensils-of-him all-of and the-altar *** and-he-anointed

bring their offerings to the
LORD, in the Desert of Sinai.

The Ordination of Aaron and His Sons

8 The LORD said to Moses,
[2]"Bring Aaron and his
sons, their garments, the
anointing oil, the bull for the
sin offering, the two rams and
the basket containing bread
made without yeast, [3]and
gather the entire assembly at
the entrance to the Tent of
Meeting." [4]Moses did as the
LORD commanded him, and
the assembly gathered at the
entrance to the Tent of Meeting.
[5]Moses said to the assembly,
"This is what the LORD has
commanded to be done."
[6]Then Moses brought Aaron
and his sons forward and
washed them with water. [7]He
put the tunic on Aaron, tied
the sash around him, clothed
him with the robe and put the
ephod on him. He also tied the
ephod to him by its skillfully
woven waistband; so it was
fastened on him. [8]He placed
the breastpiece on him and
put the Urim and Thummim
in the breastpiece. [9]Then he
placed the turban on Aaron's
head and set the gold plate, the
sacred diadem, on the front of
it, as the LORD commanded
Moses.
[10]Then Moses took the
anointing oil and anointed
the tabernacle and everything
in it, and so consecrated them.
[11]He sprinkled some of the oil
on the altar seven times,
anointing the altar and all its
utensils and the basin with its

כַּנּוֹ לְקַדְּשָׁם׃ וַיִּצֹק מִשֶּׁמֶן הַמִּשְׁחָה
the-anointing from-oil-of and-he-poured (12) to-consecrate-them stand-of-him

עַל רֹאשׁ אַהֲרֹן וַיִּמְשַׁח אֹתוֹ לְקַדְּשׁוֹ׃ וַיַּקְרֵב
then-he-brought (13) to-consecrate-him him and-he-anointed Aaron head-of on

מֹשֶׁה אֶת־ בְּנֵי אַהֲרֹן וַיַּלְבִּשֵׁם כֻּתֳּנֹת וַיַּחְגֹּר אֹתָם
them and-he-tied-around tunics and-he-put-on-them Aaron sons-of *** Moses

אַבְנֵט וַיַּחֲבֹשׁ לָהֶם מִגְבָּעוֹת כַּאֲשֶׁר צִוָּה יְהוָה אֶת־ מֹשֶׁה׃
Moses *** Yahweh he-commanded just-as headbands on-them and-he-put sash

וַיַּגֵּשׁ אֵת פַּר הַחַטָּאת וַיִּסְמֹךְ אַהֲרֹן
Aaron and-he-laid the-sin-offering bull-of *** then-he-presented (14)

וּבָנָיו אֶת־ יְדֵיהֶם עַל־ רֹאשׁ פַּר הַחַטָּאת׃
the-sin-offering bull-of head-of on hands-of-them *** and-sons-of-him

וַיִּשְׁחָט וַיִּקַּח מֹשֶׁה אֶת־ הַדָּם וַיִּתֵּן עַל־ קַרְנוֹת
horns-of on and-he-put the-blood *** Moses and-he-took and-he-slaughtered (15)

הַמִּזְבֵּחַ סָבִיב בְּאֶצְבָּעוֹ וַיְחַטֵּא אֶת־ הַמִּזְבֵּחַ וְאֶת־
and the-altar *** and-he-purified with-finger-of-him around the-altar

הַדָּם יָצַק אֶל־ יְסוֹד הַמִּזְבֵּחַ וַיְקַדְּשֵׁהוּ לְכַפֵּר
to-atone so-he-consecrated-him the-altar base-of at he-poured the-blood

עָלָיו׃ וַיִּקַּח אֶת־ כָּל־ הַחֵלֶב אֲשֶׁר עַל־ הַקֶּרֶב וְאֵת
and the-inner-part around that the-fat all-of *** and-he-took (16) for-him

יֹתֶרֶת הַכָּבֵד וְאֶת־ שְׁתֵּי הַכְּלָיֹת וְאֶת־ חֶלְבְּהֶן וַיַּקְטֵר
and-he-burned fat-of-them and the-kidneys both-of and the-liver cover-of

מֹשֶׁה הַמִּזְבֵּחָה׃ וְאֶת־ הַפָּר וְאֶת־ עֹרוֹ וְאֶת־ בְּשָׂרוֹ וְאֶת־
and flesh-of-him and hide-of-him and the-bull but (17) on-the-altar Moses

פִּרְשׁוֹ שָׂרַף בָּאֵשׁ מִחוּץ לַמַּחֲנֶה כַּאֲשֶׁר צִוָּה
he-commanded just-as of-the-camp outside in-the-fire he-burned offal-of-him

יְהוָה אֶת־ מֹשֶׁה׃ וַיַּקְרֵב אֵת אֵיל הָעֹלָה
the-burnt-offering ram-of *** then-he-presented (18) Moses *** Yahweh

וַיִּסְמְכוּ אַהֲרֹן וּבָנָיו אֶת־ יְדֵיהֶם עַל־ רֹאשׁ הָאָיִל׃
the-ram head-of on hands-of-them *** and-sons-of-him Aaron and-they-laid

וַיִּשְׁחָט וַיִּזְרֹק מֹשֶׁה אֶת־ הַדָּם עַל־ הַמִּזְבֵּחַ
the-altar on the-blood *** Moses and-he-sprinkled and-he-slaughtered (19)

סָבִיב׃ וְאֶת־ הָאַיִל נִתַּח לִנְתָחָיו וַיַּקְטֵר מֹשֶׁה אֶת־
*** Moses and-he-burned into-pieces-of-him he-cut the-ram and (20) around

הָרֹאשׁ וְאֶת־ הַנְּתָחִים וְאֶת־ הַפָּדֶר׃ וְאֶת־ הַקֶּרֶב וְאֶת־ הַכְּרָעַיִם
the-legs and the-inner-part and (21) the-fat and the-pieces and the-head

רָחַץ בַּמָּיִם וַיַּקְטֵר מֹשֶׁה אֶת־ כָּל־ הָאַיִל
the-ram whole-of *** Moses and-he-burned with-the-waters he-washed

stand, to consecrate them.
12He poured some of the
anointing oil on Aaron's head
and anointed him to consecrate him. 13Then he brought
Aaron's sons forward, put
tunics on them, tied sashes
around them and put head-
bands on them, as the LORD
commanded Moses.
14He then presented the bull
for the sin offering, and Aaron
and his sons laid their hands
on its head. 15Moses slaughtered the bull and took some of
the blood, and with his finger
he put it on all the horns of the
altar to purify the altar. He
poured out the rest of the
blood at the base of the altar.
So he consecrated it to make
atonement for it. 16Moses also
took all the fat around the inner parts, the covering of the
liver, and both kidneys and
their fat, and burned it on the
altar. 17But the bull with its
hide and its flesh and its offal
he burned up outside the
camp, as the LORD com-
manded Moses.
18He then presented the ram
for the burnt offering, and
Aaron and his sons laid their
hands on its head. 19Then
Moses slaughtered the ram
and sprinkled the blood
against the altar on all sides.
20He cut the ram into pieces
and burned the head, the
pieces and the fat. 21He
washed the inner parts and
the legs with water and
burned the whole ram on the

הַמִּזְבֵּחָה עֹלָה הוּא לְרֵיחַ־ נִיחֹחַ אִשֶּׁה הוּא
he fire-offering pleasant as-aroma-of he burnt-offering on-the-altar

לַיהוָה כַּאֲשֶׁר צִוָּה יְהוָה אֶת־ מֹשֶׁה׃ וַיַּקְרֵב אֶת־
*** then-he-presented (22) Moses *** Yahweh he-commanded just-as to-Yahweh

הָאַיִל הַשֵּׁנִי אֵיל הַמִּלֻּאִים וַיִּסְמְכוּ אַהֲרֹן וּבָנָיו
and-sons-of-him Aaron and-they-laid the-ordinations ram-of the-other the-ram

אֶת־ יְדֵיהֶם עַל־ רֹאשׁ הָאָיִל׃ וַיִּשְׁחָט | וַיִּקַּח
and-he-took then-he-slaughtered (23) the-ram head-of on hands-of-them ***

מֹשֶׁה מִדָּמוֹ וַיִּתֵּן עַל־ תְּנוּךְ אֹזֶן־ אַהֲרֹן הַיְמָנִית וְעַל־
and-on the-right Aaron ear-of lobe-of on and-he-put from-blood-of-him Moses

בֹּהֶן יָדוֹ הַיְמָנִית וְעַל־ בֹּהֶן רַגְלוֹ הַיְמָנִית׃
the-right foot-of-him big-toe-of and-on the-right hand-of-him thumb-of

וַיַּקְרֵב אֶת־ בְּנֵי אַהֲרֹן וַיִּתֵּן מֹשֶׁה מִן־ הַדָּם עַל־
on the-blood from Moses and-he-put Aaron sons-of *** and-he-brought (24)

תְּנוּךְ אָזְנָם הַיְמָנִית וְעַל־ בֹּהֶן יָדָם הַיְמָנִית וְעַל־
and-on the-right hand-of-them thumb-of and-on the-right ear-of-them lobe-of

בֹּהֶן רַגְלָם הַיְמָנִית וַיִּזְרֹק מֹשֶׁה אֶת־ הַדָּם
the-blood *** Moses then-he-sprinkled the-right foot-of-them big-toe-of

עַל־ הַמִּזְבֵּחַ סָבִיב׃ וַיִּקַּח אֶת־הַחֵלֶב וְאֶת־ הָאַלְיָה וְאֶת־
and the-fat-tail and the-fat *** and-he-took (25) around the-altar against

כָּל־ הַחֵלֶב אֲשֶׁר עַל־ הַקֶּרֶב וְאֵת יֹתֶרֶת הַכָּבֵד וְאֶת־ שְׁתֵּי
both-of and the-liver cover-of and the-inner-part around that the-fat all-of

הַכְּלָיֹת וְאֶת־ חֶלְבְּהֶן וְאֵת שׁוֹק הַיָּמִין׃ וּמִסַּל
then-from-basket-of (26) the-right thigh-of and fat-of-them and the-kidneys

הַמַּצּוֹת אֲשֶׁר | לִפְנֵי יְהוָה לָקַח חַלַּת מַצָּה אַחַת
one bread cake-of he-took Yahweh before that the-breads-without-yeast

וְחַלַּת לֶחֶם שֶׁמֶן אַחַת וְרָקִיק אֶחָד וַיָּשֶׂם עַל־ הַחֲלָבִים
the-fat-portions on and-he-put one and-wafer one oil bread and-cake-of

וְעַל שׁוֹק הַיָּמִין׃ וַיִּתֵּן אֶת־ הַכֹּל עַל כַּפֵּי אַהֲרֹן
Aaron hands-of on the-all *** and-he-put (27) the-right thigh-of and-on

וְעַל כַּפֵּי בָנָיו וַיָּנֶף אֹתָם תְּנוּפָה לִפְנֵי יְהוָה׃
Yahweh before wave-offering them and-he-waved sons-of-him hands-of and-on

וַיִּקַּח מֹשֶׁה אֹתָם מֵעַל כַּפֵּיהֶם וַיַּקְטֵר הַמִּזְבֵּחָה
on-the-altar and-he-burned hands-of-them from-on them Moses then-he-took (28)

עַל־ הָעֹלָה מִלֻּאִים הֵם לְרֵיחַ נִיחֹחַ
pleasant as-aroma-of they ordination-offerings the-burnt-offering upon

אִשֶּׁה הוּא לַיהוָה׃ וַיִּקַּח מֹשֶׁה אֶת־ הֶחָזֶה
the-breast *** Moses and-he-took (29) to-Yahweh he fire-offering

altar as a burnt offering, a pleasing aroma, an offering made to the LORD by fire, as the LORD commanded Moses.
[22]He then presented the other ram, the ram for the ordination, and Aaron and his sons laid their hands on its head.
[23]Moses slaughtered the ram and took some of its blood and put it on the lobe of Aaron's right ear, on the thumb of his right hand and on the big toe of his right foot.
[24]Moses also brought Aaron's sons forward and put some of the blood on the lobes of their right ears, on the thumbs of their right hands and on the big toes of their right feet. Then he sprinkled blood against the altar on all sides.
[25]He took the fat, the fat tail, all the fat around the inner parts, the covering of the liver, both kidneys and their fat and the right thigh.
[26]Then from the basket of bread made without yeast, which was before the LORD, he took a cake of bread, and one made with oil, and a wafer; he put these on the fat portions and on the right thigh.
[27]He put all these in the hands of Aaron and his sons and waved them before the LORD as a wave offering.
[28]Then Moses took them from their hands and burned them on the altar on top of the burnt offering as an ordination offering, a pleasing aroma, an offering made to the LORD by fire.
[29]He also took the breast—

וַיְנִיפֵהוּ תְנוּפָה לִפְנֵי יְהוָה מֵאֵיל הַמִּלֻּאִים
the-ordinations from-ram-of Yahweh before wave-offering and-he-waved-him

לְמֹשֶׁה הָיָה לְמָנָה כַּאֲשֶׁר צִוָּה יְהוָה אֶת־ מֹשֶׁה׃
Moses *** Yahweh he-commanded just-as as-share he-was for-Moses

וַיִּקַּח מֹשֶׁה מִשֶּׁמֶן הַמִּשְׁחָה וּמִן־ הַדָּם אֲשֶׁר עַל־
on that the-blood and-from the-anointing from-oil-of Moses then-he-took (30)

הַמִּזְבֵּחַ וַיַּז עַל־ אַהֲרֹן עַל־ בְּגָדָיו וְעַל־ בָּנָיו
sons-of-him and-on garments-of-him on Aaron on and-he-sprinkled the-altar

וְעַל־ בִּגְדֵי בָנָיו אִתּוֹ וַיְקַדֵּשׁ אֶת־ אַהֲרֹן אֶת־
*** Aaron *** so-he-consecrated with-him sons-of-him garments-of and-on

בְּגָדָיו וְאֶת־ בָּנָיו וְאֶת־ בִּגְדֵי בָנָיו אִתּוֹ׃
with-him sons-of-him garments-of and sons-of-him and garments-of-him

וַיֹּאמֶר מֹשֶׁה אֶל־ אַהֲרֹן וְאֶל־ בָּנָיו בַּשְּׁלוּ אֶת־ הַבָּשָׂר
the-meat *** cook! sons-of-him and-to Aaron to Moses then-he-said (31)

פֶּתַח אֹהֶל מוֹעֵד וְשָׁם תֹּאכְלוּ אֹתוֹ וְאֶת־ הַלֶּחֶם אֲשֶׁר
that the-bread and him you-eat and-there Meeting Tent-of entrance-of

בְּסַל הַמִּלֻּאִים כַּאֲשֶׁר צִוֵּיתִי לֵאמֹר אַהֲרֹן
Aaron to-say I-commanded just-as the-ordination-offerings in-basket-of

וּבָנָיו יֹאכְלֻהוּ׃ וְהַנּוֹתָר בַּבָּשָׂר
of-the-meat and-the-being-left (32) they-shall-eat-him and-sons-of-him

וּבַלָּחֶם בָּאֵשׁ תִּשְׂרֹפוּ׃ וּמִפֶּתַח אֹהֶל
Tent-of and-from-entrance-of (33) you-burn in-the-fire and-of-the-bread

מוֹעֵד לֹא תֵצְאוּ שִׁבְעַת יָמִים עַד יוֹם מְלֹאת יְמֵי
days-of to-complete day until days seven-of you-leave not Meeting

מִלֻּאֵיכֶם כִּי שִׁבְעַת יָמִים יְמַלֵּא אֶת־ יֶדְכֶם׃
hand-of-you *** he-will-fill days seven-of for ordinations-of-you

כַּאֲשֶׁר עָשָׂה בַּיּוֹם הַזֶּה צִוָּה יְהוָה לַעֲשֹׂת לְכַפֵּר
to-atone to-do Yahweh he-commanded the-this on-the-day he-did just-as (34)

עֲלֵיכֶם׃ וּפֶתַח אֹהֶל מוֹעֵד תֵּשְׁבוּ יוֹמָם וָלַיְלָה
and-night by-day you-stay Meeting Tent-of and-entrance-of (35) for-you

שִׁבְעַת יָמִים וּשְׁמַרְתֶּם אֶת־ מִשְׁמֶרֶת יְהוָה וְלֹא תָמוּתוּ כִּי־ כֵן
this for you-die so-not Yahweh requirement-of *** and-you-do days seven-of

צֻוֵּיתִי׃ וַיַּעַשׂ אַהֲרֹן וּבָנָיו אֵת כָּל־ הַדְּבָרִים
the-things all-of *** and-sons-of-him Aaron so-he-did (36) I-was-commanded

אֲשֶׁר־ צִוָּה יְהוָה בְּיַד־ מֹשֶׁה׃ וַיְהִי בַּיּוֹם
on-the-day and-he-was (9:1) Moses by-hand-of Yahweh he-commanded that

הַשְּׁמִינִי קָרָא מֹשֶׁה לְאַהֲרֹן וּלְבָנָיו וּלְזִקְנֵי
and-to-elders-of and-to-sons-of-him to-Aaron Moses he-summoned the-eighth

Moses' share of the ordination ram—and waved it before the LORD as a wave offering, as the LORD commanded Moses.
30Then Moses took some of the anointing oil and some of the blood from the altar and sprinkled them on Aaron and his garments and on his sons and their garments. So he consecrated Aaron and his garments and his sons and their garments.
31Moses then said to Aaron and his sons, "Cook the meat at the entrance to the Tent of Meeting and eat it there with the bread from the basket of ordination offerings, as I commanded, saying,[q] 'Aaron and
his sons are to eat it.' 32Then
burn up the rest of the meat
and the bread. 33Do not leave the entrance to the Tent of Meeting for seven days, until the days of your ordination are completed, for your ordination will last seven days.
34What has been done today was commanded by the LORD to make atonement for you.
35You must stay at the entrance to the Tent of Meeting day and night for seven days and do what the LORD requires, so you will not die; for that is what I have been commanded." 36So Aaron and his sons did everything the LORD commanded through Moses.

The Priests Begin Their Ministry

9 On the eighth day Moses summoned Aaron and his sons and the elders of Israel.

q31 Or *I was commanded:*

יִשְׂרָאֵל׃ וַיֹּאמֶר אֶל־אַהֲרֹן קַח־לְךָ עֵגֶל בֶּן־בָּקָר
herd young-of calf for-you take! Aaron to and-he-said (2) Israel

לְחַטָּאת וְאַיִל לְעֹלָה תְּמִימִם וְהַקְרֵב
and-present! without-defect for-burnt-offering and-ram for-sin-offering

לִפְנֵי יְהוָה׃ וְאֶל־בְּנֵי יִשְׂרָאֵל תְּדַבֵּר לֵאמֹר קְחוּ שְׂעִיר־
male-goat-of take! to-say you-say Israel sons-of then-to (3) Yahweh before

עִזִּים לְחַטָּאת וְעֵגֶל וָכֶבֶשׂ בְּנֵי־שָׁנָה תְּמִימִם
without-defect year sons-of and-lamb and-calf for-sin-offering goats

לְעֹלָה׃ וְשׁוֹר וָאַיִל לִשְׁלָמִים לִזְבֹּחַ
to-sacrifice for-fellowship-offerings and-ram and-cow (4) for-burnt-offering

לִפְנֵי יְהוָה וּמִנְחָה בְּלוּלָה בַשָּׁמֶן כִּי הַיּוֹם יְהוָה
Yahweh the-day for with-the-oil being-mixed and-grain-offering Yahweh before

נִרְאָה אֲלֵיכֶם׃ וַיִּקְחוּ אֵת אֲשֶׁר צִוָּה מֹשֶׁה אֶל־
to Moses he-commanded what *** so-they-took (5) to-you he-will-appear

פְּנֵי אֹהֶל מוֹעֵד וַיִּקְרְבוּ כָּל־הָעֵדָה וַיַּעַמְדוּ
and-they-stood the-assembly all-of and-they-came-near Meeting Tent-of front-of

לִפְנֵי יְהוָה׃ וַיֹּאמֶר מֹשֶׁה זֶה הַדָּבָר אֲשֶׁר־צִוָּה
he-commanded that the-thing this Moses then-he-said (6) Yahweh before

יְהוָה תַּעֲשׂוּ וְיֵרָא אֲלֵיכֶם כְּבוֹד יְהוָה׃ וַיֹּאמֶר
and-he-said (7) Yahweh glory-of to-you so-he-may-appear you-must-do Yahweh

מֹשֶׁה אֶל־אַהֲרֹן קְרַב אֶל־הַמִּזְבֵּחַ וַעֲשֵׂה אֶת־חַטָּאתְךָ
sin-offering-of-you *** and-sacrifice! the-altar to come! Aaron to Moses

וְאֶת־עֹלָתֶךָ וְכַפֵּר בַּעַדְךָ וּבְעַד הָעָם וַעֲשֵׂה
and-sacrifice! the-people and-for for-you and-atone! burnt-offering-of-you and

אֶת־קָרְבַּן הָעָם וְכַפֵּר בַּעֲדָם כַּאֲשֶׁר צִוָּה יְהוָה׃
Yahweh he-commanded just-as for-them and-atone! the-people offering-of ***

וַיִּקְרַב אַהֲרֹן אֶל־הַמִּזְבֵּחַ וַיִּשְׁחַט אֶת־עֵגֶל
calf-of *** and-he-slaughtered the-altar to Aaron so-he-came (8)

הַחַטָּאת אֲשֶׁר־לוֹ׃ וַיַּקְרִבוּ בְּנֵי אַהֲרֹן אֶת־
*** Aaron sons-of and-they-brought (9) for-him that the-sin-offering

הַדָּם אֵלָיו וַיִּטְבֹּל אֶצְבָּעוֹ בַּדָּם וַיִּתֵּן עַל־
on and-he-put into-the-blood finger-of-him and-he-dipped to-him the-blood

קַרְנוֹת הַמִּזְבֵּחַ וְאֶת־הַדָּם יָצַק אֶל־יְסוֹד הַמִּזְבֵּחַ׃ וְאֶת־
and (10) the-altar base-of at he-poured-out the-blood and the-altar horns-of

הַחֵלֶב וְאֶת־הַכְּלָיֹת וְאֶת־הַיֹּתֶרֶת מִן־הַכָּבֵד מִן־הַחַטָּאת
the-sin-offering from the-liver from the-cover and the-kidneys and the-fat

הִקְטִיר הַמִּזְבֵּחָה כַּאֲשֶׁר צִוָּה יְהוָה אֶת־מֹשֶׁה׃ וְאֶת־
and (11) Moses *** Yahweh he-commanded just-as on-the-altar he-burned

[2]He said to Aaron, "Take a bull calf for your sin offering and a ram for your burnt offering, both without defect, and present them before the LORD. [3]Then say to the Israelites: 'Take a male goat for a sin offering, a calf and a lamb—both a year old and without defect—for a burnt offering, [4]and a cow[r] and a ram for a fellowship offering[s] to sacrifice before the LORD, together with a grain offering mixed with oil. For today the LORD will appear to you.'"

[5]They took the things Moses commanded to the front of the Tent of Meeting, and the entire assembly came near and stood before the LORD. [6]Then Moses said, "This is what the LORD has commanded you to do, so that the glory of the LORD may appear to you."

[7]Moses said to Aaron, "Come to the altar and sacrifice your sin offering and your burnt offering and make atonement for yourself and the people; sacrifice the offering that is for the people and make atonement for them, as the LORD has commanded."

[8]So Aaron came to the altar and slaughtered the calf as a sin offering for himself. [9]His sons brought the blood to him, and he dipped his finger into the blood and put it on the horns of the altar; the rest of the blood he poured out at the base of the altar. [10]On the altar he burned the fat, the kidneys and the covering of the liver from the sin offering, as the LORD commanded Moses; [11]the

[r]4 The Hebrew word can include both male and female; also in verses 18 and 19.
[s]4 Traditionally *peace offering;* also in verses 18 and 22

הַבָּשָׂר וְאֶת־ הָעוֹר שָׂרַף בָּאֵשׁ מִחוּץ לַמַּחֲנֶה׃
of-the-camp outside in-the-fire he-burned the-hide and the-flesh

(12) וַיִּשְׁחַט אֶת־ הָעֹלָה וַיַּמְצִאוּ בְּנֵי אַהֲרֹן
Aaron sons-of and-they-handled the-burnt-offering *** then-he-slaughtered (12)

אֵלָיו אֶת־ הַדָּם וַיִּזְרְקֵהוּ עַל־ הַמִּזְבֵּחַ סָבִיב׃
around the-altar against and-he-sprinkled-him the-blood *** to-him

(13) וְאֶת־ הָעֹלָה הִמְצִיאוּ אֵלָיו לִנְתָחֶיהָ וְאֶת־ הָרֹאשׁ
the-head and by-pieces-of-her to-him they-handed the-burnt-offering and (13)

וַיַּקְטֵר עַל־ הַמִּזְבֵּחַ׃ (14) וַיִּרְחַץ אֶת־ הַקֶּרֶב וְאֶת־
and the-inner-part *** and-he-washed (14) the-altar on and-he-burned

הַכְּרָעָיִם וַיַּקְטֵר עַל־ הָעֹלָה הַמִּזְבֵּחָה׃
on-the-altar the-burnt-offering upon and-he-burned the-legs

(15) וַיַּקְרֵב אֵת קָרְבַּן הָעָם וַיִּקַּח אֶת־ שְׂעִיר
goat-of *** and-he-took the-people offering-of *** then-he-brought (15)

הַחַטָּאת אֲשֶׁר לָעָם וַיִּשְׁחָטֵהוּ וַיְחַטְּאֵהוּ
and-he-offered-him and-he-slaughtered-him for-the-people that the-sin-offering

כָּרִאשׁוֹן׃ (16) וַיַּקְרֵב אֶת־ הָעֹלָה וַיַּעֲשֶׂהָ
and-he-offered-her the-burnt-offering *** and-he-brought (16) as-the-first

כַּמִּשְׁפָּט׃ (17) וַיַּקְרֵב אֶת־ הַמִּנְחָה וַיְמַלֵּא
and-he-filled the-grain-offering *** and-he-brought (17) as-the-prescription

כַפּוֹ מִמֶּנָּה וַיַּקְטֵר עַל־ הַמִּזְבֵּחַ מִלְּבַד עֹלַת
offering-of in-addition-to the-altar on and-he-burned from-her hand-of-him

הַבֹּקֶר׃ (18) וַיִּשְׁחַט אֶת־ הַשּׁוֹר וְאֶת־ הָאַיִל זֶבַח
offering-of the-ram and the-cow *** and-he-slaughtered (18) the-morning

הַשְּׁלָמִים אֲשֶׁר לָעָם וַיַּמְצִאוּ בְּנֵי אַהֲרֹן אֶת־
*** Aaron sons-of and-they-handed for-the-people that the-fellowships

הַדָּם אֵלָיו וַיִּזְרְקֵהוּ עַל־ הַמִּזְבֵּחַ סָבִיב׃ (19) וְאֶת־
but (19) around the-altar against and-he-sprinkled-him to-him the-blood

הַחֲלָבִים מִן־ הַשּׁוֹר וּמִן־ הָאַיִל הָאַלְיָה וְהַמְכַסֶּה
and-the-fat-layer the-fat-tail the-ram and-from the-cow from the-fat-portions

וְהַכְּלָיֹת וְיֹתֶרֶת הַכָּבֵד׃ (20) וַיָּשִׂימוּ אֶת־ הַחֲלָבִים
the-fat-portions *** and-they-laid (20) the-liver and-cover-of and-the-kidneys

עַל־ הֶחָזוֹת וַיַּקְטֵר הַחֲלָבִים הַמִּזְבֵּחָה׃ (21) וְאֵת
and (21) on-the-altar the-fat-portions and-he-burned the-breasts on

הֶחָזוֹת וְאֵת שׁוֹק הַיָּמִין הֵנִיף אַהֲרֹן תְּנוּפָה לִפְנֵי
before wave-offering Aaron he-waved the-right thigh-of and the-breasts

יְהוָה כַּאֲשֶׁר צִוָּה מֹשֶׁה׃ (22) וַיִּשָּׂא אַהֲרֹן אֶת־ יָדָו
hands-of-him *** Aaron then-he-lifted (22) Moses he-commanded just-as Yahweh

flesh and the hide he burned
up outside the camp.
[12]Then he slaughtered the burnt offering. His sons handed him the blood, and he sprinkled it against the altar on all sides.
[13]They handed him the burnt offering piece by piece, including the head, and he burned them on the altar.
[14]He washed the inner parts and the legs and burned them on top of the burnt offering on the altar.
[15]Aaron then brought the offering that was for the people. He took the goat for the people's sin offering and slaughtered it and offered it for a sin offering as he did with the first one.
[16]He brought the burnt offering and offered it in the prescribed way.
[17]He also brought the grain offering, took a handful of it and burned it on the altar in addition to the morning's burnt offering.
[18]He slaughtered the cow and the ram as the fellowship offering for the people. His sons handed him the blood, and he sprinkled it against the altar on all sides.
[19]But the fat portions of the cow and the ram—the fat tail, the layer of fat, the kidneys and the covering of the liver—
[20]these they laid on the breasts, and then Aaron burned the fat on the altar.
[21]Aaron waved the breasts and the right thigh before the LORD as a wave offering, as Moses commanded.
[22]Then Aaron lifted his

°22 ק ידיו

אֶל־ הָעָם וַיְבָרְכֵם וַיֵּרֶד מֵעֲשֹׂת
from-to-sacrifice and-he-stepped-down and-he-blessed-them the-people toward

הַחַטָּאת וְהָעֹלָה וְהַשְּׁלָמִים׃
and-the-fellowship-offerings and-the-burnt-offering the-sin-offering

וַיָּבֹא מֹשֶׁה וְאַהֲרֹן אֶל־ אֹהֶל מוֹעֵד וַיֵּצְאוּ
when-they-came-out Meeting Tent-of into and-Aaron Moses then-he-went (23)

וַיְבָרֲכוּ אֶת־ הָעָם וַיֵּרָא כְבוֹד־ יְהוָה אֶל־ כָּל־
all-of to Yahweh glory-of and-he-appeared the-people *** then-they-blessed

הָעָם׃ וַתֵּצֵא אֵשׁ מִלִּפְנֵי יְהוָה וַתֹּאכַל
and-she-consumed Yahweh from-presence-of fire and-she-came-out (24) the-people

עַל־ הַמִּזְבֵּחַ אֶת־ הָעֹלָה וְאֶת־ הַחֲלָבִים וַיַּרְא כָּל־
all-of when-he-saw the-fat-portions and the-burnt-offering *** the-altar on

הָעָם וַיָּרֹנּוּ וַיִּפְּלוּ עַל־ פְּנֵיהֶם׃
faces-of-them on and-they-fell then-they-shouted the-people

וַיִּקְחוּ בְנֵי־ אַהֲרֹן נָדָב וַאֲבִיהוּא אִישׁ מַחְתָּתוֹ וַיִּתְּנוּ
and-they-put censer-of-him each and-Abihu Nadab Aaron sons-of and-they-took (10:1)

בָהֵן אֵשׁ וַיָּשִׂימוּ עָלֶיהָ קְטֹרֶת וַיַּקְרִבוּ לִפְנֵי יְהוָה
Yahweh before and-they-offered incense to-her and-they-added fire in-them

אֵשׁ זָרָה אֲשֶׁר לֹא צִוָּה אֹתָם׃ וַתֵּצֵא אֵשׁ
fire so-she-came-out (2) them he-commanded not that unauthorized fire

מִלִּפְנֵי יְהוָה וַתֹּאכַל אוֹתָם וַיָּמֻתוּ לִפְנֵי יְהוָה׃
Yahweh before and-they-died them and-she-consumed Yahweh from-presence-of

וַיֹּאמֶר מֹשֶׁה אֶל־ אַהֲרֹן הוּא אֲשֶׁר־ דִּבֶּר יְהוָה ׀ לֵאמֹר
to-say Yahweh he-spoke what this Aaron to Moses then-he-said (3)

בִּקְרֹבַי אֶקָּדֵשׁ וְעַל־ פְּנֵי כָל־ הָעָם
the-people all-of sight-of and-in I-will-show-myself-holy among-ones-near-me

אֶכָּבֵד וַיִּדֹּם אַהֲרֹן׃ וַיִּקְרָא מֹשֶׁה אֶל־
to Moses and-he-summoned (4) Aaron and-he-was-silent I-will-be-honored

מִישָׁאֵל וְאֶל אֶלְצָפָן בְּנֵי עֻזִּיאֵל דֹּד אַהֲרֹן וַיֹּאמֶר אֲלֵהֶם
to-them and-he-said Aaron uncle-of Uzziel sons-of Elzaphan and-to Mishael

קִרְבוּ שְׂאוּ אֶת־ אֲחֵיכֶם מֵאֵת פְּנֵי־ הַקֹּדֶשׁ אֶל־ מִחוּץ
outside to the-sanctuary front-of from cousins-of-you *** carry! come!

לַמַּחֲנֶה׃ וַיִּקְרְבוּ וַיִּשָּׂאֻם בְּכֻתֳּנֹתָם אֶל־
to in-tunics-of-them and-they-carried-them so-they-came (5) of-the-camp

מִחוּץ לַמַּחֲנֶה כַּאֲשֶׁר דִּבֶּר מֹשֶׁה׃ וַיֹּאמֶר מֹשֶׁה אֶל־
to Moses then-he-said (6) Moses he-commanded just-as of-the-camp outside

אַהֲרֹן וּלְאֶלְעָזָר וּלְאִיתָמָר ׀ בָּנָיו רָאשֵׁיכֶם אַל־ תִּפְרָעוּ ׀
you-uncover not heads-of-you sons-of-him and-to-Ithamar and-to-Eleazar Aaron

hands toward the people and
blessed them. And having sacrificed the sin offering, the
burnt offering and the fellowship offering, he stepped
down.
23Moses and Aaron then
went into the Tent of Meeting.
When they came out, they
blessed the people; and the
glory of the LORD appeared to
all the people. 24Fire came out
from the presence of the LORD
and consumed the burnt
offering and the fat portions
on the altar. And when all the
people saw it, they shouted for
joy and fell facedown.

The Death of Nadab and Abihu

10 Aaron's sons Nadab
and Abihu took their
censers, put fire in them and
added incense; and they
offered unauthorized fire before the LORD, contrary to his
command. 2So fire came out
from the presence of the LORD
and consumed them, and they
died before the LORD. 3Moses
then said to Aaron, "This is
what the LORD spoke of when
he said:

"'Among those who
approach me
I will show myself holy;
in the sight of all the
people
I will be honored.'"

Aaron remained silent.
4Moses summoned Mishael
and Elzaphan, sons of Aaron's
uncle Uzziel, and said to them,
"Come here; carry your cousins outside the camp, away
from the front of the sanctuary." 5So they came and carried them, still in their tunics,
outside the camp, as Moses ordered.
6Then Moses said to Aaron
and his sons Eleazar and Ithamar, "Do not let your hair
become unkempt,[f] and do not

[f]6 Or *Do not uncover your heads*

וּבִגְדֵיכֶם לֹא־ תִפְרֹמוּ וְלֹא תָמֻתוּ וְעַל כָּל־
whole-of and-with you-die so-not you-tear not and-clothes-of-you

הָעֵדָה יִקְצֹף וַאֲחֵיכֶם כָּל־ בֵּית יִשְׂרָאֵל
Israel house-of all-of but-relatives-of-you he-will-be-angry the-community

יִבְכּוּ אֶת־ הַשְּׂרֵפָה אֲשֶׁר שָׂרַף יְהוָה׃
Yahweh he-burned whom the-burnt-one *** they-may-mourn

וּמִפֶּתַח אֹהֶל מוֹעֵד לֹא תֵצְאוּ פֶּן־ תָּמֻתוּ כִּי־
because you-will-die or you-leave not Meeting Tent-of and-from-entrance-of (7)

שֶׁמֶן מִשְׁחַת יְהוָה עֲלֵיכֶם וַיַּעֲשׂוּ כִּדְבַר מֹשֶׁה׃
Moses as-word-of so-they-did on-you Yahweh anointing-of oil-of

וַיְדַבֵּר יְהוָה אֶל־אַהֲרֹן לֵאמֹר׃ יַיִן וְשֵׁכָר אַל־
not or-fermented-drink wine (9) to-say Aaron to Yahweh then-he-spoke (8)

תֵּשְׁתְּ ׀ אַתָּה ׀ וּבָנֶיךָ אִתָּךְ בְּבֹאֲכֶם אֶל־ אֹהֶל מוֹעֵד
Meeting Tent-of into when-to-go-you with-you and-sons-of-you you you-drink

וְלֹא תָמֻתוּ חֻקַּת עוֹלָם לְדֹרֹתֵיכֶם׃
for-generations-of-you lasting ordinance-of you-die so-not

וּלֲהַבְדִּיל בֵּין הַקֹּדֶשׁ וּבֵין הַחֹל וּבֵין
and-between the-profane and-between the-holy between and-to-distinguish (10)

הַטָּמֵא וּבֵין הַטָּהוֹר׃ וּלְהוֹרֹת אֶת־ בְּנֵי יִשְׂרָאֵל אֵת
*** Israel sons-of *** and-to-teach (11) the-clean and-between the-unclean

כָּל־ הַחֻקִּים אֲשֶׁר דִּבֶּר יְהוָה אֲלֵיהֶם בְּיַד־ מֹשֶׁה׃
Moses by-hand-of to-them Yahweh he-gave that the-decrees all-of

וַיְדַבֵּר מֹשֶׁה אֶל־אַהֲרֹן וְאֶל אֶלְעָזָר וְאֶל־ אִיתָמָר ׀ בָּנָיו
sons-of-him Ithamar and-to Eleazar and-to Aaron to Moses then-he-spoke (12)

הַנּוֹתָרִים קְחוּ אֶת־ הַמִּנְחָה הַנּוֹתֶרֶת
the-being-left the-grain-offering *** take! the-ones-remaining

מֵאִשֵּׁי יְהוָה וְאִכְלוּהָ מַצּוֹת אֵצֶל הַמִּזְבֵּחַ
the-altar beside without-yeast and-eat-her! Yahweh from-fire-offerings-of

כִּי קֹדֶשׁ קָדָשִׁים הִוא׃ וַאֲכַלְתֶּם אֹתָהּ בְּמָקוֹם קָדֹשׁ כִּי
for holy in-place her and-you-eat (13) she holy-ones most-holy of for

חָקְךָ וְחָק־ בָּנֶיךָ הִוא מֵאִשֵּׁי יְהוָה כִּי־
for Yahweh from-fire-offerings-of she sons-of-you and-share-of share-of-you

כֵן צֻוֵּיתִי׃ וְאֵת חֲזֵה הַתְּנוּפָה וְאֵת ׀ שׁוֹק הַתְּרוּמָה
the-presentation thigh-of and the-waved breast-of but (14) I-was-commanded so

תֹּאכְלוּ בְּמָקוֹם טָהוֹר אַתָּה וּבָנֶיךָ וּבְנֹתֶיךָ אִתָּךְ
with-you and-daughters-of-you and-sons-of-you you clean in-place you-eat

כִּי־ חָקְךָ וְחָק־ בָּנֶיךָ נִתְּנוּ מִזִּבְחֵי
from-offerings-of they-are-given children-of-you and-share-of share-of-you for

tear your clothes, or you will
die and the LORD will be angry
with the whole community.
But your relatives, all the
house of Israel, may mourn for
those the LORD has destroyed
by fire. [7]Do not leave the entrance to the Tent of Meeting
or you will die, because the
LORD's anointing oil is on
you." So they did as Moses
said.
[8]Then the LORD said to
Aaron, [9]"You and your sons
are not to drink wine or other
fermented drink whenever
you go into the Tent of Meeting, or you will die. This is a
lasting ordinance for the generations to come. [10]You must
distinguish between the holy
and the profane, between the
unclean and the clean, [11]and
you must teach the Israelites
all the decrees the LORD has
given them through Moses."
[12]Moses said to Aaron and
his remaining sons, Eleazar
and Ithamar, "Take the grain
offering left over from the
offerings made to the LORD by
fire and eat it prepared without yeast beside the altar, for it
is most holy. [13]Eat it in a holy
place, because it is your share
and your sons' share of the
offerings made to the LORD by
fire; for so I have been commanded. [14]But you and your
sons and your daughters may
eat the breast that was waved
and the thigh that was
presented. Eat them in a
ceremonially clean place; they
have been given to you and
your children as your share of

שַׁלְמֵי בְּנֵי יִשְׂרָאֵל׃ שׁוֹק הַתְּרוּמָה וַחֲזֵה
fellowships-of sons-of Israel (15) thigh-of the-presentation and-breast-of

הַתְּנוּפָה עַל אִשֵּׁי הַחֲלָבִים יָבִיאוּ לְהָנִיף
the-waved with fire-offerings-of the-fat-portions they-must-bring to-wave

תְּנוּפָה לִפְנֵי יְהוָה וְהָיָה לְךָ וּלְבָנֶיךָ
wave-offering before Yahweh and-he-will-be for-you and-for-children-of-you

אִתְּךָ לְחָק־ עוֹלָם כַּאֲשֶׁר צִוָּה יְהוָה׃ וְאֵת ׀ שְׂעִיר
with-you as-share-of regular just-as he-commanded Yahweh (16) and goat-of

הַחַטָּאת דָּרֹשׁ דָּרַשׁ מֹשֶׁה וְהִנֵּה שֹׂרָף
the-sin-offering to-inquire he-inquired Moses and-see! he-was-burned

וַיִּקְצֹף עַל־ אֶלְעָזָר וְעַל־ אִיתָמָר בְּנֵי אַהֲרֹן הַנּוֹתָרִם
so-he-was-angry with Eleazar and-with Ithamar sons-of Aaron the-ones-remaining

לֵאמֹר׃ מַדּוּעַ לֹא־ אֲכַלְתֶּם אֶת־ הַחַטָּאת בִּמְקוֹם הַקֹּדֶשׁ
to-say (17) why? not you-ate *** the-sin-offering in-area-of the-sanctuary

כִּי קֹדֶשׁ קָדָשִׁים הִוא וְאֹתָהּ ׀ נָתַן לָכֶם לָשֵׂאת אֶת־
for most-holy-of holy-ones she and-her he-gave to-you to-take-away ***

עֲוֺן הָעֵדָה לְכַפֵּר עֲלֵיהֶם לִפְנֵי יְהוָה׃ הֵן לֹא־
guilt-of the-community to-atone for-them before Yahweh (18) since not

הוּבָא אֶת־ דָּמָהּ אֶל־ הַקֹּדֶשׁ פְּנִימָה אָכוֹל
he-was-taken *** blood-of-her into the-Holy-Place inside to-eat

תֹּאכְלוּ אֹתָהּ בַּקֹּדֶשׁ כַּאֲשֶׁר צִוֵּיתִי׃
you-should-have-eaten her in-the-sanctuary just-as I-commanded

וַיְדַבֵּר אַהֲרֹן אֶל־ מֹשֶׁה הֵן הַיּוֹם הִקְרִיבוּ אֶת־
(19) and-he-replied Aaron to Moses see! the-day they-sacrificed ***

חַטָּאתָם וְאֶת־ עֹלָתָם לִפְנֵי יְהוָה
sin-offering-of-them and burnt-offering-of-them before Yahweh

וַתִּקְרֶאנָה אֹתִי כָּאֵלֶּה וְאָכַלְתִּי חַטָּאת הַיּוֹם
but-they-happened to-me such-as-the-these if-I-ate sin-offering the-day

הַיִּיטַב בְּעֵינֵי יְהוָה׃ וַיִּשְׁמַע מֹשֶׁה
would-he-be-pleased? in-eyes-of Yahweh (20) when-he-heard Moses

וַיִּיטַב בְּעֵינָיו׃ וַיְדַבֵּר יְהוָה אֶל־ מֹשֶׁה
then-he-was-satisfied in-eyes-of-him (11:1) and-he-spoke Yahweh to Moses

וְאֶל־ אַהֲרֹן לֵאמֹר אֲלֵהֶם׃ דַּבְּרוּ אֶל־ בְּנֵי יִשְׂרָאֵל לֵאמֹר זֹאת הַחַיָּה
and-to Aaron to-say to-them (2) say! to sons-of Israel to-say this the-animal

אֲשֶׁר תֹּאכְלוּ מִכָּל־ הַבְּהֵמָה אֲשֶׁר עַל־ הָאָרֶץ׃ כֹּל ׀
that you-may-eat from-all-of the-animal that on the-land (3) any-of

מַפְרֶסֶת פַּרְסָה וְשֹׁסַעַת שֶׁסַע פְּרָסֹת מַעֲלַת גֵּרָה בַּבְּהֵמָה
splitting hoof and-dividing division-of hoofs chewing-of cud among-the-animal

the Israelites' fellowship
offerings.[a] [15]The thigh that
was presented and the breast
that was waved must be
brought with the fat portions
of the offerings made by fire,
to be waved before the LORD as
a wave offering. This will be
the regular share for you and
your children, as the LORD has
commanded."

[16]When Moses inquired
about the goat of the sin
offering and found that it had
been burned up, he was angry
with Eleazar and Ithamar,
Aaron's remaining sons, and
asked, [17]"Why didn't you eat
the sin offering in the sanctuary area? It is most holy; it was
given to you to take away the
guilt of the community by
making atonement for them
before the LORD. [18]Since its
blood was not taken into the
Holy Place, you should have
eaten the goat in the sanctuary
area, as I commanded."

[19]Aaron replied to Moses,
"Today they sacrificed their
sin offering and their burnt
offering before the LORD, but
such things as this have happened to me. Would the LORD
have been pleased if I had eat-
en the sin offering today?"
[20]When Moses heard this, he
was satisfied.

Clean and Unclean Food

11 The LORD said to Moses
and Aaron, [2]"Say to the
Israelites: 'Of all the animals
that live on land, these are the
ones you may eat: [3]You may
eat any animal that has a split
hoof completely divided and
that chews the cud.

[a]14 Traditionally *peace offerings*

אֹתָהּ תֹּאכֵלוּ׃ אַךְ אֶת־ זֶה לֹא תֹאכְלוּ מִמַּעֲלֵי
from-ones-chewing-of you-must-eat not this *** only (4) you-may-eat her

הַגֵּרָה וּמִמַּפְרִיסֵי הַפַּרְסָה אֶת־ הַגָּמָל כִּי־ מַעֲלֵה
chewing-of though the-camel *** the-hoof and-from-ones-splitting-of the-cud

גֵרָה הוּא וּפַרְסָה אֵינֶנּוּ מַפְרִיס טָמֵא הוּא לָכֶם׃ וְאֶת־ הַשָּׁפָן כִּי־
though the-coney and (5) for-you he unclean splitting not-he but-hoof he cud

מַעֲלֵה גֵרָה הוּא וּפַרְסָה לֹא יַפְרִיס טָמֵא הוּא לָכֶם׃ וְאֶת־
and (6) for-you he unclean he-splits not but-hoof he cud chewing-of

הָאַרְנֶבֶת כִּי־ מַעֲלַת גֵּרָה הִוא וּפַרְסָה לֹא הִפְרִיסָה טְמֵאָה הִוא
she unclean she-splits not but-hoof she cud chewing-of though the-rabbit

לָכֶם׃ וְאֶת־ הַחֲזִיר כִּי־ מַפְרִיס פַּרְסָה הוּא וְשֹׁסַע שֶׁסַע
division-of and-dividing he hoof splitting though the-pig and (7) for-you

פַּרְסָה וְהוּא גֵּרָה לֹא־ יִגָּר טָמֵא הוּא לָכֶם׃ מִבְּשָׂרָם לֹא
not from-meat-of-them (8) for-you he unclean he-chews not cud but-he hoof

תֹאכֵלוּ וּבְנִבְלָתָם לֹא תִגָּעוּ טְמֵאִים הֵם לָכֶם׃
for-you they unclean-ones you-must-touch not or-on-carcass-of-them you-must-eat

אֶת־ זֶה תֹּאכְלוּ מִכֹּל אֲשֶׁר בַּמָּיִם כֹּל אֲשֶׁר־ לוֹ סְנַפִּיר
fin to-him that any in-the-waters that from-all you-may-eat this *** (9)

וְקַשְׂקֶשֶׂת בַּמַּיִם בַּיַּמִּים וּבַנְּחָלִים אֹתָם תֹּאכֵלוּ׃
you-may-eat them and-in-the-streams in-the-seas in-the-waters and-scale

וְכֹל אֲשֶׁר אֵין־ לוֹ סְנַפִּיר וְקַשְׂקֶשֶׂת בַּיַּמִּים וּבַנְּחָלִים
or-in-the-streams in-the-seas or-scale fin to-him not that but-any (10)

מִכֹּל שֶׁרֶץ הַמַּיִם וּמִכֹּל נֶפֶשׁ הַחַיָּה
the-living creature-of or-among-every-of the-waters swarmer-of among-every-of

אֲשֶׁר בַּמָּיִם שֶׁקֶץ הֵם לָכֶם׃ וְשֶׁקֶץ יִהְיוּ
they-are since-detestable (11) to-you they detestable in-the-waters that

לָכֶם מִבְּשָׂרָם לֹא תֹאכֵלוּ וְאֶת־ נִבְלָתָם תְּשַׁקֵּצוּ׃
you-must-detest carcass-of-them and you-must-eat not from-meat-of-them to-you

כֹּל אֲשֶׁר אֵין־ לוֹ סְנַפִּיר וְקַשְׂקֶשֶׂת בַּמָּיִם שֶׁקֶץ הוּא לָכֶם׃
to-you he detestable in-the-waters or-scale fin to-him not that any (12)

וְאֶת־ אֵלֶּה תְּשַׁקְּצוּ מִן־ הָעוֹף לֹא יֵאָכְלוּ
they-must-be-eaten not the-bird among you-must-detest these and (13)

שֶׁקֶץ הֵם אֶת־ הַנֶּשֶׁר וְאֶת־ הַפֶּרֶס וְאֵת הָעָזְנִיָּה׃
the-black-vulture and the-vulture and the-eagle *** they detestable

וְאֶת־ הַדָּאָה וְאֶת־ הָאַיָּה לְמִינָהּ׃ אֵת כָּל־
any-of *** (15) any-kind-of-her the-black-kite and the-red-kite and (14)

עֹרֵב לְמִינוֹ׃ וְאֵת בַּת הַיַּעֲנָה וְאֶת־ הַתַּחְמָס
the-screech-owl and the-horned-owl daughter-of and (16) by-kind-of-him raven

4" 'There are some that only chew the cud or only have a split hoof, but you must not eat them. The camel, though it chews the cud, does not have a split hoof; it is ceremonially unclean for you. 5The coney,[v] though it chews the cud, does not have a split hoof; it is unclean for you. 6The rabbit, though it chews the cud, does not have a split hoof; it is unclean for you. 7And the pig, though it has a split hoof completely divided, does not chew the cud; it is unclean for you. 8You must not eat their meat or touch their carcasses; they are unclean for you.

9" 'Of all the creatures living in the water of the seas and the streams, you may eat any that have fins and scales. 10But all creatures in the seas or streams that do not have fins and scales—whether among all the swarming things or among all the other living creatures in the water—you are to detest. 11And since you are to detest them, you must not eat their meat and you must detest their carcasses. 12Anything living in the water that does not have fins and scales is to be detestable to you.

13" 'These are the birds you are to detest and not eat because they are detestable: the eagle, the vulture, the black vulture, 14the red kite, any kind of black kite, 15any kind of raven, 16the horned owl, the

v5 That is, the hyrax or rock badger

וְאֶת־ הַשַּׁחַף וְאֶת־ הַנֵּץ לְמִינֵהוּ׃ וְאֶת־ הַכּוֹס וְאֶת־
and the-little-owl and (17) any-kind-of-him the-hawk and the-gull and

הַשָּׁלָךְ וְאֶת־ הַיַּנְשׁוּף׃ וְאֶת־ הַתִּנְשֶׁמֶת וְאֶת־ הַקָּאָת
the-desert-owl and the-white-owl and (18) the-great-owl and the-cormorant

וְאֶת־ הָרָחָם׃ וְאֵת הַחֲסִידָה הָאֲנָפָה לְמִינָהּ וְאֶת־ הַדּוּכִיפַת
the-hoopoe and any-kind-of-her the-heron the-stork and (19) the-osprey and

וְאֶת־ הָעֲטַלֵּף׃ כֹּל שֶׁרֶץ הָעוֹף הַהֹלֵךְ עַל־אַרְבַּע
four on the-one-walking the-flyer insect-of any-of (20) the-bat and

שֶׁקֶץ הוּא לָכֶם׃ אַךְ אֶת־ זֶה תֹּאכְלוּ מִכֹּל
from-every-of you-may-eat this *** however (21) to-you he detestable

שֶׁרֶץ הָעוֹף הַהֹלֵךְ עַל־ אַרְבַּע אֲשֶׁר־ לֹא כְרָעַיִם מִמַּעַל
from-above legs to-him that four on the-one-walking the-wing insect-of

לְרַגְלָיו לְנַתֵּר בָּהֵן עַל־ הָאָרֶץ׃ אֶת־ אֵלֶּה מֵהֶם
from-them these *** (22) the-ground on with-them to-hop to-feet-of-him

תֹּאכֵלוּ אֶת־ הָאַרְבֶּה לְמִינוֹ וְאֶת־ הַסָּלְעָם לְמִינֵהוּ
any-kind-of-him the-katydid and any-kind-of-him the-locust *** you-may-eat

וְאֶת־ הַחַרְגֹּל לְמִינֵהוּ וְאֶת־ הֶחָגָב לְמִינֵהוּ׃
any-kind-of-him the-grasshopper and any-kind-of-him the-cricket and

וְכֹל שֶׁרֶץ הָעוֹף אֲשֶׁר־ לוֹ אַרְבַּע רַגְלָיִם שֶׁקֶץ הוּא
he detestable feet four to-him that the-wing insect-of but-every-of (23)

לָכֶם׃ וּלְאֵלֶּה תִּטַּמָּאוּ כָּל־ הַנֹּגֵעַ
the-one-touching every-of you-will-become-unclean and-by-these (24) to-you

בְּנִבְלָתָם יִטְמָא עַד־ הָעָרֶב׃ וְכָל־
and-every-of (25) the-evening till he-will-be-unclean on-carcass-of-them

הַנֹּשֵׂא מִנִּבְלָתָם יְכַבֵּס בְּגָדָיו
clothes-of-him he-must-wash on-carcass-of-them the-one-picking-up

וְטָמֵא עַד־ הָעָרֶב׃ לְכָל־ הַבְּהֵמָה אֲשֶׁר
that the-animal to-every-of (26) the-evening till and-he-will-be-unclean

הִוא מַפְרֶסֶת פַּרְסָה וְשֶׁסַע ׀ אֵינֶנָּה שֹׁסַעַת וְגֵרָה אֵינֶנָּה מַעֲלָה
chewing not-she or-cud dividing not-she but-division hoof splitting she

טְמֵאִים הֵם לָכֶם כָּל־ הַנֹּגֵעַ בָּהֶם יִטְמָא׃
he-will-be-unclean on-them the-one-touching every-of to-you they unclean-ones

וְכֹל ׀ הוֹלֵךְ עַל־ כַּפָּיו בְּכָל־ הַחַיָּה
the-animal among-all-of paws-of-him on one-walking and-every-of (27)

הַהֹלֶכֶת עַל־אַרְבַּע טְמֵאִים הֵם לָכֶם כָּל־ הַנֹּגֵעַ
the-one-touching every-of to-you they unclean-ones four on the-one-walking

בְּנִבְלָתָם יִטְמָא עַד־ הָעָרֶב׃ וְהַנֹּשֵׂא
the-one-picking-up (28) the-evening till he-will-be-unclean on-carcass-of-them

screech owl, the gull, any kind
of hawk, [17]the little owl, the
cormorant, the great owl, [18]the
white owl, the desert owl, the
osprey, [19]the stork, any kind of
heron, the hoopoe and the
bat.[w]

[20]" 'All flying insects that
walk on all fours are to be detestable to you. [21]There are,
however, some winged creatures that walk on all fours
that you may eat: those that
have jointed legs for hopping
on the ground. [22]Of these you
may eat any kind of locust,
katydid, cricket or grasshop-
per. [23]But all other winged
creatures that have four legs
you are to detest.

[24]" 'You will make yourselves unclean by these; whoever touches their carcasses
will be unclean till evening.
[25]Whoever picks up one of
their carcasses must wash his
clothes, and he will be unclean
till evening.

[26]" 'Every animal that has a
split hoof not completely divided or that does not chew
the cud is unclean for you;
whoever touches ⌞the carcass
of⌟ any of them will be unclean. [27]Of all the animals that
walk on all fours, those that
walk on their paws are unclean for you; whoever
touches their carcasses will be
unclean till evening. [28]Anyone

w19 The precise identification of some of the birds, insects and animals in this chapter is uncertain.

°21 ק לו

אֶת־ נִבְלָתָם יְכַבֵּס בְּגָדָיו וְטָמֵא עַד־
till and-he-will-be-unclean clothes-of-him he-must-wash carcass-of-them ***

הָעָרֶב טְמֵאִים הֵמָּה לָכֶם׃ (29) וְזֶה לָכֶם הַטָּמֵא
the-unclean to-you and-this (29) to-you they unclean-ones the-evening

בַּשֶּׁרֶץ הַשֹּׁרֵץ עַל־ הָאָרֶץ הַחֹלֶד וְהָעַכְבָּר
and-the-rat the-weasel the-ground on the-one-moving among-the-creeper

וְהַצָּב לְמִינֵהוּ׃ (30) וְהָאֲנָקָה וְהַכֹּחַ
and-the-monitor-lizard and-the-gecko (30) any-kind-of-him and-the-great-lizard

וְהַלְּטָאָה וְהַחֹמֶט וְהַתִּנְשָׁמֶת׃ (31) אֵלֶּה
these (31) and-the-chameleon and-the-skink and-the-wall-lizard

הַטְּמֵאִים לָכֶם בְּכָל־ הַשָּׁרֶץ כָּל־ הַנֹּגֵעַ
the-one-touching every-of the-creeper among-all-of for-you the-unclean-ones

בָּהֶם בְּמֹתָם יִטְמָא עַד־ הָעָרֶב׃ (32) וְכֹל
and-anything (32) the-evening till he-will-be-unclean when-to-die-them on-them

אֲשֶׁר־ יִפֹּל־ עָלָיו מֵהֶם ׀ בְּמֹתָם יִטְמָא מִכָּל־
if-any-of he-will-be-unclean when-to-die-them from-them on-him he-falls that

כְּלִי־ עֵץ אוֹ בֶגֶד אוֹ־ עוֹר אוֹ שָׂק כָּל־ כְּלִי אֲשֶׁר־
that article any-of sackcloth or hide or cloth or wood article-of

יֵעָשֶׂה מְלָאכָה בָּהֶם בַּמַּיִם יוּבָא
he-must-be-put in-the-waters with-them work he-may-be-done

וְטָמֵא עַד־ הָעֶרֶב וְטָהֵר׃ (33) וְכָל־
but-any-of (33) then-he-will-be-clean the-evening till and-he-will-be-unclean

כְּלִי־ חֶרֶשׂ אֲשֶׁר־ יִפֹּל מֵהֶם אֶל־ תּוֹכוֹ כֹּל אֲשֶׁר
that everything inside-of-him into from-them he-falls that clay pot-of

בְּתוֹכוֹ יִטְמָא וְאֹתוֹ תִשְׁבֹּרוּ׃ (34) מִכָּל־
from-any-of (34) you-must-break and-him he-will-be-unclean inside-of-him

הָאֹכֶל אֲשֶׁר יֵאָכֵל אֲשֶׁר יָבוֹא עָלָיו מַיִם יִטְמָא
he-is-unclean waters onto-him he-comes that he-could-be-eaten that the-food

וְכָל־ מַשְׁקֶה אֲשֶׁר יִשָּׁתֶה בְּכָל־ כְּלִי יִטְמָא׃
he-is-unclean pot from-any-of he-could-be-drunk that liquid and-any-of

(35) וְכֹל אֲשֶׁר־ יִפֹּל מִנִּבְלָתָם ׀ עָלָיו יִטְמָא
he-is-unclean on-him from-carcass-of-them he-falls that and-anything (35)

תַּנּוּר וְכִירַיִם יֻתָּץ טְמֵאִים הֵם וּטְמֵאִים יִהְיוּ
they-are and-unclean-ones they unclean-ones he-must-be-broken or-pot oven

לָכֶם׃ (36) אַךְ מַעְיָן וּבוֹר מִקְוֵה־ מַיִם יִהְיֶה
he-remains waters collector-of or-cistern-of spring however (36) to-you

טָהוֹר וְנֹגֵעַ בְּנִבְלָתָם יִטְמָא׃ (37) וְכִי יִפֹּל
he-falls but-if (37) he-is-unclean on-carcass-of-them but-one-touching clean

who picks up their carcasses
must wash his clothes, and he
will be unclean till evening.
They are unclean for you.
29" 'Of the animals that
move about on the ground,
these are unclean for you: the
weasel, the rat, any kind of
great lizard, 30the gecko, the
monitor lizard, the wall lizard,
the skink and the chameleon.
31Of all those that move along
the ground, these are unclean
for you. Whoever touches
them when they are dead will
be unclean till evening.
32When one of them dies and
falls on something, that article, whatever its use, will be
unclean, whether it is made of
wood, cloth, hide or sackcloth.
Put it in water; it will be unclean till evening, and then it
will be clean. 33If one of them
falls into a clay pot, everything
in it will be unclean, and you
must break the pot. 34Any food
that could be eaten but has
water on it from such a pot is
unclean, and any liquid that
could be drunk from it is unclean. 35Anything that one of
their carcasses falls on
becomes unclean; an oven or
cooking pot must be broken
up. They are unclean, and you
are to regard them as unclean.
36A spring, however, or a cistern for collecting water remains clean, but anyone who
touches one of these carcasses
is unclean. 37If a carcass falls

מִנִּבְלָתָ֑ם עַל־ כָּל־ זֶ֥רַע זֵר֖וּעַ אֲשֶׁ֣ר יִזָּרֵ֑עַ טָה֖וֹר
clean he-will-be-planted that plant seed-of any-of on from-carcass-of-them

ה֑וּא׃ וְכִ֤י יֻתַּן־ מַ֙יִם֙ עַל־ זֶ֔רַע וְנָפַ֥ל מִנִּבְלָתָ֖ם
from-carcass-of-them and-he-falls seed on waters he-was-put but-if (38) he

עָלָ֑יו טָמֵ֥א ה֖וּא לָכֶֽם׃ וְכִ֤י יָמוּת֙ מִן־ הַבְּהֵמָ֔ה אֲשֶׁר־הִ֥יא
she that the-animal from he-dies and-if (39) for-you he unclean on-him

לָכֶ֖ם לְאָכְלָ֑ה הַנֹּגֵ֥עַ בְּנִבְלָתָ֖הּ יִטְמָ֥א עַד־
till he-will-be-unclean on-carcass-of-her the-one-touching for-food to-you

הָעָֽרֶב׃ וְהָֽאֹכֵל֙ מִנִּבְלָתָ֔הּ יְכַבֵּ֖ס
he-must-wash from-carcass-of-her and-the-one-eating (40) the-evening

בְּגָדָ֑יו וְטָמֵ֖א עַד־ הָעָ֑רֶב וְהַנֹּשֵׂא֙
and-the-one-picking-up the-evening till and-he-will-be-unclean clothes-of-him

אֶת־ נִבְלָתָ֔הּ יְכַבֵּ֥ס בְּגָדָ֖יו וְטָמֵ֥א עַד־
till and-he-will-be-unclean clothes-of-him he-must-wash carcass-of-her ***

הָעָֽרֶב׃ וְכָל־ הַשֶּׁ֖רֶץ הַשֹּׁרֵ֣ץ עַל־ הָאָ֑רֶץ
the-ground on the-one-moving the-creature and-every-of (41) the-evening

שֶׁ֥קֶץ ה֖וּא לֹ֥א יֵאָכֵֽל׃ כֹּל֩ הוֹלֵ֨ךְ עַל־ גָּח֜וֹן וְכֹ֣ל ׀
or-any-of belly on moving any-of (42) he-may-be-eaten not he detestable

הוֹלֵ֣ךְ עַל־אַרְבַּ֗ע עַ֚ד כָּל־ מַרְבֵּ֣ה רַגְלַ֔יִם לְכָל־ הַשֶּׁ֖רֶץ הַשֹּׁרֵ֣ץ
the-one-moving the-creature of-any-of feet many-of any-of or four on moving

עַל־ הָאָ֑רֶץ לֹ֥א תֹאכְל֖וּם כִּי־ שֶׁ֥קֶץ הֵֽם׃ אַל־ תְּשַׁקְּצוּ֙
you-defile not (43) they detestable for you-may-eat-them not the-ground on

אֶת־ נַפְשֹׁ֣תֵיכֶ֔ם בְּכָל־ הַשֶּׁ֖רֶץ הַשֹּׁרֵ֑ץ וְלֹ֤א
and-not the-one-creeping the-creature by-any-of selves-of-you ***

תִֽטַּמְּאוּ֙ בָּהֶ֔ם וְנִטְמֵתֶ֖ם בָּֽם׃ כִּ֣י
for (44) by-them or-you-be-made-unclean by-them you-make-yourselves-unclean

אֲנִ֣י יְהוָה֮ אֱלֹהֵיכֶם֒ וְהִתְקַדִּשְׁתֶּם֙ וִהְיִיתֶ֣ם קְדֹשִׁ֔ים כִּ֥י
for holy-ones and-you-be so-you-consecrate-yourselves God-of-you Yahweh I

קָד֖וֹשׁ אָ֑נִי וְלֹ֤א תְטַמְּאוּ֙ אֶת־ נַפְשֹׁ֣תֵיכֶ֔ם בְּכָל־ הַשֶּׁ֖רֶץ
the-creature by-any-of selves-of-you *** you-make-unclean so-not I holy

הָרֹמֵ֖שׂ עַל־ הָאָֽרֶץ׃ כִּ֣י ׀ אֲנִ֣י יְהוָ֗ה הַֽמַּעֲלֶ֤ה אֶתְכֶם֙
you the-one-bringing Yahweh I for (45) the-ground on the-one-moving

מֵאֶ֣רֶץ מִצְרַ֔יִם לִהְיֹ֥ת לָכֶ֖ם לֵאלֹהִ֑ים וִהְיִיתֶ֣ם קְדֹשִׁ֔ים כִּ֥י קָד֖וֹשׁ אָֽנִי׃
I holy for holy-ones so-you-be as-God for-you to-be Egypt from-land-of

זֹ֣את תּוֹרַ֤ת הַבְּהֵמָה֙ וְהָע֔וֹף וְכֹל֙ נֶ֣פֶשׁ
thing-of and-every-of and-the-bird the-animal regulation-of this (46)

הַֽחַיָּ֔ה הָֽרֹמֶ֖שֶׂת בַּמָּ֑יִם וּלְכָל־ נֶ֖פֶשׁ
creature and-for-every-of in-the-waters the-one-moving the-living

on any seeds that are to be planted, they remain clean.
38But if water has been put on the seed and a carcass falls on it, it is unclean for you.

39" 'If an animal that you are allowed to eat dies, anyone who touches the carcass will be unclean till evening.
40Anyone who eats some of the carcass must wash his clothes, and he will be unclean till evening. Anyone who picks up the carcass must wash his clothes, and he will be unclean till evening.

41" 'Every creature that moves about on the ground is detestable; it is not to be eaten.
42You are not to eat any creature that moves about on the ground, whether it moves on its belly or walks on all fours or on many feet; it is detestable.
43Do not defile yourselves by any of these creatures. Do not make yourselves unclean by means of them or be made unclean by them.
44I am the LORD your God; consecrate yourselves and be holy, because I am holy. Do not make yourselves unclean by any creature that moves about on the ground.
45I am the LORD who brought you up out of Egypt to be your God; therefore be holy, because I am holy.

46" 'These are the regulations concerning animals, birds, every living thing that moves in the water and every creature that moves about on the

הַשֹּׁרֶצֶת עַל־ הָאָרֶץ׃ לְהַבְדִּיל בֵּין הַטָּמֵא

the-unclean between to-distinguish (47) the-ground on the-one-moving

וּבֵין הַטָּהֹר וּבֵין הַחַיָּה הַנֶּאֱכֶלֶת וּבֵין

and-between the-being-edible the-creature and-between the-clean and-between

הַחַיָּה אֲשֶׁר לֹא תֵאָכֵל׃ וַיְדַבֵּר יְהוָה אֶל־ מֹשֶׁה

Moses to Yahweh and-he-spoke (12:1) she-may-be-eaten not that the-creature

לֵאמֹר׃ דַּבֵּר אֶל־ בְּנֵי יִשְׂרָאֵל לֵאמֹר אִשָּׁה כִּי תַזְרִיעַ

she-conceives when woman to-say Israel sons-of to say! (2) to-say

וְיָלְדָה זָכָר וְטָמְאָה שִׁבְעַת יָמִים כִּימֵי

as-days-of days seven-of then-she-will-be-unclean son and-she-bears

נִדַּת דְּוֺתָהּ תִּטְמָא׃ וּבַיּוֹם הַשְּׁמִינִי

the-eighth and-on-the-day (3) she-is-unclean monthly-of-her period-of

יִמּוֹל בְּשַׂר עָרְלָתוֹ׃ וּשְׁלֹשִׁים יוֹם וּשְׁלֹשֶׁת

and-three-of day and-thirty (4) foreskin-of-him skin-of he-must-be-circumcised

יָמִים תֵּשֵׁב בִּדְמֵי טָהֳרָה בְּכָל־ קֹדֶשׁ לֹא־

not sacred on-any-of purification in-bloods-of she-must-wait days

תִגָּע וְאֶל־ הַמִּקְדָּשׁ לֹא תָבֹא עַד־ מְלֹאת יְמֵי

days-of to-be-over until she-must-go not the-sanctuary or-to she-must-touch

טָהֳרָהּ׃ וְאִם־ נְקֵבָה תֵלֵד וְטָמְאָה

then-she-will-be-unclean she-bears daughter and-if (5) purification-of-her

שְׁבֻעַיִם כְּנִדָּתָהּ וְשִׁשִּׁים יוֹם וְשֵׁשֶׁת יָמִים תֵּשֵׁב עַל־

until she-must-wait days and-six-of day and-sixty as-period-of-her two-weeks

דְּמֵי טָהֳרָה׃ וּבִמְלֹאת ׀ יְמֵי טָהֳרָהּ

purification-of-her days-of and-when-to-be-over (6) purification bloods-of

לְבֵן אוֹ לְבַת תָּבִיא כֶּבֶשׂ בֶּן־ שְׁנָתוֹ

year-of-him son-of lamb she-must-bring for-daughter or for-son

לְעֹלָה וּבֶן־ יוֹנָה אוֹ־ תֹר לְחַטָּאת אֶל־

to for-sin-offering dove or pigeon and-young-of for-burnt-offering

פֶּתַח אֹהֶל־ מוֹעֵד אֶל־ הַכֹּהֵן׃ וְהִקְרִיבוֹ לִפְנֵי

before and-he-shall-offer-him (7) the-priest to Meeting Tent-of entrance-of

יְהוָה וְכִפֶּר עָלֶיהָ וְטָהֲרָה מִמְּקֹר

from-flow-of then-she-will-be-clean for-her and-he-shall-atone Yahweh

דָּמֶיהָ זֹאת תּוֹרַת הַיֹּלֶדֶת לַזָּכָר אוֹ

or to-the-boy the-one-giving-birth regulation-of this bloods-of-her

לַנְּקֵבָה׃ וְאִם־ לֹא תִמְצָא יָדָהּ דֵּי שֶׂה

lamb price-of hand-of-her she-can-afford not but-if (8) to-the-girl

וְלָקְחָה שְׁתֵּי־ תֹרִים אוֹ שְׁנֵי בְּנֵי יוֹנָה אֶחָד

one pigeon young-ones-of two-of or doves two-of then-she-must-bring

ground. 47You must distinguish between the unclean
and the clean, between living
creatures that may be eaten
and those that may not be eat-
en.' "

Purification After Childbirth

12 The LORD said to
Moses, 2"Say to the Is-
raelites: 'A woman who
becomes pregnant and gives
birth to a son will be
ceremonially unclean for sev-
en days, just as she is unclean
during her monthly period.
3On the eighth day the boy is
to be circumcised. 4Then the
woman must wait thirty-three
days to be purified from her
bleeding. She must not touch
anything sacred or go to the
sanctuary until the days of her
purification are over. 5If she
gives birth to a daughter, for
two weeks the woman will be
unclean, as in her period.
Then she must wait sixty-six
days to be purified from her
bleeding.
6" 'When the days of her
purification for a son or
daughter are over, she is to
bring to the priest at the entrance to the Tent of Meeting a
year-old lamb for a burnt
offering and a young pigeon
or a dove for a sin offering. 7He
shall offer them before the
LORD to make atonement for
her, and then she will be
ceremonially clean from her
flow of blood. These are the
regulations for the woman
who gives birth to a boy or a
girl.
8" 'If she cannot afford a
lamb, she is to bring two
doves or two young pigeons,

לְעֹלָה וְאֶחָד לְחַטָּאת וְכִפֶּר עָלֶיהָ
for-her so-he-will-atone for-sin-offering and-one for-burnt-offering

הַכֹּהֵן וְטָהֵרָה׃ (13:1) וַיְדַבֵּר יְהוָה אֶל־ מֹשֶׁה וְאֶל־
and-to Moses to Yahweh and-he-spoke (13:1) and-she-will-be-clean the-priest

אַהֲרֹן לֵאמֹר׃ (2) אָדָם כִּי־ יִהְיֶה בְעוֹר־ בְּשָׂרוֹ שְׂאֵת אוֹ־
or swelling flesh-of-him on-skin-of he-has when anyone (2) to-say Aaron

סַפַּחַת אוֹ בַהֶרֶת וְהָיָה בְעוֹר־ בְּשָׂרוֹ לְנֶגַע
to-infection-of flesh-of-him on-skin-of and-he-may-become bright-spot or rash

צָרָעַת וְהוּבָא אֶל־ אַהֲרֹן הַכֹּהֵן אוֹ אֶל־אַחַד
one to or the-priest Aaron to then-he-must-be-brought skin-disease

מִבָּנָיו הַכֹּהֲנִים׃ (3) וְרָאָה הַכֹּהֵן אֶת־ הַנֶּגַע
the-sore *** the-priest and-he-must-examine (3) the-priests from-sons-of-him

בְּעוֹר־ הַבָּשָׂר וְשֵׂעָר בַּנֶּגַע הָפַךְ ׀ לָבָן וּמַרְאֵה
or-appearance-of white he-turned in-the-sore if-hair the-flesh on-skin-of

הַנֶּגַע עָמֹק מֵעוֹר בְּשָׂרוֹ נֶגַע צָרַעַת הוּא
he skin-disease infection-of flesh-of-him than-skin-of deeper the-sore

וְרָאָהוּ הַכֹּהֵן וְטִמֵּא אֹתוֹ׃ (4) וְאִם־
but-if (4) him then-he-shall-pronounce-unclean the-priest when-he-examines-him

בַּהֶרֶת לְבָנָה הִוא בְּעוֹר בְּשָׂרוֹ וְעָמֹק אֵין־ מַרְאֶהָ
appearance-of-her he-is-not and-deeper flesh-of-him in-skin-of she white spot

מִן־ הָעוֹר וּשְׂעָרָה לֹא־ הָפַךְ לָבָן וְהִסְגִּיר הַכֹּהֵן
the-priest then-he-must-isolate while he-turned not and-hair the-skin than

אֶת־ הַנֶּגַע שִׁבְעַת יָמִים׃ (5) וְרָאָהוּ הַכֹּהֵן
the-priest and-he-must-examine-him (5) days seven-of the-infected-person ***

בַּיּוֹם הַשְּׁבִיעִי וְהִנֵּה הַנֶּגַע עָמַד בְּעֵינָיו
in-eyes-of-him he-is-unchanged the-infection and-if the-seventh on-the-day

לֹא־ פָשָׂה הַנֶּגַע בָּעוֹר וְהִסְגִּירוֹ הַכֹּהֵן
the-priest then-he-must-isolate-him in-the-skin the-infection he-spread not

שִׁבְעַת יָמִים שֵׁנִית׃ (6) וְרָאָה הַכֹּהֵן אֹתוֹ בַּיּוֹם
on-the-day him the-priest and-he-must-examine (6) another days seven-of

הַשְּׁבִיעִי שֵׁנִית וְהִנֵּה כֵּהָה הַנֶּגַע וְלֹא־ פָשָׂה
he-spread and-not the-infection he-faded and-if again the-seventh

הַנֶּגַע בָּעוֹר וְטִהֲרוֹ הַכֹּהֵן מִסְפַּחַת
rash the-priest then-he-shall-pronounce-clean-him in-the-skin the-infection

הִוא וְכִבֶּס בְּגָדָיו וְטָהֵר׃ (7) וְאִם־ פָּשֹׂה
to-spread but-if (7) and-he-will-be-clean clothes-of-him and-he-must-wash he

תִפְשֶׂה הַמִּסְפַּחַת בָּעוֹר אַחֲרֵי הֵרָאֹתוֹ אֶל־ הַכֹּהֵן
the-priest to to-be-shown-him after in-the-skin the-rash she-spread

one for a burnt offering and
the other for a sin offering. In
this way the priest will make
atonement for her, and she
will be clean.' "

Regulations About Infectious Skin Diseases

13 The LORD said to Moses
and Aaron, 2"When
anyone has a swelling or a
rash or a bright spot on his
skin that may become an infectious skin disease,[x] he must
be brought to Aaron the priest
or to one of his sons[y] who is a
priest. 3The priest is to examine the sore on his skin, and if
the hair in the sore has turned
white and the sore appears to
be more than skin deep,[z] it is
an infectious skin disease.
When the priest examines
him, he shall pronounce him
ceremonially unclean. 4If the
spot on his skin is white but
does not appear to be more
than skin deep and the hair in
it has not turned white, the
priest is to put the infected
person in isolation for seven
days. 5On the seventh day the
priest is to examine him, and
if he sees that the sore is unchanged and has not spread in
the skin, he is to keep him in
isolation another seven days.
6On the seventh day the priest
is to examine him again, and
if the sore has faded and has
not spread in the skin, the
priest shall pronounce him
clean; it is only a rash. The
man must wash his clothes,
and he will be clean. 7But if the
rash does spread in his skin
after he has shown himself to
the priest to be pronounced

[x]2 Traditionally *leprosy;* the Hebrew word was used for various diseases affecting the skin—not necessarily leprosy; also elsewhere in this chapter.
[y]2 Or *descendants*
[z]3 Or *be lower than the rest of the skin;* also elsewhere in this chapter

לְטָהֳרָתוֹ וְנִרְאָה שֵׁנִית אֶל־ הַכֹּהֵן׃
the-priest before again then-he-must-appear for-purification-of-him

וְרָאָה הַכֹּהֵן וְהִנֵּה פָּשְׂתָה הַמִּסְפַּחַת בָּעוֹר
in-the-skin the-rash she-spread and-if the-priest and-he-must-examine (8)

וְטִמְּאוֹ הַכֹּהֵן צָרַעַת הִוא׃
she infectious-disease the-priest then-he-shall-pronounce-unclean-him

נֶגַע צָרַעַת כִּי תִהְיֶה בְּאָדָם וְהוּבָא
then-he-must-be-brought on-anyone she-is when skin-disease infection-of (9)

אֶל־ הַכֹּהֵן׃ וְרָאָה הַכֹּהֵן וְהִנֵּה שְׂאֵת־ לְבָנָה
white swelling and-if the-priest and-he-must-examine (10) the-priest to

בָּעוֹר וְהִיא הָפְכָה שֵׂעָר לָבָן וּמִחְיַת בָּשָׂר חַי
raw flesh and-spot-of white hair she-turned and-she in-the-skin

בַּשְׂאֵת׃ צָרַעַת נוֹשֶׁנֶת הִוא בְּעוֹר בְּשָׂרוֹ
flesh-of-him in-skin-of she being-chronic skin-disease (11) in-the-swelling

וְטִמְּאוֹ הַכֹּהֵן לֹא יַסְגִּרֶנּוּ כִּי
for he-must-isolate-him not the-priest and-he-shall-pronounce-unclean-him

טָמֵא הוּא׃ וְאִם־ פָּרוֹחַ תִּפְרַח הַצָּרַעַת בָּעוֹר
over-the-skin the-disease she-breaks-out to-break-out and-if (12) he unclean

וְכִסְּתָה הַצָּרַעַת אֵת כָּל־ עוֹר הַנֶּגַע
the-infected-person skin-of all-of *** the-disease and-she-covers

מֵרֹאשׁוֹ וְעַד־ רַגְלָיו לְכָל־ מַרְאֵה עֵינֵי הַכֹּהֵן׃
the-priest eyes-of sight-of in-all-of feet-of-him even-to from-head-of-him

וְרָאָה הַכֹּהֵן וְהִנֵּה כִסְּתָה הַצָּרַעַת אֶת־ כָּל־
all-of *** the-disease she-covers and-if the-priest and-he-must-examine (13)

בְּשָׂרוֹ וְטִהַר אֶת־ הַנָּגַע כֻּלּוֹ
all-of-him the-infected-person *** then-he-shall-pronounce-clean body-of-him

הָפַךְ לָבָן טָהוֹר הוּא׃ וּבְיוֹם הֵרָאוֹת בּוֹ בָּשָׂר חַי
raw flesh on-him to-appear but-on-day (14) he clean white he-turned

יִטְמָא׃ וְרָאָה הַכֹּהֵן אֶת־ הַבָּשָׂר הַחַי
the-raw the-flesh *** the-priest when-he-sees (15) he-will-be-unclean

וְטִמְּאוֹ הַבָּשָׂר הַחַי טָמֵא הוּא
he unclean the-raw the-flesh then-he-shall-pronounce-unclean-him

צָרַעַת הוּא׃ אוֹ כִי יָשׁוּב הַבָּשָׂר הַחַי וְנֶהְפַּךְ
and-he-turns the-raw the-flesh he-changes if but (16) he infectious-disease

לְלָבָן וּבָא אֶל־ הַכֹּהֵן׃ וְרָאָהוּ
and-he-must-examine-him (17) the-priest to then-he-must-go to-white

הַכֹּהֵן וְהִנֵּה נֶהְפַּךְ הַנֶּגַע לְלָבָן וְטִהַר
then-he-shall-pronounce-clean to-white the-sore he-turned and-if the-priest

clean, he must appear before
the priest again. 8The priest is
to examine him, and if the
rash has spread in the skin, he
shall pronounce him unclean;
it is an infectious disease.
9"When anyone has an in-
fectious skin disease, he must
be brought to the priest. 10The
priest is to examine him, and
if there is a white swelling in
the skin that has turned the
hair white and if there is raw
flesh in the swelling, 11it is a
chronic skin disease and the
priest shall pronounce him
unclean. He is not to put him
in isolation, because he is already unclean.
12"If the disease breaks out
all over his skin and, so far as
the priest can see, it covers all
the skin of the infected person
from head to foot, 13the priest
is to examine him, and if the
disease has covered his whole
body, he shall pronounce that
person clean. Since it has all
turned white, he is clean. 14But
whenever raw flesh appears
on him, he will be unclean.
15When the priest sees the raw
flesh, he shall pronounce him
unclean. The raw flesh is unclean; he has an infectious disease. 16Should the raw flesh
change and turn white, he
must go to the priest. 17The
priest is to examine him, and
if the sores have turned white,
the priest shall pronounce the

הַכֹּהֵן אֶת־ הַנֶּגַע טָהוֹר הוּא׃ וּבָשָׂר כִּי־ יִהְיֶה בוֹ־
on-him he-has when and-body (18) he clean the-infected-person *** the-priest

בְעֹרוֹ שְׁחִין וְנִרְפָּא׃ וְהָיָה בִּמְקוֹם הַשְּׁחִין
the-boil in-place-of and-he-appears (19) and-he-heals boil skin-of-him

שְׂאֵת לְבָנָה אוֹ בַהֶרֶת לְבָנָה אֲדַמְדָּמֶת וְנִרְאָה אֶל־ הַכֹּהֵן׃
the-priest to then-he-must-appear reddish white spot or white swelling

וְרָאָה הַכֹּהֵן וְהִנֵּה מַרְאֶהָ שָׁפָל מִן־
than deeper appearance-of-her and-if the-priest and-he-must-examine (20)

הָעוֹר וּשְׂעָרָהּ הָפַךְ לָבָן וְטִמְּאוֹ
then-he-shall-pronounce-unclean-him white he-turned and-hair-of-her the-skin

הַכֹּהֵן נֶגַע־ צָרַעַת הִוא בַּשְּׁחִין פָּרָחָה׃
she-broke-out after-the-boil she skin-disease infection-of the-priest

וְאִם ׀ יִרְאֶנָּה הַכֹּהֵן וְהִנֵּה אֵין־ בָּהּ שֵׂעָר לָבָן
white hair in-her not and-if the-priest he-examines-her but-if (21)

וּשְׁפָלָה אֵינֶנָּה מִן־ הָעוֹר וְהִיא כֵהָה וְהִסְגִּירוֹ
then-he-shall-isolate-him faded and-she the-skin than is-not-she and-deeper

הַכֹּהֵן שִׁבְעַת יָמִים׃ וְאִם־ פָּשֹׂה תִפְשֶׂה בָּעוֹר
in-the-skin she-spreads to-spread but-if (22) days seven-of the-priest

וְטִמֵּא הַכֹּהֵן אֹתוֹ נֶגַע הִוא׃ וְאִם־
but-if (23) she infection him the-priest then-he-shall-pronounce-unclean

תַּחְתֶּיהָ תַּעֲמֹד הַבַּהֶרֶת לֹא פָשָׂתָה צָרֶבֶת הַשְּׁחִין הִוא
she the-boil scar-of she-spread not the-spot she-stays in-place-of-her

וְטִהֲרוֹ הַכֹּהֵן׃ אוֹ בָשָׂר כִּי־ יִהְיֶה
he-has when body or (24) the-priest and-he-shall-pronounce-clean-him

בְעֹרוֹ מִכְוַת־ אֵשׁ וְהָיְתָה מִחְיַת הַמִּכְוָה בַּהֶרֶת לְבָנָה
white spot the-burn raw-flesh-of and-she-appears fire burn-of skin-of-him

אֲדַמְדֶּמֶת אוֹ לְבָנָה׃ וְרָאָה אֹתָהּ הַכֹּהֵן וְהִנֵּה נֶהְפַּךְ
he-turned and-if the-priest her and-he-must-examine (25) white or reddish

שֵׂעָר לָבָן בַּבַּהֶרֶת וּמַרְאֶהָ עָמֹק מִן־ הָעוֹר צָרַעַת
infection the-skin than deeper and-appearance-of-her in-the-spot white hair

הִוא בַּמִּכְוָה פָּרָחָה וְטִמֵּא אֹתוֹ הַכֹּהֵן
the-priest him and-he-shall-pronounce-unclean she-broke-out in-the-burn she

נֶגַע צָרַעַת הִוא׃ וְאִם ׀ יִרְאֶנָּה הַכֹּהֵן וְהִנֵּה
and-if the-priest he-examines-her but-if (26) she skin-disease infection-of

אֵין־ בַּבֶּהֶרֶת* שֵׂעָר לָבָן וּשְׁפָלָה אֵינֶנָּה מִן־ הָעוֹר
the-skin than is-not-she and-deeper white hair in-the-spot there-is-no

וְהִוא כֵהָה וְהִסְגִּירוֹ הַכֹּהֵן שִׁבְעַת יָמִים׃
days seven-of the-priest then-he-must-isolate-him faded and-she

infected person clean; then he will be clean.

[18]"When someone has a boil on his skin and it heals, [19]and in the place where the boil was, a white swelling or reddish-white spot appears, he must present himself to the priest. [20]The priest is to examine it, and if it appears to be more than skin deep and the hair in it has turned white, the priest shall pronounce him unclean. It is an infectious skin disease that has broken out where the boil was. [21]But if, when the priest examines it, there is no white hair in it and it is not more than skin deep and has faded, then the priest is to put him in isolation for seven days. [22]If it is spreading in the skin, the priest shall pronounce him unclean; it is infectious. [23]But if the spot is unchanged and has not spread, it is only a scar from the boil, and the priest shall pronounce him clean.

[24]"When someone has a burn on his skin and a reddish-white or white spot appears in the raw flesh of the burn, [25]the priest is to examine the spot, and if the hair in it has turned white, and it appears to be more than skin deep, it is an infectious disease that has broken out in the burn. The priest shall pronounce him unclean; it is an infectious skin disease. [26]But if the priest examines it and there is no white hair in the spot and if it is not more than skin deep and has faded, then the priest is to put him in isolation for seven days. [27]On the

***26 Most mss have *pathah* under the second *beth* ('בַּבַּ').**

וְרָאָהוּ הַכֹּהֵן בַּיּוֹם הַשְּׁבִיעִי אִם־ פָּשֹׂה
to-spread if the-seventh on-the-day the-priest and-he-must-examine-him (27)

תִפְשֶׂה בָּעוֹר וְטִמֵּא הַכֹּהֵן אֹתוֹ
him the-priest and-he-shall-pronounce-unclean in-the-skin she-spreads

נֶגַע צָרַעַת הִוא׃ וְאִם־ תַּחְתֶּיהָ תַעֲמֹד הַבַּהֶרֶת
the-spot she-stays in-place-of-her but-if (28) she skin-disease infection-of

לֹא־ פָשְׂתָה בָעוֹר וְהִוא כֵהָה שְׂאֵת הַמִּכְוָה הִוא
she the-burn swelling-of faded and-she in-the-skin she-spread not

וְטִהֲרוֹ הַכֹּהֵן כִּי־ צָרֶבֶת הַמִּכְוָה הִוא׃
she the-burn scar-of for the-priest and-he-shall-pronounce-clean-him

וְאִישׁ אוֹ אִשָּׁה כִּי־ יִהְיֶה בוֹ נָגַע בְּרֹאשׁ אוֹ בְזָקָן׃
on-chin or on-head sore on-him he-has if woman or and-man (29)

וְרָאָה הַכֹּהֵן אֶת־ הַנֶּגַע וְהִנֵּה מַרְאֵהוּ
appearance-of-him and-if the-sore *** the-priest then-he-must-examine (30)

עָמֹק מִן־ הָעוֹר וּבוֹ שֵׂעָר צָהֹב דָּק וְטִמֵּא
then-he-shall-call-unclean thin yellow hair and-in-him the-skin than deeper

אֹתוֹ הַכֹּהֵן נֶתֶק הוּא צָרַעַת הָרֹאשׁ אוֹ הַזָּקָן הוּא׃ וְכִי־
but-if (31) he the-chin or the-head infection-of he itch the-priest him

יִרְאֶה הַכֹּהֵן אֶת־ נֶגַע הַנֶּתֶק וְהִנֵּה אֵין־ מַרְאֵהוּ
appearance-of-him not and-if the-sore infection-of *** the-priest he-examines

עָמֹק מִן־ הָעוֹר וְשֵׂעָר שָׁחֹר אֵין בּוֹ וְהִסְגִּיר
then-he-must-isolate in-him not black and-hair the-skin than deeper

הַכֹּהֵן אֶת־ נֶגַע הַנֶּתֶק שִׁבְעַת יָמִים׃ וְרָאָה
and-he-must-examine (32) days seven-of the-sore one-infected-of *** the-priest

הַכֹּהֵן אֶת־ הַנֶּגַע בַּיּוֹם הַשְּׁבִיעִי וְהִנֵּה לֹא־ פָשָׂה הַנֶּתֶק
the-itch he-spread not and-if the-seventh on-the-day the-sore *** the-priest

וְלֹא־ הָיָה בוֹ שֵׂעָר צָהֹב וּמַרְאֵה הַנֶּתֶק אֵין עָמֹק מִן־
than deeper not the-itch and-appearance-of yellow hair in-him he-is and-not

הָעוֹר׃ וְהִתְגַּלָּח וְאֶת־ הַנֶּתֶק לֹא יְגַלֵּחַ
he-must-be-shaved not the-itch but and-he-must-be-shaved (33) the-skin

וְהִסְגִּיר הַכֹּהֵן אֶת־ הַנֶּתֶק שִׁבְעַת יָמִים שֵׁנִית׃
another days seven-of the-one-infected *** the-priest and-he-must-isolate

וְרָאָה הַכֹּהֵן אֶת־ הַנֶּתֶק בַּיּוֹם הַשְּׁבִיעִי
the-seventh on-the-day the-itch *** the-priest and-he-must-examine (34)

וְהִנֵּה לֹא־ פָשָׂה הַנֶּתֶק בָּעוֹר וּמַרְאֵהוּ אֵינֶנּוּ
not-is-he and-appearance-of-him in-the-skin the-itch he-spread not and-if

עָמֹק מִן־ הָעוֹר וְטִהַר אֹתוֹ הַכֹּהֵן
the-priest him then-he-shall-pronounce-clean the-skin than deeper

seventh day the priest is to examine him, and if it is spreading in the skin, the priest shall
pronounce him unclean; it is
an infectious skin disease. [28]If,
however, the spot is un-
changed and has not spread in
the skin but has faded, it is a
swelling from the burn, and
the priest shall pronounce him
clean; it is only a scar from the
burn.
[29]"If a man or woman has a
sore on the head or on the
chin, [30]the priest is to examine
the sore, and if it appears to be
more than skin deep and the
hair in it is yellow and thin,
the priest shall pronounce that
person unclean; it is an itch,
an infectious disease of the
head or chin. [31]But if, when
the priest examines this kind
of sore, it does not seem to be
more than skin deep and there
is no black hair in it, then the
priest is to put the infected
person in isolation for seven
days. [32]On the seventh day the
priest is to examine the sore,
and if the itch has not spread
and there is no yellow hair in
it and it does not appear to be
more than skin deep, [33]he
must be shaved except for the
diseased area, and the priest is
to keep him in isolation another seven days. [34]On the
seventh day the priest is to examine the itch and if it has not
spread in the skin and appears
to be no more than skin deep,
the priest shall pronounce him

וְכִבֶּס בְּגָדָיו וְטָהֵר׃ וְאִם־ פָּשֹׂה
to-spread but-if (35) and-he-will-be-clean clothes-of-him and-he-must-wash

יִפְשֶׂה הַנֶּתֶק בָּעוֹר אַחֲרֵי טָהֳרָתוֹ׃
purification-of-him after in-the-skin the-itch he-spreads

וְרָאָהוּ הַכֹּהֵן וְהִנֵּה פָּשָׂה הַנֶּתֶק בָּעוֹר לֹא־
not in-the-skin the-itch he-spread and-if the-priest and-he-must-examine-him (36)

יְבַקֵּר הַכֹּהֵן לַשֵּׂעָר הַצָּהֹב טָמֵא הוּא׃ וְאִם־
but-if (37) he unclean the-yellow for-the-hair the-priest he-need-look

בְּעֵינָיו עָמַד הַנֶּתֶק וְשֵׂעָר שָׁחֹר צָמַח־ בּוֹ
in-him he-grew black and-hair the-itch he-is-unchanged to-eyes-of-him

נִרְפָּא הַנֶּתֶק טָהוֹר הוּא וְטִהֲרוֹ הַכֹּהֵן׃
the-priest and-he-shall-pronounce-clean-him he clean the-itch he-is-healed

וְאִישׁ אוֹ־ אִשָּׁה כִּי־ יִהְיֶה בְעוֹר־ בְּשָׂרָם בֶּהָרֹת בֶּהָרֹת
spots spots flesh-of-them on-skin-of he-is when woman or and-man (38)

לְבָנֹת׃ וְרָאָה הַכֹּהֵן וְהִנֵּה בְעוֹר־ בְּשָׂרָם
flesh-of-them on-skin-of and-if the-priest and-he-must-examine (39) white-ones

בֶּהָרֹת כֵּהוֹת לְבָנֹת בֹּהַק הוּא פָּרַח בָּעוֹר טָהוֹר הוּא׃
he clean on-the-skin he-broke-out he rash white-ones dull-ones spots

וְאִישׁ כִּי יִמָּרֵט רֹאשׁוֹ קֵרֵחַ הוּא טָהוֹר הוּא׃ וְאִם
and-if (41) he clean he bald hair-of-him he-lost when and-man (40)

מִפְּאַת פָּנָיו יִמָּרֵט רֹאשׁוֹ גִּבֵּחַ הוּא טָהוֹר הוּא׃
he clean he bald-of-forehead hair-of-him he-lost head-of-him from-front-of

וְכִי־ יִהְיֶה בַקָּרַחַת אוֹ בַגַּבַּחַת נֶגַע לָבָן
white sore on-the-bald-forehead or on-the-bald-head he-is but-if (42)

אֲדַמְדָּם צָרַעַת פֹּרַחַת הִוא בְּקָרַחְתּוֹ אוֹ בְגַבַּחְתּוֹ׃
on-forehead-of-him or on-head-of-him she breaking-out infection reddish

וְרָאָה אֹתוֹ הַכֹּהֵן וְהִנֵּה שְׂאֵת־ הַנֶּגַע לְבָנָה
white the-sore swelling-of and-if the-priest him and-he-must-examine (43)

אֲדַמְדֶּמֶת בְּקָרַחְתּוֹ אוֹ בְגַבַּחְתּוֹ כְּמַרְאֵה צָרַעַת
infection-of like-appearance-of on-forehead-of-him or on-head-of-him reddish

עוֹר בָּשָׂר׃ אִישׁ־ צָרוּעַ הוּא טָמֵא הוּא טַמֵּא
to-pronounce-unclean he unclean he being-diseased man (44) flesh skin-of

יְטַמְּאֶנּוּ הַכֹּהֵן בְּרֹאשׁוֹ נִגְעוֹ׃
sore-of-him for-head-of-him the-priest he-shall-pronounce-unclean-him

וְהַצָּרוּעַ אֲשֶׁר־ בּוֹ הַנֶּגַע בְּגָדָיו
clothes-of-him the-infection on-him that and-the-one-being-diseased (45)

יִהְיוּ פְרֻמִים וְרֹאשׁוֹ יִהְיֶה פָרוּעַ וְעַל־
and-on being-unkempt he-must-be and-hair-of-him ones-being-torn they-must-be

clean. He must wash his
clothes, and he will be clean.
[35]But if the itch does spread in
the skin after he is pro-
nounced clean, [36]the priest is
to examine him, and if the itch
has spread in the skin, the
priest does not need to look for
yellow hair; the person is unclean. [37]If, however, in his
judgment it is unchanged and
black hair has grown in it, the
itch is healed. He is clean, and
the priest shall pronounce him
clean.

[38]"When a man or woman
has white spots on the skin,
[39]the priest is to examine
them, and if the spots are dull
white, it is a harmless rash
that has broken out on the
skin; that person is clean.

[40]"When a man has lost his
hair and is bald, he is clean.
[41]If he has lost his hair from
the front of his scalp and has a
bald forehead, he is clean.
[42]But if he has a reddish-white
sore on his bald head or forehead, it is an infectious disease breaking out on his head
or forehead. [43]The priest is to
examine him and, if the swol-
len sore on his head or forehead is reddish-white like an
infectious skin disease, [44]the
man is diseased and is unclean. The priest shall pronounce him unclean because
of the sore on his head.

[45]"The person with such an
infectious disease must wear
torn clothes, let his hair be unkempt,[a] cover the lower part of

[a]45 Or *clothes, uncover his head*

שָׂפָם יַעְטֶה וְטָמֵא ׀ טָמֵא יִקְרָא׃ כָּל־ יְמֵי

days-of all-of (46) he-must-cry unclean and-unclean he-must-cover lower-face

אֲשֶׁר הַנֶּגַע בּוֹ יִטְמָא טָמֵא הוּא בָּדָד יֵשֵׁב

he-must-live alone he unclean he-is-unclean on-him the-infection that

מִחוּץ לַמַּחֲנֶה מוֹשָׁבוֹ׃ וְהַבֶּגֶד כִּי־ יִהְיֶה בוֹ

on-him he-is if now-the-clothing (47) dwelling-of-him of-the-camp outside

נֶגַע צָרָעַת בְּבֶגֶד צֶמֶר אוֹ בְּבֶגֶד פִּשְׁתִּים׃ אוֹ

or (48) linens on-clothing-of or wool on-clothing-of mildew contamination-of

בִשְׁתִי אוֹ בְעֵרֶב לַפִּשְׁתִּים וְלַצָּמֶר אוֹ בְעוֹר אוֹ

or on-leather or or-of-the-wool of-the-linens on-knitted or on-woven

בְּכָל־ מְלֶאכֶת עוֹר׃ וְהָיָה הַנֶּגַע יְרַקְרַק ׀ אוֹ

or greenish the-contamination and-he-is (49) leather product-of on-any-of

אֲדַמְדָּם בַּבֶּגֶד אוֹ בָעוֹר אוֹ־ בַשְּׁתִי אוֹ־ בָעֵרֶב

in-the-knitted or in-the-woven or in-the-leather or in-the-clothing reddish

אוֹ בְכָל־ כְּלִי־ עוֹר נֶגַע צָרַעַת הוּא

he mildew contamination-of leather article-of in-any-of or

וְהָרְאָה אֶת־ הַכֹּהֵן׃ וְרָאָה הַכֹּהֵן אֶת־

*** the-priest and-he-must-examine (50) the-priest *** and-he-must-be-shown

הַנֶּגַע וְהִסְגִּיר אֶת־ הַנֶּגַע שִׁבְעַת יָמִים׃

days seven-of the-affected-article *** and-he-must-isolate the-mildew

וְרָאָה אֶת־ הַנֶּגַע בַּיּוֹם הַשְּׁבִיעִי כִּי־ פָשָׂה

he-spread if the-seventh on-the-day the-mildew *** and-he-must-examine (51)

הַנֶּגַע בַּבֶּגֶד אוֹ־ בַשְּׁתִי אוֹ־ בָעֵרֶב אוֹ בָעוֹר

in-the-leather or in-the-knitted or in-the-woven or in-the-clothing the-mildew

לְכֹל אֲשֶׁר־ יֵעָשֶׂה הָעוֹר לִמְלָאכָה צָרַעַת מַמְאֶרֶת

destroying mildew-of for-use the-leather he-may-be-used that for-anything

הַנֶּגַע טָמֵא הוּא׃ וְשָׂרַף אֶת־ הַבֶּגֶד אוֹ אֶת־

*** or the-clothing *** and-he-must-burn (52) he unclean the-contamination

הַשְּׁתִי ׀ אוֹ אֶת־ הָעֵרֶב בַּצֶּמֶר אוֹ בַפִּשְׁתִּים אוֹ אֶת־ כָּל־

any-of *** or of-the-linens or of-the-wool the-knitted *** or the-woven

כְּלִי הָעוֹר אֲשֶׁר־ יִהְיֶה בוֹ הַנֶּגַע כִּי־ צָרַעַת

mildew-of for the-contamination in-him he-is that the-leather article-of

מַמְאֶרֶת הִוא בָּאֵשׁ תִּשָּׂרֵף׃ וְאִם יִרְאֶה

he-examines but-if (53) she-must-be-burned in-the-fire she destroying

הַכֹּהֵן וְהִנֵּה לֹא־ פָשָׂה הַנֶּגַע בַּבֶּגֶד אוֹ בַשְּׁתִי

in-the-woven or in-the-clothing the-mildew he-spread not and-see! the-priest

אוֹ בָעֵרֶב אוֹ בְּכָל־ כְּלִי־ עוֹר׃ וְצִוָּה

then-he-shall-order (54) leather article-of in-any-of or in-the-knitted or

his face and cry out, 'Unclean! Unclean!' [46]As long as he has the infection he remains unclean. He must live alone; he must live outside the camp.

Regulations About Mildew

[47]"If any clothing is contaminated with mildew—any woolen or linen clothing, [48]any woven or knitted material of linen or wool, any leather or anything made of leather— [49]and if the contamination in the clothing, or leather, or woven or knitted material, or any leather article, is greenish or reddish, it is a spreading mildew and must be shown to the priest. [50]The priest is to examine the mildew and isolate the affected article for seven days. [51]On the seventh day he is to examine it, and if the mildew has spread in the clothing, or the woven or knitted material, or the leather, whatever its use, it is a destructive mildew; the article is unclean. [52]He must burn up the clothing, or the woven or knitted material of wool or linen, or any leather article that has the contamination in it, because the mildew is destructive; the article must be burned up.

[53]"But if, when the priest examines it, the mildew has not spread in the clothing, or the woven or knitted material, or the leather article, [54]he shall

הַכֹּהֵן וְכִבְּסוּ אֵת אֲשֶׁר־ בּוֹ הַנָּגַע
the-contamination on-him what *** and-they-shall-wash the-priest

וְהִסְגִּירוֹ שִׁבְעַת־ יָמִים שֵׁנִית׃ וְרָאָה
and-he-must-examine (55) another days seven-of and-he-must-isolate-him

הַכֹּהֵן אַחֲרֵי | הֻכַּבֵּס אֶת־ הַנֶּגַע וְהִנֵּה לֹא־ הָפַךְ
he-changed not and-if the-affected-article *** he-was-washed after the-priest

הַנֶּגַע אֶת־ עֵינוֹ וְהַנֶּגַע לֹא־ פָשָׂה טָמֵא הוּא
he unclean he-spread not though-the-mildew appearance-of-him *** the-mildew

בָּאֵשׁ תִּשְׂרְפֶנּוּ פְּחֶתֶת הִוא בְּקָרַחְתּוֹ אוֹ בְגַבַּחְתּוֹ׃
on-front-of-him or on-back-of-him she mildew you-must-burn-him with-the-fire

וְאִם רָאָה הַכֹּהֵן וְהִנֵּה כֵּהָה הַנֶּגַע אַחֲרֵי
after the-mildew he-faded and-if the-priest he-examines but-if (56)

הֻכַּבֵּס אֹתוֹ וְקָרַע אֹתוֹ מִן־ הַבֶּגֶד אוֹ מִן־ הָעוֹר
the-leather from or the-clothing from him then-he-must-tear him he-was-washed

אוֹ מִן־ הַשְּׁתִי אוֹ מִן־ הָעֵרֶב׃ וְאִם־ תֵּרָאֶה עוֹד
again she-reappears but-if (57) the-knitted from or the-woven from or

בַּבֶּגֶד אוֹ־ בַשְּׁתִי אוֹ־ בָעֵרֶב אוֹ בְכָל־ כְּלִי־
article-of in-any-of or in-the-knitted or in-the-woven or in-the-clothing

עוֹר פֹּרַחַת הִוא בָּאֵשׁ תִּשְׂרְפֶנּוּ אֵת אֲשֶׁר־ בּוֹ
in-him what *** you-must-burn-him with-the-fire she spreading leather

הַנָּגַע׃ וְהַבֶּגֶד אוֹ־ הַשְּׁתִי אוֹ־ הָעֵרֶב אוֹ־ כָל־
any-of or the-knitted or the-woven or and-the-clothing (58) the-mildew

כְּלִי הָעוֹר אֲשֶׁר תְּכַבֵּס וְסָר מֵהֶם הַנָּגַע
the-mildew from-them and-he-left you-washed that the-leather article-of

וְכֻבַּס שֵׁנִית וְטָהֵר׃ זֹאת תּוֹרַת
regulation-of this (59) and-he-will-be-clean again then-he-must-be-washed

נֶגַע־ צָרַעַת בֶּגֶד הַצֶּמֶר | אוֹ הַפִּשְׁתִּים אוֹ הַשְּׁתִי אוֹ
or the-woven or the-linens or the-wool clothing-of mildew contamination-of

הָעֵרֶב אוֹ כָּל־ כְּלִי־ עוֹר לְטַהֲרוֹ אוֹ
or to-pronounce-clean-him leather article-of any-of or the-knitted

לְטַמְּאוֹ׃ וַיְדַבֵּר יְהוָה אֶל־ מֹשֶׁה לֵּאמֹר׃ זֹאת
this (2) to-say Moses to Yahweh and-he-spoke (14:1) to-pronounce-unclean-him

תִּהְיֶה תּוֹרַת הַמְּצֹרָע בְּיוֹם טָהֳרָתוֹ
cleansing-of-him on-day-of the-one-being-diseased regulaion-of she-is

וְהוּבָא אֶל־ הַכֹּהֵן׃ וְיָצָא הַכֹּהֵן אֶל־ מִחוּץ
outside to the-priest and-he-shall-go (3) the-priest to when-he-is-brought

לַמַּחֲנֶה וְרָאָה הַכֹּהֵן וְהִנֵּה נִרְפָּא נֶגַע־
infection-of he-is-healed and-if the-priest and-he-shall-examine of-the-camp

order that the contaminated
article be washed. Then he is
to isolate it for another seven
days. [55]After the affected article has been washed, the
priest is to examine it, and if
the mildew has not changed
its appearance, even though it
has not spread, it is unclean.
Burn it with fire, whether the
mildew has affected one side
or the other. [56]If, when the
priest examines it, the mildew
has faded after the article has
been washed, he is to tear the
contaminated part out of the
clothing, or the leather, or the
woven or knitted material.
[57]But if it reappears in the
clothing, or in the woven or
knitted material, or in the
leather article, it is spreading,
and whatever has the mildew
must be burned with fire.
[58]The clothing, or the woven
or knitted material, or any
leather article that has been
washed and is rid of the mildew, must be washed again,
and it will be clean."
[59]These are the regulations
concerning contamination by
mildew in woolen or linen
clothing, woven or knitted
material, or any leather article,
for pronouncing them clean or
unclean.

Cleansing From Infectious Skin Diseases

14 The LORD said to
Moses, [2]"These are the
regulations for the diseased
person at the time of his
ceremonial cleansing, when
he is brought to the priest:
[3]The priest is to go outside the
camp and examine him. If the
person has been healed of his

הַצָּרַעַת מִן־ הַצָּרוּעַ׃ (4) וְצִוָּה הַכֹּהֵן
the-priest and-he-shall-order (4) the-one-being-diseased from the-skin-disease

וְלָקַח לַמִּטַּהֵר שְׁתֵּי־ צִפֳּרִים חַיּוֹת
live-ones birds two-of for-the-one-being-cleansed and-he-shall-bring

טְהֹרוֹת וְעֵץ אֶרֶז וּשְׁנִי תוֹלַעַת וְאֵזֹב׃
and-hyssop scarlet and-yarn-of cedar and-wood-of clean-ones

(5) וְצִוָּה הַכֹּהֵן וְשָׁחַט אֶת־ הַצִּפּוֹר הָאֶחָת אֶל־
in the-one the-bird *** and-he-shall-kill the-priest then-he-shall-order (5)

כְּלִי־ חֶרֶשׂ עַל־ מַיִם חַיִּים׃ (6) אֶת־ הַצִּפֹּר הַחַיָּה יִקַּח
he-shall-take the-live the-bird *** (6) fresh-ones waters over clay pot-of

אֹתָהּ וְאֶת־ עֵץ הָאֶרֶז וְאֶת־ שְׁנִי הַתּוֹלַעַת וְאֶת־ הָאֵזֹב
the-hyssop and the-scarlet yarn-of and the-cedar wood-of and her

וְטָבַל אוֹתָם וְאֵת ׀ הַצִּפֹּר הַחַיָּה בְּדַם הַצִּפֹּר
the-bird into-blood-of the-live the-bird with them and-he-shall-dip

הַשְּׁחֻטָה עַל הַמַּיִם הַחַיִּים׃ (7) וְהִזָּה
and-he-shall-sprinkle (7) the-fresh-ones the-waters over the-one-being-killed

עַל הַמִּטַּהֵר מִן־ הַצָּרַעַת שֶׁבַע פְּעָמִים
times seven the-infection from the-one-being-cleansed on

וְטִהֲרוֹ וְשִׁלַּח אֶת־ הַצִּפֹּר הַחַיָּה
the-live the-bird *** then-he-shall-release and-he-shall-pronounce-clean-him

עַל־ פְּנֵי הַשָּׂדֶה׃ (8) וְכִבֶּס הַמִּטַּהֵר אֶת־
*** the-one-being-cleansed and-he-must-wash (8) the-field surface-of over

בְּגָדָיו וְגִלַּח אֶת־ כָּל־ שְׂעָרוֹ וְרָחַץ
and-he-must-bathe hair-of-him all-of *** and-he-must-shave clothes-of-him

בַּמַּיִם וְטָהֵר וְאַחַר יָבוֹא אֶל־ הַמַּחֲנֶה
the-camp into he-may-come and-after then-he-will-be-clean in-the-waters

וְיָשַׁב מִחוּץ לְאָהֳלוֹ שִׁבְעַת יָמִים׃ (9) וְהָיָה
and-he-will-be (9) days seven-of of-tent-of-him outside but-he-must-stay

בַיּוֹם הַשְּׁבִיעִי יְגַלַּח אֶת־ כָּל־ שְׂעָרוֹ אֶת־ רֹאשׁוֹ
head-of-him *** hair-of-him all-of *** he-must-shave the-seventh on-the-day

וְאֶת־ זְקָנוֹ וְאֵת גַּבֹּת עֵינָיו וְאֶת־ כָּל־ שְׂעָרוֹ
hair-of-him rest-of and eyes-of-him brows-of and beard-of-him and

יְגַלֵּחַ וְכִבֶּס אֶת־ בְּגָדָיו וְרָחַץ אֶת־
*** and-he-must-bathe clothes-of-him *** and-he-must-wash he-must-shave

בְּשָׂרוֹ בַּמַּיִם וְטָהֵר׃ (10) וּבַיּוֹם הַשְּׁמִינִי
the-eighth and-on-the-day (10) and-he-will-be-clean in-the-waters body-of-him

יִקַּח שְׁנֵי־ כְבָשִׂים תְּמִימִם וְכַבְשָׂה אַחַת
one and-female-lamb ones-without-blemish male-lambs two-of he-must-bring

infectious skin disease,[a] [4]the
priest shall order that two live
clean birds and some cedar
wood, scarlet yarn and hyssop
be brought for the one to be
cleansed. [5]Then the priest
shall order that one of the
birds be killed over fresh
water in a clay pot. [6]He is then
to take the live bird and dip it,
together with the cedar wood,
the scarlet yarn and the hyssop, into the blood of the bird
that was killed over the fresh
water. [7]Seven times he shall
sprinkle the one to be cleansed
of the infectious disease and
pronounce him clean. Then he
is to release the live bird in the
open fields.
[8]"The person to be cleansed
must wash his clothes, shave
off all his hair and bathe with
water; then he will be
ceremonially clean. After this
he may come into the camp,
but he must stay outside his
tent for seven days. [9]On the
seventh day he must shave off
all his hair; he must shave his
head, his beard, his eyebrows
and the rest of his hair. He
must wash his clothes and
bathe himself with water, and
he will be clean.
[10]"On the eighth day he
must bring two male lambs
and one ewe lamb a year old,
each without defect, along

[a]3 Traditionally *leprosy;* the Hebrew word was used for various diseases affecting the skin—not necessarily leprosy; also elsewhere in this chapter.

בַּת־ שְׁנָתָהּ תְּמִימָה וּשְׁלֹשָׁה עֶשְׂרֹנִים סֹלֶת
fine-flour tenths and-three without-defect year-of-her daughter-of

מִנְחָה בְּלוּלָה בַשֶּׁמֶן וְלֹג אֶחָד שָׁמֶן׃
oil one and-log with-the-oil being-mixed grain-offering

וְהֶעֱמִיד הַכֹּהֵן הַמְטַהֵר אֵת הָאִישׁ
the-man *** the-one-pronouncing-clean the-priest and-he-shall-present (11)

הַמִּטַּהֵר וְאֹתָם לִפְנֵי יְהוָה פֶּתַח אֹהֶל מוֹעֵד׃
Meeting Tent-of entrance-of Yahweh before with-them the-one-being-cleansed

וְלָקַח הַכֹּהֵן אֶת־ הַכֶּבֶשׂ הָאֶחָד
the-one the-male-lamb *** the-priest then-he-shall-take (12)

וְהִקְרִיב אֹתוֹ לְאָשָׁם וְאֶת־ לֹג הַשָּׁמֶן וְהֵנִיף
and-he-shall-wave the-oil log-of with as-guilt-offering him and-he-shall-offer

אֹתָם תְּנוּפָה לִפְנֵי יְהוָה׃ וְשָׁחַט אֶת־ הַכֶּבֶשׂ
the-lamb *** and-he-must-slaughter (13) Yahweh before wave-offering them

בִּמְקוֹם אֲשֶׁר יִשְׁחַט אֶת־ הַחַטָּאת וְאֶת־ הָעֹלָה
the-burnt-offering and the-sin-offering *** he-slaughters where in-place-of

בִּמְקוֹם הַקֹּדֶשׁ כִּי כַּחַטָּאת הָאָשָׁם הוּא
he the-guilt-offering like-the-sin-offering for the-holy in-place-of

לַכֹּהֵן קֹדֶשׁ קָדָשִׁים הוּא׃ וְלָקַח הַכֹּהֵן
the-priest and-he-must-take (14) he holy-ones most-holy-of for-the-priest

מִדַּם הָאָשָׁם וְנָתַן הַכֹּהֵן עַל־ תְּנוּךְ
lobe-of on the-priest and-he-must-put the-guilt-offering from-blood-of

אֹזֶן הַמִּטַּהֵר הַיְמָנִית וְעַל־ בֹּהֶן יָדוֹ הַיְמָנִית
the-right hand-of-him thumb-of and-on the-right the-one-being-cleansed ear-of

וְעַל־ בֹּהֶן רַגְלוֹ הַיְמָנִית׃ וְלָקַח הַכֹּהֵן
the-priest and-he-shall-take (15) the-right foot-of-him big-toe-of and-on

מִלֹּג הַשָּׁמֶן וְיָצַק עַל־ כַּף הַכֹּהֵן הַשְּׂמָאלִית׃
the-left the-priest palm-of in and-he-shall-pour the-oil from-log-of

וְטָבַל הַכֹּהֵן אֶת־ אֶצְבָּעוֹ הַיְמָנִית מִן־ הַשֶּׁמֶן
the-oil into the-right finger-of-him *** the-priest and-he-shall-dip (16)

אֲשֶׁר עַל־ כַּפּוֹ הַשְּׂמָאלִית וְהִזָּה מִן־ הַשֶּׁמֶן
the-oil from and-he-shall-sprinkle the-left palm-of-him in that

בְּאֶצְבָּעוֹ שֶׁבַע פְּעָמִים לִפְנֵי יְהוָה׃ וּמִיֶּתֶר
and-from-remainder-of (17) Yahweh before times seven with-finger-of-him

הַשֶּׁמֶן אֲשֶׁר עַל־ כַּפּוֹ יִתֵּן הַכֹּהֵן עַל־ תְּנוּךְ אֹזֶן
ear-of lobe-of on the-priest he-shall-put palm-of-him in that the-oil

הַמִּטַּהֵר הַיְמָנִית וְעַל־ בֹּהֶן יָדוֹ הַיְמָנִית
the-right hand-of-him thumb-of and-on the-right the-one-being-cleansed

with three-tenths of an
ephah[b] of fine flour mixed
with oil for a grain offering,
and one log[c] of oil. 11The priest
who pronounces him clean
shall present both the one to
be cleansed and his offerings
before the LORD at the entrance to the Tent of Meeting.
12"Then the priest is to take
one of the male lambs and
offer it as a guilt offering,
along with the log of oil; he
shall wave them before the
LORD as a wave offering. 13He
is to slaughter the lamb in the
holy place where the sin
offering and the burnt offering
are slaughtered. Like the sin
offering, the guilt offering belongs to the priest; it is most
holy. 14The priest is to take
some of the blood of the guilt
offering and put it on the lobe
of the right ear of the one to be
cleansed, on the thumb of his
right hand and on the big toe
of his right foot. 15The priest
shall then take some of the log
of oil, pour it in the palm of his
own left hand, 16dip his right
forefinger into the oil in his
palm, and with his finger
sprinkle some of it before the
LORD seven times. 17The priest
is to put some of the oil remaining in his palm on the
lobe of the right ear of the one
to be cleansed, on the thumb
of his right hand and on the

[b]10 That is, probably about 6 quarts (about 6.5 liters)

[c]10 That is, probably about 2/3 pint (about 0.3 liter); also in verses 12, 15, 21 and 24

וְעַל־ בֹּהֶן רַגְלוֹ הַיְמָנִית עַל דַּם הָאָשָׁם׃
the-guilt-offering blood-of upon the-right foot-of-him big-toe-of and-on

וְהַנּוֹתָר בַּשֶּׁמֶן אֲשֶׁר עַל־ כַּף הַכֹּהֵן יִתֵּן
he-shall-put the-priest palm-of in that of-the-oil and-the-remaining (18)

עַל־ רֹאשׁ הַמִּטַּהֵר וְכִפֶּר עָלָיו הַכֹּהֵן
the-priest for-him and-he-shall-atone the-one-being-cleansed head-of on

לִפְנֵי יְהוָה׃ וְעָשָׂה הַכֹּהֵן אֶת־ הַחַטָּאת
the-sin-offering *** the-priest then-he-must-sacrifice (19) Yahweh before

וְכִפֶּר עַל־ הַמִּטַּהֵר מִטֻּמְאָתוֹ
from-uncleanness-of-him the-one-being-cleansed for and-he-shall-atone

וְאַחַר יִשְׁחַט אֶת־ הָעֹלָה׃ וְהֶעֱלָה
and-he-shall-offer (20) the-burnt-offering *** he-shall-slaughter and-after

הַכֹּהֵן אֶת־ הָעֹלָה וְאֶת־ הַמִּנְחָה הַמִּזְבֵּחָה
on-the-altar the-grain-offering with the-burnt-offering *** the-priest

וְכִפֶּר עָלָיו הַכֹּהֵן וְטָהֵר׃ וְאִם־ דַּל
poor but-if (21) and-he-will-be-clean the-priest for-him and-he-shall-atone

הוּא וְאֵין יָדוֹ מַשֶּׂגֶת וְלָקַח כֶּבֶשׂ אֶחָד
one male-lamb then-he-must-take affording hand-of-him and-not he

אָשָׁם לִתְנוּפָה לְכַפֵּר עָלָיו וְעִשָּׂרוֹן סֹלֶת אֶחָד
one fine-flour and-tenth for-him to-atone as-wave-offering guilt-offering

בָּלוּל בַּשֶּׁמֶן לְמִנְחָה וְלֹג שָׁמֶן׃ וּשְׁתֵּי
and-two-of (22) oil and-log-of for-grain-offering with-the-oil being-mixed

תֹּרִים אוֹ שְׁנֵי בְּנֵי יוֹנָה אֲשֶׁר תַּשִּׂיג יָדוֹ
hand-of-him she-can-afford which pigeon young-ones-of two-of or doves

וְהָיָה אֶחָד חַטָּאת וְהָאֶחָד עֹלָה׃
burnt-offering and-the-other sin-offering one and-he-will-be

וְהֵבִיא אֹתָם בַּיּוֹם הַשְּׁמִינִי לְטָהֳרָתוֹ אֶל־
to for-cleansing-of-him the-eighth on-the-day them and-he-must-bring (23)

הַכֹּהֵן אֶל־ פֶּתַח אֹהֶל־ מוֹעֵד לִפְנֵי יְהוָה׃ וְלָקַח
and-he-must-take (24) Yahweh before Meeting Tent-of entrance-of at the-priest

הַכֹּהֵן אֶת־ כֶּבֶשׂ הָאָשָׁם וְאֶת־ לֹג הַשָּׁמֶן וְהֵנִיף
and-he-must-wave the-oil log-of with the-guilt-offering lamb-of *** the-priest

אֹתָם הַכֹּהֵן תְּנוּפָה לִפְנֵי יְהוָה׃ וְשָׁחַט אֶת־
*** and-he-shall-slaughter (25) Yahweh before wave-offering the-priest them

כֶּבֶשׂ הָאָשָׁם וְלָקַח הַכֹּהֵן מִדַּם
from-blood-of the-priest and-he-must-take the-guilt-offering lamb-of

הָאָשָׁם וְנָתַן עַל־ תְּנוּךְ אֹזֶן־ הַמִּטַּהֵר
the-one-being-cleansed ear-of lobe-of on and-he-must-put the-guilt-offering

big toe of his right foot, on top of the blood of the guilt offering.
18The rest of the oil in his palm the priest shall put on the head of the one to be cleansed and make atonement for him before the LORD.
19"Then the priest is to sacrifice the sin offering and make atonement for the one to be cleansed from his uncleanness. After that, the priest shall slaughter the burnt offering
20and offer it on the altar, together with the grain offering, and make atonement for him, and he will be clean.
21"If, however, he is poor and cannot afford these, he must take one male lamb as a guilt offering to be waved to make atonement for him, together with a tenth of an ephah[d] of fine flour mixed with oil for a grain offering, a log of oil,
22and two doves or two young pigeons, which he can afford, one for a sin offering and the other for a burnt offering.
23"On the eighth day he must bring them for his cleansing to the priest at the entrance to the Tent of Meeting, before the LORD.
24The priest is to take the lamb for the guilt offering, together with the log of oil, and wave them before the LORD as a wave offering.
25He shall slaughter the lamb for the guilt offering and take some of its blood and put it on the lobe of the right ear of the one to be

[d]21 That is, probably about 2 quarts (about 2 liters)

הַיְמָנִית וְעַל־ בֹּהֶן יָדוֹ הַיְמָנִית וְעַל־ בֹּהֶן רַגְלוֹ
foot-of-him big-toe-of and-on the-right hand-of-him thumb-of and-on the-right

הַיְמָנִית׃ (26) וּמִן־ הַשֶּׁמֶן יִצֹק הַכֹּהֵן עַל־ כַּף
palm-of into the-priest he-must-pour the-oil and-from (26) the-right

הַכֹּהֵן הַשְּׂמָאלִית׃ (27) וְהִזָּה הַכֹּהֵן בְּאֶצְבָּעוֹ
with-finger-of-him the-priest and-he-must-sprinkle (27) the-left the-priest

הַיְמָנִית מִן־ הַשֶּׁמֶן אֲשֶׁר עַל־ כַּפּוֹ הַשְּׂמָאלִית שֶׁבַע פְּעָמִים לִפְנֵי
before times seven the-left palm-of-him in that the-oil from the-right

יְהוָה׃ (28) וְנָתַן הַכֹּהֵן מִן־ הַשֶּׁמֶן אֲשֶׁר עַל־ כַּפּוֹ עַל־
on palm-of-him in that the-oil from the-priest and-he-must-put (28) Yahweh

תְּנוּךְ אֹזֶן הַמִּטַּהֵר הַיְמָנִית וְעַל־ בֹּהֶן יָדוֹ
hand-of-him thumb-of and-on the-right the-one-being-cleansed ear-of lobe-of

הַיְמָנִית וְעַל־ בֹּהֶן רַגְלוֹ הַיְמָנִית עַל־ מְקוֹם דַּם
blood-of place-of on the-right foot-of-him big-toe-of and-on the-right

הָאָשָׁם׃ (29) וְהַנּוֹתָר מִן־ הַשֶּׁמֶן אֲשֶׁר עַל־ כַּף
palm-of in that the-oil from and-the-remaining (29) the-guilt-offering

הַכֹּהֵן יִתֵּן עַל־ רֹאשׁ הַמִּטַּהֵר לְכַפֵּר עָלָיו
for-him to-atone the-one-being-cleansed head-of on he-shall-put the-priest

לִפְנֵי יְהוָה׃ (30) וְעָשָׂה אֶת־ הָאֶחָד מִן־ הַתֹּרִים אוֹ
or the-doves from the-one *** then-he-shall-sacrifice (30) Yahweh before

מִן־ בְּנֵי הַיּוֹנָה מֵאֲשֶׁר תַּשִּׂיג יָדוֹ׃ (31) אֵת
*** (31) hand-of-him she-can-afford from-which the-pigeon young-ones-of from

אֲשֶׁר־ תַּשִּׂיג יָדוֹ אֶת־ הָאֶחָד חַטָּאת וְאֶת־ הָאֶחָד
the-other and sin-offering the-one *** hand-of-him she-can-afford which

עֹלָה עַל־ הַמִּנְחָה וְכִפֶּר הַכֹּהֵן עַל
for the-priest so-he-will-atone the-grain-offering with burnt-offering

הַמִּטַּהֵר לִפְנֵי יְהוָה׃ (32) זֹאת תּוֹרַת אֲשֶׁר־ בּוֹ
on-him who regulation-of this (32) Yahweh before the-one-being-cleansed

נֶגַע צָרָעַת אֲשֶׁר לֹא־ תַשִּׂיג יָדוֹ
hand-of-him she-can-afford not who skin-disease infection-of

בְּטָהֳרָתוֹ׃ (33) וַיְדַבֵּר יְהוָה אֶל־ מֹשֶׁה וְאֶל־ אַהֲרֹן לֵאמֹר׃
to-say Aaron and-to Moses to Yahweh and-he-spoke (33) for-cleansing-of-him

(34) כִּי תָבֹאוּ אֶל־ אֶרֶץ כְּנַעַן אֲשֶׁר אֲנִי נֹתֵן לָכֶם לַאֲחֻזָּה
as-possession to-you giving I which Canaan land-of into you-enter when (34)

וְנָתַתִּי נֶגַע צָרַעַת בְּבֵית אֶרֶץ אֲחֻזַּתְכֶם׃
possession-of-you land-of in-house-of spreading mildew-of and-I-put

(35) וּבָא אֲשֶׁר־ לוֹ הַבַּיִת וְהִגִּיד לַכֹּהֵן
to-the-priest and-he-must-tell the-house to-him who then-he-must-go (35)

cleansed, on the thumb of his
right hand and on the big toe
of his right foot. 26The priest is
to pour some of the oil into the
palm of his own left hand,
27and with his right forefinger
sprinkle some of the oil from
his palm seven times before
the LORD. 28Some of the oil in
his palm he is to put on the
same places he put the blood
of the guilt offering—on the
lobe of the right ear of the one
to be cleansed, on the thumb
of his right hand and on the
big toe of his right foot. 29The
rest of the oil in his palm the
priest shall put on the head of
the one to be cleansed, to
make atonement for him before the LORD. 30Then he shall
sacrifice the doves or the
young pigeons, which the person can afford, 31one[e] as a sin
offering and the other as a
burnt offering, together with
the grain offering. In this way
the priest will make atonement before the LORD on behalf of the one to be cleansed."
32These are the regulations for
anyone who has an infectious
skin disease and who cannot
afford the regular offerings for
his cleansing.

Cleansing From Mildew

33The LORD said to Moses
and Aaron, 34"When you enter
the land of Canaan, which I
am giving you as your possession, and I put a spreading
mildew in a house in that
land, 35the owner of the house
must go and tell the priest, 'I

[e]31 Hebrew 31*such as the person can afford, one*

לֵאמֹר כְּנֶגַע נִרְאָה לִי בַּבָּיִת׃ (36) וְצִוָּה
and-he-must-order (36) in-the-house to-me he-appeared like-mildew to-say

הַכֹּהֵן וּפִנּוּ אֶת־ הַבַּיִת בְּטֶרֶם יָבֹא הַכֹּהֵן
the-priest he-goes-in before the-house *** and-they-must-empty the-priest

לִרְאוֹת אֶת־ הַנֶּגַע וְלֹא יִטְמָא כָּל־ אֲשֶׁר
that anything he-will-pronounce-unclean so-not the-mildew *** to-examine

בַּבָּיִת וְאַחַר כֵּן יָבֹא הַכֹּהֵן לִרְאוֹת אֶת־ הַבָּיִת׃
the-house *** to-examine the-priest he-must-go-in this and-after in-the-house

(37) וְרָאָה אֶת־ הַנֶּגַע וְהִנֵּה הַנֶּגַע בְּקִירֹת
on-walls-of the-mildew and-if the-mildew *** and-he-must-examine (37)

הַבַּיִת שְׁקַעֲרוּרֹת יְרַקְרַקֹּת אוֹ אֲדַמְדַּמֹּת וּמַרְאֵיהֶן
and-appearance-of-them reddish-ones or greenish-ones depressions the-house

שָׁפָל מִן־ הַקִּיר׃ (38) וְיָצָא הַכֹּהֵן מִן־ הַבַּיִת
the-house from the-priest then-he-shall-go-out (38) the-wall than deeper

אֶל־ פֶּתַח הַבָּיִת וְהִסְגִּיר אֶת־ הַבַּיִת שִׁבְעַת יָמִים׃
days seven-of the-house *** and-he-shall-close the-house entrance-of at

(39) וְשָׁב הַכֹּהֵן בַּיּוֹם הַשְּׁבִיעִי
the-seventh on-the-day the-priest and-he-shall-return (39)

וְרָאָה וְהִנֵּה פָּשָׂה הַנֶּגַע בְּקִירֹת הַבָּיִת׃
the-house on-walls-of the-mildew he-spread and if and-he-shall-inspect

(40) וְצִוָּה הַכֹּהֵן וְחִלְּצוּ אֶת־ הָאֲבָנִים
the-stones *** and-they-must-tear-out the-priest then-he-must-order (40)

אֲשֶׁר בָּהֵן הַנָּגַע וְהִשְׁלִיכוּ אֶתְהֶן אֶל־ מִחוּץ לָעִיר
of-the-town outside to them and-they-must-throw the-mildew on-them that

אֶל־ מָקוֹם טָמֵא׃ (41) וְאֶת־ הַבַּיִת יַקְצִעַ מִבַּיִת סָבִיב
around on-inside he-must-scrape the-house and (41) unclean place to

וְשָׁפְכוּ אֶת־ הֶעָפָר אֲשֶׁר הִקְצוּ אֶל־ מִחוּץ
outside to they-scrape-off that the-material *** and-they-must-dump

לָעִיר אֶל־ מָקוֹם טָמֵא׃ (42) וְלָקְחוּ אֲבָנִים אֲחֵרוֹת
other-ones stones then they must-take (42) unclean place into of-the-town

וְהֵבִיאוּ אֶל־ תַּחַת הָאֲבָנִים וְעָפָר אַחֵר יִקַּח
he-must-take new and-clay the-stones place-of in and-they-must-replace

וְטָח אֶת־ הַבָּיִת׃ (43) וְאִם־ יָשׁוּב הַנֶּגַע
the-mildew he-reappears but-if (43) the-house *** and-he-must-plaster

וּפָרַח בַּבַּיִת אַחַר חִלֵּץ אֶת־ הָאֲבָנִים וְאַחֲרֵי
and-after the-stones *** he-tears-out after in-the-house and-he-spreads

הִקְצוֹת אֶת־ הַבַּיִת וְאַחֲרֵי הִטּוֹחַ׃ (44) וּבָא
then-he-must-go (44) to-be-plastered and-after the-house *** to-scrape-off

have seen something that
looks like mildew in my
house.' [36]The priest is to order
the house to be emptied before
he goes in to examine the mildew, so that nothing in the
house will be pronounced unclean. After this the priest is to
go in and inspect the house.
[37]He is to examine the mildew
on the walls, and if it has
greenish or reddish depressions that appear to be deeper
than the surface of the wall,
[38]the priest shall go out of the
house and at the entrance
close up the house for seven
days. [39]On the seventh day the
priest shall return to inspect
the house. If the mildew has
spread on the walls, [40]he is to
order that the contaminated
stones be torn out and thrown
into an unclean place outside
the town. [41]He must have all
the inside walls of the house
scraped and the material that
is scraped off dumped into an
unclean place outside the
town. [42]Then they are to take
other stones to replace these
and take new clay and plaster
the house.
[43]"If the mildew reappears
in the house after the stones
have been torn out and the
house scraped and plastered,

הַכֹּהֵן וְרָאָה וְהִנֵּה פָּשָׂה הַנֶּגַע בַּבָּיִת

in-the-house the-mildew he-spread and-if and-he-must-examine the-priest

צָרַעַת מַמְאֶרֶת הִוא בַּבָּיִת טָמֵא הוּא׃ וְנָתַץ אֶת־

*** and-he-must-tear-down (45) he unclean in-the-house she destroying mildew

הַבַּיִת אֶת־ אֲבָנָיו וְאֶת־ עֵצָיו וְאֵת כָּל־ עֲפַר

plaster-of all-of and timbers-of-him and stones-of-him *** the-house

הַבַּיִת וְהוֹצִיא אֶל־ מִחוּץ לָעִיר אֶל־ מָקוֹם טָמֵא׃

unclean place to of-the-town outside to and-he-must-take the-house

וְהַבָּא אֶל־ הַבַּיִת כָּל־ יְמֵי הִסְגִּיר אֹתוֹ

him he-closes days-of any-of the-house into and-the-one-going (46)

יִטְמָא עַד־ הָעָרֶב׃ וְהַשֹּׁכֵב בַּבַּיִת

in-the-house and-the-one-sleeping (47) the-evening until he-will-be-unclean

יְכַבֵּס אֶת־ בְּגָדָיו וְהָאֹכֵל בַּבַּיִת יְכַבֵּס

he-must-wash in-the-house and-the-one-eating clothes-of-him *** he-must-wash

אֶת־ בְּגָדָיו׃ וְאִם־ בֹּא יָבֹא הַכֹּהֵן וְרָאָה

and-he-examines the-priest he-comes to-come but-if (48) clothes-of-him ***

וְהִנֵּה לֹא־ פָשָׂה הַנֶּגַע בַּבַּיִת אַחֲרֵי הִטֹּחַ אֶת־

*** to-be-plastered after in-the-house the-mildew he-spread not and-if

הַבָּיִת וְטִהַר הַכֹּהֵן אֶת־ הַבַּיִת כִּי

for the-house *** the-priest then-he-shall-pronounce-clean the-house

נִרְפָּא הַנָּגַע׃ וְלָקַח לְחַטֵּא אֶת־ הַבַּיִת שְׁתֵּי

two-of the-house *** to-purify and-he-must-take (49) the-mildew he-is-gone

צִפֳּרִים וְעֵץ אֶרֶז וּשְׁנִי תוֹלַעַת וְאֵזֹב׃

and-hyssop scarlet and-yarn-of cedar and-wood-of birds

וְשָׁחַט אֶת־ הַצִּפֹּר הָאֶחָת אֶל־ כְּלִי־ חֶרֶשׂ עַל־ מַיִם חַיִּים׃

fresh-ones waters over clay pot-of in the-one the-bird *** and-he-shall-kill (50)

וְלָקַח אֶת־ עֵץ־ הָאֶרֶז וְאֶת־ הָאֵזֹב וְאֵת ׀ שְׁנִי

yarn-of and the-hyssop and the-cedar wood-of *** then-he-must-take (51)

הַתּוֹלַעַת וְאֵת הַצִּפֹּר הַחַיָּה וְטָבַל אֹתָם בְּדַם הַצִּפֹּר

the-bird into-blood-of them and-he-must-dip the-live the-bird and the-scarlet

הַשְּׁחוּטָה וּבַמַּיִם הַחַיִּים וְהִזָּה

and-he-must-sprinkle the-fresh-ones and-in-the-waters the-one-being-killed

אֶל־ הַבַּיִת שֶׁבַע פְּעָמִים׃ וְחִטֵּא אֶת־ הַבַּיִת בְּדַם

with-blood-of the-house *** and-he-shall-purify (52) times seven the-house on

הַצִּפּוֹר וּבַמַּיִם הַחַיִּים וּבַצִּפֹּר הַחַיָּה

the-live and-with-the-bird the-fresh-ones and-with-the-waters the-bird

וּבְעֵץ הָאֶרֶז וּבָאֵזֹב וּבִשְׁנִי הַתּוֹלָעַת׃

the-scarlet and-with-yarn-of and-with-the-hyssop the-cedar and-with-wood-of

44 the priest is to go and examine it and, if the mildew has spread in the house, it is a destructive mildew; the house is unclean. 45 It must be torn down—its stones, timbers and all the plaster—and taken out of the town to an unclean place.

46 "Anyone who goes into the house while it is closed up will be unclean till evening. 47 Anyone who sleeps or eats in the house must wash his clothes.

48 "But if the priest comes to examine it and the mildew has not spread after the house has been plastered, he shall pronounce the house clean, because the mildew is gone. 49 To purify the house he is to take two birds and some cedar wood, scarlet yarn and hyssop. 50 He shall kill one of the birds over fresh water in a clay pot. 51 Then he is to take the cedar wood, the hyssop, the scarlet yarn and the live bird, dip them into the blood of the dead bird and the fresh water, and sprinkle the house seven times. 52 He shall purify the house with the bird's blood, the fresh water, the live bird, the cedar wood, the hyssop and the scarlet yarn. 53 Then he

וְשִׁלַּח אֶת־ הַצִּפֹּר הַחַיָּה אֶל־ מִחוּץ לָעִיר אֶל־
over of-the-town outside at the-live the-bird *** then-he-must-release (53)

פְּנֵי הַשָּׂדֶה וְכִפֶּר עַל־ הַבַּיִת וְטָהֵר׃
and-he-will-be-clean the-house for so-he-will-atone the-field surface-of

זֹאת הַתּוֹרָה לְכָל־ נֶגַע הַצָּרַעַת
the-skin-disease infection-of for-any-of the-regulation this (54)

וְלַנָּתֶק׃ וּלְצָרַעַת הַבֶּגֶד וְלַבָּיִת׃
or-in-the-house the-clothing for-mildew-of (55) and-for-the-itch

וְלַשְׂאֵת וְלַסַּפַּחַת וְלַבֶּהָרֶת׃
and-for-the-bright-spot and-for-the-rash and-for-the-swelling (56)

לְהוֹרֹת בְּיוֹם הַטָּמֵא וּבְיוֹם הַטָּהֹר זֹאת
this the-clean or-day-of the-unclean on-day-of to-determine (57)

תּוֹרַת הַצָּרָעַת׃ וַיְדַבֵּר יְהוָה אֶל־ מֹשֶׁה וְאֶל־ אַהֲרֹן
Aaron and-to Moses to Yahweh and-he-spoke (15:1) the-infection regulation-of

לֵאמֹר׃ דַּבְּרוּ אֶל־ בְּנֵי יִשְׂרָאֵל וַאֲמַרְתֶּם אֲלֵהֶם אִישׁ אִישׁ כִּי יִהְיֶה
he-has when any man to-them and-you-say Israel sons-of to speak! (2) to-say

זָב מִבְּשָׂרוֹ זוֹבוֹ טָמֵא הוּא׃ וְזֹאת
whether-this (3) he unclean discharge-of-him from-body-of-him discharging

תִּהְיֶה טֻמְאָתוֹ בְּזוֹבוֹ רָר בְּשָׂרוֹ אֶת־
*** body-of-him he-lets-flow in-discharge-of-him uncleanness-of-him she-is

זוֹבוֹ אוֹ־ הֶחְתִּים בְּשָׂרוֹ מִזּוֹבוֹ
from-discharge-of-him body-of-him he-blocks or discharge-of-him

טֻמְאָתוֹ הִוא׃ כָּל־ הַמִּשְׁכָּב אֲשֶׁר יִשְׁכַּב עָלָיו
on-him he-lies which the-bed any-of (4) she uncleanness-of-him

הַזָּב יִטְמָא וְכָל־ הַכְּלִי אֲשֶׁר־ יֵשֵׁב
he-sits which the-thing and-any-of he-will-be-unclean the-one-discharging

עָלָיו יִטְמָא׃ וְאִישׁ אֲשֶׁר יִגַּע בְּמִשְׁכָּבוֹ
on-bed-of-him he-touches who and-anyone (5) he-will-be-unclean on-him

יְכַבֵּס בְּגָדָיו וְרָחַץ בַּמַּיִם
with-the-waters and-he-must-bathe clothes of him he-must-wash

וְטָמֵא עַד־ הָעָרֶב׃ וְהַיֹּשֵׁב עַל־ הַכְּלִי
the-thing on and-the-one-sitting (6) the-evening till and-he-will-be-unclean

אֲשֶׁר־ יֵשֵׁב עָלָיו הַזָּב יְכַבֵּס בְּגָדָיו
clothes-of-him he-must-wash the-one-discharging on-him he-sat that

וְרָחַץ בַּמַּיִם וְטָמֵא עַד־ הָעָרֶב׃
the-evening till and-he-will-be-unclean with-the-waters and-he-must-bathe

וְהַנֹּגֵעַ בִּבְשַׂר הַזָּב יְכַבֵּס
he-must-wash the-one-discharging on-body-of and-the-one-touching (7)

is to release the live bird in the
open fields outside the town.
In this way he will make
atonement for the house, and
it will be clean."
54 These are the regulations
for any infectious skin disease, for an itch, 55 for mildew
in clothing or in a house, 56 and
for a swelling, a rash or a
bright spot, 57 to determine
when something is clean or
unclean.
These are the regulations for
infectious skin diseases and
mildew.

Discharges Causing Uncleanness

15 The LORD said to Moses
and Aaron, 2 "Speak to
the Israelites and say to them:
'When any man has a bodily
discharge, the discharge is unclean. 3 Whether it continues
flowing from his body or is
blocked, it will make him unclean. This is how his discharge will bring about uncleanness:
4 " 'Any bed the man with a
discharge lies on will be unclean, and anything he sits on
will be unclean. 5 Anyone who
touches his bed must wash his
clothes and bathe with water,
and he will be unclean till evening. 6 Whoever sits on anything that the man with a discharge sat on must wash his
clothes and bathe with water,
and he will be unclean till evening.
7 " 'Whoever touches the
man who has a discharge

בְּגָדָיו וְרָחַץ בַּמַּיִם וְטָמֵא עַד־
till and-he-will-be-unclean with-the-waters and-he-must-bathe clothes-of-him

הָעָרֶב׃ (8) וְכִי־ יָרֹק הַזָּב בַּטָּהוֹר
on-the-clean the-one-discharging to-spit and-if (8) the-evening

וְכִבֶּס בְּגָדָיו וְרָחַץ בַּמַּיִם
with-the-waters and-he-must-bathe clothes-of-him then-he-must-wash

וְטָמֵא עַד־ הָעָרֶב׃ (9) וְכָל־ הַמֶּרְכָּב אֲשֶׁר
that the-seat and-every-of (9) the-evening till and-he-will-be-unclean

יִרְכַּב עָלָיו הַזָּב יִטְמָא׃ (10) וְכָל־
and-every-of (10) he-will-be-unclean the-one-discharging on-him he-rides

הַנֹּגֵעַ בְּכֹל אֲשֶׁר יִהְיֶה תַחְתָּיו יִטְמָא עַד־
till he-will-be-unclean under-him he-was that on-anything the-one-touching

הָעָרֶב וְהַנּוֹשֵׂא אוֹתָם יְכַבֵּס בְּגָדָיו
clothes-of-him he-must-wash them and-the-one-picking-up the-evening

וְרָחַץ בַּמַּיִם וְטָמֵא עַד־ הָעָרֶב׃
the-evening till and-he-will-be-unclean with-the-waters and-he-must-bathe

(11) וְכֹל אֲשֶׁר יִגַּע־ בּוֹ הַזָּב וְיָדָיו
and-hands-of-him the-one-discharging on-him he-touches who and-anyone (11)

לֹא־ שָׁטַף בַּמָּיִם וְכִבֶּס בְּגָדָיו
clothes-of-him then-he-must-wash with-the-waters he-rinsed not

וְרָחַץ בַּמַּיִם וְטָמֵא עַד־ הָעָרֶב׃
the-evening till and-he-will-be-unclean with-the-waters and-he-must-bathe

(12) וּכְלִי־ חֶרֶשׂ אֲשֶׁר־ יִגַּע־ בּוֹ הַזָּב
the-one-discharging on-him he-touches that clay and-pot-of (12)

יִשָּׁבֵר וְכָל־ כְּלִי־ עֵץ יִשָּׁטֵף בַּמָּיִם׃
with-the-waters he-must-be-rinsed wood article-of and-any-of he-must-be-broken

(13) וְכִי־ יִטְהַר הַזָּב מִזּוֹבוֹ
from-discharge-of-him the-one-discharging he-is-cleansed and-when (13)

וְסָפַר לוֹ שִׁבְעַת יָמִים לְטָהֳרָתוֹ וְכִבֶּס
and-he-must-wash for-cleansing-of-him days seven-of to-him then-he-must-count

בְּגָדָיו וְרָחַץ בְּשָׂרוֹ בְּמַיִם חַיִּים
fresh-ones with-waters body-of-him and-he-must-bathe clothes-of-him

וְטָהֵר׃ (14) וּבַיּוֹם הַשְּׁמִינִי יִקַּח־ לוֹ
to-him he-must-take the-eighth and-on-the-day (14) and-he-will-be-clean

שְׁתֵּי תֹרִים אוֹ שְׁנֵי בְּנֵי יוֹנָה וּבָא ׀ לִפְנֵי יְהוָה
Yahweh before and-he-must-come pigeon young-ones-of two-of or doves two-of

אֶל־ פֶּתַח אֹהֶל מוֹעֵד וּנְתָנָם אֶל־ הַכֹּהֵן׃
the-priest to and-he-must-give-them Meeting Tent-of entrance-of to

must wash his clothes and
bathe with water, and he will
be unclean till evening.
8 " 'If the man with the discharge spits on someone who
is clean, that person must
wash his clothes and bathe
with water, and he will be unclean till evening.
9 " 'Everything the man sits
on when riding will be unclean, 10 and whoever touches
any of the things that were
under him will be unclean till
evening; whoever picks up
those things must wash his
clothes and bathe with water,
and he will be unclean till evening.
11 " 'Anyone the man with a
discharge touches without
rinsing his hands with water
must wash his clothes and
bathe with water, and he will
be unclean till evening.
12 " 'A clay pot that the man
touches must be broken, and
any wooden article is to be
rinsed with water.
13 " 'When a man is cleansed
from his discharge, he is to
count off seven days for his
ceremonial cleansing; he must
wash his clothes and bathe
himself with fresh water, and
he will be clean. 14 On the
eighth day he must take two
doves or two young pigeons
and come before the LORD to
the entrance to the Tent of
Meeting and give them to the

וְעָשָׂה אֹתָם הַכֹּהֵן אֶחָד חַטָּאת וְהָאֶחָד
and-the-other sin-offering one the-priest them then-he-must-sacrifice (15)

עֹלָה וְכִפֶּר עָלָיו הַכֹּהֵן לִפְנֵי יְהוָה
Yahweh before the-priest for-him so-he-will-atone burnt-offering

מִזּוֹבוֹ׃ וְאִישׁ כִּי־ תֵצֵא מִמֶּנּוּ שִׁכְבַת־ זָרַע
semen emission-of from-him she-goes when and-man (16) for-discharge-of-him

וְרָחַץ בַּמַּיִם אֶת־ כָּל־ בְּשָׂרוֹ
body-of-him whole-of *** with-the-waters then-he-must-bathe

וְטָמֵא עַד־ הָעָרֶב׃ וְכָל־ בֶּגֶד וְכָל־
or-any-of clothing and-any-of (17) the-evening till and-he-will-be-unclean

עוֹר אֲשֶׁר־ יִהְיֶה עָלָיו שִׁכְבַת־ זָרַע וְכֻבַּס
then-he-must-be-washed semen emission-of on-him he-has that leather

בַּמַּיִם וְטָמֵא עַד־ הָעָרֶב׃ וְאִשָּׁה אֲשֶׁר
when and-woman (18) the-evening till and-he-will-be-unclean with-the-waters

יִשְׁכַּב אִישׁ אֹתָהּ שִׁכְבַת־ זָרַע וְרָחֲצוּ בַמַּיִם
with-the-waters then-they-must-bathe semen emission-of with-her man he-lies

וְטָמְאוּ עַד־ הָעָרֶב׃ וְאִשָּׁה כִּי־ תִהְיֶה
she-has when and-woman (19) the-evening till and-they-will-be-unclean

זָבָה דָּם יִהְיֶה זֹבָהּ בִּבְשָׂרָהּ שִׁבְעַת יָמִים תִּהְיֶה
she-is days seven-of from-body-of-her flow-of-her he-is blood flowing

בְנִדָּתָהּ וְכָל־ הַנֹּגֵעַ בָּהּ יִטְמָא
he-will-be-unclean on-her the-one-touching and-any-of in-impurity-of-her

עַד־ הָעָרֶב׃ וְכֹל[9] אֲשֶׁר תִּשְׁכַּב עָלָיו בְּנִדָּתָהּ
during-period-of-her on-him she-lies that and-anything (20) the-evening till

יִטְמָא וְכֹל אֲשֶׁר־ תֵּשֵׁב עָלָיו יִטְמָא׃
he-will-be-unclean on-him she-sits that and-anything he-will-be-unclean

וְכָל־ הַנֹּגֵעַ בְּמִשְׁכָּבָהּ יְכַבֵּס בְּגָדָיו
clothes-of-him he-must-wash on-bed-of-her the-one-touching and-any-of (21)

וְרָחַץ בַּמַּיִם וְטָמֵא עַד־ הָעָרֶב׃
the-evening till and-he-will-be-unclean with-the-waters and-he-must-bathe

וְכָל־ הַנֹּגֵעַ בְּכָל־ כְּלִי אֲשֶׁר־ תֵּשֵׁב עָלָיו
on-him she-sat that thing on-any-of the-one-touching and-any-of (22)

יְכַבֵּס בְּגָדָיו וְרָחַץ בַּמַּיִם
with-the-waters and-he-must-bathe clothes-of-him he-must-wash

וְטָמֵא עַד־ הָעָרֶב׃ וְאִם עַל־הַמִּשְׁכָּב הוּא אוֹ עַל־
on or he the-bed on whether-if (23) the-evening till and-he-will-be-unclean

הַכְּלִי אֲשֶׁר־ הִוא יֹשֶׁבֶת־ עָלָיו בְּנָגְעוֹ־ בוֹ יִטְמָא
he-will-be-unclean on-him when-to-touch-him on-him sitting she that the-thing

priest. 15 The priest is to sacrifice them, the one for a sin
offering and the other for a
burnt offering. In this way he
will make atonement before
the LORD for the man because
of his discharge.
16 " 'When a man has an
emission of semen, he must
bathe his whole body with
water, and he will be unclean
till evening. 17 Any clothing or
leather that has semen on it
must be washed with water,
and it will be unclean till evening. 18 When a man lies with
a woman and there is an emission of semen, both must
bathe with water, and they
will be unclean till evening.
19 " 'When a woman has her
regular flow of blood, the impurity of her monthly period
will last seven days, and anyone who touches her will be
unclean till evening.
20 " 'Anything she lies on
during her period will be unclean, and anything she sits
on will be unclean. 21 Whoever
touches her bed must wash his
clothes and bathe with water,
and he will be unclean till evening. 22 Whoever touches anything she sits on must wash
his clothes and bathe with
water, and he will be unclean
till evening. 23 Whether it is the
bed or anything she was sitting on, when anyone touches
it, he will be unclean till evening.

עַד־הָעָרֶב׃ וְאִם שָׁכֹב יִשְׁכַּב אִישׁ אֹתָהּ וּתְהִי
and-she-is with-her man he-lies to-lie and-if (24) the-evening till

נִדָּתָהּ עָלָיו וְטָמֵא שִׁבְעַת יָמִים וְכָל־הַמִּשְׁכָּב
the-bed and-any-of days seven-of then-he-will-be-unclean on-him flow-of-her

אֲשֶׁר־יִשְׁכַּב עָלָיו יִטְמָא׃ וְאִשָּׁה כִּי־יָזוּב
he-discharges when and-woman (25) he-will-be-unclean on-him he-lies that

זוֹב דָּמָהּ יָמִים רַבִּים בְּלֹא עֶת־נִדָּתָהּ אוֹ כִי־
when or period-of-her time-of and-not many days blood-of-her discharge-of

תָזוּב עַל־נִדָּתָהּ כָּל־יְמֵי זוֹב טֻמְאָתָהּ
uncleanness-of-her flow-of days-of all-of period-of-her beyond she-discharges

כִּימֵי נִדָּתָהּ תִּהְיֶה טְמֵאָה הִוא׃ כָּל־הַמִּשְׁכָּב אֲשֶׁר־
that the-bed any-of (26) she unclean she-is period-of-her as-days-of

תִּשְׁכַּב עָלָיו כָּל־יְמֵי זוֹבָהּ כְּמִשְׁכַּב נִדָּתָהּ
period-of-her as-bed-of discharge-of-her days-of all-of on-him she-lies

יִהְיֶה־לָּהּ וְכָל־הַכְּלִי אֲשֶׁר תֵּשֵׁב עָלָיו טָמֵא יִהְיֶה
he-will-be unclean on-him she-sits that the-thing and-any-of to-her he-is

כְּטֻמְאַת נִדָּתָהּ׃ וְכָל־הַנּוֹגֵעַ בָּם
on-them the-one-touching and-any-of (27) period-of-her as-uncleanness-of

יִטְמָא וְכִבֶּס בְּגָדָיו וְרָחַץ
and-he-must-bathe clothes-of-him and-he-must-wash he-will-be-unclean

בַּמַּיִם וְטָמֵא עַד־הָעָרֶב׃ וְאִם־
and-when (28) the-evening till and-he-will-be-unclean with-the-waters

טָהֲרָה מִזּוֹבָהּ וְסָפְרָה לָּהּ שִׁבְעַת
seven-of to-her then-she-must-count from-discharge-of-her she-is-cleansed

יָמִים וְאַחַר תִּטְהָר׃ וּבַיּוֹם הַשְּׁמִינִי תִּקַּח־
she-must-take the-eighth and-on-the-day (29) she-will-be-unclean and-after days

לָהּ שְׁתֵּי תֹרִים אוֹ שְׁנֵי בְּנֵי יוֹנָה וְהֵבִיאָה אוֹתָם
them and-she-must-bring pigeon young-ones-of two-of or doves two-of to-her

אֶל־הַכֹּהֵן אֶל־פֶּתַח אֹהֶל מוֹעֵד׃ וְעָשָׂה
and-he-must-sacrifice (30) Meeting Tent-of entrance-of at the-priest to

הַכֹּהֵן אֶת־הָאֶחָד חַטָּאת וְאֶת־הָאֶחָד עֹלָה
burnt-offering the-other and sin-offering the-one *** the-priest

וְכִפֶּר עָלֶיהָ הַכֹּהֵן לִפְנֵי יְהוָה מִזּוֹב
for-discharge-of Yahweh before the-priest for-her so-he-will-atone

טֻמְאָתָהּ׃ וְהִזַּרְתֶּם אֶת־בְּנֵי־יִשְׂרָאֵל
Israel sons-of *** and-you-must-separate (31) uncleanness-of-her

מִטֻּמְאָתָם וְלֹא יָמֻתוּ בְּטֻמְאָתָם
in-uncleanness-of-them they-will-die so-not from-uncleanness-of-them

24 “ ‘If a man lies with her
and her monthly flow touches
him, he will be unclean for
seven days; any bed he lies on
will be unclean.
25 “ ‘When a woman has a
discharge of blood for many
days at a time other than her
monthly period or has a discharge that continues beyond
her period, she will be unclean
as long as she has the discharge, just as in the days of
her period.
26 Any bed she lies
on while her discharge continues will be unclean, as is
her bed during her monthly
period, and anything she sits
on will be unclean, as during
her period.
27 Whoever touches
them will be unclean; he must
wash his clothes and bathe
with water, and he will be unclean till evening.
28 “ ‘When she is cleansed
from her discharge, she must
count off seven days, and after
that she will be ceremonially
clean.
29 On the eighth day she
must take two doves or two
young pigeons and bring
them to the priest at the entrance to the Tent of Meeting.
30 The priest is to sacrifice one
for a sin offering and the other
for a burnt offering. In this
way he will make atonement
for her before the LORD for the
uncleanness of her discharge.
31 “ ‘You must keep the Israelites separate from things
that make them unclean, so
they will not die in their uncleanness for defiling my

בְּטַמְּאָם אֶת־ מִשְׁכָּנִי אֲשֶׁר בְּתוֹכָם׃ זֹאת
this (32) among-them which dwelling-of-me *** when-to-defile-them

תּוֹרַת הַזָּב וַאֲשֶׁר תֵּצֵא מִמֶּנּוּ שִׁכְבַת־
emission-of from-him she-goes and-whoever the-one-discharging regulation-of

זֶרַע לְטָמְאָה־ בָהּ׃ וְהַדָּוָה בְּנִדָּתָהּ
in-period-of-her and-the-woman (33) by-her to-be-made-unclean semen

וְהַזָּב אֶת־ זוֹבוֹ לַזָּכָר וְלַנְּקֵבָה
and-for-the-woman for-the-man discharge-of-him *** and-the-one-discharging

וּלְאִישׁ אֲשֶׁר יִשְׁכַּב עִם־ טְמֵאָה׃ וַיְדַבֵּר יְהוָה אֶל־
to Yahweh and-he-spoke (16:1) unclean-woman with he-lies who and-for-man

מֹשֶׁה אַחֲרֵי מוֹת שְׁנֵי בְּנֵי אַהֲרֹן בְּקָרְבָתָם לִפְנֵי־ יְהוָה
Yahweh before when-to-approach-them Aaron sons-of two-of to-die after Moses

וַיָּמֻתוּ׃ וַיֹּאמֶר יְהוָה אֶל־ מֹשֶׁה דַּבֵּר אֶל־ אַהֲרֹן אָחִיךָ
brother-of-you Aaron to tell! Moses to Yahweh and-he-said (2) and-they-died

וְאַל־ יָבֹא בְכָל־ עֵת אֶל־ הַקֹּדֶשׁ מִבֵּית
behind the-Most-Holy-Place into time at-any-of he-may-come that-not

לַפָּרֹכֶת אֶל־ פְּנֵי הַכַּפֹּרֶת אֲשֶׁר עַל־ הָאָרֹן וְלֹא
so-not the-ark on that the-atonement-cover front-of in to-the-curtain

יָמוּת כִּי בֶּעָנָן אֵרָאֶה עַל־ הַכַּפֹּרֶת׃ בְּזֹאת
as-this (3) the-atonement-cover over I-appear in-the-cloud for he-will-die

יָבֹא אַהֲרֹן אֶל־ הַקֹּדֶשׁ בְּפַר בֶּן־ בָּקָר לְחַטָּאת
for-sin-offering herd young-of with-bull the-sanctuary into Aaron he-may-enter

וְאַיִל לְעֹלָה׃ כְּתֹנֶת־ בַּד קֹדֶשׁ יִלְבָּשׁ
he-must-put-on sacred linen tunic-of (4) for-burnt-offering and-ram

וּמִכְנְסֵי־ בַד יִהְיוּ עַל־ בְּשָׂרוֹ וּבְאַבְנֵט
and-with-sash-of body-of-him next-to they-must-be linen and-undergarments-of

בַּד יַחְגֹּר וּבְמִצְנֶפֶת בַּד יִצְנֹף בִּגְדֵי־
garments-of he-must-put-on linen and-with-turban-of he-must-tie linen

קֹדֶשׁ הֵם וְרָחַץ בַּמַּיִם אֶת־ בְּשָׂרוֹ
body-of him *** with-the-waters so-he-must-bathe these sacred

וּלְבֵשָׁם׃ וּמֵאֵת עֲדַת בְּנֵי יִשְׂרָאֵל יִקַּח
he-must-take Israel sons-of community-of and-from (5) before-he-puts-on-them

שְׁנֵי־ שְׂעִירֵי עִזִּים לְחַטָּאת וְאַיִל אֶחָד לְעֹלָה׃
for-burnt-offering one and-ram for-sin-offering goats male-goats-of two-of

וְהִקְרִיב אַהֲרֹן אֶת־ פַּר הַחַטָּאת אֲשֶׁר־ לוֹ
for-him that the-sin-offering bull-of *** Aaron and-he-must-offer (6)

וְכִפֶּר בַּעֲדוֹ וּבְעַד בֵּיתוֹ׃ וְלָקַח
then-he-must-take (7) household-of-him and-for for-himself so-he-will-atone

dwelling place,[f] which is among them.' "

32These are the regulations for a man with a discharge, for anyone made unclean by an emission of semen, 33for a woman in her monthly period, for a man or a woman with a discharge, and for a man who lies with a woman who is ceremonially unclean.

The Day of Atonement

16 The LORD spoke to Moses after the death of the two sons of Aaron who died when they approached the LORD. 2The LORD said to Moses: "Tell your brother Aaron not to come whenever he chooses into the Most Holy Place behind the curtain in front of the atonement cover on the ark, or else he will die, because I appear in the cloud over the atonement cover.

3"This is how Aaron is to enter the sanctuary area: with a young bull for a sin offering and a ram for a burnt offering. 4He is to put on the sacred linen tunic, with linen undergarments next to his body; he is to tie the linen sash around him and put on the linen turban. These are sacred garments; so he must bathe himself with water before he puts them on. 5From the Israelite community he is to take two male goats for a sin offering and a ram for a burnt offering.

6"Aaron is to offer the bull for his own sin offering to make atonement for himself and his household. 7Then he is

f31 Or *my tabernacle*

אֶת־ שְׁנֵ֣י הַשְּׂעִירִ֑ם וְהֶעֱמִ֤יד אֹתָם֙ לִפְנֵ֣י יְהוָ֔ה פֶּ֖תַח
entrance-of Yahweh before them and-he-must-present the-goats two-of ***

אֹ֥הֶל מוֹעֵֽד׃ וְנָתַ֧ן אַהֲרֹ֛ן עַל־ שְׁנֵ֥י הַשְּׂעִירִ֖ם גֹּרָל֑וֹת גּוֹרָ֤ל
lot lots the-goats two-of for Aaron and-he-must-cast (8) Meeting Tent-of

אֶחָד֙ לַֽיהוָ֔ה וְגוֹרָ֥ל אֶחָ֖ד לַעֲזָאזֵֽל׃ וְהִקְרִ֤יב אַהֲרֹן֙
Aaron and-he-shall-bring (9) for-the-scapegoat other and-lot for-Yahweh one

אֶת־ הַשָּׂעִ֔יר אֲשֶׁ֨ר עָלָ֥ה עָלָ֛יו הַגּוֹרָ֖ל לַֽיהוָ֑ה וְעָשָׂ֖הוּ
and-he-shall-sacrifice-him for-Yahweh the-lot for-him he-falls that the-goat ***

חַטָּֽאת׃ וְהַשָּׂעִ֗יר אֲשֶׁר֩ עָלָ֨ה עָלָ֤יו הַגּוֹרָל֙ לַעֲזָאזֵ֔ל
as-the-scapegoat the-lot for-him he-fell that but-the-goat (10) sin-offering

יָֽעֳמַד־ חַ֛י לִפְנֵ֥י יְהוָ֖ה לְכַפֵּ֣ר עָלָ֑יו לְשַׁלַּ֥ח אֹת֛וֹ
him by-to-send for-him to-atone Yahweh before alive he-shall-be-presented

לַעֲזָאזֵ֖ל הַמִּדְבָּֽרָה׃ וְהִקְרִ֨יב אַהֲרֹ֜ן אֶת־ פַּ֤ר
bull-of *** Aaron and-he-shall-bring (11) into-the-desert as-the-scapegoat

הַֽחַטָּאת֙ אֲשֶׁר־ ל֔וֹ וְכִפֶּ֥ר בַּעֲד֖וֹ וּבְעַ֣ד
and-for for-himself and-he-shall-atone for-him that the-sin-offering

בֵּית֑וֹ וְשָׁחַ֛ט אֶת־ פַּ֥ר הַֽחַטָּ֖את אֲשֶׁר־
that the-sin-offering bull-of *** and-he-shall-slaughter household-of-him

לֽוֹ׃ וְלָקַ֣ח מְלֹֽא־ הַ֠מַּחְתָּה גַּֽחֲלֵי־ אֵ֞שׁ מֵעַ֤ל
from-on fire coals-of the-censer full-of and-he-must-take (12) for-him

הַמִּזְבֵּ֨חַ֙ מִלִּפְנֵ֣י יְהוָ֔ה וּמְלֹ֣א חָפְנָ֔יו קְטֹ֥רֶת
incense-of two-hands-of-him and-full-of Yahweh from-before the-altar

סַמִּ֖ים דַּקָּ֑ה וְהֵבִ֖יא מִבֵּ֥ית לַפָּרֹֽכֶת׃ וְנָתַ֥ן
and-he-must-put (13) to-the-curtain behind and-he-must-take ground fragrances

אֶת־ הַקְּטֹ֛רֶת עַל־ הָאֵ֖שׁ לִפְנֵ֣י יְהוָ֑ה וְכִסָּ֣ה׀ עֲנַ֣ן
smoke-of and-he-will-conceal Yahweh before the-fire on the-incense ***

הַקְּטֹ֗רֶת אֶת־ הַכַּפֹּ֛רֶת אֲשֶׁ֥ר עַל־ הָעֵד֖וּת וְלֹ֥א
so-not the-Testimony above that the-atonement-cover *** the-incense

יָמֽוּת׃ וְלָקַח֙ מִדַּ֣ם הַפָּ֔ר וְהִזָּ֧ה
and-he-must-sprinkle the-bull from-blood-of and-he-must-take (14) he-will-die

בְאֶצְבָּע֛וֹ עַל־ פְּנֵ֥י הַכַּפֹּ֖רֶת קֵ֑דְמָה וְלִפְנֵ֣י
and-before in-front the-atonement-cover front-of on with-finger-of-him

הַכַּפֹּ֗רֶת יַזֶּ֧ה שֶֽׁבַע־ פְּעָמִ֛ים מִן־ הַדָּ֖ם
the-blood from times seven he-shall-sprinkle the-atonement-cover

בְּאֶצְבָּעֽוֹ׃ וְשָׁחַ֞ט אֶת־ שְׂעִ֤יר הַֽחַטָּאת֙
the-sin-offering goat-of *** then-he-shall-slaughter (15) with-finger-of-him

אֲשֶׁ֣ר לָעָ֔ם וְהֵבִיא֙ אֶת־ דָּמ֔וֹ אֶל־ מִבֵּ֖ית לַפָּרֹ֑כֶת
of-the-curtain behind to blood-of-him *** and-he-must-take for-the-people that

to take the two goats and
present them before the LORD
at the entrance to the Tent of
Meeting. 8He is to cast lots for
the two goats—one lot for the
LORD and the other for the
scapegoat.[g] 9Aaron shall bring
the goat whose lot falls to the
LORD and sacrifice it for a sin
offering. 10But the goat chosen
by lot as the scapegoat shall be
presented alive before the
LORD to be used for making
atonement by sending it into
the desert as a scapegoat.

11"Aaron shall bring the bull
for his own sin offering to
make atonement for himself
and his household, and he is
to slaughter the bull for his
own sin offering. 12He is to
take a censer full of burning
coals from the altar before the
LORD and two handfuls of
finely ground fragrant incense
and take them behind the curtain. 13He is to put the incense
on the fire before the LORD,
and the smoke of the incense
will conceal the atonement
cover above the Testimony, so
that he will not die. 14He is to
take some of the bull's blood
and with his finger sprinkle it
on the front of the atonement
cover; then he shall sprinkle
some of it with his finger sev-
en times before the atonement
cover.

15"He shall then slaughter
the goat for the sin offering for
the people and take its blood
behind the curtain and do

g8 That is, the goat of removal; Hebrew *azazel;* also in verses 10 and 26

וְעָשָׂה אֶת־ דָּמוֹ כַּאֲשֶׁר עָשָׂה לְדַם הַפָּר
the-bull with-blood-of he-did just-as blood-of-him with and-he-must-do

וְהִזָּה אֹתוֹ עַל־ הַכַּפֹּרֶת וְלִפְנֵי הַכַּפֹּרֶת׃
the-cover and-in-front-of the-atonement-cover on him and-he-shall-sprinkle

וְכִפֶּר עַל־ הַקֹּדֶשׁ מִטֻּמְאֹת בְּנֵי
sons-of for-uncleannesses-of the-Most-Holy-Place for so-he-will-atone (16)

יִשְׂרָאֵל וּמִפִּשְׁעֵיהֶם לְכָל־ חַטֹּאתָם וְכֵן יַעֲשֶׂה
he-must-do and-same sins-of-them for-all-of and-for-rebellions-of-them Israel

לְאֹהֶל מוֹעֵד הַשֹּׁכֵן אִתָּם בְּתוֹךְ טֻמְאֹתָם׃
uncleannesses-of-them in-midst-of among-them the-staying Meeting for-Tent-of

וְכָל־ אָדָם לֹא־ יִהְיֶה ׀ בְּאֹהֶל מוֹעֵד בְּבֹאוֹ
when-to-go-in-him Meeting in-Tent-of he-may-be not person and-any-of (17)

לְכַפֵּר בַּקֹּדֶשׁ עַד־ צֵאתוֹ וְכִפֶּר
and-he-atoned to-come-out-him until in-the-Most-Holy-Place to-atone

בַּעֲדוֹ וּבְעַד בֵּיתוֹ וּבְעַד כָּל־ קְהַל יִשְׂרָאֵל׃
Israel community-of whole-of and-for household-of-him and-for for-himself

וְיָצָא אֶל־הַמִּזְבֵּחַ אֲשֶׁר לִפְנֵי־ יְהוָה וְכִפֶּר
and-he-shall-atone Yahweh before that the-altar to then-he-shall-come-out (18)

עָלָיו וְלָקַח מִדַּם הַפָּר וּמִדַּם הַשָּׂעִיר
the-goat and-from-blood-of the-bull from-blood-of and-he-shall-take for-him

וְנָתַן עַל־ קַרְנוֹת הַמִּזְבֵּחַ סָבִיב׃ וְהִזָּה
and-he-shall-sprinkle (19) around the-altar horns-of on and-he-shall-put

עָלָיו מִן־ הַדָּם בְּאֶצְבָּעוֹ שֶׁבַע פְּעָמִים וְטִהֲרוֹ
and-he-shall-cleanse-him times seven with-finger-of-him the-blood from on-him

וְקִדְּשׁוֹ מִטֻּמְאֹת בְּנֵי יִשְׂרָאֵל׃
Israel sons-of from-uncleannesses-of and-he-shall-consecrate-him

וְכִלָּה מִכַּפֵּר אֶת־ הַקֹּדֶשׁ וְאֶת־ אֹהֶל
Tent-of and the-Most-Holy-Place *** from-to-atone when-he-finishes (20)

מוֹעֵד וְאֶת־ הַמִּזְבֵּחַ וְהִקְרִיב אֶת־ הַשָּׂעִיר הֶחָי׃
the-live the-goat *** then-he-shall-bring the-altar and Meeting

וְסָמַךְ אַהֲרֹן אֶת־ שְׁתֵּי יָדָו° עַל רֹאשׁ הַשָּׂעִיר
the-goat head-of on hands-of-him both-of *** Aaron and-he-shall-lay (21)

הַחַי וְהִתְוַדָּה עָלָיו אֶת־ כָּל־ עֲוֹנֹת בְּנֵי
sons-of wickednesses-of all-of *** over-him and-he-shall-confess the-live

יִשְׂרָאֵל וְאֶת־ כָּל־ פִּשְׁעֵיהֶם לְכָל־ חַטֹּאתָם וְנָתַן
and-he-shall-put sins-of-them for-all-of rebellions-of-them all-of and Israel

אֹתָם עַל־ רֹאשׁ הַשָּׂעִיר וְשִׁלַּח בְּיַד־ אִישׁ עִתִּי
appointed man in-care-of then-he-shall-send the-goat head-of on them

°21 ק ידיו

with it as he did with the
bull's blood: He shall sprinkle
it on the atonement cover and
in front of it. [16]In this way he
will make atonement for the
Most Holy Place because of the
uncleanness and rebellion of
the Israelites, whatever their
sins have been. He is to do the
same for the Tent of Meeting,
which is among them in the
midst of their uncleanness.
[17]No one is to be in the Tent of
Meeting from the time Aaron
goes in to make atonement in
the Most Holy Place until he
comes out, having made
atonement for himself, his
household and the whole
community of Israel.
[18]"Then he shall come out to
the altar that is before the
LORD and make atonement for
it. He shall take some of the
bull's blood and some of the
goat's blood and put it on all
the horns of the altar. [19]He
shall sprinkle some of the
blood on it with his finger sev-
en times to cleanse it and to
consecrate it from the uncleanness of the Israelites.
[20]"When Aaron has finished
making atonement for the
Most Holy Place, the Tent of
Meeting and the altar, he shall
bring forward the live goat.
[21]He is to lay both hands on
the head of the live goat and
confess over it all the wickedness and rebellion of the Israelites—all their sins—and put
them on the goat's head. He
shall send the goat away into
the desert in the care of a man
appointed for the task. [22]The

הַמִּדְבָּרָה׃ וְנָשָׂא הַשָּׂעִיר עָלָיו אֶת־ כָּל־
all-of *** on-him the-goat and-he-will-carry (22) into-the-desert

עֲוֺנֹתָם אֶל־ אֶרֶץ גְּזֵרָה וְשִׁלַּח אֶת־ הַשָּׂעִיר בַּמִּדְבָּר׃
in-the-desert the-goat *** and-he-shall-release solitary place to sins-of-them

וּבָא אַהֲרֹן אֶל־ אֹהֶל מוֹעֵד וּפָשַׁט אֶת־
*** and-he-must-take-off Meeting Tent-of into Aaron then-he-must-go (23)

בִּגְדֵי הַבָּד אֲשֶׁר לָבַשׁ בְּבֹאוֹ אֶל־ הַקֹּדֶשׁ
the-Most-Holy-Place into before-to-go-him he-put-on that the-linen garments-of

וְהִנִּיחָם שָׁם׃ וְרָחַץ אֶת־ בְּשָׂרוֹ
body-of-him *** and-he-shall-bathe (24) there and-he-must-leave-them

בַמַּיִם בְּמָקוֹם קָדוֹשׁ וְלָבַשׁ אֶת־ בְּגָדָיו
garments-of-him *** then-he-shall-put-on holy in-place with-the-waters

וְיָצָא וְעָשָׂה אֶת־ עֹלָתוֹ
burnt-offering-of-him *** and-he-shall-sacrifice and-he-shall-come-out

וְאֶת־ עֹלַת הָעָם וְכִפֶּר בַּעֲדוֹ וּבְעַד
and-for for-him and-he-shall-atone the-people burnt-offering-of and

הָעָם׃ וְאֵת חֵלֶב הַחַטָּאת יַקְטִיר הַמִּזְבֵּחָה׃
on-the-altar he-shall-burn the-sin-offering fat-of also (25) the-people

וְהַמְשַׁלֵּחַ אֶת־ הַשָּׂעִיר לַעֲזָאזֵל יְכַבֵּס
he-must-wash as-the-scapegoat the-goat *** and-the-one-releasing (26)

בְּגָדָיו וְרָחַץ אֶת־ בְּשָׂרוֹ בַּמָּיִם וְאַחֲרֵי־
and-after with-the-waters body-of-him *** and-he-must-bathe clothes-of-him

כֵן יָבוֹא אֶל־ הַמַּחֲנֶה׃ וְאֵת פַּר הַחַטָּאת וְאֵת ׀ שְׂעִיר
goat-of and the-sin-offering bull-of and (27) the-camp into he-may-come this

הַחַטָּאת אֲשֶׁר הוּבָא אֶת־ דָּמָם לְכַפֵּר
to-atone blood-of-them *** he-was-brought that the-sin-offering

בַּקֹּדֶשׁ יוֹצִיא אֶל־ מִחוּץ לַמַּחֲנֶה
of-the-camp outside to he-must-take into-the-Most-Holy-Place

וְשָׂרְפוּ בָאֵשׁ אֶת־ עֹרֹתָם וְאֶת־ בְּשָׂרָם וְאֶת־
and flesh-of-them and hides-of-them *** in-the-fire and-they-must-burn

פִּרְשָׁם׃ וְהַשֹּׂרֵף אֹתָם יְכַבֵּס בְּגָדָיו
clothes-of-him he-must-wash them and-the-one-burning (28) offal-of-them

וְרָחַץ אֶת־ בְּשָׂרוֹ בַּמָּיִם וְאַחֲרֵי־ כֵן יָבוֹא
he-may-come this and-after with-the-waters body-of-him *** and-he-must-bathe

אֶל־ הַמַּחֲנֶה׃ וְהָיְתָה לָכֶם לְחֻקַּת עוֹלָם
lasting as-ordinance-of for-you and-he-shall-be (29) the-camp into

בַּחֹדֶשׁ הַשְּׁבִיעִי בֶּעָשׂוֹר לַחֹדֶשׁ תְּעַנּוּ אֶת־
*** you-must-deny of-the-month on-the-tenth the-seventh in-the-month

goat will carry on itself all
their sins to a solitary place;
and the man shall release it in
the desert.
[23]"Then Aaron is to go into
the Tent of Meeting and take
off the linen garments he put
on before he entered the Most
Holy Place, and he is to leave
them there. [24]He shall bathe
himself with water in a holy
place and put on his regular
garments. Then he shall come
out and sacrifice the burnt
offering for himself and the
burnt offering for the people,
to make atonement for himself
and for the people. [25]He shall
also burn the fat of the sin
offering on the altar.
[26]"The man who releases the
goat as a scapegoat must wash
his clothes and bathe himself
with water; afterward he may
come into the camp. [27]The bull
and the goat for the sin
offerings, whose blood was
brought into the Most Holy
Place to make atonement,
must be taken outside the
camp; their hides, flesh and
offal are to be burned up. [28]The
man who burns them must
wash his clothes and bathe
himself with water; afterward
he may come into the camp.
[29]"This is to be a lasting ordinance for you: On the tenth
day of the seventh month you
must deny yourselves[h] and

[h]29 Or *must fast*; also in verse 31

נַפְשֹׁתֵיכֶם וְכָל־ מְלָאכָה לֹא תַעֲשׂוּ הָאֶזְרָח וְהַגֵּר
or-the-alien the-native you-may-do not work and-any-of selves-of-you

הַגָּר בְּתוֹכְכֶם׃ כִּי־ בַיּוֹם הַזֶּה יְכַפֵּר עֲלֵיכֶם
for-you he-will-atone the-this on-the-day for (30) among-you the-one-living

לְטַהֵר אֶתְכֶם מִכֹּל חַטֹּאתֵיכֶם לִפְנֵי יְהוָה תִּטְהָרוּ׃
you-will-be-clean Yahweh before sins-of-you from-all-of you to-cleanse

שַׁבַּת שַׁבָּתוֹן הִיא לָכֶם וְעִנִּיתֶם אֶת־ נַפְשֹׁתֵיכֶם
selves-of-you *** and-you-must-deny to-you she rest sabbath-of (31)

חֻקַּת עוֹלָם׃ וְכִפֶּר הַכֹּהֵן אֲשֶׁר־ יִמְשַׁח אֹתוֹ
him he-anointed whom the-priest and-he-must-atone (32) lasting ordinance-of

וַאֲשֶׁר יְמַלֵּא אֶת־ יָדוֹ לְכַהֵן תַּחַת אָבִיו
father-of-him after to-be-priest hand-of-him *** he-ordained and-whom

וְלָבַשׁ אֶת־ בִּגְדֵי הַבָּד בִּגְדֵי הַקֹּדֶשׁ׃
the-sacred garments-of the-linen garments-of *** and-he-must-put-on

וְכִפֶּר אֶת־ מִקְדַּשׁ הַקֹּדֶשׁ וְאֶת־ אֹהֶל
Tent-of and the-Holy-Place Most-Holy-of *** and-he-must-atone (33)

מוֹעֵד וְאֶת־ הַמִּזְבֵּחַ יְכַפֵּר וְעַל הַכֹּהֲנִים וְעַל־ כָּל־
all-of and-for the-priests and-for he-must-atone the-altar and Meeting

עַם הַקָּהָל יְכַפֵּר׃ וְהָיְתָה־ זֹּאת לָכֶם
for-you this and-she-will-be (34) he-must-atone the-community people-of

לְחֻקַּת עוֹלָם לְכַפֵּר עַל־ בְּנֵי יִשְׂרָאֵל מִכָּל־ חַטֹּאתָם
sins-of-them for-all-of Israel sons-of for to-atone lasting for-ordinance-of

אַחַת בַּשָּׁנָה וַיַּעַשׂ כַּאֲשֶׁר צִוָּה יְהוָה אֶת־ מֹשֶׁה׃
Moses *** Yahweh he-commanded just-as and-he-did in-the-year once

וַיְדַבֵּר יְהוָה אֶל־ מֹשֶׁה לֵּאמֹר׃ דַּבֵּר אֶל־ אַהֲרֹן וְאֶל־
and-to Aaron to speak! (2) to-say Moses to Yahweh and-he-spoke (17:1)

בָּנָיו וְאֶל כָּל־ בְּנֵי יִשְׂרָאֵל וְאָמַרְתָּ אֲלֵיהֶם זֶה הַדָּבָר
the-thing this to-them and-you-say Israel sons-of all-of and-to sons-of-him

אֲשֶׁר־ צִוָּה יְהוָה לֵאמֹר׃ אִישׁ אִישׁ מִבֵּית יִשְׂרָאֵל אֲשֶׁר
who Israel from-house-of any man (3) to-say Yahweh he-commanded that

יִשְׁחַט שׁוֹר אוֹ־ כֶשֶׂב אוֹ־ עֵז בַּמַּחֲנֶה אוֹ אֲשֶׁר יִשְׁחַט מִחוּץ
outside he-sacrifices who or in-the-camp goat or lamb or cow he-sacrifices

לַמַּחֲנֶה׃ וְאֶל־ פֶּתַח אֹהֶל מוֹעֵד לֹא הֱבִיאוֹ
he-brings-him not Meeting Tent-of entrance-of and-to (4) of-the-camp

לְהַקְרִיב קָרְבָּן לַיהוָה לִפְנֵי מִשְׁכַּן יְהוָה דָּם
bloodshed Yahweh tabernacle-of in-front-of to-Yahweh offering to-present

יֵחָשֵׁב לָאִישׁ הַהוּא דָּם שָׁפָךְ וְנִכְרַת
and-he-must-be-cut-off he-shed blood the-that to-the-man he-is-considered

not do any work—whether native-born or an alien living
among you— [30]because on this
day atonement will be made
for you, to cleanse you. Then,
before the LORD, you will be
clean from all your sins. [31]It is
a sabbath of rest, and you
must deny yourselves; it is a
lasting ordinance. [32]The priest
who is anointed and ordained
to succeed his father as high
priest is to make atonement.
He is to put on the sacred lin-
en garments [33]and make
atonement for the Most Holy
Place, for the Tent of Meeting
and the altar, and for the
priests and all the people of
the community.

[34]"This is to be a lasting ordinance for you: Atonement is
to be made once a year for all
the sins of the Israelites."

And it was done, as the LORD
commanded Moses.

Eating Blood Forbidden

17 The LORD said to
Moses, [2]"Speak to
Aaron and his sons and to all
the Israelites and say to them:
'This is what the LORD has
commanded: [3]Any Israelite
who sacrifices a cow,[i] a lamb
or a goat in the camp or outside of it [4]instead of bringing
it to the entrance to the Tent of
Meeting to present it as an
offering to the LORD in front of
the tabernacle of the LORD—
that man shall be considered
guilty of bloodshed; he has
shed blood and must be cut off

[i]3 The Hebrew word can include both male and female.

הָאִ֥ישׁ הַה֖וּא מִקֶּ֥רֶב עַמּֽוֹ׃ לְמַ֡עַן אֲשֶׁר֩ יָבִ֨יאוּ
they-will-bring *** so-that (5) people-of-him from-among the-that the-man

בְּנֵ֣י יִשְׂרָאֵ֗ל אֶת־ זִבְחֵיהֶם֮ אֲשֶׁ֣ר הֵ֣ם זֹבְחִים֮ עַל־ פְּנֵ֣י
face-of in ones-making they that sacrifices-of-them *** Israel sons-of

הַשָּׂדֶה֒ וֶהֱבִיאֻ֣ם לַֽיהוָ֗ה אֶל־ פֶּ֛תַח אֹ֥הֶל מוֹעֵ֖ד
Meeting Tent-of entrance-of at to-Yahweh now-they-must-bring-them the-field

אֶל־ הַכֹּהֵ֑ן וְזָבְח֗וּ זִבְחֵ֧י שְׁלָמִ֛ים לַיהוָ֖ה
to-Yahweh fellowships offerings-of and-they-must-sacrifice the-priest to

אוֹתָֽם׃ וְזָרַ֨ק הַכֹּהֵ֤ן אֶת־ הַדָּם֙ עַל־ מִזְבַּ֣ח
altar-of against the-blood *** the-priest and-he-must-sprinkle (6) them

יְהוָ֔ה פֶּ֖תַח אֹ֣הֶל מוֹעֵ֑ד וְהִקְטִ֣יר הַחֵ֔לֶב לְרֵ֥יחַ
as-aroma-of the-fat and-he-must-burn Meeting Tent-of entrance-of Yahweh

נִיחֹ֖חַ לַיהוָֽה׃ וְלֹֽא־ יִזְבְּח֥וּ עוֹד֙ אֶת־
*** any-longer they-must-offer but-not (7) to-Yahweh pleasant

זִבְחֵיהֶ֔ם לַשְּׂעִירִ֕ם אֲשֶׁ֛ר הֵ֥ם זֹנִ֖ים אַחֲרֵיהֶ֑ם
to-them ones-prostituting they whom to-the-goat-idols sacrifices-of-them

חֻקַּ֥ת עוֹלָ֛ם תִּֽהְיֶה־ זֹּ֥את לָהֶ֖ם לְדֹרֹתָֽם׃
for-generations-of-them for-them this she-will-be lasting ordinance-of

וַאֲלֵהֶ֣ם תֹּאמַ֔ר אִ֥ישׁ אִישׁ֙ מִבֵּ֣ית יִשְׂרָאֵ֔ל וּמִן־ הַגֵּ֖ר אֲשֶׁר־
who the-alien or-from Israel from-house-of any man you-say and-to-them (8)

יָג֣וּר בְּתוֹכָ֑ם אֲשֶׁר־ יַעֲלֶ֥ה עֹלָ֖ה אוֹ־ זָֽבַח׃ וְאֶל־
and-to (9) sacrifice or burnt-offering he-offers who among-them he-lives

פֶּ֜תַח אֹ֤הֶל מוֹעֵד֙ לֹ֣א יְבִיאֶ֔נּוּ לַעֲשׂ֥וֹת אֹת֖וֹ לַיהוָ֑ה
to-Yahweh him to-sacrifice he-brings-him not Meeting Tent-of entrance-of

וְנִכְרַ֛ת הָאִ֥ישׁ הַה֖וּא מֵעַמָּֽיו׃ וְאִ֨ישׁ אִ֜ישׁ
any and-man (10) from-people-of-him the-that the-man then-he-must-be-cut-off

מִבֵּ֣ית יִשְׂרָאֵ֗ל וּמִן־ הַגֵּר֙ הַגָּ֣ר בְּתוֹכָ֔ם אֲשֶׁ֥ר יֹאכַ֖ל
he-eats who among-them the-one-living the-alien or-from Israel from-house-of

כָּל־ דָּ֑ם וְנָתַתִּ֣י פָנַ֗י בַּנֶּ֙פֶשׁ֙ הָאֹכֶ֣לֶת
the-one-eating against-the-person faces-of-me then-I-will-set blood any-of

אֶת־ הַדָּ֔ם וְהִכְרַתִּ֥י אֹתָ֖הּ מִקֶּ֥רֶב עַמָּֽהּ׃ כִּ֣י
for (11) people-of-her from-among her and-I-will-cut-off the-blood ***

נֶ֣פֶשׁ הַבָּשָׂר֮ בַּדָּ֣ם הִוא֒ וַאֲנִ֞י נְתַתִּ֤יו לָכֶם֙ עַל־ הַמִּזְבֵּ֔חַ
the-altar on to-you I-gave-him and-I she in-the-blood the-creature life-of

לְכַפֵּ֖ר עַל־ נַפְשֹׁתֵיכֶ֑ם כִּֽי־ הַדָּ֥ם ה֖וּא בַּנֶּ֥פֶשׁ יְכַפֵּֽר׃ עַל־
for (12) he-atones for-the-life he the-blood for selves-of-you for to-atone

כֵּ֤ן אָמַ֙רְתִּי֙ לִבְנֵ֣י יִשְׂרָאֵ֔ל כָּל־ נֶ֥פֶשׁ מִכֶּ֖ם לֹא־ תֹ֣אכַל דָּ֑ם
blood she-may-eat not from-you person any-of Israel to-sons-of I-say this

from his people. 5This is so the
Israelites will bring to the
LORD the sacrifices they are
now making in the open
fields. They must bring them
to the priest, that is, to the
LORD, at the entrance to the
Tent of Meeting and sacrifice
them as fellowship offerings.[j]
6The priest is to sprinkle the
blood against the altar of the
LORD at the entrance to the
Tent of Meeting and burn the
fat as an aroma pleasing to the
LORD. 7They must no longer
offer any of their sacrifices to
the goat idols[k] to whom they
prostitute themselves. This is
to be a lasting ordinance for
them and for the generations
to come.'
8"Say to them: 'Any Israelite
or any alien living among
them who offers a burnt
offering or sacrifice 9and does
not bring it to the entrance to
the Tent of Meeting to sacrifice it to the LORD—that man
must be cut off from his
people.
10" 'Any Israelite or any
alien living among them who
eats any blood—I will set my
face against that person who
eats blood and will cut him off
from his people. 11For the life
of a creature is in the blood,
and I have given it to you to
make atonement for your-
selves on the altar; it is the
blood that makes atonement
for one's life. 12Therefore I say
to the Israelites, "None of you
may eat blood, nor may an

j5 Traditionally *peace offerings*
k7 Or *demons*

וְהַגֵּר הַגָּר בְּתוֹכְכֶם לֹא־יֹאכַל דָּם׃ וְאִישׁ אִישׁ
any and-man (13) blood he-may-eat not among-you the-one-living nor-the-alien

מִבְּנֵי יִשְׂרָאֵל וּמִן־הַגֵּר הַגָּר בְּתוֹכָם אֲשֶׁר יָצוּד
he-hunts who among-them the-one-living the-alien or-from Israel from-sons-of

צֵיד חַיָּה אוֹ־עוֹף אֲשֶׁר יֵאָכֵל וְשָׁפַךְ אֶת־דָּמוֹ
blood-of-him *** then-he-must-drain he-may-be-eaten that bird or wild animal

וְכִסָּהוּ בֶּעָפָר׃ כִּי־נֶפֶשׁ כָּל־בָּשָׂר
creature every-of life-of for (14) with-the-earth and-he-must-cover-him

דָּמוֹ בְנַפְשׁוֹ הוּא וָאֹמַר לִבְנֵי יִשְׂרָאֵל דַּם כָּל־
any-of blood-of Israel to-sons-of so-I-said he in-life-of-him blood-of-him

בָּשָׂר לֹא תֹאכֵלוּ כִּי נֶפֶשׁ כָּל־בָּשָׂר דָּמוֹ הִוא
she blood-of-him creature every-of life-of for you-must-eat not creature

כָּל־אֹכְלָיו יִכָּרֵת׃ וְכָל־נֶפֶשׁ אֲשֶׁר תֹּאכַל
she-eats who person and-any-of (15) he-must-be-cut-off ones-eating-him all-of

נְבֵלָה וּטְרֵפָה בָּאֶזְרָח וּבַגֵּר וְכִבֶּס
then-he-must-wash or-the-alien whether-the-native or-torn-animal carcass

בְּגָדָיו וְרָחַץ בַּמַּיִם וְטָמֵא עַד־
till and-he-will-be-unclean with-the-waters and-he-must-bathe clothes-of-him

הָעֶרֶב וְטָהֵר׃ וְאִם לֹא יְכַבֵּס וּבְשָׂרוֹ
and-body-of-him he-washes not but-if (16) then-he-will-be-clean the-evening

לֹא יִרְחָץ וְנָשָׂא עֲוֺנוֹ׃ וַיְדַבֵּר
and-he-spoke (18:1) responsibility-of-him then-he-will-bear he-bathes not

יְהוָה אֶל־מֹשֶׁה לֵּאמֹר׃ דַּבֵּר אֶל־בְּנֵי יִשְׂרָאֵל וְאָמַרְתָּ אֲלֵהֶם אֲנִי
I to-them and-you-say Israel sons-of to speak! (2) to-say Moses to Yahweh

יְהוָה אֱלֹהֵיכֶם׃ כְּמַעֲשֵׂה אֶרֶץ־מִצְרַיִם אֲשֶׁר יְשַׁבְתֶּם־בָּהּ לֹא
not in-her you-lived where Egypt land-of as-action-of (3) God-of-you Yahweh

תַעֲשׂוּ וּכְמַעֲשֵׂה אֶרֶץ־כְּנַעַן אֲשֶׁר אֲנִי מֵבִיא אֶתְכֶם שָׁמָּה
to-there you bringing I where Canaan land-of and-as-action-of you-must-do

לֹא תַעֲשׂוּ וּבְחֻקֹּתֵיהֶם לֹא תֵלֵכוּ׃ אֶת־
*** (4) you must-follow not and-to-practices-of-them you-must-do not

מִשְׁפָּטַי תַּעֲשׂוּ וְאֶת־חֻקֹּתַי תִּשְׁמְרוּ לָלֶכֶת
to-follow you-must-be-careful decrees-of-me and you-must-obey laws-of-me

בָּהֶם אֲנִי יְהוָה אֱלֹהֵיכֶם׃ וּשְׁמַרְתֶּם אֶת־חֻקֹּתַי וְאֶת־
and decrees-of-me *** now-you-keep (5) God-of-you Yahweh I after-them

מִשְׁפָּטַי אֲשֶׁר יַעֲשֶׂה אֹתָם הָאָדָם וָחַי בָּהֶם אֲנִי יְהוָה׃
Yahweh I by-them also-he-will-live the-man them he-obeys who laws-of-me

אִישׁ אִישׁ אֶל־כָּל־שְׁאֵר בְּשָׂרוֹ לֹא תִקְרְבוּ לְגַלּוֹת
to-expose you-may-approach not body-of-him relative-of any-of to any man (6)

alien living among you eat blood."

[13]" 'Any Israelite or any alien living among you who hunts any animal or bird that may be eaten must drain out the blood and cover it with earth, [14]because the life of every creature is its blood. That is why I have said to the Israelites, "You must not eat the blood of any creature, because the life of every creature is its blood; anyone who eats it must be cut off."

[15]" 'Anyone, whether native-born or alien, who eats anything found dead or torn by wild animals must wash his clothes and bathe with water, and he will be unclean till evening; then he will be clean. [16]But if he does not wash his clothes and bathe himself, he will be held responsible.' "

Unlawful Sexual Relations

18 The LORD said to Moses, [2]"Speak to the Israelites and say to them: 'I am the LORD your God. [3]You must not do as they do in Egypt, where you used to live, and you must not do as they do in the land of Canaan, where I am bringing you. Do not follow their practices. [4]You must obey my laws and be careful to follow my decrees. I am the LORD your God. [5]Keep my decrees and laws, for the man who obeys them will live by them. I am the LORD.

[6]" 'No one is to approach any close relative to have sexual relations. I am the LORD.

עֶרְוָה אֲנִי יְהוָה׃ (7) עֶרְוַת אָבִיךָ וְעֶרְוַת
or-nakedness-of father-of-you nakedness-of (7) Yahweh I nakedness

אִמְּךָ לֹא תְגַלֵּה אִמְּךָ הִוא לֹא תְגַלֶּה עֶרְוָתָהּ׃
nakedness-of-her you-expose not she mother-of-you you-expose not mother-of-you

(8) עֶרְוַת אֵשֶׁת־ אָבִיךָ לֹא תְגַלֵּה עֶרְוַת
nakedness-of you-expose not father-of-you wife-of nakedness-of (8)

אָבִיךָ הִוא׃ (9) עֶרְוַת אֲחוֹתְךָ בַת־ אָבִיךָ
father-of-you daughter-of sister-of-you nakedness-of (9) she father-of-you

אוֹ בַת־ אִמֶּךָ מוֹלֶדֶת בַּיִת אוֹ מוֹלֶדֶת חוּץ לֹא
not elsewhere born-of or home born-of mother-of-you daughter-of or

תְּגַלֶּה עֶרְוָתָן׃ (10) עֶרְוַת בַּת־ בִּנְךָ אוֹ
or son-of-you daughter-of nakedness-of (10) nakedness-of-them you-expose

בַת־ בִּתְּךָ לֹא תְגַלֶּה עֶרְוָתָן כִּי
for nakedness-of-them you-expose not daughter-of-you daughter-of

עֶרְוָתְךָ הֵנָּה׃ (11) עֶרְוַת בַּת־ אֵשֶׁת אָבִיךָ
father-of-you wife-of daughter-of nakedness-of (11) they nakedness-of-you

מוֹלֶדֶת אָבִיךָ אֲחוֹתְךָ הִוא לֹא תְגַלֶּה עֶרְוָתָהּ׃
nakedness-of-her you-expose not she sister-of-you father-of-you born-of

(12) עֶרְוַת אֲחוֹת־ אָבִיךָ לֹא תְגַלֵּה שְׁאֵר
close-relative-of you-expose not father-of-you sister-of nakedness-of (12)

אָבִיךָ הִוא׃ (13) עֶרְוַת אֲחוֹת־ אִמְּךָ לֹא תְגַלֵּה
you-expose not mother-of-you sister-of nakedness-of (13) she father-of-you

כִּי־ שְׁאֵר אִמְּךָ הִוא׃ (14) עֶרְוַת אֲחִי־
brother-of nakedness-of (14) she mother-of-you close-relative-of for

אָבִיךָ לֹא תְגַלֵּה אֶל־ אִשְׁתּוֹ לֹא תִקְרָב דֹּדָתְךָ הִוא׃
she aunt-of-you you-approach not wife-of-him by you-expose not father-of-you

(15) עֶרְוַת כַּלָּתְךָ לֹא תְגַלֵּה אֵשֶׁת בִּנְךָ
son-of-you wife-of you-expose not daughter-in-law-of-you nakedness-of (15)

הִוא לֹא תְגַלֶּה עֶרְוָתָהּ׃ (16) עֶרְוַת אֵשֶׁת־ אָחִיךָ
brother-of-you wife-of nakedness-of (16) nakedness-of-her you-expose not she

לֹא תְגַלֵּה עֶרְוַת אָחִיךָ הִוא׃ (17) עֶרְוַת אִשָּׁה
woman nakedness-of (17) she brother-of-you nakedness-of you-expose not

וּבִתָּהּ לֹא תְגַלֵּה אֶת־ בַּת־ בְּנָהּ וְאֶת־ בַּת־
daughter-of or son-of-her daughter-of *** you-expose not and-daughter-of-her

בִּתָּהּ לֹא תִקַּח לְגַלּוֹת עֶרְוָתָהּ שַׁאֲרָה הֵנָּה
they close-relative nakedness-of-her to-expose you-take not daughter-of-her

זִמָּה הִוא (18) וְאִשָּׁה אֶל־ אֲחֹתָהּ לֹא תִקָּח לִצְרֹר
to-be-rival you-marry not sister-of-her with and-woman (18) that wickedness

[7]" 'Do not dishonor your father by having sexual relations with your mother. She is your mother; do not have relations with her.

[8]" 'Do not have sexual relations with your father's wife; that would dishonor your father.

[9]" 'Do not have sexual relations with your sister, either your father's daughter or your mother's daughter, whether she was born in the same home or elsewhere.

[10]" 'Do not have sexual relations with your son's daughter or your daughter's daughter; that would dishonor you.

[11]" 'Do not have sexual relations with the daughter of your father's wife, born to your father; she is your sister.

[12]" 'Do not have sexual relations with your father's sister; she is your father's close relative.

[13]" 'Do not have sexual relations with your mother's sister, because she is your mother's close relative.

[14]" 'Do not dishonor your father's brother by approaching his wife to have sexual relations; she is your aunt.

[15]" 'Do not have sexual relations with your daughter-in-law. She is your son's wife; do not have relations with her.

[16]" 'Do not have sexual relations with your brother's wife; that would dishonor your brother.

[17]" 'Do not have sexual relations with both a woman and her daughter. Do not have sexual relations with either her son's daughter or her daughter's daughter; they are her close relatives. That is wickedness.

[18]" 'Do not take your wife's sister as a rival wife and have

לְגַלּוֹת עֶרְוָתָהּ עָלֶיהָ בְּחַיֶּיהָ׃ וְאֶל־ אִשָּׁה
woman and-to (19) while-alive-her with-her nakedness-of-her to-expose

בְּנִדַּת טֻמְאָתָהּ לֹא תִקְרַב לְגַלּוֹת עֶרְוָתָהּ׃
nakedness-of-her to-expose you-approach not uncleanness-of-her in-period-of

וְאֶל־ אֵשֶׁת עֲמִיתְךָ לֹא־ תִתֵּן שְׁכָבְתְּךָ לְזָרַע
of-semen emission-of-you you-give not neighbor-of-you wife-of and-to (20)

לְטָמְאָה־ בָהּ׃ וּמִזַּרְעֲךָ לֹא־ תִתֵּן לְהַעֲבִיר
to-sacrifice you-give not and-from-children-of-you (21) with-her to-defile

לַמֹּלֶךְ וְלֹא תְחַלֵּל אֶת־ שֵׁם אֱלֹהֶיךָ אֲנִי יְהוָה׃
Yahweh I God-of-you name-of *** you-must-profane for-not to-the-Molech

וְאֶת־ זָכָר לֹא תִשְׁכַּב מִשְׁכְּבֵי אִשָּׁה תּוֹעֵבָה הִוא׃
that detestable woman ones-who-lie-of you-lie-with not man and (22)

וּבְכָל־ בְּהֵמָה לֹא־ תִתֵּן שְׁכָבְתְּךָ לְטָמְאָה־ בָהּ
with-her to-defile emission-of-you you-give not animal and-with-any-of (23)

וְאִשָּׁה לֹא־ תַעֲמֹד לִפְנֵי בְהֵמָה לְרִבְעָהּ תֶּבֶל
perversion to-have-relation-with-her animal to she-must-present not and-woman

הוּא׃ אַל־ תִּטַּמְּאוּ בְּכָל־ אֵלֶּה כִּי בְכָל־ אֵלֶּה
these in-all-of for these in-any-of you-defile-yourselves not (24) that

נִטְמְאוּ הַגּוֹיִם אֲשֶׁר־ אֲנִי מְשַׁלֵּחַ מִפְּנֵיכֶם׃
from-before-you driving-you I that the-nations they-became-defiled

וַתִּטְמָא הָאָרֶץ וָאֶפְקֹד עֲוֺנָהּ עָלֶיהָ
on-her sin-of-her so-I-punished the-land even-she-was-defiled (25)

וַתָּקִא הָאָרֶץ אֶת־ יֹשְׁבֶיהָ׃ וּשְׁמַרְתֶּם אַתֶּם
you but-you-keep (26) ones-inhabiting-her *** the-land and-she-vomited-out

אֶת־ חֻקֹּתַי וְאֶת־ מִשְׁפָּטַי וְלֹא תַעֲשׂוּ מִכֹּל הַתּוֹעֵבֹת
the-abominations from-any-of you-do and-not laws-of-me and decrees-of-me ***

הָאֵלֶּה הָאֶזְרָח וְהַגֵּר הַגָּר בְּתוֹכְכֶם׃ כִּי אֶת־
*** for (27) among-you the-one-living or-the-alien the-native the-these

כָּל־ הַתּוֹעֵבֹת הָאֵל עָשׂוּ אַנְשֵׁי־ הָאָרֶץ אֲשֶׁר לִפְנֵיכֶם
before-you who the-land people-of they-did the-these the-abominations all-of

וַתִּטְמָא הָאָרֶץ׃ וְלֹא־ תָקִיא הָאָרֶץ אֶתְכֶם
you the-land she-vomit-out so-not (28) the-land and-she-became-defiled

בְּטַמַּאֲכֶם אֹתָהּ כַּאֲשֶׁר קָאָה אֶת־ הַגּוֹי אֲשֶׁר לִפְנֵיכֶם׃
before-you that the-nation *** she-vomited-out just-as her when-to-defile-you

כִּי כָּל־ אֲשֶׁר יַעֲשֶׂה מִכֹּל הַתּוֹעֵבוֹת הָאֵלֶּה
the-these the-abominations from-any-of he-does who everyone indeed (29)

וְנִכְרְתוּ הַנְּפָשׁוֹת הָעֹשֹׂת מִקֶּרֶב עַמָּם׃
people-of-them from-among the-ones-doing the-persons then-they-must-be-cut-off

sexual relations with her while your wife is living.

19" 'Do not approach a woman to have sexual relations during the uncleanness of her monthly period.

20" 'Do not have intercourse with your neighbor's wife and defile yourself with her.

21" 'Do not give any of your children to be sacrificed[l] to Molech, for you must not profane the name of your God. I am the LORD.

22" 'Do not lie with a man as one lies with a woman; that is detestable.

23" 'Do not have sexual relations with an animal and defile yourself with it. A woman must not present herself to an animal to have sexual relations with it; that is a perversion.

24" 'Do not defile yourselves in any of these ways, because this is how the nations that I am going to drive out before you became defiled. 25Even the land was defiled; so I punished it for its sin, and the land vomited out its inhabitants. 26But you must keep my decrees and my laws. The native-born and the aliens living among you must not do any of these detestable things, 27for all these things were done by the people who lived in the land before you, and the land became defiled. 28And if you defile the land, it will vomit you out as it vomited out the nations that were before you.

29" 'Everyone who does any of these detestable things—such persons must be cut off from their people. 30Keep my

[l]21 *Or to be passed through* ⌊*the fire*⌋

וּשְׁמַרְתֶּם אֶת־ מִשְׁמַרְתִּי לְבִלְתִּי עֲשׂוֹת מֵחֻקּוֹת
from-customs-of to-follow not requirement-of-me *** so-you-keep (30)

הַתּוֹעֵבֹת אֲשֶׁר נַעֲשׂוּ לִפְנֵיכֶם וְלֹא
and-not before-you they-were-practiced that the-detestable-ones

תִטַּמְּאוּ בָּהֶם אֲנִי יְהוָה אֱלֹהֵיכֶם׃ וַיְדַבֵּר
and-he-spoke (19:1) God-of-you Yahweh I with-them you-defile-yourselves

יְהוָה אֶל־ מֹשֶׁה לֵּאמֹר דַּבֵּר אֶל־ כָּל־ עֲדַת בְּנֵי־ יִשְׂרָאֵל
Israel sons-of assembly-of entire-of to speak! (2) to-say Moses to Yahweh

וְאָמַרְתָּ אֲלֵהֶם קְדֹשִׁים תִּהְיוּ כִּי קָדוֹשׁ אֲנִי יְהוָה אֱלֹהֵיכֶם׃
God-of-you Yahweh I holy for you-must-be holy-ones to-them and-you-say

אִישׁ אִמּוֹ וְאָבִיו תִּירָאוּ וְאֶת־ שַׁבְּתֹתַי
Sabbaths-of-me and you-must-respect and-father-of-him mother-of-him each (3)

תִּשְׁמֹרוּ אֲנִי יְהוָה אֱלֹהֵיכֶם׃ אַל־ תִּפְנוּ אֶל־הָאֱלִילִם וֵאלֹהֵי
or-gods-of the-idols to you-turn not (4) God-of-you Yahweh I you-must-observe

מַסֵּכָה לֹא תַעֲשׂוּ לָכֶם אֲנִי יְהוָה אֱלֹהֵיכֶם׃ וְכִי
and-when (5) God-of-you Yahweh I for-you you-make not cast-metal

תִזְבְּחוּ זֶבַח שְׁלָמִים לַיהוָה לִרְצֹנְכֶם
to-be-accepted-for-you to-Yahweh fellowships offering-of you-sacrifice

תִּזְבָּחֻהוּ׃ בְּיוֹם זִבְחֲכֶם יֵאָכֵל
he-must-be-eaten sacrifice-of-you on-day-of (6) you-sacrifice-him

וּמִמָּחֳרָת וְהַנּוֹתָר עַד־ יוֹם הַשְּׁלִישִׁי בָּאֵשׁ
with-the-fire the-third day-of until and-the-remaining or-on-next-day

יִשָּׂרֵף׃ וְאִם הֵאָכֹל יֵאָכֵל בַּיּוֹם הַשְּׁלִישִׁי
the-third on-the-day he-is-eaten to-be-eaten and-if (7) he-must-be-burned

פִּגּוּל הוּא לֹא יֵרָצֶה׃ וְאֹכְלָיו עֲוֺנוֹ
responsibility-of-him and-ones-eating-him (8) he-will-be-accepted not he impure

יִשָּׂא כִּי־ אֶת־ קֹדֶשׁ יְהוָה חִלֵּל וְנִכְרְתָה
and-she-must-be-cut-off he-desecrated Yahweh holy-of *** for he-will-bear

הַנֶּפֶשׁ הַהִוא מֵעַמֶּיהָ׃ וּבְקֻצְרְכֶם אֶת־ קְצִיר
harvest-of *** and-when-to-reap-you (9) from-people-of-her the-that the-person

אַרְצְכֶם לֹא תְכַלֶּה פְּאַת שָׂדְךָ לִקְצֹר וְלֶקֶט
and-gleaning-of to-reap field-of-you corner-of you-complete not land-of-you

קְצִירְךָ לֹא תְלַקֵּט׃ וְכַרְמְךָ לֹא תְעוֹלֵל
you-pick-twice not and-vineyard-of-you (10) you-gather not harvest-of-you

וּפֶרֶט כַּרְמְךָ לֹא תְלַקֵּט לֶעָנִי
for-the-poor you-pick-up not vineyard-of-you and-fallen-grape-of

וְלַגֵּר תַּעֲזֹב אֹתָם אֲנִי יְהוָה אֱלֹהֵיכֶם׃ לֹא תִּגְנֹבוּ
you-steal not (11) God-of-you Yahweh I them you-leave and-for-the-alien

requirements and do not follow any of the detestable customs that were practiced before you came and do not defile yourselves with them. I am the LORD your God.' "

Various Laws

19 The LORD said to Moses, [2]"Speak to the entire assembly of Israel and say to them: 'Be holy because I, the LORD your God, am holy.
[3]" 'Each of you must respect his mother and father, and you must observe my Sabbaths. I am the LORD your God.
[4]" 'Do not turn to idols or make gods of cast metal for yourselves. I am the LORD your God.
[5]" 'When you sacrifice a fellowship offering[m] to the LORD, sacrifice it in such a way that it will be accepted on your behalf. [6]It shall be eaten on the day you sacrifice it or on the next day; anything left over until the third day must be burned up. [7]If any of it is eaten on the third day, it is impure and will not be accepted. [8]Whoever eats it will be held responsible because he has desecrated what is holy to the LORD; that person must be cut off from his people.
[9]" 'When you reap the harvest of your land, do not reap to the very edges of your field or gather the gleanings of your harvest. [10]Do not go over your vineyard a second time or pick up the grapes that have fallen. Leave them for the poor and the alien. I am the LORD your God.
[11]" 'Do not steal.

[m]5 Traditionally *peace offering*

וְלֹא־ תְכַחֲשׁוּ וְלֹא־ תְשַׁקְּרוּ אִישׁ בַּעֲמִיתוֹ׃ וְלֹא־
and-not (12) against-fellow-of-him man you-deceive and-not you-lie and-not

תִשָּׁבְעוּ בִשְׁמִי לַשָּׁקֶר וְחִלַּלְתָּ אֶת־ שֵׁם
name-of *** so-you-profane with-the-falsehood by-name-of-me you-swear

אֱלֹהֶיךָ אֲנִי יְהוָה׃ לֹא־ תַעֲשֹׁק אֶת־ רֵעֲךָ וְלֹא תִגְזֹל
you-rob or-not neighbor-of-you *** you-defraud not (13) Yahweh I God-of-you

לֹא־ תָלִין פְּעֻלַּת שָׂכִיר אִתְּךָ עַד־ בֹּקֶר׃ לֹא־ תְקַלֵּל
you-curse not (14) morning until with-you hired-man wage-of you-hold-back not

חֵרֵשׁ וְלִפְנֵי עִוֵּר לֹא תִתֵּן מִכְשֹׁל וְיָרֵאתָ
but-you-fear stumbling-block you-put not blind or-in-front-of deaf

מֵּאֱלֹהֶיךָ אֲנִי יְהוָה׃ לֹא־ תַעֲשׂוּ עָוֶל בַּמִּשְׁפָּט לֹא־
not of-the-justice perversion you-do not (15) Yahweh I to-God-of-you

תִשָּׂא פְנֵי־ דָל וְלֹא תֶהְדַּר פְּנֵי גָדוֹל בְּצֶדֶק תִּשְׁפֹּט
you-judge in-fairness great face-of you-favor or-not poor face-of you-lift

עֲמִיתֶךָ׃ לֹא־ תֵלֵךְ רָכִיל בְּעַמֶּיךָ לֹא תַעֲמֹד
you-stand not among-people-of-you slander you-go not (16) neighbor-of-you

עַל־ דַּם רֵעֶךָ אֲנִי יְהוָה׃ לֹא־ תִשְׂנָא אֶת־ אָחִיךָ
brother-of-you *** you-hate not (17) Yahweh I neighbor-of-you blood-of against

בִּלְבָבֶךָ הוֹכֵחַ תּוֹכִיחַ אֶת־ עֲמִיתֶךָ וְלֹא־ תִשָּׂא
you-share so-not neighbor-of-you *** you-rebuke to-rebuke in-heart-of-you

עָלָיו חֵטְא׃ לֹא־ תִקֹּם וְלֹא־ תִטֹּר אֶת־ בְּנֵי
sons-of *** you-bear-grudge or-not you-seek-revenge not (18) guilt with-him

עַמֶּךָ וְאָהַבְתָּ לְרֵעֲךָ כָּמוֹךָ אֲנִי יְהוָה׃ אֶת־
*** (19) Yahweh I as-yourself to-neighbor-of-you but-you-love people-of-you

חֻקֹּתַי תִּשְׁמֹרוּ בְּהֶמְתְּךָ לֹא־ תַרְבִּיעַ כִּלְאַיִם שָׂדְךָ
field-of-you two-kinds you-mate not animal-of-you you-keep decrees-of-me

לֹא־ תִזְרַע כִּלְאָיִם וּבֶגֶד כִּלְאַיִם שַׁעַטְנֵז לֹא יַעֲלֶה
you-wear not woven two-kinds and-clothing two-kinds you-plant-seed not

עָלֶיךָ׃ וְאִישׁ כִּי־ יִשְׁכַּב אֶת־ אִשָּׁה שִׁכְבַת־ זֶרַע וְהִוא
and-she semen emission-of woman with he-sleeps if and-man (20) on-you

שִׁפְחָה נֶחֱרֶפֶת לְאִישׁ וְהָפְדֵּה לֹא נִפְדָּתָה
she-was-ransomed not but-to-be-ransomed to-another being-promised slave-girl

אוֹ חֻפְשָׁה לֹא נִתַּן־ לָהּ בִּקֹּרֶת תִּהְיֶה לֹא יוּמְתוּ
they-must-die not she-must-be punishment to-her he-was-given not freedom or

כִּי־ לֹא חֻפָּשָׁה׃ וְהֵבִיא אֶת־ אֲשָׁמוֹ לַיהוָה אֶל־
to to-Yahweh guilt-offering-of-him *** but-he-must-bring (21) free not for

פֶּתַח אֹהֶל מוֹעֵד אֵיל אָשָׁם׃ וְכִפֶּר
and-he-shall-atone (22) guilt-offering ram-of Meeting Tent-of entrance-of

" 'Do not lie.
" 'Do not deceive one another.
12 " 'Do not swear falsely by my name and so profane the name of your God. I am the LORD.
13 " 'Do not defraud your neighbor or rob him.
" 'Do not hold back the wages of a hired man overnight.
14 " 'Do not curse the deaf or put a stumbling block in front of the blind, but fear your God. I am the LORD.
15 " 'Do not pervert justice; do not show partiality to the poor or favoritism to the great, but judge your neighbor fairly.
16 " 'Do not go about spreading slander among your people.
" 'Do not do anything that endangers your neighbor's life. I am the LORD.
17 " 'Do not hate your brother in your heart. Rebuke your neighbor frankly so you will not share in his guilt.
18 " 'Do not seek revenge or bear a grudge against one of your people, but love your neighbor as yourself. I am the LORD.
19 " 'Keep my decrees.
" 'Do not mate different kinds of animals.
" 'Do not plant your field with two kinds of seed.
" 'Do not wear clothing woven of two kinds of material.
20 " 'If a man sleeps with a woman who is a slave girl promised to another man but who has not been ransomed or given her freedom, there must be due punishment. Yet they are not to be put to death,
because she had not been freed.
21 The man, however, must bring a ram to the entrance to the Tent of Meeting for a guilt offering to the LORD.

עָלָיו הַכֹּהֵן בְּאֵיל הָאָשָׁם לִפְנֵי יְהוָה עַל־
for Yahweh before the-guilt-offering with-ram-of the-priest for-him

חַטָּאתוֹ אֲשֶׁר חָטָא וְנִסְלַח לוֹ מֵחַטָּאתוֹ
from-sin-of-him to-him and-he-will-be-forgiven he-sinned that sin-of-him

אֲשֶׁר חָטָא׃ וְכִי־ תָבֹאוּ אֶל־ הָאָרֶץ וּנְטַעְתֶּם כָּל־
any-of and-you-plant the-land into you-enter and-when (23) he-sinned that

עֵץ מַאֲכָל וַעֲרַלְתֶּם עָרְלָתוֹ אֶת־ פִּרְיוֹ
fruit-of-him *** uncircumcised-him then-you-regard-forbidden fruit tree-of

שָׁלֹשׁ שָׁנִים יִהְיֶה לָכֶם עֲרֵלִים לֹא יֵאָכֵל׃
he-must-be-eaten not ones-uncircumcised to-you he-will-be years three

וּבַשָּׁנָה הָרְבִיעִת יִהְיֶה כָּל־ פִּרְיוֹ קֹדֶשׁ
holy fruit-of-him all-of he-will-be the-fourth and-in-the-year (24)

הִלּוּלִים לַיהוָה׃ וּבַשָּׁנָה הַחֲמִישִׁת תֹּאכְלוּ אֶת־
*** you-may-eat the-fifth but-in-the-year (25) to-Yahweh praise-offerings

פִּרְיוֹ לְהוֹסִיף לָכֶם תְּבוּאָתוֹ אֲנִי יְהוָה אֱלֹהֵיכֶם׃ לֹא
not (26) God-of-you Yahweh I harvest-of-him for-you to-increase fruit-of-him

תֹאכְלוּ עַל־ הַדָּם לֹא תְנַחֲשׁוּ וְלֹא תְעוֹנֵנוּ׃
you-practice-sorcery or-not you-practice-divination not the-blood with you-eat

לֹא תַקִּפוּ פְּאַת רֹאשְׁכֶם וְלֹא תַשְׁחִית אֵת פְּאַת
edge-of *** you-clip-off or-not head-of-you side-of you-cut-hair not (27)

זְקָנֶךָ׃ וְשֶׂרֶט לָנֶפֶשׁ לֹא תִתְּנוּ בִּבְשַׂרְכֶם
in-body-of-you you-cut not for-the-dead and-cut (28) beard-of-you

וּכְתֹבֶת קַעֲקַע לֹא תִתְּנוּ בָּכֶם אֲנִי יְהוָה׃ אַל־ תְּחַלֵּל אֶת־
*** you-degrade not (29) Yahweh I on-you you-put not tattoo and-mark-of

בִּתְּךָ לְהַזְנוֹתָהּ וְלֹא־ תִזְנֶה הָאָרֶץ
the-land she-become-prostitute so-not to-make-prostitute-her daughter-of-you

וּמָלְאָה הָאָרֶץ זִמָּה׃ אֶת־ שַׁבְּתֹתַי תִּשְׁמֹרוּ
you-observe Sabbaths-of-me *** (30) wickedness the-land and-she-be-filled

וּמִקְדָּשִׁי תִּירָאוּ אֲנִי יְהוָה׃ אַל־ תִּפְנוּ אֶל־ הָאֹבֹת
the-mediums to you-turn not (31) Yahweh I you-revere and-sanctuary-of-me

וְאֶל־ הַיִּדְּעֹנִים אַל־ תְּבַקְשׁוּ לְטָמְאָה בָהֶם אֲנִי יְהוָה אֱלֹהֵיכֶם׃
God-of-you Yahweh I by-them to-be-defiled you-seek not the-spiritists or-to

מִפְּנֵי שֵׂיבָה תָּקוּם וְהָדַרְתָּ פְּנֵי זָקֵן
elderly presence-of and-you-respect you-rise aged in-presence-of (32)

וְיָרֵאתָ מֵּאֱלֹהֶיךָ אֲנִי יְהוָה׃ וְכִי־ יָגוּר אִתְּךָ
with-you he-lives and-when (33) Yahweh I for-God-of-you and-you-revere

גֵּר בְּאַרְצְכֶם לֹא תוֹנוּ אֹתוֹ׃ כְּאֶזְרָח מִכֶּם יִהְיֶה
he-must-be from-you as-native (34) him you-mistreat not in-land-of-you alien

22With the ram of the guilt offering the priest is to make atonement for him before the LORD for the sin he has committed, and his sin will be forgiven.
23" 'When you enter the land and plant any kind of fruit tree, regard its fruit as forbidden.[n] For three years you are to consider it forbidden[n]; it must not be eaten.
24In the fourth year all its fruit will be holy, an offering of praise to the LORD.
25But in the fifth year you may eat its fruit. In this way your harvest will be increased. I am the LORD your God.
26" 'Do not eat any meat with the blood still in it.
" 'Do not practice divination or sorcery.
27" 'Do not cut the hair at the sides of your head or clip off the edges of your beard.
28" 'Do not cut your bodies for the dead or put tattoo marks on yourselves. I am the LORD.
29" 'Do not degrade your daughter by making her a prostitute, or the land will turn to prostitution and be filled with wickedness.
30" 'Observe my Sabbaths and have reverence for my sanctuary. I am the LORD.
31" 'Do not turn to mediums or seek out spiritists, for you will be defiled by them. I am the LORD your God.
32" 'Rise in the presence of the aged, show respect for the elderly and revere your God. I am the LORD.
33" 'When an alien lives with you in your land, do not mistreat him.
34The alien living with you must be treated as one of your native-born.

n23 Hebrew *uncircumcised*

לָכֶם הַגֵּר ׀ הַגָּר אִתְּכֶם וְאָהַבְתָּ לוֹ כָּמוֹךָ כִּי־
for as-yourself to-him and-you-love with-you the-one-living the-alien to-you

גֵרִים הֱיִיתֶם בְּאֶרֶץ מִצְרָיִם אֲנִי יְהוָה אֱלֹהֵיכֶם׃ לֹא־תַעֲשׂוּ
you-use not (35) God-of-you Yahweh I Egypt in-land-of you-were aliens

עָוֶל בַּמִּשְׁפָּט בַּמִּדָּה בַּמִּשְׁקָל וּבַמְּשׂוּרָה׃
or-for-the-quantity for-the-weight for-the-length in-the-measure dishonesty

מֹאזְנֵי צֶדֶק אַבְנֵי־צֶדֶק אֵיפַת צֶדֶק וְהִין צֶדֶק
honest and-hin-of honest ephah-of honest weights-of honest scales-of (36)

יִהְיֶה לָכֶם אֲנִי יְהוָה אֱלֹהֵיכֶם אֲשֶׁר־הוֹצֵאתִי אֶתְכֶם מֵאֶרֶץ מִצְרָיִם׃
Egypt from-land-of you I-brought who God-of-you Yahweh I to-you he-must-be

וּשְׁמַרְתֶּם אֶת־כָּל־חֻקֹּתַי וְאֶת־כָּל־מִשְׁפָּטַי וַעֲשִׂיתֶם
and-you-do laws-of-me all-of and decrees-of-me all-of *** and-you-keep (37)

אֹתָם אֲנִי יְהוָה׃ וַיְדַבֵּר יְהוָה אֶל־מֹשֶׁה לֵּאמֹר׃ וְאֶל־בְּנֵי
sons-of now-to (2) to-say Moses to Yahweh and-he-spoke (20:1) Yahweh I them

יִשְׂרָאֵל תֹּאמַר אִישׁ אִישׁ מִבְּנֵי יִשְׂרָאֵל וּמִן־הַגֵּר ׀ הַגָּר
the-one-living the-alien or-from Israel from-sons-of any man you-say Israel

בְּיִשְׂרָאֵל אֲשֶׁר יִתֵּן מִזַּרְעוֹ לַמֹּלֶךְ מוֹת יוּמָת
he-must-die to-die to-the-Molech from-child-of-him he-gives who in-Israel

עַם הָאָרֶץ יִרְגְּמֻהוּ בָאָבֶן׃ וַאֲנִי אֶתֵּן
I-will-set and-I (3) with-the-stone they-must-stone-him the-land people-of

אֶת־פָּנַי בָּאִישׁ הַהוּא וְהִכְרַתִּי אֹתוֹ מִקֶּרֶב
from-among him and-I-will-cut the-that against-the-man faces-of-me ***

עַמּוֹ כִּי מִזַּרְעוֹ נָתַן לַמֹּלֶךְ לְמַעַן טַמֵּא
to-defile so-that to-the-Molech he-gave from-child-of-him for people-of-him

אֶת־מִקְדָּשִׁי וּלְחַלֵּל אֶת־שֵׁם קָדְשִׁי׃ וְאִם
and-if (4) holy-of-me name-of *** and-to-profane sanctuary-of-me ***

הַעְלֵם יַעְלִימוּ עַם הָאָרֶץ אֶת־עֵינֵיהֶם מִן־הָאִישׁ הַהוּא
the-that the-man from eyes-of-them *** the-land people-of they-close to-close

בְּתִתּוֹ מִזַּרְעוֹ לַמֹּלֶךְ לְבִלְתִּי הָמִית אֹתוֹ׃
him to-put-to-death not to-the-Molech from-child-of-him when-to-give-him

וְשַׂמְתִּי אֲנִי אֶת־פָּנַי בָּאִישׁ הַהוּא
the-that against-the-man faces-of-me *** I then-I-will-set (5)

וּבְמִשְׁפַּחְתּוֹ וְהִכְרַתִּי אֹתוֹ וְאֵת ׀ כָּל־הַזֹּנִים
the-ones-prostituting all-of and him and-I-will-cut and-against-family-of-him

אַחֲרָיו לִזְנוֹת אַחֲרֵי הַמֹּלֶךְ מִקֶּרֶב עַמָּם׃
people-of-them from-among the-Molech to to-prostitute with-him

וְהַנֶּפֶשׁ אֲשֶׁר תִּפְנֶה אֶל־הָאֹבֹת וְאֶל־הַיִּדְּעֹנִים
the-spiritists and-to the-mediums to she-turns who and-the-person (6)

Love him as yourself, for you were aliens in Egypt. I am the LORD your God.

[35]" 'Do not use dishonest standards when measuring length, weight or quantity. [36]Use honest scales and honest weights, an honest ephah[o] and an honest hin.[p] I am the LORD your God, who brought you out of Egypt.

[37]" 'Keep all my decrees and all my laws and follow them. I am the LORD.' "

Punishments for Sin

20 The LORD said to Moses, [2]"Say to the Israelites: 'Any Israelite or any alien living in Israel who gives[q] any of his children to Molech must be put to death. The people of the community are to stone him. [3]I will set my face against that man and I will cut him off from his people; for by giving his children to Molech, he has defiled my sanctuary and profaned my holy name. [4]If the people of the community close their eyes when that man gives one of his children to Molech and they fail to put him to death, [5]I will set my face against that man and his family and will cut off from their people both him and all who follow him in prostituting themselves to Molech.

[6]" 'I will set my face against the person who turns to mediums and spiritists to prostitute

[o]36 An ephah was a dry measure.
[p]36 A hin was a liquid measure.
[q]2 Or *sacrifices;* also in verses 3 and 4

לִזְנוֹת אַחֲרֵיהֶם וְנָתַתִּי אֶת־ פָּנַי בַּנֶּפֶשׁ
against-the-person faces-of-me *** also-I-will-set after-them to-prostitute

הַהִוא וְהִכְרַתִּי אֹתוֹ מִקֶּרֶב עַמּוֹ׃ וְהִתְקַדִּשְׁתֶּם
so-you-consecrate-selves (7) people-of-him from-among him and-I-will-cut the-that

וִהְיִיתֶם קְדֹשִׁים כִּי אֲנִי יְהוָה אֱלֹהֵיכֶם׃ וּשְׁמַרְתֶּם אֶת־
*** and-you-keep (8) God-of-you Yahweh I for holy-ones and-you-be

חֻקֹּתַי וַעֲשִׂיתֶם אֹתָם אֲנִי יְהוָה מְקַדִּשְׁכֶם׃ כִּי־ אִישׁ
man if (9) one-making-holy-you Yahweh I them and-you-follow decrees-of-me

אִישׁ אֲשֶׁר יְקַלֵּל אֶת־ אָבִיו וְאֶת־ אִמּוֹ מוֹת יוּמָת
he-must-die to-die mother-of-him or father-of-him *** he-curses who any

אָבִיו וְאִמּוֹ קִלֵּל דָּמָיו בּוֹ׃ וְאִישׁ
and-man (10) on-him bloods-of-him he-cursed or-mother-of-him father-of-him

אֲשֶׁר יִנְאַף אֶת־ אֵשֶׁת אִישׁ אֲשֶׁר יִנְאַף אֶת־
with he-commits-adultery who another wife-of with he-commits-adultery who

אֵשֶׁת רֵעֵהוּ מוֹת־ יוּמַת הַנֹּאֵף
the-man-committing-adultery he-must-die to-die neighbor-of-him wife-of

וְהַנֹּאָפֶת׃ וְאִישׁ אֲשֶׁר יִשְׁכַּב אֶת־ אֵשֶׁת
wife-of with he-sleeps who and-man (11) and-the-woman-committing-adultery

אָבִיו עֶרְוַת אָבִיו גִּלָּה מוֹת־ יוּמְתוּ
they-must-die to-die he-exposed father-of-him nakedness-of father-of-him

שְׁנֵיהֶם דְּמֵיהֶם בָּם׃ וְאִישׁ אֲשֶׁר יִשְׁכַּב אֶת־
with he-sleeps who and-man (12) on-them bloods-of-them both-of-them

כַּלָּתוֹ מוֹת יוּמְתוּ שְׁנֵיהֶם תֶּבֶל עָשׂוּ
they-did perversion both-of-them they-must-die to-die daughter-in-law-of-him

דְּמֵיהֶם בָּם׃ וְאִישׁ אֲשֶׁר יִשְׁכַּב אֶת־ זָכָר מִשְׁכְּבֵי אִשָּׁה
woman lyings-of man with he-lies who and-man (13) on-them bloods-of-them

תּוֹעֵבָה עָשׂוּ שְׁנֵיהֶם מוֹת יוּמָתוּ דְּמֵיהֶם בָּם׃
on-them bloods-of-them they-must-die to-die both-of-them they-did detestable

וְאִישׁ אֲשֶׁר יִקַּח אֶת־ אִשָּׁה וְאֶת־ אִמָּהּ זִמָּה הִוא
this wicked mother-of-her and woman *** he-marries who and-man (14)

בָּאֵשׁ יִשְׂרְפוּ אֹתוֹ וְאֶתְהֶן וְלֹא־ תִהְיֶה זִמָּה
wickedness she-will-be so-not and-them him they-must-burn in-the-fire

בְּתוֹכְכֶם׃ וְאִישׁ אֲשֶׁר יִתֵּן שְׁכָבְתּוֹ בִּבְהֵמָה מוֹת
to-die to-animal emission-of-him he-gives who and-man (15) among-you

יוּמָת וְאֶת־ הַבְּהֵמָה תַּהֲרֹגוּ׃ וְאִשָּׁה אֲשֶׁר תִּקְרַב
she-approaches who and-woman (16) you-must-kill the-animal and he-must-die

אֶל־ כָּל־ בְּהֵמָה לְרִבְעָה אֹתָהּ וְהָרַגְתָּ אֶת־ הָאִשָּׁה
the-woman *** then-you-must-kill with-her to-have-relation animal any-of to

himself by following them,
and I will cut him off from his
people.
7" 'Consecrate yourselves
and be holy, because I am the
LORD your God. 8Keep my decrees and follow them. I am
the LORD, who makes you
holy.[r]
9" 'If anyone curses his father or mother, he must be put
to death. He has cursed his father or his mother, and his
blood will be on his own head.
10" 'If a man commits adultery with another man's
wife—with the wife of his
neighbor—both the adulterer
and the adulteress must be put
to death.
11" 'If a man sleeps with his
father's wife, he has dishonored his father. Both the man
and the woman must be put to
death; their blood will be on
their own heads.
12" 'If a man sleeps with his
daughter-in-law, both of them
must be put to death. What
they have done is a perversion; their blood will be on
their own heads.
13" 'If a man lies with a man
as one lies with a woman,
both of them have done what
is detestable. They must be put
to death; their blood will be on
their own heads.
14" 'If a man marries both a
woman and her mother, it is
wicked. Both he and they
must be burned in the fire, so
that no wickedness will be
among you.
15" 'If a man has sexual relations with an animal, he must
be put to death, and you must
kill the animal.
16" 'If a woman approaches
an animal to have sexual relations with it, kill both the

[r]8 *Or who sanctifies you; or who sets you apart as holy*

וְאֶת־הַבְּהֵמָה מוֹת יוּמָתוּ דְּמֵיהֶם בָּם׃ וְאִישׁ אֲשֶׁר־

who and-man (17) on-them bloods-of-them they-must-die to-die the-animal and

יִקַּח אֶת־ אֲחֹתוֹ בַּת־ אָבִיו אוֹ בַת־

daughter-of or father-of-him daughter-of sister-of-him *** he-marries

אִמּוֹ וְרָאָה אֶת־ עֶרְוָתָהּ וְהִיא־ תִרְאֶה אֶת־

*** she-sees and-she nakedness-of-her *** and-he-sees mother-of-him

עֶרְוָתוֹ חֶסֶד הוּא וְנִכְרְתוּ לְעֵינֵי

before-eyes-of and-they-must-be-cut-off this disgrace nakedness-of-him

בְּנֵי עַמָּם עֶרְוַת אֲחֹתוֹ גִּלָּה עֲוֺנוֹ

guilt-of-him he-exposed sister-of-him nakedness-of people-of-them sons-of

יִשָּׂא׃ וְאִישׁ אֲשֶׁר־ יִשְׁכַּב אֶת־ אִשָּׁה דָּוָה וְגִלָּה אֶת־

*** and-he-exposes period woman with he-lies who and-man (18) he-must-bear

עֶרְוָתָהּ אֶת־ מְקֹרָהּ הֶעֱרָה וְהִוא גִּלְּתָה אֶת־

*** she-uncovered also-she he-uncovered flow-of-her *** nakedness-of-her

מְקוֹר דָּמֶיהָ וְנִכְרְתוּ שְׁנֵיהֶם מִקֶּרֶב

from-among both-of-them and-they-must-be-cut-off bloods-of-her flow-of

עַמָּם׃ וְעֶרְוַת אֲחוֹת אִמְּךָ וַאֲחוֹת

or-sister-of mother-of-you sister-of and-nakedness-of (19) people-of-them

אָבִיךָ לֹא תְגַלֵּה כִּי אֶת־ שְׁאֵרוֹ הֶעֱרָה

he-would-dishonor close-relative-of-him *** for you-expose not father-of-you

עֲוֺנָם יִשָּׂאוּ׃ וְאִישׁ אֲשֶׁר יִשְׁכַּב אֶת־

with he-sleeps who and-man (20) they-would-bear responsibility-of-them

דֹּדָתוֹ עֶרְוַת דֹּדוֹ גִּלָּה חֶטְאָם יִשָּׂאוּ

they-will-bear guilt-of-them he-exposed uncle-of-him nakedness-of aunt-of-him

עֲרִירִים יָמֻתוּ׃ וְאִישׁ אֲשֶׁר יִקַּח אֶת־ אֵשֶׁת

wife-of *** he-marries who and-man (21) they-will-die ones-childless

אָחִיו נִדָּה הִוא עֶרְוַת אָחִיו גִּלָּה

he-exposed brother-of-him nakedness-of this impurity brother-of-him

עֲרִירִים יִהְיוּ׃ וּשְׁמַרְתֶּם אֶת־ כָּל־ חֻקֹּתַי וְאֶת־

and decrees-of-me all-of *** now-you-keep (22) they-will-be ones-childless

כָּל־ מִשְׁפָּטַי וַעֲשִׂיתֶם אֹתָם וְלֹא־ תָקִיא אֶתְכֶם הָאָרֶץ

the-land you she-will-vomit-out so-not them and-you-follow laws-of-me all-of

אֲשֶׁר אֲנִי מֵבִיא אֶתְכֶם שָׁמָּה לָשֶׁבֶת בָּהּ׃ וְלֹא תֵלְכוּ

you-live and-not (23) in-her to-live to-there you bringing I where

בְּחֻקֹּת הַגּוֹי אֲשֶׁר־אֲנִי מְשַׁלֵּחַ מִפְּנֵיכֶם כִּי אֶת־ כָּל־ אֵלֶּה

these all-of *** for from-before-you driving I that the-nation as-custom-of

עָשׂוּ וָאָקֻץ בָּם׃ וָאֹמַר לָכֶם אַתֶּם

them to-you but-I-said (24) against-them and-I-abhorred they-did

woman and the animal. They must be put to death; their blood will be on their own heads.

[17]" 'If a man marries his sister, the daughter of either his father or his mother, and they have sexual relations, it is a disgrace. They must be cut off before the eyes of their people. He has dishonored his sister and will be held responsible.

[18]" 'If a man lies with a woman during her monthly period and has sexual relations with her, he has exposed the source of her flow, and she has also uncovered it. Both of them must be cut off from their people.

[19]" 'Do not have sexual relations with the sister of either your mother or your father, for that would dishonor a close relative; both of you would be held responsible.

[20]" 'If a man sleeps with his aunt, he has dishonored his uncle. They will be held responsible; they will die childless.

[21]" 'If a man marries his brother's wife, it is an act of impurity; he has dishonored his brother. They will be childless.

[22]" 'Keep all my decrees and laws and follow them, so that the land where I am bringing you to live may not vomit you out. [23]You must not live according to the customs of the nations I am going to drive out before you. Because they did all these things, I abhorred them. [24]But I said to you, "You

תִּירְשׁוּ אֶת־ אַדְמָתָם וַאֲנִי אֶתְּנֶנָּה לָכֶם לָרֶשֶׁת
to-inherit to-you I-will-give-her and-I land-of-them *** you-will-possess

אֹתָהּ אֶרֶץ זָבַת חָלָב וּדְבָשׁ אֲנִי יְהוָה אֱלֹהֵיכֶם אֲשֶׁר־
who God-of-you Yahweh I and-honey milk flowing-of land her

הִבְדַּלְתִּי אֶתְכֶם מִן־ הָעַמִּים׃ וְהִבְדַּלְתֶּם בֵּין־ הַבְּהֵמָה
the-animal between so-you-distinguish (25) the-nations from you I-set-apart

הַטְּהֹרָה לַטְּמֵאָה וּבֵין־ הָעוֹף הַטָּמֵא לַטָּהֹר
from-the-clean the-unclean the-bird and-between from-the-unclean the-clean

וְלֹא־ תְשַׁקְּצוּ אֶת־ נַפְשֹׁתֵיכֶם בַּבְּהֵמָה וּבָעוֹף
or-by-the-bird by-the-animal selves-of-you *** you-defile and-not

וּבְכֹל אֲשֶׁר תִּרְמֹשׂ הָאֲדָמָה אֲשֶׁר־ הִבְדַּלְתִּי לָכֶם
for-you I-set-apart which the-ground she-moves that or-by-anything

לְטַמֵּא׃ וִהְיִיתֶם לִי קְדֹשִׁים כִּי קָדוֹשׁ אֲנִי יְהוָה
Yahweh I holy for holy-ones to-me now-you-must-be (26) to-be-unclean

וָאַבְדִּל אֶתְכֶם מִן־ הָעַמִּים לִהְיוֹת לִי׃ וְאִישׁ אוֹ־ אִשָּׁה כִּי־
if woman or now-man (27) for-me to-be the-nations from you and-I-set-apart

יִהְיֶה בָהֶם אוֹב אוֹ יִדְּעֹנִי מוֹת יוּמָתוּ בָּאֶבֶן
with-the-stone they-must-die to-die spiritist or medium among-them he-is

יִרְגְּמוּ אֹתָם דְּמֵיהֶם בָּם׃ וַיֹּאמֶר יְהוָה אֶל־
to Yahweh and-he-said (21:1) on-them bloods-of-them them they-must-stone

מֹשֶׁה אֱמֹר אֶל־ הַכֹּהֲנִים בְּנֵי אַהֲרֹן וְאָמַרְתָּ אֲלֵהֶם לְנֶפֶשׁ לֹא־
not to-self to-them and-you-say Aaron sons-of the-priests to speak! Moses

יִטַּמָּא בְּעַמָּיו׃ כִּי אִם־ לִשְׁאֵרוֹ
for-relative-of-him if except (2) for-people-of-him he-must-make-unclean

הַקָּרֹב אֵלָיו לְאִמּוֹ וּלְאָבִיו וְלִבְנוֹ
or-for-son-of-him or-for-father-of-him for-mother-of-him to-him the-one-close

וּלְבִתּוֹ וּלְאָחִיו׃ וְלַאֲחֹתוֹ
or-for-sister-of-him (3) or-for-brother-of-him or-for-daughter-of-him

הַבְּתוּלָה הַקְּרוֹבָה אֵלָיו אֲשֶׁר לֹא־ הָיְתָה לְאִישׁ לָהּ
for-her to-husband she-is not who on-him the-one-dependent the-unmarried

יִטַּמָּא׃ לֹא יִטַּמָּא בַּעַל
leader he-must-make-self-unclean not (4) he-may-make-self-unclean

בְּעַמָּיו לְהֵחַלּוֹ׃ לֹא־ יִקְרְחָה קָרְחָה
baldness they-must-shave not (5) to-defile-himself among-people-of-him

בְּרֹאשָׁם וּפְאַת זְקָנָם לֹא יְגַלֵּחוּ
they-must-shave-off not beard-of-them or-edge-of on-head-of-them

וּבִבְשָׂרָם לֹא יִשְׂרְטוּ שָׂרָטֶת׃ קְדֹשִׁים יִהְיוּ
they-must-be holy-ones (6) cut they-must-cut not or-in-body-of-them

°5 ק יקרחו

will possess their land; I will give it to you as an inheritance, a land flowing with milk and honey." I am the LORD your God, who has set you apart from the nations.

25"'You must therefore make a distinction between clean and unclean animals and between unclean and clean birds. Do not defile yourselves by any animal or bird or anything that moves along the ground—those which I have set apart as unclean for you. 26You are to be holy to me[s] because I, the LORD, am holy, and I have set you apart from the nations to be my own.

27"'A man or woman who is a medium or spiritist among you must be put to death. You are to stone them; their blood will be on their own heads.'"

Rules for Priests

21 The LORD said to Moses, "Speak to the priests, the sons of Aaron, and say to them: 'A priest must not make himself ceremonially unclean for any of his people who die, 2except for a close relative, such as his mother or father, his son or daughter, his brother, 3or an unmarried sister who is dependent on him since she has no husband—for her he may make himself unclean. 4He must not make himself unclean for people related to him by marriage,[t] and so defile himself.

5"'Priests must not shave their heads or shave off the edges of their beards or cut their bodies. 6They must be

[s]26 *Or be my holy ones*
[t]4 *Or unclean as a leader among his people*

לֵאלֹהֵיהֶם וְלֹא יְחַלְּלוּ שֵׁם אֱלֹהֵיהֶם כִּי אֶת־
*** for God-of-them name-of they-must-profane and-not to-God-of-them

אִשֵּׁי יְהוָה לֶחֶם אֱלֹהֵיהֶם הֵם מַקְרִיבִם
ones-presenting they God-of-them food-of Yahweh fire-offerings-of

וְהָיוּ קֹדֶשׁ׃ אִשָּׁה זֹנָה וַחֲלָלָה לֹא יִקָּחוּ
they-must-marry not and-defiled prostitute woman (7) holy so-they-must-be

וְאִשָּׁה גְּרוּשָׁה מֵאִישָׁהּ לֹא יִקָּחוּ כִּי־ קָדֹשׁ
holy for they-must-marry not from-husband-of-her being-divorced or-woman

הוּא לֵאלֹהָיו׃ וְקִדַּשְׁתּוֹ כִּי־ אֶת־ לֶחֶם אֱלֹהֶיךָ הוּא
he God-of-you food-of *** for and-you-regard-holy-him (8) to-God-of-him he

מַקְרִיב קָדֹשׁ יִהְיֶה־ לָּךְ כִּי קָדוֹשׁ אֲנִי יְהוָה מְקַדִּשְׁכֶם׃
one-making-holy-you Yahweh I holy for to-you he-must-be holy offering

וּבַת אִישׁ כֹּהֵן כִּי תֵחֵל לִזְנוֹת אֶת־
*** to-be-prostitute she-defiles-self if priest man and-daughter-of (9)

אָבִיהָ הִיא מְחַלֶּלֶת בָּאֵשׁ תִּשָּׂרֵף׃
she-must-be-burned in-the-fire disgracing she father-of-her

וְהַכֹּהֵן הַגָּדוֹל מֵאֶחָיו אֲשֶׁר־ יוּצַק עַל־
on he-was-poured who among-brothers-of-him the-high and-the-priest (10)

רֹאשׁוֹ ׀ שֶׁמֶן הַמִּשְׁחָה וּמִלֵּא אֶת־ יָדוֹ לִלְבֹּשׁ
to-wear hand-of-him *** and-he-ordained the-anointing oil-of head-of-him

אֶת־ הַבְּגָדִים אֶת־ רֹאשׁוֹ לֹא יִפְרָע וּבְגָדָיו
or-clothes-of-him he-must-let-be-unkempt not hair-of-him *** the-garments ***

לֹא יִפְרֹם׃ וְעַל כָּל־ נַפְשֹׁת מֵת לֹא יָבֹא
he-must-go not dead bodies-of any-of and-to (11) he-must-tear not

לְאָבִיו וּלְאִמּוֹ לֹא יִטַּמָּא׃
he-must-make-self-unclean not or-for-mother-of-him for-father-of-him

וּמִן־ הַמִּקְדָּשׁ לֹא יֵצֵא וְלֹא יְחַלֵּל אֵת
*** he-must-desecrate or-not he-must-leave not the-sanctuary nor-from (12)

מִקְדַּשׁ אֱלֹהָיו כִּי נֵזֶר שֶׁמֶן מִשְׁחַת אֱלֹהָיו עָלָיו
on-him God-of-him anointing-of oil-of dedicated for God-of-him sanctuary-of

אֲנִי יְהוָה׃ וְהוּא אִשָּׁה בִבְתוּלֶיהָ יִקָּח׃ אַלְמָנָה
widow (14) he-must-marry in-virginity-of-her woman and-he (13) Yahweh I

וּגְרוּשָׁה וַחֲלָלָה זֹנָה אֶת־ אֵלֶּה לֹא יִקָּח כִּי
but he-must-marry not these *** prostitute or-defiled or-being-divorced

אִם־ בְּתוּלָה מֵעַמָּיו יִקַּח אִשָּׁה׃ וְלֹא־ יְחַלֵּל
he-will-defile so-not (15) wife he-may-marry from-people-of-him virgin only

זַרְעוֹ בְּעַמָּיו כִּי אֲנִי יְהוָה מְקַדְּשׁוֹ׃
one-making-holy-him Yahweh I for among-people-of-him offspring-of-him

holy to their God and must not profane the name of their God. Because they present the offerings made to the LORD by fire, the food of their God, they are to be holy.

7" 'They must not marry women defiled by prostitution or divorced from their husbands, because priests are holy to their God. 8Regard them as holy, because they offer up the food of your God. Consider them holy, because I the LORD, who makes you holy,[u] am holy.

9" 'If a priest's daughter defiles herself by becoming a prostitute, she disgraces her father; she must be burned in the fire.

10" 'The high priest, the one among his brothers who has had the anointing oil poured on his head and who has been ordained to wear the priestly garments, must not let his hair become unkempt[v] or tear his clothes. 11He must not enter a place where there is a dead body. He must not make himself unclean, even for his father or mother, 12nor leave the sanctuary of his God or desecrate it, because he has been dedicated by the anointing oil of his God. I am the LORD.

13" 'The woman he marries must be a virgin. 14He must not marry a widow, a divorced woman, or a woman defiled by prostitution, but only a virgin from his own people, 15so he will not defile his offspring among his people. I am the LORD, who makes him holy.[w] "

u8 Or *who sanctifies you; or who sets you apart as holy*
v10 Or *not uncover his head*
w15 Or *who sanctifies him; or who sets him apart as holy*

וַיְדַבֵּר יְהוָה אֶל־מֹשֶׁה לֵּאמֹר׃ דַּבֵּר אֶל־אַהֲרֹן לֵאמֹר אִישׁ
man to-say Aaron to say! (17) to-say Moses to Yahweh and-he-spoke (16)

מִזַּרְעֲךָ לְדֹרֹתָם אֲשֶׁר יִהְיֶה בוֹ מוּם
defect on-him he-has who for-generations-of-them from-descendant-of-you

לֹא יִקְרַב לְהַקְרִיב לֶחֶם אֱלֹהָיו׃ כִּי כָל־אִישׁ
man any-of indeed (18) God-of-him food-of to-offer he-may-come-near not

אֲשֶׁר־בּוֹ מוּם לֹא יִקְרָב אִישׁ עִוֵּר אוֹ פִסֵּחַ אוֹ חָרֻם
being-disfigured or lame or blind man he-may-come-near not defect on-him who

אוֹ שָׂרוּעַ׃ אוֹ אִישׁ אֲשֶׁר־יִהְיֶה בוֹ שֶׁבֶר רָגֶל אוֹ שֶׁבֶר
crippled or foot crippled on-him he-has who man or (19) being-deformed or

יָד׃ אוֹ־גִבֵּן אוֹ־דַק אוֹ תְבַלֻּל בְּעֵינוֹ אוֹ גָרָב
fester or in-eye-of-him defective or dwarfed or hunchbacked or (20) hand

אוֹ יַלֶּפֶת אוֹ מְרוֹחַ אָשֶׁךְ׃ כָּל־אִישׁ אֲשֶׁר־בּוֹ מוּם
defect on-him who man any-of (21) testicle damaged-of or running-sore or

מִזֶּרַע אַהֲרֹן הַכֹּהֵן לֹא יִגַּשׁ לְהַקְרִיב אֶת־
*** to-present he-may-come-near not the-priest Aaron from-descendant-of

אִשֵּׁי יְהוָה מוּם בּוֹ אֵת לֶחֶם אֱלֹהָיו לֹא
not God-of-him food-of *** on-him defect Yahweh fire-offerings-of

יִגַּשׁ לְהַקְרִיב׃ לֶחֶם אֱלֹהָיו מִקָּדְשֵׁי
from-most-holy-ones-of God-of-him food-of (22) to-offer he-must-come-near

הַקֳּדָשִׁים וּמִן־הַקֳּדָשִׁים יֹאכֵל׃ אַךְ אֶל־הַפָּרֹכֶת לֹא
not the-curtain to yet (23) he-may-eat the-holy-ones and-from the-holy-ones

יָבֹא וְאֶל־הַמִּזְבֵּחַ לֹא יִגַּשׁ כִּי־מוּם בּוֹ וְלֹא
so-not on-him defect for he-must-approach not the-altar or-to he-must-go

יְחַלֵּל אֶת־מִקְדָּשַׁי כִּי אֲנִי יְהוָה מְקַדְּשָׁם׃
one-making-holy-them Yahweh I for sanctuaries-of-me *** he-will-desecrate

וַיְדַבֵּר מֹשֶׁה אֶל־אַהֲרֹן וְאֶל־בָּנָיו וְאֶל־כָּל־בְּנֵי
sons-of all-of and-to sons-of-him and-to Aaron to Moses so-he-told (24)

יִשְׂרָאֵל׃ וַיְדַבֵּר יְהוָה אֶל־מֹשֶׁה לֵּאמֹר׃ דַּבֵּר אֶל־אַהֲרֹן וְאֶל־
and-to Aaron to tell! (2) to-say Moses to Yahweh and-he-spoke (22:1) Israel

בָּנָיו וְיִנָּזְרוּ מִקָּדְשֵׁי בְנֵי־יִשְׂרָאֵל
Israel sons-of for-sacred-offerings-of that-they-must-respect sons-of-him

וְלֹא יְחַלְּלוּ אֶת־שֵׁם קָדְשִׁי אֲשֶׁר הֵם מַקְדִּשִׁים לִי
to-me consecrating they that holy-of-me name-of *** they-will-profane so-not

אֲנִי יְהוָה׃ אֱמֹר אֲלֵהֶם לְדֹרֹתֵיכֶם כָּל־אִישׁ ׀ אֲשֶׁר־יִקְרַב
he-comes-near who man any-of for-generations-of-you to-them say! (3) Yahweh I

מִכָּל־זַרְעֲכֶם אֶל־הַקֳּדָשִׁים אֲשֶׁר יַקְדִּישׁוּ
they-consecrate that the-sacred-offerings to descendant-of-you from-any-of

[16]The LORD said to Moses,
[17]"Say to Aaron: 'For the generations to come none of your
descendants who has a defect
may come near to offer the
food of his God. [18]No man
who has any defect may come
near: no man who is blind or
lame, disfigured or deformed;
[19]no man with a crippled foot
or hand, [20]or who is hunchbacked or dwarfed, or who has
any eye defect, or who has festering or running sores or
damaged testicles. [21]No descendant of Aaron the priest
who has any defect is to come
near to present the offerings
made to the LORD by fire. He
has a defect; he must not come
near to offer the food of his
God. [22]He may eat the most
holy food of his God, as well as
the holy food; [23]yet because of
his defect, he must not go near
the curtain or approach the altar, and so desecrate my sanctuary. I am the LORD, who
makes them holy.[x]' "
[24]So Moses told this to Aaron
and his sons and to all the Israelites.

22 The LORD said to
Moses, [2]"Tell Aaron
and his sons to treat with respect the sacred offerings the
Israelites consecrate to me, so
they will not profane my holy
name. I am the LORD.
[3]"Say to them: 'For the generations to come, if any of
your descendants is ceremonially unclean and yet comes
near the sacred offerings that
the Israelites consecrate to the

[x]23 Or *who sanctifies them*; or *who sets them apart as holy*

בְּנֵי־ יִשְׂרָאֵל לַיהוָה וְטֻמְאָתוֹ עָלָיו וְנִכְרְתָה
then-she-must-be-cut on-him yet-uncleanness-of-him to-Yahweh Israel sons-of

הַנֶּפֶשׁ הַהִוא מִלְּפָנַי אֲנִי יְהוָה׃ אִישׁ אִישׁ מִזֶּרַע
from-seed-of any man (4) Yahweh I from-presence-of-me the-that the-person

אַהֲרֹן וְהוּא צָרוּעַ אוֹ זָב בַּקֳּדָשִׁים לֹא יֹאכַל
he-may-eat not from-the-sacred-offerings discharge or infection and-he Aaron

עַד אֲשֶׁר יִטְהָר וְהַנֹּגֵעַ בְּכָל־ טְמֵא־ נֶפֶשׁ
body unclean-of on-any-of and-the-one-touching he-is-cleansed when until

אוֹ אִישׁ אֲשֶׁר־ תֵּצֵא מִמֶּנּוּ שִׁכְבַת־ זָרַע׃ אוֹ־ אִישׁ אֲשֶׁר יִגַּע
he-touches who man or (5) semen emission-of from-him she-comes-out who man or

בְּכָל־ שֶׁרֶץ אֲשֶׁר יִטְמָא־ לוֹ אוֹ בְאָדָם אֲשֶׁר יִטְמָא־
he-is-unclean who on-man or by-him he-is-unclean that crawler on-any-of

לוֹ לְכֹל טֻמְאָתוֹ׃ נֶפֶשׁ אֲשֶׁר תִּגַּע־ בּוֹ
on-him she-touches who person (6) uncleanness-of-him for-any-of by-him

וְטָמְאָה עַד־ הָעָרֶב וְלֹא יֹאכַל מִן־
from he-must-eat and-not the-evening till then-she-will-be-unclean

הַקֳּדָשִׁים כִּי אִם־ רָחַץ בְּשָׂרוֹ בַּמָּיִם׃
with-the-waters body-of-him he-bathed if unless the-sacred-offerings

וּבָא הַשֶּׁמֶשׁ וְטָהֵר וְאַחַר יֹאכַל
he-may-eat and-after then-he-will-be-clean the-sun when-he-goes-down (7)

מִן־ הַקֳּדָשִׁים כִּי לַחְמוֹ הוּא׃ נְבֵלָה וּטְרֵפָה
or-torn-animal corpse (8) this food-of-him for the-sacred-offerings from

לֹא יֹאכַל לְטָמְאָה־ בָהּ אֲנִי יְהוָה׃ וְשָׁמְרוּ
now-they-must-keep (9) Yahweh I by-her to-become-unclean he-must-eat not

אֶת־ מִשְׁמַרְתִּי וְלֹא־ יִשְׂאוּ עָלָיו חֵטְא וּמֵתוּ בוֹ
for-him or-they-die guilt for-him they-bear so-not requirement-of-me ***

כִּי יְחַלְּלֻהוּ אֲנִי יְהוָה מְקַדְּשָׁם׃ וְכָל־ זָר
outsider but-any-of (10) one-making-holy-them Yahweh I they-scorned-him for

לֹא־ יֹאכַל קֹדֶשׁ תּוֹשַׁב כֹּהֵן וְשָׂכִיר לֹא־ יֹאכַל
he-may-eat not or-hired-worker priest guest-of sacred offering he-may-eat not

קֹדֶשׁ׃ וְכֹהֵן כִּי־ יִקְנֶה נֶפֶשׁ קִנְיַן כַּסְפּוֹ הוּא
he money-of-him bought-of slave he-buys if but-priest (11) sacred-offering

יֹאכַל בּוֹ וִילִיד בֵּיתוֹ הֵם יֹאכְלוּ
they-may-eat they household-of-him or-born-of with-him he-may-eat

בְלַחְמוֹ׃ וּבַת־ כֹּהֵן כִּי תִהְיֶה לְאִישׁ זָר
outsider to-man she-marries if priest and-daughter-of (12) of-food-of-him

הִוא בִּתְרוּמַת הַקֳּדָשִׁים לֹא תֹאכֵל׃ וּבַת־
but-daughter-of (13) she-may-eat not the-sacred-ones of-contribution-of she

LORD, that person must be cut
off from my presence. I am the
LORD.
4 " 'If a descendant of Aaron
has an infectious skin disease[y]
or a bodily discharge, he may
not eat the sacred offerings
until he is cleansed. He will
also be unclean if he touches
something defiled by a corpse
or by anyone who has an
emission of semen, 5 or if he
touches any crawling thing
that makes him unclean, or
any person who makes him
unclean, whatever the un-
cleanness may be. 6 The one
who touches any such thing
will be unclean till evening.
He must not eat any of the sacred offerings unless he has
bathed himself with water.
7 When the sun goes down, he
will be clean, and after that he
may eat the sacred offerings,
for they are his food. 8 He must
not eat anything found dead
or torn by wild animals, and
so become unclean through it.
I am the LORD.
9 " 'The priests are to keep
my requirements so that they
do not become guilty and die
for treating them with contempt. I am the LORD, who
makes them holy.[z]
10 " 'No one outside a priest's
family may eat the sacred
offering, nor may the guest of
a priest or his hired worker eat
it. 11 But if a priest buys a slave
with money, or if a slave is
born in his household, that
slave may eat his food. 12 If a
priest's daughter marries anyone other than a priest, she
may not eat any of the sacred
contributions. 13 But if a

y4 Traditionally *leprosy;* the Hebrew word was used for various diseases affecting the skin—not necessarily leprosy.
z9 Or *who sanctifies them;* or *who sets them apart as holy;* also in verse 16

כֹּהֵן כִּי תִהְיֶה אַלְמָנָה וּגְרוּשָׁה וְזֶרַע אֵין לָהּ
to-her he-is-not yet-child or-being-divorced widow she-becomes if priest

וְשָׁבָה אֶל־ בֵּית אָבִיהָ כִּנְעוּרֶיהָ מִלֶּחֶם
from-food-of as-youths-of-her father-of-her house-of to and-she-returns

אָבִיהָ תֹּאכֵל וְכָל־ זָר לֹא־ יֹאכַל בּוֹ׃
of-him he-may-eat not outsider but-any-of she-may-eat father-of-her

וְאִישׁ כִּי־ יֹאכַל קֹדֶשׁ בִּשְׁגָגָה וְיָסַף
then-he-must-add by-mistake sacred-offering he-eats if and-anyone (14)

חֲמִשִׁיתוֹ עָלָיו וְנָתַן לַכֹּהֵן אֶת־ הַקֹּדֶשׁ׃
the-offering *** to-the-priest and-he-must-restitute to-him fifth-of-him

וְלֹא יְחַלְּלוּ אֶת־ קָדְשֵׁי בְּנֵי יִשְׂרָאֵל אֵת
*** Israel sons-of sacred-offerings-of *** they-must-desecrate and-not (15)

אֲשֶׁר־ יָרִימוּ לַיהוָה׃ וְהִשִּׂיאוּ אוֹתָם עֲוֺן אַשְׁמָה
payment guilt-of on-them so-they-bring (16) to-Yahweh they-present that

בְּאָכְלָם אֶת־ קָדְשֵׁיהֶם כִּי אֲנִי יְהוָה מְקַדְּשָׁם׃
one-making-holy-them Yahweh I for sacred-offerings-of-them *** by-to-eat-them

וַיְדַבֵּר יְהוָה אֶל־ מֹשֶׁה לֵּאמֹר׃ דַּבֵּר אֶל־ אַהֲרֹן וְאֶל־
and-to Aaron to speak! (18) to-say Moses to Yahweh and-he-spoke (17)

בָּנָיו וְאֶל כָּל־ בְּנֵי יִשְׂרָאֵל וְאָמַרְתָּ אֲלֵהֶם אִישׁ אִישׁ
any man to-them and-you-say Israel sons-of all-of and-to sons-of-him

מִבֵּית יִשְׂרָאֵל וּמִן־ הַגֵּר בְּיִשְׂרָאֵל אֲשֶׁר יַקְרִיב קָרְבָּנוֹ
gift-of-him he-presents who in-Israel the-alien or-from Israel from-house-of

לְכָל־ נִדְרֵיהֶם וּלְכָל־ נִדְבוֹתָם אֲשֶׁר־
that freewill-offerings-of-them or-for-any-of vows-of-them for-any-of

יַקְרִיבוּ לַיהוָה לְעֹלָה׃ לִרְצֹנְכֶם
for-acceptance-of-you (19) as-burnt-offering to-Yahweh they-present

תָּמִים זָכָר בַּבָּקָר בַּכְּשָׂבִים וּבָעִזִּים׃
or-from-the-goats from-the-sheep from-the-cattle male without-defect

כֹּל אֲשֶׁר־ בּוֹ מוּם לֹא תַקְרִיבוּ כִּי־ לֹא לְרָצוֹן
for-acceptance not for you-bring not defect on-him that anything (20)

יִהְיֶה לָכֶם׃ וְאִישׁ כִּי־ יַקְרִיב זֶבַח־ שְׁלָמִים
fellowships offering-of he-brings when and-anyone (21) for-you he-will-be

לַיהוָה לְפַלֵּא־ נֶדֶר אוֹ לִנְדָבָה בַבָּקָר אוֹ
or from-the-herd as-freewill-offering or vow to-fulfill to-Yahweh

בַצֹּאן תָּמִים יִהְיֶה לְרָצוֹן כָּל־ מוּם לֹא
not blemish any-of for-acceptance he-must-be without-defect from-the-flock

יִהְיֶה־ בּוֹ׃ עַוֶּרֶת אוֹ שָׁבוּר אוֹ־ חָרוּץ אוֹ־ יַבֶּלֶת אוֹ
or with-wart or maimed or being-injured or blind (22) on-him he-must-be

priest's daughter becomes a
widow or is divorced, yet has
no children, and she returns to
live in her father's house as in
her youth, she may eat of her
father's food. No unauthorized person, however, may
eat any of it.
[14]" 'If anyone eats a sacred
offering by mistake, he must
make restitution to the priest
for the offering and add a fifth
of the value to it. [15]The priests
must not desecrate the sacred
offerings the Israelites present
to the LORD [16]by allowing them
to eat the sacred offerings and
so bring upon them guilt re-
quiring payment. I am the
LORD, who makes them
holy.' "

Unacceptable Sacrifices

[17]The LORD said to Moses,
[18]"Speak to Aaron and his
sons and to all the Israelites
and say to them: 'If any of
you—either an Israelite or an
alien living in Israel—presents
a gift for a burnt offering to the
LORD, either to fulfill a vow or
as a freewill offering, [19]you
must present a male without
defect from the cattle, sheep or
goats in order that it may be
accepted on your behalf. [20]Do
not bring anything with a defect, because it will not be accepted on your behalf. [21]When
anyone brings from the herd
or flock a fellowship offering[a]
to the LORD to fulfill a special
vow or as a freewill offering, it
must be without defect or
blemish to be acceptable. [22]Do
not offer to the LORD the blind,
the injured or the maimed, or

[a]21 Traditionally *peace offering*

גָרָב אוֹ יַלֶּפֶת לֹא־ תַקְרִיבוּ אֵלֶּה לַיהוָה וְאִשֶּׁה
and-fire-offering to-Yahweh these you-offer not running-sore or with-fester

לֹא־ תִתְּנוּ מֵהֶם עַל־ הַמִּזְבֵּחַ לַיהוָה׃ וְשׁוֹר וָשֶׂה
or-sheep but-cow (23) to-Yahweh the-altar on from-these you-make not

שָׂרוּעַ וְקָלוּט נְדָבָה תַּעֲשֶׂה אֹתוֹ
him you-may-present freewill-offering or-being-stunted being-deformed

וּלְנֵדֶר לֹא יֵרָצֶה׃ וּמָעוּךְ וְכָתוּת
or-being-crushed but-being-bruised (24) he-will-be-accepted not but-for-vow

וְנָתוּק וְכָרוּת לֹא תַקְרִיבוּ לַיהוָה וּבְאַרְצְכֶם
and-in-land-of-you to-Yahweh you-must-offer not or-being-cut or-being-torn

לֹא תַעֲשׂוּ׃ וּמִיַּד בֶּן־ נֵכָר לֹא תַקְרִיבוּ
you-must-offer not foreigner son-of and-from-hand-of (25) you-must-do not

אֶת־ לֶחֶם אֱלֹהֵיכֶם מִכָּל־ אֵלֶּה כִּי מָשְׁחָתָם בָּהֶם
on-them deformity-of-them for these from-any-of God-of-you food-of ***

מוּם בָּם לֹא יֵרָצוּ לָכֶם׃ וַיְדַבֵּר יְהוָה
Yahweh and-he-spoke (26) for-you they-will-be-accepted not on-them defect

אֶל־ מֹשֶׁה לֵּאמֹר׃ שׁוֹר אוֹ־ כֶשֶׂב אוֹ־ עֵז כִּי יִוָּלֵד וְהָיָה
then-he-must-be he-is-born when goat or sheep or cow (27) to-say Moses to

שִׁבְעַת יָמִים תַּחַת אִמּוֹ וּמִיּוֹם הַשְּׁמִינִי וָהָלְאָה
and-on the-eighth and-from-day mother-of-him with days seven-of

יֵרָצֶה לְקָרְבַּן אִשֶּׁה לַיהוָה׃ וְשׁוֹר אוֹ־ שֶׂה
sheep or but-cow (28) to-Yahweh fire as-offering-of he-will-be-acceptable

אֹתוֹ וְאֶת־ בְּנוֹ לֹא תִשְׁחֲטוּ בְּיוֹם אֶחָד׃ וְכִי־
and-when (29) same on-day you-slaughter not young-of-him with him

תִזְבְּחוּ זֶבַח־ תּוֹדָה לַיהוָה לִרְצֹנְכֶם
for-acceptance-of-you to-Yahweh thanksgiving offering-of you-sacrifice

תִּזְבָּחוּ׃ בַּיּוֹם הַהוּא יֵאָכֵל לֹא־ תוֹתִירוּ
you-leave not he-must-be-eaten the-same on-the-day (30) you-sacrifice

מִמֶּנּוּ עַד־ בֹּקֶר אֲנִי יְהוָה׃ וּשְׁמַרְתֶּם מִצְוֹתַי
commandments-of-me so-you-keep (31) Yahweh I morning till from him

וַעֲשִׂיתֶם אֹתָם אֲנִי יְהוָה׃ וְלֹא תְחַלְּלוּ אֶת־ שֵׁם
name-of *** you-profane and-not (32) Yahweh I them and-you-follow

קָדְשִׁי וְנִקְדַּשְׁתִּי בְּתוֹךְ בְּנֵי יִשְׂרָאֵל אֲנִי יְהוָה
Yahweh I Israel sons-of by for-I-must-be-acknowledged-as-holy holy-of-me

מְקַדִּשְׁכֶם׃ הַמּוֹצִיא אֶתְכֶם מֵאֶרֶץ מִצְרַיִם לִהְיוֹת
to-be Egypt from-land-of you the-one-bringing (33) one-making-holy-you

לָכֶם לֵאלֹהִים אֲנִי יְהוָה׃ וַיְדַבֵּר יְהוָה אֶל־ מֹשֶׁה לֵּאמֹר׃
to-say Moses to Yahweh and-he-spoke (23:1) Yahweh I as-God for-you

anything with warts or festering or running sores. Do not
place any of these on the altar
as an offering made to the
LORD by fire. 23You may, how
ever, present as a freewill
offering a cow[b] or a sheep that
is deformed or stunted, but it
will not be accepted in
fulfillment of a vow. 24You
must not offer to the LORD an
animal whose testicles are
bruised, crushed, torn or cut.
You must not do this in your
own land, 25and you must not
accept such animals from the
hand of a foreigner and offer
them as the food of your God.
They will not be accepted on
your behalf, because they are
deformed and have defects.' "
26The LORD said to Moses,
27"When a cow, a sheep or a
goat is born, it is to remain
with its mother for seven
days. From the eighth day on,
it will be acceptable as an
offering made to the LORD by
fire. 28Do not slaughter a cow
or a sheep and its young on
the same day.
29"When you sacrifice an
offering of thanksgiving to the
LORD, sacrifice it in such a way
that it will be accepted on your
behalf. 30It must be eaten that
same day; leave none of it till
morning. I am the LORD.
31"Keep my commands and
follow them. I am the LORD.
32Do not profane my holy
name. I must be acknowl-
edged as holy by the Israelites.
I am the LORD, who makes[c]
you holy[d] 33and who brought
you out of Egypt to be your
God. I am the LORD."

23 The LORD said to
Moses, 2"Speak to the

[b]23 The Hebrew word can include both male and female; also in verse 27.
[c]32 Or *made*
[d]32 Or *who sanctifies you;* or *who sets you apart as holy*

דַּבֵּר אֶל־ בְּנֵי יִשְׂרָאֵל וְאָמַרְתָּ אֲלֵהֶם מוֹעֲדֵי יְהוָה אֲשֶׁר־

which Yahweh feasts-of to-them and-you-say Israel sons-of to speak! (2)

תִּקְרְאוּ אֹתָם מִקְרָאֵי קֹדֶשׁ אֵלֶּה הֵם מוֹעֲדָי׃ שֵׁשֶׁת

six-of (3) feasts-of-me they these sacred assemblies-of them you-must-proclaim

יָמִים תֵּעָשֶׂה מְלָאכָה וּבַיּוֹם הַשְּׁבִיעִי שַׁבַּת שַׁבָּתוֹן

rest Sabbath-of the-seventh but-on-the-day work she-must-be-done days

מִקְרָא־ קֹדֶשׁ כָּל־ מְלָאכָה לֹא תַעֲשׂוּ שַׁבָּת הִוא לַיהוָה

to-Yahweh this Sabbath you-may-do not work any-of sacred assembly-of

בְּכֹל מוֹשְׁבֹתֵיכֶם׃ אֵלֶּה מוֹעֲדֵי יְהוָה מִקְרָאֵי קֹדֶשׁ

sacred assemblies-of Yahweh feasts-of these (4) dwellings-of-you in-all-of

אֲשֶׁר־ תִּקְרְאוּ אֹתָם בְּמוֹעֲדָם׃ בַּחֹדֶשׁ הָרִאשׁוֹן

the-first in-the-month (5) at-times-of-them them you-must-proclaim that

בְּאַרְבָּעָה עָשָׂר לַחֹדֶשׁ בֵּין הָעַרְבָּיִם פֶּסַח לַיהוָה׃

to-Yahweh Passover the-twilights at of-the-month ten on-four

וּבַחֲמִשָּׁה עָשָׂר יוֹם לַחֹדֶשׁ הַזֶּה חַג הַמַּצּוֹת

the-Unleavened-Breads Feast-of the-that of-the-month day ten and-on-five (6)

לַיהוָה שִׁבְעַת יָמִים מַצּוֹת תֹּאכֵלוּ׃ בַּיּוֹם

on-the-day (7) you-must-eat unleavened-breads days seven-of to-Yahweh

הָרִאשׁוֹן מִקְרָא־ קֹדֶשׁ יִהְיֶה לָכֶם כָּל־ מְלֶאכֶת עֲבֹדָה לֹא

not regular work-of any-of for-you he-must-be sacred assembly-of the-first

תַעֲשׂוּ׃ וְהִקְרַבְתֶּם אִשֶּׁה לַיהוָה שִׁבְעַת יָמִים

days seven-of to-Yahweh fire-offering and-you-present (8) you-must-do

בַּיּוֹם הַשְּׁבִיעִי מִקְרָא־ קֹדֶשׁ כָּל־ מְלֶאכֶת עֲבֹדָה לֹא

not regular work-of any-of sacred assembly-of the-seventh on-the-day

תַעֲשׂוּ׃ וַיְדַבֵּר יְהוָה אֶל־ מֹשֶׁה לֵּאמֹר׃ דַּבֵּר אֶל־ בְּנֵי

sons-of to speak! (10) to-say Moses to Yahweh and-he-spoke (9) you-must-do

יִשְׂרָאֵל וְאָמַרְתָּ אֲלֵהֶם כִּי־ תָבֹאוּ אֶל־ הָאָרֶץ אֲשֶׁר אֲנִי נֹתֵן לָכֶם

to-you giving I that the-land into you-enter when to-them and-you-say Israel

וּקְצַרְתֶּם אֶת־ קְצִירָהּ וַהֲבֵאתֶם אֶת־ עֹמֶר רֵאשִׁית

first-of sheaf-of *** then-you-bring harvest-of-her *** and-you-reap

קְצִירְכֶם אֶל־ הַכֹּהֵן׃ וְהֵנִיף אֶת־ הָעֹמֶר לִפְנֵי

before the-sheaf *** and-he-must-wave (11) the-priest to harvest-of-you

יְהוָה לִרְצֹנְכֶם מִמָּחֳרַת הַשַּׁבָּת יְנִיפֶנּוּ

he-must-wave-him the-Sabbath on-day-after-of for-acceptance-of-you Yahweh

הַכֹּהֵן׃ וַעֲשִׂיתֶם בְּיוֹם הֲנִיפְכֶם אֶת־ הָעֹמֶר

the-sheaf *** to-wave-you on-day and-you-must-sacrifice (12) the-priest

כֶּבֶשׂ תָּמִים בֶּן־ שְׁנָתוֹ לְעֹלָה לַיהוָה׃

to-Yahweh as-burnt-offering year-of-him son-of without-defect lamb

Israelites and say to them: 'These are my appointed feasts, the appointed feasts of the LORD, which you are to proclaim as sacred assemblies.

The Sabbath

3" 'There are six days when you may work, but the seventh day is a Sabbath of rest, a day of sacred assembly. You are not to do any work; wherever you live, it is a Sabbath to the LORD.

The Passover and Unleavened Bread

4" 'These are the LORD's appointed feasts, the sacred assemblies you are to proclaim at their appointed times: 5The LORD's Passover begins at twilight on the fourteenth day of the first month. 6On the fifteenth day of that month the LORD's Feast of Unleavened Bread begins; for seven days you must eat bread made without yeast. 7On the first day hold a sacred assembly and do no regular work. 8For seven days present an offering made to the LORD by fire. And on the seventh day hold a sacred assembly and do no regular work.' "

Firstfruits

9The LORD said to Moses, 10"Speak to the Israelites and say to them: 'When you enter the land I am going to give you and you reap its harvest, bring to the priest a sheaf of the first grain you harvest. 11He is to wave the sheaf before the LORD so it will be accepted on your behalf; the priest is to wave it on the day after the Sabbath. 12On the day you wave the sheaf, you must sacrifice as a burnt offering to the LORD a lamb a year old without

וּמִנְחָתוֹ שְׁנֵי עֶשְׂרֹנִים סֹלֶת בְּלוּלָה בַשֶּׁמֶן
with-the-oil being-mixed fine-flour tenths two-of with-grain-offering-him (13)

אִשֶּׁה לַיהוָה רֵיחַ נִיחֹחַ וְנִסְכֹּה יַיִן רְבִיעִת
fourth-of wine and-drink-offering-of-him pleasant aroma-of to-Yahweh fire-offering

הַהִין׃ וְלֶחֶם וְקָלִי וְכַרְמֶל לֹא תֹאכְלוּ עַד־
until you-must-eat not or-new-grain or-roasted-grain and-bread (14) the-hin

עֶצֶם הַיּוֹם הַזֶּה עַד הֲבִיאֲכֶם אֶת־ קָרְבַּן אֱלֹהֵיכֶם
God-of-you offering-of *** to-bring-you until the-that the-day very-of

חֻקַּת עוֹלָם לְדֹרֹתֵיכֶם בְּכֹל מֹשְׁבֹתֵיכֶם׃
dwellings-of-you in-all-of for-generations-of-you lasting ordinance-of

וּסְפַרְתֶּם לָכֶם מִמָּחֳרַת הַשַּׁבָּת מִיּוֹם
from-day the-Sabbath from-day-after-of to-you then-you-count (15)

הֲבִיאֲכֶם אֶת־ עֹמֶר הַתְּנוּפָה שֶׁבַע שַׁבָּתוֹת תְּמִימֹת תִּהְיֶינָה׃
they-must-be full-ones weeks seven the-wave-offering sheaf-of *** to-bring-you

עַד מִמָּחֳרַת הַשַּׁבָּת הַשְּׁבִיעִת תִּסְפְּרוּ חֲמִשִּׁים יוֹם
day fifty you-count the-seventh the-Sabbath to-day-after-of up (16)

וְהִקְרַבְתֶּם מִנְחָה חֲדָשָׁה לַיהוָה׃ מִמּוֹשְׁבֹתֵיכֶם
from-dwellings-of-you (17) to-Yahweh new grain-offering then-you-present

תָּבִיאוּ ׀ לֶחֶם תְּנוּפָה שְׁתַּיִם שְׁנֵי עֶשְׂרֹנִים סֹלֶת תִּהְיֶינָה
they-must-be fine-flour tenths two-of two wave-offering bread you-bring

חָמֵץ תֵּאָפֶינָה בִּכּוּרִים לַיהוָה׃ וְהִקְרַבְתֶּם עַל־
with and-you-present (18) to-Yahweh firstfruits they-must-be-baked yeast

הַלֶּחֶם שִׁבְעַת כְּבָשִׂים תְּמִימִם בְּנֵי שָׁנָה וּפַר
and-bull year sons-of ones-without-defect male-lambs seven-of the-bread

בֶּן־ בָּקָר אֶחָד וְאֵילִם שְׁנָיִם יִהְיוּ עֹלָה לַיהוָה
to-Yahweh burnt-offering they-will-be two and-rams one herd young-of

וּמִנְחָתָם וְנִסְכֵּיהֶם אִשֵּׁה רֵיחַ־
aroma-of fire-offering and-drink-offerings-of-them with-grain-offering-of-them

נִיחֹחַ לַיהוָה׃ וַעֲשִׂיתֶם שְׂעִיר־ עִזִּים אֶחָד
one goats male-goat-of then-you-sacrifice (19) to-Yahweh pleasant

לְחַטָּאת וּשְׁנֵי כְבָשִׂים בְּנֵי שָׁנָה לְזֶבַח שְׁלָמִים׃
fellowships for-offering-of year sons-of lambs and-two-of for-sin-offering

וְהֵנִיף הַכֹּהֵן ׀ אֹתָם עַל לֶחֶם הַבִּכֻּרִים
the-firstfruits bread-of with them the-priest and-he-must-wave (20)

תְּנוּפָה לִפְנֵי יְהוָה עַל־ שְׁנֵי כְּבָשִׂים קֹדֶשׁ יִהְיוּ
they-are sacred-offering lambs two-of with Yahweh before wave-offering

לַיהוָה לַכֹּהֵן׃ וּקְרָאתֶם בְּעֶצֶם ׀ הַיּוֹם הַזֶּה
the-that the-day on-same-of and-you-must-proclaim (21) for-the-priest to-Yahweh

defect, 13together with its
grain offering of two-tenths of
an ephah[f] of fine flour mixed
with oil—an offering made to
the LORD by fire, a pleasing
aroma—and its drink offering
of a fourth of a hin[g] of wine.
14You must not eat any bread,
or roasted or new grain, until
the very day you bring this
offering to your God. This is to
be a lasting ordinance for
the generations to come,
wherever you live.

Feast of Weeks

15" 'From the day after the
Sabbath, the day you brought
the sheaf of the wave offering,
count off seven full weeks.
16Count off fifty days up to the
day after the seventh Sabbath,
and then present an offering
of new grain to the LORD.
17From wherever you live,
bring two loaves made of two-
tenths of an ephah of fine
flour, baked with yeast, as a
wave offering of firstfruits to
the LORD. 18Present with this
bread seven male lambs, each
a year old and without defect,
one young bull and two rams.
They will be a burnt offering
to the LORD, together with
their grain offerings and drink
offerings—an offering made
by fire, an aroma pleasing to
the LORD. 19Then sacrifice one
male goat for a sin offering
and two lambs, each a year
old, for a fellowship offering.[h]
20The priest is to wave the two
lambs before the LORD as a
wave offering, together with
the bread of the firstfruits.
They are a sacred offering to
the LORD for the priest. 21On
that same day you are to proclaim a sacred assembly and

[f] *13* That is, probably about 4 quarts (about 4.5 liters); also in verse 17
[g] *13* That is, probably about 1 quart (about 1 liter)
[h] *19* Traditionally *peace offering*

°*13* ק ונסכו

מִקְרָא־ קֹדֶשׁ יִהְיֶה לָכֶם כָּל־ מְלֶאכֶת עֲבֹדָה לֹא תַעֲשׂוּ
you-must-do not regular work-of any-of for-you he-will-be sacred assembly-of

חֻקַּת עוֹלָם בְּכָל־ מוֹשְׁבֹתֵיכֶם לְדֹרֹתֵיכֶם׃
for-generations-of-you dwellings-of-you in-all-of lasting ordinance-of

וּבְקֻצְרְכֶם אֶת־ קְצִיר אַרְצְכֶם לֹא־ תְכַלֶּה פְּאַת
edge-of you-reap not land-of-you harvest-of *** and-when-to-reap-you (22)

שָׂדְךָ בְּקֻצְרֶךָ וְלֶקֶט קְצִירְךָ לֹא תְלַקֵּט
you-glean not harvest-of-you and-gleaning-of when-to-harvest-you field-of-you

לֶעָנִי וְלַגֵּר תַּעֲזֹב אֹתָם אֲנִי יְהוָה אֱלֹהֵיכֶם׃
God-of-you Yahweh I them you-leave and-for-the-alien for-the-poor

וַיְדַבֵּר יְהוָה אֶל־מֹשֶׁה לֵּאמֹר׃ דַּבֵּר אֶל־ בְּנֵי יִשְׂרָאֵל לֵאמֹר
to-say Israel sons-of to say! (24) to-say Moses to Yahweh then-he-spoke (23)

בַּחֹדֶשׁ הַשְּׁבִיעִי בְּאֶחָד לַחֹדֶשׁ יִהְיֶה לָכֶם שַׁבָּתוֹן
day-of-rest to-you he-will-be of-the-month on-first the-seventh in-the-month

זִכְרוֹן תְּרוּעָה מִקְרָא־ קֹדֶשׁ׃ כָּל־ מְלֶאכֶת עֲבֹדָה
regular work-of any-of (25) sacred assembly-of trumpet-blast commemoration-of

לֹא תַעֲשׂוּ וְהִקְרַבְתֶּם אִשֶּׁה לַיהוָה׃ וַיְדַבֵּר יְהוָה
Yahweh and-he-spoke (26) to-Yahweh fire-offering but-you-present you-do not

אֶל־ מֹשֶׁה לֵּאמֹר׃ אַךְ בֶּעָשׂוֹר לַחֹדֶשׁ הַשְּׁבִיעִי הַזֶּה
the-this the-seventh of-the-month on-the-tenth also (27) to-say Moses to

יוֹם הַכִּפֻּרִים הוּא מִקְרָא־ קֹדֶשׁ יִהְיֶה לָכֶם וְעִנִּיתֶם
and-you-deny for-you he-must-be sacred assembly-of he the-Atonements Day-of

אֶת־ נַפְשֹׁתֵיכֶם וְהִקְרַבְתֶּם אִשֶּׁה לַיהוָה׃ וְכָל־
and-any-of (28) to-Yahweh fire-offering and-you-present selves-of-you ***

מְלָאכָה לֹא תַעֲשׂוּ בְּעֶצֶם הַיּוֹם הַזֶּה כִּי יוֹם כִּפֻּרִים הוּא
he Atonements Day-of for the-that the-day on-same-of you-do not work

לְכַפֵּר עֲלֵיכֶם לִפְנֵי יְהוָה אֱלֹהֵיכֶם׃ כִּי כָל־ הַנֶּפֶשׁ אֲשֶׁר
who the-person any-of indeed (29) God-of-you Yahweh before for-you to-atone

לֹא־ תְעֻנֶּה בְּעֶצֶם הַיּוֹם הַזֶּה וְנִכְרְתָה
then-she-must-be-cut-off the-that the-day on-same-of she-denies-self not

מֵעַמֶּיהָ׃ וְכָל־ הַנֶּפֶשׁ אֲשֶׁר תַּעֲשֶׂה כָּל־ מְלָאכָה
work any-of she-does who the-person and-any-of (30) from-people-of-her

בְּעֶצֶם הַיּוֹם הַזֶּה וְהַאֲבַדְתִּי אֶת־ הַנֶּפֶשׁ הַהִוא
the-that the-person *** then-I-will-destroy the-that the-day on-same-of

מִקֶּרֶב עַמָּהּ׃ כָּל־ מְלָאכָה לֹא תַעֲשׂוּ חֻקַּת
ordinance-of you-shall-do not work any-of (31) people-of-her from-among

עוֹלָם לְדֹרֹתֵיכֶם בְּכֹל מֹשְׁבֹתֵיכֶם׃ שַׁבַּת
sabbath-of (32) dwellings-of-you in-all-of for-generations-of-you lasting

do no regular work. This is to be a lasting ordinance for the generations to come, wherever you live.
22" 'When you reap the harvest of your land, do not reap to the very edges of your field or gather the gleanings of your harvest. Leave them for the poor and the alien. I am the LORD your God.' "

Feast of Trumpets

23The LORD said to Moses,
24"Say to the Israelites: 'On the first day of the seventh month you are to have a day of rest, a sacred assembly commemorated with trumpet blasts.
25Do no regular work, but present an offering made to the LORD by fire.' "

Day of Atonement

26The LORD said to Moses,
27"The tenth day of this seventh month is the Day of Atonement. Hold a sacred assembly and deny yourselves,[i] and present an offering made to the LORD by fire.
28Do no work on that day, because it is the Day of Atonement, when atonement is made for you before the LORD your God.
29Anyone who does not deny himself on that day must be cut off from his people.
30I will destroy from among his people anyone who does any work on that day.
31You shall do no work at all. This is to be a lasting ordinance for the generations to come, wherever you

[i]27 Or *and fast;* also in verses 29 and 32

שַׁבָּתוֹן הוּא לָכֶם וְעִנִּיתֶם אֶת־ נַפְשֹׁתֵיכֶם בְּתִשְׁעָה לַחֹדֶשׁ
of-the-month on-ninth selves-of-you *** and-you-must-deny for-you this rest

בָּעֶרֶב מֵעֶרֶב עַד־ עֶרֶב תִּשְׁבְּתוּ שַׁבַּתְּכֶם׃
sabbath-of-you you-must-observe evening until from-evening in-the-evening

וַיְדַבֵּר יְהוָה אֶל־ מֹשֶׁה לֵּאמֹר׃ דַּבֵּר אֶל־בְּנֵי יִשְׂרָאֵל לֵאמֹר
to-say Israel sons-of to say! (34) to-say Moses to Yahweh and-he-spoke (33)

בַּחֲמִשָּׁה עָשָׂר יוֹם לַחֹדֶשׁ הַשְּׁבִיעִי הַזֶּה חַג הַסֻּכּוֹת
the-Tabernacles Feast-of the-this the-seventh of-the-month day ten on-five

שִׁבְעַת יָמִים לַיהוָה׃ בַּיּוֹם הָרִאשׁוֹן מִקְרָא־ קֹדֶשׁ כָּל־
any-of sacred assembly-of the-first on-the-day (35) to-Yahweh days seven-of

מְלֶאכֶת עֲבֹדָה לֹא תַעֲשׂוּ׃ שִׁבְעַת יָמִים תַּקְרִיבוּ אִשֶּׁה
fire-offering you-present days seven-of (36) you-do not regular work-of

לַיהוָה בַּיּוֹם הַשְּׁמִינִי מִקְרָא־ קֹדֶשׁ יִהְיֶה לָכֶם
for-you he-must-be sacred assembly-of the-eighth on-the-day to-Yahweh

וְהִקְרַבְתֶּם אִשֶּׁה לַיהוָה עֲצֶרֶת הִוא כָּל־ מְלֶאכֶת
work-of any-of she closing-assembly to-Yahweh fire-offering and-you-present

עֲבֹדָה לֹא תַעֲשׂוּ׃ אֵלֶּה מוֹעֲדֵי יְהוָה אֲשֶׁר־ תִּקְרְאוּ אֹתָם
them you-must-proclaim which Yahweh feasts-of these (37) you-do not regular

מִקְרָאֵי קֹדֶשׁ לְהַקְרִיב אִשֶּׁה לַיהוָה עֹלָה
burnt-offering to-Yahweh fire-offering to-bring sacred assemblies-of

וּמִנְחָה זֶבַח וּנְסָכִים דְּבַר־ יוֹם
day requirement-of and-drink-offerings sacrifice and-grain-offering

בְּיוֹמוֹ׃ מִלְּבַד שַׁבְּתֹת יְהוָה וּמִלְּבַד
and-in-addition-to Yahweh Sabbaths-of in-addition-to (38) for-day-of-him

מַתְּנוֹתֵיכֶם וּמִלְּבַד כָּל־ נִדְרֵיכֶם וּמִלְּבַד כָּל־
any-of and-in-addition-to vows-of-you any-of and-in-addition-to gifts-of-you

נִדְבוֹתֵיכֶם אֲשֶׁר תִּתְּנוּ לַיהוָה׃ אַךְ בַּחֲמִשָּׁה עָשָׂר יוֹם
day ten on-five so (39) to-Yahweh you-give that freewill-offerings-of-you

לַחֹדֶשׁ הַשְּׁבִיעִי בְּאָסְפְּכֶם אֶת־ תְּבוּאַת הָאָרֶץ
the-land crop-of *** after-to-gather-you the-seventh of-the-month

תָּחֹגּוּ אֶת־ חַג־ יְהוָה שִׁבְעַת יָמִים בַּיּוֹם הָרִאשׁוֹן
the-first on-the-day days seven-of Yahweh festival-of *** you-celebrate

שַׁבָּתוֹן וּבַיּוֹם הַשְּׁמִינִי שַׁבָּתוֹן׃ וּלְקַחְתֶּם לָכֶם
for-you and-you-take (40) day-of-rest the-eighth and-on-the-day day-of-rest

בַּיּוֹם הָרִאשׁוֹן פְּרִי עֵץ הָדָר כַּפֹּת תְּמָרִים וַעֲנַף
and-branch-of palms fronds-of choice tree fruit-of the-first on-the-day

עֵץ־ עָבֹת וְעַרְבֵי־ נָחַל וּשְׂמַחְתֶּם לִפְנֵי יְהוָה אֱלֹהֵיכֶם
God-of-you Yahweh before and-you-rejoice stream and-poplars-of leafy tree

live. 32It is a sabbath of rest for
you, and you must deny yourselves. From the evening of
the ninth day of the month
until the following evening
you are to observe your sabbath."

Feast of Tabernacles

33The LORD said to Moses,
34"Say to the Israelites: 'On the
fifteenth day of the seventh
month the LORD's Feast of
Tabernacles begins, and it
lasts for seven days. 35The first
day is a sacred assembly; do
no regular work. 36For seven
days present offerings made to
the LORD by fire, and on the
eighth day hold a sacred assembly and present an
offering made to the LORD by
fire. It is the closing assembly;
do no regular work.
37(" 'These are the LORD's appointed feasts, which you are
to proclaim as sacred assemblies for bringing offerings
made to the LORD by fire—the
burnt offerings and grain
offerings, sacrifices and drink
offerings required for each
day. 38These offerings are in
addition to those for the
LORD's Sabbaths and[j] in addition to your gifts and whatever you have vowed and all
the freewill offerings you give
to the LORD.)
39" 'So beginning with the
fifteenth day of the seventh
month, after you have gathered the crops of the land, celebrate the festival to the LORD
for seven days; the first day is
a day of rest, and the eighth
day also is a day of rest. 40On
the first day you are to take
choice fruit from the trees, and
palm fronds, leafy branches
and poplars, and rejoice before the LORD your God for

j38 Or *These feasts are in addition to the LORD's Sabbaths, and these offerings are*

שִׁבְעַת יָמִים׃ וְחַגֹּתֶם אֹתוֹ חַג לַיהוָה שִׁבְעַת יָמִים
days seven-of to-Yahweh festival him and-you-celebrate (41) days seven-of

בַּשָּׁנָה חֻקַּת עוֹלָם לְדֹרֹתֵיכֶם בַּחֹדֶשׁ
in-the-month for-generations-of-you lasting ordinance-of in-the-year

הַשְּׁבִיעִי תָּחֹגּוּ אֹתוֹ׃ בַּסֻּכֹּת תֵּשְׁבוּ שִׁבְעַת יָמִים
days seven-of you-live in-the-booths (42) him you-celebrate the-seventh

כָּל־ הָאֶזְרָח בְּיִשְׂרָאֵל יֵשְׁבוּ בַּסֻּכֹּת׃ לְמַעַן
so-that (43) in-the-booths he-must-live in-Israel the-native every-of

יֵדְעוּ דֹרֹתֵיכֶם כִּי בַסֻּכּוֹת הוֹשַׁבְתִּי אֶת־ בְּנֵי
sons-of *** I-made-live in-the-booths that descendants-of-you they-will-know

יִשְׂרָאֵל בְּהוֹצִיאִי אוֹתָם מֵאֶרֶץ מִצְרָיִם אֲנִי יְהוָה אֱלֹהֵיכֶם׃
God-of-you Yahweh I Egypt from-land-of them when-to-bring-me Israel

וַיְדַבֵּר מֹשֶׁה אֶת־ מֹעֲדֵי יְהוָה אֶל־ בְּנֵי יִשְׂרָאֵל׃
Israel sons-of to Yahweh feasts-of *** Moses so-he-announced (44)

וַיְדַבֵּר יְהוָה אֶל־ מֹשֶׁה לֵּאמֹר׃ צַו אֶת־ בְּנֵי יִשְׂרָאֵל
Israel sons-of *** command! (2) to-say Moses to Yahweh and-he-spoke (24:1)

וְיִקְחוּ אֵלֶיךָ שֶׁמֶן זַיִת זָךְ כָּתִית לַמָּאוֹר לְהַעֲלֹת נֵר
lamp to-burn for-the-light pressed clear olive oil-of to-you so-they-bring

תָּמִיד׃ מִחוּץ לְפָרֹכֶת הָעֵדֻת בְּאֹהֶל מוֹעֵד
Meeting in-Tent-of the-Testimony of-curtain-of outside (3) continually

יַעֲרֹךְ אֹתוֹ אַהֲרֹן מֵעֶרֶב עַד־ בֹּקֶר לִפְנֵי יְהוָה תָּמִיד
continually Yahweh before morning till from-evening Aaron him he-must-tend

חֻקַּת עוֹלָם לְדֹרֹתֵיכֶם׃ עַל הַמְּנֹרָה הַטְּהֹרָה
the-pure-gold the-lampstand on (4) for-generations-of-you lasting ordinance-of

יַעֲרֹךְ אֶת־ הַנֵּרוֹת לִפְנֵי יְהוָה תָּמִיד׃ וְלָקַחְתָּ
and-you-take (5) continually Yahweh before the-lamps *** he-must-tend

סֹלֶת וְאָפִיתָ אֹתָהּ שְׁתֵּים עֶשְׂרֵה חַלּוֹת שְׁנֵי עֶשְׂרֹנִים יִהְיֶה
he-shall-be tenths two-of loaves ten two her and-you-bake fine-flour

הַחַלָּה הָאֶחָת׃ וְשַׂמְתָּ אוֹתָם שְׁתַּיִם מַעֲרָכוֹת שֵׁשׁ הַמַּעֲרָכֶת עַל הַשֻּׁלְחָן
the-table on the-row six-of rows two them and-you-set (6) the-each the-loaf

הַטָּהֹר לִפְנֵי יְהוָה׃ וְנָתַתָּ עַל־ הַמַּעֲרֶכֶת לְבֹנָה זַכָּה
pure incense the-row along and-you-put (7) Yahweh before the-pure-gold

וְהָיְתָה לַלֶּחֶם לְאַזְכָּרָה אִשֶּׁה לַיהוָה׃
to-Yahweh fire-offering as-memorial-portion for-the-bread and-she-will-be

בְּיוֹם הַשַּׁבָּת בְּיוֹם הַשַּׁבָּת יַעַרְכֶנּוּ לִפְנֵי
before he-must-set-him the-Sabbath on-day-of the-Sabbath on-day-of (8)

יְהוָה תָּמִיד מֵאֵת בְּנֵי־ יִשְׂרָאֵל בְּרִית עוֹלָם׃
lasting covenant Israel sons-of on-behalf-of continually Yahweh

seven days. [41]Celebrate this as a festival to the LORD for seven days each year. This is to be a lasting ordinance for the generations to come; celebrate it in the seventh month. [42]Live in booths for seven days: All native-born Israelites are to live in booths [43]so your descendants will know that I had the Israelites live in booths when I brought them out of Egypt. I am the LORD your God.' "

[44]So Moses announced to the Israelites the appointed feasts of the LORD.

Oil and Bread Set Before the LORD

24 The LORD said to Moses, [2]"Command the Israelites to bring you clear oil of pressed olives for the light so that the lamps may be kept burning continually. [3]Outside the curtain of the Testimony in the Tent of Meeting, Aaron is to tend the lamps before the LORD from evening till morning, continually. This is to be a lasting ordinance for the generations to come. [4]The lamps on the pure gold lampstand before the LORD must be tended continually.

[5]"Take fine flour and bake twelve loaves of bread, using two-tenths of an ephah[k] for each loaf. [6]Set them in two rows, six in each row, on the table of pure gold before the LORD. [7]Along each row put some pure incense as a memorial portion to represent the bread and to be an offering made to the LORD by fire. [8]This bread is to be set out before the LORD regularly, Sabbath after Sabbath, on behalf of the Israelites, as a lasting covenant. [9]It

[k]5 That is, probably about 4 quarts (about 4.5 liters)

וְהָיְתָה לְאַהֲרֹן וּלְבָנָיו וַאֲכָלֻהוּ בְּמָקוֹם
in-place and-they-must-eat-him and-for-sons-of-him for-Aaron and-she-is (9)

קָדֹשׁ כִּי קֹדֶשׁ קָדָשִׁים הוּא לוֹ מֵאִשֵּׁי יְהוָה
Yahweh from-fire-offerings-of for-him he holy-ones most-holy-of for holy

חָק־ עוֹלָם׃ וַיֵּצֵא בֶּן־ אִשָּׁה יִשְׂרְאֵלִית וְהוּא בֶּן־
son-of and-he Israelite woman son-of now-he-went-out (10) regular share-of

אִישׁ מִצְרִי בְּתוֹךְ בְּנֵי יִשְׂרָאֵל וַיִּנָּצוּ בַּמַּחֲנֶה בֶּן
son-of in-the-camp and-they-fought Israel sons-of among Egyptian man

הַיִּשְׂרְאֵלִית וְאִישׁ הַיִּשְׂרְאֵלִי׃ וַיִּקֹּב בֶּן־
son-of and-he-blasphemed (11) the-Israelite and-man the-Israelite-woman

הָאִשָּׁה הַיִּשְׂרְאֵלִית אֶת־ הַשֵּׁם וַיְקַלֵּל וַיָּבִיאוּ אֹתוֹ אֶל־
to him so-they-brought and-he-cursed the-Name *** the-Israelite the-woman

מֹשֶׁה וְשֵׁם אִמּוֹ שְׁלֹמִית בַּת־ דִּבְרִי לְמַטֵּה־
from-tribe-of Dibri daughter-of Shelomith mother-of-him now-name-of Moses

דָן׃ וַיַּנִּיחֻהוּ בַּמִּשְׁמָר לִפְרֹשׁ לָהֶם עַל־ פִּי
will-of about to-them to-be-clear in-the-custody and-they-put-him (12) Dan

יְהוָה׃ וַיְדַבֵּר יְהוָה אֶל־ מֹשֶׁה לֵּאמֹר׃ הוֹצֵא אֶת־
*** take! (14) to-say Moses to Yahweh then-he-said (13) Yahweh

הַמְקַלֵּל אֶל־ מִחוּץ לַמַּחֲנֶה וְסָמְכוּ כָל־
all-of and-they-must-lay of-the-camp outside to the-one-blaspheming

הַשֹּׁמְעִים אֶת־ יְדֵיהֶם עַל־ רֹאשׁוֹ וְרָגְמוּ אֹתוֹ
him and-they-must-stone head-of-him on hands-of-them *** the-ones-hearing

כָּל־ הָעֵדָה׃ וְאֶל־ בְּנֵי יִשְׂרָאֵל תְּדַבֵּר לֵאמֹר אִישׁ אִישׁ
any man to-say you-say Israel sons-of and-to (15) the-assembly entire-of

כִּי־ יְקַלֵּל אֱלֹהָיו וְנָשָׂא חֶטְאוֹ׃
responsibility-of-him then-he-must-bear God-of-him he-curses if

וְנֹקֵב שֵׁם־ יְהוָה מוֹת יוּמָת רָגוֹם
to-stone he-must-die to-die Yahweh name-of and-one-blaspheming (16)

יִרְגְּמוּ־ בוֹ כָּל־ הָעֵדָה כַּגֵּר כָּאֶזְרָח
or-the-native whether-the-alien the-assembly entire-of on-him they-must-stone

בְּנָקְבוֹ־ שֵׁם יוּמָת׃ וְאִישׁ כִּי יַכֶּה כָּל־
any-of he-takes if and-anyone (17) he-must-die Name when-to-blaspheme-him

נֶפֶשׁ אָדָם מוֹת יוּמָת׃ וּמַכֵּה נֶפֶשׁ־ בְּהֵמָה
animal life-of and-one-taking (18) he-must-die to-die human life-of

יְשַׁלְּמֶנָּה נֶפֶשׁ תַּחַת נָפֶשׁ׃ וְאִישׁ כִּי־ יִתֵּן מוּם
injury he-gives if and-anyone (19) life for life he-must-restitute-her

בַּעֲמִיתוֹ כַּאֲשֶׁר עָשָׂה כֵּן יֵעָשֶׂה לּוֹ׃ שֶׁבֶר
fracture (20) to-him he-must-be-done so he-did just-as to-neighbor-of-him

belongs to Aaron and his sons, who are to eat it in a holy place, because it is a most holy part of their regular share of the offerings made to the LORD by fire."

A Blasphemer Stoned

10Now the son of an Israelite mother and an Egyptian father went out among the Israelites, and a fight broke out in the camp between him and an Israelite. 11The son of the Israelite woman blasphemed the name of the LORD with a curse; so they brought him to Moses. (His mother's name was Shelomith, the daughter of Dibri the Danite.) 12They put him in custody until the will of the LORD should be made clear to them.

13Then the LORD said to Moses: 14"Take the blasphemer outside the camp. All those who heard him are to lay their hands on his head, and the entire assembly is to stone him. 15Say to the Israelites: 'If anyone curses his God, he will be held responsible; 16anyone who blasphemes the name of the LORD must be put to death. The entire assembly must stone him. Whether an alien or native-born, when he blasphemes the Name, he must be put to death.

17" 'If anyone takes the life of a human being, he must be put to death. 18Anyone who takes the life of someone's animal must make restitution—life for life. 19If anyone injures his neighbor, whatever he has done must be done to him:

תַּחַת שֶׁבֶר עַיִן תַּחַת עַיִן שֵׁן תַּחַת שֵׁן כַּאֲשֶׁר יִתֵּן מוּם בָּאָדָם
to-the-other injury he-gave just-as tooth for tooth eye for eye fracture for

כֵּן יִנָּתֶן בּוֹ׃ וּמַכֵּה בְהֵמָה יְשַׁלְּמֶנָּה
he-must-restitute-her animal and-one-killing (21) to-him he-must-be-given so

וּמַכֵּה אָדָם יוּמָת׃ מִשְׁפַּט אֶחָד יִהְיֶה לָכֶם כַּגֵּר
for-the-alien to-you he-must-be same law (22) he-must-die man but-one-killing

כָּאֶזְרָח יִהְיֶה כִּי אֲנִי יְהוָה אֱלֹהֵיכֶם׃ וַיְדַבֵּר מֹשֶׁה
Moses then-he-spoke (23) God-of-you Yahweh I for he-must-be for-the-native

אֶל־בְּנֵי יִשְׂרָאֵל וַיּוֹצִיאוּ אֶת־הַמְקַלֵּל אֶל־מִחוּץ
outside to the-one-blaspheming *** and-they-took Israel sons-of to

לַמַּחֲנֶה וַיִּרְגְּמוּ אֹתוֹ אָבֶן וּבְנֵי־יִשְׂרָאֵל עָשׂוּ כַּאֲשֶׁר
just-as they-did Israel so-sons-of stone him and-they-stoned of-the-camp

צִוָּה יְהוָה אֶת־מֹשֶׁה׃ וַיְדַבֵּר יְהוָה אֶל־מֹשֶׁה בְּהַר
on-Mount-of Moses to Yahweh and-he-spoke (25:1) Moses *** Yahweh he-commanded

סִינַי לֵאמֹר׃ דַּבֵּר אֶל־בְּנֵי יִשְׂרָאֵל וְאָמַרְתָּ אֲלֵהֶם כִּי תָבֹאוּ
you-enter when to-them and-you-say Israel sons-of to speak! (2) to-say Sinai

אֶל־הָאָרֶץ אֲשֶׁר אֲנִי נֹתֵן לָכֶם וְשָׁבְתָה הָאָרֶץ שַׁבָּת
sabbath the-land then-she-must-observe to-you giving I that the-land into

לַיהוָה׃ שֵׁשׁ שָׁנִים תִּזְרַע שָׂדֶךָ וְשֵׁשׁ שָׁנִים תִּזְמֹר
you-prune years and-six field-of-you you-sow years six (3) to-Yahweh

כַּרְמֶךָ וְאָסַפְתָּ אֶת־תְּבוּאָתָהּ׃ וּבַשָּׁנָה הַשְּׁבִיעִת
the-seventh but-in-the-year (4) crop-of-her *** and-you-gather vineyard-of-you

שַׁבַּת שַׁבָּתוֹן יִהְיֶה לָאָרֶץ שַׁבָּת לַיהוָה שָׂדְךָ לֹא
not field-of-you to-Yahweh sabbath for-the-land he-must-be rest sabbath-of

תִזְרָע וְכַרְמְךָ לֹא תִזְמֹר׃ אֵת סְפִיחַ
spontaneous-growth-of *** (5) you-prune not and-vineyard-of-you you-sow

קְצִירְךָ לֹא תִקְצוֹר וְאֶת־עִנְּבֵי נְזִירֶךָ לֹא תִבְצֹר
you-harvest not untended-vine-of-you grapes-of and you-reap not crop-of-you

שְׁנַת שַׁבָּתוֹן יִהְיֶה לָאָרֶץ׃ וְהָיְתָה שַׁבַּת הָאָרֶץ
the-land sabbath-of and-she-will-be (6) for-the-land he-must-be rest year-of

לָכֶם לְאָכְלָה לְךָ וּלְעַבְדְּךָ וְלַאֲמָתֶךָ
and-for-maidservant-of-you and-for-manservant-of-you for-you for-food for-you

וְלִשְׂכִירְךָ וּלְתוֹשָׁבְךָ הַגָּרִים עִמָּךְ׃
among-you the-ones-living and-for-guest-of-you and-for-hired-worker-of-you

וְלִבְהֶמְתְּךָ וְלַחַיָּה אֲשֶׁר בְּאַרְצֶךָ תִּהְיֶה
she-will-be in-land-of-you that and-for-wild-animal and-for-stock-of-you (7)

כָל־תְּבוּאָתָהּ לֶאֱכֹל׃ וְסָפַרְתָּ לְךָ שֶׁבַע שַׁבְּתֹת
sabbaths-of seven for-you and-you-count (8) to-eat produce-of-her all-of

[20]fracture for fracture, eye for
eye, tooth for tooth. As he has
injured the other, so he is to be
injured. [21]Whoever kills an
animal must make restitution,
but whoever kills a man must
be put to death. [22]You are to
have the same law for the
alien and the native-born. I
am the LORD your God.' "
[23]Then Moses spoke to the
Israelites, and they took the
blasphemer outside the camp
and stoned him. The Israelites
did as the LORD commanded
Moses.

The Sabbatical Year

25 The LORD said to Moses
on Mount Sinai,
[2]"Speak to the Israelites and
say to them: 'When you enter
the land I am going to give
you, the land itself must observe
a sabbath to the LORD.
[3]For six years sow your fields,
and for six years prune your
vineyards and gather their
crops. [4]But in the seventh year
the land is to have a sabbath of
rest, a sabbath to the LORD. Do
not sow your fields or prune
your vineyards. [5]Do not reap
what grows of itself or harvest
the grapes of your untended
vines. The land is to have a
year of rest. [6]Whatever the
land yields during the sabbath
year will be food for you—for
yourself, your manservant
and maidservant, and the
hired worker and temporary
resident who live among you,
[7]as well as for your livestock
and the wild animals in your
land. Whatever the land produces
may be eaten.

The Year of Jubilee

[8]" 'Count off seven sabbaths

שָׁנִים שֶׁבַע שָׁנִים שֶׁבַע פְּעָמִים וְהָיוּ לְךָ יְמֵי שֶׁבַע שַׁבְּתֹת
sabbaths-of seven days-of to-you so-they-are times seven years seven years

הַשָּׁנִים תֵּשַׁע וְאַרְבָּעִים שָׁנָה׃ וְהַעֲבַרְתָּ שׁוֹפַר תְּרוּעָה
sound trumpet then-you-have-sounded (9) year and-forty nine the-years

בַּחֹדֶשׁ הַשְּׁבִעִי בֶּעָשׂוֹר לַחֹדֶשׁ בְּיוֹם הַכִּפֻּרִים
the-Atonements on-Day-of of-the-month on-the-tenth the-seventh in-the-month

תַּעֲבִירוּ שׁוֹפָר בְּכָל־ אַרְצְכֶם׃ וְקִדַּשְׁתֶּם אֵת
*** and-you-consecrate (10) land-of-you through-all-of trumpet you-sound

שְׁנַת הַחֲמִשִּׁים שָׁנָה וּקְרָאתֶם דְּרוֹר בָּאָרֶץ
through-the-land liberty and-you-proclaim year the-fiftieth year-of

לְכָל־ יֹשְׁבֶיהָ יוֹבֵל הִוא תִּהְיֶה לָכֶם
for-you she-shall-be this jubilee ones-inhabiting-her to-all-of

וְשַׁבְתֶּם אִישׁ אֶל־ אֲחֻזָּתוֹ וְאִישׁ אֶל־ מִשְׁפַּחְתּוֹ
clan-of-him to and-each family-property-of-him to each and-you-must-return

תָּשֻׁבוּ׃ יוֹבֵל הִוא שְׁנַת הַחֲמִשִּׁים שָׁנָה תִּהְיֶה
she-shall-be year the-fiftieth year-of this jubilee (11) you-must-return

לָכֶם לֹא תִזְרָעוּ וְלֹא תִקְצְרוּ אֶת־ סְפִיחֶיהָ וְלֹא
and-not spontaneous-growth-of-her *** you-reap and-not you-sow not for-you

תִבְצְרוּ אֶת־ נְזִרֶיהָ׃ כִּי יוֹבֵל הִוא קֹדֶשׁ תִּהְיֶה
she-must-be holy this jubilee for (12) untended-vines-of-her *** you-harvest

לָכֶם מִן־ הַשָּׂדֶה תֹּאכְלוּ אֶת־ תְּבוּאָתָהּ׃ בִּשְׁנַת הַיּוֹבֵל
the-Jubilee in-Year-of (13) produce-of-her *** you-eat the-field from for-you

הַזֹּאת תָּשֻׁבוּ אִישׁ אֶל־ אֲחֻזָּתוֹ׃ וְכִי־ תִמְכְּרוּ מִמְכָּר
land you-sell and-if (14) property-of-him to each you-return the-this

לַעֲמִיתֶךָ אוֹ קָנֹה מִיַּד עֲמִיתֶךָ אַל־
not countryman-of-you from-hand-of to-buy or to-countryman-of-you

תּוֹנוּ אִישׁ אֶת־ אָחִיו׃ בְּמִסְפַּר שָׁנִים אַחַר
since years by-number-of (15) other-of-him *** each you-take-advantage

הַיּוֹבֵל תִּקְנֶה מֵאֵת עֲמִיתֶךָ בְּמִסְפַּר שְׁנֵי־ תְבוּאֹת
harvests years-of by-number-of countryman-of-you from you-buy the-Jubilee

יִמְכָּר־ לָךְ׃ לְפִי ׀ רֹב הַשָּׁנִים תַּרְבֶּה
you-increase the-years many-of on-account-of (16) to-you he-must-sell

מִקְנָתוֹ וּלְפִי מְעֹט הַשָּׁנִים תַּמְעִיט מִקְנָתוֹ
price-of-him you-decrease the-years few-of and-on-account-of price-of-him

כִּי מִסְפַּר תְּבוּאֹת הוּא מֹכֵר לָךְ׃ וְלֹא תוֹנוּ אִישׁ
each you-take-advantage and-not (17) to-you selling he crops number-of for

אֶת־ עֲמִיתוֹ וְיָרֵאתָ מֵאֱלֹהֶיךָ כִּי אֲנִי יְהוָה אֱלֹהֵיכֶם׃
God-of-you Yahweh I for to-God-of-you but-you-fear countryman-of-him ***

of years—seven times seven
years—so that the seven sabbaths of years amount to a period of forty-nine years. 9Then
have the trumpet sounded
everywhere on the tenth day
of the seventh month; on the
Day of Atonement sound the
trumpet throughout your land.
10Consecrate the fiftieth year
and proclaim liberty throughout the land to all its inhabitants. It shall be a jubilee for
you; each one of you is to return to his family property
and each to his own clan.
11The fiftieth year shall be a jubilee for you; do not sow and
do not reap what grows of itself or harvest the untended
vines. 12For it is a jubilee and
is to be holy for you; eat only
what is taken directly from the
fields.

13" 'In this Year of Jubilee
everyone is to return to his
own property.

14" 'If you sell land to one of
your countrymen or buy any
from him, do not take advantage of each other. 15You are to
buy from your countryman on
the basis of the number of
years since the Jubilee. And he
is to sell to you on the basis of
the number of years left for
harvesting crops. 16When the
years are many, you are to increase the price, and when the
years are few, you are to de-
crease the price, because what
he is really selling you is the
number of crops. 17Do not take
advantage of each other, but
fear your God. I am the LORD
your God.

וַעֲשִׂיתֶם אֶת־ חֻקֹּתַי וְאֶת־ מִשְׁפָּטַי תִּשְׁמְרוּ
you-be-careful laws-of-me and decrees-of-me *** and-you-follow (18)

וַעֲשִׂיתֶם אֹתָם וִישַׁבְתֶּם עַל־ הָאָרֶץ לָבֶטַח׃ וְנָתְנָה
and-she-will-yield (19) in-safety the-land in and-you-will-live them and-you-do

הָאָרֶץ פִּרְיָהּ וַאֲכַלְתֶּם לָשֹׂבַע וִישַׁבְתֶּם
and-you-will-live to-fullness and-you-will-eat fruit-of-her the-land

לָבֶטַח עָלֶיהָ׃ וְכִי תֹאמְרוּ מַה־ נֹּאכַל בַּשָּׁנָה
in-the-year will-we-eat what? you-ask and-if (20) in-her in-safety

הַשְּׁבִיעִת הֵן לֹא נִזְרָע וְלֹא נֶאֱסֹף אֶת־ תְּבוּאָתֵנוּ׃
crop-of-us *** we-harvest or-not we-plant not if the-seventh

וְצִוִּיתִי אֶת־ בִּרְכָתִי לָכֶם בַּשָּׁנָה הַשִּׁשִּׁית
the-sixth in-the-year to-you blessing-of-me *** now-I-will-send (21)

וְעָשָׂת אֶת־ הַתְּבוּאָה לִשְׁלֹשׁ הַשָּׁנִים׃ וּזְרַעְתֶּם
while-you-plant (22) the-years for-three-of the-crop *** and-she-will-yield

אֵת הַשָּׁנָה הַשְּׁמִינִת וַאֲכַלְתֶּם מִן־ הַתְּבוּאָה יָשָׁן עַד ׀ הַשָּׁנָה
the-year until old the-crop from then-you-will-eat the-eighth the-year ***

הַתְּשִׁיעִת עַד־ בּוֹא תְּבוּאָתָהּ תֹּאכְלוּ יָשָׁן׃ וְהָאָרֶץ
and-the-land (23) old you-will-eat harvest-of-her to-come-in until the-ninth

לֹא תִמָּכֵר לִצְמִתֻת כִּי־ לִי הָאָרֶץ כִּי־ גֵרִים וְתוֹשָׁבִים
and-tenants aliens for the-land to-me for to-permanence she-must-be-sold not

אַתֶּם עִמָּדִי׃ וּבְכֹל אֶרֶץ אֲחֻזַּתְכֶם גְּאֻלָּה
redemption possession-of-you country-of and-through-all-of (24) to-me you

תִּתְּנוּ לָאָרֶץ׃ כִּי־ יָמוּךְ אָחִיךָ
countryman-of-you he-becomes-poor if (25) for-the-land you-must-provide

וּמָכַר מֵאֲחֻזָּתוֹ וּבָא גֹאֲלוֹ
one-redeeming-him then-he-must-come from-property-of-him and-he-sells

הַקָּרֹב אֵלָיו וְגָאַל אֵת מִמְכַּר אָחִיו׃
countryman-of-him sold-of *** and-he-must-redeem to-him the-one-near

וְאִישׁ כִּי לֹא יִהְיֶה־ לּוֹ גֹּאֵל וְהִשִּׂיגָה יָדוֹ
hand-of-him and-he-prospers one-redeeming to-him he-is not if and-man (26)

וּמָצָא כְּדֵי גְאֻלָּתוֹ׃ וְחִשַּׁב
and-he-must-determine (27) redemption-of-him as-sufficient-of and-he-acquires

אֶת־ שְׁנֵי מִמְכָּרוֹ וְהֵשִׁיב אֶת־ הָעֹדֵף לָאִישׁ
to-the-man the-remaining *** and-he-must-refund value-of-him years-of ***

אֲשֶׁר מָכַר־ לוֹ וְשָׁב לַאֲחֻזָּתוֹ׃ וְאִם לֹא־
not but-if (28) to-property-of-him then-he-can-go-back to-him he-sold whom

מָצְאָה יָדוֹ דֵּי הָשִׁיב לוֹ וְהָיָה
then-he-will-remain to-him to-repay means hand-of-him she-acquires

18 " 'Follow my decrees and
be careful to obey my laws,
and you will live safely in the
land. 19 Then the land will yield
its fruit, and you will eat your
fill and live there in safety.
20 You may ask, "What will we
eat in the seventh year if we
do not plant or harvest our
crops?" 21 I will send you such
a blessing in the sixth year
that the land will yield enough
for three years. 22 While you
plant during the eighth year,
you will eat from the old crop
and will continue to eat from
it until the harvest of the
ninth year comes in.

23 " 'The land must not be
sold permanently, because the
land is mine and you are but
aliens and my tenants.
24 Throughout the country that
you hold as a possession, you
must provide for the redemption of the land.

25 " 'If one of your countrymen becomes poor and sells
some of his property, his nearest relative is to come and redeem what his countryman
has sold. 26 If, however, a man
has no one to redeem it for
him but he himself prospers
and acquires sufficient means
to redeem it, 27 he is to determine the value for the years
since he sold it and refund the
balance to the man to whom
he sold it; he can then go back
to his own property. 28 But if he
does not acquire the means to
repay him, what he sold will

מִמְכָּרוֹ בְּיַד הַקֹּנֶה אֹתוֹ עַד שְׁנַת הַיּוֹבֵל
the-Jubilee Year-of until him the-one-buying in-possession-of sold-of-him

וְיָצָא בַּיֹּבֵל וְשָׁב לַאֲחֻזָּתוֹ׃
to-property-of-him and-he-can-go-back in-the-Jubilee then-he-will-return

וְאִישׁ כִּֽי־ יִמְכֹּר בֵּית־ מוֹשַׁב עִיר חוֹמָה וְהָיְתָה
then-he-retains wall city-of dwelling-of house-of he-sells if and-man (29)

גְּאֻלָּתוֹ עַד־ תֹּם שְׁנַת מִמְכָּרוֹ יָמִים תִּהְיֶה
she-may-be times sale-of-him year-of to-end until redemption-of-him

גְּאֻלָּתוֹ׃ וְאִם לֹא־ יִגָּאֵל עַד־ מְלֹאת לוֹ שָׁנָה
year by-him to-pass before he-is-redeemed not but-if (30) redemption-of-him

תְמִימָה וְקָם הַבַּיִת אֲשֶׁר־ בָּעִיר אֲשֶׁר־ לֹא חֹמָה
wall to-him that in-the-city that the-house then-he-shall-belong full

לַצְּמִיתֻת לַקֹּנֶה אֹתוֹ לְדֹרֹתָיו לֹא
not for-descendants-of-him him to-the-one-buying for-the-permanence

יֵצֵא בַּיֹּבֵל׃ וּבָתֵּי הַחֲצֵרִים אֲשֶׁר אֵין־
he-is-not that the-villages but-houses-of (31) in-the-Jubilee he-must-return

לָהֶם חֹמָה סָבִיב עַל־ שְׂדֵה הָאָרֶץ יֵחָשֵׁב
they-must-be-considered the-country open-field-of in around wall to-them

גְּאֻלָּה תִּהְיֶה־ לּוֹ וּבַיֹּבֵל יֵצֵא׃
he-must-return and-in-the-Jubilee for-him she-will-be redemption

וְעָרֵי הַלְוִיִּם בָּתֵּי עָרֵי אֲחֻזָּתָם
possession-of-them towns-of houses-of the-Levites and-towns-of (32)

גְּאֻלַּת עוֹלָם תִּהְיֶה לַלְוִיִּם׃ וַאֲשֶׁר יִגְאַל
he-may-redeem so-that (33) for-the-Levites she-is continual redemption-of

מִן־ הַלְוִיִּם וְיָצָא מִמְכַּר־ בַּיִת וְעִיר אֲחֻזָּתוֹ
holding-of-them in-town-of house sold-of and-he-must-return the-Levites from

בַּיֹּבֵל כִּי בָתֵּי עָרֵי הַלְוִיִּם הִוא אֲחֻזָּתָם
property-of-them this the-Levites towns-of houses-of for in-the-Jubilee

בְּתוֹךְ בְּנֵי יִשְׂרָאֵל׃ וּשְׂדֵה מִגְרַשׁ עָרֵיהֶם לֹא
not towns-of-them pasture-of but-land-of (34) Israel sons-of among

יִמָּכֵר כִּי־ אֲחֻזַּת עוֹלָם הוּא לָהֶם׃ וְכִי־
and-if (35) to-them he permanent possession-of for he-must-be-sold

יָמוּךְ אָחִיךָ וּמָטָה יָדוֹ
hand-of-him and-she-cannot-support countryman-of-you he-becomes-poor

עִמָּךְ וְהֶחֱזַקְתָּ בּוֹ גֵּר וְתוֹשָׁב וָחַי
so-he-can-live or-temporary-resident alien to-him then-you-help among-you

עִמָּךְ׃ אַל־ תִּקַּח מֵאִתּוֹ נֶשֶׁךְ וְתַרְבִּית וְיָרֵאתָ
but-you-fear or-usury interest from-him you-take not (36) among-you

remain in the possession of the buyer until the Year of Jubilee. It will be returned in the Jubilee, and he can then go back to his property.

29" 'If a man sells a house in a walled city, he retains the right of redemption a full year after its sale. During that time he may redeem it. 30If it is not redeemed before a full year has passed, the house in the walled city shall belong permanently to the buyer and his descendants. It is not to be returned in the Jubilee. 31But houses in villages without walls around them are to be considered as open country. They can be redeemed, and they are to be returned in the Jubilee.

32" 'The Levites always have the right to redeem their houses in the Levitical towns, which they possess. 33So the property of the Levites is redeemable—that is, a house sold in any town they hold—and is to be returned in the Jubilee, because the houses in the towns of the Levites are their property among the Israelites. 34But the pastureland belonging to their towns must not be sold; it is their permanent possession.

35" 'If one of your countrymen becomes poor and is unable to support himself among you, help him as you would an alien or a temporary resident, so he can continue to live among you. 36Do not take interest of any kind[l] from him,

[l]36 Or *take exorbitant interest*

°30 ק לו

מֵאֱלֹהֶ֑יךָ וְחֵ֥י אָחִ֖יךָ עִמָּֽךְ׃ אֶֽת־ כַּסְפְּךָ֔
money-of-you *** (37) among-you countryman-of-you so-he-may-live to-God-of-you

לֹֽא־ תִתֵּ֥ן ל֖וֹ בְּנֶ֑שֶׁךְ וּבְמַרְבִּ֖ית לֹא־ תִתֵּ֥ן אָכְלֶֽךָ׃
food-of-you you-sell not or-at-profit at-interest to-him you-lend not

אֲנִ֗י יְהוָה֙ אֱלֹהֵיכֶ֔ם אֲשֶׁר־הוֹצֵ֥אתִי אֶתְכֶ֖ם מֵאֶ֣רֶץ מִצְרָ֑יִם לָתֵ֤ת לָכֶם֙
to-you to-give Egypt from-land-of you I-brought who God-of-you Yahweh I (38)

אֶת־ אֶ֣רֶץ כְּנַ֔עַן לִהְי֥וֹת לָכֶ֖ם לֵאלֹהִֽים׃ וְכִֽי־ יָמ֥וּךְ
he-becomes-poor and-if (39) as-God to-you to-be Canaan land-of ***

אָחִ֛יךָ עִמָּ֖ךְ וְנִמְכַּר־ לָ֑ךְ לֹא־ תַעֲבֹ֥ד
you-give-work not to-you and-he-sells-self among-you countryman-of-you

בּ֖וֹ עֲבֹ֥דַת עָֽבֶד׃ כְּשָׂכִ֥יר כְּתוֹשָׁ֖ב יִהְיֶ֣ה
he-must-be as-temporary-resident as-hired-worker (40) slave work-of to-him

עִמָּ֑ךְ עַד־ שְׁנַ֥ת הַיֹּבֵ֖ל יַעֲבֹ֥ד עִמָּֽךְ׃ וְיָצָא֙
and-he-must-leave (41) for-you he-will-work the-Jubilee Year-of until among-you

מֵֽעִמָּ֔ךְ ה֖וּא וּבָנָ֣יו עִמּ֑וֹ וְשָׁב֙ אֶל־
to and-he-will-go-back with-him and-children-of-him he from-among-you

מִשְׁפַּחְתּ֔וֹ וְאֶל־ אֲחֻזַּ֥ת אֲבֹתָ֖יו יָשֽׁוּב׃ כִּֽי־
for (42) he-will-go-back forefathers-of-him property-of and-to clan-of-him

עֲבָדַ֣י הֵ֔ם אֲשֶׁר־ הוֹצֵ֥אתִי אֹתָ֖ם מֵאֶ֣רֶץ מִצְרָ֑יִם לֹ֥א
not Egypt from-land-of them I-brought whom they servants-of-me

יִמָּכְר֖וּ מִמְכֶּ֥רֶת עָֽבֶד׃ לֹא־ תִרְדֶּ֥ה ב֖וֹ בְּפָ֑רֶךְ
with-ruthlessness over-him you-rule not (43) slave sale-of they-must-be-sold

וְיָרֵ֖אתָ מֵּאֱלֹהֶֽיךָ׃ וְעַבְדְּךָ֥ וַאֲמָתְךָ֖
and-female-slave-of-you now-male-slave-of-you (44) to-God-of-you but-you-fear

אֲשֶׁ֣ר יִהְיוּ־ לָ֑ךְ מֵאֵ֣ת הַגּוֹיִ֗ם אֲשֶׁר֙ סְבִיבֹ֣תֵיכֶ֔ם מֵהֶ֥ם
from-them ones-around-you that the-nations from to-you they-are who

תִּקְנ֖וּ עֶ֥בֶד וְאָמָֽה׃ וְ֠גַם מִבְּנֵ֨י
from-children-of and-also (45) and-female-slave male-slave you-buy

הַתּוֹשָׁבִ֜ים הַגָּרִ֤ים עִמָּכֶם֙ מֵהֶ֣ם תִּקְנ֔וּ
you-may-buy from-them among-you the-ones-living the-temporary-residents

וּמִמִּשְׁפַּחְתָּם֙ אֲשֶׁ֣ר עִמָּכֶ֔ם אֲשֶׁ֥ר הוֹלִ֖ידוּ בְּאַרְצְכֶ֑ם
in-country-of-you they-bear whom among-you that and-from-clan-of-them

וְהָי֥וּ לָכֶ֖ם לַאֲחֻזָּֽה׃ וְהִתְנַחַלְתֶּ֨ם* אֹתָ֜ם
them and-you-can-will (46) as-property to-you and-they-will-become

לִבְנֵיכֶ֤ם אַחֲרֵיכֶם֙ לָרֶ֣שֶׁת אֲחֻזָּ֔ה לְעֹלָ֖ם בָּהֶ֣ם
of-them for-life property as-inheritance-of after-you to-children-of-you

תַּעֲבֹ֑דוּ וּבְאַ֨חֵיכֶ֤ם בְּנֵֽי־ יִשְׂרָאֵל֙ אִ֣ישׁ
man Israel sons-of but-over-fellows-of-you you-can-make-slave

but fear your God, so that your countryman may continue to live among you. 37You must not lend him money at interest or sell him food at a profit. 38I am the LORD your God, who brought you out of Egypt to give you the land of Canaan and to be your God.

39" 'If one of your countrymen becomes poor among you and sells himself to you, do not make him work as a slave. 40He is to be treated as a hired worker or a temporary resident among you; he is to work for you until the Year of Jubilee. 41Then he and his children are to be released, and he will go back to his own clan and to the property of his forefathers. 42Because the Israelites are my servants, whom I brought out of Egypt, they must not be sold as slaves. 43Do not rule over them ruthlessly, but fear your God.

44" 'Your male and female slaves are to come from the nations around you; from them you may buy slaves. 45You may also buy some of the temporary residents living among you and members of their clans born in your country, and they will become your property. 46You can will them to your children as inherited property and can make them slaves for life, but you must

*46 Most mss have *pathah* under the *beth* (׳נַ־).

וְכִי בְּפָרֶךְ׃ בּוֹ תִרְדֶּה לֹא־ בְּאָחִיו
and-if (47) with-ruthlessness over-him you-must-rule not over-fellow-of-him

עִמָּךְ וְתוֹשָׁב גֵּר יַד תַשִּׂיג
among-you or-temporary-resident alien hand-of she-becomes-rich

לְגֵר וְנִמְכַּר עִמּוֹ אָחִיךָ וּמָךְ
to-alien and-he-sells-self with-him countryman-of-you and-he-becomes-poor

נִמְכַּר אַחֲרֵי גֵּר׃ מִשְׁפַּחַת לְעֵקֶר אוֹ עִמָּךְ תּוֹשָׁב
he-sells-self after (48) alien clan-of to-member-of or among-you resident

יִגְאָלֶנּוּ׃ מֵאֶחָיו אֶחָד לּוֹ תִּהְיֶה־ גְּאֻלָּה
he-may-redeem-him from-relatives-of-him one for-him she-remains redemption

אוֹ־ יִגְאָלֶנּוּ דֹּדוֹ בֶן־ אוֹ דֹדוֹ אוֹ־
or he-may-redeem-him uncle-of-him son-of or uncle-of-him or (49)

אוֹ־ יִגְאָלֶנּוּ מִמִּשְׁפַּחְתּוֹ בְּשָׂרוֹ מִשְּׁאֵר
or he-may-redeem-him from-clan-of-him flesh-of-him from-relative-of

וְחִשַּׁב וְנִגְאָל׃ יָדוֹ הִשִּׂיגָה
then-he-must-count (50) then-he-may-redeem-self hand-of-him she-prospers

שְׁנַת עַד לוֹ הִמָּכְרוֹ מִשְּׁנַת קֹנֵהוּ עִם־
Year-of up-to to-him to-be-sold-him from-year-of one-buying-him with

שָׁנִים בְּמִסְפַּר מִמְכָּרוֹ כֶּסֶף וְהָיָה הַיֹּבֵל
years on-number-of release-of-him price-of and-he-will-be the-Jubilee

בַּשָּׁנִים רַבּוֹת עוֹד אִם־ עִמּוֹ׃ יִהְיֶה שָׂכִיר כִּימֵי
of-the-years many yet if (51) with-him he-would-be hired-man as-days-of

מִקְנָתוֹ׃ מִכֶּסֶף גְּאֻלָּתוֹ יָשִׁיב לְפִיהֶן
purchase-of-him from-price-of redemption-of-him he-must-pay on-account-of-them

הַיֹּבֵל שְׁנַת עַד־ בַּשָּׁנִים נִשְׁאַר מְעַט וְאִם־
the-Jubilee Year-of until of-the-years he-remains few but-if (52)

אֶת־ יָשִׁיב שָׁנָיו כְּפִי לוֹ וְחִשַּׁב־
*** and-he-must-pay years-of-him on-account-of for-him then-he-must-compute

לֹא־ עִמּוֹ יִהְיֶה בְּשָׁנָה שָׁנָה כִּשְׂכִיר גְּאֻלָּתוֹ׃
not to-him he-must-be by-year year as-hired-man-of (53) redemption-of-him

לֹא וְאִם־ לְעֵינֶיךָ׃ בְּפָרֶךְ יִרְדֶּנּוּ
not even-if (54) before-eyes-of-you with-ruthlessness he-must-rule-him

הוּא הַיֹּבֵל בִּשְׁנַת וְיָצָא בְּאֵלֶּה יִגָּאֵל
he the-Jubilee in-Year-of then-he-must-go-out by-these he-is-redeemed

עֲבָדִים יִשְׂרָאֵל בְנֵי־ לִי כִּי־ עִמּוֹ׃ וּבָנָיו
servants Israel sons-of to-me for (55) with-him and-children-of-him

יְהוָה אֲנִי מִצְרָיִם מֵאֶרֶץ אוֹתָם הוֹצֵאתִי אֲשֶׁר־ הֵם עֲבָדַי
Yahweh I Egypt from-land-of them I-brought whom they servants-of-me

not rule over your fellow Israelites ruthlessly.
47 "'If an alien or a temporary resident among you
becomes rich and one of your
countrymen becomes poor
and sells himself to the alien
living among you or to a member of the alien's clan, 48 he retains the right of redemption
after he has sold himself. One
of his relatives may redeem
him: 49 An uncle or a cousin or
any blood relative in his clan
may redeem him. Or if he
prospers, he may redeem himself. 50 He and his buyer are to
count the time from the year
he sold himself up to the Year
of Jubilee. The price for his release is to be based on the rate
paid to a hired man for that
number of years. 51 If many
years remain, he must pay for
his redemption a larger share
of the price paid for him. 52 If
only a few years remain until
the Year of Jubilee, he is to
compute that and pay for his
redemption accordingly. 53 He
is to be treated as a man hired
from year to year; you must
see to it that his owner does
not rule over him ruthlessly.
54 "'Even if he is not redeemed in any of these ways,
he and his children are to be
released in the Year of Jubilee,
55 for the Israelites belong to
me as servants. They are my
servants, whom I brought out
of Egypt. I am the LORD your

אֱלֹהֵיכֶם׃ לֹא־ תַעֲשׂוּ לָכֶם אֱלִילִם וּפֶסֶל וּמַצֵּבָה לֹא־
not or-sacred-stone or-image idols for-you you-make not (26:1) God-of-you

תָקִימוּ לָכֶם וְאֶבֶן מַשְׂכִּית לֹא תִתְּנוּ בְּאַרְצְכֶם לְהִשְׁתַּחֲוֺת
to-bow-down in-land-of-you you-place not carved and-stone for-you you-set-up

עָלֶיהָ כִּי אֲנִי יְהוָה אֱלֹהֵיכֶם׃ אֶת־ שַׁבְּתֹתַי תִּשְׁמֹרוּ
you-observe Sabbaths-of-me *** (2) God-of-you Yahweh I for before-her

וּמִקְדָּשִׁי תִּירָאוּ אֲנִי יְהוָה׃ אִם־ בְּחֻקֹּתַי תֵּלֵכוּ
you-follow to-decrees-of-me if (3) Yahweh I you-revere and-sanctuary-of-me

וְאֶת־ מִצְוֺתַי תִּשְׁמְרוּ וַעֲשִׂיתֶם אֹתָם׃ וְנָתַתִּי
then-I-will-send (4) them and-you-obey you-are-careful commands-of-me and

גִשְׁמֵיכֶם בְּעִתָּם וְנָתְנָה הָאָרֶץ יְבוּלָהּ
crop-of-her the-earth and-she-will-yield in-season-of-them rains-of-you

וְעֵץ הַשָּׂדֶה יִתֵּן פִּרְיוֹ׃ וְהִשִּׂיג
and-he-will-continue (5) fruit-of-him he-will-yield the-field and-tree-of

לָכֶם דַּיִשׁ אֶת־ בָּצִיר וּבָצִיר יַשִּׂיג אֶת־
*** he-will-continue and-grape-harvest grape-harvest *** threshing for-you

זָרַע וַאֲכַלְתֶּם לַחְמְכֶם לָשֹׂבַע וִישַׁבְתֶּם
and-you-will-live to-satisfaction food-of-you and-you-will-eat planting

לָבֶטַח בְּאַרְצְכֶם׃ וְנָתַתִּי שָׁלוֹם בָּאָרֶץ
in-the-land peace and-I-will-grant (6) in-land-of-you in-safety

וּשְׁכַבְתֶּם וְאֵין מַחֲרִיד וְהִשְׁבַּתִּי חַיָּה
beast and-I-will-remove making-afraid and-no-one and-you-will-lie-down

רָעָה מִן־ הָאָרֶץ וְחֶרֶב לֹא־ תַעֲבֹר בְּאַרְצְכֶם׃
through-country-of-you she-will-pass not and-sword the-land from savage

וּרְדַפְתֶּם אֶת־ אֹיְבֵיכֶם וְנָפְלוּ לִפְנֵיכֶם
before-you and-they-will-fall being-enemies-of-you *** and-you-will-pursue (7)

לֶחָרֶב וְרָדְפוּ מִכֶּם חֲמִשָּׁה מֵאָה וּמֵאָה
and-hundred hundred five from-you and-they-will-chase (8) by-the-sword

מִכֶּם רְבָבָה יִרְדֹּפוּ וְנָפְלוּ אֹיְבֵיכֶם
being-enemies-of-you and-they-will-fall they-will-chase ten-thousand from-you

לִפְנֵיכֶם לֶחָרֶב׃ וּפָנִיתִי אֲלֵיכֶם וְהִפְרֵיתִי
and-I-will-make-fruitful on-you and-I-will-look (9) by-the-sword before-you

אֶתְכֶם וְהִרְבֵּיתִי אֶתְכֶם וַהֲקִימֹתִי אֶת־ בְּרִיתִי אִתְּכֶם׃
with-you covenant-of-me *** and-I-will-keep you and-I-will-increase you

וַאֲכַלְתֶּם יָשָׁן נוֹשָׁן וְיָשָׁן מִפְּנֵי חָדָשׁ
new for-presence-of and-old being-old old-harvest and-you-will-eat (10)

תּוֹצִיאוּ׃ וְנָתַתִּי מִשְׁכָּנִי בְּתוֹכְכֶם וְלֹא־
and-not in-midst-of-you dwelling-of-me and-I-will-put (11) you-will-move-out

God.

Reward for Obedience

26 " 'Do not make idols or set up an image or a sacred stone for yourselves, and do not place a carved stone in your land to bow down before it. I am the LORD your God.

2" 'Observe my Sabbaths and have reverence for my sanctuary. I am the LORD.

3" 'If you follow my decrees and are careful to obey my commands,
4I will send you rain in its season, and the ground will yield its crops and the trees of the field their fruit.
5Your threshing will continue until grape harvest and the grape harvest will continue until planting, and you will eat all the food you want and live in safety in your land.

6" 'I will grant peace in the land, and you will lie down and no one will make you afraid. I will remove savage beasts from the land, and the sword will not pass through your country.
7You will pursue your enemies, and they will fall by the sword before you.
8Five of you will chase a hundred, and a hundred of you will chase ten thousand, and your enemies will fall by the sword before you.

9" 'I will look on you with favor and make you fruitful and increase your numbers, and I will keep my covenant with you.
10You will still be eating last year's harvest when you will have to move it out to make room for the new.
11I will put my dwelling place[m]

[m]11 Or *my tabernacle*

תִגְעַל נַפְשִׁי אֶתְכֶם׃ וְהִתְהַלַּכְתִּי בְּתוֹכְכֶם
in-midst-of-you and-I-will-walk (12) you spirit-of-me she-will-abhor

וְהָיִיתִי לָכֶם לֵאלֹהִים וְאַתֶּם תִּהְיוּ־ לִי לְעָם׃ אֲנִי
I (13) as-people to-me you-will-be and-you as-God to-you and-I-will-be

יְהוָה אֱלֹהֵיכֶם אֲשֶׁר הוֹצֵאתִי אֶתְכֶם מֵאֶרֶץ מִצְרַיִם מִהְיֹת לָהֶם
to-them from-to-be Egypt from-land-of you I-brought who God-of-you Yahweh

עֲבָדִים וָאֶשְׁבֹּר מֹטֹת עֻלְּכֶם וָאוֹלֵךְ אֶתְכֶם קוֹמְמִיּוּת׃
head-held-high you and-I-made-walk yoke-of-you bars-of and-I-broke slaves

וְאִם־ לֹא תִשְׁמְעוּ לִי וְלֹא תַעֲשׂוּ אֵת כָּל־
all-of *** you-carry-out and-not to-me you-listen not but-if (14)

הַמִּצְוֹת הָאֵלֶּה׃ וְאִם־ בְּחֻקֹּתַי תִּמְאָסוּ וְאִם אֶת־
*** and-if you-reject to-decrees-of-me and-if (15) the-these the-commands

מִשְׁפָּטַי תִּגְעַל נַפְשְׁכֶם לְבִלְתִּי עֲשׂוֹת אֶת־ כָּל־ מִצְוֹתַי
commands-of-me all-of *** to-carry-out not spirit-of-you she-abhors laws-of-me

לְהַפְרְכֶם אֶת־ בְּרִיתִי׃ אַף־ אֲנִי אֶעֱשֶׂה־ זֹּאת לָכֶם
to-you this I-will-do I then (16) covenant-of-me *** to-violate-you

וְהִפְקַדְתִּי עֲלֵיכֶם בֶּהָלָה אֶת־ הַשַּׁחֶפֶת וְאֶת־ הַקַּדַּחַת
the-fever and the-wasting-disease *** sudden-terror upon-you now-I-will-bring

מְכַלּוֹת עֵינַיִם וּמְדִיבֹת נָפֶשׁ וּזְרַעְתֶּם לָרִיק
in-vain and-you-will-plant life and-ones-draining eyes ones-destroying

זַרְעֲכֶם וַאֲכָלֻהוּ אֹיְבֵיכֶם׃ וְנָתַתִּי
and-I-will-set (17) being-enemies-of-you for-they-will-eat-him seed-of-you

פָנַי בָּכֶם וְנִגַּפְתֶּם לִפְנֵי אֹיְבֵיכֶם
being-enemies-of-you by so-you-will-be-defeated against-you faces-of-me

וְרָדוּ בָכֶם שֹׂנְאֵיכֶם וְנַסְתֶּם וְאֵין־
when-he-is-not and-you-will-flee ones-hating-you over-you and-they-will-rule

רֹדֵף אֶתְכֶם׃ וְאִם־ עַד־ אֵלֶּה לֹא תִשְׁמְעוּ לִי
to-me you-will-listen not these after and-if (18) you one-pursuing

וְיָסַפְתִּי לְיַסְּרָה אֶתְכֶם שֶׁבַע עַל־ חַטֹּאתֵיכֶם׃
sins-of-you for seven-time you to-punish then-I-will-continue

וְשָׁבַרְתִּי אֶת־ גְּאוֹן עֻזְּכֶם וְנָתַתִּי אֶת־
*** and-I-will-make stubborn-of-you pride-of *** and-I-will-break-down (19)

שְׁמֵיכֶם כַּבַּרְזֶל וְאֶת־ אַרְצְכֶם כַּנְּחֻשָׁה׃
like-the-bronze ground-of-you and like-the-iron skies-of-you

וְתַם לָרִיק כֹּחֲכֶם וְלֹא־ תִתֵּן
she-will-yield for-not strength-of-you in-vain and-he-will-be-spent (20)

אַרְצְכֶם אֶת־ יְבוּלָהּ וְעֵץ הָאָרֶץ לֹא יִתֵּן פִּרְיוֹ׃
fruit-of-him he-will-yield not the-land and-tree-of crop-of-her *** soil-of-you

among you, and I will not abhor you. [12]I will walk among
you and be your God, and you
will be my people. [13]I am the
LORD your God, who brought
you out of Egypt so that you
would no longer be slaves to
the Egyptians; I broke the bars
of your yoke and enabled you
to walk with heads held high.

Punishment for Disobedience

[14]" 'But if you will not listen
to me and carry out all these
commands, [15]and if you reject
my decrees and abhor my laws
and fail to carry out all my
commands and so violate my
covenant, [16]then I will do this
to you: I will bring upon you
sudden terror, wasting diseases and fever that will destroy your sight and drain
away your life. You will plant
seed in vain, because your
enemies will eat it. [17]I will set
my face against you so that
you will be defeated by your
enemies; those who hate you
will rule over you, and you
will flee even when no one is
pursuing you.

[18]" 'If after all this you will
not listen to me, I will punish
you for your sins seven times
over. [19]I will break down your
stubborn pride and make the
sky above you like iron and
the ground beneath you like
bronze. [20]Your strength will be
spent in vain, because your
soil will not yield its crops, nor
will the trees of the land yield
their fruit.

וְאִם־ תֵּלְכוּ עִמִּי קֶרִי וְלֹא תֹאבוּ לִשְׁמֹעַ לִי
to-me to-listen you-will and-not hostile toward-me you-remain and-if (21)

וְיָסַפְתִּי עֲלֵיכֶם מַכָּה שֶׁבַע כְּחַטֹּאתֵיכֶם׃
according-to-sins-of-you seven-time affliction on-you then-I-will-multiply

וְהִשְׁלַחְתִּי בָכֶם אֶת־ חַיַּת הַשָּׂדֶה
the-field animal-of *** against-you and-I-will-send (22)

וְשִׁכְּלָה אֶתְכֶם וְהִכְרִיתָה אֶת־ בְּהֶמְתְּכֶם
cattle-of-you *** and-she-will-destroy you and-she-will-make-childless

וְהִמְעִיטָה אֶתְכֶם וְנָשַׁמּוּ דַּרְכֵיכֶם׃ וְאִם־
and-if (23) roads-of-you that-they-will-be-deserted you and-she-will-make-few

בְּאֵלֶּה לֹא תִוָּסְרוּ לִי וַהֲלַכְתֶּם עִמִּי קֶרִי׃
hostile toward-me and-you-continue to-me you-are-corrected not after-these

וְהָלַכְתִּי אַף־ אֲנִי עִמָּכֶם בְּקֶרִי וְהִכֵּיתִי
and-I-will-afflict with-hostility against-you I indeed then-I-will-come (24)

אֶתְכֶם גַּם־אָנִי שֶׁבַע עַל־ חַטֹּאתֵיכֶם׃ וְהֵבֵאתִי עֲלֵיכֶם חֶרֶב
sword upon-you and-I-will-bring (25) sins-of-you for seven-time I also you

נֹקֶמֶת נְקַם־ בְּרִית וְנֶאֱסַפְתֶּם אֶל־ עָרֵיכֶם
cities-of-you into when-you-withdraw covenant vengeance-of avenging

וְשִׁלַּחְתִּי דֶבֶר בְּתוֹכְכֶם וְנִתַּתֶּם בְּיַד־
into-hand-of and-you-will-be-given in-midst-of-you plague then-I-will-send

אוֹיֵב׃ בְּשִׁבְרִי לָכֶם מַטֵּה־ לֶחֶם
bread supply-of from-you when-to-cut-off-me (26) being-enemy

וְאָפוּ עֶשֶׂר נָשִׁים לַחְמְכֶם בְּתַנּוּר אֶחָד וְהֵשִׁיבוּ
and-they-will-dole-out one in-oven bread-of-you women ten then-they-will-bake

לַחְמְכֶם בַּמִּשְׁקָל וַאֲכַלְתֶּם וְלֹא תִשְׂבָּעוּ׃
you-will-be-satisfied but-not and-you-will-eat by-the-weight bread-of-you

וְאִם־ בְּזֹאת לֹא תִשְׁמְעוּ לִי וַהֲלַכְתֶּם עִמִּי
toward-me and-you-continue to-me you-listen not after-this and-if (27)

בְּקֶרִי׃ וְהָלַכְתִּי עִמָּכֶם בַּחֲמַת־ קֶרִי
hostility in-anger-of toward-you then-I-will-continue (28) in-hostility

וְיִסַּרְתִּי אֶתְכֶם אַף־ אָנִי שֶׁבַע עַל־ חַטֹּאתֵיכֶם׃
sins-of-you for seven-time I indeed you and-I-will-punish

וַאֲכַלְתֶּם בְּשַׂר בְּנֵיכֶם וּבְשַׂר בְּנֹתֵיכֶם
daughters-of-you and-flesh-of sons-of-you flesh-of and-you-will-eat (29)

תֹּאכֵלוּ׃ וְהִשְׁמַדְתִּי אֶת־ בָּמֹתֵיכֶם וְהִכְרַתִּי
and-I-will-cut high-places-of-you *** and-I-will-destroy (30) you-will-eat

אֶת־ חַמָּנֵיכֶם וְנָתַתִּי אֶת־ פִּגְרֵיכֶם עַל־
on dead-bodies-of-you *** and-I-will-pile incense-altars-of-you ***

[21]" 'If you remain hostile toward me and refuse to listen to me, I will multiply your afflictions seven times over, as your sins deserve.
[22]I will send wild animals against you, and they will rob you of your children, destroy your cattle and make you so few in number that your roads will be deserted.

[23]" 'If in spite of these things you do not accept my correction but continue to be hostile toward me,
[24]I myself will be hostile toward you and will afflict you for your sins seven times over.
[25]And I will bring the sword upon you to avenge the breaking of the covenant. When you withdraw into your cities, I will send a plague among you, and you will be given into enemy hands.
[26]When I cut off your supply of bread, ten women will be able to bake your bread in one oven, and they will dole out the bread by weight. You will eat, but you will not be satisfied.

[27]" 'If in spite of this you still do not listen to me but continue to be hostile toward me,
[28]then in my anger I will be hostile toward you, and I myself will punish you for your sins seven times over.
[29]You will eat the flesh of your sons and the flesh of your daughters.
[30]I will destroy your high places, cut down your incense altars and pile your dead bodies on the lifeless forms of

פִּגְרֵי גִּלּוּלֵיכֶם וְגָעֲלָה נַפְשִׁי אֶתְכֶם׃
you spirit-of-me and-she-will-abhor idols-of-you lifeless-forms-of

(31) וְנָתַתִּי אֶת־ עָרֵיכֶם חָרְבָּה וַהֲשִׁמּוֹתִי אֶת־
*** and-I-will-lay-waste ruin cities-of-you *** and-I-will-turn (31)

מִקְדְּשֵׁיכֶם וְלֹא אָרִיחַ בְּרֵיחַ נִיחֹחֲכֶם׃
pleasant-of-you in-aroma-of I-will-delight and-not sanctuaries-of-you

(32) וַהֲשִׁמֹּתִי אֲנִי אֶת־ הָאָרֶץ וְשָׁמְמוּ עָלֶיהָ
at-her so-they-will-be-appalled the-land *** I and-I-will-lay-waste (32)

אֹיְבֵיכֶם הַיֹּשְׁבִים בָּהּ׃ (33) וְאֶתְכֶם אֱזָרֶה
I-will-scatter and-you (33) in-her the-ones-living being-enemies-of-you

בַגּוֹיִם וַהֲרִיקֹתִי אַחֲרֵיכֶם חָרֶב וְהָיְתָה אַרְצְכֶם
land-of-you and-she-will-be sword after-you and-I-will-draw among-the-nations

שְׁמָמָה וְעָרֵיכֶם יִהְיוּ חָרְבָּה׃ (34) אָז תִּרְצֶה הָאָרֶץ
the-land she-will-enjoy then (34) ruin they-will-be and-cities-of-you waste

אֶת־ שַׁבְּתֹתֶיהָ כֹּל יְמֵי הֳשַׁמָּה וְאַתֶּם בְּאֶרֶץ
in-country-of and-you the-desolation days-of all-of sabbaths-of-her ***

אֹיְבֵיכֶם אָז תִּשְׁבַּת הָאָרֶץ וְהִרְצָת אֶת־
*** and-she-will-enjoy the-land she-will-rest then being-enemies-of-you

שַׁבְּתֹתֶיהָ׃ (35) כָּל־ יְמֵי הָשַּׁמָּה תִּשְׁבֹּת אֵת
*** she-will-have-rest the-desolation days-of all-of (35) sabbaths-of-her

אֲשֶׁר לֹא־ שָׁבְתָה בְּשַׁבְּתֹתֵיכֶם בְּשִׁבְתְּכֶם עָלֶיהָ׃
on-her when-to-live-you during-sabbaths-of-you she-rested not that

(36) וְהַנִּשְׁאָרִים בָּכֶם וְהֵבֵאתִי מֹרֶךְ בִּלְבָבָם
in-heart-of-them fear then-I-will-bring from-you and-the-ones-being-left (36)

בְּאַרְצֹת אֹיְבֵיהֶם וְרָדַף אֹתָם קוֹל
sound-of them and-he-will-put-to-flight being-enemies-of-them in-lands-of

עָלֶה נִדָּף וְנָסוּ מְנֻסַת־ חֶרֶב וְנָפְלוּ
and-they-will-fall sword flight-of and-they-will-run being-blown leaf

וְאֵין רֹדֵף׃ (37) וְכָשְׁלוּ אִישׁ־ בְּאָחִיו
over-other-of-him one and-they-will-stumble (37) pursuing but-he-is-not

כְּמִפְּנֵי־ חֶרֶב וְרֹדֵף אָיִן וְלֹא־ תִהְיֶה לָכֶם
for-you she-will-be so-not he-is-not but-pursuing sword as-from-edges-of

תְּקוּמָה לִפְנֵי אֹיְבֵיכֶם׃ (38) וַאֲבַדְתֶּם
and-you-will-perish (38) being-enemies-of-you before standing-place

בַּגּוֹיִם וְאָכְלָה אֶתְכֶם אֶרֶץ אֹיְבֵיכֶם׃
being-enemies-of-you land-of you and-she-will-devour among-the-nations

(39) וְהַנִּשְׁאָרִים בָּכֶם יִמַּקּוּ בַּעֲוֹנָם
for-sin-of-them they-will-waste-away from-you and-the-ones-being-left (39)

your idols, and I will abhor
you. 31I will turn your cities
into ruins and lay waste your
sanctuaries, and I will take no
delight in the pleasing aroma
of your offerings. 32I will lay
waste the land, so that your
enemies who live there will be
appalled. 33I will scatter you
among the nations and will
draw out my sword and pursue you. Your land will be laid
waste, and your cities will lie
in ruins. 34Then the land will
enjoy its sabbath years all the
time that it lies desolate and
you are in the country of your
enemies; then the land will
rest and enjoy its sabbaths.
35All the time that it lies desolate, the land will have the rest
it did not have during the sabbaths you lived in it.
36" 'As for those of you who
are left, I will make their
hearts so fearful in the lands of
their enemies that the sound
of a wind-blown leaf will put
them to flight. They will run as
though fleeing from the
sword, and they will fall, even
though no one is pursuing
them. 37They will stumble over
one another as though fleeing
from the sword, even though
no one is pursuing them. So
you will not be able to stand
before your enemies. 38You
will perish among the nations;
the land of your enemies will
devour you. 39Those of you
who are left will waste away

בְּאַרְצֹת אֹיְבֵיכֶם וְאַף בַּעֲוֺנֹת אֲבֹתָם
fathers-of-them for-sins-of and-also being-enemies-of-you in-lands-of

אִתָּם יִמָּקּוּ׃ וְהִתְוַדּוּ אֶת־ עֲוֺנָם וְאֶת־
and sin-of-them *** if-they-confess (40) they-will-waste-away with-them

עֲוֺן אֲבֹתָם בְּמַעֲלָם אֲשֶׁר מָעֲלוּ־
they-were-treacherous when for-treachery-of-them fathers-of-them sin-of

בִי וְאַף אֲשֶׁר־ הָלְכוּ עִמִּי בְּקֶרִי׃ אַף־
then (41) with-hostility toward-me they-continued when and-also against-me

אֲנִי אֵלֵךְ עִמָּם בְּקֶרִי וְהֵבֵאתִי אֹתָם בְּאֶרֶץ
into-land-of them so-I-sent with-hostility toward-them I-continued I

אֹיְבֵיהֶם אוֹ־ אָז יִכָּנַע לְבָבָם הֶעָרֵל
the-uncircumcised heart-of-them he-is-humbled when then being-enemies-of-them

וְאָז יִרְצוּ אֶת־ עֲוֺנָם׃ וְזָכַרְתִּי אֶת־ בְּרִיתִי
covenant-of-me *** then-I-will-remember (42) sin-of-them *** they-pay and-when

יַעֲקוֹב וְאַף אֶת־ בְּרִיתִי יִצְחָק וְאַף אֶת־ בְּרִיתִי אַבְרָהָם
Abraham covenant-of-me *** and-also Isaac covenant-of-me *** and-also Jacob

אֶזְכֹּר וְהָאָרֶץ אֶזְכֹּר׃ וְהָאָרֶץ
for-the-land (43) I-will-remember and-the-land I-will-remember

תֵּעָזֵב מֵהֶם וְתִרֶץ אֶת־ שַׁבְּתֹתֶיהָ
sabbaths-of-her *** and-she-will-enjoy by-them she-will-be-deserted

בָּהְשַׁמָּה מֵהֶם וְהֵם יִרְצוּ אֶת־ עֲוֺנָם
sin-of-them *** they-will-pay and-they without-them when-to-be-desolate

יַעַן וּבְיַעַן בְּמִשְׁפָּטַי מָאָסוּ וְאֶת־ חֻקֹּתַי גָּעֲלָה
she-abhored decrees-of-me and they-rejected to-laws-of-me yes-because because

נַפְשָׁם׃ וְאַף־ גַּם־ זֹאת בִּהְיוֹתָם בְּאֶרֶץ
in-land-of when-to-be-them this in-spite-of and-yet (44) spirit-of-them

אֹיְבֵיהֶם לֹא־ מְאַסְתִּים וְלֹא־ גְעַלְתִּים
I-will-abhor-them or-not I-will-reject-them not being-enemies-of-them

לְכַלֹּתָם לְהָפֵר בְּרִיתִי אִתָּם כִּי אֲנִי יְהוָה אֱלֹהֵיהֶם׃
God-of-them Yahweh I for with-them covenant-of-me to-break to-destroy-them

וְזָכַרְתִּי לָהֶם בְּרִית רִאשֹׁנִים אֲשֶׁר הוֹצֵאתִי־ אֹתָם
them I-brought whom ancestors covenant-of for-them but-I-will-remember (45)

מֵאֶרֶץ מִצְרַיִם לְעֵינֵי הַגּוֹיִם לִהְיוֹת לָהֶם לֵאלֹהִים אֲנִי יְהוָה׃
Yahweh I as-God to-them to-be the-nations in-eyes-of Egypt from-land-of

אֵלֶּה הַחֻקִּים וְהַמִּשְׁפָּטִים וְהַתּוֹרֹת אֲשֶׁר נָתַן
he-established that and-the-regulations and-the-laws the-decrees these (46)

יְהוָה בֵּינוֹ וּבֵין בְּנֵי יִשְׂרָאֵל בְּהַר סִינַי בְּיַד־
by-hand-of Sinai on-Mount-of Israel sons-of and-between between-him Yahweh

in the lands of their enemies
because of their sins; also because of their fathers' sins
they will waste away.
40" 'But if they will confess
their sins and the sins of their
fathers—their treachery
against me and their hostility
toward me, 41which made me
hostile toward them so that I
sent them into the land of
their enemies—then when
their uncircumcised hearts are
humbled and they pay for
their sin, 42I will remember my
covenant with Jacob and my
covenant with Isaac and my
covenant with Abraham, and
I will remember the land. 43For
the land will be deserted by
them and will enjoy its sabbaths while it lies desolate
without them. They will pay
for their sins because they rejected my laws and abhorred
my decrees. 44Yet in spite of
this, when they are in the land
of their enemies, I will not reject them or abhor them so as
to destroy them completely,
breaking my covenant with
them. I am the LORD their God.
45But for their sake I will
remember the covenant with
their ancestors whom I
brought out of Egypt in the
sight of the nations to be their
God. I am the LORD.' "
46These are the decrees, the
laws and the regulations that
the LORD established on
Mount Sinai between himself
and the Israelites through
Moses.

מֹשֶׁה׃ וַיְדַבֵּר יְהוָה אֶל־מֹשֶׁה לֵּאמֹר׃ דַּבֵּר אֶל־בְּנֵי
sons-of to speak! (2) to-say Moses to Yahweh and-he-spoke (27:1) Moses

יִשְׂרָאֵל וְאָמַרְתָּ אֲלֵהֶם אִישׁ כִּי יַפְלִא נֶדֶר בְּעֶרְכְּךָ נְפָשֹׁת
persons by-value-of-you vow he-makes who anyone to-them and-you-say Israel

לַיהוָה׃ וְהָיָה עֶרְכְּךָ הַזָּכָר מִבֶּן עֶשְׂרִים שָׁנָה
year twenty from-son-of the-male value-of-you then-he-must-be (3) to-Yahweh

וְעַד בֶּן־שִׁשִּׁים שָׁנָה וְהָיָה עֶרְכְּךָ חֲמִשִּׁים שֶׁקֶל כֶּסֶף
silver shekel-of fifty value-of-you then-he-must-be year sixty son-of even-to

בְּשֶׁקֶל הַקֹּדֶשׁ׃ וְאִם־נְקֵבָה הִוא וְהָיָה עֶרְכְּךָ
value-of-you then-he-must-be she female and-if (4) the-sanctuary by-shekel-of

שְׁלֹשִׁים שָׁקֶל׃ וְאִם מִבֶּן־חָמֵשׁ שָׁנִים וְעַד בֶּן־עֶשְׂרִים שָׁנָה
year twenty son-of even-to years five from-son-of and-if (5) shekel thirty

וְהָיָה עֶרְכְּךָ הַזָּכָר עֶשְׂרִים שְׁקָלִים וְלַנְּקֵבָה עֲשֶׂרֶת
ten and-for-the-female shekels twenty the-male value-of-you then-he-must-be

שְׁקָלִים׃ וְאִם מִבֶּן־חֹדֶשׁ וְעַד בֶּן־חָמֵשׁ שָׁנִים וְהָיָה
he-must-be years five son-of even-to month from-son-of and-if (6) shekels

עֶרְכְּךָ הַזָּכָר חֲמִשָּׁה שְׁקָלִים כֶּסֶף וְלַנְּקֵבָה עֶרְכְּךָ
value-of-you and-for-the-female silver shekels five the-male value-of-you

שְׁלֹשֶׁת שְׁקָלִים כָּסֶף׃ וְאִם מִבֶּן־שִׁשִּׁים שָׁנָה וָמַעְלָה אִם־זָכָר
male if or-more year sixty from-son-of and-if (7) silver shekels three

וְהָיָה עֶרְכְּךָ חֲמִשָּׁה עָשָׂר שָׁקֶל וְלַנְּקֵבָה עֲשָׂרָה שְׁקָלִים׃
shekels ten and-for-the-female shekel ten five value-of-you he-must-be

וְאִם־מָךְ הוּא מֵעֶרְכֶּךָ וְהֶעֱמִידוֹ לִפְנֵי
to then-he-must-present-him than-value-of-you he being-poor and-if (8)

הַכֹּהֵן וְהֶעֱרִיךְ אֹתוֹ הַכֹּהֵן עַל־פִּי אֲשֶׁר תַּשִּׂיג
she-can-afford that amount for the-priest him and-he-will-set-value the-priest

יַד הַנֹּדֵר יַעֲרִיכֶנּוּ הַכֹּהֵן׃ וְאִם־
and-if (9) the-priest he-will-set-value-of-him the-one-making-vow hand-of

בְּהֵמָה אֲשֶׁר יַקְרִיבוּ מִמֶּנָּה קָרְבָּן לַיהוָה כֹּל אֲשֶׁר יִתֵּן
he-is-given that anything to-Yahweh offering from-her they-vowed that animal

מִמֶּנּוּ לַיהוָה יִהְיֶה־קֹּדֶשׁ׃ לֹא יַחֲלִיפֶנּוּ וְלֹא־
or-not he-must-exchange-him not (10) holy he-becomes to-Yahweh from-him

יָמִיר אֹתוֹ טוֹב בְּרָע אוֹ־רַע בְּטוֹב וְאִם־הָמֵר
to-substitute and-if for-good bad or for-bad good him he-must-substitute

יָמִיר בְּהֵמָה בִּבְהֵמָה וְהָיָה־הוּא וּתְמוּרָתוֹ
and-substitute-of-him he then-he-becomes for-animal animal he-substitutes

יִהְיֶה־קֹּדֶשׁ׃ וְאִם כָּל־בְּהֵמָה טְמֵאָה אֲשֶׁר לֹא־יַקְרִיבוּ
they-should-present not that unclean animal any-of and-if (11) holy he-becomes

Redeeming What Is the LORD's

27 The LORD said to
Moses, [2]"Speak to the
Israelites and say to them: 'If
anyone makes a special vow to
dedicate persons to the LORD
by giving equivalent values,
[3]set the value of a male between the ages of twenty and
sixty at fifty shekels[n] of silver,
according to the sanctuary
shekel[o]; [4]and if it is a female,
set her value at thirty shekels.[p]
[5]If it is a person between the
ages of five and twenty, set the
value of a male at twenty
shekels[q] and of a female at ten
shekels.[r] [6]If it is a person between one month and five
years, set the value of a male at
five shekels[s] of silver and that
of a female at three shekels[t] of
silver. [7]If it is a person sixty
years old or more, set the value
of a male at fifteen shekels[u]
and of a female at ten shekels.
[8]If anyone making the vow is
too poor to pay the specified
amount, he is to present the
person to the priest, who will
set the value for him according
to what the man making the
vow can afford.

[9]" 'If what he vowed is an
animal that is acceptable as an
offering to the LORD, such an
animal given to the LORD
becomes holy. [10]He must not
exchange it or substitute a
good one for a bad one, or a
bad one for a good one; if he
should substitute one animal
for another, both it and the
substitute become holy. [11]If
what he vowed is a ceremonially unclean animal—one that
is not acceptable as an offering

[n]3 That is, about 1 1/4 pounds (about 0.6 kilogram); also in verse 16
[o]3 That is, about 2/5 ounce (about 11.5 grams); also in verse 25
[p]4 That is, about 12 ounces (about 0.3 kilogram)
[q]5 That is, about 8 ounces (about 0.2 kilogram)
[r]5 That is, about 4 ounces (about 110 grams); also in verse 7
[s]6 That is, about 2 ounces (about 55 grams)
[t]6 That is, about 1 1/4 ounces (about 35 grams)
[u]7 That is, about 6 ounces (about 170 grams)

מִמֶּנָּה קָרְבָּן לַיהוָה וְהֶעֱמִיד אֶת־ הַבְּהֵמָה לִפְנֵי הַכֹּהֵן׃
the-priest to the-animal *** then-he-must-present to-Yahweh offering from-her

וְהֶעֱרִיךְ הַכֹּהֵן אֹתָהּ בֵּין טוֹב וּבֵין רָע
bad or-as good as her the-priest then-he-will-judge-quality (12)

כְּעֶרְכְּךָ הַכֹּהֵן כֵּן יִהְיֶה׃ וְאִם־ גָּאֹל
to-redeem and-if (13) he-will-be that the-priest as-value-of-you

יִגְאָלֶנָּה וְיָסַף חֲמִישִׁתוֹ עַל־ עֶרְכֶּךָ׃ וְאִישׁ
and-man (14) value-of-you to fifth-of-him then-he-must-add he-redeems-her

כִּי־ יַקְדִּשׁ אֶת־ בֵּיתוֹ קֹדֶשׁ לַיהוָה וְהֶעֱרִיכוֹ
then-he-must-evaluate-him to-Yahweh holy house-of-him *** he-dedicates if

הַכֹּהֵן בֵּין טוֹב וּבֵין רָע כַּאֲשֶׁר יַעֲרִיךְ אֹתוֹ הַכֹּהֵן כֵּן
so the-priest him he-sets-value just-as bad or-as good as the-priest

יָקוּם׃ וְאִם־ הַמַּקְדִּישׁ יִגְאַל אֶת־ בֵּיתוֹ
house-of-him *** he-redeems the-one-dedicating and-if (15) he-will-remain

וְיָסַף חֲמִישִׁית כֶּסֶף־ עֶרְכְּךָ עָלָיו וְהָיָה
then-he-will-become to-him value-of-you price-of fifth then-he-must-add

לוֹ׃ וְאִם | מִשְּׂדֵה אֲחֻזָּתוֹ יַקְדִּישׁ אִישׁ
man he-dedicates family-property-of-him from-land-of and-if (16) to-him

לַיהוָה וְהָיָה עֶרְכְּךָ לְפִי זַרְעוֹ זֶרַע
seed-of seed-of-him as-amount-of value-of-you then-he-must-be to-Yahweh

חֹמֶר שְׂעֹרִים בַּחֲמִשִּׁים שֶׁקֶל כָּסֶף׃ אִם־ מִשְּׁנַת הַיֹּבֵל
the-Jubilee in-Year-of if (17) silver shekel-of for-fifty barleys homer-of

יַקְדִּישׁ שָׂדֵהוּ כְּעֶרְכְּךָ יָקוּם׃ וְאִם־ אַחַר
after but-if (18) he-remains at-value-of-you field-of-him he-dedicates

הַיֹּבֵל יַקְדִּישׁ שָׂדֵהוּ וְחִשַּׁב־ לוֹ
for-him then-he-will-determine field-of-him he-dedicates the-Jubilee

הַכֹּהֵן אֶת־ הַכֶּסֶף עַל־ פִּי הַשָּׁנִים הַנּוֹתָרֹת עַד
until the-ones-remaining the-years number-of by the-price *** the-priest

שְׁנַת הַיֹּבֵל וְנִגְרַע מֵעֶרְכֶּךָ׃ וְאִם־
and-if (19) from-value-of-you and-he-will-be-reduced the-Jubilee Year-of

גָּאֹל יִגְאַל אֶת־ הַשָּׂדֶה הַמַּקְדִּישׁ אֹתוֹ וְיָסַף
then-he-must-add him the-one-dedicating the-field *** he-redeems to-redeem

חֲמִשִׁית כֶּסֶף־ עֶרְכְּךָ עָלָיו וְקָם לוֹ׃ וְאִם־
but-if (20) to-him and-he-will-be-again to-him value-of-you price-of fifth

לֹא יִגְאַל אֶת־ הַשָּׂדֶה וְאִם־ מָכַר אֶת־ הַשָּׂדֶה לְאִישׁ אַחֵר
else to-someone the-field *** he-sold or-if the-field *** he-redeems not

לֹא יִגָּאֵל עוֹד׃ וְהָיָה הַשָּׂדֶה
the-field and-he-will-become (21) ever he-can-be-redeemed not

to the LORD—the animal must
be presented to the priest,
[12]who will judge its quality as
good or bad. Whatever value
the priest then sets, that is
what it will be. [13]If the owner
wishes to redeem the animal,
he must add a fifth to its value.
[14]" 'If a man dedicates his
house as something holy to
the LORD, the priest will judge
its quality as good or bad.
Whatever value the priest
then sets, so it will remain. [15]If
the man who dedicates his
house redeems it, he must add
a fifth to its value, and the
house will again become his.
[16]" 'If a man dedicates to the
LORD part of his family land,
its value is to be set according
to the amount of seed required
for it—fifty shekels of silver to
a homer[v] of barley seed. [17]If he
dedicates his field during the
Year of Jubilee, the value that
has been set remains. [18]But if
he dedicates his field after the
Jubilee, the priest will determine the value according to
the number of years that remain until the next Year of Jubilee, and its set value will be
reduced. [19]If the man who
dedicates the field wishes to
redeem it, he must add a fifth
to its value, and the field will
again become his. [20]If, however, he does not redeem the
field, or if he has sold it to
someone else, it can never be
redeemed. [21]When the field is

[v]*16* That is, probably about 6 bushels (about 220 liters)

בְּצֵאתוֹ בַיֹּבֵל קֹדֶשׁ לַיהוָה כִּשְׂדֵה הַחֵרֶם

the-devotion like-field-of to-Yahweh holy in-the-Jubilee when-to-go-out-him

לַכֹּהֵן תִּהְיֶה אֲחֻזָּתוֹ׃ (22) וְאִם אֶת־ שְׂדֵה

field-of *** and-if (22) property-of-him she-will-become for-the-priest

מִקְנָתוֹ אֲשֶׁר לֹא מִשְּׂדֵה אֲחֻזָּתוֹ יַקְדִּישׁ

he-dedicates family-property-of-him from-land-of not that purchase-of-him

לַיהוָה׃ (23) וְחִשַּׁב־ לוֹ הַכֹּהֵן אֵת מִכְסַת

price-of *** the-priest for-him then-he-will-determine (23) to-Yahweh

הָעֶרְכְּךָ עַד שְׁנַת הַיֹּבֵל וְנָתַן אֶת־ הָעֶרְכְּךָ

the-value-of-you *** and-he-must-pay the-Jubilee Year-of to the-value-of-you

בַּיּוֹם הַהוּא קֹדֶשׁ לַיהוָה׃ (24) בִּשְׁנַת הַיּוֹבֵל יָשׁוּב

he-will-revert the-Jubilee in-Year-of (24) to-Yahweh holy the-that on-the-day

הַשָּׂדֶה לַאֲשֶׁר קָנָהוּ מֵאִתּוֹ לַאֲשֶׁר־ לוֹ אֲחֻזַּת

possession-of to-him to-whom from-him he-bought-him to-whom the-field

הָאָרֶץ׃ (25) וְכָל־ עֶרְכְּךָ יִהְיֶה בְּשֶׁקֶל הַקֹּדֶשׁ

the-sanctuary by-shekel-of he-must-be value-of-you and-every-of (25) the-land

עֶשְׂרִים גֵּרָה יִהְיֶה הַשָּׁקֶל׃ (26) אַךְ־ בְּכוֹר אֲשֶׁר־ יְבֻכַּר

he-belongs that firstborn however (26) the-shekel he-must-be gerah twenty

לַיהוָה בִּבְהֵמָה לֹא־ יַקְדִּישׁ אִישׁ אֹתוֹ אִם־ שׁוֹר אִם־ שֶׂה

sheep or cow whether him anyone he-may-dedicate not of-animal to-Yahweh

לַיהוָה הוּא׃ (27) וְאִם בַּבְּהֵמָה הַטְּמֵאָה וּפָדָה

then-he-may-buy-back the-unclean of-the-animal now-if (27) he to-Yahweh

בְעֶרְכֶּךָ וְיָסַף חֲמִשִׁתוֹ עָלָיו וְאִם־ לֹא יִגָּאֵל

he-is-redeemed not but-if to-him fifth-of-him and-he-must-add at-value-of-you

וְנִמְכַּר בְּעֶרְכֶּךָ׃ (28) אַךְ־ כָּל־ חֵרֶם אֲשֶׁר

that devoted any-of but (28) at-value-of-you then-he-must-be-sold

יַחֲרִם אִישׁ לַיהוָה מִכָּל־ אֲשֶׁר־ לוֹ מֵאָדָם וּבְהֵמָה

or-animal whether-man to-him that from-anything to-Yahweh man he-devoted

וּמִשְּׂדֵה אֲחֻזָּתוֹ לֹא יִמָּכֵר וְלֹא

or not he-may-be-sold not family property of him or-from-land-of

יִגָּאֵל כָּל־ חֵרֶם קֹדֶשׁ־ קָדָשִׁים הוּא לַיהוָה׃

to-Yahweh he holy-things most-holy-of devoted every-of he-may-be-redeemed

(29) כָּל־ חֵרֶם אֲשֶׁר יָחֳרַם מִן הָאָדָם לֹא יִפָּדֶה

he-may-be-ransomed not the-man from he-was-devoted that devoted any-of (29)

מוֹת יוּמָת׃ (30) וְכָל־ מַעְשַׂר הָאָרֶץ מִזֶּרַע

whether-grain-of the-land tithe-of and-every-of (30) he-must-die to-die

הָאָרֶץ מִפְּרִי הָעֵץ לַיהוָה הוּא קֹדֶשׁ לַיהוָה׃ (31) וְאִם־

and-if (31) to-Yahweh holy he to-Yahweh the-tree or-fruit-of the-soil

released in the Jubilee, it will become holy, like a field devoted to the LORD; it will become the property of the priests.[w]

22" 'If a man dedicates to the LORD a field he has bought, which is not part of his family land, 23the priest will determine its value up to the Year of Jubilee, and the man must pay its value on that day as something holy to the LORD. 24In the Year of Jubilee the field will revert to the person from whom he bought it, the one whose land it was. 25Every value is to be set according to the sanctuary shekel, twenty gerahs to the shekel.

26" 'No one, however, may dedicate the firstborn of an animal, since the firstborn already belongs to the LORD; whether a cow[x] or a sheep, it is the LORD's. 27If it is one of the unclean animals, he may buy it back at its set value, adding a fifth of the value to it. If he does not redeem it, it is to be sold at its set value.

28" 'But nothing that a man owns and devotes[y] to the LORD—whether man or animal or family land—may be sold or redeemed; everything so devoted is most holy to the LORD.

29" 'No person devoted to destruction[z] may be ransomed; he must be put to death.

30" 'A tithe of everything from the land, whether grain from the soil or fruit from the trees, belongs to the LORD; it is

w21 Or *priest*

x26 The Hebrew word can include both male and female.

y28 The Hebrew term refers to the irrevocable giving over of things or persons to the LORD.

z29 The Hebrew term refers to the irrevocable giving over of things or persons to the LORD, often by totally destroying them.

גָּאֹל יִגְאַל אִישׁ מִמַּעַשְׂרוֹ חֲמִשִׁיתוֹ יֹסֵף עָלָיו׃

to-him he-must-add fifth-of-him from-tithe-of-him man he-redeems to-redeem

וְכָל־ מַעְשַׂר בָּקָר וָצֹאן כֹּל אֲשֶׁר־ יַעֲבֹר תַּחַת

under he-passes that everything and-flock herd tithe-of and-entire-of (32)

הַשָּׁבֶט הָעֲשִׂירִי יִהְיֶה־ קֹּדֶשׁ לַיהוָה׃ לֹא יְבַקֵּר בֵּין־

as he-must-pick-out not (33) to-Yahweh holy he-will-be the-tenth the-rod

טוֹב לָרַע וְלֹא יְמִירֶנּוּ וְאִם־ הָמֵר

to-substitute and-if he-must-substitute-him or-not from-the-bad good

יְמִירֶנּוּ וְהָיָה־ הוּא וּתְמוּרָתוֹ יִהְיֶה־ קֹּדֶשׁ

holy he-becomes and-substitute-of-him he then-he-becomes he-substitutes-him

לֹא יִגָּאֵל׃ אֵלֶּה הַמִּצְוֹת אֲשֶׁר צִוָּה יְהוָה אֶת־

*** Yahweh he-commanded that the-commands these (34) he-can-be-redeemed not

מֹשֶׁה אֶל־ בְּנֵי יִשְׂרָאֵל בְּהַר סִינָי׃

Sinai on-Mount-of Israel sons-of for Moses

holy to the LORD. 31If a man redeems any of his tithe, he
must add a fifth of the value to
it. 32The entire tithe of the herd
and flock—every tenth animal
that passes under the shepherd's rod—will be holy to the
LORD. 33He must not pick out
the good from the bad or make
any substitution. If he does
make a substitution, both the
animal and its substitute
become holy and cannot be redeemed.' "

34These are the commands
the LORD gave Moses on
Mount Sinai for the Israelites.

וַיְדַבֵּר יְהוָה אֶל־ מֹשֶׁה בְּמִדְבַּר סִינַי בְּאֹהֶל מוֹעֵד
Meeting in-Tent-of Sinai in-Desert-of Moses to Yahweh and-he-spoke (1:1)

בְּאֶחָד לַחֹדֶשׁ הַשֵּׁנִי בַּשָּׁנָה הַשֵּׁנִית לְצֵאתָם
after-to-come-out-them the-second in-the-year the-second of-the-month on-first

מֵאֶרֶץ מִצְרַיִם לֵאמֹר׃ שְׂאוּ אֶת־ רֹאשׁ כָּל־ עֲדַת
community-of whole-of census-of *** take! (2) to-say Egypt from-land-of

בְּנֵי־ יִשְׂרָאֵל לְמִשְׁפְּחֹתָם לְבֵית אֲבֹתָם בְּמִסְפַּר שֵׁמוֹת
names by-list-of fathers-of-them by-house-of by-clans-of-them Israel sons-of

כָּל־ זָכָר לְגֻלְגְּלֹתָם׃ מִבֶּן עֶשְׂרִים שָׁנָה וָמַעְלָה כָּל־
all-of or-more year twenty from-son-of (3) by-heads-of-them male every-of

יֹצֵא צָבָא בְּיִשְׂרָאֵל תִּפְקְדוּ אֹתָם לְצִבְאֹתָם אַתָּה
you by-divisions-of-them them you-must-number in-Israel army serving

וְאַהֲרֹן׃ וְאִתְּכֶם יִהְיוּ אִישׁ אִישׁ לַמַּטֶּה אִישׁ רֹאשׁ
head each from-the-tribe one man he-must-be and-with-you (4) and-Aaron

לְבֵית־ אֲבֹתָיו הוּא׃ וְאֵלֶּה שְׁמוֹת הָאֲנָשִׁים אֲשֶׁר
who the-men names-of now-these (5) he fathers-of-him of-house-of

יַעַמְדוּ אִתְּכֶם לִרְאוּבֵן אֱלִיצוּר בֶּן־ שְׁדֵיאוּר׃ לְשִׁמְעוֹן
from-Simeon (6) Shedeur son-of Elizur from-Reuben with-you they-will-assist

שְׁלֻמִיאֵל בֶּן־ צוּרִישַׁדָּי׃ לִיהוּדָה נַחְשׁוֹן בֶּן־ עַמִּינָדָב׃
Amminadab son-of Nahshon from-Judah (7) Zurishaddai son-of Shelumiel

לְיִשָּׂשכָר נְתַנְאֵל בֶּן־ צוּעָר׃ לִזְבוּלֻן אֱלִיאָב בֶּן־ חֵלֹן׃
Helon son-of Eliab from-Zebulun (9) Zuar son-of Nethanel from-Issachar (8)

לִבְנֵי יוֹסֵף לְאֶפְרַיִם אֱלִישָׁמָע בֶּן־ עַמִּיהוּד לִמְנַשֶּׁה
from-Manasseh Ammihud son-of Elishama from-Ephraim Joseph from-sons-of (10)

גַּמְלִיאֵל בֶּן־ פְּדָהצוּר׃ לְבִנְיָמִן אֲבִידָן בֶּן־ גִּדְעֹנִי׃
Gideoni son-of Abidan from-Benjamin (11) Pedahzur son-of Gamaliel

לְדָן אֲחִיעֶזֶר בֶּן־ עַמִּישַׁדָּי׃ לְאָשֵׁר פַּגְעִיאֵל בֶּן־ עָכְרָן׃
Ocran son-of Pagiel from-Asher (13) Ammishaddai son-of Ahiezer from-Dan (12)

לְגָד אֶלְיָסָף בֶּן־ דְּעוּאֵל׃ לְנַפְתָּלִי אֲחִירַע בֶּן־ עֵינָן׃
Enan son-of Ahira from-Naphtali (15) Deuel son-of Eliasaph from-Gad (14)

אֵלֶּה קְרִיאֵי הָעֵדָה נְשִׂיאֵי מַטּוֹת
tribes-of leaders-of the-community ones-being-appointed-of these (16)

אֲבוֹתָם רָאשֵׁי אַלְפֵי יִשְׂרָאֵל הֵם׃ וַיִּקַּח מֹשֶׁה
Moses and-he-took (17) they Israel clans-of heads-of ancestors-of-them

וְאַהֲרֹן אֵת הָאֲנָשִׁים הָאֵלֶּה אֲשֶׁר נִקְּבוּ בְּשֵׁמוֹת׃ וְאֵת
and (18) by-names they-were-given whom the-these the-men *** and-Aaron

כָּל־ הָעֵדָה הִקְהִילוּ בְּאֶחָד לַחֹדֶשׁ הַשֵּׁנִי
the-second of-the-month on-first they-called-together the-community whole-of

°16 ק קרואי

The Census

1 The LORD spoke to Moses
in the Tent of Meeting in
the Desert of Sinai on the first
day of the second month of
the second year after the Israelites came out of Egypt. He
said: 2"Take a census of the
whole Israelite community by
their clans and families, list-
ing every man by name, one
by one. 3You and Aaron are to
number by their divisions all
the men in Israel twenty years
old or more who are able to
serve in the army. 4One man
from each tribe, each the head
of his family, is to help you.
5These are the names of the
men who are to assist you:

from Reuben, Elizur son of
Shedeur;
6from Simeon, Shelumiel
son of Zurishaddai;
7from Judah, Nahshon son
of Amminadab;
8from Issachar, Nethanel
son of Zuar;
9from Zebulun, Eliab son of
Helon;
10from the sons of Joseph:
from Ephraim, Elishama
son of Ammihud;
from Manasseh, Gamali-
el son of Pedahzur;
11from Benjamin, Abidan
son of Gideoni;
12from Dan, Ahiezer son of
Ammishaddai;
13from Asher, Pagiel son of
Ocran;
14from Gad, Eliasaph son of
Deuel;
15from Naphtali, Ahira son
of Enan."

16These were the men ap-
pointed from the community,
the leaders of their ancestral
tribes. They were the heads of
the clans of Israel.
17Moses and Aaron took
these men whose names had
been given, 18and they called
the whole community to-
gether on the first day of the
second month. The people

וַיִּתְיַלְדוּ עַל־ מִשְׁפְּחֹתָם לְבֵית אֲבֹתָם
fathers-of-them by-house-of clans-of-them by and-they-indicated-ancestry

בְּמִסְפַּר שֵׁמוֹת מִבֶּן עֶשְׂרִים שָׁנָה וָמַעְלָה לְגֻלְגְּלֹתָם׃
by-heads-of-them or-more year twenty from-son-of names by-list-of

(19) כַּאֲשֶׁר צִוָּה יְהוָה אֶת־ מֹשֶׁה וַיִּפְקְדֵם בְּמִדְבַּר
in-Desert-of so-he-counted-them Moses *** Yahweh he-commanded just-as (19)

סִינָי׃ (20) וַיִּהְיוּ בְנֵי־ רְאוּבֵן בְּכֹר יִשְׂרָאֵל תּוֹלְדֹתָם
records-of-them Israel firstborn-of Reuben sons-of and-they-were (20) Sinai

לְמִשְׁפְּחֹתָם לְבֵית אֲבֹתָם בְּמִסְפַּר שֵׁמוֹת לְגֻלְגְּלֹתָם
by-heads-of-them names by-list-of fathers-of-them by-house-of by-clans-of-them

כָּל־ זָכָר מִבֶּן עֶשְׂרִים שָׁנָה וָמַעְלָה כֹּל יֹצֵא צָבָא׃
army serving all-of or-more year twenty from-son-of male every-of

(21) פְּקֻדֵיהֶם לְמַטֵּה רְאוּבֵן שִׁשָּׁה וְאַרְבָּעִים אֶלֶף וַחֲמֵשׁ
and-five-of thousand and-forty six Reuben from-tribe-of numberings-of-them (21)

מֵאוֹת׃ (22) לִבְנֵי שִׁמְעוֹן תּוֹלְדֹתָם לְמִשְׁפְּחֹתָם
by-clans-of-them records-of-them Simeon from-sons-of (22) hundreds

לְבֵית אֲבֹתָם פְּקֻדָיו בְּמִסְפַּר שֵׁמוֹת לְגֻלְגְּלֹתָם
by-heads-of-them names by-list-of countings-of-him fathers-of-them by-house-of

כָּל־ זָכָר מִבֶּן עֶשְׂרִים שָׁנָה וָמַעְלָה כֹּל יֹצֵא צָבָא׃
army serving all-of or-more year twenty from-son-of male every-of

(23) פְּקֻדֵיהֶם לְמַטֵּה שִׁמְעוֹן תִּשְׁעָה וַחֲמִשִּׁים אֶלֶף
thousand and-fifty nine Simeon from-tribe-of numberings-of-them (23)

וּשְׁלֹשׁ מֵאוֹת׃ (24) לִבְנֵי גָד תּוֹלְדֹתָם לְמִשְׁפְּחֹתָם
by-clans-of-them records-of-them Gad from-sons-of (24) hundreds and-three-of

לְבֵית אֲבֹתָם בְּמִסְפַּר שֵׁמוֹת מִבֶּן עֶשְׂרִים שָׁנָה וָמַעְלָה
or-more year twenty from-son-of names by-list-of fathers-of-them by-house-of

כֹּל יֹצֵא צָבָא׃ (25) פְּקֻדֵיהֶם לְמַטֵּה גָד חֲמִשָּׁה
five Gad from-tribe-of numberings-of-them (25) army serving all-of

וְאַרְבָּעִים אֶלֶף וְשֵׁשׁ מֵאוֹת וַחֲמִשִּׁים׃ (26) לִבְנֵי יְהוּדָה
Judah from-sons-of (26) and-fifty hundreds and-six thousand and-forty

תּוֹלְדֹתָם לְמִשְׁפְּחֹתָם לְבֵית אֲבֹתָם בְּמִסְפַּר
by-list-of fathers-of-them by-house-of by-clans-of-them records-of-them

שֵׁמֹת מִבֶּן עֶשְׂרִים שָׁנָה וָמַעְלָה כֹּל יֹצֵא צָבָא׃
army serving all-of or-more year twenty from-son-of names

(27) פְּקֻדֵיהֶם לְמַטֵּה יְהוּדָה אַרְבָּעָה וְשִׁבְעִים אֶלֶף
thousand and-seventy four Judah from-tribe-of numberings-of-them (27)

וְשֵׁשׁ מֵאוֹת׃ (28) לִבְנֵי יִשָּׂשכָר תּוֹלְדֹתָם לְמִשְׁפְּחֹתָם
by-clans-of-them records-of-them Issachar from-sons-of (28) hundreds and-six

indicated their ancestry by their clans and families, and the men twenty years old or more were listed by name, one by one, [19]as the LORD commanded Moses. And so he counted them in the Desert of Sinai:

[20]From the descendants of Reuben the firstborn son of Israel:

All the men twenty years old or more who were able to serve in the army were listed by name, one by one, according to the records of their clans and families. [21]The number from the tribe of Reuben was 46,500.

[22]From the descendants of Simeon:

All the men twenty years old or more who were able to serve in the army were counted and listed by name, one by one, according to the records of their clans and families. [23]The number from the tribe of Simeon was 59,300.

[24]From the descendants of Gad:

All the men twenty years old or more who were able to serve in the army were listed by name, according to the records of their clans and families. [25]The number from the tribe of Gad was 45,650.

[26]From the descendants of Judah:

All the men twenty years old or more who were able to serve in the army were listed by name, according to the records of their clans and families. [27]The number from the tribe of Judah was 74,600.

[28]From the descendants of Issachar:

לְבֵית אֲבֹתָם בְּמִסְפַּר שֵׁמֹת מִבֶּן עֶשְׂרִים שָׁנָה וָמַעְלָה
or-more year twenty from-son-of names by-list-of fathers-of-them by-house-of

כֹּל יֹצֵא צָבָא׃ פְּקֻדֵיהֶם לְמַטֵּה יִשָּׂשכָר אַרְבָּעָה
four Issachar from-tribe-of numberings-of-them (29) army serving all-of

וַחֲמִשִּׁים אֶלֶף וְאַרְבַּע מֵאוֹת׃ לִבְנֵי זְבוּלֻן תּוֹלְדֹתָם
records-of-them Zebulun from-sons-of (30) hundreds and-four thousand and-fifty

לְמִשְׁפְּחֹתָם לְבֵית אֲבֹתָם בְּמִסְפַּר שֵׁמֹת מִבֶּן
from-son-of names by-list-of fathers-of-them by-house-of by-clans-of-them

עֶשְׂרִים שָׁנָה וָמַעְלָה כֹּל יֹצֵא צָבָא׃ פְּקֻדֵיהֶם לְמַטֵּה
from-tribe-of numberings-of-them (31) army serving all-of or-more year twenty

זְבוּלֻן שִׁבְעָה וַחֲמִשִּׁים אֶלֶף וְאַרְבַּע מֵאוֹת׃ לִבְנֵי יוֹסֵף
Joseph from-sons-of (32) hundreds and-four thousand and-fifty seven Zebulun

לִבְנֵי אֶפְרַיִם תּוֹלְדֹתָם לְמִשְׁפְּחֹתָם לְבֵית
by-house-of by-clans-of-them records-of-them Ephraim from-sons-of

אֲבֹתָם בְּמִסְפַּר שֵׁמֹת מִבֶּן עֶשְׂרִים שָׁנָה וָמַעְלָה כֹּל
all-of or-more year twenty from-son-of names by-list-of fathers-of-them

יֹצֵא צָבָא׃ פְּקֻדֵיהֶם לְמַטֵּה אֶפְרָיִם אַרְבָּעִים אֶלֶף
thousand forty Ephraim from-tribe-of numberings-of-them (33) army serving

וַחֲמֵשׁ מֵאוֹת׃ לִבְנֵי מְנַשֶּׁה תּוֹלְדֹתָם
records-of-them Manasseh from sons-of (34) hundreds and-five-of

לְמִשְׁפְּחֹתָם לְבֵית אֲבֹתָם בְּמִסְפַּר שְׁמוֹת מִבֶּן
from-son-of names by-list-of fathers-of-them by-house-of by-clans-of-them

עֶשְׂרִים שָׁנָה וָמַעְלָה כֹּל יֹצֵא צָבָא׃ פְּקֻדֵיהֶם לְמַטֵּה
from-tribe-of numberings-of-them (35) army serving all-of or-more year twenty

מְנַשֶּׁה שְׁנַיִם וּשְׁלֹשִׁים אֶלֶף וּמָאתָיִם׃ לִבְנֵי בִנְיָמִן
Benjamin from-sons-of (36) and-two-hundreds thousand and-thirty two Manasseh

תּוֹלְדֹתָם לְמִשְׁפְּחֹתָם לְבֵית אֲבֹתָם בְּמִסְפַּר
by-list-of fathers-of-them by-house-of by-clans-of-them records-of-them

שֵׁמֹת מִבֶּן עֶשְׂרִים שָׁנָה וָמַעְלָה כֹּל יֹצֵא צָבָא׃
army serving all-of or-more year twenty from-son-of names

פְּקֻדֵיהֶם לְמַטֵּה בִנְיָמִן חֲמִשָּׁה וּשְׁלֹשִׁים אֶלֶף
thousand and-thirty five Benjamin from-tribe-of numberings-of-them (37)

וְאַרְבַּע מֵאוֹת׃ לִבְנֵי דָן תּוֹלְדֹתָם לְמִשְׁפְּחֹתָם
by-clans-of-them records-of-them Dan from-sons-of (38) hundreds and-four

לְבֵית אֲבֹתָם בְּמִסְפַּר שֵׁמֹת מִבֶּן עֶשְׂרִים שָׁנָה וָמַעְלָה
or-more year twenty from-son-of names by-list-of fathers-of-them by-house-of

כֹּל יֹצֵא צָבָא׃ פְּקֻדֵיהֶם לְמַטֵּה דָן שְׁנַיִם וְשִׁשִּׁים
and-sixty two Dan from-tribe-of numberings-of-them (39) army serving all-of

All the men twenty years old or more who were able to serve in the army were listed by name, according to the records of their clans and families. 29 The number from the tribe of Issachar was 54,400.

30 From the descendants of Zebulun:
All the men twenty years old or more who were able to serve in the army were listed by name, according to the records of their clans and families. 31 The number from the tribe of Zebulun was 57,400.

32 From the sons of Joseph:
From the descendants of Ephraim:
All the men twenty years old or more who were able to serve in the army were listed by name, according to the records of their clans and families. 33 The number from the tribe of Ephraim was 40,500.

34 From the descendants of Manasseh:
All the men twenty years old or more who were able to serve in the army were listed by name, according to the records of their clans and families. 35 The number from the tribe of Manasseh was 32,200.

36 From the descendants of Benjamin:
All the men twenty years old or more who were able to serve in the army were listed by name, according to the records of their clans and families. 37 The number from the tribe of Benjamin was 35,400.

38 From the descendants of Dan:
All the men twenty years old or more who were able to serve in the army were listed by name, according to the records of their clans and families. 39 The number from the tribe of Dan was 62,700.

אֶלֶף וּשְׁבַע מֵאוֹת׃ לִבְנֵי אָשֵׁר תּוֹלְדֹתָם
records-of-them Asher from-sons-of (40) hundreds and-seven-of thousand

לְמִשְׁפְּחֹתָם לְבֵית אֲבֹתָם בְּמִסְפַּר שֵׁמֹת מִבֶּן
from-son-of names by-list-of fathers-of-them by-house-of by-clans-of-them

עֶשְׂרִים שָׁנָה וָמַעְלָה כֹּל יֹצֵא צָבָא׃ פְּקֻדֵיהֶם לְמַטֵּה
from-tribe-of numberings-of-them (41) army serving all-of or-more year twenty

אָשֵׁר אֶחָד וְאַרְבָּעִים אֶלֶף וַחֲמֵשׁ מֵאוֹת׃ בְּנֵי נַפְתָּלִי
Naphtali sons-of (42) hundreds and-five-of thousand and-forty one Asher

תּוֹלְדֹתָם לְמִשְׁפְּחֹתָם לְבֵית אֲבֹתָם בְּמִסְפַּר
by-list-of fathers-of-them by-house-of by-clans-of-them records-of-them

שֵׁמֹת מִבֶּן עֶשְׂרִים שָׁנָה וָמַעְלָה כֹּל יֹצֵא צָבָא׃
army serving all-of or-more year twenty from-son-of names

פְּקֻדֵיהֶם לְמַטֵּה נַפְתָּלִי שְׁלֹשָׁה וַחֲמִשִּׁים אֶלֶף
thousand and-fifty three Naphtali from-tribe-of numberings-of-them (43)

וְאַרְבַּע מֵאוֹת׃ אֵלֶּה הַפְּקֻדִים אֲשֶׁר פָּקַד מֹשֶׁה
Moses he-counted whom the-ones-being-counted these (44) hundreds and-four

וְאַהֲרֹן וּנְשִׂיאֵי יִשְׂרָאֵל שְׁנֵים עָשָׂר אִישׁ אִישׁ־ אֶחָד לְבֵית־
from-house-of one each man ten two Israel and-leaders-of and-Aaron

אֲבֹתָיו הָיוּ׃ וַיִּהְיוּ כָּל־ פְּקוּדֵי
ones-being-counted-of all-of and-they-were (45) they-were fathers-of-him

בְנֵי־ יִשְׂרָאֵל לְבֵית אֲבֹתָם מִבֶּן עֶשְׂרִים שָׁנָה וָמַעְלָה
or-more year twenty from-son-of fathers-of-them by-house-of Israel sons-of

כָּל־ יֹצֵא צָבָא בְּיִשְׂרָאֵל׃ וַיִּהְיוּ כָּל־ הַפְּקֻדִים
the-numberings total-of and-they-were (46) in-Israel army serving all-of

שֵׁשׁ־ מֵאוֹת אֶלֶף וּשְׁלֹשֶׁת אֲלָפִים וַחֲמֵשׁ מֵאוֹת וַחֲמִשִּׁים׃
and-fifty hundreds and-five-of thousands and-three thousand hundreds six

וְהַלְוִיִּם לְמַטֵּה אֲבֹתָם לֹא הָתְפָּקְדוּ
they-were-counted not fathers-of-them by-tribe-of now-the-Levites (47)

בְּתוֹכָם׃ וַיְדַבֵּר יְהוָה אֶל־ מֹשֶׁה לֵּאמֹר׃ אַךְ אֶת־ מַטֵּה
tribe-of *** indeed (49) to-say Moses to Yahweh and-he-spoke (48) with-them

לֵוִי לֹא תִפְקֹד וְאֶת־ רֹאשָׁם לֹא תִשָּׂא בְּתוֹךְ בְּנֵי
sons-of with you-must-take not census-of-them or you-must-count not Levi

יִשְׂרָאֵל׃ וְאַתָּה הַפְקֵד אֶת־ הַלְוִיִּם עַל־ מִשְׁכַּן הָעֵדֻת
the-Testimony tabernacle-of over the-Levites *** appoint! but-you (50) Israel

וְעַל כָּל־ כֵּלָיו וְעַל כָּל־ אֲשֶׁר־ לוֹ הֵמָּה
they to-him that all and-over furnishings-of-him all-of and-over

יִשְׂאוּ אֶת־ הַמִּשְׁכָּן וְאֶת־ כָּל־ כֵּלָיו וְהֵם
and-they furnishings-of-him all-of and the-tabernacle *** they-must-carry

[40]From the descendants of Asher:
All the men twenty years old or more who were able to serve in the army were listed by name, according to the records of their clans and families. [41]The number from the tribe of Asher was 41,500.

[42]From the descendants of Naphtali:
All the men twenty years old or more who were able to serve in the army were listed by name, according to the records of their clans and families. [43]The number from the tribe of Naphtali was 53,400.

[44]These were the men counted by Moses and Aaron and the twelve leaders of Israel, each one representing his family. [45]All the Israelites twenty years old or more who were able to serve in Israel's army were counted according to their families. [46]The total number was 603,550.

[47]The families of the tribe of Levi, however, were not counted along with the others. [48]The LORD had said to Moses: [49]"You must not count the tribe of Levi or include them in the census of the other Israelites. [50]Instead, appoint the Levites to be in charge of the tabernacle of the Testimony—over all its furnishings and everything belonging to it. They are to carry the tabernacle and all its furnishings;

יְשָׁרְתֻהוּ וְסָבִיב לַמִּשְׁכָּן יַחֲנוּ׃
they-must-encamp to-the-tabernacle and-around they-must-care-for-him

וּבִנְסֹעַ הַמִּשְׁכָּן יוֹרִידוּ אֹתוֹ הַלְוִיִּם
the-Levites him they-must-take-down the-tabernacle and-when-to-move (51)

וּבַחֲנֹת הַמִּשְׁכָּן יָקִימוּ אֹתוֹ הַלְוִיִּם
the-Levites him they-must-set-up the-tabernacle and-when-to-camp

וְהַזָּר הַקָּרֵב יוּמָת׃ וְחָנוּ בְּנֵי
sons-of and-they-must-encamp (52) he-must-die the-one-near but-the-outsider

יִשְׂרָאֵל אִישׁ עַל־מַחֲנֵהוּ וְאִישׁ עַל־דִּגְלוֹ לְצִבְאֹתָם׃
by-divisions-of-them standard-of-him under and-each camp-of-him in each Israel

וְהַלְוִיִּם יַחֲנוּ סָבִיב לְמִשְׁכַּן
to-tabernacle-of around they-must-encamp but-the-Levites (53)

הָעֵדֻת וְלֹא־יִהְיֶה קֶצֶף עַל־עֲדַת בְּנֵי יִשְׂרָאֵל
Israel sons-of community-of on wrath he-will-fall so-not the-Testimony

וְשָׁמְרוּ הַלְוִיִּם אֶת־מִשְׁמֶרֶת מִשְׁכַּן הָעֵדוּת׃
the-Testimony tabernacle-of care-of *** the-Levites and-they-are-responsible

וַיַּעֲשׂוּ בְּנֵי יִשְׂרָאֵל כְּכֹל אֲשֶׁר צִוָּה יְהוָה אֶת־מֹשֶׁה
Moses *** Yahweh he-commanded that as-all Israel sons-of so-they-did (54)

כֵּן עָשׂוּ׃ וַיְדַבֵּר יְהוָה אֶל־מֹשֶׁה וְאֶל־אַהֲרֹן לֵאמֹר׃ אִישׁ
each (2) to-say Aaron and-to Moses to Yahweh and-he-spoke (2:1) they-did so

עַל־דִּגְלוֹ בְאֹתֹת לְבֵית אֲבֹתָם יַחֲנוּ
they-must-camp fathers-of-them of-house-of with-banners standard-of-him under

בְּנֵי יִשְׂרָאֵל מִנֶּגֶד סָבִיב לְאֹהֶל־מוֹעֵד יַחֲנוּ׃
they-must-camp Meeting to-Tent-of around at-distance Israel sons-of

וְהַחֹנִים קֵדְמָה מִזְרָחָה דֶּגֶל מַחֲנֵה יְהוּדָה
Judah camp-of standard-of toward-sunrise on-east and-the-ones-camping (3)

לְצִבְאֹתָם וְנָשִׂיא לִבְנֵי יְהוּדָה נַחְשׁוֹן בֶּן־עַמִּינָדָב׃
Amminadab son-of Nahshon Judah of-people-of now-leader by-divisions-of-them

וּצְבָאוֹ וּפְקֻדֵיהֶם אַרְבָּעָה וְשִׁבְעִים אֶלֶף
thousand and-seventy four and-numberings-of-them and-division-of-him (4)

וְשֵׁשׁ מֵאוֹת׃ וְהַחֹנִים עָלָיו מַטֵּה יִשָּׂשכָר
Issachar tribe-of next-to-him and-the-ones-camping (5) hundreds and-six

וְנָשִׂיא לִבְנֵי יִשָּׂשכָר נְתַנְאֵל בֶּן־צוּעָר׃ וּצְבָאוֹ
and-division-of-him (6) Zuar son-of Nethanel Issachar of-people-of and-leader

וּפְקֻדָיו אַרְבָּעָה וַחֲמִשִּׁים אֶלֶף וְאַרְבַּע מֵאוֹת׃ מַטֵּה
tribe-of (7) hundreds and-four thousand and-fifty four and-numberings-of-him

זְבוּלֻן וְנָשִׂיא לִבְנֵי זְבוּלֻן אֱלִיאָב בֶּן־חֵלֹן׃
Helon son-of Eliab Zebulun of-people-of and-leader Zebulun

they are to take care of it and
encamp around it. 51 Whenever
the tabernacle is to move, the
Levites are to take it down,
and whenever the tabernacle
is to be set up, the Levites shall
do it. Anyone else who goes
near it shall be put to death.
52 The Israelites are to set up
their tents by divisions, each
man in his own camp under
his own standard. 53 The Levites, however, are to set up
their tents around the tabernacle of the Testimony so that
wrath will not fall on the Israelite community. The Levites
are to be responsible for the
care of the tabernacle of the
Testimony."
54 The Israelites did all this
just as the LORD commanded
Moses.

The Arrangement of the Tribal Camps

2 The LORD said to Moses
and Aaron: 2 "The Israel-
ites are to camp around the
Tent of Meeting some distance
from it, each man under his
standard with the banners of
his family."

3 On the east, toward the
sunrise, the divisions of the
camp of Judah are to en-
camp under their standard.
The leader of the people of
Judah is Nahshon son of
Amminadab. 4 His division
numbers 74,600.
5 The tribe of Issachar will
camp next to them. The
leader of the people of Issachar is Nethanel son of
Zuar. 6 His division num-
bers 54,400.
7 The tribe of Zebulun will
be next. The leader of the
people of Zebulun is Eliab
son of Helon. 8 His division

וּצְבָאוֹ וּפְקֻדָיו שִׁבְעָה וַחֲמִשִּׁים אֶלֶף
thousand and-fifty seven and-numberings-of-him and-division-of-him (8)

וְאַרְבַּע מֵאוֹת׃ כָּל־ הַפְּקֻדִים לְמַחֲנֵה יְהוּדָה
Judah to-camp-of the-ones-being-numbered all-of (9) hundreds and-four

מְאַת אֶלֶף וּשְׁמֹנִים אֶלֶף וְשֵׁשֶׁת־ אֲלָפִים וְאַרְבַּע־
and-four thousands and-six-of thousand and-eighty thousand hundred-of

מֵאוֹת לְצִבְאֹתָם רִאשֹׁנָה יִסָּעוּ׃ דֶּגֶל
standard-of (10) they-will-set-out first by-divisions-of-them hundreds

מַחֲנֵה רְאוּבֵן תֵּימָנָה לְצִבְאֹתָם וְנָשִׂיא לִבְנֵי רְאוּבֵן
Reuben of-people-of and-leader by-divisions-of-them on-south Reuben camp-of

אֱלִיצוּר בֶּן־ שְׁדֵיאוּר׃ וּצְבָאוֹ וּפְקֻדָיו שִׁשָּׁה
six and-numberings-of-him and-division-of-him (11) Shedeur son-of Elizur

וְאַרְבָּעִים אֶלֶף וַחֲמֵשׁ מֵאוֹת׃ וְהַחוֹנִם עָלָיו
next-to-him and-the-ones-camping (12) hundreds and-five-of thousand and-forty

מַטֵּה שִׁמְעוֹן וְנָשִׂיא לִבְנֵי שִׁמְעוֹן שְׁלֻמִיאֵל בֶּן־ צוּרִי־ שַׁדָּי׃
Shaddai Zuri son-of Shelumiel Simeon of-people-of and-leader Simeon tribe-of

וּצְבָאוֹ וּפְקֻדֵיהֶם תִּשְׁעָה וַחֲמִשִּׁים אֶלֶף
thousand and-fifty nine and-numberings-of-them division-of-him (13)

וּשְׁלֹשׁ מֵאוֹת׃ וּמַטֵּה גָּד וְנָשִׂיא לִבְנֵי גָד
Gad of-people-of and-leader Gad and-tribe-of (14) hundreds and-three-of

אֶלְיָסָף בֶּן־ רְעוּאֵל׃ וּצְבָאוֹ וּפְקֻדֵיהֶם חֲמִשָּׁה
five and-numberings-of-them and-division-of-him (15) Reuel son-of Eliasaph

וְאַרְבָּעִים אֶלֶף וְשֵׁשׁ מֵאוֹת וַחֲמִשִּׁים׃ כָּל־ הַפְּקֻדִים
the-numberings all-of (16) and-fifty hundreds and-six thousand and-forty

לְמַחֲנֵה רְאוּבֵן מְאַת אֶלֶף וְאֶחָד וַחֲמִשִּׁים אֶלֶף וְאַרְבַּע־
and-four thousand and-fifty and-one thousand hundred-of Reuben to-camp-of

מֵאוֹת וַחֲמִשִּׁים לְצִבְאֹתָם וּשְׁנִיִּם יִסָּעוּ׃
they-will-set-out and-second-ones by-divisions-of-them and-fifty hundreds

וְנָסַע אֹהֶל־ מוֹעֵד מַחֲנֵה הַלְוִיִּם בְּתוֹךְ
in-middle-of the-Levites camp-of Meeting Tent-of then-he-will-set-out (17)

הַמַּחֲנֹת כַּאֲשֶׁר יַחֲנוּ כֵּן יִסָּעוּ אִישׁ עַל־ יָדוֹ
place-of-him in each they-will-set-out same they-encamp just-as the-camps

לְדִגְלֵיהֶם׃ דֶּגֶל מַחֲנֵה אֶפְרַיִם לְצִבְאֹתָם
by-divisions-of-them Ephraim camp-of standard-of (18) under-standards-of-them

יָמָּה וְנָשִׂיא לִבְנֵי אֶפְרַיִם אֱלִישָׁמָע בֶּן־ עַמִּיהוּד׃
Ammihud son-of Elishama Ephraim of-people-of and-leader on-west

וּצְבָאוֹ וּפְקֻדֵיהֶם אַרְבָּעִים אֶלֶף וַחֲמֵשׁ
and-five-of thousand forty and-numberings-of-them and-division-of-him (19)

numbers 57,400.
9 All the men assigned to
the camp of Judah, according to their divisions, number 186,400. They will set
out first.

10 On the south will be the
divisions of the camp of
Reuben under their stan-
dard. The leader of the
people of Reuben is Elizur
son of Shedeur. 11 His division numbers 46,500.
12 The tribe of Simeon will
camp next to them. The
leader of the people of
Simeon is Shelumiel son of
Zurishaddai. 13 His division
numbers 59,300.
14 The tribe of Gad will be
next. The leader of the
people of Gad is Eliasaph
son of Deuel.[a] 15 His division numbers 45,650.
16 All the men assigned to
the camp of Reuben, ac-
cording to their divisions,
number 151,450. They will
set out second.

17 Then the Tent of Meet-
ing and the camp of the Levites will set out in the middle of the camps. They will
set out in the same order as
they encamp, each in his
own place under his stan-
dard.

18 On the west will be the
divisions of the camp of
Ephraim under their stan-
dard. The leader of the
people of Ephraim is Eli-
shama son of Ammihud.
19 His division numbers 40,-
500.

[a] *14* Many manuscripts of the Masoretic Text, Samaritan Pentateuch and Vulgate (see also Num. 1:14); most manuscripts of the Masoretic Text *Reuel*

**14* Most mss have *shureq* instead of *vav* with *sheva* ('וּמ).

מֵאוֹת׃ (20) וְעָלָיו מַטֵּה מְנַשֶּׁה וְנָשִׂיא לִבְנֵי
hundreds (20) and-next-to-him tribe-of Manasseh and-leader of-people-of

מְנַשֶּׁה גַּמְלִיאֵל בֶּן־ פְּדָהצוּר׃ (21) וּצְבָאוֹ
Manasseh Gamaliel son-of Pedahzur (21) and-division-of-him

וּפְקֻדֵיהֶם שְׁנַיִם וּשְׁלֹשִׁים אֶלֶף וּמָאתָיִם׃
and-numberings-of-them two and-thirty thousand and-two-hundreds

(22) וּמַטֵּה בִּנְיָמִן וְנָשִׂיא לִבְנֵי בִנְיָמִן אֲבִידָן בֶּן־
(22) and-tribe-of Benjamin and-leader of-people-of Benjamin Abidan son-of

גִּדְעֹנִי׃ (23) וּצְבָאוֹ וּפְקֻדֵיהֶם חֲמִשָּׁה וּשְׁלֹשִׁים
Gideoni (23) and-division-of-him and-numberings-of-them five and-thirty

אֶלֶף וְאַרְבַּע מֵאוֹת׃ (24) כָּל־ הַפְּקֻדִים לְמַחֲנֵה
thousand and-four hundreds (24) all-of the-ones-being-numbered to-camp-of

אֶפְרַיִם מְאַת אֶלֶף וּשְׁמֹנַת־ אֲלָפִים וּמֵאָה
Ephraim hundred-of thousand and-eight-of thousands and-hundred

לְצִבְאֹתָם וּשְׁלִשִׁים יִסָּעוּ׃ (25) דֶּגֶל מַחֲנֵה
by-divisions-of-them and-third-ones they-will-set-out (25) standard-of camp-of

דָן צָפֹנָה לְצִבְאֹתָם וְנָשִׂיא לִבְנֵי דָן אֲחִיעֶזֶר
Dan on-north by-divisions-of-them and-leader of-people-of Dan Ahiezer

בֶּן־ עַמִּישַׁדָּי׃ (26) וּצְבָאוֹ וּפְקֻדֵיהֶם שְׁנַיִם
son-of Ammishaddai (26) and-division-of-him and-numberings-of-them two

וְשִׁשִּׁים אֶלֶף וּשְׁבַע מֵאוֹת׃ (27) וְהַחֹנִים
and-sixty thousand and-seven-of hundreds (27) and-the-ones-camping

עָלָיו מַטֵּה אָשֵׁר וְנָשִׂיא לִבְנֵי אָשֵׁר פַּגְעִיאֵל בֶּן־ עָכְרָן׃
next-to-him tribe-of Asher and-leader of-people-of Asher Pagiel son-of Ocran

(28) וּצְבָאוֹ וּפְקֻדֵיהֶם אֶחָד וְאַרְבָּעִים אֶלֶף
(28) and-division-of-him and-numberings-of-them one and-forty thousand

וַחֲמֵשׁ מֵאוֹת׃ (29) וּמַטֵּה נַפְתָּלִי וְנָשִׂיא לִבְנֵי
and-five-of hundreds (29) and-tribe-of Naphtali and-leader of-people-of

נַפְתָּלִי אֲחִירַע בֶּן־ עֵינָן׃ (30) וּצְבָאוֹ וּפְקֻדֵיהֶם
Naphtali Ahira son-of Enan (30) and-division-of-him and-numberings-of-them

שְׁלֹשָׁה וַחֲמִשִּׁים אֶלֶף וְאַרְבַּע מֵאוֹת׃ (31) כָּל־ הַפְּקֻדִים
three and-fifty thousand and-four hundreds (31) all-of the-ones-being-numbered

לְמַחֲנֵה דָן מְאַת אֶלֶף וְשִׁבְעָה וַחֲמִשִּׁים אֶלֶף וְשֵׁשׁ
to-camp-of Dan hundred-of thousand and-seven and-fifty thousand and-six

מֵאוֹת לָאַחֲרֹנָה יִסְעוּ לְדִגְלֵיהֶם׃ (32) אֵלֶּה
hundreds as-the-last they-will-set-out under-standards-of-them (32) these

פְקוּדֵי בְנֵי־ יִשְׂרָאֵל לְבֵית אֲבֹתָם כָּל־ פְּקוּדֵי
countings-of sons-of Israel by-house-of fathers-of-them all-of numberings-of

20The tribe of Manasseh will be next to them. The leader of the people of Manasseh is Gamaliel son of Pedahzur. 21His division numbers 32,200.

22The tribe of Benjamin will be next. The leader of the people of Benjamin is Abidan son of Gideoni. 23His division numbers 35,400.

24All the men assigned to the camp of Ephraim, according to their divisions, number 108,100. They will set out third.

25On the north will be the divisions of the camp of Dan, under their standard. The leader of the people of Dan is Ahiezer son of Ammishaddai. 26His division numbers 62,700.

27The tribe of Asher will camp next to them. The leader of the people of Asher is Pagiel son of Ocran. 28His division numbers 41,500.

29The tribe of Naphtali will be next. The leader of the people of Naphtali is Ahira son of Enan. 30His division numbers 53,400.

31All the men assigned to the camp of Dan number 157,600. They will set out last, under their standards.

32These are the Israelites, counted according to their families. All those in the

הַמַּחֲנֹת לְצִבְאֹתָם שֵׁשׁ־ מֵאוֹת אֶלֶף וּשְׁלֹשֶׁת אֲלָפִים
thousands and-three thousand hundreds six by-divisions-of-them the-camps

וַחֲמֵשׁ מֵאוֹת וַחֲמִשִּׁים׃ וְהַלְוִיִּם לֹא הָתְפָּקְדוּ
they-were-counted not but-the-Levites (33) and-fifty hundreds and-five-of

בְּתוֹךְ בְּנֵי יִשְׂרָאֵל כַּאֲשֶׁר צִוָּה יְהוָה אֶת־ מֹשֶׁה׃ וַיַּעֲשׂוּ
so-they-did (34) Moses *** Yahweh he-commanded just-as Israel sons-of with

בְּנֵי יִשְׂרָאֵל כְּכֹל אֲשֶׁר־ צִוָּה יְהוָה אֶת־ מֹשֶׁה כֵּן־ חָנוּ
they-encamped so Moses *** Yahweh he-commanded that as-all Israel sons-of

לְדִגְלֵיהֶם וְכֵן נָסָעוּ אִישׁ לְמִשְׁפְּחֹתָיו עַל־
with with-clans-of-him each they-set-out and-so under-standards-of-them

בֵּית אֲבֹתָיו׃ וְאֵלֶּה תּוֹלְדֹת אַהֲרֹן וּמֹשֶׁה בְּיוֹם
on-day and-Moses Aaron accounts-of now-these (3:1) fathers-of-him house-of

דִּבֶּר יְהוָה אֶת־ מֹשֶׁה בְּהַר סִינָי׃ וְאֵלֶּה שְׁמוֹת בְּנֵי־
sons-of names-of and-these (2) Sinai on-Mount-of Moses *** Yahweh he-talked

אַהֲרֹן הַבְּכֹר ׀ נָדָב וַאֲבִיהוּא אֶלְעָזָר וְאִיתָמָר׃ אֵלֶּה שְׁמוֹת
names-of these (3) and-Ithamar Eleazar and-Abihu Nadab the-firstborn Aaron

בְּנֵי אַהֲרֹן הַכֹּהֲנִים הַמְּשֻׁחִים אֲשֶׁר־ מִלֵּא יָדָם
hand-of-them he-ordained whom the-ones-being-anointed the-priests Aaron sons-of

לְכַהֵן׃ וַיָּמָת נָדָב וַאֲבִיהוּא לִפְנֵי יְהוָה בְּהַקְרִבָם
when-to-offer-them Yahweh before and-Abihu Nadab but-he-died (4) to-be-priest

אֵשׁ זָרָה לִפְנֵי יְהוָה בְּמִדְבַּר סִינַי וּבָנִים לֹא־ הָיוּ
they-were not and-sons Sinai in-Desert-of Yahweh before unauthorized fire

לָהֶם וַיְכַהֵן אֶלְעָזָר וְאִיתָמָר עַל־ פְּנֵי אַהֲרֹן
Aaron presence-of during and-Ithamar Eleazar so-he-was-priest to-them

אֲבִיהֶם׃ וַיְדַבֵּר יְהוָה אֶל־ מֹשֶׁה לֵּאמֹר׃ הַקְרֵב אֶת־
*** bring! (6) to-say Moses to Yahweh and-he-spoke (5) father-of-them

מַטֵּה לֵוִי וְהַעֲמַדְתָּ אֹתוֹ לִפְנֵי אַהֲרֹן הַכֹּהֵן וְשֵׁרְתוּ
so-they-may-assist the-priest Aaron before him and-you-present Levi tribe-of

אֹתוֹ׃ וְשָׁמְרוּ אֶת־ מִשְׁמַרְתּוֹ וְאֶת־ מִשְׁמֶרֶת כָּל־
whole-of duty-of and duty-of-him *** and-they-must-perform (7) him

הָעֵדָה לִפְנֵי אֹהֶל מוֹעֵד לַעֲבֹד אֶת־ עֲבֹדַת הַמִּשְׁכָּן׃
the-tabernacle work-of *** to-do Meeting Tent-of at the-community

וְשָׁמְרוּ אֶת־ כָּל־ כְּלֵי אֹהֶל מוֹעֵד וְאֶת־
and Meeting Tent-of furnishings-of all-of *** and-they-must-take-care (8)

מִשְׁמֶרֶת בְּנֵי יִשְׂרָאֵל לַעֲבֹד אֶת־ עֲבֹדַת הַמִּשְׁכָּן וְנָתַתָּה
so-you-give (9) the-tabernacle work-of *** to-do Israel sons-of obligation-of

אֶת־ הַלְוִיִּם לְאַהֲרֹן וּלְבָנָיו נְתוּנִם נְתוּנִם
ones-being-given ones-being-given and-to-sons-of-him to-Aaron the-Levites ***

camps, by their divisions, number 603,550. [33]The Levites, however, were not counted along with the other Israelites, as the LORD commanded Moses.

[34]So the Israelites did everything the LORD commanded Moses; that is the way they encamped under their standards, and that is the way they set out, each with his clan and family.

The Levites

3 This is the account of the family of Aaron and Moses at the time the LORD talked with Moses on Mount Sinai.

[2]The names of the sons of Aaron were Nadab the firstborn and Abihu, Eleazar and Ithamar. [3]Those were the names of Aaron's sons, the anointed priests, who were ordained to serve as priests. [4]Nadab and Abihu, however, fell dead before the LORD when they made an offering with unauthorized fire before him in the Desert of Sinai. They had no sons; so only Eleazar and Ithamar served as priests during the lifetime of their father Aaron.

[5]The LORD said to Moses, [6]"Bring the tribe of Levi and present them to Aaron the priest to assist him. [7]They are to perform duties for him and for the whole community at the Tent of Meeting by doing the work of the tabernacle. [8]They are to take care of all the furnishings of the Tent of Meeting, fulfilling the obligations of the Israelites by doing the work of the tabernacle. [9]Give the Levites to Aaron and his sons; they are the Israelites who are to be given wholly to

הֵמָּה לוֹ מֵאֵת בְּנֵי יִשְׂרָאֵל׃ וְאֶת־אַהֲרֹן וְאֶת־בָּנָיו תִּפְקֹד
you-appoint sons-of-him and Aaron and (10) Israel sons-of from to-him they

וְשָׁמְרוּ אֶת־כְּהֻנָּתָם וְהַזָּר הַקָּרֵב
the-one-near but-the-outsider priesthood-of-them *** so-they-serve

יוּמָת׃ וַיְדַבֵּר יְהוָה אֶל־מֹשֶׁה לֵּאמֹר וַאֲנִי הִנֵּה לָקַחְתִּי
I-took see! now-I (12) to-say Moses to Yahweh and-he-spoke (11) he-must-die

אֶת־הַלְוִיִּם מִתּוֹךְ בְּנֵי יִשְׂרָאֵל תַּחַת כָּל־בְּכוֹר
firstborn all-of in-place-of Israel sons-of from-among the-Levites ***

פֶּטֶר רֶחֶם מִבְּנֵי יִשְׂרָאֵל וְהָיוּ לִי הַלְוִיִּם׃ כִּי
for (13) the-Levites to-me so-they-are Israel from-sons-of womb opener-of

לִי כָּל־בְּכוֹר בְּיוֹם הַכֹּתִי כָל־בְּכוֹר בְּאֶרֶץ
in-land-of firstborn all-of to-strike-down-me on-day firstborn all-of to-me

מִצְרַיִם הִקְדַּשְׁתִּי לִי כָל־בְּכוֹר בְּיִשְׂרָאֵל מֵאָדָם עַד־בְּהֵמָה
animal or whether-man in-Israel firstborn every-of for-me I-set-apart Egypt

לִי יִהְיוּ אֲנִי יְהוָה׃ וַיְדַבֵּר יְהוָה אֶל־מֹשֶׁה בְּמִדְבַּר
in-Desert-of Moses to Yahweh and-he-spoke (14) Yahweh I they-are for-me

סִינַי לֵאמֹר׃ פְּקֹד אֶת־בְּנֵי לֵוִי לְבֵית אֲבֹתָם
fathers-of-them by-house-of Levi sons-of *** count! (15) to-say Sinai

לְמִשְׁפְּחֹתָם כָּל־זָכָר מִבֶּן־חֹדֶשׁ וָמַעְלָה תִּפְקְדֵם׃
you-count-them or-more month from-son-of male every-of by-clans-of-them

וַיִּפְקֹד אֹתָם מֹשֶׁה עַל־פִּי יְהוָה כַּאֲשֶׁר צֻוָּה׃
he-was-commanded just-as Yahweh word-of at Moses them so-he-counted (16)

וַיִּהְיוּ־אֵלֶּה בְנֵי־לֵוִי בִּשְׁמֹתָם גֵּרְשׁוֹן וּקְהָת
and-Kohath Gershon by-names-of-them Levi sons-of these and-they-were (17)

וּמְרָרִי׃ וְאֵלֶּה שְׁמוֹת בְּנֵי־גֵרְשׁוֹן לְמִשְׁפְּחֹתָם לִבְנִי
Libni by-clans-of-them Gershon sons-of names-of and-these (18) and-Merari

וְשִׁמְעִי׃ וּבְנֵי קְהָת לְמִשְׁפְּחֹתָם עַמְרָם וְיִצְהָר חֶבְרוֹן
Hebron and-Izhar Amram by-clans-of-them Kohath and-sons-of (19) and-Shimei

וְעֻזִּיאֵל׃ וּבְנֵי מְרָרִי לְמִשְׁפְּחֹתָם מַחְלִי וּמוּשִׁי אֵלֶּה
these and-Mushi Mahli by-clans-of-them Merari and-sons-of (20) and-Uzziel

הֵם מִשְׁפְּחֹת הַלֵּוִי לְבֵית אֲבֹתָם׃ לְגֵרְשׁוֹן
to-Gershon (21) fathers-of-them by-house-of the-Levites clans-of they

מִשְׁפַּחַת הַלִּבְנִי וּמִשְׁפַּחַת הַשִּׁמְעִי אֵלֶּה הֵם מִשְׁפְּחֹת
clans-of they these the-Shimeite and-clan-of the-Libnite clan-of

הַגֵּרְשֻׁנִּי׃ פְּקֻדֵיהֶם בְּמִסְפַּר כָּל־זָכָר מִבֶּן־
from-son-of male every-of by-count-of numberings-of-them (22) the-Gershonite

חֹדֶשׁ וָמַעְלָה פְּקֻדֵיהֶם שִׁבְעַת אֲלָפִים וַחֲמֵשׁ מֵאוֹת׃
hundreds and-five-of thousands seven-of numberings-of-them or-more month

him.[b] 10Appoint Aaron and his
sons to serve as priests; anyone else who approaches the
sanctuary must be put to
death."

11The LORD also said to
Moses, 12"I have taken the Levites from among the Israelites in place of the first male
offspring of every Israelite
woman. The Levites are mine,
13for all the firstborn are mine.
When I struck down all the
firstborn in Egypt, I set apart
for myself every firstborn in
Israel, whether man or animal. They are to be mine. I am
the LORD."

14The LORD said to Moses in
the Desert of Sinai, 15"Count
the Levites by their families
and clans. Count every male a
month old or more." 16So
Moses counted them, as he
was commanded by the word
of the LORD.

17These were the names of the sons of Levi:
Gershon, Kohath and Merari.
18These were the names of the Gershonite clans:
Libni and Shimei.
19The Kohathite clans:
Amram, Izhar, Hebron and Uzziel.
20The Merarite clans:
Mahli and Mushi.
These were the Levite clans,
according to their families.

21To Gershon belonged the
clans of the Libnites and
Shimeites; these were the Gershonite clans. 22The number of
all the males a month old or
more who were counted was

[b]9 Most manuscripts of the Masoretic Text; some manuscripts of the Masoretic Text, Samaritan Pentateuch and Septuagint (see also Num. 8:16) *to me*

*9 Some mss and the versions above in note *b* read לִי, *to-me.*

מִשְׁפְּחֹת הַגֵּרְשֻׁנִּי אַחֲרֵי הַמִּשְׁכָּן יַחֲנוּ יָמָּה׃
on-west they-camped the-tabernacle behind the-Gershonite clans-of (23)

וּנְשִׂיא בֵית־ אָב לַגֵּרְשֻׁנִּי אֶלְיָסָף בֶּן־ לָאֵל׃
Lael son-of Eliasaph of-the-Gershonite father house-of and-leader-of (24)

וּמִשְׁמֶרֶת בְּנֵי־ גֵרְשׁוֹן בְּאֹהֶל מוֹעֵד הַמִּשְׁכָּן
the-tabernacle Meeting at-Tent-of Gershon sons-of and-responsibility-of (25)

וְהָאֹהֶל מִכְסֵהוּ וּמָסַךְ פֶּתַח אֹהֶל מוֹעֵד׃
Meeting Tent-of entrance-of and-curtain-of covering-of-him and-the-tent

וְקַלְעֵי הֶחָצֵר וְאֶת־ מָסַךְ פֶּתַח הֶחָצֵר
the-courtyard entrance-of curtain-of and the-courtyard and-curtains-of (26)

אֲשֶׁר עַל־ הַמִּשְׁכָּן וְעַל־ הַמִּזְבֵּחַ סָבִיב וְאֵת מֵיתָרָיו לְכֹל
for-all-of ropes-of-him and around the-altar and-for the-tabernacle for that

עֲבֹדָתוֹ׃ וְלִקְהָת מִשְׁפַּחַת הָעַמְרָמִי וּמִשְׁפַּחַת הַיִּצְהָרִי
the-Izharite and-clan-of the-Amramite clan-of and-to-Kohath (27) use-of-him

וּמִשְׁפַּחַת הַחֶבְרֹנִי וּמִשְׁפַּחַת הָעָזִּיאֵלִי אֵלֶּה הֵם מִשְׁפְּחֹת
clans-of they these the-Uzzielite and-clan-of the-Hebronite and-clan-of

הַקְּהָתִי׃ בְּמִסְפַּר כָּל־ זָכָר מִבֶּן־ חֹדֶשׁ וָמָעְלָה
or-more month from-son-of male every-of by-number-of (28) the-Kohathite

שְׁמֹנַת אֲלָפִים וְשֵׁשׁ מֵאוֹת שֹׁמְרֵי מִשְׁמֶרֶת
responsibility-of ones-caring-of hundreds and-six thousands eight

הַקֹּדֶשׁ׃ מִשְׁפְּחֹת בְּנֵי־ קְהָת יַחֲנוּ עַל יֶרֶךְ
side-of on they-camped Kohath sons-of clans-of (29) the-sanctuary

הַמִּשְׁכָּן תֵּימָנָה׃ וּנְשִׂיא בֵית־ אָב לְמִשְׁפְּחֹת
of-clans-of father house-of and-leader-of (30) on-south the-tabernacle

הַקְּהָתִי אֱלִיצָפָן בֶּן־ עֻזִּיאֵל׃ וּמִשְׁמַרְתָּם הָאָרֹן
the-ark and-responsibility-of-them (31) Uzziel son-of Elizaphan the-Kohathite

וְהַשֻּׁלְחָן וְהַמְּנֹרָה וְהַמִּזְבְּחֹת וּכְלֵי הַקֹּדֶשׁ
the-sanctuary and-articles-of and-the-altars and-the-lampstand and-the-table

אֲשֶׁר יְשָׁרְתוּ בָּהֶם וְהַמָּסָךְ וְכֹל עֲבֹדָתוֹ׃
use-of-him and-all-of and-the-curtain with-them they-minister that

וּנְשִׂיא נְשִׂיאֵי הַלֵּוִי אֶלְעָזָר בֶּן־ אַהֲרֹן הַכֹּהֵן
the-priest Aaron son-of Eleazar the-Levite leaders-of and-leader-of (32)

פְּקֻדַּת שֹׁמְרֵי מִשְׁמֶרֶת הַקֹּדֶשׁ׃
the-sanctuary responsibility-of ones-caring-of being-appointed-of

לִמְרָרִי מִשְׁפַּחַת הַמַּחְלִי וּמִשְׁפַּחַת הַמּוּשִׁי אֵלֶּה הֵם
they these the-Mushite and-clan-of the-Mahlite clan-of to-Merari (33)

מִשְׁפְּחֹת מְרָרִי׃ וּפְקֻדֵיהֶם בְּמִסְפַּר כָּל־ זָכָר
male every-of by-count-of and-numberings-of-them (34) Merarite clans-of

7,500. [23]The Gershonite clans
were to camp on the west, behind the tabernacle. [24]The
leader of the families of the
Gershonites was Eliasaph son
of Lael. [25]At the Tent of Meeting the Gershonites were responsible for the care of the
tabernacle and tent, its
coverings, the curtain at the
entrance to the Tent of Meeting, [26]the curtains of the courtyard, the curtain at the entrance to the courtyard surrounding the tabernacle and
altar, and the ropes—and
everything related to their use.

[27]To Kohath belonged the
clans of the Amramites, Izha-
rites, Hebronites and Uzzie-
lites; these were the Kohathite
clans. [28]The number of all the
males a month old or more
was 8,600.[c] The Kohathites
were responsible for the care
of the sanctuary. [29]The Kohathite clans were to camp on
the south side of the tabernacle. [30]The leader of the families of the Kohathite clans was
Elizaphan son of Uzziel.
[31]They were responsible for
the care of the ark, the table,
the lampstand, the altars, the
articles of the sanctuary used
in ministering, the curtain,
and everything related to their
use. [32]The chief leader of the
Levites was Eleazar son of
Aaron, the priest. He was appointed over those who were
responsible for the care of the
sanctuary.

[33]To Merari belonged the
clans of the Mahlites and the
Mushites; these were the Merarite clans. [34]The number of all

[c]*28 Hebrew; some Septuagint manuscripts 8,300*

מִבֶּן־ חֹדֶשׁ וָמַעְלָה שֵׁשֶׁת אֲלָפִים וּמָאתָיִם׃ וּנְשִׂיא
and-leader-of (35) and-two-hundreds thousands six-of or-more month from-son-of

בֵית־ אָב לְמִשְׁפְּחֹת מְרָרִי צוּרִיאֵל בֶּן־ אֲבִיחָיִל עַל יֶרֶךְ
side-of on Abihail son-of Zuriel Merari of-clans-of father house-of

הַמִּשְׁכָּן יַחֲנוּ צָפֹנָה׃ וּפְקֻדַּת מִשְׁמֶרֶת
care-of and-being-appointed-of (36) on-north they-camped the-tabernacle

בְּנֵי מְרָרִי קַרְשֵׁי הַמִּשְׁכָּן וּבְרִיחָיו וְעַמֻּדָיו
and-posts-of-him and-crossbars-of-him the-tabernacle frames-of Merari sons-of

וַאֲדָנָיו וְכָל־ כֵּלָיו וְכֹל עֲבֹדָתוֹ׃
use-of-him and-all-of equipments-of-him and-all-of and-bases-of-him

וְעַמֻּדֵי הֶחָצֵר סָבִיב וְאַדְנֵיהֶם וִיתֵדֹתָם
and-pegs-of-them and-bases-of-them around the-courtyard and-posts-of (37)

וּמֵיתְרֵיהֶם׃ וְהַחֹנִים לִפְנֵי הַמִּשְׁכָּן
the-tabernacle in-front-of and-the-ones-camping (38) and-ropes-of-them

קֵדְמָה לִפְנֵי אֹהֶל־ מוֹעֵד ׀ מִזְרָחָה מֹשֶׁה ׀ וְאַהֲרֹן
and-Aaron Moses toward-sunrise Meeting Tent-of in-front-of on-east

וּבָנָיו שֹׁמְרִים מִשְׁמֶרֶת הַמִּקְדָּשׁ לְמִשְׁמֶרֶת
on-behalf-of the-sanctuary care-of ones-being-responsible and-sons-of-him

בְּנֵי יִשְׂרָאֵל וְהַזָּר הַקָּרֵב יוּמָת׃ כָּל־
total-of (39) he-must-die the-one-near but-the-outsider Israel sons-of

פְּקוּדֵי הַלְוִיִּם אֲשֶׁר פָּקַד מֹשֶׁה וְאַהֲרֹן עַל־ פִּי
command-of at and-Aaron Moses he-counted that the-Levites numberings-of

יְהוָה לְמִשְׁפְּחֹתָם כָּל־ זָכָר מִבֶּן־ חֹדֶשׁ וָמַעְלָה שְׁנַיִם
two or-more month from-son-of male every-of by-clans-of-them Yahweh

וְעֶשְׂרִים אָלֶף׃ וַיֹּאמֶר יְהוָה אֶל־ מֹשֶׁה פְּקֹד כָּל־
every-of count! Moses to Yahweh then-he-said (40) thousand and-twenty

בְּכֹר זָכָר לִבְנֵי יִשְׂרָאֵל מִבֶּן־ חֹדֶשׁ וָמַעְלָה וְשָׂא אֵת
*** and-make! or-more month from-son-of Israel of-sons-of male firstborn-of

מִסְפַּר שְׁמֹתָם׃ וְלָקַחְתָּ אֶת־ הַלְוִיִּם לִי אֲנִי יְהוָה
Yahweh I for-me the-Levites *** and-you-take (41) names-of-them list-of

תַּחַת כָּל־ בְּכֹר בִּבְנֵי יִשְׂרָאֵל וְאֵת בֶּהֱמַת הַלְוִיִּם
the-Levites stock-of and Israel from-sons-of firstborn all-of in-place-of

תַּחַת כָּל־ בְּכוֹר בְּבֶהֱמַת בְּנֵי יִשְׂרָאֵל׃ וַיִּפְקֹד
so-he-counted (42) Israel sons-of from-stock-of firstborn all-of in-place-of

מֹשֶׁה כַּאֲשֶׁר צִוָּה יְהוָה אֹתוֹ אֶת־ כָּל־ בְּכֹר בִּבְנֵי יִשְׂרָאֵל׃
Israel of-sons-of firstborn all-of *** him Yahweh he-commanded just-as Moses

וַיְהִי כָל־ בְּכוֹר זָכָר בְּמִסְפַּר שֵׁמֹת מִבֶּן־
from-son-of names by-list-of male firstborn-of total-of and-he-was (43)

the males a month old or more
who were counted was 6,200.
[35]The leader of the families of
the Merarite clans was Zuriel
son of Abihail; they were to
camp on the north side of the
tabernacle. [36]The Merarites
were appointed to take care of
the frames of the tabernacle,
its crossbars, posts, bases, all
its equipment, and everything
related to their use, [37]as well as
the posts of the surrounding
courtyard with their bases,
tent pegs and ropes.

[38]Moses and Aaron and his
sons were to camp to the east
of the tabernacle, toward the
sunrise, in front of the Tent of
Meeting. They were responsible for the care of the sanctuary on behalf of the Israelites.
Anyone else who approached
the sanctuary was to be put to
death.

[39]The total number of Levites counted at the LORD's
command by Moses and
Aaron according to their
clans, including every male a
month old or more, was 22,-
000.

[40]The LORD said to Moses,
"Count all the firstborn Israelite males who are a month old
or more and make a list of
their names. [41]Take the Levites
for me in place of all the
firstborn of the Israelites, and
the livestock of the Levites in
place of all the firstborn of the
livestock of the Israelites. I am
the LORD."
[42]So Moses counted all the
firstborn of the Israelites, as
the LORD commanded him.
[43]The total number of firstborn
males a month old or more,

חֹדֶשׁ וָמַעְלָה לִפְקֻדֵיהֶם שְׁנַיִם וְעֶשְׂרִים אֶלֶף שְׁלֹשָׁה וְשִׁבְעִים
and-seventy three thousand and-twenty two by-numberings-of-them or-more month

וּמָאתָיִם׃ וַיְדַבֵּר יְהוָה אֶל־מֹשֶׁה לֵּאמֹר׃ קַח אֶת־
*** take! (45) to-say Moses to Yahweh and-he-spoke (44) and-two-hundreds

הַלְוִיִּם תַּחַת כָּל־בְּכוֹר בִּבְנֵי יִשְׂרָאֵל וְאֶת־בֶּהֱמַת
stock-of and Israel of-sons-of firstborn all-of in-place-of the-Levites

הַלְוִיִּם תַּחַת בְּהֶמְתָּם וְהָיוּ־לִי הַלְוִיִּם אֲנִי
I the-Levites for-me and-they-will-be stock-of-them in-place-of the-Levites

יְהוָה׃ וְאֵת פְּדוּיֵי הַשְּׁלֹשָׁה וְהַשִּׁבְעִים וְהַמָּאתָיִם
and-the-two-hundreds and-the-seventy the-three redemptions-of and (46) Yahweh

הָעֹדְפִים עַל־הַלְוִיִּם מִבְּכוֹר בְּנֵי יִשְׂרָאֵל׃
Israel sons-of from-firstborn-of the-Levites over the-ones-exceeding

וְלָקַחְתָּ חֲמֵשֶׁת חֲמֵשֶׁת שְׁקָלִים לַגֻּלְגֹּלֶת בְּשֶׁקֶל
by-shekel-of for-the-each shekels five-of five-of and-you-collect (47)

הַקֹּדֶשׁ תִּקָּח עֶשְׂרִים גֵּרָה הַשָּׁקֶל׃ וְנָתַתָּה
then-you-give (48) the-shekel gerah twenty you-collect the-sanctuary

הַכֶּסֶף לְאַהֲרֹן וּלְבָנָיו פְּדוּיֵי הָעֹדְפִים
the-ones-exceeding redemptions-of and-to-sons-of-him to-Aaron the-money

בָּהֶם׃ וַיִּקַּח מֹשֶׁה אֵת כֶּסֶף הַפִּדְיוֹם מֵאֵת
from the-redemption money-of *** Moses so-he-collected (49) over-them

הָעֹדְפִים עַל פְּדוּיֵי הַלְוִיִּם׃ מֵאֵת בְּכוֹר
firstborn-of from (50) the-Levites redemptions-of over the-ones-exceeding

בְּנֵי יִשְׂרָאֵל לָקַח אֶת־הַכָּסֶף חֲמִשָּׁה וְשִׁשִּׁים וּשְׁלֹשׁ מֵאוֹת
hundreds and-three and-sixty five the-money *** he-collected Israel sons-of

וָאֶלֶף בְּשֶׁקֶל הַקֹּדֶשׁ׃ וַיִּתֵּן מֹשֶׁה אֶת־כֶּסֶף
money-of *** Moses and-he-gave (51) the-sanctuary by-shekel-of and-thousand

הַפְּדֻיִם לְאַהֲרֹן וּלְבָנָיו עַל־פִּי יְהוָה כַּאֲשֶׁר
just-as Yahweh word-of by and-to-sons-of-him to-Aaron the-redemptions

צִוָּה יְהוָה אֶת־מֹשֶׁה׃ וַיְדַבֵּר יְהוָה אֶל־מֹשֶׁה וְאֶל־
and-to Moses to Yahweh and-he-spoke (4:1) Moses *** Yahweh he-commanded

אַהֲרֹן לֵאמֹר׃ נָשֹׂא אֶת־רֹאשׁ בְּנֵי קְהָת מִתּוֹךְ בְּנֵי לֵוִי
Levi sons-of from-among Kohath sons-of census-of *** to-take (2) to-say Aaron

לְמִשְׁפְּחֹתָם לְבֵית אֲבֹתָם׃ מִבֶּן שְׁלֹשִׁים שָׁנָה
year thirty from-son-of (3) fathers-of-them by-house-of by-clans-of-them

וָמַעְלָה וְעַד בֶּן־חֲמִשִּׁים שָׁנָה כָּל־בָּא לַצָּבָא לַעֲשׂוֹת מְלָאכָה
work to-do for-the-service coming all-of year fifty son-of even-to or-more

בְּאֹהֶל מוֹעֵד׃ זֹאת עֲבֹדַת בְּנֵי־קְהָת בְּאֹהֶל מוֹעֵד
Meeting in-Tent-of Kohath sons-of work-of this (4) Meeting in-Tent-of

listed by name, was 22,273.
44The LORD also said to
Moses, 45"Take the Levites in
place of all the firstborn of Israel, and the livestock of the
Levites in place of their livestock. The Levites are to be
mine. I am the LORD. 46To redeem the 273 firstborn Israelites who exceed the number of
the Levites, 47collect five
shekels[d] for each one, according to the sanctuary shekel,
which weighs twenty gerahs.
48Give the money for the redemption of the additional Israelites to Aaron and his
sons."
49So Moses collected the redemption money from those
who exceeded the number redeemed by the Levites. 50From
the firstborn of the Israelites
he collected silver weighing
1,365 shekels,[e] according to
the sanctuary shekel. 51Moses
gave the redemption money to
Aaron and his sons, as he was
commanded by the word of
the LORD.

The Kohathites

4 The LORD said to Moses
and Aaron: 2"Take a cen-
sus of the Kohathite branch of
the Levites by their clans and
families. 3Count all the men
from thirty to fifty years of age
who come to serve in the work
in the Tent of Meeting.
4"This is the work of the Kohathites in the Tent of Meeting: the care of the most holy

[d] *47* That is, about 2 ounces (about 55 grams)
[e] *50* That is, about 35 pounds (about 15.5 kilograms)

קֹדֶשׁ הַקֳּדָשִׁים׃ וּבָא אַהֲרֹן וּבָנָיו
and-sons-of-him Aaron then-he-must-go-in (5) the-holy-things most-holy-of

בִּנְסֹעַ הַמַּחֲנֶה וְהוֹרִדוּ אֵת פָּרֹכֶת הַמָּסָךְ
the-shield curtain-of *** and-they-must-take-down the-camp when-to-move

וְכִסּוּ־ בָהּ אֵת אֲרֹן הָעֵדֻת׃ וְנָתְנוּ
then-they-must-put (6) the-Testimony ark-of *** with-her and-they-must-cover

עָלָיו כְּסוּי עוֹר תַּחַשׁ וּפָרְשׂוּ בֶגֶד־ כְּלִיל
solid-of cloth-of and-they-must-spread sea-cow hide-of cover-of over-him

תְּכֵלֶת מִלְמָעְלָה וְשָׂמוּ בַּדָּיו׃ וְעַל ׀ שֻׁלְחַן
table-of and-over (7) poles-of-him and-they-must-put-in-place over-top blue

הַפָּנִים יִפְרְשׂוּ בֶּגֶד תְּכֵלֶת וְנָתְנוּ עָלָיו אֶת־
*** on-him and-they-must-put blue cloth-of they-must-spread the-Presences

הַקְּעָרֹת וְאֶת־ הַכַּפֹּת וְאֶת־ הַמְּנַקִּיֹּת וְאֵת קְשׂוֹת הַנָּסֶךְ
the-drink-offering jars-of and the-bowls and the-ladles and the-plates

וְלֶחֶם הַתָּמִיד עָלָיו יִהְיֶה׃ וּפָרְשׂוּ
and-they-must-spread (8) he-remains on-him the-continual and-bread-of

עֲלֵיהֶם בֶּגֶד תּוֹלַעַת שָׁנִי וְכִסּוּ אֹתוֹ בְּמִכְסֵה
with-cover-of him and-they-must-cover scarlet scarlet-of cloth-of over-them

עוֹר תָּחַשׁ וְשָׂמוּ אֶת־ בַּדָּיו׃
poles-of-him *** and-they-must-put-in-place sea-cow hide-of

וְלָקְחוּ ׀ בֶּגֶד תְּכֵלֶת וְכִסּוּ אֶת־ מְנֹרַת
lampstand-of *** and-they-must-cover blue cloth-of and-they-must-take (9)

הַמָּאוֹר וְאֶת־ נֵרֹתֶיהָ וְאֶת־ מַלְקָחֶיהָ וְאֶת־ מַחְתֹּתֶיהָ וְאֵת
and trays-of-her and wick-trimmers-of-her and lamps-of-her and the-light

כָּל־ כְּלֵי שַׁמְנָהּ אֲשֶׁר יְשָׁרְתוּ־ לָהּ בָּהֶם׃
with-them to-her they-supply that oil-of-her jars-of all-of

וְנָתְנוּ אֹתָהּ וְאֶת־ כָּל־ כֵּלֶיהָ אֶל־ מִכְסֵה עוֹר
hide-of cover-of in accessories-of-her all-of and her and-they-must-wrap (10)

תָּחַשׁ וְנָתְנוּ עַל־ הַמּוֹט׃ וְעַל ׀ מִזְבַּח
altar-of and-over (11) the-carrying-frame on and-they-must-put sea-cow

הַזָּהָב יִפְרְשׂוּ בֶּגֶד תְּכֵלֶת וְכִסּוּ אֹתוֹ בְּמִכְסֵה
with-cover-of him and-they-must-cover blue cloth-of they-must-spread the-gold

עוֹר תָּחַשׁ וְשָׂמוּ אֶת־ בַּדָּיו׃
poles-of-him *** and-they-must-put-in-place sea-cow hide-of

וְלָקְחוּ אֶת־ כָּל־ כְּלֵי הַשָּׁרֵת אֲשֶׁר יְשָׁרְתוּ־
they-minister that the-ministry articles-of all-of *** and-they-must-take (12)

בָם בַּקֹּדֶשׁ וְנָתְנוּ אֶל־ בֶּגֶד תְּכֵלֶת
blue cloth-of in and-they-must-wrap in-the-sanctuary with-them

things. [5]When the camp is to
move, Aaron and his sons are
to go in and take down the
shielding curtain and cover
the ark of the Testimony with
it. [6]Then they are to cover this
with hides of sea cows, spread
a cloth of solid blue over that
and put the poles in place.
[7]"Over the table of the Presence they are to spread a blue
cloth and put on it the plates,
ladles and bowls, and the jars
for drink offerings; the bread
that is continually there is to
remain on it. [8]Over these they
are to spread a scarlet cloth,
cover that with hides of sea
cows and put its poles in place.
[9]"They are to take a blue
cloth and cover the lampstand
that is for light, together with
its lamps, its wick trimmers
and trays, and all its jars for
the oil used to supply it. [10]Then
they are to wrap it and all its
accessories in a covering of
hides of sea cows and put it on
a carrying frame.
[11]"Over the gold altar they
are to spread a blue cloth and
cover that with hides of sea
cows and put its poles in place.
[12]"They are to take all the articles used for ministering in
the sanctuary, wrap them in a
blue cloth, cover that with

וְכִסּוּ אוֹתָם בְּמִכְסֵה עוֹר תָּחַשׁ וְנָתְנוּ עַל־
on and-they-must-put sea-cow hide-of with-cover-of them and-they-must-cover

הַמּוֹט׃ וְדִשְּׁנוּ אֶת־ הַמִּזְבֵּחַ
the-altar *** and-they-must-remove-ash (13) the-carrying-frame

וּפָרְשׂוּ עָלָיו בֶּגֶד אַרְגָּמָן׃ וְנָתְנוּ
then-they-must-place (14) purple cloth-of over-him and-they-must-spread

עָלָיו אֶת־ כָּל־ כֵּלָיו אֲשֶׁר יְשָׁרְתוּ עָלָיו בָּהֶם אֶת־
*** with-them at-him they-minister that utensils-of-him all-of *** on-him

הַמַּחְתֹּת אֶת־ הַמִּזְלָגֹת וְאֶת־ הַיָּעִים וְאֶת־ הַמִּזְרָקֹת
the-sprinkling-bowls and the-shovels and the-meatforks *** the-firepans

כֹּל כְּלֵי הַמִּזְבֵּחַ וּפָרְשׂוּ עָלָיו כְּסוּי עוֹר
hide-of cover-of over-him and-they-must-spread the-altar utensils-of all-of

תַּחַשׁ וְשָׂמוּ בַדָּיו׃ וְכִלָּה אַהֲרֹן־
Aaron when-he-finishes (15) poles-of-him and-they-must-put-in-place sea-cow

וּבָנָיו לְכַסֹּת אֶת־ הַקֹּדֶשׁ וְאֶת־ כָּל־ כְּלֵי הַקֹּדֶשׁ
the-holy articles-of all-of and the-holy-thing *** to-cover and-sons-of-him

בִּנְסֹעַ הַמַּחֲנֶה וְאַחֲרֵי־ כֵן יָבֹאוּ בְנֵי־ קְהָת לָשֵׂאת
to-carry Kohath sons-of they-must-come this then-after the-camp when-to-move

וְלֹא־ יִגְּעוּ אֶל־ הַקֹּדֶשׁ וָמֵתוּ אֵלֶּה מַשָּׂא בְנֵי־
sons-of burden-of these or-they-will-die the-holy on they-must-touch but-not

קְהָת בְּאֹהֶל מוֹעֵד׃ וּפְקֻדַּת אֶלְעָזָר ׀ בֶּן־ אַהֲרֹן הַכֹּהֵן
the-priest Aaron son-of Eleazar now-charge-of (16) Meeting in-Tent-of Kohath

שֶׁמֶן הַמָּאוֹר וּקְטֹרֶת הַסַּמִּים וּמִנְחַת
and-grain-offering-of the-fragrances and-incense-of the-light oil-of

הַתָּמִיד וְשֶׁמֶן הַמִּשְׁחָה פְּקֻדַּת כָּל־ הַמִּשְׁכָּן
the-tabernacle entire-of charge-of the-anointing and-oil-of the-regular

וְכָל־ אֲשֶׁר־ בּוֹ בְּקֹדֶשׁ וּבְכֵלָיו׃ וַיְדַבֵּר
and-he-spoke (17) and-of-articles-of-him of-holy-thing in-him that and-all

יְהוָה אֶל־ מֹשֶׁה וְאֶל־ אַהֲרֹן לֵאמֹר׃ אַל־ תַּכְרִיתוּ אֶת־ שֵׁבֶט
tribe-of *** you-cut-off not (18) to-say Aaron and-to Moses to Yahweh

מִשְׁפְּחֹת הַקְּהָתִי מִתּוֹךְ הַלְוִיִּם׃ וְזֹאת ׀ עֲשׂוּ לָהֶם
for-them do! and-this (19) the-Levites from-among the-Kohathite clans-of

וְחָיוּ וְלֹא יָמֻתוּ בְּגִשְׁתָּם אֶת־ קֹדֶשׁ
most-holy-of *** when-to-come-near-them they-die and-not so-they-may-live

הַקֳּדָשִׁים אַהֲרֹן וּבָנָיו יָבֹאוּ וְשָׂמוּ אוֹתָם
them and-they-must-assign they-must-go and-sons-of-him Aaron the-holy-things

אִישׁ אִישׁ עַל־ עֲבֹדָתוֹ וְאֶל־ מַשָּׂאוֹ׃ וְלֹא־ יָבֹאוּ
they-must-go-in but-not (20) burden-of-him and-to work-of-him to each man

hides of sea cows and put
them on a carrying frame.
13"They are to remove the
ashes from the bronze altar
and spread a purple cloth over
it. 14Then they are to place on
it all the utensils used for ministering at the altar, including
the firepans, meat forks, shovels and sprinkling bowls. Over
it they are to spread a covering
of hides of sea cows and put its
poles in place.
15"After Aaron and his sons
have finished covering the
holy furnishings and all the
holy articles, and when the
camp is ready to move, the
Kohathites are to come to do
the carrying. But they must
not touch the holy things or
they will die. The Kohathites
are to carry those things that
are in the Tent of Meeting.
16"Eleazar son of Aaron, the
priest, is to have charge of the
oil for the light, the fragrant
incense, the regular grain
offering and the anointing oil.
He is to be in charge of the
entire tabernacle and everything in it, including its holy
furnishings and articles."
17The LORD said to Moses
and Aaron, 18"See that the Kohathite tribal clans are not cut
off from the Levites. 19So that
they may live and not die
when they come near the most
holy things, do this for them:
Aaron and his sons are to go
into the sanctuary and assign
to each man his work and
what he is to carry. 20But the

לִרְאוֹת כְּבַלַּע אֶת־ הַקֹּדֶשׁ וָמֵתוּ׃
or-they-will-die the-holy-thing *** even-to-be-momentary to-look

וַיְדַבֵּר יְהוָה אֶל־ מֹשֶׁה לֵּאמֹר׃ נָשֹׂא אֶת־ רֹאשׁ בְּנֵי
sons-of census-of *** to-take (22) to-say Moses to Yahweh and-he-spoke (21)

גֵרְשׁוֹן גַּם־ הֵם לְבֵית אֲבֹתָם לְמִשְׁפְּחֹתָם׃ מִבֶּן
from-son-of (23) by-clans-of-them fathers-of-them by-house-of them also Gershon

שְׁלֹשִׁים שָׁנָה וָמַעְלָה עַד בֶּן־ חֲמִשִּׁים שָׁנָה תִּפְקֹד אוֹתָם כָּל־
every-of them you-count year fifty son-of to or-more year thirty

הַבָּא לִצְבֹא צָבָא לַעֲבֹד עֲבֹדָה בְּאֹהֶל מוֹעֵד׃ זֹאת
this (24) Meeting at-Tent-of work to-work service to-serve the-one-coming

עֲבֹדַת מִשְׁפְּחֹת הַגֵּרְשֻׁנִּי לַעֲבֹד וּלְמַשָּׂא׃ וְנָשְׂאוּ
now-they-must-carry (25) and-as-burden to-work the-Gershonite clans-of service-of

אֶת־ יְרִיעֹת הַמִּשְׁכָּן וְאֶת־ אֹהֶל מוֹעֵד מִכְסֵהוּ וּמִכְסֵה
and-cover-of cover-of-him Meeting Tent-of and the-tabernacle curtains-of ***

הַתַּחַשׁ אֲשֶׁר־ עָלָיו מִלְמָעְלָה וְאֶת־ מָסַךְ פֶּתַח אֹהֶל מוֹעֵד׃
Meeting Tent-of entrance-of curtain-of and outer over-him that the-sea-cow

וְאֵת קַלְעֵי הֶחָצֵר וְאֶת־ מָסַךְ ׀ פֶּתַח ׀ שַׁעַר
gate-of entrance-of curtain-of and the-courtyard curtains-of and (26)

הֶחָצֵר אֲשֶׁר עַל־ הַמִּשְׁכָּן וְעַל־ הַמִּזְבֵּחַ סָבִיב
surrounding the-altar and-around the-tabernacle around that the-courtyard

וְאֵת מֵיתְרֵיהֶם וְאֶת־ כָּל־ כְּלֵי עֲבֹדָתָם וְאֵת כָּל־אֲשֶׁר
that all and service-of-them equipments-of all-of and ropes-of-them and

יֵעָשֶׂה לָהֶם וְעָבָדוּ׃ עַל־ פִּי אַהֲרֹן
Aaron direction-of under (27) then-they-must-do with-them he-must-be-done

וּבָנָיו תִּהְיֶה כָּל־ עֲבֹדַת בְּנֵי הַגֵּרְשֻׁנִּי
the-Gershonite sons-of service-of all-of she-must-be-done and-sons-of-him

לְכָל־ מַשָּׂאָם וּלְכֹל עֲבֹדָתָם
work-of-them or-whether-all-of burden-of-them whether-all-of

וּפְקַדְתֶּם עֲלֵהֶם בְּמִשְׁמֶרֶת אֵת כָּל־ מַשָּׂאָם׃
burden-of-them all-of *** as-responsibility to-them and-you-shall-assign

זֹאת עֲבֹדַת מִשְׁפְּחֹת בְּנֵי הַגֵּרְשֻׁנִּי בְּאֹהֶל מוֹעֵד
Meeting at-Tent-of the-Gershonite sons-of clans-of service-of this (28)

וּמִשְׁמַרְתָּם בְּיַד אִיתָמָר בֶּן־ אַהֲרֹן הַכֹּהֵן׃
the-priest Aaron son-of Ithamar under-direction-of and-duty-of-them

בְּנֵי מְרָרִי לְמִשְׁפְּחֹתָם לְבֵית־ אֲבֹתָם תִּפְקֹד
you-count fathers-of-them by-house-of by-clans-of-them Merari sons-of (29)

אֹתָם׃ מִבֶּן שְׁלֹשִׁים שָׁנָה וָמַעְלָה וְעַד בֶּן־ חֲמִשִּׁים שָׁנָה
year fifty son-of even-to or-more year thirty from-son-of (30) them

Kohathites must not go in to look at the holy things, even for a moment, or they will die."

The Gershonites

[21]The LORD said to Moses,
[22]"Take a census also of the Gershonites by their families and clans.
[23]Count all the men from thirty to fifty years of age who come to serve in the work at the Tent of Meeting.
[24]"This is the service of the Gershonite clans as they work and carry burdens:
[25]They are to carry the curtains of the tabernacle, the Tent of Meeting, its covering and the outer covering of hides of sea cows, the curtains for the entrance to the Tent of Meeting,
[26]the curtains of the courtyard surrounding the tabernacle and altar, the curtain for the entrance, the ropes and all the equipment used in its service. The Gershonites are to do all that needs to be done with these things.
[27]All their service, whether carrying or doing other work, is to be done under the direction of Aaron and his sons. You shall assign to them as their responsibility all they are to carry.
[28]This is the service of the Gershonite clans at the Tent of Meeting. Their duties are to be under the direction of Ithamar son of Aaron, the priest.

The Merarites

[29]"Count the Merarites by their clans and families.
[30]Count all the men from thirty to fifty years of age who

תִּפְקְדֵם כָּל־ הַבָּא לַצָּבָא לַעֲבֹד אֶת־ עֲבֹדַת
work-of *** to-work to-the-service the-one-coming all-of you-count-them

אֹהֶל מוֹעֵד׃ (31) וְזֹאת מִשְׁמֶרֶת מַשָּׂאָם לְכָל־ עֲבֹדָתָם
service-of-them in-all-of burden-of-them duty-of and-this (31) Meeting Tent-of

בְּאֹהֶל מוֹעֵד קַרְשֵׁי הַמִּשְׁכָּן וּבְרִיחָיו
and-crossbars-of-him the-tabernacle frames-of Meeting at-Tent-of

וְעַמּוּדָיו וַאֲדָנָיו׃ (32) וְעַמּוּדֵי הֶחָצֵר סָבִיב
around the-courtyard and-posts-of (32) and-bases-of-him and-posts-of-him

וְאַדְנֵיהֶם וִיתֵדֹתָם וּמֵיתְרֵיהֶם לְכָל־
for-all-of and-ropes-of-them and-tent-pegs-of-them and-bases-of-them

כְּלֵיהֶם וּלְכֹל עֲבֹדָתָם וּבְשֵׁמֹת תִּפְקְדוּ אֶת־
*** you-assign and-by-names use-of-them and-for-all-of equipments-of-them

כְּלֵי מִשְׁמֶרֶת מַשָּׂאָם׃ (33) זֹאת עֲבֹדַת מִשְׁפְּחֹת בְּנֵי
sons-of clans-of service-of this (33) burden-of-them duty-of things-of

מְרָרִי לְכָל־ עֲבֹדָתָם בְּאֹהֶל מוֹעֵד בְּיַד אִיתָמָר
Ithamar under-direction-of Meeting at-Tent-of work-of-them for-all-of Merari

בֶּן־ אַהֲרֹן הַכֹּהֵן׃ (34) וַיִּפְקֹד מֹשֶׁה וְאַהֲרֹן וּנְשִׂיאֵי
and-leaders-of and-Aaron Moses so-he-counted (34) the-priest Aaron son-of

הָעֵדָה אֶת־ בְּנֵי הַקְּהָתִי לְמִשְׁפְּחֹתָם וּלְבֵית
and-by-house-of by-clans-of-them the-Kohathite sons-of *** the-community

אֲבֹתָם׃ (35) מִבֶּן שְׁלֹשִׁים שָׁנָה וָמַעְלָה וְעַד בֶּן־חֲמִשִּׁים
fifty son-of even-to or-more year thirty from-son-of (35) fathers-of-them

שָׁנָה כָּל־ הַבָּא לַצָּבָא לַעֲבֹדָה בְּאֹהֶל מוֹעֵד׃
Meeting in-Tent-of in-work to-the-service the-one-coming every-of year

(36) וַיִּהְיוּ פְקֻדֵיהֶם לְמִשְׁפְּחֹתָם אַלְפַּיִם שְׁבַע
seven-of two-thousands by-clans-of-them countings-of-them and-they-were (36)

מֵאוֹת וַחֲמִשִּׁים׃ (37) אֵלֶּה פְקוּדֵי מִשְׁפְּחֹת הַקְּהָתִי
the-Kohathite clans-of ones-being-totaled-of these (37) and-fifty hundreds

כָּל־ הָעֹבֵד בְּאֹהֶל מוֹעֵד אֲשֶׁר פָּקַד מֹשֶׁה וְאַהֲרֹן
and-Aaron Moses he-counted whom Meeting in-Tent-of the-one-serving every-of

עַל־ פִּי יְהוָה בְּיַד־ מֹשֶׁה׃ (38) וּפְקוּדֵי בְּנֵי גֵּרְשׁוֹן
Gershon sons-of and-countings-of (38) Moses by-hand-of Yahweh command-of at

לְמִשְׁפְּחוֹתָם וּלְבֵית אֲבֹתָם׃ (39) מִבֶּן שְׁלֹשִׁים
thirty from-son-of (39) fathers-of-them and-by-house-of by-clans-of-them

שָׁנָה וָמַעְלָה וְעַד בֶּן־ חֲמִשִּׁים שָׁנָה כָּל־ הַבָּא לַצָּבָא
to-the-service the-one-coming every-of year fifty son-of even-to or-more year

לַעֲבֹדָה בְּאֹהֶל מוֹעֵד׃ (40) וַיִּהְיוּ פְּקֻדֵיהֶם
countings-of-them and-they-were (40) Meeting at-Tent-of in-work

come to serve in the work at the Tent of Meeting. 31 This is their duty as they perform service at the Tent of Meeting: to carry the frames of the tabernacle, its crossbars, posts and bases, 32 as well as the posts of the surrounding courtyard with their bases, tent pegs, ropes, all their equipment and everything related to their use. Assign to each man the specific things he is to carry. 33 This is the service of the Merarite clans as they work at the Tent of Meeting under the direction of Ithamar son of Aaron, the priest."

The Numbering of the Levite Clans

34 Moses, Aaron and the leaders of the community counted the Kohathites by their clans and families. 35 All the men from thirty to fifty years of age who came to serve in the work in the Tent of Meeting, 36 counted by clans, were 2,750. 37 This was the total of all those in the Kohathite clans who served in the Tent of Meeting. Moses and Aaron counted them according to the LORD's command through Moses.

38 The Gershonites were counted by their clans and families. 39 All the men from thirty to fifty years of age who came to serve in the work at the Tent of Meeting, 40 counted

לְמִשְׁפְּחֹתָם לְבֵית אֲבֹתָם אַלְפַּיִם וְשֵׁשׁ מֵאוֹת
hundreds and-six two-thousands fathers-of-them by-house-of by-clans-of-them

וּשְׁלֹשִׁים׃ (41) אֵלֶּה פְקוּדֵי מִשְׁפְּחֹת בְּנֵי גֵרְשׁוֹן כָּל־
every-of Gershon sons-of clans-of ones-being-totaled-of these (41) and-thirty

הָעֹבֵד בְּאֹהֶל מוֹעֵד אֲשֶׁר פָּקַד מֹשֶׁה וְאַהֲרֹן עַל־
at and-Aaron Moses he-counted whom Meeting at-Tent-of the-one-serving

פִּי יְהוָה׃ (42) וּפְקוּדֵי מִשְׁפְּחֹת בְּנֵי מְרָרִי
Merari sons-of clans-of and-countings-of (42) Yahweh command-of

לְמִשְׁפְּחֹתָם לְבֵית אֲבֹתָם׃ (43) מִבֶּן שְׁלֹשִׁים שָׁנָה
year thirty from-son-of (43) fathers-of-them by-house-of by-clans-of-them

וָמַעְלָה וְעַד בֶּן־ חֲמִשִּׁים שָׁנָה כָּל־ הַבָּא לַצָּבָא
to-the-service the-one-coming every-of year fifty son-of even-to or-more

לַעֲבֹדָה בְּאֹהֶל מוֹעֵד׃ (44) וַיִּהְיוּ פְקֻדֵיהֶם
countings-of-them and-they-were (44) Meeting at-Tent-of in-work

לְמִשְׁפְּחֹתָם שְׁלֹשֶׁת אֲלָפִים וּמָאתָיִם׃ (45) אֵלֶּה פְּקוּדֵי
totalings-of these (45) and-two-hundreds thousands three by-clans-of-them

מִשְׁפְּחֹת בְּנֵי מְרָרִי אֲשֶׁר פָּקַד מֹשֶׁה וְאַהֲרֹן עַל־ פִּי יְהוָה
Yahweh command-of at and-Aaron Moses he-counted whom Merari sons-of clans-of

בְּיַד־ מֹשֶׁה׃ (46) כָּל־ הַפְּקֻדִים אֲשֶׁר פָּקַד מֹשֶׁה
Moses he-counted whom the-ones-being-counted all-of (46) Moses by-hand-of

וְאַהֲרֹן וּנְשִׂיאֵי יִשְׂרָאֵל אֶת־ הַלְוִיִּם לְמִשְׁפְּחֹתָם
by-clans-of-them the-Levites *** Israel and-leaders-of and-Aaron

וּלְבֵית אֲבֹתָם׃ (47) מִבֶּן שְׁלֹשִׁים שָׁנָה וָמַעְלָה וְעַד
even-to or-more year thirty from-son-of (47) fathers-of-them and-by-house-of

בֶּן־ חֲמִשִּׁים שָׁנָה כָּל־ הַבָּא לַעֲבֹד עֲבֹדַת עֲבֹדָה וַעֲבֹדַת
and-work-of service work-of to-do the-one-coming every-of year fifty son-of

מַשָּׂא בְּאֹהֶל מוֹעֵד׃ (48) וַיִּהְיוּ פְּקֻדֵיהֶם שְׁמֹנַת
eight-of numberings-of-them and-they-were (48) Meeting at-Tent-of carrying

אֲלָפִים וַחֲמֵשׁ מֵאוֹת וּשְׁמֹנִים׃ (49) עַל־ פִּי יְהוָה
Yahweh command-of at (49) and-eighty hundreds and-five-of thousands

פָּקַד אוֹתָם בְּיַד־ מֹשֶׁה אִישׁ אִישׁ עַל־ עֲבֹדָתוֹ וְעַל־ מַשָּׂאוֹ
burden-of-him and-to work-of-him to each man Moses by-hand-of them he-counted

וּפְקֻדָיו אֲשֶׁר־ צִוָּה יְהוָה אֶת־ מֹשֶׁה׃
Moses *** Yahweh he-commanded as so-ones-being-counted-of-him

(5:1) וַיְדַבֵּר יְהוָה אֶל־ מֹשֶׁה לֵּאמֹר׃ (2) צַו אֶת־ בְּנֵי יִשְׂרָאֵל
Israel sons-of *** command! (2) to-say Moses to Yahweh and-he-spoke (5:1)

וִישַׁלְּחוּ מִן־ הַמַּחֲנֶה כָּל־ צָרוּעַ וְכָל־ זָב
discharging or-any-of being-infected any-of the-camp from so-they-send

by their clans and families,
were 2,630. 41This was the total of those in the Gershonite
clans who served at the Tent
of Meeting. Moses and Aaron
counted them according to the
LORD's command.
42The Merarites were counted by their clans and families.
43All the men from thirty to
fifty years of age who came to
serve in the work at the Tent
of Meeting, 44counted by their
clans, were 3,200. 45This was
the total of those in the Merarite clans. Moses and Aaron
counted them according to the
LORD's command through
Moses.
46So Moses, Aaron and the
leaders of Israel counted all the
Levites by their clans and
families. 47All the men from
thirty to fifty years of age who
came to do the work of serving
and carrying the Tent of Meeting 48numbered 8,580. 49At the
LORD's command through
Moses, each was assigned his
work and told what to carry.
Thus they were counted, as
the LORD commanded Moses.

The Purity of the Camp

5 The LORD said to Moses,
2"Command the Israelites
to send away from the camp
anyone who has an infectious
skin disease[f] or a discharge of

f2 Traditionally *leprosy;* the Hebrew word was used for various diseases affecting the skin—not necessarily leprosy

וְכֹל טָמֵא לָנָפֶשׁ׃ מִזָּכָר עַד־נְקֵבָה תְּשַׁלֵּחוּ אֶל־
to you-send-away-him female to from-male (3) from-body unclean or-any-of

מִחוּץ לַמַּחֲנֶה תְּשַׁלְּחוּם וְלֹא יְטַמְּאוּ אֶת־מַחֲנֵיהֶם
camps-of-them *** they-defile so-not you-send-away-them of-the-camp outside

אֲשֶׁר אֲנִי שֹׁכֵן בְּתוֹכָם׃ וַיַּעֲשׂוּ־כֵן בְּנֵי יִשְׂרָאֵל
Israel sons-of this and-they-did (4) among-them dwelling I where

וַיְשַׁלְּחוּ אוֹתָם אֶל־מִחוּץ לַמַּחֲנֶה כַּאֲשֶׁר דִּבֶּר יְהוָה אֶל־
to Yahweh he-commanded just-as of-the-camp outside to them and-they-sent

מֹשֶׁה כֵּן עָשׂוּ בְּנֵי יִשְׂרָאֵל׃ וַיְדַבֵּר יְהוָה אֶל־מֹשֶׁה לֵּאמֹר׃
to-say Moses to Yahweh and-he-spoke (5) Israel sons-of they-did so Moses

דַּבֵּר אֶל־בְּנֵי יִשְׂרָאֵל אִישׁ אוֹ־אִשָּׁה כִּי יַעֲשׂוּ מִכָּל־
from-any-of they-commit when woman or man Israel sons-of to say! (6)

חַטֹּאת הָאָדָם לִמְעֹל מַעַל בַּיהוָה
to-Yahweh he-is-unfaithful to-be-unfaithful the-mankind wrongs-of

וְאָשְׁמָה הַנֶּפֶשׁ הַהִוא׃ וְהִתְוַדּוּ אֶת־
*** and-they-must-confess (7) the-that the-person and-she-is-guity

חַטָּאתָם אֲשֶׁר עָשׂוּ וְהֵשִׁיב אֶת־אֲשָׁמוֹ
wrong-of-him *** and-he-must-restitute they-committed that sin-of-them

בְּרֹאשׁוֹ וַחֲמִישִׁתוֹ יֹסֵף עָלָיו וְנָתַן לַאֲשֶׁר
to-whom and-he-must-give to-him he-must-add and-fifth-of-him on-head-of-him

אָשַׁם לוֹ׃ וְאִם־אֵין לָאִישׁ גֹּאֵל
relative-being-close to-the-person he-is-not but-if (8) to-him he-wronged

לְהָשִׁיב הָאָשָׁם אֵלָיו הָאָשָׁם הַמּוּשָׁב לַיהוָה
to-Yahweh the-being-restored the-wrong to-him the-wrong to-restitute

לַכֹּהֵן מִלְּבַד אֵיל הַכִּפֻּרִים אֲשֶׁר יְכַפֶּר־בּוֹ
with-him he-atones which the-atonements ram-of along-with to-the-priest

עָלָיו׃ וְכָל־תְּרוּמָה לְכָל־קָדְשֵׁי בְנֵי־
sons-of sacred-ones-of from-all-of contribution and-every-of (9) for-him

יִשְׂרָאֵל אֲשֶׁר־יַקְרִיבוּ לַכֹּהֵן לוֹ יִהְיֶה׃ וְאִישׁ אֶת־
*** and-man (10) he-is for-him to-the-priest they-bring that Israel

קֳדָשָׁיו לוֹ יִהְיוּ אִישׁ אֲשֶׁר־יִתֵּן לַכֹּהֵן לוֹ
for-him to-the-priest he-gives what man they-are to-him sacred-gifts-of-him

יִהְיֶה׃ וַיְדַבֵּר יְהוָה אֶל־מֹשֶׁה לֵּאמֹר׃ דַּבֵּר אֶל־בְּנֵי
sons-of to speak! (12) to-say Moses to Yahweh and-he-spoke (11) he-is

יִשְׂרָאֵל וְאָמַרְתָּ אֲלֵהֶם אִישׁ אִישׁ כִּי־תִשְׂטֶה אִשְׁתּוֹ
wife-of-him she-goes-astray if any man to-them and-you-say Israel

וּמָעֲלָה בוֹ מָעַל׃ וְשָׁכַב אִישׁ אֹתָהּ
with-her man and-he-sleeps (13) unfaithfulness to-him and-she-is-unfaithful

any kind, or who is ceremonially unclean because of a dead body. [3]Send away male and female alike; send them outside the camp so they will not defile their camp, where I dwell among them." [4]The Israelites did this; they sent them outside the camp. They did just as the LORD had instructed Moses.

The Test for an Unfaithful Wife

[5]The LORD said to Moses, [6]"Say to the Israelites: 'When a man or woman wrongs another in any way[h] and so is unfaithful to the LORD, that person is guilty [7]and must confess the sin he has committed. He must make full restitution for his wrong, add one fifth to it and give it all to the person he has wronged. [8]But if that person has no close relative to whom restitution can be made for the wrong, the restitution belongs to the LORD and must be given to the priest, along with the ram with which atonement is made for him. [9]All the sacred contributions the Israelites bring to a priest will belong to him. [10]Each man's sacred gifts are his own, but what he gives to the priest will belong to the priest.' "

[11]Then the LORD said to Moses, [12]"Speak to the Israelites and say to them: 'If a man's wife goes astray and is unfaithful to him [13]by sleeping

[h]6 *Or woman commits any wrong common to mankind*

שִׁכְבַת־ זֶרַע וְנֶעְלַם מֵעֵינֵי אִישָׁהּ
husband-of-her from-eyes-of and-he-is-hidden semen emission-of

וְנִסְתְּרָה וְהִיא נִטְמָאָה וְעֵד אֵין בָּהּ
against-her he-is-not and-witness she-is-impure also-she and-she-is-undetected

וְהִוא לֹא נִתְפָּשָׂה׃ וְעָבַר עָלָיו רוּחַ־ קִנְאָה
jealousy feeling-of over-him and-he-comes (14) she-was-caught not and-she

וְקִנֵּא אֶת־ אִשְׁתּוֹ וְהִוא נִטְמָאָה אוֹ־ עָבַר עָלָיו
over-him he-comes or she-is-impure and-she wife-of-him *** and-he-suspects

רוּחַ־ קִנְאָה וְקִנֵּא אֶת־ אִשְׁתּוֹ וְהִיא לֹא נִטְמָאָה׃
she-is-impure not but-she wife-of-him *** and-he-suspects jealousy feeling-of

וְהֵבִיא הָאִישׁ אֶת־ אִשְׁתּוֹ אֶל־ הַכֹּהֵן וְהֵבִיא
and-he-must-take the-priest to wife-of-him *** the-man then-he-must-take (15)

אֶת־ קָרְבָּנָהּ עָלֶיהָ עֲשִׂירִת הָאֵיפָה קֶמַח שְׂעֹרִים לֹא־
not barleys flour-of the-ephah tenth-of for-her offering-of-her ***

יִצֹק עָלָיו שֶׁמֶן וְלֹא־ יִתֵּן עָלָיו לְבֹנָה כִּי־ מִנְחַת
offering-of for incense on-him he-must-put or-not oil on-him he-must-pour

קְנָאֹת הוּא מִנְחַת זִכָּרוֹן מַזְכֶּרֶת עָוֺן׃
guilt drawing-attention reminder offering-of he jealousies

וְהִקְרִיב אֹתָהּ הַכֹּהֵן וְהֶעֱמִדָהּ לִפְנֵי יְהוָה׃
Yahweh before and-he-shall-stand-her the-priest her and-he-shall-bring (16)

וְלָקַח הַכֹּהֵן מַיִם קְדֹשִׁים בִּכְלִי־ חָרֶשׂ וּמִן־
and-from clay in-jar-of holy-ones waters the-priest then-he-shall-take (17)

הֶעָפָר אֲשֶׁר יִהְיֶה בְּקַרְקַע הַמִּשְׁכָּן יִקַּח הַכֹּהֵן
the-priest he-shall-take the-tabernacle on-floor-of he-is that the-dust

וְנָתַן אֶל־ הַמָּיִם׃ וְהֶעֱמִיד הַכֹּהֵן אֶת־
*** the-priest and-he-shall-stand (18) the-waters into and-he-shall-put

הָאִשָּׁה לִפְנֵי יְהוָה וּפָרַע אֶת־ רֹאשׁ הָאִשָּׁה
the-woman hair-of *** and-he-shall-loosen Yahweh before the-woman

וְנָתַן עַל־ כַּפֶּיהָ אֵת מִנְחַת הַזִּכָּרוֹן מִנְחַת
offering-of the-reminder offering-of *** hands-of-her in and-he-shall-place

קְנָאֹת הִוא וּבְיַד הַכֹּהֵן יִהְיוּ מֵי הַמָּרִים
the-bitter-ones waters-of they-are the-priest and-in-hand-of she jealousies

הַמְאָרְרִים׃ וְהִשְׁבִּיעַ אֹתָהּ הַכֹּהֵן
the-priest her then-he-shall-put-under-oath (19) the-ones-bringing-curse

וְאָמַר אֶל־ הָאִשָּׁה אִם־ לֹא שָׁכַב אִישׁ אֹתָךְ וְאִם־ לֹא
not and-if with-you man he-slept not if the-woman to and-he-shall-say

שָׂטִית טֻמְאָה תַּחַת אִישֵׁךְ הִנָּקִי מִמֵּי
by-waters-of be-unharmed! husband-of-you under impure you-went-astray

with another man, and this is
hidden from her husband and
her impurity is undetected
(since there is no witness
against her and she has not
been caught in the act), [14]and
if feelings of jealousy come
over her husband and he suspects his wife and she is impure—or if he is jealous and
suspects her even though she
is not impure— [15]then he is to
take his wife to the priest. He
must also take an offering of a
tenth of an ephah[i] of barley
flour on her behalf. He must
not pour oil on it or put incense on it, because it is a
grain offering for jealousy, a
reminder offering to draw attention to guilt.
[16]" 'The priest shall bring
her and have her stand before
the LORD. [17]Then he shall take
some holy water in a clay jar
and put some dust from the
tabernacle floor into the water.
[18]After the priest has had the
woman stand before the LORD,
he shall loosen her hair and
place in her hands the reminder offering, the grain
offering for jealousy, while he
himself holds the bitter water
that brings a curse. [19]Then the
priest shall put the woman under oath and say to her, "If no
other man has slept with you
and you have not gone astray
and become impure while
married to your husband, may
this bitter water that brings a

[i]15 That is, probably about 2 quarts (about 2 liters)

הַמָּרִים	הַמְאָרְרִים	הָאֵלֶּה:		וְאַתְּ	כִּי
the-bitter-ones	the-ones-bringing-curse	the-these	(20)	but-you	if

שָׂטִית	תַּחַת	אִישֵׁךְ	וְכִי	נִטְמֵאת	וַיִּתֵּן
you-went-astray	under	husband-of-you	and-if	you-defiled-self	and-he-gave

אִישׁ	בָּךְ	אֶת־	שְׁכָבְתּוֹ	מִבַּלְעֲדֵי	אִישֵׁךְ:
man	to-you	***	emission-of-him	other-than	husband-of-you

	וְהִשְׁבִּיעַ	הַכֹּהֵן	אֶת־	הָאִשָּׁה	בִּשְׁבֻעַת
(21)	then-he-must-put-under-oath	the-priest	***	the-woman	under-curse-of

הָאָלָה	וְאָמַר	הַכֹּהֵן	לָאִשָּׁה	יִתֵּן	יְהוָה	אוֹתָךְ
the-oath	and-he-shall-say	the-priest	to-the-woman	may-he-make	Yahweh	you

לְאָלָה	וְלִשְׁבֻעָה	בְּתוֹךְ	עַמֵּךְ	בְּתֵת	יְהוָה	אֶת־
as-curse	and-as-denounced	among	people-of-you	when-to-cause	Yahweh	***

יְרֵכֵךְ	נֹפֶלֶת	וְאֶת־	בִּטְנֵךְ	צָבָה:		וּבָאוּ
thigh-of-you	wasting-away	and	abdomen-of-you	swollen	(22)	and-may-they-enter

הַמַּיִם	הַמְאָרְרִים	הָאֵלֶּה	בְּמֵעַיִךְ	לַצְבּוֹת
the-waters	the-ones-bringing-curse	the-these	into-body-of-you	to-make-swell

בֶּטֶן	וְלַנְפִּל	יָרֵךְ	וְאָמְרָה	הָאִשָּׁה	אָמֵן |	אָמֵן:
abdomen	and-to-waste-away	thigh	then-she-must-say	the-woman	so-be-it	so-be-it

	וְכָתַב	אֶת־	הָאָלֹת	הָאֵלֶּה	הַכֹּהֵן	בַּסֵּפֶר
(23)	and-he-must-write	***	the-curses	the-these	the-priest	on-the-scroll

וּמָחָה	אֶל־	מֵי	הַמָּרִים:		וְהִשְׁקָה
then-he-must-wash	into	waters-of	the-bitter-ones	(24)	then-he-shall-have-drink

אֶת־	הָאִשָּׁה	אֶת־	מֵי	הַמָּרִים	הַמְאָרְרִים
***	the-woman	***	waters-of	the-bitter-ones	the-ones-bringing-curse

וּבָאוּ	בָהּ	הַמַּיִם	הַמְאָרְרִים	לְמָרִים:
and-they-will-enter	into-her	the-waters	the-ones-bringing-curse	as-bitter-ones

	וְלָקַח	הַכֹּהֵן	מִיַּד	הָאִשָּׁה	אֵת	מִנְחַת
(25)	then-he-must-take	the-priest	from-hand-of	the-woman	***	offering-of

הַקְּנָאֹת	וְהֵנִיף	אֶת־	הַמִּנְחָה	לִפְנֵי	יְהוָה	וְהִקְרִיב
the-jealousies	and-he-must-wave	***	the-offering	before	Yahweh	and-he-must-bring

אֹתָהּ	אֶל־	הַמִּזְבֵּחַ:		וְקָמַץ	הַכֹּהֵן	מִן־	הַמִּנְחָה
her	to	the-altar	(26)	then-he-must-take-handful	the-priest	from	the-offering

אֶת־	אַזְכָּרָתָהּ	וְהִקְטִיר	הַמִּזְבֵּחָה	וְאַחַר
***	memorial-offering-of-her	and-he-must-burn	on-the-altar	and-after

יַשְׁקֶה	אֶת־	הָאִשָּׁה	אֶת־	הַמָּיִם:		וְהִשְׁקָהּ
he-must-have-drink	***	the-woman	***	the-waters	(27)	when-he-makes-drink-her

אֶת־	הַמַּיִם	וְהָיְתָה	אִם־	נִטְמְאָה	וַתִּמְעֹל
***	the-waters	then-she-will-be	if	she-defiled-self	and-she-was-unfaithful

curse not harm you. [20]But if
you have gone astray while
married to your husband and
you have defiled yourself by
sleeping with a man other
than your husband"— [21]here
the priest is to put the woman
under this curse of the oath—
"may the LORD cause your
people to curse and denounce
you when he causes your
thigh to waste away and your
abdomen to swell.[j] [22]May this
water that brings a curse enter
your body so that your abdomen swells and your thigh
wastes away.[k]"
" 'Then the woman is to say,
"So be it."
[23]" 'The priest is to write
these curses on a scroll and
then wash them off into the
bitter water. [24]He shall have
the woman drink the bitter
water that brings a curse, and
this water will enter her and
cause bitter suffering. [25]The
priest is to take from her
hands the grain offering for
jealousy, wave it before the
LORD and bring it to the altar.
[26]The priest is then to take a
handful of the grain offering
as a memorial offering and
burn it on the altar; after that,
he is to have the woman drink
the water. [27]If she has defiled
herself and been unfaithful to
her husband, then when she
is made to drink the water that

j21 Or *causes you to have a miscarrying womb and barrenness*
k22 Or *body and cause you to be barren and have a miscarrying womb*

מַעַל בְּאִישָׁהּ וּבָאוּ בָהּ הַמַּיִם
the-waters into-her then-they-will-enter to-husband-of-her unfaithfulness

הַמְאָרְרִים לְמָרִים וְצָבְתָה בִטְנָהּ
abdomen-of-her and-she-will-swell as-bitter-ones the-ones-bringing-curse

וְנָפְלָה יְרֵכָהּ וְהָיְתָה הָאִשָּׁה לְאָלָה
as-curse the-woman and-she-will-become thigh-of-her and-she-will-waste-away

בְּקֶרֶב עַמָּהּ׃ (28) וְאִם־ לֹא נִטְמְאָה הָאִשָּׁה
the-woman she-defiled-self not but-if (28) people-of-her in-midst-of

וּטְהֹרָה הִוא וְנִקְּתָה וְנִזְרְעָה זָרַע׃ (29) זֹאת
this (29) child and-she-will-bear then-she-will-be-guiltless she and-clean

תּוֹרַת הַקְּנָאֹת אֲשֶׁר תִּשְׂטֶה אִשָּׁה תַּחַת אִישָׁהּ
husband-of-her under woman she-goes-astray when the-jealousies law-of

וְנִטְמָאָה׃ (30) אוֹ אִישׁ אֲשֶׁר תַּעֲבֹר עָלָיו רוּחַ קִנְאָה
jealousy feeling-of over-him she-comes when man or (30) and-she-defiles-self

וְקִנֵּא אֶת־ אִשְׁתּוֹ וְהֶעֱמִיד אֶת־ הָאִשָּׁה לִפְנֵי
before the-woman *** and-he-must-stand wife-of-him *** and-he-suspects

יְהוָה וְעָשָׂה לָהּ הַכֹּהֵן אֵת כָּל־ הַתּוֹרָה הַזֹּאת׃
the-this the-law entire-of *** the-priest to-her and-he-must-apply Yahweh

(31) וְנִקָּה הָאִישׁ מֵעָוֹן וְהָאִשָּׁה הַהִוא
the-that but-the-woman of-wrong the-husband then-he-will-be-innocent (31)

תִּשָּׂא אֶת־ עֲוֹנָהּ׃ (6:1) וַיְדַבֵּר יְהוָה אֶל־ מֹשֶׁה לֵּאמֹר׃
to-say Moses to Yahweh and-he-spoke (6:1) sin-of-her *** she-will-bear

(2) דַּבֵּר אֶל־ בְּנֵי יִשְׂרָאֵל וְאָמַרְתָּ אֲלֵהֶם אִישׁ אוֹ־ אִשָּׁה כִּי יַפְלִא
he-desires if woman or man to-them and-you-say Israel sons-of to speak! (2)

לִנְדֹּר נֶדֶר נָזִיר לְהַזִּיר לַיהוָה׃ (3) מִיַּיִן
from-wine (3) to-Yahweh to-be-separate Nazirite vow-of to-vow

וְשֵׁכָר יַזִּיר חֹמֶץ יַיִן וְחֹמֶץ
or-vinegar-of wine vinegar-of he-must-abstain or-fermented-drink

שֵׁכָר לֹא יִשְׁתֶּה וְכָל־ מִשְׁרַת עֲנָבִים לֹא
not grapes juice-of and-any-of he-must-drink not fermented-drink

יִשְׁתֶּה וַעֲנָבִים לַחִים וִיבֵשִׁים לֹא יֹאכֵל׃ (4) כֹּל
all-of (4) he-must-eat not or-dry-ones moist-ones and-grapes he-must-drink

יְמֵי נִזְרוֹ מִכֹּל אֲשֶׁר יֵעָשֶׂה מִגֶּפֶן
from-vine-of he-is-made that from-anything Nazirite-vow-of-him days-of

הַיַּיִן מֵחַרְצַנִּים וְעַד־ זָג לֹא יֹאכֵל׃ (5) כָּל־ יְמֵי נֶדֶר
vow-of days-of all-of (5) he-must-eat not skin or-even from-seeds the-wine

נִזְרוֹ תַּעַר לֹא־ יַעֲבֹר עַל־ רֹאשׁוֹ עַד־ מְלֹאת
to-be-over until head-of-him on he-may-come not razor Nazirite-of-him

brings a curse, it will go into
her and cause bitter suffering;
her abdomen will swell and
her thigh waste away,[l] and
she will become accursed
among her people. 28If, however, the woman has not
defiled herself and is free from
impurity, she will be cleared
of guilt and will be able to
have children.
29" 'This, then, is the law of
jealousy when a woman goes
astray and defiles herself
while married to her husband,
30or when feelings of jealousy
come over a man because he
suspects his wife. The priest is
to have her stand before the
LORD and is to apply this entire law to her. 31The husband
will be innocent of any
wrongdoing, but the woman
will bear the consequences of
her sin.' "

The Nazirite

6 The LORD said to Moses,
2"Speak to the Israelites
and say to them: 'If a man or
woman wants to make a
special vow, a vow of separation to the LORD as a Nazirite,
3he must abstain from wine
and other fermented drink
and must not drink vinegar
made from wine or from other
fermented drink. He must not
drink grape juice or eat grapes
or raisins. 4As long as he is a
Nazirite, he must not eat anything that comes from the
grapevine, not even the seeds
or skins.
5" 'During the entire period
of his vow of separation no razor may be used on his head.

[l]27 Or *suffering; she will have barrenness and a miscarrying womb*

הַיָּמִם אֲשֶׁר־ יַזִּיר לַיהוָה קָדֹשׁ יִהְיֶה גַּדֵּל פֶּרַע
lock-of to-be-long he-must-be holy to-Yahweh he-is-separate that the-days

שְׂעַר רֹאשׁוֹ׃ כָּל־ יְמֵי הַזִּרוֹ לַיהוָה עַל־
near to-Yahweh to-be-separate-him days-of all-of (6) head-of-him hair-of

נֶפֶשׁ מֵת לֹא יָבֹא׃ לְאָבִיו וּלְאִמּוֹ
or-for-mother-of-him for-father-of-him (7) he-must-go not dead body

לְאָחִיו וּלְאַחֹתוֹ לֹא־ יִטַּמָּא לָהֶם
for-them he-must-become-unclean not or-for-sister-of-him for-brother-of-him

בְּמֹתָם כִּי נֵזֶר אֱלֹהָיו עַל־ רֹאשׁוֹ׃ כֹּל יְמֵי
days-of all-of (8) head-of-him on God-of-him separation-of for if-to-die-them

נִזְרוֹ קָדֹשׁ הוּא לַיהוָה׃ וְכִי־ יָמוּת מֵת
one-dying he-dies and-if (9) to-Yahweh he consecrated separation-of-him

עָלָיו בְּפֶתַע פִּתְאֹם וְטִמֵּא רֹאשׁ נִזְרוֹ
dedication-of-him hair-of and-he-defiles suddenly with-suddenness by-him

וְגִלַּח רֹאשׁוֹ בְּיוֹם טָהֳרָתוֹ בַּיּוֹם
on-the-day cleansing-of-him on-day-of head-of-him then-he-must-shave

הַשְּׁבִיעִי יְגַלְּחֶנּוּ׃ וּבַיּוֹם הַשְּׁמִינִי יָבִא
he-must-bring the-eighth and-on-the-day (10) he-must-shave-him the-seventh

שְׁתֵּי תֹרִים אוֹ שְׁנֵי בְּנֵי יוֹנָה אֶל־ הַכֹּהֵן אֶל־ פֶּתַח
entrance-of at the-priest to pigeon young-ones-of two-of or doves two-of

אֹהֶל מוֹעֵד׃ וְעָשָׂה הַכֹּהֵן אֶחָד לְחַטָּאת
as-sin-offering one the-priest and-he-must-offer (11) Meeting Tent-of

וְאֶחָד לְעֹלָה וְכִפֶּר עָלָיו מֵאֲשֶׁר חָטָא עַל־
by he-sinned because for-him and-he-will-atone as-burnt-offering and-other

הַנָּפֶשׁ וְקִדַּשׁ אֶת־ רֹאשׁוֹ בַּיּוֹם הַהוּא׃
the-same on-the-day head-of-him *** and-he-must-consecrate the-body

וְהִזִּיר לַיהוָה אֶת־ יְמֵי נִזְרוֹ
separation-of-him days-of *** to-Yahweh and-he-must-be-dedicated (12)

וְהֵבִיא כֶּבֶשׂ בֶּן־ שְׁנָתוֹ לְאָשָׁם וְהַיָּמִים
and-the-days as-guilt-offering year-of-him son-of lamb and-he-must-bring

הָרִאשֹׁנִים יִפְּלוּ כִּי טָמֵא נִזְרוֹ׃
separation-of-him defiled for they-do-not-count the-previous-ones

וְזֹאת תּוֹרַת הַנָּזִיר בְּיוֹם מְלֹאת יְמֵי
days-of to-be-over in-day-of the-Nazirite law-of now-this (13)

נִזְרוֹ יָבִיא אֹתוֹ אֶל־ פֶּתַח אֹהֶל מוֹעֵד׃
Meeting Tent-of entrance-of to him he-must-bring separation-of-him

וְהִקְרִיב אֶת־ קָרְבָּנוֹ לַיהוָה כֶּבֶשׂ בֶּן־
son-of lamb to-Yahweh offering-of-him *** and-he-must-present (14)

He must be holy until the period of his separation to the LORD is over; he must let the hair of his head grow long. [6]Throughout the period of his separation to the LORD he must not go near a dead body. [7]Even if his own father or mother or brother or sister dies, he must not make himself ceremonially unclean on account of them, because the symbol of his separation to God is on his head. [8]Throughout the period of his separation he is consecrated to the LORD.

[9]" 'If someone dies suddenly in his presence, thus defiling the hair he has dedicated, he must shave his head on the day of his cleansing—the seventh day. [10]Then on the eighth day he must bring two doves or two young pigeons to the priest at the entrance to the Tent of Meeting. [11]The priest is to offer one as a sin offering and the other as a burnt offering to make atonement for him because he sinned by being in the presence of the dead body. That same day he is to consecrate his head. [12]He must dedicate himself to the LORD for the period of his separation and must bring a year-old male lamb as a guilt offering. The previous days do not count, because he became defiled during his separation.

[13]" 'Now this is the law for the Nazirite when the period of his separation is over. He is to be brought to the entrance to the Tent of Meeting. [14]There he is to present his offerings to the LORD: a year-old male lamb

שְׁנָתוֹ תָמִים אֶחָד לְעֹלָה וְכַבְשָׂה אַחַת
one and-ewe-lamb for-burnt-offering one without-defect year-of-him

בַּת־ שְׁנָתָהּ תְּמִימָה לְחַטָּאת וְאַיִל־ אֶחָד
one and-ram for-sin-offering without-defect year-of-her daughter-of

תָּמִים לִשְׁלָמִים׃ (15) וְסַל מַצּוֹת
unleavened-breads and-basket-of (15) for-fellowship-offerings without-defect

סֹלֶת חַלֹּת בְּלוּלֹת בַּשֶּׁמֶן וּרְקִיקֵי
and-wafers-of with-the-oil ones-being-mixed cakes-of fine-flour

מַצּוֹת מְשֻׁחִים בַּשָּׁמֶן וּמִנְחָתָם
and-grain-offering-of-them with-the-oil ones-being-spread unleavened-breads

וְנִסְכֵּיהֶם׃ (16) וְהִקְרִיב הַכֹּהֵן לִפְנֵי
before the-priest and-he-must-present (16) and-drink-offerings-of-them

יְהוָה וְעָשָׂה אֶת־ חַטָּאתוֹ וְאֶת־ עֹלָתוֹ׃
burnt-offering-of-him and sin-offering-of-him *** and-he-must-make Yahweh

(17) וְאֶת־ הָאַיִל יַעֲשֶׂה זֶבַח שְׁלָמִים לַיהוָה עַל
with to-Yahweh fellowships offering-of he-must-sacrifice the-ram and (17)

סַל הַמַּצּוֹת וְעָשָׂה הַכֹּהֵן אֶת־
*** the-priest and-he-must-present the-unleavened-breads basket-of

מִנְחָתוֹ וְאֶת־ נִסְכּוֹ׃ (18) וְגִלַּח
then-he-must-shave (18) drink-offering-of-him and grain-offering-of-him

הַנָּזִיר פֶּתַח אֹהֶל מוֹעֵד אֶת־ רֹאשׁ נִזְרוֹ
dedication-of-him hair-of *** Meeting Tent-of entrance-of the-Nazirite

וְלָקַח אֶת־ שְׂעַר רֹאשׁ נִזְרוֹ וְנָתַן עַל־
in and-he-must-put dedication-of-him head-of hair-of *** and-he-must-take

הָאֵשׁ אֲשֶׁר־ תַּחַת זֶבַח הַשְּׁלָמִים׃
the-fellowship-offerings sacrifice-of under that the-fire

(19) וְלָקַח הַכֹּהֵן אֶת־ הַזְּרֹעַ בְּשֵׁלָה מִן־ הָאַיִל
the-ram from boiled the-shoulder *** the-priest then-he-must-take (19)

וְחַלַּת מַצָּה אַחַת מִן־ הַסַּל וּרְקִיק מַצָּה אֶחָד
one without-yeast and-wafer-of the-basket from one without-yeast and-cake-of

וְנָתַן עַל־ כַּפֵּי הַנָּזִיר אַחַר הִתְגַּלְּחוֹ אֶת־
*** to-shave-him after the-Nazirite hands-of in and-he-must-place

נִזְרוֹ׃ (20) וְהֵנִיף אוֹתָם הַכֹּהֵן ׀ תְּנוּפָה
wave-offering the-priest them and-he-must-wave (20) dedicated-hair-of-him

לִפְנֵי יְהוָה קֹדֶשׁ הוּא לַכֹּהֵן עַל חֲזֵה הַתְּנוּפָה
the-wave-offering breast-of with for-the-priest he holy Yahweh before

וְעַל שׁוֹק הַתְּרוּמָה וְאַחַר יִשְׁתֶּה הַנָּזִיר יָיִן׃
wine the-Nazirite he-may-drink and-after the-presentation thigh-of and-with

without defect for a burnt
offering, a year-old ewe lamb
without defect for a sin
offering, a ram without defect
for a fellowship offering,[m] 15to-
gether with their grain
offerings and drink offerings,
and a basket of bread made
without yeast—cakes made of
fine flour mixed with oil, and
wafers spread with oil.

16" 'The priest is to present
them before the LORD and
make the sin offering and the
burnt offering. 17He is to
present the basket of unleavened bread and is to sacrifice
the ram as a fellowship
offering to the LORD, together
with its grain offering and
drink offering.

18" 'Then at the entrance to
the Tent of Meeting, the Nazirite must shave off the hair
that he dedicated. He is to take
the hair and put it in the fire
that is under the sacrifice of
the fellowship offering.

19" 'After the Nazirite has
shaved off the hair of his dedication, the priest is to place in
his hands a boiled shoulder of
the ram, and a cake and a wafer from the basket, both made
without yeast. 20The priest
shall then wave them before
the LORD as a wave offering;
they are holy and belong to
the priest, together with the
breast that was waved and the
thigh that was presented. After that, the Nazirite may
drink wine.

[m]14 Traditionally *peace offering;* also in verses 17 and 18

זֹאת תּוֹרַת הַנָּזִיר אֲשֶׁר יִדֹּר קָרְבָּנוֹ לַיהוָה עַל־
with to-Yahweh offering-of-him he-vows who the-Nazirite law-of this (21)

נִזְרוֹ מִלְּבַד אֲשֶׁר־תַּשִּׂיג יָדוֹ כְּפִי
in-accord-of hand-of-him she-can-afford what apart-from separation-of-him

נִדְרוֹ אֲשֶׁר יִדֹּר כֵּן יַעֲשֶׂה עַל תּוֹרַת נִזְרוֹ׃
Nazirite-vow-of-him law-of as he-must-fulfill so he-vowed that vow-of-him

וַיְדַבֵּר יְהוָה אֶל־מֹשֶׁה לֵּאמֹר׃ דַּבֵּר אֶל־אַהֲרֹן וְאֶל־
and-to Aaron to tell! (23) to-say Moses to Yahweh and-he-spoke (22)

בָּנָיו לֵאמֹר כֹּה תְבָרְכוּ אֶת־בְּנֵי יִשְׂרָאֵל אָמוֹר לָהֶם׃
to-them to-say Israel sons-of *** you-shall-bless thus to-say sons-of-him

יְבָרֶכְךָ יְהוָה וְיִשְׁמְרֶךָ׃ יָאֵר
may-he-make-shine (26) and-may-he-keep-you Yahweh may-he-bless-you (24)

יְהוָה פָּנָיו אֵלֶיךָ וִיחֻנֶּךָּ׃ יִשָּׂא
may-he-turn (26) and-may-he-be-gracious-to-you on-you faces-of-him Yahweh

יְהוָה פָּנָיו אֵלֶיךָ וְיָשֵׂם לְךָ שָׁלוֹם׃
peace to-you may-he-give toward-you faces-of-him Yahweh

וְשָׂמוּ אֶת־שְׁמִי עַל־בְּנֵי יִשְׂרָאֵל וַאֲנִי אֲבָרְכֵם׃
I-will-bless-them and-I Israel sons-of on name-of-me *** so-they-will-put (27)

וַיְהִי בְּיוֹם כַּלּוֹת מֹשֶׁה לְהָקִים אֶת־הַמִּשְׁכָּן
the-tabernacle *** to-set-up Moses to-finish on-day and-he-was (7:1)

וַיִּמְשַׁח אֹתוֹ וַיְקַדֵּשׁ אֹתוֹ וְאֶת־כָּל־כֵּלָיו וְאֶת־
and furnishings-of-him all-of and him and-he-consecrated him and-he-anointed

הַמִּזְבֵּחַ וְאֶת־כָּל־כֵּלָיו וַיִּמְשָׁחֵם וַיְקַדֵּשׁ
and-he-consecrated and-he-anointed-them utensils-of-him all-of and the-altar

אֹתָם׃ וַיַּקְרִיבוּ נְשִׂיאֵי יִשְׂרָאֵל רָאשֵׁי בֵּית
house-of heads-of Israel leaders-of then-they-made-offering (2) them

אֲבֹתָם הֵם נְשִׂיאֵי הַמַּטֹּת הֵם הָעֹמְדִים עַל־
over the-ones-being-in-charge they the-tribes leaders-of they fathers-of-them

הַפְּקֻדִים׃ וַיָּבִיאוּ אֶת־קָרְבָּנָם לִפְנֵי יְהוָה שֵׁשׁ־
six-of Yahweh before gift-of-them *** and-they-brought (3) the-ones-counted

עֶגְלֹת צָב וּשְׁנֵי עָשָׂר בָּקָר עֲגָלָה עַל־שְׁנֵי הַנְּשִׂאִים וְשׁוֹר
and-ox the-leaders two-of from cart ox ten and-two-of covered carts-of

לְאֶחָד וַיַּקְרִיבוּ אוֹתָם לִפְנֵי הַמִּשְׁכָּן׃ וַיֹּאמֶר
and-he-spoke (4) the-tabernacle before them and-they-presented from-each

יְהוָה אֶל־מֹשֶׁה לֵּאמֹר׃ קַח מֵאִתָּם וְהָיוּ לַעֲבֹד אֶת־עֲבֹדַת
work-of *** to-do so-they-may-be from-them accept! (5) to-say Moses to Yahweh

אֹהֶל מוֹעֵד וְנָתַתָּה אוֹתָם אֶל־הַלְוִיִּם אִישׁ כְּפִי
as-requirement-of each the-Levites to them and-you-give Meeting Tent-of

21"'This is the law of the
Nazirite who vows his
offering to the LORD in accordance with his separation, in
addition to whatever else he
can afford. He must fulfill the
vow he has made, according to
the law of the Nazirite.'"

The Priestly Blessing

22The LORD said to Moses,
23"Tell Aaron and his sons,
'This is how you are to bless
the Israelites. Say to them:

24"'"The LORD bless you
and keep you;
25the LORD make his face
shine upon you
and be gracious to you;
26the LORD turn his face
toward you
and give you peace."'

27"So they will put my name
on the Israelites, and I will
bless them."

Offerings at the Dedication of the Tabernacle

7 When Moses finished setting up the tabernacle, he
anointed it and consecrated it
and all its furnishings. He also
anointed and consecrated the
altar and all its utensils. 2Then
the leaders of Israel, the heads
of families who were the tribal
leaders in charge of those who
were counted, made offerings.
3They brought as their gifts
before the LORD six covered
carts and twelve oxen—an ox
from each leader and a cart
from every two. These they
presented before the tabernacle.
4The LORD said to Moses,
5"Accept these from them, that
they may be used in the work
at the Tent of Meeting. Give
them to the Levites as each

עֲבֹדָתוֹ׃ וַיִּקַּח מֹשֶׁה אֶת־הָעֲגָלֹת וְאֶת־הַבָּקָר וַיִּתֵּן אוֹתָם
them and-he-gave the-ox and the-carts *** Moses so-he-took (6) work-of-him

אֶל־הַלְוִיִּם׃ אֵת ׀ שְׁתֵּי הָעֲגָלֹת וְאֵת אַרְבַּעַת הַבָּקָר נָתַן
he-gave the-ox four-of and the-carts two-of *** (7) the-Levites to

לִבְנֵי גֵרְשׁוֹן כְּפִי עֲבֹדָתָם׃ וְאֵת ׀ אַרְבַּע הָעֲגָלֹת
the-carts four-of and (8) work-of-them as-requirement-of Gershon to-sons-of

וְאֵת שְׁמֹנַת הַבָּקָר נָתַן לִבְנֵי מְרָרִי כְּפִי עֲבֹדָתָם
work-of-them as-requirement-of Merari to-sons-of he-gave the-ox eight-of and

בְּיַד אִיתָמָר בֶּן־אַהֲרֹן הַכֹּהֵן׃ וְלִבְנֵי קְהָת
Kohath but-to-sons-of (9) the-priest Aaron son-of Ithamar under-direction-of

לֹא נָתָן כִּי־עֲבֹדַת הַקֹּדֶשׁ עֲלֵהֶם בַּכָּתֵף
on-the-shoulder on-them the-holy-thing responsibility-of for he-gave not

יִשָּׂאוּ׃ וַיַּקְרִיבוּ הַנְּשִׂאִים אֵת חֲנֻכַּת הַמִּזְבֵּחַ
the-altar dedication-of *** the-leaders and-they-brought (10) they-carry

בְּיוֹם הִמָּשַׁח אֹתוֹ וַיַּקְרִיבוּ הַנְּשִׂיאִם אֶת־קָרְבָּנָם
offering-of-them *** the-leaders and-they-presented him to-be-anointed on-day

לִפְנֵי הַמִּזְבֵּחַ׃ וַיֹּאמֶר יְהוָה אֶל־מֹשֶׁה נָשִׂיא אֶחָד לַיּוֹם
each-the-day one leader Moses to Yahweh for-he-said (11) the-altar before

נָשִׂיא אֶחָד לַיּוֹם יַקְרִיבוּ אֶת־קָרְבָּנָם
offering-of-them *** they-must-bring each-the-day one leader

לַחֲנֻכַּת הַמִּזְבֵּחַ׃ וַיְהִי הַמַּקְרִיב בַּיּוֹם
on-the-day the-one-bringing and-he-was (12) the-altar for-dedication-of

הָרִאשׁוֹן אֶת־קָרְבָּנוֹ נַחְשׁוֹן בֶּן־עַמִּינָדָב לְמַטֵּה יְהוּדָה׃
Judah from-tribe-of Amminadab son-of Nahshon offering-of-him *** the-first

וְקָרְבָּנוֹ קַעֲרַת־כֶּסֶף אַחַת שְׁלֹשִׁים וּמֵאָה מִשְׁקָלָהּ
weight-of-her and-hundred thirty one silver plate-of and-offering-of-him (13)

מִזְרָק אֶחָד כֶּסֶף שִׁבְעִים שֶׁקֶל בְּשֶׁקֶל הַקֹּדֶשׁ
the-sanctuary by-shekel-of shekel seventy silver one sprinkling-bowl

שְׁנֵיהֶם ׀ מְלֵאִים סֹלֶת בְּלוּלָה בַשֶּׁמֶן לְמִנְחָה׃
as-grain-offering with-the-oil being-mixed fine-flour ones-filled both-of-them

כַּף אַחַת עֲשָׂרָה זָהָב מְלֵאָה קְטֹרֶת׃ פַּר אֶחָד בֶּן־בָּקָר אַיִל
ram herd young-of one bull (15) incense filled gold ten one ladle (14)

אֶחָד כֶּבֶשׂ־אֶחָד בֶּן־שְׁנָתוֹ לְעֹלָה׃ שְׂעִיר־עִזִּים
goats male-goat-of (16) for-burnt-offering year-of-him son-of one lamb one

אֶחָד לְחַטָּאת׃ וּלְזֶבַח הַשְּׁלָמִים בָּקָר
ox the-fellowship-offerings and-as-sacrifice-of (17) for-sin-offering one

שְׁנַיִם אֵילִם חֲמִשָּׁה עַתּוּדִים חֲמִשָּׁה כְּבָשִׂים בְּנֵי־שָׁנָה חֲמִשָּׁה זֶה קָרְבַּן
offering-of this five year sons-of lambs five male-goats five rams two

man's work requires."
6So Moses took the carts and
oxen and gave them to the Levites. 7He gave two carts and
four oxen to the Gershonites,
as their work required, 8and
he gave four carts and eight
oxen to the Merarites, as their
work required. They were all
under the direction of Ithamar
son of Aaron, the priest. 9But
Moses did not give any to the
Kohathites, because they were
to carry on their shoulders the
holy things, for which they
were responsible.
10When the altar was anointed, the leaders brought their
offerings for its dedication
and presented them before the
altar. 11For the LORD had said
to Moses, "Each day one leader is to bring his offering for
the dedication of the altar."

12The one who brought his
offering on the first day was
Nahshon son of Amminadab
of the tribe of Judah.
13His offering was one silver plate weighing a hun-
dred and thirty shekels,[n]
and one silver sprinkling
bowl weighing seventy
shekels,[o] both according to
the sanctuary shekel, each
filled with fine flour mixed
with oil as a grain offering;
14one gold ladle weighing
ten shekels,[p] filled with incense; 15one young bull,
one ram and one male lamb
a year old, for a burnt
offering; 16one male goat for
a sin offering; 17and two
oxen, five rams, five male
goats and five male lambs a
year old, to be sacrificed as
a fellowship offering.[q] This

[n]13 That is, about 3 1/4 pounds (about 1.5 kilograms); also elsewhere in this chapter
[o]13 That is, about 1 3/4 pounds (about 0.8 kilogram); also elsewhere in this chapter
[p]14 That is, about 4 ounces (about 110 grams); also elsewhere in this chapter
[q]17 Traditionally *peace offering*; also elsewhere in this chapter

נַחְשׁוֹן בֶּן־ עַמִּינָדָב׃ בַּיּוֹם הַשֵּׁנִי הִקְרִיב נְתַנְאֵל
Nethanel he-brought the-second on-the-day (18) Amminadab son-of Nahshon

בֶּן־ צוּעָר נְשִׂיא יִשָּׂשכָר׃ הִקְרִב אֶת־ קָרְבָּנוֹ קַעֲרַת־
plate-of offering-of-him *** he-brought (19) Issachar leader-of Zuar son-of

כֶּסֶף אַחַת שְׁלֹשִׁים וּמֵאָה מִשְׁקָלָהּ מִזְרָק אֶחָד כֶּסֶף
silver one sprinkling-bowl weight-of-her and-hundred thirty one silver

שִׁבְעִים שֶׁקֶל בְּשֶׁקֶל הַקֹּדֶשׁ שְׁנֵיהֶם ׀ מְלֵאִים סֹלֶת
fine-flour ones-filled both-of-them the-sanctuary by-shekel-of shekel seventy

בְּלוּלָה בַשֶּׁמֶן לְמִנְחָה׃ כַּף אַחַת עֲשָׂרָה זָהָב מְלֵאָה
filled gold ten one ladle (20) as-grain-offering with-the-oil being-mixed

קְטֹרֶת׃ פַּר אֶחָד בֶּן־ בָּקָר אַיִל אֶחָד כֶּבֶשׂ־אֶחָד בֶּן־ שְׁנָתוֹ
year-of-him son-of one lamb one ram herd son-of one bull (21) incense

לְעֹלָה׃ שְׂעִיר־ עִזִּים אֶחָד לְחַטָּאת׃
for-sin-offering one goats male-goat-of (22) for-burnt-offering

וּלְזֶבַח הַשְּׁלָמִים בָּקָר שְׁנַיִם אֵילִם חֲמִשָּׁה
five rams two ox the-fellowship-offerings and-for-sacrifice-of (23)

עַתּוּדִים חֲמִשָּׁה כְּבָשִׂים בְּנֵי־ שָׁנָה חֲמִשָּׁה זֶה קָרְבַּן נְתַנְאֵל בֶּן־
son-of Nethanel offering-of this five year sons-of lambs five male-goats

צוּעָר׃ בַּיּוֹם הַשְּׁלִישִׁי נָשִׂיא לִבְנֵי זְבוּלֻן אֱלִיאָב בֶּן־ חֵלֹן׃
Helon son-of Eliab Zebulun of-sons-of leader the-third on-the-day (24) Zuar

קָרְבָּנוֹ קַעֲרַת־ כֶּסֶף אַחַת שְׁלֹשִׁים וּמֵאָה מִשְׁקָלָהּ
weight-of-her and-hundred thirty one silver plate-of offering-of-him (25)

מִזְרָק אֶחָד כֶּסֶף שִׁבְעִים שֶׁקֶל בְּשֶׁקֶל הַקֹּדֶשׁ
the-sanctuary by-shekel-of shekel seventy silver one sprinkling-bowl

שְׁנֵיהֶם ׀ מְלֵאִים סֹלֶת בְּלוּלָה בַשֶּׁמֶן לְמִנְחָה׃
as-grain-offering with-the-oil being-mixed fine-flour ones-filled both-of-them

כַּף אַחַת עֲשָׂרָה זָהָב מְלֵאָה קְטֹרֶת׃ פַּר אֶחָד בֶּן־ בָּקָר אַיִל
ram herd young-of one bull (27) incense filled gold ten one ladle (26)

אֶחָד כֶּבֶשׂ־אֶחָד בֶּן־ שְׁנָתוֹ לְעֹלָה׃ שְׂעִיר־ עִזִּים
goats male-goat-of (28) for-burnt-offering year-of-him son-of one lamb one

אֶחָד לְחַטָּאת׃ וּלְזֶבַח הַשְּׁלָמִים בָּקָר
ox the-fellowship-offerings and-for-sacrifice-of (29) for-sin-offering one

שְׁנַיִם אֵילִם חֲמִשָּׁה עַתֻּדִים חֲמִשָּׁה כְּבָשִׂים בְּנֵי־ שָׁנָה חֲמִשָּׁה זֶה קָרְבַּן
offering-of this five year sons-of lambs five male-goats five rams two

אֱלִיאָב בֶּן־ חֵלֹן׃ בַּיּוֹם הָרְבִיעִי נָשִׂיא לִבְנֵי רְאוּבֵן
Reuben of-sons-of leader the-fourth on-the-day (30) Helon son-of Eliab

אֱלִיצוּר בֶּן־ שְׁדֵיאוּר׃ קָרְבָּנוֹ קַעֲרַת־ כֶּסֶף אַחַת שְׁלֹשִׁים
thirty one silver plate-of offering-of-him (31) Shedeur son-of Elizur

was the offering of Nahshon son of Amminadab.

18 On the second day Nethanel son of Zuar, the leader of Issachar, brought his offering.
19 The offering he brought was one silver plate weighing a hundred and thirty shekels, and one silver sprinkling bowl weighing seventy shekels, both according to the sanctuary shekel, each filled with fine flour mixed with oil as a grain offering; 20 one gold ladle weighing ten shekels, filled with incense; 21 one young bull, one ram and one male lamb a year old, for a burnt offering; 22 one male goat for a sin offering; 23 and two oxen, five rams, five male goats and five male lambs a year old, to be sacrificed as a fellowship offering. This was the offering of Nethanel son of Zuar.

24 On the third day, Eliab son of Helon, the leader of the people of Zebulun, brought his offering.
25 His offering was one silver plate weighing a hundred and thirty shekels, and one silver sprinkling bowl weighing seventy shekels, both according to the sanctuary shekel, each filled with fine flour mixed with oil as a grain offering; 26 one gold ladle weighing ten shekels, filled with incense; 27 one young bull, one ram and one male lamb a year old, for a burnt offering; 28 one male goat for a sin offering; 29 and two oxen, five rams, five male goats and five male lambs a year old, to be sacrificed as a fellowship offering. This was the offering of Eliab son of Helon.

30 On the fourth day Elizur son of Shedeur, the leader of the people of Reuben, brought his offering.
31 His offering was one silver plate weighing a hundred and thirty shekels,

וּמֵאָה מִשְׁקָלָהּ מִזְרָק אֶחָד כֶּסֶף שִׁבְעִים שֶׁקֶל
shekel seventy silver one sprinkling-bowl weight-of-her and-hundred

בְּשֶׁקֶל הַקֹּדֶשׁ שְׁנֵיהֶם ׀ מְלֵאִים סֹלֶת בְּלוּלָה
being-mixed fine-flour ones-filled both-of-them the-sanctuary by-shekel-of

בַשֶּׁמֶן לְמִנְחָה׃ (32) כַּף אַחַת עֲשָׂרָה זָהָב מְלֵאָה קְטֹרֶת
incense filled gold ten one ladle (32) as-grain-offering with-the-oil

(33) פַּר אֶחָד בֶּן־ בָּקָר אַיִל אֶחָד כֶּבֶשׂ־אֶחָד בֶּן־ שְׁנָתוֹ
year-of-him son-of one lamb one ram herd young-of one bull (33)

לְעֹלָה׃ (34) שְׂעִיר־ עִזִּים אֶחָד לְחַטָּאת׃
for-sin-offering one goats male-goat-of (34) for-burnt-offering

(35) וּלְזֶבַח הַשְּׁלָמִים בָּקָר שְׁנַיִם אֵילִם חֲמִשָּׁה
five rams two ox the-fellowship-offerings and-for-sacrifice-of (35)

עַתֻּדִים חֲמִשָּׁה כְּבָשִׂים בְּנֵי־ שָׁנָה חֲמִשָּׁה זֶה קָרְבַּן אֱלִיצוּר בֶּן־
son-of Elizur offering-of this five year sons-of lambs five male-goats

שְׁדֵיאוּר׃ (36) בַּיּוֹם הַחֲמִישִׁי נָשִׂיא לִבְנֵי שִׁמְעוֹן שְׁלֻמִיאֵל בֶּן־
son-of Shelumiel Simeon of-sons-of leader the-fifth on-the-day (36) Shedeur

צוּרִישַׁדָּי׃ (37) קָרְבָּנוֹ קַעֲרַת־ כֶּסֶף אַחַת שְׁלֹשִׁים וּמֵאָה
and-hundred thirty one silver plate-of offering-of-him (37) Zurishaddai

מִשְׁקָלָהּ מִזְרָק אֶחָד כֶּסֶף שִׁבְעִים שֶׁקֶל בְּשֶׁקֶל
by-shekel-of shekel seventy silver one sprinkling-bowl weight-of-her

הַקֹּדֶשׁ שְׁנֵיהֶם ׀ מְלֵאִים סֹלֶת בְּלוּלָה בַשֶּׁמֶן
with-the-oil being-mixed fine-flour ones-filled both-of-them the-sanctuary

לְמִנְחָה׃ (38) כַּף אַחַת עֲשָׂרָה זָהָב מְלֵאָה קְטֹרֶת׃ (39) פַּר אֶחָד
one bull (39) incense filled gold ten one ladle (38) as-grain-offering

בֶּן־ בָּקָר אַיִל אֶחָד כֶּבֶשׂ־אֶחָד בֶּן־ שְׁנָתוֹ לְעֹלָה׃
for-burnt-offering year-of-him son-of one lamb one ram herd young-of

(40) שְׂעִיר־ עִזִּים אֶחָד לְחַטָּאת (41) וּלְזֶבַח
and-for-sacrifice-of (41) for-sin-offering one goats male-goat-of (40)

הַשְּׁלָמִים בָּקָר שְׁנַיִם אֵילִם חֲמִשָּׁה עַתֻּדִים חֲמִשָּׁה כְּבָשִׂים בְּנֵי־
sons-of lambs five male-goats five rams two ox the-fellowship-offerings

שָׁנָה חֲמִשָּׁה זֶה קָרְבַּן שְׁלֻמִיאֵל בֶּן־ צוּרִישַׁדָּי׃ (42) בַּיּוֹם
on-the-day (42) Zurishaddai son-of Shelumiel offering-of this five year

הַשִּׁשִּׁי נָשִׂיא לִבְנֵי גָד אֶלְיָסָף בֶּן־ דְּעוּאֵל׃ (43) קָרְבָּנוֹ
offering-of-him (43) Deuel son-of Eliasaph Gad of-sons-of leader the-sixth

קַעֲרַת־ כֶּסֶף אַחַת שְׁלֹשִׁים וּמֵאָה מִשְׁקָלָהּ מִזְרָק אֶחָד
one sprinkling-bowl weight-of-her and-hundred thirty one silver plate-of

כֶּסֶף שִׁבְעִים שֶׁקֶל בְּשֶׁקֶל הַקֹּדֶשׁ שְׁנֵיהֶם ׀ מְלֵאִים
ones-filled both-of-them the-sanctuary by-shekel-of shekel seventy silver

and one silver sprinkling bowl weighing seventy shekels, both according to the sanctuary shekel, each filled with fine flour mixed with oil as a grain offering;
32one gold ladle weighing ten shekels, filled with incense;
33one young bull, one ram and one male lamb a year old, for a burnt offering;
34one male goat for a sin offering;
35and two oxen, five rams, five male goats and five male lambs a year old, to be sacrificed as a fellowship offering. This was the offering of Elizur son of Shedeur.

36On the fifth day Shelumiel son of Zurishaddai, the leader of the people of Simeon, brought his offering.

37His offering was one silver plate weighing a hundred and thirty shekels, and one silver sprinkling bowl weighing seventy shekels, both according to the sanctuary shekel, each filled with fine flour mixed with oil as a grain offering;
38one gold ladle weighing ten shekels, filled with incense;
39one young bull, one ram and one male lamb a year old, for a burnt offering;
40one male goat for a sin offering;
41and two oxen, five rams, five male goats and five male lambs a year old, to be sacrificed as a fellowship offering. This was the offering of Shelumiel son of Zurishaddai.

42On the sixth day Eliasaph son of Deuel, the leader of the people of Gad, brought his offering.

43His offering was one silver plate weighing a hundred and thirty shekels, and one silver sprinkling bowl weighing seventy shekels, both according to the sanctuary shekel, each

סֹלֶת בְּלוּלָה בַשֶּׁמֶן לְמִנְחָה׃ כַּף אַחַת עֲשָׂרָה
ten one ladle (44) as-grain-offering with-the-oil being-mixed fine-flour

זָהָב מְלֵאָה קְטֹרֶת׃ פַּר אֶחָד בֶּן־ בָּקָר אַיִל אֶחָד כֶּבֶשׂ־אֶחָד בֶּן־
son-of one lamb one ram herd young-of one bull (45) incense filled gold

שְׁנָתוֹ לְעֹלָה׃ שְׂעִיר־ עִזִּים אֶחָד לְחַטָּאת׃
for-sin-offering one goats male-goat-of (46) for-burnt-offering year-of-him

וּלְזֶבַח הַשְּׁלָמִים בָּקָר שְׁנַיִם אֵילִם חֲמִשָּׁה
five rams two ox the-fellowship-offerings and-for-sacrifice-of (47)

עַתֻּדִים חֲמִשָּׁה כְּבָשִׂים בְּנֵי־ שָׁנָה חֲמִשָּׁה זֶה קָרְבַּן אֶלְיָסָף בֶּן־
son-of Eliasaph offering-of this five year sons-of lambs five male-goats

דְּעוּאֵל׃ בַּיּוֹם הַשְּׁבִיעִי נָשִׂיא לִבְנֵי אֶפְרָיִם אֱלִישָׁמָע בֶּן־
son-of Elishama Ephraim of-sons-of leader the-seventh on-the-day (48) Deuel

עַמִּיהוּד׃ קָרְבָּנוֹ קַעֲרַת־ כֶּסֶף אַחַת שְׁלֹשִׁים וּמֵאָה
and-hundred thirty one silver plate-of offering-of-him (49) Ammihud

מִשְׁקָלָהּ מִזְרָק אֶחָד כֶּסֶף שִׁבְעִים שֶׁקֶל בְּשֶׁקֶל
by-shekel-of shekel seventy silver one sprinkling-bowl weight-of-her

הַקֹּדֶשׁ שְׁנֵיהֶם ׀ מְלֵאִים סֹלֶת בְּלוּלָה בַשֶּׁמֶן
with-the-oil being-mixed fine-flour ones-filled both-of-them the-sanctuary

לְמִנְחָה׃ כַּף אַחַת עֲשָׂרָה זָהָב מְלֵאָה קְטֹרֶת׃ פַּר אֶחָד
one bull (51) incense filled gold ten one ladle (50) as-grain-offering

בֶּן־ בָּקָר אַיִל אֶחָד כֶּבֶשׂ־אֶחָד בֶּן־ שְׁנָתוֹ לְעֹלָה׃
for-burnt-offering year-of-him son-of one lamb one ram herd young-of

שְׂעִיר־ עִזִּים אֶחָד לְחַטָּאת׃ וּלְזֶבַח
and-for-sacrifice-of (53) for-sin-offering one goats male-goat-of (52)

הַשְּׁלָמִים בָּקָר שְׁנַיִם אֵילִם חֲמִשָּׁה עַתֻּדִים חֲמִשָּׁה כְּבָשִׂים בְּנֵי־
sons-of lambs five male-goats five rams two ox the-fellowship-offerings

שָׁנָה חֲמִשָּׁה זֶה קָרְבַּן אֱלִישָׁמָע בֶּן־ עַמִּיהוּד׃ בַּיּוֹם
on-the-day (54) Ammihud son-of Elishama offering-of this five year

הַשְּׁמִינִי נָשִׂיא לִבְנֵי מְנַשֶּׁה גַּמְלִיאֵל בֶּן־ פְּדָה־ צוּר׃
Zur Pedah son-of Gamaliel Manasseh of-sons-of leader the-eighth

קָרְבָּנוֹ קַעֲרַת־ כֶּסֶף אַחַת שְׁלֹשִׁים וּמֵאָה מִשְׁקָלָהּ
weight-of-her and-hundred thirty one silver plate-of offering-of-him (55)

מִזְרָק אֶחָד כֶּסֶף שִׁבְעִים שֶׁקֶל בְּשֶׁקֶל הַקֹּדֶשׁ
the-sanctuary by-shekel-of shekel seventy silver one sprinkling-bowl

שְׁנֵיהֶם ׀ מְלֵאִים סֹלֶת בְּלוּלָה בַשֶּׁמֶן לְמִנְחָה *
as-grain-offering with-the-oil being-mixed fine-flour ones-filled both-of-them

כַּף אַחַת עֲשָׂרָה זָהָב מְלֵאָה קְטֹרֶת׃ פַּר אֶחָד בֶּן־ בָּקָר אַיִל
ram herd young-of one bull (57) incense filled gold ten one ladle (56)

filled with fine flour mixed
with oil as a grain offering;
44one gold ladle weighing
ten shekels, filled with incense; 45one young bull,
one ram and one male lamb
a year old, for a burnt
offering; 46one male goat for
a sin offering; 47and two
oxen, five rams, five male
goats and five male lambs a
year old, to be sacrificed as
a fellowship offering. This
was the offering of Eliasaph
son of Deuel.

48On the seventh day Eli-
shama son of Ammihud, the
leader of the people of
Ephraim, brought his offering.
49His offering was one silver plate weighing a hun-
dred and thirty shekels,
and one silver sprinkling
bowl weighing seventy
shekels, both according to
the sanctuary shekel, each
filled with fine flour mixed
with oil as a grain offering;
50one gold ladle weighing
ten shekels, filled with incense; 51one young bull,
one ram and one male lamb
a year old, for a burnt
offering; 52one male goat for
a sin offering; 53and two
oxen, five rams, five male
goats and five male lambs a
year old, to be sacrificed as
a fellowship offering. This
was the offering of Eli-
shama son of Ammihud.

54On the eighth day Gamaliel
son of Pedahzur, the leader of
the people of Manasseh,
brought his offering.
55His offering was one silver plate weighing a hun-
dred and thirty shekels,
and one silver sprinkling
bowl weighing seventy
shekels, both according to
the sanctuary shekel, each
filled with fine flour mixed
with oil as a grain offering;
56one gold ladle weighing
ten shekels, filled with incense; 57one young bull,

*55 Most mss end verse 55 with *soph pasuq* (׃).

אֶחָד כֶּבֶשׂ־אֶחָד בֶּן־ שְׁנָתוֹ לְעֹלָה׃ שְׂעִיר עִזִּים
goats male-goat-of (58) for-burnt-offering year-of-him son-of one lamb one

אֶחָד לְחַטָּאת׃ וּלְזֶבַח הַשְּׁלָמִים בָּקָר
ox the-fellowship-offerings and-for-sacrifice-of (59) for-sin-offering one

שְׁנַיִם אֵילִם חֲמִשָּׁה עַתֻּדִים חֲמִשָּׁה כְּבָשִׂים בְּנֵי־ שָׁנָה חֲמִשָּׁה זֶה קָרְבַּן
offering-of this five year sons-of lambs five male-goats five rams two

גַּמְלִיאֵל בֶּן־ פְּדָה־ צוּר׃ בַּיּוֹם הַתְּשִׁיעִי נָשִׂיא לִבְנֵי
of-sons-of leader the-ninth on-the-day (60) Zur Pedah son-of Gamaliel

בִנְיָמִן אֲבִידָן בֶּן־ גִּדְעֹנִי׃ קָרְבָּנוֹ קַעֲרַת־ כֶּסֶף אַחַת
one silver plate-of offering-of-him (61) Gideoni son-of Abidan Benjamin

שְׁלֹשִׁים וּמֵאָה מִשְׁקָלָהּ מִזְרָק אֶחָד כֶּסֶף שִׁבְעִים שֶׁקֶל
shekel seventy silver one sprinkling-bowl weight-of-her and-hundred thirty

בְּשֶׁקֶל הַקֹּדֶשׁ שְׁנֵיהֶם ׀ מְלֵאִים סֹלֶת בְּלוּלָה
being-mixed fine-flour ones-filled both-of-them the-sanctuary by-shekel-of

בַשֶּׁמֶן לְמִנְחָה׃ כַּף אַחַת עֲשָׂרָה זָהָב מְלֵאָה קְטֹרֶת׃
incense filled gold ten one ladle (62) as-grain-offering with-the-oil

פַּר אֶחָד בֶּן־ בָּקָר אַיִל אֶחָד כֶּבֶשׂ־ אֶחָד בֶּן־ שְׁנָתוֹ
year-of-him son-of one lamb one ram herd young-of one bull (63)

לְעֹלָה׃ שְׂעִיר־ עִזִּים אֶחָד לְחַטָּאת׃
for-sin-offering one goats male-goat-of (64) for-burnt-offering

וּלְזֶבַח הַשְּׁלָמִים בָּקָר שְׁנַיִם אֵילִם חֲמִשָּׁה
five rams two ox the-fellowship-offerings and-for-sacrifice-of (65)

עַתֻּדִים חֲמִשָּׁה כְּבָשִׂים בְּנֵי־ שָׁנָה חֲמִשָּׁה זֶה קָרְבַּן אֲבִידָן בֶּן־
son-of Abidan offering-of this five year sons-of lambs five male-goats

גִּדְעֹנִי׃ בַּיּוֹם הָעֲשִׂירִי נָשִׂיא לִבְנֵי דָן אֲחִיעֶזֶר בֶּן־
son-of Ahiezer Dan of-sons-of leader the-tenth on-the-day (66) Gideoni

עַמִּישַׁדָּי׃ קָרְבָּנוֹ קַעֲרַת־ כֶּסֶף אַחַת שְׁלֹשִׁים וּמֵאָה
and-hundred thirty one silver plate-of offering-of-him (67) Ammishaddai

מִשְׁקָלָהּ מִזְרָק אֶחָד כֶּסֶף שִׁבְעִים שֶׁקֶל בְּשֶׁקֶל
by-shekel-of shekel seventy silver one sprinkling-bowl weight-of-her

הַקֹּדֶשׁ שְׁנֵיהֶם ׀ מְלֵאִים סֹלֶת בְּלוּלָה בַשֶּׁמֶן
with-the-oil being-mixed fine-flour ones-filled both-of-them the-sanctuary

לְמִנְחָה׃ כַּף אַחַת עֲשָׂרָה זָהָב מְלֵאָה קְטֹרֶת * פַּר אֶחָד
one bull (69) incense filled gold ten one ladle (68) as-grain-offering

בֶּן־ בָּקָר אַיִל אֶחָד כֶּבֶשׂ־ אֶחָד בֶּן־ שְׁנָתוֹ לְעֹלָה׃
for-burnt-offering year-of-him son-of one lamb one ram herd young-of

שְׂעִיר־ עִזִּים אֶחָד לְחַטָּאת׃ וּלְזֶבַח
and-for-sacrifice-of (71) for-sin-offering one goats male-goat-of (70)

one ram and one male lamb a year old, for a burnt offering; [58]one male goat for a sin offering; [59]and two oxen, five rams, five male goats and five male lambs a year old, to be sacrificed as a fellowship offering. This was the offering of Gamaliel son of Pedahzur.

[60]On the ninth day Abidan son of Gideoni, the leader of the people of Benjamin, brought his offering.

[61]His offering was one silver plate weighing a hundred and thirty shekels, and one silver sprinkling bowl weighing seventy shekels, both according to the sanctuary shekel, each filled with fine flour mixed with oil as a grain offering; [62]one gold ladle weighing ten shekels, filled with incense; [63]one young bull, one ram and one male lamb a year old, for a burnt offering; [64]one male goat for a sin offering; [65]and two oxen, five rams, five male goats and five male lambs a year old, to be sacrificed as a fellowship offering. This was the offering of Abidan son of Gideoni.

[66]On the tenth day Ahiezer son of Ammishaddai, the leader of the people of Dan, brought his offering.

[67]His offering was one silver plate weighing a hundred and thirty shekels, and one silver sprinkling bowl weighing seventy shekels, both according to the sanctuary shekel, each filled with fine flour mixed with oil as a grain offering; [68]one gold ladle weighing ten shekels, filled with incense; [69]one young bull, one ram and one male lamb a year old, for a burnt offering; [70]one male goat for a sin offering; [71]and two

*68 Most mss end verse 68 with *soph pasuq* (׃).

הַשְּׁלָמִים בָּקָר שְׁנַיִם אֵילִם חֲמִשָּׁה עַתֻּדִים חֲמִשָּׁה כְּבָשִׂים בְּנֵי־
sons-of lambs five male-goats five rams two ox the-fellowship-offerings

שָׁנָה חֲמִשָּׁה זֶה קָרְבַּן אֲחִיעֶזֶר בֶּן־ עַמִּישַׁדָּי׃ בַּיּוֹם עַשְׁתֵּי עָשָׂר
ten one on-day (72) Ammishaddai son-of Ahiezer offering-of this five year

יוֹם נָשִׂיא לִבְנֵי אָשֵׁר פַּגְעִיאֵל בֶּן־ עָכְרָן׃ קָרְבָּנוֹ
offering-of-him (73) Ocran son-of Pagiel Asher of-sons-of leader day

קַעֲרַת־ כֶּסֶף אַחַת שְׁלֹשִׁים וּמֵאָה מִשְׁקָלָהּ מִזְרָק אֶחָד
one sprinkling-bowl weight-of-her and-hundred thirty one silver plate-of

כֶּסֶף שִׁבְעִים שֶׁקֶל בְּשֶׁקֶל הַקֹּדֶשׁ שְׁנֵיהֶם ׀ מְלֵאִים
ones-filled both-of-them the-sanctuary by-shekel-of shekel seventy silver

סֹלֶת בְּלוּלָה בַשֶּׁמֶן לְמִנְחָה׃ כַּף אַחַת עֲשָׂרָה
ten one ladle (74) as-grain-offering with-the-oil being-mixed fine-flour

זָהָב מְלֵאָה קְטֹרֶת׃ פַּר אֶחָד בֶּן־ בָּקָר אַיִל אֶחָד כֶּבֶשׂ־אֶחָד בֶּן־
son-of one lamb one ram herd young-of one bull (75) incense filled gold

שְׁנָתוֹ לְעֹלָה׃ שְׂעִיר־ עִזִּים אֶחָד לְחַטָּאת׃
for-sin-offering one goats male-goat-of (76) for-burnt-offeirng year-of-him

וּלְזֶבַח הַשְּׁלָמִים בָּקָר שְׁנַיִם אֵילִם חֲמִשָּׁה
five rams two ox the-fellowship-offerings and-for-sacrifice-of (77)

עַתֻּדִים חֲמִשָּׁה כְּבָשִׂים בְּנֵי־ שָׁנָה חֲמִשָּׁה זֶה קָרְבַּן פַּגְעִיאֵל בֶּן־
son-of Pagiel offering-of this five year sons-of lambs five male-goats

עָכְרָן׃ בְּיוֹם שְׁנֵים עָשָׂר יוֹם נָשִׂיא לִבְנֵי נַפְתָּלִי אֲחִירַע בֶּן־ עֵינָן׃
Enan son-of Ahira Naphtali of-sons-of leader day ten two on-day (78) Ocran

קָרְבָּנוֹ קַעֲרַת־ כֶּסֶף אַחַת שְׁלֹשִׁים וּמֵאָה מִשְׁקָלָהּ
weight-of-her and-hundred thirty one silver plate-of offering-of-him (79)

מִזְרָק אֶחָד כֶּסֶף שִׁבְעִים שֶׁקֶל בְּשֶׁקֶל הַקֹּדֶשׁ
the-sanctuary by-shekel-of shekel seventy silver one sprinkling-bowl

שְׁנֵיהֶם ׀ מְלֵאִים סֹלֶת בְּלוּלָה בַשֶּׁמֶן לְמִנְחָה׃
as-grain-offering with-the-oil being-mixed fine-flour ones-filled both-of-them

כַּף אַחַת עֲשָׂרָה זָהָב מְלֵאָה קְטֹרֶת׃ פַּר אֶחָד בֶּן־ בָּקָר אַיִל
ram herd young-of one bull (81) incense filled gold ten one ladle (80)

אֶחָד כֶּבֶשׂ־אֶחָד בֶּן־ שְׁנָתוֹ לְעֹלָה׃ שְׂעִיר־ עִזִּים
goats male-goat-of (82) for-burnt-offering year-of-him son-of one lamb one

אֶחָד לְחַטָּאת׃ וּלְזֶבַח הַשְּׁלָמִים בָּקָר
ox the-fellowship-offerings and-for-sacrifice-of (83) for-sin-offering one

שְׁנַיִם אֵילִם חֲמִשָּׁה עַתֻּדִים חֲמִשָּׁה כְּבָשִׂים בְּנֵי־ שָׁנָה חֲמִשָּׁה זֶה קָרְבַּן
offering-of this five year sons-of lambs five male-goats five rams two

אֲחִירַע בֶּן־ עֵינָן׃ זֹאת ׀ חֲנֻכַּת הַמִּזְבֵּחַ בְּיוֹם
on-day the-altar dedication-offering-of this (84) Enan son-of Ahira

oxen, five rams, five male goats and five male lambs a year old, to be sacrificed as a fellowship offering. This was the offering of Ahiezer son of Ammishaddai.

72On the eleventh day Pagiel son of Ocran, the leader of the people of Asher, brought his offering.
73His offering was one silver plate weighing a hundred and thirty shekels, and one silver sprinkling bowl weighing seventy shekels, both according to the sanctuary shekel, each filled with fine flour mixed with oil as a grain offering;
74one gold ladle weighing ten shekels, filled with in-
cense; 75one young bull,
one ram and one male lamb a year old, for a burnt
offering; 76one male goat for
a sin offering; 77and two
oxen, five rams, five male goats and five male lambs a year old, to be sacrificed as a fellowship offering. This was the offering of Pagiel son of Ocran.

78On the twelfth day Ahira son of Enan, the leader of the people of Naphtali, brought his offering.
79His offering was one silver plate weighing a hundred and thirty shekels, and one silver sprinkling bowl weighing seventy shekels, both according to the sanctuary shekel, each filled with fine flour mixed with oil as a grain offering;
80one gold ladle weighing ten shekels, filled with in-
cense; 81one young bull,
one ram and one male lamb a year old, for a burnt
offering; 82one male goat for
a sin offering; 83and two
oxen, five rams, five male goats and five male lambs a year old, to be sacrificed as a fellowship offering. This was the offering of Ahira son of Enan.

84These were the offerings of the Israelite leaders for the dedication of the altar when it

הִמָּשַׁח אֹתוֹ מֵאֵת נְשִׂיאֵי יִשְׂרָאֵל קַעֲרֹת כֶּסֶף שְׁתֵּים עֶשְׂרֵה
ten two silver plates-of Israel leaders-of from him to-be-anointed

מִזְרְקֵי־כֶסֶף שְׁנֵים עָשָׂר כַּפּוֹת זָהָב שְׁתֵּים עֶשְׂרֵה׃ שְׁלֹשִׁים
thirty (85) ten two gold ladles-of ten two silver sprinkling-bowls-of

וּמֵאָה הַקְּעָרָה הָאַחַת כֶּסֶף וְשִׁבְעִים הַמִּזְרָק
the-sprinkling-bowl and-seventy silver the-each the-plate and-hundred

הָאֶחָד כֹּל כֶּסֶף הַכֵּלִים אַלְפַּיִם וְאַרְבַּע־מֵאוֹת
hundreds and-four two-thousands the-dishes silver-of all-of the-each

בְּשֶׁקֶל הַקֹּדֶשׁ׃ כַּפּוֹת זָהָב שְׁתֵּים־עֶשְׂרֵה מְלֵאֹת קְטֹרֶת
incense ones-filled ten two gold ladles-of (86) the-sanctuary by-shekel-of

עֲשָׂרָה עֲשָׂרָה הַכַּף בְּשֶׁקֶל הַקֹּדֶשׁ כָּל־ זְהַב הַכַּפּוֹת
the-ladles gold-of all-of the-sanctuary by-shekel-of the-ladle ten ten

עֶשְׂרִים וּמֵאָה׃ כָּל־ הַבָּקָר לָעֹלָה שְׁנֵים עָשָׂר
ten two for-burnt-offering the-animal total-of (87) and-hundred twenty

פָּרִים אֵילִם שְׁנֵים־עָשָׂר כְּבָשִׂים בְּנֵי־ שָׁנָה שְׁנֵים עָשָׂר וּמִנְחָתָם
and-grain-offering-of-them ten two year sons-of lambs ten two rams bulls

וּשְׂעִירֵי עִזִּים שְׁנֵים עָשָׂר לְחַטָּאת׃ וְכֹל בְּקַר ׀
animal-of and-total-of (88) for-sin-offering ten two goats and-male-goats-of

זֶבַח הַשְּׁלָמִים עֶשְׂרִים וְאַרְבָּעָה פָּרִים אֵילִם שִׁשִּׁים
sixty rams bulls and-four twenty the-fellowship-offerings sacrifice-of

עַתֻּדִים שִׁשִּׁים כְּבָשִׂים בְּנֵי־ שָׁנָה שִׁשִּׁים זֹאת חֲנֻכַּת
dedication-offering-of this sixty year sons-of lambs sixty male-goats

הַמִּזְבֵּחַ אַחֲרֵי הִמָּשַׁח אֹתוֹ׃ וּבְבֹא מֹשֶׁה אֶל־ אֹהֶל
Tent-of into Moses and-when-to-enter (89) him to-be-anointed after the-altar

מוֹעֵד לְדַבֵּר אִתּוֹ וַיִּשְׁמַע אֶת־ הַקּוֹל מִדַּבֵּר אֵלָיו
to-him speaking the-voice *** then-he-heard with-him to-speak Meeting

מֵעַל הַכַּפֹּרֶת אֲשֶׁר עַל־ אֲרֹן הָעֵדֻת מִבֵּין
from-between the-Testimony ark-of on that the-atonement-cover from-above

שְׁנֵי הַכְּרֻבִים וַיְדַבֵּר אֵלָיו׃ וַיְדַבֵּר יְהוָה אֶל־
to Yahweh and-he-spoke (8:1) with-him and-he-spoke the-cherubim two-of

מֹשֶׁה לֵּאמֹר׃ דַּבֵּר אֶל־אַהֲרֹן וְאָמַרְתָּ אֵלָיו בְּהַעֲלֹתְךָ אֶת־
*** when-to-set-up-you to-him and-you-say Aaron to speak! (2) to-say Moses

הַנֵּרֹת אֶל־ מוּל פְּנֵי הַמְּנוֹרָה יָאִירוּ שִׁבְעַת הַנֵּרוֹת׃
the-lamps seven-of they-must-light the-lampstand front-of area on the-lamps

וַיַּעַשׂ כֵּן אַהֲרֹן אֶל־מוּל פְּנֵי הַמְּנוֹרָה הֶעֱלָה נֵרֹתֶיהָ
lamps-of-her he-set-up the-lampstand front-of area on Aaron so and-he-did (3)

כַּאֲשֶׁר צִוָּה יְהוָה אֶת־ מֹשֶׁה׃ וְזֶה מַעֲשֵׂה הַמְּנֹרָה
the-lampstand make-up-of and-this (4) Moses *** Yahweh he-commanded just-as

was anointed: twelve silver
plates, twelve silver sprinkling
bowls and twelve gold ladles.
85 Each silver plate weighed a
hundred and thirty shekels,
and each sprinkling bowl seventy shekels. Altogether, the
silver dishes weighed two
thousand four hundred
shekels,[r] according to the
sanctuary shekel. 86 The twelve
gold ladles filled with incense
weighed ten shekels each, according to the sanctuary
shekel. Altogether, the gold ladles weighed a hundred and
twenty shekels.[s] 87 The total
number of animals for the
burnt offering came to twelve
young bulls, twelve rams and
twelve male lambs a year old,
together with their grain
offering. Twelve male goats
were used for the sin offering.
88 The total number of animals
for the sacrifice of the fellowship offering came to twenty-
four oxen, sixty rams, sixty
male goats and sixty male
lambs a year old. These were
the offerings for the dedication of the altar after it was
anointed.

89 When Moses entered the
Tent of Meeting to speak with
the LORD, he heard the voice
speaking to him from between
the two cherubim above the
atonement cover on the ark of
the Testimony. And he spoke
with him.

Setting Up the Lamps

8 The LORD said to Moses,
2 "Speak to Aaron and say
to him, 'When you set up the
seven lamps, they are to light
the area in front of the lampstand.' "

3 Aaron did so; he set up the
lamps so that they faced forward on the lampstand, just as
the LORD commanded Moses.
4 This is how the lampstand
was made: It was made of

[r]85 That is, about 60 pounds (about 28 kilograms)
[s]86 That is, about 3 pounds (about 1.4 kilograms)

מִקְשָׁה זָהָב עַד־ יְרֵכָהּ עַד־ פִּרְחָהּ מִקְשָׁה הִוא
she hammered blossom-of-her to base-of-her from gold hammered

כַּמַּרְאֶה אֲשֶׁר הֶרְאָה יְהוָה אֶת־מֹשֶׁה כֵּן עָשָׂה אֶת־ הַמְּנֹרָה׃
the-lampstand *** he-made so Moses *** Yahweh he-showed that like-the-pattern

(5) וַיְדַבֵּר יְהוָה אֶל־מֹשֶׁה לֵּאמֹר׃ (6) קַח אֶת־ הַלְוִיִּם מִתּוֹךְ
from-among the-Levites *** take! (6) to-say Moses to Yahweh and-he-spoke (5)

בְּנֵי יִשְׂרָאֵל וְטִהַרְתָּ אֹתָם׃ (7) וְכֹה־ תַעֲשֶׂה לָהֶם
to-them you-do and-this (7) them and-you-make-clean Israel sons-of

לְטַהֲרָם הַזֵּה עֲלֵיהֶם מֵי חַטָּאת וְהֶעֱבִירוּ
and-they-must-shave cleansing waters-of on-them sprinkle! to-purify-them

תַעַר עַל־ כָּל־ בְּשָׂרָם וְכִבְּסוּ בִגְדֵיהֶם
clothes-of-them and-they-must-wash body-of-them whole-of over razor

וְהִטֶּהָרוּ׃ (8) וְלָקְחוּ פַּר בֶּן־ בָּקָר
herd young-of bull and-they-must-take (8) so-they-purify-selves

וּמִנְחָתוֹ סֹלֶת בְּלוּלָה בַשָּׁמֶן וּפַר־
and-bull with-the-oil being-mixed fine-flour and-grain-offering-of-him

שֵׁנִי בֶן־ בָּקָר תִּקַּח לְחַטָּאת׃ (9) וְהִקְרַבְתָּ אֶת־
*** and-you-bring (9) for-sin-offering you-take herd young-of second

הַלְוִיִּם לִפְנֵי אֹהֶל מוֹעֵד וְהִקְהַלְתָּ אֶת־ כָּל־
whole-of *** and-you-assemble Meeting Tent-of to-front-of the-Levites

עֲדַת בְּנֵי יִשְׂרָאֵל׃ (10) וְהִקְרַבְתָּ אֶת־ הַלְוִיִּם לִפְנֵי יְהוָה
Yahweh before the-Levites *** and-you-bring (10) Israel sons-of community-of

וְסָמְכוּ בְנֵי־ יִשְׂרָאֵל אֶת־ יְדֵיהֶם עַל־ הַלְוִיִּם׃
the-Levites on hands-of-them *** Israel sons-of and-they-must-lay

(11) וְהֵנִיף אַהֲרֹן אֶת־ הַלְוִיִּם תְּנוּפָה לִפְנֵי יְהוָה
Yahweh before wave-offering the-Levites *** Aaron and-he-must-present (11)

מֵאֵת בְּנֵי יִשְׂרָאֵל וְהָיוּ לַעֲבֹד אֶת־ עֲבֹדַת יְהוָה׃
Yahweh work-of *** to-work so-they-may-be Israel sons-of from

(12) וְהַלְוִיִּם יִסְמְכוּ אֶת־ יְדֵיהֶם עַל רֹאשׁ הַפָּרִים
the-bulls head-of on hands-of-them *** they-must-lay and-the-Levites (12)

וַעֲשֵׂה אֶת־ הָאֶחָד חַטָּאת וְאֶת־ הָאֶחָד עֹלָה לַיהוָה
to-Yahweh burnt-offering the-other and sin-offering the-one *** then-use!

לְכַפֵּר עַל־ הַלְוִיִּם׃ (13) וְהַעֲמַדְתָּ אֶת־ הַלְוִיִּם לִפְנֵי
in-front-of the-Levites *** and-you-have-stand (13) the-Levites for to-atone

אַהֲרֹן וְלִפְנֵי בָנָיו וְהֵנַפְתָּ אֹתָם תְּנוּפָה
wave-offering them then-you-present sons-of-him and-in-front-of Aaron

לַיהוָה׃ (14) וְהִבְדַּלְתָּ אֶת־ הַלְוִיִּם מִתּוֹךְ בְּנֵי יִשְׂרָאֵל
Israel sons-of from-among the-Levites *** so-you-set-apart (14) to-Yahweh

hammered gold—from its base
to its blossoms. The lampstand
was made exactly like the pattern the LORD had shown
Moses.

The Setting Apart of the Levites

[5]The LORD said to Moses:
[6]"Take the Levites from
among the other Israelites and
make them ceremonially
clean. [7]To purify them, do this:
Sprinkle the water of cleansing on them; then have them
shave their whole bodies and
wash their clothes, and so
purify themselves. [8]Have
them take a young bull with
its grain offering of fine flour
mixed with oil; then you are to
take a second young bull for a
sin offering. [9]Bring the Levites
to the front of the Tent of
Meeting and assemble the
whole Israelite community.
[10]You are to bring the Levites
before the LORD, and the Israelites are to lay their hands on
them. [11]Aaron is to present the
Levites before the LORD as a
wave offering from the Israelites, so that they may be ready
to do the work of the LORD.
[12]"After the Levites lay their
hands on the heads of the
bulls, use the one for a sin
offering to the LORD and the
other for a burnt offering, to
make atonement for the Levites. [13]Have the Levites stand
in front of Aaron and his sons
and then present them as a
wave offering to the LORD. [14]In
this way you are to set the Levites apart from the other Israelites, and the Levites will be

וְהָיוּ לִי הַלְוִיִּם׃ וְאַחֲרֵי־ כֵן יָבֹאוּ
they-must-come this and-after (15) the-Levites to-me and-they-will-be

הַלְוִיִּם לַעֲבֹד אֶת־ אֹהֶל מוֹעֵד וְטִהַרְתָּ אֹתָם וְהֵנַפְתָּ
and-you-present them when-you-purify Meeting Tent-of *** to-work the-Levites

אֹתָם תְּנוּפָה׃ כִּי נְתֻנִים נְתֻנִים הֵמָּה לִי
to-me they ones-being-given ones-being-given for (16) wave-offering them

מִתּוֹךְ בְּנֵי יִשְׂרָאֵל תַּחַת פִּטְרַת כָּל־ רֶחֶם בְּכוֹר
firstborn-of womb every-of first-of in-place-of Israel sons-of from-among

כֹּל מִבְּנֵי יִשְׂרָאֵל לָקַחְתִּי אֹתָם לִי׃ כִּי לִי כָל־ בְּכוֹר
firstborn every-of to-me for (17) for-me them I-took Israel from-sons-of all

בִּבְנֵי יִשְׂרָאֵל בָּאָדָם וּבַבְּהֵמָה בְּיוֹם הַכֹּתִי
to-strike-me on-day or-whether-the-animal whether-the-man Israel among-sons-of

כָל־ בְּכוֹר בְּאֶרֶץ מִצְרַיִם הִקְדַּשְׁתִּי אֹתָם לִי׃ וָאֶקַּח
and-I-took (18) for-me them I-set-apart Egypt in-land-of firstborn all-of

אֶת־ הַלְוִיִּם תַּחַת כָּל־ בְּכוֹר בִּבְנֵי יִשְׂרָאֵל׃
Israel among-sons-of firstborn all-of in-place-of the-Levites ***

וָאֶתְּנָה אֶת־ הַלְוִיִּם נְתֻנִים ׀ לְאַהֲרֹן וּלְבָנָיו
and-to-sons-of-him to-Aaron ones-being-given the-Levites *** and-I-gave (19)

מִתּוֹךְ בְּנֵי יִשְׂרָאֵל לַעֲבֹד אֶת־ עֲבֹדַת בְּנֵי־ יִשְׂרָאֵל בְּאֹהֶל
at-Tent-of Israel sons-of work-of *** to-do Israel sons-of from-among

מוֹעֵד וּלְכַפֵּר עַל־ בְּנֵי יִשְׂרָאֵל וְלֹא יִהְיֶה בִּבְנֵי
on-sons-of he-will-strike so-not Israel sons-of for and-to-atone Meeting

יִשְׂרָאֵל נֶגֶף בְּגֶשֶׁת בְּנֵי־ יִשְׂרָאֵל אֶל־ הַקֹּדֶשׁ׃ וַיַּעַשׂ
so-he-did (20) the-sanctuary to Israel sons-of when-to-go-near plague Israel

מֹשֶׁה וְאַהֲרֹן וְכָל־ עֲדַת בְּנֵי־ יִשְׂרָאֵל לַלְוִיִּם
with-the-Levites Israel sons-of community-of and-whole-of and-Aaron Moses

כְּכֹל אֲשֶׁר־ צִוָּה יְהוָה אֶת־ מֹשֶׁה לַלְוִיִּם כֵּן־ עָשׂוּ
they-did so for-the-Levites Moses *** Yahweh he-commanded that as-all

לָהֶם בְּנֵי יִשְׂרָאֵל׃ וַיִּתְחַטְּאוּ הַלְוִיִּם
the-Levites and-they-purified-selves (21) Israel sons-of with-them

וַיְכַבְּסוּ בִּגְדֵיהֶם וַיָּנֶף אַהֲרֹן אֹתָם תְּנוּפָה
wave-offering them Aaron then-he-presented clothes-of-them and-they-washed

לִפְנֵי יְהוָה וַיְכַפֵּר עֲלֵיהֶם אַהֲרֹן לְטַהֲרָם׃ וְאַחֲרֵי־
and-after (22) to-purify-them Aaron for-them and-he-atoned Yahweh before

כֵן בָּאוּ הַלְוִיִּם לַעֲבֹד אֶת־ עֲבֹדָתָם בְּאֹהֶל מוֹעֵד לִפְנֵי
before Meeting at-Tent-of work-of-them *** to-do the-Levites they-came that

אַהֲרֹן וְלִפְנֵי בָנָיו כַּאֲשֶׁר צִוָּה יְהוָה אֶת־ מֹשֶׁה עַל־
for Moses *** Yahweh he-commanded just-as sons-of him and-before Aaron

mine.
15"After you have purified
the Levites and presented
them as a wave offering, they
are to come to do their work at
the Tent of Meeting. 16They
are the Israelites who are to be
given wholly to me. I have
taken them as my own in
place of the firstborn, the first
male offspring from every Israelite woman. 17Every
firstborn male in Israel,
whether man or animal, is
mine. When I struck down all
the firstborn in Egypt, I set
them apart for myself. 18And I
have taken the Levites in place
of all the firstborn sons in Israel. 19Of all the Israelites, I have
given the Levites as gifts to
Aaron and his sons to do the
work at the Tent of Meeting
on behalf of the Israelites and
to make atonement for them
so that no plague will strike
the Israelites when they go
near the sanctuary."
20Moses, Aaron and the
whole Israelite community
did with the Levites just as the
LORD commanded Moses.
21The Levites purified themselves and washed their
clothes. Then Aaron presented
them as a wave offering before
the LORD and made atonement
for them to purify them. 22Af-
ter that, the Levites came to do
their work at the Tent of Meeting under the supervision of
Aaron and his sons. They did

הַלְוִיִּם כֵּן עָשׂוּ לָהֶם׃ (23) וַיְדַבֵּר יְהוָה אֶל־מֹשֶׁה לֵּאמֹר׃
to-say Moses to Yahweh and-he-spoke (23) with-them they-did so the-Levites

(24) זֹאת אֲשֶׁר לַלְוִיִּם מִבֶּן חָמֵשׁ וְעֶשְׂרִים שָׁנָה וָמַעְלָה
or-more year and-twenty five from-son-of for-the-Levites what this (24)

יָבוֹא לִצְבֹא צָבָא בַּעֲבֹדַת אֹהֶל מוֹעֵד׃
Meeting Tent-of in-work-of service to-take-part he-shall-come

(25) וּמִבֶּן חֲמִשִּׁים שָׁנָה יָשׁוּב מִצְּבָא הָעֲבֹדָה
the-work from-service-of he-must-retire year fifty but-from-son-of (25)

וְלֹא יַעֲבֹד עוֹד׃ (26) וְשֵׁרֵת אֶת־אֶחָיו
brothers-of-him *** now-he-may-assist (26) longer he-may-work and-not

בְּאֹהֶל מוֹעֵד לִשְׁמֹר מִשְׁמֶרֶת וַעֲבֹדָה לֹא יַעֲבֹד כָּכָה תַּעֲשֶׂה
you-assign thus he-must-do not but-work duty to-perform Meeting at-Tent-of

לַלְוִיִּם בְּמִשְׁמְרֹתָם׃ (9:1) וַיְדַבֵּר יְהוָה אֶל־
to Yahweh and-he-spoke (9:1) to-responsibilities-of-them to-the-Levites

מֹשֶׁה בְמִדְבַּר־סִינַי בַּשָּׁנָה הַשֵּׁנִית לְצֵאתָם מֵאֶרֶץ
from-land-of to-come-out-them the-second in-the-year Sinai in-Desert-of Moses

מִצְרַיִם בַּחֹדֶשׁ הָרִאשׁוֹן לֵאמֹר׃ (2) וְיַעֲשׂוּ בְנֵי־
sons-of now-they-must-celebrate (2) to-say the-first in-the-month Egypt

יִשְׂרָאֵל אֶת־הַפָּסַח בְּמוֹעֲדוֹ׃ (3) בְּאַרְבָּעָה עָשָׂר־יוֹם בַּחֹדֶשׁ
of-the-month day ten on-four (3) at-time-of-him the-Passover *** Israel

הַזֶּה בֵּין הָעֲרְבַּיִם* תַּעֲשׂוּ אֹתוֹ בְּמוֹעֲדוֹ כְּכָל־
as-all-of at-time-of-him him you-celebrate the-twilights at the-this

חֻקֹּתָיו וּכְכָל־ מִשְׁפָּטָיו תַּעֲשׂוּ אֹתוֹ׃
him you-celebrate regulations-of-him and-as-all-of rules-of-him

(4) וַיְדַבֵּר מֹשֶׁה אֶל־בְּנֵי יִשְׂרָאֵל לַעֲשֹׂת הַפָּסַח׃
the-Passover to-celebrate Israel sons-of to Moses so-he-told (4)

(5) וַיַּעֲשׂוּ אֶת־הַפֶּסַח בָּרִאשׁוֹן בְּאַרְבָּעָה עָשָׂר יוֹם
day ten on-four in-the-first the-Passover *** so-they-celebrated (5)

לַחֹדֶשׁ בֵּין הָעַרְבַּיִם בְּמִדְבַּר סִינָי כְּכֹל אֲשֶׁר צִוָּה
he-commanded that as-all Sinai in-Desert-of the-twilights at of-the-month

יְהוָה אֶת־מֹשֶׁה כֵּן עָשׂוּ בְּנֵי יִשְׂרָאֵל׃ (6) וַיְהִי אֲנָשִׁים אֲשֶׁר
who men but-he-was (6) Israel sons-of they-did so Moses *** Yahweh

הָיוּ טְמֵאִים לְנֶפֶשׁ אָדָם וְלֹא־יָכְלוּ לַעֲשֹׂת־
to-celebrate they-could so-not man by-body-of unclean-ones they-were

הַפֶּסַח בַּיּוֹם הַהוּא וַיִּקְרְבוּ לִפְנֵי מֹשֶׁה וְלִפְנֵי אַהֲרֹן
Aaron and-before Moses before so-they-came the-that on-the-day the-Passover

בַּיּוֹם הַהוּא׃ (7) וַיֹּאמְרוּ הָאֲנָשִׁים הָהֵמָּה אֵלָיו אֲנַחְנוּ
we to-him the-these the-men and-they-said (7) the-that on-the-day

with the Levites just as the LORD commanded Moses.

[23]The LORD said to Moses, [24]"This applies to the Levites: Men twenty-five years old or more shall come to take part in the work at the Tent of Meeting, [25]but at the age of fifty, they must retire from their regular service and work no longer. [26]They may assist their brothers in performing their duties at the Tent of Meeting, but they themselves must not do the work. This, then, is how you are to assign the responsibilities of the Levites."

The Passover

9 The LORD spoke to Moses in the Desert of Sinai in the first month of the second year after they came out of Egypt. He said, [2]"Have the Israelites celebrate the Passover at the appointed time. [3]Celebrate it at the appointed time, at twilight on the fourteenth day of this month, in accordance with all its rules and regulations."

[4]So Moses told the Israelites to celebrate the Passover, [5]and they did so in the Desert of Sinai at twilight on the fourteenth day of the first month. The Israelites did everything just as the LORD commanded Moses.

[6]But some of them could not celebrate the Passover on that day because they were ceremonially unclean on account of a dead body. So they came to Moses and Aaron that same day [7]and said to Moses,

*3 Most mss have *pathah* under the *ayin* (הָעַרְ).

טְמֵאִים לְנֶפֶשׁ אָדָם לָמָּה נִגָּרַע לְבִלְתִּי הַקְרִב אֶת־ קָרְבַּן
offering-of *** to-present not are-we-kept why? man by-body-of unclean-ones

יְהוָה בְּמֹעֲדוֹ בְּתוֹךְ בְּנֵי יִשְׂרָאֵל׃ וַיֹּאמֶר אֲלֵהֶם מֹשֶׁה
Moses to-them and-he-answered (8) Israel sons-of with at-time-of-him Yahweh

עִמְדוּ וְאֶשְׁמְעָה מַה־ יְצַוֶּה יְהוָה לָכֶם׃ וַיְדַבֵּר
then-he-spoke (9) about-you Yahweh he-commands what and-I-will-find wait!

יְהוָה אֶל־ מֹשֶׁה לֵּאמֹר׃ דַּבֵּר אֶל־ בְּנֵי יִשְׂרָאֵל לֵאמֹר אִישׁ אִישׁ כִּי־
when any man to-say Israel sons-of to tell! (10) to-say Moses to Yahweh

יִהְיֶה־ טָמֵא ׀ לָנֶפֶשׁ אוֹ בְדֶרֶךְ רְחֹקָה לָכֶם אוֹ
or whether-you distant on-journey or by-body unclean he-is

לְדֹרֹתֵיכֶם וְעָשָׂה פֶסַח לַיהוָה׃
of-Yahweh Passover then-he-may-celebrate whether-descendants-of-you

בַּחֹדֶשׁ הַשֵּׁנִי בְּאַרְבָּעָה עָשָׂר יוֹם בֵּין הָעַרְבַּיִם
the-twilights at day ten on-four the-second in-the-month (11)

יַעֲשׂוּ אֹתוֹ עַל־ מַצּוֹת וּמְרֹרִים
and-bitter-herbs unleavened-breads with him they-must-celebrate

יֹאכְלֻהוּ׃ לֹא־ יַשְׁאִירוּ מִמֶּנּוּ עַד־ בֹּקֶר וְעֶצֶם
or-bone morning till from-him they-must-leave not (12) they-must-eat-him

לֹא יִשְׁבְּרוּ־ בוֹ כְּכָל־ חֻקַּת הַפֶּסַח
the-Passover regulation-of as-every-of in-him they-must-break not

יַעֲשׂוּ אֹתוֹ׃ וְהָאִישׁ אֲשֶׁר־ הוּא טָהוֹר וּבְדֶרֶךְ לֹא־
not and-on-journey clean he who but-the-man (13) him they-must-celebrate

הָיָה וְחָדַל לַעֲשׂוֹת הַפֶּסַח וְנִכְרְתָה הַנֶּפֶשׁ
the-person then-she-must-be-cut the-Passover to-celebrate yet-he-fails he-is

הַהִוא מֵעַמֶּיהָ כִּי ׀ קָרְבַּן יְהוָה לֹא הִקְרִיב
he-presented not Yahweh offering-of for from-people-of-her the-that

בְּמֹעֲדוֹ חֶטְאוֹ יִשָּׂא הָאִישׁ הַהוּא׃ וְכִי־
and-if (14) the-that the-man he-must-bear sin-of-him at-time-of-him

יָגוּר אִתְּכֶם גֵּר וְעָשָׂה פֶּסַח לַיהוָה
of-Yahweh Passover and-he-would-celebrate alien among-you he-lives

כְּחֻקַּת הַפֶּסַח וּכְמִשְׁפָּטוֹ כֵּן יַעֲשֶׂה חֻקָּה
regulation he-must-do so and-as-rule-of-him the-Passover as-regulation-of

אַחַת יִהְיֶה לָכֶם וְלַגֵּר וּלְאֶזְרַח הָאָרֶץ׃
the-land and-for-native-of and-for-the-alien for-you he-must-be same

וּבְיוֹם הָקִים אֶת־ הַמִּשְׁכָּן כִּסָּה הֶעָנָן אֶת־
*** the-cloud he-covered the-tabernacle *** to-set-up and-on-day (15)

הַמִּשְׁכָּן לְאֹהֶל הָעֵדֻת וּבָעֶרֶב יִהְיֶה עַל־
above he-was and-from-the-evening the-Testimony over-Tent-of the-tabernacle

"We have become unclean because of a dead body, but why
should we be kept from
presenting the LORD's offering
with the other Israelites at the
appointed time?"
8 Moses answered them,
"Wait until I find out what the
LORD commands concerning
you."
9 Then the LORD said to
Moses, 10 "Tell the Israelites:
'When any of you or your descendants are unclean because
of a dead body or are away on
a journey, they may still celebrate the LORD's Passover.
11 They are to celebrate it on the
fourteenth day of the second
month at twilight. They are to
eat the lamb, together with
unleavened bread and bitter
herbs. 12 They must not leave
any of it till morning or break
any of its bones. When they
celebrate the Passover, they
must follow all the regulations.
13 But if a man who is
ceremonially clean and not on
a journey fails to celebrate the
Passover, that person must be
cut off from his people because
he did not present the LORD's
offering at the appointed time.
That man will bear the consequences of his sin.
14 " 'An alien living among
you who wants to celebrate
the LORD's Passover must do so
in accordance with its rules
and regulations. You must
have the same regulations for
the alien and the native-
born.' "

The Cloud Above the Tabernacle

15 On the day the tabernacle,
the Tent of the Testimony,
was set up, the cloud covered
it. From evening till morning

הַמִּשְׁכָּן כְּמַרְאֵה־ אֵשׁ עַד־ בֹּקֶר׃ כֵּן יִהְיֶה תָמִיד
continually he-was so (16) morning till fire as-appearance-of the-tabernacle

הֶעָנָן יְכַסֶּנּוּ וּמַרְאֵה־ אֵשׁ לָיְלָה׃ וּלְפִי
and-at-time-of (17) night fire and-appearance-of he-covered-him the-cloud

הֵעָלֹת הֶעָנָן מֵעַל הָאֹהֶל וְאַחֲרֵי־ כֵן יִסְעוּ
they-set-out this then-after the-Tent from-above the-cloud to-be-lifted

בְּנֵי יִשְׂרָאֵל וּבִמְקוֹם אֲשֶׁר יִשְׁכָּן־ שָׁם הֶעָנָן שָׁם
there the-cloud there he-settled where and-at-place Israel sons-of

יַחֲנוּ בְּנֵי יִשְׂרָאֵל׃ עַל־ פִּי יְהוָה יִסְעוּ בְּנֵי
sons-of they-set-out Yahweh command-of at (18) Israel sons-of they-encamped

יִשְׂרָאֵל וְעַל־ פִּי יְהוָה יַחֲנוּ כָּל־ יְמֵי אֲשֶׁר יִשְׁכֹּן
he-stayed that days-of all-of they-encamped Yahweh command-of and-at Israel

הֶעָנָן עַל־ הַמִּשְׁכָּן יַחֲנוּ׃ וּבְהַאֲרִיךְ הֶעָנָן
the-cloud and-when-to-remain (19) they-encamped the-tabernacle over the-cloud

עַל־ הַמִּשְׁכָּן יָמִים רַבִּים וְשָׁמְרוּ בְנֵי־ יִשְׂרָאֵל אֶת־מִשְׁמֶרֶת
order-of *** Israel sons-of then-they-obeyed many days the-tabernacle over

יְהוָה וְלֹא יִסָּעוּ׃ וְיֵשׁ אֲשֶׁר יִהְיֶה הֶעָנָן יָמִים
days the-cloud he-stayed when and-he-was (20) they-set-out and-not Yahweh

מִסְפָּר עַל־ הַמִּשְׁכָּן עַל־ פִּי יְהוָה יַחֲנוּ וְעַל־
then-at they-encamped Yahweh command-of at the-tabernacle over few

פִּי יְהוָה יִסָּעוּ׃ וְיֵשׁ אֲשֶׁר יִהְיֶה הֶעָנָן
the-cloud he-stayed when and-he-was (21) they-set-out Yahweh command-of

מֵעֶרֶב עַד־ בֹּקֶר וְנַעֲלָה הֶעָנָן בַּבֹּקֶר
in-the-morning the-cloud when-he-was-lifted morning till from-evening

וְנָסָעוּ אוֹ יוֹמָם וָלַיְלָה וְנַעֲלָה הֶעָנָן
the-cloud when-he-was-lifted or-night by-day whether then-they-set-out

וְנָסָעוּ׃ אוֹ־ יֹמַיִם אוֹ־ חֹדֶשׁ אוֹ־ יָמִים בְּהַאֲרִיךְ
when-to-stay days or month or two-days whether (22) then-they-set-out

הֶעָנָן עַל־ הַמִּשְׁכָּן לִשְׁכֹּן עָלָיו יַחֲנוּ בְנֵי־
sons-of then-they-encamped over-him to-remain the-tabernacle over the-cloud

יִשְׂרָאֵל וְלֹא יִסָּעוּ וּבְהֵעָלֹתוֹ יִסָּעוּ׃ עַל־
at (23) they-set-out but-when-to-be-lifted-him they-set-out and-not Israel

פִּי יְהוָה יַחֲנוּ וְעַל־ פִּי יְהוָה יִסָּעוּ אֶת־
*** they-set-out Yahweh command-of and-at they-encamped Yahweh command-of

מִשְׁמֶרֶת יְהוָה שָׁמָרוּ עַל־ פִּי יְהוָה בְּיַד־ מֹשֶׁה׃
Moses by-hand-of Yahweh command-of to they-obeyed Yahweh order-of

וַיְדַבֵּר יְהוָה אֶל־ מֹשֶׁה לֵּאמֹר׃ עֲשֵׂה לְךָ שְׁתֵּי
two-of for-you make! (2) to-say Moses to Yahweh and-he-spoke (10:1)

the cloud above the tabernacle
looked like fire. 16That is how
it continued to be; the cloud
covered it, and at night it
looked like fire. 17Whenever
the cloud lifted from above the
Tent, the Israelites set out;
wherever the cloud settled, the
Israelites encamped. 18At the
LORD's command the Israelites
set out, and at his command
they encamped. As long as the
cloud stayed over the tabernacle, they remained in camp.
19When the cloud remained
over the tabernacle a long
time, the Israelites obeyed the
LORD's order and did not set
out. 20Sometimes the cloud
was over the tabernacle only a
few days; at the LORD's command they would encamp,
and then at his command they
would set out. 21Sometimes the
cloud stayed only from evening till morning, and when it
lifted in the morning, they set
out. Whether by day or by
night, whenever the cloud lifted, they set out. 22Whether the
cloud stayed over the tabernacle for two days or a month
or a year, the Israelites would
remain in camp and not set
out; but when it lifted, they
would set out. 23At the LORD's
command they encamped,
and at the LORD's command
they set out. They obeyed the
LORD's order, in accordance
with his command through
Moses.

The Silver Trumpets

10 The LORD said to
Moses: 2"Make two

חֲצוֹצְרֹת כֶּסֶף מִקְשָׁה תַּעֲשֶׂה אֹתָם וְהָיוּ לְךָ
for-you and-they-will-be them you-make hammered silver trumpets-of

לְמִקְרָא הָעֵדָה וּלְמַסַּע אֶת־ הַמַּחֲנוֹת׃
the-camps *** and-for-setting-out the-community for-calling-of

(3) וְתָקְעוּ בָּהֵן וְנוֹעֲדוּ אֵלֶיךָ כָּל־
whole-of before-you then-they-must-assemble on-them when-they-sound (3)

הָעֵדָה אֶל־ פֶּתַח אֹהֶל מוֹעֵד׃ (4) וְאִם־ בְּאַחַת יִתְקָעוּ
they-sound on-one but-if (4) Meeting Tent-of entrance-of at the-community

וְנוֹעֲדוּ אֵלֶיךָ הַנְּשִׂיאִים רָאשֵׁי אַלְפֵי יִשְׂרָאֵל׃
Israel clans-of heads-of the-leaders before-you then-they-must-assemble

(5) וּתְקַעְתֶּם תְּרוּעָה וְנָסְעוּ הַמַּחֲנוֹת הַחֹנִים
the-ones-camping the-camps then-they-must-set-out blast when-you-sound (5)

קֵדְמָה׃ (6) וּתְקַעְתֶּם תְּרוּעָה שֵׁנִית וְנָסְעוּ הַמַּחֲנוֹת
the-camps then-they-must-set-out second blast when-you-sound (6) on-east

הַחֹנִים תֵּימָנָה תְּרוּעָה יִתְקְעוּ לְמַסְעֵיהֶם׃
for-settings-out-of-them they-will-signal blast on-south the-ones-camping

(7) וּבְהַקְהִיל אֶת־ הַקָּהָל תִּתְקְעוּ וְלֹא תָרִיעוּ׃
you-signal but-not you-sound the-assembly *** and-when-to-gather (7)

(8) וּבְנֵי אַהֲרֹן הַכֹּהֲנִים יִתְקְעוּ בַּחֲצֹצְרוֹת
on-the-trumpets they-must-blow the-priests Aaron now-sons-of (8)

וְהָיוּ לָכֶם לְחֻקַּת עוֹלָם לְדֹרֹתֵיכֶם׃
for-generations-of-you lasting as-ordinance-of for-you and-they-will-be

(9) וְכִי־ תָבֹאוּ מִלְחָמָה בְּאַרְצְכֶם עַל־ הַצַּר
the-enemy against in-land-of-you battle you-go-into and-when (9)

הַצֹּרֵר אֶתְכֶם וַהֲרֵעֹתֶם בַּחֲצֹצְרוֹת
on-the-trumpets then-you-blast you the-one-oppressing

וְנִזְכַּרְתֶּם* לִפְנֵי יְהוָה אֱלֹהֵיכֶם וְנוֹשַׁעְתֶּם
and-you-will-be-rescued God-of-you Yahweh by then-you-will-be-remembered

מֵאֹיְבֵיכֶם׃ (10) וּבְיוֹם שִׂמְחַתְכֶם וּבְמוֹעֲדֵיכֶם
and-at-feasts-of-you joy-of-you and-on-day-of (10) from-being-enemies-of-you

וּבְרָאשֵׁי חָדְשֵׁיכֶם וּתְקַעְתֶּם בַּחֲצֹצְרֹת עַל
over on-the-trumpets then-you-sound months-of-you and-at-beginnings-of

עֹלֹתֵיכֶם וְעַל זִבְחֵי שַׁלְמֵיכֶם
fellowships-of-you offerings-of and-over burnt-offerings-of-you

וְהָיוּ לָכֶם לְזִכָּרוֹן לִפְנֵי אֱלֹהֵיכֶם אֲנִי יְהוָה אֱלֹהֵיכֶם׃
God-of-you Yahweh I God-of-you before as-memorial for-you and-they-will-be

(11) וַיְהִי בַּשָּׁנָה הַשֵּׁנִית בַּחֹדֶשׁ הַשֵּׁנִי בְּעֶשְׂרִים
on-twenty the-second in-the-month the-second in-the-year and-he-was (11)

trumpets of hammered silver,
and use them for calling the
community together and for
having the camps set out.
[3]When both are sounded, the
whole community is to assemble before you at the entrance
to the Tent of Meeting. [4]If only
one is sounded, the leaders—
the heads of the clans of Israel—are to assemble before you.
[5]When a trumpet blast is
sounded, the tribes camping
on the east are to set out. [6]At
the sounding of a second blast,
the camps on the south are to
set out. The blast will be the
signal for setting out. [7]To gather the assembly, blow the
trumpets, but not with the
same signal.
[8]"The sons of Aaron, the
priests, are to blow the trumpets. This is to be a lasting ordinance for you and the generations to come. [9]When you
go into battle in your own
land against an enemy who is
oppressing you, sound a blast
on the trumpets. Then you
will be remembered by the
LORD your God and rescued
from your enemies. [10]Also at
your times of rejoicing—your
appointed feasts and New
Moon festivals—you are to
sound the trumpets over your
burnt offerings and fellowship
offerings,[t] and they will be a
memorial for you before your
God. I am the LORD your God."

The Israelites Leave Sinai

[11]On the twentieth day of
the second month of the second year, the cloud lifted from

[t]10 Traditionally *peace offerings*

*9 Most mss have *sheva* under the *vav* (וְ).

בַּחֹדֶשׁ נַעֲלָה הֶעָנָן מֵעַל מִשְׁכַּן הָעֵדֻת׃
the-Testimony tabernacle-of from-above the-cloud he-was-lifted of-the-month

(12) וַיִּסְעוּ בְנֵי־ יִשְׂרָאֵל לְמַסְעֵיהֶם מִמִּדְבַּר
from-Desert-of in-travels-of-them Israel sons-of then-they-set-out (12)

סִינָי וַיִּשְׁכֹּן הֶעָנָן בְּמִדְבַּר פָּארָן׃ (13) וַיִּסְעוּ
and-they-set-out (13) Paran in-Desert-of the-cloud and-he-rested Sinai

בָּרִאשֹׁנָה עַל־ פִּי יְהוָה בְּיַד־ מֹשֶׁה׃ (14) וַיִּסַּע
and-he-set-out (14) Moses by-hand-of Yahweh command-of at at-the-first

דֶּגֶל מַחֲנֵה בְנֵי־ יְהוּדָה בָּרִאשֹׁנָה לְצִבְאֹתָם וְעַל־
and-over by-divisions-of-them at-the-first Judah sons-of camp-of standard-of

צְבָאוֹ נַחְשׁוֹן בֶּן־ עַמִּינָדָב׃ (15) וְעַל־ צְבָא מַטֵּה
tribe-of division-of and-over (15) Amminadab son-of Nahshon division-of-him

בְּנֵי יִשָּׂשכָר* נְתַנְאֵל בֶּן־ צוּעָר׃ (16) וְעַל־ צְבָא מַטֵּה
tribe-of division-of and-over (16) Zuar son-of Nethanel Issachar sons-of

בְּנֵי זְבוּלֻן אֱלִיאָב בֶּן־ חֵלֹן׃ (17) וְהוּרַד הַמִּשְׁכָּן
the-tabernacle then-he-was-taken-down (17) Helon son-of Eliab Zebulun sons-of

וְנָסְעוּ בְנֵי־ גֵרְשׁוֹן וּבְנֵי מְרָרִי נֹשְׂאֵי
ones-carrying-of Merari and-sons-of Gershon sons-of and-they-set-out

הַמִּשְׁכָּן׃ (18) וְנָסַע דֶּגֶל מַחֲנֵה רְאוּבֵן
Reuben camp-of standard-of and-he-set-out (18) the-tabernacle

לְצִבְאֹתָם וְעַל־ צְבָאוֹ אֱלִיצוּר בֶּן־ שְׁדֵיאוּר׃
Shedeur son-of Elizur division-of-him and-over by-divisions-of-them

(19) וְעַל־ צְבָא מַטֵּה בְּנֵי שִׁמְעוֹן שְׁלֻמִיאֵל בֶּן־ צוּרִי־
Zuri son-of Shelumiel Simeon sons-of tribe-of division-of and-over (19)

שַׁדָּי׃ (20) וְעַל־ צְבָא מַטֵּה בְנֵי־ גָד אֶלְיָסָף בֶּן־
son-of Eliasaph Gad sons-of tribe-of division-of and-over (20) Shaddai

דְּעוּאֵל׃ (21) וְנָסְעוּ הַקְּהָתִים נֹשְׂאֵי הַמִּקְדָּשׁ
the-holy-thing ones-carrying-of the-Kohathites then-they-set-out (21) Deuel

וְהֵקִימוּ אֶת־ הַמִּשְׁכָּן עַד־ בֹּאָם׃ (22) וְנָסַע
and-he-set-out (22) to-arrive-them before the-tabernacle *** and-they-set-up

דֶּגֶל מַחֲנֵה בְנֵי־ אֶפְרַיִם לְצִבְאֹתָם וְעַל־
and-over by-divisions-of-them Ephraim sons-of camp-of standard-of

צְבָאוֹ אֱלִישָׁמָע בֶּן־ עַמִּיהוּד׃ (23) וְעַל־ צְבָא מַטֵּה
tribe-of division-of and-over (23) Ammihud son-of Elishama division-of-him

בְּנֵי מְנַשֶּׁה גַּמְלִיאֵל בֶּן־ פְּדָהצוּר׃ (24) וְעַל־ צְבָא מַטֵּה
tribe-of division-of and-over (24) Pedahzur son-of Gamaliel Manasseh sons-of

בְּנֵי בִנְיָמִן אֲבִידָן בֶּן־ גִּדְעוֹנִי׃ (25) וְנָסַע דֶּגֶל
standard-of and-he-set-out (25) Gideoni son-of Abidan Benjamin sons-of

above the tabernacle of the Testimony. 12Then the Israelites set out from the Desert of Sinai and traveled from place to place until the cloud came to rest in the Desert of Paran. 13They set out, this first time, at the LORD's command through Moses.

14The divisions of the camp of Judah went first, under their standard. Nahshon son of Amminadab was in command. 15Nethanel son of Zuar was over the division of the tribe of Issachar, 16and Eliab son of Helon was over the division of the tribe of Zebulun. 17Then the tabernacle was taken down, and the Gershonites and Merarites, who carried it, set out.

18The divisions of the camp of Reuben went next, under their standard. Elizur son of Shedeur was in command. 19Shelumiel son of Zurishaddai was over the division of the tribe of Simeon, 20and Eliasaph son of Deuel was over the division of the tribe of Gad. 21Then the Kohathites set out, carrying the holy things. The tabernacle was to be set up before they arrived.

22The divisions of the camp of Ephraim went next, under their standard. Elishama son of Ammihud was in command. 23Gamaliel son of Pedahzur was over the division of the tribe of Manasseh, 24and Abidan son of Gideoni was over the division of the tribe of Benjamin.

25Finally, as the rear guard

*15 Most mss have *dagesh* in the *sin* (יִשּׂ).

מַחֲנֵה בְנֵי־ דָן מְאַסֵּף לְכָל־ הַמַּחֲנֹת לְצִבְאֹתָם
by-divisions-of-them the-units for-all-of being-rear-guard Dan sons-of camp-of

וְעַל צְבָאוֹ אֲחִיעֶזֶר בֶּן־ עַמִּי שַׁדָּי׃ (26) וְעַל־
and-over (26) Shaddai Ammi son-of Ahiezer division-of-him and-over

צְבָא מַטֵּה בְּנֵי אָשֵׁר פַּגְעִיאֵל בֶּן־ עָכְרָן׃ (27) וְעַל־
and-over (27) Ocran son-of Pagiel Asher sons-of tribe-of division-of

צְבָא מַטֵּה בְּנֵי נַפְתָּלִי אֲחִירַע בֶּן־ עֵינָן׃ (28) אֵלֶּה מַסְעֵי
orders-of these (28) Enan son-of Ahira Naphtali sons-of tribe-of division-of

בְנֵי־ יִשְׂרָאֵל לְצִבְאֹתָם וַיִּסָּעוּ׃ (29) וַיֹּאמֶר מֹשֶׁה
Moses now-he-said (29) so-they-set-out by-divisions-of-them Israel sons-of

לְחֹבָב בֶּן־ רְעוּאֵל הַמִּדְיָנִי חֹתֵן מֹשֶׁה נֹסְעִים ׀
ones-setting-out Moses father-in-law-of the-Midianite Reuel son-of to-Hobab

אֲנַחְנוּ אֶל־הַמָּקוֹם אֲשֶׁר אָמַר יְהוָה אֹתוֹ אֶתֵּן לָכֶם לְכָה אִתָּנוּ
with-us come! to-you I-will-give him Yahweh he-said which the-place for we

וְהֵטַבְנוּ לָךְ כִּי־ יְהוָה דִּבֶּר־ טוֹב עַל־יִשְׂרָאֵל׃
Israel to good he-promised Yahweh for with-you and-we-will-treat-well

(30) וַיֹּאמֶר אֵלָיו לֹא אֵלֵךְ כִּי אִם־ אֶל־ אַרְצִי וְאֶל־
and-to land-of-me to rather for I-will-go not to-him and-he-answered (30)

מוֹלַדְתִּי אֵלֵךְ׃ (31) וַיֹּאמֶר אַל־ נָא תַּעֲזֹב אֹתָנוּ כִּי ׀ עַל־ כֵּן
this by for us you-leave now! not but-he-said (31) I-go people-of-me

יָדַעְתָּ חֲנֹתֵנוּ בַּמִּדְבָּר וְהָיִיתָ לָּנוּ לְעֵינָיִם׃
as-eyes to-us and-you-can-be in-the-desert to-camp-us you-know

(32) וְהָיָה כִּי־ תֵלֵךְ עִמָּנוּ וְהָיָה ׀ הַטּוֹב הַהוּא
the-that the-good then-he-will-be with-us you-come if and-he-will-be (32)

אֲשֶׁר יֵיטִיב יְהוָה עִמָּנוּ וְהֵטַבְנוּ לָךְ׃ (33) וַיִּסְעוּ
so-they-set-out (33) with-you then-we-will-share to-us Yahweh he-gives which

מֵהַר יְהוָה דֶּרֶךְ שְׁלֹשֶׁת יָמִים וַאֲרוֹן בְּרִית־
covenant-of and-ark-of days three-of travel-of Yahweh from-mountain-of

יְהוָה נֹסֵעַ לִפְנֵיהֶם דֶּרֶךְ שְׁלֹשֶׁת יָמִים לָתוּר לָהֶם מְנוּחָה׃
rest-place for-them to-find days three-of travel-of before-them going Yahweh

(34) וַעֲנַן יְהוָה עֲלֵיהֶם יוֹמָם בְּנָסְעָם מִן־הַמַּחֲנֶה׃
the-camp from when-to-set-out-them by-day over-them Yahweh and-cloud-of (34)

(35) וַיְהִי בִּנְסֹעַ הָאָרֹן וַיֹּאמֶר מֹשֶׁה קוּמָה ׀ יְהוָה
Yahweh rise-up! Moses then-he-said the-ark when-to-set-out and-he-was (35)

וְיָפֻצוּ אֹיְבֶיךָ וְיָנֻסוּ
and-may-they-flee being-enemies-of-you and-may-they-be-scattered

מְשַׂנְאֶיךָ מִפָּנֶיךָ׃ (36) וּבְנֻחֹה יֹאמַר שׁוּבָה
return! he-said and-when-to-rest-her (36) from-before-you ones-hating-you

for all the units, the divisions of the camp of Dan set out, under their standard. Ahiezer son of Ammishaddai was in command. [26]Pagiel son of Ocran was over the division of the tribe of Asher, [27]and Ahira son of Enan was over the division of the tribe of Naphtali. [28]This was the order of march for the Israelite divisions as they set out.

[29]Now Moses said to Hobab son of Reuel the Midianite, Moses' father-in-law, "We are setting out for the place about which the LORD said, 'I will give it to you.' Come with us and we will treat you well, for the LORD has promised good things to Israel."

[30]He answered, "No, I will not go; I am going back to my own land and my own people."

[31]But Moses said, "Please do not leave us. You know where we should camp in the desert, and you can be our eyes. [32]If you come with us, we will share with you whatever good things the LORD gives us."

[33]So they set out from the mountain of the LORD and traveled for three days. The ark of the covenant of the LORD went before them during those three days to find them a place to rest. [34]The cloud of the LORD was over them by day when they set out from the camp.

[35]Whenever the ark set out, Moses said,

"Rise up, O LORD!
May your enemies be scattered;
may your foes flee before you."

[36]Whenever it came to rest, he said,

יְהוָ֔ה רִבְב֖וֹת אַלְפֵ֥י יִשְׂרָאֵֽל׃ וַיְהִ֤י הָעָם֙
the-people now-he-was (11:1) Israel thousands-of multitudes-of Yahweh

כְּמִתְאֹ֣נְנִ֔ים רַ֖ע בְּאָזְנֵ֣י יְהוָ֑ה וַיִּשְׁמַ֤ע יְהוָה֙
Yahweh and-he-heard Yahweh in-hearings-of hardship as-ones-complaining

וַיִּ֣חַר אַפּ֔וֹ וַתִּבְעַר־ בָּם֙ אֵ֣שׁ יְהוָ֔ה
Yahweh fire-of among-them and-she-burned anger-of-him and-he-was-aroused

וַתֹּ֖אכַל בִּקְצֵ֥ה הַֽמַּחֲנֶֽה׃ וַיִּצְעַ֥ק הָעָ֖ם אֶל־
to the-people when-they-cried (2) the-camp at-outskirt-of and-she-consumed

מֹשֶׁ֑ה וַיִּתְפַּלֵּ֤ל מֹשֶׁה֙ אֶל־ יְהוָ֔ה וַתִּשְׁקַ֖ע הָאֵֽשׁ׃
the-fire and-she-died-out Yahweh to Moses then-he-prayed Moses

וַיִּקְרָ֛א שֵֽׁם־ הַמָּק֥וֹם הַה֖וּא תַּבְעֵרָ֑ה כִּֽי־ בָעֲרָ֥ה בָ֖ם
among-them she-burned for Taberah the-that the-place name-of so-he-called (3)

אֵ֥שׁ יְהוָֽה׃ וְהָֽאסַפְסֻף֙ אֲשֶׁ֣ר בְּקִרְבּ֔וֹ הִתְאַוּ֖וּ תַּאֲוָ֑ה
craving they-craved in-midst-of-him that and-the-rabble (4) Yahweh fire-of

וַיָּשֻׁ֣בוּ וַיִּבְכּ֗וּ גַּ֚ם בְּנֵ֣י יִשְׂרָאֵ֔ל וַיֹּ֣אמְר֔וּ מִ֥י
if-only and-they-said Israel sons-of again and-they-wailed and-they-repeated

יַאֲכִלֵ֖נוּ בָּשָֽׂר׃ זָכַ֙רְנוּ֙ אֶת־ הַדָּגָ֔ה אֲשֶׁר־ נֹאכַ֥ל בְּמִצְרַ֖יִם חִנָּ֑ם
no-cost in-Egypt we-ate that the-fish *** we-remember (5) meat we-could-eat

אֵ֣ת הַקִּשֻּׁאִ֗ים וְאֵת֙ הָֽאֲבַטִּחִ֔ים וְאֶת־ הֶחָצִ֥יר וְאֶת־ הַבְּצָלִ֖ים וְאֶת־ הַשּׁוּמִֽים׃
the-garlics and the-onions and the-leek and the-melons and the-cucumbers ***

וְעַתָּ֛ה נַפְשֵׁ֥נוּ יְבֵשָׁ֖ה אֵ֣ין כֹּ֑ל בִּלְתִּ֖י אֶל־ הַמָּ֥ן
the-manna to except anything not she-went appetite-of-us but-now (6)

עֵינֵֽינוּ׃ וְהַמָּ֕ן כִּזְרַע־ גַּ֖ד ה֑וּא וְעֵינ֖וֹ
and-look-of-him he coriander like-seed-of now-the-manna (7) eyes-of-us

כְּעֵ֥ין הַבְּדֹֽלַח׃ שָׁטוּ֩ הָעָ֨ם וְלָֽקְט֜וּ
and-they-gathered the-people they-went (8) the-resin like-look-of

וְטָחֲנ֣וּ בָרֵחַ֗יִם א֤וֹ דָכוּ֙ בַּמְּדֹכָ֔ה וּבִשְּׁלוּ֙
and-they-cooked in-the-mortar they-crushed or in-the-handmills and-they-ground

בַּפָּר֔וּר וְעָשׂ֥וּ אֹת֖וֹ עֻג֑וֹת וְהָיָ֣ה טַעְמ֔וֹ כְּטַ֖עַם
like-taste-of taste-of-him and-he-was cakes him or-they-made in-the-pot

לְשַׁ֥ד הַשָּֽׁמֶן׃ וּבְרֶ֧דֶת הַטַּ֛ל עַל־ הַֽמַּחֲנֶ֖ה לָ֑יְלָה
night the-camp on the-dew and-when-to-settle (9) the-olive-oil prepared-of

יֵרֵ֥ד הַמָּ֖ן עָלָֽיו׃ וַיִּשְׁמַ֨ע מֹשֶׁ֜ה אֶת־ הָעָ֗ם
the-people *** Moses and-he-heard (10) with-him the-manna he-came-down

בֹּכֶה֙ לְמִשְׁפְּחֹתָ֔יו אִ֖ישׁ לְפֶ֣תַח אָהֳל֑וֹ וַיִּֽחַר־
and-he-burned tent-of-him at-entrance-of each by-families-of-him wailing

אַ֤ף יְהוָה֙ מְאֹ֔ד וּבְעֵינֵ֥י מֹשֶׁ֖ה רָֽע׃ וַיֹּ֨אמֶר
and-he-asked (11) trouble Moses and-in-eyes-of exceedingly Yahweh anger-of

"Return, O LORD,
to the countless
thousands of Israel."

Fire From the Lord

11 Now the people complained about their hardships in the hearing of the LORD, and when he heard them his anger was aroused. Then fire from the LORD burned among them and consumed some of the outskirts of the camp. 2When the people cried out to Moses, he prayed to the LORD and the fire died down. 3So that place was called Taberah,[u] because fire from the LORD had burned among them.

Quail From the Lord

4The rabble with them began to crave other food, and again the Israelites started wailing and said, "If only we had meat to eat! 5We remember the fish we ate in Egypt at no cost—also the cucumbers, melons, leeks, onions and garlic. 6But now we have lost our appetite; we never see anything but this manna!"

7The manna was like coriander seed and looked like resin. 8The people went around gathering it, and then ground it in a handmill or crushed it in a mortar. They cooked it in a pot or made it into cakes. And it tasted like something made with olive oil. 9When the dew settled on the camp at night, the manna also came down.

10Moses heard the people of every family wailing, each at the entrance to his tent. The LORD became exceedingly angry, and Moses was troubled.

[u]3 *Taberah* means *burning*.

מֹשֶׁה אֶל־ יְהוָה לָמָה הֲרֵעֹתָ לְעַבְדֶּךָ וְלָמָּה לֹא־
not and-why? on-servant-of-you you-brought-trouble why? Yahweh to Moses

מָצָתִי חֵן בְּעֵינֶיךָ לָשׂוּם אֶת־ מַשָּׂא כָּל־ הָעָם הַזֶּה
the-this the-people all-of burden-of *** to-put in-eyes-of-you favor I-found

עָלָי׃ הֶאָנֹכִי הָרִיתִי אֵת כָּל־ הָעָם הַזֶּה אִם־אָנֹכִי יְלִדְתִּיהוּ
I-bore-him I or the-this the-people all-of *** I-conceived I? (12) on-me

כִּי־ תֹאמַר אֵלַי שָׂאֵהוּ בְחֵיקֶךָ כַּאֲשֶׁר יִשָּׂא
he-carries just-as in-bosom-of-you carry-him! to-me you-tell that

הָאֹמֵן אֶת־ הַיֹּנֵק עַל הָאֲדָמָה אֲשֶׁר נִשְׁבַּעְתָּ לַאֲבֹתָיו׃
to-fathers-of-him you-promised that the-land to the-infant *** the-one-nursing

מֵאַיִן לִי בָּשָׂר לָתֵת לְכָל־ הָעָם הַזֶּה כִּי־ יִבְכּוּ
they-wail for the-this the-people to-all-of to-give meat to-me where? (13)

עָלַי לֵאמֹר תְּנָה־ לָּנוּ בָשָׂר וְנֹאכֵלָה׃ לֹא־אוּכַל אָנֹכִי לְבַדִּי
by-myself I I-can not (14) so-we-can-eat meat to-us give! to-say to-me

לָשֵׂאת אֶת־ כָּל־ הָעָם הַזֶּה כִּי כָבֵד מִמֶּנִּי׃ וְאִם־כָּכָה
thus so-if (15) for-me heavy for the-this the-people all-of *** to-carry

אַתְּ־ עֹשֶׂה לִּי הָרְגֵנִי נָא הָרֹג אִם־מָצָאתִי חֵן בְּעֵינֶיךָ
in-eyes-of-you favor I-found if to-kill now! kill-me! to-me treating you

וְאַל־ אֶרְאֶה בְּרָעָתִי׃ וַיֹּאמֶר יְהוָה אֶל־ מֹשֶׁה אֶסְפָה־
bring! Moses to Yahweh and-he-said (16) to-ruin-of-me let-me-face and-not

לִּי שִׁבְעִים אִישׁ מִזִּקְנֵי יִשְׂרָאֵל אֲשֶׁר יָדַעְתָּ כִּי־ הֵם זִקְנֵי
elders-of they that you-know whom Israel from-elders-of man seventy to-me

הָעָם וְשֹׁטְרָיו וְלָקַחְתָּ אֹתָם אֶל־ אֹהֶל מוֹעֵד
Meeting Tent-of to them and-you-take and-ones-leading-him the-people

וְהִתְיַצְּבוּ שָׁם עִמָּךְ׃ וְיָרַדְתִּי וְדִבַּרְתִּי
and-I-will-speak and-I-will-come-down (17) with-you there that-they-may-stand

עִמְּךָ שָׁם וְאָצַלְתִּי מִן־ הָרוּחַ אֲשֶׁר עָלֶיךָ וְשַׂמְתִּי
and-I-will-put on-you that the-Spirit from and-I-will-take there with-you

עֲלֵיהֶם וְנָשְׂאוּ אִתְּךָ בְּמַשָּׂא הָעָם וְלֹא־
so-not the-people on-burden-of with-you and-they-will-carry on-them

תִשָּׂא אַתָּה לְבַדֶּךָ׃ וְאֶל־ הָעָם תֹּאמַר
you-tell the-people and-to (18) by-yourself you you-will-carry

הִתְקַדְּשׁוּ לְמָחָר וַאֲכַלְתֶּם בָּשָׂר כִּי בְּכִיתֶם בְּאָזְנֵי
in-ears-of you-wailed for meat when-you-eat for-tomorrow consecrate-selves!

יְהוָה לֵאמֹר מִי יַאֲכִלֵנוּ בָּשָׂר כִּי־ טוֹב לָנוּ בְּמִצְרָיִם וְנָתַן
now-he-will-give in-Egypt to-us better for meat we-ate if-only to-say Yahweh

יְהוָה לָכֶם בָּשָׂר וַאֲכַלְתֶּם׃ לֹא יוֹם אֶחָד תֹּאכְלוּן וְלֹא
or-not you-will-eat one day not (19) and-you-will-eat meat to-you Yahweh

11He asked the LORD, "Why
have you brought this trouble
on your servant? What have I
done to displease you that you
put the burden of all these
people on me? 12Did I conceive
all these people? Did I give
them birth? Why do you tell
me to carry them in my arms,
as a nurse carries an infant, to
the land you promised on oath
to their forefathers? 13Where
can I get meat for all these
people? They keep wailing to
me, 'Give us meat to eat!' 14I
cannot carry all these people
by myself; the burden is too
heavy for me. 15If this is how
you are going to treat me, put
me to death right now—if I
have found favor in your
eyes—and do not let me face
my own ruin."

16The LORD said to Moses:
"Bring me seventy of Israel's
elders who are known to you
as leaders and officials among
the people. Have them come to
the Tent of Meeting, that they
may stand there with you. 17I
will come down and speak
with you there, and I will take
of the Spirit that is on you and
put the Spirit on them. They
will help you carry the burden
of the people so that you will
not have to carry it alone.

18"Tell the people: 'Consecrate yourselves in preparation for tomorrow, when you
will eat meat. The LORD heard
you when you wailed, "If only
we had meat to eat! We were
better off in Egypt!" Now the
LORD will give you meat, and
you will eat it. 19You will not
eat it for just one day, or two

יוֹמָיִם וְלֹא ׀ חֲמִשָּׁה יָמִים וְלֹא עֲשָׂרָה יָמִים וְלֹא עֶשְׂרִים יוֹם׃ עַד ׀
for (20) day twenty or-not days ten or-not days five or-not two-days

חֹדֶשׁ יָמִים עַד אֲשֶׁר־ יֵצֵא מֵאַפְּכֶם וְהָיָה לָכֶם
to-you and-he-will-be from-nostril-of-you he-comes when until days month-of

לְזָרָא יַעַן כִּי־ מְאַסְתֶּם אֶת־ יְהוָה אֲשֶׁר בְּקִרְבְּכֶם
in-midst-of-you who Yahweh *** you-rejected that because as-loathsome

וַתִּבְכּוּ לְפָנָיו לֵאמֹר לָמָּה זֶּה יָצָאנוּ מִמִּצְרָיִם׃ וַיֹּאמֶר
but-he-said (21) from-Egypt we-left this why? to-say before-him and-you-wailed

מֹשֶׁה שֵׁשׁ־ מֵאוֹת אֶלֶף רַגְלִי הָעָם אֲשֶׁר אָנֹכִי בְּקִרְבּוֹ
in-midst-of-him I that the-people on-foot thousand hundreds-of six Moses

וְאַתָּה אָמַרְתָּ בָּשָׂר אֶתֵּן לָהֶם וְאָכְלוּ חֹדֶשׁ יָמִים׃
days month-of and-they-will-eat to-them I-will-give meat you-say and-you

הֲצֹאן וּבָקָר יִשָּׁחֵט לָהֶם וּמָצָא לָהֶם
for-them would-he-be-enough for-them he-was-slaughtered and-herd if-flock (22)

אִם אֶת־ כָּל־ דְּגֵי הַיָּם יֵאָסֵף לָהֶם וּמָצָא
would-he-be-enough for-them he-was-caught the-sea fishes-of all-of *** if

לָהֶם׃ וַיֹּאמֶר יְהוָה אֶל־ מֹשֶׁה הֲיַד יְהוָה תִּקְצָר
is-she-short Yahweh arm-of? Moses to Yahweh and-he-answered (23) for-them

עַתָּה תִרְאֶה הֲיִקְרְךָ דְבָרִי אִם־ לֹא׃ וַיֵּצֵא
so-he-went (24) not or word-of-me if-he-will-come-true-for-you you-will-see now

מֹשֶׁה וַיְדַבֵּר אֶל־ הָעָם אֵת דִּבְרֵי יְהוָה וַיֶּאֱסֹף שִׁבְעִים
seventy and-he-gathered Yahweh words-of *** the-people to and-he-told Moses

אִישׁ מִזִּקְנֵי הָעָם וַיַּעֲמֵד אֹתָם סְבִיבֹת הָאֹהֶל׃
the-tent ones-around them and-he-had-stand the-people from-elders-of man

וַיֵּרֶד יְהוָה ׀ בֶּעָנָן וַיְדַבֵּר אֵלָיו וַיָּאצֶל
and-he-took with-him and-he-spoke in-the-cloud Yahweh then-he-came-down (25)

מִן־ הָרוּחַ אֲשֶׁר עָלָיו וַיִּתֵּן עַל־ שִׁבְעִים אִישׁ הַזְּקֵנִים וַיְהִי
and-he-was the-elders man seventy on and-he-put on-him that the-Spirit from

כְּנוֹחַ עֲלֵיהֶם הָרוּחַ וַיִּתְנַבְּאוּ וְלֹא יָסָפוּ׃
they-did-again but-not then-they-prophesied the-Spirit on-them as-to-rest

וַיִּשָּׁאֲרוּ שְׁנֵי־ אֲנָשִׁים ׀ בַּמַּחֲנֶה שֵׁם הָאֶחָד ׀ אֶלְדָּד
Eldad the-one name-of in-the-camp men two-of but-they-remained (26)

וְשֵׁם הַשֵּׁנִי מֵידָד וַתָּנַח עֲלֵיהֶם הָרוּחַ וְהֵמָּה
now-they the-Spirit on-them and-she-rested Medad the-other and-name-of

בַּכְּתֻבִים וְלֹא יָצְאוּ הָאֹהֱלָה וַיִּתְנַבְּאוּ
and-they-prophesied to-the-Tent they-went but-not of-the-ones-being-listed

בַּמַּחֲנֶה׃ וַיָּרָץ הַנַּעַר וַיַּגֵּד לְמֹשֶׁה וַיֹּאמַר
and-he-said to-Moses and-he-told the-young-man and-he-ran (27) in-the-camp

days, or five, ten or twenty
days, [20]but for a whole
month—until it comes out of
your nostrils and you loathe
it—because you have rejected
the LORD, who is among you,
and have wailed before him,
saying, "Why did we ever
leave Egypt?"'"
[21]But Moses said, "Here I am
among six hundred thousand
men on foot, and you say, 'I
will give them meat to eat for
a whole month!' [22]Would they
have enough if flocks and
herds were slaughtered for
them? Would they have
enough if all the fish in the sea
were caught for them?"
[23]The LORD answered Moses,
"Is the LORD's arm too short?
You will now see whether or
not what I say will come true
for you."
[24]So Moses went out and told
the people what the LORD had
said. He brought together seventy of their elders and had
them stand around the tent.
[25]Then the LORD came down in
the cloud and spoke with him,
and he took of the Spirit that
was on him and put the Spirit
on the seventy elders. When
the Spirit rested on them, they
prophesied, but they did not
do so again.[v]
[26]However, two men, whose
names were Eldad and Medad,
had remained in the camp.
They were listed among the elders, but did not go out to the
tent. Yet the Spirit also rested
on them, and they prophesied
in the camp. [27]A young man
ran and told Moses, "Eldad

[v]25 *Or prophesied and continued to do so*

אֶלְדָּד וּמֵידָד מִתְנַבְּאִים בַּמַּחֲנֶה׃ וַיַּעַן יְהוֹשֻׁעַ בִּן־
son-of Joshua and-he-spoke (28) in-the-camp ones-prophesying and-Medad Eldad

נוּן מְשָׁרֵת מֹשֶׁה מִבְּחֻרָיו וַיֹּאמַר אֲדֹנִי מֹשֶׁה
Moses lord-of-me and-he-said since-youths-of-him Moses one-aiding-of Nun

כְּלָאֵם׃ וַיֹּאמֶר לוֹ מֹשֶׁה הַמְקַנֵּא אַתָּה לִי וּמִי
if-only for-me you being-jealous? Moses to-him but-he-replied (29) stop-them!

יִתֵּן כָּל־ עַם יְהוָה נְבִיאִים כִּי־ יִתֵּן יְהוָה אֶת־
*** Yahweh he-would-put if prophets Yahweh people-of all-of he-would-make

רוּחוֹ עֲלֵיהֶם׃ וַיֵּאָסֵף מֹשֶׁה אֶל־ הַמַּחֲנֶה הוּא
he the-camp to Moses then-he-returned (30) on-them Spirit-of-him

וְזִקְנֵי יִשְׂרָאֵל׃ וְרוּחַ נָסַע מֵאֵת יְהוָה וַיָּגָז
and-he-drove-in Yahweh from he-went-out now-wind (31) Israel and-elders-of

שַׂלְוִים מִן־ הַיָּם וַיִּטֹּשׁ עַל־ הַמַּחֲנֶה כְּדֶרֶךְ יוֹם כֹּה
here day about-journey-of the-camp into and-he-brought the-sea from quails

וּכְדֶרֶךְ יוֹם כֹּה סְבִיבוֹת הַמַּחֲנֶה וּכְאַמָּתַיִם
and-about-two-cubits the-camp ones-around there day and-about-journey-of

עַל־ פְּנֵי הָאָרֶץ׃ וַיָּקָם הָעָם כָּל־ הַיּוֹם
the-day all-of the-people and-he-went-out (32) the-ground surface-of above

הַהוּא וְכָל־ הַלַּיְלָה וְכֹל יוֹם הַמָּחֳרָת וַיַּאַסְפוּ
and-they-gathered the-next day-of and-all-of the-night and-all-of the-that

אֶת־ הַשְּׂלָו הַמַּמְעִיט אָסַף עֲשָׂרָה חֳמָרִים וַיִּשְׁטְחוּ לָהֶם
to-them and-they-spread homers ten he-gathered the-being-less the-quail ***

שָׁטוֹחַ סְבִיבוֹת הַמַּחֲנֶה׃ הַבָּשָׂר עוֹדֶנּוּ בֵּין שִׁנֵּיהֶם
teeth-of-them between while-he the-meat (33) the-camp ones-around to-spread

טֶרֶם יִכָּרֵת וְאַף יְהוָה חָרָה בָעָם
against-the-people he-burned Yahweh then-anger-of he-was-consumed before

וַיַּךְ יְהוָה בָּעָם מַכָּה רַבָּה מְאֹד׃ וַיִּקְרָא
and-he-called (34) very severe plague against-the-people Yahweh and-he-struck

אֶת־ שֵׁם־ הַמָּקוֹם הַהוּא קִבְרוֹת הַתַּאֲוָה כִּי־ שָׁם קָבְרוּ אֶת־
*** they-buried there for Hattaavah Kibroth the-that the-place name-of ***

הָעָם הַמִּתְאַוִּים׃ מִקִּבְרוֹת הַתַּאֲוָה נָסְעוּ
they-traveled Hattaavah from-Kibroth (35) the-ones-craving the-people

הָעָם חֲצֵרוֹת וַיִּהְיוּ בַּחֲצֵרוֹת׃ וַתְּדַבֵּר מִרְיָם
Miriam and-she-talked (12:1) in-Hazeroth and-they-stayed Hazeroth the-people

וְאַהֲרֹן בְּמֹשֶׁה עַל־ אֹדוֹת הָאִשָּׁה הַכֻּשִׁית אֲשֶׁר לָקָח
he-married that the-Cushite the-wife reasons-of for against-Moses and-Aaron

כִּי־ אִשָּׁה כֻשִׁית לָקָח׃ וַיֹּאמְרוּ הֲרַק אַךְ־ בְּמֹשֶׁה
through-Moses indeed only? and-they-asked (2) he-married Cushite woman for

---

and Medad are prophesying in the camp."
28 Joshua son of Nun, who had been Moses' aide since youth, spoke up and said, "Moses, my lord, stop them!"
29 But Moses replied, "Are you jealous for my sake? I wish that all the LORD's people were prophets and that the LORD would put his Spirit on them!"
30 Then Moses and the elders of Israel returned to the camp.
31 Now a wind went out from the LORD and drove quail in from the sea. It brought them[w] down all around the camp to about three feet[x] above the ground, as far as a day's walk in any direction.
32 All that day and night and all the next day the people went out and gathered quail. No one gathered less than ten homers.[y] Then they spread them out all around the camp.
33 But while the meat was still between their teeth and before it could be consumed, the anger of the LORD burned against the people, and he struck them with a severe plague.
34 Therefore the place was named Kibroth Hattaavah,[z] because there they buried the people who had craved other food.
35 From Kibroth Hattaavah the people traveled to Hazeroth and stayed there.

Miriam and Aaron Oppose Moses

12 Miriam and Aaron began to talk against Moses because of his Cushite wife, for he had married a Cushite.
2 "Has the LORD spoken only through Moses?"

[w]31 Or *They flew*
[x]31 Hebrew *two cubits* (about 1 meter)
[y]32 That is, probably about 60 bushels (about 2.2 kiloliters)
[z]34 *Kibroth Hattaavah* means *graves of craving*

דִּבֶּר יְהוָה הֲלֹא גַּם־ בָּנוּ דִבֵּר וַיִּשְׁמַע יְהוָה׃
Yahweh and-he-heard he-spoke through-us also not? Yahweh he-spoke

וְהָאִישׁ מֹשֶׁה עָנָו מְאֹד מִכֹּל הָאָדָם אֲשֶׁר עַל־ פְּנֵי
face-of on who the-man more-than-any-of very humble Moses now-the-man (3)

הָאֲדָמָה׃ וַיֹּאמֶר יְהוָה פִּתְאֹם אֶל־מֹשֶׁה וְאֶל־ אַהֲרֹן וְאֶל־ מִרְיָם
Miriam and-to Aaron and-to Moses to at-once Yahweh and-he-said (4) the-earth

צְאוּ שְׁלָשְׁתְּכֶם אֶל־ אֹהֶל מוֹעֵד וַיֵּצְאוּ שְׁלָשְׁתָּם׃
three-of-them so-they-came-out Meeting Tent-of to three-of-you come-out!

וַיֵּרֶד יְהוָה בְּעַמּוּד עָנָן וַיַּעֲמֹד פֶּתַח
entrance-of and-he-stood cloud in-pillar-of Yahweh then-he-came-down (5)

הָאֹהֶל וַיִּקְרָא אַהֲרֹן וּמִרְיָם וַיֵּצְאוּ
and-they-stepped-forward and-Miriam Aaron and-he-summoned the-Tent

שְׁנֵיהֶם׃ וַיֹּאמֶר שִׁמְעוּ־ נָא דְבָרָי אִם־ יִהְיֶה
he-is when words-of-me now! listen! and-he-said (6) both-of-them

נְבִיאֲכֶם יְהוָה בַּמַּרְאָה אֵלָיו אֶתְוַדָּע בַּחֲלוֹם אֲדַבֶּר־
I-speak in-dream I-reveal-myself to-him in-the-vision Yahweh prophet-of-you

בּוֹ׃ לֹא־ כֵן עַבְדִּי מֹשֶׁה בְּכָל־ בֵּיתִי נֶאֱמָן
being-faithful house-of-me in-all-of Moses servant-of-me true not (7) to-him

הוּא׃ פֶּה אֶל־ פֶּה אֲדַבֶּר־ בּוֹ וּמַרְאֶה וְלֹא בְחִידֹת
in-riddles and-not and-clearly with-him I-speak face to face (8) he

וּתְמֻנַת יְהוָה יַבִּיט וּמַדּוּעַ לֹא יְרֵאתֶם לְדַבֵּר
to-speak you-were-afraid not so-why? he-sees Yahweh and-form-of

בְּעַבְדִּי בְמֹשֶׁה׃ וַיִּחַר אַף יְהוָה
Yahweh anger-of and-he-burned (9) against-Moses against-servant-of-me

בָּם וַיֵּלַךְ׃ וְהֶעָנָן סָר מֵעַל הָאֹהֶל
the-Tent from-above he-lifted when-the-cloud (10) and-he-left against-them

וְהִנֵּה מִרְיָם מְצֹרַעַת כַּשָּׁלֶג וַיִּפֶן אַהֲרֹן אֶל־
toward Aaron and-he-turned like-the-snow being-leprous Miriam then-see!

מִרְיָם וְהִנֵּה מְצֹרָעַת׃ וַיֹּאמֶר אַהֲרֹן אֶל־ מֹשֶׁה בִּי
please! Moses to Aaron and-he-said (11) being-leprous and-see! Miriam

אֲדֹנִי אַל־ נָא תָשֵׁת עָלֵינוּ חַטָּאת אֲשֶׁר נוֹאַלְנוּ וַאֲשֶׁר
and-that we-were-foolish that sin against-us you-hold now! not! lord-of-me

חָטָאנוּ׃ אַל־ נָא תְהִי כַּמֵּת אֲשֶׁר בְּצֵאתוֹ
when-to-come-him that as-the-stillborn let-her-be now! not (12) we-committed

מֵרֶחֶם אִמּוֹ וַיֵּאָכֵל חֲצִי בְשָׂרוֹ׃
flesh-of-him half-of then-he-is-eaten-away mother-of-him from-womb-of

וַיִּצְעַק מֹשֶׁה אֶל־ יְהוָה לֵאמֹר אֵל נָא רְפָא נָא לָהּ׃
to-her now! heal! now! God to-say Yahweh to Moses so-he-cried-out (13)

they asked. "Hasn't he also spoken through us?" And the LORD heard this.

[3](Now Moses was a very humble man, more humble than anyone else on the face of the earth.)

[4]At once the LORD said to Moses, Aaron and Miriam, "Come out to the Tent of Meeting, all three of you." So the three of them came out. [5]Then the LORD came down in a pillar of cloud; he stood at the entrance to the Tent and summoned Aaron and Miriam. When both of them stepped forward, [6]he said, "Listen to my words:

"When a prophet of the LORD is among you,
I reveal myself to him in visions,
I speak to him in dreams.
[7]But this is not true of my servant Moses;
he is faithful in all my house.
[8]With him I speak face to face,
clearly and not in riddles;
he sees the form of the LORD.
Why then were you not afraid
to speak against my servant Moses?"

[9]The anger of the LORD burned against them, and he left them.

[10]When the cloud lifted from above the Tent, there stood Miriam—leprous,[a] like snow. Aaron turned toward her and saw that she had leprosy; [11]and he said to Moses, "Please, my lord, do not hold against us the sin we have so foolishly committed. [12]Do not let her be like a stillborn infant coming from its mother's womb with its flesh half eaten away."

[13]So Moses cried out to the LORD, "O God, please heal her!"

[a]10 The Hebrew word was used for various diseases affecting the skin—not necessarily leprosy.

*9 Most mss bind these two words with *maqqeph* (וַיִּחַר־אַף).

°3 ק עניו

וַיֹּאמֶר יְהוָה אֶל־מֹשֶׁה וְאָבִיהָ יָרֹק יָרַק
he-spit to-spit if-father-of-her Moses to Yahweh and-he-replied (14)

בְּפָנֶיהָ הֲלֹא תִכָּלֵם שִׁבְעַת יָמִים תִּסָּגֵר
she-must-be-confined days seven-of she-would-be-in-disgrace not? in-face-of-her

שִׁבְעַת יָמִים מִחוּץ לַמַּחֲנֶה וְאַחַר תֵּאָסֵף׃
she-may-be-brought-back and-after of-the-camp outside days seven-of

וַתִּסָּגֵר מִרְיָם מִחוּץ לַמַּחֲנֶה שִׁבְעַת יָמִים
days seven-of of-the-camp outside Miriam so-she-was-confined (15)

וְהָעָם לֹא נָסַע עַד־הֵאָסֵף מִרְיָם׃ וְאַחַר
and-after (16) Miriam to-be-brought-back till he-moved-on not and-the-people

נָסְעוּ הָעָם מֵחֲצֵרוֹת וַיַּחֲנוּ בְּמִדְבַּר פָּארָן׃
Paran in-Desert-of and-they-encamped from-Hazeroth the-people they-left

וַיְדַבֵּר יְהוָה אֶל־מֹשֶׁה לֵּאמֹר׃ שְׁלַח־לְךָ אֲנָשִׁים
men for-you send! (2) to-say Moses to Yahweh and-he-spoke (13:1)

וְיָתֻרוּ אֶת־אֶרֶץ כְּנַעַן אֲשֶׁר־אֲנִי נֹתֵן לִבְנֵי יִשְׂרָאֵל אִישׁ
man Israel to-sons-of giving I which Canaan land-of *** so-they-may-explore

אֶחָד אִישׁ אֶחָד לְמַטֵּה אֲבֹתָיו תִּשְׁלָחוּ כֹּל נָשִׂיא בָהֶם׃
from-them leader each you-send-him ancestors-of-him from-tribe-of one man one

וַיִּשְׁלַח אֹתָם מֹשֶׁה מִמִּדְבַּר פָּארָן עַל־פִּי יְהוָה
Yahweh command-of at Paran from-Desert-of Moses them so-he-sent (3)

כֻּלָּם אֲנָשִׁים רָאשֵׁי בְנֵי־יִשְׂרָאֵל הֵמָּה׃ וְאֵלֶּה שְׁמוֹתָם
names-of-them and-these (4) they Israel sons-of leaders-of men all-of-them

לְמַטֵּה רְאוּבֵן שַׁמּוּעַ בֶּן־זַכּוּר׃ לְמַטֵּה שִׁמְעוֹן שָׁפָט
Shaphat Simeon from-tribe-of (5) Zaccur son-of Shammua Reuben from-tribe-of

בֶּן־חוֹרִי׃ לְמַטֵּה יְהוּדָה כָּלֵב בֶּן־יְפֻנֶּה׃ לְמַטֵּה
from-tribe-of (7) Jephunneh son-of Caleb Judah from-tribe-of (6) Hori son-of

יִשָּׂשכָר יִגְאָל בֶּן־יוֹסֵף׃ לְמַטֵּה אֶפְרָיִם הוֹשֵׁעַ בִּן־נוּן׃
Nun son-of Hoshea Ephraim from-tribe-of (8) Joseph son-of Igal Issachar

לְמַטֵּה בִנְיָמִן פַּלְטִי בֶּן־רָפוּא׃ לְמַטֵּה זְבוּלֻן
Zebulun from-tribe-of (10) Raphu son-of Palti Benjamin from-tribe-of (9)

גַּדִּיאֵל בֶּן־סוֹדִי׃ לְמַטֵּה יוֹסֵף לְמַטֵּה מְנַשֶּׁה גַּדִּי
Gaddi Manasseh from-tribe-of Joseph from-tribe-of (11) Sodi son-of Gaddiel

בֶּן־סוּסִי׃ לְמַטֵּה דָן עַמִּיאֵל בֶּן־גְּמַלִּי׃ לְמַטֵּה
from-tribe-of (13) Gemalli son-of Ammiel Dan from-tribe-of (12) Susi son-of

אָשֵׁר סְתוּר בֶּן־מִיכָאֵל׃ לְמַטֵּה נַפְתָּלִי נַחְבִּי בֶּן־וָפְסִי׃
Vophsi son-of Nahbi Naphtali from-tribe-of (14) Michael son-of Sethur Asher

לְמַטֵּה גָד גְּאוּאֵל בֶּן־מָכִי׃ אֵלֶּה שְׁמוֹת הָאֲנָשִׁים אֲשֶׁר־
whom the-men names-of these (16) Maki son-of Geuel Gad from-tribe-of (15)

[14]The LORD replied to Moses,
"If her father had spit in her
face, would she not have been
in disgrace for seven days?
Confine her outside the camp
for seven days; after that she
can be brought back." [15]So
Miriam was confined outside
the camp for seven days, and
the people did not move on till
she was brought back.
[16]After that, the people left
Hazeroth and encamped in
the Desert of Paran.

Exploring Canaan

13 The LORD said to
Moses, [2]"Send some
men to explore the land of Canaan, which I am giving to the
Israelites. From each ancestral
tribe send one of its leaders."
[3]So at the LORD's command
Moses sent them out from the
Desert of Paran. All of them
were leaders of the Israelites.
[4]These are their names:

from the tribe of Reuben,
Shammua son of Zaccur;
[5]from the tribe of Simeon,
Shaphat son of Hori;
[6]from the tribe of Judah,
Caleb son of Jephunneh;
[7]from the tribe of Issachar,
Igal son of Joseph;
[8]from the tribe of Ephraim,
Hoshea son of Nun;
[9]from the tribe of Benjamin,
Palti son of Raphu;
[10]from the tribe of Zebulun,
Gaddiel son of Sodi;
[11]from the tribe of Manasseh
(a tribe of Joseph), Gaddi
son of Susi;
[12]from the tribe of Dan, Ammiel son of Gemalli;
[13]from the tribe of Asher, Sethur son of Michael;
[14]from the tribe of Naphtali,
Nahbi son of Vophsi;
[15]from the tribe of Gad, Geuel
son of Maki.

[16]These are the names of the

שָׁלַח מֹשֶׁה לָתוּר אֶת־הָאָרֶץ וַיִּקְרָא מֹשֶׁה לְהוֹשֵׁעַ בִּן־
son-of to-Hoshea Moses now-he-named the-land *** to-explore Moses he-sent

נוּן יְהוֹשֻׁעַ׃ וַיִּשְׁלַח אֹתָם מֹשֶׁה לָתוּר אֶת־אֶרֶץ כְּנָעַן
Canaan land-of *** to-explore Moses them when-he-sent (17) Joshua Nun

וַיֹּאמֶר אֲלֵהֶם עֲלוּ זֶה בַּנֶּגֶב וַעֲלִיתֶם אֶת־
*** and-you-go-into through-the-Negev there go-up! to-them then-he-said

הָהָר׃ וּרְאִיתֶם אֶת־הָאָרֶץ מַה־הִוא וְאֶת־הָעָם
the-people and she what the-land *** and-you-see (18) the-hill-country

הַיֹּשֵׁב עָלֶיהָ הֶחָזָק הוּא הֲרָפֶה הַמְעַט הוּא אִם־רָב׃ וּמָה
and-what? (19) many or he if-few or-weak he if-strong in-her the-one-living

הָאָרֶץ אֲשֶׁר־הוּא יֹשֵׁב בָּהּ הֲטוֹבָה הִוא אִם־רָעָה וּמָה הֶעָרִים אֲשֶׁר־
that the-towns and-what? bad or she good? in-her living he where the-land

הוּא יוֹשֵׁב בָּהֵנָּה הַבְּמַחֲנִים אִם בְּמִבְצָרִים׃ וּמָה
and-how? (20) with-fortifications or without-walls? in-them living he

הָאָרֶץ הַשְּׁמֵנָה הִוא אִם־רָזָה הֲיֵשׁ־בָּהּ עֵץ אִם־אַיִן וְהִתְחַזַּקְתֶּם
and-you-do-best not or tree on-her is-there? poor or she fertile? the-soil

וּלְקַחְתֶּם מִפְּרִי הָאָרֶץ וְהַיָּמִים יְמֵי בִּכּוּרֵי
first-ones-of days-of for-the-days the-land from-fruit-of and-you-bring

עֲנָבִים׃ וַיַּעֲלוּ וַיָּתֻרוּ אֶת־הָאָרֶץ מִמִּדְבַּר־
from-Desert-of the-land *** and-they-explored so-they-went-up (21) grapes

צִן עַד־רְחֹב לְבֹא חֲמָת׃ וַיַּעֲלוּ בַנֶּגֶב
through-the-Negev and-they-went-up (22) Hamath Lebo Rehob as-far-as Zin

וַיָּבֹא עַד־חֶבְרוֹן וְשָׁם אֲחִימַן שֵׁשַׁי וְתַלְמַי יְלִידֵי
descendants-of and-Talmai Sheshai Ahiman now-there Hebron to and-he-came

הָעֲנָק וְחֶבְרוֹן שֶׁבַע שָׁנִים נִבְנְתָה לִפְנֵי צֹעַן מִצְרָיִם׃
Egypt Zoan before being-built years seven and-Hebron the-Anak

וַיָּבֹאוּ עַד־נַחַל אֶשְׁכֹּל וַיִּכְרְתוּ מִשָּׁם זְמוֹרָה
branch from-there then-they-cut Eshcol Valley-of to when-they-reached (23)

וְאֶשְׁכּוֹל עֲנָבִים אֶחָד וַיִּשָּׂאֻהוּ בַמּוֹט בִּשְׁנָיִם וּמִן־
and-from by-two on-the-pole and-they-carried-him one grapes and-cluster-of

הָרִמֹּנִים וּמִן־הַתְּאֵנִים׃ לַמָּקוֹם הַהוּא קָרָא
he-called the-that to-the-place (24) the-figs and-from the-pomegranates

נַחַל אֶשְׁכּוֹל עַל אֹדוֹת הָאֶשְׁכּוֹל אֲשֶׁר־כָּרְתוּ מִשָּׁם בְּנֵי
sons-of from-there they-cut that the-cluster reasons-of for Eshcol Valley-of

יִשְׂרָאֵל׃ וַיָּשֻׁבוּ מִתּוּר הָאָרֶץ מִקֵּץ אַרְבָּעִים יוֹם׃
day forty at-end-of the-land from-to-explore and-they-returned (25) Israel

וַיֵּלְכוּ וַיָּבֹאוּ אֶל־מֹשֶׁה וְאֶל־אַהֲרֹן וְאֶל־
and-to Aaron and-to Moses to and-they-came-back and-they-walked (26)

men Moses sent to explore the land. (Moses gave Hoshea son of Nun the name Joshua.)

[17]When Moses sent them to explore Canaan, he said, "Go up through the Negev and on into the hill country. [18]See what the land is like and whether the people who live there are strong or weak, few or many. [19]What kind of land do they live in? Is it good or bad? What kind of towns do they live in? Are they unwalled or fortified? [20]How is the soil? Is it fertile or poor? Are there trees on it or not? Do your best to bring back some of the fruit of the land." (It was the season for the first ripe grapes.)

[21]So they went up and explored the land from the Desert of Zin as far as Rehob, toward Lebo[b] Hamath. [22]They went up through the Negev and came to Hebron, where Ahiman, Sheshai and Talmai, the descendants of Anak, lived. (Hebron had been built seven years before Zoan in Egypt.) [23]When they reached the Valley of Eshcol,[c] they cut off a branch bearing a single cluster of grapes. Two of them carried it on a pole between them, along with some pomegranates and figs. [24]That place was called the Valley of Eshcol because of the cluster of grapes the Israelites cut off there. [25]At the end of forty days they returned from exploring the land.

Report on the Exploration

[26]They came back to Moses

[b]21 *Or toward the entrance to*
[c]23 *Eshcol* means *cluster;* also in verse 24.

כָּל־ עֲדַת בְּנֵי־ יִשְׂרָאֵל אֶל־ מִדְבַּר פָּארָן קָדֵשָׁה
at-Kadesh Paran Desert-of in Israel sons-of community-of whole-of

וַיָּשִׁבוּ אוֹתָם דָּבָר וְאֶת־ כָּל־ הָעֵדָה וַיַּרְאוּם אֶת־
*** and-they-showed-them the-assembly whole-of and report them and-they-gave

פְּרִי הָאָרֶץ׃ וַיְסַפְּרוּ־ לוֹ וַיֹּאמְרוּ בָּאנוּ אֶל־
into we-went and-they-said to-him and-they-reported (27) the-land fruit-of

הָאָרֶץ אֲשֶׁר שְׁלַחְתָּנוּ וְגַם זָבַת חָלָב וּדְבַשׁ הִוא וְזֶה־
and-here she and-honey milk flowing-of and-indeed you-sent-us where the-land

פִּרְיָהּ׃ אֶפֶס כִּי־ עַז הָעָם הַיֹּשֵׁב בָּאָרֶץ
in-the-land the-one-living the-people powerful also but (28) fruit-of-her

וְהֶעָרִים בְּצֻרוֹת גְּדֹלֹת מְאֹד וְגַם־ יְלִדֵי
descendants-of and-even very large-ones fortified-ones and-the-cities

הָעֲנָק רָאִינוּ שָׁם׃ עֲמָלֵק יוֹשֵׁב בְּאֶרֶץ הַנֶּגֶב וְהַחִתִּי
and-the-Hittite the-Negev in-land-of living Amalek (29) there we-saw the-Anak

וְהַיְבוּסִי וְהָאֱמֹרִי יוֹשֵׁב בָּהָר וְהַכְּנַעֲנִי
and-the-Canaanite in-the-hill-country living and-the-Amorite and-the-Jebusite

יֹשֵׁב עַל־ הַיָּם וְעַל יַד הַיַּרְדֵּן׃ וַיַּהַס כָּלֵב
Caleb then-he-silenced (30) the-Jordan bank-of and-along the-sea near living

אֶת־ הָעָם אֶל־ מֹשֶׁה וַיֹּאמֶר עָלֹה נַעֲלֶה
we-should-go-up to-go-up and-he-said Moses before the-people ***

וְיָרַשְׁנוּ אֹתָהּ כִּי־ יָכוֹל נוּכַל לָהּ׃ וְהָאֲנָשִׁים אֲשֶׁר־
who but-the-men (31) with-her we-can-do to-do for her and-we-should-possess

עָלוּ עִמּוֹ אָמְרוּ לֹא נוּכַל לַעֲלוֹת אֶל־ הָעָם כִּי־
for the-people against to-attack we-can not they-said with-him they-went-up

חָזָק הוּא מִמֶּנּוּ׃ וַיֹּצִיאוּ דִּבַּת הָאָרֶץ אֲשֶׁר
that the-land bad-report-of and-they-spread (32) than-us he stronger

תָּרוּ אֹתָהּ אֶל־ בְּנֵי יִשְׂרָאֵל לֵאמֹר הָאָרֶץ אֲשֶׁר עָבַרְנוּ
we-passed that the-land to-say Israel sons-of among her they-explored

בָהּ לָתוּר אֹתָהּ אֶרֶץ אֹכֶלֶת יוֹשְׁבֶיהָ הִוא וְכָל־
and-all she ones-living-in-her devouring land her to-explore through-her

הָעָם אֲשֶׁר־ רָאִינוּ בְתוֹכָהּ אַנְשֵׁי מִדּוֹת׃ וְשָׁם רָאִינוּ אֶת־
*** we-saw · and-there (33) great-sizes men-of in-her we-saw that the-people

הַנְּפִילִים בְּנֵי עֲנָק מִן־ הַנְּפִלִים וַנְּהִי
and-we-seemed the-Nephilim from Anak descendants-of the-Nephilim

בְעֵינֵינוּ כַּחֲגָבִים וְכֵן הָיִינוּ בְּעֵינֵיהֶם׃
in-eyes-of-them we-were and-same like-grasshoppers in-eyes-of-us

וַתִּשָּׂא כָּל־ הָעֵדָה וַיִּתְּנוּ אֶת־ קוֹלָם
voice-of-them *** and-they-gave the-community all-of and-she-raised (14:1)

and Aaron and the whole Israelite community at Kadesh in the Desert of Paran. There they reported to them and to the whole assembly and showed them the fruit of the
land. 27They gave Moses this account: "We went into the land to which you sent us, and it does flow with milk and
honey! Here is its fruit. 28But the people who live there are powerful, and the cities are fortified and very large. We even saw descendants of
Anak there. 29The Amalekites live in the Negev; the Hittites, Jebusites and Amorites live in the hill country; and the Canaanites live near the sea and along the Jordan."

30Then Caleb silenced the people before Moses and said, "We should go up and take possession of the land, for we can certainly do it."

31But the men who had gone up with him said, "We can't attack those people; they are
stronger than we are." 32And they spread among the Israelites a bad report about the land they had explored. They said, "The land we explored devours those living in it. All the people we saw there are of
great size. 33We saw the Nephilim there (the descendants of Anak come from the Nephilim). We seemed like grasshoppers in our own eyes, and we looked the same to them."

The People Rebel

14 That night all the people of the community raised their voices and

וַיִּבְכּוּ הָעָם בַּלַּיְלָה הַהוּא׃ וַיִּלֹּנוּ
and-they-grumbled (2) the-that through-the-night the-people and-they-wept

עַל־ מֹשֶׁה וְעַל־ אַהֲרֹן כֹּל בְּנֵי יִשְׂרָאֵל וַיֹּאמְרוּ אֲלֵהֶם
to-them and-they-said Israel sons-of all-of Aaron and-against Moses against

כָּל־ הָעֵדָה לוּ־ מַתְנוּ בְּאֶרֶץ מִצְרַיִם אוֹ בַּמִּדְבָּר
in-the-desert or Egypt in-land-of we-died if-only the-assembly whole-of

הַזֶּה לוּ־ מָתְנוּ׃ וְלָמָה יְהוָה מֵבִיא אֹתָנוּ אֶל־הָאָרֶץ הַזֹּאת
the-this the-land to us bringing Yahweh now-why? (3) we-died if-only the-this

לִנְפֹּל בַּחֶרֶב נָשֵׁינוּ וְטַפֵּנוּ יִהְיוּ לָבַז
as-plunder they-will-be and-child-of-us wives-of-us by-the-sword to-fall

הֲלוֹא טוֹב לָנוּ שׁוּב מִצְרָיְמָה׃ וַיֹּאמְרוּ אִישׁ אֶל־ אָחִיו
other-of-him to each and-they-said (4) to-Egypt to-go-back for-us better not?

נִתְּנָה רֹאשׁ וְנָשׁוּבָה מִצְרָיְמָה׃ וַיִּפֹּל מֹשֶׁה
Moses and-he-fell (5) to-Egypt and-we-should-go-back leader we-should-choose

וְאַהֲרֹן עַל־ פְּנֵיהֶם לִפְנֵי כָּל־ קְהַל עֲדַת
assembly-of gathering-of whole-of in-front-of faces-of-them on and-Aaron

בְּנֵי יִשְׂרָאֵל׃ וִיהוֹשֻׁעַ בִּן־ נוּן וְכָלֵב בֶּן־ יְפֻנֶּה מִן־
among Jephunneh son-of and-Caleb Nun son-of and-Joshua (6) Israel sons-of

הַתָּרִים אֶת־ הָאָרֶץ קָרְעוּ בִּגְדֵיהֶם׃ וַיֹּאמְרוּ
and-they-said (7) clothes-of-them they-tore the-land *** the-ones-exploring

אֶל־ כָּל־ עֲדַת בְּנֵי־ יִשְׂרָאֵל לֵאמֹר הָאָרֶץ אֲשֶׁר עָבַרְנוּ
we-passed that the-land to-say Israel sons-of assembly-of entire-of to

בָהּ לָתוּר אֹתָהּ טוֹבָה הָאָרֶץ מְאֹד מְאֹד׃ אִם־ חָפֵץ
he-is-pleased if (8) very very the-land good her to-explore through-her

בָּנוּ יְהוָה וְהֵבִיא אֹתָנוּ אֶל־ הָאָרֶץ הַזֹּאת וּנְתָנָהּ
and-he-will-give-her the-that the-land into us then-he-will-lead Yahweh with-us

לָנוּ אֶרֶץ אֲשֶׁר־הִוא זָבַת חָלָב וּדְבָשׁ׃ אַךְ בַּיהוָה אַל־
not against-Yahweh only (9) and-honey milk flowing-of she that land to-us

תִּמְרֹדוּ וְאַתֶּם אַל־ תִּירְאוּ אֶת־ עַם הָאָרֶץ כִּי לַחְמֵנוּ הֵם
they food-of-us for the-land people-of *** you-fear not and-you you-rebel

סָר צִלָּם מֵעֲלֵיהֶם וַיהוָה אִתָּנוּ אַל־
not with-us but-Yahweh from-over-them protection-of-them he-is-gone

תִּירָאֻם׃ וַיֹּאמְרוּ כָּל־ הָעֵדָה לִרְגּוֹם אֹתָם
them to-stone the-assembly whole-of but-they-talked (10) you-fear-them

בָּאֲבָנִים וּכְבוֹד יְהוָה נִרְאָה בְּאֹהֶל מוֹעֵד אֶל־
to Meeting in-Tent-of he-appeared Yahweh then-glory-of with-the-stones

כָּל־ בְּנֵי יִשְׂרָאֵל׃ וַיֹּאמֶר יְהוָה אֶל־ מֹשֶׁה עַד־ אָנָה
when? until Moses to Yahweh and-he-said (11) Israel sons-of all-of

wept aloud. 2All the Israelites grumbled against Moses and Aaron, and the whole assembly said to them, "If only we had died in Egypt! Or in this desert! 3Why is the LORD bringing us to this land only to let us fall by the sword? Our wives and children will be taken as plunder. Wouldn't it be better for us to go back to Egypt?" 4And they said to each other, "We should choose a leader and go back to Egypt."

5Then Moses and Aaron fell facedown in front of the whole Israelite assembly gathered there. 6Joshua son of Nun and Caleb son of Jephunneh, who were among those who had explored the land, tore their clothes 7and said to the entire Israelite assembly, "The land we passed through and explored is exceedingly good. 8If the LORD is pleased with us, he will lead us into that land, a land flowing with milk and honey, and will give it to us. 9Only do not rebel against the LORD. And do not be afraid of the people of the land, because we will swallow them up. Their protection is gone, but the LORD is with us. Do not be afraid of them."

10But the whole assembly talked about stoning them. Then the glory of the LORD appeared at the Tent of Meeting to all the Israelites. 11The LORD said to Moses, "How long will

יְנַאֲצֻנִי הָעָם הַזֶּה וְעַד־ אָנָה לֹא־
not when? and-until the-this the-people will-they-treat-with-contempt-me

יַאֲמִינוּ בִי בְּכֹל הָאֹתוֹת אֲשֶׁר עָשִׂיתִי בְּקִרְבּוֹ׃
among-him I-performed that the-signs despite-all-of in-me will-they-believe

(12) אַכֶּנּוּ בַדֶּבֶר וְאוֹרִשֶׁנּוּ וְאֶעֱשֶׂה
but-I-will-make and-I-will-destroy-him with-the-plague I-will-strike-him (12)

אֹתְךָ לְגוֹי־ גָּדוֹל וְעָצוּם מִמֶּנּוּ׃ (13) וַיֹּאמֶר מֹשֶׁה אֶל־
to Moses but-he-said (13) than-him and-stronger greater into-nation you

יְהוָה וְשָׁמְעוּ מִצְרַיִם כִּי־ הֶעֱלִיתָ בְכֹחֲךָ
by-power-of-you you-brought-up that Egyptians then-they-will-hear Yahweh

אֶת־ הָעָם הַזֶּה מִקִּרְבּוֹ׃ (14) וְאָמְרוּ אֶל־
to and-they-will-tell (14) from-among-him the-this the-people ***

יוֹשֵׁב הָאָרֶץ הַזֹּאת שָׁמְעוּ כִּי־ אַתָּה יְהוָה בְּקֶרֶב
in-midst-of Yahweh you that they-heard the-this the-land one-inhabiting-of

הָעָם הַזֶּה אֲשֶׁר־ עַיִן בְּעַיִן נִרְאָה | אַתָּה יְהוָה וַעֲנָנְךָ
and-cloud-of-you Yahweh you he-was-seen to-eye eye that the-this the-people

עֹמֵד עֲלֵהֶם וּבְעַמֻּד עָנָן אַתָּה הֹלֵךְ לִפְנֵיהֶם יוֹמָם
by-day before-them going you cloud and-in-pillar-of over-them staying

וּבְעַמּוּד אֵשׁ לָיְלָה׃ (15) וְהֵמַתָּה אֶת־ הָעָם הַזֶּה כְּאִישׁ
as-man the-this the-people *** if-you-kill (15) night fire and-in-pillar-of

אֶחָד וְאָמְרוּ הַגּוֹיִם אֲשֶׁר־ שָׁמְעוּ אֶת־ שִׁמְעֲךָ לֵאמֹר׃
to-say report-of-you *** they-heard who the-nations then-they-will-say one

(16) מִבִּלְתִּי יְכֹלֶת יְהוָה לְהָבִיא אֶת־ הָעָם הַזֶּה אֶל־
into the-this the-people *** to-bring Yahweh to-be-able because-not (16)

הָאָרֶץ אֲשֶׁר־ נִשְׁבַּע לָהֶם וַיִּשְׁחָטֵם בַּמִּדְבָּר׃
in-the-desert then-he-slaughtered-them to-them he-promised that the-land

(17) וְעַתָּה יִגְדַּל־ נָא כֹּחַ אֲדֹנָי כַּאֲשֶׁר דִּבַּרְתָּ לֵאמֹר׃
to-say you-declared just-as Lord strength-of now! may-he-display so-now (17)

(18) יְהוָה אֶרֶךְ אַפַּיִם וְרַב־ חֶסֶד נֹשֵׂא עָוֹן וָפָשַׁע
and-rebellion sin forgiving love and-abundant-of angers slow-of Yahweh (18)

וְנַקֵּה לֹא יְנַקֶּה פֹּקֵד עֲוֺן אָבוֹת
fathers sin-of punishing he-will-leave-unpunished not yet-to-leave-unpunished

עַל־ בָּנִים עַל־ שִׁלֵּשִׁים וְעַל־ רִבֵּעִים׃ (19) סְלַח־ נָא לַעֲוֺן
to-sin-of now! forgive! (19) fourth-ones and-to third-ones to children on

הָעָם הַזֶּה כְּגֹדֶל חַסְדֶּךָ וְכַאֲשֶׁר נָשָׂאתָה
you-pardoned and-just-as love-of-you as-greatness-of the-this the-people

לָעָם הַזֶּה מִמִּצְרַיִם וְעַד־ הֵנָּה׃ (20) וַיֹּאמֶר יְהוָה
Yahweh and-he-replied (20) now and until from Egypt the-this to-the-people

these people treat me with
contempt? How long will they
refuse to believe in me, in
spite of all the miraculous
signs I have performed among
them? [12]I will strike them
down with a plague and destroy them, but I will make
you into a nation greater and
stronger than they."
[13]Moses said to the LORD,
"Then the Egyptians will hear
about it! By your power you
brought these people up from
among them. [14]And they will
tell the inhabitants of this
land about it. They have already heard that you, O LORD,
are with these people and that
you, O LORD, have been seen
face to face, that your cloud
stays over them, and that you
go before them in a pillar of
cloud by day and a pillar of fire
by night. [15]If you put these
people to death all at one time,
the nations who have heard
this report about you will say,
[16]'The LORD was not able to
bring these people into the
land he promised them on
oath; so he slaughtered them
in the desert.'
[17]"Now may the Lord's
strength be displayed, just as
you have declared: [18]'The LORD
is slow to anger, abounding in
love and forgiving sin and rebellion. Yet he does not leave
the guilty unpunished; he
punishes the children for the
sin of the fathers to the third
and fourth generation.' [19]In
accordance with your great
love, forgive the sin of these
people, just as you have par-
doned them from the time
they left Egypt until now."
[20]The LORD replied, "I have

סָלַחְתִּי כִּדְבָרֶךָ׃ וְאוּלָם חַי־ אָנִי וְיִמָּלֵא כְבוֹד־
glory-of and-he-fills I alive but-surely (21) as-request-of-you I-forgave

יְהוָה אֶת־ כָּל־ הָאָרֶץ׃ כִּי כָל־ הָאֲנָשִׁים הָרֹאִים אֶת־
*** the-ones-seeing the-men all-of indeed (22) the-earth whole-of *** Yahweh

כְּבֹדִי וְאֶת־ אֹתֹתַי אֲשֶׁר־ עָשִׂיתִי בְמִצְרַיִם וּבַמִּדְבָּר
and-in-the-desert in-Egypt I-performed that signs-of-me and glory-of-me

וַיְנַסּוּ אֹתִי זֶה עֶשֶׂר פְּעָמִים וְלֹא שָׁמְעוּ בְּקוֹלִי׃ אִם־
not (23) to-voice-of-me they-obeyed and-not times ten now me but-they-tested

יִרְאוּ אֶת־ הָאָרֶץ אֲשֶׁר נִשְׁבַּעְתִּי לַאֲבֹתָם וְכָל־
and-all-of to-fathers-of-them I-promised that the-land *** they-will-see

מְנַאֲצַי לֹא יִרְאוּהָ׃ וְעַבְדִּי
but-servant-of-me (24) they-will-see-her not ones-treating-with-contempt-me

כָלֵב עֵקֶב הָיְתָה רוּחַ אַחֶרֶת עִמּוֹ וַיְמַלֵּא אַחֲרָי
after-me and-he-is-wholehearted in-him different spirit she-is because Caleb

וַהֲבִיאֹתִיו אֶל־ הָאָרֶץ אֲשֶׁר־ בָּא שָׁמָּה וְזַרְעוֹ
and-seed-of-him to-there he-went that the-land into then-I-will-bring-him

יוֹרִשֶׁנָּה׃ וְהָעֲמָלֵקִי וְהַכְּנַעֲנִי יוֹשֵׁב
living and-the-Canaanite now-the-Amalekite (25) he-will-inherit-her

בָּעֵמֶק מָחָר פְּנוּ וּסְעוּ לָכֶם הַמִּדְבָּר דֶּרֶךְ
route-of the-desert for-you and-set-out! turn-back! tomorrow in-the-valley

יַם־ סוּף׃ וַיְדַבֵּר יְהוָה אֶל־מֹשֶׁה וְאֶל־ אַהֲרֹן לֵאמֹר׃ עַד־
until (27) to-say Aaron and-to Moses to Yahweh and-he-said (26) Reed Sea-of

מָתַי לָעֵדָה הָרָעָה הַזֹּאת אֲשֶׁר הֵמָּה מַלִּינִים
ones-grumbling they that the-this the-wicked for-the-community when?

עָלָי אֶת־ תְּלֻנּוֹת בְּנֵי יִשְׂרָאֵל אֲשֶׁר הֵמָּה מַלִּינִים
ones-grumbling they that Israel sons-of complaints-of *** against-me

עָלַי שָׁמָעְתִּי׃ אֱמֹר אֲלֵהֶם חַי־ אָנִי נְאֻם־ יְהוָה אִם־ לֹא
surely that Yahweh declaring-of I alive to-them tell! (28) I-heard against-me

כַּאֲשֶׁר דִּבַּרְתֶּם בְּאָזְנָי כֵּן אֶעֱשֶׂה לָכֶם׃ בַּמִּדְבָּר
in-the-desert (29) to-you I-will-do so in-ears-of-me you-said just-as

הַזֶּה יִפְּלוּ פִגְרֵיכֶם וְכָל־ פְּקֻדֵיכֶם
ones-being-counted-of-you and-all-of bodies-of-you they-will-fall the-this

לְכָל־ מִסְפַּרְכֶם מִבֶּן עֶשְׂרִים שָׁנָה וָמָעְלָה אֲשֶׁר הֲלִינֹתֶם
you-grumbled who or-more year twenty from-son-of census-of-you in-every-of

עָלָי׃ אִם־ אַתֶּם תָּבֹאוּ אֶל־ הָאָרֶץ אֲשֶׁר נָשָׂאתִי אֶת־
*** I-lifted that the-land into you-will-enter you not (30) against-me

יָדִי לְשַׁכֵּן אֶתְכֶם בָּהּ כִּי אִם־ כָּלֵב בֶּן־ יְפֻנֶּה
Jephunneh son-of Caleb except only in-her you to-make-home hand-of-me

forgiven them, as you asked.
[21]Nevertheless, as surely as I
live and as surely as the glory
of the LORD fills the whole
earth, [22]not one of the men
who saw my glory and the
miraculous signs I performed
in Egypt and in the desert but
who disobeyed me and tested
me ten times— [23]not one of
them will ever see the land I
promised on oath to their
forefathers. No one who has
treated me with contempt will
ever see it. [24]But because my
servant Caleb has a different
spirit and follows me wholeheartedly, I will bring him
into the land he went to, and
his descendants will inherit it.
[25]Since the Amalekites and
Canaanites are living in the
valleys, turn back tomorrow
and set out toward the desert
along the route to the Red
Sea.[d]"
[26]The LORD said to Moses
and Aaron: [27]"How long will
this wicked community grumble against me? I have heard
the complaints of these grumbling Israelites. [28]So tell them,
'As surely as I live, declares the
LORD, I will do to you the very
things I heard you say: [29]In
this desert your bodies will
fall—every one of you twenty
years old or more who was
counted in the census and
who has grumbled against me.
[30]Not one of you will enter the
land I swore with uplifted
hand to make your home, except Caleb son of Jephunneh

[d]25 Hebrew *Yam Suph;* that is, Sea of Reeds

וִיהוֹשֻׁעַ בִּן־ נוּן׃ וְטַפְּכֶם אֲשֶׁר אֲמַרְתֶּם לָבַז
as-plunder you-said that and-child-of-you (31) Nun son-of and-Joshua

יִהְיֶה וְהֵבֵיאתִי אֹתָם וְיָדְעוּ אֶת־ הָאָרֶץ אֲשֶׁר
that the-land *** and-they-will-enjoy them now-I-will-bring-in he-would-be

מְאַסְתֶּם בָּהּ׃ וּפִגְרֵיכֶם אַתֶּם יִפְּלוּ
they-will-fall you but-bodies-of-you (32) against-her you-rejected

בַּמִּדְבָּר הַזֶּה׃ וּבְנֵיכֶם יִהְיוּ רֹעִים
ones-herding they-will-be and-children-of-you (33) the-this in-the-desert

בַּמִּדְבָּר אַרְבָּעִים שָׁנָה וְנָשְׂאוּ אֶת־ זְנוּתֵיכֶם
unfaithfulnesses-of-you *** and-they-will-suffer year forty in-the-desert

עַד־ תֹּם פִּגְרֵיכֶם בַּמִּדְבָּר׃ בְּמִסְפַּר הַיָּמִים
the-days for-number-of (34) in-the-desert bodies-of-you to-be-last until

אֲשֶׁר־ תַּרְתֶּם אֶת־הָאָרֶץ אַרְבָּעִים יוֹם יוֹם לַשָּׁנָה יוֹם לַשָּׁנָה
for-the-year day for-the-year day day forty the-land *** you-explored that

תִּשְׂאוּ אֶת־ עֲוֹנֹתֵיכֶם אַרְבָּעִים שָׁנָה וִידַעְתֶּם אֶת־
*** and-you-will-know year forty sins-of-you *** you-will-suffer

תְּנוּאָתִי אֲנִי יְהוָה דִּבַּרְתִּי אִם־ לֹא ׀ זֹאת אֶעֱשֶׂה לְכָל־
to-whole-of I-will-do this surely that I-spoke Yahweh I (35) opposition-of-me

הָעֵדָה הָרָעָה הַזֹּאת הַנּוֹעָדִים עָלָי בַּמִּדְבָּר
in-the-desert against-me the-ones-banding the-this the-wicked the-community

הַזֶּה יִתַּמּוּ וְשָׁם יָמֻתוּ׃ וְהָאֲנָשִׁים אֲשֶׁר־
whom so-the-men (36) they-will-die and-here they-will-meet-end the-this

שָׁלַח מֹשֶׁה לָתוּר אֶת־ הָאָרֶץ וַיָּשֻׁבוּ וַיַּלִּינוּ
and-they-made-grumble and-they-returned the-land *** to-explore Moses he-sent

עָלָיו אֶת־ כָּל־ הָעֵדָה לְהוֹצִיא דִבָּה עַל־ הָאָרֶץ׃
the-land about bad-report by-to-spread the-community whole-of *** against-him

וַיָּמֻתוּ הָאֲנָשִׁים מוֹצִאֵי דִבַּת־ הָאָרֶץ רָעָה
bad the-land report-of ones-spreading-of the-men so-they-died (37)

בַּמַּגֵּפָה לִפְנֵי יְהוָה׃ וִיהוֹשֻׁעַ בִּן־ נוּן וְכָלֵב בֶּן־
son-of and-Caleb Nun son-of only-Joshua (38) Yahweh before of-the-plague

יְפֻנֶּה חָיוּ מִן־ הָאֲנָשִׁים הָהֵם הַהֹלְכִים לָתוּר אֶת־
*** to-explore the-ones-going the-these the-men from they-survived Jephunneh

הָאָרֶץ׃ וַיְדַבֵּר מֹשֶׁה אֶת־ הַדְּבָרִים הָאֵלֶּה אֶל־ כָּל־
all-of to the-these the-things *** Moses when-he-reported (39) the-land

בְּנֵי יִשְׂרָאֵל וַיִּתְאַבְּלוּ הָעָם מְאֹד׃ וַיַּשְׁכִּמוּ
and-they-rose (40) bitterly the-people then-they-mourned Israel sons-of

בַבֹּקֶר וַיַּעֲלוּ אֶל־ רֹאשׁ־ הָהָר לֵאמֹר הִנֶּנּוּ
see-us! to-say the-hill-country height-of to and-they-went-up in-the-morning

°36 ק וילינו

and Joshua son of Nun. 31As
for your children that you said
would be taken as plunder, I
will bring them in to enjoy the
land you have rejected. 32But
you—your bodies will fall in
this desert. 33Your children
will be shepherds here for
forty years, suffering for your
unfaithfulness, until the last
of your bodies lies in the
desert. 34For forty years—one
year for each of the forty days
you explored the land—you
will suffer for your sins and
know what it is like to have
me against you.' 35I, the LORD,
have spoken, and I will surely
do these things to this whole
wicked community, which
has banded together against
me. They will meet their end
in this desert; here they will
die."

36So the men Moses had sent
to explore the land, who returned and made the whole
community grumble against
him by spreading a bad report
about it— 37these men responsible for spreading the bad report about the land were
struck down and died of a
plague before the LORD. 38Of
the men who went to explore
the land, only Joshua son of
Nun and Caleb son of Jephunneh survived.

39When Moses reported this
to all the Israelites, they
mourned bitterly. 40Early the
next morning they went up
toward the high hill country.

וְעָלִינוּ אֶל־ הַמָּקוֹם אֲשֶׁר־ אָמַר יְהוָה כִּי חָטָאנוּ׃
we-sinned indeed Yahweh he-promised that the-place to now-we-will-go-up

וַיֹּאמֶר מֹשֶׁה לָמָּה זֶּה אַתֶּם עֹבְרִים אֶת־ פִּי יְהוָה
Yahweh command-of *** ones-disobeying you now why? Moses but-he-said (41)

וְהִוא לֹא תִצְלָח׃ אַל־ תַּעֲלוּ כִּי אֵין יְהוָה
Yahweh he-is-not for you-go-up not (42) she-will-succeed not now-this

בְּקִרְבְּכֶם וְלֹא תִּנָּגְפוּ לִפְנֵי אֹיְבֵיכֶם׃ כִּי
for (43) being-enemies-of-you by you-will-be-defeated so-not in-midst-of-you

הָעֲמָלֵקִי וְהַכְּנַעֲנִי שָׁם לִפְנֵיכֶם וּנְפַלְתֶּם
and-you-will-fall before-faces-of-you there and-the-Canaanite the-Amalekite

בֶּחָרֶב כִּי־ עַל־ כֵּן שַׁבְתֶּם מֵאַחֲרֵי יְהוָה וְלֹא־ יִהְיֶה
he-will-be and-not Yahweh away-from you-turned this of because by-the-sword

יְהוָה עִמָּכֶם׃ וַיַּעְפִּלוּ לַעֲלוֹת אֶל־ רֹאשׁ הָהָר
the-hill-country height-of to to-go-up but-they-presumed (44) with-you Yahweh

וַאֲרוֹן בְּרִית־ יְהוָה וּמֹשֶׁה לֹא־ מָשׁוּ מִקֶּרֶב
from-within they-moved not and-Moses Yahweh covenant-of though-ark-of

הַמַּחֲנֶה׃ וַיֵּרֶד הָעֲמָלֵקִי וְהַכְּנַעֲנִי
and-the-Canaanite the-Amalekite then-he-came-down (45) the-camp

הַיֹּשֵׁב בָּהָר הַהוּא וַיַּכּוּם
and-they-attacked-them the-that in-the-hill-country the-one-living

וַיַּכְּתוּם עַד־ הַחָרְמָה׃ וַיְדַבֵּר יְהוָה אֶל־מֹשֶׁה לֵּאמֹר׃
to-say Moses to Yahweh and-he-spoke (15:1) the-Hormah to and-they-beat-them

דַּבֵּר אֶל־ בְּנֵי יִשְׂרָאֵל וְאָמַרְתָּ אֲלֵהֶם כִּי תָבֹאוּ אֶל־ אֶרֶץ
land-of into you-enter after to-them and-you-say Israel sons-of to speak! (2)

מוֹשְׁבֹתֵיכֶם אֲשֶׁר אֲנִי נֹתֵן לָכֶם׃ וַעֲשִׂיתֶם אִשֶּׁה
fire-offering and-you-present (3) to-you giving I that homes-of-you

לַיהוָה עֹלָה אוֹ־ זֶבַח לְפַלֵּא־ נֶדֶר אוֹ בִנְדָבָה
for-freewill-offering or vow to-fulfill sacrifice or burnt-offering to-Yahweh

אוֹ בְּמֹעֲדֵיכֶם לַעֲשׂוֹת רֵיחַ נִיחֹחַ לַיהוָה מִן־ הַבָּקָר
the-herd from to-Yahweh pleasant aroma-of to-present for-festivals-of-you or

אוֹ מִן־ הַצֹּאן׃ וְהִקְרִיב הַמַּקְרִיב קָרְבָּנוֹ
offering-of-him the-one-bringing then-he-shall-present (4) the-flock from or

לַיהוָה מִנְחָה סֹלֶת עִשָּׂרוֹן בָּלוּל בִּרְבִעִית הַהִין
the-hin with-fourth-of being-mixed tenth fine-flour grain-offering to-Yahweh

שָׁמֶן׃ וְיַיִן לַנֶּסֶךְ רְבִיעִית הַהִין תַּעֲשֶׂה עַל־
with you-prepare the-hin fourth-of as-the-drink-offering and-wine (5) oil

הָעֹלָה אוֹ לַזָּבַח לַכֶּבֶשׂ הָאֶחָד׃ אוֹ
or (6) the-each with-the-lamb with-the-sacrifice or the-burnt-offering

"We have sinned," they said.
"We will go up to the place the
LORD promised."
41But Moses said, "Why are
you disobeying the LORD's
command? This will not succeed! 42Do not go up, because
the LORD is not with you. You
will be defeated by your enemies, 43for the Amalekites and
Canaanites will face you there.
Because you have turned away
from the LORD, he will not be
with you and you will fall by
the sword."
44Nevertheless, in their pre-
sumption they went up
toward the high hill country,
though neither Moses nor the
ark of the LORD's covenant
moved from the camp. 45Then
the Amalekites and Canaanites who lived in that hill
country came down and at-
tacked them and beat them
down all the way to Hormah.

Supplementary Offerings

15 The LORD said to
Moses, 2"Speak to the
Israelites and say to them: 'After you enter the land I am giving you as a home 3and you
present to the LORD offerings
made by fire, from the herd or
the flock, as an aroma pleasing
to the LORD—whether burnt
offerings or sacrifices, for
special vows or freewill
offerings or festival offerings—
4then the one who brings his
offering shall present to the
LORD a grain offering of a
tenth of an ephah[e] of fine flour
mixed with a fourth of a hin[f]
of oil. 5With each lamb for the
burnt offering or the sacrifice,
prepare a fourth of a hin of
wine as a drink offering.

[e]4 That is, probably about 2 quarts (about 2 liters)

[f]4 That is, probably about 1 quart (about 1 liter); also in verse 5

לָאַיִל תַּעֲשֶׂה מִנְחָה סֹלֶת שְׁנֵי עֶשְׂרֹנִים בְּלוּלָה
being-mixed tenths two-of fine-flour grain-offering you-prepare with-the-ram

בַשֶּׁמֶן שְׁלִשִׁית הַהִין׃ וְיַיִן לַנֶּסֶךְ שְׁלִשִׁית
third-of as-the-drink-offering and-wine (7) the-hin third-of with-the-oil

הַהִין תַּקְרִיב רֵיחַ־נִיחֹחַ לַיהוָה׃ וְכִי־תַעֲשֶׂה בֶן־
young-of you-prepare and-when (8) to-Yahweh pleasant aroma-of you-offer the-hin

בָּקָר עֹלָה אוֹ־זָבַח לְפַלֵּא־נֶדֶר אוֹ־שְׁלָמִים
fellowship-offerings or vow to-fulfill sacrifice or burnt-offering herd

לַיהוָה׃ וְהִקְרִיב עַל־בֶּן־הַבָּקָר מִנְחָה סֹלֶת
flour grain-offering the-herd young-of with and-he-shall-bring (9) to-Yahweh

שְׁלֹשָׁה עֶשְׂרֹנִים בָּלוּל בַּשֶּׁמֶן חֲצִי הַהִין׃ וְיַיִן תַּקְרִיב
you-bring and-wine (10) the-hin half-of with-the-oil being-mixed tenths three

לַנֶּסֶךְ חֲצִי הַהִין אִשֵּׁה רֵיחַ־נִיחֹחַ
pleasant aroma-of fire-offering-of the-hin half-of as-the-drink-offering

לַיהוָה׃ כָּכָה יֵעָשֶׂה לַשּׁוֹר הָאֶחָד אוֹ לָאַיִל
for-the-ram or the-each for-the-bull he-must-be-done this (11) to-Yahweh

הָאֶחָד אוֹ־לַשֶּׂה בַכְּבָשִׂים אוֹ בָעִזִּים׃ כַּמִּסְפָּר
as-the-many (12) from-the-goats or from-the-lambs for-the-young or the-each

אֲשֶׁר תַּעֲשׂוּ כָּכָה תַּעֲשׂוּ לָאֶחָד כְּמִסְפָּרָם כָּל־
everyone-of (13) as-many-of-them for-the-each you-do this you-prepare that

הָאֶזְרָח יַעֲשֶׂה־כָּכָה אֶת־אֵלֶּה לְהַקְרִיב אִשֵּׁה רֵיחַ־
aroma-of fire-offering-of to-bring these *** this he-must-do the-native-born

נִיחֹחַ לַיהוָה׃ וְכִי־יָגוּר אִתְּכֶם גֵּר אוֹ אֲשֶׁר־
whoever or alien with-you he-lives and-when (14) to-Yahweh pleasant

בְּתוֹכְכֶם לְדֹרֹתֵיכֶם וְעָשָׂה אִשֵּׁה רֵיחַ־
aroma-of fire-offering-of and-he-presents for-generations-of-you among-you

נִיחֹחַ לַיהוָה כַּאֲשֶׁר תַּעֲשׂוּ כֵּן יַעֲשֶׂה׃ הַקָּהָל חֻקָּה
rule the-community (15) he-must-do so you-do exactly-as to-Yahweh pleasant

אַחַת לָכֶם וְלַגֵּר הַגָּר חֻקַּת עוֹלָם
lasting ordinance-of the-one-living and-for-the-alien for-you same

לְדֹרֹתֵיכֶם כָּכֶם כַּגֵּר יִהְיֶה לִפְנֵי יְהוָה׃
Yahweh before he-shall-be so-the-alien as-you for-generations-of-you

תּוֹרָה אַחַת וּמִשְׁפָּט אֶחָד יִהְיֶה לָכֶם וְלַגֵּר
and-to-the-alien to-you he-will-apply same and-regulation same law (16)

הַגָּר אִתְּכֶם׃ וַיְדַבֵּר יְהוָה אֶל־מֹשֶׁה לֵּאמֹר׃ דַּבֵּר
speak! (18) to-say Moses to Yahweh and-he-spoke (17) among-you the-one-living

אֶל־בְּנֵי יִשְׂרָאֵל וְאָמַרְתָּ אֲלֵהֶם בְּבֹאֲכֶם אֶל־הָאָרֶץ אֲשֶׁר
where the-land into when-to-enter-you to-them and-you-say Israel sons-of to

6" 'With a ram prepare a
grain offering of two-tenths of
an ephah[g] of fine flour mixed
with a third of a hin[h] of oil,
7and a third of a hin of wine as
a drink offering. Offer it as an
aroma pleasing to the LORD.
8" 'When you prepare a
young bull as a burnt offering
or sacrifice, for a special vow
or a fellowship offering[i] to the
LORD, 9bring with the bull a
grain offering of three-tenths
of an ephah[j] of fine flour
mixed with half a hin[k] of oil.
10Also bring half a hin of wine
as a drink offering. It will be
an offering made by fire, an
aroma pleasing to the LORD.
11Each bull or ram, each lamb
or young goat, is to be prepared in this manner. 12Do
this for each one, for as many
as you prepare.
13" 'Everyone who is native-
born must do these things in
this way when he brings an
offering made by fire as an
aroma pleasing to the LORD.
14For the generations to come,
whenever an alien or anyone
else living among you
presents an offering made by
fire as an aroma pleasing to
the LORD, he must do exactly as
you do. 15The community is to
have the same rules for you
and for the alien living among
you; this is a lasting ordinance
for the generations to come.
You and the alien shall be the
same before the LORD: 16The
same laws and regulations will
apply both to you and to the
alien living among you.' "
17The LORD said to Moses,
18"Speak to the Israelites and
say to them: 'When you enter
the land to which I am taking

g6 That is, probably about 4 quarts (about 4.5 liters)
h6 That is, probably about 1 1/4 quarts (about 1.2 liters); also in verse 7
i8 Traditionally *peace offering*
j9 That is, probably about 6 quarts (about 6.5 liters)
k9 That is, probably about 2 quarts (about 2 liters); also in verse 10

אֲנִי מֵבִיא אֶתְכֶם שָׁמָּה׃ וְהָיָה בַּאֲכָלְכֶם מִלֶּחֶם
from-food-of when-to-eat-you and-he-will-be (19) to-there you taking I

הָאָרֶץ תָּרִימוּ תְרוּמָה לַיהוָה׃ רֵאשִׁית עֲרִסֹתֵכֶם
ground-meal-of-you first-of (20) to-Yahweh portion you-must-present the-land

חַלָּה תָּרִימוּ תְרוּמָה כִּתְרוּמַת גֹּרֶן כֵּן תָּרִימוּ אֹתָהּ׃
her you-present so threshing-floor as-offering-of offering you-present cake

מֵרֵאשִׁית עֲרִסֹתֵיכֶם תִּתְּנוּ לַיהוָה תְּרוּמָה
offering to-Yahweh you-give ground-meal-of-you from-first-of (21)

לְדֹרֹתֵיכֶם׃ וְכִי תִשְׁגּוּ וְלֹא תַעֲשׂוּ
you-keep and-not you-are-unintentional now-if (22) through-generations-of-you

אֵת כָּל־הַמִּצְוֹת הָאֵלֶּה אֲשֶׁר־דִּבֶּר יְהוָה אֶל־מֹשֶׁה׃ אֵת כָּל־
any *** (23) Moses to Yahweh he-gave that the-these the-commands any-of ***

אֲשֶׁר צִוָּה יְהוָה אֲלֵיכֶם בְּיַד־מֹשֶׁה מִן־הַיּוֹם אֲשֶׁר
that the-day from Moses by-hand-of to-you Yahweh he-commanded that

צִוָּה יְהוָה וָהָלְאָה לְדֹרֹתֵיכֶם׃ וְהָיָה אִם
if and-he-is (24) through-generations-of-you and-onwards Yahweh he-commanded

מֵעֵינֵי הָעֵדָה נֶעֶשְׂתָה לִשְׁגָגָה וְעָשׂוּ
then-they-must-offer as-unintentional he-is-done the-community from-eyes-of

כָל־הָעֵדָה פַּר בֶּן־בָּקָר אֶחָד לְעֹלָה לְרֵיחַ
as-aroma-of for-burnt-offering one herd young-of bull the-community whole-of

נִיחֹחַ לַיהוָה וּמִנְחָתוֹ וְנִסְכּוֹ
and-drink-offering-of-him and-grain-offering-of-him to-Yahweh pleasant

כַּמִּשְׁפָּט וּשְׂעִיר־עִזִּים אֶחָד לְחַטָּת׃
as-sin-offering one goats and-male-goat-of as-the-prescription

וְכִפֶּר הַכֹּהֵן עַל־כָּל־עֲדַת בְּנֵי יִשְׂרָאֵל
Israel sons-of community-of whole-of for the-priest and-he-must-atone (25)

וְנִסְלַח לָהֶם כִּי־שְׁגָגָה הִוא וְהֵם הֵבִיאוּ
they-brought and-they she unintentional for to-them and-he-will-be-forgiven

אֶת־קָרְבָּנָם אִשֶּׁה לַיהוָה וְחַטָּאתָם לִפְנֵי
to and-sin-offering-of-them to-Yahweh fire-offering offering-of-them ***

יְהוָה עַל־שִׁגְגָתָם׃ וְנִסְלַח לְכָל־עֲדַת
community-of to-whole-of and-he-will-be-forgiven (26) wrong-of-them for Yahweh

בְּנֵי יִשְׂרָאֵל וְלַגֵּר הַגָּר בְּתוֹכָם כִּי לְכָל־
involving-all-of for among-them the-one-living and-to-the-alien Israel sons-of

הָעָם בִּשְׁגָגָה׃ וְאִם־נֶפֶשׁ אַחַת תֶּחֱטָא
she-sins one person but-if (27) in-unintentional-wrong the-people

בִשְׁגָגָה וְהִקְרִיבָה עֵז בַּת־שְׁנָתָהּ
year-of-her daughter-of female-goat then-she-must-bring with-no-intention

you [19]and you eat the food of the land, present a portion as an offering to the LORD. [20]Present a cake from the first of your ground meal and present it as an offering from the threshing floor. [21]Throughout the generations to come you are to give this offering to the LORD from the first of your ground meal.

Offerings for Unintentional Sins

[22]" 'Now if you unintentionally fail to keep any of these commands the LORD gave Moses— [23]any of the LORD's commands to you through him, from the day the LORD gave them and continuing through the generations to come— [24]and if this is done unintentionally without the community being aware of it, then the whole community is to offer a young bull for a burnt offering as an aroma pleasing to the LORD, along with its prescribed grain offering and drink offering, and a male goat for a sin offering. [25]The priest is to make atonement for the whole Israelite community, and they will be forgiven, for it was not intentional and they have brought to the LORD for their wrong an offering made by fire and a sin offering. [26]The whole Israelite community and the aliens living among them will be forgiven, because all the people were involved in the unintentional wrong.

[27]" 'But if just one person sins unintentionally, he must bring a year-old female goat

לְחַטָּאת׃ (28) וְכִפֶּר הַכֹּהֵן עַל־ הַנֶּפֶשׁ
for-sin-offering (28) and-he-must-atone the-priest for the-person

הַשֹּׁגֶגֶת בְּחֶטְאָה בִשְׁגָגָה לִפְנֵי יְהוָה לְכַפֵּר
the-one-erring by-to-sin with-no-intention before Yahweh when-to-atone

עָלָיו וְנִסְלַח לוֹ׃ (29) הָאֶזְרָח בִּבְנֵי יִשְׂרָאֵל
for-him then-he-will-be-forgiven to-him (29) the-native from-sons-of Israel

וְלַגֵּר הַגָּר בְּתוֹכָם תּוֹרָה אַחַת יִהְיֶה לָכֶם
and-for-the-alien the-one-living among-them law one he-applies to-you

לָעֹשֶׂה בִּשְׁגָגָה׃ (30) וְהַנֶּפֶשׁ אֲשֶׁר־ תַּעֲשֶׂה ׀
to-the-one-sinning with-no-intention (30) but-the-person who she-sins

בְּיָד רָמָה מִן־ הָאֶזְרָח וּמִן־ הַגֵּר אֶת־ יְהוָה הוּא
with-hand being-high whether the-native or-whether the-alien *** Yahweh he

מְגַדֵּף וְנִכְרְתָה הַנֶּפֶשׁ הַהִוא מִקֶּרֶב עַמָּהּ׃
blaspheming and-she-must-be-cut the-person the-that from-among people-of-her

(31) כִּי דְבַר־ יְהוָה בָּזָה וְאֶת־ מִצְוָתוֹ הֵפַר
(31) for word-of Yahweh he-despised and commandment-of-him he-broke

הִכָּרֵת ׀ תִּכָּרֵת הַנֶּפֶשׁ הַהִוא עֲוֺנָה בָהּ׃
to-be-cut-off she-must-be-cut-off the-person the-that guilt-of-her on-her

(32) וַיִּהְיוּ בְנֵי־ יִשְׂרָאֵל בַּמִּדְבָּר וַיִּמְצְאוּ אִישׁ
(32) while-they-were sons-of Israel in-the-desert then-they-found man

מְקֹשֵׁשׁ עֵצִים בְּיוֹם הַשַּׁבָּת׃ (33) וַיַּקְרִיבוּ אֹתוֹ
gathering woods on-day-of the-Sabbath (33) and-they-brought him

הַמֹּצְאִים אֹתוֹ מְקֹשֵׁשׁ עֵצִים אֶל־ מֹשֶׁה וְאֶל־ אַהֲרֹן וְאֶל כָּל־
the-ones-finding him gathering woods to Moses and-to Aaron and-to whole-of

הָעֵדָה׃ (34) וַיַּנִּיחוּ אֹתוֹ בַּמִּשְׁמָר כִּי לֹא פֹרַשׁ
the-assembly (34) and-they-kept him in-the-custody for not being-clear

מַה־ יֵּעָשֶׂה לוֹ׃ (35) וַיֹּאמֶר יְהוָה אֶל־ מֹשֶׁה מוֹת
what he-should-be-done to-him (35) then-he-said Yahweh to Moses to-die

יוּמַת הָאִישׁ רָגוֹם אֹתוֹ בָאֲבָנִים כָּל־ הָעֵדָה
he-must-die the-man to-stone him with-the-stones whole-of the-assembly

מִחוּץ לַמַּחֲנֶה׃ (36) וַיֹּצִיאוּ אֹתוֹ כָּל־ הָעֵדָה אֶל־ מִחוּץ
outside of-the-camp (36) so-they-took him whole-of the-assembly to outside

לַמַּחֲנֶה וַיִּרְגְּמוּ אֹתוֹ בָּאֲבָנִים וַיָּמֹת כַּאֲשֶׁר
of-the-camp and-they-stoned him with-the-stones and-he-died just-as

צִוָּה יְהוָה אֶת־ מֹשֶׁה׃ (37) וַיֹּאמֶר יְהוָה אֶל־ מֹשֶׁה לֵּאמֹר׃
he-commanded Yahweh *** Moses (37) and-he-said Yahweh to Moses to-say

(38) דַּבֵּר אֶל־ בְּנֵי יִשְׂרָאֵל וְאָמַרְתָּ אֲלֵהֶם וְעָשׂוּ לָהֶם
(38) speak! to sons-of Israel and-you-say to-them so-they-make for-them

for a sin offering. 28The priest
is to make atonement before
the LORD for the one who erred
by sinning unintentionally,
and when atonement has
been made for him, he will be
forgiven. 29One and the same
law applies to everyone who
sins unintentionally, whether
he is a native-born Israelite or
an alien.
30" 'But anyone who sins
defiantly, whether native-
born or alien, blasphemes the
LORD, and that person must be
cut off from his people. 31Be-
cause he has despised the
LORD's word and broken his
commands, that person must
surely be cut off; his guilt remains on him.' "

The Sabbath-Breaker Put to Death

32While the Israelites were in
the desert, a man was found
gathering wood on the Sabbath day. 33Those who found
him gathering wood brought
him to Moses and Aaron and
the whole assembly, 34and
they kept him in custody, because it was not clear what
should be done to him. 35Then
the LORD said to Moses, "The
man must die. The whole assembly must stone him outside the camp." 36So the assembly took him outside the
camp and stoned him to
death, as the LORD com-
manded Moses.

Tassels on Garments

37The LORD said to Moses,
38"Speak to the Israelites and
say to them: 'Throughout the
generations to come you are to

צִיצִת עַל־ כַּנְפֵי בִגְדֵיהֶם לְדֹרֹתָם
through-generations-of-them garments-of-them corners-of on tassel

וְנָתְנוּ עַל־ צִיצִת הַכָּנָף פְּתִיל תְּכֵלֶת׃ וְהָיָה לָכֶם
to-you and-he-will-be (39) blue cord-of the-corner tassel-of on and-they-must-put

לְצִיצִת וּרְאִיתֶם אֹתוֹ וּזְכַרְתֶּם אֶת־ כָּל־ מִצְוֺת
commands-of all-of *** so-you-will-remember him and-you-will-see as-tassel

יְהוָה וַעֲשִׂיתֶם אֹתָם וְלֹא־ תָתֻרוּ אַחֲרֵי לְבַבְכֶם וְאַחֲרֵי
and-after heart-of-you after you-go and-not them so-you-may-obey Yahweh

עֵינֵיכֶם אֲשֶׁר־אַתֶּם זֹנִים אַחֲרֵיהֶם׃ לְמַעַן תִּזְכְּרוּ
you-will-remember then (40) after-them ones-prostituting you that eyes-of-you

וַעֲשִׂיתֶם אֶת־ כָּל־ מִצְוֺתָי וִהְיִיתֶם קְדֹשִׁים
ones-consecrated and-you-will-be commands-of-me all-of *** and-you-will-obey

לֵאלֹהֵיכֶם׃ אֲנִי יְהוָה אֱלֹהֵיכֶם אֲשֶׁר הוֹצֵאתִי אֶתְכֶם מֵאֶרֶץ
from-land-of you I-brought who God-of-you Yahweh I (41) to-God-of-you

מִצְרַיִם לִהְיוֹת לָכֶם לֵאלֹהִים אֲנִי יְהוָה אֱלֹהֵיכֶם׃ וַיִּקַּח
now-he-became-insolent (16:1) God-of-you Yahweh I as-God for-you to-be Egypt

קֹרַח בֶּן־ יִצְהָר בֶּן־ קְהָת בֶּן־ לֵוִי וְדָתָן וַאֲבִירָם בְּנֵי
sons-of and-Abiram and-Dathan Levi son-of Kohath son-of Izhar son-of Korah

אֱלִיאָב וְאוֹן בֶּן־ פֶּלֶת בְּנֵי רְאוּבֵן׃ וַיָּקֻמוּ לִפְנֵי
against and-they-rose-up (2) Reuben sons-of Peleth son-of and-On Eliab

מֹשֶׁה וַאֲנָשִׁים מִבְּנֵי־ יִשְׂרָאֵל חֲמִשִּׁים וּמָאתָיִם נְשִׂיאֵי
leaders-of and-two-hundreds fifty Israel from-sons-of and-men Moses

עֵדָה קְרִאֵי מוֹעֵד אַנְשֵׁי־ שֵׁם׃ וַיִּקָּהֲלוּ
and-they-gathered (3) name men-of council ones-appointed-of community

עַל־ מֹשֶׁה וְעַל־ אַהֲרֹן וַיֹּאמְרוּ אֲלֵהֶם רַב־ לָכֶם כִּי
for to-you too-far to-them and-they-said Aaron and-against Moses against

כָל־ הָעֵדָה כֻּלָּם קְדֹשִׁים וּבְתוֹכָם יְהוָה וּמַדּוּעַ
then-why? Yahweh and-with-them holy-ones all-of-them the-community whole-of

תִּתְנַשְּׂאוּ עַל־ קְהַל יְהוָה׃ וַיִּשְׁמַע מֹשֶׁה
Moses when-he-heard (4) Yahweh assembly-of above you-set-yourselves

וַיִּפֹּל עַל־ פָּנָיו׃ וַיְדַבֵּר אֶל־ קֹרַח וְאֶל־ כָּל־
all-of and-to Korah to then-he-said (5) face-of-him on then-he-fell

עֲדָתוֹ לֵאמֹר בֹּקֶר וְיֹדַע יְהוָה אֶת־אֲשֶׁר־ לוֹ וְאֶת־
and to-him who *** Yahweh then-he-will-show morning to-say follower-of-him

הַקָּדוֹשׁ וְהִקְרִיב אֵלָיו וְאֵת אֲשֶׁר יִבְחַר־ בּוֹ
for-him he-chooses whom and to-him and-he-will-have-come-near the-holy

יַקְרִיב אֵלָיו׃ זֹאת עֲשׂוּ קְחוּ־ לָכֶם מַחְתּוֹת קֹרַח
Korah censers for-you take! do! this (6) to-him he-will-make-come-near

make tassels on the corners of your garments, with a blue cord on each tassel. 39You will have these tassels to look at and so you will remember all the commands of the LORD, that you may obey them and not prostitute yourselves by going after the lusts of your own hearts and eyes. 40Then you will remember to obey all my commands and will be consecrated to your God. 41I am the LORD your God, who brought you out of Egypt to be your God. I am the LORD your God.' "

Korah, Dathan and Abiram

16 Korah son of Izhar, the son of Kohath, the son of Levi, and certain Reubenites—Dathan and Abiram, sons of Eliab, and On son of Peleth—became insolent[l] 2and rose up against Moses. With them were 250 Israelite men, well-known community leaders who had been appointed members of the council. 3They came as a group to oppose Moses and Aaron and said to them, "You have gone too far! The whole community is holy, every one of them, and the LORD is with them. Why then do you set yourselves above the LORD's assembly?"

4When Moses heard this, he fell facedown. 5Then he said to Korah and all his followers: "In the morning the LORD will show who belongs to him and who is holy, and he will have that person come near him. The man he chooses he will cause to come near him. 6You, Korah, and all your followers are to do this: Take censers

l1 Or *Peleth—took* ⌞*men*⌟

וְכָל־ עֲדָתוֹ׃ וּתְנוּ בָהֵן ׀ אֵשׁ וְשִׂימוּ עֲלֵיהֶן ׀ קְטֹרֶת
incense in-them and-put! fire in-them and-put! (7) follower-of-him and-all-of

לִפְנֵי יְהוָה מָחָר וְהָיָה הָאִישׁ אֲשֶׁר־ יִבְחַר יְהוָה הוּא
he Yahweh he-chooses whom the-man and-he-will-be tomorrow Yahweh before

הַקָּדוֹשׁ רַב־ לָכֶם בְּנֵי לֵוִי׃ וַיֹּאמֶר מֹשֶׁה אֶל־ קֹרַח שִׁמְעוּ־
listen! Korah to Moses and-he-said (8) Levi sons-of to-you too-far the-holy

נָא בְּנֵי לֵוִי׃ הַמְעַט מִכֶּם כִּי־ הִבְדִּיל אֱלֹהֵי יִשְׂרָאֵל אֶתְכֶם
you Israel God-of he-separated that for-you enough? (9) Levi sons-of now!

מֵעֲדַת יִשְׂרָאֵל לְהַקְרִיב אֶתְכֶם אֵלָיו לַעֲבֹד אֶת־ עֲבֹדַת
work-of *** to-do to-him you to-bring-near Israel from-community-of

מִשְׁכַּן יְהוָה וְלַעֲמֹד לִפְנֵי הָעֵדָה לְשָׁרְתָם׃
to-minister-to-them the-community before and-to-stand Yahweh tabernacle-of

וַיַּקְרֵב אֹתְךָ וְאֶת־ כָּל־ אַחֶיךָ בְנֵי־ לֵוִי אִתָּךְ
with-you Levi sons-of fellows-of-you all-of and you and-he-brought-near (10)

וּבִקַּשְׁתֶּם גַּם־ כְּהֻנָּה׃ לָכֵן אַתָּה וְכָל־ עֲדָתְךָ
follower-of-you and-all-of you therefore (11) the-priesthood too but-you-seek

הַנֹּעָדִים עַל־ יְהוָה וְאַהֲרֹן מַה־הוּא כִּי תַלּוֹנוּ
you-grumble that he who? now-Aaron Yahweh against the-ones-banding-together

עָלָיו׃ וַיִּשְׁלַח מֹשֶׁה לִקְרֹא לְדָתָן וְלַאֲבִירָם
and-to-Abiram to-Dathan to-summon Moses then-he-sent (12) against-him

בְּנֵי אֱלִיאָב וַיֹּאמְרוּ לֹא נַעֲלֶה׃ הַמְעַט כִּי הֶעֱלִיתָנוּ
you-brought-us that enough? (13) we-will-come not but-they-said Eliab sons-of

מֵאֶרֶץ זָבַת חָלָב וּדְבַשׁ לַהֲמִיתֵנוּ בַּמִּדְבָּר כִּי־
now in-the-desert to-kill-us and-honey milk flowing-of from-land

תִשְׂתָּרֵר עָלֵינוּ גַּם־ הִשְׂתָּרֵר׃ אַף לֹא אֶל־ אֶרֶץ זָבַת
flowing-of land into not moreover (14) to-lord also over-us you-would-lord

חָלָב וּדְבַשׁ הֲבִיאֹתָנוּ וַתִּתֶּן־ לָנוּ נַחֲלַת שָׂדֶה
field inheritance-of to-us nor-you-gave you-brought-us and-honey milk

וָכָרֶם הַעֵינֵי הָאֲנָשִׁים הָהֵם תְּנַקֵּר לֹא נַעֲלֶה׃
we-will-come not would-you-gouge-out the-these the-men eyes-of? or-vineyard

וַיִּחַר לְמֹשֶׁה מְאֹד וַיֹּאמֶר אֶל־ יְהוָה אַל־ תֵּפֶן
you-accept not Yahweh to and-he-said very to-Moses then-he-was-angry (15)

אֶל־ מִנְחָתָם לֹא חֲמוֹר אֶחָד מֵהֶם נָשָׂאתִי וְלֹא הֲרֵעֹתִי אֶת־
*** I-wronged or-not I-took from-them one donkey not offering-of-them to

אַחַד מֵהֶם׃ וַיֹּאמֶר מֹשֶׁה אֶל־קֹרַח אַתָּה וְכָל־ עֲדָתְךָ
follower-of-you and-all-of you Korah to Moses and-he-said (16) from-them any

הֱיוּ לִפְנֵי יְהוָה אַתָּה וָהֵם וְאַהֲרֹן מָחָר׃ וּקְחוּ ׀ אִישׁ
each and-take! (17) tomorrow and-Aaron and-they you Yahweh before appear!

°11 ק תלינו

7and tomorrow put fire and incense in them before the LORD.
The man the LORD chooses will
be the one who is holy. You
Levites have gone too far!"
8Moses also said to Korah,
"Now listen, you Levites!
9Isn't it enough for you that
the God of Israel has separated
you from the rest of the Israelite community and brought
you near himself to do the
work at the LORD's tabernacle
and to stand before the community and minister to them?
10He has brought you and all
your fellow Levites near himself, but now you are trying to
get the priesthood too. 11It is
against the LORD that you and
all your followers have banded
together. Who is Aaron that
you should grumble against
him?"
12Then Moses summoned
Dathan and Abiram, the sons
of Eliab. But they said, "We
will not come! 13Isn't it enough
that you have brought us up
out of a land flowing with
milk and honey to kill us in
the desert? And now you also
want to lord it over us? 14More-
over, you haven't brought us
into a land flowing with milk
and honey or given us an inheritance of fields and vineyards. Will you gouge out the
eyes of[m] these men? No, we
will not come!"
15Then Moses became very
angry and said to the LORD,
"Do not accept their offering. I
have not taken so much as a
donkey from them, nor have I
wronged any of them."
16Moses said to Korah, "You
and all your followers are to
appear before the LORD tomorrow—you and they and
Aaron. 17Each man is to take

m14 *Or you make slaves of; or you deceive*

מַחְתָּתוֹ וּנְתַתֶּם עֲלֵיהֶם קְטֹרֶת וְהִקְרַבְתֶּם לִפְנֵי יְהוָה
Yahweh before and-you-present incense in-them and-you-put censer-of-him

אִישׁ מַחְתָּתוֹ חֲמִשִּׁים וּמָאתַיִם מַחְתֹּת וְאַתָּה וְאַהֲרֹן אִישׁ
each and-Aaron and-you censers and-two-hundreds fifty censer-of-him each

מַחְתָּתוֹ׃ (18) וַיִּקְחוּ אִישׁ מַחְתָּתוֹ וַיִּתְּנוּ עֲלֵיהֶם אֵשׁ
fire in-them and-they-put censer-of-him each so-they-took (18) censer-of-him

וַיָּשִׂימוּ עֲלֵיהֶם קְטֹרֶת וַיַּעַמְדוּ פֶּתַח אֹהֶל מוֹעֵד
Meeting Tent-of entrance-of and-they-stood incense in-them and-they-put

וּמֹשֶׁה וְאַהֲרֹן׃ (19) וַיַּקְהֵל עֲלֵיהֶם קֹרַח אֶת־ כָּל־
all-of *** Korah opposite-them when-he-gathered (19) and-Aaron with-Moses

הָעֵדָה אֶל־ פֶּתַח אֹהֶל מוֹעֵד וַיֵּרָא כְבוֹד־
glory-of then-he-appeared Meeting Tent-of entrance-of at the-following

יְהוָה אֶל־ כָּל־ הָעֵדָה׃ (20) וַיְדַבֵּר יְהוָה אֶל־ מֹשֶׁה וְאֶל־
and-to Moses to Yahweh and-he-spoke (20) the-assembly entire-of to Yahweh

אַהֲרֹן לֵאמֹר׃ (21) הִבָּדְלוּ מִתּוֹךְ הָעֵדָה הַזֹּאת
the-this the-assembly from-among separate-yourselves! (21) to-say Aaron

וַאֲכַלֶּה* אֹתָם כְּרָגַע׃ (22) וַיִּפְּלוּ עַל־ פְּנֵיהֶם
faces-of-them on but-they-fell (22) at-once them so-I-can-consume

וַיֹּאמְרוּ אֵל אֱלֹהֵי הָרוּחֹת לְכָל־ בָּשָׂר הָאִישׁ אֶחָד יֶחֱטָא
he-sins one the-man mankind of-all-of the-spirits God-of God and-they-cried

וְעַל כָּל־ הָעֵדָה תִּקְצֹף׃ (23) וַיְדַבֵּר יְהוָה
Yahweh then-he-spoke (23) you-will-be-angry the-assembly entire-of but-with

אֶל־מֹשֶׁה לֵּאמֹר׃ (24) דַּבֵּר אֶל־ הָעֵדָה לֵאמֹר הֵעָלוּ מִסָּבִיב
from-around move-away! to-say the-assembly to say! (24) to-say Moses to

לְמִשְׁכַּן־ קֹרַח דָּתָן וַאֲבִירָם׃ (25) וַיָּקָם מֹשֶׁה וַיֵּלֶךְ
and-he-went Moses and-he-got-up (25) and-Abiram Dathan Korah to-tent-of

אֶל־ דָּתָן וַאֲבִירָם וַיֵּלְכוּ אַחֲרָיו זִקְנֵי יִשְׂרָאֵל׃
Israel elders-of after-him and-they-followed and-Abiram Dathan to

(26) וַיְדַבֵּר אֶל־ הָעֵדָה לֵאמֹר סוּרוּ נָא מֵעַל אָהֳלֵי
tents-of from-near now! move-back! to-say the-assembly to and-he-warned (26)

הָאֲנָשִׁים הָרְשָׁעִים הָאֵלֶּה וְאַל־ תִּגְּעוּ בְּכָל־ אֲשֶׁר לָהֶם
to-them that on-anything you-touch and-not the-these the-wicked-ones the-men

פֶּן־ תִּסָּפוּ בְּכָל־ חַטֹּאתָם׃ (27) וַיֵּעָלוּ
so-they-moved (27) sins-of-them because-of-all-of you-will-be-swept-away or

מֵעַל מִשְׁכַּן־ קֹרַח† דָּתָן וַאֲבִירָם מִסָּבִיב וְדָתָן וַאֲבִירָם
and-Abiram now-Dathan from-around and-Abiram Dathan Korah tent-of from-near

יָצְאוּ נִצָּבִים פֶּתַח אָהֳלֵיהֶם וּנְשֵׁיהֶם
with-wives-of-them tents-of-them entrance-of ones-standing they-came-out

his censer and put incense in
it—250 censers in all—and
present it before the LORD. You
and Aaron are to present your
censers also." 18So each man
took his censer, put fire and
incense in it, and stood with
Moses and Aaron at the entrance to the Tent of Meeting.
19When Korah had gathered
all his followers in opposition
to them at the entrance to the
Tent of Meeting, the glory of
the LORD appeared to the entire assembly. 20The LORD said
to Moses and Aaron, 21"Separate yourselves from this assembly so I can put an end to
them at once."
22But Moses and Aaron fell
facedown and cried out, "O
God, God of the spirits of all
mankind, will you be angry
with the entire assembly
when only one man sins?"
23Then the LORD said to
Moses, 24"Say to the assembly,
'Move away from the tents of
Korah, Dathan and Abiram.' "
25Moses got up and went to
Dathan and Abiram, and the
elders of Israel followed him.
26He warned the assembly,
"Move back from the tents of
these wicked men! Do not
touch anything belonging to
them, or you will be swept
away because of all their
sins." 27So they moved away
from the tents of Korah, Dathan and Abiram. Dathan and
Abiram had come out and
were standing with their

*21 Most mss have *hateph pathah* under the *aleph* (וַאֲ).

†27 Most mss have *pathah* under the *resh* (קֹרַח).

וּבְנֵיהֶ֖ם וְטַפָּֽם׃ וַיֹּ֣אמֶר מֹשֶׁ֗ה בְּזֹאת֙
by-this Moses then-he-said (28) and-little-one-of-them and-children-of-them

תֵּֽדְע֔וּן כִּֽי־יְהוָ֣ה שְׁלָחַ֔נִי לַעֲשׂ֕וֹת אֵ֥ת כָּל־הַֽמַּעֲשִׂ֖ים הָאֵ֑לֶּה
the-these the-things all-of *** to-do he-sent-me Yahweh that you-will-know

כִּי־לֹ֖א מִלִּבִּֽי׃ אִם־כְּמ֤וֹת כָּל־הָֽאָדָם֙ יְמֻת֣וּן אֵ֔לֶּה
these they-die the-man every-of as-to-die if (29) from-heart-of-me not that

וּפְקֻדַּת֙ כָּל־הָ֣אָדָ֔ם יִפָּקֵ֖ד עֲלֵיהֶ֑ם לֹ֥א יְהוָ֖ה
Yahweh not by-them he-is-experienced the-man every-of and-experience-of

שְׁלָחָֽנִי׃ וְאִם־בְּרִיאָ֞ה יִבְרָ֣א יְהוָ֗ה וּפָצְתָ֨ה
and-she-opens Yahweh he-brings-about new-thing but-if (30) he-sent-me

הָאֲדָמָ֤ה אֶת־פִּ֙יהָ֙ וּבָלְעָ֤ה אֹתָם֙ וְאֶת־כָּל־אֲשֶׁ֣ר לָהֶ֔ם
to-them that everything and them and-she-swallows mouth-of-her *** the-earth

וְיָרְד֥וּ חַיִּ֖ים שְׁאֹ֑לָה וִֽידַעְתֶּ֕ם כִּ֧י נִֽאֲצ֛וּ
they-abhored that then-you-will-know to-Sheol alive-ones and-they-go-down

הָאֲנָשִׁ֥ים הָאֵ֖לֶּה אֶת־יְהוָֽה׃ וַיְהִי֙ כְּכַלֹּת֔וֹ לְדַבֵּ֕ר אֵ֥ת
*** to-say as-to-finish-him and-he-was (31) Yahweh *** the-these the-men

כָּל־הַדְּבָרִ֖ים הָאֵ֑לֶּה וַתִּבָּקַ֥ע הָאֲדָמָ֖ה אֲשֶׁ֥ר תַּחְתֵּיהֶֽם׃
under-them that the-ground that-she-was-split the-these the-things all-of

וַתִּפְתַּ֤ח הָאָ֙רֶץ֙ אֶת־פִּ֔יהָ וַתִּבְלַ֥ע אֹתָ֖ם וְאֶת־
and them and-she-swallowed mouth-of-her *** the-earth and-she-opened (32)

בָּתֵּיהֶ֑ם וְאֵ֤ת כָּל־הָֽאָדָם֙ אֲשֶׁ֣ר לְקֹ֔רַח וְאֵ֖ת כָּל־
all-of and with-Korah that the-man every-of and households-of-them

הָרְכֽוּשׁ׃ וַיֵּ֨רְד֜וּ הֵ֣ם וְכָל־אֲשֶׁ֥ר לָהֶ֛ם
to-them that and-everything they and-they-went-down (33) the-possession

חַיִּ֖ים שְׁאֹ֑לָה וַתְּכַ֤ס עֲלֵיהֶם֙ הָאָ֔רֶץ וַיֹּאבְד֖וּ
and-they-were-gone the-earth over-them and-she-closed to-Sheol alive-ones

מִתּ֥וֹךְ הַקָּהָֽל׃ וְכָל־יִשְׂרָאֵ֗ל אֲשֶׁ֛ר סְבִיבֹתֵיהֶ֖ם
ones-around-them that Israel and-all-of (34) the-community from-among

נָ֣סוּ לְקֹלָ֑ם כִּ֣י אָֽמְר֔וּ פֶּן־תִּבְלָעֵ֖נוּ
she-will-swallow-us perhaps they-shouted for at-cry-of-them they-fled

הָאָֽרֶץ׃ וְאֵ֥שׁ יָצְאָ֖ה מֵאֵ֣ת יְהוָ֑ה וַתֹּ֗אכַל אֵ֤ת
*** and-she-consumed Yahweh from she-came-out and-fire (35) the-earth

הַחֲמִשִּׁ֙ים וּמָאתַ֔יִם אִ֔ישׁ מַקְרִיבֵ֖י הַקְּטֹֽרֶת׃
the-censers ones-offering-of man and-two-hundreds the-fifty

וַיְדַבֵּ֥ר יְהוָ֖ה אֶל־מֹשֶׁ֥ה לֵּאמֹֽר׃ אֱמֹ֨ר אֶל־אֶלְעָזָ֜ר בֶּן־
son-of Eleazar to tell! (2[37]) to-say Moses to Yahweh and-he-spoke (17:1[36])*

אַהֲרֹ֣ן הַכֹּהֵ֗ן וְיָרֵ֤ם אֶת־הַמַּחְתֹּת֙ מִבֵּ֣ין הַשְּׂרֵפָ֔ה
the-smoldering-remain out-of the-censers *** so-he-takes the-priest Aaron

wives, children and little ones at the entrances to their tents.
[28]Then Moses said, "This is how you will know that the LORD has sent me to do all these things and that it was not my idea: [29]If these men die a natural death and experience only what usually happens to men, then the LORD has not sent me. [30]But if the LORD brings about something totally new, and the earth opens its mouth and swallows them, with everything that belongs to them, and they go down alive into the grave,[n] then you will know that these men have treated the LORD with contempt."
[31]As soon as he finished saying all this, the ground under them split apart [32]and the earth opened its mouth and swallowed them, with their households and all Korah's men and all their possessions. [33]They went down alive into the grave, with everything they owned; the earth closed over them, and they perished and were gone from the community. [34]At their cries, all the Israelites around them fled, shouting, "The earth is going to swallow us too!"
[35]And fire came out from the LORD and consumed the 250 men who were offering the incense.
[36]The LORD said to Moses, [37]"Tell Eleazar son of Aaron, the priest, to take the censers out of the smoldering remains

[n]30 Hebrew *Sheol*; also in verse 33

*The Hebrew numeration of chapter 17 begins with verse 36 of chapter 16 in English. The number in brackets indicates the English numeration.

וְאֶת־ הָאֵשׁ זְרֵה־ הָלְאָה כִּי קָדֵשׁוּ׃ אֵת מַחְתּוֹת
censers-of *** (3[38]) they-are-holy for at-distance scatter! the-coal and

הַחַטָּאִים הָאֵלֶּה בְּנַפְשֹׁתָם וְעָשׂוּ אֹתָם
them and-they-must-make at-lives-of-them the-these the-sinners

רִקֻּעֵי פַחִים צִפּוּי לַמִּזְבֵּחַ כִּי־ הִקְרִיבֻם לִפְנֵי־
before they-presented-them for for-the-altar overlay sheets ones-hammered-of

יְהוָה וַיִּקְדָּשׁוּ וְיִהְיוּ לְאוֹת לִבְנֵי יִשְׂרָאֵל׃
Israel to-sons-of as-sign so-let-them-be and-they-became-holy Yahweh

וַיִּקַּח אֶלְעָזָר הַכֹּהֵן אֵת מַחְתּוֹת הַנְּחֹשֶׁת
the-bronze censers-of *** the-priest Eleazar so-he-collected (4[39])

אֲשֶׁר הִקְרִיבוּ הַשְּׂרֻפִים וַיְרַקְּעוּם צִפּוּי
overlay and-they-hammered-them the-ones-being-burned they-brought that

לַמִּזְבֵּחַ׃ זִכָּרוֹן לִבְנֵי יִשְׂרָאֵל לְמַעַן אֲשֶׁר לֹא־
not *** so-that Israel for-sons-of reminder (5[40]) for-the-altar

יִקְרַב אִישׁ זָר אֲשֶׁר לֹא מִזֶּרַע אַהֲרֹן הוּא לְהַקְטִיר
to-burn he Aaron from-descendant-of not who stranger man he-should-come

קְטֹרֶת לִפְנֵי יְהוָה וְלֹא־ יִהְיֶה כְקֹרַח
like-Korah he-would-become so-not Yahweh before incense

וְכַעֲדָתוֹ כַּאֲשֶׁר דִּבֶּר יְהוָה בְּיַד־ מֹשֶׁה לוֹ׃
to-him Moses by-hand-of Yahweh he-directed just-as or-like-follower-of-him

וַיִּלֹּנוּ כָּל־ עֲדַת בְּנֵי־ יִשְׂרָאֵל מִמָּחֳרָת
on-next-day Israel sons-of community-of whole-of and-they-grumbled (6[41])

עַל־ מֹשֶׁה וְעַל־ אַהֲרֹן לֵאמֹר אַתֶּם הֲמִתֶּם אֶת־ עַם יְהוָה׃
Yahweh people-of *** you-killed you to-say Aaron and-against Moses against

וַיְהִי בְּהִקָּהֵל הָעֵדָה עַל־ מֹשֶׁה וְעַל־ אַהֲרֹן
Aaron and-against Moses against the-assembly when-to-gather but-he-was (7[42])

וַיִּפְנוּ אֶל־ אֹהֶל מוֹעֵד וְהִנֵּה כִסָּהוּ הֶעָנָן
the-cloud he-covered-him and-see! Meeting Tent-of toward and-they-turned

וַיֵּרָא כְּבוֹד יְהוָה׃ וַיָּבֹא מֹשֶׁה וְאַהֲרֹן אֶל־
to and-Aaron Moses and-he-went (8[43]) Yahweh glory-of and-he-appeared

פְּנֵי אֹהֶל מוֹעֵד׃ וַיְדַבֵּר יְהוָה אֶל־ מֹשֶׁה לֵּאמֹר׃
to-say Moses to Yahweh and-he-spoke (9[44]) Meeting Tent-of front-of

הֵרֹמּוּ מִתּוֹךְ הָעֵדָה הַזֹּאת וַאֲכַלֶּה אֹתָם
them so-I-can-consume the-this the-assembly from-among get-away! (10[45])

כְּרָגַע וַיִּפְּלוּ עַל־ פְּנֵיהֶם׃ וַיֹּאמֶר מֹשֶׁה אֶל־אַהֲרֹן
Aaron to Moses then-he-said (11[46]) faces-of-them on and-they-fell at-once

קַח אֶת־ הַמַּחְתָּה וְתֶן־ עָלֶיהָ אֵשׁ מֵעַל הַמִּזְבֵּחַ וְשִׂים
and-put! the-altar from-on fire in-her and-put! the-censer *** take!

and scatter the coals some distance away, for the censers are
holy— [38]the censers of the men
who sinned at the cost of their
lives. Hammer the censers
into sheets to overlay the altar,
for they were presented before
the LORD and have become
holy. Let them be a sign to the
Israelites."
[39]So Eleazar the priest collected the bronze censers
brought by those who had
been burned up, and he had
them hammered out to overlay the altar, [40]as the LORD directed him through Moses.
This was to remind the Israelites that no one except a descendant of Aaron should
come to burn incense before
the LORD, or he would become
like Korah and his followers.
[41]The next day the whole Israelite community grumbled
against Moses and Aaron.
"You have killed the LORD's
people," they said.
[42]But when the assembly
gathered in opposition to
Moses and Aaron and turned
toward the Tent of Meeting,
suddenly the cloud covered it
and the glory of the LORD appeared. [43]Then Moses and
Aaron went to the front of the
Tent of Meeting, [44]and the
LORD said to Moses, [45]"Get
away from this assembly so I
can put an end to them at
once." And they fell facedown.
[46]Then Moses said to Aaron,
"Take your censer and put incense in it, along with fire

*See the note on page 417.

קְטֹרֶת וְהוֹלֵךְ מְהֵרָה אֶל־ הָעֵדָה וְכַפֵּר עֲלֵיהֶם כִּי־ יָצָא
he-came-out for for-them and-atone! the-assembly to hurry and-going incense

הַקֶּצֶף מִלִּפְנֵי יְהוָה הֵחֵל הַנָּגֶף׃ (12[47]) וַיִּקַּח אַהֲרֹן
Aaron so-he-did (12[47]) the-plague he-started Yahweh from-before the-wrath

כַּאֲשֶׁר | דִּבֶּר מֹשֶׁה וַיָּרָץ אֶל־ תּוֹךְ† הַקָּהָל וְהִנֵּה
and-see! the-assembly midst-of into and-he-ran Moses he-said just-as

הֵחֵל הַנֶּגֶף בָּעָם וַיִּתֵּן אֶת־ הַקְּטֹרֶת
the-incense *** but-he-offered among-the-people the-plague he-started

וַיְכַפֵּר עַל־ הָעָם׃ (13[48]) וַיַּעֲמֹד בֵּין־ הַמֵּתִים
the-dead-ones between and-he-stood (13[48]) the-people for and-he-atoned

וּבֵין הַחַיִּים וַתֵּעָצַר הַמַּגֵּפָה׃ (14[49]) וַיִּהְיוּ
but-they-were (14[49]) the-plague and-she-stopped the-living-ones and-between

הַמֵּתִים בַּמַּגֵּפָה אַרְבָּעָה עָשָׂר אֶלֶף וּשְׁבַע מֵאוֹת
hundreds and-seven-of thousand ten four from-the-plague the-dead-ones

מִלְּבַד הַמֵּתִים עַל־ דְּבַר־ קֹרַח׃ (15[50]) וַיָּשָׁב
then-he-returned (15[50]) Korah reason-of by the-dead-ones in-addition-to

אַהֲרֹן אֶל־ מֹשֶׁה אֶל־ פֶּתַח אֹהֶל מוֹעֵד וְהַמַּגֵּפָה נֶעֱצָרָה׃
she-stopped for-the-plague Meeting Tent-of entrance-of at Moses to Aaron

(16[1]) וַיְדַבֵּר יְהוָה אֶל־מֹשֶׁה לֵּאמֹר׃ (17[2]) דַּבֵּר | אֶל־ בְּנֵי יִשְׂרָאֵל
Israel sons-of to speak! (17[2]) to-say Moses to Yahweh and-he-spoke (16[1])

וְקַח מֵאִתָּם מַטֶּה מַטֶּה לְבֵית אָב מֵאֵת כָּל־
each-of from father from-house-of staff staff from-them and-get!

נְשִׂיאֵהֶם לְבֵית אֲבֹתָם שְׁנֵים עָשָׂר מַטּוֹת אִישׁ אֶת־
*** each staffs ten two fathers-of-them by-house-of leader-of-them

שְׁמוֹ תִּכְתֹּב עַל־ מַטֵּהוּ׃ (18[3]) וְאֵת שֵׁם אַהֲרֹן תִּכְתֹּב
you-write Aaron name-of and (18[3]) staff-of-him on you-write name-of-him

עַל־ מַטֵּה לֵוִי כִּי מַטֶּה אֶחָד לְרֹאשׁ בֵּית אֲבוֹתָם׃
fathers-of-them house-of for-head-of one staff for Levi staff-of on

(19[4]) וְהִנַּחְתָּם בְּאֹהֶל מוֹעֵד לִפְנֵי הָעֵדוּת אֲשֶׁר
where the-Testimony in-front-of Meeting in-Tent-of then-you-place-them (19[4])

אִוָּעֵד לָכֶם שָׁמָּה׃ (20[5]) וְהָיָה הָאִישׁ אֲשֶׁר אֶבְחַר־ בּוֹ
to-him I-choose whom the-man and-he-will-be (20[5]) at-there with-you I-meet

מַטֵּהוּ יִפְרָח וַהֲשִׁכֹּתִי מֵעָלַי אֶת־ תְּלֻנּוֹת
grumblings-of *** from-with-me and-I-will-rid he-will-sprout staff-of-him

בְּנֵי יִשְׂרָאֵל אֲשֶׁר הֵם מַלִּינִם עֲלֵיכֶם׃ (21[6]) וַיְדַבֵּר מֹשֶׁה
Moses so-he-spoke (21[6]) against-you ones-grumbling they that Israel sons-of

אֶל־ בְּנֵי יִשְׂרָאֵל וַיִּתְּנוּ אֵלָיו | כָּל־ נְשִׂיאֵיהֶם מַטֶּה
staff leaders-of-them each-of to-him and-they-gave Israel sons-of to

from the altar, and hurry to
the assembly to make atonement for them. Wrath has
come out from the LORD; the
plague has started." [47]So
Aaron did as Moses said, and
ran into the midst of the assembly. The plague had already started among the
people, but Aaron offered the
incense and made atonement
for them. [48]He stood between
the living and the dead, and
the plague stopped. [49]But 14,-
700 people died from the
plague, in addition to those
who had died because of
Korah. [50]Then Aaron returned
to Moses at the entrance to the
Tent of Meeting, for the
plague had stopped.

The Budding of Aaron's Staff

17 The LORD said to
Moses, [2]"Speak to the
Israelites and get twelve staffs
from them, one from the leader of each of their ancestral
tribes. Write the name of each
man on his staff. [3]On the staff
of Levi write Aaron's name,
for there must be one staff for
the head of each ancestral
tribe. [4]Place them in the Tent
of Meeting in front of the Testimony, where I meet with
you. [5]The staff belonging to
the man I choose will sprout,
and I will rid myself of this
constant grumbling against
you by the Israelites."
[6]So Moses spoke to the Israelites, and their leaders gave
him twelve staffs, one for the

*See the note on page 417.

†12 Most mss have *sheva* in the *kaph* (תּוֹךְ).

לְנָשִׂיא אֶחָד מַטֶּה לְנָשִׂיא אֶחָד לְבֵית אֲבֹתָם שְׁנֵים עָשָׂר
ten two fathers-of-them of-house-of each for-leader staff each for-leader

מַטּוֹת וּמַטֵּה אַהֲרֹן בְּתוֹךְ מַטּוֹתָם׃ וַיַּנַּח
and-he-placed (22[7]) staffs-of-them in-among Aaron and-staff-of staffs

מֹשֶׁה אֶת־ הַמַּטֹּת לִפְנֵי יְהוָה בְּאֹהֶל הָעֵדֻת׃ וַיְהִי
and-he-was (23[8]) the-Testimony in-Tent-of Yahweh before the-staffs *** Moses

מִמָּחֳרָת וַיָּבֹא מֹשֶׁה אֶל־ אֹהֶל הָעֵדוּת וְהִנֵּה
and-see! the-Testimony Tent-of into Moses that-he-entered on-next-day

פָּרַח מַטֵּה־ אַהֲרֹן לְבֵית לֵוִי וַיֹּצֵא פֶרַח
sprout and-he-put-out Levi from-house-of Aaron staff-of he-sprouted

וַיָּצֵץ צִיץ וַיִּגְמֹל שְׁקֵדִים׃ וַיֹּצֵא
then-he-brought (24[9]) almonds and-he-produced blossom and-he-blossomed

מֹשֶׁה אֶת־ כָּל־ הַמַּטֹּת מִלִּפְנֵי יְהוָה אֶל־ כָּל־ בְּנֵי יִשְׂרָאֵל
Israel sons-of all-of to Yahweh from-presence-of the-staffs all-of *** Moses

וַיִּרְאוּ וַיִּקְחוּ אִישׁ מַטֵּהוּ׃ וַיֹּאמֶר יְהוָה
Yahweh and-he-said (25[10]) staff-of-him each and-they-took and-they-looked

אֶל־ מֹשֶׁה הָשֵׁב אֶת־ מַטֵּה אַהֲרֹן לִפְנֵי הָעֵדוּת לְמִשְׁמֶרֶת
to-keep the-Testimony in-front-of Aaron staff-of *** put-back! Moses to

לְאוֹת לִבְנֵי־ מֶרִי וּתְכַל תְּלוּנֹּתָם
grumblings-of-them and-she-will-put-end rebellion to-sons-of as-sign

מֵעָלַי וְלֹא יָמֻתוּ׃ וַיַּעַשׂ מֹשֶׁה כַּאֲשֶׁר
just-as Moses and-he-did (26[11]) they-will-die so-not from-against-me

צִוָּה יְהוָה אֹתוֹ כֵּן עָשָׂה׃ וַיֹּאמְרוּ בְּנֵי יִשְׂרָאֵל
Israel sons-of and-they-said (27[12]) he-did so him Yahweh he-commanded

אֶל־ מֹשֶׁה לֵאמֹר הֵן גָּוַעְנוּ אָבַדְנוּ כֻּלָּנוּ אָבָדְנוּ׃
we-are-lost all-of-us we-are-lost we-will-die see! to-say Moses to

כֹּל הַקָּרֵב ׀ הַקָּרֵב אֶל־ מִשְׁכַּן יְהוָה יָמוּת
he-will-die Yahweh tabernacle-of to the-one-near the-one-near any-of (28[13])

הַאִם תַּמְנוּ לִגְוֹעַ׃ וַיֹּאמֶר יְהוָה אֶל־ אַהֲרֹן אַתָּה
you Aaron to Yahweh and-he-said (18:1) to-die all-of-us indeed?

וּבָנֶיךָ וּבֵית־ אָבִיךָ אִתָּךְ תִּשְׂאוּ אֶת־
*** you-must-bear with-you father-of-you and-house-of and-sons-of-you

עֲוֺן הַמִּקְדָּשׁ וְאַתָּה וּבָנֶיךָ אִתָּךְ
with-you and-sons-of-you and-you the-sanctuary responsibility-of

תִּשְׂאוּ אֶת־ עֲוֺן כְּהֻנַּתְכֶם׃ וְגַם אֶת־
*** and-also (2) priesthood-of-you responsibility-of *** you-must-bear

אַחֶיךָ מַטֵּה לֵוִי שֵׁבֶט אָבִיךָ הַקְרֵב אִתָּךְ
with-you bring! father-of-you tribe-of Levi tribe-of brothers-of-you

leader of each of their ancestral tribes, and Aaron's staff was among them. [7]Moses placed the staffs before the LORD in the Tent of the Testimony.

[8]The next day Moses entered the Tent of the Testimony and saw that Aaron's staff, which represented the house of Levi, had not only sprouted but had budded, blossomed and produced almonds. [9]Then Moses brought out all the staffs from the LORD's presence to all the Israelites. They looked at them, and each man took his own staff.

[10]The LORD said to Moses, "Put back Aaron's staff in front of the Testimony, to be kept as a sign to the rebellious. This will put an end to their grumbling against me, so that they will not die." [11]Moses did just as the LORD commanded him.

[12]The Israelites said to Moses, "We will die! We are lost, we are all lost! [13]Anyone who even comes near the tabernacle of the LORD will die. Are we all going to die?"

Duties of Priests and Levites

18 The LORD said to Aaron, "You, your sons and your father's family are to bear the responsibility for offenses against the sanctuary, and you and your sons alone are to bear the responsibility for offenses against the priesthood. [2]Bring your fellow Levites from your ancestral

*See the note on page 417.

וְיִלָּווּ עָלֶיךָ וִישָׁרְתוּךָ וְאַתָּה וּבָנֶיךָ
and-sons-of-you both-you and-they-may-assist-you with-you so-they-may-join

אִתָּךְ לִפְנֵי אֹהֶל הָעֵדֻת׃ וְשָׁמְרוּ
they-must-be-responsible (3) the-Testimony Tent-of before with-you

מִשְׁמַרְתְּךָ וּמִשְׁמֶרֶת כָּל־ הָאֹהֶל אַךְ אֶל־ כְּלֵי הַקֹּדֶשׁ
the-sanctuary furnishings-of to only the-Tent all-of and-duty-of duty-of-you

וְאֶל־ הַמִּזְבֵּחַ לֹא יִקְרָבוּ וְלֹא־ יָמֻתוּ גַם־ הֵם גַּם־אַתֶּם׃
you and they both they-die so-not they-must-go-near not the-altar or-to

וְנִלְווּ עָלֶיךָ וְשָׁמְרוּ אֶת־מִשְׁמֶרֶת אֹהֶל
Tent-of care-of *** and-they-must-be-responsible with-you and-they-must-join (4)

מוֹעֵד לְכֹל עֲבֹדַת הָאֹהֶל וְזָר לֹא־ יִקְרַב אֲלֵיכֶם׃
to-you he-may-come-near not but-outsider the-Tent work-of for-all-of Meeting

וּשְׁמַרְתֶּם אֵת מִשְׁמֶרֶת הַקֹּדֶשׁ וְאֵת מִשְׁמֶרֶת הַמִּזְבֵּחַ
the-altar care-of and the-sanctuary care-of *** and-you-are-responsible (5)

וְלֹא־ יִהְיֶה עוֹד קֶצֶף עַל־ בְּנֵי יִשְׂרָאֵל׃ וַאֲנִי הִנֵּה לָקַחְתִּי
I-selected see! now-I (6) Israel sons-of on wrath again he-will-fall so-not

אֶת־ אֲחֵיכֶם הַלְוִיִּם מִתּוֹךְ בְּנֵי יִשְׂרָאֵל לָכֶם מַתָּנָה
gift for-you Israel sons-of from-among the-Levites fellows-of-you ***

נְתֻנִים לַיהוָה לַעֲבֹד אֶת־עֲבֹדַת אֹהֶל מוֹעֵד׃ וְאַתָּה
but-you (7) Meeting Tent-of work-of *** to-do to-Yahweh ones-being-dedicated

וּבָנֶיךָ אִתְּךָ תִּשְׁמְרוּ אֶת־ כְּהֻנַּתְכֶם לְכָל־
with-every-of priesthood-of-you *** you-serve with-you and-sons-of-you

דְּבַר הַמִּזְבֵּחַ וּלְמִבֵּית לַפָּרֹכֶת וַעֲבַדְתֶּם עֲבֹדַת
service-of so-you-serve of-the-curtain and-from-inside the-altar thing-of

מַתָּנָה אֶתֵּן אֶת־ כְּהֻנַּתְכֶם וְהַזָּר הַקָּרֵב יוּמָת׃
he-must-die the-one-near but-the-outsider priesthood-of-you *** I-give gift

וַיְדַבֵּר יְהוָה אֶל־אַהֲרֹן וַאֲנִי הִנֵּה נָתַתִּי לְךָ אֶת־ מִשְׁמֶרֶת
charge-of *** to-you I-put see! now-I Aaron to Yahweh then-he-said (8)

תְּרוּמֹתָי לְכָל־ קָדְשֵׁי בְנֵי־ יִשְׂרָאֵל לְךָ
to-you Israel sons-of holy-things-of from-all-of presentations-of-me

נְתַתִּים לְמָשְׁחָה וּלְבָנֶיךָ לְחָק־ עוֹלָם׃ זֶה־
this (9) regular as-share-of and-to-sons-of-you as-portion I-give-them

יִהְיֶה לְךָ מִקֹּדֶשׁ הַקֳּדָשִׁים מִן־ הָאֵשׁ כָּל־
every-of the-fire from the-holy-things from-most-holy-of for-you he-will-be

קָרְבָּנָם לְכָל־ מִנְחָתָם וּלְכָל־
and-from-every-of grain-offering-of-them from-every-of gift-of-them

חַטָּאתָם וּלְכָל־ אֲשָׁמָם אֲשֶׁר יָשִׁיבוּ
they-bring that guilt-offering-of-them and-from-every-of sin-offering-of-them

tribe to join you and assist you when you and your sons minister before the Tent of the Testimony. [3]They are to be responsible to you and are to perform all the duties of the Tent, but they must not go near the furnishings of the sanctuary or the altar, or both they and you will die. [4]They are to join you and be responsible for the care of the Tent of Meeting—all the work at the Tent—and no one else may come near where you are.

[5]"You are to be responsible for the care of the sanctuary and the altar, so that wrath will not fall on the Israelites again. [6]I myself have selected your fellow Levites from among the Israelites as a gift to you, dedicated to the LORD to do the work at the Tent of Meeting. [7]But only you and your sons may serve as priests in connection with everything at the altar and inside the curtain. I am giving you the service of the priesthood as a gift. Anyone else who comes near the sanctuary must be put to death."

Offerings for Priests and Levites

[8]Then the LORD said to Aaron, "I myself have put you in charge of the offerings presented to me; all the holy offerings the Israelites give me I give to you and your sons as your portion and regular share. [9]You are to have the part of the most holy offerings that is kept from the fire. From all the gifts they bring me as

לִי קֹדֶשׁ קֳדָשִׁים לְךָ הוּא וּלְבָנֶיךָ׃
and-for-sons-of-you he for-you holy-things most-holy-of to-me

בְּקֹדֶשׁ הַקֳּדָשִׁים תֹּאכְלֶנּוּ כָּל־ זָכָר יֹאכַל
he-shall-eat male every-of you-eat-him the-holy-things as-most-holy-of (10)

אֹתוֹ קֹדֶשׁ יִהְיֶה־ לָּךְ׃ וְזֶה־ לְּךָ תְּרוּמַת מַתָּנָם
gift-of-them set-aside-of for-you also-this (11) to-you he-must-be holy him

לְכָל־ תְּנוּפֹת בְּנֵי יִשְׂרָאֵל לְךָ נְתַתִּים
I-give-them to-you Israel sons-of wave-offerings-of from-all-of

וּלְבָנֶיךָ וְלִבְנֹתֶיךָ אִתְּךָ לְחָק־ עוֹלָם
regular as-share-of with-you and-to-daughters-of-you and-to-sons-of-you

כָּל־ טָהוֹר בְּבֵיתְךָ יֹאכַל אֹתוֹ׃ כֹּל חֵלֶב
finest-of all-of (12) him he-may-eat in-household-of-you clean everyone-of

יִצְהָר וְכָל־ חֵלֶב תִּירוֹשׁ וְדָגָן רֵאשִׁיתָם אֲשֶׁר־
that firstfruit-of-them and-grain new-wine finest-of and-all-of olive-oil

יִתְּנוּ לַיהוָה לְךָ נְתַתִּים׃ בִּכּוּרֵי כָּל־ אֲשֶׁר
that all firstfruits-of (13) I-give-them to-you to-Yahweh they-give

בְּאַרְצָם אֲשֶׁר־ יָבִיאוּ לַיהוָה לְךָ יִהְיֶה כָּל־
everyone-of he-will-be for-you to-Yahweh they-bring that in-land-of-them

טָהוֹר בְּבֵיתְךָ יֹאכְלֶנּוּ׃ כָּל־ חֵרֶם בְּיִשְׂרָאֵל
in-Israel devoted every-of (14) he-may-eat-him in-household-of-you clean

לְךָ יִהְיֶה׃ כָּל־ פֶּטֶר רֶחֶם לְכָל־ בָּשָׂר אֲשֶׁר־
that flesh from-all-of womb first-of every-of (15) he-will-be for-you

יַקְרִיבוּ לַיהוָה בָּאָדָם וּבַבְּהֵמָה יִהְיֶה־ לָּךְ אַךְ ׀
but for-you he-is and-also-the-animal both-the-man to-Yahweh they-offer

פָּדֹה תִפְדֶּה אֵת בְּכוֹר הָאָדָם וְאֵת בְּכוֹר־ הַבְּהֵמָה
the-animal firstborn-of and the-man firstborn-of *** you-must-redeem to-redeem

הַטְּמֵאָה תִּפְדֶּה׃ וּפְדוּיָו מִבֶּן־
when-son-of and-redemption-price-of-him (16) you-must-redeem the-unclean

חֹדֶשׁ תִּפְדֶּה בְּעֶרְכְּךָ כֶּסֶף חֲמֵשֶׁת שְׁקָלִים בְּשֶׁקֶל
by-shekel-of shekels five-of silver at-price-of-you you-must-redeem month

הַקֹּדֶשׁ עֶשְׂרִים גֵּרָה הוּא׃ אַךְ בְּכוֹר־ שׁוֹר אוֹ־ בְכוֹר כֶּשֶׂב
sheep firstborn-of or ox firstborn-of but (17) he gerah twenty the-sanctuary

אוֹ־ בְכוֹר עֵז לֹא תִפְדֶּה קֹדֶשׁ הֵם אֶת־ דָּמָם
blood-of-them *** they holy you-must-redeem not goat firstborn-of or

תִּזְרֹק עַל־ הַמִּזְבֵּחַ וְאֶת־ חֶלְבָּם תַּקְטִיר אִשֶּׁה לְרֵיחַ
as-aroma fire-offering you-burn fat-of-them and the-altar on you-sprinkle

נִיחֹחַ לַיהוָה׃ וּבְשָׂרָם יִהְיֶה־ לָּךְ כַּחֲזֵה
as-breast-of for-you he-is and-meat-of-them (18) to-Yahweh pleasant

most holy offerings, whether grain or sin or guilt offerings, that part belongs to you and your sons. [10]Eat it as something most holy; every male shall eat it. You must regard it as holy.

[11]"This also is yours: whatever is set aside from the gifts of all the wave offerings of the Israelites. I give this to you and your sons and daughters as your regular share. Everyone in your household who is ceremonially clean may eat it.

[12]"I give you all the finest olive oil and all the finest new wine and grain they give the LORD as the firstfruits of their harvest. [13]All the land's firstfruits that they bring to the LORD will be yours. Everyone in your household who is ceremonially clean may eat it.

[14]"Everything in Israel that is devoted[o] to the LORD is yours. [15]The first offspring of every womb, both man and animal, that is offered to the LORD is yours. But you must redeem every firstborn son and every firstborn male of unclean animals. [16]When they are a month old, you must redeem them at the redemption price set at five shekels[p] of silver, according to the sanctuary shekel, which weighs twenty gerahs.

[17]"But you must not redeem the firstborn of an ox, a sheep or a goat; they are holy. Sprinkle their blood on the altar and burn their fat as an offering made by fire, an aroma pleasing to the LORD. [18]Their meat is to be yours, just as the breast

[o]14 The Hebrew term refers to the irrevocable giving over of things or persons to the LORD, often by totally destroying them.

[p]16 That is, about 2 ounces (about 55 grams)

הַתְּנוּפָה וּכְשׁוֹק הַיָּמִין לְךָ יִהְיֶה׃ כֹּל
all-of (19) he-is for-you the-right and-as-thigh-of the-wave-offering

תְּרוּמֹת הַקֳּדָשִׁים אֲשֶׁר יָרִימוּ בְנֵי־יִשְׂרָאֵל
Israel sons-of they-present that the-holy-ones offerings-set-aside-of

לַיהוָה נָתַתִּי לְךָ וּלְבָנֶיךָ וְלִבְנֹתֶיךָ אִתְּךָ
with-you and-to-daughters-of-you and-to-sons-of-you to-you I-give to-Yahweh

לְחָק־עוֹלָם בְּרִית מֶלַח עוֹלָם הִוא לִפְנֵי יְהוָה לְךָ
for-you Yahweh before she everlasting salt covenant-of regular as-share-of

וּלְזַרְעֲךָ אִתָּךְ׃ וַיֹּאמֶר יְהוָה אֶל־אַהֲרֹן
Aaron to Yahweh and-he-said (20) with-you and-for-offspring-of-you

בְּאַרְצָם לֹא תִנְחָל וְחֵלֶק לֹא־יִהְיֶה לְךָ
for-you he-will-be not and-share you-will-inherit not in-land-of-them

בְּתוֹכָם אֲנִי חֶלְקְךָ וְנַחֲלָתְךָ בְּתוֹךְ בְּנֵי יִשְׂרָאֵל׃
Israel sons-of among and-inheritance-of-you portion-of-you I among-them

וְלִבְנֵי לֵוִי הִנֵּה נָתַתִּי כָּל־מַעֲשֵׂר בְּיִשְׂרָאֵל לְנַחֲלָה
as-inheritance in-Israel tithe all-of I-give see! Levi and-to-sons-of (21)

חֵלֶף עֲבֹדָתָם אֲשֶׁר־הֵם עֹבְדִים אֶת־עֲבֹדַת אֹהֶל מוֹעֵד׃
Meeting Tent-of service-of *** ones-doing they that work-of-them return-of

וְלֹא־יִקְרְבוּ עוֹד בְּנֵי יִשְׂרָאֵל אֶל־אֹהֶל מוֹעֵד
Meeting Tent-of to Israel sons-of ever they-must-come-near and-not (22)

לָשֵׂאת חֵטְא לָמוּת׃ וְעָבַד הַלֵּוִי הוּא אֶת־עֲבֹדַת אֹהֶל
Tent-of work-of *** he the-Levite now-he-must-do (23) to-die sin to-bear

מוֹעֵד וְהֵם יִשְׂאוּ עֲוֹנָם חֻקַּת עוֹלָם
lasting ordinance-of offense-of-them they-will-bear and-they Meeting

לְדֹרֹתֵיכֶם וּבְתוֹךְ בְּנֵי יִשְׂרָאֵל לֹא יִנְחֲלוּ
they-will-receive not Israel sons-of but-among for-generations-of-you

נַחֲלָה׃ כִּי אֶת־מַעְשַׂר בְּנֵי־יִשְׂרָאֵל אֲשֶׁר יָרִימוּ
they-present that Israel sons-of tithe-of *** instead (24) inheritance

לַיהוָה תְּרוּמָה נָתַתִּי לַלְוִיִּם לְנַחֲלָה עַל־כֵּן אָמַרְתִּי
I-said this for as-inheritance to-the-Levites I-give offering to-Yahweh

לָהֶם בְּתוֹךְ בְּנֵי יִשְׂרָאֵל לֹא יִנְחֲלוּ נַחֲלָה׃
inheritance they-will-receive not Israel sons-of among about-them

וַיְדַבֵּר יְהוָה אֶל־מֹשֶׁה לֵּאמֹר׃ וְאֶל־הַלְוִיִּם תְּדַבֵּר
you-speak the-Levites now-to (26) to-say Moses to Yahweh and-he-spoke (25)

וְאָמַרְתָּ אֲלֵהֶם כִּי־תִקְחוּ מֵאֵת בְּנֵי־יִשְׂרָאֵל אֶת־הַמַּעֲשֵׂר אֲשֶׁר
that the-tithe *** Israel sons-of from you-receive when to-them and-you-say

נָתַתִּי לָכֶם מֵאִתָּם בְּנַחֲלַתְכֶם וַהֲרֵמֹתֶם מִמֶּנּוּ
from-him then-you-must-present as-inheritance-of-you from-them to-you I-give

of the wave offering and the
right thigh are yours. [19]What-
ever is set aside from the holy
offerings the Israelites present
to the LORD I give to you and
your sons and daughters as
your regular share. It is an
everlasting covenant of salt
before the LORD for both you
and your offspring."
[20]The LORD said to Aaron,
"You will have no inheritance
in their land, nor will you
have any share among them; I
am your share and your inheritance among the Israelites.
[21]"I give to the Levites all the
tithes in Israel as their inheritance in return for the work
they do while serving at the
Tent of Meeting. [22]From now
on the Israelites must not go
near the Tent of Meeting, or
they will bear the conse-
quences of their sin and will
die. [23]It is the Levites who are
to do the work at the Tent of
Meeting and bear the responsibility for offenses against it.
This is a lasting ordinance for
the generations to come. They
will receive no inheritance
among the Israelites. [24]In-
stead, I give to the Levites as
their inheritance the tithes
that the Israelites present as
an offering to the LORD. That is
why I said concerning them:
'They will have no inheritance
among the Israelites.' "
[25]The LORD said to Moses,
[26]"Speak to the Levites and say
to them: 'When you receive
from the Israelites the tithe I
give you as your inheritance,
you must present a tenth of

תְּרוּמַת יְהוָה מַעֲשֵׂר מִן־הַמַּעֲשֵׂר׃ וְנֶחְשַׁב לָכֶם
to-you and-he-will-be-reckoned (27) the-tithe from tenth Yahweh offering-of

תְּרוּמַתְכֶם כַּדָּגָן מִן־הַגֹּרֶן וְכַמְלֵאָה
or-as-the-fullness the-threshing-floor from as-the-grain offering-of-you

מִן־הַיָּקֶב׃ כֵּן תָּרִימוּ גַם־אַתֶּם תְּרוּמַת יְהוָה
Yahweh offering-of you also you-will-present thus (28) the-winepress from

מִכֹּל מַעְשְׂרֹתֵיכֶם אֲשֶׁר תִּקְחוּ מֵאֵת בְּנֵי יִשְׂרָאֵל וּנְתַתֶּם
and-you-must-give Israel sons-of from you-receive that tithes-of-you from-all-of

מִמֶּנּוּ אֶת־תְּרוּמַת יְהוָה לְאַהֲרֹן הַכֹּהֵן׃ מִכֹּל
from-all-of (29) the-priest to-Aaron Yahweh portion-of *** from-him

מַתְּנֹתֵיכֶם תָּרִימוּ אֵת כָּל־תְּרוּמַת יְהוָה מִכָּל־
from-all-of Yahweh portion-of every-of *** you-must-present gifts-of-you

חֶלְבּוֹ אֶת־מִקְדְּשׁוֹ מִמֶּנּוּ׃ וְאָמַרְתָּ אֲלֵהֶם
to-them and-you-say (30) from-him holy-part-of-him *** best-of-him

בַּהֲרִימְכֶם אֶת־חֶלְבּוֹ מִמֶּנּוּ וְנֶחְשַׁב
then-he-will-be-reckoned from-him best-of-him *** when-to-present-you

לַלְוִיִּם כִּתְבוּאַת גֹּרֶן וְכִתְבוּאַת יָקֶב׃
winepress and-as-product-of threshing-floor as-product-of to-the-Levites

וַאֲכַלְתֶּם אֹתוֹ בְּכָל־מָקוֹם אַתֶּם וּבֵיתְכֶם כִּי־שָׂכָר
wage for and-household-of-you you place in-any-of him and-you-may-eat (31)

הוּא לָכֶם חֵלֶף עֲבֹדַתְכֶם בְּאֹהֶל מוֹעֵד׃ וְלֹא־תִשְׂאוּ
you-will-bear and-not (32) Meeting at-Tent-of work-of-you return-of for-you he

עָלָיו חֵטְא בַּהֲרִימְכֶם אֶת־חֶלְבּוֹ מִמֶּנּוּ וְאֶת־
and from-him best-of-him *** when-to-present-you guilt because-of-him

קָדְשֵׁי בְנֵי־יִשְׂרָאֵל לֹא תְחַלְּלוּ וְלֹא תָמוּתוּ׃
you-will-die and-not you-will-defile not Israel sons-of holy-things-of

וַיְדַבֵּר יְהוָה אֶל־מֹשֶׁה וְאֶל־אַהֲרֹן לֵאמֹר׃ זֹאת
this (2) to-say Aaron and-to Moses to Yahweh and-he-spoke (19:1)

חֻקַּת הַתּוֹרָה אֲשֶׁר־צִוָּה יְהוָה לֵאמֹר דַּבֵּר ׀ אֶל־בְּנֵי
sons-of to tell! to-say Yahweh he-commanded that the-law requirement-of

יִשְׂרָאֵל וְיִקְחוּ אֵלֶיךָ פָרָה אֲדֻמָּה תְּמִימָה אֲשֶׁר אֵין־בָּהּ
on-her he-is-not that without-defect red heifer to-you so-they-bring Israel

מוּם אֲשֶׁר לֹא־עָלָה עָלֶיהָ עֹל׃ וּנְתַתֶּם אֹתָהּ אֶל־אֶלְעָזָר
Eleazar to her then-you-give (3) yoke on-her he-was-on never that blemish

הַכֹּהֵן וְהוֹצִיא אֹתָהּ אֶל־מִחוּץ לַמַּחֲנֶה וְשָׁחַט
and-he-will-slaughter of-the-camp outside to her and-he-will-take the-priest

אֹתָהּ לְפָנָיו׃ וְלָקַח אֶלְעָזָר הַכֹּהֵן
the-priest Eleazar then-he-must-take (4) in-presence-of-him her

that tithe as the LORD's
offering. 27Your offering will
be reckoned to you as grain
from the threshing floor or
juice from the winepress. 28In
this way you also will present
an offering to the LORD from
all the tithes you receive from
the Israelites. From these
tithes you must give the
LORD's portion to Aaron the
priest. 29You must present as
the LORD's portion the best
and holiest part of everything
given to you.'

30"Say to the Levites: 'When
you present the best part, it
will be reckoned to you as the
product of the threshing floor
or the winepress. 31You and
your households may eat the
rest of it anywhere, for it is
your wages for your work at
the Tent of Meeting. 32By
presenting the best part of it
you will not be guilty in this
matter; then you will not
defile the holy offerings of the
Israelites, and you will not
die.' "

The Water of Cleansing

19 The LORD said to Moses
and Aaron: 2"This is a
requirement of the law that
the LORD has commanded: Tell
the Israelites to bring you a
red heifer without defect or
blemish and that has never
been under a yoke. 3Give it to
Eleazar the priest; it is to be
taken outside the camp and
slaughtered in his presence.
4Then Eleazar the priest is to

מִדָּמָהּ בְּאֶצְבָּעוֹ וְהִזָּה אֶל־ נֹכַח פְּנֵי
from-blood-of-her on-finger-of-him and-he-must-sprinkle toward front face-of

אֹהֶל־ מוֹעֵד מִדָּמָהּ שֶׁבַע פְּעָמִים׃ (5) וְשָׂרַף אֶת־
Tent-of Meeting from-blood-of-her seven times (5) and-he-must-burn ***

הַפָּרָה לְעֵינָיו אֶת־ עֹרָהּ וְאֶת־ בְּשָׂרָהּ וְאֶת־
the-heifer before-eyes-of-him *** hide-of-her and flesh-of-her and

דָּמָהּ עַל־ פִּרְשָׁהּ יִשְׂרֹף׃ (6) וְלָקַח הַכֹּהֵן
blood-of-her with offal-of-her he-must-burn (6) and-he-must-take the-priest

עֵץ אֶרֶז וְאֵזוֹב וּשְׁנִי תוֹלַעַת וְהִשְׁלִיךְ אֶל־ תּוֹךְ
wood-of cedar and-hyssop and-wool-of scarlet and-he-must-throw onto midst-of

שְׂרֵפַת הַפָּרָה׃ (7) וְכִבֶּס בְּגָדָיו הַכֹּהֵן
burning-of the-heifer (7) then-he-must-wash clothes-of-him the-priest

וְרָחַץ בְּשָׂרוֹ בַּמַּיִם וְאַחַר יָבוֹא אֶל־
and-he-must-bathe body-of-him with-the-waters then-after he-may-come into

הַמַּחֲנֶה וְטָמֵא הַכֹּהֵן עַד־ הָעָרֶב׃
the-camp but-he-will-be-unclean the-priest till the-evening

(8) וְהַשֹּׂרֵף אֹתָהּ יְכַבֵּס בְּגָדָיו בַּמַּיִם
(8) and-the-one-burning her he-must-wash clothes-of-him with-the-waters

וְרָחַץ בְּשָׂרוֹ בַּמָּיִם וְטָמֵא עַד־
and-he-must-bathe body-of-him with-the-waters and-he-will-be-unclean till

הָעָרֶב׃ (9) וְאָסַף ׀ אִישׁ טָהוֹר אֵת אֵפֶר הַפָּרָה
the-evening (9) and-he-shall-gather man clean *** ash-of the-heifer

וְהִנִּיחַ מִחוּץ לַמַּחֲנֶה בְּמָקוֹם טָהוֹר וְהָיְתָה
and-he-shall-put outside of-the-camp in-place clean and-she-shall-be

לַעֲדַת בְּנֵי־ יִשְׂרָאֵל לְמִשְׁמֶרֶת לְמֵי נִדָּה
for-community-of sons-of Israel for-use in-waters-of cleansing

חַטָּאת הִוא׃ (10) וְכִבֶּס הָאֹסֵף אֶת־ אֵפֶר
sin-purification she (10) and-he-must-wash the-one-gathering *** ash-of

הַפָּרָה אֶת־ בְּגָדָיו וְטָמֵא עַד־ הָעָרֶב
the-heifer *** clothes-of-him and-he-will-be-unclean till the-evening

וְהָיְתָה לִבְנֵי יִשְׂרָאֵל וְלַגֵּר הַגָּר בְּתוֹכָם
and-she-will-be for-sons-of Israel and-for-the-alien the-one-living among-them

לְחֻקַּת עוֹלָם׃ (11) הַנֹּגֵעַ בְּמֵת לְכָל־
as-ordinance-of lasting (11) and-the-one-touching on-dead-body on-any-of

נֶפֶשׁ אָדָם וְטָמֵא שִׁבְעַת יָמִים׃ (12) הוּא יִתְחַטָּא־
body-of man then-he-will-be-unclean seven-of days (12) he he-must-purify

בוֹ בַּיּוֹם הַשְּׁלִישִׁי וּבַיּוֹם הַשְּׁבִיעִי יִטְהָר
for-himself on-the-day the-third and-on-the-day the-seventh he-will-be-clean

take some of its blood on his finger and sprinkle it seven times toward the front of the Tent of Meeting. [5]While he watches, the heifer is to be burned—its hide, flesh, blood and offal. [6]The priest is to take some cedar wood, hyssop and scarlet wool and throw them onto the burning heifer. [7]After that, the priest must wash his clothes and bathe himself with water. He may then come into the camp, but he will be ceremonially unclean till evening. [8]The man who burns it must also wash his clothes and bathe with water, and he too will be unclean till evening.

[9]"A man who is clean shall gather up the ashes of the heifer and put them in a ceremonially clean place outside the camp. They shall be kept by the Israelite community for use in the water of cleansing; it is for purification from sin. [10]The man who gathers up the ashes of the heifer must also wash his clothes, and he too will be unclean till evening. This will be a lasting ordinance both for the Israelites and for the aliens living among them.

[11]"Whoever touches the dead body of anyone will be unclean for seven days. [12]He must purify himself with the water on the third day and on the seventh day; then he will

וְאִם־ לֹא יִתְחַטָּא בַּיּוֹם הַשְּׁלִישִׁי וּבַיּוֹם הַשְּׁבִיעִי
the-seventh and-on-the-day the-third on-the-day he-purifies-self not but-if

לֹא יִטְהָר׃ כָּל־ הַנֹּגֵעַ בְּמֵת בְּנֶפֶשׁ
on-body-of on-dead-body the-one-touching every-of (13) he-will-be-clean not

הָאָדָם אֲשֶׁר־ יָמוּת וְלֹא יִתְחַטָּא אֶת־ מִשְׁכַּן יְהוָה
Yahweh tabernacle-of *** he-purifies-self and-not he-died that the-man

טִמֵּא וְנִכְרְתָה הַנֶּפֶשׁ הַהִוא מִיִּשְׂרָאֵל כִּי מֵי
waters-of for from-Israel the-that the-person and-she-must-be-cut he-defiles

נִדָּה לֹא־ זֹרַק עָלָיו טָמֵא יִהְיֶה עוֹד טֻמְאָתוֹ
uncleanness-of-him still he-is unclean on-him he-was-sprinkled not cleansing

בוֹ׃ זֹאת הַתּוֹרָה אָדָם כִּי־ יָמוּת בְּאֹהֶל כָּל־ הַבָּא
the-one-entering any-of in-tent he-dies when person the-law this (14) on-him

אֶל־ הָאֹהֶל וְכָל־ אֲשֶׁר בָּאֹהֶל יִטְמָא שִׁבְעַת יָמִים׃
days seven-of he-will-be-unclean in-the-tent who and-anyone the-tent into

וְכֹל כְּלִי פָתוּחַ אֲשֶׁר אֵין־ צָמִיד פָּתִיל
one-fastened lid he-is-not that being-open container-of and-every-of (15)

עָלָיו טָמֵא הוּא׃ וְכֹל אֲשֶׁר־ יִגַּע עַל־ פְּנֵי הַשָּׂדֶה
the-field surface-of in he-touches who and-anyone (16) he unclean on-him

בַּחֲלַל־ חֶרֶב אוֹ בְמֵת אוֹ־ בְעֶצֶם אָדָם אוֹ בְקָבֶר
on-grave or human on-bone-of or on-dead-body or sword on-one-killed-of

יִטְמָא שִׁבְעַת יָמִים׃ וְלָקְחוּ לַטָּמֵא
for-the-unclean-one then-they-must-take (17) days seven-of he-will-be-unclean

מֵעֲפַר שְׂרֵפַת הַחַטָּאת וְנָתַן עָלָיו
on-him and-he-must-pour the-purification-offering burnt-of from-ash-of

מַיִם חַיִּים אֶל־ כֶּלִי׃ וְלָקַח אֵזוֹב וְטָבַל
and-he-must-dip hyssop then-he-must-take (18) jar into fresh-ones waters

בַּמַּיִם אִישׁ טָהוֹר וְהִזָּה עַל־ הָאֹהֶל וְעַל־ כָּל־
all-of and-on the-tent on and-he-must-sprinkle clean man in-the-waters

הַכֵּלִים וְעַל־ הַנְּפָשׁוֹת אֲשֶׁר הָיוּ־ שָׁם וְעַל־
and-on there they-were who the-people and-on the-furnishings

הַנֹּגֵעַ בַּעֶצֶם אוֹ בֶחָלָל אוֹ בַמֵּת אוֹ
or on-the-dead-body or on-the-one-killed or on-the-bone the-one-touching

בַקָּבֶר׃ וְהִזָּה הַטָּהֹר עַל־ הַטָּמֵא
the-unclean-one on the-clean-one and-he-must-sprinkle (19) on-the-grave

בַּיּוֹם הַשְּׁלִישִׁי וּבַיּוֹם הַשְּׁבִיעִי וְחִטְּאוֹ
and-he-must-purify-him the-seventh and-on-the-day the-third on-the-day

בַּיּוֹם הַשְּׁבִיעִי וְכִבֶּס בְּגָדָיו וְרָחַץ
and-he-must-bathe clothes-of-him and-he-must-wash the-seventh on-the-day

be clean. But if he does not
purify himself on the third
and seventh days, he will not
be clean. 13Whoever touches
the dead body of anyone and
fails to purify himself defiles
the LORD's tabernacle. That
person must be cut off from Israel. Because the water of
cleansing has not been sprinkled on him, he is unclean; his
uncleanness remains on him.
14"This is the law that applies when a person dies in a
tent: Anyone who enters the
tent and anyone who is in it
will be unclean for seven days,
15and every open container
without a lid fastened on it
will be unclean.
16"Anyone out in the open
who touches someone who
has been killed with a sword
or someone who has died a
natural death, or anyone who
touches a human bone or a
grave, will be unclean for sev-
en days.
17"For the unclean person,
put some ashes from the
burned purification offering
into a jar and pour fresh water
over them. 18Then a man who
is ceremonially clean is to take
some hyssop, dip it in the
water and sprinkle the tent
and all the furnishings and
the people who were there. He
must also sprinkle anyone
who has touched a human
bone or a grave or someone
who has been killed or someone who has died a natural
death. 19The man who is clean
is to sprinkle the unclean person on the third and seventh
days, and on the seventh day
he is to purify him. The person
being cleansed must wash his
clothes and bathe with water,

בַּמַּיִם וְטָהֵר בָּעָרֶב׃ וְאִישׁ אֲשֶׁר־
who but-person (20) in-the-evening and-he-will-be-clean with-the-waters

יִטְמָא וְלֹא יִתְחַטָּא וְנִכְרְתָה הַנֶּפֶשׁ
the-person then-she-must-be-cut-off he-purifies-self and-not he-is-unclean

הַהִוא מִתּוֹךְ הַקָּהָל כִּי אֶת־ מִקְדַּשׁ יְהוָה טִמֵּא
he-defiled Yahweh tabernacle-of *** for the-community from-among the-that

מֵי נִדָּה לֹא־ זֹרַק עָלָיו טָמֵא הוּא׃ וְהָיְתָה
now-she-is (21) he unclean on-him he-was-sprinkled not cleansing waters-of

לָהֶם לְחֻקַּת עוֹלָם וּמַזֵּה מֵי־
waters-of and-the-one-sprinkling lasting as-ordinance-of for-them

הַנִּדָּה יְכַבֵּס בְּגָדָיו וְהַנֹּגֵעַ בְּמֵי
on-waters-of and-the-one-touching clothes-of-him he-must-wash the-cleansing

הַנִּדָּה יִטְמָא עַד־ הָעָרֶב׃ וְכֹל אֲשֶׁר־
that and-anything (22) the-evening till he-will-be-unclean the-cleansing

יִגַּע־ בּוֹ הַטָּמֵא יִטְמָא וְהַנֶּפֶשׁ
and-the-person he-becomes-unclean the-unclean-one on-him he-touches

הַנֹּגַעַת תִּטְמָא עַד־ הָעָרֶב׃ וַיָּבֹאוּ
now-they-arrived (20:1) the-evening till she-becomes-unclean the-one-touching

בְנֵי־ יִשְׂרָאֵל כָּל־ הָעֵדָה מִדְבַּר־ צִן בַּחֹדֶשׁ הָרִאשׁוֹן
the-first in-the-month Zin Desert-of the-community whole-of Israel sons-of

וַיֵּשֶׁב הָעָם בְּקָדֵשׁ וַתָּמָת שָׁם מִרְיָם
Miriam there and-she-died at-Kadesh the-people and-he-stayed

וַתִּקָּבֵר שָׁם׃ וְלֹא־ הָיָה מַיִם לָעֵדָה
for-the-community waters he-was now-not (2) there and-she-was-buried

וַיִּקָּהֲלוּ עַל־ מֹשֶׁה וְעַל־ אַהֲרֹן׃ וַיָּרֶב
and-he-quarreled (3) Aaron and-against Moses against and-they-gathered

הָעָם עִם־ מֹשֶׁה וַיֹּאמְרוּ לֵאמֹר וְלוּ גָוַעְנוּ בִּגְוַע
when-to-die we-died if-only! to-say and-they-said Moses with the-people

אַחֵינוּ לִפְנֵי יְהוָה׃ וְלָמָה הֲבֵאתֶם אֶת־ קְהַל יְהוָה
Yahweh community-of *** you-brought now-why? (4) Yahweh before brothers-of-us

אֶל־ הַמִּדְבָּר הַזֶּה לָמוּת שָׁם אֲנַחְנוּ וּבְעִירֵנוּ׃ וְלָמָה
and-why? (5) and-livestock-of-us we here to-die the-this the-desert into

הֶעֱלִיתֻנוּ מִמִּצְרַיִם לְהָבִיא אֹתָנוּ אֶל־ הַמָּקוֹם הָרָע הַזֶּה
the-this the-terrible the-place to us to-bring from-Egypt you-brought-us

לֹא ׀ מְקוֹם זֶרַע וּתְאֵנָה וְגֶפֶן וְרִמּוֹן וּמַיִם אַיִן
there-is-no and-waters or-pomegranate or-grapevine or-fig grain place-of no

לִשְׁתּוֹת׃ וַיָּבֹא מֹשֶׁה וְאַהֲרֹן מִפְּנֵי הַקָּהָל אֶל־
to the-assembly from-before and-Aaron Moses so-he-went (6) to-drink

and that evening he will be clean. [20]But if a person who is unclean does not purify himself, he must be cut off from the community, because he has defiled the sanctuary of the LORD. The water of cleansing has not been sprinkled on him, and he is unclean. [21]This is a lasting ordinance for them.

"The man who sprinkles the water of cleansing must also wash his clothes, and anyone who touches the water of cleansing will be unclean till evening. [22]Anything that an unclean person touches becomes unclean, and anyone who touches it becomes unclean till evening."

Water From the Rock

20 In the first month the whole Israelite community arrived at the Desert of Zin, and they stayed at Kadesh. There Miriam died and was buried.

[2]Now there was no water for the community, and the people gathered in opposition to Moses and Aaron. [3]They quarreled with Moses and said, "If only we had died when our brothers fell dead before the LORD! [4]Why did you bring the LORD's community into this desert, that we and our livestock should die here? [5]Why did you bring us up out of Egypt to this terrible place? It has no grain or figs, grapevines or pomegranates. And there is no water to drink!"

[6]Moses and Aaron went

פֶּתַח אֹהֶל מוֹעֵד וַיִּפְּלוּ עַל־ פְּנֵיהֶם וַיֵּרָא
and-he-appeared faces-of-them on and-they-fell Meeting Tent-of entrance-of

כְבוֹד־ יְהוָה אֲלֵיהֶם׃ וַיְדַבֵּר יְהוָה אֶל־מֹשֶׁה לֵּאמֹר׃ קַח
take! (8) to-say Moses to Yahweh and-he-spoke (7) to-them Yahweh glory-of

אֶת־ הַמַּטֶּה וְהַקְהֵל אֶת־ הָעֵדָה אַתָּה וְאַהֲרֹן אָחִיךָ
brother-of-you and-Aaron you the-assembly *** and-gather! the-staff ***

וְדִבַּרְתֶּם אֶל־ הַסֶּלַע לְעֵינֵיהֶם וְנָתַן
and-he-will-pour-out before-eyes-of-them the-rock to and-you-speak

מֵימָיו וְהוֹצֵאתָ לָהֶם מַיִם מִן־ הַסֶּלַע
the-rock from waters for-them so-you-will-bring waters-of-him

וְהִשְׁקִיתָ אֶת־ הָעֵדָה וְאֶת־ בְּעִירָם׃ וַיִּקַּח
so-he-took (9) livestock-of-them and the-community *** and-you-will-give-drink

מֹשֶׁה אֶת־ הַמַּטֶּה מִלִּפְנֵי יְהוָה כַּאֲשֶׁר צִוָּהוּ׃
he-commanded-him just-as Yahweh from-presence-of the-staff *** Moses

וַיַּקְהִלוּ מֹשֶׁה וְאַהֲרֹן אֶת־ הַקָּהָל אֶל־ פְּנֵי הַסָּלַע
the-rock front-of in the-assembly *** and-Aaron Moses and-they-gathered (10)

וַיֹּאמֶר לָהֶם שִׁמְעוּ־ נָא הַמֹּרִים הֲמִן־ הַסֶּלַע הַזֶּה
the-this the-rock from? the-ones-rebelling now! listen! to-them and-he-said

נוֹצִיא לָכֶם מָיִם׃ וַיָּרֶם מֹשֶׁה אֶת־ יָדוֹ
arm-of-him *** Moses then-he-raised (11) waters for-you must-we-bring

וַיַּךְ אֶת־ הַסֶּלַע בְּמַטֵּהוּ פַּעֲמָיִם וַיֵּצְאוּ מַיִם
waters and-they-gushed-out twice with-staff-of-him the-rock *** and-he-struck

רַבִּים וַתֵּשְׁתְּ הָעֵדָה וּבְעִירָם׃ וַיֹּאמֶר
but-he-said (12) and-livestock-of-them the-community and-she-drank many

יְהוָה אֶל־מֹשֶׁה וְאֶל־אַהֲרֹן יַעַן לֹא־ הֶאֱמַנְתֶּם בִּי לְהַקְדִּישֵׁנִי
to-honor-as-holy-me in-me you-trusted not because Aaron and-to Moses to Yahweh

לְעֵינֵי בְּנֵי יִשְׂרָאֵל לָכֵן לֹא תָבִיאוּ אֶת־ הַקָּהָל
the-assembly *** you-will-bring not therefore Israel sons-of before-eyes-of

הַזֶּה אֶל־ הָאָרֶץ אֲשֶׁר־ נָתַתִּי לָהֶם׃ הֵמָּה מֵי מְרִיבָה
Meribah waters-of these (13) to-them I-give that the-land into the-this

אֲשֶׁר־ רָבוּ בְנֵי־ יִשְׂרָאֵל אֶת־ יְהוָה וַיִּקָּדֵשׁ
and-he-showed-himself-holy Yahweh *** Israel sons-of they-quarreled where

בָּם׃ וַיִּשְׁלַח מֹשֶׁה מַלְאָכִים מִקָּדֵשׁ אֶל־ מֶלֶךְ אֱדוֹם
Edom king-of to from-Kadesh messengers Moses and-he-sent (14) among-them

כֹּה אָמַר אָחִיךָ יִשְׂרָאֵל אַתָּה יָדַעְתָּ אֵת כָּל־ הַתְּלָאָה אֲשֶׁר
that the-hardship all-of *** you-know you Israel brother-of-you he-says this

מְצָאָתְנוּ׃ וַיֵּרְדוּ אֲבֹתֵינוּ מִצְרַיְמָה וַנֵּשֶׁב
and-we-lived into-Egypt fathers-of-us they-went-down (15) she-came-on-us

from the assembly to the entrance to the Tent of Meeting and fell facedown, and the glory of the LORD appeared to them.
[7]The LORD said to Moses,
[8]"Take the staff, and you and your brother Aaron gather the assembly together. Speak to that rock before their eyes and it will pour out its water. You will bring water out of the rock for the community so they and their livestock can drink."

[9]So Moses took the staff from the LORD's presence, just as he commanded him.
[10]He and Aaron gathered the assembly together in front of the rock and Moses said to them, "Listen, you rebels, must we bring you water out of this rock?"
[11]Then Moses raised his arm and struck the rock twice with his staff. Water gushed out, and the community and their livestock drank.

[12]But the LORD said to Moses and Aaron, "Because you did not trust in me enough to honor me as holy in the sight of the Israelites, you will not bring this community into the land I give them."

[13]These were the waters of Meribah,[q] where the Israelites quarreled with the LORD and where he showed himself holy among them.

Edom Denies Israel Passage

[14]Moses sent messengers from Kadesh to the king of Edom, saying:

"This is what your brother Israel says: You know about all the hardships that have come upon us.
[15]Our forefathers went down into Egypt, and we lived there

[q]13 *Meribah* means *quarreling*.

בְמִצְרַיִם יָמִים רַבִּים וַיָּרֵעוּ לָנוּ מִצְרַיִם וְלַאֲבֹתֵינוּ׃
and-to-fathers-of-us Egyptians to-us and-they-mistreated many days in-Egypt

וַנִּצְעַק אֶל־ יְהוָה וַיִּשְׁמַע קֹלֵנוּ וַיִּשְׁלַח מַלְאָךְ
angel and-he-sent cry-of-us and-he-heard Yahweh to but-we-cried (16)

וַיֹּצִאֵנוּ מִמִּצְרָיִם וְהִנֵּה אֲנַחְנוּ בְקָדֵשׁ עִיר קְצֵה
edge-of town at-Kadesh we now-see! from-Egypt and-he-brought-us

גְבוּלֶךָ׃ נַעְבְּרָה־ נָּא בְאַרְצֶךָ לֹא נַעֲבֹר
we-will-go not through-country-of-you now! let-us-pass (17) territory-of-you

בְּשָׂדֶה וּבְכֶרֶם וְלֹא נִשְׁתֶּה מֵי בְאֵר
well waters-of we-will-drink and-not or-through-vineyard through-field

דֶּרֶךְ הַמֶּלֶךְ נֵלֵךְ לֹא נִטֶּה יָמִין וּשְׂמֹאול עַד אֲשֶׁר־
when until or-left right we-will-turn not we-will-travel the-king highway-of

נַעֲבֹר גְּבוּלֶךָ׃ וַיֹּאמֶר אֵלָיו אֱדוֹם לֹא
not Edom to-him but-he-answered (18) territory-of-you we-passed-through

תַעֲבֹר בִּי פֶּן־ בַּחֶרֶב אֵצֵא לִקְרָאתֶךָ׃
to-attack-you I-will-march-out with-the-sword or through-me you-may-pass

וַיֹּאמְרוּ אֵלָיו בְּנֵי־ יִשְׂרָאֵל בַּמְסִלָּה נַעֲלֶה
we-will-go on-the-main-road Israel sons-of to-him and-they-replied (19)

וְאִם־ מֵימֶיךָ נִשְׁתֶּה אֲנִי וּמִקְנַי וְנָתַתִּי
then-I-will-pay or-livestock-of-me I we-drink waters-of-you and-if

מִכְרָם רַק אֵין־ דָּבָר בְּרַגְלַי אֶעֱבֹרָה׃
I-will-pass-through on-feet-of-me else nothing only price-of-them

וַיֹּאמֶר לֹא תַעֲבֹר וַיֵּצֵא אֱדוֹם
Edom then-he-came-out you-may-pass-through not but-he-answered (20)

לִקְרָאתוֹ בְּעַם כָּבֵד וּבְיָד חֲזָקָה׃ וַיְמָאֵן ׀
since-he-refused (21) powerful and-with-hand large with-army to-oppose-him

אֱדוֹם נְתֹן אֶת־ יִשְׂרָאֵל עֲבֹר בִּגְבֻלוֹ וַיֵּט יִשְׂרָאֵל
Israel and-he-turned through-territory-him to-go Israel *** to-let Edom

מֵעָלָיו׃ וַיִּסְעוּ מִקָּדֵשׁ וַיָּבֹאוּ בְנֵי־ יִשְׂרָאֵל
Israel sons-of and-they-came from-Kadesh and-they-set-out (22) from-near-him

כָּל־ הָעֵדָה הֹר הָהָר׃ וַיֹּאמֶר יְהוָה אֶל־ מֹשֶׁה
Moses to Yahweh and-he-said (23) the-Mount Hor the-community whole-of

וְאֶל־ אַהֲרֹן בְּהֹר הָהָר עַל־ גְּבוּל אֶרֶץ־ אֱדוֹם לֵאמֹר׃
to-say Edom land-of border-of near the-Mount at-Hor Aaron and-to

יֵאָסֵף אַהֲרֹן אֶל־ עַמָּיו כִּי לֹא יָבֹא אֶל־
into he-will-enter not for people-of-him to Aaron he-will-be-gathered (24)

הָאָרֶץ אֲשֶׁר נָתַתִּי לִבְנֵי יִשְׂרָאֵל עַל אֲשֶׁר־ מְרִיתֶם אֶת־
*** you-rebelled that because Israel to-sons-of I-give that the-land

many years. The Egyptians mistreated us and our fathers,
16but when we cried out to the LORD, he heard our cry and sent an angel and brought us out of Egypt.

"Now we are here at Kadesh, a town on the edge of your territory.
17Please let us pass through your country. We will not go through any field or vineyard, or drink water from any well. We will travel along the king's highway and not turn to the right or to the left until we have passed through your territory."

18But Edom answered:

"You may not pass through here; if you try, we will march out and attack you with the sword."

19The Israelites replied:

"We will go along the main road, and if we or our livestock drink any of your water, we will pay for it. We only want to pass through on foot—nothing else."

20Again they answered:

"You may not pass through."

Then Edom came out against them with a large and powerful army.
21Since Edom refused to let them go through their territory, Israel turned away from them.

The Death of Aaron

22The whole Israelite community set out from Kadesh and came to Mount Hor.
23At Mount Hor, near the border of Edom, the LORD said to Moses and Aaron,
24"Aaron will be gathered to his people. He will not enter the land I give the Israelites, because both of you rebelled against my command

פִּי לְמֵי מְרִיבָה׃ קַח אֶת־אַהֲרֹן וְאֶת־אֶלְעָזָר בְּנוֹ
son-of-him Eleazar and Aaron *** get! (25) Meribah at-waters-of command-of-me

וְהַעַל אֹתָם הֹר הָהָר׃ וְהַפְשֵׁט אֶת־אַהֲרֹן אֶת־בְּגָדָיו
garments-of-him *** Aaron *** and-remove! (26) the-Mount Hor them and-take-up!

וְהִלְבַּשְׁתָּם אֶת־אֶלְעָזָר בְּנוֹ וְאַהֲרֹן יֵאָסֵף
he-will-be-gathered and-Aaron son-of-him Eleazar *** and-you-put-on-them

וּמֵת שָׁם׃ וַיַּעַשׂ מֹשֶׁה כַּאֲשֶׁר צִוָּה יְהוָה
Yahweh he-commanded just-as Moses and-he-did (27) there and-he-will-die

וַיַּעֲלוּ אֶל־הֹר הָהָר לְעֵינֵי כָּל־הָעֵדָה׃
the-community whole-of before-eyes-of the-Mount Hor onto and-they-went-up

וַיַּפְשֵׁט מֹשֶׁה אֶת־אַהֲרֹן אֶת־בְּגָדָיו וַיַּלְבֵּשׁ אֹתָם
them and-he-put-on garments-of-him *** Aaron *** Moses and-he-removed (28)

אֶת־אֶלְעָזָר בְּנוֹ וַיָּמָת אַהֲרֹן שָׁם בְּרֹאשׁ הָהָר
the-mountain on-top-of there Aaron and-he-died son-of-him Eleazar ***

וַיֵּרֶד מֹשֶׁה וְאֶלְעָזָר מִן־הָהָר׃ וַיִּרְאוּ
when-they-learned (29) the-mountain from and-Eleazar Moses then-he-came-down

כָּל־הָעֵדָה כִּי גָוַע אַהֲרֹן וַיִּבְכּוּ אֶת־אַהֲרֹן שְׁלֹשִׁים
thirty Aaron *** then-they-mourned Aaron he-died that the-community whole-of

יוֹם כֹּל בֵּית יִשְׂרָאֵל׃ וַיִּשְׁמַע הַכְּנַעֲנִי מֶלֶךְ־עֲרָד
Arad king-of the-Canaanite when-he-heard (21:1) Israel house-of entire-of day

יֹשֵׁב הַנֶּגֶב כִּי בָּא יִשְׂרָאֵל דֶּרֶךְ הָאֲתָרִים וַיִּלָּחֶם
then-he-attacked the-Atharim road-of Israel he-comes that the-Negev living-of

בְּיִשְׂרָאֵל וַיִּשְׁבְּ ׀ מִמֶּנּוּ שֶׁבִי׃ וַיִּדַּר יִשְׂרָאֵל נֶדֶר
vow Israel and-he-vowed (2) captive from-him and-he-captured against-Israel

לַיהוָה וַיֹּאמַר אִם־נָתֹן תִּתֵּן אֶת־הָעָם הַזֶּה
the-this the-people *** you-deliver to-deliver if and-he-said to-Yahweh

בְּיָדִי וְהַחֲרַמְתִּי אֶת־עָרֵיהֶם׃ וַיִּשְׁמַע
and-he-listened (3) cities-of-them *** then-I-will-destroy into-hand-of-me

יְהוָה בְּקוֹל יִשְׂרָאֵל וַיִּתֵּן אֶת־הַכְּנַעֲנִי וַיַּחֲרֵם
and-he-destroyed the-Canaanite *** and-he-gave-over Israel to-plea-of Yahweh

אֶתְהֶם וְאֶת־עָרֵיהֶם וַיִּקְרָא שֵׁם־הַמָּקוֹם חָרְמָה׃
Hormah the-place name-of so-he-called towns-of-them and them

וַיִּסְעוּ מֵהֹר הָהָר דֶּרֶךְ יַם־סוּף לִסְבֹב
to-go-around Reed Sea-of route-of the-Mount from-Hor and-they-travelled (4)

אֶת־אֶרֶץ אֱדוֹם וַתִּקְצַר נֶפֶשׁ־הָעָם בַּדָּרֶךְ׃
on-the-way the-people spirit-of but-she-grew-impatient Edom land-of ***

וַיְדַבֵּר הָעָם בֵּאלֹהִים וּבְמֹשֶׁה לָמָה הֶעֱלִיתֻנוּ
you-brought-us why? and-against-Moses against-God the-people and-he-spoke (5)

at the waters of Meribah. [25]Get
Aaron and his son Eleazar and
take them up Mount Hor.
[26]Remove Aaron's garments
and put them on his son Eleazar, for Aaron will be gathered
to his people; he will die
there."
[27]Moses did as the LORD
commanded: They went up
Mount Hor in the sight of the
whole community. [28]Moses
removed Aaron's garments
and put them on his son Eleazar. And Aaron died there on
top of the mountain. Then
Moses and Eleazar came down
from the mountain, [29]and
when the whole community
learned that Aaron had died,
the entire house of Israel
mourned for him thirty days.

Arad Destroyed

21 When the Canaanite
king of Arad, who
lived in the Negev, heard that
Israel was coming along the
road to Atharim, he attacked
the Israelites and captured
some of them. [2]Then Israel
made this vow to the LORD: "If
you will deliver these people
into our hands, we will totally
destroy[r] their cities." [3]The
LORD listened to Israel's plea
and gave the Canaanites over
to them. They completely destroyed them and their towns;
so the place was named Hormah.[s]

The Bronze Snake

[4]They traveled from Mount
Hor along the route to the Red
Sea,[t] to go around Edom. But
the people grew impatient on
the way; [5]they spoke against
God and against Moses, and
said, "Why have you brought

r2 The Hebrew term refers to the irrevocable giving over of things or persons to the LORD, often by totally destroying them; also in verse 3.

s3 *Hormah* means *destruction*.

t4 Hebrew *Yam Suph*; that is, Sea of Reeds

מִמִּצְרַיִם לָמוּת בַּמִּדְבָּר כִּי אֵין לֶחֶם וְאֵין מַיִם
waters and-there-is-no bread there-is-no for in-the-desert to-die from-Egypt

וְנַפְשֵׁנוּ קָצָה בַּלֶּחֶם הַקְּלֹקֵל׃ וַיְשַׁלַּח
then-he-sent (6) the-miserable against-the-food she-detests and-spirit-of-us

יְהוָה בָּעָם אֵת הַנְּחָשִׁים הַשְּׂרָפִים וַיְנַשְּׁכוּ אֶת־
*** and-they-bit the-venomous-ones the-snakes *** among-the-people Yahweh

הָעָם וַיָּמָת עַם־ רָב מִיִּשְׂרָאֵל׃ וַיָּבֹא הָעָם אֶל־
to the-people and-he-came (7) from-Israel many people and-he-died the-people

מֹשֶׁה וַיֹּאמְרוּ חָטָאנוּ כִּי־ דִבַּרְנוּ בַיהוָה וָבָךְ
and-against-you against-Yahweh we-spoke when we-sinned and-they-said Moses

הִתְפַּלֵּל אֶל־יְהוָה וְיָסֵר מֵעָלֵינוּ אֶת־ הַנָּחָשׁ וַיִּתְפַּלֵּל
so-he-prayed the-snake *** away-from-us so-he-will-take Yahweh to pray!

מֹשֶׁה בְּעַד הָעָם׃ וַיֹּאמֶר יְהוָה אֶל־מֹשֶׁה עֲשֵׂה לְךָ שָׂרָף
snake for-you make! Moses to Yahweh and-he-said (8) the-people for Moses

וְשִׂים אֹתוֹ עַל־ נֵס וְהָיָה כָּל־ הַנָּשׁוּךְ וְרָאָה
when-he-sees the-one-being-bitten any-of and-he-will-be pole on him and-put!

אֹתוֹ וָחָי׃ וַיַּעַשׂ מֹשֶׁה נְחַשׁ נְחֹשֶׁת וַיְשִׂמֵהוּ
and-he-put-him bronze snake-of Moses so-he-made (9) then-he-will-live him

עַל־ הַנֵּס וְהָיָה אִם־ נָשַׁךְ הַנָּחָשׁ אֶת־ אִישׁ וְהִבִּיט אֶל־
at and-he-looked anyone *** the-snake he-bit when and-he-was the-pole on

נְחַשׁ הַנְּחֹשֶׁת וָחָי׃ וַיִּסְעוּ בְּנֵי יִשְׂרָאֵל
Israel sons-of and-they-moved-on (10) then-he-lived the-bronze snake-of

וַיַּחֲנוּ בְּאֹבֹת׃ וַיִּסְעוּ מֵאֹבֹת וַיַּחֲנוּ
and-they-camped from-Oboth then-they-set-out (11) at-Oboth and-they-camped

בְּעִיֵּי הָעֲבָרִים בַּמִּדְבָּר אֲשֶׁר עַל־ פְּנֵי מוֹאָב מִמִּזְרַח הַשָּׁמֶשׁ׃
the-sun toward-rise-of Moab face-of to that in-the-desert the-Abarim in-Iye

מִשָּׁם נָסָעוּ וַיַּחֲנוּ בְּנַחַל זָרֶד׃
Zered in-Valley-of and-they-camped they-moved-on from-there (12)

מִשָּׁם נָסָעוּ וַיַּחֲנוּ מֵעֵבֶר אַרְנוֹן אֲשֶׁר
which Arnon along-side and they-camped they-set-out from-there (13)

בַּמִּדְבָּר הַיֹּצֵא מִגְּבוּל הָאֱמֹרִי כִּי אַרְנוֹן
Arnon also the-Amorite into-territory-of the-one-extending in-the-desert

גְּבוּל מוֹאָב בֵּין מוֹאָב וּבֵין הָאֱמֹרִי׃ עַל־כֵּן יֵאָמַר
he-is-said this for (14) the-Amorite and-between Moab between Moab border-of

בְּסֵפֶר מִלְחֲמֹת יְהוָה אֶת־ וָהֵב בְּסוּפָה וְאֶת־ הַנְּחָלִים אַרְנוֹן׃
Arnon the-ravines and in-Suphah Waheb *** Yahweh Wars-of in-Book-of

וְאֶשֶׁד הַנְּחָלִים אֲשֶׁר נָטָה לְשֶׁבֶת עָר וְנִשְׁעַן
and-he-lies Ar to-site-of he-leads that the-ravines and-slope-of (15)

us up out of Egypt to die in the
desert? There is no bread!
There is no water! And we detest this miserable food!"
[6]Then the LORD sent venomous snakes among them; they
bit the people and many Israelites died. [7]The people came
to Moses and said, "We
sinned when we spoke
against the LORD and against
you. Pray that the LORD will
take the snakes away from
us." So Moses prayed for the
people.
[8]The LORD said to Moses,
"Make a snake and put it up
on a pole; anyone who is bitten can look at it and live." [9]So
Moses made a bronze snake
and put it up on a pole. Then
when anyone was bitten by a
snake and looked at the
bronze snake, he lived.

The Journey to Moab

[10]The Israelites moved on
and camped at Oboth. [11]Then
they set out from Oboth and
camped in Iye Abarim, in the
desert that faces Moab toward
the sunrise. [12]From there they
moved on and camped in the
Zered Valley. [13]They set out
from there and camped alongside the Arnon, which is in
the desert extending into Amorite territory. The Arnon is
the border of Moab, between
Moab and the Amorites.
[14]That is why the Book of the
Wars of the LORD says:

"... Waheb in Suphah[u]
and the ravines,
the Arnon [15]and[v] the
slopes of the ravines
that lead to the site of Ar

[u]14 The meaning of the Hebrew for this phrase is uncertain.
[v]14,15 Or *"I have been given from Suphah and the ravines / of the Arnon [15]to*

לִגְבוּל מוֹאָב׃ וּמִשָּׁם בְּאֵרָה הִוא הַבְּאֵר אֲשֶׁר אָמַר
he-said where the-well this to-Beer and-from-there (16) Moab along-border-of

יְהוָה לְמֹשֶׁה אֱסֹף אֶת־ הָעָם וְאֶתְּנָה לָהֶם מָיִם׃
waters to-them and-I-will-give the-people *** gather! to-Moses Yahweh

אָז יָשִׁיר יִשְׂרָאֵל אֶת־ הַשִּׁירָה הַזֹּאת עֲלִי בְאֵר עֱנוּ־
sing! well spring-up! the-this the-song *** Israel he-sang then (17)

לָהּ׃ בְּאֵר חֲפָרוּהָ שָׂרִים כָּרוּהָ נְדִיבֵי הָעָם
the-people nobles-of they-sank-her princes they-dug-her well (18) about-her

בִּמְחֹקֵק בְּמִשְׁעֲנֹתָם וּמִמִּדְבָּר מַתָּנָה׃
Mattanah then-from-desert with-staffs-of-them with-scepter

וּמִמַּתָּנָה נַחֲלִיאֵל וּמִנַּחֲלִיאֵל בָּמוֹת׃ וּמִבָּמוֹת
and-from-Bamoth (20) Bamoth and-from-Nahaliel Nahaliel and-from-Mattanah (19)

הַגַּיְא אֲשֶׁר בִּשְׂדֵה מוֹאָב רֹאשׁ הַפִּסְגָּה וְנִשְׁקָפָה עַל־
to and-she-overlooks the-Pisgah top-of Moab in-field-of that the-valley

פְּנֵי הַיְשִׁימֹן׃ וַיִּשְׁלַח יִשְׂרָאֵל מַלְאָכִים אֶל־ סִיחֹן מֶלֶךְ־
king-of Sihon to messengers Israel and-he-sent (21) the-wasteland face-of

הָאֱמֹרִי לֵאמֹר׃ אֶעְבְּרָה בְאַרְצֶךָ לֹא נִטֶּה
we-will-turn not through-country-of-you let-me-pass (22) to-say the-Amorite

בְּשָׂדֶה וּבְכֶרֶם לֹא נִשְׁתֶּה מֵי בְאֵר בְּדֶרֶךְ
along-highway-of well waters-of we-will-drink not or-into-vineyard into-field

הַמֶּלֶךְ נֵלֵךְ עַד אֲשֶׁר־ נַעֲבֹר גְּבֻלֶךָ׃ וְלֹא־
but-not (23) territory-of-you we-passed when until we-will-travel the-king

נָתַן סִיחֹן אֶת־ יִשְׂרָאֵל עֲבֹר בִּגְבֻלוֹ וַיֶּאֱסֹף
and-he-mustered through-territory-of-him to-pass Israel *** Sihon he-let

סִיחֹן אֶת־ כָּל־ עַמּוֹ וַיֵּצֵא לִקְרַאת יִשְׂרָאֵל
Israel to-oppose and-he-marched-out army-of-him entire-of *** Sihon

הַמִּדְבָּרָה וַיָּבֹא יָהְצָה וַיִּלָּחֶם בְּיִשְׂרָאֵל׃
with-Israel then-he-fought to-Jahaz when-he-came into-the-desert

וַיַּכֵּהוּ יִשְׂרָאֵל לְפִי־ חָרֶב וַיִּירַשׁ אֶת־
*** and-he-took-over sword with-edge-of Israel but-he-struck-him (24)

אַרְצוֹ מֵאַרְנֹן עַד־ יַבֹּק עַד־ בְּנֵי עַמּוֹן כִּי עַז
fortified for Ammon sons-of as-far-as Jabbok to from-Arnon land-of-him

גְּבוּל בְּנֵי עַמּוֹן׃ וַיִּקַּח יִשְׂרָאֵל אֵת כָּל־ הֶעָרִים
the-cities all-of *** Israel and-he-captured (25) Ammon sons-of border-of

הָאֵלֶּה וַיֵּשֶׁב יִשְׂרָאֵל בְּכָל־ עָרֵי הָאֱמֹרִי בְּחֶשְׁבּוֹן
in-Heshbon the-Amorite cities-of in-all-of Israel and-he-occupied the-these

וּבְכָל־ בְּנֹתֶיהָ׃ כִּי חֶשְׁבּוֹן עִיר סִיחֹן מֶלֶךְ
king-of Sihon city-of Heshbon now (26) settlements-of-her and-in-all-of

and lie along the border
of Moab."

16From there they continued
on to Beer, the well where the
LORD said to Moses, "Gather
the people together and I will
give them water."
17Then Israel sang this song:

"Spring up, O well!
Sing about it,
18about the well that the
princes dug,
that the nobles of the
people sank—
the nobles with scepters
and staffs."

Then they went from the
desert to Mattanah, 19from
Mattanah to Nahaliel, from
Nahaliel to Bamoth, 20and
from Bamoth to the valley in
Moab where the top of Pisgah
overlooks the wasteland.

Defeat of Sihon and Og

21Israel sent messengers to
say to Sihon king of the Amorites:

22"Let us pass through
your country. We will not
turn aside into any field or
vineyard, or drink water
from any well. We will
travel along the king's
highway until we have
passed through your territory."

23But Sihon would not let Israel pass through his territory.
He mustered his entire army
and marched out into the
desert against Israel. When he
reached Jahaz, he fought with
Israel. 24Israel, however, put
him to the sword and took
over his land from the Arnon
to the Jabbok, but only as far
as the Ammonites, because
their border was fortified. 25Is-
rael captured all the cities of
the Amorites and occupied
them, including Heshbon and
all its surrounding settlements. 26Heshbon was the city
of Sihon king of the Amorites,

הָאֱמֹרִי הִוא וְהוּא נִלְחַם בְּמֶלֶךְ מוֹאָב הָרִאשׁוֹן וַיִּקַּח
and-he-took the-former Moab against-king-of he-fought now-he she the-Amorite

אֶת־ כָּל־ אַרְצוֹ מִיָּדוֹ עַד־ אַרְנֹן׃ עַל־ כֵּן
this for (27) Arnon as-far-as from-hand-of-him land-of-him all-of ***

יֹאמְרוּ הַמֹּשְׁלִים בֹּאוּ חֶשְׁבּוֹן תִּבָּנֶה
let-her-be-rebuilt Heshbon come! the-ones-making-poem they-say

וְתִכּוֹנֵן עִיר סִיחוֹן׃ כִּי־ אֵשׁ יָצְאָה מֵחֶשְׁבּוֹן
from-Heshbon she-went-out fire for (28) Sihon city-of and-let-her-be-restored

לֶהָבָה מִקִּרְיַת סִיחֹן אָכְלָה עָר מוֹאָב בַּעֲלֵי בָּמוֹת
heights-of citizens-of Moab Ar-of she-consumed Sihon from-city-of blaze

אַרְנֹן׃ אוֹי־ לְךָ מוֹאָב אָבַדְתָּ עַם־ כְּמוֹשׁ נָתַן
he-gave-up Chemosh people-of you-are-destroyed Moab to-you woe! (29) Arnon

בָּנָיו פְּלֵיטִם וּבְנֹתָיו בַּשְּׁבִית לְמֶלֶךְ אֱמֹרִי
Amorite to-king-of as-the-captive and-daughters-of-him fugitives sons-of-him

סִיחוֹן׃ וַנִּירָם אָבַד חֶשְׁבּוֹן עַד־ דִּיבֹן
Dibon to Heshbon he-is-destroyed but-we-overthrew-them (30) Sihon

וַנַּשִּׁים עַד־ נֹפַח אֲשֶׁר עַד־מֵידְבָא׃ וַיֵּשֶׁב
so-he-settled (31) Medeba to that Nophah as-far-as and-we-demolished-them

יִשְׂרָאֵל בְּאֶרֶץ הָאֱמֹרִי׃ וַיִּשְׁלַח מֹשֶׁה לְרַגֵּל אֶת־ יַעְזֵר
Jazer *** to-spy Moses and-he-sent (32) the-Amorite in-land-of Israel

וַיִּלְכְּדוּ בְּנֹתֶיהָ וַיִּירֶשׁ אֶת־ הָאֱמֹרִי אֲשֶׁר־
who the-Amorite *** and-he-drove-out settlements-of-her and-they-captured

שָׁם׃ וַיִּפְנוּ וַיַּעֲלוּ דֶּרֶךְ הַבָּשָׁן
the-Bashan road-of and-they-went-up then-they-turned (33) there

וַיֵּצֵא עוֹג מֶלֶךְ־ הַבָּשָׁן לִקְרָאתָם הוּא וְכָל־
and-whole-of he to-meet-them the-Bashan king-of Og and-he-marched-out

עַמּוֹ לַמִּלְחָמָה אֶדְרֶעִי׃ וַיֹּאמֶר יְהוָה אֶל־ מֹשֶׁה אַל־
not Moses to Yahweh and-he-said (34) Edrei in-the-battle army-of-him

תִּירָא אֹתוֹ כִּי בְיָדְךָ נָתַתִּי אֹתוֹ וְאֶת־ כָּל־ עַמּוֹ וְאֶת־
and army-of-him whole-of and him I-gave into-hand-of-you for him you-fear

אַרְצוֹ וְעָשִׂיתָ לּוֹ כַּאֲשֶׁר עָשִׂיתָ לְסִיחֹן מֶלֶךְ הָאֱמֹרִי
the-Amorite king-of to-Sihon you-did just-as to-him so-you-do land-of-him

אֲשֶׁר יוֹשֵׁב בְּחֶשְׁבּוֹן׃ וַיַּכּוּ אֹתוֹ וְאֶת־ בָּנָיו וְאֶת־ כָּל־
whole-of and sons-of-him and him so-they-struck (35) in-Heshbon reigning who

עַמּוֹ עַד־ בִּלְתִּי הִשְׁאִיר־ לוֹ שָׂרִיד וַיִּירְשׁוּ אֶת־
*** and-they-possessed survivor to-him he-left not until army-of-him

אַרְצוֹ׃ וַיִּסְעוּ בְּנֵי יִשְׂרָאֵל וַיַּחֲנוּ
and-they-camped Israel sons-of then-they-traveled (22:1) land-of-him

who had fought against the former king of Moab and had taken from him all his land as far as the Arnon.
27That is why the poets say:

"Come to Heshbon and let it be rebuilt;
let Sihon's city be restored.
28"Fire went out from Heshbon,
a blaze from the city of Sihon.
It consumed Ar of Moab,
the citizens of Arnon's heights.
29Woe to you, O Moab!
You are destroyed, O people of Chemosh!
He has given up his sons as fugitives
and his daughters as captives
to Sihon king of the Amorites.

30"But we have overthrown them;
Heshbon is destroyed all the way to Dibon.
We have demolished them as far as Nophah,
which extends to Medeba."

31So Israel settled in the land of the Amorites.
32After Moses had sent spies to Jazer, the Israelites captured its surrounding settlements and drove out the Amorites who were there. 33Then they turned and went up along the road toward Bashan, and Og king of Bashan and his whole army marched out to meet them in battle at Edrei.
34The LORD said to Moses, "Do not be afraid of him, for I have handed him over to you, with his whole army and his land. Do to him what you did to Sihon king of the Amorites, who reigned in Heshbon."
35So they struck him down, together with his sons and his whole army, leaving them no survivors. And they took possession of his land.

Balak Summons Balaam

22 Then the Israelites traveled to the plains of

°32 ק ויורש

בְּעַֽרְבוֹת מוֹאָב מֵעֵבֶר לְיַרְדֵּן יְרֵחוֹ׃ וַיַּרְא בָּלָק בֶּן־
son-of Balak now-he-saw (2) Jericho of-Jordan-of along-side Moab in-plains-of

צִפּוֹר אֵת כָּל־אֲשֶׁר־עָשָׂה יִשְׂרָאֵל לָאֱמֹרִי׃ וַיָּגָר
and-he-was-terrified (3) to-the-Amorite Israel he-did that all *** Zippor

מוֹאָב מִפְּנֵי הָעָם מְאֹד כִּי רַב־הוּא וַיָּקָץ מוֹאָב
Moab and-he-was-filled-with-dread he many for very the-people because-of Moab

מִפְּנֵי בְּנֵי יִשְׂרָאֵל׃ וַיֹּאמֶר מוֹאָב אֶל־זִקְנֵי מִדְיָן עַתָּה
now Midian elders-of to Moab and-he-said (4) Israel sons-of because-of

יְלַחֲכוּ הַקָּהָל אֶת־כָּל־סְבִיבֹתֵינוּ כִּלְחֹךְ הַשּׁוֹר
the-ox as-to-lick things-around-us all-of *** the-horde they-will-lick-up

אֵת יֶרֶק הַשָּׂדֶה וּבָלָק בֶּן־צִפּוֹר מֶלֶךְ לְמוֹאָב בָּעֵת
at-the-time of-Moab king Zippor son-of now-Balak the-field grass-of ***

הַהִוא׃ וַיִּשְׁלַח מַלְאָכִים אֶל־בִּלְעָם בֶּן־בְּעוֹר פְּתוֹרָה אֲשֶׁר
that at-Pethor Beor son-of Balaam to messengers and-he-sent (5) the-that

עַל־הַנָּהָר אֶרֶץ בְּנֵי־עַמּוֹ לִקְרֹא־לוֹ לֵאמֹר הִנֵּה
see! to-say to-him to-summon people-of-him sons-of land-of the-River near

עַם יָצָא מִמִּצְרַיִם הִנֵּה כִסָּה אֶת־עֵין הָאָרֶץ וְהוּא
and-he the-land face-of *** he-covers see! from-Egypt he-came people

יֹשֵׁב מִמֻּלִי׃ וְעַתָּה לְכָה־נָּא אָרָה־לִּי אֶת־הָעָם
the-people *** for-me curse! now! come! and-now (6) next-to-me settling

הַזֶּה כִּי־עָצוּם הוּא מִמֶּנִּי אוּלַי אוּכַל נַכֶּה־
to-defeat I-will-be-able perhaps for-me he too-powerful for the-this

בּוֹ וַאֲגָרְשֶׁנּוּ מִן־הָאָרֶץ כִּי יָדַעְתִּי אֵת אֲשֶׁר־
whom *** I-know for the-country from and-I-will-drive-him against-him

תְּבָרֵךְ מְבֹרָךְ וַאֲשֶׁר תָּאֹר יוּאָר׃ וַיֵּלְכוּ
and-they-left (7) he-is-cursed you-curse and-whom being-blessed you-bless

זִקְנֵי מוֹאָב וְזִקְנֵי מִדְיָן וּקְסָמִים בְּיָדָם
in-hand-of-them and-divination-fees Midian and-elders-of Moab elders-of

וַיָּבֹאוּ אֶל־בִּלְעָם וַיְדַבְּרוּ אֵלָיו דִּבְרֵי בָלָק׃ וַיֹּאמֶר
and-he-said (8) Balak words-of to-him then-they-told Balaam to when-they-came

אֲלֵיהֶם לִינוּ פֹה הַלַּיְלָה וַהֲשִׁבֹתִי אֶתְכֶם דָּבָר כַּאֲשֶׁר
just-as answer you and-I-will-bring the-night here spend-night! to-them

יְדַבֵּר יְהוָה אֵלָי וַיֵּשְׁבוּ שָׂרֵי־מוֹאָב עִם־בִּלְעָם׃
Balaam with Moab princes-of so-they-stayed to-me Yahweh he-gives

וַיָּבֹא אֱלֹהִים אֶל־בִּלְעָם וַיֹּאמֶר מִי הָאֲנָשִׁים הָאֵלֶּה עִמָּךְ׃
with-you the-these the-men who? and-he-asked Balaam to God and-he-came (9)

וַיֹּאמֶר בִּלְעָם אֶל־הָאֱלֹהִים בָּלָק בֶּן־צִפֹּר מֶלֶךְ מוֹאָב שָׁלַח
he-sent Moab king-of Zippor son-of Balak the-God to Balaam and-he-said (10)

Moab and camped along the
Jordan across from Jericho.[w]
2Now Balak son of Zippor
saw all that Israel had done to
the Amorites, 3and Moab was
terrified because there were so
many people. Indeed, Moab
was filled with dread because
of the Israelites.
4The Moabites said to the elders of Midian, "This horde is
going to lick up everything
around us, as an ox licks up
the grass of the field."
So Balak son of Zippor, who
was king of Moab at that time,
5sent messengers to summon
Balaam son of Beor, who was
at Pethor, near the River,[x] in
his native land. Balak said:

"A people has come out
of Egypt; they cover the
face of the land and have
settled next to me. 6Now
come and put a curse on
these people, because they
are too powerful for me.
Perhaps then I will be able
to defeat them and drive
them out of the country.
For I know that those you
bless are blessed, and those
you curse are cursed."

7The elders of Moab and
Midian left, taking with them
the fee for divination. When
they came to Balaam, they told
him what Balak had said.
8"Spend the night here," Balaam said to them, "and I will
bring you back the answer the
LORD gives me." So the Moabite princes stayed with him.
9God came to Balaam and
asked, "Who are these men
with you?"
10Balaam said to God, "Balak
son of Zippor, king of Moab,

w1 Hebrew *Jordan of Jericho;* possibly an ancient name for the Jordan River
x5 That is, the Euphrates

אֵלָֽי׃ הִנֵּ֤ה הָעָם֙ הַיֹּצֵ֣א מִמִּצְרַ֔יִם וַיְכַ֖ס אֶת־

*** and-he-covers from-Egypt the-one-coming the-people see! (11) to-me

עֵ֣ין הָאָ֑רֶץ עַתָּ֗ה לְכָ֤ה קָֽבָה־ לִּי֙ אֹת֔וֹ אוּלַ֥י אוּכַ֛ל

I-will-be-able perhaps him for-me curse! come! now the-land face-of

לְהִלָּ֥חֶם בּ֖וֹ וְגֵרַשְׁתִּֽיו׃ וַיֹּ֤אמֶר אֱלֹהִים֙ אֶל־

to God but-he-said (12) and-I-will-drive-away-him against-him to-fight

בִּלְעָ֔ם לֹ֥א תֵלֵ֖ךְ עִמָּהֶ֑ם לֹ֤א תָאֹר֙ אֶת־ הָעָ֔ם כִּ֥י בָר֖וּךְ

being-blessed for the-people *** you-curse not with-them you-go not Balaam

הֽוּא׃ וַיָּ֤קָם בִּלְעָם֙ בַּבֹּ֔קֶר וַיֹּ֙אמֶר֙ אֶל־ שָׂרֵ֣י בָלָ֔ק

Balak princes-of to and-he-said in-the-morning Balaam so-he-got-up (13) he

לְכ֖וּ אֶל־ אַרְצְכֶ֑ם כִּ֚י מֵאֵ֣ן יְהוָ֔ה לְתִתִּ֖י לַהֲלֹ֥ךְ עִמָּכֶֽם׃

with-you to-go to-let-me Yahweh he-refused for country-of-you to go-back!

וַיָּק֙וּמוּ֙ שָׂרֵ֣י מוֹאָ֔ב וַיָּבֹ֖אוּ אֶל־ בָּלָ֑ק וַיֹּ֣אמְר֔וּ

and-they-said Balak to and-they-returned Moab princes-of so-they-got-up (14)

מֵאֵ֥ן בִּלְעָ֖ם הֲלֹ֥ךְ עִמָּֽנוּ׃ וַיֹּ֥סֶף ע֖וֹד בָּלָ֑ק שְׁלֹ֣חַ

to-send Balak again then-he-repeated (15) with-us to-come Balaam he-refused

שָׂרִ֔ים רַבִּ֥ים וְנִכְבָּדִ֖ים מֵאֵֽלֶּה׃

more-than-these and-ones-being-distinguished ones-numerous princes

וַיָּבֹ֖אוּ אֶל־בִּלְעָ֑ם וַיֹּ֣אמְרוּ ל֗וֹ כֹּ֤ה אָמַר֙ בָּלָ֣ק בֶּן־

son-of Balak he-says this to-him and-they-said Balaam to and-they-came (16)

צִפּ֔וֹר אַל־ נָ֥א תִמָּנַ֖ע מֵהֲלֹ֥ךְ אֵלָֽי׃ כִּֽי־ כַבֵּ֤ד

to-reward for (17) to-me from-to-come you-be-kept now! not Zippor

אֲכַבֶּדְךָ֙ מְאֹ֔ד וְכֹ֛ל אֲשֶׁר־ תֹּאמַ֥ר אֵלַ֖י אֶעֱשֶׂ֑ה וּלְכָה־

so-come! I-will-do to-me you-say that and-all handsomely I-will-reward-you

נָּא֙ קָֽבָה־ לִּ֔י אֵ֖ת הָעָ֥ם הַזֶּֽה׃ וַיַּ֣עַן בִּלְעָ֗ם

Balaam but-he-answered (18) the-this the-people *** for-me curse! now!

וַיֹּ֙אמֶר֙ אֶל־ עַבְדֵ֣י בָלָ֔ק אִם־ יִתֶּן־ לִ֥י בָלָ֛ק מְלֹ֥א

filled-of Balak to-me he-gave if Balak servants-of to and-he-said

בֵית֖וֹ כֶּ֣סֶף וְזָהָ֑ב לֹ֣א אוּכַ֗ל לַעֲבֹר֙ אֶת־ פִּי֙ יְהוָ֣ה

Yahweh command-of *** to-go-beyond I-could not and-gold silver palace-of-him

אֱלֹהָ֔י לַעֲשׂ֥וֹת קְטַנָּ֖ה א֥וֹ גְדוֹלָֽה׃ וְעַתָּ֗ה שְׁב֨וּ נָ֥א בָזֶ֛ה גַּם־אַתֶּ֖ם

you also at-here now! stay! and-now (19) great or small to-do God-of-me

הַלָּ֑יְלָה וְאֵֽדְעָ֔ה מַה־ יֹּסֵ֥ף יְהוָ֖ה דַּבֵּ֥ר עִמִּֽי׃

to-me to-tell Yahweh he-will-add what and-I-will-find-out the-night

וַיָּבֹ֨א אֱלֹהִ֥ים ׀ אֶל־בִּלְעָם֮ לַ֒יְלָה֒ וַיֹּ֣אמֶר ל֗וֹ אִם־ לִקְרֹ֤א

to-summon since to-him and-he-said night Balaam to God and-he-came (20)

לְךָ֙ בָּ֣אוּ הָאֲנָשִׁ֔ים ק֖וּם לֵ֣ךְ אִתָּ֑ם וְאַ֗ךְ אֶת־ הַדָּבָ֛ר אֲשֶׁר־

that the-thing *** but-only with-them go! rise! the-men they-came to-you

sent me this message: [11]'A people that has come out of Egypt covers the face of the land. Now come and put a curse on them for me. Perhaps then I will be able to fight them and drive them away.' "

[12]But God said to Balaam, "Do not go with them. You must not put a curse on those people, because they are blessed."

[13]The next morning Balaam got up and said to Balak's princes, "Go back to your own country, for the LORD has refused to let me go with you."

[14]So the Moabite princes returned to Balak and said, "Balaam refused to come with us."

[15]Then Balak sent other princes, more numerous and more distinguished than the first. [16]They came to Balaam and said:

"This is what Balak son of Zippor says: Do not let anything keep you from coming to me, [17]because I will reward you handsomely and do whatever you say. Come and put a curse on these people for me."

[18]But Balaam answered them, "Even if Balak gave me his palace filled with silver and gold, I could not do anything great or small to go beyond the command of the LORD my God. [19]Now stay here tonight as the others did, and I will find out what else the LORD will tell me."

[20]That night God came to Balaam and said, "Since these men have come to summon you, go with them, but do only

אֲדַבֵּר אֵלֶיךָ אֹתוֹ תַעֲשֶׂה׃ וַיָּקָם בִּלְעָם בַּבֹּקֶר
in-the-morning Balaam and-he-got-up (21) you-do him to-you I-tell

וַיַּחֲבֹשׁ אֶת־ אֲתֹנוֹ וַיֵּלֶךְ עִם־ שָׂרֵי מוֹאָב׃
Moab princes-of with and-he-went donkey-of-him *** and-he-saddled

וַיִּחַר־ אַף אֱלֹהִים כִּי־ הוֹלֵךְ הוּא וַיִּתְיַצֵּב מַלְאַךְ יְהוָה
Yahweh angel-of and-he-stood he going when God anger-of but-he-burned (22)

בַּדֶּרֶךְ לְשָׂטָן לוֹ וְהוּא רֹכֵב עַל־ אֲתֹנוֹ וּשְׁנֵי
and-two-of donkey-of-him on riding and-he against-him as-opposer in-the-road

נְעָרָיו עִמּוֹ׃ וַתֵּרֶא הָאָתוֹן אֶת־ מַלְאַךְ יְהוָה
Yahweh angel-of *** the-donkey when-she-saw (23) with-him servants-of-him

נִצָּב בַּדֶּרֶךְ וְחַרְבּוֹ שְׁלוּפָה בְּיָדוֹ
in-hand-of-him being-drawn and-sword-of-him in-the-road standing

וַתֵּט הָאָתוֹן מִן־ הַדֶּרֶךְ וַתֵּלֶךְ בַּשָּׂדֶה
into-the-field and-she-went the-road off the-donkey then-she-turned

וַיַּךְ בִּלְעָם אֶת־ הָאָתוֹן לְהַטֹּתָהּ הַדָּרֶךְ׃ וַיַּעֲמֹד
then-he-stood (24) the-road to-get-back-her the-donkey *** Balaam and-he-beat

מַלְאַךְ יְהוָה בְּמִשְׁעוֹל הַכְּרָמִים גָּדֵר מִזֶּה וְגָדֵר
and-wall on-this-side wall the-vineyards in-narrow-path-of Yahweh angel-of

מִזֶּה׃ וַתֵּרֶא הָאָתוֹן אֶת־ מַלְאַךְ יְהוָה
Yahweh angel-of *** the-donkey when-she-saw (25) on-that-side

וַתִּלָּחֵץ אֶל־ הַקִּיר וַתִּלְחַץ אֶת־ רֶגֶל בִּלְעָם אֶל־
against Balaam foot-of *** and-she-crushed the-wall to then-she-pressed-close

הַקִּיר וַיֹּסֶף לְהַכֹּתָהּ׃ וַיּוֹסֶף מַלְאַךְ־ יְהוָה
Yahweh angel-of then-he-repeated (26) to-beat-her so-he-repeated the-wall

עֲבוֹר וַיַּעֲמֹד בְּמָקוֹם צָר אֲשֶׁר אֵין־ דֶּרֶךְ לִנְטוֹת יָמִין
right to-turn room there-is-no where narrow in-place and-he-stood to-move

וּשְׂמֹאול׃ וַתֵּרֶא הָאָתוֹן אֶת־ מַלְאַךְ יְהוָה וַתִּרְבַּץ
then-she-lay-down Yahweh angel-of *** the-donkey when-she-saw (27) or-left

תַּחַת בִּלְעָם וַיִּחַר־ אַף בִּלְעָם וַיַּךְ אֶת־ הָאָתוֹן
the-donkey *** and-he-beat Balaam anger-of and-he-burned Balaam under

בַּמַּקֵּל׃ וַיִּפְתַּח יְהוָה אֶת־ פִּי הָאָתוֹן
the-donkey mouth-of *** Yahweh then-he-opened (28) with-the-staff

וַתֹּאמֶר לְבִלְעָם מֶה־ עָשִׂיתִי לְךָ כִּי הִכִּיתַנִי זֶה שָׁלֹשׁ רְגָלִים׃
times three this you-beat-me that to-you I-did what? to-Balaam and-she-said

וַיֹּאמֶר בִּלְעָם לָאָתוֹן כִּי הִתְעַלַּלְתְּ בִּי לוּ
if of-me you-made-fool because to-the-donkey Balaam and-he-answered (29)

יֶשׁ־ חֶרֶב בְּיָדִי כִּי עַתָּה הֲרַגְתִּיךְ׃ וַתֹּאמֶר
and-she-said (30) I-would-kill-you now then in-hand-of-me sword he-was

what I tell you."

Balaam's Donkey

21 Balaam got up in the morning, saddled his donkey and
went with the princes of
Moab. 22 But God was very angry when he went, and the angel of the LORD stood in the
road to oppose him. Balaam
was riding on his donkey, and
his two servants were with
him. 23 When the donkey saw
the angel of the LORD standing
in the road with a drawn
sword in his hand, she turned
off the road into a field. Balaam beat her to get her back
on the road.
24 Then the angel of the LORD
stood in a narrow path between two vineyards, with
walls on both sides. 25 When
the donkey saw the angel of
the LORD, she pressed close to
the wall, crushing Balaam's
foot against it. So he beat her
again.
26 Then the angel of the LORD
moved on ahead and stood in
a narrow place where there
was no room to turn, either to
the right or to the left. 27 When
the donkey saw the angel of
the LORD, she lay down under
Balaam, and he was angry and
beat her with his staff. 28 Then
the LORD opened the donkey's
mouth, and she said to Balaam, "What have I done to
you to make you beat me these
three times?"
29 Balaam answered the donkey, "You have made a fool of
me! If I had a sword in my
hand, I would kill you right
now."

הָאָתוֹן אֶל־בִּלְעָם הֲלוֹא אָנֹכִי אֲתֹנְךָ אֲשֶׁר־רָכַבְתָּ עָלַי

on-me you-ride which donkey-of-you I not? Balaam to the-donkey

מֵעוֹדְךָ עַד־הַיּוֹם הַזֶּה הַהַסְכֵּן הִסְכַּנְתִּי לַעֲשׂוֹת לְךָ

to-you to-do I-made-habit to-make-habit? the-this the-day to as-always-you

כֹּה וַיֹּאמֶר לֹא׃ וַיְגַל יְהוָה אֶת־עֵינֵי בִלְעָם וַיַּרְא

and-he-saw Balaam eyes-of *** Yahweh then-he-opened (31) no and-he-said this

אֶת־מַלְאַךְ יְהוָה נִצָּב בַּדֶּרֶךְ וְחַרְבּוֹ שְׁלֻפָה

being-drawn and-sword-of-him in-the-road standing Yahweh angel-of ***

בְּיָדוֹ וַיִּקֹּד וַיִּשְׁתַּחוּ לְאַפָּיו׃ וַיֹּאמֶר

and-he-asked (32) to-faces-of-him and-he-fell so-he-bowed in-hand-of-him

אֵלָיו מַלְאַךְ יְהוָה עַל־מָה הִכִּיתָ אֶת־אֲתֹנְךָ זֶה שָׁלוֹשׁ רְגָלִים

times three this donkey-of-you *** you-beat why? for Yahweh angel-of to-him

הִנֵּה אָנֹכִי יָצָאתִי לְשָׂטָן כִּי־יָרַט הַדֶּרֶךְ לְנֶגְדִּי׃

before-me the-path he-is-reckless for as-opposer I-came I see!

וַתִּרְאַנִי הָאָתוֹן וַתֵּט לְפָנַי זֶה שָׁלֹשׁ רְגָלִים

times three this away-from-me and-she-turned the-donkey and-she-saw-me (33)

אוּלַי נָטְתָה מִפָּנַי כִּי עַתָּה גַּם־אֹתְכָה הָרַגְתִּי

I-would-have-killed you indeed now then away-from-me she-turned if-not

וְאוֹתָהּ הֶחֱיֵיתִי׃ וַיֹּאמֶר בִּלְעָם אֶל־מַלְאַךְ יְהוָה

Yahweh angel-of to Balaam and-he-said (34) I-would-have-spared but-her

חָטָאתִי כִּי לֹא יָדַעְתִּי כִּי אַתָּה נִצָּב לִקְרָאתִי בַּדָּרֶךְ

in-the-road to-oppose-me standing you that I-realized not for I-sinned

וְעַתָּה אִם־רַע בְּעֵינֶיךָ אָשׁוּבָה לִּי׃ וַיֹּאמֶר

and-he-said (35) to-me I-will-go-back in-eyes-of-you displeasing if so-now

מַלְאַךְ יְהוָה אֶל־בִּלְעָם לֵךְ עִם־הָאֲנָשִׁים וְאֶפֶס אֶת־הַדָּבָר אֲשֶׁר־

that the-message *** but-only the-men with go! Balaam to Yahweh angel-of

אֲדַבֵּר אֵלֶיךָ אֹתוֹ תְדַבֵּר וַיֵּלֶךְ בִּלְעָם עִם־שָׂרֵי בָלָק׃

Balak princes-of with Balaam so-he-went you-speak him to-you I-tell

וַיִּשְׁמַע בָּלָק כִּי בָא בִלְעָם וַיֵּצֵא לִקְרָאתוֹ

to-meet-him then-he-went-out Balaam he-comes that Balak when-he-heard (36)

אֶל־עִיר מוֹאָב אֲשֶׁר עַל־גְּבוּל אַרְנֹן אֲשֶׁר בִּקְצֵה הַגְּבוּל׃

the-territory at-edge-of that Arnon border-of on that Moab town-of at

וַיֹּאמֶר בָּלָק אֶל־בִּלְעָם הֲלֹא שָׁלֹחַ שָׁלַחְתִּי אֵלֶיךָ לִקְרֹא־לָךְ

to-you to-summon to-you I-sent to-send not? Balaam to Balak and-he-said (37)

לָמָּה לֹא־הָלַכְתָּ אֵלָי הַאֻמְנָם לֹא אוּכַל כַּבְּדֶךָ׃ וַיֹּאמֶר

and-he-said (38) to-reward-you I-am-able not really? to-me you-came not why?

בִלְעָם אֶל־בָּלָק הִנֵּה־בָאתִי אֵלֶיךָ עַתָּה הֲיָכֹל אוּכַל דַּבֵּר

to-say I-am-able to-be-able? now to-you I-came see! Balak to Balaam

30The donkey said to Balaam, "Am I not your own donkey, which you have always ridden, to this day? Have I been in the habit of doing this to you?"

"No," he said.

31Then the LORD opened Balaam's eyes, and he saw the angel of the LORD standing in the road with his sword drawn. So he bowed low and fell facedown.

32The angel of the LORD asked him, "Why have you beaten your donkey these three times? I have come here to oppose you because your path is a reckless one before me.[y] 33The donkey saw me and turned away from me these three times. If she had not turned away, I would certainly have killed you by now, but I would have spared her."

34Balaam said to the angel of the LORD, "I have sinned. I did not realize you were standing in the road to oppose me. Now if you are displeased, I will go back."

35The angel of the LORD said to Balaam, "Go with the men, but speak only what I tell you." So Balaam went with the princes of Balak.

36When Balak heard that Balaam was coming, he went out to meet him at the Moabite town on the Arnon border, at the edge of his territory. 37Balak said to Balaam, "Did I not send you an urgent summons? Why didn't you come to me? Am I really not able to reward you?"

38"Well, I have come to you now," Balaam replied. "But

[y]32 The meaning of the Hebrew for this clause is uncertain.

מְא֑וּמָה הַדָּבָר אֲשֶׁר יָשִׂים אֱלֹהִים בְּפִי אֹתוֹ אֲדַבֵּר׃
I-must-speak him in-mouth-of-me God he-puts that the-message anything

(39) וַיֵּלֶךְ בִּלְעָם עִם־ בָּלָק וַיָּבֹאוּ קִרְיַת חֻצוֹת׃
Huzoth Kiriath and-they-went Balak with Balaam then-he-went (39)

(40) וַיִּזְבַּח בָּלָק בָּקָר וָצֹאן וַיְשַׁלַּח לְבִלְעָם
to-Balaam and-he-gave and-sheep cattle Balak and-he-sacrificed (40)

וְלַשָּׂרִים אֲשֶׁר אִתּוֹ׃ (41) וַיְהִי בַבֹּקֶר וַיִּקַּח
that-he-took in-the-morning and-he-was (41) with-him who and-to-the-princes

בָּלָק אֶת־ בִּלְעָם וַיַּעֲלֵהוּ בָּמוֹת בָּעַל וַיַּרְא מִשָּׁם
from-there and-he-saw Baal Bamoth and-he-took-up-him Balaam *** Balak

קְצֵה הָעָם׃ (23:1) וַיֹּאמֶר בִּלְעָם אֶל־בָּלָק בְּנֵה־ לִי בָזֶה
at-here for-me build! Balak to Balaam and-he-said (23:1) the-people part-of

שִׁבְעָה מִזְבְּחֹת וְהָכֵן לִי בָּזֶה שִׁבְעָה פָרִים וְשִׁבְעָה אֵילִים׃
rams and-seven bulls seven at-here for-me and-prepare! altars seven

(2) וַיַּעַשׂ בָּלָק כַּאֲשֶׁר דִּבֶּר בִּלְעָם וַיַּעַל בָּלָק וּבִלְעָם
and-Balaam Balak and-he-offered Balaam he-said just-as Balak so-he-did (2)

פָּר וָאַיִל בַּמִּזְבֵּחַ׃ (3) וַיֹּאמֶר בִּלְעָם לְבָלָק הִתְיַצֵּב עַל־
beside stay! to-Balak Balaam then-he-said (3) on-the-altar and-ram bull

עֹלָתֶךָ וְאֵלְכָה אוּלַי יִקָּרֵה יְהוָה לִקְרָאתִי
to-meet-me Yahweh he-will-come perhaps and-I-will-go offering-of-you

וּדְבַר מַה־ יַּרְאֵנִי וְהִגַּדְתִּי לָךְ וַיֵּלֶךְ
then-he-went to-you then-I-will-tell he-reveals-to-me whatever and-message-of

שֶׁפִי׃ (4) וַיִּקָּר אֱלֹהִים אֶל־ בִּלְעָם וַיֹּאמֶר אֵלָיו אֶת־ שִׁבְעַת
seven-of *** to-him and-he-said Balaam with God and-he-met (4) barren-height

הַמִּזְבְּחֹת עָרַכְתִּי וָאַעַל פָּר וָאַיִל בַּמִּזְבֵּחַ׃ (5) וַיָּשֶׂם
and-he-put (5) on-the-altar and-ram bull and-I-offered I-prepared the-altars

יְהוָה דָּבָר בְּפִי בִלְעָם וַיֹּאמֶר שׁוּב אֶל־ בָּלָק וְכֹה
and-this Balak to go-back! and-he-said Balaam in-mouth-of message Yahweh

תְדַבֵּר׃ (6) וַיָּשָׁב אֵלָיו וְהִנֵּה נִצָּב עַל־ עֹלָתוֹ
offering-of-him beside standing and-see! to-him so-he-went-back (6) you-speak

הוּא וְכָל־ שָׂרֵי מוֹאָב׃ (7) וַיִּשָּׂא מְשָׁלוֹ וַיֹּאמַר
and-he-said oracle-of-him then-he-uttered (7) Moab princes-of and-all-of he

מִן־ אֲרָם יַנְחֵנִי בָלָק מֶלֶךְ־ מוֹאָב מֵהַרְרֵי־ קֶדֶם לְכָה
come! east from-mountains-of Moab king-of Balak he-brought-me Aram from

אָרָה־ לִּי יַעֲקֹב וּלְכָה זֹעֲמָה יִשְׂרָאֵל׃ (8) מָה אֶקֹּב לֹא
not can-I-curse how? (8) Israel denounce! and-come! Jacob for-me curse!

קַבֹּה אֵל וּמָה אֶזְעֹם לֹא זָעַם יְהוָה׃ (9) כִּי־
for (9) Yahweh he-denounced not can-I-denounce and-how? God he-cursed-him

can I say just anything? I must
speak only what God puts in
my mouth."
39 Then Balaam went with
Balak to Kiriath Huzoth.
40 Balak sacrificed cattle and
sheep, and gave some to Balaam and the princes who
were with him. 41 The next
morning Balak took Balaam up
to Bamoth Baal, and from
there he saw part of the
people.

Balaam's First Oracle

23 Balaam said, "Build me
seven altars here, and
prepare seven bulls and seven
rams for me." 2 Balak did as Balaam said, and the two of them
offered a bull and a ram on
each altar.
3 Then Balaam said to Balak,
"Stay here beside your
offering while I go aside. Perhaps the LORD will come to
meet with me. Whatever he
reveals to me I will tell you."
Then he went off to a barren
height.
4 God met with him, and Balaam said, "I have prepared
seven altars, and on each altar
I have offered a bull and a
ram."
5 The LORD put a message in
Balaam's mouth and said, "Go
back to Balak and give him
this message."
6 So he went back to him and
found him standing beside his
offering, with all the princes of
Moab. 7 Then Balaam uttered
his oracle:

"Balak brought me from
  Aram,
 the king of Moab from
  the eastern mountains.
'Come,' he said, 'curse
  Jacob for me;
 come, denounce Israel.'
8 How can I curse
  those whom God has not
   cursed?
How can I denounce
  those whom the LORD
   has not denounced?

מֵרֹאשׁ צֻרִים אֶרְאֶנּוּ וּמִגְּבָעוֹת אֲשׁוּרֶנּוּ הֶן־ עָם
people see! I-view-him and-from-heights I-see-him rocky-ones from-peak-of

לְבָדָד יִשְׁכֹּן וּבַגּוֹיִם לֹא יִתְחַשָּׁב׃ מִי מָנָה
he-can-count who? (10) he-considers-self not and-of-the-nations he-lives apart

עֲפַר יַעֲקֹב וּמִסְפָּר אֶת־ רֹבַע יִשְׂרָאֵל תָּמֹת נַפְשִׁי
life-of-me let-her-die Israel fourth-of *** or-number Jacob dust-of

מוֹת יְשָׁרִים וּתְהִי אַחֲרִיתִי כָּמֹהוּ׃ וַיֹּאמֶר
and-he-said (11) like-of-him end-of-me and-may-she-be righteous-ones death-of

בָּלָק אֶל־בִּלְעָם מֶה עָשִׂיתָ לִי לָקֹב אֹיְבַי לְקַחְתִּיךָ
I-brought-you being-enemies-of-me to-curse to-me you-did what? Balaam to Balak

וְהִנֵּה בֵּרַכְתָּ בָרֵךְ׃ וַיַּעַן וַיֹּאמַר הֲלֹא אֵת
*** not? and-he-said and-he-answered (12) to-bless you-blessed but-see!

אֲשֶׁר יָשִׂים יְהוָה בְּפִי אֹתוֹ אֶשְׁמֹר לְדַבֵּר׃ וַיֹּאמֶר
then-he-said (13) to-speak I-must him in-mouth-of-me Yahweh he-puts what

אֵלָיו בָּלָק לְךָ־ נָא אִתִּי אֶל־מָקוֹם אַחֵר אֲשֶׁר תִּרְאֶנּוּ
you-can-see-him where another place to with-me now! come! Balak to-him

מִשָּׁם אֶפֶס קָצֵהוּ תִּרְאֶה וְכֻלּוֹ לֹא תִרְאֶה
you-will-see not but-all-of-him you-will-see part-of-him only from-there

וְקָבְנוֹ לִי מִשָּׁם׃ וַיִּקָּחֵהוּ שְׂדֵה צֹפִים אֶל־
on Zophim field-of so-he-took-him (14) from-there for-me and-curse-him!

רֹאשׁ הַפִּסְגָּה וַיִּבֶן שִׁבְעָה מִזְבְּחֹת וַיַּעַל פָּר וָאַיִל
and-ram bull and-he-offered altars seven and-he-built the-Pisgah top-of

בַּמִּזְבֵּחַ׃ וַיֹּאמֶר אֶל־ בָּלָק הִתְיַצֵּב כֹּה עַל־ עֹלָתֶךָ
offering-of-you beside here stay! Balak to and-he-said (15) on-the-altar

וְאָנֹכִי אִקָּרֶה כֹּה׃ וַיִּקָּר יְהוָה אֶל־ בִּלְעָם וַיָּשֶׂם דָּבָר
message and-he-put Balaam with Yahweh and-he-met (16) there I-meet while-I

בְּפִיו וַיֹּאמֶר שׁוּב אֶל־בָּלָק וְכֹה תְדַבֵּר׃ וַיָּבֹא
so-he-went (17) you-speak and-this Balak to go-back! and-he-said in-mouth-of-him

אֵלָיו וְהִנּוֹ נִצָּב עַל־ עֹלָתוֹ וְשָׂרֵי מוֹאָב
Moab and-princes-of offering-of-him beside standing and-see-he! to-him

אִתּוֹ וַיֹּאמֶר לוֹ בָּלָק מַה־ דִּבֶּר יְהוָה׃ וַיִּשָּׂא
then-he-uttered (18) Yahweh he-said what? Balak to-him and-he-asked with-him

מְשָׁלוֹ וַיֹּאמַר קוּם בָּלָק וּשֲׁמָע הַאֲזִינָה עָדַי בְּנוֹ
son-of-him to-me hear! and-listen! Balak arise! and-he-said oracle-of-him

צִפֹּר׃ לֹא אִישׁ אֵל וִיכַזֵּב וּבֶן־ אָדָם וְיִתְנֶחָם
that-he-changes-mind man nor-son-of that-he-lies God man not (19) Zippor

הַהוּא אָמַר וְלֹא יַעֲשֶׂה וְדִבֶּר וְלֹא יְקִימֶנָּה׃
he-fulfills-her and-not or-he-promises he-acts and-not he-speaks he?

9From the rocky peaks I see
them,
from the heights I view
them.
I see a people who live
apart
and do not consider
themselves one of the
nations.
10Who can count the dust of
Jacob
or number the fourth
part of Israel?
Let me die the death of the
righteous,
and may my end be like
theirs!"

11Balak said to Balaam,
"What have you done to me? I
brought you to curse my enemies, but you have done nothing but bless them!"
12He answered, "Must I not
speak what the LORD puts in
my mouth?"

Balaam's Second Oracle

13Then Balak said to him,
"Come with me to another
place where you can see them;
you will see only a part but not
all of them. And from there,
curse them for me." 14So he
took him to the field of Zophim on the top of Pisgah, and
there he built seven altars and
offered a bull and a ram on
each altar.
15Balaam said to Balak, "Stay
here beside your offering
while I meet with him over
there."
16The LORD met with Balaam
and put a message in his
mouth and said, "Go back to
Balak and give him this message."
17So he went to him and
found him standing beside his
offering, with the princes of
Moab. Balak asked him,
"What did the LORD say?"
18Then he uttered his oracle:

"Arise, Balak, and listen;
hear me, son of Zippor.
19God is not a man, that he
should lie,
nor a son of man, that
he should change his
mind.
Does he speak and then
not act?
Does he promise and not
fulfill?

°13 ק לכה

הִנֵּה בָרֵךְ לָקָחְתִּי וּבֵרֵךְ וְלֹא אֲשִׁיבֶנָּה׃
I-can-change-her and-not now-he-blessed I-received to-bless see! (20)

לֹא־הִבִּיט אָוֶן בְּיַעֲקֹב וְלֹא־רָאָה עָמָל בְּיִשְׂרָאֵל
in-Israel misery he-observes and-not in-Jacob misfortune he-sees not (21)

יְהוָה אֱלֹהָיו עִמּוֹ וּתְרוּעַת מֶלֶךְ בּוֹ׃ אֵל מוֹצִיאָם
bringing-them God (22) among-him King and-shout-of with-him God-of-him Yahweh

מִמִּצְרָיִם כְּתוֹעֲפֹת רְאֵם לוֹ׃ כִּי לֹא־נַחַשׁ בְּיַעֲקֹב
against-Jacob sorcery no indeed (23) to-him wild-ox as-strengths-of from-Egypt

וְלֹא־קֶסֶם בְּיִשְׂרָאֵל כָּעֵת יֵאָמֵר לְיַעֲקֹב
of-Jacob he-will-be-said at-the-now against-Israel divination and-no

וּלְיִשְׂרָאֵל מַה־פָּעַל אֵל׃ הֶן־עָם כְּלָבִיא יָקוּם
he-rises like-lioness people see! (24) God he-did what! and-of-Israel

וְכַאֲרִי יִתְנַשָּׂא לֹא יִשְׁכַּב עַד־יֹאכַל טֶרֶף וְדַם־
and-blood-of prey he-devours till he-rests not he-rouses-self and-like-lion

חֲלָלִים יִשְׁתֶּה׃ וַיֹּאמֶר בָּלָק אֶל־בִּלְעָם גַּם־קֹב לֹא
not to-curse at-all Balaam to Balak then-he-said (25) he-drinks victims

תִקֳּבֶנּוּ גַּם־בָּרֵךְ לֹא תְבָרְכֶנּוּ׃ וַיַּעַן בִּלְעָם
Balaam and-he-answered (26) you-bless-him not to-bless at-all you-curse-him

וַיֹּאמֶר אֶל־בָּלָק הֲלֹא דִּבַּרְתִּי אֵלֶיךָ לֵאמֹר כֹּל אֲשֶׁר־יְדַבֵּר יְהוָה
Yahweh he-says that all to-say to-you I-told not? Balak to and-he-said

אֹתוֹ אֶעֱשֶׂה׃ וַיֹּאמֶר בָּלָק אֶל־בִּלְעָם לְכָה־נָּא אֶקָּחֲךָ אֶל־
to let-me-take-you now! come! Balaam to Balak then-he-said (27) I-must-do him

מָקוֹם אַחֵר אוּלַי יִישַׁר בְּעֵינֵי הָאֱלֹהִים וְקַבֹּתוֹ
and-you-may-curse-him the-God in-eyes-of he-will-please perhaps another place

לִי מִשָּׁם׃ וַיִּקַּח בָּלָק אֶת־בִּלְעָם רֹאשׁ הַפְּעוֹר
the-Peor top-of Balaam *** Balak and-he-took (28) from-there for-me

הַנִּשְׁקָף עַל־פְּנֵי הַיְשִׁימֹן׃ וַיֹּאמֶר בִּלְעָם אֶל־
to Balaam and-he-said (29) the-wasteland face-of to the-one-overlooking

בָּלָק בְּנֵה־לִי בָזֶה שִׁבְעָה מִזְבְּחֹת וְהָכֵן לִי בָּזֶה שִׁבְעָה
seven at-here for-me and-prepare! altars seven at-here for-me build! Balak

פָּרִים וְשִׁבְעָה אֵילִים׃ וַיַּעַשׂ בָּלָק כַּאֲשֶׁר אָמַר בִּלְעָם
Balaam he-said just-as Balak so-he-did (30) rams and-seven bulls

וַיַּעַל פָּר וָאַיִל בַּמִּזְבֵּחַ׃ וַיַּרְא בִּלְעָם כִּי
that Balaam when-he-saw (24:1) on-the-altar and-ram bull and-he-offered

טוֹב בְּעֵינֵי יְהוָה לְבָרֵךְ אֶת־יִשְׂרָאֵל וְלֹא־הָלַךְ כְּפַעַם־
as-time he-resorted then-not Israel *** to-bless Yahweh in-eyes-of pleasing

בְּפַעַם לִקְרַאת נְחָשִׁים וַיָּשֶׁת אֶל־הַמִּדְבָּר פָּנָיו׃
faces-of-him the-desert toward but-he-turned sorceries to-use at-time

20I have received a command
to bless;
he has blessed, and I
cannot change it.
21"No misfortune is seen in
Jacob,
no misery observed in
Israel.
The LORD their God is with
them;
the shout of the King is
among them.
22God brought them out of
Egypt;
they have the strength of
a wild ox.
23There is no sorcery against
Jacob,
no divination against
Israel.
It will now be said of Jacob
and of Israel, 'See what
God has done!'
24The people rise like a
lioness;
they rouse themselves
like a lion
that does not rest till he
devours his prey
and drinks the blood of
his victims."

25Then Balak said to Balaam, "Neither curse them at all nor bless them at all!"
26Balaam answered, "Did I not tell you I must do whatever the LORD says?"

Balaam's Third Oracle

27Then Balak said to Balaam, "Come, let me take you to another place. Perhaps it will please God to let you curse them for me from there."
28And Balak took Balaam to the top of Peor, overlooking the wasteland.
29Balaam said, "Build me seven altars here, and prepare seven bulls and seven rams for me."
30Balak did as Balaam had said, and offered a bull and a ram on each altar.

24 Now when Balaam saw that it pleased the LORD to bless Israel, he did not resort to sorcery as at other times, but turned his face

וַיִּשָּׂא בִלְעָם אֶת־ עֵינָיו וַיַּרְא אֶת־יִשְׂרָאֵל שֹׁכֵן
camping Israel *** and-he-saw eyes-of-him *** Balaam when-he-lifted (2)

לִשְׁבָטָיו וַתְּהִי עָלָיו רוּחַ אֱלֹהִים׃ וַיִּשָּׂא
and-he-uttered (3) God Spirit-of on-him then-she-came by-tribes-of-him

מְשָׁלוֹ וַיֹּאמַר נְאֻם בִּלְעָם בְּנוֹ בְעֹר וּנְאֻם
and-oracle-of Beor son-of-him Balaam oracle-of and-he-said oracle-of-him

הַגֶּבֶר שְׁתֻם הָעָיִן׃ נְאֻם שֹׁמֵעַ אִמְרֵי־ אֵל
God words-of one-hearing oracle-of (4) the-eye seeing-clearly-of the-man

אֲשֶׁר מַחֲזֵה שַׁדַּי יֶחֱזֶה נֹפֵל וּגְלוּי עֵינָיִם׃ מַה־
how! (5) eyes and-being-open-of prostrating he-sees Almighty vision-of who

טֹּבוּ אֹהָלֶיךָ יַעֲקֹב מִשְׁכְּנֹתֶיךָ יִשְׂרָאֵל׃ כִּנְחָלִים
like-valleys (6) Israel dwellings-of-you Jacob tents-of-you they-are-beautiful

נִטָּיוּ כְּגַנֹּת עֲלֵי נָהָר כַּאֲהָלִים נָטַע יְהוָה
Yahweh he-plants like-aloes river beside like-gardens they-spread-out

כַּאֲרָזִים עֲלֵי־ מָיִם׃ יִזַּל־ מַיִם מִדָּלְיָו
from-buckets-of-him waters he-will-flow (7) waters beside like-cedars

וְזַרְעוֹ בְּמַיִם רַבִּים וְיָרֹם מֵאֲגַג
than-Agag and-he-will-be-greater abundant-ones with-waters and-seed-of-him

מַלְכּוֹ וְתִנַּשֵּׂא מַלְכֻתוֹ׃ אֵל מוֹצִיאוֹ
bringing-him God (8) kingdom-of-him and-she-will-be-exalted king-of-him

מִמִּצְרַיִם כְּתוֹעֲפֹת רְאֵם לוֹ יֹאכַל גּוֹיִם צָרָיו
ones-hostile-to-him nations he-devours to-him wild-ox as-strengths-of from-Egypt

וְעַצְמֹתֵיהֶם יְגָרֵם וְחִצָּיו יִמְחָץ׃
he-will-pierce and-arrows-of-him he-will-break and-bones-of-them

כָּרַע שָׁכַב כַּאֲרִי וּכְלָבִיא מִי יְקִימֶנּוּ
he-rouses-him who? and-like-lioness like-lion he-lies he-crouches (9)

מְבָרֲכֶיךָ בָרוּךְ וְאֹרְרֶיךָ אָרוּר׃
being-cursed but-one-cursing-you being-blessed one-blessing-you

וַיִּחַר־ אַף בָּלָק אֶל־ בִּלְעָם וַיִּסְפֹּק אֶת־
*** and-he-struck-together Balaam against Balak anger-of then-he-burned (10)

כַּפָּיו וַיֹּאמֶר בָּלָק אֶל־ בִּלְעָם לָקֹב אֹיְבַי
being-enemies-of-me to-curse Balaam to Balak and-he-said hands-of-him

קְרָאתִיךָ וְהִנֵּה בֵּרַכְתָּ בָרֵךְ זֶה שָׁלֹשׁ פְּעָמִים׃ וְעַתָּה
so-now (11) times three this to-bless you-blessed but-see! I-summoned-you

בְּרַח־ לְךָ אֶל־ מְקוֹמֶךָ אָמַרְתִּי כַּבֵּד אֲכַבֶּדְךָ וְהִנֵּה
but-see! I-would-reward-you to-reward I-said home-of-you to go! leave!

מְנָעֲךָ יְהוָה מִכָּבוֹד׃ וַיֹּאמֶר בִּלְעָם אֶל־בָּלָק הֲלֹא
not? Balak to Balaam and-he-answered (12) from-reward Yahweh he-kept-you

toward the desert. 2When Balaam looked out and saw Israel encamped tribe by tribe, the Spirit of God came upon him
3and he uttered his oracle:

"The oracle of Balaam son of Beor,
the oracle of one whose eye sees clearly,
4the oracle of one who hears the words of God,
who sees a vision from the Almighty,[z]
who falls prostrate, and whose eyes are opened:

5"How beautiful are your tents, O Jacob,
your dwelling places, O Israel!

6"Like valleys they spread out,
like gardens beside a river,
like aloes planted by the LORD,
like cedars beside the waters.
7Water will flow from their buckets;
their seed will have abundant water.

"Their king will be greater than Agag;
their kingdom will be exalted.

8"God brought them out of Egypt;
they have the strength of a wild ox.
They devour hostile nations
and break their bones in pieces;
with their arrows they pierce them.
9Like a lion they crouch and lie down,
like a lioness—who dares to rouse them?

"May those who bless you be blessed
and those who curse you be cursed!"

10Then Balak's anger burned against Balaam. He struck his hands together and said to him, "I summoned you to curse my enemies, but you have blessed them these three times.
11Now leave at once and go home! I said I would reward you handsomely, but the LORD has kept you from being rewarded."
12Balaam answered Balak,

z4 Hebrew *Shaddai*; also in verse 16

גַּם אֶל־ מַלְאָכֶיךָ אֲשֶׁר־ שָׁלַחְתָּ אֵלַי דִּבַּרְתִּי לֵאמֹר׃ אִם־ יִתֶּן־
he-gave if (13) to-say I-told to-me you-sent whom messengers-of-you to indeed

לִי בָלָק מְלֹא בֵיתוֹ כֶּסֶף וְזָהָב לֹא אוּכַל לַעֲבֹר
to-go-beyond I-could not and-gold silver palace-of-him filled-of Balak to-me

אֶת־ פִּי יְהוָה לַעֲשׂוֹת טוֹבָה אוֹ רָעָה מִלִּבִּי אֲשֶׁר־יְדַבֵּר יְהוָה
Yahweh he-says what from-heart-of-me bad or good to-do Yahweh command-of ***

אֹתוֹ אֲדַבֵּר׃ וְעַתָּה הִנְנִי הוֹלֵךְ לְעַמִּי לְכָה אִיעָצְךָ
let-me-warn-you come! to-people-of-me going see-I! and-now (14) I-must-say him

אֲשֶׁר יַעֲשֶׂה הָעָם הַזֶּה לְעַמְּךָ בְּאַחֲרִית הַיָּמִים׃
the-days in-coming-of to-people-of-you the-this the-people he-will-do what

וַיִּשָּׂא מְשָׁלוֹ וַיֹּאמַר נְאֻם בִּלְעָם בְּנוֹ
son-of-him Balaam oracle-of and-he-said oracle-of-him then-he-uttered (15)

בְעֹר וּנְאֻם הַגֶּבֶר שְׁתֻם הָעָיִן׃ נְאֻם
oracle-of (16) the-eye seeing-clearly-of the-man and-oracle-of Beor

שֹׁמֵעַ אִמְרֵי־ אֵל וְיֹדֵעַ דַּעַת עֶלְיוֹן מַחֲזֵה
vision-of Most-High knowledge-of and-one-knowing God words-of one-hearing

שַׁדַּי יֶחֱזֶה נֹפֵל וּגְלוּי עֵינָיִם׃ אֶרְאֶנּוּ וְלֹא
but-not I-see-him (17) eyes and-being-open-of prostrating he-sees Almighty

עַתָּה אֲשׁוּרֶנּוּ וְלֹא קָרוֹב דָּרַךְ כּוֹכָב מִיַּעֲקֹב וְקָם
and-he-will-rise from-Jacob star he-will-come near but-not I-behold-him now

שֵׁבֶט מִיִּשְׂרָאֵל וּמָחַץ פַּאֲתֵי מוֹאָב וְקַרְקַר כָּל־
all-of and-skull-of Moab foreheads-of and-he-will-crush from-Israel scepter

בְּנֵי־ שֵׁת׃ וְהָיָה אֱדוֹם יְרֵשָׁה וְהָיָה יְרֵשָׁה
conquered and-he-will-be conquered Edom and-he-will-be (18) Sheth sons-of

שֵׂעִיר אֹיְבָיו וְיִשְׂרָאֵל עֹשֶׂה חָיִל׃ וְיֵרְדְּ
and-he-will-rule (19) strong growing but-Israel being-enemy-of-him Seir

מִיַּעֲקֹב וְהֶאֱבִיד שָׂרִיד מֵעִיר׃ וַיַּרְא אֶת־ עֲמָלֵק
Amalek *** then-he-saw (20) of-city survivor and-he-will-destroy from-Jacob

וַיִּשָּׂא מְשָׁלוֹ וַיֹּאמַר רֵאשִׁית גּוֹיִם עֲמָלֵק
Amalek nations first-of and-he-said oracle-of-him and-he-uttered

וְאַחֲרִיתוֹ עֲדֵי אֹבֵד׃ וַיַּרְא אֶת־ הַקֵּינִי וַיִּשָּׂא
and-he-uttered the-Kenite *** then-he-saw (21) being-ruin to but-last-of-him

מְשָׁלוֹ וַיֹּאמַר אֵיתָן מוֹשָׁבֶךָ וְשִׂים בַּסֶּלַע
in-the-rock and-he-is-set dwelling-of-you secure and-he-said oracle-of-him

קִנֶּךָ׃ כִּי אִם־ יִהְיֶה לְבָעֵר קָיִן עַד־ מָה אַשּׁוּר
Asshur when at Kenite to-be-destroyed he-will-be yet but (22) nest-of-you

תִּשְׁבֶּךָּ׃ וַיִּשָּׂא מְשָׁלוֹ וַיֹּאמַר אוֹי מִי
who? ah! and-he-said oracle-of-him then-he-uttered (23) she-captures-you

"Did I not tell the messengers you sent me, [13]'Even if Balak gave me his palace filled with silver and gold, I could not do anything of my own accord, good or bad, to go beyond the command of the LORD—and I must say only what the LORD says'? [14]Now I am going back to my people, but come, let me warn you of what this people will do to your people in days to come."

Balaam's Fourth Oracle

[15]Then he uttered his oracle:

"The oracle of Balaam son of Beor,
the oracle of one whose eye sees clearly,
[16]the oracle of one who hears the words of God,
who has knowledge from the Most High,
who sees a vision from the Almighty,
who falls prostrate, and whose eyes are opened:

[17]"I see him, but not now;
I behold him, but not near.
A star will come out of Jacob;
a scepter will rise out of Israel.
He will crush the foreheads of Moab,
the skulls[a] of[b] all the sons of Sheth.[c]
[18]Edom will be conquered;
Seir, his enemy, will be conquered,
but Israel will grow strong.
[19]A ruler will come out of Jacob
and destroy the survivors of the city."

Balaam's Final Oracles

[20]Then Balaam saw Amalek and uttered his oracle:

"Amalek was first among the nations,
but he will come to ruin at last."

[21]Then he saw the Kenites and uttered his oracle:

"Your dwelling place is secure,
your nest is set in a rock;
[22]yet you Kenites will be destroyed
when Asshur takes you captive."

[23]Then he uttered his oracle:

[a]17 Samaritan Pentateuch (see also Jer. 48:45); the meaning of the word in the Masoretic Text is uncertain.
[b]17 Or possibly *Moab, / batter*
[c]17 Or *all the noisy boasters*

יִחְיֶה מִשֻּׂמוֹ אֵל׃ וְצִים מִיַּד כִּתִּים
Kittim from-shore-of and-ships (24) God when-to-do-him he-can-live

וְעִנּוּ אַשּׁוּר וְעִנּוּ־ עֵבֶר וְגַם־ הוּא עֲדֵי
to he but-also Eber and-they-will-subdue Asshur and-they-will-subdue

אֹבֵד׃ וַיָּקָם בִּלְעָם וַיֵּלֶךְ וַיָּשָׁב
and-he-returned and-he-went Balaam then-he-got-up (25) being-ruin

לִמְקֹמוֹ וְגַם־ בָּלָק הָלַךְ לְדַרְכּוֹ׃ וַיֵּשֶׁב
and-he-stayed (25:1) on-way-of-him he-went Balak and-also to-home-of-him

יִשְׂרָאֵל בַּשִּׁטִּים וַיָּחֶל הָעָם לִזְנוֹת אֶל־
with to-be-sexually-immoral the-people and-he-began in-the-Shittim Israel

בְּנוֹת מוֹאָב׃ וַתִּקְרֶאןָ לָעָם לְזִבְחֵי אֱלֹהֵיהֶן
gods-of-them to-sacrifices-of to-the-people and-they-invited (2) Moab women-of

וַיֹּאכַל הָעָם וַיִּשְׁתַּחֲווּ לֵאלֹהֵיהֶן׃ וַיִּצָּמֶד
so-he-joined (3) before-gods-of-them and-they-bowed the-people and-he-ate

יִשְׂרָאֵל לְבַעַל פְּעוֹר וַיִּחַר־ אַף יְהוָה בְּיִשְׂרָאֵל׃
against-Israel Yahweh anger-of and-he-burned Peor to-Baal-of Israel

וַיֹּאמֶר יְהוָה אֶל־ מֹשֶׁה קַח אֶת־ כָּל־ רָאשֵׁי הָעָם
the-people leaders-of all-of *** take! Moses to Yahweh and-he-said (4)

וְהוֹקַע אוֹתָם לַיהוָה נֶגֶד הַשָּׁמֶשׁ וְיָשֹׁב חֲרוֹן
fierce-anger-of so-he-may-turn the-daylight in before-Yahweh them and-kill!

אַף־ יְהוָה מִיִּשְׂרָאֵל׃ וַיֹּאמֶר מֹשֶׁה אֶל־ שֹׁפְטֵי יִשְׂרָאֵל
Israel ones-judging-of to Moses so-he-said (5) from-Israel Yahweh anger-of

הִרְגוּ אִישׁ אֲנָשָׁיו הַנִּצְמָדִים לְבַעַל פְּעוֹר׃ וְהִנֵּה אִישׁ
one then-see! (6) Peor to-Baal-of the-ones-joining men-of-him each kill!

מִבְּנֵי יִשְׂרָאֵל בָּא וַיַּקְרֵב אֶל־ אֶחָיו אֶת־
*** brothers-of-him to and-he-brought coming Israel from-sons-of

הַמִּדְיָנִית לְעֵינֵי מֹשֶׁה וּלְעֵינֵי כָּל־
whole-of and-before-eyes-of Moses before-eyes-of the-Midianite-woman

עֲדַת בְּנֵי־ יִשְׂרָאֵל וְהֵמָּה בֹכִים פֶּתַח אֹהֶל
Tent-of entrance-of ones weeping while-they Israel sons-of the-assembly-of

מוֹעֵד׃ וַיַּרְא פִּינְחָס בֶּן־ אֶלְעָזָר בֶּן־ אַהֲרֹן הַכֹּהֵן
the-priest Aaron son-of Eleazar son-of Phinehas when-he-saw (7) Meeting

וַיָּקָם מִתּוֹךְ הָעֵדָה וַיִּקַּח רֹמַח בְּיָדוֹ׃
in-hand-of-him spear and-he-took the-assembly from-among then-he-left

וַיָּבֹא אַחַר אִישׁ־ יִשְׂרָאֵל אֶל־ הַקֻּבָּה וַיִּדְקֹר
and-he-drove-through the-tent into Israel man-of after and-he-went (8)

אֶת־ שְׁנֵיהֶם אֵת אִישׁ יִשְׂרָאֵל וְאֶת־ הָאִשָּׁה אֶל־ קֳבָתָהּ
body-of-her into the-woman and Israel man-of *** both-of-them ***

"Ah, who can live when
God does this?[c]
24 Ships will come from the
shores of Kittim;
they will subdue Asshur
and Eber,
but they too will come to
ruin."

25 Then Balaam got up and
returned home and Balak
went his own way.

Moab Seduces Israel

25 While Israel was stay-
ing in Shittim, the men
began to indulge in sexual im-
morality with Moabite
women, 2 who invited them to
the sacrifices to their gods. The
people ate and bowed down
before these gods. 3 So Israel
joined in worshiping the Baal
of Peor. And the LORD's anger
burned against them.
4 The LORD said to Moses,
"Take all the leaders of these
people, kill them and expose
them in broad daylight before
the LORD, so that the LORD's
fierce anger may turn away
from Israel."
5 So Moses said to Israel's
judges, "Each of you must put
to death those of your men
who have joined in worshiping the Baal of Peor."
6 Then an Israelite man
brought to his family a Midianite woman right before the
eyes of Moses and the whole
assembly of Israel while they
were weeping at the entrance
to the Tent of Meeting. 7 When
Phinehas son of Eleazar, the
son of Aaron, the priest, saw
this, he left the assembly, took
a spear in his hand 8 and followed the Israelite into the
tent. He drove the spear
through both of them—
through the Israelite and into
the woman's body. Then the

[c]23 Masoretic Text; with a different word division of the Hebrew *A people will gather from the north.*

*2 Most mss have no *dagesh* in the first *vav* (חוו־).

וַתֵּעָצַר הַמַּגֵּפָה מֵעַל בְּנֵי יִשְׂרָאֵל׃ וַיִּהְיוּ
but-they-were (9) Israel sons-of from-against the-plague then-she-was-stopped

הַמֵּתִים בַּמַּגֵּפָה אַרְבָּעָה וְעֶשְׂרִים אָלֶף׃ וַיְדַבֵּר יְהוָה
Yahweh and-he-spoke (10) thousand and-twenty four in-the-plague the-ones-dead

אֶל־מֹשֶׁה לֵּאמֹר׃ פִּינְחָס בֶּן־אֶלְעָזָר בֶּן־אַהֲרֹן הַכֹּהֵן
the-priest Aaron son-of Eleazar son-of Phinehas (11) to-say Moses to

הֵשִׁיב אֶת־חֲמָתִי מֵעַל בְּנֵי־יִשְׂרָאֵל בְּקַנְאוֹ
when-to-be-zealous-him Israel sons-of from-against anger-of-me *** he-turned

אֶת־קִנְאָתִי בְּתוֹכָם וְלֹא־כִלִּיתִי אֶת־בְּנֵי־יִשְׂרָאֵל בְּקִנְאָתִי׃
in-zeal-of-me Israel sons-of *** I-put-end so-not among-them zeal-of-me with

לָכֵן אֱמֹר הִנְנִי נֹתֵן לוֹ אֶת־בְּרִיתִי שָׁלוֹם׃
peace covenant-of-me *** with-him making see-I! tell! therefore (12)

וְהָיְתָה לּוֹ וּלְזַרְעוֹ אַחֲרָיו בְּרִית
covenant-of after-him and-for-descendant-of-him for-him and-she-will-be (13)

כְּהֻנַּת עוֹלָם תַּחַת אֲשֶׁר קִנֵּא לֵאלֹהָיו וַיְכַפֵּר
and-he-atoned for-God-of-him he-was-zealous that because lasting priesthood-of

עַל־בְּנֵי יִשְׂרָאֵל׃ וְשֵׁם אִישׁ יִשְׂרָאֵל הַמֻּכֶּה אֲשֶׁר
that the-one-being-killed Israel man-of now-name-of (14) Israel sons-of for

הֻכָּה אֶת־הַמִּדְיָנִית זִמְרִי בֶּן־סָלוּא נְשִׂיא בֵית־
house-of leader-of Salu son-of Zimri the-Midianite-woman with he-was-killed

אָב לַשִּׁמְעֹנִי׃ וְשֵׁם הָאִשָּׁה הַמֻּכָּה
the-one-being-killed the-woman and-name-of (15) of-the-Simeonite father

הַמִּדְיָנִית כָּזְבִּי בַת־צוּר רֹאשׁ אֻמּוֹת בֵּית־אָב
father house-of tribes-of chief-of Zur daughter-of Cozbi the-Midianite

בְּמִדְיָן הוּא׃ וַיְדַבֵּר יְהוָה אֶל־מֹשֶׁה לֵּאמֹר׃ צָרוֹר אֶת־
*** to-be-enemy (17) to-say Moses to Yahweh and-he-spoke (16) he in-Midian

הַמִּדְיָנִים וְהִכִּיתֶם אוֹתָם׃ כִּי צֹרְרִים הֵם לָכֶם
to-you they being-enemies for (18) them and-you-kill the-Midianites

בְּנִכְלֵיהֶם אֲשֶׁר־נִכְּלוּ לָכֶם עַל־דְּבַר־פְּעוֹר וְעַל־
and-in Peor affair-of in to-you they-deceived when in-deceptions-of-them

דְּבַר כָּזְבִּי בַת־נְשִׂיא מִדְיָן אֲחֹתָם הַמֻּכָּה
the-being-killed sister-of-them Midian leader-of daughter-of Cozbi affair-of

בְיוֹם־הַמַּגֵּפָה עַל־דְּבַר־פְּעוֹר׃ וַיְהִי אַחֲרֵי הַמַּגֵּפָה
the-plague after and-he-was (19)* Peor result-of as the-plague on-day-of

וַיֹּאמֶר יְהוָה אֶל־מֹשֶׁה וְאֶל אֶלְעָזָר בֶּן־אַהֲרֹן הַכֹּהֵן
the-priest Aaron son-of Eleazar and-to Moses to Yahweh and-he-said (26:1)

לֵאמֹר׃ שְׂאוּ אֶת־רֹאשׁ ׀ כָּל־עֲדַת בְּנֵי־יִשְׂרָאֵל
Israel sons-of community-of whole-of census-of *** take! (2) to-say

plague against the Israelites
was stopped; 9but those who
died in the plague numbered
24,000.
10The LORD said to Moses,
11"Phinehas son of Eleazar, the
son of Aaron, the priest, has
turned my anger away from
the Israelites; for he was as
zealous as I am for my honor
among them, so that in my
zeal I did not put an end to
them. 12Therefore tell him I am
making my covenant of peace
with him. 13He and his descendants will have a covenant of a lasting priesthood,
because he was zealous for the
honor of his God and made
atonement for the Israelites."
14The name of the Israelite
who was killed with the Midianite woman was Zimri son
of Salu, the leader of a Simeon-
ite family. 15And the name of
the Midianite woman who
was put to death was Cozbi
daughter of Zur, a tribal chief
of a Midianite family.
16The LORD said to Moses,
17"Treat the Midianites as enemies and kill them, 18because
they treated you as enemies
when they deceived you in
the affair of Peor and their sister Cozbi, the daughter of a
Midianite leader, the woman
who was killed when the
plague came as a result of
Peor."

The Second Census

26 After the plague the
LORD said to Moses and
Eleazar son of Aaron, the
priest, 2"Take a census of the
whole Israelite community by

*19 Verse 19 in Hebrew corresponds to the first three words of verse 1 of chapter 26 in the English.

מִבֶּן עֶשְׂרִים שָׁנָה וָמַעְלָה לְבֵית אֲבֹתָם כָּל־ יֹצֵא
serving every-of fathers-of-them by-house-of or-more year twenty from-son-of

צָבָא בְּיִשְׂרָאֵל׃ וַיְדַבֵּר מֹשֶׁה וְאֶלְעָזָר הַכֹּהֵן אֹתָם
with-them the-priest and-Eleazar Moses and-he-spoke (3) in-Israel army

בְּעַרְבֹת מוֹאָב עַל־ יַרְדֵּן יְרֵחוֹ לֵאמֹר׃ מִבֶּן עֶשְׂרִים שָׁנָה
year twenty from-son-of (4) to-say Jericho Jordan-of by Moab on-plains-of

וָמַעְלָה כַּאֲשֶׁר צִוָּה יְהוָה אֶת־ מֹשֶׁה וּבְנֵי יִשְׂרָאֵל
Israel and-sons-of Moses *** Yahweh he-commanded just-as or-more

הַיֹּצְאִים מֵאֶרֶץ מִצְרָיִם׃ רְאוּבֵן בְּכוֹר יִשְׂרָאֵל בְּנֵי
sons-of Israel firstborn-of Reuben (5) Egypt from-land-of the-ones-coming

רְאוּבֵן חֲנוֹךְ מִשְׁפַּחַת הַחֲנֹכִי לְפַלּוּא מִשְׁפַּחַת הַפַּלֻּאִי׃
the-Palluite clan-of through-Pallu the-Hanochite clan-of Hanoch Reuben

לְחֶצְרֹן מִשְׁפַּחַת הַחֶצְרוֹנִי לְכַרְמִי מִשְׁפַּחַת הַכַּרְמִי׃
the-Carmite clan-of through-Carmi the-Hezronite clan-of through-Hezron (6)

אֵלֶּה מִשְׁפְּחֹת הָרֻאוּבֵנִי* וַיִּהְיוּ פְקֻדֵיהֶם שְׁלֹשָׁה
three numberings-of-them and-they-were the-Reubenite clans-of these (7)

וְאַרְבָּעִים אֶלֶף וּשְׁבַע מֵאוֹת וּשְׁלֹשִׁים׃ וּבְנֵי פַלּוּא
Pallu and-sons-of (8) and-thirty hundreds and-seven-of thousand and-forty

אֱלִיאָב׃ וּבְנֵי אֱלִיאָב נְמוּאֵל וְדָתָן וַאֲבִירָם הוּא־ דָתָן
Dathan this and-Abiram and-Dathan Nemuel Eliab and-sons-of (9) Eliab

וַאֲבִירָם קְרוּאֵי° הָעֵדָה אֲשֶׁר הִצּוּ עַל־ מֹשֶׁה
Moses against they-rebelled who the-community officials-of and-Abiram

וְעַל־ אַהֲרֹן בַּעֲדַת־ קֹרַח בְּהַצֹּתָם עַל־ יְהוָה׃
Yahweh against when-to-rebel-them Korah among-follower-of Aaron and-against

וַתִּפְתַּח הָאָרֶץ אֶת־ פִּיהָ וַתִּבְלַע אֹתָם וְאֶת־
and them and-she-swallowed mouth-of-her *** the-earth and-she-opened (10)

קֹרַח בְּמוֹת הָעֵדָה בַּאֲכֹל הָאֵשׁ אֵת חֲמִשִּׁים
fifty *** the-fire when-to-devour the-follower when-to-die Korah

וּמָאתַיִם אִישׁ וַיִּהְיוּ לְנֵס׃ וּבְנֵי־ קֹרַח לֹא־
not Korah but-sons-of (11) as-warning and-they-served man and-two-hundreds

מֵתוּ׃ בְּנֵי שִׁמְעוֹן לְמִשְׁפְּחֹתָם לִנְמוּאֵל מִשְׁפַּחַת
clan-of through-Nemuel by-clans-of-them Simeon sons-of (12) they-died-out

הַנְּמוּאֵלִי לְיָמִין מִשְׁפַּחַת הַיָּמִינִי לְיָכִין מִשְׁפַּחַת
clan-of through-Jakin the-Jaminite clan-of through-Jamin the-Nemuelite

הַיָּכִינִי׃ לְזֶרַח מִשְׁפַּחַת הַזַּרְחִי לְשָׁאוּל מִשְׁפַּחַת
clan-of through-Shaul the-Zerahite clan-of through-Zerah (13) the-Jakinite

הַשָּׁאוּלִי׃ אֵלֶּה מִשְׁפְּחֹת הַשִּׁמְעֹנִי שְׁנַיִם וְעֶשְׂרִים אֶלֶף
thousand and-twenty two the-Simeonite clans-of these (14) the-Shaulite

families—all those twenty years old or more who are able to serve in the army of Israel."
3 So on the plains of Moab by the Jordan across from Jericho,[f] Moses and Eleazar the priest spoke with them and said,
4 "Take a census of the men twenty years old or more, as the LORD commanded Moses."

These were the Israelites who came out of Egypt:

5 The descendants of Reuben, the firstborn son of Israel, were:
through Hanoch, the Hanochite clan;
through Pallu, the Palluite clan;
6 through Hezron, the Hezronite clan;
through Carmi, the Carmite clan.
7 These were the clans of Reuben; those numbered were 43,730.
8 The son of Pallu was Eliab,
9 and the sons of Eliab were Nemuel, Dathan and Abiram. The same Dathan and Abiram were the community officials who rebelled against Moses and Aaron and were among Korah's followers when they rebelled against the LORD.
10 The earth opened its mouth and swallowed them along with Korah, whose followers died when the fire devoured the 250 men. And they served as a warning sign.
11 The line of Korah, however, did not die out.

12 The descendants of Simeon by their clans were:
through Nemuel, the Nemuelite clan;
through Jamin, the Jaminite clan;
through Jakin, the Jakinite clan;
13 through Zerah, the Zerahite clan;
through Shaul, the Shaulite clan.
14 These were the clans of Simeon; there were 22,200 men.

f3 Hebrew *Jordan of Jericho*; possibly an ancient name for the Jordan River; also in verse 63

*7 Most mss have no *qibbuts* under the *resh* (הָרְאוּ־).

°9 ק קריאי

וּמָאתָיִם׃ (15) בְּנֵי גָד לְמִשְׁפְּחֹתָם לִצְפוֹן מִשְׁפַּחַת
clan-of through-Zephon by-clans-of-them Gad sons-of (15) and-two-hundreds

הַצְּפוֹנִי לְחַגִּי מִשְׁפַּחַת הַחַגִּי לְשׁוּנִי מִשְׁפַּחַת
clan-of through-Shuni the-Haggite clan-of through-Haggi the-Zephonite

הַשּׁוּנִי׃ (16) לְאָזְנִי מִשְׁפַּחַת הָאָזְנִי לְעֵרִי מִשְׁפַּחַת הָעֵרִי׃
the-Erite clan-of through-Eri the-Oznite clan-of through-Ozni (16) the-Shunite

(17) לַאֲרוֹד מִשְׁפַּחַת הָאֲרוֹדִי לְאַרְאֵלִי מִשְׁפַּחַת הָאַרְאֵלִי׃
the-Arelite clan-of through-Areli the-Arodite clan-of through-Arod (17)

(18) אֵלֶּה מִשְׁפְּחֹת בְּנֵי־גָד לִפְקֻדֵיהֶם אַרְבָּעִים אֶלֶף
thousand forty by-numberings-of-them Gad sons-of clans-of these (18)

וַחֲמֵשׁ מֵאוֹת׃ (19) בְּנֵי יְהוּדָה עֵר וְאוֹנָן וַיָּמָת עֵר וְאוֹנָן
and-Onan Er but-he-died and-Onan Er Judah sons-of (19) hundreds and-five-of

בְּאֶרֶץ כְּנָעַן׃ (20) וַיִּהְיוּ בְנֵי־יְהוּדָה לְמִשְׁפְּחֹתָם
by-clans-of-them Judah sons-of and-they-were (20) Canaan in-land-of

לְשֵׁלָה מִשְׁפַּחַת הַשֵּׁלָנִי לְפֶרֶץ מִשְׁפַּחַת הַפַּרְצִי
the-Perezite clan-of through-Perez the-Shelanite clan-of through-Shelah

לְזֶרַח מִשְׁפַּחַת הַזַּרְחִי׃ (21) וַיִּהְיוּ בְנֵי־פֶרֶץ
Perez sons-of and-they-were (21) the-Zerahite clan-of through-Zerah

לְחֶצְרֹן מִשְׁפַּחַת הַחֶצְרֹנִי לְחָמוּל מִשְׁפַּחַת הֶחָמוּלִי׃
the-Hamulite clan-of through-Hamul the-Hezronite clan-of through-Hezron

(22) אֵלֶּה מִשְׁפְּחֹת יְהוּדָה לִפְקֻדֵיהֶם שִׁשָּׁה וְשִׁבְעִים אֶלֶף
thousand and-seventy six by-numberings-of-them Judah clans-of these (22)

וַחֲמֵשׁ מֵאוֹת׃ (23) בְּנֵי יִשָּׂשכָר לְמִשְׁפְּחֹתָם תּוֹלָע מִשְׁפַּחַת
clan-of Tola by-clans-of-them Issachar sons-of (23) hundreds and-five-of

הַתּוֹלָעִי לְפֻוָה מִשְׁפַּחַת הַפּוּנִי׃ (24) לְיָשׁוּב מִשְׁפַּחַת
clan-of through-Jashub (24) the-Punite clan-of through-Puvah the-Tolaite

הַיָּשֻׁבִי לְשִׁמְרֹן מִשְׁפַּחַת הַשִּׁמְרֹנִי׃ (25) אֵלֶּה מִשְׁפְּחֹת
clans-of these (25) the-Shimronite clan-of through-Shimron the-Jashubite

יִשָּׂשכָר לִפְקֻדֵיהֶם אַרְבָּעָה וְשִׁשִּׁים אֶלֶף וּשְׁלֹשׁ מֵאוֹת׃
hundreds and-three-of thousand and-sixty four by-numberings-of-them Issachar

(26) בְּנֵי זְבוּלֻן לְמִשְׁפְּחֹתָם לְסֶרֶד מִשְׁפַּחַת הַסַּרְדִּי
the-Seredite clan-of through-Sered by-clans-of-them Zebulun sons-of (26)

לְאֵלוֹן מִשְׁפַּחַת הָאֵלֹנִי לְיַחְלְאֵל מִשְׁפַּחַת הַיַּחְלְאֵלִי׃
the-Jahleelite clan-of through-Jahleel the-Elonite clan-of through-Elon

(27) אֵלֶּה מִשְׁפְּחֹת הַזְּבוּלֹנִי לִפְקֻדֵיהֶם שִׁשִּׁים אֶלֶף
thousand sixty by-numberings-of-them the-Zebulunite clans-of these (27)

וַחֲמֵשׁ מֵאוֹת׃ (28) בְּנֵי יוֹסֵף לְמִשְׁפְּחֹתָם מְנַשֶּׁה וְאֶפְרָיִם׃
and-Ephraim Manasseh by-clans-of-them Joseph sons-of (28) hundreds and-five-of

[15]The descendants of Gad by their clans were:
through Zephon, the Zephonite clan;
through Haggi, the Haggite clan;
through Shuni, the Shunite clan;
[16]through Ozni, the Oznite clan;
through Eri, the Erite clan;
[17]through Arodi,[g] the Arodite clan;
through Areli, the Arelite clan.
[18]These were the clans of Gad; those numbered were 40,500.

[19]Er and Onan were sons of Judah, but they died in Canaan.
[20]The descendants of Judah by their clans were:
through Shelah, the Shelanite clan;
through Perez, the Perezite clan;
through Zerah, the Zerahite clan.
[21]The descendants of Perez were:
through Hezron, the Hezronite clan;
through Hamul, the Hamulite clan.
[22]These were the clans of Judah; those numbered were 76,500.

[23]The descendants of Issachar by their clans were:
through Tola, the Tolaite clan;
through Puah, the Puite[h] clan;
[24]through Jashub, the Jashubite clan;
through Shimron, the Shimronite clan.
[25]These were the clans of Issachar; those numbered were 64,300.

[26]The descendants of Zebulun by their clans were:
through Sered, the Seredite clan;
through Elon, the Elonite clan;
through Jahleel, the Jahleelite clan.
[27]These were the clans of Zebulun; those numbered were 60,500.

[28]The descendants of Joseph by their clans through Manasseh and Ephraim were:

[g]17 Samaritan Pentateuch and Syriac (see also Gen. 46:16); Masoretic Text *Arod*
[h]23 Samaritan Pentateuch, Septuagint, Vulgate and Syriac (see also 1 Chron. 7:1); Masoretic Text *through Puvah, the Punite*

בְּנֵי מְנַשֶּׁה לְמָכִיר מִשְׁפַּחַת הַמָּכִירִי וּמָכִיר
now-Makir the-Makirite clan-of through-Makir Manasseh sons-of (29)

הוֹלִיד אֶת־ גִּלְעָד לְגִלְעָד מִשְׁפַּחַת הַגִּלְעָדִי׃ אֵלֶּה
these (30) the-Gileadite clan-of through-Gilead Gilead *** he-fathered

בְּנֵי גִלְעָד אִיעֶזֶר מִשְׁפַּחַת הָאִיעֶזְרִי לְחֵלֶק מִשְׁפַּחַת הַחֶלְקִי׃
the-Helekite clan-of through-Helek the-Iezerite clan-of Iezer Gilead sons-of

וְאַשְׂרִיאֵל מִשְׁפַּחַת הָאַשְׂרְאֵלִי וְשֶׁכֶם מִשְׁפַּחַת הַשִּׁכְמִי׃
the-Shechemite clan-of and-Shechem the-Asrielite clan-of and-Asriel (31)

וּשְׁמִידָע מִשְׁפַּחַת הַשְּׁמִידָעִי וְחֵפֶר מִשְׁפַּחַת הַחֶפְרִי׃
the-Hepherite clan-of and-Hepher the-Shemidaite clan-of and-Shemida (32)

וּצְלָפְחָד בֶּן־ חֵפֶר לֹא־ הָיוּ לוֹ בָּנִים כִּי אִם־ בָּנוֹת
daughters only but sons to-him they-were not Hepher son-of now-Zelophehad (33)

וְשֵׁם בְּנוֹת צְלָפְחָד מַחְלָה וְנֹעָה חָגְלָה מִלְכָּה וְתִרְצָה׃
and-Tirzah Milcah Hoglah and-Noah Mahlah Zelophehad daughters-of and-name-of

אֵלֶּה מִשְׁפְּחֹת מְנַשֶּׁה וּפְקֻדֵיהֶם שְׁנַיִם וַחֲמִשִּׁים אֶלֶף
thousand and-fifty two and-numberings-of-them Manasseh clans-of these (34)

וּשְׁבַע מֵאוֹת׃ אֵלֶּה בְנֵי־ אֶפְרַיִם לְמִשְׁפְּחֹתָם
by-clans-of-them Ephraim sons-of these (35) hundreds and-seven-of

לְשׁוּתֶלַח מִשְׁפַּחַת הַשֻּׁתַלְחִי לְבֶכֶר מִשְׁפַּחַת הַבַּכְרִי
the-Bekerite clan-of through-Beker the-Shuthelahite clan-of through-Shuthelah

לְתַחַן מִשְׁפַּחַת הַתַּחֲנִי׃ וְאֵלֶּה בְּנֵי שׁוּתָלַח
Shuthelah sons-of and-these (36) the-Tahanite clan-of through-Tahan

לְעֵרָן מִשְׁפַּחַת הָעֵרָנִי׃ אֵלֶּה מִשְׁפְּחֹת בְּנֵי־ אֶפְרַיִם
Ephraim sons-of clans-of these (37) the-Eranite clan-of through-Eran

לִפְקֻדֵיהֶם שְׁנַיִם וּשְׁלֹשִׁים אֶלֶף וַחֲמֵשׁ מֵאוֹת אֵלֶּה
these hundreds and-five-of thousand and-thirty two by-numberings-of-them

בְנֵי־ יוֹסֵף לְמִשְׁפְּחֹתָם׃ בְּנֵי בִנְיָמִן לְמִשְׁפְּחֹתָם
by-clans-of-them Benjamin sons-of (38) by-clans-of-them Joseph sons-of

לְבֶלַע מִשְׁפַּחַת הַבַּלְעִי לְאַשְׁבֵּל מִשְׁפַּחַת הָאַשְׁבֵּלִי
the-Ashbelite clan-of through-Ashbel the-Belaite clan-of through-Bela

לַאֲחִירָם מִשְׁפַּחַת הָאֲחִירָמִי׃ לִשְׁפוּפָם מִשְׁפַּחַת
clan-of through-Shephupham (39) the-Ahiramite clan-of through-Ahiram

הַשּׁוּפָמִי לְחוּפָם מִשְׁפַּחַת הַחוּפָמִי׃ וַיִּהְיוּ
and-they-were (40) the-Huphamite clan-of through-Hupham the-Shuphamite

בְנֵי־ בֶלַע אַרְדְּ וְנַעֲמָן מִשְׁפַּחַת הָאַרְדִּי לְנַעֲמָן מִשְׁפַּחַת
clan-of through-Naaman the-Ardite clan-of and-Naaman Ard Bela sons-of

הַנַּעֲמִי׃ אֵלֶּה בְנֵי־ בִנְיָמִן לְמִשְׁפְּחֹתָם וּפְקֻדֵיהֶם
and-numberings-of-them by-clans-of-them Benjamin sons-of these (41) the-Naamite

29 The descendants of Manasseh:
through Makir, the Makirite clan (Makir was the father of Gilead);
through Gilead, the Gileadite clan.
30 These were the descendants of Gilead:
through Iezer, the Iezerite clan;
through Helek, the Helekite clan;
31 through Asriel, the Asrielite clan;
through Shechem, the Shechemite clan;
32 through Shemida, the Shemidaite clan;
through Hepher, the Hepherite clan.
33 (Zelophehad son of Hepher had no sons; he had only daughters, whose names were Mahlah, Noah, Hoglah, Milcah and Tirzah.)
34 These were the clans of Manasseh; those numbered were 52,700.

35 These were the descendants of Ephraim by their clans:
through Shuthelah, the Shuthelahite clan;
through Beker, the Bekerite clan;
through Tahan, the Tahanite clan.
36 These were the descendants of Shuthelah:
through Eran, the Eranite clan.
37 These were the clans of Ephraim; those numbered were 32,500.

These were the descendants of Joseph by their clans.

38 The descendants of Benjamin by their clans were:
through Bela, the Belaite clan;
through Ashbel, the Ashbelite clan;
through Ahiram, the Ahiramite clan;
39 through Shupham,[j] the Shuphamite clan;
through Hupham, the Huphamite clan.
40 The descendants of Bela through Ard and Naaman were:
through Ard,[k] the Ardite clan;
through Naaman, the Naamite clan.
41 These were the clans of Benjamin; those numbered were

[j] 39 A few manuscripts of the Masoretic Text, Samaritan Pentateuch, Septuagint, Vulgate and Syriac; most manuscripts of the Masoretic Text *Shephupham*

[k] 40 Samaritan Pentateuch, some Septuagint manuscripts and Vulgate; Masoretic Text does not have *through Ard,*

חֲמִשָּׁה וְאַרְבָּעִים אֶלֶף וְשֵׁשׁ מֵאוֹת׃ אֵלֶּה בְנֵי־ דָן
Dan sons-of these (42) hundreds and-six thousand and-forty five

לְמִשְׁפְּחֹתָם לְשׁוּחָם מִשְׁפַּחַת הַשּׁוּחָמִי אֵלֶּה מִשְׁפְּחֹת דָּן
Dan clans-of these the-Shuhamite clan-of through-Shuham by-clans-of-them

לְמִשְׁפְּחֹתָם׃ כָּל־ מִשְׁפְּחֹת הַשּׁוּחָמִי לִפְקֻדֵיהֶם
by-numberings-of-them the-Shuhamite clans-of all-of (43) by-clans-of-them

אַרְבָּעָה וְשִׁשִּׁים אֶלֶף וְאַרְבַּע מֵאוֹת׃ בְּנֵי אָשֵׁר לְמִשְׁפְּחֹתָם
by-clans-of-them Asher sons-of (44) hundreds and-four thousand and-sixty four

לְיִמְנָה מִשְׁפַּחַת הַיִּמְנָה לְיִשְׁוִי מִשְׁפַּחַת הַיִּשְׁוִי
the-Ishvite clan-of through-Ishvi the-Imnite clan-of through-Imnah

לִבְרִיעָה מִשְׁפַּחַת הַבְּרִיעִי׃ לִבְנֵי בְרִיעָה לְחֶבֶר
through-Heber Beriah through-sons-of (45) the-Beriite clan-of through-Beriah

מִשְׁפַּחַת הַחֶבְרִי לְמַלְכִּיאֵל מִשְׁפַּחַת הַמַּלְכִּיאֵלִי׃ וְשֵׁם
now-name-of (46) the-Malkielite clan-of through-Malkiel the-Heberite clan-of

בַּת־ אָשֵׁר שָׂרַח׃ אֵלֶּה מִשְׁפְּחֹת בְּנֵי־ אָשֵׁר לִפְקֻדֵיהֶם
by-numberings-of-them Asher sons-of clans-of these (47) Serah Asher daughter-of

שְׁלֹשָׁה וַחֲמִשִּׁים אֶלֶף וְאַרְבַּע מֵאוֹת׃ בְּנֵי נַפְתָּלִי
Naphtali sons-of (48) hundreds and-four thousand and-fifty three

לְמִשְׁפְּחֹתָם לְיַחְצְאֵל מִשְׁפַּחַת הַיַּחְצְאֵלִי לְגוּנִי מִשְׁפַּחַת
clan-of through-Guni the-Jahzeelite clan-of through-Jahzeel by-clans-of-them

הַגּוּנִי׃ לְיֵצֶר מִשְׁפַּחַת הַיִּצְרִי לְשִׁלֵּם מִשְׁפַּחַת
clan-of through-Shillem the-Jezerite clan-of through-Jezer (49) the-Gunite

הַשִּׁלֵּמִי׃ אֵלֶּה מִשְׁפְּחֹת נַפְתָּלִי לְמִשְׁפְּחֹתָם
by-clans-of-them Naphtali clans-of these (50) the-Shillemite

וּפְקֻדֵיהֶם חֲמִשָּׁה וְאַרְבָּעִים אֶלֶף וְאַרְבַּע מֵאוֹת׃ אֵלֶּה
these (51) hundreds and-four thousand and-forty five and-numberings-of-them

פְּקוּדֵי בְּנֵי יִשְׂרָאֵל שֵׁשׁ־ מֵאוֹת אֶלֶף וָאָלֶף שְׁבַע
seven-of and-thousand thousand hundreds six Israel sons-of numberings-of

מֵאוֹת וּשְׁלֹשִׁים׃ וַיְדַבֵּר יְהוָה אֶל־ מֹשֶׁה לֵּאמֹר׃ לָאֵלֶּה
to-these (53) to-say Moses to Yahweh and-he-spoke (52) and-thirty hundreds

תֵּחָלֵק הָאָרֶץ בְּנַחֲלָה בְּמִסְפַּר שֵׁמוֹת׃
names by-number-of as-inheritance the-land she-must-be-allotted

לָרַב תַּרְבֶּה נַחֲלָתוֹ וְלַמְעַט
and-to-the-small inheritance-of-him you-make-large to-the-large (54)

תַּמְעִיט נַחֲלָתוֹ אִישׁ לְפִי פְקֻדָיו
numberings-of-him by-amount-of each inheritance-of-him you-make-small

יֻתַּן נַחֲלָתוֹ׃ אַךְ־ בְּגוֹרָל יֵחָלֵק
he-must-be-distributed by-lot only (55) inheritance-of-him he-must-receive

45,600.

[42]These were the descendants
of Dan by their clans:
through Shuham, the Shuhamite clan.
These were the clans of Dan:
[43]All of them were Shuhamite
clans; and those numbered
were 64,400.

[44]The descendants of Asher by
their clans were:
through Imnah, the Imnite clan;
through Ishvi, the Ishvite clan;
through Beriah, the Beriite clan;
[45]and through the descendants of Beriah:
through Heber, the Heberite clan;
through Malkiel, the Malkielite clan.
[46](Asher had a daughter named Serah.)
[47]These were the clans of Asher; those numbered were 53,400.

[48]The descendants of Naphtali
by their clans were:
through Jahzeel, the Jahzeelite clan;
through Guni, the Gunite clan;
[49]through Jezer, the Jezerite clan;
through Shillem, the Shillemite clan.
[50]These were the clans of
Naphtali; those numbered
were 45,400.

[51]The total number of the men
of Israel was 601,730.

[52]The LORD said to Moses,
[53]"The land is to be allotted to
them as an inheritance based
on the number of names. [54]To
a larger group give a larger inheritance, and to a smaller
group a smaller one; each is to
receive its inheritance according to the number of those listed.
[55]Be sure that the land is
distributed by lot. What each

אֶת־ הָאָרֶץ לִשְׁמוֹת מַטּוֹת־ אֲבֹתָם יִנְחָלוּ׃
they-will-inherit fathers-of-them tribes-of by-names-of the-land ***

עַל־ פִּי הַגּוֹרָל תֵּחָלֵק נַחֲלָתוֹ בֵּין
among inheritance-of-him he-must-be-distributed the-lot decision-of by (56)

רַב לִמְעָט׃ וְאֵלֶּה פְקוּדֵי הַלֵּוִי לְמִשְׁפְּחֹתָם
by-clans-of-them the-Levite numberings-of and-these (57) among-small large

לְגֵרְשׁוֹן מִשְׁפַּחַת הַגֵּרְשֻׁנִּי לִקְהָת מִשְׁפַּחַת הַקְּהָתִי
the-Kohathite clan-of through-Kohath the-Gershonite clan-of through-Gershon

לִמְרָרִי מִשְׁפַּחַת הַמְּרָרִי׃ אֵלֶּה ׀ מִשְׁפְּחֹת לֵוִי מִשְׁפַּחַת
clan-of Levi clans-of these (58) the-Merarite clan-of through-Merari

הַלִּבְנִי מִשְׁפַּחַת הַחֶבְרֹנִי מִשְׁפַּחַת הַמַּחְלִי מִשְׁפַּחַת הַמּוּשִׁי
the-Mushite clan-of the-Mahlite clan-of the-Hebronite clan-of the-Libnite

מִשְׁפַּחַת הַקָּרְחִי וּקְהָת הוֹלִד אֶת־ עַמְרָם׃ וְשֵׁם ׀
and-name-of (59) Amram *** he-fathered now-Kohath the-Korahite clan-of

אֵשֶׁת עַמְרָם יוֹכֶבֶד בַּת־ לֵוִי אֲשֶׁר יָלְדָה אֹתָהּ לְלֵוִי בְּמִצְרָיִם
in-Egypt to-Levi her she-bore whom Levi daughter-of Jochebed Amram wife-of

וַתֵּלֶד לְעַמְרָם אֶת־ אַהֲרֹן וְאֶת־ מֹשֶׁה וְאֵת מִרְיָם אֲחֹתָם׃
sister-of-them Miriam and Moses and Aaron *** to-Amram and-she-bore

וַיִּוָּלֵד לְאַהֲרֹן אֶת־ נָדָב וְאֶת־אֲבִיהוּא אֶת־אֶלְעָזָר וְאֶת־אִיתָמָר׃
Ithamar and Eleazar *** Abihu and Nadab *** to-Aaron and-he-was-born (60)

וַיָּמָת נָדָב וַאֲבִיהוּא בְּהַקְרִיבָם אֵשׁ־ זָרָה
unauthorized fire-of when-to-offer-them and-Abihu Nadab but-he-died (61)

לִפְנֵי יְהוָה׃ וַיִּהְיוּ פְקֻדֵיהֶם שְׁלֹשָׁה וְעֶשְׂרִים אֶלֶף
thousand and-twenty three numberings-of-them and-they-were (62) Yahweh before

כָּל־ זָכָר מִבֶּן־ חֹדֶשׁ וָמָעְלָה כִּי ׀ לֹא הָתְפָּקְדוּ בְּתוֹךְ
along-with they-were-counted not for or-more month from-son-of male every-of

בְּנֵי יִשְׂרָאֵל כִּי לֹא־ נִתַּן לָהֶם נַחֲלָה בְּתוֹךְ בְּנֵי יִשְׂרָאֵל׃
Israel sons-of among inheritance to-them he-gave not for Israel sons-of

אֵלֶּה פְּקוּדֵי מֹשֶׁה וְאֶלְעָזָר הַכֹּהֵן אֲשֶׁר פָּקְדוּ אֶת־
*** they-counted when the-priest and-Eleazar Moses countings-of these (63)

בְּנֵי יִשְׂרָאֵל בְּעַרְבֹת מוֹאָב עַל יַרְדֵּן יְרֵחוֹ׃ וּבְאֵלֶּה
and-among-these (64) Jericho Jordan-of by Moab on-plains-of Israel sons-of

לֹא־ הָיָה אִישׁ מִפְּקוּדֵי מֹשֶׁה וְאַהֲרֹן הַכֹּהֵן אֲשֶׁר
when the-priest and-Aaron Moses from-numberings-of man he-was not

פָּקְדוּ אֶת־ בְּנֵי יִשְׂרָאֵל בְּמִדְבַּר סִינָי׃ כִּי־ אָמַר יְהוָה
Yahweh he-told for (65) Sinai in-Desert-of Israel sons-of *** they-counted

לָהֶם מוֹת יָמֻתוּ בַּמִּדְבָּר וְלֹא־ נוֹתַר מֵהֶם
from-them being-left and-not in-the-desert they-would-die to-die to-them

group inherits will be according to the names for its ancestral tribe. 56 Each inheritance is to be distributed by lot among the larger and smaller groups."

57 These were the Levites who were counted by their clans:
through Gershon, the Gershonite clan;
through Kohath, the Kohathite clan;
through Merari, the Merarite clan.

58 These also were Levite clans:
the Libnite clan,
the Hebronite clan,
the Mahlite clan,
the Mushite clan,
the Korahite clan.
(Kohath was the forefather of Amram; 59 the name of Amram's wife was Jochebed, a descendant of Levi, who was born to the Levites[l] in Egypt. To Amram she bore Aaron, Moses and their sister Miriam. 60 Aaron was the father of Nadab and Abihu, Eleazar and Ithamar. 61 But Nadab and Abihu died when they made an offering before the LORD with unauthorized fire.)

62 All the male Levites a month old or more numbered 23,000. They were not counted along with the other Israelites because they received no inheritance among them.

63 These are the ones counted by Moses and Eleazar the priest when they counted the Israelites on the plains of Moab by the Jordan across from Jericho. 64 Not one of them was among those counted by Moses and Aaron the priest when they counted the Israelites in the Desert of Sinai. 65 For the LORD had told those Israelites they would surely die in the desert, and not one of them was left except

[l] 59 Or *Jochebed, a daughter of Levi, who was born to Levi*

אִישׁ כִּי אִם־ כָּלֵב בֶּן־ יְפֻנֶּה וִיהוֹשֻׁעַ בִּן־ נוּן׃
Nun son-of and-Joshua Jephunneh son-of Caleb only except one

וַתִּקְרַבְנָה בְּנוֹת צְלָפְחָד בֶּן־ חֵפֶר בֶּן־ גִּלְעָד
Gilead son-of Hepher son-of Zelophehad daughters-of now-they-approached (27:1)

בֶּן־ מָכִיר בֶּן־ מְנַשֶּׁה לְמִשְׁפְּחֹת מְנַשֶּׁה בֶן־ יוֹסֵף וְאֵלֶּה
and-these Joseph son-of Manasseh of-clans-of Manasseh son-of Makir son-of

שְׁמוֹת בְּנֹתָיו מַחְלָה נֹעָה וְחָגְלָה וּמִלְכָּה וְתִרְצָה׃
and-Tirzah and-Milcah and-Hoglah Noah Mahlah daughters-of-him names-of

וַתַּעֲמֹדְנָה לִפְנֵי מֹשֶׁה וְלִפְנֵי אֶלְעָזָר הַכֹּהֵן וְלִפְנֵי
and-before the-priest Eleazar and-before Moses before and-they-stood (2)

הַנְּשִׂיאִם וְכָל־ הָעֵדָה פֶּתַח אֹהֶל־ מוֹעֵד לֵאמֹר׃
to-say Meeting Tent-of entrance-of the-assembly and-whole-of the-leaders

אָבִינוּ מֵת בַּמִּדְבָּר וְהוּא לֹא־ הָיָה בְּתוֹךְ הָעֵדָה
the-follower among he-was not now-he in-the-desert he-died father-of-us (3)

הַנּוֹעָדִים עַל־ יְהוָה בַּעֲדַת־ קֹרַח כִּי־ בְחֶטְאוֹ
for-sin-of-him but Korah among-follower-of Yahweh against the-ones-banding

מֵת וּבָנִים לֹא־ הָיוּ לוֹ׃ לָמָּה יִגָּרַע שֵׁם־
name-of should-he-disappear why? (4) to-him they-were not and-sons he-died

אָבִינוּ מִתּוֹךְ מִשְׁפַּחְתּוֹ כִּי אֵין לוֹ בֵּן תְּנָה־ לָּנוּ
to-us give! son to-him not because clan-of-him from-among father-of-us

אֲחֻזָּה בְּתוֹךְ אֲחֵי אָבִינוּ׃ וַיַּקְרֵב מֹשֶׁה אֶת־
*** Moses so-he-brought (5) father-of-us relatives-of among property

מִשְׁפָּטָן לִפְנֵי יְהוָה׃ וַיֹּאמֶר יְהוָה אֶל־ מֹשֶׁה לֵּאמֹר׃ כֵּן
right (7) to-say Moses to Yahweh and-he-said (6) Yahweh before case-of-them

בְּנוֹת צְלָפְחָד דֹּבְרֹת נָתֹן תִּתֵּן לָהֶם אֲחֻזַּת
property-of to-them you-give to-give ones-saying Zelophehad daughters-of

נַחֲלָה בְּתוֹךְ אֲחֵי אֲבִיהֶם וְהַעֲבַרְתָּ אֶת־ נַחֲלַת
inheritance-of *** and-you-turn father-of-them relatives-of among inheritance

אֲבִיהֶן לָהֶן׃ וְאֶל־ בְּנֵי יִשְׂרָאֵל תְּדַבֵּר לֵאמֹר אִישׁ כִּי־
if man to-say you-speak Israel sons-of and-to (8) to-them father-of-them

יָמוּת וּבֵן אֵין לוֹ וְהַעֲבַרְתֶּם אֶת־ נַחֲלָתוֹ
inheritance-of-him *** then-you-turn to-him not and-son he-dies

לְבִתּוֹ׃ וְאִם־ אֵין לוֹ בַּת וּנְתַתֶּם אֶת־
*** then-you-give daughter to-him not and-if (9) to-daughter-of-him

נַחֲלָתוֹ לְאֶחָיו׃ וְאִם־ אֵין לוֹ אַחִים
brothers to-him not and-if (10) to-brothers-of-him inheritance-of-him

וּנְתַתֶּם אֶת־ נַחֲלָתוֹ לַאֲחֵי אָבִיו׃ וְאִם־
and-if (11) father-of-him to-brothers-of inheritance-of-him *** then-you-give

Caleb son of Jephunneh and
Joshua son of Nun.

Zelophehad's Daughters

27 The daughters of Ze-
lophehad son of He-
pher, the son of Gilead, the
son of Makir, the son of
Manasseh, belonged to the
clans of Manasseh son of Joseph. The names of the daughters were Mahlah, Noah, Hoglah, Milcah and Tirzah. They
approached [2]the entrance to
the Tent of Meeting and stood
before Moses, Eleazar the
priest, the leaders and the
whole assembly, and said,
[3]"Our father died in the
desert. He was not among
Korah's followers, who banded together against the LORD,
but he died for his own sin
and left no sons. [4]Why should
our father's name disappear
from his clan because he had
no son? Give us property
among our father's relatives."
[5]So Moses brought their case
before the LORD [6]and the LORD
said to him, [7]"What Zelophehad's daughters are saying is
right. You must certainly give
them property as an inheritance among their father's
relatives and turn their father's inheritance over to
them.
[8]"Say to the Israelites, 'If a
man dies and leaves no son,
turn his inheritance over to
his daughter. [9]If he has no
daughter, give his inheritance
to his brothers. [10]If he has no
brothers, give his inheritance
to his father's brothers. [11]If his

אֵין אַחִים לְאָבִיו וּנְתַתֶּם אֶת־ נַחֲלָתוֹ
inheritance-of-him *** then-you-give to-father-of-him brothers not

לִשְׁאֵרוֹ הַקָּרֹב אֵלָיו מִמִּשְׁפַּחְתּוֹ וְיָרַשׁ אֹתָהּ
her that-he-may-possess in-clan-of-him to-him the-one-near to-relative-of-him

וְהָיְתָה לִבְנֵי יִשְׂרָאֵל לְחֻקַּת מִשְׁפָּט כַּאֲשֶׁר צִוָּה
he-commanded just-as legal as-requirement-of Israel for-sons-of now-she-must-be

יְהוָה אֶת־ מֹשֶׁה׃ וַיֹּאמֶר יְהוָה אֶל־מֹשֶׁה עֲלֵה אֶל־ הַר
mountain-of on go-up! Moses to Yahweh then-he-said (12) Moses *** Yahweh

הָעֲבָרִים הַזֶּה וּרְאֵה אֶת־ הָאָרֶץ אֲשֶׁר נָתַתִּי לִבְנֵי יִשְׂרָאֵל׃
Israel to-sons-of I-gave that the-land *** and-see! the-this the-Abarim

וְרָאִיתָה אֹתָהּ וְנֶאֱסַפְתָּ אֶל־ עַמֶּיךָ גַּם־אָתָּה
you also people-of-you to then-you-will-be-gathered her when-you-see (13)

כַּאֲשֶׁר נֶאֱסַף אַהֲרֹן אָחִיךָ׃ כַּאֲשֶׁר מְרִיתֶם
you-disobeyed just-as (14) brother-of-you Aaron he-was-gathered just-as

פִּי בְּמִדְבַּר־ צִן בִּמְרִיבַת הָעֵדָה לְהַקְדִּישֵׁנִי
to-honor-as-holy-me the-community in-rebellion-of Zin in-Desert-of command-of-me

בַמַּיִם לְעֵינֵיהֶם הֵם מֵי־ מְרִיבַת קָדֵשׁ
Kadesh-of Meribah-of waters-of these before-eyes-of-them at-the-waters

מִדְבַּר־ צִן׃ וַיְדַבֵּר מֹשֶׁה אֶל־ יְהוָה לֵאמֹר׃ יִפְקֹד
may-he-appoint (16) to-say Yahweh to Moses and-he-spoke (15) Zin Desert-of

יְהוָה אֱלֹהֵי הָרוּחֹת לְכָל־ בָּשָׂר אִישׁ עַל־ הָעֵדָה׃ אֲשֶׁר־
who (17) the-community over man mankind of-all-of the-spirits God-of Yahweh

יֵצֵא לִפְנֵיהֶם וַאֲשֶׁר יָבֹא לִפְנֵיהֶם וַאֲשֶׁר
and-who before-them he-will-come-in and-who before-them he-will-go-out

יוֹצִיאֵם וַאֲשֶׁר יְבִיאֵם וְלֹא תִהְיֶה
she-will-be so-not he-will-bring-in-them and-who he-will-lead-out-them

עֲדַת יְהוָה כַּצֹּאן אֲשֶׁר אֵין־ לָהֶם רֹעֶה׃ וַיֹּאמֶר
so-he-said (18) one-herding to-them not that like-the-sheep Yahweh people-of

יְהוָה אֶל־מֹשֶׁה קַח־ לְךָ אֶת־יְהוֹשֻׁעַ בִּן־ נוּן אִישׁ אֲשֶׁר־ רוּחַ בּוֹ
in-him spirit whom man Nun son-of Joshua *** to-you take! Moses to Yahweh

וְסָמַכְתָּ אֶת־ יָדְךָ עָלָיו׃ וְהַעֲמַדְתָּ אֹתוֹ לִפְנֵי אֶלְעָזָר
Eleazar before him and-you-stand (19) on-him hand-of-you *** and-you-lay

הַכֹּהֵן וְלִפְנֵי כָּל־ הָעֵדָה וְצִוִּיתָה אֹתוֹ
him and-you-commission the-assembly entire-of and-before the-priest

לְעֵינֵיהֶם׃ וְנָתַתָּה מֵהוֹדְךָ עָלָיו לְמַעַן
so-that to-him from-authority-of-you and-you-give (20) before-eyes-of-them

יִשְׁמְעוּ כָּל־ עֲדַת בְּנֵי יִשְׂרָאֵל׃ וְלִפְנֵי אֶלְעָזָר
Eleazar and-before (21) Israel sons-of community-of whole-of they-will-obey

father had no brothers, give
his inheritance to the nearest
relative in his clan, that he
may possess it. This is to be a
legal requirement for the Israelites, as the LORD commanded
Moses.' "

Joshua to Succeed Moses

12 Then the LORD said to
Moses, "Go up this mountain
in the Abarim range and see
the land I have given the Israelites. 13 After you have seen it,
you too will be gathered to
your people, as your brother
Aaron was, 14 for when the
community rebelled at the waters in the Desert of Zin, both
of you disobeyed my com-
mand to honor me as holy before their eyes." (These were
the waters of Meribah in Kadesh, in the Desert of Zin.)
15 Moses said to the LORD,
16 "May the LORD, the God of
the spirits of all mankind, appoint a man over this community 17 to go out and come in
before them, one who will
lead them out and bring them
in, so the LORD's people will
not be like sheep without a
shepherd."
18 So the LORD said to Moses,
"Take Joshua son of Nun, a
man in whom is the spirit,[m]
and lay your hand on him.
19 Have him stand before Eleazar the priest and the entire
assembly and commission
him in their presence. 20 Give
him some of your authority so
the whole Israelite community
will obey him. 21 He is to stand

[m]18 Or *Spirit*

הַכֹּהֵ֖ן יַעֲמֹ֔ד וְשָׁ֥אַל ל֛וֹ בְּמִשְׁפַּ֥ט הָאוּרִ֖ים

the-Urim from-decision-of for-him and-he-will-obtain he-must-stand the-priest

לִפְנֵ֣י יְהוָ֑ה עַל־ פִּ֨יו יֵצְא֜וּ וְעַל־ פִּ֣יו

command-of-him and-at they-will-go-out command-of-him at Yahweh before

יָבֹ֗אוּ ה֛וּא וְכָל־ בְּנֵֽי־ יִשְׂרָאֵ֥ל אִתּ֖וֹ וְכָל־

and-entire-of with-him Israel sons-of and-all-of he they-will-come-in

הָעֵדָֽה׃ (22) וַיַּ֣עַשׂ מֹשֶׁ֔ה כַּאֲשֶׁ֛ר צִוָּ֥ה יְהוָ֖ה אֹת֑וֹ

him Yahweh he-commanded just-as Moses so-he-did (22) the-community

וַיִּקַּ֣ח אֶת־ יְהוֹשֻׁ֗עַ וַיַּֽעֲמִדֵ֙הוּ֙ לִפְנֵי֙ אֶלְעָזָ֣ר הַכֹּהֵ֔ן וְלִפְנֵ֖י

and-before the-priest Eleazar before and-he-stood-him Joshua *** and-he-took

כָּל־ הָעֵדָֽה׃ (23) וַיִּסְמֹ֧ךְ אֶת־ יָדָ֛יו עָלָ֖יו

on-him hands-of-him *** then-he-laid (23) the-assembly whole-of

וַיְצַוֵּ֑הוּ כַּאֲשֶׁ֛ר דִּבֶּ֥ר יְהוָ֖ה בְּיַד־ מֹשֶֽׁה׃

Moses by-hand-of Yahweh he-instructed just-as and-he-commissioned-him

(28:1) וַיְדַבֵּ֥ר יְהוָ֖ה אֶל־מֹשֶׁ֥ה לֵּאמֹֽר׃ (2) צַ֚ו אֶת־ בְּנֵ֣י יִשְׂרָאֵ֔ל

Israel sons-of *** command! (2) to-say Moses to Yahweh and-he-spoke (28:1)

וְאָמַרְתָּ֖ אֲלֵהֶ֑ם אֶת־ קָרְבָּנִ֨י לַחְמִ֜י לְאִשַּׁ֗י

for-fire-offerings-of-me food-of-me offering-of-me *** to-them and-you-say

רֵ֚יחַ נִיחֹחִ֔י תִּשְׁמְר֕וּ לְהַקְרִ֥יב לִ֖י בְּמוֹעֲדֽוֹ׃

at-time-of-him to-me to-present you-see pleasant-of-me aroma-of

(3) וְאָמַרְתָּ֣ לָהֶ֔ם זֶ֚ה הָֽאִשֶּׁ֔ה אֲשֶׁ֥ר תַּקְרִ֖יבוּ

you-must-present that the-fire-offering this to-them and-you-say (3)

לַיהוָ֑ה כְּבָשִׂ֨ים בְּנֵֽי־ שָׁנָ֧ה תְמִימִ֛ם שְׁנַ֥יִם לַיּ֖וֹם

for-the-day two ones-without-defect year sons-of lambs to-Yahweh

עֹלָ֥ה תָמִֽיד׃ (4) אֶת־ הַכֶּ֥בֶשׂ אֶחָ֖ד תַּעֲשֶׂ֣ה בַבֹּ֑קֶר וְאֵת֙

and in-the-morning you-prepare one the-lamb *** (4) regular burnt-offering

הַכֶּ֣בֶשׂ הַשֵּׁנִ֔י תַּעֲשֶׂ֖ה בֵּ֥ין הָעַרְבָּֽיִם׃ (5) וַעֲשִׂירִ֧ית הָאֵיפָ֛ה

the-ephah and-tenth-of (5) the-twilights at you-prepare the-other the-lamb

סֹ֖לֶת לְמִנְחָ֑ה בְּלוּלָ֛ה בְּשֶׁ֥מֶן כָּתִ֖ית רְבִיעִ֥ת הַהִֽין׃

the-hin fourth-of pressed with-oil being-mixed for-grain-offering fine-flour

(6) עֹלַ֖ת תָּמִ֑יד הָעֲשֻׂיָה֙ בְּהַ֣ר סִינַ֔י

Sinai at-Mount-of the-one-being-instituted regular burnt-offering-of (6)

לְרֵ֣יחַ נִיחֹ֔חַ אִשֶּׁ֖ה לַיהוָֽה׃ (7) וְנִסְכּוֹ֙

and-drink-offering-of-him (7) to-Yahweh fire-offering pleasant as-aroma-of

רְבִיעִ֣ת הַהִ֔ין לַכֶּ֖בֶשׂ הָאֶחָ֑ד בַּקֹּ֗דֶשׁ הַסֵּ֛ךְ

pour-out! at-the-sanctuary the-each with-the-lamb the-hin fourth-of

נֶ֥סֶךְ שֵׁכָ֖ר לַיהוָֽה׃ (8) וְאֵת֙ הַכֶּ֣בֶשׂ הַשֵּׁנִ֔י

the-second the-lamb and (8) to-Yahweh fermented-drink drink-offering

before Eleazar the priest, who
will obtain decisions for him
by inquiring of the Urim before the LORD. At his command he and the entire community of the Israelites will go
out, and at his command they
will come in."
22 Moses did as the LORD
commanded him. He took
Joshua and had him stand before Eleazar the priest and the
whole assembly. 23 Then he
laid his hands on him and
commissioned him, as the
LORD instructed through
Moses.

Daily Offerings

28 The LORD said to
Moses, 2 "Give this
command to the Israelites and
say to them: 'See that you
present to me at the appointed
time the food for my offerings
made by fire, as an aroma
pleasing to me.' 3 Say to them:
'This is the offering made by
fire that you are to present to
the LORD: two lambs a year old
without defect, as a regular
burnt offering each day. 4 Prepare one lamb in the morning
and the other at twilight, 5 together with a grain offering of
a tenth of an ephah[n] of fine
flour mixed with a fourth of a
hin[o] of oil from pressed olives.
6 This is the regular burnt
offering instituted at Mount
Sinai as a pleasing aroma, an
offering made to the LORD by
fire. 7 The accompanying drink
offering is to be a fourth of a
hin of fermented drink with
each lamb. Pour out the drink
offering to the LORD at the
sanctuary. 8 Prepare the second

[n]5 That is, probably about 2 quarts (about 2 liters); also in verses 13, 21 and 29

[o]5 That is, probably about 1 quart (about 1 liter); also in verses 7 and 14

תַּעֲשֶׂה בֵּין הָעַרְבַּיִם כְּמִנְחַת הַבֹּקֶר
you-prepare at the-twilights as-grain-offering-of the-morning

וּכְנִסְכּוֹ תַּעֲשֶׂה אִשֵּׁה רֵיחַ נִיחֹחַ
and-as-drink-offering-of-him you-prepare fire-offering aroma-of pleasant

לַיהוָה׃ (9) וּבְיוֹם הַשַּׁבָּת שְׁנֵי־כְבָשִׂים בְּנֵי־ שָׁנָה תְּמִימִם
to-Yahweh (9) on-day-of the-Sabbath two-of lambs sons-of year ones-defectless

וּשְׁנֵי עֶשְׂרֹנִים סֹלֶת מִנְחָה בְּלוּלָה בַשֶּׁמֶן
and-two-of tenths fine-flour grain-offering being-mixed with-the-oil

וְנִסְכּוֹ׃ (10) עֹלַת שַׁבַּת בְּשַׁבַּתּוֹ
and-drink-offering-of-him (10) burnt-offering-of Sabbath on-Sabbath-of-him

עַל־ עֹלַת הַתָּמִיד וְנִסְכָּהּ׃ (11) וּבְרָאשֵׁי
beside burnt-offering-of the-regular and-drink-offering-of-her (11) and-on-firsts-of

חָדְשֵׁיכֶם תַּקְרִיבוּ עֹלָה לַיהוָה פָּרִים בְּנֵי־ בָקָר
months-of-you you-present burnt-offering to-Yahweh bulls young-ones-of herd

שְׁנַיִם וְאַיִל אֶחָד כְּבָשִׂים בְּנֵי־ שָׁנָה שִׁבְעָה תְּמִימִם׃
two and-ram one and-male-lambs sons-of year seven ones-without-defect

(12) וּשְׁלֹשָׁה עֶשְׂרֹנִים סֹלֶת מִנְחָה בְּלוּלָה בַשֶּׁמֶן
(12) and-three tenths fine-flour grain-offering being-mixed with-the-oil

לַפָּר הָאֶחָד וּשְׁנֵי עֶשְׂרֹנִים סֹלֶת מִנְחָה בְּלוּלָה
with-the-bull the-each and-two-of tenths fine-flour grain-offering being-mixed

בַשֶּׁמֶן לָאַיִל הָאֶחָד׃ (13) וְעִשָּׂרֹן עִשָּׂרוֹן סֹלֶת מִנְחָה
with-the-oil with-the-ram the-each (13) and-tenth tenth flour grain-offering

בְּלוּלָה בַשֶּׁמֶן לַכֶּבֶשׂ הָאֶחָד עֹלָה רֵיחַ
being-mixed with-the-oil with-the-lamb the-each burnt-offering aroma-of

נִיחֹחַ אִשֶּׁה לַיהוָה׃ (14) וְנִסְכֵּיהֶם חֲצִי
pleasant fire-offering to-Yahweh (14) and-drink-offerings-of-them half-of

הַהִין יִהְיֶה לַפָּר וּשְׁלִישִׁת הַהִין לָאַיִל
the-hin he-must-be with-the-bull and-third-of the-hin with-the-ram

וּרְבִיעִת הַהִין לַכֶּבֶשׂ יָיִן זֹאת עֹלַת חֹדֶשׁ
and-fourth-of the-hin with-the-lamb wine this burnt-offering-of month

בְּחָדְשׁוֹ לְחָדְשֵׁי הַשָּׁנָה׃ (15) וּשְׂעִיר עִזִּים אֶחָד
in-month-of-him at-new-moons-of the-year (15) and-male-goat-of goats one

לְחַטָּאת לַיהוָה עַל־ עֹלַת הַתָּמִיד יֵעָשֶׂה
as-sin-offering to-Yahweh beside burnt-offering-of the-regular he-must-be-made

וְנִסְכּוֹ׃ (16) וּבַחֹדֶשׁ הָרִאשׁוֹן בְּאַרְבָּעָה עָשָׂר יוֹם
with-drink-offering-of-him (16) and-on-the-month the-first on-four ten day

לַחֹדֶשׁ פֶּסַח לַיהוָה׃ (17) וּבַחֲמִשָּׁה עָשָׂר יוֹם לַחֹדֶשׁ
of-the-month Passover to-Yahweh (17) and-on-five ten day of-the-month

lamb at twilight, along with the same kind of grain offering and drink offering that you prepare in the morning. This is an offering made by fire, an aroma pleasing to the LORD.

Sabbath Offerings

9" 'On the Sabbath day, make an offering of two lambs a year old without defect, together with its drink offering and a grain offering of two-tenths of an ephah[p] of fine flour mixed with oil. 10This is the burnt offering for every Sabbath, in addition to the regular burnt offering and its drink offering.

Monthly Offerings

11" 'On the first of every month, present to the LORD a burnt offering of two young bulls, one ram and seven male lambs a year old, all without defect. 12With each bull there is to be a grain offering of three-tenths of an ephah[q] of fine flour mixed with oil; with the ram, a grain offering of two-tenths of an ephah of fine flour mixed with oil; 13and with each lamb, a grain offering of a tenth of an ephah of fine flour mixed with oil. This is for a burnt offering, a pleasing aroma, an offering made to the LORD by fire. 14With each bull there is to be a drink offering of half a hin[r] of wine; with the ram, a third of a hin[s]; and with each lamb, a fourth of a hin. This is the monthly burnt offering to be made at each new moon during the year. 15Besides the regular burnt offering with its drink offering, one male goat is to be presented to the LORD as a sin offering.

The Passover

16" 'On the fourteenth day of the first month the LORD's Passover is to be held. 17On the fifteenth day of this month

p9 That is, probably about 4 quarts (about 4.5 liters); also in verses 12, 20 and 28
q12 That is, probably about 6 quarts (about 6.5 liters); also in verses 20 and 28
r14 That is, probably about 2 quarts (about 2 liters)
s14 That is, probably about 1 1/4 quarts (about 1.2 liters)

הַזֶּה חָג שִׁבְעַת יָמִים מַצּוֹת יֵאָכֵל׃
he-must-be-eaten breads-without-yeast days seven-of festival the-this

בַּיּוֹם הָרִאשׁוֹן מִקְרָא־ קֹדֶשׁ כָּל־ מְלֶאכֶת עֲבֹדָה לֹא
not regular work-of any-of sacred assembly-of the-first on-the-day (18)

תַעֲשׂוּ׃ וְהִקְרַבְתֶּם אִשֶּׁה עֹלָה לַיהוָה פָּרִים
bulls to-Yahweh burnt-offering fire-offering and-you-present (19) you-do

בְּנֵי־ בָקָר שְׁנַיִם וְאַיִל אֶחָד וְשִׁבְעָה כְבָשִׂים בְּנֵי שָׁנָה
year sons-of male-lambs and-seven one and-ram two herd young-ones-of

תְּמִימִם יִהְיוּ לָכֶם׃ וּמִנְחָתָם
and-grain-offering-of-them (20) to-you they-must-be ones-without-defect

סֹלֶת בְּלוּלָה בַשָּׁמֶן שְׁלֹשָׁה עֶשְׂרֹנִים לַפָּר וּשְׁנֵי עֶשְׂרֹנִים
tenths and-two-of with-the-bull tenths three with-the-oil being-mixed flour

לָאַיִל תַּעֲשׂוּ׃ עִשָּׂרוֹן עִשָּׂרוֹן תַּעֲשֶׂה לַכֶּבֶשׂ הָאֶחָד
the-each with-the-lamb you-prepare tenth tenth (21) you-prepare with-the-ram

לְשִׁבְעַת הַכְּבָשִׂים׃ וּשְׂעִיר חַטָּאת אֶחָד לְכַפֵּר עֲלֵיכֶם׃
for-you to-atone one sin-offering and-goat-of (22) the-lambs with-seven-of

מִלְּבַד עֹלַת הַבֹּקֶר אֲשֶׁר לְעֹלַת
for-burnt-offering-of that the-morning burnt-offering-of in-addition-to (23)

הַתָּמִיד תַּעֲשׂוּ אֶת־ אֵלֶּה׃ כָּאֵלֶּה תַּעֲשׂוּ לַיּוֹם
by-the-day you-prepare as-the-these (24) these *** you-prepare the-regular

שִׁבְעַת יָמִים לֶחֶם אִשֵּׁה רֵיחַ־ נִיחֹחַ לַיהוָה עַל־
beside to-Yahweh pleasant aroma-of fire-offering-of food-of days seven-of

עוֹלַת הַתָּמִיד יֵעָשֶׂה וְנִסְכּוֹ׃
and-drink-offering-of-him he-must-be-prepared the-regular burnt-offering-of

וּבַיּוֹם הַשְּׁבִיעִי מִקְרָא־ קֹדֶשׁ יִהְיֶה לָכֶם כָּל־
any-of for-you he-must-be sacred assembly-of the-seventh and-on-the-day (25)

מְלֶאכֶת עֲבֹדָה לֹא תַעֲשׂוּ׃ וּבְיוֹם הַבִּכּוּרִים
the-firstfruits and-on-day-of (26) you-do not regular work-of

בְּהַקְרִיבְכֶם מִנְחָה חֲדָשָׁה לַיהוָה בְּשָׁבֻעֹתֵיכֶם
during-Feast-of-Weeks-of-you to-Yahweh new grain-offering when-to-present-you

מִקְרָא־ קֹדֶשׁ יִהְיֶה לָכֶם כָּל־ מְלֶאכֶת עֲבֹדָה לֹא תַעֲשׂוּ׃
you-do not regular work-of any-of for-you he-must-be sacred assembly-of

וְהִקְרַבְתֶּם עוֹלָה לְרֵיחַ נִיחֹחַ לַיהוָה פָּרִים
bulls to-Yahweh pleasant as-aroma-of burnt-offering and-you-present (27)

בְּנֵי־ בָקָר שְׁנַיִם אַיִל אֶחָד שִׁבְעָה כְבָשִׂים בְּנֵי שָׁנָה׃
year sons-of male-lambs seven one ram two herd young-ones-of

וּמִנְחָתָם סֹלֶת בְּלוּלָה בַשָּׁמֶן שְׁלֹשָׁה עֶשְׂרֹנִים
tenths three with-the-oil being-mixed flour and-grain-offering-of-them (28)

there is to be a festival; for seven days eat bread made without yeast.
18On the first day hold a sacred assembly and do no regular work.
19Present to the LORD an offering made by fire, a burnt offering of two young bulls, one ram and seven male lambs a year old, all without defect.
20With each bull prepare a grain offering of three-tenths of an ephah of fine flour mixed with oil; with the ram, two-tenths;
21and with each of the seven lambs, one-tenth.
22Include one male goat as a sin offering to make atonement for you.
23Prepare these in addition to the regular morning burnt offering.
24In this way prepare the food for the offering made by fire every day for seven days as an aroma pleasing to the LORD; it is to be prepared in addition to the regular burnt offering and its drink offering.
25On the seventh day hold a sacred assembly and do no regular work.

Feast of Weeks

26" 'On the day of firstfruits, when you present to the LORD an offering of new grain during the Feast of Weeks, hold a sacred assembly and do no regular work.
27Present a burnt offering of two young bulls, one ram and seven male lambs a year old as an aroma pleasing to the LORD.
28With each bull there is to be a grain offering of three-tenths of an ephah of fine flour mixed with

לַפָּר הָאֶחָד שְׁנֵי עֶשְׂרֹנִים לָאַיִל הָאֶחָד׃ עִשָּׂרוֹן עִשָּׂרוֹן
tenth tenth (29) the-each with-the-ram tenths two-of the-each with-the-bull

לַכֶּבֶשׂ הָאֶחָד לְשִׁבְעַת הַכְּבָשִׂים׃ שְׂעִיר עִזִּים אֶחָד
one goats male-goat-of (30) the-lambs with-seven-of the-each with-the-lamb

לְכַפֵּר עֲלֵיכֶם׃ מִלְּבַד עֹלַת הַתָּמִיד
the-regular burnt-offering-of in-addition-to (31) for-you to-atone

וּמִנְחָתוֹ תַּעֲשׂוּ תְּמִימִם יִהְיוּ־ לָכֶם
to-you they-must-be ones-without-defect you-prepare and-grain-offering-of-him

וְנִסְכֵּיהֶם׃ וּבַחֹדֶשׁ הַשְּׁבִיעִי בְּאֶחָד
on-first the-seventh and-in-the-month (29:1) with-drink-offerings-of-them

לַחֹדֶשׁ מִקְרָא־ קֹדֶשׁ יִהְיֶה לָכֶם כָּל־ מְלֶאכֶת עֲבֹדָה
regular work-of any-of for-you he-must-be sacred assembly-of of-the-month

לֹא תַעֲשׂוּ יוֹם תְּרוּעָה יִהְיֶה לָכֶם׃ וַעֲשִׂיתֶם
and-you-prepare (2) for-you he-is trumpet-sound day-of you-do not

עֹלָה לְרֵיחַ נִיחֹחַ לַיהוָה פַּר בֶּן־ בָּקָר אֶחָד אַיִל אֶחָד
one ram one herd young-of bull to-Yahweh pleasant as-aroma-of burnt-offering

כְּבָשִׂים בְּנֵי־ שָׁנָה שִׁבְעָה תְּמִימִם׃ וּמִנְחָתָם
and-grain-offering-of-them (3) ones-without-defect seven year sons-of lambs

סֹלֶת בְּלוּלָה בַשָּׁמֶן שְׁלֹשָׁה עֶשְׂרֹנִים לַפָּר שְׁנֵי עֶשְׂרֹנִים
tenths two-of with-the-bull tenths three with-the-oil being-mixed fine-flour

לָאָיִל׃ וְעִשָּׂרוֹן אֶחָד לַכֶּבֶשׂ הָאֶחָד לְשִׁבְעַת הַכְּבָשִׂים׃
the-lambs with-seven-of the-each with-the-lamb one and-tenth (4) with-the-ram

וּשְׂעִיר־ עִזִּים אֶחָד חַטָּאת לְכַפֵּר עֲלֵיכֶם׃ מִלְּבַד
in-addition-to (6) for-you to-atone sin-offering one goats and-male-goat-of (5)

עֹלַת הַחֹדֶשׁ וּמִנְחָתָהּ וְעֹלַת
and-burnt-offering-of and-grain-offering-of-her the-month burnt-offering-of

הַתָּמִיד וּמִנְחָתָהּ וְנִסְכֵּיהֶם
and-drink-offerings-of-them and-grain-offering-of-her the-regular

כְּמִשְׁפָּטָם לְרֵיחַ נִיחֹחַ אִשֶּׁה לַיהוָה׃
to-Yahweh fire-offering pleasant for-aroma-of as-specified-of-them

וּבֶעָשׂוֹר לַחֹדֶשׁ הַשְּׁבִיעִי הַזֶּה מִקְרָא־ קֹדֶשׁ
sacred assembly-of the-this the-seventh of-the-month and-on-tenth (7)

יִהְיֶה לָכֶם וְעִנִּיתֶם אֶת־ נַפְשֹׁתֵיכֶם כָּל־ מְלָאכָה לֹא תַעֲשׂוּ׃
you-do not work any-of selves-of-you *** and-you-must-deny for-you he-must-be

וְהִקְרַבְתֶּם עֹלָה לַיהוָה רֵיחַ נִיחֹחַ פַּר בֶּן־
young-of bull pleasant aroma-of to-Yahweh burnt-offering and-you-present (8)

בָּקָר אֶחָד אַיִל אֶחָד כְּבָשִׂים בְּנֵי־ שָׁנָה שִׁבְעָה תְּמִימִם יִהְיוּ
they-must-be ones-without-defect seven year sons-of lambs one ram one herd

oil; with the ram, two-tenths;
29and with each of the seven
lambs, one-tenth. 30Include
one male goat to make atonement for you. 31Prepare these
together with their drink
offerings, in addition to the
regular burnt offering and its
grain offering. Be sure the animals are without defect.

Feast of Trumpets

29 " 'On the first day of
the seventh month
hold a sacred assembly and do
no regular work. It is a day for
you to sound the trumpets. 2As
an aroma pleasing to the LORD,
prepare a burnt offering of one
young bull, one ram and seven
male lambs a year old, all
without defect. 3With the bull
prepare a grain offering of
three-tenths of an ephah[t] of
fine flour mixed with oil; with
the ram, two-tenths[u]; 4and
with each of the seven lambs,
one-tenth.[v] 5Include one male
goat as a sin offering to make
atonement for you. 6These are
in addition to the monthly
and daily burnt offerings with
their grain offerings and drink
offerings as specified. They are
offerings made to the LORD by
fire—a pleasing aroma.

Day of Atonement

7" 'On the tenth day of this
seventh month hold a sacred
assembly. You must deny
yourselves[w] and do no work.
8Present as an aroma pleasing
to the LORD a burnt offering of
one young bull, one ram and
seven male lambs a year old,
all without defect. 9With the

[t]3 That is, probably about 6 quarts (about 6.5 liters); also in verses 9 and 14
[u]3 That is, probably about 4 quarts (about 4.5 liters); also in verses 9 and 14
[v]4 That is, probably about 2 quarts (about 2 liters); also in verses 10 and 15
[w]7 Or *must fast*

לָכֶם׃ וּמִנְחָתָם סֹלֶת בְּלוּלָה בַשָּׁמֶן שְׁלֹשָׁה
three with-the-oil being-mixed flour and-grain-offering-of-them (9) to-you

עֶשְׂרֹנִים לַפָּר שְׁנֵי עֶשְׂרֹנִים לָאַיִל הָאֶחָד׃ עִשָּׂרוֹן עִשָּׂרוֹן
tenth tenth (10) the-one with-the-ram tenths two-of with-the-bull tenths

לַכֶּבֶשׂ הָאֶחָד לְשִׁבְעַת הַכְּבָשִׂים׃ שְׂעִיר־עִזִּים אֶחָד
one goats male-goat-of (11) the-lambs for-seven-of the-each with-the-lamb

חַטָּאת מִלְּבַד חַטַּאת הַכִּפֻּרִים וְעֹלַת
and-burnt-offering-of the-atonements sin-offering-of in-addition-to sin-offering

הַתָּמִיד וּמִנְחָתָהּ וְנִסְכֵּיהֶם׃
and-drink-offerings-of-them and-grain-offering-of-her the-regular

וּבַחֲמִשָּׁה עָשָׂר יוֹם לַחֹדֶשׁ הַשְּׁבִיעִי מִקְרָא־קֹדֶשׁ
sacred assembly-of the-seventh of-the-month day ten and-on-five (12)

יִהְיֶה לָכֶם כָּל־מְלֶאכֶת עֲבֹדָה לֹא תַעֲשׂוּ וְחַגֹּתֶם חַג
festival and-you-celebrate you-do not regular work-of any-of for-you he-must-be

לַיהוָה שִׁבְעַת יָמִים׃ וְהִקְרַבְתֶּם עֹלָה אִשֵּׁה
fire-offering-of burnt-offering and-you-present (13) days seven-of to-Yahweh

רֵיחַ נִיחֹחַ לַיהוָה פָּרִים בְּנֵי־בָקָר שְׁלֹשָׁה עָשָׂר אֵילִם שְׁנָיִם
two rams ten three herd young-ones-of bulls to-Yahweh pleasant aroma-of

כְּבָשִׂים בְּנֵי־שָׁנָה אַרְבָּעָה עָשָׂר תְּמִימִם יִהְיוּ׃
they-must-be ones-without-defect ten four year sons-of male-lambs

וּמִנְחָתָם סֹלֶת בְּלוּלָה בַשָּׁמֶן שְׁלֹשָׁה עֶשְׂרֹנִים
tenths three with-the-oil being-mixed flour and-grain-offering-of-them (14)

לַפָּר הָאֶחָד לִשְׁלֹשָׁה עָשָׂר פָּרִים שְׁנֵי עֶשְׂרֹנִים לָאַיִל
with-the-ram tenths two-of bulls ten with-three the-each with-the-bull

הָאֶחָד לִשְׁנֵי הָאֵילִם׃ וְעִשָּׂרוֹן עִשָּׂרוֹן לַכֶּבֶשׂ הָאֶחָד
the-each with-the-lamb tenth and-tenth (15) the-rams with-two-of the-each

לְאַרְבָּעָה עָשָׂר כְּבָשִׂים׃ וּשְׂעִיר־עִזִּים אֶחָד חַטָּאת מִלְּבַד
in-addition-to sin-offering one goats and-male-goat-of (16) lambs ten with-four

עֹלַת הַתָּמִיד מִנְחָתָהּ וְנִסְכָּהּ׃
and-drink-offering-of-her grain-offering-of-her the-regular burnt-offering-of

וּבַיּוֹם הַשֵּׁנִי פָּרִים בְּנֵי־בָקָר שְׁנֵים עָשָׂר אֵילִם שְׁנָיִם
two rams ten two herd young-ones-of bulls the-second and-on-the-day (17)

כְּבָשִׂים בְּנֵי־שָׁנָה אַרְבָּעָה עָשָׂר תְּמִימִם׃ וּמִנְחָתָם
and-grain-offering-of-them (18) ones-without-defect ten four year sons-of lambs

וְנִסְכֵּיהֶם לַפָּרִים לָאֵילִם וְלַכְּבָשִׂים
and-with-the-lambs with-the-rams with-the-bulls and-drink-offerings-of-them

בְּמִסְפָּרָם כַּמִּשְׁפָּט׃ וּשְׂעִיר־עִזִּים אֶחָד חַטָּאת
sin-offering one goats and-male-goat-of (19) as-the-rule by-number-of-them

bull prepare a grain offering of three-tenths of an ephah of fine flour mixed with oil; with the ram, two-tenths; [10]and with each of the seven lambs, one-tenth. [11]Include one male goat as a sin offering, in addition to the sin offering for atonement and the regular burnt offering with its grain offering, and their drink offerings.

Feast of Tabernacles

[12]" 'On the fifteenth day of the seventh month, hold a sacred assembly and do no regular work. Celebrate a festival to the LORD for seven days. [13]Present an offering made by fire as an aroma pleasing to the LORD, a burnt offering of thirteen young bulls, two rams and fourteen male lambs a year old, all without defect. [14]With each of the thirteen bulls prepare a grain offering of three-tenths of an ephah of fine flour mixed with oil; with each of the two rams, two-tenths; [15]and with each of the fourteen lambs, one-tenth. [16]Include one male goat as a sin offering, in addition to the regular burnt offering with its grain offering and drink offering.

[17]" 'On the second day prepare twelve young bulls, two rams and fourteen male lambs a year old, all without defect. [18]With the bulls, rams and lambs, prepare their grain offerings and drink offerings according to the number specified. [19]Include one male

מִלְּבַד עֹלַת הַתָּמִיד וּמִנְחָתָהּ
in-addition-to burnt-offering-of the-regular and-grain-offering-of-her

וְנִסְכֵּיהֶם׃ וּבַיּוֹם הַשְּׁלִישִׁי פָּרִים עַשְׁתֵּי־עָשָׂר
and-drink-offerings-of-them (20) and-on-the-day the-third bulls one ten

אֵילִם שְׁנָיִם כְּבָשִׂים בְּנֵי־ שָׁנָה אַרְבָּעָה עָשָׂר תְּמִימִם׃
rams two lambs sons-of year four ten ones-without-defect

וּמִנְחָתָם וְנִסְכֵּיהֶם לַפָּרִים
(21) and-grain-offering-of-them and-drink-offerings-of-them with-the-bulls

לָאֵילִם וְלַכְּבָשִׂים בְּמִסְפָּרָם כַּמִּשְׁפָּט׃
with-the-rams and-with-the-lambs by-number-of-them as-the-specified

וּשְׂעִיר חַטָּאת אֶחָד מִלְּבַד עֹלַת
(22) and-male-goat-of sin-offering one in-addition-to burnt-offering-of

הַתָּמִיד וּמִנְחָתָהּ וְנִסְכָּהּ׃
the-regular and-grain-offering-of-her and-drink-offering-of-her

וּבַיּוֹם הָרְבִיעִי פָּרִים עֲשָׂרָה אֵילִם שְׁנָיִם כְּבָשִׂים בְּנֵי־ שָׁנָה
(23) and-on-the-day the-fourth bulls ten rams two lambs sons-of year

אַרְבָּעָה עָשָׂר תְּמִימִם׃ מִנְחָתָם
four ten ones-without-defect (24) grain-offering-of-them

וְנִסְכֵּיהֶם לַפָּרִים לָאֵילִם וְלַכְּבָשִׂים
and-drink-offerings-of-them with-the-bulls with-the-rams and-with-the-lambs

בְּמִסְפָּרָם כַּמִּשְׁפָּט׃ וּשְׂעִיר־ עִזִּים אֶחָד חַטָּאת
by-number-of-them as-the-rule (25) and-male-goat-of goats one sin-offering

מִלְּבַד עֹלַת הַתָּמִיד מִנְחָתָהּ
in-addition-to burnt-offering-of the-regular grain-offering-of-her

וְנִסְכָּהּ׃ וּבַיּוֹם הַחֲמִישִׁי פָּרִים תִּשְׁעָה אֵילִם
and-drink-offering-of-her (26) and-on-the-day the-fifth bulls nine rams

שְׁנָיִם כְּבָשִׂים בְּנֵי־ שָׁנָה אַרְבָּעָה עָשָׂר תְּמִימִם׃
two lambs sons-of year four ten ones-without-defect

וּמִנְחָתָם וְנִסְכֵּיהֶם לַפָּרִים
(27) and-grain-offering-of-them and-drink-offerings-of-them with-the-bulls

לָאֵילִם וְלַכְּבָשִׂים בְּמִסְפָּרָם כַּמִּשְׁפָּט׃
with-the-rams and-with-the-lambs by-number-of-them as-the-specified

וּשְׂעִיר חַטָּאת אֶחָד מִלְּבַד עֹלַת הַתָּמִיד
(28) and-goat-of sin-offering one in-addition-to burnt-offering-of the-regular

וּמִנְחָתָהּ וְנִסְכָּהּ׃ וּבַיּוֹם
and-grain-offering-of-her and-drink-offering-of-her (29) and-on-the-day

הַשִּׁשִּׁי פָּרִים שְׁמֹנָה אֵילִם שְׁנָיִם כְּבָשִׂים בְּנֵי־ שָׁנָה אַרְבָּעָה עָשָׂר
the-sixth bulls eight rams two lambs sons-of year four ten

goat as a sin offering, in addition to the regular burnt
offering with its grain
offering, and their drink
offerings.
20" 'On the third day prepare
eleven bulls, two rams and
fourteen male lambs a year
old, all without defect. 21With
the bulls, rams and lambs, prepare their grain offerings and
drink offerings according to
the number specified. 22In-
clude one male goat as a sin
offering, in addition to the
regular burnt offering with its
grain offering and drink
offering.
23" 'On the fourth day prepare ten bulls, two rams and
fourteen male lambs a year
old, all without defect. 24With
the bulls, rams and lambs, prepare their grain offerings and
drink offerings according to
the number specified. 25In-
clude one male goat as a sin
offering, in addition to the
regular burnt offering with its
grain offering and drink
offering.
26" 'On the fifth day prepare
nine bulls, two rams and fourteen male lambs a year old, all
without defect. 27With the
bulls, rams and lambs, prepare
their grain offerings and drink
offerings according to the
number specified. 28Include
one male goat as a sin offering,
in addition to the regular
burnt offering with its grain
offering and drink offering.
29" 'On the sixth day prepare
eight bulls, two rams and fourteen male lambs a year old, all

תְּמִימִם׃ (30) וּמִנְחָתָם וְנִסְכֵּיהֶם
and-drink-offerings-of-them and-grain-offering-of-them (30) ones-without-defect

לַפָּרִים לָאֵילִם וְלַכְּבָשִׂים בְּמִסְפָּרָם כַּמִּשְׁפָּט׃
as-the-rule by-number-of-them and-with-the-lambs with-the-rams with-the-bulls

(31) וּשְׂעִיר חַטָּאת אֶחָד מִלְּבַד עֹלַת הַתָּמִיד
the-regular burnt-offering-of in-addition-to one sin-offering and-goat-of (31)

מִנְחָתָהּ וּנְסָכֶיהָ׃ (32) וּבַיּוֹם הַשְּׁבִיעִי
the-seventh and-on-the-day (32) and-drink-offering-of-her grain-offering-of-her

פָּרִים שִׁבְעָה אֵילִם שְׁנָיִם כְּבָשִׂים בְּנֵי־ שָׁנָה אַרְבָּעָה עָשָׂר תְּמִימִם׃
ones-without-defect ten four year sons-of lambs two rams seven bulls

(33) וּמִנְחָתָם וְנִסְכֵּהֶם לַפָּרִים
with-the-bulls and-drink-offerings-of-them and-grain-offering-of-them (33)

לָאֵילִם וְלַכְּבָשִׂים בְּמִסְפָּרָם כְּמִשְׁפָּטָם׃
as-specified-of-them by-number-of-them and-with-the-lambs with-the-rams

(34) וּשְׂעִיר חַטָּאת אֶחָד מִלְּבַד עֹלַת הַתָּמִיד
the-regular burnt-offering-of in-addition-to one sin-offering and-goat-of (34)

מִנְחָתָהּ וְנִסְכָּהּ׃ (35) בַּיּוֹם הַשְּׁמִינִי
the-eighth on-the-day (35) and-drink-offering-of-her grain-offering-of-her

עֲצֶרֶת תִּהְיֶה לָכֶם כָּל־ מְלֶאכֶת עֲבֹדָה לֹא תַעֲשׂוּ׃
you-do not regular work-of any-of for-you she-must-be assembly

(36) וְהִקְרַבְתֶּם עֹלָה אִשֵּׁה רֵיחַ נִיחֹחַ
pleasant aroma-of fire-offering-of burnt-offering and-you-present (36)

לַיהוָה פַּר אֶחָד אַיִל אֶחָד כְּבָשִׂים בְּנֵי־ שָׁנָה שִׁבְעָה תְּמִימִם׃
ones-without-defect seven year sons-of lambs one ram one bull to-Yahweh

(37) מִנְחָתָם וְנִסְכֵּיהֶם לַפָּר
with-the-bull and-drink-offerings-of-them grain-offering-of-them (37)

לָאַיִל וְלַכְּבָשִׂים בְּמִסְפָּרָם כַּמִּשְׁפָּט׃ (38) וּשְׂעִיר
and-goat-of (38) as-the-rule by-number-of-them and-with-the-lambs with-the-ram

חַטָּאת אֶחָד מִלְּבַד עֹלַת הַתָּמִיד
the-regular burnt-offering-of in-addition-to one sin-offering

וּמִנְחָתָהּ וְנִסְכָּהּ׃ (39) אֵלֶּה תַּעֲשׂוּ
you-prepare these (39) and-drink-offering-of-her and-grain-offering-of-her

לַיהוָה בְּמוֹעֲדֵיכֶם לְבַד מִנִּדְרֵיכֶם
from-vows-of-you addition-to at-feasts-of-you for-Yahweh

וְנִדְבֹתֵיכֶם לְעֹלֹתֵיכֶם
with-burnt-offerings-of-you and-freewill-offerings-of-you

וּלְמִנְחֹתֵיכֶם וּלְנִסְכֵּיכֶם
and-with-drink-offerings-of-you and-with-grain-offerings-of-you

without defect. 30With the
bulls, rams and lambs, prepare
their grain offerings and drink
offerings according to the
number specified. 31Include
one male goat as a sin offering,
in addition to the regular
burnt offering with its grain
offering and drink offering.
32" 'On the seventh day prepare seven bulls, two rams and
fourteen male lambs a year
old, all without defect. 33With
the bulls, rams and lambs, prepare their grain offerings and
drink offerings according to
the number specified. 34In-
clude one male goat as a sin
offering, in addition to the
regular burnt offering with its
grain offering and drink
offering.
35" 'On the eighth day hold
an assembly and do no regular
work. 36Present an offering
made by fire as an aroma
pleasing to the LORD, a burnt
offering of one bull, one ram
and seven male lambs a year
old, all without defect. 37With
the bull, the ram and the
lambs, prepare their grain
offerings and drink offerings
according to the number
specified. 38Include one male
goat as a sin offering, in addition to the regular burnt
offering with its grain offering
and drink offering.
39" 'In addition to what you
vow and your freewill
offerings, prepare these for the
LORD at your appointed feasts:
your burnt offerings, grain
offerings, drink offerings and
fellowship offerings.[x]' "

[x]39 Traditionally *peace offerings*

וּלְשַׁלְמֵיכֶם׃ וַיֹּאמֶר מֹשֶׁה אֶל־ בְּנֵי
sons-of to Moses and-he-told (30:1)* and-with-fellowship-offerings-of-you

יִשְׂרָאֵל כְּכֹל אֲשֶׁר־ צִוָּה יְהוָה אֶת־ מֹשֶׁה׃ וַיְדַבֵּר מֹשֶׁה אֶל־
to Moses and-he-spoke (2) Moses *** Yahweh he-commanded that as-all Israel

רָאשֵׁי הַמַּטּוֹת לִבְנֵי יִשְׂרָאֵל לֵאמֹר זֶה הַדָּבָר אֲשֶׁר צִוָּה
he-commands that the-thing this to-say Israel of-sons-of the-tribes heads-of

יְהוָה׃ אִישׁ כִּי־ יִדֹּר נֶדֶר לַיהוָה אוֹ־ הִשָּׁבַע שְׁבֻעָה לֶאְסֹר
to-obligate oath to-swear or to-Yahweh vow he-vows when man (3) Yahweh

אִסָּר עַל־ נַפְשׁוֹ לֹא יַחֵל דְּבָרוֹ כְּכָל־
as-every-of word-of-him he-must-break not self-of-him on pledge

הַיֹּצֵא מִפִּיו יַעֲשֶׂה׃ וְאִשָּׁה כִּי־ תִדֹּר
she-vows when and-woman (4) he-must-do from-mouth-of-him the-thing-coming

נֶדֶר לַיהוָה וְאָסְרָה אִסָּר בְּבֵית אָבִיהָ בִּנְעֻרֶיהָ׃
in-youths-of-her father-of-her in-house-of pledge or-she-obligates to-Yahweh vow

וְשָׁמַע אָבִיהָ אֶת־ נִדְרָהּ וֶאֱסָרָהּ אֲשֶׁר
which or-pledge-of-her vow-of-her *** father-of-her and-he-hears (5)

אָסְרָה עַל־ נַפְשָׁהּ וְהֶחֱרִישׁ לָהּ אָבִיהָ
father-of-her to-her but-he-says-nothing self-of-her on she-obligated

וְקָמוּ כָּל־ נְדָרֶיהָ וְכָל־ אִסָּר אֲשֶׁר־
which pledge and-every-of vows-of-her all-of then-they-will-stand

אָסְרָה עַל־ נַפְשָׁהּ יָקוּם׃ וְאִם־ הֵנִיא
he-forbids but-if (6) he-will-stand self-of-her on she-obligated

אָבִיהָ אֹתָהּ בְּיוֹם שָׁמְעוֹ כָּל־ נְדָרֶיהָ וֶאֱסָרֶיהָ
or-pledges-of-her vows-of-her all-of to-hear-him on-day her father-of-her

אֲשֶׁר־ אָסְרָה עַל־ נַפְשָׁהּ לֹא יָקוּם וַיהוָה
and-Yahweh he-will-stand not self-of-her on she-obligated which

יִסְלַח־ לָהּ כִּי־ הֵנִיא אָבִיהָ אֹתָהּ׃ וְאִם־ הָיוֹ
to-be and-if (7) her father-of-her he-forbade for from-her he-will-release

תִהְיֶה לְאִישׁ וּנְדָרֶיהָ עָלֶיהָ אוֹ מִבְטָא שְׂפָתֶיהָ
lips-of-her rash-promise-of or on-her and-vows-of-her to-husband she-is

אֲשֶׁר אָסְרָה עַל־ נַפְשָׁהּ׃ וְשָׁמַע אִישָׁהּ בְּיוֹם
on-day husband-of-her and-he-hears (8) self-of-her on she-obligated which

שָׁמְעוֹ וְהֶחֱרִישׁ לָהּ וְקָמוּ נְדָרֶיהָ
vows-of-her then-they-will-stand to-her but-he-says-nothing to-hear-him

וֶאֱסָרֶהָ אֲשֶׁר־ אָסְרָה עַל־ נַפְשָׁהּ יָקֻמוּ׃
they-will-stand self-of-her on she-obligated which or-pledges-of-her

וְאִם בְּיוֹם שְׁמֹעַ אִישָׁהּ יָנִיא אוֹתָהּ וְהֵפֵר
then-he-nullifies her he-forbids husband-of-her to-hear on-day but-if (9)

[40]Moses told the Israelites all that the LORD commanded him.

Vows

30 Moses said to the heads of the tribes of Israel: "This is what the LORD commands: [2]When a man makes a vow to the LORD or takes an oath to obligate himself by a pledge, he must not break his word but must do everything he said.

[3]"When a young woman still living in her father's house makes a vow to the LORD or obligates herself by a pledge [4]and her father hears about her vow or pledge but says nothing to her, then all her vows and every pledge by which she obligated herself will stand. [5]But if her father forbids her when he hears about it, none of her vows or the pledges by which she obligated herself will stand; the LORD will release her because her father has forbidden her.

[6]"If she marries after she makes a vow or after her lips utter a rash promise by which she obligates herself [7]and her husband hears about it but says nothing to her, then her vows or the pledges by which she obligated herself will stand. [8]But if her husband forbids her when he hears about it, he nullifies the vow that

*The Hebrew numeration of chapter 30 begins with verse 40 of chapter 29 in English; thus, there is a one-verse discrepancy throughout chapter 30.

אֶת־נִדְרָהּ אֲשֶׁר עָלֶיהָ וְאֵת מִבְטָא שְׂפָתֶיהָ אֲשֶׁר אָסְרָה
she-obligated that lips-of-her rash-promise-of or on-her that vow-of-her ***

עַל־נַפְשָׁהּ וַיהוָה יִסְלַח־לָהּ׃ וְנֵדֶר אַלְמָנָה
widow and-vow-of (10) from-her he-will-release and-Yahweh self-of-her on

וּגְרוּשָׁה כֹּל אֲשֶׁר־אָסְרָה עַל־נַפְשָׁהּ יָקוּם
he-will-bind self-of-her on she-obligates which any or-one-being-divorced

עָלֶיהָ׃ וְאִם־בֵּית אִישָׁהּ נָדָרָה אוֹ־אָסְרָה אִסָּר
pledge she-obligates or she-vows husband-of-her house-of and-if (11) on-her

עַל־נַפְשָׁהּ בִּשְׁבֻעָה׃ וְשָׁמַע אִישָׁהּ וְהֶחֱרִשׁ
but-he-says-nothing husband-of-her and-he-hears (12) under-oath self-of-her on

לָהּ לֹא הֵנִיא אֹתָהּ וְקָמוּ כָּל־נְדָרֶיהָ וְכָל־
and-every-of vows-of-her all-of then-they-will-stand her he-forbids not to-her

אִסָּר אֲשֶׁר־אָסְרָה עַל־נַפְשָׁהּ יָקוּם׃ וְאִם־
but-if (13) he-will-stand self-of-her on she-obligated which pledge

הָפֵר יָפֵר אֹתָם ׀ אִישָׁהּ בְּיוֹם שָׁמְעוֹ כָּל־
every-of to-hear-him on-day husband-of-her them he-nullifies to-nullify

מוֹצָא שְׂפָתֶיהָ לִנְדָרֶיהָ וּלְאִסַּר נַפְשָׁהּ לֹא
not self-of-her or-if-pledge-of if-vows-of-her lips-of-her thing-from

יָקוּם אִישָׁהּ הֲפֵרָם וַיהוָה יִסְלַח־
he-will-release and-Yahweh he-nullified-them husband-of-her he-will-stand

לָהּ׃ כָּל־נֵדֶר וְכָל־שְׁבֻעַת אִסָּר לְעַנֹּת נֶפֶשׁ אִישָׁהּ
husband-of-her self to-deny pledge oath-of or-any-of vow any-of (14) from-her

יְקִימֶנּוּ וְאִישָׁהּ יְפֵרֶנּוּ׃ וְאִם־
but-if (15) he-may-nullify-him or-husband-of-her he-may-confirm-him

הַחֲרֵשׁ יַחֲרִישׁ לָהּ אִישָׁהּ מִיּוֹם אֶל־יוֹם
day to from-day husband-of-her to-her he-says-nothing to-say-nothing

וְהֵקִים אֶת־כָּל־נְדָרֶיהָ אוֹ אֶת־כָּל־אֱסָרֶיהָ אֲשֶׁר
that pledges-of-her all-of *** or vows-of-her all-of *** then-he-confirms

עָלֶיהָ הֵקִים אֹתָם כִּי־הֶחֱרִשׁ לָהּ בְּיוֹם שָׁמְעוֹ׃
to-hear-him on-day to-her he-says-nothing for them he-confirms on-her

וְאִם־הָפֵר יָפֵר אֹתָם אַחֲרֵי שָׁמְעוֹ וְנָשָׂא
then-he-must-bear to-hear-him after them he-nullifies to-nullify but-if (16)

אֶת־עֲוֺנָהּ׃ אֵלֶּה הַחֻקִּים אֲשֶׁר צִוָּה יְהוָה אֶת־מֹשֶׁה
Moses *** Yahweh he-gave that the-regulations these (17) guilt-of-her ***

בֵּין אִישׁ לְאִשְׁתּוֹ בֵּין־אָב לְבִתּוֹ בִּנְעֻרֶיהָ
in-youths-of-her to-daughter-of-him father between to-wife-of-him man between

בֵּית אָבִיהָ׃ וַיְדַבֵּר יְהוָה אֶל־מֹשֶׁה לֵּאמֹר׃
to-say Moses to Yahweh and-he-spoke (31:1) father-of-her house-of

obligates her or the rash promise by which she obligates herself, and the LORD will release her.

9 "Any vow or obligation taken by a widow or divorced woman will be binding on her.

10 "If a woman living with her husband makes a vow or obligates herself by a pledge under oath
11 and her husband hears about it but says nothing to her and does not forbid her, then all her vows or the pledges by which she obligated herself will stand.
12 But if her husband nullifies them when he hears about them, then none of the vows or pledges that came from her lips will stand. Her husband has nullified them, and the
LORD will release her.
13 Her husband may confirm or nullify any vow she makes or any sworn pledge to deny herself.
14 But if her husband says nothing to her about it from day to day, then he confirms all her vows or the pledges binding on her. He confirms them by saying nothing to her when he hears about them.
15 If, however, he nullifies them some time after he hears about them, then he is responsible for her guilt."

16 These are the regulations the LORD gave Moses concerning relationships between a man and his wife, and between a father and his young daughter still living in his house.

Vengeance on the Midianites

31 The LORD said to Moses,
2 "Take vengeance on the Midianites for

*See the note on page 459.

נְקֹם נִקְמַת בְּנֵי יִשְׂרָאֵל מֵאֵת הַמִּדְיָנִים אַחַר
afterward the-Midianites on Israel sons-of vengeance-of avenge! (2)

תֵּאָסֵף אֶל־ עַמֶּיךָ׃ וַיְדַבֵּר מֹשֶׁה אֶל־ הָעָם
the-people to Moses so-he-said (3) people-of-you to you-will-be-gathered

לֵאמֹר הֵחָלְצוּ מֵאִתְּכֶם אֲנָשִׁים לַצָּבָא וְיִהְיוּ עַל־ מִדְיָן
Midian against and-they-will-go for-the-battle men from-with-you arm! to-say

לָתֵת נִקְמַת־ יְהוָה בְּמִדְיָן׃ אֶלֶף לַמַּטֶּה
from-the-tribe thousand (4) on-Midian Yahweh vengeance-of to-carry-out

אֶלֶף לַמַּטֶּה לְכֹל מַטּוֹת יִשְׂרָאֵל תִּשְׁלְחוּ לַצָּבָא׃
into-the-battle you-send Israel tribes-of from-all-of from-the-tribe thousand

וַיִּמָּסְרוּ מֵאַלְפֵי יִשְׂרָאֵל אֶלֶף לַמַּטֶּה
from-the-tribe thousand Israel from-thousands-of so-they-were-armed (5)

שְׁנֵים־עָשָׂר אֶלֶף חֲלוּצֵי צָבָא׃ וַיִּשְׁלַח אֹתָם מֹשֶׁה
Moses them and-he-sent (6) battle ones-being-supplied-of thousand ten two

אֶלֶף לַמַּטֶּה לַצָּבָא אֹתָם וְאֶת־ פִּינְחָס בֶּן־ אֶלְעָזָר
Eleazar son-of Phinehas and them into-the-battle from-the-tribe thousand

הַכֹּהֵן לַצָּבָא וּכְלֵי הַקֹּדֶשׁ וַחֲצֹצְרוֹת
and-trumpets-of the-sanctuary and-articles-of into-the-battle the-priest

הַתְּרוּעָה בְּיָדוֹ׃ וַיִּצְבְּאוּ עַל־ מִדְיָן כַּאֲשֶׁר
just-as Midian against and-they-fought (7) in-hand-of-him the-signal

צִוָּה יְהוָה אֶת־ מֹשֶׁה וַיַּהַרְגוּ כָּל־ זָכָר׃ וְאֶת־ מַלְכֵי
kings-of and (8) man every-of and-they-killed Moses *** Yahweh he-commanded

מִדְיָן הָרְגוּ עַל־ חַלְלֵיהֶם אֶת־אֱוִי וְאֶת־רֶקֶם וְאֶת־צוּר וְאֶת־חוּר
Hur and Zur and Rekem and Evi *** victims-of-them among they-killed Midian

וְאֶת־רֶבַע חֲמֵשֶׁת מַלְכֵי מִדְיָן וְאֵת בִּלְעָם בֶּן־ בְּעוֹר הָרְגוּ
they-killed Beor son-of Balaam and Midian kings-of five-of Reba and

בֶּחָרֶב׃ וַיִּשְׁבּוּ בְנֵי־ יִשְׂרָאֵל אֶת־ נְשֵׁי מִדְיָן
Midian women-of *** Israel sons-of and-they-captured (9) with-the-sword

וְאֶת־ טַפָּם וְאֵת כָּל־ בְּהֶמְתָּם וְאֶת־ כָּל־ מִקְנֵהֶם וְאֶת־
and flock-of-them all-of and herd-of-them all-of and child-of-them and

כָּל־ חֵילָם בָּזָזוּ׃ וְאֵת כָּל־ עָרֵיהֶם
towns-of-them all-of and (10) they-plundered good-of-them all-of

בְּמוֹשְׁבֹתָם וְאֵת כָּל־ טִירֹתָם שָׂרְפוּ בָּאֵשׁ׃
with-the-fire they-burned camps-of-them all-of and among-settlements-of-them

וַיִּקְחוּ אֶת־ כָּל־ הַשָּׁלָל וְאֵת כָּל־ הַמַּלְקוֹחַ בָּאָדָם
of-the-people the-spoil all-of and the-plunder all-of *** and-they-took (11)

וּבַבְּהֵמָה׃ וַיָּבִאוּ אֶל־ מֹשֶׁה וְאֶל־ אֶלְעָזָר הַכֹּהֵן
the-priest Eleazar and-to Moses to and-they-brought (12) and-of-the-animal

the Israelites. After that, you will be gathered to your people."

[3]So Moses said to the people, "Arm some of your men to go to war against the Midianites and to carry out the LORD's vengeance on them. [4]Send into battle a thousand men from each of the tribes of Israel." [5]So twelve thousand men armed for battle, a thousand from each tribe, were supplied from the clans of Israel. [6]Moses sent them into battle, a thousand from each tribe, along with Phinehas son of Eleazar, the priest, who took with him articles from the sanctuary and the trumpets for signaling.

[7]They fought against Midian, as the LORD commanded Moses, and killed every man. [8]Among their victims were Evi, Rekem, Zur, Hur and Reba—the five kings of Midian. They also killed Balaam son of Beor with the sword. [9]The Israelites captured the Midianite women and children and took all the Midianite herds, flocks and goods as plunder. [10]They burned all the towns where the Midianites had settled, as well as all their camps. [11]They took all the plunder and spoils, including the people and animals, [12]and brought the captives, spoils and plunder to Moses and

וְאֶל־ עֲדַת בְּנֵי־ יִשְׂרָאֵל אֶת־ הַשְּׁבִי וְאֶת־ הַמַּלְקוֹחַ וְאֶת־
and the-spoil and the-captive *** Israel sons-of assembly-of and-to

הַשָּׁלָל אֶל־ הַמַּחֲנֶה אֶל־ עַרְבֹת מוֹאָב אֲשֶׁר עַל־ יַרְדֵּן יְרֵחוֹ׃
Jericho Jordan-of by that Moab plains-of on the-camp at the-plunder

וַיֵּצְאוּ מֹשֶׁה וְאֶלְעָזָר הַכֹּהֵן וְכָל־ נְשִׂיאֵי
leaders-of and-all-of the-priest and-Eleazar Moses and-they-went (13)

הָעֵדָה לִקְרָאתָם אֶל־מִחוּץ לַמַּחֲנֶה׃ וַיִּקְצֹף מֹשֶׁה
Moses and-he-was-angry (14) of-the-camp outside at to-meet-them the-community

עַל פְּקוּדֵי הֶחָיִל שָׂרֵי הָאֲלָפִים וְשָׂרֵי
and-commanders-of the-thousands commanders-of the-army being-officers-of with

הַמֵּאוֹת הַבָּאִים מִצְּבָא הַמִּלְחָמָה׃ וַיֹּאמֶר
and-he-asked (15) the-war from-battle-of the-ones-returning the-hundreds

אֲלֵיהֶם מֹשֶׁה הַחִיִּיתֶם כָּל־ נְקֵבָה׃ הֵן הֵנָּה הָיוּ לִבְנֵי
to-sons-of they-came they see! (16) woman every-of you-let-live? Moses to-them

יִשְׂרָאֵל בִּדְבַר בִּלְעָם לִמְסָר־ מַעַל בַּיהוָה עַל־ דְּבַר־ פְּעוֹר
Peor matter-of in with-Yahweh away-from to-turn Balaam at-advice-of Israel

וַתְּהִי הַמַּגֵּפָה בַּעֲדַת יְהוָה׃ וְעַתָּה הִרְגוּ כָל־
every-of kill! so-now (17) Yahweh on-people-of the-plague so-she-struck

זָכָר בַּטָּף וְכָל־ אִשָּׁה יֹדַעַת אִישׁ לְמִשְׁכַּב זָכָר הֲרֹגוּ׃
kill! man to-sleep-with man knowing woman and-every-of among-the-child male

וְכֹל הַטַּף בַּנָּשִׁים אֲשֶׁר לֹא־ יָדְעוּ מִשְׁכַּב זָכָר
man sleep-with they-know not who among-the-girls the-child but-every-of (18)

הַחֲיוּ לָכֶם׃ וְאַתֶּם חֲנוּ מִחוּץ לַמַּחֲנֶה שִׁבְעַת יָמִים
days seven-of of-the-camp outside stay! and-you (19) for-you save!

כֹּל הֹרֵג נֶפֶשׁ וְכֹל ׀ נֹגֵעַ בֶּחָלָל
on-the-one-killed one-touching or-every-of anyone one-killing every-of

תִּתְחַטְּאוּ בַּיּוֹם הַשְּׁלִישִׁי וּבַיּוֹם הַשְּׁבִיעִי אַתֶּם
you the-seventh and-on-the-day the-third on-the-day you-must-purify-selves

וּשְׁבִיכֶם׃ וְכָל־ בֶּגֶד וְכָל־ כְּלִי־ עוֹר
leather thing-of and-every-of garment and-every-of (20) and-captive-of-you

וְכָל־ מַעֲשֵׂה עִזִּים וְכָל־ כְּלִי־ עֵץ תִּתְחַטָּאוּ׃
you-purify wood thing-of and-every-of goat-hairs object-of and-every-of

וַיֹּאמֶר אֶלְעָזָר הַכֹּהֵן אֶל־ אַנְשֵׁי הַצָּבָא הַבָּאִים
the-ones-going the-army men-of to the-priest Eleazar then-he-said (21)

לַמִּלְחָמָה זֹאת חֻקַּת הַתּוֹרָה אֲשֶׁר־ צִוָּה יְהוָה אֶת־מֹשֶׁה׃
Moses *** Yahweh he-gave that the-law requirement-of this into-the-battle

אַךְ אֶת־ הַזָּהָב וְאֶת־ הַכֶּסֶף אֶת־ הַנְּחֹשֶׁת אֶת־הַבַּרְזֶל אֶת־הַבְּדִיל
the-tin *** the-iron *** the-bronze *** the-silver and the-gold *** now (22)

Eleazar the priest and the Israelite assembly at their camp
on the plains of Moab, by the
Jordan across from Jericho.[y]
13 Moses, Eleazar the priest
and all the leaders of the community went to meet them
outside the camp. 14 Moses was
angry with the officers of the
army—the commanders of
thousands and commanders
of hundreds—who returned
from the battle.
15 "Have you allowed all the
women to live?" he asked
them. 16 "They were the ones
who followed Balaam's advice
and were the means of turning the Israelites away from
the LORD in what happened at
Peor, so that a plague struck
the LORD's people. 17 Now kill
all the boys. And kill every
woman who has slept with a
man, 18 but save for yourselves
every girl who has never slept
with a man.
19 "All of you who have killed
anyone or touched anyone
who was killed must stay outside the camp seven days. On
the third and seventh days
you must purify yourselves
and your captives. 20 Purify
every garment as well as
everything made of leather,
goat hair or wood."
21 Then Eleazar the priest
said to the soldiers who had
gone into battle, "This is the
requirement of the law that
the LORD gave Moses: 22 Gold,
silver, bronze, iron, tin, lead

y12 Hebrew *Jordan of Jericho;* possibly an ancient name for the Jordan River

וְאֶת־הָעֹפָֽרֶת׃ כָּל־ דָּבָר אֲשֶׁר־ יָבֹא בָאֵשׁ
against-the-fire he-can-withstand that thing any-of (23) the-lead and

תַּעֲבִירוּ בָאֵשׁ וְטָהֵר אַךְ בְּמֵי
with-waters-of also then-he-will-be-clean through-the-fire you-must-put

נִדָּה יִתְחַטָּא וְכֹל אֲשֶׁר לֹא־ יָבֹא
he-can-withstand not that and-anything he-must-be-purified cleansing

בָּאֵשׁ תַּעֲבִירוּ בַּמָּיִם׃ וְכִבַּסְתֶּם
and-you-wash (24) through-the-waters you-must-put against-the-fire

בִּגְדֵיכֶם בַּיּוֹם הַשְּׁבִיעִי וּטְהַרְתֶּם וְאַחַר
and-then and-you-will-be-clean the-seventh on-the-day clothes-of-you

תָּבֹאוּ אֶל־ הַמַּחֲנֶה׃ וַיֹּאמֶר יְהוָה אֶל־ מֹשֶׁה לֵּאמֹר׃
to-say Moses to Yahweh and-he-said (25) the-camp into you-may-come

שָׂא אֵת רֹאשׁ מַלְקוֹחַ הַשְּׁבִי בָּאָדָם וּבַבְּהֵמָה
and-of-the-animal of-the-people the-captive spoil-of amount-of *** count! (26)

אַתָּה וְאֶלְעָזָר הַכֹּהֵן וְרָאשֵׁי אֲבוֹת הָעֵדָה׃
the-community fathers-of and-heads-of the-priest and-Eleazar you

וְחָצִיתָ אֶת־ הַמַּלְקוֹחַ בֵּין תֹּפְשֵׂי הַמִּלְחָמָה
the-war ones-fighting-of between the-spoil *** and-you-divide (27)

הַיֹּצְאִים לַצָּבָא וּבֵין כָּל־ הָעֵדָה׃
the-community rest-of and-between in-the-battle the-ones-taking-part

וַהֲרֵמֹתָ מֶכֶס לַיהוָה מֵאֵת אַנְשֵׁי הַמִּלְחָמָה הַיֹּצְאִים
the-ones-going the-war men-of from to-Yahweh tribute and-you-set-apart (28)

לַצָּבָא אֶחָד נֶפֶשׁ מֵחֲמֵשׁ הַמֵּאוֹת מִן־ הָאָדָם
the-person whether the-hundreds from-five-of thing one into-the-battle

וּמִן־ הַבָּקָר וּמִן־ הַחֲמֹרִים וּמִן־ הַצֹּאן׃
the-flock or-whether the-donkeys or-whether the-cattle or-whether

מִמַּחֲצִיתָם תִּקָּחוּ וְנָתַתָּה לְאֶלְעָזָר הַכֹּהֵן תְּרוּמַת
part-of the-priest to-Eleazar and-you-give you-take from-half-of-them (29)

יְהוָה׃ וּמִמַּחֲצִת בְּנֵי־ יִשְׂרָאֵל תִּקַּח ׀ אֶחָד ׀ אָחֻז
being-taken one you-select Israel sons-of and-from-half-of (30) Yahweh

מִן־ הַחֲמִשִּׁים מִן־ הָאָדָם מִן־ הַבָּקָר מִן־ הַחֲמֹרִים
the-donkeys whether the-cattle whether the-person whether the-fifty from

וּמִן־ הַצֹּאן מִכָּל־ הַבְּהֵמָה וְנָתַתָּה אֹתָם לַלְוִיִּם
to-the-Levites them and-you-give the-animal from-every-of the-flock or-whether

שֹׁמְרֵי מִשְׁמֶרֶת מִשְׁכַּן יְהוָה׃ וַיַּעַשׂ מֹשֶׁה
Moses so-he-did (31) Yahweh tabernacle-of care-of ones-being-responsible-of

וְאֶלְעָזָר הַכֹּהֵן כַּאֲשֶׁר צִוָּה יְהוָה אֶת־ מֹשֶׁה׃ וַיְהִי
and-he-was (32) Moses *** Yahweh he-commanded just-as the-priest and-Eleazar

[23]and anything else that can
withstand fire must be put
through the fire, and then it
will be clean. But it must also
be purified with the water of
cleansing. And whatever cannot withstand fire must be put
through that water. [24]On the
seventh day wash your clothes
and you will be clean. Then
you may come into the camp."

Dividing the Spoils

[25]The LORD said to Moses,
[26]"You and Eleazar the priest
and the family heads of the
community are to count all the
people and animals that were
captured. [27]Divide the spoils
between the soldiers who took
part in the battle and the rest
of the community. [28]From the
soldiers who fought in the battle, set apart as tribute for the
LORD one out of every five
hundred, whether persons,
cattle, donkeys, sheep or goats.
[29]Take this tribute from their
half share and give it to Eleazar the priest as the LORD's
part. [30]From the Israelites'
half, select one out of every
fifty, whether persons, cattle,
donkeys, sheep, goats or other
animals. Give them to the Levites, who are responsible for
the care of the LORD's tabernacle." [31]So Moses and Eleazar
the priest did as the LORD commanded Moses.

הַמַּלְקוֹחַ יֶתֶר הַבָּז אֲשֶׁר בָּזְזוּ עַם הַצָּבָא צֹאן
sheep the-army people-of they-took that the-plunder remainder-of the-spoil

שֵׁשׁ־מֵאוֹת אֶלֶף וְשִׁבְעִים אֶלֶף וַחֲמֵשֶׁת אֲלָפִים׃ וּבָקָר
and-cattle (33) thousands and-five-of thousand and-seventy thousand hundreds six

שְׁנַיִם וְשִׁבְעִים אָלֶף׃ וַחֲמֹרִים אֶחָד וְשִׁשִּׁים אָלֶף׃
thousand and-sixty one and-donkeys (34) thousand and-seventy two

וְנֶפֶשׁ אָדָם מִן־הַנָּשִׁים אֲשֶׁר לֹא־יָדְעוּ מִשְׁכַּב זָכָר
man sleep-with they-knew not who the-women from human and-person (35)

כָּל־נֶפֶשׁ שְׁנַיִם וּשְׁלֹשִׁים אָלֶף׃ וַתְּהִי הַמֶּחֱצָה חֵלֶק
share the-half and-she-was (36) thousand and-thirty two person every-of

הַיֹּצְאִים בַּצָּבָא מִסְפַּר הַצֹּאן שְׁלֹשׁ־מֵאוֹת
hundreds three-of the-sheep number-of into-the-battle the-ones-going

אֶלֶף וּשְׁלֹשִׁים אֶלֶף וְשִׁבְעַת אֲלָפִים וַחֲמֵשׁ מֵאוֹת׃
hundreds and-five-of thousands and-seven-of thousand and-thirty thousand

וַיְהִי הַמֶּכֶס לַיהוָה מִן־הַצֹּאן שֵׁשׁ מֵאוֹת חָמֵשׁ
five hundreds six the-sheep from for-Yahweh the-tribute and-he-was (37)

וְשִׁבְעִים׃ וְהַבָּקָר שִׁשָּׁה וּשְׁלֹשִׁים אָלֶף וּמִכְסָם
and-tribute-of-them thousand and-thirty six and-the-cattle (38) and-seventy

לַיהוָה שְׁנַיִם וְשִׁבְעִים׃ וַחֲמֹרִים שְׁלֹשִׁים אֶלֶף וַחֲמֵשׁ
and-five-of thousand thirty and-donkeys (39) and-seventy two for-Yahweh

מֵאוֹת וּמִכְסָם לַיהוָה אֶחָד וְשִׁשִּׁים׃ וְנֶפֶשׁ אָדָם
human and-person (40) and-sixty one for-Yahweh and-tribute-of-them hundreds

שִׁשָּׁה עָשָׂר אָלֶף וּמִכְסָם לַיהוָה שְׁנַיִם וּשְׁלֹשִׁים נָפֶשׁ׃
person and-thirty two for-Yahweh and-tribute-of-them thousand ten six

וַיִּתֵּן מֹשֶׁה אֶת־מֶכֶס תְּרוּמַת יְהוָה לְאֶלְעָזָר הַכֹּהֵן
the-priest to-Eleazar Yahweh part-of tribute-of *** Moses and-he-gave (41)

כַּאֲשֶׁר צִוָּה יְהוָה אֶת־מֹשֶׁה׃ וּמִמַּחֲצִית בְּנֵי יִשְׂרָאֵל
Israel sons-of and-from-half-of (42) Moses *** Yahweh he-commanded just-as

אֲשֶׁר חָצָה מֹשֶׁה מִן־הָאֲנָשִׁים הַצֹּבְאִים׃ וַתְּהִי
and-she-was (43) the-ones-fighting the-men from Moses he-set-apart that

מֶחֱצַת הָעֵדָה מִן־הַצֹּאן שְׁלֹשׁ־מֵאוֹת אֶלֶף וּשְׁלֹשִׁים
and-thirty thousand hundreds three-of the-sheep from the-community half-of

אֶלֶף שִׁבְעַת אֲלָפִים וַחֲמֵשׁ מֵאוֹת׃ וּבָקָר שִׁשָּׁה
six and-cattle (44) hundreds and-five-of thousands seven-of thousand

וּשְׁלֹשִׁים אָלֶף׃ וַחֲמֹרִים שְׁלֹשִׁים אֶלֶף וַחֲמֵשׁ מֵאוֹת׃
hundreds and-five-of thousand thirty and-donkeys (45) thousand and-thirty

וְנֶפֶשׁ אָדָם שִׁשָּׁה עָשָׂר אָלֶף׃ וַיִּקַּח מֹשֶׁה מִמַּחֲצִת
from-half-of Moses and-he-selected (47) thousand ten six human and-person (46)

32 The plunder remaining
from the spoils that the soldiers took was 675,000 sheep,
33 72,000 cattle, 34 61,000 donkeys 35 and 32,000 women who
had never slept with a man.
36 The half share of those
who fought in the battle was:

337,500 sheep, 37 of which
the tribute for the
LORD was 675;
38 36,000 cattle, of which the
tribute for the LORD
was 72;
39 30,500 donkeys, of which
the tribute for the
LORD was 61;
40 16,000 people, of which
the tribute for the
LORD was 32.

41 Moses gave the tribute to
Eleazar the priest as the LORD's
part, as the LORD commanded
Moses.
42 The half belonging to the
Israelites, which Moses set
apart from that of the fighting
men— 43 the community's
half—was 337,500 sheep,
44 36,000 cattle, 45 30,500 donkeys 46 and 16,000 people.
47 From the Israelites' half,
Moses selected one out of

בְּנֵֽי־ יִשְׂרָאֵ֜ל אֶת־ הָֽאָחֻז֙ אֶחָ֣ד מִן־ הַחֲמִשִּׁ֔ים מִן־ הָאָדָ֖ם
the-person from the-fifty from one the-being-taken *** Israel sons-of

וּמִן־ הַבְּהֵמָ֑ה וַיִּתֵּ֨ן אֹתָ֜ם לַלְוִיִּ֗ם שֹֽׁמְרֵי֙
ones-being-responsible-of to-the-Levites them and-he-gave the-animal and-from

מִשְׁמֶ֙רֶת֙ מִשְׁכַּ֣ן יְהוָ֔ה כַּאֲשֶׁ֛ר צִוָּ֥ה יְהוָ֖ה אֶת־ מֹשֶֽׁה׃
Moses *** Yahweh he-commanded just-as Yahweh tabernacle-of care-of

וַֽיִּקְרְבוּ֙ אֶל־ מֹשֶׁ֔ה הַפְּקֻדִ֕ים אֲשֶׁ֖ר לְאַלְפֵ֣י
over-thousands-of that the-ones-being-officers Moses to then-they-went (48)

הַצָּבָ֑א שָׂרֵ֥י הָאֲלָפִ֖ים וְשָׂרֵ֥י הַמֵּאֽוֹת׃
the-hundreds and-commanders-of the-thousands commanders-of the-army

וַיֹּֽאמְרוּ֙ אֶל־ מֹשֶׁ֔ה עֲבָדֶ֣יךָ נָֽשְׂא֔וּ אֶת־ רֹ֛אשׁ אַנְשֵׁ֥י
men-of head-of *** they-counted servants-of-you Moses to and-they-said (49)

הַמִּלְחָמָ֖ה אֲשֶׁ֣ר בְּיָדֵ֑נוּ וְלֹֽא־ נִפְקַ֥ד מִמֶּ֖נּוּ אִֽישׁ׃
one from-him he-is-missing and-not under-command-of-us who the-war

וַנַּקְרֵ֞ב אֶת־ קָרְבַּ֣ן יְהוָ֗ה אִישׁ֩ אֲשֶׁ֨ר מָצָ֤א כְלִי־
article-of he-acquired that each Yahweh offering-of *** so-we-brought (50)

זָהָב֙ אֶצְעָדָ֣ה וְצָמִ֔יד טַבַּ֖עַת עָגִ֣יל וְכוּמָ֑ז לְכַפֵּ֥ר עַל־
for to-atone and-necklace earring signet-ring and-bracelet armlet gold

נַפְשֹׁתֵ֖ינוּ לִפְנֵ֥י יְהוָֽה׃ וַיִּקַּ֨ח מֹשֶׁ֜ה וְאֶלְעָזָ֧ר הַכֹּהֵ֛ן
the-priest and-Eleazar Moses so-he-accepted (51) Yahweh before selves-of-us

אֶת־ הַזָּהָ֖ב מֵאִתָּ֑ם כֹּ֖ל כְּלִ֥י מַעֲשֶֽׂה׃ וַיְהִ֣י ׀ כָּל־
all-of and-he-was (52) craft article-of every-of from-with-them the-gold ***

זְהַ֣ב הַתְּרוּמָ֗ה אֲשֶׁ֤ר הֵרִ֙ימוּ֙ לַֽיהוָ֔ה שִׁשָּׁ֨ה עָשָׂ֥ר אֶ֛לֶף שְׁבַע־
seven-of thousand ten six to-Yahweh they-presented that the-gift gold-of

מֵא֥וֹת וַחֲמִשִּׁ֖ים שָׁ֑קֶל מֵאֵת֙ שָׂרֵ֣י הָאֲלָפִ֔ים וּמֵאֵ֖ת
and-from the-thousands commanders-of from shekel and-fifty hundreds

שָׂרֵ֥י הַמֵּאֽוֹת׃ אַנְשֵׁי֙ הַצָּבָ֔א בָּזְז֖וּ אִ֥ישׁ לֽוֹ׃
for-him each they-plundered the-army men-of (53) the-hundreds commanders-of

וַיִּקַּ֨ח מֹשֶׁ֜ה וְאֶלְעָזָ֤ר הַכֹּהֵן֙ אֶת־ הַזָּהָ֔ב מֵאֵ֛ת
from the-gold *** the-priest and-Eleazar Moses and-he-accepted (54)

שָׂרֵ֥י הָאֲלָפִ֖ים וְהַמֵּא֑וֹת וַיָּבִ֤אוּ אֹתוֹ֙ אֶל־
into him and-they-brought and-the-hundreds the-thousands commanders-of

אֹ֣הֶל מוֹעֵ֔ד זִכָּר֥וֹן לִבְנֵֽי־ יִשְׂרָאֵ֖ל לִפְנֵ֥י יְהוָֽה׃ וּמִקְנֶ֣ה ׀
now-livestock (32:1) Yahweh before Israel for-sons-of memorial Meeting Tent-of

רַ֣ב הָיָ֞ה לִבְנֵ֧י רְאוּבֵ֛ן וְלִבְנֵי־ גָ֖ד עָצ֣וּם מְאֹ֑ד וַיִּרְא֞וּ
and-they-saw very large Gad and-to-sons-of Reuben to-sons-of he-was much

אֶת־ אֶ֤רֶץ יַעְזֵר֙ וְאֶת־ אֶ֣רֶץ גִּלְעָ֔ד וְהִנֵּ֥ה הַמָּק֖וֹם מְק֥וֹם מִקְנֶֽה׃
livestock place-of the-place and-see! Gilead land-of and Jazer land-of ***

every fifty persons and animals, as the LORD commanded him, and gave them to the Levites, who were responsible for the care of the LORD's tabernacle.
48Then the officers who were over the units of the army—the commanders of thousands and commanders of hundreds—went to Moses
49and said to him, "Your servants have counted the soldiers under our command, and not one is missing.
50So we have brought as an offering to the LORD the gold articles each of us acquired—armlets, bracelets, signet rings, earrings and necklaces—to make atonement for ourselves before the LORD."
51Moses and Eleazar the priest accepted from them the gold—all the crafted articles.
52All the gold from the commanders of thousands and commanders of hundreds that Moses and Eleazar presented as a gift to the LORD weighed 16,750 shekels.[z]
53Each soldier had taken plunder for himself.
54Moses and Eleazar the priest accepted the gold from the commanders of thousands and commanders of hundreds and brought it into the Tent of Meeting as a memorial for the Israelites before the LORD.

The Transjordan Tribes

32 The Reubenites and Gadites, who had very large herds and flocks, saw that the lands of Jazer and Gilead were suitable for livestock.

[z]52 That is, about 420 pounds (about 190 kilograms)

וַיָּבֹאוּ בְנֵי־ גָד וּבְנֵי רְאוּבֵן וַיֹּאמְרוּ אֶל־ מֹשֶׁה
(2) so-they-came sons-of Gad and-sons-of Reuben and-they-said to Moses

וְאֶל־ אֶלְעָזָר הַכֹּהֵן וְאֶל־ נְשִׂיאֵי הָעֵדָה לֵאמֹר׃ עֲטָרוֹת
and-to Eleazar the-priest and-to leaders-of the-community to-say (3) Ataroth

וְדִיבֹן וְיַעְזֵר וְנִמְרָה וְחֶשְׁבּוֹן וְאֶלְעָלֵה וּשְׂבָם וּנְבוֹ
and-Dibon and-Jazer and-Nimrah and-Heshbon and-Elealeh and-Sebam and-Nebo

וּבְעֹן׃ הָאָרֶץ אֲשֶׁר הִכָּה יְהוָה לִפְנֵי עֲדַת יִשְׂרָאֵל אֶרֶץ
and-Beon (4) the-land that he-subdued Yahweh before people-of Israel land-of

מִקְנֶה הִוא וְלַעֲבָדֶיךָ מִקְנֶה׃ וַיֹּאמְרוּ אִם־ מָצָאנוּ
livestock she and-to-servants-of-you livestock (5) and-they-said if we-found

חֵן בְּעֵינֶיךָ יֻתַּן אֶת־ הָאָרֶץ הַזֹּאת לַעֲבָדֶיךָ
favor in-eyes-of-you let-him-be-given *** the-land the-this to-servants-of-you

לַאֲחֻזָּה אַל־ תַּעֲבִרֵנוּ אֶת־ הַיַּרְדֵּן׃ וַיֹּאמֶר מֹשֶׁה
as-possession not you-make-cross-us *** the-Jordan (6) and-he-said Moses

לִבְנֵי־ גָד וְלִבְנֵי רְאוּבֵן הַאַחֵיכֶם יָבֹאוּ
to-sons-of Gad and-to-sons-of Reuben countrymen-of-you? shall-they-go

לַמִּלְחָמָה וְאַתֶּם תֵּשְׁבוּ פֹה׃ וְלָמָּה תְנוֹאוּן אֶת־ לֵב
to-the-war while-you you-sit here (7) and-why? do-you-discourage *** heart-of

בְּנֵי יִשְׂרָאֵל מֵעֲבֹר אֶל־ הָאָרֶץ אֲשֶׁר־ נָתַן לָהֶם יְהוָה׃
sons-of Israel from-to-go-over into the-land that he-gave to-them Yahweh

כֹּה עָשׂוּ אֲבֹתֵיכֶם בְּשָׁלְחִי אֹתָם מִקָּדֵשׁ בַּרְנֵעַ
(8) this they-did fathers-of-you when-to-send-me them from-Kadesh Barnea

לִרְאוֹת אֶת־ הָאָרֶץ׃ וַיַּעֲלוּ עַד־ נַחַל אֶשְׁכּוֹל
to-look-over *** the-land (9) and-they-went-up to Valley-of Eshcol

וַיִּרְאוּ אֶת־ הָאָרֶץ וַיָּנִיאוּ אֶת־ לֵב בְּנֵי יִשְׂרָאֵל
and-they-viewed *** the-land but-they-discouraged *** heart-of sons-of Israel

לְבִלְתִּי־בֹא אֶל־ הָאָרֶץ אֲשֶׁר־ נָתַן לָהֶם יְהוָה׃ וַיִּחַר־
not to-enter into the-land that he-gave to-them Yahweh (10) and-he-aroused

אַף יְהוָה בַּיּוֹם הַהוּא וַיִּשָּׁבַע לֵאמֹר׃ אִם־
anger-of Yahweh on-the-day the-that and-he-swore-oath to-say (11) not

יִרְאוּ הָאֲנָשִׁים הָעֹלִים מִמִּצְרַיִם מִבֶּן עֶשְׂרִים שָׁנָה
they-will-see the-men the-ones-coming from-Egypt from-son-of twenty year

וָמַעְלָה אֵת הָאֲדָמָה אֲשֶׁר נִשְׁבַּעְתִּי לְאַבְרָהָם לְיִצְחָק וּלְיַעֲקֹב כִּי
or-more *** the-land that I-promised to-Abraham to-Isaac and-to-Jacob for

לֹא־ מִלְאוּ אַחֲרָי׃ בִּלְתִּי כָּלֵב בֶּן־ יְפֻנֶּה
not they-were-wholehearted after-me (12) except Caleb son-of Jephunneh

הַקְּנִזִּי וִיהוֹשֻׁעַ בִּן־ נוּן כִּי מִלְאוּ אַחֲרֵי יְהוָה׃
the-Kenizzite and-Joshua son-of Nun for they-were-wholehearted after Yahweh

[2]So they came to Moses and
Eleazar the priest and to the
leaders of the community, and
said, [3]"Ataroth, Dibon, Jazer,
Nimrah, Heshbon, Elealeh,
Sebam, Nebo and Beon— [4]the
land the LORD subdued before
the people of Israel—are suitable for livestock, and your
servants have livestock. [5]If we
have found favor in your
eyes," they said, "let this land
be given to your servants as
our possession. Do not make
us cross the Jordan."
[6]Moses said to the Gadites
and Reubenites, "Shall your
countrymen go to war while
you sit here? [7]Why do you dis-
courage the Israelites from going over into the land the LORD
has given them? [8]This is what
your fathers did when I sent
them from Kadesh Barnea to
look over the land. [9]After they
went up to the Valley of Eshcol
and viewed the land, they discouraged the Israelites from
entering the land the LORD
had given them. [10]The LORD's
anger was aroused that day
and he swore this oath: [11]'Because they have not followed
me wholeheartedly, not one of
the men twenty years old or
more who came up out of
Egypt will see the land I promised on oath to Abraham,
Isaac and Jacob— [12]not one except Caleb son of Jephunneh
the Kenizzite and Joshua son
of Nun, for they followed the
LORD wholeheartedly.' [13]The

°7 ק תניאון

וַיִּחַר־ אַף יְהוָה בְּיִשְׂרָאֵל וַיְנִעֵם
and-he-made-wander-them against-Israel Yahweh anger-of and-he-burned (13)

בַּמִּדְבָּר אַרְבָּעִים שָׁנָה עַד־ תֹּם כָּל־ הַדּוֹר הָעֹשֶׂה
the-one-doing the-generation whole-of to-be-gone until year forty in-the-desert

הָרַע בְּעֵינֵי יְהוָה׃ וְהִנֵּה קַמְתֶּם תַּחַת אֲבֹתֵיכֶם
fathers-of-you in-place-of you-stand and-see! (14) Yahweh in-eyes-of the-evil

תַּרְבּוּת אֲנָשִׁים חַטָּאִים לִסְפּוֹת עוֹד עַל חֲרוֹן אַף־ יְהוָה אֶל־
against Yahweh anger-of wrath-of to more to-add sinners men brood-of

יִשְׂרָאֵל׃ כִּי תְשׁוּבֻן מֵאַחֲרָיו וְיָסַף עוֹד
again he-will-repeat from-after-him you-turn-away if (15) Israel

לְהַנִּיחוֹ בַּמִּדְבָּר וְשִׁחַתֶּם לְכָל־ הָעָם הַזֶּה׃
the-this the-people to-all-of and-you-will-destroy in-the-desert to-leave-him

וַיִּגְּשׁוּ אֵלָיו וַיֹּאמְרוּ גִּדְרֹת צֹאן נִבְנֶה
we-would-build flock pens-of and-they-said to-him then-they-came-up (16)

לְמִקְנֵנוּ פֹּה וְעָרִים לְטַפֵּנוּ׃ וַאֲנַחְנוּ נֵחָלֵץ
we-will-arm-selves but-we (17) for-child-of-us and-cities here for-stock-of-us

חֻשִׁים לִפְנֵי בְּנֵי יִשְׂרָאֵל עַד אֲשֶׁר אִם־ הֲבִיאֹנֻם
we-brought-them when that until Israel sons-of ahead-of ones-being-ready

אֶל־ מְקוֹמָם וְיָשַׁב טַפֵּנוּ בְּעָרֵי הַמִּבְצָר
the-fortification in-cities-of child-of-us but-he-will-live place-of-them to

מִפְּנֵי יֹשְׁבֵי הָאָרֶץ׃ לֹא נָשׁוּב אֶל־
to we-will-return not (18) the-land ones-inhabiting-of from-presence-of

בָּתֵּינוּ עַד הִתְנַחֵל בְּנֵי יִשְׂרָאֵל אִישׁ נַחֲלָתוֹ׃ כִּי
now (19) inheritance-of-him each Israel sons-of he-received until homes-of-us

לֹא נִנְחַל אִתָּם מֵעֵבֶר לַיַּרְדֵּן וָהָלְאָה כִּי בָאָה
she-came for and-beyond of-the-Jordan on-side with-them we-will-inherit not

נַחֲלָתֵנוּ אֵלֵינוּ מֵעֵבֶר הַיַּרְדֵּן מִזְרָחָה׃ וַיֹּאמֶר
then-he-said (20) on-east the-Jordan on-side-of to-us inheritance-of-us

אֲלֵיהֶם מֹשֶׁה אִם־ תַּעֲשׂוּן אֶת־ הַדָּבָר הַזֶּה אִם־ תֵּחָלְצוּ
you-will-arm-selves if the-this the-thing *** you-will-do if Moses to-them

לִפְנֵי יְהוָה לַמִּלְחָמָה׃ וְעָבַר לָכֶם כָּל־
every-of of-you and-he-will-go-over (21) for-the-battle Yahweh before

חָלוּץ אֶת־ הַיַּרְדֵּן לִפְנֵי יְהוָה עַד הוֹרִישׁוֹ אֶת־
*** to-drive-him until Yahweh before the-Jordan *** one-being-armed

אֹיְבָיו מִפָּנָיו׃ וְנִכְבְּשָׁה הָאָרֶץ לִפְנֵי
before the-land when-she-is-subdued (22) from-before-him being-enemies-of-him

יְהוָה וְאַחַר תָּשֻׁבוּ וִהְיִיתֶם נְקִיִּם מֵיְהוָה
from-Yahweh free-ones and-you-will-be you-may-return then-after Yahweh

LORD's anger burned against Israel and he made them wander in the desert forty years, until the whole generation of those who had done evil in his sight was gone.
14"And here you are, a brood of sinners, standing in the place of your fathers and making the LORD even more angry with Israel. 15If you turn away
from following him, he will again leave all this people in the desert, and you will be the cause of their destruction."
16Then they came up to him and said, "We would like to build pens here for our livestock and cities for our women and children. 17But we are
ready to arm ourselves and go ahead of the Israelites until we have brought them to their place. Meanwhile our women and children will live in fortified cities, for protection from the inhabitants of the land. 18We will not return to
our homes until every Israelite has received his inheritance.
19We will not receive any inheritance with them on the other side of the Jordan, because our inheritance has come to us on the east side of the Jordan."
20Then Moses said to them, "If you will do this—if you will arm yourselves before the LORD for battle, 21and if all of
you will go armed over the Jordan before the LORD until he has driven his enemies out before him— 22then when the
land is subdued before the LORD, you may return and be free from your obligation to

וּמִיִּשְׂרָאֵל וְהָיְתָה הָאָרֶץ הַזֹּאת לָכֶם לַאֲחֻזָּה
as-possession for-you the-this the-land and-she-will-be and-from-Israel

לִפְנֵי יְהוָה׃ וְאִם־ לֹא תַעֲשׂוּן כֵּן הִנֵּה חֲטָאתֶם לַיהוָה
against-Yahweh you-sin see! this you-do not but-if (23) Yahweh before

וּדְעוּ חַטַּאתְכֶם אֲשֶׁר תִּמְצָא אֶתְכֶם׃ בְּנוּ־ לָכֶם
for-you build! (24) you she-will-find-out that sin-of-you and-be-sure!

עָרִים לְטַפְּכֶם וּגְדֵרֹת לְצֹנַאֲכֶם וְהַיֹּצֵא
but-the-thing-coming for-flock-of-you and-pens for-child-of-you cities

מִפִּיכֶם תַּעֲשׂוּ׃ וַיֹּאמֶר בְּנֵי־ גָד וּבְנֵי רְאוּבֵן
Reuben and-sons-of Gad sons-of and-he-spoke (25) you-do from-mouth-of-you

אֶל־ מֹשֶׁה לֵאמֹר עֲבָדֶיךָ יַעֲשׂוּ כַּאֲשֶׁר אֲדֹנִי מְצַוֶּה׃
commanding lord-of-me just-as they-will-do servants-of-you to-say Moses to

טַפֵּנוּ נָשֵׁינוּ מִקְנֵנוּ וְכָל־ בְּהֶמְתֵּנוּ יִהְיוּ־
they-will-stay herd-of-us and-all-of flock-of-us wives-of-us child-of-us (26)

שָׁם בְּעָרֵי הַגִּלְעָד׃ וַעֲבָדֶיךָ יַעַבְרוּ
they-will-cross-over but-servants-of-you (27) the-Gilead in-cities-of here

כָּל־ חֲלוּץ צָבָא לִפְנֵי יְהוָה לַמִּלְחָמָה כַּאֲשֶׁר
just-as to-the-fight Yahweh before battle one-being-armed-of every-of

אֲדֹנִי דֹּבֵר׃ וַיְצַו לָהֶם מֹשֶׁה אֵת אֶלְעָזָר הַכֹּהֵן
the-priest Eleazar *** Moses about-them then-he-ordered (28) saying lord-of-me

וְאֵת יְהוֹשֻׁעַ בִּן־ נוּן וְאֶת־ רָאשֵׁי אֲבוֹת הַמַּטּוֹת לִבְנֵי יִשְׂרָאֵל׃
Israel of-sons-of the-tribes fathers-of heads-of and Nun son-of Joshua and

וַיֹּאמֶר מֹשֶׁה אֲלֵהֶם אִם־ יַעַבְרוּ בְנֵי־ גָד וּבְנֵי־
and-sons-of Gad sons-of they-cross-over if to-them Moses and-he-said (29)

רְאוּבֵן ׀ אִתְּכֶם אֶת־ הַיַּרְדֵּן כָּל־ חָלוּץ לַמִּלְחָמָה
for-the-battle one-being-armed every-of the-Jordan *** with-you Reuben

לִפְנֵי יְהוָה וְנִכְבְּשָׁה הָאָרֶץ לִפְנֵיכֶם וּנְתַתֶּם לָהֶם
to-them then-you-give before-you the-land when-she-is-subdued Yahweh before

אֶת־ אֶרֶץ הַגִּלְעָד לַאֲחֻזָּה׃ וְאִם־ לֹא יַעַבְרוּ
they-cross-over not but-if (30) as-possession the-Gilead land-of ***

חֲלוּצִים אִתְּכֶם וְנֹאחֲזוּ בְתֹכְכֶם בְּאֶרֶץ כְּנָעַן׃
Canaan in-land-of with-you then-they-must-possess with-you ones-being-armed

וַיַּעֲנוּ בְנֵי־ גָד וּבְנֵי רְאוּבֵן לֵאמֹר אֵת אֲשֶׁר
what *** to-say Reuben and-sons-of Gad sons-of and-they-answered (31)

דִּבֶּר יְהוָה אֶל־ עֲבָדֶיךָ כֵּן נַעֲשֶׂה׃ נַחְנוּ נַעֲבֹר
we-will-cross-over we (32) we-will-do so servants-of-you to Yahweh he-said

חֲלוּצִים לִפְנֵי יְהוָה אֶרֶץ כְּנָעַן וְאִתָּנוּ אֲחֻזַּת
property-of but-for-us Canaan land-of Yahweh before ones-being-armed

the LORD and to Israel. And
this land will be your possession before the LORD.
23"But if you fail to do this,
you will be sinning against
the LORD; and you may be sure
that your sin will find you out.
24Build cities for your women
and children, and pens for
your flocks, but do what you
have promised."
25The Gadites and Reuben-
ites said to Moses, "We your
servants will do as our lord
commands. 26Our children
and wives, our flocks and
herds will remain here in the
cities of Gilead. 27But your servants, every man armed for
battle, will cross over to fight
before the LORD, just as our
lord says."
28Then Moses gave orders
about them to Eleazar the
priest and Joshua son of Nun
and to the family heads of the
Israelite tribes. 29He said to
them, "If the Gadites and Reubenites, every man armed for
battle, cross over the Jordan
with you before the LORD,
then when the land is subdued before you, give them
the land of Gilead as their
possession. 30But if they do not
cross over with you armed,
they must accept their possession with you in Canaan."
31The Gadites and Reuben-
ites answered, "Your servants
will do what the LORD has
said. 32We will cross over before the LORD into Canaan

נַחֲלָתֵנוּ מֵעֵבֶר לַיַּרְדֵּן׃ וַיִּתֵּן לָהֶם ׀ מֹשֶׁה
Moses to-them then-he-gave (33) of-the-Jordan on-this-side inheritance-of-us

לִבְנֵי־ גָד וְלִבְנֵי רְאוּבֵן וְלַחֲצִי ׀ שֵׁבֶט ׀ מְנַשֶּׁה בֶן־
son-of Manasseh tribe-of and-to-half-of Reuben and-to-sons-of Gad to-sons-of

יוֹסֵף אֶת־ מַמְלֶכֶת סִיחֹן מֶלֶךְ הָאֱמֹרִי וְאֶת־ מַמְלֶכֶת עוֹג מֶלֶךְ
king-of Og kingdom-of and the-Amorite king-of Sihon kingdom-of *** Joseph

הַבָּשָׁן הָאָרֶץ לְעָרֶיהָ בִּגְבֻלֹת עָרֵי הָאָרֶץ
the-land cities-of in-territories with-cities-of-her the-land the-Bashan

סָבִיב׃ וַיִּבְנוּ בְנֵי־ גָד אֶת־ דִּיבֹן וְאֶת־עֲטָרֹת וְאֵת עֲרֹעֵר׃
Aroer and Ataroth and Dibon *** Gad sons-of so-they-built-up (34) around

וְאֶת־עַטְרֹת שׁוֹפָן וְאֶת־יַעְזֵר וְיָגְבְּהָה׃ וְאֶת־בֵּית נִמְרָה וְאֶת־
and Nimrah Beth and (36) and-Jogbehah Jazer and Shophan Atroth and (35)

בֵּית הָרָן עָרֵי מִבְצָר וְגִדְרֹת צֹאן׃ וּבְנֵי רְאוּבֵן
Reuben and-sons-of (37) flock and-pens-of fortified cities-of Haran Beth

בָּנוּ אֶת־ חֶשְׁבּוֹן וְאֶת־אֶלְעָלֵא וְאֵת קִרְיָתָיִם׃ וְאֶת־ נְבוֹ וְאֶת־
and Nebo and (38) Kiriathaim and Elealeh and Heshbon *** they-rebuilt

בַּעַל מְעוֹן מוּסַבֹּת שֵׁם וְאֶת־שִׂבְמָה וַיִּקְרְאוּ בְשֵׁמֹת אֶת־
*** by-names and-they-called Sibmah and name ones-being-changed-of Meon Baal

שְׁמוֹת הֶעָרִים אֲשֶׁר בָּנוּ׃ וַיֵּלְכוּ בְּנֵי מָכִיר
Makir sons-of and-they-went (39) they-rebuilt that the-cities names-of

בֶּן־ מְנַשֶּׁה גִּלְעָדָה וַיִּלְכְּדֻהָ וַיּוֹרֶשׁ אֶת־
*** and-he-drove-out and-they-captured-her to-Gilead Manasseh son-of

הָאֱמֹרִי אֲשֶׁר־ בָּהּ׃ וַיִּתֵּן מֹשֶׁה אֶת־ הַגִּלְעָד לְמָכִיר
to-Makir the-Gilead *** Moses so-he-gave (40) in-her that the-Amorite

בֶּן־ מְנַשֶּׁה וַיֵּשֶׁב בָּהּ׃ וְיָאִיר בֶּן־ מְנַשֶּׁה הָלַךְ
he-went Manasseh son-of and-Jair (41) in-her and-he-settled Manasseh son-of

וַיִּלְכֹּד אֶת־ חַוֹּתֵיהֶם וַיִּקְרָא אֶתְהֶן חַוֹּת יָאִיר׃
Jair Havvoth them and-he-called settlements-of-them *** and-he-captured

וְנֹבַח הָלַךְ וַיִּלְכֹּד אֶת־ קְנָת וְאֶת־ בְּנֹתֶיהָ
settlements-of-her and Kenath *** and-he-captured he-went and-Nobah (42)

וַיִּקְרָא לָהּ נֹבַח בִּשְׁמוֹ׃ אֵלֶּה מַסְעֵי
journeys-of these (33:1) after-name-of-him Nobah to-her and-he-called

בְנֵי־ יִשְׂרָאֵל אֲשֶׁר יָצְאוּ מֵאֶרֶץ מִצְרַיִם לְצִבְאֹתָם
by-divisions-of-them Egypt from-land-of they-came-out when Israel sons-of

בְּיַד־ מֹשֶׁה וְאַהֲרֹן׃ וַיִּכְתֹּב מֹשֶׁה אֶת־ מוֹצָאֵיהֶם
stages-of-them *** Moses and-he-recorded (2) and-Aaron Moses under-hand-of

לְמַסְעֵיהֶם עַל־ פִּי יְהוָה וְאֵלֶּה מַסְעֵיהֶם
journeys-of-them and-these Yahweh command-of at in-journeys-of-them

armed, but the property we inherit will be on this side of the
Jordan."
33Then Moses gave to the
Gadites, the Reubenites and
the half-tribe of Manasseh son
of Joseph the kingdom of Sihon king of the Amorites and
the kingdom of Og king of Bashan—the whole land with its
cities and the territory around
them.
34The Gadites built up Dibon, Ataroth, Aroer, 35Atroth
Shophan, Jazer, Jogbehah,
36Beth Nimrah and Beth Haran as fortified cities, and built
pens for their flocks. 37And the
Reubenites rebuilt Heshbon,
Elealeh and Kiriathaim, 38as
well as Nebo and Baal Meon
(these names were changed)
and Sibmah. They gave names
to the cities they rebuilt.
39The descendants of Makir
son of Manasseh went to Gilead, captured it and drove out
the Amorites who were there.
40So Moses gave Gilead to the
Makirites, the descendants of
Manasseh, and they settled
there. 41Jair, a descendant of
Manasseh, captured their settlements and called them Havvoth Jair.[a] 42And Nobah captured Kenath and its sur-
rounding settlements and
called it Nobah after himself.

Stages in Israel's Journey

33 Here are the stages in
the journey of the Isra-
elites when they came out of
Egypt by divisions under the
leadership of Moses and
Aaron. 2At the LORD's command Moses recorded the
stages in their journey. This is

[a]41 *Or them the settlements of Jair*

לְמוֹצָאֵיהֶם׃ (3) וַיִּסְעוּ מֵרַעְמְסֵס בַּחֹדֶשׁ הָרִאשׁוֹן
the-first in-the-month from-Rameses now-they-set-out (3) by-stages-of-them

בַּחֲמִשָּׁה עָשָׂר יוֹם לַחֹדֶשׁ הָרִאשׁוֹן מִמָּחֳרַת הַפֶּסַח
the-Passover on-day-after-of the-first of-the-month day ten on-five

יָצְאוּ בְנֵי־ יִשְׂרָאֵל בְּיָד רָמָה לְעֵינֵי כָּל־
all-of before-eyes-of being-lifted with-hand Israel sons-of they-marched-out

מִצְרָיִם׃ (4) וּמִצְרַיִם מְקַבְּרִים אֵת אֲשֶׁר הִכָּה יְהוָה
Yahweh he-struck-down whom *** ones-burying now-Egyptians (4) Egyptians

בָּהֶם כָּל־ בְּכוֹר וּבֵאלֹהֵיהֶם עָשָׂה יְהוָה
Yahweh he-brought and-on-gods-of-them firstborn every-of among-them

שְׁפָטִים׃ (5) וַיִּסְעוּ בְנֵי־ יִשְׂרָאֵל מֵרַעְמְסֵס וַיַּחֲנוּ
and-they-camped from-Rameses Israel sons-of and-they-left (5) judgments

בְּסֻכֹּת׃ (6) וַיִּסְעוּ מִסֻּכֹּת וַיַּחֲנוּ בְאֵתָם אֲשֶׁר
that at-Etham and-they-camped from-Succoth and-they-left (6) at-Succoth

בִּקְצֵה הַמִּדְבָּר׃ (7) וַיִּסְעוּ מֵאֵתָם וַיָּשָׁב עַל־
to and-they-turned-back from-Etham and-they-left (7) the-desert on-edge-of

פִּי הַחִירֹת אֲשֶׁר עַל־ פְּנֵי בַּעַל צְפוֹן וַיַּחֲנוּ לִפְנֵי מִגְדֹּל׃
Midgol near and-they-camped Zephon Baal east-of to that Hahiroth Pi

(8) וַיִּסְעוּ מִפְּנֵי הַחִירֹת וַיַּעַבְרוּ בְתוֹךְ־ הַיָּם
the-sea through and-they-passed Hahiroth from-before and-they-left (8)

הַמִּדְבָּרָה וַיֵּלְכוּ דֶּרֶךְ שְׁלֹשֶׁת יָמִים בְּמִדְבַּר
in-Desert-of days three-of journey-of and-they-traveled into-the-desert

אֵתָם וַיַּחֲנוּ בְּמָרָה׃ (9) וַיִּסְעוּ מִמָּרָה וַיָּבֹאוּ
and-they-went from-Marah and-they-left (9) at-Marah and-they-camped Etham

אֵילִמָה וּבְאֵילִם שְׁתֵּים עֶשְׂרֵה עֵינֹת מַיִם וְשִׁבְעִים תְּמָרִים
palm-trees and-seventy waters springs-of ten two now-in-Elim to-Elim

וַיַּחֲנוּ־ שָׁם׃ (10) וַיִּסְעוּ מֵאֵילִם וַיַּחֲנוּ עַל־ יַם־
Sea-of by and-they-camped from-Elim and-they-left (10) there and-they-camped

סוּף׃ (11) וַיִּסְעוּ מִיַּם־ סוּף וַיַּחֲנוּ בְּמִדְבַּר־
in-Desert-of and-they-camped Reed from-Sea-of and-they-left (11) Reed

סִין׃ (12) וַיִּסְעוּ מִמִּדְבַּר־ סִין וַיַּחֲנוּ בְּדָפְקָה׃
at-Dophkah and-they-camped Sin from-Desert-of and-they-left (12) Sin

(13) וַיִּסְעוּ מִדָּפְקָה וַיַּחֲנוּ בְּאָלוּשׁ׃ (14) וַיִּסְעוּ
and-they-left (14) at-Alush and-they-camped from-Dophkah and-they-left (13)

מֵאָלוּשׁ וַיַּחֲנוּ בִּרְפִידִם וְלֹא־ הָיָה שָׁם מַיִם
waters there he-was and-not at-Rephidim and-they-camped from-Alush

לָעָם לִשְׁתּוֹת׃ (15) וַיִּסְעוּ מֵרְפִידִם וַיַּחֲנוּ
and-they-camped from-Rephidim and-they-left (15) to-drink for-the-people

their journey by stages:
3 The Israelites set out
from Rameses on the
fifteenth day of the first
month, the day after the
Passover. They marched
out boldly in full view of all
the Egyptians, 4 who were
burying all their firstborn,
whom the LORD had struck
down among them; for the
LORD had brought judg-
ment on their gods.
5 The Israelites left
Rameses and camped at
Succoth.
6 They left Succoth and
camped at Etham, on the
edge of the desert.
7 They left Etham, turned
back to Pi Hahiroth, to the
east of Baal Zephon, and
camped near Migdol.
8 They left Pi Hahiroth[b]
and passed through the sea
into the desert, and when
they had traveled for three
days in the Desert of
Etham, they camped at
Marah.
9 They left Marah and
went to Elim, where there
were twelve springs and
seventy palm trees, and
they camped there.
10 They left Elim and
camped by the Red Sea.[c]
11 They left the Red Sea
and camped in the Desert
of Sin.
12 They left the Desert of
Sin and camped at Doph-
kah.
13 They left Dophkah and
camped at Alush.
14 They left Alush and
camped at Rephidim,
where there was no water
for the people to drink.
15 They left Rephidim and

[b]8 Many manuscripts of the Masoretic Text, Samaritan Pentateuch and Vulgate; most manuscripts of the Masoretic Text *left from before Hahiroth*

[c]10 Hebrew *Yam Suph*; that is, Sea of Reeds; also in verse 11

בְּמִדְבַּר סִינָי׃ (16) וַיִּסְעוּ מִמִּדְבַּר סִינַי וַיַּחֲנוּ
and-they-camped Sinai from-Desert-of and-they-left (16) Sinai in-Desert-of

בְּקִבְרֹת הַתַּאֲוָה׃ (17) וַיִּסְעוּ מִקִּבְרֹת הַתַּאֲוָה וַיַּחֲנוּ
and-they-camped Hattaavah from-Kibroth and-they-left (17) Hattaavah at-Kibroth

בַּחֲצֵרֹת׃ (18) וַיִּסְעוּ מֵחֲצֵרֹת וַיַּחֲנוּ בְּרִתְמָה׃
at-Rithmah and-they-camped from-Hazeroth and-they-left (18) at-Hazeroth

(19) וַיִּסְעוּ מֵרִתְמָה וַיַּחֲנוּ בְּרִמֹּן פָּרֶץ׃
Perez at-Rimmon and-they-camped from-Rithmah and-they-left (19)

(20) וַיִּסְעוּ מֵרִמֹּן פָּרֶץ וַיַּחֲנוּ בְּלִבְנָה׃
at-Libnah and-they-camped Perez from-Rimmon and-they-left (20)

(21) וַיִּסְעוּ מִלִּבְנָה וַיַּחֲנוּ בְּרִסָּה׃ (22) וַיִּסְעוּ
and-they-left (22) at-Rissah and-they-camped from-Libnah and-they-left (21)

מֵרִסָּה וַיַּחֲנוּ בִּקְהֵלָתָה׃ (23) וַיִּסְעוּ מִקְּהֵלָתָה
from-Kehelathah and-they-left (23) at-Kehelathah and-they-camped from-Rissah

וַיַּחֲנוּ בְּהַר־ שָׁפֶר׃ (24) וַיִּסְעוּ מֵהַר־ שָׁפֶר
Shepher from-Mount-of and-they-left (24) Shepher at-Mount-of and-they-camped

וַיַּחֲנוּ בַּחֲרָדָה׃ (25) וַיִּסְעוּ מֵחֲרָדָה וַיַּחֲנוּ
and-they-camped from-Haradah and-they-left (25) at-Haradah and-they-camped

בְּמַקְהֵלֹת׃ (26) וַיִּסְעוּ מִמַּקְהֵלֹת וַיַּחֲנוּ בְּתָחַת׃
at-Tahath and-they-camped from-Makheloth and-they-left (26) at-Makheloth

(27) וַיִּסְעוּ מִתָּחַת וַיַּחֲנוּ בְּתָרַח׃ (28) וַיִּסְעוּ
and-they-left (28) at-Terah and-they-camped from-Tahath and-they-left (27)

מִתָּרַח וַיַּחֲנוּ בְּמִתְקָה׃ (29) וַיִּסְעוּ מִמִּתְקָה
from-Mithcah and-they-left (29) at-Mithcah and-they-camped from-Terah

וַיַּחֲנוּ בְּחַשְׁמֹנָה׃ (30) וַיִּסְעוּ מֵחַשְׁמֹנָה וַיַּחֲנוּ
and-they-camped from-Hashmonah and-they-left (30) at-Hashmonah and-they-camped

בְּמֹסֵרוֹת׃ (31) וַיִּסְעוּ מִמֹּסֵרוֹת וַיַּחֲנוּ בִּבְנֵי יַעֲקָן׃
Jaakan at-Bene and-they-camped from-Moseroth and-they-left (31) at-Moseroth

(32) וַיִּסְעוּ מִבְּנֵי יַעֲקָן וַיַּחֲנוּ בְּחֹר הַגִּדְגָּד׃
Haggidgad and-Hor and-they-camped Jaakan from-Bene and-they-left (32)

(33) וַיִּסְעוּ מֵחֹר הַגִּדְגָּד וַיַּחֲנוּ בְּיָטְבָתָה׃
at-Jotbathah and-they-camped Haggidgad from-Hor and-they-left (33)

(34) וַיִּסְעוּ מִיָּטְבָתָה וַיַּחֲנוּ בְּעַבְרֹנָה׃ (35) וַיִּסְעוּ
and-they-left (35) at-Abronah and-they-camped from-Jotbathah and-they-left (34)

מֵעַבְרֹנָה וַיַּחֲנוּ בְּעֶצְיֹן גָּבֶר׃ (36) וַיִּסְעוּ מֵעֶצְיֹן
from-Ezion and-they-left (36) Geber at-Ezion and-they-camped from-Abronah

גֶּבֶר וַיַּחֲנוּ בְמִדְבַּר־ צִן הִוא קָדֵשׁ׃ (37) וַיִּסְעוּ
and-they-left (37) Kadesh that Zin in-Desert-of and-they-camped Geber

camped in the Desert of Sinai.
16 They left the Desert of Sinai and camped at Kibroth Hattaavah.
17 They left Kibroth Hattaavah and camped at Hazeroth.
18 They left Hazeroth and camped at Rithmah.
19 They left Rithmah and camped at Rimmon Perez.
20 They left Rimmon Perez and camped at Libnah.
21 They left Libnah and camped at Rissah.
22 They left Rissah and camped at Kehelathah.
23 They left Kehelathah and camped at Mount Shepher.
24 They left Mount Shepher and camped at Haradah.
25 They left Haradah and camped at Makheloth.
26 They left Makheloth and camped at Tahath.
27 They left Tahath and camped at Terah.
28 They left Terah and camped at Mithcah.
29 They left Mithcah and camped at Hashmonah.
30 They left Hashmonah and camped at Moseroth.
31 They left Moseroth and camped at Bene Jaakan.
32 They left Bene Jaakan and camped at Hor Haggidgad.
33 They left Hor Haggidgad and camped at Jotbathah.
34 They left Jotbathah and camped at Abronah.
35 They left Abronah and camped at Ezion Geber.
36 They left Ezion Geber and camped at Kadesh, in the Desert of Zin.
37 They left Kadesh and

מִקָּדֵשׁ וַיַּחֲנוּ בְּהֹר הָהָר בִּקְצֵה אֶרֶץ אֱדוֹם׃
Edom land-of on-border-of the-Mount at-Hor and-they-camped from-Kadesh

(38) וַיַּעַל אַהֲרֹן הַכֹּהֵן אֶל־הֹר הָהָר עַל־פִּי יְהוָה
Yahweh command-of at the-Mount Hor on the-priest Aaron and-he-went-up (38)

וַיָּמָת שָׁם בִּשְׁנַת הָאַרְבָּעִים לְצֵאת בְּנֵי־יִשְׂרָאֵל מֵאֶרֶץ
from-land-of Israel sons-of to-come the-fortieth in-year-of there and-he-died

מִצְרַיִם בַּחֹדֶשׁ הַחֲמִישִׁי בְּאֶחָד לַחֹדֶשׁ׃ (39) וְאַהֲרֹן בֶּן־
son-of now-Aaron (39) of-the-month on-first the-fifth in-the-month Egypt

שָׁלֹשׁ וְעֶשְׂרִים וּמְאַת שָׁנָה בְּמֹתוֹ בְּהֹר הָהָר׃
the-Mount on-Hor when-to-die-him year and-hundred-of and-twenty three

(40) וַיִּשְׁמַע הַכְּנַעֲנִי מֶלֶךְ עֲרָד וְהוּא־יֹשֵׁב בַּנֶּגֶב
in-the-Negev living now-he Arad king-of the-Canaanite and-he-heard (40)

בְּאֶרֶץ כְּנָעַן בְּבֹא בְּנֵי יִשְׂרָאֵל׃ (41) וַיִּסְעוּ מֵהֹר
from-Hor and-they-left (41) Israel sons-of that-to-come Canaan in-land-of

הָהָר וַיַּחֲנוּ בְּצַלְמֹנָה׃ (42) וַיִּסְעוּ מִצַּלְמֹנָה
from-Zalmonah and-they-left (42) at-Zalmonah and-they-camped the-Mount

וַיַּחֲנוּ בְּפוּנֹן׃ (43) וַיִּסְעוּ מִפּוּנֹן וַיַּחֲנוּ
and-they-camped from-Punon and-they-left (43) at-Punon and-they-camped

בְּאֹבֹת׃ (44) וַיִּסְעוּ מֵאֹבֹת וַיַּחֲנוּ בְּעִיֵּי הָעֲבָרִים
the-Abarim at-Iye and-they-camped from-Oboth and-they-left (44) at-Oboth

בִּגְבוּל מוֹאָב׃ (45) וַיִּסְעוּ מֵעִיִּים וַיַּחֲנוּ בְּדִיבֹן גָּד׃
Gad at-Dibon and-they-camped from-Iyim and-they-left (45) Moab on-border-of

(46) וַיִּסְעוּ מִדִּיבֹן גָּד וַיַּחֲנוּ בְּעַלְמֹן דִּבְלָתָיְמָה׃
at-Diblathaim at-Almon and-they-camped Gad from-Dibon and-they-left (46)

(47) וַיִּסְעוּ מֵעַלְמֹן דִּבְלָתָיְמָה וַיַּחֲנוּ בְּהָרֵי
in-mountains-of and-they-camped at-Diblathaim from-Almon and-they-left (47)

הָעֲבָרִים לִפְנֵי נְבוֹ׃ (48) וַיִּסְעוּ מֵהָרֵי הָעֲבָרִים
the-Abarim from-mountains-of and-they-left (48) Nebo near the-Abarim

וַיַּחֲנוּ בְּעַרְבֹת מוֹאָב עַל יַרְדֵּן יְרֵחוֹ׃ (49) וַיַּחֲנוּ
and-they-camped (49) Jericho Jordan-of by Moab on-plains-of and-they-camped

עַל־הַיַּרְדֵּן מִבֵּית הַיְשִׁמֹת עַד אָבֵל הַשִּׁטִּים בְּעַרְבֹת
in-plains-of the-Shittim Abel to the-Jeshimoth from-Beth the-Jordan along

מוֹאָב׃ (50) וַיְדַבֵּר יְהוָה אֶל־מֹשֶׁה בְּעַרְבֹת מוֹאָב עַל־יַרְדֵּן
Jordan-of by Moab on-plains-of Moses to Yahweh and-he-spoke (50) Moab

יְרֵחוֹ לֵאמֹר׃ (51) דַּבֵּר אֶל־בְּנֵי יִשְׂרָאֵל וְאָמַרְתָּ אֲלֵהֶם כִּי אַתֶּם
you when to-them and-you-say Israel sons-of to speak! (51) to-say Jericho

עֹבְרִים אֶת־הַיַּרְדֵּן אֶל־אֶרֶץ כְּנָעַן׃ (52) וְהוֹרַשְׁתֶּם אֶת־
*** then-you-drive-out (52) Canaan land-of into the-Jordan *** ones-crossing

camped at Mount Hor, on
the border of Edom. 38At the
LORD's command Aaron the
priest went up Mount Hor,
where he died on the first
day of the fifth month of
the fortieth year after the
Israelites came out of
Egypt. 39Aaron was a hun-
dred and twenty-three
years old when he died on
Mount Hor.
40The Canaanite king of
Arad, who lived in the
Negev of Canaan, heard
that the Israelites were
coming.
41They left Mount Hor
and camped at Zalmonah.
42They left Zalmonah and
camped at Punon.
43They left Punon and
camped at Oboth.
44They left Oboth and
camped at Iye Abarim, on
the border of Moab.
45They left Iyim[d] and
camped at Dibon Gad.
46They left Dibon Gad
and camped at Almon Di-
blathaim.
47They left Almon Dibla-
thaim and camped in the
mountains of Abarim, near
Nebo.
48They left the mountains
of Abarim and camped on
the plains of Moab by the
Jordan across from Jericho.[e]
49There on the plains of
Moab they camped along
the Jordan from Beth Je-
shimoth to Abel Shittim.

50On the plains of Moab by
the Jordan across from Jericho
the LORD said to Moses,
51"Speak to the Israelites and
say to them: 'When you cross
the Jordan into Canaan,
52drive out all the inhabitants

[d]45 That is, Iye Abarim
[e]48 Hebrew *Jordan of Jericho*; possibly an ancient name for the Jordan River; also in verse 50

כָּל־ יֹשְׁבֵי הָאָרֶץ מִפְּנֵיכֶם וְאִבַּדְתֶּם אֵת כָּל־
all-of *** and-you-destroy from-before-you the-land ones-inhabiting-of all-of

מַשְׂכִּיֹּתָם וְאֵת כָּל־ צַלְמֵי מַסֵּכֹתָם תְּאַבֵּדוּ וְאֵת
and you-destroy cast-ones-of-them idols-of all-of and carved-images-of-them

כָּל־ בָּמוֹתָם תַּשְׁמִידוּ׃ וְהוֹרַשְׁתֶּם אֶת־ הָאָרֶץ
the-land *** and-you-possess (53) you-demolish high-places-of-them all-of

וִישַׁבְתֶּם־ בָּהּ כִּי לָכֶם נָתַתִּי אֶת־ הָאָרֶץ לָרֶשֶׁת אֹתָהּ׃
her to-possess the-land *** I-gave to-you for in-her and-you-settle

וְהִתְנַחַלְתֶּם אֶת־ הָאָרֶץ בְּגוֹרָל לְמִשְׁפְּחֹתֵיכֶם לָרַב
to-the-large by-clans-of-you by-lot the-land *** and-you-distribute (54)

תַּרְבּוּ אֶת־ נַחֲלָתוֹ וְלַמְעַט תַּמְעִיט אֶת־
*** you-make-small and-to-the-small inheritance-of-him *** you-make-large

נַחֲלָתוֹ אֶל אֲשֶׁר־ יֵצֵא לוֹ שָׁמָּה הַגּוֹרָל לוֹ יִהְיֶה
he-will-be to-him the-lot at-there to-him he-falls whom to inheritance-of-him

לְמַטּוֹת אֲבֹתֵיכֶם תִּתְנֶחָלוּ׃ וְאִם־ לֹא תוֹרִישׁוּ אֶת־
*** you-drive-out not but-if (55) you-distribute fathers-of-you by-tribes-of

יֹשְׁבֵי הָאָרֶץ מִפְּנֵיכֶם וְהָיָה אֲשֶׁר תּוֹתִירוּ
you-let-remain whom then-he-will-be from-before-you the-land ones-inhabiting-of

מֵהֶם לְשִׂכִּים בְּעֵינֵיכֶם וְלִצְנִינִם בְּצִדֵּיכֶם
in-sides-of-you and-as-thorns in-eyes-of-you as-barbs from-them

וְצָרְרוּ אֶתְכֶם עַל־ הָאָרֶץ אֲשֶׁר אַתֶּם יֹשְׁבִים בָּהּ׃
in-her ones-living you where the-land in you and-they-will-trouble

וְהָיָה כַּאֲשֶׁר דִּמִּיתִי לַעֲשׂוֹת לָהֶם אֶעֱשֶׂה לָכֶם׃
to-you I-will-do to-them to-do I-plan just-as then-he-will-be (56)

וַיְדַבֵּר יְהוָה אֶל־ מֹשֶׁה לֵּאמֹר׃ צַו אֶת־ בְּנֵי יִשְׂרָאֵל
Israel sons-of *** command! (2) to-say Moses to Yahweh and-he-spoke (34:1)

וְאָמַרְתָּ אֲלֵהֶם כִּי־ אַתֶּם בָּאִים אֶל־ הָאָרֶץ כְּנָעַן זֹאת הָאָרֶץ
the-land this Canaan the-land into ones-entering you when to-them and-you-say

אֲשֶׁר תִּפֹּל לָכֶם בְּנַחֲלָה אֶרֶץ כְּנַעַן לִגְבֻלֹתֶיהָ׃
by-boundaries-of-her Canaan land-of as-inheritance to-you she-will-fall that

וְהָיָה לָכֶם פְאַת־ נֶגֶב מִמִּדְבַּר־ צִן עַל־ יְדֵי
borders-of along Zin from-Desert-of south side-of to-you and-he-will-be (3)

אֱדוֹם וְהָיָה לָכֶם גְּבוּל נֶגֶב מִקְצֵה יָם־ הַמֶּלַח קֵדְמָה׃
on-east the-Salt Sea-of end-of south border-of to-you and-he-will-be Edom

וְנָסַב לָכֶם הַגְּבוּל מִנֶּגֶב לְמַעֲלֵה עַקְרַבִּים
Scorpions of-Pass-of on-south the-border to-you and-he-will-cross (4)

וְעָבַר צִנָה וְהָיָה תּוֹצְאֹתָיו מִנֶּגֶב לְקָדֵשׁ
of-Kadesh on-south ends-of-him and-they-will-go to-Zin and-he-will-continue

4[a] ק והיו

of the land before you. Destroy
all their carved images and
their cast idols, and demolish
all their high places. 53Take
possession of the land and settle in it, for I have given you
the land to possess. 54Distrib-
ute the land by lot, according
to your clans. To a larger group
give a larger inheritance, and
to a smaller group a smaller
one. Whatever falls to them by
lot will be theirs. Distribute it
according to your ancestral
tribes.

55" 'But if you do not drive
out the inhabitants of the
land, those you allow to remain will become barbs in
your eyes and thorns in your
sides. They will give you trouble in the land where you will
live. 56And then I will do to
you what I plan to do to
them.' "

Boundaries of Canaan

34 The LORD said to
Moses, 2"Command
the Israelites and say to them:
'When you enter Canaan, the
land that will be allotted to
you as an inheritance will
have these boundaries:

3" 'Your southern side will
include some of the Desert of
Zin along the border of Edom.
On the east, your southern
boundary will start from the
end of the Salt Sea,[f] 4cross
south of Scorpion[g] Pass, continue on to Zin and go south of

f3 That is, the Dead Sea; also in verse 12
g4 Hebrew *Akrabbim*

בַּרְנֵעַ וְיָצָא חֲצַר־אַדָּר וְעָבַר עַצְמֹנָה׃ וְנָסַב
and-he-will-turn (5) to-Azmon and-he-will-go Addar Hazar then-he-will-go Barnea

הַגְּבוּל מֵעַצְמוֹן נַחְלָה מִצְרָיִם וְהָיוּ תוֹצְאֹתָיו
ends-of-him and-they-will-be Egypt to-Wadi-of from-Azmon the-border

הַיָּמָּה׃ וּגְבוּל יָם וְהָיָה לָכֶם הַיָּם הַגָּדוֹל
the-Great the-Sea to-you now-he-will-be west and-boundary-of (6) at-the-Sea

וּגְבוּל זֶה־יִהְיֶה לָכֶם גְּבוּל יָם׃ וְזֶה־יִהְיֶה
he-will-be and-this (7) west boundary-of to-you he-will-be this and-coast

לָכֶם גְּבוּל צָפוֹן מִן־הַיָּם הַגָּדֹל תְּתָאוּ לָכֶם הֹר
Hor for-you you-run-line the-Great the-Sea from north boundary-of to-you

הָהָר׃ מֵהֹר הָהָר תְּתָאוּ לְבֹא חֲמָת וְהָיוּ
then-they-will-go Hamath Lebo you-run-line the-Mount from-Hor (8) the-Mount

תּוֹצְאֹת הַגְּבֻל צְדָדָה׃ וְיָצָא הַגְּבֻל זִפְרֹנָה
to-Ziphron the-border and-he-will-continue (9) to-Zedad the-boundary ends-of

וְהָיוּ תוֹצְאֹתָיו חֲצַר עֵינָן זֶה־יִהְיֶה לָכֶם גְּבוּל
boundary-of to-you he-will-be this Enan Hazar ends-of-him and-they-will-go

צָפוֹן׃ וְהִתְאַוִּיתֶם לָכֶם לִגְבוּל קֵדְמָה מֵחֲצַר עֵינָן
Enan from-Hazar on-east for-boundary for-you and-you-run-line (10) north

שְׁפָמָה׃ וְיָרַד הַגְּבֻל מִשְּׁפָם הָרִבְלָה
the-Riblah from-Shepham the-boundary and-he-will-go-down (11) to-Shepham

מִקֶּדֶם לָעָיִן וְיָרַד הַגְּבוּל וּמָחָה עַל־
along and-he-will-go the-boundary and-he-will-continue of-the-Ain on-east

כֶּתֶף יָם־כִּנֶּרֶת קֵדְמָה׃ וְיָרַד הַגְּבוּל
the-boundary then-he-will-go-down (12) on-east Kinnereth Sea-of slope-of

הַיַּרְדֵּנָה וְהָיוּ תוֹצְאֹתָיו יָם הַמֶּלַח זֹאת תִּהְיֶה
she-will-be this the-Salt Sea-of ends-of-him and-he-will-be along-the-Jordan

לָכֶם הָאָרֶץ לִגְבֻלֹתֶיהָ סָבִיב׃ וַיְצַו מֹשֶׁה
Moses and-he-commanded (13) around with-boundaries-of-her the-land to-you

אֶת־בְּנֵי יִשְׂרָאֵל לֵאמֹר זֹאת הָאָרֶץ אֲשֶׁר תִּתְנַחֲלוּ אֹתָהּ בְּגוֹרָל
by-lot her you-must-assign that the-land this to-say Israel sons-of ***

אֲשֶׁר צִוָּה יְהוָה לָתֵת לְתִשְׁעַת הַמַּטּוֹת וַחֲצִי הַמַּטֶּה׃
the-tribe and-half-of the-tribes to-nine-of to-give Yahweh he-ordered that

כִּי לָקְחוּ מַטֵּה בְנֵי הָרֻאוּבֵנִי לְבֵית
by-house-of the-Reubenite sons-of tribe-of they-received for (14)

אֲבֹתָם וּמַטֵּה בְנֵי־הַגָּדִי לְבֵית אֲבֹתָם
fathers-of-them by-house-of the-Gadite sons-of and-tribe-of fathers-of-them

וַחֲצִי מַטֵּה מְנַשֶּׁה לָקְחוּ נַחֲלָתָם׃ שְׁנֵי
two-of (15) inheritance-of-them they-received Manasseh tribe-of and-half-of

Kadesh Barnea. Then it will go
to Hazar Addar and over to
Azmon, [5]where it will turn,
join the Wadi of Egypt and
end at the Sea.[h]
[6]" 'Your western boundary
will be the coast of the Great
Sea. This will be your boundary on the west.
[7]" 'For your northern
boundary, run a line from the
Great Sea to Mount Hor [8]and
from Mount Hor to Lebo[i]
Hamath. Then the boundary
will go to Zedad, [9]continue to
Ziphron and end at Hazar
Enan. This will be your
boundary on the north.
[10]" 'For your eastern boundary, run a line from Hazar
Enan to Shepham. [11]The
boundary will go down from
Shepham to Riblah on the east
side of Ain and continue
along the slopes east of the Sea
of Kinnereth.[j] [12]Then the
boundary will go down along
the Jordan and end at the Salt
Sea.
" 'This will be your land,
with its boundaries on every
side.' "
[13]Moses commanded the Israelites: "Assign this land by
lot as an inheritance. The LORD
has ordered that it be given to
the nine and a half tribes, [14]be-
cause the families of the tribe
of Reuben, the tribe of Gad
and the half-tribe of Manasseh have received their inheritance. [15]These two and a half

[h]5 That is, the Mediterranean; also in verses 6 and 7
[i]8 Or *to the entrance to*
[j]11 That is, Galilee

הַמַּטּוֹת וַחֲצִי הַמַּטֶּה לָקְחוּ נַחֲלָתָם מֵעֵבֶר
on-side inheritance-of-them they-received the-tribe and-half-of the-tribes

לְיַרְדֵּן יְרֵחוֹ קֵדְמָה מִזְרָחָה׃ וַיְדַבֵּר יְהוָה אֶל־
to Yahweh and-he-spoke (16) toward-sunrise on-east Jericho of-Jordan-of

מֹשֶׁה לֵּאמֹר׃ אֵלֶּה שְׁמוֹת הָאֲנָשִׁים אֲשֶׁר־ יִנְחֲלוּ לָכֶם אֶת־
*** for-you they-will-assign who the-men names-of these (17) to-say Moses

הָאָרֶץ אֶלְעָזָר הַכֹּהֵן וִיהוֹשֻׁעַ בִּן־ נוּן׃ וְנָשִׂיא אֶחָד נָשִׂיא
leader one and-leader (18) Nun son-of and-Joshua the-priest Eleazar the-land

אֶחָד מִמַּטֶּה תִּקְחוּ לִנְחֹל אֶת־ הָאָרֶץ׃ וְאֵלֶּה שְׁמוֹת
names-of and-these (19) the-land *** to-assign you-appoint from-tribe one

הָאֲנָשִׁים לְמַטֵּה יְהוּדָה כָּלֵב בֶּן־ יְפֻנֶּה׃ וּלְמַטֵּה
and-from-tribe-of (20) Jephunneh son-of Caleb Judah from-tribe-of the-men

בְּנֵי שִׁמְעוֹן שְׁמוּאֵל בֶּן־ עַמִּיהוּד׃ לְמַטֵּה בִּנְיָמִן אֱלִידָד
Elidad Benjamin from-tribe-of (21) Ammihud son-of Shemuel Simeon sons-of

בֶּן־ כִּסְלוֹן׃ וּלְמַטֵּה בְנֵי־ דָן נָשִׂיא בֻּקִּי בֶּן־ יָגְלִי׃
Jogli son-of Bukki leader Dan sons-of and-from-tribe-of (22) Kislon son-of

לִבְנֵי יוֹסֵף לְמַטֵּה בְנֵי־ מְנַשֶּׁה נָשִׂיא חַנִּיאֵל
Hanniel leader Manasseh sons-of from-tribe-of Joseph from-sons-of (23)

בֶּן־ אֵפֹד׃ וּלְמַטֵּה בְנֵי־ אֶפְרַיִם נָשִׂיא קְמוּאֵל בֶּן־
son-of Kemuel leader Ephraim sons-of and-from-tribe-of (24) Ephod son-of

שִׁפְטָן׃ וּלְמַטֵּה בְנֵי־ זְבוּלֻן נָשִׂיא אֱלִיצָפָן בֶּן־
son-of Elizaphan leader Zebulun sons-of and-from-tribe-of (25) Shiphtan

פַּרְנָךְ׃ וּלְמַטֵּה בְנֵי־ יִשָּׂשכָר* נָשִׂיא פַּלְטִיאֵל בֶּן־ עַזָּן׃
Azzan son-of Paltiel leader Issachar sons-of and-from-tribe-of (26) Parnach

וּלְמַטֵּה בְנֵי־ אָשֵׁר נָשִׂיא אֲחִיהוּד בֶּן־ שְׁלֹמִי׃
Shelomi son-of Ahihud leader Asher sons-of and-from-tribe-of (27)

וּלְמַטֵּה בְנֵי־ נַפְתָּלִי נָשִׂיא פְּדַהְאֵל בֶּן־ עַמִּיהוּד׃
Ammihud son-of Pedahel leader Naphtali sons-of and-from-tribe-of (28)

אֵלֶּה אֲשֶׁר צִוָּה יְהוָה לְנַחֵל אֶת־ בְּנֵי־ יִשְׂרָאֵל בְּאֶרֶץ
in-land-of Israel sons-of *** to-assign Yahweh he-commanded whom these (29)

כְּנָעַן׃ וַיְדַבֵּר יְהוָה אֶל־ מֹשֶׁה בְּעַרְבֹת מוֹאָב עַל־ יַרְדֵּן
Jordan-of by Moab on-plains-of Moses to Yahweh and-he-spoke (35:1) Canaan

יְרֵחוֹ לֵאמֹר׃ צַו אֶת־ בְּנֵי יִשְׂרָאֵל וְנָתְנוּ לַלְוִיִּם
to-the-Levites so-they-give Israel sons-of *** command! (2) to-say Jericho

מִנַּחֲלַת אֲחֻזָּתָם עָרִים לָשָׁבֶת וּמִגְרָשׁ לֶעָרִים
by-the-towns and-pasture to-live towns possession-of-them from-inheritance-of

סְבִיבֹתֵיהֶם תִּתְּנוּ לַלְוִיִּם׃ וְהָיוּ הֶעָרִים
the-towns then-they-will-be (3) to-the-Levites they-must-give ones-around-them

tribes have received their inheritance on the east side of the Jordan of Jericho,[k] toward the sunrise."

16The LORD said to Moses,
17"These are the names of the
men who are to assign the
land for you as an inheritance:
Eleazar the priest and Joshua
son of Nun. 18And appoint one
leader from each tribe to help
assign the land. 19These are
their names:

Caleb son of Jephunneh,
from the tribe of Judah;
20Shemuel son of Ammihud,
from the tribe of Simeon;
21Elidad son of Kislon,
from the tribe of Benjamin;
22Bukki son of Jogli,
the leader from the tribe of Dan;
23Hanniel son of Ephod,
the leader from the tribe of Manasseh son of Joseph;
24Kemuel son of Shiphtan,
the leader from the tribe of Ephraim son of Joseph;
25Elizaphan son of Parnach,
the leader from the tribe of Zebulun;
26Paltiel son of Azzan,
the leader from the tribe of Issachar;
27Ahihud son of Shelomi,
the leader from the tribe of Asher;
28Pedahel son of Ammihud,
the leader from the tribe of Naphtali."
29These are the men the LORD
commanded to assign the inheritance to the Israelites in the land of Canaan.

Towns for the Levites

35 On the plains of Moab by the Jordan across from Jericho,[l] the LORD said to
Moses, 2"Command the Israelites to give the Levites towns to live in from the inheritance the Israelites will possess. And give them pasturelands around the towns. 3Then they

[k]15 *Jordan of Jericho* was possibly an ancient name for the Jordan River
[l]1 Hebrew *Jordan of Jericho*; possibly an ancient name for the Jordan River

*26 Most mss have *dagesh* in the *sin* (יִשָּׂשכָר).

לָהֶם לָשָׁבֶת וּמִגְרְשֵׁיהֶם יִהְיוּ לִבְהֶמְתָּם
for-cattle-of-them they-will-be and-pastures-of-them to-live for-them

וְלִרְכֻשָׁם וּלְכֹל חַיָּתָם׃ וּמִגְרְשֵׁי
and-pasturelands-of (4) stock-of-them and-for-all-of and-for-flock-of-them

הֶעָרִים אֲשֶׁר תִּתְּנוּ לַלְוִיִּם מִקִּיר הָעִיר וָחוּצָה
and-outward the-town from-wall-of to-the-Levites you-give that the-towns

אֶלֶף אַמָּה סָבִיב׃ וּמַדֹּתֶם מִחוּץ לָעִיר אֶת־פְּאַת־
side-of *** of-the-town outside and-you-measure (5) around cubit thousand

קֵדְמָה אַלְפַּיִם בָּאַמָּה וְאֶת־פְּאַת־נֶגֶב אַלְפַּיִם בָּאַמָּה
by-the-cubit two-thousand south side-of and by-the-cubit two-thousand on-east

וְאֶת־פְּאַת־יָם ׀ אַלְפַּיִם בָּאַמָּה וְאֵת פְּאַת צָפוֹן אַלְפַּיִם
two-thousand north side-of and by-the-cubit two-thousand west side-of and

בָּאַמָּה וְהָעִיר בַּתָּוֶךְ זֶה יִהְיֶה לָהֶם מִגְרְשֵׁי
pastures-of for-them he-will-be this in-the-center and-the-town by-the-cubit

הֶעָרִים׃ וְאֵת הֶעָרִים אֲשֶׁר תִּתְּנוּ לַלְוִיִּם אֵת שֵׁשׁ־עָרֵי
cities-of six *** to-the-Levites you-give that the-towns and (6) the-towns

הַמִּקְלָט אֲשֶׁר תִּתְּנוּ לָנֻס שָׁמָּה הָרֹצֵחַ וַעֲלֵיהֶם
and-to-them the-one-killing to-there to-flee you-give that the-refuge

תִּתְּנוּ אַרְבָּעִים וּשְׁתַּיִם עִיר׃ כָּל־הֶעָרִים אֲשֶׁר תִּתְּנוּ לַלְוִיִּם
to-the-Levites you-give that the-towns all-of (7) town and-two forty you-give

אַרְבָּעִים וּשְׁמֹנֶה עִיר אֶתְהֶן וְאֶת־מִגְרְשֵׁיהֶן׃ וְהֶעָרִים אֲשֶׁר
that and-the-towns (8) pastures-of-them also with-them town and-eight forty

תִּתְּנוּ מֵאֲחֻזַּת בְּנֵי־יִשְׂרָאֵל מֵאֵת הָרַב תַּרְבּוּ
you-give-many the-many from Israel sons-of from-possession-of you-give

וּמֵאֵת הַמְעַט תַּמְעִיטוּ אִישׁ כְּפִי נַחֲלָתוֹ אֲשֶׁר
that inheritance-of-him in-proportion-of each you-give-few the-few and-from

יִנְחָלוּ יִתֵּן מֵעָרָיו לַלְוִיִּם׃ וַיְדַבֵּר
and-he-spoke (9) to-the-Levites from-towns-of-him he-must-give they-inherited

יְהוָה אֶל־מֹשֶׁה לֵּאמֹר׃ דַּבֵּר אֶל־בְּנֵי יִשְׂרָאֵל וְאָמַרְתָּ אֲלֵהֶם
to-them and-you-say Israel sons-of to speak! (10) to-say Moses to Yahweh

כִּי אַתֶּם עֹבְרִים אֶת־הַיַּרְדֵּן אַרְצָה כְּנָעַן׃ וְהִקְרִיתֶם
then-you-select (11) Canaan into-land-of the-Jordan *** ones-crossing you when

לָכֶם עָרִים עָרֵי מִקְלָט תִּהְיֶינָה לָכֶם וְנָס שָׁמָּה
to-there and-he-may-flee for-you they-will-be refuge cities-of towns for-you

רֹצֵחַ מַכֵּה־נֶפֶשׁ בִּשְׁגָגָה׃ וְהָיוּ לָכֶם
for-you and-they-will-be (12) by-accident person slaying-of one-killing

הֶעָרִים לְמִקְלָט מִגֹּאֵל וְלֹא יָמוּת הָרֹצֵחַ
the-one-killing he-may-die so-not from-one-avenging for-refuge the-cities

will have towns to live in and pasturelands for their cattle, flocks and all their other livestock.

4“The pasturelands around the towns that you give the Levites will extend out fifteen hundred feet[m] from the town wall. 5Outside the town, measure three thousand feet[n] on the east side, three thousand on the south side, three thousand on the west and three thousand on the north, with the town in the center. They will have this area as pastureland for the towns.

Cities of Refuge

6“Six of the towns you give the Levites will be cities of refuge, to which a person who has killed someone may flee. In addition, give them forty-two other towns. 7In all you must give the Levites forty-eight towns, together with their pasturelands. 8The towns you give the Levites from the land the Israelites possess are to be given in proportion to the inheritance of each tribe: Take many towns from a tribe that has many, but few from one that has few.”

9Then the LORD said to Moses: 10“Speak to the Israelites and say to them: ‘When you cross the Jordan into Canaan, 11select some towns to be your cities of refuge, to which a person who has killed someone accidentally may flee. 12They will be places of refuge from the avenger, so that a person accused of murder may not die before he

[m]4 Hebrew *a thousand cubits* (about 450 meters)
[n]5 Hebrew *two thousand cubits* (about 900 meters)

עַד־ עָמְדוֹ לִפְנֵי הָעֵדָה לַמִּשְׁפָּט׃ וְהֶעָרִים
and-the-towns (13) for-the-trial the-assembly before to-stand-him before

אֲשֶׁר תִּתֵּנוּ שֵׁשׁ־ עָרֵי מִקְלָט תִּהְיֶינָה לָכֶם׃ אֵת ׀ שְׁלֹשׁ
three-of *** (14) for-you they-will-be refuge cities-of six you-give that

הֶעָרִים תִּתְּנוּ מֵעֵבֶר לַיַּרְדֵּן וְאֵת שְׁלֹשׁ הֶעָרִים תִּתְּנוּ
you-give the-towns three-of and of-the-Jordan on-this-side you-give the-towns

בְּאֶרֶץ כְּנָעַן עָרֵי מִקְלָט תִּהְיֶינָה׃ לִבְנֵי יִשְׂרָאֵל
Israel for-sons-of (15) they-will-be refuge cities-of Canaan in-land-of

וְלַגֵּר וְלַתּוֹשָׁב בְּתוֹכָם תִּהְיֶינָה שֵׁשׁ־ הֶעָרִים
the-towns six they-will-be among-them and-for-the-visitor and-for-the-alien

הָאֵלֶּה לְמִקְלָט לָנוּס שָׁמָּה כָּל־ מַכֵּה־ נֶפֶשׁ
person one-killing-of every-of to-there to-flee for-refuge the-these

בִּשְׁגָגָה׃ וְאִם־ בִּכְלִי בַרְזֶל ׀ הִכָּהוּ וַיָּמֹת
so-he-dies he-strikes-him iron with-object-of now-if (16) by-accident

רֹצֵחַ הוּא מוֹת יוּמַת הָרֹצֵחַ׃ וְאִם
or-if (17) the-one-murdering he-shall-die to-die he one-murdering

בְּאֶבֶן יָד אֲשֶׁר־ יָמוּת בָּהּ הִכָּהוּ וַיָּמֹת
so-he-dies he-strikes-him with-her he-could-kill that hand with-stone-of

רֹצֵחַ הוּא מוֹת יוּמַת הָרֹצֵחַ׃ אוֹ בִּכְלִי
with-object-of or (18) the-one-murdering he-shall-die to-die he one-murdering

עֵץ־ יָד אֲשֶׁר־ יָמוּת בּוֹ הִכָּהוּ וַיָּמֹת
so-he-dies he-strikes-him with-him he-could-kill that hand wood-of

רֹצֵחַ הוּא מוֹת יוּמַת הָרֹצֵחַ׃ גֹּאֵל
one-avenging-of (19) the-one-murdering he-shall-die to-die he one-murdering

הַדָּם הוּא יָמִית אֶת־ הָרֹצֵחַ בְּפִגְעוֹ־ בוֹ
with-him when-to-meet-him the-one-murdering *** he-shall-kill he the-blood

הוּא יְמִיתֶנּוּ׃ וְאִם־ בְּשִׂנְאָה יֶהְדָּפֶנּוּ אוֹ־ הִשְׁלִיךְ
he-throws or he-shoves-him with-malice and-if (20) he-shall-kill-him he

עָלָיו בִּצְדִיָּה וַיָּמֹת׃ אוֹ בְאֵיבָה הִכָּהוּ
he-hits-him in-hostility or (21) so-he-dies with-intention at-him

בְיָדוֹ וַיָּמֹת מוֹת־ יוּמַת הַמַּכֶּה רֹצֵחַ
one-murdering the-one-hitting he-must-die to-die so-he-dies with-fist-of-him

הוּא גֹּאֵל הַדָּם יָמִית אֶת־ הָרֹצֵחַ
the-one-murdering *** he-shall-kill the-blood one-avenging-of he

בְּפִגְעוֹ־ בוֹ׃ וְאִם־ בְּפֶתַע בְּלֹא־ אֵיבָה
hostility with-no in-suddenness but-if (22) with-him when-to-meet-him

הֲדָפוֹ אוֹ־ הִשְׁלִיךְ עָלָיו כָּל־ כְּלִי בְּלֹא צְדִיָּה׃ אוֹ
or (23) intention with-no object any-of at-him he-throws or he-shoves-him

stands trial before the assembly. 13These six towns you give
will be your cities of refuge.
14Give three on this side of the
Jordan and three in Canaan as
cities of refuge. 15These six
towns will be a place of refuge
for Israelites, aliens and any
other people living among
them, so that anyone who has
killed another accidentally can
flee there.
16" 'If a man strikes someone
with an iron object so that he
dies, he is a murderer; the
murderer shall be put to death.
17Or if anyone has a stone in
his hand that could kill, and
he strikes someone so that he
dies, he is a murderer; the
murderer shall be put to death.
18Or if anyone has a wooden
object in his hand that could
kill, and he hits someone so
that he dies, he is a murderer;
the murderer shall be put to
death. 19The avenger of blood
shall put the murderer to
death; when he meets him, he
shall put him to death. 20If
anyone with malice afore-
thought shoves another or
throws something at him intentionally so that he dies 21or
if in hostility he hits him with
his fist so that he dies, that
person shall be put to death;
he is a murderer. The avenger
of blood shall put the murderer to death when he meets
him.
22" 'But if without hostility
someone suddenly shoves another or throws something at
him unintentionally 23or,

בְּכָל־ אֶבֶן אֲשֶׁר־ יָמוּת בָּהּ בְּלֹא רְאוֹת וַיַּפֵּל
and-he-drops to-see but-not with-her he-could-kill that stone with-any-of

עָלָיו וַיָּמֹת וְהוּא לֹא־ אוֹיֵב לוֹ וְלֹא מְבַקֵּשׁ
intending and-not to-him being-enemy not and-he so-he-dies on-him

רָעָתוֹ׃ (24) וְשָׁפְטוּ הָעֵדָה בֵּין הַמַּכֶּה
the-one-killing between the-assembly then-they-must-judge (24) harm-of-him

וּבֵין גֹּאֵל הַדָּם עַל הַמִּשְׁפָּטִים הָאֵלֶּה׃
the-these the-regulations by the-blood one-avenging-of and-between

(25) וְהִצִּילוּ הָעֵדָה אֶת־ הָרֹצֵחַ מִיַּד
from-hand-of the-one-killing *** the-assembly and-they-must-protect (25)

גֹּאֵל הַדָּם וְהֵשִׁיבוּ אֹתוֹ הָעֵדָה אֶל־ עִיר
city-of to the-assembly him and-they-must-send the-blood one-avenging-of

מִקְלָטוֹ אֲשֶׁר־ נָס שָׁמָּה וְיָשַׁב בָּהּ עַד־ מוֹת
death-of until in-her and-he-must-stay to-there he-fled that refuge-of-him

הַכֹּהֵן הַגָּדֹל אֲשֶׁר־ מָשַׁח אֹתוֹ בְּשֶׁמֶן הַקֹּדֶשׁ׃ (26) וְאִם־
but-if (26) the-holy with-oil-of him he-anointed whom the-high the-priest

יָצֹא יֵצֵא הָרֹצֵחַ אֶת־ גְּבוּל עִיר מִקְלָטוֹ
refuge-of-him city-of limit-of *** the-one-killing he-goes-out to-go-out

אֲשֶׁר יָנוּס שָׁמָּה׃ (27) וּמָצָא אֹתוֹ גֹּאֵל הַדָּם
the-blood one-avenging-of him and-he-finds (27) to-there he-fled that

מִחוּץ לִגְבוּל עִיר מִקְלָטוֹ וְרָצַח גֹּאֵל
one-avenging-of then-he-may-kill refuge-of-him city-of of-limit-of outside

הַדָּם אֶת־ הָרֹצֵחַ אֵין לוֹ דָּם׃ (28) כִּי בְעִיר
in-city-of for (28) blood to-him without the-one-killing *** the-blood

מִקְלָטוֹ יֵשֵׁב עַד־ מוֹת הַכֹּהֵן הַגָּדֹל וְאַחֲרֵי
and-after the-high the-priest death-of until he-must-stay refuge-of-him

מוֹת הַכֹּהֵן הַגָּדֹל יָשׁוּב הָרֹצֵחַ אֶל־ אֶרֶץ
land-of to the-one-killing he-may-return the-high the-priest death-of

אֲחֻזָּתוֹ׃ (29) וְהָיוּ אֵלֶּה לָכֶם לְחֻקַּת מִשְׁפָּט
legal as-requirement-of for-you these and-they-must-be (29) property-of-him

לְדֹרֹתֵיכֶם בְּכֹל מוֹשְׁבֹתֵיכֶם׃ (30) כָּל־ מַכֵּה־
one-killing-of every-of (30) dwellings-of-you in-all-of for-generations-of-you

נֶפֶשׁ לְפִי עֵדִים יִרְצַח אֶת־ הָרֹצֵחַ וְעֵד
but-witness the-one-murdering *** he-may-kill witnesses on-testimony-of person

אֶחָד לֹא־ יַעֲנֶה בְנֶפֶשׁ לָמוּת׃ (31) וְלֹא־ תִקְחוּ כֹפֶר
ransom you-accept and-not (31) to-die against-person he-may-testify not one

לְנֶפֶשׁ רֹצֵחַ אֲשֶׁר־ הוּא רָשָׁע לָמוּת כִּי־ מוֹת יוּמָת׃
he-must-die to-die for to-die guilty he who one-murdering for-life-of

without seeing him, drops a
stone on him that could kill
him, and he dies, then since
he was not his enemy and he
did not intend to harm him,
24the assembly must judge between him and the avenger of
blood according to these regulations. 25The assembly must
protect the one accused of
murder from the avenger of
blood and send him back to
the city of refuge to which he
fled. He must stay there until
the death of the high priest,
who was anointed with the
holy oil.

26" 'But if the accused ever
goes outside the limits of the
city of refuge to which he has
fled 27and the avenger of blood
finds him outside the city, the
avenger of blood may kill the
accused without being guilty
of murder. 28The accused must
stay in his city of refuge until
the death of the high priest;
only after the death of the
high priest may he return to
his own property.

29" 'These are to be legal requirements for you throughout the generations to come,
wherever you live.

30" 'Anyone who kills a person is to be put to death as a
murderer only on the testimony of witnesses. But no one
is to be put to death on the
testimony of only one witness.

31" 'Do not accept a ransom
for the life of a murderer, who
deserves to die. He must surely be put to death.

וְלֹא־ תִקְחוּ כֹפֶר לָנוּס אֶל־ עִיר מִקְלָטוֹ לָשׁוּב
to-go-back refuge-of-him city-of to to-flee ransom you-accept and-not (32)

לָשֶׁבֶת בָּאָרֶץ עַד־ מוֹת הַכֹּהֵן׃ וְלֹא־ תַחֲנִיפוּ אֶת־
*** you-pollute and-not (33) the-priest death-of before in-the-land to-live

הָאָרֶץ אֲשֶׁר אַתֶּם בָּהּ כִּי הַדָּם הוּא יַחֲנִיף אֶת־ הָאָרֶץ
the-land *** he-pollutes he the-blood for in-her you where the-land

וְלָאָרֶץ לֹא־ יְכֻפַּר לַדָּם אֲשֶׁר שֻׁפַּךְ־ בָּהּ
on-her he-was-shed that for-the-blood he-can-be-atoned not and-for-the-land

כִּי־ אִם בְּדַם שֹׁפְכוֹ׃ וְלֹא תְטַמֵּא אֶת־ הָאָרֶץ
the-land *** you-defile and-not (34) one-shedding-him by-blood-of only except

אֲשֶׁר אַתֶּם יֹשְׁבִים בָּהּ אֲשֶׁר אֲנִי שֹׁכֵן בְּתוֹכָהּ כִּי אֲנִי יְהוָה
Yahweh I for within-her dwelling I where in-her ones-living you where

שֹׁכֵן בְּתוֹךְ בְּנֵי יִשְׂרָאֵל׃ וַיִּקְרְבוּ רָאשֵׁי הָאָבוֹת
the-fathers heads-of and-they-came (36:1) Israel sons-of among dwelling

לְמִשְׁפַּחַת בְּנֵי־ גִלְעָד בֶּן־ מָכִיר בֶּן־ מְנַשֶּׁה מִמִּשְׁפְּחֹת בְּנֵי
sons-of from-clans-of Manasseh son-of Makir son-of Gilead sons-of of-clan-of

יוֹסֵף וַיְדַבְּרוּ לִפְנֵי מֹשֶׁה וְלִפְנֵי הַנְּשִׂאִים רָאשֵׁי אָבוֹת
fathers heads-of the-leaders and-before Moses before and-they-spoke Joseph

לִבְנֵי יִשְׂרָאֵל׃ וַיֹּאמְרוּ אֶת־ אֲדֹנִי צִוָּה יְהוָה
Yahweh he-commanded lord-of-me *** and-they-said (2) Israel of-sons-of

לָתֵת אֶת־ הָאָרֶץ בְּנַחֲלָה בְּגוֹרָל לִבְנֵי יִשְׂרָאֵל וַאדֹנִי
and-lord-of-me Israel to-sons-of by-lot as-inheritance the-land *** to-give

צֻוָּה בַיהוָה לָתֵת אֶת־ נַחֲלַת צְלָפְחָד אָחִינוּ
brother-of-us Zelophehad inheritance-of *** to-give by Yahweh he-was-ordered

לִבְנֹתָיו׃ וְהָיוּ לְאֶחָד מִבְּנֵי שִׁבְטֵי בְנֵי־
sons-of tribes-of from-sons-of to-one if-they-become (3) to-daughters-of-him

יִשְׂרָאֵל לְנָשִׁים וְנִגְרְעָה נַחֲלָתָן מִנַּחֲלַת
from-inheritance-of inheritance-of-them then-she-will-be-taken as-wives Israel

אֲבֹתֵינוּ וְנוֹסַף עַל נַחֲלַת הַמַּטֶּה אֲשֶׁר
that the-tribe inheritance-of to and-he-will-be-added fathers-of-us

תִּהְיֶינָה לָהֶם וּמִגֹּרַל נַחֲלָתֵנוּ יִגָּרֵעַ׃
he-will-be-taken inheritance-of-us and-from-allotment-of into-them they-marry

וְאִם־ יִהְיֶה הַיֹּבֵל לִבְנֵי יִשְׂרָאֵל וְנוֹסְפָה
then-she-will-be-added Israel for-sons-of the-Jubilee he-comes and-when (4)

נַחֲלָתָן עַל נַחֲלַת הַמַּטֶּה אֲשֶׁר תִּהְיֶינָה לָהֶם
into-them they-marry that the-tribe inheritance-of to inheritance-of-them

וּמִנַּחֲלַת מַטֵּה אֲבֹתֵינוּ יִגָּרַע
he-will-be-taken fathers-of-us tribe-of and-from-inheritance-of

32" 'Do not accept a ransom
for anyone who has fled to a
city of refuge and so allow him
to go back and live on his own
land before the death of the
high priest.
33" 'Do not pollute the land
where you are. Bloodshed pol-
lutes the land, and atonement
cannot be made for the land
on which blood has been
shed, except by the blood of
the one who shed it.
34Do not
defile the land where you live
and where I dwell, for I, the
LORD, dwell among the Israelites.' "

Inheritance of Zelophehad's Daughters

36 The family heads of the
clan of Gilead son of
Makir, the son of Manasseh,
who were from the clans of the
descendants of Joseph, came
and spoke before Moses and
the leaders, the heads of the
Israelite families.
2They said,
"When the LORD commanded
my lord to give the land as an
inheritance to the Israelites by
lot, he ordered you to give the
inheritance of our brother Zelophehad to his daughters.
3Now suppose they marry
men from other Israelite
tribes; then their inheritance
will be taken from our ancestral inheritance and added to
that of the tribe they marry
into. And so part of the inheritance allotted to us will be tak-
en away.
4When the Year of
Jubilee for the Israelites
comes, their inheritance will
be added to that of the tribe
into which they marry, and
their property will be taken
from the tribal inheritance of
our forefathers."

נַחֲלָתָן׃ וַיְצַו מֹשֶׁה אֶת־ בְּנֵי יִשְׂרָאֵל עַל־ פִּי

command-of at Israel sons-of *** Moses so-he-ordered (5) inheritance-of-them

יְהוָה לֵאמֹר כֵּן מַטֵּה בְנֵי־ יוֹסֵף דֹּבְרִים׃ זֶה הַדָּבָר

the-thing this (6) ones-saying Joseph sons-of tribe-of right to-say Yahweh

אֲשֶׁר־ צִוָּה יְהוָה לִבְנוֹת צְלָפְחָד לֵאמֹר לַטּוֹב

to-the-one-pleasant to-say Zelophehad for-daughters-of Yahweh he-commands that

בְּעֵינֵיהֶם תִּהְיֶינָה לְנָשִׁים אַךְ לְמִשְׁפַּחַת מַטֵּה

tribe-of in-clan-of as-long-as as-wives they-may-become in-eyes-of-them

אֲבִיהֶם תִּהְיֶינָה לְנָשִׁים׃ וְלֹא־ תִסֹּב נַחֲלָה

inheritance she-may-pass and-not (7) as-wives they-become father-of-them

לִבְנֵי יִשְׂרָאֵל מִמַּטֶּה אֶל־ מַטֶּה כִּי אִישׁ בְּנַחֲלַת מַטֵּה

tribe-of to-inheritance-of each for tribe to from-tribe Israel among-sons-of

אֲבֹתָיו יִדְבְּקוּ בְּנֵי יִשְׂרָאֵל׃ וְכָל־ בַּת

daughter and-every-of (8) Israel sons-of they-shall-keep fathers-of-him

יֹרֶשֶׁת נַחֲלָה מִמַּטּוֹת בְּנֵי יִשְׂרָאֵל לְאֶחָד מִמִּשְׁפַּחַת מַטֵּה

tribe-of in-clan-of to-one Israel sons-of in-tribes-of land inheriting

אָבִיהָ תִּהְיֶה לְאִשָּׁה לְמַעַן יִירְשׁוּ בְּנֵי יִשְׂרָאֵל

Israel sons-of they-will-possess so-that as-wife she-must-be father-of-her

אִישׁ נַחֲלַת אֲבֹתָיו׃ וְלֹא־ תִסֹּב נַחֲלָה

inheritance she-may-pass and-not (9) fathers-of-him inheritance-of each

מִמַּטֶּה לְמַטֶּה אַחֵר כִּי־ אִישׁ בְּנַחֲלָתוֹ יִדְבְּקוּ

they-must-keep to-inheritance-of-him each for another to-tribe from-tribe

מַטּוֹת בְּנֵי יִשְׂרָאֵל׃ כַּאֲשֶׁר צִוָּה יְהוָה אֶת־ מֹשֶׁה כֵּן

so Moses *** Yahweh he-commanded just-as (10) Israel sons-of tribes-of

עָשׂוּ בְּנוֹת צְלָפְחָד׃ וַתִּהְיֶינָה מַחְלָה תִרְצָה

Tirzah Mahlah and-they-became (11) Zelophehad daughters-of they-did

וְחָגְלָה וּמִלְכָּה וְנֹעָה בְּנוֹת צְלָפְחָד לִבְנֵי

to-sons-of Zelophehad daughters-of and-Noah and-Milcah and-Hoglah

דֹדֵיהֶן לְנָשִׁים׃ מִמִּשְׁפְּחֹת בְּנֵי־ מְנַשֶּׁה בֶן־ יוֹסֵף

Joseph son-of Manasseh sons-of in-clans-of (12) as-wives uncles-of-them

הָיוּ לְנָשִׁים וַתְּהִי נַחֲלָתָן עַל־ מַטֵּה

tribe-of in inheritance-of-them and-she-remained as-wives they-became

מִשְׁפַּחַת אֲבִיהֶן׃ אֵלֶּה הַמִּצְוֹת וְהַמִּשְׁפָּטִים אֲשֶׁר

that and-the-regulations the-commands these (13) father-of-them clan-of

צִוָּה יְהוָה בְּיַד־ מֹשֶׁה אֶל־ בְּנֵי יִשְׂרָאֵל בְּעַרְבֹת מוֹאָב

Moab on-plains-of Israel sons-of to Moses by-hand-of Yahweh he-gave

עַל יַרְדֵּן יְרֵחוֹ׃

Jericho Jordan-of by

[5]Then at the LORD's command Moses gave this order to the Israelites: "What the tribe of the descendants of Joseph is saying is right.
[6]This is what the LORD commands for Zelophehad's daughters: They may marry anyone they please as long as they marry within the tribal clan of their father.
[7]No inheritance in Israel is to pass from tribe to tribe, for every Israelite shall keep the tribal land inherited from his forefathers.
[8]Every daughter who inherits land in any Israelite tribe must marry someone in her father's tribal clan, so that every Israelite will possess the inheritance of his fathers.
[9]No inheritance may pass from tribe to tribe, for each Israelite tribe is to keep the land it inherits."
[10]So Zelophehad's daughters did as the LORD commanded Moses.
[11]Zelophehad's daughters—Mahlah, Tirzah, Hoglah, Milcah and Noah—married their cousins on their father's side.
[12]They married within the clans of the descendants of Manasseh son of Joseph, and their inheritance remained in their father's clan and tribe.
[13]These are the commands and regulations the LORD gave through Moses to the Israelites on the plains of Moab by the Jordan across from Jericho.[o]

[o]13 Hebrew *Jordan of Jericho;* possibly an ancient name for the Jordan River

אֵלֶּה הַדְּבָרִים אֲשֶׁר דִּבֶּר מֹשֶׁה אֶל־ כָּל־ יִשְׂרָאֵל בְּעֵבֶר
on-east-of Israel all-of to Moses he-spoke that the-words these (1:1)

הַיַּרְדֵּן בַּמִּדְבָּר בָּעֲרָבָה מוֹל סוּף בֵּין־ פָּארָן וּבֵין־
and-between Paran between Suph opposite in-the-Arabah in-the-desert the-Jordan

תֹּפֶל וְלָבָן וַחֲצֵרֹת וְדִי זָהָב׃ אַחַד עָשָׂר יוֹם מֵחֹרֵב
from-Horeb day ten one (2) Zahab and-Di and-Hazeroth and-Laban Tophel

דֶּרֶךְ הַר־ שֵׂעִיר עַד קָדֵשׁ בַּרְנֵעַ׃ וַיְהִי בְּאַרְבָּעִים שָׁנָה בְּעַשְׁתֵּי־
in-one year in-fortieth and-he-was (3) Barnea Kadesh to Seir Mount-of road-of

עָשָׂר חֹדֶשׁ בְּאֶחָד לַחֹדֶשׁ דִּבֶּר מֹשֶׁה אֶל־ בְּנֵי יִשְׂרָאֵל
Israel sons-of to Moses he-proclaimed of-the-month on-first month ten

כְּכֹל אֲשֶׁר צִוָּה יְהוָה אֹתוֹ אֲלֵהֶם׃ אַחֲרֵי הַכֹּתוֹ אֵת
*** to-defeat-him after (4) about-them him Yahweh he-commanded that as-all

סִיחֹן מֶלֶךְ הָאֱמֹרִי אֲשֶׁר יוֹשֵׁב בְּחֶשְׁבּוֹן וְאֵת עוֹג מֶלֶךְ הַבָּשָׁן
the-Bashan king-of Og and in-Heshbon reigning who the-Amorite king-of Sihon

אֲשֶׁר־ יוֹשֵׁב בְּעַשְׁתָּרֹת בְּאֶדְרֶעִי׃ בְּעֵבֶר הַיַּרְדֵּן בְּאֶרֶץ מוֹאָב
Moab in-land-of the-Jordan on-east-of (5) at-Edrei in-Ashtaroth reigning who

הוֹאִיל מֹשֶׁה בֵּאֵר אֶת־ הַתּוֹרָה הַזֹּאת לֵאמֹר׃ יְהוָה אֱלֹהֵינוּ
God-of-us Yahweh (6) to-say the-this the-law *** he-expounded Moses he-began

דִּבֶּר אֵלֵינוּ בְּחֹרֵב לֵאמֹר רַב־ לָכֶם שֶׁבֶת בָּהָר הַזֶּה׃
the-this at-the-mountain to-stay to-you enough to-say at-Horeb to-us he-spoke

פְּנוּ ׀ וּסְעוּ לָכֶם וּבֹאוּ הַר הָאֱמֹרִי
the-Amorite hill-country-of and-go! for-you and-advance! break-camp! (7)

וְאֶל־ כָּל־ שְׁכֵנָיו בָּעֲרָבָה בָהָר וּבַשְּׁפֵלָה
and-in-the-foothill in-the-mountain in-the-Arabah neighbors-of-him all-of and-to

וּבַנֶּגֶב וּבְחוֹף הַיָּם אֶרֶץ הַכְּנַעֲנִי וְהַלְּבָנוֹן
and-the-Lebanon the-Canaanite land-of the-sea and-by-coast-of and-in-the-Negev

עַד־ הַנָּהָר הַגָּדֹל נְהַר־ פְּרָת׃ רְאֵה נָתַתִּי לִפְנֵיכֶם
before-you I-gave see! (8) Euphrates River-of the-great the-river as-far-as

אֶת־ הָאָרֶץ בֹּאוּ וּרְשׁוּ אֶת־ הָאָרֶץ אֲשֶׁר נִשְׁבַּע יְהוָה
Yahweh he-swore that the-land *** and-possess! go-in! the-land ***

לַאֲבֹתֵיכֶם לְאַבְרָהָם לְיִצְחָק וּלְיַעֲקֹב לָתֵת לָהֶם
to-them to-give and-to-Jacob to-Isaac to-Abraham to-fathers-of-you

וּלְזַרְעָם אַחֲרֵיהֶם׃ וָאֹמַר אֲלֵכֶם בָּעֵת
at-the-time to-you and-I-said (9) after-them and-to-descendant-of-them

הַהִוא לֵאמֹר לֹא־ אוּכַל לְבַדִּי שְׂאֵת אֶתְכֶם׃ יְהוָה אֱלֹהֵיכֶם
God-of-you Yahweh (10) you to-carry by-myself I-can not to-say the-that

הִרְבָּה אֶתְכֶם וְהִנְּכֶם הַיּוֹם כְּכוֹכְבֵי הַשָּׁמַיִם לָרֹב׃
for-number the-skies as-stars-of the-day so-see-you! you he-increased

The Command to Leave Horeb

1 These are the words
Moses spoke to all Israel in
the desert east of the Jordan—
that is, in the Arabah—oppos
ite Suph, between Paran and
Tophel, Laban, Hazeroth and
Dizahab. 2(It takes eleven days
to go from Horeb to Kadesh
Barnea by the Mount Seir
road.)
3In the fortieth year, on the
first day of the eleventh
month, Moses proclaimed to
the Israelites all that the LORD
had commanded him con-
cerning them. 4This was after
he had defeated Sihon king of
the Amorites, who reigned in
Heshbon, and at Edrei had defeated Og king of Bashan, who
reigned in Ashtaroth.
5East of the Jordan in the territory of Moab, Moses began
to expound this law, saying:

6The LORD our God said to us
at Horeb, "You have stayed
long enough at this mountain.
7Break camp and advance into
the hill country of the Amorites; go to all the neighboring
peoples in the Arabah, in the
mountains, in the western
foothills, in the Negev and
along the seacoast, to the land
of the Canaanites and to Lebanon, as far as the great river,
the Euphrates. 8See, I have
given you this land. Go in and
take possession of the land
that the LORD swore he would
give to your fathers—to Abraham, Isaac and Jacob—and to
their descendants after them."

The Appointment of Leaders

9At that time I said to you,
"You are too heavy a burden
for me to carry alone. 10The
LORD your God has increased
your numbers so that today
you are as many as the stars in

יְהוָ֞ה אֱלֹהֵ֣י אֲבֽוֹתֵכֶ֗ם יֹסֵ֧ף עֲלֵיכֶ֛ם כָּכֶ֖ם אֶ֣לֶף
thousand as-you to-you may-he-increase fathers-of-you God-of Yahweh (11)

פְּעָמִ֑ים וִיבָרֵ֣ךְ אֶתְכֶ֔ם כַּאֲשֶׁ֖ר דִּבֶּ֥ר לָכֶֽם׃ אֵיכָ֥ה אֶשָּׂ֖א
can-I-bear how? (12) to-you he-promised just-as you and-may-he-bless times

לְבַדִּ֑י טָרְחֲכֶ֥ם וּמַֽשַּׂאֲכֶ֖ם וְרִֽיבְכֶֽם׃ הָב֣וּ
choose! (13) and-dispute-of-you and-burden-of-you problem-of-you by-myself

לָ֠כֶם אֲנָשִׁ֨ים חֲכָמִ֧ים וּנְבֹנִ֛ים וִידֻעִ֖ים
and-ones-being-respected and-understanding-ones wise-ones men for-you

לְשִׁבְטֵיכֶ֑ם וַאֲשִׂימֵ֖ם בְּרָאשֵׁיכֶֽם׃ וַֽתַּעֲנ֖וּ
and-you-answered (14) as-heads-of-you and-I-will-set-them from-tribes-of-you

אֹתִ֑י וַתֹּ֣אמְר֔וּ טֽוֹב־ הַדָּבָ֥ר אֲשֶׁר־ דִּבַּ֖רְתָּ לַעֲשֽׂוֹת׃ וָאֶקַּ֞ח אֶת־
*** so-I-took (15) to-do you-propose that the-thing good and-you-said me

רָאשֵׁ֣י שִׁבְטֵיכֶ֗ם אֲנָשִׁים֙ חֲכָמִ֔ים וִֽידֻעִ֔ים וָאֶתֵּ֥ן
and-I-made and-ones-being-respected wise-ones men tribes-of-you leaders-of

אֹתָ֛ם רָאשִׁ֖ים עֲלֵיכֶ֑ם שָׂרֵ֨י אֲלָפִ֜ים וְשָׂרֵ֣י מֵא֗וֹת
hundreds and-commanders-of thousands commanders-of over-you authorities them

וְשָׂרֵ֤י חֲמִשִּׁים֙ וְשָׂרֵ֣י עֲשָׂרֹ֔ת וְשֹׁטְרִ֖ים
and-ones-being-officers tens and-commanders-of fifties and-commanders-of

לְשִׁבְטֵיכֶֽם׃ וָאֲצַוֶּה֙ אֶת־ שֹׁ֣פְטֵיכֶ֔ם בָּעֵ֥ת הַהִ֖וא
the-that at-the-time ones-judging-you *** and-I-charged (16) of-tribes-of-you

לֵאמֹ֑ר שָׁמֹ֤עַ בֵּין־ אֲחֵיכֶם֙ וּשְׁפַטְתֶּ֣ם צֶ֔דֶק בֵּֽין־ אִ֥ישׁ
man between fairly and-you-judge brothers-you between to-hear to-say

וּבֵין־ אָחִ֖יו וּבֵ֥ין גֵּרֽוֹ׃ לֹֽא־ תַכִּ֨ירוּ
you-be-partial not (17) alien-of-him or-between brother-of-him and-between

פָנִ֜ים בַּמִּשְׁפָּ֗ט כַּקָּטֹן֙ כַּגָּדֹל֙ תִּשְׁמָע֔וּן לֹ֤א תָג֙וּרוּ֙
you-fear not you-hear as-the-great both-the-small in-the-judgment persons

מִפְּנֵי־ אִ֔ישׁ כִּ֥י הַמִּשְׁפָּ֖ט לֵאלֹהִ֣ים ה֑וּא וְהַדָּבָר֙ אֲשֶׁ֣ר יִקְשֶׁ֣ה
he-is-hard that and-the-case he to-God the-judgment for any from-persons-of

מִכֶּ֔ם תַּקְרִב֥וּן אֵלַ֖י וּשְׁמַעְתִּֽיו׃ וָאֲצַוֶּ֥ה אֶתְכֶ֖ם בָּעֵ֣ת
at-the-time you and-I-told (18) and-I-will-hear-him to-me you-bring for-you

הַהִ֑וא אֵ֥ת כָּל־ הַדְּבָרִ֖ים אֲשֶׁ֥ר תַּעֲשֽׂוּן׃ וַנִּסַּ֣ע
then-we-set-out (19) you-must-do that the-things all-of *** the-that

מֵֽחֹרֵ֗ב וַנֵּ֡לֶךְ אֵ֣ת כָּל־ הַמִּדְבָּ֣ר הַגָּדוֹל֩ וְהַנּוֹרָ֨א
and-the-being-dreadful the-vast the-desert all-of *** and-we-went from-Horeb

הַה֜וּא אֲשֶׁ֣ר רְאִיתֶ֗ם דֶּ֚רֶךְ הַ֣ר הָֽאֱמֹרִ֔י כַּאֲשֶׁ֥ר צִוָּ֛ה
he-commanded just-as the-Amorite hill-country-of way-of you-saw that the-that

יְהוָ֥ה אֱלֹהֵ֖ינוּ אֹתָ֑נוּ וַנָּבֹ֕א עַ֖ד קָדֵ֥שׁ בַּרְנֵֽעַ׃ וָאֹמַ֖ר אֲלֵכֶ֑ם
to-you then-I-said (20) Barnea Kadesh to so-we-reached us God-of-us Yahweh

the sky. [11]May the LORD, the
God of your fathers, increase
you a thousand times and
bless you as he has promised!
[12]But how can I bear your
problems and your burdens
and your disputes all by myself? [13]Choose some wise,
understanding and respected
men from each of your tribes,
and I will set them over you."
[14]You answered me, "What
you propose to do is good."
[15]So I took the leading men
of your tribes, wise and respected men, and appointed
them to have authority over
you—as commanders of thousands, of hundreds, of fifties
and of tens and as tribal
officials. [16]And I charged your
judges at that time: Hear the
disputes between your brothers and judge fairly, whether
the case is between brother Israelites or between one of
them and an alien. [17]Do not
show partiality in judging;
hear both small and great
alike. Do not be afraid of any
man, for judgment belongs to
God. Bring me any case too
hard for you, and I will hear it.
[18]And at that time I told you
everything you were to do.

Spies Sent Out

[19]Then, as the LORD our God
commanded us, we set out
from Horeb and went toward
the hill country of the Amorites through all that vast and
dreadful desert that you have
seen, and so we reached Kadesh Barnea. [20]Then I said to

בָּאתֶם עַד־ הַר הָאֱמֹרִי אֲשֶׁר־ יְהוָה אֱלֹהֵינוּ נֹתֵן
giving God-of-us Yahweh which the-Amorite hill-country-of to you-reached

לָנוּ׃ רְאֵה נָתַן יְהוָה אֱלֹהֶיךָ לְפָנֶיךָ אֶת־ הָאָרֶץ עֲלֵה
go-up! the-land *** before-you God-of-you Yahweh he-gave see! (21) to-us

רֵשׁ כַּאֲשֶׁר דִּבֶּר יְהוָה אֱלֹהֵי אֲבֹתֶיךָ לָךְ אַל־ תִּירָא
you-fear not to-you fathers-of-you God-of Yahweh he-told just-as possess!

וְאַל־ תֵּחָת׃ וַתִּקְרְבוּן אֵלַי כֻּלְּכֶם וַתֹּאמְרוּ
and-you-said all-of-you to-me then-you-came (22) you-be-discouraged and-not

נִשְׁלְחָה אֲנָשִׁים לְפָנֵינוּ וְיַחְפְּרוּ־ לָנוּ אֶת־ הָאָרֶץ
the-land *** for-us so-they-can-spy-out ahead-of-us men let-us-send

וְיָשִׁבוּ אֹתָנוּ דָּבָר אֶת־ הַדֶּרֶךְ אֲשֶׁר נַעֲלֶה־ בָּהּ וְאֵת
and on-her we-will-go that the-route *** report us and-they-can-bring-back

הֶעָרִים אֲשֶׁר נָבֹא אֲלֵיהֶן׃ וַיִּיטַב בְּעֵינַי
in-eyes-of-me and-he-was-good (23) to-them we-will-come that the-towns

הַדָּבָר וָאֶקַּח מִכֶּם שְׁנֵים עָשָׂר אֲנָשִׁים אִישׁ אֶחָד לַשָּׁבֶט׃
from-the-tribe one man men ten two from-you so-I-selected the-idea

וַיִּפְנוּ וַיַּעֲלוּ הָהָרָה וַיָּבֹאוּ עַד־
to and-they-came the-hill-country and-they-went-up and-they-left (24)

נַחַל אֶשְׁכֹּל וַיְרַגְּלוּ אֹתָהּ׃ וַיִּקְחוּ בְיָדָם
in-hand-of-them and-they-took (25) her and-they-explored Eshcol Valley-of

מִפְּרִי הָאָרֶץ וַיּוֹרִדוּ אֵלֵינוּ וַיָּשִׁבוּ אֹתָנוּ דָבָר
report us and-they-gave to-us and-they-brought-down the-land from-fruit-of

וַיֹּאמְרוּ טוֹבָה הָאָרֶץ אֲשֶׁר־ יְהוָה אֱלֹהֵינוּ נֹתֵן לָנוּ׃ וְלֹא
but-not (26) to-us giving God-of-us Yahweh that the-land good and-they-said

אֲבִיתֶם לַעֲלֹת וַתַּמְרוּ אֶת־ פִּי יְהוָה אֱלֹהֵיכֶם׃
God-of-you Yahweh command-of *** and-you-rebelled to-go-up you-wanted

וַתֵּרָגְנוּ בְאָהֳלֵיכֶם וַתֹּאמְרוּ בְּשִׂנְאַת יְהוָה אֹתָנוּ
us Yahweh in-hate-of and-you-said in-tents-of-you and-you-grumbled (27)

הוֹצִיאָנוּ מֵאֶרֶץ מִצְרָיִם לָתֵת אֹתָנוּ בְּיַד הָאֱמֹרִי
the-Amorite into-hand-of us to-deliver Egypt from-land-of he-brought-us

לְהַשְׁמִידֵנוּ׃ אָנָה ׀ אֲנַחְנוּ עֹלִים אַחֵינוּ הֵמַסּוּ אֶת־
*** they-made-lose brothers-of-us ones-going we where? (28) to-destroy-us

לְבָבֵנוּ לֵאמֹר עַם גָּדוֹל וָרָם מִמֶּנּוּ עָרִים גְּדֹלֹת
large-ones cities than-us and-taller stronger people to-say heart-of-us

וּבְצוּרֹת בַּשָּׁמָיִם וְגַם־ בְּנֵי עֲנָקִים רָאִינוּ שָׁם׃ וָאֹמַר
then-I-said (29) there we-saw Anakites sons-of and-also to-the-skies and-walls

אֲלֵכֶם לֹא־ תַעַרְצוּן וְלֹא־ תִירְאוּן מֵהֶם׃ יְהוָה אֱלֹהֵיכֶם
God-of-you Yahweh (30) from-them you-fear and-not you-be-terrified not to-you

you, "You have reached the
hill country of the Amorites,
which the LORD our God is
giving us. 21See, the LORD your
God has given you the land.
Go up and take possession of it
as the LORD, the God of your
fathers, told you. Do not be
afraid; do not be discouraged."
22Then all of you came to me
and said, "Let us send men
ahead to spy out the land for
us and bring back a report
about the route we are to take
and the towns we will come
to."
23The idea seemed good to
me; so I selected twelve of you,
one man from each tribe.
24They left and went up into
the hill country, and came to
the Valley of Eshcol and explored it.
25Taking with them
some of the fruit of the land,
they brought it down to us
and reported, "It is a good
land that the LORD our God is
giving us."

Rebellion Against the LORD

26But you were unwilling to
go up; you rebelled against the
command of the LORD your
God. 27You grumbled in your
tents and said, "The LORD
hates us; so he brought us out
of Egypt to deliver us into the
hands of the Amorites to destroy us.
28Where can we go?
Our brothers have made us
lose heart. They say, 'The
people are stronger and taller
than we are; the cities are
large, with walls up to the sky.
We even saw the Anakites
there.'"
29Then I said to you, "Do not
be terrified; do not be afraid of
them. 30The LORD your God,

הַהֹלֵךְ לִפְנֵיכֶם הוּא יִלָּחֵם לָכֶם כְּכֹל אֲשֶׁר עָשָׂה אִתְּכֶם
for-you he-did that as-all for-you he-will-fight he before-you the-one-going

בְּמִצְרַיִם לְעֵינֵיכֶם׃ וּבַמִּדְבָּר אֲשֶׁר רָאִיתָ אֲשֶׁר
how you-saw where and-in-the-desert (31) before-eyes-of-you in-Egypt

נְשָׂאֲךָ יְהוָה אֱלֹהֶיךָ כַּאֲשֶׁר יִשָּׂא־אִישׁ אֶת־בְּנוֹ
son-of-him *** man he-carries just-as God-of-you Yahweh he-carried-you

בְּכָל־הַדֶּרֶךְ אֲשֶׁר הֲלַכְתֶּם עַד־בֹּאֲכֶם עַד־הַמָּקוֹם הַזֶּה׃
the-this the-place to to-reach-you until you-went that the-way on-all-of

וּבַדָּבָר הַזֶּה אֵינְכֶם מַאֲמִינִם בַּיהוָה
in-Yahweh ones-trusting not-you the-this in-spite-of-the-thing (32)

אֱלֹהֵיכֶם׃ הַהֹלֵךְ לִפְנֵיכֶם בַּדֶּרֶךְ לָתוּר לָכֶם
for-you to-search on-the-journey ahead-of-you the-one-going (33) God-of-you

מָקוֹם לַחֲנֹתְכֶם בָּאֵשׁ ׀ לַיְלָה לַרְאֹתְכֶם בַּדֶּרֶךְ אֲשֶׁר תֵּלְכוּ־
you-should-go that on-the-way to-show-you night in-the-fire to-camp-you place

בָהּ וּבֶעָנָן יוֹמָם׃ וַיִּשְׁמַע יְהוָה אֶת־קוֹל
sound-of *** Yahweh when-he-heard (34) by-day and-in-the-cloud on-her

דִּבְרֵיכֶם וַיִּקְצֹף וַיִּשָּׁבַע לֵאמֹר׃ אִם־יִרְאֶה אִישׁ
one he-will-see not (35) to-say and-he-swore then-he-was-angry words-of-you

בָּאֲנָשִׁים הָאֵלֶּה הַדּוֹר הָרָע הַזֶּה אֵת הָאָרֶץ הַטּוֹבָה
the-good the-land *** the-this the-evil the-generation the-these of-the-men

אֲשֶׁר נִשְׁבַּעְתִּי לָתֵת לַאֲבֹתֵיכֶם׃ זוּלָתִי כָּלֵב בֶּן־
son-of Caleb excepting-me (36) to-fathers-of-you to-give I-swore that

יְפֻנֶּה הוּא יִרְאֶנָּה וְלוֹ־אֶתֵּן אֶת־הָאָרֶץ אֲשֶׁר
that the-land *** I-will-give and-to-him he-will-see-her he Jephunneh

דָּרַךְ־בָּהּ וּלְבָנָיו יַעַן אֲשֶׁר מִלֵּא אַחֲרֵי
after he-was-wholehearted that because and-to-sons-of-him on-her he-sets-foot

יְהוָה׃ גַּם־בִּי הִתְאַנַּף יְהוָה בִּגְלַלְכֶם לֵאמֹר גַּם־
also to-say because-of-you Yahweh he-became-angry with-me also (37) Yahweh

אַתָּה לֹא־תָבֹא שָׁם׃ יְהוֹשֻׁעַ בִּן־נוּן הָעֹמֵד לְפָנֶיךָ
to-you the-one-assisting Nun son-of Joshua (38) there you-will-enter not you

הוּא יָבֹא שָׁמָּה אֹתוֹ חַזֵּק כִּי־הוּא יַנְחִלֶנָּה
he-will-lead-to-inherit-her he for encourage! him to-there he-will-enter he

אֶת־יִשְׂרָאֵל׃ וְטַפְּכֶם אֲשֶׁר אֲמַרְתֶּם לָבַז יִהְיֶה
he-would-be as-captive you-said that and-little-one-of-you (39) Israel ***

וּבְנֵיכֶם אֲשֶׁר לֹא־יָדְעוּ הַיּוֹם טוֹב וָרָע הֵמָּה יָבֹאוּ
they-will-enter they and-bad good the-day they-knew not who and-children-of-you

שָׁמָּה וְלָהֶם אֶתְּנֶנָּה וְהֵם יִירָשׁוּהָ׃
they-will-possess-her and-they I-will-give-her and-to-them to-there

who is going before you, will
fight for you, as he did for you
in Egypt, before your very
eyes, [31]and in the desert. There
you saw how the LORD your
God carried you, as a father
carries his son, all the way you
went until you reached this
place."

[32]In spite of this, you did not
trust in the LORD your God,
[33]who went ahead of you on
your journey, in fire by night
and in a cloud by day, to
search out places for you to
camp and to show you the
way you should go.

[34]When the LORD heard what
you said, he was angry and
solemnly swore: [35]"Not a man
of this evil generation shall see
the good land I swore to give
your forefathers, [36]except
Caleb son of Jephunneh. He
will see it, and I will give him
and his descendants the land
he set his feet on, because he
followed the LORD wholeheartedly."

[37]Because of you the LORD
became angry with me also
and said, "You shall not enter
it, either. [38]But your assistant,
Joshua son of Nun, will enter
it. Encourage him, because he
will lead Israel to inherit it.
[39]And the little ones that you
said would be taken captive,
your children who do not yet
know good from bad—they
will enter the land. I will give
it to them and they will take
possession of it. [40]But as for

וְאַתֶּם פְּנוּ לָכֶם וּסְעוּ הַמִּדְבָּרָה דֶּרֶךְ יַם־ סוּף׃
Reed Sea-of route-of to-the-desert and-set-out! to-you turn! but-you (40)

וַתַּעֲנוּ ׀ וַתֹּאמְרוּ אֵלַי חָטָאנוּ לַיהוָה אֲנַחְנוּ
we against-Yahweh we-sinned to-me and-you-said then-you-replied (41)

נַעֲלֶה וְנִלְחַמְנוּ כְּכֹל אֲשֶׁר־ צִוָּנוּ יְהוָה אֱלֹהֵינוּ
God-of-us Yahweh he-commanded-us that as-all and-we-will-fight we-will-go-up

וַתַּחְגְּרוּ אִישׁ אֶת־ כְּלֵי מִלְחַמְתּוֹ וַתָּהִינוּ לַעֲלֹת
to-go-up and-you-thought-easy war-of-him weapons-of *** each so-they-put-on

הָהָרָה׃ וַיֹּאמֶר יְהוָה אֵלַי אֱמֹר לָהֶם לֹא
not to-them tell! to-me Yahweh but-he-said (42) into-the-hill-country

תַעֲלוּ וְלֹא־ תִלָּחֲמוּ כִּי אֵינֶנִּי בְּקִרְבְּכֶם וְלֹא תִּנָּגְפוּ
you-be-defeated so-not in-midst-of-you not-I for you-fight and-not you-go-up

לִפְנֵי אֹיְבֵיכֶם׃ וָאֲדַבֵּר אֲלֵיכֶם וְלֹא שְׁמַעְתֶּם
you-listened but-not to-you so-I-told (43) being-enemies-of-you before

וַתַּמְרוּ אֶת־ פִּי יְהוָה וַתָּזִדוּ וַתַּעֲלוּ
and-you-went-up and-you-were-arrogant Yahweh command-of *** and-you-rebelled

הָהָרָה׃ וַיֵּצֵא הָאֱמֹרִי הַיֹּשֵׁב
the-one-living the-Amorite and-he-came-out (44) into-the-hill-country

בָּהָר הַהוּא לִקְרַאתְכֶם וַיִּרְדְּפוּ אֶתְכֶם כַּאֲשֶׁר תַּעֲשֶׂינָה
they-do just-as you and-they-chased to-oppose-you the-that in-the-hill

הַדְּבֹרִים וַיַּכְּתוּ אֶתְכֶם בְּשֵׂעִיר עַד־ חָרְמָה׃ וַתָּשֻׁבוּ
and-you-came-back (45) Hormah to from-Seir you and-they-beat the-bees

וַתִּבְכּוּ לִפְנֵי יְהוָה וְלֹא־ שָׁמַע יְהוָה בְּקֹלְכֶם וְלֹא
and-not to-sound-of-you Yahweh he-listened but-not Yahweh before and-you-wept

הֶאֱזִין אֲלֵיכֶם׃ וַתֵּשְׁבוּ בְקָדֵשׁ יָמִים רַבִּים כַּיָּמִים אֲשֶׁר
that as-the-days many days in-Kadesh so-you-stayed (46) to-you he-turned-ear

יְשַׁבְתֶּם׃ וַנֵּפֶן וַנִּסַּע הַמִּדְבָּרָה דֶּרֶךְ
route-of to-the-desert and-we-set-out then-we-turned-back (2:1) you-stayed

יַם־ סוּף כַּאֲשֶׁר דִּבֶּר יְהוָה אֵלָי וַנָּסָב אֶת־ הַר־
hill-of *** and-we-went-around to-me Yahweh he-directed just-as Reed Sea-of

שֵׂעִיר יָמִים רַבִּים׃ וַיֹּאמֶר יְהוָה אֵלַי לֵאמֹר׃ רַב־ לָכֶם
to-you enough (3) to-say to-me Yahweh and-he-said (2) many days Seir

סֹב אֶת־ הָהָר הַזֶּה פְּנוּ לָכֶם צָפֹנָה׃ וְאֶת־ הָעָם
the-people and (4) to-north to-you turn! the-this the-hill *** to-go-around

צַו לֵאמֹר אַתֶּם עֹבְרִים בִּגְבוּל אֲחֵיכֶם בְּנֵי־
sons-of brothers-of-you through-territory-of ones-passing you to-say order!

עֵשָׂו הַיֹּשְׁבִים בְּשֵׂעִיר וְיִירְאוּ מִכֶּם וְנִשְׁמַרְתֶּם
but-you-be-careful from-you and-they-will-fear in-Seir the-ones-living Esau

you, turn around and set out toward the desert along the route to the Red Sea.[a]"

[41]Then you replied, "We have sinned against the LORD. We will go up and fight, as the LORD our God commanded us." So every one of you put on his weapons, thinking it easy to go up into the hill country.

[42]But the LORD said to me, "Tell them, 'Do not go up and fight, because I will not be with you. You will be defeated by your enemies.' "

[43]So I told you, but you would not listen. You rebelled against the LORD's command and in your arrogance you marched up into the hill country. [44]The Amorites who lived in those hills came out against you; they chased you like a swarm of bees and beat you down from Seir all the way to Hormah. [45]You came back and wept before the LORD, but he paid no attention to your weeping and turned a deaf ear to you. [46]And so you stayed in Kadesh many days—all the time you spent there.

Wanderings in the Desert

2 Then we turned back and set out toward the desert along the route to the Red Sea,[b] as the LORD had directed me. For a long time we made our way around the hill country of Seir.

[2]Then the LORD said to me, [3]"You have made your way around this hill country long enough; now turn north. [4]Give the people these orders: 'You are about to pass through the territory of your brothers the descendants of Esau, who live in Seir. They will be afraid of you, but be very careful. [5]Do

[a]40 Hebrew *Yam Suph;* that is, Sea of Reeds
[b]1 Hebrew *Yam Suph;* that is, Sea of Reeds

מְאֹד׃ אַל־ תִּתְגָּרוּ בָם כִּי לֹא־ אֶתֵּן לָכֶם
to-you I-will-give not for with-them you-make-war not (5) very

מֵאַרְצָם עַד מִדְרַךְ כַּף־ רָגֶל כִּי־ יְרֻשָּׁה לְעֵשָׂו נָתַתִּי
I-gave of-Esau possession for foot sole-of step-of even from-land-of-them

אֶת־ הַר שֵׂעִיר׃ אֹכֶל תִּשְׁבְּרוּ מֵאִתָּם בַּכֶּסֶף
with-the-silver from-them you-buy food (6) Seir hill-country-of ***

וַאֲכַלְתֶּם וְגַם־ מַיִם תִּכְרוּ מֵאִתָּם בַּכֶּסֶף וּשְׁתִיתֶם׃
and-you-drink with-the-silver from-them you-buy waters and-also and-you-eat

כִּי יְהוָה אֱלֹהֶיךָ בֵּרַכְךָ בְּכֹל מַעֲשֵׂה יָדֶךָ
hand-of-you work-of in-all-of he-blessed-you God-of-you Yahweh for (7)

יָדַע לֶכְתְּךָ אֶת־ הַמִּדְבָּר הַגָּדֹל הַזֶּה זֶה ׀ אַרְבָּעִים שָׁנָה
year forty this the-this the-vast the-desert *** to-journey-you he-watched

יְהוָה אֱלֹהֶיךָ עִמָּךְ לֹא חָסַרְתָּ דָּבָר׃ וַנַּעֲבֹר מֵאֵת
by so-we-went-past (8) anything you-lacked not with-you God-of-you Yahweh

אַחֵינוּ בְנֵי־ עֵשָׂו הַיֹּשְׁבִים בְּשֵׂעִיר מִדֶּרֶךְ הָעֲרָבָה
the-Arabah from-road-of in-Seir the-ones-living Esau sons-of brothers-of-us

מֵאֵילַת וּמֵעֶצְיֹן גָּבֶר וַנֵּפֶן וַנַּעֲבֹר דֶּרֶךְ מִדְבַּר
desert-of road-of and-we-travelled and-we-turned Geber and-from-Ezion from-Elath

מוֹאָב׃ וַיֹּאמֶר יְהוָה אֵלַי אַל־ תָּצַר אֶת־ מוֹאָב וְאַל־ תִּתְגָּר
you-provoke and-not Moab *** you-harass not to-me Yahweh then-he-said (9) Moab

בָּם מִלְחָמָה כִּי לֹא־ אֶתֵּן לְךָ מֵאַרְצוֹ יְרֻשָּׁה כִּי
for possession from-land-of-him to-you I-will-give not for war with-them

לִבְנֵי־ לוֹט נָתַתִּי אֶת־ עָר יְרֻשָּׁה׃ הָאֵמִים לְפָנִים יָשְׁבוּ
they-lived before the-Emites (10) possession Ar *** I-gave Lot to-sons-of

בָהּ עַם גָּדוֹל וְרַב וָרָם כַּעֲנָקִים׃ רְפָאִים
Rephaites (11) as-the-Anakites and-tall and-numerous strong people in-her

יֵחָשְׁבוּ אַף־ הֵם כַּעֲנָקִים וְהַמֹּאָבִים יִקְרְאוּ
they-called but-the-Moabites as-the-Anakites they also they-were-considered

לָהֶם אֵמִים׃ וּבְשֵׂעִיר יָשְׁבוּ הַחֹרִים לְפָנִים וּבְנֵי
but-sons-of before the-Horites they-lived and-in-Seir (12) Emites to-them

עֵשָׂו יִירָשׁוּם וַיַּשְׁמִידוּם מִפְּנֵיהֶם
from-before-them and-they-destroyed-them they-drove-out-them Esau

וַיֵּשְׁבוּ תַּחְתָּם כַּאֲשֶׁר עָשָׂה יִשְׂרָאֵל לְאֶרֶץ
in-land-of Israel he-did just-as in-place-of-them and-they-settled

יְרֻשָּׁתוֹ אֲשֶׁר־ נָתַן יְהוָה לָהֶם׃ עַתָּה קֻמוּ וְעִבְרוּ
and-cross! get-up! now (13) to-them Yahweh he-gave that possession-of-him

לָכֶם אֶת־ נַחַל זָרֶד וַנַּעֲבֹר אֶת־ נַחַל זָרֶד׃
Zered Valley-of *** so-we-crossed Zered Valley-of *** for-you

not provoke them to war, for I will not give you any of their land, not even enough to put your foot on. I have given Esau the hill country of Seir as his own. [6]You are to pay them in silver for the food you eat and the water you drink.' "

[7]The LORD your God has blessed you in all the work of your hands. He has watched over your journey through this vast desert. These forty years the LORD your God has been with you, and you have not lacked anything.

[8]So we went on past our brothers the descendants of Esau, who live in Seir. We turned from the Arabah road, which comes up from Elath and Ezion Geber, and traveled along the desert road of Moab.

[9]Then the LORD said to me, "Do not harass the Moabites or provoke them to war, for I will not give you any part of their land. I have given Ar to the descendants of Lot as a possession."

[10](The Emites used to live there—a people strong and numerous, and as tall as the Anakites. [11]Like the Anakites, they too were considered Rephaites, but the Moabites called them Emites. [12]Horites used to live in Seir, but the descendants of Esau drove them out. They destroyed the Horites from before them and settled in their place, just as Israel did in the land the LORD gave them as their possession.)

[13]And the LORD said, "Now get up and cross the Zered Valley." So we crossed the valley.

*9 Most mss have *pathah* under the *aleph* (אַל).

וְהַיָּמִים אֲשֶׁר־הָלַכְנוּ מִקָּדֵשׁ בַּרְנֵעַ עַד אֲשֶׁר־עָבַרְנוּ אֶת־
*** we-crossed when until Barnea from-Kadesh we-left that and-the-days (14)

נַחַל זֶרֶד שְׁלֹשִׁים וּשְׁמֹנֶה שָׁנָה עַד־תֹּם כָּל־הַדּוֹר
the-generation entire-of to-perish then year and-eight thirty Zered Valley-of

אַנְשֵׁי הַמִּלְחָמָה מִקֶּרֶב הַמַּחֲנֶה כַּאֲשֶׁר נִשְׁבַּע יְהוָה לָהֶם׃
to-them Yahweh he-swore just-as the-camp from-among the-war men-of

וְגַם יַד־יְהוָה הָיְתָה בָּם לְהֻמָּם מִקֶּרֶב
from-among to-eliminate-them against-them she-was Yahweh hand-of and-also (15)

הַמַּחֲנֶה עַד תֻּמָּם׃ וַיְהִי כַאֲשֶׁר־תַּמּוּ כָּל־
all-of they-finished just-as was-he-was (16) to-finish-them until the-camp

אַנְשֵׁי הַמִּלְחָמָה לָמוּת מִקֶּרֶב הָעָם׃ וַיְדַבֵּר יְהוָה אֵלַי
to-me Yahweh then-he-spoke (17) the-people from-among to-die the-war men-of

לֵאמֹר׃ אַתָּה עֹבֵר הַיּוֹם אֶת־גְּבוּל מוֹאָב אֶת־עָר׃ וְקָרַבְתָּ
when-you-come (19) Ar *** Moab border-of *** the-day passing you (18) to-say

מוּל בְּנֵי עַמּוֹן אַל־תְּצֻרֵם וְאַל־תִּתְגָּר בָּם כִּי לֹא־
not for with-them you-make-war and-not you-harass-them not Ammon sons-of to

אֶתֵּן מֵאֶרֶץ בְּנֵי־עַמּוֹן לְךָ יְרֻשָּׁה כִּי לִבְנֵי־לוֹט
Lot to-sons-of for possession to-you Ammon sons-of from-land-of I-will-give

נְתַתִּיהָ יְרֻשָּׁה׃ אֶרֶץ־רְפָאִים תֵּחָשֵׁב אַף־הִוא
she also she-was-considered Rephaites land-of (20) possession I-gave-her

רְפָאִים יָשְׁבוּ־בָהּ לְפָנִים וְהָעַמֹּנִים יִקְרְאוּ לָהֶם
to-them they-called but-the-Ammonites before in-her they-lived Rephaites

זַמְזֻמִּים׃ עַם גָּדוֹל וְרַב וָרָם כָּעֲנָקִים
as-the-Anakites and-tall and-numerous strong people (21) Zamzummites

וַיַּשְׁמִידֵם יְהוָה מִפְּנֵיהֶם וַיִּירָשֻׁם
and-they-drove-out-them from-before-them Yahweh but-he-destroyed-them

וַיֵּשְׁבוּ תַחְתָּם׃ כַּאֲשֶׁר עָשָׂה לִבְנֵי עֵשָׂו
Esau for-sons-of he-did just-as (22) in-place-of-them and-they-settled

הַיֹּשְׁבִים בְּשֵׂעִיר אֲשֶׁר הִשְׁמִיד אֶת־הַחֹרִי מִפְּנֵיהֶם
from-before-them the-Horite *** he-destroyed when in-Seir the-ones-living

וַיִּירָשֻׁם וַיֵּשְׁבוּ תַחְתָּם עַד הַיּוֹם הַזֶּה׃
the-this the-day to in-place-of-them and-they settled and-they-drove-out-them

וְהָעַוִּים הַיֹּשְׁבִים בַּחֲצֵרִים עַד־עַזָּה כַּפְתֹּרִים
Caphtorites Gaza as-far-as in-villages the-ones-living and-the-Avvites (23)

הַיֹּצְאִים מִכַּפְתּוֹר הִשְׁמִידֻם וַיֵּשְׁבוּ
and-they-settled they-destroyed-them from-Caphtor the-ones-coming

תַחְתָּם׃ קוּמוּ סְּעוּ וְעִבְרוּ אֶת־נַחַל אַרְנֹן רְאֵה
see! Arnon Gorge-of *** and-cross! set-out! get-up! (24) in-place-of-them

[14]Thirty-eight years passed from the time we left Kadesh Barnea until we crossed the Zered Valley. By then, that entire generation of fighting men had perished from the camp, as the LORD had sworn to them. [15]The LORD's hand was against them until he had completely eliminated them from the camp.

[16]Now when the last of these fighting men among the people had died, [17]the LORD said to me, [18]"Today you are to pass by the region of Moab at Ar. [19]When you come to the Ammonites, do not harass them or provoke them to war, for I will not give you possession of any land belonging to the Ammonites. I have given it as a possession to the descendants of Lot."

[20](That too was considered a land of the Rephaites, who used to live there; but the Ammonites called them Zamzummites. [21]They were a people strong and numerous, and as tall as the Anakites. The LORD destroyed them from before the Ammonites, who drove them out and settled in their place. [22]The LORD had done the same for the descendants of Esau, who lived in Seir, when he destroyed the Horites from before them. They drove them out and have lived in their place to this day. [23]And as for the Avvites who lived in villages as far as Gaza, the Caphtorites coming out from Caphtor[c] destroyed them and settled in their place.)

[24]"Set out now and cross the

[c]23 That is, Crete

נָתַתִּי בְיָדְךָ אֶת־סִיחֹן מֶלֶךְ־חֶשְׁבּוֹן הָאֱמֹרִי וְאֶת־אַרְצוֹ
land-of-him and the-Amorite Heshbon king-of Sihon *** into-hand-of-you I-gave

הָחֵל רָשׁ וְהִתְגָּר בּוֹ מִלְחָמָה׃ הַיּוֹם הַזֶּה אָחֵל
I-will-begin the-this the-day (25) battle with-him and-fight! possess! begin!

תֵּת פַּחְדְּךָ וְיִרְאָתְךָ עַל־פְּנֵי הָעַמִּים תַּחַת כָּל־
all-of under the-nations faces-of on and-fear-of-you terror-of-you to-put

הַשָּׁמָיִם אֲשֶׁר יִשְׁמְעוּן שִׁמְעֲךָ וְרָגְזוּ
and-they-will-tremble report-of-you they-will-hear that the-heavens

וְחָלוּ מִפָּנֶיךָ׃ וָאֶשְׁלַח מַלְאָכִים
messengers and-I-sent (26) from-presence-of-you and-they-will-be-in-anguish

מִמִּדְבַּר קְדֵמוֹת אֶל־סִיחוֹן מֶלֶךְ חֶשְׁבּוֹן דִּבְרֵי שָׁלוֹם לֵאמֹר׃
to-say peace words-of Heshbon king-of Sihon to Kedemoth from-desert-of

אֶעְבְּרָה בְאַרְצֶךָ בַּדֶּרֶךְ בַּדֶּרֶךְ אֵלֵךְ
I-will-stay on-the-road on-the-road through-land-of-you let-me-pass (27)

לֹא אָסוּר יָמִין וּשְׂמֹאול׃ אֹכֶל בַּכֶּסֶף תַּשְׁבִּרֵנִי
you-sell-me for-the-silver food (28) or-left right I-will-turn not

וְאָכַלְתִּי וּמַיִם בַּכֶּסֶף תִּתֶּן־לִי וְשָׁתִיתִי רַק
only so-I-can-drink to-me you-sell for-the-silver and-waters so-I-can-eat

אֶעְבְּרָה בְרַגְלָי׃ כַּאֲשֶׁר עָשׂוּ־לִי בְּנֵי עֵשָׂו
Esau sons-of for-me they-did just-as (29) on-feet-of-me let-me-pass-through

הַיֹּשְׁבִים בְּשֵׂעִיר וְהַמּוֹאָבִים הַיֹּשְׁבִים בְּעָר עַד אֲשֶׁר־
when until in-Ar the-ones-living and-the-Moabites in-Seir the-ones-living

אֶעֱבֹר אֶת־הַיַּרְדֵּן אֶל־הָאָרֶץ אֲשֶׁר־יְהוָה אֱלֹהֵינוּ נֹתֵן לָנוּ׃
to-us giving God-of-us Yahweh that the-land to the-Jordan *** I-cross

וְלֹא אָבָה סִיחֹן מֶלֶךְ חֶשְׁבּוֹן הַעֲבִרֵנוּ בּוֹ כִּי־
for through-him to-let-pass-us Heshbon king-of Sihon he-allowed but-not (30)

הִקְשָׁה יְהוָה אֱלֹהֶיךָ אֶת־רוּחוֹ וְאִמֵּץ
and-he-made-obstinate spirit-of-him *** God-of-you Yahweh he-made-stubborn

אֶת־לְבָבוֹ לְמַעַן תִּתּוֹ בְיָדְךָ כַּיּוֹם הַזֶּה׃
the-this as-the-day into-hand-of-you to-give-him in-order heart-of-him ***

וַיֹּאמֶר יְהוָה אֵלַי רְאֵה הַחִלֹּתִי תֵּת לְפָנֶיךָ אֶת־סִיחֹן
Sihon *** before-you to-deliver I-began see! to-me Yahweh and-he-said (31)

וְאֶת־אַרְצוֹ הָחֵל רָשׁ לָרֶשֶׁת אֶת־אַרְצוֹ׃ וַיֵּצֵא
when-he-came (32) land-of-him *** to-possess conquer! begin! land-of-him and

סִיחֹן לִקְרָאתֵנוּ הוּא וְכָל־עַמּוֹ לַמִּלְחָמָה יָהְצָה׃
at-Jahaz in-the-battle army-of-him and-all-of he to-meet-us Sihon

וַיִּתְּנֵהוּ יְהוָה אֱלֹהֵינוּ לְפָנֵינוּ וַנַּךְ אֹתוֹ וְאֶת־
and him and-we-struck before-us God-of-us Yahweh then-he-delivered-him (33)

Arnon Gorge. See, I have given into your hand Sihon the Amorite, king of Heshbon, and his country. Begin to take possession of it and engage him in battle.
25This very day I will begin to put the terror and fear of you on all the nations under heaven. They will hear reports of you and will tremble and be in anguish because of you."

Defeat of Sihon King of Heshbon

26From the desert of Kedemoth I sent messengers to Sihon king of Heshbon offering peace and saying,
27"Let us pass through your country. We will stay on the main road; we will not turn aside to the right or to the left.
28Sell us food to eat and water to drink for their price in silver. Only let us pass through on foot—
29as the descendants of Esau, who live in Seir, and the Moabites, who live in Ar, did for us—until we cross the Jordan into the land the LORD our God is giving us."
30But Sihon king of Heshbon refused to let us pass through. For the LORD your God had made his spirit stubborn and his heart obstinate in order to give him into your hands, as he has now done.

31The LORD said to me, "See, I have begun to deliver Sihon and his country over to you. Now begin to conquer and possess his land."

32When Sihon and all his army came out to meet us in battle at Jahaz,
33the LORD our God delivered him over to us

בָּנָו וְאֶת־ כָּל־ עַמּוֹ׃ וַנִּלְכֹּד אֶת־ כָּל־ עָרָיו
towns-of-him all-of *** and-we-took (34) army-of-him whole-of and sons-of-him

בָּעֵת הַהִוא וַנַּחֲרֵם אֶת־ כָּל־ עִיר מְתִם וְהַנָּשִׁים
and-the-women men city every-of *** and-we-destroyed the-that at-the-time

וְהַטָּף לֹא הִשְׁאַרְנוּ שָׂרִיד׃ רַק הַבְּהֵמָה בָּזַזְנוּ לָנוּ
for-us we-carried-off the-stock but (35) survivor we-left not and-the-child

וּשְׁלַל הֶעָרִים אֲשֶׁר לָכָדְנוּ׃ מֵעֲרֹעֵר אֲשֶׁר עַל־ שְׂפַת־
rim-of on that from-Aroer (36) we-captured that the-towns and-plunder-of

נַחַל אַרְנֹן וְהָעִיר אֲשֶׁר בַּנַּחַל וְעַד־ הַגִּלְעָד לֹא הָיְתָה
she-was not the-Gilead even-to in-the-Gorge that and-the-town Arnon Gorge-of

קִרְיָה אֲשֶׁר שָׂגְבָה מִמֶּנּוּ אֶת־ הַכֹּל נָתַן יְהוָה אֱלֹהֵינוּ
God-of-us Yahweh he-gave the-all *** for-us she-was-too-strong that town

לְפָנֵינוּ׃ רַק אֶל־ אֶרֶץ בְּנֵי־ עַמּוֹן לֹא קָרָבְתָּ כָּל־ יַד
part-of any-of you-encroached not Ammon sons-of land-of on but (37) before-us

נַחַל יַבֹּק וְעָרֵי הָהָר וְכֹל אֲשֶׁר־ צִוָּה יְהוָה
Yahweh he-commanded that and-all the-hill or-cities-of Jabbok course-of

אֱלֹהֵינוּ׃ וַנֵּפֶן וַנַּעַל דֶּרֶךְ הַבָּשָׁן וַיֵּצֵא
and-he-came the-Bashan road-of and-we-went-up next-we-turned (3:1) God-of-us

עוֹג מֶלֶךְ־ הַבָּשָׁן לִקְרָאתֵנוּ הוּא וְכָל־ עַמּוֹ לַמִּלְחָמָה
in-the-battle army-of-him and-whole-of he to-meet-us the-Bashan king-of Og

אֶדְרֶעִי׃ וַיֹּאמֶר יְהוָה אֵלַי אַל־ תִּירָא אֹתוֹ כִּי בְיָדְךָ
into-hand-of-you for him you-fear not to-me Yahweh and-he-said (2) Edrei

נָתַתִּי אֹתוֹ וְאֶת־ כָּל־ עַמּוֹ וְאֶת־ אַרְצוֹ וְעָשִׂיתָ לּוֹ
to-him so-you-do land-of-him and army-of-him whole-of and him I-handed

כַּאֲשֶׁר עָשִׂיתָ לְסִיחֹן מֶלֶךְ הָאֱמֹרִי אֲשֶׁר יוֹשֵׁב בְּחֶשְׁבּוֹן׃
in-Heshbon reigning who the-Arorite king-of to-Sihon you-did just-as

וַיִּתֵּן יְהוָה אֱלֹהֵינוּ בְּיָדֵנוּ גַּם אֶת־ עוֹג מֶלֶךְ־
king-of Og *** also into-hand-of-us God-of-us Yahweh so-he-gave (3)

הַבָּשָׁן וְאֶת־ כָּל־ עַמּוֹ וַנַּכֵּהוּ עַד־ בִּלְתִּי הִשְׁאִיר־
he-remained not until and-we-struck-him army-of-him all-of and the-Bashan

לוֹ שָׂרִיד׃ וַנִּלְכֹּד אֶת־ כָּל־ עָרָיו בָּעֵת הַהִוא
the-that at-the-time cities-of-him all-of *** and-we-took (4) survivor to-him

לֹא הָיְתָה קִרְיָה אֲשֶׁר לֹא־לָקַחְנוּ מֵאִתָּם שִׁשִּׁים עִיר כָּל־ חֶבֶל
region-of whole-of city sixty from-with-them we-took not that city she-was not

אַרְגֹּב מַמְלֶכֶת עוֹג בַּבָּשָׁן׃ כָּל־ אֵלֶּה עָרִים בְּצֻרוֹת
ones-fortified cities these all-of (5) in-the-Bashan Og kingdom-of Argob

חוֹמָה גְבֹהָה דְּלָתַיִם וּבְרִיחַ לְבַד מֵעָרֵי הַפְּרָזִי הַרְבֵּה מְאֹד׃
very to-be-many the-villager from-cities-of apart and-bar gates high wall

and we struck him down, together with his sons and his
whole army. [34]At that time we
took all his towns and completely destroyed[d] them—
men, women and children.
We left no survivors. [35]But the
livestock and the plunder from
the towns we had captured we
carried off for ourselves.
[36]From Aroer on the rim of the
Arnon Gorge, and from the
town in the gorge, even as far
as Gilead, not one town was
too strong for us. The LORD our
God gave us all of them. [37]But
in accordance with the command of the LORD our God,
you did not encroach on any
of the land of the Ammonites,
neither the land along the
course of the Jabbok nor that
around the towns in the hills.

Defeat of Og King of Bashan

3 Next we turned and went
up along the road toward
Bashan, and Og king of Bashan with his whole army
marched out to meet us in battle at Edrei. [2]The LORD said to
me, "Do not be afraid of him,
for I have handed him over to
you with his whole army and
his land. Do to him what you
did to Sihon king of the Amorites, who reigned in Heshbon."
[3]So the LORD our God also
gave into our hands Og king
of Bashan and all his army. We
struck them down, leaving no
survivors. [4]At that time we
took all his cities. There was
not one of the sixty cities that
we did not take from them—
the whole region of Argob,
Og's kingdom in Bashan. [5]All
these cities were fortified with
high walls and with gates and
bars, and there were also a
great many unwalled villages.

[d]34 The Hebrew term refers to the irrevocable giving over of things or persons to the LORD, often by totally destroying them.

°33 ק בניו

וַנַּחֲרֵם אוֹתָם כַּאֲשֶׁר עָשִׂינוּ לְסִיחֹן מֶלֶךְ חֶשְׁבּוֹן הַחֲרֵם
to-destroy Heshbon king-of to-Sihon we-did just-as them and-we-destroyed (6)

כָּל־ עִיר מְתִם הַנָּשִׁים וְהַטָּף׃ וְכָל־ הַבְּהֵמָה
the-livestock but-all-of (7) and-the-child the-women men city every-of

וּשְׁלַל הֶעָרִים בַּזּוֹנוּ לָנוּ׃ וַנִּקַּח בָּעֵת
at-the-time so-we-took (8) for-us we-carried-off the-cities and-plunder-of

הַהִוא אֶת־ הָאָרֶץ מִיַּד שְׁנֵי מַלְכֵי הָאֱמֹרִי אֲשֶׁר בְּעֵבֶר
on-east-of who the-Amorite kings-of two-of from-hand-of the-land *** the-that

הַיַּרְדֵּן מִנַּחַל אַרְנֹן עַד־ הַר חֶרְמוֹן׃ צִידֹנִים
Sidonians (9) Hermon Mount-of as-far-as Arnon from-Gorge-of the-Jordan

יִקְרְאוּ לְחֶרְמוֹן שִׂרְיֹן וְהָאֱמֹרִי יִקְרְאוּ־ לוֹ שְׂנִיר׃ כֹּל ׀
all-of (10) Senir to-him they-call and-the-Amorite Sirion to-Hermon they-call

עָרֵי הַמִּישֹׁר וְכָל־ הַגִּלְעָד וְכָל־ הַבָּשָׁן עַד־
as-far-as the-Bashan and-all-of the-Gilead and-all-of the-plateau towns-of

סַלְכָה וְאֶדְרֶעִי עָרֵי מַמְלֶכֶת עוֹג בַּבָּשָׁן׃ כִּי רַק־ עוֹג
Og only now (11) in-the-Bashan Og kingdom-of towns-of and-Edrei Salecah

מֶלֶךְ הַבָּשָׁן נִשְׁאַר מִיֶּתֶר הָרְפָאִים הִנֵּה עַרְשׂוֹ
bed-of-him see! the-Rephaites from-remnant-of he-was-left the-Bashan king-of

עֶרֶשׂ בַּרְזֶל הֲלֹה הִוא בְּרַבַּת בְּנֵי עַמּוֹן תֵּשַׁע אַמּוֹת אָרְכָּהּ
length-of-her cubits nine Ammon sons-of in-Rabbah-of she not? iron bed-of

וְאַרְבַּע אַמּוֹת רָחְבָּהּ בְּאַמַּת־ אִישׁ׃ וְאֶת־ הָאָרֶץ הַזֹּאת
the-this the-land and (12) man by-forearm-of width-of-her cubits and-four

יָרַשְׁנוּ בָּעֵת הַהִוא מֵעֲרֹעֵר אֲשֶׁר־ עַל־ נַחַל אַרְנֹן וַחֲצִי
and-half-of Arnon Gorge-of by that from-Aroer the-that at-the-time we-took

הַר־ הַגִּלְעָד וְעָרָיו נָתַתִּי לָרְאוּבֵנִי*
to-the-Reubenite I-gave and-towns-of-him the-Gilead hill-country-of

וְלַגָּדִי׃ וְיֶתֶר הַגִּלְעָד וְכָל־ הַבָּשָׁן מַמְלֶכֶת
kingdom-of the-Bashan and-all-of the-Gilead and-rest-of (13) and-to-the-Gadite

עוֹג נָתַתִּי לַחֲצִי שֵׁבֶט הַמְנַשֶּׁה כֹּל חֶבֶל הָאַרְגֹּב
the-Argob region-of whole-of the-Manasseh tribe-of to-half-of I-gave Og

לְכָל־ הַבָּשָׁן הַהוּא יִקָּרֵא אֶרֶץ רְפָאִים׃ יָאִיר
Jair (14) Rephaites land-of he-was-called the-this the-Bashan in-all-of

בֶּן־ מְנַשֶּׁה לָקַח אֶת־ כָּל־ חֶבֶל אַרְגֹּב עַד־ גְּבוּל
border-of as-far-as Argob region-of whole-of *** he-took Manasseh son-of

הַגְּשׁוּרִי וְהַמַּעֲכָתִי וַיִּקְרָא אֹתָם עַל־ שְׁמוֹ אֶת־
*** name-of-him by them and-he-called and-the-Maacathite the-Geshurite

הַבָּשָׁן חַוֹּת יָאִיר עַד הַיּוֹם הַזֶּה׃ וּלְמָכִיר נָתַתִּי אֶת־
*** I-gave and-to-Makir (15) the-this the-day to Jair Havvoth the-Bashan

6We completely destroyed[e]
them, as we had done with Sihon king of Heshbon, de-
stroying[e] every city—men,
women and children. 7But all
the livestock and the plunder
from their cities we carried off
for ourselves.
8So at that time we took from
these two kings of the Amorites the territory east of the
Jordan, from the Arnon Gorge
as far as Mount Hermon.
9(Hermon is called Sirion by
the Sidonians; the Amorites
call it Senir.) 10We took all the
towns on the plateau, and all
Gilead, and all Bashan as far as
Salecah and Edrei, towns of
Og's kingdom in Bashan.
11(Only Og king of Bashan was
left of the remnant of the Rephaites. His bed[f] was made of
iron and was more than thirteen feet long and six feet
wide.[g] It is still in Rabbah of
the Ammonites.)

Division of the Land

12Of the land that we took
over at that time, I gave the
Reubenites and the Gadites
the territory north of Aroer by
the Arnon Gorge, including
half the hill country of Gilead,
together with its towns. 13The
rest of Gilead and also all of
Bashan, the kingdom of Og, I
gave to the half tribe of
Manasseh. (The whole region
of Argob in Bashan used to be
known as a land of the Rephaites.) 14Jair, a descendant of
Manasseh, took the whole region of Argob as far as the border of the Geshurites and the
Maacathites; it was named after him, so that to this day Bashan is called Havvoth Jair.[h]
15And I gave Gilead to Makir.

[e]6 The Hebrew term refers to the irrevocable giving over of things or persons to the LORD, often by totally destroying them.
[f]11 Or *sarcophagus*
[g]11 Hebrew *nine cubits long and four cubits wide* (about 4 meters long and 1.8 meters wide)
[h]14 Or *called the settlements of Jair*

*12 Most mss have no *qibbuts* under the *resh* (לָרְאוּ׳).

הַגִּלְעָד׃ וְלָרֽאוּבֵנִי וְלַגָּדִי נָתַתִּי מִן־ הַגִּלְעָד
the-Gilead from I-gave and-to-the-Gadite but-to-the-Reubenite (16) the-Gilead

וְעַד־ נַחַל אַרְנֹן תּוֹךְ הַנַּחַל וּגְבֻל וְעַד יַבֹּק הַנַּחַל
the-River Jabbok and-to also-border the-gorge middle-of Arnon Gorge-of and-to

גְּבוּל בְּנֵי עַמּוֹן׃ וְהָעֲרָבָה וְהַיַּרְדֵּן וּגְבֻל
and-border and-the-Jordan and-the-Arabah (17) Ammon sons-of border-of

מִכִּנֶּרֶת וְעַד יָם הָעֲרָבָה יָם הַמֶּלַח תַּחַת אַשְׁדֹּת
slopes-of below the-Salt Sea-of the-Arabah Sea-of even-to from-Kinnereth

הַפִּסְגָּה מִזְרָחָה׃ וָאֲצַו אֶתְכֶם בָּעֵת הַהִוא לֵאמֹר
to-say the-that at-the-time you and-I-commanded (18) on-east the-Pisgah

יְהוָה אֱלֹהֵיכֶם נָתַן לָכֶם אֶת־ הָאָרֶץ הַזֹּאת לְרִשְׁתָּהּ
to-possess-her the-this the-land *** to-you he-gave God-of-you Yahweh

חֲלוּצִים תַּעַבְרוּ לִפְנֵי אֲחֵיכֶם בְּנֵי־ יִשְׂרָאֵל כָּל־
all-of Israel sons-of brothers-of-you ahead-of you-cross-over men-being-armed

בְּנֵי־ חָיִל׃ רַק נְשֵׁיכֶם וְטַפְּכֶם וּמִקְנֵכֶם
and-stock-of-you and-child-of-you wives-of-you however (19) able men-of

יָדַעְתִּי כִּי־ מִקְנֶה רַב לָכֶם יֵשְׁבוּ בְּעָרֵיכֶם אֲשֶׁר נָתַתִּי
I-gave that in-towns-of-you they-may-stay to-you much stock that I-know

לָכֶם׃ עַד אֲשֶׁר־ יָנִיחַ יְהוָה ׀ לַאֲחֵיכֶם כָּכֶם
as-you to-brothers-of-you Yahweh he-gives-rest when until (20) to-you

וְיָרְשׁוּ גַם־ הֵם אֶת־ הָאָרֶץ אֲשֶׁר יְהוָה אֱלֹהֵיכֶם נֹתֵן
giving God-of-you Yahweh that the-land *** they also and-they-take-over

לָהֶם בְּעֵבֶר הַיַּרְדֵּן וְשַׁבְתֶּם אִישׁ לִירֻשָּׁתוֹ
to-possession-of-him each then-you-may-go-back the-Jordan on-across to-them

אֲשֶׁר נָתַתִּי לָכֶם׃ וְאֶת־יְהוֹשׁוּעַ צִוֵּיתִי בָּעֵת הַהִוא לֵאמֹר
to-say the-that at-the-time I-commanded Joshua and (21) to-you I-gave that

עֵינֶיךָ הָרֹאֹת אֵת כָּל־אֲשֶׁר עָשָׂה יְהוָה אֱלֹהֵיכֶם לִשְׁנֵי
to-two-of God-of-you Yahweh he-did that all *** the-ones-seeing eyes-of-you

הַמְּלָכִים הָאֵלֶּה כֵּן־ יַעֲשֶׂה יְהוָה לְכָל־ הַמַּמְלָכוֹת אֲשֶׁר אַתָּה
you that the-kingdoms to-all-of Yahweh he-will-do same the-these the-kings

עֹבֵר שָׁמָּה׃ לֹא תִּירָאוּם כִּי יְהוָה אֱלֹהֵיכֶם הוּא
he God-of-you Yahweh for you-fear-them not (22) to there ones-going

הַנִּלְחָם לָכֶם׃ וָאֶתְחַנַּן אֶל־ יְהוָה בָּעֵת הַהִוא
the-that at-the-time Yahweh with and-I-pleaded (23) for-you the-one-fighting

לֵאמֹר׃ אֲדֹנָי יְהוִה אַתָּה הַחִלּוֹתָ לְהַרְאוֹת אֶת־ עַבְדְּךָ אֶת־
*** servant-of-you *** to-show you-began you Yahweh Lord (24) to-say

גָּדְלְךָ וְאֶת־ יָדְךָ הַחֲזָקָה אֲשֶׁר מִי־ אֵל בַּשָּׁמַיִם
in-the-heavens god what? for the-strong hand-of-you and greatness-of-you

16 But to the Reubenites and
the Gadites I gave the territory
extending from Gilead down
to the Arnon Gorge (the middle of the gorge being the border) and out to the Jabbok River, which is the border of the
Ammonites. 17 Its western border was the Jordan in the Arabah, from Kinnereth to the Sea of the Arabah (the Salt Sea[f]), below the slopes of Pisgah.
18 I commanded you at that
time: "The LORD your God has given you this land to take possession of it. But all your able-bodied men, armed for battle, must cross over ahead of your brother Israelites.
19 However, your wives, your children and your livestock (I know you have much livestock) may stay in the towns I have given you, 20 until the
LORD gives rest to your brothers as he has to you, and they too have taken over the land that the LORD your God is giving them, across the Jordan. After that, each of you may go back to the possession I have given you."

Moses Forbidden to Cross the Jordan

21 At that time I commanded
Joshua: "You have seen with your own eyes all that the LORD your God has done to these two kings. The LORD will do the same to all the kingdoms over there where you are going. 22 Do not be afraid of
them; the LORD your God himself will fight for you."
23 At that time I pleaded with
the LORD: 24 "O Sovereign
LORD, you have begun to show to your servant your greatness and your strong hand. For what god is there in heaven or

[f] 17 That is, the Dead Sea

וּבָאָרֶץ אֲשֶׁר־ יַעֲשֶׂה כְמַעֲשֶׂיךָ וְכִגְבוּרֹתֶךָ׃
or-as-mighty-works-of-you as-deeds-of-you he-can-do who or-on-the-earth

אֶעְבְּרָה־ נָּא וְאֶרְאֶה אֶת־ הָאָרֶץ הַטּוֹבָה אֲשֶׁר בְּעֵבֶר
on-beyond that the-good the-land *** so-I-may-see now! let-me-go-over (25)

הַיַּרְדֵּן הָהָר הַטּוֹב הַזֶּה וְהַלְּבָנֹן׃
and-the-Lebanon the-that the-fine the-hill-country the-Jordan

וַיִּתְעַבֵּר יְהוָה בִּי לְמַעַנְכֶם וְלֹא שָׁמַע אֵלָי
to-me he-listened and-not because-of-you with-me Yahweh but-he-was-angry (26)

וַיֹּאמֶר יְהוָה אֵלַי רַב־ לָךְ אַל־ תּוֹסֶף דַּבֵּר אֵלַי עוֹד
anymore to-me to-speak you-repeat not to-you enough to-me Yahweh and-he-said

בַּדָּבָר הַזֶּה׃ עֲלֵה ׀ רֹאשׁ הַפִּסְגָּה וְשָׂא עֵינֶיךָ
eyes-of-you and-lift! the-Pisgah top-of go-up! (27) the-this about-the-matter

יָמָּה וְצָפֹנָה וְתֵימָנָה וּמִזְרָחָה וּרְאֵה בְעֵינֶיךָ
with-eyes-of-you and-look! and-to-east and-to-south and-to-north to-west

כִּי־ לֹא תַעֲבֹר אֶת־ הַיַּרְדֵּן הַזֶּה׃ וְצַו אֶת־
*** but-commission! (28) the-this the-Jordan *** you-will-cross not since

יְהוֹשֻׁעַ וְחַזְּקֵהוּ וְאַמְּצֵהוּ כִּי־ הוּא יַעֲבֹר לִפְנֵי
before he-will-cross he for and-strengthen-him! and-encourage-him! Joshua

הָעָם הַזֶּה וְהוּא יַנְחִיל אוֹתָם אֶת־ הָאָרֶץ אֲשֶׁר
that the-land *** them he-will-make-inherit and-he the-this the-people

תִּרְאֶה׃ וַנֵּשֶׁב בַּגָּיְא מוּל בֵּית פְּעוֹר׃ וְעַתָּה
and-now (4:1) Peor Beth near in-the-valley so-we-stayed (29) you-will-see

יִשְׂרָאֵל שְׁמַע אֶל־ הַחֻקִּים וְאֶל־ הַמִּשְׁפָּטִים אֲשֶׁר אָנֹכִי מְלַמֵּד אֶתְכֶם
you teaching I that the-laws and-to the-decrees to listen! Israel

לַעֲשׂוֹת לְמַעַן תִּחְיוּ וּבָאתֶם וִירִשְׁתֶּם אֶת־ הָאָרֶץ
the-land *** and-you-may-possess and-you-may-go-in you-may-live so-that to-do

אֲשֶׁר יְהוָה אֱלֹהֵי אֲבֹתֵיכֶם נֹתֵן לָכֶם׃ לֹא תֹסִפוּ עַל־ הַדָּבָר
the-word to you-add not (2) to-you giving fathers-of-you God-of Yahweh that

אֲשֶׁר אָנֹכִי מְצַוֶּה אֶתְכֶם וְלֹא תִגְרְעוּ מִמֶּנּוּ לִשְׁמֹר אֶת־ מִצְוֹת
commands-of *** to-keep from-him you-subtract and-not you commanding I that

יְהוָה אֱלֹהֵיכֶם אֲשֶׁר אָנֹכִי מְצַוֶּה אֶתְכֶם׃ עֵינֵיכֶם הָרֹאֹת אֵת
*** the-ones-seeing eyes-of-you (3) you giving I that God-of-you Yahweh

אֲשֶׁר־ עָשָׂה יְהוָה בְּבַעַל פְּעוֹר כִּי כָל־ הָאִישׁ אֲשֶׁר הָלַךְ אַחֲרֵי
after he-followed who the-one every-of that Peor at-Baal Yahweh he-did what

בַעַל־ פְּעוֹר הִשְׁמִידוֹ יְהוָה אֱלֹהֶיךָ מִקִּרְבֶּךָ׃ וְאַתֶּם
but-you (4) from-among-you God-of-you Yahweh he-destroyed-him Peor Baal-of

הַדְּבֵקִים בַּיהוָה אֱלֹהֵיכֶם חַיִּים כֻּלְּכֶם הַיּוֹם׃
the-day all-of-you alive-ones God-of-you to-Yahweh the-ones-holding

on earth who can do the deeds
and mighty works you do?
25Let me go over and see the
good land beyond the Jor-
dan—that fine hill country and
Lebanon."
26But because of you the
LORD was angry with me and
would not listen to me. "That
is enough," the LORD said. "Do
not speak to me anymore
about this matter. 27Go up to
the top of Pisgah and look
west and north and south and
east. Look at the land with
your own eyes, since you are
not going to cross this Jordan.
28But commission Joshua, and
encourage and strengthen
him, for he will lead this
people across and will cause
them to inherit the land that
you will see." 29So we stayed
in the valley near Beth Peor.

Obedience Commanded

4 Hear now, O Israel, the
decrees and laws I am
about to teach you. Follow
them so that you may live and
may go in and take possession
of the land that the LORD, the
God of your fathers, is giving
you. 2Do not add to what I
command you and do not sub-
tract from it, but keep the commands of the LORD your God
that I give you.
3You saw with your own
eyes what the LORD did at Baal
Peor. The LORD your God destroyed from among you
everyone who followed the
Baal of Peor, 4but all of you
who held fast to the LORD your
God are still alive today.

רְאֵה ׀ לִמַּדְתִּי אֶתְכֶם חֻקִּים וּמִשְׁפָּטִים כַּאֲשֶׁר צִוַּנִי יְהוָה
Yahweh he-commanded-me just-as and-laws decrees you I-taught see! (5)

אֱלֹהָי לַעֲשׂוֹת כֵּן בְּקֶרֶב הָאָרֶץ אֲשֶׁר אַתֶּם בָּאִים שָׁמָּה
to-there ones-entering you that the-land with-in so to-do God-of-me

לְרִשְׁתָּהּ׃ וּשְׁמַרְתֶּם וַעֲשִׂיתֶם כִּי הִוא חָכְמַתְכֶם
wisdom-of-you this for and-you-observe and-you-be-careful (6) to-possess-her

וּבִינַתְכֶם לְעֵינֵי הָעַמִּים אֲשֶׁר יִשְׁמְעוּן אֵת
*** they-will-hear who the-nations before-eyes-of and-understanding-of-you

כָּל־ הַחֻקִּים הָאֵלֶּה וְאָמְרוּ רַק עַם־ חָכָם
wise people surely and-they-will-say the-these the-decrees all-of

וְנָבוֹן הַגּוֹי הַגָּדוֹל הַזֶּה׃ כִּי מִי־ גוֹי גָּדוֹל
great nation what? for (7) the-this the-great the-nation and-understanding

אֲשֶׁר־ לוֹ אֱלֹהִים קְרֹבִים אֵלָיו כַּיהוָה אֱלֹהֵינוּ בְּכָל־ קָרְאֵנוּ
to-pray-us when-ever-of God-of-us as-Yahweh to-him ones-near gods to-him that

אֵלָיו׃ וּמִי גּוֹי גָּדוֹל אֲשֶׁר־ לוֹ חֻקִּים וּמִשְׁפָּטִים צַדִּיקִם
righteous-ones and-laws decrees to-him that great nation and-what? (8) to-him

כְּכֹל הַתּוֹרָה הַזֹּאת אֲשֶׁר אָנֹכִי נֹתֵן לִפְנֵיכֶם הַיּוֹם׃ רַק
only (9) the-day before-you setting I that the-this the-law as-all-of

הִשָּׁמֶר לְךָ וּשְׁמֹר נַפְשְׁךָ מְאֹד פֶּן־ תִּשְׁכַּח אֶת־
*** you-forget so-not closely self-of-you and watch! to-you be-careful!

הַדְּבָרִים אֲשֶׁר־ רָאוּ עֵינֶיךָ וּפֶן־ יָסוּרוּ מִלְּבָבְךָ
from-heart-of-you they-slip and-so-not eyes-of-you they-saw that the-things

כֹּל יְמֵי חַיֶּיךָ וְהוֹדַעְתָּם לְבָנֶיךָ וְלִבְנֵי
and-to sons-of to-sons-of-you and-you-teach-them lives-of-you days-of all-of

בָנֶיךָ׃ יוֹם אֲשֶׁר עָמַדְתָּ לִפְנֵי יְהוָה אֱלֹהֶיךָ בְּחֹרֵב
at-Horeb God-of-you Yahweh before you-stood that day (10) sons-of-you

בֶּאֱמֹר יְהוָה אֵלַי הַקְהֶל־ לִי אֶת־ הָעָם וְאַשְׁמִעֵם
so-I-may-tell-them the-people *** before-me assemble! to-me Yahweh when-to-say

אֶת־ דְּבָרָי אֲשֶׁר יִלְמְדוּן לְיִרְאָה אֹתִי כָּל־ הַיָּמִים אֲשֶׁר הֵם
they that the-days all-of me to-revere they-may-learn that words-of-me ***

חַיִּים עַל־ הָאֲדָמָה וְאֶת־ בְּנֵיהֶם יְלַמֵּדוּן׃ וַתִּקְרְבוּן
and-you-came (11) they-may-teach children-of-them and the-land in ones-alive

וַתַּעַמְדוּן תַּחַת הָהָר וְהָהָר בֹּעֵר בָּאֵשׁ
with-the-fire blazing and-the-mountain the-mountain foot-of and-you-stood

עַד־ לֵב הַשָּׁמַיִם חֹשֶׁךְ עָנָן וַעֲרָפֶל׃ וַיְדַבֵּר יְהוָה
Yahweh then-he-spoke (12) and-darkness cloud black the-heavens heart-of to

אֲלֵיכֶם מִתּוֹךְ הָאֵשׁ קוֹל דְּבָרִים אַתֶּם שֹׁמְעִים וּתְמוּנָה אֵינְכֶם
not-you but-form ones-hearing you words sound-of the-fire out-of to-you

[5]See, I have taught you decrees and laws as the LORD my
God commanded me, so that
you may follow them in the
land you are entering to take
possession of it. [6]Observe
them carefully, for this will
show your wisdom and
understanding to the nations,
who will hear about all these
decrees and say, "Surely this
great nation is a wise and
understanding people." [7]What
other nation is so great as to
have their gods near them the
way the LORD our God is near
us whenever we pray to him?
[8]And what other nation is so
great as to have such righteous
decrees and laws as this body
of laws I am setting before you
today?

[9]Only be careful, and watch
yourselves closely so that you
do not forget the things your
eyes have seen or let them slip
from your heart as long as you
live. Teach them to your children and to their children after them. [10]Remember the day
you stood before the LORD
your God at Horeb, when he
said to me, "Assemble the
people before me to hear my
words so that they may learn
to revere me as long as they
live in the land and may teach
them to their children." [11]You
came near and stood at the
foot of the mountain while it
blazed with fire to the very
heavens, with black clouds
and deep darkness. [12]Then the
LORD spoke to you out of the
fire. You heard the sound of
words but saw no form; there

רֹאִים זוּלָתִי קוֹל׃ וַיַּגֵּד לָכֶם אֶת־ בְּרִיתוֹ אֲשֶׁר
that covenant-of-him *** to-you and-he-declared (13) voice only ones-seeing

צִוָּה אֶתְכֶם לַעֲשׂוֹת עֲשֶׂרֶת הַדְּבָרִים וַיִּכְתְּבֵם עַל־
on then-he-wrote-them the-commandments ten-of to-follow you he-commanded

שְׁנֵי לֻחוֹת אֲבָנִים׃ וְאֹתִי צִוָּה יְהוָה בָּעֵת הַהִוא
the-that at-the-time Yahweh he-directed and-me (14) stones tablets-of two-of

לְלַמֵּד אֶתְכֶם חֻקִּים וּמִשְׁפָּטִים לַעֲשֹׂתְכֶם אֹתָם בָּאָרֶץ אֲשֶׁר אַתֶּם
you that in-the-land them to-follow-you and-laws decrees you to-teach

עֹבְרִים שָׁמָּה לְרִשְׁתָּהּ׃ וְנִשְׁמַרְתֶּם מְאֹד
carefully and-you-watch (15) to-possess-her to-there ones-crossing

לְנַפְשֹׁתֵיכֶם כִּי לֹא רְאִיתֶם כָּל־ תְּמוּנָה בְּיוֹם דִּבֶּר יְהוָה אֲלֵיכֶם
to-you Yahweh he-spoke on-day form any-of you-saw not for to-selves-of-you

בְּחֹרֵב מִתּוֹךְ הָאֵשׁ׃ פֶּן־ תַּשְׁחִתוּן וַעֲשִׂיתֶם לָכֶם
for-you and-you-make you-become-corrupt so-not (16) the-fire out-of at-Horeb

פֶּסֶל תְּמוּנַת כָּל־ סָמֶל תַּבְנִית זָכָר אוֹ נְקֵבָה׃ תַּבְנִית כָּל־ בְּהֵמָה
animal any-of form-of (17) woman or man form-of shape any-of image-of idol

אֲשֶׁר בָּאָרֶץ תַּבְנִית כָּל־ צִפּוֹר כָּנָף אֲשֶׁר תָּעוּף בַּשָּׁמָיִם׃
in-the-skies she-flies that wing bird-of any-of form-of on-the-earth that

תַּבְנִית כָּל־ רֹמֵשׂ בָּאֲדָמָה תַּבְנִית כָּל־ דָּגָה אֲשֶׁר־
that fish any-of form-of on-the-ground one-moving any-of form-of (18)

בַּמַּיִם מִתַּחַת לָאָרֶץ׃ וּפֶן־ תִּשָּׂא עֵינֶיךָ
eyes-of-you you-lift and-so-not (19) to-the-earth at-below in-the-waters

הַשָּׁמַיְמָה וְרָאִיתָ אֶת־ הַשֶּׁמֶשׁ וְאֶת־ הַיָּרֵחַ וְאֶת־הַכּוֹכָבִים כֹּל
all-of the-stars and the-moon and the-sun *** and-you-see to-the-skies

צְבָא הַשָּׁמַיִם וְנִדַּחְתָּ וְהִשְׁתַּחֲוִיתָ לָהֶם
to-them and-you-bow-down and-you-are-enticed the-heavens array-of

וַעֲבַדְתָּם אֲשֶׁר חָלַק יְהוָה אֱלֹהֶיךָ אֹתָם לְכֹל
to-all-of them God-of-you Yahweh he-apportioned that and-you-worship-them

הָעַמִּים תַּחַת כָּל־ הַשָּׁמָיִם׃ וְאֶתְכֶם לָקַח יְהוָה וַיּוֹצִא
and-he-brought Yahweh he-took but-you (20) the-heavens all-of under the-nations

אֶתְכֶם מִכּוּר הַבַּרְזֶל מִמִּצְרַיִם לִהְיוֹת לוֹ לְעַם נַחֲלָה
inheritance as-people-of to-him to-be from-Egypt the-iron from-furnace-of your

כַּיּוֹם הַזֶּה׃ וַיהוָה הִתְאַנֶּף־ בִּי עַל־ דִּבְרֵיכֶם
reasons-of-you for with-me he-was-angry but-Yahweh (21) the-this as-the-day

וַיִּשָּׁבַע לְבִלְתִּי עָבְרִי אֶת־ הַיַּרְדֵּן וּלְבִלְתִּי־ בֹא אֶל־ הָאָרֶץ
the-land into to-enter and-not the-Jordan *** to-cross-me not and-he-swore

הַטּוֹבָה אֲשֶׁר יְהוָה אֱלֹהֶיךָ נֹתֵן לְךָ נַחֲלָה׃ כִּי אָנֹכִי
I now (22) inheritance to-you giving God-of-you Yahweh that the-good

was only a voice. 13He declared to you his covenant, the Ten Commandments, which he commanded you to follow and then wrote them on two stone tablets. 14And the LORD directed me at that time to teach you the decrees and laws you are to follow in the land that you are crossing the Jordan to possess.

Idolatry Forbidden

15You saw no form of any kind the day the LORD spoke to you at Horeb out of the fire. Therefore watch yourselves very carefully, 16so that you do not become corrupt and make for yourselves an idol, an image of any shape, whether formed like a man or a woman, 17or like any animal on earth or any bird that flies in the air, 18or like any creature that moves along the ground or any fish in the water below. 19And when you look up to the sky and see the sun, the moon and the stars—all the heavenly array—do not be enticed into bowing down to them and worshiping things the LORD your God has apportioned to all the nations under heaven. 20But as for you, the LORD took you and brought you out of the iron-smelting furnace, out of Egypt, to be the people of his inheritance, as you now are.

21The LORD was angry with me because of you, and he solemnly swore that I would not cross the Jordan and enter the good land the LORD your God is giving you as your inheritance. 22I will die in this land;

מֵת בָּאָרֶץ הַזֹּאת אֵינֶנִּי עֹבֵר אֶת־ הַיַּרְדֵּן וְאַתֶּם עֹבְרִים
ones-crossing but-you the-Jordan *** crossing not-I the-this in-the-land dying

וִירִשְׁתֶּם אֶת־ הָאָרֶץ הַטּוֹבָה הַזֹּאת׃ הִשָּׁמְרוּ לָכֶם
to-you be-careful! (23) the-this the-good the-land *** and-you-will-possess

פֶּן־ תִּשְׁכְּחוּ אֶת־ בְּרִית יְהוָה אֱלֹהֵיכֶם אֲשֶׁר כָּרַת עִמָּכֶם
with-you he-made that God-of-you Yahweh covenant-of *** you-forget so-not

וַעֲשִׂיתֶם לָכֶם פֶּסֶל תְּמוּנַת כֹּל אֲשֶׁר צִוְּךָ יְהוָה
Yahweh he-forbade-you that anything form-of idol for-you and-you-make

אֱלֹהֶיךָ׃ כִּי יְהוָה אֱלֹהֶיךָ אֵשׁ אֹכְלָה הוּא אֵל קַנָּא׃ כִּי־
after (25) jealous God he consuming fire God-of-you Yahweh for (24) God-of-you

תוֹלִיד בָּנִים וּבְנֵי בָנִים וְנוֹשַׁנְתֶּם בָּאָרֶץ
in-the-land and-you-live children and-children-of children you-bear

וְהִשְׁחַתֶּם וַעֲשִׂיתֶם פֶּסֶל תְּמוּנַת כֹּל וַעֲשִׂיתֶם הָרַע
the-evil and-you-do anything form-of idol and-you-make if-you-become-corrupt

בְּעֵינֵי יְהוָה־ אֱלֹהֶיךָ לְהַכְעִיסוֹ׃ הַעִידֹתִי בָכֶם
against-you I-call-witness (26) to-make-angry-him God-of-you Yahweh in-eyes-of

הַיּוֹם אֶת־ הַשָּׁמַיִם וְאֶת־ הָאָרֶץ כִּי־ אָבֹד תֹּאבֵדוּן מַהֵר
quickly you-will-perish to-perish that the-earth and the-heavens *** the-day

מֵעַל הָאָרֶץ אֲשֶׁר אַתֶּם עֹבְרִים אֶת־ הַיַּרְדֵּן שָׁמָּה לְרִשְׁתָּהּ
to-possess-her to-there the-Jordan *** ones-crossing you that the-land from-on

לֹא־ תַאֲרִיכֻן יָמִים עָלֶיהָ כִּי הִשָּׁמֵד תִּשָּׁמֵדוּן׃
you-will-be-destroyed to-be-destroyed but on-her days you-will-live-long not

וְהֵפִיץ יְהוָה אֶתְכֶם בָּעַמִּים וְנִשְׁאַרְתֶּם
and-you-will-survive among-the-peoples you Yahweh and-he-will-scatter (27)

מְתֵי מִסְפָּר בַּגּוֹיִם אֲשֶׁר יְנַהֵג יְהוָה אֶתְכֶם שָׁמָּה׃
to-there you Yahweh he-will-drive which among-the-nations number few-ones-of

וַעֲבַדְתֶּם־ שָׁם אֱלֹהִים מַעֲשֵׂה יְדֵי אָדָם עֵץ וָאֶבֶן אֲשֶׁר
which and-stone wood man hands-of made-of gods there and-you-will-worship (28)

לֹא־ יִרְאוּן וְלֹא יִשְׁמְעוּן וְלֹא יֹאכְלוּן וְלֹא יְרִיחֻן׃
they-smell and-not they-eat and-not they-hear and-not they-see not

וּבִקַּשְׁתֶּם מִשָּׁם אֶת־ יְהוָה אֱלֹהֶיךָ וּמָצָאתָ כִּי
if then-you-will-find God-of-you Yahweh *** from-there if-you-seek (29)

תִדְרְשֶׁנּוּ בְּכָל־ לְבָבְךָ וּבְכָל־ נַפְשֶׁךָ׃
soul-of-you and-with-all-of heart-of-you with-all-of you-look-for-him

בַּצַּר לְךָ וּמְצָאוּךָ כֹּל הַדְּבָרִים
the-things all-of and-they-happen-to-you to-you when-the-distress (30)

הָאֵלֶּה בְּאַחֲרִית הַיָּמִים וְשַׁבְתָּ עַד־ יְהוָה אֱלֹהֶיךָ
God-of-you Yahweh to then-you-will-return the-days in-later-of the-these

I will not cross the Jordan; but you are about to cross over and take possession of that good
land. [23]Be careful not to forget the covenant of the LORD your God that he made with you; do not make for yourselves an idol in the form of anything the LORD your God has forbidden. [24]For the LORD your God is a consuming fire, a jealous God.

[25]After you have had children and grandchildren and have lived in the land a long time—if you then become corrupt and make any kind of idol, doing evil in the eyes of the LORD your God and provoking him to anger,
[26]I call heaven and earth as witnesses against you this day that you will quickly perish from the land that you are crossing the Jordan to possess. You will not live there long but will certainly be destroyed.
[27]The LORD will scatter you among the peoples, and only a few of you will survive among the nations to which the LORD will drive you.
[28]There you will worship man-made gods of wood and stone, which cannot see or hear or eat or smell.
[29]But if from there you seek the LORD your God, you will find him if you look for him with all your heart and with all your
soul. [30]When you are in distress and all these things have happened to you, then in later days you will return to the LORD your God and obey him.

וְשָׁמַעְתָּ בְּקֹלוֹ׃ כִּי אֵל רַחוּם יְהוָה אֱלֹהֶיךָ
God-of-you Yahweh merciful God for (31) to-voice-of-him and-you-will-obey

לֹא יַרְפְּךָ וְלֹא יַשְׁחִיתֶךָ וְלֹא יִשְׁכַּח
he-will-forget and-not he-will-destroy-you and-not he-will-abandon-you not

אֶת־ בְּרִית אֲבֹתֶיךָ אֲשֶׁר נִשְׁבַּע לָהֶם׃ כִּי שְׁאַל־
ask! indeed (32) with-them he-confirmed that fathers-of-you covenant-of ***

נָא לְיָמִים רִאשֹׁנִים אֲשֶׁר־ הָיוּ לְפָנֶיךָ לְמִן־ הַיּוֹם
the-day about-from before-you they-were that former-ones about-days now!

אֲשֶׁר בָּרָא אֱלֹהִים׀ אָדָם עַל־ הָאָרֶץ וּלְמִקְצֵה הַשָּׁמַיִם
the-heavens and-about-from-end-of the-earth on man God he-created when

וְעַד־ קְצֵה הַשָּׁמָיִם הֲנִהְיָה כַּדָּבָר הַגָּדוֹל הַזֶּה
the-this the-great like-the-thing has-he-happened? the-heavens end-of even-to

אוֹ הֲנִשְׁמַע כָּמֹהוּ׃ הֲשָׁמַע עָם קוֹל אֱלֹהִים
God voice-of people has-he-heard? (33) like-him has-he-been-heard? or

מְדַבֵּר מִתּוֹךְ־ הָאֵשׁ כַּאֲשֶׁר־ שָׁמַעְתָּ אַתָּה וַיֶּחִי׃ אוֹ׀
or (34) and-he-lived you you-heard just-as the-fire out-of speaking

הֲנִסָּה אֱלֹהִים לָבוֹא לָקַחַת לוֹ גוֹי מִקֶּרֶב גּוֹי בְּמַסֹּת
by-tests nation out-of nation for-him to-take to-go god has-he-tried?

בְּאֹתֹת וּבְמוֹפְתִים וּבְמִלְחָמָה וּבְיָד חֲזָקָה וּבִזְרוֹעַ
and-by-arm mighty and-by-hand and-by-war and-by-wonders by-signs

נְטוּיָה וּבְמוֹרָאִים גְּדֹלִים כְּכֹל אֲשֶׁר־ עָשָׂה
he-did that like-all great-ones or-by-awesome-deeds being-outstretched

לָכֶם יְהוָה אֱלֹהֵיכֶם בְּמִצְרַיִם לְעֵינֶיךָ׃ אַתָּה הָרְאֵתָ
you-were-shown you (35) before-eyes-of-you in-Egypt God-of-you Yahweh for-you

לָדַעַת כִּי יְהוָה הוּא הָאֱלֹהִים אֵין עוֹד מִלְבַדּוֹ׃ מִן־
from (36) besides-him other there-is-no the-God he Yahweh that to-know

הַשָּׁמַיִם הִשְׁמִיעֲךָ אֶת־ קֹלוֹ לְיַסְּרֶךָּ וְעַל־
and-on to-discipline-you voice-of-him *** he-made-hear-you the-heavens

הָאָרֶץ הֶרְאֲךָ אֶת־ אִשּׁוֹ הַגְּדוֹלָה וּדְבָרָיו שָׁמַעְתָּ
you-heard and-words-of-him the-great fire-of-him *** he-showed-you the-earth

מִתּוֹךְ הָאֵשׁ׃ וְתַחַת כִּי אָהַב אֶת־ אֲבֹתֶיךָ
fathers-of-you *** he-loved that and-because (37) the-fire from-out-of

וַיִּבְחַר בְּזַרְעוֹ אַחֲרָיו וַיּוֹצִאֲךָ
then-he-brought-you after-him in-descendant-of-him and-he-chose

בְּפָנָיו בְּכֹחוֹ הַגָּדֹל מִמִּצְרָיִם׃ לְהוֹרִישׁ
to-drive-out (38) from-Egypt the-great by-strength-of-him by-Presences-of-him

גּוֹיִם גְּדֹלִים וַעֲצֻמִים מִמְּךָ מִפָּנֶיךָ לַהֲבִיאֲךָ
to-bring-you from-before-you than-you and-stronger-ones greater-ones nations

[31]For the LORD your God is a merciful God; he will not abandon or destroy you or forget the covenant with your forefathers, which he confirmed to them by oath.

The LORD Is God

[32]Ask now about the former days, long before your time, from the day God created man on the earth; ask from one end of the heavens to the other. Has anything so great as this ever happened, or has anything like it ever been heard of? [33]Has any other people heard the voice of God[j] speaking out of fire, as you have, and lived? [34]Has any god ever tried to take for himself one nation out of another nation, by testings, by miraculous signs and wonders, by war, by a mighty hand and an outstretched arm, or by great and awesome deeds, like all the things the LORD your God did for you in Egypt before your very eyes?

[35]You were shown these things so that you might know that the LORD is God; besides him there is no other. [36]From heaven he made you hear his voice to discipline you. On earth he showed you his great fire, and you heard his words from out of the fire. [37]Because he loved your forefathers and chose their descendants after them, he brought you out of Egypt by his Presence and his great strength, [38]to drive out before you nations greater and stronger than you and to bring

j33 Or *of a god*

לָתֶת־ לְךָ אֶת־ אַרְצָם נַחֲלָה כַּיּוֹם הַזֶּה׃
the-this as-the-day inheritance land-of-them *** to-you to-give

וְיָדַעְתָּ הַיּוֹם וַהֲשֵׁבֹתָ אֶל־ לְבָבֶךָ כִּי יְהוָה הוּא
he Yahweh that heart-of-you to and-you-take the-day so-you-acknowledge (39)

הָאֱלֹהִים בַּשָּׁמַיִם מִמַּעַל וְעַל־ הָאָרֶץ מִתָּחַת אֵין עוֹד׃
other there-is-no at-below the-earth and-on from-above in-the-heavens the-God

וְשָׁמַרְתָּ אֶת־ חֻקָּיו וְאֶת־ מִצְוֺתָיו אֲשֶׁר אָנֹכִי מְצַוְּךָ
giving-you I which commands-of-him and decrees-of-him *** and-you-keep (40)

הַיּוֹם אֲשֶׁר יִיטַב לְךָ וּלְבָנֶיךָ אַחֲרֶיךָ
after-you and-with-children-of-you with-you he-may-go-well that the-day

וּלְמַעַן תַּאֲרִיךְ יָמִים עַל־הָאֲדָמָה אֲשֶׁר יְהוָה אֱלֹהֶיךָ נֹתֵן
giving God-of-you Yahweh that the-land in days you-may-live-long and-so-that

לְךָ כָּל־ הַיָּמִים׃ אָז יַבְדִּיל מֹשֶׁה שָׁלֹשׁ עָרִים בְּעֵבֶר
on-east-of cities three Moses he-set-aside then (41) the-days all-of to-you

הַיַּרְדֵּן מִזְרְחָה שָׁמֶשׁ׃ לָנֻס שָׁמָּה רוֹצֵחַ אֲשֶׁר יִרְצַח
he-killed who one-killing to-there to-flee (42) sun toward-rise-of the-Jordan

אֶת־ רֵעֵהוּ בִּבְלִי־ דַעַת וְהוּא לֹא־ שֹׂנֵא לוֹ
against-him having-malice not and-he knowledge without neighbor-of-him ***

מִתְּמֹל שִׁלְשֹׁם וְנָס אֶל־ אַחַת מִן־ הֶעָרִים הָאֵל
the-these the-cites from one to and-he-could-flee previously from-before

וָחָי׃ אֶת־ בֶּצֶר בַּמִּדְבָּר בְּאֶרֶץ הַמִּישֹׁר
the-plateau in-land-of in-the-desert Bezer *** (43) and-he-would-live

לָרְאוּבֵנִי* וְאֶת־ רָאמֹת בַּגִּלְעָד לַגָּדִי וְאֶת־ גּוֹלָן
Golan and for-the-Gadite in-the-Gilead Ramoth and for-the-Reubenite

בַּבָּשָׁן לַמְנַשִּׁי׃ וְזֹאת הַתּוֹרָה אֲשֶׁר־ שָׂם מֹשֶׁה
Moses he-set that the-law and-this (44) for-the-Manassite in-the-Bashan

לִפְנֵי בְּנֵי יִשְׂרָאֵל׃ אֵלֶּה הָעֵדֹת וְהַחֻקִּים וְהַמִּשְׁפָּטִים
and-the-laws and-the-decrees the-stipulations these (45) Israel sons-of before

אֲשֶׁר דִּבֶּר מֹשֶׁה אֶל־ בְּנֵי יִשְׂרָאֵל בְּצֵאתָם מִמִּצְרָיִם׃
from Egypt when-to-come-them Israel sons-of to Moses he-gave that

בְּעֵבֶר הַיַּרְדֵּן בַּגַּיְא מוּל בֵּית פְּעוֹר בְּאֶרֶץ סִיחֹן
Sihon in-land-of Peor Beth near in-the-valley the-Jordan on-east-of (46)

מֶלֶךְ הָאֱמֹרִי אֲשֶׁר יוֹשֵׁב בְּחֶשְׁבּוֹן אֲשֶׁר הִכָּה מֹשֶׁה וּבְנֵי
and-sons-of Moses he-defeated whom in-Heshbon reigning who the-Amorite king-of

יִשְׂרָאֵל בְּצֵאתָם מִמִּצְרָיִם׃ וַיִּירְשׁוּ אֶת־ אַרְצוֹ וְאֶת־
and land-of-him *** and-they-possessed (47) from-Egypt as-to-come-them Israel

אֶרֶץ ׀ עוֹג מֶלֶךְ־ הַבָּשָׁן שְׁנֵי מַלְכֵי הָאֱמֹרִי אֲשֶׁר בְּעֵבֶר
on-east-of who the-Amorite kings-of two-of the-Bashan king-of Og land-of

you into their land to give it to
you for your inheritance, as it
is today.
[39]Acknowledge and take to
heart this day that the LORD is
God in heaven above and on
the earth below. There is no
other. [40]Keep his decrees and
commands, which I am giving
you today, so that it may go
well with you and your children after you and that you
may live long in the land the
LORD your God gives you for
all time.

Cities of Refuge

[41]Then Moses set aside three
cities east of the Jordan,
[42]where anyone who had
killed a person could flee if he
had unintentionally killed his
neighbor without malice
aforethought. He could flee
into one of these cities and
save his life. [43]The cities were
these: Bezer in the desert plateau, for the Reubenites;
Ramoth in Gilead, for the Gadites; and Golan in Bashan,
for the Manassites.

Introduction to the Law

[44]This is the law Moses set
before the Israelites. [45]These
are the stipulations, decrees
and laws Moses gave them
when they came out of Egypt
[46]and were in the valley near
Beth Peor east of the Jordan, in
the land of Sihon king of the
Amorites, who reigned in
Heshbon and was defeated by
Moses and the Israelites as
they came out of Egypt. [47]They
took possession of his land
and the land of Og king of Bashan, the two Amorite kings

*43 Most mss have no *qibbuts* under the *resh* (לָרְאוּ׳).

הַיַּרְדֵּן מִזְרַח שָׁמֶשׁ׃ מֵעֲרֹעֵר אֲשֶׁר עַל־שְׂפַת־ נַחַל אַרְנֹן וְעַד־
and-to Arnon Gorge-of rim-of on that from-Aroer (48) sun rise-of the-Jordan

הַר שִׂיאֹן הוּא חֶרְמוֹן׃ וְכָל־ הָעֲרָבָה עֵבֶר הַיַּרְדֵּן
the-Jordan east-of the-Arabah and-all-of (49) Hermon that Siyon Mount-of

מִזְרָחָה וְעַד יָם הָעֲרָבָה תַּחַת אַשְׁדֹּת הַפִּסְגָּה׃
the-Pisgah slopes-of below the-Arabah Sea-of as-far-as to-east

וַיִּקְרָא מֹשֶׁה אֶל־ כָּל־ יִשְׂרָאֵל וַיֹּאמֶר אֲלֵהֶם שְׁמַע
hear! to-them and-he-said Israel all-of to Moses and-he-summoned (5:1)

יִשְׂרָאֵל אֶת־הַחֻקִּים וְאֶת־הַמִּשְׁפָּטִים אֲשֶׁר אָנֹכִי דֹּבֵר בְּאָזְנֵיכֶם הַיּוֹם
the-day in-ears-of-you declaring I that the-laws and the-decrees *** Israel

וּלְמַדְתֶּם אֹתָם וּשְׁמַרְתֶּם לַעֲשֹׂתָם׃ יְהוָה אֱלֹהֵינוּ
God-of-us Yahweh (2) to-follow-them and-you-be-certain them so-you-learn

כָּרַת עִמָּנוּ בְּרִית בְּחֹרֵב׃ לֹא אֶת־ אֲבֹתֵינוּ כָּרַת יְהוָה
Yahweh he-made fathers-of-us with not (3) at-Horeb covenant with-us he-made

אֶת־ הַבְּרִית הַזֹּאת כִּי אִתָּנוּ אֲנַחְנוּ אֵלֶּה פֹה הַיּוֹם כֻּלָּנוּ
all-of-us the-day here these we with-us but the-this the-covenant ***

חַיִּים׃ פָּנִים ׀ בְּפָנִים דִּבֶּר יְהוָה עִמָּכֶם בָּהָר מִתּוֹךְ
out-of on-the-mountain to-you Yahweh he-spoke to-faces faces (4) ones-alive

הָאֵשׁ׃ אָנֹכִי עֹמֵד בֵּין־ יְהוָה וּבֵינֵיכֶם בָּעֵת הַהִוא
the-that at-the-time and-between-you Yahweh between standing I (5) the-fire

לְהַגִּיד לָכֶם אֶת־ דְּבַר יְהוָה כִּי יְרֵאתֶם מִפְּנֵי
of-presence-of you-were-afraid for Yahweh word-of *** to-you to-declare

הָאֵשׁ וְלֹא־ עֲלִיתֶם בָּהָר לֵאמֹר׃ אָנֹכִי יְהוָה אֱלֹהֶיךָ
God-of-you Yahweh I (6) to-say on-the-mountain you-went-up and-not the-fire

אֲשֶׁר הוֹצֵאתִיךָ מֵאֶרֶץ מִצְרַיִם מִבֵּית עֲבָדִים׃ לֹא
not (7) slaveries from-house-of Egypt from-land-of I-brought-you who

יִהְיֶה־ לְךָ אֱלֹהִים אֲחֵרִים עַל־ פָּנָיַ׃ לֹא־ תַעֲשֶׂה־
you-shall-make not (8) faces-of-me before other-ones gods to-you he-shall-be

לְךָ פֶסֶל ׀ כָּל־ תְּמוּנָה אֲשֶׁר בַּשָּׁמַיִם ׀ מִמַּעַל וַאֲשֶׁר בָּאָרֶץ
on-the-earth or-that from-above in-the-heavens that form any-of idol for-you

מִתָּחַת וַאֲשֶׁר בַּמַּיִם ׀ מִתַּחַת לָאָרֶץ׃ לֹא־ תִשְׁתַּחֲוֶה
you-shall-bow not (9) to-the-earth at-below in-the-waters or-that at-beneath

לָהֶם וְלֹא תָעָבְדֵם כִּי אָנֹכִי יְהוָה אֱלֹהֶיךָ אֵל קַנָּא
jealous God God-of-you Yahweh I for you-shall-worship-them and-not to-them

פֹּקֵד עֲוֹן אָבוֹת עַל־ בָּנִים וְעַל־ שִׁלֵּשִׁים וְעַל־ רִבֵּעִים
fourth-ones and-to third-ones even-to children on fathers sin-of punishing

לְשֹׂנְאָי׃ וְעֹשֶׂה חֶסֶד לַאֲלָפִים לְאֹהֲבַי
to-ones-loving-me to-thousands love but-showing (10) to-ones-hating-me

east of the Jordan. [48]This land extended from Aroer on the rim of the Arnon Gorge to Mount Siyon[k] (that is, Hermon), [49]and included all the Arabah east of the Jordan, as far as the Sea of the Arabah,[l] below the slopes of Pisgah.

The Ten Commandments

5 Moses summoned all Israel and said:

Hear, O Israel, the decrees and laws I declare in your hearing today. Learn them and be sure to follow them. [2]The LORD our God made a covenant with us at Horeb. [3]It was not with our fathers that the LORD made this covenant, but with us, with all of us who are alive here today. [4]The LORD spoke to you face to face out of the fire on the mountain. [5](At that time I stood between the LORD and you to declare to you the word of the LORD, because you were afraid of the fire and did not go up the mountain.) And he said:

[6]"I am the LORD your God, who brought you out of Egypt, out of the land of slavery.

[7]"You shall have no other gods before[m] me.

[8]"You shall not make for yourself an idol in the form of anything in heaven above or on the earth beneath or in the waters below. [9]You shall not bow down to them or worship them; for I, the LORD your God, am a jealous God, punishing the children for the sin of the fathers to the third and fourth generation of those who hate me, [10]but showing love to thousands who love me and

[k]48 Hebrew; Syriac (see also Deut. 3:9) *Sirion*
[l]49 That is, the Dead Sea
[m]7 Or *besides*

וּלְשֹׁמְרֵי מִצְוֹתָו׃ לֹא תִשָּׂא אֶת־ שֵׁם־
name-of *** you-shall-take not (11) commands-of-me and-to-ones-keeping-of

יְהוָה אֱלֹהֶיךָ לַשָּׁוְא כִּי לֹא יְנַקֶּה יְהוָה אֵת
*** Yahweh he-will-hold-guiltless not for for-the-misuse God-of-you Yahweh

אֲשֶׁר־ יִשָּׂא אֶת־ שְׁמוֹ לַשָּׁוְא׃ שָׁמוֹר אֶת־ יוֹם
day-of *** to-observe (12) for-the-misuse name-of-him *** he-takes who

הַשַּׁבָּת לְקַדְּשׁוֹ כַּאֲשֶׁר צִוְּךָ ׀ יְהוָה אֱלֹהֶיךָ
God-of-you Yahweh he-commanded-you just-as to-keep-holy-him the-Sabbath

שֵׁשֶׁת יָמִים תַּעֲבֹד וְעָשִׂיתָ כָּל־ מְלַאכְתֶּךָ׃
work-of-you all-of and-you-shall-do you-shall-labor days six-of (13)

וְיוֹם הַשְּׁבִיעִי שַׁבָּת ׀ לַיהוָה אֱלֹהֶיךָ לֹא תַעֲשֶׂה
you-shall-do not God-of-you to-Yahweh Sabbath the-seventh but-day-of (14)

כָל־ מְלָאכָה אַתָּה וּבִנְךָ־ וּבִתֶּךָ וְעַבְדְּךָ־
or-manservant-of-you or-daughter-of-you or-son-of-you you work any-of

וַאֲמָתֶךָ וְשׁוֹרְךָ וַחֲמֹרְךָ וְכָל־ בְּהֶמְתֶּךָ
animal-of-you or-any-of or-donkey-of-you or-ox-of-you or-maidservant-of-you

וְגֵרְךָ אֲשֶׁר בִּשְׁעָרֶיךָ לְמַעַן יָנוּחַ עַבְדְּךָ
manservant-of-you he-may-rest so-that within-gates-of-you who or-alien-of-you

וַאֲמָתְךָ כָּמוֹךָ׃ וְזָכַרְתָּ כִּי־ עֶבֶד הָיִיתָ ׀
you-were slave that and-you-remember (15) as-you and-maidservant-of-you

בְּאֶרֶץ מִצְרַיִם וַיֹּצִאֲךָ יְהוָה אֱלֹהֶיךָ מִשָּׁם בְּיָד
with-hand from-there God-of-you Yahweh and-he-brought-you Egypt in-land-of

חֲזָקָה וּבִזְרֹעַ נְטוּיָה עַל־ כֵּן צִוְּךָ יְהוָה
Yahweh he-commanded-you this for being-outstretched and-with-arm mighty

אֱלֹהֶיךָ לַעֲשׂוֹת אֶת־ יוֹם הַשַּׁבָּת׃ כַּבֵּד אֶת־ אָבִיךָ
father-of-you *** honor! (16) the-Sabbath day-of *** to-observe God-of-you

וְאֶת־ אִמֶּךָ כַּאֲשֶׁר צִוְּךָ יְהוָה אֱלֹהֶיךָ לְמַעַן ׀
so-that God-of-you Yahweh he-commanded-you just-as mother-of-you and

יַאֲרִיכֻן יָמֶיךָ וּלְמַעַן יִיטַב לָךְ עַל הָאֲדָמָה
the-land in with you he-may-go-well and-so-that days-of-you they-may-be-long

אֲשֶׁר־יְהוָה אֱלֹהֶיךָ נֹתֵן לָךְ׃ לֹא תִּרְצָח׃ וְלֹא
and-not (18) you-shall-murder not (17)* to-you giving God-of-you Yahweh that

תִּנְאָף׃ וְלֹא תִּגְנֹב׃ וְלֹא־ תַעֲנֶה
you-give and-not (20) you-shall-steal and-not (19) you-shall-commit-adultery

בְרֵעֲךָ עֵד שָׁוְא׃ וְלֹא תַחְמֹד אֵשֶׁת
wife-of you-shall-covet and-not (21) false testimony against-neighbor-of-you

רֵעֶךָ וְלֹא תִתְאַוֶּה בֵּית רֵעֶךָ שָׂדֵהוּ
land-of-him neighbor-of-you house-of you-shall-desire and-not neighbor-of-you

keep my command-
ments.
11"You shall not misuse the
name of the LORD your
God, for the LORD will not
hold anyone guiltless
who misuses his name.
12"Observe the Sabbath day
by keeping it holy, as the
LORD your God has com-
manded you. 13Six days
you shall labor and do all
your work, 14but the sev-
enth day is a Sabbath to
the LORD your God. On it
you shall not do any
work, neither you, nor
your son or daughter, nor
your manservant or
maidservant, nor your
ox, your donkey or any of
your animals, nor the
alien within your gates,
so that your manservant
and maidservant may
rest, as you do. 15Remem-
ber that you were slaves
in Egypt and that the
LORD your God brought
you out of there with a
mighty hand and an out-
stretched arm. Therefore
the LORD your God has
commanded you to ob-
serve the Sabbath day.
16"Honor your father and
your mother, as the LORD
your God has com-
manded you, so that you
may live long and that it
may go well with you in
the land the LORD your
God is giving you.
17"You shall not murder.
18"You shall not commit
adultery.
19"You shall not steal.
20"You shall not give false
testimony against your
neighbor.
21"You shall not covet your
neighbor's wife. You
shall not set your desire
on your neighbor's house

*Most Hebrew texts incorporate verses 17 through 20 into one verse, thus causing a three-verse discrepancy through the rest of this chapter. As BHS follows the English numeration rather than the Hebrew, so does the interlinear text.

°10 ק מצותי

וְעַבְדּוֹ וַאֲמָתוֹ שׁוֹרוֹ וַחֲמֹרוֹ
or-donkey-of-him ox-of-him or-maidservant-of-him or-manservant-of-him

וְכֹל אֲשֶׁר לְרֵעֶךָ׃ אֶת־ הַדְּבָרִים הָאֵלֶּה
the-these the-commandments *** (22) to-neighbor-of-you that or-anything

דִּבֶּר יְהוָה אֶל־ כָּל־ קְהַלְכֶם בָּהָר מִתּוֹךְ
from-out-of on-the-mountain assembly-of-you whole-of to Yahweh he-proclaimed

הָאֵשׁ הֶעָנָן וְהָעֲרָפֶל קוֹל גָּדוֹל וְלֹא יָסָף
he-added and-nothing loud voice and-the-darkness the-cloud the-fire

וַיִּכְתְּבֵם עַל־ שְׁנֵי לֻחֹת אֲבָנִים וַיִּתְּנֵם אֵלָי׃
to-me and-he-gave-them stones tablets-of two-of on and-he-wrote-them

וַיְהִי כְּשָׁמְעֲכֶם אֶת־ הַקּוֹל מִתּוֹךְ הַחֹשֶׁךְ
the-darkness from-out-of the-voice *** when-to-hear-you and-he-was (23)

וְהָהָר בֹּעֵר בָּאֵשׁ וַתִּקְרְבוּן אֵלַי כָּל־ רָאשֵׁי
leaders-of all-of to-me and-you-came with-the-fire blazing and-the-mountain

שִׁבְטֵיכֶם וְזִקְנֵיכֶם׃ וַתֹּאמְרוּ הֵן הֶרְאָנוּ יְהוָה
Yahweh he-showed-us see! and-you-said (24) and-elders-of-you tribes-of-you

אֱלֹהֵינוּ אֶת־ כְּבֹדוֹ וְאֶת־ גָּדְלוֹ וְאֶת־ קֹלוֹ שָׁמַעְנוּ
we-heard voice-of-him and majesty-of-him and glory-of-him *** God-of-us

מִתּוֹךְ הָאֵשׁ הַיּוֹם הַזֶּה רָאִינוּ כִּי־ יְדַבֵּר אֱלֹהִים אֶת־ הָאָדָם
the-man with God he-speaks that we-saw the-this the-day the-fire out-of

וָחָי׃ וְעַתָּה לָמָּה נָמוּת כִּי תֹאכְלֵנוּ הָאֵשׁ
the-fire she-will-consume-us for should-we-die why? but-now (25) yet-he-lives

הַגְּדֹלָה הַזֹּאת אִם־ יֹסְפִים ׀ אֲנַחְנוּ לִשְׁמֹעַ אֶת־ קוֹל יְהוָה
Yahweh voice-of *** to-hear we ones-continuing if the-this the-great

אֱלֹהֵינוּ עוֹד וָמָתְנוּ׃ כִּי מִי כָל־ בָּשָׂר אֲשֶׁר שָׁמַע
he-heard who mortal any-of who? for (26) then-we-will-die longer God-of-us

קוֹל אֱלֹהִים חַיִּים מְדַבֵּר מִתּוֹךְ־ הָאֵשׁ כָּמֹנוּ וַיֶּחִי׃ קְרַב
go! (27) and-he-survived as-we the-fire out-of speaking living God voice-of

אַתָּה וּשְׁמָע אֵת כָּל־ אֲשֶׁר יֹאמַר יְהוָה אֱלֹהֵינוּ וְאַתְּ ׀ תְּדַבֵּר
you-tell and-you God-of-us Yahweh he-says that all *** and-listen! you

אֵלֵינוּ אֵת כָּל־ אֲשֶׁר יְדַבֵּר יְהוָה אֱלֹהֵינוּ אֵלֶיךָ וְשָׁמַעְנוּ
and-we-will-listen to-you God-of-us Yahweh he-tells that all *** to-us

וְעָשִׂינוּ׃ וַיִּשְׁמַע יְהוָה אֶת־ קוֹל דִּבְרֵיכֶם
words-of-you sound-of *** Yahweh and-he-heard (28) and-we-will-obey

בְּדַבֶּרְכֶם אֵלָי וַיֹּאמֶר יְהוָה אֵלַי שָׁמַעְתִּי אֶת־ קוֹל
sound-of *** I-heard to-me Yahweh and-he-said to-me when-to-speak-you

דִּבְרֵי הָעָם הַזֶּה אֲשֶׁר דִּבְּרוּ אֵלֶיךָ הֵיטִיבוּ כָּל־ אֲשֶׁר
that all they-were-good to-you they-spoke that the-this the-people words-of

or land, his manservant
or maidservant, his ox or
donkey, or anything that
belongs to your neigh-
bor."

22These are the command-
ments the LORD proclaimed in
a loud voice to your whole assembly there on the mountain
from out of the fire, the cloud
and the deep darkness; and he
added nothing more. Then he
wrote them on two stone tablets and gave them to me.
23When you heard the voice
out of the darkness, while the
mountain was ablaze with
fire, all the leading men of
your tribes and your elders
came to me.
24And you said,
"The LORD our God has shown
us his glory and his majesty,
and we have heard his voice
from the fire. Today we have
seen that a man can live even
if God speaks with him.
25But
now, why should we die? This
great fire will consume us, and
we will die if we hear the voice
of the LORD our God any longer.
26For what mortal man has
ever heard the voice of the living God speaking out of fire,
as we have, and survived?
27Go near and listen to all that
the LORD our God says. Then
tell us whatever the LORD our
God tells you. We will listen
and obey."
28The LORD heard you when
you spoke to me and the LORD
said to me, "I have heard what
this people said to you. Everything they said was good.

*See the note on page 499.

דִּבֵּרוּ׃ מִי־ יִתֵּן וְהָיָה לְבָבָם זֶה
this heart-of-them and-he-would-be he-would-incline oh! (29) they-said

לָהֶם לְיִרְאָה אֹתִי וְלִשְׁמֹר אֶת־ כָּל־ מִצְוֹתַי כָּל־ הַיָּמִים
the-days all-of commands-of-me all-of *** and-to-keep me to-fear to-them

לְמַעַן יִיטַב לָהֶם וְלִבְנֵיהֶם לְעֹלָם׃
for-ever and-with-children-of-them with-them he-might-go-well so-that

לֵךְ אֱמֹר לָהֶם שׁוּבוּ לָכֶם לְאָהֳלֵיכֶם׃ וְאַתָּה פֹּה
here but-you (31) to-tents-of-you to-you return! to-them tell! go! (30)

עֲמֹד עִמָּדִי וַאֲדַבְּרָה אֵלֶיךָ אֵת כָּל־ הַמִּצְוָה וְהַחֻקִּים
and-the-decrees the-command all-of *** to-you so-I-may-give with-me stay!

וְהַמִּשְׁפָּטִים אֲשֶׁר תְּלַמְּדֵם וְעָשׂוּ בָאָרֶץ אֲשֶׁר
that in-the-land so-they-will-follow you-must-teach-them that and-the-laws

אָנֹכִי נֹתֵן לָהֶם לְרִשְׁתָּהּ׃ וּשְׁמַרְתֶּם לַעֲשׂוֹת כַּאֲשֶׁר
just-as to-do so-you-be-careful (32) to-possess-her to-them giving I

צִוָּה יְהוָה אֱלֹהֵיכֶם אֶתְכֶם לֹא תָסֻרוּ יָמִין וּשְׂמֹאל׃ בְּכָל־
in-all-of (33) or-left right you-turn not you God-of-you Yahweh he-commanded

הַדֶּרֶךְ אֲשֶׁר צִוָּה יְהוָה אֱלֹהֵיכֶם אֶתְכֶם תֵּלֵכוּ לְמַעַן תִּחְיוּן
you-may-live so-that you-walk you God-of-you Yahweh he-commanded that the-way

וְטוֹב לָכֶם וְהַאֲרַכְתֶּם יָמִים בָּאָרֶץ אֲשֶׁר תִּירָשׁוּן׃
you-will-possess that in-the-land days and-you-prolong to-you and-he-may-be-good

וְזֹאת הַמִּצְוָה הַחֻקִּים וְהַמִּשְׁפָּטִים אֲשֶׁר צִוָּה יְהוָה
Yahweh he-directed that and-the-laws the-decrees the-command and-this (6:1)

אֱלֹהֵיכֶם לְלַמֵּד אֶתְכֶם לַעֲשׂוֹת בָּאָרֶץ אֲשֶׁר אַתֶּם עֹבְרִים
ones-crossing you that in-the-land to-observe you to-teach God-of-you

שָׁמָּה לְרִשְׁתָּהּ׃ לְמַעַן תִּירָא אֶת־ יְהוָה אֱלֹהֶיךָ
God-of-you Yahweh *** you-may-fear so-that (2) to-possess-her to-there

לִשְׁמֹר אֶת־ כָּל־ חֻקֹּתָיו וּמִצְוֹתָיו אֲשֶׁר אָנֹכִי מְצַוֶּךָ
giving-you I that and-commands-of-him decrees-of-him all-of *** to-keep

אַתָּה וּבִנְךָ וּבֶן־ בִּנְךָ כֹּל יְמֵי חַיֶּיךָ
lives-of-you days-of all-of child-of-you and-child-of and-child-of-you you

וּלְמַעַן יַאֲרִכֻן יָמֶיךָ׃ וְשָׁמַעְתָּ יִשְׂרָאֵל
Israel so-you-hear (3) days-of-you they-will-be-long and-so-that

וְשָׁמַרְתָּ לַעֲשׂוֹת אֲשֶׁר יִיטַב לְךָ וַאֲשֶׁר
and-that with-you he-may-go-well that to-obey and-you-be-careful

תִּרְבּוּן מְאֹד כַּאֲשֶׁר דִּבֶּר יְהוָה אֱלֹהֵי אֲבֹתֶיךָ
fathers-of-you God-of Yahweh he-promised just-as greatly you-may-increase

לָךְ אֶרֶץ זָבַת חָלָב וּדְבָשׁ׃ שְׁמַע יִשְׂרָאֵל יְהוָה אֱלֹהֵינוּ
God-of-us Yahweh Israel hear! (4) and-honey milk flowing-of land-of to-you

29Oh, that their hearts would
be inclined to fear me and
keep all my commands al-
ways, so that it might go well
with them and their children
forever!
30"Go, tell them to return to
their tents. 31But you stay here
with me so that I may give you
all the commands, decrees and
laws you are to teach them to
follow in the land I am giving
them to possess."
32So be careful to do what the
LORD your God has com-
manded you; do not turn aside
to the right or to the left.
33Walk in all the way that the
LORD your God has com-
manded you, so that you may
live and prosper and prolong
your days in the land that you
will possess.

Love the LORD Your God

6 These are the commands,
decrees and laws the LORD
your God directed me to teach
you to observe in the land that
you are crossing the Jordan to
possess, 2so that you, your
children and their children after them may fear the LORD
your God as long as you live
by keeping all his decrees and
commands that I give you,
and so that you may enjoy
long life. 3Hear, O Israel, and
be careful to obey so that it
may go well with you and that
you may increase greatly in a
land flowing with milk and
honey, just as the LORD, the
God of your fathers, promised
you.
4Hear, O Israel: The LORD

*See the note on page 499.

יְהוָה׀ אֶחָד׃ וְאָהַבְתָּ אֵת יְהוָה אֱלֹהֶיךָ בְּכָל־
with-all-of God-of-you Yahweh *** and-you-must-love (5) one Yahweh

לְבָבְךָ וּבְכָל־ נַפְשְׁךָ וּבְכָל־ מְאֹדֶךָ׃
strength-of-you and-with-all-of soul-of-you and-with-all-of heart-of-you

וְהָיוּ הַדְּבָרִים הָאֵלֶּה אֲשֶׁר אָנֹכִי מְצַוְּךָ הַיּוֹם עַל־
on the-day giving-you I that the-these the-commands and-they-must-be (6)

לְבָבֶךָ׃ וְשִׁנַּנְתָּם לְבָנֶיךָ וְדִבַּרְתָּ
and-you-talk on-children-of-you and-you-impress-them (7) heart-of-you

בָּם בְּשִׁבְתְּךָ בְּבֵיתֶךָ וּבְלֶכְתְּךָ בַדֶּרֶךְ
on-the-road and-when-to-walk-you in-house-of-you when-to-sit-you about-them

וּבְשָׁכְבְּךָ וּבְקוּמֶךָ׃ וּקְשַׁרְתָּם לְאוֹת
as-symbol and-you-tie-them (8) and-when-to-get-up-you and-when-to-lie-down-you

עַל־ יָדֶךָ וְהָיוּ לְטֹטָפֹת בֵּין עֵינֶיךָ׃
eyes-of-you between as-bands and-they-must-be hand-of-you on

וּכְתַבְתָּם עַל־ מְזוּזֹת בֵּיתֶךָ וּבִשְׁעָרֶיךָ׃
and-on-gates-of-you house-of-you doorframes-of on and-you-write-them (9)

וְהָיָה כִּי יְבִיאֲךָ׀ יְהוָה אֱלֹהֶיךָ אֶל־ הָאָרֶץ אֲשֶׁר
that the-land into God-of-you Yahweh he-brings-you when and-he-will-be (10)

נִשְׁבַּע לַאֲבֹתֶיךָ לְאַבְרָהָם לְיִצְחָק וּלְיַעֲקֹב לָתֶת לָךְ
to-you to-give and-to-Jacob to-Isaac to-Abraham to-fathers-of-you he-swore

עָרִים גְּדֹלֹת וְטֹבֹת אֲשֶׁר לֹא־ בָנִיתָ׃ וּבָתִּים מְלֵאִים
ones-full and-houses (11) you-built not that and-good-ones large-ones cities

כָּל־ טוּב אֲשֶׁר לֹא־ מִלֵּאתָ וּבֹרֹת חֲצוּבִים אֲשֶׁר לֹא־ חָצַבְתָּ
you-dug not that ones-being-dug and-wells you-provided not that good all-of

כְּרָמִים וְזֵיתִים אֲשֶׁר לֹא־ נָטָעְתָּ וְאָכַלְתָּ וְשָׂבָעְתָּ׃
and-you-are-sated and-you-eat you-planted not that and-olive-groves vineyards

הִשָּׁמֶר לְךָ פֶּן־ תִּשְׁכַּח אֶת־ יְהוָה אֲשֶׁר הוֹצִיאֲךָ
he-brought-you who Yahweh *** you-forget so-not to-you be-careful! (12)

מֵאֶרֶץ מִצְרַיִם מִבֵּית עֲבָדִים׃ אֶת־ יְהוָה אֱלֹהֶיךָ
God-of-you Yahweh *** (13) slaveries from-house-of Egypt from-land-of

תִּירָא וְאֹתוֹ תַעֲבֹד וּבִשְׁמוֹ תִּשָּׁבֵעַ׃ לֹא
not (14) you-take-oath and-in-name-of-him you-serve and-him you-fear

תֵלְכוּן אַחֲרֵי אֱלֹהִים אֲחֵרִים מֵאֱלֹהֵי הָעַמִּים אֲשֶׁר סְבִיבוֹתֵיכֶם׃
ones-around-you that the-peoples after-gods-of other-ones gods after you-follow

כִּי אֵל קַנָּא יְהוָה אֱלֹהֶיךָ בְּקִרְבֶּךָ פֶּן־ יֶחֱרֶה אַף־
anger-of he-burns so-not in-among-you God-of-you Yahweh jealous God for (15)

יְהוָה אֱלֹהֶיךָ בָּךְ וְהִשְׁמִידְךָ מֵעַל פְּנֵי הָאֲדָמָה׃
the-land faces-of from-on so-he-destroys-you against-you God-of-you Yahweh

our God, the LORD is one.[n]
[5]Love the LORD your God with
all your heart and with all your
soul and with all your
strength. [6]These commandments that I give you today are
to be upon your hearts. [7]Im-
press them on your children.
Talk about them when you sit
at home and when you walk
along the road, when you lie
down and when you get up.
[8]Tie them as symbols on your
hands and bind them on your
foreheads. [9]Write them on the
doorframes of your houses
and on your gates.
[10]When the LORD your God
brings you into the land he
swore to your fathers, to Abraham, Isaac and Jacob, to give
you—a land with large, flour-
ishing cities you did not build,
[11]houses filled with all kinds of
good things you did not provide, wells you did not dig,
and vineyards and olive
groves you did not plant—
then when you eat and are satisfied, [12]be careful that you do
not forget the LORD, who
brought you out of Egypt, out
of the land of slavery.
[13]Fear the LORD your God,
serve him only and take your
oaths in his name. [14]Do not
follow other gods, the gods of
the peoples around you; [15]for
the LORD your God, who is
among you, is a jealous God
and his anger will burn
against you, and he will destroy you from the face of the

[n]4 Or *The LORD our God is one LORD;* or *The LORD is our God, the LORD is one;* or *The LORD is our God, the LORD alone*

לֹא תְנַסּוּ אֶת־ יְהוָה אֱלֹהֵיכֶם כַּאֲשֶׁר נִסִּיתֶם בַּמַּסָּה׃
at-the-Massah you-tested just-as God-of-you Yahweh *** you-test not (16)

שָׁמוֹר תִּשְׁמְרוּן אֶת־ מִצְוֹת יְהוָה אֱלֹהֵיכֶם וְעֵדֹתָיו
and-stipulations-of-him God-of-you Yahweh commands-of *** you-keep to-keep (17)

וְחֻקָּיו אֲשֶׁר צִוָּךְ׃ וְעָשִׂיתָ הַיָּשָׁר וְהַטּוֹב
and-the-good the-right and-you-do (18) he-gave-you that and-decrees-of-him

בְּעֵינֵי יְהוָה לְמַעַן יִיטַב לָךְ וּבָאתָ
and-you-may-go-in with-you he-may-go-well so-that Yahweh in-eyes-of

וְיָרַשְׁתָּ אֶת־הָאָרֶץ הַטֹּבָה אֲשֶׁר־ נִשְׁבַּע יְהוָה לַאֲבֹתֶיךָ׃
to-fathers-of-you Yahweh he-swore that the-good the-land *** and-you-may-possess

לַהֲדֹף אֶת־ כָּל־ אֹיְבֶיךָ מִפָּנֶיךָ כַּאֲשֶׁר
just-as from-before-you being-enemines-of-you all-of *** to-thrust-out (19)

דִּבֶּר יְהוָה׃ כִּי־ יִשְׁאָלְךָ בִנְךָ מָחָר לֵאמֹר מָה
what? to-say future son-of-you he-asks-you when (20) Yahweh he-said

הָעֵדֹת וְהַחֻקִּים וְהַמִּשְׁפָּטִים אֲשֶׁר צִוָּה יְהוָה
Yahweh he-commanded that and-the-laws and-the-decrees the-stipulations

אֱלֹהֵינוּ אֶתְכֶם׃ וְאָמַרְתָּ לְבִנְךָ עֲבָדִים הָיִינוּ לְפַרְעֹה
to-Pharaoh we-were slaves to-son-of-you then-you-tell (21) you God-of-us

בְּמִצְרָיִם וַיּוֹצִיאֵנוּ יְהוָה מִמִּצְרַיִם בְּיָד חֲזָקָה׃ וַיִּתֵּן
and-he-sent (22) mighty with-hand from-Egypt Yahweh but-he-brought-us in-Egypt

יְהוָה אוֹתֹת וּמֹפְתִים גְּדֹלִים וְרָעִים ׀ בְּמִצְרַיִם בְּפַרְעֹה
on-Pharaoh on-Egypt and-terrible-ones great-ones and-wonders signs Yahweh

וּבְכָל־ בֵּיתוֹ לְעֵינֵינוּ׃ וְאוֹתָנוּ הוֹצִיא
he-brought but-us (23) before-eyes-of-us household-of-him and-on-whole-of

מִשָּׁם לְמַעַן הָבִיא אֹתָנוּ לָתֶת לָנוּ אֶת־ הָאָרֶץ אֲשֶׁר נִשְׁבַּע
he-swore that the-land *** to-us to-give us to-bring-in in-order from-there

לַאֲבֹתֵינוּ׃ וַיְצַוֵּנוּ יְהוָה לַעֲשׂוֹת אֶת־ כָּל־
all-of *** to-obey Yahweh and-he-commanded-us (24) to-fathers-of-us

הַחֻקִּים הָאֵלֶּה לְיִרְאָה אֶת־ יְהוָה אֱלֹהֵינוּ לְטוֹב לָנוּ כָּל־
all-of for-us for-good God-of-us Yahweh *** to-fear the-these the-decrees

הַיָּמִים לְחַיֹּתֵנוּ כְּהַיּוֹם הַזֶּה׃ וּצְדָקָה
and-righteousness (25) the-this as-the-day to-keep-alive-us the-days

תִּהְיֶה־ לָּנוּ כִּי־ נִשְׁמֹר לַעֲשׂוֹת אֶת־ כָּל־ הַמִּצְוָה הַזֹּאת
the-this the-law all-of *** to-obey we-are-careful if for-us she-will-be

לִפְנֵי יְהוָה אֱלֹהֵינוּ כַּאֲשֶׁר צִוָּנוּ׃ כִּי יְבִיאֲךָ
he-brings-you when (7:1) he-commanded-us just-as God-of-us Yahweh before

יְהוָה אֱלֹהֶיךָ אֶל־ הָאָרֶץ אֲשֶׁר־אַתָּה בָא־ שָׁמָּה לְרִשְׁתָּהּ
to-possess-her to-there entering you that the-land into God-of-you Yahweh

land. [16]Do not test the LORD your God as you did at Massah. [17]Be sure to keep the commands of the LORD your God and the stipulations and decrees he has given you. [18]Do what is right and good in the LORD's sight, so that it may go well with you and you may go in and take over the good land that the LORD promised on oath to your forefathers, [19]thrusting out all your enemies before you, as the LORD said.

[20]In the future, when your son asks you, "What is the meaning of the stipulations, decrees and laws the LORD our God has commanded you?" [21]tell him: "We were slaves of Pharaoh in Egypt, but the LORD brought us out of Egypt with a mighty hand. [22]Before our eyes the LORD sent miraculous signs and wonders—great and terrible—upon Egypt and Pharaoh and his whole household. [23]But he brought us out from there to bring us in and give us the land that he promised on oath to our forefathers. [24]The LORD commanded us to obey all these decrees and to fear the LORD our God, so that we might always prosper and be kept alive, as is the case today. [25]And if we are careful to obey all this law before the LORD our God, as he has commanded us, that will be our righteousness."

Driving Out the Nations

7 When the LORD your God brings you into the land you are entering to possess

וְנָשַׁל גּוֹיִם־רַבִּים ׀ מִפָּנֶיךָ הַחִתִּי וְהַגִּרְגָּשִׁי
and-the-Girgashite the-Hittite from-before-you many nations and-he-drives-out

וְהָאֱמֹרִי וְהַכְּנַעֲנִי וְהַפְּרִזִּי וְהַחִוִּי
and-the-Hivite and-the-Perizzite and-the-Canaanite and-the-Amorite

וְהַיְבוּסִי שִׁבְעָה גוֹיִם רַבִּים וַעֲצוּמִים מִמֶּךָּ׃
than-you and-ones-stronger ones-larger nations seven and-the-Jebusite

וּנְתָנָם יְהוָה אֱלֹהֶיךָ לְפָנֶיךָ וְהִכִּיתָם
and-you-defeat-them before-you God-of-you Yahweh and-he-delivers-them (2)

הַחֲרֵם תַּחֲרִים אֹתָם לֹא־תִכְרֹת לָהֶם בְּרִית וְלֹא
and-not treaty with-them you-make not them you-must-destroy to-destroy

תְחָנֵּם׃ וְלֹא תִתְחַתֵּן בָּם בִּתְּךָ
daughter-of-you with-them you-intermarry and-not (3) you-show-mercy-to-them

לֹא־תִתֵּן לִבְנוֹ וּבִתּוֹ לֹא־תִקַּח לִבְנֶךָ׃
for-son-of-you you-take not and-daughter-of-him to-son-of-him you-give not

כִּי־יָסִיר אֶת־בִּנְךָ מֵאַחֲרַי וְעָבְדוּ אֱלֹהִים
gods and-they-will-serve from-after-me son-of-you *** he-will-turn for (4)

אֲחֵרִים וְחָרָה אַף־יְהוָה בָּכֶם וְהִשְׁמִידְךָ
and-he-will-destroy-you against-you Yahweh anger-of and-he-will-burn other-ones

מַהֵר׃ כִּי־אִם־כֹּה תַעֲשׂוּ לָהֶם מִזְבְּחֹתֵיהֶם תִּתֹּצוּ
you-break-down altars-of-them to-them you-do this indeed but (5) quickly

וּמַצֵּבֹתָם תְּשַׁבֵּרוּ וַאֲשֵׁירֵהֶם תְּגַדֵּעוּן
you-cut-down and-Asherah-poles-of-them you-smash and-sacred-stones-of-them

וּפְסִילֵיהֶם תִּשְׂרְפוּן בָּאֵשׁ׃ כִּי עַם קָדוֹשׁ אַתָּה לַיהוָה
to-Yahweh you holy people for (6) in-the-fire you-burn and-idols-of-them

אֱלֹהֶיךָ בְּךָ בָּחַר ׀ יְהוָה אֱלֹהֶיךָ לִהְיוֹת לוֹ לְעַם
as-people-of for-him to-be God-of-you Yahweh he-chose to-you God-of-you

סְגֻלָּה מִכֹּל הָעַמִּים אֲשֶׁר עַל־פְּנֵי הָאֲדָמָה׃ לֹא
not (7) the-earth faces-of on that the-peoples from-all-of treasure

מֵרֻבְּכֶם מִכָּל־הָעַמִּים חָשַׁק יְהוָה
Yahweh he-set-affection the-peoples than-all-of because-to-be-numerous-you

בָּכֶם וַיִּבְחַר בָּכֶם כִּי־אַתֶּם הַמְעַט מִכָּל־הָעַמִּים׃ כִּי
but (8) the-peoples of-all-of the-fewest you for to-you and-he-chose on-you

מֵאַהֲבַת יְהוָה אֶתְכֶם וּמִשָּׁמְרוֹ אֶת־הַשְּׁבֻעָה
the-oath *** and-because-to-keep-him for-you Yahweh because-of-love-of

אֲשֶׁר נִשְׁבַּע לַאֲבֹתֵיכֶם הוֹצִיא יְהוָה אֶתְכֶם בְּיָד חֲזָקָה
mighty with-hand you Yahweh he-brought-out to-fathers-of-you he-swore that

וַיִּפְדְּךָ מִבֵּית עֲבָדִים מִיַּד פַּרְעֹה מֶלֶךְ־מִצְרָיִם׃
Egypt king-of Pharaoh from-hand-of slaveries from-house-of and-he-redeemed-you

and drives out before you
many nations—the Hittites,
Girgashites, Amorites, Canaanites, Perizzites, Hivites
and Jebusites, seven nations
larger and stronger than you—
2and when the LORD your God
has delivered them over to you
and you have defeated them,
then you must destroy them
totally.[o] Make no treaty with
them, and show them no
mercy. 3Do not intermarry
with them. Do not give your
daughters to their sons or take
their daughters for your sons,
4for they will turn your sons
away from following me to
serve other gods, and the
LORD's anger will burn against
you and will quickly destroy
you. 5This is what you are to
do to them: Break down their
altars, smash their sacred
stones, cut down their
Asherah poles[p] and burn their
idols in the fire. 6For you are a
people holy to the LORD your
God. The LORD your God has
chosen you out of all the peoples on the face of the earth to
be his people, his treasured
possession.
7The LORD did not set his
affection on you and choose
you because you were more
numerous than other peoples,
for you were the fewest of all
peoples. 8But it was because
the LORD loved you and kept
the oath he swore to your
forefathers that he brought
you out with a mighty hand
and redeemed you from the
land of slavery, from the
power of Pharaoh king of

[o]2 The Hebrew term refers to the irrevocable giving over of things or persons to the LORD, often by totally destroying them; also in verse 26.
[p]5 That is, symbols of the goddess Asherah; here and elsewhere in Deuteronomy

וְיָדַעְתָּ כִּי־יְהוָה אֱלֹהֶיךָ הוּא הָאֱלֹהִים הָאֵל הַנֶּאֱמָן
the-being-faithful the-God the-God he God-of-you Yahweh that so-you-know (9)

שֹׁמֵר הַבְּרִית וְהַחֶסֶד לְאֹהֲבָיו וּלְשֹׁמְרֵי
and-to-ones-keeping-of to-ones-loving-him and-the-love the-covenant keeping

מִצְוֺתָו לְאֶלֶף דּוֹר׃ וּמְשַׁלֵּם לְשֹׂנְאָיו
to-ones-hating-him but-repaying (10) generation to-thousand commands-of-him

אֶל־פָּנָיו לְהַאֲבִידוֹ לֹא יְאַחֵר לְשֹׂנְאוֹ אֶל־
to to-ones-hating-him he-will-be-slow not to-destroy-him faces-of-him to

פָּנָיו יְשַׁלֶּם־לוֹ׃ וְשָׁמַרְתָּ אֶת־הַמִּצְוָה
the-command *** so-you-take-care (11) to-him he-will-repay faces-of-him

וְאֶת־הַחֻקִּים וְאֶת־הַמִּשְׁפָּטִים אֲשֶׁר אָנֹכִי מְצַוְּךָ הַיּוֹם לַעֲשׂוֹתָם׃
to-follow-them the-day giving-you I that the-laws and the-decrees and

וְהָיָה ׀ עֵקֶב תִּשְׁמְעוּן אֵת הַמִּשְׁפָּטִים הָאֵלֶּה וּשְׁמַרְתֶּם
and-you-are-careful the-these the-laws *** you-attend if and-he-will-be (12)

וַעֲשִׂיתֶם אֹתָם וְשָׁמַר יְהוָה אֱלֹהֶיךָ לְךָ אֶת־
*** with-you God-of-you Yahweh then-he-will-keep them and-you-follow

הַבְּרִית וְאֶת־הַחֶסֶד אֲשֶׁר נִשְׁבַּע לַאֲבֹתֶיךָ׃
to-fathers-of-you he-swore that the-love and the-covenant

וַאֲהֵבְךָ וּבֵרַכְךָ וְהִרְבֶּךָ
and-he-will-increase-you and-he-will-bless-you and-he-will-love-you (13)

וּבֵרַךְ פְּרִי־בִטְנְךָ וּפְרִי־אַדְמָתֶךָ דְּגָנְךָ
grain-of-you land-of-you and-fruit-of womb-of-you fruit-of and-he-will-bless

וְתִירֹשְׁךָ וְיִצְהָרֶךָ שְׁגַר־אֲלָפֶיךָ וְעַשְׁתְּרֹת
and-lambs-of herds-of-you calf-of and-oil-of-you and-new-wine-of-you

צֹאנֶךָ עַל הָאֲדָמָה אֲשֶׁר־נִשְׁבַּע לַאֲבֹתֶיךָ לָתֶת לָךְ׃
to-you to-give to-fathers-of-you he-swore that the-land in flock-of-you

בָּרוּךְ תִּהְיֶה מִכָּל־הָעַמִּים לֹא־יִהְיֶה
he-will-be not the-peoples more-than-any-of you-will-be being-blessed (14)

בְךָ עָקָר וַעֲקָרָה וּבִבְהֶמְתֶּךָ׃
or-among-livestock-of-you or childless-woman childless-man among-you

וְהֵסִיר יְהוָה מִמְּךָ כָּל־חֹלִי וְכָל־
and-all-of disease every-of from-you Yahweh and-he-will-keep-free (15)

מַדְוֵי מִצְרַיִם הָרָעִים אֲשֶׁר יָדַעְתָּ לֹא יְשִׂימָם
he-will-inflict-them not you-knew that the-horrible-ones Egypt diseases-of

בָּךְ וּנְתָנָם בְּכָל־שֹׂנְאֶיךָ׃ וְאָכַלְתָּ
so-you-destroy (16) ones-hating-you on-all-of but-he-will-inflict-them on-you

אֶת־כָּל־הָעַמִּים אֲשֶׁר יְהוָה אֱלֹהֶיךָ נֹתֵן לָךְ לֹא־תָחוֹס
she-must-pity not to-you giving God-of-you Yahweh whom the-peoples all-of ***

Egypt. [9]Know therefore that the LORD your God is God; he is the faithful God, keeping his covenant of love to a thousand generations of those who love him and keep his commands. [10]But

those who hate him he will
repay to their face by
destruction;
he will not be slow to
repay to their face
those who hate him.

[11]Therefore, take care to follow the commands, decrees and laws I give you today.

[12]If you pay attention to these laws and are careful to follow them, then the LORD your God will keep his covenant of love with you, as he swore to your forefathers. [13]He will love you and bless you and increase your numbers. He will bless the fruit of your womb, the crops of your land—your grain, new wine and oil—the calves of your herds and the lambs of your flocks in the land that he swore to your forefathers to give you. [14]You will be blessed more than any other people; none of your men or women will be childless, nor any of your livestock without young. [15]The LORD will keep you free from every disease. He will not inflict on you the horrible diseases you knew in Egypt, but he will inflict them on all who hate you. [16]You must destroy all the peoples the LORD your God gives over to you. Do not look on them with pity

°9 ק מצותיו

עֵינְךָ עֲלֵיהֶם וְלֹא תַעֲבֹד אֶת־אֱלֹהֵיהֶם כִּי־מוֹקֵשׁ הוּא לָךְ׃
to-you that snare for gods-of-them *** you-serve and-not on-them eye-of-you

(17) כִּי תֹאמַר בִּלְבָבְךָ רַבִּים הַגּוֹיִם הָאֵלֶּה
the-these the-nations ones-stronger in-heart-of-you you-may-say now (17)

מִמֶּנִּי אֵיכָה אוּכַל לְהוֹרִישָׁם׃ (18) לֹא תִירָא מֵהֶם
of-them you-be-afraid not (18) to-drive-out-them can-I how? than-me

זָכֹר תִּזְכֹּר אֵת אֲשֶׁר־עָשָׂה יְהוָה אֱלֹהֶיךָ לְפַרְעֹה
to-Pharaoh God-of-you Yahweh he-did what *** you-remember to-remember

וּלְכָל־מִצְרָיִם׃ (19) הַמַּסֹּת הַגְּדֹלֹת אֲשֶׁר־רָאוּ
they-saw that the-great-ones and-the-trials (19) Egypt and-to-all-of

עֵינֶיךָ וְהָאֹתֹת וְהַמֹּפְתִים וְהַיָּד הַחֲזָקָה וְהַזְּרֹעַ
and-the-arm the-mighty and-the-hand and-the-wonders and-the-signs eyes-of-you

הַנְּטוּיָה אֲשֶׁר הוֹצִאֲךָ יְהוָה אֱלֹהֶיךָ כֵּן־
same God-of-you Yahweh he-brought-out-you which the-being-outstretched

יַעֲשֶׂה יְהוָה אֱלֹהֶיךָ לְכָל־הָעַמִּים אֲשֶׁר־אַתָּה יָרֵא
fearing you that the-peoples to-all-of God-of-you Yahweh he-will-do

מִפְּנֵיהֶם׃ (20) וְגַם אֶת־הַצִּרְעָה יְשַׁלַּח יְהוָה
Yahweh he-will-send the-hornet *** and-also (20) from-presence-of-them

אֱלֹהֶיךָ בָּם עַד־אֲבֹד הַנִּשְׁאָרִים וְהַנִּסְתָּרִים
and-the-ones-hiding the-ones-surviving to-perish until among-them God-of-you

מִפָּנֶיךָ׃ (21) לֹא תַעֲרֹץ מִפְּנֵיהֶם כִּי־יְהוָה
Yahweh for from-presence-of-them you-be-terrified not (21) from-faces-of-you

אֱלֹהֶיךָ בְּקִרְבֶּךָ אֵל גָּדוֹל וְנוֹרָא׃ (22) וְנָשַׁל[9]
and-he-will-drive (22) and-being-awesome great God in-among-you God-of-you

יְהוָה אֱלֹהֶיךָ אֶת־הַגּוֹיִם הָאֵל מִפָּנֶיךָ מְעַט מְעָט
little little from-before-you the-those the-nations *** God-of-you Yahweh

לֹא תוּכַל כַּלֹּתָם מַהֵר פֶּן־תִּרְבֶּה עָלֶיךָ
around-you she-will-multiply or at-once to-eliminate-them you-can not

חַיַּת הַשָּׂדֶה׃ (23) וּנְתָנָם יְהוָה אֱלֹהֶיךָ לְפָנֶיךָ
to-you God-of-you Yahweh but-he-will-deliver-them (23) the-field animal-of

וְהָמָם מְהוּמָה גְדֹלָה עַד הִשָּׁמְדָם׃
to-be-destroyed-them until great confusion and-he-will-confuse-them

(24) וְנָתַן מַלְכֵיהֶם בְּיָדֶךָ וְהַאֲבַדְתָּ
and-you-will-wipe-out into-hand-of-you kings-of-them and-he-will-give (24)

אֶת־שְׁמָם מִתַּחַת הַשָּׁמָיִם לֹא־יִתְיַצֵּב אִישׁ
anyone he-will-stand not the-heavens from-under name-of-them ***

בְּפָנֶיךָ עַד הִשְׁמִדְךָ אֹתָם׃ (25) פְּסִילֵי אֱלֹהֵיהֶם
gods-of-them images-of (25) them to-destroy-you when against-faces-of-you

and do not serve their gods,
for that will be a snare to you.
17You may say to yourselves,
"These nations are stronger
than we are. How can we
drive them out?" 18But do not
be afraid of them; remember
well what the LORD your God
did to Pharoah and to all
Egypt. 19You saw with your
own eyes the great trials, the
miraculous signs and wonders, the mighty hand and
outstretched arm, with which
the LORD your God brought
you out. The LORD your God
will do the same to all the peoples you now fear. 20Moreover,
the LORD your God will send
the hornet among them until
even the survivors who hide
from you have perished. 21Do
not be terrified by them, for
the LORD your God, who is
among you, is a great and
awesome God. 22The LORD
your God will drive out those
nations before you, little by
little. You will not be allowed
to eliminate them all at once,
or the wild animals will multiply around you. 23But the LORD
your God will deliver them
over to you, throwing them
into great confusion until they
are destroyed. 24He will give
their kings into your hand,
and you will wipe out their
names from under heaven. No
one will be able to stand up
against you; you will destroy
them. 25The images of their

תִּשְׂרְפוּן בָּאֵשׁ לֹא־תַחְמֹד כֶּסֶף וְזָהָב עֲלֵיהֶם וְלָקַחְתָּ לָךְ
for-you so-you-take on-them and-gold silver you-covet not in-the-fire you-burn

פֶּן תִּוָּקֵשׁ בּוֹ כִּי תוֹעֲבַת יְהוָה אֱלֹהֶיךָ הוּא׃
he God-of-you Yahweh detestable-of for by-him you-will-be-ensnared or

וְלֹא־תָבִיא תוֹעֵבָה אֶל־בֵּיתֶךָ וְהָיִיתָ
or-you-will-be house-of-you into detestable-thing you-bring and-not (26)

חֵרֶם כָּמֹהוּ שַׁקֵּץ ׀ תְּשַׁקְּצֶנּוּ וְתַעֵב ׀ תְּתַעֲבֶנּוּ
you-detest-him and-to-detest you-abhor-him to-abhor as-he for-destruction

כִּי־חֵרֶם הוּא׃ כָּל־הַמִּצְוָה אֲשֶׁר אָנֹכִי מְצַוְּךָ הַיּוֹם
the-day giving-you I that the-command every-of (8:1) he for-destruction for

תִּשְׁמְרוּן לַעֲשׂוֹת לְמַעַן תִּחְיוּן וּרְבִיתֶם
and-you-may-increase you-may-live so-that to-follow you-be-careful

וּבָאתֶם וִירִשְׁתֶּם אֶת־הָאָרֶץ אֲשֶׁר־נִשְׁבַּע יְהוָה
Yahweh he-promised that the-land *** and-you-may-possess and-you-may-enter

לַאֲבֹתֵיכֶם׃ וְזָכַרְתָּ אֶת־כָּל־הַדֶּרֶךְ אֲשֶׁר הֹלִיכְךָ
he-led-you that the-way all-of *** and-you-remember (2) to-fathers-of-you

יְהוָה אֱלֹהֶיךָ זֶה אַרְבָּעִים שָׁנָה בַּמִּדְבָּר לְמַעַן עַנֹּתְךָ
to-humble-you in-order in-the-desert year forty this God-of-you Yahweh

לְנַסֹּתְךָ לָדַעַת אֶת־אֲשֶׁר בִּלְבָבְךָ הֲתִשְׁמֹר מִצְוֹתָו אִם־לֹא׃
not or commands-of-him to-keep in-heart-of-you what *** to-know to-test-you

וַיְעַנְּךָ וַיַּרְעִבֶךָ וַיַּאֲכִלְךָ אֶת־הַמָּן
the-manna *** then-he-fed-you and-he-made-hungry-you and-he-humbled-you (3)

אֲשֶׁר לֹא־יָדַעְתָּ וְלֹא יָדְעוּן אֲבֹתֶיךָ לְמַעַן הוֹדִעֲךָ
to-teach-you in-order fathers-of-you they-knew and-not you-knew not which

כִּי לֹא עַל־הַלֶּחֶם לְבַדּוֹ יִחְיֶה הָאָדָם כִּי עַל־כָּל־מוֹצָא
thing-from every-of on but the-man he-lives by-himself the-bread on not that

פִּי־יְהוָה יִחְיֶה הָאָדָם׃ שִׂמְלָתְךָ לֹא בָלְתָה
she-wore-out not clothing-of-you (4) the-man he-lives Yahweh mouth-of

מֵעָלֶיךָ וְרַגְלְךָ לֹא בָצֵקָה זֶה אַרְבָּעִים שָׁנָה׃ וְיָדַעְתָּ
so-you-know (5) year forty this she-swelled not and-foot-of-you from-on-you

עִם־לְבָבֶךָ כִּי כַּאֲשֶׁר יְיַסֵּר אִישׁ אֶת־בְּנוֹ יְהוָה
Yahweh son-of-him *** man he-disciplines just-as that heart-of-you in

אֱלֹהֶיךָ מְיַסְּרֶךָּ׃ וְשָׁמַרְתָּ אֶת־מִצְוֹת יְהוָה
Yahweh commands-of *** now-you-observe (6) disciplining-you God-of-you

אֱלֹהֶיךָ לָלֶכֶת בִּדְרָכָיו וּלְיִרְאָה אֹתוֹ׃ כִּי יְהוָה אֱלֹהֶיךָ
God-of-you Yahweh for (7) him and-to-revere in-ways-of-him to-walk God-of-you

מְבִיאֲךָ אֶל־אֶרֶץ טוֹבָה אֶרֶץ נַחֲלֵי מָיִם עֲיָנֹת וּתְהֹמֹת
and-springs pools waters streams-of land-of good land into bringing-you

gods you are to burn in the
fire. Do not covet the silver
and gold on them, do not take
it for yourselves, or you will be
ensnared by it, for it is detestable to the LORD your God.
26Do not bring a detestable
thing into your house or you,
like it, will be set apart for destruction. Utterly abhor and
detest it, for it is set apart for
destruction.

Do Not Forget the LORD

8 Be careful to follow every
command I am giving you
today, so that you may live
and increase and may enter
and possess the land that the
LORD promised on oath to your
forefathers. 2Remember how
the LORD your God led you all
the way in the desert these
forty years, to humble you and
to test you in order to know
what was in your heart,
whether or not you would
keep his commands. 3He humbled you, causing you to hunger and then feeding you with
manna, which neither you
nor your fathers had known,
to teach you that man does not
live on bread alone but on
every word that comes from
the mouth of the LORD. 4Your
clothes did not wear out and
your feet did not swell during
these forty years. 5Know then
in your heart that as a man
disciplines his son, so the
LORD your God disciplines
you.
6Observe the commands of
the LORD your God, walking in
his ways and revering him.
7For the LORD your God is
bringing you into a good
land—a land with streams and
pools of water, with springs

°2 ק מצותיו

יֹצְאִים בַּבִּקְעָה וּבָהָר׃ אֶרֶץ חִטָּה וּשְׂעֹרָה
and-barley wheat land-of (8) and-into-the-hill into-the-valley ones-flowing

וְגֶפֶן וּתְאֵנָה וְרִמּוֹן אֶרֶץ־ זֵית שֶׁמֶן וּדְבָשׁ׃ אֶרֶץ
land (9) and-honey oil olive-of land-of and-pomegranate and-fig-tree and-vine

אֲשֶׁר לֹא בְמִסְכֵּנֻת תֹּאכַל־ בָּהּ לֶחֶם לֹא־ תֶחְסַר כֹּל
anything you-will-lack not bread in-her you-will-eat in-scarcity not where

בָּהּ אֶרֶץ אֲשֶׁר אֲבָנֶיהָ בַרְזֶל וּמֵהֲרָרֶיהָ תַּחְצֹב נְחֹשֶׁת׃
copper you-can-dig and-from-hills-of-her iron rocks-of-her where land in-her

וְאָכַלְתָּ וְשָׂבָעְתָּ וּבֵרַכְתָּ אֶת־ יְהוָה אֱלֹהֶיךָ
God-of-you Yahweh *** then-you-praise and-you-are-satisfied when-you-eat (10)

עַל־ הָאָרֶץ הַטֹּבָה אֲשֶׁר נָתַן־ לָךְ׃ הִשָּׁמֶר לְךָ פֶּן־
so-not to-you be-careful! (11) to-you he-gave that the-good the-land for

תִּשְׁכַּח אֶת־ יְהוָה אֱלֹהֶיךָ לְבִלְתִּי שְׁמֹר מִצְוֹתָיו
commands-of-him to-observe not God-of-you Yahweh *** you-forget

וּמִשְׁפָּטָיו וְחֻקֹּתָיו אֲשֶׁר אָנֹכִי מְצַוְּךָ הַיּוֹם׃ פֶּן־
otherwise (12) the-day giving-you I that and-decrees-of-him and-laws-of-him

תֹּאכַל וְשָׂבָעְתָּ וּבָתִּים טֹבִים תִּבְנֶה
you-build fine-ones and-houses and-you-are-satisfied when-you-eat

וְיָשָׁבְתָּ׃ וּבְקָרְךָ וְצֹאנְךָ יִרְבְּיֻן
they-grow-large and-flock-of-you and-herd-of-you (13) and-you-settle-down

וְכֶסֶף וְזָהָב יִרְבֶּה־ לָּךְ וְכֹל אֲשֶׁר־ לְךָ יִרְבֶּה׃
he-multiplies to-you that and-all to-you he-increases and-gold and-silver

וְרָם לְבָבֶךָ וְשָׁכַחְתָּ אֶת־ יְהוָה
Yahweh *** and-you-will-forget heart-of-you then-he-will-become-proud (14)

אֱלֹהֶיךָ הַמּוֹצִיאֲךָ מֵאֶרֶץ מִצְרַיִם מִבֵּית עֲבָדִים׃
slaveries from-house-of Egypt from-land-of the-one-bringing-you God-of-you

הַמּוֹלִיכֲךָ בַּמִּדְבָּר ׀ הַגָּדֹל וְהַנּוֹרָא
and-the-being-terrible the-vast through-the-desert the-one-leading-you (15)

נָחָשׁ ׀ שָׂרָף וְעַקְרָב וְצִמָּאוֹן אֲשֶׁר אֵין־ מָיִם הַמּוֹצִיא
the-one-bringing waters not where and-dry-ground and-scorpion venomous snake

לְךָ מַיִם מִצּוּר הַחַלָּמִישׁ׃ הַמַּאֲכִלְךָ מָן
manna the-one-feeding-you (16) the-hard from-rock-of waters for-you

בַּמִּדְבָּר אֲשֶׁר לֹא־ יָדְעוּן אֲבֹתֶיךָ לְמַעַן עַנֹּתְךָ
to-humble-you in-order fathers-of-you they-knew not that in-the-desert

וּלְמַעַן נַסֹּתֶךָ לְהֵיטִבְךָ בְּאַחֲרִיתֶךָ׃
in-end-of-you to-make-go-well-with-you to-test-you and-in-order

וְאָמַרְתָּ בִּלְבָבֶךָ כֹּחִי וְעֹצֶם יָדִי
hand-of-me and-strength-of power-of-me in-heart-of-you now-you-may-say (17)

flowing in the valleys and
hills; [8]a land with wheat and
barley, vines and fig trees,
pomegranates, olive oil and
honey; [9]a land where bread
will not be scarce and you will
lack nothing; a land where the
rocks are iron and you can dig
copper out of the hills.
[10]When you have eaten and
are satisfied, praise the LORD
your God for the good land he
has given you. [11]Be careful that
you do not forget the LORD
your God, failing to observe
his commands, his laws and
his decrees that I am giving
you this day. [12]Otherwise,
when you eat and are sat-
isfied, when you build fine
houses and settle down, [13]and
when your herds and flocks
grow large and your silver and
gold increase and all you have
is multiplied, [14]then your heart
will become proud and you
will forget the LORD your God,
who brought you out of Egypt,
out of the land of slavery. [15]He
led you through the vast and
dreadful desert, that thirsty
and waterless land, with its
venomous snakes and scor-
pions. He brought you water
out of hard rock. [16]He gave you
manna to eat in the desert,
something your fathers had
never known, to humble and
to test you so that in the end it
might go well with you. [17]You
may say to yourself, "My
power and the strength of my

עָשָׂה לִי אֶת־ הַחַיִל הַזֶּה׃ וְזָכַרְתָּ אֶת־ יְהוָה
Yahweh *** but-you-remember (18) the-this the-wealth *** for-me he-produced

אֱלֹהֶיךָ כִּי הוּא הַנֹּתֵן לְךָ כֹּחַ לַעֲשׂוֹת חָיִל לְמַעַן
in-order wealth to-produce ability to-you the-one-giving he for God-of-you

הָקִים אֶת־ בְּרִיתוֹ אֲשֶׁר־ נִשְׁבַּע לַאֲבֹתֶיךָ כַּיּוֹם
as-the-day to-fathers-of-you he-swore which covenant-of-him *** to-confirm

הַזֶּה׃ וְהָיָה אִם־ שָׁכֹחַ תִּשְׁכַּח אֶת־ יְהוָה אֱלֹהֶיךָ
God-of-you Yahweh *** you-forget to-forget if and-he-will-be (19) the-this

וְהָלַכְתָּ אַחֲרֵי אֱלֹהִים אֲחֵרִים וַעֲבַדְתָּם וְהִשְׁתַּחֲוִיתָ
and-you-bow-down and-you-worship-them other-ones gods after and-you-follow

לָהֶם הַעִדֹתִי בָכֶם הַיּוֹם כִּי אָבֹד תֹּאבֵדוּן׃
you-will-perish to-perish that the-day against-you I-testify to-them

כַּגּוֹיִם אֲשֶׁר יְהוָה מַאֲבִיד מִפְּנֵיכֶם כֵּן תֹּאבֵדוּן
you-will-perish so from-before-you destroying Yahweh that like-the-nations (20)

עֵקֶב לֹא תִשְׁמְעוּן בְּקוֹל יְהוָה אֱלֹהֵיכֶם׃ שְׁמַע יִשְׂרָאֵל אַתָּה
you Israel hear! (9:1) God-of-you Yahweh to-voice-of you-obeyed not for

עֹבֵר הַיּוֹם אֶת־ הַיַּרְדֵּן לָבֹא לָרֶשֶׁת גּוֹיִם גְּדֹלִים
ones-greater nations to-dispossess to-go-in the-Jordan *** the-day crossing

וַעֲצֻמִים מִמֶּךָּ עָרִים גְּדֹלֹת וּבְצֻרֹת בַּשָּׁמָיִם׃
to-the-skies and-walls large-ones cities than-you and-ones-stronger

עַם־ גָּדוֹל וָרָם בְּנֵי עֲנָקִים אֲשֶׁר אַתָּה יָדַעְתָּ וְאַתָּה
and-you you-know you whom Anakites sons-of and-tall strong people (2)

שָׁמַעְתָּ מִי יִתְיַצֵּב לִפְנֵי בְּנֵי עֲנָק׃ וְיָדַעְתָּ
but-you-be-assured (3) Anak sons-of against he-can-stand who? you-heard

הַיּוֹם כִּי יְהוָה אֱלֹהֶיךָ הוּא־ הָעֹבֵר לְפָנֶיךָ אֵשׁ
fire ahead-of-you the-one-crossing he God-of-you Yahweh that the-day

אֹכְלָה הוּא יַשְׁמִידֵם וְהוּא יַכְנִיעֵם לְפָנֶיךָ
before-you he-will-subdue-them and-he he-will-destroy-them he devouring

וְהוֹרַשְׁתָּם וְהַאֲבַדְתָּם מַהֵר כַּאֲשֶׁר
just-as quickly and-you-will-annihilate-them and-you-will-drive-out-them

דִּבֶּר יְהוָה לָךְ׃ אַל־ תֹּאמַר בִּלְבָבְךָ בַּהֲדֹף
after-to-drive-out in-heart-of-you you-say not (4) to-you Yahweh he-promised

יְהוָה אֱלֹהֶיךָ אֹתָם ׀ מִלְּפָנֶיךָ לֵאמֹר בְּצִדְקָתִי
because-of-righteousness-of-me to-say from-before-you them God-of-you Yahweh

הֱבִיאַנִי יְהוָה לָרֶשֶׁת אֶת־ הָאָרֶץ הַזֹּאת וּבְרִשְׁעַת
but-for-wickedness-of the-this the-land *** to-possess Yahweh he-brought-me

הַגּוֹיִם הָאֵלֶּה יְהוָה מוֹרִישָׁם מִפָּנֶיךָ׃ לֹא
not (5) from-before-you driving-them Yahweh the-these the-nations

hands have produced this wealth for me." [18]But remember the LORD your God, for it is he who gives you the ability to produce wealth, and so confirms his covenant, which he swore to your forefathers, as it is today.

[19]If you ever forget the LORD your God and follow other gods and worship and bow down to them, I testify against you today that you will surely be destroyed. [20]Like the nations the LORD destroyed before you, so you will be destroyed for not obeying the LORD your God.

Not Because of Israel's Righteousness

9 Hear, O Israel. You are now about to cross the Jordan to go in and dispossess nations greater and stronger than you, with large cities that have walls up to the sky. [2]The people are strong and tall—Anakites! You know about them and have heard it said: "Who can stand up against the Anakites?" [3]But be assured today that the LORD your God is the one who goes across ahead of you like a devouring fire. He will destroy them; he will subdue them before you. And you will drive them out and annihilate them quickly, as the LORD has promised you.

[4]After the LORD your God has driven them out before you, do not say to yourself, "The LORD has brought me here to take possession of this land because of my righteousness." No, it is on account of the wickedness of these nations that the LORD is going to drive them out before you. [5]It

בְּצִדְקָתְךָ וּבְיֹשֶׁר לְבָבְךָ אַתָּה בָא
going-in you heart-of-you or-for-integrity-of for-righteousness-of-you

לָרֶשֶׁת אֶת־ אַרְצָם כִּי בְּרִשְׁעַת ׀ הַגּוֹיִם הָאֵלֶּה
the-these the-nations for-wickedness-of but land-of-them *** to-possess

יְהוָה אֱלֹהֶיךָ מוֹרִישָׁם מִפָּנֶיךָ וּלְמַעַן הָקִים
to-accomplish and-in-order from-before-you driving-them God-of-you Yahweh

אֶת־ הַדָּבָר אֲשֶׁר נִשְׁבַּע יְהוָה לַאֲבֹתֶיךָ לְאַבְרָהָם לְיִצְחָק
to-Isacc to-Abraham to-fathers-of-you Yahweh he-swore that the-thing ***

וּלְיַעֲקֹב׃ וְיָדַעְתָּ כִּי לֹא בְצִדְקָתְךָ יְהוָה
Yahweh for-righteousness-of-you not that now-you-understand (6) and-to-Jacob

אֱלֹהֶיךָ נֹתֵן לְךָ אֶת־ הָאָרֶץ הַטּוֹבָה הַזֹּאת לְרִשְׁתָּהּ כִּי
for to-possess-her the-this the-good the-land *** to-you giving God-of-you

עַם־ קְשֵׁה־ עֹרֶף אָתָּה׃ זְכֹר אַל־ תִּשְׁכַּח אֵת אֲשֶׁר־ הִקְצַפְתָּ
you-angered how *** you-forget not remember! (7) you neck stiff-of people-of

אֶת־ יְהוָה אֱלֹהֶיךָ בַּמִּדְבָּר לְמִן־ הַיּוֹם אֲשֶׁר־ יָצָאתָ ׀
you-left that the-day on-from in-the-desert God-of-you Yahweh ***

מֵאֶרֶץ מִצְרַיִם עַד־ בֹּאֲכֶם עַד־הַמָּקוֹם הַזֶּה מַמְרִים
ones-rebelling the-this the-place at to-arrive-you until Egypt from-land-of

הֱיִיתֶם עִם־ יְהוָה׃ וּבְחֹרֵב הִקְצַפְתֶּם אֶת־ יְהוָה
Yahweh *** you-aroused-wrath and-at-Horeb (8) Yahweh against you-were

וַיִּתְאַנַּף יְהוָה בָּכֶם לְהַשְׁמִיד אֶתְכֶם׃ בַּעֲלֹתִי
when-to-go-up-me (9) you to-destroy with-you Yahweh so-he-was-angry

הָהָרָה לָקַחַת לוּחֹת הָאֲבָנִים לוּחֹת הַבְּרִית
the-covenant tables-of the-stones tablets-of to-receive on-the-mountain

אֲשֶׁר־ כָּרַת יְהוָה עִמָּכֶם וָאֵשֵׁב בָּהָר אַרְבָּעִים יוֹם
day forty on-the-mountain and-I-stayed with-you Yahweh he-made that

וְאַרְבָּעִים לַיְלָה לֶחֶם לֹא אָכַלְתִּי וּמַיִם לֹא שָׁתִיתִי׃ וַיִּתֵּן
and-he-gave (10) I-drank not and-waters I-ate not bread night and-forty

יְהוָה אֵלַי אֶת־ שְׁנֵי לוּחֹת הָאֲבָנִים כְּתֻבִים
ones-being-inscribed the-stones tablets-of two-of *** to-me Yahweh

בְּאֶצְבַּע אֱלֹהִים וַעֲלֵיהֶם כְּכָל־ הַדְּבָרִים אֲשֶׁר דִּבֶּר
he-proclaimed that the-commandments as-all-of and-on-them God by-finger-of

יְהוָה עִמָּכֶם בָּהָר מִתּוֹךְ הָאֵשׁ בְּיוֹם הַקָּהָל׃
the-assembly on-day-of the-fire out-of on-the-mountain to-you Yahweh

וַיְהִי מִקֵּץ אַרְבָּעִים יוֹם וְאַרְבָּעִים לַיְלָה נָתַן יְהוָה אֵלַי
to-me Yahweh he-gave night and-forty day forty at-end-of and-he-was (11)

אֶת־ שְׁנֵי לֻחֹת הָאֲבָנִים לֻחוֹת הַבְּרִית׃ וַיֹּאמֶר
then-he-told (12) the-covenant tablets-of the-stones tablets-of two-of ***

is not because of your righteousness or your integrity that you are going in to take possession of their land; but on account of the wickedness of these nations, the LORD your God will drive them out before you, to accomplish what he swore to your fathers, to Abraham, Isaac and Jacob.
6Understand, then, that it is not because of your righteousness that the LORD your God is giving you this good land to possess, for you are a stiff-necked people.

The Golden Calf

7Remember this and never forget how you provoked the LORD your God to anger in the desert. From the day you left Egypt until you arrived here, you have been rebellious against the LORD.
8At Horeb you aroused the LORD's wrath so that he was angry enough to destroy you.
9When I went up on the mountain to receive the tablets of stone, the tablets of the covenant that the LORD had made with you, I stayed on the mountain forty days and forty nights; I ate no bread and drank no water.
10The LORD gave me two stone tablets inscribed by the finger of God. On them were all the commandments the LORD proclaimed to you on the mountain out of the fire, on the day of the assembly.
11At the end of the forty days and forty nights, the LORD gave me the two stone tablets, the tablets of the covenant.

יְהוָה אֵלַי קוּם רֵד מַהֵר מִזֶּה כִּי שִׁחֵת
he-became-corrupt for from-here at-once go-down! rise! to-me Yahweh

עַמְּךָ אֲשֶׁר הוֹצֵאתָ מִמִּצְרָיִם סָרוּ מַהֵר מִן־הַדֶּרֶךְ
the-way from quickly they-turned from-Egypt you-brought whom people-of-you

אֲשֶׁר צִוִּיתִם עָשׂוּ לָהֶם מַסֵּכָה׃ וַיֹּאמֶר יְהוָה
Yahweh and-he-said (13) cast-idol for-them they-made I-commanded-them that

אֵלַי לֵאמֹר רָאִיתִי אֶת־הָעָם הַזֶּה וְהִנֵּה עַם־קְשֵׁה־עֹרֶף
neck stiff-of people-of and-see! the-this the-people *** I-see to-say to-me

הוּא׃ הֶרֶף מִמֶּנִּי וְאַשְׁמִידֵם וְאֶמְחֶה אֶת־
*** and-I-may-blot-out so-I-may-destroy-them from-me let-alone! (14) he

שְׁמָם מִתַּחַת הַשָּׁמָיִם וְאֶעֱשֶׂה אוֹתְךָ לְגוֹי־עָצוּם
stronger into-nation you and-I-will-make the-heavens from-under name-of-them

וָרָב מִמֶּנּוּ׃ וָאֵפֶן וָאֵרֵד מִן־הָהָר
the-mountain from and-I-went-down so-I-turned (15) than-him and-larger

וְהָהָר בֹּעֵר בָּאֵשׁ וּשְׁנֵי לֻחֹת הַבְּרִית
the-covenant tablets-of and-two-of with-the-fire blazing and-the-mountain

עַל שְׁתֵּי יָדָי׃ וָאֵרֶא וְהִנֵּה חֲטָאתֶם לַיהוָה
against-Yahweh you-sinned then-see! when-I-looked (16) hands-of-me two-of in

אֱלֹהֵיכֶם עֲשִׂיתֶם לָכֶם עֵגֶל מַסֵּכָה סַרְתֶּם מַהֵר מִן־
from quickly you-turned cast-idol calf for-you you-made God-of-you

הַדֶּרֶךְ אֲשֶׁר־צִוָּה יְהוָה אֶתְכֶם׃ וָאֶתְפֹּשׂ בִּשְׁנֵי הַלֻּחֹת
the-tablets on-two-of so-I-held (17) you Yahweh he-commanded that the-way

וָאַשְׁלִכֵם מֵעַל שְׁתֵּי יָדָי וָאֲשַׁבְּרֵם לְעֵינֵיכֶם׃
before-eyes-of-you and-I-broke-them hands-of-me two-of from-in and-I-threw-them

וָאֶתְנַפַּל לִפְנֵי יְהוָה כָּרִאשֹׁנָה אַרְבָּעִים יוֹם וְאַרְבָּעִים לַיְלָה
night and-forty day forty as-the-first Yahweh before and-I-prostrated (18)

לֶחֶם לֹא אָכַלְתִּי וּמַיִם לֹא שָׁתִיתִי עַל כָּל־חַטַּאתְכֶם אֲשֶׁר
that sin-of-you all-of because-of I-drank not and-waters I-ate not bread

חֲטָאתֶם לַעֲשׂוֹת הָרַע בְּעֵינֵי יְהוָה לְהַכְעִיסוֹ׃ כִּי
for (19) to-make-angry-him Yahweh in-eyes-of the-evil to-do you-sinned

יָגֹרְתִּי מִפְּנֵי הָאַף וְהַחֵמָה אֲשֶׁר קָצַף יְהוָה
Yahweh he-was-angry for and-the-wrath the-anger from-presences-of I-feared

עֲלֵיכֶם לְהַשְׁמִיד אֶתְכֶם וַיִּשְׁמַע יְהוָה אֵלַי גַּם בַּפַּעַם
at-the-time again to-me Yahweh but-he-listened you to-destroy with-you

הַהִוא׃ וּבְאַהֲרֹן הִתְאַנַּף יְהוָה מְאֹד לְהַשְׁמִידוֹ
to-destroy-him very Yahweh he-was-angry and-with-Aaron (20) the-that

וָאֶתְפַּלֵּל גַּם־בְּעַד אַהֲרֹן בָּעֵת הַהִוא׃ וְאֶת־
and (21) the-that at-the-time Aaron on-behalf-of also but-I-prayed

12 Then the LORD told me, "Go
down from here at once, because your people whom you
brought out of Egypt have
become corrupt. They have
turned away quickly from
what I commanded them and
have made a cast idol for
themselves."
13 And the LORD said to me, "I
have seen this people, and
they are a stiff-necked people
indeed! 14 Let me alone, so that
I may destroy them and blot
out their name from under
heaven. And I will make you
into a nation stronger and
more numerous than they."
15 So I turned and went down
from the mountain while it
was ablaze with fire. And the
two tablets of the covenant
were in my hands.[q] 16 When I
looked, I saw that you had
sinned against the LORD your
God; you had made for yourselves an idol cast in the shape
of a calf. You had turned aside
quickly from the way that the
LORD had commanded you.
17 So I took the two tablets and
threw them out of my hands,
breaking them to pieces before
your eyes.
18 Then once again I fell prostrate before the LORD for forty
days and forty nights; I ate no
bread and drank no water, because of all the sin you had
committed, doing what was
evil in the LORD's sight and so
provoking him to anger. 19 I
feared the anger and wrath of
the LORD, for he was angry
enough with you to destroy
you. But again the LORD listened to me. 20 And the LORD
was angry enough with Aaron
to destroy him, but at that
time I prayed for Aaron too.

q15 Or *And I had the two tablets of the covenant with me, one in each hand*

חַטַּאתְכֶם אֲשֶׁר־ עֲשִׂיתֶם אֶת־ הָעֵגֶל לָקַחְתִּי וָאֶשְׂרֹף אֹתוֹ ׀

him and-I-burned I-took the-calf *** you-made that sinful-thing-of-you

בָּאֵשׁ וָאֶכֹּת אֹתוֹ טָחוֹן הֵיטֵב עַד אֲשֶׁר־ דַּק

he-was-fine when until to-be-fine to-grind him then-I-crushed in-the-fire

לְעָפָר וָאַשְׁלִךְ אֶת־ עֲפָרוֹ אֶל־ הַנַּחַל הַיֹּרֵד מִן־

from the-one-flowing the-stream into dust-of-him *** and-I-threw as-dust

הָהָר׃ וּבְתַבְעֵרָה וּבְמַסָּה וּבְקִבְרֹת הַתַּאֲוָה

Hattaavah and-at-Kibroth and-at-Massah and-at-Taberah (22) the-mountain

מַקְצִפִים הֱיִיתֶם אֶת־ יְהוָה׃ וּבִשְׁלֹחַ יְהוָה אֶתְכֶם

you Yahweh and-when-to-send (23) Yahweh *** you-were ones-angering

מִקָּדֵשׁ בַּרְנֵעַ לֵאמֹר עֲלוּ וּרְשׁוּ אֶת־ הָאָרֶץ אֲשֶׁר נָתַתִּי

I-gave that the-land *** and-possess! go-up! to-say Barnea from-Kadesh

לָכֶם וַתַּמְרוּ אֶת־ פִּי יְהוָה אֱלֹהֵיכֶם וְלֹא הֶאֱמַנְתֶּם

you-trusted and-not God-of-you Yahweh command-of *** but-you-rebelled to-you

לוֹ וְלֹא שְׁמַעְתֶּם בְּקֹלוֹ׃ מַמְרִים הֱיִיתֶם

you-were ones-rebelling (24) to-voice-of-him you-obeyed and-not in-him

עִם־ יְהוָה מִיּוֹם דַּעְתִּי אֶתְכֶם׃ וָאֶתְנַפַּל לִפְנֵי יְהוָה אֵת

*** Yahweh before and-I-lay-prostrate (25) you I-knew from-day Yahweh against

אַרְבָּעִים הַיּוֹם וְאֶת־ אַרְבָּעִים הַלַּיְלָה אֲשֶׁר הִתְנַפָּלְתִּי כִּי־ אָמַר יְהוָה

Yahweh he-said for I-lay-prostrate that the-night forty and the-day forty

לְהַשְׁמִיד אֶתְכֶם׃ וָאֶתְפַּלֵּל אֶל־ יְהוָה וָאֹמַר אֲדֹנָי יְהוִה אַל־

not Yahweh Lord and-I-said Yahweh to and-I-prayed (26) you to-destroy

תַּשְׁחֵת עַמְּךָ וְנַחֲלָתְךָ אֲשֶׁר פָּדִיתָ

you-redeemed that and-inheritance-of-you people-of-you you-destroy

בְּגָדְלֶךָ אֲשֶׁר־ הוֹצֵאתָ מִמִּצְרַיִם בְּיָד חֲזָקָה׃ זְכֹר

remember! (27) mighty with-hand from-Egypt you-brought that by-greatness-of-you

לַעֲבָדֶיךָ לְאַבְרָהָם לְיִצְחָק וּלְיַעֲקֹב אַל־ תֵּפֶן אֶל־

at you-look not and-to-Jacob to-Isaac to-Abraham to-servants-of-you

קְשִׁי הָעָם הַזֶּה וְאֶל־ רִשְׁעוֹ וְאֶל־

and-at wickedness-of-him and-at the-this the-people stubbornness-of

חַטָּאתוֹ׃ פֶּן־ יֹאמְרוּ הָאָרֶץ אֲשֶׁר הוֹצֵאתָנוּ

you-brought-us which the-country they-will-say otherwise (28) sin-of-him

מִשָּׁם מִבְּלִי יְכֹלֶת יְהוָה לַהֲבִיאָם אֶל־ הָאָרֶץ אֲשֶׁר־

that the-land into to-take-them Yahweh to-be-able because-not from-there

דִּבֶּר לָהֶם וּמִשִּׂנְאָתוֹ אוֹתָם הוֹצִיאָם

he-brought-them for-them and-because-of-hate-of-him to-them he-promised

לַהֲמִתָם בַּמִּדְבָּר׃ וְהֵם עַמְּךָ וְנַחֲלָתֶךָ

and-inheritance-of-you people-of-you but-they (29) in-the-desert to-kill-them

[21]Also I took that sinful thing
of yours, the calf you had
made, and burned it in the
fire. Then I crushed it and
ground it to powder as fine as
dust and threw the dust into a
stream that flowed down the
mountain.
[22]You also made the LORD
angry at Taberah, at Massah
and at Kibroth Hattaavah.
[23]And when the LORD sent
you out from Kadesh Barnea,
he said, "Go up and take
possession of the land I have
given you." But you rebelled
against the command of the
LORD your God. You did not
trust him or obey him. [24]You
have been rebellious against
the LORD ever since I have
known you.
[25]I lay prostrate before the
LORD those forty days and
forty nights because the LORD
had said he would destroy
you. [26]I prayed to the LORD and
said, "O Sovereign LORD, do
not destroy your people, your
own inheritance that you redeemed by your great power
and brought out of Egypt with
a mighty hand. [27]Remember
your servants Abraham, Isaac
and Jacob. Overlook the stub-
bornness of this people, their
wickedness and their sin.
[28]Otherwise, the country from
which you brought us will say,
'Because the LORD was not able
to take them into the land he
had promised them, and because he hated them, he
brought them out to put them
to death in the desert.' [29]But
they are your people, your inheritance that you brought out

אֲשֶׁר הוֹצֵאתָ בְּכֹחֲךָ הַגָּדֹל וּבִזְרֹעֲךָ
and-by-arm-of-you the-great by-power-of-you you-brought-out that

הַנְּטוּיָה׃ (10:1) בָּעֵת הַהִוא אָמַר יְהוָה אֵלַי
to-me Yahweh he-said the-that at-the-time (10:1) the-being-outstretched

פְּסָל־ לְךָ שְׁנֵי־ לוּחֹת אֲבָנִים כָּרִאשֹׁנִים וַעֲלֵה
and-come-up! like-the-first-ones stones tablets-of two-of for-you chisel-out!

אֵלַי הָהָרָה וְעָשִׂיתָ לְּךָ אֲרוֹן עֵץ׃ (2) וְאֶכְתֹּב
and-I-will-write (2) wood chest-of for-you and-you-make on-the-mountain to-me

עַל־ הַלֻּחֹת אֶת־ הַדְּבָרִים אֲשֶׁר הָיוּ עַל־ הַלֻּחֹת הָרִאשֹׁנִים
the-first-ones the-tablets on they-were that the-words *** the-tablets on

אֲשֶׁר שִׁבַּרְתָּ וְשַׂמְתָּם בָּאָרוֹן׃ (3) וָאַעַשׂ אֲרוֹן
chest-of so-I-made (3) in-the-chest then-you-put-them you-broke which

עֲצֵי שִׁטִּים וָאֶפְסֹל שְׁנֵי־ לֻחֹת אֲבָנִים כָּרִאשֹׁנִים
like-the-first-ones stones tablets-of two-of and-I-chiseled acacias woods-of

וָאַעַל הָהָרָה וּשְׁנֵי הַלֻּחֹת בְּיָדִי׃
in-hand-of-me the-tablets and-two-of on-the-mountain and-I-went-up

(4) וַיִּכְתֹּב עַל־ הַלֻּחֹת כַּמִּכְתָּב הָרִאשׁוֹן אֵת עֲשֶׂרֶת
ten-of *** the-first as-the-writing the-tablets on and-he-wrote (4)

הַדְּבָרִים אֲשֶׁר דִּבֶּר יְהוָה אֲלֵיכֶם בָּהָר מִתּוֹךְ
out-of on-the-mountain to-you Yahweh he-proclaimed that the-commandments

הָאֵשׁ בְּיוֹם הַקָּהָל וַיִּתְּנֵם יְהוָה אֵלָי׃ (5) וָאֵפֶן
then-I-left (5) to-me Yahweh and-he-gave-them the-assembly on-day-of the-fire

וָאֵרֵד מִן־ הָהָר וָאָשִׂם אֶת־ הַלֻּחֹת בָּאָרוֹן
in-the-chest the-tablets *** and-I-put the-mountain from and-I-came-down

אֲשֶׁר עָשִׂיתִי וַיִּהְיוּ שָׁם כַּאֲשֶׁר צִוַּנִי יְהוָה׃ (6) וּבְנֵי
now-sons-of (6) Yahweh he-commanded-me just-as there and-they-are I-made that

יִשְׂרָאֵל נָסְעוּ מִבְּאֵרֹת בְּנֵי־ יַעֲקָן מוֹסֵרָה שָׁם מֵת
he-died there Moserah Jaakan sons-of from-wells-of they-travelled Israel

אַהֲרֹן וַיִּקָּבֵר שָׁם וַיְכַהֵן אֶלְעָזָר בְּנוֹ
son-of-him Eleazar then-he-became-priest there and-he-was-buried Aaron

תַּחְתָּיו׃ (7) מִשָּׁם נָסְעוּ הַגֻּדְגֹּדָה וּמִן־
and-from the-Gudgodah they-travelled from-there (7) in-place-of-him

הַגֻּדְגֹּדָה יָטְבָתָה אֶרֶץ נַחֲלֵי מָיִם׃ (8) בָּעֵת הַהִוא
the-that at-the-time (8) waters streams-of land-of Jotbathah the-Gudgodah

הִבְדִּיל יְהוָה אֶת־ שֵׁבֶט הַלֵּוִי לָשֵׂאת אֶת־ אֲרוֹן בְּרִית־
covenant-of ark-of *** to-carry the-Levi tribe-of *** Yahweh he-set-apart

יְהוָה לַעֲמֹד לִפְנֵי יְהוָה לְשָׁרְתוֹ וּלְבָרֵךְ בִּשְׁמוֹ
in-name-of-him and-to-bless to-minister-him Yahweh before to-stand Yahweh

by your great power and your
outstretched arm."

Tablets Like the First Ones

10 At that time the LORD
said to me, "Chisel out
two stone tablets like the first
ones and come up to me on the
mountain. Also make a wood-
en chest.[r] 2I will write on the
tablets the words that were on
the first tablets, which you
broke. Then you are to put
them in the chest."
3So I made the ark out of
acacia wood and chiseled out
two stone tablets like the first
ones, and I went up on the
mountain with the two tablets
in my hands. 4The LORD wrote
on these tablets what he had
written before, the Ten Commandments he had pro-
claimed to you on the mountain, out of the fire, on the day
of the assembly. And the LORD
gave them to me. 5Then I came
back down the mountain and
put the tablets in the ark I had
made, as the LORD com-
manded me, and they are
there now.
6(The Israelites traveled from
the wells of the Jaakanites to
Moserah. There Aaron died
and was buried, and Eleazar
his son succeeded him as
priest. 7From there they traveled to Gudgodah and on to
Jotbathah, a land with streams
of water. 8At that time the
LORD set apart the tribe of Levi
to carry the ark of the covenant of the LORD, to stand before the LORD to minister and
to pronounce blessings in his

r1 That is, an ark

עַד הַיּוֹם הַזֶּה׃ עַל־כֵּן לֹא־הָיָה לְלֵוִי חֵלֶק וְנַחֲלָה
or-inheritance share to-Levi he-is not this for (9) the-this the-day to

עִם־אֶחָיו יְהוָה הוּא נַחֲלָתוֹ כַּאֲשֶׁר דִּבֶּר יְהוָה
Yahweh he-told just-as inheritance-of-him he Yahweh brothers-of-him among

אֱלֹהֶיךָ לוֹ׃ וְאָנֹכִי עָמַדְתִּי בָהָר כַּיָּמִים
as-the-days on-the-mountain I-stayed now-I (10) to-him God-of-you

הָרִאשֹׁנִים אַרְבָּעִים יוֹם וְאַרְבָּעִים לָיְלָה וַיִּשְׁמַע יְהוָה אֵלַי גַּם
also to-me Yahweh and-he-listened night and-forty day forty the-first-ones

בַּפַּעַם הַהִוא לֹא־אָבָה יְהוָה הַשְׁחִיתֶךָ׃ וַיֹּאמֶר
and-he-said (11) to-destroy-you Yahweh he-willed not the-this at-the-time

יְהוָה אֵלַי קוּם לֵךְ לְמַסַּע לִפְנֵי הָעָם וְיָבֹאוּ
so-they-may-enter the-people before on-journey go! rise! to-me Yahweh

וְיִירְשׁוּ אֶת־הָאָרֶץ אֲשֶׁר־נִשְׁבַּעְתִּי לַאֲבֹתָם לָתֵת
to-give to-fathers-of-them I-swore that the-land *** and-they-may-possess

לָהֶם׃ וְעַתָּה יִשְׂרָאֵל מָה יְהוָה אֱלֹהֶיךָ שֹׁאֵל מֵעִמָּךְ כִּי
but from-you asking God-of-you Yahweh what? Israel and-now (12) to-them

אִם־לְיִרְאָה אֶת־יְהוָה אֱלֹהֶיךָ לָלֶכֶת בְּכָל־דְּרָכָיו וּלְאַהֲבָה
and-to-love ways-of-him in-all-of to-walk God-of-you Yahweh *** to-fear only

אֹתוֹ וְלַעֲבֹד אֶת־יְהוָה אֱלֹהֶיךָ בְּכָל־לְבָבְךָ
heart-of-you with-all-of God-of-you Yahweh *** and-to-serve him

וּבְכָל־נַפְשֶׁךָ׃ לִשְׁמֹר אֶת־מִצְוֺת יְהוָה וְאֶת־
and Yahweh commands-of *** to-observe (13) soul-of-you and-with-all-of

חֻקֹּתָיו אֲשֶׁר אָנֹכִי מְצַוְּךָ הַיּוֹם לְטוֹב לָךְ׃ הֵן
see! (14) for-you for-good the-day giving-you I that decrees-of-him

לַיהוָה אֱלֹהֶיךָ הַשָּׁמַיִם וּשְׁמֵי הַשָּׁמַיִם הָאָרֶץ וְכָל־
and-all the-earth the-heavens and-heavens-of the-heavens God-of-you to-Yahweh

אֲשֶׁר־בָּהּ׃ רַק בַּאֲבֹתֶיךָ חָשַׁק יְהוָה לְאַהֲבָה אוֹתָם
them to-love Yahweh he-set-affection on-fathers-of-you yet (15) in-her that

וַיִּבְחַר בְּזַרְעָם אַחֲרֵיהֶם בָּכֶם מִכָּל־הָעַמִּים
the-nations above-all-of to-you after-them to-descendant-of-them and-he-chose

כַּיּוֹם הַזֶּה׃ וּמַלְתֶּם אֵת עָרְלַת לְבַבְכֶם
heart-of-you foreskin-of *** so-you-circumcise (16) the-this as-the-day

וְעָרְפְּכֶם לֹא תַקְשׁוּ עוֹד׃ כִּי יְהוָה אֱלֹהֵיכֶם הוּא
he God-of-you Yahweh for (17) longer you-make-stiff not and-neck-of-you

אֱלֹהֵי הָאֱלֹהִים וַאֲדֹנֵי הָאֲדֹנִים הָאֵל הַגָּדֹל הַגִּבֹּר
the-mighty the-great the-God the-lords and-Lord-of the-gods God-of

וְהַנּוֹרָא אֲשֶׁר לֹא־יִשָּׂא פָנִים וְלֹא יִקַּח שֹׁחַד׃
bribe he-accepts and-not faces he-lifts not who and-the-being-awesome

name, as they still do today.
9That is why the Levites have
no share or inheritance
among their brothers; the
LORD is their inheritance, as
the LORD your God told them.)
10Now I had stayed on the
mountain forty days and
nights, as I did the first time,
and the LORD listened to me at
this time also. It was not his
will to destroy you. 11"Go," the
LORD said to me, "and lead the
people on their way, so that
they may enter and possess
the land that I swore to their
fathers to give them."

Fear the LORD

12And now, O Israel, what
does the LORD your God ask of
you but to fear the LORD your
God, to walk in all his ways, to
love him, to serve the LORD
your God with all your heart
and with all your soul, 13and to
observe the LORD's commands
and decrees that I am giving
you today for your own good?
14To the LORD your God belong the heavens, even the
highest heavens, the earth
and everything in it. 15Yet the
LORD set his affection on your
forefathers and loved them,
and he chose you, their descendants, above all the nations, as it is today. 16Circum-
cise your hearts, therefore,
and do not be stiff-necked any
longer. 17For the LORD your
God is God of gods and Lord of
lords, the great God, mighty
and awesome, who shows no
partiality and accepts no

עֹשֶׂה מִשְׁפַּט יָתוֹם וְאַלְמָנָה וְאֹהֵב גֵּר לָתֶת לוֹ
to-him to-give alien and-loving and-widow fatherless cause-of defending (18)

לֶחֶם וְשִׂמְלָה׃ וַאֲהַבְתֶּם אֶת־ הַגֵּר כִּי־ גֵרִים הֱיִיתֶם
you-were aliens for the-alien *** so-you-love (19) and-clothing food

בְּאֶרֶץ מִצְרָיִם׃ אֶת־ יְהוָה אֱלֹהֶיךָ תִּירָא אֹתוֹ תַעֲבֹד
you-serve him you-fear God-of-you Yahweh *** (20) Egypt in-land-of

וּבוֹ תִדְבָּק וּבִשְׁמוֹ תִּשָּׁבֵעַ׃ הוּא
he (21) you-take-oath and-in-name-of-him you-hold-fast and-to-him

תְהִלָּתְךָ וְהוּא אֱלֹהֶיךָ אֲשֶׁר־ עָשָׂה אִתְּךָ אֶת־ הַגְּדֹלֹת
the-great-things *** for-you he-performed who God-of-you and-he praise-of-you

וְאֶת־ הַנּוֹרָאֹת הָאֵלֶּה אֲשֶׁר רָאוּ עֵינֶיךָ׃ בְּשִׁבְעִים
as-seventy (22) eyes-of-you they-saw that the-those the-ones-being-awesome and

נֶפֶשׁ יָרְדוּ אֲבֹתֶיךָ מִצְרָיְמָה וְעַתָּה שָׂמְךָ יְהוָה
Yahweh he-made-you and-now into-Egypt fathers-of-you they-went-down person

אֱלֹהֶיךָ כְּכוֹכְבֵי הַשָּׁמַיִם לָרֹב׃ וְאָהַבְתָּ אֵת יְהוָה
Yahweh *** so-you-love (11:1) for-the-number the-skies as-stars-of God-of-you

אֱלֹהֶיךָ וְשָׁמַרְתָּ מִשְׁמַרְתּוֹ וְחֻקֹּתָיו וּמִשְׁפָּטָיו
and-laws-of-him and-decrees-of-him requirement-of-him and-you-keep God-of-you

וּמִצְוֹתָיו כָּל־ הַיָּמִים׃ וִידַעְתֶּם הַיּוֹם כִּי ׀ לֹא
not that the-day and-you-remember (2) the-days all-of and-commands-of-him

אֶת־ בְּנֵיכֶם אֲשֶׁר לֹא־ יָדְעוּ וַאֲשֶׁר לֹא־ רָאוּ אֶת־
*** they-saw not and-who they-experienced not who children-of-you ***

מוּסַר יְהוָה אֱלֹהֵיכֶם אֶת־ גָּדְלוֹ אֶת־ יָדוֹ הַחֲזָקָה
the-mighty hand-of-him *** majesty-of-him *** God-of-you Yahweh discipline-of

וּזְרֹעוֹ הַנְּטוּיָה׃ וְאֶת־ אֹתֹתָיו וְאֶת־ מַעֲשָׂיו
deeds-of-him and signs-of-him and (3) the-being-outstretched and-arm-of-him

אֲשֶׁר עָשָׂה בְּתוֹךְ מִצְרָיִם לְפַרְעֹה מֶלֶךְ־ מִצְרַיִם וּלְכָל־
and-to-whole-of Egypt king-of to-Pharaoh Egypt in-midst-of he-performed that

אַרְצוֹ׃ וַאֲשֶׁר עָשָׂה לְחֵיל מִצְרַיִם לְסוּסָיו
to-horses-of-him Egypt to-army-of he-did and-what (4) country-of-him

וּלְרִכְבּוֹ אֲשֶׁר הֵצִיף אֶת־ מֵי יַם־ סוּף עַל־
over Reed Sea-of waters-of *** he-made-flow how and-to-chariot-of-him

פְּנֵיהֶם בְּרָדְפָם אַחֲרֵיכֶם וַיְאַבְּדֵם יְהוָה עַד
to Yahweh and-he-ruined-them after-you as-to-pursue-them faces-of-them

הַיּוֹם הַזֶּה׃ וַאֲשֶׁר עָשָׂה לָכֶם בַּמִּדְבָּר עַד־ בֹּאֲכֶם
to-come-you until in-the-desert for-you he-did and-what (5) the-this the-day

עַד־ הַמָּקוֹם הַזֶּה׃ וַאֲשֶׁר עָשָׂה לְדָתָן וְלַאֲבִירָם בְּנֵי
sons-of and-to-Abiram to-Dathan he-did and-what (6) the-this the-place to

bribes. [18]He defends the cause of the fatherless and the widow, and loves the alien, giving him food and clothing. [19]And you are to love those who are aliens, for you yourselves were aliens in Egypt. [20]Fear the LORD your God and serve him. Hold fast to him and take your oaths in his name. [21]He is your praise; he is your God, who performed for you those great and awesome wonders you saw with your own eyes. [22]Your forefathers who went down into Egypt were seventy in all, and now the LORD your God has made you as numerous as the stars in the sky.

Love and Obey the LORD

11 Love the LORD your God and keep his requirements, his decrees, his laws and his commands always. [2]Remember today that your children were not the ones who saw and experienced the discipline of the LORD your God: his majesty, his mighty hand, his outstretched arm; [3]the signs he performed and the things he did in the heart of Egypt, both to Pharaoh king of Egypt and to his whole country; [4]what he did to the Egyptian army, to its horses and chariots, how he overwhelmed them with the waters of the Red Sea[s] as they were pursuing you, and how the LORD brought lasting ruin on them. [5]It was not your children who saw what he did for you in the desert until you arrived at this place, [6]and what he did to Dathan and

[s]4 Hebrew *Yam Suph;* that is, Sea of Reeds

אֱלִיאָב בֶּן־ רְאוּבֵן אֲשֶׁר פָּצְתָה הָאָרֶץ אֶת־ פִּיהָ
mouth-of-her *** the-earth she-opened when Reuben son-of Eliab

וַתִּבְלָעֵם וְאֶת־ בָּתֵּיהֶם וְאֶת־ אָהֳלֵיהֶם וְאֵת כָּל־
all-of and tents-of-them and households-of-them and and-she-swallowed-them

הַיְקוּם אֲשֶׁר בְּרַגְלֵיהֶם בְּקֶרֶב כָּל־ יִשְׂרָאֵל׃ כִּי
but (7) Israel all-of in-middle-of under-feet-of-them that the-thing

עֵינֵיכֶם הָרֹאֹת אֶת־ כָּל־ מַעֲשֵׂה יְהוָה הַגָּדֹל אֲשֶׁר עָשָׂה׃
he-did that the-great Yahweh act-of every-of *** the-ones-seeing eyes-of-you

וּשְׁמַרְתֶּם אֶת־ כָּל־ הַמִּצְוָה אֲשֶׁר אָנֹכִי מְצַוְּךָ הַיּוֹם לְמַעַן
so-that the-day giving-you I that the-command all-of *** so-you-observe (8)

תֶּחֶזְקוּ וּבָאתֶם וִירִשְׁתֶּם אֶת־ הָאָרֶץ אֲשֶׁר
that the-land *** and-you-may-possess and-you-may-go-in you-may-be-strong

אַתֶּם עֹבְרִים שָׁמָּה לְרִשְׁתָּהּ׃ וּלְמַעַן תַּאֲרִיכוּ
you-may-live-long and-so-that (9) to-possess-her to-there ones-crossing you

יָמִים עַל־ הָאֲדָמָה אֲשֶׁר נִשְׁבַּע יְהוָה לַאֲבֹתֵיכֶם לָתֵת לָהֶם
to-them to-give to-fathers-of-you Yahweh he-swore that the-land in days

וּלְזַרְעָם אֶרֶץ זָבַת חָלָב וּדְבָשׁ׃ כִּי הָאָרֶץ
the-land now (10) and-honey milk flowing-of land and-to-descendant-of-them

אֲשֶׁר אַתָּה בָא־ שָׁמָּה לְרִשְׁתָּהּ לֹא כְאֶרֶץ מִצְרַיִם הִוא
she Egypt like-land-of not to-take-over-her to-there entering you that

אֲשֶׁר יְצָאתֶם מִשָּׁם אֲשֶׁר תִּזְרַע אֶת־ זַרְעֲךָ וְהִשְׁקִיתָ
and-you-irrigated seed-of-you *** you-planted where from-there you-came which

בְרַגְלְךָ כְּגַן הַיָּרָק׃ וְהָאָרֶץ אֲשֶׁר אַתֶּם
you that but-the-land (11) the-vegetable as-garden-of by-foot-of-you

עֹבְרִים שָׁמָּה לְרִשְׁתָּהּ אֶרֶץ הָרִים וּבְקָעֹת
and-valleys mountains land-of to-possess-her to-there ones-crossing

לִמְטַר הַשָּׁמַיִם תִּשְׁתֶּה־ מָּיִם׃ אֶרֶץ אֲשֶׁר־ יְהוָה אֱלֹהֶיךָ
God-of-you Yahweh that land (12) waters she-drinks the-heavens from-rain-of

דֹּרֵשׁ אֹתָהּ תָּמִיד עֵינֵי יְהוָה אֱלֹהֶיךָ בָּהּ מֵרֵשִׁית
from-beginning-of on-her God-of-you Yahweh eyes-of continually for-her caring

הַשָּׁנָה וְעַד אַחֲרִית שָׁנָה׃ וְהָיָה אִם־ שָׁמֹעַ תִּשְׁמְעוּ אֶל־
to you-obey to-obey if so-he-will-be (13) year end-of even-to the-year

מִצְוֹתַי אֲשֶׁר אָנֹכִי מְצַוֶּה אֶתְכֶם הַיּוֹם לְאַהֲבָה אֶת־ יְהוָה אֱלֹהֵיכֶם
God-of-you Yahweh *** to-love the-day you giving I that commands-of-me

וּלְעָבְדוֹ בְּכָל־ לְבַבְכֶם וּבְכָל־ נַפְשְׁכֶם׃
soul-of-you and-with-all-of heart-of-you with-all-of and-to-serve-him

וְנָתַתִּי מְטַר־ אַרְצְכֶם בְּעִתּוֹ יוֹרֶה
autumn-rain in-season-of-him land-of-you rain-of then-I-will-send (14)

Abiram, sons of Eliab the Reu-
benite, when the earth opened
its mouth right in the middle
of all Israel and swallowed
them up with their
households, their tents and
every living thing that belonged to them. [7]But it was
your own eyes that saw all
these great things the LORD
has done.
[8]Observe therefore all the
commands I am giving you today, so that you may have the
strength to go in and take over
the land that you are crossing
the Jordan to possess, [9]and so
that you may live long in the
land that the LORD swore to
your forefathers to give to
them and their descendants, a
land flowing with milk and
honey. [10]The land you are entering to take over is not like
the land of Egypt, from which
you have come, where you
planted your seed and irrigat-
ed it by foot as in a vegetable
garden. [11]But the land you are
crossing the Jordan to take
possession of is a land of
mountains and valleys that
drinks rain from heaven. [12]It is
a land the LORD your God cares
for; the eyes of the LORD your
God are continually on it from
the beginning of the year to its
end.
[13]So if you faithfully obey
the commands I am giving
you today—to love the LORD
your God and to serve him
with all your heart and with
all your soul— [14]then I will
send rain on your land in its
season, both autumn and

וּמַלְקוֹשׁ וְאָסַפְתָּ דְגָנֶךָ וְתִירֹשְׁךָ

and new-wine-of-you grain-of-you so-you-may-gather and-spring-rain

וְיִצְהָרֶךָ׃ וְנָתַתִּי עֵשֶׂב בְּשָׂדְךָ לִבְהֶמְתֶּךָ

for-cattle-of-you in-field-of-you grass and-I-will-provide (15) and-oil-of-you

וְאָכַלְתָּ וְשָׂבָעְתָּ׃ הִשָּׁמְרוּ לָכֶם פֶּן

or to-you be-careful! (16) and-you-will-be-satisfied and-you-will-eat

יִפְתֶּה לְבַבְכֶם וְסַרְתֶּם וַעֲבַדְתֶּם אֱלֹהִים

gods and-you-will-worship and-you-will-turn heart-of-you he-will-be-enticed

אֲחֵרִים וְהִשְׁתַּחֲוִיתֶם לָהֶם׃ וְחָרָה אַף־ יְהוָה

Yahweh anger-of then-he-will-burn (17) to-them and-you-will-bow other-ones

בָּכֶם וְעָצַר אֶת־ הַשָּׁמַיִם וְלֹא־ יִהְיֶה מָטָר

rain he-will-send so-not the-heavens *** and-he-will-shut against-you

וְהָאֲדָמָה לֹא תִתֵּן אֶת־ יְבוּלָהּ וַאֲבַדְתֶּם

and-you-will-perish produce-of-her *** she-will-yield not and-the-ground

מְהֵרָה מֵעַל הָאָרֶץ הַטֹּבָה אֲשֶׁר יְהוָה נֹתֵן לָכֶם׃ וְשַׂמְתֶּם

so-you-fix (18) to-you giving Yahweh that the-good the-land from-on soon

אֶת־ דְּבָרַי אֵלֶּה עַל־ לְבַבְכֶם וְעַל־ נַפְשְׁכֶם וּקְשַׁרְתֶּם אֹתָם

them and-you-tie mind-of-you and-in heart-of-you in these words-of-me ***

לְאוֹת עַל־ יֶדְכֶם וְהָיוּ לְטוֹטָפֹת בֵּין עֵינֵיכֶם׃

eyes-of-you between as-bands and-they-must-be hand-of-you on as-symbol

וְלִמַּדְתֶּם אֹתָם אֶת־ בְּנֵיכֶם לְדַבֵּר בָּם בְּשִׁבְתְּךָ

as-to-sit-you about-them to-talk children-of-you *** them and-you-teach (19)

בְּבֵיתֶךָ וּבְלֶכְתְּךָ בַדֶּרֶךְ וּבְשָׁכְבְּךָ

and-when-to-lie-down-you along-the-road and-when-to-walk-you at-home-of-you

וּבְקוּמֶךָ׃ וּכְתַבְתָּם עַל־ מְזוּזוֹת בֵּיתֶךָ

houses-of-you door-frames-of on and-you-write-them (20) and-when-to-get-up-you

וּבִשְׁעָרֶיךָ׃ לְמַעַן יִרְבּוּ יְמֵיכֶם וִימֵי

and-days-of days-of-you they-may-be-many so-that (21) and-on-gates-of-you

בְנֵיכֶם עַל הָאֲדָמָה אֲשֶׁר נִשְׁבַּע יְהוָה לַאֲבֹתֵיכֶם לָתֵת

to-give to-fathers-of-you Yahweh he-swore that the-land in children-of-you

לָהֶם כִּימֵי הַשָּׁמַיִם עַל־ הָאָרֶץ׃ כִּי אִם־ שָׁמֹר

to-observe if for (22) the-earth above the-heavens as-days-of to-them

תִּשְׁמְרוּן אֶת־ כָּל־ הַמִּצְוָה הַזֹּאת אֲשֶׁר אָנֹכִי מְצַוֶּה אֶתְכֶם לַעֲשֹׂתָהּ

to-follow-her you giving I that the-this the-command all-of *** you-observe

לְאַהֲבָה אֶת־ יְהוָה אֱלֹהֵיכֶם לָלֶכֶת בְּכָל־ דְּרָכָיו וּלְדָבְקָה־

and-to-hold-fast ways-of-him in-all-of to-walk God-of-you Yahweh *** to-love

בוֹ׃ וְהוֹרִישׁ יְהוָה אֶת־ כָּל־ הַגּוֹיִם הָאֵלֶּה

the-these the-nations all-of *** Yahweh then-he-will-drive-out (23) to-him

spring rains, so that you may
gather in your grain, new
wine and oil. [15]I will provide
grass in the fields for your cattle, and you will eat and be satisfied.
[16]Be careful, or you will be
enticed to turn away and worship other gods and bow
down to them. [17]Then the
LORD's anger will burn against
you, and he will shut the
heavens so that it will not rain
and the ground will yield no
produce, and you will soon
perish from the good land the
LORD is giving you. [18]Fix these
words of mine in your hearts
and minds; tie them as symbols on your hands and bind
them on your foreheads.
[19]Teach them to your children,
talking about them when you
sit at home and when you
walk along the road, when
you lie down and when you
get up. [20]Write them on the
doorframes of your houses
and on your gates, [21]so that
your days and the days of your
children may be many in the
land that the LORD swore to
give your forefathers, as many
as the days that the heavens
are above the earth.
[22]If you carefully observe all
these commands I am giving
you to follow—to love the LORD
your God, to walk in all his
ways and to hold fast to him—
[23]then the LORD will drive out
all these nations before you,

מִלִּפְנֵיכֶם וִירִשְׁתֶּם גּוֹיִם גְּדֹלִים וַעֲצֻמִים
and-ones-stronger ones-larger nations and-you-will-dispossess from-before-you

מִכֶּם׃ כָּל־ הַמָּקוֹם אֲשֶׁר תִּדְרֹךְ כַּף־ רַגְלְכֶם בּוֹ
on-him foot-of-you sole-of she-sets where the-place every-of (24) than-you

לָכֶם יִהְיֶה מִן־ הַמִּדְבָּר וְהַלְּבָנוֹן מִן־ הַנָּהָר נְהַר־
River-of the-River from and-the-Lebanon the-desert from he-will-be for-you

פְּרָת וְעַד הַיָּם הָאַחֲרוֹן יִהְיֶה גְּבֻלְכֶם׃ לֹא־
not (25) border-of-you he-will-be the-western the-Sea even-to Euphrates

יִתְיַצֵּב אִישׁ בִּפְנֵיכֶם פַּחְדְּכֶם וּמוֹרַאֲכֶם
and-fear-of-you terror-of-you against-faces-of-you man he-will-stand

יִתֵּן ׀ יְהוָה אֱלֹהֵיכֶם עַל־ פְּנֵי כָל־ הָאָרֶץ אֲשֶׁר תִּדְרְכוּ־
you-go wherever the-land whole-of face-of on God-of-you Yahweh he-will-put

בָהּ כַּאֲשֶׁר דִּבֶּר לָכֶם׃ רְאֵה אָנֹכִי נֹתֵן לִפְנֵיכֶם הַיּוֹם
the-day before-you setting I see! (26) to-you he-promised just-as in-her

בְּרָכָה וּקְלָלָה׃ אֶת־ הַבְּרָכָה אֲשֶׁר תִּשְׁמְעוּ אֶל־ מִצְוֺת יְהוָה
Yahweh commands-of to you-obey if the-blessing *** (27) and-curse blessing

אֱלֹהֵיכֶם אֲשֶׁר אָנֹכִי מְצַוֶּה אֶתְכֶם הַיּוֹם׃ וְהַקְּלָלָה אִם־ לֹא תִשְׁמְעוּ
you-obey not if and-the-curse (28) the-day you giving I that God-of-you

אֶל־ מִצְוֺת יְהוָה אֱלֹהֵיכֶם וְסַרְתֶּם מִן־ הַדֶּרֶךְ אֲשֶׁר אָנֹכִי
I that the-way from and-you-turn God-of-you Yahweh commands-of to

מְצַוֶּה אֶתְכֶם הַיּוֹם לָלֶכֶת אַחֲרֵי אֱלֹהִים אֲחֵרִים אֲשֶׁר לֹא־ יְדַעְתֶּם
you-knew not that other-ones gods after to-follow the-day you commanding

וְהָיָה כִּי יְבִיאֲךָ יְהוָה אֱלֹהֶיךָ אֶל־ הָאָרֶץ אֲשֶׁר־
that the-land into God-of-you Yahweh he-brings-you when and-he-will-be (29)

אַתָּה בָא־ שָׁמָּה לְרִשְׁתָּהּ וְנָתַתָּה אֶת־ הַבְּרָכָה עַל־
on the-blessing *** then-you-proclaim to-possess-her to-there entering you

הַר גְּרִזִים וְאֶת־הַקְּלָלָה עַל־ הַר עֵיבָל׃ הֲלֹא־הֵמָּה בְּעֵבֶר
on-across they not? (30) Ebal Mount-of on the-curse and Gerizim Mount-of

הַיַּרְדֵּן אַחֲרֵי דֶּרֶךְ מְבוֹא הַשֶּׁמֶשׁ בְּאֶרֶץ הַכְּנַעֲנִי
the-Canaanite in-territory-of the-sun set-of road west-of the-Jordan

הַיֹּשֵׁב בָּעֲרָבָה מוּל הַגִּלְגָּל אֵצֶל אֵלוֹנֵי מֹרֶה׃
Moreh trees-of near the-Gilgal vicinity-of in-the-Arabah the-one-living

כִּי אַתֶּם עֹבְרִים אֶת־ הַיַּרְדֵּן לָבֹא לָרֶשֶׁת אֶת־ הָאָרֶץ
the-land *** to-possess to-enter the-Jordan *** ones-crossing you now (31)

אֲשֶׁר־ יְהוָה אֱלֹהֵיכֶם נֹתֵן לָכֶם וִירִשְׁתֶּם אֹתָהּ וִישַׁבְתֶּם־
and-you-live her when-you-take-over to-you giving God-of-you Yahweh that

בָהּ׃ וּשְׁמַרְתֶּם לַעֲשׂוֹת אֵת כָּל־ הַחֻקִּים וְאֶת־הַמִּשְׁפָּטִים
the-laws and the-decrees all-of *** to-obey then-you-be-sure (32) in-her

and you will dispossess nations larger and stronger than
you. 24 Every place where you
set your foot will be yours:
from the desert to Lebanon,
and from the Euphrates River
to the western sea.[t] 25 No man
will be able to stand against
you. The LORD your God, as he
promised you, will put the terror and fear of you on the
whole land, wherever you go.
26 See, I am setting before you
today a blessing and a curse—
27 the blessing if you obey the
commands of the LORD your
God that I am giving you today; 28 the curse if you disobey
the commands of the LORD
your God and turn from the
way that I command you today by following other gods,
which you have not known.
29 When the LORD your God has
brought you into the land you
are entering to possess, you
are to proclaim on Mount
Gerizim the blessings, and on
Mount Ebal the curses. 30 As
you know, these mountains
are across the Jordan, west of
the road,[u] toward the setting
sun, near the great trees of
Moreh, in the territory of
those Canaanites living in the
Arabah in the vicinity of Gil-
gal. 31 You are about to cross
the Jordan to enter and take
possession of the land the
LORD your God is giving you.
When you have taken it over
and are living there, 32 be sure
that you obey all the decrees

[t] 24 That is, the Mediterranean
[u] 30 Or *Jordan, westward*

אֲשֶׁר אָנֹכִי נֹתֵן לִפְנֵיכֶם הַיּוֹם׃ אֵלֶּה הַחֻקִּים וְהַמִּשְׁפָּטִים
and-the-laws the-decrees these (12:1) the-day before-you setting I that

אֲשֶׁר תִּשְׁמְרוּן לַעֲשׂוֹת בָּאָרֶץ אֲשֶׁר נָתַן יְהוָה אֱלֹהֵי
God-of Yahweh he-gave that in-the-land to-follow you-must-be-careful that

אֲבֹתֶיךָ לְךָ לְרִשְׁתָּהּ כָּל־ הַיָּמִים אֲשֶׁר־ אַתֶּם חַיִּים עַל־
in ones-alive you that the-days all-of to-possess-her to-you fathers-of-you

הָאֲדָמָה׃ אַבֵּד תְּאַבְּדוּן אֶת־ כָּל־ הַמְּקֹמוֹת אֲשֶׁר עָבְדוּ־
they-worship that the-places all-of *** you-destroy to-destroy (2) the-land

שָׁם הַגּוֹיִם אֲשֶׁר אַתֶּם יֹרְשִׁים אֹתָם אֶת־ אֱלֹהֵיהֶם עַל־
on gods-of-them *** them ones-dispossessing you that the-nations there

הֶהָרִים הָרָמִים וְעַל־ הַגְּבָעוֹת וְתַחַת כָּל־ עֵץ
tree-of every-of and-under the-hills and-on the-high-ones the-mountains

רַעֲנָן׃ וְנִתַּצְתֶּם אֶת־ מִזְבְּחֹתָם* וְשִׁבַּרְתֶּם אֶת־
*** and-you-smash altars-of-them *** and-you-break-down (3) spreading

מַצֵּבֹתָם וַאֲשֵׁרֵיהֶם תִּשְׂרְפוּן בָּאֵשׁ
in-the-fire you-burn and-Asherah-poles-of-them sacred-stones-of-them

וּפְסִילֵי אֱלֹהֵיהֶם תְּגַדֵּעוּן וְאִבַּדְתֶּם אֶת־ שְׁמָם
name-of-them *** and-you-wipe-out you-cut-down gods-of-them and-idols-of

מִן־ הַמָּקוֹם הַהוּא׃ לֹא־ תַעֲשׂוּן כֵּן לַיהוָה אֱלֹהֵיכֶם׃
God-of-you to-Yahweh same-way you-worship not (4) the-that the-place from

כִּי אִם־ אֶל־הַמָּקוֹם אֲשֶׁר־ יִבְחַר יְהוָה אֱלֹהֵיכֶם מִכָּל־
from-all-of God-of-you Yahweh he-will-choose that the-place to rather but (5)

שִׁבְטֵיכֶם לָשׂוּם אֶת־ שְׁמוֹ שָׁם לְשִׁכְנוֹ תִדְרְשׁוּ
you-seek to-dwell-him there Name-of-him *** to-put tribes-of-you

וּבָאתָ שָׁמָּה׃ וַהֲבֵאתֶם שָׁמָּה עֹלֹתֵיכֶם
burnt-offerings-of-you to-there and-you-bring (6) to-there and-you-go

וְזִבְחֵיכֶם וְאֵת מַעְשְׂרֹתֵיכֶם וְאֵת תְּרוּמַת יֶדְכֶם
hand-of-you gift-of and tithes-of-you and and-sacrifices-of-you

וְנִדְרֵיכֶם וְנִדְבֹתֵיכֶם וּבְכֹרֹת
and-ones-firstborn-of and-freewill-offerings-of-you and-things-vowed-of-you

בְּקַרְכֶם וְצֹאנְכֶם׃ וַאֲכַלְתֶּם־ שָׁם לִפְנֵי יְהוָה אֱלֹהֵיכֶם
God-of-you Yahweh before there and-you-eat (7) and-flock-of-you herd-of-you

וּשְׂמַחְתֶּם בְּכֹל מִשְׁלַח יֶדְכֶם אַתֶּם וּבָתֵּיכֶם אֲשֶׁר
for and-families-of-you you hand-of-you work-of in-every-of and-you-rejoice

בֵּרַכְךָ יְהוָה אֱלֹהֶיךָ׃ לֹא תַעֲשׂוּן כְּכֹל אֲשֶׁר אֲנַחְנוּ עֹשִׂים
ones-doing we that as-all you-do not (8) God-of-you Yahweh he-blessed-you

פֹּה הַיּוֹם אִישׁ כָּל־ הַיָּשָׁר בְּעֵינָיו׃ כִּי לֹא־
not since (9) in-eyes-of-him the-thing-fit every-of each the-day here

and laws I am setting before you today.

The One Place of Worship

12 These are the decrees and laws you must be careful to follow in the land that the LORD, the God of your fathers, has given you to possess—as long as you live in the
land. [2]Destroy completely all the places on the high mountains and on the hills and under every spreading tree where the nations you are dispossessing worship their
gods. [3]Break down their altars, smash their sacred stones and burn their Asherah poles in the fire; cut down the idols of their gods and wipe out their names from those places.
[4]You must not worship the LORD your God in their way.
[5]But you are to seek the place the LORD your God will choose from among all your tribes to put his Name there for his dwelling. To that place you
must go; [6]there bring your burnt offerings and sacrifices, your tithes and special gifts, what you have vowed to give and your freewill offerings, and the firstborn of your herds
and flocks. [7]There, in the presence of the LORD your God, you and your families shall eat and shall rejoice in everything you have put your hand to, because the LORD your God has blessed you.
[8]You are not to do as we do
here today, everyone as he
sees fit, [9]since you have not

*3 Most mss have *sheva* under the *beth* (בְּ־).

בָּאתֶם עַד־עָתָּה אֶל־הַמְּנוּחָה וְאֶל־הַנַּחֲלָה אֲשֶׁר־יְהוָה
Yahweh that the-inheritance and-to the-resting-place to now to you-reached

אֱלֹהֶיךָ נֹתֵן לָךְ׃ וַעֲבַרְתֶּם אֶת־הַיַּרְדֵּן
the-Jordan *** but-you-will-cross (10) to-you giving God-of-you

וִישַׁבְתֶּם בָּאָרֶץ אֲשֶׁר־יְהוָה אֱלֹהֵיכֶם מַנְחִיל אֶתְכֶם
you giving-inheritance God-of-you Yahweh that in-the-land and-you-will-settle

וְהֵנִיחַ לָכֶם מִכָּל־אֹיְבֵיכֶם מִסָּבִיב
from-around being-enemies-of-you from-all-of to-you and-he-will-give-rest

וִישַׁבְתֶּם־בֶּטַח׃ וְהָיָה הַמָּקוֹם אֲשֶׁר־יִבְחַר
he-will-choose that the-place and-he-will-be (11) safety so-you-will-live

יְהוָה אֱלֹהֵיכֶם בּוֹ לְשַׁכֵּן שְׁמוֹ שָׁם שָׁמָּה תָבִיאוּ
you-bring to-there there Name-of-him to-make-dwell to-him God-of-you Yahweh

אֵת כָּל־אֲשֶׁר אָנֹכִי מְצַוֶּה אֶתְכֶם עוֹלֹתֵיכֶם וְזִבְחֵיכֶם
and-sacrifices-of-you burnt-offerings-of-you you commanding I that all ***

מַעְשְׂרֹתֵיכֶם וּתְרֻמַת יֶדְכֶם וְכֹל מִבְחַר נִדְרֵיכֶם
possessions-of-you choice-of and-all-of hand-of-you and-gift-of tithes-of-you

אֲשֶׁר תִּדְּרוּ לַיהוָה׃ וּשְׂמַחְתֶּם לִפְנֵי יְהוָה אֱלֹהֵיכֶם
God-of-you Yahweh before and-you-rejoice (12) to-Yahweh you-vowed that

אַתֶּם וּבְנֵיכֶם וּבְנֹתֵיכֶם וְעַבְדֵיכֶם
and-menservants-of-you and-daughters-of-you and-sons-of-you you

וְאַמְהֹתֵיכֶם וְהַלֵּוִי אֲשֶׁר בְּשַׁעֲרֵיכֶם כִּי אֵין לוֹ
to-him not that in-gates-of-you that and-the-Levite and-maidservants-of-you

חֵלֶק וְנַחֲלָה אִתְּכֶם׃ הִשָּׁמֶר לְךָ פֶּן־תַּעֲלֶה
you-sacrifice so-not to-you be-careful! (13) with-you or-inheritance allotment

עֹלֹתֶיךָ בְּכָל־מָקוֹם אֲשֶׁר תִּרְאֶה׃ כִּי אִם־בַּמָּקוֹם
at-the-place only for (14) you-see that place in-any-of burnt-offerings-of-you

אֲשֶׁר־יִבְחַר יְהוָה בְּאַחַד שְׁבָטֶיךָ שָׁם תַּעֲלֶה
you-offer there tribes-of-you in-one-of Yahweh he-will-choose that

עֹלֹתֶיךָ וְשָׁם תַּעֲשֶׂה כֹּל אֲשֶׁר אָנֹכִי מְצַוֶּךָּ׃
commanding-you I that all you-observe and-there burnt-offerings-of-you

רַק בְּכָל־אַוַּת נַפְשְׁךָ תִּזְבַּח ׀ וְאָכַלְתָּ
and-you-may-eat you-may-slaughter self-of-you want-of at-any-of however (15)

בָשָׂר כְּבִרְכַּת יְהוָה אֱלֹהֶיךָ אֲשֶׁר נָתַן־לְךָ בְּכָל־
within-any-of to-you he-gives that God-of-you Yahweh as-blessing-of meat

שְׁעָרֶיךָ הַטָּמֵא וְהַטָּהוֹר יֹאכְלֶנּוּ כַּצְּבִי
as-the-gazelle he-may-eat-him and-the-clean the-unclean gates-of-you

וְכָאַיָּל׃ רַק הַדָּם לֹא תֹאכֵלוּ עַל־הָאָרֶץ תִּשְׁפְּכֶנּוּ
you-pour-him the-ground on you-must-eat not the-blood but (16) or-as-the-deer

yet reached the resting place and the inheritance the LORD your God is giving you. [10]But you will cross the Jordan and settle in the land the LORD your God is giving you as an inheritance, and he will give you rest from all your enemies around you so that you will live in safety. [11]Then to the place the LORD your God will choose as a dwelling for his Name—there you are to bring everything I command you: your burnt offerings and sacrifices, your tithes and special gifts, and all the choice possessions you have vowed to the LORD. [12]And there rejoice before the LORD your God, you, your sons and daughters, your menservants and maidservants, and the Levites from your towns, who have no allotment or inheritance of their own. [13]Be careful not to sacrifice your burnt offerings anywhere you please. [14]Offer them only at the place the LORD will choose in one of your tribes, and there observe everything I command you.

[15]Nevertheless, you may slaughter your animals in any of your towns and eat as much of the meat as you want, as if it were gazelle or deer, according to the blessing the LORD your God gives you. Both the ceremonially unclean and the clean may eat it. [16]But you must not eat the blood; pour it out on the ground like water.

*9 Most mss have no *dagesh* in the *beth* (בָ׳).

כַּמָּֽיִם׃ לֹֽא־ תוּכַ֞ל לֶאֱכֹ֣ל בִּשְׁעָרֶ֗יךָ מַעְשַׂ֤ר
tithe-of within-gates-of-you to-eat you-are-able not (17) like-the-waters

דְּגָֽנְךָ֙ וְתִירֹשְׁךָ֣ וְיִצְהָרֶ֔ךָ וּבְכֹרֹ֖ת
or-ones-firstborn-of and-oil-of-you and-new-wine-of-you grain-of-you

בְּקָרְךָ֣ וְצֹאנֶ֑ךָ וְכָל־ נְדָרֶ֙יךָ֙ אֲשֶׁ֣ר תִּדֹּ֔ר
you-vowed that gifts-of-you or-any-of or-flock-of-you herd-of-you

וְנִדְבֹתֶ֖יךָ וּתְרוּמַ֥ת יָדֶֽךָ׃ כִּ֣י אִם־ לִפְנֵ֨י
before instead for (18) hand-of-you or-gift-of or-freewill-offerings-of-you

יְהוָ֣ה אֱלֹהֶ֜יךָ תֹּאכְלֶ֗נּוּ בַּמָּקוֹם֙ אֲשֶׁ֨ר יִבְחַ֜ר יְהוָ֣ה
Yahweh he-will-choose that at-the-place you-eat-him God-of-you Yahweh

אֱלֹהֶ֙יךָ֙ בּ֗וֹ אַתָּ֨ה וּבִנְךָ֤ וּבִתֶּ֙ךָ֙ וְעַבְדְּךָ֣
and-manservant-of-you and-daughter-of-you and-son-of-you you to-him God-of-you

וַאֲמָתֶ֔ךָ וְהַלֵּוִ֖י אֲשֶׁ֣ר בִּשְׁעָרֶ֑יךָ וְשָׂמַחְתָּ֗
and-you-rejoice in-gates-of-you that and-the-Levite and-maidservant-of-you

לִפְנֵי֙ יְהוָ֣ה אֱלֹהֶ֔יךָ בְּכֹ֖ל מִשְׁלַ֥ח יָדֶֽךָ׃ הִשָּׁ֣מֶר
be-careful! (19) hand-of-you work-of in-every-of God-of-you Yahweh before

לְךָ֔ פֶּֽן־ תַּעֲזֹ֖ב אֶת־ הַלֵּוִ֑י כָּל־ יָמֶ֖יךָ עַל־ אַדְמָתֶֽךָ׃
land-of-you in days-of-you all-of the-Levite *** you-neglect so-not to-you

כִּֽי־ יַרְחִיב֩ יְהוָ֨ה אֱלֹהֶ֤יךָ אֶֽת־ גְּבוּלְךָ֙ כַּאֲשֶׁ֣ר
just-as territory-of-you *** God-of-you Yahweh he-enlarges when (20)

דִּבֶּר־ לָךְ֒ וְאָמַרְתָּ֙ אֹכְלָ֣ה בָשָׂ֔ר כִּֽי־ תְאַוֶּ֥ה נַפְשְׁךָ֖
self-of-you she-craves for meat I-would-eat and-you-say to-you he-promised

לֶאֱכֹ֣ל בָּשָׂ֑ר בְּכָל־ אַוַּ֣ת נַפְשְׁךָ֔ תֹּאכַ֖ל בָּשָֽׂר׃ כִּֽי־ יִרְחַ֨ק
he-is-far if (21) meat you-may-eat self-of-you want-of at-any-of meat to-eat

מִמְּךָ֜ הַמָּק֗וֹם אֲשֶׁ֨ר יִבְחַ֜ר יְהוָ֤ה אֱלֹהֶ֙יךָ֙ לָשׂ֣וּם שְׁמוֹ֮
Name-of-him to-put God-of-you Yahweh he-chooses where the-place from-you

שָׁם֒ וְזָבַחְתָּ֞ מִבְּקָרְךָ֣ וּמִצֹּאנְךָ֗ אֲשֶׁ֨ר
that or-from-flock-of-you from-herd-of-you then-you-may-slaughter there

נָתַ֤ן יְהוָה֙ לְךָ֔ כַּאֲשֶׁ֖ר צִוִּיתִ֑ךָ וְאָֽכַלְתָּ֙ בִּשְׁעָרֶ֔יךָ
in-gates-of-you and-you-may-eat I-commanded-you just-as to-you Yahweh he-gave

בְּכֹ֖ל אַוַּ֥ת נַפְשֶֽׁךָ׃ אַ֗ךְ כַּאֲשֶׁ֨ר יֵאָכֵ֤ל אֶֽת־ הַצְּבִי֙
the-gazelle *** he-is-eaten just-as only (22) self-of-you want-of as-all-of

וְאֶת־ הָֽאַיָּ֔ל כֵּ֖ן תֹּאכְלֶ֑נּוּ הַטָּמֵא֙ וְהַטָּה֔וֹר יַחְדָּ֖ו יֹאכְלֶֽנּוּ׃
he-may-eat-him both and-the-clean the-unclean you-eat-him same the-deer or

רַ֣ק חֲזַ֗ק לְבִלְתִּי֙ אֲכֹ֣ל הַדָּ֔ם כִּ֥י הַדָּ֖ם ה֣וּא הַנָּ֑פֶשׁ וְלֹֽא־
and-not the-life he the-blood for the-blood to-eat not be-sure! but (23)

תֹאכַ֥ל הַנֶּ֖פֶשׁ עִם־ הַבָּשָֽׂר׃ לֹ֖א תֹּאכְלֶ֑נּוּ עַל־ הָאָ֖רֶץ
the-ground on you-must-eat-him not (24) the-meat with the-life you-must-eat

[17]You must not eat in your
own towns the tithe of your
grain and new wine and oil,
or the firstborn of your herds
and flocks, or whatever you
have vowed to give, or your
freewill offerings or special
gifts. [18]Instead, you are to eat
them in the presence of the
LORD your God at the place the
LORD your God will choose—
you, your sons and daughters,
your menservants and maidservants, and the Levites from
your towns—and you are to rejoice before the LORD your God
in everything you put your
hand to. [19]Be careful not to neglect the Levites as long as you
live in your land.
[20]When the LORD your God
has enlarged your territory as
he promised you, and you
crave meat and say, "I would
like some meat," then you
may eat as much of it as you
want. [21]If the place where the
LORD your God chooses to put
his Name is too far away from
you, you may slaughter animals from the herds and flocks
the LORD has given you, as I
have commanded you, and in
your own towns you may eat
as much of them as you want.
[22]Eat them as you would gazelle or deer. Both the
ceremonially unclean and the
clean may eat. [23]But be sure
you do not eat the blood, because the blood is the life, and
you must not eat the life with
the meat. [24]You must not eat
the blood; pour it out on the

תִּשְׁפְּכֶנּוּ כַּמָּיִם׃ לֹא תֹאכְלֶנּוּ לְמַעַן יִיטַב
he-may-go-well so-that you-eat-him not (25) like-the-waters you-pour-him

לְךָ וּלְבָנֶיךָ אַחֲרֶיךָ כִּי־ תַעֲשֶׂה הַיָּשָׁר
the-right-thing you-will-do for after-you and-with-children-of-you with-you

בְּעֵינֵי יְהוָה׃ רַק קָדָשֶׁיךָ אֲשֶׁר־ יִהְיוּ לְךָ
to-you they-are that consecrated-things-of-you but (26) Yahweh in-eyes-of

וּנְדָרֶיךָ תִּשָּׂא וּבָאתָ אֶל־ הַמָּקוֹם אֲשֶׁר־ יִבְחַר
he-will-choose that the-place to and-you-go you-take and-things-vowed-of-you

יְהוָה׃ וְעָשִׂיתָ עֹלֹתֶיךָ הַבָּשָׂר וְהַדָּם
and-the-blood the-meat burnt-offerings-of-you and-you-present (27) Yahweh

עַל־ מִזְבַּח יְהוָה אֱלֹהֶיךָ וְדַם־ זְבָחֶיךָ יִשָּׁפֵךְ
he-must-be-poured sacrifices-of-you and-blood-of God-of-you Yahweh altar-of on

עַל־ מִזְבַּח יְהוָה אֱלֹהֶיךָ וְהַבָּשָׂר תֹּאכֵל׃ שְׁמֹר
be-careful! (28) you-may-eat but-the-meat God-of-you Yahweh altar-of beside

וְשָׁמַעְתָּ אֵת כָּל־ הַדְּבָרִים הָאֵלֶּה אֲשֶׁר אָנֹכִי מְצַוֶּךָּ לְמַעַן
so-that giving-you I that the-these the-regulations all-of *** and-you-obey

יִיטַב לְךָ וּלְבָנֶיךָ אַחֲרֶיךָ עַד־ עוֹלָם כִּי
for always for after-you and-with-children-of-you with-you he-may-go-well

תַעֲשֶׂה הַטּוֹב וְהַיָּשָׁר בְּעֵינֵי יְהוָה אֱלֹהֶיךָ׃ כִּי־
indeed (29) God-of-you Yahweh in-eyes-of and-the-right the-good you-will-do

יַכְרִית יְהוָה אֱלֹהֶיךָ אֶת־ הַגּוֹיִם אֲשֶׁר אַתָּה בָא־
invading you that the-nations *** God-of-you Yahweh he-will-cut-off

שָׁמָּה לָרֶשֶׁת אוֹתָם מִפָּנֶיךָ וְיָרַשְׁתָּ אֹתָם
them when-you-drive-out from-before-you them to-dispossess to-there

וְיָשַׁבְתָּ בְּאַרְצָם׃ הִשָּׁמֶר לְךָ פֶּן־ תִּנָּקֵשׁ
you-are-ensnared so-not to-you be-careful! (30) in-land-of-them and-you-settle

אַחֲרֵיהֶם אַחֲרֵי הִשָּׁמְדָם מִפָּנֶיךָ וּפֶן־ תִּדְרֹשׁ
you-inquire and-not from-before-you to-be-destroyed-them after after-them

לֵאלֹהֵיהֶם לֵאמֹר אֵיכָה יַעַבְדוּ הַגּוֹיִם הָאֵלֶּה אֶת־
*** the-these the-nations do-they-serve how? to-say about-gods-of-them

אֱלֹהֵיהֶם וְאֶעֱשֶׂה־ כֵּן גַּם־ אָנִי׃ לֹא־ תַעֲשֶׂה כֵן
same you-must-worship not (31) I also same now-I-will-do gods-of-them

לַיהוָה אֱלֹהֶיךָ כִּי כָל־ תּוֹעֲבַת יְהוָה אֲשֶׁר שָׂנֵא עָשׂוּ
they-do he-hates that Yahweh detestable-of all-of for God-of-you to-Yahweh

לֵאלֹהֵיהֶם כִּי גַם אֶת־ בְּנֵיהֶם וְאֶת־ בְּנֹתֵיהֶם יִשְׂרְפוּ
they-burn daughters-of-them and sons-of-them *** even indeed for-gods-of-them

בָאֵשׁ לֵאלֹהֵיהֶם׃ אֵת כָּל־ הַדָּבָר אֲשֶׁר אָנֹכִי מְצַוֶּה
giving I that the-command all-of *** (13:1)* to-gods-of-them in-the-fire

ground like water. 25Do not eat
it, so that it may go well with
you and your children after
you, because you will be doing
what is right in the eyes of the
LORD.
26But take your consecrated
things and whatever you have
vowed to give, and go to the
place the LORD will choose.
27Present your burnt offerings
on the altar of the LORD your
God, both the meat and the
blood. The blood of your sacrifices must be poured beside
the altar of the LORD your God,
but you may eat the meat. 28Be
careful to obey all these regulations I am giving you, so that
it may always go well with
you and your children after
you, because you will be doing
what is good and right in the
eyes of the LORD your God.
29The LORD your God will cut
off before you the nations you
are about to invade and dispossess. But when you have
driven them out and settled in
their land, 30and after they
have been destroyed before
you, be careful not to be ensnared by inquiring about
their gods, saying, "How do
these nations serve their gods?
We will do the same." 31You
must not worship the LORD
your God in their way, because in worshiping their
gods, they do all kinds of detestable things the LORD hates.
They even burn their sons and
daughters in the fire as sacrifices to their gods.
32See that you do all I command you; do not add to it or

*The Hebrew numeration of chapter 13 begins with verse 32 of chapter 12 in English; thus, there is a one-verse discrepancy throughout chapter 13.

אֶתְכֶם אֹתוֹ תִּשְׁמְרוּ לַעֲשׂוֹת לֹא־ תֹסֵף עָלָיו וְלֹא תִגְרַע
you-take-away and-not to-him you-add not to-do you-be-careful him you

מִמֶּנּוּ׃ כִּי־ יָקוּם בְּקִרְבְּךָ נָבִיא אוֹ חֹלֵם חֲלוֹם
dream one-dreaming-of or prophet in-among-you he-appears if (2) from-him

וְנָתַן אֵלֶיךָ אוֹת אוֹ מוֹפֵת׃ וּבָא הָאוֹת
the-sign and-he-takes-place (3) wonder or sign to-you and-he-announces

וְהַמּוֹפֵת אֲשֶׁר־ דִּבֶּר אֵלֶיךָ לֵאמֹר נֵלְכָה אַחֲרֵי אֱלֹהִים אֲחֵרִים
other-ones gods after let-us-follow to-say to-you he-spoke which or-the-wonder

אֲשֶׁר לֹא־ יְדַעְתָּם וְנָעָבְדֵם׃ לֹא תִשְׁמַע אֶל־
to you-must-listen not (4) and-let-us-worship-them you-knew-them not that

דִּבְרֵי הַנָּבִיא הַהוּא אוֹ אֶל־ חוֹלֵם הַחֲלוֹם הַהוּא כִּי
for the-that the-dream one-dreaming-of to or the-that the-prophet words-of

מְנַסֶּה יְהוָה אֱלֹהֵיכֶם אֶתְכֶם לָדַעַת הֲיִשְׁכֶם אֹהֲבִים אֶת־ יְהוָה
Yahweh *** ones-loving whether-you to-find-out you God-of-you Yahweh testing

אֱלֹהֵיכֶם בְּכָל־ לְבַבְכֶם וּבְכָל־ נַפְשְׁכֶם׃ אַחֲרֵי
after (5) soul-of-you and-with-all-of heart-of-you with-all-of God-of-you

יְהוָה אֱלֹהֵיכֶם תֵּלֵכוּ וְאֹתוֹ תִירָאוּ וְאֶת־ מִצְוֹתָיו
commands-of-him and you-must-revere and-him you-must-follow God-of-you Yahweh

תִּשְׁמֹרוּ וּבְקֹלוֹ תִשְׁמָעוּ וְאֹתוֹ תַעֲבֹדוּ
you-must-serve and-him you-must-obey and-to-voice-of-him you must-keep

וּבוֹ תִדְבָּקוּן׃ וְהַנָּבִיא הַהוּא אוֹ חֹלֵם
one-dreaming-of or the-that and-the-prophet (6) you-must-hold-fast and-to-him

הַחֲלוֹם הַהוּא יוּמָת כִּי דִבֶּר־ סָרָה עַל־ יְהוָה
Yahweh against rebellion he-preached for he-must-die the-that the-dreams

אֱלֹהֵיכֶם הַמּוֹצִיא אֶתְכֶם ׀ מֵאֶרֶץ מִצְרַיִם וְהַפֹּדְךָ
and-the-one-redeeming-you Egypt from-land-of you the-one-bringing God-of-you

מִבֵּית עֲבָדִים לְהַדִּיחֲךָ מִן־ הַדֶּרֶךְ אֲשֶׁר צִוְּךָ
he-commanded-you that the-way from to-turn-you slaveries from-house-of

יְהוָה אֱלֹהֶיךָ לָלֶכֶת בָּהּ וּבִעַרְתָּ הָרָע מִקִּרְבֶּךָ׃
from-among-you the-evil and-you-must-purge in-her to-walk God-of-you Yahweh

כִּי יְסִיתְךָ אָחִיךָ בֶן־ אִמֶּךָ אוֹ־ בִנְךָ אוֹ־
or son-of-you or mother-of-you son-of brother-of-you he-entices-you if (7)

בִתְּךָ אוֹ ׀ אֵשֶׁת חֵיקֶךָ אוֹ רֵעֲךָ אֲשֶׁר כְּנַפְשְׁךָ
as-self-of-you who friend-of-you or love-of-you wife-of or daughter-of-you

בַּסֵּתֶר לֵאמֹר נֵלְכָה וְנַעַבְדָה אֱלֹהִים אֲחֵרִים אֲשֶׁר לֹא
not that other-ones gods and-let-us-worship let-us-go to-say in-the-secret

יָדַעְתָּ אַתָּה וַאֲבֹתֶיךָ׃ מֵאֱלֹהֵי הָעַמִּים אֲשֶׁר סְבִיבֹתֵיכֶם
around-you who the-peoples from-gods-of (8) or-fathers-of-you you you-knew

take away from it.

Worshiping Other Gods

13 If a prophet, or one who foretells by dreams, appears among you and announces to you a miraculous sign or wonder,
[2]and if the sign or wonder of which he has spoken takes place, and he says, "Let us follow other gods" (gods you have not known) "and let us worship them,"
[3]you must not listen to the words of that prophet or dreamer. The LORD your God is testing you to find out whether you love him with all your heart and with all your soul.
[4]It is the LORD your God you must follow, and him you must revere. Keep his commands and obey him; serve him and hold fast to him.
[5]That prophet or dreamer must be put to death, because he preached rebellion against the LORD your God, who brought you out of Egypt and redeemed you from the land of slavery; he has tried to turn you from the way the LORD your God commanded you to follow. You must purge the evil from among you.
[6]If your very own brother, or your son or daughter, or the wife you love, or your closest friend secretly entices you, saying, "Let us go and worship other gods" (gods that neither you nor your fathers have known,
[7]gods of the peoples around you, whether near

*See the note on page 522.

הַקְּרֹבִים אֵלֶיךָ אוֹ הָרְחֹקִים מִמֶּךָּ מִקְצֵה הָאָרֶץ וְעַד־
even-to the-land from-end-of from-you the-ones-far or to-you the-ones-near

קְצֵה הָאָרֶץ׃ (9) לֹא־ תֹאבֶה לוֹ וְלֹא תִשְׁמַע אֵלָיו וְלֹא־
and-not to-him you-listen and-not to-him you-yield not (9) the-land end-of

תָחוֹס עֵינְךָ עָלָיו וְלֹא־ תַחְמֹל וְלֹא־ תְכַסֶּה
you-shield and-not you-spare and-not to-him eye-of-you she-must-pity

עָלָיו׃ (10) כִּי הָרֹג תַּהַרְגֶנּוּ יָדְךָ תִּהְיֶה־ בּוֹ
on-him she-must-be hand-of-you you-must-kill-him to-kill but (10) over-him

בָרִאשׁוֹנָה לַהֲמִיתוֹ וְיַד כָּל־ הָעָם בָּאַחֲרֹנָה׃
as-the-next the-people all-of then-hand-of to-kill-him as-the-first

(11) וּסְקַלְתּוֹ בָאֲבָנִים וָמֵת כִּי בִקֵּשׁ לְהַדִּיחֲךָ
to-turn-you he-tried for so-he-dies with-the-stones and-you-stone-him (11)

מֵעַל יְהוָה אֱלֹהֶיךָ הַמּוֹצִיאֲךָ מֵאֶרֶץ מִצְרַיִם
Egypt from-land-of the-one-bringing-you God-of-you Yahweh away-from

מִבֵּית עֲבָדִים׃ (12) וְכָל־ יִשְׂרָאֵל יִשְׁמְעוּ
they-will-hear Israel then-all-of (12) slaveries from-house-of

וְיִרָאוּן וְלֹא־ יוֹסִפוּ לַעֲשׂוֹת כַּדָּבָר הָרָע
the-evil as-the-thing to-do they-will-repeat and-not and-they-will-be-afraid

הַזֶּה בְּקִרְבֶּךָ׃ (13) כִּי־ תִשְׁמַע בְּאַחַת עָרֶיךָ אֲשֶׁר יְהוָה
Yahweh that towns-of-you about-one-of you-hear if (13) in-among-you the-this

אֱלֹהֶיךָ נֹתֵן לְךָ לָשֶׁבֶת שָׁם לֵאמֹר׃ (14) יָצְאוּ אֲנָשִׁים בְּנֵי־
sons-of men they-rose (14) to-say there to-live to-you giving God-of-you

בְלִיַּעַל מִקִּרְבֶּךָ וַיַּדִּיחוּ אֶת־ יֹשְׁבֵי עִירָם
town-of-them ones-living-of *** and-they-led-astray from-among-you wickedness

לֵאמֹר נֵלְכָה וְנַעַבְדָה אֱלֹהִים אֲחֵרִים אֲשֶׁר לֹא־ יְדַעְתֶּם׃
you-knew not that other-ones gods let-us-worship let-us-go to-say

(15) וְדָרַשְׁתָּ וְחָקַרְתָּ וְשָׁאַלְתָּ הֵיטֵב וְהִנֵּה אֱמֶת
true and-if to-be-thorough and-you-investigate and-you-probe then-you-inquire (15)

נָכוֹן הַדָּבָר נֶעֶשְׂתָה הַתּוֹעֵבָה הַזֹּאת בְּקִרְבֶּךָ׃
in-among-you the-this the-detestable-thing she-was-done the-thing being-proved

(16) הַכֵּה תַכֶּה אֶת־ יֹשְׁבֵי הָעִיר הַהִוא לְפִי־
with-edge-of the-that the-town ones-living-of *** you-must-kill to-kill (16)

חָרֶב הַחֲרֵם אֹתָהּ וְאֶת־כָּל־אֲשֶׁר־בָּהּ וְאֶת־ בְּהֶמְתָּהּ לְפִי־ חָרֶב׃
sword with-edge-of stock-of-her and in-her that all and her destroy! sword

(17) וְאֶת־ כָּל־ שְׁלָלָהּ תִּקְבֹּץ אֶל־ תּוֹךְ רְחֹבָהּ
public-square-of-her middle-of into you-gather plunder-of-her all-of and (17)

וְשָׂרַפְתָּ בָאֵשׁ אֶת־ הָעִיר וְאֶת־ כָּל־ שְׁלָלָהּ
plunder-of-her all-of and the-town *** with-the-fire and-you-burn

or far, from one end of the land to the other), [8]do not yield to him or listen to him. Show him no pity. Do not spare him or shield him. [9]You must certainly put him to death. Your hand must be the first in putting him to death, and then the hands of all the people. [10]Stone him to death, because he tried to turn you away from the LORD your God, who brought you out of Egypt, out of the land of slavery. [11]Then all Israel will hear and be afraid, and no one among you will do such an evil thing again.

[12]If you hear it said about one of the towns the LORD your God is giving you to live in [13]that wicked men have arisen among you and have led the people of their town astray, saying, "Let us go and worship other gods" (gods you have not known), [14]then you must inquire, probe and investigate it thoroughly. And if it is true and it has been proved that this detestable thing has been done among you, [15]you must certainly put to the sword all who live in that town. Destroy it completely,[v] both its people and its livestock. [16]Gather all the plunder of the town into the middle of the public square and completely burn the town and all its plunder as a whole burnt

[v]15 The Hebrew term refers to the irrevocable giving over of things or persons to the LORD, often by totally destroying them.

*See the note on page 522.

°16 ק ההיא

כָּלִיל לַיהוָה אֱלֹהֶיךָ וְהָיְתָה תֵּל עוֹלָם לֹא
not forever ruin and-she-must-remain God-of-you to-Yahweh whole-offering

תִבָּנֶה עוֹד׃ וְלֹא־ יִדְבַּק בְּיָדְךָ מְאוּמָה
anything in-hand-of-you he-may-find and-not (18) ever she-must-be-rebuilt

מִן־ הַחֵרֶם לְמַעַן יָשׁוּב יְהוָה מֵחֲרוֹן אַפּוֹ
anger-of-her from-fierceness-of Yahweh he-will-turn so-that the-condemned from

וְנָתַן־ לְךָ רַחֲמִים וְרִחַמְךָ
and-he-will-have-compassion-on-you mercies to-you and-he-will-show

וְהִרְבֶּךָ כַּאֲשֶׁר נִשְׁבַּע לַאֲבֹתֶיךָ׃ כִּי תִשְׁמַע
you-obey for (19) to-fathers-of-you he-swore just-as and-he-will-increase-you

בְּקוֹל יְהוָה אֱלֹהֶיךָ לִשְׁמֹר אֶת־ כָּל־ מִצְוֹתָיו אֲשֶׁר אָנֹכִי
I that commands-of-him all-of *** to-keep God-of-you Yahweh to-voice-of

מְצַוְּךָ הַיּוֹם לַעֲשׂוֹת הַיָּשָׁר בְּעֵינֵי יְהוָה אֱלֹהֶיךָ׃ בָּנִים
sons (14:1) God-of-you Yahweh in-eyes-of the-right to-do the-day giving-you

אַתֶּם לַיהוָה אֱלֹהֵיכֶם לֹא תִתְגֹּדְדוּ וְלֹא־ תָשִׂימוּ קָרְחָה בֵּין
between bald you-shave and-not you-cut-selves not God-of-you of-Yahweh you

עֵינֵיכֶם לָמֵת׃ כִּי עַם קָדוֹשׁ אַתָּה לַיהוָה אֱלֹהֶיךָ
God-of-you to-Yahweh you holy people for (2) for-the-dead eyes-of-you

וּבְךָ בָּחַר יְהוָה לִהְיוֹת לוֹ לְעַם סְגֻלָּה מִכֹּל
from-all-of treasure as-people-of for-him to-be Yahweh he-chose and-to-you

הָעַמִּים אֲשֶׁר עַל־ פְּנֵי הָאֲדָמָה׃ לֹא תֹאכַל כָּל־ תּוֹעֵבָה׃
detestable-thing any-of you-eat not (3) the-earth faces-of on that the-peoples

זֹאת הַבְּהֵמָה אֲשֶׁר תֹּאכֵלוּ שׁוֹר שֵׂה כְשָׂבִים וְשֵׂה עִזִּים׃
goats and-goat-of sheep sheep-of ox you-may-eat that the-animal this (4)

אַיָּל וּצְבִי וְיַחְמוּר וְאַקּוֹ וְדִישֹׁן וּתְאוֹ
and-antelope and-ibex and-wild-goat and-roe-deer and-gazelle deer (5)

וָזָמֶר׃ וְכָל־ בְּהֵמָה מַפְרֶסֶת פַּרְסָה וְשֹׁסַעַת
and-dividing hoof splitting animal and-any-of (6) and-mountain-sheep

שֶׁסַע שְׁתֵּי פְרָסוֹת מַעֲלַת גֵּרָה בַּבְּהֵמָה אֹתָהּ תֹּאכֵלוּ׃
you-may-eat her among-the-animal cud chewing-of hoofs two-of division

אַךְ אֶת־ זֶה לֹא תֹאכְלוּ מִמַּעֲלֵי הַגֵּרָה
the-cud from-ones-chewing-of you-may-eat not this *** however (7)

וּמִמַּפְרִיסֵי הַפַּרְסָה הַשְּׁסוּעָה אֶת־ הַגָּמָל וְאֶת־
and the-camel *** the-being-divided the-hoof and-from-ones-splitting

הָאַרְנֶבֶת וְאֶת־ הַשָּׁפָן כִּי־ מַעֲלֵה גֵרָה הֵמָּה וּפַרְסָה לֹא הִפְרִיסוּ
they-split not but-hoof they cud chewing-of for the-coney and the-rabbit

טְמֵאִים הֵם לָכֶם׃ וְאֶת־ הַחֲזִיר כִּי־מַפְרִיס פַּרְסָה הוּא וְלֹא
but-not he hoof splitting for the-pig and (8) for-you they ones-unclean

offering to the LORD your God.
It is to remain a ruin forever,
never to be rebuilt. [17]None of
those condemned things
shall be found in your hands,
so that the LORD will turn from
his fierce anger; he will show
you mercy, have compassion
on you, and increase your
numbers, as he promised on
oath to your forefathers, [18]be-
cause you obey the LORD your
God, keeping all his com-
mands that I am giving you
today and doing what is right
in his eyes.

Clean and Unclean Food

14 You are the children of
the LORD your God. Do
not cut yourselves or shave the
front of your heads for the
dead, [2]for you are a people
holy to the LORD your God.
Out of all the peoples on the
face of the earth, the LORD has
chosen you to be his treasured
possession.
[3]Do not eat any detestable
thing. [4]These are the animals
you may eat: the ox, the sheep,
the goat, [5]the deer, the gazelle,
the roe deer, the wild goat, the
ibex, the antelope and the
mountain sheep.[w] [6]You may
eat any animal that has a split
hoof divided in two and that
chews the cud. [7]However, of
those that chew the cud or that
have a split hoof completely
divided you may not eat the
camel, the rabbit or the
coney.[x] Although they chew
the cud, they do not have a
split hoof; they are ceremonially unclean for you. [8]The pig
is also unclean; although it has
a split hoof, it does not chew

[w]5 The precise identification of some of the birds and animals in this chapter is uncertain.
[x]7 That is, the hyrax or rock badger

*See the note on page 522.

גֵרָה טָמֵא הוּא לָכֶם מִבְּשָׂרָם לֹא תֹאכֵלוּ וּבְנִבְלָתָם
and-on-carcass-of-them you-eat not from-meat-of-them for-you he unclean cud

לֹא תִגָּעוּ׃ אֶת־זֶה תֹּאכְלוּ מִכֹּל אֲשֶׁר בַּמָּיִם כֹּל אֲשֶׁר־
that and in-the-waters that from-all you-may-eat this *** (9) you-touch not

לוֹ סְנַפִּיר וְקַשְׂקֶשֶׂת תֹּאכֵלוּ׃ וְכֹל אֲשֶׁר אֵין־לוֹ סְנַפִּיר וְקַשְׂקֶשֶׂת
or-scale fin on-him not that and-any (10) you-may-eat or-scale fin on-him

לֹא תֹאכֵלוּ טָמֵא הוּא לָכֶם׃ כָּל־צִפּוֹר טְהֹרָה תֹּאכֵלוּ׃
you-may-eat clean bird any-of (11) for-you he unclean you-may-eat not

וְזֶה אֲשֶׁר לֹא־תֹאכְלוּ מֵהֶם הַנֶּשֶׁר וְהַפֶּרֶס
and-the-vulture the-eagle from-them you-may-eat not that but-this (12)

וְהָעָזְנִיָּה׃ וְהָרָאָה וְאֶת־הָאַיָּה וְהַדַּיָּה
and-the-falcon the-black-kite and and-the-red-kite (13) and-the-black-vulture

לְמִינָהּ׃ וְאֵת כָּל־עֹרֵב לְמִינוֹ׃ וְאֵת בַּת
daughter-of and (15) any-kind-of-him raven any-of and (14) any-kind-of-her

הַיַּעֲנָה וְאֶת־הַתַּחְמָס וְאֶת־הַשָּׁחַף וְאֶת־הַנֵּץ לְמִינֵהוּ׃
any-kind-of-him the-hawk and the-gull and the-screech-owl and the-horned-owl

אֶת־הַכּוֹס וְאֶת־הַיַּנְשׁוּף וְהַתִּנְשָׁמֶת׃ וְהַקָּאָת
the-desert-owl (17) and-the-white-owl the-great-owl and the-little-owl *** (16)

וְאֶת־הָרָחָמָה וְאֶת־הַשָּׁלָךְ׃ וְהַחֲסִידָה וְהָאֲנָפָה
and-the-heron and-the-stork (18) the-cormorant and the-osprey and

לְמִינָהּ וְהַדּוּכִיפַת וְהָעֲטַלֵּף׃ וְכֹל שֶׁרֶץ הָעוֹף
the-wing swarmer-of and-any-of (19) and-the-bat and-the-hoopoe any-kind-of-her

טָמֵא הוּא לָכֶם לֹא יֵאָכֵלוּ׃ כָּל־עוֹף טָהוֹר
clean winged-creature any-of (20) they-may-be-eaten not for-you he unclean

תֹּאכֵלוּ׃ לֹא תֹאכְלוּ כָל־נְבֵלָה לַגֵּר אֲשֶׁר־
who to-the-alien already-dead-animal any-of you-eat not (21) you-may-eat

בִּשְׁעָרֶיךָ תִּתְּנֶנָּה וַאֲכָלָהּ אוֹ מָכֹר לְנָכְרִי
to-foreigner to-sell or and-he-may-eat-her you-may-give-her in-gates-of-you

כִּי עַם קָדוֹשׁ אַתָּה לַיהוָה אֱלֹהֶיךָ לֹא־תְבַשֵּׁל גְּדִי בַּחֲלֵב
in-milk-of young-goat you-cook not God-of-you to-Yahweh you holy people but

אִמּוֹ׃ עַשֵּׂר תְּעַשֵּׂר אֵת כָּל־תְּבוּאַת
yield-of all-of *** you-give-tenth to-give-tenth (22) mother-of-him

זַרְעֶךָ הַיֹּצֵא הַשָּׂדֶה שָׁנָה שָׁנָה׃ וְאָכַלְתָּ לִפְנֵי ׀
before and-you-eat (23) year year the-field the-one-producing seed-of-you

יְהוָה אֱלֹהֶיךָ בַּמָּקוֹם אֲשֶׁר־יִבְחַר לְשַׁכֵּן שְׁמוֹ
Name-of-him to-make-dwell he-will-choose that at-the-place God-of-you Yahweh

שָׁם מַעְשַׂר דְּגָנְךָ תִּירֹשְׁךָ וְיִצְהָרֶךָ
and-oil-of-you new-wine-of-you grain-of-you tithe-of there

the cud. You are not to eat
their meat or touch their carcasses.
[9]Of all the creatures living in
the water, you may eat any
that has fins and scales. [10]But
anything that does not have
fins and scales you may not
eat; for you it is unclean.
[11]You may eat any clean
bird. [12]But these you may not
eat: the eagle, the vulture, the
black vulture, [13]the red kite,
the black kite, any kind of falcon,
[14]any kind of raven, [15]the
horned owl, the screech owl,
the gull, any kind of hawk,
[16]the little owl, the great owl,
the white owl, [17]the desert
owl, the osprey, the cormorant,
[18]the stork, any kind of
heron, the hoopoe and the bat.
[19]All flying insects that
swarm are unclean to you; do
not eat them. [20]But any
winged creature that is clean
you may eat.
[21]Do not eat anything you
find already dead. You may
give it to an alien living in any
of your towns, and he may eat
it, or you may sell it to a foreigner.
But you are a people
holy to the LORD your God.
Do not cook a young goat in
its mother's milk.

Tithes

[22]Be sure to set aside a tenth
of all that your fields produce
each year. [23]Eat the tithe of
your grain, new wine and oil,
and the firstborn of your herds
and flocks in the presence of
the LORD your God at the place
he will choose as a dwelling

וּבְכֹרֹת בְּקָרְךָ וְצֹאנֶךָ לְמַעַן תִּלְמַד

you-may-learn so-that and-flock-of-you herd-of-you and-ones-firstborn-of

לְיִרְאָה אֶת־ יְהוָה אֱלֹהֶיךָ כָּל־ הַיָּמִים׃ וְכִי־ יִרְבֶּה

he-is-distant but-if (24) the-days all-of God-of-you Yahweh *** to-revere

מִמְּךָ הַדֶּרֶךְ כִּי לֹא תוּכַל שְׂאֵתוֹ כִּי־ יִרְחַק מִמְּךָ

from-you he-is-far for to-carry-him you-are-able not so the-way from-you

הַמָּקוֹם אֲשֶׁר יִבְחַר יְהוָה אֱלֹהֶיךָ לָשׂוּם שְׁמוֹ שָׁם

there Name-of-him to-put God-of-you Yahweh he-will-choose that the-place

כִּי יְבָרֶכְךָ יְהוָה אֱלֹהֶיךָ׃ וְנָתַתָּה בַּכָּסֶף

for-the-silver then-you-exchange (25) God-of-you Yahweh he-blessed-you and

וְצַרְתָּ הַכֶּסֶף בְּיָדְךָ וְהָלַכְתָּ אֶל־ הַמָּקוֹם אֲשֶׁר

that the-place to and-you-go in-hand-of-you the-silver and-you-take

יִבְחַר יְהוָה אֱלֹהֶיךָ בּוֹ׃ וְנָתַתָּה הַכֶּסֶף

the-silver and-you-use (26) to-him God-of-you Yahweh he-will-choose

בְּכֹל אֲשֶׁר־ תְּאַוֶּה נַפְשְׁךָ בַּבָּקָר וּבַצֹּאן

or-of-the-flock of-the-cattle self-of-you she-likes that for-anything

וּבַיַּיִן וּבַשֵּׁכָר וּבְכֹל אֲשֶׁר תִּשְׁאָלְךָ

she-asks-you that or-of-anything or-of-the-fermented-drink or-of-the-wine

נַפְשֶׁךָ וְאָכַלְתָּ שָּׁם לִפְנֵי יְהוָה אֱלֹהֶיךָ וְשָׂמַחְתָּ אַתָּה

you and-you-rejoice God-of-you Yahweh before there then-you-eat self-of-you

וּבֵיתֶךָ׃ וְהַלֵּוִי אֲשֶׁר־ בִּשְׁעָרֶיךָ לֹא

not within-gates-of-you who and-the-Levite (27) and-household-of-you

תַעַזְבֶנּוּ כִּי אֵין לוֹ חֵלֶק וְנַחֲלָה עִמָּךְ׃

among-you or-inheritance allotment to-him not for you-neglect-him

מִקְצֵה ׀ שָׁלֹשׁ שָׁנִים תּוֹצִיא אֶת־ כָּל־ מַעְשַׂר תְּבוּאָתְךָ

produce-of-you tithe-of all-of *** you-bring years three at-end-of (28)

בַּשָּׁנָה הַהִוא וְהִנַּחְתָּ בִּשְׁעָרֶיךָ׃ וּבָא

so-he-may-come (29) in-towns-of-you and-you-store the-that of-the-year

הַלֵּוִי כִּי אֵין־ לוֹ חֵלֶק וְנַחֲלָה עִמָּךְ וְהַגֵּר

and-the-alien among-you or-inheritance allotment to-him not that the-Levite

וְהַיָּתוֹם וְהָאַלְמָנָה אֲשֶׁר בִּשְׁעָרֶיךָ וְאָכְלוּ

so-they-may-eat within-gates-of-you who and-the-widow and-the-fatherless

וְשָׂבֵעוּ לְמַעַן יְבָרֶכְךָ יְהוָה אֱלֹהֶיךָ

God-of-you Yahweh he-may-bless-you so-that and-they-may-be-satisfied

בְּכָל־ מַעֲשֵׂה יָדְךָ אֲשֶׁר תַּעֲשֶׂה׃ מִקֵּץ שֶׁבַע־ שָׁנִים

years seven-of at-end-of (15:1) you-do that hand-of-you work-of in-all-of

תַּעֲשֶׂה שְׁמִטָּה׃ וְזֶה דְּבַר הַשְּׁמִטָּה שָׁמוֹט

to-cancel the-cancel-of-debt way-of and-this (2) cancel-of-debt you-must-do

for his Name, so that you may
learn to revere the LORD your
God always. [24]But if that place
is too distant and you have
been blessed by the LORD your
God and cannot carry your
tithe (because the place where
the LORD will choose to put his
Name is so far away), [25]then
exchange your tithe for silver,
and take the silver with you
and go to the place the LORD
your God will choose. [26]Use
the silver to buy whatever you
like: cattle, sheep, wine or other fermented drink, or anything you wish. Then you and
your household shall eat there
in the presence of the LORD
your God and rejoice. [27]And do
not neglect the Levites living
in your towns, for they have
no allotment or inheritance of
their own.

[28]At the end of every three
years, bring all the tithes of
that year's produce and store it
in your towns, [29]so that the Levites (who have no allotment
or inheritance of their own)
and the aliens, the fatherless
and the widows who live in
your towns may come and eat
and be satisfied, and so that
the LORD your God may bless
you in all the work of your
hands.

The Year for Canceling Debts

15 At the end of every
seven years you must
cancel debts. [2]This is how it is
to be done: Every creditor

כָּל־ בַּעַל מַשֵּׁה יָדוֹ אֲשֶׁר יַשֶּׁה בְּרֵעֵהוּ לֹא־
not to-fellow-of-him he-loaned that hand-of-him loan-of creditor-of every-of

יִגֹּשׂ אֶת־ רֵעֵהוּ וְאֶת־ אָחִיו כִּי־ קָרָא
he-proclaimed for brother-of-him or fellow-of-him *** he-shall-require-payment

שְׁמִטָּה לַיהוָה׃ אֶת־ הַנָּכְרִי תִּגֹּשׂ
you-may-require-payment the-foreigner *** (3) of-Yahweh cancel-of-debt

וַאֲשֶׁר יִהְיֶה לְךָ אֶת־ אָחִיךָ תַּשְׁמֵט יָדֶךָ׃
hand-of-you she-must-cancel-debt brother-of-you *** to-you he-owes but-what

אֶפֶס כִּי לֹא יִהְיֶה־ בְּךָ אֶבְיוֹן כִּי־ בָרֵךְ
to-bless for poor among-you he-should-be not indeed however (4)

יְבָרֶכְךָ יְהוָה בָּאָרֶץ אֲשֶׁר יְהוָה אֱלֹהֶיךָ נֹתֵן־ לְךָ
to-you giving God-of-you Yahweh that in-the-land Yahweh he-will-bless-you

נַחֲלָה לְרִשְׁתָּהּ׃ רַק אִם־ שָׁמוֹעַ תִּשְׁמַע בְּקוֹל יְהוָה
Yahweh to-voice-of you-obey to-obey if only (5) to-possess-her inheritance

אֱלֹהֶיךָ לִשְׁמֹר לַעֲשׂוֹת אֶת־ כָּל־ הַמִּצְוָה הַזֹּאת אֲשֶׁר
that the-this the-command all-of *** to-follow to-be-careful God-of-you

אָנֹכִי מְצַוְּךָ הַיּוֹם׃ כִּי־ יְהוָה אֱלֹהֶיךָ בֵּרַכְךָ כַּאֲשֶׁר
just-as he-will-bless-you God-of-you Yahweh for (6) the-day giving-you I

דִּבֶּר־ לָךְ וְהַעֲבַטְתָּ גּוֹיִם רַבִּים וְאַתָּה לֹא תַעֲבֹט
you-will-borrow not but-you many nations and-you-will-lend to-you he-promised

וּמָשַׁלְתָּ בְּגוֹיִם רַבִּים וּבְךָ לֹא יִמְשֹׁלוּ׃ כִּי־
if (7) they-will-rule not but-over-you many over-nations and-you-will-rule

יִהְיֶה בְךָ אֶבְיוֹן מֵאַחַד אַחֶיךָ בְּאַחַד שְׁעָרֶיךָ
gates-of-you within-one-of brothers-of-you from-one-of poor among-you he-is

בְּאַרְצְךָ אֲשֶׁר־ יְהוָה אֱלֹהֶיךָ נֹתֵן לָךְ לֹא תְאַמֵּץ אֶת־
*** you-harden not to-you giving God-of-you Yahweh that in-land-of-you

לְבָבְךָ וְלֹא תִקְפֹּץ אֶת־ יָדְךָ מֵאָחִיךָ
toward-brother-of-you fist-of-you *** you-tighten and-not heart-of-you

הָאֶבְיוֹן׃ כִּי־ פָתֹחַ תִּפְתַּח אֶת־ יָדְךָ לוֹ וְהַעֲבֵט
and-to-lend to-him hand-of-you *** you-open to-open rather (8) the-poor

תַּעֲבִיטֶנּוּ דֵּי מַחְסֹרוֹ אֲשֶׁר יֶחְסַר לוֹ׃ הִשָּׁמֶר
be-careful! (9) for-him he-needs that need-of-him whatever you-lend-to-him

לְךָ פֶּן־ יִהְיֶה דָבָר עִם־ לְבָבְךָ בְלִיַּעַל לֵאמֹר קָרְבָה
she-is-near to-say wicked heart-of-you in thought he-comes so-not to-you

שְׁנַת־ הַשֶּׁבַע שְׁנַת הַשְּׁמִטָּה וְרָעָה עֵינְךָ
eye-of-you and-she-is-evil the-cancel-of-debt year-of the-seventh year-of

בְּאָחִיךָ הָאֶבְיוֹן וְלֹא תִתֵּן לוֹ וְקָרָא
then-he-may-appeal to-him you-give and-not the-needy toward-brother-of-you

shall cancel the loan he has made to his fellow Israelite. He shall not require payment from his fellow Israelite or brother, because the LORD's time for canceling debts has been proclaimed. [3]You may require payment from a foreigner, but you must cancel any debt your brother owes you. [4]However, there should be no poor among you, for in the land the LORD your God is giving you to possess as your inheritance, he will richly bless you, [5]if only you fully obey the LORD your God and are careful to follow all these commands I am giving you today. [6]For the LORD your God will bless you as he has promised, and you will lend to many nations but will borrow from none. You will rule over many nations but none will rule over you.

[7]If there is a poor man among your brothers in any of the towns of the land that the LORD your God is giving you, do not be hardhearted or tightfisted toward your poor brother. [8]Rather be openhanded and freely lend him whatever he needs. [9]Be careful not to harbor this wicked thought: "The seventh year, the year for canceling debts, is near," so that you do not show ill will toward your needy brother and give him nothing. He may then appeal to the LORD

עָלֶיךָ אֶל־ יְהוָה וְהָיָה בְךָ חֵטְא׃ נָתוֹן תִּתֵּן
you-give to-give (10) guilt on-you and-he-will-be Yahweh to against-you

לוֹ וְלֹא־ יֵרַע לְבָבְךָ בְּתִתְּךָ לוֹ כִּי
for to-him when-to-give-you heart-of-you he-must-hold-grudge and-not to-him

בִּגְלַל ׀ הַדָּבָר הַזֶּה יְבָרֶכְךָ יְהוָה אֱלֹהֶיךָ בְּכָל־
in-all-of God-of-you Yahweh he-will-bless-you the-this the-thing because-of

מַעֲשֶׂךָ וּבְכֹל מִשְׁלַח יָדֶךָ׃ כִּי לֹא־ יֶחְדַּל
he-will-leave not for (11) hand-of-you activity-of and-in-all-of work-of-you

אֶבְיוֹן מִקֶּרֶב הָאָרֶץ עַל־ כֵּן אָנֹכִי מְצַוְּךָ לֵאמֹר פָּתֹחַ תִּפְתַּח
you-open to-open to-say commanding-you I this for the-land from-within poor

אֶת־ יָדְךָ לְאָחִיךָ לַעֲנִיֶּךָ וּלְאֶבְיֹנְךָ
and-to-needy-of-you toward-poor-of-you toward-brother-of-you hand-of-you ***

בְּאַרְצֶךָ׃ כִּי־ יִמָּכֵר לְךָ אָחִיךָ הָעִבְרִי אוֹ
or the-Hebrew-man fellow-of-you to-you he-is-sold if (12) in-land-of-you

הָעִבְרִיָּה וַעֲבָדְךָ שֵׁשׁ שָׁנִים וּבַשָּׁנָה הַשְּׁבִיעִת
the-seventh then-in-the-year years six and-he-serves-you the-Hebrew-woman

תְּשַׁלְּחֶנּוּ חָפְשִׁי מֵעִמָּךְ׃ וְכִי־ תְשַׁלְּחֶנּוּ חָפְשִׁי
free you-release-him and-when (13) from-with-you free you-must-let-go-him

מֵעִמָּךְ לֹא תְשַׁלְּחֶנּוּ רֵיקָם׃ הַעֲנֵיק תַּעֲנִיק
you-supply to-supply (14) empty-handed you-send-away-him not from-with-you

לוֹ מִצֹּאנְךָ וּמִגָּרְנְךָ וּמִיִּקְבֶךָ
and-from-wine-vat-of-you and-from-threshing-floor-of-you from-flock-of-you to-him

אֲשֶׁר בֵּרַכְךָ יְהוָה אֱלֹהֶיךָ תִּתֶּן־ לוֹ׃ וְזָכַרְתָּ
and-you-remember (15) to-him you-give God-of-you Yahweh he-blessed-you as

כִּי עֶבֶד הָיִיתָ בְּאֶרֶץ מִצְרַיִם וַיִּפְדְּךָ יְהוָה אֱלֹהֶיךָ
God-of-you Yahweh and-he-redeemed-you Egypt in-land-of you-were slave that

עַל־ כֵּן אָנֹכִי מְצַוְּךָ אֶת־ הַדָּבָר הַזֶּה הַיּוֹם׃ וְהָיָה
but-he-will-be (16) the-day the-this the-command *** giving-you I this for

כִּי־ יֹאמַר אֵלֶיךָ לֹא אֵצֵא מֵעִמָּךְ כִּי אֲהֵבְךָ וְאֶת־
and he-loves-you for from-with-you I-would-leave not to-you he-says if

בֵּיתֶךָ כִּי־ טוֹב לוֹ עִמָּךְ׃ וְלָקַחְתָּ אֶת־ הַמַּרְצֵעַ
the-awl *** then-you-take (17) with-you for-him good for family-of-you

וְנָתַתָּה בְאָזְנוֹ וּבַדֶּלֶת וְהָיָה לְךָ
for-you and-he-will-become and-into-the-door through-ear-of-him and-you-push

עֶבֶד עוֹלָם וְאַף לַאֲמָתְךָ תַּעֲשֶׂה־ כֵּן׃ לֹא־
not (18) same you-do for-maidservant-of-you and-also for-life servant

יִקְשֶׁה בְעֵינֶךָ בְּשַׁלֵּחֲךָ אֹתוֹ חָפְשִׁי מֵעִמָּךְ כִּי
for from-with-you free him when-to-send-you in-eyes-of-you he-must-be-hard

against you, and you will be
found guilty of sin. 10Give generously to him and do so without a grudging heart; then because of this the LORD your
God will bless you in all your
work and in everything you
put your hand to. 11There will
always be poor people in the
land. Therefore I command
you to be openhanded toward
your brothers and toward the
poor and needy in your land.

Freeing Servants

12If a fellow Hebrew, a man
or a woman, is sold to you and
he serves you six years, in the
seventh year you must let him
go free. 13And when you release him, do not send him
away empty-handed. 14Supply
him liberally from your flock,
your threshing floor and your
winepress. Give to him as the
LORD your God has blessed
you. 15Remember that you
were slaves in Egypt and the
LORD your God redeemed you.
That is why I give you this
command today.

16But if your servant says to
you, "I do not want to leave
you," because he loves you
and your family and is well off
with you, 17then take an awl
and push it through his ear
lobe into the door, and he will
become your servant for life.
Do the same for your maidservant.

18Do not consider it a hardship to set your servant free,

מִשְׁנֶה שְׂכַר שָׂכִיר עֲבָדְךָ שֵׁשׁ שָׁנִים וּבֵרַכְךָ
and-he-will-bless-you years six he-served-you hired-hand worth-of twice

יְהוָה אֱלֹהֶיךָ בְּכֹל אֲשֶׁר תַּעֲשֶׂה׃ כָּל־ הַבְּכוֹר אֲשֶׁר
that the-firstborn every-of (19) you-do that in-all God-of-you Yahweh

יִוָּלֵד בִּבְקָרְךָ וּבְצֹאנְךָ הַזָּכָר תַּקְדִּישׁ
you-set-apart the-male and-in-flock-of-you in-herd-of-you he-is-born

לַיהוָה אֱלֹהֶיךָ לֹא תַעֲבֹד בִּבְכֹר שׁוֹרֶךָ וְלֹא
and-not ox-of-you of-firstborn-of you-make-work not God-of-you for-Yahweh

תָגֹז בְּכוֹר צֹאנֶךָ׃ לִפְנֵי יְהוָה אֱלֹהֶיךָ תֹאכְלֶנּוּ
you-eat-him God-of-you Yahweh before (20) flock-of-you firstborn-of you-shear

שָׁנָה בְשָׁנָה בַּמָּקוֹם אֲשֶׁר־ יִבְחַר יְהוָה אַתָּה וּבֵיתֶךָ׃
and-family-of-you you Yahweh he-will-choose that at-the-place by-year year

וְכִי־ יִהְיֶה בוֹ מוּם פִּסֵּחַ אוֹ עִוֵּר כֹּל מוּם רָע לֹא
not serious flaw any-of blind or lame defect on-him he-is and-if (21)

תִזְבָּחֶנּוּ לַיהוָה אֱלֹהֶיךָ׃ בִּשְׁעָרֶיךָ תֹּאכְלֶנּוּ
you-eat-him within-gates-of-you (22) God-of-you to-Yahweh you-sacrifice-him

הַטָּמֵא וְהַטָּהוֹר יַחְדָּו כַּצְּבִי וְכָאַיָּל׃ רַק אֶת־
*** but (23) or-as-the-deer as-the-gazelle both and-the-clean the-unclean

דָּמוֹ לֹא תֹאכֵל עַל־ הָאָרֶץ תִּשְׁפְּכֶנּוּ כַּמָּיִם׃
like-the-waters you-pour-out-him the-ground on you-eat not blood-of-him

שָׁמוֹר אֶת־ חֹדֶשׁ הָאָבִיב וְעָשִׂיתָ פֶּסַח לַיהוָה
of-Yahweh Passover and-you-celebrate the-Abib month-of *** to-observe (16:1)

אֱלֹהֶיךָ כִּי בְּחֹדֶשׁ הָאָבִיב הוֹצִיאֲךָ יְהוָה אֱלֹהֶיךָ
God-of-you Yahweh he-brought-you the-Abib in-month-of for God-of-you

מִמִּצְרַיִם לָיְלָה׃ וְזָבַחְתָּ פֶּסַח לַיהוָה אֱלֹהֶיךָ צֹאן
flock God-of-you to-Yahweh Passover and-you-sacrifice (2) night from-Egypt

וּבָקָר בַּמָּקוֹם אֲשֶׁר־ יִבְחַר יְהוָה לְשַׁכֵּן שְׁמוֹ
Name-of-him to-make-dwell Yahweh he-will-choose that at-the-place or-herd

שָׁם׃ לֹא־ תֹאכַל עָלָיו חָמֵץ שִׁבְעַת יָמִים תֹּאכַל־ עָלָיו
with-him you-eat days seven-of yeast with-him you-eat not (3) there

מַצּוֹת לֶחֶם עֹנִי כִּי בְחִפָּזוֹן יָצָאתָ מֵאֶרֶץ
from-land-of you-left in-haste for affliction bread-of breads-without-yeast

מִצְרַיִם לְמַעַן תִּזְכֹּר אֶת־ יוֹם צֵאתְךָ מֵאֶרֶץ מִצְרַיִם
Egypt from-land-of to-depart-you day *** you-may-remember so-that Egypt

כֹּל יְמֵי חַיֶּיךָ׃ וְלֹא־ יֵרָאֶה לְךָ שְׂאֹר
yeast with-you he-must-be-found and-not (4) lives-of-you days-of all-of

בְּכָל־ גְּבֻלְךָ שִׁבְעַת יָמִים וְלֹא־ יָלִין מִן־ הַבָּשָׂר אֲשֶׁר
that the-meat from he-may-remain and-not days seven-of land-of-you in-all-of

because his service to you these six years has been worth twice as much as that of a hired hand. And the LORD your God will bless you in everything you do.

The Firstborn Animals

[19]Set apart for the LORD your God every firstborn male of your herds and flocks. Do not put the firstborn of your oxen to work, and do not shear the firstborn of your sheep. [20]Each year you and your family are to eat them in the presence of the LORD your God at the place he will choose. [21]If an animal has a defect, is lame or blind, or has any serious flaw, you must not sacrifice it to the LORD your God. [22]You are to eat it in your own towns. Both the ceremonially unclean and the clean may eat it, as if it were gazelle or deer. [23]But you must not eat the blood; pour it out on the ground like water.

Passover

16 Observe the month of Abib and celebrate the Passover of the LORD your God, because in the month of Abib he brought you out of Egypt by night. [2]Sacrifice as the Passover to the LORD your God an animal from your flock or herd at the place the LORD will choose as a dwelling for his Name. [3]Do not eat it with bread made with yeast, but for seven days eat unleavened bread, the bread of affliction, because you left Egypt in haste—so that all the days of your life you may remember the time of your departure from Egypt. [4]Let no yeast be found in your possession in all your land for seven days. Do not let any of the meat you

תִּזְבַּח בָּעֶרֶב בַּיּוֹם הָרִאשׁוֹן לַבֹּקֶר׃ לֹא
not (5) until-the-morning the-first of-the-day on-the-evening you-sacrifice

תוּכַל לִזְבֹּחַ אֶת־ הַפָּסַח בְּאַחַד שְׁעָרֶיךָ אֲשֶׁר־ יְהוָה
Yahweh that gates-of-you within-any-of the-Passover *** to-sacrifice you-can

אֱלֹהֶיךָ נֹתֵן לָךְ׃ כִּי אִם־ אֶל־ הַמָּקוֹם אֲשֶׁר־ יִבְחַר
he-will-choose that the-place in only except (6) to-you giving God-of-you

יְהוָה אֱלֹהֶיךָ לְשַׁכֵּן שְׁמוֹ שָׁם תִּזְבַּח אֶת־
*** you-must-sacrifice there Name-of-him to-make-dwell God-of-you Yahweh

הַפֶּסַח בָּעֶרֶב כְּבוֹא הַשֶּׁמֶשׁ מוֹעֵד צֵאתְךָ
to-come-you anniversary the-sun when-to-go-down in-the-evening the-Passover

מִמִּצְרָיִם׃ וּבִשַּׁלְתָּ וְאָכַלְתָּ בַּמָּקוֹם אֲשֶׁר יִבְחַר
he-will-choose that at-the-place and-you-eat and-you-roast (7) from-Egypt

יְהוָה אֱלֹהֶיךָ בּוֹ וּפָנִיתָ בַבֹּקֶר וְהָלַכְתָּ
and-you-return in-the-morning then-you-go to-him God-of-you Yahweh

לְאֹהָלֶיךָ׃ שֵׁשֶׁת יָמִים תֹּאכַל מַצּוֹת וּבַיּוֹם
and-on-the-day unleavened-breads you-eat days six-of (8) to-tents-of-you

הַשְּׁבִיעִי עֲצֶרֶת לַיהוָה אֱלֹהֶיךָ לֹא תַעֲשֶׂה מְלָאכָה׃ שִׁבְעָה שָׁבֻעֹת
weeks seven (9) work you-do not God-of-you to-Yahweh assembly the-seventh

תִּסְפָּר־ לָךְ מֵהָחֵל חֶרְמֵשׁ בַּקָּמָה תָּחֵל
you-begin to-the-standing-grain sickle from-to-begin for-you you-count

לִסְפֹּר שִׁבְעָה שָׁבֻעוֹת׃ וְעָשִׂיתָ חַג שָׁבֻעוֹת לַיהוָה
to-Yahweh Weeks Feast-of then-you-celebrate (10) weeks seven to-count

אֱלֹהֶיךָ מִסַּת נִדְבַת יָדְךָ אֲשֶׁר תִּתֵּן
you-give that hand-of-you freewill-offering-of proportion-of God-of-you

כַּאֲשֶׁר יְבָרֶכְךָ יְהוָה אֱלֹהֶיךָ׃ וְשָׂמַחְתָּ לִפְנֵי ׀ יְהוָה
Yahweh before and-you-rejoice (11) God-of-you Yahweh he-blessed-you just-as

אֱלֹהֶיךָ אַתָּה וּבִנְךָ וּבִתֶּךָ וְעַבְדְּךָ
and-manservant-of-you and-daughter-of-you and-son-of-you you God-of-you

וַאֲמָתֶךָ וְהַלֵּוִי אֲשֶׁר בִּשְׁעָרֶיךָ וְהַגֵּר
and-the-alien within-gates-of-you who and-the-Levite and-maidservant-of-you

וְהַיָּתוֹם וְהָאַלְמָנָה אֲשֶׁר בְּקִרְבֶּךָ בַּמָּקוֹם אֲשֶׁר
that at-the-place in-among-you who and-the-widow and-the-fatherless

יִבְחַר יְהוָה אֱלֹהֶיךָ לְשַׁכֵּן שְׁמוֹ שָׁם׃
there Name-of-him to-make-dwell God-of-you Yahweh he-will-choose

וְזָכַרְתָּ כִּי־ עֶבֶד הָיִיתָ בְּמִצְרָיִם וְשָׁמַרְתָּ
and-you-be-careful in-Egypt you-were slave that and-you-remember (12)

וְעָשִׂיתָ אֶת־ הַחֻקִּים הָאֵלֶּה׃ חַג הַסֻּכֹּת
the-Tabernacles Feast-of (13) the-these the-decrees *** and-you-follow

sacrifice on the evening of the
first day remain until morning.
5You must not sacrifice the
Passover in any town the LORD
your God gives you 6except in
the place he will choose as a
dwelling for his Name. There
you must sacrifice the Passover in the evening, when the
sun goes down, on the anniversary[y] of your departure
from Egypt. 7Roast it and eat it
at the place the LORD your God
will choose. Then in the morning return to your tents. 8For
six days eat unleavened bread
and on the seventh day hold
an assembly to the LORD your
God and do no work.

Feast of Weeks

9Count off seven weeks from
the time you begin to put the
sickle to the standing grain.
10Then celebrate the Feast of
Weeks to the LORD your God
by giving a freewill offering in
proportion to the blessings the
LORD your God has given you.
11And rejoice before the LORD
your God at the place he will
choose as a dwelling for his
Name—you, your sons and
daughters, your menservants
and maidservants, the Levites
in your towns, and the aliens,
the fatherless and the widows
living among you. 12Remem-
ber that you were slaves in
Egypt, and follow carefully
these decrees.

y6 *Or down, at the time of day*

תַּעֲשֶׂה לְךָ שִׁבְעַת יָמִים בְּאָסְפְּךָ מִגָּרְנְךָ
from-threshing-of-you after-to-gather-you days seven-of for-you you-celebrate

וּמִיִּקְבֶךָ׃ (14) וְשָׂמַחְתָּ בְּחַגֶּךָ אַתָּה
you at-Feast-of-you and-you-rejoice (14) and-from-winepress-of-you

וּבִנְךָ וּבִתֶּךָ וְעַבְדְּךָ וַאֲמָתֶךָ
and-maidservant-of-you and-manservant-of-you and-daughter-of-you and-son-of-you

וְהַלֵּוִי וְהַגֵּר וְהַיָּתוֹם וְהָאַלְמָנָה אֲשֶׁר
who and-the-widow and-the-fatherless and-the-alien and-the-Levite

בִּשְׁעָרֶיךָ׃ (15) שִׁבְעַת יָמִים תָּחֹג לַיהוָה אֱלֹהֶיךָ
God-of-you to-Yahweh you-celebrate days seven-of (15) within-gates-of-you

בַּמָּקוֹם אֲשֶׁר־ יִבְחַר יְהוָה כִּי יְבָרֶכְךָ יְהוָה
Yahweh he-will-bless-you for Yahweh he-will-choose that at-the-place

אֱלֹהֶיךָ בְּכֹל תְּבוּאָתְךָ וּבְכֹל מַעֲשֵׂה יָדֶיךָ
hands-of-you work-of and-in-all-of harvest-of-you in-all-of God-of-you

וְהָיִיתָ אַךְ שָׂמֵחַ׃ (16) שָׁלוֹשׁ פְּעָמִים ׀ בַּשָּׁנָה יֵרָאֶה
he-must-appear in-the-year times three (16) joy complete and-you-will-have

כָל־ זְכוּרְךָ אֶת־ פְּנֵי ׀ יְהוָה אֱלֹהֶיךָ בַּמָּקוֹם אֲשֶׁר
that at-the-place God-of-you Yahweh before *** male-of-you every-of

יִבְחָר בְּחַג הַמַּצּוֹת וּבְחַג הַשָּׁבֻעוֹת
the-Weeks and-at-Feast-of the-Unleavened-Breads at-Feast-of he-will-choose

וּבְחַג הַסֻּכּוֹת וְלֹא יֵרָאֶה אֶת־ פְּנֵי יְהוָה
Yahweh before *** he-should-appear and-none the-Tabernacles and-at-Feast-of

רֵיקָם׃ (17) אִישׁ כְּמַתְּנַת יָדוֹ כְּבִרְכַּת יְהוָה
Yahweh as-blessing-of hand-of-him as-gift-of each (17) empty-handed

אֱלֹהֶיךָ אֲשֶׁר נָתַן־ לָךְ׃ (18) שֹׁפְטִים וְשֹׁטְרִים
and-ones-officiating ones-judging (18) to-you he-gave that God-of-you

תִּתֶּן־ לְךָ בְּכָל־ שְׁעָרֶיךָ אֲשֶׁר יְהוָה אֱלֹהֶיךָ נֹתֵן
giving God-of-you Yahweh that gates-of-you within-all-of for-you you-appoint

לְךָ לִשְׁבָטֶיךָ וְשָׁפְטוּ אֶת־ הָעָם מִשְׁפַּט־ צֶדֶק׃
fair judgment-of the-people *** and-they-shall-judge for-tribes-of-you to-you

(19) לֹא־ תַטֶּה מִשְׁפָּט לֹא תַכִּיר פָּנִים וְלֹא־ תִקַּח שֹׁחַד
bribe you-accept and-not faces you-regard not judgment you-pervert not (19)

כִּי הַשֹּׁחַד יְעַוֵּר עֵינֵי חֲכָמִים וִיסַלֵּף דִּבְרֵי צַדִּיקִם׃
ones-righteous words-of and-he-twists ones-wise eyes-of he-blinds the-bribe for

(20) צֶדֶק צֶדֶק תִּרְדֹּף לְמַעַן תִּחְיֶה וְיָרַשְׁתָּ אֶת־
*** and-you-may-possess you-may-live so-that you-follow justice justice (20)

הָאָרֶץ אֲשֶׁר־ יְהוָה אֱלֹהֶיךָ נֹתֵן לָךְ׃ (21) לֹא־ תִטַּע לְךָ
for-you you-set-up not (21) to-you giving God-of-you Yahweh that the-land

Feast of Tabernacles

13Celebrate the Feast of Tabernacles for seven days after
you have gathered the produce of your threshing floor
and your winepress. 14Be joy-
ful at your Feast—you, your
sons and daughters, your
menservants and maid-
servants, and the Levites, the
aliens, the fatherless and the
widows who live in your
towns. 15For seven days celebrate the Feast to the LORD
your God at the place the LORD
will choose. For the LORD your
God will bless you in all your
harvest and in all the work of
your hands, and your joy will
be complete.

16Three times a year all your
men must appear before the
LORD your God at the place he
will choose: at the Feast of Unleavened Bread, the Feast of
Weeks and the Feast of Tabernacles. No man should appear
before the LORD empty-handed: 17Each of you must bring a
gift in proportion to the way
the LORD your God has blessed
you.

Judges

18Appoint judges and
officials for each of your tribes
in every town the LORD your
God is giving you, and they
shall judge the people fairly.
19Do not pervert justice or
show partiality. Do not accept
a bribe, for a bribe blinds the
eyes of the wise and twists the
words of the righteous. 20Fol-
low justice and justice alone,
so that you may live and possess the land the LORD your
God is giving you.

Worshiping Other Gods

21Do not set up any wooden

אֲשֵׁרָה כָּל־ עֵץ אֵצֶל מִזְבַּח יְהוָה אֱלֹהֶיךָ אֲשֶׁר תַּעֲשֶׂה־

you-build that God-of-you Yahweh altar-of beside wooden any-of Asherah-pole

לָּךְ׃ וְלֹא־ תָקִים לְךָ מַצֵּבָה אֲשֶׁר שָׂנֵא יְהוָה

Yahweh he-hates that sacred-stone for-you you-erect and-not (22) for-you

אֱלֹהֶיךָ׃ לֹא־ תִזְבַּח לַיהוָה אֱלֹהֶיךָ שׁוֹר וָשֶׂה אֲשֶׁר

that or-sheep ox God-of-you to-Yahweh you-sacrifice not (17:1) God-of-you

יִהְיֶה בוֹ מוּם כֹּל דָּבָר רָע כִּי תוֹעֲבַת יְהוָה אֱלֹהֶיךָ הוּא׃

that God-of-you Yahweh detestable-of for bad flaw any-of defect on-him he-is

כִּי־ יִמָּצֵא בְקִרְבְּךָ בְּאַחַד שְׁעָרֶיךָ אֲשֶׁר־ יְהוָה

Yahweh that gates-of-you within-any-of in-among-you he-is-found if (2)

אֱלֹהֶיךָ נֹתֵן לָךְ אִישׁ אוֹ־ אִשָּׁה אֲשֶׁר יַעֲשֶׂה אֶת־ הָרַע בְּעֵינֵי

in-eyes-of the-evil *** he-does who woman or man to-you giving God-of-you

יְהוָה־ אֱלֹהֶיךָ לַעֲבֹר בְּרִיתוֹ׃ וַיֵּלֶךְ וַיַּעֲבֹד

and-he-worships and-he-goes (3) covenant-of-him to-violate God-of-you Yahweh

אֱלֹהִים אֲחֵרִים וַיִּשְׁתַּחוּ לָהֶם וְלַשֶּׁמֶשׁ ׀ אוֹ לַיָּרֵחַ אוֹ לְכָל־

to-any-of or to-the-moon or or-to-the-sun to-them and-he-bows other-ones gods

צְבָא הַשָּׁמַיִם אֲשֶׁר לֹא־ צִוִּיתִי׃ וְהֻגַּד־ לְךָ

to-you and-he-is-told (4) I-commanded not that the-heavens array-of

וְשָׁמָעְתָּ וְדָרַשְׁתָּ הֵיטֵב וְהִנֵּה אֱמֶת

true and-if to-be-thorough then-you-must-investigate and-you-heard

נָכוֹן הַדָּבָר נֶעֶשְׂתָה הַתּוֹעֵבָה הַזֹּאת בְּיִשְׂרָאֵל׃

in-Israel the-this the-detestable-thing she-was-done the-thing being-proved

וְהוֹצֵאתָ אֶת־ הָאִישׁ הַהוּא אוֹ אֶת־ הָאִשָּׁה הַהִוא אֲשֶׁר

who the-that the-woman *** or the-that the-man *** then-you-take (5)

עָשׂוּ אֶת־ הַדָּבָר הָרָע הַזֶּה אֶל־ שְׁעָרֶיךָ אֶת־ הָאִישׁ אוֹ אֶת־

*** or the-man *** gates-of-you to the-this the-evil the-deed *** they-did

הָאִשָּׁה וּסְקַלְתָּם בָּאֲבָנִים וָמֵתוּ׃ עַל־ פִּי ׀

testimony-of on (6) so-they-die with-the-stones and-you-stone-them the-woman

שְׁנַיִם עֵדִים אוֹ שְׁלֹשָׁה עֵדִים יוּמַת הַמֵּת לֹא יוּמַת

he-shall-die not the-one-dying he-shall-die witnesses three or witnesses two

עַל־ פִּי עֵד אֶחָד׃ יַד הָעֵדִים תִּהְיֶה־ בּוֹ

on-him she-must-be the-witnesses hand-of (7) one witness testimony-of on

בָרִאשֹׁנָה לַהֲמִיתוֹ וְיַד כָּל־ הָעָם בָּאַחֲרֹנָה

as-the-next the-people all-of then-hand-of to-kill-him at-the-first

וּבִעַרְתָּ הָרָע מִקִּרְבֶּךָ׃ כִּי יִפָּלֵא מִמְּךָ

for-you he-is-difficult if (8) from-among-you the-evil so-you-must-purge

דָבָר לַמִּשְׁפָּט בֵּין־ דָּם ׀ לְדָם בֵּין־ דִּין לְדִין

to-lawsuit lawsuit or to-bloodshed bloodshed whether for-the-judgment case

Asherah pole[z] beside the altar
you build to the LORD your
God, [22]and do not erect a sacred stone, for these the LORD
your God hates.

17 Do not sacrifice to the
LORD your God an ox or
a sheep that has any defect or
flaw in it, for that would be
detestable to him.

[2]If a man or woman living
among you in one of the
towns the LORD gives you is
found doing evil in the eyes of
the LORD your God in violation of his covenant, [3]and contrary to my command has
worshiped other gods, bowing
down to them or to the sun or
the moon or the stars of the
sky, [4]and this has been
brought to your attention,
then you must investigate it
thoroughly. If it is true and it
has been proved that this detestable thing has been done
in Israel, [5]take the man or
woman who has done this evil
deed to your city gate and
stone that person to death.
[6]On the testimony of two or
three witnesses a man shall be
put to death, but no one shall
be put to death on the testimony of only one witness.
[7]The hands of the witnesses
must be the first in putting
him to death, and then the
hands of all the people. You
must purge the evil from
among you.

Law Courts

[8]If cases come before your
courts that are too difficult for
you to judge—whether bloodshed, lawsuits or assaults—

[z]21 Or *Do not plant any tree dedicated to Asherah*

וּבֵין נֶגַע לָנֶגַע דִּבְרֵי רִיבֹת בִּשְׁעָרֶיךָ וְקַמְתָּ
then-you-rise in-gates-of-you judgments cases-of to-assault assault or-whether

וְעָלִיתָ אֶל־הַמָּקוֹם אֲשֶׁר יִבְחַר יְהוָה אֱלֹהֶיךָ בּוֹ׃
to-him God-of-you Yahweh he-will-choose that the-place to and-you-go

וּבָאתָ אֶל־הַכֹּהֲנִים הַלְוִיִּם וְאֶל־הַשֹּׁפֵט אֲשֶׁר יִהְיֶה
he-is who the-one-judging and-to the-Levites the-priests to and-you-go (9)

בַּיָּמִים הָהֵם וְדָרַשְׁתָּ וְהִגִּידוּ לְךָ אֵת דְּבַר
verdict-of *** to-you and-they-will-give and-you-inquire the-those in-the-days

הַמִּשְׁפָּט׃ וְעָשִׂיתָ עַל־פִּי הַדָּבָר אֲשֶׁר
that the-decision accordance-of in and-you-must-act (10) the-judgment

יַגִּידוּ לְךָ מִן־הַמָּקוֹם הַהוּא אֲשֶׁר יִבְחַר יְהוָה
Yahweh he-will-choose which the-that the-place at to-you they-give

וְשָׁמַרְתָּ לַעֲשׂוֹת כְּכֹל אֲשֶׁר יוֹרוּךָ׃ עַל־פִּי
accordance-of in (11) they-direct-you that as-all to-do and-you-be-careful

הַתּוֹרָה אֲשֶׁר יוֹרוּךָ וְעַל־הַמִּשְׁפָּט אֲשֶׁר־יֹאמְרוּ לְךָ
to-you they-give that the-decision and-by they-teach-you that the-law

תַּעֲשֶׂה לֹא תָסוּר מִן־הַדָּבָר אֲשֶׁר־יַגִּידוּ לְךָ יָמִין וּשְׂמֹאל׃
or-left right to-you they-tell that the-thing from you-turn not you-act

וְהָאִישׁ אֲשֶׁר־יַעֲשֶׂה בְזָדוֹן לְבִלְתִּי שְׁמֹעַ אֶל־הַכֹּהֵן
the-priest to to-obey not with-contempt he-acts who and-the-man (12)

הָעֹמֵד לְשָׁרֶת שָׁם אֶת־יְהוָה אֱלֹהֶיךָ אוֹ אֶל־הַשֹּׁפֵט
the-one-judging to or God-of-you Yahweh *** there to-minister the-one-standing

וּמֵת הָאִישׁ הַהוּא וּבִעַרְתָּ הָרָע מִיִּשְׂרָאֵל׃
from-Israel the-evil so-you-must-purge the-that the-man then-he-must-die

וְכָל־הָעָם יִשְׁמְעוּ וְיִרָאוּ וְלֹא
and-not and-they-will-be-afraid they-will-hear the-people and-all-of (13)

יְזִידוּן עוֹד׃ כִּי־תָבֹא אֶל־הָאָרֶץ אֲשֶׁר יְהוָה
Yahweh that the-land into you-enter when (14) again they-will-be-contemptuous

אֱלֹהֶיךָ נֹתֵן לָךְ וִירִשְׁתָּהּ וְיָשַׁבְתָּה בָּהּ וְאָמַרְתָּ
and-you-say in-her and-you-settle and-you-possess-her to-you giving God-of-you

אָשִׂימָה עָלַי מֶלֶךְ כְּכָל־הַגּוֹיִם אֲשֶׁר סְבִיבֹתָי׃
ones-around-me that the-nations like-all-of king over-me I-will-set

שׂוֹם תָּשִׂים עָלֶיךָ מֶלֶךְ אֲשֶׁר יִבְחַר יְהוָה אֱלֹהֶיךָ
God-of-you Yahweh he-chooses whom king over-you you-appoint to-appoint (15)

בּוֹ מִקֶּרֶב אַחֶיךָ תָּשִׂים עָלֶיךָ מֶלֶךְ לֹא תוּכַל
you-can not king over-you you-appoint brothers-of-you from-among to-him

לָתֵת עָלֶיךָ אִישׁ נָכְרִי אֲשֶׁר לֹא־אָחִיךָ הוּא׃ רַק לֹא־
not moreover (16) he brother-of-you not who foreigner man over-you to-place

take them to the place the
LORD your God will choose.
9Go to the priests, who are Levites, and to the judge who is
in office at that time. Inquire
of them and they will give you
the verdict. 10You must act according to the decisions they
give you at the place the LORD
will choose. Be careful to do
everything they direct you to
do. 11Act according to the law
they teach you and the decisions they give you. Do not
turn aside from what they tell
you, to the right or to the left.
12The man who shows con-
tempt for the judge or for the
priest who stands ministering
there to the LORD your God
must be put to death. You
must purge the evil from Israel. 13All the people will hear
and be afraid, and will not be
contemptuous again.

The King

14When you enter the land
the LORD your God is giving
you and have taken possession of it and settled in it, and
you say, "Let us set a king over
us like all the nations around
us," 15be sure to appoint over
you the king the LORD your
God chooses. He must be from
among your own brothers. Do
not place a foreigner over you,
one who is not a brother Israelite. 16The king, moreover,

יַרְבֶּה־ לּוֹ סוּסִים וְלֹא־ יָשִׁיב אֶת־ הָעָם
the-people *** he-must-make-return and-not horses for-him he-must-increase

מִצְרַיְמָה לְמַעַן הַרְבּוֹת סוּס וַיהוָה אָמַר לָכֶם לֹא
not to-you he-told for-Yahweh horse to-get-more to-order to-Egypt

תֹסִפוּן לָשׁוּב בַּדֶּרֶךְ הַזֶּה עוֹד׃ וְלֹא
and-not (17) again the-that on-the-way to-go-back you-must-repeat

יַרְבֶּה־ לּוֹ נָשִׁים וְלֹא יָסוּר לְבָבוֹ וְכֶסֶף
and-silver heart-of-him he-strays so-not wives to-him he-must-take-many

וְזָהָב לֹא יַרְבֶּה־ לּוֹ מְאֹד׃ וְהָיָה
and-he-will-be (18) much for-him he-must-accumulate not and-gold

כְשִׁבְתּוֹ עַל כִּסֵּא מַמְלַכְתּוֹ וְכָתַב לוֹ אֶת־
*** for-him then-he-must-write kingdom-of-him throne-of on when-to-sit-him

מִשְׁנֵה הַתּוֹרָה הַזֹּאת עַל־ סֵפֶר מִלִּפְנֵי הַכֹּהֲנִים הַלְוִיִּם׃
the-Levites the-priests from-before scroll on the-this the-law copy-of

וְהָיְתָה עִמּוֹ וְקָרָא בוֹ כָּל־ יְמֵי
days-of all-of for-him and-he-must-read with-him and-she-must-be (19)

חַיָּיו לְמַעַן יִלְמַד לְיִרְאָה אֶת־ יְהוָה אֱלֹהָיו
God-of-him Yahweh *** to-revere he-may-learn so-that lives-of-him

לִשְׁמֹר אֶת־ כָּל־ דִּבְרֵי הַתּוֹרָה הַזֹּאת וְאֶת־ הַחֻקִּים הָאֵלֶּה
the-these the-decrees and the-this the-law words-of all-of *** to-be-careful

לַעֲשֹׂתָם׃ לְבִלְתִּי רוּם־ לְבָבוֹ מֵאֶחָיו וּלְבִלְתִּי
and-not over-brothers-of-him heart-of-him to-exalt not (20) to-follow-them

סוּר מִן־ הַמִּצְוָה יָמִין וּשְׂמֹאול לְמַעַן יַאֲרִיךְ יָמִים עַל־
over days he-may-lengthen so-that or-left right the-law from to-turn

מַמְלַכְתּוֹ הוּא וּבָנָיו בְּקֶרֶב יִשְׂרָאֵל׃ לֹא־ יִהְיֶה
he-shall-be not (18:1) Israel in-among and-sons-of-him he kingdom-of-him

לַכֹּהֲנִים הַלְוִיִּם כָּל־ שֵׁבֶט לֵוִי חֵלֶק וְנַחֲלָה
or-inheritance allotment Levi tribe-of whole-of the-Levites for-the-priests

עִם־ יִשְׂרָאֵל אִשֵּׁי יְהוָה וְנַחֲלָתוֹ יֹאכֵלוּן׃
they-shall eat even-inheritance-of-him Yahweh fire-offerings-of Israel with

וְנַחֲלָה לֹא־ יִהְיֶה־ לּוֹ בְּקֶרֶב אֶחָיו יְהוָה
Yahweh brothers-of-him in-among for-him he-shall-be not and-inheritance (2)

הוּא נַחֲלָתוֹ כַּאֲשֶׁר דִּבֶּר־ לוֹ׃ וְזֶה יִהְיֶה מִשְׁפַּט
share-of he-is and-this (3) to-him he-promised just-as inheritance-of-him he

הַכֹּהֲנִים מֵאֵת הָעָם מֵאֵת זֹבְחֵי הַזֶּבַח אִם־
whether the-sacrifice ones-sacrificing-of from the-people from the-priests

שׁוֹר אִם־ שֶׂה וְנָתַן לַכֹּהֵן הַזְּרֹעַ וְהַלְּחָיַיִם
and-the-jowls the-shoulder to-the-priest now-he-must-give sheep or bull

must not acquire great numbers of horses for himself or make the people return to Egypt to get more of them, for the LORD has told you, "You are not to go back that way
again." [17]He must not take many wives, or his heart will be led astray. He must not accumulate large amounts of silver and gold.

[18]When he takes the throne of his kingdom, he is to write for himself on a scroll a copy of this law, taken from that of the
priests, who are Levites. [19]It is to be with him, and he is to read it all the days of his life so that he may learn to revere the LORD his God and follow carefully all the words of this law
and these decrees [20]and not consider himself better than his brothers and turn from the law to the right or to the left. Then he and his descendants will reign a long time over his kingdom in Israel.

Offerings for Priests and Levites

18 The priests, who are Levites—indeed the whole tribe of Levi—are to have no allotment or inheritance with Israel. They shall live on the offerings made to the LORD by fire, for that is
their inheritance. [2]They shall have no inheritance among their brothers; the LORD is their inheritance, as he promised them.

[3]This is the share due the priests from the people who sacrifice a bull or a sheep: the

וְהַקֵּבָה׃ (4) רֵאשִׁית דְּגָנְךָ תִּירֹשְׁךָ וְיִצְהָרֶךָ
and-oil-of-you new-wine-of-you grain-of-you first-of (4) and-the-inner-part

וְרֵאשִׁית גֵּז צֹאנְךָ תִּתֶּן־לוֹ׃ (5) כִּי בוֹ בָּחַר
he-chose to-him for (5) to-him you-give sheep-of-you shearing-of and-first-of

יְהוָה אֱלֹהֶיךָ מִכָּל־שְׁבָטֶיךָ לַעֲמֹד לְשָׁרֵת בְּשֵׁם־
in-name-of to-minister to-stand tribes-of-you from-all-of God-of-you Yahweh

יְהוָה הוּא וּבָנָיו כָּל־הַיָּמִים׃ (6) וְכִי־יָבֹא הַלֵּוִי
the-Levite he-moves and-if (6) the-days all-of and-sons-of-him he Yahweh

מֵאַחַד שְׁעָרֶיךָ מִכָּל־יִשְׂרָאֵל אֲשֶׁר־הוּא גָּר שָׁם וּבָא
and-he-comes there living he where Israel in-any-of gates-of-you from-one-of

בְּכָל־אַוַּת נַפְשׁוֹ אֶל־הַמָּקוֹם אֲשֶׁר־יִבְחַר יְהוָה׃
Yahweh he-will-choose that the-place to spirit-of-him earnestness-of in-all-of

(7) וְשֵׁרֵת בְּשֵׁם יְהוָה אֱלֹהָיו כְּכָל־
like-all-of God-of-him Yahweh in-name-of then-he-may-minister (7)

אֶחָיו הַלְוִיִּם הָעֹמְדִים שָׁם לִפְנֵי יְהוָה׃
Yahweh in-presence-of there the-ones-serving the-Levites fellows-of-him

(8) חֵלֶק כְּחֵלֶק יֹאכֵלוּ לְבַד מִמְכָּרָיו עַל־
from sales-incomes-of-him even-though they-shall-share as-benefit benefit (8)

הָאָבוֹת׃ (9) כִּי אַתָּה בָּא אֶל־הָאָרֶץ אֲשֶׁר־יְהוָה אֱלֹהֶיךָ
God-of-you Yahweh that the-land into entering you when (9) the-families

נֹתֵן לָךְ לֹא־תִלְמַד לַעֲשׂוֹת כְּתוֹעֲבֹת הַגּוֹיִם
the-nations as-detestable-ways-of to-imitate you-learn not to-you giving

הָהֵם׃ (10) לֹא־יִמָּצֵא בְךָ מַעֲבִיר בְּנוֹ־
son-of-him one-sacrificing among-you let-him-be-found not (10) the-those

וּבִתּוֹ בָּאֵשׁ קֹסֵם קְסָמִים מְעוֹנֵן
practicing-sorcery divinations divining in-the-fire or-daughter-of-him

וּמְנַחֵשׁ וּמְכַשֵּׁף׃ (11) וְחֹבֵר חָבֶר
spell or-casting (11) or-engaging-in-witchcraft or-interpreting-omen

וְשֹׁאֵל אוֹב וְיִדְּעֹנִי וְדֹרֵשׁ אֶל־הַמֵּתִים׃ (12) כִּי־
for (12) the-ones-dead to or-consulting or-spiritist medium or-inquiring

תוֹעֲבַת יְהוָה כָּל־עֹשֵׂה אֵלֶּה וּבִגְלַל הַתּוֹעֵבֹת
the-detestable-things and-because-of these doing every-of Yahweh detestable-of

הָאֵלֶּה יְהוָה אֱלֹהֶיךָ מוֹרִישׁ אוֹתָם מִפָּנֶיךָ׃ (13) תָּמִים
blameless (13) from-before-you them driving-out God-of-you Yahweh the-these

תִּהְיֶה עִם יְהוָה אֱלֹהֶיךָ׃ (14) כִּי ׀ הַגּוֹיִם הָאֵלֶּה אֲשֶׁר
that the-these the-nations for (14) God-of-you Yahweh before you-must-be

אַתָּה יוֹרֵשׁ אוֹתָם אֶל־מְעֹנְנִים וְאֶל־קֹסְמִים
ones-divining and-to ones-practicing-sorcery to them dispossessing you

shoulder, the jowls and the inner parts. 4You are to give
them the firstfruits of your
grain, new wine and oil, and
the first wool from the shearing of your sheep, 5for the
LORD your God has chosen
them and their descendants
out of all your tribes to stand
and minister in the LORD's
name always.
6If a Levite moves from one
of your towns anywhere in Israel where he is living, and
comes in all earnestness to the
place the LORD will choose, 7he
may minister in the name of
the LORD his God like all his
fellow Levites who serve there
in the presence of the LORD.
8He is to share equally in their
benefits, even though he has
received money from the sale
of family possessions.

Detestable Practices

9When you enter the land
the LORD your God is giving
you, do not learn to imitate the
detestable ways of the nations
there. 10Let no one be found
among you who sacrifices his
son or daughter in[a] the fire,
who practices divination or
sorcery, interprets omens, en-
gages in witchcraft, 11or casts
spells, or who is a medium or
spiritist or who consults the
dead. 12Anyone who does
these things is detestable to
the LORD, and because of these
detestable practices the LORD
your God will drive out those
nations before you. 13You
must be blameless before the
LORD your God.

The Prophet

14The nations you will dispossess listen to those who
practice sorcery or divination.

[a]10 *Or who makes his son or daughter pass through*

יִשְׁמָעוּ וְאַתָּה לֹא כֵן נָתַן לְךָ יְהוָה אֱלֹהֶיךָ׃ נָבִיא
prophet (15) God-of-you Yahweh to-you he-permitted so not but-you they-listen

מִקִּרְבְּךָ מֵאַחֶיךָ כָּמֹנִי יָקִים לְךָ יְהוָה
Yahweh for-you he-will-raise-up like-me from-brothers-of-you from-among-you

אֱלֹהֶיךָ אֵלָיו תִּשְׁמָעוּן׃ כְּכֹל אֲשֶׁר־שָׁאַלְתָּ מֵעִם
from-with you-asked that as-all (16) you-must-listen to-him God-of-you

יְהוָה אֱלֹהֶיךָ בְּחֹרֵב בְּיוֹם הַקָּהָל לֵאמֹר לֹא אֹסֵף
let-me-continue not to-say the-assembly on-day-of at-Horeb God-of-you Yahweh

לִשְׁמֹעַ אֶת־קוֹל יְהוָה אֱלֹהָי וְאֶת־הָאֵשׁ הַגְּדֹלָה הַזֹּאת לֹא־
not the-this the-great the-fire and God-of-me Yahweh voice-of *** to-hear

אֶרְאֶה עוֹד וְלֹא אָמוּת׃ וַיֹּאמֶר יְהוָה אֵלָי הֵיטִיבוּ
they-are-good to-me Yahweh and-he-said (17) I-die so-not anymore let-me-see

אֲשֶׁר דִּבֵּרוּ׃ נָבִיא אָקִים לָהֶם מִקֶּרֶב אֲחֵיהֶם
brothers-of-them from-among from-them I-will-raise prophet (18) they-say what

כָּמוֹךָ וְנָתַתִּי דְבָרַי בְּפִיו וְדִבֶּר אֲלֵיהֶם
to-them and-he-will-tell in-mouth-of-him words-of-me and-I-will-put like-you

אֵת כָּל־אֲשֶׁר אֲצַוֶּנּוּ׃ וְהָיָה הָאִישׁ אֲשֶׁר לֹא־יִשְׁמַע
he-listens not who the-man and-he-will-be (19) I-command-him that all ***

אֶל־דְּבָרַי אֲשֶׁר יְדַבֵּר בִּשְׁמִי אָנֹכִי אֶדְרֹשׁ
I-will-call-account I in-name-of-me he-speaks that words-of-me to

מֵעִמּוֹ׃ אַךְ הַנָּבִיא אֲשֶׁר יָזִיד לְדַבֵּר דָּבָר בִּשְׁמִי
in-name-of-me word to-speak he-presumes who the-prophet but (20) from-with-him

אֵת אֲשֶׁר לֹא־צִוִּיתִיו לְדַבֵּר וַאֲשֶׁר יְדַבֵּר בְּשֵׁם אֱלֹהִים
gods in-name-of he-speaks or-who to-say I-commanded-him not that ***

אֲחֵרִים וּמֵת הַנָּבִיא הַהוּא׃ וְכִי תֹאמַר
you-may-say but-now (21) the-that the-prophet then-he-must-die other-ones

בִּלְבָבֶךָ אֵיכָה נֵדַע אֶת־הַדָּבָר אֲשֶׁר לֹא־דִבְּרוֹ
to-speak-him not when the-message *** can-we-know how? in-heart-of-you

יְהוָה׃ אֲשֶׁר יְדַבֵּר הַנָּבִיא בְּשֵׁם יְהוָה וְלֹא־
and-not Yahweh in-name-of the prophet he-proclaims when (22) Yahweh

יִהְיֶה הַדָּבָר וְלֹא יָבֹא הוּא הַדָּבָר אֲשֶׁר לֹא־
not then the-thing that he-comes-true or-not the-thing he-takes-place

דִבְּרוֹ יְהוָה בְּזָדוֹן דִּבְּרוֹ הַנָּבִיא לֹא תָגוּר
you-be-afraid not the-prophet to-speak-him in-presumption Yahweh to-speak-him

מִמֶּנּוּ׃ כִּי־יַכְרִית יְהוָה אֱלֹהֶיךָ אֶת־הַגּוֹיִם אֲשֶׁר יְהוָה
Yahweh that the-nations *** God-of-you Yahweh he-destroys when (19:1) of-him

אֱלֹהֶיךָ נֹתֵן לְךָ אֶת־אַרְצָם וִירִשְׁתָּם
and-you-drive-out-them land-of-them *** to-you giving God-of-you

But as for you, the LORD your
God has not permitted you to
do so. [15]The LORD your God
will raise up for you a prophet
like me from among your own
brothers. You must listen to
him. [16]For this is what you
asked of the LORD your God at
Horeb on the day of the assembly when you said, "Let us
not hear the voice of the LORD
our God nor see this great fire
anymore, or we will die."
[17]The LORD said to me:
"What they say is good. [18]I will
raise up for them a prophet
like you from among their
brothers; I will put my words
in his mouth, and he will tell
them everything I command
him. [19]If anyone does not listen to my words that the
prophet speaks in my name, I
myself will call him to account. [20]But a prophet who
presumes to speak in my
name anything I have not
commanded him to say, or a
prophet who speaks in the
name of other gods, must be
put to death."
[21]You may say to yourselves,
"How can we know when a
message has not been spoken
by the LORD?" [22]If what a
prophet proclaims in the
name of the LORD does not
take place or come true, that is
a message the LORD has not
spoken. That prophet has
spoken presumptuously. Do
not be afraid of him.

Cities of Refuge

19 When the LORD your
God has destroyed the
nations whose land he is giving you, and when you have
driven them out and settled in

וִֽישַׁבְתָּ בְעָרֵיהֶם וּבְבָתֵּיהֶם׃ (2) שָׁלוֹשׁ עָרִים
cities three (2) and-in-houses-of-them in-towns-of-them and-you-settle

תַּבְדִּיל לָךְ בְּתוֹךְ אַרְצְךָ אֲשֶׁר יְהוָה אֱלֹהֶיךָ נֹתֵן
giving God-of-you Yahweh that land-of-you in-center-of for-you you-set-aside

לְךָ לְרִשְׁתָּהּ׃ (3) תָּכִין לְךָ הַדֶּרֶךְ וְשִׁלַּשְׁתָּ
and-you-divide-into-three the-road for-you you-build (3) to-possess-her to-you

אֶת־ גְּבוּל אַרְצְךָ אֲשֶׁר יַנְחִילְךָ יְהוָה אֱלֹהֶיךָ
God-of-you Yahweh he-makes-inherit-you that land-of-you boundary-of ***

וְהָיָה לָנוּס שָׁמָּה כָּל־ רֹצֵחַ׃ (4) וְזֶה דְּבַר
rule-of and-this (4) one-killing any-of to-there to-flee so-he-will-be

הָרֹצֵחַ אֲשֶׁר־ יָנוּס שָׁמָּה וָחָי אֲשֶׁר יַכֶּה אֶת־
*** he-kills who so-he-lives to-there he-flees who the-one-killing

רֵעֵהוּ בִּבְלִי־ דַעַת וְהוּא לֹא־ שֹׂנֵא לוֹ מִתְּמֹל
on-yesterday to-him hating not and-he intention with-no neighbor-of-him

שִׁלְשֹׁם׃ (5) וַאֲשֶׁר יָבֹא אֶת־ רֵעֵהוּ בַיַּעַר לַחְטֹב עֵצִים
woods to-cut into-the-forest neighbor-of-him with he-goes now-if (5) before

וְנִדְּחָה יָדוֹ בַגַּרְזֶן לִכְרֹת הָעֵץ וְנָשַׁל
and-he-flies-off the-tree to-fell with-the-axe hand-of-him and-she-swings

הַבַּרְזֶל מִן־ הָעֵץ וּמָצָא אֶת־ רֵעֵהוּ וָמֵת הוּא
he and-he-dies neighbor-of-him *** and-he-hits the-handle from the-head

יָנוּס אֶל־ אַחַת הֶעָרִים־ הָאֵלֶּה וָחָי׃ (6) פֶּן־
otherwise (6) and-he-will-live the-these the-cities one-of to he-may-flee

יִרְדֹּף גֹּאֵל הַדָּם אַחֲרֵי הָרֹצֵחַ כִּי־
for the-one-killing after the-blood one-avenging-of he-might-pursue

יֵחַם לְבָבוֹ וְהִשִּׂיגוֹ כִּי־ יִרְבֶּה
he-is-too-great for and-he-might-overtake-him heart-of-him he-is-enraged

הַדֶּרֶךְ וְהִכָּהוּ נָפֶשׁ וְלוֹ אֵין מִשְׁפַּט־מָוֶת
death judgment-of not though-to-him mortally and-he-might-strike-him the-distance

כִּי לֹא שֹׂנֵא הוּא לוֹ מִתְּמוֹל שִׁלְשׁוֹם׃ (7) עַל־ כֵּן אָנֹכִי מְצַוְּךָ
commanding-you I this for (7) before on-yesterday to-him he hating not for

לֵאמֹר שָׁלֹשׁ עָרִים תַּבְדִּיל לָךְ׃ (8) וְאִם־ יַרְחִיב יְהוָה
Yahweh he-enlarges and-if (8) for-you you-set-aside cities three to-say

אֱלֹהֶיךָ אֶת־ גְּבֻלְךָ כַּאֲשֶׁר נִשְׁבַּע לַאֲבֹתֶיךָ וְנָתַן
and-he-gives to-fathers-of-you he-swore just-as territory-of-you *** God-of-you

לְךָ אֶת־ כָּל־ הָאָרֶץ אֲשֶׁר דִּבֶּר לָתֵת לַאֲבֹתֶיךָ׃
to-fathers-of-you to-give he-promised that the-land whole-of *** to-you

(9) כִּי־ תִשְׁמֹר אֶת־ כָּל־ הַמִּצְוָה הַזֹּאת לַעֲשֹׂתָהּ אֲשֶׁר
that to-follow-her the-this the-law all-of *** you-are-careful because (9)

their towns and houses, 2then
set aside for yourselves three
cities centrally located in the
land the LORD your God is giving you to possess. 3Build
roads to them and divide into
three parts the land the LORD
your God is giving you as an
inheritance, so that anyone
who kills a man may flee
there.
4This is the rule concerning
the man who kills another and
flees there to save his life—one
who kills his neighbor unintentionally, without malice
aforethought. 5For instance, a
man may go into the forest
with his neighbor to cut wood,
and as he swings his ax to fell
a tree, the head may fly off and
hit his neighbor and kill him.
That man may flee to one of
these cities and save his life.
6Otherwise, the avenger of
blood might pursue him in a
rage, overtake him if the distance is too great, and kill him
even though he is not deserving of death, since he did it to
his neighbor without malice
aforethought. 7This is why I
command you to set aside for
yourselves three cities.
8If the LORD your God en-
larges your territory, as he
promised on oath to your
forefathers, and gives you the
whole land he promised them,
9because you carefully follow
all these laws I command you

אָנֹכִי מְצַוְּךָ הַיּוֹם לְאַהֲבָה אֶת־ יְהוָה אֱלֹהֶיךָ וְלָלֶכֶת
and-to-walk God-of-you Yahweh *** to-love the-day commanding-you I

בִּדְרָכָיו כָּל־ הַיָּמִים וְיָסַפְתָּ לְךָ עוֹד שָׁלֹשׁ עָרִים עַל
to cities three more for-you then-you-add the-days all-of in-ways-of-him

הַשָּׁלֹשׁ הָאֵלֶּה׃ וְלֹא יִשָּׁפֵךְ דָּם נָקִי בְּקֶרֶב
in-among innocent blood he-will-be-shed so-not (10) the-these the-three

אַרְצְךָ אֲשֶׁר יְהוָה אֱלֹהֶיךָ נֹתֵן לְךָ נַחֲלָה וְהָיָה
and-he-will-be inheritance to-you giving God-of-you Yahweh that land-of-you

עָלֶיךָ דָּמִים׃ וְכִי־ יִהְיֶה אִישׁ שֹׂנֵא לְרֵעֵהוּ וְאָרַב
and-he-waits to-neighbor-of-him hating man he-is but-if (11) bloodsheds on-you

לוֹ וְקָם עָלָיו וְהִכָּהוּ נֶפֶשׁ וָמֵת
and-he-dies mortally and-he-strikes-him against-him and-he-rises for-him

וְנָס אֶל־ אַחַת הֶעָרִים הָאֵל׃ וְשָׁלְחוּ
then-they-shall-send (12) the-these the-cities one-of to then-he-flees

זִקְנֵי עִירוֹ וְלָקְחוּ אֹתוֹ מִשָּׁם וְנָתְנוּ
and-they-shall-give from-there him and-they-shall-bring city-of-him elders-of

אֹתוֹ בְּיַד גֹּאֵל הַדָּם וָמֵת׃ לֹא־
not (13) so-he-will-die the-blood one-avenging-of into-hand-of him

תָחוֹס עֵינְךָ עָלָיו וּבִעַרְתָּ דַם־ הַנָּקִי
the-innocent blood-of so-you-must-purge to-him eye-of-you she-must-pity

מִיִּשְׂרָאֵל וְטוֹב לָךְ׃ לֹא תַסִּיג גְּבוּל
boundary-stone-of you-move not (14) for-you for-good from-Israel

רֵעֲךָ אֲשֶׁר גָּבְלוּ רִאשֹׁנִים בְּנַחֲלָתְךָ אֲשֶׁר
that in-inheritance-of-you predecessors they-set-up that neighbor-of-you

תִּנְחַל בָּאָרֶץ אֲשֶׁר יְהוָה אֱלֹהֶיךָ נֹתֵן לְךָ לְרִשְׁתָּהּ׃
to-possess-her to-you giving God-of-you Yahweh that in-the-land you-receive

לֹא־ יָקוּם עֵד אֶחָד בְּאִישׁ לְכָל־ עָוֺן וּלְכָל־
or-for-any-of crime for-any-of against-man one witness he-may-rise not (15)

חַטָּאת בְּכָל־ חֵטְא אֲשֶׁר יֶחֱטָא עַל־ פִּי ׀ שְׁנֵי
two-of testimony-of by he-committed that offense in-any-of offense

עֵדִים אוֹ עַל־ פִּי שְׁלֹשָׁה־ עֵדִים יָקוּם דָּבָר׃ כִּי־
if (16) matter he-must-establish witnesses three testimony-of by or witnesses

יָקוּם עֵד־ חָמָס בְּאִישׁ לַעֲנוֹת בּוֹ סָרָה׃
crime against-him to-accuse against-him malicious witness he-takes-stand

וְעָמְדוּ שְׁנֵי־ הָאֲנָשִׁים אֲשֶׁר־ לָהֶם הָרִיב לִפְנֵי
before the-dispute to-them who the-men two-of then-they-must-stand (17)

יְהוָה לִפְנֵי הַכֹּהֲנִים וְהַשֹּׁפְטִים אֲשֶׁר יִהְיוּ בַּיָּמִים
in-the-days they-are who and-the-ones-judging the-priests before Yahweh

today—to love the LORD your God and to walk always in his ways—then you are to set aside three more cities. [10]Do this so that innocent blood will not be shed in your land, which the LORD your God is giving you as your inheritance, and so that you will not be guilty of bloodshed.

[11]But if a man hates his neighbor and lies in wait for him, assaults and kills him, and then flees to one of these cities, [12]the elders of his town shall send for him, bring him back from the city, and hand him over to the avenger of blood to die. [13]Show him no pity. You must purge from Israel the guilt of shedding innocent blood, so that it may go well with you.

[14]Do not move your neighbor's boundary stone set up by your predecessors in the inheritance you receive in the land the LORD your God is giving you to possess.

Witnesses

[15]One witness is not enough to convict a man accused of any crime or offense he may have committed. A matter must be established by the testimony of two or three witnesses.

[16]If a malicious witness takes the stand to accuse a man of a crime, [17]the two men involved in the dispute must stand in the presence of the LORD before the priests and the judges who are in office at the time.

הָהֵם׃ וְדָרְשׁוּ הַשֹּׁפְטִים הֵיטֵב
to-be-thorough the-ones-judging and-they-must-investigate (18) the-those

וְהִנֵּה עֵד־ שֶׁקֶר הָעֵד שֶׁקֶר עָנָה בְאָחִיו׃
against-brother-of-him he-testifies lie the-witness liar witness-of and-if

וַעֲשִׂיתֶם לוֹ כַּאֲשֶׁר זָמַם לַעֲשׂוֹת לְאָחִיו
to-brother-of-him to-do he-intended just-as to-him then-you-do (19)

וּבִעַרְתָּ הָרָע מִקִּרְבֶּךָ׃ וְהַנִּשְׁאָרִים
and-the-ones-remaining (20) from-among-you the-evil so-you-must-purge

יִשְׁמְעוּ וְיִרָאוּ וְלֹא־ יֹסִפוּ לַעֲשׂוֹת עוֹד
again to-do they-will-repeat and-not and-they-will-be-afraid they-will-hear

כַּדָּבָר הָרָע הַזֶּה בְּקִרְבֶּךָ׃ וְלֹא תָחוֹס עֵינֶךָ
eye-of-you she-must-pity and-not (21) in-among-you the-this the-evil the-thing

נֶפֶשׁ בְּנֶפֶשׁ עַיִן בְּעַיִן שֵׁן בְּשֵׁן יָד בְּיָד רֶגֶל בְּרָגֶל׃
for-foot foot for-hand hand for-tooth tooth for-eye eye for-life life

כִּי־ תֵצֵא לַמִּלְחָמָה עַל־ אֹיְבֶךָ וְרָאִיתָ סוּס
horse and-you-see being-enemies-of-you against to-the-war you-go when (20:1)

וָרֶכֶב עַם רַב מִמְּךָ לֹא תִירָא מֵהֶם כִּי־ יְהוָה
Yahweh for of-them you-be-afraid not than-you greater army and-chariot

אֱלֹהֶיךָ עִמָּךְ הַמַּעַלְךָ מֵאֶרֶץ מִצְרָיִם׃ וְהָיָה
and-he-will-be (2) Egypt from-land-of the-one-bringing-you with-you God-of-you

כְּקָרָבְכֶם אֶל־ הַמִּלְחָמָה וְנִגַּשׁ הַכֹּהֵן
the-priest then-he-shall-come-forward the-battle into when-to-go-you

וְדִבֶּר אֶל־ הָעָם׃ וְאָמַר אֲלֵהֶם שְׁמַע יִשְׂרָאֵל
Israel hear! to-them and-he-shall-say (3) the-army to and-he-shall-address

אַתֶּם קְרֵבִים הַיּוֹם לַמִּלְחָמָה עַל־ אֹיְבֵיכֶם אַל־
not being-enemies-of-you against into-the-battle the-day ones-who-go you

יֵרַךְ לְבַבְכֶם אַל־ תִּירְאוּ וְאַל־ תַּחְפְּזוּ וְאַל־
and-not you-be-terrified and-not you-be-afraid not heart-of-you let-him-faint

תַּעַרְצוּ מִפְּנֵיהֶם׃ כִּי יְהוָה אֱלֹהֵיכֶם הַהֹלֵךְ עִמָּכֶם
with-you the-one-going God-of-you Yahweh for (4) from-before-them you-panic

לְהִלָּחֵם לָכֶם עִם־ אֹיְבֵיכֶם לְהוֹשִׁיעַ אֶתְכֶם׃
to-you to-give-victory being-enemies-of-you against for-you to-fight

וְדִבְּרוּ הַשֹּׁטְרִים אֶל־ הָעָם לֵאמֹר מִי־ הָאִישׁ
the-man any? to-say the-army to the-being-officers and-they-shall-say (5)

אֲשֶׁר בָּנָה בַיִת־ חָדָשׁ וְלֹא חֲנָכוֹ יֵלֵךְ וְיָשֹׁב
and-let-him-return let-him-go he-dedicated-him and-not new house he-built who

לְבֵיתוֹ פֶּן־ יָמוּת בַּמִּלְחָמָה וְאִישׁ אַחֵר יַחְנְכֶנּוּ׃
he-may-dedicate-him other and-man in-the-battle he-may-die or to-home-of-him

[18]The judges must make a thorough investigation, and if the witness proves to be a liar, giving false testimony against his brother, [19]then do to him as he intended to do to his brother. You must purge the evil from among you. [20]The rest of the people will hear of this and be afraid, and never again will such an evil thing be done among you. [21]Show no pity: life for life, eye for eye, tooth for tooth, hand for hand, foot for foot.

Going to War

20 When you go to war against your enemies and see horses and chariots and an army greater than yours, do not be afraid of them, because the LORD your God, who brought you up out of Egypt, will be with you. [2]When you are about to go into battle, the priest shall come forward and address the army. [3]He shall say: "Hear, O Israel, today you are going into battle against your enemies. Do not be faint-hearted or afraid; do not be terrified or give way to panic before them. [4]For the LORD your God is the one who goes with you to fight for you against your enemies to give you victory."

[5]The officers shall say to the army: "Has anyone built a new house and not dedicated it? Let him go home, or he may die in battle and someone else

וּמִי־ הָאִישׁ אֲשֶׁר־ נָטַע כֶּרֶם וְלֹא חִלְּלוֹ
he-began-to-enjoy-him and-not vineyard he-planted who the-man and-any? (6)

יֵלֵךְ וְיָשֹׁב לְבֵיתוֹ פֶּן־ יָמוּת בַּמִּלְחָמָה
in-the-battle he-may-die or to-home-of-him and-let-him-return let-him-go

וְאִישׁ אַחֵר יְחַלְּלֶנּוּ׃ וּמִי־ הָאִישׁ אֲשֶׁר־ אֵרַשׂ
he-became-pledged who the-man and-any? (7) he-may-enjoy-him other and-man

אִשָּׁה וְלֹא לְקָחָהּ יֵלֵךְ וְיָשֹׁב לְבֵיתוֹ
to-home-of-him and-let-him-return let-him-go he-married-her and-not woman

פֶּן־ יָמוּת בַּמִּלְחָמָה וְאִישׁ אַחֵר יִקָּחֶנָּה׃
he-may-marry-her other and-man in-the-battle he-may-die or

וְיָסְפוּ הַשֹּׁטְרִים לְדַבֵּר אֶל־ הָעָם וְאָמְרוּ
and-they-shall-say the-army to to-say the-being-officers then-they-shall-add (8)

מִי־ הָאִישׁ הַיָּרֵא וְרַךְ הַלֵּבָב יֵלֵךְ וְיָשֹׁב
and-let-him-return let-him-go the-heart or-faint-of the-afraid the-man any?

לְבֵיתוֹ וְלֹא יִמַּס אֶת־ לְבַב אֶחָיו
brothers-of-him heart-of *** he-will-trouble so-not to-home-of-him

כִּלְבָבוֹ׃ וְהָיָה כְּכַלֹּת הַשֹּׁטְרִים לְדַבֵּר
to-speak the-being-officers when-to-finish and-he-will-be (9) as-heart-of-him

אֶל־ הָעָם וּפָקְדוּ שָׂרֵי צְבָאוֹת בְּרֹאשׁ הָעָם׃
the-army at-head-of hosts commanders-of then-they-shall-appoint the-army to

כִּי־ תִקְרַב אֶל־ עִיר לְהִלָּחֵם עָלֶיהָ וְקָרָאתָ אֵלֶיהָ
to-her then-you-offer against-her to-attack city to you-march when (10)

לְשָׁלוֹם׃ וְהָיָה אִם־ שָׁלוֹם תַּעַנְךָ וּפָתְחָה לָךְ
to-you and-she-opens she-answers-you peace if and-he-will-be (11) for-peace

וְהָיָה כָּל־ הָעָם הַנִּמְצָא־ בָהּ יִהְיוּ לְךָ
for-you they-will-be in-her the-being-found the-people all-of then-he-will-be

לָמַס וַעֲבָדוּךָ׃ וְאִם־ לֹא תַשְׁלִים
she-makes-peace not but-if (12) and-they-will-serve-you for-forced-labor

עִמָּךְ וְעָשְׂתָה עִמְּךָ מִלְחָמָה וְצַרְתָּ עָלֶיהָ׃
against-her then-you-siege battle with-you and-she-engages with-you

וּנְתָנָהּ יְהוָה אֱלֹהֶיךָ בְּיָדֶךָ וְהִכִּיתָ
then-you-strike into-hand-of-you God-of-you Yahweh when-he-delivers-her (13)

אֶת־ כָּל־ זְכוּרָהּ לְפִי־ חָרֶב׃ רַק הַנָּשִׁים וְהַטַּף
and-the-child the-women only (14) sword with-edge-of man-of-her every-of ***

וְהַבְּהֵמָה וְכֹל אֲשֶׁר יִהְיֶה בָעִיר כָּל־ שְׁלָלָהּ
plunder-of-her all-of in-the-city he-is that and-all and-the-stock

תָּבֹז לָךְ וְאָכַלְתָּ אֶת־ שְׁלַל אֹיְבֶיךָ
being-enemines-of-you plunder-of *** and-you-may-use for-you you-may-take

may dedicate it. [6]Has anyone
planted a vineyard and not
begun to enjoy it? Let him go
home, or he may die in battle
and someone else enjoy it.
[7]Has anyone become pledged
to a woman and not married
her? Let him go home, or he
may die in battle and someone
else marry her." [8]Then the
officers shall add, "Is any man
afraid or faint-hearted? Let
him go home so that his brothers will not become disheart-
ened too." [9]When the officers
have finished speaking to the
army, they shall appoint commanders over it.

[10]When you march up to attack a city, make its people an
offer of peace. [11]If they accept
and open their gates, all the
people in it shall be subject to
forced labor and shall work for
you. [12]If they refuse to make
peace and they engage you in
battle, lay siege to that city.
[13]When the LORD your God delivers it into your hand, put to
the sword all the men in it.
[14]As for the women, the children, the livestock and everything else in the city, you may
take these as plunder for yourselves. And you may use the

אֲשֶׁר נֹתֵן יְהוָה אֱלֹהֶיךָ לָךְ׃ כֵּן תַּעֲשֶׂה לְכָל־
to-all-of you-must-do this (15) to-you God-of-you Yahweh he-gives that

הֶעָרִים הָרְחֹקֹת מִמְּךָ מְאֹד אֲשֶׁר לֹא־ מֵעָרֵי הַגּוֹיִם־
the-nations of-cities-of not that very from-you the-ones-distant the-cities

הָאֵלֶּה הֵנָּה׃ רַק מֵעָרֵי הָעַמִּים הָאֵלֶּה אֲשֶׁר יְהוָה
Yahweh that the-these the-nations of-cities-of however (16) nearby the-these

אֱלֹהֶיךָ נֹתֵן לְךָ נַחֲלָה לֹא תְחַיֶּה כָּל־
any-of you-leave-alive not inheritance to-you giving God-of-you

נְשָׁמָה׃ כִּי־ הַחֲרֵם תַּחֲרִימֵם הַחִתִּי
the-Hittite you-destroy-them to-destroy but (17) breathing-thing

וְהָאֱמֹרִי הַכְּנַעֲנִי וְהַפְּרִזִּי הַחִוִּי וְהַיְבוּסִי
and-the-Jebusite the-Hivite and-the-Perizzite the-Canaanite and-the-Amorite

כַּאֲשֶׁר צִוְּךָ יְהוָה אֱלֹהֶיךָ׃ לְמַעַן אֲשֶׁר לֹא־ יְלַמְּדוּ
they-teach not that in-order (18) God-of-you Yahweh he-commanded-you just-as

אֶתְכֶם לַעֲשׂוֹת כְּכֹל תּוֹעֲבֹתָם אֲשֶׁר עָשׂוּ
they-do that detestable-things-of-them after-all-of to-follow you

לֵאלֹהֵיהֶם וַחֲטָאתֶם לַיהוָה אֱלֹהֵיכֶם׃ כִּי־ תָצוּר
you-lay-siege when (19) God-of-you against-Yahweh so-you-sin for-gods-of-them

אֶל־ עִיר יָמִים רַבִּים לְהִלָּחֵם עָלֶיהָ לְתָפְשָׂהּ לֹא־ תַשְׁחִית אֶת־
*** you-destroy not to-capture-her against-her to-fight many days city to

עֵצָהּ לִנְדֹּחַ עָלָיו גַּרְזֶן כִּי מִמֶּנּוּ תֹאכֵל וְאֹתוֹ לֹא
not so-him you-can-eat from-him for axe to-him to-put tree-of-her

תִכְרֹת כִּי הָאָדָם עֵץ הַשָּׂדֶה לָבֹא מִפָּנֶיךָ בַּמָּצוֹר׃
in-the-siege from-before-you to-go the-field tree-of the-man for you-cut-down

רַק עֵץ אֲשֶׁר־ תֵּדַע כִּי־ לֹא־ עֵץ מַאֲכָל הוּא אֹתוֹ תַשְׁחִית
you-can-use him he fruit tree-of not that you-know that tree however (20)

וְכָרָתָּ וּבָנִיתָ מָצוֹר עַל־ הָעִיר אֲשֶׁר־ הִוא עֹשָׂה
making she that the-city for siege-work and-you-can-build and-you-can-cut

עִמְּךָ מִלְחָמָה עַד רִדְתָּהּ׃ כִּי־ יִמָּצֵא חָלָל בָּאֲדָמָה
in-the-land one-slain he-is-found if (21:1) to-fall-her until war against-you

אֲשֶׁר יְהוָה אֱלֹהֶיךָ נֹתֵן לְךָ לְרִשְׁתָּהּ נֹפֵל בַּשָּׂדֶה לֹא
not in-the-field lying to-possess-her to-you giving God-of-you Yahweh that

נוֹדַע מִי הִכָּהוּ׃ וְיָצְאוּ זְקֵנֶיךָ
elders-of-you then-they-shall-go-out (2) he-killed-him who being-known

וְשֹׁפְטֶיךָ וּמָדְדוּ אֶל־ הֶעָרִים אֲשֶׁר סְבִיבֹת
ones-around that the-towns to and-they-shall-measure and-ones-judging-you

הֶחָלָל׃ וְהָיָה הָעִיר הַקְּרֹבָה אֶל־ הֶחָלָל וְלָקְחוּ
that-they-shall-take the-body to the-near the-town and-he-will-be (3) the-body

plunder the LORD your God
gives you from your enemies.
15 This is how you are to treat
all the cities that are at a distance from you and do not belong to the nations nearby.
16 However, in the cities of
the nations the LORD your God
is giving you as an inheritance, do not leave alive anything that breathes.
17 Com-
pletely destroy[b] them—the
Hittites, Amorites, Canaanites, Perizzites, Hivites and
Jebusites—as the LORD your
God has commanded you.
18 Otherwise, they will teach
you to follow all the detestable
things they do in worshiping
their gods, and you will sin
against the LORD your God.
19 When you lay siege to a
city for a long time, fighting
against it to capture it, do not
destroy its trees by putting an
ax to them, because you can
eat their fruit. Do not cut them
down. Are the trees of the field
people, that you should besiege them?[c]
20 However, you
may cut down trees that you
know are not fruit trees and
use them to build siege works
until the city at war with you
falls.

Atonement for an Unsolved Murder

21 If a man is found slain,
lying in a field in the
land the LORD your God is giving you to possess, and it is
not known who killed him,
2 your elders and judges shall
go out and measure the distance from the body to the
neighboring towns.
3 Then the
elders of the town nearest the
body shall take a heifer that

[b] 17 The Hebrew term refers to the irrevocable giving over of things or persons to the LORD, often by totally destroying them.

[c] 19 *Or down to use in the siege, for the fruit trees are for the benefit of man.*

זִקְנֵי הָעִיר הַהִוא עֶגְלַת בָּקָר אֲשֶׁר לֹא־עֻבַּד בָּהּ
with-her he-was-worked not that herd heifer-of the-that the-town elders-of

אֲשֶׁר לֹא־מָשְׁכָה בְּעֹל׃ וְהוֹרִדוּ זִקְנֵי הָעִיר
the-town elders-of and-they-shall-lead (4) under-yoke she-wore not that

הַהִוא אֶת־הָעֶגְלָה אֶל־נַחַל אֵיתָן אֲשֶׁר לֹא־יֵעָבֵד
he-was-plowed not that flowing-stream valley-of to the-heifer *** the-that

בּוֹ וְלֹא יִזָּרֵעַ וְעָרְפוּ־שָׁם אֶת־הָעֶגְלָה
the-heifer *** there and-they-shall-break-neck he-was-planted and-not in-him

בַּנָּחַל׃ וְנִגְּשׁוּ הַכֹּהֲנִים בְּנֵי לֵוִי כִּי
for Levi sons-of the-priests and-they-shall-step-forward (5) in-the-valley

בָם בָּחַר יְהוָה אֱלֹהֶיךָ לְשָׁרְתוֹ וּלְבָרֵךְ בְּשֵׁם
in-name-of and-to-bless to-minister-to-him God-of-you Yahweh he-chose to-them

יְהוָה וְעַל־פִּיהֶם יִהְיֶה כָּל־רִיב וְכָל־נָגַע׃
assault and-every-of dispute every-of he-is decision-of-them and-at Yahweh

וְכֹל זִקְנֵי הָעִיר הַהִוא הַקְּרֹבִים אֶל־הֶחָלָל
the-body to the-ones-near the-that the-city elders-of then-all-of (6)

יִרְחֲצוּ אֶת־יְדֵיהֶם עַל־הָעֶגְלָה הָעֲרוּפָה
the-one-having-neck-broken the-heifer over hands-of-them *** they-shall-wash

בַנָּחַל׃ וְעָנוּ וְאָמְרוּ יָדֵינוּ לֹא
not hands-of-us and-they-shall-say and-they-shall-declare (7) in-the-valley

שָׁפְכָה° אֶת־הַדָּם הַזֶּה וְעֵינֵינוּ לֹא רָאוּ׃ כַּפֵּר
atone! (8) they-saw not and-eyes-of-us the-this the-blood *** they-shed

לְעַמְּךָ יִשְׂרָאֵל אֲשֶׁר־פָּדִיתָ יְהוָה וְאַל־תִּתֵּן דָּם
blood-of you-hold and-not Yahweh you-redeemed whom Israel for-people-of-you

נָקִי בְּקֶרֶב עַמְּךָ יִשְׂרָאֵל וְנִכַּפֵּר לָהֶם
for-them and-he-will-be-atoned Israel people-of-you against innocent

הַדָּם׃ וְאַתָּה תְּבַעֵר הַדָּם הַנָּקִי מִקִּרְבֶּךָ
from-among-you the-innocent the-blood you-will-purge so-you (9) the-bloodshed

כִּי־תַעֲשֶׂה הַיָּשָׁר בְּעֵינֵי יְהוָה׃ כִּי־תֵצֵא לַמִּלְחָמָה עַל־
against to the-war you-go when (10) Yahweh in-eyes-of the-right you-did for

אֹיְבֶיךָ וּנְתָנוֹ יְהוָה אֱלֹהֶיךָ בְּיָדֶךָ
into hand-of-you God-of-you Yahweh and-he-delivers-him being-enemies-of-you

וְשָׁבִיתָ שִׁבְיוֹ׃ וְרָאִיתָ בַּשִּׁבְיָה אֵשֶׁת
woman-of among-the-captive and-you-notice (11) captive-of-him and-you-take

יְפַת־תֹּאַר וְחָשַׁקְתָּ בָהּ וְלָקַחְתָּ לְךָ
to-her then-you-may-take to-her and-you-are-attracted form beautiful-of

לְאִשָּׁה׃ וַהֲבֵאתָהּ אֶל־תּוֹךְ בֵּיתֶךָ וְגִלְּחָה
and-she-must-shave home-of-you inside-of into then-you-bring-her (12) for-wife

has never been worked and
has never worn a yoke 4and
lead her down to a valley that
has not been plowed or
planted and where there is a
flowing stream. There in the
valley they are to break the
heifer's neck. 5The priests, the
sons of Levi, shall step forward, for the LORD your God
has chosen them to minister
and to pronounce blessings in
the name of the LORD and to
decide all cases of dispute and
assault. 6Then all the elders of
the town nearest the body
shall wash their hands over
the heifer whose neck was
broken in the valley, 7and they
shall declare: "Our hands did
not shed this blood, nor did
our eyes see it done. 8Accept
this atonement for your
people Israel, whom you have
redeemed, O LORD, and do not
hold your people guilty of the
blood of an innocent man."
And the bloodshed will be
atoned for. 9So you will purge
from yourselves the guilt of
shedding innocent blood,
since you have done what is
right in the eyes of the LORD.

Marrying a Captive Woman

10When you go to war
against your enemies and the
LORD your God delivers them
into your hands and you take
captives, 11if you notice among
the captives a beautiful
woman and are attracted to
her, you may take her as your
wife. 12Bring her into your
home and have her shave her

°7 ק שפכו

אֶת־ רֹאשָׁהּ וְעָשְׂתָה אֶת־ צִפָּרְנֶיהָ׃ וְהֵסִירָה

and-she-must-put-aside (13) nails-of-her *** and-she-must-trim head-of-her ***

אֶת־ שִׂמְלַת שִׁבְיָהּ מֵעָלֶיהָ וְיָשְׁבָה בְּבֵיתֶךָ

in-house-of-you when-she-lived from-on-her captivity-of-her clothing-of ***

וּבָכְתָה אֶת־ אָבִיהָ וְאֶת־ אִמָּהּ יֶרַח יָמִים וְאַחַר

then-after days month-of mother-of-her and father-of-her *** and-she-mourned

כֵּן תָּבוֹא אֵלֶיהָ וּבְעַלְתָּהּ וְהָיְתָה לְךָ לְאִשָּׁה׃

as-wife to-you and-she-shall-be and-you-may-marry-her to-her you-may-go this

וְהָיָה אִם־ לֹא חָפַצְתָּ בָּהּ וְשִׁלַּחְתָּהּ

then-you-let-go-her with-her you-are-pleased not if and-he-will-be (14)

לְנַפְשָׁהּ וּמָכֹר לֹא־ תִמְכְּרֶנָּה בַּכָּסֶף לֹא־

not for-the-money you-sell-her not but-to-sell as-wish-of-her

תִתְעַמֵּר בָּהּ תַּחַת אֲשֶׁר עִנִּיתָהּ׃ כִּי־ תִהְיֶיןָ

they-are if (15) you-dishonored-her that since with-her you-treat-as-slave

לְאִישׁ שְׁתֵּי נָשִׁים הָאַחַת אֲהוּבָה וְהָאַחַת שְׂנוּאָה

being-unloved but-the-other being-loved the-one wives two-of to-man

וְיָלְדוּ־ לוֹ בָנִים הָאֲהוּבָה וְהַשְּׂנוּאָה וְהָיָה

but-he-is and-the-being-unloved the-being-loved sons to-him and-they-bear

הַבֵּן הַבְּכֹר לַשְּׂנִיאָה׃ וְהָיָה בְּיוֹם הַנְחִילוֹ

to-will-him on-day and-he-will-be (16) of-the-unloved the-firstborn the-son

אֶת־ בָּנָיו אֵת אֲשֶׁר־ יִהְיֶה לוֹ לֹא יוּכַל לְבַכֵּר אֶת־

*** to-give-firstborn-right he-can not to-him he-is what *** sons-of-him ***

בֶּן־ הָאֲהוּבָה עַל־ פְּנֵי בֶן־ הַשְּׂנוּאָה הַבְּכֹר׃

the-firstborn the-being-unloved son-of preferences-of in the-being-loved son-of

כִּי אֶת־ הַבְּכֹר בֶּן־ הַשְּׂנוּאָה יַכִּיר

he-must-acknowledge the-being-unloved son-of the-firstborn *** for (17)

לָתֶת לוֹ פִּי שְׁנַיִם בְּכֹל אֲשֶׁר־ יִמָּצֵא לוֹ כִּי־הוּא רֵאשִׁית

first-of he for to-him he-is-found that of-all double share-of to-him to-give

אֹנוֹ לוֹ מִשְׁפַּט הַבְּכֹרָה׃ כִּי־ יִהְיֶה לְאִישׁ בֵּן

son to-man he-is if (18) the-firstborn right-of to-him strength-of-him

סוֹרֵר וּמוֹרֶה אֵינֶנּוּ שֹׁמֵעַ בְּקוֹל אָבִיו

father-of-him to-voice-of obeying not-him or-being-rebellious being-stubborn

וּבְקוֹל אִמּוֹ וְיִסְּרוּ אֹתוֹ וְלֹא יִשְׁמַע

he-listens but-not him and-they-discipline mother-of-him or-to-voice-of

אֲלֵיהֶם׃ וְתָפְשׂוּ בוֹ אָבִיו וְאִמּוֹ

and-mother-of-him father-of-him on-him then-they-shall-take-hold (19) to-them

וְהוֹצִיאוּ אֹתוֹ אֶל־ זִקְנֵי עִירוֹ וְאֶל־ שַׁעַר מְקֹמוֹ׃

place-of-him gate-of even-to town-of-him elders-of to him and-they-shall-bring

head, trim her nails [13]and put aside the clothes she was wearing when captured. After she has lived in your house and mourned her father and mother for a full month, then you may go to her and be her husband and she shall be your wife. [14]If you are not pleased with her, let her go wherever she wishes. You must not sell her or treat her as a slave, since you have dishonored her.

The Right of the Firstborn

[15]If a man has two wives, and he loves one but not the other, and both bear him sons but the firstborn is the son of the wife he does not love, [16]when he wills his property to his sons, he must not give the rights of the firstborn to the son of the wife he loves in preference to his actual firstborn, the son of the wife he does not love. [17]He must acknowledge the son of his unloved wife as the firstborn by giving him a double share of all he has. That son is the first sign of his father's strength. The right of the firstborn belongs to him.

A Rebellious Son

[18]If a man has a stubborn and rebellious son who does not obey his father and mother and will not listen to them when they discipline him, [19]his father and mother shall take hold of him and bring him to the elders at the gate of his town. [20]They shall

וְאָמְרוּ אֶל־ זִקְנֵי עִירוֹ בְּנֵנוּ זֶה סוֹרֵר
being-stubborn this son-of-us town-of-him elders-of to and-they-shall-say (20)

וּמֹרֶה אֵינֶנּוּ שֹׁמֵעַ בְּקֹלֵנוּ זוֹלֵל
one-squandering to-voice-of-us listening not-him and-being-rebellious

וְסֹבֵא׃ וּרְגָמֻהוּ כָּל־ אַנְשֵׁי עִירוֹ
town-of-him men-of all-of then-they-shall-stone-him (21) and-drinking

בָאֲבָנִים וָמֵת וּבִעַרְתָּ הָרָע מִקִּרְבֶּךָ וְכָל־
and-all-of from-among-you the-evil so-you-purge so-he-dies with-the-stones

יִשְׂרָאֵל יִשְׁמְעוּ וְיִרָאוּ׃ וְכִי־ יִהְיֶה בְאִישׁ
to-man he-is and-if (22) and-they-will-be-afraid they-will-hear Israel

חֵטְא מִשְׁפַּט־ מָוֶת וְהוּמָת וְתָלִיתָ אֹתוֹ עַל־ עֵץ׃
tree on him and-you-hang and-he-is-killed death judgment-of guilt-of

לֹא־ תָלִין נִבְלָתוֹ עַל־ הָעֵץ כִּי־ קָבוֹר תִּקְבְּרֶנּוּ
you-bury-him to-bury but the-tree on body-of-him you-leave-overnight not (23)

בַּיּוֹם הַהוּא כִּי־ קִלְלַת אֱלֹהִים תָּלוּי וְלֹא תְטַמֵּא אֶת־
*** you-desecrate and-not being-hung God curse-of for the-that on-the-day

אַדְמָתְךָ אֲשֶׁר יְהוָה אֱלֹהֶיךָ נֹתֵן לְךָ נַחֲלָה׃ לֹא־
not (22:1) inheritance to-you giving God-of-you Yahweh that land-of-you

תִרְאֶה אֶת־ שׁוֹר אָחִיךָ אוֹ אֶת־ שֵׂיוֹ נִדָּחִים
ones-straying sheep-of-him *** or brother-of-you ox-of *** you-see

וְהִתְעַלַּמְתָּ מֵהֶם הָשֵׁב תְּשִׁיבֵם לְאָחִיךָ׃
to-brother-of-you you-take-back-them to-take-back from-them and-you-ignore

וְאִם־ לֹא קָרוֹב אָחִיךָ אֵלֶיךָ וְלֹא יְדַעְתּוֹ
you-know-him or-not to-you brother-of-you near not and-if (2)

וַאֲסַפְתּוֹ אֶל־ תּוֹךְ בֵּיתֶךָ וְהָיָה עִמְּךָ עַד
until with-you and-he-will-be home-of-you inside-of to then-you-take-him

דְּרֹשׁ אָחִיךָ אֹתוֹ וַהֲשֵׁבֹתוֹ לוֹ׃ וְכֵן
and-same (3) to-him then-you-give-back-him for-him brother-of-you to-look

תַּעֲשֶׂה לַחֲמֹרוֹ וְכֵן תַּעֲשֶׂה לְשִׂמְלָתוֹ וְכֵן תַּעֲשֶׂה
you-do and-same for-cloak-of-him you-do and-same for-donkey-of-him you-do

לְכָל־ אֲבֵדַת אָחִיךָ אֲשֶׁר־ תֹּאבַד מִמֶּנּוּ וּמְצָאתָהּ
and-you-find-her from-him she-is-lost that brother-of-you lost-of for-any-of

לֹא תוּכַל לְהִתְעַלֵּם׃ לֹא־ תִרְאֶה אֶת־ חֲמוֹר אָחִיךָ אוֹ
or brother-of-you donkey-of *** you-see not (4) to-ignore you-can not

שׁוֹרוֹ נֹפְלִים בַּדֶּרֶךְ וְהִתְעַלַּמְתָּ מֵהֶם הָקֵם
to-help-up from-them and-you-ignore on-the-road ones-being-fallen ox-of-him

תָּקִים עִמּוֹ׃ לֹא־ יִהְיֶה כְלִי־ גֶבֶר עַל־ אִשָּׁה וְלֹא־
and-not woman on man clothing-of he-shall-be not (5) with-him you-help-up

say to the elders, "This son of ours is stubborn and rebellious. He will not obey us. He is a profligate and a drunkard."
21Then all the men of his town shall stone him to death. You must purge the evil from among you. All Israel will hear of it and be afraid.

Various Laws

22If a man guilty of a capital offense is put to death and his body is hung on a tree,
23you must not leave his body on the tree overnight. Be sure to bury him that same day, because anyone who is hung on a tree is under God's curse. You must not desecrate the land the LORD your God is giving you as an inheritance.

22 If you see your brother's ox or sheep straying, do not ignore it but be sure to take it back to him.
2If the brother does not live near you or if you do not know who he is, take it home with you and keep it until he comes looking for it. Then give it back to him.
3Do the same if you find your brother's donkey or his cloak or anything he loses. Do not ignore it.
4If you see your brother's donkey or his ox fallen on the road, do not ignore it. Help him get it to its feet.
5A woman must not wear men's clothing, nor a man

יִלְבַּשׁ גֶּבֶר שִׂמְלַת אִשָּׁה כִּי תוֹעֲבַת יְהוָה אֱלֹהֶיךָ
God-of-you Yahweh detestable-of for woman clothing-of man he-shall-wear

כָּל־ עֹשֵׂה אֵלֶּה׃ כִּי יִקָּרֵא קַן־ צִפּוֹר | לְפָנֶיךָ בַּדֶּרֶךְ
beside-the-road before-you bird nest-of he-is-found if (6) these doing any-of

בְּכָל־ עֵץ | אוֹ עַל־ הָאָרֶץ אֶפְרֹחִים אוֹ בֵיצִים וְהָאֵם רֹבֶצֶת
sitting and-the-mother eggs or young-ones the-ground on or tree in-any-of

עַל־ הָאֶפְרֹחִים אוֹ עַל־הַבֵּיצִים לֹא־ תִקַּח הָאֵם עַל־ הַבָּנִים׃
the-young-ones with the-mother you-take not the-eggs on or the-young-ones on

שַׁלֵּחַ תְּשַׁלַּח אֶת־ הָאֵם וְאֶת־ הַבָּנִים תִּקַּח־
you-may-take the-young-ones and the-mother *** you-let-go to-let-go (7)

לָךְ לְמַעַן יִיטַב לָךְ וְהַאֲרַכְתָּ יָמִים׃ כִּי
when (8) days and-you-may-have-long with-you he-may-go-well so-that for-you

תִבְנֶה בַּיִת חָדָשׁ וְעָשִׂיתָ מַעֲקֶה לְגַגֶּךָ וְלֹא־ תָשִׂים
you-bring so-not around-roof-of-you parapet then-you-make new house you-build

דָּמִים בְּבֵיתֶךָ כִּי־ יִפֹּל הַנֹּפֵל מִמֶּנּוּ׃ לֹא־
not (9) from-him the-one-falling he-falls if on-house-of-you bloodsheds

תִזְרַע כַּרְמְךָ כִּלְאָיִם פֶּן־ תִּקְדַּשׁ הַמְלֵאָה הַזֶּרַע אֲשֶׁר
that the-seed the-crop you-defile or two-kinds vineyard-of-you you-plant

תִּזְרָע וּתְבוּאַת הַכָּרֶם׃ לֹא־ תַחֲרֹשׁ בְּשׁוֹר־
with-ox you-plow not (10) the-vineyard and-fruit-of you-planted

וּבַחֲמֹר יַחְדָּו׃ לֹא תִלְבַּשׁ שַׁעַטְנֵז צֶמֶר וּפִשְׁתִּים
and-linens wool mixed-fabric you-wear not (11) together and-with-donkey

יַחְדָּו׃ גְּדִלִים תַּעֲשֶׂה־ לָּךְ עַל־אַרְבַּע כַּנְפוֹת כְּסוּתְךָ אֲשֶׁר
that cloak-of-you corners-of four on for-you you-make tassels (12) together

תְּכַסֶּה־ בָּהּ׃ כִּי־ יִקַּח אִישׁ אִשָּׁה וּבָא אֵלֶיהָ
with-her and-he-lies wife man he-takes if (13) with-her you-cover

וּשְׂנֵאָהּ׃ וְשָׂם לָהּ עֲלִילֹת דְּבָרִים
things ones-slanderous to-her and-he-accuses (14) and-he-dislikes-her

וְהוֹצִיא עָלֶיהָ שֵׁם רָע וְאָמַר אֶת־ הָאִשָּׁה הַזֹּאת לָקַחְתִּי
I-married the-this the-woman *** and-he-says bad name to-her and-he-gives

וָאֶקְרַב אֵלֶיהָ וְלֹא־ מָצָאתִי לָהּ בְּתוּלִים׃
proofs-of-virginity with-her I-found then-not to-her when-I-approached

וְלָקַח אֲבִי הַנַּעֲרָ וְאִמָּהּ
and-mother-of-her the-girl father-of then-he-shall-take (15)

וְהוֹצִיאוּ אֶת־ בְּתוּלֵי הַנַּעֲרָ אֶל־ זִקְנֵי הָעִיר
the-town elders-of to the-girl proofs-of-virginity-of *** and-they-shall-bring

הַשָּׁעְרָה׃ וְאָמַר אֲבִי הַנַּעֲרָ אֶל־ הַזְּקֵנִים אֶת־
*** the-elders to the-girl father-of then-he-will-say (16) at-the-gate

wear women's clothing, for
the LORD your God detests
anyone who does this.
6If you come across a bird's
nest beside the road, either in
a tree or on the ground, and
the mother is sitting on the
young or on the eggs, do not
take the mother with the
young. 7You may take the
young, but be sure to let the
mother go, so that it may go
well with you and you may
have a long life.
8When you build a new
house, make a parapet around
your roof so that you may not
bring the guilt of bloodshed
on your house if someone falls
from the roof.
9Do not plant two kinds of
seed in your vineyard; if you
do, not only the crops you
plant but also the fruit of the
vineyard will be defiled.[d]
10Do not plow with an ox
and a donkey yoked together.
11Do not wear clothes of
wool and linen woven to-
gether.
12Make tassels on the four
corners of the cloak you wear.

Marriage Violations

13If a man takes a wife and,
after lying with her, dislikes
her 14and slanders her and
gives her a bad name, saying,
"I married this woman, but
when I approached her, I did
not find proof of her virginity," 15then the girl's father and
mother shall bring proof that
she was a virgin to the town
elders at the gate. 16The girl's
father will say to the elders, "I

d9 Or *be forfeited to the sanctuary*

°15a ק הנערה , °15b ק הנערה
°16 ק הנערה

בִּתִּי נָתַתִּי לָאִישׁ הַזֶּה לְאִשָּׁה וַיִּשְׂנָאֶהָ׃
but-he-dislikes-her as-wife the-this to-the-man I-gave daughter-of-me

וְהִנֵּה־ הוּא שָׂם עֲלִילֹת דְּבָרִים לֵאמֹר לֹא־ מָצָאתִי
I-found not to-say things ones-slanderous he-accused he now-see! (17)

לְבִתְּךָ בְּתוּלִים וְאֵלֶּה בְּתוּלֵי
proofs-of-virginity-of but-these proofs-of-virginity with-daughter-of-you

בִתִּי וּפָרְשׂוּ הַשִּׂמְלָה לִפְנֵי זִקְנֵי הָעִיר׃
the-town elders-of before the-cloth then-they-shall-display daughter-of-me

וְלָקְחוּ זִקְנֵי הָעִיר־ הַהִוא אֶת־ הָאִישׁ
the-man *** the-that the-town elders-of and-they-shall-take (18)

וְיִסְּרוּ אֹתוֹ׃ וְעָנְשׁוּ אֹתוֹ מֵאָה כֶסֶף
silver hundred him and-they-shall-fine (19) him and-they-shall-punish

וְנָתְנוּ לַאֲבִי הַנַּעֲרָה כִּי הוֹצִיא שֵׁם רָע עַל בְּתוּלַת
virgin-of to bad name he-gave for the-girl to-father-of and-they-shall-give

יִשְׂרָאֵל וְלוֹ־ תִהְיֶה לְאִשָּׁה לֹא־ יוּכַל לְשַׁלְּחָהּ כָּל־
all-of to-divorce-her he-can not as-wife she-will-continue and-to-him Israel

יָמָיו׃ וְאִם־ אֱמֶת הָיָה הַדָּבָר הַזֶּה לֹא־ נִמְצְאוּ
they-can-be-found not the-this the-charge he-is true but-if (20) days-of-him

בְתוּלִים לַנַּעֲרָ׃ וְהוֹצִיאוּ אֶת־ הַנַּעֲרָ אֶל־
to the-girl *** then-they-shall-bring (21) of-the-girl proofs-of-virginity

פֶּתַח בֵּית־ אָבִיהָ וּסְקָלוּהָ אַנְשֵׁי עִירָהּ
town-of-her men-of and-they-shall-stone-her father-of-her house-of door-of

בָּאֲבָנִים וָמֵתָה כִּי־ עָשְׂתָה נְבָלָה בְּיִשְׂרָאֵל לִזְנוֹת
to-be-promiscuous in-Israel disgrace she-did for so-she-dies with-the-stones

בֵּית אָבִיהָ וּבִעַרְתָּ הָרָע מִקִּרְבֶּךָ׃ כִּי־
if (22) from-among-you the-evil so-you-purge father-of-her house-of

יִמָּצֵא אִישׁ שֹׁכֵב | עִם־ אִשָּׁה בְעֻלַת־ בַּעַל וּמֵתוּ
then-they-must-die husband being-married-of woman with sleeping man he-is-found

גַּם־ שְׁנֵיהֶם הָאִישׁ הַשֹּׁכֵב עִם־ הָאִשָּׁה וְהָאִשָּׁה
and-the-woman the-woman with the-one-sleeping the-man both-of-them indeed

וּבִעַרְתָּ הָרָע מִיִּשְׂרָאֵל׃ כִּי יִהְיֶה נַעֲרָ בְתוּלָה מְאֹרָשָׂה
being-pledged virgin girl he-is if (23) from-Israel the-evil so-you-purge

לְאִישׁ וּמְצָאָהּ אִישׁ בָּעִיר וְשָׁכַב עִמָּהּ׃
with-her and-he-sleeps in-the-town man and-he-meets-her to-man

וְהוֹצֵאתֶם אֶת־ שְׁנֵיהֶם אֶל־ שַׁעַר | הָעִיר הַהִוא
the-that the-town gate-of to both-of-them *** then-you-shall-take (24)

וּסְקַלְתֶּם אֹתָם בָּאֲבָנִים וָמֵתוּ אֶת־ הַנַּעֲרָ עַל־
for the-girl *** so-they-die with-the-stones them and-you-shall-stone

gave my daughter in marriage
to this man, but he dislikes
her. [17]Now he has slandered
her and said, 'I did not find
your daughter to be a virgin.'
But here is the proof of my
daughter's virginity." Then
her parents shall display the
cloth before the elders of the
town, [18]and the elders shall
take the man and punish him.
[19]They shall fine him a hundred shekels of silver[e] and
give them to the girl's father,
because this man has given an
Israelite virgin a bad name.
She shall continue to be his
wife; he must not divorce her
as long as he lives.

[20]If, however, the charge is
true and no proof of the girl's
virginity can be found, [21]she
shall be brought to the door of
her father's house and there
the men of her town shall
stone her to death. She has
done a disgraceful thing in Israel by being promiscuous
while still in her father's
house. You must purge the evil
from among you.

[22]If a man is found sleeping
with another man's wife, both
the man who slept with her
and the woman must die. You
must purge the evil from Israel.

[23]If a man happens to meet
in a town a virgin pledged to
be married and he sleeps with
her, [24]you shall take both of
them to the gate of that town
and stone them to death—the

[e]19 That is, about 2 1/2 pounds (about 1 kilogram)

°20 ק לנערה ,°21 ק הנערה
°23 ק נערה ,°24 ק הנערה

דְּבַר אֲשֶׁר לֹא־ צָעֲקָה בָעִיר וְאֶת־ הָאִישׁ עַל־ דְּבַר אֲשֶׁר־
that reason-of for the-man and in-the-town she-screamed not that reason-of

עִנָּה אֶת־ אֵשֶׁת רֵעֵהוּ וּבִעַרְתָּ הָרָע מִקִּרְבֶּךָ׃
from-among-you the-evil so-you-purge fellow-of-him wife-of *** he-violated

(25) וְאִם־ בַּשָּׂדֶה יִמְצָא הָאִישׁ אֶת־ הַנַּעֲרָ° הַמְאֹרָשָׂה
the-being-pledged the-girl *** the-man he-meets in-the-country but-if (25)

וְהֶחֱזִיק־ בָּהּ הָאִישׁ וְשָׁכַב עִמָּהּ וּמֵת
then-he-shall-die with-her and-he-lies the-man over-her and-he-overpowers

הָאִישׁ אֲשֶׁר־ שָׁכַב עִמָּהּ לְבַדּוֹ׃ (26) וְלַנַּעֲרָ° לֹא־ תַעֲשֶׂה דָבָר
thing you-do not but-to-the-girl (26) only-him with-her he-lay who the-man

אֵין לַנַּעֲרָ° חֵטְא מָוֶת כִּי כַּאֲשֶׁר יָקוּם אִישׁ עַל־ רֵעֵהוּ
neighbor-of-him against man he-rises just-as for death sin-of to-the-girl not

וּרְצָחוֹ נֶפֶשׁ כֵּן הַדָּבָר הַזֶּה׃ (27) כִּי בַשָּׂדֶה
in-the-country for (27) the-this the-case same mortally and-he-murders-him

מְצָאָהּ צָעֲקָה הַנַּעֲרָ° הַמְאֹרָשָׂה וְאֵין מוֹשִׁיעַ
one-rescuing but-not the-being-betrothed the-girl she-screamed he-found-her

לָהּ׃ (28) כִּי־ יִמְצָא אִישׁ נַעֲרָ° בְתוּלָה אֲשֶׁר לֹא־ אֹרָשָׂה
being-pledged not who virgin girl man he-meets if (28) to-her

וּתְפָשָׂהּ וְשָׁכַב עִמָּהּ וְנִמְצָאוּ׃
and-they-are-discovered with-her and-he-lies and-he-forces-her

(29) וְנָתַן הָאִישׁ הַשֹּׁכֵב עִמָּהּ לַאֲבִי הַנַּעֲרָ°
the-girl to-father-of with-her the-one-lying the-man then-he-shall-pay (29)

חֲמִשִּׁים כָּסֶף וְלוֹ־ תִהְיֶה לְאִשָּׁה תַּחַת אֲשֶׁר עִנָּהּ לֹא־
not he-violated-her that because as-wife she-must-be and-to-him silver fifty

יוּכַל שַׁלְּחָהּ כָּל־ יָמָיו׃ (23:1)* לֹא־ יִקַּח אִישׁ אֶת־
*** man he-must-marry not (23:1)* days-of-him all-of to-divorce-her he-can

אֵשֶׁת אָבִיו וְלֹא יְגַלֶּה כְּנַף אָבִיו׃ (2) לֹא־
not (2) father-of-him bed-of he-must-dishonor and-not father-of-him wife-of

יָבֹא פְצוּעַ־ דַּכָּא וּכְרוּת שָׁפְכָה בִּקְהַל
to-assembly-of genital of-being-cut-of crushing being-wounded-of he-may-enter

יְהוָה׃ (3) לֹא־ יָבֹא מַמְזֵר בִּקְהַל יְהוָה גַּם
even Yahweh to-assembly-of one-illegitimate he-may-enter not (3) Yahweh

דּוֹר עֲשִׂירִי לֹא־ יָבֹא לוֹ בִּקְהַל יְהוָה׃ (4) לֹא־
not (4) Yahweh in-assembly-of of-him he-may-enter not tenth generation

יָבֹא עַמּוֹנִי וּמוֹאָבִי בִּקְהַל יְהוָה גַּם דּוֹר עֲשִׂירִי
tenth generation even Yahweh to-assembly-of or-Moabite Ammonite he-may-enter

לֹא־ יָבֹא לָהֶם בִּקְהַל יְהוָה עַד־ עוֹלָם׃ (5) עַל־ דְּבַר אֲשֶׁר
that reason-of for (5) ever for Yahweh in-assembly-of of-them he-may-enter not

girl because she was in a town
and did not scream for help,
and the man because he violated another man's wife.
You must purge the evil from
among you.
[25]But if out in the country a
man happens to meet a girl
pledged to be married and
rapes her, only the man who
has done this shall die. [26]Do
nothing to the girl; she has
committed no sin deserving
death. This case is like that of
someone who attacks and
murders his neighbor, [27]for
the man found the girl out in
the country, and though the
betrothed girl screamed, there
was no one to rescue her.
[28]If a man happens to meet a
virgin who is not pledged to
be married and rapes her and
they are discovered, [29]he shall
pay the girl's father fifty
shekels of silver.[f] He must
marry the girl, for he has violated her. He can never divorce her as long as he lives.
[30]A man is not to marry his
father's wife; he must not dishonor his father's bed.

Exclusion From the Assembly

23 No one who has been
emasculated by crush-
ing or cutting may enter the
assembly of the LORD.
[2]No one born of a forbidden
marriage[g] nor any of his descendants may enter the assembly of the LORD, even
down to the tenth generation.
[3]No Ammonite or Moabite
or any of his descendants may
enter the assembly of the
LORD, even down to the tenth
generation. [4]For they did not

f29 That is, about 1 1/4 pounds (about 0.6 kilogram)
g2 Or *one of illegitimate birth*

*The Hebrew numeration of chapter 23 begins with verse 30 of chapter 22 in English; thus, there is a one-verse discrepancy throughout chapter 23.

°25 ק הנערה , °26a ק לנערה
°26b ק הנערה , °27 ק לנערה
°28 ק נערה , °29 ק הנערה

לֹא־קִדְּמוּ אֶתְכֶם בַּלֶּחֶם וּבַמַּיִם בַּדֶּרֶךְ בְּצֵאתְכֶם

as-to-come-you on-the-way and-with-the-waters with-the-bread you they-met not

מִמִּצְרַיִם וַאֲשֶׁר שָׂכַר עָלֶיךָ אֶת־בִּלְעָם בֶּן־בְּעוֹר מִפְּתוֹר

from-Pethor Beor son-of Balaam *** against-you he-hired and-that from-Egypt

אֲרַם נַהֲרַיִם לְקַלְלֶךָּ׃ וְלֹא־אָבָה יְהוָה אֱלֹהֶיךָ לִשְׁמֹעַ

to-listen God-of-you Yahweh he-would but-not (6) to-curse-you Naharaim Aram

אֶל־בִּלְעָם וַיַּהֲפֹךְ יְהוָה אֱלֹהֶיךָ לְּךָ אֶת־הַקְּלָלָה לִבְרָכָה

to-blessing the-curse *** for-you God-of-you Yahweh but-he-turned Balaam to

כִּי אֲהֵבְךָ יְהוָה אֱלֹהֶיךָ׃ לֹא־תִדְרֹשׁ שְׁלֹמָם

peace-of-them you-seek not (7) God-of-you Yahweh he-loves-you for

וְטֹבָתָם כָּל־יָמֶיךָ לְעוֹלָם׃ לֹא־תְתַעֵב אֲדֹמִי כִּי

for Edomite you-abhor not (8) for-ever days-of-you all-of or-good-of-them

אָחִיךָ הוּא לֹא־תְתַעֵב מִצְרִי כִּי־גֵר הָיִיתָ בְאַרְצוֹ׃

in-land-of-him you-were alien for Egyptian you-abhor not he brother-of-you

בָּנִים אֲשֶׁר־יִוָּלְדוּ לָהֶם דּוֹר שְׁלִישִׁי יָבֹא

they-may-enter third generation to-them they-are-born that children (9)

לָהֶם בִּקְהַל יְהוָה׃ כִּי־תֵצֵא מַחֲנֶה עַל־

against camp you-set-up when (10) Yahweh to-assembly-of of-them

אֹיְבֶיךָ וְנִשְׁמַרְתָּ מִכֹּל דָּבָר רָע׃ כִּי־

if (11) impure thing from-every-of then-you-keep-away being-enemies-of-you

יִהְיֶה בְךָ אִישׁ אֲשֶׁר לֹא־יִהְיֶה טָהוֹר מִקְּרֵה־לָיְלָה וְיָצָא

then-he-must-go night from-emision-of clean he-is not who man among-you he-is

אֶל־מִחוּץ לַמַּחֲנֶה לֹא יָבֹא אֶל־תּוֹךְ הַמַּחֲנֶה׃

the-camp midst-of into he-may-enter not of-the-camp outside to

וְהָיָה לִפְנוֹת־עֶרֶב יִרְחַץ בַּמָּיִם

with-the-waters he-must-wash evening to-approach but-he-will-be (12)

וּכְבֹא הַשֶּׁמֶשׁ יָבֹא אֶל־תּוֹךְ הַמַּחֲנֶה׃ וְיָד

and-place (13) the-camp midst-of into he-may-return the-sun and-when-to-set

תִּהְיֶה לְךָ מִחוּץ לַמַּחֲנֶה וְיָצָאתָ שָׁמָּה חוּץ׃

outside to-there so-you-can-go of-the-camp outside for-you she-must-be

וְיָתֵד תִּהְיֶה לְךָ עַל־אֲזֵנֶךָ וְהָיָה

and-he-will-be equipment-of-you with for-you she-must-be and-digger (14)

בְּשִׁבְתְּךָ חוּץ וְחָפַרְתָּה בָהּ וְשַׁבְתָּ

and-you-return with-her then-you-shall-dig outside when-to-relieve-you

וְכִסִּיתָ אֶת־צֵאָתֶךָ׃ כִּי יְהוָה אֱלֹהֶיךָ מִתְהַלֵּךְ ׀

moving God-of-you Yahweh for (15) excrement-of-you *** and-you-cover

בְּקֶרֶב מַחֲנֶךָ לְהַצִּילְךָ וְלָתֵת אֹיְבֶיךָ

being-enemies-of-you and-to-deliver to-protect-you camp-of-you in-among

come to meet you with bread
and water on your way when
you came out of Egypt, and
they hired Balaam son of Beor
from Pethor in Aram Naha-
raim[h] to pronounce a curse on
you. 5However, the LORD your
God would not listen to Balaam but turned the curse into
a blessing for you, because the
LORD your God loves you. 6Do
not seek peace or good relations with them as long as you
live.

7Do not abhor an Edomite,
for he is your brother. Do not
abhor an Egyptian, because
you lived as an alien in his
country. 8The third generation
of children born to them may
enter the assembly of the
LORD.

Uncleanness in the Camp

9When you are encamped
against your enemies, keep
away from everything im-
pure. 10If one of your men is
unclean because of a noctur-
nal emission, he is to go outside the camp and stay there.
11But as evening approaches
he is to wash himself, and at
sunset he may return to the
camp.

12Designate a place outside
the camp where you can go to
relieve yourself. 13As part of
your equipment have some-
thing to dig with, and when
you relieve yourself, dig a hole
and cover up your excrement.
14For the LORD your God
moves about in your camp to
protect you and to deliver your

h4 That is, Northwest Mesopotamia

*See the note on page 548.

לְפָנֶיךָ וְהָיָה מַחֲנֶיךָ קָדוֹשׁ וְלֹא־ יִרְאֶה בְךָ
among-you he-will-see so-not holy camps-of-you so-he-must-be before-you

עֶרְוַת דָּבָר וְשָׁב מֵאַחֲרֶיךָ׃ לֹא־ תַסְגִּיר
you-hand-over not (16) away-from-you and-he-will-turn thing indecent-of

עֶבֶד אֶל־ אֲדֹנָיו אֲשֶׁר־ יִנָּצֵל אֵלֶיךָ מֵעִם אֲדֹנָיו׃
master-of-him from-with with-you he-took-refuge that master-of-him to slave

עִמְּךָ יֵשֵׁב בְּקִרְבְּךָ בַּמָּקוֹם אֲשֶׁר־ יִבְחַר
he-chooses that in-the-place in-among-you let-him-live with-you (17)

בְּאַחַד שְׁעָרֶיךָ בַּטּוֹב לוֹ לֹא תּוֹנֶנּוּ׃ לֹא־
not (18) you-oppress-him not to-him as-the-good gates-of-you within-any-of

תִהְיֶה קְדֵשָׁה מִבְּנוֹת יִשְׂרָאֵל וְלֹא־
and-not Israel from-daughters-of temple-prostitute she-shall-become

יִהְיֶה קָדֵשׁ מִבְּנֵי יִשְׂרָאֵל׃ לֹא־ תָבִיא
you-bring not (19) Israel from-sons-of temple-prostitute he-shall-become

אֶתְנַן זוֹנָה וּמְחִיר כֶּלֶב בֵּית יְהוָה אֱלֹהֶיךָ
God-of-you Yahweh house-of dog or-hire-of female-prostitute earning-of

לְכָל־ נֶדֶר כִּי תוֹעֲבַת יְהוָה אֱלֹהֶיךָ גַּם־ שְׁנֵיהֶם׃
both-of-them indeed God-of-you Yahweh detestable-of for vow for-any-of

לֹא־ תַשִּׁיךְ לְאָחִיךָ נֶשֶׁךְ כֶּסֶף נֶשֶׁךְ
interest-of money interest-of to-brother-of-you you-charge-interest not (20)

אֹכֶל נֶשֶׁךְ כָּל־ דָּבָר אֲשֶׁר יִשָּׁךְ׃ לַנָּכְרִי
to-foreigner (21) he-may-earn-interest that thing any-of interest-of food

תַשִּׁיךְ וּלְאָחִיךָ לֹא תַשִּׁיךְ לְמַעַן
so-that you-charge-interest not but-to-brother-of-you you-may-charge-interest

יְבָרֶכְךָ יְהוָה אֱלֹהֶיךָ בְּכֹל מִשְׁלַח יָדֶךָ עַל־
in hand-of-you work-of in-every-of God-of-you Yahweh he-may-bless-you

הָאָרֶץ אֲשֶׁר־ אַתָּה בָא־ שָׁמָּה לְרִשְׁתָּהּ׃ כִּי־ תִדֹּר נֶדֶר
vow you-vow if (22) to-possess-her to-there entering you that the-land

לַיהוָה אֱלֹהֶיךָ לֹא תְאַחֵר לְשַׁלְּמוֹ כִּי־ דָרֹשׁ
to-demand for to-pay-him you-be-slow not God-of-you to-Yahweh

יִדְרְשֶׁנּוּ יְהוָה אֱלֹהֶיךָ מֵעִמָּךְ וְהָיָה בְךָ
on-you and-he-will-be from-with-you God-of-you Yahweh he-will-demand-him

חֵטְא׃ וְכִי תֶחְדַּל לִנְדֹּר לֹא־ יִהְיֶה בְךָ חֵטְא׃
guilt on-you he-will-be not from-to-vow you-refrain but-if (23) guilt

מוֹצָא שְׂפָתֶיךָ תִּשְׁמֹר וְעָשִׂיתָ כַּאֲשֶׁר נָדַרְתָּ
you-vowed just-as and-you-do you-be-sure lips-of-you thing-from (24)

לַיהוָה אֱלֹהֶיךָ נְדָבָה אֲשֶׁר דִּבַּרְתָּ בְּפִיךָ׃ כִּי
if (25) with-mouth-of-you you-promised that freely God-of-you to-Yahweh

enemies to you. Your camp must be holy, so that he will not see among you anything indecent and turn away from you.

Miscellaneous Laws

[15]If a slave has taken refuge with you, do not hand him over to his master. [16]Let him live among you wherever he likes and in whatever town he chooses. Do not oppress him.

[17]No Israelite man or woman is to become a temple prostitute. [18]You must not bring the earnings of a female prostitute or of a male prostitute[i] into the house of the LORD your God to pay any vow, because the LORD your God detests them both.

[19]Do not charge your brother interest, whether on money or food or anything else that may earn interest. [20]You may charge a foreigner interest, but not a brother Israelite, so that the LORD your God may bless you in everything you put your hand to in the land you are entering to possess.

[21]If you make a vow to the LORD your God, do not be slow to pay it, for the LORD your God will certainly demand it of you and you will be guilty of sin. [22]But if you refrain from making a vow, you will not be guilty. [23]Whatever your lips utter you must be sure to do, because you made your vow freely to the LORD your God with your own mouth.

[i]18 Hebrew *of a dog*

*See the note on page 548.

תָבֹא בְּכֶרֶם רֵעֶךָ וְאָכַלְתָּ עֲנָבִים

grapes then-you-may-eat neighbor-of-you into-vineyard-of you-enter

כְּנַפְשְׁךָ שָׂבְעֶךָ וְאֶל־ כֶּלְיְךָ לֹא תִתֵּן׃ (26) כִּי

if (26) you-put not basket-of-you but-in want-of-you as-desire-of-you

תָבֹא בְּקָמַת רֵעֶךָ וְקָטַפְתָּ מְלִילֹת

kernels then-you-may-pick neighbor-of-you into-grainfield-of you-enter

בְּיָדֶךָ וְחֶרְמֵשׁ לֹא תָנִיף עַל קָמַת רֵעֶךָ׃

neighbor-of-you standing-grain-of to you-put not but-sickle with-hand-of-you

(24:1) כִּי־ יִקַּח אִישׁ אִשָּׁה וּבְעָלָהּ וְהָיָה אִם־לֹא תִמְצָא־

she-finds not if and-he-is and-he-marries-her woman man he-takes if (24:1)

חֵן בְּעֵינָיו כִּי־ מָצָא בָהּ עֶרְוַת דָּבָר

thing indecent-of about-her he-finds because in-eyes-of-him favor

וְכָתַב לָהּ סֵפֶר כְּרִיתֻת וְנָתַן בְּיָדָהּ

in-hand-of-her and-he-gives divorce certificate-of for-her and-he-writes

וְשִׁלְּחָהּ מִבֵּיתוֹ׃ (2) וְיָצְאָה מִבֵּיתוֹ

from-house-of-him and-she-leaves (2) from-house-of-him and-he-sends-her

וְהָלְכָה וְהָיְתָה לְאִישׁ־ אַחֵר׃ (3) וּשְׂנֵאָהּ הָאִישׁ

the-man and-he-dislikes-her (3) another to-man and-she-becomes and-she-goes

הָאַחֲרוֹן וְכָתַב לָהּ סֵפֶר כְּרִיתֻת וְנָתַן

and-he-gives divorce certificate-of for-her and-he-writes the-second

בְּיָדָהּ וְשִׁלְּחָהּ מִבֵּיתוֹ אוֹ כִי יָמוּת הָאִישׁ

the-man he-dies if or from-house-of-him and-he-sends-her in-hand-of-her

הָאַחֲרוֹן אֲשֶׁר־ לְקָחָהּ לוֹ לְאִשָּׁה׃ (4) לֹא־ יוּכַל

he-is-allowed not (4) as-wife for-him he-took-her that the-second

בַּעְלָהּ הָרִאשׁוֹן אֲשֶׁר־ שִׁלְּחָהּ לָשׁוּב לְקַחְתָּהּ לִהְיוֹת

to-be to-take-her to-return he-divorced-her who the-first husband-of-her

לוֹ לְאִשָּׁה אַחֲרֵי אֲשֶׁר הֻטַּמָּאָה כִּי־ תוֹעֵבָה הִוא לִפְנֵי יְהוָה

Yahweh before that detestable for she-was-defiled when after as-wife to-him

וְלֹא תַחֲטִיא אֶת־ הָאָרֶץ אֲשֶׁר יְהוָה אֱלֹהֶיךָ נֹתֵן לְךָ

to-you giving God-of-you Yahweh that the-land *** you-bring-sin so-not

נַחֲלָה׃ (5) כִּי־ יִקַּח אִישׁ אִשָּׁה חֲדָשָׁה לֹא יֵצֵא בַּצָּבָא וְלֹא־

or-not to-the-war he-must-go not recent wife man he-takes if (5) inheritance

יַעֲבֹר עָלָיו לְכָל־ דָּבָר נָקִי יִהְיֶה לְבֵיתוֹ שָׁנָה אֶחָת

one year at-home-of-him he-must-be free duty as-any-of on-him he-must-lay

וְשִׂמַּח אֶת־ אִשְׁתּוֹ אֲשֶׁר־ לָקָח׃ (6) לֹא־

not (6) he-married that wife-of-him *** and-he-must-bring-happiness

יַחֲבֹל רֵחַיִם וָרָכֶב כִּי־ נֶפֶשׁ הוּא חֹבֵל׃

being-security that livelihood for or-upper two-millstones you-take-as-security

24If you enter your neighbor's vineyard, you may eat all
the grapes you want, but do
not put any in your basket. 25If
you enter your neighbor's
grainfield, you may pick kernels with your hands, but you
must not put a sickle to his
standing grain.

24 If a man marries a
woman who becomes
displeasing to him because he
finds something indecent
about her, and he writes her a
certificate of divorce, gives it
to her and sends her from his
house, 2and if after she leaves
his house she becomes the
wife of another man, 3and her
second husband dislikes her
and writes her a certificate of
divorce, gives it to her and
sends her from his house, or if
he dies, 4then her first husband, who divorced her, is not
allowed to marry her again after she has been defiled. That
would be detestable in the
eyes of the LORD. Do not bring
sin upon the land the LORD
your God is giving you as an
inheritance.

5If a man has recently married, he must not be sent to
war or have any other duty
laid on him. For one year he is
to be free to stay at home and
bring happiness to the wife he
has married.

6Do not take a pair of mill-
stones—not even the upper
one—as security for a debt, because that would be taking a
man's livelihood as security.

*See the note on page 548.

מִבְּנֵי יִשְׂרָאֵל מֵאֶחָיו נֶפֶשׁ גֹּנֵב אִישׁ יִמָּצֵא כִּֽי־
Israel from-sons-of of-brothers-of-him one kidnapping man he-is-caught if (7)

הַגַּנָּב וּמֵת וּמְכָרוֹ בּוֹ וְהִתְעַמֶּר־
the-kidnapper then-he-must-die or-he-sells-him to-him and-he-treats-as-slave

בְּנֶֽגַע־ הִשָּׁמֶר מִקִּרְבֶּֽךָ׃ הָרָע וּבִעַרְתָּ הַהוּא
about-disease-of be-careful! (8) from-among-you the-evil so-you-purge the-that

אֶתְכֶם יוֹרוּ אֲשֶׁר־ כְּכֹל וְלַעֲשׂוֹת מְאֹד לִשְׁמֹר הַצָּרַעַת
you they-instruct that as-all and-to-do very to-be-careful the-leprosy

לַעֲשֽׂוֹת׃ תִּשְׁמְרוּ צִוִּיתִם כַּאֲשֶׁר הַלְוִיִּם הַכֹּהֲנִים
to-follow you-be-careful I-commanded-them just-as the-Levites the-priests

בַּדֶּרֶךְ לְמִרְיָם אֱלֹהֶיךָ יְהוָה עָשָׂה אֵת אֲשֶׁר־ זָכוֹר
along-the-way to-Miriam God-of-you Yahweh he-did what *** to-remember (9)

בְרֵֽעֲךָ* תַשֶּׁה כִּֽי־ מִמִּצְרָֽיִם׃ בְּצֵאתְכֶם
to-neighbor-of-you you-make-loan when (10) from-Egypt after-to-come-you

עֲבֹטֽוֹ׃ לַעֲבֹט בֵּיתוֹ אֶל־ תָבֹא לֹא־ מְאוּמָה מַשַּׁאת
pledge-of-him to-get-pledge house-of-him into you-go not any-kind loan-of

יוֹצִיא בּוֹ נֹשֶׁה אַתָּה אֲשֶׁר וְהָאִישׁ תַּעֲמֹד בַּחוּץ
let-him-bring to-him loaning you whom and-the-man you-stay on-the-outside (11)

תִשְׁכַּב לֹא הוּא עָנִי אִישׁ וְאִם־ הַחֽוּצָה׃ הַעֲבוֹט אֶֽת־ אֵלֶיךָ
you-sleep not he poor man and-if (12) to-the-outside the-pledge *** to-you

כְּבֹא הָעֲבוֹט אֶֽת־ לוֹ תָּשִׁיב הָשֵׁב בַּעֲבֹטֽוֹ׃
as-to-set the-pledge *** to-him you-return to-return (13) with-pledge-of-him

וּלְךָ וּבֵֽרְכֶךָּ בְּשַׂלְמָתוֹ וְשָׁכַב הַשֶּׁמֶשׁ
and-to-you then-he-will-thank-you in-cloak-of-him so-he-may-sleep the-sun

תַעֲשֹׁק לֹא־ אֱלֹהֶֽיךָ׃ יְהוָה לִפְנֵי צְדָקָה תִּהְיֶה
you-take-advantage not (14) God-of-you Yahweh before righteous-act she-will-be

אֲשֶׁר מִגֵּרְךָ אוֹ מֵאַחֶיךָ וְאֶבְיוֹן עָנִי שָׂכִיר
who from-alien-of-you or from-brothers-of-you and-needy poor hired-man

וְֽלֹא־ שְׂכָרוֹ תִתֵּן בְּיוֹמוֹ בִּשְׁעָרֶֽיךָ׃ בְּאַרְצְךָ
and-not wage-of-him you-pay on-day-of-him (15) in-gates-of-you in-land-of-you

נַפְשׁוֹ אֶת־ נֹשֵׂא הוּא וְאֵלָיו הוּא עָנִי כִּי הַשֶּׁמֶשׁ עָלָיו תָבוֹא
life-of-him *** basing he and-on-him he poor for the-sun on-him she-may-set

לֹא־ חֵֽטְא׃ בְךָ וְהָיָה יְהוָה אֶל־ עָלֶיךָ יִקְרָא וְלֹֽא־
not (16) guilt on-you and-he-will-be Yahweh to against-you he-may-cry so-not

עַל־ יוּמְתוּ לֹא־ וּבָנִים בָּנִים עַל־ אָבוֹת יוּמְתוּ
for they-shall-die not and-children children for fathers they-shall-die

מִשְׁפַּט תַטֶּה לֹא יוּמָֽתוּ׃ בְּחֶטְאוֹ אִישׁ אָבוֹת
justice-of you-deprive not (17) they-shall-die for-sin-of-him each fathers

7 If a man is caught kidnapping one of his brother Israelites and treats him as a slave or sells him, the kidnapper must die. You must purge the evil from among you.

8 In cases of leprous[j] diseases be very careful to do exactly as the priests, who are Levites, instruct you. You must follow carefully what I have commanded them. 9 Remember what the LORD your God did to Miriam along the way after you came out of Egypt.

10 When you make a loan of any kind to your neighbor, do not go into his house to get what he is offering as a pledge. 11 Stay outside and let the man to whom you are making the loan bring the pledge out to you. 12 If the man is poor, do not go to sleep with his pledge in your possession. 13 Return his cloak to him by sunset so that he may sleep in it. Then he will thank you, and it will be regarded as a righteous act in the sight of the LORD your God.

14 Do not take advantage of a hired man who is poor and needy, whether he is a brother Israelite or an alien living in one of your towns. 15 Pay him his wages each day before sunset, because he is poor and is counting on it. Otherwise he may cry to the LORD against you, and you will be guilty of sin.

16 Fathers shall not be put to death for their children, nor children put to death for their fathers; each is to die for his own sin.

17 Do not deprive the alien or

j8 The Hebrew word was used for various diseases affecting the skin—not necessarily leprosy.

*10 Most mss have the accent *tiphhah* under the *kaph* (בְרֵעֲךָ).

גֵּר יָתוֹם וְלֹא תַחֲבֹל בֶּגֶד אַלְמָנָה׃ וְזָכַרְתָּ
and-you-remember (18) widow cloak-of you-take-pledge and-not fatherless alien

כִּי עֶבֶד הָיִיתָ בְּמִצְרַיִם וַיִּפְדְּךָ יְהוָה אֱלֹהֶיךָ מִשָּׁם
from-there God-of-you Yahweh and-he-redeemed-you in-Egypt you-were slave that

עַל־כֵּן אָנֹכִי מְצַוְּךָ לַעֲשׂוֹת אֶת־הַדָּבָר הַזֶּה׃ כִּי תִקְצֹר
you-harvest when (19) the-this the-thing *** to-do commanding-you I this for

קְצִירְךָ בְשָׂדֶךָ וְשָׁכַחְתָּ עֹמֶר בַּשָּׂדֶה לֹא
not in-the-field sheaf and-you-overlook in-field-of-you harvest-of-you

תָשׁוּב לְקַחְתּוֹ לַגֵּר לַיָּתוֹם וְלָאַלְמָנָה
and-for-the-widow for-the-fatherless for-the-alien to-get-him you-go-back

יִהְיֶה לְמַעַן יְבָרֶכְךָ יְהוָה אֱלֹהֶיךָ בְּכֹל מַעֲשֵׂה
work-of in-all-of God-of-you Yahweh he-may-bless-you so-that he-is

יָדֶיךָ׃ כִּי תַחְבֹּט זֵיתְךָ לֹא תְפַאֵר אַחֲרֶיךָ
after-you you-go-over not olive-tree-of-you you-beat when (20) hands-of-you

לַגֵּר לַיָּתוֹם וְלָאַלְמָנָה יִהְיֶה׃ כִּי תִבְצֹר
you-harvest when (21) he-is and-for-the-widow for-the-fatherless for-the-alien

כַּרְמְךָ לֹא תְעוֹלֵל אַחֲרֶיךָ לַגֵּר לַיָּתוֹם
for-the-fatherless for-the-alien after-you you-go-over-vine not vineyard-of-you

וְלָאַלְמָנָה יִהְיֶה׃ וְזָכַרְתָּ כִּי־עֶבֶד הָיִיתָ בְּאֶרֶץ
in-land-of you-were slave that and-you-remember (22) he-is and-for-the-widow

מִצְרָיִם עַל־כֵּן אָנֹכִי מְצַוְּךָ לַעֲשׂוֹת אֶת־הַדָּבָר הַזֶּה׃ כִּי־
when (25:1) the-this the-thing *** to-do commanding-you I this for Egypt

יִהְיֶה רִיב בֵּין אֲנָשִׁים וְנִגְּשׁוּ אֶל־הַמִּשְׁפָּט
the-court to then-they-must-go men between dispute he-is

וּשְׁפָטוּם וְהִצְדִּיקוּ אֶת־הַצַּדִּיק
the-innocent *** and-they-will-acquit and-they-will-judge-them

וְהִרְשִׁיעוּ אֶת־הָרָשָׁע׃ וְהָיָה אִם־בִּן
deserving-of if and-he-will-be (2) the-guilty *** and-they-will-condemn

הַכּוֹת הָרָשָׁע וְהִפִּילוֹ הַשֹּׁפֵט
the-one-judging then-he-shall-make-lie-down him the-guilty to-beat

וְהִכָּהוּ לְפָנָיו כְּדֵי רִשְׁעָתוֹ בְּמִסְפָּר׃
in-number crime-of-him as-deserving-of before-him and-he-shall-flog-him

אַרְבָּעִים יַכֶּנּוּ לֹא יֹסִיף פֶּן־יֹסִיף
he-gives-more if he-shall-give-more not he-shall-flog-him forty (3)

לְהַכֹּתוֹ עַל־אֵלֶּה מַכָּה רַבָּה וְנִקְלָה אָחִיךָ
brother-of-you then-he-will-be-degraded many lash these than to-flog-him

לְעֵינֶיךָ׃ לֹא־תַחְסֹם שׁוֹר בְּדִישׁוֹ׃ כִּי־יֵשְׁבוּ
they-live if (5) while-to-tread-him ox you-muzzle not (4) in-eyes-of-you

the fatherless of justice, or take
the cloak of the widow as a
pledge. [18]Remember that you
were slaves in Egypt and the
Lord your God redeemed you
from there. That is why I command you to do this.
[19]When you are harvesting
in your field and you overlook
a sheaf, do not go back to get
it. Leave it for the alien, the
fatherless and the widow, so
that the Lord your God may
bless you in all the work of
your hands. [20]When you beat
the olives from your trees, do
not go over the branches a second time. Leave what remains
for the alien, the fatherless
and the widow. [21]When you
harvest the grapes in your
vineyard, do not go over the
vines again. Leave what remains for the alien, the fatherless and the widow. [22]Remem-
ber that you were slaves in
Egypt. That is why I command
you to do this.
25 When men have a dis-
pute, they are to take it
to court and the judges will decide the case, acquitting the
innocent and condemning the
guilty. [2]If the guilty man deserves to be beaten, the judge
shall make him lie down and
have him flogged in his presence with the number of
lashes his crime deserves, [3]but
he must not give him more
than forty lashes. If he is
flogged more than that, your
brother will be degraded in
your eyes.
[4]Do not muzzle an ox while
it is treading out the grain.

אַחִים יַחְדָּו וּמֵת אַחַד מֵהֶם וּבֵן אֵין־ לוֹ לֹא־
not to-him there-is-no and-son of-them one and-he-dies together brothers

תִהְיֶה אֵשֶׁת־ הַמֵּת הַחוּצָה לְאִישׁ זָר
stranger to-man on-the-outside the-one-dead widow-of she-must-marry

יְבָמָהּ יָבֹא עָלֶיהָ וּלְקָחָהּ לוֹ
to-him and-he-must-take-her to-her he-must-come brother-of-husband-to-her

לְאִשָּׁה וְיִבְּמָהּ׃ וְהָיָה הַבְּכוֹר
the-firstborn and-he-will-be (6) and-he-must-do-duty-of-brother-in-law-of-her as-wife

אֲשֶׁר תֵּלֵד יָקוּם עַל־ שֵׁם אָחִיו הַמֵּת וְלֹא־
so-not the-dead brother-of-him name-of on he-shall-carry she-bears whom

יִמָּחֶה שְׁמוֹ מִיִּשְׂרָאֵל׃ וְאִם־ לֹא יַחְפֹּץ הָאִישׁ
the-man he-wants not but-if (7) from-Israel name-of-him he-is-blotted-out

לָקַחַת אֶת־ יְבִמְתּוֹ וְעָלְתָה יְבִמְתּוֹ
wife-of-brother-of-him then-she-shall-go wife-of-brother-of-him *** to-marry

הַשַּׁעְרָה אֶל־ הַזְּקֵנִים וְאָמְרָה מֵאֵין* יְבָמִי
brother-of-husband-of-me he-refuses and-she-shall-say the-elders to to-the-gate

לְהָקִים לְאָחִיו שֵׁם בְּיִשְׂרָאֵל לֹא אָבָה יַבְּמִי׃
to-fulfill-duty-to-me he-will not in-Israel name for-brother-of-him to-carry-on

וְקָרְאוּ־ לוֹ זִקְנֵי־ עִירוֹ וְדִבְּרוּ
and-they-shall-talk city-of-him elders-of for-him and-they-shall-summon (8)

אֵלָיו וְעָמַד וְאָמַר לֹא חָפַצְתִּי לְקַחְתָּהּ׃ וְנִגְּשָׁה
then-she-shall-go (9) to-marry-her I-want not and-he-says if-he-persists to-him

יְבִמְתּוֹ אֵלָיו לְעֵינֵי הַזְּקֵנִים וְחָלְצָה
and-she-shall-take-off the-elders before-eyes-of to-him widow-of-brother-of-him

נַעֲלוֹ מֵעַל רַגְלוֹ וְיָרְקָה בְּפָנָיו
in-faces-of-him and-she-shall-spit foot-of-him from-on sandal-of-him

וְעָנְתָה וְאָמְרָה כָּכָה יֵעָשֶׂה לָאִישׁ אֲשֶׁר לֹא־
not who to-the-man he-is-done this and-she-shall-say and-she-shall-speak

יִבְנֶה אֶת־ בֵּית אָחִיו׃ וְנִקְרָא
and-he-will-be-known (10) brother-of-him family-line-of *** he-will-build-up

שְׁמוֹ בְּיִשְׂרָאֵל בֵּית חֲלוּץ הַנָּעַל׃ כִּי־ יִנָּצוּ
they-fight if (11) the-sandal being-removed-of family-of in-Israel name-of-him

אֲנָשִׁים יַחְדָּו אִישׁ וְאָחִיו וְקָרְבָה אֵשֶׁת הָאֶחָד לְהַצִּיל
to-rescue the-one wife-of and-she-comes and-brother-of-him man together men

אֶת־ אִישָׁהּ מִיַּד מַכֵּהוּ וְשָׁלְחָה
and-she-reaches-out one-assaulting-him from-hand-of husband-of-her ***

יָדָהּ וְהֶחֱזִיקָה בִּמְבֻשָׁיו׃ וְקַצֹּתָה
then-you-cut-off (12) on-private-parts-of-him and-she-seizes hand-of-her

5If brothers are living together and one of them dies
without a son, his widow
must not marry outside the
family. Her husband's brother
shall take her and marry her
and fulfill the duty of a brother-in-law to her. 6The first son
she bears shall carry on the
name of the dead brother so
that his name will not be blot-
ted out from Israel.
7However, if a man does not
want to marry his brother's
wife, she shall go to the elders
at the town gate and say, "My
husband's brother refuses to
carry on his brother's name in
Israel. He will not fulfill the
duty of a brother-in-law to
me." 8Then the elders of his
town shall summon him and
talk to him. If he persists in
saying, "I do not want to marry her," 9his brother's widow
shall go up to him in the presence of the elders, take off one
of his sandals, spit in his face
and say, "This is what is done
to the man who will not build
up his brother's family line."
10That man's line shall be
known in Israel as The Family
of the Unsandaled.
11If two men are fighting and
the wife of one of them comes
to rescue her husband from
his assailant, and she reaches
out and seizes him by his private parts, 12you shall cut off

*7 Most mss have no *yod* (מֵאַן).

אֶת־ כַּפָּהּ לֹא תָחוֹס עֵינֶךָ׃ לֹא־ יִהְיֶה לְךָ

to-you he-must-be not (13) eye-of-you she-must-pity not hand-of-her ***

בְּכִיסְךָ אֶבֶן וָאָבֶן גְּדוֹלָה וּקְטַנָּה׃ לֹא־ יִהְיֶה לְךָ

to-you he-must-be not (14) and-light heavy and-weight weight in-bag-of-you

בְּבֵיתְךָ אֵיפָה וְאֵיפָה גְּדוֹלָה וּקְטַנָּה׃ אֶבֶן שְׁלֵמָה

accurate weight (15) and-small large and-measure measure in-house-of-you

וָצֶדֶק יִהְיֶה־ לָּךְ אֵיפָה שְׁלֵמָה וָצֶדֶק יִהְיֶה־ לָּךְ

to-you he-must-be and-honest accurate measure to-you he-must-be and-honest

לְמַעַן יַאֲרִיכוּ יָמֶיךָ עַל הָאֲדָמָה אֲשֶׁר־ יְהוָה אֱלֹהֶיךָ

God-of-you Yahweh that the-land in days-of-you they-may-be-long so-that

נֹתֵן לָךְ׃ כִּי תוֹעֲבַת יְהוָה אֱלֹהֶיךָ כָּל־ עֹשֵׂה אֵלֶּה

these doing any-of God-of-you Yahweh detestable-of for (16) to-you giving

כֹּל עֹשֵׂה עָוֶל׃ זָכוֹר אֵת אֲשֶׁר־ עָשָׂה לְךָ עֲמָלֵק

Amalek to-you he-did what *** to-remember (17) dishonestly dealing any-of

בַּדֶּרֶךְ בְּצֵאתְכֶם מִמִּצְרָיִם׃ אֲשֶׁר קָרְךָ בַּדֶּרֶךְ

on-the-journey he-met-you when (18) from-Egypt when-to-come-you along-the-way

וַיְזַנֵּב בְּךָ כָּל־ הַנֶּחֱשָׁלִים אַחֲרֶיךָ* וְאַתָּה עָיֵף

weary and-you behind-you the-ones-lagging all-of from-you and-he-cut-off

וְיָגֵעַ וְלֹא יָרֵא אֱלֹהִים׃ וְהָיָה בְּהָנִיחַ

when-to-give-rest and-he-will-be (19) God he-feared and-not and-worn-out

יְהוָה אֱלֹהֶיךָ ׀ לְךָ מִכָּל־ אֹיְבֶיךָ מִסָּבִיב

from-around being-enemies-of-you from-all-of to-you God-of-you Yahweh

בָּאָרֶץ אֲשֶׁר יְהוָה־ אֱלֹהֶיךָ נֹתֵן לְךָ נַחֲלָה לְרִשְׁתָּהּ

to-possess-her inheritance to-you giving God-of-you Yahweh that in-the-land

תִּמְחֶה אֶת־ זֵכֶר עֲמָלֵק מִתַּחַת הַשָּׁמָיִם לֹא תִּשְׁכָּח׃

you-forget not the-heavens from-under Amalek memory-of *** you-shall-blot-out

וְהָיָה כִּי־ תָבוֹא אֶל־ הָאָרֶץ אֲשֶׁר יְהוָה אֱלֹהֶיךָ

God-of-you Yahweh that the-land into you-enter when and-he-will-be (26:1)

נֹתֵן לְךָ נַחֲלָה וִירִשְׁתָּהּ וְיָשַׁבְתָּ בָּהּ׃

in-her and-you-settle and-you-possess-her inheritance to-you giving

וְלָקַחְתָּ מֵרֵאשִׁית ׀ כָּל־ פְּרִי הָאֲדָמָה אֲשֶׁר תָּבִיא

you-produce that the-soil fruit-of all-of from-firstfruit-of then-you-take (2)

מֵאַרְצְךָ אֲשֶׁר יְהוָה אֱלֹהֶיךָ נֹתֵן לָךְ וְשַׂמְתָּ

and-you-put to-you giving God-of-you Yahweh that from-land-of-you

בַטֶּנֶא וְהָלַכְתָּ אֶל־הַמָּקוֹם אֲשֶׁר יִבְחַר יְהוָה אֱלֹהֶיךָ

God-of-you Yahweh he-will-choose that the-place to then-you-go in-the-basket

לְשַׁכֵּן שְׁמוֹ שָׁם׃ וּבָאתָ אֶל־ הַכֹּהֵן אֲשֶׁר יִהְיֶה

he-is who the-priest to and-you-go (3) there name-of-him to-make-dwell

her hand. Show her no pity.
[13]Do not have two differing weights in your bag—one heavy, one light. [14]Do not have two differing measures in your house—one large, one small. [15]You must have accurate and honest weights and measures, so that you may live long in the land the LORD your God is giving you. [16]For the LORD your God detests anyone who does these things, anyone who deals dishonestly.

[17]Remember what the Amalekites did to you along the way when you came out of Egypt. [18]When you were weary and worn out, they met you on your journey and cut off all who were lagging behind; they had no fear of God. [19]When the LORD your God gives you rest from all the enemies around you in the land he is giving you to possess as an inheritance, you shall blot out the memory of Amalek from under heaven. Do not forget!

Firstfruits and Tithes

26 When you have entered the land the LORD your God is giving you as an inheritance and have taken possession of it and settled in it, [2]take some of the firstfruits of all that you produce from the soil of the land the LORD your God is giving you and put them in a basket. Then go to the place the LORD your God will choose as a dwelling for his Name [3]and say to the

*18 Most mss have no *hateph pathah* under the *beth* (אַחֲ׳).

בַּיָּמִים הָהֵם וְאָמַרְתָּ אֵלָיו הִגַּדְתִּי הַיּוֹם לַיהוָה
to-Yahweh the-day I-declare to-him and-you-say the-those in-the-days

אֱלֹהֶיךָ כִּי־בָאתִי אֶל־הָאָרֶץ אֲשֶׁר נִשְׁבַּע יְהוָה לַאֲבֹתֵינוּ
to-fathers-of-us Yahweh he-swore that the-land into I-came that God-of-you

לָתֶת לָנוּ׃ וְלָקַח הַכֹּהֵן הַטֶּנֶא מִיָּדֶךָ
from-hand-of-you the-basket the-priest and-he-shall-take (4) to-us to-give

וְהִנִּיחוֹ לִפְנֵי מִזְבַּח יְהוָה אֱלֹהֶיךָ׃ וְעָנִיתָ
then-you-declare (5) God-of-you Yahweh altar-of in-front-of and-he-shall-set-him

וְאָמַרְתָּ לִפְנֵי יְהוָה אֱלֹהֶיךָ אֲרַמִּי אֹבֵד אָבִי
father-of-me wandering Aramean God-of-you Yahweh before and-you-say

וַיֵּרֶד מִצְרַיְמָה וַיָּגָר שָׁם בִּמְתֵי מְעָט וַיְהִי־
and-he-became few with-people-of there and-he-lived to-Egypt and-he-went-down

שָׁם לְגוֹי גָּדוֹל עָצוּם וָרָב׃ וַיָּרֵעוּ אֹתָנוּ
us but-they-mistreated (6) and-numerous powerful great into-nation there

הַמִּצְרִים וַיְעַנּוּנוּ וַיִּתְּנוּ עָלֵינוּ עֲבֹדָה קָשָׁה׃
hard labor on-us and-they-put and-they-made-suffer-us the-Egyptians

וַנִּצְעַק אֶל־יְהוָה אֱלֹהֵי אֲבֹתֵינוּ וַיִּשְׁמַע יְהוָה אֶת־
*** Yahweh and-he-heard fathers-of-us God-of Yahweh to then-we-cried (7)

קֹלֵנוּ וַיַּרְא אֶת־עָנְיֵנוּ וְאֶת־עֲמָלֵנוּ וְאֶת־לַחֲצֵנוּ׃
oppression-of-us and toil-of-us and misery-of-us *** and-he-saw voice-of-us

וַיּוֹצִאֵנוּ יְהוָה מִמִּצְרַיִם בְּיָד חֲזָקָה וּבִזְרֹעַ
and-with-arm mighty with-hand from-Egypt Yahweh so-he-brought-out-us (8)

נְטוּיָה וּבְמֹרָא גָּדֹל וּבְאֹתוֹת וּבְמֹפְתִים׃
and-with-wonders and-with-signs great and-with-terror being-outstretched

וַיְבִאֵנוּ אֶל־הַמָּקוֹם הַזֶּה וַיִּתֶּן־לָנוּ אֶת־הָאָרֶץ
the-land *** to-us and-he-gave the-this the-place to and-he-brought-us (9)

הַזֹּאת אֶרֶץ זָבַת חָלָב וּדְבָשׁ׃ וְעַתָּה הִנֵּה הֵבֵאתִי אֶת־
*** I-bring see! and-not (10) and-honey milk flowing-of land the-this

רֵאשִׁית פְּרִי הָאֲדָמָה אֲשֶׁר־נָתַתָּה לִּי יְהוָה וְהִנַּחְתּוֹ
then-you-place-him Yahweh to-me you-gave that the-soil fruit-of first-of

לִפְנֵי יְהוָה אֱלֹהֶיךָ וְהִשְׁתַּחֲוִיתָ לִפְנֵי יְהוָה אֱלֹהֶיךָ׃
God-of-you Yahweh before and-you-bow-down God-of-you Yahweh before

וְשָׂמַחְתָּ בְכָל־הַטּוֹב אֲשֶׁר נָתַן־לְךָ יְהוָה אֱלֹהֶיךָ
God-of-you Yahweh to-you he-gave that the-good in-all-of and-you-rejoice (11)

וּלְבֵיתֶךָ אַתָּה וְהַלֵּוִי וְהַגֵּר אֲשֶׁר בְּקִרְבֶּךָ׃
in-among-you who and-the-alien and-the-Levite you and-to-household-of-you

כִּי תְכַלֶּה לַעְשֵׂר אֶת־כָּל־מַעְשַׂר תְּבוּאָתְךָ
produce-of-you tenth-of all-of *** to-set-aside you-finish when (12)

priest in office at the time, "I
declare today to the LORD your
God that I have come to the
land the LORD swore to our
forefathers to give us." 4The
priest shall take the basket
from your hands and set it
down in front of the altar of
the LORD your God. 5Then you
shall declare before the LORD
your God: "My father was a
wandering Aramean, and he
went down into Egypt with a
few people and lived there and
became a great nation, powerful and numerous. 6But the
Egyptians mistreated us and
made us suffer, putting us to
hard labor. 7Then we cried out
to the LORD, the God of our fathers, and the LORD heard our
voice and saw our misery, toil
and oppression. 8So the LORD
brought us out of Egypt with a
mighty hand and an out-
stretched arm, with great terror and with miraculous signs
and wonders. 9He brought us
to this place and gave us this
land, a land flowing with milk
and honey; 10and now I bring
the firstfruits of the soil that
you, O LORD, have given me."
Place the basket before the
LORD your God and bow down
before him. 11And you and the
Levites and the aliens among
you shall rejoice in all the good
things the LORD your God has
given to you and your
household.
12When you have finished
setting aside a tenth of all your

בַּשָּׁנָה הַשְּׁלִישִׁת שְׁנַת הַמַּעֲשֵׂר וְנָתַתָּה לַלֵּוִי
to-the-Levite then-you-give the-tithe year-of the-third in-the-year

לַגֵּר לַיָּתוֹם וְלָאַלְמָנָה וְאָכְלוּ בִשְׁעָרֶיךָ
in-gates-of-you so-they-may-eat and-to-the-widow to-the-fatherless to-the-alien

וְשָׂבֵעוּ׃ וְאָמַרְתָּ לִפְנֵי יְהוָה אֱלֹהֶיךָ בִּעַרְתִּי
I-removed God-of-you Yahweh before then-you-say (13) and-they-may-be-satisfied

הַקֹּדֶשׁ מִן־ הַבַּיִת וְגַם נְתַתִּיו לַלֵּוִי
to-the-Levite I-gave-him and-also the-house from the-sacred-portion

וְלַגֵּר לַיָּתוֹם וְלָאַלְמָנָה כְּכָל־ מִצְוָתְךָ
command-of-you as-all-of and-to-the-widow to-the-fatherless and-to-the-alien

אֲשֶׁר צִוִּיתָנִי לֹא־ עָבַרְתִּי מִמִּצְוֹתֶיךָ וְלֹא שָׁכָחְתִּי׃
I-forgot and-not from-commands-of-you I-turned not you-commanded-me that

לֹא־ אָכַלְתִּי בְאֹנִי מִמֶּנּוּ וְלֹא־ בִעַרְתִּי מִמֶּנּוּ
from-him I-removed and-not from-him in-mourning-of-me I-ate not (14)

בְּטָמֵא וְלֹא־ נָתַתִּי מִמֶּנּוּ לְמֵת שָׁמַעְתִּי בְּקוֹל
to-voice-of I-obeyed for-dead from-him I-offered and-not in-uncleanness

יְהוָה אֱלֹהָי עָשִׂיתִי כְּכֹל אֲשֶׁר צִוִּיתָנִי׃ הַשְׁקִיפָה
look-down! (15) you-commanded-me that as-all I-did God-of-me Yahweh

מִמְּעוֹן קָדְשְׁךָ מִן־ הַשָּׁמַיִם וּבָרֵךְ אֶת־ עַמְּךָ
people-of-you *** and-bless! the-heavens from holy-of-you from-dwelling-of

אֶת־ יִשְׂרָאֵל וְאֵת הָאֲדָמָה אֲשֶׁר נָתַתָּה לָנוּ כַּאֲשֶׁר נִשְׁבַּעְתָּ
you-promised just-as to-us you-gave that the-land and Israel ***

לַאֲבֹתֵינוּ אֶרֶץ זָבַת חָלָב וּדְבָשׁ׃ הַיּוֹם הַזֶּה יְהוָה
Yahweh the-this the-day (16) and-honey milk flowing-of land to-fathers-of-us

אֱלֹהֶיךָ מְצַוְּךָ לַעֲשׂוֹת אֶת־ הַחֻקִּים הָאֵלֶּה וְאֶת־ הַמִּשְׁפָּטִים
the-laws and the-these the-decrees *** to-follow commanding-you God-of-you

וְשָׁמַרְתָּ וְעָשִׂיתָ אוֹתָם בְּכָל־ לְבָבְךָ וּבְכָל־
and-with-all-of heart-of-you with-all-of them and-you-observe and-you-be-careful

נַפְשֶׁךָ׃ אֶת־ יְהוָה הֶאֱמַרְתָּ הַיּוֹם לִהְיוֹת לְךָ לֵאלֹהִים
as-God to-you to-be the-day you-declared Yahweh *** (17) soul-of-you

וְלָלֶכֶת בִּדְרָכָיו וְלִשְׁמֹר חֻקָּיו וּמִצְוֹתָיו
and-commands-of-him decrees-of-him and-to-keep in-ways-of-him and-to-walk

וּמִשְׁפָּטָיו וְלִשְׁמֹעַ בְּקֹלוֹ׃ וַיהוָה הֶאֱמִירְךָ
he-declared-you and-Yahweh (18) to-voice-of-him and-to-obey and-laws-of-him

הַיּוֹם לִהְיוֹת לוֹ לְעַם סְגֻלָּה כַּאֲשֶׁר דִּבֶּר־ לָךְ
to-you he-promised just-as treasure as-people-of to-him to-be the-day

וְלִשְׁמֹר כָּל־ מִצְוֹתָיו׃ וּלְתִתְּךָ עֶלְיוֹן עַל כָּל־
all-of above high and-to-set-you (19) commands-of-him all-of and-to-keep

produce in the third year, the
year of the tithe, you shall give
it to the Levite, the alien, the
fatherless and the widow, so
that they may eat in your
towns and be satisfied. [13]Then
say to the LORD your God: "I
have removed from my house
the sacred portion and have
given it to the Levite, the
alien, the fatherless and the
widow, according to all you
commanded. I have not
turned aside from your commands nor have I forgotten
any of them. [14]I have not eaten
any of the sacred portion
while I was in mourning, nor
have I removed any of it while
I was unclean, nor have I
offered any of it to the dead. I
have obeyed the LORD my
God; I have done everything
you commanded me. [15]Look
down from heaven, your holy
dwelling place, and bless your
people Israel and the land you
have given us as you promised
on oath to our forefathers, a
land flowing with milk and
honey."

Follow the LORD's Commands

[16]The LORD your God commands you this day to follow
these decrees and laws; carefully observe them with all
your heart and with all your
soul. [17]You have declared this
day that the LORD is your God
and that you will walk in his
ways, that you will keep his
decrees, commands and laws,
and that you will obey him.
[18]And the LORD has declared
this day that you are his
people, his treasured possession as he promised, and that
you are to keep all his commands. [19]He has declared that

הַגּוֹיִם אֲשֶׁר עָשָׂה לִתְהִלָּה וּלְשֵׁם וּלְתִפְאָרֶת וְלִהְיֹתְךָ
and-to-be-you and-in-honor and-in-fame in-praise he-made that the-nations

עַם־ קָדֹשׁ לַיהוָה אֱלֹהֶיךָ כַּאֲשֶׁר דִּבֵּר׃ וַיְצַו
and-he-commanded (27:1) he-promised just-as God-of-you to-Yahweh holy people

מֹשֶׁה וְזִקְנֵי יִשְׂרָאֵל אֶת־ הָעָם לֵאמֹר שָׁמֹר אֶת־ כָּל־
all-of *** to-keep to-say the-people *** Israel and-elders-of Moses

הַמִּצְוָה אֲשֶׁר אָנֹכִי מְצַוֶּה אֶתְכֶם הַיּוֹם׃ וְהָיָה בַּיּוֹם אֲשֶׁר
that on-the-day and-he-will-be (2) the-day you commanding I that the-command

תַּעַבְרוּ אֶת־ הַיַּרְדֵּן אֶל־ הָאָרֶץ אֲשֶׁר־ יְהוָה אֱלֹהֶיךָ נֹתֵן לָךְ
to-you giving God-of-you Yahweh that the-land into the-Jordan *** you-cross

וַהֲקֵמֹתָ לְךָ אֲבָנִים גְּדֹלוֹת וְשַׂדְתָּ אֹתָם בַּשִּׂיד׃
with-the-plaster them and-you-coat large-ones stones for-you then-you-set-up

וְכָתַבְתָּ עֲלֵיהֶן אֶת־ כָּל־ דִּבְרֵי הַתּוֹרָה הַזֹּאת
the-this the-law words-of all-of *** on-them and-you-write (3)

בְּעָבְרֶךָ לְמַעַן אֲשֶׁר תָּבֹא אֶל־ הָאָרֶץ אֲשֶׁר־ יְהוָה אֱלֹהֶיךָ ׀
God-of-you Yahweh that the-land into you-enter when so-that when-to-cross-you

נֹתֵן לְךָ אֶרֶץ זָבַת חָלָב וּדְבַשׁ כַּאֲשֶׁר דִּבֶּר יְהוָה
Yahweh he-promised just-as and-honey milk flowing-of land to-you giving

אֱלֹהֵי־ אֲבֹתֶיךָ לָךְ׃ וְהָיָה בְּעָבְרְכֶם אֶת־
*** when-to-cross-you and-he-will-be (4) to-you fathers-of-you God-of

הַיַּרְדֵּן תָּקִימוּ אֶת־ הָאֲבָנִים הָאֵלֶּה אֲשֶׁר אָנֹכִי מְצַוֶּה אֶתְכֶם הַיּוֹם
the-day you commanding I that the-these the-stones *** you-set-up the-Jordan

בְּהַר עֵיבָל וְשַׂדְתָּ אוֹתָם בַּשִּׂיד׃ וּבָנִיתָ שָּׁם מִזְבֵּחַ
altar there and-you-build (5) with-the-plaster them and-you-coat Ebal on-Mount-of

לַיהוָה אֱלֹהֶיךָ מִזְבַּח אֲבָנִים לֹא־ תָנִיף עֲלֵיהֶם בַּרְזֶל׃ אֲבָנִים
stones (6) iron-tool on-them you-use not stones altar-of God-of-you to-Yahweh

שְׁלֵמוֹת תִּבְנֶה אֶת־ מִזְבַּח יְהוָה אֱלֹהֶיךָ וְהַעֲלִיתָ עָלָיו
on-him and-you-offer God-of-you Yahweh altar-of *** you-build natural-ones

עוֹלֹת לַיהוָה אֱלֹהֶיךָ׃ וְזָבַחְתָּ שְׁלָמִים
fellowship-offerings and-you-sacrifice (7) God-of-you to-Yahweh burnt-offerings

וְאָכַלְתָּ שָּׁם וְשָׂמַחְתָּ לִפְנֵי יְהוָה אֱלֹהֶיךָ׃ וְכָתַבְתָּ
and-you-write (8) God-of-you Yahweh before and-you-rejoice there and-you-eat

עַל־ הָאֲבָנִים אֶת־ כָּל־ דִּבְרֵי הַתּוֹרָה הַזֹּאת בַּאֵר הֵיטֵב׃
to-be-good to-be-clear the-this the-law words-of all-of *** the-stones on

וַיְדַבֵּר מֹשֶׁה וְהַכֹּהֲנִים הַלְוִיִּם אֶל כָּל־ יִשְׂרָאֵל
Israel all-of to and-the-Levites and-the-priests Moses then-he-spoke (9)

לֵאמֹר הַסְכֵּת ׀ וּשְׁמַע יִשְׂרָאֵל הַיּוֹם הַזֶּה נִהְיֵיתָ לְעָם
as-people you-became the-this the-day Israel and-listen! be-silent! to-say

he will set you in praise, fame
and honor high above all the
nations he has made and that
you will be a people holy to the
LORD your God, as he promised.

The Altar on Mount Ebal

27 Moses and the elders of
Israel commanded the
people: "Keep all these commands that I give you today.
2When you have crossed the
Jordan into the land the LORD
your God is giving you, set up
some large stones and coat
them with plaster. 3Write on
them all the words of this law
when you have crossed over to
enter the land the LORD your
God is giving you, a land flowing with milk and honey, just
as the LORD, the God of your
fathers, promised you. 4And
when you have crossed the
Jordan, set up these stones on
Mount Ebal, as I command
you today, and coat them with
plaster. 5Build there an altar to
the LORD your God, an altar of
stones. Do not use any iron
tool upon them. 6Build the altar of the LORD your God with
fieldstones and offer burnt
offerings on it to the LORD
your God. 7Sacrifice fellowship
offerings[k] there, eating them
and rejoicing in the presence
of the LORD your God. 8And
you shall write very clearly all
the words of this law on these
stones you have set up."

Curses From Mount Ebal

9Then Moses and the priests,
who are Levites, said to all Israel, "Be silent, O Israel, and
listen! You have now become
the people of the LORD your

[k]7 Traditionally *peace offerings*

לַיהוָה אֱלֹהֶיךָ׃ וְשָׁמַעְתָּ בְּקוֹל יְהוָה אֱלֹהֶיךָ
God-of-you Yahweh to-voice-of and-you-obey (10) God-of-you to-Yahweh

וְעָשִׂיתָ אֶת־ מִצְוֺתוֹ וְאֶת־ חֻקָּיו אֲשֶׁר אָנֹכִי מְצַוְּךָ
giving-you I that decrees-of-him and commands-of-him *** and-you-follow

הַיּוֹם׃ וַיְצַו מֹשֶׁה אֶת־ הָעָם בַּיּוֹם הַהוּא לֵאמֹר׃
to-say the-that on-the-day the-people *** Moses and-he-commanded (11) the-day

אֵלֶּה יַעַמְדוּ לְבָרֵךְ אֶת־ הָעָם עַל־ הַר גְּרִזִים
Gerizim Mount-of on the-people *** to-bless they-shall-stand these (12)

בְּעָבְרְכֶם אֶת־ הַיַּרְדֵּן שִׁמְעוֹן וְלֵוִי וִיהוּדָה וְיִשָּׂשכָר
and-Issachar and-Judah and-Levi Simeon the-Jordan *** when-to-cross-you

וְיוֹסֵף וּבִנְיָמִן׃ וְאֵלֶּה יַעַמְדוּ עַל־ הַקְּלָלָה
the-curse for they-shall-stand and-these (13) and-Benjamin and-Joseph

בְּהַר עֵיבָל רְאוּבֵן גָּד וְאָשֵׁר וּזְבוּלֻן דָּן וְנַפְתָּלִי׃
and-Naphtali Dan and-Zebulun and-Asher Gad Reuben Ebal on-Mount-of

וְעָנוּ הַלְוִיִּם וְאָמְרוּ אֶל־ כָּל־ אִישׁ
person-of every-of to and-they-shall-say the-Levites and-they-shall-recite (14)

יִשְׂרָאֵל קוֹל רָם׃ אָרוּר הָאִישׁ אֲשֶׁר יַעֲשֶׂה פֶסֶל וּמַסֵּכָה
or-cast-idol image he-makes who the-man being-cursed (15) loud voice Israel

תּוֹעֲבַת יְהוָה מַעֲשֵׂה יְדֵי חָרָשׁ וְשָׂם בַּסָּתֶר
in-the-secret and-he-sets-up craftsman hands-of work-of Yahweh detestable-of

וְעָנוּ כָל־ הָעָם וְאָמְרוּ אָמֵן׃
amen and-they-shall-say the-people all-of then-they-shall-answer

אָרוּר מַקְלֶה אָבִיו וְאִמּוֹ
or-mother-of-him father-of-him one-dishonoring being-cursed (16)

וְאָמַר כָּל־ הָעָם אָמֵן׃ אָרוּר מַסִּיג
one-moving being-cursed (17) amen the-people all-of then-he-shall-say

גְּבוּל רֵעֵהוּ וְאָמַר כָּל־ הָעָם אָמֵן׃
amen the-people all-of then-he-shall-say neighbor-of-him boundary-stone-of

אָרוּר מַשְׁגֶּה עִוֵּר בַּדָּרֶךְ וְאָמַר
then-he-shall-say on-the-road blind one-leading-astray being-cursed (18)

כָּל־ הָעָם אָמֵן׃ אָרוּר מַטֶּה מִשְׁפַּט גֵּר־
alien justice-of one-withholding being-cursed (19) amen the-people all-of

יָתוֹם וְאַלְמָנָה וְאָמַר כָּל־ הָעָם אָמֵן׃ אָרוּר
being-cursed (20) amen the-people all-of then-he-shall-say or-widow fatherless

שֹׁכֵב עִם־ אֵשֶׁת אָבִיו כִּי גִלָּה כְּנַף אָבִיו
father-of-him bed-of he-dishonors for father-of-him wife-of with one-sleeping

וְאָמַר כָּל־ הָעָם אָמֵן׃ אָרוּר שֹׁכֵב
one-having-relation being-cursed (21) amen the-people all-of then-he-shall-say

God. [10]Obey the LORD your
God and follow his commands
and decrees that I give you today."
[11]On the same day Moses
commanded the people:
[12]When you have crossed the
Jordan, these tribes shall stand
on Mount Gerizim to bless the
people: Simeon, Levi, Judah,
Issachar, Joseph and Benjamin. [13]And these tribes shall
stand on Mount Ebal to pronounce curses: Reuben, Gad,
Asher, Zebulun, Dan and
Naphtali.
[14]The Levites shall recite to
all the people of Israel in a loud
voice:

[15]"Cursed is the man who
carves an image or casts an
idol—a thing detestable to
the LORD, the work of the
craftsman's hands—and
sets it up in secret."
Then all the people shall
say, "Amen!"
[16]"Cursed is the man who
dishonors his father or his
mother."
Then all the people shall
say, "Amen!"
[17]"Cursed is the man who
moves his neighbor's
boundary stone."
Then all the people shall
say, "Amen!"
[18]"Cursed is the man who
leads the blind astray on
the road."
Then all the people shall
say, "Amen!"
[19]"Cursed is the man who
withholds justice from the
alien, the fatherless or the
widow."
Then all the people shall
say, "Amen!"
[20]"Cursed is the man who
sleeps with his father's
wife, for he dishonors his
father's bed."
Then all the people shall
say, "Amen!"
[21]"Cursed is the man who
has sexual relations with

°10 ק מצותיו

עִם־ כָּל־ בְּהֵמָה וְאָמַר כָּל־ הָעָם אָמֵן׃ אָרוּר
being-cursed (22) amen the-people all-of then-he-shall-say animal any-of with

שֹׁכֵב עִם־ אֲחֹתוֹ בַּת־ אָבִיו אוֹ בַת־
daughter-of or father-of-him daughter-of sister-of-him with one-sleeping

אִמּוֹ וְאָמַר כָּל־ הָעָם אָמֵן׃ אָרוּר
being-cursed (23) amen the-people all-of then-he-shall-say mother-of-him

שֹׁכֵב עִם־ חֹתַנְתּוֹ וְאָמַר כָּל־ הָעָם
the-people all-of then-he-shall-say mother-in-law-of-him with one-sleeping

אָמֵן׃ אָרוּר מַכֵּה רֵעֵהוּ בַּסָּתֶר
in-the-secret neighbor-of-him one-killing being-cursed (24) amen

וְאָמַר כָּל־ הָעָם אָמֵן׃ אָרוּר לֹקֵחַ
one-accepting being-cursed (25) amen the-people all-of then-he-shall-say

שֹׁחַד לְהַכּוֹת נֶפֶשׁ דָּם נָקִי וְאָמַר כָּל־ הָעָם
the-people all-of and-he-shall-say innocent blood-of person to-kill bribe

אָמֵן׃ אָרוּר אֲשֶׁר לֹא־ יָקִים אֶת־ דִּבְרֵי הַתּוֹרָה־ הַזֹּאת
the-this the-law words-of *** he-upholds not whoever being-cursed (26) amen

לַעֲשׂוֹת אוֹתָם וְאָמַר כָּל־ הָעָם אָמֵן׃ וְהָיָה
and-he-will-be (28:1) amen the-people all-of then-he-shall-say them to-carry-out

אִם־ שָׁמוֹעַ תִּשְׁמַע בְּקוֹל יְהוָה אֱלֹהֶיךָ לִשְׁמֹר לַעֲשׂוֹת
to-follow to-be-careful God-of-you Yahweh to-voice-of you-obey to-obey if

אֶת־ כָּל־ מִצְוֹתָיו אֲשֶׁר אָנֹכִי מְצַוְּךָ הַיּוֹם וּנְתָנְךָ
then-he-will-set-you the-day giving-you I that commands-of-him all-of ***

יְהוָה אֱלֹהֶיךָ עֶלְיוֹן עַל כָּל־ גּוֹיֵי הָאָרֶץ׃ וּבָאוּ
and-they-will-come (2) the-earth nations-of all-of above high God-of-you Yahweh

עָלֶיךָ כָּל־ הַבְּרָכוֹת הָאֵלֶּה וְהִשִּׂיגֻךָ כִּי
if and-they-will-accompany-you the-these the-blessings all-of upon-you

תִשְׁמַע בְּקוֹל יְהוָה אֱלֹהֶיךָ׃ בָּרוּךְ אַתָּה בָּעִיר
in-the-city you being-blessed (3) God-of-you Yahweh to-voice-of you-obey

וּבָרוּךְ אַתָּה בַּשָּׂדֶה׃ בָּרוּךְ פְּרִי־ בִטְנְךָ
womb-of-you fruit-of being-blessed (4) in-the-country you and-being-blessed

וּפְרִי אַדְמָתְךָ וּפְרִי בְהֶמְתֶּךָ שְׁגַר אֲלָפֶיךָ
herds-of-you calf-of stock-of-you and-young-of land-of-you and-crop-of

וְעַשְׁתְּרוֹת צֹאנֶךָ׃ בָּרוּךְ טַנְאֲךָ
basket-of-you being-blessed (5) flock-of-you and-lambs-of

וּמִשְׁאַרְתֶּךָ׃ בָּרוּךְ אַתָּה בְּבֹאֶךָ
when-to-come-in-you you being-blessed (6) and-kneading-trough-of-you

וּבָרוּךְ אַתָּה בְּצֵאתֶךָ׃ יִתֵּן יְהוָה אֶת־
*** Yahweh and-he-will-grant (7) when-to-go-out-you you and-being-blessed

any animal."
Then all the people shall say, "Amen!"
22"Cursed is the man who sleeps with his sister, the daughter of his father or the daughter of his mother."
Then all the people shall say, "Amen!"
23"Cursed is the man who sleeps with his mother-in-law."
Then all the people shall say, "Amen!"
24"Cursed is the man who kills his neighbor secretly."
Then all the people shall say, "Amen!"
25"Cursed is the man who accepts a bribe to kill an innocent person."
Then all the people shall say, "Amen!"
26"Cursed is the man who does not uphold the words of this law by carrying them out."
Then all the people shall say, "Amen!"

Blessings for Obedience

28 If you fully obey the LORD your God and carefully follow all his commands I give you today, the LORD your God will set you high above all the nations on earth.
2All these blessings will come upon you and accompany you if you obey the LORD your God:

3You will be blessed in the city and blessed in the country.
4The fruit of your womb will be blessed, and the crops of your land and the young of your livestock—the calves of your herds and the lambs of your flocks.
5Your basket and your kneading trough will be blessed.
6You will be blessed when you come in and blessed when you go out.

7The LORD will grant that the

אֹיְבֶיךָ הַקָּמִים עָלֶיךָ נִגָּפִים לְפָנֶיךָ
before-you ones-being-defeated against-you the-ones-rising being-enemies-of-you

בְּדֶרֶךְ אֶחָד יֵצְאוּ אֵלֶיךָ וּבְשִׁבְעָה דְרָכִים יָנוּסוּ
they-will-flee directions but-in-seven at-you they-will-come one from-direction

לְפָנֶיךָ׃ יְצַו יְהוָה אִתְּךָ אֶת־ הַבְּרָכָה בַּאֲסָמֶיךָ
on-barns-of-you the-blessing *** to-you Yahweh he-will-send (8) from-you

וּבְכֹל מִשְׁלַח יָדֶךָ וּבֵרַכְךָ בָּאָרֶץ אֲשֶׁר־
that in-the-land and-he-will-bless-you hand-of-you work-of and-on-all-of

יְהוָה אֱלֹהֶיךָ נֹתֵן לָךְ׃ יְקִימְךָ יְהוָה לוֹ
for-him Yahweh and-he-will-establish-you (9) to-you giving God-of-you Yahweh

לְעַם קָדוֹשׁ כַּאֲשֶׁר נִשְׁבַּע־ לָךְ כִּי תִשְׁמֹר אֶת־ מִצְוֺת יְהוָה
Yahweh commands-of *** you-keep if to-you he-promised just-as holy as-people

אֱלֹהֶיךָ וְהָלַכְתָּ בִּדְרָכָיו׃ וְרָאוּ כָּל־
all-of then-they-will-see (10) in-ways-of-him and-you-walk God-of-you

עַמֵּי הָאָרֶץ כִּי שֵׁם יְהוָה נִקְרָא עָלֶיךָ וְיָרְאוּ
and-they-will-fear on-you he-is-called Yahweh name-of that the-earth peoples-of

מִמֶּךָּ׃ וְהוֹתִרְךָ יְהוָה לְטוֹבָה בִּפְרִי
in-fruit-of to-prosperity Yahweh and-he-will-grant-you (11) from-you

בִטְנְךָ וּבִפְרִי בְּהַמְתְּךָ* וּבִפְרִי אַדְמָתֶךָ עַל
in ground-of-you and-in-crop-of stock-of-you and-in-young-of womb-of-you

הָאֲדָמָה אֲשֶׁר נִשְׁבַּע יְהוָה לַאֲבֹתֶיךָ לָתֶת לָךְ׃
to-you to-give to-fathers-of-you Yahweh he-swore that the-land

יִפְתַּח יְהוָה׀ לְךָ אֶת־ אוֹצָרוֹ הַטּוֹב אֶת־
*** the-bountiful storehouse-of-him *** for-you Yahweh and-he-will-open (12)

הַשָּׁמַיִם לָתֵת מְטַר־ אַרְצְךָ בְּעִתּוֹ וּלְבָרֵךְ אֵת
*** and-to-bless in-season-of-him land-of-you rain-of to-send the-heavens

כָּל־ מַעֲשֵׂה יָדֶךָ וְהִלְוִיתָ גּוֹיִם רַבִּים וְאַתָּה לֹא
not but-you many nations and-you-will-lend hand-of-you work-of all-of

תִלְוֶה׃ וּנְתָנְךָ יְהוָה לְרֹאשׁ וְלֹא לְזָנָב
as-tail and-not as-head Yahweh and-he-will-make-you (13) you-will-borrow

וְהָיִיתָ רַק לְמַעְלָה וְלֹא תִהְיֶה לְמָטָּה כִּי־ תִשְׁמַע אֶל־
to you-attend if at-bottom you-will-be and-not at-top always and-you-will-be

מִצְוֺת׀ יְהוָה אֱלֹהֶיךָ אֲשֶׁר אָנֹכִי מְצַוְּךָ הַיּוֹם לִשְׁמֹר
to-be-careful the-day giving-you I that God-of-you Yahweh commands-of

וְלַעֲשׂוֹת׃ וְלֹא תָסוּר מִכָּל־ הַדְּבָרִים אֲשֶׁר אָנֹכִי מְצַוֶּה
giving I that the-commands from-any-of you-turn and-not (14) and-to-follow

אֶתְכֶם הַיּוֹם יָמִין וּשְׂמֹאול לָלֶכֶת אַחֲרֵי אֱלֹהִים אֲחֵרִים לְעָבְדָם׃
to-serve-them other-ones gods after to-follow or-left right the-day you

enemies who rise up against you will be defeated before you. They will come at you from one direction but flee from you in seven.
8The LORD will send a blessing on your barns and on everything you put your hand to. The LORD your God will bless you in the land he is giving you.
9The LORD will establish you as his holy people, as he promised you on oath, if you keep the commands of the LORD your God and walk in his
ways. 10Then all the peoples on earth will see that you are called by the name of the LORD, and they will fear you.
11The LORD will grant you abundant prosperity—in the fruit of your womb, the young of your livestock and the crops of your ground—in the land he swore to your forefathers to give you.
12The LORD will open the heavens, the storehouse of his bounty, to send rain on your land in season and to bless all the work of your hands. You
will lend to many nations but will borrow from none. 13The
LORD will make you the head, not the tail. If you pay attention to the commands of the LORD your God that I give you this day and carefully follow them, you will always be at the top, never at the bottom.
14Do not turn aside from any of the commands I give you today, to the right or to the left, following other gods and serving them.

*11 Most mss have *segol* under the *he* (בְּהֶמְ׳).

וְהָיָה אִם־לֹא תִשְׁמַע בְּקוֹל יְהוָה אֱלֹהֶיךָ
God-of-you Yahweh to-voice-of you-obey not if but-he-will-be (15)

לִשְׁמֹר לַעֲשׂוֹת אֶת־כָּל־מִצְוֺתָיו וְחֻקֹּתָיו אֲשֶׁר
that and-decrees-of-him commands-of-him all-of *** to-follow to-be-careful

אָנֹכִי מְצַוְּךָ הַיּוֹם וּבָאוּ עָלֶיךָ כָּל־הַקְּלָלוֹת הָאֵלֶּה
the-these the-curses all-of on-you then-they-will-come the-day giving-you I

וְהִשִּׂיגוּךָ׃ אָרוּר אַתָּה בָּעִיר וְאָרוּר
and-being-cursed in-the-city you being-cursed (16) and-they-will-overtake-you

אַתָּה בַּשָּׂדֶה׃ אָרוּר טַנְאֲךָ וּמִשְׁאַרְתֶּךָ׃
and-kneading-trough-of-you basket-of-you being-cursed (17) in-the-country you

אָרוּר פְּרִי־בִטְנְךָ וּפְרִי אַדְמָתֶךָ שְׁגַר
calf-of land-of-you and-crop-of womb-of-you fruit-of being-cursed (18)

אֲלָפֶיךָ וְעַשְׁתְּרוֹת צֹאנֶךָ׃ אָרוּר אַתָּה בְּבֹאֶךָ
when-to-come-you you being-cursed (19) flock-of-you and-lambs-of herds-of-you

וְאָרוּר אַתָּה בְּצֵאתֶךָ׃ יְשַׁלַּח יְהוָה ׀ בְּךָ אֶת־
*** on-you Yahweh he-will-send (20) when-to-go-out-you you and-being-cursed

הַמְּאֵרָה אֶת־הַמְּהוּמָה וְאֶת־הַמִּגְעֶרֶת בְּכָל־מִשְׁלַח יָדְךָ
hand-of-you work-of in-all-of the-rebuke and the-confusion *** the-curse

אֲשֶׁר תַּעֲשֶׂה עַד הִשָּׁמֶדְךָ וְעַד־אֲבָדְךָ מַהֵר
suddenly to-be-ruined-you and-until to-be-destroyed-you until you-do that

מִפְּנֵי רֹעַ מַעֲלָלֶיךָ אֲשֶׁר עֲזַבְתָּנִי׃ יַדְבֵּק יְהוָה
Yahweh he-will-plague (21) you-forsook-me when deeds-of-you evil because-of

בְּךָ אֶת־הַדָּבֶר עַד כַּלֹּתוֹ אֹתְךָ מֵעַל הָאֲדָמָה אֲשֶׁר־אַתָּה
you that the-land from-on you to-destroy-him until the-disease *** on-you

בָא־שָׁמָּה לְרִשְׁתָּהּ׃ יַכְּכָה יְהוָה
Yahweh he-will-strike-you (22) to-possess-her to-there entering

בַּשַּׁחֶפֶת וּבַקַּדַּחַת וּבַדַּלֶּקֶת
and-with-the-inflammation and-with-the-fever with-the-wasting-disease

וּבְחַרְחֻר וּבַחֶרֶב וּבַשִּׁדָּפוֹן וּבַיֵּרָקוֹן
and-with-the-mildew and-with-the-blight and-with-the-drought and-with-the-heat

וּרְדָפוּךָ עַד אָבְדֶךָ׃ וְהָיוּ שָׁמֶיךָ
skies-of-you and-they-will-be (23) to-perish-you until and-they-will-plague-you

אֲשֶׁר עַל־רֹאשְׁךָ נְחֹשֶׁת וְהָאָרֶץ אֲשֶׁר־תַּחְתֶּיךָ בַּרְזֶל׃
iron beneath-you that and-the-ground bronze head-of-you over that

יִתֵּן יְהוָה אֶת־מְטַר אַרְצְךָ אָבָק וְעָפָר מִן־
from and-powder dust country-of-you rain-of *** Yahweh he-will-turn (24)

הַשָּׁמַיִם יֵרֵד עָלֶיךָ עַד הִשָּׁמְדָךְ׃ יִתֶּנְךָ
he-will-cause-you (25) to-be-ruined-you until on-you he-will-come-down the-skies

Curses for Disobedience

15 However, if you do not
obey the LORD your God and
do not carefully follow all his
commands and decrees I am
giving you today, all these
curses will come upon you and
overtake you:

16 You will be cursed in
the city and cursed in the
country.
17 Your basket and your
kneading trough will be
cursed.
18 The fruit of your womb
will be cursed, and the
crops of your land, and the
calves of your herds and
the lambs of your flocks.
19 You will be cursed
when you come in and
cursed when you go out.

20 The LORD will send on you
curses, confusion and rebuke
in everything you put your
hand to, until you are destroyed and come to sudden
ruin because of the evil you
have done in forsaking him.[l]
21 The LORD will plague you
with diseases until he has destroyed you from the land you
are entering to possess. 22 The
LORD will strike you with
wasting disease, with fever
and inflammation, with
scorching heat and drought,
with blight and mildew,
which will plague you until
you perish. 23 The sky over
your head will be bronze, the
ground beneath you iron.
24 The LORD will turn the rain of
your country into dust and
powder; it will come down
from the skies until you are
ruined.
25 The LORD will cause you to

l20 Hebrew *me*

יְהוָה ׀ נִגָּף לִפְנֵי אֹיְבֶיךָ בְּדֶרֶךְ אֶחָד
one from-direction being-enemies-of-you before being-defeated Yahweh

תֵּצֵא אֵלָיו וּבְשִׁבְעָה דְרָכִים תָּנוּס לְפָנָיו
from-him you-will-flee directions but-in-seven at-him you-will-come

וְהָיִיתָ לְזַעֲוָה לְכֹל מַמְלְכוֹת הָאָרֶץ׃
the-earth kingdoms-of to-all-of as-horror and-you-will-become

וְהָיְתָה נִבְלָתְךָ לְמַאֲכָל לְכָל־ עוֹף הַשָּׁמַיִם
the-skies bird-of for-every-of as-food carcass-of-you and-she-will-be (26)

וּלְבֶהֱמַת הָאָרֶץ וְאֵין מַחֲרִיד׃ יַכְּכָה
and-he-will-afflict-you (27) one-frightening and-not the-earth and-for-beast-of

יְהוָה בִּשְׁחִין מִצְרַיִם וּבַעְפֹלִים* וּבַגָּרָב
and-with-the-festering-sore and-with-the-tumors Egypt with-boil-of Yahweh

וּבֶחָרֶס אֲשֶׁר לֹא־ תוּכַל לְהֵרָפֵא׃ יַכְּכָה
and-he-will-afflict-you (28) to-be-cured you-can not that and-with-the-itch

יְהוָה בְּשִׁגָּעוֹן וּבְעִוָּרוֹן וּבְתִמְהוֹן לֵבָב׃
mind and-with-confusion-of and-with-blindness with-madness Yahweh

וְהָיִיתָ מְמַשֵּׁשׁ בַּצָּהֳרַיִם כַּאֲשֶׁר יְמַשֵּׁשׁ הָעִוֵּר
the-blind-man he-gropes just-as at-the-midday groping and-you-will-be (29)

בָּאֲפֵלָה וְלֹא תַצְלִיחַ אֶת־ דְּרָכֶיךָ וְהָיִיתָ אַךְ
also and-you-will-be ways-of-you *** you-will-succeed and-not in-the-dark

עָשׁוּק וְגָזוּל כָּל־ הַיָּמִים וְאֵין מוֹשִׁיעַ׃
one-rescuing but-not the-days all-of and-being-robbed being-oppressed

אִשָּׁה תְאָרֵשׂ וְאִישׁ אַחֵר יִשְׁגָּלֶנָּה† בַּיִת
house he-will-ravish-her another but-man you-will-be-pledged woman (30)

תִּבְנֶה וְלֹא־ תֵשֵׁב בּוֹ כֶּרֶם תִּטַּע וְלֹא
but-not you-will-plant vineyard in-him you-will-live but-not you-will-build

תְחַלְּלֶנּוּ׃ שׁוֹרְךָ טָבוּחַ לְעֵינֶיךָ
before-eyes-of-you being-slaughtered ox-of-you (31) you-will-begin-to-enjoy-him

וְלֹא תֹאכַל מִמֶּנּוּ חֲמֹרְךָ גָּזוּל מִלְּפָנֶיךָ וְלֹא
and-not from-before-you being-taken donkey-of-you from-him you-will-eat but-not

יָשׁוּב לָךְ צֹאנְךָ נְתֻנוֹת לְאֹיְבֶיךָ
to-being-enemies-of-you ones-being-given sheep-of-you to-you he-will-return

וְאֵין לְךָ מוֹשִׁיעַ׃ בָּנֶיךָ וּבְנֹתֶיךָ
and-daughters-of-you sons-of-you (32) one-rescuing to-you and-not

נְתֻנִים לְעַם אַחֵר וְעֵינֶיךָ רֹאוֹת
ones-watching and-eyes-of-you another to-nation ones-being-given

וְכָלוֹת אֲלֵיהֶם כָּל־ הַיּוֹם וְאֵין לְאֵל יָדֶךָ׃
hand-of-you with-power and-not the-day all-of for-them and-ones-worn-out

be defeated before your enemies. You will come at them from one direction but flee from them in seven, and you will become a thing of horror to all the kingdoms on earth.
26Your carcasses will be food for all the birds of the air and the beasts of the earth, and there will be no one to frighten them away.
27The LORD will afflict you with the boils of Egypt and with tumors, festering sores and the itch, from which you cannot be cured.
28The LORD will afflict you with madness, blindness and confusion of mind.
29At midday you will grope about like a blind man in the dark. You will be unsuccessful in everything you do; day after day you will be oppressed and robbed, with no one to rescue you.
30You will be pledged to be married to a woman, but another will take her and ravish her. You will build a house, but you will not live in it. You will plant a vineyard, but you will not even begin to enjoy its fruit.
31Your ox will be slaughtered before your eyes, but you will eat none of it. Your donkey will be forcibly taken from you and will not be returned. Your sheep will be given to your enemies, and no one will rescue them.
32Your sons and daughters will be given to another nation, and you will wear out your eyes watching for them day after day, powerless to lift a hand.

*27 The *Ketbib* and *Qere* are synonyms.

†30 The *Ketbib* is a more violent word than the *Qere*.

°27 ק ובטחרים

°30 ק ישכבנה

פְּרִי אַדְמָתְךָ וְכָל־ יְגִיעֲךָ יֹאכַל עַם אֲשֶׁר
that people he-will-eat labor-of-you and-all-of land-of-you produce-of (33)

לֹא־ יָדָעְתָּ וְהָיִיתָ רַק עָשׁוּק וְרָצוּץ כָּל־
all-of and-being-crushed being-oppressed only and-you-will-be you-know not

הַיָּמִים׃ וְהָיִיתָ מְשֻׁגָּע מִמַּרְאֵה עֵינֶיךָ
eyes-of-you from-sight-of being-driven-mad and-you-will-be (34) the-days

אֲשֶׁר תִּרְאֶה׃ יַכְּכָה יְהוָה בִּשְׁחִין רָע עַל־
on painful with-boil Yahweh and-he-will-afflict-you (35) you-see that

הַבִּרְכַּיִם וְעַל־ הַשֹּׁקַיִם אֲשֶׁר לֹא־ תוּכַל לְהֵרָפֵא מִכַּף
from-sole-of to-be-cured you-can not that the-legs and-on the-knees

רַגְלְךָ וְעַד קָדְקֳדֶךָ׃ יוֹלֵךְ יְהוָה אֹתְךָ וְאֶת־ מַלְכְּךָ
king-of-you and you Yahweh he-will-drive (36) head-of-you even-to foot-of-you

אֲשֶׁר תָּקִים עָלֶיךָ אֶל־ גּוֹי אֲשֶׁר לֹא־ יָדַעְתָּ אַתָּה וַאֲבֹתֶיךָ
or-fathers-of-you you you-know not that nation to over-you you-will-set that

וְעָבַדְתָּ שָּׁם אֱלֹהִים אֲחֵרִים עֵץ וָאָבֶן׃ וְהָיִיתָ
and-you-will-be (37) and-stone wood other-ones gods there and-you-will-worship

לְשַׁמָּה לְמָשָׁל וְלִשְׁנִינָה בְּכֹל הָעַמִּים
the-nations to-all-of and-as-object-of-ridicule as-object-of-scorn as-horror

אֲשֶׁר־ יְנַהֶגְךָ יְהוָה שָׁמָּה׃ זֶרַע רַב תּוֹצִיא
you-will-sow much seed (38) to-there Yahweh he-will-drive-you that

הַשָּׂדֶה וּמְעַט תֶּאֱסֹף כִּי יַחְסְלֶנּוּ הָאַרְבֶּה׃
the-locust he-will-devour-him for you-will-harvest but-little the-field

כְּרָמִים תִּטַּע וְעָבָדְתָּ וְיַיִן לֹא־ תִשְׁתֶּה
you-will-drink not but-wine and-you-will-cultivate you-will-plant vineyards (39)

וְלֹא תֶאֱגֹר כִּי תֹאכְלֶנּוּ הַתֹּלָעַת׃ זֵיתִים
olive-trees (40) the-worm she-will-eat-him for you-will-gather and-not

יִהְיוּ לְךָ בְּכָל־ גְּבוּלֶךָ וְשֶׁמֶן לֹא תָסוּךְ כִּי
for you-will-use not but-oil country-of-you in-all-of to-you they-will-be

יִשַּׁל זֵיתֶךָ׃ בָּנִים וּבָנוֹת תּוֹלִיד וְלֹא־
but-not you-will-bear and-daughters sons (41) olive-of-you he-will-drop-off

יִהְיוּ לָךְ כִּי יֵלְכוּ בַּשֶּׁבִי׃ כָּל־
every-of (42) into-the-captivity they-will-go for with-you they-will-stay

עֵצְךָ וּפְרִי אַדְמָתֶךָ יְיָרֵשׁ הַצְּלָצַל׃
the-locust-swarm he-will-take-over land-of-you and-crop-of tree-of-you

הַגֵּר אֲשֶׁר בְּקִרְבְּךָ יַעֲלֶה עָלֶיךָ מַעְלָה מָּעְלָה
to-higher to-higher above-you he-will-rise in-among-you who the-alien (43)

וְאַתָּה תֵרֵד מַטָּה מָּטָּה׃ הוּא יַלְוְךָ וְאַתָּה לֹא
not but-you he-will-lend-to-you he (44) lower lower you-will-sink but-you

33A people that you do not
know will eat what your land
and labor produce, and you
will have nothing but cruel
oppression all your days. 34The
sights you see will drive you
mad. 35The LORD will afflict
your knees and legs with
painful boils that cannot be
cured, spreading from the
soles of your feet to the top of
your head.
36The LORD will drive you
and the king you set over you
to a nation unknown to you or
your fathers. There you will
worship other gods, gods of
wood and stone. 37You will
become a thing of horror and
an object of scorn and ridicule
to all the nations where the
LORD will drive you.
38You will sow much seed in
the field but you will harvest
little, because locusts will devour it. 39You will plant vineyards and cultivate them but
you will not drink the wine or
gather the grapes, because
worms will eat them. 40You
will have olive trees throughout your country but you will
not use the oil, because the olives will drop off. 41You will
have sons and daughters but
you will not keep them, because they will go into captivity. 42Swarms of locusts will
take over all your trees and the
crops of your land.
43The alien who lives among
you will rise above you higher
and higher, but you will sink
lower and lower. 44He will
lend to you, but you will not

תַלְוֶנּוּ הוּא יִהְיֶה לְרֹאשׁ וְאַתָּה תִּהְיֶה לְזָנָב׃
as-tail you-will-be but-you as-head he-will-be he you-will-lend-to-him

וּבָאוּ עָלֶיךָ כָּל־ הַקְּלָלוֹת הָאֵלֶּה
the-these the-curses all-of upon-you and-they-will-come (45)

וּרְדָפוּךָ וְהִשִּׂיגוּךָ עַד הִשָּׁמְדָךְ
to-be-destroyed-you until and-they-will-overtake-you and-they-will-pursue-you

כִּי־ לֹא שָׁמַעְתָּ בְּקוֹל יְהוָה אֱלֹהֶיךָ לִשְׁמֹר מִצְוֹתָיו
commands-of-him to-observe God-of-you Yahweh to-voice-of you-obeyed not for

וְחֻקֹּתָיו אֲשֶׁר צִוָּךְ׃ וְהָיוּ בְךָ לְאוֹת
as-sign to-you and-they-will-be (46) he-gave-you that and-decrees-of-him

וּלְמוֹפֵת וּבְזַרְעֲךָ עַד־ עוֹלָם׃ תַּחַת אֲשֶׁר לֹא־
not that because (47) forever to and-to-descendant-of-you and-as-wonder

עָבַדְתָּ אֶת־ יְהוָה אֱלֹהֶיךָ בְּשִׂמְחָה וּבְטוּב לֵבָב
heart and-with-gladness-of with-joy God-of-you Yahweh *** you-served

מֵרֹב כֹּל׃ וְעָבַדְתָּ אֶת־ אֹיְבֶיךָ אֲשֶׁר
that being-enemies-of-you *** so-you-will-serve (48) great in-prosperity

יְשַׁלְּחֶנּוּ יְהוָה בָּךְ בְּרָעָב וּבְצָמָא וּבְעֵירֹם
and-in-nakedness and-in-thirst in-hunger against-you Yahweh he-sends-him

וּבְחֹסֶר כֹּל וְנָתַן עֹל בַּרְזֶל עַל־ צַוָּארֶךָ עַד
until neck-of-you on iron yoke-of and-he-will-put dire and-in-poverty

הִשְׁמִידוֹ אֹתָךְ׃ יִשָּׂא יְהוָה עָלֶיךָ גּוֹי מֵרָחֹק
from-far-away nation against-you Yahweh he-will-bring (49) you to-destroy-him

מִקְצֵה הָאָרֶץ כַּאֲשֶׁר יִדְאֶה הַנָּשֶׁר גּוֹי אֲשֶׁר לֹא־
not that nation the-eagle he-swoops-down just-as the-earth from-end-of

תִשְׁמַע לְשֹׁנוֹ׃ גּוֹי עַז פָּנִים אֲשֶׁר לֹא־
not that faces fierce-of nation (50) language-of-him you-understand

יִשָּׂא פָנִים לְזָקֵן וְנַעַר לֹא יָחֹן׃ וְאָכַל
and-he-will-devour (51) he-pities not and-young of-old faces he-respects

פְּרִי בְהֶמְתְּךָ וּפְרִי־ אַדְמָתְךָ עַד הִשָּׁמְדָךְ אֲשֶׁר
that to-be-destroyed-you until land-of-you and-crop-of stock-of-you young-of

לֹא־ יַשְׁאִיר לְךָ דָּגָן תִּירוֹשׁ וְיִצְהָר שְׁגַר אֲלָפֶיךָ
herds-of-you calf-of or-oil new-wine grain to-you he-will-leave not

וְעַשְׁתְּרֹת צֹאנֶךָ עַד הַאֲבִידוֹ אֹתָךְ׃ וְהֵצַר
and-he-will-lay-siege (52) you to-ruin-him until flock-of-you or-lambs-of

לְךָ בְּכָל־ שְׁעָרֶיךָ עַד רֶדֶת חֹמֹתֶיךָ הַגְּבֹהוֹת
the-high-ones walls-of-you to-fall-down until gates-of-you to-all-of to-you

וְהַבְּצֻרוֹת אֲשֶׁר אַתָּה בֹּטֵחַ בָּהֵן בְּכָל־ אַרְצֶךָ
land-of-you in-all-of in-them trusting you which and-the-fortified-ones

lend to him. He will be the
head, but you will be the tail.
45All these curses will come
upon you. They will pursue
you and overtake you until
you are destroyed, because
you did not obey the LORD
your God and observe the
commands and decrees he
gave you. 46They will be a sign
and a wonder to you and your
descendants forever. 47Because
you did not serve the LORD
your God joyfully and gladly
in the time of prosperity,
48therefore in hunger and
thirst, in nakedness and dire
poverty, you will serve the
enemies the LORD sends
against you. He will put an
iron yoke on your neck until
he has destroyed you.
49The LORD will bring a nation against you from far
away, from the ends of the
earth, like an eagle swooping
down, a nation whose lan-
guage you will not under-
stand, 50a fierce-looking nation without respect for the
old or pity for the young.
51They will devour the young
of your livestock and the crops
of your land until you are destroyed. They will leave you
no grain, new wine or oil, nor
any calves of your herds or
lambs of your flocks until you
are ruined. 52They will lay
siege to all the cities throughout your land until the high
fortified walls in which you

וְהֵצַר לְךָ בְּכָל־ שְׁעָרֶיךָ בְּכָל־ אַרְצְךָ אֲשֶׁר
that land-of-you in-all-of gates-of-you to-all-of to-you and-he-will-besiege

נָתַן יְהוָה אֱלֹהֶיךָ לָךְ׃ (53) וְאָכַלְתָּ פְרִי־ בִטְנְךָ
womb-of-you fruit-of and-you-will-eat (53) to-you God-of-you Yahweh he-gives

בְּשַׂר בָּנֶיךָ וּבְנֹתֶיךָ אֲשֶׁר נָתַן־ לְךָ יְהוָה
Yahweh to-you he-gave whom and-daughters-of-you sons-of-you flesh-of

אֱלֹהֶיךָ בְּמָצוֹר וּבְמָצוֹק אֲשֶׁר־ יָצִיק לְךָ
on-you he-inflicts that and-because-of-suffering because-of-siege God-of-you

אֹיְבֶךָ׃ (54) הָאִישׁ הָרַךְ בְּךָ וְהֶעָנֹג מְאֹד
most and-the-sensitive among-you the-gentle the-man (54) being-enemy-of-you

תֵּרַע עֵינוֹ בְאָחִיו וּבְאֵשֶׁת חֵיקוֹ
loved-of-him and-to-wife-of to-brother-of-him eye-of-him she-will-be-evil

וּבְיֶתֶר בָּנָיו אֲשֶׁר יוֹתִיר׃ (55) מִתֵּת ׀ לְאַחַד
to-one not-to-give (55) he-remains who children-of-him and-to-survivor-of

מֵהֶם מִבְּשַׂר בָּנָיו אֲשֶׁר יֹאכֵל מִבְּלִי הִשְׁאִיר־
he-remains because-not he-eats that children-of-him from-flesh-of of-them

לוֹ כֹּל בְּמָצוֹר וּבְמָצוֹק אֲשֶׁר יָצִיק
he-will-inflict that and-because-of-suffering because-of-siege anything to-him

לְךָ אֹיִבְךָ בְּכָל־ שְׁעָרֶיךָ׃ (56) הָרַכָּה
the-gentle-woman (56) gates-of-you on-all-of being-enemy-of-you on-you

בְךָ וְהָעֲנֻגָּה אֲשֶׁר לֹא־ נִסְּתָה כַף־ רַגְלָהּ
foot-of-her sole-of she-would-venture not who and-the-sensitive among-you

הַצֵּג עַל־ הָאָרֶץ מֵהִתְעַנֵּג וּמֵרֹךְ תֵּרַע
she-will-be-evil and-from-gentleness from-to-be-sensitive the-ground on to-touch

עֵינָהּ בְּאִישׁ חֵיקָהּ וּבִבְנָהּ וּבְבִתָּהּ׃
and-to-daughter-of-her and-to-son-of-her loved-of-her to-husband-of eye-of-her

(57) וּבְשִׁלְיָתָהּ הַיּוֹצֵת ׀ מִבֵּין רַגְלֶיהָ
feet-of-her from-between the-one-coming and-to-afterbirth-her (57)

וּבְבָנֶיהָ אֲשֶׁר תֵּלֵד כִּי־ תֹאכְלֵם בְּחֹסֶר־ כֹּל
great in-want she-will-eat-them for she-bears whom and-to-children-of-her

בַּסֵּתֶר בְּמָצוֹר וּבְמָצוֹק אֲשֶׁר יָצִיק לְךָ
on-you he-will-inflict that and-in-distress in-siege in-the-secret

אֹיִבְךָ בִּשְׁעָרֶיךָ׃ (58) אִם־ לֹא תִשְׁמֹר לַעֲשׂוֹת אֶת־
*** to-follow you-are-careful not if (58) on-gates-of-you being-enemy-of-you

כָּל־ דִּבְרֵי הַתּוֹרָה הַזֹּאת הַכְּתוּבִים בַּסֵּפֶר הַזֶּה
the-this in-the-book the-ones-being-written the-this the-law words-of all-of

לְיִרְאָה אֶת־ הַשֵּׁם הַנִּכְבָּד וְהַנּוֹרָא הַזֶּה אֵת
*** the-this and-the-being-awesome the-being-glorious the-name *** to-revere

trust fall down. They will besiege all the cities throughout the land the LORD your God is giving you.

[53]Because of the suffering that your enemy will inflict on you during the siege, you will eat the fruit of the womb, the flesh of the sons and daughters the LORD your God has given you. [54]Even the most gentle and sensitive man among you will have no compassion on his own brother or the wife he loves or his surviving children, [55]and he will not give to one of them any of the flesh of his children that he is eating. It will be all he has left because of the suffering your enemy will inflict on you during the siege of all your cities. [56]The most gentle and sensitive woman among you—so sensitive and gentle that she would not venture to touch the ground with the sole of her foot—will begrudge the husband she loves and her own son or daughter [57]the afterbirth from her womb and the children she bears. For she intends to eat them secretly during the siege and in the distress that your enemy will inflict on you in your cities.

[58]If you do not carefully follow all the words of this law, which are written in this book, and do not revere this glorious and awesome name—

יְהוָה אֱלֹהֶיךָ׃ וְהִפְלָא יְהוָה אֶת־מַכֹּתְךָ וְאֵת
and plagues-of-you *** Yahweh and-he-will-make-fearful (59) God-of-you Yahweh

מַכּוֹת זַרְעֶךָ מַכּוֹת גְּדֹלוֹת וְנֶאֱמָנוֹת
and-being-prolonged-ones harsh-ones disasters descendant-of-you plagues-of

וָחֳלָיִם רָעִים וְנֶאֱמָנִים׃ וְהֵשִׁיב בְּךָ
upon-you and-he-will-bring (60) and-lingering-ones severe-ones and-illnesses

אֵת כָּל־מַדְוֵה מִצְרַיִם אֲשֶׁר יָגֹרְתָּ מִפְּנֵיהֶם וְדָבְקוּ
and-they-will-cling from-them you-dreaded that Egypt disease-of all-of ***

בָּךְ׃ גַּם כָּל־חֳלִי וְכָל־מַכָּה אֲשֶׁר לֹא
not that disaster and-every-of sickness every-of also (61) to-you

כָתוּב בְּסֵפֶר הַתּוֹרָה הַזֹּאת יַעְלֵם יְהוָה עָלֶיךָ
on-you Yahweh he-will-bring-them the-this the-Law in-Book-of being-recorded

עַד הִשָּׁמְדָךְ׃ וְנִשְׁאַרְתֶּם בִּמְתֵי מְעָט תַּחַת אֲשֶׁר
that because few as-men-of and-you-will-be-left (62) to-be-destroyed-you until

הֱיִיתֶם כְּכוֹכְבֵי הַשָּׁמַיִם לָרֹב כִּי־לֹא שָׁמַעְתָּ בְּקוֹל
to-voice-of you-obeyed not but in-number the-skies as-stars-of you-were

יְהוָה אֱלֹהֶיךָ׃ וְהָיָה כַּאֲשֶׁר־שָׂשׂ יְהוָה עֲלֵיכֶם
about-you Yahweh he-pleased just-as and-he-will-be (63) God-of-you Yahweh

לְהֵיטִיב אֶתְכֶם וּלְהַרְבּוֹת אֶתְכֶם כֵּן יָשִׂישׂ יְהוָה עֲלֵיכֶם
about-you Yahweh he-will-please so you and-to-increase you to-make-prosper

לְהַאֲבִיד אֶתְכֶם וּלְהַשְׁמִיד אֶתְכֶם וְנִסַּחְתֶּם מֵעַל הָאֲדָמָה
the-land from-in and-you-will-be-uprooted you and-to-destroy you to-ruin

אֲשֶׁר־אַתָּה בָא־שָׁמָּה לְרִשְׁתָּהּ׃ וֶהֱפִיצְךָ
then-he-will-scatter-you (64) to-possess-her to-there entering you that

יְהוָה בְּכָל־הָעַמִּים מִקְצֵה הָאָרֶץ וְעַד־קְצֵה
end-of even-to the-earth from-end-of the-nations among-all-of Yahweh

הָאָרֶץ וְעָבַדְתָּ שָׁם אֱלֹהִים אֲחֵרִים אֲשֶׁר לֹא־יָדַעְתָּ אַתָּה
you you-knew not that other-ones gods there and-you-will-worship the-earth

וַאֲבֹתֶיךָ עֵץ וָאָבֶן׃ וּבַגּוֹיִם הָהֵם לֹא
not the-those and-among-the-nations (65) and-stone wood or-fathers-of-you

תַרְגִּיעַ וְלֹא־יִהְיֶה מָנוֹחַ לְכַף־רַגְלֶךָ
foot-of-you for-sole-of resting-place he-will-be and-not you-will-repose

וְנָתַן יְהוָה לְךָ שָׁם לֵב רַגָּז וְכִלְיוֹן עֵינַיִם
eyes and-longing anxious mind there to-you Yahweh and-he-will-give

וְדַאֲבוֹן נָפֶשׁ׃ וְהָיוּ חַיֶּיךָ תְּלֻאִים
ones-being-in-suspense lives-of-you and-you-will-live (66) heart and-despairing

לְךָ מִנֶּגֶד וּפָחַדְתָּ לַיְלָה וְיוֹמָם וְלֹא תַאֲמִין
you-will-be-sure and-not and-by-day night and-you-will-dread in-front to-you

the LORD your God— [59]the
LORD will send fearful plagues
on you and your descendants,
harsh and prolonged disasters, and severe and lingering
illnesses. [60]He will bring upon
you all the diseases of Egypt
that you dreaded, and they
will cling to you. [61]The LORD
will also bring on you every
kind of sickness and disaster
not recorded in this Book of
the Law until you are de-
stroyed. [62]You who were as
numerous as the stars in the
sky will be left but few in
number, because you did not
obey the LORD your God. [63]Just
as it pleased the LORD to make
you prosper and increase in
number, so it will please him
to ruin and destroy you. You
will be uprooted from the land
you are entering to possess.
[64]Then the LORD will scatter
you among all nations, from
one end of the earth to the other. There you will worship
other gods—gods of wood and
stone, which neither you nor
your fathers have known.
[65]Among those nations you
will find no repose, no resting
place for the sole of your foot.
There the LORD will give you
an anxious mind, eyes weary
with longing, and a despair-
ing heart. [66]You will live in
constant suspense, filled with
dread both night and day,

בְּחַיֶּיךָ׃ בַּבֹּקֶר תֹּאמַר מִֽי־יִתֵּן
he-would-come if-only! you-will-say in-the-morning (67) of-lives-of-you

עֶרֶב וּבָעֶרֶב תֹּאמַר מִֽי־יִתֵּן בֹּקֶר
morning he-would-come if-only! you-will-say and-in-the-evening evening

מִפַּחַד לְבָבְךָ אֲשֶׁר תִּפְחָד וּמִמַּרְאֵה עֵינֶיךָ
eyes-of-you and-from-sight-of you-will-dread that heart-of-you from-terror-of

אֲשֶׁר תִּרְאֶה׃ וֶהֱשִֽׁיבְךָ יְהוָה ׀ מִצְרַיִם בָּאֳנִיּוֹת
in-ships Egypt Yahweh and-he-will-send-back-you (68) you-will-see that

בַּדֶּרֶךְ אֲשֶׁר אָמַרְתִּי לְךָ לֹא־תֹסִיף עוֹד לִרְאֹתָהּ
to-see-her again you-should-repeat not to-you I-said that on-the-journey

וְהִתְמַכַּרְתֶּם שָׁם לְאֹיְבֶיךָ לַעֲבָדִים
as-male-slaves to-being-enemies-of-you there and-you-will-sell-yourselves

וְלִשְׁפָחוֹת וְאֵין קֹנֶה׃ אֵלֶּה דִבְרֵי הַבְּרִית
the-covenant terms-of these (69)* one-buying but-not and-as-female-slaves

אֲשֶׁר־צִוָּה יְהוָה אֶת־מֹשֶׁה לִכְרֹת אֶת־בְּנֵי יִשְׂרָאֵל בְּאֶרֶץ
in-land-of Israel sons-of with to-make Moses *** Yahweh he-commanded that

מוֹאָב מִלְּבַד הַבְּרִית אֲשֶׁר־כָּרַת אִתָּם בְּחֹרֵב׃
at-Horeb with-them he-made that the-covenant in-addition-to Moab

וַיִּקְרָא מֹשֶׁה אֶל־כָּל־יִשְׂרָאֵל וַיֹּאמֶר אֲלֵהֶם אַתֶּם רְאִיתֶם
you-saw you to-them and-he-said Israel all-of to Moses and-he-summoned (29:1)

אֵת כָּל־אֲשֶׁר עָשָׂה יְהוָה לְעֵינֵיכֶם בְּאֶרֶץ מִצְרַיִם לְפַרְעֹה
to-Pharaoh Egypt in-land-of before-eyes-of-you Yahweh he-did that all ***

וּלְכָל־עֲבָדָיו וּלְכָל־אַרְצוֹ׃ הַמַּסּוֹת
the-trials (2) land-of-him and-to-all-of officials-of-him and-to-all-of

הַגְּדֹלֹת אֲשֶׁר רָאוּ עֵינֶיךָ הָאֹתֹת וְהַמֹּפְתִים
and-the-wonders the-signs eyes-of-you they-saw that the-great-ones

הַגְּדֹלִים הָהֵם׃ וְלֹא־נָתַן יְהוָה לָכֶם לֵב לָדַעַת
to-understand mind to-you Yahweh he-gave but-not (3) the-those the-great-ones

וְעֵינַיִם לִרְאוֹת וְאָזְנַיִם לִשְׁמֹעַ עַד הַיּוֹם הַזֶּה׃ וָאוֹלֵךְ אֶתְכֶם
you when-I-led (4) the-this the-day to to-hear or-ears to-see or-eyes

אַרְבָּעִים שָׁנָה בַּמִּדְבָּר לֹא־בָלוּ שַׂלְמֹתֵיכֶם מֵעֲלֵיכֶם
from-on-you clothes-of-you they-wore-out not through-the-desert year forty

וְנַעַלְךָ לֹא־בָלְתָה מֵעַל רַגְלֶךָ׃ לֶחֶם לֹא אֲכַלְתֶּם
you-ate not bread (5) foot-of-you from-on she-wore-out not and-sandal-of-you

וְיַיִן וְשֵׁכָר לֹא שְׁתִיתֶם לְמַעַן תֵּדְעוּ כִּי אֲנִי
I that you-might-know so-that you-drank not or-fermented-drink and-wine

יְהוָה אֱלֹהֵיכֶם׃ וַתָּבֹאוּ אֶל־הַמָּקוֹם הַזֶּה וַיֵּצֵא
then-he-came-out the-this the-place to when-you-reached (6) God-of-you Yahweh

never sure of your life. [67]In the morning you will say, "If only it were evening!" and in the evening, "If only it were morning!"—because of the terror that will fill your hearts and the sights that your eyes will see. [68]The LORD will send you back in ships to Egypt on a journey I said you should never make again. There you will offer yourselves for sale to your enemies as male and female slaves, but no one will buy you.

Renewal of the Covenant

29 These are the terms of the covenant the LORD commanded Moses to make with the Israelites in Moab, in addition to the covenant he had made with them at Horeb.

[2]Moses summoned all the Israelites and said to them:

Your eyes have seen all that the LORD did in Egypt to Pharaoh, to all his officials and to all his land. [3]With your own eyes you saw those great trials, those miraculous signs and great wonders. [4]But to this day the LORD has not given you a mind that understands or eyes that see or ears that hear. [5]During the forty years that I led you through the desert, your clothes did not wear out, nor did the sandals on your feet. [6]You ate no bread and drank no wine or other fermented drink. I did this so that you might know that I am the LORD your God.

[7]When you reached this

*The Hebrew numeration of chapter 29 begins with verse 2 in English; thus, there is a one-verse discrepancy throughout the chapter.

סִיחֹן מֶלֶךְ־ חֶשְׁבּוֹן וְעוֹג מֶלֶךְ־ הַבָּשָׁן לִקְרָאתֵנוּ לַמִּלְחָמָה
in-the-fight to-meet-us the-Bashan king-of and-Og Heshbon king-of Sihon

וַנַּכֵּם׃ וַנִּקַּח אֶת־ אַרְצָם וַנִּתְּנָהּ
and-we-gave-her land-of-them *** and-we-took (7) but-we-defeated-them

לְנַחֲלָה לָרֻאוּבֵנִי וְלַגָּדִי וְלַחֲצִי שֵׁבֶט
tribe-of and-to-half-of and-to-the-Gadite to-the-Reubenite as-inheritance

הַמְנַשִּׁי׃ וּשְׁמַרְתֶּם אֶת־ דִּבְרֵי הַבְּרִית הַזֹּאת
the-this the-covenant terms-of *** now-you-be-careful (8) the-Manassite

וַעֲשִׂיתֶם אֹתָם לְמַעַן תַּשְׂכִּילוּ אֵת כָּל־ אֲשֶׁר תַּעֲשׂוּן׃ אַתֶּם
you (9) you-do that all *** you-may-prosper so-that them and-you-follow

נִצָּבִים הַיּוֹם כֻּלְּכֶם לִפְנֵי יְהוָה אֱלֹהֵיכֶם רָאשֵׁיכֶם
leaders-of-you God-of-you Yahweh before all-of-you the-day ones-standing

שִׁבְטֵיכֶם זִקְנֵיכֶם וְשֹׁטְרֵיכֶם כֹּל אִישׁ יִשְׂרָאֵל׃
Israel man-of every-of and-being-officials-of-you elders-of-you chiefs-of-you

טַפְּכֶם נְשֵׁיכֶם וְגֵרְךָ אֲשֶׁר בְּקֶרֶב מַחֲנֶיךָ
camps-of-you in-among who and-alien-of-you wives-of-you child-of-you (10)

מֵחֹטֵב עֵצֶיךָ עַד שֹׁאֵב מֵימֶיךָ׃
waters-of-you one-drawing-of to woods-of-you from-one-cutting-of

לְעָבְרְךָ בִּבְרִית יְהוָה אֱלֹהֶיךָ וּבְאָלָתוֹ
and-into-oath-of-him God-of-you Yahweh into-covenant-of to-enter-you (11)

אֲשֶׁר יְהוָה אֱלֹהֶיךָ כֹּרֵת עִמְּךָ הַיּוֹם׃ לְמַעַן הָקִים־ אֹתְךָ
you to-confirm in-order (12) the-day with-you making God-of-you Yahweh that

הַיּוֹם ׀ לוֹ לְעָם וְהוּא יִהְיֶה־ לְּךָ לֵאלֹהִים כַּאֲשֶׁר דִּבֶּר־
he-promised just-as as-God to-you he-will-be and-he as-people to-him the-day

לָךְ וְכַאֲשֶׁר נִשְׁבַּע לַאֲבֹתֶיךָ לְאַבְרָהָם לְיִצְחָק וּלְיַעֲקֹב׃
and-to-Jacob to-Isaac to-Abraham to-fathers-of-you he-swore and-just-as to-you

וְלֹא אִתְּכֶם לְבַדְּכֶם אָנֹכִי כֹּרֵת אֶת־ הַבְּרִית הַזֹּאת
the-this the-covenant *** making I by-selves-of-you with-you and-not (13)

וְאֶת־הָאָלָה הַזֹּאת׃ כִּי אֶת־ אֲשֶׁר יֶשְׁנוֹ פֹּה עִמָּנוּ
with-us here there-is-him whom with indeed (14) the-this the-oath and

עֹמֵד הַיּוֹם לִפְנֵי יְהוָה אֱלֹהֵינוּ וְאֵת אֲשֶׁר אֵינֶנּוּ פֹּה
here there-is-not-him whom and-with God-of-us Yahweh before the-day standing

עִמָּנוּ הַיּוֹם׃ כִּי־ אַתֶּם יְדַעְתֶּם אֵת אֲשֶׁר־ יָשַׁבְנוּ בְּאֶרֶץ מִצְרָיִם
Egypt in-land-of we-lived how *** you-know you for (15) the-day with-us

וְאֵת אֲשֶׁר־ עָבַרְנוּ בְּקֶרֶב הַגּוֹיִם אֲשֶׁר עֲבַרְתֶּם׃
you-passed-through that the-nations through-midst-of we-passed how and

וַתִּרְאוּ אֶת־ שִׁקּוּצֵיהֶם וְאֵת גִּלֻּלֵיהֶם עֵץ
wood idols-of-them and detestable-images-of-them *** and-you-saw (16)

place, Sihon king of Heshbon
and Og king of Bashan came
out to fight against us, but we
defeated them. 8We took their
land and gave it as an inheritance to the Reubenites, the
Gadites and the half-tribe of
Manasseh.
9Carefully follow the terms
of this covenant, so that you
may prosper in everything
you do. 10All of you are standing today in the presence of
the LORD your God—your leaders and chief men, your elders
and officials, and all the other
men of Israel, 11together with
your children and your wives,
and the aliens living in your
camps who chop your wood
and carry your water. 12You
are standing here in order to
enter into a covenant with the
LORD your God, a covenant the
LORD is making with you this
day and sealing with an oath,
13to confirm you this day as his
people, that he may be your
God as he promised you and
as he swore to your fathers,
Abraham, Isaac and Jacob. 14I
am making this covenant,
with its oath, not only with
you 15who are standing here
with us today in the presence
of the LORD our God but also
with those who are not here
today.
16You yourselves know how
we lived in Egypt and how we
passed through the countries
on the way here. 17You saw
among them their detestable
images and idols of wood and

*See the note on page 568.

וְאֶבֶן כֶּסֶף וְזָהָב אֲשֶׁר עִמָּהֶם׃ פֶּן־ יֵשׁ בָּכֶם אִישׁ
man among-you there-is not (17) among-them that and-gold silver and-stone

אוֹ־ אִשָּׁה אוֹ מִשְׁפָּחָה אוֹ־שֵׁבֶט אֲשֶׁר לְבָבוֹ פֹנֶה הַיּוֹם מֵעִם
from-with the-day turning heart-of-him that tribe or clan or woman or

יְהוָה אֱלֹהֵינוּ לָלֶכֶת לַעֲבֹד אֶת־ אֱלֹהֵי הַגּוֹיִם הָהֵם פֶּן־
not the-those the-nations gods-of *** to-worship to-go God-of-us Yahweh

יֵשׁ בָּכֶם שֹׁרֶשׁ פֹּרֶה רֹאשׁ וְלַעֲנָה׃ וְהָיָה
and-he-is (18) and-bitterness poison producing root-of among-you there-is

בְּשָׁמְעוֹ אֶת־ דִּבְרֵי הָאָלָה הַזֹּאת וְהִתְבָּרֵךְ
then-he-blesses-himself the-this the-oath words-of *** when-to-hear-him

בִּלְבָבוֹ לֵאמֹר שָׁלוֹם יִהְיֶה־ לִּי כִּי בִּשְׁרִרוּת
in-stubbornness-of though to-me he-will-be safety to-say in-heart-of-him

לִבִּי אֵלֵךְ לְמַעַן סְפוֹת הָרָוָה אֶת־הַצְּמֵאָה׃ לֹא־
not (19) the-dry *** watered-land to-bring-disaster so-that I-go heart-of-me

יֹאבֶה יְהוָה סְלֹחַ לוֹ כִּי אָז יֶעְשַׁן אַף־ יְהוָה
Yahweh wrath-of he-will-burn always for to-him to-forgive Yahwh he-will-want

וְקִנְאָתוֹ בָּאִישׁ הַהוּא וְרָבְצָה בּוֹ כָּל־
all-of on-him and-she-will-fall the-that against-the-man and-zeal-of-him

הָאָלָה הַכְּתוּבָה בַּסֵּפֶר הַזֶּה וּמָחָה יְהוָה
Yahweh and-he-will-blot-out the-this in-the-book the-being-written the-curse

אֶת־ שְׁמוֹ מִתַּחַת הַשָּׁמָיִם׃ וְהִבְדִּילוֹ יְהוָה
Yahweh and-he-will-single-out-him (20) the-heavens from-under name-of-him ***

לְרָעָה מִכֹּל שִׁבְטֵי יִשְׂרָאֵל כְּכֹל אָלוֹת הַבְּרִית
the-covenant curses-of as-all-of Israel tribes-of from-all-of for-disaster

הַכְּתוּבָה בְּסֵפֶר הַתּוֹרָה הַזֶּה׃ וְאָמַר
and-he-will-say (21) the-this the-Law in-Book-of the-being-written

הַדּוֹר הָאַחֲרוֹן בְּנֵיכֶם אֲשֶׁר יָקוּמוּ מֵאַחֲרֵיכֶם
from-after-you they-follow who children-of-you the-later the-generation

וְהַנָּכְרִי אֲשֶׁר יָבֹא מֵאֶרֶץ רְחוֹקָה וְרָאוּ אֶת־
*** when-they-see distant from-land he-comes who and-the-foreigner

מַכּוֹת הָאָרֶץ הַהִוא וְאֶת־ תַּחֲלֻאֶיהָ אֲשֶׁר־ חִלָּה יְהוָה
Yahweh he-afflicted that diseases-of-her and the-this the-land calamities-of

בָּהּ׃ גָּפְרִית וָמֶלַח שְׂרֵפָה כָל־ אַרְצָהּ לֹא תִזָּרַע
she-is-planted not land-of-her all-of burnt-waste and-salt sulfur (22) on-her

וְלֹא תַצְמִחַ וְלֹא־ יַעֲלֶה בָהּ כָּל־ עֵשֶׂב כְּמַהְפֵּכַת
as-destruction-of vegetation any-of on-her she-grows and-not she-sprouts and-not

סְדֹם וַעֲמֹרָה אַדְמָה וּצְבִיִּם אֲשֶׁר הָפַךְ יְהוָה בְּאַפּוֹ
in-anger-of-him Yahweh he-overthrew which and-Zeboiim Admah and-Gomorrah Sodom

stone, of silver and gold.
18Make sure there is no man or
woman, clan or tribe among
you today whose heart turns
away from the LORD our God
to go and worship the gods of
those nations; make sure there
is no root among you that produces such bitter poison.
19When such a person hears
the words of this oath, he in-
vokes a blessing on himself
and therefore thinks, "I will
be safe, even though I persist
in going my own way." This
will bring disaster on the watered land as well as the dry.[m]
20The LORD will never be willing to forgive him; his wrath
and zeal will burn against that
man. All the curses written in
this book will fall upon him,
and the LORD will blot out his
name from under heaven.
21The LORD will single him out
from all the tribes of Israel for
disaster, according to all the
curses of the covenant written
in this Book of the Law.
22Your children who follow
you in later generations and
foreigners who come from distant lands will see the calamities that have fallen on the
land and the diseases with
which the LORD has afflicted it.
23The whole land will be a
burning waste of salt and sulfur—nothing planted, nothing
sprouting, no vegetation
growing on it. It will be like
the destruction of Sodom and
Gomorrah, Admah and Ze-
boiim, which the LORD overthrew in fierce anger. 24All the

m19 Or way, in order to add drunkenness to thirst."

*See the note on page 568.

°22 ק וצבוים

וּבַחֲמָתוֹ׃ וְאָמְרוּ כָּל־ הַגּוֹיִם עַל־ מֶה עָשָׂה
he-did why? for the-nations all-of and-they-will-ask (23) and-in-wrath-of-him

יְהוָה כָּכָה לָאָרֶץ הַזֹּאת מֶה חֳרִי הָאַף הַגָּדוֹל הַזֶּה׃
the-this the-fierce the-anger burning-of why? the-this to-the-land this Yahweh

וְאָמְרוּ עַל אֲשֶׁר עָזְבוּ אֶת־ בְּרִית יְהוָה
Yahweh covenant-of *** they-abandoned that because and-they-will-answer (24)

אֱלֹהֵי אֲבֹתָם אֲשֶׁר כָּרַת עִמָּם בְּהוֹצִיאוֹ אֹתָם
them when-to-bring-him with-them he-made that fathers-of-them God-of

מֵאֶרֶץ מִצְרָיִם׃ וַיֵּלְכוּ וַיַּעַבְדוּ אֱלֹהִים אֲחֵרִים
other-ones gods and-they-worshiped and-they-went-off (25) Egypt from-land-of

וַיִּשְׁתַּחֲווּ† לָהֶם אֱלֹהִים אֲשֶׁר לֹא־ יְדָעוּם וְלֹא חָלַק לָהֶם׃
to-them he-gave and-not they-knew-them not that gods to-them and-they-bowed

וַיִּחַר־ אַף יְהוָה בָּאָרֶץ הַהִוא לְהָבִיא עָלֶיהָ
on-her to-bring the-this against-the-land Yahweh anger-of so-he-burned (26)

אֶת־ כָּל־ הַקְּלָלָה הַכְּתוּבָה בַּסֵּפֶר הַזֶּה׃
the-this in-the-book the-being-written the-curse all-of ***

וַיִּתְּשֵׁם יְהוָה מֵעַל אַדְמָתָם בְּאַף וּבְחֵמָה
and-in-fury in-anger land-of-them from-in Yahweh and-he-uprooted-them (27)

וּבְקֶצֶף גָּדוֹל וַיַּשְׁלִכֵם אֶל־ אֶרֶץ אַחֶרֶת כַּיּוֹם הַזֶּה׃
the-this as-the-day another land into and-he-thrust-them great and-in-wrath

הַנִּסְתָּרֹת לַיהוָה אֱלֹהֵינוּ וְהַנִּגְלֹת
but-the-things-being-revealed God-of-us to-Yahweh the-things-being-hidden (28)

לָנוּ וּלְבָנֵינוּ עַד־ עוֹלָם לַעֲשׂוֹת אֶת־ כָּל־ דִּבְרֵי הַתּוֹרָה
the-law words-of all-of *** to-follow forever to and-to-children-of-us to-us

הַזֹּאת׃ וְהָיָה כִי־ יָבֹאוּ עָלֶיךָ כָּל־ הַדְּבָרִים
the-things all-of on-you they-come when and-he-will-be (30:1) the-this

הָאֵלֶּה הַבְּרָכָה וְהַקְּלָלָה אֲשֶׁר נָתַתִּי לְפָנֶיךָ וַהֲשֵׁבֹתָ אֶל־
to and-you-take before-you I-set that and-the-curse the-blessing the-these

לְבָבֶךָ בְּכָל־ הַגּוֹיִם אֲשֶׁר הִדִּיחֲךָ יְהוָה אֱלֹהֶיךָ
God-of-you Yahweh he-disperses-you where the-nations among-all-of heart-of-you

שָׁמָּה׃ וְשַׁבְתָּ עַד־ יְהוָה אֱלֹהֶיךָ וְשָׁמַעְתָּ בְקֹלוֹ
to-voice-of-him and-you-obey God-of-you Yahweh to and-you-return (2) to-there

כְּכֹל אֲשֶׁר־אָנֹכִי מְצַוְּךָ הַיּוֹם אַתָּה וּבָנֶיךָ בְּכָל־
with-all-of and-children-of-you you the-day commanding-you I that as-all

לְבָבְךָ וּבְכָל־ נַפְשֶׁךָ׃ וְשָׁב יְהוָה
Yahweh then-he-will-restore (3) soul-of-you and-with-all-of heart-of-you

אֱלֹהֶיךָ אֶת־ שְׁבוּתְךָ וְרִחֲמֶךָ
and-he-will-have-compassion-on-you captivity-of-you *** God-of-you

nations will ask: "Why has the LORD done this to this land? Why this fierce, burning anger?"

[25]And the answer will be: "It is because this people abandoned the covenant of the LORD, the God of their fathers, the covenant he made with them when he brought them out of Egypt. [26]They went off and worshiped other gods and bowed down to them, gods they did not know, gods he had not given them. [27]Therefore the LORD's anger burned against this land, so that he brought on it all the curses written in this book. [28]In furious anger and in great wrath the LORD uprooted them from their land and thrust them into another land, as it is now."

[29]The secret things belong to the LORD our God, but the things revealed belong to us and to our children forever, that we may follow all the words of this law.

Prosperity After Turning to the LORD

30 When all these blessings and curses I have set before you come upon you and you take them to heart wherever the LORD your God disperses you among the nations, [2]and when you and your children return to the LORD your God and obey him with all your heart and with all your soul according to everything I command you today, [3]then the LORD your God will restore your fortunes[n] and have compassion on you and

[n]3 Or *will bring you back from captivity*

*See the note on page 568.

†25 Most mss have no *dagesh* in the first *vav* (וּ־).

וְשָׁב וְקִבֶּצְךָ מִכָּל־ הָעַמִּים אֲשֶׁר
where the-nations from-all-of and-he-will-gather-you and-he-will-restore

הֱפִיצְךָ יְהוָה אֱלֹהֶיךָ שָׁמָּה׃ אִם־ יִהְיֶה נִדַּחֲךָ
banishing-of-you he-is if (4) to-there God-of-you Yahweh he-scattered-you

בִּקְצֵה הַשָּׁמָיִם מִשָּׁם יְקַבֶּצְךָ יְהוָה אֱלֹהֶיךָ
God-of-you Yahweh he-will-gather-you from-there the-heavens to-end-of

וּמִשָּׁם יִקָּחֶךָ׃ וֶהֱבִיאֲךָ יְהוָה
Yahweh and-he-will-bring-back-you (5) he-will-bring-back-you and-from-there

אֱלֹהֶיךָ אֶל־ הָאָרֶץ אֲשֶׁר־ יָרְשׁוּ אֲבֹתֶיךָ
fathers-of-you they-possessed that the-land to God-of-you

וִירִשְׁתָּהּ וְהֵיטִבְךָ וְהִרְבְּךָ
and-he-will-increase-you and-he-will-make-prosper-you and-you-will-possess-her

מֵאֲבֹתֶיךָ׃ וּמָל יְהוָה אֱלֹהֶיךָ אֶת־
*** God-of-you Yahweh and-he-will-circumcise (6) more-than-fathers-of-you

לְבָבְךָ וְאֶת־ לְבַב זַרְעֶךָ לְאַהֲבָה אֶת־ יְהוָה אֱלֹהֶיךָ
God-of-you Yahweh *** to-love descendant-of-you heart-of and heart-of-you

בְּכָל־ לְבָבְךָ וּבְכָל־ נַפְשְׁךָ לְמַעַן חַיֶּיךָ׃
lives-of-you so-that soul-of-you and-with-all-of heart-of-you with-all-of

וְנָתַן יְהוָה אֱלֹהֶיךָ אֵת כָּל־ הָאָלוֹת הָאֵלֶּה עַל־
on the-these the-curses all-of *** God-of-you Yahweh and-he-will-put (7)

אֹיְבֶיךָ וְעַל־ שֹׂנְאֶיךָ אֲשֶׁר רְדָפוּךָ׃
they-persecute-you who ones-hating-you and-on being-enemies-of-you

וְאַתָּה תָשׁוּב וְשָׁמַעְתָּ בְּקוֹל יְהוָה
Yahweh to-voice-of and-you-will-obey you-will-return and-you (8)

וְעָשִׂיתָ אֶת־ כָּל־ מִצְוֺתָיו אֲשֶׁר אָנֹכִי מְצַוְּךָ הַיּוֹם׃
the-day giving-you I that commands-of-him all-of *** and-you-will-follow

וְהוֹתִירְךָ יְהוָה אֱלֹהֶיךָ בְּכֹל ׀ מַעֲשֵׂה
work-of in-all-of God-of-you Yahweh then-he-will-make-prosper-you (9)

יָדֶךָ בִּפְרִי בִטְנְךָ וּבִפְרִי בְהֶמְתְּךָ וּבִפְרִי
and-in-crop-of stock-of-you and-in-young-of womb-of-you in-fruit-of hand-of-you

אַדְמָתְךָ לְטֹבָה כִּי ׀ יָשׁוּב יְהוָה לָשׂוּשׂ עָלֶיךָ לְטוֹב
to-prosperity in-you to-delight Yahweh he-will-return then for-good land-of-you

כַּאֲשֶׁר־ שָׂשׂ עַל־ אֲבֹתֶיךָ׃ כִּי תִשְׁמַע בְּקוֹל יְהוָה
Yahweh to-voice-of you-obey if (10) fathers-of-you in he-delighted just-as

אֱלֹהֶיךָ לִשְׁמֹר מִצְוֺתָיו וְחֻקֹּתָיו הַכְּתוּבָה
the-being-written and-decrees-of-him commands-of-him to-keep God-of-you

בְּסֵפֶר הַתּוֹרָה הַזֶּה כִּי תָשׁוּב אֶל־ יְהוָה אֱלֹהֶיךָ בְּכָל־
with-all-of God-of-you Yahweh to you-turn if the-this the-Law in-Book-of

gather you again from all the
nations where he scattered
you. [4]Even if you have been
banished to the most distant
land under the heavens, from
there the LORD your God will
gather you and bring you
back. [5]He will bring you to the
land that belonged to your fathers, and you will take
possession of it. He will make
you more prosperous and numerous than your fathers.
[6]The LORD your God will circumcise your hearts and the
hearts of your descendants, so
that you may love him with all
your heart and with all your
soul, and live. [7]The LORD your
God will put all these curses on
your enemies who hate and
persecute you. [8]You will again
obey the LORD and follow all
his commands I am giving
you today. [9]Then the LORD
your God will make you most
prosperous in all the work of
your hands and in the fruit of
your womb, the young of your
livestock and the crops of your
land. The LORD will again delight in you and make you
prosperous, just as he delighted in your fathers, [10]if you
obey the LORD your God and
keep his commands and de-
crees that are written in this
Book of the Law and turn to
the LORD your God with all

לְבָבְךָ וּבְכָל־ נַפְשֶׁךָ׃ כִּי הַמִּצְוָה הַזֹּאת אֲשֶׁר
that the-this the-command now (11) soul-of-you and-with-all-of heart-of-you

אָנֹכִי מְצַוְּךָ הַיּוֹם לֹא־ נִפְלֵאת הִוא מִמְּךָ וְלֹא רְחֹקָה
distant and-not for-you she being-too-difficult not the-day commanding-you I

הִוא׃ לֹא בַשָּׁמַיִם הִוא לֵאמֹר מִי יַעֲלֶה־ לָּנוּ
for-us he-will-ascend who? to-say she in-the-heavens not (12) she

הַשָּׁמַיְמָה וְיִקָּחֶהָ לָּנוּ וְיַשְׁמִעֵנוּ אֹתָהּ
her and-he-will-proclaim-to-us for-us so-he-will-get-her into-the-heavens

וְנַעֲשֶׂנָּה׃ וְלֹא־ מֵעֵבֶר לַיָּם הִוא לֵאמֹר מִי
who? to-say she of-the-sea on-beyond and-not (13) so-we-may-obey-her

יַעֲבָר־ לָנוּ אֶל־ עֵבֶר הַיָּם וְיִקָּחֶהָ לָּנוּ
for-us so-he-will-get-her the-sea beyond to for-us he-will-cross

וְיַשְׁמִעֵנוּ אֹתָהּ וְנַעֲשֶׂנָּה׃ כִּי־ קָרוֹב אֵלֶיךָ
to-you near for (14) so-we-may-obey-her her and-he-will-proclaim-to-us

הַדָּבָר מְאֹד בְּפִיךָ וּבִלְבָבְךָ לַעֲשֹׂתוֹ׃ רְאֵה נָתַתִּי
I-set see! (15) to-obey-him and-in-heart-of-you in-mouth-of-you very the-word

לְפָנֶיךָ הַיּוֹם אֶת־ הַחַיִּים וְאֶת־ הַטּוֹב וְאֶת־ הַמָּוֶת וְאֶת־
and the-death and the-prosperity and the-lives *** the-day before-you

הָרָע׃ אֲשֶׁר אָנֹכִי מְצַוְּךָ הַיּוֹם לְאַהֲבָה אֶת־ יְהוָה
Yahweh *** to-love the-day commanding-you I for (16) the-destruction

אֱלֹהֶיךָ לָלֶכֶת בִּדְרָכָיו וְלִשְׁמֹר מִצְוֺתָיו
commands-of-him and-to-keep in-ways-of-him to-walk God-of-you

וְחֻקֹּתָיו וּמִשְׁפָּטָיו וְחָיִיתָ וְרָבִיתָ
and-you-will-increase then-you-will-live and-laws-of-him and-decrees-of-him

וּבֵרַכְךָ יְהוָה אֱלֹהֶיךָ בָּאָרֶץ אֲשֶׁר־ אַתָּה בָא־
entering you where in-the-land God-of-you Yahweh and-he-will-bless-you

שָׁמָּה לְרִשְׁתָּהּ׃ וְאִם־ יִפְנֶה לְבָבְךָ וְלֹא
and-not heart-of-you he-turns-away but-if (17) to-possess-her to-there

תִשְׁמָע וְנִדַּחְתָּ וְהִשְׁתַּחֲוִיתָ לֵאלֹהִים אֲחֵרִים
other-ones to-gods and-you-bow-down and-you-are-drawn-away you-obey

וַעֲבַדְתָּם׃ הִגַּדְתִּי לָכֶם הַיּוֹם כִּי אָבֹד
to-be-destroyed that the-day to-you I-declare (18) and-you-worship-them

תֹּאבֵדוּן לֹא־ תַאֲרִיכֻן יָמִים עַל־ הָאֲדָמָה אֲשֶׁר אַתָּה
you that the-land in days you-will-have-long not you-will-be-destroyed

עֹבֵר אֶת־ הַיַּרְדֵּן לָבֹא שָׁמָּה לְרִשְׁתָּהּ׃ הַעִידֹתִי
I-call-witness (19) to-possess-her to-there to-enter the-Jordan *** crossing

בָכֶם הַיּוֹם אֶת־ הַשָּׁמַיִם וְאֶת־ הָאָרֶץ הַחַיִּים וְהַמָּוֶת
and-the-death the-lives the-earth and the-heavens *** the-day against-you

your heart and with all your
soul.

The Offer of Life or Death

11Now what I am command-
ing you today is not too
difficult for you or beyond
your reach. 12It is not up in
heaven, so that you have to
ask, "Who will ascend into
heaven to get it and proclaim
it to us so we may obey it?"
13Nor is it beyond the sea, so
that you have to ask, "Who
will cross the sea to get it and
proclaim it to us so we may
obey it?" 14No, the word is
very near you; it is in your
mouth and in your heart so
you may obey it.

15See, I set before you today
life and prosperity, death and
destruction. 16For I command
you today to love the LORD
your God, to walk in his ways,
and to keep his commands,
decrees and laws; then you
will live and increase, and the
LORD your God will bless you
in the land you are entering to
possess.

17But if your heart turns
away and you are not obedi-
ent, and if you are drawn
away to bow down to other
gods and worship them, 18I declare to you this day that you
will certainly be destroyed.
You will not live long in the
land you are crossing the Jordan to enter and possess.

19This day I call heaven and
earth as witnesses against you
that I have set before you life

נָתַתִּי לְפָנֶיךָ הַבְּרָכָה וְהַקְּלָלָה וּבָחַרְתָּ בַּחַיִּים
to-the-lives now-you-choose and-the-curse the-blessing before-you I-set

לְמַעַן תִּחְיֶה אַתָּה וְזַרְעֶךָ׃ לְאַהֲבָה אֶת־יְהוָה אֱלֹהֶיךָ
God-of-you Yahweh *** to-love (20) and-child-of-you you you-may-live so-that

לִשְׁמֹעַ בְּקֹלוֹ וּלְדָבְקָה־בוֹ כִּי הוּא חַיֶּיךָ
lives-of-you he for to-him and-to-hold-fast to-voice-of-him to-listen

וְאֹרֶךְ יָמֶיךָ לָשֶׁבֶת עַל־הָאֲדָמָה אֲשֶׁר נִשְׁבַּע יְהוָה
Yahweh he-swore that the-land in to-dwell days-of-you and-length-of

לַאֲבֹתֶיךָ לְאַבְרָהָם לְיִצְחָק וּלְיַעֲקֹב לָתֵת לָהֶם׃
to-them to-give and-to-Jacob to-Isaac to-Abraham to-fathers-of-you

וַיֵּלֶךְ מֹשֶׁה וַיְדַבֵּר אֶת־הַדְּבָרִים הָאֵלֶּה אֶל־כָּל־
all-of to the-these the-words *** and-he-spoke Moses then-he-went-out (31:1)

יִשְׂרָאֵל׃ וַיֹּאמֶר אֲלֵהֶם בֶּן־מֵאָה וְעֶשְׂרִים שָׁנָה אָנֹכִי הַיּוֹם
the-day I year and-twenty hundred son-of to-them and-he-said (2) Israel

לֹא־אוּכַל עוֹד לָצֵאת וְלָבוֹא וַיהוָה אָמַר אֵלַי לֹא
not to-me he-said and-Yahweh and-to-come-in to-go-out longer I-am-able not

תַעֲבֹר אֶת־הַיַּרְדֵּן הַזֶּה׃ יְהוָה אֱלֹהֶיךָ הוּא עֹבֵר
crossing he God-of-you Yahweh (3) the-this the-Jordan *** you-shall-cross

לְפָנֶיךָ הוּא־יַשְׁמִיד אֶת־הַגּוֹיִם הָאֵלֶּה מִלְּפָנֶיךָ
from-before-you the-these the-nations *** he-will-destroy he ahead-of-you

וִירִשְׁתָּם יְהוֹשֻׁעַ הוּא עֹבֵר לְפָנֶיךָ כַּאֲשֶׁר דִּבֶּר
he-said just-as ahead-of-you crossing he Joshua and-you-will-possess-them

יְהוָה׃ וְעָשָׂה יְהוָה לָהֶם כַּאֲשֶׁר עָשָׂה לְסִיחוֹן וּלְעוֹג
and-to-Og to-Sihon he-did just-as to-them Yahweh and-he-will-do (4) Yahweh

מַלְכֵי הָאֱמֹרִי וּלְאַרְצָם אֲשֶׁר הִשְׁמִיד אֹתָם׃
them he-destroyed that and-to-land-of-them the-Amorite kings-of

וּנְתָנָם יְהוָה לִפְנֵיכֶם וַעֲשִׂיתֶם לָהֶם
to-them and-you-must-do over-to-you Yahweh and-he-will-deliver-them (5)

כְּכָל־הַמִּצְוָה אֲשֶׁר צִוִּיתִי אֶתְכֶם׃ חִזְקוּ וְאִמְצוּ
and-be-courageous! be-strong! (6) you I-commanded that the-command as-all-of

אַל־תִּירְאוּ וְאַל־תַּעַרְצוּ מִפְּנֵיהֶם כִּי יְהוָה אֱלֹהֶיךָ
God-of-you Yahweh for because-of-them you-be-terrified and-not you-fear not

הוּא הַהֹלֵךְ עִמָּךְ לֹא יַרְפְּךָ וְלֹא יַעַזְבֶךָּ׃
he-will-forsake-you and-not he-will-leave-you not with-you the-one-going he

וַיִּקְרָא מֹשֶׁה לִיהוֹשֻׁעַ וַיֹּאמֶר אֵלָיו לְעֵינֵי כָל־
all-of before-eyes-of to-him and-he-said to-Joshua Moses then-he-summoned (7)

יִשְׂרָאֵל חֲזַק וֶאֱמָץ כִּי אַתָּה תָּבוֹא אֶת־הָעָם
the-people with you-must-go you for and-be-courageous! be-strong! Israel

and death, blessings and curses. Now choose life, so that you and your children may live 20 and that you may love the LORD your God, listen to his voice, and hold fast to him. For the LORD is your life, and he will give you many years in the land he swore to give to your fathers, Abraham, Isaac and Jacob.

Joshua to Succeed Moses

31 Then Moses went out and spoke these words to all Israel: 2 "I am now a hundred and twenty years old and I am no longer able to lead you. The LORD has said to me, 'You shall not cross the Jordan.' 3 The LORD your God himself will cross over ahead of you. He will destroy these nations before you, and you will take possession of their land. Joshua also will cross over ahead of you, as the LORD said. 4 And the LORD will do to them what he did to Sihon and Og, the kings of the Amorites, whom he destroyed along with their land. 5 The LORD will deliver them to you, and you must do to them all that I have commanded you. 6 Be strong and courageous. Do not be afraid or terrified because of them, for the LORD your God goes with you; he will never leave you nor forsake you."

7 Then Moses summoned Joshua and said to him in the presence of all Israel, "Be strong and courageous, for you must go with this people

הַזֶּה אֶל־ הָאָרֶץ אֲשֶׁר נִשְׁבַּע יְהוָה לַאֲבֹתָם לָתֵת
to-give to-fathers-of-them Yahweh he-swore that the-land into the-this

לָהֶם וְאַתָּה תַּנְחִילֶנָּה אוֹתָם׃ וַיהוָה הוּא ׀
he and-Yahweh (8) to-them you-must-divide-as-inheritance-her and-you to-them

הַהֹלֵךְ לְפָנֶיךָ הוּא יִהְיֶה עִמָּךְ לֹא יַרְפְּךָ וְלֹא
and-not he-will-leave-you not with-you he-will-be he before-you the-one-going

יַעַזְבֶךָּ לֹא תִירָא וְלֹא תֵחָת׃ וַיִּכְתֹּב
so-he-wrote (9) you-be-discouraged and-not you-fear not he-will-forsake-you

מֹשֶׁה אֶת־ הַתּוֹרָה הַזֹּאת וַיִּתְּנָהּ אֶל־ הַכֹּהֲנִים בְּנֵי לֵוִי
Levi sons-of the-priests to and-he-gave-her the-this the-law *** Moses

הַנֹּשְׂאִים אֶת־ אֲרוֹן בְּרִית יְהוָה וְאֶל־ כָּל־ זִקְנֵי
elders-of all-of and-to Yahweh covenant-of ark-of *** the-ones-carrying

יִשְׂרָאֵל׃ וַיְצַו מֹשֶׁה אוֹתָם לֵאמֹר מִקֵּץ ׀ שֶׁבַע שָׁנִים
years seven at-end-of to-say them Moses then-he-commanded (10) Israel

בְּמֹעֵד שְׁנַת הַשְּׁמִטָּה בְּחַג הַסֻּכּוֹת׃
the-Tabernacles during-Feast-of the-cancel-of-debt year-of at-time-of

בְּבוֹא כָל־ יִשְׂרָאֵל לֵרָאוֹת אֶת־ פְּנֵי יְהוָה אֱלֹהֶיךָ
God-of-you Yahweh before *** to-appear Israel all-of when-to-come (11)

בַּמָּקוֹם אֲשֶׁר יִבְחָר תִּקְרָא אֶת־ הַתּוֹרָה הַזֹּאת נֶגֶד
before the-this the-law *** you-shall-read he-will-choose that at-the-place

כָּל־ יִשְׂרָאֵל בְּאָזְנֵיהֶם׃ הַקְהֵל אֶת־ הָעָם הָאֲנָשִׁים
the-men the-people *** assemble! (12) in-ears-of-them Israel all-of

וְהַנָּשִׁים וְהַטַּף וְגֵרְךָ אֲשֶׁר בִּשְׁעָרֶיךָ לְמַעַן
so-that in-gates-of-you who and-alien-of-you and-the-child and-the-women

יִשְׁמְעוּ וּלְמַעַן יִלְמְדוּ וְיָרְאוּ אֶת־ יְהוָה
Yahweh *** so-they-will-fear they-can-learn and-so-that they-can-listen

אֱלֹהֵיכֶם וְשָׁמְרוּ לַעֲשׂוֹת אֶת־ כָּל־ דִּבְרֵי הַתּוֹרָה
the-law words-of all-of *** to-follow so-they-will-be-careful God-of-you

הַזֹּאת׃ וּבְנֵיהֶם אֲשֶׁר לֹא־ יָדְעוּ יִשְׁמְעוּ
they-must-hear they-know not who and-children-of-them (13) the-this

וְלָמְדוּ לְיִרְאָה אֶת־ יְהוָה אֱלֹהֵיכֶם כָּל־ הַיָּמִים אֲשֶׁר אַתֶּם
you that the-days all-of God-of-you Yahweh *** to-fear and-they-must-learn

חַיִּים עַל־ הָאֲדָמָה אֲשֶׁר אַתֶּם עֹבְרִים אֶת־ הַיַּרְדֵּן שָׁמָּה
to-there the-Jordan *** ones-crossing you that the-land in ones-alive

לְרִשְׁתָּהּ׃ וַיֹּאמֶר יְהוָה אֶל־ מֹשֶׁה הֵן קָרְבוּ
they-are-near see! Moses to Yahweh and-he-said (14) to-possess-her

יָמֶיךָ לָמוּת קְרָא אֶת־ יְהוֹשֻׁעַ וְהִתְיַצְּבוּ בְּאֹהֶל מוֹעֵד
Meeting at-Tent-of and-present-yourselves! Joshua *** call! do-die days-of-you

into the land that the LORD swore to their forefathers to give them, and you must divide it among them as their inheritance. [8]The LORD himself goes before you and will be with you; he will never leave you nor forsake you. Do not be afraid; do not be discouraged."

The Reading of the Law

[9]So Moses wrote down this law and gave it to the priests, the sons of Levi, who carried the ark of the covenant of the LORD, and to all the elders of Israel. [10]Then Moses commanded them: "At the end of every seven years, in the year for canceling debts, during the Feast of Tabernacles, [11]when all Israel comes to appear before the LORD your God at the place he will choose, you shall read this law before them in their hearing. [12]Assemble the people—men, women and children, and the aliens living in your towns—so they can listen and learn to fear the LORD your God and follow carefully all the words of this law. [13]Their children, who do not know this law, must hear it and learn to fear the LORD your God as long as you live in the land you are crossing the Jordan to possess."

Israel's Rebellion Predicted

[14]The LORD said to Moses, "Now the day of your death is near. Call Joshua and present yourselves at the Tent of Meeting, where I will commission

וַאֲצַוֶּנּוּ וַיֵּלֶךְ מֹשֶׁה וִיהוֹשֻׁעַ וַיִּתְיַצְּבוּ
and-they-presented-selves and-Joshua Moses so-he-came and-I-will-commission-him

בְּאֹהֶל מוֹעֵד׃ וַיֵּרָא יְהוָה בָּאֹהֶל בְּעַמּוּד עָנָן
cloud in-pillar-of at-the-Tent Yahweh then-he-appeared (15) Meeting at-Tent-of

וַיַּעֲמֹד עַמּוּד הֶעָנָן עַל־ פֶּתַח הָאֹהֶל׃ וַיֹּאמֶר
and-he-said (16) the-Tent entrance-of over the-cloud pillar-of and-he-stood

יְהוָה אֶל־ מֹשֶׁה הִנְּךָ שֹׁכֵב עִם־ אֲבֹתֶיךָ וְקָם
and-he-will-rise fathers-of-you with resting see-you! Moses to Yahweh

הָעָם הַזֶּה וְזָנָה ׀ אַחֲרֵי ׀ אֱלֹהֵי נֵכַר־ הָאָרֶץ
the-land foreign-of gods-of after and-he-will-prostitute the-this the-people

אֲשֶׁר הוּא בָא־ שָׁמָּה בְּקִרְבּוֹ וַעֲזָבַנִי וְהֵפֵר
and-he-will-break and-he-will-forsake-me in-among-him to-there entering he that

אֶת־ בְּרִיתִי אֲשֶׁר כָּרַתִּי אִתּוֹ׃ וְחָרָה אַפִּי
anger-of-me and-he-will-burn (17) with-him I-made that covenant-of-me ***

בוֹ בַיּוֹם־ הַהוּא וַעֲזַבְתִּים וְהִסְתַּרְתִּי
and-I-will-hide and-I-will-forsake-them the-that on-the-day against-him

פָנַי מֵהֶם וְהָיָה לֶאֱכֹל וּמְצָאֻהוּ
and-they-will-come-on-him to-destroy and-he-will-be from-them faces-of-me

רָעוֹת רַבּוֹת וְצָרוֹת וְאָמַר בַּיּוֹם הַהוּא הֲלֹא
not? the-that on-the-day and-he-will-ask and-difficulties many disasters

עַל כִּי־ אֵין אֱלֹהַי בְּקִרְבִּי מְצָאוּנִי הָרָעוֹת
the-disasters they-came-on-me in-midst-of-me God-of-me not because for

הָאֵלֶּה׃ וְאָנֹכִי הַסְתֵּר אַסְתִּיר פָּנַי בַּיּוֹם הַהוּא
the-that on-the-day faces-of-me I-will-hide to-hide and-I (18) the-these

עַל כָּל־ הָרָעָה אֲשֶׁר עָשָׂה כִּי פָנָה אֶל־אֱלֹהִים אֲחֵרִים׃
other-ones gods to he-turned when he-did that the-wickedness all-of for

וְעַתָּה כִּתְבוּ לָכֶם אֶת־הַשִּׁירָה הַזֹּאת וְלַמְּדָהּ אֶת־ בְּנֵי־
sons-of *** and-teach-her! the-this the-song *** for-you write! and-now (19)

יִשְׂרָאֵל שִׂימָהּ בְּפִיהֶם לְמַעַן תִּהְיֶה־ לִּי הַשִּׁירָה הַזֹּאת
the-this the-song for-me she-may-be so-that in-mouth-of-them put-her! Israel

לְעֵד בִּבְנֵי יִשְׂרָאֵל׃ כִּי־ אֲבִיאֶנּוּ אֶל־הָאֲדָמָה ׀
the-land into I-bring-him when (20) Israel against-sons-of as-witness

אֲשֶׁר־ נִשְׁבַּעְתִּי לַאֲבֹתָיו זָבַת חָלָב וּדְבַשׁ וְאָכַל
and-he-eats and-honey milk flowing-of to-fathers-of-him I-promised that

וְשָׂבַע וְדָשֵׁן וּפָנָה אֶל־ אֱלֹהִים אֲחֵרִים
other-ones gods to then-he-will-turn and-he-thrives and-he-is-full

וַעֲבָדוּם וְנִאֲצוּנִי וְהֵפֵר אֶת־
*** and-he-will-break and-they-will-reject-me and-they-will-worship-them

him." So Moses and Joshua came and presented themselves at the Tent of Meeting.
15Then the LORD appeared at the Tent in a pillar of cloud, and the cloud stood over the entrance to the Tent.
16And the LORD said to Moses: "You are going to rest with your fathers, and these people will soon prostitute themselves to the foreign gods of the land they are entering. They will forsake me and break the covenant I made with them.
17On that day I will become angry with them and forsake them; I will hide my face from them, and they will be destroyed. Many disasters and difficulties will come upon them, and on that day they will ask, 'Have not these disasters come upon us because our God is not with us?'
18And I will certainly hide my face on that day because of all their wickedness in turning to other gods.
19"Now write down for yourselves this song and teach it to the Israelites and have them sing it, so that it may be a witness for me against them.
20When I have brought them into the land flowing with milk and honey, the land I promised on oath to their forefathers, and when they eat their fill and thrive, they will turn to other gods and worship them, rejecting me and

בְּרִיתִי׃ וְהָיָה כִּי־ תִמְצֶאןָ אֹתוֹ רָעוֹת רַבּוֹת

many disasters upon-him they-come when and-he-will-be (21) covenant-of-me

וְצָרוֹת וְעָנְתָה הַשִּׁירָה הַזֹּאת לְפָנָיו

against-him the-this the-song then-she-will-testify and-difficulties

לְעֵד כִּי לֹא תִשָּׁכַח מִפִּי זַרְעוֹ

descendant-of-him from-mouth-of she-will-be-forgotten not for as-witness

כִּי יָדַעְתִּי אֶת־ יִצְרוֹ אֲשֶׁר הוּא עֹשֶׂה הַיּוֹם בְּטֶרֶם אֲבִיאֶנּוּ

I-bring-him even-before the-day doing he that way-of-him *** I-know for

אֶל־ הָאָרֶץ אֲשֶׁר נִשְׁבָּעְתִּי׃ וַיִּכְתֹּב מֹשֶׁה אֶת־ הַשִּׁירָה הַזֹּאת

the-this the-song *** Moses so-he-wrote (22) I-promised that the-land into

בַּיּוֹם הַהוּא וַיְלַמְּדָהּ אֶת־ בְּנֵי יִשְׂרָאֵל׃ וַיְצַו

and-he-commanded (23) Israel sons-of *** and-he-taught-her the-that on-the-day

אֶת־ יְהוֹשֻׁעַ בִּן־ נוּן וַיֹּאמֶר חֲזַק וֶאֱמָץ כִּי אַתָּה

you for and-be-courageous! be-strong! and-he-said Nun son-of Joshua ***

תָּבִיא אֶת־ בְּנֵי יִשְׂרָאֵל אֶל־ הָאָרֶץ אֲשֶׁר־ נִשְׁבַּעְתִּי לָהֶם

to-them I-promised that the-land into Israel sons-of *** you-will-bring

וְאָנֹכִי אֶהְיֶה עִמָּךְ׃ וַיְהִי ׀ כְּכַלּוֹת מֹשֶׁה לִכְתֹּב אֶת־

*** to-write Moses after-to-finish and-he-was (24) with-you I-will-be and-I

דִּבְרֵי הַתּוֹרָה־ הַזֹּאת עַל־ סֵפֶר עַד תֻּמָּם׃ וַיְצַו

then-he-commanded (25) to-end-them until book in the-this the-law words-of

מֹשֶׁה אֶת־ הַלְוִיִּם נֹשְׂאֵי אֲרוֹן בְּרִית־ יְהוָה לֵאמֹר׃

to-say Yahweh covenant-of ark-of ones-carrying-of the-Levites *** Moses

לָקֹחַ אֵת סֵפֶר הַתּוֹרָה הַזֶּה וְשַׂמְתֶּם אֹתוֹ מִצַּד

at-side-of him and-you-place the-this the-Law Book-of *** to-take (26)

אֲרוֹן בְּרִית־ יְהוָה אֱלֹהֵיכֶם וְהָיָה־ שָׁם בְּךָ

against-you there and-he-will-remain God-of-you Yahweh covenant-of ark-of

לְעֵד׃ כִּי אָנֹכִי יָדַעְתִּי אֶת־ מֶרְיְךָ וְאֶת־ עָרְפְּךָ הַקָּשֶׁה

the-stiff neck-of-you and rebellion-of-you *** I-know I for (27) as-witness

הֵן בְּעוֹדֶנִּי חַי עִמָּכֶם הַיּוֹם מַמְרִים הֱיִתֶם עִם־ יְהוָה

Yahweh against you-are ones-rebelling the-day with-you alive if-still-me see!

וְאַף כִּי־ אַחֲרֵי מוֹתִי׃ הַקְהִילוּ אֵלַי אֶת־

*** before-me assemble! (28) death-of-me after when then-how-much-more?

כָּל־ זִקְנֵי שִׁבְטֵיכֶם וְשֹׁטְרֵיכֶם וַאֲדַבְּרָה

so-I-can-speak and-being-officials-of-you tribes-of-you elders-of all-of

בְּאָזְנֵיהֶם אֵת הַדְּבָרִים הָאֵלֶּה וְאָעִידָה בָּם

against-them so-I-can-call-witness the-these the-words *** in-ears-of-them

אֶת־ הַשָּׁמַיִם וְאֶת־ הָאָרֶץ׃ כִּי יָדַעְתִּי אַחֲרֵי מוֹתִי כִּי־

that death-of-me after I-know for (29) the-earth and the-heavens ***

breaking my covenant. [21]And
when many disasters and
difficulties come upon them,
this song will testify against
them, because it will not be
forgotten by their descend
ants. I know what they are
disposed to do, even before I
bring them into the land I
promised them on oath." [22]So
Moses wrote down this song
that day and taught it to the
Israelites.
[23]The LORD gave this command to Joshua son of Nun:
"Be strong and courageous, for
you will bring the Israelites
into the land I promised them
on oath, and I myself will be
with you."
[24]After Moses finished writing in a book the words of this
law from beginning to end,
[25]he gave this command to the
Levites who carried the ark of
the covenant of the LORD:
[26]"Take this Book of the Law
and place it beside the ark of
the covenant of the LORD your
God. There it will remain as a
witness against you. [27]For I
know how rebellious and
stiff-necked you are. If you
have been rebellious against
the LORD while I am still alive
and with you, how much
more will you rebel after I die!
[28]Assemble before me all the
elders of your tribes and all
your officials, so that I can
speak these words in their
hearing and call heaven and
earth to testify against them.
[29]For I know that after my
death you are sure to become
utterly corrupt and to turn
from the way I have com-
manded you. In days to come,

הַשְׁחֵת תַּשְׁחִתוּן וְסַרְתֶּם מִן־ הַדֶּרֶךְ אֲשֶׁר
that the-way from and-you-will-turn you-will-become-corrupt to-be-corrupt

צִוִּיתִי אֶתְכֶם וְקָרָאת אֶתְכֶם הָרָעָה בְּאַחֲרִית הַיָּמִים
the-days in-coming-of the-disaster on-you and-she-will-fall you I-commanded

כִּי־ תַעֲשׂוּ אֶת־ הָרַע בְּעֵינֵי יְהוָה לְהַכְעִיסוֹ בְּמַעֲשֵׂה
by-work-of to-anger-him Yahweh in-eyes-of the-evil *** you-will-do for

יְדֵיכֶם׃ (30) וַיְדַבֵּר מֹשֶׁה בְּאָזְנֵי כָּל־ קְהַל יִשְׂרָאֵל
Israel assembly-of all-of in-ears-of Moses and-he-recited (30) hands-of-you

אֶת־ דִּבְרֵי הַשִּׁירָה הַזֹּאת עַד תֻּמָּם׃ (32:1) הַאֲזִינוּ הַשָּׁמַיִם
the-heavens listen! (32:1) to-end-them until the-this the-song words-of ***

וַאֲדַבֵּרָה וְתִשְׁמַע הָאָרֶץ אִמְרֵי־ פִי׃ (2) יַעֲרֹף
let-him-fall (2) mouth-of-me words-of the-earth and-you-hear and-I-will-speak

כַּמָּטָר לִקְחִי תִּזַּל כַּטַּל אִמְרָתִי
word-of-me like-the-dew let-her-descend teaching-of-me like-the-rain

כִּשְׂעִירִם עֲלֵי־ דֶשֶׁא וְכִרְבִיבִים עֲלֵי־ עֵשֶׂב׃ (3) כִּי שֵׁם
name-of for (3) plant on and-like-abundant-rains grass on like-showers

יְהוָה אֶקְרָא הָבוּ גֹדֶל לֵאלֹהֵינוּ׃ (4) הַצּוּר תָּמִים
perfect the-Rock (4) of-God-of-us greatness praise! I-will-proclaim Yahweh

פָּעֳלוֹ כִּי כָל־ דְּרָכָיו מִשְׁפָּט אֵל אֱמוּנָה וְאֵין עָוֶל
wrong and-without faithful God just ways-of-him all-of indeed work-of-him

צַדִּיק וְיָשָׁר הוּא׃ (5) שִׁחֵת לוֹ לֹא בָּנָיו
children-of-him not toward-him he-acted-corruptly (5) he and-just upright

מוּמָם דּוֹר עִקֵּשׁ וּפְתַלְתֹּל׃ (6) הַ־ לַיהוָה תִּגְמְלוּ־ זֹאת
this you-repay to-Yahweh ? (6) and-crooked warped generation shame-of-them

עַם נָבָל וְלֹא חָכָם הֲלוֹא־ הוּא אָבִיךָ קָּנֶךָ הוּא
he he-created-you Father-of-you he not? wise and-not foolish people

עָשְׂךָ וַיְכֹנְנֶךָ׃ (7) זְכֹר יְמוֹת עוֹלָם בִּינוּ שְׁנוֹת
years-of consider! old days-of remember! (7) and-he-formed-you he-made-you

דּוֹר־ וָדוֹר שְׁאַל אָבִיךָ וְיַגֵּדְךָ
and-he-will-tell-you father-of-you ask! and-generation generation

זְקֵנֶיךָ וְיֹאמְרוּ לָךְ׃ (8) בְּהַנְחֵל
when-to-give-inheritance (8) to-you and-they-will-explain elders-of-you

עֶלְיוֹן גּוֹיִם בְּהַפְרִידוֹ בְּנֵי אָדָם יַצֵּב גְּבֻלֹת
boundaries-of he-set-up man sons-of when-to-divide-him nations Most-High

עַמִּים לְמִסְפַּר בְּנֵי יִשְׂרָאֵל*׃ (9) כִּי חֵלֶק יְהוָה עַמּוֹ
people-of-him Yahweh portion-of for (9) *Israel sons-of by-number-of peoples

יַעֲקֹב חֶבֶל נַחֲלָתוֹ׃ (10) יִמְצָאֵהוּ בְּאֶרֶץ מִדְבָּר
desert in-land-of he-found-him (10) inheritance-of-him allotment-of Jacob

disaster will fall upon you because you will do evil in the sight of the LORD and provoke him to anger by what your hands have made."

The Song of Moses

[30]And Moses recited the words of this song from beginning to end in the hearing of the whole assembly of Israel:

32 Listen, O heavens,
and I will speak;
hear, O earth, the words
of my mouth.
[2]Let my teaching fall like
rain
and my words descend
like dew,
like showers on new grass,
like abundant rain on
tender plants.

[3]I will proclaim the name of
the LORD.
Oh, praise the greatness
of our God!
[4]He is the Rock, his works
are perfect,
and all his ways are just.
A faithful God who does
no wrong,
upright and just is he.

[5]They have acted corruptly
toward him;
to their shame they are
no longer his children,
but a warped and
crooked generation.[n]
[6]Is this the way you repay
the LORD,
O foolish and unwise
people?
Is he not your Father, your
Creator,[o]
who made you and
formed you?
[7]Remember the days of old;
consider the generations
long past.
Ask your father and he will
tell you,
your elders, and they will
explain to you.
[8]When the Most High gave
the nations their
inheritance,
when he divided all
mankind,
he set up boundaries for
the peoples
according to the number
of the sons of Israel.[p]
[9]For the LORD's portion is
his people,
Jacob his allotted
inheritance.

[10]In a desert land he found
him,

[n]5 Or *Corrupt are they and not his children, / a generation warped and twisted to their shame*
[o]6 Or *Father, who bought you*
[p]8 Masoretic Text; Dead Sea Scrolls (see also Septuagint) *sons of God*

*8 The Dead Sea Scrolls read בְּנֵי אֵל, *God sons-of.*

וּבְתֹהוּ יְלֵל יְשִׁמֹן יְסֹבְבֶנְהוּ יְבוֹנְנֵהוּ
and-in-barren and-howling waste he-shielded-him he-cared-for-him

יִצְּרֶנְהוּ כְּאִישׁוֹן עֵינוֹ׃ (11) כְּנֶשֶׁר יָעִיר קִנּוֹ
he-guarded-him as-pupil-of eye-of-him (11) like-eagle he-stirs-up nest-of-him

עַל־ גּוֹזָלָיו יְרַחֵף יִפְרֹשׂ כְּנָפָיו יִקָּחֵהוּ
over young-ones-of-him he-hovers he-spreads wings-of-him he-catches-him

יִשָּׂאֵהוּ עַל־ אֶבְרָתוֹ׃ (12) יְהוָה בָּדָד יַנְחֶנּוּ וְאֵין
he-carries-him on pinion-of-him (12) Yahweh alone he-led-him and-not

עִמּוֹ אֵל נֵכָר׃ (13) יַרְכִּבֵהוּ עַל־ בָּמֳתֵי° אָרֶץ וַיֹּאכַל
with-him god foreign (13) he-made-ride-him on heights-of land and-he-ate

תְּנוּבֹת שָׂדָי וַיֵּנִקֵהוּ דְבַשׁ מִסֶּלַע וְשֶׁמֶן מֵחַלְמִישׁ
fruits-of field and-he-nourished-him honey-of from-rock and-oil from-flinty

צוּר׃ (14) חֶמְאַת בָּקָר וַחֲלֵב צֹאן עִם־ חֵלֶב כָּרִים וְאֵילִים
crag (14) curd-of herd and-milk-of flock with fat-of lambs and-rams

בְּנֵי־ בָשָׁן וְעַתּוּדִים עִם־ חֵלֶב כִּלְיוֹת חִטָּה וְדַם־ עֵנָב
sons-of Bashan and-goats with finest-of kernels-of wheat and-blood-of grape

תִּשְׁתֶּה־ חָמֶר׃ (15) וַיִּשְׁמַן יְשֻׁרוּן וַיִּבְעָט שָׁמַנְתָּ
you-drank wine (15) and-he-grew-fat Jeshurun and-he-kicked you-were-filled

עָבִיתָ כָּשִׂיתָ וַיִּטֹּשׁ אֱלוֹהַ* עָשָׂהוּ
you-became-heavy you-became-sleek and-he-abandoned God he-made-him

וַיְנַבֵּל צוּר יְשֻׁעָתוֹ׃ (16) יַקְנִאֻהוּ
and-he-rejected Rock-of Savior-of-him (16) they-made-jealous-him

בְּזָרִים בְּתוֹעֵבֹת יַכְעִיסֻהוּ׃ (17) יִזְבְּחוּ
with-foreign-gods with-detestable-idols they-angered-him (17) they-sacrificed

לַשֵּׁדִים לֹא אֱלֹהַ* אֱלֹהִים לֹא יְדָעוּם חֲדָשִׁים מִקָּרֹב
to-the-demons not God gods not they-knew-them recent-ones from-near

בָּאוּ לֹא שְׂעָרוּם אֲבֹתֵיכֶם׃ (18) צוּר יְלָדְךָ
they-appeared not they-feared-them fathers-of-you (18) Rock he-fathered-you

תֶּשִׁי וַתִּשְׁכַּח אֵל מְחֹלְלֶךָ׃ (19) וַיַּרְא יְהוָה
you-deserted and-you-forgot God one-bearing-you (19) and-he-saw Yahweh

וַיִּנְאָץ מִכַּעַס בָּנָיו וּבְנֹתָיו׃
and-he-rejected because-of-anger-of sons-of-him and-daughters-of-him

(20) וַיֹּאמֶר אַסְתִּירָה פָנַי מֵהֶם אֶרְאֶה מָה
(20) and-he-said I-will-hide faces-of-me from-them I-will-see what

אַחֲרִיתָם כִּי דוֹר תַּהְפֻּכֹת הֵמָּה בָּנִים לֹא־ אֵמֻן
end-of-them for generation-of perverse-ones they children not faithful

בָם׃ (21) הֵם קִנְאוּנִי בְלֹא־ אֵל כִּעֲסוּנִי
among-them (21) they they-made-jealous-me by-not god they-angered-me

in a barren and howling
waste.
He shielded him and cared
for him;
he guarded him as the
apple of his eye,
11like an eagle that stirs up
its nest
and hovers over its
young,
that spreads its wings to
catch them
and carries them on its
pinions.
12The LORD alone led him;
no foreign god was with
him.
13He made him ride on the
heights of the land
and fed him with the
fruit of the fields.
He nourished him with
honey from the rock,
and with oil from the
flinty crag,
14with curds and milk from
herd and flock
and with fattened lambs
and goats,
with choice rams of Bashan
and the finest kernels of
wheat.
You drank the red blood of
the grape.
15Jeshurun[q] grew fat and
kicked;
filled with food, he
became heavy and
sleek.
He abandoned the God
who made him
and rejected the Rock his
Savior.
16They made him jealous
with their foreign gods
and angered him with
their detestable idols.
17They sacrificed to demons,
which are not God—
gods they had not
known,
gods that recently
appeared,
gods your fathers did not
fear.
18You deserted the Rock,
who fathered you;
you forgot the God who
gave you birth.
19The LORD saw this and
rejected them
because he was angered
by his sons and
daughters.
20"I will hide my face from
them," he said,
"and see what their end
will be;
for they are a perverse
generation,

q15 *Jeshurun* means *the upright one*, that is, Israel.

*15, 17 Most mss have *mappiq* in the *he* (הַ).

°13 ק במותי

בְּהַבְלֵיהֶם וַאֲנִי אַקְנִיאֵם בְּלֹא־עָם
people by-not I-will-make-jealous-them so-I with-worthless-idols-of-them

בְּגוֹי נָבָל אַכְעִיסֵם׃ כִּי־אֵשׁ קָדְחָה
she-was-kindled fire for (22) I-will-anger-them foolish by-nation

בְאַפִּי וַתִּיקַד עַד־שְׁאוֹל תַּחְתִּית וַתֹּאכַל אֶרֶץ
earth and-she-will-devour below Sheol to and-she-burns by-wrath-of-me

וִיבֻלָהּ וַתְּלַהֵט מוֹסְדֵי הָרִים׃
mountains foundations-of and-she-will-set-afire and-harvest-of-her

אַסְפֶּה עָלֵימוֹ רָעוֹת חִצַּי אֲכַלֶּה־בָּם׃
against-them I-will-spend arrows-of-me calamities on-them I-will-heap (23)

מְזֵי רָעָב וּלְחֻמֵי רֶשֶׁף וְקֶטֶב מְרִירִי
deadly and-plague pestilence and-ones-consuming-of famine ones-wasting-of (24)

וְשֶׁן־בְּהֵמוֹת אֲשַׁלַּח־בָּם עִם־חֲמַת זֹחֲלֵי
ones-gliding-of venom-of with against-them I-will-send wild-beasts and-fang-of

עָפָר׃ מִחוּץ תְּשַׁכֶּל־חֶרֶב וּמֵחֲדָרִים אֵימָה
terror and-in-homes sword she-will-make-childless on-outside (25) dust

גַּם־בָּחוּר גַּם־בְּתוּלָה יוֹנֵק עִם־אִישׁ שֵׂיבָה׃ אָמַרְתִּי
I-said (26) gray-hair man-of with infant young-woman and young-man both

אַפְאֵיהֶם אַשְׁבִּיתָה מֵאֱנוֹשׁ זִכְרָם׃ לוּלֵי
but (27) memory-of-them from-mankind I-would-erase I-would-scatter-them

כַּעַס אוֹיֵב אָגוּר פֶּן־יְנַכְּרוּ צָרֵימוֹ
adversary-of-them they-misunderstand lest I-dreaded being-enemy taunt-of

פֶּן־יֹאמְרוּ יָדֵינוּ רָמָה וְלֹא יְהוָה פָּעַל כָּל־זֹאת׃
this all-of he-did Yahweh and-not triumphing hands-of-us they-say lest

כִּי־גוֹי אֹבַד עֵצוֹת הֵמָּה וְאֵין בָּהֶם תְּבוּנָה׃ לוּ
if! (29) discernment in-them and-not they senses lacking nation indeed (28)

חָכְמוּ יַשְׂכִּילוּ זֹאת יָבִינוּ לְאַחֲרִיתָם׃
about-end-of-them they-would-discern this they-would-understand they-were-wise

אֵיכָה יִרְדֹּף אֶחָד אֶלֶף וּשְׁנַיִם יָנִיסוּ
they-could-put-to-flight or-two thousand one could-he-chase how? (30)

רְבָבָה אִם־לֹא כִּי־צוּרָם מְכָרָם וַיהוָה הִסְגִּירָם׃
he-gave-up-them and-Yahweh he-sold-them Rock-of-them that not if ten-thousand

כִּי לֹא כְצוּרֵנוּ צוּרָם וְאֹיְבֵינוּ פְּלִילִים׃
conceders and-being-enemies-of-us rock-of-them like-Rock-of-us not for (31)

כִּי־מִגֶּפֶן סְדֹם גַּפְנָם וּמִשַּׁדְמֹת עֲמֹרָה
Gomorrah and-from-fields-of vine-of-them Sodom from-vine-of for (32)

עֲנָבֵמוֹ עִנְּבֵי־רוֹשׁ אַשְׁכְּלֹת מְרֹרֹת לָמוֹ׃ חֲמַת
venom-of (33) to-them bitter-ones clusters poison grapes-of grape-of-them

children who are
unfaithful.
21They made me jealous by
what is no god
and angered me with
their worthless idols.
I will make them envious
by those who are not a
people;
I will make them angry
by a nation that has
no understanding.
22For a fire has been kindled
by my wrath,
one that burns to the
realm of death[r] below.
It will devour the earth and
its harvests
and set afire the
foundations of the
mountains.

23"I will heap calamities
upon them
and spend my arrows
against them.
24I will send wasting famine
against them,
consuming pestilence
and deadly plague;
I will send against them
the fangs of wild
beasts,
the venom of vipers that
glide in the dust.
25In the street the sword will
make them childless;
in their homes terror will
reign.
Young men and young
women will perish,
infants and gray-haired
men.
26I said I would scatter them
and erase their memory
from mankind,
27but I dreaded the taunt of
the enemy,
lest the adversary
misunderstand
and say, 'Our hand has
triumphed;
the LORD has not done all
this.' "

28They are a nation without
sense,
there is no discernment
in them.
29If only they were wise and
would understand this
and discern what their
end will be!
30How could one man chase
a thousand,
or two put ten thousand
to flight,
unless their Rock had sold
them,
unless the LORD had
given them up?
31For their rock is not like
our Rock,
as even our enemies
concede.
32Their vine comes from the
vine of Sodom

[r]22 Hebrew *to Sheol*

תַּנִּינִם יֵינָם וְרֹאשׁ פְּתָנִים אַכְזָר׃ הֲלֹא־הוּא
this not? (34) deadly cobras and-poison-of wine-of-them serpents

כָּמֻס עִמָּדִי חָתֻם בְּאוֹצְרֹתָי׃ לִי נָקָם
vengeance to-me (35) in-vaults-of-me being-sealed with-me being-reserved

וְשִׁלֵּם לְעֵת תָּמוּט רַגְלָם כִּי קָרוֹב יוֹם
day-of near for foot-of-them she-will-slip in-time and-repayment

אֵידָם וְחָשׁ עֲתִדֹת לָמוֹ׃ כִּי־ יָדִין יְהוָה
Yahweh he-will-judge for (36) upon-them dooms and-he-rushes disaster-of-them

עַמּוֹ וְעַל־ עֲבָדָיו יִתְנֶחָם כִּי יִרְאֶה
he-sees when he-will-have-compassion servants-of-him and-on people-of-him

כִּי־ אָזְלַת יָד וְאֶפֶס עָצוּר וְעָזוּב׃
or-being-free being-slave and-none strength she-is-gone that

וְאָמַר אֵי אֱלֹהֵימוֹ צוּר חָסָיוּ בוֹ׃
in-him they-took-refuge rock gods-of-them where? and-he-will-say (37)

אֲשֶׁר חֵלֶב זְבָחֵימוֹ יֹאכֵלוּ יִשְׁתּוּ יֵין
wine-of they-drank they-ate sacrifices-of-them fat-of who (38)

נְסִיכָם יָקוּמוּ וְיַעְזְרֻכֶם יְהִי עֲלֵיכֶם
for-you let-him-be and-let-them-help-you let-them-rise drink-offering-of-them

סִתְרָה׃ רְאוּ ׀ עַתָּה כִּי אֲנִי אֲנִי הוּא וְאֵין אֱלֹהִים עִמָּדִי אֲנִי
I besides-me gods and-there-is-no He myself I that now see! (39) shelter

אָמִית וַאֲחַיֶּה מָחַצְתִּי וַאֲנִי אֶרְפָּא וְאֵין
and-no-one I-will-heal and-I I-wounded and-I-bring-to-life I-put-to-death

מִיָּדִי מַצִּיל׃ כִּי־ אֶשָּׂא אֶל־ שָׁמַיִם יָדִי
hand-of-me heavens to I-lift indeed (40) delivering from-hand-of-me

וְאָמַרְתִּי חַי אָנֹכִי לְעֹלָם׃ אִם־ שַׁנּוֹתִי בְּרַק חַרְבִּי
sword-of-me flashing-of I-sharpen when (41) for-ever I alive and-I-declare

וְתֹאחֵז בְּמִשְׁפָּט יָדִי אָשִׁיב נָקָם
vengeance I-will-take hand-of-me in-judgment and-she-grasps

לְצָרָי וְלִמְשַׂנְאַי אֲשַׁלֵּם׃ אַשְׁכִּיר
I-will-make-drunk (42) I-will-repay and-to-ones-hating-me on-adversaries-of-me

חִצַּי מִדָּם וְחַרְבִּי תֹּאכַל בָּשָׂר מִדַּם חָלָל
slain from-blood-of flesh she-devours and-sword-of-me with-blood arrows-of-me

וְשִׁבְיָה מֵרֹאשׁ פַּרְעוֹת אוֹיֵב׃ הַרְנִינוּ גוֹיִם
nations rejoice! (43) being-enemy leaders-of from-head-of and-captive

עַמּוֹ כִּי דַם־ עֲבָדָיו יִקּוֹם וְנָקָם
and-vengeance he-will-avenge servants-of-him blood-of for * people-of-him

יָשִׁיב לְצָרָיו וְכִפֶּר אַדְמָתוֹ עַמּוֹ׃
people-of-him land-of-him and-he-will-atone on-enemies-of-him he-will-take

and from the fields of
Gomorrah.
Their grapes are filled with
poison,
and their clusters with
bitterness.
33 Their wine is the venom of
serpents,
the deadly poison of
cobras.

34 "Have I not kept this in
reserve
and sealed it in my
vaults?
35 It is mine to avenge; I will
repay.
In due time their foot
will slip;
their day of disaster is near
and their doom rushes
upon them."
36 The LORD will judge his
people
and have compassion on
his servants
when he sees their strength
is gone
and no one is left, slave
or free.
37 He will say: "Now where
are their gods,
the rock they took refuge
in,
38 the gods who ate the fat of
their sacrifices
and drank the wine of
their drink offerings?
Let them rise up to help
you!
Let them give you
shelter!
39 "See now that I myself am
He!
There is no god besides
me.
I put to death and I bring
to life,
I have wounded and I
will heal,
and no one can deliver
from my hand.
40 I lift my hand to heaven
and declare:
As surely as I live
forever,
41 when I sharpen my
flashing sword
and my hand grasps it in
judgment,
I will take vengeance on
my adversaries
and repay those who
hate me.
42 I will make my arrows
drunk with blood,
while my sword devours
flesh:
the blood of the slain and
the captives,
the heads of the enemy
leaders."

*43 אלהים (כל) לו והשתחוו
angels (all-of) to-him and-worship!
The Dead Sea Scrolls and Septuagint have this phrase, apparently quoted in Hebrews 1:6.

וַיָּבֹא מֹשֶׁה וַיְדַבֵּר אֶת־ כָּל־ דִּבְרֵי הַשִּׁירָה־ הַזֹּאת
the-this the-song words-of all-of *** and-he-spoke Moses and-he-came (44)

בְּאָזְנֵי הָעָם הוּא וְהוֹשֵׁעַ בִּן־ נוּן׃ וַיְכַל מֹשֶׁה
Moses when-he-finished (45) Nun son-of and-Hoshea he the-people in-ears-of

לְדַבֵּר אֶת־ כָּל־ הַדְּבָרִים הָאֵלֶּה אֶל־ כָּל־ יִשְׂרָאֵל׃ וַיֹּאמֶר
and-he-said (46) Israel all-of to the-these the-words all-of *** to-recite

אֲלֵהֶם שִׂימוּ לְבַבְכֶם לְכָל־ הַדְּבָרִים אֲשֶׁר אָנֹכִי מֵעִיד
solemnly-declaring I that the-words to-all-of heart-of-you take-to! to-them

בָּכֶם הַיּוֹם אֲשֶׁר תְּצַוֻּם אֶת־ בְּנֵיכֶם לִשְׁמֹר
to-be-careful children-of-you *** you-may-command-them that the-day to-you

לַעֲשׂוֹת אֶת־ כָּל־ דִּבְרֵי הַתּוֹרָה הַזֹּאת׃ כִּי לֹא־ דָבָר רֵק הוּא
he idle word not for (47) the-this the-law words-of all-of *** to-obey

מִכֶּם כִּי־ הוּא חַיֵּיכֶם וּבַדָּבָר הַזֶּה תַּאֲרִיכוּ
you-will-live-long the-this and-by-the-word lives-of-you he indeed for-you

יָמִים עַל־ הָאֲדָמָה אֲשֶׁר אַתֶּם עֹבְרִים אֶת־ הַיַּרְדֵּן שָׁמָּה
to-there the-Jordan *** ones-crossing you that the-land in days

לְרִשְׁתָּהּ׃ וַיְדַבֵּר יְהוָה אֶל־ מֹשֶׁה בְּעֶצֶם הַיּוֹם הַזֶּה
the-that the-day on-same Moses to Yahweh and-he-spoke (48) to-possess-her

לֵאמֹר׃ עֲלֵה אֶל־ הַר הָעֲבָרִים הַזֶּה הַר־ נְבוֹ אֲשֶׁר
that Nebo Mount-of the-this the-Abarim Range-of to go-up! (49) to-say

בְּאֶרֶץ מוֹאָב אֲשֶׁר עַל־ פְּנֵי יְרֵחוֹ וּרְאֵה אֶת־ אֶרֶץ כְּנַעַן
Canaan land-of *** and-view! Jericho faces-of across that Moab in-land-of

אֲשֶׁר אֲנִי נֹתֵן לִבְנֵי יִשְׂרָאֵל לַאֲחֻזָּה׃ וּמֻת בָּהָר
on-the-mountain and-die! (50) as-possession Israel to-sons-of giving I that

אֲשֶׁר אַתָּה עֹלֶה שָׁמָּה וְהֵאָסֵף אֶל־ עַמֶּיךָ כַּאֲשֶׁר־ מֵת
he-died just-as people-of-you to and-be-gathered! on-there climbing you that

אַהֲרֹן אָחִיךָ בְּהֹר הָהָר וַיֵּאָסֶף אֶל־ עַמָּיו׃
people-of-him to and-he-was-gathered the-Mount on-Hor brother-of-you Aaron

עַל אֲשֶׁר מְעַלְתֶּם בִּי בְּתוֹךְ בְּנֵי יִשְׂרָאֵל
Israel sons-of in-presence-of with-me you-broke-faith that because (51)

בְּמֵי־ מְרִיבַת קָדֵשׁ מִדְבַּר־ צִן עַל אֲשֶׁר לֹא־ קִדַּשְׁתֶּם
you-upheld-as-holy not that for Zin Desert-of Kadesh Meribah-of at-waters-of

אוֹתִי בְּתוֹךְ בְּנֵי יִשְׂרָאֵל׃ כִּי מִנֶּגֶד תִּרְאֶה אֶת־
*** you-will-see from-distance therefore (52) Israel sons-of among me

הָאָרֶץ וְשָׁמָּה לֹא תָבוֹא אֶל־ הָאָרֶץ אֲשֶׁר־ אֲנִי נֹתֵן
giving I that the-land into you-will-enter not but-to-there the-land

לִבְנֵי יִשְׂרָאֵל׃ וְזֹאת הַבְּרָכָה אֲשֶׁר בֵּרַךְ מֹשֶׁה אִישׁ
man-of Moses he-pronounced that the-blessing and-this (33:1) Israel to-sons-of

43 Rejoice, O nations, with
his people,[r,s]
for he will avenge the
blood of his servants;
he will take vengeance on
his enemies
and make atonement for
his land and people.

44 Moses came with Joshua[t]
son of Nun and spoke all the
words of this song in the hearing of the people. 45 When
Moses finished reciting all
these words to all Israel, 46 he
said to them, "Take to heart all
the words I have solemnly declared to you this day, so that
you may command your children to obey carefully all the
words of this law. 47 They are
not just idle words for you—
they are your life. By them you
will live long in the land you
are crossing the Jordan to possess."

Moses to Die on Mount Nebo

48 On that same day the LORD
told Moses, 49 "Go up into the
Abarim Range to Mount Nebo
in Moab, across from Jericho,
and view Canaan, the land I
am giving the Israelites as
their own possession. 50 There
on the mountain that you
have climbed you will die and
be gathered to your people,
just as your brother Aaron
died on Mount Hor and was
gathered to his people. 51 This
is because both of you broke
faith with me in the presence
of the Israelites at the waters
of Meribah Kadesh in the
Desert of Zin and because you
did not uphold my holiness
among the Israelites. 52 Therefore, you will see the land only
from a distance; you will not
enter the land I am giving to
the people of Israel."

Moses Blesses the Tribes

33 This is the blessing
that Moses the man of
God pronounced on the Israelites before his death. 2 He said:

[r] 43 Or *Make his people rejoice, O nations*
[s] 43 Masoretic Text; Dead Sea Scrolls (see also Septuagint) *people, / and let all the angels worship him /*
[t] 44 Hebrew *Hoshea,* a variant of *Joshua*

הָאֱלֹהִים אֶת־ בְּנֵי יִשְׂרָאֵל לִפְנֵי מוֹתוֹ׃ וַיֹּאמַר יְהוָה
Yahweh and-he-said (2) death-of-him before Israel sons-of *** the-God

מִסִּינַי בָּא וְזָרַח מִשֵּׂעִיר לָמוֹ הוֹפִיעַ מֵהַר
from-Mount-of he-shone over-them from-Seir and-he-dawned he-came from-Sinai

פָּארָן וְאָתָה מֵרִבְבֹת קֹדֶשׁ מִימִינוֹ אֵשְׁדָּת
*mountain-slope from-south-of-him holy-one with-myriads-of and-he-came Paran

לָמוֹ׃ אַף חֹבֵב עַמִּים כָּל־ קְדֹשָׁיו בְּיָדֶךָ
in-hand-of-you holy-ones-of-him all-of peoples one-loving surely (3) to-them

וְהֵם תֻּכּוּ לְרַגְלֶךָ יִשָּׂא מִדַּבְּרֹתֶיךָ׃
from-instructions-of-you he-receives at-foot-of-you they-bow and-they

תּוֹרָה צִוָּה־ לָנוּ מֹשֶׁה מוֹרָשָׁה קְהִלַּת יַעֲקֹב׃ וַיְהִי
and-he-was (5) Jacob assembly-of possession Moses to-us he-gave law (4)

בִישֻׁרוּן מֶלֶךְ בְּהִתְאַסֵּף רָאשֵׁי עָם יַחַד שִׁבְטֵי יִשְׂרָאֵל׃
Israel tribes-of with people leaders-of when-to-assemble king over-Jeshurun

יְחִי רְאוּבֵן וְאַל־ יָמֹת וִיהִי מְתָיו מִסְפָּר׃
few men-of-him nor-let-him-be let-him-die and-not Reuben let-him-live (6)

וְזֹאת לִיהוּדָה וַיֹּאמַר שְׁמַע יְהוָה קוֹל יְהוּדָה וְאֶל־
and-to Judah cry-of Yahweh hear! and-he-said about-Judah and-this (7)

עַמּוֹ תְּבִיאֶנּוּ יָדָיו רָב לוֹ וְעֵזֶר
and-help with-him he-defends hands-of-him you-bring-him people-of-him

מִצָּרָיו תִּהְיֶה׃ וּלְלֵוִי אָמַר תֻּמֶּיךָ
Thummim-of-you he-said and-about-Levi (8) you-be against-foes-of-him

וְאוּרֶיךָ לְאִישׁ חֲסִידֶךָ אֲשֶׁר נִסִּיתוֹ בְּמַסָּה
at-Massah you-tested-him whom favored-of-you to-man and-Urim-of-you

תְּרִיבֵהוּ עַל־ מֵי מְרִיבָה׃ הָאֹמֵר לְאָבִיו
to-father-of-him the-one-saying (9) Meribah waters-of at you-contended-with-him

וּלְאִמּוֹ לֹא רְאִיתִיו וְאֶת־ אֶחָיו לֹא הִכִּיר
he-recognized not brothers-of-him and I-regard-him not and-to-mother-of-him

וְאֶת־ בָּנָו לֹא יָדָע כִּי שָׁמְרוּ אִמְרָתֶךָ
word-of-you they-watched-over but he-acknowledged not children-of-him or

וּבְרִיתְךָ יִנְצֹרוּ׃ יוֹרוּ מִשְׁפָּטֶיךָ לְיַעֲקֹב
to-Jacob precepts-of-you they-teach (10) they-guarded and-covenant-of-you

וְתוֹרָתְךָ לְיִשְׂרָאֵל יָשִׂימוּ קְטוֹרָה בְּאַפֶּךָ וְכָלִיל
and-offering before-face-of-you incense they-offer to-Israel and-law-of-you

עַל־ מִזְבְּחֶךָ׃ בָּרֵךְ יְהוָה חֵילוֹ וּפֹעַל יָדָיו
hands-of-him and-work-of skill-of-him Yahweh bless! (11) altar-of-you on

תִּרְצֶה מְחַץ מָתְנַיִם קָמָיו וּמְשַׂנְאָיו
and-ones-hating-him ones-rising-against-him loins smite! you-be-pleased

"The LORD came from Sinai
and dawned over them
from Seir;
he shone forth from
Mount Paran.
He came with[u] myriads of
holy ones
from the south, from his
mountain slopes.[v]
3Surely it is you who love
the people;
all the holy ones are in
your hand.
At your feet they all bow
down,
and from you receive
instruction,
4the law that Moses gave us,
the possession of the
assembly of Jacob.
5He was king over
Jeshurun[w]
when the leaders of the
people assembled,
along with the tribes of
Israel.

6"Let Reuben live and not
die,
nor[x] his men be few."

7And this he said about
Judah:

"Hear, O LORD, the cry of
Judah;
bring him to his people.
With his own hands he
defends his cause.
Oh, be his help against
his foes!"

8About Levi he said:

"Your Thummim and Urim
belong
to the man you favored.
You tested him at Massah;
you contended with him
at the waters of
Meribah.
9He said of his father and
mother,
'I have no regard for
them.'
He did not recognize his
brothers
or acknowledge his own
children,
but he watched over your
word
and guarded your
covenant.
10He teaches your precepts to
Jacob
and your law to Israel.
He offers incense before
you
and whole burnt
offerings on your altar.
11Bless all his skills, O LORD,

[u]2 Or *from*
[v]2 The meaning of the Hebrew for this phrase is uncertain.
[w]5 *Jeshurun* means *the upright one,* that is, Israel; also in verse 26.
[x]6 Or *but let*

°2 ק אש דת
*2 *law fire(-of)* [?] (*Qere* translation)

°9 ק בניו

מִן־יְקוּמוּן (12) לְבִנְיָמִן אָמַר יְדִיד יְהוָה יִשְׁכֹּן

let-him-rest Yahweh beloved-of he-said about-Benjamin (12) they-rise not

לָבֶטַח עָלָיו חֹפֵף עָלָיו כָּל־הַיּוֹם וּבֵין

and-between the-day all-of over-him one-shielding in-him in-security

כְּתֵפָיו שָׁכֵן׃ (13) וּלְיוֹסֵף אָמַר מְבֹרֶכֶת יְהוָה

Yahweh blessing he-said and-about-Joseph (13) he-rests shoulders-of-him

אַרְצוֹ מִמֶּגֶד שָׁמַיִם מִטָּל וּמִתְּהוֹם רֹבֶצֶת תָּחַת׃

below lying and-with-deep-water with-dew heavens with-precious-of land-of-him

(14) וּמִמֶּגֶד תְּבוּאֹת שָׁמֶשׁ וּמִמֶּגֶד גֶּרֶשׁ יְרָחִים׃

moons yield-of and-with-finest-of sun produce-of and-with-best-of (14)

(15) וּמֵרֹאשׁ הַרְרֵי־קֶדֶם וּמִמֶּגֶד גִּבְעוֹת

hills-of and-with-fruit-of ancient mountains-of and-with-choicest-of (15)

עוֹלָם׃ (16) וּמִמֶּגֶד אֶרֶץ וּמְלֹאָהּ וּרְצוֹן

and-favor-of and-fullness-of-her earth and-with-best-of (16) everlasting

שֹׁכְנִי סְנֶה תָּבוֹאתָה לְרֹאשׁ יוֹסֵף וּלְקָדְקֹד

and-on-brow-of Joseph on-head-of you-let-rest-her burning-bush one-dwelling-of

נְזִיר אֶחָיו׃ (17) בְּכוֹר שׁוֹרוֹ הָדָר לוֹ

to-him majesty bull-of-him firstborn-of (17) brothers-of-him prince-of

וְקַרְנֵי רְאֵם קַרְנָיו בָּהֶם עַמִּים יְנַגַּח יַחְדָּו

even he-will-gore nations with-them horns-of-him wild-ox and-horns-of

אַפְסֵי־אָרֶץ וְהֵם רִבְבוֹת אֶפְרַיִם וְהֵם אַלְפֵי מְנַשֶּׁה׃

Manasseh thousands-of so-they Ephraim ten-thousands-of so-they earth ends-of

(18) וְלִזְבוּלֻן אָמַר שְׂמַח זְבוּלֻן בְּצֵאתֶךָ

in-to-go-out-you Zebulun rejoice! he-said and-about-Zebulun (18)

וְיִשָּׂשכָר בְּאֹהָלֶיךָ׃ (19) עַמִּים הַר־יִקְרָאוּ שָׁם

there they-will-summon mountain peoples (19) in-tents-of-you and-Issachar

יִזְבְּחוּ זִבְחֵי־צֶדֶק כִּי שֶׁפַע יַמִּים

seas abundance-of and righteousness sacrifices-of they-will-offer

יִינָקוּ וּשְׂפֻנֵי טְמוּנֵי חוֹל׃

sand ones-being-treasured-of and-ones-being-hidden-of they-will-feast

(20) וּלְגָד אָמַר בָּרוּךְ מַרְחִיב גָּד כְּלָבִיא שָׁכֵן

he-lives like-lion Gad one-enlarging being-blessed he-said and-about-Gad (20)

וְטָרַף זְרוֹעַ אַף־קָדְקֹד׃ (21) וַיַּרְא רֵאשִׁית לוֹ כִּי־שָׁם

there indeed for-him best and-he-chose (21) head or arm and-he-tears

חֶלְקַת מְחֹקֵק סָפוּן וַיֵּתֵא רָאשֵׁי עָם

people heads-of when-he-assembled being-kept one-leading portion-of

צִדְקַת יְהוָה עָשָׂה וּמִשְׁפָּטָיו עִם־יִשְׂרָאֵל׃

Israel to and-judgments-of-him he-carried-out Yahweh righteousness-of

and be pleased with the
work of his hands.
Smite the loins of those
who rise up against
him;
strike his foes till they
rise no more."
12About Benjamin he said:
"Let the beloved of the
LORD rest secure in
him,
for he shields him all day
long,
and the one the LORD
loves rests between his
shoulders."
13About Joseph he said:
"May the LORD bless his
land
with the precious dew
from heaven above
and with the deep waters
that lie below;
14with the best the sun
brings forth
and the finest the moon
can yield;
15with the choicest gifts of
the ancient mountains
and the fruitfulness of
the everlasting hills;
16with the best gifts of the
earth and its fullness
and the favor of him
who dwelt in the
burning bush.
Let all these rest on the
head of Joseph,
on the brow of the
prince among[y] his
brothers.
17In majesty he is like a
firstborn bull;
his horns are the horns
of a wild ox,
with them he will gore the
nations,
even those at the ends of
the earth.
Such are the ten thousands
of Ephraim;
such are the thousands of
Manasseh."
18About Zebulun he said:
"Rejoice, Zebulun, in your
going out,
and you, Issachar, in
your tents.
19They will summon peoples
to the mountain
and there offer sacrifices
of righteousness;
they will feast on the
abundance of the seas,
on the treasures hidden
in the sand."
20About Gad he said:
"Blessed is he who enlarges
Gad's domain!
Gad lives there like a
lion,
tearing at arm or head.

y16 Or *of the one separated from*

וּלְדָן אָמַר דָּן גּוּר אַרְיֵה יְזַנֵּק מִן־הַבָּשָׁן׃
the-Bashan from he-springs lion cub-of Dan he-said and-about-Dan (22)

וּלְנַפְתָּלִי אָמַר נַפְתָּלִי שְׂבַע רָצוֹן וּמָלֵא
and-he-is-full favor abundant-of Naphtali he-said and-about-Naphtali (23)

בִּרְכַּת יְהוָה יָם וְדָרוֹם יְרָשָׁה׃ וּלְאָשֵׁר אָמַר
he-said and-about-Asher (24) inherit! and-south lake Yahweh blessing-of

בָּרוּךְ מִבָּנִים אָשֵׁר יְהִי רְצוּי אֶחָיו
brothers-of-him being-favored-of let-him-be Asher of-sons being-blessed

וְטֹבֵל בַּשֶּׁמֶן רַגְלוֹ׃ בַּרְזֶל וּנְחֹשֶׁת מִנְעָלֶךָ
gate-bolts-of-you and-bronze iron (25) foot-of-him in-the-oil and-bathing

וּכְיָמֶיךָ דָּבְאֶךָ׃ אֵין כָּאֵל יְשֻׁרוּן
Jeshurun like-the-God-of no-one (26) strength-of-you and-as-days-of-you

רֹכֵב שָׁמַיִם בְּעֶזְרֶךָ וּבְגַאֲוָתוֹ שְׁחָקִים׃ מְעֹנָה
refuge (27) clouds and-in-majesty-of-him in-help-of-you heavens riding

אֱלֹהֵי קֶדֶם וּמִתַּחַת זְרֹעֹת עוֹלָם וַיְגָרֶשׁ
and-he-will-drive-out everlasting arms-of and-at-under eternal God-of

מִפָּנֶיךָ אוֹיֵב וַיֹּאמֶר הַשְׁמֵד׃ וַיִּשְׁכֹּן
so-he-will-live (28) destroy! and-he-will-say being-enemy from-before-you

יִשְׂרָאֵל בֶּטַח בָּדָד עֵין יַעֲקֹב אֶל־אֶרֶץ דָּגָן וְתִירוֹשׁ אַף־
also and-new-wine grain land-of in Jacob spring-of alone safely Israel

שָׁמָיו יַעַרְפוּ־טָל׃ אַשְׁרֶיךָ יִשְׂרָאֵל מִי כָמוֹךָ עַם
people like-you who? Israel blessed-you (29) dew they-drop heavens-of-him

נוֹשַׁע בַּיהוָה מָגֵן עֶזְרֶךָ וַאֲשֶׁר־חֶרֶב גַּאֲוָתֶךָ
glorious-of-you sword and-who helper-of-you shield by-Yahweh being-saved

וְיִכָּחֲשׁוּ אֹיְבֶיךָ לָךְ וְאַתָּה עַל־
on and-you before-you being-enemies-of-you and-they-will-cower

בָּמוֹתֵימוֹ תִדְרֹךְ׃ וַיַּעַל מֹשֶׁה
Moses then-he-climbed (34:1) you-will-trample high-places-of-them

מֵעַרְבֹת מוֹאָב אֶל־הַר נְבוֹ רֹאשׁ הַפִּסְגָּה אֲשֶׁר עַל־פְּנֵי
faces-of across that the-Pisgah top-of Nebo Mount-of to Moab from-plains-of

יְרֵחוֹ וַיַּרְאֵהוּ יְהוָה אֶת־כָּל־הָאָרֶץ אֶת־הַגִּלְעָד עַד־דָּן׃
Dan to the-Gilead *** the-land whole-of *** Yahweh and-he-showed-him Jericho

וְאֵת כָּל־נַפְתָּלִי וְאֶת־אֶרֶץ אֶפְרַיִם וּמְנַשֶּׁה וְאֵת כָּל־אֶרֶץ
land-of all-of and and-Manasseh Ephraim land-of and Naphtali all-of and (2)

יְהוּדָה עַד הַיָּם הָאַחֲרוֹן׃ וְאֶת־הַנֶּגֶב וְאֶת־הַכִּכָּר בִּקְעַת
Valley-of the-region and the-Negev and (3) the-western the-sea to Judah

יְרֵחוֹ עִיר הַתְּמָרִים עַד־צֹעַר׃ וַיֹּאמֶר יְהוָה אֵלָיו זֹאת
this to-him Yahweh then-he-said (4) Zoar to the-Palms City-of Jericho

21 He chose the best land for himself;
the leader's portion was kept for him.
When the heads of the people assembled,
he carried out the LORD's righteous will,
and his judgments concerning Israel."

22 About Dan he said:

"Dan is a lion's cub,
springing out of Bashan."

23 About Naphtali he said:

"Naphtali is abounding with the favor of the LORD
and is full of his blessing;
he will inherit southward to the lake."

24 About Asher he said:

"Most blessed of sons is Asher;
let him be favored by his brothers,
and let him bathe his feet in oil.
25 The bolts of your gates will be iron and bronze,
and your strength will equal your days.
26 "There is no one like the God of Jeshurun,
who rides on the heavens to help you
and on the clouds in his majesty.
27 The eternal God is your refuge,
and underneath are the everlasting arms.
He will drive out your enemy before you,
saying, 'Destroy him!'
28 So Israel will live in safety alone;
Jacob's spring is secure
in a land of grain and new wine,
where the heavens drop dew.
29 Blessed are you, O Israel!
Who is like you,
a people saved by the LORD?
He is your shield and helper
and your glorious sword.
Your enemies will cower before you,
and you will trample down their high places.[z]"

The Death of Moses

34 Then Moses climbed Mount Nebo from the plains of Moab to the top of Pisgah, across from Jericho. There the LORD showed him the whole land—from Gilead

[z]29 Or *will tread upon your bodies*

הָאָרֶץ אֲשֶׁר נִשְׁבַּעְתִּי לְאַבְרָהָם לְיִצְחָק וּֽלְיַעֲקֹב לֵאמֹר
to-say and-to-Jacob to-Isaac to-Abraham I-promised that the-land

לְזַרְעֲךָ אֶתְּנֶנָּה הֶרְאִיתִיךָ בְעֵינֶיךָ
with-eyes-of-you I-let-see-you I-will-give-her to-descendant-of-you

וְשָׁמָּה לֹא תַעֲבֹר׃ וַיָּמָת שָׁם מֹשֶׁה עֶֽבֶד־
servant-of Moses there and-he-died (5) you-will-cross not but-to-there

יְהוָה בְּאֶרֶץ מוֹאָב עַל־ פִּי יְהוָה׃ וַיִּקְבֹּר אֹתוֹ בַגַּיְ
in-the-valley him and-he-buried (6) Yahweh saying-of as Moab in-land-of Yahweh

בְּאֶרֶץ מוֹאָב מוּל בֵּית פְּעוֹר וְלֹא־ יָדַע אִישׁ אֶת־ קְבֻרָתוֹ עַד
to grave-of-him *** man he-knows and-not Peor Beth opposite Moab in-land-of

הַיּוֹם הַזֶּה׃ וּמֹשֶׁה בֶּן־ מֵאָה וְעֶשְׂרִים שָׁנָה בְּמֹתוֹ
when-to-die-him year and-twenty hundred son-of and-Moses (7) the-this the-day

לֹא־ כָהֲתָה עֵינוֹ וְלֹא־ נָס לֵחֹה׃
strength-of-him he-was-gone and-not eye-of-him she-was-weak not

וַיִּבְכּוּ בְנֵי יִשְׂרָאֵל אֶת־ מֹשֶׁה בְּעַרְבֹת מוֹאָב שְׁלֹשִׁים יוֹם
day thirty Moab in-plains-of Moses *** Israel sons-of and-they-grieved (8)

וַיִּתְּמוּ יְמֵי בְכִי אֵבֶל מֹשֶׁה׃ וִיהוֹשֻׁעַ
now-Joshua (9) Moses mourning-of weeping-of days-of then-they-were-over

בִּן־ נוּן מָלֵא רוּחַ חָכְמָה כִּֽי־ סָמַךְ מֹשֶׁה אֶת־ יָדָיו
hands-of-him *** Moses he-laid for wisdom spirit-of he-was-filled Nun son-of

עָלָיו וַיִּשְׁמְעוּ אֵלָיו בְּנֵי־ יִשְׂרָאֵל וַיַּעֲשׂוּ כַּאֲשֶׁר
just-as and-they-did Israel sons-of to-him so-they-listened on-him

צִוָּה יְהוָה אֶת־ מֹשֶׁה׃ וְלֹא־ קָם נָבִיא עוֹד בְּיִשְׂרָאֵל
in-Israel since prophet he-rose and-not (10) Moses *** Yahweh he-commanded

כְּמֹשֶׁה אֲשֶׁר יְדָעוֹ יְהוָה פָּנִים אֶל־פָּנִים׃ לְכָל־ הָאֹתוֹת
the-signs with-all-of (11) faces to faces Yahweh he-knew-him whom like-Moses

וְהַמּוֹפְתִים אֲשֶׁר שְׁלָחוֹ יְהוָה לַעֲשׂוֹת בְּאֶרֶץ מִצְרָיִם לְפַרְעֹה
to-Pharaoh Egypt in-land-of to-do Yahweh he-sent-him that and-the-wonders

וּלְכָל־ עֲבָדָיו וּלְכָל־ אַרְצוֹ׃
land-of-him and-to-whole-of officials-of-him and-to-all-of

וּלְכֹל הַיָּד הַחֲזָקָה וּלְכֹל הַמּוֹרָא
the-being-awesome and-with-all-of the-mighty the-hand and-with-all-of (12)

הַגָּדוֹל אֲשֶׁר עָשָׂה מֹשֶׁה לְעֵינֵי כָּל־ יִשְׂרָאֵל׃
Israel all-of before-eyes-of Moses he-performed that the-great-deed

to Dan, 2all of Naphtali, the
territory of Ephraim and
Manasseh, all the land of
Judah as far as the western
sea,[a] 3the Negev and the whole
region from the Valley of Jericho, the City of Palms, as far as
Zoar. 4Then the LORD said to
him, "This is the land I promised on oath to Abraham,
Isaac and Jacob when I said, 'I
will give it to your descendants.' I have let you see it with
your eyes, but you will not
cross over into it."
5And Moses the servant of
the LORD died there in Moab,
as the LORD had said. 6He buried him[b] in Moab, in the valley opposite Beth Peor, but to
this day no one knows where
his grave is. 7Moses was a
hundred and twenty years old
when he died, yet his eyes
were not weak nor his
strength gone. 8The Israelites
grieved for Moses in the
plains of Moab thirty days,
until the time of weeping and
mourning was over.
9Now Joshua son of Nun
was filled with the spirit[c] of
wisdom because Moses had
laid his hands on him. So the
Israelites listened to him and
did what the LORD had commanded Moses.
10Since then, no prophet has
risen in Israel like Moses,
whom the LORD knew face to
face, 11who did all those
miraculous signs and wonders
the LORD sent him to do in
Egypt—to Pharaoh and to all
his officials and to his whole
land. 12For no one has ever
shown the mighty power or
performed the awesome deeds
that Moses did in the sight of
all Israel.

[a]2 That is, the Mediterranean
[b]6 Or *He was buried*
[c]9 Or *Spirit*